15,858

5,776 + 82

15,858

Remedies
Cases and Materials
Sixth Edition

GENERAL EDITOR

Jeffrey Berryman
Faculty of Law
University of Windsor

Vaughan Black
Faculty of Law
Dalhousie University

Jamie Cassels
Faculty of Law
University of Victoria

Michael Pratt
Faculty of Law
Queen's University

Kent Roach
Faculty of Law
University of Toronto

Stephen M. Waddams
Faculty of Law
University of Toronto

2012
Emond Montgomery Publications
Toronto, Canada

Emond Montgomery Publications Limited
60 Shaftesbury Avenue
Toronto, ON M4T 1A3
http://www.emp.ca/lawschool

Printed in Canada.
17 16 15 14 13 12 11   1 2 3 4 5

We acknowledge the financial support of the Government of Canada through the Canada Book Fund for our publishing activities.

Acquisitions editor: Bernard Sandler
Marketing manager: Christine Davidson
Supervising editor: Jim Lyons
Copy and production editor: Nancy Ennis
Proofreader: David Handelsman

Library and Archives Canada Cataloguing in Publication

Remedies : cases and materials / Jeffrey Berryman ... [et al.]. -- 6th ed.

Includes bibliographical references.
ISBN 978-1-55239-470-0

1. Remedies (Law) — Canada — Cases.   2. Damages — Canada — Cases.
I. Berryman, Jeffrey Bruce

KE1232.R46 2011   347.71'077   C2011-907216-5
KF1250.R46 2011

Acknowledgments

This book, like others of its nature, contains extracts from published materials. We have attempted to request permission from and to acknowledge in the text all sources of such material. We wish to make specific reference here to the authors, publishers, journals, and institutions that have been generous in giving their permission to reproduce works in this text. If we have inadvertently overlooked any acknowledgment, we offer our sincere apologies and undertake to rectify the omission in any further editions.

M.G. Baer   M.G. Baer, "The Assessment of Damages for Breach of Contract—Loss of Profit" (1973), 51 *Canadian Bar Review* 490, at 490, 493-99.

Cambridge Law Journal   Sir Robin Cooke, "Remoteness of Damages and Judicial Discretion" (1978), 37 *Cambridge Law Journal* 288.

Cambridge Law Journal   J.A. Jolowicz, "Damages in Equity—A Study of Lord Cairns' Act" (1975), 34 *Cambridge Law Journal* 224, at 224-30.

Canadian Bar Review   M.G. Baer, "The Assessment of Damages for Breach of Contract—Loss of Profit" (1973), 51 *Canadian Bar Review* 490, at 490, 493-99.

Carswell   Jeffrey B. Berryman, "Anton Piller Injunctions: An Update" (1985), 2 *Intellectual Property Journal* 49, at 58. Reprinted by permission of Carswell, a division of Thomson Canada Limited.

Carswell   Donald H. Clark, "Rethinking the Role of Specific Relief in the Contractual Setting," in Jeffrey B. Berryman, ed., *Remedies: Issues and Perspectives* (Scarborough, ON: Carswell, 1991), 139, at 139-42, 156-73. Reprinted by permission of Carswell, a division of Thomson Canada Limited.

Carswell   Ken Cooper-Stephenson, *Personal Injury Damages in Canada*, 2nd ed. (Scarborough, ON: Carswell, 1996), 205-6. Reprinted by permission of Carswell, a division of Thomson Canada Limited.

Carswell   Robert J. Sharpe, *Injunctions and Specific Performance*, 2nd ed. (Aurora, ON: Canada Law Book), paragraphs 4.440-4.580 (looseleaf). Reprinted by permission of Carswell, a division of Thomson Canada Limited.

Carswell   Stephen M. Waddams, *The Law of Damages* (Aurora, ON: Canada Law Book), paragraphs 5.10-5.140 (looseleaf). Reprinted by permission of Carswell, a division of Thomson Canada Limited.

Columbia Law Review   E. Allan Farnsworth, "Legal Remedies for Breach of Contract" (1970), 70 *Columbia Law Review* 1145, at 1149-56.

Emond Montgomery Publications   S.M. Waddams, ed., *Milner's Cases and Materials on Contracts*, 4th ed. (Toronto: Emond Montgomery Publications, 1985).

Her Majesty's Stationery Office   The Law Commission, *Personal Injury Compensation: How Much Is Enough? A Study of the Compensation Experiences of Victims of Personal Injury* (London: LAW COM. no. 225: HMSO, 1994), 262-65. Crown copyright is reproduced with the permission of the Controller of Her Majesty's Stationery Office and the Queen's Printer for Scotland.

Indiana University Press   Owen M. Fiss, *The Civil Rights Injunction* (Bloomington, IN: Indiana University Press, 1978), 38. Reprinted with permission of Indiana University Press.

Insurance Bureau of Canada   Insurance Bureau of Canada, "Compulsory No-fault Auto Insurance Coverage in Canada" (Toronto: Insurance Bureau of Canada, updated August 30, 2011). Chart reproduced with the permission of Insurance Bureau of Canada. The information provided in this chart is intended for educational purposes and is only current to the last updated date.

Irwin Law Incorporated   Jeffrey B. Berryman, *Equitable Remedies* (Toronto: Irwin Law, 2000), 101-3. Reprinted by permission of the publisher.

Kluwer Law International   H.W. Arthurs, D.D. Carter, J. Fudge, H.J. Glasbeek, and G. Trudeau, *Labour Law and Industrial Relations in Canada,* 4th ed. (Deventer, the Netherlands: Kluwer Law International, 1993), 309-11, 313-14. Reprinted/adapted with the permission of Kluwer Law International.

LexisNexis Butterworths   Sir Gordon Borrie and Nigel Lowe, *Law of Contempt*, 2nd ed. (London: Butterworths, 1983), 128, 135, and 138. Reproduced by permission of Reed Elsevier (UK) Limited, trading as LexisNexis.

LexisNexis Canada   Kent Roach, "Principled Remedial Discretion Under the Charter" (2004), 25 *Supreme Court Law Review* (2d) 101, at 106-13.

Manitoba Law Journal   Dale Gibson, "Repairing the Law of Damages" (1978), 8 *Manitoba Law Journal* 637, at 650-51.

John P.S. McLaren   John P.S. McLaren, "The Common Law Nuisance Actions and the Environmental Battle—Well Tempered Swords or Broken Reeds?" (1972), 10 *Osgoode Hall Law Journal* 505, at 511-16.

David J. Mullan   David J. Mullan, "Damages for Violation of Constitutional Rights—A False Spring?" (1995), 6 *National Journal of Constitutional Law* 105, at 114-19.

National Hockey League   National Hockey League, "Standard Player's Contract" (2005 Form) (New York: National Hockey League, 2005).

A.I. Ogus   A.I. Ogus, *The Law of Damages* (London: Butterworths, 1973), at 346-54.

Oxford University Press   A.S. Burrows, *Remedies for Torts and Breach of Contract*, 2nd ed. (London: Butterworths, 1994), 250-54.

Oxford University Press Incorporated   Don DeWees, David Duff, and Michael Trebilcock, *Exploring the Domain of Accident Law: Taking the Facts Seriously* (New York: Oxford University Press, 1996), 412-14. Copyright by Oxford University Press Incorporated. Used by permission of Oxford University Press Incorporated.

Marilyn L. Pilkington   Marilyn L. Pilkington, "Monetary Redress for Charter Infringement," in Robert J. Sharpe, ed., *Charter Litigation* (Toronto: Butterworths, 1987), 308-10.

Richard A. Posner   Richard A. Posner, *Economic Analysis of Law*, 2nd ed. (Boston: Little, Brown and Company, 1977), 88-93 and 95-97.

Queen's Printer for Ontario   Ministry of Financial Institutions, *Final Report of the Task Force on Insurance* ("Slater Commission Report") (© May 1986), 60-70. Reproduced with permission.

Queen's Printer for Ontario   Ontario Law Reform Commission, *Report on Sale of Goods* (© 1979), 409, at 409-10, 422, and 501-2. Reproduced with permission.

Robert J. Sharpe   Robert J. Sharpe, "Injunctions and the Charter" (1984), 22 *Osgoode Hall Law Journal* 473, at 476-79.

Sweet & Maxwell Limited   Hanbury, *Modern Equity*, 8th ed. (London: Stevens & Sons, 1962), c. 23, at 547-50. Reprinted by permission of Sweet & Maxwell Limited, a division of The Thomson Corporation.

Sweet & Maxwell Limited   Harry Street, *Principles of the Law of Damages* (London: Sweet & Maxwell Limited, 1962), 259-66. Reprinted by permission of Sweet & Maxwell Limited, a division of The Thomson Corporation.

University of Toronto Press   Jeffrey B. Berryman, "Anton Piller Orders: A Canadian Common Law Approach" (1984), 34 *University of Toronto Law Journal* 1, at 7-9, 18-25. Reprinted by permission of University of Toronto Press Incorporated (www.utpjournals.com).

University of Toronto Press   R. Grant Hammond, "Interlocutory Injunctions: Time for a New Model?" (1980), 30 *University of Toronto Law Journal* 241, at 241-44, 249, 266-67. Reprinted by permission of University of Toronto Press Incorporated (www.utpjournals.com).

University of Toronto Press   Lewis N. Klar, "New Zealand's Accident Compensation Scheme: A Tort Lawyer's Perspective" (1983), 30 *University of Toronto Law Journal* 80, at 105-7. Reprinted by permission of University of Toronto Press Incorporated (www.utpjournals.com).

University of Toronto Press   D.M. Paciocco, "Anton Piller Orders: Facing the Threat of the Privilege Against Self-Incrimination" (1984), 34 *University of Toronto Law Journal* 26, at 26-27. Reprinted by permission of University of Toronto Press Incorporated (www.utpjournals.com).

Stephen M. Waddams   Stephen M. Waddams, "Damages for Breach of Contract," in Law Society of Upper Canada Special Lectures, *New Developments in Law of Remedies* (Toronto: The Law Society of Upper Canada, 1981), 267, at 259-63.

Sir Arthur Owen Woodhouse   Sir Arthur Owen Woodhouse, *A Challenge to the Law—Personal Injuries Compensation* (Calgary: Burroughs and Company, 1979).

Yale Law Journal   L.L. Fuller and William R. Perdue Jr., "The Reliance Interest in Contract Damages" (1936), 46 *Yale Law Journal* 52, at 52-57.

Preface to the Sixth Edition

Five years have passed since the publication of the fifth edition. At the suggestion of our publishers, we have undertaken the necessary updating to present this sixth edition. Fortunately, there has been no change in the editorial team. Nevertheless, there has been some rearranging of chapter responsibility. Jamie Cassels has taken over responsibility for chapter 5 on personal injury damages, and relinquished responsibility for chapters 6 and 7, dealing with injunctions, to Jeff Berryman. Similarly, Michael Pratt has assumed responsibility for chapter 10, Financial Relief in Equity. These changes are to better align editorial responsibility with the current academic interests of editors. The changes to the actual text have not been dramatic as a result of these rearrangements.

As with previous editions, we have kept to the original format set by the founding editors, David Mullan and Stanley Sadinsky. The book is a collection of contemporary material to be used as a teaching resource. Instructors can pick and choose from the material and fashion a course to their own particular needs with the knowledge that the materials provide up-to-date treatment across all areas of the law of remedies.

The changes in this edition are evolutionary rather than revolutionary. In the past five years the Supreme Court of Canada has been quite active in a number of areas touching on the law of remedies. We have included in these materials the Supreme Court's treatment of Anton Piller orders (*Celanese Canada Inc. v. Murray Demolition Corp.* and *British Columbia (Attorney General) v. Malik*); its treatment of non-pecuniary loss in *Sun Life Insurance v. Fidler*; the acceptance of vindicatory damages for breach of Charter rights in *Vancouver (City) v. Ward*; and the changes to quantifying damages in wrongful dismissal suits resulting from *Honda v. Keays*. The flow-on effects of the court's decision in *Semelhago v. Paramadevan* on the availability of specific performance are also referenced.

Beyond the inclusion of recent Supreme Court of Canada decisions, we have taken the opportunity of a new edition to enrich the notes and text accompanying the cases. The notes can be relied on to highlight differing perspectives, contentious issues, and opportunities for more detailed reflection.

We welcome feedback from all users of this casebook. Our hope is to keep the material contemporary and interesting; befitting an important area of law, the law of remedies.

As always, thanks are owed to the wonderful staff at Emond Montgomery for their continuing support of the casebook. In particular, Bernard Sandler and Nancy Ennis are to be thanked for keeping the project together and on time and David Handelsman for his editorial work.

Jeff Berryman
October 2011

Preface to the Fifth Edition

The publishing of this fifth edition heralds a significant change in the editorial personnel of the casebook. The two founding editors, David Mullan and Stanley Sadinsky, as a result of retiring from active teaching at Queen's University, have decided to leave the editorial board. The remaining editors wish to record their deepest and sincerest gratitude to David and Stanley for both taking the initiative to create a remedies casebook and diligently seeing each of the last four editions through to publication. In addition to David and Stanley leaving the editorial board, Thomas Cromwell has also decided to withdraw from active editorship. Readers will know that Thomas was appointed to the bench of the Nova Scotia Court of Appeal, a task that has left him little time to continue editing his chapters of the book.

Jeff Berryman has assumed the general editorship, and he and Jamie Cassels and Stephen Waddams, two of the original editors, have been joined by Vaughan Black, Michael Pratt, and Kent Roach. We are glad to have such highly respected scholars in remedies join the editorial team. Vaughan has assumed control of chapters 3 and 4, vacated by Thomas Cromwell; Michael has direction over chapters 9 and 11, vacated by David Mullan and Stanley Sadinsky; and Kent takes over control of chapter 12, on Charter remedies. With new blood have come new ideas for the casebook.

David and Stanley envisaged a casebook that would act as a comprehensive resource tool, combining academic commentary, case reports, and detailed notes on the subject of remedies. Their conception was a casebook that could be adapted to the particular focus and interests of individual instructors. Thus, for an instructor who wished to focus only on equitable remedies, the material commencing at part II of the text would provide all that is necessary to ensure complete coverage of the area. The current editors remain true to that original vision. Our experience leads us to believe that most remedies courses taught in Canada combine elements of both common law and equitable remedies, although emphasis may vary as to whether interlocutory injunctions, Charter remedies, or damages for personal injury are covered. The choice is left to individual instructors, who will find in this casebook appropriate material to meet all particular needs.

The fifth edition of the casebook is evolutionary, rather than revolutionary, in its accommodation of new jurisprudence. We have avoided the temptation simply to expand the amount of materials to reflect recent cases, but have, by careful editing, consciously tried to reduce the size of the casebook, while maintaining its topical relevance and comprehensive coverage. In chapter 1, the Supreme Court of Canada's important treatment on punitive damages in *Whitten* has warranted extensive excerpts. In chapter 5, on personal injuries, much of the public policy material on approaches to compensation has been deleted. While legislatures continue to talk about comprehensive reform in this area, their efforts are more piecemeal and directed to injuries resulting from automobile accidents. Judicial pronouncements in this area remain important and more space has been created to include recent developments in areas such as compensating women for loss of working capacity. In chapter 9, the treatment on the doctrine of part-performance has been removed. This material overlapped with much that is taught in first year contract law courses. In chapter 11, a new section on the enforcement of keep-open covenants in business contracts has been added. Chapter 12, on Charter remedies, has undergone significant revision, including the addition of the Supreme Court of Canada's decision in *Doucet-Boudreau v. Nova Scotia (Minister of Education)*, which tentatively advances structural injunctions. While the basic cases have remained fairly constant, readers will note considerable addition to the notes and legislative updating throughout the text.

Faculty in Canadian law schools understood from an early point in time the value accorded the systematic studying of remedies, and the importance of making space in an otherwise crowded curriculum for a dedicated course devoted to the subject. Throughout the 18 years since publication of the first edition, this casebook has been a source of materials to shape and instill an understanding of the central role that remedies play in comprehending and realizing rights. We hope this new edition remains as relevant and topical as its predecessors.

As always, thanks are owed to the wonderful staff at Emond Montgomery for the continuing support of the casebook, particularly Peggy Buchan and David Stokaluk; to Nancy Ennis at WordsWorth Communications, for skilful and careful editing; and Christopher Pavlov, for arranging copyright releases. Here, at Windsor, I wish to thank Tanya Brogan, my executive assistant, for keeping me on track.

Jeff Berryman
March 2006

Table of Contents

Detailed Table of Contents

PART II   EQUITABLE REMEDIES

Table of Cases

A page number in boldface type indicates that the text of the case or a portion thereof is reproduced. A page number in lightface type indicates that the case is merely quoted briefly or discussed. Cases mentioned within excerpts are not listed.

PART I

Monetary Relief

CHAPTER ONE

General Principles of Damages

INTRODUCTION

The purpose of an award of damages, it has often been said, is to put the party complaining in the position that he or she would have occupied if the wrong had not been done. The most widely quoted statement is that of Lord Blackburn in *Livingstone v. Rawyards Coal Co.* (1880), 5 App. Cas. 25, at 39 (HL (Sc.)):

> I do not think that there is any difference of opinion as to its being the general rule that, where any injury is to be compensated by damages, in settling the sum of money to be given for reparation of damages you should as nearly as possible get at that sum of money which will put the party who has been injured, or who has suffered, in the same position as he would have been in if he had not sustained the wrong for which he is now getting his compensation or reparation.

But this principle, like all general principles that concern the law, is not self-applying. It has always been found that some restrictions must necessarily be placed on the search for perfect compensation. The law of damages constantly reveals a tension between, on the one hand, an investigation into precisely what position the plaintiff would have occupied if the wrong had not been done (necessarily a hypothetical inquiry), and, on the other hand, the adoption of principles that are capable of consistent, fair, and reasonably inexpensive application. Consider the following statement of Dr. Lushington, in a ship collision case, *The "Columbus"* (1849), 3 W Rob. 158, at 162; 166 ER 922, at 923 (HC Admir.).

> [N]ot only in this Court [the High Court of Admiralty] but in all other Courts, I apprehend the general rule of law is, that where an injury is committed by one individual to another ... the party receiving the injury is entitled to an indemnity for the same. But although this is the general principle of law, all Courts have found it necessary to adopt certain rules for the application of it; and it is utterly impossible, in all the various cases that may arise, that the remedy which the law may give should always be the precise amount of the loss or injury sustained. In many cases it will, of necessity, exceed, in others fall short of the precise amount.

The chief limiting principles are uncertainty, remoteness, and mitigation. The plaintiff must establish, on the balance of probabilities, that he or she has suffered a loss, and that the loss has been caused by the defendant's wrong. But if all such losses were to be compensated, defendants would be liable for very unexpected consequences. Willes J in *British Columbia and Vancouver's Island Spar Lumber & Saw-Mill Co. Ltd. v. Nettleship* (1868), LR 3 CP 499, at 508 gave the example of "a case said to have been decided about two centuries and a half ago, where a man going to be married to an heiress, his horse having cast a shoe on the journey, employed a blacksmith to replace it, who did the work so unskillfully that the horse was lamed, and, the rider not arriving in time, the lady married another; and the blacksmith was held liable for the loss of the marriage." Willes J called the imposition of liability an "absurdity," and, since the 19th century, it has been recognized that a limit is necessary, but it has not been found easy to formulate a principle to explain and predict which kinds of losses will be classified as legally too remote, and which will not.

The issues of remoteness and causation are also relevant with respect to the equitable remedy of compensation and further material can be found in chapter 10, "Financial Relief in Equity," where that remedy is addressed specifically. There, consideration is given to the proposition that equitable compensation is not subject in quite the same way to the limitations on recovery resulting from principles of remoteness and causation as apply in the domains of contract and tort damages.

REMOTENESS

H. Parsons (Livestock) Ltd. v. Uttley Ingham & Co. Ltd.
[1978] QB 791 (CA)

[The defendant sold a hopper for storing pig food to the plaintiff for the plaintiff's pigs. In installing the hopper, the defendant failed to open a ventilator, with the result that the pignuts became mouldy and the pigs were affected by the intestinal infection known as "E. coli."]

SCARMAN LJ (at 810-13): … The outbreak of E. coli, which did the damage, was, as found by the judge and now conceded by the defendants, caused by the mouldy condition of the nuts fed from the hopper. It is also conceded, as the judge also found, that the lack of top ventilation in the hopper caused this condition. But it is the defendants' case that at the time of the contract the parties could not have reasonably contemplated that nuts, rendered mouldy by lack of hopper ventilation, would cause serious illness, such as E. coli, in the pigs that fed on them.

A formidable volume of expert evidence upon this point was deployed for the consideration of the judge. His findings as to the contemplatability of E. coli [were] as follows:

> I would not consider that I would be justified in finding that in the spring of 1971 at the time of the contract either a farmer in the position of the plaintiffs or a hopper manufacturer in the position of the defendants would reasonably have contemplated that there was either a very substantial degree of possibility or a real danger or serious possibility that the feeding of mouldy pignuts in the condition described by Mr. Parsons would cause illness in the pigs that ate them, even on an intensive farm such as that of the plaintiffs.

The plaintiffs, by their respondent's notice, challenge this finding. I have done my best to study the evidence as it appears from the detailed and lucid judgment under appeal. I confess that I think I might well have reached a different conclusion, but bearing in mind the inevitable limitations upon an appellate court's consideration of such a question and the great advantages available to the judge, and most assuredly used to the full by him, I think it would be wrong to disturb his finding.

But it is necessary to note the essence—and the limits—of the finding. It is a finding that the parties could not reasonably be supposed to have had in contemplation that there was a serious possibility of mouldy nuts causing illness in the plaintiffs' pigs. It is not a finding that they could not reasonably have had in contemplation that a hopper unfit for its purpose of storing food in a condition suitable for feeding to the pigs might well lead to illness.

The judge's other findings of fact may be summarized as follows. He found that there was a warranty—its existence is not disputed by the defendants—to the effect that the hopper should be reasonably fit for the purpose of storing pignuts in a condition suitable for feeding to the plaintiffs' pigs. He found that the hopper, being unventilated, was not so fit; and this defect was a breach of the warranty, and that the pignuts were unfit by reason of the breach. He found that the plaintiffs' loss was caused by the breach of warranty. Upon the basis of these findings, the judge held that since the first question is whether "the damage" claimed arises in the ordinary course of things from the breach, "there is no need to have recourse to the question of the presumed contemplation." He then considered the meaning of the implied term "pleaded and admitted" that the hopper should be reasonably fit for the purpose of storing pignuts to be fed to the plaintiffs' pigs and reached the conclusion, which I respectfully think was inevitable, that it meant that, in so far as proper storage could achieve it, the hopper would keep the pignuts in a condition such as not to make the plaintiffs' pigs ill. He stressed the importance to be attached to the particular nature of this herd of pigs—a very different set of animals from the ordinary farmyard pig—and to the intensive nature of the plaintiffs' farming operation, all of which matters were made known to the defendants before contract. He stated his conclusion in these words:

> On this interpretation the inevitable conclusion from the findings I have already made would be that this hopper was not reasonably fit for that purpose and that this caused the nuts to become toxic and that the illness of the pigs was a direct and natural consequence of such breach and toxicity, and that the plaintiffs do not have to prove that the toxicity or its results were foreseeable to either party. To put it another way, once the question of foreseeability of the breach is eliminated, as it is by the absolute warranty, the consequences of the breach flow naturally from it.

Mr. Drake criticises strongly this part of the judgment. He says it is based on a misunderstanding of *Hadley v. Baxendale*, 9 Exch. 341; 156 ER 145 and he referred us to the well-known passage in Lord Reid's speech in *C. Czarnikow Ltd. v. Koufos*, [1969] 1 AC 350 (HL (Eng.)) where he said that it is not enough that in fact the plaintiff's loss was directly caused by the defendant's breach of contract. Lord Reid said, at p. 385:

> The crucial question is whether, on the information available to the defendant when the contract was made, he should, or the reasonable man in his position would, have realised that such loss was sufficiently likely to result from the breach of contract to make it proper to hold that the loss flowed naturally from the breach or that loss of that kind should have been within his contemplation.

Notwithstanding his choice of language, I think the judge was making the approach which, according to Lord Reid, is the correct one. He was saying, in effect, that the parties to this contract must have appreciated that, if, as happened in the event, the hopper, unventilated, proved not to be suitable for the storage of pignuts to be fed to the plaintiffs' pigs, it was not unlikely, there was a serious possibility, that the pigs would become ill. The judge put it this way:

> The *natural* result of feeding toxic food to animals is damage to their health and may be death, which is what occurred, albeit from a hitherto unknown disease and to particularly susceptible animals. There was therefore no need to invoke the question of *reasonable* contemplation in order to make the defendant liable (my emphasis).

The judge in this critical passage is contrasting a natural result, i.e. one which people placed as these parties were would consider as a serious possibility, with a special, specific result, i.e. E. coli disease, which, as he later found, the parties could not at the time of contract reasonably have contemplated as a consequence. He distinguished between "presumed contemplation" based on a special knowledge from ordinary understanding based upon general knowledge and concludes that the case falls within the latter category. He does so because he has held that the assumption, or hypothesis, to be made is that the parties had in mind at the time of contract not a breach of warranty limited to the delivery of mouldy nuts but a warranty as to the fitness of the hopper for its purpose. The assumption is of the parties asking themselves not what is likely to happen if the nuts are mouldy but what is likely to happen to the pigs if the hopper is unfit for storing nuts suitable to be fed to them. While, on his finding, nobody at the time of contract could have expected E. coli to ensue from eating mouldy nuts, he is clearly—and, as a matter of common sense, rightly—saying that people would contemplate, upon the second assumption, the serious possibility of injury and even death among the pigs.

And so the question becomes: was he right to make the assumption he did? In my judgment, he was: see *Grant v. Australian Knitting Mills Ltd.*, [1936] AC 85 (PC (Aust.)), and particularly the well-known passage in the speech of Lord Wright at pp. 97-100.

I would agree with *McGregor on Damages* (London: Sweet & Maxwell, 13th ed., 1972) at pp. 131-132 that

> … in contract as in tort, it should suffice that, if physical injury or damage is within the contemplation of the parties, recovery is not to be limited because the degree of physical injury or damage could not have been anticipated.

This is so, in my judgment, not because there is, or ought to be, a specific rule of law governing cases of physical injury but because it would be absurd to regulate damages in such cases upon the necessity of supposing the parties had a prophetic foresight as to the exact nature of the injury that does in fact arise. It is enough if upon the hypothesis predicated physical injury must have been a serious possibility. Though in loss of market or loss of profit cases the factual analysis will be very different from cases of physical injury, the same principles, in my judgment, apply. Given the situation of the parties at the time of contract, was the loss of profit, or market, a serious possibility, something that would have been in their minds had they contemplated breach?

It does not matter, in my judgment, if they thought that the chance of physical injury, loss of profit, loss of market, or other loss as the case may be, was slight, or that the odds were against it, provided they contemplated as a serious possibility the type of consequence, not necessarily the specific consequence, that ensued upon breach. Making the assumption as to breach that the judge did, no more than common sense was needed for them to appreciate that food affected by bad storage conditions might well cause illness in the pigs fed upon it.

As I read the judgment under appeal, this was how the judge, whose handling of the issues at trial was such that none save one survives for our consideration, reached this decision. In my judgment, he was right, upon the facts as found, to apply the first rule in *Hadley v. Baxendale* or, if the case be one of breach of warranty, as I think it is, the rule in section 53(2) of the *Sale of Goods Act 1893* without inquiring as to whether, upon a juridical analysis, the rule is based upon a presumed contemplation. At the end of a long and complex dispute the judge allowed common sense to prevail. I would dismiss the appeal.

LORD DENNING MR (at 801-03):

The Law as to Remoteness

Remoteness of damage is beyond doubt a question of law. In *C. Czarnikow Ltd. v. Koufos*, [1969] AC 350 (HL (Eng.)) the House of Lords said that, in remoteness of damage, there is a difference between contract and tort. In the case of a *breach of contract*, the court has to consider whether the consequences were of such a kind that a reasonable man, at the time of making the contract, would *contemplate* them as being of a very substantial degree of probability. (In the House of Lords various expressions were used to describe this degree of probability, such as, not merely "on the cards" because that may be too low: but as being "not unlikely to occur" (see pp. 383 and 388); or "likely to result or at least not unlikely to result" (see p. 406); or "liable to result" (see p. 410); or that there was a "real danger" or "serious possibility" of them occurring (see p. 415).)

In the case of a *tort*, the court has to consider whether the consequences were of such a kind that a reasonable man, at the time of the tort committed, would *foresee* them as being of a much lower degree of probability. (In the House of Lords various expressions were used to describe this, such as, it is sufficient if the consequences are "liable to happen in the most unusual case" (see p. 385) or in a "very improbable" case (see p. 389); or that "they may happen as a result of the breach, however unlikely it may be, unless it can be brushed aside as far-fetched" (see p. 422).)

I find it difficult to apply those principles universally to all cases of contract or to all cases of tort: and to draw a distinction between what a man "contemplates" and what he "foresees." I soon begin to get out of my depth. I cannot swim in this sea of semantic exercises— to say nothing of the different degrees of probability—especially when the cause of action can be laid either in contract or in tort. I am swept under by the conflicting currents. I go back with relief to the distinction drawn in legal theory by Professors Hart and Honore in their book *Causation in the Law* (Oxford: Clarendon Press, 1959), at pp. 281-287. They distinguish between those cases in contract in which a man has suffered no damage to person or property, but only *economic loss*, such as loss of profit or loss of opportunities for gain in some future transaction: and those in which he claims damages for an *injury actually done* to his person or *damage actually done* to his property (including his livestock) or for ensuing expense (*damnum emergens*) to which he has actually been put. In the law of *tort*, there is emerging a distinction between economic loss and physical damage: see *Spartan Steel & Alloys Ltd. v. Martin & Co. (Contractors) Ltd.*, [1973] QB 27 (CA) at pp. 36-37. It underlies the words of Lord Wilberforce in *Anns v. Merton London Borough Council*, [1978] AC 728 (HL (Eng.)) at 759 recently, where he classified the recoverable damage as "material, physical damage." It has been much considered by the Supreme Court of Canada in *Rivtow Marine Ltd. v. Washington Iron Works and Walkem Machinery & Equipment Ltd.*, [1974] SCR 1189 and by the High Court of Australia in *Caltex Oil (Australia) Pty. Ltd. v. Dredge Willemstad* (1976), 136 CLR 529.

Loss of Profit Cases

I would suggest as a solution that in the former class of case—loss of profit cases—the defaulting party is only liable for the consequences if they are such as, at the time of the contract, he ought reasonably to have *contemplated* as a *serious* possibility or real danger. You must assume that, at the time of the contract, he had the very kind of breach in mind—such a breach as afterwards happened, as for instance, delay in transit—and then you must ask: ought he reasonably to have *contemplated* that there was a *serious* possibility that such a breach would involve the plaintiff in loss of profit? If yes, the contractor is liable for the loss unless he has taken care to exempt himself from it by a condition in the contract—as, of course, he is able to do if it was the sort of thing which he could reasonably contemplate. The law on this class of case is now covered by the three leading cases of *Hadley v. Baxendale*; *Victoria Laundry (Windsor) Ltd. v. Newman Industries Ltd.*, [1949] 2 KB 528 (CA); and *C. Czarnikow Ltd. v. Koufos*. These were all "loss of profit" cases: and the test of "reasonable contemplation" and "serious possibility" should, I suggest, be kept to that type of loss or, at any rate, to economic loss.

Physical Damage Case

In the second class of case—the physical injury or expense case—the defaulting party is liable for any loss or expense which he ought reasonably to have *foreseen* at the time of the breach as a possible consequence, even if it was only a *slight* possibility. You must assume that he was aware of his breach, and then you must ask: ought he reasonably to have foreseen, at the time of the breach, that something of this kind might happen in consequence of it? This is the test which has been applied in cases of tort ever since *The Wagon Mound* cases, [1961] AC 388 (PC (NSW)), and [1967] 1 AC 617 (PC (NSW)). But there is a long line of cases which support a like test in cases of contract.

[Orr LJ agreed with Scarman LJ.]

The appeal was dismissed.

Kienzle v. Stringer
(1981), 35 OR (2d) 85 (CA)

ZUBER JA: This is an appeal by the plaintiff from a judgment of Mr. Justice Cromarty [14 RPR 29] awarding the plaintiff the sum of $17,459.48 plus costs on a solicitor-and-client basis.

The sole issue at trial and on this appeal is the quantum of the plaintiff's damages. The defendant Stringer is a solicitor and the plaintiff was his client; from this relationship there flowed the problems that now confront this Court. Even though liability is not an issue, some reference to the facts is necessary to understand the problems raised on this appeal.

The plaintiff's parents Otis and Catherine Kienzle were the owners of a farm in the Town of Norwich in the County of Oxford (the "Oxford farm"). Catherine Kienzle died in 1943, leaving her husband and three children: the plaintiff and his two sisters Annie Ashbaugh and Velma Allin. No steps were taken in the estate of Catherine Kienzle until 1973 when letters of administration were issued to her husband. However, before any further steps were taken, Otis Kienzle died a widower on June 22, 1974. In 1977, letters of administration in the father's estate and letters of administration *de bonis non* in the mother's estate were issued to Annie Ashbaugh.

Shortly before the death of Otis Kienzle, the plaintiff, at his father's request, began working with him on the Oxford farm. He continued to work the farm up until his father's death and thereafter until the time of trial. In 1974 he rented an additional 78 acres of nearby land to work with the Oxford farm to render the operation economical.

In 1977, the plaintiff elected to buy the Oxford farm and offered the sum of $55,000 which was accepted by Mrs. Ashbaugh as administratrix of both estates. The defendant who had acted as the solicitor for both estates also acted as solicitor for the plaintiff. The defendant prepared a deed dated July 12, 1977 conveying the Oxford farm from Annie Ashbaugh as administratrix of both estates to the plaintiff. Mrs. Ashbaugh did not join in the conveyance in her personal capacity. Mrs. Allin did not join in the conveyance at all. In due course, each sister was paid one-third of the $55,000 and the plaintiff also received his one-third share. The defendant certified in the traditional language that the plaintiff had "a good and marketable title."

The title to the Oxford farm was neither good nor marketable. Since three years had expired since the date of Otis Kienzle's death and no appropriate steps had been taken, title to the farm had vested in the three next of kin, the plaintiff and his two sisters. The deed of the administratrix without the concurrence of the two sisters in their personal capacities was of little or no value.

The plaintiff, however (at least for the time being), was unaware of his title problems but encountered others. He found that it was increasingly difficult to operate the Oxford farm on a profitable basis and as a result planned to buy a larger farm. In the spring of 1978 he found such a farm in the Kincardine area (the "Kincardine farm") which he agreed to buy at a price of $119,800. This agreement was conditional upon his being able to sell the Oxford farm. Shortly thereafter he received and accepted an offer to sell the Oxford farm at a price of $76,000. In anticipation of these two sales, the lease for the 78 acres near the Oxford farm was not renewed.

The plaintiff was, of course, unable to convey good title to the Oxford farm. Mrs. Ashbaugh, having received her one-third of the $55,000 was prepared to convey her one-third to the plaintiff. However, Mrs. Allin was not prepared to do so. As a result, the sale of the Oxford farm collapsed. The plaintiff then lacked the funds to complete the purchase of the Kincardine farm and that purchase was lost.

The learned trial judge awarded the plaintiff the amount of money necessary to buy out the Allin interest ($15,509.48), the return of the legal fees paid to the defendant ($1,200) and legal fees paid to another solicitor who attempted to unravel the title problems ($750). The plaintiff claims, however, that he is entitled to much more, namely damages for loss of income when the plaintiff was obliged to remain on the Oxford farm while it was no longer a viable operation without the additional leasehold property and damages for the lost purchase of the Kincardine farm the value of which had risen to $164,000 at the time of trial.

The learned trial judge was of the view that he was bound by the case of *Messineo v. Beale* (1978), 20 OR (2d) 49 (CA), and that his award of damages was therefore limited to the difference between the contract price and the market value of what was received. I take it to be clear as well that the market value spoken of is the market value at the time of the transaction, otherwise rising values would wipe out the plaintiff's damages but leave him with his problems unresolved. On this premise the trial judge calculated the plaintiff's damages to be $15,509.48. In addition, he awarded a certain amount for legal costs already described.

In my respectful view, *Messineo v. Beale* is not authority for such a broad proposition. In *Messineo v. Beale*, the plaintiff agreed to buy several parcels of property, among them a particular piece called Murch's Point. The defendant's solicitor searched the title, closed the transaction and presented to the plaintiff a deed which included Murch's Point. A month later it was discovered that the purchaser had not received title to Murch's Point because the vendor had never owned it. However, the value of the land received exceeded the purchase price. The plaintiff was therefore awarded only nominal damages.

In my respectful opinion, *Messineo v. Beale* decides only that the defendant did not *cause* the plaintiff any damage. Since the vendor did not own Murch's Point, the defendant's solicitor did not cause its loss. The solicitor caused the plaintiff to complete a transaction that he would otherwise have avoided but no loss resulted from this. The plaintiff could have resold as soon as he discovered that he had not obtained Murch's Point and would have suffered no loss at all. It would have been far different if the vendor had owned Murch's Point and the solicitor had omitted the property from the deed or in some other way had caused the plaintiff to lose the property. In that case, the plaintiff's damage would have been the value of the missing property despite the fact that the value of what he had received was greater than the purchase price.

It appears that in many of the cases, as a matter of fact, the damages amount to no more than the difference between the purchase price and the market value of what is received, but I find no case binding on this Court compelling the acceptance of such a measure as a rule of law.

In my view the law should not support a rule which gives exceptional protection to solicitors from the general principles of damages which flow from either contractual or tortious responsibilities.

One problem that intrudes but briefly in this case is whether the liability of the solicitor is based in contract alone or in tort as well. (See again, *Messineo v. Beale*.) However, in this case, the question is of little consequence. Liability is admitted, no limitation period intervenes; the sole question is the question of damages. The extent of recovery for damages from breach of contract is described in the classic words of Baron Alderson in *Hadley v. Baxendale* (1854), 9 Exch. 341 at p. 355, 156 ER 145 at p. 151:

> Where two parties have made a contract which one of them has broken, the damages which the other party ought to receive in respect of such breach of contract should be such as may fairly

and reasonably be considered either arising naturally, i.e., according to the usual course of things, from such breach of contract itself, or such as may reasonably be supposed to have been the contemplation of both parties, at the time they made the contract, as the probable result of the breach of it.

In tort, the measure is reasonable foreseeability. It is, I think, apparent that neither of these tests is a measure of precision and I number myself among those who are unable to see any real difference between them. (See H. *Parsons (Livestock) Ltd. v. Uttley Ingham & Co. Ltd.*, [1978] QB 791 (CA).)

For the purpose of simplicity, I shall use the term "reasonable foreseeability" as embracing the test in both tort and contract. Using this measure, we come to the case at hand. There is no denial that the plaintiff is entitled to the sum of money needed to put the title to the Oxford farm in good order. It was disclosed on this appeal that it actually required $750 more (for her costs) to settle with Mrs. Allin than the sum of $15,509.48 estimated by the trial judge. This item of damages must, therefore, be increased. The plaintiff is, of course, entitled to the other items allowed by the trial judge.

The first substantial item of consequential loss asserted by the appellant flows from the fact that the appellant, relying on the marketability of the Oxford farm, shut down the effective operation of that farm by letting go the surrounding leasehold property. When the sale fell through, the plaintiff was obliged to keep the Oxford farm without being able to do much with it. Even his credit position had been adversely affected by the discovery of the faulty title. His profit from the Oxford farm dropped drastically. The plaintiff, however, was obliged to mitigate his damages and could not simply stay in this position forever. In my view, a reasonable period for him to untangle himself from the web in which he found himself would be a period of one year and for that period his loss of profits should be assessed at $10,000. This loss is directly and immediately connected to the defective title and consequent lack of marketability of the Oxford farm, and would have occurred if the plaintiff had chosen only to sell the Oxford farm without any plan to purchase another farm. I conclude, therefore, that this loss is within the ambit of reasonable foreseeability.

The far more difficult problem that arises is the lost profit on the purchase of the Kincardine farm. Mr. Cherniak asked that the appellant's award be increased to reflect this loss. The contract price of the Kincardine farm was $119,800; by the time of trial it had advanced to $164,000, a difference of $44,200. During this same period, the value of the Oxford farm rose from $76,000 to $100,000. Mr. Cherniak claims on behalf of his client the loss on the Kincardine sale, diminished by the gain on the retention of the Oxford farm, i.e., $20,200.

The question that then arises is whether or not this loss is "reasonably foreseeable" and it becomes apparent that this measure is far from precise.

It may be helpful to recognize that in using the terms "reasonably foreseeable" or "within the reasonable contemplation of the parties" courts are not often concerned with what the parties in fact foresaw or contemplated. (I leave aside those cases where the disclosure of special facts may lead to the conclusion that a party has assumed an extraordinary risk.) The governing term is reasonable and what is reasonably foreseen or reasonably contemplated is a matter to be determined by a court. These terms necessarily include more policy than fact as courts attempt to find some fair measure of compensation to be paid to those who suffer damages by those who cause them. (See Barry J. Reiter & John Swan, *Studies in Con-*

tract Law (Toronto: Butterworths, 1980) at p. 61, study 3, Katherine Swinton, "Foreseeability: Where Should the Award of Contract Damages Cease?")

In the ordinary course, a client relies on his solicitor to guarantee the title that he certifies. The fee charged is calculated upon the sale price of the title certified and arguably the size of the risk assumed. It is not unreasonable to add to that risk consequential damages immediately concerned with the failure of marketability.

This reliance, however, does not or should not extend to the loss of profits from secondary transactions which may be fuelled by funds expected from the marketing of the subject real property. This range of secondary transactions is unpredictable and limitless and so are the losses that may flow therefrom. If the ambit of reasonable foreseeability takes us into this area of secondary transactions it is difficult, if not impossible, to know where a boundary may be found. In my view, the damages that flow from the loss of profits from a secondary bargain lie on the far side of a Rubicon that should not be crossed; reasonable foreseeability takes us only to the shore. I except again those cases in which particular disclosure may lead to the assumption of additional risks. In this case, of course, there was no such disclosure that the Oxford farm was to be the basis of future purchases.

I conclude that the plaintiff should not recover his loss resulting from his inability to purchase the Kincardine farm.

In declining to extend the ambit of the plaintiff's recovery to the Kincardine transaction I have chosen not to rely upon the weakest reason for so doing, *i.e.*, the plaintiff's impecuniosity. That classic argument would say that the plaintiff should have completed the purchase of the Kincardine farm by drawing upon his theoretically limitless funds; the fact that he had no such funds is not the fault of the defendant. But, in this case, the plaintiff's financial problems were in large part caused by his title problems. However, it is not necessary to decide whether impecuniosity alone would have precluded the plaintiff from recovering his Kincardine loss and I say no more about it.

For the foregoing reasons, I would allow in part the plaintiff's appeal and would vary the trial judgment by increasing the amount awarded by $10,750. The appellant is entitled to his costs of this appeal.

Sir Robin Cooke, "Remoteness of Damages and Judicial Discretion"
(1978), 37 *Cambridge Law Journal* 288

The purpose of the law is to ensure, as far as money can, that the plaintiff is in the same position as he would have enjoyed if his rights had not been violated by the defendant. Any damage of which the defendant's tort or breach of contract is a substantial cause is prima facie recoverable. Nevertheless, as between the parties it may be just, on the facts of any given case, to limit the damages by excluding certain heads; and in determining that question in any given case the court should have regard to a range of considerations. The main relevant considerations have already emerged from the case law and are somewhat as follows:

(i) The degree of likelihood that such damage, or damage of broadly the same kind, would be caused by such an act or omission. In all cases this should be considered from the point of view of a reasonable man in the defendant's position immediately before the act or omission in question; but in contract an assessment as at the date of the contract will also be relevant.

(ii) The directness or otherwise of the causation and its potency. Intervening human action comes in under this head.

(iii) The nature of the damage—whether to person, property or purely economic interests.

(iv) The degree of the defendant's culpability: for example, whether his action was deliberate or grossly negligent at the one extreme or in venial breach of a minor but strict contractual duty on the other.

(v) Whether the defendant had a reasonable opportunity of limiting his liability by an agreed term.

. . .

An avowed discretionary approach would not necessarily make the law any more certain, in the sense of making the results of cases more predictable. But perhaps it would do something in that direction by reducing distraction and bringing into a more direct light the kind of considerations which tend to sway decisions. It should have the definite advantage of making it easier for a court to do justice without straining to fit the facts into old or new formulae. And it should also make decisions at first instance rather less vulnerable to challenge. The ordinary principles governing appellate review of discretionary decisions, liberal enough at the present day, would apply. A decision could be set aside if—but only if—it gave no or insufficient weight to relevant considerations or were shown to have resulted in an injustice. Perhaps an appellate judge may be permitted to say that such limitations on the appellate court as are involved in that proposition are not unhealthy.

NOTE

In *Transfield Shipping Inc. v. Mercator Shipping Inc. (The Achilleas)*, [2009] 1 AC 61, the House of Lords held that the charterer of a ship was not liable for the loss, caused by late re-delivery of the ship, of an exceptionally profitable contract made by the owner with another charterer to start after the end of the current charter. Though the loss of such a follow-on contract was readily foreseeable in general terms, it was held by Lords Hoffmann and Hope, with whom Lord Walker agreed, not to be the type of loss for which the charterer could be taken to have assumed responsibility. It is not absolutely clear, however, that this reason commanded the assent of a majority, because Lord Rodger, with whom Lord Walker also agreed, avoided the language of assumption of responsibility and Baroness Hale expressly preferred the approach of Lord Rodger.

CERTAINTY AND CAUSATION

Schrump v. Koot
(1977), 82 DLR (3d) 553 (Ont. CA)

LACOURCIÈRE JA: The interesting and important issue in this case, raised directly for the first time in this Court, is whether "possibilities," as contrasted with "probabilities," of future loss or damage resulting from a present injury are to be taken into account in assessment of a plaintiff's damages.

The defendants appeal from a judgment of Morden J, based on a jury's answer to a question submitted to them respecting the general damages suffered by the female plaintiff, the respondent Mary Schrump. The appellants had admitted liability for a motor vehicle collision which occurred on January 3, 1974. The respondent, a 61-year-old housewife at the time of trial with a life expectancy of 20.5 years, suffered, in addition to less serious injuries, a severe compression fracture of the 5th lumbar vertebra (L 5) compressed to about one-half the normal height.

The course of hospitalization and treatment and the prolonged disability of the respondent are not in dispute at this stage of the litigation. While the experts who gave evidence at trial were in agreement that the respondent suffers from a permanent, persistent backache, they expressed differing prognoses on her future expectations. At the trial the respondent's expert expressed it this way:

> Q. When you saw Mrs. Schrump in January of 1975, at that time what is your prognosis for her future? A. I felt then there was a ninety to ninety-five percent probability that she would have persisting and long-term back problems, and she may, particularly with pain upon excessive activity and damp weather intolerance.
>
> What I am saying, arthritic-type significant back pain.
>
> Q. Yes? A. I also felt that there was a *twenty-five to fifty per cent probability* that she would have significant worsening future problems that may require a discectomy [*sic*] and/or back fusion.

(Emphasis added.)

In contrast, the distinguished orthopaedic surgeon called at trial on behalf of the defendants was of the view that the possibility of future surgery was very remote. In his view there were no objective signs of disc rupture and therefore no likelihood that she could require disc surgery. He also stated that the pain was not sufficient for a spinal fusion and, in any event, he did not consider her a suitable candidate for that operation because she would complain of pain even if a solid fusion were obtained.

In his charge, the learned trial Judge properly instructed the jury on how to deal with the evidence of expert witnesses and with the principles relating to the assessment of damages. He carefully reviewed all the evidence in an extremely fair, accurate and complete manner, and focused on the medical evidence of the two doctors, repeatedly quoting accurately significant parts of their testimony as summarized above, and the cross-examinations thereon.

The appellants' only criticism of the charge is that the learned trial Judge erred in failing to direct the jury to ignore and disregard the possibility of future surgery. Mr. Raphael contends that, since the medical evidence most favourable to the respondent indicated only a possibility and not a probability of surgery in the future, the jury should have been told to exclude it from their consideration. He contended that "damages in a personal injury case are to be assessed upon the basis of the injury suffered as it manifests itself at the date of the trial making due allowance for the probable future developments but excluding such matters as remain in the sphere of possibility," relying on *Corrie v. Gilbert*, [1965] SCR 457 and *Turenne v. Chung* (1962), 36 DLR (2d) 197.

In *Corrie v. Gilbert* the Court had to consider an assessment of damages in a case where a mild permanent disability, pre-existing before the accident became, as a result of the defendant's conduct, a serious permanent disability due to phlebitis. Speaking for the majority in favour of varying the amount of damages, Ritchie J said at p. 461:

> In my opinion the trial judge, having correctly instructed the jury that their verdict was to be based upon "probability," sufficiently illustrated the difference between "probabilities" and possibilities" in relation to the present case and there was no misdirection in this regard. I do not, however, think that there was any evidence in the record to warrant the instruction to the jury that they might consider the serious "possibilities" as a factor contributing to the plaintiff's nervous tension. To so direct the jury was, in my view, having regard to the evidence, to invite speculation.
>
> It is my opinion that the damages in the present case are to be assessed upon the basis of the injury suffered by Mrs. Corrie as it manifested itself at the date of the trial, making due allowance for the probable future developments but excluding such matters as remain in the sphere of possibility, and that upon this basis the verdict of the jury was inordinately high.

The Court reduced the amount of general damages on the basis that no jury acting judicially could have reached the verdict if they had confined themselves to the existing injury and its probable future development.

In *Turenne v. Chung* the Manitoba Court of Appeal held that the trial Judge had erred in principle in considering the mere possibility, rather than the probability, of prospective damage—specifically, the likelihood or otherwise of future degenerative changes due to arthritis consequent upon the injuries sustained in the accident. Miller CJM, at pp. 198-9, stated that:

> Damages should not be awarded on the basis of conjecture or speculation. Loss reasonably to be anticipated is a proper basis upon which to award damages. Is a mere possibility of loss, as distinct from a probability, sufficient? In our view it is not.

The *Turenne* case supports the appellants' proposition, but of course is not binding on this Court. This cannot be said of the *Corrie v. Gilbert* decision, which has been followed in several Canadian cases: see *Davidson v. Melendy* (1965), 54 DLR (2d) 416 (BC CA).

In my respectful view, the passage which I have quoted from *Corrie v. Gilbert* does not stand for the broad proposition advanced by the appellants. The words quoted, "probable future developments," are used in the context of a discussion as to what possibilities should be considered by a jury as a factor contributing to the increase in the plaintiff's nervous tension. The medical evidence referred to in the report is very scant, and this may support the view that the Court was dealing with remote possibilities. To direct the jury that *remote* possibilities of amputation or death from a pulmonary embolism could be considered as a factor in the plaintiff's continuing nervous tension was an invitation to speculate.

In this area of the law relating to the assessment of damages for physical injury, one must appreciate that though it may be necessary for a plaintiff to prove, on the balance of probabilities, that the tortious act or omission was the effective cause of the harm suffered, it is not necessary for him to prove, on the balance of probabilities, that future loss or damage *will* occur, but only that there is a reasonable chance of such loss or damage occurring. The distinction is made clear in the following passages in 12 Hals., 4th ed., pp. 437, 483-4:

> 1137. *Possibilities, probabilities and chances.* Whilst issues of fact relating to liability must be decided on the balance of probability, the law of damages is concerned with evaluating, in terms of money, future possibilities and chances. In assessing damages which depend on the court's view as to what will happen in the future, or would have happened in the future if something had not happened in the past, the court must make an estimate as to what are the chances that a particular thing will happen or would have happened and reflect those chances, *whether they are more or less than even*, in the amount of damages which it awards. …
>
> 1199. *Proof of damage.* … The plaintiff must prove his damage on a balance of probabilities. In many cases, however, the court is called upon to evaluate chances, such as the chance of a plaintiff suffering further loss or damage in the future; in these cases the plaintiff need only establish that he has a *reasonable*, as distinct from a *speculative*, chance of suffering such loss or damage, and the court must then assess the value of that chance.

(Emphasis added.)

The principle concisely stated in the passage quoted is directly applicable in this case. Speculative and fanciful possibilities unsupported by expert or other cogent evidence can be removed from the consideration of the trier of fact and should be ignored, whereas substantial possibilities based on such expert or cogent evidence must be considered in the assessment of damages for personal injuries in civil litigation. This principle applies regardless of the percentage of possibility, as long as it is a substantial one, and regardless of whether the possibility is favourable or unfavourable. Thus, future contingencies which are less than probable are regarded as factors to be considered, provided they are shown to be substantial and not speculative: they may tend to increase or reduce the award in a proper case.

The proper test to be applied is discussed in *Davies v. Taylor*, [1974] AC 207 (HL (Eng.)). This case involved an assessment of damages under fatal accident legislation. It was held that the plaintiff, who had deserted her husband some time before his death, had to prove that there was a significant prospect as opposed to a mere speculative possibility, of a reconciliation with her husband if he had lived. Lord Reid observed at pp. 212-13:

> When the question is whether a certain thing is or is not true—whether a certain event did or did not happen—then the court must decide one way or the other. There is no question of chance or probability. Either it did or it did not happen. But the standard of civil proof is a balance of probabilities. If the evidence shows a balance in favour of it having happened then it is proved that it did in fact happen.
>
> But here we are not and could not be seeking a decision either that the wife would or that she would not have returned to her husband. You can prove that a past event happened, but you cannot prove that a future event will happen and I do not think that the law is so foolish as to

suppose that you can. All that you can do is to evaluate the chance. Sometimes it is virtually 100 per cent.: sometimes virtually nil. But often it is somewhere in between. And if it is somewhere in between I do not see much difference between a probability of 51 per cent. and a probability of 49 per cent.

"Injury" in the *Fatal Accidents Act* does not and could not possibly mean loss of a certainty. It must and can only mean loss of a chance. The chance may be a probability of over 99 per cent. but it is still only a chance. So I can see no merit in adopting here the test used for proving whether a fact did or did not happen. There it must be all or nothing.

If the balance of probability were the proper test what is to happen in the two cases which I have supposed of a 60 per cent. and a 40 per cent. probability. The 40 per cent. case will get nothing but what about the 60 per cent. case. Is it to get a full award on the basis that it has been proved that the wife would have returned to her husband? That would be the logical result. I can see no ground at all for saying that the 40 per cent. case fails altogether but the 60 per cent. case gets 100 per cent. But it would be almost absurd to say that the 40 per cent. case gets nothing while the 60 per cent. case award is scaled down to that proportion of what the award would have been if the spouses had been living together. That would be applying two different rules to the two cases. So I reject the balance of probability test in this case.

The same approach is found in the judgment of the British Columbia Court of Appeal (Davey, CJBC, Bull and Robertson JJA) in *Kovats v. Ogilvie* (1970), 17 DLR (3d) 343, [1971] 1 WWR 561. On this point, the judgment of the Court given by Robertson JA is accurately summarized in the headnote [WWR]:

> In assessing damages for personal injuries the award may cover not only all injuries actually suffered and disabilities proved as of the date of trial, but also the "risk" or "likelihood" of future developments attributable to such injuries. It is not the law that a plaintiff must prove on a balance of probabilities the probability of future damage; he may be compensated if he proves in accordance with the degree of proof required in civil matters that there is a possibility or a danger of some adverse future development.

The Court held that the trial Judge was in error in awarding nothing for the future disability of the plaintiff where the medical evidence had placed the possibility of disabling arthritis at somewhere between 33 and 50%. Robertson JA said at p. 346:

> In my respectful opinion, the learned Judge misdirected himself. It is a fundamental rule that in civil cases questions of fact are to be decided on a balance of probabilities; this is a matter of proof. But it is not equally true that damages in respect of things which have not yet developed may only be awarded if it is probable that they will develop and may not be awarded if it is only possible that they will develop. One can decide on a balance of probabilities that something in the future is a possibility, and in appropriate circumstances that possibility can be taken into account in assessing damages; in such a case it is not essential, before damages can be assessed for the thing, to decide on a balance of probabilities that the thing in future is a probability. When the word "probability" is used in such a context there is an inclination to contrast it with the word "possibility." That can be avoided by using instead the word "risk," or perhaps "danger" or "likelihood." Then one can say, without the danger of being misunderstood, that one can decide on a balance of probabilities that there is a risk of something happening in the future. In an appropriate case such a risk can be taken into account in assessing damages for the wrongful

act or default that caused it. As put by Cartwright J, on behalf of himself and Rand, Kellock and Fauteux JJ, in *Archibald v. Nesting and Dalton*, [1954] 1 DLR 347 at p. 361, [1953] 2 SCR 423:

> … the innocent person who has been gravely injured by the fault of another should not be called upon to bear all the risk of the uncertainties of the future.

The degree of risk, danger or likelihood in each case will, of course, be taken into account in assessing damages as a matter aggravating the injury. When "probability" and "possibility" are used, which term fits the circumstances cannot be decided by any mathematical proposition.

The learned Judge did not interpret the words of Ritchie J, in *Corrie v. Gilbert*, [1965] SCR 457, as deciding anything different from the passage immediately quoted. I entirely agree with this view.

Adverting to the medical evidence in the present case, the plaintiff's expert felt that "there was a 25 to 50% probability" of future surgery. Since the risk is no greater than 50%, the expert's opinion might better be regarded as prognosticating the possibility only of future surgery. But, as in the *Kovats* case, *supra*, the semantic distinction between the words "probability" and "possibility" is not decisive. Rather, it is the "risk, danger or likelihood" of future surgery as established by the evidence which is crucial to the decision. The Court in *Kovats*, *supra*, was free to draw its inferences from the medical evidence, as the case had been tried by a Judge without a jury. Here, in a situation involving a jury award which is attacked as being inordinately high, this Court must assume that the jury drew from the medical evidence inferences favourable to the respondent. In particular, the jury must have concluded that, at the time of trial, there was a real and substantial possibility or risk that the respondent would require a discotomy or fusion.

Mr. Raphael, who was defendants' counsel at trial, placed the argument presented in this appeal before the trial Judge. We have obtained a transcript of the exchange which took place in the absence of the jury. The learned trial Judge was familiar with the case of *Corrie v. Gilbert* and commented upon it as follows:

> Yes, that's right but I do not think when one looks at the general damages issue that is an exhaustive statement of the law and if you were acting for the plaintiff, Mr. Raphael, I do not think you would be inclined to say that. I just do not see how you could then accommodate the well understood fact that has been acted on that someone who by reason of an accident has an increased susceptibility to some kind of illness or future operation is a less well person than before, it is just—it depends on how strong the susceptibility is, does it not?

He concluded, thus:

> Gentlemen, I fear that I may do more harm in trying to lay down a blanket analysis for the jury and I have attempted thus far to explain the burden of proof as accurate[ly] as I can and to deal with the evidence as clearly as I can and I do not propose to recharge the jury on that issue. I fear I may do more harm than good, I don't know to which party.

We do not find error in the learned trial Judge's charge in his decision not to recall the jury. In the general part of his charge, he had explained to the jury that they could draw logical inferences from the evidence, but that this did not mean that they could make findings of fact on mere speculation or conjecture. The possibility of future surgery upon the respondent's back was left fairly and quite properly to the jury. We must assume that the jury considered the possibility as a serious factor aggravating the respondent's permanent disability.

In charging the jury, the presiding Judge will, in a proper case, warn them to exclude from their consideration remote, fanciful or speculative possibilities. He will leave for their consideration any real and substantial risk, with the higher degree or the greater chance or risk of a future development attracting a higher award. In the present case, the risk of future surgery was substantial and supported by medical evidence. It follows that the award of $20,000 was not an inordinately high one, and therefore did not represent a wholly erroneous assessment of the respondent's general damages. I would dismiss the appeal.

In his statement and argument, respondents' counsel failed to refer to any case law or to develop any argument based on general principle, and the Court was left without any help in meeting the strong argument put forward on behalf of the appellants. In the exercise of my discretion, I would not allow the respondents any costs of the appeal.

Farrell v. Snell
[1990] 2 SCR 311

SOPINKA J: The issue of law in this case is whether the plaintiff in a malpractice suit must prove causation in accordance with traditional principles or whether recent developments in the law justify a finding of liability on the basis of some less onerous standard. The practical effect of a determination of this issue will be whether the appellant was liable for the loss by the respondent of the vision in her right eye.

Facts

The respondent, age 70 at the time of trial, consulted the appellant with respect to problems with her vision. The appellant is a medical doctor specializing in the field of ophthalmology. The respondent was "legally blind" in her right eye. She was advised that she had a cataract which should be surgically removed. After the appellant had explained the operation and the risks involved, the respondent consented. The accepted procedure for elderly patients consisted of local anaesthetization, to avoid risks associated with general anaesthetic, followed by removal of the cataract and implantation of a prosthetic lens into the anterior chamber of the eye behind the cornea.

The procedure is first to anaesthetize the eyelid to prevent blinking. Then a needle is inserted underneath the eyeball to inject anaesthetic into the retrobulbar muscles behind the eyeball to prevent movement and pain. These muscles control eye movement and surround the optic nerve. One complication, which occurs in 1% to 3% of cases, is haemorrhage in the retrobulbar area caused by inserting the needle. There is no treatment for such haemorrhage but to let it be reabsorbed naturally. A common result of such haemorrhage is pressure behind the eyeball, which can cause the contents of the eye to be expelled when an incision is made in the cornea during the procedure to remove the cataract. Both experts testifying at trial stated that if retrobulbar haemorrhage occurs, the operation should not be continued. They also testified that an incision into the eye would remove the tamponade effect created by an intact eyeball, allowing a retrobulbar haemorrhage to flow more freely.

The classic symptoms of retrobulbar haemorrhage are redness of the eyelids where they touch the eyeball, and hardness of the eye. After injecting the anaesthetic into the retrobulbar area of the eye, Doctor Farrell noticed a small discoloration, one to two centimeters in diameter, at the puncture site below the eye on the surface of the skin. On discovery he stated that this was a very small retrobulbar bleed. He palpated the eye, finding that it was not hard, and there were no other signs of retrobulbar haemorrhage. After waiting 30 minutes he proceeded with the surgery. The operation went normally. The trial judge accepted Mrs. Snell's evidence that Dr. Farrell told another doctor assisting him that he would have to hurry the operation.

Following the surgery Mrs. Snell developed excruciating pain and was given pain killers. That evening Dr. Farrell removed the patch on Mrs. Snell's eye, finding more blood than at the time of surgery. A retrobulbar bleed had obviously occurred. Dr. Farrell found there to be pressure on the eye, although it was not too great and he did not accurately measure it until a month later. There was blood in the anterior chamber, which cleared rapidly, and blood in the vitreous chamber, which took some nine months to clear. When the vitreous chamber cleared Dr. Farrell was able to see for the first time that the optic nerve had atrophied, resulting in the loss of sight in Mrs. Snell's right eye.

Atrophy results from a loss of the optic nerve's blood supply. One possible cause is pressure due to retrobulbar haemorrhage. The plaintiff's expert, Dr. Samis, examined Mrs. Snell in 1985 (about 17 months after the operation) finding new blood vessel formation in the iris, which indicated that she had suffered a stroke in the back of the eye at some point. He could not identify what caused the stroke. He testified that a major cause of optic nerve atrophy is a stroke in the eye itself, which is most likely in a patient with cardiovascular disease, high blood pressure or diabetes. Mrs. Snell suffered from the latter two conditions, although only to the extent that they were controlled by diet rather than medication. Mrs. Snell also suffered from severe glaucoma, which over a long period can also cause optic nerve atrophy. The plaintiff's expert testified that it was unusual to have chronic glaucoma in just one eye, like Mrs. Snell, unless there has been an intervention of some type. The only intervention of which the expert was aware was the operation itself.

Neither expert was able to express with certainty an opinion as to what caused the atrophy in this case or when it occurred.

The respondent succeeded in an action against the appellant in the Court of Queen's Bench of New Brunswick, the trial judge finding that the appellant was liable in negligence: 77 NBR (2d) 222. The appellant's appeal to the Court of Appeal of New Brunswick was dismissed: 84 NBR (2d) 401.

Judgments

Court of Queen's Bench (Turnbull J)

The respondent sued claiming both in negligence and battery. Considering his conclusion with respect to negligence, the trial judge did not make a finding with respect to battery.

The trial judge accepted the appellant's evidence that the respondent did not develop the hardening of the eye ordinarily associated with a retrobulbar bleed. He concluded, however, that the appellant had thought that there was a small retrobulbar bleed and that he would have to work quickly before it exerted pressure on the content of the eye. He remarked that the appellant's decision "went beyond the judgment call" and he accepted the evidence of the expert Dr. Samis that, where there is bleeding other than the obvious pinprick of the needle, the operation should be aborted as it is impossible to determine the location of the bleeding.

Turnbull J was of the opinion that once the appellant had made the decision to proceed with the operation the onus shifted to him under the doctrine of *res ipsa loquitur*. In so concluding, he relied upon the decision of the Supreme Court of Canada in *Finlay v. Auld*, [1975] 1 SCR 338. However, as the defendant could provide an explanation of the occurrence equally consistent with there being no negligence, the plaintiff could not succeed under this doctrine.

Although neither of the expert witnesses called by the parties could say whether the operation had caused the injury, the trial judge was satisfied that the facts of the case at bar brought it "within an emerging branch of the law of causation" whereby the onus to disprove causation shifts to the defendant in certain circumstances. In this regard, he relied on the decision of the House of Lords in *McGhee v. National Coal Board*, [1973] 1 WLR 1 (HL (Sc.)). He concluded that the respondent had *prima facie* proved that the appellant's actions had caused her injury and that the appellant had not satisfied the onus that had shifted to him. Therefore causation, and negligence, was made out.

Court of Appeal (Hoyt JA for the Court)

In the opinion of the Court of Appeal, the evidence supported the trial judge's conclusion that the appellant recognized a small retrobulbar haemorrhage following his administration of the anaesthetic. Hoyt JA considered *Wilsher v. Essex Area Health Authority*, [1987] QB 730 (CA), and approved of the analysis of *McGhee, supra*, by Mustill LJ. According to Mustill LJ, if it is established that conduct of a certain kind materially adds to the risk of injury, if the defendant engages in such conduct in breach of a common-law duty, and if the injury is the kind to which the conduct related, then the defendant is taken to have caused the injury even though the existence and extent of the contribution made by the breach cannot be ascertained. The Court of Appeal found that Turnbull J was correct in applying the decision of the House of Lords in *McGhee*. The conduct of the appellant, in not aborting the operation, made it more likely that the respondent, to whom the appellant owed a duty, would lose the sight in her right eye.

The Issues

1. Is the burden of proof of causation in a medical malpractice case on the plaintiff and, if so, how is it satisfied?

2. If the burden of proof of causation is on the plaintiff, did the trial judge infer causation in this case and, if not, ought he to have done so?

Causation: Principles

Both the trial judge and the Court of Appeal relied on *McGhee*, which (subject to its reinterpretation in the House of Lords in *Wilsher* [[1988] AC 1074 (HL (Eng.))]) purports to depart from traditional principles in the law of torts that the plaintiff must prove on a balance of probabilities that, but for the tortious conduct of the defendant, the plaintiff would not have sustained the injury complained of. In view of the fact that *McGhee* has been applied by a number of courts in Canada to reverse the ordinary burden of proof with respect to causation, it is important to examine recent developments in the law relating to causation and to determine whether a departure from well-established principles is necessary for the resolution of this appeal.

The traditional approach to causation has come under attack in a number of cases in which there is concern that due to the complexities of proof, the probable victim of tortious conduct will be deprived of relief. This concern is strongest in circumstances in which, on the basis of some percentage of statistical probability, the plaintiff is the likely victim of the combined tortious conduct of a number of defendants, but cannot prove causation against a specific defendant or defendants on the basis of particularized evidence in accordance with traditional principles. The challenge to the traditional approach has manifested itself in cases dealing with non-traumatic injuries such as man-made diseases resulting from the widespread diffusion of chemical products, including product liability cases in which a product which can cause injury is widely manufactured and marketed by a large number of corporations. The developments in this area are admirably surveyed by Professor John G. Fleming in "Probabilistic Causation in Tort Law" (1989), 68 Can. Bar Rev. 661. Except for the United States, this challenge has had little impact in the common law jurisdictions. Even in the United States, its effect has been sporadic. In the area referred to above, courts in some states have experimented with a theory of probability which requires proof on the basis of probability at less than 51%, and apportionment of liability among defendant manufacturers of the product in question on the basis of market share: see Fleming, *op. cit.*; *Sindell v. Abbott Laboratories*, 607 P2d 924 (Cal. 1980).

Although, to date, these developments have had little impact in other common law countries, it has long been recognized that the allocation of the burden of proof is not immutable. The legal or ultimate burden of proof is determined by the substantive law "upon broad reasons of experience and fairness": J.H. Wigmore, *Evidence in Trials at Common Law*, (Boston: Little, Brown & Co., 4th ed., 1981), s. 2486, at p. 292. In a civil case, the two broad principles are:

1. that the onus is on the party who asserts a proposition, usually the plaintiff;

2. that where the subject-matter of the allegation lies particularly within the knowledge of one party, that party may be required to prove it.

This court has not hesitated to alter the incidence of the ultimate burden of proof when the underlying rationale for its allocation is absent in a particular case: see *National Trust Co. v. Wong Aviation Ltd.*, [1969] SCR 481. This flexibility extends to the issue of causation. In *Cook v. Lewis*, [1951] SCR 830, the plaintiff was struck by a bullet fired from the gun of one of his two companions. The evidence supported the theory that they fired simultaneously in the plaintiff's direction when they knew his location. The plaintiff could not prove which shot struck him and, therefore, on traditional rules, he would fail. The basic premises referred to above did not make good legal sense in this instance. Both defendants were negligent and each asserted that his negligence did not cause the injury. Since the plaintiff could establish that one of them caused the injury, why should not the defendants be required to exculpate themselves by proving their assertions, and failing that, be held equally liable? Applying the reasoning in *Summers v. Tice* (1948), 5 ALR (2d) 91, this court concluded that if it could not be determined which defendant fired the shot which struck the plaintiff, both defendants must be found liable.

Proof of causation in medical malpractice cases is often difficult for the patient. The physician is usually in a better position to know the cause of the injury than the patient. On the basis of the second basic principle referred to above, there is an argument that the burden of proof should be allocated to the defendant. In some jurisdictions, this has occurred to an extent by operation of the principle of *res ipsa loquitur*: *Cross on Evidence* (London: Butterworths, 6th ed., 1985), at p. 138. In Canada, the rule has been generally regarded as a piece of circumstantial evidence which does not shift the burden of proof: see *Interlake Tissue Mills Co. v. Salmon*, [1948] OR 950 (CA); *Cudney v. Clements Motor Sales Ltd.*, [1969] 2 OR 209 (CA); *Kirk v. McLaughlin Coal & Supplies Ltd.*, [1968] 1 OR 311 (CA); *Jackson v. Millar*, [1973] 1 OR 399 (CA). As the rule was properly held not to be applicable in this case and no argument was directed to this issue, I will refrain from commenting further upon it.

This brings me to the *McGhee* case and its influence on subsequent cases, particularly in the medical malpractice field. ...

The question that this court must decide is whether the traditional approach to causation is no longer satisfactory in that plaintiffs in malpractice cases are being deprived of compensation because they cannot prove causation where it in fact exists.

Causation is an expression of the relationship that must be found to exist between the tortious act of the wrongdoer and the injury to the victim in order to justify compensation of the latter out of the pocket of the former. Is the requirement that the plaintiff prove that the defendant's tortious conduct caused or contributed to the plaintiff's injury too onerous? Is some lesser relationship sufficient to justify compensation? I have examined the alternatives arising out of the *McGhee* case. They were that the plaintiff simply prove that the defendant created a risk that the injury which occurred would occur. Or, what amounts to the same thing, that the defendant has the burden of disproving causation. If I were convinced that defendants who have a substantial connection to the injury were escaping liability because plaintiffs cannot prove causation under currently applied principles, I would not hesitate to adopt one of these alternatives. In my opinion, however, properly applied, the principles relating to causation are adequate to the task. Adoption of either of the proposed alternatives would have the effect of compensating plaintiffs where a substantial connection between the injury and the defendant's conduct is absent. Reversing the burden of proof may be justified where two defendants negligently fire in the direction of the plaintiff and then by their tortious conduct destroy the means of proof at his disposal. In such a case it is clear that the injury was not caused by neutral conduct. It is quite a different matter to compensate a plaintiff by reversing the burden of proof for an injury that may very well be due to factors unconnected to the defendant and not the fault of anyone.

The experience in the United States tells us that liberalization of rules for recovery in malpractice suits contributed to the medical malpractice crisis of the 1970s: see Glen O. Robinson, "The Medical Malpractice Crisis of the 1970s: A Retrospective" (1986), 49 Law & Contemp. Probs., 5 at p. 18. Insurance premiums in some states increased up to 500%. Some major commercial insurers withdrew from the market entirely, creating serious problems of availability of insurance: see James R. Posner, "Trends in Medical Malpractice Insurance, 1970-85" (1986), 49 Law & Contemp. Probs., 37 at p. 38.

In Britain, proposals to reverse the burden of proof in malpractice cases which gained momentum by virtue of the *McGhee* case were not adopted. In 1978, the Royal Commission on Civic Liability and Compensation for Personal Injury (Pearson Report, vol. I, London: H.M. Stationery Off., 1978), reported as follows (at p. 285):

> Some witnesses suggested that, if the burden of proof were reversed, the patient's difficulties in obtaining and presenting his evidence would be largely overcome. It was said that doctors were in a better position to prove absence of negligence than patients were to establish liability. At the Council of Europe colloquy, however, although it was agreed that the patient was at a disadvantage when he sought to establish a claim, serious doubts were expressed on the desirability of making a radical change in the burden of proof. We share these doubts. We think that there might well be a large increase in claims, and although many would be groundless, each one would have to be investigated and answered. The result would almost certainly be an increase in defensive medicine.

The *Wilsher* decision in the House of Lords which followed ensured that the common law did not undermine this recommendation.

I am of the opinion that the dissatisfaction with the traditional approach to causation stems to a large extent from its too rigid application by the courts in many cases. Causation need not be determined by scientific precision. It is, as stated by Lord Salmon in *Alphacell Ltd. v. Woodward*, [1972] AC 824 (HL (Eng.)), at p. 847, "… essentially a practical question of fact which can best be answered by ordinary common sense rather than abstract metaphysical theory." Furthermore, as I observed earlier, the allocation of the burden of proof is not immutable. Both the burden and the standard of proof are flexible concepts. In *Blatch v. Archer* (1774), 1 Cowp. 63 at p. 65, 98 ER 969 at p. 970, Lord Mansfield stated: "It is certainly a maxim that all evidence is to be weighed according to the proof which it was in the power of one side to have produced, and in the power of the other to have contradicted."

In many malpractice cases, the facts lie particularly within the knowledge of the defendant. In these circumstances, very little affirmative evidence on the part of the plaintiff will justify the drawing of an inference of causation in the absence of evidence to the contrary. This has been expressed in terms of shifting the burden of proof. …

These references speak of the shifting of the secondary or evidential burden of proof or the burden of adducing evidence. I find it preferable to explain the process without using the term secondary or evidential burden. It is not strictly accurate to speak of the burden shifting to the defendant when what is meant is that evidence adduced by the plaintiff may result in an inference being drawn adverse to the defendant. Whether an inference is or is not drawn is a matter of weighing evidence. The defendant runs the risk of an adverse inference in the absence of evidence to the contrary. This is sometimes referred to as imposing on the defendant a provisional or tactical burden: see Cross, *op. cit.*, at p. 129. In my opinion, this is not a true burden of proof, and use of an additional label to describe what is an ordinary step in the fact-finding process is unwarranted.

The legal or ultimate burden remains with the plaintiff, but in the absence of evidence to the contrary adduced by the defendant, an inference of causation may be drawn, although positive or scientific proof of causation has not been adduced. If some evidence to the contrary is adduced by the defendant, the trial judge is entitled to take account of Lord Mansfield's famous precept. This is, I believe, what Lord Bridge had in mind in *Wilsher* when he referred to a "robust and pragmatic approach to the ... facts" (p. 1090).

It is not, therefore, essential that the medical experts provide a firm opinion supporting the plaintiff's theory of causation. Medical experts ordinarily determine causation in terms of certainties whereas a lesser standard is demanded by the law. As pointed out in D.W. Louisell, 3 *Medical Malpractice* (by Charles Kramer, New York: Matthew Bender, 1977-90), at pp. 25-57, the phrase "in your opinion with a reasonable degree of medical certainty," which is the standard form of question to a medical expert, is often misunderstood. The author explains that:

> Many doctors do not understand the phrase ... as they usually deal in "certainties" that are 100% sure, whereas "reasonable" certainties which the law requires need only be more probably so, *i.e.*, 51%.

In D.M. Harvey, *Medical Malpractice* (Indianapolis: A. Smith, 1973), at p. 169, the learned author states:

> Some courts have assumed an unrealistic posture in requiring that the medical expert state conclusively that a certain act caused a given result. Medical testimony does not lend itself to precise conclusions because medicine is not an exact science.

The respective functions of the trier of fact and the expert witness are distinguished by Justice Brennan of the United States Supreme Court in the following passage in *Sentilles v. Inter-Caribbean Shipping Corp.*, 361 US 107 (1959) at pp. 109-10:

> The jury's power to draw the inference that the aggravation of petitioner's tubercular condition, evident so shortly after the accident, was in fact caused by that accident, was not impaired by the failure of any medical witness to testify that it was in fact the cause. Neither can it be impaired by the lack of medical unanimity as to the respective likelihood of the potential causes of the aggravation, or by the fact that other potential causes of the aggravation existed and were not conclusively negated by the proofs. The matter does not turn on the use of a particular form of words by the physicians in giving their testimony. The members of the jury, not the medical witnesses, were sworn to make a legal determination of the question of causation. They were entitled to take all the circumstances, including the medical testimony, into consideration.

With respect, it was the failure to appreciate this distinction which led Lord Wilberforce in *McGhee* to suggest bridging the evidential gap by reversing the burden of proof. He writes (at p. 7): "... to bridge the evidential gap by inference seems to me something of a fiction, since it was precisely this inference which the medical expert declined to make."

In *Wilsher, supra*, Lord Bridge gave effect to this difference when he explained *McGhee* (at p. 1088):

> ... where the layman is told by the doctors that the longer the brick dust remains on the body, the greater the risk of dermatitis, although the doctors cannot identify the process of causation scientifically, there seems to be nothing irrational in drawing the inference, as a matter of *common sense*, that the consecutive periods when brick dust remained on the body contributed

cumulatively to the causation of the dermatitis. I believe that a process of inferential reasoning on these general lines underlies the decision of the majority in *McGhee's* case.

(Emphasis added.)

The issue, then, in this case is whether the trial judge drew an inference that the appellant's negligence caused or contributed to the respondent's injury, or whether, applying the above principles, he would or ought to have drawn such an inference.

Causation in This Case

The trial judge found that the appellant was negligent in continuing with the operation when retrobulbar bleeding occurred. This finding is not contested and is fully supported by the evidence. An opinion expressed by both the appellant and his assistant, Dr. Quinn, that what occurred was a "lid bleed" was rejected by the trial judge. It was common ground that the respondent's blindness occurred due to atrophy or death of the optic nerve which was occasioned by a stroke. A stroke is the destruction of a blood vessel due to an interruption of the blood supply. There were two possible causes of the stroke, one of which was natural and the other due to continuing the operation. Dr. Regan, the appellant's expert, testified as follows on cross-examination:

> Q. But it's not the only thing. As you indicated earlier in your testimony a retrobulbar hemorrhage can also place pressure on the optic nerve.
> A. Yes.
> Q. And if it becomes aggravated for whatever reason or in whatever fashion it can eventually harm the optic nerve, even cause stroke?
> A. Could.
> Q. Well the stroke could occur due to some systemic disease of the patient as well, couldn't it?
> A. By stroke you're talking about destruction of a vessel?
> Q. Yes.
> A. Yes.
> Q. That could happen either as a result of a retrobulbar bleed which continued or got aggravated, or naturally. It could occur naturally without any traumatic interference.
> A. That's correct.

Earlier in chief, Dr. Regan gave the following answer:

> Q. Is it possible to tell what caused the atrophy of the optic nerve in your opinion?
> A. I would think probably the base cause is the retrobulbar hemorrhage, the fact that there was enough pressure behind the eye at some point that caused all this bleeding, that this may have been sufficient to compromise the blood supply to the optic nerve and result in the optic damage, but I can't tell you this for sure, it's just a … in reading the charts this may well be what it is. Certainly there are people that have retrobulbar hemorrhages who do not have any compromise of the vascular supply and do not end up with nerve damage.

The appellant testified in cross-examination as follows:

Q. Right. But we're on common ground that the most likely cause of blindness in Mrs. Snell's case was an ocular occlusion or an occlusion, a stroke, affecting the blood supply to the optic nerve.

A. Yes.

Q. The most reasonable explanation.

In re-examination he gave the following answer:

Q. The question, doctor, is that there's no evidence, is there, that anything other than the operation, the whole operation, was a factor in causing the stroke which Mrs. Snell suffered. There's no evidence of anything external to the operation that caused that stroke, is there?

A. Well it's partially semantics here but there's a very ... in medical terms there's a very distinct definition or distinction between the operation and the anesthetic so that if you're including the anesthetic in your general term operation, then fine, I can agree, but in particular, there's no evidence that the operation per se, other than the anesthetic, involved or caused a problem with the stroke. There are the other systemic problems that Mrs. Snell has that may possibly have caused the stroke *but there's no indication that they did.*

(Emphasis added.)

The anaesthetic, of course, was the needle which caused the retrobulbar bleeding. The trial judge found that it should have been recognized as such and the operation terminated. If it had, the bleeding would have been stanched. Continuing with the operation permitted the bleeding to continue undetected because the eye was occluded by blood and patched. Palpation of the eye to test for hardness apparently failed to disclose the haemorrhaging. A crucial finding of the trial judge was the following (at pp. 228-9):

Neither Dr. Samis nor Dr. Regan could give an opinion as to what caused the atrophy to the optic nerve. Neither doctor could state when the atrophy occurred since it was some eight months before Dr. Farrell could see the optic nerve because of the blood in the anterior chamber. It was atrophied when he first saw it in August 1984. Neither doctor was able to express an opinion that the operation contributed to the atrophy *except to the extent that the retrobulbar hemorrhage which may have been stanched may have been reopened by the operation.* Perhaps what eventually did happen was going to happen once the injection was completed. The retrobulbar bleeding commenced at that time. It may have been a slow hemorrhage that had not stopped and was not going to stop. *The hemorrhage would have been allowed to flow more freely with the removal of the tamponade effect of opening the cornea.* I cannot go beyond this since neither doctor did and I should not speculate in matters of medical opinion. Both doctors agree that the atrophy resulted from a loss of its own blood supply. *This may have been a result of natural causes although I am not inclined to this view. The operation would assist bleeding while the cornea remained open.*

(Emphasis added.)

It is significant that this finding virtually rules out natural causes, as did the appellant. The trial judge then continued (at p. 241):

Dr. Farrell greatly increased the risk of injury to Mrs. Snell's eye by operating when he knew she had a retrobulbar bleed. *Bleeding in the retrobulbar area was facilitated during the operation.* No one can say what happened or with certainty when it happened, because the bleeding from the cataract removal prohibited the doctors from seeing the optic nerve. I am of the opinion that the defendant was "asking for trouble" by operating when he knew his patient had a retrobulbar bleed and that the increased risk was followed by injury in the same area of risk.

I am of the opinion that the plaintiff has prima facie proved that the defendant's actions caused the plaintiff's injury and that the defendant has not satisfied the onus that shifted to him.

(Emphasis added.)

The finding in the last paragraph can be read as a finding of causation inferred from the circumstances and, in the absence of evidence to the contrary, in satisfaction of the evidential burden cast upon the defendant. Or it could be interpreted as accepting Lord Wilberforce's formulation in *McGhee* which reverses the ultimate burden upon finding that a risk was created and an injury occurred within the area of risk. If the former was intended, I am of the opinion that such an inference was fully warranted on the evidence. On the other hand, if the latter is the interpretation to be placed on that statement, and I am inclined to think that it is, then I am satisfied that had the trial judge applied the principles referred to above he would have drawn an inference of causation between the appellant's negligence and the injury to the respondent.

The appellant was present during the operation and was in a better position to observe what occurred. Furthermore, he was able to interpret from a medical standpoint what he saw. In addition, by continuing the operation which has been found to constitute negligence, he made it impossible for the respondent or anyone else to detect the bleeding which is alleged to have caused the injury. In these circumstances, it was open to the trial judge to draw the inference that the injury was caused by the retrobulbar bleeding. There was no evidence to rebut this inference. The fact that testing the eye for hardness did not disclose bleeding is insufficient for this purpose. If there was any rebutting evidence, it was weak, and it was open to the trial judge to find causation, applying the principles to which I have referred.

I am confident that had the trial judge not stated that "I cannot go beyond this since neither doctor did and I should not speculate," he would have drawn the necessary inference. In stating the above, he failed to appreciate that it is not essential to have a positive medical opinion to support a finding of causation. Furthermore, it is not speculation but the application of common sense to draw such an inference where, as here, the circumstances, other than a positive medical opinion, permit.

While this court does not ordinarily make findings of fact, this course is fully justified in this case. First, I am of the opinion that the trial judge either made the necessary finding or would have but for error of law. Second, it would be a disservice to all to send this case back for a new trial when the evidence is not essentially in conflict. I note that in *Wilsher*, the House of Lords refrained from deciding the case only because the evidence of the experts was seriously in conflict. That is not the case here.

In the result, I would dismiss the appeal with costs.

Laferrière v. Lawson
[1991] 1 SCR 541

GONTHIER J: This case deals with the legal consequences of a doctor's failure to inform his patient of a cancerous condition and, subsequently, to follow up on the patient's health in the appropriate manner. The court is asked to consider whether an action can succeed even where it is not proven that the patient's fate would have been different absent the doctor's fault. In particular, the court must examine the theory of *"perte de chance,"* or loss of chance, and determine whether it should be introduced into the civil law of Quebec in matters of medical responsibility.

I Facts and Proceedings

The respondent, Me Nicole Laferrière, acts in her capacity as testamentary executor of the late Mrs. Mireille Fortier-Dupuis. Mrs. Dupuis began proceedings against the appellant, Dr. Ray Lawson, in November 1975, claiming the sum of $150,000 as damages arising out of the alleged non-fulfilment by Dr. Lawson of his obligations as a medical professional. Mrs. Dupuis died in 1978, before these proceedings had been completed. She was, however, able to testify before her death and did so, at the request of the appellant, on June 21, 1976. Following a judgment of Guerin J on September 23, 1981, Me Laferrière was authorized to continue the suit on behalf of Mrs. Dupuis. A re-amended declaration, dated November 23, 1983 claimed a total of $250,000.

In 1970, Mrs. Dupuis, at that time 48 years of age, became increasingly concerned about the presence of an abnormal nodule or lump in her right breast. She consulted her gynecologist who recommended a mammogram, the results of which proved negative. Apparently, these results did not allay Mrs. Dupuis' anxiety. In March 1971, she read an article about Dr. Ray Lawson in the week-end magazine of a Montreal newspaper. She noted that he was an international authority on the treatment of breast cancer, that he used the most up-to-date equipment for the detection of breast cancer and that his progressive approach to treatment of such cancer avoided any unnecessary removal of breast tissue. Mrs. Dupuis contacted Dr. Lawson at his Westmount Breast Centre and made an appointment for March 10, 1971.

At the Centre, Mrs. Dupuis underwent a number of diagnostic procedures, including mammogram and thermogram. As a result of these tests, Dr. Lawson recommended an excisional biopsy, or surgical removal of the abnormal mass for more accurate diagnosis. Mrs. Dupuis accepted this proposal.

On April 12, 1971, Mrs. Dupuis was admitted to the Royal Victoria Hospital. Two days later, Dr. Lawson performed the surgery, described in the hospital records as "breast biopsy and excision of lump of right breast." The pathology report, dated April 20, 1971, indicated "intraductal carcinoma with infiltrative growth," that is, cancer of the breast.

Mrs. Dupuis was discharged from the hospital on April 15, 1971. She later saw Dr. Lawson at an out-patient clinic and discussed routine matters such as the healing of the scar left after surgery. According to the trial judge's findings, she was not informed that the lump in her breast was cancerous, and she was not advised as to the appropriate post-operative treatments. No long-term follow-up was arranged for her by Dr. Lawson.

From 1971 to 1974, Mrs. Dupuis underwent regular gynecological check-ups and had no cause during that time to worry about her health. In the fall of 1974, her health began to deteriorate and by March 1975, an eyelid disorder (known as the Claude Bernard-Horner syndrome) developed which caused her doctors to suspect that a cancerous condition had taken hold. One of her doctors looked more closely into his patient's history and by obtaining records from the Royal Victoria Hospital discovered the 1971 diagnosis of cancer of the breast. This information was made known to Mrs. Dupuis in April 1975.

Subsequently, Mrs. Dupuis underwent surgery to remove nodules which had newly appeared on the right breast. This intervention revealed systemic metastases or generalized cancer requiring removal of the ovaries. Following surgery, Mrs. Dupuis received various treatments, including chemotherapy. She died on January 27, 1978.

[The action was dismissed at trial on the ground that the plaintiff had suffered no loss in consequence of the defendant's failure to inform the patient. The Quebec Court of Appeal awarded damages for loss of the chance of obtaining proper treatment, and for the distress suffered by the patient on learning the truth. Gonthier J considered the law in several civil law jurisdictions, and concluded:]

By way of summary, I would make the following brief, general observations:

- The rules of civil responsibility require proof of fault, causation and damage.
- Both acts and omissions may amount to fault and both may be analyzed similarly with regard to causation.
- Causation in law is not identical to scientific causation.
- Causation in law must be established on the balance of probabilities, taking into account all the evidence: factual, statistical and that which the judge is entitled to presume.
- In some cases, where a fault presents a clear danger and where such a danger materializes, it may be reasonable to presume a casual link, unless there is a demonstration or indication to the contrary.
- Statistical evidence may be helpful as indicative but is not determinative. In particular, where statistical evidence does not indicate causation on the balance of probabilities, causation in law may none the less exist where evidence in the case supports such a finding.
- Even where statistical and factual evidence do not support a finding of causation on the balance of probabilities with respect to particular damage (*e.g.*, death or sickness), such evidence may still justify a finding of causation with respect to lesser damage (*e.g.*, slightly shorter life, greater pain).
- The evidence must be carefully analyzed to determine the exact nature of the fault or breach of duty and its consequences as well as the particular character of the damage which has been suffered, as experienced by the victim.

- If after consideration of these factors a judge is not satisfied that the fault has, on his or her assessment of the balance of probabilities, caused any real damage, then recovery should be denied.

2. Application to the Facts in This Case

I have reviewed the detailed evidence submitted by the parties and have considered the findings of the trial judge. I agree with the majority of the Court of Appeal that the trial judge focused primarily on the surgical technique employed by the appellant in 1971 rather than on those procedures and treatments which should have been available to the patient had she been appropriately informed and followed up on by her doctor. I cannot, however, endorse the conclusions of the Court of Appeal as to the extent of the damages.

Jacques JA bases his award of $50,000 in damages on the small hope of survival which medical science held out to Mrs. Dupuis had she been informed, followed more closely and consequently treated in a timely and proper fashion. For reasons which I have set out earlier, I do not feel that it is appropriate to focus on the degree of probability of success and to compensate accordingly; it is at least necessary that such a probability, or here, at most, a small possibility, translate into a concrete benefit for the patient which she can be said to have lost as a result of the doctor's fault.

In my view, the evidence amply supports the trial judge's finding that the appellant's fault could not be said to have caused Mrs. Dupuis' death seven years after the first diagnosis of cancer of the breast. Unfortunately, I must agree with the trial judge that all the evidence clearly confirms the stubborn and virulent nature of this disease.

I am less convinced, however, by the judge's implicit findings regarding the pain, anguish and suffering which the appellant's fault allegedly caused to Mrs. Dupuis. I have decided as a matter of law that proper causal analysis requires the judge to examine closely all elements of the damage, and with the greatest respect for the trial judge who was faced with a complex and difficult case, I find it necessary to reconsider his findings in this more narrow respect.

First, I am convinced that Mrs. Dupuis experienced a type of psychological suffering which was directly related to the appellant's failure to inform his patient of her condition. From 1975 until her death, she experienced the horrible rhythms of her disease and the regular and seemingly ineffectual treatments and medications in the knowledge that things might have been different had she known earlier and been treated earlier. Her chances may not have been sufficient for the law, but they were very real to her, no doubt. I think that it was also probable that the pain which she experienced as a result of the advancing disease was all the more distressing given that knowledge. While she was a person who was concerned with her health and prepared to seek the best medical evidence and abide by it, she was denied the opportunity and choice of doing so by reason of the appellant's failure to inform her. This led, for instance, to her continued use of contraception pills which she would have been advised against had her condition been known. I would therefore agree with Vallerand JA's specific recognition of psychological damages, and, given the exceptional nature of this case, I would increase the amount in question to $10,000.

Furthermore, I am of the view that while the death caused by cancer was not caused by the appellant's failure to follow up on his patient, it is probable that Mrs. Dupuis was denied the benefit of earlier treatment which would have translated into some real improvement in her admittedly terminal condition. I note, for example, that expert witnesses for both parties stated that proper and timely treatment would probably have provided for the patient a better quality of life even in the face of such a malignant condition.

Dr. Jacques Cantin, expert witness for the respondent, stated the following in the course of his testimony (translation):

> There is a second aspect to patient follow-up, namely the notion of quality of life.
>
> Certainly, patients have been followed very regularly and die all the same, but if they are properly followed, and recurrences are detected early, the patient may have a better quality of life. I will explain.
>
> If, for example, you have a patient whose first recurrence of the disease is one or two pulmonary metastases, if the problem is taken at the start, when there are two or three small images on the lung, it is an easier problem for us to handle, the situation is not as serious for the patient as if, for example, the patient comes to us with water in her lungs: her quality of life will not be the same. We will prevent her having a lot of problems.
>
> If, for example, this patient—I suggest it is possible that if we catch it when she only has these small local recurrences, well, the problems that she has are fewer than theoretically if we wait until she has an invasion of the cervical plexus with a Claude Bernard Horner, and the other dimension that I would like to pass on to the judge, it is not true that this will necessarily cure more people, but in any case often the quality of patients' lives at the time they suffer recurrences can be better.

Dr. Roger Poisson, one of the appellant's expert witness, was even more confident on this score (translation):

> ... [Patients] live for several years in a more comfortable way than in the past, without the rate of survival being necessarily improved that much. I think it is mainly ... the quality of life which is improved. ...
>
> Now, to answer the judge ... it has to be admitted that survival rates in breast cancer ... have unfortunately not improved very much ... and, you know, it is ironic because despite the advance in surgery, radiotherapy and so on ... survival rates unfortunately remain too stable. On the other hand, quality of life has I think improved a great deal.

The improvement in the quality of life may not have been great, but I believe that deprivation of such a real and probable improvement should be recognized and compensated. I believe that $7,500 would be appropriate for the damage represented by the diminished quality of life which Mrs. Dupuis experienced as a result of the appellant's fault.

V Disposition

I would allow the appeal in part and order the appellant to pay respondent $17,500 with interest and the additional indemnity pursuant to art. 1078.1 *CL* beginning April 1, 1983, and with costs throughout.

[La Forest J dissented, adopting the view of the Quebec Court of Appeal.]

NOTE

In *Cottrelle v. Gerrard* (2003), 67 OR (3d) 737, the Ontario Court of Appeal reached a similar conclusion in respect of Ontario law. In *Gregg v. Scott*, [2005] UKHL 2, a medical negligence case where the adverse effect had not materialized at the time of the judgment, the House of Lords, by a 3-2 majority, denied recovery for loss of chance.

In *Hanke v. Resurfice Corp.*, [2007] 1 SCR 333, the Supreme Court of Canada reasserted the "but for" test as the primary test of causation.

Sunrise Co. Ltd. v. The "Lake Winnipeg"
[1991] 1 SCR 3

L'HEUREUX-DUBÉ J: On June 7, 1980, the "Kalliopi L," while downbound on the St. Law-rence River, met but did not collide with, the upbound "Lake Winnipeg." Immediately after the meeting, the "Kalliopi L" went aground. The trial judge found that the "Lake Winnipeg" and her owners were entirely responsible for this grounding. In proceeding to an anchorage area, the "Kalliopi L" again, though through no fault of the "Lake Winnipeg," went aground and suffered further damage. The second incident was unrelated to the first. Each grounding alone would have required the "Kalliopi L" to proceed immediately to dry dock for repairs once her cargo had been discharged. The time in dry dock necessitated by damage repairs occasioned by both incidents was 27 days. The detention in dry dock for repairs from the first incident alone would have required the full 27 days. If, however, repairs relating to the second incident were carried out separately, only 14 days in dry dock would have been necessary.

Liability for the cost of repairs is not an issue in the principal appeal as each party as-sumed responsibility for these costs. The loss in dispute is that resulting from the detention of the ship. Accordingly, the sole issue raised by the principal appeal is who is responsible for the loss of profit resulting from the detention for 27 days of the "Kalliopi L." ...

[Discussion followed of *The Haversham Grange*, [1905] P 307, and of *Carslogie Steamship Co. v. Royal Norwegian Government*, [1952] AC 292 (HL (Eng.)).]

I will briefly comment on the comparison of loss of profit cases in the shipping area with personal injury cases. While, as my colleague McLachlin J points out at p. 28, *post*, of her reasons, the general principles may be the same, their application is of necessity different. Inherent differences in the nature of the injuries sustained militate against any meaningful comparisons between the two areas. The problems that may arise upon such an attempt can be seen in the difficulties experienced by the court in the personal injuries case referred to by McLachlin J in *Baker v. Willoughby*, [1970] AC 467 (HL (Eng.)).

Another example in the case law of an attempted comparison can be found in *Stene v. Evans* (1958), 14 DLR (2d) 73 (Alta. CA). At trial, *The "Carslogie"* was held to be inapplic-able. On appeal, McBride JA implicitly warned against such comparisons. At p. 77 he spoke of his inability to find any meaningful similarities in the shipping cases:

> I find it difficult to see any similarity or parallel between a seaworthy motor vessel damaged but still requiring further repairs because of original collision damage, then later and further se-

verely damaged in mid-Atlantic, and the plaintiff Stene's position after the doctors had done all they could for him with respect to the first accident and he had made his maximum recovery and had started to learn accountancy.

It seems to me that a more meaningful use of the principles in the shipping cases occurs in *Performance Cars Ltd. v. Abraham*, [1962] 1 QB 33 (CA), in that, as in the shipping cases, the issue revolved around property damage. In this case, a car was involved in two collisions. The damage done was slight although the first collision necessitated the respraying of the whole lower part of the car. As the plaintiff was unable to recover the amount needed for respraying from the first tortfeasor, he reasoned that, as the damage caused by the second tortfeasor would have independently required respraying, he would look to the second tortfeasor for recovery of this cost. Lord Evershed MR in coming to a conclusion, relied partly on the reasoning in *The "Carslogie"* and *The "Haversham Grange."* At p. 40, he concluded:

> In my judgment in the present case the defendant should be taken to have injured a motor-car that was already in certain respects (that is, in respect of the need for respraying) injured; *with the result that to the extent of that need or injury the damage claimed did not flow from the defendant's wrongdoing.*

(Emphasis added.) While in the case before us liability for the cost of repairs is not in issue, I have referred to this case to illustrate what is, in my opinion, a more appropriate context for meaningful use to be made of those principles laid down in the shipping cases. The conclusion reached by Lord Evershed MR is also helpful in the search for a principled conclusion in the case presently before us. ...

It is not sufficient in this case merely to determine that the damage caused by the second incident was a cause of the detention. Notwithstanding an affirmative answer to this question, one must, on the principles set out above, answer the further and more important question of liability for loss of profit. While the second incident caused time in dry dock it did not have as a consequence any loss of profit. This conclusion is necessitated both on principle and on the clear reasons on this point offered by the House of Lords. The profit-making enterprise was brought to a halt by the meeting with the "Lake Winnipeg." Repairs due to the second incident were completed within the 27 days' detention required by the first incident. The second incident did not, therefore, have as a consequence a diminution in profit-earning. Thus, this further question in the determination of liability must be answered in the negative.

As was made clear above, the nature of the second casualty, be it tortious or otherwise, is irrelevant in this determination. It does not seem useful then, in focusing on the nature of the second incident, to characterize this case as a *"Carslogie"*-type case as does my colleague McLachlin J, at p. 31, *post*, of her reasons: *"Carslogie* ... unlike *The 'Haversham Grange'* but like the case at bar, was a case where the intervening event was not the act of another tortfeasor." Such a characterization has little place in what is, in my respectful opinion, the proper analytical framework. At p. 31 of his factum the appellant states:

> ... [I]f the first casualty directly prevented the vessel from continuing her profit-making venture and the length of the period of repairs arising from the first casualty exceeded that of any repairs resulting from any other cause, such as a second incident, then the detention and dry

docking expenses fall upon the party responsible for the first accident, whether the second accident was caused by the fault of the ship owner, the fault of a third party or the fault of no one, such as heavy weather.

In my opinion, the appellant has, on the facts of this case, asserted a correct proposition of law, one that commends itself to me both on the cases and on principle. On my interpretation of the case law in reaching a result in this case, there is no need to "conjure up explanations aimed at reconciling the disparate results in *The 'Haversham Grange'* and *The 'Carslogie.'* " When one adopts the view I take of the cases, in my opinion, the result is clear.

In summary, there is no causal link between the second incident and the loss of profit suffered by the owners of the "Kalliopi L," such damage being merely coincidental. The "Lake Winnipeg" must, as a consequence, bear the responsibility for the full 27 days' detention in dry dock.

For the foregoing reasons, I would dismiss the cross-appeal with costs, set aside the judgment of the Court of Appeal as regards the principal appeal and restore the findings of the trial judge, the whole with costs both in the Court of Appeal and in this court.

[McLachlin and Gonthier JJ dissented, favouring apportionment of responsibility for the 14 days in issue.]

MITIGATION

Introduction

Mitigation is used in several senses in the law of damages. Its principal meaning is to refer to conduct of the plaintiff that might have diminished the loss complained of, or to events that have in fact diminished the loss.

Provocation in Intentional Torts

Landry v. Patterson
(1978), 22 OR (2d) 335 (CA)

MACKINNON ACJO: The appellant appeals a judgment of His Honour Judge Coo whereby the learned trial Judge awarded to the respondent damages in the amount of $3,178.06 for an assault committed on the respondent by the appellant. The main ground of appeal argued was that the provocation was so great that the assault under the circumstances was justified and was not excessive.

The trial Judge, in his careful and thorough reasons for judgment, although sympathetic to the appellant's position, concluded on this particular point as follows:

The law is entirely clear that a person in a position such as that in which the defendant found himself is not obliged to measure to a nicety just precisely how he ought to respond, and I have no doubt at all that a Court ought to take a broad, generous and even sympathetic view of the difficulties with which the defendant was confronted.

Also it must be borne in mind that the fact of the nature of the injury indeed suffered by the plaintiff, standing entirely alone, cannot and should not be [the] determinative factor.

Against the background of all that, I have come to the conclusion that the conduct of the defendant in responding to the plaintiff's activities as I have found he did represented on the part of the defendant an unreasonable and excessive use of force in the circumstances. I must say that this conclusion has for me not been one arrived at easily or without very major concern, for reasons which I trust are entirely obvious from the foregoing recital of the facts as I find them.

We are not persuaded that, on the facts as found by him, the learned trial Judge erred in his conclusion that there had been an unreasonable and excessive use of force on the part of the respondent and, accordingly, this argument must fall.

Counsel for the appellant put a further submission to the court which we had difficulty in appreciating. He pointed out that the judgment of this Court in *Shaw v. Gorter* (1977), 16 OR (2d) 19 (CA) was not released until after the completion of the trial in the instant case. In that case the Court held that provocation could only be argued and used in mitigation of punitive damages and not of general damages. Counsel submitted that if the learned trial Judge had given his judgment immediately rather than reserving the matter, he would not have felt bound by *Shaw v. Gorter* (because it had not as yet been decided) and he would have reduced the respondent's general damages by 50% due to, as it was put by the trial Judge, "the enormous provocation offered by the plaintiff [respondent]." As I said, we have some difficulty in appreciating the force of this submission but we were assured by counsel for the appellant that he was not seeking to distinguish *Shaw v. Gorter* nor to argue that it had been given *per incuriam* nor that it was in error. We pointed out to counsel during the course of the argument that if he agreed that *Shaw v. Gorter* was binding authority on the trial Judge, then it was the law which he had to apply, regardless of when it came to his attention, and there is no merit in the submission made.

We note that the judgment in *Lane v. Holloway*, [1968] 1 QB 379 (CA), relied upon by this Court in *Shaw v. Gorter*, has since been "distinguished" by the English Court of Appeal in *Murphy v. Culhane*, [1977] QB 94 (CA). This later judgment so distinguishes *Lane v. Holloway* as to make it virtually meaningless as a precedent for the principle it appeared to stand for. Arnup JA, speaking for the Court in *Shaw v. Gorter*, said the following (pp. 20-1):

Provocation as a factor reducing the damages was discussed in *Griggs v. Southside Hotel Ltd.*, [1947] OR 674 (HC and aff'd. CA), a judgment of Mr. Justice LeBel at trial, and in *Hartlen v. Chaddock* (1957), 11 DLR (2d) 705, a judgment at trail of Chief Justice Ilsley in Nova Scotia, but the distinction now made here was not discussed. The point had been discussed in New Zealand in *Green v. Costello*, [1961] NZLR 1010, where it was held provocation operated in mitigation of both punitive and general damages, and by the High Court of Australia in *Fontin v. Katapodis* (1962), 108 CLR 177, where it was held provocation operated only in relation to the punitive damages.

In 1967 the matter came up squarely for decision by the English Court of Appeal in *Lane v. Holloway*, [1968] 1 QB 379 (CA). In that case it was unanimously held that the Australian case was to be followed in preference to the New Zealand and Canadian cases, and that provocation was to be taken into account, in assessing damages, only in mitigation, reduction or extinction of punitive damages and not in reduction of what Lord Denning called "the real damages."

Both counsel before us agreed that the judgment in *Lane v. Holloway* is reasonable and ought to be adopted by this Court. We accept the proposition as laid down by the English Court of Appeal. We are therefore left with a case in which a trial Judge who suffered in this respect from the lack of assistance of counsel, has charged the jury in a way which left it open to the jury to conclude that they were entitled to treat provocation as a factor which could reduce not only the punitive damages, but also the general damages. We do not know, and could only speculate, as to the result which might have been reached by a jury properly charged with respect to this unusual and narrow distinction.

The English Court of Appeal came back to the problem in *Murphy v. Culhane*. In that case the defendant had been convicted of the manslaughter of the plaintiff's husband. The plaintiff subsequently sued the defendant claiming that the defendant had unlawfully assaulted and killed her husband and claimed damages under the *Fatal Accidents Acts*. The defendant admitted his plea of guilty to manslaughter but alleged that the assault had occurred during a criminal affray which the plaintiff's husband had initiated with others for the purpose of assaulting the defendant. He raised as his grounds of defence *ex turpi causa non oritur actio* and *volenti non fit injuria*. He also pleaded contributory negligence. The plaintiff succeeded in having judgment as to liability entered against the defendant on the basis of the admissions contained in the defence. The defendant appealed to the Court of Appeal. In distinguishing the cases of *Fontin v. Katapodis* (1962), 108 CLR 177, and *Lane v. Holloway*, Lord Denning MR (who was a member of the Court which had decided *Lane v. Holloway*), said (p. 535):

> ... those were cases where the conduct of the injured man was trivial—and the conduct of the defendant was savage—entirely out of proportion to the occasion. So much so that the defendant could fairly be regarded as solely responsible for the damage done. I do not think they can or should be applied where the injured man, by his own conduct, can fairly be regarded as partly responsible for the damage he suffered. So far as general principle is concerned, I would like to repeat what I said in the later case of *Gray v. Barr*, [1971] 2 QB 554 (CA) at p. 569:
>
> > In an action for assault, in awarding damages, the judge or jury can take into account, not only circumstances which go to aggravate damages, but also those which go to mitigate them.
>
> That is the principle I prefer rather than the earlier cases.

As I read *Fontin v. Katapodis*, and indeed Lord Denning's own reasons for judgment in *Lane v. Holloway*, there does not appear to be any suggestion that the unavailability of provocation in mitigation of general damages is limited to cases where the conduct of the plaintiff was "trivial." The High Court of Australia in *Fontin v. Katapodis*, dealt with the issue as a matter of principle and came to the conclusion that once the tort was established then the plaintiff was entitled to receive compensatory damages for the injuries done to him. However, if the jury or Judge were inclined to punish the defendant by way of punitive damages for his acts then, in mitigation of those damages, provocation could be raised.

In *Lane v. Holoway*, Lord Denning said the following in applying *Fontin v. Katapodis* (p. 387):

I think that the Australian High Court should be our guide. The defendant has done a civil
wrong and should pay compensation for the physical damage done by it. Provocation by the
plaintiff can properly be used to take away any element of aggravation. But not to reduce the
real damages.

Salmon LJ, in the same case, agreed (p. 392):

> There are many cases from the Commonwealth Law Reports in which the question has been
> considered as to whether or not the fact that the plaintiff behaved badly can diminish damages
> which are awarded as compensation for physical injury. Some of these decisions are conflicting.
> For my part I entirely accept what was said in the High Court of Australia in *Fontin v. Katapo-
> dis*. It was an exceptionally strong court consisting of Sir Owen Dixon CJ, McTiernan and
> Owen JJ. The case seems to me, for all practical purposes, indistinguishable from the present
> and it states in the plainest terms what, as I have already said, I should have been prepared to
> hold without any authority, namely, that on principle, when considering what damages a plain-
> tiff is entitled to as compensation for physical injury, the fact that the plaintiff may have be-
> haved badly is irrelevant. I think it is important to remember this. Some of the older English
> authorities and some of the Commonwealth cases appear to fall into the error, which until re-
> cently had by no means been eliminated, of thinking that damages for tort were partly to pun-
> ish the defendant.

In *Fontin*, Owen J stated the principle, without the gloss now put on it by *Murphy v.
Culhane, supra*, in these words (p. 187):

> In an action for assault, as in many other cases of tort, the conduct and motives of the parties
> may be taken into account either to aggravate or mitigate damages. In a proper case the dam-
> ages recoverable are not limited to compensation for the loss sustained but may include exem-
> plary or punitive damages as, for example, where the defendant has acted in a high-handed
> fashion or with malice. But the rule by which the defendant in an action in which exemplary
> damages are recoverable is entitled to show that the plaintiff's own conduct was responsible for
> the commission of the tortious act and to use this fact to mitigate damages has no application
> to damages awarded by way of compensation. It operates only to prevent the award of exem-
> plary damages or to reduce the amount of such damages which, but for the provocation, would
> have been awarded.

It appears that the English Court of Appeal has now so limited the effect of *Lane v. Holloway, supra*, as to, for most intents and purposes, reverse it. The question that immediately
arises is what is the effect on *Shaw v. Gorter* of that severe limitation on the principle enunciated in *Lane v. Holloway*?: see *Re Maskewycz and Maskewycz* (1973), 2 OR (2d) 713 (CA).
The answer to that question appears to me to be that *Lane v. Holloway* has not been overruled, nor indeed has *Fontin v. Katapodis*, whose reasoning was also relied on by this Court,
and *Shaw v. Gorter* stands as an authority binding on us.

In *Check v. Andrews Hotel Co. Ltd.* (1974), 56 DLR (3d) 364 (Man. CA), Matas JA, speaking for himself and Freedman CJM, in a thorough and helpful review of the authorities in
this field, emphasized the logic of the principle accepted by this Court and enunciated in
Fontin v. Katapodis, and *Lane v. Holloway*. The dissenting reasons for judgment of Hall JA,
in *Check v. Andrews Hotel Co. Ltd.*, give the other side of the coin and state the logic of the

position now adopted by the English Court of Appeal in *Murphy v. Culhane*. As noted by Hall JA, other jurisdictions in this country and some earlier authorities in the Province have held that provocation which occurs at the time or shortly before the assault, and which causes the defendant to lose his self-control, can be considered in mitigation of the general damages. There is much to be said for the argument that, if the injured party in large part brought the injuries upon himself by his provocative behaviour, then that behaviour should be considered when general damages are being assessed.

As I said earlier, counsel did not speak to distinguish *Shaw v. Gorter*, *supra*, and we are bound by that decision which is in line with most modern authorities. It may be that the time has come for the Court of final resort in this country to resolve the issue so that there will be unanimity in the way in which the Courts of the various Provinces deal with this problem.

The appeal is dismissed, but under all the circumstances without costs.

NOTE

In *Hurley v. Moore* (1993), 107 DLR (4th) 664 (Nfld. CA) and in *Bruce v. Coliseum Management Ltd.* (1998), 165 DLR (4th) 473 (BC CA), damages were reduced on account of provocation.

Valuation of Chance of Avoiding Loss

Janiak v. Ippolito
[1985] 1 SCR 146

WILSON J: The central issue in this case is how damages for personal injury are to be assessed where the victim of the accident unreasonably refuses to undergo the recommended surgery.

1. The Facts

On March 31, 1976, the respondent sustained serious back injuries when his automobile was struck from behind by a vehicle driven by the appellant. Prior to that date the respondent had been employed for 11 years as a crane operator. Since the accident he has been disabled to such an extent that it has been impossible for him to return to work. Liability for negligent driving was admitted by the appellant and the trial was confined to the issue of damages.

The respondent's main injury, according to the medical evidence presented at trial, consisted of a disc protrusion of the cervical spine. Several medical experts testified to the effect that the recommended course of treatment for such an injury would be the surgical excision of the disc together with a spinal fusion. The trial judge accepted the evidence that this type of operation entails an approximately 70% chance of success and that, if successful, could result in an almost 100% recovery for the respondent who could thereafter return to work as a crane operator. The respondent, however, appears to have suffered from a great fear of surgery of any kind and insisted on assurance of a 100% chance of success before consenting to undergo the recommended procedure. As neither his family physician nor his orthopaedic surgeon was able to provide such an absolute guarantee for this or any other type of surgery, the respondent refused to heed the medical advice. Accordingly, his back injuries have not improved and he continues to be disabled and out of work.

2. The Courts Below

At trial, Callaghan J found that the respondent (plaintiff in the original action) had acted unreasonably in refusing to undergo the recommended surgery. Having made this finding he went on to state that any individual claiming damages for personal injuries has "a duty to mitigate his loss by obtaining proper medical treatment" and that he is not entitled to damages in respect of "any pain, suffering, loss of amenities, or loss of earnings consequent upon an unreasonable refusal to undergo medical treatment or surgical operation." Taking into account the estimated period of convalescence from a spinal fusion operation, Mr. Justice Callaghan found that, had the respondent acted reasonably, he would have been able to return to work by the end of March 1978. Accordingly, he found the appellant responsible for the respondent's loss of income for the two years between the date of the accident and March 31, 1978, which loss amounted to a total of $33,000. In addition, he assessed general damages for pain and suffering in sustaining the injuries at $25,000. When these awards were reduced to reflect the insurance benefits the respondent had received, the total amount for which the respondent received judgment at trial was $47,900 plus interest from November 25, 1977.

In the Ontario Court of Appeal Blair JA (with whom Goodman JA concurred) agreed generally with the line of reasoning pursued by the trial judge, but differed in his calculation of damages to the extent that he did not cut off the appellant's responsibility for lost earnings at the date when the respondent might have been expected to recuperate from the operation and return to work [see (1981), 34 OR (2d) 151 (CA)]. Rather, he took into account the fact that the recommended surgery entailed only a 70% chance of success and adjusted the award for loss of income upward in order to take into account the fact that, even if the respondent had acted reasonably in the circumstances, his recovery would not have been assured. After making a series of adjustments to reflect the contingencies entailed in the surgery and the respondent's future job prospects had he undergone the operation, Blair JA awarded damages for loss of earnings in the amount of $81,661. He then deducted the insurance benefits which the respondent had received and added the $25,000 representing general damages for pain and suffering. This produced a total award of $103,651.

A strong dissent in the Court of Appeal was voiced by MacKinnon ACJO based on his analysis of the English case-law on the issue of the refusal of a tort victim to seek medical care. The principle he elicited from the English authorities is that a tort victim's unreasonable refusal to undergo medical treatment constitutes an intervening cause which effectively cuts off the liability of the initial tortfeasor. Accordingly, as applied by MacKinnon ACJO, this principle has the effect of barring the respondent from any claim for loss of income beyond the date on which he might reasonably be expected to have returned to work had he undergone the surgery and the surgery had been a success. While MacKinnon ACJO was prepared to take account of the approximately 30% chance of the operation's failure in assessing the reasonableness of the respondent's refusal of the surgery, he was not prepared to factor this percentage into the quantum of loss awarded once the respondent was held to have acted unreasonably. Although he would have varied the damages calculation in some minor respects, the overall thrust of his dissent was to approve the approach taken by Callaghan J at trial.

3. *Unreasonable Refusal of Treatment*

The single most noteworthy fact with which this appeal is concerned is that the trial judge found the respondent to have been unreasonable in his refusal to accept the recommended medical treatment. As noted by each of the members of the House of Lords in *Steele v. Robert George & Co. (1937) Ltd.*, [1942] AC 497 (HL (NI)), this question is most appropriately left to the trier of fact to decide. There is no reason to conclude that Callaghan J committed an error of law in determining this issue in the case at bar. Both the majority and the dissent in the Ontario Court of Appeal were of the view that there was sufficient evidence to support the trial judge's finding and, in the absence of any suggestion that he misdirected himself or applied the wrong test to the facts presented to him, there is no basis on which this court can interfere with his finding. He alone had the opportunity to assess the evidence and determine the issue of the respondent's reasonableness at first hand.

It may, however, be opportune, since this court now has the concept of reasonableness in relation to a refusal of medical or surgical treatment before it, to make reference to some of the difficult elements involved in a finding of unreasonableness before considering precisely how such a finding affects the legal principles otherwise applicable on an assessment of damages.

(1) Unreasonableness and the "Thin Skull" Doctrine

The first difficult issue which arises in assessing the reasonableness or otherwise of a plaintiff's refusal of medical treatment is the extent, if any, to which subjective attributes of the plaintiff may be taken into account by the court. In the case at bar it was submitted by the respondent that, whether or not his refusal of treatment was perceived as objectively unreasonable, its source lay in an innate fear of surgery which he could not be expected to overcome. Accordingly, he invoked a variation of the long accepted principle that "if the wrong is established the wrongdoer must take the victim as he finds him": *per* Lord Wright in *Hay or Bourhill v. Young*, [1943] AC 92 (HL (Sc.)) at pp. 109-10. It followed from this, he argued, that the injuries resulting from his inordinate fear, which might otherwise have been avoided if a reasonable decision regarding medical treatment had been made, were analogous to the type of aggravated injuries which might be suffered by a haemophiliac inflicted with a bleeding wound or any other victim with a predisposed physiological over-sensitivity: *Bishop v. Arts & Letters Club of Toronto* (1978), 18 OR (2d) 471.

It is, of course, well established that damages for aggravated injuries consequent on some pre-existing infirmity of the plaintiff are recoverable even if the infirmity is of a psychological nature: see, *e.g.*, *Love v. Port of London Authority*, [1959] 2 Lloyd's Rep. 541 (QB); *Gray v. Cotic*, [1983] 2 SCR 2. As Geoffrey Lane J said in *Malcolm v. Broadhurst*, [1970] 3 All ER 508 at p. 511, "there is no difference in principle between an egg-shell skull and an egg-shell personality." Indeed, it would seem that the *locus classicus* of the "thin skull rule," the decision of Kennedy J in *Dulieu v. White & Sons*, [1901] 2 KB 669, was in fact a case of aggravated injuries which were triggered by the impact of the defendant's tortious act on the plaintiff's inchoate psychological hypersensitivity.

The key word, however, is *pre-existing*. Once it is acknowledged that there is such a thing as a "psychological thin skull," the inquiry shifts to (a) the timing and (b) the nature of the alleged psychological infirmity.

(a) Timing

With regard to *timing*, it would seem that the very concept of a thin-skulled plaintiff embodies within it the notion that the oversensitive condition was pre-existing at the time of the injury. That is to say, where the ultimate consequence of which the plaintiff complains is not due to the impact of the defendant's wrongful act on some existing sensitivity of the plaintiff, but rather arises only subsequent to the injury and independent of any intrinsic physiological or psychological problem for which the tortious act has served as a catalyst, the ordinary rules of recoverability apply. By way of illustration, where a blow to the plaintiff's chest inflicted by the defendant ultimately results in the development of a malignancy, but there is no evidence of any pre-existing susceptibility to such a disease in the plaintiff, then the ordinary rules of causation apply: *Blackstock v. Foster*, [1938] SR (NSW) 341. On the other hand, where the defendant's negligent act results in the plaintiff's lip being burned and, due to a rare pre-malignant condition of the plaintiff, this burn turns into a fatal malignant growth, then the pre-existing "thin skull" serves to displace the otherwise applicable rules of causation: *Smith v. Leech Brain & Co. Ltd.*, [1962] 2 QB 405.

The same dichotomy must presumably apply to cases of a psychological thin-skulled plaintiff. A significant distinction has to be made between persons who subsequent to an accident develop an emotional or psychological infirmity and those who bring a pre-existing emotional or psychological infirmity to the accident. The question posed by the kind of case we have here is: do persons in the latter group have to meet the objective test of reasonableness when their refusal of medical help is being assessed by the trier of the fact or are their subjective attributes to be given due consideration?

In *Marcroft v. Scruttons, Ltd.*, [1954] 1 Lloyd's Rep. 395 (CA), the plaintiff, a dock labourer, was unloading cargo from a steamship at the Liverpool docks when the wire of a derrick which was unloading cargo from part of the lower hold fouled the hatch beam. The hatch cover on which the plaintiff was standing was dislodged and he fell about ten feet into the hold. He suffered no physical injuries apart from bruises but anxiety neurosis and depression following the shock incapacitated him from work. Liability was not contested by the plaintiff; the only issue was damages.

The plaintiff saw his panel doctor who referred him to a psychologist. She saw him on several occasions and observed that he had tremors of the hand, mouth, eyelids, general shaking of the body, severe depression and lack of confidence. She recommended that he go to the Rainhill Mental Hospital for electric shock treatment. He refused to go because it was a mental hospital. The trial judge found that this was unreasonable. When the case went to appeal Lord Justice Singleton said it was one of the most difficult cases on the assessment of damages that he had encountered in a long time. He adverted to the fact that some of the doctors who gave evidence testified "that this man was of a type who might be more readily affected by an accident of this kind than other men would be." He also referred to the medical evidence that many people have a natural antipathy to entering mental hospitals. He had to deal with the contention made by counsel for the plaintiff that the plaintiff's condition really was such that he could not make up his mind. Dr. Evans, one of the defendant's witnesses, said at p. 398:

I felt he was incapable of really coherent thought when I saw him. I did not think he was really capable of reasoning the thing out. I think it was just a matter of taking fright at the mere mention of mental hospital.

Lord Justice Singleton dealt with that in the following way at p. 399:

A man who is in an anxiety state may have difficulty in making up his mind, but on a question as to the treatment which he should have his mind is, or ought to be, made up for him by his own medical adviser. That is one of the purposes of having medical advisors. The patient would not know what he ought to do; the patient takes medical advice, and the patient ought to be guided by his medical advisers.

His Lordship concluded at the same page:

I do not wish to say anything that would hurt the feelings of a plaintiff in a case of this kind, but I believe it to be the duty of this Court to say that if a man is recommended by his own medical advisers and by others to undergo a course of treatment, he ought to undergo it; if he is advised that it gives him a reasonable chance of recovery, and if the treatment is reasonable, he ought to undergo it; if he will not, he must see that it is a little hard upon the defendants if they are to be asked to pay damages in respect of a period extending afterwards. If the general opinion is that treatment would cure him, or, at least, render him in a much better state in every way, then he ought to undergo the treatment.

It is interesting to note that Lord Justice Denning in his concurring reasons indicates that the plaintiff had, "unbeknown to him, a constitutional weakness which made it very serious for him, because the accident operating on that weakness produced in him a very severe nervous shock, trembling from head to foot" (p. 401). He nevertheless found that this factor had to be disregarded. He said at p. 401:

Viewing the matter objectively, he was quite unreasonable in refusing to follow their advice; but viewing the matter subjectively, the man's attitude was quite understandable. *He was an uneducated, ignorant man who did not realize that a mental hospital nowadays is very different from what it was 30 or 40 years ago; and moreover, owning to his anxiety neurosis, he was not in a fit state to make reasonable decisions. The difficult question in the case is whether we are to admit this subjective condition of his as a reason for refusing medical treatment. I think not.* We should do great harm if we allowed him to go on receiving compensation for the rest of his life because of his refusal to accept medical treatment. Persons who suffer from an anxiety state have more chance of recovery if they are treated as responsible human beings and are expected to behave reasonably, rather than as weaklings who can give way to their weakness and expect to get paid for it.

(Emphasis added.)

The court in *Marcroft* clearly refused to permit subjective attributes to enter into the question of the reasonableness of the plaintiff's refusal of medical treatment. Their Lordships' conclusion that the plaintiff was more vulnerable than most prior to the accident to the effects of shock does not appear to have affected the outcome either in terms of the reasonableness of his refusal of medical treatment or in relation to aggravated damages.

By way of contrast, in *Elloway v. Boomars* (1968), 69 DLR (2d) 605 (BC SC), the plaintiff who suffered minor injuries in an automobile accident developed a psychosis of a schizophrenic nature which by the time of trial was largely disabling. McIntyre J found the medical evidence that the plaintiff suffered from a pre-existing condition which predisposed him to schizophrenic illness and that the accident, operating on that predisposition, brought about the full schizophrenic illness. The plaintiff had been advised to take treatment for his condition but he refused. McIntyre J concluded, however, that *his psychosis was itself a factor in his refusal* and he could not therefore be held responsible for the worsening of his condition. Damages must be assessed on the basis that he had not wilfully failed in his duty to mitigate.

In *McGrath v. Excelsior Life Ins. Co.* (1973), 6 Nfld. & PEIR 203 (Nfld. SC, TD), the plaintiff, an unskilled labourer, injured his back while working as a painter's helper. He was in continuous pain. One specialist recommended a spinal fusion to alleviate the pain. Another said it would not help. The plaintiff decided not to have it and the insurance company discontinued his disability benefits. Higgins J said at p. 208:

> The position therefore is that Dr. Shapter and Dr. Russell, both specialists in their respective fields, are in complete disagreement as to the benefits which might result from surgery. Faced with this conflict of expert opinion, it is not to be wondered at that the patient, *an unlettered man*, would be reluctant to agree to an operation. I do not regard his refusal, in these circumstances, as unreasonable.

(Emphasis added.)

In *Morgan v. T. Wallis Ltd.*, [1974] 1 Lloyd's Rep. 165 (QB), the plaintiff, aged 33, was employed by the defendants as a lighterman of the River Thames. In January 1970, a stevedore employed by the defendants on the ship "Cymric" threw some wire rope on to an adjoining barge on which the plaintiff was working. While trying to avoid this the plaintiff fell into the hold and injured his back. There was no dispute as to liability. Special damages were agreed. General damages were disputed on the ground that the plaintiff unreasonably refused to undergo tests and an operation out of a genuine, though misplaced, fear. The evidence indicated that the fear was beyond his control. Mr. Justice Browne found that the plaintiff's refusal to undergo the tests and the operation was unreasonable. Quoting from his reasons at p. 170:

> Everybody agrees, and I emphasize strongly, that the plaintiff in the present case is not in the slightest degree a malingerer, and is a completely honest man who genuinely holds the beliefs and fears about which he has told us in evidence. But in deciding whether the defendants have proved that he has unreasonably refused to have the investigation and operation in question here, it seems to me clear from the authorities to which I have referred, that *I must apply an objective test, in this sense, would a reasonable man in all the circumstances, receiving the advice which the plaintiff did receive, have refused the operation?* I think this question must be considered as at the times when his decision was made and on the basis of the advice he then received. If the plaintiff preferred and prefers to go on as he is rather than to have the operation no-one can blame him. But the question I have to consider is not, "Is the plaintiff to blame for refusing the operation?" but, "Is it fair and reasonable to make the defendants pay for his refusal?"

(Emphasis added.)

It is, however, of interest to note that at p. 173 Browne J states:

> As I have said several times, I entirely accept that the plaintiff's fear and his inability to bring himself to agree to the operation are absolutely genuine. *But in my view there is no evidence that this is due to any physical or mental or psychological disability which existed before the accident and which would entitle the plaintiff to say that the defendants must take the plaintiff as they find him.*

(Emphasis added.) He concluded at the same page:

> As I have said, I think one must decide the question whether the plaintiff's refusal was unreasonable by the objective standard of the reasonable man, and the fact that this particular plaintiff has got himself into an emotional state where he finds it impossible to agree to the operation is, in my view, no ground for saying that his refusal was not unreasonable.

It would appear then on the English authorities that a psychological "thin skull" developed subsequent to the tortious act is not a factor that can be considered in relation to reasonableness: the objective test prevails in the absence of any pre-existing condition.

(b) Nature

The other element that has to be considered in determining whether the objective test of reasonableness applies to the decision made by the alleged thin-skulled plaintiff is the *nature* of the pre-existing psychological infirmity. It is evident that not every pre-existing state of mind can be said to amount to a psychological thin skull. It seems to me that the line must be drawn between those plaintiffs who are capable of making a rational decision regarding their own care and those who, due to some pre-existing psychological condition, are not capable of making such a decision. As pointed out by Professor Fleming, a plaintiff cannot by making an unreasonable decision in regard to his own medical treatment "unload upon his defendant the consequences of his own stupidity or irrational scruples": J.G. Fleming, *The Law of Torts* (Sydney: Law Book Co., 6th ed., 1983) at p. 226. Accordingly, non-pathological but distinctive subjective attributes of the plaintiff's personality and mental composition are ignored in favour of an objective assessment of the reasonableness of his choice. So long as he is capable of choice the assumption of tort damages theory must be that he himself assumes the cost of any unreasonable decision. On the other hand, if due to some pre-existing psychological condition he is incapable of making a choice at all, then he should be treated as falling within the thin-skull category and should not bear the cost once it is established that he has been wrongfully injured.

I believe that Lord Justice Singleton's concern in *Marcroft v. Scruttons*, stemmed from his doubt as to whether the plaintiff in that case was capable of making a rational decision. Not only that, there was some indication in the medical evidence that his incapacity may have been itself a consequence of the trauma induced by the accident. If this is so, it would appear manifestly unjust to cut off his recovery for failure to mitigate his damages through a rational decision as to treatment. The reasons of Lord Justice Denning are even more baffling. He attributes the plaintiff's traumatic state after the accident to a pre-existing constitutional weakness and says it rendered the plaintiff incapable of making reasonable decisions. Yet he concluded that this was a subjective factor that could not be considered. This would appear to be carrying the objective test too far in that it overrides the "thin skull" principle altogether.

The position in the United States would appear to be that a great number of personal attributes falling short of a constitutional incapacity to act reasonably can be taken into account in evaluating the plaintiff's post-injury behaviour. This position is best summed up in Dan B. Dobbs, *Law of Remedies* (St. Paul, Minn.: West, 1973), p. 580, as follows:

> In such cases the courts have spoken of "the reasonable and prudent man" or "reasonable care" by the plaintiff as a test, but this term is probably too narrow. Personal preferences of the plaintiff, personal finances of the plaintiff, and even irrational fears of the plaintiff are given due weight in deciding what he is expected to do to minimize damages. The standard, then, is not so much the objective standard of the hypothetical reasonable man as it is subjective standard based on what can be reasonably expected of the particular plaintiff.

In their text on *Personal Injury Damages in Canada* (Toronto: Carswell, 1981), Professors Cooper-Stephenson and Saunders point out that no clear position has emerged from the Canadian jurisprudence in this area although cases such as *Elloway* and *McGrath* suggest that a plaintiff in Canada may not be held to an objective standard of reasonableness which it is beyond his capacity to attain. This position would appear to most appropriately complement Fleming's assertion that where a plaintiff does not suffer from a constitutional incapacity to act reasonably he cannot make the defendant bear the burden of his unreasonable behaviour. Thus, the analytic focus in each case is on the *capacity* of the plaintiff to make a reasonable choice.

(2) Unreasonableness and Conflicting Medical Opinions

Another problem trial judges face in assessing the reasonableness of a plaintiff's decision whether or not to have medical or surgical treatment is the way in which he is expected to handle conflicting medical opinions.

In *Asamera Oil Corp. Ltd. v. Sea Oil & Gen'l Corp.; Baud Corp., N.V. v. Brook*, [1979] 1 SCR 633 at p. 649, Estey J stated that "a plaintiff need not take all possible steps to reduce his loss." He is only bound to act like "a reasonable and prudent man": *British Westinghouse Electric & Mfg. Co. Ltd. v. Underground Electric R. Co. of London Ltd.*, [1912] AC 673 (HL (Eng.)). The steps he takes, Lord Macmillan said in *Banco de Portugal v. Waterlow & Sons, Ltd.*, [1932] AC 452 (HL (Eng.)) at p. 506, "ought not to be weighed in nice scales."

What guidance, if any, do these very general observations afford an injured plaintiff confronted with conflicting medical advice and varying prognoses for the outcome of treatment? In *Savage v. T. Wallis Ltd.*, [1966] 1 Lloyd's Rep. 357 (CA), the doctors disagreed as to whether a slight operation would get rid of the plaintiff's headaches. It was held that the plaintiff in refusing the surgery had not failed in his duty to mitigate. In *McGrath v. Excelsior Life Ins. Co.*, supra, medical opinion was divided as to whether a spinal fusion would reduce the plaintiff's pain. It was held that the plaintiff did not fail in his duty to mitigate by refusing to have the surgery. In *Steele v. Robert George & Co. (1937) Ltd.*, [1942] AC 497 (HL (NI)), Viscount Simon L said at p. 500:

> It may in some cases be quite reasonable for a man to decide not to undergo an operation if his own doctor advises against it, for it is the conclusion reached by his doctor which governs his decision much more than the logic by which his doctor has reached the conclusion.

As to the possibility of medical opinions conflicting with that of his own doctor Viscount Simon said (p. 501):

... that where the workman has been advised against the operation by a skilled medical man in whom he has confidence, it would be necessary to bring home to the workman an extremely strong body of expert advice to the contrary before the onus which rests on the employer of proving that the refusal was unreasonable should be regarded as discharged.

These cases are, however, to be contrasted with cases such as *Marcroft v. Scrutton*, and *McAuley v. London Transport Executive*, [1957] 2 Lloyd's Rep. 500 (CA) where the refusal of surgery was held to be unjustified. It would appear from the authorities that as long as a plaintiff follows any one of several courses of treatment recommended by the medical advisers he consults he should not be said to have acted unreasonably.

As a qualification to the general principle that a plaintiff's actions must not be subjected to an overly critical standard of review, the English courts have suggested that in determining what steps he ought to take the plaintiff should consider the defendant's interests as well as his own. In *Darbishire v. Warran*, [1963] 1 WLR 1067 (CA), the court pointed out that, while the plaintiff may have acted reasonably as far as he was concerned, the true question was whether the plaintiff acted reasonably as between himself and the defendant and in view of his duty to mitigate the damages: *per* Harman LJ at p. 1072; Pearson LJ at p. 1076. It should be noted that this rule has never been adopted in Canada, and the English courts in the context of the law of contracts have held that a plaintiff "is not bound to nurse the interests of the contract breaker": *Harlow & Jones, Ltd. v. Panex (Int'l), Ltd.*, [1967] 2 Lloyd's Rep. 509 (QB), *per* Roskill J at p. 530.

In making his finding as to the reasonableness or otherwise of a refusal of medical treatment, the trier of fact will also, of course, take into consideration the degree of risk to the plaintiff from the surgery (*Taylor v. Addems and Addems*, [1932] 1 WWR 505 (Sask. CA)), the gravity of the consequences of refusing it (*Masny v. Carter-Hall-Aldinger Co. Ltd.*, 24 SLR 216 (Sask. KB)), and the potential benefits to be derived from it (*Matters v. Baker & Fawcett*, [1951] SASR 91 (SC)).

(3) The Onus of Proof of Reasonableness

While a plaintiff has the burden of proving both the fact that he has suffered damage and the quantum of that damage, the burden of proof moves to the defendant if he alleges that the plaintiff could have and should have mitigated his loss. That this is the law in Canada has been clearly stated by this court in *Red Deer College v. Michaels*, [1976] 2 SCR 324, and more recently reaffirmed by Estey J in the *Asamera Oil* case. In *Red Deer* Laskin CJC said at p. 331:

> If it is the defendant's position that the [plaintiff] could reasonably have avoided some part of the loss claimed, it is for the defendant to carry the burden of that issue, subject to the defendant being content to allow the matter to be disposed of on the trial Judge's assessment of the plaintiff's evidence on avoidable consequences.

Two Australian cases are instructive in this area. In *Buczynski v. McDonald*, [1971] 1 SASR 569, the plaintiff was shown to be suffering from a compensation neurosis as a result of personal injuries sustained in an automobile accident caused by the defendant's negligence. The report of the case deals only with a problem that arose in the assessment of damages as to the plaintiff's duty to mitigate his loss. It was proved in evidence that there is no treatment that would relieve the plaintiff's neurosis and it was therefore of the utmost urgency that his claim be tried since the chances of his recovery from his condition would "get less and less as the time from the date of his original injury increases." The trial was expedited accordingly. Quoting from the judgment of Walters J at p. 573:

> I turn now to the question whether the plaintiff has done all that he could reasonably have done to alleviate his condition of compensation neurosis. The principle to be applied with respect to the mitigation of damages in the case of tort is clear. The plaintiff is "bound to act not only in his own interests, but in the interests of the party who would have to pay damages, and keep down the damages, so far as it is reasonable and proper, by acting reasonably in the matter" (*Smailes & Sons v. Hans Dessen & Co.* ((1905), 94 LT 492 (KB): on appeal (1906), 95 LT 809 (CA)), per Channel J at p. 493. And as Mayo J said in *Fishlock v. Plummer* ([1950] SASR 176), at p. 181: "If any part of his [the plaintiff's] damage was sustained by reason of his own negligent or unreasonable behaviour, the plaintiff will not be recouped as to that part." However, "the question what is reasonable for the plaintiff to do in mitigation of damages is not a question of law, but one of fact in the circumstances of each particular case, the burden of proof being upon the defendant" (*Halsbury's Laws of England*, 3rd ed. vol. 11, para. 477, p. 290). The authorities show that once the plaintiff has "made out a prima facie case of damages, actual or prospective, to a given amount," the burden lies upon the defendant to prove circumstances whereby the loss could have been diminished. Not only must the defendant discharge the onus of showing that the plaintiff could have mitigated his loss if he had reacted reasonably, but he must also show how and to what extent that loss could have been minimized (*Roper v. Johnson* (1873), LR 8 CP 167, per Grove J at p. 184; *Criss v. Alexander (No. 2)* (1928), 28 SR (NSW) 587; per Street CJ at p. 596).

Walters J then dealt with the defendant's submission that the plaintiff's duty to mitigate in a case of compensation neurosis included a duty to bring on the action for an early trial. He said at p. 574:

> It cannot be disputed that the plaintiff could have taken earlier steps to expedite the trial of the action, but it was equally open to the defendant to have done so, at least by October 1970. Moreover, in the period between April 1970 and June 1970, there had been a delay of two months on the part of the defendant in answering the interrogatories delivered for his examination, and until the answers had been filed, application could not have been made for entry of the action for trial. And it is to be noticed that a summons for leave to enter the action for trial was issued three days following the filing of the answers to the interrogatories. Another matter which I am unable to overlook is the initial delay on the part of the defendant in filing his defence to the statement of claim.
>
> Looking at the conduct of the parties, I am unable to say that any blame lies with one side rather than the other, and I am not persuaded that any mischief done can be solely ascribed to the plaintiff. In any case, apart from the prognosis given in evidence by Mr. Schaeffer, there is not a great deal to show to what extent the plaintiff's neurosis might have been relieved if the action had been brought to trial sooner. I cannot speculate as to the extent to which the plaintiff might have minimized his loss by bringing on his action for an earlier trial. And in all the circumstances, I do not think that the defendant has persuaded me that the plaintiff has been unreasonable in failing to take steps to minimize his damages, or that it has been proved that he is responsible for consequences of his injuries which might have been avoided or materially lessened, so that his damages ought to be calculated at a time prior to the actual date of assess-

ment. It seems to me that after looking to all that has happened, there can be no warrant for abating the award of general damages.

In *Plenty v. Argus*, [1975] WAR 155, Jackson CJ referred to the two aspects of the defendant's burden of proof. He said at pp. 157-8:

> There can be no doubt but that upon this issue the onus was at trial upon the respondent to this appeal and the learned trial Judge so held. In the course of argument before us, however, it did appear that doubt did exist as to what was involved in the discharge of that onus. The question giving rise to that doubt can be posed by asking whether in such a case as this the defendant in order to discharge the onus that the plaintiff had failed to mitigate his damage must prove, on the balance of probabilities, that the plaintiff acted unreasonably in not submitting himself to the advised treatment, and in addition, and to the same standard of persuasion that the treatment, if carried out, would cure, or, to a certain degree cure the plaintiff's condition, or whether on the other hand, the issue to which the onus attaches is but the single issue, it being whether the plaintiff in refusing the treatment had failed to do something which in reason he ought to have done to mitigate his damage. *In all the personal injury negligence cases so far reported, it appears to have been established on the balance of probabilities both that the plaintiff had acted unreasonably and that had the operation been carried out, the incapacity would have been removed or reduced to a certain degree. In such cases the onus is discharged on either view and with the result that damages are assessed "as they would properly have been assessable if he had, in fact, undergone the operation and secured the degree of recovery to be expected from it"*: McAuley v. London Transport Executive, [1957] 2 Lloyd's Rep. 500 at 505 per Jenkins LJ.

(Emphasis added.)

A recent English case which is hard to reconcile with the Canadian and Australian authorities and, indeed, with earlier English authorities, is *Selvanayagam v. University of West Indies*, [1983] 1 WLR 585 (PC (Trin. and Tob.)). In that case the Privy Council held that a plaintiff who rejects a medical recommendation in favour of surgery must, in order to discharge the burden on him to prove that he acted reasonably in regard to his duty to mitigate his damage, prove that his refusal was reasonable. The trial judge had placed the onus on the plaintiff (appellant) and the Court of Appeal had treated this as a basis for review. Lord Scarman said they were wrong. Quoting from his reasons at p. 589:

> The rule that a plaintiff who rejects a medical recommendation in favour of surgery must show that he acted reasonably is based on the principle that a plaintiff is under a duty to act reasonably so as to mitigate his damage.

While this articulation of the duty to mitigate is obviously correct, Lord Scarman's placing of the burden of proof of mitigation on the plaintiff seems to be in sharp contrast to a long line of earlier English authority and, as has been seen, is contrary to the general principles of mitigation of damages enunciated by this court in *Red Deer, supra*, and *Asamera Oil, supra*.

4. The Consequences of an Unreasonable Refusal of Treatment

Turning now to the implication of finding unreasonableness for the plaintiff's recovery, it is clear that the so-called "duty to mitigate" derives from the general proposition that a plaintiff cannot recover from the defendant damages which he himself could have avoided by the taking of reasonable steps. As Pearson LJ pointed out in *Darbishire v. Warran* it is not a "duty" in the strict sense. A breach of it is not actionable. Quoting from his reasons at p. 1075:

> … [I]t is important to appreciate the true nature of the so-called "duty to mitigate the loss" or "duty to minimize the damage." The plaintiff is not under any actual obligation to adopt the cheaper method: if he wishes to adopt the more expensive method, he is at liberty to do so and by doing so he commits no wrong against the defendant or anyone else. The true meaning is that the plaintiff is not entitled to charge the defendant by way of damages with any greater sum than that which he reasonably needs to expend for the purpose of making good the loss. In short, he is fully entitled to be as extravagant as he pleases but not at the expense of the defendant.

Mitigation has to do with post-accident events. In this respect it should perhaps be contrasted with contributory negligence and perceived as more closely aligned with *novus actus interveniens*. It differs from the latter, however, in that the *novus actus* may be the act of a third party whereas mitigation (or its failure) is exclusively the act of the claimant. Overhanging all three concepts, mitigation, contributory negligence and *novus actus*, are the general principles of foreseeability and remoteness as they apply to post-accident events.

The appellant in the case at bar invoked some of these general doctrines of tort law. He submitted "that the majority of the Court of Appeal have failed to take into account the fact that the plaintiff's unreasonable refusal was not reasonably foreseeable and the damages claimed are too remote." I do not find such an approach helpful in a case of this kind. It seems to me that by hypothesis the whole of the plaintiff's damages are reasonably foreseeable and would be recoverable were it not for the additional fact that a portion of them was reasonably avoidable by the plaintiff. I have difficulty in seeing how the failure to avoid what is a reasonably avoidable loss can in and of itself make the remaining unavoidable loss unforeseeable. Nor, it seems to me, does the doctrine of proximate cause, also invoked by the appellant, elucidate the problem. References to "proximate cause" and "intervening cause," in my opinion, predetermine the legal issue but do not provide a rationale for it. I find the following passage from 22 Amer. Jur., 2nd, at p. 52, more illuminating:

> Other courts have suggested that the doctrine of avoidable consequence is an extension of the proximate cause principle—that is, if the plaintiff could reasonably have avoided the damages which resulted, then the activity of the defendant can no longer be considered the proximate cause of those damages. While this statement can be accepted as theoretically valid (since "proximate cause" probably means nothing more than the cause which is recognized by law as the cause of the damages), it is not precise enough to express the ideal contained in the doctrine of avoidable consequences. For example, if defendant's negligent activity caused plaintiff's broken leg and much of plaintiff's pain could have been avoided by consulting a doctor, it is unnecessarily ambiguous to state that the failure to consult a doctor prevented the negligent activity from being the proximate cause of a portion of the pain, but not from being the proximate cause of the rest of the pain. It is more precise to state that consulting a doctor would have avoided a certain portion of the pain and, thus, damages cannot be recovered for the avoidable pain.

Essentially the same point may be made with respect to *novus actus interveniens*. The concept does not advance the analysis in any helpful way. Obviously mitigation and *novus actus* may coincide in cases such as the case at bar but talking in terms of *novus actus* is, in my view, of little assistance in defining the scope of the duty to mitigate.

What then counts as an unavoidable loss in a case like this where there has been found to be an unreasonable refusal of surgery? The answer given by MacKinnon ACJO is that one looks to what would have happened on a balance of probabilities had the operation in fact taken place. The majority approach, on the other hand, is to determine what damages are avoidable by assuming that the plaintiff has agreed to an operation which has not yet been performed. If the majority is correct, then the courts would normally take account of any "substantial possibility" of failure and the amount by which full compensation would be discounted—in this case 70%—would represent his avoidable loss.

There is a paucity of direct authority on this issue. The following passage from the judgment of Jenkins LJ in *McAuley, supra,* may be viewed as support for the approach taken by the majority (p. 505):

> If he receives medical advice to the effect that an operation will have a 90 per cent chance of success, and is strongly recommended to undergo the operation and does not do so, then the result must be, I think, that he has acted unreasonably, and that the damages ought to be assessed as they would properly have been assessable if he had, in fact, undergone the operation *and secured the degree of recovery to be expected from it.*

(Emphasis added.) It seems to me not only to be implicit in the English authorities but also to be common ground between the majority and the dissent in the Court of Appeal in this case that, even after an unreasonable refusal of surgery, the plaintiff is still entitled to claim unavoidable losses assuming, of course, that they are otherwise recoverable. MacKinnon ACJO would, it is true, deny all subsequent recovery in this case where on the balance of probabilities (70%) surgery would lead to a full recovery, but if there was a 50-100% chance of no more than an 80% recovery at the outside, it seems to me that his approach would necessarily permit a plaintiff to recover the remaining 20% of his damages as unavoidable loss.

As Blair JA points out, support is also to be found for the majority approach in a number of Australian cases, notably *Newell v. Lucas,* [1964-65] NSWR 1597. In *Plenty v. Argus,* Burt J seems to have adopted it in the following *obiter* statement at p. 159:

> And if a finding is made that a plaintiff in the face of an uncertain prognosis acted unreasonably in not submitting himself to surgery or treatment, then it would seem that his damages would be assessed having regard to his condition as it is, discounted by the evaluation of the lost chance, or as one would if the assessment were made in advance of the carrying out of the advised treatment.

In my view the majority approach is consistent with first principles as expressed by Lord Diplock in *Mallet v. McMonagle,* [1970] AC 166 (HL (NI)) at p. 176:

> The role of the court in making an assessment of damages which depends upon its view as to what will be and what would have been is to be contrasted with its ordinary function in civil actions of determining what was. In determining what did happen in the past a court decides on the balance of probabilities. Anything that is more probable than not it treats as certain. But in assessing damages which depend upon its view as to what will happen in the future or would have happened in the future if something had not happened in the past, the court must make an estimate as to what are the chances that a particular thing will or would have happened and reflect those chances, whether they are more or less than even, in the amount of damages which it awards.

See also Lord Reid in *Davies v. Taylor*, [1974] AC 207 (HL (Eng.)) at pp. 212-13. This position is essentially the one adopted by Lacourcière JA in *Schrump v. Koot et al.* (1977), 18 OR (2d) 337 (CA), which Blair JA cites in support of his position. MacKinnon ACJO attempts to distinguish this latter case on the ground that it applies only to assessing the risk of likelihood of future developments but, as the passage from Lord Diplock makes clear, the balance of probabilities test is confined to determining what did *in fact* happen in the past. In assessing damages the court determines not only what will happen but what *would have* happened by estimating the chance of the relevant event occurring, which chance is then to be directly reflected in the amount of damages. The general rule stated by Lord Diplock would therefore seem to be applicable to this case, suggesting that the majority approach is at least *prima facie* correct. The issue then becomes, it seems to me, a question of whether there are any reasons to take this particular type of case outside the general rule.

MacKinnon ACJO suggests that the majority approach bypasses the trial judge's initial finding of unreasonableness. With respect, I think he must be in error in this since the respondent is precluded by that finding from claiming full compensation for the losses he has already suffered. The same response can be made to the appellant's submission that the uncertainty in the evidence results from the plaintiff's unreasonable conduct and that he ought not to be able to "profit" from it. The finding that his refusal to undergo surgery was unreasonable and precludes the plaintiff from recovering his actual loss. To hold that his remaining compensation should be determined on the basis of principles higher than those normally applied in assessing tort damages would, it seems to me, be to punish him for not undergoing surgery. This would be contrary to the general judicial policy that "it is not the prerogative of the court to require that any person undergo surgery to any degree": *McCarthy v. MacPherson's Estate* (1977), 14 Nfld. & PEIR 294 (PEI CA) at p. 297.

Nor am I swayed by the appellant's submission that a respondent may, because he is free to change his mind about the surgery, effectively be overcompensated. As long as he is *bona fide* in his present claim that he does not intend to have the operation and is not deliberately taking a calculated risk that he will come out ahead by recovering 30% of his damages now and then after have the surgery with a 70% chance of complete success (an intention which would amount to fraud on the court in any event), there does not seem to me to be any problem arising from the fact that he might change his mind in the future and be overcompensated in the result. The potential for over or under compensation is, it seems to me, a pervasive difficulty with the present "once and for all" method of awarding tort damages. The situation presented by this case is only one example of that more comprehensive problem; it does not, in and of itself, call for a special solution of any sort. It should also be kept in mind that, while it is true that if the respondent does decide to have the operation at some future time there is a 70% chance that he will be somewhat overcompensated, it is also true that there exists a 30% possibility that he will be very substantially undercompensated.

I would respectfully adopt the approach of the majority of the Court of Appeal to this issue.

5. *Conclusions*

The case-law makes it clear that the question of whether a refusal of treatment is reasonable or not is for the trier of fact. Since the respondent (appellant by cross-appeal) did not in the

Court of Appeal expressly impugn the objective test applied by the trial judge, the Court of Appeal was correct in refusing to interfere with the trial judge's finding. The respondent cannot be permitted to impugn the objective test for the first time in this court.

For the reasons given I would dismiss the appeal. Counsel are agreed, however, that Blair JA made a mathematical error in his calculations and that the overall figure for damages, instead of being $103,651, should have been $96,146. The dismissal of the appeal is therefore subject to this variation in the Court of Appeal's order.

I would also dismiss the respondent's cross-appeal which was directed to Blair JA's method of calculation of the respondent's damages. While it is not entirely clear from his reasons how he used the more detailed breakdown of possible results from the surgery to arrive at the second discount of one-third, I do not believe that this kind of determination is susceptible of precise calculation. It would, however, have been of assistance to the respondent on the cross-appeal if Blair JA had attempted to relate the percentage predictions of result to the discount.

Leave to appeal was granted in this case in terms that the appellant pay the costs of the appeal on a solicitor-client basis in any event of the cause forthwith after taxation thereof. Costs in the courts below were left to the disposition of this court.

I cannot accept the submission of counsel for the respondent that the costs of the cross-appeal are covered by the order on the leave application. There is nothing in the order to indicate that a cross-appeal was contemplated although I do not doubt the respondent's right to proceed with one once leave to appeal was granted to the appellant. I would therefore dismiss the cross-appeal with costs. I would not interfere with the disposition of costs in the courts below.

Appeal and cross-appeal dismissed;
Court of Appeal's order as to damages varied.

Anticipatory Breach

Sells Ltd. v. Thomson Stationery Co. Ltd.
(1914), 19 BCLR 400 (CA)

MACDONALD CJA: The defendant, a company of booksellers doing business in Vancouver, ordered from the plaintiffs, a publishing company doing business in London, England, but licensed in this province, twenty-five volumes of a book having the title of "British Columbia," etc. These volumes were to be taken out of stock, and would have to be appropriated to the contract in order to pass the property therein to the defendants. The contract falls within rule 5, sub-sec. (1) of the *Sale of Goods Act*, ch. 203. RSBC, 1911, ch. 26, which reads as follows:

> Where there is a contract for the sale of unascertained or future goods by description, and goods of that description and in a deliverable state are unconditionally appropriated to the contract, either by the seller with the assent of the buyer, or by the buyer with the assent of the seller, the property in the goods thereupon passes to the buyer. Such assent may be express or implied, and may be given either before or after the appropriation is made.

I take it that in this case there would be an implied assent to the appropriation of the goods by the seller. Until such an appropriation the contract would be an executory one of bargain and sale.

The defendant cabled to the plaintiff cancelling the order for a balance of 13 volumes which had not then been sent out. Counsel for the plaintiffs admitted that no appropriation of these had been made prior to the receipt of the cablegram. The plaintiff nevertheless thereafter appropriated 13 volumes to this contract, and the defendant having refused to accept the books action was brought for the price as upon a contract for goods sold and delivered. I have therefore to ask myself whether or not the implied assent of the defendant, to the future appropriation of goods, to the contract, was withdrawn or destroyed by the notification that they would not accept the goods; in other words, whether or not the plaintiff, after receipt of that notification, could proceed to convert the executory agreement into an executed one by setting the goods apart as applicable to the contract and thus pass the property in them to the defendant against their will. I have not been able to find any direct authority upon this point. I am, however, of opinion that the implied assent to an appropriation of the goods was withdrawn by the notice, and that the plaintiff could not thereafter without defendant's assent convert the executory contract into an executed one.

Finelli v. Dee
[1968] 1 OR 676 (CA)

LASKIN JA (orally): This case arises out of a written contract between the plaintiffs and the male defendant, for the paving of the driveway at the defendant's home. The contract was made on June 18, 1966, and while a price was fixed and other terms included, it did not fix any particular time for the commencement or completion of the work. It appears from the evidence that the parties agreed that the work would not begin immediately because the defendant was then in no position to pay for it, but that it would be performed sometime in October or about that time, in 1966.

There is evidence, which was accepted by the trial Judge, that the defendant telephoned the office of the plaintiffs, after the contract was made and before any performance was contemplated, cancelling the contract, and that the plaintiffs' sales manager at the office who received the telephone call, agreed that it would be cancelled. On or about November 1, 1966, when the defendants were away from home, the plaintiffs carried out the contract and the defendants were confronted with the completed work on their return to their premises in the evening. The plaintiffs sued for the price of the work done under the contract but their claim was rejected by the trial Judge.

On appeal, a question was raised whether the cancellation of the contract amounted to rescission or simply represented a repudiation by the defendant. Of course, if there was rescission (and I should say that, notwithstanding the contrary argument of the plaintiffs' counsel, rescission could be effected by oral agreement even though the contract in question was in writing), then there would be no basis on which an action to enforce the provision as to price could be founded. If, on the other hand, the cancellation amounted to repudiation, a question arises as to the applicability of the principles canvassed by the House of Lords in *White & Carter (Councils) Ltd. v. McGregor*, [1962] AC 413 (HL (Sc.)). It was the view of the majority of Court that a repudiation by one party to a contract does not preclude the innocent party from carrying out the contract and suing for the price, at least where this can be done without assent or cooperation of the party in breach. I am not, of course, bound by this judgment, but, respecting as I do the considered opinion of the majority, I must say that I am attracted by the reasons of the two dissenting members of the Court. Repudiation is not something that calls for acceptance when there is no question of rescission, but merely excuses the innocent party from performance and leaves him free to sue for damages. But, even accepting the majority view in the *McGregor* case, I should point out that it was a case in which the innocent party could carry out the contract notwithstanding the repudiation, without the assent or co-operation of the party in breach. This is not the situation here.

In the first place, it was necessary for the plaintiffs to enter upon the defendants' land in order to perform; and without wishing to embark on any issue as to trespass, the plaintiffs, in my view, were obliged to give previous intimation to the defendant that they were prepared to do the work called for by the contract and proposed to do it on a certain day. This, of course, was not done.

It follows that whether the cancellation amounts to rescission or merely to repudiation by the defendant, the plaintiffs are not entitled to recover the contract price. Accordingly, I would dismiss the appeal with costs and with a counsel fee of $25 to the defendants.

NOTE

Some cases have suggested that if the plaintiff lacks the financial resources to mitigate her loss, the loss is not recoverable. It is not clear, however, whether this suggestion rests on the assumption that the loss in such a case is likely to be too remote, or whether it is an independent rule of law. It seems difficult to support any such rule on general principles of mitigation (that the plaintiff could, acting reasonably, have avoided the loss) because, by hypothesis, the plaintiff had not the means to avoid it. It will be noted that, in *Kienzle v. Stringer*, above, Zuber JA expressly left the question open.

Avoided Loss

Erie County Natural Gas and Fuel Company Ltd. v. Carroll
[1911] AC 105 (PC (Ont.))

[The defendant wrongfully withheld a supply of gas needed by the plaintiffs for use in their business. The plaintiffs acquired other gas leases, constructed new works to secure their supply of gas, and later sold them at a profit.]

LORD ATKINSON (at pp. 115-19): ... The Master by his report, dated April 20, 1907, found:

1. That the plaintiffs were entitled to have the works operated by them supplied with natural gas from the mains of the Provincial Company from November 15, 1894 to August 1, 1902.

2. That the company consumed 911,722,303 cubic feet of their own gas for that purpose within the above-mentioned period.

3. That this gas was worth 12½ cents per 1000 cubic feet, amounting to $113,965.29 in all, which sum he found the Provincial Company (not both the companies) liable to pay to the plaintiffs. The result in money if this award held good would, if the figures $60,000 and $75,000 be accurate, be something like this.

If the defendants had discharged their obligation the plaintiffs would have got from them gas presumably sufficient to operate their plant without paying for it anything extra. The defendants, however, failed to discharge that obligation for about 7¾ years, and the plaintiffs by constructing works at a cost of less than $60,000 procured the necessary gas from elsewhere. After having this gas and worked their plant they sold these works presumably for $75,000, about $15,000 more than they cost; yet, because of the temporary default of the defendants, the plaintiffs are, notwithstanding their use and enjoyment of the substituted gas, to receive in addition the sum of $113,965.22 as damages, thereby making a profit by the defendants' breach of their obligation of about $128,965.22, a somewhat grotesque result.

Britton J in delivering the judgment of the Supreme Court of Ontario apparently approved of the principle upon which the damages were assessed by the Master, and agreed with him as to the price at which it should be taken that the plaintiffs could have sold the gas which they had used, namely 12½ cents per 1000 cubic feet, but thought the quantity found by the Master to have been produced was excessive, and reduced the damages to $54,031.82, less than half the sum at which they had been assessed by the Master. The Court of Appeal concurred in opinion with him, affirmed his judgment and decision, and dismissed the appeal of the defendants and the cross-appeal of the plaintiffs with costs.

Their Lordships are quite unable to adopt these conclusions. In their opinion they are erroneous; and they think the error is due to the fact that the Court of Appeal did not take a true view of the nature of the transaction embodied in the agreement of April 6, 1891, and the conveyance of the 20th of the same month as amended, or of the rights which in the circumstances of the case sprung from it.

It is plain, on the face of these documents, that the parties to them contemplated that more gas should be obtained from the properties leased than would be sufficient to operate the plant of the plaintiffs, and the reservation contained in the agreement and subsequently embodied in the conveyance merely amounts, in their Lordships' opinion, to a contract on the part of the Erie County Natural Gas and Fuel Company to supply the plaintiffs, out of this larger volume of gas, with sufficient to operate their plant. Upon the execution of the conveyance of July 18, 1894, that contract, of course, became binding on the defendants, the Provincial Natural Gas and Fuel Company, Limited; but the amount of gas to be supplied was not specifically set apart for or appropriated to the plaintiffs' use, or had ever become their property. Had the plaintiffs without the consent of the defendants tapped the latter's mains and helped themselves, they would, according to *The Queen v. White* (1853), 22 LJ (MC) 123, a case of the highest authority, and *The Queen v. Firth* (1869), LR 1 CCR 173, have been liable to be convicted of larceny, and certainly would have been liable in trover. They were merely in the position of a person who had, for instance, purchased from the owner of a large quantity of grain in bulk a portion of it, while the portion purchased remained part of the bulk and before it had been in any way set apart or identified. The defendants have admittedly broken their contract. They are liable for damages for that breach. The only question for decision is what, in the circumstances of the case, is the true measure of those damages. It would have been competent for the plaintiffs to have abstained from procuring gas in substitution for that which the defendants should have supplied to them, and have sued the defendants for damages for breach of their contract. They did not take that course. They chose to perform on behalf of the defendants, in a reasonable way, that contract for them and to obtain from an independent source a sufficient quantity of gas, similar as near as might be in character and quality to that which they were entitled to receive. In such cases it is well established that the measure of damages is the cost of procuring the substituted article, not at all the price at which the substituted article when procured could have been sold by the person who has procured it. In *Hamlin v. Great Northern Ry. Co.* (1856), 26 LJ (Ex.) 20 at p. 23 Alderson B thus lays down the law applicable to these cases: "The principle is that if the party does not perform his contract the other may do so for him, as near as may be, and charge him for the expenses incurred in so doing." In *Le Blanche v. London and North Western Ry. Co.* (1876), 1 CPD 286, at p. 302, Lord Esher (then Brett LJ) thus expresses himself: "We think it may properly be said that if the party bound to perform a contract does not perform it the other party may do so for him, as reasonably near as may be, and charge him for the reasonable expense incurred in so doing," but whether the thing done was a reasonable thing to do must be determined having regard to all the circumstances. James, Mellish, and Baggallay LJJ expressly approve of the principle laid down by Alderson B, with this qualification, however, that the second party must not take a course which as regards the party in default would be unreasonable or oppressive. This principle appears to be generally accepted and applied: Sedgwick on Damages, 8th ed., vol. 1, pp. 322-325.

Where the contract is one for the sale of goods, one of the modes in which a party to it may, on the default of the party bound to perform it, perform it for him is by going into the market and buying goods of a description and quality similar to those contracted for; but if he purchases at a sum equal to or less than the contract price, he can only recover nominal damages, because, the cost of procuring the substituted article not being greater than the contract price, he has got goods equal to those contracted for and at the same or a less cost, and has therefore suffered no loss: *Valpy v. Oakeley* (1851), 16 QB 941, 117 ER 1142; *Griffiths v. Perry* (1859), 1 E & E 680; 120 ER 1065. The case of *Western Wagon and Property Co. v. West*, [1892] 1 Ch. 271 is an illustration of the same principle.

The same rule must apply whether the substituted goods or commodities are manufactured, or mined for, or otherwise produced, or purchased in open market. In the latter case the cost of procuring the goods is the price at which they were bought; in the former cases the cost of procuring them is the cost of their production. The method adopted to procure them cannot make any difference.

If then the cost to which the plaintiffs were put to acquire gas to operate their plant during the 7¾ years mentioned be the true test of damages in this case, as it clearly is, the next question to consider is what have the plaintiffs shewn to be the amount of the initial gross cost to which they were put, and what deductions, if any, the defendants have shewn should be made from that amount in order to ascertain the net cost, and consequently the actual loss, and therefore the sum recoverable. The plaintiffs have vouched expenditure to the amount of $58,297.52 in their before-mentioned statement of damages, and it was stated by

Mr. Eldon Bankes, and not disputed, that this amount covered labour, materials, and sums paid for superintendence. The answers to certain questions in the record would go to shew that it included the expenses of the plaintiffs. It is not suggested that it included interest on the money spent. It may possibly not have included maintenance. A reference to the statement of damages shews that the main expenditure took place in the years 1898 and 1902. Even if the outlay be taken at $60,000, the interest at 5 per cent on the different sums expended from the dates given in evidence could not, as has been already point out, well exceed $12,000, but that is a mere matter of arithmetic which could be readily ascertained. If these works cost the plaintiffs more than this it was their business to shew it. They cannot be permitted to recover damages on guesswork or surmise. They have failed to shew it. Mr. Simon, on their behalf, contended that as the defendants by their conduct had compelled the plaintiffs to become producers of gas, they are bound to pay the latter for their courage and enterprise. There is no authority for such a proposition. The contention is in their Lordships' opinion unsound. It may well be that if several reasonable but abortive attempts had been made to procure this gas the cost of these would have been properly treated as part of the cost of ultimately obtaining it, but that question does not arise in the case. The works having admittedly been sold, something must have been obtained for them. It is clear that if the defendants are to pay for the cost of making those works and of thereby supplying the plaintiffs with the gas the works produced they must get credit for the sum for which these works, after having supplied the gas, were sold, otherwise the plaintiffs would make by the defendants' breach of contract a profit equal to the price obtained on sale. The prima facie inference to be drawn from a document printed in the record is that $75,000 was the amount of it. That inference, unless rebutted, should in justice to the defendants be acted upon. The burden of rebutting it lay upon the plaintiffs. They have, in their Lordships opinion, failed to discharge that burden, and should not be permitted, by leaving the matters in obscurity, to recover more than they have lost. The plaintiffs have not sued for the loss of their contract. They have only sued for the damages caused to them by the temporary deprivation of the gas. They have got the substituted article, identical in description and quality, have used it, and have failed to shew that it has not in the result been obtained by them free of cost. They are therefore, according to the principles established by the authorities already cited, only entitled to nominal damages.

Cockburn v. Trusts & Guarantee Co.
(1917), 55 SCR 264

[The plaintiff, who had been wrongfully dismissed by his employer when it went into liquidation, bought assets at the liquidation sale, and sold them at a profit of $11,000. The trial judge awarded damages for wrongful dismissal, but the Ontario Appellate Division substituted an award of nominal damages. A further appeal to the Supreme Court of Canada was dismissed.]

ANGLIN J (at 268-71): ... The fundamental basis of the assessment of damages for breach of contract—compensation for pecuniary loss naturally flowing from the breach—and its qualification—that the plaintiff cannot recover any part of the damages due to his own failure to take all reasonable steps to mitigate his loss—are too well settled to admit of controversy. The application of this qualified rule, however, sometimes presents difficulty. The qualification does not impose on the plaintiff claiming damages for the breach "an obligation to take any steps which a reasonable and prudent man would not ordinarily take in the course of his business": nevertheless, when in the course of his business he has taken action arising out of the transaction, which action has diminished his loss, the effect in actual diminution of the loss he has suffered may be taken into account even though there was no duty on him to act.

The applicability of the principles expressed in these passages from the judgment of Lord Chancellor Haldane in *British Westinghouse Elec. & Manufacturing Co. v. Underground Elec. Rlys. Co. of London*, [1912] AC 673 (HL (Eng.)), at 689, to breaches of contract for personal services is shewn by the authorities cited by Hodgins J, in delivering the judgment of the Appellate Division—notably in *Beckman v. Drake* (1849), 2 HL Cas. 579 at p. 608; 9 ER 1213 at pp. 1223-24 (HL (Eng.)).

The action of the appellant in acquiring and disposing at a profit of a considerable part of the manufactured stock of his former employers arose out of his relations with them. It involved the employment by him of time, labour and ability which he had engaged to give to them. For his loss of an opportunity to use these in earning a salary from those employers he is now asking that the respondent shall be compelled to pay by way of damages. It would seem to be manifestly unfair that, if the appellant is thus to be remunerated on a contractual basis by way of damages, he should not be held accountable in mitigation for money made by using for his own purposes the time, labour and ability so to be paid for. The $11,000 profit which he made, although the making of it required some assumption of risk and responsibility and also an expenditure clearly beyond anything which it was his duty to them, or to the respondent, to undertake, is within the rule of accountability stated by Lord Haldane. The action which produced it arose out of his former employment in the sense in which the Lord Chancellor uses the phrase "arising out of the transaction," as is shewn by his illustration from *Staniforth v. Lyall* (1830), 7 Bing. 169; 131 ER 65 (CP). Again to quote his Lordship (p. 691): "The transaction was … one in which the person whose contract was broken took a reasonable and prudent course quite naturally arising out of the circumstances in which he was placed by the breach."

By devoting his time, energy and skill for 2 years to the service of his former employers the appellant would have earned $10,000. A breakdown in his health, or other foreseen contingencies might have prevented his doing so. Excused from that service, he was enabled by a happy combination of making use of the time, labour and ability thus set free and taking advantage of the opportunity afforded by his employer's misfortune within 66 days to make a clear profit of $11,000—and he still had at his disposal, in which to add to his earnings, if so inclined, or to amuse himself if he preferred doing so, the remaining year and 299 days. Were he to be now awarded not the $10,000 claimed in his action but the $4,000 allowed him by the trial judge, he would, as a result of his employers' disaster, be better off by at least $5,000 than he would have been had he put in his 2 years of service—"a somewhat grotesque result," as Lord Atkinson put it in *Erie County Natural Gas and Fuel Co. v. Carroll*, [1911] AC 105 (PC (Ont.)) at p. 115. Making due allowance for extra time and trouble expended and all other elements proper to be considered involved in the efforts which resulted in the plaintiff's securing the profit of $11,000, and taking into account the year and

299 days left at his disposal after that was accomplished, it seems reasonably clear that he did not sustain any actual damage as a result of losing his position. He was probably, on the whole, better off.

Upon the facts, when "allowed to speak for themselves," not only is the conclusion reached by the Appellate Division in conformity with legal principles and the authorities but any other would shock the common sense of justice.

Jamal v. Moolla Dawood Sons & Co.
[1916] 1 AC 175 (PC (Burma))

LORD WRENBURY: ... Under six contracts made at various dates between April and August 1911, the plaintiff (the appellant) was seller to the defendants of certain 23,500 shares at prices amounting in the aggregate to Rs. 184,125.10. The date for delivery was December 30, 1911. The contract notes contained a term providing that in the event of the buyer not making payment on the settlement day the seller should have the option of reselling the shares by auction, and any loss arising should be recoverable from the buyer. In some cases the words ran, "by auction at the Exchange at the next meeting."

By December 30 the shares had fallen largely in value. On that day the vendor tendered the shares and asked payment of the price, adding, "Failing compliance with this request by to-day our client will be forced to sell the said shares by public auction on or about the 2nd proximo, responsible for all losses sustained thereby." The purchasers did not pay the sum demanded. They set up a contention that the seller was indebted to them on another transaction, and they sent cheques for the differential sum of Rs. 75,925.10, and called for a transfer of the shares. On January 2, 1912, the seller repudiated the claim to a set-off, and repeated, "We have now to give you notice that our client intends to resell these shares and to institute a suit against you for the recovery of any loss which may result from that course." The purchasers stopped payment of the cheques, and nothing turns upon the fact that they were given.

Negotiations ensued between the parties which extended to February 26, 1912. On that day the seller, by his agents, wrote to the purchaser a letter as follows: "We are instructed by Mr. A.K.A.S. Jamal that he has not hitherto taken any steps to enforce his claim against you for failing to pay for and take delivery of 23,500 shares in the British Burma Petroleum Company, Limited, at your request, in order that his claim might, if possible, be settled. It now appears that no active steps are being taken to settle the matter but that much time is being lost. Our client will therefore now proceed to enforce his rights by suit unless the sum of Rs. 109,219.6 is paid to him by way of compensation before the end of this week. The amount claimed is arrived at by deducting Rs. 74,906.4, the value of 23,500 shares at 4s. 3d., from Rs. 184,125.10, the agreed price of the shares." The 4s. 3d. a share there mentioned was the market price of the shares on December 30.

On March 22 the seller commenced a suit to recover Rs. 109,218.12 as damages for breach measured by the difference between the contract price of the shares and their market price (4s. 3d. a share) on the date of the breach, December 30, 1911. This is (with a trifling variance) the same sum and arrived at in the same way as the Rs. 109,219.6 mentioned in the letter.

Immediately after the letter of February 26, 1912, namely, on February 28, the seller commenced to make sale of the shares. He sold them all at various dates from February 28 onwards. In one case the sale was at less than 4s. 3d. (namely, at 4s.). In one case it was at 4s. 3d. In every other case it was at a higher price.

The decision under appeal is one which gives the purchaser the benefit of the increased prices which the shares realized, by giving him credit in reduction of the damages for the increased prices in fact realized over the market price at December 30, the date of the breach. The appellant contends that this is wrong.

Their Lordships will first deal with the contractual term as to resale. Upon breach by the purchaser his contractual right to the shares fell to the ground. There arose a right to damages, and the stipulation in question was in their Lordships' opinion only a stipulation that the seller might, if he thought fit, liquidate the damages by ascertaining the value of the shares at the date of the breach by an auction sale as specified. If the seller availed himself of that option he was not selling the purchaser's shares with a consequential obligation to account to him for the price but was selling shares belonging to the seller which the purchaser ought to, but failed to, take up and pay for in order to ascertain what was the loss arising by reason of the purchaser not completing at the contract price. Their Lordships are unable to agree with the original judge that the plaintiff's letters of December 30 and January 2 amounted to an election to take a measure of damages to be arrived at by a resale. Moreover, there never was any sale by auction under the option. Nothing turns upon this provision as to resale.

The question therefore is the general question and may be stated thus: In a contract for sale of negotiable securities, is the measure of damages for breach the difference between the contract price and the market price at the date of the breach—with an obligation on the part of the seller to mitigate the damages by getting the best price he can at the date of the breach—or is the seller bound to reduce the damages, if he can, by subsequent sales at better prices? If he is, and if the purchaser is entitled to the benefit of subsequent sales, it must also be true that he must bear the burden of subsequent losses. The latter proposition is in their Lordships' opinion impossible, and the former is equally unsound. If the seller retains the shares after the breach, the speculation as to the way the market will subsequently go is the speculation of the seller, not of the buyer; the seller cannot recover from the buyer the loss below the market price at the date of the breach if the market falls, nor is he liable to the purchaser for the profit if the market rises.

It is undoubted law that the plaintiff who sues for damages owes the duty of taking all reasonable steps to mitigate the loss consequent upon the breach and cannot claim as damages any sum which is due to his own neglect. But the loss to be ascertained is the loss *at the date of the breach*. If at that date the plaintiff could do something or did something which mitigated the damage, the defendant is entitled to the benefit of it. *Staniforth v. Lyall* (1830), 7 Bing. 169; 131 ER 65 is an illustration of this. But the fact that by reason of the loss of the contract which the defendant has failed to perform the plaintiff obtains the benefit of another contract which is of value to him does not entitle the defendant to the benefit of the latter contract: *Yates v. Whyte* (1838), 4 Bing. NC 272; 132 ER 793; *Bradburn v. Great Western Railway* (1874), LR 10 Ex. 1; *Jebsen v. East and West India Dock Co.* (1875), LR 10 CP 300.

The decision in *Rodocanachi v. Milburn* (1886), 18 QBD 67 (CA), that market value at the date of the breach is the decisive element, was upheld in the House of Lords in *Williams*

Brothers v. Agius, [1914] AC 510 (HL (Eng.)). The breach in *Rodocanachi v. Milburn* was a breach by the seller to deliver, but in their Lordships' opinion the proposition is equally true where the breach is committed by the buyer.

The respondents further contend that ss. 73 and 107 of the *India Contract Act*, or one of them, is in their favour. As regards s. 107 their Lordships are unable to see that it has any application in the present case. It deals with cases in which a seller has a lien on goods or has stopped them *in transitu*. The section follows upon sections dealing with those subject-matters. The present case is not one which falls under either of those heads. The seller was and remained the legal holder of the shares. As regards s. 73 it is but declaratory of the right to damages which has been discussed in the course of this judgment.

Their Lordships find that upon the appeal the officiating Chief Judge rested his judgment on a finding that the seller reduced his loss by selling the shares at a higher price than obtained at the date of the breach. This begs the question by assuming that loss means loss generally, not loss at the date of the breach. The seller's loss at the date of the breach was and remained the difference between contract price and market price at that date. When the buyer committed this breach the seller remained entitled to the shares, and became entitled to damages such as the law allows. The first of these two properties, namely, the shares, he kept for a time and subsequently sold them in a rising market. His pocket received benefit, but his loss at the date of the breach remained unaffected.

Their Lordships will humbly advise His Majesty that this appeal ought to be allowed, and the orders in the original Court and in the Appeal Court discharged, and judgment entered for the plaintiff according to his plaint, and that the respondent ought to pay the costs in the Courts below and of this appeal.

Campbell Mostyn (Provisions) Ltd. v. Barnett Trading Company
[1954] 1 Lloyd's Rep. 65 (CA)

[The plaintiff sold 350 cans of ham that the defendants wrongfully refused to accept. On October 24, the date of the refusal to accept, the market price was below the contract price, but the market price suddenly rose in November, and the plaintiff resold the ham at a price above the contract price.]

SOMERVELL LJ (at 67-69): … The goods tendered were not sold on October 24. The goods were South African tinned ham of a particular brand, which was said to be not a popular brand on the market. Early in that year, 1951, recapitulating part of the Master's findings of fact, there had been considerable imports of tinned ham; the best varieties, one gathers, coming from Germany and Belgium. The market became somewhat overcharged and prices fell. The fact that the market was inactive affected, apparently, the Dominion ham, particularly the brand in question, more than the German brand. There was undoubtedly a fall in price. Subsequently, after the breach, within a fortnight, the Government, which had been then recently elected and had taken office, made an announcement with regard to imposing an extra measure of control on imports from Continental countries. That, with Christmas not very far off, improved the market for ham and with it the less popular Dominion brands, with one of which we are concerned. In fact, the sellers sold these 18 oz. tins after Nov. 7 at a sum in excess of the market price, and therefore, on the face of it, suffered no damage. One can understand, in those circumstances, the buyers thinking that that was the end of it and feeling aggrieved if the provisions of the law held them liable to pay a sum in damages.

The learned Master and Divisional Court have held that the defendants are liable to pay damages, notwithstanding the events, which I have recounted, on the principle which is stated concisely in the Privy Council opinion in *A.K.A.S. Jamal v. Moolla Dawood, Sons & Co.*, [1916] 1 AC 175 (PC (Burma.)) at p. 179. That dealt, as will be seen, with negotiable securities, but in my opinion the principle is equally applicable to the sale of goods:

> The question therefore is the general question and may be stated thus: In a contract for sale of negotiable securities, is the measure of damages for breach the difference between the contract price and the market price at the date of the breach—with an obligation on the part of the seller to mitigate the damages by getting the best price he can at the date of the breach—or is the seller bound to reduce the damages, if he can, by subsequent sales at better prices? If he is, and if the purchaser is entitled to the benefit of subsequent sales, it must also be true that he must bear the burden of subsequent losses. The latter proposition is in their Lordships' opinion impossible, and the former is equally unsound. If the seller retains the shares after the breach, the speculation as to the way the market will subsequently go is the speculation of the seller, not of the buyer; the seller cannot recover from the buyer the loss below the market price at the date of the breach if the market falls, nor is he liable to the purchaser for the profit if the market rises.

No doubt it is small comfort to the defendants in this case to know that if the market had gone even worse than it was on Oct. 24 they would not have been liable to pay more than whatever sum was fixed, assuming there was a market, for the market price on that day.

This appeal is a curious one in this way. The appellants are in effect asking this Court, as they asked the Master and as they asked the Divisional Court, to disregard the evidence given by their own witnesses and to find that there was no market. ... Just reading the note of the evidence, it would seem fairly clear that, as it were, all the witnesses went into the box with the idea of assisting the Master to find out what was the market price on Oct. 24. The plaintiffs, who put in their claim on the basis that the price was 45s. per dozen, were seeking to say that it was a poor market for this type of goods; the sort of man you would have got to buy might well have been described as a speculator and they, the plaintiffs, would have been lucky to get 40s. The witnesses for the defendants, on the other hand, went into the box and they drew a much more rosy picture of the market. One of them said: "The demand was there in October. It is an astounding suggestion that the market remained flooded until Nov. 7. If I had been asked to handle 350 cases in October I could have disposed of them at about 1s. less than the German."

Mr. Shaw, who appeared for the defendants, as I have said, took the point at that stage, and it was taken before the Divisional Court and before us, that, relying on what had happened and on certain answers given by Mr. Wand for the plaintiffs, there was no market within the meaning of the *prima facie* rule. Though we have not heard the other side, I will assume for the purposes of this judgment that if it could have been established that there had been no market within the meaning of the rule the appellants would have succeeded and the Court would have taken the actual ultimate transaction as the measure. Certainly if Mr. Beyfus had satisfied me that there was no market within the meaning of the rule I would have wanted to hear the other side. But he has failed to do so, and I must state my reasons.

I will read the passages on which he very rightly relies. Mr. Wand, after giving a general account of the market which I have summarized, said: "If we had had to sell 350 cases of 36 it would have been to a speculative buyer who would have paid far less ... If we had put the 350 cases in this action on the market then I doubt whether a speculator would have given me 3s. a lb." Mr. Beyfus relied very much on the word "speculator," but I do not think that helps very much. Then Mr. Wand says this in cross-examination, which is rather the other way: "At the beginning of October the market was extremely quiet." However, going back to the passage the appellants rely on, "On or about Oct. 24, we wrote or telephoned to our agents to try and sell the goods," the name of the agent for some reason was not written down. No light has been thrown on that and it was not disclosed and I do not think we can derive any help from the non-disclosure. If the defendants had wanted to know, they should have taken that up before the Master. "Our market man would have been offering them (Mr. Case, not with us now)." Then Mr. Wand says in re-examination, "So far as I know attempts were being made to sell the goods in October 1951." Then this is, I think, an important answer: "Before writing the letter of Oct. 26 we tried to find out the market price. As we could not get what we thought was a fair price we did not sell." Then there is another sentence: "We had bought from a French company. We were both trying to sell."

The Master in a full and careful judgment comes to deal with this point and he uses words which Mr. Beyfus relies on as showing that he had misdirected himself. He finds that there was a market for these goods and he finds the market price. He later is dealing with this argument. He refers to the fact that Mr. Shaw had a sentence in his note which the learned Master had not got in his: "There was no market then for these goods. I cannot remember anyone making an offer for these goods." The Master goes on:

> Nevertheless the mere fact that the plaintiffs did not [—and these are the words relied on—] or could not get an offer is not conclusive of the matter, and if Mr. Wand did say "There was no market," I think the words must be taken in conjunction with his previous answer, "As we couldn't get what *we thought* was a fair price we didn't sell." The matter is, I think, put beyond question by the evidence of the defendants' own witnesses Mr. Churchman and Mr. Dewar, whose evidence in effect was that 350 cases would have been a mere bagatelle and that there would have been no difficulty in disposing of them.

Those words "or could not get an offer," taken out of their context, might suggest a misdirection, but they must be read with the rest of the judgment and with regard to the words which follow, where the Master is saying that Mr. Wand did say "There was no market" in connection with the other answer "As we couldn't get what we thought was a fair price." Therefore, having done my best to consider the point put by Mr. Beyfus, I think the Master came to the right conclusion and that he was entitled to find on this evidence that there was a market.

On the basis that he was entitled to find that there was a market, Mr. Beyfus does not seek to disturb the actual figure which he arrived at. Mr. Beyfus submitted that there might, and I am not saying there might not, be a sort of half-way house where it could not be said that you could not sell at a sacrifice but where it was reasonable not to sell. I think there might be difficulty in taking such a case out of what I will call the principle in the *Jamal v. Moolla* case unless the buyer who was available was given a chance of agreeing, because on this basis the damages might be increased. I do not think those complications arise here, because I think on the evidence, particularly that of the defendants which the learned Master was entitled to accept, there was a market within the terms of the *prima facie* rule, and the answers relied on in Mr. Wand's evidence are explicable in the way I have tried to indicate.

For these reasons, I think this appeal fails.

Slater v. Hoyle & Smith Ltd.
[1920] 2 KB 11 (CA)

WARRINGTON LJ: The plaintiffs are the sellers, and the defendants are the buyers under a contract dated June 20, 1918, for the sale and purchase of certain goods, to wit, 3000 pieces of cotton cloth of a description mentioned in the contract. After 1625 pieces had been delivered the defendants refused to accept the remaining 1375, alleging that the cloth already delivered had been persistently of a quality not in accordance with the contract and that they were entitled to assume that future deliveries would be as bad, and to treat the plaintiffs as repudiating the contract. The plaintiffs sued the defendants for non-acceptance of the undelivered goods, and the defendants counterclaimed for damages, for the non-delivery of the undelivered goods; and for breach of warranty of quality in respect of the goods delivered.

The learned judge decided the main issue in the defendants' favour, and on the counterclaim he awarded no damages for non-delivery, on the ground that the market price at the date of the breach was below the contract price; but as damages for breach of warranty he awarded the difference between the value at the date of delivery of the goods actually delivered and the value they would have had if they had answered to the warranty, eliminating from consideration certain sub-contracts made by the defendants, which I will refer to more particularly in a moment, in partial fulfilment of which 691 pieces of the cloth delivered by the plaintiffs had been employed. On the main question I agree with the judgment of Greer J and Bankes LJ, and have nothing to add. I also agree that taking, as he did, $4\frac{1}{2}$ *d.* a yard as the difference in the two values, the judge was doing the best he could on the materials before him, and we ought not to interfere.

But the plaintiffs say that as to the 691 pieces delivered under the sub-contracts, the learned judge ought to have taken into account the prices realized by the defendants under the sub-contracts, and that as those prices were equal to or exceeded the contract price, the defendants in fact suffered no damage and ought to have had none awarded to them. There were two sub-contracts, both with the West Somerset and Devon Manufacturing Co., one dated December 14, 1917, before the date of the contract in question, and the other dated June 26, 1918. The price under the first was $8\frac{1}{2}$ *d.* a yard, and under the second 1*s.* 3*d.* The cloth to be delivered under the head contract was to be unbleached, or "grey" cloth, that under the sub-contracts, was, as I understand, to be bleached. The plaintiffs knew nothing of these contracts, and the defendants were under no obligation to their purchasers to deliver the plaintiffs' goods. Under these circumstances the question is: Was the learned judge right in the course he took?

The general principle on which he acted is that laid down by s. 53, sub-s. 3, of the *Sale of Goods Act, 1893*, and this appears to be clearly the right principle where goods are delivered not of the right quality and the buyer elects not to reject them but to claim damages. Into the calculation for the purpose of applying this principle the contract price as such does not enter at all, though I suppose it may be an element in assessing the value.

The defendants rely on the rule laid down by Lord Esher MR in *Rodocanachi v. Milburn* (1886), 18 QBD 67 (CA) at p. 77. He said: "It is well settled that in an action for non-delivery or non-acceptance of goods under a contract of sale the law does not take into account in estimating the damages anything that is accidental as between the plaintiff and the defendant, as for instance an intermediate contract entered into with a third party for the purchase or sale of the goods." In those cases the elements for comparison are, in general, the contract price and the market price at the date when the goods should have been delivered or accepted, as the case may be, and if in such cases sub-contracts are not to be taken into account I do not see why they should be in such a case as the present. Indeed on the facts of the case there are special reasons against doing so. The sub-contracts were not for the identical goods, being for bleached instead of grey cloth, and they might or might not be performed by delivering the goods the subject of the head contract. The decision in *Rodocanachi v. Milburn* was followed in the House of Lords in *Williams v. Agius*, [1914] AC 510 (HL (Eng.)).

But it is said that the present case is governed by *Wertheim v. Chicoutimi Pulp Co.*, [1911] AC 301 (PC (Qué.)). That was an action for delayed delivery of goods. The purchaser had sold the goods, the subject of the head contract, at a price exceeding that prevailing at the date of delivery, and it was held that the higher price so obtained must be substituted for the lower one as one of the elements of comparison. I do not think the present case is governed by *Wertheim's Case*. The purchaser here has received inferior goods of smaller value than those he ought to have received. He has lost the difference in the two values, and it seems to me immaterial that by some good fortune, with which the plaintiffs have nothing to do, he has been able to recoup himself what he paid for the goods. If the goods had been of the quality contracted for he might have sold them at a higher price and made a profit. In truth, as I have already pointed out, in the class of case we are dealing with, the contract price does not directly enter into the calculation at all.

Ontario Law Reform Commission
(1979), 2 *Report on Sale of Goods*, at 409-10, 422, and 501-2 (footnotes omitted)

Seller's Remedies (Right of Resale) (at 409-10)

The points requiring clarification are as follows. In the first place, it is not clear whether the seller is bound by the results of a resale in claiming damages as measured under the provisions of UCC 2-708, which employs a market price test. The commentators are divided on the issue, although there is substantial historical evidence that the Code draftsmen envisaged the right of resale enuring only for the seller's benefit. To permit the seller to ignore the results of the resale and to claim damages based on the difference between the market price and the contract price could, however, lead to undesirable consequences. It could provide the seller with an unjustifiable windfall, thus violating the general principle in UCC 1-106 that the object of the Code's remedial provisions is to put an aggrieved party in the same position as if the other party had fully performed. It could also leave the buyer in an uncertain state. UCC 2-706 requires the seller to give the buyer notice of his intention to resell and, in the case of a public sale, of the time and place of the sale. It would be pointless for the buyer to attend the sale, or to take other protective steps, if he had no assurance that the seller would be bound by the results of the sale.

In the Commission's opinion, where a seller has exercised his right of resale, he should be bound by the results of the resale in claiming his damages, and we so recommend. To ensure this result, the recommended general provision in the revised Act dealing with the computation and measure of the seller's damages should provide that, where the seller re-sells, he is not entitled to sue for the difference between the contract price and the price that we later recommend for adoption in lieu of the market price, if his actual loss is less than this difference. Some of the implications of this restatement of the compensatory principle of contract damages are examined later in this chapter; suffice it to say for the moment that it is broad enough to answer the problem at hand. Implicit, also, in this recommendation is our rejection of the concept that the market price test provides a liquidated measure of dam-ages which the seller (and, in a converse case where the seller is in breach, the buyer) should be entitled to recover as a statutory minimum.

Seller's Remedies (Damages) (at 422)

We have touched earlier on one aspect of the problem of overcompensation in recommend-ing, in the context of UCC 2-706, that the seller should not be entitled to invoke the test that we later recommend in lieu of the market price test where he has actually resold the goods for a price higher than market, but that he should be bound by the results of the resale. This recommendation is consistent with the reasoning of the Privy Council in *Wertheim v. Chi-coutimi Pulp Co.*, [1911] AC 301 (PC (Qué.)), which involved a claim for damages by a buyer. The question whether a defaulting buyer should be able to resist a market price claim, or a similar claim for damages, by the seller on the ground that the seller's cost of produc-tion would have exceeded the contract price appears to be unsettled. If the compensatory basis of contract damages is taken to its logical conclusion, the buyer's defence should suc-ceed unless the market price test is regarded as establishing a minimum, liquidated form of measure of damages. The reasoning in *Wertheim* implicitly rejects such a characterization, as does our Draft Bill.

Buyer's Remedies (Damages) (at 501-2)

The second question is the extent to which the seller can take advantage of the buyer's actual resale or compensating purchase, as the case may be, in order to show that the buyer's actual loss was *less* than the figure that would otherwise be arrived at by the market price formula. The rule in the *Rodocanachi* case [*Rodocanachi Sons & Co. v. Milburn Brothers* (1887), 18 QBD 67 (CA)], just referred to, does not furnish an automatic answer to this question, be-cause it fails to take into account the buyer's general obligation to mitigate his damages, which arises *after* he has learned of the seller's breach. The point does not appear to be cov-ered by authority, but textwriters generally take a negative view. We have earlier recom-mended that a provision equivalent to UCC 2-712, which confers upon the buyer a right to "cover," should be incorporated into the revised Act. If this recommendation is accepted, then the mitigation issue will resolve itself in cases where the buyer has made a compensating purchase. The reason is that the covering price will measure the extent of the buyer's damages, whether the price is lower or higher than the prevailing market price.

Our recommended right to cover does not, however, provide a complete answer to the broad policy issue presented by the question under discussion. The right to cover is by its nature limited to a post-breach event and does not relate to events that occur prior to breach. To what extent should evidence of such pre-breach events be admissible? Our response to this policy issue is contained in our Draft Bill which, following the controversial decision of the Privy Council in *Wertheim v. Chicoutimi Pulp Co.*, limits the aggrieved party to such damages as he has actually suffered without distinguishing between events occurring before or after the date of breach. We have adopted this position because, in our view, the criticism of the *Wertheim* case confuses two separate issues. If the question is whether the aggrieved party should be entitled to recover enhanced damages because of loss of, or liability under, a sub-contract, the foreseeability of such damages is a relevant issue. But foreseeability has nothing to do with the question whether damages higher than those actually suffered should be recoverable. We agree with the Privy Council that the compensatory purpose of damages should be as applicable here as in other branches of contract law. Admittedly, this may lead to a lesser award than would otherwise be the case, but, in our view, this possibility is irrelevant. What is relevant is that the judgment leaves the aggrieved party in approximately the same position as if the contract had been performed, and this is what a damage award is supposed to do. We recognize that a market price test is easier to apply and that it has the appearance of being even-handed. However, its equitable nature disappears once it is conceded that the buyer's damages may be based on the results of a covering purchase. The question then becomes whether only post-breach factors may be taken into account, or whether the admissible evidence may also include antecedent events. For the reasons we have given we prefer the rule that is more generous to the seller. Accordingly, we recommend that the buyer should be limited to such damages as he has actually suffered without distinguishing between events occurring before or after the date of breach.

Collateral Benefits

In *Ratych v. Bloomer*, [1990] 1 SCR 940, the plaintiff, a police officer, was injured by the defendant's negligence. He was unable to work for a period during which his pay continued, pursuant to the terms of a collective agreement. The Supreme Court of Canada held that the continued pay had to be taken into account, with the result that no damages were recoverable from the defendant in respect of lost pay. The court said that the result might be different in case of receipts by way of gift, or pursuant to insurance, or if the employer had a right to repayment from the proceeds of the award, by subrogation or otherwise.

Cunningham v. Wheeler
[1994] 1 SCR 359

CORY J: These three appeals were heard together. They raise the following questions. First, should payments received by a plaintiff pursuant to a private policy of insurance be deducted from the amount recovered for loss of wages? Second, if private policies of insurance are to be exempt from deduction, then should disability benefits negotiated under a collective agreement also be exempted from deduction? Third, if disability benefits provided by a collective agreement are to be exempt from deduction, what proof is required of the payment for the benefits by the plaintiff-employee? ...

Cunningham v. Wheeler

Factual Background

Some confusion may arise from the designation of the parties as appellants or respondents. I will therefore refer to those seeking to recover lost wages without deduction of their insurance or disability benefits as the plaintiffs, and those arguing for deduction as the defendants.

On November 14, 1988, the plaintiff Bradwell Cunningham was injured when he was struck by a car while he was walking across a road. At the time he was 46 years old and had been employed by BC Rail, for about 25 years. He was in hospital for nine days and off work for almost 20 weeks. During this period, pursuant to the provisions of a collective bargaining agreement, he collected disability benefits which amounted to $5,327.15.

No deductions were made from his pay for the disability benefits. However, there was evidence accepted by the trial judge which demonstrated that collateral benefits formed an important aspect of the negotiations between the company and its various unions. A union representative and the company vice-president of human resources explained that if the indemnity coverage was increased, there would be a proportionate decrease in either the hourly wages or the other collateral benefits paid to the employees. Put another way, it was said that under the collective bargaining agreement the employees were entitled to receive an hourly wage package. That package was made up of an hourly rate of pay together with the collateral benefits. If the disability benefits were to be abandoned, then the hourly wage rate would be proportionately higher. The company held the funds for the disability payments and turned them over to the Aetna Group Canada for management. Mr. Cunningham was not required to repay the weekly disability benefits he recovered from the defendants either to BC Rail or to Aetna Group Canada.

Decision at Trial

The trial judge found that the evidence established the disability benefits paid to Cunningham were directly paid for by him [summarized 23 ACWS (3d) 296]. He noted that any increase in the disability benefits would result in a proportionate decrease in the hourly wage rate or other benefits.

He considered the decision of this court in *Ratych v. Bloomer*, [1990] 1 SCR 940. He concluded that the plaintiff Cunningham had established that the indemnity benefits were paid for by him as part of his wage package. He therefore determined that the weekly disability payments should not be deducted in calculating the amount payable by the defendants for the wages lost by the plaintiff as a result of his injuries.

The Court of Appeal

The Court of Appeal ((1991), 95 DLR (4th) 655) determined that since there was no subrogation right in the employer, and the direct funding for the disability benefits came from the employer, the plan was not in the nature of a private insurance policy. As a result, the court held that the funds received should be deducted from the damage award. The position was put this way (at p. 674):

> It is quite true, as was pointed out by Mr. Justice Anderson in his judgment in *Cunningham v. Wheeler*, that there are trade-offs in wage negotiations and, in the case of BC Rail, it might well be willing to raise the wages of its employees if the disability plan was abandoned.
>
> But I have no reason to think that the Peel Regional Board of Commissioners of Police did not look at the costs of paying the salaries of injured policemen as part of the wage cost to the board. The right of Constable Ratych against the board was of no different order than the right of Mr. Cunningham against BC Rail.

The Private Insurance Policy: Its History of Exemption from Deduction and Its Present Status

For over 119 years, the courts of England and Canada have held that payments received for loss of wages pursuant to a private policy of insurance should not be deducted from the lost wages claim of a plaintiff. The first question to be considered is whether the rationale for this exemption persists. In my view, there are convincing reasons both for the existence of the policy and for its continuation.

At the outset, it may be well to state once again the principle of recovery in an action for tort. Simply, it is to compensate the injured party as completely as possible for the loss suffered as a result of the negligent action or inaction of the defendant. However, the plaintiff is not entitled to a double recovery for any loss arising from the injury. How then has the insurance exception arisen? It was first formally recognized in *Bradburn v. Great Western Rail Co.* (1874), LR 10 Ex. 1, [1874-80] All ER Rep. 195 (Ex. Div.). In that case the plaintiff had been injured as a result of the negligence of the defendant railway company. The plaintiff had received a sum of money from a private insurer to compensate him for lost income as a result of the accident. It was held that the plaintiff was entitled to full damages from the defendant as well as the payment from the insurer. That is to say, there was to be no deduction of the insurance proceeds received from his recovery from the defendant. This result was explained by stating that there would be no justice in setting off an amount to which the plaintiff had entitled himself under a contract of insurance such as any prudent man would make. The justification for the rule is explained in these words at p. 197 [All ER Rep.] in the reasons of Pigott B:

> ... I think that there would be no justice or principle in setting off an amount which the plaintiff has entitled himself to under a contract of insurance, such as any prudent man would make on the principle of, as the expression is, "laying by for a rainy day." He pays the premiums upon a contract which, if he meets with an accident, entitles him to receive a sum of money. It is not because he meets with the accident, but because he made a contract with, and paid premiums to, the insurance company, for that express purpose, that he gets the money from them. It is true that there must be the element of accident in order to entitle him to the money; but it is under and by reason of his contract with the insurance company, that he gets the amount; and I think that it ought not, upon any principle of justice, to be deducted from the amount of the damages proved to have been sustained by him through the negligence of the defendants.

The decision of the court in that case was founded on the ground that the accident was not the *causa causans* of the receipt of the insurance benefits, but merely a *causa sine qua non*.

Later, the basis for the exemption was shifted from the causal reason set out in *Bradburn* to one based on the fact that the plaintiff had paid for the insurance benefit and that benefit thus paid for should not enure to the benefit of the defendant. This was the approach adopted by Asquith LJ for the Court of Appeal in *Shearman v. Folland*, [1950] 1 All ER 976 at p. 978:

> What in a given case is, and what is not, "collateral"? Insurance affords the classic example of something which is treated in law as collateral. Where X is insured by Y against injury which comes to be wrongfully inflicted on him by Z, Z cannot set up in mitigation or extinction of his own liability X's right to be recouped by Y or the fact that X has been recouped by Y: *Bradburn v. Great Western Ry. Co. [supra]* and *Simpson v. Thomson* [(1877), 3 App. Cas. 279]. There are special reasons for this. If the wrongdoer were entitled to set-off what the plaintiff was entitled to recoup or had recouped under his policy, he would, in effect, be depriving the plaintiff of all benefit from the premiums paid by the latter and appropriating that benefit to himself.

This reasoning was adopted by the House of Lords in *Parry v. Cleaver, infra.*

The English courts have in some cases narrowly interpreted the non-deductibility rule, but the application of the *Bradburn* rule to private insurance has never been questioned. In *Browning v. War Office*, [1962] 3 All ER 1089 (CA), the majority of the Court of Appeal held that the plaintiff's disability pension should be deducted in assessing his damages for lost earnings. However, both Lord Denning MR and Diplock LJ cited the *Bradburn* rule as an exception to the principle that a plaintiff should be compensated for his or her full loss, but no more.

In *Parry v. Cleaver*, [1969] 1 All ER 555, the majority of the House of Lords reversed *Browning* and held that a police officer's disability pension should not be taken into account in assessing his damages for loss of income. Their reasons affirmed the importance of the *Bradburn* rule, and justified it in terms of fairness. Lord Reid stated at p. 558:

> As regards moneys coming to the plaintiff under a contract of insurance, I think that the real and substantial reason for disregarding them is that the plaintiff has bought them and that it would be unjust and unreasonable to hold that the money which he prudently spent on premiums and the benefit from it should enure to the benefit of the tortfeasor. Here again I think that the explanation that this is too remote is artificial and unreal. Why should the plaintiff be left worse off than if he had never insured?

Lord Pearce stated at pp. 575-6:

> One must, I think, start with the firm basis that *Bradburn v. Great Western Ry. Co.* was rightly decided and that the benefits from a private insurance by the plaintiff are not to be taken in account.
>
> The Australian cases have accepted *Bradburn's* case as correct. So, too, the Canadian cases. It has never been criticised in our courts. It accords with the view of the American Restatement. And counsel for the respondent has not assailed it here.
>
> One may put the justification of *Bradburn's* case on various grounds. Pigott B, in deciding it said:

... [T]here would be no justice or principle in setting off an amount which the plaintiff has entitled himself to under a contract of insurance, such as any prudent man would make on the principle of, as the expression is "laying by for a rainy day." ... It is true that there must be the element of accident in order to entitle him to the money; but it is under and by reason of his contract with the insurance company, that he gets the amount; and I think it ought not, upon any principle of justice, to be deducted from the amount of the damages proved to have been sustained by him through the negligence of the defendants.

In *Shearman v. Folland* the court in a judgement given by Asquith LJ, in discussing what benefits were merely "collateral" said of *Bradburn's* case:

If the wrongdoer were entitled to set-off what the plaintiff was entitled to recoup or had recouped under his policy, he would, in effect, be depriving the plaintiff of all benefit from the premiums paid by the latter and appropriating that benefit to himself.

In *Hussain v. New Taplow Paper Mills Ltd.*, [1988] 1 All ER 541, the House of Lords once again affirmed the importance of the *Bradburn* rule. At pp. 544-5, Lord Bridge stated: "... where a plaintiff recovers under an insurance policy for which he has paid the premiums, the insurance moneys are not deductible from damages payable by the tortfeasor ... ."

The *Bradburn* rule has been consistently applied by Canadian courts. It has been affirmed by appellate courts in Saskatchewan (*Tubb v. Lief*, [1932] 3 WWR 245 (Sask. CA); *Dawson v. Sawatzky*, [1946] 1 DLR 476 (Sask. CA)); New Brunswick (*Bourgeois v. Tzrop* (1957), 9 DLR (2d) 214 (NB CA)); Ontario (*Boarelli v. Flannigan* (1973), 36 DLR (3d) 4 (CA)); and British Columbia (*Chan v. Butcher* (1984), 11 DLR (4th) 233 (CA)). In *Canadian Pacific Ltd. v. Gill*, [1973] SCR 654, and in *Guy v. Trizec Equities Ltd.*, [1979] 2 SCR 756, this court affirmed the principle first set out in *Bradburn's* case and adopted in *Parry v. Cleaver* that the proceeds of insurance should not be deducted from a plaintiff's damages.

I think the exemption for the private policy of insurance should be maintained. It has a long history. It is understood and accepted. There has never been any confusion as to when it should be applied. More importantly, it is based on fairness. All who insure themselves for disability benefits are displaying wisdom and forethought in making provision for the continuation of some income in case of disabling injury or illness. The acquisition of the policy has social benefits for those insured, their dependants and indeed their community. It represents forbearance and self-denial on the part of the purchaser of the policy to provide for contingencies. The individual may never make a claim on the policy and the premiums paid may be a total loss. Yet the policy provides security.

Recovery in tort is dependent on the plaintiff establishing injury and loss resulting from an act of misfeasance or nonfeasance on the part of the defendant, the tortfeasor. I can see no reason why a tortfeasor should benefit from the sacrifices made by a plaintiff in obtaining an insurance policy to provide for lost wages. Tort recovery is based on some wrongdoing. It makes little sense for a wrongdoer to benefit from the private act of forethought and sacrifice of the plaintiff.

There is a good reason why the courts should be slow to change a carefully considered long-standing policy that no deductions should be made for insurance moneys paid for lost wages. If any action is to be taken, it should be by legislatures. It is significant that in general no such action has been taken.

Although in Ontario the non-deductibility principle was abandoned in relation to motor vehicle accidents when a no-fault motor vehicle insurance regime was enacted, the general rule in other tort litigation of non-deductibility has not been altered: s. 267 of the *Insurance Act*, RSO 1990, c. I.8. It is significant that this was done in the context of creating a new system for compensating victims of motor vehicle accidents, largely outside traditional tort law. The non-deductibility rule in respect to tort damages has not been altered in any of the other provinces.

Even more significantly, the Quebec legislators, after careful consideration of the advantages and disadvantages, specifically provided that there was to be no deductibility. The provision of the *Civil Code of Quebec*, SQ 1991, c. 64, and the Attorney-General's commentaries are instructive. They are as follows:

Article 1608:
The obligation of the debtor to pay damages to the creditor is neither reduced nor altered by the fact that the creditor receives a prestation from a third person, as a result of the injury he has sustained, except so far as the third person is subrogated to the rights of the creditor.

Commentary on Article 1608 (translation):
This article adopts, with a few changes and making its application more general, the rule regarding insurance contracts stated in art. 2494 CCLC.

It is intended to resolve the question of whether the obligation on a debtor to compensate can be reduced or altered by payments made to the creditor by a third party, whether those payments are gratuitous or for consideration. This would be the case if, for example, without being required to do so, the creditor's employer continued to pay him his salary while he was unable to work; it would also be the case if the creditor's insurer paid him, in his capacity as an insured, the proceeds of an insurance policy he had taken out.

Giving a negative answer to this question may sometimes result in giving the creditor double compensation—what he receives from the third party and what he is paid by the debtor—and so conferring an enrichment on him; such an answer may also seem contrary to the principle of compensation for injury, since in some cases the injury may no longer exist as the third party may have already given compensation for it.

On the other hand, an affirmative answer seems contrary to the preventive function of the obligation to compensate, and may also lead to the somewhat disturbing result of relieving the debtor of any obligation to compensate solely as the result of the good will of a third party or the creditor's foresight in protecting himself at his own expense against the possibility of the injury.

The article comes down in favour of a negative answer to this question of whether the debtor's obligation to compensate may be reduced or altered by payments the creditor receives from a third party; but so as to avoid the principal cases in which double compensation would result, it expressly excludes situations where the third party is legally or by agreement subrogated to the creditor's rights.

This is the solution which seems fairest in the circumstances, especially as most of the payments made by third parties—social security indemnities, insurance payments or payments resulting from collective labour agreements—are not really in the nature of an indemnity and in any case are not meant to compensate for the injury sustained by the creditor.

(Quebec, *Code Civil du Quebec: Commentaries du ministre de la Justice* (Montreal: DACFO Inc., 1993).)

Should the insurance exception apply in the situation where disability benefits are obtained not privately but pursuant to a collective bargaining agreement?

The Court of Appeal refused to exempt the disability payments received by the plaintiff because they were obtained as a result of a collective bargaining agreement, rather than by way of a direct deduction from his pay. That, I think, is too narrow an exception. They were bargained for and obtained as a result of a reduction in the hourly rate of pay. These benefits were therefore obtained and paid for by the plaintiff just as much as if he had bought and privately paid for a policy of disability insurance.

The scheme in this case can qualify as an insurance exception on the basis of the reasons of the majority in *Ratych v. Bloomer, supra*. In that case, McLachlin J writing for the majority specifically limited her comments to benefits which were not in the nature of insurance or gratuitous payments in these words (at p. 54): "These comments should not be taken as extending to types of collateral benefits other than lost earnings, such as insurance paid for by the plaintiff and gratuitous payments made by third parties."

To say that the exception applies only to private insurance, where actual premiums are paid to the insurance company, would create barriers that are unfair and artificial. It would mean that top management and professionals who could well afford to purchase their own insurance would have the benefit of the insurance exception, while those who made the same provision and made relatively greater financial sacrifices to provide for the disability payments through their collective bargaining agreement would be denied the benefits of the insurance exception. This would be manifestly unfair. There is no basis for such a socially regressive distinction.

Union representation and collective bargaining are recognized as a means for working people to protect their interests. The benefits for which employees have bargained in good faith should not be sacrificed simply because the mode of payment for the disability benefit is different from that in private insurance contracts. Where evidence is adduced that an employee-plaintiff has paid in some manner for his or her benefits under a collective agreement or contract of employment, the insurance exception should apply. It would be unjust to deprive employees of the benefits which, through prudence and thrift, they have provided for themselves.

On the facts of *Ratych v. Bloomer*, McLachlin J found that it could not be established that the plaintiff in that case had paid for the benefits at issue, thus making them in the nature of private insurance. However, she held that if there were evidence that the plaintiff had paid for the benefits, they might not be deductible. At pp. 46-7, she stated:

> I accept that if an employee can establish that he or she has suffered a loss in exchange for obtaining wages during the time he or she could not work, the employee should be compensated for that loss. Thus in *Lavigne v. Doucet* the New Brunswick Court of Appeal quite rightly allowed damages for loss of accumulated sick benefits. I also accept that if an employee can establish that he or she directly paid for a policy in the nature of insurance against unemploy-

ment, equivalent to a private insurance, he or she may be able to recover the benefits of that policy, although I would leave resolution of this question for another case.

These are two different exceptions. The first has nothing to do with the insurance exception, but covers a situation where although the employee continues to receive a salary while off work, he or she has to give up something else to receive it. An example of such a loss, provided by McLachlin J, is sick leave. The employee continues to receive wages, but gives up sick days, which he or she could have used at some other time. In such a situation the insurance exception does not arise, because there is in fact no double compensation problem. The employee who uses up his sick leave to get wages while he or she is off work loses the sick benefits, and so should be compensated for them. Or alternatively, the employee could decide not to use his or her sick days, and not get paid. There is also a loss in such a case.

The second exception McLachlin describes is an application of the insurance exception. However, she held that proof was required that the employee had paid for the benefit in some way to make it akin to private insurance.

McLachlin J, although recognizing the rule for personal insurance, questioned whether, aside from the evidentiary requirement, there was some substantive reason for there to be deductibility in cases where the benefits arise out of a contract of employment. At pp. 47-8 she wrote:

> The foregoing comments rest primarily on evidentiary considerations. Approaching the problem from a substantive point of view, it may be that there is a valid distinction between cases where a person has prudently obtained and paid for personal insurance and cases where the benefits flow from the employer/employee relationship. The law has long recognized that in the first situation an exception should be made to the usual rule against double recovery. The existence of such an exception does not mean it should be extended to situations where personal prudence and deprivation are not demonstrated. In the latter case there is little to be weighed in the balance against the general policy of the law against double compensation.

The substantive concern is, I think, inextricably linked with the evidentiary requirement. Once the evidentiary requirement is met, the substantive concern for personal prudence and deprivation will also be satisfied. If the plaintiff can show that he or she has paid for the benefits in the nature of insurance against unemployment akin to private insurance, that same proof will also demonstrate personal prudence and deprivation. Indeed, such a deprivation for an employee will often be proportionately very much higher than that of the executive or professional person acquiring personal insurance.

In my view *Ratych v. Bloomer, supra*, simply placed a burden upon plaintiffs to establish that they had paid for the provision of disability benefits. I think the manner of payment may be found, for example, in evidence pertaining to the provisions of a collective bargaining agreement just as clearly as in a direct payroll deduction.

Further, the presence or absence of a third party carrier for the insurance will not affect the non-deductibility of the benefits from the wage claim. A requirement of a third party carrier as a necessary condition for non-deductibility was considered, and in my view properly rejected, by the House of Lords in *Parry v. Cleaver*. At p. 558, Lord Reid asks and answers this question:

Then I ask—why should it make any difference that he be insured by arrangement with his employer rather than with an insurance company? In the course of the argument the distinction came down to be as narrow as this: if the employer says nothing or merely advises the man to insure and he does so, then the insurance money will not be deductible; but if the employer makes it a term of the contract of employment that he shall insure himself and he does so, then the insurance money will be deductible. There must be something wrong with an argument that drives us to so unreasonable a conclusion.

It is often more economical for large corporations to self-insure than to purchase insurance from a third party carrier. Risk can be spread among the employees, who are the policyholders of the self-insurance. The law should not discourage the efficiencies of self-insurance within large corporations or government agencies.

What proof is required to establish payment for the disability benefits by the plaintiff? In other words, what proof is necessary to establish the insurance policy nature of the disability benefits?

In *Ratych v. Bloomer*, there was no evidence put forward that the plaintiff had paid for the disability benefits. What type of proof will be required to show that the benefits are in the nature of insurance? It is my opinion that what is required by the *Ratych* decision is that there be evidence adduced of some type of consideration given up by the employee in return for the benefit. The method or means of payment of the consideration is not determinative. Evidence of a contribution to the plan by the employee, whether paid for directly or by a reduced hourly wage reflected in a collective bargaining agreement, will be sufficient.

Generally speaking, any of the following examples, by no means an exhaustive list, provide the sort of evidence that could well be sufficient to establish that the employee paid for the benefit:

(1) Evidence that there were trade-offs in the collective bargaining process, which demonstrate that the employee has forgone higher wages or other benefits in return for the disability benefits. In such a case, the employee has paid for the benefits through wages forgone.

(2) Evidence of some money forgone by the employee in return for the benefits. For example if the employees gave up the return of a percentage of their Unemployment Insurance Plan premiums in return for the benefits.

(3) Evidence of a direct contribution by the employee, in a form such as payroll deductions, in return for the benefits. Such a contribution need not be 100% of the premium.

(4) Evidence of payments by the employer for the benefits made on behalf of the employee which shows that those payments were part of the employee's wages, and thus the employee provided work for the employer in order to have the premium paid. For example, if the employer's contribution is listed on the employee's pay slip or statement of benefits, it can reasonably be inferred that the contribution is part of the employee's wage package.

The application of the insurance exception to benefits received under a contract of employment should not be limited to cases where the plaintiff is a member of a union and bargains collectively. Benefits received under the employment contracts of non-unionized employees will also be non-deductible if proof is provided of payment in some manner by the employee for the benefits. Although there may not be evidence of negotiations for the wage/benefits package which makes up the employee's remuneration, evidence that the employer takes the cost of benefits into account in determining wages would adequately establish that the employee contributed by way of a trade-off against higher wages. Clearly, if the non-union employee contributed to the plan by means of payroll deductions, that would prove the employee's contribution. Again, these suggested methods of proof are not an exhaustive list.

In this appeal, there is evidence that the plaintiff paid for the benefits pursuant to his collective agreement through the trade-off of a reduced hourly wage rate. For this reason, this case is distinguishable from *Ratych v. Bloomer*, since there is evidence to bring him within the insurance exception.

Disposition of the Cunningham Appeal

In the result, the collateral benefits obtained by Cunningham as a result of his collective bargaining agreement are in the nature of a private policy of insurance. The benefits obtained under the collective agreement, like those obtained under a private policy of insurance, should not be deducted from the claim for lost wages. The order of the Court of Appeal should be amended accordingly. The plaintiff should have his costs throughout.

II. Miller v. Cooper

Factual Background

On September 4, 1987 Mariea Cooper was injured in a motor vehicle accident. At that time she had been employed for nine years by MacMillan Bloedel in its Port Alberni Pulp Mill. After the accident she attempted unsuccessfully to return to work. At the time of the trial, three years after the accident, she was still totally disabled. The trial judge found that she would continue to be so for a further one and one-half years.

Mrs. Cooper as a member of a union was a party to a collective bargaining agreement. That agreement provided both long-term and short-term disability plans. Her share of the cost of each of these plans was 30 percent, paid by means of deductions from her pay, set out in her pay slips. The employer paid the balance.

Before trial, Mrs. Cooper received $26,102.86 in short-term disability benefits, and was entitled to further sums post-trial if her disability continued. The plaintiff was not obligated to repay the short-term disability benefits, either to MacMillan Bloedel or the insurance carrier Crown Life Insurance Company.

Judgment at Trial and on Appeal

The trial judge considered *Ratych v. Bloomer* and decided that the disability provisions were paid for in part by the employee and in part by the employer pursuant to the collective bargaining agreement. He determined that the company deducted its costs of the disability benefits from the hourly wage paid to the employees. It was his opinion that even though there was no subrogation provision, as a result of the payment by the plaintiff of 30 percent of the premium cost of the insurance she came within the category of those who had bought insurance. As a result, he concluded that her benefits should not be deducted from her recovery for lost wages.

The Court of Appeal as well concluded that in light of the payments made by the plaintiff, the disability benefit provisions were in the nature of a private contract of insurance and should not be deducted from her recovery for loss of wages.

Analysis

It is clear that the disability benefits were in the nature of an insurance policy. As such they should not be deducted from the lost wages recovered from the defendant.

The evidence put forward in this case demonstrates, in my view, the wisdom of the policy of non-deductibility of disability payments such as these. The plaintiff paid 30 percent of the costs of the benefits, while the employer paid 70 percent. Yet the evidence given by a union representative and a negotiator for the pulp and paper companies established that the employer negotiated the entire contract on the basis of the cost per hour per employee. Whatever sums the employer contributed to fringe benefits such as the disability payments were deducted from the total hourly wage that would otherwise have been paid to the employee. Thus the entire cost of the benefits was in fact paid by the employee. It is interesting to consider the amounts paid by the employee during the course of her 11 years of employment up to the time of trial. With regard to the long-term benefits, the collective agreement provided that the employer would retain the employee's $5/12$th share of the reduction in premiums which resulted from the provision of the long-term disability benefits. Thus the employee paid for the long-term disability benefits by way of foregoing the return of the unemployment insurance premium as well as the 30 percent payroll deduction.

All of the employer's share of payments for the plan was in essence deducted from the hourly wages that would otherwise have been paid to the plaintiff. Specifically the employer paid $840 per year towards the short-term benefits. That, coupled with the annual deductions of $360 from the employee for the short-term benefits, amounted to the sum of $1,200 per year. For the long-term payments, the employer paid approximately $727 per year which, coupled with the employee's payment of $311, amounted to a total of $1,038 per year. The total cost of the short- and long-term disability insurance to Mrs. Cooper was over $2,200 per year. Clearly, there was a considerable amount paid by her for this insurance. The disability benefits represented a significant portion of her annual wages and represented a very real self-denial. The cost to her of this form of insurance would be considerably higher proportionally than would the cost of premiums for private insurance paid by a company executive or professional person. Her sacrifice was correspondingly greater.

Socially, these disability payments represented a significant safeguard for her. They meant that she could live and remain independent without resort to social assistance. Nor should it be forgotten that the insurance itself represents a gamble for the insured person. It might well be that Mrs. Cooper could have worked her entire career without any disabling injury and retired without ever having resorted to disability payments. It follows that for the reasons expressed in the Cunningham appeal there should not be any deduction from any recovery for lost wages. If it could be said to be double recovery, it constitutes a very small reward for the self-denial which the heavy cost of premiums represents for the individual assured. There is a benefit received by society resulting from the purchase of these disability benefits by the plaintiff. The long history of the non-deductibility of the proceeds of private insurance should be maintained for all disability insurance paid for by the plaintiff.

III. Shanks v. McNee

Factual Background

As a result of injuries received in a motor vehicle accident on February 13, 1988, Samuel Shanks was unable to return to work for a period of approximately two years.

At the time of the accident, Mr. Shanks had been employed as a first aid attendant by Canadian Pacific Forest Products for some two years. He was a member of a bargaining unit represented by the International Woodworkers of America. By the terms of his collective agreement, Mr. Shanks was a member of both a short-term and a long-term disability plan. From 1986 to 1988, the long-term plan was funded 70 percent by the employer and 30 percent by the employee through payroll deductions. In the 1988 through 1991 collective agreement the percentages were changed to 50 percent paid by the employer and 50 percent paid by the employee. The disability plans were underwritten by an outside carrier.

There was no payroll deduction for the short-term disability plan. However the collective agreement provided that if the short-term disability plan met "the standard requirements for full premium reduction for 'wage loss replacement plan under the *Unemployment Insurance Act*'" the employee's 5/12th share of the Unemployment Insurance Plan premium reduction was to be retained by the employer as payment for the short-term indemnity plan. The evidence indicated that the short-term indemnity plan did meet those requirements and that the employer kept the premiums which would otherwise have been returned to the employee.

There was a subrogation clause in the long-term disability plan, and Mr. Shanks testified that it was his understanding that he was required to repay any of the sums he had received under the long-term disability plan if they were recovered from the defendants. There was no subrogation clause in the short-term disability plan, and Mr. Shanks testified that he was not required to repay any sums he received under the short-term disability plan. Mr. Shanks received $24,408 under the short-term disability plan and $9,317.56 under the long-term plan. At trial he was awarded a total of $73,459 for lost wages. No deduction was made for his disability benefits.

Trial Judgment

The trial judge found that the disability payments were in the nature of insurance paid for by the employee. As a result of this finding, he did not deduct the benefits received from the wages lost which were to be recovered from the defendants. He further held that there was to be no deduction from the lost wages for the income tax which would have been paid on the lost wages if the plaintiff had received them while he was working. He concluded that the case law was clear that such deduction should not be made.

The Court of Appeal

In the Court of Appeal, it was decided that since the employees contributed 30 percent of the cost of the premiums of the long-term disability plan, those benefits were in the nature of insurance paid for by the employee and should not be deducted. However, the court concluded that since there was no direct contribution made by the employee to the short-term disability plan, and there was no subrogation clause pertaining to these benefits, they were not in the nature of insurance and should be deducted.

On the issue of a deduction for the income tax, it was held that although such a deduction was logical, in light of the decisions of this Court, it should not be made.

Analysis

The Nature of the Benefits

There can be no question that the long-term disability benefits were in the nature of an insurance paid for by the employee and should not have been deducted. Contrary to the decision of the Court of Appeal, I am of the view that the short-term benefits were also in the nature of insurance and should not have been deducted.

It is true that in the *Shanks* case, no evidence was called as to the collective bargaining process whereby the hourly wage rate was reduced in exchange for the provision of the collateral benefits such as these. However, Mr. Cy Pederson, the president of the union local, testified that the 1986 contract containing the short-term disability plan was arrived at after a four-and-one-half month strike. These benefits were confirmed in the 1988 agreement. In my view it must be inferred from this evidence that the collective bargaining agreement could only have been reached after a lengthy and difficult bargaining process. There must have been trade-offs made by the employees in return for the collateral benefits which were received. It is hard to imagine that Mr. Shanks' employer was in any different position from BC Rail, the employer of the plaintiff Cunningham. That is to say, the collective agreement must have been based upon a total wage package for the employees. That wage package could either reflect higher hourly wages or lower hourly wages and increased collateral benefits. It would, I think, be cruelly insensitive and unrealistic to think that this was not the case after such a long strike.

In any event, there is evidence of a direct contribution by the plaintiff to both the long-term and the short-term benefits in this case. There was a payroll deduction made for the employee's contribution to the long-term disability plan. The employee agreed to give up to the employer the return of the Unemployment Insurance premiums for the short-term disability plan. There is thus evidence of an employee contribution to both plans which is sufficient to bring them into the insurance exception. The evidence in this case establishes that both disability plans meet the evidentiary requirements of *Ratych v. Bloomer, supra*. As an aside, it is interesting to note that the plaintiff testified that he had thought about purchasing private disability insurance, but felt that there was no need to do so, since he was covered under the collective agreement.

In my view, when employees choose to negotiate through their union representatives for benefits in the nature of insurance, and it is proven that they paid for those benefits in some manner, then they have demonstrated the same personal choice as to the expenditure of their funds, the same forbearance, sacrifice, prudence and thrift which is the mark of the purchase of a private policy of insurance and the basis for the Bradburn rule. Where the evidence demonstrates that the plaintiff paid for the wage indemnity or disability benefits, either monetarily by payroll deductions, or indirectly, through trade-offs such as lower wages, then the wage indemnity/disability benefits received should not be deductible. It follows that in this case no deductions should have been made for either the short-term or the long-term disability plan.

Subrogation

Generally, subrogation has no relevance in a consideration of the deductibility of the disability benefits if they are found to be in the nature of insurance. However, if the benefits are not "insurance" then the issue of subrogation will be determinative. If the benefits are not shown to fall within the insurance exception, then they must be deducted from the wage claim that is recovered. However, if the third party who paid the benefits has a right of subrogation then there should not be any deduction. It does not matter whether the right of subrogation is exercised or not. The exercise of the right is a matter that rests solely between the plaintiff and the third party. The failure to exercise the right cannot in any way affect the defendant's liability for damages. However, different considerations might well apply in a situation where the third party has formally released its subrogation right.

[McLACHLIN J (La Forest and L'Heureux-Dubé JJ concurring) (dissenting in part):]

… In short, the ideal of the law in negligence cases is fully restorative but non-punitive damages. The ideal of compensation which is at the same time full and fair is met by awarding damages for all the plaintiff's actual losses, and no more. The watchword is restoration; what is required to restore the plaintiff to his or her pre-accident position. Double recovery is not permitted.

Cory J and I agree on the basic principle of recovery in a tort action. As he states, it is simply to compensate the plaintiff as fully as money may do for the loss suffered as a result of the tortfeasor's negligence. The plaintiff is not, we both agree, generally entitled to double recovery (Cory J [*ante*, p. 7]). However, Cory J suggests that the case is governed by an exception to the general principles called the private insurance exception.

My colleague and I part company on the issue of whether the present case falls within the private insurance exception. Cory J seems to assume that the benefits in question fall within the private insurance exception; the issue as he sees it is rather whether the private insurance exception should be maintained. … I, on the other hand, do not question that the insurance exception (if indeed it is an exception) should be maintained. The questions which arise, as I see the matter, are the scope of the so-called insurance exception to the rule against double recovery, and whether employment plans such as those here at issue fall within that exception. …

D. Conclusion on the Law

I conclude that principle, precedent and policy all favour the conclusion that wage benefits paid pursuant to employment plans should be deducted from damages for loss of earnings claimed against the tortfeasor, except where it is established that a right of subrogation will be exercised, thereby avoiding double recovery. The only exceptions that should be endorsed are charity and cases of non-indemnity insurance or pensions. Any benefits which indemnify the plaintiff against wage loss must be brought into account in a damage claim for that loss against a tortfeasor because, to the extent the plaintiff has been indemnified, no loss arises. On the other hand, benefits which are not in the nature of indemnification for the loss claimed against the tortfeasor need not be brought into account.

E. Application to the Facts of This Case

The benefits under the plans at issue on these appeals were paid in lieu of wages to the plaintiffs. Having been compensated for these lost wages, neither Shanks, Miller nor Cunningham can claim that they suffered a loss for those amounts. For the reasons I have suggested, the benefits should not be held to fall under any of the exceptions to the principle of compensatory damages. It follows that they must be brought into account in calculating damages.

The Court of Appeal held that notwithstanding the fact that generally the benefits must be deducted from the damages, this should not happen in the case of Shanks' long-term disability benefits because the employer was subrogated to them. It did the same in the case of Miller, even though there appears to have been no subrogation in that case. The latter conclusion appears to have been in error. I would dismiss the appeals, except in the Miller action, where the appeal should be allowed.

[Sopinka, Iacobucci, and Major JJ concurred with Cory J.]

NOTE

In *M.B. v. British Columbia*, [2003] 2 SCR 477, welfare benefits were held to be deductible from awards of damages.

Insurance Act
RSNS 1989, c. 231

Medical and Other Expense Coverage

140(1) Every motor vehicle liability policy shall provide

(a) medical, rehabilitation, loss of income, death and funeral expense benefits; and
(b) other benefits,

set forth in set forth in regulations made by the Governor in Council, which shall be printed in every policy under the heading "Section B—Accident Benefits."

(2) Where an insurer makes a payment under a provision of a contract of insurance referred to in subsection (1), the payment constitutes, to the extent of such payment, a release by the insured person or his personal representatives of any claim that the insured person or his personal representatives or a person claiming through or under him or by virtue of the Fatal Injuries Act may have against the insurer and any other person who may be liable to the insured person or his personal representatives if that other person is insured under a contract of the same type as is specified in subsection (1), but nothing in the subsection precludes an insurer from demanding, as a condition precedent to payment, a re-

lease to the extent of the payment from the person insured or his personal representative or any other person.

[See also RSA 2000, c. I-3, s. 651; RSBC 1996, c. 226, ss. 168-69; RSM 1987, c. I40, ss. 264-65; RSNB 1973, c. I-12, ss. 256-57; RSN 1990, c. A-22, ss. 34-35; RSO 1990, c. I.8, s. 274 (as am. by SO 1996, c. 21, s. 33); RSPEI 1988, c. I-4, ss. 246-47; and RSS 1978, c. S-26, ss. 256-57.]

Subrogation

149(1) An insurer who makes any payment or assumes liability therefor under a contract is subrogated to all rights of recovery of the insured against any person and may bring action in the name of the insured to enforce those rights [as inserted by SNS 1966, c. 79, s. 4].

[See also RSA 2000, c. I-3, s. 553(1), s. 336(1); RSBC 1996, c. 226, s. 178(1); RSM 1987, c. I40, s. 273(1); RSNB 1973, c. I-12, s. 266(1); RSN 1990, c. A-22, s. 45(1); RSO 1990, c. I.8, s. 278; RSPEI 1988, c. I-4, s. 255(1); and RSS 1978, c. S-26, s. 225(1).]

Health Services and Insurance Act
RSNS 1989, c. 197

Right of Recovery by Injured Person

18(1) Where, as a result of the negligence or wrongful act or omission of another, a person suffers personal injuries for which the person received insured hospital services, benefits under the Insured Prescription Drug Plan, ambulance services to which the Province has made payment, home-care services, care for a person in a home for special care or child-care facility to which the Province has made payment, insured professional services under this Act, or any other care, services or benefits designated by regulation, including the future costs of any such care, services or benefits, the person

(a) has the same right to recover the sum paid for the care, services or benefits against the person who was negligent or was responsible for the wrongful act or omission as the person would have had if that person had been required to pay for the care, services or benefits; and

(b) if the person makes any claim for the personal injuries suffered against the person who was negligent or who was responsible for the wrongful act or omission, shall claim and seek to recover the costs of the care, services or benefits.

(2) Where, under subsection (1), a person recovers a sum in respect of insured hospital services, benefits under the Insured Prescription Drug Plan, ambulance services to which the Province has made payment or insured professional services received by him under this Act, he shall forthwith pay the sum recovered to the Minister.

(3) Her Majesty in right of the Province shall be subrogated to the rights of a person under this Section to recover any sum paid by the Minister for insured hospital services, benefits under the Insured Prescription Drug Plan, ambulance services to which the Province has made payment or insured professional services provided to that person, and an

action may be maintained by Her Majesty, either in Her own name or in the name of that person, for the recovery of such sum.

[See also RSA 2000, c. H-12, s. 62; RSBC 1996, c. 204, s. 25 (as am. by RSBC 1996 (Supp.), c. 204, s. 10); RSM 1987, c. H35, ss. 97 (as am. by SM 1991-92, c. 8, s. 20; SM 1992, c. 35, s. 37; SM 1993, c. 36, s. 6; SM 2001, c. 21, s. 10), 99 (as am. by SM 1992, c. 35, s. 11), 106 (as am. by SM 1991-92, c. 8, s. 24; SM 1992, c. 35, s. 41); RSNB 1973, c. H-9, s. 10 (as am. by SNB 1985, c. 13, s. 2); SNB 1986, c. 42, s. 1; SNB 1988, c. 18, s. 2; SNB 1992, c. 81, s. 2); RSN 1990, c. H-7, s. 5 (as am. by SN 1994, c. 43, s. 2); RSO 1990, c. H.6, ss. 30-36 (as am. by SO 1993, c. 10, s. 53; SO 1996, c. 21, s. 51); and RSPEI 1988, c. H-2, s. 22 (as substituted by SPEI 1999, c. 27, s. 3).]

Guy v. Trizec Equities Ltd.
[1979] 2 SCR 756

RITCHIE J: This is an appeal brought with leave of the Appeal Division of the Supreme Court of Nova Scotia from a judgment rendered by it allowing an appeal from a judgment of Cowan CJTD, varying the award of damages made by him and dismissing the cross-appeal entered by the present appellant.

The facts giving rise to this case have been carefully and exhaustively described in the reasons for judgment rendered by Macdonald JA on behalf of the majority of the Appeal Division which are now conveniently reported in (1978), 26 NSR 1 at p. 7 *et seq.*, which also embodies the dissenting judgment of Cooper JA at p. 41 NSR *et seq.*, and the reasons for judgment delivered at trial by Cowan CJTD (1977), 26 NSR (2d) 48. I find it necessary, however, in order to make these reasons more intelligible, to recite the circumstances giving rise to the questions of law raised in this appeal.

The appellant was injured on December 4, 1974, when a piece of plywood fell from the roof of an office building in Halifax owned and occupied by the respondent Trizec Equities Limited while repairs were being effected thereon by the respondent, Fundy Construction Company Limited, which in turn subcontracted for this work to be done by the respondent Maritime Form Work Limited.

A construction shack was being erected on the roof of this building by employees of Maritime Form Work Limited when a piece of plywood was dropped falling to the unprotected sidewalk below and hitting the appellant on the neck and back resulting in the serious injuries giving rise to the present litigation.

The appellant, who was the executive vice-president and general manager of Nova Scotia Savings and Loan Company, and as such was in receipt of a salary in excess of $40,000 per annum, suffered a severe strain of the neck and mid and lower back as a result of this accident which also produced psychological side effects and resulted in his being prevented from continuing work, according to the testimony of a number of medical experts who gave evidence at the trial.

On December 31, 1975, the appellant officially retired from his work and there is no doubt that his retirement was occasioned by the injuries he sustained as a result of being struck by the falling plywood. Upon his retirement he received a company pension of approximately $14,000 per annum and his services as a director, for which he had theretofor received no salary, were compensated by a payment of $2,000 per annum plus $50 per meeting. After an extensive review of the evidence, Cowan CJTD found the injuries to have been occasioned by the negligence of the respondents and this finding was not disturbed in the Appeal Division or seriously questioned in this Court. In varying the award of $250,000 made by Cowan CJTD, Macdonald JA, speaking for the majority of the Appeal Division, reduced this amount to $133,000, while his brother Judge Cooper JA in dissent, would have fixed the damages at a total of $195,166.80.

The learned trial Judge found that the appellant would not have continued working until the normal age of retirement, *i.e.*, 65 years, even if there had been no accident, but he made no findings as to the date at which the appellant's retirement would take place and his failure to do so is characterized as error by the Appeal Division.

In this regard, Macdonald JA made the following observation at p. 18:

> With respect, it seems to me that once he decided that the respondent would have retired early in any event the trial Judge should have indicated when, in his opinion, this would have occurred. His failure to do so, in my opinion, was an error of omission that amounted, under the circumstances, to an error in principle that entitles, indeed requires, this Court to determine as best we can when such premature retirement would have taken place.

The majority opinion of the Appeal Division was expressed by Macdonald JA in the following terms at p. 32:

> Giving all latitude to the respondent I do not think he would have continued working for the company after age 60. The trial Judge, as mentioned, found that the probabilities are that Mr. Guy would not have continued at age 65. Some date prior to this must be determined and on balance I am of the view that to fix early retirement at age 60, for assessment purposes, is fair and reasonable.

And Macdonald JA later said, at p. 34:

> I know that the appellant ceased work as of December 31, 1975. In view of the finding by the trial Judge that the probabilities were that the appellant would have taken early retirement it was necessary for me to determine as best I could when this would have taken place. I found on a preponderance of probabilities that it would have occurred at the end of 1978 when the appellant would be within a few weeks of his 60th birthday.

Cooper JA, on the other hand, expressed a dissenting view at p. 44, where he said:

> I now face the question—when would the respondent have retired if he had not had the accident? My answer, having regard to all the relevant evidence and the finding of the trial Judge to which I have referred, is December 31, 1980, being 20 days short of the respondent's 62nd birthday. I think this date is one which does justice to the respondent and is also fair to the wrongdoers responsible for his injuries.

With respect for the learned dissenting Judge, I do not think it appropriate at this stage to overrule the finding made by the majority of the Appeal Division in this regard.

A more important question of law to which the judgment of Cowan CJTD gives rise was occasioned by the fact that after reviewing the evidence he assessed the damages for both pecuniary and non-pecuniary loss on a global basis at $250,000 and in so doing he was at variance with judgments subsequently delivered in this Court in *Andrews v. Grand & Toy Alberta Ltd.*, [1978] 2 SCR 229; *Thornton v. Board of School Trustees of School District No. 57 (Prince George)*, [1978] 2 SCR 267; *Arnold v. Teno*, [1978] 2 SCR 287 and *Keizer v. Hanna*, [1978] 2 SCR 342. In this regard my brother Dickson, speaking for this Court in *Andrews v. Grand & Toy Alberta Ltd.* summarized what is now recognized as the proper method of assessing general damages when he said, at pp. 235-6:

> The method of assessing general damages in separate amounts, as has been done in this case, in my opinion, is a sound one. It is the only way in which any meaningful review of the award is possible on appeal and the only way of affording reasonable guidance in future cases. Equally important, it discloses to the litigants and their advisers the components of the overall award, assuring them thereby that each of the various heads of damage going to make up the claim has been given thoughtful consideration.

It is appreciated that this method had not been so clearly articulated at the time of the trial of the present action and the learned Chief Justice did not have the benefit of the guidelines established in the cases last referred to which had not been decided when he adopted the global approach. I think, however, that it can be said with assurance that the Appeal Division was correct in adopting the method outlined by Dickson J, and if this method is to be followed, it is obvious that it was necessary to make a finding as to the probable date of the appellant's retirement if no accident had occurred.

In determining the amount to be awarded in respect of loss of future earnings, the majority of the Appeal Division proceeded on the basis that the appellant had been deprived of his earnings from the date of retirement, *i.e.*, December 31, 1975, until December 31, 1978, a period of three years, and in this regard Mr. Justice Macdonald said, at p. 36:

> Because of the foregoing known facts and bearing in mind that the respondent is to be compensated fully for loss of earnings, it seems to me that the practical approach is to award him for the years 1976, 1977 and 1978 what he would have earned according to his actuarial witness based on an annual escalation rate of 5%. From such amount I would, like the actuary, and for the reasons given, deduct the director's fees for the years 1976 and 1977. I would not deduct them for the current year because I have no way of knowing if the respondent will continue to be a director of the company or whether he will resign his directorship or be voted off the board. The pension is received by the respondent as of right and I would therefore propose that it be deducted for the three years with which I am concerned.
>
> Based on the following approach for the year 1976 I would round the respondent's salary to $50,000 from which must be deducted pension benefits of $13,901.16, which I round to $14,000, and director's fees of $4,500, making a total deduction of $18,500, for a net loss of earnings in 1976 of $31,500.
>
> With respect of the year 1977, I would round salary to $53,000. The combined pension benefits of $14,000 and director's fees of $4,725 amount to $18,725 which, when deducted from salary leaves a net of $34,275 for earnings lost for the year 1977.
>
> With respect to the current year the respondent's projected salary will be $55,979. As mentioned I do not think it proper to deduct director's fees but would reduce such salary by the

amount of the pension, namely $14,000, leaving a net of $41,979, which I would calculate as loss of future earnings for the year 1978.

I agree with the Appeal Division that the director's fees for the years 1976 and 1977 should be deducted in making provision for loss of earnings, but I am unable to share the opinion that the pension benefits should be deducted in the manner proposed because I take the view that this contributory pension is derived from the appellant's contract with his employer and that the payments made pursuant to it are akin to payments under an insurance policy. This view is in accord with the judgment of the House of Lords in *Parry v. Cleaver*, [1970] AC 1 (HL (Eng.)), which was expressly approved in this Court in the reasons for judgment of Mr. Justice Spence in *Canadian Pacific Ltd. v. Gill*, [1973] SCR 654 at pp. 667-8, where he said, speaking of the reasons for judgment rendered by Nemetz JA, on behalf of the majority of the Court of Appeal for British Columbia [26 DLR (3d) 650] in that case:

> Nemetz JA gave the reasons for the majority in coming to the conclusion that the pension payments under the Canada Pension Plan should not be deducted from the award of damages. In doing so, he relied most strongly on the recent decision of the House of Lords in *Parry v. Cleaver*, [1970] AC 1 (HL (Eng.)). That was an appeal dealing with a claim by a police constable for damages due to injuries and was not a fatal accident case as is the present one. *However, the ratio used in the House of Lords, Nemetz JA found and, with respect, I agree with him, was most convincing.* In the House of Lords the majority of the Law Lords composed of Lord Reid, Lord Pearce and Lord Wilberforce were of the opinion that the pension payment should not be deducted. Lord Pearson and Lord Morris of Borth-y-Gest dissented. It is sufficient to quote two short extracts. Lord Reid said at p. 16:

> > What, then, is the nature of a contributory pension? Is it in reality a form of insurance or is it something quite different? [Example quoted is omitted.] … The products of the sums paid into the pension fund are in fact delayed remuneration for his current work. That is why pensions are regarded as earned income.
> >
> > But the man does not get back in the end the accumulated sums paid into the fund on his behalf. This is a form of insurance. Like every other kind of insurance, what he gets back depends on how things turn out. He may never be off duty and may die before retirement age, leaving no dependents. Then he gets nothing back. Or he may, by getting a retirement or disablement pension, get much more back than has been paid in on his behalf. I can see no relevant difference between this and any form of insurance. So, if insurance benefits are not deductible in assessing damages and remoteness is out of the way, why should his pension be deductible?

> Lord Pearce said at p. 37:

> > If one starts on the basis that *Bradburn's* case (1874), LR 10 Ex. 1, decided on fairness and justice and public policy, is correct in principle, one must see whether there is some reason to except from it pensions which are derived from a man's contract with his employer. These, whether contributory or non-contributory, flow from the work which a man has done. They are part of what the employer is prepared to pay for his services. The fact that they flow from past work equates them to rights which flow from an insurance privately effected by him. He has simply paid for them by weekly work instead of weekly premiums.

> Is there anything else in the nature of these pension rights derived from work which puts them into a different class from pension rights derived from private insurance? Their "character" is the same, that is to say, they are intended by payer and payee to benefit the workman and not to be subvention for wrongdoers who will cause him damage.

The italics are my own.

I agree with Macdonald JA that the pension payments for the three years in question amounted to $14,000 per annum, and accordingly, had the Appeal Division applied the reasoning established in *Parry v. Cleaver*, instead of deducting these payments, the amount of the award for loss of future earnings would have been increased by $42,000, from the $108,000 fixed by the Appeal Division, to $150,000, and in view of the above, I would increase this award accordingly.

The argument was advanced in the factum of the appellant that, in assessing damages for loss of earnings, account should have been taken of the fact that the early retirement brought about by the accident had the effect of depriving the appellant of the years of work which he would have contributed to the company had he been continually employed until the normal date of retirement, *i.e.*, age 65, and that by being deprived of these working years the appellant was denied the opportunity to make additional pension contributions which would have resulted in an increased pension for the balance of his life. The contention is that this is a loss for which the appellant is entitled to compensation, but the proposition does not appear to have been considered either at trial or on appeal, and having regard to the insufficiency of evidence to support it in the record, I can see no ground for embarking upon it for the first time in this Court.

As I have pointed out, Cowan CJTD made no separate finding representing damages for non-pecuniary loss and Macdonald JA was content to assess damages under this head at $25,000. Cooper JA, on the other hand, at pp. 46-8, reviewed the elements of pain and suffering and general debility resulting from the accident and speaking of the trial Judge observed, at p. 48:

> Although the damage award of the learned trial Judge must be reduced it is obvious that he who saw and heard the witnesses was convinced that the pain and suffering undergone by the respondent was very serious indeed and I do not think that this factor can be entirely lost sight of.

A very extensive and detailed review of the appellant's injuries and his resulting disabilities is to be found in the judgment at trial, reported at pp. 60-7 of the report.

Having considered these passages, I am satisfied, as was Cooper JA, that the trial Judge made a substantial allowance for non-pecuniary loss although he did not make any separate finding in this regard. It would be inappropriate in my view for me to suggest any figure not previously considered by way of compensation under this heading, but I am satisfied to adopt the figure of $40,000 which the learned dissenting Judge would have awarded for non-pecuniary loss as it appears to me that an amount of at least these proportions must have been included in the global award of $250,000 made by the learned trial Judge and, like Cooper JA, I think account must be taken of the advantage of having seen and heard the witnesses which was enjoyed by the Chief Justice at trial and denied to the Appeal Division and this Court.

In view of all the above, I would allow this appeal and vary the judgment below by leaving the pension payments out of account in determining loss of earnings and increasing the award for non-pecuniary loss. In the result, the appellant will recover $108,000 plus the $42,000 pension payments previously deducted for an award of $150,000 in respect of loss of earnings together with an award of $40,000 for non-pecuniary loss, making a total of $190,000.

Jack Cewe Ltd. v. Jorgenson
[1980] 1 SCR 812

PIGEON J: Judgment was rendered at trial against the appellant ("the Company") in an action for wrongful dismissal brought by the respondent. The trial Judge held that the proper amount of damages to be awarded was a full year's salary. From this, he deducted amounts received from various sources during the relevant 12 months, including unemployment insurance benefits in the amount of $1,330. An appeal by the Company was unanimously dismissed by the Court of Appeal for British Columbia (1978), 9 BCLR 292. On respondent's cross-appeal, it was held that the unemployment insurance benefits should not be deducted. From this judgment, the Company appeals by leave of this Court on two points only: (1) a deduction should be made for income tax; and (2) unemployment insurance benefits should be deducted in proportion to the Company's contribution.

With respect to income tax, the Company's submission rests on the premise that respondent is not liable to income tax on the damages awarded. This is based on the judgment of the Federal Court of Appeal in *The Queen v. Atkins* (1976), 68 DLR (3d) 187, affirming the judgment of Collier J, 59 DLR (3d) 276. This judgment is contrary to the decision of Cattanach J in *Quance v. The Queen*, [1974] CTC 225, as to which Jackett CJ said, speaking for the Federal Court of Appeal [at 188-89]:

> Having regard to the weight placed by the appellant on the decision of the Trial Division in *Quance v. The Queen*, [1974] CTC 225, I deem it advisable to state in my own words what I regard as the basic fallacy in the appellant's position.
>
> Once it is conceded, as the appellant does, that the respondent was dismissed "without notice," monies paid to him (pursuant to a subsequent agreement) "in lieu of notice of dismissal" cannot be regarded as "salary," "wages" or "remuneration" or as a benefit "received or enjoyed by him … in respect of, in the course of, or by virtue of the office or employment." Monies so paid (*i.e.*, "in lieu of notice of dismissal") are paid in respect of the "breach" of the contract of employment and are not paid as a benefit under the contract or in respect of the relationship that existed under the contract before that relationship was wrongfully terminated.

I have grave doubt as to the validity of this reasoning. Damages payable in respect of the breach of a contract of employment are certainly due only by virtue of this contract; I fail to see how they can be said not to be paid as a benefit under the contract. They clearly have no other source. In *Livesley v. Horst Co.*, [1924] SCR 605, Duff J said, speaking for the Court (at p. 607):

In principle, it is difficult to discover a solid ground for refusing to classify the right to damages for breach of contract with other rights arising under the proper law of the contract, and recognizable and enforceable as such.

The basic principle governing the award of damages for breach of contract is that "the party complaining should, so far as it can be done by money, be placed in the same position as he would have been in if the contract had been performed." I fail to see any reason why this would not hold true towards the tax collector as well as towards the parties to the contract. In *The Queen v. Jennings*, [1966] SCR 532, where the damages awarded were in tort and mainly for permanent disability, Judson J gave the reasons for declining to follow *British Transport Com'n v. Gourley*, [1957] AC 185 (HL (Eng.)), where a deduction for income tax had been made. Before coming to that conclusion, he said (at p. 544):

> *Gourley* was decided upon an admission of counsel that the damages were a non-taxable capital receipt. This admission was taken to be an accurate reflection of the law and of the practice of the Inland Revenue.
>
> For what it is worth, my opinion is that an award of damages for impairment of earning capacity would not be taxable under the Canadian *Income Tax Act*. To the extent that an award includes an identifiable sum for loss of earnings up to the date of judgment the result might well be different. But I know of no decisions where these issues have been dealt with and until this had been done in proceedings in which the Minister of National Revenue is a party, any expression of opinion must be insecure. Such litigation would have to go through the Board of Tax Appeals or direct to the Exchequer Court with a final appeal, in appropriate cases, to this Court.

In my view, the present situation with respect to income tax on this award of "an identifiable sum for loss of earnings" must be considered legally insecure. This Court might well disagree with the conclusion reached by the Federal Court of Appeal in *Atkins, supra*. In this respect, I will note that in that case consideration appears to have been given only to the question whether the damages for wrongful dismissal were income "from an office or employment" within the meaning of ss. 5 and 25 of the *Income Tax Act*, RSC 1952, c. 148 [am. 1970-71-72, c. 63]. No consideration appears to have been given to the broader question whether they might not be income from an unspecified source under the general provision of s. 3.

Counsel for the appellant referred to *Parsons v. B.N.M. Laboratories Ltd.*, [1964] 1 QB 95 (CA). In that case the English Court of Appeal relied on a specific provision of the British Act making such payments taxable above the stated amount; this was held to imply that under such amount they were not taxable. As to the reasons for the ultimate conclusion that the employer should in such a situation get the benefit of the income tax that the dismissed employee would not have to pay, the majority rely on *Gourley, supra*, by which they consider themselves bound but which this Court has firmly rejected in *Jennings*. I find much more persuasive the reasons given by Sellers LJ for making no such deduction than the reasons given for the majority for making it. He says (at pp. 111-12):

> The justification for regarding tax in assessing damages is at least more questionable when looked at in terms of contract. The employer has at all times during the subsistence of a service agreement to pay the employee the contractual sum, no contractual provision is made for any deduction of or reduction by tax. It is true that the sum the employee receives when it comes to be distributed by him has to meet the requirements of income tax which for the convenience of admin-

istration under our P.A.Y.E. scheme is, in effect, handed back to the employer to pay over to the Inland Revenue on behalf of the employee, the taxpayer. It seems unnecessary to say that that is the employee's expenditure and payment to meet his contribution to the services he receives from the state and to which he may have to make further contribution by way of surtax. If his salary were less, the employee would no doubt pay less tax, but whatever he pays in taxes in no way reduces the contractual obligation on the employer to pay the whole of the agreed sum. ...

... [I]ncome tax might appropriately have been made payable by the employee on the damages received, for he will have had his earnings so computed, and the tax could be assessed on the basis of probable liability, as *Gourley's* case contemplates it will be where *Gourley's* case applies, or on some other basis, and either paid by the employer to the revenue or collected direct from the taxpayer, but as it chances (and it may possibly be a "flaw" or omission in our taxation law) the grossed up lost income is treated as a capital sum and is not subject to some recent provisions which call for consideration, exigible to income tax. This is a fortuitous circumstance which has nothing to do with the employer or his contract of service with the employee and cannot, as I see it, enure to his benefit so as to result in his contract being treated as one not to pay the sum stipulated by some lesser sum which might vary between a number of employees all having a common form of contract for, say £2,000 a year but each having a different tax liability.

These observations were answered by the majority in holding *Gourley* binding and undistinguishable. Having rejected *Gourley* we must hold this to be no answer. Even on the assumption that respondent will escape income tax on the damages awarded to him, it would be illogical to allow his employer a deduction for income tax not payable.

I cannot dismiss this point without referring to *Florence Realty Co. Ltd. v. The Queen*, [1968] SCR 42, a decision which came less than two years after *Jennings*. In that case compensation had been assessed in the Exchequer Court for the loss of a private railway siding. It was determined, as upon an expropriation, at the amount which a prudent owner would have paid rather than lose the rail service. In thus estimating the value of a permanent asset used for profit making purposes, the annual profit lost was taken into account net of income tax. This Court held that its judgment in *Jennings* was not applicable to exclude such deduction in the assessment of the compensation. It is unnecessary to consider whether this is consistent with expropriation compensation principles and cases generally; this decision concerning compensation for the loss of a permanent asset has no possible application in the assessment of a loss of personal earnings any more than in the assessment of a loss of personal earning capacity.

Turning now to the unemployment benefits, I find the Company's contention untenable. The payment of unemployment insurance contributions by the employer was an obligation incurred by reason of respondent's employment, therefore, to the extent that the payment of those contributions resulted in the provision of unemployment benefits, these are a consequence of the contract of employment and, consequently, cannot be deducted from damages for wrongful dismissal. The situation is similar to contributory pension benefits which this Court recently decided should not be deducted in assessing compensation for loss of earnings. In *Guy v. Trizec Equities Ltd.*, [1979] 2 SCR 756, Ritchie J said, expressing the unanimous opinion of the full Court (at p. 762):

> ... I am unable to share the opinion that the pension benefits should be deducted in the manner proposed because I take the view that this contributory pension is derived from the appellant's

contract with his employer and that the payments made pursuant to it are akin to payments under an insurance policy. This view is in accord with the judgment of the House of Lords in *Parry v. Cleaver*, [1970] AC 1, which was expressly approved in this Court in the reasons for judgment of Mr. Justice Spence in *Canadian Pacific Ltd. v. Gill*, [1973] SCR 654. ...

Furthermore, it appears that damages for wrongful dismissal are "earnings" for unemployment insurance purposes, being defined by the *Unemployment Insurance Regulations* as income "arising out of employment." In *Re A.-G. Can. and Walford*, [1979] 1 FC 768 (CA), the Federal Court of Appeal reversed an Umpire's decision holding that a payment of damages for wrongful dismissal was not income. The judgment in *The Queen v. Atkins, supra*, was held not to be an authority in the interpretation of the *Unemployment Insurance Regulations*. The anomaly of considering damages for wrongful dismissal as income for unemployment insurance purposes but not for income tax purposes is an additional reason for doubting the correctness of the decision in *Atkins*.

I do not find it necessary to consider whether, due to the time element, respondent will be entitled to retain the unemployment insurance benefits which were allowed to him at a time when he was being denied compensation for his wrongful dismissal. Even if it should happen that he will not now be obliged to reimburse them, this is a matter between him and the unemployment insurance authorities; it does not concern the appellant company.

TIME OF ASSESSMENT

The classic statement of the aim of contract damages is that of Parke B in *Robinson v. Harman* (1848), 1 Ex. 850, at 855; 154 ER 363, at 365.

> The rule of the common law is, that where a party sustains a loss by reason of a breach of contract, he is, so far as money can do it, to be placed in the same situation with respect to damages, as if the contract had been performed.

Does this remain the guiding principle? If no, what is the aim of contract damages? If yes, historic reasons apart, why should specific performance ever be denied? It is the surest way of guaranteeing that the plaintiff gets what he or she bargained for. These questions will be addressed in part II, "Equitable Remedies," below. They are, however, intimately linked with questions of mitigation, and the time for assessment of damages, as is illustrated by the case of a rise in the value of property purchased, between the date of the breach and the date of judgment.

Asamera Oil Corp. Ltd. v. Sea Oil & General Corp.; Baud Corp., N.V. v. Brook
[1979] 1 SCR 633

ESTEY J: These appeals arise out of a long series of agreements concerning the shares and operations of the appellant, Asamera Oil Corporation Ltd. (hereinafter referred to as "Asamera"), which company was in one way or another involved in exploration for oil in Indonesia. Three separate actions were commenced by the parties.

1. *Baud Corporation, N.V. (Plaintiff) v. Thomas L. Brook (Defendant)* (commenced on July 26, 1960), wherein "Baud," as it shall hereinafter be called (which is a wholly owned subsidiary of the Sea Oil & General Corporation), sought the return of 125,000 Asamera shares from the respondent, Brook (who at all material times was the president and chief officer of Asamera). Baud alleged that 125,000 Asamera shares were loaned by it in October and November 1957, to the respondent, Brook, under an agreement dated November 10, 1958, requiring their return by the end of 1959. In addition, Baud claimed damages in the sum of $150,750 representing the difference in the market value of the 125,000 shares between the date upon which they were to have been returned and the date of the writ.

2. *Asamera Oil Corporation Ltd. (Plaintiff) v. Sea Oil & General Corporation and Baud Corporation, N.V. (Defendant)* (commenced on July 27, 1960). This action was instituted the day after action No. 1. In it Asamera sought rescission of the basic agreement between the two groups of entrepreneurs represented by Baud on the one hand, and Brook on the other. The effect of rescission, if granted, would be the cancellation of treasury shares issued by Asamera to Baud and Sea Oil & General Corporation Ltd. pursuant to this agreement.

3. *Baud Corporation, N.V. (Plaintiff) v. Thomas L. Brook, (Defendant)* (commenced on December 6, 1966). In this action, Baud repeated its allegations as asserted in action No. 1, and claimed the return of 125,000 Asamera shares, which the respondent, Brook, was required to return under the agreements mentioned in action No. 1. The third action arose out of the allegation by the respondent in action No. 1 that the first action was premature since the date for the return of the shares had been extended by the parties until December 31, 1960. In addition to its claim for the return of the shares, Baud claimed damages in the sum of $400,000. An amendment of the statement of claim whereby the damage claim was raised to $6,000,000 was allowed at trial. In this action, the respondent, Brook, counterclaimed for substantially the same relief sought by him in action No. 2.

In action No. 2 Asamera alleged a total failure of consideration under the basic agreement and, accordingly, claimed that the agreement was null and void *ab initio*. In the alternative Asamera claimed that the performance of the agreement had been frustrated, and thus that the contract was voidable at its option. The learned trial Judge dismissed this action, finding that the parties had settled their differences in respect of action No. 2 by an agreement dated October 28, 1958. The Supreme Court of Alberta, Appellate Division, reached the same conclusion [(1973), 40 DLR (3d) 418]. ...

The evidence in the record amply supports, in my respectful view, this finding of the learned trial Judge relating to the scope and effect of the settlement agreement. This finding was confirmed on appeal. I would dismiss the appeal to this Court with respect to the second action and the counterclaim by the respondent in action No. 3.

The first action was dismissed by the learned trial Judge when he found that there was indeed an agreement extending the loan of the 125,000 Asamera shares beyond the original expiry date, December 31, 1959, until December 31, 1960. The record includes considerable evidence in support of such a finding which was confirmed on appeal. There being no demonstration of any error in law in the Courts below in so disposing of action No. 1, I would dismiss the appeal with reference to that action.

This leaves outstanding only the question of the remedy or remedies open to Baud in the third action. The action apparently proceeded on the basis that Brook, by his wrongful retention of the shares, was open to an action by Baud in detinue or, alternatively, in conversion because Brook had wrongfully disposed of the shares loaned to him. Brook admitted in his statement of defence, filed on July 6, 1967, that these shares had been sold, and further admitted on examination for discovery in May 1968, that the sale had occurred in 1958. The trial Judge found that the brokers, in an effort to protect their position, had sold shares of Asamera for the Brook account in December 1957, and in January and February 1958.

This phase of the matter is somewhat complicated by the fact that an injunction was issued by McLaurin CJTD, in the Supreme Court of Alberta on July 27, 1960, which might be construed as restraining Brook from selling the 125,000 shares loaned to him by Baud. Brook's interpretation of his position under the injunction order was that he remained in compliance therewith so long as he held not less than 125,000 shares. There is nothing to indicate that on this interpretation he was in breach of the injunction. Baud, on the other hand, took the position that, as regards the action of detinue or conversion, it had the right to insist that Brook make whatever arrangements may have been necessary with the broker to retain the actual certificates forwarded to him by Baud. The order itself is ambiguous as to whether some retention *in specie* or a mere credit balance is required for compliance by Brook. The injunction issued by Chief Justice McLaurin in 1960 enjoins Brook from voting or disposing of or dealing with "the 125,000 shares ... referred to in paragraphs 2 and 3 of the Statement of Claim." Baud's reference in its statement of claim is directed to the 125,000 shares loaned to Brook in 1957. The injunction therefore may be construed as restraining dealing by Brook with those specific 125,000 shares. But this relation of the history of the transaction does not dispose of the matter. In the course of the trial the appellant moved for an order that the shares be deposited in Court by Brook. This application was dismissed by the trial Judge, apparently on the basis that the retention of 125,000 shares by Brook would be sufficient compliance with the order. Since all the shares of Asamera are identical in class and conditions attaching thereto, no practical consideration arises which required retention *in specie*, if that be technically possible, of the actual 125,000 shares loaned to Brook. The background against which the loan of the shares was made and the subsequent option granted for their purchase lead one to the view that, should a determination of this issue become necessary, Baud is protected by the order and Brook from its contravention by the retention by Brook of a like number of shares of Asamera. To other aspects of this issue I will return later.

It is trite law that under the applicable statutes and common law a certificate is not in itself a share or shares of the corporation but only evidence thereof: *vide Solloway, Mills v. Blumberger*, [1933] SCR 163 at p. 167, *per* Rinfret J. These shares are intangible, incorporeal property rights represented or evidenced by share certificates. They are not in themselves capable of individual identification and isolation from all other shares of the corporation of the same class. Therefore, once these shares were pledged by Brook in fully negotiable form and placed in the name of the broker, as was the evidence here, it was not possible to determine whether some or all of these 125,000 shares had been sold even presuming that at any time a specific share of a corporation as distinct from the certificate representing the share can be isolated and given an existence separate and apart from all other shares of the same class. ...

The learned trial Judge dismissed Baud's claims in detinue and conversion and assessed damages on the basis that Brook's failure to deliver constituted a breach of contract. The action in substance is a simple case of breach of contract to return 125,000 Asamera shares and, in my view, the claims made and the issues arising in this action should be disposed of on that basis. That being so, we come to the only real issue in this appeal, namely, to what recovery is the appellant Baud in these circumstances entitled and, if the appropriate relief be a monetary award, the quantum of damages?

Baud has asked this Court to award specific performance of the agreement to return 125,000 Asamera shares, and in particular, in its statement of claim has requested an order directing the return or replacement of the shares. The jurisdiction to award specific performance of contractual obligations is ordinarily exercised only where damages would be inadequate to compensate a plaintiff for his losses. As the original 125,000 shares are indistinguishable from all other Asamera shares, and since there has been no suggestion that corporate control is at issue in this case, or that shares were not readily available in the stock market, an order for delivery of shares would merely be another method or form for the payment of any judgment awarded. Asamera shares are listed on the public stock exchanges and consequently some estimate of their market value can be readily ascertained from day to day. The parties themselves therefore throughout the 21 years since these transactions began have had the benefit of the daily assessment by the stock market of the value of these shares. It is obvious that damages are an adequate remedy and that the Courts in such circumstances do not resort to the equitable remedy of specific performance.

The assessment of the quantum of damages for this breach of contract is somewhat complex. The calculation of damages relating to a breach of contract is, of course, governed by well-established principles of common law. Losses recoverable in an action arising out of the non-performance of a contractual obligation are limited to those which will put the injured party in the same position as he would have been in had the wrongdoer performed what he promised.

Not all kinds of losses are recoverable in actions for breach of contract. The limitations on damages recoverable in contract were discussed in *Victoria Laundry (Windsor) Ltd. v. Newman Industries Ltd.*, [1949] 2 KB 528 (CA), wherein Asquith LJ, at p. 539, went to great lengths to explain such limits.

> (1.) It is well settled that the governing purpose of damages is to put the party whose rights have been violated in the same position, so far as money can do so, as if his rights had been observed: (*Sally Wertheim v. Chicoutimi Pulp Company*, [1911] AC 301 (PC (Que.)). This purpose, if relentlessly pursued, would provide him with a complete indemnity for all loss de facto resulting from a particular breach, however improbable, however unpredictable. This, in contract at least, is recognized as too harsh a rule. Hence,
>
> (2.) In cases of breach of contract the aggrieved party is only entitled to recover such part of the loss actually resulting as was at the time of the contract reasonably foreseeable as liable to result from the breach.
>
> (3.) What was at that time reasonably so foreseeable depends on the knowledge then possessed by the parties or, at all events, by the party who later commits the breach.

Three additional rules or refinements of the above rules are thereupon enumerated by Asquith LJ, but these are not here relevant. The principle set out in para. 2 above was thereafter modified somewhat by the House of Lords in *Koufos v. C. Czarnikow Ltd. (The "Heron II")*, [1969] 1 AC 350 (HL (Eng.)), where it was determined that the proper test for remoteness was not the "reasonable foreseeability" of the head of damages claimed as in an action in tort, but whether the probability of the occurrence of the damage in the event of breach should have been within the reasonable contemplation of the contracting parties at the time of the entry into the contract: *vide Brown & Root Ltd. v. Chimo Shipping Ltd.*, [1967] SCR 642 at p. 648, *per* Ritchie J.

These principles were most recently discussed in *Parsons (Livestock) Ltd. v. Uttley Ingham & Co. Ltd.*, [1978] QB 791 (CA), where, subject to qualifications raised in the judgment, it was concluded by all members of the Court of Appeal that the appropriate legal rules relating to remoteness will not depend upon the classification of the action as being one of contract or tort. The case has already been the subject of comment: *vide* Note (1978), 94 LQR 171. Scarman LJ, at p. 807 stated:

> As to the first problem, I agree with Lord Denning MR in thinking that the law must be such that, in a factual situation where all have the same actual or imputed knowledge and the contract contains no term limiting the damages recoverable for breach, the amount of damages recoverable does not depend upon whether, as a matter of legal classification, the plaintiff's cause of action is breach of contract or tort. It may be that the necessary reconciliation is to be found, notwithstanding the strictures of Lord Reid at pp. 466 and 389-90, in holding that the difference between "reasonably foreseeable" (the test in the tort) and "reasonably contemplated" (the test in contract) is semantic, not substantial. Certainly Lord Justice Asquith in *Victoria Laundry v. Newman*, [1949] 2 KB 528 (CA) at p. 535 and Lord Pearce in *Czarnikow v. Koufos* thought so: and I confess I think so too.

[O]r more succinctly at p. 806:

> ... [T]he law is not so absurd as to differentiate between contract and tort save in situations where the agreement, or the factual relationship, of the parties with each other requires it in the interests of justice.

(Leave to appeal to the House of Lords was granted by the Court of Appeal.)

In any event the damage flowing from the wrongful act of the respondent in this case, that is the loss of the opportunity to resell the shares at a profit, is recoverable under any of the tests set out above.

In cases dealing with the measure of damages for non-delivery of goods under contracts for sale, the application over the years of the above-mentioned principles has given the law some certainty, and it is now accepted that damages will be recoverable in an amount representing what the purchaser would have had to pay for the goods in the market, less the contract price, at the time of the breach. This rule, which was authoritatively stated in *Barrow v. Arnaud* (1846), 8 QB 595, 115 ER 1000, may be seen as a combination of two principles. The first, as stated earlier, is the right of the plaintiff to recover all of his losses which are reasonably contemplated by the parties as liable to result from the breach. The second is the responsibility imposed on a party who has suffered from a breach of contract to take all reasonable steps to avoid losses flowing from the breach. This responsibility to mitigate was explained by Laskin CJC, in *Red Deer College v. Michaels*, [1976] 2 SCR 324 at pp. 330-1:

> It is, of course, for a wronged plaintiff to prove his damages, and there is therefore a burden upon him to establish on a balance of probabilities what his loss is. The parameters of loss are governed by legal principle. The primary rule in breach of contract cases, that a wronged plain-

tiff is entitled to be put in as good a position as he would have been in if there had been proper performance by the defendant, is subject to the qualification that the defendant cannot be called upon to pay for avoidable losses which would result in an increase in the quantum of damages payable to the plaintiff. The reference in the case law to a "duty" to mitigate should be understood in this sense.

In short, a wronged plaintiff is entitled to recover damages for the losses he has suffered but the extent of those losses may depend on whether he has taken reasonable steps to avoid their unreasonable accumulation.

[A]nd later in the judgment at p. 331:

If it is the defendant's position that the plaintiff could reasonably have avoided some part of the loss claimed, it is for the defendant to carry the burden of that issue, subject to the defendant being content to allow the matter to be disposed of on the trial Judge's assessment of the plaintiff's evidence on avoidable consequences.

Thus, if one were to adopt, without reservation, in the settlement of Baud's damage claims, the rules governing recovery for non-delivery of goods in sales contracts, the *prima facie* measure of damages in the case at bar would be the value of the shares on the date of breach, that is, December 31, 1960. The learned trial Judge found the market price on December 31, 1960 to be 29¢ per share. The value of the 125,000 shares wrongfully retained by Brook, and thus the loss to Baud by reason of its not being in possession of those shares, on that date therefore was $36,250 assuming, for the purposes of discussion only, the market price to be constant throughout the purchase or sale of such a number of shares. To this must be added other expenses which could reasonably be said to be incidental to steps taken to mitigate the damages flowing from the breach. ...

Assuming for the moment that the breach of contract occurred on December 31, 1960 and that the appellant's right to damages came into being at that time, and assuming that it should then have acted to forestall the accumulation of avoidable losses, what action did the law then require of the appellant by way of mitigation of damages? A plaintiff need not take all possible steps to reduce his loss and, accordingly, it is necessary to examine some of the special circumstances here present. The appellant argues that there exist in this case clear circumstances which render the duty to purchase 125,000 Asamera shares an unreasonable one. The first of these has its foundations in the established principle that a plaintiff need not put his money to an unreasonable risk including a risk not present in the initial transaction in endeavouring to mitigate his losses. This principle was demonstrated in *Lesters Leather & Skin Co. v. Home & Overseas Brokers* (1948), 64 TLR 569 (CA), and in *Jewelowski v. Propp*, [1944] KB 510, as well as in *Pilkington v. Wood*, [1953] Ch. 770. The appellant here was placed in the unusual position where mitigative action would require that it purchase as replacement property, shares of a company engaged in a speculative undertaking under the effective control and under the promotional management of a person in breach of contract, the respondent, Brook, who thereafter was in an adversarial position in relation to the appellant.

On the evidence adduced at trial, the market value of shares in Asamera had fallen from $3 shortly before the dates on which Baud first loaned the two blocs of shares to Brook to between $1.62 and $1.87 in November 1958 and to 29¢ per share on December 31, 1960. Evidence of share values after that date indicates only that there was a relatively small recovery in value to about $1.21 a share by March 1965, when the fortunes of the company improved. The appellant argues that it could not have been expected in December 1960 to purchase shares in mitigation of its losses where the value of these shares had fallen as rapidly as is indicated in the evidence.

A more important circumstance which might render unreasonable any requirement that Baud purchase shares in the market was the existence of the aforementioned injunction issued on July 27, 1960, restraining the respondent from selling 125,000 Asamera shares. The appellant contends that it is inconceivable that the law should require a party, who has suffered a misappropriation of his property and who has requested and been afforded the considerable protection of an injunction granted by a Court of Equity, to ignore the force and effect of that injunction and to go out and acquire the same number of shares as Brook was required to retain, however the terms of the injunction be construed.

Even if one accepts that submission, it must be acknowledged that the right of Baud to rely on the injunction as a shield against an obligation to minimize its losses is not absolute. In the first place, Baud was informed by Brook in his pleadings of July 6, 1967 that shares which were subject to the injunction had been sold. As of that date the shares were selling at $4.30 to $4.35 and had been rising in value since April 1965, and at a median price of $4.33 would have cost Baud $541,250. Accordingly, at least by July 1967, it could not be said that Baud would reasonably be discouraged from replacing the 125,000 shares in the open market because of the low price of an inactive company, nor could it be said that thereafter it could reasonably refrain from prosecuting its claim for damages because of the order enjoining the disposition of the shares by Brook. It remains the case, however, that the market price for such speculative shares as those of an oil-exploration company was subject to wide price fluctuations sometimes inspired by management which itself held, as did Brook, a considerable number of shares.

The learned trial Judge referred to a number of English authorities in support of the proposition that in the case of a loan of shares a plaintiff need not mitigate his losses either by purchasing shares on the market or even by bringing a suit for recovery of damages within a reasonable time. The result under these authorities where the market value of the shares has risen or fallen between breach and trial, has been an award of damages representing the value of the shares at the time of the breach or of the trial at the election of the plaintiff: *vide Harrison v. Harrison* (1824), 1 C & P 412, 171 ER 1253 (CP); *Shepherd v. Johnson* (1802), 2 East. 211, 102 ER 349 (KB); *McArthur v. Lord Seaforth* (1810), 2 Taunt. 257, 127 ER 1076 (CP); *Saunders v. Kentish* (1799), 8 Term. Rep. 162, 101 ER 1323 (KB). These cases were adopted in Canada and other jurisdictions: *vide Vicary v. Foley* (1891), 17 VLR 407 (Australia); *Galigher v. Jones* (1889), 129 US 193, and cases cited therein. These authorities raise no responsibility in the plaintiff to mitigate his losses: *Shepherd v. Johnson, supra, per* Grose J at p. 212 (350 (ER)). The application of the principle developed in these early cases would produce damages calculated at the end of the trial or perhaps at the highest point prior to that date. The trial proceeded intermittently from June 1969 to December 1971, and final judgment was pronounced in May 1972. The latter price would be about $21 a share and the highest price attained was about $46.50 per share, allowing recovery of approximately $2,625,000 and $5,812,500 respectively.

A proper analysis of these cases is made difficult by reason of their antiquity, and after serious consideration, I have concluded that they ought not to be followed by this Court. In the first place, they were decided long before modern principles of contractual remedies had been developed. Secondly, they are not in accord with recent decisions of this Court. Thirdly, they ignore the all-important and overriding considerations which have led to the judicial recognition of the desirability and indeed the necessity that a plaintiff mitigate his losses arising on a breach of contract. There is a fourth consideration. This old principle produces an arbitrary, albeit a readily ascertainable result because it lacks the flexibility needed to take into account the infinite range of possible circumstances in which the parties may find themselves at the time of the breach and before a trial can in practice take place. The pace of the market place and the complexities of business have changed radically since this rule or principle was developed in the early 19th century.

Before proceeding further with the analysis of the nature and extent of damages in the field of contract law, it will be helpful to examine briefly the principles which have evolved in analogous situations in the law of torts. In conversion, the measure of damages has been said to be the value of the shares at the date of conversion, and in addition, consequential damages represented by the loss of the opportunity to dispose of the shares at the highest price attained prior to the end of the trial: *vide McNeil v. Fultz* (1906), 38 SCR 198, *per* Duff J at 205; *The Queen in right of Alberta v. Arnold*, [1971] SCR 209 at p. 230, *per* Spence J. I am aware of course that these cases were for the most part dealing with the wrongful refusal of a person under the liability of a trustee to deliver property to a beneficiary, but on principle the result would be the same in simple cases of conversion: *vide McGregor on Damages*, 13th ed. (London: Sweet & Maxwell, 1972), at p. 671.

In detinue, the measure of damages has been said to be the value of the shares at the end of the trial and, in addition, damages for the detention. The value of the shares at the end of the trial must be awarded on the basis that the action in detinue is, in fact, a *quasi*-proprietary action for return of the plaintiff's goods. If that cannot be done, then the clearest approximation of the plaintiff's loss is the value of those goods when they would have been recovered, that is, at the end of trial. In addition, an award must compensate the plaintiff for damages flowing from the wrongful detention of his property, which it seems must be assessed on the basis of the highest value of the goods between the date at which the plaintiff ought to have recovered possession and the end of trial. In *McGregor on Damages* at p. 699, the case is put this way:

> As with conversion there is no clear case of a market rise followed by a market fall between the time of the initial detention and the time of judgment. Although in *Williams v. Peel River Co.* (1887), 55 LT 689 (CA) the market appears to have risen and then fallen, it seems that the plaintiff was only claiming, as damages for detention, the value at initial default less the value at judgment. In *Archer v. Williams* (1846), 2 C & K 26; 175 ER 11 (Nisi Prius), in detinue for scrip certificates, Cresswell J directed the jury that "the measure of damages is the highest sum the scrip could have been sold for from the time of the detention till the time when it was returned," but on appeal the case was argued only on whether the plaintiff was entitled to recover the amount by which the market value of the scrip certificates had fallen between the defendant's refusal to deliver and his actual delivery. It is submitted that the highest price which the market had attained before the time when the plaintiff ought to have sued should control here also.

One should pause here to point out that I have advisedly referred to the cut-off time as being the end of the trial. In some cases and texts, reference is made to "judgment." No authority has come to my attention where a significant factual change has occurred during the gap between the end of trial and judgment. Protracted difficulties could arise if the books must be kept open for a last-value measurement after trial and before settlement of the final judgment. Therefore I would apply the principle as closing off valuation considerations at the end of the trial. Holland J, in *Metropolitan Trust Co. of Canada v. Pressure Concrete Services Ltd.*, [1973] 3 OR 629; affirmed 9 OR (2d) 375 (CA), directed the assessment officer to take into account damages incurred beyond the end of trial to the date reserved judgment was delivered. In the course I propose to follow herein, this point need not be determined.

The application of the basic principles of remoteness and causality enunciated in the leading cases mentioned earlier points to the conclusion that Baud may have, in the absence of a duty to mitigate, a right of recovery in damages for breach of contract represented by the highest value attained by the shares between the date of breach and the end of trial, that is, $46.50 or $5,812,500. ...

It is very likely that Brook would have foreseen the probable loss to be suffered by Baud on the non-return of its property, particularly bearing in mind his activity as a stock broker and his own dealings in Asamera shares. In the absence of a contrary indication he may be taken to have assumed the risk of its occurrence. Such a loss is not speculative; neither is it so improbable nor so remote as to remove it from the kind of damages recoverable in an action in contract. As to quantum of damages, it is not unreasonable to scale the recovery for the loss suffered by Baud by virtue of its loss of the opportunity to sell the shares to a price or prices at least approaching the median point between breach and trial, subject to the varying influences of the many relevant factors to be discussed below.

The application of another basic principle relating to the computation of contract damages, namely, that the plaintiff should be, so far as money may do so, placed in the same position as he would have enjoyed had the breach not occurred, produces a like result. Had Brook returned the shares when the contract provided, Baud would then have been in a position to dispose of those shares during the period of market appreciation. The range of damages on such a basis would be from 29¢ or, more realistically, $2 per share to $46.50 per share. The $2 per share is more properly the baseline for computation of value because that is the option price agreed upon between the parties for the period ending at the time the breach of contract occurred. Since it is entirely unrealistic to assume that the peak price was attainable for a block sale of 125,000 Asamera shares, and as it is most unlikely that Baud or anyone else would enjoy such perspicacity, a median range of $20 to $25 for the period from mid-1967 to the end of trial is more appropriate: *vide Fales v. Canada Permanent Trust Co.*, [1977] 2 SCR 302 at p. 322, *per* Dickson J. This would produce damages of about $3,000,000 before any consideration is given to the required mitigation. ...

The cases which establish the exceedingly technical rules relating to recovery of damages for the non-return of shares turn on the theory that only where a breach of contract gives rise to an asset in the hands of the plaintiff will the law require him to mitigate his losses by employing that asset in a reasonable manner. Thus if an employer wrongfully dismisses an employee the breach results in the employee obtaining an asset, an ability to work for another employer, or at least the opportunity to offer his services to that end, which he did not enjoy prior to the dismissal. This is no more than a philosophical explanation of the simple test of fairness and reasonableness in establishing the presence and extent of the burden to mitigate in varying circumstances. ...

It follows that a contrary result should arise where damages are recoverable for a breach of contract by a vendor on a *sale of shares*. There the breach would normally allow a buyer the use of his funds formerly committed to the purchase and consequently damages should be calculated on the basis that he ought to have taken steps to avoid his losses by the purchase of shares on the market at the time of the breach. ...

A different consideration arises where the plaintiff-buyer has prepaid the contract price and has not received delivery. As in the case of non-return of shares, the breach does not give rise to any asset in the hands of the plaintiff since he has already parted with his funds, and on that basis some Courts have held that the injured party need not purchase like goods in the market. ...

The creation of an "asset" on a breach of contract cannot be an invariable prerequisite to the operation of the principle that a party injured by a breach of contract must respond in mitigation to avoid an unconscionable accumulation of losses. Nor should the absence of such an "asset" invariably exonerate a plaintiff from taking mitigative action. The presence or absence of such an "asset" is but one of many factors which bear on the task of determining in a particular case what is or is not reasonable on the part of the injured party in all the circumstances. ...

In short, it would appear that the principles of mitigation in respect of contracts for the sale of goods generally may not be applied without reservation to the determination of the duty to mitigate arising in respect of contracts for the sale of shares and, in any case, differ fundamentally from the case of a breach of a contract for the return of shares. It is inappropriate in my view simply to extend the old principles applied in the detinue and conversion authorities to the non-return of shares with the result that a party whose property has not been returned to him could sit by and await an opportune moment to institute legal proceedings, all the while imposing on a defendant the substantial risk of market fluctuations between breach and trial which might very well drive him into bankruptcy. Damages which could have been avoided by the taking of reasonable steps in all the circumstances should not and, indeed, in the interests of commercial enterprise, must not be thrown onto the shoulders of a defendant by an arbitrary although nearly universal rule for the recovery of damages on breach of the contract for redelivery of property.

We start of course with the fundamental principle of mitigation authoritatively stated by Viscount Haldane LC, in *British Westinghouse Electric & Mfg. Co., Ltd. v. Underground Electric R. Co. of London, Ltd.*, [1912] AC 673 (HL (Eng.)) at p. 689:

> The fundamental basis is thus compensation for pecuniary loss naturally flowing from the breach; but this first principle is qualified by a second, which imposes on a plaintiff the duty of taking all reasonable steps to mitigate the loss consequent on the breach, and debars him from claiming any part of the damage which is due to his neglect to take such steps. In the words of James LJ in *Dunkirk Colliery Co. v. Lever* (1898), 9 Ch. D 20 (CA) at p. 25: "The person who has broken the contract is not to be exposed to additional cost by reason of the plaintiffs not doing what they ought to have done as reasonable men, and the plaintiffs not being under any obligation to do anything otherwise than in the ordinary course of business."

As James LJ indicates, this second principle does not impose on the plaintiff an obligation to take any step which a reasonable and prudent man would not ordinarily take in the course of his business. But when in the course of his business he has taken action arising out of the transaction, which action has diminished his loss, the effect in actual diminution of the loss he has suffered may be taken into account even though there was no duty on him to act.

The principle has been applied in the case of conversion of shares, as well as in the case of breach of contract to sell shares, and should, for the reasons developed above, be applied according to the circumstances to the case of a breach of contract to return shares. ...

While the circumstances of the case prompted the Court to direct if not to confine its direction to conversion of the shares and its consequences, the broader principle is simply the right to damages arising on the breach of contract to redeliver whatever the reason for breach might have been, that is with or without a conversion. The application of such a principle to the circumstances arising herein following the breach to redeliver raises some additional considerations.

This Court in *The Queen in right of Alberta v. Arnold*, [1971] SCR 209, considered in some detail the limitations to be placed on the damages recoverable in conversion upon a failure to return securities. The majority dismissed the plaintiff's claim for reasons not here relevant. Spence J would have allowed the claim in part and in doing so stated at p. 230:

> Surely a plaintiff whose securities have been converted cannot wait to issue process for their recovery or damages for the conversion until just before the period of limitation lapses, then be entitled to claim damages fixed at the highest value of those securities within the six-year limitation term.

Spence J concluded that the plaintiff could not recover losses which might have been avoided by the purchase of alternate shares. The majority judgment by Martland J, and I have noted, did not have to deal with damages but concluded at p. 220:

> ... but, if I had had to deal with that issue, I would have concurred in the views expressed by my brother Spence.

... The same principle was applied in assessing damages for conversion of personal property other than corporate securities in *Sachs v. Miklos*, [1948] 2 KB 23 (CA). There may, as already discussed, be instances where mitigation will not require a plaintiff to incur the significant risk and expense of purchasing replacement property, but in any case the plaintiff must crystallize his claim either by replacement acquisition or in some circumstances by prompt litigation expeditiously prosecuted which will enable the Court to establish the damage with reference to the mitigative measures imposed by law. The failure of the appellant either to mitigate or litigate promptly makes difficult the task of applying these principles to the circumstances of this case.

In the light of the enormous hardships sometimes occasioned by the application of the old doctrine of damage assessment, and in view of the massive distortion which may follow when the principles of mitigation are, as in the older authorities, made inapplicable to nondelivery of shares, I have come to the conclusion that the authorities cited from the early 1800s, principally from the Courts of England, which in effect allow recovery of "avoidable losses" ought not to be followed. Rather the lead furnished by *The Queen v. Arnold*, should be taken. Subject always to the precise circumstances of each case, this will impose on the injured party the obligation to purchase like shares in the market on the date of breach (or knowledge thereof in the plaintiff) or, more frequently, within a period thereafter which is reasonable in all the circumstances. The implementation of this principle must take cognizance of the realities of market operations, including the nature of the shares in question, the strength of the market when called upon to digest large orders to buy or sell, the number of shares qualified for public trading, the recent volatility of the price, the recent volume of trading, the general state of the market at the time, the susceptibility of the price of the shares to the current operation of the corporation and similar considerations.

Some classes of property, including shares, whose value is subject to sudden and constant fluctuations of unpredictable amplitude, and whose purchase is not lightly entered into, call for a modification of the general rule that the value of the property on the "date of breach" be taken as the starting point for the calculation of damages. There is some authority for this view in English law as well. In P.J. Atiyah, *Sale of Goods* (London: Pitman, 4th ed., 1974) at p. 294, the learned author has this to say:

> Although the market price rule is now firmly established in English law it may be observed that there are cases in which it does not do full justice to the buyer. In particular it is unrealistic to suppose that a buyer will in practice be able to buy goods on the market on the very day on which the seller fails to deliver. The buyer will often wish to consider his position, or to negotiate with the seller on breach and some delay before he buys substitute goods is likely to be the rule rather than the exception.

… It is contended by the appellant, Baud, however, that the peculiar circumstances of this case rendered the purchase of highly speculative shares in a company controlled by its adversary unreasonable in all of the circumstances, particularly the injunction obtained by the appellant restraining the sale of 125,000 Asamera shares held by Brook. None the less, it remains the case that at least some of the losses claimed by the appellant could have been avoided by the taking of other reasonable steps. The most obvious of these would have been to move with reasonable speed to institute and proceed with legal action in an effort either to recover the shares and, if that was not possible, then to recover damages. …

One must not become so lost in the technicalities of damages in the law of contract as to lose sight of the practical consideration of the cost of money and of the reality of the risks to be imposed on a plaintiff by a requirement of complete mitigating measures. In this case the magnitude of the operation, in the range of $800,000 to $1,000,000 if the shares were to cost $7 to $8 each, leads one to conclude that a "reasonable" time for mitigative action must be allowed after the appropriate point of time in law has been isolated.

The appellant bases its contention that it has no obligation to purchase shares in the market in part on the ground that it ought to be allowed to seek specific performance of the contract to return the shares, and while relying on an injunction restraining their disposition it need not have any concern with losses occasioned by its inaction. Counsel for the appellant did not refer this Court to any cases in which the principle of mitigation has interacted and conflicted with recovery by way of specific performance, and such authority as I have been able to discover supports the common sense view that the principle of mitigation should, unless there is a substantial and legitimate interest represented by specific performance, prevail in such a case.

This conflict sometimes occurs on the interaction of the principle of mitigation and an award of damages in lieu of or in addition to specific performance in equity. In decisions relating to damages the Courts of Equity have acted on the authority of *Lord Cairns' Act* (more properly cited as the *Chancery Amendment Act*, 1858 (UK), c. 27, s. 2), which empowers a Court of Equity to award damages "either in addition to or in substitution for ... specific performance." Accordingly, in a number of cases concerning contracts for the sale of land, damages calculated on the value of the land as of the date of judgment, as opposed to the date of breach, have been awarded: *vide Wroth v. Tyler; Metropolitan Trust Co. of Canada v. Pressure Concrete Services Ltd.*; *Calgary Hardwood & Veneer Ltd. v. C.N.R. Co.* (1977), 5 AR 582 (SC TD). The Supreme Court of New Zealand in *Hickey v. Bruhns*, [1977] 2 NZLR 71, had occasion to review *Wroth v. Tyler*, and the earlier authorities and, after concluding that specific performance was inappropriate, held that an award of damages in substitution for specific performance must take into account the conduct of the parties, particularly when inordinate delay has occurred thereby making critical the date selected for the computation of damages: *vide Kaunas v. Smyth* (1976), 15 OR (2d) 237.

On principle it is clear that a plaintiff may not merely by instituting proceedings in which a request is made for specific performance and/or damages thereby shield himself and block the Court from taking into account the accumulation of losses which the plaintiff by acting with reasonable promptness in processing his claim could have avoided. Similarly, the bare institution of judicial process in circumstances where a reasonable response by the injured plaintiff would include mitigative replacement of property, will not entitle the plaintiff to the relief which would be achieved by such replacement purchase and prompt prosecution of the claim. Before a plaintiff can rely on a claim to specific performance so as to insulate himself from the consequences of failing to procure alternative property in mitigation of his losses, some fair, real and substantial justification for his claim to performance must be found. Otherwise its effect will be to cast upon the defendant all the risk of aggravated loss by reason of delay in bringing the issue to trial. The appellant in this case contends that it ought to be allowed to rely on its claim for specific performance and the injunction issued in support of it, and thus recover avoidable losses. After serious consideration, I have concluded that this argument must fail.

It is, of course, an eminently reasonable position to take if, as Lord Reid suggests in *White & Carter (Councils) Ltd. v. McGregor*, [1962] AC 413 (HL (Sc.)), in the case of anticipatory breach, there is a substantial and legitimate interest in looking to performance of a contractual obligation. So a plaintiff who has agreed to purchase a particular piece of real estate, or a block of shares which represent control of a company, or has entered into performance of his own obligations, and where to discontinue performance might aggravate his losses, might well have sustained the position that the issuance of a writ for specific performance would hold in abeyance the obligation to avoid or reduce losses by acquisition of replacement property. Yet, even in these cases, the action for performance must be instituted and carried on with due diligence. This is but another application of the ordinary rule of mitigation which insists that the injured party act reasonably in all of the circumstances. Where those circumstances reveal a substantial and legitimate interest in seeking performance as opposed to damages, then a plaintiff will be able to justify his inaction and on failing in his plea for specific performance might then recover losses which in other circumstances might be classified as avoidable and thus unrecoverable; but such is not the case here.

Having regard to the complex issues raised in all three actions (and the period devoted to this litigation must take into account more than the simple action for the recovery of shares loaned to Brook) and taking into account the other circumstances mentioned, it would be unreasonable to hold the appellant to any timetable which contemplated the trial of these many issues prior to the end of 1966 or early in 1967. If litigation may represent an alternative to the investment by a plaintiff of substantial funds to avoid the accumulation of losses, the Courts cannot apply in the computation of damages a principle recognizing some relevance of the fluctuating value of the *res* of the contract between breach and trial and not at the same time maintain a strict surveillance on the assiduity of a plaintiff in bringing his claim to judgment.

When Brook pleaded (on July 6, 1967) (a) his right to refuse return of the shares, and (b) the previous sale of shares by Brook, the shares were trading from $4.30 to $4.35 per share. The volume of trading was very low. By the end of 1967 the price had climbed to $7.25 but the volume of trading remained low. Unfortunately there is no evidence of the depth or strength of the market, but it is reasonable to conclude from the small volume of trade over a lengthy period of time that the market was thin and probably could not have absorbed large purchases or sustained the quoted prices in the face of large sales. By the time of the examination for discovery in May 1968, the price per share had reached a range from $7.60 to $8.20. The volume of trading had increased markedly over the preceding year but was sporadic. By the end of the year the price quoted on the Exchange was $27, in comparatively active trading. The price of Asamera shares peaked at $46.50 in 1969 during the opening session of the trial. By the time of the issuance of the reasons for judgment in April 1971, as mentioned above, the price had declined to $22 per share and, when final issues were disposed of and formal judgment entered in May 1972, the price of Asamera shares on the Stock Exchange was about $21.

The Courts below determined from different approaches that the critical date for assessment of damages was the date of the breach of the contract to return the shares on December 31, 1960. The price was then 29¢ on the open market. Each Court observed as well that the parties had agreed that the purchase price (if the option be exercised) on that date was $2 and, accordingly, damages could not be assessed at less. Furthermore, the evidence indicated that Brook, on the sale of a like number of shares in 1957 and 1958, had realized prices ranging from $1.50 to $1.80 so that an award based on the market price on the date of breach would allow Brook to profit from his wrongdoing. It would appear from the judgments in the Courts below that Brook's enrichment through his breach of contract played an important role in the assessment of damages. Accordingly damages were assessed at $2 per share or $250,000 in gross.

It seems to me that the motives or unjust enrichment of the defendant on breach are generally of no concern in the assessment of contractual damages: *vide* G.H. Treitel, *The Law of Contract* (London: Stevens, 4th ed., 1975), at p. 618:

> In general, damages are based on loss to the plaintiff and not on gain to the defendant. They are not, in other words, based on any profit which the defendant may have made out of the breach.

An appellate tribunal in such an appeal as this is in an invidious position. The record at trial is deficient. In the result precise evidence as to market conditions, credit facilities, rates of interest, borrowing power of the appellant, effect on market price of mitigative action by it, the time reasonably required to acquire by purchase such a volume of shares on the open market, and other evidence relevant to the assessment of damages is not before this Court. On the other hand, the transaction occurred 20 years ago, and the trial which was extensive and no doubt expensive, was completed seven years ago. To direct a reassessment of the damages would be time-consuming, difficult to carry out after such a lapse of time, and expensive for the parties. Faced with these unsatisfactory alternatives, an appellate Court must discern if at all possible from the record the elements necessary to permit the completion of the assessment process.

We therefore approach the matter of the proper appraisal of the damages assessable in the peculiar circumstances of this case on the following basis: that the same principles of remoteness will apply to the claims made whether they sound in tort or contract subject only to special knowledge, understanding or relationship of the contracting parties or to any terms express or implied of the contractual arrangement relating to damages recoverable on breach; that Baud was under the general duty to mitigate its losses and may not escape this duty by relying on the 1960 injunction interminably; that the specific duty to mitigate and to crystallize its claim for damages within a reasonable time of the breach of contract by bringing action seeking appropriate remedies and to prosecute such action with due diligence, was qualified or postponed by Brook's request of Baud some time prior to 1966 to refrain from enforcing its claims; that any postponement of such requirement to prosecute and to acquire replacement shares had come to an end at the latest on the awareness of Baud that the defaulting party was not only in breach of the duty to return the shares but had disposed of shares at least equal in number to those loaned by Baud; that any postponement of the duty to acquire replacement shares, which may have been due to the sharp reduction in the value of the shares which occurred during the loan, was ended with the revival in values on the public market at least by the end of 1966; that a plaintiff in the position of Baud may not successfully assert throughout the years of litigation a right to specific performance of the contract to redeliver the subject-matter of the contract and at the same time seek to avoid or reduce his losses on the grounds that to do so by buying replacement shares would involve him in investing his funds in the shares of a company managed or dominated by his adversary, Brook; that having regard to the nature of a common share, neither the terms of the injunction or the loan contract, nor the action by Brook in disposing of shares in number equal to those loaned, have any effect on the characterization of the rights of Baud or the obligation of Brook throughout this long and tortuous transaction; that damages are an adequate remedy, and that a Court in these complex and particular circumstances will not invoke the extraordinary remedies of equity.

The application of these principles and determinations to the particular circumstances in this case requires, in my respectful view, a determination of the damages payable by Brook on the assumption that Baud ought to have crystallized these damages by the acquisition of replacement shares so as to minimize the avoidable losses flowing from the deprivation by Brook of Baud's opportunity to market the 125,000 shares. Such share purchases should have taken place within a reasonable time after the date of breach. Having regard to all the above-noted special circumstances, the time for purchase in my opinion was the fall of 1966, when Baud was, by its own admission, free from any agreed restraint not to press its claim against Brook. It would be unreasonable to impose on Baud the burden of going into the market and acquiring replacement shares at a time when the litigation of its claims was in a dormant state at Brook's request. Furthermore, Baud acknowledged that by the fall of 1966 the fortunes of Asamera had improved and this had begun to be reflected in the market price of its shares. In short, the appellant is not, in my view, entitled in law to any compensation for the loss of opportunity to sell its shares after that date. Thereafter its loss of this opportunity is of its own making. The theory of such a damage award is to provide the funds needed to replace the shares at the time the law required it to do so in order to avoid an accumulating claim. There should be an allowance of a reasonable time to permit the organization of the finances and the mechanics required for the careful acquisition of 125,000 shares either by a series of relatively small purchases or by negotiated block purchases. This would carry the matter into the fall of 1967. By this time the price had risen to a range of $5 to $6. Making allowance for the upward pressure on the market price which would be generated by the purchase of such a large number of shares on a relatively low-volume stock, the purchase price would surely have exceeded the $6 price reached in mid-1967 without any market intervention by Baud. For this factor, in my best consideration, an allowance of $1 per share should be made. Taking into account the effect of market intervention by Baud, the median price during the period from late 1966 to mid-1967, adjusted accordingly, would be about $6.50, and in my view, the damages should be awarded to Baud on that basis, that is, the total damages for breach of agreement to return the Asamera shares should amount to $812,500. In weighing the magnitude of this award one should not lose sight of the essential fact that Brook at any time right down to trial could, if he had remained in compliance with the injunction of July 1960, have avoided this result or the risk of this award by delivering from any source 125,000 Asamera shares.

Brook has below and before this Court asserted a claim for damages in respect of the undertaking given by Baud upon the issuance of the interim injunction in July 1960. This claim was dismissed by the learned trial Judge and in this dismissal the Supreme Court of Alberta, Appellate Division, concurred. Nothing has been advanced in this Court to indicate error below, and therefore I would dismiss this cross-appeal by Brook.

I would therefore allow the appeal and vary the judgment below by awarding damages payable by Brook to Baud in the amount of $812,500, together with costs to Baud throughout.

PROBLEM

The following is an extract from a trial judgment. You are instructed to appeal on behalf of the defendant. What are the arguments? Will you succeed?

> The plaintiff engaged the services of the defendant, a building contractor for the construction of a building. When the building had been completed, the plaintiff realized that the defendant had failed to meet contract specifications as to reinforced steel in the roof and immediately brought this action against the defendant alleging damages. After bringing the action, the plaintiff was able to sell the building to a purchaser for whom the reinforcing was unimportant and acquired another building which fully met the plaintiff's own needs. It is clear on the evidence that the price was fully equal to the price which would have been obtained had the defendant fully performed the contract. It is also clear that the special needs of the plaintiff for a reinforced roof have been met as the plaintiff has been able to acquire another satisfactory site for its operation. Indeed, the plaintiff appears to have got just enough from the sale to cover all costs of acquiring

and moving to the alternate site. The fundamental principle of contract remedies is that the innocent party should be put in the position he would have been in had the contract been performed. Had this contract been performed, the plaintiff would have had constructed a building with proper steel reinforcing. Accordingly, the proper measure of damages is the difference in cost of the actual work done and the work specified. This is not a departure from the fundamental principle of compensation. The fact that the plaintiff has sold the property advantageously is irrelevant to his dispute with this defendant. The defendant should not be allowed to profit from his breach and the plaintiff's skilful mitigation efforts. The amount which the defendant saved through breach is properly owed to the plaintiff since the plaintiff has already paid the defendant the full contract price.

Dodd Properties v. Canterbury City Council
[1980] 1 WLR 433 (CA)

MEGAW LJ: This is an appeal from a judgment of Cantley J.

The first plaintiffs, Dodd Properties (Kent) Ltd., are the owners of a building in Rose Lane, Canterbury, known as Marlowe Garage. The second plaintiffs, Marlowe Garage (Canterbury) Ltd., have been the occupiers of Marlowe Garage as lessees of the first plaintiffs. They carry on their business there as motor car dealers and they sell petrol, oil and accessories.

In 1968 the first defendants, the mayor, aldermen and citizens of the city of Canterbury, erected a large multi-storey car park close to Marlowe Garage. The second defendants, Truscon Ltd., were the main contractors; the third defendants, Frankipile Ltd., were their subcontractors for the foundations of the car park. As a result of their operations, damage was caused to the plaintiffs' building. Liability was for long denied, but shortly before the action came on for hearing before Cantley J in 1978 liability was admitted in nuisance by the second and third defendants, though the extent of the damage was in issue and also the basis of assessment of the amount of damages to which the plaintiffs were entitled. The first defendants did not formally admit liability, but they took no part in the proceedings, having received an undertaking of indemnity from the other defendants.

Cantley J held that the first defendants also were liable. They are not parties to the appeal. There is no dispute as to liability. The issues are as to damages.

No question of fact is now in dispute; Cantley J's findings of fact are accepted as to the extent of the physical damage and as to other matters.

On the question of the extent of the damage, Cantley J to a large degree accepted the evidence of the defendants' experts. On their evidence, the necessary repairs would, at the prices prevailing at the time of the hearing in 1978, cost about £30,000. On the evidence of the plaintiffs' expert, the repairs required were much greater and the cost much higher.

The question which remained, and which is the primary issue before us, is this: by reference to which of two dates is the cost of the repairs to be ascertained, for purposes of arriving at the amount of the defendants' liability for their tort? The plaintiffs say that the relevant date for this purpose is the date of the hearing, or of the judgment: that is, that the 1978 prices are relevant and decisive. The defendants say that the relevant date is 1970 and the relevant prices are the 1970 prices. As a result of inflation, the difference between the computations at those respective dates is very large. The 1978 figure, for the repairs which Cantley J held to be required, is £30,327. The 1970 figure, for the same work, is approximately £11,375.

The second plaintiffs also have a claim. It gives rise to the same issue as to the proper date of assessment. The second plaintiff's claim arises out of prospective interruption of their business during the time that would be required for the carrying out of the appropriate repairs, if and when that work is done. The figure, if the repairs were to be carried out in 1978, would be £11,951. In 1970 the corresponding amount would have been £4,108.

Taking the first and second plaintiff's potential entitlements together, the sums payable by the defendants as damages (apart from any question of interest) would be: on the 1970 assessment, £15,483; on the 1978 assessment, £42,278.

Cantley J held that in law, in the circumstances, judgment had to be given on the 1970 basis. He also awarded interest, making the total payable by the defendants to the first and second plaintiffs £22,974.20.

Against the judgment, the plaintiffs appeal and the defendants cross-appeal. The plaintiffs say that Cantley J was wrong in law to make his assessment of damages on the basis of the cost of the repairs in 1970. They say that he should have taken the 1978 computation. They say, in the alternative, that, if they should be wrong on this, which is their first and main contention, then he ought to have awarded interest from an earlier date and at a higher rate. They accept that, if they are right on their first contention—that is, the acceptance of 1978 as the date by reference to which the cost of the repairs is to be assessed—then they could not claim interest.

The defendants' cross-appeal raises an issue affecting the damages of the second plaintiffs only. The defendants say that, since Cantley J held that it was only "just about established" that it was probable that the repairs would in fact be carried out after his judgment, he ought not to have awarded to the second plaintiffs the full amount of the prospective loss to them arising from the interruption of their business which would be caused by those potential repairs. He, say the defendants, should have awarded the second plaintiffs only, say 60 per cent of the total prospective loss by interruption, because the chance that the loss would in fact occur was no greater than a chance of that order.

On the first, and main, issue raised by the plaintiffs, it is necessary to see what Cantley J found were the reasons why the repairs for this damage to Marlowe Garage, caused in 1968, had still not been carried out when the action was heard in 1978. Because I think it is important to see precisely what Cantley J held in this respect, I shall quote his own words, ante, p. 442E-F:

> I find that the first plaintiffs could probably have raised the money for repairs but this would have increased their annual losses and their financial stringency. As a commercial decision, judged exclusively from the point of view of the immediate and short-term welfare of the companies, it was reasonable to postpone incurring the very considerable expense of these repairs while no harm was being done to the building by the delay in repairing it and while these three rich defendants with apparent if not genuine belief in the validity of their defences were firmly denying liability to make even a contribution.

Cantley J then referred to the well-known, much discussed, case, *The Liesbosch*, [1933] AC 449 (HL (Eng.)). He said, ante, p. 443C: "In the case of destruction of a chattel, the normal measure of the damage is the market value at the time of the loss. That was the measure of damage applied in *The Liesbosch*." He then cited from the judgment of Denning LJ in *Philips v. Ward*, [1956] 1 WLR 471 (CA), at p. 474:

> The general principle of English law is that damages must be assessed as at the date when the damage occurs, which is usually the same day as the cause of action arises, ... A fall thereafter in the value of money does not in law affect the figure, for the simple reason that sterling is taken to be constant in value. ...

Although this may not affect the statement of "the general principle," I think that the reasoning as to sterling having to be taken to be constant in value is unfortunately no longer good law, having regard to the facts of life and the recent authoritative decisions, including *Miliangos v. George Frank (Textiles) Ltd.*, [1976] AC 443 (HL (Eng.)).

Cantley J then said:

> No authority has been cited to me, and in my very limited opportunity lately I have discovered none for myself, where a court has considered the time at which damages are to be assessed in the cases of buildings damaged and put in need of repair by a tortious act. If there is no authority on that precise point, it may be because no one has ever before thought to contend that the general principle did not apply to it. The general principle is that damages must be assessed as at the date when the damage occurs. In my view, that general principle applies here. It is not, of course, to be rigidly applied as a rule of thumb, fixing the time rigidly by the calendar and the clock. The damage may be concealed by some fault of the wrongdoer or not reasonably discoverable by the victim until some time after it has first appeared: see, for example, *East Ham Corporation v. Bernard Sunley & Sons Ltd.*, [1966] AC 406 (HL (Eng.)) and *Applegate v. Moss*, [1971] 1 QB 406. Moreover, repairs cannot usually be put in hand at once and at prices ruling at the very date of damage. There may have to be inspections and specifications and tenders and an available contractor may have to be found before the work can be started. Furthermore, the nature and circumstances of the damage may be such that it would be imprudent and possibly wasteful to begin the work before waiting longer to ensure that no further damage is going to develop from the same cause. This is particularly true when the foundations of a building have been disturbed by vibrations. I would put it in this way. The appropriate damages are the cost of repairs at the time when it was reasonable to begin repairs. Whether the time is reasonable must be judged objectively and not taking into account such matters as impecuniosity or financial stringency which, in the words of Lord Wright in *The Liesbosch*, [1933] AC 449 (HL (Eng.)) at pp. 460-61, are extrinsic.

He then held that it had been reasonable for the plaintiffs not to begin repairs until 1970 even though the damage had all occurred, and had been known, in 1968. On that basis he adopted "as the measure of damage the cost of repairs ... on the prices ruling in 1970"; that is, £11,375.

There is no dispute in this case but that the appropriate measure of damages on this claim of the first plaintiffs is by reference to the cost of the repairs required.

The defendants do not challenge Cantley J's acceptance of the 1970 figures. That means that they do not now contend that he should have taken the lower prices for the repair work prevailing in 1968 when the tort was committed.

It is important to bear in mind that we are not concerned with any suggestion that the plaintiffs were under a duty towards the defendants to repair the premises damaged by the defendants' wrongdoing. The plaintiffs did not lose their right to recover damages from the defendants because they did not effect the repairs. True, in certain circumstances with which we are not concerned here, such as the building being destroyed by fire before the repairs had been carried out, the amount of the plaintiffs' entitlement to damages might have become nil. But what we are concerned with here is: by reference to what date is the amount of the recoverable loss to be calculated, during a period when the cost of the necessary work is rising as time goes on? Since the defendants do not suggest that Cantley J was wrong in taking the 1970 prices instead of the 1968 prices, it is accepted, and I think necessarily and rightly accepted, by the defendants that there are circumstances in which the proper amount of damages, where, as here, the damages are to be computed by reference to the cost of repairs, has to be computed by reference to that cost at a date later than the date of the wrongdoing which caused the damage.

The general principle, referred to in many authorities, has recently been recognised by Lord Wilberforce in *Miliangos v. George Frank (Textiles) Ltd.*, [1976] AC 443 (AC (Eng.)) at p. 468, namely, that "… as a general rule in English law damages for tort or for breach of contract are assessed as at the date of the breach … ." But in the very passage in which this "general rule" is there stated, it is stressed that it is not a universal rule. That it is subject to many exceptions and qualifications is clear. Cantley J in the present case rightly recognised that that was so, in the passage from his judgment which I have recently read.

Indeed, where, as in the present case, there is serious structural damage to a building, it would be patently absurd, and contrary to the general principle on which damages fall to be assessed, that a plaintiff, in a time of rising prices, should be limited to recovery on the basis of the prices of repair at the time of the wrongdoing, on the facts here being two years, at least, before the time when, acting with all reasonable speed, he could first have been able to put the repairs in hand. Once that is accepted, as it must be, little of practical reality remains in postulating that, in a tort such as this, the "general rule" is applicable. The damages are not required by English law to be assessed as at the date of breach.

The true rule is that, where there is a material difference between the cost of repair at the date of the wrongful act and the cost of repair when the repairs can, having regard to all relevant circumstances, first reasonably be undertaken, it is the latter time by reference to which the cost of repair is to be taken in assessing damages. That rule conforms with the broad and fundamental principle as to damages, as stated in Lord Blackburn's speech in *Livingstone v. Rawyards Coal Co.* (1880), 5 App. Cas. 25 (HL (Sc.)) at p. 39, where he said that the measure of damages is

> … that sum of money which will put the party who has been injured, or who has suffered, in the same position as he would have been in if he had not sustained the wrong for which he is now getting his compensation or reparation.

In any case of doubt, it is desirable that the judge, having decided provisionally as to the amount of damages, should, before finally deciding, consider whether the amount conforms with the requirement of Lord Blackburn's fundamental principle. If it appears not to conform, the judge should examine the question again to see whether the particular case falls within one of the exceptions of which Lord Blackburn gave examples, or whether he is obliged by some binding authority to arrive at a result which is inconsistent with the fundamental principle. I propose to carry out that exercise later in this judgment.

Cantley J has held, in a passage which I have already read, that as a commercial decision, judged exclusively from the plaintiffs' point of view, it was reasonable to postpone incurring expense of the repairs up to—for so I understand what Cantley J says—the time when the action had been heard and liability decided, resulting in a judgment which, when complied with, would have put the plaintiffs in funds. The reasons why that deferment of repairs was reasonable from the plaintiffs' point of view included the fact, not that they were "impecunious," meaning poverty-stricken or unable to raise the necessary money, but that the provision of the money for repairs would have involved for them a measure of "financial stringency." Other reasons, consistent with commercial good sense, why the repairs should have been deferred include those mentioned in evidence by a director of the plaintiff companies, whose evidence was accepted by Cantley J as truthful and reliable. If there had been no money problem, he said, he would still not have spent money on the building before he was sure of recovering the cost from the defendants. It would not have made commercial sense to spend this money on a property which would not produce corresponding additional income. So long as there was a dispute, either as to liability or as to the amount of compensation, he would have done no more than to keep the building weatherproof and "in working order."

If that was, as Cantley J held, reasonable from the point of view of the plaintiffs as being grounds for deferring the carrying out of repairs, and if the time at which the cost of the repairs falls to be computed in order to ascertain the amount of damages is the time when it has become reasonable to do the repairs, why did Cantley J reject 1978, for which the plaintiffs contended, and accept 1970 for which the defendants contended?

There are, as I see it, two possible answers to that question. The first answer is that what is reasonable has to be looked at from the point of view of both parties and a balance struck. Cantley J's finding of reasonableness of the deferment from the point of view of the plaintiffs does not, therefore, conclude the matter. But I do not think that that was the answer intended to be given by Cantley J. He nowhere refers to the question in any such form and there is no indication of any attempt by him to strike a balance. If a balance had to be struck, surely it would be right, even in a climate of indulgence to contract-breakers or tortfeasors, that the scales should move heavily in the favour of the innocent party as against the wrongdoer, in any comparison of respective disadvantages or unfairness? It has to be borne in mind that these were defendants who were wrongly maintaining a denial of any liability and thereby leaving the plaintiffs faced with all the potentially heavy expenditure of money required for the mere purpose of establishing by litigation what we now know to have been their rights. Moreover, as the plaintiffs concede, they could not claim interest on the amount of their compensation starting to run before the date when the money was expended on repairs. So the defendants, being liable, as we now know, to recompense the plaintiffs for the tort which the defendants committed in 1968, will have enjoyed the free use for their own account of the money which would have been the appropriate compensation at that date, with the opportunity of earning compound interest thereon, from 1968 until the date of judgment. If that were the ground on which Cantley J held in favour of the defendants on this issue, I would respectfully hold that it was a wrong ground. But I do not think that he did so hold.

The second possible answer is that which I believe to have influenced Cantley J. He thought that the decision in *The Liesbosch* precluded him from taking into account, in considering the reasonableness of the deferment of repairs, any part of the deferment which was caused by "financial stringency."

The Liesbosch has been the subject of much debate and much speculation, and a consider-able measure of disagreement, as to its *ratio decidendi* and the scope of its application, par-ticularly in the light of later House of Lords decisions: see, for example, the discussion of the case by the learned author of the article on "Damages" in *Halsbury's Laws of England*, 4th ed., vol. 12 (1975), para. 1144, footnote 4. I agree with the analysis of *The Liesbosch* and the com-ments thereon in the judgment which Donaldson LJ will deliver hereafter. I do not think that, on any fair view of the *ratio decidendi* of *The Liesbosch*, it applies to the issue with which we are concerned. Amongst other reasons, there are these two. First, it was not "financial strin-gency," let alone "impecuniousness" as in *The Liesbosch*, which on any fair view, on Cantley J's findings, was *the* cause, or even, I think, an effective cause, of the decision to postpone re-pairs. The "financial stringency" which would have been created by carrying out the repairs was merely one factor among a number of factors which together produced the result that commercial good sense pointed towards deferment of the repairs. The second reason which I would mention is that, once it is accepted that the plaintiff was not in any breach of any duty owed by him to the defendant in failing to carry out repairs earlier than the time when it was reasonable for the repairs to be put in hand, this becomes, for all practical purposes, if not in theory, equated with a plaintiff's ordinary duty to mitigate his damages. Lord Wright in his speech in *The Liesbosch*, at p. 461, accepted Lord Collin's dictum in *Clippens Oil Co. Ltd. v. Edinburgh and District Water Trustees*, [1907] AC 291 (HL (Sc.)) at p. 303:

> [I]n my opinion the wrongdoer must take his victim *talem qualem*, and if the position of the latter is aggravated because he is without the means of mitigating it, so much the worse for the wrongdoer. …

I agree with the observations of Oliver J in *Radford v. De Froberville*, [1977] 1 WLR 1262 (Ch. D) at p. 1268 as to the relationship between the duty to mitigate and the measure, or amount, of damages in relation to a question such as the question with which we are here concerned. A plaintiff who is under a duty to mitigate is not obliged, in order to reduce the damages, to do that which he cannot afford to do: particularly where, as here, the plaintiffs' "financial stringency," so far as it was relevant at all, arose, as a matter of common sense, if not as a matter of law, solely as a consequence of the defendant's wrongdoing.

My provisional answer to the question raised in the first issue would, thus, be that the dam-ages in this case are to be assessed by reference to the 1978 cost of repairs. I now carry out that exercise which I mentioned earlier. Once it is accepted, as it is accepted by the parties, that the damages fall to be computed by reference to the cost of repairs to the building, and once *The Liesbosch*, [1933] AC 449 (HL (Eng.)) and *Philips v. Ward*, [1956] 1 WLR 471 (CA) are out of the reckoning, there is no exception of which I am aware which is relevant here to exclude application of Lord Blackburn's fundamental principle. On the relevant facts as found by Cantley J, the 1978 cost of the repairs gives the answer which accords with that principle. The calculation of damages by reference to the 1970 cost of repairs would not so accord.

On that issue, I would allow the appeal.

The result is that the plaintiff's alternative ground of appeal, as to the appropriate calcula-tion of interest, does not arise. For it is a necessary part of their submission on the first issue that, damages being referable to the deferment of repairs, interest is not payable up to the date of the hearing. In the circumstances, I think it better to say nothing on that point, on which the argument on either side was commendably brief. …

BROWNE LJ: I agree that this appeal should be allowed and the cross-appeal dismissed, for the reasons given by Megaw LJ and the reasons which will be given by Donaldson LJ in the judgment he will deliver very soon. I can summarise my own reasons fairly shortly, because they are in substance the same as theirs.

The first principle for the assessment of damages is that the injured person should, so far as money can do it, be put in the same position as if the wrong—in this case the tort—had not been committed against him: see *Halsbury's Laws of England*, 4th ed., vol. 12, title "Damages," para. 1129, and—for example—the authority cited by Megaw LJ, *Livingstone v. Rawyards Coal Co.* (1880), 5 App. Cas. 25 (HL (Sc.)), *per* Lord Blackburn, at p. 39. This the damages of £11,375 awarded to the first plaintiffs, for the cost of repairs in 1970, glaringly fail to do. By the time of the hearing in 1978 the cost had risen to £30,327. In fact, the repairs had not been done by that time, and the cost will probably have risen still further by the time they are done, but the plaintiffs do not make any further claim beyond the cost at the date of the hearing.

It is not disputed that in this case the measure of the first plaintiffs' damages is the cost of repair, as opposed to the other possible measure in a case of this sort, *i.e.* the diminution of the value of the building. The only question is the time as at which that cost shall be taken.

The general rule, both in contract and tort, is that damages should be assessed as at the date when the cause of action arises, but they may be assessed as at some later date. In my view, Cantley J was plainly right in saying, ante, pp. 444H-445A: "The appropriate damages are the cost of repairs at the time when it was reasonable to begin repairs." In *Johnson v. Agnew*, [1980] AC 367 (HL (Eng.)), Lord Wilberforce said, at pp. 400-01:

> The general principle for the assessment of damages is compensatory, i.e. that the innocent party is to be placed, so far as money can do so, in the same position as if the contract had been performed. Where the contract is one of sale, this principle normally leads to assessment of damages as at the date of the breach—a principle recognised and embodied in section 51 of the *Sale of Goods Act 1893*. But this is not an absolute rule: if to follow it would give rise to injustice, the court has power to fix such other date as may be appropriate in the circumstances. In cases where a breach of a contract for sale has occurred, and the innocent party reasonably continues to try to have the contract completed, it would to me appear more logical and just rather than tie him to the date of the original breach, to assess damages as at the date when (otherwise than by his default) the contract is lost. Support for this approach is to be found in the cases. In *Ogle v. Earl Vane* (1867), LR 2 QB 275; (1868), LR 3 QB 272 the date was fixed by reference to the time when the innocent party, acting reasonably, went into the market; in *Hickman v. Haynes* (1875), LR 10 CP 598 at a reasonable time after the last request of the defendants (buyers) to withhold delivery. In *Radford v. De Froberville*, [1977] 1 WLR 1262 (Ch. D), where the defendant had covenanted to build a wall, damages were held measurable as at the date of the hearing rather than at the date of the defendant's breach, unless the plaintiff ought reasonably to have mitigated the breach at an earlier date.

Lord Wilberforce, of course, was there speaking of damages for breach of contract, but I have no doubt that the same principle applies to this case, where it is common ground that the measure of damages is the cost of repairs. I think this view is supported by analogy by the decision of the House of Lords in *West Midland Baptist (Trust) Association (Inc.) v. Birmingham Corporation*, [1970] AC 874 (HL (Eng.)).

In this case, it was common ground, and Cantley J accepted that it had been reasonable to postpone the doing of the repairs from 1968, when damage had first been discovered, until 1970, and that 1970 was the earliest date as at which the cost of repairs should be assessed. The defendants contended that the assessment should not be any further postponed; Cantley J accepted this contention, and assessed the damages on the cost of repairs in 1970.

In the course of the passage in his judgment which Megaw LJ has already read, *ante*, pp. 442E-F, 449C-D, he held that:

> As a commercial decision, judged exclusively from the point of view of the immediate and short-term welfare of the companies, it was reasonable to postpone incurring the very considerable expense of these repairs. ...

Like Megaw LJ, I understand this to mean that it was in this sense reasonable to postpone doing the repairs until after the hearing. This was based on the evidence of Mr. Smith, a director of both the plaintiff companies and a chartered accountant, which is set out in Cantley J's judgment and has been summarised already by Megaw LJ. Cantley J gave a number of reasons for the decision. Only one of what he said were the relevant factors was financial, and I think that his finding on this point falls far short of "impecuniosity" or "financial embarrassment" in the *Liesbosch* sense.

Cantley J said, ante, pp. 444E-445A:

> Whether the time is reasonable must be judged objectively and not taking into account such matters as impecuniosity or financial stringency which, in the words of Lord Wright in *The Liesbosch*, [1933] AC 449 at pp. 460-461, are extrinsic.

I am afraid I do not clearly understand what Cantley J meant by "objectively" in that sentence. If he meant that the decision to postpone, although reasonable from the point of view of the plaintiff companies, was not reasonable from the point of view of a hypothetical reasonable commercial man, I cannot agree; it seems to me that any commercial man in the circumstance with which Mr. Smith was faced could reasonably, and probably would, have come to the same decision.

The judge relied on *Philips v. Ward*, [1956] 1 WLR 471 (CA) and *Clark v. Woor*, [1965] 1 WLR 650 (QB), in which Lawton J simply followed and applied *Philips v. Ward*. I agree with Megaw LJ that the reasoning of Lord Denning MR in *Philips v. Ward*, at p. 474, can no longer be regarded as good law.

That leaves only *The Liesbosch*. I do not propose to analyse that difficult case, because I entirely agree with Megaw LJ and Donaldson LJ that, for the reasons they give, it did not compel Cantley J to take the 1970 cost of repairs. I will only say that, like Megaw LJ, I agree with the observations of Oliver J in *Radford v. De Froberville*, [1977] 1 WLR 1262 at p. 1272 as to the relationship between the duty to mitigate and the measure of damages in a case such as this.

I would, therefore, allow the first plaintiffs' appeal and vary the judgment by substituting £30,327 for £11,375.

Perry v. Sidney Phillips & Sons
[1982] 1 WLR 1297 (CA)

LORD DENNING MR: In 1976 the plaintiff, Mr. Perry, was minded to buy a house. He saw what looked like a very attractive property. It was Kyre Bank Cottage, Kyre, near Tenbury Wells, in Worcestershire. He made an offer of £27,000 subject to survey and contract. He employed a firm of surveyors, Messrs. Sidney Phillips & Son, the defendants, to carry out the survey. They surveyed the property and prepared a report. Mr. Perry read the report. On the faith of it—although it did disclose some defects in the property—he was satisfied that the cottage was a sound buy. So, on July 2, 1976, he completed the contract of sale for £27,000.

Unfortunately, after Mr. Perry took possession, he found many defects. They had not been mentioned in the report. In particular, there were serious defects in the roof and in the septic tank. The surveyors had not noticed them. The roof leaked and the rain came in. The septic tank gave off an offensive odour. Mr. Perry consulted a different firm of surveyors. They made a report showing that there were many defects which had not been mentioned by Messrs. Sidney Phillips & Son in their report. Mr. Perry instructed solicitors. They wrote to Messrs. Sidney Phillips & Son listing the defects. Messrs. Sidney Phillips & Son instructed their own solicitors. The upshot was that the surveyors denied any liability.

This placed Mr. Perry in a quandary. He simply did not have the money to undertake major repairs. He carried out what minor repairs he could on a "do-it-yourself" basis. As Messrs. Sidney Phillips & Son were denying liability, he could not risk doing the repairs on borrowed money.

On his solicitors' advice, Mr. Perry brought an action against Messrs. Sidney Phillips & Son for damages for their negligence in making their report. The claim was put both in breach of contract and in negligence. In 1981 the case was tried by Mr. Patrick Bennett QC sitting as a deputy High Court judge. He dealt with liability before considering the quantum of damages. At that stage Mr. Perry and his wife were still living in the cottage.

The judge found that the surveyors were negligent in making their report. He held that damages should be assessed according to the cost of repairing the defects in 1981 when the action was tried. He also held that Mr. Perry ought to be awarded damages for vexation—that is, the worry, discomfort and distress which he had suffered by reason of the house being in poor condition. The defendants appeal to this court.

But then the unexpected happened. After the trial and pending the appeal, Mr. Perry decided to sell the house. After the trial in April 1981 Mr. Perry found himself in financial difficulties. He had received bills from his solicitors for £4,788 costs. He could not get any assurance as to the date when damages would be assessed. He was faced with the prospect of the appeal and long-drawn-out hearings as to damages. So Mr. Perry put the cottage on the market without doing any of the repairs. He sold it for £43,000.

Mr. Perry made an affidavit to explain why he had found it necessary to sell the cottage. In August 1981 he had been offered a job as a clerk with stockjobbers on the London Stock Exchange. It was necessary that he should live nearer to his new place of work. So he sold the cottage and bought a house at Fittleworth in Sussex.

We now have to consider how the damages are to be assessed. The cases show up many differences. I need only draw attention to these:

First, where there is a contract to build a wall or a house, or to do repairs to it, then if the contractor does not do the work or does it badly, the employer is entitled, by way of damages, to recover the reasonable cost of doing such work as is reasonable to make good the breach. The cost is to be assessed at the time when it would be reasonable for the employer to do it, having regard to all the circumstances of the case, including therein any delay due to a denial of liability by the contractor or the financial situation of the employer. The work may not have been done even up to the date of trial. If the cost has increased in the meantime since the breach—owing to inflation—then the increased cost is recoverable, but no interest is to be allowed for the intervening period (see *Radford v. De Froberville*, [1977] 1 WLR 1262 (Ch. D) and *William Cory & Son Ltd. v. Wingate Investments (London Colney) Ltd.* (1980), 17 BLR 104 (CA)); likewise if a wrongdoer damages his neighbour's house by nuisance or negligence, and the neighbour is put to expense in the repairing of it: see *Dodd Properties (Kent) Ltd. v. Canterbury City Council*, [1980] 1 WLR 433 (CA).

Second, where there is a contract by a prospective buyer with a surveyor under which the surveyor agrees to survey a house and make a report on it—and he makes it negligently—and the client buys the house on the faith of the report, then the damages are to be assessed at the time of the breach, according to the difference in price which the buyer would have given if the report had been carefully made from that which he in fact gave owing to the negligence of the surveyor. The surveyor gives no warranty that there are no defects other than those in his report. There is no question of specific performance. The contract has already been performed, albeit negligently. The buyer is not entitled to remedy the defects and charge the cost to the surveyor. He is only entitled to damages for the breach of contract or for negligence. It was so decided by this court in *Philips v. Ward*, [1956] 1 WLR 471 (CA), followed in *Simple Simon Catering Ltd. v. Binstock Miller & Co.* (1973), 117 SJ 529 (CA).

The former case was concerned with breach of contract by surveyors. It is their duty to use reasonable care and skill in making a proper report on the house. In our present case Messrs. Sidney Phillips & Son failed in that duty in 1976 when they made the negligent report. Mr. Perry acted on the report in 1976 when he bought the house in July 1976. The general rule of law is that you assess the damages at the date of the breach: so as to put the plaintiff in the same position as he would have been in if the contract had been properly performed. Even if the claim be laid in tort against the surveyor, the damages should be on the same basis.

So you have to take the difference in valuation. You have to take the difference between what a man would pay for the house in the condition in which it was reported to be and what he would pay if the report had been properly made showing the defects as they were. In other words, how much more did he pay for the house by reason of the negligent report than he would have paid had it been a good report? That being the position, the difference in valuation should be taken at the date of the breach in 1976. We were given some approximate figures of the difference in the valuation. The plaintiff's figure was £6,000. The defendants' figure was £2,250.

I would go on to say—and this is important—that although the date for the assessment of damages is 1976, there is some compensation for inflation because those damages carry interest. Probably 9 per cent., 10 per cent. or even 11 per cent. would be awarded nowadays from 1976 until the date when the damages are paid: or, at least, up until judgment is given and then afterwards at the judgment rate.

The second point is as to the distress, worry, inconvenience and all the trouble to which Mr. Perry was put during the time when he was in the house. Mr. Hicks sought to say before us that damages ought not to be recoverable under this head at all. He referred to the *The Liesbosch*, [1933] AC 449 (HL (Eng.)). In that case Lord Wright said at p. 460 that the loss due to the impecuniosity of the plaintiffs was not recoverable. I think that that statement must be restricted to the facts of *The Liesbosch*. It is not of general application. It is analysed and commented upon in this court in *Dodd Properties (Kent) Ltd. v. Canterbury City Council*, [1980] 1 WLR 433 (CA). It is not applicable here. It seems to me that Mr. Perry is entitled to damages for all the vexation, distress and worry which he has been caused by reason of the negligence of the surveyor. If a man buys a house—for his own occupation—on the surveyor's advice that it is sound—and then he finds out that it is in a deplorable condition, it is reasonably foreseeable that he will be most upset. He may, as here, not have the money to repair it and this will upset him all the more. That too is reasonably foreseeable. All this anxiety, worry and distress may nowadays be the subject of compensation. Not excessive, but modest compensation. That appears from such cases as *Jarvis v. Swans Tours Ltd.*, [1973] QB 233 (CA); *Jackson v. Horizon Holidays Ltd.*, [1975] 1 WLR 1468; *Heywood v. Wellers*, [1976] QB 446 (CA) and *Hutchinson v. Harris* (1978), 10 BLR 19 (CA). In our present case, the judge said [1982] 1 All ER 1005 at pp. 1016-1017:

> I think it was reasonably foreseeable that, if Mr. Perry bought the house in such a condition that he was exposed to the incursion of water, the anxiety resulting from the question of when the repairs should be done and the odour and smell from the defective septic water tank would cause him distress and discomfort which I have gathered together under the term "vexation." ... In my view, the plaintiff is entitled ... to damages for such discomfort, distress and the like which he has suffered as a result of the defendants' negligence in, in effect, giving this house a clean bill of health. ... I am satisfied that he has not acted unreasonably and he has not failed to mitigate his damage and that the consequences which have flowed from the defendants' breach of contract and/or negligence were foreseeable, are direct and have not been diminished or extinguished by any failure on the part of Mr. Perry to mitigate his loss.

Mr. Perry is entitled to damages on that score also. The quantum of damages is to be assessed by an official referee later on.

In the circumstances, I think that the appeal must be allowed in so far as it affects the date at which damages are to be assessed, but dismissed on the question of vexation.

OLIVER LJ: I agree with the order which Lord Denning MR has proposed. It is not now suggested that the measure of damages which was proposed by the deputy judge ought to be sustained in its totality, not because of any error in his reasoning—although no doubt the defendants would have wished to challenge that if the matter had proceeded on that basis—but because it has been overtaken by events, the house having now been sold by the plaintiff at a price very considerably in excess of that which the plaintiff paid for it in 1976. In these circumstances, the cost of repairs, which have not in fact been carried out, cannot any longer be an appropriate measure; and the debate before us has concentrated on two points. The first is the question whether the appropriate measure of damage on the basis of what the deputy judge described as "differential in valuation" is, as Mr. Hicks submits, the difference between the price paid by the plaintiff and the value at the date of its acquisition—the property which he actually got—or whether it is, as Mr. Lantham suggests, the difference between the value of the house at the date of the trial in its defective condition and the value which it would then have had if it had been in the condition in which on the basis of the surveyor's report it should have been. Speaking for myself, I have no doubt whatever that the basis suggested by Mr. Hicks is the right one. What Mr. Latham contends for in effect makes the surveyors warrant the value of the property surveyed, and indeed the deputy judge seems so to have thought. He said, [1982] 1 All ER 1005 at p. 1011:

> Counsel for the defendants, in the course of an extremely helpful address, warned me against putting the surveyor into the shoes of the vendor, that is warranting the condition of the property and requiring, if that warranty is breached, the surveyor to pay compensation to the purchaser.

I interpose to say that I do not believe for a moment that vendors normally do do that and it may be that this is a misprint for "valuer." The judge then goes on to say:

> In reality the surveyor is not far removed from that situation. The purchaser is relying upon his skill, his expertise and his care to ensure that what he, the purchaser, is buying is worth what he is paying for it. In that sense, the surveyor is describing the property which is being bought.

With the greatest respect to the deputy judge, I cannot agree with that. The position as I see it is simply this, that the plaintiff has been misled by a negligent survey report into paying more for the property than that property was actually worth. The position, as I see it, is exactly the same as that which arose in *Philips v. Ward*, [1956] 1 WLR 471 (CA), to which Lord Denning MR has already referred, and in the subsequent case of *Ford v. White & Co.*, [1964] 1 WLR 885 (Ch. D). It is said by Mr. Latham that this proposition is supported in some way by a more recent case, *Dodd Properties (Kent) Ltd. v. Canterbury City Council*, [1980] 1 WLR 433 (CA). That was a case in which the plaintiffs were claiming damages in tort against the defendants, they having removed a support to the plaintiffs' premises. It could not be suggested in that case that there was any other measure of damages than the cost of repair, the only question being the date at which the repairs ought to have been carried out; and the debate there was as to the date at which it was reasonable for the plaintiffs to have carried out the repairs. As I read the case, it merely exemplifies the general principle which is set out in the headnote to the case:

> [T]he fundamental principle as to damages was that the measure of damages was that sum of money that would put the injured party in the same position as that in which he would have been if he had not sustained the injury. …

and the question was what loss the plaintiff, acting reasonably, had actually suffered.

I see nothing in that case which justifies the proposition for which Mr. Latham contends that damages are to be assessed on the basis of some hypothetical value at the date of the trial because the plaintiff has chosen—as he did in this case—to retain the property and not to cut his loss by reselling it. I therefore am of the same view as Lord Denning MR that the right measure of damage is the measure suggested in both *Philips v. Ward*, [1956] 1 WLR 471 (CA) and *Ford v. White & Co.*, [1964] 1 WLR 885 (Ch. D), which is simply the difference between what the plaintiff paid for the property and its value at the date when he obtained it.

Courts of Justice Act

RSO 1990, c. C.43

Damages in Lieu of Injunction or Specific Performance

99. A court that has jurisdiction to grant an injunction or order specific performance may award damages in addition to, or in substitution for, the injunction or specific performance.

[See also RSA 2000, c. J-2, ss. 19 and 20; CCSM c. C280, s. 36; and RSS 1998, c. Q-1.01, s. 66.]

Wroth v. Tyler

[1974] Ch. 30

[The defendant, Tyler, lived with his wife and daughter in a bungalow in Surrey. His title to the bungalow was registered at the Land Registry as absolute, and the bungalow was mortgaged to a building society. In or around March 1971 the defendant decided to sell the bungalow and to buy another bungalow in Norfolk. His wife and daughter were not enthusiastic about the proposed move.

After the bungalow was placed in the hands of estate agents, the plaintiffs visited the bungalow with a view to buying it. During that visit, the defendant's wife explained to the plaintiffs the working of the cooker, gas drier, etc. The plaintiffs eventually agreed to buy the bungalow for £6,050; this amount included £50 for fittings, etc. They visited the bungalow on two or three other occasions following the first visit. The defendant's wife may have been there on at least one of those occasions. On May 27, 1971 contracts were exchanged for the sale of the bungalow, the defendant as beneficial owner contracting to sell with vacant possession at the agreed price, and completion to take place on or before October 31. On the same day, the defendant entered into a contract to purchase the Norfolk bungalow. On May 28 the defendant's wife, without the defendant's knowledge, entered in the charges register against the defendant's title at the Land Registry a notice of her rights of occupation under ss. 1 and 2 of the *Matrimonial Homes Act 1967*. The defendant's wife had at no time given any indication to the plaintiffs that she was unwilling to leave the bungalow. Neither the defendant's wife nor the Land Registry disclosed the registration of the notice directly to the defendant, but on June 11 the building society wrote to the defendant's solicitors enclosing a notice of the wife's rights of occupation, which had been received by them from the Land Registry. On June 18 the defendant learned of the notice when he received notification of the registration from his solicitors. An argument followed between the defendant and his wife over the notice. The next day, the defendant instructed his solicitors to withdraw from his contract with the plaintiffs and to cancel the purchase of the Norfolk bungalow. Although the defendant made several attempts to persuade his wife to withdraw her notice, she steadfastly refused. On July 13 the defendant's solicitors wrote to the plaintiffs' solicitors confirming that the defendant would not complete the contract with the plaintiffs. October 31 passed without completion taking place and in January 1972 the plaintiffs issued a writ claiming, among other things, specific performance of the contract and damages in lieu or in addition. At the date set for completion of the contract, the market value of the house was

£7,500; at the date of judgment in January 1973 the value of the house had risen to £11,500, an amount far above the contract price. Although the parties had contemplated that there would be a rise in house prices, they had not anticipated that the market price of the bungalow would have risen so rapidly during the following year and a half.]

MEGARRY J [having recited the facts]: … By his defence the defendant admits that at the date for completion and at the date of the defence he was unable to give vacant possession of the bungalow, and that he was thereby in breach of his agreement; and he states his willingness to submit to an enquiry as to damages for the breach. By an amendment made on 13th November, shortly before the hearing began, the defendant contends that if (which is denied) the plaintiffs are otherwise entitled to judgment for specific performance, they have disentitled themselves to it by delay. The plaintiffs' primary claim is to specific performance, with damages as an alternative.

The issues before me may be summarised as follows. (1) Delay apart, are the plaintiffs entitled to specific performance of the contract with vacant possession? If they are, a form of order is sought that will require the defendant to make an application to the court for an order against his wife terminating her rights of occupation under the *Matrimonial Homes Act 1967*, in accordance with s. 1(2). (2) Delay apart, are the plaintiffs, as an alternative, entitled to specific performance of the contract subject to the rights of occupation of the defendant's wife, with damages or an abatement of the purchase price in respect thereof? If they are, they will be able to make the application to the court under the 1967 Act, by virtue of ss. 1(2) and 2(3). (3) If, apart from delay, the plaintiffs would be entitled to an order for specific performance under either of these two heads, is their right to it barred by delay? (4) If the plaintiffs have no right to specific performance, then it is common ground that they are entitled to damages. There is, however, an acute conflict as to the measure of damages. The primary contention of the defendant is that the damages are limited by the rule in *Bain v. Fothergill* (1874), LR 7 HL 158 (HL (Eng.)), so that the defendant need only release the deposit to the plaintiffs and pay their costs of investigating title, and is not liable to them for more than nominal damages for loss of their bargain. Is this contention sound? (5) If *Bain v. Fothergill* does not apply, then the defendant accepts that damages for loss of the bargain are payable; but there is a dispute as to the computation of those damages. The defendant says that the damages must be assessed as at the date of the breach, in accordance with the normal rule; the plaintiffs say that this is a case where damages must be assessed as at the date of assessment, that is, today, if I assess the damages. The valuers on each side have not given evidence, but very sensibly they have agreed [on] a graph which shows the figures at successive dates, and counsel put this in as an agreed document. I can ignore £50 of the contract price, for that was for the various fittings and chattels; and on that footing the contract price was £6,000. It is agreed that at the date fixed for completion the bungalow was worth £7,500; and it is agreed that at the time of the hearing before me it was worth £11,500. Damages assessed as at the date of the breach would be £1,500, but as at the date of the hearing would be £5,500. At which figure should damages for the loss of the bargain be assessed? The defendant says that the former figure applies, in accordance with the general rule, but the plaintiffs say that the latter figure applies, for unless it does, they will be unable to acquire an equivalent house at today's prices. …

[Having reviewed the statutory provisions affording the wife the right to claim a right to remain in the home, he continued:]

... I may summarise my conclusions as to the essentials of the right given by the Act to an occupying spouse as follows. The right is in essence a personal and non-assignable statutory right not to be evicted from the matrimonial home in question during marriage or until the court otherwise orders; and this right constitutes a charge on the estate or interest of the owning spouse which requires protection against third parties by registration. For various reasons, the right may be said to be one which readily fits into no category known to conveyancers before 1967; the phrase *sui generis* seems apt, but of little help.

With that in mind, I turn to the first question before me. Delay apart, are the plaintiffs entitled to specific performance of the contract with vacant possession? If they are, the form of order sought will require the defendant to make an application to the court under s. 1(2) to terminate his wife's rights of occupation which arose and became a charge on the defendant's estate on 1st January 1968, and were protected by registration on 28th May 1971. ...

It seems to me that where a third party has some rights over the property to be sold, there are at least three categories of cases. First, there are those cases where the vendor is entitled as of right to put an end to the rights of the third party, or compel his concurrence or cooperation in the sale. Second, and at the other extreme, there are cases where the vendor has no right to put an end to the third party's rights, or compel his concurrence or co-operation in the sale, and can do no more than try to persuade him to release his rights or to concur in the sale. An example of the first category would be the vendor's right, as mortgagor, to pay off a mortgage, or his right, as a mortgagee, to obtain possession from the mortgagor. An example of the second category would be when the third party is entitled to an easement over the land.

In between those two categories there is a third category, namely, where the vendor cannot as of right secure the requisite discharge or concurrence, but if it is refused he can go to the court, which has power, on a proper case being shown, to secure the release or concurrence. Examples would be a restrictive covenant which may be modified or discharged under the *Law of Property Act 1925*, s. 34 (as amended), or the requisite consent of a landlord to an assignment of a lease where there is a contractual or statutory requirement that the landlord's consent is not to be unreasonably withheld. The powers of the court under s. 1(2) of the 1967 Act seem to me to bring the present case within this third and intermediate category. ...

Persuasion having failed, I think that the court should be slow to grant a decree of specific performance that would require an unwilling husband to make an application to the court under s. 1(2) of the 1967 Act, particularly as the decision of the court depends on the application of phrases such as "just and reasonable" under s. 1(3). In any case, the court would be reluctant to make an order which requires a husband to take legal proceedings against his wife, especially while they are still living together. Accordingly, although this is a contract of a type which the court is normally ready to enforce by a decree of specific performance, in my judgment it would, in Lord Redesdale L's phrase, be "highly unreasonable" to make such a decree if there is any other form of order that could do justice; and that I must consider in due course. Let me add that I would certainly not regard proceedings under the Act by the defendant against his wife as being without prospects of success. As the evidence stands (and of course I have not heard the defendant's wife) there is at least a real prospect of success for the defendant. He does not in any way seek to deprive his wife of a home; the difference between them is a difference as to where the matrimonial home is to be. In that, the conduct of the wife towards the plaintiffs and the defendant must play a substantial part.

I turn to the second main question, that of counsel for the plaintiffs' alternative claim to specific performance for which he contended if he failed in his main claim to specific performance, and if he also was limited either to *Bain v. Fothergill* damages, or else to damages assessed as at the date of the breach. This alternative claim was for specific performance of the contract, but with the plaintiffs taking subject to the charge in favour of the defendant's wife, and receiving damages or an abatement of the purchase money. ...

There is at least a real possibility that a decree of specific performance subject to the wife's right not to be evicted or excluded would enable the plaintiffs, by taking suitable proceedings, to evict the defendant and perhaps the daughter, and thus split up the family. These circumstances seem to me to make the case one in which the court should be slow to decree specific performance if any reasonable alternative exists. I shall accordingly turn in due course to the question of damages to see whether they would provide the plaintiffs with an adequate remedy.

Before I consider damages, I must deal with the third main point, that of laches, which is a defence to specific performance, although not, of course, to damages. In the end, counsel for the defendant relied only on the delay between 17th August 1971 and the issue of the writ on 25th January 1972. On 17th August the plaintiffs' solicitors wrote to the defendant's solicitors saying that they were taking counsel's advice and would write further when they obtained it. Not until 30th November 1971 did the plaintiffs' solicitors write to the defendant's solicitors to say that proceedings for specific performance or damages (or both) would be instituted shortly, and that the delay had been occasioned by the plaintiff's unsuccessful application for legal aid. The period in question was thus some 3½ months or 5½ months, according to whether the *terminus ad quem* was the letter before action, or the writ. Counsel for the defendant's strongest cases were *Huxham v. Llewellyn* (1873), 21 WR 570 (Ch.) and *Glasbrook v. Richardson* (1874), 23 WR 51 (Ch.), where periods of unexplained delay for over five months and some 3½ months respectively were held to be a bar to specific performance. However, as counsel for the plaintiffs pointed out, in this case the date fixed for completion was 31st October 1971, and it must, he said, at least be open to the plaintiffs to refrain from suing for specific performance until the defendant had broken the contract. Time therefore ought to run not from 17th August but from 31st October, with a consequent reduction of some 2½ months in each of the periods. In any case, the authorities cited were cases of the sale of interests in a colliery, and so sales of highly speculative interests, approaching a trade, to which special considerations applied. It seems plain to me that there has been no unexplained delay of an order which, in the circumstances of this case, would justify holding the remedy of specific performance barred by laches or acquiescence.

I turn to damages. The fourth main point is whether the damages are limited to those recoverable under the rule in *Bain v. Fothergill*. The rule is conveniently stated in *Williams's Contracts of Sale of Land* (London: Butterworths, 1930):

> Where the breach of contract is occasioned by the vendor's inability, without his own fault, to show a good title, the purchaser is entitled to recover as damages his deposit, if any, with interest,

and his expenses incurred in connection with the agreement, but not more than nominal damages for the loss of his bargain.

What is said by counsel for the defendant is, quite simply, that the statutory charge in favour of the defendant's wife is a defect in title within the rule, just as much as any other charge would be, whether legal or equitable, and so the rule applies.

In *Bain v. Fothergill* itself, a distinction was drawn between matters of conveyancing and matters of title. Lord Hatherley said at p. 209:

> Whenever it is a matter of conveyancing, and not a matter of title, it is the duty of the vendor to do everything that he is enabled to do by force of his own interest, and also by force of the interest of others whom he can compel to concur in the conveyance.

This was said in relation to *Engell v. Fitch* (1868), LR 4 QB 659, where the principle of *Bain v. Fothergill*, as exemplified in its ancestor, *Flureau v. Thornhill* (1776), 2 Wm. Bl. 1078, was held not to apply to mortgagees who sold with vacant possession but refused to evict the mortgagor who was in possession. The right to vacant possession may be regarded as a matter of conveyancing rather than of title, in that vacant possession is required to be delivered only on completion, and a title may be in perfect order even though the vendor is out of possession. By contrast, in *Bain v. Fothergill* the vendor had a mere equitable title to the lease of the mining royalty that he had contracted to sell, and he unexpectedly failed to obtain the lessor's consent to the assignment that would have enabled him to convey what he had contracted to sell. That was plainly a matter of title, and the rule applied. That in turn may be contrasted with *Day v. Singleton*, [1899] 2 Ch. 320 (CA), where the lessor's consent was requisite for the assignment of the lease which had been sold, and, as I have mentioned, the vendor either did not really try to obtain the consent, or else had induced the lessors to withhold it. The Court of Appeal held that damages for loss of the bargain were recoverable in that the vendor had failed in his duty to obtain the lessor's consent. Lord Lindley MR and Rigby LJ said (at p. 329) of the rule in *Bain v. Fothergill* that it was—

> an anomalous rule based upon and justified by difficulties in shewing a good title to real property in this country, but one which ought not to be extended to cases in which the reasons on which it is based do not apply.

Certainly the courts have proved ready to find grounds for holding that cases do not fall within the rule. In *Re Daniel, Daniel v. Vassall*, [1917] 2 Ch. 405, a testator had, before his death, contracted to sell land which, with other property, was comprised in a mortgage. The mortgagees refused to release the land on payment of an appropriate fraction of what was due under the mortgage, and the testator's estate was insufficient to pay off the entire mortgage. Sargant J held that the rule in *Bain v. Fothergill* did not apply, for the failure of the executors to perform the contract was not due to any defect in title, but to the insufficiency of the testator's estate, and he refused to extend the anomalous rule in *Bain v. Fothergill* (or *Flureau v. Thornhill*) to a case which was not within the spirit of the rule. In *Braybrooks v. Whaley*, [1919] 1 KB 435, a mortgagee contracted to sell land, but without obtaining, either before or after the contract, the leave of the court made requisite by the *Courts (Emergency Powers) Act 1914*. Again the rule was held not to apply. Horridge J said that the failure to seek leave of the court was not a matter of title within the rule, but a matter of completing the contract by conveyance, and Salter J held that the contention that the application, if made, would have failed had not been established. Counsel for the defendant submitted that this decision was wrong, at all events insofar as it proceeded on the footing that the vendor was under a duty to take proceedings to remove the obstacle to completion, for he had no clear right to the grant of leave by the court but merely a hope or prospect that the discretionary powers of the court would be exercised in his favour.

Various other cases were cited, including *Thomas v. Kensington*, [1942] 2 KB 181, and *J.W. Cafés Ltd. v. Brownlow Trust Ltd.*, [1950] 1 All ER 894 (KB), but I do not think I need discuss them. None of the cases cited to me plainly covers the facts of the present case, or answers the question whether the wife's right is a defect in title within the principle of *Bain v. Fothergill*. At one stage counsel for the defendant observed that her right was a very strange right, but whatever it was, it was a defect in title within the rule; and counsel for the plaintiffs was constrained to accept that it constituted some sort of defect in title, though he said that it was not a defect of a type which brought *Bain v. Fothergill* into play, particularly as the rule was anomalous and ought not to be extended.

Let me consider the consequences of holding that the rule applies, in days when a new verb of doubtful etymology has been attracting considerable attention, namely, the verb "to gazump." The most helpful approach seems to me to take the matter by stages. First, if the mere existence of the wife's charge, before registration, creates a defect in title within the rule, then Parliament has at a blow imposed a defect in title on many millions of homes vested in one or other of the parties to a marriage. On 1st January 1968 millions of perfectly good titles became defective. I should be slow indeed to impute to Parliament any intention to produce this result. This is all the more striking in the case of registered land, where the operation of the rule in *Bain v. Fothergill* might be expected to be minimal; for the main purpose of the *Land Registration Acts* is to simplify titles and conveyancing. Furthermore, if the mere existence of an unregistered charge under the 1967 Act constitutes a defect in title, it is a singularly impotent defect, for on completion of a sale it will be void against the purchaser for want of registration. If instead the vendor refused to complete, plainly he would be refusing to take a step which would remove the defect from his title; and on the principle of *Day v. Singleton* he would appeal to *Bain v. Fothergill* in vain. As at the date of the contract in this case, I therefore cannot see how the rule in *Bain v. Fothergill* could have applied. In other words, looking at matters immediately after the contract had been made, the case could not, in my judgment, be said to fall within either the spirit or the letter of the rule in *Bain v. Fothergill*.

When in this case the wife's rights were registered the day after the contract had been made, a different situation arose; for then her rights could no longer be destroyed by completing the sale. On the footing that the wife's rights thereupon became capable of attracting the rule in *Bain v. Fothergill*, does the rule apply to cases where, at the date of the contract, the necessary conditions for the application of the rule did not exist, but those conditions first came into being after the contract had been made? It has not been suggested that there is any authority bearing directly on this point. The action is an action for damages for breach of contract, and I should be slow to hold that some supervening event could bring within the rule a case initially outside it. Furthermore, the basis of the rule is that of the contract having been made against a background of the uncertainty of titles to land in England; see, for example, *Bain v. Fothergill*, per Lord Hatherley. In *Engell v. Fitch* Kelly CB said that the rule was—

founded entirely on the difficulty that a vendor often finds in making a title to real estate, not from any default on his part, but from his ignorance of the strict legal state of his title.

As I have indicated, a rule laid down for defects in title which lay concealed in title deeds which were often, in the phrase attributed to Lord Westbury, "difficult to read, disgusting to touch, and impossible to understand," seems singularly inapposite to the effect of a modern statute on registered land, with its aseptic certainty and clarity of title.

Furthermore, the rule is anomalous, and, as was shown by the Court of Appeal in *Re Compton, Powell v. Compton*, [1945] Ch. 123 (CA) at pp. 139-40 (in an entirely different field), where the court encounters an anomalous rule, it is in general better to confine the anomaly within its established sphere than to extend the anomaly to analogous cases. Here, the wife's rights are the creature of statute, imposed generally, and in no way dependent on the vicissitudes of a particular title to property. The charge itself is *sui generis*. The wife has personal rights of occupation which she cannot deal with, thus differing greatly from other charges, such as legal or equitable charges for money. If her rights are rights of property at all, they are at least highly idiosyncratic. They do not seem to me to fall within the spirit or intendment of the rule in *Bain v. Fothergill*; and so I hold.

That brings me to the fifth main point. If *Bain v. Fothergill* does not apply, what is the measure of damages? It was common ground that the normal rule is that the general damages to which a purchaser is entitled for breach of a contract for the sale of land are basically measured by the difference between the contract price and the market price of the land at the date of the breach, normally the date fixed for completion. On the facts of this case, the damages under this rule would be of the order of £1,500. The real issue was whether that rule applies to this case, or whether some other rule applies.

Now the principle that has long been accepted is that stated by Parke B in *Robinson v. Harman* (1848), 1 Exch. 850; 154 ER 363, in which, incidentally, the rule in *Flureau v. Thornhill* was considered. Parke B said at p. 855:

> The rule of the common law is, that where a party sustains a loss by reason of a breach of contract, he is, so far as money can do it, to be placed in the same situation, with respect to damages, as if the contract had been performed.

In the present case, if the contract had been performed, the plaintiffs would at the date fixed for completion have had the house, then worth £7,500, in return for the contractual price of £6,000. If in lieu of the house they had been paid £1,500 damages at that date, they could, with the addition of the £6,000 that they commanded, have forthwith bought an equivalent house. I am satisfied on the evidence that the plaintiffs had no financial resources of any substance beyond the £6,000 that they could have put together for the purchase of the defendant's bungalow, and that the defendant knew this when the contract was made. The plaintiffs were therefore, to the defendant's knowledge, unable at the time of the breach to raise a further £1,500 in order to purchase an equivalent house forthwith, and so, as events have turned out, mitigate their loss. Today, to purchase an equivalent house they need £5,500 in addition to their £6,000. How, then, it may be asked, would the award today of £1,500 damages place them in the same situation as if the contract had been performed? The result that would have been produced by paying £1,500 damages at the date of the breach can today be produced only by paying £5,500 damages, with in each case the return of the deposit. On facts such as these, the general rule of assessing damages as at the date of the breach seems to defeat the general principle, rather than carry it out. In the ordinary case of a buyer of goods which the seller fails to deliver, the buyer can at once spend his money in purchasing equivalent goods from another, as was pointed out in *Gainsford v. Carroll* (1824), 2 B & C 624; 107 ER 516 (KBD), and so the rule works well enough; but that is a very different case. It therefore seems to me that on the facts of this case there are strong reasons for applying the principle rather than the rule. The question is whether it is proper to do so.

I do not think that I need enquire whether such an award could be made at common law. It may be that it could. The rule requiring damages to be ascertained as at the date of the breach does not seem to be inflexible, and in any case the rule may be one which, though normally carrying out the principle, does on occasion fail to do so; and on those occasions the rule may have to be modified so as to accord with the principle. However, as I have said, I do not think I need explore that; for it seems to me that this case, in which there is a proper claim for specific performance, falls within the *Chancery Amendment Act 1858* (better known as *Lord Cairns' Act*), and that damages assessed under that Act are to be ascertained in accordance with that Act on a basis which is not identical with that of the common law. That Act provides, by s. 2, that:

> In all cases in which the Court of Chancery has jurisdiction to entertain an application for an injunction against a breach of any covenant, contract, or agreement, or against the commission or continuance of any wrongful act, or for the specific performance of any covenant, contract, or agreement, it shall be lawful for the same court, if it shall think fit, to award damages to the party injured, either in addition to or in substitution for such injunction or specific performance, and such damages may be assessed in such manner as the court shall direct.

The 1858 Act itself has been repealed, but in *Leeds Industrial Co-operative Society Ltd. v. Slack*, [1924] AC 851 (HL (Eng.)), the House of Lords established that statute has maintained in force the jurisdiction conferred by s. 2. I should say that Fry's Specific Performance (London: Stevens, 6th ed., 1921) at p. 602 states:

> It is apprehended that where damages are awarded under this Act in substitution for specific performance, the measure of damages would be the same as in an action at Common law for breach of the contract. So, where the damages at Common Law would be nominal, they would also, it is submitted, be nominal under the statute.

That, however, was written before the *Leeds* case had been decided, though there were other authorities on the point which perhaps had not been borne in mind.

In the case before me, the *Leeds* case is both relevant and important. It shows that *Lord Cairns' Act* extended the field of damages. In the *Leeds* case the House of Lords, by a majority, held that the Act allowed damages to be awarded *quia timet*. An injunction had been sought to restrain a threatened obstruction of ancient lights; and although no actual obstruction had taken place, and so there could be no claim for damages at common law, the Act was held to have empowered the court to award damages for the whole of the threatened injury. That case, of course, was concerned with the award of damages under the 1858 Act which could not be awarded at common law, and not with the quantum of damages in a case where damages could be claimed at common law. The same may be said of *Eastwood v. Lever* (1863), 4 De GJ & Sm. 114; 46 ER 859 (Ch.). That case suggests that damages could be awarded under the 1858 Act when the right infringed was a purely equitable right and the remedy of an injunction had been lost by acquiescence or delay. Yet in a sense the contention that there is jurisdiction to award damages on a scale different from that applicable at law is a fortiori the established jurisdiction to award damages when no claim at all lies at law.

On the wording of the section, the power "to award damages to the party injured ... in substitution for such ... specific performance" at least envisages that the damages awarded will in fact constitute a true substitute for specific performance. Furthermore, the section is speaking of the time when the court is making its decision to award damages in substitution for specific performance, so that it is at that moment that the damages must be a substitute. The fact that a different amount of damages would have been a substitute if the order had been made at the time of the breach must surely be irrelevant. In the case before me, I cannot see how £1,500 damages would constitute any true substitute for a decree of specific performance of the contract to convey land which at the time of the decree is worth £5,500 more than the contract price. A choice between the inadequate and the equivalent seems to me to be no real choice at all. It may seem strange that nearly 115 years should have elapsed before this aspect of *Lord Cairns' Act* should have emerged; but the economic conditions which reveal its significance have not been with us long.

There are dicta in the *Leeds* case which support this view, or are at least consistent with it. In a speech with which the Earl of Birkenhead expressed his agreement, Viscount Finlay said (at p. 859):

> [T]he power to give damages in lieu of an injunction must in all reason import the power to give an equivalent for what is lost by the refusal of the injunction; for this purpose compensation only for what has passed would be futile.

He added:

> It has been urged that the word "damages" must be used as denoting compensation for what has already happened. It is, of course, true that a Court of common law gives damages as compensation for past wrongs, but the word "damages" is perfectly apt to denote compensation for the damage which will be sustained if a building is allowed to proceed so as to obstruct ancient lights. If an injunction is granted the obstruction will never take place. If damages are given instead of the injunction, they must be in respect of an injury which is still in the future.

Lord Dunedin expressly concurred in Lord Finlay's speech; but he also said (at p. 865) that the words referring to damages in substitution for an injunction—

> clearly point to a pecuniary payment equalling the loss to be occasioned by the act against which, but for the provision in question, an injunction would have been obtained. ...

I must, of course, have care in applying dicta uttered in a case where the problem before me was obviously not in view, even though s. 2 of the Act lays down the same rule for injunctions and specific performance alike. Yet on principle I would say simply that damages "in substitution" for specific performance must be a substitute, giving as nearly as may be what specific performance would have given. There are, moreover, certain other authorities which provide assistance. In *Fritz v. Hobson* (1880), 14 Ch. D 542, it was held that damages awarded under the 1858 Act in substitution for an injunction were not confined to damages down to the issue of the writ, as at law, but included damages down to the hearing. Fry J said (at p. 556):

Now it is manifest that damages cannot be an adequate substitute for an injunction unless they cover the whole area which would have been covered by the injunction. …

In *Chapman, Morsons & Co. v. Guardians of Auckland Union* (1889), 23 QBD 294 (CA), the Court of Appeal approved the view taken by Fry J in *Fritz v. Hobson.* In *Dreyfus v. Peruvian Guano Co.* (1889), 43 Ch. D 316 at p. 342 Fry LJ said of *Lord Cairns' Act*:

I am clear that the statue often enables the Court, where a wrong has been done, to give damages upon a different scale from what was done by the Courts of Common Law, because it may give them in substitution for an injunction. …

Cotton LJ who had previously delivered the leading judgment, then said that he agreed with what Fry LJ had said about *Lord Cairns' Act.*

I should say at once that these additional authorities were not discussed before me, but as they support the view which I took without their aid, it seems proper for me to cite them without incurring the costs and delay of restoring the case for further argument. There seems to me to be adequate authority for the view that damages under *Lord Cairns' Act* may be awarded in cases in which there is no claim at all at law, and also that the quantum of damages is not limited by the rules at law. No doubt in exercising the jurisdiction conferred by the 1858 Act a court with equitable jurisdiction will remember that equity follows the law, and will in general apply the common law rules for the assessment of damages; but this is subject to the overriding statutory requirement that damages shall be "in substitution for" the injunction or specific performance. In the words of Cardozo CJ, "Equity follows the law, but not slavishly nor always": see *Graf v. Hope Building Corporation* (1930), 254 NY 1 at p. 9. Obedience to statute, whether in its precise words or in its spirit, is an excellent and compelling reason for not following the law.

In my judgment, therefore, if under *Lord Cairns' Act* damages are awarded in substitution for specific performance, the court has jurisdiction to award such damages as will put the plaintiffs into as good a position as if the contract had been performed, even if to do so means awarding damages assessed by reference to a period subsequent to the date of the breach. This seems to me to be consonant with the nature of specific performance, which is a continuing remedy, designed to secure, inter alia, that the purchaser receives in fact what is his in equity as soon as the contract is made, subject to the vendor's right to the money, and so on. On the one hand, a decree may be sought before any breach of contract has occurred, and so before any action lies for common law damages; and on the other hand the right to a decree may continue long after the breach has occurred. On the facts of this case, the damages that may be awarded are not limited to the £1,500 that is appropriate to the date of the breach, but extend to the £5,500 that is appropriate at the present day, when they are being awarded in substitution for specific performance. I should add that no contention has been advanced (in my judgment, quite rightly) that the case does not fall within *Lord Cairns' Act.* The sale of a house is a case par excellence in which the court "has jurisdiction to entertain an application … for the specific performance" of a contract, and the plaintiffs have done nothing to disentitle themselves to a decree. The undesirability of granting the decree if any suitable alternative exists springs from the position of the defendant and his wife.

That brings me to a subsidiary point which counsel for the defendant urged on me. He contended that an award of damages of the order of £5,500 was precluded by the operation of what is often called the "second rule" in *Hadley v. Baxendale* (1854), 9 Exch. 341; 156 ER 145, relating to what was in the contemplation of the parties. I was very properly referred to that case in the light of the discussion in later cases set out in McGregor on Damages (London: Sweet & Maxwell, 13th ed., 1972) at pp. 124-32. It was beyond question that a rise in the price of houses was in the contemplation of the parties when the contract was made in this case. But counsel for the defendant took it further. He contended that what a plaintiff must establish is not merely a contemplation of a particular head of damage, but also of the quantum under that head. Here, the parties contemplated a rise in house prices, but not a rise of an amount approaching that which in fact took place. A rise which nearly doubled the market price of the property was, as the evidence showed, outside the contemplation of the parties, and so it could not be recovered. Thus ran the argument.

I do not think that this can be right. On principle, it seems to me to be quite wrong to limit damages flowing from a contemplated state of affairs to the amount that the parties can be shown to have had in contemplation, for to do this would require evidence of the calculation in advance of what is often incalculable until after the event. The function of the so-called "second rule" in *Hadley v. Baxendale* seems to me to be not so much to add to the damages recoverable as to exclude from them any liability for any type or kind of loss which could not have been foreseen when the contract was made. No authority was put before me which appeared to me to provide any support for the alleged requirement that the quantum should have been in contemplation. So far as it went, the language used in the authorities that were cited seems to me to have been directed to the heads of damage rather than to quantum. Thus one finds phrases such as "special circumstances" and the "type" or "kind" of damage. I would therefore on principle reject the defendant's contention, and hold that a plaintiff invoking the so-called "second rule" in *Hadley v. Baxendale* need show only a contemplation of circumstances which embrace the head or type of damage in question, and need not demonstrate a contemplation of the quantum of damages under that head or type. Accordingly, in my judgment, this subsidiary contention of the defendant fails, even if it is one that would apply, either directly or by analogy, to damages under *Lord Cairns' Act*.

During the argument it seemed to me surprising that the point should not be covered by authority; yet the only authority put before me that seemed to bear on the point was *Vacwell Engineering Co. Ltd. v. B D H Chemicals Ltd.*, [1971] 1 QB 88. Counsel for the defendant referred me to this case in performance of his duty of assisting the court, although it was against him. The point does not seem to have been argued there in terms, but it was held that where the parties to a contract could reasonably have foreseen that there might be a small or minor explosion, with some damage to property, if a proper warning was not given as to the precautions to be taken in handling the chemical sold, but could not reasonably have foreseen the major explosion which in fact occurred, killing a scientist and doing extensive damage to property, the vendors were nevertheless liable for the whole of the damage done. As Rees J said (at p. 110):

> [T]he explosion and the type of damage being foreseeable, it matters not in the law that the magnitude of the former and the extent of the latter were not.

An appeal was settled: see [1971] 1 QB 111 at p. 112 (Note).

That case, however, does not stand alone. In *Great Lakes Steamship Co. v. Maple Leaf Milling Co. Ltd.* (1924), 41 TLR 21 (PC (Ont.)), the respondents, in breach of contract, had failed "to lighter immediately" the appellants' vessel on its arrival at the respondents' wharf on Lake Erie. Three days later, before any lightering had taken place, the vessel settled on the bottom as a result of a fall in the level of the water in the lake that was within the contemplation of the parties. Unknown to either party, a large anchor was resting on the bottom at that point, projecting two feet above the rock floor which there formed the bottom. This anchor caused serious injuries to the hull, for which the appellants claimed over $40,000 damages. In delivering the advice of the Judicial Committee, Lord Carson said (at p. 23):

> There can be no doubt that it was from breach of the contract immediately to lighter that the vessel grounded by reason of the lowering of the water, the very thing which it was anticipated might occur and which rendered the immediate lightering so important, and it must, in their Lordships' opinion, be held that it was the breach of contract in not lightering the vessel which was the immediate cause of the damage, and the fact that such damage might not have occurred if the anchor had not been sunk can make no difference. If grounding takes place in breach of contract, the precise nature of the damage incurred by grounding is immaterial.

That case seems to provide strong support for the view that I take. In the present case, the argument is directed purely to quantum. The precise head of damage, a general rise in the price of houses, was admittedly in contemplation: all that could be said to be outside the contemplation was the full amount, or the higher stages of the rise from £6,000 to £11,500. In the *Great Lakes* case, what was in contemplation was the fact that delay in lightering might cause the vessel to rest on the bottom by the wharf, a bottom consisting of rock; nobody contemplated the anchor, yet the damages recoverable included those stemming from the anchor. On the authority of that case, the case before me seems a fortiori. I therefore find confirmation in that case of the view that at the hearing I took without its aid.

The conclusion that I have reached, therefore, is that as matters stand I ought to award damages to the plaintiffs of the order of £5,500, in substitution for decreeing specific performance, with all the doubts and difficulties and probably undesirable consequences that a decree in either form would produce. An award of damages on this scale, I accept, will bear hardly on the defendant. Although he is able in one way or another to raise £1,500 without selling his bungalow, £5,500 is another matter; in all probability he could not raise that sum without selling the bungalow with vacant possession, and he has no power to do this. If, however, he becomes bankrupt, then his trustee in bankruptcy can sell the bungalow free from the wife's rights, even though they are registered: see the 1967 Act, s. 2(5). With the money so raised, the trustee in bankruptcy will then be able to pay the plaintiffs their damages, one hopes in full; or it may be possible for the plaintiffs to take the bungalow in satisfaction of their claim. This is a dismal prospect for the defendant, but if the plaintiffs obtain neither a decree of specific performance nor £,5,500 by way of damages, theirs also is a dismal prospect. Having made a binding contract to purchase for £6,000 a bungalow now worth £11,500, they would recover neither the bungalow nor damages that would enable them to purchase anything like its equivalent. It is the plaintiffs who are wholly blameless. Nothing whatever can be said against them, or has been, save as to the contention that delay barred them from a decree of specific performance; and that I have rejected. Nor do I think that there was any delay on their part that could affect the measure of damages.

The ultimate truth as between the defendant and his wife I do not know. As the evidence stands, his wife did nothing whatever to warn the plaintiffs that she was not willing to leave the bungalow, but conducted herself so as to lead them to believe that she concurred in the sale. So far as the defendant was concerned, his wife was very cool about the move, and it may well be that the move was one which a strong-willed husband was in effect imposing on a reluctant yet secretive wife. Nevertheless, the consequences of disputes between husband and wife, whether open or concealed, ought not to be visited on innocent purchasers.

In these circumstances, I think that what I ought to do is make no order today, but, subject to what counsel may have to say, to adjourn the case until the first day of next term. In ordinary circumstances, I would adjourn the case for only a week, but unfortunately the impending vacation makes this impossible. During the adjournment I hope that the defendant and his wife will take advice, separately or together. When I resume the hearing, it may be that the defendant's wife will not have changed her mind about her charge. In that case, I shall award the plaintiffs damages against the defendant of the order of £5,500, even though the probable consequence will be the bankruptcy of the defendant and the sale of the bungalow with vacant possession by his trustee in bankruptcy, free from the wife's rights. On the other hand, the defendant's wife may by then have changed her mind, and rather than force her husband into bankruptcy without avoiding having to vacate the bungalow, she may have taken effective steps to enable the defendant to convey the bungalow to the plaintiffs free from her rights. In that case I shall decree specific performance of the contract. In this way the plaintiffs will obtain either the bungalow that they bought or else an amount of damages which will enable them to purchase its equivalent. I may add that of course I give each side liberty to apply in the meantime; and I should say that I shall be available until 4.00 pm today. As I have indicated, I feel much sympathy for the defendant as well as for the plaintiffs at being embroiled in this way. Yet as between the two sides both the law and the merits seem to me to point to the plaintiffs as being the parties who should be as little hurt as possible; and they have already suffered considerably, not least in relation to their temporary accommodation pending these proceedings. Counsel will no doubt assist me with any submissions that they may have on this proposed adjournment, which was not mooted during the argument.

11th January. The defendant's wife refusing to remove her notice, his Lordship ordered that the defendant pay damages to the plaintiffs to be quantified as at the date of judgment, i.e. 11th January. Counsel having agreed that as no increase in prices had taken place since the date of hearing, damages were assessed at £5,500.

Judgment accordingly.

Metropolitan Trust Co. of Canada v. Pressure Concrete Services Ltd.
[1973] 3 OR 629

HOLLAND J: ... This is an action for specific performance of an agreement of purchase and sale between the Montreal Trust Company, as trustee, purchaser, and Pressure Concrete Services Limited, vendor, of certain real property described in the agreement of purchase and sale, which agreement is dated July 22, 1970. The action is, in the alternative, for damages for breach of the said agreement. ...

Pressure Concrete was at all material times the owner of real property known municipally as 3691 Weston Rd. upon which was erected a freezer plant. Robichaud was at all material times the president and beneficial owner of Pressure Concrete. Some time prior to July 8, 1970, Tremblay, who was familiar with the holdings of Robichaud and who had acted on prior occasions as a mortgage broker for Robichaud in his transactions, approached Robichaud with the suggestion that, in order to provide additional capital, Robichaud consider a sale of the property with a lease back. Robichaud was interested and, as a result, Tremblay entered into negotiations with Metropolitan Trust, who were at the time trustees for certain German interests and in particular Canada Fonds. As a result of these negotiations a memorandum of agreement was entered into, ex. 1, dated July 8, 1970, whereby Pressure Concrete agreed to sell to the client of Metropolitan Trust the above referred to real property at a price of $1,830,000. The purchase price was made up of cash of $600,000, and the assumption of a first mortgage to British Mortgage and a second mortgage to I.A.C. The agreement further provided:

> Purchaser will enter into a lease upon completion of the sale with Associated Freezers of Canada Limited, for a period of 20 years at an annual rental of Two Hundred and Five Thousand, Three Hundred and Twenty ($205,320) Dollars calculated to yield the Purchaser nine and one-half percent (9½%) on the amount of cash invested, in addition to principal and interest payments under the first and second mortgage loans.

The principal and interest payments under the first and second mortgage loans amounted to $148,320, giving a cash return of $57,000 on a cash investment of $600,000. The agreement provided for a cost of living increment on the cash return and further provided in part as follows:

> The Offer to Purchase will be ready for signature by July 17, 1970 and the transaction will close as soon as all the legal documentation including the drafting of the head lease are completed, but not later than July 31, 1970.

[The contract was subject to the vendor obtaining the consent of a mortgagee, I.A.C., to the head lease. The vendor failed to use his best efforts to obtain that consent.]

It may be helpful at this point to summarize the main facts, which facts are really uncontradicted:

(1) The parties entered into an agreement of purchase and sale dated July 22, 1970, with the transaction to close on August 14th.

(2) The time for closing was extended from August 14th to August 21st and again to August 27th.

(3) Neither party was ready to close on August 27th and that date went by without repudiation or tender.

(4) Robichaud on behalf of the vendor repudiated the contract on August 31st.

(5) The solicitors for the purchaser fixed a date for closing, being September 4th and on that date tendered all documents necessary to complete the transaction and this tender was refused.

(6) I.A.C., whose consent was required to the surrender of the existing lease did not, in fact, consent, although I.A.C. had submitted the necessary documents for an opinion to their solicitors. The solicitors did not receive those documents until about the time of the repudiation by Robichaud of the agreement. ...

The obligation to close was subject to a true condition precedent which was not performed. Any judgment for specific performance could be thwarted by the actions of I.A.C. in refusing to consent to the surrender of the existing lease. It was urged upon me that I grant specific performance under the direction of the Master of this Court and require the vendor to attempt to obtain the consent of I.A.C. and permit the purchaser to assist in obtaining such consent. Counsel for the purchaser stated that he could find no case in Canada or in England where this type of order had been made. I was referred, however, to three American authorities: *Franko v. Olszewski* (1947), 25 NW 2d 593 (Mich. SC); *Watson Bros. Transp. Co. Inc. v. Jaffa* (1944), 143 F2d 340 (Circ. CA, 8th); *Renner v. Crisman* (1964), 127 NW 2d 717 (SDSC). These American authorities can be distinguished on their facts. The situation was discussed by Megarry J, in *Wroth v. Tyler*, [1974] Ch. 30 at pp. 47-48, where the following appears:

> It seems to me that where a third party has some rights over the property to be sold, there are at least three categories of cases. First, there are those cases where the vendor is entitled as of right to put an end to the rights of the third party, or compel his concurrence or co-operation in the sale. Second, and at the other extreme, there are cases where the vendor has no right to put an end to the third party's rights or compel his concurrence or co-operation in the sale, and can do no more than to try to persuade him to release his rights or to concur in the sale. An example of the first category would be the vendor's right, as mortgagor, to pay off a mortgage, or his right, as a mortgagee, to obtain possession from the mortgagor. An example of the second category would be when the third party is entitled to an easement over the land.
>
> In between those two categories there is a third category, namely, where the vendor cannot as of right secure the requisite discharge or concurrence, but if it is refused he can go to the court, which has power, upon a proper case being shown, to secure the release or concurrence.

And further at p. 48:

> The modern doctrine seems to me to be stated in *Fry* at p. 466:
>
>> As the consent of a third party is, or may be, a thing impossible to procure, a defendant who has entered into a contract to the performance of which such consent is necessary, will not, in case such consent cannot be procured, be decreed to obtain it, and thus perform an impossibility.

In my view, for the above reason alone specific performance should be refused. ...

The plaintiff, not being entitled to specific performance, is entitled to damages for breach of the obligations undertaken by the vendor above referred to. The question remains whether the damage flowing from the failure of the vendor to perform its obligation under para. 3(e) of the agreement of purchase and sale, and to perform its implied obligation to use its best efforts to obtain the consent of I.A.C. to the surrender of the existing lease, is the same as the damage flowing from breach of an obligation to complete the transaction. It appears to me that had the vendor used its best efforts to obtain the consent of I.A.C., bearing in mind the telephone assurance that the consent would be granted, as set out in ex. 3, and the provisions of cl. 9 of the mortgage, marked as sch. E to the agreement of purchase and sale, referred to above, such would have been forthcoming. I am therefore of the opinion that the damages for the breach of the obligation to obtain the consent of I.A.C. in this case should be assessed on the same basis as if the vendor had breached its obligation to complete the transaction. ...

There is insufficient evidence before me upon which I can make an assessment of damages and the matter will therefore have to be referred to the Master to assess damages. It is necessary, however, to give the Master some direction as to the assessment, with particular reference to any claim for damages for loss of the bargain in that the value of the property has increased since 1970.

A helpful decision in this connection is *Wroth v. Tyler*. ...

Megarry J applied the common law principle that when a party sustains a loss by reason of breach of contract, he is, so far as money can do it, to be placed in the same situation with respect to damages as if the contract had been performed and assessed the damages as the difference in value from the date of the breach to the date of the judgment: see also *Horsnail v. Shute* (1921), 30 BCR 189 (CA); *Day v. Singleton*, [1899] 2 Ch. 320 (CA); *Harvey Foods Ltd. v. Reid* (1971), 3 NBR (2d) 444 (SC, App. Div.); *Remer Bros. Investment Corp. v. Robin*, [1966] SCR 506.

I am of the opinion that in this case the plaintiffs are entitled as part of their damages to any increase in the value of the property from August 31, 1970 to the date of this judgment. ...

[An appeal from the decision of Holland J was dismissed: (1975), 9 OR (2d) 375. On the issue of damages, Schroeder JA (for the court) said as follows (at 377-78)]:

The learned Judge granted an award of damages for breach of contract in lieu of specific performance and directed that such damages should be determined on a reference to the Master. He also gave a direction as to the measure of damages to be applied on the reference. He stated in his reasons [at p. 651]: "I am of the opinion that in this case the plaintiffs are entitled as part of their damages to any increase in the value of the property from August 31, 1970 to the date of this judgment." In so doing he adopted and applied the principle enunciated by Mr. Justice Megarry in *Wroth v. Tyler*, [1974] Ch. 30.

Having regard to our view that the only real and substantial ground for refusal of the relief sought by way of specific performance was the one first stated by the learned trial Judge, namely, that performance of the contract was dependent upon the consent or action of a third party, the circumstances of this coincide with the circumstances existing in *Wroth v. Tyler*. The learned trial Judge was therefore justified in giving such direction as to the measure of damages to be applied by the Master.

We are respectfully of the opinion that on the facts and circumstances disclosed in *Wroth v. Tyler*, the principle there enunciated was valid and was appropriately applied in the present case.

Johnson v. Agnew
[1980] AC 367 (HL (Eng.))

[In November 1973, the plaintiff vendors entered into a written agreement to sell their properties. At the time, they were in arrears with the repayments of mortgages on those properties.
The purchaser agreed to pay a price that exceeded the amounts required to discharge the
mortgages and a loan raised by the vendors to enable them to buy another property. The
purchaser failed to complete the contract, and in November 1974 the vendors obtained a
summary order for specific performance. The order for specific performance was not carried out, and in July 1975 the mortgagees of the properties enforced their securities by selling the properties. The proceeds realized by the mortgagees were inadequate to discharge
the mortgages in full, and the vendors moved for an order for the purchaser to pay the balance of the purchase price to the vendors, credit being given for the amounts realized by the
mortgagees' sales. The judge made no order on the motion. The Court of Appeal allowed the
vendors' appeal. The court held that the order for specific performance should be discharged and damages awarded in lieu.]

LORD WILBERFORCE: … My Lords, this appeal arises in a vendors' action for specific performance of a contract for the sale of land, the appellant being the purchaser and the vendors respondents. The factual situation is commonplace, indeed routine. An owner of land
contracts to sell it to a purchaser; the purchaser fails to complete the contract; the vendor
goes to the court and obtains an order that the contract be specifically performed; the purchaser still does not complete; the vendor goes back to the court and asks for the order for
specific performance to be dissolved, for the contract to be terminated or "rescinded," and
for an order for damages. One would think that the law as to so typical a set of facts would
be both simple and clear. It is no credit to our law that it is neither. Learned judges in the
Chancery Division and in the Court of Appeal have had great difficulty in formulating a
rule and have been obliged to reach differing conclusions. That this is so is due partly to the
mystification which has been allowed to characterise contracts for the sale of land, as contrasted with other contracts, partly to an accumulated debris of decisions and text book
pronouncements which has brought semantic confusion and misunderstandings into an
area capable of being governed by principle. I hope that this may be an opportunity for a
little simplification. …

[Having reviewed the facts, he continued:]

In this situation it is possible to state at least some uncontroversial propositions of law.

First, in a contract for the sale of land, after time has been made, or has become, of the
essence of the contract, if the purchaser fails to complete, the vendor can *either* treat the
purchaser as having repudiated the contract, accept the repudiation, and proceed to claim
damages for breach of the contract, both parties being discharged from further performance
of the contract; *or* he may seek from the court an order for specific performance with damages for any loss arising from delay in performance. (Similar remedies are of course available to purchasers against vendors.) This is simply the ordinary law of contract applied to
contracts capable of specific performance.

Secondly, the vendor may proceed by action for the above remedies (viz. specific performance or damages) in the alternative. At the trial he will however have to elect which remedy to pursue.

Thirdly, if the vendor treats the purchaser as having repudiated the contract and accepts the repudiation, he cannot thereafter seek specific performance. This follows from the fact that, the purchaser having repudiated the contract and his repudiation having been accepted, both parties are discharged from further performance.

At this point it is important to dissipate a fertile source of confusion and to make clear that although the vendor is sometimes referred to in the above situation as "rescinding" the contract, this so-called "rescission" is quite different from rescission *ab initio*, such as may arise for example in cases of mistake, fraud or lack of consent. In those cases, the contract is treated in law as never having come into existence. (Cases of a contractual right to rescind may fall under this principle but are not relevant to the present discussion.) In the case of an accepted repudiatory breach the contract has come into existence but has been put an end to or discharged. Whatever contrary indications may be disinterred from old authorities, it is now quite clear, under the general law of contract, that acceptance of a repudiatory breach does not bring about "rescission ab initio." I need only quote one passage to establish these propositions.

In *Heyman v. Darwins Ltd.*, [1942] AC 356 (HL (Eng.)), Lord Porter said, at p. 399:

> To say that the contract is rescinded or has come to an end or has ceased to exist may in individual cases convey the truth with sufficient accuracy, but the fuller expression that the injured party is thereby absolved from future performance of his obligations under the contract is a more exact description of the position. Strictly speaking, to say that on acceptance of the renunciation of a contract the contract is rescinded is incorrect. In such a case the injured party may accept the renunciation as a breach going to the root of the whole of the consideration. By that acceptance he is discharged from further performance and may bring an action for damages, but the contract itself is not rescinded.

See also *Boston Deep Sea Fishing & Ice Co. v. Ansell* (1888), 39 Ch. D 339 (CA) at p. 365, *per* Bowen LJ; *Mayson v. Clouet*, [1924] AC 980 (PC (Sing.)) at p. 985, *per* Lord Dunedin and *Lep Air Services Ltd. v. Rolloswin Ltd.*, [1973] AC 331 (HL (Eng.)) at p. 345, *per* Lord Reid and p. 350, *per* Lord Diplock. I can see no reason, and no logical reason has ever been given, why any different result should follow as regards contracts for the sale of land, but a doctrine to this effect has infiltrated into that part of the law with unfortunate results. I shall return to this point when considering *Henty v. Schröder* (1879), 12 Ch. D 666 and cases which have followed it down to *Barber v. Wolfe*, [1945] Ch. 187 and *Horsler v. Zorro*, [1975] Ch. 302.

Fourthly, if an order for specific performance is sought and is made, the contract remains in effect and is not merged in the judgment for specific performance. This is clear law, best illustrated by the judgment of Sir Wilfrid Greene MR in *Austins of East Ham Ltd. v. Macey*, [1941] Ch. 338 (CA) at p. 341 in a passage which deals both with this point and with that next following. It repays quotations in full.

> The contract is still there. Until it is got rid of, it remains as a blot on the title, and the position of the vendor, where the purchaser has made default, is that he is entitled, not to annul the contract by the aid of the court, but to obtain the normal remedy of a party to a contract which

the other party has repudiated. He cannot, in the circumstances, treat it as repudiated except by order of the court and the effect of obtaining such an order is that the contract, which until then existed, is brought to an end. The real position, in my judgment, is that, so far from proceeding to the enforcement of an order for specific performance, the vendor, in such circumstances is choosing a remedy which is alternative to the remedy of proceeding under the order for specific performance. He could attempt to enforce that order and could levy an execution which might prove completely fruitless. Instead of doing that, he elects to ask the court to put an end to the contract, and that is an alternative to an order for enforcing specific performance.

Fifthly, if the order for specific performance is not complied with by the purchaser, the vendor may *either* apply to the court for enforcement of the order, *or* may apply to the court to dissolve the order and ask the court to put an end to the contract. This proposition is as stated in *Austins of East Ham Ltd. v. Macey* (and see *Singh (Sudagar) v. Nazeer*, [1979] Ch. 474 at p. 480, *per* Megarry V-C) and is in my opinion undoubted law, both on principle and authority. It follows, indeed, automatically from the facts that the contract remains in force after the order for specific performance and that the purchaser has committed a breach of it of a repudiatory character which he has not remedied, or as Megarry V-C puts it (at p. 480), that he is refusing to complete.

These propositions being, as I think they are, uncontrovertible, there only remains the question whether, if the vendor takes the latter course, i.e. of applying to the court to put an end to the contract, he is entitled to recover damages for breach of the contract. On principle one may ask "Why ever not?" If, as is clear, the vendor is entitled, after, and notwithstanding that an order for specific performance has been made, if the purchaser still does not complete the contract, to ask the court to permit him to accept the purchaser's repudiation and to declare the contract to be terminated, why, if the court accedes to this, should there not follow the ordinary consequences, undoubted under the general law of contract, that on such acceptance and termination the vendor may recover damages for breach of contract?

I now consider the arguments which are said to support the negative answer.

(1) The principal authority lies in the case of *Henty v. Schröder* (1879), 12 Ch. D 666 (CA) at p. 667 in which Sir George Jessel MR is briefly reported as having laid down that a vendor "could not at the same time obtain an order to have the agreement rescinded and claim damages against the defendant for breach of the agreement." The unsatisfactory nature of this statement has often been remarked upon. It is unsupported by reasons, and is only reported *in oratio obliqua*. It is in direct conflict with previous authorities—*Sweet v. Meredith* (1863), 4 Giff. 207, 66 ER 680 (Ch.); *Watson v. Cox* (1873), LR 15 Eq. 219 (more fully in 42 LJ Ch. 279); yet no reason is given why these authorities are not followed, nor is it said that they are overruled. If it were not for the great authority of the Master of the Rolls, I can hardly believe that so fragile and insecure a foundation for the law would ever have survived. Explanations have been canvassed—that Sir George Jessel was confusing discharge of a contract by accepted repudiation with rescission ab initio, a desperate hypothesis; that (much more plausibly) the statement was procedural in character, the emphasis being on "at the same time"; there was indeed authority that, at that time, in order to obtain damages a separate bill had to be filed; see *Hythe Corporation v. East* (1866), LR 1 Eq. 620. But it is not profitable to pursue these: the authority, weak as it is, is there and has been followed: it is necessary to see what strength it has gained in the process. ...

Textbook authority in general supports the decision. George Russell Northcote (ed.), *Fry on Specific Performance* (London: Stevens, 6th ed., 1921) at p. 548 mentions the proposition with lack of enthusiasm but the main pillars in this case are Mr. T. Cyprian Williams' books on *The Contract of Sale of Land* (London: Butterworths, 1930) and on *Vendor and Purchaser* (4th ed., 1936). In the former work (p. 121) he firmly commits himself to the theory of rescission plus *restitutio in integrum* as remedies for breach of the contract. In the latter, a well-known book of reference on conveyancing matters, he equally firmly denies a right to damages. The learned author writes, at pp. 1025-1026 of vol. 2:

> And if he obtains an order for specific performance of the contract, that will be a bar to his recovering damages for the breach; for in equity the plaintiff suing on a breach of contract was required, as a rule, to elect which remedy he would pursue; and a man entitled to alternative remedies is barred, after judgment on the one, from asserting the other.

See also p. 1004.

My Lords, this passage is almost a perfect illustration of the dangers, well perceived by our predecessors but tending to be neglected in modern times, of placing reliance on textbook authority for an analysis of judicial decisions. It is on the face of it a jumble of unclear propositions not logically related to each other. It is "supported" by footnote references to cases (two of this House and one of the Privy Council) which are not explained or analysed. It would be tedious to go through them in detail. ...

The state of authority then, so far as English law is concerned, is that, starting from a judgment in which no reasons are given, and which may rest upon any one of several foundations, of which one is unsound and another obsolete, a wavering chain of precedent has been built up, relying upon that foundation, which is itself unsound. Systems based upon precedent unfortunately often develop in this way and it is sometimes the case that the resultant doctrine becomes too firmly cemented to be dislodged.

This is however the first time that this House has had to consider the right of an innocent party to a contract for the sale of land to damages on the contract being put an end to by accepted repudiation, and I think that we have the duty to take a fresh look. I should certainly be reluctant to invite your Lordships to endorse a line of authority so weak and unconvincing in principle. Fortunately there is support for a more attractive and logical approach from another bastion of the common law whose courts have adopted a robuster attitude. I quote first from a judgment of Dixon J in *McDonald v. Dennys Lascelles Ltd.* (1933), 48 CLR 457 which with typical clarity sets out the principle—this, be it observed, in a case concerned with a contract for the sale of land. Dixon J says, at pp. 476-477:

> When a party to a simple contract, upon a breach by the other contracting party of a condition of the contract, elects to treat the contract as no longer binding upon him, the contract is not rescinded as from the beginning. Both parties are discharged from the further performance of the contract, but rights are not divested or discharged which have already been unconditionally acquired. Rights and obligations which arise from the partial execution of the contract and causes of action which have accrued from its breach alike continue unaffected. When a contract is rescinded because of matters which affect its formation, as in the case of fraud, the parties are to be rehabilitated and restored, so far as may be, to the position they occupied before the contract was made. But when a contract, which is not void or voidable at law, or liable to be set

aside in equity, is dissolved at the election of one party because the other has not observed an essential condition or has committed a breach going to its root, the contract is determined so far as it is executory only and the party in default is liable for damages for its breach.

Closer to the present case, in *Holland v. Wiltshire* (1954), 90 CLR 409 the High Court was directly concerned with a question of damages for breach of contract for the sale of land. The purchaser having failed to complete, the vendor claimed damages. Dixon CJ said, at p. 416:

> The proper conclusion is that the vendor proceeded not under the contractual provision but on the footing that the purchasers had discharged him from the obligations of the contract. It follows that he is entitled to sue for unliquidated damages. Some suggestion was made for the defendants appellants that once the contract was treated by the vendor as discharged he could not recover for breach. This notion, however, is based on a confusion with rescission for some invalidating cause. It is quite inconsistent with principle and has long since been dissipated. It is enough to refer to the note upon the subject in Mr. *Voumard's Sale of Land in Victoria* (1939), at page 499.

Voumard's Sale of Land—judicially approved—p. 508—is explicit that damages can be recovered.

Then, in a case very similar to the present, *McKenna v. Richey*, [1950] VLR 360, it was decided by O'Bryan J in the Supreme Court of Victoria that, after an order for specific performance had been made, which in the events could not be carried into effect, even though this was by reason of delay on the part of the plaintiff, the plaintiff could still come to the court and ask for damages on the basis of an accepted repudiation. The following passage is illuminating, at p. 372:

> The apparent inconsistency of a plaintiff suing for specific performance and for common law damages in the alternative arises from the fact that, in order to avoid circuitry of action, there is vested in the one court jurisdiction to grant either form of relief. The plaintiff, in effect, is saying: "I don't accept your repudiation of the contract but am willing to perform my part of the contract and insist upon your performing your part—but if I cannot successfully insist on your performing your part, I will accept the repudiation and ask for damages." Until the defendant's repudiation is accepted the contract remains on foot, with all the possible consequences of that fact. But if, from first to last, the defendant continues unwilling to perform her part of the contract, then, if for any reason the contract cannot be specifically enforced, the plaintiff may, in my opinion, turn round and say: "Very well, I cannot have specific performance; I will now ask for my alternative remedy of damages at common law." This, in my opinion, is equally applicable both before and after decree whether the reason for the refusal or the failure of the decree of specific performance is due to inability of the defendant to give any title to the property sold, or to the conduct of the plaintiff which makes it inequitable for the contract to be specifically enforced. …

And later the learned judge said, at p. 376:

> It is an appropriate case for a court of equity to say: "As a matter of discretion, this contract should not now be enforced specifically, but, in lieu of the decree for specific performance, the court will award the plaintiff such damages as have been suffered by her in consequence of the defendant's breach. That is the best justice that can be done in this case."

The learned judge in his judgment fully discussed and analyses the English cases but nevertheless reaches this view.

My Lords, I am happy to follow the latter case. In my opinion *Henty v. Schröder* (1879), 12 Ch. D 666 cannot stand against the powerful tide of logical objection and judicial reasoning. It should no longer be regarded as of authority: the cases following it should be overruled.

In particular *Barber v. Wolfe*, [1945] Ch. 187 and *Horsler v. Zorro*, [1975] Ch. 302 cannot stand so far as they are based on the theory of "rescission ab initio" which has no application to the termination of a contract on accepted repudiation.

The second basis for denying damages in such cases as the present is that which underlies the judgment of the Court of Appeal in *Swycher's* case [*Capital and Suburban Properties Ltd. v. Swycher*, [1976] Ch. 319 (CA)]. This is really a rationalisation of *Henty v. Schröder*, the weakness of which case the court well perceived. The main argument there accepted was that by deciding to seek the remedy of specific performance the vendor (or purchaser) has made an election which either is irrevocable or which becomes so when the order for specific performance is made. A second limb of this argument (but in reality a different argument) is that the vendor (or purchaser) has adequate remedies under the order for specific performance so that there is no need, or equitable ground, for allowing him to change his ground and ask for damages.

In my opinion, the argument based on irrevocable election, strongly pressed by the appellant's counsel in the present appeal, is unsound. Election, though the subject of much learning and refinement, is in the end a doctrine based on simple considerations of common sense and equity. It is easy to see that a party who has chosen to put an end to a contract by accepting the other party's repudiation cannot afterwards seek specific performance. This is simply because the contract has gone—what is dead is dead. But it is no more difficult to agree that a party, who has chosen to seek specific performance, may quite well thereafter, if specific performance fails to be realised, say, "Very well, then, the contract should be regarded as terminated." It is quite consistent with a decision provisionally to keep alive, to say "Well, this is no use—let us now end the contract's life." A vendor who seeks (and gets) specific performance is merely electing for a course which may or may not lead to implementation of the contract—what he elects for is not eternal and unconditional affirmation, but a continuance of the contract under control of the court which control involves the power, in certain events, to terminate it. If he makes an election at all, he does so when he decides not to proceed under the order for specific performance, but to ask the court to terminate the contract: see the judgment of Sir Wilfrid Greene MR in *Austins of East Ham Ltd. v. Macey*, [1941] Ch. 338 (CA) quoted above. The fact is that the election argument proves too much. If it were correct it would deny the vendor not just the right to damages, but the right to "rescind" the contract, but there is no doubt that this right exists: what is in question is only the right on "rescission," to claim damages.

The authority most relied on to support this argument is in the end the passage already quoted from *Williams on Vendor and Purchaser*, 4th ed.—I have commented on this. The cases cited relate to different situations where an election might well be regarded as creating a new situation from which subsequent departure would be impossible. Cases relating to acceptance of defective goods, or to waiver or enforcement of forfeiture, or to a decision to sue one set of parties rather than another: *Scarf v. Jardine* (1882), 7 App. Cas. 345 (HL (Eng.)), or to a case of fraud, to be asserted or waived: *Clough v. London and North Western Railway Co.* (1871), LR 7 Ex. 26, are examples, and there are many others, where an election creates, or recognises, a situation from which consequences flow and when the election is irrevocable. But this is clearly not such a case, or the right to "rescind" after an order for specific performance would not have been recognised.

So far as regards the subsidiary argument, it is equally the case that it proves too much, for if correct it would result in a denial of the undoubted power to "rescind." Moreover the argument is itself refuted by the action taken by the Court of Appeal itself, for after allowing the vendors to rescind they awarded damages under *Lord Cairns' Act*. So clearly there was nothing inappropriate or unnecessary in granting the vendors "rescission" and damages. As Goff LJ pointed out, it was not possible to leave the vendors to "work out" the decree for specific performance—their only remedy (if any) must lie in an award of damages.

In my respectful opinion therefore *Swycher's* case whether it should be regarded as resting upon *Henty v. Schröder*, or upon an independent argument based on election was wrongly decided in so far as it denied a right to contractual damages and should so far be overruled. The vendors should have been entitled, upon discharge of the contract, on grounds of normal and accepted principle, to damages appropriate for a breach of contract.

There is one final point, on this part of the case, on which I should make a brief observation. Once the matter has been placed in the hands of a court of equity, or one exercising equity jurisdiction, the subsequent control of the matter will be exercised according to equitable principles. The court would not make an order dissolving the decree of specific performance and terminating the contract (with recovery of damages) if to do so would be unjust, in the circumstances then existing, to the other party, in this case to the purchaser. (To this extent, in describing the vendor's right to an order as *"ex debito justitiae"* Clauson LJ may have put the case rather too strongly: *John Barker & Co. Ltd. v. Littman*, [1941] Ch. 405 (CA) at p. 412.) This is why there was, in the Court of Appeal, rightly, a relevant and substantial argument, repeated in this House, that the non-completion of the contract was due to the default of the vendors: if this had been made good, the court could properly have refused them the relief sought. But the Court of Appeal came to the conclusion that this non-completion, and the ultimate impossibility of completion, was the fault of the purchaser. I agree with their conclusion and their reasons on this point and shall not repeat or add to them.

It is now necessary to deal with questions relating to the measure of damages. The Court of Appeal, while denying the vendors' right to damages at common law, granted damages under *Lord Cairns' Act*. Since, on the view which I take, damages can be recovered at common law, two relevant questions now arise. (1) Whether *Lord Cairns' Act* provides a different measure of damages from the common law: if so, the respondents would be in a position to claim the more favourable basis to them. (2) If the measure of damages is the same, on what basis they should be calculated.

Since the decision of this House, by majority, in *Leeds Industrial Co-operative Society Ltd. v. Slack*, [1924] AC 851 (HL (Eng.)) it is clear that the jurisdiction to award damages in accordance with section 2 of *Lord Cairns' Act* (accepted by the House as surviving the repeal of the Act) may arise in some cases in which damages could not be recovered at common law: examples of this would be damages in lieu of a *quia timet* injunction and damages for breach of a restrictive covenant to which the defendant was not a party. To this extent the

Act created a power to award damages which did not exist before at common law. But apart from these, and similar cases where damages could not be claimed at all at common law, there is sound authority for the proposition that the Act does not provide for the assessment of damages on any new basis. The wording of section 2 "may be assessed in such manner as the court shall direct" does not so suggest, but clearly refers only to procedure.

In *Ferguson v. Wilson* (1866), LR 2 Ch. 77, 88 Turner LJ sitting in a court which included Sir Hugh Cairns himself expressed the clear opinion that the purpose of the Act was to enable a court of equity to grant those damages which another court might give; a similar opinion was strongly expressed by Kay J in *Rock Portland Cement Co. Ltd. v. Wilson* (1882), 52 LJ Ch. 214, and George Russell Northcote (ed.), *Fry on Specific Performance* (London: Stevens, 6th ed., 1921) at p. 602 is of the same opinion. In *Wroth v. Tyler*, [1974] Ch. 30, however, Megarry J, relying on the words "in lieu of specific performance" reached the view that damages under the Act should be assessed as on the date when specific performance could have been ordered, in that case as at the date of the judgment of the court. This case was followed in *Grant v. Dawkins*, [1973] 1 WLR 1406 (Ch.). If this establishes a different basis from that applicable at common law, I could not agree with it, but in *Horsler v. Zorro*, [1975] Ch. 302 at p. 316 Megarry J went so far as to indicate his view that there is no inflexible rule that common law damages must be assessed as at the date of the breach. Furthermore, in *Malhotra v. Choudhury*, [1980] Ch. 52 (CA) the Court of Appeal expressly decided that, in a case where damages are given in substitution for an order for specific performance, both equity and the common law would award damages on the same basis—in that case as on the date of judgment. On the balance of these authorities and also on principle, I find in the Act no warrant for the court awarding damages differently from common law damages, but the question is left open on what date such damages, however awarded, ought to be assessed.

(2) The general principle for the assessment of damages is compensatory, i.e. that the innocent party is to be placed, so far as money can do so, in the same position as if the contract had been performed. Where the contract is one of sale, this principle normally leads to assessment of damages as at the date of the breach—a principle recognised and embodied in section 51 of the *Sale of Goods Act 1893*. But this is not an absolute rule: if to follow it would give rise to injustice, the court has power to fix such other date as may be appropriate in the circumstances.

In cases where a breach of a contract for sale has occurred, and the innocent party reasonably continues to try to have the contract completed, it would to me appear more logical and just rather than tie him to the date of the original breach, to assess damages as at the date when (otherwise than by his default) the contract is lost. Support for this approach is to be found in the cases. In *Ogle v. Earl Vane* (1867), LR 2 QB 275; LR 3 QB 272 the date was fixed by reference to the time when the innocent party, acting reasonably, went into the market; in *Hickman v. Haynes* (1875), LR 10 CP 598 at a reasonable time after the last request of the defendants (buyers) to withhold delivery. In *Radford v. de Froberville*, [1977] 1 WLR 1262 (Ch.), where the defendant had covenanted to build a wall, damages were held measurable as at the date of the hearing rather than at the date of the defendant's breach, unless the plaintiff ought reasonably to have mitigated the breach at an earlier date.

In the present case if it is accepted, as I would accept, that the vendors acted reasonably in pursuing the remedy of specific performance, the date on which that remedy became aborted (not by the vendors' fault) should logically be fixed as the date on which damages should be assessed. Choice of this date would be in accordance both with common law principle, as indicated in the authorities I have mentioned, and with the wording of the Act "in substitution for … specific performance." The date which emerges from this is April 3, 1975—the first date on which mortgagees contracted to sell a portion of the property. I would vary the order of the Court of Appeal by substituting this date for that fixed by them—viz. November 26, 1974. The same date (April 3, 1975) should be used for the purpose of limiting the respondents' right to interest on damages. Subject to these modifications I would dismiss the appeal.

QUESTIONS

Are any of the following statements correct with respect to the *Wroth v. Tyler* situation?

1. The Wroths did not recover enough to compensate them for their loss. They had a particular interest in acquiring the Tylers' house. All they got was enough to buy another similar house. They should have got more to compensate for the deprivation of their "consumer surplus" in the very house they were after.

2. The Wroths recovered too much. They received double compensation to the extent that had the Tylers closed at the date fixed, the Wroths would have been paying (and the Tylers receiving) interest on the purchase price. Hence, the inflationary increase after the date of breach would not have been cost-free to the Wroths. Therefore, their damage award should be reduced by the amount of interest they would have paid between the date for closing and the date of judgment.

3. The Wroths got exactly what they should have got
   a. for the correct reasons
   b. for the wrong reasons.

In an ordinary specific performance decree, should the plaintiff-purchaser have to pay interest to the defendant-vendor on the balance required to complete? Should the vendor have to account to the purchaser for the rents or use he has made of the property up to completion? Should the same rules apply to commercial as non-commercial property? The ramifications of *Wroth v. Tyler* and *Johnson v. Agnew* and the general topic of equitable damages are revisited in chapter 10, "Financial Relief in Equity," under the heading "Equitable Damages."

PROBLEM

The following is an extract from a trial judgment that you, on behalf of the defendants, have been instructed to appeal. What arguments would you make? What degree of success do you expect?

In this action, the plaintiff (vendor) sues for specific performance, and in the alternative damages, in respect of an agreement of purchase and sale of land, namely a restaurant operation. It is clear that the defendant is in breach of its obligation under the agreement of purchase and sale and the only question is that of the remedy to which the plaintiff is entitled. The agreement was to close in June 1976. At that time, the value of the property on the evidence produced was $150,000. In late 1977, the plaintiff resold the property for the price of $100,000. The contract price was $200,000. It is clear that the defendant realized shortly after he had made the agreement that he had over-valued the property and moreover that the property value was diminishing due to general market conditions. At first the plaintiff made no efforts to resell the property although it was clear to everyone that the value was declining. Apparently, the plaintiff had a sentimental attachment to the fact that pursuant to the agreement between the parties, the defendant undertook to carry on the restaurant business in the name of the plaintiff. He had worked long and hard to build up the business and although he had no commercial or economic reason, wanted his name to remain before the public as a restauranteur. Accordingly, upon the defendant's breach, he sued immediately for specific performance, but in 1977 was finally persuaded by his family and his solicitor to resell at a loss. Naturally, at the outset of the trial, the plaintiff abandoned his claim for specific performance and elected as his remedy damages. It appears to me that the crucial factor here is whether or not the party in the position of the plaintiff has kept the contract alive following its breach. In this case, the vendor had a right to specific performance and asserted that right. I do not think that he should be held to the risk of declining value of the property after the date of the breach. To award him anything but the difference between the contract price and the resale price would not achieve what is after all the goal of the contract remedies, namely, to put him in the position he would have been in had there not been any breach. Accordingly, there will be judgment for the plaintiff in the amount of $100,000.

When a buyer of property obtains an award of damages based on an increased value at the date of judgment, the question arises whether the buyer should give credit for interest on the unpaid purchase price. In *306793 Ontario Ltd. in Trust v. Rimes* (1979), 25 OR (2d) 79, the Ontario Court of Appeal declined to reduce the buyer's damages on this account.

Semelhago v. Paramadevan
[1996] 2 SCR 415

[S contracted with P to purchase a house under construction. The price was $205,000. S had $75,000 cash and was going to meet the balance of $130,000 by a mortgage on his present residence (worth $190,000 at that time). The vendor reneged on the transaction and transferred title in the property to a third party. S then commenced an action for specific performance of the contract with a claim in the alternative for damages. At the commencement of the trial, S elected to forgo his claim for specific performance and confined himself to a damages claim based on the difference between the purchase price of $205,000 and the value of the property at the date of trial ($325,000), an amount of $120,000 plus legal and appraisal fees incurred on the abortive transaction. (By that time, his own house, which he had retained, was worth $300,000.)

The trial judge, feeling bound by the decision of the Ontario Court of Appeal in *306793 Ontario Ltd. in Trust v. Rimes*, awarded the amount sought with the exception of the legal and appraisal fees. P appealed against this judgment and S cross-appealed against the denial of his claim for the fees. The Ontario Court of Appeal allowed the appeal in part and also allowed the cross-appeal: (1994), 19 OR (3d) 479. In so doing, it held that *Rimes* had not obliged the trial judge to award $120,000. Rather, discounts had to be applied to that figure reflecting the interest that S had notionally earned on his $75,000 in the meantime and the charges associated with carrying a mortgage of $130,000 to the date of trial as well as the legal costs that would have been associated with closing the transaction. However, this discount had to be offset by the legal and appraisal fees actually paid by the plaintiff. This produced an award of $80,810.21. Putting it another way, the plaintiff recovered damages on the following basis:

> ((current value of house − purchase price) + legal and appraisal fees) − (interest from completion date to date of trial on $70,000 + interest from completion date to date of trial on $130,000 mortgage + legal costs that would have been incurred on closing)

P obtained leave to appeal to the Supreme Court of Canada. (There was no cross-appeal.) He contended that the damages should have been reduced even further because not only had S avoided costs as a result of the transaction not coming to fruition but he had also benefited by the contemporaneous increase in value of his existing residence. It was argued that, as a consequence, damages were more appropriately calculated by reference either to the current difference in value between the two properties ($25,000) or perhaps even the difference between the extent to which the two properties had risen in value ($5,000).

Among the facts found by the trial judge were the following: S intended to sell his own house on the completion of the transaction, the $130,000 mortgage being a bridge to that event. Both parties were sophisticated property dealers. The house in question, while intended for occupation by the purchaser, was not "unique." She also suggested, though this was not argued by the defendant, that this was not a proper case for advancing a claim to specific performance.]

SOPINKA J (delivering the judgment of himself, Gonthier, Cory, McLachlin, Iacobucci, and Major JJ):

The trial judge expressed reservations about the propriety of an award of specific performance in this case. While I share those reservations and will return to the question as to the circumstances under which specific performance is an appropriate remedy, this appeal should be disposed of on the basis that specific performance was appropriate. The case was dealt with by the parties in both courts below and in this Court on the assumption that specific performance was an appropriate remedy.

A party who is entitled to specific performance is entitled to elect damages in lieu thereof. The jurisdiction to award damages in lieu of specific performance was conferred on the Court of Chancery by *The Chancery Amendment Act, 1858* (UK), 21 & 22 Vict., c. 27 (known as *Lord Cairns' Act*). Although the Act was repealed, in *Leeds Industrial Co-operative Society Ltd. v. Slack*, [1924] AC 851, the House of Lords established that the jurisdiction to award damages in lieu of specific performance was maintained. This jurisdiction exists as part of the law of Ontario by virtue of the *Courts of Justice Act*, RSO 1990, c. C.43, s. 99, which provides:

> 99. A court that has jurisdiction to grant an injunction or order specific performance may award damages in addition to, or in substitution for, the injunction or specific performance.

Lord Cairns' Act permits damages to be awarded in some circumstances in which no claim for damages could be entertained at common law. See *Leeds*, *supra*, and *Wroth v. Tyler*, [1974] 1 Ch. 30, at p. 57. In cases in which damages could also be claimed at common law, the principles generally applicable are those of the common law. In *Johnson v. Agnew*, [1980] AC 367, at pp. 400-1, Lord Wilberforce stated that:

(2) The general principle for the assessment of damages is compensatory, *i.e.*, that the innocent party is to be placed, so far as money can do so, in the same position as if the contract had been performed. Where the contract is one of sale, this principle normally leads to assessment of damages as at the date of the breach—a principle recognised and embodied in section 51 of the *Sale of Goods Act 1893*. But this is not an absolute rule: if to follow it would give rise to injustice, the court has power to fix such other date as may be appropriate in the circumstances.

The rationale for assessing the damages at the date of breach in the case of breach of contract for the sale of goods is that if the innocent purchaser is compensated on the basis of the value of the goods as of the date of breach, the purchaser can turn around and purchase identical or equivalent goods. The purchaser is therefore placed in the same financial situation as if the contract had been kept.

Different considerations apply where the thing which is to be purchased is unique. Although some chattels such as rare paintings fall into this category, the concept of uniqueness has traditionally been peculiarly applicable to agreements for the purchase of real estate. Under the common law every piece of real estate was generally considered to be unique. Blackacre had no readily available equivalent. Accordingly, damages were an inadequate remedy and the innocent purchaser was generally entitled to specific performance. Given the flexibility of the rule at common law as to the date for the assessment of damages, it would not be appropriate to insist on applying the date of breach as the assessment date when the purchaser of a unique asset has a legitimate claim to specific performance and elects to take damages instead (see *Wroth v. Tyler*; *Johnson v. Agnew*; and *Mavretic v. Bowman*, [1993] 4 WWR 329). The rationale that the innocent purchaser is fully compensated, if provided with the amount of money that would purchase an asset of the same value on the date of the breach, no longer applies. This disposition would not be a substitute for an order of specific performance. The order for specific performance may issue many months or even years after the breach. The value of the asset may have changed. Moreover, the claim for specific performance revives the contract to the extent that the defendant who has failed to perform can avoid a breach if at any time up to the date of judgment, performance is tendered. In cases such as the one at bar, where the vendor reneges in anticipation of performance, the innocent party has two options. He or she may accept the repudiation and treat the agreement as being at an end. In that event, both parties are relieved from performing any outstanding obligations and the injured party may commence an action for damages. Alternatively, the injured party may decline to accept the repudiation and continue to insist on performance. In that case, the contract continues in force and neither party is relieved of their obligations under the agreement. As is elaborated in *McGregor on Damages* (13th ed. 1972), at p. 149:

> Where a party to a contract repudiates it, the other party has an option to accept or not to accept the repudiation. If he does not accept it there is still no breach of contract, and the contract subsists for the benefit of both parties and no need to mitigate arises. On the other hand, if the repudiation is accepted this results in an anticipatory breach of contract in respect of which suit can be brought at once for damages. ...

Thus, the claim for specific performance can be seen as reviving the contract to the extent that the defendant who has failed to perform can avoid a breach if, at any time up to the date of judgment, performance is tendered. In this way, a claim for specific performance has the effect of postponing the date of breach.

For all of these reasons, it is not inconsistent with the rules of the common law to assess damages as of the date of trial. It must be remembered that the rules of the common law did not contemplate awarding damages as a substitute for specific performance. The rules of the common law must be applied in light of the statutory imperative contained in s. 99 of the *Courts of Justice Act*. The damages that are awarded must be a true substitute for specific performance. This point is forcefully made by Megarry J in *Wroth v. Tyler*. In that case, the purchaser had contracted for the purchase of a house for £6,000. The vendor defaulted. On the closing date, the property was worth £7,500. As of the date of trial the property was worth £11,500. In assessing damages as of the date of trial, Megarry J stated, at p. 58:

> On the wording of the section, the power "to award damages to the party injured, … in substitution for such … specific performance," at least envisages that the damages awarded will in fact constitute a true substitute for specific performance. Furthermore, the section is speaking of the time when the court is making its decision to award damages in substitution for specific performance, so that it is at that moment that the damages must be a substitute. The fact that a different amount of damages would have been a substitute if the order had been made at the time of the breach must surely be irrelevant. In the case before me, I cannot see how £1,500 damages would constitute any true substitute for a decree of specific performance of the contract to convey land which at the time of the decree is worth £5,500 more than the contract price.

At p. 59 Megarry J added:

> Yet on principle I would say simply that damages "in substitution" for specific performance must be a substitute, giving as nearly as may be what specific performance would have given.

This was also the basis upon which *Rimes* was decided by the Ontario Court of Appeal. The reasons for judgment of MacKinnon ACJO cite *Wroth v. Tyler* with approval, pointing out that that case was not overruled by *Johnson v. Agnew*, *supra*. I agree with that observation. In *Johnson v. Agnew*, Lord Wilberforce, speaking for the House of Lords, concluded that in view of the flexibility of the common law rule with respect to the date for the assessment of damages to which I have referred, the view taken by Megarry J in *Wroth v. Tyler* was consistent with the common law.

I therefore conclude that, in the circumstances of this case, the appropriate date for the assessment of damages is the date of trial as found by the trial judge. Technically speaking, the date of assessment should be the date of judgment. That is the date upon which specific performance is ordered. For practical purposes, however, the evidence that is adduced which is relevant to enable damages to be assessed will be as of the date of trial. It is not usually possible to predict the date of judgment when the evidence is given.

The difference between the contract price and the value "given close to trial" as found by the trial judge is $120,000. I would not deduct from this amount the increase in value of the respondent's residence which he retained when the deal did not close. If the respondent had received a decree of specific performance, he would have had the property contracted for and retained the amount of the rise in value of his own property. Damages are to be substituted for the decree of specific performance. I see no basis for deductions that are not related to the value of the property which was the subject of the contract. To make such deductions would depart from the principle that damages are to be a true equivalent of specific performance.

This approach may appear to be overly generous to the respondent in this case and other like cases and may be seen as a windfall. In my opinion, this criticism is valid if the property agreed to be purchased is not unique.

[The judgment here dealt with the law governing the availability of specific performance in the case of contracts for the disposition of an interest in land. These parts of the judgment may be found in chapter 9, "Specific Performance."]

The trial judge was of the view in this case that the property was not unique. She stated that, "It was a building lot under construction which would be interchangeable in all likelihood with any number of others." Notwithstanding this observation, she felt constrained by authority to find that specific performance was an appropriate remedy. While I would be inclined to agree with the trial judge as to the inappropriateness of an order for specific performance, both parties were content to present the case on the basis that the respondent was entitled to specific performance. The case was dealt with on this basis by the Court of Appeal. In the circumstances, this Court should abide by the manner in which the case has been presented by the parties and decided in the courts below. In future cases, under similar circumstances, a trial judge will not be constrained to find that specific performance is an appropriate remedy.

This takes me to the deductions made by the Court of Appeal. While I have some reservations about the propriety of these deductions, there was no cross-appeal by the respondent with respect to the award of damages. No argument was presented with respect to these deductions. My reservations relate to the basis upon which the Court of Appeal distinguished *Rimes*. In this regard, the Court stated (at p. 481):

> Those are not the facts of the case now before the court. In this case, the purchaser is not a shell and the trial judge found that the evidence established what probably would have happened had the transaction closed.

On my reading of the reasons of MacKinnon ACJO in *Rimes*, the principal reason for deciding not to deduct the carrying charges was that to do so would be inconsistent with adopting the date of trial as the assessment date. I am not convinced that there is an inconsistency but would prefer not to express any further opinion on the question inasmuch as there is no cross-appeal and these matters are not in issue here.

The Court of Appeal added out-of-pocket expenses of $673.75 for legal fees and $250 for appraisal fees, amounts which were apparently inadvertently omitted from the judgment at trial. There was no dispute about these items.

Disposition

In the result, the appeal is dismissed with costs.

LA FOREST J: I have had the advantage of reading the reasons of my colleague, Justice Sopinka, and I agree with his proposed disposition in the circumstances of this case. However, given the assumption under which the case was argued, I prefer not to deal with the circumstances giving rise to entitlement to specific performance or generally the interpretation that should be given to the legislation authorizing the award of damages in lieu of specific performance. In considering modification to existing law, both these interdependent factors may well require examination, and the arguments in this case were not made in those terms.

This case is considered again in chapter 9, "Specific Performance."

NOTES AND QUESTIONS

1. Why might the defendant have not put in issue the legitimacy of the plaintiff's pursuit until trial of a claim for specific performance? What would have been the impact on the plaintiff's entitlement to damages of a finding that he did not have a legitimate interest in pursuing such a claim? What factors or considerations would have undermined the legitimacy of that claim?

2. Why does the court reject the defendant's contention that the plaintiff's expectations were defeated here only to the extent that the investment opportunity on the one house exceeded the investment value of the other house by only $5,000? Is there any justification for awarding more when a plaintiff before trial forgoes voluntarily his claim to specific performance even if there was initially a legitimate reason for making such a claim? By retaining his residence in a rising market, has the plaintiff not in effect mitigated his damages particularly when it appears as though he was intending to occupy the house under construction as his residence? Are there any countervailing facts or assumptions that can be made to strengthen any claim for damages at the level awarded by the Court of Appeal and sustained by the Supreme Court of Canada?

3. What is the authority of *Rimes* after this judgment? Does it leave open the possibility that, in a case such as this, the even higher level of recovery awarded in *Rimes* (no deductions for interest earned or interest avoided) could still be available? After all, as Sopinka J notes, the plaintiff did not cross-appeal. By reference to what policies or facts might a *Rimes*-level claim be advanced in this class of case or, indeed, in any class of case?

4. The law governing specific performance of contracts for the transfer of an interest in land is addressed directly in chapter 9, "Specific Performance," where the *dicta* on this subject in *Semelhago* are put in context. See also chapter 10, "Financial Relief in Equity."

MITIGATION, EFFICIENT BREACH, AND THE MEASURE OF DAMAGES

Another problem that compels inquiry into the relationship between specific performance and damages is the case where the cost of making good the wrong exceeds the value to the plaintiff of doing so.

Richard A. Posner, *Economic Analysis of Law*
2d ed. (Boston: Little, Brown, 1977), at 88-93 and 95-97 (footnotes omitted)

When a breach of contract is established, the issue becomes one of the proper remedy. A starting point for analysis is Holmes's view that it is not the policy of the law to compel adherence to contracts but only to require each party to choose between performing in accordance with the contract and compensating the other party for any injury resulting from a failure to perform. This view contains an important economic insight. In many cases it is uneconomical to induce the completion of a contract after it has been breached. I agree to purchase 100,000 widgets custom-ground for use as components in a machine that I manufacture. After I have taken delivery of 10,000, the market for my machine collapses. I promptly notify my supplier that I am terminating the contract, and admit that my termination is a breach of the contract. When notified of the termination he has not yet begun the custom grinding of the other 90,000 widgets, but he informs me that he intends to complete his performance under the contract and bill me accordingly. The custom-ground widgets have no use other than in my machine, and a negligible scrap value. Plainly, to grant the supplier any remedy that induced him to complete the contract after the breach would result in a waste of resources. The law is alert to this danger and, under the doctrine of mitigation of damages, would refuse to permit the supplier to recover any costs he incurred in continuing production after my notice of termination.

Let us change the facts. I need 100,000 custom-ground widgets for my machine but the supplier, after producing 50,000, is forced to suspend production because of a mechanical failure. Other suppliers are in a position to supply the remaining widgets that I need, but I insist that the original supplier complete his performance of the contract. If the law compels completion, the supplier will probably have to make arrangements with other widget producers to complete his contract with me. But it may be more costly for him to procure an alternative supplier than for me to do so directly; indeed, were it cheaper for him than for me, he would do it voluntarily in order to minimize his liability for breach of contract. To compel completion of the contract would again result in a waste of resources and again the law does not compel completion but remits the victim to a simple damages remedy. ...

The objective of giving the party to a contract an incentive to fulfill his promise unless the result would be an inefficient use of resources (the production of the unwanted widgets in the first example, the roundabout procurement of a substitute supplier in the second) can usually be achieved by allowing the victim of a breach to recover his expected profit on the transaction. If the supplier in the first example receives his expected profit from completing the 10,000 widgets, he will have no incentive to produce the remaining 90,000. We do not want him to produce them; no one wants them. In the second example, if I receive my expected profit from dealing with the original supplier, I become indifferent to whether he completes his performance.

In these examples the breach was in a sense involuntary. It was committed only to avert a larger loss. The breaching party would have been happier had there been no occasion to commit a breach. But in some cases a party would be tempted to breach the contract simply because his profit from breach would exceed his expected profit from completion of the contract. If his profit from breach would also exceed the expected profit to the other party from completion of the contract, and if damages are limited to loss of expected profit, there will be an incentive to commit a breach. There should be. The opportunity cost of completion to the breaching party is the profit that he would make from a breach, and if it is greater than his profit from completion, then completion will involve a loss to him. If that loss is greater than the gain to the other party from completion, breach would be value-maximizing and should be encouraged. And because the victim of the breach is made whole for his loss, he is indifferent; hence encouraging breaches in these circumstances will not deter people from entering into contracts in the future.

An arithmetical illustration may be helpful here. I sign a contract to deliver 100,000 custom-ground widgets at $.10 apiece to A, for use in his boiler factory. After I have delivered 10,000, B comes to me, explains that he desperately needs 25,000 custom-ground widgets at once since otherwise he will be forced to close his pianola factory at great cost, and offers me $.15 apiece for 25,000 widgets. I sell him the widgets and as a result do not complete timely delivery to A, who sustains $1000 in lost profits from my breach. Having obtained an additional profit of $1250 on the sale to B, I am better off even after reimbursing A for his loss. Society is also better off. Since B was willing to pay me $.15 per widget, it must mean that each widget was worth at least $.15 to him. But it was worth only $.14 to A—the $.10 that he paid plus his expected profit of $.04 ($1000 divided by 25,000). Thus the breach resulted in a transfer of the 25,000 widgets from a less to a more valuable use. To be sure, had I refused to sell to B, he could have gone to A and negotiated an assignment of part of A's contract with me to him. But this would have introduced an additional step and so imposed additional transaction costs.

Thus far the emphasis has been on the economic importance of not awarding damages in excess of the lost expectation. It is equally important, however, not to award less than the expectation loss. Suppose A contracts to sell B for $100,000 a machine that is worth $110,000 to B, i.e., that would yield him a profit of $10,000. Before delivery C comes to A and offers him $109,000 for the machine promised B. A would be tempted to breach were he not liable to B for B's loss of expected profit. Given that measure of damages, C will not be able to induce a breach of A's contract with B unless he offers B more than $110,000, thereby indicating that the machine really is worth more to him than to B. The expectation rule thus assures that the machine ends up where it is most valuable.

In *Groves v. John Wunder Co.* the defendant, as part of a larger deal, had agreed to level some land owned by the plaintiff, but willfully failed to carry out his agreement. The cost of leveling would have been $60,000 and the value of the land, after leveling, no more than $12,000. The court awarded the plaintiff $60,000, reasoning that he was entitled to get the performance he had contracted for and that it was no business of the defendant whether, or how much, his performance enhanced the market value of the plaintiff's property. However, this was not a case, familiar to us from our discussion of just compensation in the last chapter, where value and market price were different. The land in question was a commercial parcel. If the plaintiff had wanted the performance rather than the $60,000, he would probably have brought an action for specific performance. He did not bring such an action and, even more telling, he did not use the money he won from the defendant to level the land. The measure of damages was incorrect from an economic standpoint because, had it been known to the defendant from the outset, it would have made him indifferent as between breaching his agreement to level the land and performing it, whereas efficiency dictated breach: the $60,000 worth of labor and materials that would have been consumed in leveling the land would have purchased a less than $12,000 increase in value.

The court never alluded to the real economic issue in the case, which was how the contract allocated the risk of a fall in the market for real estate, the Depression of the 1930s having occurred after the contract was signed. Since the plaintiff as owner of the land would have enjoyed the benefit of any general increase in real estate values, the parties probably contemplated that he would also bear the cost of a general decline in those values. The effect of the court's judgment was to give the plaintiff a cushion, for which he had not contracted, against the impact of the Depression on land values.

One superficially attractive alternative to measuring contract damages by loss of expectation (i.e., lost profits) is to measure them by the reliance loss, especially in cases where liability is imposed not to induce performance but to penalize careless behavior. And even in the case where the breach is deliberate, it is arguable that expectation damages may overcompensate the victim of the breach. Suppose I sign a contract to deliver 10,000 widgets in six months, and the day after the contract is signed I default. The buyer's reliance loss—the sum of the costs he has irretrievably incurred as a result of the contract—is, let us say, zero, but his lost profit $1,000. Why should be he allowed to reap a windfall gain by the use of a measure of damages that does not correspond to any actual social cost?

One answer has already been given: the lost-profit measure is necessary to assure that the only breaches made are those that promote efficiency. But there is another answer: that on average, though not in every case, the lost-profit method will give a better approximation than the reliance measure to the actual social costs of contract breach. In long-run competitive equilibrium, the total revenues of the sellers in a market are just equal to their total costs; there are no "profits" in the economic sense. What law and accounting call profits are frequently not profits in that sense at all, but rather reimbursement of the costs of capital, of entrepreneurial effort, and of other imputs. These items of cost are excluded by the reliance measure of damages, which will therefore tend to understate the true social costs of breach.

There are exceptions, however, some sufficiently clear to deserve, and receive, legal recognition. Compare the following cases: (1) A tenant defaults and the landlord promptly rents the property to another tenant at a rental only slightly below that of the defaulting tenant. In a suit against the defaulting tenant for the rental due on the balance of the tenant's lease, should the landlord be required to deduct the rental of the substitute tenant? (2) A manufacturer of widgets receives an order for 1000 widgets from X, but X refuses to accept delivery and the manufacturer resells the widgets to Y at a price only slightly lower than what X had agreed to pay. In a suit against X for the profits that were lost on the sale, should the manufacturer be required to deduct the profits he received on the substitute sale to Y?

The law answers yes in the first case and no in the second, and these answers are correct from an economic standpoint. The good supplied by the landlord is fixed in the short run: he cannot add a room because one more family wants to lease from him. The rental that he receives from the substitute tenant in our first case is a gain *enabled* by the breach of contract by the first tenant. His true loss is, therefore the difference between the two rentals. But a manufacturer can usually vary his output, at least somewhat, in the short run. X's default did not enable the manufacturer to obtain a profit from selling to Y: if X had not defaulted, the manufacturer could still have supplied Y with 1000 widgets. The profit on the sale to Y is a gain that the manufacturer would have obtained regardless of the default, so his true loss is the entire expected profit from the sale to X. ...

... The existence of a variety of equitable remedies, such as specific performance, for breach of contract may seem inconsistent with our proposition that expected profit should be the measure of contract damages. However, consider a typical real estate case (where specific performance is allowed as a matter of course): I have a contract to buy a house and the seller defaults. The estimation of damages may be very difficult, since, as we have seen, I may value the house a good deal more than the market does. To remit a purchaser to damages in such cases might result in a systematic undervaluation of the costs of breach, since a court will perforce be guided by market price and be sceptical of a buyer's claim that the house is worth more to him. Although this problem can be solved by decreeing specific performance, another economic problem is created. The fact that the seller defaulted may indicate that there is another transaction that increases value by even more than would completion of the sale to me; if so, we want to encourage the breach. The results of decreeing specific performance are not catastrophic, since the seller can always pay me to surrender my right of specific performance and presumably will do so if a substitute transfer would yield him a higher price. But to require the seller to conduct this additional negotiation does impose additional transaction costs.

It would probably be a mistake, however, to authorize injunctive remedies generally in contract cases. Suppose that in a case of physical impossibility in which discharge was not warranted, the promisee could obtain a decree ordering the promisor to complete the performance due under the contract. Although the promisor could pay the promisee to remove the injunction (as an alternative to suffering the penalties, sometimes quite severe, for disobeying an injunction), the amount of the payment would bear little or no relation to the costs to the promisee of the promisor's failure to perform.

The general problem illustrated by this example is that the reason behind a breach of contract is, one conjectures, less often the bad faith of the promisor than the occurrence of some event (or the discovery of some preexisting condition) which makes performance uneconomical. Since an injunction would in principle require the promisor to incur possibly unlimited costs (infinite, in a case of true physical impossibility) to comply with the contract, the promisor might, depending on the costs of defying an injunction, have to yield his entire wealth to the promisee in order to obtain a release from his obligation, even though nonperformance might have imposed only trivial costs on the promisee. In fact, he is unlikely to have to pay *that* much; the lesser of his wealth and of the cost of defying the injunction would merely be the upper limit of the range within which bargaining would occur between the parties to the contract. (What would be the lower limit?) In short, the effect of equitable remedies in this case is to create a bilateral monopoly—a source of high transaction costs.

NOTE

For conflicting views as to the efficiency of specific performance, see Anthony T. Kronman, "Specific Performance" (1978), 45 *University of Chicago Law Review* 351 and Alan Schwartz, "The Case for Specific Performance" (1980), 89 *Yale Law Journal* 271.

The principles governing the award of specific performance are also discussed in G.H. Treitel, "Specific Performance in the Sale of Goods," [1966] *Journal of Business Law* 211; Donald Harris, Anthony Ogus, and Jennifer Phillips, "Contract Remedies and the Consumer Surplus" (1979), 95 *Law Quarterly Review* 581; and Robert J. Sharpe, "Specific Relief for Contract Breach," in Barry J. Reiter and John Swan, eds., *Studies in Contract Law* (Toronto: Butterworths, 1980), chapter 5, at 123.

In *Bank of America Canada v. Mutual Trust Co.*, [2002] 2 SCR 601, the court said, at para. 31, that "[e]fficient breach should not be discouraged by the courts. This lack of disapproval emphasizes that a court will usually award money damages for breach of contract equal to the value of the bargain to the plaintiff."

Radford v. DeFroberville
[1977] 1 WLR 1262 (Ch. D)

[Plaintiff sued for breach of a contract to erect a boundary wall on defendant's property.]

OLIVER J: ... The cost of erecting a wall of the appropriate specification at the date when it should have been erected under the contract was about £1,200 and is now about £3,400. On the other hand the absence of a physical barrier on the boundary, although it may cause some slight inconvenience to the occupiers of the plaintiff's flats (because the plot is now becoming overgrown and tends to be used as a short-cut by trespassing pedestrians) cannot be said to cause any serious discomfort and—certainly in these days of scarce accommodation—would be unlikely to bring about any significant diminution in letting value. Indeed the defendant's expert witness has expressed an opinion that the presence of an adjoining open space actually enhances the value of the plaintiff's property. ...

[I]f the contract had been performed according to its terms, the plaintiff would have had his property bounded and enclosed by a wall of a particular height which did not obtrude into his land; which was maintainable wholly by his neighbour and which was constructed to a specification and design approved by the plaintiff as suitable for his adjoining property. What he is left with in fact, after eight years of patient endeavour and fours years of exasperated litigation, is no wall at all, no right to demand one, no control over what is erected along his boundary, the expense of putting up a wall or fence of his own if he wants one and, for his trouble, the sum of 40 shillings or its decimal equivalent and the consolation of knowing that he has parted irrevocably with his adjoining land and his right of pre-emption for a consideration part of which has, in the event, turned out to be totally illusory.

Now, if that is right, it produces, as it seems to me, a result so strange and so monstrously unjust that Mr. Bumble's animadversion on the nature of the law seems, by contrast a model of restrained understatement. The purpose of the law is to remedy wrongs, not to perpetuate injustices. ...

I must consider the effect of the decision of Field and Cave JJ in the Queen's Bench Divisional Court in *Wigsell v. School for Indigent Blind* (1882), 8 QBD 357, a case which, until recently, has enjoyed modest obscurity—it is not even mentioned in the current edition of the volume on damages of *Halsbury's Laws of England*, 4th ed, vol. 12 (1975), although it receives a worthier treatment in *McGregor on Damages* (London: Sweet & Maxwell, 13th ed., 1972), where it is cited both in connection with damages for breach of a covenant to build and also in the analogous context of covenants between lessor and lessee. Certainly it is fair to say than in *McGregor on Damages* in paragraphs 766 and 770 it is cited to support a general principle. In paragraph 766 it appears under the heading "Covenant for working the premises" and the author says:

> In covenants to build, to mine or to farm, the measure of damages is the amount of the diminu-
> tion in the market value of the premises, and this will be so whether the action is brought dur-
> ing the term or at its determination. There is little authority but what there is supports this
> proposition, which is after all based upon general principle. The only alternative measure that
> could command any support is the cost of executing the building, mining or farming that the
> lessee has wrongly failed to do. The reasons for the rejection of this have never been better put
> than by Field J in *Wigsell v. School for Indigent Blind.* ...

He then cites a passage that I will come to in a moment. At paragraph 771, under the heading "Covenant in Respect of User and Alteration of the Premises," the author says:

> The prima facie measure of damages remains the diminution in the value of the reversion, for
> this represents the lessor's basic loss, the amount by which he is pecuniarily worse off by the
> breach of covenant. If however he intends to alter the condition of the premises to comply with
> the contract, and this can be regarded as a reasonable course for him to take in the circum-
> stances, then he ought to be awarded as damages the cost of such alteration. Such damages
> become in effect the alternative to a decree of specific performance and should therefore only
> be awarded where a court would be prepared to grant such a decree. ...

The plaintiffs in *Wigsell's* case were the executors of a certain Colonel Wigsell who had been the owner of a substantial area of building land at Coulsdon and who had, in 1872, sold an area of some 12 acres to the defendants who were proposing to erect on it a school or asylum for the blind. In the conveyance to them the defendants covenanted with the vendor that they would enclose and keep enclosed the land sold within a wall or railings to a height of seven feet. There was also a provision that if, within ten years, the defendants desired to sell the whole or any part of it, they should first offer it to the vendor at a price (in the case of the whole) about £500 less and (in the case of a part) about £48 an acre less than that which they had paid for it. They did not, in fact, build either the school or the wall, and, having abandoned the project, they offered the land back to the plaintiffs. That offer was refused. Notice was given to the defendants requiring them to build the enclosing wall, but it was not complied with and the plaintiffs commenced an action for damages. ...

What Field J said was:

> The first head of damage, however, was very strongly contended for by Mr. Wills, who cited
> many authorities in support of it, but we are of opinion that it cannot be supported. It must be
> remembered that remedies for a breach of contract such as this are of two kinds. First, the
> plaintiffs, if they really wished to have the wall built in accordance with the contract, so that
> they might have the very thing contracted for, and nothing else, might have claimed in the
> Chancery Division specific performance of the covenant, and, in that event, if the court had
> come to the conclusion that the damages to be recovered in an action for damages, upon the
> principles applicable to such action, would [not] adequately protect the plaintiffs' rights and

interests, it might have ordered the defendants to build the wall, and so no question could have arisen as the extent or otherwise of any injury sustained by the plaintiffs from the absence of it. But it was also open to the plaintiffs to do what they have done viz., bring this action for damages, in which event they will be under no obligation whatever to expend the amount recovered in erecting the wall, and most probably would never think for a moment of any such expenditure, which, to us at least, would seem a simple waste of money. The effect, however, of electing to bring the action for damages, is to convert the right to the performance of the contract into a right to have compensation in money, and the rule in such a case, stated in its most general terms, is that the plaintiff is entitled to have his damages assessed at the pecuniary amount of the difference between the state of the plaintiff upon the breach of the contract and what it would have been if the contract had been performed (*per* Parke B in *Robinson v. Harman* (1848), 1 Exch. 850; 154 ER 363 adopted in *Lock v. Furze* (1866), LR 1 CP 441).

In the present case the only difference between the two states is that twenty acres of the plaintiffs' land are said to be of less value than they would have been if the wall had been built, and for that difference, whatever it may be, the defendants admit that they are liable. But in what way does the cost of the wall or fence become the measure of that difference? If it had been oak paling the damages would have been less, although such a fence is equally effective for the purposes of the contract; if the fence had been limited by the contract to the alternative iron railing, the damages would have been £3,013, equal nearly to the fee simple value of the twenty acres, at the price at which the plaintiffs were entitled to buy the 12 acres back. The element of cost to the defendants, which may thus vary, cannot be the measure of the difference to the plaintiffs, which is one thing—it represents in no sense that difference. Upon principle, therefore, such a basis of assessment seems to us to be inadmissible, and it must needs be seen if it can be supported upon authority.

… The plaintiffs had not proceeded for specific performance and there was no suggestion that they had the slightest intention of laying out any damages recovered in building. Nor does it appear from the argument that counsel was seeking to justify the award on this ground. …

It is, as it seems to me, in the light of these submissions, and of the fact that no one was contending or thought for a moment that the wall would ever be built, that the judgment falls to be considered. The court began by putting a gloss on the general principle of Parke B which has much the same effect as that for which Mr. Sher contends. That was no doubt quite justified because on the view that they took of the facts, the only difference between the plaintiffs' actual state and that contemplated by the contract was that the plaintiffs owned land which was not separated from the defendants' by a physical barrier. And, of course, the cost of a wall which, *ex hypothesi*, was never going to be built could not be the measure of that difference. But the rule as they stated it was not the same either in terms or in effect as the rule stated by Parke B or as Blackburn J enunciated it in *Lock v. Furze* (1866), LR 1 CP 441 at p. 453. Blackburn J expressed it thus: "… the person injured by the breach is to be placed as far as money can do it in the same position as he would have been in if the contract had been fulfilled." And that, of course, is not the same—or not necessarily the same—as saying that he will be put in "as good a financial position as he would have been in had the contract been performed. …"

Now, I am, of course, very conscious of the doctrine of *stare decisis* and of the duty of a judge to adopt and apply the *rationes decidendi* of decisions of superior courts—the more so in the light of the speeches in the House of Lords in *Miliangos v. George Frank (Textiles) Ltd.*, [1976] AC 443 (HL (Eng.)). But what, I ask myself, is the true *ratio decidendi* in *Wigsell's* case? Is it—can it be—anything more than an application of the general principle of compensation in cases of breach of contract to a particular and individual factual situation, bearing in mind that the House of Lords has, on several occasions, said that there can be no rigid rules in this area? I can find no such general principle in the case as is contended for. So far as the court put the matter on the basis of the authorities they were merely stating, as is plainly the case, that the authorities did not support counsel's contention that they established the cost of building as an absolute measure regardless of circumstances. So far as they treated the matter as one of principle, they seem to me to be saying no more than this that one who has the benefit of a specifically enforceable covenant and who declines specific performance but *elects* his remedy in damages will be confined to the normal contractual measure of damages—that is to say, he submits to the inquiry "What have you actually lost?"—an inquiry which has to be approached in light of the deliberate election which the plaintiff has made. As it seems to me, the court, far from seeking to establish an absolute measure in all cases of breach of covenant, did just the reverse. It looked at what the plaintiffs had actually lost and it did so in the light both of the fact that they had elected not to sue for specific performance and of the great improbability of their ever even thinking of building the wall for themselves—circumstances which were otherwise wholly irrelevant but which are expressly referred to in the judgment. Then, having stated the general principle, they concluded that "in the present case" the only loss which the plaintiffs had suffered was the diminution in value of their adjoining 20 acres. ...

[*Wigsell's* case was] considered at some length by Megarry V-C in the course of his judgment in *Tito v. Waddell (No. 2)*, [1977] Ch. 106 (better known, perhaps, as the *Ocean Island* case). ...

I am fortified in the view which I have formed as to the true effect of *Wigsell's* case by the fact that the reference to *Tito v. Waddell* showed that it coincided with the view of Megarry V-C expressed in the following passage from his judgment, at p. 334:

> In *Wigsell v. School for Indigent Blind*, of course, the only conviction that could have existed was that the wall would never be built. The object of requiring the wall to be built was plainly to protect the vendor's land against the proposed asylum. The proposal to build an asylum had been abandoned; and by suing for damages and not specific performance the vendors executors were doing little more than recognise the reality that the wall would never be erected. On that footing the executors could not establish that the cost of building the wall represented any loss that they had suffered.

Referring to the observations of Field J on the plaintiff's election and to the general proposition already referred to in paragraph 766 of *McGregor*, Megarry V-C said, at p. 331:

> I can see many difficulties in this. I should watch with interest the progress of an action for specific performance of a contract to farm or to mine; and if a plaintiff decided to sue for damages instead, I think most Chancery practitioners would ascribe his decision to prudence rather than a choice between available remedies. For contracts to build, I do not understand how or

why a covenant to build and a covenant to repair can or should be distinguished for this purpose: yet *Joyner v. Weeks*, [1891] 2 QB 31 (CA) is clear authority for the cost of repairs being the normal measure for damages at the end of the term for breach of a covenant in a lease to deliver up the premises in repair. I do not think that footnote 69 on p. 528 in *McGregor on Damages* is sound or is supported by the authority cited. In any case, I doubt very much whether a suitable test exists or can be devised which depends on what it is that has been contracted to be done. Certainly I do not think that *Wigsell's* case can be generalised into supporting the proposition in *McGregor on Damages* that I have mentioned.

Megarry V-C rejected the suggestion that the consideration of whether or not the plaintiff sued for, or was able to sue for, specific performance was necessarily decisive and gave as an example a recluse who sold part of his land on terms that the purchaser would enclose the retained land with a high wall. I gratefully and respectfully adopt this passage from his judgment. He said, at p. 332:

His land may be worth more on the market without the wall than with it, but I cannot see that either this or the fact that he is not suing for specific performance ought to debar him from obtaining damages equal to the cost of building the wall. Whether the wall to be taken for this purpose is to be the actual wall, if reasonable, or the contractual wall, I need not discuss. If, without erecting the wall, he sues merely for damages, but establishes that he will spend the money on erecting a wall, preferring to have nothing more to do with the faithless purchaser, I do not see why the result should not be the same.

Megarry V-C then set out four general propositions specifically in relation to the type of contract with which I am concerned in the instant case. It would be a work of supererogation for me to paraphrase them in less felicitous language and I, therefore, quote and adopt them in full. He said, at p. 332:

In the absence of any clear authority on the matter before me, I think I must consider it as a matter of principle. I do this in relation to the breach of a contract to do work on the land of another, whether to build, repair, replant or anything else: and I put it very broadly. First, it is fundamental to all questions of damages that they are to compensate the plaintiff for his loss or injury by putting him as nearly as possible in the same position as he would have been in had he not suffered the wrong. The question is not one of making the defendant disgorge what he has saved by committing the wrong, but one of compensating the plaintiff.

He then quotes from the judgment of O'Connor LJ in *Murphy v. Wexford County Council*, [1921] 2 IR 230 (CA) at p. 240 and continues:

Second, if the plaintiff has suffered monetary loss, as by a reduction in the value of his property by reason of the wrong, that is plainly a loss that he is entitled to recoup. On the other hand, if the defendant has saved himself money, as by not doing what he has contracted to do, that does not of itself entitle the plaintiff to recover the saving as damages; for it by no means necessarily follows that what the defendant has saved the plaintiff has lost.

Third, if the plaintiff can establish that his loss consists of or includes the costs of doing work which in breach of contract the defendant has failed to do, then he can recover as damages the sum equivalent to that cost. It is for the plaintiff to establish this: the essential question is what his loss is.

Fourth, the plaintiff may establish that the cost of doing the work constitutes part or all of his loss in a variety of ways. The work may already have been done before he sues. Thus, he may have had it done himself as in *Jones v. Herxheimer*, [1950] 2 KB 106 (CA). Alternatively, he may be able to establish that the work will be done. This, I think, must depend on all the circumstances, and not merely on whether he sues for specific performance. An action for specific performance is doubtless one way of manifesting a sufficient intention that the work shall be done: but there are others. Thus, the plaintiff may be contractually bound to a third party to do the work himself, as in *Conquest v. Ebbetts*, [1896] AC 490 (HL (Eng.)). Other cases of what may be called extraneous coercion may easily be imagined, such as the enforcement by a local authority of some statutory obligation.

I do not, however, think that this head is confined to cases of coercion. I have already mentioned the case of the plaintiff who does the work himself before he sues: I cannot see that it matters that he did it without his being under obligation to do so. After all, he contracted for valuable consideration that it should be done. Suppose, then, that he has not done it but states that he intends to do it. Of course, he may not be believed: but if he is, why should not his loss be measured by what it will cost him to do the thing that the defendant ought to have done but did not do? In some cases, the circumstances may demonstrate a sufficient fixity of intention in the plaintiff's resolve, as where the property is his home and it will be highly inconvenient or nearly uninhabitable until the work is done. In such a case I cannot think that it matters that the house could be made convenient or inhabitable by doing cheaper or less idiosyncratic work: what matters is the work to which the plaintiff is entitled under the contract.

He concluded, at p. 334: "In the end, the question seems to me to come down to a very short point. The cost is a loss if it is shown to be a loss."

In the instant case, the plaintiff says in evidence that he wishes to carry out the work on his own land and there are, as it seems to me, three questions that I have to answer. First, am I satisfied on the evidence that the plaintiff has a genuine and serious intention of doing the work? Secondly, is the carrying out of the work on his own land a reasonable thing for the plaintiff to do? Thirdly, does it make any difference that the plaintiff is not personally in occupation of the land but desires to do the work for the benefit of his tenants? I see no reason to disbelieve the plaintiff's evidence, but in any event Mr. McDonnell is prepared, as I understand it, to protect the position by a suitable form of undertaking. That was a course which was suggested by Kelly CB in *Wigsell's* case. He said, at p. 222:

> Supposing, then, an action to lie by the covenantee against the covenantor on a covenant of this nature, just as if it had been a covenant to pay a certain sum of money at a certain specified time, and assuming the covenant to be an absolute one, and that it has been broken by the defendants' refusal to build the wall, and damages to be recovered in consequence, there can be no doubt that a court of equity would call upon the plaintiffs on the one side to proceed to build the wall with the money so recovered, and upon the defendants on the other side to afford all facilities in the way of approaches to the spot for the purpose of enabling the plaintiffs to build it.

Once again I have to acknowledge my debt to Megarry V-C who has dealt with this point also in the course of his judgment in *Tito v. Waddell (No. 2)*, [1977] Ch. 106. He said, at p. 333:

In other cases, if the circumstances fail to indicate sufficiently that the work will be done, the court might accept an undertaking by the plaintiff to do the work; and this, as in the business tenancy cases, would surely "compel fixity of intention." Whatever the circumstances, if the plaintiff establishes that the contractual work has been or will be done, then in all normal circumstances it seems to me that he has shown that the cost of doing it is, or is part of, his loss, and is recoverable as damages. Even if it is open to question whether the plaintiff will do the work, the cost of doing it may afford a starting figure, though it should be scaled down according to the circumstances, the real question being that of the loss to the plaintiff.

As he pointed out, short of an undertaking, there can, in most cases, be no absolute certainty that the work will be done, for supervening events may alter the position. Nevertheless, he observed, at p. 334:

I do not think that the plaintiffs' rights are affected by any such absence of certainty. Just as Lord Herschell, in the circumstances, of *Conquest v. Ebbetts*, [1896] AC 490 (HL (Eng.)) at p. 495, denied the defendant the right to "demand that a speculative inquiry shall be entered upon as to what may possibly happen and what arrangements it may be possible to come to," so I think the court should refuse to speculate on other possibilities of this sort. The court ought to be ready to act on evidence which, without assuring certainty, nevertheless carries conviction.

In the instant case, I am entirely satisfied that the plaintiff genuinely wants this work done and that he intends to expend any damages awarded on carrying it out. In my judgment, therefore, the damages ought to be measured by the cost of the work, unless there are some other considerations which point to a different measure.

That brings me to the second question, which is really one of mitigation. Mr. Sher submits that the purpose of the wall is to keep out weeds and trespassers, these being the matters of which the plaintiff specifically complains in his evidence. A prefabricated boundary fence would, he submits, be just as effective for that purpose and would cost much less. This would, therefore, he submits, be the reasonable way of mitigating the plaintiff's loss and the damages ought to be measured by the cost of this cheaper substitute. To build a wall is a waste, he suggests, because at some time in the future the owner of the plot may erect a house the northern flank wall of which will, so far as it extends, render the plaintiff's wall superfluous and perhaps even inconvenient. I think that there are a number of answers to this. First, a prefabricated fence is in no sense a permanent structure and I have to bear in mind that it is the plaintiff who would have to maintain it. Secondly, and perhaps more important, it was not what the plaintiff stipulated for and what, in effect, he paid for when he sold the plot. I know of no principle of damages which would dictate that a plaintiff who has stipulated for an article of a certain quality should be fobbed off with an inferior substitute merely because it is cheaper for a defendant who has broken his contract to supply it. Thirdly, although I appreciate that there may come a time when the third party or some other owner of the plot may erect a house there, I have to bear in mind that the covenant in the present case is 12-years-old and no house has been erected yet nor is there any certainty that one ever will be erected. Indeed, it seems to me that there may now be difficulties in obtaining planning permission. A plaintiff may be willing to accept a less expensive method of performance but I see nothing unreasonable in his wishing to adhere to the contract specification.

Groves v. John Wunder Co.
(1939), 205 Minn. 163, 286 NW 235 (Minn. SC)

STONE J: Action for breach of contract. Plaintiff got judgment for a little over $15,000. Sorely disappointed by that sum, he appeals.

In August 1927, S.J. Groves & Sons Company, a corporation (hereinafter mentioned simply as Groves), owned a tract of 24 acres of Minneapolis suburban real estate. It was served or easily could be reached by railroad trackage. It is zoned as heavy industrial property. But for lack of development of the neighborhood its principal value thus far may have been in the deposit of sand and gravel which it carried. The Groves company had a plant on the premises for excavating and screening the gravel. Near by defendant owned and was operating a similar plant.

In August 1927, Groves and defendant made the involved contract. For the most part it was a lease from Groves, as lessor, to defendant as lessee; its term seven years. Defendant agreed to remove the sand and gravel and to leave the property "at a uniform grade, substantially the same as the grade now existing at the roadway ... on said premises, and that in stripping the overburden ... it will use said overburden for the purpose of maintaining and establishing said grade."

Under the contract defendant got the Groves screening plant. The transfer thereof and the right to remove the sand and gravel made the consideration moving from Groves to defendant, except that defendant incidentally got rid of Groves as a competitor. On defendant's part it paid Groves $105,000. So that from the outset, on Groves' part the contract was executed except for defendant's right to continue using the property for the stated term. (Defendant had a right to renewal which it did not exercise.)

Defendant breached the contract deliberately. It removed from the premises only "the richest and best of the gravel" and wholly failed, according to the findings, "to perform and comply with the terms, conditions, and provisions of said lease ... with respect to the condition in which the surface of the demised premises was required to be left." Defendant surrendered the premises, not substantially at the grade required by the contract "nor at any uniform grade." Instead, the ground was "broken, rugged, and uneven." Plaintiff sues as assignee and successor in right of Groves.

As the contract was construed below, the finding is that to complete its performance 288,495 cubic yards of overburden would need to be excavated, taken from the premises, and deposited elsewhere. The reasonable cost of doing that was found to be upwards of $60,000. But, if defendant had left the premises at the uniform grade required by the lease, the reasonable value of the property on the determinative date would have been only $12,160. The judgment was for that sum, including interest, thereby nullifying plaintiff's claim that cost of completing the contract rather than difference in value of the land was the measure of damages. The gauge of damage adopted by the decision was the difference between the market value of plaintiff's land in the condition it was when the contract was made and what it would have been if defendant had performed. The one question for us arises upon plaintiff's assertion that he was entitled, not to that difference in value, but to the reasonable cost to him of doing the work called for by the contract which defendant left undone.

1. Defendant's breach of contract was wilful. There was nothing of good faith about it. Hence, that the decision below handsomely rewards bad faith and deliberate breach of contract is obvious. That is not allowable. Here the rule is well settled, ... that where the contractor wilfully and fraudulently varies from the terms of a construction contract he cannot sue thereon and have the benefit of the equitable doctrine of substantial performance. That is the rule generally. ...

2. In reckoning damages for breach of a building or construction contract, the law aims to give the disappointed promisee, so far as money will do it, what he was promised. ...

Never before, so far as our decisions show, has it even been suggested that lack of value in the land furnished to the contractor who had bound himself to improve it any escape from the ordinary consequences of a breach of the contract. ...

Even in case of substantial performance in good faith, the resulting defects being remediable, it is error to instruct that the measure of damage is "the difference in value between the house as it was and as it would have been if constructed according to contract." The "correct doctrine" is that the cost of remedying the defect is the "proper" measure of damages. ...

Value of the land (as distinguished from the value of the intended product of the contract, which ordinarily will be equivalent to its reasonable cost) is no proper part of any measure of damages for wilful breach of a building contract. The reason is plain.

The summit from which to reckon damages from trespass to real estate is its actual value at the moment. The owner's only right is to be compensated for the deterioration in value caused by the tort. That is all he has lost. But not so if a contract to improve the same land has been breached by the contractor who refuses to do the work, especially where, as here, he has been paid in advance. The summit from which to reckon damages for that wrong is the hypothetical peak of accomplishment (not value) which would have been reached had the work been done as demanded by the contract.

The owner's right to improve his property is not trammeled by its small value. It is his right to erect thereon structures which will reduce its value. If that be the result, it can be of no aid to any contractor who declines performance. As said long ago in *Chamberlain v. Parker* (1871), 45 NY 569 (NY SC) at p. 572:

> A man may do what he will with his own, ... and if he chooses to erect a monument to his caprice or folly on his premises, and employs and pays another to do it, it does not lie with a defendant who has been so employed and paid for building it, to say that his own performance would not be beneficial to the plaintiff.

To the same effect is *Restatement, Contracts*, s. 346, p. 576. Illustrations of Subsection (1), para. 4.

Suppose a contractor were suing the owner for breach of a grading contract such as this. Would any element of value, or lack of it, in the land have any relevance in reckoning damages? Of course not. The contractor would be compensated for what he had lost, i.e., his profit. Conversely, in such a case as this, the owner is entitled to compensation for what he has lost, that is, the work or structure which he has been promised, for which he has paid, and of which he has been deprived by the contractor's breach.

To diminish damages recoverable against him in proportion as there is presently small value in the land would favor the faithless contractor. It would also ignore and so defeat plaintiff's right to contract and build for the future. To justify such a course would require more of the prophetic vision than judges possess. This factor is important when the subject matter is trackage property in the margin of such an area of population and industry as that of the Twin Cities. ...

[Under] a construction contract, the thing lost by a breach such as we have here is a physical structure or accomplishment, a promised and paid for alteration in land. That is the "injury" for which the law gives him compensation. Its only appropriate measure is the cost of performance.

It is suggested that because of little or no value in his land the owner may be unconscionably enriched by such a reckoning. The answer is that there can be no unconscionable enrichment, no advantage upon which the law will frown, when the result is but to give one party to a contract only what the other has promised; particularly where, as here, the delinquent has had full payment for the promised performance.

3. It is said by the Restatement, Contracts, s. 346, Comment b:

> Sometimes defects in a completed structure cannot be physically remedied without tearing down and rebuilding, at a cost that would be imprudent and unreasonable. The law does not require damages to be measured by a method requiring such economic waste. If no such waste is involved, the cost of remedying the defect is the amount awarded as compensation for failure to render the promised performance.

The "economic waste" declaimed against by the decisions applying that rule has nothing to do with the value in money of the real estate, or even with the product of the contract. The waste avoided is only that which would come from wrecking a physical structure completed, or nearly so, under the contract. ... Absent such waste, as it is in this case, the rule of the Restatement, Contracts, s. 346, is that "the cost of remedying the defect is the amount awarded as compensation for failure to render the promised performance." That means that defendants here are liable to plaintiff for the reasonable cost of doing what defendants promised to do and have wilfully declined to do. ...

The judgment must be reversed with a new trial to follow.

JULIUS J. OLSEN J (dissenting): ... Since there is no issue of fact, we should limit our inquiry to the single legal problem presented: What amount in money will adequately compensate plaintiff for his loss caused by defendant's failure to render performance? ...

As the rule of damages to be applied in any given case has for its purpose compensation, not punishment, we must be ever mindful that, "if the application of a particular rule for measuring damages to given facts results in more than compensation, it is at once apparent that the wrong rule has been adopted." *Crowley v. Burns Boiler Co.* (1907), 100 Minn. 178 at p. 187; 110 NW 969 at p. 973 (Minn. SC).

We have here then a situation where, concededly, if the contract had been performed, plaintiff would have had property worth, in round numbers, no more than $12,000. If he is to be awarded damages in an amount exceeding $60,000 he will be receiving at least 500 per cent more than his property, properly leveled to grade by actual performance, was intrinsically worth when the breach occurred. To so conclude is to give him something far beyond what the parties had in mind or contracted for. There is no showing made, nor any finding suggested, that this property was unique, specially desirable for a particular or personal use, or of special value as to location or future use different from that of other property surrounding it. Under the circumstances here appearing, it seems clear that what the parties contracted for was to put the property in shape for general sale. And the lease contemplates just that, for by the terms thereof defendant agreed "from time to time, as the sand and gravel are removed from the various lots … leased, it will surrender said lots to the lessor" if of no further use to defendant "in connection with the purposes for which this lease is made."

The theory upon which plaintiff relies for application of the cost of performance rule must have for its basis cases where property or the improvement to be made is unique or personal instead of being of the kind ordinarily governed by market values. His action is one at law for damages, not for specific performance. As there was no affirmative showing of any peculiar fitness of this property to a unique or personal use, the rule to be applied is, I think, the one applied by the court. The cases bearing directly upon this phase so hold. Briefly, the rule here applicable is this: Damages recoverable for breach of a contract to construct is the difference between the market value of the property in the condition it was when delivered to and received by plaintiff and what its market value would have been if defendant had fully complied with its terms. …

No one doubts that a party may contract for the doing of anything he may choose to have done (assuming what is to be done is not unlawful) "although the thing to be produced had no marketable value." In *Restatement, Contracts*, s. 346, pp. 576, 577, Illustrations of Subsection (1), para. 4, the same thought is thus stated:

> A contracts to construct a monumental fountain in B's yard for $5,000, but abandons the work after the fountain has been laid and $2,800 has been paid by B. The contemplated fountain is so ugly that it would decrease the number of possible buyers of the place. The cost of completing the fountain would be $4,000. B can get judgment for $1,800, the cost of completion less the part of price unpaid.

But that is not what plaintiff's predecessor in interest contracted for. Such a provision might well have been made, but the parties did not. They could undoubtedly have provided for liquidated damages for nonperformance … or they might have determined in money what the value of performance was considered to be and thereby have contractually provided a measure for failure of performance.

The opinion also suggests that this property lies in an area where the owner might rightly look for future development, being in a so-called industrial zone, and that as such he should be privileged to so hold it. This he may of course do. But let us assume that on May 1, 1934, condemnation to acquire this area had so far progressed as to leave only the question of price (market value) undetermined; that the area had been graded in strict conformity with the contract but that the actual market value of the premises was only $12,160, as found by the court and acquiesced in by plaintiff, what would the measure of his damages be? Obviously, the limit of his recovery could be no more than the then market value of his property. In that sum he has been paid with interest and costs; and he still has the fee title to the premises, something he would not possess if there had been condemnation. In what manner has plaintiff been hurt beyond the damages awarded? As to him "economic waste" is not apparent. Assume the defendant abandoned the entire project without taking a single yard of gravel therefrom but left the premises as they were when the lease was made, could plaintiff recover damages upon the basis here established? The trouble with the prevailing opinion is that here plaintiff's loss is not made the basis for the amount of his recovery but rather what it would cost the defendant. No case has been decided upon that basis until now. Plaintiff asserts that he knows of no rule "giving a different measure of damages for public contracts and for private contracts in case of nonperformance." It seems to me there is a clear distinction to be drawn with respect to the application of the rule for recoverable damages in case of breach of a public works contract from that applicable to contracts between private parties. The construction of a public building, a sewer, drainage ditch, highway, or other public work, permits of no application of the market value doctrine. There simply is and can be no "market value" as to such. And for this cogent reason there can be but one rule of damages to apply, that of cost of completion of the thing contracted to be done. I think the judgment should be affirmed.

[STONE J delivered the judgment of the court save that Hilton and Loring JJ took no part, and Holt J joined in the dissenting judgment.]

NOTE

In *Peevyhouse v. Garland Coal & Mining Co.* (1963), 382 P2d 109 (Okla. SC), the Supreme Court of Oklahoma refused to follow *Groves v. John Wunder Co.* in a case where the plaintiff sought damages for breach of a promise to restore a strip mining site.

Miles v. Marshall
(1975), 7 OR (2d) 544

[A claim was made by a landlord for damages for breach of a tenant's obligation to surrender the premises in good repair.]

WEATHERSTON J: A peculiar difficulty arises as to the proper method of assessing damages. Mr. Orkin argues that the plaintiffs by counterclaim are entitled to the full cost of repair of the premises, even though some repairs are unnecessary for the enjoyment of the premises for their intended purpose. The law was settled in England by *Joyner v. Weeks*, [1891] 2 QB 31. In the Divisional Court, Wright J said at pp. 36-7:

> Two measures have been suggested, the first the amount of money which it will cost the lessor to do the repairs, with some allowance for loss of rent or occupation during the time of reparation and with some deduction where proper by reason of substitution of new for old; the second, the diminution of the value of the lessor's estate by reason of the non-repair. In general they will both come to the same thing, and it can seldom be the case that the diminution in value can be more than the cost of repair. It may, however, often be the case that the diminution in value by reason of some or all of the tenant's defaults is much less than the cost of making them good. A part of the structure may have been designed for a purpose which has become obsolete, or a building may for many reasons be found at the end of a term to be as valuable, or

nearly as valuable, in a partially as in a completely repaired state. In such cases, which measure is to be preferred? The former, the cost of repairing, is adopted with more or less positiveness in the following cases: ...

[He then recited a long list of cases.]

It appears to us that the better measure is the amount of the diminution of value, but not exceeding the cost of doing the repairs (with the addition or deduction as above suggested), and that in the cases which appear to adopt the other test it was not intended to decide that the cost of repairing ought to be or can properly be given so far as it exceeds the diminution of value.

But in the Court of Appeal, Lord Esher MR said at p. 43:

A great many cases have been cited, of which one only was directly in point, though another was as nearly as possible in point; and a series of dicta of learned judges have been referred to, which seem to me to shew that for a very long time there has been a constant practice as to the measure of damages in such cases. Such an inveterate practice amounts, in my opinion, to a rule of law. That rule is that, when there is a lease with a covenant to leave the premises in repair at the end of the term, and such covenant is broken, the lessee must pay what the lessor proves to be a reasonable and proper amount for putting the premises into the state of repair in which they ought to have been left. It is not necessary in this case to say that is an absolute rule applicable under all circumstances; but I confess that I strongly incline to think that it is so. It is a highly convenient rule. It avoids all the subtle refinements with which we have been indulged to-day, and the extensive and costly inquiries which they would involve. It appears to me to be a simple and businesslike rule; and, if I were obliged to decide that point, I am very much inclined to think that I should come to the conclusion that it is an absolute rule.

That authority stood until 1927 when the *Landlord and Tenant Act* was amended to provide that the measure of damages should be as stated by Wright J. *Joyner v. Weeks* has been followed in two cases in the Exchequer Court of Canada: *Royal Trust Co. v. The King*, [1924] Ex. CR 121, and *National Trust Co. Ltd. v. The King*, [1949] 2 DLR 472. But I am unable to find that in this Province there has been an inveterate practice such as Lord Esher said existed in England, and I see no reason to depart from the general rule that damages are limited to the actual loss sustained by an injured party. I think my view on this point is confirmed by *Montreal Trust Co. v. Hercules Sales Ltd.*, [1969] 1 OR 661. I propose, therefore, to assess damages at the diminution of the value of the property by reason of the non-repair.

Dewees v. Morrow
(1932), 45 BCLR 154 (CA)

[This was an appeal from a judgment awarding the cost of repairing an automobile damaged by the defendant's negligence.]

MacDONALD CJBC: I think that *Lodge Holes Colliery Co. v. Wednesbury Corp.*, [1908] AC 323 (HL (Eng.)) is decisive of this appeal. The finding of the trial Judge was held to be conclusive on the question of fact. There had been a subsidence of part of a road by reason of mining operations. The company proposed to repair it to less than its former state and at less cost of such repair. The Colliery Co. submitted that it could be repaired to a condition just as convenient to the public though not to its original condition at a much lower sum. The trial Judge held that that cost was the measure of damages. On appeal by the corporation to the Court of Appeal the judgment was reversed and on appeal to the House of Lords, the House reversed the Court of Appeal and restored the judgment of the trial Judge. The Lord Chancellor on pp. 325-6 said that:—

> They (the plaintiffs) did not in fact consider how they could make an equally commodious road without unnecessary expense. Their position was that they were in law entitled to raise the road to its old level and to charge the defendants with the cost of so raising it. At the trial, as an afterthought, they also contended that the road would not in fact be so commodious to the public if it were made up on the lower level at the smaller cost. ...
>
> My Lords, I regard the finding of Jelf J (the trial Judge) as conclusive on the question of fact. ...
>
> The point of law which was advanced by the plaintiffs, namely, that they were entitled to raise the road to the old level, cost what it might and whether it was more commodious to the public or not, will not, in my opinion, bear investigation. Such a rule might lead to a ruinous and wholly unnecessary outlay. There is no authority for it, though there is authority to shew that as between the owners of a public road and the adjacent lands the former may be entitled to restore the ancient level. Even those who have been wronged must act reasonably. ...
>
> Accordingly, with the utmost respect to the Court of Appeal, I think the judgment of Jelf J should be restored.

Lord Macnaghten and Lord Atkinson concurred.

The position of the corporation there was analogous to that of the plaintiff in this case. Here he insists upon putting the car back into the same condition it was in before injury. That, it is admitted, will cost more than the car was worth. Now had the car been utterly destroyed the measure of damages would be the fair market value of the car at the time. It was contended here that the fair market value was what a car of a similar kind in similar condition could have been bought for second-hand. In fact it was sought to apply the rule applicable to a contract for the sale of goods of which there was a breach and in which the purchaser or vendor could go into the market and buy a similar article and claim the difference in the cost of it and the cost of the goods contracted for as the measure of his damages. That rule, I think, is not applicable to this case.

It is impossible to find another article of the kind and in the condition of this car in the market. It can be said that there is no real market for such cars but it is admitted that cars equal in class and in second-hand condition can be bought on the market and are constantly sold on the market at a much lower price than this car would have cost to repair. I think the rule to apply is that the plaintiff is entitled to the fair value of his car just before it was injured which brings this case rather closely within the case of a broken contract but in a different way. Evidence was called here to prove that a similar car in a like condition could have been bought for $900. The learned Judge made this finding:—

> Plaintiff's car at the time of the accident was in first-class shape mechanically, and in appearance. It will cost $1458.05 to place it in like condition. If this were done the car could not be sold, as second-hand cars are usually marketed, for more than $900 at the outside.

That I think is a finding of the fair value of the car before its injury. No sentimental consideration enters into this case and the plaintiff can replace his car by another equally as good for $900. The case is analogous to the case above cited where the cost of a road equally commodious substituted for the original one was allowed as the reasonable measure of damages.

There are many cases pro and con on this subject but I am of opinion that the decision in such cases should be consistent with reason and when an amount can be arrived at which in all the circumstances is reasonable that amount should be adopted as the fair market value. The injured car is worth $100 as scrap, which deducted from the $900 above mentioned leaves the plaintiff's damages at $800. The damages are reduced accordingly.

C.R. Taylor (Wholesale) Ltd. v. Hepworths Ltd.
[1977] 1 WLR 659 (QB)

MAY J: ... At all material times in this case the defendants were the owners and occupiers of premises at 11 Market Place, Nuneaton, in the centre of Nuneaton; joining it from the south is a street known as Coventry Street.

[His Lordship referred to premises owned or occupied by the second, third, and fourth plaintiffs and continued:]

Prior to October 26, 1970, the first plaintiffs owned and occupied premises comprising, first, three lock-up shops fronting on to Coventry Street. Of these nos. 17 and 21-23 Coventry Street, the latter comprising what had originally been two single shops, were unlet and empty. No. 19 Coventry Street was occupied by a Mrs. Neil as a wool shop. She was holding over as tenant after the expiry of a lease which had been granted for a term of three years from Christmas 1959 at a rent of £175 per year. As the first plaintiff's solicitors wrote in the fourth paragraph of their letter of September 20, 1976 to the defendants' solicitors:

> No formal documents extending the lease appear to have been executed, however, and we understand from Peter Bromwich, Horne and Co. (the first plaintiffs' estate agents and surveyors) that the arrangement that existed between Mrs. Neil and the first plaintiffs was that she should continue in occupation until such time as the property was required for development.

Secondly and behind these three lock-up shops was an old billiard hall. This was vacant on October 26, 1970, and I shall have to relate more of its history a little later in this judgment.

The length of the frontage to Coventry Street of the premises was 65 feet. To the northeast of those premises there was a small alley-way which had a frontage of 4 feet to Coventry Street. This alley-way was open from the road back to about the level of the boundary between nos. 11 and 12 Market Place, and was then either covered or built on for the remainder of its length, except perhaps for another small open portion at the rear. Precisely how the alley-way was covered or built over was not clear on the evidence, but it seems that part may have been occupied by the second plaintiffs under some arrangement with the first plaintiffs who were also the freeholders of the alley-way throughout its length. The complete premises, therefore, of which the first plaintiffs were at material times the owners in fee had a frontage to Coventry Street of 69 feet.

On the evening of October 26, 1970, some servant or agent of the defendants burnt some rubbish in the open part of the alley-way at the rear of their own premises, 11, Market Place. This fire got out of control and did substantial damage to the various premises of the various plaintiffs which I have described. Until shortly before the trial in this action began the defendants continued to dispute their liability for such damage. By their solicitors' letter of October 8, 1976, however, liability was admitted and, save in respect of the first plaintiffs, agreement has been reached on the quantum of the damages payable by the defendants to the various plaintiffs. It is agreed that the second plaintiffs are entitled to judgment for the sum of £16,809; that the third plaintiffs are entitled to judgment for the sum of £4,885; and that the fourth plaintiffs are entitled to judgment for the sum of £385.

In so far as the first plaintiffs are concerned, the defendants accept their liability to pay the two sums of £74 and £650 respectively pleaded under the particulars of damage of the first plaintiffs in paragraph 9 of the re-amended statement of claim, and also now concede that the latter are entitled to a further £2,643.63, as I shall indicate hereafter. No further agreement, however, has been possible in respect of the first plaintiffs' claim in this action, and in the end this has been the only issue which I have had to try. For the remainder of this judgment, therefore, I propose to describe the first plaintiffs as just "the plaintiffs" save where the context necessarily requires me to do otherwise.

As the result of the fire the billiard hall which comprised by far the largest part of the plaintiffs' site was for practical purposes destroyed. It was never rebuilt, but in so far as it may be relevant it is agreed as a figure between the plaintiffs and the defendants that the cost of reinstating the billiard hall after the fire, giving credit for any betterment that such reinstatement would have produced, would have been the sum of £28,956.95. Fortunately the fire caused no damage to the three shops on the Coventry Street frontage of the plaintiffs' site and Mrs. Neil continued to occupy 19, Coventry Street until she gave up possession in 1973 in circumstances which I shall have to relate hereafter. After the fire certain repairs on the boundaries or "fringes" of the plaintiffs' site had to be carried out at a cost of £2,487.24. In addition it was necessary to demolish parts of the billiard hall itself and to board it up and padlock it against trespassers; this minor work cost £156.39. The defendants now agree that these two items of work had to be carried out on the premises as a result of the fire; they agree the cost of each of them; and they consequently also agree that whatever may be my decision upon the principal issue in this case, the defendants are in any event liable to the first plaintiffs for the aggregate of these two sums, namely £2,643.63.

That principal issue is what is the correct measure of damages in law to which the plaintiffs are entitled in all the circumstances of the case in respect of the very substantial damage that the fire caused to the actual billiard hall. Although I have not seen the relevant policy, it is not disputed that the plaintiffs were themselves insured in respect of their whole premises at the time of the fire. The chartered loss adjuster acting on behalf of the plaintiffs' insurers, Mr. Lewis, gave evidence before me and it was he who prepared the report of September 1971. In respect of the billiard hall, as appears from the report and as Mr. Lewis deposed to in evidence which I accept, his insured, that is to say the plaintiffs, elected to accept for their loss what was described as "an indemnity settlement." Apparently, under the terms of their policy the plaintiffs were entitled either to require their insurers to reinstate the damaged premises in fact, or alternatively to be paid by those insurers what it would have cost to have reinstated them, making all due allowance for betterment and any other relevant considerations. To this end, quantity surveyors were instructed to prepare bills of quantities for the theoretical reinstatement of the billiard hall and after adjustment agreement was reached between the plaintiffs and their insurers that the theoretical cost of reinstatement was £32,896.61. Due allowance for betterment was then made and agreed and ultimately the plaintiffs' insurers paid to the plaintiffs the total sum of $28,956.95, in addition to the aggregate sum of £2,643.63 to which I have already referred, in respect of the fire damage to their premises. This is therefore a subrogated action and in truth a dispute between the plaintiffs' insurers on the one hand and the defendants' insurers on the other, although this has no relevance in so far as my ultimate decision on the facts and law is concerned. I must and do treat this case as a claim by the plaintiffs personally against the defendants personally and I must assess upon the facts as I find them to be and upon the law as I think it is the sum of money which the plaintiffs are entitled to recover from the defendants, putting out of my mind any question of the respective insurances.

In brief, the dispute between the parties can be put in this way. The plaintiffs first contend that the proper measure of damages for the loss which they sustained as the result of the destruction of the billiard hall by the fire is its theoretical cost of reinstatement. They therefore contend that in addition to the various smaller agreed items to which I have referred they are entitled to recover from the defendants the sum of £28,956.95 as the cost of reinstatement, and consequently to a total sum of £32,324.58 as originally pleaded in the particulars of damage of these plaintiffs in paragraph 9 of the re-amended statement of claim. For their part, the defendants submit that upon the evidence to which I shall shortly refer the plaintiffs never had any intention of reinstating the billiard hall on their site. This site, so the defendants contend, was one which in planning jargon was "ripe for development," and that consequently the proper measure of damage is not the estimated theoretical cost of reinstating the premises after the fire, but the diminution in the market value of those premises caused by the fire. The defendants' argument continues that as this was at all material times a development site, its market value was its value as such, and that this in truth was in no way affected by the fire or by the damage due to it, save only in the sense favourable to the plaintiffs in that instead of having to clear the site prior to development the fire in effect did this for them. In these circumstances the defendants submit that their only liability to the plaintiffs in this case is the aggregate of the various agreed smaller items.

In the course of the trial Mr. Otton on behalf of the plaintiffs sought and obtained leave to re-amend the statement of claim to allege in the alternative that if he were wrong in his first submission that the proper measure of damages in law was the reinstatement cost, and that the defendants were correct in contending that the proper measure of damages was the difference between the pre- and post-fire market value of the premises, then the value of his clients' site before the fire was £58,125 and that its value after the fire was a mere £22,588. The diminution in value was then £35,537. However, in order properly to assess damages on this basis, credit must be given for what it would have cost to clear the site, an operation which the fire effected free for the plaintiffs. This cost on the evidence he submitted would have amounted to about £3,000, but per contra there should be added back the sum of £2,643.63 for the necessary immediate repairs and security measures which had to be made and taken. In the result, Mr. Otton submitted that if Mr. O'Brien's submissions on the defendants' behalf were correct in law, nevertheless on the evidence the plaintiffs were entitled to £35,904.63 a sum rather greater than the damages to which they contended they were entitled in the first instance.

I now turn to the evidence which was adduced before me and to the findings of fact which I am able to make upon it. The first witness called on behalf of the plaintiffs was Mr. Dudley. He is a Fellow of the Royal Institute of Chartered Surveyors and had practised in the Nuneaton and Coventry districts for the past 40 years. He had practised for the past 22 years on his own account at premises at 1, Coton Road in Nuneaton. Mr. Dudley, therefore, had substantial experience not only as a chartered surveyor but also of the actual area of Nuneaton in which the plaintiffs' premises were. Indeed, he had been in the business as such on his own account at premises only some 70 yards or so from the billiard hall and the adjoining shops for the last 22 years. Whatever view one may take of other parts of Mr. Dudley's evidence, I have no doubt that his history of the relevant area is to be accepted and indeed it was not seriously disputed by the defendants or their witnesses.

The plaintiffs' billiard hall and shops were built in 1919. The billiard hall remained in use as such until the outbreak of the last war in 1939. It was then occupied by a hosiery firm, but they ceased to use it at the end of the war. It then became a warehouse which was for some time assimilated with the occupation of 12, Market Place, which it will be remembered was owned by the third plaintiffs and let and occupied by the second plaintiffs at the time of the fire as a supermarket. The use of the billiard hall as a warehouse with 12, Market Place ceased, however, some years before the fire. From time to time thereafter it was used casually as a warehouse, for instance at Christmas or when an occupier had surplus stock which he wished to store for a period, but even this desultory use stopped and the billiard hall remained vacant for about three years before the fire on October 26, 1970. Originally the shops on the Coventry Street frontage were let and occupied. Mr. Dudley remembered no. 17 occupied as a camera shop and confirmed that no. 19 was occupied as a wool shop. However, no. 17 became vacant two years or thereabouts before the fire; thereafter it remained empty except for short temporary periods, for instance during elections. The other two shops, nos. 21 and 32, had been a double unit for many years, but they too had been unoccupied for some five or six years before the fire occurred. So much for the undisputed part of Mr. Dudley's evidence.

The part of his evidence which was disputed, however, was that despite the history which I have outlined and despite the position of the plaintiffs' site in or near to the business and commercial centre of Nuneaton, nevertheless the plaintiffs' site was not one ripe for development.

[His Lordship considered the evidence of Mr. Dudley and expert witnesses called by the plaintiffs and the defendants on the question of the site's potential development, and continued:]

On all the evidence, therefore, the conclusions to which I have come are as follows. Immediately prior to the fire on October 26, 1970, I do not think that anyone could realistically or did indeed regard the plaintiffs' premises as otherwise than a potential redevelopment site. I am quite satisfied that the chance of letting the premises in whole or in part, as distinct from redevelopment, was minimal, save for isolated instances for short periods. I am satisfied that the plaintiffs made no attempt to let any part of their premises for some years before the fire. As I have said, I think that these premises and indeed the plaintiff company itself were in reality only a small part of the overall business interests of their actual proprietors. For this reason, and also because those concerned saw the development potential in the premises, I do not think that any substantial effort was made even to sell them before the fire. I think that the plaintiffs and their agents were content to await any offers that came in, and if any seemed to be sufficiently attractive then to consider and perhaps accept them. In my view Mr. Stevens, a chartered surveyor who was called to give evidence by the defendants, was being unnecessarily generous to the plaintiffs in putting a value of £50,000 on their premises immediately before the fire occurred. He did this on the basis that they had some investment value for letting which, as I have already indicated, I do not think was the fact. I am prepared to accept that the premises were rather more valuable before the fire than they were after the fire, and I think that the realistic and correct view to take is that the value of the plaintiffs' premises before the fire was £42,500 and that their value after the fire was £40,000. For any proposing redeveloper who had bought the premises before the fire for £42,500 I think that it would have cost £3,000 to clear the site to the condition to which it had been cleared by the fire when the latter occurred. Nevertheless, once the fire had occurred the sum of £2,643.63 had to be spent to make the premises safe and to do necessary immediate works to what I have called the "fringe" buildings. In the result, whereas the theoretical cost of reinstating the plaintiffs' premises after the fire is shown and agreed to have been £28,956.95, I think that in so far as their then value to the plaintiffs was concerned the fire on October 26, 1970, only reduced this by £2,500.

What principles of law, therefore, have to be applied to these findings of fact? This is a case in which the issue between the parties is the proper measure of damages to be paid by one to the other for the damage caused to the latter's premises by the legal fault of the former. I have been referred to a number of cases concerned with the measure of damages for torts affecting land, principally trespass. In some of them damages have been assessed upon what has been said to be the prima facie measure of damages, that is to say the amount of the diminution of the value of the land. Examples of this type of case are *Jones v. Gooday* (1841), 8 M & W 146; 151 RR 985 (Exch.); *Moss v. Christchurch Rural District Council*, [1925] 2 KB 750 and *Hole & Son (Sayers Common) Ltd. v. Harrisons of Thurnscoe Ltd.*, [1973] 1 Lloyd's Rep. 345 (QB).

The other, and perhaps more recent line of authority to which I have also been referred is that in which the measure of damages has been held to be the actual cost of reinstating the land and the buildings on it, whether or not any credit is given for what is described as betterment. Examples of this type of case are *Hollebone v. Midhurst and Fernhurst Builders Ltd.*, [1968] 1 Lloyd's Rep. 38 (QB) and *Harbutt's "Plasticine" Ltd. v. Wayne Tank and Pump Co. Ltd.*, [1970] 1 QB 447 (CA). It is true to say that the latter case was strictly one in contract, but the nature of the damage and the circumstances in which it occurred were such that in my opinion no real distinction can be drawn between it and those cases in which the cause of action lies properly in tort.

In R.F.V. Heuston (ed.), *Salmond on the Law of Torts* (London: Sweet & Maxwell, 16th ed., 1973) p. 574, it is said:

> When a trespass has caused physical damage to the land, the measure of damages is the loss thereby caused to the plaintiff, which in all ordinary cases is measured by the resulting diminution in the value of the property. The measure of damages is not the cost of reinstatement ... a cost which may greatly exceed the actual diminution in the value of the land. Thus if an old

building is pulled down, the plaintiff cannot recover the cost of putting up a new one, but merely the value of the old, unless his house was unique.

Finally, in *McGregor on Damages* (London: Sweet & Maxwell, 13th ed., 1972) in paras. 1059-61 there are these passages:

> It was for long said that the normal measure of damages was the amount of the diminution of the value of the land, a proposition based on what was generally considered to be the leading, but somewhat ancient, case of *Jones v. Gooday* (1841), 8 M & W 146; 151 ER 985 (Exch.) where the alternative measure of cost of replacement or repair, i.e. the sum which it would take to restore the land to its original state, was rejected. ... However, as was pointed out in the 12th edition of this work, not only is *Jones v. Gooday* the sole case where a plaintiff in possession and with full ownership was refused the cost to him of replacement or repair of the damage done but Alderson B's remark there suggests that the cost of replacement or repair may be an inappropriate measure only because it is out of all proportion to the injury to the plaintiff. That this is the true reason of the result in *Jones v. Gooday* is now supported by *Hollebone v. Midhurst and Fernhurst Builders Ltd.*, [1968] 1 Lloyd's Rep. 38 (QB), a decision which has been adopted by the Court of Appeal, in the context of a claim for breach of contract, in *Harbutt's "Plasticine" Ltd. v. Wayne Tank and Pump Co. Ltd.*, [1970] 1 QB 447 (CA). ... The difficulty in deciding between diminution in value and cost of reinstatement arises from the fact that the plaintiff may want his property in the same state as before the commission of the tort but the amount required to effect this may be substantially greater than the amount by which the value of the property has been diminished. The test which appears to be the appropriate one is the reasonableness of the plaintiff's desire to reinstate the property; this will be judged in part by the advantages to him of reinstatement in relation to the extra cost to the defendant in having to pay damages for reinstatement rather than damages calculated by the diminution in the value of the land.

I think that these passages which I have just read from *McGregor on Damages* correctly reflect the state of the law. The various decided cases on each side of the line to which my attention has been drawn, and to some of which I have referred in this judgment, show in my opinion merely the application in them of two basic principles of law to the facts of those various cases. These two basic principles are, first, that whenever damages are to be awarded against a tortfeasor or against a man who has broken a contract, then those damages shall be such as will, so far as money can, put the plaintiff in the same position as he would have been had the tort or breach of contract not occurred. But secondly, the damages to be awarded are to be reasonable, reasonable that is as between the plaintiff on the one hand and the defendant on the other. That these are the underlying principles is I think quite clear, for instance, from the judgments in *Jones v. Gooday* (1841), M & W 146; 151 ER 985 (Exch.) and in particular from the judgment of Alderson B. In *Moss v. Christchurch Rural District Council*, [1925] 2 KB 750 the plaintiff was the reversioner and could reasonably be and was put into the same position in so far as money was concerned as he would have been had the relevant tort not occurred by the award to him of the diminution in value of his property caused by the fire which was the subject matter of that case. That all these cases do really only reflect the application of the two basic principles to which I have referred to their special facts can, if I may say so, be demonstrated by adopting the judgment of O'Connor LJ in the Irish case of *Hepenstall v. Wicklow County Council*, [1921] 2 IR 165 (CA), from the bottom of p. 174 onwards. Again in *Hole & Son (Sayers Common) Ltd. v. Harrisons of Thurnscoe Ltd.*, [1973] 1 Lloyd's Rep. 345 (QB) the facts were that before the relevant accident the plaintiffs had intended to demolish the cottages which were extensively damaged by the lorry that ran into them. At no time had they intended to repair them but so soon as the statutory tenancy in one of the cottages had been determined it had been their intention to redevelop the site by building new and different premises upon it in place of the cottages. On the facts of that case clearly the damage suffered by the plaintiffs was only the cost of temporary repairs and any proved loss of rent. To have awarded them the cost of reinstating the premises would have put them in a better position than they would have been from a monetary point of view had the collision by the lorry never occurred, and would in any event clearly have been unreasonable as between the plaintiffs and the defendants.

On the other hand, in *Hollebone v. Midhurst and Fernhurst Builders Ltd.*, [1968] 1 Lloyd's Rep. 38 (QB) the plaintiff was the freehold owner of the damaged premises actually in occupation of them as his dwellinghouse, and that house was itself unique. The judge found as a fact that the diminution in value due to the relevant fire was just under £15,000. Nevertheless in order to repair the premises and so allow the plaintiff and his family to continue to occupy their own home would have cost nearly £19,000. On these facts the judge came to the conclusion that the proper application of the relevant principles to which I have referred required him to award the larger of the two sums. On the facts of that case such a sum was required to put that particular plaintiff in the same position, so far as money could, as he would have been had the tort not occurred and the award of that amount was not unreasonable in all the circumstances as between the two parties. The judge referred to the words of Viscount Dunedin in *Admiralty Commissioners v. S.S. Susquehanna (Owners) (The Susquehanna)*, [1926] AC 655 (HL (Eng.)) at p. 662, namely that no rigid rule or rules that apply in all cases can be laid down, but that one must consider all the relevant circumstances. He referred also to the proposition of Lord Sumner in *Admiralty Commissioners v. S.S. Chekiang (The Chekiang)*, [1926] AC 637 (HL (Eng.)) at p. 643:

> The measure of damages ought never to be governed by mere rules of practice, nor can such rules override the principles of law on this subject.

Finally, the judge quoted the observations of Denning LJ in *Phillips v. Ward*, [1956] 1 WLR 471 (CA) at p. 473:

> It all depends on the circumstances of the case. … The general rule is that the injured person is to be fairly compensated for the damage he has sustained, neither more nor less.

—and then concluded his judgment in this way, at p. 41:

> For the reasons which I have endeavoured to set out, in my judgment the cost of repair is the correct measure of damage in the circumstances of this case, as providing fair and proper restitution for the damage sustained.

Similarly, in *Harbutt's* case merely to have awarded the plaintiffs the diminution in value of their factory premises caused by fire would not have been reasonable in so far as they were concerned. Theirs were factory premises, they were in production and it was only reasonable that they should get back into production and into full production as soon as they could. It was found as a fact that they acted reasonably in rebuilding the premises as they did; they sought to obtain nothing effectively better or more valuable than they had before the fire. In these circumstances the court held that in order to put the plaintiffs into the same position as they would have been had the fire not occurred it was in truth necessary to award them the cost of rebuilding the damaged part of the factory, although this was rebuilt differently from what had been there before, and that such an award of damages was on the facts of that case reasonable as between plaintiff and defendant.

Whereas, as is stated in *Halsbury's Laws of England*, 4th ed., vol. 12 (1975), para. 1168:

> The prima facie measure of damages for all torts affecting land is the diminution in value to the plaintiff or, in the case of a plaintiff in possession with full ownership, the cost of reasonable reinstatement.

—may well be correct, this is not in my opinion really the statement of any legal principle, it is merely the factual result in the majority of cases of the application of the two basic rules to which I have referred to cases of torts affecting land. Given appropriate facts, there may well be exceptions.

What then is the result of applying the basic principles to the facts of the present case as I have found them, bearing in mind of course the assistance that I can and do obtain from the earlier cases, but remembering that they were decisions on their own particular facts?

First, it is irrelevant for my decision that the plaintiffs have been paid over £28,000 by their own insurers as the theoretical cost of reinstating their premises after the fire on October 26, 1970. They were no doubt entitled to this pursuant to the contract which they had made with their insurers. That they had made that contract and that it had that result is of no relevance in so far as the present claim is concerned. There is no doubt that in the present case at the time of the fire the plaintiffs were the freeholders in possession of their premises, with the minor exception of shop no. 19 which cannot affect the overall position. I have found as a fact that the plaintiffs' premises immediately before the fire occurred were not worth something of that order of £58,000 as deposed to by Mr. Dudley. As I have indicated, I think that the value of the plaintiff's premises at that time was £42,500. After the fire I think that the value of the plaintiffs' premises was £40,000 and that accordingly the diminution in value caused by the fire was £2,500. Are the plaintiffs only entitled to this figure or are they entitled to the notional cost of restoring the billiard hall to its pre-fire condition? I think that they are merely entitled to the former. To award the plaintiffs the cost of reinstatement, theoretical or not, if it is intended thereby to put them into the same position as they would have been had the fire not occurred, in so far as money can, and also be reasonable as between themselves and the defendants, one must at least be able to contemplate the possibility, if not the probability, that the plaintiffs were indeed minded to rebuild their billiard hall and shops. For the reasons which I have indicated, had the defendants gone to the plaintiffs the day after the fire and offered to reinstate the premises themselves at their own cost for the plaintiffs, the latter would, I think, have immediately told them to do no such thing. They would have said that it would only be a waste of money, because not only had the premises not been occupied for some years before but also they had no intention of occupying themselves or letting them for occupation to others: they were merely holding on to the premises in only one particular sense as an investment, that is to say an investment which might over the years show capital appreciation by way of increase in development value. That development value lay in the site itself, not in the buildings whole or destroyed which had previously been erected upon it. In these circumstances, it would in my opinion not only be totally unrealistic, but also unreasonable as between the plaintiffs and the defendants, to award the former the notional cost of reinstating the premises. To do so would be to put them in a far better position, from the point of view of money, than they were immediately before the fire occurred. Whereas in another case in the same field of law it might be irrelevant to consider any special purpose to which an owner of premises had intended to put them immediately prior to a fire which gutted them, nevertheless as between the owners of the premises and the persons responsible for the fire, it is both relevant and reasonable to consider of what nature were the premises alleged to have been damaged. The premises in the present case comprised a site the building on which it was intended in the fullness of time would be razed to the ground by developers' bulldozers for the purposes of redevelopment without any investment letting, in Mr. Dudley's meaning of the phrase, in the meantime.

Prima facie, therefore, the plaintiffs would have been entitled to the sum of £2,500 as the diminution in value of their property as damages for the injury to those premises by the fire. However, as I have already indicated, the evidence clearly is that it would have cost the plaintiffs at least this amount to clear the site for development purposes to the extent that it was cleared by the fire. In respect of this head of damage, therefore, I do not think that the plaintiffs are entitled to recover anything from the defendants. They are, however, entitled to recover the cost of the immediate necessary remedial and safety work namely £2,643.63. In addition they are entitled to the agreed figure of £74 for damage to trade fixtures and fittings, and to the further agreed sum of £650 in respect of the cost of the removal of debris.

PUNITIVE DAMAGES

Cassell & Co. Ltd. v. Broome
[1972] AC 1027 (HL Eng.))

LORD REID: ... My Lords, the appellants published a book "The Destruction of Convoy PQ17" which according to their advertisement on the dust jacket was the result of five intensive years of meticulous research by the author. It contained many statements about the conduct of Captain Broome who was the naval officer in command of the convoy. He sued the appellants and the author for damages for libel. After a trial which lasted for some 17 days a number of questions were left to the jury. They found that the words complained of were defamatory of Captain Broome, and were not true in substance and in fact. They were asked what compensatory damages they awarded, and they awarded £15,000. Then they were asked "Has the plaintiff proved that he is entitled to exemplary damages?" Their answer was Yes against both defendants. Next they were asked "What additional sum should be awarded him by way of exemplary damages?" Their answer was £25,000. So judgment was entered against both defendants for £40,000.

Others of your Lordships have dealt in detail with these statements and I do not think it necessary to say more than that in my opinion the jury were well entitled to find that they conveyed imputations of the utmost gravity against the character and conduct of Captain Broome as a naval officer. Indeed the appellants do not now seek to disturb the award of £15,000 as "compensatory damages." Their contention before your Lordships is twofold: first that the jury were not entitled to award any exemplary damages and secondly that the amount awarded under this head was much too great. As no objection was taken at the time to the form of the question there cannot now be any objection to the jury having been asked in this case to consider separately compensatory and exemplary damages.

The whole matter of exemplary damages was dealt with in this House in *Rookes v. Barnard*, [1964] AC 1129 (HL (Eng.)) in a speech by Lord Devlin with which all who sat with him, including myself, concurred. The Court of Appeal dealing with the present case held that if they applied the law as laid down in *Rookes v. Barnard* the appellants' appeal must fail and the jury's verdict must stand. They could have stopped there, but they chose to go on and attack the decision of this House as bad law. They were quite entitled to state their views and reasons for reaching that conclusion but very unfortunately Lord Denning MR, apparently with the concurrence of his two colleagues, went on to say, [1971] 2 QB 354 (CA) at p. 384:

> This case may, or may not, go on appeal to the House of Lords. I must say a word, however, for the guidance of judges who will be trying cases in the meantime. I think the difficulties presented by *Rookes v. Barnard* are so great that the judges should direct the juries in accordance with the law as it was understood before *Rookes v. Barnard*. Any attempt to follow *Rookes v. Barnard* is bound to lead to confusion.

It seems to me obvious that the Court of Appeal failed to understand Lord Devlin's speech, but whether they did or not I would have expected them to know that they had no power to give any such direction and to realise the impossible position in which they were seeking to put those judges in advising or directing them to disregard a decision of this House. That aberration of the Court of Appeal has made it necessary to re-examine the whole subject and incidentally has greatly increased the expense to which the parties to this case have been put.

The very full argument which we have had in this case has not caused me to change the views which I held when *Rookes v. Barnard* was decided or to disagree with any of Lord Devlin's main conclusions, but it has convinced me that I and my colleagues made a mistake in simply concurring with Lord Devlin's speech. With the passage of time I have come more and more firmly to the conclusion that it is never wise to have only one speech in this House dealing with an important question of law. My main reason is that experience has shown that those who have to apply the decision to other cases and still more those who wish to criticise it seem to find it difficult to avoid treating sentences and phrases in a single speech as if they were provisions in an Act of Parliament. They do not seem to realize that it is not the function of noble and learned Lords or indeed of any judges to frame definitions or to lay down hard and fast rules. It is their function to enunciate principles and much that they say is intended to be illustrative or explanatory and not to be definitive. When there are two or more speeches they must be read together and then it is generally much easier to see what are the principles involved and what are merely illustrations of it.

I am bound to say that, in reading the various criticisms of Lord Devlin's speech to which we have been referred, I have been very surprised at the failure of its critics to realise that it was intended to state principles and not to lay down rules. But I suppose that those of us who merely concurred with him ought to have foreseen that this might happen and to have taken steps to prevent it. So I shall try to repair my omission by stating now in a different way the principles which I, and I believe also Lord Devlin, had in mind. I do not think that he would have disagreed with any important part of what I am now about to say.

Damages for any tort are or ought to be fixed at a sum which will compensate the plaintiff, so far as money can do it, for all the injury which he has suffered. Where the injury is material and has been ascertained it is generally possible to assess damages with some precision. But that is not so where [the plaintiff] has been caused mental distress or when his reputation has been attacked—where to use the traditional phrase he has been held up to hatred, ridicule or contempt. Not only is it impossible to ascertain how far other people's minds have been affected, it is almost impossible to equate the damage to a sum of money. Any one person trying to fix a sum as compensation will probably find in his mind a wide bracket within which any sum could be regarded by him as not unreasonable—and different people will come to different conclusions. So in the end there will probably be a wide gap between the sum which on an objective view could be regarded as the least and the sum which could be regarded as the most to which the plaintiff is entitled as compensation.

It has long been recognised that in determining what sum within that bracket should be awarded, a jury, or other tribunal, is entitled to have regard to the conduct of the defendant. He may have behaved in a high-handed, malicious, insulting or oppressive manner in committing the tort or he or his counsel may at the trial have aggravated the injury by what they there said. That would justify going to the top of the bracket and awarding as damages the largest sum that could fairly be regarded as compensation.

Frequently in cases before *Rookes v. Barnard* when damages were increased in that way but were still within the limit of what could properly be regarded as compensation to the plaintiff, it was said that punitive, vindictive or exemplary damages were being awarded. As a mere matter of language that was true enough. The defendant was being punished or an example was being made of him by making him pay more than he would have to pay if his conduct had not been outrageous. But the damages although called punitive were still truly compensatory; the plaintiff was not being given more than his due.

On the other hand when we came to examine the old cases we found a number which could not be explained in that way. The sums awarded as damages were more—sometimes much more—than could on any view be justified as compensatory, and courts, perhaps without fully realising what they were doing, appeared to have permitted damages to be measured not by what the plaintiff was fairly entitled to receive but by what the defendant ought to be made to pay as punishment for his outrageous conduct. That meant that the plaintiff, by being given more than on any view could be justified as compensation, was being given a pure and undeserved windfall at the expense of the defendant, and that insofar as the defendant was being required to pay more than could possibly be regarded as compensation he was being subjected to pure punishment.

I thought and still think that that is highly anomalous. It is confusing the function of the civil law which is to compensate with the function of the criminal law which is to inflict deterrent and punitive penalties. Some objection has been taken to the use of the word "fine" to denote the amount by which punitive or exemplary damages exceed anything justly due to the plaintiff and is purely punitive.

Those of us who sat in *Rookes v. Barnard* thought that the loose and confused use of words like "punitive" and "exemplary" and the failure to recognise the difference between

damages which are compensatory and damages which go beyond that and are purely punitive had led to serious abuses, so we took what we thought was the best course open to us to
limit those abuses. Theoretically we might have held that as purely punitive damages had
never been sanctioned by any decision of this House (as to which I shall say more later)
there was no right under English law to award them. But that would have been going beyond the proper function of this House. There are many well established doctrines of the
law which have not been the subject of any decision by this House. We thought we had to
recognise that it had become an established custom in certain classes of case to permit
awards of damages which could not be justified as compensatory, and that that must remain
the law. But we thought and I still think it well within the province of this House to say that
that undesirable anomaly should not be permitted in any class of case where its use was not
covered by authority. In order to determine the classes of case in which this anomaly had
become established it was of little use to look merely at the words which had been used by
the judges because, as I have said, words like "punitive" and "exemplary" were often used
with regard to damages which were truly compensatory. We had to take a broad view of the
whole circumstances.

I must now deal with those parts of Lord Devlin's speech which have given rise to difficulties. He set out two categories of cases which in our opinion comprised all or virtually all
the reported cases in which it was clear that the court had approved of an award of a larger
sum of damages than could be justified as compensatory. Critics appear to have thought that
he was inventing something new. That was not my understanding. We were confronted with
an undesirable anomaly. We could not abolish it. We had to choose between confining it
strictly to classes of cases where it was firmly established, although that produced an illogical result, or permitting it to be extended so as to produce a logical result. In my view it is
better in such cases to be content with an illogical result than to allow any extension.

It will be seen that I do not agree with Lord Devlin's view that in certain classes of case
exemplary damages serve a useful purpose in vindicating the strength of the law. That view
did not form an essential step in his argument. Concurrence with the speech of a colleague
does not mean acceptance of every word which he has said. If it did there would be far fewer
concurrences than there are. So I did not regard disagreement on this side issue as preventing me from giving my concurrence.

I think that the objections to allowing juries to go beyond compensatory damages are
overwhelming. To allow pure punishment in this way contravenes almost every principle
which has been evolved for the protection of offenders. There is no definition of the offence
except that the conduct punished must be oppressive, high-handed, malicious, wanton or
its like—terms far too vague to be admitted to any criminal code worthy of the name. There
is no limit to the punishment except that it must not be unreasonable. The punishment is
not inflicted by a judge who has experience and at least tries not to be influenced by emo-
tion; it is inflicted by a jury without experience of law or punishment and often swayed by
considerations which every judge would put out of his mind. And there is no effective appeal against sentence. All that a reviewing court can do is quash the jury's decision if it
thinks the punishment awarded is more than any 12 reasonable men could award. The court
cannot substitute its own award. The punishment must then be decided by another jury and
if they too award heavy punishment the court is virtually powerless. It is no excuse to say
that we need not waste sympathy on people who behave outrageously. Are we wasting sym-

pathy on vicious criminals when we insist on proper legal safeguards for them? The right to give punitive damages in certain cases is so firmly embedded in our law that only Parliament can remove it. But I must say that I am surprised by the enthusiasm of Lord Devlin's critics in supporting this form of palm tree justice.

Lord Devlin's first category is set out in the passage where he said (at p. 1226):

> The first category is oppressive, arbitrary or unconstitutional action by the servants of the government. I should not extend this category—I say this with particular reference to the facts of this case—to oppressive action by private corporations or individuals.

This distinction has been attacked on two grounds: first, that it only includes Crown servants and excludes others like the police who exercise governmental functions but are not Crown servants and, secondly, that it is illogical since both the harm to the plaintiff and the blameworthiness of the defendant may be at least equally great where the offender is a powerful private individual. With regard to the first I think that the context shows that the category was never intended to be limited to Crown servants. The contrast is between "the government" and private individuals. Local government is as much government as national government, and the police and many other persons are exercising governmental functions. It was unnecessary in *Rookes v. Barnard* to define the exact limits of the category. I should certainly read it as extending to all those who by common law or statute are exercising functions of a governmental character.

The second criticism is I think misconceived. I freely admit that the distinction is illogical. The real reason for the distinction was, in my view, that the cases showed that it was firmly established with regard to servants of "the government" that damages could be awarded against them beyond any sum justified as compensation, whereas there was no case except one that was overruled where damages had been awarded against a private bully or oppressor to an amount that could not fairly be regarded as compensatory, giving to that word the meaning which I have already discussed. I thought that this House was therefore free to say that no more than that was to be awarded in future.

We are particularly concerned in the present case with the second category. With the benefit of hindsight I think I can say without disrespect to Lord Devlin that it is not happily phrased. But I think the meaning is clear enough. An ill disposed person could not infrequently deliberately commit a tort in contumelious disregard of another's rights in order to obtain an advantage which would outweigh any compensatory damages likely to be obtained by his victim. Such a case is within this category. But then it is said, suppose he commits the tort not for gain but simply out of malice why should he not also be punished. Again I freely admit there is no logical reason. The reason for excluding such a case from the category is simply that firmly established authority required us to accept this category however little we might like it, but did not require us to go farther. If logic is to be preferred to the desirability of cutting down the scope for punitive damages to the greatest extent that will not conflict with established authority then this category must be widened. But as I have already said I would, logic or no logic, refuse to extend the right to inflict exemplary damages to any class of case which is not already clearly covered by authority. On that basis I support this category.

In my opinion the conduct of both defendants in this case was such that the jury were clearly entitled, if properly directed, to hold that it brought them within the second category.

Again, I do not intend to cover ground already covered by my noble and learned friends. So I say no more than that the jury were fully entitled to hold that the appellants knew when they committed this tort that passages in this book were highly defamatory of Captain Broome and could not be justified as true and that it could properly be inferred that they thought that it would pay them to publish the book and risk the consequences of any action Captain Broome might take. It matters not whether they thought that they could escape with moderate damages or that the enormous expense involved in fighting an action of this kind would prevent Captain Broome from pressing his claim.

It was argued that to allow punitive damages in this case would hamper other publishers or limit their freedom to conduct their business because it can always be inferred that publishers publish any book because they expect a profit from it. But punitive damages could not be given unless it was proved that they knew that passages in the book were libellous and could not be justified or at least deliberately shut their eyes to the truth. I would hope that no publisher would publish in such circumstances. There is no question of curtailing the freedom of a reputable publisher.

The next passage in Lord Devlin's speech which has caused some difficulty is what has been called the "if, but only if" paragraph (at p. 1228). I see no difficulty in it but again I shall set out the substance of it in my own words. The difference between compensatory and punitive damages is that in assessing the former the jury or other tribunal must consider how much the plaintiff ought to receive whereas in assessing the latter they must consider how much the defendant ought to pay. It can only cause confusion if they consider both questions at the same time. The only practical way to proceed is first to look at the case from the point of view of compensating the plaintiff. He must not only be compensated for proved actual loss but also for any injury to his feelings and for having to suffer insults, indignities and the like. And where the defendant has behaved outrageously very full compensation may be proper for that. So the tribunal will fix in their minds what sum would be proper as compensatory damages. Then if it has been determined that the case is a proper one for punitive damages the tribunal must turn its attention to the defendant and ask itself whether the sum which it has already fixed as compensatory damages is or is not adequate to serve the second purpose of punishment or deterrence. If they think that that sum is adequate for the second purpose as well as for the first they must not add anything to it. It is sufficient both as compensatory and as punitive damages. But if they think that sum is insufficient as a punishment then they must add to it enough to bring it up to a sum sufficient as punishment. The one thing which they must not do is to fix sums as compensatory and as punitive damages and add them together. They must realize that the compensatory damages are always part of the total punishment.

It was argued that the jury were not properly directed by the trial judge on this matter. I agree with your Lordships that the argument must fail. A judge's direction to a jury is not to be considered *in vacuo*. It must be read in light of all the circumstances as they then existed and I cannot believe that the jury were left in any doubt as to how they must deal with this matter.

Next there are questions arising from the fact there were two defendants. When dealing with compensatory damages the law is quite clear. There was one tort of which both defendants were guilty. So one sum is fixed as compensation and judgment is given for that sum against both defendants leaving it to the plaintiff to sue whichever he chooses and then leaving it to the defendant who has paid to recover a contribution if he can from the other. But when we come to punitive damages the position is different. Although the tort was committed by both only one may have been guilty of the outrageous conduct or if two or more are so guilty they may be guilty in different degrees or owing to one being rich and another poor punishment proper for the former may be too heavy for the latter.

Unless we are to abandon all pretence of justice, means must be found to prevent more being recovered by way of punitive damages from the least guilty than he ought to pay. We cannot rely on his being able to recover some contribution from the other. Suppose printer, author and publisher of a libel suit are all sued. The printer will probably be guiltless of any outrageous conduct but the others may deserve punishment beyond compensatory damages. If there has to be one judgment against all three then it would be very wrong to allow any element of punitive damages at all to be included because very likely the printer would have to pay the whole and the others might not be worth suing for a contribution. The only logical way to deal with the matter would be first to have a judgment against all the defendants for the compensatory damages and then to have a separate judgment against each of the defendants for such additional sum as he should pay as punitive damages. I would agree that that is impracticable. The fact that is impracticable to do full justice appears to me to afford another illustration of how anomalous and indefensible is the whole doctrine of punitive damages. But as I have said before we must accept it and make the best we can of it.

So, in my opinion, the jury should be directed that, when they come to consider what if any addition is to be made to the compensatory damages by way of punitive damages, they must consider each defendant separately. If any one of the defendants does not deserve punishment or if the compensatory damages are in themselves sufficient punishment for any one of the defendants, then they must not make any addition to the compensatory damages. If each of the defendants deserves more punishment than is involved in payment of the compensatory damages then they must determine which deserves the least punishment and only add to the compensatory damages such additional sum as that defendant ought to pay by way of punishment. I do not pretend that that achieves full justice but it is the best we can do without separate awards against each defendant.

It was argued that here again there was misdirection of the jury because all that was not made plain to them. But again I agree with your Lordships that in the whole circumstances we ought not to hold the direction of the learned trial judge to be inadequate. Again the jury can have been in no doubt as to what was required of them.

There remains what is perhaps the most difficult question in this case—whether the additional award of £25,000 as punitive damages is so excessive that we can interfere. I think that it is much too large, but that is not the test. I would like to be able to hold that the court has more control over an award of punitive damages than it has over an award of compensatory damages. As regards the latter it is quite clear that a court can only interfere if satisfied that no 12 reasonable men could have awarded so large a sum and the reason for that is plain. The court has no power to substitute its own assessment for the verdict of a jury. If it interferes it can only send the matter back to another jury. So before it can interfere it must be well satisfied that no other jury would award so large a sum. I do not see how this House could arrogate to itself any wider power with regard to punitive damages. We could not deprive the plaintiff of his right to a new trial so we must adhere to the established test. Any diminution or abolition of the functions of a jury in libel cases can only come from Parliament. If this case brings nearer the day when Parliament does take action I for one shall not be sorry.

Whether or not we can interfere with this award is a matter which is not capable of much elaboration. In considering how far 12 reasonable men might go, acting as jurors commonly do act, one has to bear in mind how little guidance the court is entitled to give them. All that they can be told is that they must not award a sum which is unreasonable. In answer to questions whether anything more definite could properly be said neither counsel in this case was able to make any suggestion and I have none to offer. The evidence in this case is such that the jury could take an extremely unfavourable view of the conduct of both defendants. I do not say that they ought to have done so, but they were entitled to do so. And they must have done so. I find it impossible to say that no jury of reasonable men, inexperienced but doing their best with virtually no guidance, could reach the sum of £25,000. Or, to put it another way, I would feel no confidence that if the matter were submitted to another jury they must reach a substantially different result. So with considerable regret I must hold that it would be contrary to our existing law and practice if this House refused to uphold this verdict.

It is true that in this case the parties agreed that if the verdict for £25,000 were quashed they would leave it to this House to substitute another figure. But that agreement cannot justify us in doing otherwise than we would have done if the parties had stood on their legal rights. The obvious reason for that agreement was a common desire to avoid the enormous expense of a new trial. This is not the first occasion on which I have felt bound to express my concern about the undue prolixity and expense of libel actions. I would not blame any individuals. It may arise from the conduct of a trial before a jury being more expensive than a trial before a judge. If so that is an additional argument for taking these cases away from juries. Or it may be that it suits wealthy publishers of newspapers, books and periodicals that the cost of fighting a libel action is so great that none but a person with large financial backing can sue them effectively. Whatever be the reason the costs of this case have already reached a figure which many laymen would call scandalous. I think that those in a position to take effective action might take note.

Finally, I must say something about a strange misconception which appears in the judgments of the Court of Appeal in this case. Somehow they reached the conclusion that the decision of this House in *Rookes v. Barnard* was made per incuriam, was *ultra vires*, and had produced an unworkable position. It must be noted that in at least three earlier cases the Court of Appeal were able without difficulty or question to apply that decision (*McCarey v. Associated Newspapers Ltd. (No. 2)*, [1965] 2 QB 86 (CA), *Broadway Approvals Ltd. v. Odhams Press Ltd. (No. 2)*, [1965] 1 WLR 805 (CA) and *Fielding v. Variety Incorporated*, [1967] QB 841). What has caused their change of mind does not appear but I must deal with their new view. As regards the present position being unworkable, of course many difficulties remain in this branch of the law, but these difficulties are an inheritance from the confusion of the past. I have dealt fairly fully with the proper interpretation of *Rookes v. Barnard* and it appears to me that that decision removes many old difficulties, and creates few, if any, new ones.

I need not deal separately with the novel idea that a decision of this House can be *ultra vires* because that charge appears to be consequential on the charge that this House acted per incuriam in reaching its decision. It is perfectly legitimate to think and say that we were wrong but how anyone could say we acted per incuriam in face of the passage in which reference is made (at p. 1037) to *Ley v. Hamilton* (1935), 153 LT 384 (HL (Eng.)) I fail to understand.

This charge is really based on what appears to be to be a misreading by the Court of Appeal of two decisions of this House, *E. Hulton & Co v. Jones*, [1910] AC 20 (HL (Eng.)) and *Ley v. Hamilton*. *Hulton's* case has always been regarded as the leading authority for the proposition that a defamatory description intended to apply to a fictional person may in fact be a libel on a real person and therefore a subject for damages. I see nothing in the speeches in this House to indicate that punitive damages in the modern sense were being considered. It was said that there was an element of recklessness in the failure of the defendants to realise that there was a real Artemus Jones and that this justified a rather high sum of damages but I see nothing to indicate any view that the damages went beyond anything that could be justified as compensation and could only be justified as being punitive in the modern sense.

Ley v. Hamilton requires rather fuller consideration. But again I see nothing to indicate that this House held that the damages went beyond compensation or that there had been outrageous conduct justifying a punitive award which went beyond compensation. The majority in the Court of Appeal certainly held that the £5,000 damages awarded was punitive in the modern sense. They held that the real damage was trifling and the rest punishment. Greer LJ said ((1934), 151 LT 360 (CA) at p. 369) that if Mr. Hamilton had been prosecuted for criminal libel it was inconceivable that he would have been fined £5,000. Maugham LJ said (at p. 374) that the damages could not be described as a fair and reasonable compensation but were in the nature of a fine. In this House only Lord Atkin delivered a speech. I read it as intended to show that elements properly included in compensatory damages were far wider than the majority in the Court of Appeal had thought and that the whole of the £5,000 was in fact justified as being compensatory. He said (at p. 386):

> The fact is that the criticism with great respect seems based upon an incorrect view of the assessment of damages for defamation. They are not arrived at as the Lord Justice seems to assume by determining the "real" damage and adding to that a sum by way of vindictive or punitive damages. It is precisely because the "real" damage cannot be ascertained and established that the damages are at large. It is impossible to track the scandal, to know what quarters the poison may reach: it is impossible to weigh at all closely the compensation which will recompense a man or a woman for the insult offered or the pain of a false accusation. No doubt in newspaper libels juries take into account the vast circulations which are justly claimed in present times. The "punitive" element is not something which is or can be added to some known factor which is non-punitive. In particular it appears to present no analogy to punishment by fine for the criminal offence of publishing a defamatory libel.

By saying that compensation for insult or the pain of a false accusation cannot be weighed at all closely and that there was nothing here analogous to punishment by fine, he was to my mind making it as clear as words can make it that the whole of this £5,000 was truly compensatory in character. So I think that Lord Devlin was perfectly right in saying that there is no decision of this House which recognises punitive damages in the modern sense of something which goes beyond compensation. Where the Court of Appeal went wrong was in failing to realise that in the older cases damages were frequently referred to as exemplary or punitive although they were in reality compensatory.

On the whole matter I would dismiss this appeal.

NOTE

One of the limited situations in which the House of Lords in *Rookes v. Barnard* was prepared to concede the availability of punitive or exemplary damages in English law was that of "oppressive, arbitrary or unconstitutional actions by servants of the government." That particular exception raises questions about the extent to which punitive damages should be available in Canada for constitutional violations and, in particular, infringements of the *Canadian Charter of Rights and Freedoms*, part I of the *Constitution Act, 1982*, RSC 1985, app. II, no. 44. We return to that subject in chapter 12, "Charter Remedies."

Whiten v. Pilot Insurance Co.
[2002] 1 SCR 595

BINNIE J (McLachlin CJC, L'Heureux-Dubé, Gonthier, Major, and Arbour JJ concurring):

[1] This case raises once again the spectre of uncontrolled and uncontrollable awards of punitive damages in civil actions. The jury was clearly outraged by the high-handed tactics employed by the respondent, Pilot Insurance Company, following its unjustified refusal to pay the appellant's claim under a fire insurance policy (ultimately quantified at approximately $345,000). Pilot forced an eight-week trial on an allegation of arson that the jury obviously considered trumped up. It forced the appellant to put at risk her only remaining asset (the insurance claim) plus approximately $320,000 in legal costs that she did not have. The denial of the claim was designed to force her to make an unfair settlement for less than she was entitled to. The conduct was planned and deliberate and continued for over two years, while the financial situation of the appellant grew increasingly desperate. Evidently concluding that the arson defence from the outset was unsustainable and made in bad faith, the jury added an award of punitive damages of $1 million, in effect providing the appellant with a "windfall" that added something less than treble damages to her actual out-of-pocket loss. The respondent argues that the award of punitive damages is itself outrageous.

[2] The appellant, Daphne Whiten, bought her home in Haliburton County, Ontario, in 1985. Just after midnight on January 18, 1994, when she and her husband Keith were getting ready to go to bed, they discovered a fire in the addition to their house. They and their daughter, who had been upstairs, fled the house wearing only their nightclothes. It was minus 18 degrees Celsius. Mr. Whiten gave his slippers to his daughter to go for help and suffered serious frostbite to his feet for which he was hospitalized. He was thereafter confined to a wheelchair for a period of time. The fire totally destroyed the Whitens' home and its contents, including their few valuable antiques and many items of sentimental value and their three cats.

[3] The appellant was able to rent a small winterized cottage nearby for $650 per month. Pilot made a single $5,000 payment for living expenses and covered the rent for a couple of months or so, then cut off the rent without telling the family, and thereafter pursued a hostile and confrontational policy which the jury must have concluded was calculated to force the appellant (whose family was in very poor financial shape) to settle her claim at substantially less than its fair value. The allegation that the family had torched its own home was contradicted by the local fire chief, the respondent's own expert investigator, and its initial

expert, all of whom said there was no evidence whatsoever of arson. The respondent's position, based on wishful thinking, was wholly discredited at trial. Pilot's appellate counsel conceded here and in the Ontario Court of Appeal that there was no air of reality to the allegation of arson.

[4] A majority of the Ontario Court of Appeal allowed the appeal in part and reduced the punitive damage award to $100,000. In my view, on the exceptional facts of this case, there was no basis on which to interfere with the jury award. The award, though very high, was rational in the specific circumstances disclosed in the evidence and within the limits that a jury is allowed to operate. The appellant was faced with harsh and unreasoning opposition from an insurer whose policy she had purchased for peace of mind and protection in just such an emergency. The jury obviously concluded that people who sell peace of mind should not try to exploit a family in crisis. Pilot, as stated, required the appellant to spend $320,000 in legal costs to collect the $345,000 that was owed to her. The combined total of $665,000 at risk puts the punitive damage awards in perspective. An award of $1 million in punitive damages is certainly at the upper end of a sustainable award on these facts but not beyond it. I would allow the appeal and restore the jury award of $1 million punitive damages. ...

[5] The facts surrounding the fire itself have already been briefly mentioned. The origin of the fire was never discovered but everyone who investigated the fire in the six months after it occurred concluded that it was accidental. The first persons to investigate the fire were the fire chief and firefighters called to the scene. The fire chief thought, and he was eventually shown to be correct, that the fire was caused at a single point of origin by a malfunctioning kerosene heater in the porch of the addition. This was where the fire was first observed and also the area which had sustained the most fire damage. The firefighters saw no evidence of arson and therefore they did not request the Fire Marshal's office to investigate.

[6] Pilot retained an experienced independent insurance adjuster, Derek Francis, to investigate the loss. Francis inspected the site and interviewed the Whitens, who freely acknowledged that they had both been unemployed and had financial difficulties. Francis also interviewed the firefighters about the speed at which the fire spread, a key indicator of arson. Both the physical evidence and the Whitens' conduct satisfied Francis that the fire was accidental and on February 3, 1994 he reported to Pilot that "there is no suspicion of arson on behalf of the insureds or any members of their family." ...

[25] The Whitens lived in a small community. People were aware that their home was not being rebuilt because the insurer was alleging arson. The stigma persisted. Pilot continued to allege arson throughout the trial. Pilot now concedes that the evidence as a whole unequivocally demonstrates that the fire was accidental. ...

[36] Punitive damages are awarded against a defendant in exceptional cases for "malicious, oppressive and high-handed" misconduct that "offends the court's sense of decency": *Hill v. Church of Scientology of Toronto*, [1995] 2 SCR 1130 [126 DLR (4th) 129], at para. 196. The test thus limits the award to misconduct that represents a marked departure from ordinary standards of decent behaviour. Because their objective is to punish the defendant rather than compensate a plaintiff (whose just compensation will already have been assessed), punitive damages straddle the frontier between civil law (compensation) and criminal law (punishment).

[37] Punishment is a legitimate objective not only of the criminal law but of the civil law as well. Punitive damages serve a need that is not met either by the pure civil law or the pure

criminal law. In the present case, for example, no one other than the appellant could rationally be expected to invest legal costs of $320,000 in lengthy proceedings to establish that on this particular file the insurer had behaved abominably. Overcompensation of a plaintiff is given in exchange for this socially useful service.

[38] Nevertheless, the hybrid nature of punitive damages offends some jurists who insist that legal remedies should belong to one jurisprudential field or the other. That is one major aspect of the controversy, often framed in the words of Lord Wilberforce's comments, dissenting, in *Broome v. Cassell & Co.*, [1972] AC 1027 (HL), at p. 1114:

> It cannot lightly be taken for granted, even as a matter of theory, that the purpose of the law of tort is compensation, still less that it ought to be, an issue of large social import, or that there is something inappropriate or illogical or anomalous (a question-begging word) in including a punitive element in civil damages, or, conversely, that the criminal law, rather than the civil law, is in these cases the better instrument for conveying social disapproval, or for redressing a wrong to the social fabric, or that damages in any case can be broken down into the two separate elements. As a matter of practice English law has not committed itself to any of these theories: it may have been wiser than it knew.

[39] A second major aspect of the controversy surrounding punitive damages is related to the quantum. Substantial awards are occasionally assessed at figures seemingly plucked out of the air. The usual procedural protections for an individual faced with potential punishment in a criminal case are not available. Plaintiffs, it is said, recover punitive awards out of all proportion to just compensation. They are subjected, it is said, to "palm tree justice": *Cassell, supra,* at p. 1078. They are handed a financial windfall serendipitously just because, coincidentally with their claim, the court desires to punish the defendant and deter others from similar outrageous conduct. Defendants on the other hand say they suffer out of all proportion to the actual wrongs they have committed. Because the punishment is tailored to fit not only the "crime" but the financial circumstances of the defendant (i.e., to ensure that it is big enough to "sting"), defendants complain that they are being punished for who they are rather than for what they have done. The critics of punitive awards refer *in terrorem* to the United States experience where, for example, an Alabama jury awarded $4 million in punitive damages against a BMW dealership for failure to disclose a minor paint job to fix a cosmetic blemish on a new vehicle in *BMW of North America, Inc. v. Gore*, 517 US 559 (1996). In 1994, a jury in New Mexico awarded 81-year-old Stella Liebeck $160,000 in compensatory damages and $2.7 million in punitive damages against McDonald's Restaurants for burns resulting from a spilled cup of coffee, notwithstanding that she tried to open the cup while balancing it on her lap in the passenger seat of a car (*Liebeck v. McDonald's Restaurants, P.T.S. Inc.*, 1995 WL 360309 (NM Dist.)). Critics of punitive damages warn against an "Americanization" of our law that, if adopted, would bring the administration of justice in this country into disrepute.

[40] These are serious concerns, but in fact, the punitive damage controversies have little if anything to do with Americanization of our law. Jury awards of punitive damages in civil actions have a long and important history in Anglo-Canadian jurisprudence. They defy modern attempts at neat classification of remedies. The jury is invited to treat a plaintiff as a public interest enforcer as well as a private interest claimant. Almost 240 years ago, government agents broke into the premises of a Whig member of Parliament and pamphleteer, John Wilkes, to seize copies of a publication entitled *The North Briton, No. 45*, which the

Secretary of State regarded as libellous. Lord Chief Justice Pratt (later Lord Camden LC) on that occasion swept aside the government's defence. "If such a [search] power is truly invested in a Secretary of State," he held, "and he can delegate this power, it certainly may affect the person and property of every man in this kingdom, and is totally subversive of the liberty of the subject." As to punitive damages, he affirmed that:

> [A] jury have it in their power to give damages for more than the injury received. Damages are designed not only as a satisfaction to the injured person, but likewise as a punishment to the guilty, to deter from any such proceeding for the future, and as a proof of the detestation of the jury to the action itself.

(*Wilkes v. Wood* (1763), Lofft. 1, 98 ER 489 (KB), at pp. 498-99.)

[41] Long before the days of Lord Pratt CJ, the related idea of condemning a defendant to a multiple of what is required for compensation (in the present appeal, as stated, the punitive damages were roughly triple the award of compensatory damages) reached back to the Code of Hammurabi, Babylonian law, Hittite law (1400 BC), the Hindu Code of Manu (200 BC), ancient Greek codes, the Ptolemaic law in Egypt and the Hebrew Covenant Code of Mosaic law (see Exodus 22:1: "If a man shall steal an ox, or a sheep, and kill it, or sell it; he shall restore five oxen for an ox, and four sheep for a sheep"). Roman law also included provisions for multiple damages. Admittedly, in these early systems, criminal law and civil law were not always clearly differentiated. The United States Supreme Court in *BMW*, *supra*, referred at p. 581 to "65 different enactments [in English statutes] during the period between 1275 and 1753 [that] provided for double, treble, or quadruple damages."

[42] Even in terms of quantum, the use of punitive damages in the eighteenth century was aggressive. In *Huckle v. Money* (1763), 2 Wils. KB 205, 95 ER 768 (KB), the journeyman Huckle (who had actually printed the pamphlet *The North Briton, No. 45* at issue in *Wilkes*, *supra*) won a cause of action for trespass, assault and false imprisonment and received 300 pounds in damages from the jury despite the comfortable and short six-hour duration of his confinement. The government's motion for a new trial on the basis that the award was "outrageous" was denied, even though actual damages totalled only 20 pounds (i.e., a multiplier of 15) (p. 768 ER). The Lord Chief Justice, in introducing the expression "exemplary damages," thought there was no precedent for judges "intermeddling" with damages awarded by juries.

[43] The three objectives identified by Lord Chief Justice Pratt, in *Wilkes*, *supra*—punishment, deterrence and denunciation ("proof of the detestation")—are with us still, even though some scholarly critics have argued that these rationales "have very particular and divergent implications" that occasionally wind up undermining each other: B. Chapman and M. Trebilcock, "Punitive Damages: Divergence in Search of a Rationale" (1989), 40 *Ala. L Rev.* 741, at p. 744. No doubt, as a matter of language, the word "punishment" includes both retribution and denunciation, and the three objectives should perhaps better be referred to as retribution, deterrence and denunciation.

[44] The notion of private enforcers (or "private Attorneys General"), particularly where they act for personal gain, is worrisome unless strictly controlled. Thus, while the availability of punitive damages in Canada was affirmed early on by this Court in *Collette v. Lasnier* (1886), 13 SCR 563, a patent case, they were not widely awarded until the 1970s. Since then the awards have multiplied in number and escalated in amount. A report on punitive damages by the Ontario Law Reform Commission, issued in 1991, which examined research

begun in 1989, predicted limited and principled development in the law of punitive damages in Canada: Ontario Law Reform Commission, *Report on Exemplary Damages*, June 1, 1991, at pp. 93 and 98. By 1998, the report's research director, Dean Bruce Feldthusen, conceded that the law was "certainly developing quite differently in Canada than one would have predicted only a short time ago" and that "many of the doctrinal pillars on which the Report's predictions of limited and principled development in the law governing punitive damages were based have since cracked or collapsed": B. Feldthusen, "Punitive Damages: Hard Choices and High Stakes," [1998] *NZ L Rev.* 741, at p. 742. Contrary to expectations, the awards were much larger, more frequent, appeared to rely more often on the defendant's wealth in support, and included more high profile jury awards. The kinds of causes of action had expanded; punitive damages were the "norm" and had "proliferated" in actions in sexual battery, were now "clearly available" for breach of fiduciary duty, and "persisted" in contract actions. Prior criminal convictions, he concluded, no longer automatically barred punitive awards. He added: "Perhaps most significantly, the courts seem to have accepted general deterrence, not retributive punishment, as the dominant purpose behind punitive damage awards in a number of important decisions" (p. 742).

[45] This Court more recently affirmed a punitive damage award of $800,000 in *Hill*, *supra*. On that occasion some guidelines were set out to keep this remedy within reasonable limits. The Court on this occasion has an opportunity to clarify further the rules governing whether an award of punitive damages ought to be made and if so, the assessment of a quantum that is fair to all parties. ...

[66] For present purposes, I draw the following assistance from the experience in other common law jurisdictions which I believe is consistent with Canadian practice and precedent.

[67] First, the attempt to limit punitive damages by "categories" does not work and was rightly rejected in Canada in *Vorvis v. Insurance Corp. of British Columbia*, [1989] 1 SCR 1085, at pp. 1104-6. The control mechanism lies not in restricting the category of case but in rationally determining circumstances that warrant the addition of punishment to compensation in a civil action. It is in the nature of the remedy that punitive damages will largely be restricted to intentional torts, as in *Hill*, *supra*, or breach of fiduciary duty as in *M. (K.) v. M. (H.)*, [1992] 3 SCR 6 [96 DLR (4th) 289], but *Vorvis* itself affirmed the availability of punitive damages in the exceptional case in contract. In *Denison v. Fawcett*, [1958] OR 312 [12 DLR (2d) 537], the Ontario Court of Appeal asserted in *obiter* that on proper facts punitive damages would be available in negligence and nuisance as well. In *Robitaille v. Vancouver Hockey Club Ltd.* (1981), 124 DLR (3d) 228, the British Columbia Court of Appeal awarded punitive damages in a negligence case on the principle that they ought to be available whenever "the conduct of the defendant [was] such as to merit condemnation by the [c]ourt" (p. 250). This broader approach seems to be in line with most common law jurisdictions apart from England.

[68] Second, there is a substantial consensus that coincides with Lord Pratt CJ's view in 1763 that the general objectives of punitive damages are punishment (in the sense of retribution), deterrence of the wrongdoer and others, and denunciation (or, as Cory J put it in *Hill*, *supra*, at para. 196, they are "the means by which the jury or judge expresses its outrage at the egregious conduct").

[69] Third, there is recognition that the primary vehicle of punishment is the criminal law (and regulatory offences) and that punitive damages should be resorted to only in ex-

ceptional cases and with restraint. Where punishment has actually been imposed by a criminal court for an offence arising out of substantially the same facts, some jurisdictions, such as Australia and New Zealand, bar punitive damages in certain contexts ... but the dominant approach ... is to treat it as another factor, albeit a factor of potentially great importance .... The Ontario Law Reform Commission ... recommended that the "court should be entitled to consider the fact and adequacy of any prior penalty imposed in any criminal or other similar proceeding brought against the defendant." ...

[70] Fourth, the incantation of the time-honoured pejoratives ("high-handed," "oppressive," "vindictive," etc.) provides insufficient guidance (or discipline) to the judge or jury setting the amount. Lord Diplock in *Cassell, supra*, at p. 1129, called these the "whole gamut of dyslogistic judicial epithets." A more principled and less exhortatory approach is desirable.

[71] Fifth, all jurisdictions seek to promote rationality. In directing itself to the punitive damages, the court should relate the facts of the particular case to the underlying purposes of punitive damages and ask itself how, in particular, an award would further one or other of the objectives of the law, and what is the lowest award that would serve the purpose, i.e., because any higher award would be irrational.

[72] Sixth, it is rational to use punitive damages to relieve a wrongdoer of its profit where compensatory damages would amount to nothing more than a licence fee to earn greater profits through outrageous disregard of the legal or equitable rights of others.

[73] Seventh, none of the common law jurisdictions has adopted (except by statute) a formulaic approach, as advocated by the intervener the Insurance Council of Canada in this appeal, such as a fixed cap or fixed ratio between compensatory and punitive damages. The proper focus is not on the plaintiff's loss but on the defendant's misconduct. A mechanical or formulaic approach does not allow sufficiently for the many variables that ought to be taken into account in arriving at a just award.

[74] Eighth, the governing rule for quantum is proportionality. The overall award, that is to say compensatory damages plus punitive damages plus any other punishment related to the same misconduct, should be rationally related to the objectives for which the punitive damages are awarded (retribution, deterrence and denunciation). Thus there is broad support for the "if, but only if" test formulated, as mentioned, in *Rookes, supra*, and affirmed here in *Hill, supra*.

[75] Ninth, it has become evident that juries can and should receive more guidance and help from the judges in terms of their mandate. They should be told in some detail about the function of punitive damages and the factors that govern both the award and the assessment of a proper amount. Juries should not be thrown into their assignment without any help, then afterwards be criticized for the result.

[76] Tenth, and finally, there is substantial consensus (even the United States is moving in this direction) that punitive damages are not at large (as pointed out by Cory J in *Hill, supra*) and that an appellate court is entitled to intervene if the award exceeds the outer boundaries of a rational and measured response to the facts of the case.

[77] With the benefit of these general principles, I now turn to the specific issues raised by this appeal.

(1) Punitive Damages for Breach of Contract

[78] This, as noted, is a breach of contract case. In *Vorvis, supra*, this Court held that punitive damages are recoverable in such cases provided the defendant's conduct said to give rise to the claim is itself "an actionable wrong" (p. 1106). The scope to be given this expression is the threshold question in this case, i.e., is a breach of an insurer's duty to act in good faith an actionable wrong independent of the loss claim under the fire insurance policy? *Vorvis* itself was a case about the employer's breach of an employment contract. This is how McIntyre J framed the rule at pp. 1105-6:

> When then can punitive damages be awarded? It must never be forgotten that when awarded by a judge or a jury, a punishment is imposed upon a person by a Court by the operation of the judicial process. What is it that is punished? It surely cannot be merely conduct of which the Court disapproves, however strongly the judge may feel. Punishment may not be imposed in a civilized community without a justification in law. *The only basis for the imposition of such punishment must be a finding of the commission of an actionable wrong which caused the injury complained of by the plaintiff.* [Emphasis added.]

This view, McIntyre J said (at p. 1106), "has found approval in the *Restatement on the Law of Contracts 2d* in the United States," which reads as follows:

> Punitive damages are not recoverable for a breach of contract unless the conduct constituting the breach is also a *tort* for which punitive damages are recoverable. [Emphasis added.]

Applying these principles in *Vorvis*, McIntyre J stated, at p. 1109:

> Each party had the right to terminate the contract without the consent of the other, and where the employment contract was terminated by the employer, the appellant was entitled to reasonable notice of such termination or payment of salary and benefits for the period of reasonable notice. The termination of the contract on this basis by the employer is not *a wrong in law* and, where the reasonable notice is given or payment in lieu thereof is made, the plaintiff—subject to a consideration of aggravated damages which have been allowed in some cases but which were denied in this case—is entitled to no further remedy. … [Emphasis added.]

Wilson J, with whom L'Heureux-Dubé J concurred, dissented. She did not agree "that punitive damages can only be awarded when the misconduct is in itself an 'actionable wrong.'" She stated, at p. 1130:

> In my view, the correct approach is to assess the conduct in the context of all the circumstances and determine whether it is deserving of punishment because of its shockingly harsh, vindictive, reprehensible or malicious nature. Undoubtedly some conduct found to be deserving of punishment will constitute an actionable wrong but other conduct might not.

[79] In the case at bar, Pilot acknowledges that an insurer is under a duty of good faith and fair dealing. Pilot says that this is a contractual duty. *Vorvis*, it says, requires a tort. However, in my view, a breach of the contractual duty of good faith is independent of and in addition to the breach of contractual duty to pay the loss. It constitutes an "actionable wrong" within the *Vorvis* rule, which does not require an independent tort. I say this for several reasons.

[80] First, McIntyre J chose to use the expression "actionable wrong" instead of "tort" even though he had just reproduced an extract from the *Restatement* which does use the word tort. It cannot be an accident that McIntyre J chose to employ a much broader expression when formulating the Canadian test.

[81] Second, in *Royal Bank of Canada v. W. Got & Associates Electric Ltd.*, [1999] 3 SCR 408 [178 DLR (4th) 385], at para. 26, this Court, referring to McIntyre J's holding in *Vorvis*, said "the circumstances that would justify punitive damages for breach of contract *in the absence* of actions also constituting *a tort* are rare" (emphasis added). Rare they may be, but the clear message is that such cases do exist. The Court has thus confirmed that punitive damages can be awarded in the absence of an accompanying tort.

[82] Third, the requirement of an independent tort would unnecessarily complicate the pleadings, without in most cases adding anything of substance. *Central Trust Co. v. Rafuse*, [1986] 2 SCR 147 [31 DLR (4th) 481], held that a common law duty of care sufficient to found an action in tort can arise within a contractual relationship, and in that case proceeded with the analysis in tort instead of contract to deprive an allegedly negligent solicitor of the benefit of a limitation defence. To require a plaintiff to formulate a tort in a case such as the present is pure formalism. An independent actionable wrong is required, but it can be found in breach of a distinct and separate contractual provision or other duty such as a fiduciary obligation.

[83] I should add that insurance companies have also asserted claims for punitive damages against their insured for breach of the mutual "good faith" obligation in insurance contracts. ...

[91] The appellant also pleaded that Pilot's manner of dealing with her claim had created "hardship" of which "the Defendants, through their agents and employees always had direct and ongoing knowledge" (para. 8). In para. 14 she pleaded that "as a result of the actions of the Defendants, the Plaintiff has suffered and continues to suffer great emotional stress" (although there was no claim for aggravated damages). The respondent specifically denied acting in bad faith (Statement of Defence and Counterclaim of the Defendant, at para. 6). The statement of claim was somewhat deficient in failing to relate the plea for punitive damages to the precise facts said to give rise to the outrage, but Pilot was content to go to trial on this pleading and I do not think it should be heard to complain about it at this late date.

[92] As to the respondent's objection that the pleading does not allege separate and distinct damages flowing from the independent actionable wrong, the respondent's argument overlooks the fact that punitive damages are directed to the quality of the defendant's conduct, not the quantity (if any) of the plaintiff's loss. As Cory J observed in *Hill, supra*, at para. 196: "Punitive damages bear no relation to what the plaintiff should receive by way of compensation. Their aim is not to compensate the plaintiff, but rather to punish the defendant. It is the means by which the jury or judge expresses its outrage at the egregious conduct of the defendant." In any event, there is a good deal of evidence of emotional stress and financial cost over and above the loss that would have been incurred had the claim been settled in good faith within a reasonable time. ...

(3) Was the Jury Charge Adequate?

[93] The respondent argues that the trial judge did not give the jury adequate guidance on how to assess punitive damages. There is considerable merit in this submission. The judge's charge on this point was skeletal. It is my view, for the reasons already discussed, that the charge on punitive damages should not be given almost as an afterthought but should be understood as an important source of control and discipline. The jurors should not be left to guess what their role and function is.

[94] To this end, not only should the pleadings of punitive damages be more rigorous in the future than in the past …, but it would be helpful if the trial judge's charge to the jury included words to convey an understanding of the following points, even at the risk of some repetition for emphasis. (1) Punitive damages are very much the exception rather than the rule, (2) imposed only if there has been high-handed, malicious, arbitrary or highly reprehensible misconduct that departs to a marked degree from ordinary standards of decent behaviour. (3) Where they are awarded, punitive damages should be assessed in an amount reasonably proportionate to such factors as the harm caused, the degree of the misconduct, the relative vulnerability of the plaintiff and any advantage or profit gained by the defendant, (4) having regard to any other fines or penalties suffered by the defendant for the misconduct in question. (5) Punitive damages are generally given only where the misconduct would otherwise be unpunished or where other penalties are or are likely to be inadequate to achieve the objectives of retribution, deterrence and denunciation. (6) Their purpose is not to compensate the plaintiff, but (7) to give a defendant his or her just desert (retribution), to deter the defendant and others from similar misconduct in the future (deterrence), and to mark the community's collective condemnation (denunciation) of what has happened. (8) Punitive damages are awarded only where compensatory damages, which to some extent are punitive, are insufficient to accomplish these objectives, and (9) they are given in an amount that is no greater than necessary to rationally accomplish their purpose. (10) While normally the state would be the recipient of any fine or penalty for misconduct, the plaintiff will keep punitive damages as a "windfall" in addition to compensatory damages. (11) Judges and juries in our system have usually found that moderate awards of punitive damages, which inevitably carry a stigma in the broader community, are generally sufficient.

[95] These particular expressions are not, of course, obligatory. What is essential in a particular case will be a function of its particular circumstances, the need to emphasize the nature, scope and exceptional nature of the remedy, and fairness to both sides.

[96] The trial judge should keep in mind that the standard of appellate review applicable to punitive damages ultimately awarded, is that a reasonable jury, properly instructed, could have concluded that an award in that amount, and no less, was rationally required to punish the defendant's misconduct, as discussed below.

[97] If counsel can agree on a "bracket" or "range" of an appropriate award, the trial judge should convey these figures to the jury, but at the present time specific figures should not be mentioned in the absence of such agreement (*Hill, supra, per* Cory J, at paras. 162-63. This prohibition may have to be re-examined in future, based on further experience). Counsel should also consider the desirability of asking the trial judge to advise the jury of awards of punitive damages made in comparable circumstances that have been sustained on appeal.

[98] The foregoing suggestions are put forward in an effort to be helpful rather than dogmatic. They grow out of the observation in *Hill* that punitive damages are not "at large"

(para. 197). Unless punitive damages can be approached rationally they ought not to be awarded at all. To the extent these suggestions are considered useful, they will obviously have to be both modified and elaborated to assist the jury on the facts of a particular case. The point, simply, is that jurors should not be left in any doubt about what they are to do and how they are to go about it.

[99] It is evident that I am suggesting a more ample charge on the issue of punitive damages than was given in this case. Finlayson JA said that he was "not entirely happy with the trial judge's charge to the jury on the issue of punitive damages" (p. 661), and Laskin JA agreed that "[t]he trial judge might have given the jury more help than he did" (p. 656). However, both Finlayson and Laskin JJA agreed that the jury charge covered the essentials, however lightly. This conclusion is reinforced by the fact that no objection was made by either counsel. With some hesitation, I agree with the Court of Appeal, unanimous on this point, that in the circumstances this ground of appeal should be rejected. ...

(4) Reviewing the Jury Award

(a) Whether the Award of Punitive Damages in This Case Was a Rational Response to the Respondent's Misconduct

[100] The applicable standard of review for "rationality" was articulated by Cory J in *Hill, supra*, at para. 197:

> Unlike compensatory damages, punitive damages are not at large. Consequently, courts have a much greater scope and discretion on appeal. The appellate review should be based upon the court's estimation as to whether the punitive damages serve a rational purpose. In other words, was the misconduct of the defendant so outrageous that punitive damages were rationally required to act as deterrence?

[101] The "rationality" test applies both to the question of whether an award of punitive damages should be made at all, as well as to the question of its quantum.

[102] The respondent claims that an insurer is entirely within its rights to thoroughly investigate a claim and exercise caution in evaluating the circumstances. It is not required to accept the initial views of its investigators. It is perfectly entitled to pursue further inquiries. I agree with these points. The problem here is that Pilot embarked on a "train of thought" as early as February 25, 1994 ... that led to the arson trial, with nothing to go on except the fact that its policyholder had money problems.

[103] The "train of thought" mentioned in the letter to Pilot from Derek Francis kept going long after the requirements of due diligence or prudent practice had been exhausted. There is a difference between due diligence and wilful tunnel vision. The jury obviously considered this case to be an outrageous example of the latter. In my view, an award of punitive damages (leaving aside the issue of quantum for the moment) was a rational response on the jury's part to the evidence. It was not an inevitable or unavoidable response, but it was a rational response to what the jury had seen and heard. The jury was obviously incensed at the idea that the respondent would get away with paying no more than it ought to have paid after its initial investigation in 1994 (plus costs). It obviously felt that something more was required to demonstrate to Pilot that its bad faith dealing with this loss claim was not a wise or profitable course of action. The award answered a perceived need for retribution, denunciation and deterrence.

[104] The intervener, the Insurance Council of Canada, argues that the award of punitive damages will over-deter insurers from reviewing claims with due diligence, thus lead to the payment of unmeritorious claims, and in the end drive up insurance premiums. This would only be true if the respondent's treatment of the appellant is not an isolated case but is widespread in the industry. If, as I prefer to believe, insurers generally take seriously their duty to act in good faith, it will only be rogue insurers or rogue files that will incur such a financial penalty, and the extra economic cost inflicted by punitive damages will either cause the delinquents to mend their ways or, ultimately, move them on to lines of work that do not call for a good faith standard of behaviour.

[105] The Ontario Court of Appeal was unanimous that punitive damages in some amount were justified and I agree with that conclusion. This was an exceptional case that justified an exceptional remedy. The respondent's cross-appeal will therefore be dismissed. ...

(ii) Proportionate to the Degree of Vulnerability of the Plaintiff

[115] I add two cautionary notes on the issue of vulnerability [of the plaintiff]. First, this factor militates *against* the award of punitive damages in most commercial situations, particularly where the cause of action is contractual and the problem for the Court is to sort out the bargain the parties have made. Most participants enter the marketplace knowing it is fuelled by the aggressive pursuit of self-interest. Here, on the other hand, we are dealing with a homeowner's "peace of mind" contract.

[116] Second, it must be kept in mind that punitive damages are not compensatory. Thus the appellant's pleading of emotional distress in this case is only relevant insofar as it helps to assess the oppressive character of the respondent's conduct. Aggravated damages are the proper vehicle to take into account the additional harm caused to the plaintiff's feelings by reprehensible or outrageous conduct on the part of the defendant. Otherwise there is a danger of "double recovery" for the plaintiff's emotional stress, once under the heading of compensation and secondly under the heading of punishment. ...

(6) Conclusion on "Rationality"

[128] I would not have awarded $1 million in punitive damages in this case but in my judgment the award is within the rational limits within which a jury must be allowed to operate. The award was not so disproportionate as to exceed the bounds of rationality. It did not overshoot its purpose. I have already outlined the reasons why I believe this to be the case.

[129] The jury followed the "if but only if" model, i.e., punitive damages should be awarded "if but only if" the compensatory award is insufficient. The form and order of the questions put to the jury required them first of all to deal with compensation for the loss of the plaintiff's house (replacement or cash value), its contents, and any increase in her living and moving expenses. Only after those matters had been dealt with was the jury instructed to turn their minds to a final question on punitive damages. They were clearly aware that compensatory damages might well be sufficient punishment to avoid a repetition of the offence and a deterrent to others. In this case, the jury obviously concluded that the compensatory damages ($345,000) were not sufficient for those purposes. It was no more than the respondent had contractually obligated itself to pay under the insurance policy. In this case,

the power imbalance was highly relevant. Pilot holds itself out to the public as a sure guide to a "safe harbour." In its advertising material it refers to itself as "Your Pilot" and makes such statements as:

> At Pilot Insurance Company, guiding people like you into safe harbours has been our mission for nearly 75 years.

Insurance contracts, as Pilot's self-description shows, are sold by the insurance industry and purchased by members of the public for peace of mind. The more devastating the loss, the more the insured may be at the financial mercy of the insurer, and the more difficult it may be to challenge a wrongful refusal to pay the claim. Deterrence is required. The obligation of good faith dealing means that the appellant's peace of mind should have been Pilot's objective, and her vulnerability ought not to have been aggravated as a negotiating tactic. It is this relationship of reliance and vulnerability that was outrageously exploited by Pilot in this case. The jury, it appears, decided a powerful message of retribution, deterrence and denunciation had to be sent to the respondent and they sent it.

[130] The respondent points out that there is no evidence this case represents a deliberate corporate strategy as opposed to an isolated, mishandled file that ran amok. This is true, but it is also true that Pilot declined to call evidence to explain why this file ran amok, and what steps, if any, have been taken to prevent a recurrence.

[131] The respondent also argues that at the end of the day, it did not profit financially from its misbehaviour. This may also be true, but if so, that result was not for want of trying. The respondent clearly hoped to starve the appellant into a cheap settlement. ... That it failed to do so is due in no small part to appellant's counsel who took a hotly contested claim into an eight-week jury trial on behalf of a client who was effectively without resources of her own; and who obviously could have been starved into submission but for his firm's intervention on her behalf.

[132] While, as stated, I do not consider the "ratio" test to be an appropriate indicator of rationality, the ratio of punitive damages to compensatory damages in the present case would be either a multiple of three (if only the insurance claim of $345,000 is considered) or a multiple of less than two (if the claim plus the award of solicitor-client costs is thought to be the total compensation). Either way, the ratio is well within what has been considered "rational" in decided cases.

[133] The majority opinion of the Ontario Court of Appeal recognized that punitive damages are not "at large" and appellate courts have "much greater scope and discretion on appeal" than they do in the case of general damages (*Hill, supra*, at para. 197). If the court considers the award or its quantum to be irrational, it is its duty to interfere.

[134] This was the view taken by the majority judgment of Finlayson JA. The appellant complains that Finlayson JA applied a standard of "simply too high" (p. 61). It is true that he thought the award was too high, but that observation must be understood in light of other comments made in the course of his reasons. Finlayson JA concluded there was "no justification for such a radical departure from precedent" (pp. 661-62), which revealed awards in the range of $7,500 to $15,000. In his view, an appropriate figure for quantum requires a "balancing of factors such as those enumerated by Blackmun J" (p. 667) in *Pacific Mutual Life Insurance Co.* [*Pacific Mutual Life Insurance Co. v. Haslip*, 499 US 1 (1991)] ... . Finlayson JA looked at "the degree of reprehensibility of the defendant's conduct" (p. 666) and

concluded that "[t]his case does not demonstrate that there was such insidious, pernicious and persistent malice as would justify an award of this magnitude" (p. 666).

[135] With respect to precedent, it must be remembered that the respondent's trial counsel objected to any range or "bracket" of appropriate figures being given to the jury. Had the jury been given the information, it may have influenced their views. The respondent itself appears to have been unimpressed by the size of prior awards of punitive damages. In its factum, commenting on Crabbe's letter of June 9, 1994, counsel states, "However, it should also be noted that Mr. Crabbe was clearly attempting to allay Pilot's concern about the Whiten's bad faith claim at a time when punitive damage awards against insurers were in the range of $7,500 to $15,000." Pilot's concern may have been easy to allay when the expected exposure to punitive damages was only $15,000.

[136] The respondent objects that, prior to this judgment, the highest previous award in an insurer bad faith case was $50,000. However, prior to the $800,000 award of punitive damages upheld in *Hill, supra*, the highest award in punitive damages in a libel case in Canada was $50,000. ... One of the strengths of the jury system is that it keeps the law in touch with evolving realities, including financial realities. ...

[140] Having accepted with some hesitation the adequacy of the trial judge's instructions to the jury, and there being no convincing demonstration that the jury's subsequent imposition and assessment of punitive damages were irrational, I would affirm the award of punitive damages. ...

[141] I would allow the appeal and restore the jury award of $1 million in punitive damages, with costs in this Court and in the Court of Appeal on a party-and-party basis.

[142] The respondent's cross-appeal against the award of any punitive damages is dismissed with costs to the appellant, also on a party-and-party basis.

LE BEL J (dissenting):

[147] The purpose of this part of our legal system remains to make good the loss suffered, no less, no more. ...

[148] The award of punitive damages in discussion here leads us far away from that principle. It tends to turn tort law upside down. It transmogrifies what should have remained an incident of a contracts case into the central issue of the dispute. ... [T]he main purpose of the action becomes the search for punishment, not compensation.

NOTES

1. In *Sylvan Lake Golf & Tennis Club Ltd. v. Performance Industries Ltd.*, [2002] 1 SCR 678, decided concurrently with the *Whiten* case, the court unanimously upheld the setting aside of an award of $200,000 punitive damages for fraud, on the ground that the award would serve no rational purpose. Binnie J said, at para. 87, "fraud is generally reprehensible, but only in exceptional cases does it attract punitive damages."

2. The economic concept of "efficient breach," discussed earlier, was approved in *Bank of America Canada v. Mutual Trust Co.*, [2002] 2 SCR 601, decided two months after *Whiten*.

3. See Berryman, "The Case for Restitutionary Damages Over Punitive Damages: Teaching the Wrongdoer That Tort Does Not Pay" (1994), 73 *Canadian Bar Review* 320.

4. Punitive damages were refused by the Supreme Court of Canada in *Fidler v. Sun Life Assurance Co. of Canada*, [2006] 2 SCR 3, and in *Honda Canada Inc. v. Keays*, [2008] 2 SCR 362, excerpted in chapter 3.

COMPENSATION FOR LOSS OF MONEY

Damages and Inflation

Leitch Transport Ltd. v. Neonex International Ltd.
(1979), 27 OR (2d) 363 (CA)

BY THE COURT: ...

Allowance for Inflation

The trial Judge allowed $1,149,398 to compensate the plaintiff for the fact that the damages under the first five heads of damage (the trial Judge did not allow anything under the fourth heading) were being assessed as of the date of the breach, but judgment was not being given until 1978. In the meantime inflation had eroded the value of the Canadian dollar and to provide for payment to the plaintiff in 1978 dollars would not compensate it for its actual loss. He therefore awarded an inflationary allowance for four years at 3½% per annum, not compounded, upon the sum total of the five (*sic*) heads of damage, in the amount of $1,149,398.

Mr. Carthy took the position on the appeal that nothing should be allowed under this heading. Mr. Thomson has cross-appealed and submitted that the allowance should have been calculated at the rate of 7½% per annum for part of the seven-year period since the breach. This would be accomplished, in his submission, by allowing 4% per annum for a period of four years, and 7½% per annum for a further three years, compounded, on the full amount of the damages awarded to Leitch Transport.

This latter submission was made to the trial Judge. In effect the plaintiff was claiming an inflationary allowance running from the date of the breach. The trial Judge decided that he was "not prepared to go back to the date of the breach" but since it was almost four years, at the time of the trial, since Leitch Transport had acquired 100% of the shares of Upper Lakes, he thought that a four-year period would be reasonable. He declined to compound the inflationary factor. He used a rate of 3½% because of his finding that the evidence clearly indicated that inflation at the rate of 3½% to 4% was within the contemplation of business at the time the contract was negotiated, although the actual rate of inflation turned out to be in the range of 7%.

Mr. Thomson indicated that he was not prepared to support the reasons of the trial Judge in this regard, but said that "the award [for inflation] was reasonable."

In considering what legal basis there might be for the making of such an award, the trial Judge referred to *Mitchell v. Mulholland (No. 2)*, [1972] 1 QB 65 (CA); A.G. Guest, ed., *Chitty on Contracts* (London: Sweet & Maxwell, 24th ed., 1977) at p. 747, para. 1581, and to the text by F.A. Mann, *The Legal Aspect of Money* (3rd ed., 1971) at pp. 101-2 and 113-4. He questioned whether *Bishop v. Cunard White Star Ltd.*, [1950] P 240, was now supportable in the light of judgment of Widgery LJ, in *Mitchell v. Mulholland*.

Before we express our views as to the legal foundation of an award in respect of inflation, reference should be made to the factual basis put forward by the plaintiff in support of the claim. No witness who was a party to the actual negotiations indicated that there was any discussion whatever with respect to future inflation nor that he had the subject in mind. The plaintiff sought to support factually the second rule in *Hadley v. Baxendale* (1854), 9 Ex. 341; 156 ER 145, as commented upon in *Koufos v. C. Czarnikow Ltd.*, [1969] 1 AC 350 (HL (Eng.)); applying the rule to the facts, the plaintiff sought to prove that to reasonable businessmen it would have appeared not unlikely at the date of the making of the contract that if either party failed to carry it out, the effect of inflation would erode the dollar amount of damages that might be occasioned to the innocent party.

To accomplish this, the plaintiff called Dr. Lawrence Berk Smith, the Associate Chairman of the Department of Political Economy of the University of Toronto, an economist of impeccable academic qualifications and who had done certain consulting work in the area of economics, as well as being the author of a number of books and publications. Dr. Smith testified concerning what forecasts and other published data were available in 1970 from which one could endeavour to reach a conclusion as to the probable degree of future inflation. He gave evidence on what factors were taken into account in deciding whether inflation was a reality, the most important of which was indicated by interest rates. He said that in general the value of money deteriorated more quickly than anyone would have foreseen in 1970.

At the conclusion of the cross-examination, and at a point where the witness had not really testified with precision to the key fact that the plaintiff was seeking to establish, there ensued these two questions and answers, at the instance of the trial Judge:

HIS LORDSHIP:

Q. If I may ask you a question or two, Doctor. As I understand the tenor of your evidence, you said in 1970 it would have been reasonably foreseeable to a businessman that a four per cent rate of inflation would continue into the next number of reasonably foreseeable years?

A. Yes, sir.

Q. But that it would not be within the contemplation of a reasonable businessman to foresee the seven and a half per cent which did in fact occur?

A. That's right.

In fact the witness had not so testified in these terms, but his answer is clear and unambiguous, and counsel who was leading his evidence quite naturally decided he had no questions to ask in reply.

It is of course obvious that Dr. Smith was giving his evidence eight years after the time as of which the inquiry was directed, namely, the negotiation stage. Nevertheless this is obviously the evidence upon which the trial Judge relied. There was no other evidence.

A substantial obstacle facing the plaintiff with respect to this claim is that what may be termed its secondary difficulties were not caused by inflation—a misfortune it shared with all Canadians—but by simply being kept out of money to which it was entitled, for which the normal recompense is interest. The distinction is made very clearly by the House of Lords in *Pickett v. British Rail Engineering Ltd.*, [1980] AC 136 (HL (Eng.)), where Lord Wilberforce said at p. 151:

Increase for inflation is designed to preserve the "real" value of money; interest to compensate for being kept out of that "real" value.

Prior to the 1977 amendment to the *Judicature Act*, RSO 1970, c. 228, made by 1977 (Ont.), c. 51, s. 3(1), interest could not have been allowed in the circumstances of this case, and by s. 3(2) of the 1977 Act no interest can be awarded for a period before the new s. 38 came into force (on November 25, 1977). The writ in the action was issued on July 7, 1971. Hence the new provision is not applicable.

Even if the new section had been available, it would have been at best debatable whether the delay in bringing the action to trial was the fault of the defendant alone.

Mr. Thomson conceded at trial and again before us that interest before judgment could not be allowed in this case, and we think he was correct.

Turning to the question whether an award to compensate for inflation is justified in law, the short answer, from our point of view, is that the question was squarely raised and clearly decided in the case before this Court of *Genessee Holdings Ltd. et al. v. West York Motors Canada (Ltd.)* (1978), 6 CPC 63 (Ont. CA). The case was decided just two days before Montgomery J delivered his judgment and obviously was not and could not have been brought to his attention. In that case the plaintiff had had a new muffler installed on his truck by the defendant. The truck took fire and was lost with its cargo. The plaintiff paid for the repairs to the truck and paid the customers whose goods were lost in the fire. He sued the defendant. The damages were assessed by a Master on a reference. On the reference, the plaintiff "asked to be paid in dollars which included a sum for inflation which occurred since he paid out these monies." By coincidence, the moneys were expended in 1970. The Master made an allowance for inflation, saying in part (as quoted by Brooke JA, in giving the judgment of this Court) [at 64]:

> Further, being expected to spend hard dollars to mitigate his damages, it is hardly right and just that he be forced to accept compensation in the comparatively soft dollar of today. In truth, the "dollar of loss" was a *1971 dollar*, and the plaintiff is entitled to be compensated in *that* dollar, which is admittedly approximately 1.44 by today's standard.

The report of the Master was upheld by Donohue J from whose judgment an appeal was taken to this Court. The Court was unanimously of the view that the judgment could not stand (the Master had not allowed the full 44% but had assessed the allowance for inflation at $20,000). Brooke JA said at p. 64:

> His conclusion is that some, and not all of the inflation is a sound basis for consideration. This is so uncertain that it is arbitrary. It is true that general damages today reflect contemporary values, and it is true that damages assessed in actions such as a claim for specific performance in which damages are given in lieu thereof, reflect contemporary values. It is also true that it is proper to consider inflationary trends in the estimation of future expenses. Reference to *Arnold v. Teno*, [1978] 2 SCR 287 a judgment recently released in the Supreme Court of Canada. *But this principle has never been applied to damages for moneys expended or advanced in the past.*

(Emphasis added.) While this was an oral judgment, its binding effect is the same as that of a reserved judgment unless it is made to appear—which is not so in this case—that the Court has misapprehended the facts or the issues: *Levy v. Manley*, [1975] 2 SCR 70 at pp. 72-3.

Since the judgment at trial in this case, the question of an allowance for inflation in the case of a claim sounding in tort has been considered by the British Columbia Court of Appeal in *McCaig v. Reys* (1978), 7 BCLR 367 (CA). The judgment of the majority was given by McIntyre JA, with whom Seaton JA agreed. There the trial Judge had assessed the general damages at $23,000 and added $6,349 "as an allowance to adjust for inflation." Evidence was given by an actuary that the equivalent purchasing power of $23,000 in 1972 would be $29,349 at the date of trial in March 1975.

McIntyre JA pointed out that in *Stephens v. Gulf Oil Canada Ltd.* (1974), 3 OR (2d) 241 Henry J had made an allowance for inflation in a case of breach of contract, but the judgment was reversed on appeal on other grounds [(1975), 11 OR (2d) 129] and it was unnecessary for the Court of Appeal to deal with the point. The only other authority referred to was the judgment of the trial Judge in the present case. At p. 380 McIntyre JA dealt with the matter in this short passage:

> While a tendency seems to have developed to allow for inflationary trends in damage awards, there is no compelling authority which has been referred to us upon the subject. At trial and before this Court it was considered that the award of $23,000, prior to the application of the inflation allowance, was in accordance with authority. The only question before us is whether the inflationary allowance should have been applied. It is my opinion that no such allowance should be made here.

In the result therefore the majority of the Court reduced the award by the amount of the inflationary allowance. Craig JA dissented on this point. He stated (at p. 380) that he had not been able to find any authority which would preclude the Court from taking inflation into account in making an award in circumstances similar to those in the case before him. He referred to *Andrews v. Grand & Toy Alberta Ltd.*, [1978] 2 SCR 229 at pp. 239-40, and said [at 380-81]:

> Logically, and in fairness, therefore, a plaintiff who establishes that he has suffered a pecuniary loss because of the wrongful conduct of the defendant should be entitled to have judgment in an amount which has a comparable value at the date of the trial with the value of the amount of the pecuniary loss at the time the cause of action arose, providing he proves that there has been an alteration in value and the amount of it and providing that he has not been responsible for any delay in getting to trial, otherwise he is not getting full compensation—*restitutio in integrum*. Conversely, of course, the defendant should have the same right in the case of increased purchasing power of the dollar. Inflation has been taken into consideration in determining the size of an award for future pecuniary costs (loss), *e.g.*, *Andrews v. Grand & Toy*. Logically, I can see no reason why it should not be taken into consideration when determining the amount of an award for the period from when the loss occurred to the date of the trial. In the case of non-pecuniary losses, too, the Courts, without necessarily mentioning the subject, take into consideration the significant drop in the purchasing price of the dollar over the past few years. Why, then, should not inflation be taken into consideration in connection with pretrial pecuniary loss? In these circumstances the Court is still measuring the loss as of the date of the wrong, but is merely insuring that the plaintiff receives full compensation for his loss.
>
> With respect, I think that certain remarks of Lord Wilberforce in *Miliangos v. George Frank (Textiles) Ltd.*, [1976] AC 443 (HL (Eng.)) at p. 468, are apt. He said as follows:

It is for the courts, or for arbitrators, to work out a solution in each case best adapted to giving the injured plaintiff that amount in damages which will most fairly compensate him for the wrong which he has suffered.

Thus at the present time in Canada there appears to have been no case, prior to this one, in which an allowance was made for inflation with respect to damages for a breach of contract, assessed as at the date of the breach, but payable at or after judgment. It is only quite recently that an allowance has been made for inflation with respect to future pecuniary loss, culminating in the well-known trilogy of cases in the Supreme Court of Canada, of which *Teno v. Arnold* and *Andrews v. Grand & Toy*, are two. No suggestion is found in the judgments in the Supreme Court of Canada that an allowance should be made with respect to special damages, *i.e.*, pecuniary losses and expenditures incurred to the date of trial.

The matter has been much debated in England in recent years in cases involving personal injuries ... . [From] *Lim Poh Choo v. Camden & Islington Area Health Authority*, [1979] QB 196 (CA), substantially affirmed [1980] AC 174 (HL (Eng.)) it appears that the law (or practice) in England is different from that which has developed in Canada, and an allowance for inflation, even in respect of an award for future care, is the exception rather than the norm.

Such textbook authority as exists simply indicates that there is no authority for the proposition that an allowance for inflation should be made in the case of breach of contract, where the damages are assessed as at the date of the breach. Since the argument in this case, an article titled "Inflation and the Duty to Mitigate," written by David Feldman of the University of Bristol and D.F. Libling of the Bar of New South Wales has appeared in (1979), 95 *LQ Rev.* 270. It puts forward a strong argument that an allowance for inflation should be made, as part of carrying out the principle that a plaintiff is entitled to be fully compensated for loss caused him by the defendant's breach of contract, and to do this compensation must be assessed in terms of the value of money at the time of payment.

The policy of the law has changed in England with respect to payment of obligations in a foreign currency. It has now been decided that an English Court may give judgment for a sum of money expressed in a foreign currency and that the conversion to sterling should be at the date when the Court authorized enforcement of the judgment in terms of sterling: *Miliangos v. George Frank (Textiles) Ltd.*, [1976] AC 443 (HL (Eng.)). In that case Lord Wilberforce and Lord Cross expressly left open the question whether there should be a similar rule with respect to claims for damages for breach of contract.

There are expressions in the judgments in *Miliangos*, which, if applied by analogy to the case of a claim for an allowance for inflation, could be said to lend support to such a claim. Lord Wilberforce at p. 463:

[O]ne of the arguments against making orders for payment of foreign currency in specie has been that damages are an adequate remedy ... . But if, in the circumstances of today, damages are not an adequate remedy, as they clearly may not be if the breach date rule is applied in times of floating currencies, this argument, in any case nothing more than an appeal to discretion, loses its force. ...

2. The situation as regards currency stability has substantially changed even since 1961. Instead of the main world currencies being fixed and fairly stable in value, subject to the risk of periodic re- or devaluations, many of them are now "floating," i.e., they have no fixed exchange value even from day to day. This is true of sterling. This means that, instead of a situation in

which changes of relative value occurred between the "breach date" and the date of judgment or payment being the exception, so that a rule which did not provide for this case could be generally fair, this situation is now the rule. So the search for a formula to deal with it becomes urgent in the interest of justice.

At p. 468:

> [T]he mere fact that as a general rule in English law damages for tort or for breach of contract are assessed as at the date of the breach need not preclude, in particular cases, the conversion into sterling of an element in the damages, which arises and is expressed in foreign currency, as at some later date. It is for the courts, or for arbitrators, to work out a solution in each case best adapted to giving the injured plaintiff that amount in damages which will most fairly compensate him for the wrong which he has suffered.

Lord Fraser of Tullybelton at p. 503:

> I would add that I am not entirely satisfied that difficulty, and even injustice, may not occur if the rule continues to be that damages are converted at the breach date while foreign debts are converted at the date of payment.

In 1978 the House of Lords carried the matter forward into the area left open in *Miliangos* and held that in a claim based on tort, judgment could be given in a foreign currency, and that the currency to be chosen was that in which the owners of the "plaintiff" ship conducted their business. The same principle was applied in the companion case dealing with breach of contract (a charter party): see *Owners of M.V. "Eleftherotria" v. Owners of M.V. "Despina R,"* [1979] AC 685 (HL (Eng.)); and see commentary (1979), 42 *Mod. L Rev.* 452.

At pp. 700-01 Lord Wilberforce, after noting that *Miliangos* had held that a judgment in contractual and other cases could be given in a currency other than sterling, said:

> Whether it should be, and, in a case where there is more than one eligible currency, in which currency, must depend on general principles of the law of contract and on rules of conflict of laws. The former require application, as nearly as possible, of the principle of *restitutio in integrum*, regard being had to what was in the reasonable contemplation of the parties. ...
>
> If then the contract fails to provide a decisive interpretation, the damage should be calculated in the currency in which the loss was felt by the plaintiff or "which most truly expresses his loss" [language used by Lord Denning MR in the court below]. ... In ascertaining which this currency is, the court must ask what is the currency, payment in which will as nearly as possible compensate the plaintiff in accordance with the principle of restitution, and whether the parties must be taken reasonably to have had this in contemplation.

Lord Russell of Killowen said at p. 705:

> My Lords, in this case also the goal of *restitutio in integrum* is the aim. In cases such as this for damages for breach of contract—subject of course to questions of remoteness—the question is what is truly the claimant's loss resulting from the breach of contract? True, the direct disbursement was in cruzeiros: but in order to make that disbursement the respondent had perforce to expend francs, against which by the time of the award cruzeiros had steeply (and indeed predictably) declined. The arbitrators found:

It was reasonable to contemplate that the charterers, being a French corporation and having their place of business in Paris, would have to use French francs to purchase other currencies to settle cargo claims arising under the bills of lading.

In my opinion the award was properly made in French francs, and I would dismiss this appeal.

Mr. Thomson puts his case along the same broad lines. No Court in England, to our knowledge, has expressed views on the precise question in terms of considering an allowance for inflation to "truly express the plaintiff's loss."

If we were called upon to decide the matter *de novo* we would have to consider some very serious problems in trying to lay down a principle to be followed in this and future cases. It is one thing to be able to find that the parties to a contract for the sale and purchase of a house had in contemplation a rise in the price of houses over the period following the agreed date of closing, as Megarry J was able to do in *Wroth v. Tyler*, [1974] Ch. 30. It is much more difficult to be able to arrive at the conclusion that reasonable businessmen in the position of the parties ought to have had in contemplation that it was not unlikely that the purchasing power of the dollar would decline sharply over the next four years. It is even more difficult to accept, at its complete literal wording, the opinion of a professor of economics that reasonable businessmen ought so to have foreseen the future. It seems to us that this would involve consideration, in every case, of the extent to which persons in the business, trade or profession concerned had occasion to consider the future of the value of the dollar, had information available from which an informed conclusion could be reached, and whether it was customary in that trade or business to pay any attention to considerations of that sort.

This Court in the *Genessee* case thought the assessment of the Master in awarding somewhat less than half of the actual decline in the value of the dollar was arbitrary. In the present case, as in that one, there was actual evidence as to the approximate rate of inflation from 1970 to the date of the trial, but the trial Judge thought that only part of such decline was foreseeable. It is true he based his estimate on the evidence of the professor, but the professor himself had said "there is no measure of inflation," which meant, he went on to explain, that there was no accurate way in which one could say, mathematically, that the rate of inflation was (his illustration) 7.23% or some other equally precise rate.

If such an award is to be allowed, consideration would have to be given to the question of how the measure of inflation is to be determined. Is the Court to have primary regard to the Consumer Price Index? The rate of interest from time to time? The Composite Wage Index? If it is the Consumer Price Index, whose index is going to be used? When the proper measure of inflation is determined, how is the calculation of the inflation credit to be made? Is it to be calculated daily? weekly? monthly? annually? Is it to be compounded? What period of time should it cover?

Since we are bound by authority in this Province to disallow the claim for an allowance for inflation, we are not required to answer these very difficult questions. The award of the trial Judge in this regard must be set aside and there will be no allowance for inflation upon the damages to be awarded to the plaintiff.

NOTE

The table on pages 207-8 from Dale Gibson, "Repairing the Law of Damages" (1978), 8 *Manitoba Law Journal* 637, at 650-51 shows the relationship, over a 12-year period, between inflation and interest.

Pre-Judgment Interest

Courts of Justice Act
RSO 1990, c. C.43

Prejudgment and Postjudgment Interest Rates

Definitions

127(1) In this section and in sections 128 and 129,

"bank rate" means the bank rate established by the Bank of Canada as the minimum rate at which the Bank of Canada makes short-term advances to banks listed in Schedule I to the *Bank Act* (Canada);

"date of the order" means the date the order is made, even if the order is not entered or enforceable on that date, or the order is varied on appeal, and in the case of an order directing a reference, the date the report on the reference is confirmed;

"postjudgment interest rate" means the bank rate at the end of the first day of the last month of the quarter preceding the quarter in which the date of the order falls, rounded to the next higher whole number where the bank rate includes a fraction, plus 1 per cent;

"prejudgment interest rate" means the bank rate at the end of the first day of the last month of the quarter preceding the quarter in which the proceeding was commenced, rounded to the nearest tenth of a percentage point;

"quarter" means the three-month period ending with the 31st day of March, 30th day of June, 30th day of September or 31st day of December.

Calculation and Publication of Interest Rates

(2) After the first day of the last month of each quarter, a person designated by the Deputy Attorney General shall forthwith,

(a) determine the prejudgment and postjudgment interest rate for the next quarter; and

(b) publish in the prescribed manner a table showing the rate determined under clause (a) for the next quarter and the rates determined under clause (a) or under a predecessor of that clause for all the previous quarters during the preceding 10 years.

Year & Quarter	Interest Rates					Inflation	Earning Rate
	90-Day Commercial Paper	3-5-Year Government Bonds	10-Year-and-Over Government Bonds	McLeod, Young, Weir Industrials	Average	Year-Over-Year % Change in Consumer Price Index	% Excess of Average Annual Interest Rate Over Average Annual Inflation
1965:1	4.43	4.62	5.06	5.50	4.90	2.0	
1965:2	4.81	4.87	5.16	5.64	5.12	2.3	
1965:3	5.22	5.09	5.32	5.83	5.37	2.5	
1965:4	6.09	5.23	5.40	6.05	5.69	2.9	
1965					5.27	2.43	2.84
1966:1	6.07	5.37	5.58	6.22	5.81	3.4	
1966:2	6.28	5.39	5.66	6.30	5.91	3.8	
1966:3	6.40	5.76	5.75	6.83	6.19	3.9	
1966:4	6.63	5.58	5.76	6.83	6.20	3.9	
1966					6.03	3.75	2.28
1967:1	5.39	4.76	5.48	6.65	5.57	3.0	
1967:2	5.54	5.68	5.87	7.07	6.04	3.3	
1967:3	5.95	6.10	6.19	7.43	6.42	4.0	
1967:4	6.57	6.48	6.54	7.59	6.80	3.8	
1967					6.21	3.53	2.68
1968:1	7.39	7.12	6.91	7.93	7.34	4.5	
1968:2	7.20	6.79	6.62	8.05	7.17	4.1	
1968:3	6.19	6.25	6.60	7.82	6.72	3.6	
1968:4	6.65	7.06	7.27	8.18	7.29	4.2	
1968					7.13	4.10	3.03
1969:1	7.04	7.27	7.22	8.43	7.49	3.8	
1969:2	7.82	7.62	7.50	8.89	7.96	4.8	
1969:3	8.43	8.06	7.81	8.91	8.30	4.9	
1969:4	9.17	8.29	8.33	9.29	8.77	4.5	
1969					8.13	4.50	3.63
1970:1	7.89	7.32	7.93	9.24	8.10	4.7	
1970:2	7.31	7.07	8.09	9.24	7.93	3.7	
1970:3	6.68	7.12	7.88	9.19	7.72	3.0	
1970:4	5.58	5.42	6.99	8.83	6.71	2.2	
1970					7.62	3.40	4.22
1971:1	3.53	5.19	6.76	8.37	5.96	1.7	
1971:2	3.98	6.02	7.30	8.52	6.46	2.2	
1971:3	4.99	5.63	6.97	8.32	6.48	3.2	
1971:4	4.32	5.09	6.56	8.24	6.05	4.2	
1971					6.24	2.83	3.41
1972:1	5.15	6.29	7.24	8.24	6.73	4.8	
1972:2	5.16	6.68	7.45	8.34	6.91	4.3	
1972:3	5.01	6.57	7.46	8.46	6.88	4.8	
1972:4	5.15	6.00	7.12	8.15	6.61	5.2	
1972					6.78	4.78	2.00

[The table is concluded on the next page]

		Interest Rates				Inflation	Earning Rate
Year & Quarter	90-Day Commercial Paper	3-5-Year Government Bonds	10-Year-and-Over Government Bonds	McLeod, Young, Weir Industrials	Average	Year-Over-Year % Change in Consumer Price Index	% Excess of Average Annual Interest Rate Over Average Annual Inflation
1973:1	5.24	6.50	7.30	8.22	6.82	5.8	
1973:2	7.40	7.19	7.74	8.40	7.68	7.3	
1973:3	8.95	7.25	7.72	8.62	8.14	8.2	
1973:4	10.25	7.25	7.70	8.81	8.50	9.0	
1973					7.79	7.58	.21
1974:1	9.20	7.57	8.19	9.26	8.56	9.7	
1974:2	11.70	9.24	9.46	10.45	10.21	10.8	
1974:3	11.04	8.89	9.67	10.99	10.15	11.0	
1974:4	10.25	6.96	8.77	10.72	9.18	12.0	
1974					9.53	10.88	_1.35
1975:1	6.86	6.71	8.47	10.15	8.05	11.7	
1975:2	7.25	7.49	8.88	10.57	8.55	10.5	
1975:3	8.94	8.86	9.70	11.40	9.73	10.9	
1975:4	9.34	8.39	9.35	11.06	9.54	10.2	
1975					8.97	10.83	_1.86
1976:1	9.99	8.55	9.39	10.82	9.69	9.3	
1976:2	9.20	8.47	9.35	10.74	9.44	8.5	
1976:3	9.47	8.40	9.16	10.33	9.34	6.5	
1976:4	8.16	7.57	8.47	9.83	8.51	5.9	
1976					9.25	7.55	1.70
1977:1	7.77	7.78	8.83	9.88	8.57	6.8	
1977:2	6.99	7.64	8.72	9.63	8.25	7.6	
1977:3	7.25	7.81	8.61	9.55	8.31	8.4	
1977:4	7.23	8.10	8.77	9.71	8.45	9.1	
1977					8.40	7.98	.42
				Average for total period surveyed			1.79

Regulations

(3) The Attorney General may, by regulation, prescribe the manner in which the table described in clause (2)(b) is to be published.

Prejudgment Interest

128(1) A person who is entitled to an order for the payment of money is entitled to claim and have included in the order an award of interest thereon at the prejudgment interest rate, calculated from the date the cause of action arose to the date of the order.

Exception for Non-pecuniary Loss on Personal Injury

(2) Despite subsection (1), the rate of interest on damages for non-pecuniary loss in an action for personal injury shall be the rate determined by the rules of court made under clause 66(2)(w).

Special Damages

(3) If the order includes an amount for past pecuniary loss, the interest calculated under subsection (1) shall be calculated on the total past pecuniary loss at the end of each six-month period and at the date of the order.

Exclusion

(4) Interest shall not be awarded under subsection (1),
   (a) on exemplary or punitive damages;
   (b) on interest accruing under this section;
   (c) on an award of costs in the proceeding;
   (d) on that part of the order that represents pecuniary loss arising after the date of the order and that is identified by a finding of the court;
   (e) with respect to any advance payment that has been made towards settlement of the claim, for the period after the advance payment has been made;
   (f) where the order is made on consent, except by consent of the debtor; or
   (g) where interest is payable by a right other than under this section.

Discretion of Court

130(1) The court may, where it considers it just to do so, in respect of the whole or any part of the amount on which interest is payable under section 128 or 129,
   (a) disallow interest under either section;
   (b) allow interest at a rate higher or lower than that provided in either section;
   (c) allow interest for a period other than that provided in either section.

Idem

(2) For the purpose of subsection (1), the court shall take into account
   (a) changes in market interest rates;
   (b) the circumstances of the case;
   (c) the fact that an advance payment was made;
   (d) the circumstances of medical disclosure by the plaintiff;
   (e) the amount claimed and the amount recovered in the proceeding;
   (f) the conduct of any party that tended to shorten or to lengthen unnecessarily the duration of the proceeding; and
   (g) any other relevant consideration.

[See also *Judgment Interest Act*, SA 1984, c. J-0.5, ss. 2-5; *Court Order Interest Act*, RSBC 1996, c. 78, ss. 1-6; *Court of Queen's Bench Act*, RSM 1987, c. C280, ss. 80-84; *Judicature Act*,

RSNB 1973, c. J-2, ss. 45-46; *Judgment Interest Act*, RSN 1990, c. J-2, ss. 3-4; *Interest on Judgments Act*, RSNS 1989, c. 233; *Supreme Court Act*, RSPEI 1988, c. S-10, ss. 49-50; and *Pre-Judgment Interest Act*, SS 1984-85-86, c. P-22.2.]

NOTE

In *Bank of America Canada v. Mutual Trust Co.*, [2002] 2 SCR 601, the Supreme Court of Canada held, despite s. 128(4)(b) above, that compound interest could be awarded in some circumstances at common law.

Foreign Currency Obligations

Miliangos v. George Frank (Textiles) Ltd.
[1976] AC 433 (HL (Eng.))

LORD WILBERFORCE: … My Lords, the facts in this case are as simple as in *In re United Railways of Havana and Regla Warehouses Ltd.*, [1961] AC 1007 (HL (Eng.)) they were complex. It is concerned with a contract made in May 1971 for the sale of 90,718 kilogrammes of polyester yarn at a price of 12.56 Swiss francs per kilogramme, price to be paid within 30 days of invoice. The proper law of this contract was Swiss law and the money of account and of payment was Swiss francs. The respondent, the seller, is a national of Switzerland and the yarn was produced by his firm in Switzerland. It was delivered in the autumn of 1971 under five invoices, each of which stated the price in Swiss francs, payment to be made within 30 days to a Swiss bank. The appellant company did not pay any part of the price. It accepted, by way of part payment, two bills of exchange drawn in Switzerland for a total sum of 300,000 Swiss francs payable on January 31, 1972, but these were dishonoured on presentation.

The action was begun by writ on April 20, 1972. In his statement of claim the respondent claimed the amount of the price or, alternatively, the amount due on the bills expressed, in each case, in the sterling equivalent of the sum due in Swiss francs as at the dates when payment should have been made. The appellant delivered a defence and a counterclaim alleging that the yarn was defective and there followed a number of interlocutory steps arising out of this allegation. But on November 22, 1974, just before the action was due to come on for trial the appellant wrote to say that it abandoned the defence and counterclaim and would submit to judgment.

Thereafter the proceedings took a remarkable course. On November 26, 1974, the Court of Appeal (Lord Denning MR, Lawton LJ, and Foster J) announced their decision in a case involving a claim in German currency—*Schorsch Meier GmbH v. Hennin*, [1975] QB 416 (CA). Although they were faced with a unanimous decision of this House in *In re United Railways of Havana and Regla Warehouses Ltd.*, that, on a foreign currency claim, judgment can only be given in sterling, to which the foreign currency must be converted as at the date when the debt became due, the court held by a majority that an English court could give a money judgment in a foreign currency, when that currency was the currency of the contract. Lawton LJ, dissenting, considered that he was bound by the *Havana Railways* case. Unanimously, as a second ground of decision, the court held that where the creditor resided in an EEC country, an English court was obliged [sic] by article 106 of the Treaty of Rome to give a judgment in the currency of the creditor, if that was the currency of the contract.

This decision was naturally welcomed by the respondent. So when this action came on for hearing on December 2, 1974, he applied to amend his statement of claim so as to claim the amount due to him in Swiss francs. This amendment was allowed by Bristow J so that the claim became one for 415,522.45 Swiss francs for the price plus 621.75 the cost of protesting the two bills, making together 416,144.20 Swiss francs. Since, between the date in 1971 when payment was due and the date of the hearing, sterling had fallen in value as against the Swiss franc from Sw.Frs. 9.90 to 6.00 (approximately) to the £, this meant that if the respondent could obtain judgment in Swiss francs he could recover in sterling terms some £60,000, whereas if he had to accept the sterling equivalent at the 1971 rate he could recover only some £42,000.

This amendment having been made, the action (together with a second action into which it is unnecessary to enter) came for trial. The learned judge found himself in a difficult position. On the one hand there was the decision of this House in the *Havana Railways* case which clearly precluded him from giving judgment in Swiss francs or from awarding the sterling equivalent of the sum due converted at any other date than the date when the sum claimed was due. On the other hand there was the decision of the Court of Appeal in *Schorsch Meier*, which had declined to apply the *Havana Railways* decision. In these circumstances he decided that he ought to follow the decision of this House and that the decision in *Schorsch Meier* was given *per incuriam*.

An appeal was brought to the Court of Appeal and was heard in February 1975 by Lord Denning MR, Stephenson and Goeffrey Lane LJJ. It was submitted that the court, on indistinguishable facts, was bound by and should follow the *Havana Railways* case, but the court declined to do so. It held that the majority decision in *Schorsch Meier* was not given *per incuriam* (the unanimous alternative was not directly relevant since Switzerland is not an EEC member) and that it was binding upon the court. It therefore varied the judgment of Bristow J so as to give judgment for the respondent for the sum claimed in Swiss francs. From this judgment appeal has come to this House. There has been no appeal in the *Schorsch Meier* case but since it was applied by the Court of Appeal in these proceedings I shall have to comment upon it.

My Lords, it is clear from this account that some distortion of the judicial process has been brought about. As Bristow J said [1975] QB 487 at p. 492:

> I am faced with a judgment of a majority of the Court of Appeal, which in its application to the issue raised before me says that a rule of English law taken for granted by the Court of Appeal and the House of Lords for some 350 years is no longer a rule of English law. The speeches of the House of Lords in *Broome v. Cassell & Co. Ltd.*, [1972] AC 1027 (HL (Eng.)) constrain me in the circumstances to hold that the rule of law that my judgment can only be expressed in sterling is still of full force and effect, since Parliament has not altered it, nor has the House of Lords itself under its 1966 declaration: see *Practice Statement (Judicial Precedent)*, [1966] 1 WLR 1234.

It has to be reaffirmed that the only judicial means by which decisions of this House can be reviewed is by this House itself, under the declaration of 1966. Whether it can or should do so is a difficult enough question, which I shall now examine.

My Lords, although the "breach date rule" has a long history, possibly, but, I think, not clearly, extending back to the Year Books, consideration of it at the present time as regards foreign money debts must start from the *Havana Railways* case. For that was a case of a money debt as to which it was sought to persuade this House that a different rule should be applied from that which was admitted to be relevant to claims for damages for tort or for breach of contract. The claim there was for a debt (or debts) in US dollars, due under a contract the proper law of which was held to be the law of Pennsylvania. The debtor (the United Havana Railways Co.) was English: the creditor was American. The proceedings were by way of proof in the liquidation of the debtor, not by action by writ, but it was not suggested that this made any difference, and I say at once that I do not think that any distinction can be drawn on this ground. On the arguments presented which were at least strenuous, and after examination of the cases extending over a long period, the House unanimously decided that the provable sum in US dollars had to be converted into sterling at the rates of exchange prevailing when the relevant sums fell due and were not paid. They rejected the counter-suggestion that conversion should be made at the date of judgment. They did not take up or accept suggestions which had been made in some earlier cases that a separate rule applied to foreign money claims.

My Lords, even if I were inclined to question some of the arguments used in the speeches, I should find it inappropriate and unnecessary to say that, in the circumstances of the time and on the arguments and authorities presented, the decision was wrong or is open to distinction or explanation.

What we can do, and what is our responsibility, is to consider whether this decision, clear and comparatively recent, should be regarded as a binding precedent in today's circumstances. For that purpose it is permissible to examine the speeches in order to understand the considerations upon which the opinions there reached were based, for the ultimate purpose of seeing whether there have emerged fresh considerations which might have appealed to those who gave those opinions and so may appeal to their successors. ...

[His Lordship then examined the *Havana Railways* case.]

My Lords, I have quoted extensively from these opinions, not only because they embody the standing authority on the question now at issue, but also in order to make clear what, I think, appears from all of them to be the basic presupposition. This is that procedurally an action cannot be brought here for recovery or payment of a sum expressed in foreign currency, and that, in effect, it can only be brought for a sum expressed in sterling, recoverable by way of damages. I now have to ask, what is the position at the present time? Have any fresh considerations of any substance emerged which should induce your Lordships to follow a different rule? I will endeavour to state those which appear to me to be significant.

1. The courts have evolved a procedure under which orders can be made for payment of foreign currency debts in the foreign currency. The Court of Appeal has given its approval to the form: "It is adjudged ... that the defendant do pay to the plaintiff [the sum in foreign currency] or the sterling equivalent at the time of payment." (See *Schorsch Meier GmbH v.*

Hennin at p. 425 *per* Lord Denning MR.) I can find no reason in principle why such orders cannot be made. The courts have generally power to order delivery in specie whenever, in their opinion, damages are an inadequate remedy. In cases such as the present, indeed, one of the arguments against making orders for payment of foreign currency in specie has been that damages are an adequate remedy (see particularly *Lloyd Royal Belge S.A. v. Louis Dreyfus & Co.* (1927), 27 Ll. L Rep. 288 (QB) at p. 294 *per* Romer J). But if, in the circumstances of today, damages are not an adequate remedy, as they clearly may not be if the breach date rule is applied in times of floating currencies, this argument, in any case nothing more than an appeal to discretion, loses its force. The jurisdiction is clear, on general principle: how the court's discretion is to be exercised depends on the circumstances. I return to this later. Further, I can find nothing in the Rules of the Supreme Court which prevents such orders being made: indeed, though I do not attach the same importance to the change as did the learned Master of the Rolls, the present form of the rules (RSC, 42, r. 1, Ord. 45 and Forms 45 et seq., Appendix A) is somewhat more favourable to the making of orders in this form than was the version in force in 1961. Lord Denning MR adhered to this position in the present case after further argument upon the rules, by which time any serious inconveniences or practical difficulties would have come to light. I shall return to this subject later with particular reference to the question of the date of conversion. At the present stage what is relevant is that orders in this form are jurisdictionally legitimate and procedurally workable.

2. The situation as regards currency stability has substantially changed even since 1961. Instead of the main world currencies being fixed and fairly stable in value, subject to the risk of periodic re- or devaluations, many of them are now "floating," i.e., they have no fixed exchange value even from day to day. This is true of sterling. This means that, instead of a situation in which changes of relative value occurred between the "breach date" and the date of judgment or payment being the exception, so that a rule which did not provide for this case could be generally fair, this situation is now the rule. So the search for a formula to deal with it becomes urgent in the interest of justice. This leads to the next point.

3. The state of facts referred to under 2 has become recognised in those commercial circles which are closely concerned with international contracts. The reaction to them appears in the field of arbitration. In 1969 two of the most experienced arbitrators in the City of London made an award expressed in terms of U.S. dollars and the validity of this came to be tested in the courts: *Jugoslavenska Oceanska Plovidba v. Castle Investment Co. Inc.*, [1974] QB 292 (CA). In reserved judgments the Court of Appeal (Lord Denning MR, Cairns and Roskill LJJ), disagreeing with observations made in that court in *The Teh Hu*, [1970] P 106 (CA) at p. 129, held that the award was valid. What is more, and relevant in the present context, they held that it could be enforced under section 26 of the *Arbitration Act 1950* which enables an award to be enforced "in the same manner as a judgment or order to the same effect." They pointed out that this was also the case as regards foreign awards which under section 36(1) of the same Act "shall be enforceable" in the same manner as an award "is enforceable under section 26." Roskill LJ, who has great experience in these matters, said that awards of this kind made in the City have been entirely satisfactory and honoured all over the world. He also referred to inquiries made by Kerr J, at first instance, of the Central Office of the High Court which showed that there is no difficulty in practice in enforcing foreign currency awards: the foreign currency is simply converted into sterling at the rate prevailing at the date of the award.

I regard this development as of great importance for two reasons. First, it goes a long way towards removing the practical objections as regards enforcement which weighed so heavily in the *Havana Railways* case. If an award in a foreign currency case can be readily enforced, after conversion into a sterling sum, and since an award is enforceable as a judgment, it should follow that a judgment in a foreign currency can be similarly enforced, after conversion into a sterling sum. Secondly, it would be an intolerable situation if a different rule were to prevail as regards arbitrations upon debts expressed in foreign currency on the one hand and actions upon similar debts on the other. Counsel for the appellants was therefore obliged to argue that if he was to succeed the decision in the *Jugoslavenska* case must either be overruled, or narrowly confined. I can find no limits within which it can be confined which would not still enclose the present case, so, if the appeal were to be allowed, the case would have to be overruled. But if I am faced with the alternative of forcing commercial circles to fall in with a legal doctrine which has nothing but precedent to commend it or altering the doctrine so as to conform with what commercial experience has worked out, I know where my choice lies. The law should be responsive as well as, at times, enunciatory, and good doctrine can seldom be divorced from sound practice.

4. Further recognition of the need for, and practicality of, making orders in terms of foreign currencies was given in *The Halcyon the Great*, [1975] 1 WLR 515 (QB), where an order was made in Admiralty for the sale of a ship for US dollars, and for the lodgment of the price in a separate dollar account. The judgment of Brandon J contains a clear acceptance (contrary to the appellant's arguments here) of the proposition that US dollar currency may be regarded as "money" within the meaning of English procedural rules and that the courts can easily adapt their procedure so as to give effect to foreign money claims in specie. The case indeed prompts the reflection that a similar procedure might have been regarded as acceptable in the *Havana Railways* case, the factual situation (i.e., a debt in foreign currency secured upon a sum expressed in foreign currency) being in many respects similar.

5. I should mention at this stage the argument based upon article 106 of the EEC Treaty of Rome. I can understand the temptation, in the search for an argument why the *Havana Railways* case should not now be followed, to fasten upon the important development which the treaty represents. Although Switzerland is not an EEC member, the argument unanimously accepted by the Court of Appeal in *Schorsch Meier* was invoked by the respondent in this appeal and correspondingly attacked by the appellants. It cannot therefore be passed over in silence, all the less since there is a risk that it may be quoted as a precedent. There are two reasons for dealing with it here with restraint. First, there is no direct appeal against the decision in *Schorsch Meier*: secondly, the issue of the applicability and interpretation of article 106, if it were to be considered by this House, would necessitate a reference to the European Court under article 177 of the treaty. But nevertheless I feel bound to say that I entertain the strongest reservations concerning the use made by the Court of Appeal of article 106 in the present context, and I cannot believe that, if the court had heard argument on the other side (corresponding to that of the present appellants), very weighty arguments would not have been brought forward concerning such questions as the direct applicability of this article, its bearing on any question of the currency in which claims may be made in the courts of member States or its relevance at all to the ascertainment of the date of conversion of such claims, which arguments seem to have been unappreciated. Any other court in which such issues may arise would be well advised to refer them to the European Court for

clarification. In this appeal, in my opinion, no argument based directly or indirectly upon article 106 of the treaty should be considered as available to the respondent.

6. Finally, I wish to express my agreement as to what my noble and learned friend Lord Simon of Glaisdale has said about the maxim "*cessante ratione*," etc. [*cessante ratione, cessat ipsa lex*—when the reason for it ceases, the rule itself must cease.]

My Lords, before attempting the task of deciding where, in the end, this House should stand as regards the *Havana Railways* rule there are some other general observations I think should be made.

First, I do not for myself think it doubtful that, in a case such as the present, justice demands that the creditor should not suffer from fluctuations in the value of sterling. His contract has nothing to do with sterling: he has bargained for his own currency and only his own currency. The substance of the debtor's obligations depends upon the proper law of the contract (here Swiss law): and though English law (*lex fori*) prevails as regards procedural matters, it must surely be wrong in principle to allow procedure to affect, detrimentally, the substance of the creditor's rights. Courts are bound by their own procedural law and must obey it, if imperative, though to do so may seem unjust. But if means exist for giving effect to the substance of a foreign obligation, conformably with the rules of private international law, procedure should not unnecessarily stand in the way.

There is, unfortunately, as Lord Radcliffe pointed out in the *Havana Railways* case, a good deal of confusion in English cases as to what the creditor's rights are. Appeal has been made to the principle of nominalism, so as to say that the creditor must take the pound sterling as he finds it. Lord Denning said so in the *Havana Railways* case (pp. 1069-70) and I can safely and firmly disagree with him in that because he has himself, since then, come to hold another view. The creditor has no concern with pounds sterling: for him what matters is that a Swiss franc for good or ill should remain a Swiss franc. This is substantially the reasoning of Holmes J in the important judgment of the US Supreme Court in *Deutsche Bank Filiale Nürnberg v. Humphrey* (1926), 272 US 517. Another argument is that the "breach date" makes for certainty whereas to choose a later date makes the claim depend on currency fluctuations. But this is only a partial truth. The only certainty achieved is certainty in the sterling amount—but that is not in point since sterling does not enter into the bargain. The relevant certainty which the rule ought to achieve is that which gives the creditor neither more nor less than he bargained for. He bargained for 415,522.45 Swiss francs: whatever this means in (unstipulated) foreign currencies, whichever way the exchange into those currencies may go, he should get 415,522.45 Swiss francs or as nearly as can be brought about. That such a solution, if practicable, is just, and adherence to the "breach date" in such a case unjust in the circumstances of today, adds greatly to the strength of the argument for revising the rule or, putting it more technically, it adds strength to the case for awarding delivery in specie rather than giving damages. ...

[His Lordship then examined the line of cases disallowing judgments in foreign currency.]

This brings me to the declaration made by this House in 1966. Under it, the House affirmed its power to depart from a previous decision when it appears right to do so, recognising that too rigid adherence to precedent might lead to injustice in a particular case and unduly restrict the proper development of the law. My Lords, on the assumption that to depart from the *Havana Railways* case would not involve undue practical difficulties, that a new and more satisfactory rule is capable of being stated, I am of opinion that the present case falls within the terms of the declaration. To change the rule would, for the reasons already explained, avoid injustice in the present case. To change it would enable the law to keep in step with commercial needs and with the majority of other countries facing similar problems. The latter proposition is well vouched by Dr. F.A. Mann's work, *The Legal Aspect of Money* (3rd ed., 1971), Chapter X.

I return then to the two preconditions.

1. Can a better rule be stated? I would make it clear that, for myself, I would confine my approval at the present time of a change in the breach-date rule to claims such as those with which we are here concerned, i.e., to foreign money obligations, sc. obligations of a money character to pay foreign currency arising under a contract whose proper law is that of a foreign country and where the money of account and payment is that of that country, or possibly of some other country but not of the United Kingdom.

I do not think that we are called upon, or would be entitled in this case, to review the whole field of the law regarding foreign currency obligations: that is not the method by which changes in the law by judicial decision are made. In my opinion it should be open for future discussion whether the rule applying to money obligations, which can be a simple rule, should apply as regards claims for damages for breach of contract or for tort. It is only because it has been thought that the same rule need apply to all these situations that we have been forced into strait-jacket solutions based on concepts, or on forms of action ("archaic legalistic nonsense" in the words of Lawton LJ in *Schorsch Meier* at p. 430). But the principles on which damages are awarded for tort or breach of contract are both very intricate and not the same in each case, involve questions of remoteness (cf. the speech of Lord Parmoor in *S.S. Celia (Owners) v. S.S. Volturno (Owners) (The Volturno)*, [1921] 2 AC 544 (HL (Eng.)) and have no direct relevance to claims for specific things, in which I include specific foreign currency. To take one familiar point. Whereas in the case of the inevitable contract to supply a foreign cow, the intending purchaser has to be treated as going into the market to buy one as at the date of breach, this doctrine cannot be applied to a foreign money obligation, for the intending creditor has nothing to buy his own currency with—except his own currency. I therefore see no need to overrule or criticise or endorse such cases as *The Volturno*, [1921] 2 AC 544 (HL (Eng.)) or *Di Ferdinando v. Simon, Smits & Co. Ltd.*, [1920] 3 KB 409 (CA). I would only say, in agreement with Scrutton LJ (*The Baarn*, [1933] P 251 (CA) at p. 266), that the former case leaves a number of difficulties unsolved and that the mere fact that as a general rule in English law damages for tort or for breach of contract are assessed as at the date of the breach need not preclude, in particular cases, the conversion into sterling of an element in the damages, which arises and is expressed in foreign currency, as at some later date. It is for the courts, or for arbitrators, to work out a solution in each case best adapted to giving the injured plaintiff that amount in damages which will most fairly compensate him for the wrong which he has suffered. As examples in which acceptance of this principle might have led to a juster result I may refer to *The Teh Hu*, [1970] P 106 (CA) and *Nederlandsch-Amerikaansche Stoomvaart Maatchppij N.V. v. Royal Mail Lines Ltd.*, [1958] 1 Lloyd's Rep. 412 (QB), and as an example where it did so to *In re Dawson, decd.*, [1966] 2 NSWR 211.

As regards foreign money obligations (defined above), it is first necessary to establish the form of the claim to be made. In my opinion acceptance of the argument already made requires that the claim must be specifically for the foreign currency—as in this case for a sum stated in Swiss francs. To this may be added the alternative "or the sterling equivalent at the date of …" (see below). As regards the conversion date to be inserted in the claim or in the judgment of the court, the choice, as pointed out in the *Havana Railways* case, is between (i) the date of action brought, (ii) the date of judgment, (iii) the date of payment. Each has its advantages, and it is to be noticed that the Court of Appeal in *Schorsch Meier* and in the present case chose the date of payment meaning, as I understand it, the date when the court authorises enforcement of the judgment in terms of sterling. The date of payment is taken in the convention annexed to the *Carriage of Goods by Road Act 1965* (article 27(2)). This date gets nearest to securing to the creditor exactly what he bargained for. The date of action brought, though favoured by Lord Reid and Lord Radcliffe in the *Havana Railways* case, seems to me to place the creditor too severely at the mercy of the debtor's obstructive defences (cf. this case) or the law's delay. It may have been based on an understanding of the judgment of Holmes J in the *Deutsche Bank* case now seen to be probably mistaken (see Mann, *The Legal Aspect of Money*, at p. 355 and cases cited). The date of judgment is shown to be a workable date in practice by its inclusion in the Carriage by *Air Act 1961* which gave effect to The Hague Convention of 1965 varying, on this very point, the Warsaw Convention of 1929, but, in some cases, particularly where there is an appeal, may again impose on the creditor a considerable currency risk. So I would favour the payment date, in the sense I have mentioned. In the case of a company in liquidation, the corresponding date for conversion would be the date when the creditor's claim in terms of sterling is admitted by the liquidator. In the case of arbitration, there may be a minor discrepancy, if the practice which is apparently adopted (see the *Jugoslavenska* case at p. 305) remains as it is, but I can see no reason why, if desired, that practice should not be adjusted so as to enable conversion to be made as at the date when leave to enforce in sterling is given.

2. A rule in the form suggested above would not, in my opinion, give rise to any serious procedural difficulty. Suggestions were made at the Bar that as regards such matters as set off, counterclaim, payment into court, it would be difficult or impossible to apply. I would say as to these matters that I see no reason why this should be so: it would be inappropriate to discuss them here in detail and unnecessary since the Court of Appeal has assessed the procedural implications and has not been impressed with any difficulty. I have no doubt that practitioners, with the assistance of the Supreme Court, can work out suitable solutions— not overlooking the provisions of the *Exchange Control Act 1947*. I would only add that while the rule I have suggested would fit perfectly well into such a situation as existed in *Société des Hôtels Le Touquet Paris-Plage v. Cummings*, [1922] 1 KB 451 (CA) it would not be reconcilable with the later case of *Madeleine Vionnet et Cie. v. Wills*, [1940] 1 KB 72 (CA). I do not think that case can any longer be followed.

My Lords, in conclusion I would say that, difficult as this whole matter undoubtedly is, if once a clear conclusion is reached as to what the law ought now to be, declaration of it by this House is appropriate. The law on this topic is judge-made: it has been built up over the years from case to case. It is entirely within this House's duty, in the course of administering justice, to give the law a new direction in a particular case where, on principle and in reason, it appears right to do so. I cannot accept the suggestion that because a rule is long established only legislation can change it—that may be so when the rule is so deeply entrenched that it has infected the whole legal system, or the choice of a new rule involves more far-reaching research than courts can carry out. A recent example of the House changing a very old established rule is *West Midland Baptist (Trust) Association (Inc.) v. Birmingham Corporation*, [1970] AC 874 (HL (Eng.)). Lord Reid thought that it was proper to re-examine a judge-made rule of law based on an assumption of fact (as to the stability of money) when the rule was formulated but which was no longer true and which in many cases caused serious injustice. So in that case the House selected a new date and did not think it necessary or right to wait for legislation and I would not think it necessary or right here. Indeed, from some experience in the matter, I am led to doubt whether legislative reform, at least prompt and comprehensive reform, in this field of foreign currency obligation, is practicable. Questions as to the recovery of debts or of damages depend so much upon individual mixtures of facts and merits as to make them more suitable for progressive solutions in the courts. I think that we have an opportunity to reach such a solution here. I would accordingly depart from the *Havana Railways* case and dismiss this appeal.

LORD SIMON OF GLAISDALE (dissenting): My Lords, "… if there is one thing clear in our law, it is that the claim must be made in sterling and the judgment given in sterling," said Lord Denning in *In re United Railways of Havana and Regla Warehouses* at pp. 1068-69. This was apparently still the law when *Jugoslavenska Oceanska Plovidba v. Castle Investment Co. Inc.* was decided on July 6, 1973 (see especially Lord Denning MR at p. 299D-F). But by the time the judgments in *Schorsch Meier GmbH v. Hennin* came to be delivered by the Court of Appeal some 17 months later the things that had been clearest in our law were no longer apparent: in fact the rules of law had been clearly reversed; and it was held that a claim could be made in our courts in a foreign currency and judgment could be given in that currency by an English court. Of course, the fact that a rule of law is clear and of long standing and has been reiterated by a long series of great lawyers does not preclude its abrogation when it is found to work injustice or no longer to accord with changed social or economic conditions or with changed ideologies or sensibilities or with newly dominant theories. But it has been generally accepted that a revolutionary change in the law prompted by such factors is within the proper and exclusive province of Parliament advised by the executive (and often, appropriately, by a Royal Commission or a departmental or interdepartmental committee); because Parliament, so advised, is in general the constitutional organ best fitted to weigh such factors. It is true that since 1966 your Lordships have power to depart from a previous decision of your Lordship's House; although, in view of the limited resources available to decision-making by a court of law, it is a power which your Lordships have exercised with due restraint. But the statement of Lord Gardiner LC of July 26, 1966 [*Practice Statement (Judicial Precedent)*, [1966] 1 WLR 395], expressly asserted that it was "not intended to affect the operation of the rule of precedent elsewhere than" in your Lordships' House; and it is clear law that the Court of Appeal is bound by a decision of your Lordships' House and (at least on its civil side) by a previous decision of the Court of Appeal itself …. Any change in this respect would require legislation. …

Notwithstanding the great authority and the high lineage of the *Havana* case, notwithstanding all its juridical adhesions, notwithstanding my lack of confidence that I am capable of weighing the full potentialities of the situation and the full repercussions of the decision, I might be tempted to join in overruling *Havana* if I were convinced that that would on balance conduce to justice. I do not think that the *Havana* rules do justice in the present case—

it was envisaged that they (like all others put forward) might not in every case. But take the following example.

John Mitchell is a newly and greatly enriched dividend-stripper and property speculator in England. He conceives that a notable art collection would be a desirable adjunct and mark of his new position in society. His art agent learns that Count Commenus has the finest collection in Central Europe, accumulated by his enlightened family over the centuries; and that the estates of the count are so heavily encumbered that he is reluctantly faced with the necessity of selling his family collection. The deal is clinched. John Mitchell agrees to buy the collection for 10 million Ruritanian talers. The taler is gold-backed, and the sum is equivalent to £1 million. The collection is duly shipped to England, but the purchaser fails to pay on the due date. It is not his fault. War has broken out, and strict exchange control has been imposed. Towards the end of the war a revolution takes place in Ruritania. Count Commenus is glad to escape with his bare life, and arrives penniless in this country. In the meantime, the Ruritanian taler, no longer gold-backed, has become worth only the accumulating paper it is printed on. Count Commenus remembers his debt from Mr. Mitchell and that his magnificent collection is now the principal ornament of the Mitchell mansions. He claims £1 million. Mr. Mitchell tenders him a lorry filled with 10 million worthless Ruritanian talers. Is it justice that Mr. Mitchell should succeed, the proud possessor of a valuable collection acquired for nothing, and that the count should starve? ...

Afterword. There are three more general questions which are raised by this important appeal.

(1) Overruling *Havana* involves that the law must be deemed always to have been as my noble and learned friends now declare it. This may affect the *vires* of some Rules of Court; but beyond this there has been, so far as I can see, no consideration of what consequences the retrospective alteration of the law (for, let us face it, that is the reality) may have. I would be more ready to go along with my noble and learned friends if the decision had prospective effect only. One of the several reasons why radical law reform is in general more appropriately carried out by Parliament is that a statute can (and usually does) operate prospectively. I venture once again to plead that consideration should be given to the various forms of prospective overruling such as obtain in some other common law systems.

(2) The type of law reform by the judiciary which is here exemplified, and which has been exemplified in some other recent cases, is a very considerable social responsibility. Of course, no worthwhile judge is afraid of responsibility. But I presume to suggest that consideration should be given to the desirability of the Lords of Appeal sitting in banc in such circumstances—at least where the overruling of a *recent* decision of your Lordships' House is in question.

(3) The main ground of my dissent from the opinions of my noble and learned friends is that this type of issue is unsuitable for law reform by the judiciary. It is the sort of case where, in my view, a wide range of advice, official especially but also commercial, is required. The training and experience of a judge is unsuitable for this type of decision-making unaided; his circumspection is too narrow; his very qualities of keen perception of his immediate problem tend to militate against sound judgment of the wider and more general issues involved. But if courts are to undertake legislative responsibilities, something might be done to equip them better for the type of decision-making which is involved. Official

advice and a balanced executive view might be made available by a law officer or his counsel acting as *amicus curiae*. I venture to suggest consideration of some such machinery.

Batavia Times Publishing Co. v. Davis
(1978), 20 OR (2d) 437 (HC), aff'd. (1979), 26 OR (2d) 249 and 800n (CA)

CARRUTHERS J: … Counsel for the parties have now made their representations concerning the issue of what rate of exchange, if any, is to be applied as of what date in computing the amount owed by the defendant under the judgment I gave on December 21, 1977.

Both counsel are in agreement that s. 11 of the *Currency and Exchange Act*, RSC 1970, c. C-39, requires all money judgments granted by Courts in Canada to be expressed in the currency of Canada. Section 11 [now s. 12 of the *Currency Act*] reads as follows:

> 11. All public accounts throughout Canada shall be kept in the currency of Canada; and any statement as to money or money value in any indictment or legal proceeding shall be stated in the currency of Canada.

I was referred to the decision of *Baumgartner v. Carsley Silk Co. Ltd.* (1971), 23 DLR (3d) 255 (Qué. CA). There, Montgomery JA concluded that a judgment of the Supreme Court of the District of Montreal whereby the defendant was ordered to pay a sum of money expressed in "U.S. dollars" violated the provisions of s. 11 and could not stand. I note that, as in the present case, there was no suggestion made there that s. 11 of the *Currency and Exchange Act* cannot be so applied for constitutional reasons. I do not intend here to pursue that matter further because in a final analysis and, in any event, I have to agree with Montgomery JA when he states that all judgments must be "susceptible of execution." I think notwithstanding the fact that we do not have in Ontario a provision such as is contained in art. 469 of the *Code of Civil Procedure*, 1965 (Qué.), c. 80, to which Montgomery JA referred, the same difficulty would confront Sheriff's officers here in attempting to execute a judgment which called for the payment of a sum expressed only in a foreign currency. I do not believe that similar problems would arise if a judgment of this Court could be expressed in terms which included a specified sum of foreign currency and provision for the payment of an equivalent amount of Canadian dollars.

In the present case we are dealing with the enforcement in Ontario of a judgment originally obtained in the State of Pennsylvania and which calls for the defendant to pay an amount expressed in United States currency. The parties agree that I am able to apply an exchange rate so that the amount of my judgment as expressed in Canadian dollars reflects more accurately the value of the debt upon which the original cause of action was based. The parties are not able to agree on what rate should be chosen, and this raises the problem of determining a proper date for conversion, for the rate of exchange prevailing on that date will be applied. Having regard to the economic climate of fluctuating currencies which I know has existed for some time the choice can be very significant to the parties. No evidence has yet been led on what the rate of exchange was on the various dates available to be chosen. If when I have determined the date for conversion no agreement as to the rate has been reached between the parties, I will accept the statement from a Canadian chartered bank over the signature of an officer or manager.

From the authorities which I have read I have concluded that the choice of proper date of conversion that has been made is a product of judicial decision-making, and, in so far as Canadian cases dealing with the subject-matter are concerned they indicate that Canadian Courts have followed the English case law. The English Courts in cases involving an action brought to enforce a foreign judgment appear to have dealt with a choice of conversion date on a basis different than where the action was proceeding on the original cause of action, and where the Court was required to assess damages or give judgment in terms of or on the basis of foreign currency. It is to be noted that the English Courts until 1975 have always proceeded on the premise that they had possessed no ability in any case to grant judgment that was expressed in a foreign currency.

Scott v. Bevan (1831), 2 B & Ad. 78, 109 ER 1073 (KB), is one of the earlier decisions on this subject of conversion rate. It has been confirmed by subsequent cases as a precedent for holding in cases involving an action to enforce a foreign judgment that the date as of which the exchange rate is to be applied is the date of the foreign judgment. The case involved an action that was instituted in England on a judgment obtained in Jamaica for recovery of a debt. The Court held the plaintiff should recover a sum of money expressed in that amount of sterling which the currency would have produced according to the actual rate of exchange between the two countries at the date of the Jamaican judgment.

Scott v. Bevan was referred to by Viscount Simonds in the House of Lords decision of *Re United Railways of Havana and Regal Warehouses Ltd.*, [1961] AC 1007 (HL (Eng.)) at p. 1046 as one of "certain landmarks in the case law" on the subject of conversion rate, and Lord Denning in the same decision referred to it with approval.

Sellers J in the case of *East India Trading Co. Inc. v. Carmel Exporters & Importers Ltd.*, [1952] 2 QB 439 followed *Scott v. Bevan*. In that case, the plaintiff sued on a foreign judgment obtained in the State of New York awarding damages for breach of contract. In the interval, the English currency had been devalued. The judgment was sufficient if the rate of exchange was calculated as of the date of actual breach, but a further sum would be due if the date of judgment in the New York Court was adopted. Sellers J accepted the date of the foreign judgment as the relevant date.

The *East India Trading* case was the most recent English authority brought to my attention that involved an action in which a foreign judgment was being enforced and where it was necessary to determine the date of conversion for the purposes of applying an appropriate rate of exchange. I have been referred to no Canadian cases dealing with this situation. Ordinarily, then, under these circumstances I would by reason of the persuasive authority of these English cases to which I have referred apply the rule adopted in those cases and, accordingly, fix the date of the judgment of the Pennsylvania Court as the pertinent date. I do not, however, think that such an approach should be taken without first having regard to the recent developments which have occurred in England concerning the rule to be applied in action where the plaintiff is suing on the original cause of action.

With the exception of an action brought upon a debt expressed in foreign currency, no question had existed for over 300 years that the English Courts would, where required, choose as a relevant time for conversion the date of the original breach, whether that was in an action for breach of contract or tort. This has been referred to as the "breach-day" rule. The *United Railways of Havana* case was the first occasion upon which the House of Lords had been asked to consider the subject of conversion rate. The result was a confirmation of the rule and a clarification that it extended to all cases including cases where a plaintiff sued for a debt due in a foreign currency. Prior to that decision there had been many cases which had dealt with the question of the conversion rate, including two decisions of the Judicial Committee of the Privy Council. One was *Owners of Steamship "Celia" v. Owners of Steamship "Volturno,"* [1921] 2 AC 544 (HL (Eng.)) and another was *Syndic in Bankruptcy of Salim Nasrallah Khoury v. Khayat*, [1943] AC 507 (HL (Eng.)) at pp. 512-3, where Lord Wright said:

> At what dates must the rate of exchange be calculated? There can, their Lordships apprehend, be now no doubt as to the English law on this point. It is true that different views have been taken at different times and by different systems of law. Indeed, there are at least four different rules which might be adopted. The rate of exchange might be determined as at the date at which payment was due, or at the date of actual payment, or at the date of the commencement of proceedings to enforce payment, or at the date of judgment. English law has adopted the first rule, not only in regard to obligations to pay a sum certain at a particular date, but also in regard to obligations the breach of which sounds in damages, as for an ordinary breach of contract, and also in regard to the satisfaction of damages for a wrongful act or tort.

In the *United Railways* case, Viscount Simonds said, at pp. 1048-9:

> We are engaged in settling the law upon a question in which any rule is artificial and to some extent arbitrary. In other systems of law different rules have been adopted, there is no doubt that one system may benefit one creditor and another another. No rule can do perfect justice in every case. In this country the rule is settled so as to bind all courts that where the claim is in damages for breach of contract, or for a tortious act, the date of conversion is the date of that breach or that act. It would, in my opinion, introduce a sort of refinement into the law, against which I have striven and shall ever strive, if a different rule were adopted in the case of a foreign debt.

In the same case Lord Reid said, at p. 1052:

> The reason for the existing rule is, I think, primarily procedural. A plaintiff cannot sue in England for payment of dollars, and he cannot get specific performance of a contract to pay dollars—it would not be right that he should.

At p. 1053, Lord Reid continued:

> So even if this were still an open question, I would have to come to the conclusion that in every case where a plaintiff sues for a debt due in a foreign currency, that debt should be converted into sterling at the rate of exchange current when the debt fell due. That rule may in some cases be artificial, it may even be unjust, but it has been accepted for a long time, it is clear and certain, and no other rule could be relied on to produce a more just result: indeed, no other rule is really practicable.

As of 1961 then the decision of the House of Lords in *Re United Railways of Havana* was the authority binding upon all English Courts. It is to be noted that the reason for the rule, as discussed in that decision was primarily practical or procedural it being thought a plaintiff could not in England sue to recover a foreign currency or damages expressed in a foreign currency, because the defendant could not be forced to pay the same in England.

In 1975 the Court of Appeal in England departed from this rule and gave judgment in Deutschmarks, stipulating that if payment of the judgment was made in sterling, the conversion should be made as of the date of payment. The case of *Schorsch Meier GmbH v. Hennin*, [1975] QB 416 (CA), concerned a debt for sale and delivery of goods pursuant to a contract which provided for payment in German funds. Following the date of the breach by the English debtor, the value of sterling declined relative to the value of German currency. The Court of Appeal based its decision primarily on certain provisions of the Treaty of Rome which authorized payment for goods supplied in the currency of the creditor's own State if that was the currency of the contract. Of greater interest for the purposes of the present case is the fact that the English Court of Appeal also supported its judgment on the basis that the economic and legal conditions underlying the House of Lords' decision in *Re United Railways of Havana* no longer existed. According to Lord Denning, who had spoken as a member of the House of Lords in the *Re United Railways of Havana* case, the rule restricting payment to English currency evolved because of two factors, faith in the stability of sterling and procedural difficulties, the latter being the prime factor. As sterling "floats in the wind" and procedural changes had since altered the form of judgment and permitted the specific performance of a contract to pay money expressed in foreign currency, Lord Denning was compelled to change a rule he considered obsolete by economic changes. At p. 156 of the report he stated: "Seeing that the reasons no longer exist, we were at liberty to discard the rule itself. *Cessante ratione legis cessat ipsa lex.*"

It is doubtful that the English Court of Appeal was entitled to depart from the rule of law confirmed by the House of Lords in the *Re United Railways* case on the basis put forward by Lord Denning. The principle of *stare decisis* required then as now that until reviewed by the House of Lords a rule of law which it had pronounced remained to be followed by all lower Courts in England. The review did not take place until later that year in the decision of *Miliangos v. George Frank (Textiles) Ltd.*, [1976] AC 443 (HL (Eng.)). The majority of the members of the House of Lords in *Miliangos* opted for a more realistic approach to modern economic conditions. In that case a Swiss seller and an English buyer contracted for the sale of goods according to Swiss law with payment to be made in Swiss francs. The plaintiff sued in England for payment of the sterling equivalent of the contract price at the date payment was due. Between the time of the breach and trial, sterling fell in value against the Swiss franc. Undoubtedly mindful of the *Schorsch Meier* case, the plaintiff had obtained leave to amend its statement of claim, so as to claim an amount due in Swiss francs.

In order to bring about a departure Lord Wilberforce had to overcome the reasoning behind the decision in *Re United Railways of Havana*, where the House of Lords were guided by the premise described there as being primarily procedural in nature that in an action for damages the plaintiff could not recover a sum in a foreign currency but only a sum expressed in sterling. Lord Wilberforce in *Miliangos* felt that the Court had the power to order delivery *in specie* wherever damages were inadequate as might be the case if the "breach-day" rule was applied in times of floating currencies. At p. 463 of the report he stated that the argument concerning the adequacy of damages as a remedy in this situation was "nothing more than an appeal to discretion" and "loses its force." With respect to the proper conversion date, Lord Wilberforce noted that changes in the value of currency between the breach date and date of judgment or payment were the rule rather than the exception. Having regard to the current economic conditions then existing and recognizing a need for the law to conform to commercial realities, he remarked at p. 464:

But if I am faced with the alternative of forcing commercial circles to fall in with a legal doctrine which has noting but precedent to commend it or altering the doctrine so as to confirm with what commercial experience has worked out, I know where my choice lies. *The law should be responsive as well as, at times, enunciatory, and good doctrine can seldom be divorced from sound practice.*

(The emphasis is mine.)

The date of payment, not the date of breach was chosen by the House of Lords in *Miliangos* as the most appropriate date to apply the exchange rate. In the words of Lord Wilberforce at p. 467: "To change the rule would ... avoid injustice in the present case" and "enable the law to keep in step with commercial needs and with the majority of other countries facing similar problems."

It is to be noted that in reversing the decision of the *Re United Railways of Havana* case and departing from the date of breach rule for the purposes of conversion, the majority of the members of the House of Lords in the *Miliangos* case limited their reasoning to the problem before them, that is, claims for foreign money obligations arising under a contract whose proper law was that of a foreign State and where the money of account and payment was of that country or some other country other than the one in which the action was then being brought. Lord Wilberforce said, at pp. 467-68:

> I do not think that we are called on, or would be entitled in this case, to review the whole field of law regarding foreign currency obligations; that is not the method by which changes in the law by judicial decision are made. In my opinion it should be open for future discussion whether the rule applying to money obligations, which can be a simple rule, should apply as regards claims for damages for breach of contract or for tort. ... It is for the courts, or for arbitrators, to work out a solution in each case best adapted to giving the injured plaintiff that amount in damages which will most fairly compensate him for the wrong which he has suffered.

Those Canadian cases which I considered have followed the English law as it existed prior to the *Miliangos* decision. The Supreme Court of Canada in the case of *The Custodian v. Blucher*, [1927] SCR 420, decided that the rate of exchange for conversion into Canadian currency of dividends payable in United States funds to the respondent was the rate prevailing at the time when each dividend became due and payable to the Custodian, the lawful recipient of the moneys and not the date when the respondent became entitled to receive them. Newcombe J said at p. 426:

> As to the time for conversion, I think the learned judge of the Exchequer Court was right in principle, and upon the authority of the decisions, which in England have been substantially uniform, that the rate is that which ruled at the time when each of the quarterly dividends became due or payable to the Custodian. ...

In *Gatineau Power Co. v. Crown Life Ins. Co.*, [1945] SCR 655, Rand J, in giving the judgment of the Supreme Court of Canada and dealing with the ground of appeal concerning the date of conversion into Canadian funds, the action having been brought on bond, said at pp. 658-9:

> In such a case the rule laid down in *The Custodian v. Blucher*, [1927] SCR 420 and in *S.S. Celia v. S.S. Volturno*, [1921] 2 AC 544 (HL (Eng.)) at p. 528 is that conversion into the currency of

the forum is to be made as of the date of the breach and that rule was followed in the Court of King's Bench. But even if it were to take the date of judgment as controlling, the amount recoverable would be the same.

I was not referred to, nor did I find any Canadian case in which the Court was asked to decide the date of conversion in an action where the plaintiff was proceeding to enforce a foreign judgment. All of the cases dealt with actions based on the original cause of action, and, all with one exception, apply the "breach-day" rule. The one exception is the decision of the Ontario Court of Appeal, *Quartier v. Farah* (1921), 49 OLR 186 (CA). This was an action by a French solicitor in Ontario to recover an amount due for services upon the taking of evidence under a foreign commission in France. The majority of the Court of Appeal applied as the date of conversion, the date of judgment. Meredith CJO found that although by statute the judgment was to be expressed in Canadian currency he found no reason why the prevailing rate of exchange should not be applied. He reviewed many prior English and Canadian decisions and then, speaking for the majority, found that the case law which supported the "breach-day" rule involved claims for moneys that were payable at a fixed or definite date or for damages for breach of contract and because the action before the Court there was for neither of those types of claims he decided that the date of judgment was appropriate. Apparently, the Ontario Court of Appeal felt that the "breach-day" rule did not apply to actions based on a foreign debt. That feeling had prevailed for some time in England and, in fact, it remained until the House of Lords decision in *Re United Railways of Havana*, which decided that actions on a foreign debt were not unlike actions for damages for breach of contract and the "breach-day" rule applied.

The most recent Canadian case that I have found is the *Baumgartner v. Carsley Silk Co. Ltd.* decision of the Quebec Court of Appeal, in 1971, 23 DLR (3d) 255 (Qué. CA), and to which I have referred above. In that case, Lajoie JA remarked that there was no evidence in the case of the equivalent in Canadian dollars of the American dollars "at the relevant time." He did not say what date he considered to be relevant.

The decision of the House of Lords in *Miliangos* has reversed the English cases, and in particular, the rule of law upon which the Canadian cases, including those of the Supreme Court of Canada to which I have referred, have proceeded. Although strictly speaking *Miliangos* has not overruled those decisions of the Supreme Court of Canada including the decision of the Judicial Committee of the Privy Council [*sic*] in *Owners of Steamship "Celia" v. Owners of Steamship "Volturno,"* [1921] 2 AC 544 (HL (Eng.)), and they therefore remain today as authorities binding upon the lower Courts of Canada, I find it difficult to accept that those cases should now be applied by the lower Courts. Apart from the fact that the "breach-day" rule which they applied no longer exists in England, when I consider that justice requires that a creditor should not suffer by reason of a depreciation of the value of currency between the due date on which the debtor should have met his obligation and the date when the creditor was eventually able to obtain judgment, I think what Lord Wilberforce had to say, at p. 469 of the *Miliangos* case, is most pertinent:

> The law on this topic is judge made; it has been built up over the years from case to case. It is entirely within this House's duty, in the course of administering justice, to give the law a new direction in a particular case where, on principle and in reason, it appears right to do so. I cannot accept the suggestion that because a rule is long-established only legislation can change it—that

may be so when the rule is so deeply entrenched that it has infected the whole legal system, or the choice of a new rule involves more far-reaching research than courts can carry out.

I have noted above Lord Denning in *Schorsch Meier GmbH v. Hennin* felt that he was entitled to disregard a decision of the House of Lords which was binding on the English Court of Appeal. Lord Wilberforce described this approach as a "distortion of the judicial process" and Lord Simon questioned if the principle of binding precedents was not paramount so as to require a lower Court to wait until the higher Court had dealt with the matter even though the reason for its decision in the outstanding authority no longer existed. I feel I must be concerned about these remarks because there has been some suggestion in the English cases that although there appears to be a distinction between those cases involving a plaintiff suing on their original cause of action and those where a foreign judgment is being enforced, there actually is not. The suggestion is that the foreign judgment is the debt being sued upon, and its date is therefore the date of breach thereby making that situation consistent with the other line of cases. In *East India Trading Co. Inc. v. Carmel Exporters and Importers Ltd.*, at p. 444, Sellers J said: "The American judgment is the immediate source from which the defendants' liability flows in the present action, and no earlier date can be called into consideration." This was said by him after he expressly refused to accept the contention that the date of the breach of contract should be taken as the material date, and after he said at p. 443:

> In the case of the enforcement of a foreign judgment I would follow the most recent decision of *Madeleine Vionnet et Cie v. Wills*, [1940] 1 KB 72 (CA), which decided that the correct date on which to convert a debt in foreign currency sued for in this country is the date on which the debt became due. This is in accord with *Scott v. Bevan*, which, after all these years, should be followed unless there are impelling reasons to the contrary.

In following *Madeleine Vionnet v. Wills*, [1940] 1 KB 72 (CA), Sellers J followed a decision which involved a claim for damages for breach of contract, and where Clauson LJ, after indicating that there was no distinction in principle between a claim for breach of contract *via* damages and a claim *via* judgment for a fixed sum, applied the "breach-day" rule. In saying: "This is in accord with *Scott v. Bevan*," I can only conclude that in accepting the date of the foreign judgment as the date for conversion, Sellers J felt the two situations were the same. I find this reasoning difficult to follow. A judgment enforcing a foreign judgment does not merge the original cause of action. The action to enforce is not based on the original cause of action. The original cause of action remains and, accordingly, there is still a date of breach for the Court to consider if it wished to do so, and such breach date is not the date of the foreign judgment. In my opinion, the decisions of the Supreme Court of Canada in *The Custodian v. Blucher* and *Gatineau Power v. Crown Life* and the decision of the Judicial Committee of the Privy Council in *"Celia" v. "Volturno"* cannot be applied in cases involving the enforcement of a foreign judgment so as to require me to follow that which was done in *Scott v. Bevan* and *East India Trading Co.* I hold this view without considering that those cases would not now in my opinion likely be followed in England.

As I find the situation in Canada at this time, then, there are no authorities which bind me in determining the conversion date in a case such as we are dealing with here. I am then in my opinion free to adopt that date which in my view "avoids an injustice" and is "in step with commercial needs." Neither of the parties should be adversely affected by fluctuating currencies.

I do not believe that the Courts of Canada are able to move to the date of effective payment as providing the rate of exchange as the English Courts have now done in cases involving circumstances similar to those outlined in *Miliangos*. As I have indicated above I can see no reason why the English Courts will not, as it was left open for them to do by the House of Lords, take the same approach in all cases where the date of conversion rate is material, including actions to enforce a foreign judgment. I tend to agree with the learned author J.-G. Castel where he says in p. 533 of his text *Canadian Conflict of Laws* (Toronto: Butterworths, 1975), vol. 1:

> It would be difficult for Canadian courts to adopt the rate of exchange prevailing on the date of effective payment since, on the one hand, they cannot render a decision expressed in a foreign currency and, on the other hand, they do not know the rate of exchange which will prevail on that day. ...
>
> In view of federal legislation, the adoption of the rate of exchange prevailing at the time when the second judgment is given, as unsatisfactory as it may be, is certainly a lesser evil, so long as no machinery is found for the adoption of the effective payment-day rule. Where the local currency has depreciated after the day when the original judgment was given, it is unjustifiable to impose on a creditor a loss through depreciation caused by the debtor's fault. The date of second-judgment rule would at least produce the same result as the date of effective payment rule if the judgment is paid at once.

If I could be satisfied that there are not procedural or practical problems and that the *Currency and Exchange Act* either did not apply to judgments or did not prevent a judgment being given for a sum of foreign currency and its equivalent in Canadian dollars, as the English Courts are now doing, I would adopt the effective date of payment as being the date for determining the rate of exchange. Because I am not certain that there are no problems and because I assume that the *Currency and Exchange Act* does not permit judgments to be given as they are now being given in England, I will use the rate of exchange as prevailing at the date of the second judgment herein, the date of my judgment, December 21, 1977, in determining the amount which the defendant here owes to the plaintiff. As I have said above if the parties cannot agree upon what the rate of exchange was on December 21, 1977, I will accept on behalf of the plaintiff a statement of any chartered bank of Canada signed by an officer or manager thereof which sets out the rate of exchange on that date.

There will, therefore, be judgment before the plaintiff in the amount of that number of Canadian dollars which as of December 21, 1977 will be the equivalent of $16,940.63 United States dollars together with interest at the rate of 5% per annum calculated on the amount from August 26, 1970 to December 21, 1977, inclusive. The plaintiff is to have its costs of this action forthwith after taxation thereof.

Clinton v. Ford
(1982), 37 OR (2d) 448 (CA)

[On the question of the date for conversion in an action on a foreign judgment, Houlden JA said (at 453-54) for the court:]

HOULDEN JA: The defendant alleged that Judge Sullivan should not have used the exchange rate for the South African rand as at the date of the statement of claim. He argued that the amount of the judgment should have been converted into Canadian dollars at the conversion rate existing on the date of judgment.

The writ of summons pleaded that the rate of exchange as quoted by the Canadian Imperial Bank of Commerce at the date of the issue of the writ was 1.4927 Canadian dollars for each 1.000 South African rand and stated that on the date of judgment that amount would be converted to Canadian dollars at the rate quoted by the Canadian Imperial Bank of Commerce. The defendant defended the specially endorsed writ, and the plaintiff had to proceed with the action. In the statement of claim, the plaintiff pleaded that the rate of exchange at the date of the statement of claim was 1.5771 Canadian dollars for each 1.000 South African rand. This is the only information that was before Judge Sullivan on the motion for judgment. No material was put before him as to the rate of exchange at the date of judgment.

In the recent case of *Batavia Times Publishing Co. v. Davies* (1978), 20 OR (2d) 437, affirmed 26 OR (2d) 800 (CA), Carruthers J stated (at p. 446) that the judge granting judgment on a foreign judgment should be free "to adopt that date which … 'avoids an injustice' and is 'in step with commercial needs.' " While Judge Sullivan might have used the rate of exchange prevailing at the date of judgment, I am unable to say that, on the material before him, he erred in using the rate prevailing at the date of the statement of claim.

NOTES

1. In *Williams & Glyn's Bank Ltd. v. Belkin Packaging Ltd.*, [1983] 1 SCR 661, at 682, where the trial court had followed *Batavia Times v. Davis*, the Supreme Court of Canada, deciding the case on another ground, found it "not necessary to consider the issue" of the conversion date. In *Brown & Root v. Aerotech Herman Nelson Inc. et al.* (2004), 238 DLR (4th) 594, the Manitoba Court of Appeal held, by a majority, that conversion of foreign currency at the date of judgment was permissible, and appropriate in that case.

2. For a full discussion, see V. Black, *Foreign Currency Claims in the Conflict of Laws* (Oxford: Hart Publishing, 2010).

Courts of Justice Act
RSO 1990, c. C.43

Foreign Money Obligations

121(1) Subject to subsections (3) and (4), where a person obtains an order to enforce an obligation in foreign currency, the order shall require payment of an amount in Canadian currency sufficient to purchase the amount of the obligation in the foreign currency at a bank in Ontario listed in Schedule I to the *Bank Act* (Canada) at the close of business on the first day on which the bank quotes a Canadian dollar rate for purchase of the foreign currency before the day payment of the obligation is received by the creditor.

Multiple Payments

(2) Where more than one payment is made under an order referred to in subsection (1), the rate of conversion shall be the rate determined as provided in subsection (1) for each payment.

Discretion of Court

(3) Subject to subsection (4), where, in a proceeding to enforce an obligation in a foreign currency, the court is satisfied that conversion of the amount of the obligation to Canadian currency as provided in subsection (1) would be inequitable to any party, the order may require payment of an amount in Canadian currency sufficient to purchase the amount of the obligation in the foreign currency at a bank in Ontario on such other day as the court considers equitable in the circumstances.

Other Obligations That Include Conversion

(4) Where an obligation enforceable in Ontario provides for a manner of conversion to Canadian currency of an amount in a foreign currency, the court shall give effect to the manner of conversion in the obligation.

Enforcement by Seizure or Garnishment

(5) Where a writ of seizure and sale or notice of garnishment is issued under an order to enforce an obligation in a foreign currency, the day the sheriff, bailiff or clerk of the court receives money under the writ or notice shall be deemed, for the purposes of this section and any obligation referred to in subsection (4), to be the day payment is received by the creditor.

CHAPTER TWO

Awards Measured by Benefit to Defendant

Two remedies, the first equitable in origin and the second deriving from the common law, permit the plaintiff to recover on the basis of the gain accruing to the defendant rather than the actual damage sustained. The equitable remedy, account, is described as follows.

Harry Street, *Principles of the Law of Damages*
(London: Sweet & Maxwell, 1962), at 259-66 (footnotes omitted)

Account

In many circumstances the plaintiff is entitled to an account of the profits made by the defendant. Equity developed this remedy, and since the *Judicature Acts* a common-law court can also give it on the same conditions as those previously recognized in equity alone.

A plaintiff who seeks an account, then, must have some ground for seeking equitable relief.

1. He may be making a purely equitable demand, such as rescission for fraud, or setting up a constructive trust.

2. He may already be in equity because he seeks some equitable relief such as injunction, whereupon equity will administer complete relief.

3. Legal remedies may be inadequate, for example, accounts may be so complicated that a bill of discovery would have been granted under the old rules.

4. The proceedings may be of a character entrusted to Chancery jurisdiction in order to strike a balance between parties: guardians, receivers, joint tenants, partnership.

The plaintiff must bring his action within one of these four heads before he can justify a claim for an account: it is not enough, for example, for him to prove a tort.

The significance of account in the present context is like that of quasi-contract. When the remedy is ordered, the plaintiff is not limited to his own loss, his damages are measured instead by the profit which the wrongdoer has made.

Such inexplicably little use is made of account that it is difficult to produce English authorities which mark its limits with precision. Perhaps its most venerable application is in waste. If the plaintiff sues for equitable waste, he will be entitled to an account, even though an injunction is not competent, for he falls within Rule 1 above. Whatever the kind of waste, if an injunction will lie to restrain it, an account of past waste will be ordered. If the waste is not equitable, and in the circumstances there is nothing on which an injunction can operate, an account will not be ordered unless the plaintiff can bring himself within another of the four heads. For instance, where a tenant for life was executrix of a preceding tenant for life, both being impeachable for waste, and both having committed waste of timber, although an injunction and an account were granted against the existing tenant for life, it was held that, as no injunction could be granted against the preceding tenant for life, an account could not be ordered against her executrix for waste committed by the preceding tenant for life. On the other hand, where a remainderman in fee colluded with the tenant for life in cutting timber before the birth of the contingent remainderman, so that equity jurisdiction alone would be able to redress the wrong, the unavailability of an injunction did not prevent the ordering of an account. Where the accounts will have the complexity of an account in trade, this is in itself reason for granting an account in equity. Thus, even though no injunction is possible, waste in the form of extracting coal will be remedied by account, whereas if the object of the waste were timber, the courts used to refuse an account on the ground that no trade was involved. When a tenant in common commits destructive waste on the common property, for example, by working a mine, he is liable to account to his co-owners for their shares of the moneys so obtained.

The most important area for the account today is that of economic torts. As long ago as 1843, where the plaintiff's copyright had been infringed the Court of Chancery ordered an account, Wigram V-C saying "the court ... takes from the wrongdoer all his profits, and gives them to the person who is wronged, though the court in so doing may give a party more than he is entitled to, for *non constat* that a single copy more would have been sold by the plaintiff, if the injury had not been committed." If the defendant passes off the plaintiff's product as his own, whether or not his conduct be innocent, the plaintiff can claim an account of the defendant's profits. In other allied wrongs, such as infringement of trade marks, patents and designs, and injurious falsehood, the plaintiff will sometimes be able to claim an account. He will ordinarily get into equity by seeking an injunction. There seems no reason why, in cases like *Hivac, Ltd. v. Park Royal Scientific Instruments, Ltd.*, [1946] Ch. 169 (CA) where the plaintiffs obtained an injunction restraining their business rivals from employing their servants because of their "know-how" in their spare time, an account of profits should not also be obtained. Similarly where an injunction is obtained to restrain continued disclosure of trade secrets, an account of profits should lie; English cases are rare, but in *Green v. Folgham* (1823), 1 Sim & St. 398; 57 ER 159 (Ch.) an account was directed against a trustee who appropriated a trade secret. The principle is accepted in the United States. English law also recognises that the victim of deceit, instead of rescinding, can in effect ratify the fraud and seek an account on the basis of the principal-agent relationship thereby created.

It is submitted that if the plaintiff can bring himself within the jurisdiction of equity for any of the four reasons given earlier he can claim an account of the profits resulting to the defendant from his wrong, whatever it may be. For instance, where the defendant in an action for defamation was restrained from attacking the plaintiff's trading reputation, an account could also be ordered. An American case of particular interest in view of the decision in *Phillips v. Homfray* is *Edwards v. Lee's Administrator* (1936), 265 Ky. 418:

> The plaintiff and defendant were owners of adjoining lands above the "Great Onyx Cave," the entrance to which was on the defendant's land. The defendant conducted sightseeing tours of the cave upon payment, thereby trespassing upon the plaintiff's land. The plaintiff was granted an injunction and an account of profits. He was given one-third of the profits, based on the relative area of his part of the cave and the attractions therein.

Whatever difficulties there might be in the way of a successful action in England for quasi-contract on such facts, it is submitted that, once they were overcome, an English court would have followed the American court in granting an account of profits on a rateable proportion. Of course, if the plaintiff has sustained a naked injury without any corresponding benefit to the defendant account will not lie: there is no profit to account. So, where a tenant for life wrongfully pulled down a mansion house and built a new house with the materials of the old one on another part of the estate, no account was granted; it would have been otherwise had the tenant for life sold any of the materials.

It is difficult to formulate rules for the assessment of profits which are of general application to account. In account of mines and minerals the courts have followed the common-law rules of trespass by deducting the cost of severance and bringing to the surface where the conduct is innocent, and by deducting the cost of raising to the surface but not of extraction where the conduct is fraudulent. It is a question of some importance what expenses, *e.g.*, advertising, proportionate share of overheads, taxes, will be deducted when an account is directed of profits for economic torts, but there is a surprising and regrettable absence of authority.

It is remarkable how little use is made of account. Passing off is illustrative. One would have thought that where the plaintiff is in business in a small way and the defendant palms off his product and, using his superior marketing organisation, effects sales greatly in excess of any contemplated by the plaintiff, account would be his obvious remedy. It used to be thought that the court had a discretion to refuse an account where the plaintiff would otherwise be over-compensated in a manner unjust to the defendant. The House of Lords decisively rejected that view in *Weingarten Bros. v. Charles Bayer, Ltd.* (1905), 22 RPC 341 (HL (Eng.)):

> The Court of Appeal refused an account, because it would be grossly unjust to the defendant who was a large trader, and would over-compensate the plaintiff whose anticipated profits were small. The House of Lords reversed the decision on the ground that the plaintiff always has the right to ask for an account of profits in addition to his injunction, and ordered an account.

And yet account remains rare in passing off.

It is almost invariably stated that the plaintiff cannot claim both account and damages. If this were so, it would of course be a serious restriction on account. Before 1858 there was no power in Chancery to award damages, so that account and damages could not both be awarded in Chancery. After the passing of *Lord Cairns' Act* in 1858, which for the first time authorised the award of damages in Chancery, the court awarded an account of profits for minerals extracted and also in the same action awarded damages where other harm had been caused to the plaintiff's land. It follows, therefore, that there is no procedural obstacle to recovering damages and account in the same suit. Obviously, one could not have both for the same head of damage; a plaintiff could not claim an account of profits for minerals extracted and also damages for conversion of the coal.

There is, however, considerable authority for the view that account and damages cannot both be claimed in trade torts. In *Neilson v. Betts* (1871), LR 5 HL 1 (Eng.) the claim was for infringement of patent. After plaintiff had succeeded on the substantive ground, Lord Westbury referred to a point which had not been argued, the form of the decree in which the plaintiff sought both damages and account of profits, and said that the plaintiff must make his election, for "if you take an account of profits you condone the infringement." In associated proceedings a decision of the House of Lords on this opinion was sought [*De Vitre v. Betts* (1873), 6 HL 319 (Eng.)]. The House of Lords confirmed Lord Westbury's view. Lord Cairns said that "the recent power given to the Court of Chancery to grant an inquiry as to damages was not intended to be superadded to, and could not co-exist with, the old relief administered by the Court of Chancery of granting an inquiry as to profits." This decision probably does not overrule the cases on mines cited above: on the other hand it is binding authority for all economic torts that the effect of the Act of 1858 was not to allow a plaintiff in Chancery to claim in one suit both damages and profits in respect of the unlawful appropriation by the defendant. It has since been assumed, not surprisingly, that the point is unarguable, and that the reason for the rule is that the plaintiff would be taking up inconsistent positions if he challenged the infringement by seeking damages and condoned the defendant's infringement by requiring him to account for his profits.

But what is the precedent status of *De Vitre v. Betts*? It is merely a decision on the interpretation of the Act of 1858: that the Act did not authorise a court of Chancery to award at one and the same time damages for industrial torts in addition to the existing power to award an account of profits. The Act of 1858 has been repealed, and section 24 of the *Judicature Act* of 1873 now authorises all divisions to grant "such and the same relief" as that formerly given by courts of Chancery. It is arguable therefore that *De Vitre v. Betts* is a dead letter. What would continue to count would be pre-1873 decisions in Chancery that account cannot be given if damages have already been given, or ones deciding at common law that damages cannot be given if account has already been given in Chancery, for they would have restricted the relief given by section 24. There are, however, no such House of Lords decisions, or indeed any other traceable ones. One can therefore consider the question untrammeled by force of binding precedent.

Obviously, then, one must look to the argument of Lord Westbury that to seek account is to condone the infringement. In *Caxton Publishing Co. v. Sutherland Publishing Co., Ltd.,* [1939] AC 178 (HL (Eng.)) the House of Lords, after stating this principle of Lord Westbury, added at p. 199:

> For the same reason, namely, that by doing so the plaintiff affirms the action of the converter, it is possible for a plaintiff to lose his remedy in conversion by electing to sue for money had and received and so waiving the tort: *Smith v. Baker*.

Next came *United Australia, Ltd. v. Barclays Bank, Ltd.*, [1941] AC 1 (HL (Eng.)). The House of Lords held that *Smith v. Baker* was wrongly decided. They exposed the fallacy that by suing for money had and received you condone the wrong: the previous error was failure to realise that these were merely different remedies for the same wrong. There is no compulsion to choose between alternative remedies. As Lord Porter said in the earlier case, the analogy between account and damages on the one hand, and damages and money had and received on the other, is in this respect exact. Does it not follow that the House of Lords has necessarily rejected Lord Westbury's view that to seek account is to condone the wrong? Not only is there no binding authority preventing the plaintiff from seeking both, but the alleged reason for denying it has been authoritatively exposed as fallacious. Of course the plaintiff cannot recover both an account of the defendant's profits and the damage in the form of loss of profits which he has sustained, for there is another principle, left intact, that a man cannot be compensated twice over. There are, however, circumstances in economic torts where the plaintiff suffers damage other than loss of profits on sales: he may have suffered loss of goodwill, or business reputation. In the United States the plaintiff can recover such damages in addition to an account of profits. It is submitted that the English rule is the same. *United Australia, Ltd. v. Barclays Bank, Ltd.*, shows that there is no difficulty in claiming both simultaneously.

No doubt, then, a plaintiff who has sued in conversion cannot maintain a subsequent action for money had and received. No doubt also a plaintiff who has recovered one head of damages cannot bring a second action for the same tort in order to recover another head of damages—he could not recover damages for loss of profits and then have an account of profits. But equally clearly two different heads of damages (provided always that they do not overlap) are recoverable in one proceeding.

It is true that Lord Atkin said that when the plaintiff relies both on conversion and money had and received "he can take judgment only for the one, and his cause of action on both will then be merged in the one" (at p. 30). But are the remedies of account and damages for passing off separate causes of action in the sense that money had and received and conversion are? And in any case is Lord Atkin merely saying that the notion of estoppel involved in merger of judgment only operates to prevent successive actions on the same facts or the recovery of double compensation?

It is submitted therefore that this doctrine of merger does not prevent a plaintiff from recovering both an account of profits and damages other than those connected with profits. The American courts have held that both are recoverable in one action, and English courts should exercise their freedom to reach the same conclusion. Lord Westbury's dictum should no longer be heeded.

NOTE

Compare the *Copyright Act*, RSC 1985, c. C-42:

35(1) Where a person infringes copyright, the person is liable to pay such damages to the owner of the copyright as the owner has suffered due to the infringement and, in addition to those damages, such part of the profits that the infringer has made from the infringement and that were not taken into account in calculating the damages as the court considers just.

(2) In proving profits,

(a) the plaintiff shall be required to prove only receipts or revenues derived from the infringement; and

(b) the defendant shall be required to prove every element of cost that the defendant claims.

The nature of waiver of tort is discussed in the following case.

United Australia Ltd. v. Barclays Bank, Ltd.
[1941] AC 1 (HL (Eng.))

[In November 1934, debtors of United Australia Ltd. sent to the company a crossed cheque for £1900 payable to their order. The cheque was purportedly endorsed by one Emons, secretary for United Australia Ltd., in favour of MFG Trust Ltd. The cheque was then presented at Barclays Bank for payment into the account of MFG Trust Ltd. In May 1935 United Australia Ltd. issued a writ against MFG Trust Ltd. for £1900 claiming that because Emons had acted without authority, the receipt of the moneys amounted to either a loan to MFG Trust Ltd., or money had and received to United Australia Ltd.'s use. The action never proceeded because in the interim MFG Trust Ltd. went into liquidation. Subsequently, on reviewing the cheque and seeing that it had been cleared by Barclays Bank, United Australia Ltd. commenced proceedings against Barclays Bank for conversion of the cheque, or, alternatively, negligence. The issue before the court was whether the proceedings which had been commenced against MFG Trust Ltd. constituted a defence for Barclays Bank and so relieved it of liability. The lower courts held in favour of Barclays Bank on the ground that because United Australia Ltd. had framed its cause of action against MFG Trust Ltd. as one sounding as a loan, this amounted to a ratification of the actions by Emons, and thus constituted a "waiver of tort" of the conversion and negligence actions brought against Barclays Bank. United Australia Ltd. appealed to the House of Lords.]

LORD ATKIN: ... My Lords, we are thus compelled to consider the law relating to waiver of tort: and two questions arise: (1). Did the plaintiffs waive the conversion by M.F.G. Trust, Ld., by suing them and proving in their liquidation for money lent or money had and received? (2). If they did waive conversion by the M.F.G. Trust, Ld., was that a waiver by them of the conversion by the defendant bank?

I do not propose to discuss at any length the history of the claim in *indebitatus assumpsit*, and the cases through which that history has been traced. Very much learning has been devoted to this subject, and lawyers are indebted to Professor Ames, Sir William Holdsworth, and Professor Winfield for the light they have thrown upon the subject in well known works: and I should not like to omit the work of Mr. R.M. Jackson on "The History of Quasi-Contract in English Law," published in 1936 in the Cambridge Studies in English Legal History, from which I have derived assistance. There is also what I hope I may respectfully call a valuable contribution to the discussion in the articles recently published by my noble and learned friend Lord Wright on *Sinclair v. Brougham*, [1914] AC 398 (HL (Eng.)), and a review of the American Restatement of the Law of Restitution at pp. 1 to 65 of Legal Essays and Addresses published in 1939. I have myself consulted most of the cases referred to in these works with the exception of the cases from the Year Books which I have accepted from the authors.

The story starts with the action of debt which was not necessarily based upon the existence of a contract, for it covered claims to recover sums due for customary dues, penalties for breaches of by-laws, and the like. The action of debt had its drawbacks, the chief being that the defendant could wage his law. There followed the application of the action on the case of assumpsit to debt. "The defendant being indebted then promised." At first there must be an express promise; then the Courts implied a promise from an executory contract:

Slade's case (1602), 4 Coke 92(b); 76 ER 1074 (KB). *Slade's* case was not a claim in *indebitatus* assumpsit, but the principle was applied, and it became unnecessary to prove an express promise in those cases. Then the action was allowed in respect of cases where there was no contract, executory or otherwise, as in the cases where debt would have lain for customary fees and the like; and by a final and somewhat forced application to cases where the defendant had received money of the plaintiff to which he was not entitled. These included cases where the plaintiff had intentionally paid money to the defendant, e.g., claims for money paid on a consideration that wholly failed and money paid under a mistake: cases where the plaintiff had been deceived into paying money, cases where money had been extorted from the plaintiff by threats or duress of goods. They also included cases where money had not been paid by the plaintiff at all but had been received from third persons, as where the defendant had received fees under colour of holding an office which in fact was held by the plaintiff: and finally cases like the present where the defendant had been wrongfully in possession of the plaintiff's goods, had sold them and was in possession of the proceeds. Now to find a basis for the actions in any actual contract whether express or to be implied from the conduct of the parties was in many of the instances given obviously impossible. The cheat or the blackmailer does not promise to repay to the person he has wronged the money which he has unlawfully taken: nor does the thief promise to repay the owner of the goods stolen the money which he has gained from selling the goods. Nevertheless, if a man so wronged was to recover the money in the hands of the wrongdoer, and it was obviously just that he should be able to do so, it was necessary to create a fictitious contract: for there was no action possible other than debt or assumpsit on the one side and action for damages for tort on the other. The action of *indebitatus* assumpsit for money had and received to the use of the plaintiff in the cases I have enumerated was therefore supported by the imputation by the Court to the defendant of a promise to repay. The fiction was so obvious that in some cases the judge created a fanciful relation between the plaintiff and the defendant. Thus in cases where the defendant had wrongly sold the plaintiff's goods and received the proceeds it was suggested in some cases, not in all, that the plaintiff chose to treat the wrongdoer as having sold the goods as his agent and so being under an implied contract to his principal to repay. Even here in the relatively more recent cases where this explanation is given by Grose J in *King v. Leith* (1787), 2 Term. Rep. 141 at p. 145: 100 ER 77 at pp. 78-79 (KB) and *Marsh v. Keating* (1834), 1 Bing. NC 198 at p. 215; 131 ER 1094 at p. 1100 (HL (Eng.)) by Park J in delivering the opinion of the judges in the House of Lords the wrongdoer had in fact in both cases purported to sell the goods as the agent of his principal. But the fiction is too transparent. The alleged contract by the blackmailer and the robber never was made and never could be made. The law, in order to do justice, imputed to the wrongdoer a promise which alone as forms of action then existed could give the injured person a reasonable remedy. But while it was just that the plaintiff in such cases should be able to recover the money in the possession of the other party, he was not bound to exercise this remedy: in cases where the money had been received as the result of a wrong he still had the remedy of claiming damages for tort in action for trespass, deceit, trover, and the like. But he obviously could not compel the wrongdoer to recoup him his losses twice over. Hence he was restricted to one of the two remedies: and herein as I think arose the doctrine of "waiver of the tort." Having recovered in contract it is plain that the plaintiff cannot go on to recover in tort. *Transit in rem judicatam.* The doctrine has thus alternatively been said to be based on election: i.e., election between two remedies and the stage at which this election takes place was the subject of discussion in the argument in the present case. I will treat of election later. But at present I wish to deal with the waiver of the tort which is said to arise whenever the injured person sues in contract for money received. If the plaintiff in truth treats the wrongdoer as having acted as his agent, overlooks the wrong, and by consent of both parties is content to receive the proceeds this will be a true waiver. It will arise necessarily where the plaintiff ratifies in the true sense an unauthorized act of an agent: in that case the lack of authority disappears, and the correct view is not that the tort is waived, but by retroaction of the ratification has never existed. But in the ordinary case the plaintiff has never the slightest intention of waiving, excusing or in any kind of way palliating the tort. If I find that a thief has stolen my securities and is in possession of the proceeds, when I sue him for them I am not excusing him. I am protesting violently that he is a thief and because of his theft I am suing him: indeed he may be in prison upon my prosecution. Similarly with the blackmailer: in such a case I do not understand what can be said to be waived. The man has my money which I have not delivered to him with any real intention of passing to him the property. I sue him because he has the actual property taken: and I suggest that it can make no difference if he extorted a chattel which he afterwards sold. I protest that a man cannot waive a wrong unless he either has a real intention to waive it, or can fairly have imputed to him such an intention, and in the cases which we have been considering there can be no such intention either actual or imputed. These fantastic resemblances of contracts invented in order to meet requirements of the law as to forms of action which have now disappeared should not in these days be allowed to affect actual rights. When these ghosts of the past stand in the path of justice clanking their mediaeval chains the proper course for the judge is to pass through them undeterred.

Concurrently with the decisions as to waiver of tort there is to be found a supposed application of election: and the allegation is sometimes to be found that the plaintiff elected to waive the tort. It seems to me that in this respect it is essential to bear in mind the distinction between choosing one of two alternative remedies, and choosing one of two inconsistent rights. As far as remedies were concerned, from the oldest time the only restriction was on the choice between real and personal actions. If you chose the one you could not claim on the other. Real actions have long disappeared: and, subject to the difficulty of including two causes of action in one writ which has also now disappeared, there has not been and there certainly is not now any compulsion to choose between alternative remedies. You may put them in the same writ: or you may put one in first, and then amend and add or substitute another. I will cite one authority which has to deal with the question whether a claim for injury to a passenger was founded on contract or tort for the purposes of the *County Courts Act.*

> At the present time a plaintiff may frame his claim in either way, but he is not bound by the pleadings, and if he puts his claim on one ground and proves it on another he is not now embarrassed by any rules as to departure.

per Lord Esher in *Kelly v. Metropolitan Ry. Co.*, [1895] 1 QB 944 (CA) at p. 946.

On the other hand, if a man is entitled to one of two inconsistent rights it is fitting that when with full knowledge he has done an unequivocal act showing that he has chosen the one he cannot afterwards pursue the other, which after the first choice is by reason of the inconsistency no longer his to choose. Instances are the right of a principal dealing with an agent for an undisclosed principal to choose the liability of the agent or the principal: the right of a landlord where forfeiture of a lease has been committed to exact the forfeiture or to treat the former tenant as still tenant and the like. To those cases the statement of Lord Blackburn in *Scarf v. Jardine* (1882), 7 App. Cas. 345 (HL (Eng.)) at p. 360 applies:

> [W]here a man has an option to choose one or other of two inconsistent things when once he has made his election it cannot be retracted.

In a later passage (at 311) Lord Blackburn speaks of a man choosing between two remedies: but it is plain that he is speaking of remedies in respect of the inconsistent things as stated above. The case was one where the plaintiff had a right of recourse against two former partners, or against two new partners: but obviously not against both. Lord Blackburn quotes *Dumpor's* case (1601), 4 Co. Rep. 119 b; 76 ER 1110 (KB) which was a plain case of inconsistent rights, the question of waiver of a forfeiture. I therefore think that on a question of alternative remedies no question of election arises until one or other claim has been brought to judgment. Up to that stage the plaintiff may pursue both remedies together, or pursuing one may amend and pursue the other: but he can take judgment only for the one, and his cause of action on both will then be merged in the one. This seems to me to be the decision of both Lord Russell of Killowen CJ and of Vaughan Williams LJ in *Rice v. Reed*, [1900] 1 QB 54 (CA): and I cannot agree with the dictum of A.L. Smith LJ at pp. 65-66 that to bring an action for money had and received waives the tort. He founded himself upon words used by Bovill CJ in *Smith v. Baker* (1873), LR 8 CD 350 at p. 355. The dictum was unnecessary, for in that case the plaintiff had obtained an order from the Court of Bankruptcy to hand over the proceeds of a conversion and had been paid the money. The dictum of Bovill CJ is in my opinion incorrect.

    In the present case, therefore, I find the plaintiffs were at no stage in the proceedings they took against M.F.G. Trust called to make an election, and, if it were necessary so to hold, in fact made no election, to claim in contract and not to claim in tort: and the foundation of the defendant's defence disappears. But I think it necessary to add that even if the tort had been waived, or the plaintiff had made any final election against M.F.G. Trust, Ld., I fail to see why that should have any effect upon their claims against the bank. If a thief steals the plaintiff's goods worth 500*l.* and sells them to a receiver for 50*l.* who sells them to a fourth party for 400*l.*, if I find the thief and he hands over to me the 50*l.* or I sue him for it and recover judgment I can no longer sue him for damages for the value of the goods, but why should that preclude me from suing the two receivers for damages? I shall not be misunderstood as imputing dishonesty in this case but the instance illustrates the point. I can see no justice in the contention: and I know of no authority in support of it. The case of *Vershures Creameries, Ld. v. Hull and Netherlands Steamship Co., Ld.*, [1921] 2 KB 608 (CA), upon which both the Courts below founded their decision has with great respect very little bearing on the matter. A firm of carriers being authorized by the plaintiffs to carry goods to A delivered them to B. The plaintiffs invoiced the goods to B, sued him for the price, recovered judgment and took bankruptcy proceedings against him. They afterwards sued the carriers for misdelivery. It was the plainest case of ratification of an act done by the carriers purporting to deliver on behalf of the plaintiffs; and as such there could be no complaint against the carriers for breach of authority. There are statements made in some of the judgments on "approbating and reprobating": but these words have had their proper meaning attributed to them in the judgment of my noble and learned friend Viscount Maugham in *Lissenden v. C.A.V. Bosch, Ld.*, [1940] AC 412 (HL (Eng.)) at p. 417, and will probably now become unfashionable.

I think that authority for the opposite view is to be found both in *Rice v. Reed*, [1900] 1 QB 54 and in *Hunter v. Prinsep* (1808), 10 East 378; 103 ER 818 (KB). In that case the charterer had loaded a cargo of wood at Honduras for London, freight to be paid on delivery in London. The ship had an adventurous voyage, for, having been captured and recaptured, she was wrecked at St. Kitts. There the captain without authority obtained an order from the Vice-Admiralty Court for sale of the cargo: and the proceeds of sale were remitted to the shipowners. On being sued by the charterers for money had and received they set up a cross claim for freight *pro rata itineris*. It was contended by the shipowners that by suing for money had and received the plaintiffs had adopted and confirmed the act of the master and had acquiesced therefore in preventing further conveyance and the earnings of the full freight. But Lord Ellenborough held [at 391 (824 ER)] that

> the fallacy of the argument on the part of the defendants appears to us to consist in attributing more effect to the mere form of this action than really belongs to it. In bringing an action for money had and received, instead of trover, the plaintiff does no more than waive any complaint, with a view to damages of the tortious act by which the goods were converted into money; and takes to the neat proceeds of the sale as the value of the goods.

He decided therefore, that the shipowners were not excused for their failure to deliver the goods and were not entitled to the freight claimed. This decision which applies to the case of the party from whom money had and received was claimed and whose tort was on the hypothesis waived, seems capable of application a fortiori to an independent wrongdoer.

I think, therefore, that the defence of the bank fails on all grounds. I notice, however, that the judgment of the Court of Appeal gives to the members the comforting reflection that they have arrived at a decision which is not only right in law but is just in fact. I see no kind of injustice in the present result which enables the plaintiffs to recover a sum of money which, but for the want of ordinary care on the part of the bank officials, they would probably never have lost. I think that the appeal should be allowed, the judgment of Goddard J set aside and judgment entered for the plaintiffs with costs here and below for 1900*l.* together with such interest, if any, that the House shall decide to give them.

Phillips v. Homfray
(1883), 24 Ch. D 439 (CA)

[This suit was brought in 1866 by the plaintiffs against S. Homfray and other persons, including the deceased R. Fothergill. The defendants had been mining the minerals under the lands adjoining the plaintiffs' farm for some time when the plaintiffs discovered that the defendants were also mining the minerals under the plaintiffs' farm and using the plaintiffs' roads and passages to transport the minerals. The plaintiffs sought a declaration that the defendants were liable for minerals extracted from under the plaintiffs' farm; an account of the minerals that they extracted from under the plaintiffs' farm; and an account of the minerals transported from the defendants' own mines through roads and passages under the plaintiffs' farm. They also sought an order that the defendants be required to pay for minerals illegally extracted from the plaintiffs' farm, a wayleave (right of use) rent or compensation for use of the plaintiffs' roads and passages, compensation for damage done to the surface of the plaintiffs' farm, and other relief.]

BOWEN LJ (Cotton LJ concurring): ... The Plaintiffs' claim is for compensation for the secret and tortious use made by the deceased *R. Fothergill* and others during his lifetime of the underground ways and passages under the Plaintiffs' farm for the purpose of conveying the coal and ironstone of *R. Fothergill* and his co-trespassers. The judgment of Mr. Justice *Pearson* as to these two inquiries is based upon the view that this description of claim did not abate upon *R. Fothergill's* death, but was capable of being prosecuted against the assets in the hands of his executrix. That it is in form a claim in the nature of a claim for trespass, the damages for which were to be measured by the amount of wayleave which the Defendants would have had to pay for permission to use the Plaintiffs' ways and passages, cannot be disputed. But Mr. Justice *Pearson* was of opinion that this was one of the class of cases in which a deceased man's estate remained liable for a profit derived by it out of his wrongful acts during his lifetime. The learned Judge founded his opinion upon certain language of Lord *Mansfield* in the case of *Hambly v. Trott* (1776), 1 Comp. 372 at p. 374; 98 ER 1136 at p. 1137 (KB), to the effect that, so far as the act of the offender had been beneficial to himself, his assets ought to be answerable. We have therefore to consider, in the first place, what is the true limit and meaning of the rule that a personal action dies upon a defendant's death, and whether there is, or can be, in the circumstances raised by the case, a profit received by his assets, which the Plaintiffs can follow.

The only cases in which, apart from questions of breach of contract, express or implied, a remedy for a wrongful act can be pursued against the estate of a deceased person who has done the act, appear to us to be those in which property, or the proceeds or value of property, belonging to another, have been appropriated by the deceased person and added to his own estate or moneys. In such cases, whatever the original form of action, it is in substance brought to recover property, or its proceeds or value, and by amendment could be made such in form as well as in substance. In such cases the action, though arising out of a wrongful act, does not die with the person. The property or the proceeds or value which, in the lifetime of the wrongdoer, could have been recovered from him, can be traced after his death to his assets, and recaptured by the rightful owner there. But it is not every wrongful act by which a wrongdoer indirectly benefits that falls under this head, if the benefit does not consist in the acquisition of property, or its proceeds or value. Where there is nothing among the assets of the deceased that in law or in equity belongs to the plaintiff, and the damages which have been done to him are unliquidated and uncertain, the executors of a wrongdoer cannot be sued merely because it was worth the wrongdoer's while to commit the act which is complained of, and an indirect benefit may have been reaped thereby. ...

It was urged before us on behalf of the Plaintiffs that they were entitled in the present case to waive the tort which had been committed against them by the deceased, and to treat the claim as substantially one of implied contract or account, upon the theory of an implied promise by him to pay for what he had done, or at all events on the principle that his estate had reaped some measurable benefit or profit from the wrong, which the executrix was not entitled as against the Plaintiffs to retain. Reference was made to the analogy of the cases where an action for money had and received has been held to be maintainable for the proceeds of goods wrongfully sold, and to a more doubtful class of authorities in which it has been suggested that use and occupation would lie for the enjoyment of lands occupied, even in the absence of any demise by the plaintiff. It seems to us, as we have said, that the profits arising from a wrong done by a deceased man which can be followed against his estate are only such profits as take the shape of property or the proceeds or value of property withdrawn from the rightful owner and acquired by the wrongdoer.

We do not believe that the principle of waiving a tort and suing in contract can be carried further than this—that a plaintiff is entitled, if he chooses it, to abstain from treating as a wrong the acts of the defendant in cases where, independently of the question of wrong, the plaintiff could make a case for relief. …

The difficulties of extending the above principle to the present case appear to us insuperable. The deceased, *R. Fothergill*, by carrying his coal and ironstone in secret over the Plaintiffs' roads took nothing from the Plaintiffs. The circumstances under which he used the road appear to us to negative the idea that he meant to pay for it. Nor have the assets of the deceased Defendant been necessarily swollen by what he has done. He saved his estate expense, but he did not bring into it any additional property or value belonging to another person. … As far as we can see the equity authorities relied upon in argument by the Plaintiffs do not assist them. …

BAGGALLAY LJ (dissenting): … The circumstances under which the wrongful act with which we at present have to deal was committed may be concisely stated as follows:—In the year 1866 the Plaintiffs were the owners of a farm in *Monmouthshire*, and the Defendants, *Homfray, Fothergill*, and *Forman*, who carried on business under the style of the *Tredegar Iron Company*, had for some time past been working the minerals underlying lands adjoining the Plaintiffs' farm, and in the course of that year the Plaintiffs discovered that the Defendants were not only getting minerals from under the farm but were using roads and passages made by them through the Plaintiffs' lands for the conveyance of minerals gotten by the Defendants from their own mines. In the observations I am about to make it is important to bear in mind the nature of the wrongful act in respect of which the Plaintiffs claim redress; but I deem it unnecessary to further refer to the institution and progress of the suit, as those have been sufficiently detailed in the judgment which has just been delivered. It has hardly been disputed on the present appeal that a remedy for a wrongful act can be pursued against the estate of a deceased person by whom the act has been committed, when property, or the proceeds of property, belonging to another have been appropriated by the deceased person, in other words that the action in such cases, though arising out of a wrongful act, does not die with the person; but it has been urged that the principle thus enunciated is limited to cases in which property, or the proceeds of property, have been appropriated by the dead person, and that it does not apply to a case in which the deceased person has derived any other benefit from his wrongdoing than property or the proceeds of property, and in particular that it does not apply to a case in which the benefit derived has not been in the form of an actual acquisition of property, but of a saving of expenditure which must otherwise have been incurred by the wrongdoer, as in the present case, in which, for the purpose of the present argument, it must be assumed that by the use by the Defendants, for the carriage of their minerals, of the roads and passages under the Plaintiffs' farm, there was a saving to them of an expenditure which they must otherwise have incurred.

Speaking with much diffidence, as my views in this respect differ from those of my colleagues, I feel bound to say that I cannot appreciate the reasons upon which it is insisted that although executors are bound to account for any accretions to the property of their testator derived directly from his wrongful act, they are not liable for the amount or value of any other benefit which may be derived by his estate from or by reason of such wrongful act.

NOTE

Phillips v. Homfray is often said to stand for the proposition that it is only where the plaintiff has been deprived of some property that can be followed into the defendant's hands that waiver of tort will lie: see Lord Goff and Gareth Jones, *The Law of Restitution*, 6th ed. (London: Sweet & Maxwell, 2002), at 36-002, where this result is criticized.

It should be noted, however, that the question in issue was whether the action survived the wrongdoer's death. No doubt was cast on the decision in earlier proceedings that Fothergill personally would have been liable to pay a fair rent for the use of the underground passages (wayleave). In the earlier proceedings, (1871), LR 6 Ch. App. 770, Lord Hatherley LC had said (at 780-81):

> I at first felt some doubt as to compensation for wayleave; but on further consideration I think that on principle it ought to be given, whether the cases have as yet gone that length or not. Here is a man doing a surreptitious act, which cannot be discovered except through the medium of a bill. Under the old practice there would have been a bill for discovery of the thing, and then an action for damages in respect of it would have been brought; but this Court has now the power to grant compensation in respect of a continuously accruing damage *de die in diem*, arising from a continuous trespass underground, which can only be stopped by injunction restraining any further conveyance of coal through the Respondents' property. These damages cannot be better assessed than by an inquiry into what is fit and proper to be paid for wayleave for the coals carried through the property. I therefore affirm that part of the decree.

Whitwham v. Westminster Brymbo Coal and Coke Company
[1896] 2 Ch. 538 (CA)

[The plaintiff sued for an injunction and damages, the defendant having trespassed on the plaintiff's land by tipping spoil on it from their colliery. The trial judge held that the damages were to be measured not merely by the diminution in value to the plaintiff's land, but by the value derived by the wrongdoer from the tort.]

LINDLEY LJ: In this case we are all agreed that the principle acted upon by the learned judge is right. Let us consider what the defendants have done. They have done two things. They have, first of all, so used the plaintiffs' land as to diminish its value, say by 200*l*. Mr. Russell admits that the defendants must pay that, but contends that they are to pay no more. That leaves out of sight what more the defendants have done. What they have done more is this—

they have been using the land for years. Why are not the plaintiffs to be entitled to some compensation in respect of that user? The plaintiffs have been injured in two respects. First, they have had the value of their land diminished; secondly, they have lost the use of their land, and the defendants have had it for their own benefit. It is unjust to leave out of sight the use which the defendants have made of this land for their own purposes, and that lies at the bottom of what are called the way-leave cases. Those cases are based upon the principle that, if one person has without leave of another been using that other's land for his own purposes, he ought to pay for such user. The law is now settled by *Jegon v. Vivian* (1871), LR 6 Ch. App. 742, which has been approved of by the House of Lords in *Livingstone v. Rawyards Coal Co.* (1880), 5 App. Cas. 25 (HL (Sc.)). It proceeds upon the principle which Lord Hatherley LC stated in *Phillips v. Homfray* (1871), LR 6 Ch. App. 770 at p. 780. It must be borne in mind that if one man runs trucks on rails over another man's land it does not do any harm whatever, and there is no pecuniary damage. I will read what he says: "I at first felt some doubt as to compensation for way-leave; but on further consideration I think that on principle it ought to be given, whether the cases have as yet gone that length or not. Here is a man doing a surreptitious act which cannot be discovered except through the medium of a bill. Under the old practice there would have been a bill for discovery of the thing, and then an action for damages in respect of it would have been brought; but this Court has now the power to grant compensation in respect of a continuously accruing damage *de die in diem*, arising from a continuing trespass underground, which can only be stopped by injunction restraining any further conveyance of coal through the respondents' property." Applying that reasoning to this case, on what principle of justice can it be said that these defendants are to use the plaintiffs' land for years for their own purposes, and to pay nothing for it, in addition to the injury that they have done to the land? Chitty J has proceeded upon that principle, and, the principle being right, the figures are not disputed. The appeal must be dismissed with costs.

[Lopes and Rigby LJJ concurred separately.]

Wrotham Park Estate Co. Ltd. v. Parkside Homes Ltd.
[1974] 1 WLR 798 (Ch.)

[The defendant built on land in breach of a restrictive covenant. Brightman J refused a mandatory injunction that would have required the house to be demolished.]

BRIGHTMAN J: I turn to the consideration of the quantum of damages. I was asked by the parties to assess the damages myself, should the question arise, rather than to direct an inquiry. The basic rule in contract is to measure damages by that sum of money which will put the plaintiff in the same position as he would have been in if the contract had not been broken. From that basis, the defendants argue that the damages are nil or purely nominal, because the value of the Wrotham Park Estate as the plaintiffs concede is not diminished by one farthing in consequence of the construction of a road and the erection of 14 houses on the allotment site. If, therefore, the defendants submit, I refuse an injunction I ought to award no damages in lieu. That would seem, on the face of it, a result of questionable fair-

ness on the facts of this case. Had the offending development been the erection of an advertisement hoarding in defiance of protest and writ, I apprehend (assuming my conclusions
on other points to be correct) that the court would not have hesitated to grant a mandatory
injunction for its removal. If, for social and economic reasons, the court does not see fit in
the exercise of its discretion, to order demolition of the 14 houses, is it just that the plaintiffs
should receive no compensation and that the defendants should be left in undisturbed possession of the fruits of their wrongdoing? Common sense would seem to demand a negative
answer to this question. A comparable problem arose in wayleave cases where the defendant
had trespassed by making use of the plaintiff's underground ways to the defendant's profit
but without diminishing the value of the plaintiff's property. The plaintiff, in such cases,
received damages assessed by reference to a reasonable wayleave rent. This principle was
considered and extended in *Whitwham v. Westminster Brymbo Coal and Coke Co.*, [1896] 2
Ch. 538 (CA). For six years the defendant wrongfully tipped colliery waste onto the plaintiff's land. At the trial the defendant was directed to cease tipping and give up possession.
The question then arose what damages should be awarded for the wrongful act done to the
plaintiff during the period of the defendant's unauthorised user of the land. The official
referee found that the diminution in the value of the plaintiff's land was only £200, but that
the value of the plaintiff's land to the defendant in 1888 for tipping purposes for six years
was some £900. It was held that the proper scale of damages was the higher sum on the
ground that the trespasser should not be allowed to make use of another person's land without in some way compensating that other person for the user.

A like principle was applied by the House of Lords in a Scottish case, *Watson, Laidlaw &
Co. Ltd. v. Pott, Cassels and Williamson* (1914), 31 RPC 104 (HL (Sc.)). A patentee elected
to sue an infringer for damages rather than for an account of profits. Part of the infringement had taken place in Java. There was evidence that the patentee could not have competed
successfully in that island. It was submitted that no damages ought to be awarded in respect
of the Java infringement. Lord Shaw said, at pp. 119-120:

> It is at this state of the case ... that a second principle comes into play. It is not exactly the prin-
> ciple of restoration, either directly or expressed through compensation, but it is the principle
> underlying price or hire. It plainly extends—and I am inclined to think not infrequently ex-
> tends—to patent cases. But, indeed, it is not confined to them. For wherever an abstraction or
> invasion of property has occurred, then, unless such abstraction or invasion were to be sanc-
> tioned by law, the law ought to yield a recompense under the category or principle, as I say,
> either of price or of hire. If A, being a liveryman, keeps his horse standing idle in the stable, and
> B, against his wish or without his knowledge, rides or drives it out, it is no answer to A for B to
> say: "Against what loss do you want to be restored? I restore the horse. There is no loss. The
> horse is none the worse; it is the better for the exercise." I confess to your Lordships that this
> seems to me to be precisely in principle the kind of question and retort which underlay the
> argument of the learned counsel for the appellants about the Java trade. ... [I]n such cases it
> appears to me that the correct and full measure is only reached by adding that a patentee is also
> entitled, on the principle of price or hire, to a royalty for the unauthorised sale or use of every
> one of the infringing machines in a market which the infringer, if left to himself, might not have
> reached. Otherwise, that property which consists in the monopoly of the patented articles
> granted to the patentee has been invaded, and indeed abstracted, and the law, when appealed
> to, would be standing by and allowing the invader or abstractor to go free.

The same principle was applied in detinue in *Strand Electric and Engineering Co. Ltd. v. Brisford Entertainments Ltd.*, [1952] 2 QB 246 (CA). The defendant came into possession of portable switchboards which were part of the stock-in-trade of the plaintiff. The defendant used them for its own profit for 43 weeks. The trial judge, Pilcher J, ordered the return of the switchboards and awarded damages. The damages took into account the fact that if the defendant had not wrongfully retained the switchboards the plaintiff would be unlikely to have hired out every one for the full period of 43 weeks. It was held by the Court of Appeal that the plaintiff was entitled to recover as damages the full market rate of hire for the whole period of detention. ...

The facts of the cases I have mentioned are a long way from the facts of the case before me. Should I, as invited by the plaintiffs, apply a like principle to a case where the defendant Parkside, in defiance of protest and writ, has invaded the plaintiffs' rights in order to reap a financial profit for itself? In *Leeds Industrial Co-operative Society Ltd. v. Slack*, [1924] AC 851 (HL (Eng.)) Lord Sumner said, at p. 870:

> [N]o money awarded in substitution can be justly awarded, unless it is at any rate designed to be a preferable equivalent for an injunction and therefore an adequate substitute for it. ...

This was said in a dissenting speech but his dissent did not arise in the context of that observation.

In the present case I am faced with the problem what damages ought to be awarded to the plaintiffs in the place of mandatory injunctions which would have restored the plaintiffs' rights. If the plaintiffs are merely given a nominal sum, or no sum, in substitution for injunctions, it seems to me that justice will manifestly not have been done.

As I have said, the general rule would be to measure damages by reference to that sum which would place the plaintiffs in the same position as if the covenant had not been broken. Parkside and the individual purchasers could have avoided breaking the covenant in two ways. One course would have been not to develop the allotment site. The other course would have been for Parkside to have sought from the plaintiffs a relaxation of the covenant. On the facts of this particular case the plaintiffs, rightly conscious of their obligations towards existing residents, would clearly not have granted any relaxation, but for present purposes I must assume that it could have been induced to do so. In my judgment a just substitute for a mandatory injunction would be such a sum of money as might reasonably have been demanded by the plaintiffs from Parkside as a quid pro quo for relaxing the covenant. The plaintiffs submitted that that sum should be a substantial proportion of the development of the land. This is currently put at no less that £10,000 per plot, i.e. £140,000 on the assumption that the plots are undeveloped. Mr. Parker gave evidence that a half or a third of the development value was commonly demanded by a landowner whose property stood in the way of a development. I do not agree with that approach to damages in this type of case. I bear in mind the following factors:

(1) The lay-out covenant is not an asset which the estate owner ever contemplated he would have either the opportunity or the desire to turn to account. It has no commercial or even nuisance value. For it cannot be turned to account except to the detriment of the existing residents who are people the estate owner professes to protect.

(2) The breach of covenant which has actually taken place is over a very small area and the impact of this particular breach on the Wrotham Park Estate is insignificant. The validity of the covenant over the rest of area 14 is unaffected.

I think that in a case such as the present a landowner faced with a request from a developer which, it must be assumed, he feels reluctantly obliged to grant, would have first asked the developer what profit he expected to make from his operations. With the benefit of foresight the developer would, in the present case, have said about £50,000 for that is the profit which Parkside concedes it made from the development. I think that the landowner would then reasonably have required a certain percentage of that anticipated profit as a price for the relaxation of the covenant, assuming, as I must, that he feels obliged to relax it. In assessing what would be a fair percentage I think that the court ought, on the particular facts of this case, to act with great moderation. For it is to be borne in mind that the plaintiffs were aware, before the auction took place, that the land was being offered for sale as freehold building land for 13 houses, and they knew that they were not going to consent to any such development. They could have informed the Potters Bar Urban District Council of their attitude in advance of the auction, or could have given the like information to Parkside prior to completion of the contract for sale. In either event it seems highly unlikely that Parkside would have parted with its £90,000, at any rate unconditionally. I think that damages must be assessed in such a case on a basis which is fair and, in all the circumstances, in my judgment a sum equal to five per cent of Parkside's anticipated profit is the most that is fair. I accordingly award the sum of £2,500 in substitution for mandatory injunctions. I think that this amount should be treated as apportioned between the 14 respective owners or joint owners of the plots and Parkside (as the owner of the road) in ¹⁄₁₅th shares, so that the damages awarded will be £166 odd in each case. In fact, I apprehend that by virtue of the arrangement between Parkside and the insurance office the entirety of the £2,500 will ultimately be recoverable from Parkside, so that the apportionment does not have any real significance. I will also grant a declaration in appropriate terms after I have heard submissions from counsel as to such terms.

Order accordingly.

NOTE

In *Surrey County Council v. Bredero Homes Ltd.*, [1993] 1 WLR 1361 (CA) the defendant had, in breach of a restrictive covenant of which the plaintiff was the beneficiary, built 77 houses in a housing development, instead of the 72 permitted. The breach of the covenant caused no diminution in the value of the plaintiff's own property. The English Court of Appeal held that the plaintiff was entitled to nominal damages only. The argument that the plaintiff had been deprived of an opportunity to bargain was dismissed by Steyn LJ as "a fiction." *Wrotham Park Estate Co. Ltd. v. Parkside Homes Ltd.* was explained as "only defensible on the basis of the ... restitutionary principle." The court, unwilling to extend restitution to breach of contract generally, thought it inapplicable in the *Bredero* case, which was characterized simply as a case of "breach of contract."

The English Court of Appeal later reconsidered this question, and held that the *Wrotham Park* case was rightly decided, and was, after all, rightly to be understood as resting on compensatory not restitutionary principles. The facts in *Jaggard v. Sawyer*, [1995] 1 WLR 269 were that the defendant had built a house on land adjoining land affected by a restrictive covenant, and in breach of the covenant, of which the plaintiff was one of the beneficiaries, had given a right of access to the new house over the land affected by the covenant. The defendant was also in breach of the covenant by giving access to the new house over the roadway opposite the plaintiff's house, a breach that could be characterized as a trespass, as well as a breach of contract. As usual in these cases, the plaintiff's house was not diminished in value by the new building, and so there was no obvious loss. The plaintiff wanted an injunction to prevent access to the new house, and in fact herself argued, as a reason in support of this result, that damages, properly assessed, would only be nominal. But the court, refusing the injunction as unduly oppressive to the defendant, held that the plaintiff was entitled to a money award, measured by her share of the reasonable licence fee that the defendant would probably have agreed to pay for permission to build the house. Sir Thomas Bingham MR said that the "*Wrotham Park* approach was appropriate even on pure compensatory principles."

Attorney General v. Blake
[2000] 3 WLR 625 (HL (Eng.))

[George Blake, while an employee of the British secret service, betrayed British secrets to the Soviet Union. He was convicted of spying and sentenced to 42 years in prison, but subsequently escaped to Moscow. In 1989 he wrote his autobiography, in which he revealed information that he had obtained in the course of his employment. The information was no longer confidential in 1989, but publication was still a breach of contract, and a breach of the *Official Secrets Act*. The Crown sought an order for payment of all money received and to be received by Blake from the publisher. The trial judge held that there was no private law remedy available to the Crown. The public law aspects were not argued at trial. In the Court of Appeal, however, argument was permitted on the public law, and it was held that the attorney general was entitled to an injunction to restrain Blake from receiving any future royalties on the ground that they were the fruits of crimes under the *Official Secrets Act*. The claim for restitution for breach of contract was not argued, but the Court of Appeal nevertheless gave extensive consideration to the question. The court said that the general rule was that damages for breach of contract were compensatory, but that there were exceptional cases in which restitution was available for breach of contract. Two such cases were mentioned: first, where the defendant had "skimped" performance of the contract (by using cheaper means of performance than promised while causing no loss to the plaintiff) and, second, cases where the defendant had obtained a profit by doing the very thing that he had contracted not to do. The *Blake* case was held to fall into the second category, the court saying that there was a "direct connection" between the breach and the profit. In the House of Lords, the decision was upheld on the basis of account of profits for breach of contract.]

LORD NICHOLLS: ... I turn to the decision of the Court of Appeal in *Surrey County Council v. Bredero Homes Ltd.* ... This is a difficult decision. It has attracted criticism from academic commentators and also in judgments of Sir Thomas Bingham MR and Millett LJ in *Jaggard v. Sawyer*, [1995] 1 WLR 269. I need not pursue the detailed criticisms. In the *Bredero* case Dillon LJ himself noted, at p. 1364, that had the covenant been worded differently, there could have been provision for payment of an increased price if a further planning permission were forthcoming. That would have been enforceable. But, according to the *Bredero* decision, a covenant not to erect any further houses without permission, intended to achieve the same result, may be breached with impunity. That would be a sorry reflection on the law. Suffice to say, in so far as the *Bredero* decision is inconsistent with the approach adopted in the *Wrotham Park* case, the latter approach is to be preferred.

The *Wrotham Park* case, therefore, still shines, rather as a solitary beacon, showing that in contract as well as tort, damages are not always narrowly confined to recoupment of financial loss. In a suitable case damages for breach of contract may be measured by the benefit gained by the wrongdoer from the breach. The defendant must make a reasonable payment in respect of the benefit he has gained. In the present case the Crown seeks to go further. The claim is for all the profits of Blake's book which the publisher has not yet paid him. This raises the question whether an account of profits can ever be given as a remedy for breach of contract. The researches of counsel have been unable to discover any case where the court has made such an order on a claim for breach of contract. In *Tito v. Waddell (No. 2)*, [1977] Ch. 106, 332, a decision which has proved controversial, Sir Robert Megarry V-C said that, as a matter of fundamental principle, the question of damages was "not one of making the defendant disgorge" his gains, in that case what he had saved by committing the wrong, but "one of compensating the plaintiff." In *Occidental Worldwide Investment Corpn. v. Skibs A/S Avanti*, [1976] 1 Lloyd's Rep. 293, 337, Kerr J summarily rejected a claim for an account of profits when ship owners withdrew ships on a rising market.

There is a light sprinkling of cases where courts have made orders having the same effect as an order for an account of profits, but the courts seem always to have attached a different label. A person who, in breach of contract, sells land twice over must surrender his profits on the second sale to the original buyer. Since courts regularly make orders for the specific performance of contracts for the sale of land, a seller of land is, to an extent, regarded as holding the land on trust for the buyer: *Lake v. Bayliss*, [1974] 1 WLR 1073. In *Reid-Newfoundland Co. v. Anglo-American Telegraph Co., Ltd.*, [1912] AC 555 a railway company agreed not to transmit any commercial messages over a particular telegraph wire except for the benefit and account of the telegraph company. The Privy Council held that the railway company was liable to account as a trustee for the profits it wrongfully made from its use of the wire for commercial purposes. In *British Motor Trade Association v. Gilbert*, [1951] 2 All ER 641 the plaintiff suffered no financial loss but the award of damages for breach of contract effectively stripped the wrongdoer of the profit he had made from his wrongful venture into the black market for new cars.

These cases illustrate that circumstances do arise when the just response to a breach of contract is that the wrongdoer should not be permitted to retain any profit from the breach. In these cases the courts have reached the desired result by straining existing concepts. Professor Peter Birks has deplored the "failure of jurisprudence when the law is forced into this kind of abusive instrumentalism": see (1993), 109 LQR 518, 520. Some years ago Professor Dawson suggested there is no inherent reason why the technique of equity courts in land contracts should not be more widely employed, not by granting remedies as the by-product of a phantom "trust" created by the contract, but as an alternative form of money judgment remedy. That well known ailment of lawyers, a hardening of the categories, ought not to be an obstacle: see "Restitution or Damages" (1959), 20 Ohio LJ 175.

My conclusion is that there seems to be no reason, in principle, why the court must in all circumstances rule out an account of profits as a remedy for breach of contract. I prefer to avoid the unhappy expression "restitutionary damages." Remedies are the law's response to a wrong (or, more precisely, to a cause of action). When, exceptionally, a just response to a breach of contract so requires, the court should be able to grant the discretionary remedy of requiring a defendant to account to the plaintiff for the benefits he has received from his breach of contract. In the same way as a plaintiff's interest in performance of a contract may render it just and equitable for the court to make an order for specific performance or grant an injunction, so the plaintiff's interest in performance may make it just and equitable that the defendant should retain no benefit from his breach of contract.

The state of the authorities encourages me to reach this conclusion, rather than the reverse. The law recognises that damages are not always a sufficient remedy for breach of contract. This is the foundation of the court's jurisdiction to grant the remedies of specific performance and injunction. Even when awarding damages, the law does not adhere slavishly to the concept of compensation for financially measurable loss. When the circumstances require, damages are measured by reference to the benefit obtained by the wrongdoer. This applies to interference with property rights. Recently, the like approach has been adopted to breach of contract. Further, in certain circumstances an account of profits is ordered in preference to an award of damages. Sometimes the injured party is given the choice: either compensatory damages or an account of the wrongdoer's profits. Breach of confidence is an instance of this. If confidential information is wrongfully divulged in breach of a non-disclosure agreement, it would be nothing short of sophistry to say that an account of profits may be ordered in respect of the equitable wrong but not in respect of the breach of contract which governs the relationship between the parties. With the established authorities going thus far, I consider it would be only a modest step for the law to recognise openly that, exceptionally, an account of profits may be the most appropriate remedy for breach of contract. It is not as though this step would contradict some recognised principle applied consistently throughout the law to the grant or withholding of the remedy of an account of profits. No such principle is discernible.

The main argument against the availability of an account of profits as a remedy for breach of contract is that the circumstances where this remedy may be granted will be uncertain. This will have an unsettling effect on commercial contracts where certainty is important. I do not think these fears are well founded. I see no reason why, in practice, the availability of the remedy of an account of profits need disturb settled expectations in the commercial or consumer world. An account of profits will be appropriate only in exceptional circumstances. Normally the remedies of damages, specific performance and injunction, coupled with the characterisation of some contractual obligations as fiduciary, will provide an adequate response to a breach of contract. It will be only in exceptional cases, where those remedies are inadequate, that any question of accounting for profits will arise. No fixed rules can be prescribed. The court will have regard to all the circumstances, including the subject matter of the contract, the purpose of the contractual provision which has been breached, the circumstances in which the breach occurred, the consequences of the breach and the circumstances in which relief is being sought. A useful general guide, although not exhaustive, is whether the plaintiff had a legitimate interest in preventing the defendant's profit-making activity and, hence, in depriving him of his profit.

It would be difficult, and unwise, to attempt to be more specific. In the Court of Appeal Lord Woolf MR suggested there are at least two situations in which justice requires the award of restitutionary damages where compensatory damages would be inadequate: see [1998] Ch. 439, 458. Lord Woolf was not there addressing the question of when an account of profits, in the conventional sense, should be available. But I should add that, so far as an account of profits is concerned, the suggested categorisation would not assist. The first suggested category was the case of "skimped" performance, where the defendant fails to provide the full extent of services he has contracted to provide. He should be liable to pay back the amount of expenditure he saved by the breach. This is a much discussed problem. But a part refund of the price agreed for services would not fall within the scope of an account of profits as ordinarily understood. Nor does an account of profits seem to be needed in this context. The resolution of the problem of cases of skimped performance, where the plaintiff does not get what was agreed, may best be found elsewhere. If a shopkeeper supplies inferior and cheaper goods than those ordered and paid for, he has to refund the difference in price. That would be the outcome of a claim for damages for breach of contract. That would be so, irrespective of whether the goods in fact served the intended purpose. There must be scope for a similar approach, without any straining of principle, in cases where the defendant provided inferior and cheaper services than those contracted for.

The second suggested category was where the defendant has obtained his profit by doing the very thing he contracted not to do. This category is defined too widely to assist. The category is apt to embrace all express negative obligations. But something more is required than mere breach of such an obligation before an account of profits will be the appropriate remedy.

Lord Woolf, at [1998] Ch. 439, 457, 458, also suggested three facts which should not be a sufficient ground for departing from the normal basis on which damages are awarded: the fact that the breach was cynical and deliberate; the fact that the breach enabled the defendant to enter into a more profitable contract elsewhere; and the fact that by entering into a new and more profitable contract the defendant put it out of his power to perform his contract with the plaintiff. I agree that none of these facts would be, by itself, a good reason for ordering an account of profits.

The Present Case

The present case is exceptional. The context is employment as a member of the security and intelligence services. Secret information is the lifeblood of these services. In the 1950s Blake deliberately committed repeated breaches of his undertaking not to divulge official information gained as a result of his employment. He caused untold and immeasurable damage to the public interest he had committed himself to serve. In 1990 he published his autobiography, a further breach of his express undertaking. By this time the information disclosed was no longer confidential. In the ordinary course of commercial dealings the disclosure of non-confidential information might be regarded as venial. In the present case disclosure was also a criminal offence under the *Official Secrets Acts*, even though the information was no longer confidential. Section 1 of the *Official Secrets Act 1989* draws a distinction in this regard between members of the security and intelligence services and other Crown servants.

Under section 1(3) a person who is or has been a Crown servant is guilty of an offence if without lawful authority he makes "a damaging disclosure" of information relating to security or intelligence. The offence is drawn more widely in the case of a present or past member of the security and intelligence services. Such a person is guilty of an offence if without lawful authority he discloses "any information" relating to security or intelligence which is or has been in his possession by virtue of his position as a member of those services. This distinction was approved in Parliament after debate when the legislation was being enacted.

Mr. Clayton submitted that section 1(1) is drawn too widely and infringes article 10 of the European Convention of Human Rights. Section 1(1) criminalises disclosure of information when no damage results. It focuses on the status of the individual who makes the disclosure, rather than on the nature of the information itself. A non-damaging disclosure by a member of the security and intelligence services is criminal, but the identical non-damaging disclosure by a Crown servant is not.

This argument was raised for the first time in this House. Your Lordships are not equipped with the material necessary to decide the point. In the event this does not matter, because there is in the present case another consideration which is sufficient for the purposes of the Attorney General. When he joined the Secret Intelligence Service Blake expressly agreed in writing that he would not disclose official information, during or after his service, in book form or otherwise. He was employed on that basis. That was the basis on which he acquired official information. The Crown had and has a legitimate interest in preventing Blake profiting from the disclosure of official information, whether classified or not, while a member of the service and thereafter. Neither he, nor any other member of the service, should have a financial incentive to break his undertaking. It is of paramount importance that members of the service should have complete confidence in all their dealings with each other, and that those recruited as informers should have the like confidence. Undermining the willingness of prospective informers to co-operate with the services, or undermining the morale and trust between members of the services when engaged on secret and dangerous operations, would jeopardise the effectiveness of the service. An absolute rule against disclosure, visible to all, makes good sense.

In considering what would be a just response to a breach of Blake's undertaking the court has to take these considerations into account. The undertaking, if not a fiduciary obligation, was closely akin to a fiduciary obligation, where an account of profits is a standard remedy in the event of breach. Had the information which Blake has now disclosed still been confidential, an account of profits would have been ordered, almost as a matter of course. In the special circumstances of the intelligence services, the same conclusion should follow even though the information is no longer confidential. That would be a just response to the breach. I am reinforced in this view by noting that most of the profits from the book derive indirectly from the extremely serious and damaging breaches of the same undertaking committed by Blake in the 1950s. As already mentioned, but for his notoriety as an infamous spy his autobiography would not have commanded royalties of the magnitude Jonathan Cape agreed to pay.

As a footnote I observe that a similar conclusion, requiring the contract-breaker to disgorge his profits, was reached in the majority decision of the United States Supreme Court in *Snepp v. United States* (1980), 444 US 507. The facts were strikingly similar. A former employee of the Central Intelligence Agency, whose conditions of employment included a promise not to divulge any information relating to the agency without pre-publication clearance, published a book about the agency's activities in Vietnam. None of the information was classified, but an agent's violation of his non-disclosure obligation impaired the agency's ability to function properly. The court considered and rejected various forms of relief. The actual damage was not quantifiable, nominal damages were a hollow alternative, and punitive damages after a jury trial would be speculative and unusual. Even if recovered they would bear no relation to either the government's irreparable loss or Snepp's unjust gain. The court considered that a remedy which required Snepp "to disgorge the benefits of his faithlessness," was swift and sure, tailored to deter those who would place sensitive information at risk and, since the remedy reached only funds attributable to the breach, it could not saddle the former agent with exemplary damages out of all proportion to his gain. In order to achieve this result the court "imposed" a constructive trust on Snepp's profits. In this country, affording the plaintiff the remedy of an account of profits is a different means to the same end.

The Form of the Order

The Attorney General's entitlement to an account of Blake's profits does not, in this case, confer on the Crown any proprietary interest in the debt due to Blake from Jonathan Cape. The Crown is entitled, on the taking of the account, to a money judgment which can then be enforced by attachment of the debt in the usual way. These formal steps may be capable of being short-circuited. Despite the niceties and formalities once associated with taking an account, the amount payable under an account of profits need not be any more elaborately or precisely calculated than damages. But in this case there is a complication. Blake has brought third party proceedings against Jonathan Cape, seeking payment of £90,000 (less tax). In the third-party proceedings Jonathan Cape has sought to deduct legal expenses incurred in resisting a defamation claim and in resisting the Crown's claim. Accordingly, the appropriate form of order on this appeal is a declaration that the Attorney General is entitled to be paid a sum equal to whatever amount is due and owing to Blake from Jonathan Cape under the publishing agreement of 4 May 1989. The injunction granted by the Court of Appeal will remain in force until Jonathan Cape duly makes payment to the Attorney General. I would dismiss this appeal.

LORD HOBHOUSE (dissenting): Where the plaintiff has failed to obtain or failed to apply for an injunction, he has to be content with a remedy in damages. What has happened in such cases is that there has either actually or in effect been a compulsory purchase of the plaintiff's right of refusal. (The award of damages in tort for the conversion or detinue of goods is also an example of compulsory purchase as is demonstrated by the common law rule that the payment of the damages vests the title in the goods in the defendant.) What the plaintiff has lost is the sum which he could have exacted from the defendant as the price of his consent to the development. This is an example of compensatory damages. They are damages for breach. They do not involve any concept of restitution and so to describe them is an error. The error comes about because of the assumption that the only loss which the plaintiff can have suffered is a reduction in the value of the dominant tenement. It is for this reason that I agree with my noble and learned friend Lord Nicholls that the decision in *Wrotham*

Park Estate Co. Ltd. v. Parkside Homes Ltd., [1974] 1 WLR 798 is to be preferred to that in *Surrey C.C. v. Bredero Homes Ltd.*, [1993] 1 WLR 1361: see also *Jaggard v. Sawyer*, [1995] 1 WLR 269. I would however add that the order proposed by your Lordships does not reflect this principle; it goes further. It does not award to the Crown damages for breach of contract assessed by reference to what would be the reasonable price to pay for permission to publish. It awards the Crown damages which equal the whole amount owed by Jonathan Cape to Blake. That is a remedy based on proprietary principles when the necessary proprietary rights are absent.

The principle of compensation is both intellectually sound as the remedy for breach and provides the just answer. The examples discussed in my noble and learned friend's speech do not on the correct analysis disclose the supposed need to extend the boundaries of remedies for breach of contract. The reason why the Crown should not recover damages in the present case derives from the exceptional public law nature of the undertaking which Blake gave. If the relationship had been a commercial one it is probable that by 1989 the undertaking would be regarded as spent or no longer enforcible, but if still enforcible the breach of it would have supported compensatory damages on the "compulsory purchase" basis. ...

I must also sound a further note of warning that if some more extensive principle of awarding non-compensatory damages for breach of contract is to be introduced into our commercial law the consequences will be very far reaching and disruptive. I do not believe that such is the intention of your Lordships but if others are tempted to try to extend the decision of the present exceptional case to commercial situations so as to introduce restitutionary rights beyond those presently recognised by the law of restitution, such a step will require very careful consideration before it is acceded to.

My Lords, Mr. Clayton was right to say that the exceptional facts of this case have been critical to its decision. The policy which is being enforced is that which requires Blake to be punished by depriving him of any benefit from anything connected with his past deplorable criminal conduct. Your Lordships consider that this policy can be given effect to without a departure from principle. I must venture to disagree. I would allow the appeal and dismiss the cross-appeal.

Strand Electric Engineering Co. Ltd. v. Brisford Entertainments Ltd.
[1952] 2 QB 246 (CA)

[In 1949, the defendants, Brisford Entertainments Ld., were negotiating for the sale of a theatre to the Bedford Theatre (London) Ld., and that company was permitted to go into possession before completion of the purchase. Under a contract made by it with the plaintiffs, the Bedford Theatre (London) Co. were lent by the plaintiffs certain portable switchboards, pending the manufacture and installation by the plaintiffs of permanent switchboards. No hire was charged in the first instance, but as the Bedford Theatre Co. failed to take delivery of the permanent switchboards, but desired to retain the portable apparatus, it was agreed that as from January 1, 1951, the company should pay the plaintiffs' usual charge of £9 6s. 8d. per week. The hiring out of portable switchboards was a normal part of the plaintiffs' business. On January 8 the defendants, Brisford Entertainments Ld., took possession of the theatre and gave instructions that nothing whatsoever must be removed, and the Bedford Theatre Co. disclaimed any responsibility for the plaintiffs' hire equipment as from that date.

Between January and March, 1951, the plaintiffs wrote a number of letters to the defendants, demanding the return of their equipment, but received neither their property nor any satisfactory reply. On March 17, 1951, the plaintiffs issued a writ claiming the return of their equipment or its value, and damages for the period of its detention, which at the trial was shown to be for 43 weeks.]

DENNING LJ: In assessing damages, whether for a breach of contract or for a tort, the general rule is that the plaintiff recovers the loss he has suffered, no more and no less. This rule is, however, often departed from. Thus in cases where the damage claimed is too remote in law the plaintiff recovers less than his real loss: *Liesbosch Dredger (Owners) v. Edison S.S. (Owners)*, [1933] AC 449 (HL (Eng.)). In other cases the plaintiff may get more than his real loss. Thus, where the damage suffered by the plaintiff is recouped or lessened owing to some reason with which the defendant is not concerned, the plaintiff gets full damages without any deduction on that account: *Slater v. Hoyle & Smith Ld.*, [1920] 2 KB 11 (CA); *Smiley v. Townshend*, [1950] 2 KB 311 (CA); *Haviland v. Long*, [1952] 2 QB 80 (CA). Again, in cases where the defendant has obtained a benefit from his wrongdoing he is often made liable to account for it, even though the plaintiff has lost nothing and suffered no damage: *Reading v. Attorney-General*, [1951] AC 507 (HL (Eng.)).

The question in this case is: What is the proper measure of damages for the wrongful detention of goods? Does it fall within the general rule that the plaintiff only recovers for the loss he has suffered or within some other, and if so what, rule? It is strange that there is no authority upon this point in English law; but there is plenty on the analogous case of detention of land. The rule there is that a wrongdoer, who keeps the owner out of his land, must pay a fair rental value for it, even though the owner would not have been able to use it himself or to let it to anyone else. So also a wrongdoer who uses land for his own purposes without the owner's consent, as, for instance, for a fair ground, or as a wayleave, must pay a reasonable hire for it, even though he has done no damage to the land at all: *Whitwham v. Westminster Brymbo Coal Company*, [1896] 2 Ch. 538 (CA). I see no reason why the same principle should not apply to detention of goods.

If the wrongdoer has made use of goods for his own purposes, then he must pay a reasonable hire for them, even though the owner has in fact suffered no loss. It may be that the owner would not have used the goods himself, or that he had a substitute readily available, which he used without extra cost to himself. Nevertheless the owner is entitled to a reasonable hire. If the wrongdoer had asked the owner for permission to use the goods, the owner would be entitled to ask for a reasonable remuneration as the price of his permission. The wrongdoer cannot be better off because he did not ask permission. He cannot be better off by doing wrong than he would be by doing right. He must therefore pay a reasonable hire. This will cover, of course, the wear and tear which is ordinarily included in a hiring charge; but for any further damage the wrongdoer must pay extra. I do not mean to suggest that an owner who has suffered greater loss will not be able to recover it. Suppose that a man used a car in his business, and owing to its detention he had to hire a substitute at an increased cost, he would clearly be able to recover the cost of the substitute. In such cases the plaintiff recovers his actual loss. I am not concerned with those cases.

I am here concerned with the cases where the owner has in fact suffered no loss, or less loss than is represented by a hiring charge. In such cases if the wrongdoer has in fact used the goods he must pay a reasonable hire for them. Nor do I mean to suggest that a wrongdoer who has merely detained the goods and not used them would have to pay a hiring charge. The damages for detention recoverable against a carrier or a warehouseman have never been measured by a hiring charge. They are measured by the loss actually sustained by the plaintiff, subject, of course, to questions of remoteness. They are like cases of injury to a ship or a car by negligence. If it is put out of action during repair the wrongdoer is only liable for the loss suffered by the plaintiff. (See the principles set out in the *The Susquehanna*, [1926] AC 655 (HL (Eng.)) and many other cases.) The claim for a hiring charge is therefore not based on the loss to the plaintiff, but on the fact that the defendant has used the goods for his own purposes. It is an action against him because he has had the benefit of the goods. It resembles, therefore, an action for restitution rather than an action of tort. But it is unnecessary to place it into any formal category. The plaintiffs are entitled to a hiring charge for the period of detention, and that is all that matters. I can imagine cases where an owner might be entitled to the profits made by a wrongdoer by the use of a chattel, but I do not think this is such a case.

If the goods are retained by the wrongdoer up till judgment, the hiring charge runs up to that time, and in addition the owner will get the return of the goods or their value at the time of judgment (*Rosenthal v. Alderton & Sons Ld.*, [1946] KB 374 (CA)); but if the goods have been disposed of by the wrongdoer the hiring charge will cease at the time of such disposal, but the owner will get in addition damages for the loss he has sustained by the conversion, which is usually the value at the time of conversion. (See *S.S. Celia v. S.S. Volturno*, [1921] 2 AC 544 (HL (Eng.)) and cf. *Sachs v. Miklos and Others*, [1948] 2 KB 23 (CA).) In the present case the defendants retained the goods until judgment, but have returned them in pursuance of the judgment. In these circumstances the hiring charge runs up to the date when the goods were returned. It starts from the very moment when the defendants took possession of the goods. They had, it is true, a reasonable time to make inquiries as to title, but once that time expired and they wrongly decided to retain them, then the wrong related back to the first taking. It became wrongful *ab initio*. ...

In my opinion the plaintiffs in this case are entitled to the full hiring charge for the full period of 43 weeks, without any of the deductions allowed by the judge. I agree that the appeal should be allowed.

[Somervell and Romer LJJ delivered separate concurring opinions.]

Peter Pan Manufacturing Corporation v. Corsets Silhouette Ltd.
[1964] 1 WLR 96 (Ch.)

[Peter Pan was an American company that had designed and manufactured brassieres for a considerable period of time. From their original patterns a new design of brassiere had evolved which was called U25 and U15. In 1953, Peter Pan entered into a licensing agreement with Silhouette, an English company which also manufactured women's underwear garments, to produce and sell its designs in the United Kingdom. Under this agreement,

Peter Pan shared its designs, patterns, and processes with Silhouette in complete confidence. In 1958, a Silhouette designer made a site visit to the United States and was shown the U25 and U15 designs by Peter Pan. In 1959, Silhouette commenced manufacturing its own U25 and U15 inspired brassieres. In 1960, Peter Pan commenced proceedings for an injunction to restrain Silhouette from manufacturing, selling, advertising, and distributing U25 and U15 brassieres or any style that presented a colourable imitation. In addition, Peter Pan sought damages or an account of profits. Peter Pan was successful at trial and elected to take an account of profits. Only the portion of Pennycuick J's judgment dealing with the question of remedy is reproduced here.]

PENNYCUICK J: [T]he effect of my judgment is that the manufacture and sale of brassières of styles U15 and U25 involves confidential information, and therefore Silhouette is not entitled to manufacture those styles. From that it follows as a matter of right that Peter Pan is entitled at their option to claim damages in respect of such invasion of their rights as has already taken place, or alternatively, an account of the profits made by manufacture and sale of brassières in invasion of their rights. It is unnecessary to go through a number of authorities which have been cited, and it will be sufficient to refer to the case of *Lever v. Goodwin* (1887), 36 Ch. D 1 (CA). The headnote is:

> The defendants, who were soap manufacturers, brought out their soap in packets so closely resembling those in which the plaintiffs, who were also soap manufacturers, had been in the habit of bringing out their soap, as to be calculated to deceive purchasers: Held, by Chitty J, that although the retail dealers who bought soap from the defendants would not be deceived, the defendants by their imitation of the plaintiffs' packets put into the hands of the retail dealers an instrument of fraud, and ought to be restrained by injunction. An injunction was accordingly granted, and an account was directed of the profits made by the defendants in selling soap in the form in which it was held that they were not entitled to sell it: Held, on appeal, that the injunction had been rightly granted, and that the account was in the proper form, and ought not to be limited by excluding from it soap which the retail dealers sold to persons who bought it as the defendants' soap.

The actual issue in the case was a somewhat different one, but the order made by Chitty J was:

> An account of the profits made by the defendants in selling or disposing of soap made by or for the defendants in any wrapper such as that contained in the exhibits marked JSS1, JSS4, and BB1, and in the form of those exhibits.

It seems to me on a plain reading of that order that the account would have been of the profits made by the defendants from selling tablets of soap in wrappers of any of the three specified forms; that is to say—How much had it cost to manufacture that soap? What was the price received on its sale? And the difference was the profit.

The case went to the Court of Appeal where the form of account ordered by Chitty J was challenged. The Court of Appeal upheld the order. Cotton LJ said (at p. 7):

> It is well known that, both in trade-mark cases and patent cases, the plaintiff is entitled, if he succeeds in getting an injunction, to take either of two forms of relief; he may either say, "I claim from you the damage I have sustained from your wrongful act," or "I claim from you the

profit which you have made by your wrongful act." ... The profit for which the defendants must account is the profit which they have made by the sale of soap in that fraudulent dress to the middlemen. It is immaterial how the middlemen deal with it.

I have been referred to a number of forms of order in *Seton's Judgments and Orders* (7th ed., 1912), vol. 1, in which an account of profits has been ordered. They were patent cases, trade mark cases, or otherwise, and in each case the account was in this simple form, e.g. (at p. 615):

And it is ordered that an account be taken of the profits made by the defendants in manufacturing and selling, and in selling shirts under the mark or title of "Eureka";

or (at p. 616):

An account of the profits made by the defendants in selling or disposing of soap,

which is *Lever v. Goodwin* which I have already read; and there are one or two others, for example (at p. 655):

An account of the number of copies of the defendants' directory so printed, and of the number thereof so published by the defendant W. as aforesaid, which the defendants or any other person etc., by their or any of their order, or for their or any of their use, have sold or disposed of; and the number of copies now remaining on hand unsold, or undisposed of. An account of all and every sum or sums of money received by the defendants, and each of them, or by any other person etc., upon or by the sale of such copies

and then an order

[t]hat the defendants do pay to the plaintiff what upon taking the said account shall be certified to be the net profit arising from the printing and publication of the defendants' said directory.

It seems to me that on the plain terms of those orders, what a plaintiff who elects in favour of an account of profits is entitled to, is simply an account of profits in the sense which I have indicated, that is, what has the plaintiff expended on manufacturing these goods? What is the price which he has received on their sale? And the difference is profit. That is what Peter Pan claims in the order for an account as formulated by it; that is simply an account of the profits made by Silhouette in the manufacture and sale of the brassières U15 and U25.

Counsel for Silhouette has said that that is not the true meaning of the order for an account in the various cases to which I have referred, and that the true meaning of the order, if I understand him, is an account of the amount by which the profit made by the defendant from manufacturing articles with the aid of patents, trademarks, confidential information, or whatever it may be, which he has in fact used exceeds the amount of the profit which he would have made if he had manufactured the same article without the aid of that material. It seems to me quite impossible to construe the orders made in the various cases as bearing that meaning, and further, so far as I can see, it is perfectly impossible to take as one factor in an account the amount of profit which Silhouette would have made by manufacturing brassières in the styles U15 and U25 without the use of confidential information, since the manufacture of brassières of those styles necessarily and inevitably involves the use of confidential information. Indeed, counsel very aptly said that an account in the only form which he says that Peter Pan is entitled to an account would be impracticable. I am quite unsatisfied by any authorities which have been cited to me that that is the only account to which Peter Pan is entitled, or that the account to which I have held it is entitled would present any serious difficulty in its working out.

I should, I think, mention that one of the cases cited to me by counsel for Silhouette was *Siddell v. Vickers* (1892), 9 RPC 152 (CA). In that case on the particular facts of the case the Court of Appeal laid down that

> [t]he true test of comparison was with what the defendants would probably have used instead of the invention, looking at all the circumstances of the case.

That means only this, that the defendants could have manufactured the product in question by other means, but were able to manufacture more economically by making use of a particular appliance which they were not entitled to use. The position there seems to be wholly different from that in the present case, where the manufacture of the article in question of itself involved the use of the confidential information and Silhouette could not have manufactured that article at all without the use of the confidential information. So again it seems to me that the proper order for an account is in the terms which Peter Pan have put forward, which is the time-honoured form, and I do not see myself any reason why that form should not be adopted.

Seager v. Copydex, Ltd. (No. 2)
[1969] 1 WLR 809 (CA)

[Seager, the plaintiff, was an engineer who had designed a carpet grip. Information on the design of the carpet grip had been given in confidence to Copydex, the defendant, who had then promptly manufactured its own carpet grip under the name "Invisigrip." The plaintiff commenced proceedings against the defendant alleging that it had acted in breach of confidence. The plaintiff sought an injunction to restrain the defendant from making use of the information and for an inquiry as to damages, or an account of profits, for breach of confidence.]

LORD DENNING MR: In April 1967 we heard a case which the plaintiff, Mr. Seager, brought against the defendant company, Copydex, Ltd., alleging that they had taken confidential information relating to a design for a carpet grip. We found in favour of the plaintiff. Now a question has arisen as to the principles on which the damages are to be assessed. They are to be assessed, as we said, at the value of the information which the defendant company took. If I may use an analogy, it is like damages for conversion. Damages for conversion are the value of the goods. Once the damages are paid, the goods become the property of the defendant. A satisfied judgment in trover transfers the property in the goods. So, here, once the damages are assessed and paid, the confidential information belongs to the defendant company.

The difficulty is to assess the value of the information taken by the defendant company. We have had a most helpful discussion about it. The value of the confidential information depends on the nature of it. If there was nothing very special about it, that is, if it involved no particular inventive step but was the sort of information which could be obtained by employing any competent consultant, then the value of it was the fee which a consultant would charge for it; because in that case the defendant company, by taking the information, would only have saved themselves the time and trouble of employing a consultant. But, on the other hand, if the information was something special, as, for instance, if it involved an inventive step or something so unusual that it could not be obtained by just going to a consultant, then the value of it is much higher. It is not merely a consultant's fee, but the price which a willing buyer—desirous of obtaining it—would pay for it. It is the value as between a willing seller and a willing buyer. In this case, the plaintiff says that the information was very special. People had been trying for years to get a carpet grip and then he hit on this idea of a dome-shaped prong. It was, he said, an inventive step. And he is supported in this issue by the fact that the defendant company themselves have applied for a patent for it. Furthermore, if he is to be regarded as a seller, it must be remembered that he had a patent for another carpet grip called "Klent"; and, if he was selling the confidential information (which I will call the "Invisigrip" information), then the sales of the "Klent" might be adversely affected. The sales of the "Klent" would be reduced owing to the competition of the "Invisigrip." So he would ask for a higher price for the confidential information in order to compensate him for the reduction in the "Klent." In these circumstances, if the plaintiff is right in saying that the confidential information was very special indeed, then it may well be right for the value to be assessed on the footing that, in the usual way, it would be remunerated by a royalty. The court, of course, cannot give a royalty by way of damages; but it could give an equivalent by a calculation based on a capitalisation of a royalty. Thus it could arrive at a lump sum. Once a lump sum is assessed and paid, then the confidential information would belong to the defendant company in the same way as if they had bought and paid for it by an agreement of sale. The property, so far as there is property in it, would vest in them. They would have the right to use that confidential information for the manufacture of carpet grips and selling of them. If it is patentable, they would be entitled to the benefit of the patent as if they had bought it. In other words, it would be regarded as a real outright purchase of the confidential information. The value should, therefore, be assessed on that basis; and damages awarded accordingly.

In these circumstances, I do not think that we should make any such declaration as the defendant company ask. It is sufficient for us to say that, on a satisfied judgment for damages, the confidential information belongs to the defendant company.

There is one thing more. We have been told that patent proceedings are pending by the defendant company. They are applying for a patent and the plaintiff is opposing it. That cannot affect directly the matters which we have had to decide today. But the matters are so linked together that I think that the damages should be assessed not by a master in the Chancery Division but by a patent judge. I hope that one patent judge will deal with the patent proceedings as well as these damages. The only order which I would make on the motion is simply to say that the damages are to be assessed in conformity with our judgments.

[Salmon and Winn LJJ delivered separate concurring judgments.]

Townsview Properties Ltd. v. Sun Construction & Equipment Co. Ltd.
(1973), 2 OR (2d) 213 (HC)

STARK J: The plaintiffs bring this action against the defendants, which is described in the statement of claim as being an action based upon trespass and the maintenance of a nuisance, claiming damages to their property including exemplary and punitive damages. The circumstances giving rise to the action occurred in 1964 and 1965. The land owned by the plaintiff Townsview Properties Limited consists of a parcel of vacant land with a frontage of 45 ft. on St. Clair Ave. E., in the City of Toronto, a short distance from Yonge St., with a depth of 109 ft. and with certain air rights over a Toronto Transportation Commission loop on the west, of some 35 ft. The parcel owned by the plaintiff Yonge Pleasant Holdings Limited lies at the rear of this property and extends to Pleasant Blvd. The two plaintiffs are acting in concert in this matter, being both represented by the same counsel, and both acquired ownership of their lands at approximately the same time.

Immediately adjoining the plaintiffs' lands on the east are the properties owned, or more correctly leased under a 120-year lease, by the defendant Don Mills Developments Limited. Upon this property, the said defendant through its contractor, Sun Construction and Equipment Company Limited, planned to erect and did erect a substantial apartment and shopping complex known as Towne Mall. The building was constructed within one inch of the property line separating the plaintiffs' lands from the lands of Don Mills Developments Limited. In building the foundation walls, the defendants instead of confining their activities to their own property excavated upon the plaintiffs' properties to a varying width of some 20 ft. and to a depth of over 20 ft. In addition they used the plaintiffs' properties for the storage of materials and for convenient egress and ingress to their property. The claims of the plaintiffs are for damages for these alleged wrongful acts, and for punitive or exemplary damages for their conduct. ...

The evidence indicated that the defendants effected a substantial saving to themselves by making use of the plaintiffs' land. The alternate procedure would have been to erect the foundation walls by a shoring process on their own property. It was estimated that the saving by reason of the excavating on the neighbouring property, would be a figure ranging from $7,000 to $11,000, and that a further saving in time, of possibly two weeks, would also be effected. ...

[Having found that a trespass had been committed] ...

There remains to consider the amount of the damages. Considerable expert evidence was given as to the extent and nature of the soil disturbance caused by the excavation. The defendants did fill in the excavation and took steps to ensure that the fill was properly packed. The plaintiffs' experts submitted that their soil testing revealed variations in the results indicating the need for deeper and more extensive foundations than would normally be required if a building were to be erected. The defendants' experts also conducted soil tests and felt that the plaintiffs' apprehensions as to future building requirements were exaggerated. It is not disputed that excavated soil is not the same quality as undisturbed land. But the evidence also indicated that to reach a firm conclusion in this regard it would be necessary to conduct further and more extensive tests. The fact is that the plaintiffs have no immediate intention of building upon this vacant land and it has remained idle ever since. The plaintiff Townsview Properties Limited had at one time engaged an architect to prepare preliminary plans for the erection of a one-storey type building on the property, but these plans were not proceeded with, for a variety of reasons not pertinent to this action. There is no immediate intention to build on the property. The only special damage that the plaintiffs can point to at the moment is the cost of the soil tests which they had arranged at a cost of $479.33 and for which reimbursement is justified. In the matter of general damages, I have allowed the sum of $500 for the cost of future soil tests which will be required before construction of a building could be commenced.

Since I regard the defendants' action as an inexcusable and unwarranted trespass upon the plaintiffs' property, without justification, I consider this a proper matter to take into consideration in fixing the general damages. In my view, this is a case for the inclusion of punitive or exemplary damages in my award. By their trespass, the defendants have gained a substantial saving in the construction of their own building, the amount and nature of which I have described elsewhere. Accordingly, I fix the general damages herein at the sum of $5,500, to which should be added the special damages of $479.37, for a total of $5,979.37. The award should be divided between the two plaintiffs in proportion to the extent of their holdings as affected by the trespass, and I understand that such a division is not in dispute between them. The plaintiffs are, of course, also entitled to their costs.

Judgment for plaintiffs.

The judgment was varied by the Court of Appeal (1974), 7 OR (2d) 666 (CA) with respect to a matter not relevant here. The award of exemplary damages was upheld as justified on the basis of the arrogant conduct on the part of the defendant (at 671).

NOTE

In *Rookes v. Barnard*, [1964] AC 1129, at 1226 (HL (Eng.)), Lord Devlin described one category of case appropriate for exemplary damages as follows:

> Cases in the second category are those in which the defendant's conduct has been calculated by him to make a profit for himself which may well exceed the compensation payable to the plaintiff. ...
>
> It is a factor also that is taken into account in damages for libel; one man should not be allowed to sell another man's reputation for profit. Where a defendant with a cynical disregard for a plaintiff's rights has calculated that the money to be made out of his wrongdoing will probably exceed the damages at risk, it is necessary for the law to show that it cannot be broken with impunity. This category is not confined to moneymaking in the strict sense. It extends to cases in which the defendant is seeking to gain at the expense of the plaintiff some object—perhaps some property which he covets—which either he could not obtain at all or not obtain except at a price greater than he wants to put down. Exemplary damages can properly be awarded whenever it is necessary to teach a wrongdoer that tort does not pay.

This was elaborated in *Broome v. Cassell & Co. Ltd.*, as follows:

Broome v. Cassell & Co. Ltd.
[1972] AC 1027 (HL (Eng.))

LORD HAILSHAM (at 1078): … When one comes to the second category, we reach a field which was more exhaustively discussed in the case before us. It soon became apparent that a broad rather than a narrow interpretation of Lord Devlin's words was absolutely essential, and that attempts to narrow the second category by a quotation out of context of one sentence from the passage wherein it is defined simply will not do. Lord Devlin [in *Rookes v. Barnard*] founded his second category on a sequence of cases beginning with *Bell v. Midland Railway Co.* (1861), 10 CBNS 287; 142 ER 462 (CP) and on the judgment of Maule J in *Williams v. Currie* (1845), 1 CB 841 at p. 848; 135 ER 774 at pp. 776-77 (CP) and the dictum of Martin B in *Crouch v. Great Northern Railway* (1856), 11 Exch. 742 at p. 759; 156 ER 1031 at p. 1038. None of these were examples of precise calculation of the balance sheet type. Then he said, at p. 1227:

> [The motive of making a profit] is a factor also that is taken into account in damages for libel; one man should not be allowed to sell another man's reputation for profit. Where a defendant with a cynical disregard for a plaintiff's rights has calculated that the money to be made out of his wrongdoing will probably exceed the damages at risk, it is necessary for the law to show that it cannot be broken with impunity. *This category is not confined to moneymaking in the strict sense. It extends to cases in which the defendant is seeking to gain at the expense of the plaintiff some object—perhaps some property which he covets—which either he could not obtain at all or not obtain except at a price greater than he wants to put down. Exemplary damages can properly be awarded whenever it is necessary to teach a wrongdoer that tort does not pay.* (Italics mine.)

Even a casual reading of the above passage shows that the sentence: "Where a defendant with a cynical disregard for a plaintiff's rights has calculated that the money to be made out of his wrongdoing will probably exceed the damages at risk, it is necessary for the law to show that it cannot be broken with impunity" is not intended to be exhaustive but illustrative, and is not intended to be limited to the kind of mathematical calculations to be found on a balance sheet. The sentence must be read in its context. The context occurs immediately after the sentence: "one man should not be allowed to sell another man's reputation for profit," where the word "calculation" does not occur. The context also includes the final sentence: "Exemplary damages can properly be awarded whenever it is necessary to teach a wrongdoer that tort does not pay." The whole passage must be read sensibly as a whole, together with the authorities on which it is based.

It is true, of course, as was well pointed out by Widgery J in *Manson v. Associated Newspapers Ltd.*, [1965] 1 WLR 1038 at p. 1045, that the mere fact that a tort, and particularly a libel, is committed in the course of a business carried on for profit is not sufficient to bring a case within the second category. Nearly all newspapers, and most books, are published for profit. What is necessary in addition is (i) knowledge that what is proposed to be done is against the law or a reckless disregard whether what is proposed to be done is illegal or legal, and (ii) a decision to carry on doing it because the prospects of material advantage outweigh the prospects of material loss. It is not necessary that the defendant calculates that the plaintiff's damages if he sues to judgment will be smaller than the defendant's profit. This is simply one example of the principle. The defendant may calculate that the plaintiff will not sue at all because he has not the money (I suppose the plaintiff in a contested libel action like the present must be prepared nowadays to put at least £30,000 at some risk), or because he may be physically or otherwise intimidated. What is necessary is that the tortious act must be done with guilty knowledge for the motive that the chances of economic advantage outweigh the chances of economic, or perhaps physical, penalty.

LORD DIPLOCK (at 1130): I have no similar doubts about the retention of the second category. It too may be a blunt instrument to prevent unjust enrichment by unlawful acts. But to restrict the damages recoverable to the actual gain made by the defendant if it exceeded the loss caused to the plaintiff would leave a defendant contemplating an unlawful act with the certainty that he had nothing to lose to balance against the chance that the plaintiff might never sue him or, if he did, might fail in the hazards of litigation. It is only if there is a prospect that the damages may exceed the defendant's gain that the social purpose of this category is achieved—to teach a wrong-doer that tort does not pay.

To bring a case within this category it must be proved that the defendant, at the time that he committed the tortious act, knew that it was unlawful or suspecting it to be unlawful deliberately refrained from taking obvious steps which, if taken, would have turned suspicion into certainty. While, of course, it is not necessary to prove that the defendant made an arithmetical calculation of the pecuniary profit he would make from the tortious act and of the compensatory damages and costs to which he would render himself liable, with appropriate discount for the chances that he might get away with it without being sued or might settle the action for some lower figure, it must be a reasonable inference from the evidence that he did direct his mind to the material advantages to be gained by committing the tort and came to the conclusion that they were worth the risk of having to compensate the plaintiff if he should bring an action.

NOTES

1. In Robert Sharpe and S.M. Waddams, "Damages for Lost Opportunity To Bargain" (1982), 2 *Oxford Journal of Legal Studies* 290, the authors suggest that in many of the cases under consideration the plaintiff had suffered a real loss—namely, loss of opportunity to bargain. The relation of this idea to wrongdoing and to unjust enrichment has been the subject of controversy. In Waddams, *Dimensions of Private Law: Categories and Concepts in Anglo-American Legal Reasoning* (Cambridge: Cambridge University Press, 2003), at 108-9, one of the authors attempted to restate the point:

> Another dimension of the question is the argument that in many of the cases the plaintiff *has* suffered a real loss, though one that is difficult to quantify, by being deprived of the opportunity to bargain with the wrongdoer for a rent, licence charge, or fee. This consideration might in some cases, though not in all, support an award purely on compensatory principles, but, even where it does not, it has not been wholly irrelevant: even if the court's primary objective is taken to be the elimination of the defendant's profit, it cannot weaken the plaintiff's claim to show that an award will also *simultaneously* perform a compensatory function. To put the point at its very lowest, the idea that the plaintiff has suffered an actual but unquantifiable loss has tended to strengthen the

claim to some degree, and it has, together with other considerations, been influential in supporting awards related in some measure to the defendant's profit.

2. Claims based on unjust enrichment, although individually for small amounts, have assumed a new significance in the context of class actions. See *Heward v. Eli Lilly & Co.* (2007), 295 DLR (4th) 175 (Div. Ct.) and *The Queen v. Elder Advocates Society*, 2011 SCC 24.

CHAPTER THREE

Damages for Breach of Contract

THE INTERESTS PROTECTED AND THE PURPOSES PURSUED

L.L. Fuller and William R. Perdue Jr., "The Reliance Interest in Contract Damages"
(1936), 46 *Yale Law Journal* 52, at 52-62 (edited; footnotes omitted)

The proposition that legal rules can be understood only with reference to the purposes they serve would today scarcely be regarded as an exciting truth. The notion that law exists as a means to an end has been commonplace for at least half a century. There is, however, no justification for assuming, because this attitude has now achieved respectability, and even triteness, that it enjoys a pervasive application in practice. Certainly there are even today few legal treatises of which it may be said that the author has throughout clearly defined the purposes which his definitions and distinctions serve. We are still all too willing to embrace the conceit that it is possible to manipulate legal concepts without the orientation which comes from the simple inquiry: toward what end is this activity directed? Nietzsche's observation, that the most common stupidity consists in forgetting what one is trying to do, retains a discomforting relevance to legal science.

In no field is this more true than in that of damages. In the assessment of damages the law tends to be conceived, not as purposive ordering of human affairs, but as a kind of juristic mensuration. The language of the decisions sounds in terms not of command but of discovery. We *measure* the *extent* of the injury; we *determine* whether it was *caused* by the defendant's act; we *ascertain* whether the plaintiff has included the *same item* of damage twice in his complaint. One unfamiliar with the unstated premises which language of this sort conceals might almost be led to suppose that Rochester produces some ingenious instrument by which these calculations are accomplished.

It is, as a matter of fact, clear that the things which the law of damages purports to "measure" and "determine"—the "injuries," "items of damage," "causal connections," etc.—are in considerable part its own creations, and that the process of "measuring" and "determining" them is really a part of the process of creating them. This is obvious when courts work on the periphery of existing doctrine, but it is no less true of fundamental and established principles. For example, one frequently finds the "normal" rule of contract damages (which awards to the promisee the value of the the expectancy, "the lost profit") treated as a mere corollary of a more fundamental principle, that the purpose of granting damages is to make "compensation" for injury. Yet in this case we "compensate" the plaintiff by giving him something he never had. This seems on the face of things a queer kind of "compensation." We can, to be sure, make the term "compensation" seem appropriate by saying that the defendant's breach "deprived" the plaintiff of the expectancy. But this is in essence only a metaphorical statement of the effect of the legal rule. In actuality the loss which the plaintiff suffers (deprivation of the expectancy) is not a datum of nature but the reflection of a normative order. It appears as a "loss" only by reference to an unstated *ought*. Consequently, when the law gauges damages by the value of the promised performance it is not merely measuring a quantum, but is seeking an end, however vaguely conceived this end may be.

It is for this reason that it is impossible to separate the law of contract damages from the larger body of motives and policies which constitutes the general law of contracts. It is, unfortunately for the simplicity of our subject, impossible to assume that the purposive and policy-directed element of contract law has been exhausted in the rules which define contract and breach. If this were possible the law of contract damages would indeed be simple, and we would have but one measure of recovery for all contracts. Of course this is not the case. What considerations influence the setting up of different measures of recovery for different kinds of contracts? What factors explain the rather numerous exceptions to the normal rule which measures damages by the value of the expectancy? It is clear that these questions cannot be answered without an inquiry into the reasons which underlie (or may underlie) the enforcement of promises generally.

In our own discussion we shall attempt first an analysis of the purposes which may be pursued in awarding contract damages or in "enforcing" contracts generally; then we shall attempt to inquire to what extent, and under what circumstances, these purposes have found expression in the decisions and doctrinal discussions. As the title suggests, the primary emphasis will be on what we call "the reliance interest" as a possible measure of recovery in suits for breach of contract.

The Purposes Pursued in Awarding Contract Damages

It is convenient to distinguish three principal purposes which may be pursued in awarding contract damages. These purposes, and the situations in which they become appropriate, may be stated briefly as follows:

First, the plaintiff has in reliance on the promise of the defendant conferred some value on the defendant. The defendant fails to perform his promise. The court may force the defendant to disgorge the value he received from the plaintiff. The object here may be termed the prevention of gain by the defaulting promisor at the expense of the promisee; more briefly, the prevention of unjust enrichment. The interest protected may be called the *restitution interest*. For our present purposes it is quite immaterial how the suit in such a case be classified, whether as contractual or quasi-contractual, whether as a suit to enforce the contract or as a suit based upon a rescission of the contract. These questions relate to the superstructure of the law, not to the basic policies with which we are concerned.

Secondly, the plaintiff has in reliance on the promise of the defendant changed his position. For example, the buyer under a contract for the sale of land has incurred expense in the investigation of the seller's title, or has neglected the opportunity to enter other contracts. We may award damages to the plaintiff for the purpose of undoing the harm which his reliance on the defendant's promise has caused him. Our object is to put him in as good a position as he was in before the promise was made. The interest protected in this case may be called the *reliance interest*.

Thirdly, without insisting on reliance by the promisee or enrichment of the promisor, we may seek to give the promisee the value of the expectancy which the promise created. We may in a suit for specific performance actually compel the defendant to render the promised performance to the plaintiff, or, in a suit for damages, we may make the defendant pay the money value of this performance. Here our object is to put the plaintiff in as good a position as he would have occupied had the defendant performed his promise. The interest protected in this case we may call the *expectation interest*.

It will be observed that what we have called the *restitution interest* unites two elements: (1) reliance by the promisee, [and] (2) a resultant gain to the promisor. It may for some purposes be necessary to separate these elements. In some cases a defaulting promisor may after his breach be left with an unjust gain which was not taken from the promisee (a third party furnished the consideration), or which was not the result of reliance by the promisee (the promisor violated a promise not to appropriate the promisee's goods). Even in those cases where the promisor's gain results from the promisee's reliance it may happen that the damages will be assessed somewhat differently, depending on whether we take the promisor's gain or the promisee's loss as the standard of measurement. Generally, however, in the cases we shall be discussing, gain by the promisor will be accompanied by a corresponding and, so far as its legal measurement is concerned, identical loss to the promisee, so that for our purposes the most workable classification is one which presupposes in the restitution interest a correlation of promisor's gain and promisee's loss. If, as we shall assume, the gain involved in the restitution interest results from and is identical with the plaintiff's loss through reliance, then the restitution interest is merely a special case of the reliance interest; all of the cases coming under the restitution interest will be covered by the reliance interest, and the reliance interest will be broader than the restitution interest only to the extent that it includes cases where the plaintiff has relied on the defendant's promise without enriching the defendant.

It should not be supposed that the distinction here taken between the reliance and expectation interests coincides with that sometimes taken between "losses caused" (*damnum emergens*) and "gains prevented" (*lucrum cessans*). In the first place, though reliance ordinarily results in "losses" of an affirmative nature (expenditures of labor and money) it is also true that opportunities for gain may be foregone in reliance on a promise. Hence the reliance interest must be interpreted as at least potentially covering "gains prevented" as well as "losses caused." (Whether "gains prevented" through reliance on a promise are properly compensable in damages is a question not here determined. Obviously, certain scruples concerning "causality" and "foreseeability" are suggested. It is enough for our present purpose to note that there is nothing in the definition of the reliance interest itself which would exclude items of this sort from consideration.) On the other hand, it is not possible to make the expectation interest entirely synonymous with "gains prevented." The disappointment of an expectancy often entails losses of a positive character.

It is obvious that the three "interests" we have distinguished do not present equal claims to judicial intervention. It may be assumed that ordinary standards of justice would regard the need for judicial intervention as decreasing in the order in which we have listed the three interests. The "restitution interest," involving a combination of unjust impoverishment with unjust gain, presents the strongest case for relief. If, following Aristotle, we regard the purpose of justice as the maintenance of an equilibrium of goods among members of society, the restitution interest presents twice as strong a claim to judicial intervention as the reliance interest, since if A not only causes B to lose one unit but appropriates that unit to himself, the resulting discrepancy between A and B is not one unit but two.

On the other hand, the promisee who has actually relied on the promise, even though he may not thereby have enriched the promisor, certainly presents a more pressing case for relief than the promisee who merely demands satisfaction for his disappointment in not getting what was promised him. In passing from compensation for change of position to compensation for loss of expectancy we pass, to use Aristotle's terms again, from the realm of corrective justice to that of distributive justice. The law no longer seeks merely to heal a disturbed status quo, but to bring into being a new situation. It ceases to act defensively or restoratively, and assumes a more active role. With the transition, the justification for legal relief loses its self-evident quality. It is as a matter of fact no easy thing to explain why the normal rule of contract recovery should be that which measures damages by the value of the promised performance. Since this "normal rule" throws its shadow across our whole subject it will be necessary to examine the possible reasons for its existence. It may be said parenthetically that the discussion which follows, though directed primarily to the normal measure of recovery where damages are sought, also has relevance to the more general question, why should a promise which has not been relied on ever be enforced at all, whether by a decree of specific performance or by an award of damages?

It should also be said that our discussion of "reasons" does not claim to coincide in all particulars with the actual workings of the judicial mind, certainly not with those of any single judicial mind. It is unfortunately very difficult to discuss the possible reasons for rules of law without unwittingly conveying the impression that these "reasons" are the things which control the daily operations of the judicial process. This has had the consequence, at a time when men stand in dread of being labelled "unrealistic," that we have almost ceased to talk about reasons altogether. Those who find unpalatable the rationalistic flavor of what follows are invited to view what they read not as law but as an excursus into legal philosophy, and to make whatever discount that distinction may seem to them to dictate.

Why Should the Law Ever Protect the Expectation Interest?

Perhaps the most obvious answer to this question is one which we may label "psychological." This answer would run something as follows: The breach of a promise arouses in the promisee a sense of injury. This feeling is not confined to cases where the promisee has relied on the promise. Whether or not he has actually changed his position because of the promise, the promisee has formed an attitude of expectancy such that a breach of the promise causes him to feel that he has been "deprived" of something which was "his." Since this sentiment is a relatively uniform one, the law has no occasion to go back of it. It accepts it as a datum and builds its rule about it.

The difficulty with this explanation is that the law does in fact go back of the sense of injury which the breach of a promise engenders. No legal system attempts to invest with juristic sanction all promises. Some rule or combination of rules effects a sifting out for enforcement of those promises deemed important enough to society to justify the law's concern with them. Whatever the principles which control this sifting out process may be, they are not convertible into terms of the degree of resentment which the breach of a particular kind of promise arouses. Therefore, though it may be assumed that the impulse to assuage disappointment is one shared by those who make and influence the law, this impulse can hardly be regarded as the key which solves the whole problem of the protection accorded by the law to the expectation interest.

A second possible explanation for the rule protecting the expectancy may be found in the much-discussed "will theory" of contract law. This theory views the contracting parties as exercising, so to speak, a legislative power, so that the legal enforcement of a contract becomes merely an implementing by the state of a kind of private law already established by the parties. If A has made, in proper form, a promise to pay B one thousand dollars, we compel A to pay this sum simply because the rule or *lex* set up by the parties calls for this payment. *Uti lingua nuncupassit, ita jus esto.*

It is not necessary to discuss here the contribution which the will theory is capable of making to a philosophy of contract law. Certainly some borrowings from the theory are discernible in most attempts to rationalize the bases of contract liability. It is enough to note here that while the will theory undoubtedly has some bearing on the problem of contract damages, it cannot be regarded as dictating in all cases a recovery of the expectancy. If a contract represents a kind of private law, it is a law which usually says nothing at all about what shall be done when it is violated. A contract is in this respect like an imperfect statute which provides no penalties, and which leaves it to the courts to find a way to effectuate its purposes. There would, therefore, be no necessary contradiction between the will theory and a rule which limited damages to the reliance interest. Under such a rule the penalty for violating the norm established by the contract would simply consist in being compelled to compensate the other party for detrimental reliance. Of course there may be cases where the parties have so obviously anticipated that a certain form of judicial relief will be given that we can, without stretching things, say that by implication they have "willed" that this relief should be given. This attitude finds a natural application to promises to pay a definite sum of money. But certainly as to most types of contracts it is vain to expect from the will theory a ready-made solution for the problem of damages.

A third and more promising solution of our difficulty lies in an economic or institutional approach. The essence of a credit economy lies in the fact that it tends to eliminate the distinction between present and future (promised) goods. Expectations of future values become, for purposes of trade, present values. In a society in which credit has become a significant and pervasive institution, it is inevitable that the expectancy created by an enforceable promise should be regarded as a kind of property, and breach of the promise as an injury to that property. In such a society the breach of a promise works an "actual" diminution of the promisee's assets—"actual" in the sense that it would be so appraised according to modes of thought which enter into the very fiber of our economic system. That the promisee had not "used" the property which the promise represents (had not relied on the promise) is as immaterial as the question whether the plaintiff in trespass *quare clausum fregit* was using his property at the time it was encroached upon. The analogy to ordinary forms of property goes further, for even in a suit for trespass the recovery is really for an expectancy, an expectancy of possible future uses. Where the property expectancy is limited (as where the plaintiff has only an estate for years) the recovery is reduced accordingly. Ordinary property differs from a contract right chiefly in the fact that it lies within the power of more persons to work a direct injury to the expectancy it represents. It is generally only the promisor or some one working through or upon him who is able to injure the contract expectancy in a direct enough manner to make expedient legal intervention.

The most obvious objection which can be made to the economic or institutional explanation is that it involves a *petitio principii*. A promise has present value, why? Because the law enforces it. "The expectancy," regarded as a present value, is not the cause of legal intervention but the consequence of it. This objection may be reinforced by a reference to legal history. Promises were enforced long before there was anything corresponding to a general system of "credit," and recovery was from the beginning measured by the value of the promised performance, the "agreed price." It may therefore be argued that the "credit system" when it finally emerged was itself in large part built on the foundations of a juristic development which preceded it.

The view just suggested asserts the primacy of law over economics; it sees law not as the creature but as the creator of social institutions. The shift of emphasis thus implied suggests the possibility of a fourth explanation for the law's protection of the unrelied-on expectancy, which we may call *juristic*. This explanation would seek a justification for the normal rule of recovery in some policy consciously pursued by courts and other lawmakers. It would assume that courts have protected the expectation interest because they have considered it wise to do so, not through a blind acquiescence in habitual ways of thinking and feeling, or through an equally blind deference to the individual will. Approaching the problem from this point of view, we are forced to find not a mere explanation for the rule in the form of some sentimental, volitional, or institutional datum, but articulate reasons for its existence.

What reasons can be advanced? In the first place, even if our interest were confined to protecting promisees against an out-of-pocket loss, it would still be possible to justify the rule granting the value of the expectancy, both as a cure for, and as a prophylaxis against, losses of this sort.

It is a cure for these losses in the sense that it offers the measure of recovery most likely to reimburse the plaintiff for the (often very numerous and very difficult to prove) individual acts and forbearances which make up his total reliance on the contract. If we take into account "gains prevented" by reliance, that is, losses involved in foregoing the opportunity to enter other contracts, the notion that the rule protecting the expectancy is adopted as the most effective means of compensating for detrimental reliance seems not at all far-fetched. Physicians with an extensive practice often charge their patients the full office call fee for broken appointments. Such a charge looks on the face of things like a claim to the promised fee; it seems to be based on the "expectation interest." Yet the physician making the charge will quite justifiably regard it as compensation for the loss of the opportunity to gain a similar fee from a different patient. This foregoing of other opportunities is involved to some extent in entering most contracts, and the impossibility of subjecting this type of reliance to any kind of measurement may justify a categorical rule granting the value of the expectancy as the most effective way of compensating for such losses.

The rule that the plaintiff must after the defendant's breach take steps to mitigate damages tends to corroborate the suspicion that there lies hidden behind the protection of the expectancy a concern to compensate the plaintiff for the loss of the opportunity to enter other contracts. Where after the defendant's breach the opportunity remains open to the plaintiff to sell his services or goods elsewhere, or to fill his needs from another source, he is bound to embrace that opportunity. Viewed in this way the rule of "avoidable harms" is a qualification on the protection accorded the expectancy, since it means that the plaintiff, in those cases where it is applied, is protected only to the extent that he has in reliance on the contract foregone other equally advantageous opportunities for accomplishing the same end.

But, as we have suggested, the rule measuring damages by the expectancy may also be regarded as a prophylaxis against the losses resulting from detrimental reliance. Whatever tends to discourage breach of contract tends to prevent the losses occasioned through reliance. Since the expectation interest furnishes a more easily administered measure of recovery than the reliance interest, it will in practice offer a more effective sanction against contract breach. It is therefore possible to view the rule measuring damages by the expectancy in a quasi-criminal aspect, its purpose being not so much to compensate the promisee as to penalize breach of promise by the promisor. The rule enforcing the unrelied-on promise finds the same justification, on this theory, as an ordinance which fines a man for driving through a stoplight when no other vehicle is in sight.

In seeking justification for the rule granting the value of the expectancy there is no need, however, to restrict ourselves by the assumption, hitherto made, that the rule can only be intended to cure or prevent the losses caused by reliance. A justification can be developed from a less negative point of view. It may be said that there is not only a policy in favor of promoting and undoing the harms resulting from reliance, but also a policy in favor of promoting and facilitating reliance on business agreements. As in the case of the stop-light ordinance we are interested not only in preventing collisions but in speeding traffic. Agreements can accomplish little, either for their makers or for society, unless they are made the basis for action. When business agreements are not only made but are also acted on, the division of labor is facilitated, goods find their way to the places where they are most needed, and economic activity is generally stimulated. These advantages would be threatened by any rule which limited legal protection to the reliance interest. Such a rule would in practice tend to discourage reliance. The difficulties in proving reliance and subjecting it to pecuniary measurement are such that the business man knowing, or sensing, that these obstacles stood in the way of judicial relief would hesitate to rely on a promise in any case where the legal sanction was of significance to him. To encourage reliance we must therefore dispense with its proof. For this reason it has been found wise to make recovery on a promise independent of reliance, both in the sense that in some cases the promise is enforced though not relied on (as in the bilateral business agreement) and in the sense that recovery is not limited to the detriment incurred in reliance.

The juristic explanation in its final form is then twofold. It rests the protection accorded the expectancy on (1) the need for curing and preventing the harms occasioned by reliance, and (2) on the need for facilitating reliance on business agreements. From this spelling out of a possible juristic explanation, it is clear that there is no incompatibility between it and the economic or institutional explanation. They view the same phenomenon from two different aspects. The essence of both of them lies in the word "credit." The economic explanation views credit from its institutional side; the juristic explanation views it from its rational side. The economic view sees credit as an accepted way of living; the juristic view invites us to explore the considerations of utility which underlie this way of living, and the part which conscious human direction has played in bringing it into being.

NOTE

Fuller and Perdue's article is one of the best-known, most-cited law review articles of all time. It is a classic of American legal realism. The authors identify three interests of the plaintiff that might be protected by an award of damages. As you know, the general rule in contract damages is to compensate the plaintiff for the loss of the value of the bargain. This is reflected in the statement that the award of damages seeks, in money terms, to put the plaintiff in the position that he or she would have reached had the contract been performed. This involves both prediction and evaluation. The court must predict where it is that the plaintiff would have reached had the contract been performed, working within the limits prescribed by the doctrines of remoteness and certainty. It must then evaluate that position by assigning a money amount to represent its value to the plaintiff. This involves decisions about *how* to measure this value as well as decisions about *how to apply* the selected measures to the particular situation. The materials that follow explore some of these issues about how the expectation interest of the plaintiff should be measured, as well as looking at some cases in which the other interests identified by Fuller and Perdue are protected by compensation instead of or in addition to compensation for loss of the expectation interest.

The following case will serve as a first illustration of the application of the general rule of protecting the expectation interest in a situation where arguments about remoteness and, perhaps, certainty of damage were made by the defendant.

Canlin Ltd. v. Thiokol Fibres Canada
(1983), 40 OR (2d) 687 (CA)

CORY JA (for the court): Can a plaintiff recover damages for the estimated loss of future profits caused by the defendant's breach of warranty? That is the question that must be determined on this appeal.

Factual Background

The trial judge gave extensive and careful reasons on the issue of liability which favoured the plaintiff, respondent ("Canadian Tarpoly") [summarized 14 ACWS (2d) 423]. Although the finding of liability is not challenged by the defendant, appellant ("Thiokol"), something must be said of the nature of the contract between the parties in order to understand the problem which arises in the award of damages.

Canadian Tarpoly has been in the business of manufacturing and sale of various plastic products since 1968. In 1971, this company began to manufacture and sell solid swimming-pool covers which kept out debris, dirt and water. In 1974, Canadian Tarpoly was satisfied that there was a ready market in the USA for the sale of mesh pool covers. These covers would keep debris and dirt out of a pool but water could pass through them. A competitor of Canadian Tarpoly was meeting this demand and Canadian Tarpoly was anxious to enter this market and share in the profits to be derived from it.

Thiokol manufactured polypropylene, polyolefin and polyethylene fabric and had supplied material to Canadian Tarpoly since 1971. In September of 1974, representatives of Canadian Tarpoly inquired of Thiokol whether they were interested in supplying the required polypropylene fabric for the mesh pool covers. Tarpoly specifically advised Thiokol that it would be offering its customers a three-year guaranty and that the material supplied would be required to meet the following conditions:

(a) that it be similar in appearance and colour to that of Canadian Tarpoly's American competitor;

(b) that it have a minimum life of two winter seasons;

(c) that it contain sufficient ultraviolet inhibitors to avoid deterioration from prolonged exposure to sunlight, and

(d) that it be made available to Canadian Tarpoly, especially early in 1975 to enable that company to manufacture and sell the covers to its customers prior to September, a month when pool covers are traditionally installed by pool users.

Thiokol was aware of the nature of Canadian Tarpoly's business, the nature and extent of the guaranty, and with that background undertook to meet the Tarpoly requirements and supply the fabric.

With its supply of material secured the Tarpoly company undertook a promotional campaign for the sale of the mesh covers. The sale of the covers began in the spring of 1975. One complaint was received in November of 1975 but a single complaint with a new product would hardly be considered out of the way. However, in the spring of 1976, particularly in the month of May of that year, Canadian Tarpoly was deluged with complaints. They were so voluminous and vituperative that it was necessary for Canadian Tarpoly to secure warehouse space in Buffalo to store the mesh covers returned by dissatisfied customers. It was found that the covers disintegrated so that parts of the fabric found their way into not only the pool filters but the pool heaters. The situation was aptly described by the trial judge as a "fiasco." Canadian Tarpoly ceased its manufacture of the mesh covers from the Thiokol fabric in the summer of 1976. By this time, grievous damage had been done to the reputation of Tarpoly. At a convention of the pool supply industry in 1977, distributors were advised not to use Tarpoly equipment.

The trial judge concluded that Tarpoly, as the buyer, had expressly made known to the seller, Thiokol, the particular purposes for which the goods were required and relied upon Thiokol's skill to supply the required material. There was thus an implied condition that the goods would be reasonably fit for Tarpoly's purposes. The material supplied by Thiokol was not fit for the purposes for which it was intended and Thiokol was thus in breach of its warranty.

Damages Awarded at Trial

In very brief reasons the trial judge then assessed the damages against Thiokol for breach of its warranty under the following headings:

Credit notes and write-offs converted to Canadian dollars....	$ 84,009
Other expenses...	3,500
Replacement covers....................................	5,500
Projected loss of future business........................	100,000
Total:..	$193,009

The claim for projected loss of future profits was put forward at $482,401. This figure was based on the projected sales and increase in sales that would have been made to customers of Tarpoly, had these customers not cancelled their business with the company as a result of their disastrous experience with the disintegrating pool covers. There was evidence given on behalf of Tarpoly and apparently accepted by the trial judge that it was not reasonable for it to re-enter the pool cover business in the United States until 1980.

The trial judge recognized the difficulty Tarpoly faced in obtaining satisfactory proof of the loss of profits. It would have been required to call witnesses from its customers in the United States who in turn would need to produce records of their sales. The task would be well-nigh impossible for business relations between Tarpoly and its American customers had virtually ceased to exist between 1976 and 1980. In essence, it was found at trial that there was a substantial loss which was impossible to calculate with any accuracy. Thus, the figure of $100,000 represented the trial judge's estimate of this head of damage.

The Appellant's Position

It is the position of the appellant Thiokol that the loss of future business profits was not a foreseeable consequence of a breach of warranty. Alternatively, it is said that such a loss is not a consequence directly and naturally resulting from the breach of warranty.

Some General Comments on the Appellant's Position

The appellant's proposition appears to me to be one that flies in the face of reason and common sense. Most commercial contracts pertaining to the sale and delivery of material or goods must, of necessity, be entered into with a view to making a profit in the future. To say otherwise amounts to a denial of the profit motive in the free enterprise system. The case at bar is a prime example. The plaintiff made known to the defendant that it was in business selling to distributors in the United States and that it wished to manufacture and sell a specific type of pool cover. It had determined that there was a profit to be made. It was to secure such a profit that it entered into a contract with Thiokol to supply the material for the manufacture of the pool covers.

Let us consider the unlikely scenario wherein the executive or board of directors of Thiokol sat down and discussed what was likely to happen if they supplied defective material to Tarpoly. In my view, the result would be the same in this case and should be the same in all cases whether the question the executives of Thiokol posed was framed as it would be for a tort case or one involving breach of contract. If these executives asked the "tort" question, what can we reasonably "foresee" as likely to befall Tarpoly if we supply inadequate material, the answer of reasonable men of business would be to the effect that Tarpoly would lose the profits it might expect to make on the sale of pool covers. If the "contract" question was phrased, what can we reasonable "contemplate" as a result directly flowing from our breach of warranty, the answer would be to precisely the same effect. The Thiokol executives would have foreseen or contemplated the very effects that befell Tarpoly.

Why should not damages be awarded for the loss of that contemplated future profit? The court, I believe, would be shirking its duty if it were to say that no damages should flow because of the difficulty of calculating and assessing such damages and that they are therefore too remote. An assessment of future loss of profits must, of necessity, be an estimate.

Whether such damages are awarded will depend entirely upon the court's assessment of the evidence put forward. The clearest case might base the loss of future profits upon past history of sales to the same or similar customers for same or similar items. It may be developed from evidence given by customers of a plaintiff as to what orders they would have given had the product not been defective over a period of time in the future which is deemed by the court to be reasonable and proper. The task will always be difficult but not insurmountable. It poses no greater obstacle to a court than the assessment of general damages in a serious personal injury claim.

Are there then any obstacles to the court proceeding in this way?

Authorities Relied Upon by the Appellant

In support of its position the appellant relies upon two cases decided in the English Court of Appeal. The first of these cases is *Simon v. Pawsons and Leaf, Ltd.* (1932), 38 Com. Cas. 151 (CA). In that case the plaintiff carried on a small dressmaking business. By arrangement with a school she was to make uniforms for the girls attending the school. She obtained her materials from the defendant. The material was defective and the uniforms were rejected. The defendant failed to supply the proper material within the time required to make the uniforms. As a result, the school authorities cancelled the plaintiff's appointment to make uniforms.

At trial the plaintiff recovered damages both for the defective material and the loss of her appointment to make the uniforms for the school. On appeal it was held that the damages claimed for the loss of appointment were too remote. Scrutton LJ, at p. 157, indicated that in his considerable experience of contracts for the sale of goods he did not remember any cases wherein claims for losses of repeat orders from the customer had been allowed. He appeared to consider such losses too remote.

Later decisions of the English Court of Appeal may have varied this position but, in any event, it seems to me that the facts are such that the case is clearly distinguishable from the one presently before the court. From the reasons of Greer LJ it is apparent that the unfortunate dressmaker did have access to alternate material which she could have obtained in time to fulfil her obligation to make the uniforms. In any event, there are limitations to the extent to which this case should be relied upon in light of the next authority relied upon by the appellant.

In *H. Parsons (Livestock) Ltd. v. Uttley Ingham & Co. Ltd.*, [1978] QB 791 (CA) the Court of Appeal again considered whether an award for future loss of profits was appropriate in a case involving a breach of warranty. All members of the court were in agreement that, generally speaking, in the absence of either special knowledge of either of the parties or of a special contractual clause, the amount of damages recoverable was the same whether the plaintiff's cause of action was the breach of the contract or tort. However, the court was divided as to the damages recoverable for loss of future profits.

Lord Denning MR was of the view that there is a distinction to be drawn in cases in which the plaintiff had suffered physical injury to his personal property from those cases in which the plaintiff had suffered only economic loss. He was of the opinion that in cases of physical injury, the defendant was liable for all damages which could reasonably have been foreseen at the date of the breach. In the case of economic loss, the defendant was liable only if the damages were such that at the time of the contract he could reasonably have contemplated them as a serious possibility in the event of a breach occurring.

On the other hand, the other members of the court, Orr and Scarman LJJ, were of the view that the plaintiff could recover loss in an action for damages for breach of contract if the loss which occurred could reasonably be supposed to be in the parties' contemplation as a serious possibility in the event of a breach. They believed that it was not necessary that the parties should have had it within their contemplation that the loss which in fact occurred was likely to occur in the event of a breach. At p. 813, Scarman LJ stated that the court should approach the question of the loss of profits by posing this question:

> Given the situation of the parties at the time of contract, was the loss of profit, or market, a serious possibility, something that would have been in their minds had they contemplated breach?

In my view, the majority of the court in the above case appears to support the respondent's position on this case and not that of the appellant.

Sale of Goods Act and Canadian Authorities

Section 51(2) of the *Sale of Goods Act*, RSO 1980, c. 462, applies to this case. It is a codification of the common law and provides:

> 51(2) The measure of damages for breach of warranty is the estimated loss directly and naturally resulting in the ordinary course of events from the breach of warranty.

Whether damages for loss of profit is a "loss directly and naturally resulting in the ordinary course of events from the breach of warranty" has been considered on at least two occasions in the Supreme Court of Canada. In *Richmond Wineries Western Ltd. et al. v. Simpson et al.*, [1940] SCR 1, the Supreme Court of Canada upheld the findings of the trial judge awarding damages which included the profits that the plaintiff's might have been expected to make on sale of the wine which the defendants did not deliver to them. The trial judge found that the measure of damages was the estimated loss directly and naturally resulting, in the ordinary course of events, from the sellers' breach of contract; that the plaintiffs were entitled to recover the profits which the court considered they might have been expected to make on the sale of the gallons of wine which the defendants failed to deliver.

In a more recent case, *Sunnyside Greenhouses Ltd. v. Golden West Seeds Ltd.* (1972), 27 DLR (3d) 434 (Alta. CA), affirmed [1973] SCR v, Clement JA, speaking for the Alberta Court of Appeal, at p. 441 stated:

> I think that the correct principle is that loss of profit (or similar loss) which is the direct and natural consequence of the breach, may be claimed for the period during which the breach is the effective cause of the loss, in addition to other heads of damage which fairly come within s. 53 [Alberta *Sale of Goods Act*, which is the same as s. 51(2) of the Ontario *Sale of Goods Act*].

Clement JA, on the facts of that case, determined that the loss of profit for a period of one year was appropriate compensation. The Supreme Court of Canada dismissed an appeal from this judgment and adopted the reasons given by Clement JA.

There is then strong and binding authority to the effect that damages for loss of future profits may, in proper cases, be awarded as damages to be included in "the estimated loss directly and naturally resulting in the ordinary course of events from a breach of warranty." ...

Conclusions

In earlier times, the view of the courts, at least in the United Kingdom, seems to have been that damages for expected loss of profits arising out of a breach of contract could not be recovered on the ground that they were too remote or speculative. There is now binding authority that such damages are recoverable. The following principles can be gathered from the more recent authorities:

(1) Section 51(2) of the *Sale of Goods Act* is a legislative codification of the common law. For ease of reference, I set out that section again:

> 51(2) The measure of damages for breach of warranty is the estimated loss directly and naturally resulting in the ordinary course of events from the breach of warranty.

(2) The test of determining what is a loss that directly and naturally results in the ordinary course of events from the breach of warranty may be phrased in the classical contract question, namely, are the consequences of the breach of contract such that a reasonable man at the time of the making of the contract would contemplate them as being liable to result or to be a serious possibility; or, in the classical tort question, namely, are the consequences of the act such that a reasonable man at the time the tort was committed would foresee that damages are likely to result. The questions are in reality the same. The affirmative answer to either question should lead to the same result. There is no difference between what a reasonable man might reasonably contemplate and what a reasonable man might reasonably foresee: see *Parsons v. Uttley, supra,* 11, *Williston on Contracts,* at pp. 238-39 and 242, *Kienzle v. Stringer* (1981), 35 OR (2d) 85 at p. 89, *Robert Simpson Co. Ltd. v. Foundation Co. of Canada Ltd.* (1982), 36 OR (2d) 97 (CA) at pp. 109-10. This conclusion would not apply if the contracting parties were specifically aware of certain conditions or if precise contractual provisions fixed the quantum of damages in case of a breach.

(3) Most commercial contracts are entered into with a view to making future profits. The loss of future profits arising from a breach of such a contract are recoverable if they should have been within the contemplation of the parties or ought reasonably to have been foreseen by the parties.

(4) The proof of the loss of the respective profits rests, of course, upon the plaintiff. The amount of future profits and the period for which they should be allowed will depend upon the facts of each individual case. Although such damages may be difficult to assess, it must be remembered that they arise as a result of the breach of the defendant and the court should make all reasonable efforts to assess those damages.

Application of Principles to the Present Case

There can be no doubt that Thiokol could and should reasonably have contemplated that damages would flow from a breach of contract. Those damages would include loss of future or prospective profits.

The assessment for loss of profits made by the trial judge was very reasonable in the circumstances. It was based upon the past history of Canadian Tarpoly with various customers and upon an estimate of the future business it expected to do with those customers. It was deprived not only of that business but also of goodwill and reputation as a result of the breach. The time over which the loss of profits was estimated was reasonable in the circumstances.

Evidence before the trial judge which he could and did accept was that it was unreasonable for the plaintiff to re-enter the field until 1980. It was thus appropriate to award damages for loss of profit for the period from 1976 to 1980. That assessment should not be interfered with by this court.

There are certain other complaints about the assessment put forward by the appellant. It was said that the plaintiff should have stopped selling the goods earlier than it did. It will be remembered that the bulk of the complaints came in May of 1976 and in June of 1976 Tarpoly was writing to Thiokol with regard to the problem. Ninety per cent of all its sales excepting one customer were made before the summer of 1976. Eighty per cent of the sales to the remaining customer were made before the summer of 1976. Tarpoly seems to have acted with reasonable expedition and there is no merit to this submission.

It was said, as well, that the trial judge should have taken into account the write-off of certain accounts and the fact that Tarpoly usually had a 2% to 3% return of pool covers. There are two grounds for discounting these submissions. Firstly, all the returns resulted from the defective material supplied by Thiokol. Thus, there is no basis for making any deduction for the "usual" returns of pool covers. More importantly, the trial judge's conservative estimate of loss of profits would seem to take into account all contingencies, including write-offs and returns. In the circumstances it was not necessary for the trial judge to state that he was making due allowance for these specific contingencies.

Thiokol also contends that its counterclaim should not have been dismissed. There is no merit to this submission. The goods supplied were grossly defective. They were of no value; rather they created a disastrous situation for Tarpoly. Under these circumstances, there is nothing payable to Thiokol on its counterclaim. In any event, the cost of material was taken into account in assessing the estimated loss of future profits.

QUESTIONS

1. Do you agree with Cory JA that the question of remoteness should be the same whether "framed as it would be for a tort case or one involving breach of contract"?

2. Cory JA says, "The court, I believe, would be shirking its duty if it were to say that no damages should flow because of the difficulty of calculating and assessing such damages." What, if anything, justifies this degree of tolerance of inaccuracy? Is something else than a desire to "compensate" the plaintiff involved?

3. Why should courts award damages measured by the anticipated value of the bargain? In the following excerpt, Professor Waddams reviews some of the arguments for and against this approach.

S.M. Waddams, *The Law of Damages*
(Aurora, ON: Canada Law Book, December 1999) (looseleaf), at paras. 5.10-5.140
(footnotes omitted)

One of the most significant of all economic interests is the benefit of a favourable contract. A person who has made a good bargain is treated by the law for many purposes as one who has a present right, the value of which is measured by the value of the promised performance. The primary manifestation of this approach is reflected in the measure of damages for breach of contract; the contract breaker is bound to make good the loss caused by the breach, a loss measured by the value of the performance promised. The notion of an enforceable contract as a present valuable right affects many other branches of the law where the measure of damages naturally reflects the primary measure for breach of contract. Thus, assignments of contractual rights are common and the measure of damages for wrongful failure to assign would be based upon the value of the contractual right. Actions for breach of warranty of authority and for including breach of contract also lead to damages measured by the value of the contract lost to the plaintiff.

It is commonly said that the measure of damages for breach of contract differs from that in tort in that contract damages, but not tort damages, give to the plaintiff the benefit of the bargain. The most generally accepted formulations of compensatory principles, however, are wide enough to embrace both contract and tort. Thus, it is usually said that the object of compensatory damages is to put the party complaining in the position that would have been occupied "if his rights had been observed." It will be seen that these formulations are quite capable of supporting a rule of contract damages that gives to the promisee the benefit of the bargain, for if the wrong had not been done the contract would have been performed and the promisee would have received the benefit of performance.

It may be objected that there is an element of circularity in this. No wrong would have been done to the plaintiff if no contract had been made in the first place. To describe the wrong as the breaking of the contract, rather than as the making of a contract that is not kept, is to beg the question. Independent justification is still needed for a rule measuring compensation by the value of the contractual benefit. Several writers have indeed questioned the necessity and the desirability of maintaining the present rule, and the arguments will be discussed below in the following paragraphs. So far as the courts are concerned the general rule continues to be asserted as the normal rule of contract damages that the promisee is entitled to the full value of the promised performance. In *Robinson v. Harman* (1848), 1 Exch. 850; 154 ER 363, Park B said: "The rule of the common law is, that where a party sustains a loss by reason of a breach of contract, he is, so far as money can do it, to be placed in the same situation, with respect to damages, as if the contract had been performed (at p. 855). A very similar statement, from a Canadian Privy Council case, frequently cited in Canadian courts, appears in *Wertheim v. Chicoutimi Pulp Co.*, [1911] AC 301 (PC (Qué.)):

> And it is the general intention of the law that, in giving damages for breach of contract, the party complaining should, so far as it can be done by money, be placed in the same position as he would have been in if the contract had been performed. ... That is a ruling principle. It is a just principle (at p. 307).

From time to time writers have asked whether this rule is indeed a just rule. It may be argued that the main social purpose of the law of contracts is to protect reliance, and that thought should be given to changing the present rule, at least in cases where it is clear that the plaintiff has not altered his position in reliance on the defendant's promise. Answers can be given to the various arguments that have been adduced in support of enforcement. First the argument that reasonable expectations ought to be protected is met by pointing out its circulatory and its tendency to prove too much by being theoretically applicable beyond the realm of promises. Professor Atiyah has written:

To raise an expectation and then to decline to fulfil it is, in some measure, to worsen the position of the promisee, certainly an individual promisee. Prima facie this is something that should be avoided, other things being equal. But I am bound to say that it does appear to me to be a very weak ground for the enforcement of executory contracts, and one that could very easily be counterbalanced by proof that other things are not equal. ... [I]t might well be thought by most people that the inconvenience to the promisor of being held to his contract would be enough to outweigh the prima facie desirability of not disappointing the promisee. [P.S. Atiyah, "Contracts, Promises, and the Law of Obligations" (1978), 94 *Law Quarterly Review* 193, at 214-15.]

A second argument, that enforcing all promises as a matter of principle even where there has been no reliance, will better protect reliance when reliance occurs, can be met by proposing a change in the onus of proof. If the reason for enforcement is reliance, it can be argued that the promisee's position is sufficiently protected by a requirement that the promisor is bound unless reliance is disproved.

The argument that contracts are deliberate allocations of risk can be met by pointing out that not all contracts can be so categorized. The moral argument for enforceability can be met by pointing out that, from a moral point of view, no distinction can be drawn between purely gratuitous promises and executory promises that have not been relied on.

In his later book, *The Rise and Fall of Freedom of Contract* (Oxford: Clarendon Press, 1979), Professor Atiyah returns to the same theme. He writes (at pp. 763-64):

Nevertheless, it remains true in current law, generally speaking, that expectations are the basis of the damages which will be awarded for breach of contract where such liability does exist. Even where there has been some element of reliance, or some benefit rendered, and where it might have been thought that the damages would be confined to the element of reliance or the value of the benefit, this is not generally the case. Doubtless, there are arguments for maintaining the traditional principle here (see Fuller and Perdue, "The Reliance Interest in Contract Damages") though it might be better to recognize them frankly for what they are. Frequently, the best justification for awarding such expectation damages is not that the plaintiff's expectations in fact deserve such handsome protection, but that proof of the losses flowing from reliance would be too difficult or costly, and that if the damages are excessive by way of compensation, then this is a deserved penalty on the defendant anyhow. But in view of the declining belief in the idea that the law should actually deter parties from breaking their contracts, it would not be surprising if future developments tend to show a still further whittling down of expectation damages.

Professor Atiyah concludes his book (at p. 799) with this comment: "So too, the role of expectations, their relationship to promises, and their importance even where they arise without promises, must be reexamined. ... The task is one to which I hope to return."

A change in the present rule would, however, raise a number of difficulties. First, if specific performance is available to enforce some contracts without a need for reliance, it seems difficult to contemplate a measure of damages that is not in principle of equivalent value. If the *prima facie* measure of damages ceased to be the value of the promised performance, there would be increased incentive to claim specific performance, an argument that damages were never "adequate" compensation and an anomalous discrepancy in economic result between cases where specific performance was awarded and cases where damages were given. A change in the basic measure of damages, therefore, would require a corresponding narrowing of the circumstances in which specific enforcement is available.

Secondly, in the case of a formal contract, for example a gift promise under seal, it has generally been accepted that the appropriate measure of enforcement is the value of the promise. It would be anomalous if formal contracts were fully enforceable but informal contracts only to the extent of reliance.

Thirdly, it must surely be conceded that completed exchanges, after execution, are final. The result of exchanges is often to confer a benefit on one of the parties. It is difficult to contemplate a rule permitting the rescission of executed transactions on the ground that one party has benefited to a greater extent than his reliance. If this is a sound position, it is hard to see why, in principle, parties should not agree in respect to a future planned exchange that the legal relationship between the two shall now be as though the exchange were actually effected. If this can be done expressly it can surely be done by implication, and arguably such an implication is a fair one in the case of the usual exchange transaction. If the parties do not intend to commit themselves to the full extent of the exchange they can always, under present law, make express provision. If the law normally only protected reliance, a new class of contracts would surely emerge where the promisor fully guaranteed performance. Following normal rules of contract construction such a guarantee could be implicit, as well as express, and this would bring us back to the present position. In other words, the argument is that the normal measure of contract damages simply reflects the usual implications of a contractual transaction.

This point is strengthened, it is submitted, by the existence of the doctrine of consideration as the normal test of contract enforcement. One of the reasons for allowing the promisee to recover the value of the promised performance is that he has "bought" the right to it. It is widely acknowledged that some measure of enforcement should be, and has been given, to promises that have not been bought (*i.e.*, where there is no consideration), but it is in just those cases that, as has been argued elsewhere, the measure of damages ought to be restricted to the protection of reliance. When the promisee has not brought the right to performance, there is much less reason to allow recovery of its value.

Fourthly, it would generally be conceded that risk allocation contracts ought to be enforced. It does not seem that a ready means is available to distinguish "risk allocation" contracts from other contracts. Every agreed exchange can be said to allocate risks of error in assessing the comparative value of the properties to be exchanged. One of the simplest explanations of the theoretical basis of contract law is that it enables persons to make their future less uncertain; this explanation also provides a strong support for a remedial scheme that protects the promisee's expectations, for uncertainty about the future is only removed if the promisee can count on a legal remedy that will give him the anticipated benefit of performance.

Lastly, Fuller and Perdue's argument that only a measure of expectation damages can adequately protect reliance does not seem fully to be met by putting the onus of proof upon the promisor to disprove reliance. A promisee who had made a beneficial bargain would know that reliance on performance of the promise was not safe until losses (not disprovable) or expenses equivalent to the contractual advantage had been incurred. Similarly, it would be profitable for the promisor to break a promise as long as the promisor calculated that it could be shown that such losses had not been incurred. These considerations would inhibit reliance and encourage the manufacture of otherwise unnecessary evidence of reliance for purposes of possible litigation. Furthermore, there is almost always reliance in the shape of foregone alternative opportunities that is very hard to measure. If a reversal of the onus of proof combined with consideration of the possibility that the promisee might have foregone other opportunities to contract will make it practically impossible for the promisor to disprove reliance, the present position will remain in substance unchanged in which case the present rule might as well be preserved. If, on the other hand, it is envisaged that reliance can be readily disproved on a showing that the promisee would probably not have found another opportunity to make a similar contract it may be objected that reliance, in the form of a possibility (up to a probability of .49) of the promisee's making an alternative contract will be left unprotected.

For these reasons there seems to be insufficient reason to advocate the judicial or legislative change of the present rule.

QUESTION

Do any of these arguments assist you with the questions posed at the end of the *Canlin* case, above?

SOME PROBLEMS OF DETERMINING THE VALUE OF THE BARGAIN

Avoiding Double Recovery

R.G. McLean Ltd. v. Canadian Vickers Ltd.
[1971] 1 OR 207 (CA)

ARNUP JA (for the court): This is an appeal by the defendants from the judgment of Wilson J, dated February 18, 1969. There were originally cross-actions between the parties, with a counterclaim in one of the actions, but the issues were the same in each action and they were consolidated. For convenience I will herein refer to R.G. McLean Limited throughout as "plaintiff" and the two defendants collectively as "the defendant." After the transactions giving rise to the issues in this action, Canadian Vickers Limited sold its "George Mann Division" to the defendant R.W. Crabtree & Sons (Canada) Limited, and whatever may be the rights of the latter company as against Canadian Vickers Ltd., the matter was argued before this Court as if the two defendants were one and I do not propose to refer again to R.W. Crabtree & Sons (Canada) Ltd.

The action arises from the sale by the defendant to the plaintiff of a two-colour press. The plaintiff had previously purchased from the Mann company a two-colour press and, after considerable discussion between the parties, it was decided that the plaintiff should purchase a second press as identical as possible to the first one, with the idea of running them in tandem. By using both presses it would be possible to print two-colour material using one press and an additional two colours using the other, and thereby turn out a finished product in four colours. The parties entered into a written contract dated September 30, 1964, covering the sale by the defendant to the plaintiff of the second press at a price of

$75,850, plus applicable taxes, with an adjustment in the price dependent upon the rate of exchange. The agreement was expressed to be "subject to the conditions of sale of goods attached hereto … ."

It contemplated that a conditional sales agreement would subsequently be executed and, in pursuance of this, such an agreement dated August 18, 1965 was entered into. That contract contained the following provision:

9. THERE are no representations, warranties, collateral agreements, conditions, express or implied, statutory or otherwise with respect to the machine or this agreement or affecting the rights of the parties other than as specifically contained herein and other than those contained in paragraphs numbered 12 and 13 of the Vendor's standard conditions of sale, a copy of which is attached hereto.

It is common ground that, of the "standard conditions of sale" referred to in both agreements, cl. 12 is the most important. This clause reads as follows:

12. Warranty

(a) Subject to fair and proper use we undertake to repair or replace all parts of our manufacture which shall, during the twelve months immediately following the date on which the goods are despatched, be found to be defective due either to faulty workmanship or the use of defective material.

(b) In any such case you shall (unless otherwise arranged) despatch within fourteen days the part or parts alleged to be defective and our Works free and carriage paid together with a full report thereon. Should it be found that the defect is due to faulty workmanship or defective materials we will repair or replace the part or parts and return them to you carriage paid. Any customs dues or import charges payable however in connection with the repaired or replacement part shall be to your account. We shall not be responsible for dismantling or re-assembly or any charges in connection therewith.

· · ·

(e) This condition No. 12 is in substitution for and excludes all express conditions warranties or liabilities of any kind relating to the goods sold whether as to fitness or otherwise and whether arising under the *Sale of Goods Act, 1893* or other statute or in tort or by implication of law or otherwise. In no event shall we be liable for any direct or indirect loss or damage (whether special, consequential or otherwise) or any other claims except as provided for in these conditions.

· · ·

The learned trial Judge correctly found on the evidence [[1969] 2 OR 249, at 251] that "the new press was expected to turn out the highest quality offset lithographic printing. Anything less was not within the contemplation of the buyer or seller." Following the installation of the new press in the plaintiff's premises in Toronto, a long series of difficulties ensued. Some of these were capable of being repaired and were minor in nature, and were, in fact, repaired by the defendant or the plaintiff itself. Problems continued, however, throughout the fall of 1965 and the early winter of 1966. Representatives of the defendant were sent out from England to try to locate the source of the trouble. Many things were tried but in the end it became obvious to the defendant that, whatever the trouble was, it could not be pinpointed and they were unable to fix it.

It was at this point (which was shortly before March 30, 1966) that the defendant finally offered to take back the press and to refund the payments made by the plaintiff. The plaintiff refused this suggestion, pointing out that it had already incurred more than $36,000 in expenses and direct losses. The offer, however, was not conditional upon the plaintiff agreeing to forego any claim for damages. This becomes significant in considering the question of damages, which I shall deal with later.

The learned trial Judge, after considering the totality of the defects, both those which had been fixed and those which could not either be found or fixed, concluded [at 253] that the machine had "never operated as anticipated by both the vendor and purchaser on any proper commercial basis for the production of very high quality lithographing offset prints, in spite of genuine and sincere efforts made by employees of the vendor and purchaser working together to produce the desired results." While he does not in terms make a finding that the defects in their totality were such as to constitute a "fundamental breach of contract" on the part of the defendant, it is clear that such was his intention: ...

I therefore conclude, on the issue of liability, that there was a fundamental breach of the contract by the defendant; that the plaintiff did not, as it might have done, treat the contract as ended and sue for damages; that, construing the contract as a whole, the plaintiff is not precluded from asserting a cause of action for breach of warranty, which cause of action it is compelled to assert, notwithstanding that the breach was in law a breach of condition. In the circumstances of this case, the plaintiff was obliged to treat, and did treat, the breach of condition as a breach of warranty.

The next question therefore is: what damages should be awarded to the plaintiff on the basis of these findings? In effect, the award by the learned trial Judge in favour of the plaintiff falls into three categories:

(i) He dismissed entirely the claim of the defendant for the purchase price of the machine. This claim was for $59,782.75.

(ii) He awarded $50,549.47 in respect of a list of items which he appears to have thought were in the nature of special damages. These are as follows at p. 261:

losses on Ontario 66 book	$18,338.25
losses due to lost press hours	6,968.00
	5,769.79
losses incurred while Canadian mechanic of G. Mann Co. testing for print	643.50
loss incurred while mechanic from England G. Mann Co. working on press	8,190.00
13,750 sheets used in testing press	1,616.00
1,500 sheets used in testing press	129.59
plate making time, plate metal test plates	244.00
blankets spoiled	600.00
supervision and plant engineer's time spent with mechanics of George Mann Co.	2,286.27
installation cost on No. 7 press	4,542.46
loss incurred while press being tested during visit of L. Wright, George Mann. Co.	1,221.42
	$50,549.28

(iii) He allowed $50,554.50 for "loss of business profits."

Dealing with item (iii) first, the learned trial Judge stated [at 264] that he had been furnished, during the trial, and after the accountants for both sides had examined the plaintiff's records, "with a statement (ex. 87) showing the various items of damage and the amounts, the amounts being agreed to, as I understand it, as accurate." He further said that that statement showed the loss of business as $50,554.50.

In this the learned Judge was clearly under a misapprehension. While the figure of $50,554.50 for loss of business profits continued to be shown in a column on ex. 87, it was made quite clear at the trial by counsel for the plaintiff that that amount was *not* being agreed to and that the issue with respect to it was at large. The learned trial Judge's allowance, under this heading, being based entirely upon a mistaken impression of the agreement between counsel, therefore cannot stand, and, while I have endeavoured on the basis of the record and the evidence as it exists to ascertain what a suitable allowance would be for loss of business profits, or indeed whether any such allowance should be made at all, I have found it impossible to do so on this record. This is partly due to the fact that in my view, as will appear, the basis upon which the over-all claim for damages was put forward is erroneous.

Turning next to the dismissal of the claim for the price, this could only have been done on the basis that a claim for breach of warranty had been established in an amount which exceeded the claim for the price. The plaintiff was quite entitled to set up the breach of warranty in diminution or extinction of the purchase price, and to claim any amount of damages over and above the amount of the price which he could establish, but in this case the learned trial Judge has not taken into account, in otherwise assessing the plaintiff's damages, the fact that he had in effect already allowed the plaintiff $59,782.75 by way of damages for breach of warranty when he dismissed the claim against the plaintiff for the price.

Since the damages are to be assessed on the basis that the contract was still in force, the plaintiff is entitled to be compensated (subject to questions of mitigation) to the extent that it will be in approximately the same position as it would have been in if the contract had been performed according to its terms: *Wertheim v. Chicoutimi Pulp Co.*, [1911] AC 301 (PC (Qué.)) at p. 307, and see the cases referred to in *Sunshine Exploration Ltd. et al. v. Dolly Varden Mines Ltd. (N.P.L.)*, [1970] SCR 2. If the contract had been performed, and profits earned by use of the machine, the plaintiff would have had to pay the purchase price. In any calculation of damages, on a basis as if the contract had been performed, the purchase price must stand as a debit against the plaintiff: any damages awarded in its favour can be used to extinguish the purchase price, but only the excess can then be allowed to the plaintiff by way of further damages.

This conclusion is supported by the judgment of the English Court of Appeal in *Cullinane v. British "Rema" Manufacturing Co. Ltd.*, [1954] 1 QB 292 (CA). Mr. Starr attacked the reasoning of the majority of the Court in that case and invited us to adopt instead the reasons for judgment of Morris LJ (as he then was), in his dissenting judgment at p. 313. A close reading of the case does not indicate that the divergence of opinion between the majority and Morris LJ on the point involved here was as great as was indicated by Mr. Starr, but, in any event, I do not think that case assists Mr. Starr so far as the actual purchase price of the machine is concerned. There is a useful discussion of the case in Harry Street, *Principles of the Law of Damages* (London: Sweet & Maxwell, 1962) at pp. 243-5. While the learned author criticizes the actual decision of the majority on the facts of that case, he does indicate at p. 244 that to give a purchaser both a refund of the purchase price and expenditures made would be double compensation.

Coming then to item (ii), it seems quite clear to me that there is overlapping as to at least three items in this list into the heading of damages "loss of business profits." These items are:

losses on Ontario 66 book	$18,338.25
losses due to lost press hours	6,968.00
losses due to lost press hours	5,769.79

These items in themselves total $31,076.04.

It was further argued before us that other items in this list, while treated by the plaintiff as being direct loss through expense incurred, or as outlays made for which no return was received, nevertheless included supervision and overhead (including supervision and overhead on the "Ontario 66 book job" itself), and hence further overlapping has taken place. There is much force in this argument but, since, for the reasons I have already stated, it is not possible for me to arrive at the assessment which I think would have been proper in this case, I do not pursue the mathematics of this matter further.

Before arriving at my final conclusion with respect to damages, I must deal with the arguments advanced to us that the plaintiff had failed to mitigate its damages. It was suggested that once the plaintiff had realized the difficulties being encountered with the new press, it should have run certain work on the old press instead of continuing to run it on the new one. I regard this as a counsel of perfection, particularly since some of these damages as claimed were sustained before it had become clear that nothing but trouble could ensue from further attempts to use the new press.

The more serious points of mitigation, however, arise from the argument of the defendant that by February 1966, the plaintiff had concluded that there were serious problems with the press, yet went ahead knowing of these problems and of sufficient facts that any prudent person in the position of the plaintiff should have known that the press could never properly perform its function. The first proposition made by counsel for the defendant is founded on the offer of the defendant, already referred, to remove the press and refund the purchase price. No evidence was referred to in the argument which would indicate that there was any condition, express or implied, that the plaintiff must accept such offer in full settlement and forego any claim for damages. The plaintiff's answer to this contention was that it had already spent so much money and had sustained such losses that it could not afford to buy another press to replace the one purchased from the defendant. In my opinion, this argument cannot prevail. The plaintiff could not refuse the unconditional offer made, retain the obviously defective press and "run damages" to the prejudice of the defendant. The frailties (if any) of the plaintiff's credit, or its inability to purchase a new press from available assets, cannot be set up to destroy the effect of the defendant's offer. If the plaintiff had a good cause of action for damages by March 1966 (and I have already found that it had), any delay in actually collecting such damages would not in law be the fault of the defendant nor a valid excuse for the plaintiff's failure to mitigate its damages by accepting the offer.

The second point arises independently of the offer, but on facts existing at approximately the same time. As I have indicated, the plaintiff should have known by February or March 1966, that the difficulties concerning the press were so serious that it was entitled to treat the breach of contract as a fundamental one, enabling it to treat the contract as at an end, and demand back its money (only a portion of the purchase price had then been paid), and sue for damages. In my opinion, once the innocent party is in a position to make this election, in a case where the other party has purported to complete its performance, he cannot make an election which has the effect of increasing the burden upon the wrongdoer. The effect in law is almost precisely the same as the effect of the offer, *i.e.*, the plaintiff could not elect to keep the press, knowing it could never properly perform its function and that its continued operation would only result in future losses, and thereby "run up the damages" against the defendant. This seems to me to be the clear and logical conclusion which follows from the conclusion that the right of election arose.

The situation would undoubtedly be different in a case of an instalment contract, or one requiring the performance of a series of future acts. In such case, when fundamental breach occurs, the innocent party may decide he wants the rest of the contract performed and he is entitled to require that that be done. In this case no further acts of performance on the part of the defendant were called for by the contract; it was what had already been done that either was, or was not, a performance of its contractual obligations.

I am therefore of the opinion that the plaintiff did fail to mitigate its damages and that in the assessment of damages a date which I will arbitrarily take as being March 30, 1966 should be treated as being the "cutoff date"; no damages should be payable by the defendant in respect of events occurring after that date.

Finally, it was argued before us that there was no evidence to show what work was lost to the plaintiff by reason of the press being shut down, or what work was available for tender by it. Instead, the accountant who gave evidence on behalf of the plaintiff appears to have based his figures on precontract estimates rather than actual contracts performed. He made estimates based on the number of available hours of press run and the estimated profit which might have been made by running at full capacity during those available hours, and from this he arrived at a mathematical conclusion. Furthermore, in taking into consideration the assessment of "loss of business profits," the profit picture for this company in the four years preceding 1966 was not such as to make certain by any means that the purchase of a second press identical to the one it already had was going to change its profit position (which had varied from small losses to small profits) into one of very substantial profit.

I therefore conclude that there must be a new assessment of damages in this case. Having regard to the extent to which the issues have already been canvassed with respect to damages, I see no reason to send this matter back to a trial Judge for a reassessment of damages, and I therefore would refer it to the Master at Toronto to assess the damages arising from the breach of contract. In so doing the Master will observe these principles:

1. The plaintiff is to be treated as being liable to pay the balance of the purchase price, if it elects to assert a claim for damages for breach of warranty in excess of the price.

2. No damages should be allowed in respect of any matter occurring subsequent to March 30, 1966.

3. The Master, when he comes to deal with "loss of business profits" generally, is to ensure that there is no duplication with items claimed for losses within the plant which include an allowance for supervision and overhead.

4. In assessing any claim that may be asserted for "loss of business profits" the Master will satisfy himself that work sufficient to earn the profits claimed was in fact available in the periods in question, and could have been obtained and performed by the plaintiff.

5. In assessing such loss of profits, the Master should take into account the work which was actually done, so that any estimate of the work which could have been done but for the defects in the machine will not include (as the estimates of the accountant at this trial clearly did include) the expenses and time of work actually done.

In the result the appeal will be allowed with costs, the judgment in appeal will be set aside, and in lieu thereof there will be a declaration that the plaintiff is entitled to damages for breach of contract on the basis that the machine delivered was quite unfit for the purposes for which, in the contemplation of the parties, it was required, and there will be a reference to the Master to ascertain the account of such damages, upon the principles set out in this judgment.

The plaintiff will be entitled to the costs of the first trial and to the costs of the reference.

Appeal allowed in part.

M.G. Baer, "The Assessment of Damages for Breach of Contract—Loss of Profit"
(1973), 61 *Canadian Bar Review* 490, at 490, 493-99 (edited; footnotes omitted)

Seldom have so many important issues concerning the assessment of damages for breach of contract been presented together as they were in the recent remarkably similar cases of *Freedhoff v. Pomalift Industries Ltd.*, [1971] 2 OR 773 (CA) and *R.G. McLean Ltd. v. Canadian Vickers*, [1971] 1 OR 207 (CA); seldom has more confusion and bad law been generated as a result. Some, but not all, of the confusion and bad law might have been avoided if the cases had proceeded in a normal fashion with a firm determination of the relevant facts and the applicable law. Instead the trial and appeal judgments in both cases are marked by a cavalier treatment of sums and dates. The vagueness of some of the trial judges' findings allowed the Court of Appeal to find difficulty without the usual qualms about second guessing the trier of facts. In both cases the appeal court overruled the trial judge's findings of fact in conclusive terms with no extensive reference to the evidence. As well, since both cases had to be sent to the Master for the ultimate assessment of damages, appeal decisions were rendered enunciating general principles before all the facts had been clearly determined.

Both cases involved the purchase of revenue generating equipment which when delivered, failed to perform satisfactorily. In both cases the equipment was central to the purchasers business and its failure left him financially unable to extricate himself. ...

II. Election of Remedies and the Application of the "Rema" Case

Running through the appeal decisions are two separate notions of election which should be distinguished. One is the familiar principle found at both common law and equity that where there has been repudiation (in the sale of goods, a breach of condition) or innocent misrepresentation, the innocent injured party can elect to treat the contract as at an end. He can accept the repudiation (in the sale of goods, reject the goods) or obtain rescission depending on whether his remedy is at common law or equity. If he has paid money under the contract he is entitled to its return. Alternatively he can choose to affirm the contract and, at least at common law, pursue a remedy in damages. The second principle is fairly novel and involves the notion that in claiming damages the plaintiff must elect between two methods for assessing his damages. This latter election of remedies doctrine stems from the "*Rema*" case [*Cullinane v. British "Rema" Manufacturing Co. Ltd.*, [1954] 1 QB 292 (CA)] and may in part result from confusion in the application of the more traditional doctrine. To throw some light on this confusion these two notions will be examined separately. After discussing the courts' ruling concerning the more traditional concept of election, the right to accept repudiation and reject the goods, the second more novel concept of election will be discussed in relation to the courts' method of assessing damages. ...

[See chapter 10, "Financial Relief in Equity," for a discussion about the election of remedies with regard to specific performance and damages.]

B. Assessment of Damages and the Need for Second Election of Remedies

Most lawyers would accept the general proposition that in assessing damages for breach of contract, the common law courts try to put the injured party in as favourable a position as he would have been if the contract had been performed according to its terms. Not only is the injured party entitled to recoup out of pocket expenses but he is also entitled to any sum he could have expected to receive if the contract had been performed—his expectancy interest. For example, if a retailer purchased machinery at $1,000 for the purpose (known to his vendor) of resale at $1,500 and the machinery delivered was worthless, the retailer could not only recover the $1,000 purchase price, but could also collect from his vendor the $500 profit he would have made on the resale. In addition if he had incurred additional expenses in a reasonable but unsuccessful attempt to make the machinery work, he would be entitled to recover that. If he had not paid for the machinery he would have a good defence to a claim for the purchase price and in addition could counterclaim for his expenses and loss of profit. Subject to the duty of the injured party to mitigate his damages, these are long standing results which have been codified in the *Sale of Goods Act*. Most lawyers will be surprised to learn that these seemingly obvious results have now been thrown in doubt by the Ontario Court of Appeal in *McLean* which has stated that "to give a purchaser both a refund of the purchase price and expenditures would be double compensation," [at 214-15] and "In any calculation of damages, on a basis as if the contract had been performed, the purchase price must stand as a debit against the plaintiff. ... [at 214]." They have in effect held that in a case like our example where the retailer has not yet paid the purchase price he can only collect damages for expenses and loss of profit in his counterclaim to the extent that these damages exceed the purchase price.

How could such a result, totally contrary to the general theory for assessing damages for breach of contract, and in total disregard for section 51 of the *Sale of Goods Act* occur? The decision is the result of two errors both of which the court adopted from the "*Rema*" case. The second error is the ruling that the plaintiff must elect to either prove his damages in the form of lost revenue *or* to claim a return of the purchase price. This is a mistaken deduction from a more general idea that the plaintiff can either demand to be put back into his original position or can demand to be put into the position he would have been in if the contract had been performed according to its terms.

In accepting the defendant's argument that the plaintiff could not both succeed on the counterclaim and claim loss of profit, the court cited the "*Rema*" case with apparent approval. In both cases the courts readily accept the facile statement that in order to earn profit, the plaintiff would have had to pay for the machine. Hence the purchase price must be deducted from the claim for lost profit. This shows some confusion about what is claimed under the term "loss of profit." Of course if the plaintiff is claiming the loss of gross income that the machine would have generated if it had functioned as contracted, this figure must be reduced by the amounts the plaintiff would have had to spend to generate that income. That is, in arriving at profit, expenses (both operating and capital) must be deducted from income. Naturally in the simple example mentioned above, the retailer could not claim the return of the purchase price ($1,000) and $1,500 for loss of income. He could only get the return of the purchase price (or have a good defence to a claim for it) plus his loss of *profit* which is calculated by deducting his expense from his gross income." But it is almost too elementary for printing in the *Review* that you do not deduct the purchase price from his profit a second time to arrive at his loss.

Of course the *McLean* case is somewhat more complex than our example in that the machinery was not bought for resale but for use. If the damage for loss profit covered the entire useful life of the machine, this difference would not be significant. The capital cost of the machine would have to be deducted along with the operating expenses from expected revenue to arrive at the profit which would have been earned. However, in view of the purchaser's obligation to mitigate his damage he will seldom be in a position to claim for the loss of profit for the entire life of the chattel. To calculate his loss of profit for a limited period, both operating and capital expenses for that period must be deducted from his expected income. The capital expense for a particular period is normally calculated by depreciating the total capital cost over the life of the chattel.

Mr. Justice Arnup's judgment is not clear as to whether the sum claimed by the plaintiff as lost profit was derived by deducting part of the capital cost of the press as depreciation. However, even assuming the plaintiff was not claiming lost profit but rather the difference between gross potential revenue and operating expenses, the court was in error. While it would at least not be deducting the capital cost from potential revenue twice as some statements in the case suggest, it would be attributing the entire capital expense to the first two years of operation (the period for which loss of profits was allowed). This is an error, because if the contract had been carried out, the plaintiff at the end of two years would have had two years' profit *plus* a valuable two year old machine (whose value is the purchase price less two years' depreciation).

In fact the court's error seems to go further. The court appears to be saying that the plaintiff cannot claim as damages any expenditures made without deducting the purchase price. That is, even amounts spent by the plaintiff to try to cure the machine's defects, which would not have been necessary if the contract had not been breached, cannot be claimed in addition to a refund of the purchase price. This error cannot be attributed to confusion about the term "profit" nor to a superficial application of the fatuous notion that you must deduct the purchase price from all claims for expectant benefits, on the basis that the expectancy would not happen without payment of the price. These claims are for out of pocket expenses actually incurred because the contract was breached, not for benefits that would have been received had the contract been carried out.

Perhaps this confusion would have been avoided if the Ontario court had been referred to the decision of the High Court of Australia in *T Industrial Plant Pty. Ltd. v. Roberts Q.L.D. Pty. Ltd.* (1963), 37 ALJR 289 (HCA). The Australian court demonstrates what if any general principle can be salvaged from the "*Rema*" case. By a neat algebraic equation they show how the plaintiff's claim in the "*Rema*" case was the same as the amount the court said it would have been entitled to if its claim had been properly framed and proved.

In the "*Rema*" case the plaintiff purchased a clay pulverizing machine from the defendant which did not pulverize clay at the warranted rate. The plaintiff sued for breach of warranty and its claim was submitted to an official referee under five heads. Heads A, B and C were capital expenditures, head D was a claim for interest on A, B and C for three years and head E was a claim for loss of profit for three years. E was arrived at by taking the estimated receipts for the warranted output and subtracting not only running costs, office expenses and interest but also depreciation at ten percent per annum. The official referee allowed heads A, B, C and D and also E but without subtracting depreciation. That plainly was not right and was not what the plaintiff asked for. The majority of the English Court of Appeal held that the plaintiff could claim either its loss of capital or its "loss of profit" but not both. However, they would have called as "loss of profit" the expected income less expected operating expenses (if the plaintiff had pleaded and proved them). The court stated that in calculating loss of profit "depreciation has nothing whatever to do with it." Obviously the court was using the term "profit" idiosyncratically to mean expected net revenue, after deducting operating expenses only. Hence any general statement in the case that a plaintiff must choose between claiming loss of capital or loss of profit must be used with some care.

In effect once you understand the way in which the court was using the term "profit" in "*Rema*," its objection was not to the amount but rather the method of calculating the plaintiff's loss. Since either method (as the Australian High Court has demonstrated) comes to the same result, it would not seem to matter which is used. However, the method adopted by the English Court of Appeal only reflects the total loss if the gross revenue for the life of the machine is known and can be proved. Since the plaintiff has a duty to mitigate his damage, he will always be limited to a claim for loss of profit for only a limited period out of the potential life of the machine. To allow the plaintiff only his potential net income (potential revenue less operating expenses) for that period *or* his lost capital (return of the purchase price) does not allow him to recover his loss in full. To repeat, if the contract had been properly performed in *McLean* the plaintiff would not only have made a profit for two years but he would also have had a valuable two year old machine.

While the plaintiff can sometimes elect between rescission or rejection and damages, once he has lost his right to reject as the plaintiff in *McLean* had, his damages are those which directly and naturally result from the breach. The notion that there are two ways (and only two ways) of assessing these damages and that the plaintiff must elect between them results in the plaintiff recovering less than his loss. Such a novel notion is contrary to both *Hadley v. Baxendale* [(1854), 9 Exch. 341; 156 ER 145] and the *Sale of Goods Act* and should have been rejected by the Ontario courts as it has been in Australia.

NOTES AND QUESTIONS

1. What definition of profit underlies the court's decision in *McLean*? Is it correct? Do the arguments advanced in favour of the general rule awarding damages for the value of the bargain support the court's approach?

2. The court's award in *McLean* makes no allowance for the fact that the press as delivered was considerably less valuable than the press contracted for. Would there be an element of double compensation if such allowance were awarded *in addition* to the award for loss of profit?

3. *McLean* shows the interrelation of the expectancy rule and the principle of mitigation. Bearing the reasons for the expectancy rule in mind, do the two work at cross-purposes? Explain.

4. Review the judgments of the Ontario Court of Appeal in *306793 Ontario Ltd. v. Rimes* and *Semelhago v. Paramadevan*, both of which are elaborated on in the judgment of the Supreme Court of Canada in *Semelhago* extracted in chapter 1, "General Principles of Damages." Which approach is preferable and why? Which approach is more consistent with *McLean*? Is the only issue measurement of compensation or do other considerations influence the decisions?

Ticketnet Corp. v. Air Canada
(1998), 154 DLR (4th) 271 (Ont. CA); application for leave to appeal to SCC
dismissed 161 DLR (4th) viii

[The plaintiff had created an Internet-based ticket-booking service for arts organizations. The plaintiff believed such software would be of interest to the defendant and approached it with a view to enter into a joint development project. Air Canada was interested and opened negotiations on a development agreement. Both parties committed resources to the project and an agreement was eventually reached. The defendant repudiated the agreement, a repudiation that was subsequently found wrongful by the trial judge. The plaintiff then brought an action for damages for breach of contract, and, in particular, for loss of profits and lost business opportunity. At trial the plaintiff was awarded $11.5 million. On appeal the award was reduced to $10.16 million. The Court of Appeal confirmed that while the burden of proof was always on the plaintiff to prove its damages, where the defendant's wrong prevented precise proof, the plaintiff could rely upon projections discounted to reflect certain contingencies.]

LASKIN JA: ...

4. The Proper Measure of Value

The acquisition agreement dated June 30, 1986 provided that American would acquire the shares of Ticketnet. American was to pay $750,000 on closing and "Earn Outs" on tickets sold to an "annual cap" of $666,667 for a maximum of ten years, assume liabilities of approximately $1.4 million and enter into five-year employment contracts with Lamarre and Clark. In return, American was to receive not only the software but the marketing plan of Ticketnet, the research tax credits and all other assets of the company including Uniticket.

Air Canada submits that the cash payment of $750,000 to be made by American is the proper measure of the value of the software and therefore of Ticketnet's damages. Air Canada argues that although this was to be a share sale, not an asset sale, $750,000 still reflects the value of Ticketnet's net assets. Air Canada bolsters this argument by pointing to the acquisition agreement dated November 20, 1986. When the June 30 agreement did not close because the software was not delivered, American entered into a new agreement on November 20 to acquire the shares of Ticketnet. The terms of the two acquisition agreements were almost the same, but there were at least two important differences: the November 20 agreement expressly recognized that Air Canada had refused to deliver the software and the November 20 agreement did not call for a cash payment on closing. These two differences, Air Canada argues, show that the software was valued at $750,000.

The trial judge rejected this argument because, in his view, the purchase price of shares from shareholders who were under great financial pressure did not adequately represent the value of the business of Ticketnet. He wrote at p. 163:

> I note that this was an analysis concerned with buying the shares of Ticketnet from shareholders who were already stretched beyond belief. *It is not an analysis of what the value of the business was to Ticketnet; it must be recognized that Ticketnet was the plaintiff and not the stressed out shareholders of Ticketnet.* [Emphasis in original.]

And at p. 164:

> The consideration pursuant to this November agreement was identical to the consideration contained in the June 30, 1986 agreement with the exception that the $750,000 cash payment was no longer to be made. According to AC, what the principals of Ticketnet therefore "lost" by reason of the non-delivery of the software by AC was the $750,000 upfront payment which American would otherwise have made. *However, again it should be noted that the plaintiff is Ticketnet, not its then principals.* [Emphasis in original.]

Air Canada relies on the principle that the capital value of property reflects the present value of future use, so that if complete compensation is given to Ticketnet for the value of the software, there is no room for any additional claim (see Lord Wright in *Liesbosch v. Edison*, [1933] AC 449 (HL (Eng.))). This principle was accepted by this court in *Ronald Elwyn Lister Ltd. v. Dayton Tire Canada Ltd.* (1985), 52 OR (2d) 88 (CA), but expressed by Morden JA as follows at p. 112:

> I turn now to the matter of double recovery or duplication. … Lister Limited cannot recover both the value of its business as a going concern and, also, damages based on the value of its assets that were convened. The latter are, logically, contained in the former. They were reflected in the profit-earning potential of the company which is embodied in the capitalization approach. To give both net asset value and the value of the business as a going concern would be contrary to the business practice reflected in … the law respecting damages.

The concern that founds this principle in damages law is that a party claiming loss of use, or loss of business opportunity, should not obtain "double recovery." A party is not entitled to both the net asset value and the value of the business as a going concern because the value of the business as a going concern reflects the net asset value. The result in *Lister, supra,* shows that a plaintiff is entitled to have damages to a business assessed on whatever basis results in a higher recovery.

Ticketnet is not seeking "double recovery" in its action against Air Canada. It is not seeking damages for the past or present value of the software; instead, it seeks to recover the present value of its lost business opportunity, an opportunity which was effectively destroyed by Air Canada's breach of the SDA and subsequent injunction.

Air Canada's submission implies that the value of Ticketnet's lost business opportunity is equal to the value of the software, and no more. The trial judge, however, explicitly found that the $750,000 difference between the consideration attached to the two agreements did not reflect the value of Ticketnet's lost business opportunity in the software. This was a share sale, in which Ticketnet, as a business, was to change hands. In his view, $750,000 could not be the proper measure of damages because the transaction was conducted when Ticketnet's shareholders were under extreme financial pressure and eager to mitigate their losses. I agree that the evidence shows that the principals of Ticketnet were under financial pressure, caused by Air Canada's failure to honour it contractual commitments. A forced sale price is not a good indication of value. Air Canada should not profit from the poor bargaining position that it imposed on the principals of Ticketnet. ...

The Cross-Appeal on Damages

The Smith and Gain report shows that, in the three-and-one-half year period between January 1, 1985 and June 30, 1988, Ticketnet incurred actual or out-of-pocket expenses of $3,513,550. Of this amount, the trial judge included $500,000 in his damages award. The difference, $3,013,550, is in issue on Ticketnet's cross-appeal.

Of the $3,513,550 in expenses, $1,971,000 was incurred before Air Canada repudiated the SDA on August 1, 1986. Against these pre-repudiation expenses, Ticketnet received a tax credit of $352,000, leaving a balance of $1,619,000. The trial judge did not include any part of the $1,619,000 in his damages award. Ticketnet claims that between August 1, 1986 and June 30, 1988 it incurred additional costs of $1,894,550. Of this amount, the trial judge awarded Ticketnet $500,000 for its out-of-pocket costs "truly expended in an effort to mitigate its damages," leaving a balance of $1,394,550. On its cross-appeal, Ticketnet therefore claims pre- and post-repudiation expenses totalling $3,013,550 ($1,619,000 + $1,394,550).

Ticketnet makes three submissions on its cross-appeal:

(i)   by not including the $3,013,550 in expenses in his damages award, the trial judge failed to put Ticketnet in the position it would have been in had Air Canada not breached the SDA. In other words, by not including these expenses, the trial judge double counted them;

(ii) alternatively, if Ticketnet's expenses after repudiation are limited to the $500,000 awarded at trial, the trial judge erred by failing to include in his damages award the $1,619,000 in expenses incurred before repudiation;

(iii) in the alternative, the trial judge erred by discounting Ticketnet's out-of-pocket expenses for the first two years. If full credit were given for these expenses, the damages award would be increased by $547,000.

As I have already stated, the trial judge's award of damages for loss of business' opportunity should have placed Ticketnet in the position it would have been in if Air Canada had not breached the SDA: see *Wertheim v. Chicoutimi, supra*, and *Freedhoff v. Pomalift, supra*. The trial judge generally accepted Smith and Gain's valuation. Smith and Gain determined the present value of seven years of projected lost profits. They estimated Ticketnet's loss of profits by deducting projected expenses and taxes from projected revenues. They did not include Ticketnet's out-of-pocket expenses of $3,513,550 in profit projections. In other words, they calculated lost profits separately from Ticketnet's actual expenses. Then, to make Ticketnet whole, they added these actual expenses—both pre- and post-repudiation—to their loss of profit projections. They explained this methodology in their report:

> 43. The loss of profits represent the estimated income that would have been generated by the implementation of Ticketnet's business plan had Air Canada not repudiated the software development agreement and prevented Ticketnet from completing the development by obtaining an interlocutory injunction to stop further development and marketing by Ticketnet. The out-of-pocket costs represent the costs incurred by Ticketnet during the development stage and costs incurred subsequent to Air Canada's repudiation of the contract. The loss of profits are measured based on the net earnings determined by deducting the projected expenses and income taxes from projected revenues. To the extent that expenses were incurred with no offsetting revenue, these out-of-pocket costs must be added to the estimated loss of profits to fully compensate Ticketnet for its losses. This has the effect of compensating Ticketnet for the out-of-pocket costs as well as the foregone net earnings.

Smith elaborated on this methodology in his evidence:

> Q. Okay. Now, you've calculated the loss of—loss of profits separately?
> A. Yes.
> Q. And in addition to the out-of-pocket claim?
> A. Yes.
> Q. Why is that?
> A. Well, there are two elements to a measurement of loss of earnings. One is the earnings that would have been made after all—after considering all operating expenses that would have been incurred or were incurred, all of the costs associated with that earnings stream. To that you must add those costs that were in fact incurred to get the true measure of the loss. You can work it two ways, in accounting lingo, it is the bottom up or the top down. From the bottom up, you take the loss of profit after all operating expenses and you add the expenses that were incurred, which is what's done here. You get exactly the same result if you had started with the top number, the revenue loss, and deducted from that those operating costs which would have been incurred, but which were saved, in other words, which were not incurred. And that's what we've—so that this takes the approach, if you will, of the bottom up.

Ticketnet submits that these actual expenses were wasted expenditures because they did not generate any offsetting revenue and because the software had no residual value. Therefore, they must be added to the damage award to avoid double counting.

The trial judge rejected the claim for out-of-pocket expenses, except those incurred to try to mitigate losses because, in his view, expenses to complete the software were "part of the ticket of admission to earn the projected revenue." He made the following findings on Ticketnet's claim for out-of-pocket expenses at p. 165:

> I must confess that I still do not understand their concept of claiming for out-of-pocket expenses when it appears that these expenses are to be used to generate the anticipated revenues. In my view these expenses (except to the extent mitigate losses) are already taken into account in the profit projections. These "ordinary" (and planned) expenses would be Ticketnet's ticket of admission to the industry.

And at pp. 166-167:

> I do not think that on that basis Ticketnet's damages would include its out of pocket costs except to the extent that such were truly expended in an effort to mitigate damages. In this respect, I would think that any expenditures to complete the software would be part of the ticket of admission to earn the projected revenue. To the extent that there is any double counting with respect to the estimated cost to complete, as indicated by Bedford and which I have taken into account immediately following, this should be coordinated so there is only a single "deduction." I may be spoken to on this by counsel within 40 days of the release of these reasons. Otherwise it would appear that only about $0.5 million (which I would allow at $350,000 for fiscal 1987 and $150,000 for fiscal 1988) could be said to be extra expenses incurred by Ticketnet over and above what Smith and Gain projected as "ordinary" expenses (see schedule 7 to their report related to professional fees and some miscellaneous expenses; to the extent that such are legal fees, such should not be included in the award of costs). In my view one should not confuse cash outlay with a valuation based on projected revenues.

And at pp. 182-183:

> Given my views on the "ticket of admission" expenses, there is no award for expenses incurred to the date of the breach: see *R.G. McLean v. Canadian Vickers Ltd.*, *supra*, at p. 214; *Cullinane v. British "Rema" Manufacturing Co. Ltd.*, [1954] 1 QB 292 (CA) at p. 308; and *Anglia Television Ltd. v. Reed*, [1971] 3 All ER 690 (CA) at p. 692.

My difficulty with the trial judge's reasoning is that the projected expenses were already included in the Smith and Gain loss of profits estimate. By not awarding Ticketnet its actual expenses in addition to the present value of its loss of projected profits, the trial judge may have double counted these expenses. As Mr. Bell submitted during oral argument, accepting that out-of-pocket expenses were the "ticket of admission," Ticketnet was not obliged to buy two tickets.

The trial judge's approach is supportable by adopting the proposition that a party claiming damages for breach of contract must elect between claiming for loss of profits or for wasted expenditures. It cannot claim both. This proposition was succinctly stated by Lord Denning in *Anglia Television Ltd. v. Reed*, [1971] 3 All ER 690 (CA) at p. 692, a case cited by the trial judge:

> It seems to me that a plaintiff in such a case as this had an election: he can either claim for his loss of profits; or for his wasted expenditure. But he must elect between them. He cannot claim both. If he has not suffered any loss of profits—or if he cannot prove what his profits would have

been—he can claim in the alternative the expenditure which has been thrown away, that is, wasted, by reason of the breach.

I do not see the need for an election in a case like this one, where loss of profits are claimed and actual expenses are not included in projected profits. I agree with the following observation of Professor Waddams in his text *The Law of Contracts* (Toronto: Canada Law Book, 3rd ed., 1993):

> A second question that arises in many of these case is that of expenses incurred by the buyer. If the buyer incurs expenses in connection with the goods, for example installation costs, can the buyer combine a recovery of these with a claim for loss of profit? The seller's argument may be that the expenses would have had to be incurred in any event and therefore cannot be combined with loss of profits. The logical answer appears to be that wasted expenses may be claimed provided that they are not claimed twice over by being included also in the measure of the potential profits. That is, the profits must be net profits, not gross potential income. [Footnote omitted.]

This passage implicitly endorses the methodology used by Smith and Gain. This methodology is discussed in detail in Biger and Rosen, "A Framework for the Assessment of Business Damages for Breach of Contract" (1980-81), 5 CBLJ 302, in which the authors reduced their discussion to a simple formula at p. 307:

> It is true that capital and profits are different concepts and must be treated as such. However, avoidance of double-counting can best be accomplished by focusing on the general principle governing damages assessment: place the innocent party in as good a position as he would have been in if the contract had been performed. That is, measure the injured party's expected post-contract position, measure his actual position, and compute the difference. Following this scheme will automatically incorporate capital and profit aspects of the damages and eliminate any potential for doublecounting. [Under this formula, any offsetting revenue and any residual value to the income earning asset would have to be taken into account.]

Thus applying the methodology used by Smith and Gain, as the trial judge did, out-of-pocket expenses must also be considered to avoid double counting those expenses. To that extent, I agree that the trial judge erred in his treatment of Ticketnet's actual costs. Nonetheless, in my view, the trial judge's allowance of only $500,000 for out-of-pocket expenses is supportable on other grounds.

Time of Assessment

Golden Strait Corp. v. Nippon Yusen Kubishka Kaisha
[2007] UKHL 12, [2007] AC 353

[Golden Strait chartered its tanker to Nippon Yusen for seven years. One of the terms of the charter would have permitted Nippon Yusen to cancel the contract if war broke out between the United States and Iraq. Nippon Yusen then repudiated the contract in December 2001 and in March 2003 the Second Gulf War began. The question arose whether the calculation of damages should take into account the fact that, subsequent to Nippon Yusen's breach, an

event occurred which would have permitted Nippon Yusen to terminate the contract without paying damages. The plaintiff shipowners argued that the outbreak of the Second Gulf
War should be ignored and that damages should be awarded for the entire remaining term
of the charter. A majority of the House of Lords rejected the owners' argument on this point.
In the words of Lord Scott (at para. 38):]

> The arguments of the Owners offend the compensatory principle. They are seeking compensa-
> tion exceeding the value of the contractual benefits of which they were deprived. Their case
> requires the assessor to speculate about what might happen over the period 17 December 2001
> to 6 December 2005 regarding the occurrence of a clause 33 event and to shut his eyes to the
> actual happening of a clause 33 event in March 2003. The argued justification for thus offending
> the compensatory principle is that priority should be given to the so-called principle of cer-
> tainty. My Lords there is, in my opinion, no such principle. Certainty is a desideratum and a
> very important one, particularly in commercial contracts. But it is not a principle and must give
> way to principle. Otherwise incoherence of principle is the likely result. The achievement of
> certainty in relation to commercial contracts depends, I would suggest, on firm and settled
> principles of the law of contract rather than on the tailoring of principle in order to frustrate
> tactics of delay to which many litigants in many areas of litigation are wont to resort. Be that as
> it may, the compensatory principle that must underlie awards of contractual damages is, in my
> opinion, clear and requires the appeal in the case to be dismissed.

[Lord Walker and Lord Bingham dissented. The latter wrote, at para. 22:]

> The thrust of the charterers' argument was that the owners would be unfairly over-compensated
> if they were to recover as damages sums which, with the benefit of hindsight, it is now known
> that they would not have received had there been no accepted repudiation by the charterers.
> There are, in my opinion, several answers to this. The first is that contracts are made to be per-
> formed, not broken. It may prove disadvantageous to break a contract instead of performing it.
> The second is that if, on their repudiation being accepted, the charterers had promptly hon-
> oured their secondary obligation to pay damages, the transaction would have been settled well
> before the Second Gulf War became a reality. The third is that the owners were … entitled to be
> compensated for the value of what they had lost on the date it was lost, and it could not be
> doubted that what the owners lost at that date was a charterparty with slightly less than four
> years to run. This was a clear and, in my opinion, crucial finding, but it was not mentioned in
> either of the judgments below, nor is it mentioned by any of my noble and learned friends in
> the majority. On the arbitrator's finding, it was marketable on that basis. I can readily accept
> that the value of a contract in the market may be reduced if terminable on an event which the
> market judges to be likely but not certain, but that was not what the arbitrator found to be the
> fact in this case. There is, with respect to those who think otherwise, nothing artificial in this
> approach. If a party is compensated for the value of what he has lost at the time when he loses
> it, and its value is at that time for any reason depressed, he is fairly compensated. That does not
> cease to be so because adventitious later events reveal that the market at that time was de-
> pressed by the apprehension of risks that did not eventuate. A party is not, after all, obliged to
> accept a repudiation: he can, if he chooses, keep the contract alive, for better or worse.

QUESTION AND NOTE

1. How do we square the decision in *Golden Strait* with the cases in chapter 1 that say that normally damages are assessed as of the date of breach?

2. The Supreme Court of Canada dealt with a similar matter almost a century ago: *Findlay v. Howard* (1919), 58 SCR 516. Mignault J wrote (at 544):

> Where future damages are claimed, future conditions must necessarily be considered, and what better evidence of conditions, which were in the future at the date of the breach, can be made than by shewing, at the date of trial, what has actually occurred since the breach of contract?

Cost of Substituted Performance or Diminution in Market Value?

This issue was explored in both contract and tort cases in chapter 1. As you read the following two cases, can you identify the factors that led to the result in each?

Sunshine Exploration Ltd. v. Dolly Varden Mines Ltd. (N.P.L.)
[1970] SCR 2

MARTLAND J (for the court): This appeal is in an action for damages for breach of contract brought by the respondent against the appellants. The breach is admitted and the sole issue before the Court is as to the measure of damages.

The respondent, hereinafter referred to as "Dolly Varden," entered into an agreement made on March 4, 1964, and dated, for reference, February 1, 1964, with the appellant, Sunshine Exploration Ltd., an Alberta company, registered in British Columbia. This company is a wholly owned subsidiary of Sunshine Mining Company, incorporated in the State of Idaho, which could not be registered in British Columbia as its name was similar to another company, already registered in that Province. Because of this, the agreement was made by the subsidiary company, but the parent company agreed with Dolly Varden and with the subsidiary that the subsidiary was an agent of the parent to perform the mining operations required under the agreement and that the parent should be liable to Dolly Varden as though it had executed the agreement.

For the purposes of this appeal, the legal situation of both appellants is the same and I will refer to them both, jointly, as "Sunshine" as though they constituted, together, one party to the agreement.

By the terms of the agreement, Dolly Varden, which is the owner of certain mining properties in British Columbia, described in the agreement, granted to Sunshine an exclusive right, at Sunshine's expense, to explore and develop those properties. The agreement contemplated four stages of development. The first was exploratory, to enable Sunshine to determine what mining operations it was prepared to conduct during later stages. The second stage involved further exploration and was to continue until commercial production was obtained. The third stage was a period for the recovery, out of production, of the respective investments of the parties. The fourth stage was defined as "the remaining life of the agreement" (for a maximum of 50 years) during which the parties would share equally any profits realized from production.

Sunshine was given the right to elect whether or not it would proceed from the first to the second stage, and, as matters turned out, it never did so proceed.

Dolly Varden agreed, on the closing date, to assign and convey to Sunshine one half of its interest in the mining properties described in the agreement. Sunshine agreed to deposit, with an escrow agent, documents to evidence a complete reconveyance of the half interest to Dolly Varden, which were to be delivered to that company if Sunshine terminated the agreement or failed to give notice of its intention to proceed to the second development stage. In the event, these documents were so delivered.

The first development period was defined as follows:

> The First Stage or the first Development Period shall mean the period commencing from the Closing Date and ending on December 31, 1964 unless extended by written notice given by the Operator (Sunshine) to the Company (Dolly Varden) before November 30, 1964 whereupon the First Development Period shall end on June 30, 1965.

> 6. The Operator covenants with the Company that:

> 6.01 Forthwith after the Closing Date it will enter upon the Mining Property and undertake the development program which is generally described in Schedule F hereto (herein referred to as "the development program") provided that in any event the Operator shall be free during the First Development Period to accelerate, retard or vary such program as it progresses.

> 6.02 Notwithstanding any termination provision herein contained the Operator will expend in the development program as set out in Schedule F hereto during the period ending December 31, 1964 not less than $250,000 and will maintain the Mining Property during the First Development Period, reasonable wear and tear and loss by fire and the elements excepted.

> 6.03 If the Operator shall have notified the Company of its intention to extend the First Development Period to June 30, 1965 it shall thereupon be obligated to expend in development in each quarterly period or any part thereof between January 1, 1965 and June 30, 1965 not less than $60,000 which shall include the maintenance of the Mining Property during such extension period.

Sunshine also agreed to consult with an officer of Dolly Varden on all phases of the development programme; to give him progress reports at least monthly; and to give him reports, on request, as to the results of drilling, sampling and other engineering data. Sunshine was required to maintain complete records and sufficient surveys, assays, maps and logs so that Dolly Varden would be fully informed as to the nature and character of the mine workings and the operations performed.

Between March and October 1964, exploration work was done and Sunshine expended some $348,000. However, this work was not done to the satisfaction of Dolly Varden, which complained that it was not being provided with proper reports of expenditures and on work done, and that Sunshine had changed materially the emphasis of the drilling programme.

On November 30, 1964, Dolly Varden received notice that Sunshine proposed to enter the second development period. On January 14, 1965, Dolly Varden gave notice of default to Sunshine, specifying a large number of points in respect of which defaults under the agreement were alleged.

Thereafter, there were various meetings between the directors of Dolly Varden and of Sunshine, as a result of which, finally, an amending agreement was executed, dated, formally, January 22, 1965. Under the provisions of this latter agreement:

1. Sunshine withdrew and cancelled its notice of intention to enter the second period of development.

2. Dolly Varden withdrew its notice of default and excused Sunshine from any further work on the programme described in sch. F to the principal agreement.

3. The first development period was extended to September 30, 1965, with Sunshine having the right, by giving notice before August 31, 1965, to extend it further to December 31, 1966.

4. Sunshine further covenanted as follows:

> Notwithstanding any termination provision herein contained, the Operator, during the remainder of the First Development Period but prior to October 1, 1965, will perform the work outlined in Schedule "A" hereto, it will proceed therewith continuously and at no time during the performance of the work outlined in Schedule "A" hereto will the properties be left with no exploration or development work in progress. In the event that the work outlined in Schedule "A" hereto shall not be completed prior to October 1, 1965, the Company shall have the right to terminate the Principal Agreement by giving notice in writing of such termination to the Operator and upon the Company giving such notice the Principal Agreement shall thereupon be at an end subject however to the Operator's continuing obligations with respect to termination as provided in Clause 15 of the Principal Agreement. Provided however, that such termination shall not relieve the Operator from the obligations to complete the work outlined in Schedule "A."

5. The provisions of the principal agreement, subject to the amendments made by the amending agreement, were confirmed.

Schedule A to the amending agreement called for the undertaking of an agreed programme of diamond drilling and unwatering of the Torbrit mine (one of the mining properties described in the principal agreement); the testing of the downward plunge of the Torbrit ore body; testing by diamond drilling of the width of mineralization in the east end of the Torbrit mine; completion of approximately 5,000 ft. of diamond drilling on the Wolf property (another of the mining properties covered by the principal agreement); and completion of approximately 500 ft. of diamond drilling on the Sussex claims (another mining property covered by the principal agreement).

Although some preparatory organizational work was done to implement the amending agreement, nothing was done by Sunshine on the ground to carry out the work called for by sch. A. Sunshine shut down the operation.

Under the provisions of the principal agreement, as amended, the first development period expired on September 30, 1965, unless extended by Sunshine by notice given prior to August 31, 1965, or unless, prior to that date, Sunshine gave notice of intention to enter upon the second development period. No notice of extension was given, nor did Sunshine give notice of intention to undertake the second development period.

It is admitted, in the argument in this Court, that the agreement came to an end, and that Sunshine was in breach of its contractual obligation to carry out the work prescribed in sch. A which it had agreed to perform.

Dolly Varden commenced action against Sunshine for damages for breach of the agreement. The action was tried between January 30 and February 17, 1967 inclusive. Following the hearing, further documents were filed and argument submitted respecting the consequences of an agreement which took effect on March 9, 1967 between Dolly Varden and Newmont Mining Corporation of Canada Limited (hereinafter referred to as "Newmont").

Briefly, this agreement provided that Dolly Varden would give to Newmont exclusive possession, management and control of the mining properties of Dolly Varden, so as to conduct drilling, exploration and development work thereon. Newmont agreed to conduct a geological survey of the property, in such manner as it decided, and a geophysical survey of such portion of the property as it considered advisable. These surveys were to be completed by December 31, 1967. If this work were completed, as provided, Newmont had the right to terminate the agreement, or to extend its rights for a year, in which event it would be committed to expend not less than $200,000 on or for the benefit of the property. Two further periods of extension, for one year, were similarly provided for, at the option of Newmont, involving expenditure in each year of not less than $300,000. Thereafter Newmont had the right either to terminate the agreement or to equip the property for mining, in which event it would acquire title to the property for the joint venture. Profits of operation would be divided equally after reimbursement to the parties of their respective expenditures. There was no covenant by Newmont to do the work described in sch. A to the amending agreement with Sunshine.

The learned trial Judge [(1967), 64 DLR (2d) 283 (BCSC)] gave judgment for damages for breach of contract, the award for nonperformance of the sch. A work being $314,051 based on evidence as to the cost of performing such work.

Sunshine's appeal from this judgment was dismissed, unanimously, by the Court of Appeal [(1968), 69 DLR (2d) (BCCA)] and a cross-appeal by Dolly Varden seeking an increase in this award was allowed, the damages being increased by $64,976.

The appeal to this Court is based solely on the issue of the measure of damages, it being contended that Dolly Varden had neither proved nor suffered any damage by reason of the non-performance of the sch. A work. It was submitted that it was an error in law to award an amount equivalent to the cost of performance of that work.

The learned trial Judge found, as a fact, that [at 316-17]:

I am of the opinion that the completion of the schedule "A" work was a necessary and economic step in the development of the Torbrit mine.

In the light of this finding and his finding that the officers of Dolly Varden intended the completion of the sch. A work, the learned trial Judge held that the damages should be assessed upon the same basis as was approved by this Court in the case of *Cunningham v. Insinger*, [1924] SCR 8. In that case a mine owner gave to a mine operator an option to purchase a mine for a cash amount, payable in instalments. When the first instalment fell due, the operator negotiated for an extension of time. This extension was granted by the owner in consideration of the operator agreeing to do certain development work not mentioned in the option, consisting mainly of the driving of certain tunnels. The operator failed to pay, relinquished possession of the mine, and surrendered the option without having done the work. The owner sued for damages in the amount of the cost of this work. This Court decided that he was entitled to recover this amount. Idington J dissented. Counsel for the operator, Mr. Lafleur, contended that the owner was only entitled to recover the pecuniary advantage he would have obtained by performance of the contract, which, in this case, would be the equivalent of any increase in the value of the mine arising therefrom.

Duff J (as he then was) said, at p. 14:

> It would be inadvisable, I think to attempt to lay down any general rule for ascertaining the damages to which a mine-owner is entitled for a breach of covenant to perform development work or exploratory work by a person holding an option of purchase. Cases may no doubt arise in which the test suggested by Lafleur's argument would be the only proper test, and difficult and intricate as the inquiry might be, it would be the duty of the Court to enter upon an examination of the effect of doing the work upon the value of the property.
>
> On the other hand, cases must arise in which the plaintiff's right is plainly to recover at least the cost of doing the work. If it were conclusively made out, for example, that the work to be done formed part and a necessary part of some plan of exploration or development requisite, from the miner's point of view, for developing the property as a working mine, and necessary, from the point of view of businesslike management, so that it might fairly be presumed that in the event of the option lapsing the owner would in the ordinary course have the work completed, then the damages arising in the ordinary course would include the cost of doing the work and would accordingly be recoverable under the rule.

Anglin J (as he then was) said, at p. 16:

> Acting on the advice of M.S. Davys, a mining engineer, the plaintiff insisted on the promise by Cunningham to undertake and prosecute this work immediately and continuously as the basis of any extension to be given him. Davys deposes that he and Moore had agreed that the work in question should be done. The plaintiff relied upon Davys, and it is a fair inference not only that he regards the work as essential but that it is work which he will have done. It is probably necessary to reach that conclusion in order to justify the departure made by the trial Judge from the ordinary rule that the measure of damages for breach by a defendant of a contract to perform work on the plaintiff's land is the actual pecuniary loss sustained by the plaintiff as a result of such breach, *i.e.*, the difference between what would have been the value of the premises had the work contracted for been done and their value with it unperformed. The question is by no means free from difficulty and, as presently advised, it is only because I think the learned trial judge must have dealt with it on the footing indicated and because his having done so was warranted by the evidence that I accept the measure of damages as determined.
>
> Reference may be had to *Pell v. Shearman* (1855), 10 Exch. 766, 156 ER 650; *Mayne on Damages*, 9th ed., pp. 237-8; *Sedgwick on Damages*, 9th ed., s. 610; *Wigsell v. School for Indigent Blind* (1882), 8 QBD 357; *Joyner v. Weeks*, [1891] 2 QB 31 (CA). In the last cited case the Court of Appeal (p. 43) treated the breach of a tenant's covenant to yield up premises in good repair as subject to a convenient rule of inveterate practice ordinarily applicable specially to such cases and tantamount to a rule of law that the measure of the lessor's damages should be the cost of making the omitted repairs. A recent decision of an Appellate Divisional Court in Ontario may also be adverted to *O'Brien Ltd. v. Freedman* (1923), 25 OWN 210.

Mignault J said, at p. 17:

> In my opinion, on the construction of the agreement entered into by the parties, by their letters
> of October 19, October 26, and November 2, 1918, the carrying on of the development work
> mentioned in para. 3 of the appellant's letter of October 10 was the consideration of the exten-
> sion of time granted by the respondent for the payment of the balance of the first instalment
> under the option contract between the parties. It was in no wise a condition of the original op-
> tion to be unenforceable in case the option to purchase was not exercised by the appellant. On
> the contrary, the only possible interest the respondent could have in view when he stipulated
> for this development work was in case the appellant relinquished his option. If he purchased
> the property, and paid for it, it would be a matter of indifference to the respondent what develop-
> ment work had been done. Moreover, the letter stated that the work should begin immediately.

Counsel for Sunshine contends that the learned trial Judge should have applied the decision
of this Court in *Cotter v. General Petroleums Ltd. and Superior Oils Ltd.*, [1951] SCR 154,
and should have awarded only nominal damages.

In that case, Cotter had granted to General Petroleums Limited and Superior Oils, Limited an option on petroleum and natural gas in certain lands held under lease by Cotter.
Clause 2 of the agreement provided for the exercise of the option within a stipulated period
by commencing the drilling of a well upon the land described and by notifying Cotter of the
exercise of the option. Under cl. 3 of the agreement, the companies covenanted to exercise
the option within the period prescribed in cl. 2. It was provided that on their failure to do
so, Cotter, notwithstanding the lapse of the option, could be entitled to exercise any legal
remedies available for breach of the covenant, which, the parties agreed, was given as the
substantial consideration for the granting of the option.

The companies did not fulfil their covenant, and Cotter sued them for damages. At trial
[[1949] 1 WWR 193 (Alta. SC TD)] he was awarded an amount equivalent to the cost of
drilling a well. On appeal, the Appellate Division of the Supreme Court of Alberta [[1949]
3 DLR 634 (Alta. SC AD)] found that cl. 3 of the agreement was void for repugnancy and
must be rejected as destructive of the object of the instrument, a view which was shared by
Locke J in this Court.

Rinfret J and Kerwin J (as he then was), while disagreeing with this conclusion, held that
there was no covenant by the companies to drill a well. Kerwin J, who wrote the reasons,
said at p. 159:

> The allowance by the trial Judge was made on the basis of reading together the head lease, the
> agreement in question, and the form of lease attached thereto and construing the covenant sued
> upon as one to dig a well. I am unable to agree that this is the proper way of approaching the
> matter. Clause 4 of the agreement provides that the optioner shall grant to the optionees the
> sublease "in the event of the exercise of the said option" and I cannot read the document as
> equivalent to a simple agreement for a lease. Such a result could follow only if the option had in
> fact been exercised. It appears to me that cl. 3 was drawn having in mind that the option had in
> fact been exercised and provided that, if the optionees neglected or failed to exercise it, certain
> results should follow. It was only if the option was exercised that the lease was to be entered into.

Notwithstanding that the appellant's case was put as if the respondents' covenant was to dig a well, which as I have indicated is not in my view its proper construction, the appellant is entitled to more than nominal damages.

In the present case there was a specific agreement to perform the sch. A work and a clear breach of that undertaking.

Cartwright J (as he then was), with whose reasons Fauteux J concurred, held that cls. 2 and 3 were not repugnant to each other, and further held that the companies had covenanted to drill a well. He said, at p. 172:

> I think that, read as a whole, the agreement of April 21, 1948 with its schedules discloses the intention of the parties to agree that on or before August 1, 1948, the respondents would commence to drill a well in the manner set out in para. 2 of the agreement, that forthwith on such commencement the parties would execute the sublease and that the respondents would carry on the drilling of the well to completion in the manner set out in the sublease. I think that the respondents were bound in contract not only to commence but to complete the drilling of the well within the time and in the manner prescribed, and that such obligations bound them from the moment that the agreement of April 21, 1948 was executed.

He then sent on to hold that Cotter was not entitled, in the circumstances of the case, for breach of the covenant to drill a well, to recover the expense of such drilling. His reasoning is as follows (at p. 174):

> It remains to be considered on what principle and at what amount the damages should be assessed.
>
> The underlying principle is expressed by Lord Atkinson in *Wertheim v. Chicoutimi Pulp Co.*, [1911] AC 301 (PC (Qué.)) at p. 307: "And it is the general intention of the law that, in giving damages for breach of contract, the party complaining should, so far as it can be done by money, be placed in the same position as he would have been in if the contract had been performed. ... That is a ruling principle. It is a just principle." In the case at bar if the respondents had carried out the contract the appellant would not have had to pay the $1,000 for a 6 months' extension which he did in fact pay to the head-lessor. The circumstances as to the necessity of making such payment were known to the parties and I agree with the learned trial Judge that that sum is recoverable. What further benefits would have resulted to the appellant from the performance of the contract? If the respondents had drilled the well to the prescribed depth and it had proved a producer, the appellant would have received, (a) his share of the proceeds and, (b) the benefit of having the head lease validated, by the performance of the lessee's covenant to drill, not only to the 80 acres described in the sublease but as to the whole 160 acres described in the head lease. If on the other hand, as, from the evidence of the geologists, would seem much more probable, the well had proved a failure the appellant would not have received benefit (a) but would have received benefit (b). It must be remembered however that as a result of the respondents' breach the appellant holds the whole 160 acres free from any claim of the respondents. No part of the consideration which under the contract would have passed to the respondents had passed, except that from April 21, 1948 until some time in June 1948, when they repudiated the agreement, the respondents had rights in the 80 acres and the appellant was not free to deal therewith. Under these circumstances, I do not think that the cost of drilling is

the proper measure of damages. Suppose that instead of the consideration set out in the contract the appellant had agreed to pay the respondents $58,500 to drill the well and the respondents had repudiated the contract before the date set for the commencement of the work and before any monies had been paid to them. In such a case by analogy to the rule in the case of building contracts the measure of damages would seem to be the difference (if any) between the price of the work agreed upon and the cost to which the appellant was actually put in its completion. I think it will be found that these cases in which it has been held that the cost of drilling is the proper measure of damages are cases where the consideration to be given for the drilling had actually passed to the defendant. Examples of such cases are *Cunningham v. Insinger*, [1924] SCR 8 and *Pell v. Shearman* (1855), 10 Exch. 766, 156 ER 650 (a contract to sink a shaft).

It will be noted, from the passages above cited, that the obligation of the companies to drill a well (as distinct from commencing to drill a well) would arise only if the option had been exercised and they had been granted a sublease. The consideration for the drilling was to be the granting of the sublease and that consideration had not passed to them. In the present case, the consideration for the undertaking of the sch. A work had been received by Sunshine in full. Sunshine had received, under the principal agreement, the transfer to it of a one-half interest in the mining properties. Under the amending agreement, it had received from Dolly Varden the consideration stipulated in that agreement, namely, withdrawal of the notice of default, waiver of the performance of further work under sch. F of the principal agreement, waiver of any prior defaults, and an extension of the term of the first development period. For that consideration Sunshine had given a firm commitment to perform the sch. A work, which it failed and refused to perform.

For these reasons, I do not consider that the reasoning in the *Cotter* case is of assistance to Sunshine in the present appeal.

Davey CJBC, in the Court of Appeal, agreed with the judgment at trial that Dolly Varden was entitled to receive the expense involved in performing the sch. A work. He reached this conclusion for reasons somewhat different from those of the learned trial Judge. He points out that the view of Duff J, in the *Cunningham* case, as to the inadvisability of attempting to lay down a general rule of law for ascertaining the damages sustained by a mine owner for breach of a covenant to perform exploratory or development work is supported by high authority, and he cites the following statements of the law [69 DLR (2d), at 217-18]:

> In *Wertheim v. Chicoutimi Pulp Co.*, [1911] AC 301 (PC (Qué.)) which was cited in *Cotter v. General Petroleums Ltd.*, *supra*, Lord Atkinson stated at p. 307:
>
> > And it is the general intention of the law that, in giving damages for breach of contract, the party complaining should, so far as it can be done by money, be placed in the same position as he would have been in if the contract had been performed: *Irvine v. Midland Ry. Co. (Ireland)* (1880), 6 LR Ir. at p. 63, approved of by Palles CB in *Hamilton v. Magill* (1883), 12 LR Ir. at p. 202. That is a ruling principle. It is a just principle. The rule which prescribes as a measure of damages the difference in market prices at the respective times above mentioned is merely designed to apply this principle and, as stated in one of the American cases cited, it generally secures a complete indemnity. The market value is taken because it is presumed to be the true value of the goods to the purchaser. In the case of non-delivery, where the purchaser does not get the goods he purchased, it is as-

sumed that these would be worth to him, if he had them, what they would fetch in the open market; and that, if he wanted to get others in their stead, he could obtain them in that market at that price.

In British Westinghouse Electric & Mfg. Co. Ltd. v. Underground Electric Railways Co. of London, Ltd., [1912] AC 673 (HL (Eng.)), Lord Haldane LC, at pp. 688-9, stated:

> In order to come to a conclusion on the question as to damages thus raised, it is essential to bear in mind certain propositions which I think are well established. In some of the cases there are expressions as to the principles governing the measure of general damages which at first sight seem difficult to harmonize. The apparent discrepancies are, however, mainly due to the varying nature of the particular questions submitted for decision. The quantum of damage is a question of fact, and the only guidance the law can give is to lay down general principles which afford at times but scanty assistance in dealing with particular cases. The judges who give guidance to juries in these cases have necessarily to look at their special character, and to mould, for the purposes of different kinds of claim, the expression of the general principles which apply to them, and this is apt to give rise to an appearance of ambiguity.
>
> Subject to these observations I think that there are certain broad principles which are quite well settled. The first is that, as far as possible, he who has proved a breach of a bargain to supply what he contracted to get is to be placed, as far as money can do it, in as good a situation as if the contract had been performed.
>
> The fundamental basis is thus compensation for pecuniary loss naturally flowing from the breach. ...

In *Monarch Steamship Co., Ltd. v. Karlshamns Oljefabriker A/B*, [1949] AC 190 (HL (Eng.)), the House of Lords followed the principle applied in *Wertheim v. Chicoutimi Pulp Co.*, and by Duff J in *Cunningham v. Insinger*, which is founded upon *Hadley v. Baxendale* (1854), 9 Ex. 341, 156 ER 145. At pp. 222-3, Lord Wright repeated the passage from Viscount Haldane's speech which I have quoted above.

The following passage from the speech of Lord Du Parcq at p. 232 puts the particular rules for measuring damages in their proper light, as simply methods of solving what is after all essentially a question of fact, and that this application must vary according to the circumstances of each case:

> I do not doubt the wisdom of the judges who, in *Hadley v. Baxendale* and the many later cases which interpreted or explained that classic decision, have laid down rules or principles for the guidance of those whose duty it is, as judges or jurymen, to assess damages. When those rules or principles are applied, however, it is essential to remember what my noble and learned friend Lord Wright, and Lord Haldane in the passage cited by him, have emphasized, that in the end what has to be decided is a question of fact, and therefore a question proper for a jury. Circumstances are so infinitely various that, however carefully general rules are framed, they must be construed with some liberality, and not too rigidly applied. It was necessary to lay down principles lest juries should be persuaded to do injustice by imposing an undue, or perhaps an inadequate, liability on a defendant. The court must be careful, however, to see that the principles laid down are

never so narrowly interpreted as to prevent a jury, or judge of fact, from doing justice between the parties. So to use them would be to misuse them.

Applying these principles, Davey CJBC reaches the following conclusions [at 219-20]:

So in the result the appellants have received from the respondent everything they bargained for under the principal and amending agreement as the consideration for their contract to do the work specified in schedule "F" as modified by schedule "A," but have done nothing they agreed to do under schedule "A." The respondent has been denied the information it would have got if the work had been done under schedule "A," for which it had paid by fulfilling all its obligations under the principal and amending agreements.

If appellant had performed its obligations respondent would have received valuable information about the Torbrit property. True the information might have shown the property to be of great value, or valueless, but even in the latter case the information would have been valuable to the respondent to enable it to adopt a realistic policy, and save expense of carrying worthless claims.

It seems quite clear that the direct and natural consequence of the appellant's default was to deprive the respondent of essential information about the value of its properties for which it had paid. The measure of that loss is the value of the information that respondent would have obtained from the performance by appellant of its contract to do the drilling. The value of that information cannot be determined by what it would have disclosed, for that is not known, but by what it would cost the respondent to obtain it, following the analogy of determining the value to the purchaser of goods bought but not delivered by the cost of replacing them: *Wertheim v. Chicoutimi Pulp Co.* quoted *supra*.

The reasons of Branca JA for supporting the judgment at trial are substantially similar to those of the Chief Justice. Nemetz JA agreed with the learned trial Judge that, on its facts, this case was similar to the *Cunningham* case and that the same measure of damages ought to be applied.

The submissions made on behalf of Sunshine in this Court have failed to persuade me that, in the circumstances of the case, the Courts below were in error in awarding to Dolly Varden damages equivalent to the expense involved in performing the sch. A work which Sunshine contracted to perform and deliberately failed to carry out. As stated by Lord du Parcq in the passage cited earlier, what has to be decided, in determining damages, is a question of fact, and the *Cunningham* case certainly establishes that there is no rule of law which precludes the application of the method of assessing damages which was adopted by the learned trial Judge in this case, when the Court considers it to be appropriate. For the reasons already stated, I do not think that the *Cotter* case is of any assistance to Sunshine in this appeal.

It was contended, for Sunshine, that Dolly Varden was only entitled to receive, by way of damages, the difference between the value of the premises if the work had been performed, and their value with the work unperformed, and that there was no evidence to establish any damage upon this basis. In the circumstances of this case I do not think that this was a proper test for ascertaining damages.

Counsel for Sunshine, in this connection, relied upon two cases, *Wigsell v. School for Indigent Blind* (1881), 8 QBD 357 and *James v. Hutton and J. Cook & Sons Ltd.*, [1950] 1 KB 9 (CA).

In the former case, a grantee of land had covenanted to construct around the land conveyed, on all sides where it abutted on the grantor's land, a 7-ft. brick wall. The wall was not erected and action was brought for damages. It appeared that the value of the adjoining land was not decreased by the non-erection of the wall to anything like the amount required to construct it.

The Court refused to award damages equivalent to the cost of constructing the wall.

This was a case of a purchaser's covenant, similar to a restrictive covenant, taken by the seller for the protection of his adjoining land, and the measure of damages in such cases is usually the diminution in value of the adjoining land resulting from non-performance. In cases of this kind, the grantor has available the remedy of specific performance, where damages would not adequately protect his rights.

The latter case involved a covenant by a lessee, who under licence, made an alteration to the front of the store he had leased. The lessee undertook, on request, to restore the building to its original condition on the expiration of the lease. The lessee failed to comply with such a request by the lessor. There was no evidence that the restoration would make the premises suitable for any particular purpose or business or that the premises were adversely affected or made less valuable by reason of the new store front which replaced the old.

The Court held that the lessor was only entitled to recover the damage he had actually suffered, which, in this case, was merely nominal. The Court, however, expressly disclaimed that it was suggested that the plaintiff could not give evidence that he desired to use the premises for a purpose for which the new front was unsuitable.

I do not regard these cases as being analogous to the circumstances of the present case. The covenant of the grantee in the *Wigsell* case was given for the benefit of the adjacent lands retained by the grantor. The extent to which the value of those lands was affected by breach of the covenant was not, in the circumstances of that case, determinable by reference to the cost of construction of the wall. Similarly, in the *James* case, the covenant given by the lessee under the licence granted to him by the lessor, was for the benefit of the reversionary interest of the lessor. In the absence of evidence that breach of the covenant affected the use to which the lands were to be put, or their value, after the expiration of the lease, the lessor was held not entitled to recover the cost of restoration of the store front to its previous condition.

The agreements in the present case related to a joint venture for exploration, development and production of minerals underlying the mining properties. These properties were known to have good prospects. Stage one of the principal agreement provided Sunshine with an opportunity to ascertain whether these properties offered a potential return to it sufficient to warrant a decision to proceed further into stage two. Dolly Varden's interest was in having Sunshine proceed with the various stages into commercial production, but, failing such further progress, it would obtain, pursuant to the provisions of the agreement, full information as to the work done, the results thereof and the cost involved. In a sense, although the agreement provided that it should not be construed as creating a partnership, the parties were partners in a joint venture.

The work described in sch. A to the amending agreement was work which Sunshine had decided would be of advantage, after conducting a study of the Torbrit mine and on the recommendation of its chief geologist. It committed itself to do that work for the consideration given by Dolly Varden, which Sunshine received in full. Sunshine committed itself to perform that work, obviously because it considered the results of it would be of value. Dolly

Varden gave the stipulated consideration because, if the results were favourable, it would obtain the further development of its property, and, if Sunshine was not satisfied with the results, it would be the recipient of useful information about its property. Clearly, in this case, both parties considered that the work, contracted to be performed, would be worth the expense of doing it. This is an entirely different situation from the covenants given in the two cases mentioned, which would be of advantage only, if at all, to the grantor and the lessor respectively.

When Sunshine, later, deliberately breached its contract to perform the work, what was the measure of Dolly Varden's damage? If it had paid cash for the work, it would clearly be entitled to a repayment of it, and would also have a claim in damages. The consideration was not in cash, but Sunshine, when it executed the amending agreement, considered it to be of sufficient value to warrant the expenditure necessary to perform the work.

It is pointless, in these circumstances, to suggest that a comparison be made between the value of the mining property with and without the work being done. The result of the sch. A work is unknown, and it is unknown because Sunshine elected to break the contract for its performance. But when Sunshine, by entering the agreement, acknowledged that, in the light of its future potential benefits under the agreement, its own suggested programme of work was worth the cost of consideration for its performance, I consider that it was entirely proper for the learned trial Judge to assess the damage resulting from the breach as being equivalent to the cost of doing the work. In so doing he was seeking to fulfil the underlying principle stated by Lord Atkinson in *Wertheim v. Chicoutimi Pulp Co.*, [1911] AC 301 (PC (Qué.)) at p. 307, and cited by Cartwright J in the *Cotter* case in the passage already quoted [at 174]:

> And it is the general intention of the law that, in giving damages for breach of contract, the party complaining should, so far as it can be done by money, be placed in the same position as he would have been if the contract had been performed.

Having reached this conclusion, I must go on to consider whether the right to receive damages, determined in this manner, is affected by Dolly Varden having entered into the agreement with Newmont, which did not become effective until after Dolly Varden had asserted its right to damages against Sunshine, and after that action had been tried.

In this Court, counsel for Sunshine did not contend that the benefits accruing to Dolly Varden under that contract should be considered by way of mitigation of damages. His position was that no question of mitigation arises because, he said, Dolly Varden had not established any damages. I have already indicated my reasons for disagreeing with this latter assertion. His submission was that the Newmont agreement was relevant as showing that, from its effective date, Dolly Varden had abandoned any power or intention of doing the sch. A work itself, and, on this basis, this case was not analogous to the *Cunningham* case.

The same submission was made at trial and, in respect of it, the learned trial Judge made the following finding [64 DLR (2d), at 318]:

> However, I have found that the work was economic and necessary as a part of the over-all scheme of development of Torbrit. I also accept the evidence of the officers of the plaintiff company to the effect that they intend the completion of the schedule "A" work.
>
> The fact that the new agreement with Newmont does not make specific reference to the work and does not provide for its completion at once does not mean that the plaintiff does not

intend to do the work or have it done or exclude the possibility that it will be done, and the work being a necessary step in the development of the mining properties the introduction of a new principal cannot justify a finding, by itself, that the work would not be done.

I am not prepared to disturb this finding. Furthermore, I do not regard the Newmont agreement as having any bearing in this case. The agreement with Sunshine terminated at the end of the first development stage. Sunshine had not given notice of intent to extend that period or to enter the next development stage. It abandoned the agreement. Immediately upon the termination of the agreement, in my opinion, for the reasons already given, Dolly Varden had a valid claim in damages equivalent to the expense of doing the sch. A work, which it asserted by action against Sunshine. On such termination Dolly Varden had the mining property on its hands, and, later, it was able to obtain the agreement with Newmont for its development. Under that contract, the work to be done by Newmont was in its discretion, subject to its commitment, if it entered the second and later stages, to expend stipulated amounts of money "for the benefit of the property." It was not obligated to perform the sch. A work. In view of these circumstances, I do not see how this contract can affect the cause of action of Dolly Varden to recover damages equivalent to the cost of the sch. A work, arising out of Sunshine's failure to do that work, which cause of action arose on the termination of the Sunshine agreement.

I would dismiss this appeal, with costs.

Appeal dismissed.

QUESTIONS

1. Martland J notes that Sunshine "deliberately breached its contract to perform the work." What effect, if any, should this have on the assessment of damages?

2. Martland J says, "It is pointless ... to suggest that a comparison be made between the value of the mining property with and without the work being done. The result of ... the work is unknown." Recall, however, that Cory JA said in *Canlin*, above, that "[t]he Court ... would be shirking its duty if it were to say that no damages should flow because of the difficulty of calculating and assessing such damages." Do you see any conflict between these statements and, if so, can they be reconciled?

3. Is the court's decision in *Dolly Varden* sound when viewed in the light of the reasons supporting the expectancy rule?

Ruxley Electronics and Construction Ltd. v. Forsyth
[1996] 1 AC 344 (HL (Eng.))

LORD KEITH of Kinkel, LORD BRIDGE of Harwich, LORD JAUNCEY of Tullichettle, LORD MUSTILL and LORD LLOYD of Berwick: The defendant (the owner) contracted with the two plaintiff companies, R and L (the builders), to build a swimming pool in his garden and a building to enclose it for a total price of £70,178.74. The contract expressly provided that the maximum depth of the pool should be 7 ft 6 in. After the work had been completed, the

owner discovered that the maximum depth was only 6 ft 9 in and that at the point where
people would dive into the pool the depth was only 6 ft. The owner paid various sums on
account and after certain agreed credits the balance of the price due for the construction of
the pool and the enclosure amounted to £39,072. The builders claimed the balance of the
contract price and the owner counterclaimed for breach of contract. Although it was accepted that the failure to provide the required depth was a breach of contract, the trial judge
found that the shortfall in depth had not decreased the value of the pool and gave judgment
for R in the sum of £3,903 and for L in the sum of £36,874 but awarded the owner £2,500
general damages for loss of amenity on his counterclaim. The owner appealed, contending
that the judge should have awarded damages in respect of the breach or deducted a sum
from the contract price to reflect the cost of reconstructing the swimming pool to conform
to the original contractual specification and that by itself the award of general damages was
too low if he received no other compensation for the breach. The Court of Appeal allowed
the appeal, holding that it was not unreasonable to award as damages the cost of replacing
the swimming pool in order to make good the breach of contract, even though the shortfall
in the depth of the pool had not decreased its value. The court awarded the owner £21,560
damages against R. R appealed to the House of Lords. ...

LORD KEITH OF KINKEL: My Lords, I have had the advantage of reading in draft the
speeches to be delivered by my noble and learned friends Lord Jauncey of Tullichettle, Lord
Mustill and Lord Lloyd of Berwick. I agree with them and for the reasons they give would
allow this appeal.

LORD BRIDGE OF HARWICH: My Lords, damages for breach of contract must reflect, as
accurately as the circumstances allow, the loss which the claimant has sustained because he
did not get what he bargained for. There is no question of punishing the contract-breaker.
Given this basic principle, the court, in assessing the measure of the claimant's loss, has ultimately to determine a question of fact, although the law has of course developed detailed
criteria which are to be applied in ascertaining the appropriate measure of loss in a wide
variety of commonly occurring situations. Since the law relating to damages for breach of
contract has developed almost exclusively in a commercial context, these criteria normally
proceed on the assumption that each contracting party's interest in the bargain was purely
commercial and that the loss resulting from a breach of contract is measurable in purely
economic terms. But this assumption may not always be appropriate. ...

The cogent argument of Mr. Jacob for the respondent, reduced to its bare essentials, can,
I think be summarised in three propositions. (1) The judge's award of £2,500 damages to the
respondent for "loss of amenity" demonstrates that the respondent suffered a real loss for
which he is entitled to be compensated. (2) In a building contract case there is no admissible
head of damages capable of assessment by reference to such concepts as loss of amenity,
inconvenience or loss of aesthetic satisfaction. These are imponderables which the court can
only evaluate by plucking figures out of the air. If a possible head of damage of this nature
were to be admitted in building contract cases, this would introduce chaotic uncertainty into
the law and undermine clear and well-settled principles. (3) By these well-settled principles
damages in a building contract case can only be assessed by reference to diminution in value

or cost of reinstatement. There being here no diminution in value, the only available measure of damages to compensate the respondent for his real loss is the cost of reinstatement.

Attractive as was Mr. Jacob's development of this argument, it seems to me to suffer from an inherent logical flaw in that it leads from the premise that a loss has been suffered which is incapable of economic measurement to the conclusion that it must be compensated by reference to a measure of economic loss, namely the cost of reinstatement, which has not been and will not be incurred.

It is no doubt correct that, in the absence of any cross-appeal against the judge's award, the propriety of that award is strictly not in issue. But since the attack on the principle of the award was central to Mr. Jacob's argument, I think the issue is one which we may properly address and I agree with my noble and learned friend Lord Mustill in the reasons he gives for concluding that there is no reason in principle why the court should not have power to award damages of the kind in question and indeed that in some circumstances such power may be essential to enable the court to do justice.

But, quite independently of these conclusions, to hold in a case such as this that the measure of the building owner's loss is the cost of reinstatement, however unreasonable it would be to incur that cost, seems to me to fly in the face of common sense.

LORD JAUNCEY OF TULLICHETTLE: … The trial judge made the following findings which are relevant to this appeal: (1) the pool as constructed was perfectly safe to dive into; (2) there was no evidence that the shortfall in depth had decreased the value of the pool; (3) the only practicable method of achieving a pool of the required depth would be to demolish the existing pool and reconstruct a new one at a cost of £21,560; (4) he was not satisfied that the respondent intended to build a new pool at such a cost; (5) in addition such cost would be wholly disproportionate to the disadvantage of having a pool of a depth of only 6 ft as opposed to 7 ft 6 in and it would therefore be unreasonable to carry out the works; and (6) that the respondent was entitled to damages for loss of amenity in the sum of £2,500.

The general principles applicable to the measure of damages for breach of contract are not in doubt. In a very well-known passage Parke B in *Robinson v. Harman* (1848), 1 Exch. 850 at p. 855:

> The next question is: What damages is the plaintiff entitled to recover? The rule of the common law is that where a party sustains a loss by reason of a breach of contract, he is, so far as money can do it, to be placed in the same situation, with respect to damages, as if the contract had been performed.

In *British Westinghouse Electric and Manufacturing Co. Ltd. v. Underground Electric Railways Co. of London Ltd.* [1912] AC 673 (HL (Eng.)) at pp. 688-689, Viscount Haldane LC said:

> The quantum of damage is a question of fact, and the only guidance the law can give is to lay down general principles which afford at times but scanty assistance in dealing with particular cases. … Subject to these observations I think that there are certain broad principles which are quite well settled. The first is that, as far as possible, he who has proved a breach of a bargain to supply what he contracted to get is to be placed, as far as money can do it, in as good a situation

as if the contract had been performed. The fundamental basis is thus compensation for pecuniary loss naturally flowing from the breach; but this first principle is qualified by a second, which imposes on a plaintiff the duty of taking all reasonable steps to mitigate the loss consequent on the breach. ...

More recently, in what is generally accepted as the leading authority on the measure of damages for defective building work, Lord Cohen in *East Ham BC v. Bernard Sunley & Sons Ltd.*, [1966] AC 406 (HL (Eng.)) at pp. 434–435 said:

> ... [T]he learned editors of HUDSON'S BUILDING AND ENGINEERING CONTRACTS (8th edn., 1959) say, at p. 319, that there are in fact three possible bases of assessing damages, namely, (a) the cost of reinstatement; (b) the difference in cost to the builder of the actual work done and work specified; or (c) the diminution in value of the work due to the breach of contract. They go on (ibid.): "There is no doubt that wherever it is reasonable for the employer to insist upon re-instatement the courts will treat the cost of re-instatement as the measure of damage." In the present case it could not be disputed that it was reasonable for the employers to insist on re-instatement and in these circumstances it necessarily follows that on the question of damage the trial judge arrived at the right conclusion.

Lord Upjohn likewise stated that in a case of defective building work reinstatement was the normal measure of damages (see [1966] AC 406 at p. 445).

Mr. McGuire QC for the appellant argued that the cost of reinstatement was only allowable where (1) the employer intended as a matter of probability to rebuild if damages were awarded, and (2) that it was reasonable as between him and the contractor so to do. Since the judge had found against the respondent on both these matters the appeal should be allowed. Mr. Jacob on the other hand maintained that reasonableness only arose at the stage when a real loss had been established to exist and that where that loss could only be met by damages assessed on one basis there was no room for consideration of reasonableness. Such was the case where a particular personal preference was part of the contractual objective—a situation which did not allow damages to be assessed on a diminution of value basis.

I start with the question of reasonableness in the context of reinstatement. There is a considerable body of authority dealing with this matter. Lord Cohen in the passage in *East Ham BC v. Bernard Sunley & Sons Ltd.* quoted above referred to the reasonableness of insisting on reinstatement. In *Imodco Ltd. v. Wimpey Major Projects Ltd.* (1987), 40 BLR 1 at p. 19 Glidewell LJ stated that the cost of work to put pipes in the position contracted for would be recoverable if there was an intention to carry out the work and if it was reasonable so to do. In *Minscombe Properties Ltd. v. Sir Alfred McAlpine & Sons Ltd.* (1986), 2 Const. LJ 303 at p. 309 O'Connor LJ applied the test of reasonableness in determining whether the cost of reinstatement of land to its contracted for condition should be recoverable as damages. In *Radford v. De Froberville* [1977] 1 WLR 1262 at p. 1283 Oliver J said:

> In the instant case, the plaintiff says in evidence that he wishes to carry out the work on his own land and there are, as it seems to me, three questions that I have to answer. First, am I satisfied on the evidence that the plaintiff has a genuine and serious intention of doing the work? Secondly, is the carrying out of the work on his own land a reasonable thing for the plaintiff to do? Thirdly, does it make any difference that the plaintiff is not personally in occupation of the land but desires to do the work for the benefit of his tenants?

In *C.R. Taylor (Wholesale) Ltd. v. Hepworths Ltd.* [1977] 1 WLR 659 at p. 667 May J referred with approval to a statement in *McGregor On Damages* (13th edn., 1972) at paras. 1059-1061 that in deciding between diminution in value and cost of reinstatement the appropriate test was the reasonableness of the plaintiff's desire to reinstate the property and remarked that the damages to be awarded were to be reasonable as between plaintiff and defendant. He concluded that in the case before him to award the notional cost of reinstatement would be unreasonable since it would put the plaintiffs in a far better financial position than they would have been before the fire occurred (see [1977] 1 WLR 659 at p. 670). In *McGregor* (15th edn., 1988) at para. 1092, after a reference to the cost of reinstatement being the normal measure of damages in a case of defective building, it is stated:

> If, however, the cost of remedying the defect is disproportionate to the end to be attained, the damages fall to be measured by the value of the building had it been built as required by the contract less its value as it stands.

In *Bellgrove v. Eldridge* (1954), 90 CLR 613 at pp. 617-618 the High Court of Australia in a judgment of the court, after referring with approval to the rule stated in *Hudson on Building Contracts* (7th edn., 1946) p. 343 that—

> [t]he measure of the damages recoverable by the building owner for the breach of a building contract is ... the difference between the contract price of the work or building contracted for and the cost of making the work or building conform to the contract. ...

and referring to a number of cases supporting this proposition, continued:

> In none of these cases is anything more done than that work which is required to achieve conformity and the cost of the work, whether it be necessary to replace only a small part, or a substantial part, or, indeed, the whole of the building is, subject to the qualification which we have already mentioned and to which we shall refer, together with any appropriate consequential damages, the extent of the building owner's loss. The qualification, however, to which this rule is subject is that, not only must the work undertaken be necessary to produce conformity, but that also, it must be a reasonable course to adopt.

A similar approach to reasonableness was adopted by Cardozo J delivering the judgment of the majority of the Court of Appeals of New York in *Jacob & Youngs Inc. v. Kent* (1921), 230 NY 239 at pp. 244-245.

Damages are designed to compensate for an established loss and not to provide a gratuitous benefit to the aggrieved party, from which it follows that the reasonableness of an award of damages is to be linked directly to the loss sustained. If it is unreasonable in a particular case to award the cost of reinstatement it must be because the loss sustained does not extend to the need to reinstate. A failure to achieve the precise contractual objective does not necessarily result in the loss which is occasioned by a total failure. This was recognised by the High Court of Australia in the passage in *Bellgrove v. Eldridge* cited above where it was stated that the cost of reinstatement work subject to the qualification of reasonableness was the extent of the loss, thereby treating reasonableness as a factor to be considered in determining what was that loss rather than, as the respondents argued, merely a factor in determining which of two alternative remedies were appropriate for a loss once established.

Further support for this view is to be found in the following passage in the judgment of Megarry V-C in *Tito v. Waddell (No 2)* [1977] Ch 106 at p. 332:

> Per contra, if the plaintiff has suffered little or no monetary loss in the reduction of value of his land, and he has no intention of applying any damages towards carrying out the work contracted for, or its equivalent, I cannot see why he should recover the cost of doing work which will never be done. It would be a mere pretence to say that this cost was a loss and so should be recoverable as damages.

Megarry V-C was, as I understand it, there saying that it would be unreasonable to treat as a loss the cost of carrying out work which would never in fact be done.

I take the example suggested during argument by my noble and learned friend Lord Bridge of Harwich. A man contracts for the building of a house and specifies that one of the lower courses of brick should be blue. The builder uses yellow brick instead. In all other respects the house conforms to the contractual specification. To replace the yellow bricks with blue would involve extensive demolition and reconstruction at a very large cost. It would clearly be unreasonable to award to the owner the cost of reconstructing because his loss was not the necessary cost of reconstruction of his house, which was entirely adequate for its design purpose, but merely the lack of aesthetic pleasure which he might have derived from the sight of blue bricks. Thus in the present appeal the respondent has acquired a perfectly serviceable swimming pool, albeit one lacking the specified depth. His loss is thus not the lack of a usable pool with consequent need to construct a new one. Indeed were he to receive the cost of building a new one and retain the existing one he would have recovered not compensation for loss but a very substantial gratuitous benefit, something which damages are not intended to provide.

What constitutes the aggrieved party's loss is in every case a question of fact and degree. Where the contract breaker has entirely failed to achieve the contractual objective it may not be difficult to conclude that the loss is the necessary cost of achieving that objective. Thus if a building is constructed so defectively that it is of no use for its designed purpose the owner may have little difficulty in establishing that his loss is the necessary cost of reconstructing. Furthermore, in taking reasonableness into account in determining the extent of loss it is reasonableness in relation to the particular contract and not at large. Accordingly, if I contracted for the erection of a folly in my garden which shortly thereafter suffered a total collapse it would be irrelevant to the determination of my loss to argue that the erection of such a folly which contributed nothing to the value of my house was a crazy thing to do. As Oliver J said in *Radford v. De Froberville* [1977] 1 WLR 1262 at p. 1270:

> If he contracts for the supply of that which he thinks serves his interests, be they commercial, aesthetic or merely eccentric, then if that which is contracted for is not supplied by the other contracting party I do not see why, in principle, he should not be compensated by being provided with the cost of supplying it through someone else or in a different way, subject to the proviso, of course, that he is seeking compensation for a genuine loss and not merely using a technical breach to secure an uncovenanted profit.

However, where the contractual objective has been achieved to a substantial extent the position may be very different.

It was submitted that where the objective of a building contract involved satisfaction of a personal preference the only measure of damages available for a breach involving failure to achieve such satisfaction was the cost of reinstatement. In my view this is not the case. Personal preference may well be a factor in reasonableness and hence in determining what loss has been suffered but it cannot per se be determinative of what that loss is.

My Lords, the trial judge found that it would be unreasonable to incur the cost of demolishing the existing pool and building a new and deeper one. In so doing he implicitly recognised that the respondent's loss did not extend to the cost of reinstatement. He was, in my view, entirely justified in reaching that conclusion. It therefore follows that the appeal must be allowed.

It only remains to mention two further matters. The appellant argued that the cost of reinstatement should only be allowed as damages where there was shown to be an intention on the part of the aggrieved party to carry out the work. Having already decided that the appeal should be allowed I no longer find it necessary to reach a conclusion on this matter. However, I should emphasise that in the normal case the court has no concern with the use to which a plaintiff puts an award of damages for a loss which has been established. Thus, irreparable damage to an article as a result of a breach of contract will entitle the owner to recover the value of the article irrespective of whether he intends to replace it with a similar one or to spend the money on something else. Intention, or lack of it, to reinstate can have relevance only to reasonableness and hence to the extent of the loss which has been sustained. Once that loss has been established intention as to the subsequent use of the damages ceases to be relevant.

The second matter relates to the award of £2,500 for loss of amenity made by the trial judge. The respondent argued that he erred in law in making such award. However, as the appellant did not challenge it, I find it unnecessary to express any opinion on the matter.

LORD MUSTILL: My Lords, I agree that this appeal should be allowed for the reasons stated by my noble and learned friends Lord Jauncey of Tullichettle and Lord Lloyd of Berwick. I add some observations of my own on the award by the trial judge of damages in a sum intermediate between on the one hand the full cost of reinstatement and on the other the amount by which the malperformance has diminished the market value of the property on which the work was done: in this particular case, nil. This is a question of everyday practical importance to householders who have engaged contractors to carry out small building works, and then find (as often happens) that performance has fallen short of what was promised. I think it proper to enter on the question here, although there is no appeal against the award, because the possibility of such a recovery in a suitable case sheds light on the employer's claim that reinstatement is the only proper measure of damage.

The proposition that these two measures of damage represent the only permissible bases of recovery lies at the heart of the employer's case. From this he reasons that there is a presumption in favour of the cost of restitution, since this is the only way in which he can be given what the contractor had promised to provide. Finally, he contends that there is nothing in the facts of the present case to rebut this presumption.

The attraction of this argument is its avoidance of the conclusion that, in a case such as the present, unless the employer can prove that the defects have depreciated the market value of the property the householder can recover nothing at all. This conclusion would be unacceptable to the average householder, and it is unacceptable to me. It is a common feature of small building works performed on residential property that the cost of the work is not fully reflected by an increase in the market value of the house, and that comparatively minor deviations from specification or sound workmanship may have no direct financial effect at all. Yet the householder must surely be entitled to say that he chose to obtain from the builder a promise to produce a particular result because he wanted to make his house more comfortable, more convenient and more conformable to his own particular tastes; not because he had in mind that the work might increase the amount which he would receive if, contrary to an expectation, he thought it expedient in the future to exchange his home for cash. To say that in order to escape unscathed the builder has only to show that to the mind of the average onlooker, or the average potential buyer, the results which he has produced seem just as good as those which he had promised would make a part of the promise illusory and unbalance the bargain. In the valuable analysis contained in *Radford v. De Froberville*, [1977] 1 WLR 1262 at p. 1270 Oliver J emphasised that it was for the plaintiff to judge what performance he required in exchange for the price. The court should honour that choice. *Pacta sunt servanda*. If the appellant's argument leads to the conclusion that in all cases like the present the employer is entitled to no more than nominal damages, the average householder would say that there must be something wrong with the law.

In my opinion there would indeed be something wrong if, on the hypothesis that cost of reinstatement and the depreciation in value were the only available measures of recovery, the rejection of the former necessarily entailed the adoption of the latter; and the court might be driven to opt for the cost of reinstatement, absurd as the consequence might often be, simply to escape from the conclusion that the promisor can please himself whether or not to comply with the wishes of the promisee which, as embodied in the contract, formed part of the consideration for the price. Having taken on the job the contractor is morally as well as legally obliged to give the employer what he stipulated to obtain, and this obligation ought not to be devalued. In my opinion, however, the hypothesis is not correct. There are not two alternative measures of damage, at opposite poles, but only one: namely the loss truly suffered by the promisee. In some cases the loss cannot be fairly measured except by reference to the full cost of repairing the deficiency in performance. In others, and in particular those where the contract is designed to fulfil a purely commercial purpose, the loss will very often consist only of the monetary detriment brought about by the breach of contract. But these remedies are not exhaustive, for the law must cater for those occasions where the value of the promise to the promisee exceeds the financial enhancement of his position which full performance will secure. This excess, often referred to in the literature as the "consumer surplus" (see e.g. the valuable discussion by Harris, Ogus and Phillips, "Contract Remedies and the Consumer Surplus" (1979), 95 LQR 581) is usually incapable of precise valuation in terms of money, exactly because it represents a personal, subjective and non-monetary gain. Nevertheless, where it exists the law should recognise it and compensate the promisee if the misperformance takes it away. The lurid bathroom tiles, or the grotesque folly instanced in argument by my noble and learned friend Lord Keith of Kinkel, may be so discordant with general taste that in purely economic terms the builder may be said to do the employer a favour by failing to instal them. But this is too narrow and materialistic a view of the transaction. Neither the contractor nor the court has the right to substitute for the employer's individual expectation of performance a criterion derived from what ordinary people would regard as sensible. As my Lords have shown, the test of reasonableness plays a central part in determining the basis of recovery, and will indeed be decisive in a case such as the present when the cost of reinstatement would be wholly disproportionate to the non-monetary loss suffered by the employer. But it would be equally unreasonable to deny all recovery for such a loss. The amount may be small, and since it cannot be quantified directly there may be room for difference of opinion about what it should be. But in several fields the judges are well accustomed to putting figures to intangibles, and I see no reason why the imprecision of the exercise should be a barrier, if that is what fairness demands.

My Lords, once this is recognised, the puzzling and paradoxical feature of this case, that it seems to involve a contest of absurdities, simply falls away. There is no need to remedy the injustice of awarding too little by unjustly awarding far too much. The judgment of the trial judge acknowledges that the employer has suffered a true loss and expresses it in terms of money. Since there is no longer any issue about the amount of the award, as distinct from the principle, I would simply restore his judgment by allowing the appeal.

Appeal allowed.

QUESTION

Can you reconcile *Dolly Varden* with *Ruxley*?

ALTERNATIVE PERFORMANCE

We speak of contract damages being measured by the plaintiff's expectation. However, it is important to recognize that the relevant benchmark is not what the plaintiff *actually* expected by way of contractual performance, but rather what the plaintiff had a *right* to expect. Take the example of a plaintiff who hires a worker because she believes, based on reports and reputation, that the worker always performs superior work. If the contract only requires the worker to perform up to a standard of reasonable competence and the worker attains that standard (but does not perform to a superior standard), then there will be no breach of contract, despite the plaintiff's expectation that the worker always performs to a higher standard. Now imagine that the same worker completes the job but the standard of work is poor. Under those circumstances there is a breach of contract, but the measure of damages will not be the monetary equivalent of the difference between the poor work that the worker did and the superior work that the plaintiff expected. Rather, it will be the monetary equivalent of the difference between the poor work that the worker did and the reasonably competent work that the plaintiff had a legal right to expect pursuant to the contract.

In some contracts one party may have the option of performing its duties in more than one way. What happens if that party does not perform at all? Do we measure the non-breaching party's loss by looking to the mode of performance that the breaching party would most probably have rendered had it decided to perform? That was the argument advanced by the plaintiff in *Hamilton v. Open Window Bakery Ltd.*, [2004] 1 SCR 303, 235 DLR (4th) 193. There the plaintiff argued, at para. 14, that damages should be assessed by inquiring into "how the defendant would likely have performed his or her obligations under the contract, hypothetically, but for his or her repudiation." The Supreme Court, cleaving to the principle set out in the previous paragraph, unanimously rejected that argument. It noted, at para. 20, that an

> assessment of damages required only a determination of the minimum performance the plaintiff was entitled to under the contract, *i.e.*, the performance which was least burdensome for the defendant.

Do you think the following case is still good law after *Hamilton v. Open Window Bakery*?

Ditmars v. Ross Drug Co. Ltd.
(1971), 3 NBR (2d) 139 (QB)

DICKSON J: In this action the plaintiff claims damages in respect of his alleged wrongful dismissal from employment by the defendant. The defendant pleads that the plaintiff was not in fact dismissed but left his employment of his own accord and, alternatively, that if he was dismissed the dismissal was for cause and in any event was made with sufficient notice.

The pertinent circumstances as indicated by the evidence are as hereunder set out and I so find.

The defendant company has for some years operated a number of retail drugstores including several at the City of Fredericton. The president of the company has for the past twelve years or so been one C.H. Forbes of Fredericton who has during that period, and earlier, had supervision of the Fredericton stores. In February 1953 the defendant, through Mr. Forbes, engaged the plaintiff, a pharmacist of long standing, as manager of one of its stores which was operated in conjunction with a medical clinic, and for eighteen years, until March of the present year, he continued employment with the defendant, at various times as either manager-pharmacist or as pharmacist. Several years after 1953 he was transferred to the "clinic" store at a new location. In March 1969 he was moved to a new store located in the K-Mart shopping center. There he served as chief pharmacist until September when he was assigned also the duties of manager.

The original terms of employment were arranged between Mr. Forbes and the plaintiff orally and with little formality. He was initially paid $140 every two weeks. In January 1954 this was altered to $140 every half month. In March of that year the rate of pay was increased to $333 a month and pay for the calendar month was thenceforth paid at mid-month. Various increases were subsequently made, viz., to $355 in 1956, to $376 in 1957, to $398 in 1958, to $438 in 1960, to $546 in 1963, to $588 in 1966, and finally, under an arrangement which involved future discontinuance of certain bonus payments, to $833 as of October 1, 1969. In each year the plaintiff received a Christmas bonus, as did all other staff members. In most recent years this amounted in his case to $100. On several occasions over the years he received special "Rexall" bonuses in negligible amounts. In addition he received in each year from and including 1956, always in either March or April, a bonus. These bonuses were fixed annually by the Board of Directors of the defendant company. Those received by the plaintiff were as follows: 1956 – $150; 1957 – $275; 1958 – $600; 1959 – $900; 1960 – $1,100; 1961 – $737; 1962 – $1,378; 1963 – $1,207; 1964 – $2,953; 1965 – $2,609; 1966 – $3,000; 1967 – $3,000; 1968 – $3,000; 1969 – $2,500. The 1964 bonus included a special $500 company anniversary bonus.

The system of bonus payments to certain employees was adopted by the defendant company in 1939 as a sort of "incentive" system. Originally a sum of money calculated as a percentage of profits was paid to store managers who were relied upon to allocate the monies equitably to staff members. Some years later, because the store managers were allocating what the company management considered an inordinately disproportionate share to themselves, the arrangement was altered and the management undertook to allocate payments directly to managers, pharmacists and perhaps certain other classifications of employees. In 1962 the company for the first time treated the bonuses as earnings of the recipients and deducted income tax on such amounts at source. While in the early years the bonuses paid could undoubtedly be considered incentive payments to induce employees to increase their efforts on behalf of their employer, it is apparent that in recent years the purpose of the bonuses was essentially to adjust the recipients' wages to those generally prevailing in the trade.

Those bonuses paid in 1969 were in respect of services rendered in 1968. At a meeting of the defendant's directors in September 1969 the decision was taken, on the advice of the company's auditors and presumably prompted by tax considerations, to discontinue the bonus system and to revise the salary schedule upward "in October 1969." At the same time the decision was taken to pay a bonus for the six month period January to June 1969. This decision was reflected in a resolution adopted by the directors. Those bonuses paid as a result of such decision were not in fact paid until March or April 1970. On October 1st the wages of the plaintiff were increased from the rate of about $7,058 a year to $10,000 a year. It will be noted that the increase in the plaintiff's case about corresponded to the amount of bonus paid over each of the years 1966 to 1968 inclusive.

On February 9, 1970 the plaintiff, who is now seventy years of age, was obliged to enter hospital for an operation. He was discharged on February 23rd and undertook a period of convalescence at his home. On Sunday evening March 8th Mr. Forbes called him by phone and requested him to attend at work the next morning. The plaintiff indicated that the next day he was due to see his doctor again. He did not report for work on the morning of the 9th whereupon Mr. Forbes called him again and told him to "turn in his key and pick up his cheque." ...

I find without hesitation that the plaintiff was in fact dismissed summarily by Mr. Forbes on March 9th. ...

I also find that the dismissal did not amount to dismissal for cause such as would disentitle the plaintiff to notice of termination. Mr. Forbes in his evidence admits as much. ...

On balance in the instant case I feel that the plaintiff was entitled to three months notice. ...

I find that his loss of weekly remuneration has amounted to $500 and that he is entitled to this amount by way of damages in recompense therefore. He is also entitled to the sum of $78.20 for vacation pay for the period January 1st to March 9th 1970.

It only remains to be considered whether the plaintiff is entitled, as he claims, to further damages by reason of non-payment of any bonus given in respect of the six month period January to July 1969. The defendant, through counsel, contends that because the bonus was voluntary on the part of the company and not contemplated by the parties at the time of hiring such cannot be considered. In this regard my attention has been directed to the dictum of McRuer CJHC on a similar issue raised in the *Bardal* case ... [(1960), 24 DLR (2d) 140 (Ont. HC)]. It is my view that the circumstances here are sufficiently different that the *Bardal* decision should be distinguished. While criticizing in no way the finding in the *Bardal* case

I cannot see that where the original engagement took place many years ago and under circumstances perhaps substantially different from those prevailing today, and where a bonus system was subsequently adopted and utilized over a long period to adjust wages to prevailing levels, one can have regard only for what might have been in the contemplation of the parties at the time of hiring. Surely in a case such as this payment of the annual bonus, although never originally contemplated, has in recent years become such an integral part of this employer's wage structure that its payment must be considered virtually a matter of right on the part of those employees ordinarily accustomed to receive it.

The only equitable view the law can take in such circumstances is that it is not the original terms of engagement which must be considered but those terms under which, with the passage of time and the inevitable change in circumstances, the engagement was continued. Surely the only way in which the defendant was able over recent years to engage and to retain pharmacists at wages on basic levels which can only be considered substandard was to hold out the inducement of a sizable bonus each year, almost as a matter of guarantee, to those employees. Surely also it would be the equivalent of giving recognition to labour practices abandoned a century ago to suggest that an employer could in this day and age arbitrarily exclude a senior employee from sharing in such a bonus after having gained for its own benefit the fruits of his labour. Here it has been suggested by the defendant that the bonus was payable only to pharmacists in those of its stores which showed a profit and that because the K-mart store, where the plaintiff was employed for just over half of the period in question, failed to show a profit he would not therefore be included. Does this mean to suggest that the defendant would contend that by transferring any one of its pharmacists during the last day or so of a bonus sharing period from one of its profit making stores to a non profit making one it could thereby arbitrarily debar such employee from collecting 30% of the annual income which he had every reason to believe he would receive?

The evidence indicates to me clearly that had the plaintiff continued to be employed, as in the absence of notice he was entitled to be employed, through March and April he would have received a sizable bonus from his employer, as other employees serving in similar capacity with the company in fact did, for the first half of 1969. Denial of payment to him was an arbitrary and unjustifiable act on the part of the defendant. His loss of a bonus must be considered an item of damage directly flowing from his unlawful dismissal. There is not direct and explicit evidence as to what amount he might have expected to receive for that period by way of bonus. In the circumstances I can only base an assessment of the damages suffered by the plaintiff in this regard on the amount by which his wages were in October 1969 increased to compensate for the future non-payment of bonus. I fix such damages in the sum of $1,500.

I may only add that in fixing the earlier amount of $500 for loss of basic wage I have deliberately disregarded Mr. Forbes' admitted intention to pay full wages for April, for such intention was obviously based on an accompanying intention to deprive the plaintiff of the bonus.

The plaintiff is entitled to enter judgment against the defendant in the total sum of $2,078.20, together with the costs of the action to be taxed under the appropriate column of the tariff.

Judgment for the plaintiff.

NOTES AND QUESTIONS

1. In *Bardal v. Globe and Mail Ltd.* (1960), 24 DLR (2d) 140 (Ont. HC), McRuer CJHC refused to award compensation for loss of an expected bonus, saying, "The ... bonus was a purely voluntary gift distributed among the employees as a matter of good will" (at 146). It seems that in predicting where the plaintiff would have been had the contract been performed, the court is making an assumption about the employer's conduct. Is the assumption justified? Is Dickson J's approach in *Ditmars* more satisfactory?

2. In *Paula Lee Ltd. v. Robert Zehil*, [1983] 2 All ER 390 (QB), the court agreed that where, under the contract, the defendant had the right to select alternative methods of performance, damages should be assessed on the assumption that the defendant would have selected the most favourable. However, the court added that there is an implied contractual term that the method selected be reasonable in all of the circumstances.

3. For an argument that the minimum performance rule adopted by the Supreme Court of Canada in *Hamilton v. Open Window Bakery* is wrong, see Michael Pratt, "Damages for Breach of Contracts with Alternative Performance," in Jeff Berryman and Rick Bigwood, eds., *The Law of Remedies: New Directions in the Common Law* (Toronto: Irwin Law, 2010) chapter 4.

DEPARTURES FROM THE EXPECTANCY RULE

Non-Pecuniary Loss in Contract

S.M. Waddams, "Damages for Breach of Contract"
in *New Developments in the Law of Remedies* (1981), *Law Society of Upper Canada Special Lectures* 257, at 259-63 (footnotes omitted)

Until 1972, it was thought that no damages were available for mental distress caused by breach of contract. The case usually cited for this proposition was *Addis v. Gramophone Co. Ltd.*, [1909] AC 488 (HL (Eng.)) where the House of Lords rejected an award of damages to an employee for wrongful dismissal "in respect of the harsh and humiliating way in which he was dismissed, including, presumably, the pain he experienced by reason, it is alleged, of the imputation upon him conveyed by the manner of his dismissal (at p. 493)." In an action by a client against a solicitor, Lord Denning MR said:

> It can be foreseen that there will be injured feelings: mental distress; anger; and annoyance; but for none of these can damages be recovered. It was so held in *Groom v. Crocker* on the same lines as *Addis v. Gramophone Company, Cook v. Swinfen*, [1967] 1 WLR 455 (CA) at p. 461.

Six years later, however, in *Jarvis v. Swans Tours Ltd.*, [1973] QB 233 (CA), the same Court awarded damages against a travel agent both for the loss of the expected enjoyment of the holiday promised, and for the mental distress and disappointment caused by the breach of contract, Lord Denning MR said (at p. 237):

What is the right way of assessing damages? It has often been said that on a breach of contract damages cannot be given for mental distress. ... The courts in those days only allowed the plaintiff to recover damages if he suffered physical inconvenience. ...

I think that those limitations are out of date. In a proper case damages for mental distress can be recovered in contract, just as damages for shock can be recovered in tort. One such case is a contract for a holiday, or any other contract to provide entertainment and enjoyment. If the contracting party breaks his contract, damages can be given for the disappointment, the distress, the upset and frustration caused by the breach.

The measurement of damages poses an obvious difficulty. This, however, did not deter the English Court of Appeal. Lord Denning continued (at p. 238):

I know that it is difficult to assess in terms of money, but it is no more difficult than the assessment which the courts have to make every day in personal injury cases for loss of amenities.

The price paid for the holiday had been £63. Lord Denning assessed the damages as follows (p. 238):

Looking at the matter quite broadly, I think the damages in this case should be the sum of £125.

As one commentator said, it seems rather generous to allow the plaintiff 100% profit on his disappointment! In a subsequent case, *Jackson v. Horizon Holidays Ltd.*, [1975] 1 WLR 1468 (CA), the English Court of Appeal reaffirmed the principle established in the *Jarvis* case. In *Jackson*, the plaintiff recovered damages not only for his own distress and disappointment, but for that of his wife and children. On the question of damage assessment Lord Denning MR said (p. 1473):

Applying the principles to this case, I think that the figure of £1,100 was about right. It would, I think, have been excessive if it had been awarded only for the damages suffered by Mr. Jackson himself. But when extended to his wife and children, I do not think it is excessive. People look forward to a holiday. They expect the promises to be fulfilled. When it fails, they are greatly disappointed and upset. It is difficult to assess in terms of money; but it is the task of the judges to do the best they can.

These cases have been applied several times in the Canadian courts. Subsequent cases have shown that the principle is by no means limited to cases of lost holidays, where peace of mind might be said to be the very thing bargained for. In *Heywood v. Wellers*, [1976] QB 446 (CA), the English Court of Appeal extended the doctrine to the case of a solicitor who failed, in breach of contract, to secure protection for a client against molestation. Lord Denning indicated that earlier decisions denying recovery for mental distress in actions by clients against solicitors might have to be reconsidered, though it should be noted that mental distress on the part of a client is more likely to be foreseeable where the solicitor is employed to protect the client against molestation than in the case where the solicitor undertakes to convey land or to prosecute litigation. However, to take the latter example, it is well known that litigation causes mental stress to the parties, and it could well be held to be within the contemplation of a reasonable solicitor that, if he failed to conduct litigation properly, the client would be liable to suffer unnecessary mental distress.

In *Newell v. Canadian Pacific Airlines, Ltd.* (1976), 14 OR (2d) 752 (Co. Ct.), Borins Co. Ct. J applied the principle of the *Jarvis* case to the owner of pet dogs who were injured by breach of a contract of carriage. In *Dunn v. Disc Jockey Unlimited Co. Ltd.* (1978), 20 OR (2d) 309 (Small Claims Ct.), a Small Claims Court Judge awarded damages to compensate the plaintiff for the defendant's failure to supply entertainment at the plaintiff's wedding.

In some cases damages have been awarded for wrongful dismissal of employees. In a recent Ontario case, *Pilon v. Peugeot Canada Ltd.* (1980), 29 OR (2d) 711 (HC), an employee was wrongfully dismissed. The employee had served the company loyally for many years, and the company had led him to expect permanent security of employment. Because the plaintiff had mitigated his loss quite successfully, he was held to be entitled only to damages of about $1,000 in respect of the period for which he ought to have been given notice. Nevertheless the Ontario High Court awarded damages for mental distress of $7,500. The case is interesting and significant both in its application to employment contracts, and in its departure from the comparatively modest level of damage awards manifested by previous cases on mental distress. It has been suggested by some writers that punitive considerations are entering the calculation of damages in these cases. Another possible explanation of the *Pilon* case is that the Court intended to give compensation for the employee's expectation of permanent employment, even though unwilling to find an enforceable contract to that effect.

A related point concerns the question of injury to reputation. It was held by the House of Lords in *Addis v. Gramophone Co. Ltd.*, that damages for breach of an employment contract could not be enhanced by a claim for loss of reputation. Lord Atkinson said (at page 496):

> I can conceive nothing more objectionable and embarrassing in litigation than trying in effect an action of libel or slander as a matter of aggravation in an action for illegal dismissal, the defendant being permitted, as he must in justice be permitted, to traverse the defamatory sense, rely on privilege, or raise every point which he could raise in an independent action brought for the alleged libel or slander itself.

This conclusion has been accepted in several Canadian cases. In *Tippett v. International Typographical Union Local 226* (1976), 71 DLR (3d) 146 (BCSC), however, the British Columbia Supreme Court awarded damages against a union for injury to reputation caused to a member by wrongful expulsion.

Since the rationale for excluding damages for loss of reputation appears to be basically one of procedural convenience, it seems unwise to rely on the exclusion of such damages as a firm rule in all cases. Well established cases have awarded damages as a firm rule in all cases. Well established cases have awarded damages against banks that fail to honour a customer's cheque causing loss of reputation, and in favour of actors for loss of expected advertisement. It seems, therefore, that there is no overwhelming difficulty in compensating injury to reputation caused by a breach of contract where it appears to the court procedurally convenient to do so. It may well be that future cases will lead to an erosion of this rule, like the former rule denying damages for mental distress.

See *Vorvis v. Insurance Corporation of British Columbia*, [1989] 1 SCR 1085.

QUESTIONS AND NOTE

1. What reasons are advanced for the reluctance to award non-pecuniary damages in contract? Are these reasons consistent with the expectancy rule?

2. In what sense can damages for a so-called non-pecuniary loss be "compensatory"? You may wish to reconsider this issue after you have dealt with non-pecuniary loss in personal injury cases in chapter 5, "Damages for Personal Injury or Death."

3. In recent years the Supreme Court of Canada has made non-pecuniary damages in contract somewhat more readily available, as the following case shows.

Fidler v. Sun Life Assurance Co. of Canada
2006 SCC 30, [2006] 2 SCR 3

[For over five years the defendant insurance company wrongfully denied Fidler disability benefits to which it was eventually determined she was entitled. In addition to those benefits the trial judge awarded her $20,000 in damages for mental distress arising from breach of the insurance contract. The Court of Appeal for British Columbia upheld that and added punitive damages of $100,000.]

McLACHLIN CJ and ABELLA J (Bastarache, Binnie, LeBel, Deschamps, Fish, and Charron JJ concurring):

[27] Damages for breach of contract should, as far as money can do it, place the plaintiff in the same position as if the contract had been performed. However, at least since the 1854 decision of the Court of Exchequer Chamber in *Hadley v. Baxendale* (1854), 9 Ex. 341, 156 ER 145, at p. 151, it has been the law that these damages must be "such as may fairly and reasonably be considered either arising naturally ... from such breach of contract itself, or such as may reasonably be supposed to have been in the contemplation of both parties."

[28] Until now, damages for mental distress have not been welcome in the family of remedies spawned by this principle. The issue in this appeal is whether that remedial ostracization continues to be warranted.

[29] In *Hadley v. Baxendale*, the court explained the principle of reasonable expectation as follows:

Where two parties have made a contract which one of them has broken, the damages which the other party ought to receive in respect of such breach of contract should be such as may fairly and reasonably be considered either arising naturally, i.e., according to the usual course of things, *from such breach of contract itself, or such as may reasonably be supposed to have been in the contemplation of both parties, at the time they made the contract, as the probable result of the breach of it.* Now, if the special circumstances under which the contract was actually made were communicated by the plaintiffs to the defendants, and thus known to both parties, the damages resulting from the breach of such a contract, which they would reasonably contemplate, would be the amount of injury which would ordinarily follow from a breach of contract under these special circumstances so known and communicated. But, on the other hand, if these special circumstances were wholly unknown to the party breaking the contract, he, at the most, could only be supposed to have had in his contemplation the amount of injury which would arise generally, and in the great multitude of cases not affected by any special circumstances, from such a breach of contract. [Emphasis added; p. 151.]

[30] *Hadley v. Baxendale* makes no distinction between the types of loss that are recoverable for breach of contract. The principle of reasonable expectation is stated as a general principle. Nevertheless, subsequent cases purported to rule out damages for mental distress for breach of contract except in certain defined situations.

[31] While courts have always accepted that some non-pecuniary losses arising from breach of contract are compensable, including physical inconvenience and discomfort, they have traditionally shied away from awarding damages for mental suffering caused by the contract breach.

[32] This tradition of refusing to award damages for mental distress was launched in *Hobbs v. London and South Western Rail. Co.* (1875), LR 10 QB 111, and *Hamlin v. Great Northern Railway Co.* (1856), 1 H & N 408, 156 ER 1261 (Ex.). In 1909, in the case of *Addis v. Gramophone Co.*, [1909] AC 488, the House of Lords "cast a long shadow over the common law" when it rejected a claim for mental distress because the conduct said to cause the distress was not actionable: *Eastwood v. Magnox Electric plc*, [2004] 3 All ER 991, [2004] UKHL 35, at para. 1.

[33] To this day, *Addis* is cited for the proposition that mental distress damages are not generally recoverable for breach of contract: see *Malik v. Bank of Credit and Commerce International S.A.*, [1998] AC 20 (HL), *per* Lord Nicholls, at p. 38; *Wallace v. United Grain Growers Ltd.*, [1995] 9 WWR 153 (Man. CA), at para. 81, var'd [1997] 3 SCR 701; *Morberg v. Klassen* (1991), 49 CLR 124 (BCSC); *Taylor v. Gill*, [1991] 3 WWR 727 (Alta. QB); *Chitty on Contracts* (29th ed. 2004), vol. II, at p. 1468; and see S.M. Waddams, *The Law of Damages* (4th ed. 2004), at p. 222.

[34] In short, the foundational concepts of reasonable expectations had a ceiling: mental distress. As Bingham LJ said in *Watts v. Morrow*, [1991] 1 WLR 1421 (CA), at p. 1445:

A contract-breaker is not in general liable for any distress, frustration, anxiety, displeasure, vexation, tension or aggravation which his breach of contract may cause to the innocent party. *This rule is not, I think, founded on the assumption that such reactions are not foreseeable, which they surely are or may be, but on considerations of policy.* [Emphasis added.]

[35] A number of policy considerations have been cited in support of this restriction. One is the perceived minimal nature of mental suffering:

[A]s a matter of ordinary experience, it is evident that, while the innocent party to a contract will generally be disappointed if the defendant does not perform the contract, the innocent party's disappointment and distress are seldom so significant as to attract an award of damages on that score. (*Baltic Shipping Co. v. Dillon* (1993), 176 CLR 344 (Austl. HC), at p. 365, *per* Mason CJ.)

[36] Others have suggested that a "stiff upper lip" expectation in commercial life is the source of the prohibition. In *McGregor on Damages* (17th ed. 2003), the author explains:

The reason for the general rule is that contracts normally concern commercial matters and that mental suffering on breach is not in the contemplation of the parties as part of the business risk of the transaction. [p. 63]

This resonated in *Johnson v. Gore Wood & Co.*, [2001] 2 WLR 72 (HL), at p. 108, where Lord Cooke observed: "Contract-breaking is treated as an incident of commercial life which players in the game are expected to meet with mental fortitude."

[37] This Court's jurisprudence has followed the restrictive interpretation of *Addis*, generally requiring that a claim for compensation for mental distress be grounded in independently actionable conduct. The general rule that damages for mental distress should not be awarded for breach of contract was thus preserved: *Peso Silver Mines Ltd. (N.P.L.) v. Cropper*, [1966] SCR 673.

[38] Without resiling from the general rule that damages for mental suffering could not be awarded at contract, the courts in the 1970s acknowledged that the reasons of principle and policy for the rule did not always apply, and began to award such damages where the contract was one for pleasure, relaxation or peace of mind. The charge was led, as so many were, by Lord Denning. In *Jarvis v. Swans Tours Ltd.*, [1973] 1 All ER 71 (CA), the plaintiff had contracted with the defendant to arrange a holiday. The defendant breached the contract by providing a terrible vacation. Acknowledging but declining to follow what he referred to as the "out of date" decisions in *Hamlin* and *Hobbs*, which had sired *Addis*, Lord Denning held that mental distress damages could be recovered for certain kinds of contracts:

> In a proper case damages for mental distress can be recovered in contract, just as damages for shock can be recovered in tort. One such case is a contract for a holiday, or any other contract to provide entertainment and enjoyment. If the contracting party breaks his contract, damages can be given for the disappointment, the distress, the upset and frustration caused by the breach. [p. 74]

[39] This holding in *Jarvis* emerged from the common law chrysalis as the "peace of mind exception" to the general rule against recovery for mental distress in contract breaches. This exception was confined to contracts which had as their object the peace of mind of a contracting party. Bingham LJ in *Watts v. Morrow* stated: "Where the very object of [the] contract is to provide pleasure, relaxation, peace of mind or freedom from molestation, damages will be awarded" (p. 1445).

[40] More recently, the House of Lords in *Farley v. Skinner*, [2001] 4 All ER 801, [2001] UKHL 49, loosened the peace of mind exception so as to permit recovery of mental distress not only when pleasure, relaxation, or peace of mind is the "very object of the contract," but also when it is a "major or important object of the contract" (para. 24).

[41] The right to obtain damages for mental distress for breach of contracts that promise pleasure, relaxation or peace of mind has found wide acceptance in Canada. Mental distress damages have been awarded not only for breach of vacation contracts, but also for breaches of contracts for wedding services (*Wilson v. Sooter Studios Ltd.* (1988), 33 BCLR (2d) 241 (CA)), and for luxury chattels (*Wharton v. Tom Harris Chevrolet Oldsmobile Cadillac Ltd.* (2002), 97 BCLR (3d) 307, 2002 BCCA 78). Some courts have included disability insurance contracts: see *Warrington* and *Thompson v. Zurich Insurance Co.* (1984), 7 DLR (4th) 664 (Ont. HCJ). The Ontario Court of Appeal has endorsed contractual damages for mental distress where peace of mind is the "very essence" of the promise: see *Prinzo v. Baycrest Centre for Geriatric Care* (2002), 60 OR (3d) 474, at para. 34.

[42] In *Vorvis v. Insurance Corp. of British Columbia*, [1989] 1 SCR 1085, this Court described the line of cases awarding mental distress damages as standing for the proposition

that "in some contracts the parties may well have contemplated at the time of the contract that a breach in certain circumstances would cause a plaintiff mental distress" (p. 1102). It is thus clear that an independent actionable wrong has not always been required, contrary to Sun Life's arguments before us.

[43] The view taken by this Court in *Vorvis* that damages for mental distress in "peace of mind" contracts should be seen as an expression of the general principle of compensatory damages of *Hadley v. Baxendale*, rather than as an exception to that principle, is shared by others. In *Baltic Shipping*, Mason CJ of the High Court of Australia questioned whether one should confine mental distress claims for breach of contract to particular categories, noting:

> [T]he fundamental principle on which damages are awarded at common law is that the injured party is to be restored to the position (not merely the financial position) in which the party would have been had the actionable wrong not taken place. Add to that the fact that anxiety and injured feelings are recognized as heads of compensable damage, at least outside the realm of the law of contract. Add as well the circumstance that the general rule has been undermined by the exceptions which have been engrafted upon it. We are then left with a rule which rests on flimsy policy foundations and conceptually is at odds with the fundamental principle governing the recovery of damages, the more so now that the approaches in tort and contract are converging. [p. 362]

Similarly, Professor J.D. McCamus argues, in *The Law of Contracts* (2005), at p. 877, that once peace of mind is understood as a reflection of, or "proxy" for the reasonable contemplation of the contracting parties, "there is no compelling reason not to simply apply the foreseeability test itself." At this point, the apparent inconsistency between the general rule in *Hadley v. Baxendale* and the exception vanishes. See also: S.K. O'Byrne, "Damages for Mental Distress and Other Intangible Loss in a Breach of Contract Action" (2005), 28 *Dal. LJ* 311, at pp. 346-47, and R. Cohen and S. O'Byrne, "Cry Me a River: Recovery of Mental Distress Damages in a Breach of Contract Action—A North American Perspective" (2005), 42 *Am. Bus. LJ* 97.

[44] We conclude that damages for mental distress for breach of contract may, in appropriate cases, be awarded as an application of the principle in *Hadley v. Baxendale*: see *Vorvis*. The court should ask "what did the contract promise?" and provide compensation for those promises. The aim of compensatory damages is to restore the wronged party to the position he or she would have been in had the contract not been broken. As the Privy Council stated in *Wertheim v. Chicoutimi Pulp Co.*, [1911] AC 301, at p. 307: "[T]he party complaining should, so far as it can be done by money, be placed in the same position as he would have been in if the contract had been performed." The measure of these damages is, of course, subject to remoteness principles. There is no reason why this should not include damages for mental distress, where such damages were in the reasonable contemplation of the parties at the time the contract was made. This conclusion follows from the basic principle of compensatory contractual damages: that the parties are to be restored to the position they contracted for, whether tangible or intangible. The law's task is simply to provide the benefits contracted for, whatever their nature, if they were in the reasonable contemplation of the parties.

[45] It does not follow, however, that all mental distress associated with a breach of contract is compensable. In normal commercial contracts, the likelihood of a breach of contract

causing mental distress is not ordinarily within the reasonable contemplation of the parties. It is not unusual that a breach of contract will leave the wronged party feeling frustrated or angry. The law does not award damages for such incidental frustration. The matter is otherwise, however, when the parties enter into a contract, an object of which is to secure a particular psychological benefit. In such a case, damages arising from such mental distress should in principle be recoverable where they are established on the evidence and shown to have been within the reasonable contemplation of the parties at the time the contract was made. The basic principles of contract damages do not cease to operate merely because what is promised is an intangible, like mental security.

[46] This conclusion is supported by the policy considerations that have led the law to eschew damages for mental suffering in commercial contracts. As discussed above, this reluctance rests on two policy considerations—the minimal nature of the mental suffering and the fact that in commercial matters, mental suffering on breach is "not in the contemplation of the parties as part of the business risk of the transaction": *McGregor on Damages*, at p. 63. Neither applies to contracts where promised mental security or satisfaction is part of the risk for which the parties contracted.

[47] This does not obviate the requirement that a plaintiff prove his or her loss. The court must be satisfied: (1) that an object of the contract was to secure a psychological benefit that brings mental distress upon breach within the reasonable contemplation of the parties; and (2) that the degree of mental suffering caused by the breach was of a degree sufficient to warrant compensation. These questions require sensitivity to the particular facts of each case.

[48] While the mental distress as a consequence of breach must reasonably be contemplated by the parties to attract damages, we see no basis for requiring it to be the dominant aspect or the "very essence" of the bargain. As the House of Lords noted in *Farley*, the law of contract protects all significant parts of the bargain, not merely those that are "dominant" or "essential." Lord Steyn rejected this kind of distinction as "a matter of form and not substance" (para. 24). Lord Hutton added:

> I can see no reason in principle why, if a plaintiff who has suffered no financial loss can recover damages in some cases if there has been a breach of the principal obligation of the contract, he should be denied damages for breach of an obligation which, whilst not the principal obligation of the contract, is nevertheless one which he has made clear to the other party is of importance to him. [para. 51]

Principle suggests that as long as the promise in relation to state of mind is a part of the bargain in the reasonable contemplation of the contracting parties, mental distress damages arising from its breach are recoverable. This is to state neither more nor less than the rule in *Hadley v. Baxendale*.

[49] We conclude that the "peace of mind" class of cases should not be viewed as an exception to the general rule of the non-availability of damages for mental distress in contract law, but rather as an application of the reasonable contemplation or foreseeability principle that applies generally to determine the availability of damages for breach of contract.

[50] One further point should be added.

[51] It may be useful to clarify the use of the term "aggravated damages" in the context of damages for mental distress arising from breach of contract. "Aggravated damages," as

defined by Waddams (*The Law of Damages* (1983), at pp. 562-63), and adopted in *Vorvis*, at p. 1099, describ[e] an award that aims at compensation, but takes full account of the intangible injuries, such as distress and humiliation, that may have been caused by the defendant's insulting behaviour. As many writers have observed, the term is used ambiguously. The cases speak of two different types of "aggravated" damages.

[52] The first are true aggravated damages, which arise out of aggravating circumstances. They are not awarded under the general principle of *Hadley v. Baxendale*, but rest on a separate cause of action—usually in tort—like defamation, oppression or fraud. The idea that damages for mental distress for breach of contract may be awarded where an object of a contract was to secure a particular psychological benefit has no effect on the availability of such damages. If a plaintiff can establish mental distress as a result of the breach of an independent cause of action, then he or she may be able to recover accordingly. The award of damages in such a case arises from the separate cause of action. It does not arise out of the contractual breach itself, and it has nothing to do with contractual damages under the rule in *Hadley v. Baxendale*.

[53] The second are mental distress damages which do arise out of the contractual breach itself. These are awarded under the principles of *Hadley v. Baxendale*, as discussed above. They exist independent of any aggravating circumstances and are based completely on the parties' expectations at the time of contract formation. With respect to this category of damages, the term "aggravated damages" becomes unnecessary and, indeed, a source of possible confusion.

[54] It follows that there is only one rule by which compensatory damages *for breach of contract* should be assessed: the rule in *Hadley v. Baxendale*. The *Hadley* test unites all forms of contractual damages under a single principle. It explains why damages may be awarded where an object of the contract is to secure a psychological benefit, just as they may be awarded where an object of the contract is to secure a material one. It also explains why an extended period of notice may have been awarded upon wrongful dismissal in employment law: see *Wallace v. United Grain Growers Ltd.*, [1997] 3 SCR 701. In all cases, these results are based on what was in the reasonable contemplation of the parties at the time of contract formation. They are not true aggravated damages awards.

[55] The recognition that *Hadley v. Baxendale* is the single and controlling test for compensatory damages in cases of breach of contract therefore refutes any argument that an "independent actionable wrong" is a prerequisite for the recovery of mental distress damages. Where losses arise from the breach of contract itself, damages will be determined according to what was in the reasonable contemplation of the parties at the time of contract formation. An independent cause of action will only need to be proved where damages are of a different sort entirely: where they are being sought on the basis of aggravating circumstances that extend beyond what the parties expected when they concluded the contract.

[56] Turning to the case before us, the first question is whether an object of this disability insurance contract was to secure a psychological benefit that brought the prospect of mental distress upon breach within the reasonable contemplation of the parties at the time the contract was made? In our view it was. The bargain was that in return for the payment of premiums, the insurer would pay the plaintiff benefits in the case of disability. This is not a mere commercial contract. It is rather a contract for benefits that are both tangible, such as payments, and intangible, such as knowledge of income security in the event of disability. If

disability occurs and the insurer does not pay when it ought to have done so in accordance with the terms of the policy, the insurer has breached this reasonable expectation of security.

[57] Mental distress is an effect which parties to a disability insurance contract may reasonably contemplate may flow from a failure to pay the required benefits. The intangible benefit provided by such a contract is the prospect of continued financial security when a person's disability makes working, and therefore receiving an income, no longer possible. If benefits are unfairly denied, it may not be possible to meet ordinary living expenses. This financial pressure, on top of the loss of work and the existence of a disability, is likely to heighten an insured's anxiety and stress. Moreover, once disabled, an insured faces the difficulty of finding an economic substitute for the loss of income caused by the denial of benefits. See D. Tartaglio, "The Expectation of Peace of Mind: A Basis for Recovery of Damages for Mental Suffering Resulting from the Breach of First Party Insurance Contracts" (1983), 56 *S. Cal. L Rev.* 1345, at pp. 1365-66.

[58] People enter into disability insurance contracts to protect themselves from this very financial and emotional stress and insecurity. An unwarranted delay in receiving this protection can be extremely stressful. Ms. Fidler's damages for mental distress flowed from Sun Life's breach of contract. To accept Sun Life's argument that an independent actionable wrong is a precondition would be to sanction the "conceptual incongruity of asking a plaintiff to show *more* than just that mental distress damages were a reasonably foreseeable consequence of breach" (O'Byrne, at p. 334 (emphasis in original)).

[59] The second question is whether the mental distress here at issue was of a degree sufficient to warrant compensation. Again, we conclude that the answer is yes. The trial judge found that Sun Life's breach caused Ms. Fidler a substantial loss which she suffered over a five-year period. He found as a fact that Ms. Fidler "genuinely suffered significant additional distress and discomfort *arising out of the loss of the disability coverage*" (para. 30 (emphasis added)). This finding was amply supported in the evidence, which included extensive medical evidence documenting the stress and anxiety that Ms. Fidler experienced. He concluded that merely paying the arrears and interest did not compensate for the years Ms. Fidler was without her benefits. His award of $20,000 seeks to compensate her for the psychological consequences of Sun Life's breach, consequences which are reasonably in the contemplation of parties to a contract for personal services and benefits such as this one. We agree with the Court of Appeal's decision not to disturb it.

NOTES

1. The Supreme Court went on to consider punitive damages and held that in accordance with its reasoning in *Whiten v. Pilot Insurance* (above, chapter 1) no such damages should be awarded because the defendant had not acted in bad faith.

2. *Fidler* represents a significant doctrinal shift, one that sets Canada apart from the United Kingdom on this point. It remains to be seen whether a concept as general and open-ended as foreseeability is adequate to determine when damages for mental distress should be available for breach of contract.

3. One case mentioned in *Fidler* was *Vorvis v. Insurance Corporation of British Columbia*, [1989] 1 SCR 1085, which concerned mental distress damages in the context of unjust dismissal. The following case, decided two years after *Fidler*, takes up the question of mental

distress damages in the contract of employment. In particular, it considers whether the generally applicable notice period, which is multiplied by the wage to arrive at the amount of compensatory damages, may be lengthened by the manner in which notice of dismissal is communicated and the motivation for that dismissal. These are sometimes referred to as *Wallace* damages, after the Supreme Court's judgment in *Wallace v. United Grain Growers*, also discussed in *Fidler*.

Honda Canada Inc. v. Keays
2008 SCC 39, [2008] 2 SCR 362

[After working for Honda Canada for 14 years Kevin Keays was fired, allegedly for cause. He sued for wrongful dismissal and the trial found that there was no cause for the termination and he was entitled to a notice period of 15 months. The trial then considered additional damages dependent on the manner of dismissal and bad faith that motivated it (so-called *Wallace* damages) and increased the notice period to 24 months. In addition, the trial judge awarded punitive damages against Honda in the amount of $500,000. The Ontario Court of Appeal unanimously upheld the finding of wrongful termination as well as the regular damages and the *Wallace* damages. A majority also ordered that the quantum of punitive damages be reduced from $500,000 to $100,000. The Supreme Court considered the evidence at length and concluded that the lower courts were wrong to find that Honda had acted in bad faith. It continued.]

BASTARACHE J (McLachlin CJ and Binnie, Deschamps, Abella, Charron, and Rothstein JJ concurring):

[50] An action for wrongful dismissal is based on an implied obligation in the employment contract to give reasonable notice of an intention to terminate the relationship in the absence of just cause. Thus, if an employer fails to provide reasonable notice of termination, the employee can bring an action for breach of the implied term (*Wallace*, at para. 115). The general rule, which stems from the British case of *Addis v. Gramophone Co.*, [1909] AC 488 (HL), is that damages allocated in such actions are confined to the loss suffered as a result of the employer's failure to give proper notice and that no damages are available to the employee for the actual loss of his or her job and/or pain and distress that may have been suffered as a consequence of being terminated. This Court affirmed this rule in *Peso Silver Mines Ltd. (N.P.L.) v. Cropper*, [1966] SCR 673, at p. 684:

> [T]he damages cannot be increased by reason of the circumstances of dismissal whether in respect of the [employee's] wounded feelings or the prejudicial effect upon his reputation and chances of finding other employment.

[51] Later in *Vorvis v. Insurance Corp. of British Columbia*, [1989] 1 SCR 1085, McIntyre J stated at p. 1103:

> ... I would conclude that while aggravated damages may be awarded in actions for breach of contract in appropriate cases, this is not a case where they should be given. The rule long established in the *Addis* and *Peso Silver Mines* cases has generally been applied to deny such damages,

and the employer/employee relationship (in the absence of collective agreements which involve consideration of the modern labour law régime) has always been one where either party could terminate the contract of employment by due notice, and therefore the only damage which could arise would result from a failure to give such notice.

[52] The Court in *Vorvis* nevertheless left open the possibility of allocating aggravated damages in wrongful dismissal cases where the acts complained of were also independently actionable. McIntyre J stated at p. 1103:

> I would not wish to be taken as saying that aggravated damages could never be awarded in a case of wrongful dismissal, particularly where the acts complained of *were also independently actionable*, a factor not present here. [Emphasis added.]

[53] In *Wallace*, Iacobucci J endorsed a strict interpretation of the *Vorvis* "independently actionable wrong" approach, rejecting both an implied contractual duty of good faith and a tort of bad faith discharge. At para. 73, he said:

> Relying upon the principles enunciated in *Vorvis*, *supra*, the Court of Appeal held that any award of damages beyond compensation for breach of contract for failure to give reasonable notice of termination "must be founded on a separately actionable course of conduct" (p. 184). *Although there has been criticism of Vorvis ... this is an accurate statement of the law. ...* An employment contract is not one in which peace of mind is the very matter contracted for (see e.g. *Jarvis v. Swans Tours Ltd.*, [1973] 1 QB 233 (CA)) and so, *absent an independently actionable wrong, the foreseeability of mental distress or the fact that the parties contemplated its occurrence is of no consequence. ...* [Emphasis added.]

[54] This brings us to *Fidler*, where the Court, *per* McLachlin CJ and Abella J, concluded that it was no longer necessary that there be an independent actionable wrong before damages for mental distress can be awarded for breach of contract, whether or not it is a "peace of mind" contract. It stated at para. 49:

> We conclude that the "peace of mind" class of cases should not be viewed as an exception to the general rule of the non-availability of damages for mental distress in contract law, but rather as an application of the reasonable contemplation or foreseeability principle that applies generally to determine the availability of damages for breach of contract.

This conclusion was based on the principle, articulated in *Hadley v. Baxendale* (1854), 9 Ex. 341, 156 ER 145, that damages are recoverable for a contractual breach if the damages are "such as may fairly and reasonably be considered either arising naturally ... from such breach of contract itself, or such as may reasonably be supposed to have been in the contemplation of both parties" (p. 151). The court in *Hadley* explained the principle of reasonable expectation as follows:

> Now, if the special circumstances under which the contract was actually made were communicated by the plaintiffs to the defendants, and thus known to both parties, the damages resulting from the breach of such a contract, which they would reasonably contemplate, would be the amount of injury which would ordinarily follow from a breach of contract under these special circumstances so known and communicated. But, on the other hand, if these special circumstances were wholly unknown to the party breaking the contract, he, at the most, could only be

supposed to have had in his contemplation the amount of injury which would arise generally, and in the great multitude of cases not affected by any special circumstances, from such a breach of contract. [p. 151]

[55] Thus, in cases where parties have contemplated at the time of the contract that a breach in certain circumstances would cause the plaintiff mental distress, the plaintiff is entitled to recover (*Fidler*, at para. 42; *Vorvis*, at p. 1102). This principle was reaffirmed in para. 54 of *Fidler*, where the Court recognized that the *Hadley* rule explains the extended notice period in Wallace:

> It follows that there is only one rule by which compensatory damages for breach of contract should be assessed: the rule in *Hadley v. Baxendale*. The *Hadley* test unites all forms of contractual damages under a single principle. It explains why damages may be awarded where an object of the contract is to secure a psychological benefit, just as they may be awarded where an object of the contract is to secure a material one. It also explains why an extended period of notice may have been awarded upon wrongful dismissal in employment law: see *Wallace v. United Grain Growers Ltd.*, [1997] 3 SCR 701. In all cases, these results are based on what was in the reasonable contemplation of the parties at the time of contract formation. [Emphasis deleted.]

[56] We must therefore begin by asking what was contemplated by the parties at the time of the formation of the contract, or, as stated in para. 44 of *Fidler*: "[W]hat did the contract promise?" The contract of employment is, by its very terms, subject to cancellation on notice or subject to payment of damages in lieu of notice without regard to the ordinary psychological impact of that decision. At the time the contract was formed, there would not ordinarily be contemplation of psychological damage resulting from the dismissal since the dismissal is a clear legal possibility. The normal distress and hurt feelings resulting from dismissal are not compensable.

[57] Damages resulting from the manner of dismissal must then be available only if they result from the circumstances described in *Wallace*, namely where the employer engages in conduct during the course of dismissal that is "unfair or is in bad faith by being, for example, untruthful, misleading or unduly insensitive" (para. 98).

[58] The application of *Fidler* makes it unnecessary to pursue an extended analysis of the scope of any implied duty of good faith in an employment contract. *Fidler* provides that "as long as the promise in relation to state of mind is a part of the bargain in the reasonable contemplation of the contracting parties, mental distress damages arising from its breach are recoverable" (para. 48). In *Wallace*, the Court held employers "to an obligation of good faith and fair dealing in the manner of dismissal" (para. 95) and created the expectation that, in the course of dismissal, employers would be "candid, reasonable, honest and forthright with their employees" (para. 98). At least since that time, then, there has been expectation by both parties to the contract that employers will act in good faith in the manner of dismissal. Failure to do so can lead to foreseeable, compensable damages. As aforementioned, this Court recognized as much in *Fidler* itself, where we noted that the principle in *Hadley* "explains why an extended period of notice may have been awarded upon wrongful dismissal in employment law" (para. 54).

[59] To be perfectly clear, I will conclude this analysis of our jurisprudence by saying that there is no reason to retain the distinction between "true aggravated damages" resulting

from a separate cause of action and moral damages resulting from conduct in the manner of termination. Damages attributable to conduct in the manner of dismissal are always to be awarded under the *Hadley* principle. Moreover, in cases where damages are awarded, no extension of the notice period is to be used to determine the proper amount to be paid. The amount is to be fixed according to the same principles and in the same way as in all other cases dealing with moral damages. Thus, if the employee can prove that the manner of dismissal caused mental distress that was in the contemplation of the parties, those damages will be awarded not through an arbitrary extension of the notice period, but through an award that reflects the actual damages. Examples of conduct in dismissal resulting in compensable damages are attacking the employee's reputation by declarations made at the time of dismissal, misrepresentation regarding the reason for the decision, or dismissal meant to deprive the employee of a pension benefit or other right, permanent status for instance (see also the examples in *Wallace*, at paras. 99-100).

[60] In light of the above discussion, the confusion between damages for conduct in dismissal and punitive damages is unsurprising, given that both have to do with conduct at the time of dismissal. It is important to emphasize here that the fundamental nature of damages for conduct in dismissal must be retained. This means that the award of damages for psychological injury in this context is still intended to be compensatory. The Court must avoid the pitfall of double-compensation or double-punishment that has been exemplified by this case.

3.2.2.2 Application of the Revised Test to This Case

[61] I have reviewed the major overriding and palpable errors which undermine the trial judge's finding that Honda acted in "bad faith" when terminating Keays. There was, in my opinion, no such breach and no justification for an award of damages for conduct in dismissal.

NOTES

1. The majority also overturned the award of punitive damages. It held that there was no independent actionable wrong and no bad faith.

2. LeBel J delivered a dissent in which Fish J concurred. Like the majority, he would not have awarded punitive damages. He differed from the majority in thinking that Honda had acted in bad faith. This justified the *Wallace* damages that the lower courts had awarded—that is, lengthening the notice period from 15 to 24 months and increasing damages accordingly. For an argument that the finding of bad faith was justified and that the damages awarded by the majority were insufficient to deter discriminatory employers, see Dianne Pothier, "Wrongful Termination Claims in the Supreme Court of Canada: Coming Up Short" (2011) 34 *Dal LJ*.

Actions for Non-Payment of Money

A.I. Ogus, *The Law of Damages*
(London: Butterworths, 1973), at 304-7 (footnotes omitted)

3 Actions for Non-Payment of Money

The second rule limits the recovery of the expectation interest in actions for the non-payment of money. The starting point is the basic proposition that in an action for the non-payment of a debt at common law a plaintiff can recover neither interest nor damages for the detention of the debt. In fact the rule has been considerably undermined by exceptions both statutory and judicial. It is proposed first to give a brief historical introduction to the rule, then to examine its scope, finally to consider its rationale.

(a) History

The general disinclination to favour the creditor in these actions was part of a general attack on usury, and in the medieval period recovery of the expectation interest was strictly barred. But the specific rule that in an action for the non-payment of money only nominal damages might be recovered appears to date only from the eighteenth century as a result of the complex feud between the old action for debt and the ever-expanding action of assumpsit. In the area of commerce the rule was clearly of great inconvenience and could not survive. As has already been seen, the law by gradual steps overcame its inhibitions sufficiently to permit the award of interest, but since the sixteenth century all claims for compensation beyond this have failed. The ghost of usury appears still to loom in the distance, though in a recent case the Court of Appeal appeared willing to rid themselves of it.

(b) Exceptions to Rule

If, in theory, the principle still prevails that damages for the expectation interest may not be awarded in cases where the defendant fails to pay a sum due, its impact has been substantially reduced by exceptions.

(i) Breach of a Different Obligation

If the creditor is able to characterize his action as one for the breach of another contractual obligation the rule will not apply. In *Trans Trust S.P.R.L. v. Danubian Trading*, [1952] 2 QB 297 (CA).

> Ds contracted to buy steel from Ps. For the purposes of payment, Ds also agreed to procure credit in favour of X from whom Ps were to buy the steel. Ds failed to procure the opening of credit and repudiated the contract. Ds argued that their breach was a failure to pay money and damages beyond interest could not be awarded. But it was held that substantial damages could be awarded: Ds were in breach not of an obligation to pay money, but of an obligation to open credit.

Similarly expectation interest damages can be awarded for failure to maintain or honour the plaintiff's credit, and for breach of a promise to lend the plaintiff money. A purchaser of goods who has repudiated the contract may be sued for damages in an action for non-acceptance of the goods. An improperly dismissed employee will recover his lost earnings by claiming in an action for wrongful dismissal that the employer refused to accept performance. There are special statutory provisions governing actions for dishonouring bills of exchange and promissory notes.

(ii) Interest

Interest may be recovered *as of right* where the parties have expressly or impliedly agreed that it should be paid, or *at the court's discretion* under section 3(1) of the *Law Reform (Miscellaneous Provisions) Act 1934.*

(iii) Exceptional Cases

In the *Trans Trust* case two members of the Court of Appeal *obiter* questioned whether the rule that prohibited the award of substantial damages for the non-payment of a debt was an absolute one. Denning LJ did not think "that the law has ever taken up such a rigid standpoint." Remoteness is "the only real ground on which damages can be refused for non-payment of money (at p. 306)." Romer LJ agrees: he was not "as at present advised, prepared to subscribe to the view that in no case can damages be recovered for non-payment of money (at p. 307)." The door has been opened. It remains to be seen whether a judge will be prepared to venture through it.

(c) Rationale

The alleged reasons for the existence of the rule tend to be even more unsatisfactory than those adduced for the rule in *Bain v. Fothergill.*

(i)   It has been argued that it is merely an illustration of the remoteness doctrine. This ignores the historical background to the rule and the plain language of the judges applying it. The rationale of the rule certainly has deeper foundations than this.

(ii)   One writer attributes it to "the policy of having a measure of damages of easy and certain application." It may be conceded that this is indeed the chief historical reason for the rule. But the desire to facilitate procedure should not by itself be a ground for refusing to award damages for provable losses, and is, in any case, hardly appropriate in modern conditions where the doctrine of certainty exists to deal with this same difficulty.

(iii) Doubtless, at one time the rule was an effective weapon against usury, but today more sophisticated armoury exists.

(iv)   All that remains is the disturbing fact that if the plaintiff is able to characterize his action in terms of the breach of a different obligation his award is not so limited. The method of pleading a case is an improper criterion for any rule of substantive law. The forms of action should not continue to rule us from the grave.

Hungerfords v. Walker
(1989), 171 CLR 125 (HC (Aust.)) (footnotes omitted)

[The plaintiffs operated an electrical appliance rental business, initially as a partnership, and, later, as an incorporated company. The defendant was an accountant engaged by the plaintiffs to complete both personal and partnership accounts. The defendant made an error in calculating depreciation allowances, which resulted in the plaintiffs' income being over-stated and thus the tax paid on the income. The same mistake was repeated in subsequent years until it was realized by a new accountant who had been engaged by the plaintiffs to advise on incorporation. The plaintiff was able to amend its tax returns for the current year and to recover the overpaid tax from the Commission of Taxation. However, the plaintiffs were statute barred from reclaiming overpaid tax for any of the preceding years. The plain-tiffs then brought a suit against the defendant for negligence. In that claim, in addition to recovering the actual overpaid taxes, the plaintiff claimed a sum for the loss of the use of the overpaid taxes. The latter claim was made as an alternative to claiming compound interest on the overpaid taxes. The trial judge held that the law did not allow interest to be awarded as damages, but did allow the alternative claim for loss of use of the money. The trial judge further held that the plaintiffs would have put most of the overpaid money back into the partnership business and that they could have produced a profit fairly assessed at a rate of 10 percent per annum on the money. The plaintiffs appealed, and the defendant cross-appealed to the Full Court of the Supreme Court of South Australia. The court affirmed the trial judge's decision but increased the rate of interest (20 percent) on the basis that the funds would have been used to repay loans bearing a higher interest or invested back in the busi-ness to earn profits at a higher rate of interest. The accountants appealed to the High Court.]

MASON CJ and WILSON J: This appeal raises the important question whether, at common law, a court, when awarding damages for breach of contract or negligence, can include in its award damages, assessed by reference to appropriate interest rates, for the loss of the use of money which the plaintiff paid away and lost as a direct consequence of the defendant's breach of contract or negligence. There is the further question whether the presence of s. 30c of the *Supreme Court Act 1935* (SA) ("the Act") inhibits any development of common law principles which would favour an affirmative answer to the primary question. The ap-pellants would be entitled to an award of interest under s. 30c in the absence of good cause shown. However, it has not been suggested that the relevant component of the damages awarded to the appellant could be accommodated within the ambit of the power conferred by the section: but *cf. Wheeler v. Page* [(1982), 31 SASR 1, at 5 (SC (*in banco*))].

The appellants appeal to this Court against, among other things, the award of damages for the loss of the use of money assessed by reference to an annual compound interest rate of 20 per cent. The respondents seek to cross-appeal against the ruling that some of the overpaid amounts would not have been used in the business and the consequential reduc-tion in the award of damages for the loss of the use of money. It is convenient to begin with the appellants' contentions and then to turn to the cross-appeal.

Before us Mr. Bennett QC, for the appellants, submitted that, where a purely financial loss is inflicted, damages caused by the consequential unavailability of money should not be awarded. This, he asserted, is the first time that a court has awarded damages for loss of use of money caused by a negligently inflicted loss of money. Mr. Bennett also argued that, because the legislature has intervened by enacting s. 30c, interest should not be awarded otherwise than in accordance with that provision.

It is certainly true to say that the common law hitherto has turned its face against awarding interest as compensation for the late payment of damages. It has been considered that the decision of the House of Lords in *London, Chatham & Dover Railway Co. v. South Eastern Railway Co.* [[1893] AC 429 (HL (Eng.))] necessarily denied the entitlement of a plaintiff to such an award. What is meant by the expression "late payment of damages" in this context and whether the respondents' claim for loss of the use of money in this case is for the late payment of damages are central questions for decision.

This is not the occasion to trace the tortuous path by which the common law of England arrived at the position that interest will not be awarded for the late payment of damages: see *Tehno-Impex v. Gebr. Van Weelde* [[1981] QB 648, at 660 *et seq.* (CA)]. However, it is necessary to mention, if only very briefly, the common law attitude towards interest before *Lord Tenterden's Act 1833* (UK) made statutory provision for the award of interest in some cases. In mediaeval times religious hostility to usury meant that the law gave little encouragement to the recovery of interest directly or by way of damages for late payment. As late as 1807 the reporter of *De Havilland v. Bowerbank* [(1807), 1 Camp. 50, at 52; 170 ER 872, at 873 (NP)] commented:

> It would fortunately be a very difficult matter to fix upon another point of English law, on which the authorities are so little in harmony with each other.

Lord Tenterden's decision in *Page v. Newman* [(1829), 9 B & C 378; 109 ER 140 (KB)] confirmed the traditional rule that a creditor was not entitled to interest, in the absence of agreement, when the borrower failed to repay money lent on the due date. Lord Tenterden CJ said [at 381 (B & C); 141 (ER)] it would be "productive of great inconvenience" if a rule were adopted that "interest is due wherever the debt has been wrongfully withheld after the plaintiff has endeavoured to obtain payment of it" because "it might frequently be made a question at Nisi Prius whether proper means had been used to obtain payment of the debt, and such as the party ought to have used." His Lordship referred to "the long-established rule" against awards of interest in such cases.

Page v. Newman led to the enactment of *Lord Tenterden's Act* in 1833. Sections 28 and 29 of that Act qualified the common law by granting the court a discretion to award interest on "debts or sums certain" in certain torts and in claims upon policies of insurance.

It was against this background that the House of Lords decided in *London, Chatham & Dover Railway Co.* that the plaintiff could not recover an award of interest on a provisional amount payable under an agreement because there was no debt or sum certain payable by virtue of a written instrument at a certain time within the meaning of s. 28 of the Act of 1833. Their Lordships also decided that the plaintiff could not recover interest by way of damages for detention of the debt, the law on that subject, unsatisfactory though it was, having been too long settled to permit of departure. Although Lord Herschell LC considered that the ground assigned in *Page v. Newman* was not "a satisfactory reason for excluding altogether any claim to interest by way of damages in cases where justice requires that it should be awarded," he thought that the course of authority and the fact of limited legislative intervention precluded judicial review of the common law [[1893] AC 429, at 440 (HL

(Eng.))]. His Lordship reached this conclusion reluctantly because he thought that the rule should be:

> [W]hen money is owing from one party to another and that other is driven to have recourse to legal proceedings in order to recover the amount due to him, the party who is wrongfully withholding the money from the other ought not in justice to benefit by having that money in his possession and enjoying the use of it, when the money ought to be in the possession of the other party who is entitled to its use [at 437].

The decision stands for the proposition that in England, at common law, in the absence of any agreement or statutory provision for the payment of interest, a court has no power to award interest, simple or compound, as compensation for the late payment of a debt: *President of India v. La Pintada Compania Navigacion S.A.* [[1985] AC 104, at 115 (HL (Eng.))]. For a long time the decision was regarded as applying to any form of damages, including special as well as general damages. ...

It was not until 1952 that it was recognized that loss due to the late payment of a debt or damages might be recoverable in accordance with *Hadley v. Baxendale*. It was then acknowledged that loss of this kind might constitute special damage within the contemplation of the parties under the second limb in *Hadley v. Baxendale*. In *Trans Trust S.P.R.L. v. Danubian Trading Co. Ltd.* [[1952] 2 QB 297 (CA)] the Court of Appeal recognized that a failure to pay money would give rise to an entitlement to damages for breach of contract if a special loss was foreseeable at the time of the contract as the consequence of non-payment. Denning LJ asserted that the ground on which the law refused interest for late payment of a debt or damages was that interest was " 'generally presumed not to be within the contemplation of the parties': see Bullen & Leake, 3rd ed., at p. 51" [at 306]. Denning LJ went on to say: "That is, I think, the only real ground on which damages can be refused for non-payment of money. It is because the consequences are as a rule too remote."

Subsequently in *Wadsworth v. Lydall* [[1981] 1 WLR 598 (CA)] the Court of Appeal, applying what had been said in *Trans Trust S.P.R.L.*, held that a plaintiff was entitled to recover as special damages the loss suffered by him as the result of the failure of the defendant to pay a sum of £10,000 due to him under a contract, the circumstances being that the defendant ought to have known that the plaintiff would need to acquire another farm or smallholding, using the £10,000 payable under the contract for the purpose, and that if the £10,000 was not paid the plaintiff would be compelled to incur expense in arranging alternative finance and paying interest. The Court of Appeal distinguished *London, Chatham & Dover Railway Co.* on the ground that it was concerned with the first, but not the second, limb in *Hadley v. Baxendale*. Brightman LJ said [at 603] of the action in *London, Chatham & Dover Railway Co.*:

> The action was an action for an account. The House was concerned only with a claim for interest by way of general damages. If a plaintiff pleads and can prove that he has suffered special damage as a result of the defendant's failure to perform his obligation under a contract, and such damage is not too remote on the principle of *Hadley v. Baxendale* [(1854), 9 Ex. 341], I can see no logical reason why such special damage should be irrecoverable merely because the obligation on which the defendant defaulted was an obligation to pay money and not some other type of obligation.

In *La Pintada* [[1985] AC 104, at 127 (HL (Eng.))] the House of Lords approved *Wadsworth v. Lydall* and the distinction drawn by Brightman LJ between that case and *London, Chatham & Dover Railway Co.* The House of Lords, though acknowledging the injustices caused by the old common law rule as confirmed by its 1893 decision, concluded that it could not depart from that decision. This was because Parliament had chosen to remedy some of those injustices in certain circumstances and because the rule had been judicially qualified by limiting its application to claims for general, as opposed to special, damages [at 129-31].

In confining the authority of its earlier decision, the House of Lords opened the way to a logical and principled development of the law of damages on the topic now under consideration. The means by which this initiative was achieved—asserting that the 1893 decision was concerned only with the first limb in *Hadley v. Baxendale* [(1854), 9 Ex. 341; 156 ER 145]—enabled the House of Lords to escape from the rigours of *stare decisis*. *London, Chatham & Dover Railway Co.* [[1893] AC 429 (HL (Eng.))] does not confront us quite so starkly, but *Norwest Refrigeration* [(1984), 157 CLR 149] presents a similar problem, with which we shall deal in due course.

However, for the moment, it is necessary to examine the distinction made by the House of Lords along with the consequence that the distinction entails. In the first place, the distinction is a gloss on *London, Chatham & Dover Railway Co.* which proceeded on the broad footing that interest by way of damages was too remote, without discriminating between the refinements of *Hadley v. Baxendale* of which no mention was made. Secondly, and more importantly, the circumstances which are now held to attract the second limb in *Hadley v. Baxendale*—take, for example, those in *Wadsworth v. Lydall*—are very often circumstances which in any event would attract the first limb. If a plaintiff sustains loss or damage in relation to money which he has paid out or foregone, why is he not entitled to recover damages for loss of the use of money—when the loss or damage sustained was reasonably foreseeable as liable to result from the relevant breach of contract or tort? After all, that is the fundamental rule governing the recovery of damages, according to the first limb in *Hadley v. Baxendale Ltd.* (see *Victoria Laundry (Windsor) Ltd. v. Newman Industries Ltd.* [[1949] 2 KB 528, at 539 (CA)]) and, subject to proximity, in negligence. The object of the second limb in *Hadley v. Baxendale* was to include loss arising from special circumstances of which the defendant had actual knowledge when that loss does not fall within the first limb because it does not arise from "the ordinary course of things" of which the defendant has imputed knowledge: see *Victoria Laundry* [*supra*, at 539]. To allow a plaintiff to recover special, but not general, damages, is illogical, subverts the second limb in *Hadley v. Baxendale* from its intended purpose and introduces a new element into the general measure of damages for negligence.

If the distinction between the two limbs is to be rigorously applied in claims for damages for loss of the use of money, a plaintiff who actually incurs the expense of interest on borrowed money to replace money paid away or withheld from him will be entitled to recover that cost, so long as the defendant was aware of the special circumstances, but not otherwise. The expense must fall within the second limb of *Hadley v. Baxendale* in order to be compensable. It cannot fall within the first limb because the defendant cannot be fixed with imputed knowledge of the plaintiff's financial situation and of his need to incur expense by borrowing money. Furthermore, a plaintiff who is not compelled to borrow money by way of replacement of money paid away or withheld will not be entitled to recover for the opportunity lost to him, i.e., lost opportunity to invest or to maintain an investment. This is because in the ordinary course of things the defendant appreciates that the plaintiff will replace from his other resources the money lost, so that opportunity cost falls more readily within the first limb of *Hadley v. Baxendale*. How can this difference in treatment be justified? In each case the plaintiff sustains a loss and, *ex hypothesi*, the defendant's wrongful act or omission is the effective cause of that loss, at least if we put *Liesbosch, Dredger* [[1933] AC 449 (HL (Eng.))] to one side.

In Canada it seems that a plaintiff is entitled to recover interest charges actually incurred on money borrowed on the defendant's default or if the plaintiff owes money to anyone equal to the amount of the claim and is paying interest on it: Waddams, *Law of Damages* (Aurora, ON: Canada Law Book, 1983), §833; and see *Atlantic Salvage Ltd. v. City of Halifax* [(1978), 94 DLR (3d) 513 (NS SCAD)] where the plaintiff's claim for interest succeeded on the ground that it had been indebted to its bank for a sum exceeding the amount of the claim throughout the period. But it has been acknowledged that it is anomalous to allow interest only to a plaintiff who has an overdraft: *Municipal Spraying & Contracting Ltd. v. J. Harris & Sons Ltd.* [(1979), 35 NSR (2d) 237 (SCTD)]. If a justification exists for the difference in treatment, it must have its genesis in a policy that encourages recovery of expense actually incurred and discourages or denies recovery of opportunity cost. Yet it is not easy to see any cogent reason for the adoption of such a policy; the award of compensation for opportunity cost would not expose the courts to insuperable problems in fact-finding.

Indeed, such a policy would be at odds with the fundamental principle that a plaintiff is entitled to *restitutio in integrum*. According to that principle, the plaintiff is entitled to full compensation for the loss which he sustains in consequence of the defendant's wrong, subject to the rules as to remoteness of damage and to the plaintiff's duty to mitigate his loss. In principle he should be awarded the compensation which would restore him to the position he would have been in but for the defendant's breach of contract or negligence. Judged from a commercial viewpoint, the plaintiff sustains an economic loss if his damages are not paid promptly, just as he sustains such a loss when his debt is not paid on the due date. The loss may arise in the form of the investment cost of being deprived of money which could have been invested at interest or used to reduce an existing indebtedness. Or the loss may arise in the form of the borrowing cost, *i.e.*, interest payable on borrowed money or interest foregone because an existing investment is realized or reduced.

The requirement of foreseeability is no obstacle to the award of damages, calculated by reference to the appropriate interest rates, for loss of the use of money. Opportunity cost, more so than incurred expense, is a plainly foreseeable loss because, according to common understanding, it represents the market price of obtaining money. But, even in the case of incurred expense, it is at least strongly arguable that a plaintiff's loss or damage represented by this expense is not too remote on the score of foreseeability. In truth, it is an expense which represents loss or damage flowing naturally and directly from the defendant's wrongful act or omission, particularly when that act or omission results in the withholding of money from a plaintiff or causes the plaintiff to pay away money.

The truism that there is no cause of action for the late payment of damages is sometimes proffered as a justification for not compensating loss by way of incurred expense and opportunity cost for money paid away or withheld. True, a defendant commits no tort by contesting the plaintiff's claim for damages or for that matter by contesting the plaintiff's claim to recover a debt. But the problem is not concerned with finding a cause of action; rather it is a problem of defining the limits of recoverable damages for an established cause of action. The argument for denying the recovery of incurred expense and opportunity cost in the sense already discussed rests on the more limited proposition that a plaintiff is not entitled to compensation for late payment of damages otherwise than in the form of interest in accordance with the relevant statutory provisions. As a matter of logic and principle, as well as commercial reality, this proposition has little to commend it in the circumstances of the present case.

Incurred expense and opportunity cost arising from paying money away or the withholding of moneys due to the defendant's wrong are something more than the late payment of damages. They are pecuniary losses suffered by the plaintiff as a result of the defendant's wrong and therefore constitute an integral element of the loss for which he is entitled to be compensated by an award of damages. Fitzgerald J made this very point in *Sanrod v. Dainford* [(1984), 54 ALR 179, at 191 (FCA)] when he said:

> [W]hatever may be the position otherwise in respect of damages under the *[Trade Practices] Act*, I can myself perceive no difficulty in accepting that, when money is paid in consequence of misleading conduct, the loss suffered by that conduct includes not only the money paid but also the cost of borrowing that money or the loss from its investment, as the case may be: *cf. Frith v. Gold Coast Mineral Springs Pty. Ltd.* [(1983), ATPR 40-339]; aff'd. [(1983), 47 ALR 547 (FCA)]. Interest awarded as a component of damages in such circumstances is not for loss of the use of the money awarded as damages, but for loss of the use of the money paid over in consequence of the misleading conduct and is directly related to the misleading conduct.

Notwithstanding that these remarks were made in relation to the payment of money in consequence of misleading conduct, the underlying principle is one of wider application. The point is that the loss of the use of the money paid away is so directly related to the wrong that the loss cannot be classified simply as due to the late payment of damages: see also *General Securities Ltd. v. Don Ingram Ltd.* [[1940] SCR 670] (the plaintiff recovered a business loss incurred as a borrower in consequence of the lender's breach of obligation to advance the money) and *Pelletier v. Pe Ben Industries Co. Ltd.* [[1976] 6 WWR 640 (BCSC)] (damages awarded on a contract to purchase a truck in consequence of the defendant's wrongful dismissal of the plaintiff from his employment). These cases proceed on the proposition that the cost of borrowing money to avoid a loss caused by a breach of contract is recoverable and not too remote. ...

Once it is accepted that the cost of borrowing money to replace money paid away or withheld is not too remote, it is pointless to insist on a distinction between the award of damages for loss of the use of money in the case of a liquidated claim and the award of such interest in an unliquidated claim. The award of damages in accordance with *Hadley v. Baxendale* is unrelated to, and free from, any requirement that there is, or should be, any "wrongful" withholding of money, be it a debt or damages.

There can be no objection to the recovery of the cost of borrowing as consequential loss by reference to the notion that the loss is one which arises after the plaintiff's cause of action accrues or becomes complete. Such a notion is by no means an absolute bar to recovery for loss arising after that date. It was acknowledged by this Court in *Johnson v. Perez* [(1988), 166 CLR 351] that the rule that damages for breach of contract or tort are assessed at the date of breach or when the cause of action arises is not universal. *Wenham v. Ella* [(1972),

127 CLR 454] is a striking illustration of a plaintiff recovering loss which accrued after his cause of action became complete. There the plaintiff recovered damages for the loss of income he sustained by reason of the defendant's breach of contract for refusing to transfer income-producing land pursuant to the contract between the parties, the loss being within the contemplation of the parties [at 461, 463, 467, and 472]. In that case the Court took account of the fact that the plaintiff had paid the entire consideration payable by him as purchaser and of the fact that the defendant had had the use of the plaintiff's money. Menzies J noted [at 463]:

> In the interval between the breach and judgment, the purchaser would be out of pocket, and the vendor in pocket, by the amount of the return from the land.

The significance of the decision is that by reason of the breach the plaintiff lost income after breach and damages were awarded for that head of loss. Gibbs J observed that it was immaterial whether the damages came within the first or second limb of *Hadley v. Baxendale* "or indeed whether both are applicable" [(1972), 127 CLR 454, at 472]. There was no suggestion that the plaintiff's loss was to be attributed to the late payment of damages.

We turn now to examine the distinction made in *Lips Maritime* [[1988] AC 395 (HL (Eng.))] between a claim for interest on a debt and a claim for interest on damages. Properly understood the plaintiff's claim in *Lips Maritime* … was for interest by way of damages for the late payment of damages and as such the claim failed. The demurrage clause liquidated exchange losses according to a stipulated formula. The plaintiff sought interest on the unpaid liquidated losses. A claim for interest on unpaid liquidated losses or damages is of necessity a claim for late payment of damages and one which goes beyond the measure of damages agreed between the parties. Accordingly *Lips Maritime* … is not inconsistent with the award of damages assessed by reference to appropriate interest rates as a component or head of loss in the assessment of a plaintiff's damages.

Norwest Refrigeration [(1984), 157 CLR 149] presents a different problem. The remarks in the joint judgment about the non-award of damages by way of interest at common law were obiter. The plaintiff's claim for interest was based on the statutory provisions, which had been amended during the course of the litigation, not on the common law. Moreover, no reference was made in argument to *Trans Trust* or to *Wadsworth v. Lydall* and the decision antedated *La Pintada* and *Lips Maritime*. Furthermore, *Norwest Refrigeration* did not involve a claim for damages for the loss of the use of money paid away or withheld as a result of breach of contract or negligence. For these reasons it is not an obstacle to an award of interest in favour of the respondents. …

Accordingly, we would vary the grant of special leave to appeal by confining it in the manner indicated, dismiss the appeal, and refuse special leave to cross-appeal.

THE RELIANCE INTEREST

Introduction

The general rule of damages for breach of contract is that the plaintiff ought to be placed, so far as money can place the plaintiff, where he or she would have been had the contract been performed. As we have seen, the main element of an award based on this rule will be damages to compensate for the loss of the value of the bargain, the plaintiff's expectation interest. However, damage to the plaintiff's other interests may be compensated, either in addition to or instead of the expectation interest. The following material explores, although very briefly, some of the circumstances in which this may occur.

As an introduction to this material, consider once again the *McLean* case in this chapter. Review the losses claimed by the plaintiff and classify them as, for example, "expectation" or "reliance." In his note on the case, Professor Baer suggests that the court in *McLean* put the plaintiff to an election "to either prove damages in the form of lost revenue *or* to claim a return of the purchase price." How would you characterize this election in terms of the interests that it protects? As you review the material that follows, consider what factors might justify giving the plaintiff such an election. A further issue arising from this "election" is whether to permit a claim for damages based on loss of revenue *as well as* a claim based on return of the purchase price would be to award double compensation. Can you characterize this issue in the light of the plaintiff's interests that are being compensated? As you review the following material, consider how a decision to compensate some interest of the plaintiff *in addition* to the expectation interest might lead to double compensation and how such a result might be avoided.

A.I. Ogus, *The Law of Damages*
(London: Butterworths, 1973), at 346-54 (footnotes omitted)

An inquiry into the role of the reliance interest in the English law of damages involves entering into a murky area where only a few outlines are visible and where much remains uncharted. For some considerable time judicial discussion of the question was non-existent. So-called damages for "wasted expenses" were often awarded but more often instinctively than in accordance with established legal principles. In the United States of America the subject has been extensively treated. It is only within recent years that it has received academic and judicial attention in this country.

The basic notion of the reliance interest is a simple one: in relying on the defendant's promise to perform, the plaintiff has acted to his own detriment usually by the outlay of some money. While awaiting completion of a conveyance the purchaser of a house may have purchased furniture or fittings. A manufacturer, while awaiting delivery of special parts, may have commenced work on a machine, or engaged special labour forces. Should the defendant fail to perform, these expenses will be wasted.

It is important to appreciate that damages for the plaintiff's reliance interest may be awarded for two different purposes: (i) they may be awarded as an *alternative* to damages for loss of the expectation interest; or (ii) they may be awarded to *complement* damages for the loss of the expectation interest. In (i) the object of compensation will not be, as with the expectation interest, to put the plaintiff in the position he would have been in if the defendant had satisfactorily performed his contract. Instead it will be to put him in the position he would have been *if he had not entered into the contract*. It is the basic compensatory principle of actions in tort: *restitutio in integrum*. As measure of damages in a contractual situation it is a double-edged sword, for it can operate either to the advantage or to the disadvantage of the plaintiff. If he has made a profitable bargain, then should it replace compensation based on the expectation interest, it will prevent him reaping the benefits. If, on the other hand, he has made a bad bargain, as against expectation interest damages, it will protect him against the consequences of his folly. It is necessary to add, however, that if the law considers the latter consequence to be undesirable—if, in short, it seeks never to put the plaintiff in a better position than he would have been in if the contract had been performed—then it will place a limit on recovery of the reliance interest, such that a plaintiff may never recover more than the extent of this expectation interest. As will appear, it is not yet clear whether English law imposes this limitation, and as a result the policy considerations behind the award of the reliance interest remain largely unexplored. As regards (ii) where the reliance interest is used to complement the expectation interest, there can be no doubt that the object of the award is the more effectively to put the plaintiff in the position he would have been in if the contract had been performed. It deals, in such circumstances, with losses which on another view might well have entered into the calculation of the expectation interest itself. Where the reliance interest is used for this purpose care must be taken that the plaintiff does not benefit from double recovery.

2 Reliance Interest as Alternative to Expectation Interest

It is proposed first to consider the scope and recoverability of the reliance interest as an alternative to the expectation interest.

(a) Losses Other Than Expenses

In most cases the loss for compensation of which the defendant is sued comprises money spent by the plaintiff in reliance on the defendant's promise to perform. But the remedy will extend to cases where he assigns some valuable property to or performs some valuable service for another. In *Hydraulic Engineering Co. v. McHaffie* (1878), 4 ABD 670 (CA),

> Ps contracted to deliver to X a piece of machinery part of which was to be manufactured by Ds. Ds failed to deliver on time. Ps lost the contract with X. They recovered damages *inter alia* for the cost of making other parts of the machinery and also for painting it.

(b) Overlap with Restitution Interest

The plaintiff usually changes his position by paying money to or conferring something of value on a third party. Yet during the currency of the contract he is, of course, also likely to confer something of value on the defendant himself. This, though it may be regarded as part of the reliance interest, is treated under the restitution interest.

(c) Time and Purpose of Expenses

The most important category of loss which directly comes within the ambit of the reliance interest covers those expenses which were necessarily incurred by the plaintiff in performance of his part of the contract and the payments of which took place during the currency of the contract. It is sometimes said that in order to recover compensation for the reliance interest, the doctrine of remoteness must be satisfied. In the ordinary case of expenses necessary for performance (what have conveniently been described as constituting the "essential reliance interest") the requirement will always be satisfied. A defendant should always foresee what the plaintiff *must* do under the contract. Recovery of other losses is less certain.

(i) Incidental Expenses

The expenses incurred may be incidental to, rather than necessary for, performance of the contract: for example, a purchaser of land acquiring stock or furniture. The principle emerging clearly from the case-law is that compensation for these wasted expenses is recoverable provided they were reasonably within the contemplation of the defendant at the time of making the contract. This is well illustrated by *Lloyd v. Stanbury*, [1971] 1 WLR 535 (Ch.).

> D agreed to sell to P a plot of land, knowing that P intended to use it for poultry farming. It was a term of the contract that D could occupy a caravan to be brought onto the land by P until alternative accommodation was ready. In anticipation of completion by D, P (a) moved the caravan onto the land, (b) installed a chemical toilet for use in connection with it, (c) purchased a chicken house and wire netting for use on the land, (d) transported some of his furniture, (e) spent some money in improving the roadway and cutting the grass. The expenses incurred in (a) and (b) were recoverable as being items of essential reliance interest. The remaining items were incidental to P's performance of the contract and of these only (c) and (d) were recovered as (e) was not reasonably within the contemplation of D at the time of the contract.

(ii) Expenses Incurred After Breach

Any reliance interest expenses which the plaintiff incurs after breach are governed by the doctrine of mitigation. Once he has notice of breach he may not reasonably incur expenses in reliance on the defendant's performance, and such expenses if incurred will not be recoverable. Thus in *Lloyd v. Stanbury* (above) when the plaintiff had already issued a writ for breach of contract, hoping for a decree of specific performance, he installed a power control, a television aerial and a telephone. It was, however, held that he had already repudiated the contract, and hence that these expenses were unreasonable and could not be recovered.

(iii) Expenses Incurred Before Contract

The question then arises whether the plaintiff might recover any expenses incurred before the contract with the defendant was made. It must first be observed that where a plaintiff claims the expenses *in addition* to profits, that is as part of his expectation interest, they should be taken into account. In the calculation of lost profits, an allowance is made for expenses necessarily incurred, and it would seem unreasonable to exclude consideration of overheads and other expenses which related to the profitable transaction but which were incurred before the contract. Where, however, the reliance interest is claimed as an *alternative* to the expectation interest, the position appears to be different. Here the object is to put the plaintiff in the position he would have been in if the contract had not been made, and on that hypothesis the expenses would still have been incurred. There is, indeed, no causal connection between the loss (the wasted expenses) and either the making of the contract or its breach. On these grounds American authorities have rejected claims for pre-contract expenditure. English law seems to have taken a different path. Until recently, recovery was allowed only within very narrow limits. In contracts for the sale of land where a vendor had failed to complete, the disappointed purchaser could recover the expenses of executing the contract. In a recent case within this area, Brightman J extended the ambit of recovery to cover "the costs of performing an act required to be done by the contract" (*Lloyd v. Stanbury* at p. 546). Finally in *Anglia Television v. Reed*, [1972] 1 QB 60 (CA) a completely new principle was introduced. On the breach of *any* class of contract, the plaintiff could recover *all* pre-contract expenditure which "was such as would reasonably be in the contemplation of the parties as likely to be wasted if the contract was broken" (at p. 64). Now it may be conceded that dogmatically to insist that there may be recovery of expenditure incurred only from the moment that the contract was completed might lead to artificial results. If the parties had clearly reached agreement on the substance of the contract and all that remained was for their legal advisers to draft and execute the contract, it would be unfair to the plaintiff to disallow a claim for expenses which had been incurred at this stage. But the broad principle of *Reed's* case surely goes too far. The doctrine of *restitutio in integrum* which lies at the heart of the reliance interest award dictates that while a contract is still being negotiated a party who incurs expenditure does so at his own risk. Perhaps the best solution would be for the reliance interest award to comprise those expenses incurred as from the time when there was substantial agreement between the parties.

(d) Election and Limitation by the Expectation Interest

Although this section deals with the reliance interest as an "alternative" to expectation interest damages, it is to be observed that in certain circumstances, it will represent the plaintiff's only chance of substantial damages. Such is the case where there is a rule of law preventing the award of the expectation interest, as under *Bain v. Fothergill* (1974), LR 7 HL 158 (HL (Eng.)). But the same is also true where loss of profits is too remote, or the existence and extent of the expectation interest remain so speculative and uncertain that the court is not prepared to award damages on this basis. The well-known Australian case of *McRae v. Commonwealth Disposals Commission* (1951), 84 CLR 377 provides an excellent illustration.

> Ds sold to Ps the wreck of an oil tanker lying on a reef about 100 miles north of Samarai. At considerable expense Ps fitted out a salvage expedition and proceeded to the location but found no tanker there. They successfully sued Ds for breach of contract. Ps were awarded not their expectation interest (the value of the ship and its contents) which was so speculative as to make quantification impossible, but their reliance interest: the wasted expenditure.

The principle has recently been asserted that a plaintiff may elect between expectation interest damages and reliance interest damages. If the plaintiff claims his reliance interest, the question then arises as to whether his remedy should in any way be limited by reference to his expectation interest. English case-law provides no guidance on the point and yet it goes to the very root of the reliance interest and its rationale. The objection to allowing recovery unaffected by the expectation interest is that it may be too generous to the plaintiff. By seeking to put the plaintiff in the position he would have been in if the contract had not been made, it may protect him against the consequences of having entered into a bad bargain. He may be put in a better position than if the defendant had performed his contract. For example:

> D agrees to supply materials for P, a property developer, to build a house. In necessary preparation for the work P spends £3,000. Because of prevailing market conditions, D is able to show that P would have made a net loss on the sale of the house of £200 (i.e. P's expectation interest is £-200). On breach by D, P elects to claim his wasted expenditure of £3,000. If he recovers this

sum he will be in the position he would have been in if he had not entered into the contract with D, but he will be £200 better off than if D had performed his contract.

It may be sought to defend this result on the ground that it does not lie in the mouth of a person who has broken his contract to complain if the plaintiff is put in the position he would have been in if he had not entered into a contract with the defendant. But this view involves by implication some punitive consideration. The opposing view that a plaintiff should never be put in a better position than if the contract had been performed, seems to be more consistent with the true principle of compensation. If this conclusion is accepted, the principle emerges, as formulated by the American Restatement that "if full performance would have resulted in a net loss to the plaintiff, the amount of this loss must be deducted ..." s. 333 d. The objection might then be brought that if damages are to be assessed on this basis, there would be no point in the plaintiff electing to sue for his reliance interest—the remedy would have no advantage over expectation interest damages. If the expectation interest shows a net profit, he might as well sue for that, while if it shows a net loss, the rule will compel the court to take it into account in assessing reliance interest damages. The answer to this objection is that, when suing for his reliance interest, the plaintiff will have the advantage of the burden of proof. In a claim for expectation interest damages the plaintiff must prove to the satisfaction of the court that he has sustained a loss which is capable of quantification. Where, in the alternative, the reliance interest is claimed, then should the defendant seek to limit the award on the principle stated above, it will be for him to prove that the plaintiff would have made a net loss on the transaction.

3 Reliance Interest as a Complement to Expectation Interest

It cannot be doubted that when the reliance interest is used to complement the expectation interest the ordinary object of putting the plaintiff in the position he would have been in if the contract had been performed is to be pursued. It may at first sight seem strange that if that be the object of damages the plaintiff should be entitled to both his reliance and his expectation interest. It would seem that the plaintiff has to spend the reliance interest in order to earn the expectation interest, and therefore to award both would amount to a double recovery. It is on this ground that the courts have insisted that the plaintiff is not entitled to *both* wasted expenditure *and* loss of profits. But this principle, as stated, is ambiguous and misleading for in every case whether or not the reliance interest may complement the expectation interest depends on how the expectation interest has been calculated, in short on what is meant by "profits" in this context.

(i)   Where the expectation interest is based on the "net profit," that is, where the plaintiff's expenses have been deducted from his receipts he will be entitled both to his wasted expenses and to the "net profit" lost, for clearly the "net profit" does not allow for the fact that the price he will get on eventual sale or dealing will include reimbursement of the expenses.

(ii) Where the expectation interest is calculated simply by reference to "gross profit," that is to receipts on eventual sale or dealings without deduction for expenses, then the plaintiff is not entitled to both the "gross profit" and the wasted expenses, for, in order to earn that profit those expenses would have been incurred.

There are, therefore, two methods of calculating damages. Their contrasting application may be seen in the following illustration (based on the facts in *Hydraulic Engineering Co. v. McHaffie*):

> D agrees to supply materials to P for £100. P is to incorporate these materials in the manufacture of a machine which he will sell to X for £1,200. In addition to the price of the materials P must spend another £900 in part performance of his contract with X, but as D fails to deliver the special materials, the machine is useless and the contract with X is lost.

On *Method* (i) it would be said that P's "net profit" is:

> £1,200 [minus] (£900 + £100) = £200

Assuming that P has paid £100 to D for the materials, he will be entitled to compensation for his real loss which is wasted expenses plus "net profit":

> £900 + £100 + £200 = £1,200

On *Method* (ii) it would be said that P's "gross profit" is £1,200 (his receipts on sale of the machine to X). Assuming that P has paid £100 to D for the materials, he will be entitled only to his "gross profit" without any addition for his wasted expenses = £1,200.

Whether in any given case, the expectation interest will be calculated on the basis of the "net profits" or the "gross profits" will depend on various factors including the nature of the contract, the nature of the expenses, the nature of the eventual profit, and accountancy practice. Unhappily it is not always clear in the decided cases on what basis "profits" have been calculated. The result has been some considerable confusion. The award of both "profits" and expenses in *Hydraulic Engineering v. McHaffie* has been criticized for allowing double recovery and yet defended by an Australian court on the ground that the "profits" referred to in the judgments were "net profits" and not "gross profits." In truth, it is impossible to ascertain from the facts as reported which was intended. Even greater difficulty arises from *Cullinane v. British "Rema" Manufacturing Co.*, [1954] 1 QB 292 (CA).

> D sold and delivered to P a clay pulverizing plant warranting that it would process clay at six tons per hour. In fact it could handle clay at only two tons per hour. P claimed (a) wasted expenditure *viz.* the capital cost of the plant, the cost of installing it, and the cost of an ancillary plant less the residual value of the plant *and* (b) loss of "net profits" *viz.* estimated receipts after deducting for depreciation, interest, maintenance and other expenses.

Now clearly in accordance with the principles discussed above, the claim did not infringe the double recovery rule: it sought to recover damages on the basis of method (i) and not method (ii). However the majority of the Court of Appeal refused to allow recovery of both heads of damages. They seemingly failed to appreciate that there was any difference between the two methods for, having made the unexceptional statement that a plaintiff cannot recover both wasted expenditure and "gross profits" (at pp. 302 and 308), they concluded that this was a conclusive ground for rejecting the plaintiff's claim. The point was, however, taken by Morris LJ in his dissenting judgment: the plaintiff might claim either his "gross profits" or his "net profits" plus expenditure. In this case, he claimed the latter, and as such his claim was "permissible and logical" (at p. 315). It is to be hoped that in future cases the courts will adopt his reasoning rather than that of the majority.

Bowlay Logging Ltd. v. Domtar Ltd.
[1978] 4 WWR 105, 87 DLR (3d) 325 (BCSC); (1982), 37 BCLR 195 (CA)

[Bowlay contracted with Domtar to log a 10,000-cunit timber sale. Bowlay was to cut, skid, and load the logs for $15 per cunit. Domtar was to haul them, but in breach of its contract failed to provide sufficient trucks. Bowlay sued for damages, claiming $124,776.43 on the basis that those were its expenditures in partly performing the contract. The trial judge cited Fuller and Perdue's "The Reliance Interest in Contract Damages" (above) for the proposition that in a suit for reimbursement for losses due to breach of contract a court should not knowingly put the plaintiff in a position better than that it would have occupied had the contract been performed. He concluded that, had the contract been performed, Bowlay would have lost money. Accordingly, he awarded Bowlay only nominal damages. Bowlay appealed.]

SEATON JA (for the court): In these proceedings the appellant did not ask to be put in the position it would have been in had there been no breach. It asked to be put in the position it would have been in had it never entered into the contract. It says that it incurred expenditures of $232,905, that it was paid $108,128.57 by the respondent and that it is entitled to recover the difference as expenditures rendered futile by the respondent's breach.

There was a suggestion that the appellant was forced to this position because the job was not profitable and was not going to become profitable. The suggestion comes from the use of the term "lost profits" in *Anglia Television Ltd. v. Reed*, [1972] 1 QB 60 (CA). I do not think that an unprofitable venturer that was injured is precluded from recovering damages for breach of contract. If its loss was greater by reason of the breach than it otherwise would have been, the increase in the loss is the amount necessary to put the plaintiff in the position it would have been in had there been no breach. That amount should be recoverable whether or not it can be accurately described as lost profit.

In this case, the appellant offered no evidence of a loss. It simply showed the expenditures it had incurred and revenue it had received. It then claimed the balance as the loss incurred when it was obliged by the respondent's breach to abandon the project. The respondent does not take issue with the manner in which the appellant formulates its claim. It simply says that the expenditures admittedly incurred were not lost as a result of the breach. It says that no loss was caused by the breach; that the expenditures were rendered futile by the combination of an improvident contract and inefficient execution. The trial Judge agreed with that. He said:

> The law of contract compensates a plaintiff for damages resulting from the defendant's breach; it does not compensate a plaintiff for damages resulting from his making a bad bargain. Where it can be seen that the plaintiff would have incurred a loss on the contract as a whole, the expenses he has incurred are losses flowing from entering into the contract, not losses flowing from the defendant's breach. In these circumstances, the true consequence of the defendant's breach is that the plaintiff is released from his obligation to complete the contract—or in other words, he is saved from incurring further losses.

And later:

The onus is on the defendant. But the onus has been met. The only conclusion that I can reach on the evidence is that if the plaintiff had fully performed the contract its losses would have continued at the rate that the figures show they were running at up to the time when the logging operation was closed down.

The case at bar takes the matter farther than any of the cases cited, because here the defendant has shown that the losses the plaintiff would have incurred on full performance exceed the expenditures actually made in part performance. No award for loss of outlay can therefore be made. There is no escaping the logic of this: see *Corbin on Contracts* (1964), at pp. 205-6:

> If, on the other hand, it is proved that full performance would have resulted in a net loss to the plaintiff, the recoverable damages should not include the amount of this loss. *If the amount of his expenditure at the date of breach is less than the expected net loss, he should be given judgment for nominal damages only.* If the expenditures exceed this loss, he should be given judgment for the excess.

The appellant made a number of attacks on the judgment. Most focus on the calculations that led the trial Judge to conclude that the losses would have been incurred by the appellant with or without the respondent's breach.

The appellant argues that the trial Judge ought to have taken into account that some of the work was done under circumstances made more difficult by the breach. I think that the Judge was justified in rejecting that contention. The evidence does not indicate that the excessive costs were brought about or even significantly contributed to by the breach.

Next it is said that the trial Judge ought to have taken from his figures start-up costs and capital costs when he weighed the question whether the loss would have been incurred in any event. The 10,000 cunits in the timber sale at $15 each would have yielded about $150,000 to the appellant if it had completed the job. It spent $232,905 and the respondent was required to pay something over $5,000 to clean up the property and pay Workers' Compensation Board assessments. The work done was worth about $180,000.

The accountant referred to costs prior to the first shipment of logs as start-up costs. There was no evidence of start-up costs that should not have been absorbed, at least substantially, in the first half of the work. I have read the whole of the evidence respecting damages and have concluded that the trial Judge did not err when he failed to make an allowance for start-up costs.

Capital costs raise a more difficult question. The appellant claims them as expenditures made on this project but says that they were not an expense on this project and therefore should not be taken into account in the projection of the loss that would have been incurred with or without the breach. The trial Judge dealt with this matter on a motion to reopen for further argument (unreported). He said this:

> The motion is founded on the contention that in my reasons for judgment I failed to apply properly to the evidence in the case the rule derived from the American authorities, *i.e.*, that the defendant is entitled to offset against the plaintiff's claim for expenses made in reliance on the contract which has been breached the loss the plaintiff would have suffered on the contract had there been no breach.
>
> Two complaints are made:

1. that in calculating the loss that the plaintiff would have suffered on the contract had there been no breach, I included expenses attributable to the breach that would have been incurred had there been no breach; and

2. that capital expenditures incurred by the plaintiff should not have [been] included in calculating the loss the plaintiff would have suffered had there been no breach.

As to the first contention, I am not persuaded that it has been made out. As to the second contention, it is a fair characterization of the way in which the principle derived from the American authorities was applied. I considered whether it should be applied in that way, and I was of the view it ought to be. Since the principle that the plaintiff relies upon allows such expenses to be claimed as damages, it seems reasonable that the defendant should be allowed to include them in any calculation of the loss the plaintiff would have suffered had there been no breach. In any event, the parties only contracted in the case at bar for the plaintiff to log the timer sale in question. The plaintiff incurred capital expenditures at its peril. I am not persuaded, therefore, that the principle derived from the American authorities was wrongly applied.

There was a modest capital investment. Some equipment was being rented with a provision for purchase, a vehicle was being purchased and some other things were bought outright. There was an element of capital in some payments but that element would be offset, at least in part, by a proper depreciation allowance.

The appellant was prevented from completing this one project which normally would have been finished in the fall. But the respondent's breach did not cause the collapse of the appellant's plans to undertake other logging projects. Those plans were abandoned because of the losses the appellant had incurred; losses that would have been greater had there not been a breach that permitted it to close down the project.

The appellant supported its claim for capital expended with an allegation that it was to have contracts each year. Thus it said that expenditures made with a view to a series of contracts were rendered futile by the breach of the first contract. The trial Judge, rightly in my view, rejected that approach as raising claims that were "too uncertain and remote."

The inquiry is not an accounting process, it is a matter of judgment to be exercised after weighing all of the evidence. I am persuaded that the trial Judge reached the right conclusion on the evidence.

The central question in this case is one of fact. The trial Judge found that the losses that were being incurred prior to the breach would have continued and that in the end, if there had been no breach, the loss would have been even greater. I take that to be what the trial Judge meant when he said: "… here the defendant has shown that the losses the plaintiff would have incurred on full performance exceed the expenditures actually made in part performance."

On the evidence it seems clear that the appellant was losing heavily; not because of the respondent's breach, but because of an improvident contract and grossly inefficient work practices. The appellant's claim that it expended $232,905 partially completing a project that was to yield $150,000, demonstrates the extent to which it was losing money. The result of the breach was to release the appellant from further performance that would have resulted in further losses. In short, no damage was sustained by the appellant as a consequence of the respondent's breach.

The appellant's final argument fell only slightly short of a claim for exemplary damages. The argument is that the respondent breached the contract, took the benefit of the breach, and should not be permitted to escape with impunity. The respondent was penalized by having to absorb some costs that would have been charged to the appellant if the job had been completed, but the appellant has much larger amounts in mind as suitable in the circumstances.

The answer to the final argument is clear. There was not the conduct on which to base a case for exemplary damages, and the appellant suffered no loss as a consequence of the breach on which to found a claim for compensatory damages.

I conclude that the trial Judge's award of damages should be upheld and the appeal dismissed.

Appeal dismissed.

NOTE

In *Omak Maritime Ltd v. Mamola Challenger Shipping Co.*, [2010] EWHC 2026, [2011] 1 Ll. Rep. 47, a charterer had repudiated the charter of a ship when, unusually, the market rate of hire was higher than the contractual rate. The shipowners, who were thus enabled to rent out their ship at a rate greater than that in the repudiated contract, nevertheless claimed for their expenses in preparing to perform the charterparty with the defendant. An arbitrator allowed the owners' claim and the charterer appealed. In allowing the appeal Teare J held wrote (at para. 65):

> The tribunal's error was to regard a claim for wasted expenses and a claim for loss of profits as two separate and independent claims which could not be "mixed." But the weight of authority clearly shows that both claims are illustrations of, and governed by, the fundamental principle stated by Baron Parke in *Robinson v. Harman*. That principle requires the court to make a comparison between the claimant's position and what it would have been had the contract been performed. Where steps have been taken to mitigate the loss which would otherwise have been caused by a breach of contract that principle requires the benefits obtained by mitigation to be set against the loss which would otherwise have been sustained. To fail to do so would put the claimant in a better position than he would have been in had the contract been performed.

Sunshine Vacation Villas Ltd. v. Governor and Company of Adventurers of England Trading Into Hudson's Bay
(1984), 58 BCLR 33 (CA)

BY THE COURT: The respondent, Sunshine Vacation Villas (Sunshine Vacation), was incorporated in 1976 to pursue the idea of a travel agency concentrating on retail tour packages and operating from large department store locations. The trial judge awarded damages to Sunshine Vacation for the failure of the Hudson's Bay Company (the Bay) to carry out the promises made to allow the concept to be put into practice.

The Bay has appealed both the finding of liability and the amount of damages. As is well known, the Bay owns department stores in many centres in Canada, and, based upon size, a store is classified as either "A," "B," or "C." In 1976, in the lower part of British Columbia, there were four stores in the largest of the classifications, "A." These four stores were the prime objectives sought by the group of five persons who incorporated Sunshine Vacation.

The central person in that group was William Robinson. He had been working for 17 years in the travel industry, and he was the one who proposed to the Bay that there were profits to be made by a different approach to the sale of travel services. Earlier, the Bay had granted licences to a firm called "Ask Mr. Foster" (Foster) to operate travel agencies in the four "A" stores in Vancouver, Victoria, Lougheed Mall and North Surrey. The Bay was dissatisfied with Foster for several reasons, and its officials were very interested in Robinson's ideas.

Those ideas involved sale outlets in all of the Bay stores in British Columbia in a ratio of 1:2:2 of "A," "B" and "C" stores. The stores in the "B" and "C" categories were located in the northern and interior areas of the province. A number of meetings took place. The trial judge (unreported) made these critical findings on the outcome of those meetings:

> I am further of the view that my initial impression of the frankness of the plaintiff's five directors has not been shaken and, accordingly, I accept the plaintiff's version of the events where they are materially in conflict with the defendant's witnesses concerning the discussions that occurred on both September 7 and 21, 1976.
>
> It is, therefore, my finding that at the September 7, 1976 meeting that Mr. Peterson said to Mr. Bill Robinson and Mr. Harrison that if they would take the six western region outlets at that time that in the spring of 1977 they would get the "Ask Mr. Foster" outlets, providing that the plaintiff met the three criteria of productivity, low customer complaints and increased use of the Bay credit cards. I further find that the plaintiff's directors subsequently met and decided to accept Mr. Peterson's proposal. I am also of the view that if no such proposal had been made the plaintiff would not have dealt further with the defendant. The licensing agreement was subsequently drafted, discussed, and revised and at the September 21, 1976 meeting the substance of what Mr. Peterson had proposed and the plaintiff company had accepted was confirmed in the presence of Mr. Lorimer. I further find that the written licensing agreement, executed on or about September 23, 1976, does not contain the full agreement between the parties. It is apparent from the written agreement itself, which contains the references to rental rates for class "A" stores, that there was more agreed upon between the parties than just that six outlets which were scheduled to have the plaintiff open by mid-November of 1976. In addition to the "Ask Mr. Foster" stores which were to become available in the spring of 1977, I find that it was verbally agreed that new stores, as they became available, would be made available to the plaintiff.

Sunshine Vacation opened retail outlets in six Bay stores in Prince George, Kelowna, Vernon, Penticton, Kamloops and Trail in November and December 1976. The initial three or four months of the licence was covered by a letter of understanding to which was annexed the formal licence which would come into effect February 1, 1977.

In April 1977, Sunshine Vacation received information that the Bay had renewed the Foster licences and that the new "A" store in the Park Royal Shopping Centre in West Vancouver was not to be made available to Sunshine Vacation as an outlet. From that point to the withdrawal by Sunshine Vacation from the six locations in July 1977, unsuccessful efforts were made by both parties to achieve a settlement of the dispute that developed. No purpose will be served by giving the details of those efforts. ...

[The court concluded that the appeal with respect to liability failed.]

Damages

Some additional reference to the facts is necessary to an understanding of the issues relating to damages. As previously stated, the principals of Sunshine Vacation learned in April 1977 that the Bay had renewed the Foster licences and that the new "A" store at Park Royal was not to be made available as an outlet. Sunshine Vacation was then aware that the Bay was in breach of its promise to make available the four large outlets. During the next two months, extensive negotiations took place directed towards the possibility of Sunshine Vacation becoming the Bay's exclusive travel agent in western Canada. In the hope that those negotiations would succeed, Sunshine Vacation carried through with its plans to open an outlet in Cranbrook in June but, by the end of that month, negotiations had broken down. Sunshine Vacation decided in early July that it did not wish to continue doing business with the Bay and advised the latter of its intention to close out the seven outlets then operating and cease business. That intention was carried out with the result that all offices were closed in August 1977.

The damage award was in the total amount of $275,956.19 plus prejudgment interest. The award was made up of two elements:

- Loss of capital—$175,956.19
- Loss of profit—$100,000

The Bay submits that the award for loss of capital is wrong in principle, that the circumstances of the case do not support an award under that head and that no loss of profit was proved so that only nominal damages should have been awarded.

The award for loss of capital is made up of two components. One is the sum of $80,000 invested in the company at the outset by the five shareholders. The second is the increase in the bank line of credit from April 2, 1977, which was assumed to be the date of breach, to August 31, 1977, by which time all operations had terminated. That loan stood at $19,043.81 on April 2nd and, by the end, had risen to $115,000. The trial judge awarded the difference between those two figures ($95,956.19) which he held to be in the same category as the original capital of $80,000.

It should be understood that the reference in this case to "lost capital" is in the sense of unrecovered working capital. It is not an outlay for capital purposes but is rather a measure of the expenses incurred by Sunshine Vacation which, by reason of the breach by the Bay, could not be recovered. They were expenses incurred by Sunshine Villa in part performance of the contract.

In this court, Sunshine Vacation has cross-appealed seeking an increase in the damages in the amount of $19,043.81. Mr. Nathanson, for the Bay, did not dispute that, if loss of capital is a properly allowable head of damage, the deduction of $19,043.81 was not justified. He accepts that, in the circumstances of this case, the combination of the initial shareholders' investment and the ultimate overdraft balance fairly represents the capital loss. He submits, however, as he did at trial, that loss of capital is not a proper approach to assessing damages. Alternatively, he submits that it is only available as an alternative to loss of profit and that it is wrong in principle to make an award, as here, based upon a mixture of those approaches.

The alternative submission is right. One method of assessment, the return of expenses or loss of capital, approaches the matter by considering what Sunshine Vacation's position would have been had it not entered into the contract. The other, loss of profit, approaches it by considering what the position would have been had the Bay carried out its bargain. The two approaches must be alternatives. *McGregor on Damages*, 14th ed. (London: Sweet & Maxwell, 1980), p. 21, para. 24, states that the "normal measure of damages in contract" is:

> If one party makes default in performing his side of the contract, then the basic loss to the other party is the market value of the benefit of which he has been deprived through the breach. Put shortly, the plaintiff is entitled to compensation for the loss of his bargain. That is what may best be called the normal measure of damages in contract.

At p. 32 (para. 42) he says:

> Just as expenses rendered futile by the breach may generally be claimed as an alternative to the normal measure of damages, so they may also be claimed as an alternative to recovering for gains prevented by the breach. Again, it is important to realize that such expenses form an alternative and not an additional head of damage, since they represent part of the price that the plaintiff was to incur in order to secure the gain. Sometimes this has been lost sight of, and a double recovery involving an inconsistency of compensation has been allowed.

The trial judge, in holding that Sunshine Vacation could recover both lost profits and capital, relied on two cases, one English and one Canadian. He referred first to *Cullinane v. British "Rema" Manufacturing Co. Ltd.*, [1954] 1 QB 292 (CA), a decision of the Court of Appeal of England which supports the law as stated in the passages set out above. He went on to say:

> A more recent judgment of that court, *Esso Petroleum Co. Ltd. v. Mardon*, [1976] 1 QB 801 (CA), although not referring to *Cullinane*, seems to me to be inconsistent as in the latter case loss of profits were considered in addition to lost capital without any reference being made to election of remedies.

The trial judge also relied upon *Haack v. Martin*, [1927] SCR 413, a case of wrongful termination of the lease of a farm and, in particular, the following passage in the judgment of Rinfret J at p. 417:

> When the respondent and the appellants in this case got together on February 26, 1924, and made the agreement whereby the respondent leased his lands and the appellants promised to pay the yearly rental of one-third of the crop, no doubt the crop each party anticipated was the average crop grown on these lands during the previous years; and the value to each of them of such average crop may reasonably be considered as representing the damages within the contemplation of the parties, if for some reason they happened to be deprived of their share or portion of the yearly rental. *Such therefore, in this case, is the measure whereby the damages must be computed, in addition to any actual loss or expense that may be established.*

(Emphasis added.)

The last sentence of that paragraph should not, in our view, be taken as authorizing the award of damages for loss of profits as well as for any actual losses incurred. The reference to "any actual loss or expense" is explained by the facts of the case. The plaintiff had, in addition to his claim for loss of profit which would have been earned from the crops in the remaining years of the lease, a claim for a separate sum for work actually done by him in summer-fallowing. It is that claim which gave rise to the actual loss and expense.

Nor should *Esso Petroleum Co. Ltd. v. Mardon, supra,* be regarded as establishing any general principle contrary to the basic rule that claims for loss of capital and loss of profits are in the alternative. In that case, there was a claim by a lessee of a service station which had just been built at the time of the lease. The operation proved consistently unprofitable, despite efforts by both parties over several years to improve the position. The lessee had entered into the lease on the strength of the lessor's honest but negligent representation that the potential annual throughput was 200,000 gallons. For reasons which the lessor should have appreciated before it made the representation, the throughput never got to 50% of that figure. The lessor terminated the lease and sued for possession. The lessee counterclaimed for damages for breach of warranty and for negligent misrepresentation. At trial he succeeded on the ground of misrepresentation. All three members of the Court of Appeal, in separate judgments, held that he was entitled to succeed for breach of warranty as well as on the basis of misrepresentation. On the question of damages, Lord Denning MR said at p. 822:

> On this footing, the loss which he has suffered would seem to be as follows (subject to further argument by the parties): Capital loss: cash put into the business and lost, £6,720; overdraft incurred in running the business, £7,774. Loss of earnings to be discussed. There will be interest to be added for a period to be discussed.

Shaw LJ concurred to make the majority judgment on the question. The reference to "earnings" appears to relate to an observation, at the foot of p. 821, to the effect that it may be assumed that the plaintiff would have made a reasonable return by way of earnings for his own work had he not entered into the contract. Ormrod LJ at p. 829 gave reasons for agreeing that the sums of £6,270 and £4,000 were recoverable and that there should also be an allowance for interest. He added: "The claim for loss of profits is, in my opinion, virtually incapable of proof, and I will not deal with that."

The final assessment, as appears at p. 834, was adjourned to allow for possible settlement and was settled at a figure not set out in the reports, which the court indicated was "in line with" that at which it would have arrived.

The case is one in which, on its particular circumstances, the court held that the loss of capital invested was an appropriate basis for assessment. It is clearly a case in which the court approached assessment on the basis of putting the plaintiff in the position in which he would have been had he never entered into the contract. That is true even of the reference by Lord Denning to "loss of earnings." The earnings are those which the plaintiff, who apparently took no wages out of the business while he was operating it, would have been able to earn in other endeavours had he not entered into the contract. The case is not an authority for making an award based on a combination of viewing the matter as if the plaintiff had never entered into the contract and as if the defendant had carried out its bargain. No consideration was given to the question of principle and it is not even clear that, in the result, any allowance was made for loss of earnings—it was "to be discussed."

The principal submission of the Bay is that there was no proper basis for making a substantial award for either loss of capital or loss of profits. That submission is based on the contention that the trial judge should have found that Sunshine Vacation could not have earned a profit, that it was bound to fail, and that only nominal damages should have been awarded.

The authority relied upon in support of that submission is *Bowlay Logging Ltd. v. Domtar Ltd.* (1978), 87 DLR (3d) 325; affirmed (1982), 37 BCLR 195 (CA). That was a case in which a logging contract was terminated when the defendant timber owner breached its obligation to make trucks available. Mr. Justice Berger, at trial, held that the plaintiff could elect to claim its expenses but that, if the owner could show that the plaintiff would have incurred a loss had it completed the contract, nominal damages only should be awarded. He said at p. 335:

> If the law of contract were to move from compensating for the consequences of breach to compensating for the consequences of entering into contracts, the law would run contrary to the normal expectations of the world of commerce. The burden of risk would be shifted from the plaintiff to the defendant. The defendant would become the insurer of the plaintiff's enterprise. Moreover, the amount of the damages would increase not in relation to the gravity or consequences of the breach but in relation to the inefficiency with which the plaintiff carried out the contract. The greater his expenses owing to inefficiency, the greater the damages.
>
> The fundamental principle upon which damages are measured under the law of contract is *restitutio in integrum*. The principle contended for here by the plaintiff would entail the award of damages not to compensate the plaintiff but to punish the defendant. So it has been argued that a defendant ought to be able to insist that the plaintiff's damages should not include any losses that would have been incurred if the contract had been fully performed. According to G.H. Treitel, *Law of Contract* (London: Stevens, 3rd ed., 1970), at p. 798:
>
> > It is uncertain whether the plaintiff can recover his entire expenses if those exceed the benefit which he would have derived from the contract, had there been no breach.
>
> Ogus, in *The Law of Damages* (1973), has said at p. 347 that, "it is not yet clear whether English law imposes this limitation."
>
> The tendency in American law is to impose such a limitation. And I think Canadian law ought to impose it too.
>
> The onus is on the defendant.

Mr. Justice Berger went on to hold that the onus had been met and that the plaintiff should therefore recover only nominal damages.

On appeal to this court, the decision and the reasoning of the trial judge were affirmed. Mr. Justice Seaton, for the court, held that the damages recoverable, in the case of an unprofitable enterprise, will be the amount, if any, by which the plaintiff's loss is greater than it would have been had there been no breach. He quoted [at 181] with approval this passage from *Corbin on Contracts*, vol. 5A (St. Paul: West Publishing Co., 1964) at pp. 205-6, para. 1033:

> If, on the other hand, it is proved that full performance would have resulted in a net loss to the plaintiff, the recoverable damages should not include the amount of this loss. If the amount of his expenditure at the date of breach is less than the expected net loss, he should be given judgment for nominal damages only. If these expenditures exceed this loss, he should be given judgment for the excess.

The crucial finding of fact in *Bowlay* is that the amount of the plaintiff's expenditure to the date of breach was less than the net loss which would have been incurred had the contract been completed. The onus of establishing that state of fact rests upon the defendant. It has not been discharged in this case.

To explain that, some reference to the basis of the claim for loss of profit, and the conclusions of the trial judge with respect to it, is necessary. The claim was based on projections as to the profit which Sunshine Vacation would have earned had the Bay kept its bargain and granted Sunshine Vacation a licence for the four "A" stores for three years from April 2, 1977. The three-year period was chosen because it was the fixed period of the licence agreed to be given by the Bay. The projections put forward by Sunshine Vacation indicated a profit, at the end of that period, of $348,982.

The Bay did not dispute the methodology employed by Sunshine Vacation in calculating loss of profits but challenged the assumptions upon which the calculation was based. It called expert evidence seeking to establish that the factual assumptions made by witnesses for Sunshine Vacation were unrealistic and indicating that, on the basis of what its witnesses said were more realistic assumptions, Sunshine Vacation would have been in a loss position at the end of the three-year period.

The trial judge concluded, on the basis of the conflicting evidence, that the projections of Sunshine Vacation were essentially reliable. He accepted a major adjustment put forward by the Bay's accounting witness affecting the total projected profit and deducted from the figure of $348,982 the sum of $119,198 which was the accumulated deficit before taxes at April 2, 1977. He rounded down the gross claim for lost profits to $200,000 in recognition of the element of guesswork necessarily involved in all such calculations and then reduced that figure by 50% to make allowance for what he held was the failure of Sunshine Vacation to mitigate its damages by seeking out and opening alternative locations in which to promote its new marketing concept. Sunshine Vacation takes no issue with the 50% reduction or the basis of it. For present purposes, it is of some importance to recognize that it was based upon a finding of fact that Sunshine Vacation, had it sought out alternative locations for operating the major outlets represented by the Bay's four "A" stores, could have found adequate alternate locations about halfway through the three-year period. In reaching that conclusion, the trial judge laid some stress upon his view that Sunshine Vacation had a "viable business concept" to market. That conclusion was reached after a careful analysis of the evidence and arguments put forward by the Bay.

The principal issue in relation to the loss of profit award was whether the trial judge, in accepting in substance the projections of Sunshine Vacation with very little adjustment, was excessively favourable to it. The principal witness for the Bay was Mr. Gani. Although he was accepted by the trial judge as a reliable witness, his major contentions were not accepted for reasons which, the Bay asserts, indicate a failure to appreciate some aspects of the evidence. For instance, Mr. Gani said that no new operation would be likely to be profitable in the first five years and that the three-year period of the licence was therefore inadequate to establish a profitable operation. The trial judge accepted that evidence "in general terms" but disposed of it by pointing out that Mr. Gani's company, after taking over the four locations, made a profit in its second year of operation so "why should the plaintiff similarly not have been profitable." One answer to that which is disclosed by the evidence is that Mr. Gani's company did not attempt a novel concept but continued in the traditional manner to accept whatever business came along, a method of business which would be expected to produce much larger gross revenues than the specialized concept of Sunshine Vacation. That, the Bay contends, is a fatal weakness in the projection of Sunshine Vacation being based upon the actual revenues of Nortrav, Mr. Gani's company. Another point which has a similar effect is that relating to the projected range of percentages of revenue to gross sales. The trial judge noted that, if the projected percentages were reduced by only 1% and all other figures were accepted, Sunshine Vacation would have been in a substantial loss position. But he accepted the projections without major modification. Mr. Nathanson stresses that the evidence of Mr. Gani was to the effect that no one had ever achieved percentages as high as those upon which the projections made by Sunshine Vacation in 1977 for the purposes of negotiations with the Bay; it used a percentage well below that in the trial projections. Mr. Nathanson also points to the fact that the actual performance in the six small stores was considerably below the level used in the projections at trial. Those matters, he submits, were ignored by the trial judge.

On the other hand, Mr. Harbottle for Sunshine Vacation points to a number of indications in its evidence that the trial projections were prepared on a conservative basis. It must also be kept in mind that the trial judge made a substantial deduction from the projected figure in recognition of uncertainties and that his deduction of some $119,000 from the projected three-year profit figure may not have been correct in principle if no allowance was to be made in the award for loss of capital.

We conclude that some weight should have been given to the points made by Mr. Gani and, because that was not done, it is reasonable to conclude that, if there was error in the assessment of loss of profit, it favoured Sunshine Vacation. Even if the deduction of $119,000 were to be added back into the calculation on the side of Sunshine Vacation the result would be to determine loss of profit at a lesser figure than the loss of capital.

On the other hand, on any view of the matter, it cannot be concluded that the trial judge should have found that Sunshine Vacation would have operated at a loss. He gave great weight, as he was entitled to do, to his considered conclusion that Mr. Robinson was an able and energetic manager and that the marketing concept of Sunshine Vacation was a good one, and that it was therefore probable that the operation would have been profitable.

The shortcomings of this aspect of the Bay's case can be illustrated by reference to $230,000 in partially completing a contract which, had it been completed, would have produced revenues of $150,000. To the point of termination, it had earned $108,000. Had it been required to complete the contract, its additional expenditures would have exceeded the additional income. So the reality of the situation was that the defendant did the plaintiff a favour by giving it an opportunity to get out of having to complete. On the basis, it was held that nominal damages only should be awarded. The factual situation in the case at bar is entirely different and, as a result, the Bay cannot discharge the onus of establishing that Sunshine Vacation would have suffered a loss.

Sunshine Vacation, on the other hand, has not established that a proper award for loss of profits would have exceeded the amount of the lost capital. That being so, the amount of lost capital is, in all the circumstances of this case, the appropriate amount to award as damages for breach of contract.

That amount represents, in the circumstances of this case, the expenses incurred by Sunshine Vacation and not recovered by it. That approach to assessment is particularly appropriate in this case. The breach was one which went to the root of the contract. After Sunshine Vacation had incurred large expenses in carrying out obligations which were recognized to be the unprofitable portion of the contract, the Bay refused to carry out its promises in relation to the profitable part. Because of the nature of the enterprise and the point at which the breach took place, the assessment of damages for loss of profits is more than usually speculative. In those respects, the case is similar to *Anglia Television Ltd. v. Reed*, [1972] 1 QB 60 (CA). A useful discussion of that case, and of the relationship of the principle relied on in it to the decision of this court in *Bowlay Logging, supra*, is to be found in S.M. Waddams, *The Law of Damages* (Toronto: Canada Law Book, 1983), at pp. 318-21.

It follows the damage award should be reduced from $275,956.19 to $195,000, being the amount of loss of capital after restoring the amount of $19,043.81 deducted by the trial judge. In all other respects the appeal and cross-appeal should be dismissed.

Appeal allowed in part.

A.S. Burrows, *Remedies for Torts and Breach of Contract*
3d ed. (Oxford: Oxford University Press, 2004), at 66-70
(selected footnotes incorporated)

May the Reliance Interest Be Protected Even When Direct Protection of the Expectation Interest Is Not Barred?

Dicta of the majority of the Court of Appeal in *Cullinane v. British Rema Manufacturing Co. Ltd.*, [[1954] 1 QB 292 (CA)] and of the unanimous Court of Appeal in *Anglia Television Ltd. v. Reed* supported the view that the claimant is always free to claim protection of his reliance interest. As Lord Denning said in the later case, "[T]he plaintiff … has an election; he can either claim for loss of profits or for his wasted expenditure." [[1972] 1 QB 60 (CA), at 63, 64. Clearly the profits referred to were gross and not net.] The decision in *Lloyd v. Stanbury* [[1971] 1 WLR 535 (Ch.). The damages awarded here extended beyond "wasted expenses," strictly construed, to include a sum for the claimant's loss of earnings] could also be regarded as supporting this although it concerned a contract for the sale of land and such contracts could, arguably, be regarded as special particularly given the *Bain v. Fothergill* rule. But the answer to this question has now been put beyond doubt by Hutchison J's comments in *CCC Films (London) Ltd. v. Impact Quadrant Films Ltd.* [1985 QB 16]. The defendants had there granted a licence to the claimants to exploit three films and the claimants had paid the agreed consideration of $12,000 for that licence. By the contract the defendants were to send to the claimants video tapes of the films and were to insure them. In breach of contract the defendants sent the video tapes by ordinary post and uninsured and they were lost. The defendants were also in breach of contract in failing to deliver replacement tapes. The claimants could not prove any loss of profits and instead claimed damages in respect of the expenses of $12,000. Hutchison J held that they could recover those damages. Moreover he squarely addressed the question of whether a claimant's choice to claim reliance expenses is unfettered and said:

[T]he plaintiff has an unfettered choice; it is not only where he establishes by evidence that he cannot prove loss of profit or that such loss of profit as he can prove is small that he is permitted to frame his claim as one for wasted expenditure … . I consider that those cases [*Cullinane v. British Rema Manufacturing Co. Ltd.* and *Anglia Television Ltd. v. Reed*] are authority for the proposition that a plaintiff may always frame his claim in the alternative way if he chooses. [[1985] QB 16 at 32]

But the crucial question that then arises is whether this means that the courts will allow a claimant to escape from what is clearly a bad bargain by recovering damages protecting his reliance interest. The answer, as laid down in *C & P Haulage v. Middleton* [[1983] 1 WLR 1161] and *CCC Films (London) v. Impact Quadrant Films Ltd.*, is that they will not. In the former case, the respondents had granted a contractual licence to the appellant to use their yard for his car-repair business. With ten weeks remaining of a second six-month licence the respondents, in breach of contract, terminated the licence. Proceedings were begun by the respondents but the real controversy centred on the appellant's counterclaim for reimbursement of £1,767.51 to cover labour and material used in building a wall enclosing the yard, laying on electricity and transferring a telephone. The Court of Appeal refused to award the appellant anything beyond nominal damages. If we adopt the reliance interest interpretation, the reasoning was that a court will not award damages protecting a claimant's reliance interest if this will knowingly put him in a better position than he would have been in if the contract had been performed. To have awarded the appellant the damages he claimed would have contravened this because the respondents could have lawfully terminated the licence at the end of the next ten weeks and presumably the appellant could not during that period of time, nor indeed during a full six months, have recouped in profits his expenditure on the yard; but, in any case, as the local authority had permitted him to work from home the appellant had been able fully to mitigate his loss of profits during those ten weeks. Indeed his profits would be higher working at home since he was spared paying for the use of the yard.

In deciding that a claimant cannot escape from a known bad bargain by claiming protection of his reliance interest, the Court of Appeal took the same view as that prevailing in the US and Canada. Indeed Ackner LJ, giving the principal judgment, relied heavily on the decision of the British Columbia Supreme Court in *Bowlay Logging Ltd. v. Domtar Ltd.* [[1978] 4 WWR 105] which in turn had cited with approval *L. Albert & Son v. Armstrong Rubber Co.* [178 F2d 182 (1949)] the classic US authority on this point. In the former, Berger J admirably summarised the underlying rationale of these cases in the following passage:

Where it can be seen that the plaintiff would have incurred a loss on the contract as a whole, the expenses he incurred are losses flowing from entering into the contract, not losses flowing from the defendant's breach … . The principle contended for … would entail the award of damages not to compensate the plaintiff but to punish the defendant. [[1978] 4 WWR 105 at 117]

C & P Haulage v. Middleton was applied in *CCC Films*, where Hutchison J went on to stress, relying on the same Canadian and US authorities, that where the claimant claims reliance damages, the burden of proving that he has made a bad bargain, that is that he would not have recouped his expenses if the contract had been performed, is on the defendant.

The upshot of all this is that where the defendant (D) cannot prove that the claimant (C) has made a bad bargain and C's reliance loss exceeds the expectation loss that C can prove, it will be to C's advantage to claim reliance damages. But where D can prove that C has made a bad bargain C's "free choice" to claim protection of the reliance interest is of no advantage to C because he will be confined to his lower expectation damages.

Ultimately, then, the reliance interest bows to the expectation interest. This is only right since it is the breaking of the promise, disappointing the claimant's expectations, that renders the defendant's conduct wrongful. As such, damages for tortious misrepresentation provide an interesting contrast. The very objection to misrepresentation is that the defendant ought not to have induced the claimant to rely on an untrue statement. If in reliance on the misrepresentation the claimant has, for example, entered into what is a bad bargain, he can and ought to be able to escape from it by recouping all his losses because if the defendant had not wrongfully made the representation the claimant would not have entered into the contract. In other words, unlike a contract-breaker who acts wrongfully when he breaks his contractual promise and not when he induces the claimant to enter into the contract, the misrepresentor commits a wrong when he induces the claimant by his statement to act to his detriment by, for example, entering into a losing contract.

In the difficult Australian case of *Commonwealth of Australia v. Amann Aviation Pty Ltd.* [[1991], 66 ALJR 123; Treitel, "Damages for Breach of Contract in the High Court of Australia" (1992), LQR 226] the primary question in issue was the standard of proof faced by a defendant who seeks to discharge the burden of showing that the claimant has made a bad bargain (i.e., that the claimant would not have recouped his reliance loss).

The claimant had won a contract to conduct aerial coastal surveillance for the defendant. It committed large sums of money in acquiring the necessary specially equipped aircraft. Several months after the contract commenced, and at a time when the claimant was itself in breach by having insufficient aircraft available, the defendant committed a repudiatory breach by serving an invalid termination notice. That breach entitled the claimant to terminate the contract and sue for damages, which it did. The majority of the High Court of Australia (Mason CJ, Dawson J, Brennan J, Gaudron J) held that it was entitled to full reliance damages of some $5.5 million (plus interest). Although the defendant had shown that there was a 20% chance that the defendant would otherwise have validly terminated the contract for the claimant's own breach, in which event the claimant's reliance losses would not have been recouped, the majority felt that no discount should be made for that chance because it was unlikely. A balance of probabilities, all or nothing, standard of proof therefore seems to have been applied. In contrast, the three minority judges thought that a discount should be made. Intriguingly each of them adopted different reasoning and conclusions. Deane J thought the appropriate discount from full reliance damages should be the 20% chance that the defendant would have validly terminated. Toohey J considered that, taking account of all the contingencies in the case, the discount should be 50%. On the other hand, McHugh J thought that reliance damages were inappropriate and that instead normal expectation damages, reduced by the 20% chance, should be awarded.

4. The Justification for Reliance Damages for Breach of Contract

As the courts will not knowingly award reliance damages which put the claimant into a better position than if the contract had been performed, the best interpretation of the cases awarding reliance damages is that they are concerned to protect the claimant's expectation interest, albeit in a different way than the expectation interest is normally protected. That is, one can say that the law accepts an alternative way of putting the claimant into as good a position as if the contract had been performed, because it allows the claimant the benefit of a presumption, rebuttable by the defendant, that the claimant has not made a bad bargain. Hence where the claimant can prove its reliance expenses, this rebuttable presumption enables it to recover that amount on the ground that if the contract had been performed it would at the very least have made gains to cover those expenses. This was the interpretation strongly favoured by at least five judges of the High Court of Australia in *Commonwealth of Australia v. Amann Aviation Pty Ltd*.

The great merit of this analysis is that it provides the only convincing explanation for why the courts do not allow claimants to escape from a known bad bargain by claiming reliance damages. If one were concerned to protect the reliance interest because that provides an alternative and valid aim of compensation for breach of contract (as suggested by Fuller and Perdue), it is hard to see why it should be limited by a known lower expectation interest.

On the other hand, it may at first sight appear puzzling why, on this interpretation, the courts are willing to give the claimant the benefit of a rebuttable presumption that it would have recouped its expenses. But it is submitted that this is simply a consequence of the fact that the defendant is a contract-breaker. It is as a result of breach by the defendant that one does not know what the position would have been had the contract been performed. It is therefore only fair and proper that the problems of proving that the claimant would not have recouped its reliance loss should fall on the contract-breaker and not on the innocent claimant.

One should also note that, as Berger J stressed in the passage cited above, there is simply no causal link between a breach of contract and damages protecting the reliance interest. The expenses would have been incurred even if there had been no breach. This is another way of expressing the point that expectation, and not reliance, protection is the natural measure of compensation for breach of contract.

NOTES AND QUESTIONS

1. In *Sunshine*, did the court base the award on the plaintiff's expectation or reliance interest? What assumption about the "value" of the bargain was the court prepared to make?

2. Compare the approach in *Sunshine* with that in *Bowlay Logging*. Can you reconcile the approaches and, if so, how?

3. In *Sunshine*, the court said:

> One method of assessment, the return of expenses or loss of capital, approaches the matter by considering what Sunshine Vacation's position would have been had it not entered into the contract. The other, loss of profit, approaches it by considering what the position would have been had the Bay carried out its bargain. *The two approaches must be alternatives* (emphasis added).

Is this statement correct?

4. Why was the plaintiff not allowed to recover on the alternative basis of where it "would have been had it not entered into the contract" in *Bowlay*?

5. It seems that, in some cases, the expectation interest will set an upper limit on the plaintiff's recovery. But in others, it will not. Can you explain why this is so, and generate a statement of when each approach would be appropriate? Are the reasons based completely on the notion of compensation or are other facts relevant?

6. For an interesting analysis of the "reliance interest" that comments on the misunderstanding that surrounds terminology, see David McLauchlan, "Reliance Damages for Breach of Contract," in Jeff Berryman and Rick Bigwood, eds., *The Law of Remedies: New Directions in the Common Law* (Toronto: Irwin Law, 2010) chapter 2.

DAMAGES FOR NEGLIGENT PERFORMANCE OF A CONTRACT, NEGLIGENT MISSTATEMENT, AND COMPENSATION FOR BREACH OF FIDUCIARY DUTY

Introduction

It is true that in some later cases opinions were expressed that the measure of damages is the same in tort as it is in contract .... In my view these opinions must now be regarded as erroneous.

Koufos v. C. Czarnikow Ltd.
[1969] 1 AC 350 (HL (Eng.)), *per* Lord Reid, at 387

Courts should strive to treat similar wrongs similarly regardless of the particular cause or causes of action that may have been pleaded. ... In other words, the courts should look to the harm suffered from the breach of the given duty, and apply the appropriate remedy.

Hodgkinson v. Simms
[1994] 2 SCR 377, *per* La Forest J, at 444

These quotations are only 25 years apart in time, but they represent a dramatic shift in the approach to remedies for breach of civil obligations. To Lord Reid in 1969, it was obvious that the focus for determining the remedy was the cause of action. The legal classification of the duty carried with it certain remedial consequences. It was equally obvious to La Forest J, 25 years later, that the focus should be on the harm suffered, not the legal category through which it is sought to be redressed. This new remedial flexibility helps ensure that similar harms receive similar remedies regardless of the legal category into which the case falls. What is called for is an approach founded on basic principles, not mechanical application of the traditional rules.

In the field of monetary compensation for breach of obligations, the task of coming to grips with the new remedial flexibility can be enormously challenging. This is particularly true in areas of concurrent liability where the traditional approaches to compensation differ depending on the cause of action. Part of the reason for the difficulty is the overlap between questions of liability and damages. It is hard to liberate remedies from the traditional categories without also reconsidering the bases of liability. As Professor Waddams points out with respect to tort:

> In torts ... it is impossible to draw a clear dividing line between questions of liability and damages. ... A test of reasonable foresight is used in negligence cases to determine whether the defendant owed a duty, whether there was breach of the duty, and whether the damage claimed is too remote. As Denning LJ said, ... "[Y]ou will find that the three questions, duty, causation, and remoteness, run continually into one another. It seems to be that they are simply three different ways of looking at one and the same problem."

See S.M. Waddams, *The Law of Damages* (Aurora, ON: Canada Law Book, December 1999) (looseleaf), at 14-21.

There is similar overlap in fiduciary duty claims: the Supreme Court of Canada has made it clear that there is a range of fiduciary obligations the breach of which may require different remedial responses. See *Canson Enterprises v. Boughton & Co.*, [1991] 3 SCR 534, at 587-88.

Binnie J made the same point, speaking for the Supreme Court of Canada in *Cadbury Schweppes Inc. v. FBI Foods Ltd.*, [1999] 1 SCR 142, a case concerning breach of confidence, at para. 21:

> While the only controversies still alive in this Court turn on the principles on which financial compensation is to be calculated ... *the disagreement among the parties on the remedies reflect their differing views as to the true nature and scope of the cause of action* .... This appeal therefore requires us to examine more closely the character of the interest protected ... and on that basis to assess the appropriateness of the remedy.

In this section, we will touch on money remedies in four types of cases with a contractual element but which involve negligence and/or breach of fiduciary duty:

1. negligent misstatement inducing a contract;

2. negligent performance of a contractual duty;

3. negligent performance of a service apart from contract; and

4. breach of a fiduciary duty where there is also a contract between the parties.

Before turning to these four types of cases, it may be helpful to recall some general remedial principles. In contract, as we have seen, the successful plaintiff generally is awarded *expectation damages*—that is, damages based on the assumption that the contract has been performed. The goal is to give the plaintiff the anticipated economic benefits of the bargain. In negligence, an award to the successful plaintiff generally is based on detriment flowing from the tortfeasor's acts—that is, the award should restore the plaintiff to the position he or she would have been in had the negligent act not been committed. This is sometimes referred to as an award to compensate the plaintiff for adverse changes in his or her position in *reliance* on the defendant. For breach of trust, the remedy is generally *restitutionary*—that is, based on the prevention of gain to the defendant arising from the breach.

While these general principles are straightforward, the real world is more complicated. Three examples, two of which we have already examined, illustrate the point:

- In *Sunshine Vacation Villas v. Governor and Company of Adventurers of England Trading Into Hudson's Bay* (1984), 58 BCLR 33 (CA), the Bay was found liable in contract for failing to carry out its promises to allow the plaintiff to pursue the idea of a travel agency concentrating on retail tour packages operating from large department store locations. The Court of Appeal awarded the plaintiff damages equivalent to its lost capital investment. In other words, the effect of the award was to put the plaintiff in the position it would have been in if the contract had never been entered into rather than where it would have been had the contract been performed.

- In *V.K. Mason Construction v. Bank of Nova Scotia*, [1985] 1 SCR 271, the plaintiff succeeded in an action based on the bank's negligent misrepresentation that sufficient financing would be provided to a developer to cover the construction of a proposed development. In reliance on that assurance, the plaintiff had entered into a construction contract with the developer and completed the work, but was not fully paid. The Supreme Court of Canada awarded damages against the bank that included an allowance for loss of profit on the contract. The damages in negligent misstatement were based on the expected profit under the contract induced by the misstatement even though there would have been no contract but for the negligent misstatement.

- In *Canson Enterprises v. Boughton* (see chapter 10, "Financial Relief in Equity"), a solicitor was found to have breached a fiduciary duty to his client by failing to inform the client of the solicitor's involvement with other clients on the transaction. The effect was that the plaintiff thought it was purchasing land directly when, in fact, there was an intermediate purchaser who made a substantial profit on the intervening "flip" of the land. The plaintiff thereafter lost a good deal of money in its attempts to develop the land as a result of the negligence of a soil engineer and a firm hired to drive pilings. The plaintiff was not able to recover all of its losses from those tortfeasors. The Supreme Court of Canada refused to allow the plaintiff to recover this shortfall from the solicitor and upheld the lower courts' award of damages based on the measure applied in cases of deceit—that is, the difference between the amount paid and the value of the land plus consequential damages equal to expenses incurred on the development project prior to the wrongful acts of the engineers and pile-drivers.

For a thorough discussion of the cases in Canada, the United Kingdom, and Australia, see Laura C.H. Hoyano, "The Profit Paradox: Protecting Legitimate Expectations in Tort" (1999), 78 *Canadian Bar Review* 363.

Negligent Misstatements Inducing a Contract

The traditional view of the difference in the measure of damages in contract and negligent misstatement was summarized by Bayda CJS in the following case.

Beaver Lumber Co. v. McLenaghan
(1982), 21 Sask. R 65 (CA)

BAYDA CJS (for the court): The plaintiffs, the respondents in this appeal, recovered a judgment for $7,500 for damages for negligent misrepresentation. The defendant company appealed on the issues of liability and quantum of damages. The respondents, by notice to vary, have asked that the damages be increased. ... The issue relating to damages involves a determination of the proper measure of damages in *Hedley Byrne* situations: should the tortious (reliance) measure prevail or the contractual (expectation) measure?

The material facts are not substantially in dispute. The respondents purchased from the appellant a package of components for a prefabricated house. The terms of sale were expressed in a written agreement. Contemporaneously, the respondents entered into a written agreement with a certain Mr. Nixon for the assembly of the components and the construction of the house. Mr. Nixon, too, was sued but his liability is not in issue in this appeal. It is common ground that Mr. Nixon's workmanship proved faulty, but there is a dispute about the degree of seriousness of that faulty workmanship.

Before the respondents entered into their contract with Mr. Nixon, a Mr. Griffiths, the appellant's agent, represented Mr. Nixon to them as "the man for the job" and as one who had experience erecting the appellant's houses. The respondents claim that a special relationship existed between them and the appellant imposing a duty of care upon the latter when giving advice and information to them; that they relied upon the appellant's advice and information; and that the advice and information given to them by Mr. Griffiths about Mr. Nixon constituted misrepresentation. The respondents claim further that the misrepresentation was made negligently. They contend that given Mr. Nixon's total lack of experience as a contractor—he had not previously acted as a contractor, but was then negotiating for the first time in the capacity of a contractor to construct a house for a Corporal Gordon—the appellant should have taken some positive steps to determine if Mr. Nixon was the "man for the job." It was not sufficient, they say, that Mr. Nixon previously was successfully employed as a carpenter, under some other person's supervision, erecting the appellant's houses.

The appellant does not dispute the respondent's claims, and the trial judge's findings, respecting the special relationship and the reliance by the respondents upon the appellant's advice and information. The appellant contends, however, that the representations by Mr. Griffiths, the appellant's agent, were not misrepresentations and if they were, there is no evidence that they were made negligently. ...

[The court dismissed the appeal with respect to liability.]

I turn now to the issue of damages, and in that respect, it is necessary first to refer briefly to the evidence of four witnesses.

Mr. Grenke, who was called by the respondents, was employed by the Director of the *Veterans' Land Act* for 26 years, and during many of those years was involved in the inspection of homes under construction. In his appraisal report on the respondents' house, he said in part:

> I have never seen poorer workmanship in some 30 years as an appraiser. There is little or no market for this house in its present condition at the present time. However to say it has no value is not acceptable. A number of these functional obsolescence factors could be cured by replacement and repair to make the house livable. However this would prove to be quite expensive and as it would not be satisfactory for private ownership and occupation, it could be used as a revenue potential as the average renter would be satisfied to overlook these objectional features and be prepared to pay a reasonable rental for the property.

Using the cost approach, he appraised the value of the property "constructed to plan and Specifications with satisfactory workmanship" at $37,709.20, made up of a land value of $8,000 and a building value of $29,709.20. However, given the deficiencies in the building, his opinion was that a fair market value of the property as it stood was $17,000, made up of a land value of $8,000 and a building value of $9,000. The trial judge rejected Mr. Grenke's assessment of the condition of the building in these words:

> On the evidence before me, I am not prepared to accept the appraiser's view that the home cannot be placed in a condition which would be satisfactory for "private ownership and occupation."

Mr. Gampe, who, too, was called by the respondents, is a carpenter and a former foreman for a construction company and has had considerable experience in the construction of houses. He described the deficiencies in the house and estimated the cost to fix and finish the house at $26,000. The trial judge, in finding Mr. Gampe's evidence unreliable, expressed himself thus:

> While I am not implying that Mr. Gampe's evidence was untruthful, I felt that during his examination-in-chief, cross-examination and in his rebuttal evidence, his friendship with the plaintiff was, to some extent, influencing his evidence.

Mr. Kowalski, also called by the respondents, is a carpenter of eight years' standing and experience in constructing houses. In his opinion, the best way to remedy the defects in the house is to tear down the house and reconstruct it. His estimate for so doing was $10,000 to $20,000 "a couple of years ago" and as of the date of the trial, at "twenty, thirty thousand."

Mr. Johnson was called by the appellant. He is a professional engineer who, for 25 years, has been involved in the design of residential buildings and in the inspection of homes for the purpose of providing "remedial work." He described the deficiencies in the house and estimated the cost of remedial work at $3,000 and the cost of finishing the house at $3,000.

The trial judge decided that the damages "should not be in an amount to provide for the demolition and reconstruction of the home" for the house still had a value, as Mr. Grenke testified. He made reference to Mr. Gampe's estimate of $26,000 (erroneously referred to by him as Mr. Kowalski's evidence) to fix and finish the house and to Mr. Johnson's estimate of $6,000 and found the costs of "doing such work" (presumably to "fix and finish") to be much closer to the $6,000 figure. He concluded:

> I am of the view that based on the evidence, an expenditure of $7,500 will bring this home into the condition of a normal 900-square foot three or four-year-old home. I therefore award damages to the plaintiffs against the defendant in the amount of $7,500.

The appellant's complaint is that a portion of the $7,500 represented the cost of finishing the house. That portion, the appellant contends, is $3,000. The remainder of $4,500 is attributable to fixing the house. The appellant's submission is that while the item for fixing the house is claimable, the item for finishing is not; and, that the trial judge's failure to recognize this distinction renders his assessment wrong in principle, justifying this court to interfere and lower the award.

The respondents contend that the damages should be increased. Their submission is that the trial judge should have found that their loss consisted of the difference between the value of the house they would have got had Mr. Nixon turned out to be a "good man"

($37,000) and the value of the house they actually got ($17,000), the difference being $20,000. That submission directly put into issue the proper measure of damages in these cases. It is that issue I now address.

Where the negligent misrepresentation induces the plaintiff to enter into a contract with the representor or a third party, is the proper measure of damages for that negligent misrepresentation the tortious (reliance) measure or the contractual (expectation) measure? The distinction between the two measures is important and is this: the tortious measure aims at restoring the *status quo ante* and the contractual measure at putting the plaintiff in the position he would have been in had the misrepresentation been true. Thus, where a misrepresentation induces the plaintiff to enter into a contract, the tortious measure (and I am concerned here only with pecuniary loss) would be the difference between the value of the property or services received under the contract and the amount paid for that property or those services, plus his consequential losses, that is, his out-of-pocket loss but not his loss of bargain or prospective loss of profits. In other words, the damages should put the plaintiff in the position he would have been in had he not entered into the contract. The contractual measure, on the other hand (and here, also, I am concerned only with pecuniary loss), where the representation amounts to a warranty, would seek to put the plaintiff in the position he would have been in had the warranty been fulfilled. Such an award would include loss of bargain, that is, loss of expected profits.

There appears to be no Saskatchewan case that has squarely faced the issue of appropriate measure. In other jurisdictions, the courts tend to favour the tortious measure. In *Esso Petroleum Co. Ltd. v. Mardon*, [1976] QB 801 (CA), while the issue of a proper measure of damages for negligent misrepresentation was somewhat obscured by a finding that the misstatement could have been either a breach of warranty or a negligent misrepresentation, the English Court of Appeal appears to have opted for the tortious measure. Lord Denning MR (with whose formulation of the computation of damages Shaw LJ agreed) at pp. 820-1 said:

> Mr. Mardon [the claimant] is not to be compensated here for "loss of a bargain." He was given no bargain that the throughput *would* amount to 200,000 gallons a year. He is only to be compensated for having been induced to enter into a contract which turned out to be disastrous for him. Whether it be called breach of warranty or negligent misrepresentation, its effect was *not* to warrant the throughput, but only to induce him to enter the contract. So the damages in either case are to be measured by the loss he suffered. Just as in *Doyle v. Olby (Ironmongers) Ltd.*, [1969] 2 QB 158 (CA) at p. 167 he can say: "... I would not have entered into this contract at all but for your representation. Owing to it, I have lost all the capital I put into it. I also incurred a large overdraft. I have spent four years of my life in wasted endeavour without reward: and it will take me some time to re-establish myself."
>
> For all such loss he is entitled to recover damages. It is to be measured in a similar way as the loss due to a personal injury. You should look into the future so as to forecast what would have been likely to happen if he had never entered into this contract: and contrast it with his position as it is now as a result of entering into it. The future is necessarily problematical and can only be a rough-and-ready estimate. But it must be done in assessing the loss.

It is noted that in relying upon *Doyle*, Lord Denning seems to make no distinction between cases where the misrepresentation stems from fraud and those where it stems from negligence.

In British Columbia, Anderson J in *Uncle Ben's Tartan Holdings Ltd. v. Northwest Sports Enterprises Ltd.* (1974), 46 DLR (3d) 280 (BCSC) at p. 287 adopted the tortious measure, and like Lord Denning, did so by relying upon the *Doyle* decision. In this respect, reference is also made to *West Coast Finance Ltd. v. Gunderson, Stokes, Walton & Co.* (1975), 56 DLR (3d) 460 (BC CA) at pp. 464-5.

In *Capital Motors Ltd. v. Beecham*, [1975] 1 NZLR 576 (SC), a New Zealand case involving a plaintiff who paid $1,400 for a car, the true market value of which was $1,300, Cooke J, in awarding $100 damages, stated [at 581]:

> In an action for fraudulent misrepresentation on a sale the measure of damage is prima facie the difference between the price paid and the fair value at the time of purchase .... . When an action lies for negligent misrepresentation inducing a sale, I think a similar measure may be appropriate.

With respect, I agree with the decisions reached in these cases to use the tortious measure, and I agree with the following view expressed by the learned author of *McGregor on Damages* (London: Sweet & Maxwell, 14th ed., 1980) at para. 1489, p. 1002:

> Once it has been decided that the tortious measure of damages prevails in deceit and no loss of bargain damages are available to the plaintiff—and the decision for the tortious measure was clearly and deliberately taken by the Court of Appeal in *Doyle v. Olby (Ironmongers)* before any of the above cases on the *Misrepresentation Act 1967* had appeared—it cannot conceivably be right to allow loss of bargain damages to a plaintiff who complains only of a negligent misrepresentation.

It is true that this view was expressed in the context of a discussion respecting a proper measure of damages for negligent misrepresentation as envisaged by s. 2(1) of the English *Misrepresentation Act, 1967* (UK), c. 7. Nevertheless, the words apply equally to negligent misrepresentation under the common law.

The Supreme Court of Canada in *Hepting v. Schaaf*, [1964] SCR 100, affirmed that the measure of damages for fraudulent misrepresentation is the tortious measure (the matter of consequential losses did not arise in that case) and that, of course, is the law in this jurisdiction. There is no good reason why the same measure should not govern damages for negligent misrepresentation.

Thus far I have been dealing with the situation where the negligent misrepresentation induces the plaintiff to enter into a contract with the representor or a third party. It is of some benefit to deal briefly with the measure of damages where the plaintiff's change of position consequent upon the misrepresentation is not the conclusion of a contract. That measure, too, is the tortious measure and is the amount necessary to restore the plaintiff to the position in which he would have been had the misrepresentation never been made, subject, of course, to the usual rules of remoteness, that is, the damages must be direct and foreseeable. This was the measure adopted in *Nelson Lumber Co. Ltd. v. Koch* without a discussion of the point. Reference is also made to *Porky Packers Ltd. v. Town of The Pas* (1974), 46 DLR (3d) 83 (Man. CA); reversed on issue of liability, [1977] 1 SCR 51, and to *McGregor*, para. 1481, p. 996.

In the present case, the negligent misrepresentation induced the respondents to enter into a contract with Mr. Nixon obligating them to pay $3,170 to him for certain specified services. He was entitled to be paid an additional sum for "extras." The respondents paid to him a total of $3,235. Under the first tortious measure discussed above (where the negligent misrepresentation induces a contract), the respondents would be entitled to the difference between the value of Mr. Nixon's services and the amount paid to him for the services, plus consequential losses. No evidence was given respecting the value of Mr. Nixon's services, but even if one were to assume that they were totally worthless, the only amount the plaintiff could claim in this respect is the amount paid for the services, namely $3,235, plus consequential losses.

What are the consequential losses? At the very most, the consequential losses consist of the total additional amounts the respondents spent on the house and lot, less the value of the property they ended up with. Those additional amounts, according to the evidence of the respondent's wife, came to $21,197. The value of the property, if one were to take Mr. Grenke's valuation—a valuation favourable to the respondents, but not wholly accepted by the trial judge—was $17,000. Thus, the consequential losses at most came to $4,497. Accordingly, an application of this measure of damages produces a maximum loss of $7,732. In that case, the trial judge's award of $7,500 should not be interfered with by this court.

It is perhaps more reasonable to treat the estimate of fixing the deficiencies as the appropriate sum for consequential losses. Mr. Johnson's estimate was $3,000, a sum that the trial judge was reluctant to accept unreservedly. On the assumption that Mr. Nixon's services were valueless, that approach results in a loss of $6,235. Such a conclusion, too, would not justify an interference by this court of the award of $7,500.

An application of the second tortious measure discussed above (where the negligent misrepresentation does not result in a contract) would produce a result approximating a loss of $7,500.

All of these calculations are based on the assumption that Mr. Nixon's services were worthless—an assumption that was not made by the trial judge and is not warranted by the evidence. Accordingly, on the basis of the tortious measure of damages, the evidence, when assessed in a light most favourable to the respondents, does not warrant an increase of the damages award.

The respondent's submission on the issue of damages, namely, that their loss should be calculated as the difference between the value of the house they would have got had Mr. Nixon turned out to be a "good man" and the value of the house they actually got, amounts to a submission that the contractual (expectation) measure is the proper one. For the reasons I have outlined, that submission must fail.

I turn briefly to the appellant's claim that the award should be decreased.

Mr. Johnson testified as follows:

> Q. And all this would cost how much?
>
> A. ... To completely remedy, and bring it back to the stage of construction that it is now in, a maximum of $3,000. Now, to finish the project up to but not including the finished flooring, but adding all the finished carpentry and everything else, another $3,000, and the project will be complete and satisfactory to anybody with an ordinary discriminatory attitude.

Two observations are apposite: First, the learned trial judge was not prepared to unreservedly accept Mr. Johnson's figures. Second, $3,000 "to finish the project up" would appear to consist to a large extent of finish carpentry. This part of Mr. Johnson's evidence was not explored in examination-in-chief or cross-examination. An examination of the contract that the respondents entered into with Mr. Nixon shows that he was responsible for completing the "interior finishing." What portion of the $3,000 was ascribed by Mr. Johnson to material and what portion to labour was not made clear. Indeed, the whole issue of "finishing" was left in an entirely unsatisfactory state. To reduce the award based on such incomplete and unsatisfactory evidence would be unjustifiable.

In the result, the appeal and the application to vary are dismissed.

The matter of costs gives me cause for concern. The respondents raised the question of appropriate measure of damages, but unfortunately, the issue was not dealt with adequately in the factum or in argument before us. As a result, judgment had to be reserved and the issue researched. The respondents should not be awarded their full costs of the appeal. There will be an order that the respondents will have 70% of their taxed costs of the appeal.

Appeal and application to vary dismissed.

Consider the correctness of the *Beaver Lumber* decision in the light of the following two cases.

V.K. Mason Construction Ltd. v. Bank of Nova Scotia
[1985] 1 SCR 271

[Mason, a building construction company, entered into a contract to build an office retail complex for Courtot. The Bank of Nova Scotia (BNS) provided finance to Courtot for the development. Mason had only agreed to enter into the development contract on the basis of a letter provided by BNS that Courtot was adequately financed to meet all its payments. During construction, it became clear that Courtot would not be able to cover all the costs of completion of the development. Mason eventually lodged a mechanics' lien and BNS exercised its power of sale as mortgagee. Mason settled its mechanics' lien action with Courtot, but after BNS asserted its priority as mortgagee over the proceeds of sale there were insufficient funds to fully pay Mason's mechanics' lien action. Mason then commenced an action against BNS alleging breach of contract and negligence. Mason also argued that by virtue of s. 4 of the *Interest Act*, RSC 1970, c. 1-18, BNS was limited to interest at the rate of 5 percent. If this rate were applied, there would be sufficient funds from the proceeds of sale to cover the settlement of its mechanics' lien action. The trial judge agreed with the later argument. The trial judge also held that BNS was in breach of contract with Mason, and, further, that BNS was also liable for negligent misrepresentation to Mason. The trial judge awarded $1,057,941 for breach of contract, and, alternatively, $897,941 for negligent misrepresentation; the latter amount was determined by subtracting the projected profits of $160,000 from the value of the contract damages. The Ontario Court of Appeal dismissed an appeal on liability for breach of contract and did not find it necessary to comment on the negligence claim. The court allowed the appeal on the application of the *Interest Act*, which it held was not applicable to limit BNS's interest to 5 percent. On further appeal to the Supreme Court of Canada, BNS was not liable in contract, there being insufficient certainty to found a contract. BNS was not bound to limit its interest by the *Interest Act* provisions.

However, BNS was liable for negligent misrepresentation. On the assessment of damages for negligent misrepresentation Wilson J for the court gave the following judgment.]

WILSON J (for the court): ...

(2) Negligent Misrepresentation

It seems to me that a negligent misrepresentation analysis properly focuses attention on the gravamen of the cause of action in this case, namely, the fact that the Bank's representation to Mason was false. The parties are in agreement that the applicable law is to be found in the decision of the House of Lords in *Hedley Byrne & Co. Ltd. v. Heller & Partners Ltd.*, [1964] AC 465 (HL (Eng.)). Mr. Sopinka sums up the requirements for liability as follows: (a) there must be an untrue statement; (b) it must have been made negligently; (c) there must be a special relationship giving rise to a duty of care; and (d) there must be reliance which is foreseeable. His submission to the court comprised a reconstruction of the facts to show that none of these prerequisites was present. His problem is that Mr. Justice O'Leary made very clear findings of fact against the Bank on all four requirements.

The main difficulty I have with Mr. Sopinka's approach to the facts is that he attempts to isolate them from their context when it is the context that gives them meaning. For example, with respect to the falsity of the September 8, 1972 letter, Mr. Sopinka attempts to show that, on the basis of Courtot's estimates of total project costs minus soft costs, the Bank was justified in representing that it was loaning Courtot sufficient money to complete the project. This seems to me to completely overlook the fact that what Mason was seeking was an assurance that Courtot would have sufficient funds at a time when Mason already knew the basic terms of the Bank's loan to Courtot. In other words, the September 8, 1972 letter would, as the Bank knew, be construed as an assurance of something over and above the terms of the loan, yet the Bank went ahead and gave that assurance relying solely on the terms of the loan and Courtot's cost estimates. Mr. Hway may have felt at the time that he was justified in his hope that the soft costs would not materialize before permanent financing had been secured, but he was not justified in assuring Mason that there would be sufficient funds without informing them that his assurance was based on the assumption that soft costs would not be incurred.

The same general comment can be made with respect to Mr. Sopinka's submissions on negligence, particularly in relation to special relationship and reliance. The Bank had a special relationship with Mason because it was inducing Mason to sign a contract with Courtot in reliance on the Bank's assurance of adequate financing. The statement was negligent because it was made without revealing that the Bank was giving an assurance based solely on a loan arrangement which Mason had already said was insufficient assurance to it of the existence of adequate financing.

Not only was the Bank's misrepresentation made negligently but it is clear from the finding of fact of Mr. Justice O'Leary that Mason relied on it and that such reliance was foreseeable by the Bank. I believe therefore that all the requirements for negligent misrepresentation are met in this case.

One of the interesting legal issues with respect to negligent misrepresentation is the issue of damages. Mason cross-appealed on this issue. The Bank concedes that in principle the proper aim of a damage award is to restore the plaintiff to the position in which he would have been if the negligent misrepresentation had never been made: see Harvey McGregor, *McGregor on Damages* (London: Sweet and Maxwell, 14th ed., 1988) at p. 996. The Bank argues that Mason would have lost money in any event even if the misrepresentation had not been made because it would have lost money in severing its relationship with Courtot. The problem with this submission is that the trial judge made an express finding to the contrary. What we have to assume, I believe, is that but for the misrepresentation Mason would have ceased work for Courtot, recovered its expenses for work already done and found another construction project to work on.

The learned trial judge awarded damages for misrepresentation on the basis that they were equal to contract damages minus Mason's anticipated profit. Counsel for Mason submits that the trial judge was wrong in subtracting the anticipated profit because damages in contract and tort are the same. He also submitted that interest should have been awarded on the damages at 12% from the completion of the project on October 7, 1974. While I tend to the view that there is a conceptual difference between damages in contract and in tort, I believe that in many instances the same quantum will be arrived at, albeit by somewhat different routes.

I agree with the submission of counsel for Mason that the trial judge was wrong in subtracting profit. I believe that in principle one is entitled to assume that Mason would have found a profitable means of employing itself had it not been induced to work on the Courtot project by the Bank's misrepresentation. This, in my view, is a reasonably foreseeable head of damage: see *Patrick L. Roberts Ltd. v. Sollinger Industries Ltd. and Ontario Development Corp.* (1978), 19 OR (2d) 44 (CA). In equating Mason's lost profit with the profit estimated on the Courtot project we are simply saying that this is a reasonable estimate of what Mason would have been likely to have made if it had decided to abandon the Courtot project and find other work. That is to say, the lost profit on *this* contract represents the lost opportunity for profit on *any* contract. If Mason had made an exceptional profit on the Courtot project it might be disentitled to an award of the entire amount of that profit in tort damages, but this would be so only because it was not reasonably foreseeable that it would have made a similarly exceptional profit on some other contract.

On the basis of the same reasoning it seems to me that Mason ought to be entitled to prejudgment interest as of the date of completion of the project. In other words, to put Mason in the position it would have been in absent the misrepresentation we must assume that it would have in hand at the time it completed the project that amount of outlay and anticipated profit which it lost in completing the project. It seems to me to be only reasonable to assume that it would have been able to put that money to profitable use. Interest is the court's way of compensating Mason for the loss of the opportunity to invest that money.

I note that in connection with the issue of negligent misrepresentation the learned trial judge found that the Bank had a duty to warn Mason in April 1974 that Court did not have enough money to complete the project. This, in my view, is a separate (although related) head of liability. However, because the original negligent misrepresentation encompasses a greater liability than the duty to warn, I do not consider it necessary to deal with this aspect of the case.

Rainbow Industrial Caterers Ltd. v. CNR Co.
[1991] 3 SCR 3

[The plaintiff responded to a call for tenders issued by the defendant for the catering of meals nationwide for its track crews. It was estimated that 1,092,500 meals would be required, and the plaintiff lodged a bid of $4.94 per meal. The defendant then reduced the number of estimated meals by 15 percent and the plaintiff lodged a new bid of $5.02 per meal, which bid was accepted. It turned out that far fewer meals were required, there being a reduction in the order of a further 30 percent. The contract was not a financial success for the plaintiff and it suffered a loss of over $1,000,000 by the time it terminated the contract on 30 days' notice, as provided in the terms of the contract. The plaintiff then brought an action against the defendant for breach of contract and in negligence. The trial judge found the defendant liable for negligence and awarded $1,194,525 damages being the plaintiff's actual operating losses on the contract. On appeal, the Court of Appeal upheld liability in negligence but ordered a new trial on the assessment of damages. At issue was whether there had been a finding that but for the negligent misrepresentation by the defendant, the plaintiff would not have entered into the contract, and thus all the losses of the contract were recoverable; or, whether, if the plaintiff had been furnished accurate estimates, it would have submitted a different bid but at a higher per meal price, in which case, the plaintiff had been tricked out of the additional remuneration on each meal rather than its whole investment outlay. At the new trial, before the original trial judge, no new evidence was adduced, and thus the assessment of damages did not change. The second appeal to the BC Court of Appeal was dismissed.]

SOPINKA J (for La Forest, L'Heureux-Dubé, Gonthier, Stevenson, and Iacobucci JJ): ...

5. Assessment of Damages

The plaintiff seeking damages in an action for negligent misrepresentation is entitled to be put in the position he or she would have been in if the misrepresentation had not been made. In G.H.L. Fridman, 2 *The Law of Torts in Canada* (Toronto: Carswell, 1990), the author says (at p. 136):

> What sort of economic loss is recoverable in an action for negligent misrepresentation is still to be resolved conclusively, although the accepted test seems to be restoration of the plaintiff to the position in which he would have been if the negligent misrepresentation had never been made. Some cases suggest that what the plaintiff can recover is what might be termed "out of pocket expenses." In other words, he is entitled to be reimbursed for those costs and expenses which he has incurred and has expended in reliance on the misrepresentation.

To the same effect is the statement in "Assessment of Damages for Misrepresentations Inducing Contracts" by D.W. McLauchlan (1987), 6 Otago LR 370 at p. 388:

> It is axiomatic that the object of damages is to put the party whose rights have been violated in the same position, so far as money can do so, as if his rights had been observed. Therefore, in a tort action the object is to put the plaintiff in the position he would have been in if the tort had not been committed.

What that position would have been is a matter that the plaintiff must establish on a balance of probabilities. In a case in which a material negligent misrepresentation has induced the plaintiff to enter into a transaction, the plaintiff's position is usually that, absent the misrepresentation, the plaintiff would not have entered into the transaction. The plaintiff was restored to the position he would have occupied had he never entered the transaction in the following cases: *Friesen v. Berta* (1979), 100 DLR (3d) 91 (BC SC); *Irving Oil Ltd. v. Adams* (1984), 46 Nfld. & PEIR 234 (Nfld. CA); *H.B. Nickerson & Sons Ltd. v. Wooldridge* (1980), 40 NSR (2d) 388 (SC, AD); and *Steer v. Aerovox Inc.* (1984), 65 NSR (2d) (SC, TD).

Once the loss occasioned by the transaction is established, the plaintiff has discharged the burden of proof with respect to damages. A defendant who alleges that a plaintiff would have entered into a transaction on different terms sets up a new issue. It is an issue that requires the court to speculate as to what would have happened in a hypothetical situation. It is an area in which it is usually impossible to adduce concrete evidence. In the absence of evidence to support a finding on this issue, should the plaintiff or defendant bear the risk of non-persuasion? Must the plaintiff negative all speculative hypotheses about his position if the defendant had not committed a tort or must the tortfeasor who sets up this hypothetical situation establish it?

Although the legal burden generally rests with the plaintiff, it is not immutable: see *National Trust Co. v. Wong Aviation, Ltd.*, [1969] SCR 481 and *Snell v. Farrell*, [1990] 2 SCR 311. Valid policy reasons will be sufficient to reverse the ordinary incidence of proof. In my opinion, there is good reason for such reversal in this kind of case. The plaintiff is the innocent victim of a misrepresentation which has induced a change of position. It is just that the plaintiff should be entitled to say "but for the tortious conduct of the defendant, I would not have changed my position." A tortfeasor who says, "Yes, but you would have assumed a position other than the *status quo ante*," and thereby asks a court to find a transaction whose terms are hypothetical and speculative, should bear the burden of displacing the plaintiff's assertion of the *status quo ante*.

The operation of a similar principle can be found in cases in which a secured creditor unlawfully disposes of the debtor's goods. The loss to the debtor is the market value of the goods. A creditor who alleges that in the debtor's hands they would have less value must prove it: see *National Bank of Canada v. Corbeil*, [1991] 1 SCR 117 and *Banque Provinciale du Canada v. Gagnon*, [1981] 2 SCR 98.

Applying the foregoing to this I observe that Rainbow established the following:

(a) it was the victim of a negligent misrepresentation;

(b) but for this misrepresentation it would not have entered into this contract on these terms; and,

(c) this contract resulted in the loss that was awarded by the trial judge.

The appellant CN alleged that the loss was not all attributable to the misrepresentation because Rainbow would have entered into a different contract on other terms which would have resulted in at least some of the loss. What the respondent would have done had it not been for the tortious act requires a great deal of speculation, and, on the basis of the principles which I have reviewed above, I would apply the legal burden of proof against the appellant. The trial judge declined to make a finding in favour of the appellant on this issue.

The judgment of the majority of the Court of Appeal found no error on the part of the trial judge in this regard. Indeed, they seem to have expressly approved it. Alternatively, the passage to which I made reference above suggests that it was implicit in the findings of the trial judge that he found in favour of the plaintiff on this issue.

It was argued by CN that much of the loss was not caused by the misrepresentation and would have been suffered even had the estimate been accurate. CN pointed out that Rainbow itself, in para. 49 of its statement of claim, alleged that losses were caused by certain conduct of CN and its employees during the performance of the contract, such as taking too much food. Those claims were in breach of contract, and have never been adjudicated. But CN's position is that the losses caused by such conduct cannot be recoverable in the misrepresentation claim.

But I have concluded that CN bore the burden of proving that Rainbow would have bid even if the estimate had been accurate. That was not proved, and so it is taken as a fact that Rainbow would *not* have contracted had the estimate been accurate. The conduct referred to in para. 49 would not have occurred if there had been no contract, and therefore the loss caused thereby, like all other losses in the proper execution of the contract by Rainbow, is directly related to the negligent misrepresentation. The entering into of the contract is a link in the chain with respect to the para. 49 losses. These losses are causally and directly connected to the contract and the contract is causally connected to the negligent misrepresentation. Finally, in my view these damages were foreseeable and therefore are not remote. For these reasons, I conclude that the trial judge correctly assessed the damages and the Court of Appeal was right to affirm his judgment.

In the result, the appeal is dismissed with costs.

McLACHLIN J (dissenting): ... The trial judge found a negligent misrepresentation likely to induce a representee to act on it. This entitled him to infer that the plaintiffs relied on the misrepresentation leading it to enter into the contract.

This brings us to the next question: what portion of the plaintiffs' losses on the contract were caused by the negligent misrepresentation? The defendant led evidence that some of the loss had been caused by factors other than its negligent misrepresentation. If the trial judge had found that a portion of the plaintiffs' loss was caused by factors other than the negligent misrepresentation, then the chain of causation would have been broken and there would have been no recovery for losses caused by these factors. The trial judge, however, made no finding as to the effect on the total contract loss of acts of the plaintiffs, third parties, or other factors unrelated to the defendant's tortious act. He apparently took the view that these matters were irrelevant. In fact, they were relevant on the issue of causation of the loss. The matter must be remitted to trial to permit the necessary findings on this issue.

To amplify, the plaintiffs' losses may have been caused by: (a) the defendant's negligent misrepresentation; (b) other wrongful acts or omissions of the defendant, whether in negligence or breach of contract; (c) the plaintiffs' acts or omissions; (d) the acts of third parties; and/or (e) factors unrelated to the fault of either the plaintiffs or the defendant. The defendant is responsible for losses flowing from (a) or (b), but not for losses flowing from (c), (d) and (e). The trial judge wrongly assumed that all the plaintiffs' contract losses must be attributed to (a) and made no findings with respect to the other possibilities, notwithstanding the fact that the defendant CN led evidence on them. These findings must be made if justice is to be done.

Loss found to be caused by the defendant's misrepresentation must meet the further test of foreseeability; that is, it must not be too remote. The question is: was the loss caused by the misrepresentation the reasonably foreseeable consequence of the misrepresentation at the time it was made. This rule comes into play only after it has been established that the defendant's misrepresentation in fact caused the loss. Given that I would remit this case to trial for proper determination of the issue of causation, the rule of remoteness need not be considered at this stage. However, were it necessary to consider it, I would find that losses caused by factors other than the tortious misstatement would not have been foreseeable at the time the representation was made, given that the defendant was entitled to assume that the plaintiffs in bidding would make allowance for all factors relevant to the cost of executing the contract (excluding the defendant's wrongful acts), and that the plaintiff would not exacerbate the loss by its own acts.

I conclude the matter must be remitted to trial.

Additional Observations

The appeal as presented focused on whether the trial judge should have considered whether the plaintiffs had adduced evidence that they would not have contracted but for the representation. It will be apparent from the foregoing that I agree with the trial judge that, in the absence of rebutting evidence, he was entitled to infer reliance inducing the contract. While I agree with Justice Sopinka that such an inference may be drawn, in my view this flows from the authorities, and is not dependent upon the policy dictates of a particular case.

I also share the trial judge's view that speculation about what the plaintiffs would have bid had they known the truth is not necessary in a tort action for negligent misrepresentation. The aim in tort is simply to restore the plaintiff to the position it would have been in had the tortious act not been committed. The only question is whether it can be found (or inferred) that the plaintiffs would not have contracted but for the misrepresentation.

In contract the matter is otherwise. In contract the aim of damages is to put the plaintiff in the position it would have been in had the representation been true; *i.e.*, to compensate the plaintiff for its contractual expectation. It therefore becomes necessary to determine what would have happened had the representation made as to the number of meals been true. Even this inquiry, however, does not require the court to speculate on what the plaintiff would have bid had it known the true facts (the test proposed by Sopinka J).

In short, I conclude that the trial judge applied the appropriate general test for damages, given that he was considering the action in tort and not in contract. He also properly inferred reliance, notwithstanding the absence of a statement by the plaintiffs that they would not have contracted had they known the truth. The trial judge's only error was that identified by Southin JA in her reasons below: he failed to consider whether all the losses on the contract were caused by the defendant's tortious misrepresentation, or whether, on the contrary, some of the losses were caused by other factors.

The authorities do not suggest that all contractual losses are inevitably recoverable in an action for negligent or fraudulent misrepresentation inducing a contract. In *Esso Petroleum Co. v. Mardon, supra,* and *Doyle v. Olby (Ironmongers) Ltd.*, [1969] 2 QB 158 (CA), general contractual losses were recoverable. However, as Southin JA pointed out, there was no allegation in those cases that part of the loss had been caused by the plaintiffs' acts. The defendant is obliged to compensate the plaintiffs for losses caused by the defendant's wrongful act, but not for losses caused by the acts of others. Were it otherwise, the measure of damages in tort might significantly exceed the measure in contract. I agree with Southin JA that as a matter of practical justice, the damages awarded for a given wrongful act should be the same, whether the act is seen as a tort or a breach of contract.

Disposition

I would remit the matter to trial for determination of whether any part of the loss was caused by factors unrelated to the defendant's misrepresentation.

NOTES AND QUESTIONS

1. In *Banque Bruxelles Lambert SA v. Eagle Star Insurance Co.*, [1997] AC 191, the House of Lords had a different analysis of the problem. It turned to the concept of the duty of care in tort and held that the duty question must be addressed prior to the causation issue—that is, we might approach a case like *Rainbow Caterers* by saying that, regardless of what losses were in fact caused by CNR's misrepresentation, CNR had a duty only with respect to those losses attributable to its incorrect estimate of the number of meals that would be required; it had no duty with respect to any of Rainbow's losses attributable to other factors (such as Rainbow's miscalculation as to how much food railway workers consume). What effect does such an approach have on the question of which party has the onus of proving responsibility for that portion of the losses due to factors other than CNR's negligent estimate of the number of meals that would be required? For analysis of *Banque Bruxelles*, *Rainbow Caterers*, and other cases on this issue, see Nicholas Rafferty, "Damages for Market Losses" (2000), 33 *Canadian Business Law Journal* 38.

2. What reasons support awarding damages in the "tortious" measure in *Beaver*? Why could the loss of increased value of the house not be treated as an item of consequential loss even assuming the rest of the court's analysis were sound?

3. Assume the same facts as in *Beaver*, except that the McLenaghans were just about to sign a contract with a responsible contractor when Mr. Griffiths bursts into the room and shouts "Stop! I know a better man, Mr. Nixon." As a result, the McLenaghans hire Nixon. Assume that the McLenaghans can prove that the contractor they were just about to engage before Griffiths' intervention would have satisfactorily completed the house for the same price as that charged by Nixon. Would (should) the assessment of damages be different in the light of these new facts?

4. Is there a clear line between the "tortious" and the "contractual" measure, as the court in *Beaver* suggests? Should there be?

5. Does the following passage from John G. Fleming, *The Law of Torts*, 8th ed. (Sydney: The Law Book Co., 1992) accurately summarize the applicable principles?

> As in the case of deceit, damages for negligent misrepresentation are restricted to reliance losses and do not include expectation losses (loss of bargain) as could a claim for breach of warranty. Thus a plaintiff who had been misled into buying an insurance, in the belief that it contained a

certain cover in the event of injury, recovered nothing because the policy he purchased was worth (even without that cover) what he paid for it. The court allowed, however, that he would have prevailed if he could have proved that he forwent an opportunity to purchase elsewhere a policy containing the extra cover. Similarly, when a mistaken certificate from a local authority led a prospective purchaser to believe that the land was zoned for subdivision, his damages were assessed on the basis of its lesser value (plus conveyancing costs) but not including profits from any subdivision. These would have been recoverable only on proof that he lost an opportunity of buying another property which would have earned profits. While the possibility of recovering opportunity costs moves the tort measure closer to the expectancy measure of contracts, it is not identical with it. In case of a promise by a seller that the property yielded a certain return, the promisee's recovery (in contract) will be measured by the expected gains, whereas in tort for misrepresentation it would be the (usually lesser) return of an alternative investment.

6. Another difference traditionally said to exist between damages in contract and tort is in the area of remoteness of damages. Review the cases of *Kienzle v. Stringer* and *Asamera Oil Corp. Ltd. v. Sea Oil & General Corp.; Baud Corp., N.V. v. Brook* in chapter 1, "General Principles of Damages," and *Canlin Ltd. v. Thiokol Fibres Canada* in this chapter. Is there now any life left in the traditional distinction? Should there be?

7. Another traditional distinction between contract and negligence is that apportionment of liability (and damages) was not possible in contract. In *Smith v. McInnis*, [1978] 2 SCR 1357, a solicitor's negligence case, two judges of the Supreme Court of Canada considered this point in judgments dissenting from the majority of the court on the issue of liability of the solicitors Smith, Matthews; the majority did not address the apportionment issue. Speaking for the two dissenting judges, Pigeon J said:

> The Court of Appeal held that Smith, Matthews' contribution should be one-third. There is a cross-appeal against this division and it raises two questions:
>
> 1. Should the division of responsibility be modified?
>
> 2. Is a division justified in law? …
>
> The second question requires consideration of the legal basis for the apportionment of liability. This point was not considered in the Court of Appeal. After finding that Matthews had failed to discharge his duties to Meehan, Coffin JA only said that he did not feel he "should have the sole responsibility" and would apportion one-third against his firm. In this Court it was submitted that the liability was in contract, the *Contributory Negligence Act*, RSNS 1967, c. 54 was inapplicable to such liability and therefore there was no legal basis for an apportionment of liability.
>
> I have to agree that the liability of a solicitor to his client for negligence in his duty to give advice, or otherwise, is in contract only, not in tort. [Note: This is no longer the law. See *Central Trust v. Rafuse*, [1986] 2 SCR 147.] I adhere to the view I have previously expressed in other cases, that a breach of duty may constitute a tort only if it is a breach of a duty owed independently of any contract with the claimant, "an independent tort" as I said in *Nunes Diamonds v. Dominion Electric Protection*, [1972] SCR 769 at p. 777. In the case of a solicitor retained to give advice, his duty to advise properly arises only under contract and I do not see how liability can arise otherwise than on a contractual basis as was held in the case of a consulting engineer in *Halvorson v. McLellan Co.*, [1973] SCR 65 at p. 74. Breach of contract appears to be the basis on which a solicitor

was found liable by the House of Lords in *Nocton v. Ashburton*, [1914] AC 932 (HL (Eng.)), and by the English Court of Appeal in *Groom v. Crocker*, [1939] 1 KB 194 (CA).

Even assuming the *Contributory Negligence Act* is inapplicable to contractual liability, it does not seem to me that this means that there is no basis for the apportionment of liability. The reason for which at common law there could be no apportionment in actions founded on negligence was that any contributory negligence was a complete defence. It never was so in contract as far as I have been able to ascertain. In *Corpus Juris Secundum* under Contracts, para. 525, one reads:

> … [P]laintiff's contributory negligence is not a defense to an action for breach of contract, but plaintiff's negligence may be material where he seeks to hold defendant liable for damage to the property which constitutes the subject matter of the contract, unless such negligence is not the proximate cause of the damage.

There are not many cases cited in support of the above statement and they all appear to do no more than repeat it. The most recent is *Rotman v. Hirsch* (1972), 199 NW (2d) 53, a judgment of the Supreme Court of Iowa in which previous decisions are referred to (at p. 56). In *Joint Torts and Contributory Negligence* (London: Stevens, 1951) at p. 328 Glanville Williams, submits "that at common law the defence of contributory negligence applied in substance (whatever the precise language used) to actions in contract as well as to actions in tort (para. 59)." With respect, I do not find his reasoning and authorities persuasive. Having read all the cases he cites, I find that they only go on to show that a plaintiff's negligence may, in a proper case, be set up as a defence to an action founded on a contract. For instance, in *London Joint Stock Bank Limited v. MacMillan*, [1918] AC 777 (HL (Eng.)), the House of Lords held that when a cheque had been written in a way which made it easy to increase the amount for which it was drawn, the loss could not be recovered from the bank. As in other similar cases, it was an all or nothing situation. There was thus no occasion to decide whether the doctrine of contributory negligence as understood in actions in tort, was applicable in actions on contract so as to negate the possibility of apportionment when both parties were at fault.

In the same book, Glanville Williams expresses the opinion that the *Law Reform (Contributory Negligence) Act*, 1945, is applicable to liability in contract as well as in tort. I must point out that this English statute is far from identical with the Nova Scotia *Contributory Negligence Act*. While it similarly uses the word "fault" in the cardinal provision calling for apportionment of liability, it includes a definition of the term as follows:

> "[F]ault" means negligence, breach of statutory duty or other act or omission which gives rise to a liability in tort or would, apart from this Act, give rise to the defence of contributory negligence.

The *Contributory Negligence Act* of Nova Scotia, although originally adopted in 1954, does not take its inspiration from the United Kingdom Act. Section 1, the basic provision, is practically a verbatim copy of the New Brunswick *Contributory Negligence Act* in the form in which it appeared in the Revised Statutes of New Brunswick 1952, c. 36. As in other similar acts of other Canadian provinces, the wording is a re-arrangement, in slightly revised form, of the uniform *Contributory Negligence Act* prepared by the Conference of Commissioners on Uniformity of Legislation which was adopted by several Canadian provinces, including British Columbia in 1936, and Saskatchewan in 1944. The first *Contributory Negligence Act* had been adopted by Ontario in 1924 (c. 32) followed by similar statutes in New Brunswick and in British Columbia in 1925 (New Brunswick, c. 41, British Columbia, c. 8).

In all those enactments, the word "fault" (undefined) is used to describe what may occasion a division of liability. In some early statutes the expression was "fault or negligence"; however, in the *Uniform Act* as in all present statutes, the word "fault" is used by itself as in the Nova Scotia enactment where section 1 reads:

> 1(1) Where by the fault of two or more persons damage or loss is caused to one or more of them, the liability to make good the damage or loss is in proportion to the degree in which each person was at fault but if, having regard to all the circumstances of the case, it is not possible to establish different degrees of fault, the liability shall be apportioned equally.
>
> (2) Nothing in this Section operates so as to render any person liable for any damage or loss to which his fault has not contributed.

Fault, it should be noted, is the word used in the civil law to designate not only every culpable act or omission giving rise to delictual or quasi-delictual liability, but also any violation of a contractual obligation. In the civil law, the division of liability on the basis of the respective degrees of fault is effected by application of the principle of causality without any specific provision in that regard. To the extent that the damage suffered by a plaintiff is due to his own fault, it is held not to have been caused by the fault of the defendant. As at common law there is joint and several liability between the joint authors of fault causing the damage, but this solidarity among the joint authors does not exist as between them and the claimant. To the extent that the latter is the author of his own misfortune, he has to bear his loss but of his share only, because in the civil law nothing prevents a joint author of a delictual or quasi-delictual act from recovering from another such joint author his proper share of the loss; in other words, the situation is as under the *Tortfeasors Act*. (See what was said under the heading "Consequences of the common fault" in *Hôpital Notre-Dame de l'Espérance v. Laurent*, [1978] 1 SCR 605 at pp. 618-619.) It appears to me that the use of the word "fault" in the *Contributory Negligence Act* is evidence of the origin of the rule and of the intention to adopt the civil law principle with respect to the division of liability in proportion to the respective degrees of fault in all cases.

In the case of liability in contract, I think that even if the *Contributory Negligence Act* was applicable the same result would obtain at common law, because there never was in contractual liability the rule that prevented one tortfeasor from suing another. This I think was the true basis of the doctrine of contributory negligence: if the plaintiff was himself negligent he was in the situation of a joint tortfeasor who could have no recourse against another tortfeasor. The loss having fallen on him he had to bear it in full. In my opinion the authors of *Corpus Juris Secundum* are correct in their view that the doctrine of contributory negligence, does not apply in contract liability. The result is that the principle of causality must be applied and, therefore, there has to be an apportionment in the rare case of separate breaches of contract having contributed to a single loss.

Negligent Performance of a Contractual Duty

As we have seen, where a negligent misstatement induces a contract, the general measure of damages assumes that the contract would not have been entered into. However, it may be possible for the plaintiff to recover damages for other profitable opportunities that have been foregone on the strength of the misstatement, or to show that, but for the misstatement, the contract would have been entered into on more profitable terms.

The same holds true in the award of damages for professional negligence. The major difference between this group of cases and the first is that here, there is a contractual duty to use reasonable care and skill in providing the service. The application of the traditional reliance measure is appropriate where the professional negligence deprives the plaintiff of information permitting him or her to avoid a loss. The reliance measure may not be appropriate, however, if the professional negligence is itself the cause of the loss of some anticipated benefit. Three solicitor negligence cases illustrate the point.

In *Messineo v. Beale* (1978), 20 OR (2d) 49 (CA), the plaintiff entered into a contract to buy a number of pieces of land. The defendant solicitor negligently failed to advise the plaintiff that the vendor did not own one of them. The market value of the land actually conveyed by the vendor, even though it did not include this piece, was more than the purchase price. The Court of Appeal held the plaintiff could not recover damages because the proper measure of damages was the difference between the market value of the land received and the contract price. This result is defensible because the negligent advice of the solicitor was responsible only for the plaintiff not knowing that one of the pieces could not be conveyed by the vendor. The solicitor was not responsible for the vendor not having title to that piece. In other words, even if the solicitor had not been negligent, the vendor would not have received title to that piece because the vendor, due to no fault of the solicitor, did not have title to convey. Consider the following case.

Toronto Industrial Leaseholds Limited v. Posesorski et al.; Solway, Third Party
(1994), 21 OR (3d) 1 (CA)

[In 1979, the clients purchased a piece of industrial property for $325,000. S., their solicitor, acted for them and for the vendor. The clients knew that the property was subject to a long-term lease until 1984, but did not know that TILCO had obtained an option to rent the property for ten years beginning when the existing lease expired. That option provided for rent which was substantially below current market rents. S. knew about the option but had forgotten about it and did not tell the clients of its existence before they completed the transaction. His negligence in failing to do so was admitted. The clients learned of the option in 1981 when they received notice from TILCO that it intended to exercise its option. They consulted S., who told them that it was his opinion that the option was not a valid one. They retained new solicitors, who gave them the same advice as S. S.'s insurer was also of the opinion that the option was not valid.

In 1982, TILCO brought an action against the clients, seeking a declaration that the option was valid. The clients joined S. as a third party claiming contribution and indemnity based upon solicitor's negligence. In 1984, when the existing lease terminated, the tenants moved out leaving the clients with an empty building which they were unable to rent because of the option. The clients sold the property and as part of the sale proceeds took back a mortgage. TILCO had consented to the sale on condition that the clients would hold the principal of the mortgage in trust as security for any damages which TILCO might recover in the action against them. A settlement of TILCO's claim was negotiated. A consent judgment in the amount of $260,000 inclusive of damages, interest and costs was entered in TILCO's favour against the clients. S.'s insurer funded the settlement by paying the judgment. The condition of that funding was that the mortgage would continue to be held in trust pending the determination of the third party issue between the clients and S.

The trial judge found that, because of the option, the property had a true market value of $225,000 in 1979, $100,000 less than the price paid by the clients. She also found that during the two years when the clients owned the property before learning of the option, the real market value of the property declined by a further $5,000. She held that the measure of the clients' damages was the difference between the price paid for the property and its market value at the time of purchase. She adjusted the difference by $5,000 to compensate the clients for the further diminution in the property's value until 1981 when they learned of the option. She therefore assessed the clients' damages at $105,000 and ordered them to pay S. the sum of $155,000, being the excess of the funding provided by S.'s insurer over their assessed damages.

The clients appealed.]

GALLIGAN JA (dissenting in part): ... It is common ground, and found as a fact by the trial judge, that had the clients known of the existence of TILCO's option they would not have purchased the property. In 1979 they were interested in buying a property for investment purposes but would not have bought this one subject as it was to TILCO's option. ...

The Trial Judge's Assessment of the Clients' Damages

Over one-half of the time at trial was taken up with the evidence of two experts in the value of real estate. One was called by each side. Their testimony is voluminous, contradictory, at times incomprehensible and often speculative. Nevertheless the trial judge was able to glean something out of it all.

She found that, because of the option, the property had a true market value of $225,000 in 1979. This was $100,000 less than the price paid by the clients. She also found that during the two years when the clients owned the property before learning of the option the real market value of the property declined by a further $5,000.

The trial judge held that the measure of the clients' damages was the difference between the price paid for the property and its market value at the time of purchase. She based that holding upon the decision of this court in *Messineo v. Beale* (1978), 20 OR (2d) 49, 86 DLR (3d) 713. She adjusted that difference by the sum of $5,000 to compensate the clients for the further diminution in the property's value until 1981 when they learned of the option "and could therefore take corrective measures if they felt it appropriate." She therefore assessed the clients' damages at $105,000.

I am in respectful disagreement with the trial judge's approach to the assessment of the damages in this case and will set out my reasons for that disagreement. However, if I were in agreement with her basic approach, I think that she erred in not allowing interest on the notional loss of $100,000 as an element of her assessment of damages. If the trial judge was correct in fixing that amount as the clients' loss it seems to me that they were deprived of the use of $100,000 from 1979 until the property was sold at the end of 1984. If they had spent $100,000 less for the purchase of the property they would have had the $100,000 to place in other investments. It is reasonably foreseeable to anticipate that they would have earned income from the investment of that $100,000. I am of the opinion that their damages should include the interest which they would have earned on that $100,000. It does not appear that this claim was raised before the trial judge.

If I had agreed with the trial judge's approach to the assessment of the clients' damages I would have allowed their appeal to the extent of adding interest for the years 1979 through 1984 to their damages. Because of the view which I take of the case it is not necessary for me to quantify the amount of that interest.

Is Messineo v. Beale the Correct Measure of Damages in This Case?

Counsel for Mr. Solway agreed with the general proposition that the object of the assessment of damages was to restore the clients, so far as money could, to the position which they would have been in had it not been for the solicitor's negligence. Mr. Solway's negligence caused the clients to purchase a property subject to an option. That option reduced the value of the property by almost one-third.

It seems to me that there were two ways by which the clients could have been put in the position they would have been in had it not been for Mr. Solway's negligence. The first was to allow them damages equivalent to the reduction in market value caused by the option. This was the method chosen by the trial judge. The other was to remove the option. The removal of the option would restore the value of the property to what it would have been had there not been the option. In theory either method would accomplish the same thing. Where I part company with the trial judge is her conclusion that in the circumstances of this case the law recognized only one way, the difference between what they paid for it and its market value.

Messineo v. Beale, supra, was an unusual case. The client had entered into an agreement to purchase a number of pieces of property including Murch's Point. In fact the vendor did not own and could not convey Murch's Point. The solicitor failed to notice the defect and permitted his client to close the transaction by taking a conveyance of lands from the vendor which purported to include Murch's Point. Later it was learned that the client did not receive title to Murch's Point because the vendor did not own it. By happy coincidence the market value of the lands which the client did receive was $8,500 more than the price he actually paid for them.

It was in those circumstances that Arnup JA, speaking for this court, said at p. 52:

> The measure of damages is the difference in money between the amount paid by the client to the vendor and the market value of the land to which the client received a good title.

In that case no money was required to put the client in the position he would have been in had it not been for the solicitor's negligence. He suffered no damages. He had something worth more than he paid for it. In this case, however, the clients have suffered damages. They received something worth a great deal less than they paid for it.

Two years after Messineo v. Beale this court was required to revisit the problem of the assessment of damages in a solicitor's negligence case. It did so in Kienzle v. Stringer (1981), 35 OR (2d) 85. The circumstances in that case were somewhat more complicated than they were in *Messineo v. Beale*. I do not think it is necessary to review them in great detail. When the client purchased a property known as the Oxford Farm the solicitor certified to him that he had a "good and marketable title" to it. In fact there were serious defects in the title. Later, when the client went to sell the Oxford Farm, the transaction fell through because of the defects in title. The client lost the sale of the Oxford Farm, he lost the purchase of another property, the Kincardine Farm which he had intended to buy with the proceeds of the sale, and he suffered consequential damages resulting from having to continue to operate the Oxford Farm after having planned to leave it. The issue in the appeal was whether the client was entitled to the consequential damages and to damages for the loss of the purchase of the Kincardine Farm. The solicitor's position was, based upon *Messineo v. Beale*, that the client's damages were restricted to the difference between the contract price and the market value of the property at the time of its purchase. The trial judge had agreed with the solicitor that *Messineo v. Beale* restricted damages in such cases to the difference between the market value and what was paid for the property.

The appeal was allowed. The court was unanimous in allowing the consequential damages. In addition to the consequential damages, Wilson JA would have allowed the damages for the loss of the purchase of the Kincardine Farm. When Zuber JA, who was a member of the court which decided *Messineo v. Beale*, spoke about *Messineo v. Beale* he was speaking for the unanimous court. He said at p. 88:

> The learned trial judge was of the view that he was bound by the case of *Messineo v. Beale* (1978), 20 OR (2d) 49, and that his award of damages was therefore limited to the difference between the contract price and the market value of what was received. ...
>
> In my respectful view, *Messineo v. Beale* is not authority for such a broad proposition. ...
>
> It appears that in many of the cases, as a matter of fact, the damages amount to no more than the difference between the purchase price and the market value of what is received, *but I find no case binding on this Court compelling the acceptance of such a measure as a rule of law.*
>
> In my view the law should not support a rule which gives exceptional protection to solicitors from the general principles of damages which flow from either contractual or tortious responsibilities.

(Emphasis added.)

In the light of those comments I do not think that it is now open to this court to hold that, in solicitor's negligence cases, the measure of damages must be the difference between the purchase price and the market value of the property. That measure is one which is appropriate in some cases but not necessarily so in all. I do not think that it was an appropriate measure in this case. ...

The Appropriate Measure of Damages in This Case

I stated earlier that in my opinion there were two ways by which the clients could have been put in the position which they would have been in had it not been for Mr. Solway's negligence. The first was by paying them the difference between what they paid for the property and its market value. The second was getting rid of the option. That would involve paying the cost of removing the option. Since I have rejected the first, a process of elimination brings me to the second.

There is authority which justifies the second method of assessing the clients' damages. While in England, as a general rule, the diminution in value method is used to assess the damages in cases like this, where that method is not appropriate, the cost of reinstatement or of making good the negligent error can be allowed as damages: see *County Personnel Ltd. v. Alan R. Pulver & Co.*, [1987] 1 WLR 916 (CA), where the following appears in the judgment of Bingham LJ at p. 925:

> (2) On the authorities as they stand the diminution in value rule appears almost always, if not always, to be appropriate where property is acquired following negligent advice by surveyors. Such cases as *Philips v. Ward*, [1956] 1 WLR 471 (CA); *Pilkington v. Wood*, [1953] Ch. 770; *Ford v. White & Co.*, [1964] 1 WLR 885 (Ch.); and *Perry v. Sidney Phillips & Son*, [1982] 1 WLR 1297 (CA) lay down that rule and illustrate its application in cases involving both surveyors and solicitors.
>
> (3) That is not, however, an invariable approach, at least in claims against solicitors, and should not be mechanistically applied in circumstances where it may appear inappropriate. In *Simple Simon Catering Ltd. v. Binstock Miller & Co.* (1973), 228 EG 527 the Court of Appeal favoured a more general assessment, taking account of the "general expectation of loss." In other cases the cost of repair or reinstatement may provide the appropriate measure: the *Dodd Properties* case, [1980] 1 WLR 433 (CA), at p. 456, per Donaldson LJ. In other cases the measure of damage may properly include the cost of making good the error of a negligent adviser: examples are found in *Braid v. W.L. Highway & Sons* (1964), 191 EG 433, and *G. & K. Ladenbau (U.K) Ltd. v. Crawley de Reya*, [1978] 1 WLR 266 (QB).

(Emphasis added.)

The clients could have been reinstated by having the option removed and the negligent error could have been made good by its removal. The settlement with TILCO did both.

There was no reason for the clients to attempt to establish what the option's value might have been at any time before 1987 because until then the three sets of solicitors were of the opinion that it was not valid. There is no evidence about what it might have cost at an earlier time to get rid of the option. The amount of the settlement is not only the best evidence but it is the only evidence of what it would have cost to get rid of that option at any time. I think the cost of that settlement is the appropriate measure of damages to be applied in this case. There is another reason why I think $260,000 is the correct measure of the clients' damages. Mr. Solway's negligence was the direct cause of the clients being bound by TILCO's option. That option put them in peril of being sued by TILCO. TILCO did sue them and obtained judgment against them for $260,000. It seems to me inescapable that Mr. Solway's negligence led directly to the clients being subjected to a liability of $260,000. That judgment establishes the clients' damages. From another point of view it might be said that the $260,000 was paid to get rid of the option. From either point of view the result is the same. The clients suffered $260,000 in damages as a result of Mr. Solway's negligence.

The Clients' Claim for Special Damages

It will be remembered that when the existing lease expired in 1984 the clients were unable to lease the property because of TILCO's option. The property was vacant until it was sold. That sale was completed in late 1984 or early 1985. The clients had expenses in maintaining the vacant property from the end of the lease until the closing of the sale. The clients incurred those expenses because there was no rental income to cover them. Liability for those expenses is denied by Mr. Solway but their quantum is agreed to in the amount of $39,422.57.

Mr. Solway's position is that the proper measure of damages is the difference between the price paid and the market value of the property at the date of purchase. Therefore expenses incurred in 1984 can form no part of the clients' damages. The trial judge held;

> Their claim for special damages in the range of $39,000 cannot be sustained. These costs were incurred during the period where the property was vacant after the long term lease expired in 1984 and before the defendants were successful in selling the property.

In my opinion Mr. Solway's position that the clients' damages are restricted to the difference between the price paid and the market value at the time of purchase cannot be sustained in the light of *Kienzle v. Stringer*. That case is also authority for the proposition that consequential damages are recoverable if they are reasonably foreseeable. When I held that the clients' damages in this case ought to have been assessed at $260,000, I am not to be taken as holding that their damages are restricted to that amount. That amount is an important element of their damages, but it is not necessarily the only one.

Kienzle v. Stringer establishes that the test for assessing damages in a solicitor's negligence case is that of reasonable foreseeability. At p. 89 Zuber JA said:

> One problem that intrudes but briefly in this case is whether the liability of the solicitor is based in contract alone or in tort as well. (See again, *Messineo v. Beale, supra.*) However, in this case, the question is of little consequence. Liability is admitted, no limitation period intervenes: the sole question is the question of damages. The extent of recovery for damages from breach of contract is described in the classic words of Baron Alderson in *Hadley v. Baxendale* (1854), 9 Exch. 341 at p. 355, 156 ER 145 at p. 151:
>
> > Where two parties have made a contract which one of them has broken, the damages which the other party ought to receive in respect of such breach of contract should be such as may fairly and reasonably be considered either arising naturally, i.e., according to the usual course of things, from such breach of contract itself, or such as may reasonably be supposed to have been in the contemplation of both parties, at the time they made the contract, as the probable result of the breach of it.
>
> In tort, the measure is reasonable foreseeability. It is, I think, apparent that neither of these tests is a measure of precision and I number myself among those who are unable to see any real difference between them. (See *H. Parsons (Livestock) Ltd. v. Uttley Ingham & Co. Ltd.*, [1978] QB 791 (CA).)
>
> For the purpose of simplicity, I shall use the term "reasonable foreseeability" as embracing the test in both tort and contract. Using this measure, we come to the case at hand.

(Emphasis added.)

In that case the client had shut down the effective operation of the Oxford Farm because he thought he had sold it. When the sale fell through the client could not "do much with" the farm and his profit from it "dropped drastically." His lost profit was assessed and allowed as a consequential damage because it was found to be within the "ambit of reasonable foreseeability."

The option to rent at a rate which was not economical in 1984 would affect the clients' ability to rent the property profitably. That inability would clearly be within the ambit of reasonable foreseeability. It was reasonably foreseeable that the existence of the option could cause economic loss to the clients in the operation of their investment property. I am unable to find any distinction in principle between this case and *Kienzle v. Stringer*. It follows, therefore, that the clients' expenses were recoverable consequential damages and, in my opinion, ought to have been allowed. ...

I would allow the clients' special damages as claimed at $39,422.57. Those expenses were substantially incurred by the end of 1984. I would therefore allow prejudgment interest from January 1, 1985 as provided for in the relevant provisions of the *Courts of Justice Act*, RSO 1990, c. C.43.

Since the preparation of these reasons I have had the opportunity of reading in draft the comprehensive reasons for judgment prepared by my colleague Doherty JA. I maintain my difference of opinion with him in regard to the basis of assessing the major part of the clients' damages. However, I agree with him that the clients are entitled to recover, as an element of their special damages, their costs of challenging the validity of the option including the defence of the action brought against them by TILCO. They are, in my opinion, entitled to full indemnification for those legal expenses. If the parties cannot agree upon the amount of such costs they should be assessed by an assessment officer.

There does not appear to be any reason why the clients are not entitled to prejudgment interest upon those costs. It would seem to me that the amount of them must have crystallized at the time of the TILCO judgment. The consent judgment was granted on July 16, 1987. I would therefore allow prejudgment interest upon the amount of those costs from July 16, 1987 as provided for in the appropriate provisions of the *Courts of Justice Act*.

The Cross-Appeal

It follows from the reasons which I have set out above that I am of the opinion that the cross-appeal must be dismissed. ...

Disposition

1. In accordance with these reasons I would allow the appeal with costs and would set aside the judgment entered at trial. In its place I would enter judgment for the clients as follows:

(a) Declaring that the clients' damages exceed the sum of $260,000 paid on their behalf by Mr. Solway and that therefore the clients are not bound to reimburse any amount to him.

(b) Ordering Mr. Solway to pay to the clients:

(i) $39,422.57 plus prejudgment interest from January 1, 1985 calculated according to the appropriate provisions of the *Courts of Justice Act*;

(ii) their costs of challenging the option which costs are to be assessed by an assessment officer if they cannot be agreed upon plus prejudgment interest on the amount of those costs from July 16, 1987 calculated according to the appropriate provisions of the *Courts of Justice Act.*

(c) Ordering Mr. Solway to pay to the clients their costs of the action on a party and party scale.

2. I would dismiss the cross-appeal with costs.

DOHERTY JA (Laskin JA concurring): I have had the benefit of reading the persuasive reasons of Galligan JA. I agree with his reasons with respect to the amendment sought by the appellants. Also, like Galligan JA, I would allow the appeal and increase the damages awarded to the clients. I would, however, assess those damages differently than does my colleague.

I begin with the proposition that damages should, to the extent possible, restore the clients to the position they would have been in had the solicitor properly discharged his duty. I take this to be the aim regardless of whether the claim is for breach of contract or negligent performance of a professional service. After setting out the same principle Galligan JA writes at p. 8:

> It seems to me that there were two ways by which the clients could have been put in the position they would have been in had it not been for Mr. Solway's negligence. The first was to allow them damages equivalent to the reduction in market value caused by the option. This was the method chosen by the trial judge. The other was to remove the option. The removal of the option would restore the value of the property to what it would have been had there not been the option. In theory either method would accomplish the same thing. Where I part company with the trial judge is her conclusion that in the circumstances of this case the law recognized only one way, the difference between what they paid for it and its market value.

In my opinion, the two approaches identified by Galligan JA do not achieve the same result. The first awards the clients the monetary difference between the value of what the clients thought they were purchasing and the value of what, in fact, they purchased. The second method awards the clients the cost of removing the undisclosed liability some eight years after the purchase. The fact that the two approaches yield significantly different amounts indicates to me that they do not put the clients in the same position.

The removal of the option would not put the clients in the same position they would have been in had Mr. Solway properly performed his duties. His wrong, whether it be founded in negligence or breach of contract, rested in his failure to alert his clients to the existence of the option. Mr. Solway was under no obligation as part of his services to remove that option. Nor did he promise that he would remove the option or warrant that there was no option on the property. Mr. Solway's failure to perform properly that job did not create the option or cause it to remain in place when the clients purchased the property.

Mr. Solway's negligence also did not deny the clients the opportunity to purchase the property without the option for $325,000. That opportunity never existed. The vendor offered to sell the property complete with the option for $325,000. According to the evidence, the price was non-negotiable. There is no basis for concluding that but for Mr. Solway's negligence the clients could have acquired the property without the option for $325,000. That is, however, the effect of awarding the clients the amount required to buy out the option holder. On this view of the case, Mr. Solway is required to pay the cost of removing the option, and the clients end up with an asset—the property without the option—which they could not have had if Mr. Solway had properly performed his job.

Had Mr. Solway alerted his clients to the option, they would have had two alternatives. They could have refused to close, in which case they would have suffered no loss, or they could have attempted to negotiate a new price taking the option into consideration. The clients could not have purchased the property without the option for $325,000. The approach taken by Galligan JA goes beyond restoration and puts the clients in a better position than they would have been in had Mr. Solway properly performed his duties as their solicitor.

I distinguish a case like this one from one in which the solicitor's error results in an encumbrance remaining on title. In those cases, had the solicitor not been negligent, the client would have acquired the property without the encumbrance and his or her damages should include the cost of removing the encumbrance. *Kienzle v. Stringer* (1980), 14 RPR 29 (Ont. HCJ), var'd. (1981), 35 OR (2d) 85 (CA) is such a case. As a result of the solicitor's negligence in that case, property was mistakenly conveyed from an estate to the client, when in fact by the time of the conveyance the beneficiaries of the estate owned the property in their personal capacities. As a result of the solicitor's error, the deed conveyed nothing to the client. Had the solicitor drawn the deed properly, the client would have acquired the entire interest in the property. The client eventually acquired a two-thirds interest in the property at no additional cost. However, the owner of the remaining one-third interest refused to convey that interest to the client at the amount agreed on when the initial conveyance occurred. The client sued his solicitor. The trial judge held that the client was entitled to recover damages equal to the net cost of buying out the remaining one-third interest calculated as of the trial date. In so holding, the trial judge assessed the damages and the amount needed to give the client the monetary equivalent of what he would have had after the conveyance had the solicitor not been negligent, that is, a full interest in the land.* The Court of Appeal affirmed this part of the trial judgment with a minor mathematical correction (at p. 89).

The trial judge's approach in *Kienzle*, which is in fact the approach used by Galligan JA in this case, was appropriate in *Kienzle* because as a result of the solicitor's error, the client did not acquire a property interest which he would have acquired but for that error. In my view, it does not apply where the property interest acquired by the client is the very property interest offered for sale by the vendor, but had the solicitor not been negligent the client would not have purchased that interest. Indeed, Zuber JA in *Kienzle*, *supra*, at p. 88 makes that very distinction. In distinguishing the former type of case as represented by *Kienzle*, *supra*, from the latter type of case as represented by *Messineo*, *supra*, Zuber JA said at p. 88:

> In my respectful opinion, *Messineo v. Beale* decides only that the defendant did not *cause* the plaintiff any damage. Since the vendor [in *Messineo*] did not own Murch's Point the defendant's solicitor did not cause its loss. The solicitor caused the plaintiff to complete a transaction that he would otherwise have avoided but no loss resulted from this. The plaintiff could have resold

---

* The trial judge purported to apply *Messineo v. Beale* (1978), 20 OR (2d) 49 (CA), aff'g. (1976), 13 OR (2d) 329 (HC) in assessing the client's damages. In fact, as Professor J. Swan points out in his annotation to the trial judge's reasons (at 29 (RPR)), the trial judge did not use the *Messineo* approach, but rather looked to the monetary value of the property interest the client would have had but for the solicitor's error.

as soon as he discovered that he had not obtained Murch's Point and would have suffered no loss at all. It would have been far different if the vendor had owned Murch's Point and the solicitor had omitted the property from the deed or in some other way had caused the plaintiff to lose the property. In that case the plaintiff's damage would have been the value of the missing property despite the fact that the value of what he had received was greater than the purchase price.

(Emphasis in original.)

I, therefore, conclude that the approach adopted by Galligan JA, while appropriate had the solicitor's error caused the option to remain on title is not appropriate where the error did not go to the continued existence of the option, but rather caused the clients to enter into a transaction which they otherwise would not have entered into.

The parties agreed at trial that had Mr. Solway told the clients about the option, they would not have purchased the property. Perfect restitution would therefore appear to require a notional undoing of the transaction some ten years after it was completed, coupled with an attempt to determine the net benefit or loss suffered by the clients as a result of entering into the transaction. Sometimes the evidence permits a relatively accurate reconstruction of events on the assumption that certain things would or would not have occurred had there been no breach (see, *e.g.*, *Semelhago v. Paramadevan* (1994), 19 OR (3d) 479 (CA)). In this case, it is impossible to perform that reconstruction. There are too many variables, many of which were not addressed in the evidence, presumably because the parties were satisfied that an attempt to unravel the transaction and establish the clients' position on the assumption that the transaction had not occurred was so complicated as to defy performance.

Absent the ability to make perfect restitution, a court, in assessing damages, must do the best it can. In my view, the loss flowing from Mr. Solway's negligence falls under three heads. First, the clients paid more for the property than it was actually worth. Second, they lost the use of the funds represented by that overpayment for a period of five years. Third, the clients incurred certain additional costs and expenses which were a reasonably foreseeable consequence of Mr. Solway's negligence. The clients should recover all of those losses. I will quantify each in turn.

A. The Overpayment (The Diminution in Value)

The clients agreed to pay $325,000 for the property, believing that it was subject to a five-year lease. They in fact got something different than they thought they were purchasing. They received a property with a five-year lease, but one also encumbered by a further ten-year lease option at commercially undesirable rates. The clients are entitled to recover the difference between the amount paid by them and the fair market value of the property with the option. Like the trial judge, I would hold that *Messineo v. Beale, supra*, governs that assessment.

In *Messineo*, the clients believed that they were obtaining title to a parcel of land including an area known as Murch's Point. In fact, the vendor owned the land on both sides of Murch's Point but did not own the Point and could not convey it to the clients. Because of their solicitor's error, the clients were not told that Murch's Point was not included in the transaction. They learned of the error several months after the purchase was completed and sued their solicitor, claiming a loss equal to the actual value of Murch's Point. The trial judge and this court rejected that submission. Arnup JA observed at p. 51:

In my view, it is obvious that the defendant's breach of duty was not the cause of the plaintiff's getting no title to Murch's Point. The vendor had no title to Murch's Point, and could give none. Nothing the defendant could have done would have changed the situation.

Arnup JA went on to hold at p. 52:

> The measure of damages is the difference in money between the amount paid by the client to the vendor and the market value of the land to which the client received a good title.

Zuber JA, in a concurring judgment, wrote at p. 54:

> The negligence of the defendant did not cause the plaintiffs to lose Murch's Point. Since Finley, the vendor in the subject transaction never had title to Murch's Point it was never within the grasp of the plaintiffs, and hence could not have been lost. The defendant's negligence simply caused the plaintiffs to complete a transaction that they otherwise would have avoided. Therefore, it is the responsibility of the defendant to compensate the plaintiffs for the loss suffered as a result of entering this transaction.

Justice Zuber agreed that compensation should be calculated in the manner described by Justice Arnup.

Justice Zuber's words have direct application to this case. The clients were not deprived of the property minus the option because of Mr. Solway's negligence. The property without the option could not have been conveyed to the clients. As in *Messineo*, the solicitor's negligence caused the clients to complete a transaction they would not have entered into had the solicitor done his job properly. As in *Messineo*, the clients are entitled to recover the overpayment, if any, resulting from the solicitor's failure to alert them to the "defect" in the property. The overpayment is the difference between the price actually paid for the property and the market value of the property with the option. ...

In accepting the approach in *Messineo* as the norm, I do not mean to suggest that the *Messineo* formula provides the only method of assessing damages in cases where clients have entered into real estate transactions as a result of negligent advice from their solicitors. As the English cases demonstrate, there will be instances where other approaches more effectively achieve a full restoration: *County Personnel Ltd. v. Alan R. Pulver & Co.*, [1987] 1 All ER 289 (CA) at p. 297; *Hayes v. James & Charles Dodd*, [1990] 2 All ER 815 (CA) at p. 819. These cases, however, establish that the measure of damages used in *Messineo* is the appropriate one absent some basis in the evidence for holding that some other means more effectively restores the wronged party to the position he or she would have been in but for the solicitor's error.

As predictability in the assessment of damages fosters early and fair settlements of claims, I see great value in promoting that certainty. The *Messineo* approach to damages has been widely accepted as a proper measure of damages in cases like this one and should be applied unless the party promoting a different approach can demonstrate that the alternative approach more effectively achieves the restitutionary goal underlying the law of damages. For the reasons set out above, I think the alternative put forward by the clients, that is, the cost of the removal of the option, goes beyond restitution and does not offer a satisfactory alternative to the *Messineo* approach.

I would also emphasize that the measure of damages described in *Messineo* is not necessarily exhaustive of the full measure of damages suffered by clients in every case. The negligent solicitor is responsible for all reasonably foreseeable damages caused by his or her negligence. In some cases, there may be consequential damages in addition to those reflected in the difference between the amount paid by the client and the market value of the property. If those consequential damages are reasonably foreseeable, then the client is entitled to be compensated for those losses on top of any award assessed using the *Messineo* formula.

Kienzle, supra, is instructive with respect to the assessment of consequential damages. As indicated above, the trial judge had purported (wrongly, in my view) to apply *Messineo* in assessing the client's damages. The trial judge went on to hold that with a very limited exception, *Messineo* provided the full measure of the client's damages. The Court of Appeal did not consider whether the trial judge's quantification of the damages was in fact an accurate reflection of the *Messineo* approach, but instead focused on his holding that the *Messineo* approach provided an exhaustive measure of those damages.

Zuber JA summarized the trial judgment at p. 88:

> The learned trial judge was of the view that he was bound by the case of *Messineo v. Beale* [citations omitted] and that his award of damages was therefore limited to the difference between the contract price and the market value of what was received.

Zuber JA expressly held that *Messineo* was not authority for the broad proposition that the trial judge had taken from the case. After summarizing the holding in *Messineo*, Zuber JA said at p. 88:

> It appears that in many of the cases, as a matter of fact, the damages amount to no more than the difference between the purchase price and the market value of what is received, but I find no case binding on this Court compelling the acceptance of such a measure as a rule of law.

Zuber JA then went on to consider whether the additional damages claimed by the plaintiffs, which his Lordship referred to as "consequential losses," were a reasonably foreseeable result of the solicitor's breach of his duty. Zuber JA, joined by Goodman JA, held that certain losses relating to the operation of the farm were reasonably foreseeable, but that losses relating to the Kienzles' inability to purchase another farm were not reasonably foreseeable. Justice Wilson disagreed and regarded both losses as reasonably foreseeable and therefore recoverable.

With respect to the contrary view, I do not regard *Kienzle* as a departure from *Messineo*. As indicated above, the two cases demonstrate that the initial measure of damages will depend in part on the nature of the solicitor's error. If the error caused the client to lose an interest in property he or she otherwise would have had, *Kienzle* is the appropriate starting point. If the error did not cause the client to lose an interest in property, but instead caused the client to enter into a transaction he or she would otherwise not have entered into, then *Messineo* is the appropriate starting point in the assessment of the client's damages. Further, as the Court of Appeal in *Kienzle* indicates, even where *Messineo* is the appropriate starting point, that measure of damages does not necessarily exhaust the client's claim. Consequential damages are recoverable if they were reasonably foreseeable. The Court of Appeal judgments in *Messineo* and *Kienzle* work together to describe the client's measure of damages.

Messineo addresses the loss suffered by the initial overpayment, and *Kienzle* speaks to the solicitor's liability for reasonably foreseeable consequential losses caused by the solicitor's negligence and occurring subsequent to the ill-advised purchase. There are consequential damages in this case and I will address those later in these reasons.

Galligan JA holds that *Messineo* applies only where it can be said that it would have been reasonable for the client to sell the property upon learning of the solicitor's error. My colleague goes on to hold that it would have been unreasonable for these clients to sell in 1981 when they learned of the existence of the option because of the advice they received from Mr. Solway and their own solicitors to the effect that the option was not valid.

I have two difficulties with this position. First, nothing in *Messineo* suggests that the approach used in that case turned on whether it was reasonable for the clients to sell the property when they learned that they did not own Murch's Point. In fact, the clients had not sold the property and the judgment makes only brief reference to their minimal efforts to sell the property (at p. 52). Neither Arnup JA nor Zuber JA suggests that the measure of damages settled upon in *Messineo* was dependent on a finding of fact that it would have been reasonable for the clients to sell the property when they learned of their solicitor's error. Nor did the trial judge make that finding. ...

These clients ... were free to allow (sic) any of several courses of conduct after they learned of Mr. Solway's error. ... [They] chose to fix the problem by removing it, and thereby acquired something which they would not have been entitled to had Solway properly performed his job. The clients chose to put themselves in a different position than they would have been had Mr. Solway performed his job properly. They were, of course, fully entitled to do so, but Mr. Solway cannot be required to pay the costs of putting them in that different position.

My second concern with the finding that it was unreasonable for the clients to sell the property before they did, is that no such finding was made at trial. ...

As I am satisfied that *Messineo* controls the assessment of damages in so far as they relate to the clients' overpayment on the purchase price, I turn now to the trial judge's calculation of those damages. She accepted the clients' expert's evidence as to the value of the property with the lease in 1979 and found that the clients had paid $100,000 more than the property was worth with the lease. The trial judge also found that the value of the property decreased from $225,000 to $215,000 between the date of sale and 1981, when the clients learned of the existence of the option. That decrease in value was attributed directly to the existence of the option. The trial judge calculated the clients' loss by subtracting the 1981 value ($215,000) from the amount paid by the clients in 1979 ($325,000). The trial judge fixed the resulting amount at $105,000. It would appear that she made an arithmetical error and that the actual loss was $110,000 ($325,000 − $215,000).

In using the value of the property as of the date of discovery of the error as opposed to the date of the purchase, the trial judge appears to have ploughed new ground. ...

Where the value of the property decreases between the purchase date and the date of discovery of the error and the decrease is directly attributable to the fact that it was not disclosed to the client, then, in my view, the negligent solicitor should bear the burden of that decrease in value. I too would fix the value of the property as of 1981 and would hold that the clients paid $110,000 more for the property than it was worth. That is the measure of their damages according to the *Messineo* formula.

B. *The Monetary Value of the Loss of the Use of Funds Represented by the Overpayment*

Mr. Solway's negligence caused the clients to pay $100,000 more than they should have for the property. By 1981 when the clients were made aware of Mr. Solway's error, the amount of the overpayment had climbed to $110,000. But for Mr. Solway's breach, the clients would have had the amount represented by the overpayment and could have used that money to earn more money. The clients are entitled to be paid the amount they could have earned by investing the overpayment: *Watts v. Morrow*, ... [[1991] 4 All ER 937 (CA)], at pp. 958-60; *Perry v. Sidney Phillips & Son, supra*, at pp. 708-12. The clients were effectively deprived of the amount represented by their overpayment until December 1984 when the property was sold for $700,000. The clients received $310,000 cash and took back a mortgage in the amount of $390,000. That mortgage was held in trust pending the resolution of the option holder's claim; however, the clients received the interest payments on the mortgage. In my view, this arrangement effectively gave the clients the use of the amount represented by their overpayment after December 1984. I would, therefore, hold that the clients are entitled to the amount they could have earned by investing the overpayment during the five-year per-iod between the purchase (October 1979) and the sale (December 1984).

Interest rates fluctuated considerably during that time. Bank rates ranged from a high of 22.25 per cent to a low of 11 per cent. Using those rates as a guideline, I would apply a 15 per cent rate of return in calculating this part of the clients' loss and would fix that loss at $81,000. In doing so, I do not treat this as a matter governed by the statutory provisions relating to prejudgment interest, but rather as the amount needed to compensate the clients for the loss of the use of the funds represented by the overpayment.

In my opinion, the damages awarded should have included the amount set out above. Although no such claim was made at trial, I see no prejudice to Mr. Solway in permitting that claim to be advanced now.

C. *Consequential Damages*

It was reasonably foreseeable that the clients would seek legal advice upon learning of Mr. Solway's error. They needed legal assistance in untangling themselves from the mess created by Mr. Solway's negligence. The clients are entitled to be compensated for the cost of that legal advice: *Kienzle v. Stringer, supra*, at p. 87.

The clients obtained legal advice. That advice, entirely consistent with the position taken by Mr. Solway and counsel for his insurers, was to contest the validity of the option. The contest led to litigation which was not ultimately resolved until 1987. In my opinion, the clients are entitled to be compensated for their own legal costs associated with retaining new counsel and challenging the validity of the option. Compensation in this context must mean full indemnification for all reasonable fees and disbursements. In so holding, I observe that no issue was taken with respect to the reasonableness of the conduct of the new solicitors in respect of their efforts to challenge the validity of the lease.

Given the way the parties advanced their respective claims before the trial judge, that amount is not quantified in the trial record. I do not think that this should deny the clients their right to recover that amount. I would hope that the parties could agree on the costs of those services. If they cannot, I would direct that the assessment officer determine those costs.

The clients' consequential damages do not stop with the indemnification for the costs associated with their new lawyer's attempts to extract the clients from the problem created by Mr. Solway's negligence. As is to be expected, the clients followed that advice, and that too cost them money. In my view, it was reasonably foreseeable not only that the clients would seek out new legal advice, but that they would follow any reasonable advice given to them by their new lawyers. Mr. Solway can hardly challenge the reasonableness of that advice here since the advice and the steps taken pursuant to that advice were entirely consistent with the position he and the lawyers for his insurer took between 1981 and 1987.

As a result of following their new lawyer's advice, the clients eventually became liable, as part of the settlement with the option holder, to pay some of the costs incurred by the option holder in advancing its claim with respect to the option. These costs were a direct product of following the advice given by the new lawyers and were a reasonably foreseeable consequence of Mr. Solway's breach. The clients are entitled to recover that amount from Mr. Solway: *Braid v. W.L. Highway & Sons* (1964), 191 EG 433 (QB); *Moorcroft v. Doraty* ... [(1990), 65 DLR (4th) 315 (Ont. HC)], at p. 320. The record does not disclose the actual amount of the option holders' legal fees paid by the clients although it consists of some part of the $40,000 paid to the option holder on account of interest and legal fees. I would hope that the parties can agree on what part of that $40,000 constituted legal fees. If they cannot, I would refer this matter to the assessment officer.

By following the advice given to them by their new lawyers, the clients incurred one further monetary loss. Because the clients challenged the validity of the lease, the status of the property was uncertain in August of 1984 when the five-year lease expired. This uncertainty scuppered arrangements the clients had made to lease the property after the five-year lease expired. As a result, the property was vacant for several months and the clients incurred expenses in the amount of $39,422.57. As it was reasonably foreseeable that the clients would follow the reasonable legal advice given to them by their new lawyers, and as the expenses associated with maintaining the vacant property were a direct result of following that advice, I would hold that these too constituted consequential damages properly payable to the clients by Mr. Solway. I would also allow prejudgment interest on this amount as described by Galligan JA in his reasons.

D. Summary of Damages

I would assess the clients' damages as follows:

1. Overpayment	$110,000	
2. Monetary value of the loss of the use of the funds constituting the overpayment	81,000	
3. Consequential damages		
(i) Indemnification for costs associated with retaining new lawyers and challenging the validity of the option	To be agreed upon or fixed by the assessment officer	
(ii) The amount paid on account of legal fees incurred by the option holder	To be agreed upon or fixed by the assessment officer	
(iii) Expenses associated with maintaining the vacant property	39,422 plus interest	

As is evident, my approach, like that of Galligan JA, would significantly increase the clients' damages. His approach results in a somewhat larger increase.

E. The Cross-Appeal

My proposed disposition of the appeal dooms the cross-appeal. I would dismiss the cross-appeal.

F. Costs at Trial

For the reasons provided by Galligan JA, I would hold that the clients are entitled to their costs at trial on a party-and-party basis.

G. Disposition

I would allow the appeal with costs, set aside the judgment entered at trial and substitute a declaration that the clients are entitled to the amount calculated in accordance with the summary of damages set out above. If that amount does not exceed $260,000, the clients shall pay the difference to Mr. Solway. If the amount exceeds $260,000, Mr. Solway shall pay the difference to the clients.

I would dismiss the cross-appeal with costs.

Appeal allowed.

These cases may be contrasted with situations in which the professional negligence does deprive the plaintiff of a profitable opportunity. *Kienzle v. Stringer* (1981), 35 OR (2d) 85 (CA) (leave to appeal to SCC refused March 4, 1982), chapter 1, "General Principles of Damages," is an example. There, the solicitor's error resulted in the conveyance conveying nothing and the Court of Appeal upheld a damage award based on the amount of money necessary to acquire what would have been conveyed but for the solicitor's mistake.

Negligent Rendering of a Service Apart from Contract

In these types of cases, the provision of services causes injury to third parties who have no contractual relationship with the service provider. So, for example, in *White v. Jones*, [1995] 1 All ER 691 (HL), where a solicitor drew up a will and, as a result of his negligence, the intended beneficiary was deprived of a legacy, the solicitor was held liable for the loss. The basis of the holding is that where, as in *White*, the negligent performance of a service causes a loss of an advantage that would have resulted from the proper performance of the service, damages are assessed by giving the financial equivalent of the lost advantage. In this regard, Lord Goff said at p. 711:

> I do not consider that damages for loss of an expectation are excluded in cases of negligence arising under the principle in Hedley Byrne, simply because the cause of action is classified as tortious. Such damages may in principle be recoverable in cases of contractual negligence; and I cannot see that, for present purposes, any relevant distinction can be drawn between the two forms of action. In particular, an expectation loss may well occur in cases where a professional

man, such as a solicitor, has assumed responsibility for the affairs of another; and I for my part can see no reason in principle why the professional man should not, in an appropriate case, be liable for such loss under the Hedley Byrne principle (emphasis added).

This is consistent with the approach taken in the solicitors' negligence cases. The choice of expectation or reliance damages depends on the loss caused by the negligent act. In all cases, the goal is to put the plaintiff in the position that would have been reached had proper advice or service been provided.

Breach of Fiduciary Duty Where There Is Contract Between the Parties

There is considerable overlap among cases involving liability for breach of contract, negligent performance of a contractual duty, and breach of fiduciary duty. For example, in relationships that are inherently fiduciary, such as principal and agent, there will usually also be contractual obligations and tort duties of care. In such cases of concurrent liability, the choice of the proper remedy may be intricate. If the traditional categories are applied, the restitutionary approach of fiduciary duty, the reliance approach of negligence, and the expectation approach of contract may lead to different remedies. (For excellent discussions, see Jeff Berryman, "Equitable Compensation for Breach of Fact-Based Fiduciaries" (1999), 37 *Alberta Law Review* 95; Paul M. Perell, "Compensation and the Scope of Equity's Remedial and Restitutionary Generosity" (1999), 37 *Alberta Law Review* 114.)

The Supreme Court of Canada has very recently reaffirmed its commitment to remedial flexibility exercised according to the assessment of the harm suffered and the underlying policy objectives of the substantive law giving rise to liability. As Binnie J put it in *Cadbury Schweppes Inc. v. FBI Foods Ltd.*, [1999] 1 SCR 142, at para. 26 in the context of an action for breach of confidence:

> While none of the judges who decided Lac Minerals advocated common law or statutory remedies for an action for breach of confidence, they did look to the underlying policy objectives of the various potential causes of action. They fastened on the particular circumstances that gave rise to liability in the case before them as governing the choice of remedy. That having been said, La Forest J, at p. 677, was at pains to avoid a "Chancellor's foot" approach to the choice of remedy:
>
> > I do not countenance the view that a proprietary remedy can be imposed whenever it is "just" to do so, unless further guidance can be given as to what those situations may be. To allow such a result would be to leave the determination of proprietary rights to "some mix of judicial discretion … subjective views about which party 'ought to win' …, and 'the formless void of individual moral opinion.'" …
>
> The emphasis on matching the remedy to underlying policy objectives was reiterated in *M.(K.) v. M.(H.)*, [1992] 3 SCR 6, per La Forest J at p. 81, and per McLachlin J at p. 86. It is in this sense, I think, that Sopinka J's statement in *Lac Minerals* (at p. 615) that "[t]he jurisdictional basis supporting the particular claim is relevant in determining the appropriate remedy," must be understood. *In short, whether a breach of confidence in a particular case has a contractual, tortious, proprietary or trust flavour goes to the appropriateness of a particular equitable remedy* but does not

limit the court's jurisdiction to grant it. Such a view is consistent with earlier cases in this Court, including *Pre-Cam Exploration & Development Ltd. v. McTavish*, [1966] SCR 551 (emphasis added).

Compensation for breach of equitable duties is addressed in chapter 10, "Financial Relief in Equity." In taking up Justice Binnie's challenge to match the remedy to the underlying policy objective, it will be helpful to reflect on the policy considerations relating to damages for breach of contract.

REVIEW PROBLEM

Ms. Developer retains Mr. Solicitor to act for her in connection with her purchase of an apartment building in downtown Sleepyville. Mr. Solicitor, negligently and in breach of contract, fails to obtain the correct signatures on the conveyance and as well to discharge a mortgage on the property. The result is that Ms. Developer pays the full purchase price of $1 million and obtains nothing in return. She sues Mr. Solicitor concurrently in contract and tort. Assume the following additional facts:

1. The apartment building produced a net profit (ignoring the cost of acquiring the building) of $200,000 per year.

2. Shortly after the transaction, the economy of Sleepyville skyrockets. The value of the apartment building soars to $3 million.

3. But for the solicitor's negligence and breach of contract, Developer would have obtained good title to the property.

4. Solicitor sought advice about the transaction from Professor Property, a lawyer teaching real property at the Sleepyville Law School, and Solicitor has commenced third-party proceedings against Property.

5. The dramatic upturn in the Sleepyville economy was not within the reasonable contemplation of Developer or Solicitor at the time Solicitor was retained, but the loss to Developer by virtue of that upturn was a loss of the type that was foreseeable at that time.

6. Developer suffered a nervous collapse as a result of the transaction.

How should damages be assessed in both contract and tort in this situation? What award should the court make?

CHAPTER FOUR

Damages for Invasion of Property Interests

The following material deals with the assessment of damages where the plaintiff's real or personal property has been damaged, destroyed, or misappropriated. As in other instances in the law of damages, the concept of the market is a central one and you should pay special attention to how the concept is used and how it is defined in these cases. You should also consider how the approaches adopted in these cases seem designed to achieve compensation or whether other objectives are incidentally or deliberately relevant to the outcomes.

DESTRUCTION OF PROPERTY

Liesbosch Dredger v. Edison S.S.
[1933] AC 449 (HL (Eng.))

[On November 26, 1928, the respondents' steamship *Edison* fouled the moorings of the appellants' dredger *Liesbosch* and did not free them until she had carried the *Liesbosch* into the open sea, where it filled with water, sank, and was a total loss.]

LORD WRIGHT: ... I agree with the conclusion of the Court of Appeal that the Registrar and Langton J proceeded on a wrong basis and that the damages must be assessed as if the appellants had been able to go into the market and buy a dredger to replace *Liesbosch*. On that basis it is necessary to decide between the conflicting views put forward, on the one hand by the respondents, that all that is recoverable is the market price of the dredger, together with cost of transport to Patras and interest, and on the other hand by the appellants that they are also entitled to damages in addition for loss during the period of inevitable delay before the substituted dredger could arrive and start work at Patras. The respondents in support of their contention relied on *The Columbus* (1849), 3 W Rob. 158 (Admir.) at p. 164; 166 ER 922 at p. 924, in which Dr. Lushington refused in respect of a fishing vessel any compensation save on the basis of the smack's market value with interest; he gave as an illustration of the same principle the case of an East Indiaman with a valuable freight on board sunk in collision by a wrongdoing vessel; in that case, as in the case of the humble fishing vessel, the compensation would in his opinion be thus limited. He said:

> The true rule of law in such a case would, I conceive, be this, viz., to calculate the value of the property destroyed at the time of the loss, and to pay it to the owners, as a full indemnity to

them for all that may have happened, without entering for a moment into any other consideration. If the principle to the contrary, contended for by the owners of the smack in this case, were once admitted, I see no limit in its application to the difficulties which would be imposed upon the Court. It would extend to almost endless ramifications and in every case I might be called upon to determine, not only the value of the ship, but the profits to be derived on the voyage in which she might be engaged, and indeed even to those of the return voyage, which might be said to have been defeated by the collision.

But, for all the eminence of Dr. Lushington, the simple but arbitrary rule he thus enunciated has not prevailed at least as regards ships under profitable freight engagement. Perhaps it was felt that, in the words afterwards used by Lord Sumner in *Admiralty Commissioners v. S.S. Chekiang (Owners)*, [1926] AC 637 (HL (Eng.)) at p. 643: "The measure of damages ought never to be governed by mere rules of practice, nor can such rules override the principles of the law on this subject." Lord Sumner also distinguishes "a rule of thumb" from what is binding law. In these cases the dominant rule of law is the principle of *restitutio in integrum*, and subsidiary rules can only be justified if they give effect to that rule. A view of the practice of the Admiralty Court differing from that of Dr. Lushington was stated by Sir Robert Phillimore in *The Northumbria* (1869), LR 3 A & E 6 (Admir.), and in *The Kate*, [1899] P 165 it was expressly held that in the case of a vessel being totally lost by collision, while on her way in ballast to load under a charter, the proper measure of damages against the vessel solely liable for the collision was the value of the vessel at the end of her voyage, plus the profits lost under the charterparty. The same principle was extended in *The Racine*, [1906] P 273 (CA) to a vessel sunk while on her voyage under charter from her home port to a foreign port, from which port she was chartered to proceed to another port, from which again she was chartered back to her home port; it was held that the owner was entitled to recover the presumed net loss of freight on all three charters less 10 per cent for contingencies and her value on her return to the home port at the end of the three charters. But in *The Philadelphia*, [1917] P 101 (CA) it was decided that the value must be determined as at the time of the loss (the market had in that case risen between the date of the loss and the presumed date of her arrival at the end of the voyage) together with the proper net sum in respect of her existing charters, subject to allowance for contingencies. It is now clear, accordingly, that the arbitrary rule suggested by Dr. Lushington is not law, though the decisions just cited, however just in the result, cannot be regarded as logical or complete. The true rule seems to be that the measure of damages in such cases is the value of the ship to her owner as a going concern at the time and place of the loss. In assessing that value regard must naturally be had to her pending engagements, either profitable or the reverse. The rule, however, obviously requires some care in its application; the figure of damage is to represent the capitalized value of the vessel as a profit-earning machine, not in the abstract but in view of the actual circumstances. The value of prospective freights cannot simply be added to the market value but ought to be taken into account in order to ascertain the total value for purpose of assessing the damage, since if it is merely added to the market value of a free ship, the owner will be getting *pro tanto* his damages twice over. The vessel cannot be earning in the open market, while fulfilling the pending charter or charters. Again, the present valuation of a future charter becomes a difficulty in the case even of successive charters, still more in the case of long charters, such for instance as that in the *Lord Strathcona Steamship*

Co. v. Dominion Coal Co., [1926] AC 108 (PC (NS)), which was for ten St. Lawrence seasons, with extension at the charterers' option for further eight seasons. The assessment of the value of such a vessel at the time of loss, with her engagements, may seem to present an extremely complicated and speculative problem. But different considerations apply to the simple case of a ship sunk by collision when free of all engagements, either being laid up in port or being a seeking ship in ballast, though intended for employment, if it can be obtained, under charter or otherwise. In such a case the fair measure of damage will be simply the market value, on which will be calculated interest at and from the date of loss, to compensate for delay in paying for the loss. But the contrasted cases of a tramp under charter or a seeking tramp do not exhaust all the possible problems in which must be sought an answer to the question what is involved in the principle of *restitutio in integrum*. I have only here mentioned such cases as a step to considering the problem in the present case. Many, varied and complex are the types of vessels and the modes of employment in which their owners may use them. Hence the difficulties constantly felt in defining rules as to the measure of damages. I think it impossible to lay down any universal formula. A ship of war, a supply ship, a lightship, a dredger employed by a public authority, a passenger line, a trawler, a cable ship, a tug boat (to take a few instances), all may raise quite different questions before their true value can be ascertained.

The question here under consideration is again different; the *Liesbosch* was not under charter nor intended to be chartered, but in fact was being employed by the owners in the normal course of their business as civil engineers, as an essential part of the plant they were using in performance of their contract at Patras. Just as in the other cases considered, so in this, what the Court has to ascertain is the real value to the owner as part of his working plant, ignoring remote considerations at the time of loss. If it had been possible without delay to replace a comparable dredger exactly as and where *Liesbosch* was, at the market price, the appellants would have suffered no damage save the cost of doing so, that is in such an assumed case the market price, the position being analogous to that of the loss of goods for which there is a presently available market. But that is in this case a merely fanciful idea. Apart from any consideration of the appellants' lack of means, some substantial period was necessary to procure at Patras a substituted dredger; hence, I think, the appellants cannot be restored to their position before the accident unless they are compensated (if I may apply the words of Lord Herschell in *The Greta Holme*, [1897] AC 596 (HL (Eng.)) at p. 605), "in respect of the delay and prejudice caused to them in carrying out the works entrusted to them." He adds: "It is true these damages cannot be measured by any scale." Lord Herschell was there dealing with damages in the case of a dredger which was out of use during repairs, but in the present case I do not think the Court are any more entitled to refuse, on the ground that there is difficulty in calculation, to consider as an element in the value to the appellants of the dredger the delay and the prejudice in which its loss involved them; nor is it enough to take the market value, that is, the purchase price (say, in Holland), even increased by the cost of transport, and add to that 5 per cent interest as an arbitrary measure. It is true that the dredger was not named in the contract with the Patras Harbour authority, nor appropriated to it; but it was actually being used, and was intended to be used, by the appellants for the contract work. I am not clear if that view is what is meant by Scrutton LJ in his judgment in this case, when he quotes the word of Gorell Barnes J in *The Harmonides*, [1903] P 1 at p. 16: "The real test ... is ... what is the value" of the vessel "to the owners, as a going concern, at the time the vessel was sunk"; and the Lord Justice continues: "I should add, 'at that place,' for if the vessel had to be replaced at Patras, expense and time might have been added to the cost of the vessel replaced." In *The Harmonides* Gorell Barnes J had to consider in the case of an Atlantic passenger liner not her mere value in the general market, but her actual value to her owner in a business sense; he refused to confirm the Registrar's Report putting her value in the market at 18,000*l*., but heard fresh evidence and fixed the value at 31,000*l*. as being the real value to the owners. The problem there was in principle the same as the problem in this case. A nearer parallel is afforded by *Clyde Navigation Trustees v. Bowring Steamship Co.* (1928), 32 Ll. L Rep. 35 (Outer House), aff'd. (1929), 34 Ll. L Rep 319 (Scot. Ct. Sess.), in which the Court of Session in Scotland, affirming Lord Morison, held that the pursuers, whose dredger had been rendered a total loss by the negligent navigation of the defenders' vessel, were entitled, if they were to be placed in the same position as if the injury had not been done them, to have a value placed on their dredger as the value to them, based on three elements: (1.) The cost of procuring a comparable dredger; (2.) cost of adapting it to their requirements; (3.) compensation for loss of user. The Court rejected the contention that there was any absolute rule fixing the compensation at the market value with interest from the date of the collision. The late Mr. Registrar Roscoe, in his valuable work on "Measure of Damages in Maritime Collisions," cites at p. 42 of the 3rd ed. the case of *The Pacaure* (1912), Shipping Gazette (Dec. 1912), a lightship which was sunk in collision; the owners, the Mersey Docks and the Harbour Board, were allowed, in addition to the value of the sunken vessel, the cost of a substituted vessel for 366 days. I should prefer to state that such extra cost was an element in assessing the loss of value to the owners of the lightship, though it may be no different result would follow from the difference in statement.

In my judgment similar principles are applicable to the present case; the difficulty in applying them is that the evidence called before, and the findings made by, the Registrar and Merchants were directed, as explained above, to a different measure of damage: Scrutton LJ thus sums up the position, [1932] P 52 (CA) at p. 67: "But what the owners have lost is their dredger. If the Court gives them the value of their dredger at the time and place of the loss as a profit-earning dredger, and gives them interest on that value from the time of the loss till judgment, I do not see any room for a further award of profits"; and he goes on to describe the indirect losses which they claim in expense thrown away over the whole period during which they were without a dredger and the heavy outlay incurred in hiring and working the *Adria*, and for loss of profits. What Scrutton LJ in fact awards as the value of the dredger to the appellants at the time and place of loss is 9177*l*., which was what was paid for the *Adria* in September 1930, but, as the Lord Justice points out, that fact is not evidence of the market value of the *Liesbosch* in November 1928, when the *Liesbosch* was lost, any more than is the cost to them of the *Liesbosch* when they bought her, or the amount for which she was insured. It might seem to follow that Scrutton LJ is intending to give some compensation, beyond the actual cost of replacing the *Liesbosch*, for delay and prejudice in the contract work; if not, I do not see how he is giving the value of the dredger to the owners at Patras as a factor in their business as a going concern. It is on the true value so ascertained that the interest at 5 per cent from the date of the collision will run, as further damages, on the principles of the Court of Admiralty stated by Sir Charles Butt in *The Kong Magnus*, [1891] P 233 that is, damages for the loss of the use of the money representing the lost vessel as from the date of the loss until payment. Mr. Raeburn has pressed that the matter should be sent back to the Registrar and Merchants for the amount of damages to be assessed on the principles accepted by this House. I have felt grave doubt about this, as I am not quite sure on what principle the Court of Appeal have arrived at the sum they have awarded. But the best opinion I can form is that they intended to give simply the replacement cost, without including in the value any allowance for disturbance and prejudice during the necessary period of delay. If that is so, though I agree with their disallowance of the claim as put forward, I do not agree with the disallowance, in ascertaining the value, of anything beyond the cost of replacement. I do not think in a case like this interest is a compensation for that factor, because I think that factor must be something to be taken into account in arriving at the figure of value on which interest must run. On the whole I think Mr. Raeburn is right in urging that the matter should be referred back to the Registrar and Merchants to ascertain the true value on the principles I have stated. From these it follows that the value of the *Liesbosch* to the appellants, capitalized as at the date of the loss, must be assessed by taking into account: (1.) the market price of a comparable dredger in substitution; (2.) costs of adaptation, transport, insurance, etc., to Patras; (3.) compensation for disturbance and loss in carrying out their contract over the period of delay between the loss of the *Liesbosch* and the time at which the substituted dredger could reasonably have been available for use in Patras, including in that loss such items as overhead charges, expenses of staff and equipment, and so forth thrown away, but neglecting any special loss due to the appellants' financial position. On the capitalized sum so assessed, interest will run from the date of the loss.

The result is that the appellants have substantially failed in the appeal, because they have failed in their claim that the judgment of Langton J should be restored, and accordingly they should have to pay to the respondents three-quarters of their costs of this appeal. The order of the Court of Appeal will be varied by substituting for the judgment for 9177*l*. 3*s*. 4*d*. a judgment for such sum as the Registrar and Merchants may find on reference back to them. Save as so varied the order of the Court of Appeal will stand. I cannot help expressing a hope that the parties may now compose this remaining difference without further proceeding in the Registry.

Order of the Court of Appeal varied by substituting for the judgment for such sum as the Admiralty Registrar may find on reference back to him; subject to such variation the said order affirmed.
Cause remitted to the Registrar with a direction to assess the true measure of damage on the principles laid down by this House.
The appellants to pay to the respondents three-quarters of the costs incurred by them in respect of the said appeal.

[The other law lords concurred in Lord Wright's speech.]

NOTES AND QUESTIONS

1. In his speech, Lord Wright says: "The value of prospective freights cannot simply be added to the market value but ought to be taken into account in order to ascertain the total value for the purpose of assessing the damage, since if it is merely added to the market value of a free ship, the owner will be getting *pro tanto* his damages twice over." Can you define

with more precision the element of double compensation alluded to by Lord Wright? How might the extent of this double compensation be assessed?

2. The House permitted the *Liesbosch*'s owners to recover "the cost of procuring a comparable dredger" as well as "the cost of adapting it to their requirements." How would you express this result in terms of the market value of the dredger, and how would such market be defined?

3. In *Liesbosch*, the measure of the loss takes account of the owner's particular situation and requirements. But when the House of Lords considers damages for delay between the loss of the dredger and its replacement, the owners are restricted to recovery for a period of time within which a replacement "could reasonably have been available … neglecting any special loss due to the appellant's financial position." What justified the use of a fairly subjective approach to the assessment with respect to the dredger itself but a fairly objective assessment of the damages for delay? Would the result have been the same if the owners had been using an unnecessarily sophisticated (and therefore expensive) dredger at the time of loss? Why, or why not?

4. Lord Wright's statement that in calculating damages a court must ignore "any special loss due to the plaintiff's financial position" seems to indicate that the plaintiff's impecuniosity is no excuse for its failure to mitigate. In other words, we must treat the reasonable person as having the means to mitigate. It is not clear that such a strict rule was ever the law, since some pre-*Liesbosch* cases indicated that impecuniosity might be an excuse for a failure to mitigate: see, for example, *Clippins Oil Co. v. Edinburgh and District Water Trustees*, [1907] AC 291 (HL). Regardless of what the old law was, two important subsequent decisions have altered the scene. In *Alcoa Minerals of Jamaica v. Broderick*, [2001] 1 AC 371, the Privy Council took the view that whether a plaintiff's impecuniosity amounts to an excuse for a failure to mitigate is essentially a question of foreseeability. That is, if both the plaintiff's injury and the lack of the means to mitigate were foreseeable, then impecuniosity can amount to an excuse for a failure to mitigate. That case held that the foreseeability question was behind Lord Wright's statement in *Liesbosch*—that is, that Lord Wright had not intended to lay down any general rule. Three years later the House of Lords went further. In *Lagden v. O'Connor*, [2004] 1 AC 1067, Lord Hoffmann referred to Lord Wright's words in *Liesbosch* and wrote (at 1073) that they "can no longer be taken as authoritative. They must now be regarded as overtaken by subsequent developments in the law." Like *Alcoa v. Broderick*, *Lagden v. O'Connor* held that whether a plaintiff's impecuniosity could be an excuse for its failure to mitigate was a question of foreseeability.

James Street Hardware and Furniture Co. v. Spizziri
(1987), 62 OR (2d) 385 (CA)

[The defendant was a welder whose negligent work was responsible for extensive fire damage to a building. The plaintiff rebuilt the damaged part of the building in a superior form, exact restoration being prohibited by the building code. The section of the court's reasons dealing with liability is omitted. The trial judge apportioned damages with the result that the plaintiff was awarded 55 percent of $475,338. The plaintiff appealed.]

Damages

We turn to the matter of damages. Following the fire, the appellant did not restore the building to its pre-fire condition but, rather, rebuilt it as a different and larger structure. The *Building Code Act* prohibited restoring the building to its pre-fire condition.

A breakdown of the damages awarded by the trial judge is as follows [(1985), 51 OR (2d) 641, at 657]:

Building claim	$306,000.00
Clean-up costs	9,952.00
Rental of alternative accommodation	13,000.00
Damage to inventory	140,000.00
Advertising	6,386.00
Total Damages	$475,338.00

With respect to the building claim, the trial judge accepted "without hesitation" the evidence of D.P. Short, "an architect of great experience with impressive powers of analysis and articulation," who established that the cost of restoring the building to its pre-fire state was $340,000. The trial judge deducted $34,000 from this amount to cover the "enhancement" in the appellant's position. This related to the concern of the respondents that "they not be required to pay for a better building than the plaintiff had at the time of the fire."

Mr. Short also gave evidence, which the trial judge accepted, that the additional cost of rebuilding to ensure compliance with the standards of the *Building Code Act* was $49,394. The trial judge held, however, that the appellant was not entitled to this additional amount.

The respondents adduced expert evidence that the cost of rebuilding was $282,000 and that the depreciation of the materials in the appellant's building at the time of the fire was $95,000. The trial judge, as may be gathered from what has already been said, did not accept this evidence with respect to building costs and, further, had difficulty accepting the evidence respecting depreciation. After refusing to make the deduction sought on account of depreciation, he said that the respondents' concern respecting the enhancement in the appellant's position could be met by the $34,000 deduction from the $340,000 cost of restoration.

In its appeal on damages, the appellant has made three submissions. They are that the trial judge erred:

(a) by deducting $34,000 from the $340,000 cost to replace the building;

(b) by refusing to allow the $49,394 as the cost of compliance with the *Building Code Act*, and

(c) by allowing only $13,000 as the cost of four and one-half months' rental of alternative accommodation for the store, instead of the cost of nine months' rental, $29,250.

On the argument before us no submissions were made in support of the third matter. The conclusion of the trial judge on this point is clearly supported by the evidence and we accept it.

In their cross-appeal the respondents submit that the trial judge erred in not deducting $95,000 for depreciation and, with respect to the damage to the inventory ($140,000), that he erred in not reducing it by a profit of $124,925 received on the sale of this inventory.

The appellants' submissions respecting the deduction of $34,000 and the respondents' submissions respecting the deduction of $95,000 both relate to the same basic issue and therefore will be considered together.

The Betterment/Depreciation Issue

In support of its argument that the trial judge erred in deducting $34,000 from the award, the appellant relies upon the judgment of the Court of Appeal of England in *Harbutt's "Plasticine" Ltd. v. Wayne Tank & Pump Co. Ltd.*, [1970] 1 QB 447. In this case the plaintiff's factory was destroyed by fire. Under the applicable planning law the plaintiff was not allowed to rebuild according to the same structure and design as the destroyed building. The replacement building had two storeys. The old factory had five storeys. The cost of replacement was £146,581. The difference in value of the factory before and after the fire was £116,785. Each of the three judges addressed the damages issue succinctly.

At p. 468 Lord Denning MR said:

> The defendants said it should be the difference in value before and after the fire, relying on *Philips v. Ward*, [1956] 1 WLR 471. The plaintiffs said it should be the cost of replacement, relying on *Hollebone v. Midhurst & Fernhurst Builders Ltd.*, [1968] 1 Lloyd's Rep. 38.
>
> The destruction of a building is different from the destruction of a chattel. If a second-hand car is destroyed, the owner only gets its value; because he can go into the market and get another second-hand car to replace it. He cannot charge the other party with the cost of replacing it with a new car. But when this mill was destroyed, the plasticine company had no choice. They were bound to replace it as soon as they could, not only to keep their business going, but also to mitigate the loss of profit (for which they would be able to charge the defendants). They replaced it in the only possible way, without adding any extras. I think they should be allowed the cost of replacement. True it is that they got new for old; but I do not think the wrongdoer can diminish the claim on that account. If they had added extra accommodation or made extra improvements, they would have to give credit. But that is not this case. I think the judge was right on this point.

Widgery LJ said at pp. 472-3:

> I must now turn to the issues raised as to the measure of damage. The distinction between those cases in which the measure of damage is the cost of repair of the damaged article, and those in which it is the diminution in value of the article, is not clearly defined. In my opinion each case depends on its own facts, it being remembered, first, that the purpose of the award of damages is to restore the plaintiff to his position before the loss occurred, and secondly, that the plaintiff must act reasonably to mitigate his loss. If the article damaged is a motor car of popular make, the plaintiff cannot charge the defendant with the cost of repair when it is cheaper to buy a similar car on the market. On the other hand, if no substitute for the damaged article is available and no reasonable alternative can be provided, the plaintiff should be entitled to the cost of repair. It was clear in the present case that it was reasonable for the plaintiffs to rebuild their factory, because there was no other way in which they could carry on their business and retain their labour force. The plaintiffs rebuilt their factory to a substantially different design, and if this had involved expenditure beyond the cost of replacing the old, the difference might not have been recoverable, but there is no suggestion of this here. Nor do I accept that the plaintiffs

must give credit under the heading of "betterment" for the fact that their new factory is modern in design and materials. To do so would be the equivalent of forcing the plaintiffs to invest their money in the modernising of their plant which might be highly inconvenient for them. Accordingly I agree with the sum allowed by the trial judge as the cost of replacement.

Finally, Cross LJ said at pp. 475-6:

… [B]ut in my judgment the value of the building and of the plant and machinery before the fire throws no light on the true measure of damage in a case like this where it was obviously right for the plaintiffs to rebuild and re-equip their factory and start business again as soon as possible. Further, I do not think that the defendants are entitled to claim any deduction from the actual cost of rebuilding and re-equipping simply on the ground that the plaintiffs have got new for old. It is not in practice possible to rebuild and re-equip a factory with old and worn materials and plant corresponding to what was there before, and such benefit as the plaintiffs may get by having a new building and new plant in place of an old building and old plant is something in respect of which the defendants are not, as I see it, entitled to any allowance. I can well understand that if the plaintiffs in rebuilding the factory with a different and more convenient lay-out had spent more money than they would have spent had they rebuilt it according to the old plan, the defendants would have been entitled to claim that the excess should be deducted in calculating the damages. But the defendants did not call any evidence to make out a case of betterment on these lines and we were told that in fact the planning authorities would not have allowed the factory to be rebuilt on the old lines. Accordingly, in my judgment, the capital sum awarded by the judge was right.

Before dealing specifically with the question of betterment, it is useful to consider matters and principles of a more general nature. The "general rule from which one must always start in resolving a question as to the measure of damages" (Harvey McGregor, *McGregor on Damages* (London: Sweet and Maxwell, 14th ed., 1980) at p. 7) is that the damages are the amount that will put the plaintiff "in the same position as he would have been in if he had not sustained the wrong for which he is now getting his compensation or reparation": *Livingstone v. Rawyards Coal Co.* (1880), 5 App. Cas. 25 (HL (Eng.)) at p. 39. No one quarrels with this as a general starting point proposition. Differences often arise with respect to its application in particular cases.

Dealing directly with the measure of damages with respect to torts affecting land, *McGregor on Damages* (at p. 761 *et seq.*) deals with the differing approaches to the measure of damages which were referred to by Widgery LJ in *Harbutt's "Plasticine" Ltd. v. Wayne Tank & Pump Co. Ltd.*, [1970] 1 QB 447 (CA), as (1) the amount of the diminution of the value of the land, on the one hand, and (2) the cost of replacement or repair, on the other. *McGregor* reviews the cases, including *Harbutt's "Plasticine,"* and then says at p. 763:

The difficulty in deciding between diminution in value and cost of reinstatement arises from the fact that the plaintiff may want his property in the same state as before the commission of the tort but the amount required to effect this may be substantially greater than the amount by which the value of the property has been diminished. The test which appears to be the appropriate one is the reasonableness of the plaintiff's desire to reinstate the property; this will be judged in part by the advantages to him of reinstatement in relation to the extra cost to the defendant in having to pay damages for reinstatement rather than damages calculated by the diminution in value of the land.

The cost of replacement approach often brings with it the question of betterment or enhancement. *McGregor* deals with it on a general plane in relation to the starting point proposition that damages are to restore a plaintiff to the position he or she would have been in if the tort had not been committed. Having pointed out (p. 8) that there are "a number of important limits" engrafted on the general rule, the text goes on to say (p. 9) that "[a]t the other end of the scale there are certain circumstances in which the plaintiff will recover more than his loss as defined by the general rule ... ." It describes (p. 11) one kind of case in this latter category as follows:

> The second variety stems from the frequent impossibility of repairing damaged property without putting it into better condition than it was before the damage had been inflicted, since repairing with old and worn materials is not a practical possibility. In these circumstances the question arises whether there should be a deduction from the cost of repair of the amount by which the property, after repair, is more valuable than beforehand. The first cases tended to hold that there should indeed be such a deduction, this solution appearing both in cases where land was tortiously damaged and in cases where lessees were in breach of covenants to repair. But, at a comparatively early date, the cases concerning damage to ships rejected the argument that there must be a deduction on account of "new for old" since, as was well expressed by Dr. Lushington [from his reasons in *The Gazelle* (1844), 2 W Rob. (Adm.) 279, at 281], if the plaintiff "derives incidentally a greater benefit than mere indemnification, it arises only from the impossibility of otherwise effecting such indemnification without exposing him to some loss or burden, which the law will not place on him." This approach has been adopted in modern times in relation to damage to land whether caused tortiously or through breach of contract.

McGregor goes on to say at pp. 11-2:

> On the other hand, where the necessity of the case does not demand reinstatement, plaintiffs may find themselves limited to claiming for the diminution of the value of the property in question.

Returning, for the moment, to the facts of this case, it cannot be seriously argued that the appellant did not act reasonably in deciding to continue its retail business on the location of the damaged premises. In this respect, it was in virtually the same position as the plaintiff in *Harbutt's "Plasticine" Ltd. v. Wayne Tank & Pump Co. Ltd.* The fact that it built a different and larger building, thereby obliging it to establish its repair costs on the basis of estimates rather than actual costs, is not put forward as a ground for depriving it of basing its claim on the replacement cost approach, and we do not think that it reasonably could have this effect.

If the proper approach to the measure of damages was the before-and-after one, *i.e.,* the diminution in the value of the property occasioned by the fire, the question of the degree of depreciation in the pre-fire building would, of course, be directly relevant. It is not directly relevant where the cost of replacement approach is used, except in so far as it may relate to the question of betterment.

The trial judge, as we have indicated, rejected the depreciation evidence offered in this case. It is submitted by the respondents that he was wrong in doing this because he reached his conclusion on the basis that "[d]epreciation is essentially an accounting concept." In the light of the particular evidence that was called, we do not think that he rejected the $95,000 deduction for depreciation simply on this basis. The evidence was an unsatisfactory basis for determining the degree of betterment resulting from the rebuilding according to the cost estimates filed. It was based on the arbitrary assumption that all of the component parts of the building to which it related (*e.g.*, ceiling tile, paint on walls, wall coverings, flooring, and built-up roofing) had been fully depreciated, *i.e.*, had no value. The expert witness who gave this evidence did not know when the parts were installed in the building. He assumed that all of the parts had been in the building since its original construction in 1953 and, also, that none of them had any value at the time of the fire. This is not necessarily a criticism of the witness who gave this evidence, as he did not have more particular information at his disposal. None the less, it cannot be said that the trial judge was wrong in not relying upon his evidence. We also note that this evidence did not purport to establish the actual increase in the value of the building with the new materials in it or its increased life span, if any.

We return to the question of the principle of a deduction for betterment. The trial judge referred to the treatment of the question in S.M. Waddams, *The Law of Damages* (Toronto: Canada Law Book Co., 1983). We shall quote the same passage from Waddams that appears in the trial judge's reasons [at 655-56] and one further one:

> It commonly occurs that a plaintiff, in making good damage to property, will not be able to restore himself to his pre-loss position without improving it. If the plaintiff's ten-year-old roof is damaged, he will not be able to purchase a replacement ten-year-old roof. The only reasonable course will be to replace with a new roof. If roofs have a life of twenty years, and the defendant is compelled to pay the full cost of the replacement, the plaintiff will be in a better position after satisfaction of the judgment than if the damages had not occurred in the first place. It would seem, therefore, that the damages should be reduced by the value of the improvement of the plaintiff's position. The contrary argument is that it is the defendant's wrong that has caused the need for replacement, and that the plaintiff should not be compelled against his will to invest his money in a replacement he might not have chosen to make. These arguments, however, do not appear to be conclusive. The fact that the plaintiff is forced to make an unwanted investment can be met by conceding the point and increasing the damages by any loss suffered by the plaintiff's making such an investment. The plaintiff's interest can be met by putting the onus of proof on the defendant to show that the plaintiff does not suffer any loss by this reason [paragraph 281]. ...

> These cases [cases concerned with the principle of mitigation of the plaintiff's loss] seem inconsistent with a rule that improvements to the plaintiff's position by effecting repairs are to be ignored. The increase in the plaintiff's wealth is one that could not have occurred in the absence of the wrong. It is suggested, therefore, that an anticipated benefit accruing to the plaintiff on repairing damaged property ought to be taken into account to reduce damages, with compensation, however, for the cost to the plaintiff of the unexpected expenditure required of him, and with the onus of proof upon the defendant in case of doubt on this question, or on the value of the benefit [paragraph 287].

We appreciate the logic of the reasoning in *Harbutt's "Plasticine"* and of the statement of Dr. Lushington in *The "Gazelle"* (1844), 2 W Rob. 279, 166 ER 759, which is contained in one of the passages from *McGregor* that we have quoted. Quite simply, if a plaintiff, who is entitled to be compensated on the basis of the cost of replacement, is obliged to submit to a deduction from that compensation for incidental and unavoidable enhancement, he or she will not be fully compensated for the loss suffered. The plaintiff will be obliged, if the difference is paid for out of his or her own pocket, whether borrowed or already possessed, to submit to "some loss or burden," to quote from Dr. Lushington. Widgery LJ in *Harbutt's "Plasticine"* called it "forcing the plaintiffs to invest their money in the modernising of their plant which might be highly inconvenient for them."

These considerations, however, do not necessarily mean that in cases of this kind the plaintiff is entitled to damages which include the element of betterment. As Waddams suggests, the answer lies in compensating the plaintiff for the loss imposed upon him or her in being forced to spend money he or she would not otherwise have spent—at least as early as was required by the damages occasioned to him by the tort. In general terms, this loss would be the cost (if he has to borrow) or value (if he already has the money) of the money equivalent of the betterment over a particular period of time.

Before considering the application of this approach to the case before us, it would be well to reiterate what has been said in so many previous decisions on the assessment of damages and that is that each case turns on its own facts and that the process of assessing damages should be a practical one designed to do justice between the parties. The process should not be unnecessarily complicated or rule-ridden. The rules applied should be responsive to the particular facts of the case. For example, in some cases, perhaps many, the repair or replacement of property (the mere substituting of new for old) may well not involve any increase in the value of the property as a whole: see, *e.g., Barrette v. Franki Compressed Pile Co. of Canada Ltd.*, [1955] OR 413 at p. 430 and *Jens v. Mannix Co. Ltd.* (1978), 89 DLR (3d) 351 (BCSC). None the less, in cases where there is a serious issue of betterment, the approach outlined in Waddams offers a useful guide to accommodating the interests of the defendant who wishes to avoid paying for a windfall and of a plaintiff who wishes to avoid being forced to spend money that he or she may or may not have. We add the reservation that, where the plaintiff alleges a loss with respect to being required to make an unexpected expenditure, the onus of proof with respect to it should lie on him or her.

In the present case there is no satisfactory evidence on the life expectancy of the building, either before the fire or what it would have been after being repaired—nor was there any evidence as to the amount of the increase in value, if any, after the fire. In this respect the evidence in the case of *City of North York v. Kert Chemical Industries Inc.* (1985), 32 ACWS (2d) 271 (Ont. HC) referred to in the trial judge's reasons may be contrasted. The trial judge in the present case assumed that there was some betterment and, in making his best effort fairly to assess the damages, he deducted $34,000, or 10% of the $340,000 cost of restoration.

Having regard to the principle that in cases of doubt it is for the defendant to prove the value of an alleged improvement, we think that the trial judge erred in making this deduction. He had rejected the respondents' evidence respecting depreciation. In view of the fact that the respondents' expert did not know how long the components which he fully depreciated had been in the building and there being no evidence on the effect of the replacement of the new for old components on the value of the building, we do not think that this evidence affords a reasonable basis for deduction.

Further, in making the deduction, the trial judge does not appear to have considered the concomitant question of loss flowing to the appellant when its compensation is reduced by the deduction for enhancement.

Having regard to the foregoing, and to the matter we shall discuss in the following paragraphs, we think that the sum of $34,000 should not have been deducted from the damages under this head of the claim.

The Repair Costs Relating to the Cost of Complying with the Building Code Act

We turn now to the refusal of the trial judge to increase the repair costs by $49,394 to cover the cost of complying with the current *Building Code Act* standards. The trial judge rejected this claim on the basis that: (a) it was conceptual, piling "artificiality upon artificiality"; (b) it was difficult to see how it reasonably flowed from the defendants' negligence; and (c) to require the defendants to pay for the code-required improvements would be to give the plaintiff a better property than it had immediately before the fire at the defendants' expense.

The difficulty in considering this issue, of course, is that the appellant did not rebuild the building according to its pre-fire design, but instead used a different design. If it had rebuilt according to its pre-fire design and, in doing so, had necessarily incorporated the changes required by law, we think it would have been entitled to recover these additional costs subject, if relevant, to the application of the principles respecting betterment which we have earlier discussed. If the appellant had not rebuilt at all, we are inclined to think that this additional "cost" would not have been recoverable. Indeed, in these circumstances, the appropriate measure of damages might simply be the diminution in the value of the property rather than cost of replacement.

However, in following the course it did, *i.e.*, replacing the damaged building with a different building, it must be assumed that the appellant incurred part of the costs related to compliance with the *Building Code Act* requirements, *e.g.*, using incombustible materials in place of combustible finish and new drywall to obtain appropriate fire rating in place of fibre tile ceiling and beam furrings. Therefore, it cannot be said that, in fact, the increased costs relating to the *Building Code Act* are entirely conceptual, artificial, or do not flow from the defendants' negligence. The particular difficulty, however, is that of assessing how much increased cost relating to compliance is relevant. The appellant made no attempt to do so and, on the evidence, we think that it would have been difficult for it to do so. All that can be said is that the cost of compliance is not irrelevant to this claim and that any injustice resulting from the failure to take it into account in the appellant's favour may be balanced by the possible overcompensation of the appellant by the costs resulting in a better building—the value of the improvement itself not being quantified.

Damage to Inventory

The reasons of the trial judge on this particular part of the claim read as follows [at 657]:

That damage occurred to the merchandise that was in the store on the date of the fire is not in dispute. The plaintiff chose itself to sell the salvageable articles to the public rather than sell them as salvage. It conducted a large sale, in respect of which it conducted an advertising campaign, at the Memorial Gardens. Complicating the determination of damages under this head is the fact that, to make the sale successful, it brought in from its other branch stores and from elsewhere, new articles. The records do not enable a distinction to be made between receipts for the sale of articles that came from the Queen St. E. store and receipts for the sale of other articles.

It is for that reason that I am unable to accept, as helpful, the evidence of Mr. T.W. Massicotte, a chartered accountant called by the defendants, who testified that the plaintiff made a net profit on the fire sale in the sum of $124,925. It is impossible to relate that figure to the damaged stock. The evidence called by the plaintiff supports as eminently reasonable its claim for the damages to the contents of the building or loss of inventory in the sum of $140,000.

The appellant's claim was based on the opinion evidence of a representative of a salvage company that the fire reduced the value of its inventory of some $270,000 by the amount of $140,000. According to this approach, its salvage value was, therefore, $130,000.

The evidence of Mr. Massicotte, referred to in the trial judge's reasons, was based on information received from the appellant. In broad terms it was that the gross revenue from the fire sale was $397,000 and the cost of the goods sold was $247,000 (comprising the salvage value of $130,000 of the fire damaged goods, referred to above, and $117,000 as the cost of new goods from other sources that were also sold at the sale). The expenses of the sale were $42,075 and "Carrying Charge Income" to be added in the calculation was $17,000. The resulting net profit was $124,925.

In the light of the introduction of $117,000 worth of additional merchandise into the sale, it is true that the $124,925 profit cannot be related entirely to the fire damaged stock. On the other hand, there is no reason to attribute it entirely to the additional merchandise. The difficulty is caused by the failure of the appellant, who had a duty to mitigate its loss, to keep its records in such a way that it would be possible to determine, with accuracy, the parts of the profit attributable to each source. Although, as far as comparison of the cost figures is concerned ($130,000 salvage inventory and $117,000 new inventory) there may have been more salvage merchandise sold than new merchandise, it is also the case that the margin of profit on the new inventory may well have been greater than that on the salvage inventory. In these circumstances it is not unreasonable to assume that it is likely that about one-half of the profit, $62,500, was attributable to the sale of the salvage goods. Accordingly, a more appropriate figure for the loss on inventory would be $140,000 minus $62,500, or $77,500.

Conclusion on Damages

In the light of the foregoing the total damages should be recalculated by adding $34,000 and deducting $62,500. The resulting amount is $446,838.

Conclusion

Both the appeal and the cross-appeal are allowed, each with costs, with the result that the amount of the appellant's recovery will be varied from $261,435.90 to $446,838. The balance of the trial judgment, after giving effect to this variance, will stand.

Appeal and cross-appeal allowed in part.

NOTES

1. For a helpful discussion of these issues, see J. Berryman, "Betterment Before Canadian Common Law Courts" (1993), 72 *Canadian Bar Review* 54.

2. The Ontario Court of Appeal refined the calculation of the deduction for betterment in *Upper Lakes Shipping v. St. Lawrence Cement* (1992), 89 DLR (4th) 722. The case of *Safe Step Building Treatments v. 1382680 Ontario Inc.* (2004), 37 CLR 3d 281 (Ont. SCJ) offers a helpful summary (at paras. 78-79):

> The deduction is determined according to a two-step process. The first step is to determine the "extra" or "surplus" lifespan of the new equipment or structure, should the full cost of performance (with the added "betterment") be awarded. The betterment is then quantified by calculating the interest accrued during the "extra" life expectancy on the funds that the injured party would otherwise have spent to replace the original structure or equipment. For example, if a machine, purchased in 1988, would need to be replaced in 1998, but the plaintiff receives a new machine (with the same life expectancy) in 1993, as a result of the defendant's breach, the plaintiff's machine has received an increase in life expectancy of 5 years. Had the plaintiff replaced the original machine in 1998, he or she would have expended a certain sum of money; by deferring the purchase of a new machine for an additional 5 years, the plaintiff has the opportunity to invest that sum. Interest is, therefore, calculated on that sum during those 5 additional years. This interest sum is then prima facie deductible from the award for damages.

> The second step limits or mitigates the effect of the first step in awarding the plaintiff an amount representing an "interest cost" on the betterment sum from the date of breach until the date the original equipment or structure would have been replaced or repaired. By recognizing that the injured party will typically incur extra costs in repairing or replacing a structure or equipment earlier than expected (in the hypothetical example, the machinery is replaced in 1993 instead of 1998) as a result of the breach, the second step aims to partially compensate the plaintiff for the deduction achieved in the first step. The overall effect is that the "betterment deduction" (to prevent a plaintiff's unfair windfall) is slightly offset by compensating the plaintiff for unexpected costs and expenses.

DAMAGE TO PROPERTY

As you review the following two cases, consider how the court in each defines the "market" that is the basis of the assessment and whether the court approaches the assessment subjectively or objectively. Can the two cases be reconciled?

O'Grady v. Westminster Scaffolding Ltd.
[1962] 2 Lloyd's Rep. 238 (QB)

In this case, the plaintiff, Mr. John Dudley Alexander O'Grady, claimed against the defendants, Westminster Scaffolding, Ltd., in respect of damage caused to his M.G. motor car on July 13, 1960, when it was struck by falling steel scaffolding erected by the defendants in Great Marlborough Street, W.1.

The defendants originally denied negligence, but at the trial they admitted negligence and contested the case solely on the question of the proper measure of damages.

In his statement of claim, the plaintiff said that on July 13, 1960, at about 10 a.m., his motor car was standing on the carriageway on the north side of Great Marlborough Street,

London, W.I., adjacent to the shop premises occupied by Dickins & Jones, Ltd. He said that
the defendants were engaged in the erection of steel scaffolding on the side of the shop
premises facing Great Marlborough Street when a large quantity of the scaffolding fell into
the street, causing damage to his motor car.

The plaintiff alleged that the accident was caused by the negligence of the defendants,
their servants or agents, and claimed as follows:

	£	s.	d.
Cost of repairs to motor car	253	0	6
Hire of motor vehicles during the period of repairs:			
Hire of motor car from Sunny-side Garages			
from 14th July, 1960 to 26th July, 1960	33	0	0
Hire of motor car from Victor Britain Limited			
from 26th July 1960 to 3rd November 1960	174	0	4
Expense of taxis on 13th July, 1960	1	4	6
	461	5	4

The defendants admitted liability for their negligence, but contended, by their defence,
that the value of the plaintiff's motor car immediately prior to the accident was the sum of
£175 to £185 or thereabouts and the salvage value thereof immediately thereafter was of the
order of £35 to £40 or thereabouts; that, therefore, in having the car repaired as alleged and
for the alleged length of time the plaintiff acted unreasonably; and that, accordingly, the
amount of the plaintiff's claim was excessive and unreasonable.

Judgment

EDMUND DAVIES J: To the romantically minded, this might seem a touching tale of loyalty
and devotion. To be more prosaic, it is an action about a motor car. In these proceedings the
plaintiff seeks to recover compensation for the damage caused to his motor car on July 13,
1960, when it was struck by a large quantity of steel scaffolding erected by the defendants,
which fell from the premises of Dickins & Jones, Ltd., in Great Marlborough Street. Although negligence by the defendants was originally denied, it is now admitted, and the sole
question is as to the proper measure of damages.

The car was a 1938 or 1939 M.G. open tourer of the T.B. model. The plaintiff had bought
it in 1947 for £475 and it had received his loving care and assiduous attention ever since.
Clearly it was his pride and joy, and it—or perhaps I should say "she," for the car was affec-
tionately known as "Hortensia"—repaid his attentions by serving him well in his work as a
commercial traveller covering between 10,000 and 15,000 miles per annum. Quite clearly,
he thought there was no other car like it. I mention these matters at the outset, for they have
to be borne in mind in determining the reasonableness or otherwise of the plaintiff's conduct
after the accident. Despite the heavy damage sustained by the car, what the plaintiff did was
to proceed to have it repaired and to hire substitute vehicles meanwhile, and he now seeks to
recover the sum of £461 5s. 4d. which was the total cost of these items. Although the plaintiff did not have possession of the car until Nov. 26, 1960, his claim terminates on Nov. 3.

Where a chattel is negligently damaged, the normal measure of compensation is the difference between the value of the chattel before the damage and its value as damaged. In this

case of a partial loss, this will usually be (a) the cost of repairing; (b) the difference (if any) between the value of the chattel before the accident and after it was repaired, and (c) such consequential loss as the reasonable cost of hiring another chattel while repairs are being effected. The defendants in the present case accept these propositions, but dispute their applicability, on the grounds that every injured party is obliged to act reasonably and that this plaintiff has acted unreasonably. Relying on the passage in *Mayne and McGregor on Damages*, 12th ed., at p. 633, to the effect that the cost of repairs affords the measure of damages

> ... provided that in the circumstances it is reasonable for the plaintiff to effect the repair: it might be cheaper to buy a replacement on the market and sell the damaged goods for what they will fetch. ...

The defendants submit that that is precisely what the plaintiff should have done and failed to do. In essence, their case is that the car had a pre-accident value of £175 to £185, and a post-accident scrap value of £35 to £40, that it was accordingly wholly unreasonable for the plaintiff to incur repair costs exceeding £250 and meanwhile to hire other cars for many weeks. They maintain that a reasonably similar and suitable vehicle was readily obtainable in the market and that this is an inflated claim.

The defendants, however, accept that a plaintiff who proceeds to have his damaged chattel repaired is *prima facie* acting reasonably and is entitled to recover the cost thereof and the cost of hiring another vehicle meanwhile, provided that the charges and the period involved are themselves reasonable. They further accept (and rightly so, in my judgment), that the onus is upon them

> ... to show both that the damage has been increased by the plaintiff's unreasonable conduct and that it would probably have been less if the plaintiff had acted reasonably.

See *Halsbury's Laws of England*, 3rd ed., Vol. II, at p. 292 and the cases there cited.

I prefer, however, to decide this case not an any narrow ground as to whether a particular burden has been established by the party upon whom it rests, but by asking myself whether on the generality of the evidence the plaintiff has satisfied me that he acted reasonably in all the circumstances and, if so, to what damages is he entitled.

I turn to consider firstly the pre-accident value of the car and the possibility of the plaintiff's purchasing another to replace it. As to the latter point, it is clear that, however devoted the plaintiff was to his car, the law does not permit him to murmur in a Dowsonian adaptation, "I will be faithful to thee Hortensia in my fashion," and refuse to buy another reasonably suitable vehicle if it is available. I have, therefore, been mindful of his obvious attachment to her in assessing his testimony that she was irreplaceable—or, at least, could not be replaced at a figure less than the total amount claimed here. As I have said, in 1947 she cost him £475, and I attach little or no importance to the fact that that figure has remained her stated value for insurance purposes ever since. But it is clear that she was regularly maintained by a competent firm of motor engineers and the defendants did not seek to dispute that this cost him some £300 to £400 per annum. During the period of his ownership, her engine was replaced on three occasions, an entirely new one having been put in in the year before the accident at a cost of £162 10s. and that same year the coachwork had been completely renewed for the sum of £180. Work had also recently been done on, among other things, the wheels, the steering column and the hood. Taking the matter quite generally, I am satisfied that the car had been very well maintained and was in good condition at the time of the accident, and neither of these matters is in dispute. I do not, however, think that I should attach any weight to the plaintiff's assertion that a gentleman in Minnesota has twice since the accident offered him £500 for "Hortensia," in the absence of that gentleman from the witness-box.

What happened after the accident was this. On July 22, 1960, University Motors, Ltd. (who had serviced the car throughout), estimated that certain necessary engineering work would cost £8 6s., the coachwork repairs £118 4s. 6d., and in addition there would be specialists' charges for repairs to certain parts and the cost of itemized new parts. On Aug. 9, the defendants' engineer inspected and on Aug. 12 their insurers informed the plaintiff's insurance brokers that the car has a pre-accident market value of about £180, that the cost of repairs would greatly exceed that sum and that the car must be regarded as a constructive total loss with a salvage value of £35 to £40. The plaintiff refused to accept any of these statements and proceeded to have the car repaired, as I have stated, and no dispute arises as to the reasonableness of the cost of such repairs.

Should he have done otherwise and proceeded to buy another reasonably similar car in the market? Could he have done so? I do not think that he ever directly addressed the latter question to himself, but he is a knowledgeable man about such matters and had gone about looking for needed new parts for "Hortensia" after the accident and in so doing saw the sorts and conditions of the M.G. cars on the market at that time. He claims that none of the many M.G. cars then being advertised for sale was anything like as good as "Hortensia," or could have been rendered as attractive and suitable as she was for a sum below the repairs and hiring charges now sought to be recovered. On the other hand, the defendants rely on the evidence of Mr. Silverthorn, an automobile assessor, who estimated the pre-accident value at £175 to £185 and its salvage value at £35 to £40. But he had never seen "Hortensia" before the accident, and did not even know that she had had a new engine fitted only a year before and of the other work then done. Bearing these new matters in mind, he hazarded in the witness-box that an "enthusiast" would have paid "£250 plus" for this car, which he described as having a "specialist" attraction. He also quoted from a trade journal for July 1960, containing advertisements of various M.G. cars at prices ranging from £130 to £240, but again he had seen none of them, and I do not feel I can place reliance on his evidence that a car similar to "Hortensia" could then have been bought for £250. The defendants also call in aid a passage in a letter from University Motors, Ltd., of Dec. 20, 1960, that is well after the repairs had been executed, which reads as follows:

> As to the value of this car at the time of the accident; as it had been so well maintained and in such excellent condition, we are of the opinion that we would have no difficulty in selling the car for upwards of £200 retail. ...

Pausing there, one may observe that the pre-accident market value of chattels affords a guide to the measure of compensation when, and only when, a similar chattel can be obtained in the open market, and as to this the remainder of the letter significantly adds:

> ... [W]e appreciate that this figure [—that is £200—] is in excess of what a car of this type would normally fetch, but owing to its condition [—and I stress that word—] it could be considered as unique and it is doubtful whether a car in similar condition would be available.

It is against the background of that evidence that I ask myself whether the plaintiff appears to have acted reasonably in incurring when he did the cost of repairs and hiring charges which are here claimed. In my judgment, that question calls for an affirmative answer. Alternatively, I am certainly not satisfied that he acted unreasonably in following the line of conduct which he adopted. I propose, accordingly, to award him in full the £253 0s. 6d. for repairs and the further undisputed small item of £1 4s. 6d.

I now turn to the two items of £33 and £174 for hiring charges. The first covers a period of 12 days, and the defendants submit that, although the plaintiff originally acted unreasonably in hiring from a nearby garage at £18 to £19 per week, he should have found a car to hire at the cheaper rate of about £13 3s. a week charged by the second hirers before the 12 days had expired. I do not think that this submission is made out. The plaintiff is a busy man, travelling long distances for which a car was imperative, this was the holiday period when cars for hire were in short supply, and I consider that he showed fair and proper regard for the defendants' interests in obtaining a cheaper car on July 26. I accordingly, propose to award him the full sum of £33.

But the claim for £174, which covered a period of some 14 weeks and two days, stands on a different footing. It is undisputed that the repairs began on Sept. 26 and ended on Nov. 25 and that these 5½ weeks constituted a reasonable period to allow for their execution. But why they were not begun until Sept. 26, that is some 11 weeks after the accident, is unexplained. In my judgment, this delay was unreasonable and, although the plaintiff is as personally free from blame in the matter as the defendants are and could not reasonably have been expected to anticipate that the repairs would take so long, someone acting on his behalf was at fault and therefore the plaintiff must bear the loss. In my judgment, repairs should have begun within a few days after the defendants' letter of Aug. 12, say, on Aug. 17, and on that basis they would have ended on about Sept. 24 and the car then ready to be used. Precision is impossible, but it appears to me that the plaintiff is entitled to recover roughly 8½ weeks' cost of hiring from Victor Britain, Ltd., and no more, and I propose to award him £100 under this head. The total amount for hiring is £133 instead of the £207 originally claimed.

From these various awards a deduction must be made for the avoidance of wear and tear on the car during the period of its immobilization. All I can here attempt is, as defendants' Counsel invited me, an "intelligent guess," and I propose to deduct the sum of £15 to make allowance for this factor.

In the result, the plaintiff has satisfied me that he is entitled to recover the items of £253 0s. 6d.; £33; £100 and £1 4s. 6d., making a total of £387 5s., but less the £15 referred to. There will, accordingly, be judgment for the plaintiff for £372 5s.

Darbishire v. Warran
[1963] 1 WLR 1067 (CA)

HARMAN LJ: The facts of this case are simple and except on one point, a matter of quantum, not seriously in dispute. The plaintiff's car was in collision with the defendant's and was seriously damaged by what was admittedly entirely the defendant's fault. The plaintiff therefore sued the defendant in damages. These damages he based on the cost to him of repairing his car. The defence is that the cost of doing this was unreasonable and not recoverable from the defendant having regard to the duty lying upon the plaintiff to mitigate his damages which in the circumstances it is said were not more than the market value of the car at the time of the accident together with some damages for the loss of its use while he was reasonably engaged in looking out for a comparable one.

The facts are that the plaintiff's car was a 1951 Lea Francis which he had bought in the year 1958 for the sum of £330. He is by profession a mechanical engineer and had always kept the car by his own efforts in a high state of efficiency having regard to its age. He had done a number of mechanical repairs and renewals and at the time of the accident was in the course of repairing a damaged door which was actually off the car at the time. The market value, that is to say, the replacement value, of the car according to the ordinary guide in use in the trade was at the time £80. The garage to which the plaintiff took the car originally took the view that repairs were uneconomic or, as the manager said, not an economic proposition. The engineer called by the defendants took the same view and the insurance company advised against repairs. The insurance company valued the car at £85 and, as the plaintiff was liable under his policy for the first £5 of damages, he was paid £80.

Notwithstanding the advice he received, the plaintiff determined to have the car repaired and this he did at a cost of £192. He took the view that the car was worth that to him. It suited his needs and the needs of his family and his opinion was that he could not buy a car of the same worth to him for less than £192. He accordingly gave the defendant credit for the £80 received from the insurance company and sued for the balance together with the cost of hiring a car during the period of repair of his own. The county court judge made certain deductions from the hire charges owing to delay in doing the repairs and awarded £25 under this head together with £5, being the first £5 of the insurance: otherwise, the judge in effect acceded to the plaintiff's claim, which, however, he reduced to £100 and gave the plaintiff judgment of £130, that is to say, £100 for repairs plus the £5 and the £25. The defendant appeals.

The law of damages arising out of collisions on land has been developed out of the Admiralty rule on collisions at sea and the rule of liability is the same in Admiralty and common law cases: see Lord Dunedin's speech in *The Susquehanna (Admiralty Commissioners v. S.S. Susquehanna)*, [1926] AC 655 (HL (Eng.)). The principle is that of *restitutio in integrum*, that is to say, to put the plaintiff in the same position as though the damage had not happened. It has come to be settled that in general the measure of damage is the cost of repairing the damaged article; but there is an exception if it can be proved that the cost of repairs greatly exceeds the value in the market of the damaged article. This arises out of the plaintiff's duty to minimise his damages. Were it otherwise it would be more profitable to destroy the plaintiff's article than to damage it. In the latter cases the measure is the value of the article in the market and this, of course, supposes that there is a market in which the article can be bought. If there is none, then the cost of repairs may still be claimed. …

The Judge here held that the plaintiff was reasonable in having the car repaired notwithstanding that the cost was more than twice the value. It may well be that the plaintiff, so far as he himself was concerned, did act reasonably and that what he got was of more value to him than the damages represented by the value of the car. The plaintiff, however, did not show that he had any special use for which this car alone was suitable, as, for instance, in his business, or anything more than that it was a sound car very well maintained and suited to his ordinary life. In my opinion the judge asked himself the wrong question. The true question was whether the plaintiff acted reasonably as between himself and the defendant and in view of his duty to mitigate the damages. The evidence was that a Lea Francis 1951 car might be difficult to find but that other similar estate cars were on the market and could be had for between £85 and £100 which the plaintiff himself stated to be the value of his car. The judge relied on *O'Grady v. Westminster Scaffolding Ltd.*, [1962] 2 Lloyd's Rep. 238 (QB) where Edmund Davies J held the plaintiff entitled to the cost of repairing his car at a cost considerably exceeding its market value. This case, of course, is not binding on us but if it be right, it may be supported perhaps on the ground that the car there in question was unique and could not be replaced. It was a remarkable vehicle, having been supplied by the plaintiff, the apple of whose eye it was, with no less than three new engines, a new body, and other replacements. In my judgment the facts are very different from those in the present case.

[Pearson LJ and Pennycuick J delivered concurring judgments.]

NOTE

For a comparable Canadian decision, see *Scobie v. Wing* (1992), 63 BCLR (2d) 76 (CA).

Jens v. Mannix Co.
(1978), 89 DLR (3d) 351 (BCSC)

MEREDITH J: The plaintiffs seek compensation for damage to a house, its contents, a garage and surrounding land owned by the plaintiffs and situated at 100 Mile House, British Columbia. The defendant admits liability. The issue is as to the amount to be awarded.

The accident occurred in July 1972, when the buildings and land were saturated with crude oil which escaped from a nearby pipeline. Notwithstanding concerted efforts to correct the condition the house still oozes oil, and the yard is saturated to a depth of five and one-half feet. The disagreeable odour of the oil permeates the house. The evidence of Mr. Harker, a witness called on behalf of the defendant, is to the effect that the oil spill "rendered the subject residence uninhabitable." In the months following the accident the plaintiffs, forced from the house, used a cottage owned by them in Lac la Hache, some miles north of 100 Mile House. But since that time I understand they have been able to live in the house and endure the odour. No doubt the enjoyment of the house has been much reduced.

The plaintiffs ask for an amount sufficient to replace the buildings, amounting, they say, to $50,032 (this amount is in issue); another $12,515 (the amount is agreed upon) to remove and replace the surrounding trees and topsoil; and compensation for the inconvenience they have been put to. The defendant concedes liability in the sum of $10,863 for the clean-up and other costs.

The defendant says that the plaintiffs are not entitled to anything for the replacement of the buildings, the soil and the trees, because that part of the property upon which they are located is zoned for and suited to commercial use and that the market value of that part of the property, if sold for commercial purposes, exceeds its value for residential purposes, with or without the buildings. Thus the defendant maintains that the value of the property is not diminished by the fact that the house is uninhabitable.

The plaintiffs reply that the property has a special practical and sentimental value to them as a place to live.

Mr. Jens is a retired lumberman in his early sixties. He is a pioneer resident of 100 Mile House. The Jens have three children and a number of grandchildren living in the area. Although they spend much of each year elsewhere, they plan to continue to make 100 Mile House their principal home for the rest of their lives.

The house in question is situated on a lot having a frontage of 100 feet on the Cariboo Highway and a depth of 200 feet. The house was built in 1955 by Mr. Jens and his brother on the front half of the lot. On the rear of the lot a hangar had been constructed to house aircraft owned by the Jens (although he does not now pilot an aircraft Mr. Jens retains an interest in flying and has an affinity to the airport which abuts the property).

In 1969 Mr. Jens began collecting vintage cars. He originally housed the collection in the hangar. In 1976 the hangar was enlarged to accommodate the growing collection at a cost of some $65,000. The resulting structure now occupies much of the back half of the property. The 32 cars forming the present collection may well be worth some $500,000. The village council recognizes the collection and structure as a "car museum." The cars are frequently on display to visitors and tourists. When he is at home Mr. Jens is frequently called upon to conduct tours. He shows the cars without charge. His sons fill in when he is away. The house, situated as it is close by the museum, enables the Jens while they are at home to keep a close eye on the collection. The village zoning (Highway Commercial IV) which otherwise would not permit a use of this sort, specifically provides that this property may be used for purposes of a "car museum." Mr. Jens has obtained from the village council as well a special concession which would enable him to demolish the present house and build a new one even though, as the property is zoned for commercial use, rebuilding would not otherwise be allowed. I think this amounts to official recognition that the residence is at least not inappropriate as a permanent adjunct to the museum, now a community asset of significant value.

I pause to observe that the main defence presupposes that the front half of the property upon which the house and garage are situated can in fact be severed from the back half by legal subdivision of the whole lot. However, on the evidence, it seems open to some doubt that a subdivision would be approved by the village. The reason is that subdivision would create a parcel on the back half which may not conform to the village requirements as to building set backs. Of course, if subdivision were not permitted the front half of the lot could not be sold separately for commercial or any other use. But I proceed, nevertheless, on the basis that subdivision is possible and that the plaintiffs could sell the front half for commercial use.

The defendant says that, if I should hold against the contention that no damages should be awarded for loss of the house and garage and the surrounding soil, then I should at least find that the liability of the defendant extends only to reimbursing the plaintiffs for the depreciated value of the structures, that is to say, the current replacement cost less depreciation. Otherwise, the defendant says, the plaintiffs will be benefited at the defendant's expense by the provision of a new home. On the other hand the plaintiffs say that payment of less than the full money value of a new house will not reinstate them in the position that they were before the spill.

I turn then to the law relating to both questions.

In *McGregor on Damages* (London: Sweet & Maxwell, 13th ed., 1972) at paras. 1059-61, pp. 711-3, the author discusses the current state of the law:

It was for long said that the normal measure of damages was the amount of the diminution of the value of the land, a proposition based on what was generally considered to be the leading, but somewhat ancient, case of *Jones v. Gooday* (1814), 8 M & W 146; (1814), 151 ER 985 (Ex.) where the alternative measure of cost of replacement or repair, *i.e.* the sum which it would take to restore the land to its original state, was rejected. ...

However, as we pointed out in the 12th edition of this work, not only is *Jones v. Gooday* the sole case where a plaintiff in possession and with full ownership was refused the cost to him of replacement or repair of the damage done but Alderson B's remark there suggests that the cost of replacement or repair may be an inappropriate measure only because it is out of all proportion to the injury to the plaintiff. That this is the true reason of the result in *Jones v. Gooday* is now supported by *Hollebone v. Midhurst and Fernhurst Builders*, [1968] 1 Lloyd's Rep. 38 (QB), a decision which has been adopted by the Court of Appeal in the context of a claim for breach of contract, in *Harbutt's Plasticine v. Wayne Tank and Pump Co.*, [[1970] 1 QB 447 (CA)]. ...

The difficulty in deciding between diminution in value and cost of reinstatement arises from the fact that the plaintiff may want his property in the same state as before the commission of the tort but the amount required to effect this may be substantially greater than the amount by which the value of the property has been diminished. The test which appears to be the appropriate one is the reasonableness of the plaintiff's desire to reinstate the property; this will be judged in part by the advantages to him of reinstatement in relation to the extra cost to the defendant in having to pay damages for reinstatement rather than damages calculated by the diminution in value of the land.

The foregoing passages were discussed by May J, in the recent case of *C.R. Taylor (Wholesale) Ltd. v. Hepworths Ltd.*, [1977] 1 WLR 659 (QB).

[His Lordship reviewed and quoted extensively from the judgment, which is reproduced in chapter 1, "General Principles of Damages."]

I do not find in the Canadian cases cited in argument law that would preclude me awarding damages based on replacement cost. *Montreal Trust Co. v. Hercules Sales Ltd.*, [1969] 1 OR 661 (CA) and *Waterloo Warehousing & Storage Ltd. v. Swenco Mfg. Ltd.* (1975), 8 OR (2d) 404, like the *Taylor* case, involved buildings essentially valueless because they were situated on redevelopment sites. There the appropriate measure of damages was the difference between the market value of the property before and after destruction of the buildings—a relatively small amount. In *Barrette v. Franki Compressed Pile Co. of Canada Ltd.*, [1955] OR 413 and *Regnier v. Nelson* (1956), 64 Man. R 56, the Courts granted damages based on the cost of repairs but deducted the amount by which the plaintiffs benefited by the improved structure. It is true that in those cases, although the awards were based on the cost of repairs, the Courts adhered to the value "before and after" principle. And in *Stevens v. Abbotsford Lumber Mining & Development Co.* (1924), 33 BCR 299 (CA), Macdonald CJA stated at p. 301 that "the true value of the property destroyed was the measure of damages." I am not by these cases prevented from applying the basic legal principles expressed by May J to the particular circumstances of the case at bar. Certainly cases involving claims under policies of insurance, based as they are upon contractual terms, are no guide to an award in this case.

Here, then, the first consideration must be whether the plaintiffs' claim to replacement of the building is reasonable "as between the plaintiff on the one hand and the defendant on the other." If so, the second question is whether the plaintiffs are entitled to full recovery for replacement or whether the amount should be reduced if it can be said that a new house would give the plaintiffs something "effectively better or more valuable than they had before."

The plaintiffs want to stay where they are because this has been their home for many years. They would not be able to find a residential lot in 100 Mile House of the size that suits them and the location is attractive to them for reasons which principally include the proximity to the museum. The village council, in sanctioning the building of a new house on the lot, in effect confirms that a house is an appropriate permanent adjunct of the museum. And I would judge that, from the standpoint of the village, the continued existence of the house goes a long way to ensuring the continued existence of the museum. Thus I think it altogether reasonable that the plaintiffs should be given an amount sufficient to replace the house at present value.

The evidence does not establish that a new home, even though it were to differ in many respects from the old, would be worth any more to the plaintiffs than the old. In fact several features of the old house—for instance, the plastered walls which are attractive to the plaintiffs—probably cannot be duplicated. Thus in some respects a new home, in the eyes of the plaintiffs, will have less value, not more. The longer life of the new building adds nothing to its value from the plaintiffs' point of view and probably will not enhance the ultimate value of the lot as a whole. Thus I conclude that there should be no deduction for depreciation or for benefit conferred.

I would feel more secure in awarding the plaintiffs full recovery for replacement if they had actually built a new house by now. The fact is they have suffered out the pollution and lived in the house off and on for the past four years. It is conceivable, I suppose, that they would prefer to leave the house as it is and treat the award as simply compensation for their continued discomfort. However, I conclude that, as the defendant concedes that the house is uninhabitable, I must proceed on the footing that it has in effect been destroyed.

I come then to the amount that is required to replace the buildings. The appraiser for the defendant calculated the cost of replacement to be $40,377 as compared with the $50,032 given by the plaintiffs' appraiser. The defendant's appraiser sought to verify his figures by sales statistics of a number of comparable homes in the Kamloops area. These show that if those sales were made at cost to the builder-vendor, then each of the houses must have cost less than $40,000 to build. On the other hand the plaintiffs' appraiser produced two estimates of contractors working in the 100 Mile House area. The contractors themselves gave evidence. Boyko Bros.' estimate of August 30, 1977 was in the sum of $57,153; Kai's Homes Ltd. estimated $51,800. I think these last estimates, made as they were by local contractors, verify that the estimate of the plaintiffs' appraiser is the more reliable.

The plaintiffs have suffered a good deal of inconvenience as a result of the oil saturation. This not only includes putting up with the unpleasant odour itself but they lost the use of the house for some months in 1973, and they have had the very considerable inconvenience of cleaning up. For this I award them the sum of $3,000.

On the evidence as it stands, then, the plaintiffs are entitled to judgment in the following sums:

Special damages as agreed	10,863.00
Replacement of trees and turf	13,515.00
Replacement of house and garage	50,032.00
General damages	3,000.00
	$77,410.00

Logically, the plaintiffs should be entitled to the cost of the demolition of the old buildings, but as no evidence was proffered as to this I can make no award.

The plaintiffs will have their costs of the action.

Assessment accordingly.

[The defendant appealed to the Court of Appeal (1979), 30 DLR (4th) 260 (BCCA).]

HINKSON JA: ... Two issues were raised on the appeal. The first was whether depreciation should be deducted from the award made by the learned trial judge in respect of the damage to the house; and, secondly, the date upon which damages for that loss should be awarded.

At trial, the learned judge concluded that damages should be awarded on the basis of replacement, and the appeal has been presented by the appellant accepting that that was the appropriate principle on which to assess the damages for the loss of the house, under the circumstances of this case. The learned trial judge heard evidence from contractors and experts as to the replacement cost of the residence. Two contractors who operate in the 100 Mile House area gave evidence as to the cost of replacement at a date in August 1977, some four years after the damage occurred. An expert called by the respondents gave evidence, based partly on the evidence of the contractors, as to the replacement cost of the home as at the date of trial. The trial judge accepted that evidence and awarded the sum of $50,032 for the cost of replacement of the house and garage.

There was evidence before the learned trial judge of an expert called on behalf of the plaintiffs, Mr. Morley, as to the replacement cost of the house as at July 1973. Mr. Morley testified that that cost at that date was $37,474. He further testified that the appropriate factor for depreciation at that time was 16% and, applying that figure to the replacement cost, he would deduct $5,996, to arrive at a total of $31,478. The learned trial judge did not apply the depreciated replacement cost at the time of the loss but, rather, as I have indicated, gave full replacement, without depreciation, as at the date of trial.

Counsel for the respondents contends that there was no error made by the learned trial judge in adopting that approach. The basis upon which he makes the submission is that, because of the unusual occurrence in July of 1973, the house was saturated with oil and it took a considerable time to determine what methods could be adopted to overcome the effect of the oil saturation and that, after a considerable period of time and after various experts had inspected the property, it was concluded that no satisfactory methods were available to overcome the effects of the oil saturation and that, in effect, the house had become uninhabitable.

At trial, the defendant, the appellant company here, admitted liability for the loss and conceded that the house was in fact uninhabitable; but, because that concession was not made at a much earlier date, counsel for the respondents contends that the trial judge properly selected the trial date as the time for assessing damages.

In my view, the appropriate time for assessing the damages to be awarded was the date of the loss, that is, July of 1973, and the various factors urged by counsel for the respondents have not persuaded me that the ordinary rule should be departed from in this particular case. Therefore, the starting point, it seems to me, is July 1973.

There was a conflict at trial in the evidence of Mr. Morley and an expert called on behalf of the appellant. Counsel for the appellant does not contend that the trial judge was not entitled to prefer the evidence of Mr. Morley. He bases his submission on that evidence. Accepting that evidence, therefore, the appropriate award of damages for replacement cost as at the date of the loss was $37,474.

Turning to the second issue, counsel for the appellant contends that, on the basis of a number of authorities, particularly Canadian decisions, where replacement cost is determined to be the proper basis for the award of damages, depreciation should also be taken into account. Again, counsel for the respondents contends that, in view of the unique character of this property, the respondents should be fully restored to the same position as before the break in the pipeline and that no deduction ought to be made for depreciation. In particular, counsel for the respondents relies upon the decision in *Hollebone v. Midhurst & Fernhurst Builders, Eastman & White of Midhurst Ltd.*, [1968] 1 Lloyd's Rep. 38 (QB Ref. Div.). In that case the learned county court judge, on the particular facts before him, concluded that it was appropriate to make no deduction for depreciation. The facts in that case involved repairs to a residence.

I am not persuaded, on the facts in this particular case, that this is an appropriate case to apply the decision in *Hollebone*. Rather, it seems to me that, having regard to the nature of this property and to the type of loss that has occurred, that the usual principle should be applied and that depreciation should be taken into account and ought to have been taken into account by the learned trial judge.

In those circumstances, the evidence of Mr. Morley would indicate that the appropriate figure for depreciation would be $5,996, so that the depreciated value for replacement of the house and garage would be $31,478.

Accordingly, I would allow the appeal and reduce the one item that is in contention from $50,032 to $31,478. There were other items contained in the award of the learned trial judge which are not in issue on this appeal.

BULL JA: I agree.

TAGGART JA: I agree.

QUESTIONS

1. Should the result have been different if the defendants had established to the court's satisfaction that the land was worth more as vacant land sold for commercial purposes? Would your answer be different if

a. the plaintiffs' land had been expropriated and the issue was the amount of compensation to be paid to them by the expropriating authority?

b. the plaintiffs intended to sell their property for commercial purposes anyway?

c. the plaintiffs, although intending to rebuild at the time of judgment, changed their minds thereafter and sold for commercial purposes?

If any of these changes in fact lead you to change your initial answer, can you explain your changes in the light of any consistent theory of compensation? If other factors are relevant, what are they?

2. If you were required to express the court's decision in terms of market value how would the market be defined?

3. The plaintiffs resided in the house for four years during which it was, as the defendant conceded, uninhabitable. They were awarded damages on this account. Was it reasonable for the plaintiff to reside in those conditions for that length of time? If not, and in the light of the result in the *Liesbosch*, is the assessment of damages correct?

4. What does the Court of Appeal mean when it makes allowance for depreciation? Is its approach consistent with that taken in *James Street Hardware*?

MISAPPROPRIATION OF PROPERTY

Personal Property

General and Finance Facilities Ltd. v. Cooks Cars (Romford) Ltd.
[1963] 1 WLR 644 (CA)

In November 1958, the plaintiffs, General and Finance Facilities Ltd., let a mobile crane by a hire-purchase agreement to a company called All Star Cars Ltd. The cash price was £1,000; the hire-purchase price was £1,120; All Star Cars Ltd. paid a deposit of £300 and by September 1959 had paid instalments amounting to £377 2s. 6d., the remainder of the hire-purchase price being £442 17s. 6d. In breach of the hire-purchase agreement All Star Cars Ltd. purported to sell the crane to a man called Gooch, and afterwards, in 1960, Gooch purported to sell it to Romford Scrap and Salvage Co. Ltd. for £200. Romford Scrap and Salvage Co. Ltd. then instructed the defendants, Cooks Cars (Romford) Ltd., to do certain repairs to the crane, and delivered it to them for that purpose. The repairs appeared to have been carried out, and the defendants sent an account dated October 24, 1960, addressed to the Romford Scrap and Salvage Co. Ltd. for an amount of £488, including £250 for a 5LW Gardiner engine. The plaintiffs, who had lost trace of the crane, found where it was, and their managing director, one Saunders, went to see it in April 1961.

On May 8, 1961, the plaintiffs' solicitors wrote the defendants saying:

Dear Sirs, Re Thorneycroft Crane OMF 347, I am instructed by my clients, General and Finance Facilities Ltd., that you are in possession of the above mobile crane. This crane is owned by my clients who let it on hire-purchase to All Star Cars Ltd. who later disposed of the crane in breach of their hire-purchase agreement. This crane subsequently came into the possession of

Romford Scrap and Salvage Company Ltd. who of course had no rights to the crane at all who sent it to you for repairs. My clients wish to repossess the crane at present at your premises and request that you treat this letter as a demand that you deliver up the said crane to them or their representative forthwith, failing which proceedings will be instituted against you for its return.

The reply dated May 15, 1961 to that letter said:

With reference to your letter concerning the above we must point out that we have a lien on this vehicle as already noted to your client, General and Finance Facilities Ltd., and when this is discharged we will willingly deliver up the vehicle.

This lien was not effective against the plaintiffs.

On June 2, 1961, the plaintiffs issued a specially indorsed writ claiming "the return of the mobile crane Index No. OMF 347 or its value and damages for detaining the same." The particulars claimed (1) the return of the crane or £2,000, its value; (2) damages for conversion; (3) loss of hire for the crane from May 15, 1961, at £40 per week, which for 33 weeks until January 12, 1962 amounted to £1,320. On September 1, 1961, the plaintiffs' solicitors wrote a letter to the defendants' solicitors setting out a great many defects in the crane.

The plaintiffs made an application under RSC, Ord. 14, for leave to sign final judgment and Master Diamond granted leave, the judgment signed on April 13, 1962, being

that the plaintiffs do have return of the mobile crane OMF 347 or recover against the defendants its value and damages to be assessed.

On July 20, 1962, Master Clayton ordered that

[u]pon hearing counsel for the plaintiffs and defendants upon the plaintiffs' application to assess the amount of damages pursuant to the judgment of Master Diamond dated April 13, 1962, it is ordered that the amount of damages be assessed at £150.

After the hearing before Master Clayton, the master indicated that the plaintiffs were not to have the crane returned to them.

The plaintiffs appealed, contending, *inter alia*, that there should have been separate figures for the value of the crane and for damages, so as to enable them, if they preferred the return of the crane to payment of its assessed value, to apply for a writ of delivery. At the hearing of the appeal, counsel for the plaintiffs stated that they only wished to recover £442 17s. 6d., the balance of the full hire-purchase price, in respect of their claim for damages and loss of hire.

DIPLOCK LJ: This appeal raises a neat point as to the remedies available to a plaintiff who sues for the wrongful detention of goods. The plaintiffs by a specially endorsed writ claimed "the return of a mobile crane Index No. OMF 347 or its value and damages for detaining the same." They pleaded their title to the crane and relied upon a demand for its delivery up dated May 8, 1961. The prayer included an alternative claim for damages for conversion.

There are important distinctions between a cause of action in conversion and a cause of action in detinue. The former is a single wrongful act and the cause of action accrues at the date of the conversion; the latter is a continuing cause of action which accrues at the date of the wrongful refusal to deliver up the goods and continues until delivery up of the goods or judgment in the action for detinue. It is important to keep this distinction clear, for confusion sometimes arises from the historical derivation of the action of conversion from detinue sur bailment and detinue sur trover; of which one result is that the same facts may constitute both detinue and conversion. Demand for delivery up of the chattel was an essential requirement of an action in detinue, and detinue lay only when at the time of the demand for delivery up of the chattel made by person entitled to possession the defendant was either in actual possession of it or was estopped from denying that he was still in possession. Thus if there had been an actual bailment of the chattel by the plaintiff to the defendant, the latter was estopped from asserting that he had wrongfully delivered the chattel to a third person or had negligently lost it before demand for delivery up, and the plaintiff could sue in detinue notwithstanding that the defendant was not in actual possession of the chattel at the time of the demand. (See *Jones v. Dowie* (1841), 9 M & W 19; 152 ER 9 (Exch.); *Reeve v. Palmer* (1858), 5 CBNS 84; 141 ER 33 (Exch.).) Alternatively the plaintiff could sue in conversion for the actual wrongful delivery of the chattel to the third person, though not for its loss. In the absence of bailment, an unqualified refusal to comply with a demand for delivery up of a chattel made by the person entitled to possession may amount to conversion as an alternative to detinue if the defendant at the time of the refusal was in actual possession of the chattel. If he has wrongfully delivered it to a third person before the date of the demand the prior wrongful delivery constitutes the conversion, not the subsequent refusal to comply with the demand. (See *Sachs v. Miklos*, [1948] 2 KB 23 (CA).) But even where, as in the present case, the chattel is in the actual possession of the defendant at the time of the demand to deliver up possession, so that the plaintiff has alternative causes of action in detinue or conversion based upon the refusal to comply with that demand, he has a right to elect which cause of action he will pursue (see *Rosenthal v. Alderton & Sons Ltd.*, [1946] 1 KB 374 at p. 379) and the remedies available to him will differ according to his election.

The action in conversion is a purely personal action and results in a judgment for pecuniary damages only. The judgment is for a single sum of which the measure is generally the value of the chattel at the date of the conversion together with any consequential damage flowing from the conversion and not too remote to be recoverable in law. With great respect to the dictum of Goddard LJ in *Sachs v. Miklos* (at p. 38) this is not necessarily the same as the measure of damages for detinue where the same act constitutes detinue as well as conversion, although in many cases this will be so. This dictum was based upon the headnote to *Rosenthal v. Alderton & Sons Ltd.* which, in my view, misrepresents the effect of the last paragraph of the actual judgment. The law is in my view correctly stated in *Salmond on Torts* (London: Sweet & Maxwell, 13th ed., 1961) at pp. 287 and 288. Notwithstanding that judgment for damages for conversion does not, until satisfied, divest the plaintiff of his property in the chattel (see the analysis of the cases in *Ellis v. John Stenning & Son*, [1932] 2 Ch. 81), it does not entitle the plaintiff to the assistance of the court or the executive, *videlicet* the sheriff, in recovering possession of the chattel.

On the other hand the action in detinue partakes of the nature of an action *in rem* in which the plaintiff seeks specific restitution of his chattel. At common law it resulted in a judgment for delivery up of the chattel or payment of its value as assessed, and for payment of damages for its detention. This, in effect, gave the defendant an option whether to return the chattel or to pay its value, and if the plaintiff wished to insist on specific restitution of the chattel he had to have recourse to Chancery. (See *In re Scarth, per* Mellish LJ (1854), 10 Ch.

App. 234 at p. 235.) The *Common Law Procedure Act*, 1854, s. 78, gave the court power to order delivery up of the chattel by the defendant without giving him the option to pay its value as assessed. Such an order was enforceable by execution, and if the chattel could not be found distraint could be had upon the defendant's lands and goods until he delivered up the specific chattel, or at the option of the plaintiff distraint could be had of the defendant's goods for the assessed value of the chattel. This, in effect, where the court thought fit to make such an order, gave the plaintiff an option to insist upon specific restitution of his chattel if the defendant did not deliver it up voluntarily; but this remedy was not available unless and until the value of the chattel had been assessed. (See *Chilton v. Carrington* (1885), 15 CB 730; 139 ER 612 (Ex. Ch.).) This remedy continues to exist under the modern law, but if the plaintiff does not wish to exercise his option to recover the assessed value of the chattel the assessment of its value is no longer a condition precedent to an order for specific restitution. (See *Hymas v. Ogden*, [1905] 1 KB 246 (DC); RSC, Ord. 48, r. 1.) In addition to an order for specific restitution of the chattel or for payment of its value as assessed, the plaintiff was always entitled to damages for wrongful detention of the chattel.

In the result an action in detinue today may result in a judgment in one of three different forms: (1) for the value of the chattel as assessed and damages for its detention; or (2) for return of the chattel or recovery of its value as assessed and damages for its detention; or (3) for return of the chattel and damages for its detention.

A judgment in the first form is appropriate where the chattel is an ordinary article in commerce, for the court will not normally order specific restitution in such a case, where damages are an adequate remedy. (See *Whiteley Ltd. v. Hilt*, [1918] 2 KB 808 at pp. 819 and 824.) A judgment in this form deprives the defendant of the option which he had under the old common law form of judgment of returning the chattel; but if he has failed to do so by the time of the judgment the plaintiff, if he so elects, is entitled to a judgment in this form as of right (cf. RSC, Ord. 13, r. 6). In substance this is the same as the remedy in conversion, although the sum recoverable, as I have indicated, may not be the same as damages for conversion, for the cause of action in detinue is a continuing one up to the date of judgment and the value of the chattel is assessed as at that date. (See *Rosenthal v. Alderton & Sons Ltd.*) A final judgment in such a form is for a single sum of money.

A judgment in the second form gives to the defendant the option of returning the chattel, but it also gives to the plaintiff the right to apply to the court to enforce specific restitution of the chattel by writ of delivery, or attachment or sequestration as well as recovering damages for its detention by writ of *fieri facias* (RSC, Ord. 42, r. 6). This is an important right and it is essential to its exercise that the judgment should specify separate amounts for the assessed value of the chattel and for the damages for its detention, for if the plaintiff wishes to proceed by writ of delivery for which he can apply *ex parte* (RSC, Ord. 48, r. 1) he has the option of distraining for the assessed value of the chattel if the chattel itself is not recovered by the sheriff. He would be deprived of this option if the value of the chattel were not separately assessed.

A judgment in the third form is unusual, but can be given. (See *Hymas v. Ogden*.) Under it the only pecuniary sum recoverable is damages for detention of the chattel. Its value need not be assessed and the plaintiff can only obtain specific restitution of the chattel by writ of delivery, attachment or sequestration. He has no option under the writ of delivery to distrain for the value of the chattel.

In the ordinary way where an action goes to trial, the issues of liability, assessment of value of the chattel, and damages for its detention are dealt with at the hearing, and final judgment in one or other of the above forms is entered. In the present case, however, proceedings were brought under RSC, Ord. 14, and on April 13, 1962, the plaintiffs upon leave obtained from Master Diamond signed final judgment "that the plaintiff do have return of the mobile crane OMF 347 or recover against the defendant its value and damages to be assessed." No appeal was brought against this judgment. It is a final judgment granting the plaintiff relief in the second form referred to above and entitling the plaintiff, upon the assessment of the value of the chattel and of the damages for its detention, to select and enforce his appropriate remedies by execution.

The assessment of the value of the chattel and of the damages for its detention was referred to Master Clayton under RSC, Ord. 36B, rr. 3 and 6. It thereupon became his duty to assess both these amounts separately at the date of the assessment (see RSC, Ord. 36B, r. 7) and to certify each amount (RSC, Ord. 36B, r. 8). He did not do this; what he did instead was to order that "the amount of damages be assessed at £150." He made no separate assessment of the value of the crane. We are informed that after the hearing counsel returned and asked the master whether he intended that the plaintiffs should have their crane back and that he replied "No." It would seem, therefore, that the sum of £150 was intended to include both the value of the crane and damages for its detention, and I agree with Pearson LJ that it was open to him upon the evidence to come to that conclusion. But an order assessing a single sum of money would be justifiable only under a judgment in the first form discussed above, whereas the plaintiffs' entitlement to a judgment in the second form discussed above was already *res judicata* under the earlier judgment of Master Diamond. Master Clayton had no jurisdiction to deprive the plaintiffs of that and the consequent options which a judgment in that form secures to a plaintiff. His sole jurisdiction and his duty under Master Diamond's order was to assess separately both the value of the crane and the damages for its detention and to certify these two amounts.

Although I share Pearson LJ's regret that this litigation should be further protracted, the matter is one of substance, not merely of form, for Master Clayton's order prevents the plaintiffs from exercising an option to which they are in law entitled under the judgment of Master Diamond, videlicet of choosing whether to seek specific restitution of the crane or to recover its value. The matter must accordingly go back to Master Clayton with a direction to assess separately (1) the value of the crane at the date of the assessment and (2) the damages sustained by the plaintiffs by its detention up to the date of the assessment.

[Pearson LJ agreed in the result.]

Steiman v. Steiman
(1982), 18 Man. R (2d) 203 (CA)

O'SULLIVAN JA (Monnin JA dissenting in part; Hall JA concurring): The plaintiff has judgment for $186,786.66 for damages for conversion of jewellery and other items together with costs of $10,100 plus disbursements. The award is made up of the following amounts:

(a) Agreed upon value of non-jewellery items in 1976.....................	$ 8,500.00
(b) Interest thereon at 10% between April 1976 and June 1981 (the date of judgment)...	4,391.66
(c) Agreed upon value of missing jewellery as of June 1981 (date of trial)	31,850.00
(d) Value of missing jewellery not agreed upon, valued at date of trial	132,360.00
(e) Sales tax on (a) and (d)	7,043.00
(f) Letter box...	50.00
(g) Sales tax on (c)	1,592.00
(h) Exemplary damages...	1,000.00
	$186,786.66

There is no dispute as to liability in this appeal but the appellants say the award is too high. Quantum is attacked on three main grounds: (1) the award of interest is unwarranted; (2) the jewellery was valued by the learned trial judge at the date of trial rather than at the date when it could have been replaced by the plaintiff; and (3) individual pieces of jewellery were overvalued. ...

As to the second ground, it was agreed by the parties that some missing jewellery had a value at the date of trial of $31,850. The defendants did not agree that this was a suitable date for ascertaining such value but acknowledged that this amount was the value at the date of trial. The learned trial judge was invited to determine the value of the other missing jewellery, amounting to 14 pieces. He heard evidence and decided these 14 items were worth $132,360 at the time of trial; he included in his award both figures of $31,850 and $132,360. He also awarded 5% of the value of the missing items to cover sales tax [(1981), 11 Man. R (2d) 376].

Counsel for the appellants submits that the learned trial judge erred in valuing the missing jewellery at the date of the trial. He submits the value should be determined as of the date of the conversion (or more strictly the date at which the jewellery could reasonably have been replaced following the conversion). All parties agreed that the value of jewellery at the date of conversion was one-third of the 1981 values. Plaintiff's appraiser, Stephen Powell, in his evaluation had said 1976 values would be between 30% and 35% of the values shown as of the date of his appraisal, April 7, 1981. As I say, counsel agreed that we could take it that the 1976 values, the values at the time of conversion, were one-third of the 1981 values. So, if the learned trial judge erred in selecting the date of trial as the appropriate time for measuring damages, then the award as to item (c) should be reduced from $31,850 to $10,616.67 and the award as to item (d) should be reduced from $132,360 to $44,120. In both cases the reduced awards would carry 5% for sales tax and, if interest is payable, the interest rate would be 10% per year.

The learned trial judge said [at 381]:

[S]urely it is reasonable and just to fix the date of valuation as of the time of judgment as opposed to conversion. The rationale is simply that had the goods not been converted from the plaintiff but left in her possession, or returned to her, then she would have had the benefit not only of the use of the jewellery but also of any increase in the value to date.

With respect, it seems to me this reasoning is flawed. A person who finds his goods taken may continue to regard the goods as his own and sue in detinue for their return but if he elects to claim damages for conversion his damages must be based on the supposition that he has replaced the missing goods at market prices.

The victim who replaces converted goods will not lose any appreciation in value by reason of a rising market. If the victim were permitted to recover damages as of the date of trial for goods which he has in fact replaced by purchase, he would gain twice from appreciation—once on the goods converted and once on the goods purchased.

Thousands of cases are settled every day on the basis that a wrongdoer who destroys a chattel is bound to pay only that amount which will cover the cost of replacing the chattel at the time of the tort (or a reasonable time thereafter) plus loss of use limited to the period of time required to find a replacement. In insurance law, motor vehicle law, many branches of the law, this principle is accepted as basic.

It is true that where there is a wrongful taking the victim may have the alternative of claiming in detinue, where the unsuccessful defendant must replace the goods or pay the value at the time of the trial. But the plaintiff then runs the risk of a falling market and of depreciation in value; the defendant's option to restore the goods continues to judgment and maybe even to execution.

In the case before us, the pleadings were drawn in such a way as to support a judgment in detinue as well as in conversion but the plaintiff has taken judgment in conversion. Perhaps the plaintiff preferred to have money damages rather than risk the restoration of the jewellery which has since the trial fallen dramatically in price. In any event, it seems clear that the plaintiff's judgment is one for conversion.

On the appeal, counsel for the plaintiff submitted that the measure of damages is the same in conversion as in detinue and the learned trial judge was of the same view. There have been some judicial pronouncements to the same effect. Thus, for example, Lord Goddard CJ in *Sachs v. Miklos*, [1948] 2 KB 23 (CA) at p. 39, said:

> It seems to me that in assessing damages for detinue or for conversion (and, for myself, I do not see where the distinction is to be drawn between those two causes of action for this purpose) the damages are not necessarily and in all cases the value of the goods at the date of judgment.

But in *General & Finance Facilities Ltd. v. Cooks Cars (Romford) Ltd.*, [1963] 1 WLR 644 (CA) at p. 648, a decision of the English Court of Appeal, Diplock LJ said:

> There are important distinctions between a cause of action in conversion and a cause of action in detinue. The former is a single wrongful act and the cause of action accrues at the date of the conversion; the latter is a continuing cause of action which accrues at the date of the wrongful refusal to deliver up the goods and continues until delivery up of the goods or judgment in the action for detinue.

And at p. 649:

> The action in conversion is a purely personal action and results in a judgment for pecuniary damages only. The judgment is for a single sum of which the measure is generally the value of the chattel at the date of the conversion together with any consequential damage flowing from the conversion and not too remote to be recoverable in law. With great respect to the dictum of Goddard LJ in *Sachs v. Miklos* [[1948] 2 KB 23 (CA), at 38], this is not necessarily the same as the measure of damages for detinue where the same act constitutes detinue as well as conversion,

although in many cases this will be so. This dictum was based upon the headnote to *Rosenthal v. Alderton & Sons Ltd.*, [1946] 1 KB 374, which, in my view, misrepresents the effect of the last paragraph of the actual judgment.

In *Asamera Oil Corp. Ltd. v. Sea Oil & General Corp.*, [1979] 1 SCR 633, Estey J for the Supreme Court examined briefly the principles which have evolved in the law of torts. He said at p. 652:

> In conversion, the measure of damages has been said to be the value of the shares at the date of conversion, and in addition, consequential damages represented by the loss of the opportunity to dispose of the shares at the highest price attained prior to the end of trial: *vide McNeil v. Fults et al.* (1906), 38 SCR 198, *per* Duff J, at p. 205; *The Queen in right of Alberta v. Arnold*, [1971] SCR 209 at p. 230, *per* Spence J.

He went on to say:

> I am aware of course that these cases were for the most part dealing with the wrongful refusal of a person under the liability of a trustee to deliver property to a beneficiary, but on principle the result would be the same in simple cases of conversion: *vide McGregor on Damages* (London: Sweet & Maxwell, 13th ed., 1972) at p. 671.

Although these remarks are *obiter dicta*, considering their source, they are entitled to great respect. However, I think it is clear from an examination of the cases that the weight of authority is in favour of the proposition that in simple cases of conversion there is no right to be awarded as consequential damages the difference between the market value at the time when it would have been reasonable to replace the converted goods and either their value at the time of trial or their highest value at some intermediate point.

Indeed, in *The Queen in right of Alberta v. Arnold*, [1971] SCR 209, referred to with approval by Estey J, I think that Spence J rejected the idea that a victim of conversion can claim as consequential damages the difference between the replacement cost of the goods at the time he became aware of the conversion and some subsequent date. The reasons of Spence J were dissenting reasons in the sense that he and Hall J thought that an award should be sustained as to liability while the majority reversed the award on this point, but I think Estey J is right when he says that what was said by Spence J accurately states the law. In the view Spence J took of the facts, the plaintiff had suffered loss by reason of the conversion of 4,500 shares in 1959. The Appellate Division of the Supreme Court of Alberta had assessed damages on the basis of $21.50 per share being the highest market value between the times when the shares were converted and the date the action was commenced (less the amounts realized on the actual sales and credited to him). In his reasons for judgment, Spence J said the Alberta Appellate Division was wrong. At pp. 231-2, he pointed out that the plaintiff knew of the sale of his shares in early 1960. Applying the test set out by Lord Goddard in *Sachs v. Miklos, supra*, he said at p. 232:

> … I have come to the conclusion that the respondent's damages should be calculated with reference to the price of the shares when he was notified of the conversion. There is no doubt that he could at that time have purchased other shares in their place and have claimed from the appellants the cost of such replacement purchase.

While there was no clear evidence as to the market price of the shares on any specific date in 1960, Spence J accepted the evidence of a statistician that the shares ranged from $3.40 to $6.75 in the year 1960. He said at p. 232:

If we were to take the average of that high and low price, the result would be $5.07½ per share. Four thousand, five hundred shares at that rate would have sold for $22,837.50 and, in my opinion, the respondent's damages should be assessed at that amount.

After deducting credits to which the appellant was entitled, he would therefore have reduced the judgment appealed from by varying the award of $96,750.00–$13,220.56 and substituting an award of $22,837.50–$13,220.56. He would also have given the plaintiff interest on the net recovery at 5% from the date of the issuance of the statement of claim.

In my opinion, if what Spence J says is good law, and I think it is, then the plaintiff in the case before us can recover for item (c) $10,616.67 rather than $31,850 and for item (d) at most $44,120 rather than the $132,360 awarded to her by the learned trial judge. To this would be added sales tax and interest at 10% in accordance with the provisions of s. 72(3) of the *Queen's Bench Act* from the time of conversion, April 1, 1976.

In *Sachs v. Miklos* at p. 40, Lord Goddard CJ put the matter of consequential damages in this way:

[I]t seems to me that if he knew, or ought to have known, of this conversion in or about July 1944, the damage which he now says that he has suffered owing to the rise in price is damage for which the defendants are not liable because it has not flowed from their act; it has flowed from his act.

Counsel for the plaintiff referred us in argument to a number of textbooks which seem to give a view of the law different from that of Spence J but the textbook writers have not been uniform in their treatment of this question. In *Ley v. Lewis*, [1952] VLR 119, the Supreme Court of Victoria has made a useful analysis of the various authorities and of the differing views of textbook writers as of the date of the case. In England the law has been drastically altered by the *Torts (Interference with Goods) Act*, 1977 (UK), c. 32, which simply abolished detinue and conversion and substituted for them a new tort of wrongful interference with goods. For this reason late editions of English textbooks and English authorities must be read with caution so far as concerns their applicability to Canada and particularly to this province where detinue and conversion both remain as alternative remedies. ...

There should be added to the value of the goods at the time of conversion interest at 10% per year from the date of conversion pursuant to s. 72(3) of the *Queen's Bench Act*.

Accordingly, I would vary the judgment appealed from by substituting for the amounts therein set out the following award:

Value of non-jewellery items	$ 8,500.00
Value of missing jewellery	44,064.67
5% for sales tax on above	2,628.24
	$55,192.91
Letter box	50.00
Exemplary damages	1,000.00
	$56,242.91

plus interest at the rate of 10% per year on $55,192.91 from April 21, 1976 to the date of the certificate of judgment in this court together with costs of $10,000 plus disbursements to be taxed. The appellants shall have their costs in this court with a factum fee of $100.

Appeal allowed; judgment appealed from varied.

NOTES AND QUESTIONS

1. What theory of compensation supports the court's refusal to award damages for the loss of increase in the value of the goods from the date of conversion to the date of trial?

2. Statutes and/or rules of court often provide special interim remedies for wrongful detention of personal property (such as replevin) and may affect the common law measure of recovery. See, for example, Nova Scotia Civil Procedure Rule 48.

3. Do the differences between the causes of action in detinue and conversion justify different rules for the assessment of damages? Do the cases of *Semelhago v. Paramadevan* and *306793 Ontario Ltd. v. Rimes* (outlined in *Semelhago* in chapter 1) shed any light on this question? Does the case of *Jamal v. Moolla Dawood Sons & Co.* in chapter 1, "General Principles of Damages," assist?

4. Should the assessment of damages be influenced by the sentimental value of the property? In *Mason v. Westside Cemeteries* (1996), 135 DLR (4th) 361 (Ont. Gen. Div.), a cemetery misplaced the ashes of the plaintiff's parents and he sued for damages. The trial judge, Molloy J, analyzed the damages issue as set out in the following paragraphs. Do you agree?

1. Special Damages

The calculation of damages in an action based on the loss of property is normally based on the value of the property lost. This is the case whether the cause of action is founded on bailment, contract or negligence. Accordingly, in considering the special damages claim I will not distinguish between the alternative causes of action.

The plaintiff paid $50 for the interment of his parents' ashes at Westminster. He received no value for that payment. Accordingly, he is entitled to the return of that $50 together with interest from August 2, 1979.

The plaintiff is also entitled to special damages based on the value of the property lost. The usual method of determining that value is by reference to the price at which the property could likely be sold to an arms-length purchaser, i.e., its market value. Clearly, this method of valuation is of no use in the case at hand. Even if cremated human remains were a commodity capable of being bought and sold, there would be no arms-length purchaser who would want to buy them. There is no ascertainable "market price" for human ashes.

There have been cases in the past dealing with property which is difficult to valuate because it is so rare or unusual in character that there is no established market value. That is quite different, in my view, from a situation in which there is no market at all. In the former situation, there is a market price but it is difficult to calculate because of its rarity. In the latter, if nobody would purchase the property in question, it has no market value at all.

The plaintiff argues that in determining the value of his parents' ashes, consideration must be given to their special value to him. There are cases in which the value of the property at issue has been adjusted upwards somewhat to reflect its real value to its owner over and above the market value: *Buchanan v. Cook* (1958), 11 DLR (2d) 638 (Sask. CA), dealing with a used rug; *Clarke v. Fullerton* (1871), 8 NSR 348 (CA), dealing with a telescope presented to the plaintiff's father for heroism; *McNair v. Collins* (1912), 6 DLR 510 (Ont. Div. Ct.), awarding $125 for the loss of a half-breed dog who was a pet as well as a farm and watch dog even though there was evidence of "pups being worth $10 a dozen"; *Chappell v. Barati* (1982), 30 CCLT 137 (Ont. HCJ), assessing damages for value of trees lost in a fire although the market value of the land was unaffected by their loss. In all of these cases the property in question had a real value apart from the owner's special interest in it. The ashes that were lost in this case, however, had little or no intrinsic monetary value. They had a value to the plaintiff, but only because of his emotional connection to them. I am not aware of any case in which a value has been placed on an object based entirely on the plaintiff's emotional attachment to it. Indeed, as a general principle the sentimental value ascribed to an object by its owner is not recoverable in damages. I agree with Professor Waddams' statement of this principle, as follows:

> There is little authority on the problem of what is called "sentimental value." It may be that the plaintiff would not have sold his pet dog or his mother's locket at any price, but this does not entitle him to infinite damages. References to market value in the older cases suggest that a value entirely idiosyncratic to the plaintiff would be ignored, and it cannot be satisfactory to measure damages by the price the plaintiff would in fact have demanded for the property, not only because of the unreliability of the testimony on such an issue, but also because of the apparent inequity of compensating persons who have lost similar property at different rates according to the strength of their sentiments.

S.M. Waddams, *The Law of Damages* (Toronto: Canada Law Book, 2d ed., 1994), at pp. 1-17.

Even in *Clark v. Fullerton*, the case most often cited as authority for taking sentimental value into account, the court did not base the damages solely on the sentimental value of the telescope. In fact, the appellate court reduced the $350 award given by the jury at trial to $100. Although, $100 was more than the telescope's appraised value, the court expressly stated that damages could not be set based merely on the "ideal estimate" of the plaintiff because that would be "too vague and uncertain to form our measure of value." However, the court did go on to say (at p. 358):

> This principle ought not, however, in my opinion, to be entirely lost sight of, if we are to adjust the damages in our discretion, *in view of the circumstances under which this plaintiff was deprived of the possession.*

(Emphasis added.) Likewise, although the Saskatchewan Court of Appeal in *Buchanan v. Cook* took into account the value of the rug to the plaintiff, it also endorsed the principle that the owner of property "is not entitled to a fanciful price which he may for special reasons place upon it" (*supra*, at p. 640 [DLR]).

Interestingly, many of the cases which take sentimental value into account in assessing damages for loss of property involve deliberate acts of wrongdoing by the defendant. This point was made by the Alberta Supreme Court in *Jennings v. Wolfe*, [1950] 3 DLR 442, a bailment case against a taxidermist for the negligent loss of the plaintiff's much prized grizzly bear hide. In *Jennings* the court allowed only the market value of the bearskin and nothing for its sentimental value to the plaintiff as a hunting trophy. The court declined to follow *Clarke v. Fullerton* because there was no "wrongful motive" by the taxidermist in the case before it. In *Clarke v. Fullerton* the subject telescope had been stolen and sold privately by the defendant. In *McNair v. Collins* the subject dog was deliberately shot by a neighbour. It appears that in some of these cases there has been an overlapping of sentimental value with punitive or exemplary damages and these cases must therefore be viewed with caution.

I accept that the difficulty of assessing damages based on the value of the goods involved does not absolve a trial judge from his or her duty to nevertheless arrive at an assessment. In the case before me, however, the quantification of value goes beyond "difficult." It is impossible. In my opinion the cremated remains of the plaintiff's parents have no monetary value whatsoever. Further, I do not consider it appropriate to affix a completely arbitrary monetary value to the ashes based solely on the plaintiff's emotional attachment to them. Indeed, I find the very idea of putting a monetary value on the ashes of human beings to be somewhat distasteful. I would therefore assign the nominal value of $1 to the ashes and award the plaintiff $2 for the loss of both urns.

Alternatively, even if it were in theory appropriate to assess a larger amount for sentimental value, I would not consider this an appropriate case in which to do so. In saying this, I wish to make it clear that I am drawing a distinction between the sentimental value that the plaintiff attached to the ashes themselves and the distress that the plaintiff has experienced as a result of their loss. I accept that the plaintiff is genuinely distressed that the ashes are missing. I do not accept that the plaintiff had any emotional attachment to the ashes themselves. His mother's ashes sat on a shelf at the funeral home for nine years and his father's ashes sat there for five years. He only moved them to the cemetery in 1979 at the urging of the funeral home that he do something. He had the opportunity to take personal possession of the ashes but did not do so because he said he would be uncomfortable having them around. He never visited or memorialized the ashes in any way for 23 years. He has never even seen them. One has to question how great his attachment to the ashes themselves can possibly be. I hasten to add that this is by no means a criticism of the plaintiff. Some people attach a significance to visiting burial sites, erecting monuments and otherwise honouring the remains of their loved ones, and other people do not. The plaintiff did not. But this has nothing to do with his love for his parents, his grief at their death or his genuine distress that their remains have been lost. It does, however, affect the amount at which I would assess the value of the ashes if I were to take into account their special value to the plaintiff. In my opinion, the ashes themselves were of very little, if any, value to the plaintiff. If I had to assign a value to it I would fix it at $250 for each urn. However for the reasons already expressed above, I do not consider this amount to be recoverable at law.

2. General Damages for Mental Distress

(i) Impact of the Loss on the Plaintiff

I accept the plaintiff's evidence that he has experienced, and will continue to experience, considerable emotional upset as a result of the loss of his parents' ashes. At first blush this may seem to be at odds with the fact that he paid no attention to the ashes for 23 years. However, the plaintiff testified that he saw no particular need to visit or honour the ashes as objects. What was important to him, he said, was that he always knew where they were and that ultimately, when he died, his parents' remains would be interred next to his own and those of his other family members. That is what was important to the plaintiff. And that is what he has lost. The point was made on cross-examination that the plaintiff has not required any professional care or medication as a result of this emotional distress, to which the plaintiff responded that he had survived four years in a prisoner of war camp in World War II and that he is not the sort of person that breaks down. I recognize that real emotional hurt can be present without significant outward manifestations and I accept that the plaintiff is the type of individual who may not openly show his feelings, even ones that are quite deep. That does not necessarily negate the reality or intensity of those emotions. It is clear that the emotional impact has not been devastating in the sense that the plaintiff has had a complete breakdown. However, he has been quite shaken and unsettled and this will not go away. He has, in a very real sense, lost peace of mind.

(ii) Recoverability of Damages for Mental Distress

There is very little case law dealing with fact situations similar to this one. Furthermore, the cases that do exist are too few and too varied to extract any principles of general application except to say that plaintiffs whose cases are founded on trespass tend to have been more successful than plaintiffs in negligence or contract cases.

In *Phillips v. Montreal General Hospital* (1908), 33 Que. SC 483, the Quebec Superior Court upheld the existence of a cause of action based in trespass arising from an unlawful autopsy performed upon the plaintiff's deceased husband. While the court seemed to suggest that compensation for the injury to the widow's feelings would be appropriate, there is no discussion of quantum as the decision relates only to whether the cause of action exists.

Similarly, the Alberta Court of Appeal held in *Edmonds v. Armstrong Funeral Home Ltd.*, [1931] 1 DLR 676 that a husband has the right to the custody and control of the remains of his deceased wife and that any unauthorized interference with that right, including an unauthorized autopsy, would give rise to a cause of action. Although the quantum of damages is not mentioned, the court clearly recognized that damages for mental distress were recoverable because of the wilful misconduct of the defendant. The court reasoned that since mental suffering can be considered in assessing damages for assault, defamation, malicious prosecution and seduction, there was no good reason to exclude it in a case of this nature. However, the court clearly distinguished the situation of an intentional tort from a case of negligence, reasoning that damages for wounded feelings in a case involving wilful misconduct are awarded in part to punish the defendant and not merely to compensate the plaintiff.

In *Edmonds v. Armstrong Funeral Home* the Alberta Court of Appeal was careful to distinguish its earlier decision in a negligence case, *Miner v. CPR* (1911), 3 Alta. LR 408. In that case the plaintiff had arranged a funeral for her deceased son to be held in "Bawlf" and the defendant was shipping the corpse by rail to that location. Unfortunately, the defendant's employees misread the destination and put the corpse off the train at "Banff" by mistake. As a result the corpse did not arrive in Bawlf in time for the funeral, causing great distress to the mother. However the court held that damages for mental suffering alone were not recoverable in a negligence action and dismissed the action.

In *Loach & Son Ltd. v. Kennedy* (1952), 103 L Jo. 76, an English County Court awarded damages against an undertaker for breach of contract. The undertaker had been instructed to pick up a body from the hospital mortuary on the day scheduled for its funeral and transport it to the cemetery. To suit their own convenience, the undertakers picked up the body on Saturday and stored it in their machine shop until the funeral on Monday. The family learned of this after the funeral and sued for breach of contract. The court awarded £15 for the "anxiety and distress" caused to the family.

In 1938, the English King's Bench in *Owens v. Liverpool Corp.*, [1939] 1 KB 394 upheld the decision of a lower court which awarded damages in a negligence action for nervous shock to various members of the family of a deceased. There was a funeral procession in which the family members were in a carriage following a hearse containing the corpse. The hearse was struck by a tramcar negligently operated by the defendant, causing the coffin to be overturned and nearly ejected onto the road. The trial judge made a factual finding that the relatives who witnessed this were "horrified" and sustained "severe shock." Damages were awarded based on the varying degrees of shock in the amounts of £75, £15, £100 and £11. The Court of King's Bench found that there was no error of law in making such an award. The court held at p. 400:

> On principle we think that the right to recover damages for mental shock caused by the negligence of a defendant is not limited to cases in which apprehension as to human safety is involved. The principle must be that mental or nervous shock, if in fact caused by the defendant's negligent act, [does just as real] damage to the sufferer as a broken limb—less obvious to the layman, but nowadays equally ascertainable by the physician. That alleged shock results from apprehension as to a less important matter may well be material in considering whether the allegation be proved. But fear that unfounded claims may be put forward, and may result in erroneous conclusions of fact, ought not to influence us to impose legal limitations as to the nature of the facts that it is permissible to prove. As Kennedy J said in *Dulieu v. Mite & Sons (I)*: "I should be sorry to adopt a rule which would bar all such claims on grounds of policy alone, and in order to prevent the possible success of unrighteous or groundless actions. Such a course involves the denial of redress in meritorious cases, and it necessarily implies a certain degree of distrust, which I do not share, in the capacity of legal tribunals to get at the truth in this class of claim."

With respect to the quantum of damages, the court ruled at pp. 400-1:

> It may be that the plaintiffs are of that class which is peculiarly susceptible to the luxury of woe at a funeral so as to be disastrously disturbed by any untoward accident to the trappings of mourning. But one who is guilty of negligence to another must put up with idiosyncrasies of his victim that increase the likelihood or extent of damage to him: it is no answer to a claim for a fractured skull that its owner had an unusually fragile one.

The most recent Canadian case I have seen dealing with this subject area is a 1976 British Columbia Supreme Court decision, *McNeil v. Forest Lawn Memorial Services Ltd.* (1976), 72 DLR (3d) 556. The plaintiffs were the parents of a young woman who died violently and in suspicious circumstances, possibly murdered. The plaintiff retained the defendant funeral director to obtain the body of their dead daughter and take it to the funeral home where there was to be viewing by the mother and father only. After the viewing by the parents, the body was to be cremated. The parents purchased a dress for $35 to be used to clothe their daughter's body prior to the viewing. Due to a breakdown in internal communications at the funeral home, the body was cremated before the parents saw it. The trial judge found that the deprivation of seeing their daughter's body was only a minute fraction of the mental agony sustained by the parents in connection with their daughter's death. He assessed general damages for the mental distress caused by the funeral home's actions at $750 for each parent. However he then went on to find that these damages were not compensable as a question of law. In so finding, the trial judge held that there was no basis for a cause of action in tort or trespass and that there had been no wilful misconduct on the part of the defendant so as to attract punitive damages. Since the cause of action rested entirely in contract, the court found that damages for mental distress were not recoverable. Gould J held at p. 562:

> The claim is for mental anguish only. Such anguish would certainly be foreseeable by any funeral director who failed to afford relatives a view of the body, when they wanted and had contracted for such. In breach of contract of marriage cases exemplary or punitive damages may be given, presumably for mental anguish, in addition to the damages for pecuniary loss. In this case there is nothing to warrant any consideration of punitive or exemplary damages. The only pecuniary loss which arose from the defendant's breach of contract here was the purchase of the dress, for $35, by Mr. McNeil. The rest of the claim is exclusively for mental anguish arising out of breach of contract, and such is not compensable.

As I said earlier, it is difficult to determine from these cases what principles should be applied in determining the recoverability of mental distress damages. While some courts awarded such damages, others refused to do so in the absence of wilful misconduct by the defendant. Also, some of the cases were decided prior to relatively recent developments in the general case law as to the recoverability of damages for mental distress. It is therefore necessary to turn to general principles in order to decide whether damages for mental distress should be awarded in the case before me.

I was not directed to and am not aware of any judicial authority dealing with damages for mental distress in a case of bailment. There are cases dealing with the availability of such damages for breach of contract and there are cases dealing with mental distress damages for negligence. Although in recent years there has been a gradual merger of the legal principles applicable to contract and tort, this process has not as yet evolved fully for mental distress damages. On the current state of the law, damages for mental distress would appear to be more readily recoverable for breach of contract than for negligence.

The general rule for assessment of damages in contract, as established by *Hadley v. Baxendale* (1854), 9 Ex. 341, 156 ER 145, is that the plaintiff is entitled to recover damages for that which may reasonably have been supposed to be in the contemplation of the parties at the time they made the contract as the probable result of the contract being breached. It had long been the law that damages could not be recovered in contract for disappointment or mental distress caused by the breach. This principle was fundamentally altered by Lord Denning's landmark decision in *Jarvis v. Swans Tours Ltd.*, [1973] 1 QB 233 (CA), in which Mr. Jarvis was awarded damages for his loss of enjoyment, disappointment and distress when the holiday he booked with the defendant turned out to be far less than was promised. Since then, courts have fairly readily awarded damages for mental distress in situations where such distress would have been within the contemplation of the parties as a foreseeable consequence of a breach of the contract between them.

This principle was applied by Borins J in *Newell v. Canadian Pacific Airlines Ltd.* (1976), 74 DLR (3d) 574 (Ont. Co. Ct.), in which the defendant airline agreed to transport the plaintiffs' two pet dogs from Toronto to Mexico City. The airline was aware of the plaintiffs' emotional attachment to the dogs and of their concern for their pets' safety and well-being. However, due to the defendant's negligence, when the airplane arrived in Mexico, one dog was dead and the other in a comatose state. In addition to compensating the plaintiffs for their pecuniary losses, Borins J awarded general damages of $500 for the mental distress caused to the plaintiff as a result of the injury and death of their dogs. In reaching this decision, Borins J applied the following test [at 592]:

Was the contract such that the parties must have contemplated that its breach might entail mental distress, such as frustration, annoyance or disappointment?

Having answered that question in the affirmative, he found that damages for mental distress were recoverable.

Adapting that test to the case before me, I must consider whether the relationship between Westminster and the plaintiff was such that Westminster must have contemplated that the loss of the plaintiff's parents' ashes would cause him mental distress. The answer is obvious. Westminster was fully aware that the next of kin would likely be upset if the remains of their loved ones went missing. That being the case, I can see no basis for denying recovery of damages to a person in the plaintiff's position. If damages are recoverable for upset over the loss of a dog or for the disappointment of a ruined holiday, surely the distress caused by loss of the remains of someone's deceased parents is likewise compensable.

In tort cases, courts have for the most part refused to award damages for emotional upset unless this has caused physical symptoms or some recognizable psychiatric illness. It has repeatedly been said that grief alone is not compensable in damages: see Allen M. Linden, *Canadian Tort Law* (Toronto: Butterworths, 5th ed., 1993), at pp. 363-79. Where damages for mental shock have been awarded, this has tended to be in addition to damages for physical injuries sustained or as a result of somebody having witnessed the injury or death of a loved one: *Abramzik v. Brenner* (1967), 65 DLR (2d) 651 (Sask. CA); *Heighington v. Ontario* (1987), 41 DLR (4th) 208 (Ont. HC), aff'd. on other grounds, (1989), 61 DLR (4th) 190 (CA). It is difficult to rationalize awarding damages for physical scratches and bruises of a minor nature but refusing damages for deep emotional distress which falls short of a psychiatric condition. Trivial physical injury attracts trivial damages. It would seem logical to deal with trivial emotional injury on the same basis, rather than by denying the claim altogether. Judges and juries are routinely required to fix monetary damages based on pain and suffering even though it is well-known that the degree of pain is a subjective thing incapable of concrete measurement. It is recognized that emotional pain is just as real as physical pain and may, indeed, be more debilitating. I cannot see any reason to deny compensation for the emotional pain of a person who, although suffering, does not degenerate emotionally to the point of actual psychiatric illness. Surely emotional distress is a more foreseeable result from a negligent act than is a psychiatric illness. I agree with the observations and conclusions of Southin J in *McDermott v. Ramadanovic Estate* (1988), 44 CCLT 249 (BCSC), awarding damages of $20,000 to a 13-year-old plaintiff for emotional scars caused by watching the death of her parents in a car accident. Although the plaintiff's emotional suffering did not amount to a psychiatric condition, it was nevertheless real and more painful to her than the physical injuries she sustained (the pain and suffering award for the physical injuries being assessed at $5,000). Southin J observed that damages are awarded for physical scars even if there is no ongoing pain or associated pecuniary loss. She then stated [at 259]:

> But what is the logical difference between a scar on the flesh and a scar on the mind? If a scar on the flesh is compensable although it causes no pecuniary loss why should a scar on the mind be any the less compensable?

I agree. And I would add that it seems equally illogical to me that mental distress damages should be recoverable in a case based on contract but not in a negligence case. I recognize the undesirability of lawsuits based on nothing more than fright or mild upset. However, in my view the more appropriate way to control these frivolous actions is by limiting recovery based on foreseeability (and perhaps proximity or directness) and by awarding limited damages and imposing cost sanctions in cases of a trivial nature.

In the case at hand, it was foreseeable to Westminster that if it was negligent in the handling of the remains entrusted to it, the likely result was mental distress to the next of kin. The plaintiff was clearly within the group of people whom the defendant could expect would suffer emotional harm as a result of its negligence. Although the plaintiff did not suffer a complete mental breakdown or psychiatric illness, his emotional pain was real, foreseeable and, in my opinion, compensable.

I am not aware of any case dealing with the issue of mental distress damages in a bailment situation. Bailment may arise from a contract but may also arise in other circumstances. The English Queen's Bench held in *Chesworth v. Farar*, [1967] 1 QB 407 that "the circumstances, contractual or otherwise, which give rise to a bailment do not of themselves determine the nature of proceedings brought by the parties thereto in relation to its subject-matter" (at p. 407). Rather, it is necessary to look at the substance of the claim to determine whether it is in actuality a contract claim or a negligence claim. Further, if the claim could be said to be equally poised in contract or tort, the plaintiff is entitled to rely upon that aspect which is most favourable in the circumstances (at p. 416). In the case before me, the plaintiff's claim could be said to be based in contract or could equally be described as a negligence claim. It seems utterly nonsensical to me that the damages to which the plaintiff may be entitled should depend on what is essentially in this context a meaningless characterization. The facts giving rise to the claim and the legal duty of Westminster is precisely the same whether the cause of action is considered as negligence or as a contract of bailment. Under contract law principles as I have referred to above, damages for mental distress are recoverable. The plaintiff is entitled, therefore, to treat the bailment as more akin to contract than negligence so as to obtain that benefit. Alternatively, even if the substance of the claim is negligence, I would still award damages for mental distress on the basis set out above.

(iii) Quantum of Damages for Mental Distress

There is very little case law which is of any assistance in determining the quantum of damages in a case such as this one. In 1976 the trial judge in *McNeil v. Forest Lawn* (body cremated before parents saw it) assessed general damages for mental distress at $750 (although finding it not compensable). The English County Court in *Loach & Sons Ltd. v. Kennedy* (body stored in a machine shop) awarded £15 for anxiety and distress in 1952. In 1938 one of the plaintiffs in *Owens v. Liverpool* (accident with a hearse) was awarded £75 but she was described as having suffered "severe shock and collapse." In *Newell v. Canadian Pacific Airlines* (1976), the plaintiffs were awarded $500 for the mental distress caused by the death and injury of their dogs.

While none of these cases is the same as the one before me, it is apparent that the general theme is that damages for mental distress, when allowed, have been relatively low. That seems to me to be appropriate. The plaintiff in this case is genuinely and understandably upset. He has lost some peace of mind. However, in the general scheme of things, his suffering has not been extreme. Indeed, I would place this case within the general category of claims for relatively minor mental distress which are so trivial in nature that they ought not to be encouraged. It is important in our society that all citizens have access to our courts of civil justice to redress wrongs committed against them. That does not mean that a civil action for damages is the appropriate solution to every instance of emotional upset or hurt feelings caused by somebody else's civil wrong. While those claims may, on the application of general legal principles, be valid, if the injury suffered is trivial in nature, the damages awarded should reflect that fact. The plaintiff in this case ignored his parents ashes for 23 years. While he clearly is upset, I consider the emotional harm done to him to be minor. I would assess his general damages for mental distress at $1,000 in total.

5. Molloy J mentions the *Newell* case, where the parties received general damages in respect of injury to and death of their pets. Many persons are deeply attached to their companion animals and regard them as almost family members. Yet in the eyes of the law non-human animals are their owners' property. The tension between these opposing conceptualizations has traditionally been resolved in favour of the traditional classification of animals as property. However, some recent cases have seen higher damages awards that, at least in part, appear to recognize a pet owner's loss when a companion animal is killed. For discussion, see Jessica Dellow, "Valuing Companion Animals: Alternatives to Market Value" (2008), 17 *Dal. J Leg. Stud.* 175. Some American states have sought to address this problem by statute. Here is the key provision in Tennessee's statute *Tenn. Code Ann.* ¶ 44-17-403 (2000):

> If a person's pet is killed or sustains injuries that result in death caused by the unlawful and intentional, or negligent, act of another or the animal of another, the trier of fact may find the individual causing the death or the owner of the animal causing the death liable for up to five thousand dollars ($5,000) in noneconomic damages; provided, that if the death is caused by the negligent act of another, the death or fatal injury must occur on the property of the deceased pet's owner or caretaker, or while under the control and supervision of the deceased pet's owner or caretaker.

There are no equivalent legislative provisions in Canada.

Real Property

Bracewell v. Appleby
[1975] Ch. 408

[The defendant bought one of six houses in a cul-de-sac development in which access to the properties was over a private road. The plaintiffs owned other houses in the development. Access to all six properties was secured by rights of way secured over the properties, and which created the private road. Subsequent to his original purchase, the defendant was able to acquire, at very low cost, a piece of vacant land adjoining his own property. This property was effectively landlocked and had no road access. With this additional land added to his own property the defendant sought planning approval, which was granted, to build a new home partly on his existing land and partly on the recently acquired landlocked land. The plaintiffs objected, claiming that the defendant's right of way, which gave access to his existing property, did not give a right of access to the recently acquired landlocked property. The plaintiffs threatened to bring interlocutory injunction proceedings but delayed in doing so. By the time proceedings were initiated, the defendant's new home was in an advanced stage of construction. Pennycuick VC dismissed the plaintiffs' motion for an interlocutory injunction based on the delay in commencing proceedings. On the original suit, Graham J held that the defendant's existing right of way could not be extended to the landlocked land; thus, the defendant was committing a trespass. Graham J affirmed that an injunction was an inappropriate remedy because the effect would be to make the defendant's new home uninhabitable, and thus granted damages in lieu of an injunction.]

GRAHAM J: ... I come now to the question of relief. As already stated, I am unwilling in the circumstances to grant an injunction, but as, in my judgment, the plaintiffs have established their legal right, and by reason of the *Chancery Amendment Act 1858 (Lord Cairns' Act)* they can ask for, and the court can grant, damages in lieu of an injunction. The defendant accepted that such was the position if I was thus far in the plaintiffs' favour. After consideration I propose to approach the question of damages and assess the amount, which I was requested to do by both parties, along the same lines as those followed by Brightman J in *Wrotham Park Estate Co. Ltd. v. Parkside Homes Ltd.*, [1974] 1 WLR 798 (Ch. D) at p. 812 *et seq.* It seems to me that the defendant must be liable to pay an amount of damages which in so far as it can be estimated is equivalent to a proper and fair price which would be payable for the acquisition of the right of way in question. In dealing with the case before him, Brightman J said, at p. 815:

> In my judgment a just substitute for a mandatory injunction would be such a sum of money as might reasonably have been demanded by the plaintiffs from Parkside as a quid pro quo for relaxing the covenant.

Then, after rejecting the approach which aimed at obtaining half or a third of the development value, he went on:

> I think that in a case such as the present a landowner faced with a request from a developer which, it must be assumed, he feels reluctantly obliged to grant, would have first asked the developer what profit he expected to make from his operations.

The profit in that case was large, being of the order of £50,000 and in the end the damages were assessed at £2,500, being 5 per cent of the profit.

In the present case, the plaintiffs, for amenity reasons, did not want an extra house built in the cul-de-sac and I think it is right to regard them also as "reluctant" just as Brightman J did in the case of the plaintiffs before him. On the other hand, in all the circumstances, I think that for the purpose of estimating damages they and the other servient owners in Hill Road, albeit reluctant, must be treated as being willing to accept a fair price for the right of way in question and must not be treated as if they were in the extremely powerful bargaining position which an interlocutory injunction would have given them if it had been obtained before the defendant started operations and incurred expense. Such is to my mind the penalty of standing by until the house is built.

On the evidence here the probable figure of notional profit which the defendant has made, being the difference between the overall cost of the new house and its present-day value seems to be somewhere between £4,000 and £6,000 and I think it is fair to take £5,000 as about as accurate a figure as one can get. The circumstances here are very different from those in the *Wrotham Park* case and I think that the proper approach is to endeavour to arrive at a fair figure which, on the assumption made, the parties would have arrived at as one which the plaintiffs would accept as compensating them for loss of amenity and increased user, and which at the same time, whilst making the blue land a viable building plot would not be so high as to deter the defendant from building at all. The defendant was not a speculative builder and in fact wanted to live in, and does now live in, 2A himself and I think he would have been prepared to pay what is relatively to his notional profit quite a large sum for the right of way in question and to achieve the building of his new home. This was a time of rising property values and I think he would have been prepared to pay £2,000 to get his right of way and if he had made such an offer, I think the other five owners in Hill Road ought also to have been prepared to accept it. The plaintiffs are, of course, only entitled to their appropriate share of this figure, namely, ⅕th each and I therefore award them £400 each by way of damages for the exercise of a right of way over their respective pieces of land.

Judgment for plaintiffs for £400 each with costs.

NOTES AND QUESTIONS

1. How does the court define the notional "market" that forms the basis of the assessment? Of what relevance is the defendant's notional profit on the transaction? Does the assessment take sufficient notice of the plaintiffs' unwillingness to sell? Is the assessment consistent with the theory underlying market value assessment?

2. Can this decision be reconciled with *O'Grady v. Westminster Scaffolding Ltd.*, in this chapter? If so, how?

3. In *Costello et al. v. City of Calgary* (1997), 152 DLR (4th) 453 (Alta. CA), leave to appeal to SCC denied 154 DLR (4th) ix, the court discussed the proper assessment of damages for trespass. The city took possession of the owners' property in 1974, believing that it had validly expropriated the property. Nine years later, it was finally determined that the purported expropriation was void and the city was found liable in trespass. Picard JA, for the court, set out the following principles for the assessment of damages:

V. Damage Assessment

The primary issue on appeal is remedial. Given that the City trespassed upon the Ranch Site, what measure of compensation is appropriate?

The trial judge calculated damages with reference to the principle of *restitutio in integrum* and sought to place the respondents in the position that they would have enjoyed if the appellant had not committed the wrong. In doing so, he followed settled principles (*Marsan v. Grand Trunk Pacific Railway Co.* (1912), 1 DLR 850 (Man. CA)) and relied upon a factual finding to the effect that, if the City had not trespassed on the Ranch Site, the Costellos would have developed a 40-unit motel on the property by 1 January 1976. Despite the fact that the Costellos once again were registered as owners of the property on 17 October 1983, the trial judge extended the period of damages to 31 December 1985 to reflect the time that it would have taken the Costellos to develop the property upon its return, had they wished to do so.

It is important to appreciate the nature of the appeal under this heading. The City accepts that if the trial judge was correct in finding that, but for the trespass, the Costellos would have developed a 40-unit motel on the Ranch Site, he also was correct with respect to the period for which damages must be awarded and with respect to the basic calculation of damages (leaving aside the questions of mitigation and interest). In fact, however, the City disputes the trial judge's fundamental finding that the Costellos would have developed the property as proposed if they had not been wrongfully dispossessed.

The appellant's position essentially is that the respondents never would have been permitted to develop a 40-unit motel on the Ranch Site. To reiterate, City Council adopted a resolution in 1968 that contemplated the construction of a major traffic interchange at 50th Avenue and Macleod Trail, the location of the Ranch Site. On the basis of that fact, the City presented a number of arguments to the effect that the trial judge erred in his determination of what the Costellos' position would have been if they had not been subject to a tort. Those arguments conveniently can be addressed under the rubric of three questions. (i) Did the 1968 Plan prohibit development of the Ranch Site? (ii) Would the City validly have expropriated if it had not invalidly expropriated? (iii) Would the Planning Commission have refused the Costellos' development permit application?

(i) The 1968 Plan

The 1968 Plan was merely a blueprint for possible future development. It did not irreversibly commit the City to any particular course of action, nor to any particular development schedule. The contemplated interchange might never have been developed, and even if it was developed, construction might have been delayed for many years, during which time the Costellos could have operated their proposed 40-unit motel. (Although the point is not relevant to my decision, I note in passing that the interchange still has not been built.) Consequently, although the City argued that the 1968 Plan effected a general "freeze" on development, I am inclined to the view that the plan, in itself, did not constitute an insurmountable barrier to the Costellos' intentions.

That view is supported by the existence of the *City Transportation Act*, SA 1970, c. 19. Several provisions are relevant. Section 5 of that Act stated (in part):

5(1) The city council shall by by-law establish a transportation system in accordance with the transportation study report and by by-law shall designate the transportation system.

(2) The by-law shall include a map showing the approximate location of the transportation facilities and such other items as may be required by the regulations.

Section 10(1) of the Act stated:

10(1) Where the city intends to acquire any area of land for a transportation system, either immediately or over a period of time as it becomes available or is needed, the city may by by-law declare that area of land to be a transportation protection area.

With respect to "transportation protected areas," s. 15 of the Act further stated that development could be undertaken only upon receipt of a permit from a protection area officer and that such a permit was a condition precedent to the approval of a development permit application under the *Planning Act*, RSA 1970, c. 276. Finally, s. 20 of the Act stated that:

20(1) The city may acquire land within a transportation protection area as it is required or in advance of its being required.

(2) Land acquired within a transportation area may be acquired by the city

(a) by purchase, where the owner of the land and the city agree as to the price, or

(b) by expropriation, where the owner of the land and the city cannot agree as to price or where the owner of the land requests that the land be expropriated or consents to expropriation, or

(c) by gift.

(3) Land which has been within a transportation protection area for a period of three years or longer must, upon the request of the owner of the land, be acquired by the city either

    (a) by purchase, where the owner of the land and the city agree as to the price, or

    (b) by expropriation, where the owner of the land and the city cannot agree as to price or where the owner of the land requests that the land be expropriated or consents to expropriation in which case expropriation proceedings shall be commenced within 60 days of the request for expropriation or the consent to expropriation.

The intention of the statute appears clear. The legislature sought to introduce a fair and orderly scheme under which a city could acquire land for the purpose of developing a transportation system. I note in particular that s. 10 allowed a city to earmark land for future development by declaring it to be a "transportation protection area." However, I also note that s. 20(3) conferred upon an affected landowner the right to compel a city to acquire such land within three years of such a declaration. The result was that land could not be "frozen" indefinitely. While a city was entitled to arrest development for a three-year period, it could be compelled to acquire affected property after such time.

The City never made a declaration under s. 10 of the *City Transportation Act* to the effect that the Ranch Site fell within a "transportation protection area." Nevertheless, it argued that it effectively had subjected that property to an indefinite development "freeze" by virtue of adopting the 1968 Plan. I do not agree. If that argument was correct, the scheme created by the Act would be greatly undermined and the safeguards enacted by the legislature for the protection of landowners such as the Costellos would be illusory. Such parties would lose both the ability to limit a development "freeze" to three years and the ability to compel acquisition of affected property after that time. Essentially, if the City's argument is correct, it would be able to enjoy all of the benefits, without bearing any of the burdens, of the Act. I do not believe that that is what the legislature had in mind.

In response to an argument presented orally by counsel for the City, I also reject the suggestion that the scheme created by the Act merely presented the City with an option. I recognize that s. 10(1) states that a city "may" declare an area that it intends to acquire for a transportation system to be a "transportation protection area." However, unless a city does so, it has no basis under s. 15 for prohibiting development on such land. Again, the City must take the good with the bad. If it wished to "freeze" the Ranch Site, it was required to make a proper declaration and to accept all the obligations attendant upon such a course of action. ... The City also argued that the trial judge erred in his estimation of the position that the Costellos would have enjoyed if a trespass had not been committed because he failed to recognize that the City would have expropriated the Ranch Site as a means of preventing the development of a 40-unit motel.

As a matter of logic, I concede that that argument has some appeal. Damages in trespass are intended to place the plaintiff in the position that she would have enjoyed if the wrong had not been committed. In that regard, I am willing to assume for the purpose of the argument that the City gets things right more often than it gets things wrong, and that it usually succeeds when it attempts to expropriate. Consequently, it seems reasonable (at least superficially) to say that if the City had not invalidly expropriated the Ranch Site, it validly would have done so. That proposition is supported by the fact that the purported expropriation was not doomed to failure from the outset. The City undoubtedly had the authority to expropriate under the *Municipal Government Act*, RSA 1970, c. 246, and if it had given proper notice to Mrs. Dickhoff, it might well have legally acquired the land.

As a matter of law, however, I reject the City's argument. "The life of the law has not been logic: it has been experience": O.W. Holmes, *The Common Law* (Boston: Little, Brown, 1881), at p. 1.

And experience strongly suggests a need to provide incentives to lawful behaviour. In the present context, it has long been held that an authority that assumes possession of land following an invalid expropriation generally cannot resist damages in trespass on the ground that it could have effected a valid expropriation. The policy rationale of that rule, while not stated expressly in the case law, is clear. If such a defence was available, an expropriating authority would have little reason to comply with the detailed procedural requirements set out in the *Expropriation Act*. Regardless of such compliance, it could take land at the cost of expropriation damages, as opposed to trespass damages. Assuming that an authority would be entitled to retain the property upon payment of the former, its final position would be the same in either event. Of course, such a result would be contrary to the philosophy that underlies the law of expropriation. Legislatures and courts, recognizing both the general sanctity of property rights and the extraordinary nature of the power of expropriation, demand strict compliance with procedural requirements. Indeed, that attitude clearly was illustrated by the Supreme Court of Canada when it declared the City's purported expropriation invalid. McIntrye J emphatically rejected the suggestion that the difference between the notice prescribed by the Act (three weeks) and the notice actually received by Mrs. Dickhoff (seventeen days) was insignificant in the circumstances and hence insufficient to impugn the validity of the expropriation: *Costello v. Calgary* (1983), 23 Alta. LR (2d) 380 at pp. 391-392.

The preceding analysis receives generous support in the case law and it will suffice to provide but one example. In *Inverness Railway and Coal Co. v. McIsaac* (1905), 37 SCR 134, the respondent rail company entered upon the appellants' property and removed gravel and timber. It undoubtedly had statutory authority to expropriate land for such purposes if it gave notice of its intentions to the landowners. Despite an opportunity to provide such notice, however, it failed to do so. The Supreme Court of Canada ignored the possibility of compliance, held the railway to have committed a trespass and awarded damages accordingly. See also *R v. Lee* (1917), 38 DLR 695 (Ex. Ct.), aff'd. (1919) 59 SCR 652; *Dominion Iron & Steel Co. v. Burt*, [1917] AC 179 (PC NS); *Re Vancouver Charter; Re Arbitration Act; Re Magnone* (1957), 23 WWR 415 (BCSC); *Parkdale (Village) v. West* ... [(1887), 12 App. Cas. 602, (PC (Can.))]; *Lethbridge Northern Irrigation District v. Maunsell*, ... [[1926] SCR 603]; *Leahy v. Town of North Sydney* ... [(1906), 37 SCR 464]; *Hanley v. Toronto, Hamilton and Buffalo RW Co.* ... [(1905), 11 OLR 91 (HC)]. Similarly in the present appeal, the fact that the City could have validly expropriated the Ranch Site is no answer to the Costellos' claim in tort and does not provide a basis upon which to reduce damages.

It is true, as the City argued, that the preceding analysis is not invariably followed. In exceptional circumstances, an authority that commits a trespass following an invalid taking may be held liable for expropriation, rather than tort, damages. Two such situations can be identified. In the first, an authority unlawfully takes possession of land, but executes a valid expropriation before the landowner's action in trespass reaches the court: see *e.g. Re Ruttan and Canadian Northern RW Co.* (1906), 12 OLR 187 (HC). Of course, the facts in the present appeal clearly are distinguishable from that situation in so far as the City never validly expropriated the Ranch Site. The second situation in which a court may recognize a *de facto* expropriation and refuse to award tort damages occurs when it is impossible or highly impractical for the land to be returned to the owner (for example, because the property has been developed into a significant public harbour or a military installation): see *e.g. Jalbert v. The King in right of Canada*, [1937] SCR 51; *Malone v. The*

Queen (1977), 79 DLR (3d) 677 (FCTD). In such circumstances, the courts may allow the public authority to expropriate the land and pay compensation accordingly. Of course, the case on appeal once again is clearly distinguishable. The City did not, while unlawfully in possession, make significant and irreversible improvements to the Ranch Site; it merely leased the property to a third party for the purpose of operating the 10-unit motel. Consequently, there is no basis upon which to treat the City's occupation of the Ranch Site as a "technical" trespass sounding only in expropriation damages.

In conclusion on this point, then, I am of the view that the Costellos are entitled to compensatory damages in trespass and that the measure of relief should not be reduced to reflect the fact that the City could have validly expropriated the Ranch Site and thereby prevented development of the proposed 40-unit motel. In that regard, I find no error in the decision below.

Kates v. Hall
(1991), 53 BCLR (2d) 322 (CA)

[The plaintiff owned a three-acre property in Vancouver. Along the boundary line that adjoined the defendant's property grew a number of mature Hemlock trees that shaded the defendant's swimming pool. Without permission, the defendant entered the plaintiff's property and cut down 13 of the mature trees. The plaintiff, who spent little time on the property, brought suit claiming as damages the cost to transplant mature trees of similar size on the property. The plaintiff's experts gave evidence that to undertake the transplanting would require the attachment of guy-wires to the trees for a period of two years with some of the anchors crossing onto the defendant's property. No assurance could be given that the transplanted trees would survive. The cost of the procedure was put at between $195,000 and $210,000. The trial judge rejected this approach stating that it was plainly unreasonable. The trial judge also rejected the approach advocated by the defendant's experts, namely, a proposal to plant 8 to 10 smaller trees and a hedge, the cost of which was put at $11,000. The trial judge then awarded the plaintiff the cost of restoration in the amount of $21,000, plus an additional $1,000 per tree loss of amenity value. Finally, to reflect the high-handed and outrageous way the defendant had acted, the trial judge awarded an additional $2,000 per tree as punitive damages. The plaintiff appealed and the defendant cross-appealed. Both appeal and cross-appeal were dismissed by the court for the reasons given by Proudfoot JA.]

PROUDFOOT JA: ... In their factum the appellants set out six errors in judgment. In my opinion, the appellants in essence advance three main issues to be dealt with on this appeal. First, they say compensatory damages should have been measured by the cost of doing the work that the appellants felt would accomplish complete restoration of the property. Second, they say those damages should have been awarded in an amount that directly reflected one of the expert's reports or failing that then the award should have been itemized. Finally the appellants submit in the alternative that the learned trial judge erred by not awarding an amount sufficient to replace the 40-foot trees with 20-foot trees and including an amount for the associated loss of amenities.

In support of the first issue the appellants argue that because a wilful trespass occurred they are entitled to an award sufficient to cover the cost of replicating the status quo as nearly as possible, irrespective of the cost or likelihood of success. Counsel for the appellants went so far as to say that the restoration plan can be unreasonable and can even be inadvisable if it is physically possible to replace the trees.

More specifically the appellants argue that the trial judge applied the wrong test when he dealt with the award on the basis of a reasonable person in the plaintiffs' position. It was submitted that where there is a wilful trespass, as in the case at bar, the test is not that of a reasonable person but that of the "express wishes" of the appellants. They say the appellants are entitled to be unreasonable. In support of this proposition three cases were cited: *Livingstone v. Rawyards Coal Co.* (1880), 5 App. Cas. 25 (HL (Eng.)); *Carr-Harris v. Schacter*, [1956] OR 944 (HC); and *Peters v. Diamond*, [1964] 1 OR 139 (Co. Ct.).

The appellants relied specifically on the last of these cases. Not only are these authorities not binding on this court, especially *Peters*, but these cases do not go that far.

In *Livingstone*, the defendant coal company mined coal out from under the plaintiff's property. The case is often cited for the general principle as stated by Lord Blackburn at p. 39 that:

> [W]here any injury is to be compensated by damages, in settling the sum of money to be given for reparation of damages you should as nearly as possible get at that sum of money which will put the party who has been injured, or who has suffered, in the same position as he would have been in if he had not sustained the wrong for which he is now getting his compensation or reparation. That must be qualified by a great many things which may arise. ...

This passage must be interpreted in light of what the court actually did. In determining the actual sum to be awarded as compensation Lord Blackburn emphasized that it should be the "fair" value of the unmined coal. The House of Lords used a "reasonable" royalty rate as the appropriate measure of that value.

In *Carr-Harris* the defendant builder intentionally trespassed upon and excavated under the plaintiff's land. The excavation resulted in the subsidence of the plaintiff's land and the loss of some trees and flowerbeds. As in the case at bar the court there was unable to find that there was any measurable decrease in the value of the plaintiff's property. The court characterized the plaintiff's claim as "the most suitable repair reasonably possible in the circumstances." The repair did not amount to exact restoration and the court relied upon the evidence of the plaintiff's expert, who had been given "fair" instructions by the plaintiff, to arrive at the appropriate amount of compensation.

Finally, in *Peters*, employees of the defendant developer trespassed on the plaintiff's property and cut down some apple trees. After referring to *Carr-Harris* the court awarded an amount sufficient to put the plaintiff "in the same position as he was before suffering the damage." The award was based upon alternatives presented that would replace the screen and privacy and restore the beauty lost as opposed to replication of the trees lost.

In any event, the *Livingstone* and the *Carr-Harris* cases were dealt with in the case of *Dykhuizen v. Saanich (Dist.)*, No. V177184, 25th October 1989 [now reported (1989), 63 DLR (4th) 211], decided by this court. In that case Mr. Justice Taylor said for the court at p. 6 [at 215]:

The damages in such cases may extend to the cost of restoration or restitution, within reasonable bounds, together with compensation for loss of amenity to the extent that complete restoration cannot reasonably be affected.

The appellants pointed to the words "possible" and "practicable" in *Peters v. Diamond* and said that that was the only limit on restoration. The case law simply does not support this proposition.

Indeed what the appellants seek as relief is, according to their experts, possible and practicable only with great difficulty. It is hardly reasonable or fair, in my view, for several reasons. First, the cost is totally out of proportion to the negligible reduction in value of the property, especially in light of how little time the appellants spend there. Second, the time, logistics and damage involved in implementing the proposal. Third, the use of guy-wires to anchor the trees for a two-year period which would, of necessity, have to be placed on the respondent's property. And the appellants were unable to point to any authority for the proposition that this court should order the respondent to have huge anchors placed in the ground on his property from which guy-wires would lead to the trees on the appellants' property. Finally, as stated by the experts, survival of trees of the size suggested by the appellants is not guaranteed. One can only envisage one tree dying and the whole process starting all over again. ...

The law in British Columbia following *Dykhuizen* requires the court to ask what is reasonable in the circumstances, not, as argued by counsel for the appellants, what are the "express wishes" of the appellants. As the trial judge said:

> The authorities clearly establish that there are limits imposed on the extent to which a trespasser who causes damage can be required to restore land to its previous state. A court will not require the trespasser to finance restorative measures which are plainly unreasonable.

It is important that several other matters not be overlooked when dealing with the principle of reasonableness. It was agreed here that there was no measurable diminution in value of the property. In this circumstance the courts will consider the difference in cost between "meticulous restoration" and reasonable repairs. And the courts will balance the actual benefits to the plaintiff of meticulous reinstatement against the extra cost to the defendant over and above damages based on the diminution in value of the land. See, for example, *Lodge Holes Colliery Co. v. Wednesbury Corp.*, [1908] AC 323 (HL (Eng.)), and *Dodd Properties (Kent) Ltd. v. Canterbury City Council*, [1980] 1 WLR 433 (CA).

One of the factors the courts consider in the balancing process is the use to which the injured party has and will put the property. The trees in question were providing privacy for only a limited portion of the residence, chiefly a bedroom. The appellants spent little time in the home. On the grounds there remain many more trees and many shrubs. The loss of privacy can be restored by a less costly approach than that proposed by the appellants. I do not say that the wishes of the owner are irrelevant. However, I do say they are subordinate to the overall consideration of what is reasonable, practical and fair in all of the circumstances. The trial judge considered these factors when he concluded at p. 5:

> In deciding what is reasonable the court must have regard to the wishes of Mr. and Mrs. Kates, rather than those which the ordinary or average person would entertain in the circumstances.

But the court must, I think, be satisfied, before seeking to give effect to the expressed wishes of Mr. and Mrs. Kates, that these are wishes reasonably directed to the enjoyment of their land, and not to making the largest possible demand on Mr. Hall's purse.

I mean that in dealing with the compensatory damage claim the court must be concerned with reinstatement rather than retribution.

I can see no error in that conclusion.

Before I move to the appellants' second argument I would make one further observation. At the trial the evidence was that nothing had yet been done by the appellants toward effecting any repairs or restoration. The trial judge in his judgment stated it was obvious nothing would be done by the appellants unless the respondent paid for it. When the appeal was heard still no restoration had taken place. The court has to wonder whether these property owners are genuinely interested in restoring their privacy or whether they seek only retribution against the respondent. …

In summary then it is my opinion that the trial judge did not err in his determination of the appropriate amount of compensatory damages or in his award of damages for loss of amenities.

After hearing all the witnesses and considering all of the evidence, including the wishes of the appellants, he properly awarded compensatory damages in a sum representing the cost of remedial work that a reasonable person in the appellants' position and with no money constraints would have done. He then awarded an additional amount in recognition of the loss of use and enjoyment that the appellants would suffer as a result of less than perfect reinstatement.

He also, quite properly, considered the nature of the respondent's conduct under the separate head of punitive damages.

It follows from my conclusions that this appeal should be dismissed.

Cross-Appeal

… The remaining issue deals solely with the quantum of the punitive damages awarded. The respondent rightly admits that this is a proper case for such an award. He argued that the case law establishes an appropriate range for punitive damages when the conduct was not malicious and that the $26,000 award here falls beyond that range and is therefore excessive.

The trial judge did not err in his application of the appropriate legal principles in making the award for exemplary or punitive damages. The amount of $26,000 is not excessively high. In fact, in my opinion, the amount could well have been higher, and this court should not interfere with that award.

I would dismiss the cross-appeal.

Disposition

I would dismiss both the appeal and the cross-appeal.

Inverugie Investments Ltd. v. Hackett
[1995] 3 All ER 841 (PC)

[The plaintiff, Hackett, held 99-year leases on 30 apartments that formed part of the defendant's hotel in the Bahamas. The leases were executed in 1970. However, in 1974 the plaintiff was ejected by Inverugie, the defendants. The plaintiff commenced proceedings in 1975 for possession. The proceedings were finally concluded in 1986 when the plaintiff won an order for possession; however, Inverugie only gave up possession in 1990, some 15¹/₂ years after the original ejectment. The plaintiff sought mesne profits for the continuing trespass. The registrar opted for a different assessment and awarded the plaintiff interest on his initial investment of $300,000 at 12¹/₂ percent for the entire 15¹/₂ years, amounting to $577,500. The plaintiff appealed and the defendant cross-appealed. A majority of the Bahamas Court of Appeal awarded the plaintiff $1,813,269 mesne profits being the notional gross revenue of the 30 apartments assuming 100 percent occupancy for the entire period ($3,872,790) of the trespass minus the total expenses relating to the 30 apartments ($2,059,521). The actual occupancy rate during the period of the trespass was 35 percent; and, in fact, the hotel had run at a continuing loss. The third member of the Court of Appeal assessed the damages at $2,437,843 on the basis that this was the reasonable rental rate for the 30 apartments over the period of the trespass. This rate was assessed on the basis that the defendant had the exclusive use of the apartments for the entire period of the trespass regardless of whether the defendant had in fact made use of the apartments in its hotel operation. The owners appealed to the Privy Council, contending that the damages had to reflect the fact that the actual occupancy rate of the hotel had been 35 percent. The following judgment of the board was delivered.]

LORD LLOYD OF BERWICK: ... Before stating their own conclusions on the facts, their Lordships should say a brief word on the law. The cases to which they have already referred establish, beyond any doubt, that a person who lets out goods on hire, or the landlord of residential property, can recover damages from a trespasser who has wrongfully used his property whether or not he can show that he would have let the property to anybody else, and whether or not he would have used the property himself. The point is well expressed by Megaw LJ in *Swordheath Properties Ltd. v. Tabet*, [1979] 1 WLR 285 (CA) at p. 288 as follows:

> It appears to me to be clear, both as a matter of principle and of authority, that in a case of this sort the plaintiff, when he has established that the defendant has remained on as a trespasser in residential property, is entitled, without bringing evidence that he could or would have let the property to someone else in the absence of the trespassing defendant, to have as damages for the trespass the value of the property as it would fairly be calculated; and, in the absence of anything special in the particular case it would be the ordinary letting value of the property that would determine the amount of damages.

It is sometimes said that these cases are an exception to the rule that damages in tort are compensatory. But this is not necessarily so. It depends how widely one defines the "loss" which the plaintiff has suffered. As the Earl of Halsbury LC pointed out in *Mediana (owners) v. Comet (owners), The Mediana*, [1900] AC 113 (HL (Eng.)) at p. 117, [1900-3] All ER Rep

126 at 129, it is no answer for a wrongdoer who has deprived the plaintiff of his chair to point out that he does not usually sit in it or that he has plenty of other chairs in the room.

In *Stoke-on-Trent City Council v. W. & J. Wass Ltd.*, [1988] 1 WLR 1406 (CA) at p. 1416 Nicholls LJ called the underlying principle in these cases the "user principle." The plaintiff may not have suffered any *actual* loss by being deprived of the use of his property. But under the user principle he is entitled to recover a reasonable rent for the wrongful use of his property by the trespasser. Similarly, the trespasser may not have derived any *actual* benefit from the use of the property. But under the user principle he is obliged to pay a reasonable rent for the use which he has enjoyed. The principle need not be characterised as exclusively compensatory, or exclusively restitutionary; it combines elements of both.

If this is the correct principle, how does it apply to the facts of the present case? Mr. Mowbray argues that it makes no difference whether there were 30 apartments, or only one. If there had been only one, Inverugie would have been obliged to pay a reasonable rent for the use of the apartment for 365 days in the year, even though the apartment might not be taken by a tour operator, or otherwise occupied, for more than 35% of the time. The same must apply, says Mr. Mowbray, to each of the 30 apartments.

Mr. Price argues that the unusual facts of the present case take it outside the normal rule. Inverugie is a hotel operator. If one assumes that the parties had negotiated a notional rent for the 30 apartments as a whole, they would have taken account of the average occupancy. What has to be valued is the chance of Inverugie making a profit from the letting of the 30 apartments to tour operators, not the rent which an individual person would pay per apartment. On the basis of $3.00 per day per apartment—the figure calculated by the registrar—a hotel proprietor would not have been prepared to pay more than $400 per apartment per year. In this way Mr. Price arrives at $159,360 as the appropriate measure of damages.

The point is not altogether easy. But their Lordships have concluded that Mr. Mowbray's argument is to be preferred. If a man hires a concrete mixer, he must pay the daily hire, even though he may not in the event have been able to use the mixer because of rain. So also must a trespasser who takes the mixer without the owner's consent. He must pay the going rate, even though in the event he has derived no benefit from the use of the mixer. It makes no difference whether the trespasser is a professional builder or a do-it-yourself enthusiast.

The same applies to residential property. In the present case Inverugie have had the use of all 30 apartments for 15½ years. Applying the user principle, they must pay the going rate, even though they have been unable to derive actual benefit from all the apartments for all the time. The fact that Inverugie is a hotel operator does not take the case out of the ordinary rule. Mr. Hackett was not asking for an account of profits. The chance of making a profit from the use of the apartments is not the correct test for arriving at a reasonable rent.

It follows that their Lordships cannot agree with the judgment of the majority in the court below. *McArthur & Co. v. Cornwall*, [1892] AC 75 (PC (Fiji)) is not in point since the assessment of damages in that case was not for wrongful occupation of land but for conversion of produce. Their Lordships find themselves in full agreement with the approach adopted by Rowe JA.

What then is a reasonable rental value for the 30 apartments for 365 days a year? Rowe JA might have taken the published rates for each of the apartments. But as has been seen, he took instead the "wholesale" rate paid by tour operators, that is to say, the published rate less 35% in the winter, and 65% in the summer. Their Lordships see no reason to take a different view. For the reasons already explained, it is wholly irrelevant that Mr. Hackett would not himself have been able to let the apartments to tour operators for 365 days in the year.

The final question is what, if any, deductions should be set off against the reasonable rental value of the 30 apartments. Mr. Mowbray concedes that Inverugie are entitled to set off the sums which would have been payable under the lease. The relevant provisions are to be found in the fourth schedule to the lease dated 5 June 1970. Rowe JA deducted $226,800 for ground rent and $950,331 for the cost of maintaining and refurbishing the common areas, making $1,177,131 in all. Mr. Mowbray agrees that these were correct deductions. Rowe JA also deducted $974,574 for electricity, and Mr. Hackett's share of the cost of interior maintenance and repairs. This appears to have been conceded below. But Mr. Mowbray does not accept this deduction. Mr. Price submits that Rowe JA was right to make this deduction, and should also have deducted $387,279 for 10% management commission and $1,832,721 for Mr. Hackett's share of the general expenses of running the hotel.

For the reasons given by Rowe JA, he was plainly right not to deduct anything for general expenses. They are not a set-off against rent. The same applies to the management commission. The position with regard to electricity and the cost of interior maintenance and repairs is not so clear. But it matters not. For even if $974,574 was correctly deducted, the final figure on Rowe JA's approach comes to well in excess of the $1,800,000 awarded by the majority. Inverugie has thus failed to show that the figure should be reduced.

Accordingly, their Lordships will humbly advise Her Majesty that the appeal should be dismissed. Inverugie must pay the plaintiff's costs before the Board. The orders for costs in the courts below will stand.

Appeal dismissed.

QUESTION

The Supreme Court of the United Kingdom revisited *Inverugie* in *Star Energy Weald Basin v. Bocardo SA*, [2010] UKSC 35. There the defendant had committed trespass by drilling under the plaintiff's land to access some oil. However, there was a statute that would have permitted the defendant to apply for the right to drill. That right would have been granted subject to statutorily determined compensation paid by the defendant to the plaintiff. An administrative board would have set the level of compensation. The Supreme Court held that damages for trespass should not be determined on the *Inverugie* basis, but rather by reference to the legislation: what sort of compensation would the statutorily created administrative body have awarded had the defendant, instead of trespassing, made an application for the right to drill?

CHAPTER FIVE

Damages for Personal Injury or Death

APPROACHES TO COMPENSATION

Introduction

Damages for personal injury are unlike any other damage assessment action. You would have observed in previous chapters that the law distinguishes between the level of compensation provided for pure economic loss and that provided for damage to property. In terms of the interests protected, it should come as no surprise that our law favours compensation for personal injuries over and above property and economic loss—albeit with some effort to balance the goal of compensation with the need to foster predictability and control unduly large damage awards.

The goals of compensation, predictability, and balance are not easy to achieve. At the same time as being "generously" disposed toward personally injured plaintiffs, courts have experienced tremendous difficulties in assessing these damages. Difficulties arise over the need to forecast a plaintiff's future income losses attributable to the injury, and future health care costs, a particularly onerous task for the severely injured or quadriplegic plaintiff. Such forecasts require courts to review the state of the economy to determine long-term inflation and interest rates, the plaintiff's prognosis, and a host of other contingencies that may affect or, had the plaintiff not been injured, would have had an effect upon his or her future ability to earn income.

It is very difficult to obtain accurate statistics on personal injuries. What can be obtained are startling. The most comprehensive compilation of personal injury statistics in Canada, *Accidents in Canada* (General Social Survey Analysis Series, Minister of Supply and Services Canada, 1991), by W. Millar and O. Adams, reveals that in 1987 there were 1.7 million motor vehicle accidents causing injury, representing 33 percent of all injuries in that year; 1.1 million (21 percent) workplace injuries; 1.2 million (23 percent) sports injuries; and 670,000 (13 percent) at-home injuries in Canada.

The growing recognition of the inevitability of personal injury in modern society has given rise to a plethora of ways to handle the problem. In the following pages, some of these approaches are outlined.

The following commentary discusses some of the issues and problems associated with a civil tort litigation system for handling personal injury.

463

Ontario Task Force on Insurance
Ministry of Financial Institutions, *Final Report of the Task Force on Insurance*
("Slater Commission Report") (May 1986), at 60-70 (footnotes omitted)

IV *The Need for a Fundamentally Different Approach to Accident Compensation*

The Tort System in Context

Many people believe that the tort system plays a central role in injury reparation. The tort system is but one part of a multi-faceted compensation system. Most injuries are dealt with outside the court system, on a no-tort basis. In a study completed for the Task Force, Osborne describes the existing array of federal and provincial no-tort compensation programs.

The most obvious example, of course, is the Workers' Compensation Plan, which has been providing no-tort injury compensation since its enactment in 1914. Another is the Ontario Health Insurance Plan. A third is the range of no-fault benefits that have been "added on" to bolster automobile insurance coverage. Other examples are found in the disability benefits found under the unemployment insurance, Canada Pension Plan and veterans' allowance programs, provincial injury compensation schemes for victims of crime, and injury benefits that are available to many Canadians under private disability insurance plans.

For most Canadians compensation for personal injury is handled without the use of judges, lawyers or courts. Compensation is paid directly to the injured first-party on a no-tort basis. The social and economic significance of these first-party no-tort injury compensation schemes is substantial: over $5 billion is paid out annually under these programs to accident victims in Canada. The proportional importance of tort within this larger context is relatively small: of the $2.5 billion that was paid out under various Ontario accident compensation schemes in 1981 to injury victims, only $250 million was paid through tort. No-tort injury compensation, or what is popularly but somewhat inaccurately referred to as "no-fault" compensation, is not a novel notion in the overall Canadian context. Indeed, for most injuries, it is the norm.

Nonetheless, it is fair to say that the tort litigation fragment continues to assume a pre-eminent role in the compensation delivery system. It continues to attract attention not because it is central but because it is inherently uncertain.

The Incoherence of Modern Tort Law: The Insurance-Deterrence Dilemma

Modern tort law, both in the United States and in Canada, has in recent years undergone a major transformation. In the personal injury area it has been dramatically transformed from a mechanism primarily concerned with deterrence to one whose main purpose is compensation. The Osborne study described this transformation as follows:

> Since the turn of the century the tort of negligence has expanded from a relatively narrow and circumscribed field of civil liability to a generalized remedy for virtually all victims of negligent conduct. The duty of care now extends to almost all persons involved in activities which involve a risk to life and limb. This expansion of the scope of the tort [of] negligence has been accompanied by a steady reformulation of the rules of liability to withstand the scope of compensation and to minimize the difficulties of the plaintiff in proving his or her case. The development has been typically judicial—cautious, incremental and broadly within the boundaries of the

fault concept. Nevertheless, the sum of the individual changes is a massive transformation of the fault system.

Both in the United States and in Canada tort law has seen the judicial expansion of negligence liability to include new areas of activity and injury. In a study completed for the Task Force, Trebilcock describes the Canadian and American developments in some detail. It is sufficient to note here that, notwithstanding the formal distinctions described earlier, fundamentally the differences between the American and Canadian tort systems are differences of degree, not differences in kind. The American and Canadian judiciaries have both learned to manipulate highly malleable negligence doctrines in order to respond to the changing needs of modern society. Both judiciaries have learned to use tort for loss distribution.

Why has this transformation taken place? Here lies the irony. The basic reason for the dramatic transformation from deterrence to compensation is the phenomenon of modern liability insurance.

> The massive transformation of the fault system ... is a change which is explicable only on the basis of liability insurance and judicial compassion for the victims of social progress. Judges who in their written judgments give no indication of the prevalence of liability insurance are in fact keenly aware that in almost all cases the defendant is not paying, and that they are in the last analysis deciding whether or not the plaintiff should be compensated from insurance monies. ... The prevalence of liability insurance fundamentally altered the moralistic nature of the loss-shifting function of fault. The loss-shifting mechanism was converted into a loss-spreading mechanism and it became more realistic to speak of the fault system as a fault-insurance system. The punitive and deterrent aspects of fault were diminished and compensation became the predominant function of tort law.

We discuss in more detail below the reasons why insurance was bound to undermine deterrence. These findings have now been documented in the literature to which we will turn shortly. But the judiciary, in both the US and Canada, seem to have recognized intuitively the implications of insurance.

Because of insurance, the analytical sequence in the judicial determination of "fault" has been reversed; rather than proceeding from a finding of liability to an award of compensation, the pervasiveness of insurance now has moved courts inevitably to look first to insurance and then to liability. The Trebilcock study found that "many judges even within a negligence regime are influenced by this revised sequence of insurance to liability in making determinations of negligence." Thus tort was effectively transformed into a system of social insurance for a wide range of societal risks, and it is the ultimate irony of the present insurance crisis that it was in the very success of modern liability insurance that the seeds were planted for the inevitable failure of tort.

With liability insurance, and a progressive and conscientious judiciary, the insurance-deterrence conundrum is made complete. The courts know they cannot deter; they also know they cannot fully and completely compensate all victims for all accidental injury. Thus, a "radical indeterminacy" is inevitably introduced into tort and, hence, an inherent instability.

In more human terms, the contradictory demands of the insurance-transformed tort system place an enormous strain upon the integrity of its judges. In a recent speech, Mr. Justice Krever of the Ontario Court of Appeal openly reflected on the incoherence of modern tort law and the inevitable pressures that sometimes lead judges into "intellectual dishonesty." Mr. Justice Krever noted that judges will tend to find "fault" where none exists, so that totally innocent plaintiffs who suffer catastrophic injury can be adequately compensated by the wealthier insurers of equally blameless defendants. Mr. Justice Krever expressed a view that is undoubtedly shared by many of his colleagues:

> It is not satisfactory to continue to base compensation only on the necessity to find fault because [there] is a propensity—in those cases where there will be no real compensation, unless there is fault—towards intellectual dishonesty.

This is bad enough. But further tension is created when compensation has to be denied a seriously injured plaintiff simply because the elastic doctrines of modern negligence law have run out of elasticity and "fault" cannot be found. This happened in a recent case in which Mr. Justice Krever himself had sat as the trial judge. A 58-year-old milkman was rendered a quadriplegic as a result of a non-negligently administered angiogram. He could not afford to hire help to turn him over two or three times at night as his medical condition required, and thus his 70-year-old wife had to do it herself. He could not afford to build ramps, or change the doorways where he lived, even to permit his wheelchair to be wheeled into the bathroom. The court found that "for all practical purposes, he became a virtual prisoner in the apartment." Nonetheless, despite the serious injury and the difficult consequences, Mr. Justice Krever had to deny compensation; "fault" could not be found and thus compensation could not be awarded. Mr. Justice Krever reflected on his decision:

> Here['s] a person who, through no fault of his own, entrusting himself to the health care system, became incapable of supporting himself and his wife and living an ordinary life, incapable of relieving his wife of the obligation of getting up in the night to turn him over. All of these things could have been made available by an award of damages, but you have to find fault.

He referred to his dilemma in the course of his reasons for judgment:

> I confess to a feeling of discomfort over the state of affairs in an enlightened and compassionate society in which a patient who undergoes a necessary procedure and who cannot afford to bear the entire loss, through no fault of his own, and reposing full confidence in our system of medical care, suffers catastrophic disability but is not entitled to be compensated because of the absence of fault on the part of those involved in his care. ... While it may be that there [is] no remedy for this unfortunate and brave plaintiff and that this shortcoming cannot be corrected ... , there is in my view an urgent need for correction.

The decision was appealed to the Ontario Court of Appeal, but the Court again had no alternative but to deny compensation. The Court of Appeal then said this:

> We [would] not want to leave this case without adding that we are in complete sympathy and agreement with ... the learned trial judge's reasons. ... We agree that in situations such as the instant one, "an enlightened and compassionate society," to use the words of the learned trial judge, should do more.

In many ways the modern tort system, at least in the personal injury area, has reached the limits of its capacity. It cannot continue to operate as a compensation mechanism using notions of negligence or fault. This will only deepen the incoherence, instability and continuing unpredictability.

Any proposals for tort reform that continue to obscure the fundamental tension between insurance and deterrence should be rigorously resisted. The answer is not in adding illogic to incoherence, but in understanding that the tort system should not be asked to do the impossible. It cannot promote socially optimal insurance and deterrence objectives simultaneously. This is the present dilemma. There is no good reason to dig the courts into a deeper hole.

The Need for Reform

The answer lies in separating the compensation function from the deterrence function. The appropriate direction for reform would be in the design of a compensation system that works and also a deterrence system that works. Compensation should be principled and prompt. Deterrence should be principled and precise.

Although we have already suggested that in the personal injury area, the modern tort system cannot be counted on to perform these separate functions simultaneously, what if measures were taken to separate the compensation function from the deterrence function and then allow the tort system to continue doing one *or* the other? Could it succeed in either area?

This matter has been explored extensively both theoretically and empirically. The literature is voluminous. Suffice it here to draw the reader's attention to the most salient conclusions on these points. First, the deterrence function.

The Tort System and Deterrence

The inability of the tort-insurance system to achieve a significant deterrence objective has been documented in the literature. In 1979, the Ontario Law Reform Commission concluded that "tort law is a haphazard and inefficient means of deterrence." In 1984, the New South Wales Law Reform Commission went even further: "It is difficult to find any empirical evidence which proves that ... fault operates as an effective deterrent." A recent Canadian study summarized the reasons why the existing tort-insurance system cannot be expected to perform a deterrence role:

> The root assumption, and one that puts into serious question the overall utility of tort law ability deterrence theory, is that our system of common law adjudication is efficient. This threshold assumption of the efficiency of our courts and their determination and imposition of liability is crucial. The precision and sensitivity (the "efficiency") required for market deterrence to be a workable concept in practice is extraordinary. What you need is nothing less than a responsive, sophisticated, perfectly informed and litigationally motivated plaintiff; a fully informed judiciary with a confident capability in differential calculus; a litigation process that precludes below-social-cost settlement practices and ensures the accurate and immediate imposition of liability upon the appropriate supplier; a suppliers' marketplace that in fact does internalize the full brunt of the liability judgment and then reflects this internalization in subsequent product-pricing decisions; and, at the very least, a sophisticated insurance industry that is technologically able to resuscitate the deterrent effect of an insurance-covered tort judgment by means of a carefully calibrated and supplier-individualized rate-making procedure.

In sum, market deterrence to be at all workable requires a high degree of product information, victim initiative, judicial care and capability, supplier responsiveness, and insurance industry precision.

The same study went on to explain this analysis and reiterate the many findings worldwide as to why it is that the tort-insurance system cannot and does not achieve a significant deterrent objective. The reasons include the following:

— most injured people do not sue—even when there is a reasonable basis for believing that the "fault" of another could be established;

— for the small percentage of injury claims that actually proceed to litigation the parties are soon confronted with the highly elastic doctrinal norms of modern negligence law and with the realization that "fault" is not a self-defining concept, adding further imprecision and unpredictability to the process;

— years may pass as the lawsuit winds its way through court with further delays that further dilute deterrence;

— when judgment is finally delivered and damages are awarded there is no relationship between the severity of the sanction (the damage award) and the degree of "fault";

— the judgment that is finally handed down by a well-intentioned court is rarely paid by the individual wrongdoer; in 9 cases out of 10 insurance fully absorbs the impact of the judicial decision;

— any residual impact that might notionally remain is at most by way of an adjustment or increase in the insurance premium, years later, and as a study of the New York Insurance Department concluded in its report on automobile insurance, "individual last moment driver mistakes—undeterred by fear of death, injury, imprisonment, fine of loss of license—surely cannot be deterred by fear of civil liability against which one is insured," or, one could add, by fear of a belated and imprecise adjustment in one's insurance premium.

Finally, even if these inefficiencies and obstacles could be cleared by a Herculean reform of the tort system, the question of deterrence, given the reality of modern insurance, is one that can be answered outside of tort. To the extent that modern insurance coverage means that in most situations deterrence will be achieved or will be achievable through the vehicle of premium variability or "experience rating," this very mechanism exists and can be worked into any first-party no-tort accident compensation plan. That is, deterrence via higher premium pricing or "penalty rating" is a common feature of many existing first-party no-tort schemes and could easily be incorporated and developed as a component of the no-tort scheme that we set out in more detail below.

In sum, the best evidence we have today suggests that deterrence alone cannot justify the retention of the tort litigation fragment for non-work injuries. The theoretical foundations for the tort-market deterrence model are shaky, the practical problems as described above are insurmountable and, given the pervasiveness of modern liability insurance and the need for deterrence through premium variability, the tort-deterrence debate is ultimately irrelevant.

The Tort System and Compensation

If deterrence must be discarded as a rationale for preserving tort, the only other rationale that remains and one that ironically continues to drive the tort system today, in the personal injury area at least, is compensation. Here, the modern theoretical and empirical literature in its evaluation of tort as a compensation mechanism is even more compelling. The compensation rationale, put simply, fails both in theory and in practice.

The fundamental flaw in using tort to compensate through efficient insurance principles was explained in the Trebilcock study. The study correctly observed that efficient insurance cannot be delivered by the tort system because the system yields no coherent theory of how to identify the most efficient insurer. Given this incoherence and the uncertainties attendant on it, it would be futile to attempt to reform the tort system with insurance objectives or compensation objectives as the operative criteria.

The practical difficulties of continuing to utilize tort primarily as a compensation mechanism in the personal injury area have been documented extensively. The Osborne study discusses the findings in detail and the reader is referred to it for further amplification. But here a brief summary may be useful. The basic reasons why the tort-insurance system remains an ineffective and inadequate compensation mechanism are:

(1) Under tort, compensation is paid on an irrational basis. Even given the highly elastic and inevitably expanding "fault" liability doctrines, the seriously injured plaintiffs would still slip through the judicial net. For example, the 58-year-old milkman who was rendered a quadriplegic through the non-negligently administered angiogram discussed earlier should have been compensated. All of the judges hearing the case agreed that he should have been compensated, yet compensation was denied because "fault" could not be found. But if the compensation mechanism is intended to compensate for accidental injury, it should compensate for all accidental injury, whether slipping on a sidewalk, being hit by a car, or stupidly but tragically walking through a glass door.

(2) Under tort, more than half of all modern injuries go uncompensated. The best evidence that we have today indicates that only ⅓ to ½ of accident victims get any compensation through the tort system. Others, including those who are seriously or catastrophically injured, are left behind or slip through the cracks.

(3) Under tort, there is enormous delay. The tort system as it presently operates does not pay compensation promptly even to the winners. Evidence shows that it is not unusual for some cases to drag through the court system from 2 to 13 years. In the much-discussed *Brampton* decision, if liability is upheld on appeal, a further 3 or 4 years will go by before substantial compensation is actually paid—in total some 13 years after the accident occurred. And these are the "winners" in the system.

In a recent study, Feldthusen and McNair examined how the Canadian tort system treats the "winners." They studied one of the trilogy decisions of 1978, *Teno v. Arnold*, where the Supreme Court of Canada awarded $540,000 in damages to the parents of a severely disabled girl for injuries she sustained when hit by an ice cream truck that was driving through the neighbourhood. The case wound its way through the courts for nine years. Finally, the

Supreme Court of Canada awarded the parents $540,000. Did the Tenos "win"? The Feld-thusen and McNair study provides a troubling answer:

> The strength of the tort system ... seemed to lie in how well it treats its "winners"—they are persons who not only secure a judgment in their favour, but whose lump sum award by pure chance proves adequate to meet their lifetime needs. But ask whether Mrs. Teno, with her daughter's best interests at heart, would not rationally have preferred assured future care expenses and basic income for life, payable more or less routinely without a trial in 1969, [over] almost 9 years of uncertainty and expense, culminating finally in 1978. Would not many successful plaintiffs trade the "justice" and "satisfaction" of litigation and the non-pecuniary damages for the relatively low-cost, fast and secure benefits that would be available under a no-tort compensation scheme? If this is true of the "winner" of one of the largest Canadian awards ever, what of the "losers"—the unsuccessful plaintiffs, the victims of non-tortious accidents, and the tortfeasors themselves?

(4) The present tort-insurance system, although run by a well-intentioned and compassionate judiciary, remains riddled with uncertainty and unpredictability—so much so that many commentators have described tort litigation as a "lottery." In the leading study of this question, O'Connell summarized the various factors that combine to make tort litigation very much like a game of chance.

> The operation of the tort system is akin to a lottery. The most crucial criteria of payment are largely controlled by chance:
>
> a) Whether one is "lucky" enough to be injured by someone whose conduct or product can be proved faulty;
>
> b) Whether that party's insurance limits or assets are sufficient to promise an award or settlement commensurate with losses and expenses;
>
> c) Whether one's own innocence of faulty conduct can be proved; and
>
> d) Whether one has the good fortune to retain a lawyer who can exploit all the variables before an impressionable judge or jury, including graphically portraying whatever pain one has suffered.

(5) Even if all of the other deficiencies described above could be eliminated, the final one is the most serious; the inordinate financial cost of continuing to use tort for injury compensation. A large portion of every premium dollar is eaten up by the transactions costs of the tort-insurance system. More than 50 cents of every premium dollar is absorbed in the administrative and legal costs of running the system.

Less than 50 cents of the premium dollar is actually paid out in compensation under tort, compared with 80 to 90 cents that are paid out under no-tort insurance plans. As a recent Canadian study concluded:

> If you sat down to design a system for wasting and dissipating precious medical and insurance resources, you could not do any better than what we have now.

The Trebilcock study came to the same conclusion:

Compensation administered through the tort system—in large part because of the uncertainties entailed—is appallingly expensive. Victims receive only a little more than ⅓ of the monies entering the system, compared to 80 or 90 per cent under most forms of first party or social insurance. ... As a system of insurance or compensation, the current tort system is, on most criteria, an abject failure.

In the personal injury area, tort should not be used either for deterrence or for compensation objectives. The former should be clarified and reinforced through a combination of regulatory initiatives at both the premium-pricing level (via a bonus-malus system described in more detail in Part C below) and at the public safety and Criminal Code enforcement level. The latter, compensation, should be dealt with separately in the context of a fair and more expeditious no-tort insurance system.

The importance of separating compensation objectives from quality-control concerns in the design of a modern health and safety program was stressed in a recent study that was conducted for the federal Department of Health and Welfare on the "Potential Effect of Liability Claims on the Canadian Public Health-Care System." The study examined the current crisis in the health-care system and, in particular, the difficulties in the medical malpractice area: the changing nature of medical malpractice litigation, the increasing numbers of actions that are being brought against doctors, the spiralling increases in legal costs, and the growing delay in the processing and settlement of medical injury claims. The study concluded that "the civil liability system for the compensation of the disabled is cumbersome, complex and expensive" and urged that an alternative to litigation for the compensation of those disabled by medical injury had to be sought. The study said this:

> We should compensate the disabled regardless of how their disability was caused. We should ensure that their quality of life is maintained. ... The legal system does not ensure that the disabled are compensated unless negligence can be proved. As well, the tort system does not and cannot deal effectively with the health-care professional who practices sub-standard care. Nor can it deal effectively with a negligent hospital or with negligence in the health products industry. ... The issue of compensation for the disabled should be clearly separated from the issue of the regulatory requirements for maintaining the standards of health care. ... An alternative to litigation for the compensation of the disabled has to be sought.

Towards a No-Tort System of Accident Compensation

The fundamental solution lies in recognizing that compensation and deterrence must be separated and that the compensation job must be done through a more efficient and equitable first-party no-tort accident insurance system. The modern-day problem of injury compensation should be dealt with more efficiently and expeditiously—not through tort but through insurance. Whether the reforms proposed below are to be instituted incrementally or more generally is a matter that must be left for the legislature. The Task Force will set out its views on this matter in more detail below.

First, however, it is important to emphasize the following three points:

(1) The *design* of the new insurance compensation system should proceed on a no-tort basis. This does not, however, mean a "no-fault" basis. Compensation, to be sure, will be provided on a "no-fault" basis, but fault will remain relevant and deterrence

will be achieved through a more refined and rigorous penalty-rating or premium-pricing mechanism, as described earlier.

(2) The *delivery* of the no-tort accident compensation system should remain primarily in the hands of the private insurance industry—at least so long as private insurance can demonstrate that it has the financial capacity to design and administer such a scheme at affordable premium levels.

The basic scheme that is envisaged by the Task Force is a no-tort accident insurance policy designed and delivered by private industry, providing unlimited medical and rehabilitation benefits, including cost of care, and income replacement benefits at levels that would be reasonably adequate for the vast majority of Ontario citizens.

(3) Additional coverage for income replacement benefits in excess of the basic insurance package would be obtained on a first-party basis, through the voluntary purchase of additional "layers."

To return then to the question of degree of implementation: the Task Force sees three basic choices once the principles of no-tort accident compensation has been accepted. They are as follows:

(1) No-Tort Injury Compensation for Automobile Accident Injury Only

This would involve the redesign of the existing and compulsory automobile insurance scheme by raising the no-tort or "no-fault" benefits to accommodate the basic principle developed above and then to provide for the purchase of additional layers for those individuals who choose to obtain excess coverage above the basic norm. The province of Quebec has had a no-tort automobile accident insurance plan in operation since 1978. However, it is important to note that the Quebec scheme is government-run. The Task Force believes that in Ontario the private insurance industry should have the opportunity to demonstrate whether and to what extent it can be counted on to deliver the insurance product.

(2) No-Tort Injury Compensation for All Accidents

In many ways this is the logical reform in the redesign of the Ontario injury compensation system. If workers' compensation remains as it is—a government-run first-party no-tort compensation scheme—and if a no-tort automobile accident plan can be designed and delivered by private industry, then all that remains is an additional insurance dimension that would deal with the non-work, non-automobile injury. All accidents could then be covered.

The notion of a universal accident compensation scheme is not an unfamiliar one. New Zealand has had such a system since 1974 and by all reports it continues to operate efficiently, expeditiously and fairly. We have included a summary of the New Zealand system in Appendix 15 to provide readers with a better sense of what universal accident compensation would entail. However, here again, it is important to stress that unlike New Zealand, the Ontario compensation scheme would be designed and delivered by the private insurance industry.

(3) No-Tort Compensation for All Disability

This is really the logical extension of injury compensation: the extension to include not just "accidental" injuries but indeed all disability—accidental injury, sickness and disease. The literature has demonstrated that there is no principled basis upon which to differentiate accidental injury from congenital defects or disease-related disability.

There would certainly be considerable advantage to a comprehensive approach to the needs of those disabled by accident and disease. As set out in Appendix 16, the uneven patchwork nature of the present system of disability benefits in Ontario is particularly disturbing. For some time now, officials of the federal and provincial governments have had ongoing discussions about the possibility of a comprehensive disability scheme. Phase I of the study was completed in 1983 and the First Report submitted to the Ministers of Social Services in September 1983. It outlined the serious problems with Canada's disability income protection system and possible options for reform. In the second phase of the study, the Task Force was asked to develop and cost specific models. The draft Second Report was completed in November 1985 and is now under consideration.

For all practical purposes, however, although a comprehensive disability program was endorsed by the recent Macdonald Commission, it appears that universal disability may have to await a much wealthier economic base for its implementation and also a complicated process of rationalization between federal and provincial authorities and private insurers of the vast array of no-tort compensation schemes described earlier. In many ways then, universal disability compensation, although logically compelling, is realistically unattainable in the short-to-medium term.

Some strengths of the civil litigation model are noted in the following.

Lewis N. Klar, "New Zealand's Accident Compensation Scheme: A Tort Lawyer's Perspective"
(1983), 33 *University of Toronto Law Journal* 80, at 105-7 (footnotes omitted)

One of the advantages of the common law action in tort has been its flexibility and adaptability. Over the years the courts have been able to expand and contract liability, to recognize new needs, to set new standards, and to recognize new economic realities. One of the disadvantages in legislating programs is that this tends to perpetuate the status quo. In New Zealand, the accident compensation bureaucracy has become a rather inflexible and insensitive institution. It has been attacked as being too "insurance-oriented" and for having lost sight of the original goals of its founders. Reform of the compensation process has been taken away from the courts and placed into the hands of politicians and bureaucrats. One has only to witness the recent attempts at reform of the program to realize how political the issue has become. Not only must reform be acceptable to a range of vested interests, but it must now be acceptable to the bureaucracy itself. Palmer notes how proposals made by him in 1975 for co-ordinating the welfare effort and for extending the accident compensation program to sickness were resisted by the Accident Compensation Commission: "The Accident

Compensation Commission resisted the development and was successful in excluding from the terms of reference any mention of the manner in which the *Accident Compensation Act* was working, and any revisions in the legislation."

If one examines the development of common law rights in Canada in the few years since the accident compensation scheme was introduced into New Zealand (1972), one can see that there has been recognition in Canada of important new protections for individuals, some of which might never occur in the context of an accident compensation program. Medical patients have been given new rights; Canadian doctors are legally obliged to inform their patients fully of all unusual, special, or material risks associated with medical procedures under contemplation for their patients. These new rights are a direct result of litigation brought by patients. Directions have been given to school boards and physical education instructors with respect to the need for greater caution in carrying out physical education classes; this has reportedly resulted in a change in the nature of these programs. Prison guards and police officers have been called to task by individual citizens for their abusive and sometimes violent behaviour. Those engaged in sport have been taught that the sporting arena is not immune from basic tenets of decency. Those who engage in ultra-hazardous activities must bear the responsibility for the injurious results of their activities, even if they are not "unusual." Those who are in authority cannot deprive persons of their freedoms and liberty by abusing their statutory authority. The tort of "nuisance" has been expanded to encompass interferences with a person's "peace of mind." An action in privacy has been claimed for mental and physical harassment and invasion of privacy. Responsibility for highway traffic accidents does not rest only on the drivers involved but may also rest on government agencies responsible for keeping the roads in good repair or for erecting adequate safety barriers. A distributor of a defective product was held liable to a consumer who was injured while using the product. While New Zealand has abolished the right of spouses to sue for loss of consortium, Alberta has reinforced it. Many more examples could be noted. In areas of particular weakness, the common law has attempted to reform. As a result of recent Supreme Court decisions in Canada, inflation is taken into account in the assessment of damages, there is a limit to the lump-sum awards for non-pecuniary losses, and victims are entitled to real compensation for their injuries, even if this means providing quadriplegic victims with individually adapted homes. To counter some of the negative effects of large lump-sum payments, the "structured settlement" is being increasingly used. Where the common law is unable or unwilling to react, the legislatures can intervene. Canadian jurisdictions have introduced seat belt legislation and occupier's liability statutes and have abolished guest passenger restrictions and inter-spousal tort immunities.

In the future, society will require increased protection from activities which, although potentially beneficial, will entail great risks. It is difficult to believe that many of the protections which we now enjoy, and will in the future demand, can be assured with the assistance of a civil cause of action.

NOTE

A further example of the adaptability of personal injuries damages is the recent growth in suits brought by the victims of sexual assault who sue their assailants in civil court. See *Myers v. Haroldson*, [1989] 3 WWR 604 (Sask. QB); *M.(K.) v. M.(H.)*, [1992] 3 SCR 6, noted in chapter 10;

and the article by K. Sutherland, "Measuring Pain: Quantifying Damages in Civil Suits for Sexual Assault," in K. Cooper-Stephenson and E. Gibson, eds., *Tort Theory* (North York: Captus Press, 1993), at 212.

Workers' Compensation Schemes

Injury to workers accounts for approximately 30 percent of all injuries suffered. Most of these injuries are compensated within the framework of provincial workers' compensation schemes.

The origin of these schemes lies in the initial lack of sympathy courts expressed toward workers in the late 19th century, and the general inadequacy of applying fault-based liability to new more industrialized manufacturing processes. The doctrine of negligence itself had the effect of transferring attention away from the injured onto the offending party. A host of other essentially employment-related doctrines further restricted the right of injured workers to receive compensation.

As early as 1914, Ontario was one of the first jurisdictions to pass a comprehensive workers' compensation scheme. The author of the scheme, Sir William Meredith, in a report to the Ontario legislature in 1913, outlined what were then considered radical departures from the common law position. Those principles were: (1) no-fault compensation—compensation was to be paid whether negligence contributed to the accident or not; (2) assurance of payments to injured workers who were eligible for compensation for as long as their disability lasted, and assurance of compensation pensions; (3) financing of this compensation scheme by employers; and (4) an independent commission or board to administer the compensation scheme without recourse to the adversarial system of the courts.

The significance of Meredith's scheme was commented upon by Sir Arthur Owen Woodhouse, the author of New Zealand's Accident Compensation Scheme, in the 1978 Lloyd H. Fenerty Memorial Lecture delivered at the University of Calgary.

Sir Arthur Owen Woodhouse, *A Challenge to the Law— Personal Injuries Compensation*
(Calgary: Burroughs and Co., 1979), at 18-19 (footnotes omitted)

You may wonder why I dwell tonight on an aspect of personal injury that has been established and given nation-wide support in this country for so long. I have three reasons:

The first is to say that it is, I believe, a remarkable achievement that more than 60 years ago your predecessors appreciated that the problem of industrial injuries involved not legal but social issues. And avoiding half-measures they took action to substitute an entirely new system for the old.

In doing it they swept away the common law action for damages with the beneficent effect that during the years that have passed by since then all the cost that is associated with the court process has been channelled into systems that are the envy of the workmen's compensation world. No doubt from time to time the local citizen has recognized problems of detail within the various provincial schemes. But in this field Canada has certainly led the way. The fact was given the attention it rightly deserves in the Report on Personal Injury presented to the New Zealand Government in 1967, following the work of the Royal Commission of Inquiry set up in the previous year.

I have a second reason for reminding you of this Canadian achievement. The mutual insurance character of the workmen's compensation schemes results in the end in acceptance of general responsibility by the community for those who are injured, for it is the community which finally pays. And it is done by a means of a state monopoly with an achievement in terms of administrative efficiency which has ensured that there is the optimum relationship of cost to benefits. It all reflects a just and sensible application of the community conscience to a major social problem.

There is the third reason. So far as an onlooker is able to judge the opinion of Sir William Meredith that the negligence action could have no desirable part to play for those injured at work seems to have won general agreement in Canada. Apparently it is thought that if the tort system were to operate in this field it would reintroduce the "nuisance of litigation" which Meredith described in his report; and it would involve a diversion of funds and effort with consequential extravagance of administration. May I remind you of the conclusions reached upon these matters by Mr. Justice Middleton in 1932. A year earlier he had been directed to review the Ontario *Workmen's Compensation Act*, by then in operation for 18 years. He said:

> This scheme of compensation in the place of legal liability based upon negligence has worked well and has given complete satisfaction to all those concerned. It has been a great advantage to the general public for it has avoided the expense incident to the litigation which prevailed under the former system. To the workmen it has brought compensation without the burden of establishing negligence. The employer has been relieved from the uncertainty arising from litigation and has had substituted for it a fixed payment which he can regard as part of his overhead expense. He has the further satisfaction of knowing that practically all the money paid by the employers reaches the hands of the workmen injured.

The Ontario scheme formed a model for the other provinces (Nova Scotia, 1915; British Columbia and Manitoba, 1916; Alberta and New Brunswick, 1918; Saskatchewan, 1929; Quebec, 1931; Prince Edward Island, 1949; and Newfoundland, 1950).

Workers' compensation schemes have had their fair share of critics and on numerous occasions commissions of inquiry have been established to inquire as to their operation. One of the broadest ranging inquiries was undertaken by Paul C. Weiler, *Reshaping Workers' Compensation for Ontario* (Toronto: Ministry of Government Services, 1980).

Automobile Insurance Schemes

Road accidents account for approximately 25-30 percent of all personal injuries. It is not surprising then, that all provinces have legislated some form of no-fault benefits and compulsory liability insurance. In Quebec and Manitoba, comprehensive and compulsory no-fault schemes have been enacted. Under these schemes, the right to sue in tort for bodily injury or death as a result of an automobile accident has been abolished. In its place, a number of fixed entitlements are granted covering all medical expenditures, and providing income replacement indemnity and a lump sum indemnity for victims who sustain disfigurement, dismemberment, or loss of enjoyment in life. There are fixed monetary parameters within which the victim's losses are quantified.

In all the remaining common law provinces, various compromises between no-fault benefits and tort liability exist. Under these schemes, a victim is entitled to a number of no-fault benefits automatically. However, his or her right to sue at common law is also preserved subject only to a set-off of any no-fault benefits paid.

These compromise schemes still allow tort actions and it is from these that the majority of reported court decisions on personal injuries emanate. As the gap between no-fault benefits and court-awarded compensation grows, there is an incentive for victims to pursue civil litigation or to purchase optional extensions on insurance coverage. For example, in some of the provinces, the no-fault income replacement benefits are now well below the minimum wage levels.

Periodically, alarm by the insurance industry has been raised at the escalating damages awarded by courts and the industry's inability to make accurate forecasts on future economic conditions. Consumers have also been alarmed at the rapid increase in automobile insurance premiums above the rate of inflation. In the Maritimes and Ontario, automobile insurance has become a political football. In the late 1980s, the Ontario legislature set up a task force on insurance to make recommendations in the area of automobile insurance. The task force recommendations resulted in the introduction of a partial no-fault scheme (*Insurance Act*, RSO 1990, c. I.8). Under the scheme persons injured in an automobile could only claim against their insurers on a first-party basis. The right to sue in court was lost unless the extent of the person's injury resulted in death, or a serious disfigurement or "permanent serious impairment of a bodily function caused by continuing injury which is physical in nature," in which case a tortious action could have been brought. In 1994, the scheme was again amended. The limited right to sue was completely abrogated with respect to economic losses (at the same time the level of income-replacement benefits was substantially increased), but it was partially restored for non-pecuniary losses, where the plaintiff could prove that he or she had suffered a "serious disfigurement, or serious impairment of an important physical, mental, or psychological function." Yet again, the Ontario government changed the automobile insurance scheme in 1996. The government reintroduced a right to sue for economic loss in excess of the no-fault benefits. (See the chart on pages 478-82.)

A Final Assessment

It may seem surprising that in an area of law in which there has been so much discussion and analytical research there are few studies that have actually looked at how successful plaintiffs who have recovered damages through the tort litigation process have actually fared after leaving the courthouse. One such study has been that undertaken by the United Kingdom Law Commission. The study reviewed 761 successful cases where the injury had occurred at least two years prior to the survey.

Compulsory No-fault Auto Insurance Coverage in Canada

Note 1: Content includes tort coverage where applicable. Alberta, Atlantic Provinces, BC and Saskatchewan (under Tort option) allow policyholders to sue for benefits that exceed the compulsory minimum no-fault amounts.

	British Columbia	Alberta	Saskatchewan *Tort*	Saskatchewan *No-fault*	Manitoba
Minimum 3rd Party Liability	$200,000	$200,000	$200,000	$200,000	$200,000
Medical Payments (time limit varies and depends on nature of injury)	$150,000	$50,000[a]	$23,841 (non-catastrophic) $178,838 (catastrophic)	$6,098,358	No limit
Disability income time limits apply					
% of income	75% gross weekly income	80% gross weekly income (to $400 max/ week)	$360/wk max 2 years, total disability $180/wk max 2 years, partial disability	90% net income based on $79,273 max insurable earnings/year	90% net income based on $83,000 max insurable earnings/year
Max/per week	$300/wk	$400/wk	See above	See above	See above
Home support (Max/per week)	$145	$135 (total disability)	No	$770 full or $386 (reduced living assistance)	$4,142 max/month
Funeral Expense[c]	$2,500	$5,000	$5,962	$9,148	$7,527
Minor Injury Cap (maximum award)	n/a	$4,500 (indexed) Current = $4,559	n/a	n/a	n/a

Note 2: Death benefits are mandatory in all provinces. They are not included in this table as terms for death benefits vary widely depending upon the number of dependents and age of dependents.

Ontario	Quebec	New Brunswick	Nova Scotia	Prince Edward Island	Newfound-land & Labrador
$200,000	$50,000	$200,000	$500,000	$200,000	$200,000
$50,000 Buy-up options available	No limit	$50,000	$25,000	$25,000	$25,000[b] (optional)
70% gross weekly income	90% net income based on $64,000 max/year	80% gross weekly income	80% gross weekly income	80% gross weekly income n/a	80% gross weekly income
$400 $185	See above $784 max	$250/wk $100	$140/wk $70	$140/wk $70	$140/wk $70
$6,000 (indexed) Current = $8,264	$4,695	$2,500	$1,000	$1,000	$1,000
$3,500	n/a	$2,500 (under review in 2011)	$7,500 (indexed) Current = $7,665	$2,500	n/a

	British Columbia	Alberta	Saskatchewan *Tort*	Saskatchewan *No-fault*	Manitoba
CAT (catastrophic impairment) limits	$150,000 Med/Rehab	n/a	$178,838 Med/Rehab	$213,443 Permanent Impairment	$4,947[d] max/month Personal Care
lump sum or maximum amounts			$154,992 Permanent Impairment		$138,073 non-catastrop. Permanent Impairment
					$216,290 Permanent Impairment
					$1,000,000 (lifetime) Transitional Expense Coverage
Right to Sue	Yes	Yes	Yes (subject to deductible[f])	No (with exceptions)	
Controls on Health Care Costs[h]	Yes	No	Yes	Yes	Yes

[a] In Alberta, as part of the $50,000 medical benefits there are sub-limits on chiropractics ($750), massage therapy ($750) and acupuncture ($250). In addition, Alberta offers physical, psychological and occupational therapy, as well as grief counseling on death benefits.

[b] Accident benefit coverages are not mandatory in Newfoundland & Labrador.

[c] The amounts provided under funeral and death benefits can vary with the CPI (Consumer Price Index), if the indexation optional benefit is purchased within the auto insurance policy. The indexed amount will vary depending on when the accident occurred.

[d] The amount is approximate.

Ontario	Quebec	New Brunswick	Nova Scotia	Prince Edward Island	Newfound-land & Labrador
$1,000,000[e] Med/Rehab $1,000,000 Attendant Care	Maximums vary (based on age, income level, injury, etc.)	n/a	n/a	n/a	n/a
Yes (subject to threshold)	No	Yes	Yes	Yes	Yes (subject to deductible[g])
Yes	Yes	No	No	No	No

[e] Includes assessments.

[f] There is a $5,000 deductible for pain and suffering.

[g] There is a $2,500 deductible for pain & suffering.

[h] Controls on health care costs are based on limits of workers' compensation or provincial health insurance plans.

Sources: Standard Automobile Policies for each jurisdiction; MPI, SGI, ICBC & SAAQ auto plan brochures; provincial automobile insurance legislation; etc.

AUTOMOBILE INSURANCE NOTES
SOME AUTOMOBILE INSURANCE COVERAGES EXPLAINED

ACCIDENT BENEFITS: This coverage provides compensation, regardless of fault, if you, your passengers, or pedestrians suffer injury or death in an automobile collision. Accident benefits coverage is compulsory in all provinces and territories, except Newfoundland and Labrador.

BODILY INJURY CAUSED BY UNINSURED OR UNIDENTIFIED AUTOMOBILE: This coverage provides up to $200,000 ($500,000 in Nova Scotia) if you are injured or killed through the fault of a motorist who has no insurance, or by an unidentified vehicle. You receive payment under this protection through the Uninsured Automobile coverage in your policy—unless the Canadian province, territory or U.S. state where you were injured has a special fund from which to claim. You will be reimbursed for the money you would otherwise be entitled to recover from the uninsured/unidentified motorist.

DIRECT COMPENSATION—PROPERTY DAMAGE: In Quebec, Ontario and New Brunswick, your own insurer compensates you for the share of the loss of use of your vehicle and the damage caused to your vehicle (including contents) for which another driver would be legally responsible. You deal with your own insurer, not the other person's; this speeds up the payment process. If an identified insured motorist is responsible for the collision, you can collect from your own insurer regardless of whether or not you have purchased optional physical damage coverage for your own car. There are rules, however, for Direct Compensation to apply. If these conditions cannot be fulfilled, then you may have to rely on your collision insurance (if you have it).

QUEBEC—OVERVIEW

The automobile insurance system in Quebec has two main parts: bodily injury, which is covered by a public plan administered by the *Société de l'assurance automobile du Québec* (SAAQ), and damage to property, which is covered by private insurers. SAAQ will compensate Quebec residents for bodily injury arising from an automobile accident anywhere in the world, regardless of fault, just as if the accident had happened in Quebec. Such an accident may involve any vehicle. After six months' absence from Quebec, however, other coverage is required. The SAAQ plan also covers non-residents to the extent they were not at fault. Private insurers in Quebec offer "Endorsement 34" to supplement the SAAQ no-fault bodily injury compensation plan; it covers, to varying degrees, the named insured and his or her spouse and dependent children. Under certain conditions, SAAQ compensates victims for bodily injury or property damage caused by an unidentified third party.

**Personal Injury Compensation: How Much Is Enough? A Study of the
Compensation Experiences of Victims of Personal Injury**
(1994), The Law Commission (LAW COM. no. 225: London, HMSO), 262-65
(footnotes omitted)

Overview of Research Findings

This research has generated a wealth of data about the long-term effects of accidents on jobs, income, family and social life. Against this background an assessment has been presented of the extent to which damages prove to be adequate in meeting past and future losses and extra expenses. This information provides a factual basis upon which the remedy of damages can be appraised and it is worth focusing on some notable findings of the survey, and considering their implications. Before so doing, however, it is important not to lose the sense of the wider context of accidental injury.

Compensated Accident Victims in Context

In Chapter 1 it was noted that the findings of this Report refer to the population of *compensated* accident victims, and not to *all* accident victims. The accident victims included in this study are those who have made a claim for damages through the tort system and succeeded with that claim. In this respect they may be considered a "fortunate" minority. It is well known that only a fraction of all victims of accidental injury seek and obtain compensation for their injuries. The most recent estimate of the proportion of accident victims (sustaining more than minor injuries) who obtain damages through the tort system is twelve per cent. The widespread failure to commence a claim for damages, or to succeed with a claim, results from a number of factors including: lack of claims consciousness; lack of knowledge of the legal system; the inability to finance a claim or the unwillingness to risk the substantial cost of losing an action among those ineligible for legal aid; and, importantly, the fact that in many cases the tort system offers no remedy for accident victims because there has been no negligence in the circumstances of the accident. Even among the minority who commence claims for damages, a proportion abandon their claims without achieving a settlement, for example, because of evidential difficulties, or the pressure of mounting legal costs combined with the customary resistance of claims by defendants.

The majority of those who have the misfortune to suffer accidental injury, therefore, do *not* receive damages through the tort system to compensate for their losses and extra expenses. Although their injuries will have the same impact on their ability to work, the same impact on their ability to function independently, and the same impact on their family and social life as the injuries of compensated accident victims, "uncompensated" accident victims and their families must simply depend on their own savings and social security benefits to cover the losses and extra expenses resulting from their injuries. In focusing on the experiences and perceptions of compensated accident victims, it is important not to lose sight of the wider issues.

Delay in the Litigation Process

The problem of delay in the civil litigation process has been the subject of comment, research and procedural reform over many years. Few would dissent from the view that the cost and delay of civil proceedings present major challenges to the administration of civil justice. This study confirms that there are substantial delays in the settlement of personal injury claims, and reveals that the larger the amount of damages in issue, the longer accident victims are forced to wait for their compensation. Although some degree of delay is inevitable while the parties wait for the medical condition of the plaintiff to stabilize, it is notable that a substantial proportion of cases, both large and small, remain unresolved four years after the date of the accident. There are a number of important implications of this delay. During the litigation process victims and their families face a prolonged period of financial difficulty during which savings are depleted, debts accumulate and legal costs increase. These extended periods of financial hardship, in addition to physical suffering, affect levels of satisfaction with damages and perceptions of adequacy. Delay in receiving damages also influences choices about the use of money, as accident victims seek to make up for the material comforts that they have lacked in the years while they waited for their case to be settled.

Accident victims whose lives have been shattered in an instant by the carelessness of others feel keenly the unfairness of their misfortune. A system which forces them to wait unacceptably long periods for compensation that will help to rebuild their lives, or at least alleviate financial hardship, appears to compound the unfairness. Equally important, the strain of litigation, and uncertainty about the future, may delay recovery, which has an impact on the likelihood that accident victims will eventually be able to return to the labour force and find suitable work.

The Relationship Between Injury, Effects, and Damages

In Chapter 1 attention was drawn to the fact that the amount of damages received by accident victims who succeed with a tort claim is a reflection of past and future losses and expenses, and not a measure of the seriousness of their injury and degree of continuing impairment. The findings of this study highlight the fact that relatively serious injuries may not necessarily result in substantial settlements and that minor injuries may have unexpectedly severe consequences. Within the lower settlement bands there were respondents who had suffered serious injuries that had a substantial impact on their work and family lives, but who had received only modest settlements, for example because of their age, their pre-accident activity status or other factors. Also within the lower settlement bands were respondents who had suffered relatively minor injuries that had resulted in surprisingly serious consequences. This is reflected in the analyses of long-term health problems and work histories following accidents.

The Failure To Return to Work and Adequacy of Damages

A particular concern is the high proportion of accident victims in all settlement ranges who did not return to work at all after their accident, or who returned for a period and were then forced to leave work as a result of the continuing effects of their injuries. For many of these victims, the amount of damages received did not cover their past losses and will not cover their future loss of earnings and the extra expenses resulting from their injury. It is notable that many accident victims fail to realise, in the period after settlement, just how little they have received, relative to their potential losses, and for how long they are likely to be affected by their injuries. Accident victims are often not aware of the extent to which they will be dependant on their damages in the future. In this respect, victims of catastrophic injury may be in a more favourable position because their permanent inability to carry out normal work is evident at the time of settlement. For many others, however, it appears that at the time of settlement their own expectations of their ability to return to work in the future are unrealistic. It is not entirely clear whether this is because experts fail to anticipate the extent of future incapacity, or whether the effect of a prolonged recovery period reduces the chances of finding work, or whether appropriate work is unavailable. What is clear, however, is that many respondents are unprepared for the impact of their injuries on their long-term capacity for work.

This problem is reflected clearly in respondents' changing perceptions of the value of damages. Although most respondents are satisfied at settlement when presented with what appears to be a very substantial sum of money, this sense of satisfaction alters dramatically over time as accident victims are faced with the reality of long-term ill-effects of their injuries and a reduced capacity for work.

The Need for Independent Financial Advice

Although most respondents are keen to preserve the value of their damages for the future, the evidence of the survey suggests that accident victims on the whole are not in the best position to yield the maximum returns from their damages. The research indicated that the availability of independent financial advice is patchy; while some respondents were deluged by advisers, others had little idea where to seek advice or from whom. Although the majority of accident victims received some advice, it is striking that among those receiving settlements of between £20,000 and £49,999 almost one-half had not received advice about the management of their damages, and among those receiving between £50,000 and £99,999 one-third received no advice.

There are also questions to be asked about the sources of advice used. The most common source of advice was from banks and building societies and the most common means of saving or investing damages was bank or building society accounts. The responses in the survey and in qualitative interviews suggest that banks are consulted because they are easily accessible, and equally important, because banks and building societies are viewed as "safe" choices. Some of the responses manifest an image of banks as more cosy, more independent and more interested in the individual's well-being than other sources of investment advice. The reality of the investment services offered by banks is, of course, that they operate in a similar way to other institutions and charge for their services. It is not clear, however, that accident victims who simply take their damages in to their local branch necessarily understand this to be the case.

What is clear, is that given the need for the value of damages to be preserved for as long as possible, even those who receive relatively modest settlements would benefit from genuinely independent and expert advice about how to deal with their damages. Although accident victims are not profligate, they may regret the choices that they make, both about savings and expenditure. Good quality advice at an early stage would not reduce the control over damages that appears to be so valued by accident victims, but it would ensure that decisions about the use of damages were well-informed.

The Burden of Unpaid Care

The research also provides ample evidence of the past and future burden of unpaid care shouldered by the parents, spouses, friends and neighbours of injured victims. Although questions were not asked during the survey about the impact of caring on spouses and relatives, other than to identify situations in which carers had been forced to give up paid employment, information given during qualitative interviews provided evidence about the strain to which long-term carers are exposed. The impact of providing long-term care can be dramatic, damaging the work prospects of those providing the care, and placing carers under considerable physical and emotional strain.

Looking Forward

Qualitative interviews revealed a conspicuous lack of advice or counselling for victims of accidental injury. This is true for psychological and emotional difficulties, and for employment difficulties, as well as for the management of damages already discussed. Although accident victims have considerable contact with experts during settlement negotiations, attention at this stage naturally concentrates on those matters relevant to the claim. After years of focus on the circumstances of the accident, on the effects of injuries, on the reduced capacity to work, and the inability to perform hundreds of small daily tasks, there is a need for attention to be constructively diverted toward the future. There is a need for psychological support; there is a need to address the problem of the debilitating effects of pain; and there is a need to re-train those who are no longer able to undertake their normal work. In short, there is a need to help accident victims to adjust to their circumstances and to envisage a useful and productive future for themselves, albeit different from their pre-accident expectations.

In an important contribution to the debate on the appropriateness of tort law Professors Dewees, Duff, and Trebilcock have brought together previously published empirical and analytical studies on personal injury assessment in five different areas—automobile accidents, medical accidents, product-related accidents, environmental injuries, and workplace injuries—and have used this research to determine the extent to which, within each category, the normative goals of deterrence, compensation, and corrective justice are met by existing assessment practices. The following brief excerpt provides a summary of their conclusions. Their book is compelling reading for law reformers.

D. Dewees, D. Duff, and M. Trebilcock, *Exploring the Domain of Accident Law*
(Oxford: Oxford University Press, 1996), at 412-14 (footnotes omitted)

Over the past 20 years or so, tort scholarship has been dominated by theoretical debates about the appropriate normative goals of the tort system and the doctrinal implications that each entails. These debates have centered around three major goals: deterrence, compensation, and corrective justice. We believe that these debates cannot be resolved in the abstract, but require close attention to empirical evidence on how the tort system, and alternatives to it, actually perform. We believe that the central normative question should not be which of these goals, or values, is superior to which other, but rather which legal or policy instruments are best equipped to vindicate which values. In other words, we accept the legitimacy of all of these goals and focus our analysis on identifying the means that best achieve each goal.

In this respect, the empirical evidence has convinced us that a single instrument, the tort system, cannot successfully achieve all three of the major goals claimed for it, and attempting to use it in pursuit of objectives for which it is not well suited is both costly and damaging to its ability to perform well with respect to other goals that it is better able to realize. Almost a century ago, the tort system was abandoned for workplace accidents and replaced by an administrative workers' compensation system to perform the compensation function with a regulatory system emerging to deter some types of hazardous workplace behavior. Since the middle of this century, no-fault compensation systems have been adopted in various jurisdictions to compensate victims of automobile accidents, complementing regulatory systems for reducing risks to motorists. We endorse these moves and propose extensions of them with three caveats: compensation schemes must be separately funded in each of the accident areas; premiums for compensation schemes must be risk-rated to preserve deterrence incentives; and tort should not be entirely displaced, but should have a residual role in cases of egregious behavior causing serious harm. However, we do not see these compensation schemes operating in the areas of product or environmental injuries.

The conclusions and implications that we have drawn from our empirical research are summarized in the following principal points that are supported more fully in the following two sections of this chapter:

1. The tort system performs so poorly in compensating most victims of personal injury that we should abandon tort as a means of pursuing this compensation objective, turning instead to other instruments.

2. The tort system performs unevenly in deterring the causes of personal injuries, so its scope should be restricted to situations where its effect seems likely to justify its high cost.

3. The regulatory system has achieved varying success in reducing personal injuries; its performance can be improved by reducing its use in areas in which it is ineffective, by expanding its use where it is more effective, and by improving its design.

4. Compensation systems can create substantial deterrent incentives through risk-rating of premiums and through the design of benefits to reduce moral hazard problems.

5. Wherever feasible, accident costs should be internalized to classes of activities and to individual actors through the design of appropriate insurance arrangements, rather than through the tort system.

6. Compensation of most victims in the motor vehicle and medical malpractice fields would best be achieved through no-fault insurance which incorporates as essential features: risk-rating of premiums, the elimination of non-pecuniary damages,

deductibles for short-term pecuniary loss, compensation for medical and rehabilitation costs, and reasonably complete wage-loss replacement. This implies separate systems separately funded, each with features similar to existing workers' compensation schemes. Tort liability would be retained only for the few cases in which intentional, reckless, or grossly negligent infliction of serious injury could be proven.

7. Workers' compensation should be retained for workplace injuries, with more attention to risk-rating of premiums, but product liability suits for workplace-related injuries should be prohibited.

8. Product liability should be governed by negligence doctrines, not strict liability, and should not be available for workplace cases covered by workers' compensation.

9. Environmental injuries should continue to be controlled primarily through government regulation, with tort playing a residual role in situations where causation can readily be proven.

10. Many personal injuries occur in situations outside both the tort system and the compensation schemes that we recommend here, and these victims are often currently undercompensated for medical costs, lost income, and costs of rehabilitation, especially in the case of permanent total or partial disability. These accidents are quite diverse, and we have no recommendations regarding deterrence. The compensation problem might best be attacked by a comprehensive medical insurance system like that in Canada and by more comprehensive long-term wage-loss disability coverage.

We have focused on a number of institutions that contribute to the three objectives discussed in this volume, each making some contribution to one or more objectives. The role of the tort system has expanded greatly in the United States during the last three decades, far more than in other jurisdictions. The results of this expansion have been disappointing. With the benefit of hindsight and a review of the facts, we believe that tort has expanded far beyond the areas in which it is cost effective; it must be substantially contracted.

The resources released by reduced tort litigation will allow more money to be paid to victims; will reduce uncertainty for many individuals, firms, and insurance companies who defend these claims; and will allow many able lawyers to apply their talents to more productive activities. The regulatory system also expanded during this time, achieving somewhat greater success, but again at high cost. Some adjustment of the regulatory system could reduce its costs and increase its effectiveness. The expansion of no-fault insurance systems can achieve compensation objectives at far lower cost than is achieved through the present tort system, while sacrificing little deterrence and sometimes enhancing it by appropriate rating and benefit design features.

We believe that the systems performing the three normative objectives that we have focused on in this study have become seriously unbalanced in the United States during the last three decades, and that the solution is to bring them back into balance. Balance will be achieved not by turning back the clock, but by moving forward to replace tort with new systems that perform better and more efficiently. Canada has already taken some of the steps that we recommend, providing useful experience as to their performance. We believe that our recommendations would provide substantial net benefits for Americans.

Our substantive conclusions also lead us to some reflections on the activity of economists, lawyers, and other analysts who have written about these problems over the last two decades. As noted in these chapters, many assertions in the academic literature about the efficacy of the tort system have been supported principally by theory and assumption with little or no empirical analysis. We have tried to redress this balance by assembling the available empirical evidence and testing the theoretical hypotheses. The great disappointment that the deterrent effect of tort is limited and uneven or cannot be established by existing studies suggests that considerable intellectual effort has been expended on models that omit some crucial facts about the real world, including high transaction costs and imperfect information. The implication for academics is that theory can take us only so far; at some point it is essential to gather data to test the most basic parameters of the systems in which we are interested—that is, to take the facts seriously.

For the legal profession there is another lesson. The tort system expanded in response to powerful demands for victim compensation and a belief that large corporations and insurance companies are appropriate risk-spreaders. The result has largely been a failure: compensation remains very uneven. It is time to admit that tort does not and cannot perform this general compensation function well and to turn to other instruments that are more appropriate for compensation, leaving tort to focus more directly on its traditional corrective justice objective.

ADDITIONAL READINGS

P. Atiyah, *The Damages Lottery* (Oxford: Hart Publishing, 1997).

Peter Cane, *Atiyah's Accidents, Compensation and the Law*, 6th ed. (London: Weidenfeld and Nicolson, 1999).

Compensation for Personal Injury in New Zealand (Wellington: Government Printing Office, 1967) ("Woodhouse Report").

Terence G. Ison, *Accident Compensation: A Commentary on the New Zealand Scheme* (London: Croom Helm, 1980).

————— *The Forensic Lottery* (London: Staples, 1967).

————— *Compensation Systems for Injury and Disease: The Policy Choices* (Toronto: Butterworths, 1994).

Jeffrey O'Connell and Roger C. Henderson, *Tort Law, No-Fault and Beyond* (New York: M. Bender, 1975).

Geoffrey W.R. Palmer, *Compensation for Incapacity* (Wellington, NZ: Oxford University Press, 1979).

Royal Commission on Civil Liability and Compensation for Personal Injury ("Pearson Commission Report") (London: HMSO Cmd. 7054, 1978).

Special Edition of the Victoria University of Wellington Law Review, "Looking Back at Accident Compensation: Finding Lessons for the Future" (2003), 34 VUWLR.

CIVIL LITIGATION AND PERSONAL INJURY DAMAGES ASSESSMENT

Introduction

Although the majority of personal injury claims are dealt with under workers' compensation and automobile compulsory insurance, there is still a significant role served by the civil litigation model of personal injury damages assessment. In particular, awards made under a tort litigation scheme are often seen as setting a comparator against which public no-fault schemes are measured. This comparison is not always welcome by those advocates for comprehensive no-fault schemes. See G. Palmer, "The Design of Compensation Systems: Tort Principles Rule, OK?" (1995), 29 *Valparaiso UL Rev.* 1115. In this section, the mechanics of court assessment will be explored.

The majority of cases in this section deal with severely injured plaintiffs, either paraplegics or quadriplegics. The severity of their injuries results in large damages awards that receive a great deal of media attention. These cases are only the tip of the iceberg. To gain the right perspective, take time to browse through Robert Stonehouse, ed., *Goldsmith's Damages for Personal Injuries and Death in Canada* (Toronto: Carswell, 1978), where you will find all the reported decisions categorized by type of injury and listing the exact amounts awarded. Are you still surprised by the amounts awarded?

If you have looked at any of the periodical literature on personal injuries you may have seen a reference to the "Supreme Court trilogy." The trilogy refers to three important decisions that were delivered by the Canadian Supreme Court in 1978: *Andrews v. Grand & Toy Alberta Ltd.*, [1978] 2 SCR 229; *Thornton v. Board of School Trustees (Prince George)*, [1978] 2 SCR 267; and *Teno v. Arnold*, [1978] 2 SCR 287.

Andrews v. Grand & Toy Alberta Ltd.
[1978] 2 SCR 229

DICKSON J: This is a negligence action for personal injury involving a young man rendered a quadriplegic in a traffic accident for which the respondent Anderson and his employer, Grand & Toy Alberta Ltd., have been found partially liable. Leave to appeal to this Court was granted on the question whether the Appellate Division of the Supreme Court of Alberta erred in law in the assessment of damages. At trial Mr. Justice Kirby awarded $1,022,477.48 [(1974), 54 DLR (3d) 85]; the Appellate Division reduced that sum to $516,544.48 [(1975), 64 DLR (3d) 663].

The amount awarded in each Court under each of the several heads of damages is set out below:

Pecuniary Loss

(a) *Cost of Future Care*	*Appellate Trial*	*Division*
— special equipment	$ 14,200	$ 14,200
— monthly amount.....................	4,135	1,000
— contingencies	20%	30%
— capitalization rate....................	5%	5%
— life expectancy	45 years	45 years
	$735,594	$164,200

(b) Loss of Prospective Earnings

— level of earnings	$ 830	$ 1,200
— basic deduction to avoid duplication between the award for future care and that part of the lost earnings that would have been spent on living expenses	440	—
Net	$ 390	$ 1,200
— contingencies	20%	20%
— work span	30.81	30.81
— capitalization rate	5%	5%
Total	$59,539	$175,000

Non-Pecuniary Loss

— Pain and Suffering	$150,000	$100,000
— Loss of Amenities		
— Loss of Expectation of Life		

Special Damages	$ 77,344	$ 77,344

Liability is not an issue. The trial Judge found that the fault was entirely that of the respondents. The Appellant Division (McDermid JA dissenting on this issue) found the appellant James Andrews 25% contributorily negligent. Those findings do not arise for discussion in this appeal. Nor does the question of special damages.

This Court is called upon to establish the correct principles of law applicable in assessing damages in cases such as this where a young person has suffered wholly incapacitating injuries and faces a lifetime of dependency on others. The question of "million dollar" awards has not arisen in Canada until recently, but within the past several years four such cases have been before the Courts, namely: (i) the case at bar; (ii) *Thornton v. Board of School Trustees of School District No. 57 (Prince George)* (1975), 57 DLR (3d) 438 (BC SC); varied (1976), 73 DLR (3d) 35 (BC CA), at present under appeal to this Court [*post*], in which the award at trial was $1,534,058, reduced on appeal to $649,628; (iii) *Teno v. Arnold* (1974), 7 OR (2d) 276; reversed in part (1976), 11 OR (2d) 585 (CA), also under appeal to this Court [*post*], in which the award for general damages at trial was $950,000, reduced on appeal to $875,000; (iv) *McLeod v. Hodgins* (unreported), in which Mr. Justice Robins, of the Ontario High Court, awarded at trial an amount of $1,041,197, of which $1,000,000 were general damages.

Let me say in introduction what has been said many times before, that no appellate Court is justified in substituting a figure of its own for that awarded at trial simply because it would have awarded a different figure if it had tried the case at first instance. It must be satisfied that a wrong principle of law was applied, or that the overall amount is a wholly erroneous estimate of the damage; *Nance v. BC Electric R Co.*, [1951] AC 601 (PC (BC)).

The method of assessing general damages in separate amounts, as has been done in this case, in my opinion, is a sound one. It is the only way in which any meaningful review of the award is possible on appeal and the only way of affording reasonable guidance in future cases. Equally important, it discloses to the litigants and their advisers the components of the overall award, assuring them thereby that each of the various heads of damage going to make up the claim has been given thoughtful consideration.

The subject of damages for personal injury is an area of the law which cries out for legislative reform. The expenditure of time and money in the determination of fault and of damage is prodigal. The disparity resulting from lack of provision for victims who cannot establish fault must be disturbing. When it is determined that compensation is to be made, it is highly irrational to be tied to a lump-sum system and a once-and-for-all award.

The lump-sum award presents problems of great importance. It is subject to inflation; it is subject to fluctuation on investment; income from it is subject to tax. After judgment new needs of the plaintiff arise and present needs are extinguished; yet, our law of damages knows nothing of periodic payment. The difficulties are greatest where there is a continuing need for intensive and expensive care and long-term loss of earning capacity. It should be possible to devise some system whereby payments would be subject to periodic review and variation in the light of the continuing needs of the injured person and the cost of meeting those needs. In making this comment I am not unaware of the negative recommendation of the British Law Commission (Law Com. 56—*Report on Personal Injury Litigation—Assessment of Damages*) following strong opposition from insurance interests and the plaintiffs' bar.

The apparent reliability of assessments provided by modern actuarial practice is largely illusionary, for actuarial science deals with probabilities, not actualities. This is in no way to denigrate a respected profession, but it is obvious that the validity of the answers given by the actuarial witness, as with a computer, depends upon the soundness of the postulates from which he proceeds. Although a useful aid, and a sharper tool than the "multiplier-multiplicand" approach favoured in some jurisdictions, actuarial evidence speaks in terms of group experience. It cannot, and does not purport to, speak as to the individual sufferer. So long as we are tied to lump-sum awards, however, we are tied also to actuarial calculations as the best available means of determining amount.

In spite of these severe difficulties with the present law of personal injury compensation, the positive administrative machinery required for a system of reviewable periodic payments, and the need to hear all interested parties in order to fashion a more enlightened system, both dictate that the appropriate body to act must be the Legislature, rather than the Courts. Until such time as the Legislature acts, the Courts must proceed on established principles to award damages which compensate accident victims with justice and humanity for the losses they may suffer.

I proceed now to a brief recital of the injuries sustained by the appellant James Andrews in the present case. He suffered a fracture with dislocation of the cervical spine between the fifth and sixth cervical vertebrae, causing functional transection of the spinal cord, but leaving some continuity; compound fracture of the left tibia and left humerus; fracture of the left patella. The left radial nerve was damaged. The lesion of the spinal cord left Andrews with paralysis involving most of the upper limbs, spine and lower limbs. He has lost the use of his legs, his trunk, essentially his left arm and most of his right arm. To add to the misery, he does not have normal bladder, bowel and sex functions. He suffers from spasticity in both upper and lower limbs. He has difficulty turning in bed and must be re-positioned every two hours. He needs regular physiotherapy and should have someone in close association with him at all times, such as a trained male orderly. The only functioning muscles of respiration are those of the diaphragm and shoulders. There is much more in the evidence but it need not be recited. Andrews is severely, if not totally disabled. Dr. Weir, a specialist in neurosurgery, said of Andrews' condition that "there is no hope of functional improvement." For the rest of his life he will be dependent on others for dressing, personal hygiene, feeding and, indeed, for his very survival. But, of utmost importance, he is not a vegetable or a piece of cordwood. He is a man of above average intelligence and his mind is unimpaired. He can see, hear and speak as before. He has partial use of his right arm and hand. With the aid of a wheelchair he is mobile. With a specially designed van he can go out in the evening to visit friends, or to the movies, or to a pub. He is taking driving lessons and proving to be an apt pupil. He wants to live as other human beings live. Since May 31, 1974, he has resided in his own apartment with private attendant care. The medical long-term care required is not at a sophisticated level but rather at a practical care level.

Andrews was 21 years of age and unmarried on the date of the accident. On that date he was an apprentice carman employed by the Canadian National Railways in the City of Edmonton.

I turn now to consider assessment of the damages to which Andrews is entitled.

1. Pecuniary Loss

(a) Future Care

(i) Standard of Care

While there are several subsidiary issues to be decided in this case, there is one paramount issue: in a case of total or near-total disability should the future care of the victim be in an institutional or a home-care environment? The trial judge chose home care. The Appellate Division agreed that home care would be better but denied it to him. Chief Justice McGillivray who delivered the judgment of the Court on this issue said [at 698]:

> All the evidence called supports the proposition that psychologically and emotionally Andrews would be better in a home of his own, where he would be lord of the manor, as it were.

Some evidence even indicated the medical superiority of a home environment.

The trial Judge found that it would take $4,135 per month to provide care for Andrews in a home environment. The Appellate Division considered that this standard of care was unreasonably and unrealistically high. Without giving any reason for selecting the particular figure chosen, the Appellate Division substituted $1,000 per month. Obviously, here is the heart of the controversy. On other matters there was substantial agreement between the lower Courts.

In my opinion, the Court of Appeal erred in law in the approach it took. After the statement quoted above, that Andrews would be better psychologically and emotionally in a home of his own, Chief Justice McGillivray referred to some of the evidence supporting that proposition. He quoted the following passage from the evidence of Dr. Weir [at 698]:

> Well, I think that the greatest problem they have and the greatest burden of their affliction is the fact that they are all depressed because not only have they lost the potential for many normal and enjoyable human activities. In fact up until the present they pretty well have been converted into lifelong inhabitants of a hospital institution and an institution is an institution, it is virtually a life sentence and has been to this date. I would say that if you really, you know,

if you wanted to give him the optimal potential it would be in a home environment in which he had some, in which he had the control of it to the same extent that the rest of us have control over our own homes and dwelling places. I don't really think that any hospital or medical institution has the potential to give someone that same feeling that they are in fact the lords and masters of their own castle.

The Chief Justice noted that Andrews had said he would not live in an institution and the following excerpts from the evidence were quoted [at 699]:

Q. Tell us, Jim, would you be prepared to live in an auxiliary hospital?

A. Never.

Q. Would you elaborate on that?

A. Well there is just no way that I would go into an auxiliary hospital that is—I don't know, I think that is one step into a grave, that is all it is, too many old folks that have nothing to do but reminisce, you know, I don't know, but just from what I have heard of auxiliary hospitals.

Q. Well how about other disabled people, do you have any difficulty getting along with them, would you be prepared to live with them, say if they were even younger?

A. My age?

Q. Yes.

A. With my same disability?

Q. Yes, if you were in some place with people that have disabled problems?

A. No, because it is the same thing, people get into a state of depression and they throw it on the group, like even now in the hospital like the way it is now there is a group of younger people and, you know, even friction can be created amongst us because of one person's bad day kind of thing, and I wouldn't want to live with other disabled persons, not at all.

I am hesitant to enter upon a detailed analysis of the reasons advanced by the Appellate Division for its decision, but in view of the importance of the matters raised in this litigation, not only for the appellant Andrews but for others in a similar plight, I do not think any other course is open.

Following the passage from the evidence of Andrews which I have quoted, Chief Justice McGillivray said:

In having a home of his own, it is stated that Andrews needs at least 20 hours a day care. He has to be turned at night every two hours, he has to have constant attention, and it is on this footing that two orderlies and a house-keeper and the cost of operating a three-bedroom home are advanced as being reasonable costs. Now, while the proposition that to the extent that money can do it, a plaintiff should be put into the position he would have been in, but for the accident, this does not mean that the plaintiff does not have to be reasonable and mitigate damage.

With respect, I agree that a plaintiff must be reasonable in making a claim. I do not believe that the doctrine of mitigation of damages, which might be applicable, for example, in an action for conversion of goods, has any place in a personal injury claim. In assessing damages in claims arising out of personal injuries, the ordinary common law principles apply. The basic principle was stated by Viscount Dunedin in *Admiralty Com'rs v. S.S. "Susquehanna,"* [1926] AC 655 (HL (Eng.)) at p. 661 (cited with approval in *H. West & Son Ltd. v. Shephard*, [1964] AC 326 (HL (Eng.)) at p. 345), in these words:

... [T]he common law says that the damages due either for breach of contract or for tort are damages which, so far as money can compensate, will give the injured party reparation for the wrongful act. ...

The principle was phrased differently by Lord Dunedin in the earlier case of *Admiralty Com'rs v. S.S. "Valeria,"* [1922] 2 AC 242 (HL (Eng.)) at p. 248, but to the same effect:

... [I]n calculating damages you are to consider what is the pecuniary sum which will make good to the sufferer, so far as money can do so, the loss which he has suffered as the natural result of the wrong done to him.

The principle that compensation should be full for pecuniary loss is well-established: see *McGregor on Damages* (London: Sweet & Maxwell, 13th ed., 1972) at pp. 738-9, para 1097:

The plaintiff can recover, subject to the rules of remoteness and mitigation, full compensation for the pecuniary loss he has suffered. This is today a clear principle of law.

To the same effect, David A.M. Kemp & Margaret S. Kemp, *Quantum of Damages* (London: Sweet & Maxwell, 3rd ed., 1967), vol. 1, p. 4: "The person suffering the damage is entitled to full compensation for the financial loss suffered." This broad principle was propounded by Lord Blackburn at an early date in *Livingstone v. Rawyards Coal Co.* (1880), 5 App. Cas. 25 (HL (Sc.)) at p. 39, in these words:

I do not think there is any difference of opinion as to its being a general rule that, where any injury is to be compensated by damages, in settling the sum of money to be given for reparation of damages you should as nearly as possible get at that sum of money which will put the party who has been injured, or who has suffered, in the same position as he would have been in if he had not sustained the wrong for which he is now getting his compensation or reparation.

In theory a claim for the cost of future care is a pecuniary claim for the amount which may reasonably be expected to be expended in putting the injured party in the position he would have been in if he had not sustained the injury. Obviously, a plaintiff who has been gravely and permanently impaired can never be put in the position he would have been in if the tort had not been committed. To this extent, *restitutio in integrum* is not possible. Money is a barren substitute for health and personal happiness, but to the extent, within reason, that money can be used to sustain or improve the mental or physical health of the injured person it may properly form part of a claim.

Contrary to the view expressed in the Appellate Division of Alberta, there is no duty to mitigate, in the sense of being forced to accept less than real loss. There is a duty to be reasonable. There cannot be "complete" or "perfect" compensation. An award must be moderate, and fair to both parties. Clearly, compensation must not be determined on the basis of sympathy, or compassion for the plight of the injured person. What is being sought is compensation, not retribution. But, in a case like the present, where both Courts have favoured a home environment, "reasonable" means reasonableness in what is to be provided in that home environment. It does not mean that Andrews must languish in an institution which on all evidence is inappropriate for him.

The reasons for judgment of the Appellate Division embodied three observations which are worthy of brief comment. The first [at 699]:

> [I]t is the choice of the respondent to live in a home of his own, and from the point of view of advancing a claim of damages, it is a most salutary choice, because it is vastly the most expensive.

I am not entirely certain as to what is meant by this observation. If the import is that the appellant claimed a home life for the sole purpose of inflating his claim, then I think the implication is both unfair and unsupported by the evidence. There is no doubt upon the medical and other evidence that a home environment would be salutary to the health of the appellant and productive of good effects. It cannot be unreasonable for a person to want to live in a home of his own.

The next observation [at 699-700]:

> Secondly, it should be observed that in many cases, particularly in Alberta, where damages have been awarded, the persons injured were going to live with their families. Here, the evidence (in spite of the fact that the respondent's mother advanced a claim for $237 which represented a towing charge for the motor-cycle and parking, taxis and bus fare expended on visits to her son in the hospital for approximately a nine-month period prior to the issue of the statement of claim) is that the respondent and his mother were not close before the accident, and matters proceeded on the footing that the mother's natural love and affection should have no part in Andrews' future. Again, this situation is the most expensive from the point of view of the respondent.

The evidence showed that the mother of the appellant James Andrews was living alone, in a second-floor apartment and that relations between Andrews and his mother were strained at times. This should have no bearing in minimizing Andrews' damages. Even if his mother had been able to look after Andrews in her home, there is now ample authority for saying that dedicated wives or mothers who choose to devote their lives to looking after infirm husbands or sons are not expected to do so on a gratuitous basis. The second observation is irrelevant.

The third observation was in these words:

> Thirdly, it should be observed that the learned trial Judge has referred with approval to the English authorities which held that full compensation for pecuniary loss must be given. It does not, however, follow that every conceivable expense which a plaintiff may conjure up is a pecuniary loss. On the evidence, then, should this Court consider that Andrews should live in a home of his own for the next 45 years at the expense of the appellant?

I agree that a plaintiff cannot "conjure up every conceivable expense." I do not think that a request for home care falls under that rubric.

Each of the three observations seems to look at the matter solely from the point of view of the respondents and the expense to them. An award must be fair to both parties but the ability of the defendant to pay has never been regarded as a relevant consideration in the assessment of damages at common law. The focus should be on the injuries of the innocent party. Fairness to the other party is achieved by assuring that the claims raised against him are legitimate and justifiable.

The Appellate Division relied upon *Cunningham v. Harrison*, [1973] QB 942 (CA). In that case, as a result of an accident, the plaintiff was permanently paralyzed in his body and all four limbs. The trial Judge found that the plaintiff was a self-opinionated person who should, if possible, live in some dwelling of his own where he would be looked after by a housekeeper and the persons who did the nursing. The Court of Appeal held that the plaintiff's entitlement to reasonable expenses for nursing and accommodation appropriate to a normal person should not be increased by reason of his exceptional personality. The Court of Appeal in reducing the award from £72,616 to £59,316, took into account three factors: (i) the difficulty of obtaining a housekeeper and nurses; (ii) that ground floor flats specially designed for handicapped persons were being built in the borough; (iii) that the plaintiff might accept the aid of statutory and voluntary organizations at much less cost. None of these factors is significant in the present case. Although it reduced the award, the Court nevertheless affirmed that the award included provision for a housekeeper and nursing services and also for extra accommodation. The case does not stand for the proposition that though home care is better, it will not be provided because the cost is excessive. In the present case, the Appellate Division asked [at 700-7]:

> If Andrews does have a home of his own, however, should he not so locate that orderly services from existing hospitals could be available to him at night and in the daytime for his hygienic and getting-up periods? Is it to be assumed that in a Province such as Alberta, orderly services could not be given outside the four walls of an institution if the subject of the service is a nearby resident?

The respondents did not raise the possibility about which the Court speculated. There was no evidence as to the feasibility of such a proposal, no evidence as to the availability or cost of outpatient care.

With respect to Andrews' disinclination to live in an institution, the Court commented:

> He might equally say that he would not live in Alberta, as he did not wish to face old friends, or for any other reasons, and that he wished to live in Switzerland or the Bahamas.

Andrews is not asking for a life in Europe or in the Caribbean. He asks that he be permitted to continue to live in Alberta and to see his old friends, but in his own home or apartment, not in an institution.

The Court then expressed the view that the standard accepted by the trial Judge was the equivalent of supplying a private hospital. The phrase "private hospital" is both pejorative and misleading. It suggests an extravagant standard of care. The standard sought by the appellant is simply practical nursing in the home. The amount Andrews is seeking is, without question, very substantial, but essentially it means providing two orderlies and a housekeeper. The amount is large because the victim is young and because life is long. He has 45 years ahead. That is a long time.

In reducing the monthly amount to $1,000, the Appellate Division purported to apply a "final test" which was expressed in terms of the expenses that reasonably minded people would incur, assuming sufficient means to bear such expense. It seems to me difficult to conceive of any reasonably minded person of ample means who would not be ready to incur the expense of home care, rather than institutional care, for himself or for someone in the condition of Andrews for whom he was responsible. No other conclusion is open upon the evidence adduced in this case. If the test enunciated by the Appellate Division is simply a plea for moderation then, of course, no one would question it. If the test was intended to suggest that reasonably minded people would refuse to bear the expense of home care, there is simply no evidence to support that conclusion.

The Appellate Division, seeking to give some meaning to the test, said that it should be open to consider "standards of society as a whole as they presently exist." As instances of such standards the Court selected the daily allowances provided under the *Workmen's Compensation Act* 1973 (Alta.), c. 87, s. 56, and the federal *Pension Act*, RSC 1970, c. P-7, s. 28 [rep. & sub. RSC 1970, c. 22 (2nd Supp.), s. 14(1)]. The standard of care expected in our society in physical injury cases is an elusive concept. What a Legislature sees fit to provide in the cases of veterans and in the cases of injured workers and the elderly is only of marginal assistance. The standard to be applied to Andrews is not merely "provision," but "compensation," *i.e.*, what is the proper compensation for a person who would have been able to care for himself and live in a home environment if he had not been injured? The answer must surely be home care. If there were severe mental impairment, or in the case of an immobile quadriplegic, the results might well be different; but, where the victim is mobile and still in full control of his mental faculties, as Andrews is, it cannot be said that institutionalization in an auxiliary hospital represents proper compensation for his loss. Justice requires something better.

Other points raised by the Appellate Division in support of its reversal of the trial Judge, may be briefly noted [at 704]: (i) "It seems to me probable that there will be, at Government expense, people employed to look after quadriplegics. In the United States, there are now a few institutions which have special apartments as part of the hospital setting, where patients can receive attention and, at the same time, have privacy." There is no evidence that the Government of Alberta at present has any plans to provide special care or institutions for quadriplegics. Any such possibility is speculation. (ii) "... [W]ill the respondent, in fact, operate a home of his own?" The Court expressed the fear that Andrews would take the award, then go into an auxiliary hospital and have the public pay. It is not for the Court to conjecture upon how a plaintiff will spend the amount awarded to him. There is always the possibility that the victim will not invest his award wisely but will dissipate it. That is not something which ought to be allowed to affect a consideration of the proper basis of compensation within a fault-based system. The plaintiff is free to do with that sum of money as he likes. Financial advice is readily available. He has the flexibility to plan his life and to plan for contingencies. The preference of our law to date has been to leave this flexibility in the plaintiff's hands: see John G. Fleming, "Damages: Capital or Rent?" (1969), 19 *U of Toronto LJ* 295. Save for infants and the mentally incompetent, the Courts have no power to control the expenditure of the award. There is nothing to show that the dangers the Appellate Division envisaged have any basis in fact.

In its conclusion, the Appellate Division held that the damages awarded by the trial judge were "unreasonably and unrealistically high" and an award which would result in the appellant receiving approximately $1,000 a month for cost of care would be entirely adequate and would constitute a generous award. The Appellate Division further reduced the award by 30% for potential contingencies. Why $1,000? The main issue at trial was the choice between home care and institutional care. There is no question but that Andrews could be taken care of in an auxiliary hospital, but both Courts below concluded that home care was the appropriate standard. The trial Judge made an award reflecting the cost of home care. The Appellate Division made an award related to neither home care nor institutional care. The effect is to compel a youthful quadriplegic to live the rest of life in an auxiliary hospital. In my opinion, the Appellate Division failed to show that the trial Judge applied any wrong principle of law or that the overall amount awarded by him was a wholly erroneous estimate of the damage. With great respect, the irrelevant considerations which the Appellate Division took into account were errors in law.

Is it reasonable for Andrews to ask for $4,135 per month for home care? Part of the difficulty of this case is that 24-hour orderly care was not directly challenged. Counsel never really engaged in consideration of whether, assuming home care, such care could be provided at lesser expense. Counsel wants the Court, rather, to choose between home care and auxiliary hospital care. There are unanimous findings below that home care is better. Although home care is expensive, auxiliary hospital care is so utterly unattractive and so utterly in conflict with the principle of proper compensation that this Court is offered no middle ground.

The basic argument, indeed the only argument, against home care is that the social cost is too high. In these days the cost is distributed through insurance premiums. In this respect, I would adopt what was said by Salmon LJ, in *Fletcher v. Autocar & Transporters Ltd.*, [1968] 2 QB 322 (CA) at p. 363, where he stated:

> Today, however, virtually all defendants in accident cases are insured. This certainly does not mean compensation should be extravagant, but there is no reason why it should not be realistic … . It might result in some moderate increase in premium rates, which none would relish, but of which no-one, in my view, could justly complain. It would be monstrous to keep down premiums by depressing damages below their proper level, i.e., a level which ordinary men would regard as fair—unprejudiced by its impact on their own pockets.

I do not think the area of future care is one in which the argument of the social burden of the expense should be controlling, particularly in a case like the present, where the consequences of acceding to it would be to fail in large measure to compensate the victim for his loss. Greater weight might be given to this consideration where the choice with respect to future care is not so stark as between home care and an auxiliary hospital. Minimizing the social burden of expense may be a factor influencing a choice between acceptable alternatives. It should never compel the choice of the unacceptable.

(ii) Life Expectancy

At trial, figures were introduced which showed that the life expectancy of 23-year-old persons in general is 50 years. As Chief Justice McGillivray said in the Appellate Division, it would be more useful to use statistics on the expectation of life of quadriplegics. A statistical average is helpful only if the appropriate group is used. At trial, Dr. Weir and Dr. Gingras testified that possibly five years less than normal would be a reasonable expectation of life for a quadriplegic. The Appellate Division accepted this figure. On the evidence I am willing to accept it.

(iii) Contingencies of Life

The trial Judge did, however, allow a 20% discount for "contingencies and hazards of life." The Appellate Division allowed a further 10% discount. It characterized the trial Judge's discount as being for "life expectancy" or "duration of life," and said that this ignored the contingency of "duration of expense," i.e., that despite any wishes to the contrary, Andrews in the years to come may be obliged to spend a great deal of time in hospital for medical reasons or because of the difficulty of obtaining help. With respect, the Appellate Division appears to have misunderstood what the trial Judge did. The figure of 20% as a discount for contingencies was arrived at first under the heading of "Prospective Loss of Earnings" and then simply transferred to the calculation of "Costs of Future Care." It was not an allowance for a decreased life expectancy, for this had already been taken into account by reducing the normal 50-year expectancy to 45 years. The "contingencies and hazards of life" in the context of future care are distinct. They relate essentially to duration of expense and are different from those which might affect future earnings, such as unemployment, accident, illness. They are not merely to be added to the latter so as to achieve a cumulative result. Thus, so far as the action taken by the Appellate Division is concerned, in my opinion, it was an error to increase by an extra 10% the contingency allowance of the trial Judge.

This whole question of contingencies is fraught with difficulty, for it is in large measure pure speculation. It is a small element of the illogical practice of awarding lump-sum payments for expenses and losses projected to continue over long periods of time. To vary an award by the value of the chance that certain contingencies may occur is to assure either over-compensation or under-compensation, depending on whether or not the event occurs. In light of the considerations I have mentioned, I think it would be reasonable to allow a discount for contingencies in the amount of 20%, in accordance with the decision of the trial Judge.

(iv) Duplication with Compensation for Loss of Future Earnings

It is clear that a plaintiff cannot recover for the expense of providing for basic necessities as part of the cost of future care while still recovering fully for prospective loss of earnings. Without the accident, expenses for such items as food, clothing and accommodation would have been paid for out of earnings. They are not an additional type of expense occasioned by the accident.

When calculating the damage award, however, there are two possible methods of proceeding. One method is to give the injured party an award for future care which makes no deduction in respect of the basic necessities for which he would have had to pay in any event. A deduction must then be made for the cost of such basic necessities when computing the award for loss of prospective earnings, i.e., the award is on the basis of net earnings and not gross earnings. The alternative method is the reverse, i.e., to deduct the cost of basic necessities when computing the award for future care and then to compute the earnings award on the basis of gross earnings.

The trial judge took the first approach, reducing loss of future earnings by 53%. The Appellate Division took the second. In my opinion, the approach of the trial Judge is to be preferred. This is in accordance with the principle which I believe should underlie the whole consideration of damages for personal injuries: that proper future care is the paramount goal of such damages. To determine accurately the needs and costs in respect of future care, basic living expenses should be included. The costs of necessaries when in an infirm state may well be different from those when in a state of health. Thus, while the types of expenses would have been incurred in any event, the level of expenses for the victim may be seen as attributable to the accident. In my opinion, the projected cost of necessities should, therefore, be included in calculating the cost of future care, and a percentage attributable to the necessities of a person in a normal state should be reduced from the award for future earnings. For the acceptability of this method of proceeding see the judgment of this Court in *The Queen v. Jennings*, [1966] SCR 532 at pp. 540-1; affirming, [1965] OR 285, *sub nom. Jennings v. Crousberry*, and also *Bisson v. District of Powell River* (1967), 66 DLR (2d) 226 (BC CA) at pp. 239-40.

(v) Cost of Special Equipment

In addition to his anticipated monthly expenses, Andrews requires an initial capital amount for special equipment. Both Courts below held that $14,200 was an appropriate figure for the cost of this equipment. In my opinion, this assessment is correct in principle, and I would therefore accept it.

(b) Prospective Loss of Earnings

We must now gaze more deeply into the crystal ball. What sort of a career would the accident victim have had? What were his prospects and potential prior to the accident? It is not loss of earnings but, rather, loss of earnings capacity of which compensation must be made: *The Queen v. Jennings*, *supra*. A capital asset has been lost: what was its value?

(i) Level of Earnings

The trial Judge fixed the projected level of earnings of Andrews at $830 per month, which would have been his earnings on January 1, 1973. The Appellate Division raised this to $1,200 per month, a figure between his present salary and the maximum for his type of work of $1,750 per month. Without doubt the value of Andrews' earning capacity over his working life is higher than his earnings at the time of the accident. Although I am inclined to view even that figure as somewhat conservative, I would affirm the holding of the Appellate Division that $1,200 per month represents a reasonable estimate of Andrews' future average level of earnings.

(ii) Length of Working Life

Counsel for the appellants objected to the use of 55 rather than 65 as the projected retirement age for Andrews. It is agreed that he could retire on full pension at 55 if he stayed with his present employer, Canadian National Railways. I think it is reasonable to assume that he would, in fact, retire as soon as it was open for him to do so on full pension.

One must then turn to the mortality tables to determine the working life expectancy for the appellant over the period between the ages of 23 and 55. The controversial question immediately arises whether the capitalization of future earning capacity should be based on the expected working life span prior to the accident, or the shortened life expectancy. Does one give credit for the "lost years"? When viewed as the loss of a capital asset consisting of income-earning capacity rather than a loss of income, the answer is apparent: it must be the loss of that capacity which existed prior to the accident. This is the figure which best fulfils the principle of compensating the plaintiff for what he has lost: see *Mayne and McGregor on Damages* (London: Sweet & Maxwell, 12th ed., 1961) at p. 659; Kemp & Kemp, *Quantum of*

Damages, 3rd ed., vol. 1 (Supp.) c. 3, p. 28; *Skelton v. Collins* (1966), 115 CLR 94. In the instant case, the trial Judge refused to follow the *Oliver v. Ashman*, [1962] 2 QB 210 (CA) approach, the manifest injustice of which is demonstrated in the much-criticized case of *McCann v. Sheppard*, [1973] 1 WLR 540 (CA), and in this I think the judge was right. I would accept his decision that Andrews had a working life expectancy of 30.81 years.

(iii) Contingencies

It is a general practice to take account of contingencies which might have affected future earnings, such as unemployment, illness, accidents and business depression. In the *Bisson* case, which also concerned a young quadriplegic, an allowance of 20% was made. There is much support for the view that such a discount for contingencies should be made: see, *e.g.*, *Warren v. King*, [1964] 1 WLR 1 (CA); *McKay v. Board of Govan School Unit No. 29 of Saskatchewan*, [1968] SCR 589. There are, however, a number of qualifications which should be made. First, in many respects, these contingencies implicitly are already contained in an assessment of the projected average level of earnings of the injured person, for one must assume that this figure is a projection with respect to the real world of work, vicissitudes and all. Second, not all contingencies are adverse, as the above list would appear to indicate. As is said in *Bresatz v. Przibilla* (1962), 108 CLR 541, in the Australian High Court, at p. 544: "Why count the possible buffets and ignore the rewards of fortune?" Finally, in modern society there are many public and private schemes which cushion the individual against adverse contingencies. Clearly, the percentage deduction which is proper will depend on the facts of the individual case, particularly the nature of the plaintiff's occupation, but generally it will be small: see J.H. Prevett, "Actuarial Assessment of Damages: The Thalidomide Case—I" (1972), 35 Mod. L Rev. 140 at p. 150.

In reducing Andrews' award by 20% Mr. Justice Kirby gives no reasons. The Appellate Division also applied a 20% reduction. It seems to me that actuarial evidence could be of great help here. Contingencies are susceptible to more exact calculation than is usually apparent in the cases; see A.T. Traversi, "Actuaries and the Courts" (1956), 29 Aust. Law J 557. In my view, some degree of specificity, supported by evidence, ought to be forthcoming at trial.

The figure used to take account of contingencies is obviously an arbitrary one. The figure of 20% which was used in the lower Courts (and in many other cases), although not entirely satisfactory, should, I think, be accepted.

(iv) Duplication of the Cost of Future Basic Maintenance

As discussed, since basic needs such as food, shelter, and clothing have been included in the cost of future care, a deduction must be made from the award for prospective earnings to avoid duplication. The injured person would have incurred expenses of this nature even if he had not suffered the injury. At trial evidence was given that the cost of basics for a person in the position of Andrews prior to the accident would be approximately 53% of income. I would accept this figure and reduce his anticipated future monthly earnings accordingly to a figure of $564.

(c) Considerations Relevant to Both Heads of Pecuniary Loss

(i) Capitalization Rate: Allowance for Inflation and the Rate of Return on Investments

What rate of return should the Court assume the appellant will be able to obtain on his investment of the awards? How should the Court recognize future inflation? Together these considerations will determine the discount rate to use in actuarially calculating the lump sum award.

The approach at trial was to take as a rate of return the rental value of money which might exist during periods of economic stability, and consequently to ignore inflation. This approach is widely referred to as the Lord Diplock approach, as he lent it his support in *Mallett v. McMonagle*, [1970] AC 166 (HL (NI)). Although this method of proceeding has found favour in several jurisdictions in this country and elsewhere, it has an air of unreality. Stable, non-inflationary economic conditions do not exist at present, nor did they exist in the recent past, nor are they to be expected in the foreseeable future. In my opinion, it would be better to proceed from what known factors are available rather than to ignore economic reality. Analytically, the alternate approach to assuming a stable economy is to use existing interest rates and then make an allowance for the long-term expected rate of inflation. At trial the expert actuary, Mr. Grindley, testified as follows:

> Yes, as I mentioned yesterday, I was comfortable with that assumption 5% interest because it produces the same result as for example 8% interest and 3% inflation. ...
>
> I would be happy to use either of the following two packages of assumption, either an 8% interest rate combined with provision for amounts which would increase 3% in every year in the future or a 5% interest rate and level amount, that is no allowance for inflation.

One thing is abundantly clear: present interest rates should not be used with no allowance for future inflation. To do so would be patently unfair to the plaintiff. It is not, however, the level of inflation in the short term for which allowance must be made, but that predicted over the long term. It is this expectation which is built into present interest rates for long-term investments. It is also this level of inflation which may at present be predicted to operate over the lifetime of the plaintiff to increase the cost of care for him at the level accepted by the Court, and to erode the value of the sum provided for lost earning capacity.

In *Bisson v. District of Powell River*, the British Columbia Court of Appeal held that there had been a misdirection, or non-direction amounting to misdirection, in the trial Judge's charge to the jury with respect to quantum of damages for the plaintiff's personal injuries. Bull JA listed several instances of misdirection, including failure to instruct the jury that although they might give some thought to possibilities of future inflation, it was wrong to include any built-in inflation factors in the actuarial calculations with respect to the sums for future care and loss of prospective earnings. An appeal to this Court was dismissed, [1968] SCR (v), Cartwright CJC giving short oral reasons as follows:

> We are all of opinion that the Court of Appeal [66 DLR (2d) 226; 62 WWR 707] were right in holding that they were justified in setting aside the assessment of damages made by the jury. In such circumstances they had jurisdiction under Rule 36 of the British Columbia Court of Appeal Rules to reduce the damages instead of ordering a new trial. We find ourselves unable to

say that in fixing the amount of damages the Court of Appeal erred in principle or that the figure at which they arrived was such as to represent a wholly erroneous estimate.

In my opinion, this cannot be taken as an express endorsement by this Court of the method of calculation expressed by Bull JA. When discussing this issue, Bull JA stated that the correct procedure was to use a capitalization rate of 5% or 6%, since there was evidence that 6% was a normal and available rate of return on first-class securities, and not to build in any inflation rate at all. With respect, I cannot understand how the thought is to be given to the possibility of inflation in calculating the award if no inflation factor is to be built into the calculation of the award. In his judgment, Bull JA further states, at p. 242:

> If inflationary trends appear, it may well be that the use to which the money is put, whatever it may be, will itself increase its own amount as part of an inflationary process. It is well known that interest rates, or the "wages" of money, rise in times of inflation.

One might offer two comments: First, the words "If inflationary trends appear" reflect economic conditions in 1967 when serious inflation was only on the horizon. During the past ten years, inflation has become one of the most serious Canadian problems. The Court, in *Reference re Anti-Inflation Act*, [1976] 2 SCR 373, recognized the *Anti Inflation Act*, 1974-75 (Can.), c. 75, as a measure necessary to meet a situation of economic crisis imperilling the well-being of the people of Canada as a whole. Second, the passage immediately above-quoted accepts the proposition that interest rates or the "wages" of money rise in times of inflation. This rise is attributable, at least in part, to the erosion of the dollar. Accepting the highly unlikely proposition that the appellant will be able to invest for the balance of his lifetime at current high rates the capital sum awarded to him, this investment will provide him with a constant number of dollars each year, but the services which those dollars will provide will become more costly by the year. If current high interest rates abate with a re-duction of inflationary pressures and return, say, to the 1967 rates of 5% or 6%, it is obvious that reinvestment from time to time in later years of the equities or fixed income securities comprising the capital sum will be at rates which fall far short of those at present available. Then, even the number of dollars the appellant gets will be less than *even the present cost of care*. With respect, the economic analysis in *Bisson* proceeds on the erroneous basis that the cost of services decreases as the rate of inflation decreases. On the contrary, a decrease in the rate of inflation merely results in a lower rate of increase in the cost of these services.

In *Schroth v. Innes* (1976), 71 DLR (3d) 647 (CA), Bull JA, delivering the judgment of the Court, repeated his views on this matter. Again, the relevance of inflation was recognized in principle but was excluded from the calculation of the award. At p. 657 Bull JA states, "... it is today's money to which the respondent Shiels is entitled in damages." With respect, we are not concerned only with today's money. The real concern is in determining what that money will provide in the way of services over the next 45 years.

Bull JA voiced his disapproval of any recognition for inflation, whether by building in an inflation factor while using current rates of return, or by using a hypothetical "stable state." The learned Judge attempted to refute the conclusion that inflation should be included. He said, at pp. 659-60:

> With the greatest deference, I do not agree with the basic premises of those conclusions. To me what was really said was that current interest rates, much higher than those prevailing in the

> old days of the so-called "stable economy," exist only because of an existing inflated economy and of current fear of future inflation; and hence should not be used unless future inflation estimates or factors are fed into the computer also. That may also be so in England but I am not prepared to accede to that proposition with respect to this country. I think it general knowledge that interest rates in Canada for many years have reached higher levels because of the desire and need to attract new capital from abroad to create and service our expanding industrial and commercial economy. But I content myself with saying that I am satisfied that the current high rates of interest (which have been with us for years with only modest variations up and down) reflect today the present value of already inflated money in exactly the same way as do current high wages and prices generally. They live together, and the use of a high level of wages as one side of the coin and a low level of interest for the other is, in my respectful view, wrong.

In my opinion, this analysis is manifestly in error. Fear of future inflation is not confined to England. It is such as to have constituted a national emergency in this country. The current high rates of interest do not merely reflect the present value of already inflated money. They reflect the present expectation of *future* inflation. This is not the only factor which determines the existing interest rate, but it is without doubt one of the major factors. In my opinion, recognition of this fact must be made in the calculations of a damage award.

The approach which I would adopt, therefore, is to use present rates of return on long-term investments and to make some allowance for the effects of future inflation. Once this approach is adopted, the result, in my opinion, is different from the 5% discount figure accepted by the trial Judge. While there was much debate at trial over a difference of half to one percentage point, I think it is clear from the evidence that high quality long-term investments were available at time of trial at rates of return in excess of 10%. On the other hand, evidence was specifically introduced that the former head of the Economic Council of Canada, Dr. Deutsch, had recently forecast a rate of inflation of $3\frac{1}{2}$% over the long-term future. These figures must all be viewed flexibly. In my opinion, they indicate that the appropriate discount rate is approximately 7%. I would adopt that figure. It appears to me to be the correct result of the approach I have adopted, *i.e.*, having regard to present investment market conditions and making an appropriate allowance for future inflation. I would, accordingly, vary to 7% the discount rate to be used in calculating the present value of the awards for future care and loss of earnings in this case. The result in future cases will depend upon the evidence adduced in those cases.

(ii) Allowance for Tax

In *The Queen v. Jennings* this Court held that an award for prospective income should be calculated with no deduction for tax which might have been attracted had it been earned over the working life of the plaintiff. This results from the fact that it is earning capacity and not lost earnings which is the subject of compensation. For the same reason, no consideration should be taken of the amount by which the income from the award will be reduced by payment of taxes on the interest, dividends, or capital gain. A capital sum is appropriate to replace the lost capital asset of earning capacity. Tax on income is irrelevant either to decrease the sum for taxes the victim would have paid on income from his job, or to increase it for taxes he will now have to pay on income from the award.

In contrast with the situation in personal injury cases, awards under the *Fatal Accident Acts* should reflect tax considerations, since they are to compensate dependants for the loss of support payments made by the deceased. These support payments could only come out of take-home pay, and the payments from the award will only be received net of taxes: see the contemporaneous decision of this Court in *Keizer v. Hanna*, [1978] 2 SCR 342.

The impact of taxation upon the income from the capital sum for future care is mitigated by the existence of s. 110(1)(c)(iv.1) [enacted 1973-74, c. 14, s. 35] of the *Income Tax Act*, RSC 1952, c. 148 (as amended by 1970-71-72, c. 63), in respect of the deduction of medical expenses, which provides that medical expenses in excess of 3% of the taxpayer's income includes "remuneration for one full-time attendant upon an individual who was a taxpayer ... in a self-contained domestic establishment in which the cared for person lived." This exemption, I should think, permits a deduction for the payment of one full-time attendant for seven days a week, regardless of whether this attendance is provided by several attendants working over 24-hour periods, or one person working 24-hour shifts seven days a week.

The exact tax burden is extremely difficult to predict, as the rate and coverage of taxes swing with the political winds. What concerns us here is whether some allowance must be made to adjust the amount assessed for future care in light of the reduction from taxation. No such allowance was made by the Courts below. Elaborate calculations were provided by the appellant to give an illusion of accuracy to this aspect of the wholly speculative projection of future costs. Because of the provision made in the *Income Tax Act* and because of the position taken in the Alberta Courts, I would make no allowance for that item. The Legislature might well consider a more generous income tax treatment of cases where a fund is established by judicial decision and the sole purpose of the fund is to provide treatment or care of an accident victim.

One subsidiary point should be affirmed with respect to the determination of the present value of the cost of future care. The calculations should provide for a self-extinguishing sum. To allow a residual capital amount would be to over-compensate the injured person by creating an estate for him. This point was accepted by the lower Courts and not challenged by the parties.

2. Non-Pecuniary Losses

Andrews used to be a healthy young man, athletically active and socially congenial. Now he is a cripple, deprived of many of life's pleasures and subjected to pain and disability. For this, he is entitled to compensation. But the problem here is qualitatively different from that of pecuniary losses. There is no medium of exchange for happiness. There is no market for expectation of life. The monetary evaluation of non-pecuniary losses is a philosophical and policy exercise more than a legal or logical one. The award must be fair and reasonable, fairness being gauged by earlier decisions; but the award must also of necessity be arbitrary or conventional. No money can provide true restitution. Money can provide for proper care: this is the reason that I think the paramount concern of the Courts when awarding damages for personal injuries should be to assure that there will be adequate future care.

However, if the principle of the paramountcy of care is accepted, then it follows that there is more room for the consideration of other policy factors in the assessment of damages for non-pecuniary losses. In particular, this is the area where the social burden of large awards deserves considerable weight. The sheer fact is that there is no objective yardstick for translating non-pecuniary losses, such as pain and suffering and loss of amenities, into monetary terms. This area is open to widely extravagant claims. It is in this area that awards in the United States have soared to dramatically high levels in recent years. Statistically, it is the area where the danger of excessive burden of expense is greatest.

It is also the area where there is the clearest justification for moderation. As one English commentator has suggested, there are three theoretical approaches to the problem of non-pecuniary loss (A.I. Ogus, "Damages for Lost Amenities: For a Foot, a Feeling or a Function?" (1972), 35 Mod. L Rev. 1). The first, the "conceptual" approach, treats each faculty as a proprietary asset with an objective value, independent of the individual's own use or enjoyment of it. This was the ancient "bot," or tariff system, which prevailed in the days of King Alfred, when a thumb was worth 30 shillings. Our law has long since thought such a solution unsubtle. The second, the "personal" approach, values the injury in terms of the loss of human happiness by the particular victim. The third, or "functional" approach, accepts the personal premise of the second, but rather than attempting to set a value on lost happiness, it attempts to assess the compensation required to provide the injured person "with reasonable solace for his misfortune." "Solace" in this sense is taken to mean physical arrangements which can make his life more endurable rather than "solace" in the sense of sympathy. To my mind, this last approach has much to commend it, as it provides a rationale as to why money is considered compensation for non-pecuniary losses such as loss of amenities, pain and suffering, and loss of expectation of life. Money is awarded because it will serve a useful function in making up for what has been lost in the only way possible, accepting that what has been lost is incapable of being replaced in any direct way. As Windeyer J said in *Skelton v. Collins* (1966), 115 CLR 94 at p. 13:

> [H]e is, I do not doubt, entitled to compensation for what he suffers. Money may be compensation for him if having it can give him pleasure or satisfaction … . But the money is not then a recompense for a loss of something having a money value. It is given as some consolation or solace for the distress that is the consequence of a loss on which no monetary value can be put.

If damages for non-pecuniary loss are viewed from a functional perspective, it is reasonable that large amounts should not be awarded once a person is properly provided for in terms of future care for his injuries and disabilities. The money for future care is to provide physical arrangements for assistance, equipment and facilities directly related to the injuries. Additional money to make life more endurable should then be seen as providing more general physical arrangements above and beyond those relating directly to the injuries. The result is a coordinated and interlocking basis for compensation, and more rational justification for non-pecuniary loss compensation.

However one may view such awards in a theoretical perspective, the amounts are still largely arbitrary or conventional. As Lord Denning MR said in *Ward v. James*, [1966] 1 QB 273 (CA), there is a great need in this area for assessability, uniformity and predictability. In my opinion, this does not mean that the courts should not have regard to the individual situation of the victim. On the contrary, they must do so to determine what has been lost. For example, the loss of a finger would be a greater loss of amenities for an amateur pianist than for a person not engaged in such an activity. Greater compensation would be required to provide things and activities which would function to make up for this loss. But there should be guidelines for the translation into monetary terms of what has been lost. There must be an exchange rate, albeit conventional. In *Warren v. King*, [1964] 1 WLR 1 (CA) at p. 10 the following dictum of Harman LJ appears, which I would adopt, in respect of the assessment of non-pecuniary loss for a living plaintiff:

> It seems to me that the first element in assessing such compensation is not to add up items [such] as loss of pleasures, of earnings, of marriage prospects, of children and so on, but to consider the matter from the other side, what can be done to alleviate the disaster to the victim, what will it cost to enable her to live as tolerably as may be in the circumstances.

Cases like the present enable the Court to establish a rough upper parameter on these awards. It is difficult to conceive of a person of his age losing more than Andrews has lost. Of course, the figures must be viewed flexibly in future cases in recognition of the inevitable differences in injuries, the situation of the victim, and changing economic conditions.

The amounts of such awards should not vary greatly from one part of the country to another. Everyone in Canada, wherever he may reside, is entitled to a more or less equal measure of compensation for similar non-pecuniary loss. Variation should be made for what a particular individual has lost in the way of amenities and enjoyment of life, and for what will function to make up for this loss, but variation should not be made merely for the Province in which he happens to live.

There has been a significant increase in the size of awards under this head in recent years. As Moir JA, of the Appellate Division of the Alberta Supreme Court, has warned: "To my mind, damages under the head of loss of amenities will go up and up until they are stabilized by the Supreme Court of Canada": *Hamel v. Prather* (1976), 66 DLR (3d) 109 at p. 127. In my opinion, this time has come.

It is customary to set only one figure for all non-pecuniary loss, including such factors as pain and suffering, loss of amenities, and loss of expectation of life. This is a sound practice. Although these elements are analytically distinct, they overlap and merge at the edges and in practice. To suffer pain is surely to lose an amenity of a happy life at that time. To lose years of one's expectation of life is to lose all amenities for the lost period, and to cause mental pain and suffering in the contemplation of this prospect. These problems, as well as the fact that these losses have the common trait of irreplaceability, favour a composite award for all non-pecuniary losses.

There is an extensive review of authorities in the Court of Appeal judgment in this case as well as in the *Thornton* and *Teno* cases, *supra*, to which I have referred. I need not review these past authorities. What is important is the general picture. It is clear that until very recently damages for non-pecuniary losses, even from very serious injuries such as quadriplegia, were substantially below $100,000. Recently, though, the figures have increased markedly. In *Jackson v. Millar*, [1976] 1 SCR 225, this Court affirmed a figure of $150,000 for non-pecuniary loss in an Ontario case of a paraplegic. However, this was done essentially on the principle of non-interference with awards allowed by provincial Courts of Appeal. The need for a general assessment with respect to damages for non-pecuniary loss, which is now apparent, was not as evident at that time. Even in Ontario, prior to these recent cases, general damages allocable for non-pecuniary loss, such as pain and suffering and loss of amenities, were well below $100,000.

In the present case, $150,000 was awarded at trial, but this amount was reduced to $100,000 by the Appellate Division. In *Thornton* and *Teno* $200,000 was awarded in each case, unchanged in the provincial Courts of Appeal.

I would adopt as the appropriate award in the case of a young adult quadriplegic like Andrews the amount of $100,000. Save in exceptional circumstances, this should be regarded as an upper limit of non-pecuniary loss in cases of this nature.

Total Award

This is largely a matter of arithmetic. Of course, in addition, it is customary for the Court to make an overall assessment of the total sum. This, however, seems to me to be a hangover from the days of global sums for all general damages. It is more appropriate to make an overall assessment of the total under each head of future care, prospective earnings, and non-pecuniary loss, in each case in light of general considerations such as the awards of other Courts in similar cases and an assessment of the reasonableness of the award.

In the result I would assess general damages for the appellant Andrews as follows:

1. PECUNIARY LOSS
   (a) *Cost of future care*
       — special equipment .... $ 14,200
       — amount for monthly payments (monthly amount $4,135;
       life expectancy 45 years; contingencies 20%;
       capitalization rate 7%) 557,232
   (b) *Prospective loss of earnings*
       (monthly amount $564; work span 30.81 years; contingencies 20%;
       capitalization rate 7%) 69,981
2. NON-PECUNIARY LOSS
   — compensation for physical and mental pain and suffering endured
   and to be endured, loss of amenities and enjoyment of life, loss of
   expectation of life 100,000

Total General Damages $741,413

Rounded off at $740,000

To arrive at the total damage award, the special damages of $77,344 must be added to give a final figure of $817,344.

The appellant Andrews will have judgment for 75% of that amount, that is $613,008.

The appellants should have their costs in this Court and in the trial Court. The respondents should have their costs in the Court of Appeal as they achieved substantial success in that Court in respect of the finding of contributory negligence on the part of Andrews.

NOTES

1. The trilogy heralded a number of significant changes in damages assessment. The prior practice of making global awards has been abandoned in favour of an itemization approach under four headings: pecuniary loss occurring before the trial, non-pecuniary loss, loss of

earning capacity, and cost of future care. The apparent rationale for this movement was to increase predictability and consistency among awards and assist appellate review.

2. The respective role of trial and appellate courts in personal injury assessment is discussed in *Pickering v. Deakin* (1984), 58 BCLR 145, *per* Lambert JA, at 149-51 (CA):

> I propose to refer now to the general approach that must be taken, first, by a trial judge, and second, by a Court of Appeal, in assessing damages in the case of a gravely injured plaintiff.
>
> The general approach to be taken by a trial judge is set out in *Andrews v. Grand & Toy Alta. Ltd.*, [1978] 2 SCR 229 at p. 235, and *Lewis v. Todd*, [1980] 2 SCR 694 at p. 707. The damages should be assessed as separate amounts under the various relevant heads of damages. But when that has been done, the trial judge is to be accorded a large discretionary area of freedom to deal with the expert evidence and to adjust both the separately assessed amounts and the total award upward or downward if the expert evidence and resulting calculations provide either separate headings or an overall total that seem to the trial judge to be either much too low or much too high.
>
> The approach to be taken by a Court of Appeal remains unchanged since *Nance v. BC Elec. Ry.*, [1951] AC 601 (PC (BC)). That approach was reaffirmed by the Supreme Court of Canada in *Andrews v. Grand & Toy*, at p. 235, and in *Woelk v. Halvorson*, [1980] 2 SCR 430, at p. 435, where McIntyre J puts it in these words:
>
> > It is well settled that a Court of Appeal should not alter a damage award made at trial merely because, on its view of the evidence, it would have come to a different conclusion. It is only where a Court of Appeal comes to the conclusion that there was no evidence upon which a trial judge could have reached this conclusion, or where he proceeded upon a mistaken or wrong principle, or where the result reached at the trial was wholly erroneous, that a Court of Appeal is entitled to intervene.
>
> If none of the conditions are present that permit a Court of Appeal to reconsider a damage award, then that ends the matter. It is not open to a Court of Appeal to reassess the damages and reach a different figure than the trial judge by repeating the functions of the trial judge. On the other hand, if there is a mistake in calculation or an error in principle, or some other reviewable error, a Court of Appeal is obliged to reconsider the questions of damages. But that reconsideration should not start from the beginning again. Wherever the assessments made by the trial judge under individual headings are untainted by the error, then the assessments under those headings should be retained. And if the trial judge's findings of fact are independent from the error and would be equally relevant if the error had not occurred, then the Court of Appeal ought to accept those findings of fact in just the same way as it would be required to accept the findings if there had been no reviewable error.
>
> But sometimes the identification and correction of an error in principle require the Court of Appeal to consider whether the trial judge would have made different findings of fact or additional findings of fact if he had applied the correct principle. And in those circumstances, the Court of Appeal must look again at the evidence. But, still, it should do so with a consciousness of any findings of credibility that the trial judge has made, and with due regard to the weight that the trial judge has decided should be attached to the testimony of individual witnesses.
>
> Then, after applying the principle that the Court of Appeal considers correct to the facts derived in this way from the evidence and from the reasons and findings of the trial judge, the Court of Appeal must make whatever adjustments are necessary to the award of the trial judge.

At that stage the Court of Appeal must exercise anew the functions that the trial judge was required to exercise as laid down in *Lewis v. Todd*. The Court of Appeal must decide whether the adjustment that it has made to the assessment of the trial judge is such that either the individual heading that has been adjusted or the whole award itself has now become, by reason of the adjustment, either much too high or much too low.

3. Section 119 of the Ontario *Courts of Justice Act*, RSO 1990, c. C.43 states that on appeal from an award of damages for personal injury, the court may, if it considers it just, substitute its own assessment of the damages. The power to substitute its own award for that of the trial court has also been recognized by the BC Court of Appeal in *DaSilva v. Dudas* (1989), 38 BCLR (2d) 104 (CA). See also *Lawrence and Lawrence v. Good* (1985), 33 Man. R (2d) 312 (CA). In *White v. Nuraney* (2000), 80 BCLR (3d) 307 (CA), the BC Court of Appeal stated that an appellate court can interfere with a jury award where the award is "internally inconsistent or contradictory." In *Padfield v. Martin* (2003), 64 (3d) 577, the Ontario Court of Appeal described the circumstances where it would be appropriate for an appellate court to substitute its own evaluation of the damages in place of a jury's award pursuant to s. 119. Where the jury has simply arrived at an inappropriate assessment on the evidence, an appellate court should substitute its own assessment. However, where the jury's assessment has been derived from a misconduct of the trial, or misdirection by the judge, an order for a new trial is more likely appropriate.

4. Section 118 of the Ontario *Courts of Justice Act*, RSO 1990, c. C.43 states that in an action for damages for personal injury, the court may give guidance to the jury on the amount of damages to be awarded. In *Foreman v. Foster* (2001), 84 BCLR (3d) 184 (CA), at para. 73, Lambert JA undertook an extensive review of the law in a number of jurisdictions as to when it is appropriate for a judge to give guidance to a jury. He concluded:

> The law has been modified in Canada (Saskatchewan, Ontario, and *Crosby v. O'Reilly* in the Supreme Court of Canada). It has been modified in similar ways in England, Australia, and New Zealand. In each jurisdiction the Courts have tried to strike a balance in which "the need for fairness, consistency, and rationality in damage awards" is coupled with the independence of judgment of the jury on questions of fact. In every jurisdiction in which the balance has been struck, the trial judge is given the discretion to choose whether to give guidance on the appropriate range for a conventional award, or not. That decision depends on whether the interests of justice would be more likely to be served than thwarted by the guidance. If the findings of fact open to the jury on the evidence are so diverse as to complicate any guidance instruction to the point of potential confusion, then giving guidance may be more confusing than enlightening. But a greater measure of consistency in damage awards is an important goal in the administration of justice.

Lambert JA then adopted the approach suggested by Vancise JA in *Junek v. Ede*, [1991] 1 WWR 60 (Sask. CA), at 69:

> (1) The judge should receive submissions from counsel as to the appropriate range of damages, in the absence of the jury. Those submissions can be in the form of written briefs submitted prior to trial or during the trial which will then form the basis for argument, having regard to the evidence proved at trial, which will be made to the judge in the absence of the jury before the judge instructs the jury. Counsel are not permitted to make submissions regarding damages directly to the jury, as that is the function of the trial judge, and the submissions will assist the trial judge in formulating an appropriate range of damages.

(2) If counsel agree on the appropriate range of damages, and the trial judge is of the view that it will be helpful, he shall instruct the jury on the agreed range of damages.

(3) If counsel do not agree, and the trial judge is of the view that it would be helpful, he shall instruct the jury as to the range of damages he considers appropriate having regard to the evidence and the submissions of counsel.

(4) In instructing the jury as to damages, the trial judge should state in clear and unequivocal terms that it is the jury's function to determine damages and that his function is to assist them in their task. He should make it clear that the range which is being put to them is for their guidance and assistance and is not a hard-and-fast upper and lower limit but a range which the trial judge considers wide enough in the circumstances, having regard to the evidence, to encompass the damages suffered by the plaintiff, and that they alone will determine the appropriate amount. It is the jury's function, not the trial judge's function, to decide the proper measure of damages.

5. The Supreme Court also approved the use of actuarial and statistical evidence of probable pre- and post-accident life spans of the injured person, and forecasts for the assessment of present and future economic conditions. However, the court did point out that actuarial figures were based on the general population's experiences and not those of particular individuals. The use of statistical evidence can mask many undesirable social realities. For example, the use of statistic evidence to identify loss of working capacity, if broken down by gender, will result in less compensation for females. See the discussion in J. Cassels, "(In)equality and the Law of Tort: Gender, Race, and the Assessment of Damages" (1995), 17 *Advocates' Q* 158, and J. Cassels and E. Adjin-Tettey, *Remedies: The Law of Damages*, 2d ed. (Toronto: Irwin Law, 2008), at 146.

6. The use of expert testimony for predicting future events both of the plaintiff and the economy has been severely criticized in *MacDonald v. Alderson* (1982), 15 Man. R (2d) 35, *per* O'Sullivan JA, at 50-52 (CA) (leave to appeal refused (1982), 17 Man. R (2d) 180 (SCC)):

It now seems to be the law that the capital sum awarded to cover future expenses and loss of income must be calculated with reference to future inflation, with actuarial and economists' assistance, on the hypothesis that the award will be invested in interest-bearing securities. This means that during a trial of an action for damages involving very serious injuries much time is now taken with economists and actuaries offered by both sides. I do not think the courts are well-equipped to assess their evidence, and the time and expense of such trials has been enormously increased.

I am particularly concerned that courts are being invited to come to a decision, based on the evidence presented case by case, as to future economic trends. Economists are invited to give their opinions on future rates of inflation and on future nominal interest rates for fixed-income securities. Some economists, while disclaiming the possibility of scientifically predicting the future at all, yet contend that it can be proved there is a fairly constant spread between anticipated future rates of inflation and nominal interest rates prevailing in the market at any given time. I confess that I find their theory unconvincing, particularly in light of the recent history of interest rates, which have gyrated spectacularly, even while anticipated future inflation rates have remained relatively stable.

According to the principles of evidence, as I understood them, the courts receive the opinions of experts only where there is some scientific or rational basis for such opinions. Fortune-tellers are not allowed to come to court to predict the future, because there is no rational basis for their predictions. I do not mean to downgrade the science of economics, but I know of no scientific or rational basis for accepting their predictions of the future.

Then too, I have some difficulty with the idea that a lump sum should be calculated in such a way that it will be used up over an assigned life expectancy. Hardly anyone lives an average life expectancy or an anticipated life expectancy. Some live shorter and some live longer. It would be imprudent for the recipient of a damage award to invest and spend it on the basis that his award would be exhausted over the period of his assigned life expectancy; if he did so, he would be a pauper at the end of the period of his anticipated life; how could he survive if he lived longer than his expected years? In fatal accident awards the case is quite different. What is there determined is the amount which compensates for loss of support from the deceased; his average life expectancy and those of his dependants are relevant to the determination of the probable loss of support; in the damage actions, what is sought to be given to the plaintiff is an amount that is likely to enable the plaintiff to be compensated for as long as he suffers damage from the tortfeasor, over the length of his actual life.

I would have preferred if the courts had avoided resort to economists and other futurologists; since the courts have been invited to listen to their evidence, they must do the best they can; it would be appreciated, I am sure, if the Supreme Court of Canada were to offer more clarification as to the criteria by which the opinion of one expert is to be preferred to that of another expert. It surely cannot depend on the demeanor or testimonial conduct of the experts.

When calculating a lump sum to cover future anticipated expenses, a further problem arises where the award is for less than 100 per cent. In the case before us, the learned trial judge has based his award on the assumption that the plaintiff will live independently, in a house, with an attendant. However, since the plaintiff was contributorily negligent, he will in fact receive only one-half of the amount needed to enable him to live in a house, with an attendant. He has no other funds than those awarded. This means that, if the data on which the award is calculated are correct, the plaintiff will not have a sum sufficient to meet his anticipated needs, but a sum sufficient to meet only half his needs. If, with a 100 per cent award, he can have a house of his own and an attendant, with a 50 per cent award he can have only half a house and half an attendant. But he cannot live independently with only half a house and half an attendant. So the hypothesis on which the global sum is calculated is not likely to be realized in actuality.

The effect of income tax is not, I take it, to be taken into account, although its effect is very real. If $1,000,000, spent, with interest, over an anticipated lifetime, will produce sufficient to provide expenditures over that anticipated lifetime, no account being taken of income tax on income, the same sum will not at all provide the same future expenditure if future income tax is taken into account.

I mention these concerns that I have with the law as now laid down for us by the Supreme Court of Canada.

In a number of jurisdictions, the need for case-by-case expert evidence has been reduced somewhat by setting discount rates legislatively and through rules of court (for example, Ontario Rules of Civil Procedure, r. 53.09; BC *Law and Equity Act*, RSBC 1996, c. 253, s. 56).

7. In *Dubé (Litigation Guardian of) v. Penlon Ltd.* (1994), 21 CCLT (2d) 268 (Ont. Gen. Div.), at para. 16, Zuber J described the requisite level of care a victim of personal injury could expect in the following terms:

> With respect to those who testified with respect to levels of care, cost of housing, cost of recreation and educative devices and similar matters, it appeared to me that the witnesses testified from a variety of theoretical premises. There was firstly what might be described as the subsistence level; with what could a plaintiff simply make do. There was secondly the level of care that might be provided by the community to care for one of its badly injured members. This notion of course involves the expenditure of limited public funds. Thirdly, there is a level of care a victim may expect as part of compensation within a fault-based system. Fourthly, there is a high level of care which includes all the care, housing and hardware that a victim could wish for or absorb.
>
> I further take it to be obvious that the first and fourth alternatives are wrong premises. I conclude that while it is not so obvious that the second alternative is also wrong. What communities or government may provide is only of marginal assistance. The standard is compensation not provision (see *Andrews v. Grand & Toy* (1978), 2 SCR 229 at 246). It is therefore the third alternative which must be the basis for the award in this case. Within this basis the principle that compensation should be full for pecuniary loss is well established. It is also clear that there is no duty to mitigate in the sense of being forced to accept less than real loss (see *Andrews v. Grand & Toy*, *supra*, at 229). The overriding principle is that damages should be reasonable, neither extravagant nor generated by sympathy or compassion but neither should they be niggardly or parsimonious.

Non-Pecuniary Losses

Non-pecuniary losses are designed to compensate three areas—loss of amenities, pain and suffering, and loss of expectation of life.

In the trilogy, the Supreme Court of Canada was clearly concerned with placing limits on the amounts recoverable for non-pecuniary losses. In the following case, the court further explored the issue.

Lindal v. Lindal
[1981] 2 SCR 629

DICKSON J: This is another tragic personal injury case. Liability is no longer in issue. The only question on appeal is whether the Court of Appeal of British Columbia erred in reducing from $135,000 to $100,000 the award for pain and suffering and loss of amenities of life.

This Court, in recent years, has sought to fashion a body of rational and cohesive principles to guide trial Courts in the assessment of damages in personal injury cases. The broad outline of these principles was sketched in three judgments delivered on January 19, 1978, sometimes referred to as the "trilogy": *Andrews v. Grand & Toy Alberta Ltd.*, [1978] 2 SCR 229; *Arnold v. Teno*, [1978] 2 SCR 287; *Thornton v. Board of School Trustees of School District No. 57 (Prince George)*, [1978] 2 SCR 267. The outline was further clarified and refined in *Lewis v. Todd*, [1980] 2 SCR 694. The present case affords an opportunity to continue the exposition.

The issue here is narrow: under what circumstances should a trial Judge exceed the rough upper limit of $100,000 for non-pecuniary loss established by the Court in the trilogy?

I

The appellant, Brian Lindal, claimed against his brother, the respondent Kenneth Lindal, for damages sustained by the appellant as a result of negligence of the respondent in the operation of a motor vehicle on May 18, 1975, at River Rd. in the Municipality of Delta, Province of British Columbia. The respondent lost control of the motor vehicle, in which the appellant was a passenger, and collided with a telephone pole resulting in severe physical and other injuries to the appellant. He was comatose for a period of almost three months. He suffered extensive damage to brain and brain stem resulting in severe dysarthria (speech impairment) due to loss of control of the muscles of the lips, tongue and palate. He suffered also from ataxic (irregularity of function) and spastic (sudden convulsive movement) double hemiplegia (loss of control of the muscles of the arms and hands and legs). In addition to the physical disability flowing from the loss of brain function there is appreciable personal and emotional disorder. The appellant lacks the capacity to reconcile himself mentally to his condition. He is emotionally labile, irritable, erratic and given to fits of depression. As at the date of trial, the appellant did not have any pain as a result of his injuries.

In assessing damages the trial Judge, Fulton J, in reasons reported in [1978] 4 WWR 592, carefully reviewed the decisions I have mentioned. He considered the appellant was not as severely paralyzed as either Andrews or Thornton, but in the end result was less mobile than they, for they apparently were able to move about freely in wheelchairs and one of them, Andrews, was able to drive a specially equipped van whereas here the appellant was limited to extremely slow, unsteady and difficult walking. More importantly, the appellant has suffered loss of brain function with resultant speech impairment and other consequences, whereas both Andrews and Thornton were left with mental functions unimpaired. In the *Teno* case, the infant plaintiff had also suffered severe brain injury but in *Teno* there did not appear to have been the personality disorders and constant frustration shown by Brian Lindal as a result of inability to make the mental adjustment.

Mr. Justice Fulton noted that this Court, in the trilogy, had established a normal upper limit of $100,000 for damages for non-pecuniary loss. However, in Fulton J's opinion, the door had been left open for a higher award in an "exceptional case." The trial Judge referred [[1978] 4 WWR, at 602] to the following passage from the judgment in *Andrews*, *supra*, p. 265, in support of this proposition:

> I would adopt as the appropriate award in the case of a young adult quadriplegic like Andrews the amount of $100,000. Save in exceptional circumstances, this should be regarded as an upper limit of non-pecuniary loss in cases of this nature.

The Judge felt that "exceptional circumstances" were present in the case of Brian Lindal. Brian Lindal, because of his damaged brain, has no chance of adjusting and leading a useful life; this possibility was open to the plaintiffs in *Andrews* and *Thornton* where there was no loss of brain function.

The Judge concluded that in *Andrews* this Court had fixed the normal upper limit of an award under the head of non-pecuniary damages in very severe personal injury cases, but that this was "not an absolute ceiling fixed and for all time." The following passage from *Andrews, supra*, at p. 263, was quoted [at 602]:

> It is difficult to conceive of a person of his age losing more than Andrews has lost. Of course, the figures must be viewed flexibly in future cases in recognition of the inevitable differences in injuries, the situation of the victim, and changing economic conditions.

The Judge found what he referred to as "compelling reasons" for fixing a higher sum. He considered that the consequences of Brian Lindal's injuries—lack of mobility, lack of ability to communicate, personality disorders—were substantially more serious than in the *Andrews* and *Thornton* cases. Two additional facts were relied on—(i) evidence of extreme depression and suicidal tendencies and (ii) the taking of a drug called dantrium, which had undesirable side effects, to relieve the effects of spasticity in the muscles. Damages for non-pecuniary loss loss were fixed at $135,000.

II

The sole issue on the appeal to the Court of Appeal of British Columbia was whether the trial Judge had erred in awarding a sum in excess of $100,000 for non-pecuniary loss. The Court of Appeal, speaking through Taggart JA, could not accept the conclusion that Brian Lindal was less mobile than Thornton and Andrews; Thornton and Andrews were, in the opinion of the Court, immeasurably worse off than Lindal. The impairment of Lindal's mental faculties was a most serious disability, one not suffered by Andrews and Thornton, but, when one had regard to the injuries sustained by the child in *Teno*, not so serious as to warrant an award in excess of $100,000. The following passage sums up the views of the Court [(1980), 25 BCLR 381, at 391 (CA)]:

> It will never be possible to make a precise comparison between persons who suffer non-pecuniary losses as a result of personal injuries. Their personalities will differ as will the circumstances obtaining both before and after the accident giving rise to their injuries. The effect of their injuries on them even though those injuries be similar will also vary because of their differing abilities to adjust to the altered circumstances in which they find themselves. I think it is because there is no possibility of making a precise comparison that Dickson J in *Andrews* and *Thornton* and Spence J in *Teno* used general language in fixing the rough upper limit of $100,000 as the amount to be awarded for non-pecuniary losses. I think that also led them to say that it should be only in exceptional cases that that limit should be exceeded. In my view this is not an exceptional case but rather one in which the limit fixed by Dickson J in *Thornton* and *Andrews* and by Spence J in *Teno* should prevail.

The Court allowed the appeal and reduced the amount awarded for non-pecuniary damages from $135,000 to $100,000.

Counsel for Brian Lindal advanced without success an alternative argument, in an attempt to sustain the higher award. He submitted that changes in economic conditions, that is to say, inflation, between the date of judgment at trial in April 1978 and date of judgment on appeal in October 1980, militated in favour of increasing the award from $100,000 to $135,000. The Court declined to hear this submission on the ground that it would have been necessary for counsel to refer to statistical and other materials not introduced in evidence at trial and there had been no application before the Court to introduce new evidence. The Court added [at 391]:

> We sit as a Court of review and not for the purpose of retrying a case. If we were to take account of the factors suggested by counsel for the respondent it seems to me we would be following the latter course. That is not to say that where evidence of an economic nature is adduced at trial which supports a conclusion that the case is one where an award in excess of the $100,000 level fixed in *Andrews, Thornton* and *Teno* should be made we cannot have regard for that evidence. I say simply that the material to which counsel for the respondent wished to refer was not before the trial Judge and forms no part of the record which is before us. For those reasons we declined to hear counsel for the respondent on this aspect of his argument.

III

In the trilogy, this Court reaffirmed the basic principle that the purpose of awarding damages for personal injury is compensation not punishment. The goal is to put the plaintiff in the position he would have been in had the injury not been suffered. The principle of compensation ensures a measure of fairness to both parties (*Andrews*, at pp. 243-4):

> The focus should be on the injuries of the innocent party. Fairness to the other party is achieved by assuring that the claims raised against him are legitimate and justifiable.

A number of secondary principles flow from the basic precept of compensation. The first is that anything having a money value which the plaintiff has lost should be made good by the defendant. If the plaintiff is unable to work, then the defendant should compensate him for his lost earnings. If the plaintiff has to pay for expensive medical or nursing attention, then this cost should be borne by the defendant. These costs are "losses" to the plaintiff, in the sense that they are expenses which he would not have had to incur but for the accident. The amount of the award under these heads of damages should not be influenced by the depth of the defendant's pocket or by sympathy for the position of either party. Nor should arguments over the social costs of the award be controlling at this point. The first and controlling principle is that the victim must be compensated for his loss.

Different considerations are paramount in the matter of damages for non-pecuniary loss. The principle *restitutio in integrum* can find only limited application in the matter of non-pecuniary losses. A lost limb or a lost mind are not assets that can be valued in monetary terms. Money cannot repair brain damage or obliterate anguish and suffering. As the Court put it in *Andrews* at p. 261:

> There is no medium of exchange for happiness. There is no market for expectation of life. The monetary evaluation of non-pecuniary losses is a philosophical and policy exercise more than a legal or logical one.

Pain and suffering and loss of amenities are intangibles. They are not possessions that have an objective, ascertainable value. Professor Otto Kahn-Freund in his brilliant essay "Expectation of Happiness" (1941), 5 Mod. LR 81, cites the example of the Stoic philosopher Poseidonios, who, when tormented by pain, is reported to have exclaimed [at 86] "Pain, thou shalt not defeat me. I shall never admit that thou art an evil." How, Professor Kahn-Freund asks, could we award damages for pain and suffering to this philosopher who welcomed his misery as a test of his own power to resist it? Is the stoic entitled to less compensation than the weak-willed person who recoils at the slightest suggestion of pain or unhappiness? These examples only reinforce the conclusion that it is fruitless to attempt to put a dollar value on the loss of a faculty in the way that we put a dollar value on the loss of a piece of property.

These problems were identified and discussed by the Court in the trilogy. In *Andrews*, three theoretical approaches to the problem of non-pecuniary loss were canvassed. The first two approaches, the "conceptual," which treats each faculty as a proprietary asset with an objective value, and the "personal," which would measure loss in terms of human happiness of the particular individual, both seek, in varying ways, to place a dollar value on human faculties and human happiness. The Court adopted the third approach, the "functional," which, rather than attempting to set a value on lost happiness, attempts to assess the compensation required to provide the injured person with reasonable solace for his misfortune. Money is awarded, not because lost faculties have a dollar value, but because money can be used to substitute other enjoyments and pleasures for those that have been lost. The matter is discussed in *Andrews* in these terms at p. 262:

> [I]t provides a rationale as to why money is considered compensation for non-pecuniary losses such as loss of amenities, pain and suffering, and loss of expectation of life. Money is awarded because it will serve a useful function in making up for what has been lost in the only way possible, accepting that what has been lost is incapable of being replaced in any direct way. As Windeyer J said in *Skelton v. Collins* (1966), 115 CLR 94 at p. 131:
>
> > [H]e is, I do not doubt, entitled to compensation for what he suffers. Money may be compensation for him if having it can give him pleasure or satisfaction … . But the money is not then a recompense for a loss of something having a money value. It is given as some consolation or solace for the distress that is the consequence of a loss on which no monetary value can be put.
>
> If damages for non-pecuniary loss are viewed from a functional perspective, it is reasonable that large amounts should not be awarded once a person is properly provided for in terms of future care for his injuries and disabilities. The money for future care is to provide physical arrangements for assistance, equipment and facilities directly related to the injuries. Additional money to make life more endurable should then be seen as providing more general physical arrangements above and beyond those relating directly to the injuries. The result is a coordinated and interlocking basis for compensation and a more rational justification for non-pecuniary compensation.

Thus the amount of an award for non-pecuniary damage should not depend alone upon the seriousness of the injury but upon its ability to ameliorate the condition of the victim considering his or her particular situation. It therefore will not follow that in considering what part of the maximum should be awarded the gravity of the injury alone will be determinative. An appreciation of the individual's loss is the key and the "need for solace will not necessarily correlate with the seriousness of the injury" (Kenneth D. Cooper-Stephenson and Iwan B. Saunders, *Personal Injury Damages in Canada* (Toronto: Carswell, 1981) at p. 373). In dealing with an award of this nature it will be impossible to develop a "tariff." An award will vary in each case "to meet the specific circumstances of the individual case": *Thornton*, at p. 284.

Mr. Justice Spence, in *Arnold v. Teno*, at pp. 333-4, approached the matter of non-pecuniary loss on the same footing:

> If, as did my brother Dickson, one realizes that it is impossible to compensate for the losses of the various elements involved in non-pecuniary damages and that it is reasonable, none the less, to make an award then gauge that award by attempting to set up a fund from which the plaintiff may draw, not to compensate for those losses, but to provide some substitute for those amenities. As Harman LJ put it so well in *Warren et al. v. King*, [1964] 1 WLR 1 (CA) at p. 10, "... what can be done to alleviate the disaster to the victim, what will it cost to enable her to live as tolerably as may be in the circumstances?"

The following comments on the functional approach are found in a recent article by Professor Beverley M. McLachlin, "What Price Disability? A Perspective on the Law of Damages of Personal Injury" (1981), 59 Can. Bar Rev. 1 at pp. 11-2 and 48:

> The essential point is that the plaintiff must demonstrate a reasonable or fair function which the money claimed will serve. As these examples illustrate, what is a reasonable or fair function may involve reference to the restitutionary concept of what the plaintiff would have enjoyed or have been able to provide for his dependants had he not been injured. This reflects the fact that the functional approach to damages is not in conflict with the ideal of *restitutio in integrum*, but rather provides a basis for calculating the closest practical equivalent to the goal of restoring the plaintiff to his original position. Viewed thus, the functional approach shows a promise of providing the comprehensive and just rationale for the calculation of damages for personal injuries which has heretofore been wanting. ...
>
> The attractions of a functional approach to the assessment of non-pecuniary damages are considerable. It provides a much needed rationale for such damages. It solves the problem inherent in the traditional compensation model of what the compensation is for. And it is in conformity with the conclusion of Lord Pearson's Commission:
>
> > We think the approach should be to [award] non-pecuniary damages only where they can serve some useful purpose, for example, by providing the plaintiff with an alternative source of satisfaction to replace one that he has lost.

The functional approach in the assessment of damages for non-pecuniary loss was adopted by the Pearson Commission in England (Royal Commission on Civil Liability and Compensation for Personal Injury, (1978) Cmnd. 7054-I). The commissioners stated that the main aim of any system for the award for pecuniary damages should be to make good the loss. Non-pecuniary damages should be awarded only when they can serve some useful purpose, for example, by providing the plaintiff with an alternative source of satisfaction to replace one that he has lost (vol. 1, para. 397). This led the commissioners to recommend that a permanently unconscious plaintiff should not receive any damages for non-pecuniary loss since the money award could serve no useful purpose (vol. 1, para. 398).

I have already indicated that the social costs of the award cannot be controlling when assessing damages for loss of income and the cost of future care. The plaintiff must be provided with a fund of money which will provide him with adequate, reasonable care for the rest of his life. The social impact of the award must be considered, however, in calculating the damages for non-pecuniary loss. There are a number of reasons for this. First, the claim of a severely injured plaintiff for damages for non-pecuniary loss is virtually limitless. This is particularly so if we adopt the functional approach and award damages according to the use which can be made of the money. There are an infinite number of uses which could be suggested in order to improve the lot of the crippled plaintiff. Moreover, it is difficult to determine the reasonableness of any of these claims. There are no accurate measures available to guide decisions in this area.

A second factor that must be considered is that we have already fully compensated the plaintiff for his loss of future earnings. Had he not been injured, a certain portion of these earnings would have been available for amenities. Logically, therefore, even before we award damages under the head of non-pecuniary loss, the plaintiff has certain funds at his disposal which can be used to provide a substitute for lost amenities. This consideration indicates that a moderate award for non-pecuniary damages is justified.

A third factor is that damages for non-pecuniary loss are not really "compensatory." The purpose of making the award is to substitute other amenities for those that have been lost, not to compensate for the loss of something with a money value. Since the primary function of the law of damages is compensation, it is reasonable that awards for non-pecuniary loss, which do not fulfil this function, should be moderate.

The social impact and possible effect, in practical terms, of very large awards for non-pecuniary loss was considered by Mr. Justice Spence in the *Teno* case, *supra*, at p. 333:

> The very real and serious social burden of these exorbitant awards has been illustrated graphically in the United States in cases concerning medical malpractice. We have a right to fear a situation where none but the very wealthy could own or drive automobiles because none but the very wealthy could afford to pay the enormous insurance premiums which would be required by insurers to meet such exorbitant awards.

This Court, while recognizing that limits are by their very nature arbitrary and conventional, endorsed the concept of an upper limit for awards of non-pecuniary loss in personal injury cases. The Court felt this to be desirable for the reasons outlined above and in the *Andrews* judgment, *supra*, from which I quote the following at p. 261:

> However, if the principle of the paramountcy of care is accepted, then it follows that there is more room for the consideration of other policy factors in the assessment of damages for non-pecuniary losses. In particular, this is the area where the social burden of large awards deserves considerable weight. The sheer fact is that there is no objective yardstick for translating non-pecuniary losses, such as pain and suffering and loss of amenities, into monetary terms. This area is open to widely extravagant claims. It is in this area that awards in the United States have soared to dramatically high levels in recent years. Statistically, it is the area where the danger of excessive burden of expense is the greatest.
>
> It is also the area where there is the clearest justification for moderation.

I would here reaffirm, for all the reasons outlined above, a rough upper limit of $100,000 for non-pecuniary loss in cases of severe personal injury, as providing a measure of uniformity and predictability in this difficult area. None of us, however, is unaware of, or unaffected by, the inflationary trend and the erosion in the value of money since the trilogy of cases was decided by this Court. The value of money has been steadily declining. It seems only reasonable therefore to reaffirm the statement in *Andrews*, at p. 263, that the figures must be viewed flexibly in recognition of, *inter alia*, "changing economic conditions." Such amount of $100,000 should be subject to increase upon proof of, or agreement as to, the effect of inflation on the value of money since the decisions of this Court in *Andrews*, *Teno* and *Thornton*. A Court may take judicial notice of the fact that an inflationary trend exists, but I should not think that the precise monthly or yearly inflation rate is normally a fact of which such notice may be taken.

IV

Mr. Justice Fulton made no reference to functional considerations in making his award of $135,000 for Brian Lindal's non-pecuniary loss. He referred to those passages in *Andrews* which discuss the need for "flexibility" in the assessment of non-pecuniary damages. He concentrated on demonstrating that the plaintiff Lindal was in a worse position than the plaintiffs in *Andrews* and *Thornton*, in concluding that $35,000 was a "reasonable and proper measure" of the difference between Lindal and Andrews and Thornton.

With great respect, in the case at bar, Mr. Justice Fulton appears to have misapprehended fundamentally the significance of the award of a conventional sum of $100,000 for non-pecuniary loss made by this Court to the three plaintiffs in the trilogy. He seems to have assumed that the figure of $100,000 was a measure of the "lost assets" of the plaintiffs in those cases. The issue was seen as one of quantifying and comparing the losses sustained. Once this premise is accepted, the question then becomes whether the plaintiff Lindal has lost more "assets" than did the plaintiffs in the earlier cases. If the answer to this question is in the affirmative, then it naturally follows that Brian Lindal deserves an award of over $100,000 under the head of non-pecuniary loss. The excess will represent the difference in value between what Lindal has lost and what the plaintiffs Andrews and Thornton have lost.

The difficulty with this approach is with the initial premise. The award of $100,000 for non-pecuniary loss in the trilogy was not in any sense a valuation of the assets which had been lost by Andrews, Thornton and Teno. As has been emphasized, these assets do not have a money value, and thus an objective valuation is impossible. The award of $100,000 was made, as earlier indicated, in order to provide more general physical arrangements above and beyond those directly relating to the injuries in order to make life more endurable. This is reflected in the fact that an identical sum was awarded to each of the three plaintiffs in those cases, even though their injuries were quite different. James Andrews, for example, suffered a lesion of the spinal cord which paralyzed most of his upper limbs, spine and lower limbs. He no longer had normal bladder, bowel and sex functions. Andrews was severely, if not totally, disabled. By way of contrast, Diane Teno had suffered a severe brain injury. Her speech was affected and she had a severe spastic paralysis on her left hand and arm. She was able to walk by herself but she did so clumsily.

No one would suggest that the injuries suffered by these two individuals were precisely identical. The Court recognized that their situations were in many ways quite different. Notwithstanding these differences, the Court awarded the same sum for non-pecuniary loss. Equally, the fact that Brian Lindal's injuries are different from and arguably more severe than those of James Andrews does not justify an award of more than $100,000 in this case.

It is true that the Court in *Andrews* spoke of exceeding the limit of $100,000 in "exceptional circumstances." The variety of possible fact situations is limitless, and it would be unwise to foreclose the possibility of ever exceeding the guide-line of $100,000. But, if the purpose of the guide-line is properly understood, it will be seen that the circumstances in which it should be exceeded will be rare indeed. We award non-pecuniary damages because the money can be used to make the victim's life more bearable. The limit of $100,000 was not selected because the plaintiff could only make use of $100,000 and no more. Quite the opposite. It was selected because without it, there would be no limit to the various uses to which a plaintiff could put a fund of money. The defendant, and ultimately society at large, would be in the position of satisfying extravagant claims by severely injured plaintiffs.

It is apparent, therefore, that there was no justification for exceeding the limit of $100,000 in the case of Brian Lindal. While his injuries were different from those of the plaintiffs in the trilogy, this alone does not justify exceeding the upper limit.

V

The plaintiff argued in the Court of Appeal and in this Court that, even assuming that the trial Judge erroneously exceeded the limit of $100,000, changes in economic circumstances since judgment was given in April 1978, justified an award of $135,000.

Account may be taken of inflation in awarding damages and it is not suggested that the figure of $100,000 should not vary in response to economic conditions, in particular, the debasement of purchasing power as a result of inflation.

In the present case, inflation is not a significant factor. The trial judgment was delivered in April 1978, some four months after the judgments in the trilogy and it is conceded there was no measurable increase in inflation during this brief period. I do not think in the circumstances that the award of the trial Judge can be supported on the basis of inflation.

In the result, in my view, the disposition of the Court of Appeal was correct. The appropriate level of damages for non-pecuniary loss in this case is $100,000.

VI

I would dismiss the appeal with costs. In response to the request and agreement of counsel, I would also order that the damages awarded by the trial Judge for loss of future income be increased by adding interest set out in the British Columbia *Court Order Interest Act*, RSBC 1979, c. 76, less 5%, calculated from the date of the trial judgment until payment.

Appeal dismissed.

NOTES AND QUESTIONS

1. The adoption of the functional approach can be contrasted with the conceptual approach (also termed diminution-of-value approach), still operating in the United Kingdom (even despite the exhortations of the "Pearson Commission" (*Report of the Royal Commission on Civil Liability and Compensation for Personal Injury* (London: HMSO Cmnd. 7054, 1978), paragraph 389). In *Lim Poh Choo v. Camden and Islington Area Health Authority*, [1980] AC 174 (HL (Eng.)), the plaintiff, who had suffered irremediable brain damage that left her barely

sentient, was awarded £20,000 for pain and suffering and loss of amenities. The English approach to non-pecuniary losses is explained by Lord Scarman (at 188):

> My Lords, I think it would be wrong now to reverse by judicial decision the two rules which were laid down by the majority of the House in *H. West & Son Ltd. v. Shephard*, [1964] AC 326 (HL (Eng.)), namely: (1) that the fact of unconsciousness does not eliminate the actuality of the deprivation of the ordinary experiences and amenities of life (see the formulation used by Lord Morris of Borth-y-Gest, at 349); (2) that, if damages are awarded upon a correct basis, it is of no concern to the court to consider any question as to the use that will thereafter be made of the money awarded. The effect of the two cases (*Wise v. Kaye*, [1962] 1 QB 638 (CA) being specifically approved in *H. West & Son Ltd. v. Shephar d*) is two-fold. First, they draw a clear distinction between damages for pain and suffering and damages for loss of amenities. The former depend upon the plaintiff's personal awareness of pain, her capacity for suffering. But the latter are awarded for the fact of deprivation—a substantial loss, whether the plaintiff is aware of it or not. Secondly, they establish that the award in *Benham v. Gambling*, [1941] AC 157 (HL (Eng.)) (assessment in fatal cases of damages for loss of expectation of life) is not to be compared with, and has no application to, damages to be awarded to a living plaintiff for loss of amenities.

The United Kingdom Law Commission reviewed the state of English law concerning the award of damages for non-pecuniary loss and reaffirmed the conceptual or diminution-in-value approach. It rejected the functional approach on the basis that it placed too high a burden on claimants to produce evidence of pecuniary loss in order to receive damages for non-pecuniary loss; that substitute pleasures do not account for all forms of non-pecuniary loss; and, that the functional approach was inimical to creating a tariff because the amount awarded depended upon quantifying a myriad of ways to give an individual solace. However, the Law Commission did recommend that the level of awards for non-pecuniary loss should be increased by a factor of 50 percent. *Law Commission Report: Damages for Personal Injury—Non-Pecuniary Loss* (London: Law Com. No. 257, 1999), para. 2.5. In *Heil v. Rankin*, [2001] QB 272, the English Court of Appeal raised the upper limit on non-pecuniary damages to between £150,000 and 200,000. D. Harris, *Remedies in Contract and Tort*, 2nd ed. (Chicago: Northwestern University Press, 2001), describes this judgment as legislation masquerading as judgment amounting to a scandal.

2. The functional approach, applied to the unaware plaintiff, a person who is biologically alive but permanently unconscious, has the potential, at least, to result in a zero award under this head of damages. Intuitively, this is a difficult resolution for courts: see *Knutson v. Farr* (1984), 55 BCLR 145 (CA); *Wipfli v. Britten* (1984), 56 BCLR 273 (CA); leave to appeal to SCC granted (1983), 13 DLR (4th) 169n; and the case comment by G. Mew (1986), 64 *Canadian Bar Review* 562. Where a plaintiff experiences diminished capacity to be fully aware of what he or she has lost, but is still capable of sensory experiences, damages for non-pecuniary loss have generally not been reduced. See *Rothwell v. Raes* (1988), 66 OR (2d) 449 (HC); aff'd. (1990), 76 (4th) 280 (Ont. CA); leave to appeal to SCC refused [1991] 1 SCR xiii, and *Granger (Litigation Guardian of) v. Ottawa General Hospital* (1996), 7 OTC 81 (Gen. Div.).

Can you recognize the differences between the conceptual, personal, and functional approaches and do you think that the Supreme Court of Canada has given full effect to the latter approach? See Lewis N. Klar, "Developments in Tort Law: The 1981-82 Term" (1983), 5 *Supreme Court Law Review* 273, at 274 ("Lindal v. Lindal: Mixed Signals from the Supreme

Court") and Beverley M. McLachlin, "What Price Disability? A Perspective on the Law of Damages for Personal Injury" (1981), 59 *Canadian Bar Review* 1.

3. The $100,000 limitation imposed in the trilogy has been lifted by subsequent courts to take account of inflation. In *ter Neuzen v. Korn*, [1995] 3 SCR 674 the plaintiff became infected by HIV following an artificial insemination program run by the defendant obstetrician and gynaecologist. The majority of the judgment deals with the issue of liability and whether, at the time of the insemination, the defendant had fallen below a reasonable standard of care. However, the Supreme Court did address the issue of non-pecuniary damages and whether the upper limit imposed by the trilogy was applicable in this type of case. Sopinka J (giving the decision of the court, at 722) said:

> In *Andrews*, this Court set out the rationale for the upper limit placed on the assessment of non-pecuniary damages for pain and suffering. It is simply impossible to put a money value on the non-pecuniary losses which have been suffered by the plaintiff. Therefore, the award of non-pecuniary damages "is a philosophical and policy exercise more than a legal or logical one" (p. 261). This Court has adopted the "functional" approach to assessing such damages. That is, rather than attempting to evaluate the loss of happiness, non-pecuniary damages seek to provide the plaintiff with reasonable solace for the misfortune suffered. Money acts as a substitute for the pleasure and enjoyment which has been lost and endeavours to alleviate, as far as possible, the pain and suffering that the plaintiff has endured and will have to endure in the future.
>
> The amount of the award depends on the ability of money to ameliorate the condition of the victim in his or her particular situation. Non-pecuniary damages should only be awarded to the extent that they can serve a useful purpose by providing an alternative source of satisfaction.
>
> However, as Dickson J observed in *Andrews*, once non-pecuniary damages are viewed from a functional perspective, excessively large amounts should not be awarded once an individual is fully compensated in terms of future care and other pecuniary losses. Awards for non-pecuniary loss are inherently arbitrary or conventional. Therefore, once the future care of the plaintiff is adequately addressed, it is more appropriate to consider policy issues in limiting damage awards. In particular, the social burdens of excessive awards must be considered, as extravagant claims can pose a significant burden on society. In fact, in *Arnold v. Teno*, [1978] 2 SCR 287, it was observed that the real social cost of exorbitant damage awards had been particularly evident in the United States with respect to medical malpractice cases. In *Lindal*, this Court reiterated the sentiments expressed in the *Andrews* trilogy, recognizing that the claim for non-pecuniary damages in the case of a severely injured plaintiff can potentially be limitless.

The Supreme Court also indicated that at the time of judgment in this case (1995) the upper limit for non-pecuniary damages stood at $240,000. Sopinka J also indicated that it was appropriate for a trial judge to instruct a jury on the upper limit for non-pecuniary damages. L'Heureux-Dubé J disagreed on this point. In her opinion, the determination of the level of damages was a question that should be left exclusively for the jury and only be reduced by a trial judge where the award was excessive.

In Ontario, in the *Courts of Justice Act*, RSO 1990, c. C.43, s. 118, the parties may make submissions to the jury, and the court may give guidance on the appropriate level of damages in personal injury actions.

The current cap on non-pecuniary damages stands at approximately $300,000. See *Crawford (Litigation Guardian of) v. Penney* (2003), 14 CCLT (3d) 60; aff'd. (2004), 26 CCLT (3d) 246 (Ont. CA); *Lee v. Dawson* (2006), 51 BCLR (4th) 221 (BCCA).

4. The BC Law Reform Commission (LRC) has recommended the abolition of the upper limit on non-pecuniary damages. See *Report on Compensation for Non-Pecuniary Loss*, LRC 76 (1984) and S.M. Waddams, "Compensation for Non-Pecuniary Loss: Is There a Case for Legislative Intervention?" (1985), 63 *Canadian Bar Review* 734. The Ontario Law Reform Commission (OLRC) has recommended no change in the existing approach to non-pecuniary damages as applied in the trilogy. See *Report on Compensation for Personal Injuries and Death*, [1987] OLRC, at 84. In the time since the trilogy, the issue has been raised whether the cap on non-pecuniary losses for personal injury will be carried over into other forms of action where similar types of losses are experienced. For instance, it has now been established that in the case of defamation the cap will not be applied to limit non-pecuniary damages. See *Hill v. Church of Scientology of Toronto*, [1995] 2 SCR 1130. Similarly, the Supreme Court of Canada has also held that the cap does not apply in the case of compensation for mental distress, upholding a $430,000 award for the distress caused by a negligent false allegation of child abuse; see *Young v. Bella*, 2006 SCC 3. There is conflicting jurisprudence on whether the ceiling on non-pecuniary damages applies in cases of sexual assault. The BC Court of Appeal did not apply the cap in a case dealing with non-pecuniary damages flowing from a sexual assault. See *Y.(S.) v. C.(F.G.)* (1996), 26 BCLR (3d) 155. Courts in other provinces have taken different approaches. In *G. (B.M.) v. Nova Scotia (Attorney General)* (2007), 288 DLR (4th) 88, the Nova Scotia Court of Appeal affirmed the use of the functional approach to non-pecuniary damages in sexual assault cases and also held that there should be a range of awards with a ceiling comparable to other personal injury cases. In *Padfield v. Martin* (2003), 64 OR (3d) 577 (CA), the Ontario Court of Appeal refused to lift the cap on non-pecuniary damages for a plaintiff who argued that, because he would be inadequately compensated for his pecuniary loss, he was thus entitled to greater non-pecuniary damages. The plaintiff had been injured in a motor vehicle accident and thus his income replacement compensation fell to be determined under the statutory no-fault automobile scheme. The plaintiff, who was a student at the time of his accident, argued that he had the expectation of pursuing professional volleyball and the potential to earn a university scholarship. These expectations had been shattered as a result of the accident. The pecuniary award under the no-fault benefits did not give adequate recognition to these losses. In terms of a claim for loss of amenities as part of non-pecuniary loss, the jury had, to the surprise of everyone, awarded the plaintiff $500,000 damages. The trial judge had reduced these to $274,000, the maximum under the cap on non-pecuniary damages. On appeal these were further lowered to $150,000. In comparison to other similar losses experienced by competitive athletes, and bearing in mind the settlement offers that had been discussed prior to trial, an award of $274,000 was seen as excessive.

Loss of Working Capacity

The trilogy spoke of loss of earning capacity. This terminology tends to mask the real issue of providing compensation for loss of working capacity. Ken Cooper-Stephenson encapsulates the issues in the following excerpt.

Ken Cooper-Stephenson, *Personal Injury Damages in Canada*
2d ed. (Toronto: Carswell, 1996), at 205 (footnotes omitted)

(i) The Theoretical Problem

The ongoing dispute as to the title of this head of damages is often merely terminological, although some aspects of it are fundamentally substantive and illustrate the importance of language as a creator of perceptions—the power of "naming." It now seems clear that neither the notion of "earnings" nor "earning capacity" underlies this head of damages, but rather "work value" or "working capacity" in a sense that evaluates all the pecuniary losses that flow from the plaintiff's inability to work. Hence the emerging sub-heads: (1) loss of earnings; (2) loss of homemaking capacity; (3) loss of shared family income; and (possibly) (4) loss of shared family homemaking. It is becoming increasingly understood that the idea of "earning capacity," although descriptively acceptable in some circumstances, is unhelpful and may be misleading from a practical and substantive point of view. Either its meaning and content must make reference to the actual earnings that would have been received by the plaintiff or the actual work that would have been accomplished; or it evaluates an abstract ability that is divorced from reality and which may depreciate and denigrate the value of the work that has been lost.

The issue of substance behind the terminological debate begins with the question whether damages for remunerated work should be assessed on the basis of what the plaintiff as a *matter of prediction would in fact have earned*, or whether, on the other hand, the assessment should be based on what the plaintiff *had a capacity to earn, irrespective of whether he or she would have exercised that capacity*. In resolving the issue one is led to conclude that "earnings" as such should not be the focus of the inquiry, but instead valuable "work." However, even accepting this conceptual shift it remains necessary to resolve the question whether the plaintiff's abstract capacity to perform valuable work is the focus of assessment, or whether a prediction of what valuable work would in fact have been accomplished is the appropriate inquiry. It now seems clear that the latter is conceptually sound as the appropriate underpinning for the losses under this head. The essence of the task under this head of damages is to award compensation for any pecuniary loss which will result from an inability to work. "Loss of the value of work" is the substance of the claim-loss of the value of any work the plaintiff would have done but for the accident but now will be unable to do. The loss framed in this way may be measured in different ways. Sometimes it will be measured by reference to the *actual earnings* the plaintiff would have received; sometimes by a *replacement cost evaluation of tasks* which the plaintiff will now be unable to perform; sometimes by an assessment of reduced *company profits*; and sometimes by the amount of secondary income lost, such as *shared family income*.

Teno v. Arnold
[1978] 2 SCR 287

SPENCE J: ... I turn next to the consideration of an award to cover the income which the infant plaintiff would have earned had she grown to womanhood and joined the work force.

This amount was not separately assessed or considered by the learned trial judge although he did emphasize in discussing the global award that it would have to be made to cover the plaintiff's own living costs even apart from the award to cover the special care, with which I have already dealt, as "she has been deprived of any opportunity to provide for herself" [at 306].

Zuber JA, in his reasons for the Court of Appeal for Ontario, assigned the sum of $115,000 to cover this loss of future income. His reasons for doing so are set out in one paragraph which I quote [at 602]:

> Diane Teno is entitled to be compensated for the loss of future income she would have earned but for this accident. Inherent in this statement, there is the obvious difficulty of selecting the income she would have earned. In view of Diane's age, obviously no evidence could be tendered as to what in fact her potential earnings might have been. It was disclosed in evidence that Diane's mother, Yvonne, was a teacher, earning in excess of $10,000. In the absence of any other guide, the trial Judge rightly used this as some indication of Diane's potential. It would not be unreasonable to assume that she would begin earning money at age 19 and continue to a retirement age of 65. The capital sum required as of the date of trial, to produce that income, between those ages, using a 5% interest rate, is $115,500. It is now settled law that in arriving at an award to compensate for future loss of income, the effect of income tax is not to be considered: *Regina v. Jennings*.

The allowance of an amount for loss of future income in the present case is extremely difficult. The plaintiff at the time of her injury was a 4½-year-old child. There can be no evidence whatsoever which will assist us in determining whether she ever would have become a member of the work force or whether she would have grown up in her own home and then married. There can be no evidence upon which we may assess whether she would have had a successful business future or have been a failure. Since the court is bound not to act on mere speculation, I do not see how this court could approve the course taken by Zuber JA, which simply amounted to assuming, as he quite frankly said, in "the absence of any other guide," that the infant plaintiff would follow the course of her mother who was a primary school teacher with an income of $10,000 per year. On the other hand, I do not think we can assume that a bright little girl would not grow up to earn her living and would be a public charge, and we are not entitled to free the defendants, who have been found guilty of negligence, from the payment of some sum which would be a present value of the future income which I think we must assume that the infant plaintiff would earn. It must be remembered that the allowance for future care provides only for the cost of attendants and that like everyone else the infant plaintiff has to eat, clothe herself and shelter herself.

If there is no allowance for the loss of future income, then the fund from which her ordinary living costs would be supplied would have to come from the amount awarded for non-pecuniary damages, and there can be no excuse for depriving the infant plaintiff of an allowance for those non-pecuniary damages, fixed in a fashion which I shall discuss hereafter, by requiring her to use those non-pecuniary damages to live on. The problem has caused concern in many other cases. Lord Denning in *Taylor v. Bristol Omnibus Co.*, [1975] 1 WLR 1054 (CA) dealt with a claim for loss of future income by a boy 3½ years old at the time of the accident. At p. 1059 he said:

3 Loss of Future Earnings

The judge assumed that Paul would start earning at the age of 19. He took the yardstick of his father's position. He took an average figure of £2,000 a year and used a multiplier of 16. Thus making £32,000. Less one-half for present payment: making £16,000.

Counsel for the defendants urged us to adopt a new attitude in regard to babies who are injured. He suggested that the loss of future earnings was so speculative that, instead of trying to calculate it, we should award a conventional sum of say £7,500. He suggested that we might follow the advice given by Lord Devlin in *H. West & Son Ltd. v. Shephard*, [1964] AC 326 (HL (Eng.)) at 357, that is: (i) give him such a sum as will ensure that for the rest of his life, this boy will not, within reason, want for anything that money can buy; (ii) give him, too, compensation for pain and suffering and loss of amenities; (iii) but do not, in addition, give him a large sum for loss of future earnings. At this very young age these are speculative in the extreme. Who can say what a baby boy will do with his life? He may be in charge of a business and make much money. He may get into a mediocre groove and just pay his way. Or he may be an utter failure. It is even more speculative with a baby girl. She may marry and bring up a large family, but earn nothing herself. Or, she may be a career woman, earning high wages. The loss of future earnings for a baby is so speculative that I am much tempted to accept the suggestion of counsel for the defendants.

In David A. McI. Kemp and Margaret Sylvia Kemp on *The Quantum of Damages* (London: Sweet & Maxwell, 1975) at p. 135, in a paragraph entitled "Where the plaintiff is a child or youth and has not commenced on any career, and so there is no figure for net annual loss at the date of the trial," it is stated that in that class of case the court is really reduced to pure guesswork. Lord Denning, in the statement of *Taylor v. Bristol Omnibus Co.* which I have quoted, cites the argument of counsel that there should be awarded "a conventional sum of say £7,500."

As I have said, I think we must make an award of some sum but we have no guidance whatsoever in the fixation of that sum. It would seem to me that we are entitled to say that the infant plaintiff would not have become a public charge. To award an annual loss of income of the sum of $5,000 is to make an award of an amount which, in the present economic state, is merely on the poverty level, yet I cannot justify an award based on an amount of $10,000 as did Zuber JA. I think that we would be doing justice to both plaintiff and defendants, and I find it equitable, to determine that the infant plaintiff would, at least, have earned $7,500 per year for her business life.

As I have already pointed out, this court in *Regina v. Jennings* found that there should be no deduction for income tax from the amount allowed for loss of future income.

I am of the view that annual amounts should only be calculated from the time the infant plaintiff would have reached 20 years of age until she would have reached the normal retirement age in industry today of 65 years. Moreover, when we assume that the plaintiff would have been a wage earner, we must also consider that all wage earners are faced with possibilities of failure through illness short of death, financial disasters, personality defects, and other causes. I, therefore, believe that we should allow a 20 per cent contingency deduction from the $7,500 to make a net annual loss of income of $6,000, and then calculate the present value of payments of $6,000 commencing at the time the infant plaintiff would have attained the age of 20 years and continuing until she would have reached 65 years. That present value, in my view, should be calculated at the same discount rate of 7 per cent as the present value of the amount provided for future care for the reasons which I have discussed above. This calculation appears hereafter in my summary.

NOTES

The issue of how to quantify the loss of working capacity of young children has come before the courts on a number of occasions. Courts have sanctioned a number of factors that may give guidance in determining what appropriate career and future income stream may have eventuated. For example, in *Dubé (Litigation Guardian of) v. Penlon Ltd.* (1994), 21 CCLT (2d) 268 (Ont. Gen. Div.), the court looked at the educational attainments of the plaintiff's parents and siblings. In *Houle v. Calgary (City)* (1985), 60 AR 366 (CA), the court accepted the following as relevant: youth's school and motivation, his or her family income; father's occupation, education, and income; the plaintiff's own IQ; social class; the mother's education; the number and place in the birth order of siblings; and the stability of his or her family life.

Another emerging problem is whether the assessment process should simply mirror inequalities in earning levels between men and women and how should changes in the labour markets that have tended to close the gap in salary levels be accommodated in the damage assessment process for young children. Consider the varying approach of the trial and appellate courts with respect to this issue in the following case.

MacCabe v. Westlock Roman Catholic School District No. 110
[2002] 1 WWR 610, 2001 ABCA 257

[The plaintiff, who was 16 at the time of her tragic accident, was injured while taking part in a gymnastics class at school. The accident rendered the plaintiff a quadriplegic. By the time her case came on for trial the plaintiff had completed a university degree in Recreational Administration. The main issue on appeal was the appropriateness of using male earning tables and contingency deductions in quantifying compensation for loss of working capacity.]

WITTMANN JA:

[80] The only aspect of the damages award under appeal is the learned trial judge's method of calculating MacCabe's loss of future earning capacity.

[81] In assessing loss of future earning capacity, the learned trial judge found MacCabe would have been able to attain her pre-accident desire to become a physiotherapist had the accident not occurred. In addition, she also found, despite very serious injuries, MacCabe finished high school and continued on to successfully complete a university degree in Recreational Administration. At the time of the trial, MacCabe had additional academic goals including pursuit of a master's degree.

[82] The probability of MacCabe securing long-term employment in her post-accident condition generated extensive evidence at trial. There was conflicting expert evidence in this regard. Dr. Christopher Bruce, an economist, was of the view MacCabe's long-term employability was severely compromised by her disabilities rendering her competitively unemployable (at 112 para. 443).

[83] The learned trial judge did not accept MacCabe would never work as this was, in her view, contrary to the evidence. She found (at 112 para. 446) MacCabe demonstrated high motivation, a very strong academic performance and a strong desire to work. Nonetheless, she also found MacCabe had severe limitations on her ability to work due to fatigue and various other medical conditions related to her injury. Considering all of these factors, the learned trial judge determined MacCabe's employability potential was at best 50 per cent. In addition, due to many constraints on MacCabe's time and energy, she found (at 113 para. 449) MacCabe would likely work 60 per cent of full time, retire at age 52, and work in the area of health promotion or recreation administration during her working life. None of these findings were appealed.

[84] The controversial aspect of the learned trial judge's calculation of damages is the quantification of MacCabe's loss of future earning capacity. As has been said many times, this determination involves some crystal ball gazing as the court is burdened with the task of deciding what career path and other life choices MacCabe would have taken which could have impacted her earnings. As this Court recently stated in *Olson v. General Accident Assurance Co. of Canada*, [2001] AJ No. 414 at para. 24:

> Damages for loss of earning capacity are awarded when there is evidence demonstrating that the injuries will, or are likely to, impair a plaintiff's future earning capacity with regard to his previous occupation: *Cook v. Benson Lobster Co. Ltd.* (1990), 105 NBR (2d) 265 (CA). The proof need not be that the future loss will likely occur, but that there is a "real and substantial possibility and not mere speculation" that the loss will occur: *Athey* ..., at 470; *Graham v. Rourke* (1990), 74 DLR (4th) 1 (Ont. CA) at 12-13.

[85] A trial judge's determination of the future loss need not be precise. This Court will not intervene on the basis that a different, reasonable way to allow for losses or calculate damages is possible. The test is whether the method to quantify the future loss adopted by a trial judge was "unreasonable by such a clear margin that an appeal court, which saw none of the witnesses, should intervene": *Madge v. Meyer*, [2001] AJ No. 492 (CA) at para. 11.

[86] Based on MacCabe's stated intentions, the learned trial judge determined at 119 [para. 477] had the accident not occurred, MacCabe would have become a physiotherapist, secured long term employment at a hospital and retired at age 65. This was quantified as the amount MacCabe would have earned as a physiotherapist at a hospital.

1. Male Versus Female Data

[87] The appellants urged the court to use female specific earning tables. MacCabe argued that use of female tables is potentially discriminatory. The learned trial judge agreed and refused to adopt female specific statistics. I quote from her reasons at 117-8 (paras. 469-470) at length as her approach is unique:

> It is entirely inappropriate that any assessment I make continues to reflect historic wage inequities. I cannot agree more with Chief Justice McEachern of the British Columbia Court of Appeal in *Tucker* [(*Public Trustee of*) v. *Asleson* (1993), 78 BCLR (2d) 173 (BCCA)] that the courts must ensure as much as possible that the appropriate weight be given to societal trends in the labour market in order that the future loss of income properly reflects future circumstances. Where we differ is that I will not sanction the "reality" of pay inequity. The societal trend is and

must embrace pay equity given our fundamental right to equality which is entrenched in the constitution. The courts have judicially recognized in tort law the historical discriminatory wage practices between males and females. The courts have endeavoured to alleviate this discrimination with the use of male or female wage tables modified with either negative or positive contingencies. However, I am of the view that these approaches merely mask the problem; how can the court embrace pay inequity between males and females? I cannot apply a flawed process which perpetuates a discriminatory practice. The application of the contingencies, although in several cases reduce the wage gap, still sanction the disparity.

A growing understanding of the extent of discriminatory wage practices and the effect of the societal inequity must lead the court to retire an antiquated or limited judicial yardstick and embrace a more realistic and expansive measurement legally grounded in equality. Equality is now a fundamental constitutional value in Canadian society … .

… The court cannot sanction future forecasting if it perpetuates the historic wage disparity between men and women. Accordingly, if there is a disparity between the male and female statistics in the employment category I have determined for the plaintiff the male statistics shall be used, subject to the relevant contingencies. Once again if the contingencies are gender specific, then the contingencies applicable to males shall be used except in the case of life expectancy, for obvious reasons.

[88] The appellants contested this reasoning before this Court framing the issue as:

Did the learned trial judge err in finding that male earnings statistics and male contingences should be used in calculating the female respondent's future loss of income?

[89] The appellants made a variety of submissions why it was inappropriate to use male earning data in calculating MacCabe's loss of future earnings. In their view, applying male statistics, particularly, male contingencies, unrealistically inflated MacCabe's potential earnings. In addition, they argued that in attempting to rectify the social wrong of pay inequity, the learned trial judge ignored the tort principle of compensatory damages, the *restitutio in integrum* principle. The appellants argued if the discrepancy in women's compensation is a matter of evidence reflecting reality, they should not have to pay higher damages as a result of these inequities.

2. Evidence of Gender Earning Discrepancies

[90] In Alberta, physiotherapists, employed in a hospital setting, as union members subject to a collective agreement, are remunerated regardless of gender. The base line income used in this case was not controversial. All other things being equal, male and female physiotherapists employed in an Alberta hospital are paid the same. The problem arises in the application of negative contingencies, particularly, non-participation rates, generally called contingencies, for female, as opposed to male physiotherapists, unemployment and part time work in general.

[91] The court was provided with numerous tables. One table set out male contingencies and another, female contingencies applicable to the work of physiotherapists. Other tables set out MacCabe's post-accident earning potential in the fields of recreation administration and health promotion. The figures for MacCabe's post-accident earnings were calculated to comply with the findings that she was 50 per cent employable, would work part time at 60

per cent and would retire at age 52. To determine MacCabe's actual loss of future earnings, her likely post-accident earnings must be subtracted from her pre-accident earning potential. In calculating MacCabe's post-accident earnings, the parties took the mid-point between recreational administration and health promotion earnings, the two careers determined to be the most likely for MacCabe.

[92] The numbers below were provided by counsel to the court as calculated by Gerry Taunton of PETA Consultants Ltd. As the base line salary between male and female physio-therapists is the same, the only differences are the negative contingencies:

Pre-Accident—Present Value:
Physiotherapist I—working in a hospital setting until age 65
    Male contingencies—$1,016,428   Female contingencies—$828,008

Post-Accident—Present Value:
Recreation administration—working 40% part-time at 50% employability until age 52
    Male contingencies—$178,747   Female contingencies—$158,080

Health promotion—working 40% part-time at 50% employability until age 52
    Male contingencies—$202,485   Female contingencies—$163,778

Average or mid-point between recreational administration and health promotion:
    Male contingencies—$190,616   Female contingencies—$160,929

Total Loss of Earnings Calculation:
Male calculation: $1,016,428 [minus] $190,616 = $825,812
Female calculation: $828,008 [minus] $160,929 = $667,079

Total Difference Between Male and Female Calculations
$825,812 [minus] $667,079 = $158,733

[93] Given the total value of this claim, over $4 million, the difference of $158,733 be-tween the male and female contingencies is not large. The parties led evidence and the trial proceeded on the basis that either male or female contingencies would apply.

[94] Determination of negative contingencies based upon a classification according to sex is not unreasonable in these circumstances. The situation is analogous to the use of ac-tuarial tables based on sex, age or marital status to determine insurance premium rates for drivers of motor vehicles.

[95] In *Zurich Insurance Co. v. Ontario (Human Rights Commission)*, [1992] 2 SCR 321, a complaint had been made that the practice of the insurance company which charged un-married, under 25 years of age male drivers higher car insurance rates, engaged in prohibited discrimination practices. The Supreme Court of Canada recognized that insurance rates based on statistics relating to the degree of risk associated with a class or group of persons ran counter to the human rights concept that an individual has a right to be dealt with on his or her own merits and not on the basis of group characteristics. An important principle of insurance premium determination is that premiums charged to policy holders should vary in accordance with the degree of risk posed by the policy holder. The majority held that to determine the degree of risk, it is necessary to determine risk on the basis of groups sharing

characteristics material to the risk. In some cases, individuals would not share the average characteristics and the rate discriminated against them. However, an insurance rating scheme based on class or group classifications is a permissible conflict with human rights legislation when it was based on sound and accepted insurance practice and there is no practical alternative.

[96] Similarly, in the case of contingencies, the use of statistical tables is employed to make a prediction of the future loss of income for an injured plaintiff. Different calculations of future loss are based upon different class or group characteristics. The plaintiff's membership in a particular class or group is used as a basis to make a prediction which reflects the individual. Depending on the evidence, particularly the lack of evidence about the individual, it is usually appropriate to resort to class or group tables. In this case, there was no practical alternative to the use of statistical tables predicting the time spent outside the paid workforce based upon an individual's gender.

[97] In reviewing the decision below, the first step is to consider what evidence and argument the learned trial judge had before her to determine the appropriateness of applying male contingencies.

3. Negative Contingencies

[98] There are three negative contingencies applicable to both men and women in the tables provided. These are non-participation in the labour force, unemployment and part-time work. In his report dated September 20, 1997, Taunton described these contingencies and his method of calculation as follows (AB3987-3988):

Non-Participation in the Labour Force—this is the first of three negative labour market contingencies which have been incorporated into the analysis. Participation rates measure the propensity of individuals to be working or (if not working) actively seeking work.

Factors normally explaining withdrawal from the labour market include voluntary retirement, temporary absences to care for other family members or to pursue other interests (i.e. education, travel) and involuntary withdrawal for reasons of illness/sickness/disability.

Unemployment—data are available from the 1991 census, documenting rates of unemployment amongst Alberta females with a bachelor's degree (other than law) by five year age cohort. These rates were converted to single year values through simple mathematical interpolation and adjusted by the ratio of the long-term rate of unemployment in Alberta to the rate prevailing in the 1991 Census year.

Part-Time Work—the part-time factor for Alberta females with a bachelor's degree (other than law) are derived from 1991 Census data, with conversion to single year data using simple mathematical interpolation.

The September 1997 report differed from the numbers set out above (in para. 94) because the latter was produced with specific direction from the trial judge. In addition, Taunton had 1996-97 Census data available for the later report. Nonetheless, these descriptions assist in understanding what the negative contingencies address.

[99] In assessing the applicability of the negative contingencies, the court and the expert witness also had relevant information from MacCabe herself. She indicated a desire to have

as many as four children and that she might stay home with those children until they were in school (AB 1703-1704). According to MacCabe, this would have been her "ideal wish" (AB 1703). When cross examined on this, MacCabe said:

> Q Okay. Ms. MacCabe, you told Suzanne Lancaster that it was your wish to have four children?
>
> A Ideal wish, yes.
>
> Q I'm sorry?
>
> A An ideal wish, yes.
>
> Q And your experience thus far with children has been holding other people's small children?
>
> A Since my injury, yes. Prior to that with my sister's children, yeah.
>
> Q Okay. Now, I believe you've indicated to us earlier that your goal before the accident was to go on to university and to work in the rehabilitation field?
>
> A That's right.
>
> Q Okay. Prior to the accident, had you considered what you would do if you had children later on?
>
> A No concrete plans. I had maybe thought of following the same protocols that my sisters had followed, which they stayed home until their kids went to school and then went back to work, but I haven't made any concrete plans, no.

[100] How is this "ideal wish" to be factored in? What is the probability that this is the course MacCabe's life would have taken? It is rare for families to have four children in modern Canadian society; in addition, many families depend on two incomes making it difficult for either parent to choose to stay at home.

[101] Additionally, evidence from Dr. Bruce established that while women continue to be more likely than men to work part time, working part time declines as education increases (AB 1818). Further, Dr. Bruce testified that women's participation rates in the work force have increased dramatically over the last 20 to 30 years and again, those participation rates rise with education and income. MacCabe, who is very highly educated with plans to pursue even more education, would likely form a strong attachment to her work. Because of these factors, Dr. Bruce felt it reasonable to present the court with data that reflected what she would have earned if she had followed the pattern of a typical male, "which is that she didn't work part-time and that she didn't leave the labour force for a significant number of years" (AB 1819:40-42).

[102] However, MacCabe's stated preferences do not follow a typical male pattern. She testified that she wanted several children and would consider staying home with them. While I do not simply accept this statement as a certain prediction of what MacCabe would have done, this was evidence which cannot be ignored.

[103] How then do we balance MacCabe's stated intentions with the learned trial judge's concerns that courts should not sanction pay inequity and discriminatory labour practices? While the issue of pay equity per se is not at issue here (since male and female physiotherapists working in a hospital are paid on the same negotiated scale), inequitable and discriminatory societal forces impact negative contingencies. In other words, participation rates, unemployment and part-time work are not devoid of discriminatory influences.

[104] Women, by and large, continue to be and are expected to be the primary child caregivers in the family. This impinges on the way in which women work in Canadian society. As Professor Elaine Gibson articulated in "The Gendered Wage Dilemma" in K. Cooper-Stephenson and E. Gibson eds., *Tort Theory* (North York: Captus University Press, 1993) at 197-198:

> Women are constrained at present by societal roles. Primary responsibility for childrearing, homemaking, and extended family obligations provides Canadian women with less time on average to devote to wage labour and inclines them toward lower-paying but more flexible work arrangements. The typical workplace is set up to function based on traditional male labour arrangements in terms of hours of work, job security, seniority (women take time out and are disadvantaged by such interruptions as maternity leave) and ability to block out other aspects of life that are co-ordinated predominantly by women. As well, male models of competence, dress code, objectification of women in the workplace, networking and hierarchical relationships disadvantage women's opportunities for promotion. The areas of work conventionally allocated to women are seriously undervalued.
>
> [Footnotes omitted.]

[105] The learned trial judge, wrestling with these very issues, concluded it was inappropriate for the court to play any role in sanctioning, perpetuating or even accepting these "realities" of women's access to the paid labour market. In her opinion, it would be contrary to the principles of equality articulated in the *Canadian Charter of Rights and Freedoms* for the court to take this approach.

[106] The Supreme Court of Canada has stated that the common law, and therefore, tort law, must be interpreted in a manner consistent with Charter principles: *Dolphin Delivery*, [1986] 2 SCR 573. Cory J went even further to suggest revisions to the law may be appropriate when he stated in *Hill v. Church of Scientology of Toronto*, [1995] 2 SCR 1130 at 1138:

> Historically the common law evolved as a result of the courts making those incremental changes which were necessary in order to make the law comply with current societal values. The Charter represents a restatement of the fundamental values which guide and shape our democratic society and our legal system. It follows that it is appropriate for the courts to make such incremental revisions to the common law as may be necessary to have it comply with the values enunciated in the Charter.

[107] While I accept that the common law must try to be consistent with Charter values including equality, this consistency cannot be at the expense of the fundamental purposes of compensatory damages in tort law. In this case, to strictly adopt the approach taken by the learned trial judge runs the risk of ignoring, or at the very least, minimizing the essential purpose of compensatory damages in tort law.

[108] The Latin phrase *restitutio in integrum* embodies the purpose of tort damages. This phrase was explained in the frequently cited judgment of Lord Blackburn in *Livingstone v. Rawyards Coal Ltd.* (1880), 5 App. Cas. 25 (HL), where he said at 39:

> I do not think there is any difference of opinion as to its being a general rule that, where any injury is to be compensated by damages, in settling the sum of money to be given for reparation of damages you should as nearly as possible get at that sum of money which will put the party

who has been injured, or who has suffered, in the same position as he would have been in if he had not sustained the wrong for which he is now getting compensation. ...

[109] Given this accepted principle, I find that applying male contingencies ignores the stated desire of MacCabe to have children and stay at home. Ignoring such evidence potentially inflates her damage award by putting her in a better position than if she had not "sustained the wrong." The situation may be different if she had testified she had no desire to have children or if she stated an intention not to absent herself from the workforce for any reason. If that were the case, it may be inappropriate to rely on female contingencies known to have a discriminatory element. Indeed, counsel for the appellants conceded in argument that there may be cases where male actuarial tables ought to be applied to female victims, if the evidence supports it.

[110] Quantifying damages requires examining the evidence to determine what the individual in question likely would have earned. In this case, the evidence we have, upon which to decide some of the negative contingencies appropriate for this individual, is her uncontradicted testimony. This contrasts with many of the cases cited which have contended with the use of male and female earning tables where such evidence is different or lacking. Still, it is instructive to observe how other courts have dealt with similar issues.

4. Jurisprudence on Gendered Earnings

[111] Several cases have dealt with the appropriateness of gendered earning tables. One much discussed case is the decision in *Toneguzzo-Norvell (Guardian ad litem of) v. Burnaby Hospital* (SCC); reversing, in part, (1992), 73 BCLR (2d) 116 (BCCA); reversing, in part, [1991] BCJ No. 2206, June 24, 1991, Doc. Vancouver C893067 (BCSC). In that case, the plaintiff, Jessica Toneguzzo-Norvell, suffered extreme oxygen deprivation during birth as a result of the attending physician's negligence. Jessica was severely brain damaged rendering her deaf and blind, incapable of voluntary motor activity, lacking any cognitive ability and prone to life threatening epileptic seizures. One issue was the quantum of damages Jessica should receive for her lost earning capacity.

[112] At trial, the court was presented with several tables of projected earnings. These tables forecast income levels for women with a high school diploma, women with post-secondary non-university training and comparable tables for men. The tables included discounts for unemployment, part time and non-participation rates. Tables were also provided for single women in these categories without deducting the "voluntary" part time work for females. The trial court decided to award loss of earning capacity based on the table for women with post-secondary non-university training. Evidence at trial was that this table represented women who were inclined to focus more on family than on career, whereas the tables for single women represented women who focussed primarily on career. The court treated the possibility that earning levels for women may increase over time to become more on par with male earnings as a positive contingency to be considered along with other positive and negative contingencies. In the result, the court awarded $292,758 under this head of damages.

[113] At the Court of Appeal, this amount was reduced by 50 per cent to reflect deductions for living expenses. Before the Supreme Court of Canada, one issue was whether it was

appropriate for the trial judge to have relied on the gendered earning tables at all and whether the tables for male earnings would have been more appropriate.

[114] The Supreme Court declined to decide this issue since the appropriate evidence had not been placed before the trial judge and therefore, they could not decide whether or not male earning tables should have been used. The Supreme Court restored the trial judge's assessment of life expectancy, but maintained the 50 per cent reduction implemented by the Court of Appeal against her lost earnings award. Although all three courts faced questions regarding reliance on gendered earning capacity tables, no resolution was reached. Arguably, however, *Toneguzzo* opened the door for such arguments to be made.

[115] The appropriateness of gendered earning tables was more fully addressed in *Tucker v. Aselson* (1991), 86 DLR (4th) 73 (BCSC); affirmed, (1993), 102 DLR (4th) 518 (BCCA). There, the plaintiff, an eight-year-old girl, suffered a permanent and disabling brain injury from a motor vehicle accident. The plaintiff argued that she would have been capable of achieving any goal and any career and thus, the appropriate measure of damages was the average lifetime earnings of a male university graduate in British Columbia: $947,000. The defendant argued the appropriate measure was the lifetime earnings of female university graduates in BC which was $302,000.

[116] The trial court accepted, at 137-138, that "the measure of the plaintiff's earning capacity should not be limited by statistics based upon her sex" and used, as a starting point, the figure provided for average male incomes. However, the trial judge dramatically reduced the award by 63 per cent to reflect the contingency the plaintiff would not reach her potential and would not attain a university degree. The final award under this head of damages was $350,000, barely over the amount indicated on the female earning tables.

[117] The decision was upheld on appeal, but a strong dissent was written by McEachern CJBC rejecting the idea of basing a female plaintiff's lost earnings on actuarial evidence of male earnings. McEachern CJBC, however, allowed for the positive contingency that women will likely move closer to wage parity with men in the future.

[118] More recent cases confronted with this issue include *Terranciano (Guardian ad litem of) v. Etheridge*, [1997] BCJ No. 1051 (SC), where a 16-year-old girl was rendered a paraplegic in a motor vehicle accident. The defendant urged the court to adopt average female earnings as the appropriate measure of loss of future income. The court rejected this approach at para. 80 saying:

> Apart from the fact that these statistics perpetuate historical inequality between men and women in average earning ability, and that they have hidden in them various discounts for lower and sporadic participation in the labour market which are duplicated by many of the negative contingencies used only by economists to massage the numbers downward, such statistics may provide little assistance in predicting the future of a particular female plaintiff.

[119] In the recent British Columbia Supreme Court decision, *Audet (Guardian ad litem of) v. Bates*, [1998] BCJ No. 678, the female plaintiff asphyxiated during birth due to the attending physician's negligence. The resulting cerebral palsy meant she would never be able to work. The court was faced with quantifying her loss of future earning capacity. Evidence before the court included earning tables calculating the present value of future earnings for men and women. The earning tables indicated that a female of the plaintiff's age who obtained a university degree would make $489,000 based on present values, while a male

would make $833,000. Assuming more than one year of post-secondary education, a female would earn $466,000, while a male would earn $766,000. The court found at para. 76 "no logical or compelling reason to differentiate between male and female earning capacity when making an assessment in relation to an infant whose work and education prospects cannot be identified or characterized with any precision." Regardless of this conclusion, the court took into account that the plaintiff might choose to marry and raise a family and discounted the award by 30 per cent for total of $560,000. Reasons for the 30 per cent discount were vague. No justification for choosing the particular number were given and the trial judge merely indicated it represented contingencies for lifestyle choice and the possibility the plaintiff may at some time engage in some type of employment.

[120] In *Gray v. Macklin*, [2000] OJ No. 4603 (SC), the trial judge dealing with the appropriateness of using female or male earning tables, focussed on the likelihood that wage parity would soon exist in Canada. On this point, Shaughnessy J said at para. 197:

> I find that there has been sufficient evidence adduced to indicate that wage parity will occur in the future. However, what is not predictable, is when it will occur. On balance it is open to the Court to view the wage parity as a positive contingency, which justifies an award higher than might otherwise be the case, or alternatively, to adopt the male tables and then apply a negative contingency to reflect that the goal of wage parity may not be completely achieved for a number of years in the future. On balance I prefer and choose to use the statistical male wage tables and apply a negative contingency. In my opinion it reflects the fairest approach in the circumstances consistent with the evidence. In doing so I am mindful that it is inappropriate for an assessment of damages to reflect historic wage inequities.

[121] While adopting male earning tables, the trial judge in *Gray v. Macklin* also applied several negative contingencies, deducting 10 per cent to reflect the possibility that wage parity would not be achieved and at para. 203, deducting 20 per cent as a general contingency "to take into account labour force interruptions, early retirement, sickness, accident, career changes or unemployment." No comment was made whether there was evidence to support this 20 per cent number or whether it was gender specific. The court described this negative contingency as a usual general contingency of life which was likely to be the common future of us all. This language suggests there was no gender specificity in the quantification, although one may query whether so high a percentage would have been applied to a male plaintiff.

[122] These cases show that courts generally accept that wage statistics reflect historic wage inequities. The applications of contingencies have been inconsistent because the evidence and arguments presented to the courts have been inconsistent, but Canadian courts have been more sympathetic to applying male statistics when awarding damages for loss of future earning capacity where the plaintiff is a catastrophically injured infant with no opportunity to express a view on the course her life might have taken.

5. Conclusion on Damages

[123] Assessing damages for loss of future earning capacity involves the hazardous exercise of predicting a person's future had he or she not been injured. This task is more difficult when the person is young and without an established earning pattern from which to make

a projection. The learned trial judge in this case also sought to avoid using wage statistics that she said perpetuate inequities in the labour market and in society's treatment of women.

[124] The appellants invited guidelines from this Court on the appropriateness of using male earning statistics and male negative contingencies to assess damages for a female because, as evident from the wide variety of approaches taken in the cases cited above, there is no uniform methodology. However, I need not make that determination because in this case, the application of female contingencies would not perpetuate or sanction historical and societal discrimination. Further, wage statistics perpetuate nothing. Valid data reflects historical reality.

[125] In general, tort law and in particular, the quantification of damages necessitates an individual approach. This is where I find the learned trial judge erred. In attempting to rectify potential inequities in the methods for quantifying damages, the learned trial judge neglected to focus on the evidence and the individual actually before her. While principles of equality should inform tort law, the learned trial judge's application of equitable principles resulted in her ignoring some of the relevant material facts.

[126] In this case, based on the evidence, it was not reasonable to calculate MacCabe's damages based on male contingencies. MacCabe stated she wanted to have children and would have preferred to stay at home with them for some period. This meant she would not have worked a pattern typical for male physiotherapists. There was no evidence to indicate it was more likely that MacCabe would not have had children and chosen not to take time off from full time paid employment as a physiotherapist. Thus, it would be inappropriate to apply male contingencies to her when there was no evidentiary basis that she would have worked a typical male pattern.

[127] While I do not forecast that MacCabe would have had four children and stayed at home until all of them were in school, the fact that she expressed this preference cannot be ignored and supports the appropriateness of applying female contingencies since they reflect the likelihood that women will take time out of the paid workforce, and in particular, more accurately reflect that this individual female likely would have taken time out of the paid workforce.

IX. Relief

[128] The appeal is allowed on the issue of contributory negligence, resulting in 25 per cent assessed against the respondent, and 75 per cent against the appellants. The appeal on the quantum of damages for loss of future earnings is allowed to the extent that the female negative contingencies for non-participation, unemployment and part time work are to be applied to the loss of future earnings claim. According to my calculation, the loss of future earnings claim, therefore, is assessed at $667,079.

NOTES

See also J. Cassels, "(In)equality and the Law of Tort: Gender, Race, and the Assessment of Damages" (1975), 17 *Advocates' Q* 158; E. Adjin-Tettey, "Replicating and Perpetuating Inequalities in Personal Injury Claims Through Female-Specific Contingencies" (2004), 49 *McGill LJ* 309; E. Gibson, "The Gendered Wage Dilemma in Personal Injury Damages," in K. Cooper-

Stephenson and E. Gibson, eds., *Tort Theory* (Toronto: Captus Press, 1993), 185; and M. Mc-Innes, "The Gendered Earnings Proposal in Tort Law" (1998), 77 *Can. Bar Rev.* 152.

A problem similar to that of assessing a young person's future income profile is experienced in determining the loss of earning capacity of a homemaker. Consider the quantification of damages under this head in the following case.

Fenn v. City of Peterborough
(1979), 25 OR (2d) 399, at 454 (CA); aff'd. [1981] 2 SCR 613

(d) Basic Costs of Living: Lost Earning Capacity

It is now appropriate to return to an issue which the learned trial Judge doubtless had in mind when he allowed an unspecified amount for loss of income within the assessment of general damages at $250,000. The amounts assessed under the prior heading of future care include nothing for the basic cost of living, *i.e.*, food and shelter, etc., until Sandra Fenn reaches 65 years of age, at which point the cost of institutional care is provided.

Prior to the explosion, Sandra Fenn was not employed in the sense that she earned a wage from an outside source. She was, however, employed, and one might say gainfully, in the care of her family and the management of her household. This household, funded by the earnings of Gerard Fenn, provided Sandra Fenn with a modest but comfortable living. The explosion destroyed not only the Fenn house but the household as well. The marriage was unable to withstand the tragedy heaped upon it and without the fault of either Gerard or Sandra Fenn, crumbled. The plaintiff Sandra Fenn is now left without support or any realistic likelihood of ever being supported by her husband. Her injuries have rendered her utterly incapable of supporting herself.

It appears that this issue can be approached in either one of two ways and each leads to substantially the same result. The funds necessary to provide for the basic living costs can be classed simply as part of the cost of future care made necessary as a result of the explosion. Dickson J, in *Andrews*, having spoken of moderation in the assessment of non-pecuniary damages, included this significant sentence at p. 261:

> Money can provide for proper care: this is the reason that I think the paramount concern of the courts when awarding damages for personal injuries should be to assure that there will be adequate future care.

The loss of basic living expenses is a pecuniary loss. The appellants who seek moderation in non-pecuniary damages in accord with the principles enunciated in *Andrews*, *Teno* and *Thornton*, must surely yield to the counterbalancing principle of full compensation for pecuniary losses.

On the other hand, the matter might be approached as an assessment of damages for the lost earning capacity of Sandra Fenn. Support for this approach is found in the words of Spence J, in *Teno*, who said at p. 328:

> I turn next to the consideration of an award to cover the income which the infant plaintiff would have earned had she grown to womanhood and joined the work force. This amount was not separately assessed or considered by the learned trial judge although he did emphasize in

> discussing the global award that it would have to be made to cover the plaintiff's own living costs even apart from the award to cover the special care with which I have already dealt as "she had been deprived of an opportunity to provide for herself."

And at pp. 329-30:

> If there is no allowance for the loss of future income, then the fund from which her ordinary living costs would be supplied would have to come from the amount awarded for non-pecuniary damages and there can be no excuse for depriving the infant plaintiff of an allowance for those non-pecuniary damages fixed in a fashion which I shall discuss hereafter by requiring her to use those non-pecuniary damages to live on.

The remaining problem is the selection of an amount. There is no helpful employment history of Sandra Fenn to be used as a guide. We select the figure of $6,000 per year as a reasonable estimate of her earning capacity, a figure barely above the poverty level and a figure which is consistent with the approach used by Spence J in *Teno*. Further, the sum of $6,000 a year is a reasonable, if somewhat arbitrary, estimate of her basic living expenses. Thus this sum, it seems to us, can be justified on either basis. Using the actuarial evidence supplied, the provision of this sum from the date of trial until Sandra Fenn reaches age 65, using a 3% discount rate, would cost $154,105. Age 65 is significant as the customary end of one's working life expectancy and in this case the age at which the trial Judge estimated Sandra Fenn would require institutional care. Thus, the termination date will be the same whether this annual sum is classed as the cost of basic living expenses or as lost earning capacity.

The way to quantify damages for impairment of housekeeping capacity has been discussed in *Fobel v. Dean* (1991), 83 DLR (4th) 385 (Sask. CA), leave to appeal to SCC denied (1992), 87 DLR (4th) vii (note). In that case, the plaintiff's injuries, which left her experiencing chronic pain, resulted in her being unable to perform most of her employment duties in a family-owned bakery and substantially reduced her capacity to perform housekeeping work. Speaking for the majority, Vancise JA said (at 396):

> This case requires us to define housekeeping capacity and determine the criteria to be used to calculate or quantify the loss of housekeeping capacity. ...
>
> The Supreme Court of Canada in *St. Lawrence & Ottawa R Co. v. Lett* (1885), 11 SCR 422 (albeit in another context), recognized that household services included more than domestic services and included the "care and management of a household" in an award of damages. The recognition of that fact has not, however, resulted in compensation being awarded for such loss of capacity to care and manage for the family. Awards tend to minimize the importance of such contribution and work by homemakers. The literature is full of articles which have considered the problem of fair and just compensation for loss of housekeeping capacity but awards of compensation have not reflected that concern: see Kenneth D. Cooper-Stephenson and Iwan B. Saunders, *Personal Injury Damages in Canada* (Toronto: Carswell, 1981), at pp. 213-24, fns. 49, 50, 60, 61, and 62. In examining Cooper-Stephenson and Saunders, as well as the literature, a number of approaches to quantify the loss of housekeeping capacity have been suggested:

(1) Replacement of Earning Capacity

The injured homemaker is compensated for earnings based on what she would have been able to earn had she worked outside the home. The difficulty with this approach is that compensation is determined by reference to outside activities.

(2) Opportunity Cost

The value of the homemaking is calculated in terms of benefits that the victim gave up, that is, the alternate career, in order to be able to remain or to devote time to homemaking. The obvious difficulty with such a theory is that the value of homemaking is determined not by the home-making activity itself but by some extraneous activity that could lead to widely disparate results.

(3) Replacement Cost

The homemaker is compensated for the replacement cost of substituting the functions which the homemaker would have performed had she been able to do so. Such value is determined by the marketplace.

(4) Substitute Homemaker

The homemaker is compensated for what it would cost to replace an injured homemaker to perform "all of the tasks," not just domestic labour, performed by a person of equal ability and qualifications.

(5) Catalogue of Services

A homemaker's time is assigned to a number of occupations such as chef, nurse, counsellor, etc., and that time is then multiplied by the community's fair market salary of each occupation and totalled to arrive at a weekly salary. This is an attempt to quantify non-economic activities performed inside the home by reference to comparable activities in the marketplace.

In my opinion, a combination of the substitute homemaker/catalogue services approach would permit the courts to fairly value homemaking services and award realistic compensation for such loss. One starts with the proposition that the service, even though performed inside the home and outside the marketplace, has an economic value capable of quantification. To award damages on this basis it is necessary to identify the various elements or components of home-making. To do that I have separated the homemaking function into two parts: (i) direct labour, and (ii) management. Included under the heading of direct labour are those elements which are traditionally known as "ordinary housekeeping matters" which are readily capable of replacement by paid domestic help. This category includes such things as: food preparation, cleaning, clothing and linen care, maintenance, gardening, and physical child care. The heading of management includes intangible items such as the management and organization of the household, which would include the following matters, which is not intended to be an exhaustive list: marketing (in the broadest sense including shopping for all items required for the efficient organization and operation of a home), food planning (including the determination of menus and quality and amount of food), tutorial child care, activity co-ordination and organization, health care and counselling.

It will be seen that the injured party may be physically incapacitated and unable to do those things with a direct labour component, such as physical child care, cleaning and laundry, but could perform certain managerial functions that do not require physical activity. It would be for the trial judge to determine on the facts of each case which elements or components have been impaired or lost.

How then does one compensate for such loss? So far as replacement labour is concerned, it is relatively simple and straightforward. In so far as the management component is concerned, it is not capable of precise calculation but figures and economic models exist which would assist the court in arriving at a realistic value of homemaking capacity. Various economic models have been constructed in an effort to arrive at such a valuation. ...

What one needs to do is to provide meaningful evidence to the court which enables it to evaluate the homemaking capacity in all its aspects so as to fully compensate the victim for the loss suffered. There is ample economic statistical evidence available of the amount of time spent by homemakers in the home and the economic benefit which they provide to a family which would permit a court using the approach that I have outlined to properly assess the damages and award fair and just compensation.

The OLRC in its *Report on Compensation for Personal Injuries and Death* (1987), at 48, recommended a different approach to that outlined in *Fobel v. Dean, supra*. Guided by practical concerns to assist in easy quantification of the damages for lost household services, the commission favoured a linkage between loss of capacity to perform household services with reference to the average weekly earnings in Ontario.

The quantification of damages for loss of homemaking capacity challenges a number of conceptual hurdles. As *Fobel v. Dean* reveals, most courts have accepted that loss of homemaking capacity is to be regarded as a pecuniary loss even though it is a service provided outside the money economy. This change in approach raises another question touching what services are to be included in homemaking capacity. For example, some people find gardening a pleasure, while for others it is a necessary evil. Should the inability to do gardening be included as a loss of homemaking capacity, and, if so, should it be treated as a non-pecuniary loss or a pecuniary loss? If gardening is included, should the inability to undertake volunteer work also be included, and if so, how? These questions have been the subject of debate in the respective judgments of the BC Court of Appeal in *Kroeker v. Jansen* (1995), 4 BCLR (3d) 178 (CA) and *McTavish v. MacGillivray* (2000), 74 BCLR (3d) 281 (CA).

Another hurdle arises where either other family members or the employment of outside services has not replaced the work of the homemaker. The fact that the work of the homemaker has not been replaced may indicate that it is a service that is not valued, or that it has not in fact been lost. This problem commonly occurs in claims for loss of homemaking capacity experienced before trial. Some courts treat this as a non-pecuniary loss, which will be affected by the cap on such damages. See *Lyne v. McClarty* (2003), 170 Man. R (2d) 161 (CA). Others treat it as a pecuniary loss that is calculated on a replacement services basis, regardless of the fact that the plaintiff has not incurred that expenditure. To do otherwise would penalize those without resources to purchase replacement services pending the outcome of the trial. See *McTavish v. MacGillivray*, above.

NOTES AND QUESTIONS

1. In *Teno*, the young child's loss of earning capacity was quantified as being $7,500 *per annum* which was then subject to a 20 percent contingency deduction placing her close to the poverty level. In *Fenn*, the plaintiff was given $6,000 per annum, again close to the poverty line. Do you believe these to be the appropriate levels of compensation under this heading?

2. In *Fenn*, the Ontario Court of Appeal indicated that damages for lost earning capacity and funds to provide basic living costs would each lead to substantially the same result. Is this necessarily correct and what assumptions does it make about the lost earning capacity of homemakers? What alternative ways of assessing damages for lost earning capacity of homemakers can you suggest? See Kenneth D. Cooper-Stephenson and Iwan B. Saunders, *Personal Injury Damages in Canada*, 2d ed. (Toronto: Carswell, 1996), at 288 *et seq.* and S.M. Waddams, *The Law of Damages* (Aurora, ON: Canada Law Book, 1999) (looseleaf), at paragraph 3.810 *et seq.*

3. Loss of earning capacity is calculated on a pre-accident life expectancy rather than post-accident life expectancy, which for a severely handicapped individual can be considerably shortened. The difference in life expectancies is called the "lost years." With respect to the lost years, personal living expenses are to be deducted from gross income since the plaintiff, by hypothesis, will have no living expenses during those years. In effect, the plaintiff should be left with only his or her probable savings for the period of the lost years. See Waddams, *The Law of Damages* (looseleaf), at paragraph 3.910 *et seq.* and Cooper-Stephenson, *supra*, at 357 *et seq.* The Supreme Court has recently approved the deduction of personal living expenses from the award of lost earnings during the lost years. See *Toneguzzo-Norvell v. Burnaby Hospital*, [1994] 1 SCR 114.

4. Recently, recognition has been given to claims based on "loss of shared family income." These claims are built on the argument that people who live together in a permanent relationship experience a pecuniary advantage over those living alone. The loss of opportunity to marry or enter a permanent relationship as a result of a personal injury is a real loss to a plaintiff who is therefore entitled to compensation for its loss. Lambert JA commented on this type of claim in *Reekie v. Messervey* (1989), 59 DLR (4th) 481. As the result of a car accident, the plaintiff, a 21-year-old woman, suffered injuries that rendered her a paraplegic. On the lost opportunity to marry, Lambert JA said (at 494):

Loss of Opportunity To Marry

Mr. Justice Locke, the trial judge, awarded damages of $50,000 under this heading. On this appeal, counsel for the defendants argued that no award should have been made for loss of opportunity to marry.

This aspect of the damage award was called "[l]oss of opportunity to marry" by counsel and by the trial judge. But marriage itself is not the significant point. The significance lies in the loss of an opportunity to form a permanent interdependency relationship which may be expected to produce financial benefits in the form of shared family income. Such an interdependency might have been formed with a close friend of either sex or with a person with whom a plaintiff might have lived as husband and wife, but without any marriage having taken place. Permanent financial interdependency, not marriage, is the gist of the claim. For the sake of simplicity and consistency, I will now usually call this head of loss "[l]ost opportunity of family income."

(a) Three Preliminary Points

The first point to note is that the plaintiff is entitled to be compensated for her full pecuniary loss caused by the accident. The cases where loss of opportunity to marry is discussed do not suggest otherwise. If a financial loss is suffered and it arose from the accident, then compensation must be awarded equal to the best estimate of that financial loss. The difficulty suggested by the cases is the difficulty of proving that any loss at all arose under this heading: see *Blackstock v. Patterson*,

[1982] 4 WWR 519 at p. 534, 35 BCLR 231 (BC CA); *Abbott v. Silver Star Sports Ltd.* (1986), 6 BCLR (2d) 83 (BC SC); *Newell v. Hawthornthwaite* (1988), 26 BCLR (2d) 105, 10 ACWS (3d) 21 (BC SC); and *Scarff v. Wilson* (November 25, 1988, CA006987, *per* McEachern CJBC at p. 28 [now reported 55 DLR (4th) 247, at 263; [1989] 3 WWR 259; 33 BCLR (2d) 290 (CA)].

The second point to note is that there is both a pecuniary and a non-pecuniary aspect to loss of opportunity to form a permanent interdependency relationship. The proper course is to consider the non-pecuniary aspect in the award for non-pecuniary damages, and the pecuniary aspect in the award for other pecuniary losses. Care must be taken to distinguish the two and care must be taken to avoid double compensation. Loss of the rich emotional benefits of a loving relationship must be compensated for under the heading of "non-pecuniary loss" or not at all. "Lost opportunity of family income" deals only with the financial aspects of the loss of an opportunity to form such a relationship.

The third point to note is that the existence of a marriage or the prospect of a marriage, with resultant financial benefits, is taken into account to reduce the amount of an award in fatal accident cases (see, for example, *Chapman v. Verstraete*, [1977] 4 WWR 214) and in calculating the cost of future care where some of the care will be provided by a spouse (see, for example, *Pickering v. Deakin*, [1985] 1 WWR 289 at pp. 299-300, 58 BCLR 145). So the courts have recognized, in calculations of damages, the financial benefits that may flow from a permanent interdependency relationship.

(b) The Place of Family Income Loss in the Scheme of the Whole Award

The importance of separating an award for general damages into its separate integral components was discussed by Mr. Justice Dickson in *Andrews v. Grand & Toy Alberta Ltd.* (1978), 83 DLR (3d) 452 at pp. 457-8, [1978] 2 SCR 229, [1978] 1 WWR 577 (SCC), in these words:

> The method of assessing general damages in separate amounts, as has been done in this case, in my opinion, is a sound one. It is the only way in which any meaningful review of the award is possible on appeal and the only way of affording reasonable guidance in future cases. Equally important, it discloses to the litigants and their advisers the components of the overall award, assuring them thereby that each of the various heads of damage going to make up the claim has been given thoughtful consideration.

The breakdown in the *Andrews* case was into "Non-Pecuniary Loss," "Cost of Future Care" and "Loss of Prospective Earnings." That breakdown has become standard. Each of those three headings, properly considered, contains a distinct type of loss which is not compensated for in the other heads.

But I do not understand that Mr. Justice Dickson was recommending any further breakdown of the three heads. For example, I do not think that anything is added to a consideration of non-pecuniary loss by breaking the award itself under that heading into component parts for pain and suffering, loss of amenities, and loss of expectation of life. Those three aspects must all be considered. But they are so interrelated that the usual practice, and I think the best practice, is to consider them all and then to make one single award for non-pecuniary loss.

The award for cost of future care is somewhat different. Properly considered, this award includes only the extra costs that would not have been incurred in normal living, but for the accident. Those extra costs can often be separately quantified, and that should be done wherever possible. It should be possible to make separate calculations for medical attendants, for domestic help, for a vehicle, for the adaptation of a house for use with a wheelchair, for prosthetic devices, and the like. In the end, one overall award is usually made under the head of "Cost of Future Care," but it is composed of those separate parts added together.

The third heading of general damages is financial loss arising from income foregone as a result of the accident. The major, and in many cases, the exclusive item under this heading is the item variously called "Lost Earning Capacity" and "Loss of Prospective Earnings." But, if there are other losses on the income side of the equation, as opposed to the expenditure side, they should be included under this heading.

Let me put an example. Suppose a person usually worked for wages in the fishing season in a fish-cannery for, say, eight months of the year, on average, but in the remaining four months that person usually worked at home knitting sweaters for sale. Suppose the person was injured and could pursue no occupation at all for gain. Would it be the proper course to assess the lost earning capacity arising from the fish-canning work separately from the lost earning capacity arising from home-knitting? Not necessarily. It might well be best to look at the whole future income as it would have been without the accident, and the whole future income as it may be expected to be as a result of the accident, and to subtract one from the other and so reach a figure for loss of future income as a result of the accident.

I think that the composite approach applies even more readily in the case of loss of family income arising from the lost opportunity to form a permanent interdependency. Most women starting out on marriage in the 1980s will expect to remain in the labour force after marriage and to move in and out of the labour force for the remainder of their working lives. When they are working they will have earnings. They will also have savings from the sharing of expenditures in the family group. And they will contribute to those expenditures. When they are not working they will have the benefit of family income being spent on them and being provided by the other member of the interdependency.

In many cases the best and most reasonable way to measure the losses on the income side of the equation is to take the total inflow from all sources, namely, earnings, family support payments, and reductions in costs from family economies, all as they would have been but for the accident, and to take the total inflow and any savings in normal daily living as they may be expected to be following the accident, and to subtract one from the other to arrive at the total loss over the plaintiff's life expectancy, reduced to present value.

It is particularly advantageous to adopt this approach where there could have been expected to have been a fair amount of movement in and out of the labour force because of marriage itself or because of child-bearing or child-rearing. In those circumstances the benefits flowing from family income tend to be at their greatest just when the contingency of non-employment is making the greatest erosion in earning capacity or prospective earnings.

Indeed, in many cases it is impossible to make an informed estimate of loss of prospective earnings without taking into account the financial impact of family formation and child-bearing and child-rearing. One result of not marrying may well be an increased interest in, and availability for, participation in the labour force, with an increased likelihood of being in a state of employment, or of being employed at a higher level. Another consequence of not marrying is a decreased likelihood of having dependent children, with similar earnings consequences.

So, support from family income and support from earnings are intimately interrelated and it is often unrealistic to separate them out under different headings for the purposes of calculation of losses on the financial inflow side of the equation.

My conclusion is that diminishment of an opportunity to form a more or less permanent relationship of interdependency has definite financial consequences, some positive and some negative. Those consequences are closely associated with the person's employment status. So an endeavour should be made to assess the net pecuniary effect of the interconnected financial consequences. Sometimes they will be more significant than at other times. The assessment will usually depend on both statistical evidence and a particular assessment of the individual. And it will, in most cases, be the best course to make the damage award reflect the relationship between losses flowing from the loss of the opportunity to create an interdependency, on the one hand, and loss of earning capacity and other income-achieving capacity, on the other hand, and to make only one assessment covering the whole of the income side of the plaintiff's future loss, including cost savings forgone.

5. Loss of opportunity to marry is now termed "loss of interdependent relationship." For a recent decision awarding these damages see *Walker v. Ritchie* (2005), 197 OAC 81.

6. Yet another head of loss is "loss of competitive advantage." This loss flows from the realization that a person who has experienced a partial disability, but still retains a capacity to work, will, nevertheless, experience greater difficulty in securing and retaining employment arising from the preference of employers to favour an able-bodied person over one who has a disability. See *Dikih v. Via Rail Canada Inc.*, [1987] OJ No. 272 (HCJ) (QL); *Branch v. Martini* (1998), 62 OTC 161 (Gen. Div.); *Pallos v. Insurance Corp. of British Columbia* (1995), 100 BCLR (2d) 260 (CA); and *Moeliker v. A. Reyrolle & Co Ltd.*, [1977] 1 All ER 9.

Cost of Future Care

Dickson J indicated in *Andrews* that a plaintiff is entitled to the level of care appropriate to his or her needs. The plaintiff does not have to languish in an institution when home care would provide the optimal solution. Cost to a defendant is not a relevant consideration. The only limits on a plaintiff's claim is that he or she must act within the boundary of reasonableness. Thus, medical expenses (subject to a subrogated claim in some provincial medical insurance schemes), cost of adapting a house to the individual's special needs, and provision of nursing and other attendants' services are all compensable. The Supreme Court of Canada has reaffirmed its position on favouring home care where that is the optimal solution over less expensive institutional care: see *Watkins v. Olafson*, [1989] 2 SCR 750. In *Krangle (Guardian ad litem of) v. Brisco*, [2002] 1 SCR 205, the Supreme Court required the defendant to meet "the normal and reasonable expectations" of the plaintiff. The classification of whether an expenditure flows as an act of required and desired rehabilitation or is an improvement on the plaintiff's style of living from that which would have been expected had the injury not occurred can significantly affect the damages awarded. For example, costs can vary appreciably depending on whether the severely injured plaintiff is entitled to home care in a specially built home or simple modification of an existing home, or is likely to be resident in institutional or shared care. In *Dubé (Litigation Guardian of) v. Penlon Ltd.* (1994), 21 CCLT (2d) 268 (Ont. Gen. Div.), the court allowed the plaintiff the cost of a covered in-ground swimming pool, stating that it was needed as part of a rehabilitation plan, and that there was a scarcity of heated public pools in the plaintiff's vicinity. In *Crawford (Litigation Guardian of) v. Penney* (2003), 14 CCLT (3d) 60; aff'd. on appeal (2004), 26 CCLT (3d) 246 (Ont. CA), the court allowed only modification of the plaintiff's home rather than acceding to the plaintiff's wishes of a move to a purpose-built new home, stating that the alteration was all that was "necessary and reasonable." However, this case is notable for awarding one of the largest personal injury awards in the country, just over $10 million.

Cost of future care is determined by looking at the plaintiff's post-accident life span.

Overlap Between Cost of Future Care and Loss of Working Capacity

If a person is compensated fully for his or her future care, there is the potential for double recovery if a deduction for the cost of necessities of life (food, shelter, and clothing) is not made from the damages for loss of future working capacity. A deduction between 30 and 50 percent is normal. A further problem occurs because the loss of future working capacity is determined by looking at the plaintiff's pre-accident life span, while the plaintiff's future care costs are determined on a post-accident life span. The period between these two determinations in known as the "lost years." In *Toneguzzo-Norvell (Guardian ad litem of) v. Burnaby Hospital*, [1994] 1 SCR 114, McLachlin J indicated that a similar deduction of living expenses should be made during the period of the "lost years" to avoid the spectre of simply unjustly enriching the plaintiff's heirs. On occasion, the amount deducted during the lost years has risen to 70 percent, using an approach that measures the savings the plaintiff would have accumulated during the period of the lost years. See *Granger (Litigation Guardian of) v. Ottawa General Hospital* (1996), 7 OTC 81 (Gen. Div.).

Another area that raises the issue of potential double recovery concerns the overlap between damages assessed for either lost earning capacity or future care, and state welfare and health programs or privately arranged disability insurance. With respect to privately arranged insurance or other employment-related disability benefits, these are generally considered as collateral benefits that are not to inure to the defendant in reduction of the damages assessed. Private insurance or acts of benevolence have traditionally been exceptions to the collateral benefit rule, which favours deductibility of any benefits received. With respect to government welfare, health, and other universal benefits, whether they reduce the defendant's damages depends on the wording of the legislation creating the scheme and, in particular, whether the legislation provides for subrogation. See chapter 1, "General Principles of Damages," and Waddams, *The Law of Damages* (looseleaf), at paragraph 3.1490 *et seq*. See also OLRC, *Report on Compensation for Personal Injuries and Death* (1987), chapter 6; J. Cassels and E. Adjin-Tettey, *Remedies: The Law of Damages*, 2d ed. (Toronto: Irwin Law, 2008), chapter 13, "Collateral Benefits"; Law Commission (UK), *Damages for Personal Injury: Medical, Nursing and Other Expenses: Collateral Benefits* (Law Com. 262, 1999); and *M.B. v. British Columbia*, [2003] 2 SCR 477.

The following issues are common both to loss of future earning capacity and cost of future care.

Contingencies

Most personal injury awards deduct a percentage from loss of future earning capacity and cost of future care to cover contingencies. Deductions for contingencies are supposed to represent the possible changes in circumstances that a plaintiff may have experienced in income profile had he or she not been injured (for example, unemployment, illness, accidents, economic decline in the industry of employment), and the change in circumstances that may eventuate in the plaintiff's post-accident life (for example, the possibility of later institutionalization should the plaintiff's condition deteriorate, progress in medical science resulting in improvements in the plaintiff's condition, or premature death of the plaintiff).

It is difficult to find any discussion of the principles behind contingency deductions, yet their impact can be dramatic. For example, a plaintiff whose compensation has been assessed on the basis of providing home care may be deprived of the funds to pay for it after a 20 percent contingency deduction is made.

In *Penso v. Solowan and Public Trustee*, Anderson JA provides a set of guidelines respecting contingencies.

Penso v. Solowan and Public Trustee
(1982), 35 BCLR 250 (CA)

[The plaintiff had been severely injured in a motor vehicle accident when she was 38 years of age. The injuries to her skull had brought about a personality change marked by "depression, emotional lability and decreased social ability." She also suffered problems in communicating and loss of motor coordination. She had been twice divorced prior to the accident, the first marriage lasting 15 years, the second only one month.]

ANDERSON JA (at 253ff.): ... With respect to contingencies, the law has been well settled by the Supreme Court of Canada in recent decisions.

In one of the "trilogy" cases, *Andrews v. Grand & Toy*, Dickson J said at p. 253:

(iii) Contingencies

It is a general practice to take account of contingencies which might have affected future earnings, such as unemployment, illness, accidents and business depression. In the *Bisson v. Powell River* (1967), 66 DLR (2d) 226 (BC CA), affirmed without written reasons (1968), 68 DLR (2d) 765n (SCC), case, which also concerned a young quadriplegic, an allowance of 20% was made. There is much support for the view that such a discount for contingencies should be made: see, e.g. *Warren v. King*, [1964] 1 WLR 1 (CA); *McKay v. Bd. of Govan School Unit No. 29*, [1968] SCR 589. There are, however, a number of qualifications which should be made. First, in many respects, these contingencies implicitly are already contained in an assessment of the projected average level of earnings of the injured person, for one must assume that this figure is a projection with respect to the real world of work, vicissitudes and all. Second, not all contingencies are adverse, as the above list would appear to indicate. As is said in *Bresatz v. Przibilla* (1962), 108 CLR 541, in the Australian High Court, at p. 544: "Why count the possible buffets and ignore the rewards of fortune?" Finally, in modern society there are many public and private schemes which cushion the individual against adverse contingencies. Clearly, the percentage deduction which is proper will depend on the facts of the individual case, particularly the nature of the plaintiff's occupation, but generally it will be small: see J.H. Prevett, "Actuarial Assessment of Damages: The Thalidomide case—I" (1972), 35 Mod. L Rev. 140 at p. 150.

In reducing Andrews' award by 20% Mr. Justice Kirby gives no reasons. The Appellate Division also applied a 20% reduction. It seems to me that actuarial evidence could be of great help here. Contingencies are susceptible to more exact calculation than is usually apparent in the cases: see A.T. Traversi, "Actuaries and the Courts" (1956), 29 Aust. Law J 557. In my view, some degree of specificity, supported by evidence, ought to be forthcoming at trial.

The figure used to take account of contingencies is obviously an arbitrary one. The figure of 20% which was used in the lower Courts (and in many other cases), although not entirely satisfactory, should, I think, be accepted.

In *Keizer v. Hanna*, [1978] 2 SCR 342 at p. 351, Dickson J said:

It is, of course, true that a trial judge must consider contingencies tending to reduce the ultimate award and give those contingencies more or less weight. It is equally true there are contingencies tending to increase the award to which a judge must give due weight. At the end of the day the only question of importance is whether, in all circumstances, the final award is fair and adequate. Past experience should make one realize that if there is to be error in the amount of an award it is likely to be one of inadequacy.

In *Lewis v. Todd*, [1980] 2 SCR 694 at p. 708, Dickson J said:

Third, the award of damages is not simply an exercise in mathematics which a Judge indulges in, leading to a "correct" global figure. The evidence of actuaries and economists is of value in arriving at a fair and just result. That evidence is of increasing importance as the niggardly approach sometimes noted in the past is abandoned, and greater amounts are awarded, in my view properly, in cases of severe personal injury or death. If the Courts are to apply basic principles of the law of damages and seek to achieve a reasonable approximation to pecuniary *restitutio in integrum* expert assistance is vital. But the trial Judge, who is required to make the decision, must be accorded a large measure of freedom in dealing with the evidence presented by the experts. If the figures lead to an award which in all circumstances seems to the Judge to be inordinately high it is his duty as I conceive it, to adjust those figures downward; and in like manner to adjust them upward if they lead to what seems to be an unusually low award.

He also said at pp. 714-15:

(c) Contingencies

In principle, there is no reason why a Court should not recognize, and give effect to, those contingencies, good or bad, which may reasonably be foreseen. This is not to say that the Courts are justified in imposing an automatic contingency deduction. Not all contingencies are adverse. The Court must attempt to evaluate the probability of the occurrence of the stated contingency. It is here that actuarial evidence may be of aid. I merely repeat what was said in *Andrews* (at p. 253): "... actuarial evidence would be of great help here. Contingencies are susceptible to more exact calculation than is usually apparent in the cases."

In this case the actuarial tables projected a joint life expectancy but not a working expectancy for the deceased; thus it was not inappropriate to take into account general contingencies such as those mentioned by the trial judge.

A trial judge should consider whether there is *any* evidence which takes the deceased's situation outside the "average"; whether there are any features of which no account was taken in the actuarial tables, either because the factor is entirely personal to the individual or, because the "average" is not adapted for the category or class to which the person belongs, *e.g.*, police officers.

At trial, actuarial evidence on the probable life expectancy of Constable Lewis and his wife was adduced. There was no evidence with respect to any of the other contingencies considered by the trial Judge. The trial Judge resisted the temptation to use a "conventional figure of 20%" and explicitly noted that "all contingencies do not necessarily work against the interest of the plaintiff." In his judgment, less than 10% should be deducted for adverse contingencies.

The Court of Appeal held that 10% was an appropriate contingency deduction. This conclusion is stated without any reason as to why the determination of the trial Judge was inappropriate. It may be that the Court was simply "rounding off" the deduction made by the trial Judge. In the result, I would restore the finding of the trial Judge.

In summary, the above cases appear to set out the following guidelines:

(1) The courts are not justified in applying automatic contingency deductions.

(2) The courts should avoid making large contingency deductions which are not justified by the evidence.

(3) Past experience has shown that if there is to be an error in the amount of the award, it is likely to be one of inadequacy.

(4) If the trial judge, after reviewing all the evidence, reaches the conclusion that the award is inordinately high or low, he may make an upward or downward adjustment.

(5) Twenty per cent appears to be the maximum contingency deduction in the absence of unusual factors.

(6) Contingencies are susceptible to more exact calculation than is usually apparent in the cases.

(7) Actuarial advice is very helpful and should be relied upon wherever possible.

(8) The reasons for judgment should express the evidentiary basis upon which contingency allowances are made.

As the amount awarded by the learned trial judge for loss of future earning capacity is clearly inadequate, we must endeavour to ascertain the proper amount to be awarded. The evidence with respect to this issue is sparse and may be summarized as follows:

(1) The employment record of the plaintiff is spotty. In 1973 she had gross earnings of $5,000 and in 1975 about $2,900 (apart from unemployment insurance benefits).

(2) Except for a very short period she never received social assistance.

(3) She has been supported in large measure by her husbands or by the men with whom she lived.

(4) Since the accident she has not formed any lasting relationships with men.

It seems to me that on the facts of the case on appeal, we must approach the matter on the basis suggested in *Fenn v. Peterborough* (1979), 25 OR (2d) 399 (CA) and *Arnold v. Teno*, [1978] 2 SCR 287.

In *Arnold v. Teno*, Spence J said at p. 329:

> The allowance of an amount for loss of future income in the present case is extremely difficult. The plaintiff at the time of her injury was a four and a half-year-old child. There can be no evidence whatsoever which will assist us in determining whether she ever would have become a member of the work force or whether she would have grown up in her own home and then married. There can be no evidence upon which we may assess whether she would have had a successful business future or have been a failure. Since the Court is bound not to act on mere speculation, I do not see how this Court could approve the course taken by Zuber JA, which simply amounted to assuming, as he quite frankly said, "in the absence of any other guide," that the infant plaintiff would follow the course of her mother who was a primary school teacher with an income of $10,000 per year. On the other hand, I do not think we can assume that a bright little girl would not grow up to earn her living and would be a public charge, and we are not entitled to free the defendants, who have been found guilty of negligence, from the payment of some sum which would be a present value of the future income which I think we must assume the infant plaintiff would earn.

In *Fenn*, at p. 455 the reasons for judgment of the court read in part as follows:

> The remaining problem is the selection of an amount. There is no helpful employment history of Sandra Fenn to be used as a guide. We select the figure of $6,000 per year as a reasonable estimate of her earning capacity, a figure barely above the poverty level and a figure which is consistent with the approach used by Spence J in *Teno*. Further, the sum of $6,000 a year is a reasonable, if somewhat arbitrary, estimate of her basic living expenses. Thus this sum, it seems to us, can be justified on either basis. Using the actuarial evidence supplied, the provision of this sum from the date of trial until Sandra Fenn reaches 65, using a three per cent discount rate, would cost $154,105. Age 65 is significant as the customary end of one's working life expectancy and in this case the age at which the trial Judge estimated Sandra Fenn would require institutional care. Thus, the termination date will be the same whether this annual sum is classed as the cost of basic living expenses or as lost earning capacity.

While I am of the opinion that the above approach is applicable here, we must make some moderate deduction for the unlikely chance that the plaintiff might have sought to live on welfare or that she may again find a lasting relationship with another man.

The actuarial evidence indicates that if the earnings of the appellant amounted to $6,000 per annum using a discount rate of $3\frac{1}{2}$ per cent, her loss would amount to $92,000. While no evidence was adduced as to the "poverty" level or as to the amount which the appellant now received by way of social assistance, I am of the opinion that the figure of $6,000 is a conservative one and should be used for the purpose of assessing loss of future earning capacity.

I would make a deduction of $17,600 to cover the following matters:

(a) Usual contingencies;

(b) The contingency that the plaintiff may seek to live on welfare or form a lasting relationship with another man;

(c)   The uncertainty caused by the fact that no evidence was adduced as to the amount which the plaintiff would be required to earn to reach the "poverty level."

I would, therefore, fix the award for loss of future earning capacity at $75,000.

[Note the criticism of this case in J. Cassels, "Damages for Lost Earning Capacity: Women and Children Last!" (1992), 71 *Can. Bar Rev.* 445, at 459, for its treatment of women and the prospect of remarriage as a negative contingency.]

NOTES

1. Assembling lists of contingencies is proving to be a profitable and imaginative field for litigants. Check some of the continuing legal education literature for lists of contingencies—for example, Continuing Legal Education Society of British Columbia, *Damages* (September 1984), material prepared by J. Camp and *Insight: Current Issues and Developments in Personal Injury and Death Claims* (Toronto: November 1984), material prepared by R. O'Donnell.

2. Contingency deductions normally fall into the 10-20 percent range, although some have risen to 60 percent (see *McNichol v. Mardell*, [1983] 3 WWR 299 (Alta. QB), varied on other issues, [1984] 5 WWR 117, leave to appeal refused (1984), 58 AR 38 (SC)) while others have evenly balanced positive and negative contingencies arriving at no deduction (see *Nielson v. Kaufmann* (1984), 28 CCLT 54 (Ont. HC)). On appeal, this point was not disputed by the court as being appropriate in this case ((1986), 54 OR (2d) 188 (CA)). See also the discussion in *Paine v. Donovan* (1994), 118 Nfld. & PEIR 91, at 203 (PEI TD) and moderate contingency rate of 2.5 percent.

Discount Rate

An award that is made up of damages for future losses must be paid in today's money, which in turn may be invested. The discount rate is an attempt to convert the damages awarded for future losses into present-day value. The choice of discount rate is based on the difference in forecasts between the effect of long-term inflation and long-term interest rates.

The impact of varying discount rates is aptly illustrated in Bruce Feldthusen and Keith McNair, "General Damages in Personal Injury Suits: The Supreme Court Trilogy" (1978), 28 *University of Toronto Law Journal*, at 390:

> Even small differences in the discount rate selected can have an enormous effect upon the lump sum award ultimately obtained by the plaintiff. In *Teno v. Arnold*, Spence J referred to the significance of the discount rate selected, pointing out that the present value of $1,000 per year for 66.9 years would vary from $21,563, if a 4.5% rate were used, to $9,100 if the rate applied were 11%. An increase in the discount rate from 4.5% to 6.5% would reduce the present value from $21,563 to $15,685. Assuming that these figures were applied to a calculated cost for future medical care of $21,000 *per annum*, the award for this period, using a 4.5% discount rate, would amount to $452,823, while if 6.5% were used the amount would be $329,385. Differences of this magnitude indicate the importance of an appropriate discount rate.

Lewis v. Todd
[1980] 2 SCR 694, at 709-12

DICKSON J: ... It is clear that the discount rate is a critical factor in determining quantum in any fatal accident, or serious personal injury, litigation. Some confusion seems to have attended this Court's acceptance of a 7% discount rate in the "trilogy" and a 6½% rate in *Keizer v. Hanna*. Some Courts have interpreted the question of discount rate as a matter of law and have applied the 7% rate utilized in the trilogy. Others have given effect to the Court's statement in *Andrews v. Grand & Toy Alberta Ltd.*, that "the result in future cases will depend upon the evidence adduced in those cases" (at p. 258), and have felt free to depart from the 7% figure. It is important, I think, that the Court affirm the principle that the discount rate is normally a factual issue which will turn on the evidence advanced in individual cases.

It would be useful to recall precisely the function which the "discount rate" is intended to serve. In the case of a fatal accident the Court is endeavouring to compensate the dependents of the deceased for loss of a future stream of income which the dependents might have expected to receive but for the death of the deceased. As it is not open to a Court, in the absence of enabling legislation, to order periodic payments adjusted to future needs, the dependents receive immediately a capital sum roughly approximating the present value of the income they would have received had the deceased survived. They are able to invest this capital sum and earn interest thereon. A proportion of the interest received may be offset by the effect of inflation. To the extent that the interest payments exceed the rate of inflation, there is conferred on the dependents, through payment today of a stream of future income, a benefit which can be expressed as the "real rate of return." There would clearly be enrichment of the plaintiff at the expense of the defendant if the Court did not take this benefit into account in making an award. Accordingly, the court applies a so-called "discount factor," *i.e.*, the real rate of return which the plaintiff can expect to receive on the damage award. This is what the Court was suggesting in *Andrews* when it was stated "the approach which I would adopt, therefore, is to use present rates of return on long-term investments and to make some allowance for the effects of future inflation" (at p. 258).

It has been suggested at various times that there is no need for a Court to hear evidence on expected rates of interest and inflation as the relationship between these two factors and thus the real rate of return, is constant: see generally Dale Gibson, "Repairing the Law of Damages" (1978), 8 Man. LJ 637 at p. 651; M. Braniff and A. Pratt, "Tragedy in the Supreme Court of Canada: New Developments in the Assessment of Damages for Personal Injuries" (1979), 37 UT Fac. L Rev. 1 at p. 26. Such an approach has been termed the "Lord Diplock approach" or "modified Lord Diplock approach," following *Mallet v. McMonagle*, [1970] AC 166 (HL (NI)).

I know of no authority by which this Court, if so minded, could legislate a fixed discount rate, applicable for all cases. Even if such authority were present, I would be loath to exercise it in the present case. At trial, the plaintiff called one economist and one actuary to give evidence on future trends in inflation and interest rates. It would be irresponsible for this Court to make an immutable pronouncement on a complex issue on the basis of such limited evidence. The findings made herein should, in justice, only bind the parties to the present litigation.

The principle remains that, absent legislation (see the *Judicature Amendment Act*, 1979 (Ont.), c. 65, s. 6(5)) which directs the manner of calculating discount rate (*e.g.*, by setting a figure or by pegging the interest rate to return on specific investment vehicles and inflation to a particular index), the discount rate will vary according to the expert testimony led at trial.

This does not mean that there will never be any uniformity in the selection of discount rates. As litigants in these cases produce more thorough and rigorous economic data and as the judiciary becomes more familiar with this data, a certain uniformity will no doubt emerge.

As I have earlier indicated, the trial Judge selected 8.25% as the reasonable rate of return for high-grade investments of long-term duration. This was balanced against inflation (4%) and yielded a real rate of return of 4.25%. A productivity factor of 2% was then introduced. The Court of Appeal did not deal at any length with the evidence on this issue. Rather, it overturned the trial Judge's finding on the sole basis that this Court had adopted a 7% discount rate in *Teno v. Arnold*, and there was "a basis" for adopting a similar rate in the present case. In imposing a 7% discount rate, the Court of Appeal did not explicitly state the assumptions which supported such a figure. It is not clear, for example, whether the Court was eliminating the 2% productivity factor included by the trial Judge; nor is it clear what nominal rate of return the Court considered the plaintiff would receive through investment of the damage award.

With respect, the Court of Appeal erred in treating the discount rate adopted in *Teno* as, virtually, a matter of law. The Court turned to the evidence in the case only to determine whether there was "a basis" for adopting a similar rate here. The Court should have commenced its inquiry with the finding of the trial Judge and evidence adduced at trial, and should have left those findings undisturbed if supported on the evidence. The "trilogy" of cases was available for guidance on the basic questions of principle.

Turning to that evidence, it is true there was testimony which could have supported a higher discount rate. There was, however, ample evidence to support the trial Judge's finding that inflation would run at approximately 4% and long-term investment rates would average 8.25%. Productivity was not raised as a factor in the "trilogy" but I consider it an appropriate component of a damage award in a proper case. There was evidence to support the 2% figure selected by the trial Judge.

In the result, I would reverse the judgment of the Court of Appeal on this point and restore the finding at trial.

NOTES AND QUESTIONS

1. In the above extract, Dickson J makes reference to a further reduction in the discount rate to accommodate a productivity factor. A productivity factor recognizes that in certain occupations real gains over and above inflation have been made in wages or salaries. See Weatherston JA in *Dziver v. Smith* (1983), 41 OR (2d) 385 (CA) for discussion.

2. In most jurisdictions, a statutory discount rate has been legislated. In Ontario, r. 53.09 of the Rules of Civil Procedure states:

> 53.09(1) The discount rate to be used in determining the amount of an award in respect of future pecuniary damages, to the extent that it reflects the difference between estimated investment and price inflation rates, is

(a) for the 15-year period that follows the start of the trial, the average of the value for the last Wednesday in each month of the real rate of interest on long-term Government of Canada real return bonds (Series V121808, formerly Series B113911), as published in the *Bank of Canada Weekly Financial Statistics* for the 12 months ending on August 31 in the year before the year in which the trial begins, less 1 per cent and rounded to the nearest per cent; and

(b) for any later period covered by the award, 2.5 per cent per year.

For a trial commencing in 2005, the 15-year discount rate in Ontario was 1.5%.

A similar provision to the Ontario rule exists in Nova Scotia (Rules of Civil Procedure, r. 31.10(2)) and New Brunswick (Rules of Court, r. 54.10(2)). British Columbia has a similar provision: *Law and Equity Act*, RSBC 1996, c. 253, s. 56:

51(2) The Chief Justice of the Supreme Court may make regulations prescribing

(a) a discount rate which shall be deemed to be the future difference between the investment rate of interest and the rate of increase of earnings due to inflation and general increases in productivity, and

(b) a discount rate which shall be deemed to be the future difference between the investment rate of interest and the rate of general price inflation.

The rates have been set at 2½ and 3½ percent respectively: BC reg. 351/81, and see the criticism in *Pickering v. Deakin* (1984), 58 BCLR 145, *per* Lambert JA, at 160 (CA). In Manitoba and Saskatchewan, the rate is set at 3 percent: *Manitoba (Court of Queen's Bench Act)*, CCSM, c. C280, ss. 83(1) and (2); Saskatchewan Queen's Bench Rules, r. 284 B(1)(b). The court has power to vary the discount rate from that stipulated in the rules, particularly when the discount rate can be predicted with reasonable accuracy and where it is dramatically different from the rule. See *McDermid v. Ontario* (1985), 53 OR (2d) 495 (HC).

3. To what extent do you believe the economic forecasts on which the discount rate is determined are accurate? See W. Landsea, "How Workable Are Net Discount Rates?" (1982), 28 *McGill Law Journal* 102; G. Bale, "Adding Insult to Injury: The Inappropriate Use of Discount Rates to Determine Damage Awards" (1982), 28 *McGill Law Journal* 1015; and C. Bruce, "The Introduction of Economic Factors into Litigation Cases: Ontario's 2½ Percent Solution" (1982), 60 *Can. Bar Rev.* 677.

4. See also *Townsend v. Kroppmanns*, [2004] 1 SCR 315.

Management Fees

Where the plaintiff is incapable of managing his or her own award, through either mental or physical incapacity, or age, the court will often award an amount to employ professional money managers. This award will be made by either an additional lump sum amount, or by altering the discount rate by one-half percent.

The Supreme Court of Canada has endorsed the practice of including a management fee or investment counselling fee in the lump sum award. In *Mandzuk v. Insurance Corporation of British Columbia*, [1988] 2 SCR 650, a plaintiff who had been rendered a quadriplegic had been denied any management or investment counselling fee by the BC Supreme Court on the basis that the plaintiff had not suffered any mental or intellectual impairment as a result of the accident. On appeal, the Court of Appeal had granted $40,000 as an investment counselling fee. The Supreme Court of Canada thought the actual award was on the high side but dismissed the appeal. In passing, Sopinka J, speaking for the court, said:

> SOPINKA J: We are all of the opinion that the appeal should be dismissed. The issue in this appeal is whether or not in serious personal injury cases an amount for an investment counselling fee should be awarded to the plaintiff. This is essentially a question of fact in each case. The only principle that appears to be applicable is that the defendant must take the plaintiff as he finds him, including his state of intelligence. Whether this is low by reason of the injuries complained of or its natural state, a management fee or an investment counselling fee should be awarded if the plaintiff's level of intelligence is such that he is either unable to manage his affairs or lacks the acumen to invest funds awarded for future care so as to produce the requisite rate of return. ...
>
> A plaintiff seeking to recover either a management fee or an investment counselling fee should provide a factual basis to the trier of fact, including:
>
> (i) evidence that management assistance is in fact necessary;
>
> (ii) evidence that investment advice is in fact necessary in the circumstances;
>
> (iii) evidence as to the cost of such services.

In *Townsend v. Kroppmanns*, [2004] 1 SCR 315, the plaintiff, as a result of an automobile accident, suffered a personal injury for which she was awarded damages of $1,445,000. Half this sum was paid to the plaintiff, who then used part of the award to purchase a house and to pay her legal expenses. Five years after this initial payment, the issue of appropriate discount rates, management fees, and tax gross-up remained unresolved. The defendant argued that because a management fee was granted, the expected return on the plaintiff's award should be greater than the standardized assumptions made to determine the discount rate. As a result, a further deduction in the amount of the award should be made. The Supreme Court rejected this argument on the ground that this would necessarily entail the reintroduction of expert evidence to determine appropriate rates of return that could be achieved through using financial management consultants. The legislative interventions on standardizing discount rates to avoid the need to call expert evidence would thus be undermined. The defendant also argued that both management rates and tax gross-up should be calculated on the residual funds that the plaintiff had available after paying legal fees and purchasing a house, rather than on the initial award. The defendant argued that the subsequent actions of the plaintiff reveal that neither a management fee nor tax gross-up would be necessary on that part of the funds already spent. The Supreme Court rejected this argument on three grounds. Deschamp J (at 324) for the court said:

> First, damages are assessed and not calculated ... . In assessing damages, courts do not take into consideration what victims actually do with the award. The fact that the respondent here had to wait for almost five years before management fees were assessed creates an atypical situation, but these exceptional circumstances should not justify a departure of the usual rules. Notional amounts cannot be mixed with actual amounts when assessing future damages.
>
> Secondly, damages are awarded in a lump sum in order to respect the principle of finality: ... . The award should not be reassessed every time reality reveals a discrepancy with the forecast. Therefore, monitoring the respondent's use of the award or adjusting it with her changing circumstances would create more uncertainty than the present rule, would undermine the purpose

of the statutory discount rate, and would improperly interfere with the third principle of damages relevant to this case.

This final and most important principle is that the plaintiff has property of the award [and] … that it is not relevant to inquire into how the plaintiff chooses to spend the amounts recovered for the assessment of damages for management fees and tax gross-up. Consequently, management fees and tax gross-up are to be assessed based on the first assessment of damages and not according to the amount available for investment as eventually found at some indeterminate future date. In other words, the appropriate basis for calculation is the one determined at trial, without considering what happens thereafter. It is improper for a trial judge to consider what the plaintiff does with awarded damages.

Taxation

You will have noticed that in the assessment of lost earning capacity courts ignore the incidence of taxation when determining a plaintiff's probable income profile. The rationale for this approach is explained in *The Queen in Right of Ontario v. Jennings*.

The Queen in Right of Ontario v. Jennings
[1966] SCR 532, at 544

[In this case, the Supreme Court of Canada declined to follow the English House of Lords' decision in *British Transportation Commission v. Gourley*, [1956] AC 185 (HL (Eng.)). In that case, the House of Lords, by a majority, held that a person's lost earning capacity compensation should be calculated on the net after-tax income of the plaintiff, on the basis that the plaintiff could not have received more than this amount had the wrong not been committed.]

JUDSON J: … I would, however, put my rejection upon broader grounds. I agree with the dissenting opinion of Lord Keith in the *Gourley* case and the minority views expressed in the 7th Report of the Law Reform Committee on the effect of tax liability on damages, published in August of 1958. These are stated in the following paragraphs [at 4]:

(a) Damages should, so far as any monetary award can do so, restore the plaintiff to the position in which he would have stood but for the defendant's wrongdoing. On this basis they should represent compensation for loss of earning capacity and not for loss of earnings. In a case of personal injuries, what the plaintiff has lost is the whole or part, as the case may be, of his natural capital equipment and to tax him on this is contrary to generally accepted principles of taxation.

(b) What the plaintiff would have done or have been required to do with this money had he not suffered the injury complained of is, so far as the defendant is concerned, irrelevant. Tax is not a charge on income before it is received and there is no more reason for taking it into account than rates, mortgage interest and any other liabilities which the plaintiff may have to meet. To do so means that the defendant is making something less than full restitution for the injury. In other words, each £1 of income lost is worth £1 *to the plaintiff*, either to spend on himself, or to discharge his liabilities, including that for income tax.

(c) The net sum representing what the plaintiff would have received after deduction of tax is not adequate compensation for loss of the ability to deal freely with the gross sum. Not only is the plaintiff deprived of his chance of dealing with his income as he thinks fit and so reducing his liability to tax, but third parties who might otherwise have benefited from such arrangements as the plaintiff might be disposed to make are unable to do so.

(d) The present law operates in some cases in a way which is contrary to public policy. Thus it is now frequently more profitable to pay damages for the breach of a contract of service than to perform the contract, because by paying damages the employer saves the amount of the tax on the employee's salary.

It has been said that if the incidence of taxation on future earnings is ignored, the plaintiff is being overcompensated. With this I do not agree. A lump sum award under this head is at best no more than rough-and-ready compensation. There must be very few plaintiffs who are compelled to take a lump sum who would not be better off with their earning capacity unimpaired or a periodic reassessment of the effect of its impairment. There is, as things are at present, no possibility of such a reassessment. But mathematical precision is impossible in assessing the lump sum, and where large amounts and serious permanent disability are involved, I think that the award is usually a guess to the detriment of the plaintiff.

To assess another uncertainty—the incidence of income tax over the balance of the working life of a plaintiff—and then deduct the figure reached from an award is, in my opinion, an undue preference for the case of the defendant or his insurance company. The plaintiff has been deprived of his capacity to earn income. It is the value of that capital asset which has to be assessed. In making that determination it is proper and necessary to estimate the future income earning capacity of the plaintiff, that is, his ability to produce dollar income, if he had not been injured. This estimate must be made in relation to his net income, account being taken of expenditures necessary to earn the income. But income tax is not an element of cost in earning income. It is a disposition of a portion of the earned income required by law. Consequently, the fact that the plaintiff would have been subject to tax on future income, had he been able to earn it, and that he is not required to pay tax upon the award of damages for his loss of capacity to earn income does not mean that he is over-compensated if the award is not reduced by an amount equivalent to the tax. It merely reflects the fact that the state has not elected to demand payment of tax upon that kind of a receipt of money. It is not open to the defendant to complain about this consequence of tax policy and the Courts should not transfer this benefit to the defendant or his insurance company.

The speculative and unsatisfactory result that may follow from a deduction for future income tax may be illustrated from the *Gourley* case itself. As pointed out in Harry Street, *Principles of the Law of Damages* (London: Sweet & Maxwell, 1962) at p. 102, if Gourley had been able to postpone the trial for two years, he would inevitably have received several thousand pounds more by way of damages.

The practical difficulties that arise from the application of the principle are many and they have been noticed. What is to be done with the young plaintiff who had a promising career ahead of him? If he is unmarried or newly married, how does the Court deal with his potential exemptions? How does it deal with the complexities that may arise from a wife's separate income? Why should it be assumed that investment income is necessarily permanent or that it will always remain taxable in the hands of the plaintiff? What will be done with the foreign plaintiff and foreign systems of taxation?

In this country there are additional difficulties. Each of the Provinces has the power to impose taxation upon income, and there is no assurance that the total impact of Federal and provincial tax upon taxpayers in each of the Provinces will remain the same. At the same time there is a considerable and increasing movement of people from one Province to another. To deduct from an award of damages for loss of earning capacity an amount based upon the existing tax rates in the Province in which he lived at the time of his injury might well create a hardship for a man who might reasonably have anticipated, in the future, a transfer of his employment to another Province in which the rate of taxation is less.

In the litigation itself there are practical difficulties. There will be discovery on income tax matters with its possibilities of oppressive and endless examination. There are also problems of onus of proof. I notice that *West Suffolk County Council v. W. Rought Ltd.*, [1957] AC 403 (HL (Eng.)), put the burden on the plaintiff. The Ontario Court of Appeal, in the present case, put the burden on the defendant. Finally, how does the principle fit in with lump sum awards either from a Judge or jury or with jury trials at all in these cases?

I agree with Cartwright J that the appeal should be dismissed with costs but I think that we should say now that we reject the principle stated in *Gourley*.

NOTE

The approach in *Jennings* was criticized by the Nova Scotia Court of Appeal in *Guy v. Trizec Equities Ltd.* (1978), 26 NSR (2d) 1 (CA). On appeal, the Supreme Court of Canada declined to review its earlier decision, [1979] 2 SCR 756.

The Supreme Court has reaffirmed its position in *Jennings* with respect to using gross earnings in *Cunningham v. Wheeler* (1994), 113 DLR (4th) 1, at 20 (SCC) (a case that also appears in chapter 1, "General Principles of Damages," because of its treatment of the issue of collateral benefits).

A further taxation problem arises when we consider the incidence of taxation on the lump sum awarded. While tax on the actual award is not payable, tax on the interest earned in subsequent years is payable. The lump sum award for future care is, as we have seen, designed to produce an annual amount to cover care costs for the future years of the injured person's life. To create this income stream, the investment return on the lump sum is factored into the calculation of the award itself. To ignore the effect of taxation on the income generated from investing the lump sum will exhaust the sum for future care at a much earlier date than originally contemplated.

Realizing this potential for undercompensation, some courts, particularly in Ontario, commenced a practice of "grossing up" the future care costs to allow for taxation. See *Fenn v. City of Peterborough*, *supra*, and *McErlean v. Sarel* (1987), 61 OR (2d) 396 (CA), leave to appeal refused [1988] 1 SCR xi. This practice was not followed by other courts. See, for example, *Scarff v. Wilson* (1988), 33 BCLR (2d) 290 (CA), but overruled on appeal [1989] 2 SCR 776, and *Watkins v. Olafson* (1987), 48 Man. R (2d) 81 (CA), but overruled on appeal [1989] 2 SCR 750.

The Supreme Court of Canada has decided to adopt the approach taken by the Ontario Court of Appeal and has concluded that a gross-up for tax liability is appropriate for future care costs. In *Watkins v. Olafson*, [1989] 2 SCR 750, speaking for the court, McLachlin J said (at 767):

> Those who argue against making an allowance for taxation in calculating the cost of future care do so, not on the ground that the allowance is not required if the plaintiff is to be adequately provided for, but mainly on the basis that the calculation is so speculative that it should not be attempted. I cannot accept that allowance for taxation is so inherently speculative that it should not be taken into account. In the first place, difficulty of calculation is a weak basis for refusing to award a plaintiff damages to which he or she is in principle entitled. The entire exercise of assessing damages for future care over a period of decades is fraught with uncertainty; yet the courts do their best to calculate an appropriate award. Where there is a right, there must also be a remedy: *Ashby v. White* (1703), 2 Ld. Raym. 938 at p. 953; 92 ER 126 at p. 136, *per* Holt CJ. ...
>
> A second reason is advanced for declining to take taxation into account in calculating the award for future care; it is said that to do so would be anomalous since no allowance for tax is made on lost earning capacity: *The Queen in right of Ontario v. Jennings*, [1966] SCR 532 (where the effect would be to reduce the award rather than increase it). But it should not be overlooked that the award for lost earning capacity is also discounted for the earnings on income in the earlier years, and that such earnings are taxable. Thus the plaintiff is in fact paying tax on the award for lost earning capacity.
>
> I conclude that an allowance should be made for the impact of taxation on the award for cost of future care where the evidence supports it, and that the evidence in this case meets that requirement.

The Ontario *Courts of Justice Act*, RSO 1990, c. C.43, s. 116(5) states that a court shall include an amount to offset liability for income tax on income from investment of an award where the court does not make an order for a periodic payment in a personal injury claim. Under s. 66(2)(v) of the same Act, power has been given to the rules committee to make rules determining the method to calculate the damages to offset liability for income tax on income from investment of the award. Rule 53.09(2) now provides a formula linked to the yield on government of Canada bonds to determine the tax gross-up. The BC LRC has also recommended standardized assumptions to calculate the tax gross-up. In addition, the commission has also recommended that on the assessment of loss of earnings, the damages should be calculated on "net" after-tax earnings and then grossed up to take account of the tax on the interest earned of the award. See *Report on Standardised Assumptions for Calculating Tax Gross-up and Management Fees in Assessing Damages* (1994, LRC 133) and *Report on Taxation and the Assessment of Income Related Damages Awards* (1994, LRC 134).

In Ontario, under s. 116 of the *Courts of Justice Act*, the court can order a periodic payment scheme where the parties consent, or where the plaintiff is seeking a tax gross-up on the lump sum award. Once the plaintiff makes such a request, the defendant can suggest an alternative periodic award. The lower cost of such an award is the incentive for a defendant to invoke s. 116. If the plaintiff wishes to persevere with a lump-sum award, he or she must prove to the court that such a lump sum would be in his or her best interest. The Ontario Court of Appeal has described the section as being poorly drafted. See *Wilson v. Martinello* (1995), 23 OR (3d) 417.

Alberta has recently altered the way compensation for loss of working capacity is to be calculated with respect to automobile accidents. Under the *Insurance Act*, RSA 2000, c. I-3, s. 626.1(2), after-tax income is to be used to quantify earnings replacement.

Fatal Injuries and Third-Party Claims

There are two distinct claims from which third parties may benefit in a fatal injury situation: (1) through being a beneficiary of the deceased's estate, where the estate has a survival action, (2) as a claimant entitled under fatal accidents legislation.

The former will not be dealt with in this casebook. The type and extent of damages recoverable by the estate are very much influenced by the particular provincial legislation concerned. However, particular attention should be paid to the recommendations of the OLRC, *Report on Compensation for Personal Injuries and Death* (1987), at 29, where it recommended the total repeal of s. 61 of the *Family Law Act*, set out below. The commission's recommendations are to channel all claims for lost capacity to earn income through the deceased's estate, although the scheme of distribution in fatal accidents would accord third parties some rights and not automatically follow the normal distribution of a deceased's estate. For further details, see Waddams, *Law of Damages* (looseleaf), chapter 6 or Cooper-Stephenson, *Personal Injury Damages in Canada*, chapter 12. The latter grants a certain designated class of claimants an independent action against a defendant. In all provinces, this action arises out of legislation: *Family Compensation Act*, RSBC 1996, c. 126; *Fatal Accidents Act*, RSS 1978, c. F-11; *Fatal Accidents Act*, RSA 2000, c. F-8; *Fatal Accidents Act*, RSNB 1997, c. F-7; *Fatal Injuries Act*, RSNS 1989, c. 163; *Fatal Accidents Act*, RSPEI 1988, c. F-5; *Fatal Accidents Act*, RSN 1990, c. F-6; *Fatal Accidents Act*, CCSM, c. F50.

Most provinces have some provision with respect to non-pecuniary damages or equivalent. In Ontario, Manitoba, and Prince Edward Island damages can be awarded for "loss of care, guidance and companionship"; in Nova Scotia for non-pecuniary loss including "guidance, care and companionship"; and in New Brunswick for "companionship and grief." In British Columbia, Newfoundland, and Saskatchewan, non-pecuniary losses are not recoverable. Alberta has enacted a provision that sets damages for bereavement, which includes loss-of-care guidance and companionship, at $75,000 for the loss of a spouse or partner, or for a parent's loss of a child, and $45,000 to a child who has lost a parent. See *Fatal Accidents Act*, RSA 2000, c. F-8, s. 8(2). Manitoba has enacted similar legislation but at lower rates. See *Fatal Accidents Act*, CCSM, c. F50, s. 3.1(2), and Cooper-Stephenson, at 697.

Family Law Act
RSO 1990, c. F.3

Right of Dependants To Sue in Tort

61(1) If a person is injured or killed by the fault or neglect of another under circumstances where the person is entitled to recover damages, or would have been entitled if not killed, the spouse, as defined in Part III (Support Obligations), children, grandchildren, parents, grandparents, brothers and sisters of the person are entitled to recover their pecuniary loss resulting from the injury or death from the person from whom the person injured or killed is entitled to recover or would have been entitled if not killed, and to maintain an action for the purpose in a court of competent jurisdiction.

Damages in Case of Injury

(2) The damages recoverable in a claim under subsection (1) may include,

(a) actual expenses reasonably incurred for the benefit of the person injured or killed;

(b) actual funeral expenses reasonably incurred;

(c) a reasonable allowance for travel expenses actually incurred in visiting the person during his or her treatment or recovery;

(d) where, as a result of the injury, the claimant provides nursing, housekeeping or other services for the person, a reasonable allowance for loss of income or the value of the services; and

(e) an amount to compensate for the loss of guidance, care and companionship that the claimant might reasonably have expected to receive from the person if the injury or death had not occurred.

Contributory Negligence

(3) In an action under subsection (1), the right to damages is subject to any apportionment of damages due to contributory fault or neglect of the person who was injured or killed. ...

Offer To Settle for Global Sum

62(1) The defendant may make an offer to settle for one sum of money as compensation for his or her fault or neglect to all plaintiffs, without specifying the shares into which it is to be divided.

Apportionment

(2) If the offer is accepted and the compensation has not been otherwise apportioned, the court may, on motion, apportion it among the plaintiffs.

Payment Before Apportionment

(3) The court may direct payment from the fund before apportionment.

Payment May Be Postponed

(4) The court may postpone the distribution of money to which minors are entitled.

Assessment of Damages, Insurance

63. In assessing damages in an action brought under this Part, the court shall not take into account any sum paid or payable as a result of the death or injury under a contract of insurance.

There are marked similarities and differences between fatal and personal injury damage assessments. The significant differences follow: (1) the claim is based on determining the degree of dependency a claimant had on the deceased, to the extent that the deceased had surplus resources over and above what he or she expended on himself or herself; (2) taxation, ignored in personal injury calculations on loss of earning capacity, is deducted in fatal injury assessment; (3) damages for fatal injury covers only pecuniary losses save where the legislation provides for compensation for "loss of guidance, care and companionship"; and (4) the types of contingencies differ.

Some of these issues are explored in the following cases.

Keizer v. Hanna
[1978] 2 SCR 342

DICKSON J: I have had the advantage of reading the reasons for judgment prepared by Mr. Justice Spence and by Mr. Justice Grandpré in this appeal. There are two issues: (i) the deductibility of income tax in arriving at an award of damages; (ii) quantum. Although as a member of the Court, I shared in the decision in *Gehrmann v. Lavoie*, [1976] 2 SCR 561, I have concluded, upon reading the reasons for judgment to which I have referred, and upon further reflection, that Mr. Justice de Grandpré is correct in law and that the impact of income tax should be taken into account in assessing a damage award under the *Fatal Accidents Act*, RSO 1970, c. 164.

On point (ii), however, "quantum," I have come to a conclusion other than that arrived at by my brother de Grandpré. I would allow the appeal, and like my brother Spence, award the amount of $100,000 claimed in the statement of claim but deduct therefrom the amount of $6,500 insurance benefits already received by the appellant under the accident and death benefits provision found in Sch. E of the deceased's insurance policy. In the result, the award of general damages would amount to $93,500.

The accident in which Mr. Keizer was killed occurred on July 16, 1973. At that date he was 33 years of age with a life expectancy of 38.55 years. He was a tool-room foreman for the Town of Renfrew, capable, conscientious, industrious and in good health. He had been married for nine years to the appellant who, at the date of his death was 27 years of age with a life expectancy of 49.60 years. Mr. and Mrs. Keizer had one child, an infant of six months.

The trial Judge projected average earnings of $15,000 for a working expectancy of 31 years. From this figure he deducted $3,200 for income tax, $1,800 for personal use, and $3,000 for personal support leaving disposable income for dependants in the amount of $7,000. The Judge made a deduction for income tax with which the Court of Appeal agreed and which, in my view, was proper. The Court of Appeal did not question the Judge's finding that the deceased would expend $1,800 for his personal use and $3,000 for his personal support. Thus, as a result, $7,000 would be available as disposable income for dependants. The evidence was that he contributed his pay cheque weekly to his family reserving only nominal sums and odd-job earnings for his own use. Having concluded that $7,000 per year would have been available to the appellant and her child each year, the Judge said [(1975), 7 OR (2d) 327, at 336 (Co. Ct.)]:

Actuarial tables filled as ex. 1 herein at 9% and 10% compound interest show the present value of $1 to age 65 for the male as $9.9375 and $9.1381 respectively. I believe a more realistic interest rate would be the approximate amount of 6½% which would materially inflate these figures; for example, at 4% the factor is 18.66461. One must consider income tax as a reality of modern life and its depreciating impact along with the contingencies hereinbefore alluded to is reflected in my assessment. Under the provisions of the *Fatal Accidents Act* I award the plaintiff the sum of $120,000, of which sum I apportion $17,500 for the infant Mitchel Stephen.

It is difficult, if not impossible, to know what use, if any, the trial Judge made of actuarial tables to which he was referred. It would seem, however, that he proceeded on an exhausting fund basis, with a discount rate of approximately 6½%. He made an allowance in respect of the income tax which the deceased would have had to pay on his earnings, had he lived, and he further reduced the award by a contingency allowance. He referred to the contingencies which might bear on assessment, as follows [at 333-34]:

(a) Possibility of remarriage;

(b) Possibility of widow's death before expiry of joint expectancy period;

(c) Possibility of deceased's dying under other circumstances prior to expiry of said joint expectancy period;

(d) Possibility of deceased husband's retiring before expiry of joint expectancy period;

(e) Acceleration of inheritance to widow—bearing in mind likelihood of increased inheritance in event death had not occurred;

(f) Possibility the infant child may not be a burden to the father or require additional benefits for the full period of his calculated working life.

On the question of prospects of remarriage, the judge adopted the apt comments of Phillimore J in *Buckley v. John Allen & Ford (Oxford), Ltd.*, [1967] 2 QB 637, including the statement that Judges should act on evidence rather than guesswork and, there being no evidence of any existing interest or attachment, concluded [at 335]: "I therefore accord no material significance to this prospect by way of deduction." He does not say that he is according no weight to the contingency.

As to the possibility of the early demise of either husband or wife, the Judge said:

All of the evidence indicates excellent health prospects and I rule that relatively little real significance can be attached to this contingency by way of reduction.

Again, it is not a question of refusing to consider a particular contingency. The judge considered the contingency, but decided it merited little significance. I do not think he can be faulted on this account.

With respect to the possibility of acceleration of the inheritance to the appellant, the Judge had this to say:

So far as the acceleration of her inheritance is concerned, I am readily satisfied that same should have no reducing effect as in these circumstances I am assured it is more than offset by the substantial loss she has suffered in future realization from this source.

Finally, the possibility that the infant child might not be a burden during his father's working life. On this point, the Judge said that he would give this fact material consideration in considering his award. These are his words:

> Unquestionably, there is the probability that the child Mitchel Stephen would not have been a burden to his father for anything like the 30 years or so of his working expectancy and I give this fact material consideration in considering this award.

The quantum of the award came before the Court of Appeal for Ontario. In that Court, reference was made by Mr. Justice Arnup, for the Court, to the six contingencies to which the trial Judge referred. Mr. Justice Arnup observed that the trial Judge might have added "possibility of incapacity to earn, occasioned by industrial or other accident, or by illness." He then continued [(1975), 10 OR (2d) 597, at 604 (CA)]:

> Having listed these contingencies, the trial Judge decided he should make no deduction for any of them. In so doing, he erred. A contingency, in the context of damages under the *Fatal Accidents Act*, is obviously an event that may or may not happen. A defendant is entitled to have contingencies taken into account by way of reduction from the result that would be reached if every contingency turned out favourably to the dependants, although due weight must be given in each case to the probability, or otherwise, of the contingent event actually happening.

I have been unable to find in the trial judgment any statement by the trial Judge that he had decided he should not make any deduction for any of the contingencies. The evidence, as I read it, is to the contrary. It is true that the trial Judge might have considered the possibility of the deceased husband becoming unable to earn, but I do not think it can be said that failure to express himself on this point amounts to reversible error. The award of $120,000 exceeded the amount claimed of $100,000 but that does not preclude an award of $100,000.

In making a gross award of $65,000 the Court of Appeal was content with the following cryptic statement:

> In my view, the appropriate award of general damages in all of the circumstances of this case, as disclosed by the evidence, would have been $65,000.

The judgment does not assist us, or the parties, by explaining why $65,000 should be considered to be the appropriate award. From this amount the Court of Appeal deducted the $6,500 to which I have referred and directed that $10,000 be paid into Court for the infant. In the result, the widow would receive from the defendants for her support and maintenance for the next fifty years the sum of $48,500. This, plus $6,500 already received, totals $55,000.

It is, of course, true that a trial Judge must consider contingencies tending to reduce the ultimate award and give those contingencies more or less weight. It is equally true there are contingencies tending to increase the award to which a Judge must give due weight. At the end of the day the only question of importance is whether, in all the circumstances, the final award is fair and adequate. Past experience should make one realize that if there is to be error in the amount of an award it is likely to be one of inadequacy.

In my opinion, in the circumstances of this case, an award of $55,000 to the appellant can only be described as niggardly. The appellant is entitled to an award of such amount as will assure her the comforts and station in life which she would have enjoyed but for the untimely death of her husband. If one is speaking of contingencies, I think it is not unreasonable to give primary attention to the contingencies, and they are many, the occurrence of which would result in making the award, in the light of events, entirely inadequate. An assessment must be neither punitive nor influenced by sentimentality. It is largely an exercise of business judgment. The question is whether a stated amount of capital will provide, during the period in question, having regard to contingencies tending to increase or decrease the award, a monthly sum at least equal to that which might reasonably have been expected during the continued life of the deceased.

The proper method of calculating the amount of a damage award under the *Fatal Accidents Act* is similar to that used in calculating the amount of an award for loss of future earnings, or for future care, in cases of serious personal injury. In each, the Court is faced with the task of determining the present value of a lump sum which, if invested, would provide payments of the appropriate size over a given number of years in the future, extinguishing the fund in the process. This matter has been discussed in detail in the decisions of this Court in *Andrews v. Grand & Toy Alberta Ltd.*; *Thornton v. Board of School Trustees of School District No. 57 (Prince George)*; and *Arnold v. Teno*, which are being delivered with the decision in the present case.

The object here is to award a sum which will replace present-day payments of $7,000 per year for a future period of 31 years, with some reduction for contingencies. The trial Judge used a discount rate of 6½% without explaining this choice except to say that it was a "more realistic" rate than 9% or 10%. As I have said in *Andrews* and *Thornton*, in my opinion the discount rate should be calculated on the basis of present rates of return on long-term investments with an allowance for the effects of future inflation. Evidence on these matters was not introduced at trial in the present case. However, the 6½% chosen by the Judge can be tested by the fact that present-day investment rates reach about 10½%, and Dr. Deutsch of the Economic Council of Canada forecasted an inflation rate of about 3½% over the long-term future. These two figures suggest that an appropriate discount rate is approximately 7%. This is only marginally different from the rate used by the trial Judge. Ignoring, for the moment, the other factors to be taken into consideration, the sum required to produce $7,000 per year for 31 years, payable monthly, discounted at 6½%, is slightly less than $95,000. The award should be reduced somewhat to account for contingencies although, as I have mentioned, this amount will probably not be large. On the other hand, in order to yield the sum required net of taxes a greater sum would obviously be called for. The resulting amount would not reach the figure of $120,000 which the trial Judge chose. The sum of $100,000, the amount claimed, can be justified, however, with reasonable allowance made for income tax impact and contingency deduction.

I would allow the appeal, set aside the judgment of the Court of Appeal and direct that the appellant recover from the defendants the sum of $93,500. Out of that sum there should be paid to Marilyn E. Keizer the sum of $78,500 and there should be paid into Court to the credit of the infant, Mitchel Stephen Keizer, the sum of $15,000, to be paid out to the said infant when he attains the age of 18 years, or upon further order of a Judge of the County Court of the County of Renfrew. The appellant is also entitled to her award of $1,600 under the provisions of the *Trustee Act*, RSO 1970, c. 470, in respect of funeral expenses and the value of an automobile.

I would allow the appellant her costs at trial against both defendants and her costs in this Court and in the Court of Appeal against the defendant Buch.

DE GRANDPRÉ J (dissenting in part): I have read with great interest the reasons for judgment prepared for delivery by my brother Spence. With respect, I am unable to reach the same conclusion on the quantum of damages.

Appellant has made two submissions on this point:

(1) the trial Judge having made no error in principle in his examination of the contingencies, the Court of Appeal should not have varied the decision of the trial Judge on the point;

(2) both the trial Judge and the Court of Appeal were wrong in taking into consideration the impact of the income tax on the gross earnings of the deceased.

The first submission cannot succeed. As pointed out by my brother Spence, the trial Judge did commit an error in principle in his examination of the question of contingencies, thus opening the door to a full re-examination of the subject-matter by the Court of Appeal. In such circumstances, the duty of this Court is to refrain from interfering in the absence of an error in principle by the Court of Appeal. The rule has been expressed by my brother Judson in *Hossack v. Hertz Drive Yourself Stations of Ontario Ltd.*, [1966] SCR 28 at p. 34:

> It is highly desirable that this power of review of reasonably wide scope should exist in the Court of Appeal and that this Court, if it recognizes that the case is one for review, should be slow to interfere. Everyone concerned is aware of the difficulties that surround an assessment of damages and its review in the Court of Appeal, and the volume of litigation in personal injury cases under the *Fatal Accidents Act* demonstrates the need for an experienced reviewing tribunal with reasonably wide powers. The Court of Appeal has this experience. They know better than anyone else what an award should be both in the interests of justice to the particular litigants and interest of some principle of uniformity, to the extent that this is attainable. Any further reviewing tribunal should be slow to interfere unless it is convinced that there is error in principle.

One aspect of any assessment of damages is the actuarial calculation. In the case at bar, plaintiff chose to obtain expert assistance and in August 1974, through her counsel, requested the Wyatt Company to conduct the necessary investigation on data supplied by plaintiff. The report of that firm, dated September 9, 1974, some three months before the trial, was filed by consent of the parties and is the only evidence on the point. The expert assumes a compound interest of 9% and 10% and plaintiff was content to submit her case on that basis. The record does not disclose any other information about these calculations.

Upon this aspect of the case, the trial Judge had this to say [7 OR (2d) 327, at 336 (Co. Ct.)]:

> Actuarial tables filed as ex. 1 herein at 9% and 10% compound interest show the present value of $1 to age 65 for the male as $9.9375 and $9.1381 respectively. I believe a more realistic interest rate would be in the approximate amount of 6½% which would materially inflate these figures; for example, at 4% the factor is 18.66461.

To which the Court of Appeal added this comment [10 OR (2d) 597, at 604]:

> There was no evidence before him as to the cost of an annuity in the market place, nor of the interest factor on which the purchase price of annuities was based at the relevant time.

There is no doubt that the inflationary trends of our time have in principle to be taken into consideration when determining the proper rate of interest to be used when capitalizing the loss of support. However, that principle no longer applies when as in the present instance plaintiff chooses to adduce evidence of calculations based on high interest rates, without any qualification, and enters into an agreement with the defence, the net result of which is to make that evidence the only one on the point. In these circumstances, the hands of the Judges are tied and the case must be decided without recourse to other information or prior judicial knowledge.

Thus the Court of Appeal was right in its approach to the question of damages. I cannot find any error in principle in its judgment with the possible exception of the issue of income tax to which I now turn.

In the case at bar, the deceased left a widow and one child. At the time of his death, his gross income was $12,000 but there is a finding that two or three years later, that figure would have been $15,000. It is on that basis that the damages have been calculated:

Gross income		$15,000
Less: Personal use and support	$4,800	
Income tax	$3,200	
		$ 8,000
Disposable income		$ 7,000

As already mentioned, appellant takes issue with the deduction for income tax submitting that *Gehrmann v. Lavoie*, [1976] 2 SCR 561, has decided the point in her favour. I sat in that case and expressly reserved my consideration of the matter, feeling at the time that the appeal could be dismissed on other grounds. I must now examine the question.

My starting point will be the general attitude of Bench and Bar throughout the years. An expression of that attitude is to be found in the Special Lectures of the Law Society of Upper Canada on *Damages for Personal Injuries* in 1958, where Stewart J expressed, while discussing awards for personal injuries, his views on *British Transport Com'n v. Gourley*, [1956] AC 185 (HL (Eng.)) in very clear terms: "I will not follow it." Still another lecturer, P.B.C. Pepper, at p. 23, when discussing the calculation of damages for loss of a husband, stated unequivocally that they should be calculated on the net earnings: "By net earnings, I mean gross earnings after deduction of income tax at source."

A number of cases could be cited in support of that statement but it is not necessary to do so. Suffice it to say that the Courts have until *Gehrmann* come to the same conclusion. A very relevant example is *May v. Municipality of Metropolitan Toronto*, [1969] 1 OR 419, where Addy J makes a study in depth of the questions, underlining the basic distinction between the situation in personal injuries cases as decided in the *The Queen in right of Ontario v. Jennings*, [1966] SCR 532 and the situation under the *Fatal Accidents Act*, now RSO 1970, c. 164. The following extract from p. 422 summarizes his thoughts:

I feel it is quite clear, however, that the *Jennings* case does not apply to the case at bar in any event, for the present case is not taken by the person who would be earning the income but by the person who would be receiving a benefit from the net income. It is obvious that the widow at no time was entitled to the income and at no time was she ever able to receive or could she count on receiving either as of right or as a gratuitous payment anything more than the net income of the deceased after deducting income tax and all of the other expenses of the deceased.

This reasoning was adopted in so many words by the Court of Appeal of Ontario in *Hawryluk v. Hodgins*, [1972] 3 OR 741 (CA) at p. 748 (*per* MacKay JA). It is of interest to note that two of the three Judges in *Hawryluk*, namely, MacKay and Kelly JJA, were also sitting in *Jennings*, [1965] 2 OR 285, where, in a personal injury case, they came to another conclusion, namely, that the impact of the income tax on the gross earnings of the injured party should not be taken into consideration, a conclusion which was affirmed in this Court.

That there is a fundamental distinction between a personal injury claim and a fatal accident one has repeatedly been underlined in a variety of cases. A recent example involving proceedings under the *Trustee Act*, RSA 1955, c. 346, s. 32 is to be found in *Crosby v. O'Reilly*, [1975] 2 SCR 381.

En passant, I would also underline that in *Canadian Pacific Ltd. v. Gill*, [1973] SCR 654, the trial Judge had, in his calculations, deducted from the gross earnings the income tax payable by the deceased. The point was not mentioned in the Court of Appeal nor in this Court where, on the question of damages, the only problem raised was that of the pension payments under the Canada Pension Plan.

It is not only in Canada that the views were unanimous on the point. *McGregor on Damages* (London: Sweet & Maxwell, 13th ed., 1972) at p. 291, para. 407, gives the situation in England which still holds true to this date:

> (b) *Injuries resulting in death*. Even before *Gourley's* case it had been accepted in actions by or on behalf of a deceased's dependants under the *Fatal Accidents Acts* that what the deceased would have had to pay in tax must be taken into account in assessing the damages. While in a physically injured plaintiff's claim for his loss of earnings it was possible to regard any tax which would be levied on them as representing a collateral liability which should be ignored, as the claim of a deceased's dependants is for their loss of that portion of the deceased's earnings which would have been used for their support, and therefore for an amount which would already have suffered tax in the deceased's hands before it came to be applied for their benefit, no question of the liability to tax being merely collateral could ever arise.

See also Melford Stevenson, QC and Alan Orr, "The Tax Element in Damages," [1956] *British Tax Review* 6; Harry Street, *The Law of Torts* (London: Butterworths, 6th ed., 1976) at p. 414.

J.G. Fleming, *The Law of Torts* (Sydney: Law Book Co., 4th ed., 1971), tells us that the situation is the same in Australia (p. 586):

> Compensation is due, and due only, for loss of support, measured by the claimant's reasonable expectation of pecuniary benefit. Where the person killed was the breadwinner, the principal source of pecuniary detriment is the loss of the deceased's net earnings, present and future. The basis of calculation is, therefore, the amount of his wages or other income from which must be deducted an estimated amount of what the deceased required for his own personal and living expenses.

The word "net" in footnote No. 49 is defined "income tax deducted."

In South Africa, that view appears to be accepted without question. In a note on "Income Tax and Damages in Delict" in (1950), 67 *South African Law Journal*, CJJ writes (p. 296):

(b) The matter also becomes of importance in cases where an action is brought by dependants for damages in respect of the death of the breadwinner. It is submitted that in these cases the income tax which would have been paid by the breadwinner must clearly be taken into account in assessing the damages to be awarded to the plaintiffs. Here the plaintiffs are entitled to damages in the amount which it is anticipated they would have received by way of support from the breadwinner but for his decease. There can, it is suggested, be no doubt but that in assessing the amount which would have been made available by the deceased for their support, the amount which he would have been obliged to devote to his own purposes, including the discharge of his obligation to pay income tax, must be taken into account by deduction from the anticipated amount of his total earnings, in arriving at the damages to be awarded to the plaintiffs.

This unanimity at first sight is very persuasive. Still the reasons behind those views must be examined. Under the *Fatal Accidents Act*, what must be determined is the pecuniary benefit lost by the plaintiff because of the untimely death of the deceased: *Littley v. Brooks*, [1932] SCR 462 at p. 470; *Proctor v. Dyck*, [1953] 1 SCR 244. It seems to me that what the widow and the child have lost in this case is the support payments made by the deceased, support payments which could only come out of funds left after deducting the cost of maintaining the husband, including the amount of tax payable on his income. I cannot see how this pecuniary loss could be evaluated on any other basis than the take-home pay, that is the net pay after deductions on many items, including income tax.

In *Proctor* just mentioned, Cartwright J, as he then was, speaking for the Court, underlined that a child of the deceased, although not depending on the latter at the time of death, had nevertheless a right of indemnity if he had "a reasonable expectation of deriving pecuniary advantage" (at p. 249) from his father. In the circumstances of that case, the expectation was based on the deceased's steadily increasing net worth resulting from savings and capital profits. In this context, savings can only exist after payment of income tax.

It is trite law that the *Fatal Accidents Act* has created a right of action which did not exist at common law and, as mentioned above, that the loss that can be recovered is the financial loss. This was not the approach in *Jennings* where it was stated: "The plaintiff has been deprived of his capacity to earn income. It is the value of that capital asset which has to be assessed" (*per* Judson J, at p. 546). I cannot consider that the deceased here was a capital asset.

There is more. Respondent submits that the whole subject-matter of the impact of the income tax in a fatal accident case must be examined not only in the narrow confines of the situation in the case at bar but also by reference to other factual situations. He has submitted figures for gross incomes of $100,000 and $50,000 where the tax bite would have been in round figures for the year 1973, $50,000 and $20,000 respectively. In chart form:

Gross income	Tax	Net income
$100,000	$50,000	$50,000
$ 50,000	$20,000	$30,000

It is quite obvious that basing an award under the *Fatal Accidents Act* on gross income would fail to take into consideration the realities of life in a modern state and would, in some cases, give to the dependants a fund greatly in excess of their financial loss. Income tax must therefore be taken into consideration and the Court of Appeal was right in accepting the trial Judge's approach in that respect.

I now turn to a point that has no bearing on the result in the case at bar but which could be major in other cases: by what mechanics do the Courts provide for the tax to be paid by the defendants on the income produced by the fund? Two approaches are to be found in the jurisprudence, one is that outlined by Chief Justice Cowan in *Spurr v. Naugler; Co-Operative Fire & Casualty Co., Third Party* (1974), 11 NSR (2d) 637 (SC, TD), and another in the decision of the House of Lords in *Taylor v. O'Connor*, [1971] AC 115 (HL (Eng.)). In the *Spurr* case, Chief Justice Cowan deducted the income tax "on that part of the gross income not available for the widow and other dependents." In *Taylor*, we find the following in the speech of Lord Reid (at pp. 126-27):

> But take the present case. The respondent will have the £10,000 to which I have referred and damages in respect of: (a) loss of her dependency; and (b) loss of her interest in the savings which the husband would have made. The damages for the loss of dependency ought to be such that she will have available to spend each year free of tax a sum equal to the amount of the dependency. But if the damages are calculated without a reference to income tax that will not be so. Suppose the damages are sufficient to buy an ordinary annuity for her life of that amount. Part of each year's annuity payment will be a return of capital and will not be taxable; but that part which is truly income will have to bear tax. So the amount available to her to spend will fall short of what it should be by the amount of that tax. The damages will, therefore, have to be increased by an amount necessary to counteract this shortfall. This shortfall will be increased by the present high rates of interest.

To my mind, both approaches stem from the same philosophy but the means chosen by the House of Lords are to be preferred. The method outlined in *Spurr* only gives an exact result if care is taken not to pro-rate the income tax between the deceased and the dependants. Keeping in mind the progressive feature of the taxing statute, the greater bite of the tax should be on the deceased's share because the remainder coming to the dependants attracts a lower rate. In the case at bar, the impact of the income tax on the dependants is minimal. In any event, as already underlined, the award of the Court of Appeal is generous enough.

For these reasons, I would dismiss the appeal and the cross-appeal with costs, subject to the correction of the clerical error mentioned by my brother Spence as to the sum of $1,600 mentioned by Arnup JA in his reasons but not included in the formal judgment.

Appeal allowed in part.

To v. Toronto Board of Education
(2001), 55 OR (3d) 641 (CA)

OSBORNE ACJO:

[1] After a 28-day jury trial, in which both liability and damages were in issue, Dyson J gave judgment for the plaintiffs further to answers to questions submitted to the jury as part of the trial judge's charge. No issue is taken with the trial judge's charge or with the jury's

liability findings. What is in issue on the defendant Toronto Board of Education's appeal is the jury's assessment of damages for the loss of guidance, care and companionship under the *Family Law Act*, RSO 1990, c. F.3, s. 61 in respect of the 14-year old deceased's father, mother and sister. The assessments in issue are $100,000 for each of the deceased's father and mother and $50,000 for his sister. ...

Overview

[3] On February 26, 1992, Binh Hoy To (the deceased), a 14-year old Grade 9 student, was doing pull ups on the steel crossbar of a large European handball net in the gymnasium during a physical education class at Harbord Collegiate. He was killed when the net toppled over and crushed his head between the steel frame of the net and the gymnasium floor. He was survived by his father Quoc Luong To (Mr. To), his mother, Kiet Linh Luong To (Mrs. To) and his younger sister, Mary To.

[4] In due course the deceased's mother, father and sister sued the Toronto Board of Education and the vendor of the equipment in question, Sports Equipment of Toronto Limited. The defendant Queonto Ltd. did not take part in the trial.

[5] The trial commenced before Dyson J and a jury on September 15, 1998. On October 23, 1998, in response to questions put to them, the jury returned a verdict finding negligence on the part of the Board (75%) and the deceased (25%). The jury found no negligence on the part of Sports Equipment of Toronto Limited. In answer to the damages questions put to them, the jury assessed damages as follows:

- Pecuniary loss—$11,582

- Loss of future support (economic loss)—$0

- Loss of guidance, care and companionship

  Mr. To—$100,000

  Mrs. To—$100,000

  Mary To—$50,000

. . .

[7] In its appeal, the appellant Board submits that the damages assessed by the jury for guidance, care and companionship are inordinately high and that the trial judge erred in exercising his discretion on costs by awarding the plaintiffs solicitor-and-client costs of the trial even though there were no Rule 49 offers which would support a solicitor-and-client costs order.

The Evidence

[8] Some reference to the evidence led at trial is required in order to deal with the issue of the jury's assessment of damages for guidance, care and companionship. The evidence to which I refer largely concerns the relationship between the deceased and his mother, father and sister.

[9] The deceased was born in 1977 in South Vietnam. Shortly after his birth, his father and mother determined that as persons of Chinese descent in South Vietnam, recently

overtaken by Communist North Vietnam, the To family would have a very difficult future. They thus arranged to escape from South Vietnam by travelling without the required papers to North Vietnam, from there to China and then to the South China Sea, where they arranged to board a small boat destined for Hong Kong with about 30 other people.

[10] Mr. and Mrs. To, with their young son, immigrated to Canada in 1980, where they established themselves and became independent in a financial sense by working in restaurants and eventually by becoming restaurant owners. In due course, they became Canadian citizens. Mary To, the sister of the deceased, was born shortly after the To family arrived in Canada, when the deceased was about three years old.

[11] There was considerable evidence led at trial about the particular culture into which the deceased was born, particularly with respect of the relationship between the deceased and his family. This evidence concerned, among other things, the important place occupied by a first-born son. It was expected from the outset that the deceased as the To's first-born son would excel scholastically and graduate from a university with a view to obtaining highly remunerative employment. It was also expected that he would be obedient and provide financial and social support for his parents and direct assistance to his sister, Mary. Mr. and Mrs. To were devoted to, and relied upon, the deceased in many ways. Their goals for him were shared and high.

[12] From the evidence adduced at trial, it is apparent that the deceased fit comfortably into the expected mould. He excelled at school, he was devoted to his parents and they to him. The deceased helped his father with both business and personal correspondence because Mr. To did not read English. The deceased was in many ways his father's contact with the English-speaking world. By the age of 14, he had become a trusted companion and adviser to his father. There is ample evidence of both guidance and companionship in the deceased's relationship with his father and mother. I will comment on the meaning of guidance and companionship later in these reasons.

[13] The deceased's relationship with his sister, Mary was extremely close, almost paternal. The deceased was devoted to his mother, father and sister. He recognized the need to meet his parents' high expectations. He accepted responsibility for ensuring that his sister's homework was properly completed. He also helped her with her school work. He would comfort and care for her if his parents were not at home. He was also consistently available to her to discuss problems she had. The deceased was a surrogate father to his sister and an integral part of her life.

[14] Because Mr. and Mrs. To often worked very long hours in the family business, the deceased was often required to care for his sister. Mrs. To testified that the deceased was of considerable assistance to Mary in school. In addition, there was evidence from Anh Honh Trinh that the deceased consistently helped his sister do her homework. Mrs. To testified that Mary's academic performance has declined since the deceased's death.

[15] The deceased and Mary provided considerable companionship to one another. They were inseparable until Mary was six years old. Anh Honh Trinh testified that when the family came to Canada "they are all the time together, and the brother is always taking care of the sister because the sister was much younger." She testified that when the two attended the same school, they walked home together and that even when the deceased moved to another school, they were still "always together." Mary testified that she and the deceased

planned to live near each other as adults, and that they were as close as a brother and sister could be.

[16] The deceased's tragic death had a devastating effect on his mother, father and sister. He was not buried until approximately three weeks after his death, when an appropriate date in the Chinese calendar was reached. His family moved out of the family home for about one year. After his death, the family travelled every weekend from their home to the Cam Sham Temple on Bayview Avenue in Toronto where incense was burned. Mrs. To prepared the deceased's favourite foods, which she believed his spirit could smell but not eat. At some risk to her own health, Mrs. To tried on two occasions to produce another son. She made inquiries about fertilization. In the end, she had complications, and eventually required a hysterectomy. After her hysterectomy, Mrs. To offered to divorce Mr. To because she no longer could bear him a son.

[17] Mr. To has a partnership interest in two restaurants with his older brother. His time was reasonably flexible since he was the person in charge of the administrative aspects of the business. Mrs. To did not have a fixed schedule. She regularly picked the deceased and his sister up from school to accompany them home from school, after which she prepared dinner. The deceased and his sister were almost always accompanied to and from school by one of their parents.

[18] The deceased was a fun-loving, outgoing, popular, hardworking teenager who was committed to school and who cared for his family and his friends at Harbord Collegiate. He was an excellent student. Although he was a hockey fan, he did not play hockey or any other sport because his goals did not permit him time to pursue such hobbies.

[19] On the evidence led at trial, most of which was uncontradicted, it was clearly open to the jury to conclude that the To family was extremely close and that the family's expectations were that the deceased would proceed to a university education, likely to post-graduate work and a professional career. In short, there was an abundance of evidence that the deceased provided, and would have continued to provide, guidance and companionship to his mother and father and guidance, care and companionship to his sister.

Statutory Damages for Loss of Guidance, Care, and Companionship

[20] The statutory scheme permitting recovery for damages for the loss of guidance, care and companionship became part of the law of Ontario in 1978 with the introduction of the *Family Law Reform Act*, 1978, SO 1978, c. 2. Section 60(2) of the *Family Law Reform Act* (now *Family Law Act*, s. 61(2)(e)) provided that damages recoverable in a fatal accident claim "may include" damages for the loss of guidance, care and companionship.

[21] Section 61 of the *Family Law Act*, makes provision for compensation for the loss of guidance, care and companionship:

> 61(1) If a person is injured or killed by the fault or neglect of another under circumstances where the person is entitled to recover damages, or would have been entitled if not killed, ... children, grandchildren, parents, grandparents, brothers and sisters of the person are entitled to recover their pecuniary loss resulting from the injury or death from the person from whom the person injured or killed is entitled to recover or would have been entitled to recover if not killed, and to maintain an action for the purpose in a court of competent jurisdiction.

(2) The damages recoverable in a claim under subsection (1) may include, ...

(e) an amount to compensate for the loss of guidance, care and companionship that the claimant might reasonably have been expected to receive from the person if the injury or death had not occurred.

[22] The introduction of the *Family Law Reform Act* represented a major change in the scope of the quantum of recovery of damages in fatal accident claims. At common law, no action lay for any loss in circumstances where the tortious conduct of the defendant caused another person's death. However, in 1846 in England, through *An Act for Compensating Families of Persons Killed by Accidents* (9 and 10 Vict., C.93), (made part of the law of Ontario and Quebec in 1847 with the introduction of the *Fatal Accidents Act* (10 and 11 Vict., C.6), the tortfeasor was liable to an action for damages to certain prescribed persons in particular relationships with the deceased. The *Fatal Accidents Act* was not interpreted to permit compensation for grief, mental distress or solatium. Companionship was limited to pecuniary loss. It was eventually held that the *Fatal Accidents* Act permitted the granting of compensation to a child for the loss of his/her parents' companionship. See *Vana v. Tosta*, [1968] SCR 71. The prevailing fiction was that a child's loss of a parent's companionship was a pecuniary loss.

[23] In 1969, the Ontario Law Reform Commission in its *Report on Family Law* (Toronto: Department of Justice, 1969) Vol. 1 at p. 109, recommended that a full study be undertaken of losses, including losses which were non-pecuniary in their character, in both personal injury and fatal accident claims. The Commission recommended in its brief report that the legislation, which was then contemplated, limit recovery of damages in fatal accident claims to pecuniary losses, as the Commission assumed was the case under the *Fatal Accidents Act*.

[24] The *Family Law Reform Act* was proclaimed in force in 1978. It provided for the recovery of "pecuniary loss" in respect of personal injury and fatal accident claims. However, s. 60(2) of the *Act* provided that recoverable losses by certain relatives of the deceased, expanded in the *Family Law Reform Act* to include siblings, may include an amount to compensate for the loss of guidance, care and companionship.

[25] The question quickly arose whether a compensable damages for the loss of guidance, care or companionship, included essentially non-pecuniary losses. This court's judgment in *Mason v. Peters* (1982), 39 OR (2d) 27, put that debate to rest. In that case, the trial judge assessed guidance, care and companionship compensation for a mother whose 11-year old son was killed in an accident in April 1978 at $45,000. He assessed the deceased's sister's damages at $5,000. Robins JA, after reviewing the relatively meagre damages awarded in cases involving the death of children under the former *Fatal Accidents Act*, focused on companionship. He said, at p. 33:

Whatever the situation may have been in earlier times when children were regarded as an economic asset, in this day and age, the death of a child does not often constitute a monetary loss or one measurable in pecuniary terms. The most significant loss suffered, apart from the sorrow, grief and anguish that always ensues from such deaths, is not potential economic gain, but deprivation of the society, comfort and protection which might reasonably be expected had the child lived—in short, the loss of the rewards of association which flow from the family relationship and are summarized in the word "companionship."

[26] Subsequent cases (decided under both the *Family Law Reform Act* and the *Family Law Act*) revealed a great disparity in guidance, care and companionship damage awards. See for example, *Reidy v. McLeod*, (1986), 54 OR (2d) 661 (CA), rev'g (1984), 47 OR (2d) 313 (HCJ); *Hamilton v. Canadian National Railway Co.*, (1991), 80 DLR (4th) 470 (Ont. CA); and *Macartney v. Warner* (2000), 46 OR 669 (CA).

[27] Because guidance, care and companionship damages assessments were not consistent, in the interest of certainty, some called for conventional awards. See *Gervais v. Richard*, (1984), 48 OR (2d) 191 (HCJ). As it turned out the call was not heeded. Cases like *Nielsen v. Kaufmann*, (1986), 54 OR (2d) 188 (CA) and *Zdasiuk v. Lucas*, (1987), 58 OR (2d) 443 (CA) established that in assessing guidance, care and companionship damages the particular family circumstances in each case must be taken into account by the trier of fact. Even when guidance, care and companionship damages awards were reduced on appeal, the reduction was not premised on accepted "conventional" awards. For example, in *Reidy, supra*, this court reduced the trial judge's assessment of guidance, care and companionship damages but it did not suggest that these assessments should be conventional.

[28] The result of a case-by-case analysis of family relationships has led to a range of guidance, care and companionship assessments so broad as to defy description as conventional. The range of these assessments will, of course, expand if we continue to permit juries to assess these damages.

[29] I regard the existing disparity in guidance, care and companionship awards as the inevitable result of choices made by the courts and the Legislature. The courts could have established conventional guidance, care and companionship awards, or could have imposed rough upper limits as the Supreme Court of Canada did in respect of non-pecuniary general damages in personal injury cases. See *Andrews v. Grand and Toy Alberta Ltd.*, [1978] 2 SCR 229. That has not happened. Alternatively, the Legislature could have moved towards a legislative scheme such as exists in Alberta where the *Alberta Fatal Accidents Act*, RSA 1980, c. F-5, s. 8 (as amended), provides that in the event of the death of a child under 18 years of age, the court is directed to award $43,000 to each of the child's parents for grief and loss of guidance, care and companionship. This is done without reference to other damages or evidence of damage.

[30] Although one might quibble with the numbers, in my view, this system merits serious consideration. However, that is a matter for the Legislature. As matters now stand, as I have said, each case must be given separate consideration to measure what Krever J viewed as "immeasurable" and "incalculable" in *Gervais, supra*, at p. 201. Judges and juries are left to do the best they can in each case where the assessment of damages for guidance, care and companionship is required.

The Standard of Appellate Review

[31] It is against that general background that I turn to consider the standard of appellate review as it relates to the jury's assessment of damages of the deceased's mother, father and sister for the loss of guidance, care and companionship. It is manifest, merely because I would have assessed guidance, care and companionship damages lower than the jury's assessment, does not justify this court's intervention with the jury's assessment. In the circumstances where there was no error in the charge so that the jury can be taken to have considered and

applied the proper factors and principles, the jury's assessment must be so inordinately high (or low) as to constitute a wholly erroneous estimate of the guidance, care and companionship loss. See *Woelk v. Halvorson*, [1980] 2 SCR 430; *Macartney, supra*; and *Scott v. Musial* (1959), 3 All ER 193 (CA). While reference to other guidance, care and companionship assessments involving deaths of children is helpful to test the reasonableness of the award, it is not determinative. Each case must be considered in light of the evidence material to the guidance, care and companionship claims in that case. When this is done, for the reasons that follow, in my view, the $100,000 guidance, care and companionship assessments of Mr. and Mrs. To are not so inordinately high as to justify this court's interference. In my opinion, the assessment of $50,000 for the deceased's sister is outside the range of reasonableness and is inordinately high.

The Guidance, Care, and Companionship Claim of the Deceased's Mother and Father

[32] This court has consistently held that the guidance, care and companionship compensation in each case must be assessed in an objective and unemotional way. See *Hamilton, supra*; and *Macartney, supra*. Since each case must be considered in light of the particular family relationship involved, assessments will, of course, vary. An appellate court will not lightly interfere with a properly instructed jury's assessment of damages; however, the reasonableness of the jury's assessment will be tested but by comparison with assessments in other cases. This latter exercise leads to establishing a range of damages. These issues were referred to by Krever and Finlayson JJA in *Hamilton, supra*, pp. 472-73:

> We are mindful that *this is a jury award and that we should not lightly interfere with it*. However, in viewing the evidence in this case in its totality and in a light most favourable to the claims, we are of the opinion that the quantum of damages set by the jury cannot be justified. *The quantum of damages here far exceeds the general range of damages that has been awarded by our courts in cases involving the death of minor children* ... . [Emphasis added.]

[33] In the result, in *Hamilton, supra*, this court (Galligan JA dissenting) reduced the jury's assessment of damages for the deceased's mother from $150,000 to $50,000; the assessment for the deceased's two brothers was reduced from $15,000 to $7,500 and the assessment for the deceased's sister, who was the closest to her, was reduced from $25,000 to $10,000.

[34] In *Macartney, supra*, a non-jury case involving the death of a 19-year old boy, the damage assessments were alleged to be too low. Rosenberg JA, after recognizing that the amount of guidance, care and companionship compensation in a particular case will depend on the facts and circumstances in evidence in that case, referred to an accepted range of damages at p. 674:

> While it is my view that [the trial judge's guidance, care and companionship damages assessments] are low, they were within the accepted range for this type of case, albeit at the very bottom of that range. The limits of appellate review of damage awards are well settled. The Court of Appeal should not interfere merely because it would have come to a different conclusion ... .

[35] In both *Hamilton, supra*, and *Macartney, supra*, there was no evidence that would take the case out of the general range of guidance, care and companionship damages that

had been awarded in cases involving the death of teenage children. Both cases reveal a reluctance to interfere with a trial judge's assessment of damages. The same reluctance prevails in respect of jury assessments of damages. In *Hamilton*, this court did interfere because it concluded that the guidance, care and companionship assessments were higher than the accepted range. In *Macartney*, this court did not interfere because the damages, although low, came within the accepted range.

[36] Companionship, as it was defined in *Mason v. Peters* in a fatal accident context, consists of the deprivation of the society, comfort and protection which might reasonably be expected had the child lived. Robins JA described it as "the loss of the rewards of association which flow from the family relationship." Care was referred to by Linden J in *Thornborrow v. MacKinnon* (1981), 32 OR (2d) 740 (HCJ) as including "feeding, clothing, cleaning, transporting, helping and protecting another person." *Thornborrow* was cited with approval by Robins JA in *Mason v. Peters*. See also *Huggins v. Ramtej*, [1999] OJ No. 1696 (Ont. SCJ) (QL). In *Thornborrow*, Linden J described guidance as including such things as education, training, discipline and moral teaching.

[37] The assessments of $100,000 for each of Mr. and Mrs. To might be viewed as being at the high end of an accepted range of guidance, care and companionship damages. The question that must be considered is whether those assessments are outside the accepted range of damages. In my view, the $100,000 assessments for Mr. and Mrs. To are not outside the range. Expressed in constant dollars, the $100,000 assessments for Mr. and Mrs. To are roughly comparable to the $45,000 guidance, care and companionship assessment in *Mason v. Peters*. In April 1978, (the month of the *Mason v. Peters* accident) the consumer price index for Canada was at 54.6. In February 1992, the month of the deceased's death, the consumer price index was at 127.1. Given that increase in the consumer price index, it would take $104,753 in February 1992 dollars to purchase the same basket of good purchased for $45,000 in 1978. I view *Mason v. Peters* to be an acceptable comparator for the purpose of assessing a range of "accepted damages." In addition, I note that the $45,000 *Mason v. Peters* guidance, care and companionship assessment was referred by Robins JA as "modest" and an assessment that could "in no sense be considered excessive." Although I think that the jury's guidance, care and companionship assessments for Mr. and Mrs. To are high, they are not so high as to justify this court's intervention. In my opinion, there was evidence in this case that would support a conclusion that damages for guidance, care and companionship in respect of the mother, father and sister were justifiably assessed at the high end of what one might describe as an accepted range of damages. There was evidence of an extremely close relationship between the deceased and his mother and father. It was open to the jury to find that Mr. and Mrs. To suffered a substantial loss of society, comfort and protection, all benefits that flow from the family relationship. I would not give effect to this ground of appeal.

[38] I should address two further points. First, there was some confusion as to whether counsel at trial referred to the assessment of guidance, care and companionship damages in another case. This turned out to be a non-issue on the appeal; however, to avoid future problems, I should make it clear that counsel should not refer to other cases when making submissions to the jury. See *Thomas (Committee of) v. Bell Helmets* (1999), 40 CPC (4th) 31 (Ont. CA). This will serve only to deflect the jury from the required analysis of the evidence in the case before them. Second, the constant dollar comparison of the guidance, care and companionship assessments in this case with the *Mason v. Peters* assessment was the subject

matter of affidavit evidence that the respondents sought to tender as fresh evidence. In my opinion, this "evidence" (the accuracy of which was accepted) is best viewed as an acceptable aid to oral argument, not as fresh evidence. Thus, I would dismiss the motion to introduce fresh evidence without costs.

The Deceased's Sister Guidance, Care, and Companionship Claim

[39] As I have said, the jury assessed the deceased's sister Mary's claim for the loss of guidance, care and companionship at $50,000. As is the case with the claim of the deceased's mother and father, Mary To's entitlement to guidance, care and companionship compensation must be considered in light of the particular relationship between her and the deceased.

[40] There is no doubt that the evidence supports a finding that Mary To suffered a loss of guidance, care and companionship as a result of her brother's death. The question then is simply whether the jury's assessment is so inordinately high as to require this court's intervention.

[41] At the time of her brother's death, Mary was 11 years old. There was evidence that Mary and her brother were close and that the deceased was "always taking care of her." Mrs. To described her children's relationship as "very good." She said that they never fought, and that "he tried to yield to his sister." Mr. To testified that his son was a companion to all members of the family. He described the family unit as "very, very happy."

[42] The general or accepted range of damages in sibling claims for the loss of guidance, care and companionship in roughly comparable cases is very broad but the assessments are consistently lower than $50,000. The facts in *Rintoul v. Linde Estate* (1997), 32 OR (3d) 704 (Gen. Div.) are closest to this case. In *Rintoul*, the deceased was 16 years old when he died. He was survived by one sister who was 12 at the time of the deceased's death. The family was close and supportive. Before the tragic accident, the deceased and his sister discussed taking over the family farm together. The trial judge, Salhany J, held that the facts of that case were "unique." He concluded that the deceased's sister relied on him for guidance, even at his young age. The trial judge awarded the sister $20,000 for her guidance, care and companionship loss. In other guidance, care and companionship sibling assessment cases, the awards are lower. See for example, *Frawley v. Asselstine*, (1990), 73 OR (2d) 525 (HCJ); *Koncovy v. Hodulik*, [1986] OJ No. 864 (HCJ) (QL); *Thompson Estate v. Bigham*, [1985] OJ No. 726 (HCJ) (QL); *Radovini v. HOJ National Leasing Ltd.*, [1986] OJ No. 196 (HCJ)(QL); *Ashley Estate v. Goodman*, [1994] OJ No. 1672 (Gen. Div.) (QL); *Vahey v. Farrell*, [1994] OJ No. 459 (Gen. Div.) (QL); and *Hechavarria v. Reale*, (2000), 51 OR (3d) 364 (SCJ).

[43] As was the case in *Rintoul, supra*, the deceased in this case was an older sibling and the only male child in the family, a fact that is particularly significant in Chinese culture. He was mature, responsible and enjoyed a very close relationship with his sister, Mary. He was her role model.

[44] Although Mary To suffered a significant loss of guidance and companionship as a result of the death of her brother, she will in all probability go on to establish a life of her own and likely a family of her own.

[45] As the majority stated in *Hamilton, supra*, the assessment in question must fall somewhere within the range of damages established in comparable cases involving the deaths of minor children. In my opinion, a $50,000 guidance, care and companionship as-

sessment exceeds the accepted range of damages to a degree that requires this court's intervention. To put it another way, the assessment is inordinately high.

[46] I accept that there was a very close relationship between the deceased and his sister, and that she suffered a significant loss of guidance, care and companionship as a result of her brother's death. As was the case in *Rintoul, supra,* the circumstances of this case support a substantial assessment of guidance, care and companionship damages for the deceased's sister. Since it would make no sense to prolong these proceedings and since this court has authority to vary the assessment in issue (see s. 119 of the *Courts of Justice Act,* RSO 1990, c. C.43), recognizing that the jury was prepared to be generous, I would vary the assessment of Mary To's guidance, care and companionship damages by reducing it from $50,000 to $25,000.

NOTES AND QUESTIONS

1. The Ontario legislation limits the class of third-party claimants to children, grandchildren, parents, grandparents, brothers and sisters, and spouse. S.M. Waddams, *Law of Damages* (looseleaf), at paragraph 6.990:

> Another problem is the definition of the statutory class of claimants. With the changing social view of family relationships there is constant pressure to enlarge the class of claimants. Amendments in most jurisdictions have included illegitimate and adopted children; some have included foster children and *de facto* spouses. But there is no persuasive reason to stop at that point. It is foreseeable that with the declining significance of the marriage relationship as such, there will be an extension of the statutory benefits to homosexual relationships and to non-sexual household arrangements. Quite a strong case can then theoretically be made for including remote dependent relatives and unrelated dependent persons especially if they are elderly or handicapped.

Prince Edward Island appears to provide the broadest class of claimants by including the following provision:

> section 1 "dependant" ...
>
> f. means any other person who for a period of at least three years immediately prior to the death of the deceased was dependent upon the deceased for maintenance and support.

2. Because the claim of a spouse is based on proof of actual pecuniary loss, courts have been obliged to consider the state of a claimant's marriage before the accident, as well as the possibility of future remarriage after the accident. To what extent do you believe this is relevant? Section 7 of the *Fatal Accidents Act,* RSPEI 1988, c. F-5, states that in the assessment of damages under the Act no impact should be accorded

> the probability that a dependant may marry or the effects of such probability on any other dependant.

See also in the United Kingdom the *Administration of Justice Act,* 1982, c. 53, s. 3(3) (amending the *Fatal Accidents Act,* 1976), which contains this provision:

> 3(3) In an action under this Act where there fall to be assessed damages payable to a widow in respect of the death of her husband there shall not be taken account the re-marriage of the widow or her prospects of re-marriage.

See also *Sharp-Barker v. Fehr* (1982), 39 BCLR 19 and *Lamb v. Brandt* (1984), 56 BCLR 74 (CA).

3. Both *Keizer* and *Mason* use the term "dependant" to describe the class of claimants. How appropriate is this term as a description of contemporary spousal relationships? See S.M. Waddams, *Law of Damages* (looseleaf), at paragraph 6.990 (footnotes omitted):

> All these considerations raise a broader issue, that is, whether the concept of dependency is really useful or appropriate in the context of modern family relationships. In fact, *Lord Campbell's Act* did not use the word "dependant"; dependency has never been a strict requirement for recovery. Financial loss caused by the death is the test and from the earliest cases it has been held that an earner can recover for the loss of his spouse's household services. Yet it cannot be doubted that in the social context of 1846 the Act was seen as designed to benefit widows and children, and courts and writers have always used the words "dependants" and "dependency" in discussing the Act and calculating the amount recoverable. In modern times, however, it is often not obvious that one spouse is dependent upon the other, and the decline of the concept of dependency calls into question the soundness of the concept of enabling one spouse to collect damages for the death of the other. In 1846 there was a general consensus that a wife suffered a financial loss on the death of her husband. Today, the *Fatal Accidents Act* requires the court in calculating damages for the loss of a spouse to venture into territory where any social consensus is conspicuous by its absence. The difficulties are illustrated not only by the matters already discussed, but by the most basic calculation of all—the annual value of the dependency. This is usually calculated by deducting from the net income of the deceased money that would have been spent on the deceased, and savings. But where the claimant also has earnings, it is not clear whether the claimant's own maintenance is deemed to come first from the claimant's own earnings, enhancing the deceased's savings, or whether the claimant can claim support as a first charge on the deceased's income, allocating earnings to savings. It seems very artificial for the result to turn on the particular manner in which the claimant and the deceased, during their life together chose to allocate their income to current expenses. There is also the difficult problem of how to treat the claimant's future earning capacity. In short, the assumption that the loss of earning power of one spouse automatically affects the future wealth of the other is not always justified where both are earners and is likely to be less often justified in the future. A claim under *Lord Campbell's Act* may require assertion of a dependency that the claimant might vigorously have repudiated during the deceased's lifetime. Many recent family law cases have preferred the analogy of partnership to that of dependency. Yet there is a decision specifically rejecting a claim under *Lord Campbell's Act* for loss of business income to a husband and wife partnership. These problems will not disappear on the repeal of *Lord Campbell's Act*, for the extent of the estate's recovery will vary in response to some of these questions. But a claim against the deceased's estate by a survivor, not requiring the assertion or proof of dependency will, it is suggested, ease the task of the courts and fit better into modern family law.

4. In *Macartney v. Warner* (2000), 183 DLR (4th) 345 (Ont. CA), a majority of the Ontario Court of Appeal upheld the right of plaintiffs to bring a claim under s. 61(1) for lost income experienced because the plaintiffs could no longer return to work having suffered nervous shock arising from the death of their son in an automobile accident. The plaintiffs had no right to bring an independent tortuous action for nervous shock, but claimed an entitlement under the *Family Law Act*. Thus, the claim for pecuniary loss was not of any direct pecuniary benefit they could hope to have received from their deceased child had he lived, but was of

their own pecuniary loss that had resulted from their son's death. In essence, this pecuniary loss flows from an extreme reaction to the grieving process, and is in addition to any damages for loss of care, guidance, and companionship.

5. Bowlby J defined "care, guidance and companionship," as it relates to a parent's loss of a child in *Reidy v. McLeod* (1984), 47 OR (2d) 313, var'd. on appeal (1986), 54 OR (2d) 661n, at 320 (CA), where he said:

> In awarding damages for the loss of care, guidance and companionship of a child whose life has been taken due to the negligence of another, each word must be examined separately when considering what compensation is to be awarded and related to the facts as called at trial relevant to the position the child held in the family unit, both to his brothers and sisters, if any, and to his mother and father, if living.
>
> The changes enacted by the legislators become hollow gestures made to rectify social inequities in our past law if we as judges do not put flesh and meaning to their intentions. The words of s. 60 form the skeleton which, with imaginative pens, we as judges must bedeck with a suitable and deserving raiment.
>
> Each case must be scrupulously and carefully examined. An award following the death of one child, when applying s. 60 of the *Family Law Reform Act*, might and perhaps will offer little guidance to a court considering the death of a child in another. Families differ greatly in the closeness which exists between their members and the atmosphere of "love" generated by such unit.
>
> Each word (care, guidance and companionship) must be examined separately to explore what the Legislature intended or how this most important enactment should be interpreted.
>
> "Care" is a factor which must cause the judge to project his mind to the future. Does the evidence satisfy him that the child who was killed would, in the years to come, bestow care upon his parents or his or her brother or sister, should such be needed? One should reflect on how many times we have heard the words of proud parents speaking of how one of their children has cared for them in times of stress, be it emotional or pecuniary.
>
> The element of care is closely wedded to the element of guidance as when the child takes the hand of the elderly parent who so many times took his during his youth.
>
> It is not just in oriental or other ethnic societies or environments that this ultimate repayment for love given can be seen; but, to an ever-growing extent, in western culture as well. The "care and guidance" given to the elderly parent is hopefully to be less and less forfeited to the "old age home," but preserved in the atmosphere where it flourishes and is not stunted by loneliness. In my view, this fact was not lost sight of by the framers of the legislation.
>
> The case of *Mason v. Peters* (1982), 39 OR (2d) 385, is not in my view to be used as the highest range of compensation involved in the translating of the word "care" into a damage award because its facts were so dramatically discernible (*i.e.*, care involved in the attending to a mother who was tragically paralyzed). A son or daughter may provide a myriad of acts of assistance of greater and lesser degree, motivated by love of which the aged parent is the proud and thankful beneficiary. The court should closely examine the facts of each case and determine would this child, now deceased, have been likely to provide this type of care and guidance and, having made this decision, then be resolute that it is reflected in its award. Before leaving this portion of my judgment, reflect on the number of times we have heard a parent or even a sibling ask of a member of his family, "Should I buy this home …"; "The man wants to sell me such and such, would I be wise to buy …"; "Would you help me with my gardening, or shopping, or getting ready

for a short trip … ." The list is endless of the joy and benefit gained by the help made tenfold by the love which motivated it.

Perhaps the most readily understood loss which the Legislature has now made compensable is that of "companionship." A great observer of life's scene once penned:

> No man is an iland intire of itselfe. Every man is a peece of the continent a part of the maine; if Clod bee washed away from the sea, Europe is the lesse as well as if a promontorie were, as well as if a mannor of thy friends or thine owne were; any man's death diminishes me because I am involved in mankinde; and therefore never send to know for whom the bell tolls; it tolls for thee.

meaning that companionship is one of life's greatest needs and forces. It is this companionship which may lift our lives if it be rewarding, to the heights of beauty or can shatter it, if it be otherwise.

It is the "nexus" of the existence between two or more human beings, or which can give existence meaning, hope and indeed purpose. It is my judgment that it is in this context that the word finds its way into the *Family Law Reform Act*.

In short, the words "care, guidance and companionship" correct the arid wasteland of the verbiage to be found in the *Fatal Accidents Act*.

While the Court of Appeal did not disagree with Bowlby J's interpretation of the section, it did significantly reduce the amounts he had awarded under this heading, describing the damages as "excessive."

6. The response of some legislatures to rising awards of damages for loss of care guidance and companionship has been to cap the amount. At the same time, the plaintiff has been relieved of the evidential burden to prove this loss. See *Fatal Accidents Act*, CCSM, c. F50, s. 3.1(2) and inflation index under s. 3.1(5) and *Fatal Accidents Act*, RSA 2000, c. F-8, s. 8(2).

7. Where the deceased spouse was a homemaker, courts have normally assessed a claimant's loss on the basis of what it would cost to replace those services. Can you suggest any other method? See Janet Yale, "The Valuation of Household Services in Wrongful Death Actions" (1984), 34 *University of Toronto Law Journal* 283.

Structured Settlements

A development in personal injury damages assessment has been the structured settlement. The structured settlement attempts to overcome some of the deficiencies of lump-sum awards by providing for periodic payments. The structured settlement is not a means to have periodic reassessment; it is simply a device to stage payments, usually by the purchase of an annuity.

The main advantages to a structured settlement are:

(a) In the hands of the plaintiff, any payments are not taxable. Thus, the plaintiff benefits from having the investment income earned off the lump sum.

(b) The possibility of a plaintiff dissipating his or her award is minimized.

(c) The awarding of a tax gross-up can be avoided where a structured settlement is approved by the court, thus lowering the defendant's damages.

NOTES

1. The first reported case approving a structured settlement was *Yepremian v. Scarborough General Hospital (No. 2)* (1981), 31 OR (2d) 384. For a general discussion, see J.P. Weir, *Structured Settlements* (Toronto: Carswell, 1984) and E.G. Upenieks, "Structured Settlements: Are They Here to Stay?" (1981-82), 3 *Advocates' Q* 393.

2. As a result of the Osborne Report and the OLRC's *Report on Compensation for Personal Injuries and Death* (1987), s. 116 was added to the Ontario *Courts of Justice Act*, RSO 1990, c. C.43:

> 116(1) In a proceeding where damages are claimed for personal injuries or under Part V of the *Family Law Act* for loss resulting from the injury to or death of a person, the court,
>
> > (a) if all affected parties consent, may order the defendant to pay all or part of the award for damages periodically on such terms as the court considers just; and
> >
> > (b) if the plaintiff requests that an amount be included in the award to compensate for income tax payable on the award, shall order the defendant to pay all or part of the award periodically on such terms as the court considers just.
>
> (2) An order under clause (1)(b) shall not be made if the parties otherwise consent or if the court is of the opinion that the order would not be in the best interests of the plaintiff, having regard to all the circumstances of the case.
>
> (3) In considering the best interests of the plaintiff, the court shall take into account,
>
> > (a) whether the defendant has sufficient means to fund an adequate scheme of periodic payments;
> >
> > (b) whether the plaintiff has a plan or a method of payment that is better able to meet the interests of the plaintiff than periodic payments by the defendant; and
> >
> > (c) whether a scheme of periodic payments is practicable having regard to all the circumstances of the case.
>
> (4) In an order made under this section, the court may, with the consent of all the affected parties, order that the award be subject to future review and revision in such circumstances and on such terms as the court considers just.
>
> (5) If the court does not make an order for periodic payment under subsection (1), it shall make an award for damages that shall include an amount to offset liability for income tax on income from investment of the award.

See also Saskatchewan *Automobile Accident Insurance Act*, RSS 1978, c. A-35, s. 103(3)(a)(i), as am. by the *Automobile Accident Insurance Amendment Act*, SS 1994, c. 34, s. 18, British Columbia *Insurance (Motor Vehicle) Act*, RSBC 1996, c. 231, s. 55(1), Alberta *Insurance Act*, RSA 2000, c. I-3, s. 650.2(1), and Manitoba, *Court of Queen's Bench Act*, SM 1988-89, c. 4, CSM c. C280, s. 88.2, as am. by SM 1993, c. 19, s. 6.

Section 116 has been interpreted by the Ontario Court of Appeal in *Wilson v. Martinello* (1995), 23 OR (3d) 417. The plaintiff's wife and daughter had been killed in a motor-vehicle accident in which the defendant was held liable. The plaintiff was awarded approximately $200,000 in pecuniary damages and an additional $173,000 in tax gross-up. The defendant appealed on the basis that the plaintiff was required to accept a periodic payment scheme where the plaintiff was seeking a tax gross-up. The plaintiff argued that he wanted to use the award to buy a donut franchise and thus a periodic payment scheme was not in his "best interests" as provided by the statute.

The Court of Appeal described s. 116 as being poorly drafted. However, once the plaintiff seeks a lump-sum award with a tax gross-up, the defendant can either choose to pay the total award by consent or put up a scheme of periodic payments for the consideration of the court. Where the gross-up is requested, a periodic payment scheme is mandatory unless the plaintiff can show that such a scheme is not in his or her best interests. In this case the court accepted the plaintiff's wish to buy a donut franchise. The plaintiff, who was in fact a teacher, had investigated the cost of the franchise from a friend but had done nothing more. The court noted that the onus on the plaintiff was rather low and that it did not require the plaintiff to propose a superior payment scheme to that proposed by the defendant. The court also indicated that in this case the award was to a husband who did not have any on-going obligations to provide for a family that had been taken from him through the accident. Nor did he have any ongoing health-care costs for himself. Against this was the plaintiff's liberty to spend the award the way he chose and the fact that the lump sum was the only way that he could buy the franchise. Once the court has determined the issue of best inter-ests, the calculation of the actual tax gross-up must be done according to the section and the rules. The section contemplates an income stream from fixed income securities. That income stream may be quite different from the income stream that the plaintiff is contemplating with the award, and which would lead to a totally different set of income tax issues. The court said that the actual tax issues as contemplated by the plaintiff were to be ignored, and the section alone provided for the way the tax liability gross-up was to be calculated.

This case appears to beg the question why the plaintiff was entitled to a tax gross-up in the first place. If his intentions were to start a donut franchise with the award, he would have exhausted the fund within the first few months. The plaintiff would not have incurred any tax liability through keeping the fund to pay for the losses that it was originally intended to compensate—namely, loss of future dependency and ongoing housekeeping services. Clearly, the plaintiff did not value the damages to meet these particular losses.

3. In *Steeves v. Fitzsimmons* (1975), 11 OR (2d) 387 (HC), the parties gave their consent, and the court approved a review of the plaintiff's injuries prior to his seventh birthday.

4. In *Watkins v. Olafson* (1987), 48 Man. R (2d) 81 (CA), the court approved a structured judgment in which the Manitoba government, one of the defendants, was required to en-trust a trustee with sufficient funds each year to cover the plaintiff's actual care expenses. On appeal, [1989] 2 SCR 750, the Supreme Court of Canada would not permit a court to impose a periodic payment scheme on a plaintiff in the absence of any enabling legislation or con-sent of the parties. While the court saw merit in periodic schemes, it believed that for such a far-reaching development in the law to come through judicial fiat was beyond the traditional role of courts.

5. Where the plaintiff is a minor, the appointment of a litigation guardian is required and court approval of any settlement must be obtained. In giving approval, the court must aban-don its normal umpire-like role and assume a more interventionist mode. See *Tsaoussis (Liti-gation Guardian of) v. Baetz* (1998), 41 OR (3d) 257 (CA).

PART II

Equitable Remedies

CHAPTER SIX

Injunctions and Specific Performance

INTRODUCTION

The following chapters examine the remedies of injunction and specific performance. These are commonly referred to as "specific," as opposed to substitutionary, forms of relief, or equitable, as opposed to common law, remedies. Specific performance is a contract remedy whereby the court may, instead of awarding damages, order the defendant actually to perform the contract. An injunction is an order, available to protect a wide array of substantive legal rights, requiring a person to refrain from or to take a course of action. A failure to obey such orders may result in a citation for contempt of court and a fine or imprisonment.

Injunctions and specific performance are equitable remedies. Equity is the existing body of rules, principles, and remedies developed in the Court of Chancery and now administered by the regular courts. Some bodies of modern substantive law, such as the law of trusts, are derived almost entirely from equity. Others incorporate many equitable principles. For example, in contract law, the law of mistake, rescission, rectification, undue influence, and unconscionability can be traced in whole or in part to the principles fashioned in the Court of Chancery. While the principles of equity and common law are now administered in unison by the regular courts, the origins of equity and many features of modern equitable principles can be understood only in their historical context.

THE ORIGINS OF EQUITY

As S.F.C. Milsom points out (*Historical Foundations of the Common Law* (London: Butterworths, 1981)), the origins of "equity" are shrouded in mystery; and certainly the notion that equity was originally a substantive body of law, different from and more "just" than the common law, is something of a romantic fiction. Equity, like common law, had its origin in petitions addressed to the king, requesting the exercise of his prerogative powers to resolve some conflict or correct some abuse, inadequacy, or injustice. By the 14th century, the administration of justice had largely been established through the formal institutions of common law. The three superior courts, King's Bench, Common Pleas, and Exchequer, administered the law of the land. But the jurisdiction of these courts was neither exhaustive nor exclusive. The law remained grounded in the king's justice and the sovereign did not relinquish his ultimate authority to consider individual petitions and dispense justice (though the scope of this residual jurisdiction was to become a source of considerable political controversy). Thus, in addition to the three courts, citizens had the legal right to petition the king directly where it was alleged that justice could not be obtained in the common law courts.

The Chancery was not originally a "court." Rather it was a department of government that did the "paperwork" of the state. The Chancellor, historically a cleric, was the custodian of the royal seal used for the authentication of all government documents (including the common law writs), and was responsible for many of the internal affairs of the country. As petitions to the king became more numerous they were frequently referred to the Chancellor who, exercising delegated powers, gradually assumed a prominent role in the administration of royal justice. As the Chancellor's judicial role became better established, individuals alleging some defect or abuse in the common law courts would petition him directly for assistance. Such petitions might allege the dishonesty of local judicial officers or juries, the poverty of the petitioner or, more frequently with the increasing inflexibility of the common law writ system, some unfairness in the substantive or procedural law. Where satisfied of the justice of the petitioner's case, the Chancellor might issue a new common law writ to direct the courts to provide some redress or, with increasing frequency, would issue an appropriate order directly to the offender to abide by the dictates of conscience.

The Chancellor's "conscience" often inclined in a direction opposite to the result reached by the common law. In fact, one of the earliest uses of the injunction was to restrain unfair proceedings in the common law courts. Of equal importance was the enforcement by the Chancellor of uses or trusts, which the common law refused to recognize. However, the Chancellor was not thought to be administering a separate system of rules, or overriding the common law, but instead was simply "perfecting" the administration of the king's justice. And while the orders of the Chancellor might, at times, run counter to the results reached in the common law courts, these orders, directed only to the affected parties and not a matter of record, did not alter the general rules of common law. The explanation eventually adopted to explain the relationship between the common law and equity rested on the Aristotelian notion that equitable justice is a necessary correction of the defects of legal justice resulting from the universality of the latter. General rules will on occasion work injustice and it would be against conscience to allow this to occur. As Lord Ellesmere said in *Earl of Oxford's Case* (1615), 1 Rep. Ch. 1, at 6; 21 ER 485, at 486:

> That men's actions are so diverse and infinite that it is impossible to make any general law which may aptly meet with every particular and not fail in some circumstances. The office of the Chancellor is to correct men's consciences for frauds, breaches of trust, wrongs and oppressions of what nature so ever they be, and to soften and mollify the extremity of the law.

Nevertheless, the relationship between law and equity did not remain a harmonious one. As J.H. Baker points out, "[t]he anomaly that a politician should hold the highest judicial office in the land was compounded by the undefined nature of the Chancellor's jurisdiction" (*An Introduction to English Legal History*, 2d ed. (London: Butterworths, 1979), at 86). Perhaps not surprisingly, common law lawyers began to object to the apparently arbitrary nature of the Chancellor's jurisdiction and the relationship between the common law courts and the Chancellor became increasingly uneasy. The mounting antagonism (which may also have had something to do with the fact that judicial revenues depended upon the volume of litigation) eventually assumed the proportions of a constitutional crisis in 1616 in the form of a clash between the Chancellor, Lord Ellesmere, and the Chief Justice of the King's Bench, Sir

Edward Coke. While Coke lost the battle, the stage was set for the formalization of the relationship between law and equity. Equity was said to be superior to common law in that, where the two conflicted, equity would prevail; however, subsequent Chancellors took greater care to define their jurisdiction and to introduce greater certainty and predictability into equity. The increasing appointment of common lawyers (particularly Lord Nottingham, 1673–1682) to the position of Chancellor further accelerated the trend to delineate the jurisdiction of Chancery by rules and principles and to rely on binding precedent. The familiarity with, and deference to, the common law by the Chancellors further cemented the principle that while equity is superior to common law, it is but corrective and supplementary. The reporting of the Chancellor's decisions also played a role in the transformation of equity from an expression of subjective conscience to a body of rules. By the time of the publication of *Blackstone's Commentaries* (1765–1769) equity, no less than common law, was considered to be a part of the positive substantive law of the land and capable of systematic exposition.

The reconciliation of law and equity was achieved at a price. As you will see, the "regularization" of equitable principles has arguably resulted in the same type of inflexibility in this area of law that equity was originally designed to remedy. At the very least, there remains a tension in equity between "conscience" and "rule" and the nature of equitable discretion is an important jurisprudential question (see, for example, R. Dworkin, *Taking Rights Seriously* (Cambridge: Harvard University Press, 1978), at 14-45). Perhaps of greater historical importance, the growing number of Chancery petitions, the increasing formalization of equity, and the institutional and procedural limitations of Chancery procedure led eventually to the dismal situation described by Dickens in *Bleak House* (though this book was not published until some time after the darkest hours of Chancery). Under the tutelage of the unfortunate Lord Eldon (1801–1827), the Chancery had become unworkable. A series of reforms beginning in the early 19th century allowed for the appointment of more judges to assist the beleaboured Chancellor (until 1813 there had been only two judges in Chancery). Sweeping changes to Chancery procedure in the middle of the century widened the powers of the Chancery and streamlined its procedures. As we shall see, one of the most important of these reforms was *Lord Cairns' Act* (*Chancery Amendment Act*, 1858, 21 & 22 Vict., c. 27), which gave the Chancery jurisdiction to award damages. Similarly, common law courts were given the power to take notice of certain equitable principles and to award equitable remedies. The increasing similarity of procedure in common law and equity and the overlapping powers of the two systems of courts paved the way finally for the reforms of the *Judicature Acts* in 1873 and 1875 whereby the dual system of courts was abolished and the Supreme Court of Judicature was established having authority to administer both bodies of law.

These reforms were, by and large, followed in Canada. The four western provinces, newer to the confederation, never had a dual court system, but happily administered both equity and common law. By way of contrast, the Supreme Court of New Brunswick declared in 1842 that it had no equity jurisdiction (*AG v. Baillie* (1842), 3 NBR 443). In the maritime provinces, equity was administered by the governor as Chancellor and later by a separate court or a division of the Supreme Court. Similarly, in Ontario, a Court of Chancery was established in 1837. Following the English reforms, most provinces enacted variants of the *Judicature Act* unifying the administration of law and equity (see B. Laskin, *The British Tradition in Canadian Law* (London: Stevens, 1969)).

In some respects, the unification of the administration of common law and equity has paved the way for the unification of the substantive law. Thus, for example, in contract law it makes little difference now that the rules with respect to penalties and forfeitures, duress, and undue influence derive from Chancery practice. Nevertheless, the historical origins of equitable principles continue to illuminate the character of modern equity and the method by which such principles are applied. This is particularly true when we turn explicitly to the remedies of injunction and specific performance and the principles of remedial selection.

REMEDIAL SELECTION AND THE METHOD OF EQUITY

It would be misleading at this point to suggest that there is one "method" of remedial selection. However, the process of determining the appropriate remedy in any case can be organized around several central concerns. The court must be satisfied first, that there is a substantive cause of action or violation of the plaintiff's rights; second, that substitutionary relief would not adequately vindicate those rights; and finally, that no discretionary factors incline against specific relief. As Turner LJ said in *AG v. Sheffield Gas Consumers Co.* (1852), 3 De. GM & G 304, at 321, 43 ER 119, at 126 (CA Ch.), the question is "whether this is a case in which the remedy at law is so inadequate that the court ought to interfere, having regard to the legal remedy, the rights and interests of the parties, and the consequence of this court's interference."

Rights

It might be thought that the question of the plaintiff's rights is a preliminary issue, decided before the remedial question is addressed and unaffected by remedial principles. But this would be misleading. In a very important sense, issues of rights cannot be decided in a remedial vacuum. It makes little sense to speak of a right without a remedy, and the nature and scope of rights depend very much upon the nature of the remedy that will be made available to vindicate those rights. Rights are fashioned in order to protect certain favoured interests and they are also limited for the sake of other interests. One way in which rights are limited is through remedial choice, and while it is a commonplace that the nature of the right will partly determine the appropriate remedy, so will the available remedies affect the way in which substantive issues are adjudicated. While the language of law sometimes suggests that the question of remedial choice is an almost automatic process flowing from a decision about the parties' rights, as L.L. Fuller and W.R. Perdue suggest, the process of selecting remedies to protect interests "is really part of the process of creating them." ("The Reliance Interest in Contract Damages" (1936), 46 *Yale Law Journal* 52, at 52.) In some instances, remedial adjudication clearly creates new rights. So, for example, later chapters deal with recent developments in interlocutory injunctions where the courts have fashioned new remedies to protect the interests of litigants even before the rights of the parties are established at trial. Similarly, it might be suggested that as the courts grant remedies to individuals to enforce legislation, they are in the process creating new rights. In other cases, the effect of remedial selection is more subtle. Legal history and common sense suggest that the courts are more or less willing to protect certain interests depending upon the effect of the available remedy. Thus, for example, if specific performance were the only contract remedy, the substantive law of contract might look very different today. Similarly, if the injunction were the only remedy for the protection of property interests, such interests might be more narrowly defined than they are today. It is simply impossible to separate the questions of what rights people do and should have from the question of what remedies are or should be available to protect those rights. Remedial issues cannot be treated as straightforward procedural responses, but are intimately connected to the underlying purposes of the substantive law.

The Concept of Irreparable Harm

It is usually said to be a first principle of equity that specific remedies are available only when damages would be inadequate. This idea is sometimes expressed as a requirement that the plaintiff must demonstrate that irreparable harm would be suffered if specific relief were not granted. The explanation for this "hierarchical" approach to remedial choice is largely historical, accounted for by the subordinate or supplementary role of the Court of Chancery prior to the fusion of the administration of law and equity. Yet the principle is still frequently affirmed. Indeed, it is one of the paradoxes of the reforms referred to above that equitable principles, originally developed to define the relationship between two systems of courts, became frozen in the substantive law when those courts were merged. An important issue raised by the following materials is whether the inadequacy prerequisite serves any substantive purpose and whether there remains any good reason for the hierarchical approach to remedial choice.

The requirement of irreparable harm is easier to state than to apply. Consider a number of possible meanings:

1. damage to person or property that is impossible to repair;

2. damage to an interest that is not easily susceptible to economic measurement;

3. a legal wrong that causes no financial or economic harm;

4. damages are ascertainable but unlikely to be recovered;

5. a threat to an interest that is so important that a substitutionary remedy (damages) is inappropriate;

6. an injury that has not yet occurred or a wrong that is continuing.

The idea of irreparable harm is obviously capable of a large number of meanings and the principle is differently applied in different ways. The question whether damages are inadequate immediately raises the question "inadequate for what purpose?" And the answer to this question can only be found in an examination of the nature of the interests at stake, the purposes of the underlying substantive law, and the advantages and disadvantages of different remedies.

See D. Rendleman, "The Inadequate Remedy at Law Prerequisite for an Injunction" (1981), 33 *University of Florida Law Review* 346.

Discretion and the Balance of Convenience

Another frequently affirmed principle is that equitable remedies are available only at the court's discretion. While, on occasion, the language of equity suggests that specific relief may be had almost as of right when damages are inadequate, this obscures the more subtle nature of remedial selection and design. The interests of the plaintiff are not the only relevant considerations. Other elements must be weighed in the balance. The courts are also concerned about the interests of the defendant and in the efficacy and efficiency of their own processes. While some of these concerns may be treated as part of the process of determining irreparable harm, they are of sufficient importance to keep analytically distinct. The desire to decide disputes with finality and to discourage a "multiplicity of actions" are factors that are important in choosing the appropriate remedy. Similarly, concern for their own processes and the interests of both parties make the courts reluctant to issue orders that are difficult to define and supervise, or unlikely to be obeyed. The courts recognize that equitable remedies are often highly intrusive and burdensome. They will, on occasion, balance the benefit of specific relief to the plaintiff against the burden of that form of relief to the defendant. The balancing of the costs and benefits of equitable relief is a common theme when the courts are asked to enjoin a nuisance or order specific performance of a contract. Likewise, in the case of interlocutory injunctions the courts are loath to unfairly paralyze the activities of the defendant or to give the plaintiff unfair bargaining leverage in forthcoming litigation. A similar concern for the interests of the defendant is reflected in the principle of mutuality that, in the case of contracts, requires the courts to ensure that the interests of the defendant in the plaintiff's own performance can be adequately secured. Finally, there are defences based on unfairness, delay, hardship, the conduct of the plaintiff, and considerations of public policy. All of these are merely examples of the discretionary factors that will invariably influence the process of remedial choice. The materials included in the following chapters explore these considerations as well as the moral, economic, and procedural factors that influence the choice and design of appropriate remedies.

ADDITIONAL READINGS

Two excellent Canadian textbooks deal with equitable remedies:

Jeffrey Berryman, *The Law of Equitable Remedies* (Toronto: Irwin Law, 2000).

Robert J. Sharpe, *Injunctions and Specific Performance* (Aurora, ON: Canada Law Book, 2009) (looseleaf).

CHAPTER SEVEN

Injunctions

INTRODUCTION

This chapter examines the remedy of the injunction. An injunction is an order, originally fashioned by the courts of equity, requiring a person to refrain from or to take a course of action. While the courts are not always precise or consistent in their terminology, the following vocabulary might be found useful.

A *prohibitive injunction* orders a person to refrain from specified conduct. A *mandatory injunction* orders a person to take positive action to right a wrong or repair damage done. Injunctions may be permanent or temporary. The most usual forms of the latter are pre-trial injunctions, which, in cases of urgency, preserve the status quo until the rights of the parties may be finally determined at trial. Pre-trial injunctions are further classified as interim or interlocutory. An *interim injunction* is valid only for a specified period. An *interlocutory injunction* is binding until trial. Pre-trial injunctions are dealt with in chapter 8, "Interlocutory Injunctions."

An injunction is normally sought to restrain a continuing violation of the applicant's rights, but may also be sought *quia timet*, before the wrong has occurred or before any damage has been suffered.

In cases of urgency, injunctions may be sought on an *ex parte* basis; that is, in the absence of the respondent.

QUIA TIMET INJUNCTIONS AND THE PROBLEM OF RIPENESS

When a plaintiff seeks injunctive relief before a wrong has been committed, the action is said to be *quia timet*, "since he fears." While similar considerations apply to this type of order as to any other permanent injunction, the fact that relief is sought before the harm has been suffered introduces some of these considerations in a particularly clear fashion. The following materials introduce the limitations imposed on the availability of injunctive relief and explore the purposes served by those limitations. Note that the additional conditions discussed below apply to *quia timet* injunctions as a permanent order of the court. This is to be distinguished from interlocutory orders, which often have the effect of a *quia timet* injunction in that they suspend the further incursion of harm, but the suspension only operates for the duration of the interlocutory proceedings and may not create a permanent restraint on the defendant.

Fletcher v. Bealey
(1885), 28 Ch. D 688

PEARSON J: The plaintiff complains that the Defendants are placing upon a piece of land on the bank of the River *Irwell*, higher up the river than his works, a large mass of a substance called "vat waste," the existence of which in that particular spot will, he says, imperil his trade. He has carried on business for many years at the *Kearsley Paper Mills*, which are situated upon the bank of the River *Irwell*. The Defendants are alkali manufacturers, their works being on the same river, about six miles higher up the stream. The Plaintiff is a manufacturer of papers of a peculiar description. He says, in one of his affidavits, "I have for many years past especially excelled in trade in the productions of the very finest classes of paper which are made in *England*, such as cigarette paper, the finer kinds of copying papers, and fine and delicate tissues of all kinds. For the purposes of my works I use in the making of paper very high class waste and linen, and in the first processes this has to be bleached, after being boiled and beaten up, to as pure a white as it is possible to get, and this is the secret of my success in trade, that I have, by long experience and care in the use of water and chemicals, succeeded in getting a great purity of white to start the process of paper making. Unless I am able to get this pure white for what is known in the trade as bottom, no amount of washing or use of chemicals in the later processes will enable me to get the delicacy of colour shewn in some of the sample-books now produced, and if, in order to get rid of deleterious matter, I have to use too much chemicals in the later processes of washing, it quite spoils the paper by rendering the fibre too tender." The Defendants, as I have said, are alkali manufacturers. In the process of manufacturing alkali, a very large quantity is produced of a refuse which is denominated "vat waste." It contains a considerable amount of sulphur, and is hot, and when heaped up it gets, as I conclude, hotter, and unless great care is taken it will ignite, and if a large heap of this "vat waste" should ignite, the result, as one of the witnesses told me, would be to suffocate all the people in the neighbourhood. It is, therefore, a very dangerous material, and the alkali manufacturers are obliged to be exceedingly careful in the handling of it, and, after a large heap of it, the product possibly of many years, has been stored, there flows from it a liquid of a greenish colour, which contains very destructive chemical elements. The Defendants for some years got rid of this refuse by carting it bodily into the River *Irwell*, but, I think in the year 1881, they were restrained by injunction at the suit of the *Salford* corporation from continuing that process, and, not having any land in the immediate neighbourhood of their works which is suitable for storing this refuse, they have taken for the purpose, from the *Lancashire and Yorkshire Railway Company*, a piece of land comprising three and a half acres, adjoining the *Bolton, Bury, and Manchester Canal*, which belongs to that company, at *Nob End Wharf*, which is on the bank of the river, and one mile and 740 yards above the Plaintiff's works. The Plaintiff says that if the Defendants proceed to deposit this refuse on this land, depositing, as they do at the present moment, at the rate of 1000 tons a month, the result will be that, sooner or later, there will necessarily come from the heap a large quantity of this green liquid, which will find its way into the River *Irwell*, and, finding its way into the river, it will be carried down to his works, and when he pumps the water from the river he will take in with it this chemical matter which will be destructive to his paper. There is no dispute between the parties that in process of time a liquid of that character does come from these heaps. There is no dispute that if any reasonably large quantity of that liquid should find its way into the Plaintiff's bleaching works, that is, if it should be pumped by him from the river into his reservoir, it would be very destructive to his manufacture. But the Defendants say: "You need be under no apprehension. We have not the slightest intention of injuring you; we intend to conduct our works in such a way that no appreciable quantity of that liquid shall find its way into the *Irwell*, and consequently no appreciable quantity will find its way from our heap into your works."

The hearing of this case was commenced in August last; it was continued in December; and neither in August nor in December was there any allegation that the Plaintiff had, in fact, received any injury from the Defendants' operations. It is admitted that the action is brought, not to obtain damages for a past injury, but to prevent that which is feared as a future injury, or, to use the more technical expression, the action is a *quia timet* action.

That being so, the objection has been taken that, under the particular circumstances of this case, a *quia timet* action will not lie, and, as that seems to me to be really the only point in the case, I think that I had better consider, first, what are the rules which have been laid down with regard to *quia timet* actions, and then I will consider whether the evidence in this case brings it within those circumstances which have been held to justify such an action. I need not refer to many of the cases which have been cited, because there is really no dispute as to the law.

The first case I will mention is *Earl of Ripon v. Hobart* (1834), 3 My. & K 169; 40 ER 65 (Ch.). In that case the parliamentary commissioners for cleansing and improving the river *Witham* and its navigation, and the drainage of the adjacent lands, asked for an injunction against the defendants, who were the trustees for draining another district, and who were commencing to erect a steam engine for pumping water from the fens into the river *Witham*, substituting a steam engine for the power which they had previously obtained by windmills, which had up to that time been used for the purpose. It was said that the steam engine intended to be employed would be equivalent in power to twenty-seven windmills, and that the effect of using a steam engine of that power would be to pump so much water into the navigation as to overpower it altogether. Lord *Broughham* LC said (at p. 176 (My. & K); p. 67 (ER)):

> If, indeed, this be a work which not only gives the power of doing mischief, but cannot be used, or can hardly, in the common course of things, be used without working mischief; if, in short, it be a thing which can scarcely be used without being abused, the case comes to be very different, For, in matters of this description, the law cannot make over-nice distinctions, and refuse the relief merely because there is a bare possibility that the evil may be avoided. Proceeding upon practical views of human affairs, the law will guard against risks which are so imminent that no prudent person would incur them, although they do not amount to absolute certainty of damage. Nay, it will go further, according to the same practical and rational view, and, balancing the magnitude of the evil against the chances of its occurrence, it will even provide against a somewhat less imminent probability in cases where the mischief, should it be done, would be vast and overwhelming. Accordingly, if it appeared that the works in question could hardly be used without damage to the inferior districts, I might hold that erecting them was, in itself, a beginning of injury, though there might be a possibility of otherwise using them; and, if the damage, should it happen at all, were the destruction of the navigation, and the subjecting of the lower districts to a deluge, I might scrutinize less narrowly the probability of the engines being injuriously worked.

In *Attorney-General v. Corporation of Kingston* (1865), 13 WR 888 (Ch.) an information had been filed against the corporation of *Kingston*, because they were proceeding to pour a large quantity of sewage into the River *Thames*. They were connecting their own system of drainage with a new main sewer, in such a way as greatly to enlarge the quantity of sewage coming into the River *Thames*. After discussing the Acts of Parliament under which the corporation had power to do this, and concluding that, if they did create a nuisance, they were not justified by the Acts under which they were incorporated, *Wood* VC said: "It remained then to be considered whether there was evidence of an actual nuisance committed, or evidence of the extreme probability of a nuisance, if that which was being done was allowed to continue. The difficulty in the way of the plaintiffs was that it was necessary for them to establish the existence of an actual immediate nuisance, and not a mere *quia timet* case of injury a hundred years hence, when chemical contrivances might have been discovered for preventing the evil."

Again, in *Salvin v. North Brancepeth Coal Company* (1873), LR 9 Ch. App. 705, which was a case of alleged injury to trees and grounds generally by fumes from a chemical factory, and which both *Jessel* MR and the Court of Appeal considered was not made out by the evidence, *Mellish* LJ said (at p. 712):

> The question to be determined is, whether the plaintiff has made out that in an action at law he could recover substantial damages for the nuisance alleged in the bill; and the only real difficulty is in distinguishing how much that proposition depends upon questions of fact, and how much upon questions of law. There is a difficulty in distinguishing precisely what is a question of fact from what is a question of law in these proceedings about nuisances. Indeed, when certain inferences of fact have been established by numerous cases, they become, to a great extent, very nearly of the same authority as if they were propositions of law. For instance, it is not correct to say, as a strict proposition of law, that, if the plaintiff has not sustained, or cannot prove that he has sustained, substantial damage, this Court will give no relief; because, of course, if it could be proved that the plaintiff was certainly about to sustain very substantial damage by what the defendant was doing, and there was no doubt about it, this Court would at once stop the defendant, and would not wait until the substantial damage had been sustained. But in nuisance of this particular kind, it is known by experience that unless substantial damage has actually been sustained, it is impossible to be certain that substantial damage ever will be sustained, and, therefore, with reference to this particular description of nuisance, it becomes practically correct to lay down the principle, that, unless substantial damage is proved to have been sustained, this Court will not interfere.

I do not think, therefore, that I shall be very far wrong if I lay it down that there are at least two necessary ingredients for a *quia timet* action. There must, if no actual damage is proved, be proof of imminent danger, and there must also be proof that the apprehended damage will, if it comes, be very substantial. I should almost say it must be proved that it will be irreparable, because, if the danger is not proved to be so imminent that no one can doubt that, if the remedy is delayed, the damage will be suffered, I think it must be shewn that, if the damage does occur at any time, it will come in such a way and under such circumstances that it will be impossible for the Plaintiff to protect himself against it if relief is denied to him in a *quia timet* action.

Now the circumstances of the present case are these. In the first place, it is said that, do what the Defendants may, if they proceed to cover, as they propose to do, two acres and a half of the land with this refuse, at the rate of 1000 tons a month, necessarily, although not immediately, there will ooze from the heap a large quantity of this pernicious liquid. More-over, it is said that, inasmuch as the Defendants have taken a lease of the land from the railway company only for the purpose of depositing this refuse on it, and they have the power of giving up the lease when they have made as much use of the land as they can for the purpose, at the end of ten years, at which time it is reasonably concluded they will have deposited on the land as much of the refuse as it will hold, they will give up the lease, and then the heap will be left without any person whose duty is to take care of it, and the liquid will continue to ooze out of it for a period of forty or fifty years, or even longer, and the Plaintiff will be under a risk, an increasing risk, certainly a much greater risk than he incurs at the present moment, of having the water of the *Irwell* polluted, and of pumping into his works the water which is so polluted. The quantity of water which the Plaintiff takes from the *Irwell* is very large indeed, amounting, I think, sometimes to one-third of the water in the river; 1,000,000 gallons in the twenty-four hours.

Now, if that stood alone, would there be a sufficient ground for a *quia timet* action? I think not. There was some conflict in the evidence as to what amount of the liquid would be sufficient to pollute the water so as to injure the Plaintiff. According to the evidence of the Plaintiff, one gallon in 10,000 would be sufficient to produce injury, and it is also in evidence that, if at the end of ten years there were 120,000 tons of the refuse deposited on the land, there would not be less of the liquid oozing from the heap and capable of getting into the *Irwell* than one gallon in a little more than 5000, and of course, if one gallon in 10,000 would be injurious, one gallon in 5000 would be highly injurious. But the answer of the Defend-ants is this. They do not intend that any appreciable amount of this liquid should get into the *Irwell*, and, inasmuch as it is perfectly practicable, according to all that we know, to prevent the liquid which comes from the heap from getting into the *Irwell*, I cannot think that at the present moment the evidence on this point is sufficient to justify the Court in interfering. In *Attorney-General v. Corporation of Kingston* (at p. 888), Wood VC spoke of injurious results at the end of 100 years. If an injury does result in the present case it will result in a much shorter time, and, if the heap were left alone without any protection to the river to prevent the liquid from oozing into it, I have no doubt that at the end of ten years the water would be polluted sufficiently to do a great amount of injury to the Plaintiff. But Wood V, pointed out that in 100 years' time chemical processes might be invented which would prevent the sewage from doing any injury to the River *Thames*, and I think that in ten years time it is highly probable that science (which is now at work on the subject) may have discovered some means for rendering this green liquid innocuous. But, even if no such discovery should be made in that time, I cannot help seeing that there are contrivances, such as tanks and pumps, and other things of that kind, by which the liquid may, as the Defend-ants say, be kept out of the river altogether. Therefore, upon that ground alone, I do not think that the action can be supported.

There is another observation to be made on this point of the case. In the first place I think the danger is not imminent, because it must be some years before any such quantity of the liquid will be found issuing from the heap as would pollute the *Irwell* to the detriment of the Plaintiff. And, in the next place, if any such quantity of the liquid did get into the river so as to injure the Plaintiff, I think it would be discovered immediately, and it would be perfectly possible for him then to apply to the Court for relief, and to obtain an immediate injunction restraining the Defendants from allowing the liquid to get into the river. For both these reasons I think there is not sufficient in this part of the case to sustain a *quia timet* action. ...

[Pearson J then went on to discuss the plaintiff's evidence regarding the likelihood of the contaminated land slipping into the river and concluded that this situation posed no serious threat to the plaintiff.]

I think the Plaintiff has been premature in bringing his action, and that, according to the rules which have been laid down (and I cannot go beyond precedent), I must refuse to grant an injunction, and I believe, according to the practice in these cases, I have no choice but to dismiss the action with costs. But I observe that in *Attorney-General v. Corporation of Kingston, Wood* VC guarded the dismissal of the information by a declaration of the right of the plaintiff to bring another action thereafter if there should be actual damage, or damage which he could prove to be imminent or likely to be irreparable. The Vice-Chancellor said (at p. 842):

> The proper course would be to dismiss the information, such dismissal being prefaced by a declaration that the Court was of opinion that the evidence did not establish the existence of any nuisance in respect of the works executed, or intended to be executed, by the defendants, or any case for the interference of the Court in respect of nuisance to be apprehended, if such works were carried into effect. The order would be without prejudice to any future proceedings on the part of the Attorney-General in case the works should occasion a nuisance.

Though I do not think it is necessary, yet, if the Plaintiff's counsel desire it, I have no objection to inserting a similar declaration in the order which I am now making.

NOTES AND QUESTIONS

1. In what way do the issues raised in a *quia timet* application differ from those that are raised in an ordinary application (for example, to restrain a nuisance)? Is it relevant that some harm has or has not occurred?

2. What considerations are present in a case like *Fletcher v. Bealey* that militate against an injunction? What harm would be done by granting an injunction in a case where the court is convinced that if the harm did occur it would be actionable? What interest of the defendant is the court concerned in protecting by denying the injunction?

3. The relief claimed by the plaintiff was an "injunction to restrain the defendants from sending 'vat waste,' or refuse, or other matter whatsoever, from their chemical works, or otherwise, into the river, or on to the ground adjacent thereto, or in any way so as to pollute the water" to his injury. Could the problem of prematurity have been avoided by a differently worded order?

4. In *Mendez v. Palazzi* (1976), 12 OR (2d) 270 (Co. Ct.), the plaintiff alleged that the growing roots of her neighbour's poplar trees were destroying her rock garden, lawn, and patio, and were threatening her septic system and house foundations. Hollingworth Co. Ct. J held that the roots were a nuisance, but that the damage so far done was not sufficiently substan-

tial to award a mandatory injunction to remove the trees. Following *Fletcher v. Bealey*, he stated (at 278-79):

> I would say it must be proved damage will be irreparable; if the danger is not proved to be so imminent that no one can doubt that if the remedy is delayed the damage will be suffered, I think it must be shown that, if the damage does occur at any time, it will come in such a way and under such circumstances, that it will be impossible for the plaintiffs to protect themselves against it if relief is denied to them in a *quia timet* action.
>
> Here, there was no evidence at all that the roots had reached the tile bed. Although one root shoot was found near the house, there is no probative evidence before me that the basement has settled or has been damaged as a result of root action.

The plaintiffs were awarded $500 damages for the nuisance.

In *Jagtoo v. 407 ETR Concession Co.*, [1999] OJ no. 4944, the Ontario Superior Court considered an application by property owners for an interlocutory *quia timet* injunction against the construction of a highway near their property. Following *Fletcher v. Bealey* the application was denied. Although the court held there would be irreparable harm that could not be quantified in monetary terms (that is, deteriorated air quality, contaminated ground water, and increased noise), this harm was not imminent, and was especially not so immediate that it would have to be remedied by an interlocutory injunction. At para. 38, the court stated: "Although the construction of the Highway 407 Extension is expected to be completed in the next couple of years, some of the effects of the Extension claimed by the plaintiffs will not be felt for a number of years. Indeed, some may never be felt. … I do not believe that irreparable harm will be done to the plaintiffs between the commencement of construction and the beginning of the trial."

5. Today, a situation such as *Fletcher v. Bealey* might be dealt with under existing provincial environmental legislation. Often such legislation allows the minister or another official to issue stop-work orders to prevent environmental harm from occurring or continuing to occur. In British Columbia, for example, under s. 34 of the *Environmental Assessment Act*, SBC 2002, c. 43, the minister is entitled to order a reviewable project or activity to cease if it is not in compliance with the project approval certificate, or if a project approval certificate has not yet been issued. Similarly, Ontario's *Environmental Protection Act*, RSO 1990, c. E.19 allows the director to issue a stop-work order when a contaminant has entered the natural environment and is an immediate danger to health, life, or property. The relevant provisions are reproduced below.

> 8(1) When the Director, upon reasonable and probable grounds, is of the opinion that a source of contaminant is discharging into the natural environment any contaminant that constitutes, or the amount, concentration or level of which constitutes, an immediate danger to human life, the health of any persons, or to property, the Director may issue a stop order directed to,
>
> (a) an owner or previous owner of the source of contaminant;
>
> (b) a person who is or was in occupation of the source of contaminant; or
>
> (c) a person who has or had the charge, management or control of the source of contaminant. …
>
> 12. Despite the issue of a program approval or order, when the Director is of the opinion, based upon reasonable and probable grounds, that it is necessary or advisable for the protection

or conservation of the natural environment, the prevention or control of an immediate danger to human life, the health of any persons or to property, the director may issue a stop order or a control order directed to the person responsible.

Another significant piece of legislation from Ontario is the *Environmental Bill of Rights*, SO 1993, c. 28. Section 84 empowers private citizens to launch actions to prevent a contravention or imminent contravention of the Act that has caused or will imminently cause serious harm to a public resource. Section 93 of the Act then allows the court to award an injunction if the person is successful in the action. The relevant provisions are detailed below.

84(1) Where a person has contravened or will imminently contravene an Act, regulation or instrument prescribed for the purposes of Part V and the actual or imminent contravention has caused or will imminently cause significant harm to a public resource of Ontario, any person resident in Ontario may bring an action against the person in the court in respect of the harm and is entitled to judgment if successful.

(2) Despite subsection (1), an action may not be brought under this section in respect of an actual contravention unless the plaintiff has applied for an investigation into the contravention under Part V and,

(a) has not received one of the responses required under sections 78 to 80 within a reasonable time, or

(b) has received a response under sections 78 to 80 that is not reasonable. ...

(6) Subsections (2) and (4) do not apply where the delay involved in complying with them would result in significant harm or serious risk of significant harm to a public resource. ...

93(1) If the court finds that the plaintiff is entitled to judgment in an action under section 84, the court may,

(a) grant an injunction against the contravention; ...

(d) make any other order, including an order as to costs, that the court considers appropriate.

(2) No award of damages shall be made under subsection (1).

Palmer v. Nova Scotia Forest Industries
(1984), 60 NSR (2d) 271 (TD)

[The plaintiffs applied for an injunction to prevent the spraying of herbicides 2,4-D, and 2,4,5-T in the vicinity of their homes and farms. They were concerned that the herbicides, which contained the dioxin TCDD, would drift onto their lands and also contaminate their drinking water. The presentation of expert evidence consumed nearly 21 days.]

NUNN J [after extensively summarizing the evidence]: ... The relief claimed is set forth in the statement of claim as follows: ...

(b) a permanent injunction enjoining the defendant from spraying the phenoxy herbicides 2,4-D and 2,4,5-T at the sites,

(c) a declaration that the plaintiffs have the right to be free of exposure to the phenoxy herbicides 2,4-D and 2,4,5-T,

(d) the costs of this action,

(e) such other relief as this Honourable Court thinks just.

The legal causes of action on which the relief is claimed are alleged to arise from the proposed spraying by the defendant and fall within the following categories:

(i) private nuisance;

(ii) trespass to land;

(iii) the rule in *Rylands v. Fletcher* (1868), LR 3 HL 330;

(iv) the right of riparian owners to water undiminished in quality;

(v) the right of landowners to groundwater free of chemical contamination;

(vi) breach of the *Fisheries Act*, RSC 1970, c. F-14, and particularly ss. 30, 31(1) and 33(2).

I shall first dispose of two of the matters raised by the plaintiffs.

First, the relief claimed of a declaration that the plaintiffs have the right to be free of exposure to the phenoxy herbicides 2,4-D and 2,4,5-T is not one within the power of this court to grant. Exposure may come from many sources and in many different situations, while I am dealing only with rights between these plaintiffs and this defendant. What is being sought is not justiciable between these parties. What the plaintiffs are seeking here is a societal matter and therefore a matter for government or regulatory agency. The function of a court was clearly set forth by MacKeigan CJNS in *A-G NS v. Bedford Service Com'n* (1976), 18 NSR (2d) 132 (SCAD) at pp. 147-8:

> A Court of law is exactly that, a Court *of law*, to administer the law, to adjudicate on legal rights, and to determine justiciable questions. It has no power to act as a sort of ombudsman, or general overseer of political or administrative bodies or officials, or to act as a commission of inquiry into economic, social or ecological matters.

Obviously the relief claimed goes beyond the activities of this defendant and reaches the realm of a broad social right applicable not only to these plaintiffs but to all members of society. Its basis rests in the political arena and not in the court ...

[Nunn J then proceeded to discuss the elements of the substantive causes of action relied on by the applicant. On the basis of *R v. Saskatchewan Wheat Pool*, [1983] 1 SCR 205 he rejected the claim of breach of statutory duty. He noted that nuisance required proof of "substantial interference with enjoyment of property" and that in the present case, proof of danger to health would suffice. Trespass, on the other hand, required proof only of a direct physical interference and the deposit of any substance on the applicants' land would therefore be trespass.]

The complete burden of proof, of course, rests upon the plaintiffs throughout for all issues asserted by them. If the spraying had actually occurred, they would have to prove by a preponderance of probabilities the essential elements of either or all of the alleged causes of action as I have set them out. However, the spraying has not occurred and this application is for a *quia timet* injunction. This can be translated as "which he fears." In other words, a plaintiff does not have to wait until actual damage occurs. Where such damage is apprehended, an application for a *quia timet* injunction is an appropriate avenue to obtain a remedy which will prevent the occurrence of the harm. That remedy also, however, is not without its limitations.

In *Attorney-General v. Corporation of Manchester*, [1893] 2 Ch. 87, Chitty J states at p. 92:

> The principle which I think may be properly and safely extracted from the *quia timet* authorities is, that the plaintiff must shew a strong case of probability that the apprehended mischief will, in fact, arise.

This passage was approved by Anglin J in the Supreme Court of Canada in *Matthew v. Guardian Ass'ce Co.* (1918), 58 SCR 47 at p. 61, and is still the proper principle to consider in an application of this kind.

It was argued by the plaintiffs that the principle as expressed in *Salmond & Heuston on the Law of Torts, supra* [R.F.V. Heuston, *Salmond on the Law of Torts*, 18th ed. (London: Sweet & Maxwell, 1981)], is more appropriate. At p. 555 they state as follows:

> In all cases, however, it seems necessary that there shall be a sufficient degree of probability that the injury will be substantial and will be continued, repeated, or committed at no remote period, and damages will not be a sufficient or adequate remedy.

It was suggested that this demonstrates that there is no set standard of proof that has to be met—simply that the risk that the plaintiff's right will be breached be significantly great in all circumstances.

I fail to see the difference suggested. A "strong case of probability" and "a sufficient degree of probability" create only a semantic difference and not a difference in substance. I prefer the former as more clearly setting forth the proper principle. This does not impose an impossible burden nor does it deprive the court of its ability to consider the balance of convenience or inconvenience or hardship between the parties nor the size or amount of the injury or distress which might occur. All of these are factors which are woven into the fabric of "a strong probability" and are considered in determining whether the burden of proof has been met.

The plaintiffs must, however, prove the essential elements of a regular injunction, namely, irreparable harm and that damages are not an adequate remedy as they are also essential elements of the *quia timet* injunction.

Finally, any injunction is a discretionary remedy and sufficient grounds must be established to warrant the exercise by the court of its discretion.

I am satisfied that a serious risk to health, if proved, would constitute irreparable harm and that damages would not be an adequate remedy. Further, recognizing the great width and elasticity of equitable principles, I would have no hesitation in deciding that such a situation would be one of the strongest which would warrant the exercise of the court's discretion to restrain the activity which would create the risk.

This matter thus reduces itself now to the single question. Have the plaintiffs offered sufficient proof that there is a serious risk of health and that such serious risk of health will occur if the spraying of the substances here is permitted to take place?

Before answering this question, there are a number of matters which must be considered.

This action is to restrain the spraying of two particular phenoxy herbicides, namely, 2,4-D and 2,4,5-T, and perhaps a third, if a mixture of 2,4-D and 2,4,5-T known under the trade name Esteron 3-3E is considered to be a separate herbicide. More particularly, the evidence submitted by the defendant indicated a specific quantity and mix of these substances it intended to use and it is this evidence which is of relevance to the issues here.

Because of the nature of the issues in dispute, the witnesses produced and the testimony given, the enormous publicity attached to the trial and the public interest involved, the evidence went far beyond the particular substances involved and related to all the phenoxy herbicides and their derivatives. The whole trial took on the aura of a scientific inquiry as to whether the world should be exposed to dioxins. Scientists from all over North America, as well as from Sweden were called and testified. Scientific reports and studies from scientists the world over were filed as part of the evidence. In order to give both sides full opportunity to present their cases fully, it was necessary to grant this latitude although both parties were aware that the final decision would have to relate to the particular facts between the parties before the court.

As to the wider issues relating to the dioxin issue, it hardly seems necessary to state that a court of law is no forum for the determination of matters of science. Those are for science to determine, as facts, following the traditionally accepted methods of scientific inquiry. A substance neither does nor does not create a risk to health by court decree and it would be foolhardy for a court to enter such an inquiry. If science itself is not certain, a court cannot resolve the conflict and make the thing certain.

Essentially a court is engaged in the resolution of private disputes between parties and in the process follows certain time-honoured and well-established procedures and applies equally well-established principles of law, varying and altering them to adjust to an ever-changing society. Part of the process is the determination of facts and another part the application of the law to those facts, once determined, and designing the remedy. As to the occurrence of events, the court is concerned with "probability" and not with "possibility."

I have, as I have said, set out a reasonably complete summary of the evidence heard by me, as well as some of the documentary evidence and I have done so specifically because of the nature of this trial, recognizing that it may be somewhat unorthodox to set out the evidence in such detail when there is so much. I believe it to be important in this case, that it be obvious just what the evidence was so that the approach and reasoning of the court be more easily understood.

While this dispute is between the parties to the action and will depend upon the facts and their relevance as I find them, this case is unique by its nature and the world-wide interest in its result. Apparently it is the first time that the leading scientists of opposing views regarding dioxin have met in court where the chemicals involved are at the very centre of the dispute.

As a result, this in one of those very rare cases where, I believe, the court owes a duty which goes beyond the parties, to make clear its findings so as to give some assistance, one way or another, which will help the understanding of those so vitally interested in this substance.

By way of background, the phenoxy herbicides are a group of herbicides which have been widely used in many parts of the world since the late 1940's and early 1950's. They are selective in that they affect only certain types of vegetation, namely, broadleaved plants, and have no, or little effect on conifers. They are a family of compounds having similar chemical and biological properties but each member compound differs in effect on individual plants. The two family members concerned here are 2,4-D (2,4-dichlorophenoxyacetic acid) and 2,4,5-T (2,4,5-trichlorophenoxyacetic acid).

2,4,5-T and all of its derivative herbicides contain a chemical contaminant formed in the manufacturing process, unavoidably to the present time and of no value, known as 2,3,7,8-tetrachlorodibenzo-p-dioxin and referred to as TCDD. Originally the quantity of TCDD in the manufactured product was in the range of 80 parts per million but, over the years, improvements in manufacturing techniques have reduced this amount to less than 0.1 parts per million. In fact the present supply of 2,4,5-T held by the defendant has been formulated with a TCDD content indicated as "non-detectable" at 0.01 parts per million.

The herbicide 2,4-D is free of any TCDD contamination.

Both herbicides have been widely used in Canada, and elsewhere, upon agricultural crops, forests, roadside and railroad rights-of-way in vast quantities and, only until recently, without too much precaution. In comparison to other uses, forestry has used only a small percentage of the total used.

Phenoxy herbicides are used to discriminate between the unwanted plants and those desired to be retained or encouraged. In a forestry site they are used to release the young conifers from competition. In Nova Scotia those competitors are the hardwoods, such as aspen, birch and maple, and raspberry. Their use is not designed to kill all competition but to permit light to reach the young conifers and decrease competition for soil nutrients and moisture. After a few years the young conifers will outgrow the competition and be permanently released. In Nova Scotia the evidence is, and I accept it, that the situation requires one treatment, and perhaps a second after three to five years, over a 40-year period.

Treatment is usually applied in early summer when susceptibility is greatest but it can be applied in late summer or early fall.

The benefits, of course, are a greater yield over a shorter period of time of the conifer forest.

The contaminant TCDD is one of the most toxic chemicals known to man. One witness described it as "exquisitely toxic." Much has been written on TCDD and its effects. It has been indicated that there are upwards of 40,000 different articles on the subject. A great number of those were submitted to the court. It is not my intention to summarize those, nor is it necessary, as almost every scientific witness as well as the regulatory agencies have already done that. While there are opposing views, and the whole field is not without some uncertainty, there is no dearth of writings. So there can be no doubt that everything submitted was considered by me, I have read every article submitted to me, a formidable task in itself, and I now join the group who has reviewed all the relevant literature, although I am far from convinced that this volume of documents was necessary for this case.

Having mentioned regulatory agencies, it is appropriate to indicate that most countries, including Canada, have regulatory agencies, whose function it is to regulate and control the use of new chemical compounds before they are exposed to the environment. In Canada this is done through various divisions of Health and Welfare Canada. Drs. Riedel and Krewski, two of the defendant's witnesses, testified in this area. In the United Kingdom there is the Advisory Committee on Pesticides and other Toxic Chemicals of which Dr. Kilpatrick, another of the defendant's witnesses, is chairman. In the United States, their legislation in this field and the approach taken is so different that little help can be gained by further considering the EPA.

As to Canada and the United Kingdom, both have registered 2,4-D and 2,4,5-T for forestry use with a maximum TCDD level of 0.1 parts per million. Registration for use in Canada for 2,4-D was in 1947 and 2,4,5-T in 1952. In both jurisdictions reviews are made periodically after reviews of the literature and independent study by highly trained and competent scientists. The evidence indicates this to be an ongoing process. In both countries registration for use is still in effect and neither jurisdiction has accepted that there are valid studies which would cause them to cancel the registration.

The provincial Department of Environment is also involved in this ongoing process as it relates to Nova Scotia and that department has not restricted the use of these herbicides.

I do not mention regulatory agencies of other countries but there are some countries, notably Sweden, where 2,4,5-T is either restricted or prohibited. However, I have no evidence before me indicating that any such restriction or prohibition is the result of a scientific inquiry. All seem to be political decisions made for whatever reason. Even in the United States no such inquiry has been made and completed. Those decisions, therefore, are of no help to me.

To some extent this case takes on the nature of an appeal from the decision of the regulatory agency and any such approach through the courts ought to be discouraged in its infancy. Opponents to a particular chemical ought to direct their activities towards the regulatory agencies or, indeed, to government itself where broad areas of social policy are involved. It is not for the courts to become a regulatory agency of this type. It has neither the training nor the staff to perform this function. Suffice it to say that this decision will relate to, and be limited to, the dispute between these parties. ...

Having accepted Mr. Ross' testimony and accepting the evidence of Donald Freer and ex. D-70 that the defendant's supply of 2,4,5-T is formulated with a TCDD content of "nondetectable" at 0.01 parts per million, it is obvious that the amount of TCDD to be sprayed in Nova Scotia by the defendant is infinitesimally small. After hearing Lt. Col. Thalken I do not accept Dr. Wulfman's suggestion that storage may affect the product in any way.

It is, therefore, in the light of this concentration of TCDD that I must consider whether the plaintiffs have met the burden of proof.

The plaintiffs, I should add, also claimed a second family of evil contaminants of both 2,4-D and 2,4,5-T besides the dioxins and those were the family of "furans" or, more properly, the dibenzofurans. They also alleged that there was still the possibility of risk to health from, if I might use the term, pure 2,4-D and 2,4,5-T. However, almost the whole of the evidence related to TCDD. I am satisfied that I have not heard sufficient evidence of a probable risk to health of the furans or pure 2,4-D or pure 2,4,5-T to warrant any fear of risk to health, particularly when considering the quantity of these substances to be used here. The totality of evidence in this regard does not even come close to establishing any probability, let alone a strong probability, of risk to health to warrant the granting of *quia timet* injunctive relief.

A great deal of the evidence submitted related to animal studies where TCDD was reported to have caused various effects indicating it to be, among other things, foetotoxic, teratagenic, carcinogenic and to cause immunological deficiencies, enzymatic changes, liver problems and the like. Also it is alleged to bioaccumulate and be persistent both in soil and in tissue. I do not pretend to have included all of its effects, but those are the most major. I was asked to make findings of fact in all of these areas, but I decline to do so. Nothing would be added to the body of scientific fact by any such determination by this court. That TCDD has had all of these effects is undoubtedly true in the experiments described, but, in every case, the effect must be related to dose. In the animal studies the doses are extremely high and, in all cases, many, many thousands of times greater than any dose which could be received in Nova Scotia.

Human studies are a different matter because actual testing is not an acceptable process in our society. I do note that Dr. Newton, another of the defence witnesses, participated in some actual testing on himself and several others, without any apparent harmful result. The human information comes from a number of studies made in various countries of the world. Some resulted from industrial accidents, some from the Vietnam experiences and some from massive industrial exposure. It was in this area that a great deal of the evidence was directed. I am satisfied that in all these cases the exposure was massive, either through accident or industrial exposure or the Vietnam War.

The use of these products in Vietnam bears some comment. They are defoliants and their use in Vietnam was to defoliate areas as completely and as quickly as possible. As a result, Agent Orange, a mixture of 2,4-D and 2,4,5-T, was sprayed without dilution in massive quantities as were Agent White, 2,4-D with pichloran (this latter contained no known dioxins). Between 1967 and 1970, 44 million litres of Agent Orange and 20 million litres of Agent White were sprayed on South Vietnam. After this the Vietnamese sprayed the considerable remaining stocks. This is the famous operation Ranch Hand.

While these amounts were sprayed pure and without dilution and without too much care, there is no scientifically acceptable proof of risk to health. There are studies, particularly Dr. Long's, which suggest some effects but these studies are widely accepted as flawed and therefore prove nothing. There are other contradictory studies suggesting no evidence of risk to health. Therefore, despite the quantity of these substances released into the Vietnam environment, there are, at present, no conclusions which can be drawn. One outstanding point, however, is that with the quantity used and the toxicity alleged, one would have expected that, at least, some of the alleged effects would have been obvious.

The studies from which the opponents of dioxin gained the most support and entrenched their position were the Hardell studies in Sweden. They are amply referred to by many of the witnesses and I do not intend to repeat them or discuss them in detail. They claim to prove an increased carcinogenic risk from exposure. It is not for the court to accept or reject their validity, but despite the defence of the validity of the studies by Dr. Erikkson, I am satisfied that a substantial group of informed scientists, including those who testified on behalf of the defendant, consider them to be flawed and unacceptable as proof of the results claimed. I do not deny their importance nor the zeal of the scientists involved in them, but I accept the evidence which indicates that they cannot be taken at face value. I am not alone in this regard as the United Kingdom Advisory Committee has not seen fit to alter its course as a result of these studies nor has Health and Welfare Canada, both of whom have considered them fully.

Were I to consider each and every study and attempt to balance them, one against the other, volumes would be written and the larger dispute would not likely be resolved. However, I need not do so for I am satisfied that, on the whole of the evidence, where risk to health is claimed in any study, the circumstance has been one of massive exposure and such are not of significant probative value in light of the actual low possible exposure here. ...

This brings me to the next suggestion by the plaintiffs which is that cancer, as a disease, has a long incubation period and the effects of dioxin cannot be known until time passes, approximately 40 years, so that it can be determined whether dioxin is indeed carcinogenic in humans. This again is not my function. I am to determine only if there is a probability of risk to health. To this point in time there is not sufficient acceptable evidence despite 35 years of use. One of the plaintiffs' witnesses, Dr. Daum, suggested that the only approach is to wait that period without permitting any further use. I cannot accept that. She is working from the premise that any substance should be proved absolutely safe before use but, as commendable as that may be, it is not practical nor is it in conformity with currently accepted determinations for use of many substances. I doubt very much if any substance can be proved absolutely safe.

If all substances which are carcinogenic or otherwise toxic were removed from use, we would have no air to breathe or potable water and many common everyday products, necessary to our life, would be removed. The key to the use of all these is dosage. Where it can be determined that there is a safe dosage, according to acceptable scientific standards, then a substance can be used. Our regulatory agencies and scientists around the world are daily involved in this very area. ...

It would be a Herculean task to go through the evidence of each witness indicating which particular facts were accepted or rejected. However, it is not necessary, for reasons already stated. I will say though, as a general point, that I accept the evidence of the defendant's witnesses as representing the generally accepted view of responsible scientists, and also as indicative of the risks involved. Each of them categorically states that neither 2,4-D nor 2,4,5-T, nor the concentration of TCDD presently in 2,4,5-T, nor the mixture of 2,4-D and 2,4,5-T in the concentrations to be sprayed on Nova Scotia forests pose any health hazard whatsoever. I am unable to accept that the plaintiffs have proved any strong probability or a sufficient degree of probability of risk to health to warrant the granting of the remedy sought, a *quia timet* injunction.

Having made this finding, it is unnecessary for me to consider the matter of riparian rights or groundwater rights. Since I have accepted that no risk to health has been proved, I need not consider these areas. Were I required to do so, and perhaps to allay public fears, I will add that the strongest evidence indicates that these substances sprayed in the Nova Scotia environment will not get into or travel through the rivers or streams, nor will they travel via groundwater to any lands of the plaintiffs who are adjacent to or near the sites to be sprayed.

Further, if any did the amount would be so insignificant that there would be no risk.

I need not consider whether any particular area need be sprayed, whether other substances should be used, or whether manual release is a better approach. While considerable evidence was adduced in this regard, it is not the court's function to direct how the defendant should manage its affairs or carry out its activities. My only concern is whether or not the defendant should be restrained from the proposed activity. While those factors may have been considered in the wide discretionary area if an injunction were to be granted, they do not arise when the plaintiffs have not proved the grounds for an injunction.

There is, accordingly, no nuisance, real or probable. As to trespass, none has been proved as probable to occur. Possibilities do not constitute proof. Similarly, there has been no basis established for the application of the rule in *Rylands v. Fletcher*, as neither the danger of the substance nor the likelihood of its escape to the plaintiffs' lands has been proved.

Therefore, the answer to the single remaining question I posed earlier which has two parts—have the plaintiffs offered sufficient proof that there is a serious risk to health and that such serious risk to health will occur if the spraying of the substances here is permitted to take place—is, for each part, in the negative.

One final comment is warranted. This decision could have been much shorter and, I am sure, the parties would have accepted that it was on the basis of the evidence presented, and that all was considered. It was obvious throughout that the subject is of vital interest to the public. It still is, as is evidenced by events in this province after the trial itself. For this reason I felt it incumbent upon me to set forth this detail of fact and my own observations so as to make clear that all the evidence available has been presented by the parties, and that, based on this evidence, fully weighed and considered, this court is of the opinion that these spraying operations can be carried out in safety and without risk to the health of the citizens of this province.

The plaintiffs, therefore, fail in this action and the defendant is entitled to its costs, to be taxed.

Since the defendant has claimed damages and the parties agreed to set aside the matter of damages until after the decision on the main issue, I shall hear the parties as to damages at their convenience.

Judgment to be entered accordingly.

Action dismissed.

NOTE

In chapter 12, "Charter Remedies," we take up the question of whether the same test should apply for *quia timet* injunctions where constitutional rights are at stake.

Hooper v. Rogers
[1975] Ch. 43 (CA)

[The plaintiff and defendant were owners of adjacent farmhouses and co-owners and co-occupiers of a tract of land beside the plaintiff's house. This land sloped steeply down from the plaintiff's house. The defendant bulldozed a track below the plaintiff's house, thereby exposing the slope to soil erosion and the possibility that the plaintiff's farmhouse would be deprived of support and eventually collapse. At trial, the plaintiff was awarded damages in lieu of a mandatory injunction ordering the defendant to restore the natural angle of the slope. The defendant appealed on the ground that the damage to the farmhouse was not imminent and that damages could not be awarded at common law because there is no tort until the damage has been sustained.]

RUSSELL LJ: It is, I apprehend, clear that in respect of the support of the farmhouse no damages at common law could have been awarded. It is established by authority binding upon this court (a) that damage is the gist of the action in nuisance, (b) that in an action for damages based upon deprivation of support to land or buildings it is necessary to establish that the land or buildings have been physically damaged by the withdrawal of support, and (c) that damages cannot be awarded at common law in a case of probable or even future physical damage to the land or buildings from loss of support based upon a present decline in the market value of the land due to such probable or certain future physical damage. But this is a case in which a mandatory order was sought upon the defendant to take such steps as were necessary to reinstate the excavated track to its former condition as to restore to the slope the angle or repose of the soil and thus avert the threat of future removal of support to the farmhouse. The award of damages could only be supported as equitable damages under the *Chancery Amendment Act 1858* (*Lord Cairns's Act*) in lieu of such an injunction. The injunction, mandatory in character, would be *quia timet*, as preventing an apprehended legal wrong, the legal wrong requiring in this case physical damage to the farmhouse for its constitution or (save the mark) perfection. ...

The case in this court therefore boils down to the question whether it is one in which the judge could have (however unwisely in the context of the relationship of unremitting hostility between the parties) made a mandatory order for the reinstatement of the natural angle of repose of the slope, having regard to the evidence of the probable ultimate outcome, in terms of removal of support to the farmhouse, of the defendant's interference with that natural angle of repose. The whole contention of counsel on behalf of the defendant is that there was here no case on which a mandatory order could have been made—*quia timet*: and, consequently, there was no scope for an award of equitable damages in lieu under *Lord Cairns's Act*. ...

Mr. Borton, a surveyor, inspected the site on behalf of the plaintiff in January 1972. He inspected again in January and June 1973, and observed erosion from the west of the track. He considered that there was a long-term danger to the plaintiff's farmhouse by the process that I have already described. He said that if (as had been done) you dig out the bottom, the top follows. He could not give a time when the erosion would reach the farmhouse. His remedy was either to fill back the track and consolidate or (more expensively) build a retaining wall on the west edge of the track as dug out.

The judgment contains these passages:

> The evidence of Mr. Borton, which I accept, is that there is a real probability, not just a possibility—a real probability—of prejudice to the plaintiff's house if nothing is done. He says that when you take out the bottom, then the top follows. ... The trees at the top of the bank will be in jeopardy with the continual erosion, and there is a long-term danger to the building. ... I do not agree that it is all speculative. I am satisfied that unless something is done, judging by what has happened already since December 1971, particularly with regard to the terrain, the trees on the bank to the west of the track will certainly be in jeopardy as continuing falls of soil and shillet occur and continuing erosion occurs, and that unless the soil on that bank is retained there is, as Mr. Borton says, a probability in the course of time that the plaintiff's premises will be in jeopardy. ... I accept the evidence of Mr. Borton as to the reality of the risk, and I find there is a real risk.

The situation is, therefore, as found by the judge, that there is a real probability that in time the activities of the defendant will result in actual damage to the plaintiff's house by removal of support unless the activities are prevented from having that effect by infilling the track and consolidating. No evidence was called to suggest that at a later stage, when the threat became more imminent in point of time, preventive measures would be available higher up the slope nearer to the farmhouse. In those circumstances, was there jurisdiction to make a mandatory order on the defendant to take those steps had the judge in his discretion decided to do so? The defendant contends not. For the defendant it was contended that a mandatory injunction could not have been ordered because the injury to the farmhouse was, on the evidence, neither certain nor "imminent." Reliance was placed upon passages in the judgment of Brougham L in *Earl of Ripon v. Hobart* (1834), 3 My. & K 169; 40 ER 65 (Ch.), in particular at pp. 176 and 177 (ER at pp. 67-68) as showing that imminence was a requirement. That was an application on affidavit evidence for an interlocutory injunction to restrain the defendants from operating a steam engine to drain certain lands on the ground that its operation would throw so much water into the River Witham that it would damage the banks: there was voluminous and conflicting evidence on whether damage would result. I do not regard the use of the word "imminent" in those passages as negativing a power to grant a mandatory injunction in the present case: I take the use of the word to indicate that the injunction must not be granted prematurely. But here the operation has been performed, and there was no evidence that any other step would avoid the proven probability of damage to the farmhouse than the step sought by way of mandatory injunction: it could not be said to be premature.

Our attention was next drawn to *Fletcher v. Bealey* (1885), 28 Ch. D 688, a decision of Pearson J. A paper manufacturer was anxious lest a deposit of vat waste from alkali works on land upstream should leak into the river and pollute the water which the plaintiff used in his manufacture. At the trial he sought an injunction *quia timet* to restrain the dumping of vat waste. The decision, as summarised in the headnote, was as follows:

> Held, that, it being quite possible by the use of due care to prevent the liquid from flowing into the river, and it being also possible that, before it began to flow from the heap, some method of rendering it innocuous might have been discovered, the action could not be maintained, and must be dismissed with costs. But the dismissal was expressly declared to be without prejudice to the right of the plaintiff to bring another action hereafter, in case of actual injury or imminent danger.

Pearson J said at p. 698:

> There must, if no actual damage is proved, be proof of imminent danger, and there must also be proof that the apprehended damage will, if it comes, be very substantial. I should almost say it must be proved that it will be irreparable, because, if the damage is not proved to be so imminent that no one can doubt that, if the remedy is delayed, the damage will be suffered, I think it must be shown that, if the damage does occur at any time, it will come in such a way and under such circumstances that it will be impossible for the plaintiff to protect himself against it if relief is denied to him in a *quia timet* action.

Again it seems to me that "imminent" is used in the sense that the circumstances must be such that the remedy sought is not premature; and again I stress that there is no suggestion that in the present case any other step than reconstituting the track will be available to save the farmhouse from the probable damage.

In different cases differing phrases have been used in describing circumstances in which mandatory injunctions and *quia timet* injunctions will be granted. In truth it seems to me that the degree of probability of future injury is not an absolute standard: what is to be aimed at is justice between the parties, having regard to all the relevant circumstances. I am not prepared to hold that on the evidence in this unusual case the judge was wrong in considering that he could have ordered the defendant to fill in and consolidate the road at the suit of the plaintiff as owner of the farmhouse, or that he was wrong in ordering damages in lieu of such an order. I would dismiss the appeal.

NOTES AND QUESTIONS

1. The award of damages in this case is available only on the assumption that an injunction would have been available. Why does the court not simply award the injunction?

2. Prior to 1858, the Court of Chancery had no power to award damages, and common law courts could award damages for past injuries only. The court in *Hooper* found its jurisdiction to award damages in the *Chancery Amendment Act 1858 (Lord Cairns' Act)*, one of the most important pieces of Chancery reform legislation. This statute granted to Chancery the power to award damages and provided that:

> In all cases in which the Court of Chancery has jurisdiction to entertain an application for an injunction against a breach of any covenant, contract or agreement, or against the commission or continuance of any wrongful act, or the specific performance of any covenant, contract or agreement, it shall be lawful for the same court, if it shall think fit, to award damages to the injured party, either in addition to or in substitution for such injunction or specific performance, and such damages may be assessed in such a manner as the court shall direct.

Canadian courts have the same power to award damages, with a number of provincial legislatures having adopted the provisions of *Lord Cairns' Act*. See, for example: *Judicature Act*, RSA 2000, c. J-1, s. 19; *Court of Queen's Bench Act*, SM 1988-89, c. 4, CCSM c. C280, s. 36; *Queen's Bench Act*, SS 1998, c. Q-1.01, s. 66; *Courts of Justice Act*, RSO 1990, c. C.43, s. 99; *Supreme Court Act*, RSPEI 1988, c. S-10, s. 32.

The power to award "equitable damages" added considerably to the remedial flexibility of the courts. In particular, the courts could now award damages in respect of continuing wrongs and prospective injuries. In a later part of these materials, we examine the discretionary considerations that the court will take into account in deciding whether it is appropriate to award damages in lieu of an injunction. Later, in chapter 10, "Financial Relief in Equity," we also return to a direct consideration of *Lord Cairns' Act*, principally in the context of specific performance actions.

3. How would the damages be calculated in *Hooper v. Rogers*?

4. In *Holland America Cruises NV v. Gralewicz* (1976), 60 DLR (3d) 512 (BC SC), the BC Supreme Court granted a *quia timet* injunction to restrain the defendant union from carrying out a threat to picket the plaintiff's cruise ship. The defendant union represented the crew of a ship that the plaintiff had recently sold. The new ship was to be manned by an Indonesian crew that was not subject to the collective agreement and paid lower wages. Bouck J declined at the interlocutory stage to rule on the defendant's argument that the union had successor rights with respect to the new ship. He held that the union's proposed activity would amount to civil conspiracy and that a *quia timet* injunction was appropriate. He said (at 521-22):

Although a high standard of probability of damage to the plaintiff was necessary in *quia timet* actions based on the tort of nuisance, this test may no longer apply to other causes of action. ...

The reason why the law on *quia timet* actions has in the past required such proof may have been due to the nature of the tort of nuisance. For example, a nuisance could be committed by dumping waste into a stream to the detriment of a person using the water further on down. Since there were few of the sophisticated scientific instruments available to society at the stage when the law on this subject was developing, it became a matter of some speculation as to the probable damage and the amount of damage to the downstream user. Today the means of proof are more readily available and it is doubtful that we should apply the same standard of proof to other torts where technical evidence is not a part of the method of proof.

MANDATORY INJUNCTIONS: DEFINITION AND SUPERVISION

In this section we examine the mandatory injunction. Again, while similar principles apply to the choice of remedy in these cases as in any other application for injunctive relief, the mandatory injunction raises certain problems in a particularly acute manner. In particular, we see judges demonstrating a concern for the burden of injunctions on "innocent" defendants, and also courts recognizing their own institutional limitations as considerations to be taken into account.

Redland Bricks v. Morris
[1970] AC 652 (HL (Eng.))

LORD UPJOHN: My Lords, this appeal raises some interesting and important questions as to the principles upon which the court will grant *quia timet* injunctions, particularly when mandatory.

The facts may be simply stated. The respondents, Mr. and Mrs. Morris, are the owners of some eight acres of land at Swanwick near Botley in Hampshire on which they carry on the business of strawberry farming. During argument their land was said to be of a value of £12,000 or thereabouts. This land slopes downwards towards the north and the owners of the land on the northern boundary are the appellants who use this land, which is clay bearing, to dig for clay for their brick-making business.

The appellants naturally quarry down to considerable depths to get the clay, so that there is always a danger of withdrawing support from their neighbours' land if they approach too near or dig too deep by that land. Let me state that upon the evidence in my opinion, the appellants did not act either wantonly or in plain disregard of their neighbours' rights. Their chief engineer and production director in evidence said that he considered that they left a safe margin for support of the respondents' land. In this he was in fact wrong. But the appellants had retained for twelve years a distinguished geologist, who gave evidence, to advise them on these problems, though there is no evidence that he was called in to advise them before their digging operations in this area.

The appellants ceased their excavations on their land in 1962 and about Christmas, 1964, some of the respondents' land started slipping down into the appellants' land, admittedly due to lack of support on the part of the appellants. Further slips of land took place in the winter of 1965-66. So in July, 1966, the respondents issued their plaint in the county court against the appellants claiming damages (limited to £500) and injunctions, and the matter came on for hearing before His Honour Judge Talbot (as he was then) in September and October, 1966. Between these hearings a further slip of land occurred. After a full hearing with expert evidence on either side he granted an injunction restraining the appellants from withdrawing support from the respondents' land without leaving sufficient support and he ordered that:

> The [appellants] do take all necessary steps to restore the support to the [respondents'] land within a period of six months.

He also gave damages to the respondents for the injury already done to their land by the withdrawal of support, in the sum of £325. On May 1, 1967, the appellants' appeal against this decision was dismissed by a majority of the Court of Appeal, [1967] 1 WLR 967 (CA) (Danckwerts and Sachs LJJ, Sellers LJ dissenting).

My Lords, the only attack before your Lordships made upon the terms of the order of the county court judge was in respect of the mandatory injunction.

It is, of course, quite clear and was settled in your Lordships' House nearly a hundred years ago in *Darley Main Colliery Co. v. Mitchell* (1886), 11 App. Cas. 127 (HL (Eng.)), that if a person withdraws support from his neighbour's land that gives no right of action at law to that neighbour until damage to his land has thereby been suffered; damage is the gist of the action. When such damage occurs the neighbour is entitled to sue for the damage suffered to his land and equity comes to the aid of the common law by granting an injunction to restrain the continuance or recurrence of any acts which may lead to a further withdrawal of support in the future.

The neighbour may not be entitled as of right to such an injunction, for the granting of an injunction is in its nature a discretionary remedy, but he is entitled to it "as of course" which comes to much the same thing and at this stage an argument on behalf of the tortfeasor, who has been withdrawing support that this will be very costly to him, perhaps by rendering him liable for heavy damages for breach of contract for failing to supply e.g., clay or gravel, receives scant, if any, respect. A similar case arises when injunctions are granted in the negative form where local authorities or statutory undertakers are enjoined from polluting rivers; in practice the most they can hope for is a suspension of the injunction while they have to take, perhaps, the most expensive steps to prevent further pollution.

But the granting of an injunction to prevent further tortious acts and the award of compensation for damage to the land already suffered exhausts the remedies which at law and (under this heading) in equity the owner of the land is entitled. He is not prejudiced at law for if, as a result of the previous withdrawal of support, some further slip of his land occurs he can bring a fresh action for this new damage and ask for damages and injunctions.

But to prevent the jurisdiction of the courts being stultified equity has invented the *quia timet* action, that is an action for an injunction to prevent an apprehended legal wrong, though none has occurred at present, and the suppliant for such an injunction is without any remedy at law.

My Lords, *quia timet* actions are broadly applicable to two types of cases: first, where the defendant has as yet done no hurt to the plaintiff but is threatening and intending (so the plaintiff alleges) to do works which will render irreparable harm to him or his property if carried to completion. Your Lordships are not concerned with that and those cases are normally, though not exclusively, concerned with negative injunctions. Secondly, the type of case where the plaintiff has been fully recompensed both at law and in equity for the damage he has suffered but where he alleges that the earlier actions of the defendant may lead to future causes of action. In practice this means the case of which that which is before your Lordships' House is typical, where the defendant has withdrawn support from his neighbour's land or where he has so acted in depositing his soil from his mining operations as to constitute a menace to the plaintiff's land. It is in this field that the undoubted jurisdiction of equity to grant a mandatory injunction, that is an injunction ordering the defendant to carry out positive works, finds its main expression, though of course it is equally applicable to many other cases. Thus, to take the simplest example, if the defendant, the owner of land, including a metalled road over which the plaintiff has a right of way, ploughs up that land so that it is no longer usable, no doubt a mandatory injunction will go to restore it; damages are not a sufficient remedy, for the plaintiff has no right to go upon the defendant's land to remake his right of way.

The cases of *Isenberg v. East India House Estate Co. Ltd.* (1863), 3 De GJ & S 263; 46 ER 637 (Ch.) and *Durell v. Pritchard* (1865), 1 Ch. App. 244 have laid down some basic principles, and your Lordships have been referred to some other cases which have been helpful. The grant of a mandatory injunction is, of course, entirely discretionary and unlike a negative injunction can never be "as of course." Every case must depend essentially upon its own particular circumstances. Any general principles for its application can only be laid down in the most general terms:

1. A mandatory injunction can only be granted where the plaintiff shows a very strong probability upon the facts that grave damage will accrue to him in the future. As Lord Dunedin said in 1919 it is not sufficient to say "timeo." [*Attorney-General for the Dominion of Canada v. Ritchie Contracting and Supply Co.*, [1919] AC 999, at 1005 (PC (Can.)).] It is a jurisdiction to be exercised sparingly and with caution but in the proper case unhesitatingly.

2. Damages will not be a sufficient or adequate remedy if such damage does happen. This is only the application of a general principle of equity; it has nothing to do with *Lord Cairns' Act* or *Shelfer's* case, [1895] 1 Ch. 287 (CA).

3. Unlike the case where a negative injunction is granted to prevent the continuance or recurrence of a wrongful act the question of the cost to the defendant to do works to prevent or lessen the likelihood of a future apprehended wrong must be an element to be taken into account:

   (a) where the defendant has acted without regard to his neighbour's rights, or has tried to steal a march on him or has tried to evade the jurisdiction of the court or, to sum it up, has acted wantonly and quite unreasonably in relation to his neighbour he may be ordered to repair his wanton and unreasonable acts by doing positive work to restore the status quo even if the expense to him is out of all proportion to the advantage thereby accruing to the plaintiff. As illustrative of this see *Woodhouse v. Newry Navigation Co.*, [1898] 1 IR 161 (CA);

(b) but where the defendant has acted reasonably, though in the event wrongly, the cost of remedying by positive action his earlier activities is most important for two reasons. First, because no legal wrong has yet occurred (for which he has not been recompensed at law and in equity) and, in spite of gloomy expert opinion, may never occur or possibly only upon a much smaller scale than anticipated. Secondly, because if ultimately heavy damage does occur the plaintiff is in no way prejudiced for he has his action at law and all his consequential remedies in equity.

So the amount to be expended under a mandatory order by the defendant must be balanced with these considerations in mind against the anticipated possible damage to the plaintiff and if, on such balance, it seems unreasonable to inflict such expenditure upon one who for this purpose is no more than a potential wrongdoer then the court must exercise its jurisdiction accordingly. Of course, the court does not have to order such works as upon the evidence before it will remedy the wrong but may think it proper to impose upon the defendant the obligation of doing certain works which may upon expert opinion merely lessen the likelihood of any further injury to the plaintiff's land. Sargant J pointed this out in effect in the celebrated "Moving Mountain" case, *Kennard v. Cory Bros. & Co. Ltd.*, [1922] 1 Ch. 265 at the foot of p. 274 (his judgment was affirmed in the Court of Appeal [1922] 2 Ch. 1).

4. If in the exercise of its discretion the court decides that it is a proper case to grant a mandatory injunction, then the court must be careful to see that the defendant knows exactly in fact what he has to do and this means not as a matter of law but as a matter of fact, so that in carrying out an order he can give his contractors the proper instructions.

This has been well settled for a long time and I regret that I cannot agree with Danckwerts LJ ([1967] 1 WLR 967 (CA) at p. 974 B), that the observations of Joyce J, in *Attorney General v. Staffordshire County Council*, [1905] 1 Ch. 336 at p. 342 have not been followed in practice. My experience had been quite the opposite. There may be some cases where, to revert to the simple illustration I gave earlier, the defendant can be ordered "to restore the right of way to its former condition." This is so simple as to require no further elucidation in the court order. But in anything more complicated the court must in fairness to the defendant tell him what he has to do, though it may well be by reference to plans prepared by some surveyor, as pointed out by Sargant J, in the passage in the "Moving Mountain" case to which I have already referred. The principle is summed up by Maugham LJ, in *Fishenden v. Higgs & Hill Ltd.* (1935), 153 LT 128 (CA) at p. 142:

I should like to observe, in the first place, that I think a mandatory injunction, except in very exceptional circumstances, ought to be granted in such terms that the person against whom it is granted ought to know exactly what he has to do.

My Lords, I shall apply these principles or conditions to this case, and I can do so very shortly.

1. As a matter of expert evidence supported by the further slip of land during the hearing it is obvious that this condition, which must be one of fact in each case, is satisfied and, indeed, is not disputed.

2. Damages obviously are not a sufficient remedy, for no one knows whether any further damage will occur and, if so, upon what scale—upon the expert evidence it might be very substantial.

3. The appellants have not behaved unreasonably but only wrongly. Upon the facts of this case the judge, in my opinion would have been fully justified in imposing upon the appellants an obligation to do some reasonable and not too expensive works which might have a reasonable chance of preventing further damage. He did not do so and it is not surprising that in the county court this was not further explored. Alternatively he might have given leave to apply for a mandatory injunction.

4. But in making his mandatory order in my opinion the judge totally disregarded this necessary and perfectly well settled condition. The terms of the order imposed upon the appellants an absolutely unqualified obligation upon them to restore support without giving them any indication of what was to be done. The judge might have ordered the appellants to carry out the remedial works described by the respondents' expert in his evidence though it would have to be set out in great detail. I could have understood that, but as it was thought to cost £30,000 that would have been most unreasonable and would have offended principle 3, but the order in fact imposed went much further; it imposed an unlimited and unqualified obligation upon the appellants, and I do not know how they could have attempted to comply with it. The expenditure of the sum of £30,000 which I have just mentioned would not necessarily have complied with it for though it would in all probability have prevented any further damage it was not guaranteed to do so and that is what in effect the mandatory order of the learned judge required. My Lords, in my opinion that part of the order of the county court judge cannot stand and the appeal must be allowed.

I have given anxious consideration to the question whether some order could not be made with a view to imposing upon the appellants some obligation to make a limited expenditure (by which I mean a few thousand pounds) to lessen the likelihood of further land slips to the respondents' land but, not without reluctance, I do not think this would be a helpful course. First, the matter would have to be tried de novo as a matter of expert evidence because the trial judge is not available and because two and a half years have elapsed since the trial, without, so far as their Lordships know, any further land slips and upon that expert evidence may have something to say. The costs of such a further enquiry would be very heavy and the enquiry possibly inconclusive. Secondly, the respondents are not unduly prejudiced, for in the event of a further land slip all their remedies at law and in equity will be open to them and they will no doubt begin in a more appropriate forum than the county court.

For these reasons I would allow the appeal. The appellants, however, must pay the respondents' costs here and below in accordance with their undertaking.

NOTES AND QUESTIONS

1. The possibility of further slippage in this case left the plaintiffs with the risk that one acre of their property, with a market value of £1,500 might be deprived of support. Why

should the plaintiffs be left with this risk? Would an award of the market value of the property provide adequate compensation to the plaintiffs?

2. Could the plaintiffs have obtained a *quia timet* injunction before the defendant began excavating?

3. Why is it important that the court be able to define closely what is required of the defendant before granting a mandatory order? What type of information will the court require to satisfy this requirement? Who is in the best position to provide this information?

4. In *AG v. Weston Plank Road Co.* (1853), 4 Gr. 211 (Upper Canada Chancery), the court refused to order the defendant company to repair roads, stating (at 218):

> To admit such a jurisdiction would be, in effect, to constitute this court the general superintendent of roads throughout the province; for, if it be our duty to direct the defendants to repair this particular highway, it must be equally our duty to grant relief in every other case of neglect—which is, I think, absurd.

5. In *Vane v. Barnard* (1716), 2 Vern. 738, 23 ER 1082 (Ch.), the defendant, upon his son's marriage, conveyed Raby Castle to his son, reserving to himself a life estate. Having taken some "displeasure" against the son, the defendant hired 200 workers and in several days stripped the castle of the lead, iron, glass doors, boards, etc. The court awarded a mandatory injunction against the defendant, ordering that it be restored to its former condition and also ordered, at the expense of the defendant, the appointment of a commission and master to determine what repairs had to be made and to supervise the work.

6. In *Redland Bricks*, Lord Upjohn suggests that in the case of a mandatory injunction one factor that the court should take into account is the cost to the defendant of complying with the order. Why? He also suggests that the cost of compliance is not a factor to be taken into account where the plaintiff is simply seeking a negative injunction or a mandatory injunction where the defendant has acted wantonly or unreasonably.

In *Lim v. Titov*, [1998] 5 WWR 495 (Alta. QB), the applicants alleged a retaining wall built by the respondent crossed over the property line both above and below ground, and sued the respondents for trespass. The applicants applied for a mandatory injunction requiring the respondents to remove the wall. The court denied the injunction with respect to the subterranean trespass. Deyell J stated:

> The evidence before me leads me to the inexorable conclusion that this is a case in which I am entitled to exercise my discretion to refuse the application for a mandatory injunction. In saying so, I am not unmindful of the authorities which emphasize the sacrosanct nature of property rights and the fact that actual harm to the plaintiff need not be illustrated for an injunction to be granted. However, in determining whether to issue a mandatory injunction, I am entitled to consider all the factors. One of these factors is that the subterranean intrusion of the retaining wall is a small infringement upon the Applicants' rights. It occurs in an area far removed from the house at the base of a hill in an unimproved area and occurs up to a maximum of about seven inches, much of which occurs underground. Furthermore, the very purpose of the retaining wall is to prevent the subsidence of the Applicants' land onto the Respondents' property.
>
> In addition, there is no evidence before me to convince me that the Respondents wilfully and deliberately trespassed upon the Applicants' land in building the retaining wall. Although the

property line had been marked out, I am not persuaded that the Applicants were involved in the trespass.

7. Where the conduct of the defendant is careless or otherwise blameworthy, the courts are not so sympathetic. In *Gross v. Wright*, [1923] SCR 214, the defendant built a party wall pursuant to an agreement with the plaintiff. While the basement and first storey conformed to the specifications in the agreement, the walls on the second and third floor were too narrow by four and eight inches respectively. On the plaintiff's side, the wall was perpendicular, though it was unclear whether it would be thick enough to allow the plaintiff to construct an adjoining building. After several years, the plaintiff discovered the problem and sought specific performance of the agreement or an injunction. The trial judge ordered demolition of the non-conforming portions of the wall, but stayed the injunction for two years to enable the parties to rectify the situation. The Court of Appeal reversed this judgment, holding that there had been only a breach of contract and that damages were the appropriate remedy. The Supreme Court of Canada upheld the trial judgment, holding that the conduct of the defendant was not only in breach of contract but also constituted trespass because the wall on the plaintiff's property was constructed under false pretences. The conduct of the defendant was deceitful and showed a wanton disregard for the rights of the plaintiff. Duff J said (at 226) that the case

> falls within the class dealing with the responsibilities of persons who, having obtained an advantage on faith of an undertaking to do something for the benefit of another seeks to retain the advantage while escaping the obligation through some technical loophole. Equity has always, in such cases, insisted upon the performance of the duty where the advantage could not be surrendered.

Duff J compared the case to *Goodson v. Richardson*, suggesting that damages reflecting the diminished value of the plaintiff's land might not be adequate since "a very important element in the value of land may be the right to exclude a particular trespasser or the right of the owner to have specific works erected."

8. In *Krehl v. Burrell* (1878), 7 Ch. D 551, the court ordered the defendant to tear down a building that obstructed the plaintiff's right-of-way. The plaintiff had indicated that he would accept an offer of alternate access and compensation of £800. The defendant refused to pay that sum. Jessel MR granted the injunction. He said (at 553-54):

> [C]onsidering the position of the parties, I thought it desirable to give the Defendant an opportunity of coming to terms before I delivered judgment. I thought it more likely that he would make good terms before judgment than he would afterwards; and in mercy to the Defendant, so as not to put him entirely in the power of the Plaintiff, I allowed the case to stand over. It seems that some terms have been proposed offering a substituted right of way, which the Plaintiff is willing to accept, provided the sum of £800 is paid to him as damages ... . At all events the sum in question does not appear to me to come at all within the description of extortion, especially considering the enormous benefit which would accrue to the Defendant by allowing this expensive building to remain. So far I think my object has been accomplished. But, however, the Defendant declines to pay the damages, and prefers, if necessary, to submit to an injunction.

Jessel MR rejected the defendant's argument that damages should be awarded instead of the injunction, stating (at 554) that:

> [T]he question I have to consider is, whether the Court ought to exercise the discretion given by [*Lord Cairns' Act*] by enabling the rich man to buy the poor man's property without his consent, for that is what it really comes to. If with notice of the right belonging to the Plaintiff, and in defiance of that notice, without any reasonable ground, and after action brought, the rich Defendant is entitled to build up a house of enormous proportions, at an enormous expense, and then to say in effect to the Court, "You will injure me a great deal more by pulling it down than you will benefit the poor man by restoring his right,"—of course that simply means that the Court in every case, at the instance of the rich man, is to compel the poor man to sell his property at a valuation. That would be the real result of such a decision. It appears to me that it never could have been intended by the Legislature to bring such a result about.

Notice how forcefully Jessel MR expresses the idea, yet how qualified the language of the decision is. Which of these qualifications are part of the rule in this case? In what circumstances may the court order damages instead of an injunction in such a case?

Should the plaintiff have a right of "self-help" in a case like *Krehl*? What would be the legal position of the parties if the plaintiff simply tore down the offending structure?

9. Sometimes a defendant, or the court, will in fact prefer a mandatory injunction over damages because of a concern that the damages may not, in fact, be an accurate or fair way to protect a plaintiff's interest. There may be a concern that the damages overcompensate or overstate the plaintiff's real loss, that they are out of proportion, or that they will not actually be used for the purpose of reinstating the plaintiff's position. For example, in *Payjack v. Springhill Farms*, [2002] MJ no. 123 (Man. QB) the court found the defendant liable for dumping contaminated litter on the plaintiff's farm. The plaintiff claimed damages, measured by the costs of removal, or a mandatory injunction. The court acceded to the defendant's argument that a mandatory injunction was preferable, on the basis that it could remove the material itself at a much lower cost than the damages estimate.

10. In *Kerlenmar Holdings Ltd. v. Corporation of the District of Matsqui* (1989), 40 BCLR (2d) 230, var'd. (1991), 56 BCLR (2d) 377 (CA), the plaintiff sued the municipality for damage caused to its farmland by flooding. It claimed damages for lost income and for the cost of doing work to prevent the flooding.

At trial, the flooding was found to be the result of increased urbanization in the area and was held by the court to be a nuisance. Toy J (the trial judge) granted damages to the plaintiff for past loss of farming income, but refused to award the cost of doing the work because of a concern that the plaintiff might not use the funds for this purpose. Instead, he granted a mandatory injunction requiring the municipality to construct dykes on the plaintiff's lands to prevent further flooding. He estimated that the cost of complying with the injunction would be under $145,000, whereas the diminished value of the plaintiff's land as a result of the flooding was between $200,000 and $450,000.

The Court of Appeal upheld the trial judge's decision, but dissolved the mandatory injunction. It held that the order might affect third parties who were not before the court (because the dykes might simply divert the flooding to other lands). The court quoted from *Miller v. Jackson*, [1977] QB 966 (CA), set out later in this chapter:

Courts of equity will not ordinarily and without special necessity interfere by injunction where the injunction will have the effect of very materially injuring the rights of third persons not before the court.

In place of the trial judge's order, the Court of Appeal, at the plaintiff's request and with the consent of the defendant, granted a new mandatory injunction ordering the defendant to purchase the plaintiff's property at a price fixed by valuing the land in its "unflooded state" ($490,000). Compare *Spur Industries Inc. v. Del E. Webb Development Co.* (1972), 494 P2d 700 (Ariz. SC), set out later in this chapter.

11. Mandatory injunctions are also becoming a featured remedy in Charter litigation and, in particular, there is much controversy about the place of structural injunctions (with their highly intrusive mandatory component) in Canadian law. We deal with this aspect in chapter 12, "Charter Remedies."

PROBLEM

In July, Susan purchased a small piece of property intending to build a house. The lot adjoins that of her new next-door neighbour Alexander. Susan had her property surveyed and staked out where she intended to excavate the foundations for her house.

When Alexander noticed where Susan had marked the property, he immediately objected. He claimed that her house would encroach upon his property by about four feet. Unfortunately for both, what began as a friendly discussion rapidly evolved into a heated argument, both parties insisting that they were right. The conversation ended with Alexander saying, "You'll be hearing from my lawyer," and Susan responding, "That's fine by me. I'll see you in court."

Neither Susan nor Alexander did anything for a week. They were not on speaking terms. At the end of the week, Susan called her surveyor and was assured that her initial survey was correct. Susan called in the contractors in August and by August 15 the excavation was completed and the foundations were laid. Meanwhile, Alexander consulted his lawyer and a writ was issued on August 20.

On the advice of her lawyer, Susan suspended construction of her house. By that time, the contractors had begun the frame and she had spent $12,000. The matter has now come to trial and it has been determined that Susan's survey was incorrect and that one corner of her house did encroach on Alexander's property. Alexander has requested a mandatory injunction to have the house removed. The encroachment (of approximately 10 square feet) has diminished the value of his property by $500. Susan's surveyor is without insurance and is unlikely to have sufficient assets to satisfy any judgment against him. Should the order be granted and are there any alternative remedies?

See *Bracewell v. Appleby*, [1975] Ch. 408; *Clark v. McKenzie* (1930), 42 BCLR 449 (CA); and *Earle v. Martin* (1998), 528 APR 105 (Nfld. TD).

INJUNCTIONS TO PROTECT PROPERTY INTERESTS

Introduction

While the courts constantly reiterate the principle that equitable remedies are available only when damages would be inadequate to protect the plaintiff's rights, when it comes to the protection of property rights, the injunction is the preferred remedy and it is only in exceptional cases that the plaintiff will be limited to damages. So, for example, injunctions are almost always available to restrain trespass and nuisance. In fact, it might be suggested that the very definition of "property" depends on whether injunctive relief is available to protect the interest asserted. Indeed, instead of distinguishing between proprietary and non-proprietary rights, some writers distinguish between rights protected by property rules and those protected by liability rules (Guido Calabresi and A. Douglas Melamed, "Property Rules, Liability Rules and Inalienability: One View of the Cathedral" (1972), 85 *Harvard Law Review* 1089).

The preference for injunctive relief in the case of property stems in part from the historical tenderness that the law has evinced towards land and from early procedural restrictions. Until 1858, the courts had no power to award damages for a continuing or future injury. Thus, in the absence of an injunction, the only remedy available to a plaintiff for a continuing wrong would be an action for past damages and the highly undesirable prospect of future actions in respect of the same wrong for as long as it continued. As noted earlier, this remedial inflexibility was removed in 1858 by *Lord Cairns' Act* (*Chancery Amendment Act*), 1858 (UK), which gave to the Chancery power to award damages in lieu of an injunction. Yet, as many of the following cases demonstrate, this legislation did not eliminate the judicial preference for injunctive relief. (For a discussion of the social and political importance of property and its impact on the law of remedies, see David Cohen, "The Relationship of Contractual Remedies to Political and Social Status: A Preliminary Inquiry" (1982), 32 *University of Toronto Law Journal* 31.)

Perhaps more important, as Professor Sharpe suggests (*Injunctions and Specific Performance* (Toronto: Canada Law Book, 2009) (looseleaf), at 4.20), injunctive remedies correspond most closely with the very notion of a property right. He explains, "It is the very essence of the concept of property that the owner should not be deprived without consent." The notion of property has traditionally implied the power to exclude others and to deal with the interest at the owner's discretion. "An injunction brings to bear coercive powers to vindicate that right. Compensatory damages for a continuous and wrongful interference with a property interest offers only limited protection in that the plaintiff is, in effect, deprived of his property without consent at an objectively determined price. Special justification is required for damages rather than an injunction if the principle of autonomous control over property is to be preserved."

This insight does not, however, answer the question of remedial choice. First, because "property" is a legal concept, there would be a certain circularity of thought involved in the assumption that the question of remedial choice turns simply on whether the interest at stake is a proprietary one. In a sense, this is the very question that the courts are asked to decide. Indeed, there is some evidence that concepts of property have expanded and contracted according to the remedial conclusions reached by courts. Second, the idea that specific remedies are available only to protect property interests has now been put to rest. Property rights are not the only interests that attract the protection of equity. Conversely, as you will see, the principle of autonomous control over property is not absolute, and there are circumstances in which it may give way to other goals. It must not be assumed, therefore, that the question of whether injunctive relief will be available to protect a particular interest turns simply upon an *a priori* examination of the classification of the interest for which the plaintiff is seeking protection.

Questions of remedial choice can only be answered by an examination of the nature of the interest being asserted by the plaintiff, against the background of the purposes of substantive and remedial law. So, for example, we might ask with Sharpe, "is this the type of interest over which the plaintiff should be given the power of autonomous control and which she should not be deprived of without her consent?" Or are there competing considerations and policies that override this principle? As you read the materials in this chapter you should attempt to articulate the considerations that the courts take into account in answering this crucial question.

Chattels

Where an article has a special or unique value to the owner as, for example, a rare piece of art, an injunction will ordinarily be granted to protect the owner's interest. Where, however, the property is an ordinary article of commerce and easily replaceable, the right to equitable relief is more problematic.

In *Cook v. Rogers* (1946), 46 SR (NSW) 229, the plaintiff and defendant were involved in a dispute over the ownership of an automobile. The plaintiff was the last of five owners of the car. The defendant, on the instructions of the original owner, repossessed the car on the basis that the second purchaser had defaulted on his payments. The plaintiff sought an injunction to restrain the defendant from dealing with the car in any manner prejudicial to the plaintiff's rights.

Roper J held that the plaintiff would not be entitled to the injunction requested. He said (at 232-33):

> Normally, the wrongful detention of goods gives no equity to the person entitled to possession. His remedy is at common law. Where the goods have a peculiar value and damages at law would not be an adequate remedy, an equity does arise. The article in question here is a motor car of no peculiar value other than that attaching to motor cars generally ... . It has been put, however, that as the demand for motor cars now exceeds supply (of which there is no evidence strictly before me), and as prices are fixed, damages in this case would not be an adequate remedy, and that the plaintiff therefore has a remedy in equity. I do not agree with this proposition. There would be an extraordinary extension of the jurisdiction in equity if it were attracted to cases in which it would otherwise be absent merely by the fact that goods were temporarily in short supply and difficult to obtain, or by that fact together with the additional fact that the prices of the goods were fixed by law. If this were so the remedies of injunction and specific performance would at the present time presumably be available in a very large number of ordinary mercantile contracts. In my opinion, the existence of market difficulties of an apparently temporary nature does not give a jurisdiction to this Court which it would not otherwise have, even though it might be difficult to predict when the difficulties will disappear.

I.C.F. Spry (*Equitable Remedies*, 7th ed. (North Ryde: Law Book Co., 2007), at 387) criticizes this approach and argues that an injunction should be available even when the property is not unique. He suggests that the courts should not rely on cases involving specific performance where the right asserted by the plaintiff is based only on an agreement to acquire new property; that different considerations arise when the injunction is sought to protect a pre-existing interest in property.

In most provinces, the rules of court now provide for pre-trial injunctions to restrain the disposition of assets that are the subject matter of the litigation. In chapter 9, "Specific Performance," we turn to the question of specific performance and injunctions to enforce contracts for the sale of goods.

Trespass to Land: General Principles

The cases in this section deal primarily with the problem of trespass to property. Cases considering both prohibitive and mandatory injunctions are grouped together for, while somewhat different considerations may be relevant to each, they raise similar fundamental issues.

Goodson v. Richardson
(1874), LR 9 Ch. App. 221

S. Goodson, the Plaintiff in this case, was owner in fee of an undivided moiety of lands in the *Isle of Thanet*, abutting upon the highway from *Broadstairs* to *Ramsgate*, and as such was owner in fee of an undivided moiety of the adjoining half of the highway. He was also shareholder in a waterworks company at *Ramsgate*. The Defendant, *R. Richardson*, owned some houses at *Ramsgate*, and, being dissatisfied with the waterworks company, proceeded to construct waterworks for the supply of his houses. He applied to the Highway Board of the *Isle of Thanet* for permission to lay down pipes along the highway, which, after some time and discussion and opposition form the waterworks company, was, on the 8th of April, 1873, granted to him; the clerk to the board at the same time informing him that the board could only give permission subject to the rights of the owners of the lands. The Defendant had on the 4th of April begun to lay the pipes along the highway, and (apparently in the course of the day of the 9th of April) he laid the pipes in the soil of the side of the road adjoining the land of which the Plaintiff has an undivided moiety. On the same 9th of April the Plaintiff and other landowners served the Defendant with notice not to lay pipes in their lands, and that they intended to apply for an injunction. There was a dispute as to the exact times when the pipes were laid, and when the notice was received.

On the 21st of April the bill in this suit was filed, praying for a perpetual injunction to restrain the Defendant from so laying any pipes and from allowing them to remain. The Master of the Rolls, Sir *G. Jessel*, made a decree for a perpetual injunction, and the Defendant appealed. ...

LORD SELBORNE LC: In this case the Master of the Rolls has thought it right, in the exercise of that discretion which, as Mr. *Beaumont* very properly said, is a judicial and not an arbitrary discretion, to grant an injunction restraining the continuance of certain water-pipes which the Defendant has placed in the Plaintiff's land.

Now, it is undoubtedly true that where a legal remedy exists, this Court, in determining whether it will leave the parties to that legal remedy or will interfere by way of injunction, has regard to the circumstances of each particular case, and amongst those circumstances are, no doubt, the time at which the work was executed, and also what will be the result to the parties of the interference of the Court, on the one hand, or of leaving them to their legal rights and liabilities, on the other hand. But I apprehend that the Court has nowhere said that when a trespass of this kind has been committed under circumstances at all similar to those in the present case, the mere fact of the trespass being complete at the time when the bill was filed will prevent an injunction against the continuance of the trespass.

The Plaintiff is the owner of the soil through which these pipes have been laid, and no one has a right to take that soil for such a purpose, except under contract with the owner, or with his consent. At the same time the Plaintiff has not the right of an unlimited owner in respect of that soil, because the upper surface is dedicated to the public for the purpose of a public highway, which is under the management of local authorities; and the Plaintiff cannot use the soil, or deal with it by breaking it open, or in any other manner, so as to interfere with the use of it by the public for the purpose of a highway.

These pipes, therefore, being laid below the surface, the Plaintiff might not, without exposing himself to difficulties with the public authorities who are the guardians of the highway, be able to redress the injury in the easy and simple manner which he could if the same thing had been done in an ordinary field.

It is said that the objection of the Plaintiff to the laying of these pipes in his land is an unneighbourly thing, and that his right is one of little or no value, and one which Parliament, if it were to deal with the question, might possibly disregard. What Parliament might do, if it were to deal with the question, is, I apprehend, not a matter for our consideration now, as Parliament has not dealt with the question. Parliament is, no doubt, at liberty to take a higher view upon a balance struck between private rights and public interests than this Court can take. But with respect to the suggested absence of value of the land in its present situation, it is enough to say that the very fact that no interference of this kind can lawfully take place without his consent, and without a bargain with him, gives his interest in this land, even in a pecuniary point of view, precisely the value which that power of veto upon its use creates, when such use is to any other person desirable and an object sought to be obtained. Besides which, I am not prepared to accede to the proposition that it is an unneighbourly proceeding in a man, whose motive for desiring to prevent a particular act may be collateral to the interest in his land—such, for instance, as his being a proprietor of waterworks which may be injured by the proposed use of it—to say to his neighbour who wishes to compete with him in that business, "You are perfectly at liberty to enter into competition with me as a seller of water to the public of *Ramsgate* in any lawful manner; but you are not at liberty to take my land without my consent for the purpose of competing with me, and I shall object to your doing so." In that, I confess, I see nothing unneighbourly whatsoever.

Then what are the actual circumstances of this case? The Plaintiff has certainly been guilty of neither acquiescence nor delay. ...

[His Lordship then stated the facts of the case.]

In that state of things, and looking to the nature of the work, and that it was capable of being so quickly done, and done in that manner, I have no hesitation in saying that I think this Court is bound to deal with the case exactly as it would have done if this bill had been filed, not as it was a few days afterwards, but on the morning of the day, and before any part of the work had been done.

I cannot look upon this case otherwise than as a deliberate and unlawful invasion by one man of another man's land for the purpose of a continuing trespass, which is in law a series of trespasses from time to time, to the gain and profit of the trespasser, without the consent of the owner of the land; and it appears to me, as such, to be a proper subject for an injunction.

The cases which have been referred to are either cases of ancient lights, such as *Durell v. Pritchard* (1865), LR 1 Ch. App. 244, or cases of covenants, such as *Bowes v. Law* (1870), LR 9 Eq. 636, where a man had, once for all, done upon his own land something which exposed him to an action by the other party. In those cases the thing was finished, and in the judgment of the Court it was more equitable, having regard to the consequences of interference or non-interference, to leave the parties to their legal rights and liabilities, or to give damages, rather than to interfere by injunction. No doubt in such a state of things the *quantum* of damage to the Plaintiff, as compared with the *quantum* of loss to the Defendant, is a material consideration; but that consideration does not appear to me to arise in the present case.

NOTES AND QUESTIONS

So great, moreover, is the regard of the law for private property, that it will not authorize the least violation of it; no, not even for the general good of the whole community.

Blackstone, *Commentaries*, Book I, c. 1.

There is nothing which so generally strikes the imagination and engages the affections of mankind, as the right of property; or that sole and despotic dominion which one man claims and exercises over the external things of the world, in total exclusion of the right of any other individual in the universe.

Blackstone, *Commentaries*, Book II, c. 1.

1. Bentham defined property as "nothing but a basis of expectation ... being able to draw such or such an advantage from the thing possessed" (*Theory of Legislation: Principles of the Civil Code*, Book II, c. 1). What are these expectations and how are they created? Are they absolute?

2. If the plaintiff's property would suffer no material damage and the plaintiff would incur no monetary loss as a result of the defendant's trespass, what interest of the plaintiff is being protected by the award of the injunction in this case?

3. Might *Goodson v. Richardson* have been differently decided if the defendant had been unaware of the plaintiff's ownership of the property until after the pipes had been installed?

4. Recall the case of *Mayor of Bradford v. Pickles*, [1895] AC 587 (HL (Eng.)) in which the House of Lords refused to enjoin a landowner from disturbing the city's water supply by intercepting the water as it percolated through his land. Lord Macnaghten summed up (at 601) the court's reasoning by recognizing that Mr. Pickles

prefers his own interests to the public good. He may be churlish, selfish, and grasping. His conduct may seem shocking to a moral philosopher. But where is the malice? Mr. Pickles has no spite against the people of Bradford. He bears no ill will to the corporation. They are welcome to the water, and to his land too, if they will pay the price for it.

5. Compare the treatment of the concept of equity by Aristotle. In the *Nichomachean Ethics* (Book 5, c. 10), he suggests that equitable justice is a correction of legal justice. "The reason is that all law is universal but about some things it is not possible to make a universal statement which shall be correct … . And this is the nature of the equitable, a correction of law where it is defective owing to its universality." He concludes, "It is plain, then, what the equitable is, and that it is just and is better than one kind of justice. It is evident also from this who the equitable man is; the man who chooses and does such acts, and is no stickler for his rights in a bad sense but tends to take less than his share though he has the law on his side, is equitable, and this state of character is equity."

6. In *Behrens v. Richards*, [1905] 2 Ch. 614, the plaintiff purchased a tract of remote coastal land. The local people were used to using paths across this land as a means of access to the beach for the purposes of fishing, seaweed harvesting, and recreation. The plaintiff blocked the paths and sought an injunction to restrain the defendants from trespassing on his land. The defendants argued that they had established a public right-of-way.

Buckley J held that the defendants had not established a public right-of-way and that they were technically trespassers but indicated that he would nevertheless have refused the injunction (the plaintiff having dropped the claim for specific relief). He said (at 621-22):

> From the fact, however, that I arrive at the conclusion that the defendants have not established the common public rights which they claim, it does not, in my opinion, follow that the plaintiff is entitled to the formidable weapon of the injunction of this Court … . No doubt it is the law that upon the foreshore of this country and the rough cliff paths which exist in many places along the coast the public have not a right of way recognized by the law, and no doubt it is true that rights of property are as a general proposition entitled to protection by, if necessary, an injunction of this Court. … The existing security of the tenure of land in this country is largely maintained by the fact that the owners of the land behave reasonably in the matter of its enjoyment. It would, in my judgment, be a disastrous thing, not for the public only, but for the landowners also, if this Court, at the caprice of the landowner, not because circumstances have altered, but merely because he was minded that it should be so, entertained every trivial application to restrain persons by injunction from using paths which, though not public highways, have in fact been used by the permission of the owners for many generations, and whose user is no injury to the owner of the land.

Buckley J refused to grant the injunction. The plaintiff was awarded nominal damages and no costs were awarded.

7. A modern equivalent of *Behrens* is *Jarnouin v. Parvais* (1997), 122 Man. R (2d) 223 (QB). The plaintiff sought an injunction to prevent the defendant's cattle from straying onto his fields and causing damage to his crops. The plaintiff was awarded damages, but the injunction was denied as the defendant had taken steps to prevent the trespasses from reoccurring. Schulman J concluded that "[t]he occasional straying of an animal is commonplace in this municipality, and most farmers are able to resolve the problem with a telephone call to the offending farmer."

8. See also the case of *Jerome v. Ross* (1823), 7 John Ch. R 315, in which the plaintiff sought an injunction to restrain the defendant from trespassing upon his land for the purpose of removing rock to build a dam. Chancellor Kent refused the injunction noting that the rock was not of particular value to the plaintiff and while the loss of the rock was irreparable in the sense that it could not be replaced, it could be perfectly compensated in money. He held that an injunction should only issue where the trespass threatens the value or character of the property and stated (at 332-33) that

[t]he objection to the injunction, in cases of private trespass, except under very special circumstances, is, that it would be productive of public inconvenience, by drawing cases of ordinary trespass within the cognisance of equity, and by calling forth, upon all occasions, its power to punish by attachment, fine and imprisonment, for a further commission of trespass, instead of the more gentle common law remedy by action, and the assessment of damages by a jury. In ordinary cases, this latter remedy has been found amply sufficient for the protection of property.

9. See also *Douglas v. Bullen* (1912), 22 OWR 837. An interim injunction against trespass (where a proposed building might encroach on neighbouring land by a few inches) was refused because the amount of the land in dispute was small and its value insignificant.

10. Where a person has mistakenly built on another's land, s. 37(1) of the *Conveyancing and Law of Property Act*, RSO 1990, c. C.34 provides:

Where a person makes lasting improvements on land under the belief that it is the person's own, the person or the person's assigns are entitled to a lien upon it to the extent of the amount by which its value is enhanced by the improvements, or are entitled or may be required to retain the land if the Superior Court of Justice is of opinion or requires that this should be done, according as may under all circumstances of the case be most just, making compensation for the land, if retained, as the court directs.

However, also note that where the trespass has been advertent the court may, in addition to ordering a mandatory injunction to remove the trespass, also award punitive damages. See *Zambri v. Grammelhofer*, [2009] OJ no. 5043 (SCJ).

Woollerton and Wilson Ltd. v. Richard Costain Ltd.
[1970] 1 WLR 411 (Ch.)

STAMP J: The plaintiff company owns a factory and warehouse on the west side of Clyde Street in the city of Leicester. On the east side of the street the defendant company, a wholly owned subsidiary of the well-known building contractors, Richard Costain Ltd., are in course of constructing a building for the use of the General Post Office which will be 300 feet in height when completed. The project upon which they are engaged is an important and considerable one. The new building will occupy almost the whole of the site upon which it is being erected and working space is most exceptionally limited. The operations of the defendants have caused congestion in Clyde Street, which has been the cause of complaint by the plaintiffs. Near the south west corner of the building which is being constructed there is a tower crane which was installed on September 13 or 14, 1969. It is so placed that when in operation the jib of the crane swings not merely over Clyde Street but over the plaintiffs' factory. When it is not in operation it has to be left free to swing and if the wind is in the direction to cause that result it also then swings over the plaintiffs' factory. Loads are not carried over the plaintiffs' property. The mast of the crane is about 160 feet high. Approximately 35 feet of this is below street level and approximately 15 feet above jib level. The radius of the jib arm at its maximum overhangs the plaintiffs' premises by about 50 feet. The jib when over the plaintiffs' premises is about 50 feet above roof level.

It is no part of the plaintiffs' case that the crane incommodes them or their servants in the slightest degree or is in any way a nuisance. The plaintiffs do not claim that they are in any fear or apprehension. But they claim an interlocutory injunction to restrain what is conceded to be an invasion of their air space and a trespass.

The plaintiffs, while not complaining of any damage, apprehension or inconvenience have, so they would have the court believe, only one object in these proceedings, namely, to prevent the jib of the crane swinging over their premises; and something more than £250 which the defendants have offered would have been required to induce them to change their mind.

It is the plaintiffs' case that the absence of any damage caused by the trespass, either present or apprehended, is no reason for refusing the injunction, for which they ask. It is their further contention that since the tort of trespass is admitted and is threatened to be continued there is no good reason for refusing interlocutory relief on the ground of balance of convenience. In my judgment both these submissions are well founded.

It is in my judgment well established that it is no answer to a claim for an injunction to restrain a trespass that the trespass does no harm to the plaintiff. Indeed, the very fact that no harm is done is a reason for rather than against the granting of an injunction: for if there is no damage done the damage recovered in the action will be nominal and if the injunction is refused the result will be no more nor less than a licence to continue the tort of trespass in return for a nominal payment. Furthermore, the very fact that the plaintiff is the owner of the property

> that no interference of this kind can lawfully take place without his consent, and without a bargain with him, gives his interest in this land, even in a pecuniary point of view, precisely the value which the power of veto upon its use creates, when such use is to any other person desirable and an object sought to be obtained.

See the judgment of Lord Selborne L in *Goodson v. Richardson* (1874), LR 9 Ch. App. 211 at p. 224.

Sir George Jessel MR in *Eardley v. Granville* (1876), 3 Ch. D 826 at p. 832, remarked of the defendant in that case:

> [H]e is a mere trespasser and he being a trespasser comes within the well established doctrine of *Goodson v. Richardson* and *Rochdale Canal Company v. King* (1851), 14 QB 122, where damages would be no compensation for a right to property, and the plaintiffs are entitled to prohibit him by injunction. There may be little or no injury to the estate, but if they restrain him he will be glad to pay a way-leave.

Mr. Harman referred me to a number of cases the effect of which, he submitted, was to modify the principle or rule so stated in *Eardley v. Granville* (1876), 3 Ch. D 826 and to justify the court in refusing an injunction in a case such as the present. These were cases in which the claim was based on nuisance not on trespass. The gist of an action for nuisance is damage. And since the tort of nuisance can only exist if there be damage, in an action for nuisance damage can be obtained which will be measured by the extent of the nuisance and the plaintiff in such a case is not in a situation of a plaintiff in an action for trespass who may recover only nominal damages. In an action of nuisance the licence which the court by refusing an injunction may be said to give the defendant to continue the nuisance will be compensated by the damage which the plaintiff will receive on his claim for damages. In *Shelfer v. City of London Electric Lighting Co.*, [1895] 1 Ch. 287, A.L. Smith LJ in a well-known passage of his judgment stated as a good working rule, at p. 322:

(1) If the injury to the plaintiff's legal rights is small,
(2) and is one which is capable of being estimated in money,
(3) and is one which can be adequately compensated by a small money payment,
(4) and the case is one in which it would be oppressive to the defendant to grant an injunction:

then damages in substitution for an injunction may be given. The case which the Lord Justice was considering was, however, a case of nuisance; and in my view that passage cannot be regarded as applicable where the complaint is of a trespass in respect of which only nominal damages can be recovered. There is no suggestion whatever in any of the cases of nuisance to which Mr. Harman referred that *Rochdale Canal Co. v. King*; *Goodson v. Richardson*; and *Eardley v. Granville* were not good law. There are dicta in the judgment of McNair J in *Kelson v. Imperial Tobacco Co.*, [1957] 2 QB 334, suggesting that the classic remarks of A.L. Smith LJ are applicable as well to an action for trespass as to one for nuisance, but in fact McNair J followed *Goodson v. Richardson*, remarking towards the end of his judgment at p. 347:

If I were to decide that an appropriate remedy would be a small money payment of nominal damages, I would be, in effect, saying that although such implied licence, if any, as the defendants have has been determined, nevertheless the defendants are entitled to continue to display their sign.

As to the balance of convenience which is normally to be considered where application is made for an interlocutory injunction, it is sufficient that I should refer to the judgment of James LJ in *Stocker v. Planet Building Society* (1878), 27 WR 877 (CA) at p. 878:

Balance of convenience has nothing to do with a case of this kind; it can only be considered where there is some question which must be decided at the hearing. Here the defendants say "Allow us to commit a trespass." I think the injunction is quite right.

The question, therefore, as I see it is not whether the plaintiffs ought to have an injunction until the trial but whether they ought to have an injunction.

If the trespass was one which was to be continued indefinitely the plaintiffs would in my judgment in accordance with principle be entitled to the injunction which they claim, subject to consideration of the question whether the circumstances were such that the operation of the injunction should be postponed for an appropriate period. I could approach the problem in this way by granting the plaintiffs the injunction which they seek and postponing its operation if I thought that I ought in the exercise of my discretion on the facts of this case so to do; and I think this is the correct approach notwithstanding that the trespass will, so it is said, in any event come to an end next November. But whether I approach the problem in this way or consider simply whether I ought now to grant the injunction which the plaintiffs seek, probably makes no difference: for I have come to the conclusion on the facts of this case that I ought in the exercise of this discretion, which it is common ground that I have, to withhold an immediate injunction.

The erection of the building was begun as long ago as last October. It was planned upon the basis that a tower crane of the type of which complaint is made would be employed in the erection. There is uncontradicted evidence that a tower crane was a practical necessity for reasons connected with the fact that the site is a most restricted one and that a mobile crane would cause a complete blockage in Clyde Street and the installation of other types of crane would be impracticable. The only place in which the tower crane can be placed is precisely where it is. There is also uncontradicted evidence that if the tower crane was required to be removed from where it is, all building operations would be brought to a halt while the job was replanned. It is the opinion of the defendants' contracts manager that the building would have to be redesigned and that this would result in the contract period being extended by at least 6 and probably 12 months. The plaintiffs have been offered £250 for the right to continue to trespass while the crane is there; and although as a matter of law the plaintiffs are no doubt entitled to exploit to the full the fact that the air space in which the jib of the crane swings has by reason of these defendants' vital requirements suddenly assumed a very artificial value, the court may, I think, properly take into account in considering whether an immediate injunction ought to be granted the fact that they have been offered a sum of money which is at least substantial so that when they started this action they were not in the position of a plaintiff whose only remedy other than an injunction was nominal damages. In considering whether or not an injunction should be granted and, if so, on what terms, the court may consider the behaviour of the parties. Nor do I think I ought to ignore in considering whether an immediate injunction ought to be granted the fact that the air space in question has only assumed any value at all by reason of those particular defendants' necessities. This is not a case such as was before McNair J in *Kelson v. Imperial Tobacco Co.* where the air space could be let to a party other than the defendant company which was trespassing on it and it is not a case where the defendants have been insisting upon the right to swing the crane over the plaintiffs' land as a matter of right. Furthermore, it is the evidence of Mr. Waters, the general manager employed by the defendants that on no occasion in his experience has any neighbouring proprietor over whose property the jib of a tower crane has passed sought to obtain an injunction to prevent this happening or to claim compensation for the crane swinging over his air space. Nor, says Mr. Waters, is he aware that any other contractor has encountered difficulties of this nature. He says that on previous occasions the Costain Group has provided neighbouring proprietors with insurance cover against the possibility of any damage being caused and this has always satisfied them. Finally, he adds that on no occasion has any claim been made against this insurance cover. On this evidence I can only hold that the defendants have got themselves into the position of being, so to speak, held up to ransom, not by a flagrant disregard of the plaintiffs' proprietary rights but by inadvertence. A contractor in the future will be warned not to enter into a building contract involving the erection of one of these cranes in such a position as to swing upon the land of an adjoining owner without first obtaining permission from that adjoining owner. Much has been made in this case of the importance of work being done by the defendants; but if I had thought that the defendants in this case had deliberately proceeded upon the footing that the importance of the work would prevent the court from granting an injunction, I would have made an order different from that which I will presently make. Taking all factors to which I have called attention into consideration, I conclude that I ought in the exercise of my discretion to grant the injunction which the plaintiffs seek until trial of the action, but to postpone its operation until the end of November of next year. I am conscious that by so doing I am giving with one hand and taking away with the other. But by so doing I give effect to the process by which I have come to my conclusion that in principle there ought to be an injunction but on the particular facts of this case not until the defendants have had a proper opportunity of finishing the job. If for any reason the job would not be finished in November next, application could be made, with what result I know not, to extend the suspension of the order.

Order accordingly. Costs in the cause.

NOTES AND QUESTIONS

1. Why were no damages awarded in this case?

2. In *Woollerton*, Stamp J refers to *Shelfer v. City of London Electric Lighting Co.*, [1895] 1 Ch. 287 (CA), in which A.L. Smith LJ considered the court's jurisdiction under *Lord Cairns' Act*. A.L. Smith LJ stated (at 322) that the "working rule" was to substitute damages:

  (1) If the injury to the plaintiff's legal right is small,
  (2) and is one which is capable of being estimated in money,
  (3) and is one which can be adequately compensated by a small money payment,
  (4) and the case is one in which it would be oppressive to the defendant to grant an injunction.

In *Shelfer*, the defendants had installed an electricity plant near the plaintiff's home. The plaintiff had a 20-year lease. Noise and vibrations from the plant kept the plaintiff awake at night and caused some structural damage to the plaintiff's house. At trial, Kekewich J held that the defendant's operation was a nuisance, but since the plaintiff had suffered no financial loss, and because of the very large loss that would be suffered as a result of shutting down the defendant's operation, the case was an appropriate one for an award of damages only. This decision was reversed by the Court of Appeal. After stating the "working rule" governing damages in lieu of an injunction, A.L. Smith LJ admitted that the rule was difficult to apply, but that the discomfort caused to the plaintiff, which would continue for the remaining 19 years of his lease, was not a "small injury" nor one that was capable of being estimated in money. He concluded (at 324):

  In order to constitute a real assessment it appears to me that the principle of purchasing the Plaintiff's interest in his lease for the unexpired term will have to be adopted as the basis upon which the assessment is to be made, and as I have before stated, this is never sanctioned by the Court at the instance of a tortfeasor.

For a case involving similar facts with a similar result, see *340909 Ont. Ltd. v. Huron Steel Products (Windsor) Ltd.* (1990), 73 OR (2d) 641 (HC), aff'd. (1992), 10 OR (3d) 95 (CA).

3. Stamp J suggests that the rule in *Shelfer* is applicable only in cases of nuisance and could not, therefore, be applied in *Woollerton*. Why does he make this distinction?

4. In *Charrington v. Simons & Co. Ltd.*, [1971] 1 WLR 598 (CA), the defendant had acquired a parcel of property from the plaintiff, intending to resurface a track on the land, but covenanting not to raise the road surface above the level of the plaintiff's adjacent land. The defendant breached this covenant and the raised roadway interfered with the plaintiff's land by making it hazardous to operate farm equipment near the concrete track and more difficult to drive trucks on and off the track.

At trial, the judge granted a mandatory injunction to compel the removal of the track, but suspended its operation for three years to enable the defendant to carry out specified remedial work as an alternative—that is, raising the level of the plaintiff's property, building a sloping shoulder, etc. The order also envisaged the possibility that these measures might not perfectly remedy the problem and provided further that at the end of the three years the defendant might be ordered to remove the track or pay damages to the plaintiff. The Court of Appeal deleted the suspension from the injunction and ordered that the track be removed. Russell LJ said (at 603) that the judge had required the plaintiff to submit to a continuing trespass and had

> travelled beyond the bounds within which discretion may be judicially exercised; for in effect he sought to force on a reluctant plaintiff something like a settlement involving operations by the defendant company on the plaintiff's land.

5. In *Lewvest Ltd. v. Scotia Towers Ltd.* (1981), 126 DLR (3d) 239 (Nfld. SC) the plaintiff sought an injunction to prevent the defendant from swinging a crane over his property in the course of constructing a building. Goodridge J granted the injunction on the basis that the overswinging crane was a trespass. In the course of his judgment he agreed that the maxim *cujus est solum est usque ad coleum* was long overdue for revision, but even such revision would probably not assist the defendant. He stated (at 240) that

> [u]nder our system of law, property rights are sacrosanct. For that reason, the rules that generally apply to injunctions do not apply in cases such as this. The balance of convenience and other matters may have to take second place to the sacrosanctity of property rights in matters of trespass.
>
> What has happened here is that the third defendant, by trespassing on property of Lewvest Limited, can save itself, according to the evidence, close to half a million dollars. If it can save that money, so be it, but the Court is not going to give it a right to use the plaintiff's property. That is a right that it must negotiate with the plaintiff.

6. Compare *Bernstein of Leigh (Baron) v. Skyviews & General Ltd.*, [1978] QB 479, in which Griffiths J refused to grant an injunction to prevent the defendants from flying over Lord Bernstein's land to take photographs, reasoning that such an overflight could not be a trespass, but at most a nuisance. See also *Didow v. Alberta Power Co.*, [1988] 5 WWR 606 (Alta. CA) in which the court approved the reasoning in *Bernstein* but concluded that low level overhanging arms of a power line pole constituted a trespass. The court distinguished between transient interferences and permanent structures over land.

Didow was followed, in turn, in *Kingsbridge Development Inc. v. Hanson Needler Corp.* (1990), 71 OR (2d) 636 (HC). This case also involved an application for an interlocutory injunction to prevent a crane from swinging over the plaintiff's parking lot during the construction of an apartment building. The plaintiff had sold the land to the defendant knowing that the defendant would be constructing a building. The court followed *Didow*, holding that an overswinging crane should no longer be considered a trespass, but rather a nuisance. In any event, the court held that the plaintiff's interest could adequately be compensated in damages.

John Trenberth Ltd. v. National Westminster Bank Ltd.
(1979), 39 P & CR 104 (Ch.)

WALTON J: In this case the plaintiffs and the first defendant own adjoining property in Bute Street, Cardiff, the plaintiffs' property being 117 Bute Street, Cardiff. Next door to them, the premises to the south are owned by the first defendant, the National Westminster Bank Ltd. The first defendant has found itself in a very unfortunate situation because the building which it occupies is apparently in a dangerous condition; or the bulk of it was in a dangerous condition, so far as the frontage of it was concerned at any rate, because that consisted of stone slabs with metalwork behind, water had penetrated between the metalwork and the stone slabs forming an accumulation of rust, which occupies a greater volume than the metal itself, and the stones have been therefore pushed forward and are to some extent dangerous. Therefore, the building had become in a dangerous condition.

Mr. Powell-Jones, who has said everything that can possibly be said on behalf of the defendants, has submitted to me that it was the first defendant's duty to remedy the defective state of their building, and that I readily accept. At common law there is a duty to maintain premises adjacent to the highway, and these premises were adjacent to Bute Street, in a safe condition; and he also called my attention to section 58(1) of the *Public Health Act 1936*, whereby if one does not comply with the notice to make a defective building safe certain penalties follow. Therefore, he said, the first defendant found itself in this dilemma: that their building is so constructed that it cannot be effectively repaired without to some extent trespassing upon the plaintiff's land. And so, not wishing if they could to commit a trespass, but realising that they might in order to repair the premises cheaply and efficiently have to do so, they in fact entered into a correspondence with the plaintiffs starting by a letter of May 30, 1978, and pursued thereafter down to December 8, 1978, after which the plaintiffs did not answer any more letters.

Mr. Powell-Jones has submitted that the first defendant, the owners of the property, and their contractors for putting the building right, E. Turner & Sons Ltd., behaved throughout perfectly properly, not in flagrant disregard of the plaintiffs' rights but offering full indemnities against any accidents that might happen, full assurances that nothing would happen, and so on and so forth. And ultimately, whatever they asked for and however they put it, the reply of the plaintiffs to the request for permission was a flat, "No."

It may be or it may not be, and I do not think I am really concerned with that, that the refusal of the plaintiffs to grant permission was irrational. But it certainly was made in good faith and it certainly was not made, as the evidence makes perfectly clear, as a bargaining counter in order to extract concessions from the defendants. It was a genuine belief and desire on the part of the plaintiffs—they did not want their property to be trespassed upon by the defendants.

The situation at the end of that correspondence when the defendants, according to Mr. Powell-Jones, and I accept his formulation as being absolutely accurate, felt they were never going to get the plaintiffs' permission to carry out their works—that is to say, the plaintiffs' permission to trespass on the plaintiffs' land in order to carry out their works. Therefore, Mr. Powell-Jones says, the defendants (particularly the first defendant) were in an impossible position. There was on the one hand the Scylla of the dangerous building and there was on the other hand the Charybdis of trespassing upon the plaintiffs' land, and they chose, says Mr. Powell-Jones, to go ahead and trespass. And he says that the defendants were not thereby acting unreasonably in pressing ahead and completing works, in so far as they have been completed, to make the building safe.

I can see fully and I can sympathise with the dilemma in which the defendants (particularly the first defendants) found themselves, but on Mr. Powell-Jones' own summary of the evidence, and what happened, it is clear beyond peradventure that the defendants, knowing that they had not and were not likely to get permission to trespass upon the land of the plaintiffs, nevertheless went ahead and trespassed. And if flagrant invasion of another's rights of property of that nature is not sufficient to call forth the interposition of a court of equity, I do not know what invasion ever could be said so to do.

Mr. Powell-Jones has said that the invasion was not for the commercial benefit of the first defendant, but was merely to ensure that the property was made safe so as not to be dangerous to third parties, including the plaintiffs themselves. I do not accept that for one moment. The defendants wished to use their building as a building, possibly for aught I know as a bank. If the building was dangerous, another alternative could easily be to pull it down and start all over again. But, of course, that course would be one which would cost them a great deal of money, and so they deliberately chose the less expensive course of trespassing upon the plaintiffs' land.

Therefore, it seems to me that this is a case, there being nothing else in the facts which raise the faintest shadow of a cloud upon the plaintiffs' title to relief, on which the injunction must at any rate in a normal case go. So, far from acceding to Mr. Powell-Jones' first real submission, that this was not a clear case for an injunction and it is inconceivable it would be granted, it appears to me the clearest possible case for an injunction and inconceivable that it would not be granted.

He then says, well, supposing his submission is not accepted, his second submission is that the plaintiffs can be compensated in damages; that to obtain an injunction would be obtaining an injunction for an injunction's sake, and that it would be a great hardship to the first defendants if the injunction were to go. I do not accept that either. Indeed, it may be that there are special circumstances here which will ultimately result in the plaintiffs obtaining aggravated damages. I must not be taken to express any opinion upon that at all. But it is perfectly clear that the actual damage, apart from any question of aggravation, caused by the mere trespass, both by oversailing the front of the plaintiffs' property and by actually resting upon the rear of the plaintiffs' property, is comparatively slight; so slight that if an action were brought for it, it would hardly command the smallest coin in the realm. But so far from that being a reason why an injunction should not be granted, it has been said in many of the cases to which Mr. Munby drew my attention that the fact that any damage would be trifling is the very reason why an injunction should be granted. People are not to infringe the property rights of others and then say, "And I am entitled to go on doing it because I am really doing you no tangible harm, and fivepence will amply compensate you for that harm."

Mr. Powell-Jones' third point was on the question of suspension. He said, and he rightly says, that in a proper case the court can always suspend the operation of an injunction. He referred me in this connection to *Stollmeyer v. Trinidad Lake Petroleum Co. Ltd.*, [1918] AC 485 (PC (Trin.)) a case in the Privy Council. Now, I would remark that that case in fact does not do very much for his proposition because that was a case of nuisance and not a case of trespass; and as has been well pointed out so far as nuisance is concerned, damage being the gist of the action it is possible, normally, to compensate the plaintiff—at any rate for a short suspension—in damages. Moreover, one has to look at the nature of the works required in that case, which were obviously going to be very very considerable indeed, dealing with property which had been put up to exploit Trinidad's then burgeoning petroleum industry. That is a totally different sort of case from the present, where half a day's work, if that, is all that will be required to remove entirely the trespass to the plaintiffs' property.

I think I must refer in this connection to *Woollerton and Wilson Ltd. v. Richard Costain Ltd.*, [1970] 1 WLR 411 (Ch.) where, on facts which in some ways bear a great resemblance to the present case, Stamp J granted an injunction, but then suspended it for a couple of years. I find that that case is not one which, on the question of suspension, has received universal approbation; and, indeed, in *Charrington v. Simons & Co. Ltd.*, [1971] 1 WLR 498 (CA) there occurs in the judgment of Russell LJ these words [at 503]: "Further we wish to reserve our opinion whether the decision in *Woollerton and Wilson Ltd. v. Richard Costain Ltd.* was correct. Neither counsel seemed to think that it was."

I therefore think that this must be a case where Homer nodded, and that *Woollerton and Wilson Ltd. v. Richard Costain Ltd.* cannot be relied upon so far as suspension is concerned. And I think the reason it cannot be relied upon was well illustrated by Mr. Munby in his submissions to me when he said that in a sense, when one is dealing with the direct physical invasion of a right of property by a trespass one is very close to the line of cases stemming from *Doherty v. Allman* (1878), 3 App. Cas. 709 (HL (I)) which decide that an injunction to enforce a negative stipulation in a contract goes almost as of course. The parties, having agreed that something shall not be done, the court simply says that what the parties have agreed shall not be done.

The matter can be tested, I think, very simply in this way. Supposing that instead of putting up that scaffolding, as the second defendants doubtless did, taking their time about it in the normal way, supposing they had signalled notice of their intention well in advance so that it was quite clear what was going to happen if it was not restrained, and the plaintiffs had applied to the court for an injunction *quia timet*; what conceivable ground could have been put forward by the defendants in answer to the claim for such an injunction? There is not the faintest shadow of a reason they could have advanced why they should not be restrained from committing the trespass. Can it then be any better that they have actually committed it? Does the fact of their having committed it and it being, I doubt not from a structural point of view and commercially, highly advantageous to them that they should be able to go on and complete their building make the matter better from their point of view? Does that give them any right at all to have a suspension of the injunction which, if the plaintiffs had been able to come realising what was going to happen earlier, they would have got without the faintest difficulty at all? The answer must clearly be "No," there can be no conceivable reason for such postponement at all.

Therefore, for those reasons it appears to me that the negative injunctions which are sought, and which I gave to the plaintiffs by way of *ex parte* relief on March 29, 1979, must be continued until judgment in the action or further order.

NOTES AND QUESTIONS

1. In *Bertram v. Builders' Association of North Winnipeg* (1915), 23 DLR 534 (Man. KB), the plaintiff sought damages and an injunction against the defendants who, in the course of an excavation next to the plaintiff's property, had caused minor slippage of the plaintiff's land. A portion of an old fence fell in. A new fence could be put up for $30. Galt J characterized the dispute as "petty" and said (at 539-40):

> In this country, where an adjoining landowner is desirous of erecting a building upon his prop-
> erty, it is inevitable that to a certain extent the workmen will frequently and almost of necessity
> do acts which in the strict eye of the law are legal trespasses upon the adjoining owner; but in
> such cases one would have supposed that people would have already learned the lesson recog-
> nized in the last quoted case [*Behrens v. Richards*], and would apply their reason, common sense
> and ordinary forbearance, rather than go to law over trifles.

The judge awarded $36 damages without costs.

2. Contrast the case of *Cash and Carry Cleaners Ltd. v. Delmas* (1973), 7 NBR (2d) 101 (CA). The defendants trespassed on neighbouring property in the course of rebuilding their prem-
ises following a fire. Among other things, they excavated an alleyway over which they had a right-of-way but that was owned by the defendant. The plaintiff also complained that the defendants' tenants sometimes parked on its property. The plaintiff claimed damages and an injunction. The New Brunswick Court of Appeal held that while the plaintiff showed an "excessive sensitivity of its property rights, there was clearly no justification for the defendants excavating the alleyway as they did." The court granted $500 in punitive damages. The court also held that while the other forms of trespass (unauthorized parking) were trifling, it never-
theless reluctantly upheld the injunction "only because of the absence of any other satisfac-
tory remedy for dealing with petty trespasses."

3. Is a more sensible approach to the type of problem that existed in the *Trenberth* case found in legislation such as s. 132 of the *Municipal Act*, SO 2001, c. 25? That section reads as follows:

> 132(1) A local municipality may authorize the owner or occupant of land to enter adjoining
> land, at any reasonable time, for the purpose of making repairs or alterations to any building,
> fence or other structures on the land of the owner or occupant but only to the extent necessary
> to carry out the repairs or alterations.

Conditions

> (2) The following apply to a power of entry under a by-law under this section:
>
> 1. The power of entry may be exercised by an employee or agent of the owner or occupant
>   of land.
>
> 2. A person exercising the power of entry must display or, on request, produce proper
>   identification.
>
> 3. Nothing in a by-law under this section authorizes entry into a building.
>
> 4. The owner or occupant shall provide reasonable notice of the proposed entry to the
>   occupier of the adjoining land.

5. The owner or occupant of land shall, in so far as is practicable, restore the adjoining land to its original condition and shall provide compensation for any damages caused by the entry or by anything done on the adjoining land.

4. In *The Transformation of American Law, 1780-1860* (Cambridge: Harvard University Press, 1977), at 31-34, Morton J. Horwitz suggests that the Blackstonian concept of absolute dominion over property was developed in a static agrarian economy in which a low level of economic activity made land use conflicts rare. He suggests that a more rapidly developing economy placed this conception under increasing pressure in the 19th century; and he describes how, in the name of economic efficiency, common law and legislative reforms gradually replaced such notions as absolute dominion, natural use, and priority of rights with notions of reasonable use and interest balancing.

5. If the harm that would be suffered by the plaintiff in trespass cases is the lost opportunity to bargain with the defendant for a price for the use of the property, is it true that a damages remedy could not be devised to compensate this loss? See Robert J. Sharpe and S.M. Waddams, "Damages for Lost Opportunity to Bargain" (1982), 2 *Oxford Journal of Legal Studies* 290.

A NOTE ON POST-JUDGMENT BARGAINING: COMPENSATION OR EXTORTION?

Especially where the defendant has already embarked on the project that interferes with the plaintiff's rights, the granting of an injunction will place the plaintiff in a better bargaining position than he would have been in had the defendant approached the plaintiff for permission earlier on. The plaintiff can potentially demand from the defendant an amount almost equal to the full cost of complying with the injunction. In what situations should the plaintiff be given this strong bargaining leverage? Should the court inquire into the plaintiff's motives for seeking an injunction? Can placing the plaintiff in this strong bargaining position serve a useful purpose or does it amount simply to a licence to extort money from the defendant?

See Barton H. Thompson Jr., "Injunction Negotiations: An Economic, Moral, and Legal Analysis" (1975), 27 *Stanford Law Review* 1563.

In *Colls v. Home and Colonial Stores Ltd.*, [1904] AC 179 (HL (Eng.)), the House of Lords refused to grant a mandatory injunction to order the defendant to tear down a building that interfered with the plaintiff's ancient lights. Their Lordships noted the chilling effect that an absolute protection of ancient lights would have on development. Lord Macnaghten also expressed doubts that an injunction would be an appropriate remedy, stating (at 192-93):

It has been said that an injunction ought to be granted when substantial damages would be given at law. I have some difficulty in following out this rule. I observe that in some cases juries have been directed to give 1s. damages as a notice to the defendant to remove the obstruction complained of. And then if the obstruction was not removed, in a subsequent action the damages were largely increased. In others a substantial sum has been awarded, to be reduced to nominal damages on removal of the obstruction. But the recovery of damages, whatever the amount may be, indicates a violation of a right, and in former times, unless there were something special in the case, would have entitled the plaintiff as of course to an injunction in equity. I rather doubt whether the amount of the damages which may be supposed to be recoverable at law affords a satisfactory test. In some cases, of course, an injunction is necessary—if, for instance, the injury cannot fairly be compensated by money—if the defendant has acted in a high-handed manner—if he has endeavoured to steal a march upon the plaintiff or to evade the jurisdiction of the Court. In all these cases an injunction is necessary, in order to do justice to the plaintiff and as a warning to others. But if there is really a question as to whether the obstruction is legal or not, and if the defendant has acted fairly and not in an unneighbourly spirit, I am disposed to think that the Court ought to incline to damages rather than to an injunction. It is quite true that a man ought not to be compelled to part with his property against his will, or to have the value of his property diminished, without an Act of Parliament. On the other hand, the Court ought to be careful not to allow an action for the protection of ancient lights to be used as a means of extorting money. Often a person who is engaged in a large building scheme has to pay money right and left in order to avoid litigation, which will put him to even greater expense by delaying his proceedings. As far as my own experience goes, there is quite as much oppression on the part of those who invoke the assistance of the Court to protect some ancient lights, which they have never before considered of any great value, as there is on the part of those who are improving the neighbourhood by the erection of buildings that must necessarily to some extent interfere with the light of adjoining premises.

In *Isenberg v. East India House Estate Co. Ltd.* (1863), 3 De GJ & S 263, 46 ER 637 (Ch.), the defendant, disregarding the plaintiff's objections, constructed a building across from the plaintiff's shop, which interfered with the light. The defendant argued that it had offered to come to terms with the plaintiff by appointing an arbitrator to determine how the building might be modified to increase the plaintiff's light, or to determine the amount of compensation that should be paid to the plaintiff for the interference, but that the plaintiff had refused all overtures "insisting on our paying him a sum of money, hinting at a sum which clearly shewed his object to be extortion of money and nothing else." The plaintiff argued that if the court refused to award an injunction it would protect "the power and willingness of these large companies to use their status to crush individuals with practical impunity. And if the Court in this case sanctions that all they have to fear is payment of damages, the rights of individuals are practically at an end."

Westbury L set aside the mandatory injunction that had been granted in the court below. He said (at 271-74 (De GJ & S); 241-42 (ER)):

Every one of this class of cases must depend upon its own peculiar circumstances.

The common law remedy for a grievance of this description is an action for damages; an action liable to be resorted to as long as the cause of damage continues. Upon that ground, and by reason also of the damage in many cases not admitting of being estimated in money, this Court has assumed jurisdiction.

The jurisdiction of this Court, so far as it partakes of the nature of a preventive remedy, that is, prohibition of further damage or an intended damage, is a jurisdiction that may be exercised without difficulty, and rests upon the clearest principles.

But there has been superadded to that the power of the Court to grant what has been denominated a mandatory injunction, that is, an order compelling a Defendant to restore things to the condition in which they were at the time when the Plaintiff's complaint was made. The exercise of that power is one that must be attended with the greatest possible caution. I think, without intending to lay down any rule, that it is confined to cases in which the injury done to the

Plaintiff cannot be estimated and sufficiently compensated by a pecuniary sum. Where it admits of being so estimated, and where the evil sustained by the Plaintiff may be abundantly compensated in money there appears to me to be no necessity to superadd the exercise of that extraordinary power of this Court.

I can easily understand cases in which an ancient mansion or family seat may be prejudicially affected, and where the remedy therefore can hardly be other than that of restoring things to their former condition. I can imagine the interruption of a supply of water that would entirely stop a flourishing manufactory, whereas it is impossible to estimate the future profits of the trade, so that it would be difficult to define at the moment a sum of money which might be a sufficient compensation for all injury thereafter. But that is not the case before me.

In this case I think it a matter of very doubtful result whether any damage has been sustained; but it is a case in which beyond all question, without taking into consideration the confession of the parties, the whole of the injury that has been sustained by the Plaintiff or that is likely to be sustained by the Plaintiff, the whole of the prejudice and damage to the Plaintiff's premises by the erection of the Defendant's buildings may be abundantly compensated in money. To what end, then, should I exercise a jurisdiction which in such a case as this would simply be mischievous to the Defendants, without being attended with corresponding benefit to the Plaintiff, unless, indeed, I could approve of the Plaintiff taking advantage of the mischief and loss that the Defendants would have to sustain, in order to aggravate his claim to pecuniary compensation.

This is a case in which the benefit of the recent statute giving power to this Court to assess and ascertain damages is peculiarly felt; and I hold it, therefore, to be the duty of the Court in such a case as the present not, by granting a mandatory injunction, to deliver the Defendants over to the Plaintiff bound hand and foot, in order to be made subject to any extortionate demand that he may by possibility make, but to substitute for such mandatory injunction an inquiry before itself, in order to ascertain the measure of damage that has been actually sustained.

I shall not forget the fact which has been properly pressed upon me, that the Defendants, after having notice of the Plaintiff's complaint, carried on their works. I cannot, however, rest upon that at all judicially. They had the power of doing so. But it may be taken as a confession on their part that what they were doing would certainly be attended with some injury to the Plaintiff. That, I think, is not to be lost sight of in the estimation of that injury.

NOTES AND QUESTIONS

1. Does the distinction between preventive and mandatory injunctions solve the question of when damages should be awarded in substitution for an injunction?

2. How can Westbury L be confident that the whole of the injury suffered by the plaintiff can be ascertained and compensated by money? How would you define the injury suffered by the plaintiff?

3. To what extent does the choice of remedy in these cases reflect the court's view of the merits of the dispute between the parties, or the wisdom of the substantive law which the court is bound to apply?

4. In *Phonographic Performance Limited v. Maitra*, [1998] 1 WLR 870 (CA), the English Court of Appeal rejected the notion that an injunction should be refused or rejected because the plaintiff could use it as a bargaining tool. In this case, the first instance judge was concerned that the plaintiff could use a permanent injunction as leverage to compel musical copyright

infringers to pay past fees at a higher rate than the original licence fees. The plaintiff's practice on receipt of such an injunction was to require defendants to pay for future licencing rights and to pay for past rights at a higher rate than the original licence fees. The trial judge therefore restricted the injunction. The Court of Appeal disagreed, stating:

> A person who exploits his property right by licensing is entitled, unless there are special circumstances, to prevent another from using that property right without his licence and to refuse to grant a licence save on his terms and conditions as to payment and use. In a case, such as the present, where the Defendant did not contest the allegation in the PPL's Statement of Claim, was well aware of PPL's rights and that he was infringing and shows an intention to continue to infringe, we can see no reason why the use of an injunction in the normal form to prevent further infringement could be an abuse. No doubt the consequence is that a Defendant is forced to pay if he wishes to use the repertoire, but PPL are entitled to use the rights assigned to them for the purpose of requiring payment of fees in return for a licence to do what would, in the absence of a licence, be an infringement of the rights. ...
>
> Use of an injunction by PPL to obtain money to which they are not entitled would be an abuse, but there is no evidence that that ever occurs. Where unauthorised use of PPL's copyright is taking place, we do not believe it is an abuse to refuse to licence that copyright without an appropriate payment for past use and an agreement for future use. Nor do we consider it an abuse for PPL to require compliance with an injunction either by the person refraining from using the repertoire or by paying for such use that has taken place and will take place.

Alternatives to Injunctive Relief

In *MacDonald v. Lawrence and Lawrence* (1980), 38 NSR (2d) 319 (TD) (remedy reported in 40 NSR (2d) 626), the defendant erected a wall that encroached upon the plaintiff's property. The plaintiff claimed an injunction requiring removal of the wall or, in the alternative, damages equal to the cost of restoring the status quo prior to the encroachment. The encroachment was due to a surveyor's error which was not discovered until the wall had been partially built. The evidence indicated that the cost of removing the wall would be $1,400 and the cost of rebuilding it would be $3,650. Glube J stated, "When dealing with land, wherever possible, the court should not interject itself as an expropriating authority requiring a party to give up any portion of their land unless they are mutually willing to reach that accommodation." She awarded a mandatory injunction requiring the wall to be removed and concluded (at 629):

> If the defendants do not complete the removal and repairs within 30 days, the defendant shall pay to the plaintiff the sum of $3,650 which shall be used to abate the encroachment and restoration of the plaintiff's premises as well as the construction of a proper retaining wall for the purpose of preventing any continuing trespass or nuisance by reason of collapse of fill material from the defendant's lot.

In *Dempsey v. J.E.S. Developments Ltd.* (1976), 15 NSR (2d) 448, the defendant, over the plaintiff's protests, constructed a building which encroached on 35 square feet of the plaintiff's property. The cost of the defendant's building was $600,000. MacIntosh J declined to grant an order requiring the building to be removed on the basis that it "would involve the defendant in great costs." In considering the quantum of damages he said (at 454):

While the damage to the plaintiff's land is not extensive, the Court must not be placed in the position of sanctioning a wrong doing on the part of the encroacher. If in its discretion, the Court decides that damages are the proper remedy, then they should be such that in no way can it be said that the Court has not properly considered all relevant factors. One of the relevant factors in determining appropriate damages must be the use to which the defendant has put the land. Here the additional land means additional rental income to the defendant. Rental of commercial property in this area has a maximum value of $10.00 per square foot.

MacIntosh J also held that the defendant had acted in an abusive and contemptuous manner and had committed the trespass in the belief that the savings "made the trespass a potential profitable operation." He awarded damages, including exemplary damages, of $5,000, directing that upon payment of the sum the plaintiff would release her interest in the lands in issue.

See also *Townsview Properties Ltd. v. Sun Construction & Equipment Co. Ltd.* (1973), 2 OR (2d) 213, aff'd. (1974), 7 OR (2d) 666 (CA).

In *Gallant v. MacDonald* (1970), 3 NSR (2d) 137 (TD), the defendants' house encroached on 25 feet of a lakefront property owned by the plaintiff. The encroachment diminished the value of the plaintiff's lot by $4,800 and made it impossible for the plaintiff to obtain a building permit to construct a house. Cowan CJTD granted an injunction requiring the defendants to remove the encroaching portion of their house. He said (at 160):

> [T]his is not a case where the defendants by committing a wrongful act, albeit unintentionally, are thereby entitled to ask the Court to sanction that wrongful act by purchasing the neighbour's rights by assessing damages and leaving the neighbours, namely the plaintiffs, with lands of no present value. … the injury to the plaintiffs' legal rights is not small. It is not one which is capable of being accurately estimated in money. I can determine, as indicated above, the diminution in value of the plaintiffs' lands and the additional expenses to which they have been put, but this, admittedly, leaves the plaintiffs with lands of no real value at the present time … . The case is not one in which it would be oppressive to the defendants to grant an injunction.

The Chief Justice, however, suspended the operation of the injunction for six months in order to give the parties an opportunity to settle the matter. He suggested that the plaintiffs might sell their property to the defendants or that the parties might arrange, with the cooperation of other neighbouring landowners, a rearrangement of property lines to satisfy the planning requirements for a building permit. He also indicated that had he assessed damages, they would have reflected the diminution in the value of the property, plus the plaintiffs' expenses, plus $1,000 damages for trespass, and that if damages were assessed the plaintiffs would be required to execute a release in favour of the defendant. At the end of the case, the Department of Veterans Affairs, which held the mortgage on the plaintiffs' land, purchased the plaintiffs' lots for about double their market value. The department then made an arrangement with all of the neighbours to realign the boundaries and then sold the balance of lots 8 and 8A to the defendants so that they owned the lands on which their house sat.

Recall also *Wrotham Park Estate Co. Ltd. v. Parkside Homes Ltd.*, [1974] 1 WLR 798 (Ch.) in chapter 2, "Awards Measured by Benefit to Defendant." In that case the court fashioned a restitutionary remedy in lieu of a mandatory injunction. See also *Arbutus Park Estates Ltd. v. Fuller* (1976), 74 DLR (3d) 257 (BC SC); *Bracewell v. Appleby*, [1975] Ch. 408; and Robert J. Sharpe and S.M. Waddams, "Damages for Lost Opportunity To Bargain" (1982), 2 *Oxford Journal of Legal Studies* 290.

NUISANCE

The following section deals with the question of remedial choice in nuisance litigation. As you will see, many of the issues raised are similar to those that are present in trespass, though arguably the courts display greater flexibility in dealing with nuisance disputes. This may be due to the fact that the very definition of what constitutes a nuisance is a fluid one and requires the courts to balance the interests of the affected parties. It may also be due to the fact that in many cases (for example, widespread industrial pollution) the range of the affected interests is wider, and more complex policy and value choices must be made. In particular, the costs of nuisance and the economic and social consequences of injunctive relief are highly problematic. The section therefore includes an examination of the economic aspects of nuisance and its accompanying legal remedies.

Miller v. Jackson
[1977] QB 966 (CA)

LORD DENNING MR: In summertime village cricket is the delight of everyone. Nearly every village has its own cricket field where the young men play and the old men watch. In the village of Lintz in County Durham they have their own ground, where they have played these last 70 years. They tend it well. The wicket area is well rolled and mown. The outfield is kept short. It has a good club house for the players and seats for the onlookers. The village team play there on Saturdays and Sundays. They belong to a league, competing with the neighbouring villages. On other evenings after work they practise while the light lasts. Yet now after these 70 years a judge of the High Court has ordered that they must not play there any more. He has issued an injunction to stop them. He has done it at the instance of a newcomer who is no lover of cricket. This newcomer has built, or has had built for him, a house on the edge of the cricket ground which four years ago was a field where cattle grazed. The animals did not mind the cricket. But now this adjoining field has been turned into a housing estate. The newcomer bought one of the houses on the edge of the cricket ground. No doubt the open space was a selling point. Now he complains that when a batsman hits a six the ball has been known to land in his garden or on or near his house. His wife has got so upset about it that they always go out at weekends. They do not go into the garden when cricket is being played. They say that this is intolerable. So they asked the judge to stop the cricket being played. And the judge, much against his will, has felt that he must order the cricket to be stopped: with the consequences, I suppose, that the Lintz Cricket Club will disappear. The cricket ground will be turned to some other use. I expect for more houses or a factory. The young men will turn to other things instead of cricket. The whole village will be much the poorer. And all this because of a newcomer who has just bought a house there next to the cricket ground.

I must say that I am surprised that the developers of the housing estate were allowed to build the houses so close to the cricket ground. No doubt they wanted to make the most of their site and put up as many houses as they could for their own profit. The planning authorities ought not to have allowed it. The houses ought to have been so sited as not to interfere with the cricket. But the houses have been built and we have to reckon with the consequences.

At the time when the houses were built it was obvious to the people of Lintz that these new houses were built too close to the cricket ground. It was a small ground, and there might be trouble when a batsman hit a ball out of the ground. But there was no trouble in finding purchasers. Some of them may have been cricket enthusiasts. But others were not. In the first three years—1972, 1973, and 1974—quite a number of balls came over or under the boundary fence and went into the gardens of the houses: and the cricketers went round to get them. Mrs. Miller [the second plaintiff] was very annoyed about this. To use her own words:

> … when the ball comes over, they [the cricketers] either ring or come round in twos and threes and ask if they can have the ball back, and they never ask properly. They just ask if they can have the ball back, and that's it. … They have been very rude, very arrogant and very ignorant, … and very deceitful

and that to get away from any problems they made a point of going out on Wednesdays, Fridays and the week-ends.

Having read the evidence, I am sure that was a most unfair complaint to make of the cricketers. They have done their very best to be polite. It must be admitted, however, that on a few occasions before 1974 a tile was broken or a window smashed. The householders made the most of this and got their rates reduced. The cricket club then did everything possible to see that no balls went over. In 1975, before the cricket season opened, they put up a very high protective fence. The existing concrete fence was only six feet high. They raised it to nearly 15 feet high by a galvanised chain-link fence. It cost £700. They could not raise it any higher because of the wind. The cricket ground is 570 feet above sea level. During the winter even this high fence was blown down on one occasion and had to be repaired at a cost of £400. Not only did the club put up this high protective fence. They told the batsmen to try to drive the balls low for four and not hit them up for six. This greatly reduced the number of balls that got into the garden. So much so that the rating authority no longer allowed any reduction in rates.

Despite these measures, a few balls did get over. The club made a tally of all the sixes hit during the seasons of 1975 and 1976. In 1975 there were 2,221 overs, that is 13,326 balls bowled. Of them there were 120 six hits on all sides of the ground. Of these only six went over the high protective fence and into this housing estate. In 1976 there were 2,616 overs, that is 15,696 balls. Of them there were only 160 six hits. Of these only nine went over the high protective fence and into this housing estate.

No one has been hurt at all by any of these balls, either before or after the high fence was erected. There has, however, been some damage to property, even since the high fence was erected. The cricket club have offered to remedy all the damage and pay all expenses. They have offered to supply and fit unbreakable glass in the windows, and shutters or safeguards for them. They have offered to supply and fit a safety net over the garden whenever cricket is being played. In short, they have done everything possible short of stopping playing cricket on the ground at all. But Mrs. Miller and her husband have remained unmoved. Every offer by the club has been rejected. They demand the closing down of the cricket club. Nothing else will satisfy them. They have obtained legal aid to sue the cricket club.

In support of the case, the plaintiffs rely on the dictum of Lord Reid in *Bolton v. Stone*, [1951] AC 850 (HL (Eng.)) at p. 867: "If cricket cannot be played on a ground without creating a substantial risk, then it should not be played there at all." I would agree with that saying if the houses or road was there first, and the cricket ground came there second. We would not allow the garden of Lincoln's Inn to be turned into a cricket ground. It would be too dangerous for windows and people. But I would not agree with Lord Reid's dictum when the cricket ground has been there for 70 years and the houses are newly built at the very edge of it. I recognise that the cricket club are under a duty to use all reasonable care consistently with the playing of the game of cricket, but I do not think the cricket club can be expected to give up the game of cricket altogether. After all they have their rights in their cricket ground. They have spent money, labour and love in the making of it: and they have the right to play upon it as they have done for 70 years. Is this all to be rendered useless to them by the thoughtless and selfish act of an estate developer in building right up to the edge of it? Can the developer or a purchaser of the house say to the cricket club: "Stop playing. Clear out." I do not think so. And I will give my reasons. ...

[Lord Denning then went on to discuss the law in the 19th century. He concluded that anytime that a batsman hit the ball over the fence so that it landed in the garden, he would be guilty of trespass as would the committee of the cricket club for encouraging this behaviour. He also concluded that the law of trespass was unbending and that the cricket club would have little defence to this action. However, Lord Denning did raise the doctrine of derogation from grant as a possible defence for the cricket club.]

The Law in the 20th Century

The case here was not pleaded by either side in the formulae of the 19th century. The plaintiffs did not allege trespass. The defendants did not raise the doctrine of derogation from grant. The case was pleaded in negligence or alternatively nuisance. That was, I think, quite right, having regard to the decision of the House of Lords in *Bolton v. Stone*. Miss Stone had just stepped out of her garden gate on to the pavement when she was hit by a cricket ball. She did not sue in trespass to the person. That would be quite out of date. As I said in *Letang v. Cooper*, [1965] 1 QB 232 (CA) at p. 239:

> If [the defendant] does not inflict injury intentionally, but only unintentionally, the plaintiff has
> no cause of action today in trespass. His only cause of action is in negligence, and then only on
> proof of want of reasonable care.

Miss Stone did seek to put her case on the doctrine of *Rylands v. Fletcher* (1868), LR 3 HL 330 (HL (Eng.)). She suggested that a cricket ball was a dangerous thing which the defendants had brought on to the cricket ground and it had escaped. That suggestion was dismissed by the House of Lords out of hand. Lord Reid said: "... there is no substance in this argument": at p. 867. She also suggested that the club were liable in nuisance: but this was not pressed in the House of Lords, because nuisance was not distinguishable from negligence. Lord Porter remarked at p. 860 that "in the circumstances of this case nuisance cannot be established unless negligence is proved."

In our present case, too, nuisance was pleaded as an alternative to negligence. The tort of nuisance in many cases overlaps the tort of negligence. The boundary lines were discussed in two adjoining cases in the Privy Council *Overseas Tankship (U.K.) Ltd. v. Miller Steamship Co. Pty. (The Wagon Mound (No. 2))*, [1967] 1 AC 617 (PC (NSW)), 639 and *Goldman v. Hargrave*, [1967] 1 AC 645 (PC (Aust.)) 657.

But there is at any rate one important distinction between them. It lies in the nature of the remedy sought. Is it damages? Or an injunction? If the plaintiff seeks a remedy in damages for injury done to him or his property, he can lay his claim either in *negligence* or *nuisance*. But if he seeks an injunction to stop the playing of cricket altogether, I think he must take his claim in nuisance. The books are full of cases where an injunction has been granted to restrain the continuance of a nuisance. But there is no case, so far as I know, where it has been granted so as to stop a man being negligent. At any rate in a case of this kind where an occupier of a house or land seeks to restrain his neighbour from doing something on his own land, the only appropriate cause of action on which to base the remedy of an injunction is nuisance: see the report of the Law Commission on *Civil Liability for Dangerous Things and Activities*; Law Commission Report No. 32 (1970), p. 25. It is the very essence of a private nuisance that it is the unreasonable use by a man of his land to the detriment of his neighbour. He must have been guilty of the fault, not necessarily of negligence, but of the unreasonable use of the land: see *The Wagon Mound (No. 2)* at p. 639, by Lord Reid.

It has been often said in nuisance cases that the rule is sic utere tuo ut alienum non laedas. But that is a most misleading maxim. Lord Wright put it in its proper place in *Sedleigh-Denfield v. O'Callaghan*, [1940] AC 880 (HL (Eng.)), at p. 903:

> [It] is not only lacking in definiteness but is also inaccurate. An occupier may make in many ways a use of his land which causes damage to the neighbouring landowners and yet be free from liability ... a useful test is perhaps what is reasonable according to the ordinary usages of mankind living in society, or more correctly in a particular society.

I would, therefore, adopt this test. Is the use by the cricket club of this ground for playing cricket a reasonable use of it? To my mind it is a most reasonable use. Just consider the circumstances. For over 70 years the game of cricket has been played on this ground to the great benefit of the community as a whole, and to the injury of none. No one could suggest that it was a nuisance to the neighbouring owners simply because an enthusiastic batsman occasionally hit a ball out of the ground for six to the approval of the admiring onlookers. Then I would ask: does it suddenly become a nuisance because one of the neighbours chooses to build a house on the very edge of the ground—in such a position that it may well be struck by the ball on the rare occasion when there is a hit for six? To my mind the answer is plainly No. The building of the house does not convert the playing of cricket into a nuisance when it was not so before. If and in so far as any damage is caused to the house or anyone in it, it is because of the position in which it was built. Suppose that the house had not been built by a developer, but by a private owner. He would be in much the same position as the farmer who previously put his cows in the field. He could not complain if a batsman hit a six out of the ground, and by a million to one chance it struck a cow or even the farmer himself. He would be in no better position than a spectator at Lord's or the Oval or at a motor rally. At any rate, even if he could claim damages for the loss of the cow or the injury, he could not get an injunction to stop the cricket. If the private owner could not get an injunction, neither should a developer or a purchaser from him.

It was said, however, that the case of the physician's consulting room was to contrary: *Sturges v. Bridgman* (1879), 11 Ch. D 852. But that turned on the old law about easements and prescriptions, and so forth. It was in the days when rights of property were in the ascendant and not subject to any limitations except those provided by the law of easements. But nowadays it is a matter of balancing the conflicting interests of the two neighbours. That was made clear by Lord Wright in *Sedleigh-Denfield v. O'Callaghan* at p. 903, when he said:

> A balance has to be maintained between the right of the occupier to do what he likes with his own, and the right of his neighbour not to be interfered with.

In this case it is our task to balance the right of the cricket club to continue playing cricket on their cricket ground—as against the right of the householder not to be interfered with. On taking the balance, I would give priority to the right of the cricket club to continue playing cricket on the ground, as they have done for the last 70 years. It takes precedence over the right of the newcomer to sit in his garden undisturbed. After all he bought the house four years ago in mid-summer when the cricket season was at its height. He might have guessed that there was a risk that a hit for six might possibly land on his property. If he finds that he does not like it, he ought, when cricket is played, to sit on the other side of the house or in the front garden, or go out: or to take advantage of the offers the club have made to him of fitting unbreakable glass, and so forth. Or, if he does not like that, he ought to sell his house and move elsewhere. I expect there are many who would gladly buy it in order to be near the cricket field and open space. At any rate he ought not to be allowed to stop cricket being played on this ground.

This case is new. It should be approached on principles applicable to modern conditions. There is a contest here between the interest of the public at large; and the interest of a private individual. The *public* interest lies in protecting the environment by preserving our playing fields in the face of mounting development, and by enabling our youth to enjoy all the benefits of outdoor games, such as cricket and football. The *private* interest lies in securing the privacy of his home and garden without intrusion or interference by anyone. In deciding between these two conflicting interests, it must be remembered that it is not a question of damages. If by a million to one chance a cricket ball does go out of the ground and cause damage, the cricket club will pay. There is no difficulty on that score. No, it is a question of an injunction. And in our law you will find it repeatedly affirmed that an injunction is a discretionary remedy. In a new situation like this, we have to think afresh as to how discretion should be exercised. On the one hand, Mrs. Miller is a very sensitive lady who has worked herself up into such a state that she exclaimed to the judge: "I just want to be allowed to live in peace. ... Have I got to wait until someone is killed before anything can be done?" If she feels like that about it, it is quite plain that, for peace in the future, one or other has to move. Either the cricket club has to move: but goodness knows where. I do not suppose for a moment there is any field in Lintz to which they could move. Or Mrs. Miller must move elsewhere. As between their conflicting interests, I am of opinion that the public interest should prevail over the private interest. The cricket club should not be driven out. In my opinion the right exercise of discretion is to refuse an injunction; and, of course, to refuse damages in lieu of an injunction. Likewise as to the claim for past damages. The club were entitled to use this ground for cricket in the accustomed way. It was not a nuisance, nor was it negligent of them so to run it. Nor was the batsman negligent when he hit the ball for six. All were doing simply what they were entitled to do. So if the club had put it to the test, I would have dismissed the claim for damages also. But as the club very fairly say that they are willing to pay for any damage, I am content that there should be an award of £400 to cover any past or future damage. I would allow the appeal, accordingly.

GEOFFREY LANE LJ:

[Geoffrey Lane LJ canvassed the facts noting that even after the cricket club had built its fence, several cricket balls per year landed in the plaintiffs' back garden, and others in their neighbours'. He concluded that "on almost every Saturday during the summer when the weather was fine the houses and gardens in Brackenridge and anyone in them would be at risk." He held that there was a real and foreseeable risk of injury to person and property and that the defendants were guilty of negligence. He rejected as fallacious the defendants' argument that because they had done all they could to prevent injury they were not negligent. So long as such measures did not eliminate the risk, the activity of the defendants is negligent. Geoffrey Lane LJ went on to discuss nuisance.]

Was there here a use by the defendants of their land involving an unreasonable interference with the plaintiffs' enjoyment of *their* land? There is here in effect no dispute that there has been and is likely to be in the future an interference with the plaintiffs' enjoyment of no. 20 Brackenridge. The only question is whether it is unreasonable. It is a truism to say that this is a matter of degree. What that means is this. A balance has to be maintained between on the one hand the rights of the individual to enjoy his house and garden without the threat of damage and on the other hand the rights of the public in general or a neighbour to engage in lawful pastimes. Difficult questions may sometimes arise when the defendants' activities are offensive to the senses, for example, by the way of noise. Where, as here, the damage or potential damage is physical the answer is more simple. There is, subject to what appears hereafter, no excuse I can see which exonerates the defendants from liability in nuisance for what they have done or from what they threaten to do. It is true that no one has yet been physically injured. That is probably due to a great extent to the fact that the householders in Brackenridge desert their gardens while cricket is in progress. The danger of injury is obvious and is not slight enough to be disregarded. There is here a real risk of serious injury.

There is, however, one obviously strong point in the defendants' favour. They or their predecessors have been playing cricket on this ground (and no doubt hitting sixes out of it) for 70 years or so. Can someone, by building a house on the edge of the field in circumstances where it must have been obvious that balls might be hit over the fence, effectively stop cricket being played? Precedent apart, justice would seem to demand that the plaintiffs should be left to make the most of the site they have elected to occupy with all its obvious advantages and all its equally obvious disadvantages. It is pleasant to have an open space over which to look from your bedroom and sitting room windows, so far as it is possible to see over the concrete wall. Why should you complain of the obvious disadvantages which arise from the particular purpose to which the open space is being put? Put briefly, can the defendants take advantage of the fact that the plaintiffs have put themselves in such a position by coming to occupy a house on the edge of a small cricket field, with the result that what was not a nuisance in the past now become a nuisance? If the matter were *res integra*, I confess I should be inclined to find for the defendants. It does not seem just that a long-established activity—in itself innocuous—should be brought to an end because someone chooses to build a house nearby and so turn an innocent pastime into an actionable nuisance. Unfortunately, however, the question is not open. In *Sturges v. Bridgman* this very problem arose. The defendant had carried on a confectionery shop with a noisy pestle and mortar for more than 20 years. Although it was noisy, it was far enough away from neighbouring premises not to cause trouble to anyone, until the plaintiff who was a physician built a consulting room on his own land but immediately adjoining the confectionery shop. The noise and vibrations seriously interfered with the consulting room and became a nuisance to the physician. The defendant contended that he had acquired the right either at common law or under the *Prescription Act 1832* by uninterrupted use for more than 20 years to impose the inconvenience. It was held by the Court of Appeal, affirming the judgment of Sir George Jessel MR, that use such as this which was, prior to the construction of the consulting room, neither preventible nor actionable, could not found a prescriptive right. That decision involved the assumption, which so far as one can discover has never been questioned, that it is no answer to a claim in nuisance for the defendant to show that the plaintiff brought the trouble on his own head by building or coming to live in a house so close to the defendant's premises that he would inevitably be affected by the defendant's activities, where no one had been affected previously: see also *Bliss v. Hall* (1838), 4 Bing. (NC) 183; 132 ER 758 (CP). It may be that this rule works injustice, it may be that one would decide the matter differently in the absence of authority. But we are bound by the decision in *Sturges v. Bridgman* and it is not for this court as I see it to alter a rule which stood for so long.

Injunction

Given that the defendants are guilty of both negligence and nuisance, is it a case where the court should in its discretion give relief, or should the plaintiffs be left to their remedy in damages? There is no doubt that if cricket is played damage will be done to the plaintiff's tiles or windows or both. There is a not inconsiderable danger that if they or their son or their guests spend any time in the garden during the weekend afternoons in the summer they may be hit by a cricket ball. So long as this situation exists it seems to me that damages cannot be said to provide an adequate form of relief. Indeed, quite apart from the risk of physical injury, I can see no valid reason why the plaintiffs should have to submit to the inevitable breakage of tiles and/or windows, even though the defendants have expressed their willingness to carry out any repairs at no cost to the plaintiffs. I would accordingly uphold the grant of the injunction to restrain the defendants from committing nuisance. However, I would postpone the operation of the injunction for 12 months to enable the defendants to look elsewhere for an alternative pitch.

So far as the plaintiffs are concerned, the effect of such postponement will be that they will have to stay out of their garden until the end of the cricket season but thereafter will be free to use it as they wish.

I have not thought it necessary to embark upon any discussion of the possible rights of the defendants arising from matters which were neither pleaded nor argued.

CUMMING BRUCE LJ:

[He agreed that the activities of the defendants amounted to negligence and nuisance and that *Sturges v. Bridgman* was binding and proceeded to consider the appropriate remedy.]

The only problem that arises is whether the judge is shown to be wrong in deciding to grant the equitable remedy of an injunction which will necessarily have the effect that the ground which the defendants have used as a cricket ground for 70 years can no longer be used for that purpose.

Reeve J correctly directed himself that the principles which apply are those described by Lord Evershed MR in *Pride of Derby and Derbyshire Angling Association Ltd. v. British Celanese Ltd.*, [1953] Ch. 149 at p. 181 (CA), and by A.L. Smith LJ in *Shelfer v. City of London Electric Lighting Co. Ltd.*, [1895] 1 Ch. 287 at p. 322 (CA). Did he correctly apply those principles to the facts of the case? There is authority that in considering whether to exercise a judicial discretion to grant an injunction the court is under a duty to consider the interests of the public. So said Lord Romilly MR over 100 years ago in *Raphael v. Thames Valley Railway Co.* (1866), LR 2 Eq. 37 at p. 46; but the conflict of interest there was between proprietary private rights and inconvenience to be suffered by users of railway: see also *Wood v. Sutcliffe* (1851), 2 Sim. NS 163 at p. 165; 61 ER 303 at p. 303 (Ch.). Courts of equity will not ordinarily and without special necessity interfere by injunction where the injunction will have the effect of very materially injuring the rights of third persons not before the court. The principle has recently been accurately stated in a text book:

> Regard must be had "not only to the dry strict rights of the plaintiff and the defendant, but also the surrounding circumstances, to the rights or interests of other persons which may be more or less involved." So it is that where the plaintiff has prima facie a right to specific relief, a court of equity will, if occasion should arise, weigh the disadvantage or hardship which he will suffer if relief were refused against any hardship or disadvantage which would be caused to third persons or to the public generally if relief were granted:

see I.C.F. Spry, *Equitable Remedies* (London: Sweet & Maxwell, 1971) at p. 365, and the cases referred to in the footnote. Putting it in a slightly different way, Lord Wright said that a useful test is perhaps what is reasonable according to the ordinary usages of mankind living in society, or more correctly in a particular society: *Sedleigh-Denfield v. O'Callaghan*, [1940] AC 880 at p. 903 (HL (Eng.)).

So on the facts of this case a court of equity must seek to strike a fair balance between the right of the plaintiffs to have quiet enjoyment of their house and garden without exposure to cricket balls occasionally falling like thunderbolts from the heavens, and the opportunity of the inhabitants of the village in which they live to continue to enjoy the manly sport which constitutes a summer recreation for adults and young persons, including one would hope and expect the plaintiffs' son. It is a relevant circumstance which a court of equity should take into account that the plaintiffs decided to buy a house which in June 1972 when completion took place was obviously on the boundary of a quite small cricket ground where cricket was played at weekends and sometimes on evenings during the working week. They selected a house with the benefit of the open space beside it. In February, when they first saw it, they did not think about the use of this open space. But before completion they must have realised that it was the village cricket ground, and that balls would sometimes be knocked from the wicket into their garden, or even against the fabric of the house. If they did not realise it, they should have done. As it turns out, the female plaintiff has developed a somewhat obsessive attitude to the proximity of the cricket field and the cricketers who visit her to seek to recover their cricket balls. The evidence discloses a hostility which goes beyond what is reasonable, although, as the judge found, she is reasonable in her fear that if the family uses the garden while a match is in progress they will run risk of serious injury if a great hit happens to drive a ball up to the skies and down into their garden. It is reasonable to decide that during matches the family must keep out of the garden. The risk of damage to the house can be dealt with in other ways, and is not such as to fortify significantly the case for an injunction stopping play on this ground.

With all respect, in my view the judge did not have regard sufficiently to these considerations. He does not appear to have had regard to the interest of the inhabitants of the village as a whole. Had he done so he would in my view have been led to the conclusion that the plaintiffs having accepted the benefit of the open space marching with their land should accept the restrictions upon enjoyment of their garden which they may reasonably think necessary. That is the burden which they have to bear in order that the inhabitants of the village may not be deprived of their facilities for an innocent recreation which they have so long enjoyed on this ground. There are here special circumstances which should inhibit a court of equity from granting the injunction claimed. If I am wrong in that conclusion, I agree with Geoffrey Lane LJ that the injunction should be suspended for one year to enable the defendants to see if they can find another ground.

Appeal allowed. Past and future damages increased to £400.
No order for costs in Court of Appeal or below save legal aid taxation.

NOTES AND QUESTIONS

1. The judges in *Miller* view the rule in *Sturges v. Bridgman* with apparent disfavour. What might the rationale for that rule be? How might the interests of persons who are "first in time" be protected?

2. A short comment on *Miller v. Jackson* concludes with the following thoughts:

> To have regard to the interests of the inhabitants of the village in this manner and thereby deprive the plaintiffs of a remedy to which they would normally be entitled is to open a new ground of public policy. That is notoriously difficult to bridle and maintain. Is their interest truly in the maintenance of the ground for cricket as opposed to other forms of recreation? Moreover, is any weight to be given to the reason why the situation has arisen: an increase in population, a desire to prevent indiscriminate building in the countryside, a demand on the part of all people in the village, and not just the lord of the manor, for more living space than they were prepared to put up with 70 years ago?

(Notes (1977), 93 *Law Quarterly Review* 481, at 483. See also (1978), 94 *Law Quarterly Review* 178.)

3. On the appeal to the Court of Appeal, because the precedential importance of this case was so potentially significant for many cricket grounds across the country, the costs of the club's appeal were underwritten by the National Cricket Association and the Test and County Cricket Board. Does this fact affect your views about the court's consideration of the public interest? Incidentally, after the case was decided, Lord Denning's clerk informed a reporter from the "Daily Telegraph" that the judge was "not a sporting man" and that his pas-

sions were confined to "rice pudding and the law." (See John Scott, *Caught in Court* (London: Andre Deutsch, 1989), at 235-37.)

4. In *Kennaway v. Thompson*, [1981] QB 88 (CA), the Court of Appeal had an opportunity to consider a similar case. The plaintiff sought an injunction against speed-boat racing on the lake on which she owned her cottage. At trial, damages were awarded in substitution for an injunction, *inter alia* on the basis that there was considerable public interest in the racing club. This decision was reversed by the Court of Appeal. Lawton LJ expressed some doubt about Lord Denning MR's suggestion in *Miller v. Jackson* that the public interest should prevail over the private in such a case, pointed out that each judge had based his decision in that case upon a different ground, and refused to follow it. However, Lawton LJ also noted that some racing existed on the lake at the time the plaintiff bought the property, and discussed the inevitability of a certain amount of annoyance under modern conditions and the importance of a spirit of "give and take, live and let live." He stated that his task was "to decide on a form of order which will protect the plaintiff from the noise which the judge found to be intolerable but which will not stop the club from organizing activities about which she cannot reasonably complain." He then itemized the number and length of the international, national and local events which the club might organize in each year, and granted an injunction against noise levels over 75 decibels except during those specified events.

5. *Ward v. Magna International Inc.*, [1994] OJ no. 1123, 28 CPC (3d) 327 is a good example of the balancing act judges may sometimes be called on to perform in nuisance cases when two valuable uses of adjoining property collide. In this case, the judge adopted a hands-on approach, including the offer of continued judicial supervision, in order to resolve a nuisance dispute. The plaintiff alleged that his quiet enjoyment of his property was unduly impaired by the noises from the neighbouring park (a facility developed by the defendant company for its employees). Recognizing the need to balance the interest of the plaintiff in peaceful enjoyment of his property with the significant benefits of the defendant's recreational park facilities for its employees, the judge provided detailed parameters within which he suggested the parties craft the terms of a settlement or final order. Those parameters included suggestions regarding the permissible sporting and entertainment activities in the park and their frequency; the construction of noise barriers; the renovation of buildings for the purpose of noise insulation; and permissible levels of music from, for example, radios. When the parties were still unable to agree on such terms, the judge crafted a final and detailed order along these lines (see [1994] OJ no. 1781). The judge recognized that, because of the detailed nature of the order, some further judicial supervision might yet be required. See also the call for a balancing approach that entailed a certain degree of "give and take" in *Cattell v. Great Plains Leaseholds Ltd.* (2008), 311 Sask. R 70 (CA), which concerned a plaintiff seeking an injunction to prevent the nuisance from erratically hit golf balls flying onto his property.

6. The addition of objective performance standards as part of the injunction order has become more frequent in nuisance cases, particularly those concerning noise. In *Suzuki v. Munroe*, [2009] BCJ no. 2019 (SC), 87 RPR (4th) 68, the court ordered a defendant either to discontinue using an air conditioner located close to the plaintiffs' home or to lower the noise it produced to below 55 dB(A) during the day and 45 dB(A) at night. In addition, the defendant was required to reposition surveillance cameras so as not to monitor the plaintiffs' property. For another amusing noise case, see *Hsu v. Weddings Etc. Ltd.*, [2009] NZHC 949 in which

the defendant was restrained from mowing his lawn during periods when the plaintiff held outdoor wedding ceremonies on its property.

7. Sensitivity over odour nuisances generated from intensive farming practices has resulted in the passage of right-to-farm legislation restricting courts' jurisdiction to grant injunctions. Section 2(2) of the *Farming and Food Production Protection Act*, SO 1998, c. 1 provides:

> No court shall issue an injunction or other order that prohibits a farmer from carrying on the agricultural operation because it causes or creates a disturbance.

See also *Farm Practices Protection (Right to Farm) Act*, RSBC 1996, c. 131, s. 2(1)(b).

Robert J. Sharpe, *Injunctions and Specific Performance*
(Aurora, ON: Canada Law Book, 2009) (looseleaf), at 4.440-4.580
(footnotes omitted)

3. Economic Analysis

Economists have turned their attention to the question of remedial choice in nuisance cases, and while lawyers may find the analysis unfamiliar, there is benefit to be derived from seeing legal problems subjected to the analytic techniques of another discipline.

The starting point of economic analysis in this area is the so-called Coase theorem which contains a valuable insight into the relationship between legal rights and efficiency. Ordinarily, property rights can be bought and sold. The thrust of the Coase theorem is that whatever initial assignment of rights is made by the law, economic forces will operate so that the person who most values the right will acquire it in the end. Thus, market forces will tend to produce the most efficient allocation of resources whether or not the law gives a right to use that resource to the party who can put it to the most efficient use. Such a result is said to be "efficient" in that it maximizes net social wealth: the gain to the party acquiring the right exceeds the loss to the party giving it up. The theory assumes that both parties conduct themselves so as to maximize their own wealth, and on that hypothesis, transactions will occur until the gains from trading are exhausted. Thus, while the legal approach is to determine who is in the "right," economic forces will "correct" judicial decisions which produce inefficient results. In the context of nuisance disputes, the focus of economic analysis is "whether the gain from preventing the harm is greater than the loss which would be suffered elsewhere as a result of stopping the action which produces harm."

The analysis suggested by the Coase theorem may be illustrated by the following example. Assume a factory which creates a nuisance and derives a $100,000 benefit from increased production directly attributable to the nuisance-creating activity. The home-owner beside the factory is bothered by the nuisance, but would be prepared to put up with it if paid $80,000. Thus, it can be said that the value to the home-owner of being free of the nuisance is $80,000. The efficient allocation of resources would be to permit the factory to go on polluting, because it is worth $20,000 more to the factory to pollute than it is to the home-owner to breathe clean air. That allocation of the resource will in fact occur, according to the Coase theorem, whether the law says that the home-owner has the right to be free of pollution or whether the factory has the right to pollute. Even if the home-owner gets an injunction against the factory, the factory will be willing to pay him up to $100,000 in exchange for his right to enforce the injunction. If the figures are reversed, and freedom from nuisance is worth more to the home-owner than creating the nuisance is to the factory, then even if the home-owner has no legal right to stop the nuisance, he will pay the factory up to $100,000 to stop, as he would still be better off by the equivalent of $20,000 to be free of the nuisance.

If the Coase theorem told the whole story, the law could ignore the goal of efficiency as a consideration in resolving disputes. The problem of social costs would be solved by economic forces whatever goals the law sought to pursue in the initial assignment of rights and determination of appropriate remedies. Clearly, however, as Coase himself pointed out, the theory is based upon the usually unrealistic assumption of perfect market conditions. In this blissful economic state, transactions occur without cost. In the real world, where there usually are costs in striking bargains, those costs must be taken into account in the overall calculation of social gains and losses. When there are costs associated with transactions, a bargain which would otherwise benefit both parties will not be struck if the gains from the bargain do not exceed the costs of reaching the bargain.

While economists do not appear to have derived a settled definition of "transaction costs," the economic analysis of law literature identifies certain sources relevant to the nuisance problem. Numerous parties in the same interest are said to produce "holdout" and "freerider" problems. Thus, where pollution would be worth $100,000 to the factory in increased production, and the 100 residents affected value freedom from pollution at $800 each, the efficient allocation of resources would be to allow the factory to continue polluting, as it values pollution by $20,000 more than the residents value being free of pollution. However, assuming an initial inefficient assignment is made to the 100 residents, some of them will try to get a share of the full $100,000 that the factory derives from pollution, and will conceal their true valuation and "hold out" for more than $800. The factory will incur costs in discovering their true valuation and bargaining with them. If the amount it takes to buy them out together with the cost of the transaction exceeds $100,000, then the transaction will not occur, although, *ex hypothesi*, a bargain would be efficient. Conversely, if the factory is given the entitlement and the figures are reversed, and each of the 100 residents values clean air at $1,000 and pollution is worth $80,000 to the factory, "freeriders" will refuse to disclose their true valuation, hoping that the $80,000 will be made up by others. In either case, strategic behaviour may generate prohibitive transaction costs, and the "market" will fail to produce the efficient outcome.

At this point, there is an important shift in economic analysis. In the absence of transaction costs, the law can ignore efficiency, and pursue whatever goals seem appropriate. However, in the real world of high transaction costs, the legal system cannot rely on the market to correct "errors"—from the efficiency point of view—in the initial assignment of rights. Economic analysis becomes prescriptive and suggests that if the goal of efficiency is to be pursued, the law must consciously develop a strategy aimed at achieving that goal.

The starting point is the identification of three levels of protection and four remedial possibilities. While this categorization was adopted to facilitate the development of the economic model, it is also usefully employed in more traditional legal analysis, and has influenced recent thinking on remedies, as is evident from other parts of this book. The three levels of protection or types of "entitlement" are:

(1) a property rule, that is: "someone who wishes to remove the entitlement from its holder must buy it from him in a voluntary transaction in which the value of the entitlement is agreed upon by the seller";

(2) a liability rule allowing the defendant to "destroy the initial entitlement if he is willing to pay an objectively determined value for it";

(3) inalienability, that is, "that its transfer is not permitted between a willing buyer and a willing seller."

The four remedial possibilities are as follows:

(1) An injunction. The polluter is restrained and the plaintiff is fully protected. In this situation, the plaintiff is said to be given a property-type protection in that his right to be free of pollution can only be taken away from him if he chooses to sell, and then it must be paid for at an agreed price.

(2) Damages. The polluter is liable but the plaintiff is merely compensated. The polluter may go on polluting and the effect of the order is to "buy out" the plaintiff at an objective and judicially determined price rather than at a price agreed to by the plaintiff and the defendant. The plaintiff is given a liability-type of protection only.

(3) No liability. This choice may be described as a property-type protection in favour of the polluter. He is permitted to go on polluting and can be stopped only if the plaintiff buys him out at an agreed price. This third choice is the reverse of the first.

(4) Compensated injunction. This final remedial choice is one which has many attractions but which has been rarely employed. The property owner is protected by an injunction, but only on the condition that he buy out the polluter at a judicially determined price, usually fixed to compensate the polluter for relocation expenses and the loss of sunk costs. This is the reverse of the second possibility, and may be said to make the property owner "liable" for the cost of removing the source of the harm.

As indicated above, in the absence of transaction costs, an efficient allocation will occur as a result of post-judgment bargaining, even if the court opts for an apparently inefficient result by granting or refusing an injunction, and thereby imposes burdens on the loser out of proportion with the benefit derived by the winner. Where, however, there are transaction costs which would preclude such a bargain, a court motivated solely to attain the efficient result must pursue a conscious strategy to that end.

Assuming that there are high transaction costs, and that the choice of remedy is to be governed solely by the goal of efficiency, economic analysis is said to yield the following result. If the court is certain that one party can avoid or reduce the cost of the conflicting property use more cheaply than the other, then a "property" rule is called for, which assigns the entitlement to the latter so as to induce the former to adopt cost-minimizing precautions (injunction in favour of the polluted, no liability on polluter, as appropriate). Because the court is certain that one party is the least cost avoider, there is no need to incur the judicial and administrative costs inherent in a liability rule which requires assessment of the value of the nuisance.

Where there is doubt as to which party is the least cost avoider (and this is likely to be so in most pollution cases), a property rule should be avoided. If the court is wrong in its guess, transaction costs will prevent the market from correcting the error. What the court must do here is construct a hypothetical market, and through a damages award, determine objectively the valuation which would have been made had there been no market failure. Almost invariably, this means imposing liability on the polluter, and awarding damages in compensation. So long as the amount of damages is an accurate reflection of the injury caused, efficiency will be satisfied. The damages award, taking place of the market transaction which circumstances prevent, will put the conflict to the efficiency test: can the polluter's enterprise pay damages and still operate profitably, or does the value to the property owners (objectively measured) exceed the value in production gained by polluting? Theoretically, a similar result can be obtained from the fourth possible choice, that of a compensated injunction. Making the affected party pay the costs that an injunction imposes upon the polluter weighs the relative values of the parties in a similar way.

Thus, in terms of actual results, the economic model outlined here would probably produce more damage awards than does the existing case-law. Economic analysis avoids injunctions which cannot, as a practical matter, be bargained around. Many nuisance cases involve harmful effects on a large number of parties, and thus market failure due to high transaction costs suggests damages as the effective remedy. Assuming high transaction costs, an injunction will be awarded against a polluter only where he is clearly the least cost avoider. This is a much narrower range of case than presented by the case-law. Plaintiffs who are least cost avoiders would also be disfavoured by economic analysis: if the court determines that the value of pollution exceeds the value of being pollution free, the plaintiff would be denied relief altogether and the polluter would have the "remedy" of no liability.

Clearly, there are substantial objections and major difficulties in the way of implementing this economic model as the sole standard for the resolution of nuisance disputes. The law tends to focus on righting past wrongs and preventing future wrongs, whereas the economist's concern is to provide the appropriate structure of incentives to encourage the efficient allocation of resources. While the pursuit of efficiency is also an important legal goal, it is a pursuit qualified by the concept of rights which may not be superseded merely because the general social welfare would be advanced. To take perhaps the most obvious example emerging from the foregoing discussion, a concept of rights renders inconceivable a result whereby the plaintiff is told by the court that he has lost because he is clearly the least cost avoider, or even that he is being denied an injunction and being judicially expropriated for an objectively measured amount because transaction costs are high. Taken to its logical conclusion and if fully implemented as a legal principle, efficiency analysis would appear to make expropriation legislation unnecessary. It would provide justification for allocating and altering property rights solely on the basis of efficiency. The jurisprudential limit upon the value of efficiency is not a subject within the scope of this book; suffice it to say that it is rarely suggested that justice can be defined in terms of efficiency alone.

The economic model is also based on certain assumptions which cause difficulty if the model is to be used as a means of resolving concrete problems. The most important from the legal perspective is first, that the motive for all behaviour can be explained as a desire to maximize wealth, and second, that the existing distribution of wealth must be taken as a given. Few will accept that human behaviour can be entirely or adequately explained, for legal purposes, on the basis of the theory of wealth maximization. The other important point is the fact that the differences in wealth and ability to bargain render efficiency analysis much less precise than it first appears to be. The ability and willingness to pay is clearly affected by wealth, and hence, for every different distribution of wealth, there is a different efficient outcome. Since efficiency analysis is determined in part by the respective wealth of the parties, it surely follows that efficiency alone is unlikely to produce a result which can be described as just, once distributive issues are taken into account.

Economists do not, in fact, believe that all people always behave in a rational, economic and wealth-maximizing way, or that the existing distribution of wealth must not be tampered with. These assumptions are merely devices to make possible the construction of theoretical models which will reveal certain patterns or relationships which might not otherwise be seen. The analysis is at a general and abstract level; it is not intended to solve particular problems. The lawyer's immediate objection to such assumptions derives from the legal need to develop theories and rules which allow him to solve each particular problem. A general theory which rests on such assumptions cannot be relied upon for this purpose.

At the same time, however, these criticisms are not a reason for totally rejecting economic analysis, but rather suggest that it must be viewed critically and employed cautiously. Some of the leading exponents of economic analysis are explicit about the shortcomings of the formal analytic model-building approach. Similarly, lawyers should be conscious of the advantages of an analysis which does tend to highlight or identify certain relationships and general theoretical points which might otherwise not be apparent. Economic analysis of the pollution problem provides no panacea; neither is it an exercise that the law should ignore. From the earlier discussion of the case law, it does seem clear that the goal of efficiency plays an important part in the resolution of nuisance disputes, including the selection of the appropriate remedy. To the extent economists can help improve analysis already undertaken, that contribution should be welcomed. In particular, the perception that greater explicit attention should be paid to the fact that market forces will operate in some cases to alter the legal result is an important one. The degree to which consideration of post-judgment bargaining helps explain and elucidate the significance of legal results suggests that courts and lawyers can benefit from taking economic analysis into account.

Boomer v. Atlantic Cement Co. Ltd.
257 NE 2d 870 (NY CA 1970) (footnotes omitted)

BERGAN J: Defendant operates a large cement plant near Albany. These are actions for injunction and damages by neighboring land owners alleging injury to property from dirt, smoke and vibration emanating from the plant. A nuisance has been found after trial, temporary damages have been allowed; but an injunction has been denied.

The public concern with air pollution arising from many sources in industry and in transportation is currently accorded ever wider recognition accompanied by a growing sense of responsibility in State and Federal Governments to control it. Cement plants are obvious sources of air pollution in the neighborhoods where they operate.

But there is now before the court private litigation in which individual property owners have sought specific relief from a single plant operation. The threshold question raised by the division of view on this appeal is whether the court should resolve the litigation between the parties now before it as equitably as seems possible; or whether, seeking promotion of the general public welfare, it should channel private litigation into broad public objectives.

A court performs its essential function when it decides the rights of parties before it. Its decision of private controversies may sometimes greatly affect public issues. Large questions of law are often resolved by the manner in which private litigation is decided. But this is normally an incident to the court's main function to settle controversy. It is rare exercise of judicial power to use a decision in private litigation as a purposeful mechanism to achieve direct public objectives greatly beyond the rights and interests before the court.

Effective control of air pollution is a problem presently far from solution even with the full public and financial powers of government. In large measure adequate technical procedures are yet to be developed and some that appear possible may be economically impracticable.

It seems apparent that the amelioration of air pollution will depend on technical research in great depth; on a carefully balanced consideration of the economic impact of close regulation; and of the actual effect on public health. It is likely to require massive public expenditure and to demand more than any local community can accomplish and to depend on regional and interstate controls.

A court should not try to do this on its own as a by-product of private litigation and it seems manifest that the judicial establishment is neither equipped in the limited nature of any judgment it can pronounce nor prepared to lay down and implement an effective policy for the elimination of air pollution. This is an area beyond the circumference of one private lawsuit. It is a direct responsibility for government and should not thus be undertaken as an incident to solving a dispute between property owners and a single cement plant—one of many—in the Hudson River valley.

The cement making operations of defendant have been found by the court at Special Term to have damaged the nearby properties of plaintiffs in these two actions. That court, as it has been noted, accordingly found defendant maintained a nuisance and this has been affirmed at the Appellate Division. The total damage to plaintiffs' properties is, however, relatively small in comparison with the value of defendant's operation and with the consequences of the injunction which plaintiffs seek.

The ground for the denial of injunction, notwithstanding the finding both that there is a nuisance and that the plaintiffs have been damaged substantially, is the large disparity in economic consequences of the nuisance and of the injunction. This theory cannot, however, be sustained without overruling a doctrine which has been consistently reaffirmed in several leading cases in this court and which has never been disavowed here, namely that where a nuisance has been found and where there has been any substantial damage shown by the party complaining an injunction will be granted.

The rule in New York has been that such a nuisance will be enjoined although marked disparity be shown in economic consequence between the effect of the injunction and the effect of the nuisance. ...

Although the court at Special Term and the Appellate Division held that injunction should be denied, it was found that plaintiffs had been damaged in various specific amounts up to the time of the trial and damages to the respective plaintiffs were awarded for those amounts. The effect of this was, injunction having been denied, plaintiffs could maintain successive actions at law for damages thereafter as further damage was incurred.

The court at Special Term also found the amount of permanent damage attributable to each plaintiff, for the guidance of the parties in the event both sides stipulated to the payment and acceptance of such permanent damage as a settlement of all the controversies among the parties. The total permanent damages to all plaintiffs thus found was $185,000. This basis of adjustment has not resulted in any stipulation by the parties.

This result at Special Term and at the Appellate Division is a departure from a rule that has become settled; but to follow the rule literally in these cases would be to close down the plant at once. This court is fully agreed to avoid that immediately drastic remedy; the difference in view is how best to avoid it. [Respondent's investment in the plant is in excess of $45,000,000. There are over 300 people employed there.]

One alternative is to grant the injunction but postpone its effect to a specified future date to give opportunity for technical advances to permit defendant to eliminate the nuisance; another is to grant the injunction conditioned on the payment of permanent damages to plaintiffs which would compensate them for the total economic loss to their property present and future caused by defendant's operations. For reasons which will be developed the court chooses the latter alternative.

If the injunction were to be granted unless within a short period—e.g., 18 months—the nuisance be abated by improved methods, there would be no assurance that any significant technical improvement would occur.

The parties could settle this private litigation at any time if defendant paid enough money and the imminent threat of closing the plant would build up the pressure on defendant. If there were no improved techniques found, there would inevitably be applications to the court at Special Term for extensions of time to perform on showing of good faith efforts to find such techniques.

Moreover, techniques to eliminate dust and other annoying by-products of cement making are unlikely to be developed by any research the defendant can undertake within any short period, but will depend on the total resources of the cement industry nationwide and throughout the world. The problem is universal wherever cement is made.

For obvious reasons the rate of the research is beyond control of defendant. If at the end of 18 months the whole industry has not found a technical solution a court would be hard put to close down this one cement plant if due regard be given to equitable principles.

On the other hand, to grant the injunction unless defendant pays plaintiffs such permanent damages as may be fixed by the court seems to do justice between the contending parties. All of the attributions of economic loss to the properties on which plaintiffs' complaints are based will have been redressed.

The nuisance complained of by these plaintiffs may have other public or private consequences, but these particular parties are the only ones who have sought remedies and the judgment proposed will fully redress them. The limitation of relief granted is a limitation only within the four corners of these actions and does not foreclose public health or other public agencies from seeking proper relief in a proper court.

It seems reasonable to think that the risk of being required to pay permanent damages to injured property owners by cement plant owners would itself be a reasonable effective spur to research for improved techniques to minimize nuisance.

The power of the court to condition on equitable grounds the continuance of an injunction on the payment of permanent damages seems undoubted. ...

The damage base here suggested is consistent with the general rule in those nuisance cases where damages are allowed. "Where a nuisance is of such a permanent and unabatable character that a single recovery can be had, including the whole damage past and future resulting therefrom, there can be but one recovery" (66 CJS Nuisances §140, p. 947). It has been said that permanent damages are allowed where the loss recoverable would obviously be small as compared with the cost of removal of the nuisance (*Kentucky-Ohio Gas Co. v. Bowling* (1936), 264 Ky. 470 at p. 477, 95 SW 2d 1). ...

[Bergan J went on to consider a number of nuisance cases, mostly involving public utilities and railways in which the courts neither awarded an injunction nor forced the defendant to resort to condemnation proceedings, but instead ordered permanent damages.]

The judgment, by allowance of permanent damages imposing a servitude on land, which is the basis of the actions, would preclude future recovery by plaintiffs or their grantees. ...

This should be placed beyond debate by a provision of the judgment that the payment by defendant and the acceptance by plaintiffs of permanent damages found by the court shall be in compensation for a servitude on the land.

Although the Trial Term has found permanent damages as a possible basis of settlement of the litigation, on remission the court should be entirely free to re-examine this subject. It may again find the permanent damage already found; or make new findings.

The orders should be reversed, without costs, and the cases remitted to Supreme Court, Albany County to grant an injunction which shall be vacated upon payment by defendant of such amounts of permanent damage to the respective plaintiffs as shall for this purpose be determined by the court.

JASEN J (dissenting): I agree with the majority that a reversal is required here, but I do not subscribe to the newly enunciated doctrine of assessment of permanent damages, in lieu of an injunction, where substantial property rights have been impaired by the creation of a nuisance.

It has long been the rule in this State, as the majority acknowledges, that a nuisance which results in substantial continuing damage to neighbors must be enjoined. To now change the rule to permit the cement company to continue polluting the air indefinitely upon the payment of permanent damages is, in my opinion, compounding the magnitude of a very serious problem in our State and Nation today.

In recognition of this problem, the Legislature of this State has enacted the *Air Pollution Control Act* (Public Health Law, Consol. Laws, c. 45, §§1264 to 1299-m) declaring that it is the State policy to require the use of all available and reasonable methods to prevent and control air pollution (Public Health Law §1265).

The harmful nature and widespread occurrence of air pollution have been extensively documented. Congressional hearings have revealed that air pollution causes substantial property damage, as well as being a contributing factor to a rising incidence of lung cancer, emphysema, bronchitis and asthma.

The specific problem faced here is known as particulate contamination because of the fine dust particles emanating from defendant's cement plant. The particular type of nuisance is not new, having appeared in many cases for at least the past 60 years. ... It is interesting to note that cement production has recently been identified as a significant source of particulate contamination in the Hudson Valley. This type of pollution, wherein very small particles escape and stay in the atmosphere, has been denominated as the type of air pollution which produces the greatest hazard to human health. We have thus a nuisance which not only is damaging to the plaintiffs, but also is decidedly harmful to the general public.

I see grave dangers in overruling our long-established rule of granting an injunction where a nuisance results in substantial continuing damage. In permitting the injunction to become inoperative upon the payment of permanent damages, the majority is, in effect, licensing a continuing wrong. It is the same as saying to the cement company, you may continue to do harm to your neighbors so long as you pay a fee for it. Furthermore, once such permanent damages are assessed and paid, the incentive to alleviate the wrong would be eliminated, thereby continuing air pollution of an area without abatement.

It is true that some courts have sanctioned the remedy here proposed by the majority in a number of cases, but none of the authorities relied upon by the majority are analogous to the situation before us. In those cases, the courts, in denying an injunction and awarding money damages, grounded their decision on a showing that the use to which the property was intended to be put was primarily for the public benefit. Here, on the other hand, it is clearly established that the cement company is creating a continuing air pollution nuisance primarily for its own private interest with no public benefit.

This kind of inverse condemnation ... may not be invoked by a private person or corporation for private gain or advantage. Inverse condemnation should only be permitted when the public is primarily served in the taking or impairment of property. ... The promotion of the interests of the polluting cement company has, in my opinion, no public use or benefit.

Nor is it constitutionally permissible to impose servitude on land, without consent of the owner, by payment of permanent damages where the continuing impairment of the land is for a private use. ... This is made clear by the State Constitution (art. I, §7, subd. [a]) which provides that "[p]rivate property shall not be taken for *public use* without just compensation" (emphasis added). It is, of course, significant that the section makes no mention of taking for a *private use*.

In sum, then, by constitutional mandate as well as by judicial pronouncement, the permanent impairment of private property for private purposes is not authorized in the absence of clearly demonstrated public benefit and use.

I would enjoin the defendant cement company from continuing the discharge of dust particles upon its neighbor's properties unless, within 18 months, the cement company abated this nuisance.

It is not my intention to cause the removal of the cement plant from the Albany area, but to recognize the urgency of the problem stemming from this stationary source of air pollution, and to allow the company a specified period of time to develop a means to alleviate this nuisance.

I am aware that the trial court found that the most modern dust control devices available have been installed in defendant's plant, but, I submit, this does not mean that *better* and more effective dust control devices could not be developed within the time allowed to abate the pollution.

Moreover, I believe it is incumbent upon the defendant to develop such devices, since the cement company, at the time the plant commenced production (1962), was well aware of the plaintiffs' presence in the area, as well as the probable consequences of its contemplated operation. Yet, it still chose to build and operate the plant at this site.

In a day when there is a growing concern for clean air, highly developed industry should not expect acquiescence by the courts, but should, instead, plan its operations to eliminate contamination of our air and damage to its neighbors.

Accordingly, the orders of the Appellate Division, insofar as they denied the injunction, should be reversed, and the actions remitted to Supreme Court, Albany County to grant an injunction to take effect 18 months hence, unless the nuisance is abated by improved techniques prior to said date.

[Fuld CJ and Burke and Scileppi JJ concurred with Bergan J.]

[Jasen J dissented in part and voted to reverse in a separate opinion.]

[Breitel and Gibson JJ took no part.]

NOTES AND QUESTIONS

1. Does the economic analysis of remedial choice explained by Sharpe suggest a rationale for the distinction between trespass and nuisance?

2. Is it true that a rule allowing damages awards in this type of case would not provide an incentive to improve pollution control? Does the threat of an injunction provide such an incentive? Would a hard and fast rule against damages in such a situation provide an incentive?

3. What is Bergan J's view of the proper role of the court in this type of dispute? Is he faithful to this view?

4. Jasen J distinguishes between private and public benefit. What is this distinction?

5. What type of information does the court require in nuisance litigation to "balance the equities"? Is the court a competent institution to engage in this process?

6. In *Manchester v. Farnworth*, [1930] AC 171 (HL (Eng.)) a nuisance action against a coal-fired electrical generating station, Lord Blanesburgh said (at 203-4):

> Very readily would I decide, if I felt at liberty to do so, that the loss resulting to the plaintiff from the defendant's operation should without any qualification be borne by the Corporation. That loss is truly just as much part of the cost of generating electrical energy as is, for example, the cost of the coal whose combustion is the original source of all the mischief. In a question between plaintiff on the one hand and the Corporation on the other I can discover no sound principle why the loss should not be theirs.

Do you agree with this statement of the economics and morality of pollution? If so, does it provide any guidance in choosing between damages and injunctions? In "The Problem of Social Cost" (1980), 3 *Journal of Law and Economics* 1, R.H. Coase suggests that this way of stating the problem obscures the real nature of the social choice that has to be made. He argues (at 2) that:

> The question is commonly thought of as one in which A inflicts harm on B and what has to be decided is: how should we restrain A? But this is wrong. We are dealing with a problem of a reciprocal

nature. To avoid the harm to B would inflict harm on A. The real question that has to be decided is: should A be allowed to harm B or should B be allowed to harm A? The problem is to avoid the more serious harm.

Coase concludes with a discussion of the view that the "externalities" of pollution-generating activities are anti-social and should be restrained. He suggests that such activities may or may not be anti-social depending upon the harm that they cause when measured against the good that results. He concludes that "[n]othing could be more 'anti-social' than to oppose any action which causes harm to anyone."

7. In *McKie v. The K.V.P. Co. Ltd.*, [1948] OR 398, at 410-11, McRuer CJHC granted to the plaintiffs, who were riparian owners on the Spanish River, an injunction to restrain a pulp mill from discharging waste into the river. He said (at 410-11):

> Some evidence was given on behalf of the defendant to show the importance of its business in the community, and that it carried it on in a proper manner. Neither of these elements is to be taken into consideration in a case of this character, nor are the economic interests of the defendant relevant … . In my view, if I were to consider and give effect to an argument based on the defendant's economic position in the community, or its financial interests, I would in effect be giving to it a veritable power of expropriation of the common law rights of the riparian owners, without compensation.

This decision was upheld in the Supreme Court of Canada: [1949] SCR 698. The Ontario legislature immediately passed a statute (*An Act Respecting The K.V.P. Company Ltd.*, SO 1950, c. 33) that dissolved the injunction. The right of the plaintiffs to damages was preserved. The Act also provided that the plaintiffs might submit their claims to arbitration and that the Research Council of Ontario should develop methods to abate the pollution of the Spanish River.

Is the analogy of "expropriation" helpful in the context of a nuisance action or does it simply assume the answer to the question that the court must address? Which of the plaintiff and defendant is seeking to expropriate the rights of the other?

8. In *Canada Paper Co. v. Brown* (1921), 63 SCR 243, the Supreme Court of Canada affirmed an injunction against the defendant pulp mill, prohibiting the use of materials that polluted the air with sulphate fumes. Idington J stated that for mere commercial reasons the appellants had disregarded the rights of the respondents and objected to the "mass of irrelevant evidence" that had been introduced in support of the "remarkable conclusion that because the prosperity of said town or village would be enhanced by the use of the new process therefore the respondent has no rights upon which to rest his rights of property." He stated further (at 248):

> The invasion of rights incidental to the ownership of property, or the confiscation thereof, may suit the grasping tendencies of some and incidentally the needs or desires of the majority in any community benefitting thereby; yet such a basis or principle of action should be stoutly resisted by our courts, in answer to any such like demands or assertions of social right unless and until due compensation made by due process of law.

Duff J agreed that the injunction should be granted, but noted that he was not convinced by the evidence that an injunction against the sulphate process would close down the plant. He also commented that he could not accept that considerations touching on the impact of the injection upon the local community were irrelevant to the question of whether an injunction should issue. The granting of an injunction is discretionary,

not, that is to say, an arbitrary choice or a choice based upon the personal views of the judge, but a discretion regulated in accordance with judicial principles as illustrated by the practice of the courts in giving and withholding that remedy. An injunction will not be granted where, having regard to all the circumstances, to grant it would be unjust; and the disparity between the advantage to the plaintiff to be gained by the granting of that remedy and the inconvenience and disadvantage which the defendant and others would suffer in consequence thereof may be a sufficient ground for refusing it. ... This is not, as was suggested in argument, equivalent to subjecting the plaintiff to a process of expropriation, it is merely applying the limitations and restrictions which the law imposes in relation to the pursuit of this particular form of remedy in order to prevent it becoming an instrument of injustice and oppression (at 252).

9. While injunctive relief appears to be the preferred remedy in respect of nuisance, it has been denied in a number of Canadian cases where the economic and social consequences of an injunction appeared to the judge to be extreme. See *Black v. Canadian Copper Co.* (1917), 12 OWN 243 (HC), aff'd. (1920), 17 OWN 399 (Div. Ct.) and *Bottom v. Ontario Leaf Tobacco Co. Ltd.*, [1935] OR 205 (CA).

10. In *Stephens v. Village of Richmond Hill*, [1955] OR 806, aff'd. [1956] OR 88 (CA), Stewart J granted an injunction against municipal sewage disposal in a local river. He stated (at 812-13):

[I]t is not for the judiciary to permit the doctrine of utilitarianism to be used as a make-weight in the scales of justice. In civil matters, the function of the Court is to determine rights between parties. ... It is the duty of the state (and of statesmen) to seek the greatest good for the greatest number.

Is this an accurate statement of the function of civil adjudication and the difference between the courts and the legislature? Are you familiar with any areas of the common law in which the utilitarian calculus is used as a make-weight in the scales of justice? Does it follow from the fact that a person has a right that that right must be protected by injunction? See R. Dworkin, *Taking Rights Seriously* (Cambridge: Harvard University Press, 1978) and R. Epstein, "Nuisance Law: Corrective Justice and Its Utilitarian Constraints" (1979), 8 *Journal of Legal Studies* 49.

On the history of the relationship between nuisance law and economic development, see Morton Horwitz, *The Transformation of American Law* (Cambridge: Harvard University Press, 1977) and J.P.S. McLaren, "Nuisance Law and the Industrial Revolution—Some Lessons From Social History" (1983), 3 *Oxford Journal of Legal Studies* 155.

Spur Industries Inc. v. Del E. Webb Development Co.
494 P2d 700 (Ariz. SC 1972)

CAMERON VJ: From a judgment permanently enjoining the defendant, Spur Industries, Inc., from operating a cattle feedlot near the plaintiff Del. E. Webb Development Company's Sun City, Spur appeals. Webb cross-appeals. Although numerous issues are raised, we feel that it is necessary to answer only two questions. They are:

1. Where the operation of a business, such as a cattle feedlot is lawful in the first instance, but becomes a nuisance by reason of a nearby residential area, may the feedlot operation be enjoined in an action brought by the developer of the residential area?

2. Assuming that the nuisance may be enjoined, may the developer of a completely new town or urban area in a previously agricultural area be required to indemnify the operator of the feedlot who must move or cease operation because of the presence of the residential area created by the developer? ...

[Sun City is located some 14 to 15 miles from Phoenix, Arizona. Plans for this development were drawn in May 1959, and 20,000 acres of farmland were purchased for $15,000,000 or $750 per acre. This price was considerably less than the price of land located near the urban area of Phoenix.

The area in which the development was planned had been farmland since 1911 and there had been feedlots in the vicinity since 1956. In September 1959, Del Webb, the developers of Sun City, began to develop their property south, in the direction of the Spur feedlots. In 1960, Spur began to expand, and developed lands both north and south of the original feedlot. By 1962, Spur's expansion program was completed and had expanded from approximately 35 acres to 114 acres.

Del Webb continued to develop in a southerly direction until sales resistance resulting from the odours from the feedlots became so great that the parcels of land became difficult if not impossible to sell.]

By December 1967, Del Webb's property had extended south to Olive Avenue and Spur was within 500 feet of Olive Avenue to the north. See Exhibit B above. Del Webb filed its original complaint alleging that in excess of 1,300 lots in the southwest portion were unfit for development for sale as residential lots because of the operation of the Spur feedlot.

Del Webb's suit complained that the Spur feeding operation was a public nuisance because of the flies and the odor which were drifting or being blown by the prevailing south to north wind over the southern portion of Sun City. At the time of the suit, Spur was feeding between 20,000 and 30,000 head of cattle, and the facts amply support the finding of the trial court that the feed pens had become a nuisance to the people who resided in the southern part of Del Webb's development. The testimony indicated that cattle in a commercial feedlot will produce 35 to 40 pounds of wet manure per day, per head, or over a million pounds of wet manure per day for 30,000 head of cattle, and that despite the admittedly good feedlot management and good housekeeping practices by Spur, the resulting odor and flies produced an annoying if not unhealthy situation as far as the senior citizens of southern Sun City were concerned. There is no doubt that some of the citizens of Sun City were unable to enjoy the outdoor living which Del Webb had advertised and that Del Webb was faced with sales resistance from prospective purchasers as well as strong and persistent complaints from the people who had purchased homes in that area. ...

May Spur Be Enjoined?

The difference between a private nuisance and a public nuisance is generally one of degree. A private nuisance is one affecting a single individual or a definite small number of persons in the enjoyment of private rights not common to the public, while a public nuisance is one affecting the rights enjoyed by citizens as a part of the public. To constitute a public nuisance, the nuisance must affect a considerable number of people or an entire community or neighborhood. ... Where the injury is slight, the remedy for minor inconveniences lies in an action for damages rather than in one for an injunction. ... Moreover, some courts have held, in the "balancing of conveniences" cases, that damages may be the sole remedy. See *Boomer v. Atlantic Cement Co.* (1970), 26 NY 2d 219, 309 NYS 2d 312, 257 NE 2d 870, 40 ALR 3d 590, and annotation comments, 40 ALR 3d 601.

Thus, it would appear from the admittedly incomplete record as developed in the trial court that, at most, residents of Youngtown would be entitled to damages rather than injunctive relief.

We have no difficulty, however, in agreeing with the conclusion of the trial court that Spur's operation was an enjoinable public nuisance as far as the people in the southern portion of Del Webb's Sun City were concerned.

§36-601, subsec. A reads as follows:

§36-601. Public nuisances dangerous to public health

A. The following conditions are specifically declared public nuisances dangerous to the public health:

1. Any condition or place in populous areas which constitutes a breeding place for flies, rodents, mosquitoes and other insects which are capable of carrying and transmitting disease-causing organisms to any person or persons.

By this statute, before an otherwise lawful (and necessary) business may be declared a public nuisance, there must be a "populous" area in which people are injured:

[I]t hardly admits a doubt that, in determining the question as to whether a lawful occupation is so conducted as to constitute a nuisance as a matter of fact, the locality and surroundings are of the first importance. (citations omitted) A business which is not per se a public nuisance may become such by being carried on at a place where the health, comfort, or convenience of a populous neighborhood is affected. ... What might amount to a serious nuisance in one locality by reason of the density of the population, or character of the neighborhood affected, may in another place and under different surroundings be deemed proper and unobjectionable. ...

MacDonald v. Perry (1927), 32 Ariz. 39 at pp. 49-50; 255 P 494 at p. 497.

It is clear that as to the citizens of Sun City, the operation of Spur's feedlot was both a public and a private nuisance. They could have successfully maintained an action to abate the nuisance. Del Webb, having shown a special injury in the loss of sales, had a standing to bring suit to enjoin the nuisance. ... The judgment of the trial court permanently enjoining the operation of the feedlot is affirmed.

Must Del Webb Indemnify Spur?

A suit to enjoin a nuisance sounds in equity and the courts have long recognized a special responsibility to the public when acting as a court of equity:

> §104. Where public interest is involved.
>
> Courts of equity may, and frequently do, go much further both to give and withhold relief in furtherance of the public interest than they are accustomed to go when only private interests are involved. Accordingly, the granting or withholding of relief may properly be dependent upon considerations of public interest. …

27 Am. Jur. 2d, Equity, page 626.

In addition to protecting the public interest, however, courts of equity are concerned with protecting the operator of a lawfully, albeit noxious, business from the result of a knowing and willful encroachment by others near his business.

In the so-called "coming to the nuisance" cases, the courts have held that the residential landowner may not have relief if he knowingly came into a neighborhood reserved for industrial or agricultural endeavors and has been damaged thereby:

> Plaintiffs chose to live in an area uncontrolled by zoning laws or restrictive covenants and remote from urban development. In such an area plaintiffs cannot complain that legitimate agricultural pursuits are being carried on in the vicinity, nor can plaintiffs, having chosen to build in an agricultural area, complain that the agricultural pursuits carried on in the area depreciate the value of their homes. The area being *primarily agricultural*, any opinion reflecting the value of such property must take this factor into account. The standards affecting the value of residence property in an urban setting, subject to zoning controls and controlled planning techniques, cannot be the standards by which agricultural properties are judged.
>
> People employed in a city who build their homes in suburban areas of the county beyond the limits of a city and zoning regulations do so for a reason. Some do so to avoid the high taxation rate imposed by cities, or to avoid special assessments for street, sewer and water projects. They usually build on improved or hard surface highways, which have been built either at state or county expense and thereby avoid special assessments for these improvements. It may be that they desire to get away from the congestion of traffic, smoke, noise, foul air and the many other annoyances of city life. But with all these advantages in going beyond the area which is zoned and restricted to protect them in their homes, they must be prepared to take the disadvantages. …

And:

> [A] party cannot justly call upon the law to make that place suitable for his residence which was not so when he selected it. …

Gilbert v. Showerman (1871), 23 Mich. 448 at p. 455; 2 Brown 158.

Were Webb the only party injured, we would feel justified in holding that the doctrine of "coming to the nuisance" would have been a bar to the relief asked by Webb, and, on the other hand, had Spur located the feedlot near the outskirts of a city and had the city grown toward the feedlot, Spur would have to suffer the cost of abating the nuisance as to those people locating within the growth pattern of the expanding city:

The case affords, perhaps, an example where a business established at a place remote from population is gradually surrounded and becomes part of a populous center, so that a business which formerly was not an interference with the rights of others has become so by the encroachment of the population. ...

City of Ft. Smith v. Western Hide & Fur Co. (1922), 153 Ark. 99 at p. 103, 239 SW 724 at p. 726.
We agree, however, with the Massachusetts court that:

The law of nuisance affords no rigid rule to be applied in all instances. It is elastic. It undertakes to require only that which is fair and reasonable under all the circumstances. In a commonwealth like this, which depends for its material prosperity so largely on the continued growth and enlargement of manufacturing of diverse varieties, "extreme rights" cannot be enforced. ...

Stevens v. Rockport Granite Co. (1914), 216 Mass. 486 at p. 488, 104 NE 371 at p. 373.
There was no indication in the instant case at the time Spur and its predecessors located in western Maricopa County that a new city would spring up, full-blown, alongside the feeding operation and that the developer of that city would ask the court to order Spur to move because of the new city. Spur is required to move not because of any wrongdoing on the part of Spur, but because of a proper and legitimate regard of the courts for the rights and interests of the public.

Del Webb, on the other hand, is entitled to the relief prayed for (a permanent injunction), not because Webb is blameless, but because of the damage to the people who have been encouraged to purchase homes in Sun City. It does not equitably or legally follow, however, that Webb, being entitled to the injunction, is then free of any liability to Spur if Webb has in fact been the cause of the damage Spur has sustained. It does not seem harsh to require a developer, who has taken advantage of the lesser land values in a rural area as well as the availability of large tracts of land on which to build and develop a new town or city in the area, to indemnify those who are forced to leave as a result.

Having brought people to the nuisance to the foreseeable detriment of Spur, Webb must indemnify Spur for a reasonable amount of the cost of moving or shutting down. It should be noted that this relief to Spur is limited to a case wherein a developer has, with foreseeability, brought into a previously agricultural or industrial area the population which makes necessary the granting of an injunction against a lawful business and for which the business has no adequate relief.

It is therefore the decision of this court that the matter be remanded to the trial court for a hearing upon the damages sustained by the defendant Spur as a reasonable and direct result of the granting of the permanent injunction. Since the result of the appeal may appear novel and both sides have obtained a measure of relief, it is ordered that each side will bear its own costs.

NOTES AND QUESTIONS

1. What moral or legal justification is there for imposing the burden of cleaning up the environment on the "victim" of pollution? Are there any assumptions necessary to support the solution achieved in *Spur*?

2. Why did the court in this case not simply refuse the injunction? The parties could then have struck a bargain. The economic literature suggests that if the developer sufficiently valued the land free of pollution a mutually advantageous bargain might have been achieved. If not, then a court-imposed bargain would be inefficient. Is there any reason apart from economics why the court would choose to force the parties into an agreement?

3. Is anyone getting a "free ride" as a result of the remedy fashioned in this case?

4. Would the remedy fashioned in *Spur* be workable in other pollution cases? What are the limits of this approach?

5. *Spur v. Del Webb* illustrates an important point about remedial selection, especially in nuisance litigation. In adjudicating any conflict there are two questions: what should be done to resolve the conflict (how should the resource be allocated), and who should bear the costs of that resolution? A recognition that these two questions are analytically distinct may enhance remedial flexibility and allow the courts to fashion more sophisticated solutions that respond better to the sometimes apparently conflicting demands of utility, fairness, and efficiency. See E. Rabin, "Nuisance Law: Rethinking Fundamental Assumptions" (1977), 63 *Virginia Law Review* 1299.

6. Compare *Sullivan and Sullivan Farms Ltd. v. Desrosiers* (1987), 76 NBR (2d) 271 (CA). The defendant has been operating a farm since 1975 in an area that included similar operations. Increasingly, the defendant concentrated on raising hogs until by 1980, he had 140 sows and 1,000 feeder hogs. The farm also included a large "manure lagoon" to capture the 260 cubic feet of liquid waste produced each day. Twenty-five neighbours, living in homes built mostly since 1975, brought an action in nuisance claiming an injunction and damages. The farm burned down in 1984 (during the litigation), and the lagoon was finally filled in in 1985. The trial judge and court of appeal were satisfied that the operation resulted in an odour that seriously and unreasonably interfered with the plaintiffs' use and enjoyment of their property. The neighbours were awarded $1,500 each. Because of the fire, the nuisance had ceased and the injunction was therefore not granted. Neither level of court accepted that the plaintiffs had come to the nuisance. The expansion of the defendant's operation and the construction of the housing took place roughly over the same period.

See also *340909 Ont. Ltd. v. Huron Steel Products (Windsor) Ltd.* (1990), 73 OR (2d) 641 (HC). This case involved a claim in nuisance by the owner of an apartment building against a nearby stamping plant. The defendant had installed new presses in 1979 and 1983 and the plaintiff complained that the noise and vibration was driving away tenants. The court held that the plant was a nuisance, analyzing the facts in terms of the following factors: the severity of the interference; the character of the locale; the utility of the defendant's conduct; and the sensitivity of the use interfered with. The court placed some importance on the fact that the first press did not comply with the sound guidelines in the *Environmental Protection Act*. The neighbourhood was now one of mixed use; the noise from the factory had increased along with the growing residential use; and, at any rate, Potts J held that it is no defence to a nuisance action that the plaintiff has moved to the nuisance. He accepted that the utility of the defendant's enterprise and its value to the community were relevant considerations, though going to the leniency of the remedy rather than to liability, and held that there were improvements to the building that could reduce the nuisance. Potts J awarded damages for lost rental revenue and also for the diminished value of the building. At his suggestion the parties agreed on remedial works to be undertaken and an injunction was ordered in these terms on condition that if the work was not completed by a certain date the defendant would be prohibited from operating the press.

ADDITIONAL READINGS

R.E. Hawkins, "In and of Itself: Some Thoughts on the Assignment of Property Rights in Nuisance Cases" (1978), 36 *University of Toronto Faculty of Law Review* 209.

A.D. Melamed and G. Calabresi, "Property Rules, Liability Rules and Inalienability: One View of the Cathedral" (1972), 85 *Harvard Law Review* 1089.

A.I. Ogus and G.M. Richardson, "Economics and the Environment: A Study of Private Nuisance" (1977), 36 *Cambridge Law Journal* 284.

S. Tromans, "Nuisance—Prevention or Payment?" (1982), 41 *Cambridge Law Journal* 87.

INJUNCTIONS TO PROTECT OTHER PERSONAL RIGHTS

Domestic Violence and the Family Home

A potentially important use of the injunction is to prevent violence, particularly in the domestic situation. While this is not a remedy designed to enforce property rights, proprietary notions appear to have had a significant influence. In *Duggan v. Duggan*, [1965] 2 OR 651 the plaintiff sought an injunction to restrain her husband from entering the matrimonial home or molesting her and her children pending divorce proceedings. The affidavit evidence alleged conduct that, in the eyes of Ferguson J, if proved, "would amount to cruelty of a very serious nature." Ferguson J discussed the equitable right of the non-owning spouse to remain in the matrimonial home, and considered a number of cases in which that right had been protected by injunction. He concluded that in a situation where the husband is the legal owner of the house, the wife's equitable interest confers upon her the right to stay in the home, but not to exclude the husband unless he has been guilty of desertion and cruelty and is likely to drive her out of the home, thus "bullying her out of her rights." Ferguson J distinguished most of the cases in which an injunction had been granted to the wife on the basis that she was the legal owner of the home. He characterized the very few cases in which the successful applicant was not the legal owner as "extreme cases" where the husband was guilty of desertion as well as cruelty and adultery, and where there was a danger that if the order was not granted the wife would be bullied out of her right. He concluded that on the facts of the present case, while the husband may have been guilty of "ill-treatment of a serious nature," because he was a joint owner of the property, he could not be prevented from living in the house.

See also *Donoghue v. Donoghue* (1973), 11 RFL 305 (Ont. HC), where such an order was granted to the wife notwithstanding that her husband owned the house, and *Hersog v. Hersog* (1976), 22 RFL 380 (BC SC), in which the husband, who was the owner of the home obtained an injunction against his wife. Meredith J noted that while the wife was a co-owner of the home, it had been owned by the husband for 12 years before they were married and that he had conveyed a half interest in it to her only upon her request and to make her feel "more secure in the community." The test adopted by the judge for granting the application, based on English precedent, was that "the shared use of the property is a practical impossibility and, secondly, that he should be preferred as occupant since on balance he will suffer much the greater hardship if denied the use of the premises." The applicant was held to be the preferred occupier because of his use of the home for business purposes. See "Domestic Violence: Legislative and Judicial Remedies" (1979), 2 *Harvard Women's Law Journal* 167; *Kendrick v. Kendrick*, [1990] FCR 780 (CA); *Spindlow v. Spindlow*, [1978] 3 WLR 777 (CA); and *Davis v. Johnson*, [1979] AC 214 (HL (Eng.)).

Provincial family law legislation now authorizes the court to make an order of exclusive possession of the matrimonial home, notwithstanding legal ownership. See, for example, *Family Law Act*, RSO 1990, c. F.3, s. 24 and *Family Relations Act*, RSBC 1996, c. 128, ss. 124, 126. BC's *Family Relations Act*, for example, provides that a court may order that one spouse be given exclusive occupancy of the family residence (s. 124). In addition, a court may restrict contact by ordering that one spouse shall not enter premises while the premises are occupied by the other spouse or a child in the custody of the other spouse (s. 126). This provision applies regardless of whether the spouse against whom the order is made owns or has a right to possession of the premises.

In *Campeau v. Elliot*, Vic. Reg. No. 91/1147, April 15, 1991, BC SC, the plaintiff common law wife had left the home with her children because of the defendant common law husband's threats of violence. The plaintiff applied for exclusive occupation of the home. The defendant claimed the plaintiff could not have exclusive occupation because the home was rented. The BC Supreme Court held that the plaintiff could have sole possession of the matrimonial home, even though the premises was rented.

An order for one spouse to have exclusive occupation of the matrimonial home under the *Family Relations Act* need not, of course, involve domestic violence. In *Hock v. Hock*, New Westminster Reg. No. D035782, September 29, 1995, BC SC, the Supreme Court held that the plaintiff wife could have sole and exclusive occupation of the matrimonial home. The defendant husband had moved out of the home when he and the plaintiff had separated. After commencing divorce proceedings, the defendant moved back into the home against the wishes of the plaintiff and their children, and refused to leave. The court held that even though there had been no violence, the plaintiff ought to be given exclusive occupation as the presence of the defendant had been upsetting and traumatic to the children and the plaintiff. See also *Seed v. Seed* (1980), 25 BCLR 139 (SC).

Another statutory provision that serves to prevent domestic violence is s. 810 of the *Criminal Code*. Section 810(1) allows an information to be laid before a justice of the peace by or on behalf of any individual who, with reasonable grounds, fears another person will cause personal injury to him or her, or to his or her child. The court may order the individual to attend a hearing and, if it is found that there are reasonable grounds, the individual may be ordered to enter into a recognizance to keep the peace and be of good behaviour, and comply with other reasonable conditions prescribed by the court or justice. Section 810(3.2) details other conditions with which a court or justice can require the defendant to comply. Section 810(3.2) provides that the justice or court may prohibit the defendant from being at, or within, a specified distance from a place where the complainant or complainant's child is regularly found. Further, the court or justice can also prohibit the defendant from communicating directly or indirectly with the complainant or the complainant's child. Section 810 is a special preventive remedy that does not involve the laying of a formal charge.

Reputational Interests

While there is a reluctance to impose "prior restraint" on free speech, injunctions can be used to restrain defamation (libel and slander) in clear cases. One example is the case of *Barrick Gold Corp. v. Lopehandia* (2004), 71 OR (3d) 416. In this case, the defendant, through email and Web postings, conducted a defamatory campaign against the plaintiff. The Ontario Court of Appeal granted the plaintiff both damages and a permanent injunction to restrain the defamation. A further interesting aspect of this case is that, while the defendant conducted his campaign from British Columbia, where he lived, the use of the Internet, and its impact on the plaintiff's reputation in Ontario, was held by the court to be sufficient to establish both a real and substantial connection between Ontario and the plaintiff and defendant and an *in personam* jurisdiction over the out-of-province defendant for the purpose of binding him by injunction.

CRIMINAL EQUITY: INJUNCTIONS TO PROTECT PUBLIC RIGHTS

The Role of the Attorney General and the Courts

At one time, it could be confidently asserted that equity had no jurisdiction over crime, and the courts would not grant an injunction to restrain criminal conduct. Property lay at the heart of the early equitable jurisdiction and it has been suggested that the cautious approach adopted by the Chancery to criminal matters was motivated by a concern that it not be viewed in the same light as the old Star Chamber (E.S. Mack, "The Revival of Criminal Equity" (1903), 16 *Harvard Law Review* 398 and "Developments in the Law—Injunctions" (1965), 78 *Harvard Law Review* 993).

Early exceptions to this rule were developed in the area of public nuisance, which, while considered a common law crime, could in some instances be said to interfere with property. Perhaps also, because of a tempting similarity of terminology with private nuisance, the Chancery felt free to extend its jurisdiction to public nuisance. As Prosser has said of nuisance, "[f]ew terms have afforded so excellent an illustration of the familiar tendency of the courts to seize upon a catchword as a substitute for any analysis of a problem" (*The Law of Torts*, 5th ed. (St. Paul, MN: West Pub. Co., 1984), at 616-17).

Notwithstanding these early extensions, the traditional reluctance to enjoin crime remained strong. So, for example, in *Robinson v. Adams* (1924), 56 OLR 217 (CA), the Ontario Court of Appeal refused to grant an injunction to restrain picketing that the plaintiff argued amounted to the crime of watching and besetting. Middleton JA stated (at 224):

> The equitable jurisdiction of a civil court cannot properly be invoked to suppress crime. Unlawful acts which are an offence against the public, and so fall within the criminal law, may also be the foundation of an action based upon the civil wrong done to an individual, but when Parliament has, in the public interest, forbidden certain acts, and made them an offence against the law of the land, then, unless a right of property is affected, the civil courts should not attempt to interfere and forbid by injunction that which has already been forbidden by Parliament itself. Much less should the courts interfere when the thing complained of is not within the terms of the criminal law, although it may be rightly regarded as objectionable or even immoral, for then the civil

courts by injunction are attempting to enlarge and amend the criminal law. Government by injunction is a thing abhorrent to the law of England and of this Province.

The following materials illustrate that in recent years the courts have liberalized their approach to the "criminal injunction." However, the concerns expressed in *Robinson* remain important factors taken into account in the choice of remedy. It remains important to consider the suitability of the civil process as an instrument for the enforcement of "public rights."

There are two main issues when the court is asked to grant an injunction to protect public rights: who should have standing to obtain such an order and in what circumstances should the order be made? The first question goes to the jurisdiction and discretion of the Attorney General (and of individuals) to enforce the law; the second question goes to the jurisdiction and discretion of the courts to award injunctions. The following case addresses both of these issues. We then examine in more depth the issue of the courts' jurisdiction and discretion and finally return to the issue of individual standing.

Gouriet v. Union of Post Office Workers
[1978] AC 435 (HL (Eng.))

LORD WILBERFORCE: My Lords, these appeals relate to certain orders made by the Court of Appeal in January 1977. The Attorney-General, Mr. J.P. Gouriet, and the two Post Office unions are each appealing against portions of these orders. It is difficult to summarise at all accurately the exact issues at stake because the record is in a state of procedural confusion due to improvisations and changes of direction by the court and the parties. But, briefly, the issues which have emerged for decision by this House are:

1. Whether, in spite of the refusal of the Attorney-General to consent to the use of his name in relator proceedings, Mr. Gouriet, as a private citizen, was entitled to come to the court and ask for an injunction against the Post Office unions from soliciting interference with the mail to or with communications with the Republic of South Africa, and/or for a declaration that it would be unlawful for the unions to take such action.

2. Whether Mr. Gouriet's claim against the Post Office unions to such injunctions or declarations is maintainable or ought to be struck out.

The present proceedings are interlocutory only, so that Mr. Gouriet should be allowed to go on with his action unless it is manifestly ill-founded in law.

The facts are that Mr. Gouriet who, though supported by an association, appears simply as a citizen, on January 13, 1977, discovered that the executive of the Union of Post Office Workers (UPW) had resolved to call on its members not to handle mail from this country to South Africa during the week starting at midnight, Sunday, January 16. The general secretary of the UPW, Mr. Tom Jackson, appeared on television that evening (13th) and said that the legality of such action had never been tested in the courts: the relevant laws dated from Queen Anne and were more appropriate for dealing with highwaymen and footpads. On January 14 "The Times" reported the passing of the UPW resolution and also reported that the Post Office Engineering Union (POEU) had said that they would instruct their members not to provide or maintain circuits to South Africa except in a matter of "life and death."

On January 14 (Friday) Mr. Gouriet applied to H.M. Attorney-General for consent to an action in the name of the Attorney-General at the relation of Mr. Gouriet against the UPW for an injunction against soliciting or procuring any person wilfully to delay any postal package in the course of transmission between this country and South Africa. The Attorney-General refused his consent to this application in the following terms:

> Having considered all the circumstances including the public interest relating to the application for my consent ... I have come to the conclusion that in relation to this application I should not give my consent.

Mr. Gouriet thereupon issued a writ in his own name against the UPW and immediately applied for an interim injunction against it in the terms mentioned above. This application was supported by an affidavit deposing to the facts as I have stated them. After a hearing, Stocker J dismissed the application on the ground that he had no power to make the order requested. I have no doubt that on the authorities he was perfectly correct in so doing. Mr. Gouriet appealed to the Court of Appeal which sat specially to hear the appeal on January 15 (Saturday). In the course of the argument the court expressed itself critically of the decision of the Attorney-General. Ultimately, the Court of Appeal allowed the appeal and granted an interim injunction as asked until Tuesday, January 18. Then they gave the plaintiff leave to join the POEU as a party and granted an injunction against that union. This followed the wording of the *Telegraph Act 1863*, section 45, set out below. Thirdly, leave was given to add the Attorney-General as a defendant. The plaintiff did this and, following indications which had been given in the argument, claimed against the Attorney-General a declaration that in refusing his consent to the plaintiff to bring relator proceedings the Attorney-General acted improperly and wrongfully exercised his discretion—I refer to this as declaration X.

On the resumed hearing on January 18, the Attorney-General appeared and contested the court's right to review the exercise of his discretion. After substantial argument, the plaintiff conceded that he was not entitled to declaration X. The Court of Appeal reserved judgment on the matters before it until January 27. On that day judgments were given in which:

1. By a majority (Lawton LJ and Ormrod LJ) it was held that the court had no power to review the decision of the Attorney-General in refusing consent to relator proceedings. Lord Denning MR held that the court had this power to review at least indirectly.

2. By a majority (as above) it was held that, consent having been refused to bring relator proceedings, the plaintiff was not entitled to permanent injunction in the terms previously mentioned. Lord Denning MR dissented.

3. All three members of the court held that the plaintiff could claim declarations in the form mentioned and that, pending a decision on this claim, the court could grant interim injunctions as sought. However, in fact, the court discharged the injunctions as being no longer necessary. The plaintiff had not, at this stage, asked for declarations, but the Court of Appeal gave leave for him to (re)amend his claim so as to do so. This he did. He also amended his claim against the Attorney-General so as to seek a declaration that notwithstanding his refusal to allow relator proceedings, the plaintiff is entitled to proceed with his claim against the unions for declarations and interim relief. The unions and the Attorney-General were then treated as having

applied to the court to strike out all the plaintiff's claims and such putative applications were dismissed. Leave to appeal to this House was then granted.

This narrative shows that the proceedings involved a high degree of improvisation, even of fiction. But this must not obscure the important real issues which underlie these hurried proceedings. These the parties to this appeal have fully and frankly argued, and our main task is to decide them. I shall make such observations as are necessary on the procedure at a later stage.

It is, first, convenient to set out the statutory provisions relevant to the workings of Post Office services. These are:

(i) *Post Office Act 1953*, section 58(1):

If any officer of the Post Office, contrary to his duty … wilfully detains or delays, or procures or suffers to be detained or delayed, any … postal packet [in course of transmission by post], he shall be guilty of a misdemeanour and be liable to imprisonment [for a term not exceeding two years] or to a fine, or to both: …

(ii) Section 68:

If any person solicits or endeavours to procure any other person to commit an offence punishable on indictment under this Act, he shall be guilty of a misdemeanour and be liable to imprisonment for a term not exceeding two years.

(iii) *Telegraph Act 1863*, section 45:

If any person in the employment of the [Post Office]—wilfully or negligently omits or delays to transmit or deliver any message; or by any wilful or negligent act or omission prevents or delays the transmission or delivery of any message; … he shall for every such offence be liable to a penalty not exceeding £20. …

When Parliament decides to prohibit certain conduct (e.g. delaying the mail) it enacts legislation defining the prohibited act (*e.g. Post Office Act 1953*, sections 58, 68). To violation or disregard of the prohibition it attaches a sanction—prosecution as for a misdemeanour with a possible sentence of two years' imprisonment. Enforcement of the law means that any person who commits the relevant offence is prosecuted. So it is the duty either of the Post Office itself, or of the Director of Public Prosecutions or of the Attorney-General, to take steps to enforce the law in this way. Failure to do so, without good cause, is a breach of their duty (for a recent formulation of this duty see the statement of Sir Hartley Shawcross A-G (1951) in J.L.J. Edwards, *The Law Officers of the Crown* (London: Sweet & Maxwell, 1964) at p. 223). The individual, in such situations, who wishes to see the law enforced has a remedy of his own: he can bring a private prosecution. This historical right which goes right back to the earliest days of our legal system, though rarely exercised in relation to indictable offences, and though ultimately liable to be controlled by the Attorney-General (by taking over the prosecution and, if he thinks fit, entering a *nolle prosequi*) remains a valuable constitutional safeguard against inertia or partiality on the part of authority. This is the true enforcement process and it must be clear that an assertion of a right to invoke it is of no help to Mr. Gouriet here. His case is not based on the committal of offence plus a refusal to prosecute, it is based on a right to take preventive action in a civil court which could have been taken but was not taken by the Attorney-General in relator proceedings. This involves consideration of the "relator action" and of the Attorney-General's part in it.

A relator action—a type of action which has existed from the earliest times—is one in which the Attorney-General, on the relation of individuals (who may include local authorities or companies) brings an action to assert a public right. It can properly be said to be a fundamental principle of English law that private rights can be asserted by individuals, but that public rights can only be asserted by the Attorney-General as representing the public. In terms of constitutional law, the rights of the public are vested in the Crown, and the Attorney-General enforces them as an officer of the Crown. And just as the Attorney-General has in general no power to interfere with the assertion of private rights, so in general no private person has the right of representing the public in the assertion of public rights. If he tries to do so his action can be struck out. ...

Lord Denning MR, in his judgment, invoked two cases from overseas, *Thorson v. Attorney-General of Canada (No. 2)*, [1975] 1 SCR 138 and *Flast v. Cohen* (1968), 392 US 83. The first of these recognises the English law on enforcement of public rights, but distinguishes it where constitutionality of legislation is involved. The second turns wholly upon the position under the US Constitution and has no discussion of English authorities. These are unimpressive support.

In contrast with these inconclusive passages I will cite one of many in which the contrary has been affirmed. In the *Stockport District Waterworks Co. v. Manchester Corporation* (1862), 9 Jur. NS 266 (CA Ch.) Lord Westbury L said at p. 267:

> [T]hose are a few of the reasons which might be assigned, showing how desirable it is not to allow any private individual to usurp the right of representing the public interest. The only arguments which I am disposed to accept from those which I have heard today, are arguments founded upon the public interest, and the general advantage of restraining an incorporated company within its proper sphere of action. But, in the present case, the transgression of those limits inflicts no private wrong upon these plaintiffs; and although the plaintiffs, in common with the rest of the public, might be interested in the larger view of the question, yet the constitution of the country has wisely intrusted the privilege with a public officer, and has not allowed it to be usurped by a private individual.

That it is the exclusive right of the Attorney-General to represent the public interest—even where individuals might be interested in a larger view of the matter—is not technical, not procedural, not fictional. It is constitutional. I agree with Lord Westbury L that it is also wise.

From this general consideration of the nature of relator actions, I pass to the special type of relator action with which this appeal is concerned. It is of very special character, and it is one in which the predominant position of the Attorney-General is *a fortiori* the general case.

This is a right, of comparatively modern use, of the Attorney-General to invoke the assistance of *civil courts* in aid of the *criminal law*. It is an exceptional power confined, in practice, to cases where an offence is frequently repeated in disregard of a, usually, inadequate penalty—see *Attorney-General v. Harris*, [1961] 1 QB 74 (CA); or to cases of emergency—see *Attorney-General v. Chaudry*, [1971] 1 WLR 1614 (CA). It is one not without its difficulties and these may call for consideration in the future.

If Parliament has imposed a sanction (e.g. a fine of £1), without an increase in severity for repeated offences, it may seem wrong that the courts—civil courts—should think fit, by granting injunctions, breaches of which may attract unlimited sanctions, including imprisonment, to do what Parliament has not done. Moreover, where Parliament has (as here in the *Post Office Act 1953*) provided for trial of offences by indictment before a jury, it may seem wrong that the courts, applying a civil standard of proof, should in effect convict a subject without the prescribed trial. What would happen if, after punishment for contempt, the same man were to be prosecuted in a criminal court? That Lord Eldon L was much oppressed by these difficulties is shown by the discussions in *Attorney-General v. Cleaver* (1811), 18 Ves. Jun. 211; 34 ER 297 (Ch.).

These and other examples which can be given show that this jurisdiction—though proved useful on occasions—is one of great delicacy and is one to be used with caution. Further, to apply to the court for an injunction at all against the threat of a criminal offence, may involve a decision of policy with which conflicting considerations may enter. Will the law best be served by preventive action? Will the grant of an injunction exacerbate the situation? (Very relevant this in industrial disputes.) Is the injunction likely to be effective or may it be futile? Will it be better to make it clear that the law will be enforced by prosecution and to appeal to the law-abiding instinct, negotiations, and moderate leadership, rather than provoke people along the road to martyrdom? All these matters—to which Devlin J justly drew attention in *Attorney-General v. Bastow*, [1957] 1 QB 514 at p. 519, and the exceptional nature of this *civil* remedy, point the matter as one essentially for the Attorney-General's preliminary discretion. Every known case, so far, has been so dealt with: in no case hitherto has it ever been suggested than an individual can act, though relator actions for public nuisance which may also involve a criminal offence, have been known for 200 years.

There are two arguments put forward for permitting individual citizens to take this action.

The first points to the private prosecution. All citizens have sufficient interest in the enforcement of the law to entitle them to take this step. Why then should this same interest not be sufficient to support preventive action by way of injunction—subject it may be, to ultimate control by the Attorney-General? At one time I was attracted by this argument. But I have reached the conclusion that I cannot accept it.

The Attorney-General's right to seek, in the civil courts, anticipatory prevention of a breach of the law, is a part or aspect of his general power to enforce, in the public interest, public rights. The distinction between public rights, which the Attorney-General can and the individual (absent special interest) cannot seek to enforce, and private rights, is fundamental in our law. To break it, as the plaintiff's counsel frankly invited us to do, is not a development of the law, but a destruction of one of its pillars. Nor, in my opinion, at least in this particular field, would removal of the distinction be desirable. More than in any other field of public rights, the decision to be taken before embarking on a claim for injunctive relief, involving as it does the interests of the public over a broad horizon, is a decision which the Attorney-General alone is suited to make: see *Attorney-General v. Bastow*, [1957] 1 QB 514.

This brings me to the *second* argument. Surely, it is said, since the whole matter is discretionary it can be left to the court. The court can prevent vexations or frivolous, or multiple actions: the court is not obliged to grant an injunction: leave it in the court's hands. I cannot accept this either. The decisions to be made as to the public interest are not such as courts are fitted or equipped to make. The very fact, that, as the present case very well shows, decisions are of the type to attract political criticism and controversy, shows that they are outside the range of discretionary problems which the courts can resolve. Judges are equipped to find legal rights and administer, on well-known principles, discretionary remedies. These matters are widely outside those areas. ...

VISCOUNT DILHORNE: The Attorney-General has many powers and duties. He may stop any prosecution on indictment by entering a *nolle prosequi*. He merely has to sign a piece of paper saying that he does not wish the prosecution to continue. He need not give any reasons. He can direct the institution of a prosecution and direct the Director of Public Prosecutions to take over the conduct of any criminal proceedings and he may tell him to offer no evidence. In the exercise of these powers he is not subject to direction by his ministerial colleagues or to control and supervision by the courts. ...

In deciding whether or not to prosecute "there is only one consideration which is altogether excluded," Sir Hartley Shawcross said, "and that is the repercussion of a given decision upon my personal or my party's or the Government's political fortunes." (See Edwards at pp. 222-23.) In the discharge of any of the duties to which I have referred, it is, of course, always possible that an Attorney-General may act for reasons of this kind and may abuse his powers. One does not know the reasons for the Attorney-General's refusal in this case but it should not be inferred from his refusal to disclose them that he acted wrongly. For all one knows he may have attached considerable importance to the fact that the injunction sought did no more than repeat the language of the sections of the *Post Office Act 1953*. On the Friday he may indeed have thought that to start proceedings so speedily for an injunction which did no more than that was not likely to serve any useful purpose and might indeed exacerbate the situation. Instances of applications by Attorneys-General to the civil courts for aid in enforcing the criminal law are few in number and exceptional in character. In the Court of Appeal a number of observations were made as to the inability of the courts to "enforce the law" if the Attorney-General refused his consent to an application for such an injunction. A breach of the law was impending according to Lord Denning MR "Are the courts to stand idly by?" was the question he posed on the Saturday. On January 27 he said, [1977] QB 729 (CA) at p. 761:

> If he (the Attorney-General) does not act himself—or refuses to give his consent to his name being used—then the law will not be enforced. If one Attorney-General after another does this, if each in his turn declines to take action against those who break the law—then the law becomes a dead letter.

With great respect the criminal law does not become a dead letter if proceedings for injunctions to restrain the commission of offences or for declarations that certain conduct is unlawful are not brought. The criminal law is enforced in the criminal courts by the conviction and punishment of offenders, not in the civil courts. The jurisdiction of the civil courts is mainly as to the determination of disputes and claims. They are not charged with responsibility for the administration of the criminal courts. The question "Are the courts to stand idly by?" might be supposed by some to suggest that the civil courts have some executive authority in relation to the criminal law. The line between the functions of the executive and the judiciary should not be blurred.

There are a number of statutory offences for the prosecution of which the consent of the Attorney-General or of the Director of Public Prosecutions is required but apart from these offences, anyone can if he wishes start a prosecution without obtaining anyone's consent. The enforcement of the criminal law does not rest with the civil courts or depend on the Attorney-General alone.

The enactment by Parliament defining and creating a criminal offence amounts to an injunction by Parliament restraining the commission of the acts made criminal. If the injunction in the Act is not obeyed—and in these days it frequently is not—the statute normally states the maximum punishment that can be awarded on conviction. If in addition to the enactment, an injunction is granted in the civil courts to restrain persons from doing the acts already made criminal by Parliament, an injunction which does no more than embody the language of the statute, has that any greater potency than the injunction by Parliament contained in the Act? An injunction in the terms sought when the application in this case was made to the Attorney-General does not appear to me to be one that can with any accuracy of language be regarded as "enforcing the law." Repetition is not enforcement. The granting of such an injunction merely imposes a liability to fine or imprisonment for contempt additional to the maximum Parliament has thought fit to prescribe on conviction for the same conduct.

Great difficulties may arise if "enforcement" of the criminal law by injunction became a regular practice. A person charged, for instance, with an offence under section 58 or 68 of the *Post Office Act 1953* has the right of trial by jury. If, before he commits the offence, an injunction is granted restraining him from committing an offence under those sections and he is brought before the civil courts for contempt, his guilt will be decided not by a jury but by a judge or judges. If he is subsequently tried for the criminal offence, might not the finding of guilt by a judge or judges prejudice his trial? This question is not to my mind satisfactorily answered by saying that juries can be told to ignore certain matters. It was suggested that this difficulty might be overcome by adjourning the proceedings for contempt until after the conclusion of the criminal trial. If that was done, the question might arise then as to the propriety of imposing a punishment in the contempt proceedings additional to that imposed on conviction for the same conduct in the criminal court.

Such considerations may have been present to the mind of the Attorney-General when he considered Mr. Gouriet's application on the Friday and may have provided valid grounds for his refusal of consent. Whether they did so or not, one does not know but I have mentioned them as they seem to me to suffice to show that even if good legal reasons for his decision were not immediately apparent, the inference that he abused or misused his powers is not one that should be drawn.

An Attorney-General is not subject to restrictions as to the applications he makes, either ex officio or in relator actions, to the courts. In every case it will be for the court to decide whether it has jurisdiction to grant the application and whether in the exercise of its discretion it should do so. It has been and in my opinion should continue to be exceptional for the aid of the civil courts to be invoked in support of the criminal law and no wise Attorney-General will make such an application or agree to one being made in his name unless it appears to him that the case is exceptional.

One category of cases in which the Attorney-General has successfully sought an injunction to restrain the commission of criminal acts is where the penalties imposed for the offence have proved wholly inadequate to deter its commission: see *Attorney-General v. Sharp*, [1931] 1 Ch. 121 (CA); *Attorney-General v. Premier Line Ltd.*, [1932] 1 Ch. 303; *Attorney-General v. Bastow*, [1957] 1 QB 514 and *Attorney-General v. Harris*, [1961] 1 QB 74 (CA) where the defendant had been convicted on no less than 142 occasions of breaches of the *Manchester Police Regulation Act 1844*.

In *Attorney-General v. Chaudry*, [1971] 1 WLR 1614 (CA) an injunction was granted at the instance of the Attorney-General in a relator action to restrain the defendant from using a building as a hotel without a certificate under the *London Building Acts*. There was a serious fire risk and it was not possible to secure the early hearing of a summons charging the defendant with a criminal offence in so using the building without a certificate. In those circumstances an interlocutory injunction was granted prohibiting the use of the building as a hotel until the necessary certificate was granted.

I do not wish to suggest that the cases to which I have referred are the only types of cases in which the civil courts can and should come to the aid of the criminal law by granting injunctions at the instance of the Attorney-General but they, I think, serve to show that the exercise of that jurisdiction at the instance of the Attorney-General is exceptional.

It was also urged that if, as is undoubtedly the case, any person can start a prosecution for a criminal offence without, save in those cases where the consent of the Attorney-General or the Director of Public Prosecutions is required by statute, the consent of anyone, why should not any member of the public be entitled to apply to the civil courts for an injunction in an endeavour to prevent the commission of an offence? Why when the Attorney-General is not the only person who can start a prosecution, should he be the only person who can apply for such an injunction?

The reply to this made on behalf of the Attorney-General and the unions was that Mr. Gouriet was not qualified to act on behalf of the public to prevent injury to public rights and the courts had not jurisdiction to entertain his claim.

Mr. Gouriet does not as I have said assert a private right of any kind. He does not claim that he would have suffered any loss or damage by reason of the interruption of postal services to and from South Africa. If he had suffered any such loss or damage, he would have no cause of action against the Post Office or in tort against the unions and their members: see the *Post Office Act 1969*, sections 9(4) and 29(1).

It is not necessary therefore to consider the long line of cases dealing with the rights of individuals to secure injunctions and declarations when their private rights are threatened though it is not without interest to note that in *Springhead Spinning Co. v. Riley* (1868), LR 6 Eq. 551 it was held that an injunction could be granted at the instance of a person to prevent the commission of a crime if, but only if, that person would be damaged thereby. In that case Malins V-C said, at p. 558:

> [I]f these acts amount to the commission of a crime only, it is clear that this court has no jurisdiction to restrain them. In the celebrated case of *Gee v. Pritchard* (1818), 2 Sw. 402 at p. 413, 36 ER 670 at p. 674 (Ch.) the object of which was to restrain the publication of letters written by the plaintiff to the defendant, Lord Eldon says "The publication of a libel is a crime, and I have no jurisdiction to prevent the commission of crimes, excepting, of course, such cases as belong to the protection of infants where a dealing with an infant may amount to a crime—an exception arising from the peculiar jurisdiction of this court." ... The jurisdiction of this court

is to protect property, and it will interfere by injunction to stay any proceedings, whether connected with crime or not, which go to the immediate, or tend to the ultimate, destruction of property, or to make it less valuable or comfortable for use or occupation. ...

In *Cutler v. Wandsworth Stadium Ltd.*, [1949] AC 398 (HL (Eng.)) Lord Simonds, referring to the *Betting and Lotteries Act 1934*, observed, at p. 408:

> [T]he sanction of criminal proceedings emphasises that this statutory obligation, like many others which the Act contains, is imposed for the public benefit and that the breach of it is a public not a private wrong.

So here in my opinion the sanction of criminal proceedings in sections 58 and 68 of the *Post Office Act 1953* and in section 45 of the *Telegraph Act 1863* was imposed for the public benefit and breach of them is a public and not a private wrong. ...

The conclusion to which I have come in the light of the many authorities to which we were referred is that it is the law, and long established law, that save and in so far as the *Local Government Act 1972*, section 222, gives local authorities a limited power so to do, only the Attorney-General can sue on behalf of the public for the purpose of preventing public wrongs and that a private individual cannot do so on behalf of the public though he may be able to do so if he will sustain injury as a result of a public wrong. In my opinion the cases establish that the courts have no jurisdiction to entertain such claims by a private individual who has not suffered and will not suffer damage.

If these conclusions are right, then when the Attorney-General gives his consent to a relator action, he is enabling an action to be brought which an individual alone could not bring. When he refuses his consent, he is not denying the right of any individual and barring his access to the courts for the courts have no jurisdiction to entertain a claim by an individual whose only interest is as a member of the public in relation to a public right. Consequently, any suggestion that his refusal constitutes a challenge to the rule of law appears to me to be entirely misconceived, and though views may differ as to where the balance of public interest lies, it should not be lightly assumed that his refusal of consent in a particular case was unjustified and not grounded on considerations of public interest. ...

In conclusion, as I see it, we were asked not just to extend the existing law but to override a mass of authority and to say that long established law should no longer prevail. That is a question for the legislature to consider and in the light of what I have said about the exceptional character of requests by the Attorney-General to the civil courts to come to the aid of the criminal law and of the occasions when that has been given, I must confess to considerable doubt whether it would be in the public interest that private individuals such as Mr. Gouriet should be enabled to make such applications in cases where such interest as they have is in common with all other members of the public and when the object is the enforcement of public rights.

For these reasons in my opinion the appeals of the Attorney-General and the unions should be allowed and that of Mr. Gouriet dismissed. His claim should be struck out and, the Attorney-General not seeking costs in this House, Mr. Gouriet should pay the unions' costs here in addition to the costs in the courts below which were ordered to be costs in cause.

LORD DIPLOCK: My Lords, at the heart of the issues in these appeals lies the difference between private law and public law. It is the failure to recognise this distinction that has in my view led to some confusion and an unaccustomed degree of rhetoric in this case. …

The ordinary way of enforcing criminal law is by punishing the offender after he has acted in breach of it. Commission of the crime precedes the invocation of the aid of a court of criminal jurisdiction by a prosecutor. The functions of the court whose aid is then invoked are restricted to (1) determining (by verdict of a jury in indictable cases) whether the accused is guilty of the offence that he is charged with having committed and, (2) if he is found guilty, decreeing what punishment may be inflicted on him by the executive authority. In English public law every citizen still has the right, as he once had a duty (though of imperfect obligation), to invoke the aid of courts of criminal jurisdiction for the enforcement of the criminal law by this procedure. It is a right which nowadays seldom needs to be exercised by an ordinary member of the public, for since the formation of regular police forces charged with the duty in public law to prevent and detect crime and to bring criminals to justice, and the creation in 1879 of the office of Director of Public Prosecutions, the need for prosecutions to be undertaken (and paid for) by private individuals has largely disappeared; but it still exists and is a useful constitutional safeguard against capricious, corrupt or biased failure or refusal of those authorities to prosecute offenders against the criminal law.

Mr. Gouriet could have initiated a private prosecution against the UPW; but he would have had to wait until an offence under section 68 of the *Post Office Act 1953* had been committed; and it is doubtful whether that could be proved until the officials of the union had acted on the resolution by actually sending out to its members instructions to "black" all South African mail.

So much for the ordinary way of enforcing the criminal law. There are, however, two procedures by which the aid of a court of justice may be anticipatively invoked before any crime, even inchoate, has actually been committed. Both these procedures are exceptional and in some respects anomalous. Of the first, the power of a magistrate to bind over a person to be of good behaviour, I need say very little. It has its origin in the *Justice of the Peace Act 1361* when the distinction between the executive and the judicial functions of these dignitaries was still blurred. The power was extended to all courts of criminal jurisdiction by the *Administration of Justice Act 1969*, but it is debatable whether it should properly be classified as appertaining to criminal or to public law.

The second exceptional procedure is that which has given rise to these appeals: the application to a court of civil jurisdiction for an injunction to restrain a potential offender from doing something in the future which although if done it would give the applicant no right to redress in private law, would nevertheless be a criminal offence.

My Lords, there is ample authority already cited by Lord Wilberforce that this procedure is undoubtedly available if applied for by the Attorney-General either *ex officio* or *ex relatione*; but it is no less anomalous than that of binding over to be of good behaviour a person who has not been proved to have committed any offence. It is in my view appropriate to be used only in the most exceptional of cases. It is not accurate to describe it as preventive justice. It is a deterrent and punitive procedure; but this is characteristic too of the enforcement of criminal law through the ordinary courts of criminal jurisdiction. The very creation by Parliament of a statutory offence constitutes a warning to potential offenders that if they are found guilty by a court of criminal jurisdiction of the conduct that is proscribed, they will be liable to suffer punishment up to a maximum authorised by the statute. When a court of civil jurisdiction grants an injunction restraining a potential offender from committing what is a crime but not a wrong for which there is redress in private law, this in effect is warning him that he will be in double jeopardy, for if he is found guilty by the civil court of committing the crime he will be liable to suffer punishment of whatever severity that court may think appropriate, whether or not it exceeds the maximum penalty authorised by the statute and notwithstanding that he will also be liable to be punished again for the same crime if found guilty of it by a court of criminal jurisdiction. Where the crime that is the subject matter of the injunction is triable on indictment the anomalies involved in the use of this exceptional procedure are enhanced. The accused has the constitutional right to be tried by jury and his guilt established by reference to the criminal standard of proof. If he is proceeded against for contempt of court he is deprived of these advantages.

I mention these matters, obvious though they may be, for two reasons. First, in justice to the Attorney-General against whom it has been hinted that there could be no reasons that were not partizan for his refusal to authorise the bringing of a relator action against the UPW when asked to do so by Mr. Gouriet on January 14. The matters I have referred to are juristic considerations proper to be taken into account, no doubt with others of a less juristic character, in determining whether the public interest was likely to be best served by resorting to this exceptional and anomalous procedure for the enforcement of the criminal law.

The second reason why they are important is that they are relevant to the distinction between an injunction in restraint of crime *simpliciter* and an injunction to restrain conduct which, although amounting to a crime, would also infringe some right belonging to the plaintiff who is applying for the injunction, which is enforceable by him in private law. The supercession of private revenge for wrongs by remedies obtainable from courts of justice and enforceable by the executive authority of the state lies in the common origin both of the criminal law and of the civil private law of tort. So from the outset there have been many crimes which at common law were private wrongs to the person who suffered particular damage from them as well as public wrongs; and the policy of the law has been not to deprive the victim of a private wrong of his redress in civil private law against the wrongdoer merely because the wrongdoer is subject also to punitive sanctions under the criminal law for the same conduct; although until the recent abolition of the distinction between felonies and misdemeanours if the facts relied upon by the plaintiff as constituting a private wrong amounted also to the graver crime, a felony, the plaintiff was barred from proceeding with his civil remedy until after the wrongdoer had been prosecuted in a criminal court.

In modern statutes whose object is to protect the health or welfare of a section of the public by prohibiting conduct of a particular kind, it is not infrequently the case that the prohibited conduct is made both a criminal offence and a civil wrong for which a remedy in private law is available to any individual member of that section of the public who has suffered damage as a result of it. So it creates a private right to be protected from loss or damage caused by the prohibited conduct.

For the protection of the private right created by such a statute a court of civil jurisdiction has jurisdiction to grant to the person entitled to the private right, *but to none other*, an injunction to restrain a threatened breach of it by the defendant. Upon the application for the injunction the issues are neither technically nor actually the same as they would be upon a subsequent prosecution for the criminal offence once the threat had been translated into action. They would still not be technically the same upon the application to the civil court to commit the defendant for contempt of court for breach of the injunction; though proof of commission of an offence would be a necessary step in the proof of the contempt where the only civil wrong involved was conduct prohibited by the penal provisions of the statute. This is a consideration that it would be proper for the court to bear in mind in exercising its discretion whether or not to grant an injunction in this type of case; but however sparingly it should be exercised, where the court is satisfied that *grave and irreparable harm would otherwise be done to the plaintiff's private rights for which damages could not provide adequate compensation,* it has undoubted jurisdiction to grant one.

The words italicised in the last paragraph are important words for they draw attention to the fact that the jurisdiction of a civil court to grant remedies in private law is confined to the grant of remedies to litigants whose rights in private law have been infringed or are threatened with infringement. To extend that jurisdiction to the grant of remedies for unlawful conduct which does not infringe any rights of the plaintiff in private law, is to move out of the field of private into that of public law with which analogies may be deceptive and where different principles apply.

There is nothing that I desire to add to what my noble and learned friends Lord Wilberforce and Viscount Dilhorne have already said about the exclusive right of the Attorney-General to represent the public interest in litigation, or about the development of the practice of his seeking *ex officio* or *ex relatione* a civil remedy by injunction against unlawful conduct that would cause public harm. I do desire, however, to comment briefly upon the exercise of the jurisdiction to grant a remedy by injunction on the application of the Attorney-General in cases where what makes conduct sought to be restrained unlawful as well as harmful is because it constitutes a criminal offence. Resort to this jurisdiction is of respectable antiquity. It was first used in cases of public nuisance as a more effective and expeditious remedy than was provided by indictment or criminal information. Nevertheless the extension of its use to statutory offences is modern, and has hitherto been confined by the consistent practice of successive Attorneys-General to statutes whose objects are to promote the health, the safety or the welfare of the public and to particular cases under such statutes either where the prescribed penalty for the summary offences has proved to be insufficient to deter the offender from numerous repetitions of the offence, as in *Attorney-General v. Sharp*, [1931] 1 Ch. 121; *Attorney-General v. Premier Line Ltd.*, [1932] 1 Ch. 303 and *Attorney-General v. Harris*, [1961] 1 QB 74 (CA); or where the defendant's disobedience to the statutory prohibition may cause grave and irreparable harm, as in *Attorney-General v. Chaudry*, [1971] 1 WLR 1614 (CA). The use of this procedure for the reasons I have already given ought not in my view to be extended beyond those limits. ...

LORD EDMUND-DAVIES: I have to say that none of the grounds advanced on behalf of the Attorney-General and trade unions have satisfied me that in the circumstances predicated it must necessarily be in the public interest to deny such a claim by a private citizen. For example, it was urged that any change in the present law would open what were called the "floodgates" to a multiplicity of claims by busybodies. But it is difficult to see why such people should be more numerous or active than private prosecutors are at the present day, and they are few and far between, though this fact may be attributable in part to the power of the Attorney-General to enter a "*nolle prosequi*" in any criminal case or to order the Director of Public Prosecutions to take it over and then to offer no evidence. It was also urged that the granting of an injunction could prejudice the subsequent jury trial of the wrongdoer, turning as it would upon a different standard of proof than that applied in the civil proceedings, and that great complications could arise if (an injunction having been granted, the breach of which could lead to a committal for contempt and might, indeed, already have done so) the defendant was later tried and acquitted of the criminal charge. But exactly the same observations can be made at the present time in, for example, cases of public nuisances (which are crimes), in relation to which the Attorney-General not infrequently seeks and secures injunctions. And it would always be open to the Attorney-General himself to intervene and make representations in civil proceedings brought by a private individual if he considered that the public interest required him to do so.

Be that as it may, there is nevertheless a massive body of law supporting the proposition that only the Attorney-General can seek and obtain injunctive relief in relation to criminal acts, whether threatened or committed, which do not also involve the invasion of private rights of person or property, though it is clearly desirable that he should take extreme care before deciding to exercise it. ...

The law being perfectly clear, does the public interest require that it be changed? All three members of the Court of Appeal sternly condemned the Attorney-General's conduct. He had acted "contrary to the whole spirit of the law of England," and, by refusing to explain his refusal, he had made "a direct challenge to the rule of law." So said Lord Denning MR, [1977] QB 729 (CA) at pp. 753A and 758G, quoting Baggallay LJ, who had said in *Attorney-General v. Great Eastern Railway Co.* (1879), 11 Ch. D 449 (CA) at p. 500, that:

> It is the interest of the public that the law should in all respects be respected and observed, and if the law is transgressed or threatened to be transgressed ... it is the duty of the Attorney-General to take the necessary steps to enforce it, nor does it make any difference whether he sues ex officio, or at the instance of relators.

But it is *not* the law that every criminal act must lead to a prosecution (*Buckoke v. Greater London Council*, [1971] Ch. 655 (CA), *per* Lord Denning MR, at p. 668D-H) and, even if it were, the Attorney-General is unquestionably entitled to halt prosecutions in the manner already indicated. In other words, it is ultimately a matter for his unfettered discretion. The Court of Appeal regarded the manner of its exercise in the present case as so inexplicable that, in the words of Lawton LJ, at p. 739:

> ... [U]ntil such times as there is some explanation as to why the Attorney-General did not intervene, then on the face of it his failure to do so must have been for some reason which was not a good reason in law.

And yet lip-service was paid to the proposition that the Attorney-General's exercise of his discretion cannot be reviewed by the courts. For my part, I venture to reiterate by way of a contrast the striking fact that my noble and learned friend, Viscount Dilhorne, has expressed the affirmative view that the Attorney-General may well have acted in the public interest in withholding his consent. This highlights the undesirability of making the matter one of disputation in the courts, instead of in Parliament.

NOTES AND QUESTIONS

1. Are the concerns expressed by the House of Lords with respect to injunctions relevant only when an individual is seeking to enforce a statute or are they also applicable when the applicant is the attorney general?

2. Are the courts really incapable of exercising their discretion to deny relief to individuals when the public interest would not be served? What remedies are available to individuals if the attorney general refuses unreasonably to enforce the criminal law? On the issue of private prosecutions and the ability of the attorney general to intervene and stay the actions, see B. Tingle, "The Strange Case of the Crown Prerogative Over Private Prosecutions or Who Killed Public Interest Law Enforcement?" (1994), 28 *University of British Columbia Law Review* 309.

3. What is the distinction between "public" and "private" rights? Does this distinction determine when individuals may have standing, or do the rules about standing determine this distinction?

4. Would this case have been differently decided if Gouriet had asserted a "private interest" in the subject matter of the dispute (for example, if he was a frequent user of the mail service to South Africa, or if his business depended upon that service)?

5. Does the threat of a contempt conviction for violation of an injunction to enforce the criminal law really increase the penalties for the offence or raise the problem of double jeopardy? Section 11(h) of the *Canadian Charter of Rights and Freedoms* provides that individuals have the right "if finally acquitted of the offence, not to be tried for it again and, if finally found guilty and punished for the offence, not to be tried or punished for it again."

6. For a detailed comment on *Gouriet*, see D. Feldman, "Injunctions and the Criminal Law" (1979), 42 *Modern Law Review* 369.

7. How might *Gouriet* fare in Canada after *Finlay v. Minister of Finance (Canada)*, [1986] 2 SCR 607 and its recognition of public interest standing in administrative law cases? Other recent cases on standing in public interest litigation include *Canadian Council of Churches v. Canada*, [1992] 1 SCR 236 and *Coalition of Citizens for a Charter Challenge v. Metropolitan Authority* (1993), 103 DLR (4th) 409 (NS SC), rev'd. (1993), 125 NSR (2d) 241 (CA). These cases have sounded a somewhat more cautious note, expressing the need for courts to take into account scarce judicial resources and for the matter to raise a serious and justiciable issue. In the latter case the Nova Scotia Court of Appeal denied standing to a group seeking to challenge municipal waste incineration. In particular, the court held that the matter was not "ripe" because no plan had been approved and the proposal had first to pass through an environmental assessment. Chipman JA held that to allow a challenge to the project before going through this process, or to allow a challenge to municipal incineration programs in the abstract, would be a waste of judicial resources.

The question of standing is considered in more detail later in this chapter.

Attorney-General of Alberta v. Plantation Indoor Plants Ltd.
(1982), 34 AR 348 (CA)

McCLUNG JA: This is an appeal by the Attorney-General of Alberta from the refusal of a Judge in Chambers to grant an interim injunction to restrain the respondent "from unlawfully selling goods contrary to the *Lord's Day Act*."

The respondent operates a retail store in the City of Edmonton. It has been convicted on five charges of unlawfully carrying on the sale of goods contrary to s. 4 of the *Lord's Day Act*, RSC 1970, c. L-13, which provides:

> 4. It is not lawful for any person on the Lord's Day, except as provided herein, or in any provincial Act or law in force on or after the 1st day of March 1907, to sell or offer for sale or purchase any goods, chattels, or other personal property, or any real estate, or to carry on or transact any business of his ordinary calling, or in connection with such calling, or for gain to do, or employ any other person to do, on that day, any work, business or labour.

The dates of the offences and of the convictions together with the fines levied are set out below:

Date of Offence	Date of Conviction	Fine
March 4/79	June 7/79	$40.00
June 24/79	Nov. 13/79	$40.00
July 1/79	Oct. 1/79	$1.00
July 15/79	Nov. 13/79	$40.00
July 29/79	Nov. 13/79	$40.00

It is established beyond doubt that Plantation Indoor Plants Limited, the respondent, has carried on its business and intends to do so in cold disregard of the strictures of the *Lord's Day Act*, RSC 1970, c. L-13. Repeated prosecutions and convictions brought under s. 12 of the Act, which provides for a fine upon conviction not exceeding $40, have not deterred the respondent, hence the Attorney-General of the Province of Alberta has brought action and applied to the Court of Queen's Bench for interim injunctive relief curtailing the respondent's practices pending trial. It was refused [(1981), 29 AR 477]. No exception to the constitutional status of the Attorney-General of Alberta to bring this application is taken.

Plantation's position here and below is basically threefold. First, it is said that injunctive relief should not issue in aid of the enforcement of the criminal law and that, at least, protection of some property or economic right must be in issue. Lord's Day legislation, whatever its popular appeal, is legislation pertaining to the criminal law. It has been accepted as such since *A-G Ont. v. Hamilton St. R Co.*, [1903] AC 524 (PC (Ont.)). However, the proposition that injunctive relief will not lie in aid of the criminal law, despite some historical support: *vide Robinson v. Adams* (1924), 56 OLR 217 (CA), no longer enjoys general acceptance. When the Attorney-General—as opposed to a private citizen—sees fit to bring the application, the usual prohibitions against invoking the equitable jurisdiction of the Court to suppress crime may be put aside. This was underlined by Matas JA in *Re Regina and Odeon Morton Theatres Ltd.* (1973), 42 DLR (3d) 471 (Man. CA).

There the conduct sought to be enjoined was the continuing exhibition of a movie alleged to be obscene contrary to the *Criminal Code*. The injunction was refused simply because the exhibitor had gained a trial acquittal and there was, therefore, no crime to be suppressed at the time of the Attorney-General's application which was brought pending an appeal of the acquittal. The objection, including the subordinate requirement that financial or property rights had to be infringed, was quickly rejected by Stevenson J (as he then was) in *United Nurses of Alberta v. A-G Alta.* (1980), 25 AR 69, following *A-G Ont. v. Grabarchuk* (1976), 11 OR (2d) 607 (HC, Div. Ct.) at p. 612, in which case the Ontario Court of Appeal [*sic*] noted:

> There are numerous precedents in England and Australia for the proposition that the Attorney-General, as protector of public rights and the public interest, may obtain an injunction where the law as contained in a public statute is being flouted. This is so notwithstanding that, (a) the statute itself may contain penalties of a different kind, and (b) all possible alternate remedies have not been exhausted. The position of the Attorney-General as custodian of the public interest is the same whether one speaks of England, Australia or Canada.

I would dismiss the initial objections.

Secondly, the respondent urges that s. 5(1)(b) of the *Criminal Code* and the traditional prohibitions against duplication of punishment militate against supplemental injunctive relief in these cases. It is said that if the injunction issues Plantation would be exposed to the sanction of proceedings for civil contempt of the order as well as the penalties provided in the *Lord's Day Act.*

Section 5(1)(b) of the *Criminal Code* provides:

> 5(1) Where an enactment creates an offence and authorizes a punishment in respect thereof. ...
>
> (b) a person who is convicted of that offence is not liable to any punishment in respect thereof other than the punishment prescribed by this Act or by the enactment that creates the offence.

In my opinion, s. 5(1)(b) does not bar this motion. Proceedings for contempt and the statutory sanctions provided for a breach of the *Lord's Day Act* are separate remedies for separate delicts, as they would be in the case of an assault committed in the face of a domestic restraining order. Moreover, s. 5(1)(b) of the *Criminal Code* deals only with mode or form of punishment now permitted by law recognizing that certain anomalous and anti-quated punishments carried out at common law have now been abolished: *R v. Turcotte*, [1970] SCR 843. I would dismiss this objection.

Remaining and apparently foremost among the reasons given by the learned Chambers Judge is his consideration of certain factors touching the exercise of his judicial discretion [at 482]:

> An injunction being an equitable remedy should only be resorted to where there is not (*sic*) other remedy available to the plaintiff [he said]. I am satisfied that the plaintiff has not ex-hausted its remedies before the Provincial Court or by way of an appeal to the Court of Queen's Bench and I therefore decline to grant the injunction sought by the Attorney-General.

First, it must be noted that appeals to the Court of Queen's Bench from the fines imposed would have been fruitless. Plantation was apparently charged under s. 12 of the Act and the $40 fines imposed in four of the five prosecutions were the maximum allowed. That leaves the possibility of other prosecutions. In argument we were treated to the unprepossessing pageant of the wrongdoer minimizing the efficacy of the Attorney-General's responses to date. We were told that five separate convictions is not enough. To this must be added Plantation's admission that it has been in business on "most Sundays" since October, 1978. It is argued that the failure of the Attorney-General to proceed against Plantation as a transgressing employer or corporate employer under ss. 13 or 14 of the *Lord's Day Act*, which might expose Plantation to greater fines, serves as a barrier to the discretionary success of this application. These sections provide:

> 13. Every employer who authorizes or directs anything to be done in violation of this Act, is for each offence liable, on summary conviction, to a fine not exceeding one hundred dollars and not less than twenty dollars, in addition to any other penalty prescribed by law for the same offence.
>
> 14. Every corporation that authorizes, directs or permits its employees to carry on any part of the business of such corporation in violation of this Act, is liable, on summary conviction before two justices of the peace, for the first offence, to a penalty not exceeding two hundred and fifty dollars and not less than fifty dollars, and, for each subsequent offence, to a penalty not exceeding five hundred dollars and not less than one hundred dollars, in addition to any other penalty prescribed by law for the same offence.

No doubt the Attorney-General has considered this alternative and has rejected it. It is not difficult to see why. Real and insurmountable difficulties in the proof of the precise employer–employee relationship that exists at a given time may be anticipated. This is so notwithstanding the definition of "employer" furnished by s. 2 of the Act. Kindred obstacles were encountered in the pursuit of the wrongdoing principals in *A-G Ont. v. Grabarchuk*. However that may be, it is for the law officers of the Crown and, as is the adequacy of any other relief, primarily for the administrative discretion of the Attorney-General. In *Attorney-General v. Bastow*, [1957] 1 QB 514, Devlin J (as he then was) observed at p. 520:

> That still leaves the second question, whether or not this is a proper case for the grant of an injunction by this court. It is plain that this court is not concerned with the reasons which have seemed good to the Attorney-General in causing him to bring this action. Obviously if, on every occasion that an offence were committed which involved the invasion of a public right, and which is normally dealt with by a magistrates' court by the imposition of a small fine, the Attorney-General were to take the matter up and ask for an injunction in this court, the work of the court would become impossible, but it is for the Attorney-General to decide with which cases he considers it right to deal in this way.

Lord Devlin continued (at p. 521):

> One of the circumstances to which it is alleged that the court should have regard, and I think properly, is whether there are or are not other remedies open either to the Attorney-General or to the relator which might be just as effective. I think that is a point to which the court ought to have regard, but in having regard to it, the court must bear this in mind: the Attorney-General is the person who is primarily responsible for the enforcement of the law, he is the first law officer of the Crown and I think that, if he considers it necessary to come into the court by way of a relator action to ask for the assistance of the court in enforcing obedience to a clear provi-

sion of the law, the court, although retaining its discretion, ought to be very slow to say that the Attorney-General ought to have exhausted other remedies before he came to the court.

It is not to be assumed, on authority or principle, that injunctive relief in these cases will issue upon the bald application of the Attorney-General. There must be much more. As indicated in *Attorney-General v. Lees & Courtney*, [1932] 3 WWR 533 (Alta. SC) the history of the matter must clearly demonstrate, as it does here, an open and continuous disregard of an imperative public statute and its usual sanctions which is unlikely to be thwarted without the intervention of the Court.

Of further significance to the discretion that attaches to the disposition of the Attorney-General's application are the provisions of s. 16 of the *Lord's Day Act* which I quote:

> 16. No action or prosecution for a violation of this Act shall be commenced without the leave of the Attorney General, or his lawful deputy, for the province in which the offence is alleged to have been committed, nor after the expiration of sixty days from the time of the commission of the alleged offence.

To me the reference to "action" in s. 16 is an anticipation of the grant of injunctive relief in an appropriate case. It is difficult to envision other relief of civil consequence that might be attracted. At the least a reading of the whole Act does not preclude the right of the Attorney-General to so apply. This was deemed relevant in *Attorney-General v. Lees & Courtney*, [1932] 3 WWR 533, where it was demonstrated that disregard of the legislation in question—the prohibitions under the *Dental Association Act*—was open and continuous and that the defendants intended to continue as in the past unless restrained by the Court from so doing. McGillivray JA in enjoining the defendants, concluded at p. 542: "In these circumstances I think I should exercise my discretion in favour of granting an injunction." It is true that in *Attorney-General v. Lees* the injunction was not sought in aid of the enforcement of the criminal law but that distinction has, as I have indicated, now been removed.

In *Goodyear Tire & Rubber Co. of Canada Ltd. v. The Queen*, [1956] SCR 303, constitutional challenge was taken against an order made under an enabling provision of the *Combines Investigation Act*, RSC 1927, c. 26, s. 31, now RSC 1970, c. C-23, s. 30(1)(b) whereby a convicting Court may enjoin the repetition of the trade practices prohibited by the Act which were the subject of the conviction. This is in addition to the specific penalties available. In upholding the enactment's validity the Supreme Court of Canada observed that the power to legislate in relation to the criminal law was not restricted to defining offences and providing penalties for their commission. The power of Parliament extends to legislation designed for the prevention of crime as well as the punishment of crime. Rand J added at pp. 311-2:

> What has called for the device of injunction and punishment for its contravention is undoubtedly the experience in dealing with these offences. The burden of proving the combination and its operation is, for obvious reasons, complicated and time-consuming and the procedure of enforcement by conviction and fine has tended to exhibit a course of things bearing a close likeness to periodic licensing of illegality. That sanctions cannot be made more effective, that an offence by its nature continuing cannot be dealt with as criminal law by an enjoining decree that will facilitate enforcement might go far towards enabling self-confessed lawlessness to set the will of Parliament at defiance.

The granting of injunctive direction in support of the enforcement of the criminal law of Canada is neither foreign nor offensive. Within the *Criminal Code* itself it is available and commonly resorted to, in statutory course, in many instances. Injunctive prohibitions are encouraged in the making of probation and judicial interim release orders. The whole philosophy of the preventive detention of dangerous offenders is anchored to the enjoinment of the likely commission of further serious crimes. Recognizances to keep the peace are similarly designed.

With respect, I view the refusal of the injunction sought, given the proven history of the correspondent's dedicated disregard of the prohibitions of the Act and the Attorney-General's duty to protect the vitality of public statutes by their even enforcement as invitive of the periodic licensing of illegality apprehended by Rand J in *Goodyear Tire & Rubber Co. of Canada Ltd. v. The Queen.*

In conclusion, I believe that the injunction should have issued. The history of Plantation's pointed disregard of the *Lord's Day Act* and the relief contemplated by it are decisive. I take this view notwithstanding the marginal significance—and utility—of the other suggested remedies. With respect, the discretion employed by the learned Chambers Judge in the initial refusal was rooted to irrelevant considerations. I would allow the appeal and direct the issuance of an interlocutory injunction restraining until the trial or other disposition of the action the respondent Plantation Indoor Plants Limited and every person bound to conform to its orders or direction and any person or corporation acting on its behalf from carrying on business, either directly or indirectly, in contravention of the *Lord's Day Act.*

Costs to the appellant throughout.

On appeal to the SCC ([1985] 1 SCR 366), McIntyre J, without expressing any view on the validity of the injunction when granted (January 27, 1982), declared the injunction invalid as of April 19, 1982, because the *Lord's Day Act* was held to be unconstitutional by reason of its infringement of the "freedom of religion" provisions of the *Canadian Charter of Rights and Freedoms*. See *R v. Big M Drug Mart Ltd.*, [1985] 1 SCR 295, for the decision regarding the constitutionality of the *Lord's Day Act*.

NOTES AND QUESTIONS

1. What is the defect in the *Lord's Day Act* that the injunction in this case was designed to remedy? Why should the courts be concerned that the defendant is "flouting" a statute? Another series of cases involving the refusal of a merchant to close on a statutory holiday involved orders granted under Ontario's *Retail Business Holidays Act*, RSO 1980, c. 453, as am. The litigation is summarized in *Hy and Zel's Inc. v. Ontario (Attorney-General); Paul Magder Furs Ltd. v. Ontario (Attorney-General)*, [1993] 3 SCR 675, at 684-88.

2. McClung JA takes note of the traditional reluctance of the courts to enjoin crime but suggests that when the applicant is the attorney general, the usual concerns about such injunctions may be put aside. Why? For an argument that courts should not give up their discretion even when the request is from the attorney general, see L. Friedlander, "Must the Law Be Obeyed? The Attorney-General's Response to Flouting" (1995), 17 *Advocates' Q* 80.

3. Should the courts be more hesitant to grant the injunction when there is an issue of the constitutionality of the law sought to be enforced? What is the legal position of the defendants if they choose to ignore the injunction pending appeal, arguing (as they successfully did in this case) that the law is unconstitutional? Should an individual be able to obtain an injunction to prevent enforcement of a law which is arguably unconstitutional? See *Morgentaler v. Ackroyd* (1983), 42 OR (2d) 659 (HC). (We return to the issue of injunctions in such cases in chapter 12, "Charter Remedies.")

4. In *Attorney General for Ontario v. Grabarchuk* (1976), 11 OR (2d) 607 (Div. Ct.), Reid J granted an injunction to restrain the defendant from carrying on its transport business without a licence. The Act provided for fines up to $1,000 and the defendant had been convicted on numerous occasions. Reid J stated (at 612) that "[t]here are numerous precedents in England and Australia for the proposition that the Attorney-General, as the protector of public rights and the public interest, may obtain an injunction where the law as contained in a public statute is being flouted. This is so notwithstanding that, (a) the statute itself may contain penalties of a different kind, and (b) all possible alternative remedies have not been exhausted. ... One who knowingly and deliberately flouts the plain law can hardly argue that it is not just that he be stopped."

5. In *Attorney-General v. Able*, [1984] QB 795, the attorney general sought to prevent the defendants from distributing a book on how to commit suicide. Rather than resort to the criminal law, the attorney general sought a declaration that any future distribution of the books would be a criminal offence. In refusing the application, the court expressed concern that such an order would usurp the jurisdiction of the criminal courts and the function of the jury. Woolf J commented (at 808) that "[w]hile of course recognizing the advantage of the application of the law being clear in relation to future conduct, it would only be proper to grant a declaration if it is clearly established that there is no risk of it treating conduct as criminal which is not clearly in contravention of the criminal law."

6. In *Attorney General v. Harris*, [1960] 1 QB 31, rev'd. [1961] 1 QB 74 (CA), the attorney general sought to enjoin the defendants from operating a sidewalk flower stall in contravention of a municipal bylaw. The defendant had been ticketed 237 times and the small fines were paid each week. At trial, Solomon J refused the injunction, expressing concern about the reasons for the application: competitors had influenced and exerted pressure upon city council. He held that as the defendants were causing no damage or inconvenience to the public and no public nuisance, an injunction would be inappropriate. Finally, he stated that the court had discretion to refuse the injunction and that discretion was not removed because of the fact that it was the attorney general seeking the order.

This decision was reversed on appeal. Responding to Solomon J's suggestion that the injunction was being sought for improper reasons, Sellers LJ stated (at 86) that "[i]t cannot, in my opinion be anything other than a public detriment for the law to be so defied, week by week, and the offender to find it profitable to pay the fine and continue to flout the law."

Pearce LJ wrote a concurring judgment, stating (at 93-94):

> It is not, of course, desirable that Parliament should habitually rely upon the High Court to deter the law breaker by other means than the statutory penalties instead of taking the legislative step of making the penalties adequate to prevent the offence which it created. Especially this is so when the offences are of a trivial nature. Yet it is, on the other hand, highly undesirable that some

member of the public should with impunity flout the law and deliberately continue acts forbidden by Parliament. And in cases where, under the existing law, this court alone can provide a remedy, it should in general lend its aid to enforce obedience to the law when that aid is invoked by the Attorney-General on behalf of the public.

7. In *Attorney General for Ontario v. Harry* (1979), 22 OR (2d) 321 (HC), the court granted an injunction to prevent the sale of land pursuant to a scheme devised to circumvent the requirements of the provincial planning legislation. The legislation contained no penalties for violation and the injunction was granted, in part, to protect innocent third parties who might purchase the land.

The interlocutory injunction granted in *Harry* was made permanent in *Attorney General for Ontario v. Yeotes* (1980), 28 OR (2d) 577 (HC), in which Montgomery J summarized the law (at 585) as follows:

(1) Where the rights of the public are involved by reason of the illegal action of the defendant, there is jurisdiction to grant an injunction at the instance of the Attorney-General notwithstanding the fact that there are other remedies available, if such remedies are inadequate.

(2) The conduct in question need not be restricted to acts which constitute an invasion of any right of property, but can extend to a mere invasion of the community's general right to have laws obeyed.

(3) By virtue of the fact that the conduct necessarily involves the public, the dispute is no longer between individuals and therefore engenders an exception to the general rule that the punishment prescribed by a statute is to be the only remedy.

(4) The authority of the Court is discretionary, but cognizance must be given to the fact that the action is brought by the Attorney-General and therefore the injunction will be refused only in exceptional circumstances.

(5) Deliberate and persistent breaches of the law are facts which also go to the question of the exercise of discretion unless the matter is too trivial, or injustice would be caused, or there is good reason for refusing to enforce the general right of the public to have the laws obeyed.

An appeal of this decision was allowed by the Court of Appeal on the merits: (1981), 31 OR (2d) 589 (CA), leave to appeal to SCC refused (1981), 37 NR 356n. In *Attorney General for Ontario v. Harry; Attorney General for Ontario v. Yeotes* (1982), 35 OR (2d) 248 (HC), Montgomery J decided against ordering the attorney general to account for damages sustained by the defendant as a result of the previous injunctions granted. Holding that there were "special circumstances" that exempted the case from the ordinary requirement to account, he concluded (at 251) that "[t]hese actions were brought by the Attorney-General for the protection of the public and the prevention of public injury. The checkerboard scheme used by the defendants succeeded because of a 'loophole' in the *Planning Act*. … The defendants have their subdivision; let them make their profit on it and not at the expense of the defenders of the public interest."

The role of the damage undertaking is considered in more detail later when we turn to consider interlocutory injunctions.

8. Following the decision in *R v. Morgentaler*, [1988] 1 SCR 30, which declared unconstitutional the abortion offence in the *Criminal Code*, a number of provinces responded by enacting their own legislation. This legislation itself gave rise to various injunction applications. For example, in *Nova Scotia (Attorney General) v. Morgentaler* (1989), 93 NSR (2d) 202, aff'd. (1990), 96 NSR (2d) 54 (CA), the court granted an injunction against operation of the defendant's abortion clinic pending the outcome of criminal charges under the province's *Medical Services Act*, SNS 1989, c. 9. Criminal charges against Morgentaler under the Nova Scotia legislation were dismissed on the basis that the legislation was unconstitutional (*R v. Morgentaler* (1991), 99 NSR (2d) 293 (Prov. Ct.), aff'd. (1991), 104 NSR (2d) 361 (CA), aff'd. [1993] 3 SCR 463).

Attorney General of British Columbia v. Couillard
(1985), 59 BCLR 102

McEACHERN CJSC (orally): I grew up in this city, and I have always lived here. Although I have never been a resident of the West End, it has obviously been one of the most interesting and liveable areas in the city. It is said to be the most densely populated residential area in Canada as it is within easy walking distance of downtown Vancouver. What has happened in the West End is an urban tragedy that should never have occurred.

What has happened is that a small but persistent and probably changing group of young men and women have taken over the streets and sidewalks of a part of the West End for the purpose of prostitution to the great discomfort of the neighbourhood. It is argued that they have a legal right to do this. We hear much of individual rights in these courts, and I take second place to no one in my defence of lawful legal rights, but even the rights and freedoms enshrined in our Charter are expressly subject to such reasonable limits prescribed by law as can be demonstrably justified in a free and democratic society.

It is not necessary in this case to decide whether anyone has the right to be a prostitute. All private rights are subject to reasonable limits, the principal limitation often being the correlative rights of other citizens and of society itself. As Holmes J said in *Schenck v. United States* (1919), 249 US 47 at p. 52:

> The most stringent protection of free speech would not protect a man in falsely shouting fire in a theatre and causing a panic. It does not even protect a man from an injunction against uttering words that may have all the effect of force.

What is in question in this case is whether prostitution may be practised at the expense of a neighbourhood.

The Attorney-General, on behalf of all the citizens of British Columbia, including those living in the West End, has established beyond the slightest shadow of a doubt that all of the named defendants served with this notice and many others were, at the commencement of these proceedings, using the streets, lanes, sidewalks and other public and private amenities of the West End for the purposes of public aggressive and disorderly male and female and transsexual prostitution.

The Attorney-General has further established that such conduct, in the circumstances described in the affidavits, constitutes an obvious and serious public nuisance.

None of the respondents on this motion have filed any material in any way denying either the conduct as described in the affidavits or questioning in any way the basic facts from which I have concluded a public nuisance has existed. In fact, most counsel for the respondents have very properly expressed sympathy and concern for the residents of the West End.

In these circumstances, the Attorney-General seeks an interim injunction restraining until trial and further order the conduct constituting this public nuisance in a specific residential portion of the West End bounded by Thurlow, Beach, Bidwell and Nelson Sts., which the Attorney-General says is a residential community.

Some time after the Attorney-General commenced this action and just a few days before this motion was to be heard, many or all of the respondents and all or almost all other prostitutes removed themselves from and discontinued their impudent conduct in the residential area in question, but the material discloses that they propose to carry on these activities in another nearby area in down-town Vancouver. The respondents by their counsel and others first said they do not propose to return to the residential West End for the purposes of prostitution, but counsel did not foreclose the possibility that the respondents may at some time resume their activities in this area.

Counsel for the respondents oppose the application on numerous grounds relying in part upon the language of some of the Law Lords in *Gouriet v. Union of Post Office Workers*, [1978] AC 435 (HL (Eng.)), particularly the speeches of Lord Wilberforce at p. 481, and of Viscount Dilhorne at p. 491. The respondents particularly stress that an injunction in a case such as this is unprecedented, such activities never having previously been banned anywhere in the western world.

While I doubt that that is a completely accurate assertion, I have instructed myself in accordance with their lordships' admonitions. I note, however, that the applicant in *Gouriet* was not the Attorney-General, and at p. 491 Viscount Dilhorne said:

> An Attorney-General is not subject to restrictions as to the applications he makes, either *ex officio* or in relator actions to the courts. In every case it will be for the court to decide whether it has jurisdiction to grant the application and whether in the exercise of its discretion it should do so. It has been and in my opinion should continue to be exceptional for the aid of the civil courts to be invoked in support of the criminal law and no wise Attorney-General will make such an application or agree to one being made in his name unless it appears to him that the case is exceptional.

In answer to the submission of the respondents, I can say that so far as I know, blatant aggressive disorderly prostitution has never before been practised or tolerated in a residential area and, to the extent that special, exceptional or even very special circumstances are required, I have no hesitation in finding that the circumstances I have mentioned are not just special or very special, but extraordinary.

With respect, I must reject Mr. Corrigan's submission that because Canada is a federal State, the Attorney-General is limited to actions designed to enforce or support matters falling within provincial jurisdiction. He says that this action in its pith and substance is to ban prostitution, a federal matter, and that the Attorney-General therefore has no standing to bring this action.

While I do not think this distinction is of any significance in the disposition I propose to make of this application, I understand that, in a proper case, the Attorney General has standing to bring proceedings for enforcing any law within the province. The real question is not the standing of the Attorney-General, but rather the jurisdiction of the court.

It was argued by Mr. Giles that the Attorney-General is in a special position and that, as he represents the public as a whole, the court will normally, but in the exercise of its discretion, grant an application made by the Attorney-General for an injunction to restrain public nuisance: *Attorney-General v. Harris*, [1961] 1 QB 74 (CA).

I do not have to dwell or rely upon that interesting proposition because in this case I am content to apply the usual tests for the granting of an injunction described in *American Cyanamid Co. v. Ethicon*, [1975] AC 396 (HL (Eng.)), and many other judgments of our Court of Appeal, namely, the court must be satisfied that the claim is not frivolous or vexatious in the sense that there is a serious question to be tried.

Thompson-Schwab v. Costaki, [1956] 1 WLR 335 (CA), is direct authority for the proposition that conduct for the interim injunction has been made out and subject to what I am about to say, an injunction must, as a debt of justice to the citizens of British Columbia generally and to the residents of the West End particularly, be forthwith issued enjoining the particulars of this public nuisance.

All counsel for the respondents pointed out that the affidavits do not implicate their clients in any specific activity—just that they are prostitutes and they have been observed in the West End. As I mentioned during counsel's argument, I do not think a jury would have the slightest difficulty inferring as I do that the individual respondents contributed to the nuisance, particularly in the absence of any denial by any of them regarding their activities.

It is sufficient to refer to two textbook authorities on this point. In J.G. Fleming, *The Law of Torts*, 5th ed. (Sydney: Law Book Co., 1977) at p. 393, the learned editors say:

> Because of the large variety of situations encompassed by the term [nuisance], the crucial point is easily obscured that nuisance is a field of tort liability rather than any particular type of tortious conduct. Its unifying element resides in the general kind of harm caused, not in any particular kind of conduct causing it.

In R.F.V. Heuston (ed.), *Salmond on the Law of Torts* (London: Sweet & Maxwell, 18th ed., 1981) at p. 66, it is stated:

> Two or more persons may jointly create or continue a nuisance and then they will be joint tortfeasors. But it is also no defence that the act of the Defendant would not amount to a nuisance unless other persons acting independently of him did the same thing at the same time. Thus if twenty factories pour out smoke and fumes into the atmosphere, the contribution of each may be so small and its detrimental effect so inappreciable that it does not per se amount to a nuisance. Yet the aggregate quantity may be the cause of serious harm or discomfort. In such a case each of the contributors is liable in nuisance and for his own proportion of the total damage.

In addition, as this is only an application for an interim injunction, the Attorney-General need only show there is a serious question to be tried and that test has been satisfied.

Before I turn to the terms of my order, I wish to make it clear that I do not base by judgment solely on the ground that the West End is a residential area. That prostitutes should invade a residential community is, as I have said, an extraordinary circumstance, but a public nuisance in any area would equally be enjoinable upon proper circumstances being shown. The streets and sidewalks belong to all of us.

For reasons which are not material to this application, it is apparent that a small group of prostitutes have assumed, quite incorrectly, that causing public inconvenience for the purpose of prostitution is lawful subject only to prosecution under the *Criminal Code*. Authorities such as *Hutt v. The Queen*, [1978] 2 SCR 476, suggest that there may be some practical problems in the prosecution of soliciting under the *Criminal Code* at the present time, but that does not mean that public misconduct is lawful. It is not, and if it amounts to a public nuisance anywhere in the province, it may be enjoined upon a proper application being made by the Attorney-General.

Those who would defile our city must understand that in addition to the criminal law, the citizens of this country are protected by the common law which is a statement of the accumulated wisdom of history. But it is a dynamic force which is always ready to respond to the reasonable requirements of civilization.

Over 90 years ago, Noyes PJ, a Pennsylvania judge, said in *Hague v. Wheeler* (1893), 27 A 714, that the common law is a growing tree, its principles must be continually adapted to new facts and the changing conditions of modern life.

Noyes PJ went on to say that the legislatures have the responsibility to change the law, that the courts have the duty to ensure that the law remains current with the times. The case at bar is a perfect example of how the common law supplements legislation for the protection of the public. Public nuisance for the purpose of prostitution has had too long a grasp upon this city and it is time for its dreadful regime to come to an end. If the legislative branch of the government has failed in this regard, the common law will not be found wanting.

I turn next to the terms of the injunction which the court will pronounce. The Attorney-General asked me to restrain the respondents and anyone having knowledge of the injunction from engaging in or causing a nuisance in the defined residential area, and for greater certainty, but without restricting the generality of the foregoing, from:

(1) purchasing or attempting to purchase sexual services of any kind;

(2) selling or attempting to sell sexual services of any kind;

(3) engaging in any conduct or activity, including soliciting, pimping, pandering or procuring, which is done for the purposes of male or female prostitution;

(4) using any public or private property, including streets and alleys, for the purposes of male or female prostitution;

(5) engaging in any other conduct, including:

   (i) loitering, littering, fighting, screaming, shouting or swearing;

   (ii) using insulting, abusive, suggestive or obscene language or gestures;

   (iii) assaulting, harassing, impeding, obstructing, threatening with violence or otherwise intimidating any person or child;

   (iv) defecating, urinating or any form of carnal copulation including *fellatio* and sodomy;

so as to constitute or cause a nuisance.

I think there is merit in the submissions of counsel for the respondents who urge me not to attempt to enjoin prostitution, which is what paras. 1, 2 and 4 of the notice of motion would prohibit. Parliament has never sought to prohibit prostitution. Instead, Parliament has at different times prohibited various offensive public activities, and I think I should follow that course in the first instance, not because of any philosophical or constitutional concerns, but merely because I think the court should proceed cautiously. Because of the exaggerated and totally indiscreet conduct of the respondents and others in the past, I am going to go further than otherwise might be the case, but the respondents have brought this on themselves.

It may be a matter of comment that what I am about to order is directed only at male and female prostitutes and not at their customers. This is because I think it is the responsibility of Parliament, not the court, to extend the sanction of the law in that direction if Parliament decides to do so. It is to be hoped that this entire question will receive the attention of Parliament at a very early date. In any event, I wish to make it clear that I regard the peaceful integrity of a community to be more important than policy considerations, and if what I am about to order is deficient, then upon application I shall be prepared to consider rephrasing my order in different language. No one should be in any doubt that prostitution as it has been practised in the West End must be discontinued.

The order I propose to make shall be in the form of the first unnumbered paragraph of the notice of motion, but the particulars shall be as follows. I will not read the first paragraph as it is substantially in the form set out in the notice of motion. The particulars will be:

1. engaging in any public conduct or activity apparently for the purposes of male or female prostitution, or any public conduct or activity which is calculated by itself or in conjunction with any conduct or activity by another person or persons to cause or contribute to a nuisance;

2. publicly offering themselves or publicly appearing to offer themselves directly or indirectly for the purposes of male or female prostitution by words or without words, or by actions, gestures, loitering or otherwise;

3. using or trespassing upon any public property including streets, lanes, sidewalks, boulevards, parks or school properties for the purposes of male or female prostitution;

4. trespassing upon any private property for the purposes of male or female prostitution;

5. engaging in any other conduct, including:

    (i) loitering, littering, fighting, screaming, shouting or swearing;

    (ii) using insulting, abusive, suggestive or obscene language or gestures;

    (iii) assaulting, harassing, impeding, obstructing, threatening with violence or otherwise intimidating any person or child;

    (iv) defecating, urinating or any form of carnal copulation including *fellatio* and sodomy;

    so as to constitute or cause a nuisance.

Lastly, with respect to the geographical limits of my order, I am naturally concerned about the affidavit filed by a respondent and sworn by a lady who says she is a co-founder of an alliance of prostitutes. She says that the prostitutes who created this nuisance have decided to move *en masse* to an area bounded by Drake, Nelson, Burrard and Pacific Blvd. I cannot help but recognize that if these respondents and others can move *en masse* to that location, they may also move to other areas inside or outside the area described by the Attorney-General in his notice of motion, and the court is not disposed to secure such portion of the West End at the expense of another portion or of an adjacent area. Neither is the court prepared to tolerate such an artificial attempt to evade its authority. To paraphrase Winston Churchill, what kind of people do these prostitutes and their associates think British Columbians are that they would tolerate such indecency on a continuing basis? The answer is that by and large, we are peaceful, law-abiding people who respect the rights of others under the rule of law, and we expect others to do the same. Those who are prohibited from unlawful conduct in one area should not presume to carry on such lawlessness across the street or down the block or anywhere else.

But even in the face of such an affront to decency, the court must proceed with caution. The West End of Vancouver is a geographic unit. While there may be differences of opinion about its eastern boundary, it is not completely arbitrary to say that it begins at the east property line of Granville St. The area covered by the injunction, if the Attorney-General requests it, will therefore be the area of downtown Vancouver north of False Creek and English Bay, and west of the east property line to Granville St. As mentioned, the court will not be reluctant to extend its protection to any other area where a nuisance may arise, and in such cases I would expect the court to extend the territorial operation of this order, if at all, not by streets or blocks, but rather to large geographic areas of the city as may be required or threatened.

If the threat just mentioned is carried out by these or any prostitutes having notice of this injunction, I shall entertain an immediate application to extend this order not just to the threatened area, but to the large geographic unit of which such area is a part. If the Attorney-General does not seek the wider territorial operation of this order as I have described it, then he may take an order for the area described in the notice of motion. The order, of course, is effective immediately, but in the circumstances I think I should actually sign the order.

Judgment accordingly.

NOTES AND QUESTIONS

1. In *Hutt v. The Queen*, [1978] 2 SCR 476, the Supreme Court held that before being guilty of the offence of soliciting under what was then s. 195.1 (now s. 213) of the *Criminal Code* the accused must exhibit conduct that is "pressing or persistent." Does the same restriction apply to persons enjoined by the order made in *Couillard*? Should it?

2. What does the injunction granted in this case add to the existing criminal law?

3. Are the customers of prostitutes bound by the wording of the order in this case? Does McEachern CJ believe that they are bound? What facts would have to be established to convict a customer of contempt?

4. In *Westendorp v. The Queen*, [1983] 1 SCR 43, the Supreme Court struck down a Calgary bylaw which prohibited the presence of persons on city streets for the purpose of prostitution. The court held that the bylaw invaded the federal authority to legislate with respect to criminal law. In the absence of any reference in the bylaw to interference with property, Laskin CJ characterized as "baffling" the city's argument that the bylaw was an exercise of the provincial power to control the streets and eliminate public nuisance.

5. Within six days of the judgment in *Couillard*, 134 persons had been served with the order and it was reported that the streets of the West End of Vancouver were free of prostitution. The newspapers reported that the police had "spread new hooker dragnet" and that prostitutes, not just in the West End, but everywhere in the city, were "getting the boot in the wake of this week's court decision." See J. Cassels, "Prostitution and Public Nuisance: Desperate Measures and the Limits of Civil Adjudication" (1985), 63 *Can. Bar Rev.* 764.

6. At the time of the application in *Couillard*, the Fraser Committee was preparing its report on prostitution (Report of the Special Committee on Pornography and Prostitution, *Pornography and Prostitution in Canada* (Ottawa: Supply and Services Canada, 1985)). This report, while recognizing the nuisance aspects of prostitution, rejected "draconian" solutions. Legislation had also been drafted. That legislation (SC 1985, c. 50, s. 1), which replaced s. 195.1 (s. 213), now provides that every person

who in a public place or in any place open to public view

(a) stops or attempts to stop any motor vehicle,

(b) impedes the free flow of pedestrian or vehicular traffic or ingress or to egress from premises adjacent to that place, or

(c) stops or attempts to stop any person or in any manner communicates or attempts to communicate with any person

for the purpose of engaging in prostitution or of obtaining the sexual services of a prostitute is guilty of an offence.

7. In *Stein v. Gonzales* (1984), 58 BCLR 110 (SC), McLachlin J denied an injunction against prostitution to a Vancouver hotel owner. The plaintiff's hotel was adjacent to the area subject to the order made in *Couillard* and prostitution-related activities in the area had "greatly increased" since that order had been issued. McLachlin J denied the plaintiff's application on two grounds: first, that the activities of the defendants were not a private nuisance since they did not sufficiently interfere with the plaintiff's use of his property; second, that the plaintiff did not have standing to request an injunction to enjoin a public nuisance since he was suffering no "special or peculiar damage" different from that suffered by other members of the community.

This case and the issue of standing are considered in more detail in the next section.

Attorney General of Nova Scotia v. Beaver
(1985), 67 NSR (2d) 281 (CA)

HART JA: On October 25, 1984, the appellant, the Attorney-General of Nova Scotia, representing Her Majesty the Queen in the right of the Province of Nova Scotia, commenced an action against 47 women said to be prostitutes operating in the downtown area of the City of Halifax claiming that their activities constituted a public nuisance and seeking a permanent injunction to abate the same. The particular acts of nuisance are set forth in the statement of claim as follows:

(a) Accosting and propositioning pedestrians and motorists for the purpose of prostitution;

(b) selling or offering sexual services of all kinds;

(c) using public and private property, including streets, parking lots, driveways and parks, for the purpose of prostitution;

(d) loitering, littering, fighting, screaming, shouting, swearing, using insulting, suggestive or obscene language or gestures, impeding, obstructing and assaulting members of the public, defecating, urinating, and all forms of carnal copulation including fellatio.

It was alleged that the defendants' activities injuriously affected the quiet enjoyment of property by tenants and landowners in the downtown area and it caused the area to deteriorate and property values to diminish.

On December 3, 1984, an application was made to the court on behalf of the Attorney-General to obtain an interlocutory injunction against the defendants to prevent them from engaging in or causing a nuisance by way of the following activities in the downtown area of the city prior to trial:

1) engaging in any public conduct apparently for the purpose of prostitution, or any public conduct which by itself, or in conjunction with the conduct of another person, causes or contributes to nuisance;

2) publicly offering or appearing to offer themselves directly or indirectly for prostitution by words, actions, gestures, loitering or otherwise;

3) using or trespassing upon any public property for the purpose of prostitution or related activity;

4) using or trespassing upon any private property for the purpose of prostitution or related activity;

5) engaging in any other conduct, including:

 (i) loitering, littering, fighting, screaming, shouting or swearing;

 (ii) using insulting, abusive, suggestive or obscene language or gestures;

 (iii) assaulting, harassing, impeding, obstructing, threatening with violence or otherwise intimidating any person;

 (iv) impeding or obstructing traffic;

 (v) defecating, urinating in an offensive manner;

 (vi) carnal copulation, including fellatio, for the purpose of prostitution.

In support of the application, which came on for hearing before Mr. Justice MacIntosh, 34 affidavits were filed by the Crown. Many of these affidavits were from residents who claimed that they were bothered by the activities of the prostitutes, their pimps, their customers and curious onlookers, who together caused a great deal of noise, heavy traffic, interference with their passage in the streets, trespassing and a devaluation of their properties. The affidavits of two police officers indicated that the presence of the prostitutes on the streets was often accompanied by shouts and fighting over territorial control between the prostitutes and their pimps, and that many women of the area, were often mistaken for prostitutes and bothered by their customers. On cross-examination, however, the officers admitted that only two members of the 300-member city police force were assigned to the morality squad, and although most of the activities complained of were criminal offences that very little effort was made to suppress the problems by ordinary criminal procedures.

Thirty-five affidavits were filed on behalf of the defendants in which other residents of the downtown area claimed that they were familiar with the presence of prostitutes, but at no time were bothered by them or other associated activities. It was further argued by the defendants that the downtown area had many beverage-rooms and lounges which contributed to the heavy traffic in the evening hours, and the patrons of these establishments were often the cause of noisy activities on the streets.

Mr. Justice MacIntosh, after considering the evidence before him, reached the conclusion that there were at the time of the application only about twenty prostitutes carrying on their activities in the downtown area. He further found that much of the so-called "nuisance" was emanating from the licensed drinking establishments and that the police were hampered not only by the interpretation of the meaning of soliciting under s. 195.1 of the *Criminal Code* under the decision of *Hutt v. The Queen*, [1978] 2 SCR 476, but also by the reluctance of the complaining residents to participate as witnesses in any prosecutions. For these and other reasons little was being done by the civic authorities to control the activities complained of.

Mr. Justice MacIntosh then reviewed the general principles upon which courts exercise their discretion to grant or withhold interlocutory injunctions and, in particular, injunctions for the abatement of a public nuisance. He then entered upon a consideration of whether or not those principles would be applicable in a case where the type of conduct sought to be prevented was of a criminal nature rather than civil. Reference was made to *Westendorp v. The Queen*, [1983] 1 SCR 43, where the Supreme Court of Canada held that the City of Calgary could not make prostitution an offence under a by-law for the control of its streets, since prostitution was in essence a subject that fell under the federal jurisdiction in relation to criminal law. MacIntosh J then went on to say:

> There is no doubt in my mind that this application is an attempt to control prostitution. The pith and substance of the application relates to prostitution. The Attorney-General is attempting to control street prostitution in downtown Halifax by civil procedure. It is of no significance whether a province or a municipality attempts to usurp criminal jurisdiction by way of legislation or injunction. The point is that they are not free to invade federal jurisdiction in these matters by any means.

Mr. Justice MacIntosh then proceeded to consider whether he should exercise his discretion against the granting of the injunction for another reason, that is, because there were other means available to overcome the problem. He said:

If the activities of the respondents are as outlined in the applicant's affidavits, then as pointed out, the following sections of the *Criminal Code* are available to deal with them:

Section 169—Indecent Acts
Section 170—Nudity
Section 171—Causing a Disturbance
Section 173—Trespassing at Night
Section 176—Nuisance
Section 193—Keeping a Common Bawdy House
Section 195—Procuring
Section 244—Assault
Section 387—Mischief

In addition to these federal *Criminal Code* provisions, much of the unlawful conduct set forth in the applicant's affidavits are covered by provincial or municipal laws such as the *Protection of Property Act*, 1982 (NS), c. 13, the *Motor Vehicle Act*, RSNS 1967, c. 191, and others. In other words, there are already remedies available to the authorities to correct the alleged situation existing in the so-called "downtown" Halifax. The court cannot accept the contention of a Halifax police constable that they are powerless. If such is the case, it is little wonder where in a city of this size a morality squad of two men only are allotted to look after this problem.

Surely this court is entitled to ask the applicant—why apply to this court where there are already remedies in place in the *Criminal Code* and provincial laws to most of your problems? A bit more diligence is indicated.

Mr. Justice MacIntosh then turned to consider whether the criminal law should be enforced by the civil remedy of injunction, and after setting forth some of the inherent dangers in so doing as revealed in the case-law, he decided to reject the application for the injunction and in doing so stated:

All persons summoned to court for criminal misconduct in this country have an inalienable right to be tried by due process of criminal law with all its attendant protective procedural protections. On the other hand, there are those represented by the Attorney-General who are entitled to a resolution of their problem. Unfortunately for the latter, I do not consider an interim injunction to be proper procedure in this particular instance. The application is therefore denied with costs which shall be for the determination at trial.

It is from this decision that the Attorney-General has applied for leave to appeal, and since a confirmation of the decision would in fact be equivalent to a dismissal of the action, I would consider it appropriate to grant the leave requested.

The grounds of appeal are that the trial judge erred:

(i) in finding that the application of the Attorney-General was an attempt to usurp exclusive federal jurisdiction in the sphere of criminal law, and that it was of "no significance whether a province or a municipality attempts to usurp criminal jurisdiction by way of legislation or injunction" … and

(ii) in finding that "injunctions will not be granted to restrain *Criminal Code* offences. …"

. . .

[Hart JA then discussed the general law of nuisance and the right of the attorney general to seek an injunction.]

In the case at bar there is no challenge to the Attorney-General's right to bring his action for an alleged nuisance, but the Crown alleges that the trial judge improperly exercised his discretion in refusing the Attorney-General's request. The first ground of appeal suggests that the trial judge was wrong in considering that the application was an attempt by the Attorney-General to usurp exclusive federal jurisdiction in the sphere of criminal law rather than a valid attempt to abate a real public nuisance. This is a concept peculiar to Canada where there is a division of legislative powers between the federal government and the provinces, and no assistance can be obtained from the English decisions.

The trial judge relied heavily upon the decision of the Supreme Court of Canada in *Westendorp v. The Queen*, [1983] 1 SCR 43, which held a Calgary by-law prohibiting people from being on the street for the purpose of prostitution *ultra vires* the powers of the province and, therefore, the municipality, as an invasion of the field of criminal law. Laskin CJ, speaking for the court, said [at 53]:

> In examining the submission of counsel for the accused that the by-law was a colourable attempt to deal, not with a public nuisance but with the evil of prostitution, Kerans JA observed that the evil of prostitution is a matter of public morality and, if the pith and substance of this legislation were an attack on this evil, it might well be a matter beyond the competence of the Legislature of Alberta. He then went on to say that (1982), 35 AR 228 at p. 244:
>
>> ... the by-law does not strike at prostitution as such; it does not seek to suppress the market for sexual favours; it seeks only to protect the citizens who use the streets from the irritation and embarrassment of being unwilling participants in that market.
>
> This assessment of "pith and substance" is to me baffling when regard is had to the terms of s. 6.1. It becomes doubly baffling when Kerans JA says this [at 247]:
>
>> I concede that the Calgary legislation makes it an offence for a prostitute simply to enter upon a street for the purpose of prostitution, *i.e.*, without yet doing anything. But this is not an attack on prostitution as such. This is an attempt, by preventative measure, to regulate the activities of the prostitutes and their customers on the streets. It is, as it were, a pre-emptive strike. And as such is troubling. But it is insufficiently troubling to change the pith and substance of the legislation.
>
> What appears to me to emerge from Keran JA's consideration of the by-law is to establish a concurrency of legislative power, going beyond any double aspect principle and leaving it open to a Province or to a municipality authorized by a Province to usurp exclusive federal legislative power. If a Province or municipality may translate a direct attack on prostitution into street control through reliance on public nuisance, it may do the same with respect to trafficking in drugs. And, may it not, on the same view, seek to punish assaults that take place on city streets as an aspect of street control!
>
> However desirable it may be for the municipality to control or prohibit prostitution, there has been an over-reaching in the present case which offends the division of legislative powers.

I would, accordingly, allow the appeal, set aside the judgment of the Alberta Court of Appeal and restore the acquittal directed by the provincial court judge.

Mr. Justice MacIntosh had no doubt that the Attorney-General's application was an attempt to control prostitution and went on to say that it matters not whether this attempt is by legislation or by civil action for an injunction.

The Crown takes the position that the *Westendorp* decision relates solely to the legislative division of powers and does not in any way restrict the Attorney-General's ancient right to apply to the civil courts for the remedy of injunction and the abatement of a public nuisance.

This question was raised many years ago in *People's Holding Co. v. A-G Que.*, [1931] SCR 452. In that case the Attorney-General of Quebec sought to prevent a federally incorporated company from acting beyond its powers so as to defraud the public. The question for decision by the Supreme Court of Canada was whether the Attorney-General of Quebec had the right to seek such an abatement when the regulation of these companies was within federal jurisdiction. Rinfret J said [at 457]:

> But the objection of the appellant goes deeper and it says: The People's Holding Co. is a federal corporation whose status cannot be impaired by provincial authority. The respondent, as an executive officer of the Province, is not empowered to conduct litigation in respect of any subject within the authority or jurisdiction of the Dominion. He cannot, as such, grant a fiat for the issue of a writ to annul federal letters patent, nor can he take out such a writ himself without permission from the proper federal authority. In brief, Article 978 CPC, on which the respondent relies, does not apply to federal companies or, if it does apply in such cases, then the proceedings can only be brought by the Attorney-General of Canada or, in the alternative, if the article is meant to apply to federal companies and if it should be interpreted as giving the alleged power to the Attorney-General of Quebec, then it is *pro tanto ultra vires*.
>
> There are no decisions of the higher Courts precisely in point.

Rinfret J continued [at 458]:

> The allegations of the petition all point to violations of the law or of the Acts by which the appellant is governed, with the object of defrauding the public and of endangering the public welfare. The prosecution tends to abate the alleged violations and is declared to be instituted and carried on in the general public interest of the people of the Province of Quebec in particular.
>
> Now the Crown, as *parens patriae*, represents the interest of the whole of His Majesty's subjects, and we can discover no reason why the Attorney-General for the Province, acting as the officer of the Crown, should not be empowered to go before the Courts to prevent the violation of the rights of the public of that Province, even if the perpetrator of the deeds complained of be a creature of the federal authority. In the words of Surveyer J in the present case: "*le procureur-général d'une province a le droit et le devoir de réprimer les délits civils qui se commettent dans les limites de sa province.*"
>
> This accords with the position taken at bar by the Attorney-General of Canada who stated that he did "not desire to contest the right of an Attorney-General of a Province to take such proceedings as may be open to him to take, according to the practice of the Courts of the Province, for the purpose of compelling the observance within the Province of any law, federal or provincial, which may be in force therein."

The Supreme Court of Canada has here recognized the right of a provincial Attorney-General to take proceedings in the civil court for the prevention of damage being caused to the citizens of that province by breaches of the law enacted under either federal or provincial legislative powers. The constitutional restriction on the right to pass laws does not impede the province's right to demand their observance.

Although the *People's Holding Co.* decision referred to the violation of the rights of the people of a province by virtue of the commission of civil offences, I can see nothing wrong in principle in extending the same jurisdiction to an Attorney-General with relation to breaches of penal statutes, including the *Criminal Code*. The enforcement of the provisions of the *Criminal Code* rest, of course, with the provincial Attorney-General in any event.

I would conclude therefore that the Attorney-General's application here, which has been found by the trial judge to be in reality an attempt to control prostitution, a topic within the federal criminal legislation jurisdiction, is not for that reason alone improper. The fact that the activity sought to be controlled is really criminal in nature may, however, be a factor that the trial judge should take into consideration in deciding whether the remedy sought is appropriate under all of the circumstances.

There is one other aspect of this issue that may have been in the mind of the trial judge. An injunction is, of course, an equitable remedy and should not ordinarily be granted if the application is in reality for an oblique motive. Here the Attorney-General alleges that members of the public in downtown Halifax are being damaged and inconvenienced by the activities of the defendants and their associates. The court has been asked to tell the defendants that they cannot ply their trade even though the federal Parliament that has the jurisdiction to do so has failed to make prostitution, *per se*, an offence. If the injunction action should be considered a direct attempt to ban prostitution rather than abate the nuisance caused thereby this factor could well be considered by the judge in deciding whether to exercise his discretion for or against the application.

In the second ground of appeal the Crown alleges that Mr. Justice MacIntosh erred in holding that an injunction was not an appropriate remedy for the enforcement of the criminal law. Since prostitution is not of itself a criminal offence, the judge in referring to this issue must have had reference to the many infractions of the *Criminal Code* which were alleged to take place by the defendants themselves and other persons associated with them in their trade. MacIntosh J relied upon the decision of the Appellate Division of Ontario in *Robinson v. Adams* (1924), 56 OLR 217 (App. Div.). In that case, in setting aside an interim injunction to prevent the picketing of a theatre and accompanying union activities, Middleton JA said [at 224-25]:

> The equitable jurisdiction of a civil Court cannot properly be invoked to suppress crime. Unlawful acts which are an offence against the public, and so fall within the criminal law, may also be the foundation of an action based upon the civil wrong done to an individual, but when Parliament has, in the public interest, forbidden certain acts and made them an offence against the law of the land, then, unless a right to property is affected, the civil Courts should not attempt to interfere and forbid by their injunction that which has already been forbidden by Parliament itself. Much less should the Courts interfere when the thing complained of is not within the terms of the criminal law, although it may be rightly regarded as objectionable or even immoral, for then the civil Courts by injunction are attempting to enlarge and amend the

criminal law. Government by injunction is a thing abhorrent to the law of England and of this Province.

The fact that the criminal law emanates from the Dominion, and the civil law from the Province, and that our Courts are created by the Province, only serves to manifest the desirability of refraining from any assumption by the civil Courts of a power to regulate public conduct.

The questions of trades unionism and of the open shop and of how far those who advocate the one as against the other should be permitted to go in endeavouring to uphold and enforce their views, are essentially matters for Parliament and quite foreign to civil Courts.

The Court of Chancery, notwithstanding all this, asserted its rights to protect property by means of its injunction. This jurisdiction was based entirely upon the idea of protecting the property of the plaintiff against the wrongful act of the defendant, and was quite independent of any consideration of the nature of the act complained of as viewed from the standpoint of the criminal law. This jurisdiction is exemplified in nuisance cases.

It is safe to say that the Court of Chancery never granted an injunction in aid of the criminal law, or as supplementing the criminal law, if it was found to be inefficient. ...

[Hart JA then considered *Gouriet v. UPW* at length as well as *AG Alta. v. Plantation Indoor Plants Ltd.*]

There are these and other decisions in which courts have permitted the enforcement of penal and criminal statutes by means of civil injunction, but the various judges have been careful to preserve the discretion that must remain with the court in doing so. In my opinion, a judge when being asked by an Attorney-General to grant such an injunction must consider whether it is really necessary in the light of other procedures available to accomplish the same end. He should consider, as well, the dangers of eliminating criminal conduct without the usual safeguards of criminal procedure available to an accused. He should also consider whether the evil complained of should more properly be eliminated by a change in legislation. Only in very exceptional cases where by reason of lack of time or otherwise no other suitable remedy is available should such an injunction be granted to prevent the commission of a crime.

If Mr. Justice MacIntosh had based the exercise of his discretion solely on the ground that the Attorney-General was attempting to usurp exclusive federal jurisdiction in the sphere of criminal law or on the ancient equitable doctrine that injunctions should not be used for the enforcement of criminal law, as alleged in the notice of appeal, I would find that his discretion had been improperly exercised. It appears to me from reading his decision as a whole, however, that much more was involved. He started with the assumption that prostitution *per se* was not against the law and then recognized the difficulties of prosecuting cases of soliciting, because of the *Hutt* decision, *supra*. He found that the application was in pith and substance an attempt to control prostitution rather than for the purposes of abating a public nuisance. He referred to the activities alleged to constitute the nuisance and showed that they, for the most part, amounted to individual offences against the *Criminal Code*, for the commission of which the persons named as defendants or other persons actually committing them could be prosecuted and penalized. It should be noted that none of the defendants has ever been charged with any of these offences. He referred to other provincial laws that could be utilized to control the situation, and the fact that only a minimal police effort was used by the City of Halifax to assist in controlling the problem.

Mr. Justice MacIntosh also referred to the evidence indicating much of the so-called "disturbance" emanated from sources other than the defendants, and that the region in which the injunction is sought was only to a very limited extent residential. He considered whether an injunction was the appropriate type of remedy and made reference to the warnings about enforcing criminal law in this manner recently referred to in the House of Lords. In conclusion he rejected the application as he did not consider an interim injunction to be a proper procedure under all the circumstances.

In a somewhat similar application by the Attorney-General of British Columbia the discretion of the trial judge was exercised in favour of the injunction. In that case, *A-G BC v. Couillard* (1984), 59 BCLR 102 at p. 105, McEachern CJSC stated:

> In answer to the submissions of the respondents, I can say that so far as I know, blatant aggressive disorderly prostitution has never before been practised or tolerated in a residential area and, to the extent that special, exceptional or even very special circumstances are required. I have no hesitation in finding that the circumstances I have mentioned are not just special or very special, but extraordinary.

I understand that this case is now on appeal, and I mention it only to show that two judges in somewhat similar circumstances have exercised their discretion in the one case for and in the other case against the granting of injunctive relief.

All the authorities to which I have referred have repeatedly spoken of the wide latitude that must be given to the exercise of a trial judge's discretion in deciding whether an injunction of this type should be granted. In my opinion the matters considered by Mr. Justice MacIntosh fall generally within that latitude, and I cannot say that his discretion was not exercised in accordance with proper principles. I would therefore dismiss the appeal with costs.

Appeal dismissed.

NOTES AND QUESTIONS

1. Especially where the respondent may be able to assert a constitutional interest, courts appear to be reasserting their discretion in injunction cases brought by the attorney general. This is particularly apparent in cases involving civil disobedience. One example is the case of *Attorney General for Ontario v. Dieleman* (1994), 20 OR (3d) 229 (Gen. Div.). Here, the attorney general of Ontario sought an injunction, based on public nuisance, to prohibit anti-abortion protest activity within 500 feet of 23 locations. Adams J's lengthy consideration of the merits of the application was premised on the recognition that such an injunction should not be granted automatically. He stated (at 238):

> Central to this matter is an assessment of the impact of the protest activity on women patients and on their medical service providers in the context of an equally full appreciation of the role of free speech in a democratic society.

Adams J held that the injunction requested was a *prima facie* interference with the Charter guarantee of freedom of speech (s. 2(b)) and that only a more limited order could be justified as a reasonable limitation under s. 1. He did find that the protest activities jeopardized the privacy, health, and security of patients and abortion service providers and that the government had a legitimate interest in preventing these harms. In the result, he granted more limited orders prohibiting protesting and "counselling" within certain zones around clinics and physicians' offices and residences. The injunction order was still capturing those who offended its terms as late as 2009. See *R v. Gibbons*, [2011] OJ no. 1889 (CJ).

For a discussion of *Dieleman*, see Paul Horwitz, "Anti-Abortion Protests and the Public Forum: Ontario (Attorney General) v. Dieleman" (1995), 17 *Advocates' Q* 466.

2. In British Columbia, the issue that arose in *Dieleman* has been addressed by legislation, the *Access to Abortion Services Act*, RSBC 1996, c. 1. This statute provides for the creation of "access zones," or what have been commonly referred to as "bubble zones," around facilities that provide abortions, the residences of doctors who perform abortions, the residences of service providers who assist in abortions, and the offices of doctors who perform abortions. By regulation, the lieutenant governor in council may set up an access zone surrounding a facility up to a distance of 50 metres from its boundaries. An access zone of 160 metres is established around the residences of doctors. As well, by regulation the lieutenant governor in council may establish an access zone around the residence of a service provider. A 10-metre access zone is also established for the office of every doctor who provides abortion services. Within these access zones, any type of protest is severely restricted. In the access zone, an individual cannot engage in sidewalk interference, protest, or physically interfere with or attempt to intimidate a patient, service provider, or doctor who performs abortions. Further, within the access zone, an individual cannot continuously or repeatedly observe or place oneself close to a patient, service provider, or doctor who performs abortions. As well, no pictures may be taken or sketches drawn of any doctor, patient or service provider within the access zone for the purpose of dissuading the use of or provision of abortion services.

The Act also serves to limit the harassment of doctors, patients and service providers. The Act forbids repeatedly following or threatening a person, including repeated communication via phone or fax for the purpose of dissuading the use or provision of abortion services.

This legislation has been challenged in court by a protester who had been charged under the Act. The defendant claimed that the Act violated s. 2 of the *Charter of Rights and Freedoms*, by infringing on the freedom of conscience and religion, freedom of expression, and freedom of association. The legislation was, however, upheld by the Supreme Court of British Columbia in *R v. Lewis* (1996), 139 DLR (4th) 480 (BCSC).

NOTE ON PUBLIC RIGHTS INJUNCTIONS IN LABOUR MATTERS

1. In *Re British Columbia Government Employees' Union* (1983), 48 BCLR 1; 48 BCLR 5 (SC), aff'd. (1985), 64 BCLR 113 (CA), aff'd. [1988] 2 SCR 264, McEachern CJ, on his own motion, granted an injunction to restrain courthouse workers from picketing the courthouse during a legal strike. He reasoned that the picketing was calculated to interfere with the administration of justice and, as such, constituted a contempt of court, especially insofar as it might deter witnesses, jurors, or lawyers from entering courthouses to discharge their duties. The union

moved to set aside the order several days later and the matter was fully argued by the BCGEU and the attorney general (representing the public interest and in support of the injunction).

In upholding the order, McEachern CJ reasoned that the courts had an inherent jurisdiction to protect their own process and could, in the face of contempt, exercise that jurisdiction in a summary fashion and on the judge's own motion. The union argued that the provincial labour legislation provided for the designation of essential services and that in the absence of such designation a union has a right to picket during a legal strike. The legislation also gave to the labour board exclusive jurisdiction to restrain picketing (*Labour Code*, RSBC 1979, c. 212, s. 31). McEachern CJ rejected these arguments on the basis that the legislation did not (and perhaps could not as a matter of constitutional law) deprive the court of its jurisdiction to protect its authority against criminal contempt. If picketing, otherwise lawful under the legislation, violates the civil or criminal law the courts retain their jurisdiction to restrain it.

This decision was upheld on appeal. The Court of Appeal affirmed the importance of judicial independence and the right of the citizen to full and unimpeded access to the courts. The court agreed that the picketing was calculated to obstruct the course of justice and that the courts retained the jurisdiction to enjoin this as a criminal contempt. The court rejected the further submission that the injunction infringed the picketers' freedom of assembly and expression on the basis that the restriction was a reasonable limit on those freedoms under s. 1 of the *Canadian Charter of Rights and Freedoms*. This holding was subsequently affirmed by the Supreme Court of Canada: [1988] 2 SCR 264.

2. In *Attorney General for Ontario v. Canadian Union of Public Employees* (1981), 31 OR (2d) 618 (HC), Cromarty J granted an injunction against hospital employees who were striking in violation of the *Hospital Labour Disputes Arbitration Act*, RSO 1970, c. 208. The defendant argued that an injunction was premature as other available remedies had not been exhausted. Cromarty J rejected this argument on the basis that the decisions of the attorney general, as the first law officer of the Crown, ought not to be lightly disregarded. The defendant further objected that the statutory requirements (*Judicature Act*, RSO 1970, c. 228, s. 20) governing the availability of injunctions in "labour disputes" had not been satisfied. Cromarty J held (at 622) that

> the dispute before me is not really a labour matter but is a matter of the chief law officer of the Crown seeking to enjoin the union members from continuing to breach the laws of Ontario and the same rules apply to that as if the Attorney-General was seeking to prevent the flouting of any other statute other than the *Labour Relations Act*. The difference may be subtle but it is real and it was for those reasons that I said earlier that s. 20 [of the *Judicature Act*] did not apply to this application.

3. In June 1987, organized labour in British Columbia held a 24-hour general strike. Fearing a repetition, the attorney general sought an injunction to prevent persons from "circulating any writing advocating the use of force, including work stoppages, slow-downs, study sessions … as a means of accomplishing governmental change in the Province." This wording was based on the sedition provisions of the *Criminal Code* (ss. 59–61). The application was dismissed, ostensibly on technical grounds regarding the pleadings: *British Columbia (Attorney General) v. Georgetti* (1987), 14 BCLR (2d) 119 (SC).

The issue of labour injunctions is considered in further detail in chapter 8, "Interlocutory Injunctions."

Private Actions: Standing and Other Procedural Issues

A second manifestation of the traditional caution of the courts in the area of criminal equity is found in the rules about standing. You have already read *Gouriet*, and as the foregoing materials indicate, it is normally the attorney general, as guardian of the public interest, who may bring the action. With the permission of the attorney general an interested citizen may bring a "relator action." Otherwise, the traditional rule is that an individual may sue in respect of a public nuisance or other violation of public rights only when the wrong complained of also amounts to a violation of that individual's private rights (for example, where the conduct of the defendant also amounts to a tort) or where, as a result of the defendant's conduct, the plaintiff suffers "special and peculiar damage." The classic statement of this rule was given by Buckley J in *Boyce v. Paddington Borough Council*, [1903] 1 Ch. 109, at 114:

> A plaintiff can sue without joining the Attorney-General in two cases: first, where the interference with the public right is such that some private right of his is at the same time interfered with (e.g., where an obstruction is so placed in a highway that the owner of premises abutting upon the highway is specially affected by reason that the obstruction interferes with his private right to access from and to his premises to and from the highway); and, secondly, where no private right is interfered with, but the plaintiff, in respect of his public right, suffers special damage peculiar to himself from the interference with the public right.

The law regarding standing in constitutional matters is considerably different and more liberal. See *Thorson v. AG Canada*, [1975] 1 SCR 138; *Nova Scotia Board of Censors v. McNeil*, [1976] 2 SCR 265; *Minister of Justice of Canada v. Borowski*, [1981] 2 SCR 575; *Canadian Council of Churches v. Canada*, [1992] 1 SCR 236; and *Hy and Zel's Inc. v. Ontario (Attorney General)*, [1993] 3 SCR 675. But in non-constitutional cases, Canadian courts have followed *Boyce* and *Gouriet* on many occasions.

Another illustrative case is *League for Life in Manitoba v. Morgentaler* (1985), 34 Man. R (2d) 91 (QB). Kroft J declined to grant an injunction to restrain the defendant from operating an abortion clinic allegedly in violation of s. 251 of the *Criminal Code*. Kroft J commented on the emotional nature of the issue and noted that the defendant had been tried and acquitted of the offence on previous occasions, that he had been charged with the offence in Manitoba, and that the charge had been stayed pending the outcome of an appeal of an acquittal of the defendant of the same charge in Ontario. The attorney general had not consented to a relator action and Kroft J held that the plaintiffs, alleging neither special damage nor violation of a private right, had no standing to bring the action.

Kroft J also considered *Thorson v. AG Canada*, [1975] 1 SCR 138; *Nova Scotia Board of Censors v. McNeil*, [1976] 2 SCR 265; and *Minister of Justice of Canada v. Borowski*, [1981] 2 SCR 575. The plaintiff argued that these cases had liberalized the law of standing in Canada, for in each of them the Supreme Court of Canada had granted standing to an interested citizen to challenge the constitutional validity of legislation. The court had distinguished the nuisance cases and discounted the fear of floodgates and officious intermeddlers. Kroft J confined these cases to situations in which the plaintiff is seeking a declaration with respect to the constitutional validity of a statute and refused to extend them to the present case on the basis that he had been given no "compelling reason why one citizen should be granted the standing to sue another and to invoke civil remedies simply on his assertion that the enforcement of the criminal law is inherently good and therefore sustainable in the civil courts."

Kroft J went on to state that even if the plaintiffs had standing he would not have granted the injunction. He endorsed the cautious approach exemplified by *Robinson v. Adams* and suggested that criminal injunctions should largely be confined to situations in which the defendant continually violates the statute because the penalty is inadequate as a deterrent, or cases in which there is a threat to the health, safety, or environment of the general public. He noted that the defendant had never been convicted under the *Criminal Code* and that if convicted the threat of life imprisonment was an adequate deterrent. He concluded (at 102):

> If this court were to do as requested it would, as already stated, be doing no more than repeating the injunction that Parliament has already made. Such a move would be worse than useless. If the court order were made and if it were ignored, then the remedy would be to cite Dr. Morgentaler for contempt. If he denied his contempt he would be entitled to a trial in accordance with criminal standards in which he could raise all of the defences which will be available when the charges under s. 251 are heard. The proceedings would differ only in that there would be no jury. Aside from the futility of that procedure, one might ask whether it would be a contravention of constitutional and other rights.

See also *Dehler v. Ottawa Civic Hospital* (1979), 25 OR (2d) 748 (HC), aff'd. (1980), 29 OR (2d) 677 (CA) and *Carruthers v. Langley* (1984), 57 BCLR 373 (SC), aff'd. (1985), 69 BCLR 24 (CA).

A different approach was adopted in *College of Physicians and Surgeons of Manitoba v. Morgentaler* (1985), 36 Man. R (2d) 97, in which the college was granted standing to seek an injunction to close the defendant's free-standing abortion clinic. Wilson J distinguished *League for Life* on the basis that there the applicant was simply a citizen group with no interest different from the general public. In the present case, the college had a statutory mandate to protect the public and therefore had standing. The application was successful because the defendant had not obtained the college's approval for the clinic as required by the provincial *Medical Act*, SM 1980-81, c. 11 (CSM, c. M90).

Canadian courts still jealously guard against extending standing to those who wish to enforce penal statutes or who claim to represent the public interest without a commensurate infringement of some private interest. In *Reece v. Edmonton (City)*, [2011] AJ No. 876 (CA), the Alberta Court of Appeal upheld the trial judge who had held that it would be an abuse of process to allow the applicant to seek a declaration concerning whether Edmonton City was in breach of the *Animal Protection Act*, RSA 2000, c. A-41. The city operated a zoo in which a lone Asian elephant was housed. The applicant believed the elephant's conditions violated the Act and wanted it moved to an elephant sanctuary in a warmer climate. Similarly, in *Cassells v. University of Victoria* (2010), 323 DLR (4th) 180 the applicant was held to lack standing where she sought to argue that the university's management plan to deal with an infestation of wild rabbits allegedly violated the provisions of the *Wildlife Act*, RSBC 1996, c. 488. The applicant claimed to suffer special damage peculiar to herself on the basis that she was a social activist and politician who had campaigned to relocate and save the rabbit population. On this argument A.F. Cullen J commented (at para. 64):

> I would not give effect to that submission, although it had some initial attractiveness. As I see it, the private interest or special damage which gives rise to standing, must flow from the impact of the asserted public wrong on the petitioner independently of the political or social activism which she undertook to oppose it. Otherwise standing could be manufactured by the unilateral action of any person choosing to incur a fiduciary obligation, to put their reputation at issue, or

even to contribute money to a cause which is subject to public law. That, it seems to me, would undermine the purpose of a standing requirement.

The following case provides an example of standing based on an infringement of both public and private rights; it also sets out certain procedural rules regarding addressing injunctions to unnamed persons, police enforcement of "private" injunctions, and the nature of contempt proceedings when an injunction is disobeyed.

MacMillan Bloedel Ltd. v. Simpson
[1996] 2 SCR 1048

McLACHLIN J (for the court): This case raises the issue of the power of the courts to grant injunctions against members of the public engaged in protests that interfere with the private rights of others. Can the courts make orders against unidentified persons not named in the action or named only in proxy as "Jane Doe" and "John Doe"? Or must the persons enjoined be sued and named before an order is enforceable against them?

I. Facts

The appeal arises out of protests against the logging operations of the MacMillan Bloedel Forest Products Company on Vancouver Island in the Clayoquot Sound region of British Columbia. MacMillan Bloedel was engaged in harvesting trees on its properties in the Bulson Creek Watershed. Following a government decision to permit certain harvesting of old-growth forest, the logging of the Pacific Rain Forest in which MacMillan Bloedel and others were engaged became the focus of controversy. People opposed to the harvest of the forests mounted protests. One form of protest was to block public roads in order to prevent the logging trucks from sending cut logs out of the forest area.

MacMillan Bloedel took legal action to end these blockades. On September 17, 1991, it brought an action to restrain the protesters from blocking the roads on which it trucked its logs. It named as defendants the appellant Valerie Langer, four other named individuals, and "John Doe, Jane Doe and Persons Unknown," seeking damages for trespass, nuisance, intimidation, interference with contractual relations and conspiracy, as well as injunctive relief.

The day after its action was launched, MacMillan Bloedel proceeded to apply for and obtain an *ex parte* order enjoining "all persons having notice" of the order from impeding MacMillan Bloedel's logging operations on the Bulson Creek Watershed. In a series of subsequent applications the order was amplified, refined, and extended both in duration and to include other sites: Spencer J added arrest and detention provisions on September 20, 1991; Bouck J converted the interim injunction to an interlocutory injunction on September 25, 1991; Hamilton J expanded the geographical scope of the injunction on June 30, 1992; following further protest activities in July 1992, Tysoe J granted an interim injunction of one year's duration covering yet more territory; and on July 16, 1993, Esson CJSC extended the injunction to August 31, 1993. Public demonstrations escalated from July 5, 1993 onwards, with 56 persons ultimately being charged with contempt. Their trial was set for August 30, 1993.

On August 26, 1993, the application which gives rise to the order under appeal was brought. It came on before Hall J. He granted an interim injunction prohibiting the named defendants, as well as "John Doe, Jane Doe and Persons Unknown" and "all persons having notice of th[e] Order" from engaging in conduct which interfered with MacMillan Bloedel's operations at specified locations: (1993), 106 DLR (4th) 556. He also extended the injunctions granted by Esson CJSC and Hamilton J to August 31, 1994. The appellants appealed from this order. The British Columbia Court of Appeal dismissed the appeal, Wood JA dissenting: (1994), 96 BCLR (2d) 201. The appellants now appeal to this Court.

The injunction barred members of the public from blocking the Kennedy River bridge and authorized the police to remove offenders in the following terms:

> AND THIS COURT FURTHER ORDERS that any persons attending at or near the Kennedy River Bridge during working hours of the Plaintiff and while vehicles are travelling along the travelled roadway in such area shall situate themselves off that roadway and shall not attend within fifteen feet of that roadway;
>
> AND THIS COURT FURTHER ORDERS that any peace officer be authorized to arrest and remove any person who the peace officer has reasonable and probable grounds to believe is contravening or has contravened the provisions of this order.

The police arrested over 800 individuals during the summer and fall of 1993 of violating the interlocutory orders obtained by MacMillan Bloedel. The vast majority of the people arrested were not named as defendants in the Statement of Claim. Six hundred and twenty-six people were convicted of criminal contempt of court and sanctioned by fines of up to $3,000 and jail terms of up to 60 days. The individuals arrested came from all parts of Canada and a number of other countries. The evidence establishes that before arresting a protester, the police followed the practice of handing the injunction to the protester and then reading its contents to him or her. Upon this being done, most protesters peacefully left the blockade.

Throughout this period, the Attorney General of British Columbia followed a policy of not laying criminal charges against environmental groups or individuals engaged in civil disobedience, leaving it instead to the affected private parties to seek civil relief through the courts.

MacMillan Bloedel has not brought the main action on for trial. Its counsel did not suggest that it ever would. The government policy has changed and the protests have died down. The injunctions have long since expired.

II. Judgments for the British Columbia Courts

Hall J granted the order in terms similar to previous orders made in this matter by other justices of the Supreme Court of British Columbia.

The Court of Appeal upheld the order, Wood JA dissenting. The majority of the Court of Appeal was satisfied that the Supreme Court, as a court of inherent jurisdiction, had jurisdiction to make orders binding on non-parties and that the use of such power was justified to preserve the respondent's property rights in the face of mass obstruction. Wood JA dissented on the ground that court orders are binding only on named parties to the action, and that the epithets "John Doe, Jane Doe and Persons Unknown" did not make members of the public parties to the action. In his view, the proper remedy when mass action threatens to overrun private rights is for the Attorney General to enforce the criminal law.

III. The Issues

The appellants make one main point: the court, in the context of civil litigation between private parties, does not have the power to grant an injunction which binds non-parties or the general public. Nor can the problem be cured, in their view, by the use of terms like "John Doe," "Jane Doe" or "Persons Unknown." The appellant Valerie Langer argues that if the courts have the power to make orders against non-parties, it is not appropriate to include provisions authorizing the police to arrest and detain strangers to the litigation. Three issues, therefore, arise:

(1) Do the courts have the power in the context of civil litigation between private parties to enjoin non-parties or members of the public from designated conduct?

(2) If so, can such orders be made using terms like "John Doe" or "Jane Doe" or "Persons Unknown"?

(3) If the courts can make such orders, is it appropriate to include in them provisions authorizing the police to arrest and detain strangers to the litigation?

IV. Analysis

A) Do the Courts Have Jurisdiction To Make Orders Binding on Non-Parties?

This case, like most, rests on a fundamental conflict. The conflict is between the right to express public dissent on the one hand, and the exercise of property and contractual rights on the other. Thus the appellants are wrong in asserting that the orders in question are nothing more than "government by injunction" aimed at suppressing public dissent. The respondent is equally wrong in asserting that this case has nothing to do with the public expression of dissenting views and pertains only to private property. This case is about truth. In a society that prizes both the right to express dissent and the maintenance of private rights, a way to reconcile both interests must be found. One of the ways this can be done is through court orders like the one at issue in this case. The task of the courts is to find a way to protect the legitimate exercise of lawful private rights while preserving maximum scope for the lawful exercise of the right of expression and protest.

At issue in this case is the power of the courts to use an injunction granted in private litigation to regulate or curtail public conduct. The protesters, members of the public, were blocking public roads. The injunction ordered them not to do so and provided for their arrest if they persisted. The submission of the appellant Greenpeace comes down to this: private parties cannot use the courts to curtail the activity of members of the public because private litigation is confined to named, identifiable parties. If members of the public violate the law, disturb the peace or interfere with the lawful exercise of private rights, it is a matter for the Attorney General to prosecute under the criminal law or seek an injunction in the public interest.

It is accepted by all that the British Columbia Supreme Court, as a court of inherent jurisdiction, possesses the power required to maintain the rule of law. More specifically, the broad power of the Court to grant interlocutory injunctions is confirmed by the *Law and Equity Act*, RSBC 1979, c. 224, s. 36, which provides for their grant "in all cases in which it appears to the court to be just or convenient that the order should be made ... on terms and conditions the court thinks just." Relying on these powers, MacMillan Bloedel argues that where a court of inherent jurisdiction has jurisdiction over a dispute or *lis* by reason of private litigation, it can make all orders necessary to preserve the rights of the parties, including orders against unknown persons where this is necessary to make the relief effective. Citing this Court's recent decision in *Weber v. Ontario Hydro*, [1995] 2 SCR 929, MacMillan Bloedel argues that if the rule of law is to be maintained, it must not be deprived of an effective remedy. MacMillan Bloedel contends that the sole purpose of the injunction at issue was to remove the physical blockades that prevented it from exercising the property rights asserted in the action. Having made out a *prima facie* case that its property rights were being violated, MacMillan Bloedel takes the position that it was entitled to an interim order protecting those rights. An order going merely against named parties, *i.e.*, those who had blocked the road in the past, would be ineffective because new people were arriving daily to participate in the blockades. Since the only effective way to protect its rights was, in MacMillan Bloedel's submission, by means of an order directed at unknown persons, it contends that the British Columbia Supreme Court had jurisdiction to grant the order sought.

Against this position, the appellants raise two arguments. The first is that the courts have no inherent jurisdiction to make orders against members of the public in criminal law matters. The second is that the courts have no jurisdiction to make orders against unnamed parties. I will consider each in turn.

(1) The Criminal Law Argument

The appellant Langer argues that there was no need for the BC Supreme Court to assume jurisdiction over unknown parties because an alternative remedy was available. MacMillan Bloedel's "most obvious" remedy, she submits, was to "prevail upon law enforcement officials to enforce the *Criminal Code*."

On a practical level, this remedy offered little assistance to MacMillan Bloedel in the summer of 1993. The Attorney General of British Columbia had a specific policy *not* to lay criminal charges against environmental groups engaging in civil disobedience, but to leave it to affected parties to seek injunctive relief. MacMillan Bloedel submits that it was precisely because the Attorney General was not acting that it needed the protection of an interim injunction.

Underlying the argument that the proper remedy lay in the criminal law is the proposition that, as a matter of law, it is for the Attorney General alone to decide whether and how to deal with conduct of a criminal nature. If the Attorney General decides that it is not in the public interest for the government to act, it is not open to a private party to enlist the aid of the courts to stop the conduct. The appellant Langer relies on *Robinson v. Adams* (1924), 56 OLR 217 (CA) and *Gouriet v. Union of Post Office Workers*, [1978] AC 435 (HL (Eng.)), in support of this contention.

I cannot accept the appellant's position. The mere fact that conduct may be characterized as criminal does not deprive a person whose private rights are affected from seeking relief in the civil courts. *Robinson* and *Gouriet* deal with the narrower issue whether a person who asserts no private right has standing to advance the public interest without first obtaining the consent of the Attorney General. Where, as here, a private litigant's rights are affected by criminal conduct, there is no question that the litigant has such standing: Sharpe, *Injunctions and Specific Performance* (Aurora, ON: Canada Law Book, 2nd ed., 1995 (loose-leaf)), c. 4; *Robinson, supra; Gouriet, supra*. More specifically, where criminal conduct affects property rights, the person so affected may invoke the equitable jurisdiction of the court to obtain an injunction prohibiting the conduct: Sharpe, *supra*, at p. 3-32; *Hurtig v. Reiss*, [1937] 3 WWR 549 (Man. CA). Sharpe cites the following passage from *Boyce v. Paddington Borough Council*, [1903] 1 Ch. 109, at p. 114, rev'd, [1903] 2 Ch. 556 (CA), rev'd [1906] AC 1 (HL (Eng.)), as a classic statement of the right of a private individual to seek relief from criminal conduct in the civil courts:

> A plaintiff can sue without joining the Attorney-General in two cases: first, where the interference with the public right is such as that some private right of his is at the same time interfered with (e.g., *where an obstruction is so placed in a highway that the owner of premises abutting upon the highway is specially affected by reason that the obstruction interferes with his private right to access from and to his premises to and from the highway*); and secondly, where no private right is interfered with, but the plaintiff, in respect of his public right, suffers special damage peculiar to himself from the interference with the public right. [Emphasis added.]

Section 11 of the *Criminal Code*, RSC 1985, c. C-46, codifies this principle in unqualified terms: "No civil remedy for an act or omission is suspended or affected by reason that the act or omission is a criminal offence."

I conclude that the fact that the conduct of blocking the roads can be characterized as criminal does not deprive the British Columbia Supreme Court of the right to grant an injunction against potential offenders in a civil action.

(2) The Problem of Unidentified Persons

The second jurisdictional attack on the interim injunction is the assertion that the courts do not have the jurisdiction to make orders binding on non-parties. On this submission, an order can bind only parties named in the action. Wood JA accepted this argument. In his view, it is "a principle fundamental to our notion of justice" (p. 231) that "the single-minded purpose of the modern day writ of summons and its ancestors has been to give the defendant notice of the proceedings against him, by virtue of which notice the courts then had jurisdiction to grant relief at the behest of the plaintiff" (pp. 231-32). Relying on English authority, Wood JA concluded that, absent a writ directed against an individual personally, the court lacks jurisdiction to make an order against that person.

I propose to consider this argument in two ways: first, from the perspective of the authorities, and second, from the perspective of the effect that such a rule would have on maintaining the rule of law in Canadian society. I turn first to the authorities. I conclude that while the relevant principles have been articulated somewhat differently in England and Canada, the practical effect is the same: in both countries, non-parties who violate injunctions may be found in contempt of court. Hence, non-parties may be seen as being, if not technically *bound by the order, bound to obey the order*. The same rule, it will be seen, has been accepted in other countries with legal systems similar to our own.

It is important at the outset to keep one distinction firmly in mind, as the failure to do so led to some confusion in the submissions before us. I refer to the distinction between the question whether an order may refer to classes of unnamed persons, and the quite separate question whether an order can bind persons not party to the litigation. The first is a procedural question, a matter of pleading. The second is the real question raised by the dissenting opinion of Wood JA. It is with the second question that I am concerned at this point.

The argument that the jurisdiction of the courts is confined to parties named and served in the action rests on the notion that the courts can act only *in personam*; that is, against named individuals. In *Marengo v. Daily Sketch and Sunday Graphic, Ltd.*, [1948] 1 All ER 406 (HL (Eng.)), Lord Uthwatt cited *Iveson v. Harris* (1802), 7 Ves. 251, 32 ER 102 at p. 104, for the proposition that a court is not competent "to hold a man bound by an injunction, who is not a party in the cause for the purpose of the cause." He went on to say (at p. 407):

> The reference to servants, workmen, and agents in the common form is nothing other than a warning against wrongdoing to those persons who may by reason of their situation be thought easily to fall into the error of implicating themselves in a breach of the injunction by the defendant. There its operation, in my opinion, ends.

The traditional English rule thus appears to be that only named parties can be bound by a court order. While general terminology referring to others may be included in the order, this is done only to capture the idea that the named party—often a corporation—is enjoined from committing the specified act both directly and through the actions of others, such as servants and agents, whom it may direct. The general terminology also serves to provide a warning to third parties who might otherwise implicate themselves in a breach of the order.

If third parties are not bound by an order, it would seem logically to follow that they cannot personally be held responsible for breaching it. Nevertheless, the English courts accept that non-parties may be held guilty of contempt for violating court orders. The House of Lords has recently confirmed that a person not named in an order may be held in contempt of court for doing the act prohibited by the order, even when acting independently and not aiding or abetting the named defendant: *Attorney-General v. Times Newspapers Ltd.*, [1991] 2 WLR 994 (HL (Eng.)); see also *In re Supply of Ready Mixed Concrete*, [1991] 3 WLR 707 (CA) at p. 718. In this sense, it may be argued that the English authorities, despite an apparent rule to the contrary, in fact hold that injunctions are binding on persons other than the parties to the action.

How is the fact that non-parties can be found guilty of violating court orders and sent to prison therefor to be reconciled with the assertion of the English authorities that only parties to the litigation can be bound by court orders? On the level of theory, these apparently contradictory positions are reconciled by the distinction between being bound by an injunction as a party to the action and being guilty of contempt of court by obstructing justice. Only parties are "bound" by the injunction. But anyone who disobeys the order or interferes with its purpose may be found to have obstructed the course of justice and hence be found guilty of contempt of court. Thus in *Seaward v. Paterson*, [1897] 1 Ch. 545 (CA), Lindley LJ wrote (at p. 555):

> A motion to commit a man for breach of an injunction, which is technically wrong unless he is bound by the injunction, is one thing; and a motion to commit a man for contempt of Court, not because he is bound by the injunction by being a party to the cause, but because he is conducting himself so as to obstruct the course of justice, is another and a totally different thing.

On the level of practice, the distinction seems to be a distinction without a difference since in either case, a person not named in the action who violates the injunction may be brought before the courts, tried, and penalized. The difference vanishes in the Canadian context where the practice is to charge non-parties with contempt rather than for violating the injunction. In the case at bar, for example, the 626 people convicted under the various injunctions were convicted not of violating the injunction, but of criminal contempt.

It thus emerges that Wood JA correctly asserts the existence of the English rule that injunctions bind only parties to the action. The assertion, however, is of little consequence because third parties who violate or interfere with the injunction may be prosecuted for contempt of court. The case at bar does not raise the issue whether non-parties are bound by an injunction in the technical sense discussed by Wood JA; it does raise the issue whether non-parties can be found in contempt of court for violating an injunction. On the English authorities, the answer to that question is indubitably affirmative.

Canadian judges considering the problem of mass violations of private rights have made less of the distinction between being bound by an injunction (confined to parties) and being bound to obey an injunction (not confined to parties). In *Bartle & Gibson Co. v. Retail, Wholesale and Department Store Union, Local 580*, [1971] 2 WWR 449 (BCCA), Tysoe JA, considering a submission that non-parties should not be described in an order, stated (at p. 455):

> I find it a little difficult to understand why, if it is true—and it is, of course, quite true that persons who, with knowledge of an order, take any steps to assist in contravening it, may be proceeded against for contempt of court—why the order should not provide that it covers somebody who, having knowledge of the order, disobeys it.

A similar recognition that anyone who violates a court order, whether a party or not, may be charged with contempt of court seems to underlie the comment of Estey J, speaking for this Court in *International Longshoremen's Association, Local 273 v. Maritime Employers' Association*, [1979] 1 SCR 120 at p. 144:

> However [language enjoining non-parties] has, for many years, been adopted in these injunctions ... no doubt for the good reason that *it makes the impact and sense of the order clear to all those likely to be affected thereby* and, in any event, such wording can hardly be said to harm *any of the persons in law affected by the order*. [Emphasis added.]

In other words, since persons other than named parties may be affected by the order, and be held in contempt for violating it, it makes good sense to use language which alerts those people to that risk. More recent English authority suggests that courts there, too, may be coming to see the practical value of such an approach. Thus, in *Attorney General v. Newspaper Publishing plc*, [1987] 3 All ER 276 (CA) at pp. 314-15, Balcombe LJ commented that in an appropriate case it may be "preferable" for the court to make its initial protective order in terms which make it clear to members of the public who may be affected by the order that they also are required to obey it.

It may be confidently asserted, therefore, that both English and Canadian authorities support the view that non-parties are bound by injunctions: if non-parties violate injunctions, they are subject to conviction and punishment for contempt of court. The courts have jurisdiction to grant interim injunctions which all people, on pain of contempt, must obey. The only issue—and one which has preoccupied courts both in England and, to a lesser extent, here—is whether the wording of the injunction should warn non-parties that they, too, may be affected by including language enjoining the public, or classes of the public, from committing the prohibited acts. On this point I share the view of Tysoe JA in *Bartle & Gibson, supra,* and Estey J in *International Longshoremen's Association, supra*: if members of the public may be bound to respect court orders in private suits on pain of being held in contempt, it seems appropriate that the order apprise them of that fact.

It remains to consider a final argument raised by the appellants. Underlying both their submissions and the dissenting reasons of Wood JA is the suggestion that it is improper to use private litigation for the sole purpose of obtaining an injunction to constrain public action. Hence the emphasis on the fact that MacMillan Bloedel's main action against the named defendants has never proceeded to trial. Having given this concern my most serious consideration, I conclude that it provides no basis for invalidating the order made in this case. MacMillan Bloedel sued and named as defendants five persons identified at the first blockades. MacMillan Bloedel was entitled to claim against them such relief as the law allows. Although it contented itself with obtaining interim injunctions, MacMillan Bloedel could have proceeded to trial to obtain permanent injunctions and damages against them. The fact that it chose not to pursue the fullest remedy available is not a basis for denying it any other relief allowed by law. The interlocutory injunctions obtained against the named defendants for blocking the logging roads also bound members of the public at large. There is nothing new in this. Canadian courts have for decades followed the practice of issuing orders directed at prohibiting interference with private property rights, which orders affect not only the named parties but also the general public. ...

Having considered the authorities, I turn to the practical consequences of ruling that courts cannot issue injunctions which non-parties are required to respect. Wood JA, having concluded that the courts have no such authority, was required to face this problem. He wrote (at p. 248):

> Can the courts stand by and watch helplessly when the private rights of the individual are overrun by the mob? Should we turn our backs on the person who looks to us for help in such circumstances over an issue so apparently technical as jurisdiction? If there were no alternative solution to that individual's dilemma, I would be quick to answer "no" to both questions. The progress of the law is an ever-evolving journey which must respond to new challenges lying within its path. Much of the jurisdiction which the Supreme Court exercises today was born out of just such necessitous circumstances.
>
> However, in my view there is an alternative solution. It lies in the proper discharge of the obligations which attach to the office of the Attorney General.

Wood JA went on to state that it is "the responsibility of the Attorney General as the chief law enforcement officer ... to see to it that the criminal law is enforced" (p. 249).

Every citizen would endorse these words. Yet, as this case demonstrates, to state the obligation of the Attorney General is not to ensure that it will be discharged in such a way as to provide the required protection to citizens injured by the conduct of others. It is to fill this gap that the equitable remedy of injunctions—injunctions which not only the parties but also all others must respect on peril of being found in contempt of court—has developed.

What then of the other side? What are the dangers of empowering the courts to make orders to protect private interests which all must obey on pain of contempt? It is fundamental that no state founded on the rule of law can permit members of the public to be detained and punished for violating an order of which they are ignorant. If members of the public are to be charged with obstruction of justice for having disobeyed an injunction, they must first be apprised of the existence and terms of the order and be given an opportunity to comply. That is precisely what was done in enforcing the injunctions here. Before a protester was arrested, he or she was handed a copy of the order and its terms were read to him or her. The protester was then asked to quit the blockade. Most complied. Only those who refused were arrested. It is also desirable, as this Court suggested in *International Longshoremen, supra,* that the order's terms speak of the duty of non-parties to respect it. This, too, was done here. Finally, it is necessary that the orders be carefully worded and constrained to ensure that they are fair and not unduly broad. This requirement, too, was met in the case at bar. Over the months, a number of justices reviewed and amended the terminology of the injunctions to make them clearer and fairer. For example, in July 1993, Esson CJSC removed language enjoining "creating a nuisance"—legal language which some members of the public might not have understood—and replaced it by more precise language specifying that what was prohibited was "physical" obstruction. Words could be used, signs could be paraded; what could not be done was to physically block the road.

(3) Summary on Jurisdiction

I conclude that the British Columbia Supreme Court had jurisdiction to make orders binding on persons who are not parties to the action.

B) Suing Unnamed Persons

The second issue is whether the use of terminology such as "John Doe," "Jane Doe" and "Persons Unknown" in the style of cause invalidates the order. The appellants argue that these terms represent an attempt to sue the general public, and that such terms are not justified under the British Columbia Rules of Practice and the principles developed under the Rules.

The practice of using terms like "John Doe" is directed at permitting a plaintiff to sue a person whose name the plaintiff does not know: *Jackson v. Bubela and Doe,* [1972] 5 WWR 80 (BC CA). Under the British Columbia Rules, the procedure for objecting to such an appellation is to apply to have the terms struck out. Alternatively, an application by the plaintiff to have the defendant's name substituted for "John Doe" for the purpose of obtaining relief against him may be dismissed if the use of the "John Doe" designation is found to have been inappropriate. We have been referred to no authority suggesting that an order made under a valid action is invalid because the style of cause of the action included a reference to "John Doe, Jane Doe and Persons Unknown."

In fact, the use of "John Doe, Jane Doe and Persons Unknown" in the present action appears to be surplusage. As discussed above, a person who is not a party to an action is bound to respect an order made in the action, on pain of being found in contempt of court. This was the procedure used to enforce the order here at issue. None of the protesters was charged or sued as a party to the action. So the question whether relief may be obtained against them *in the action* on the basis of having sued them as "John Doe, Jane Doe and Persons Unknown" never arose. Accordingly, it is unnecessary for this Court to decide whether, as a matter of pleading, the use of these terms in the style of cause could validly engage members of the public served with the writ.

C) Provisions Authorizing Arrest and Detention

The appellant Valerie Langer has questioned the appropriateness of including a provision authorizing the police to arrest and detain persons breaching the injunction. She argues that no authorization or direction from the court is necessary to enable the police to act. The respondent accepts that the authorization is superfluous, and states that it is included only because the police have requested such wording. No objection to this term was made before Hall J and it is not suggested that it vitiates the order. In these circumstances, this Court need not consider it further. I observe only that the inclusion of police authorization appears to follow the Canadian practice of ensuring that orders which may affect members of the public clearly spell out the consequences of non-compliance. Members of the public need not take the word of the police that the arrest and detention of violators is authorized because this is clearly set out in the order signed by the judge. Viewed thus, the inclusion does no harm and may make the order fairer.

V. Conclusion

I conclude that the British Columbia Supreme Court has jurisdiction to make orders enjoining unknown persons from violating court orders. Such orders are enforceable on the long-standing principle that persons who are not parties to the action, but who violate an order of the court, may be found guilty of contempt for interfering with justice. Provided that contempt is the only remedy sought, it is not necessary to join all unknown persons in the action under the designation, "John Doe, Jane Doe and Persons Unknown." Nor, strictly speaking, is it essential that the order refer to unknown persons at all. However, the long-standing Canadian practice of doing so is commendable because it brings to the attention of such persons the fact that the order may constrain their conduct. Similarly to be commended is the practice followed by the courts in this case of ensuring that the wording of the orders is clear and that their effect is properly circumscribed.

I would dismiss the appeal with costs.

NOTES

1. The Supreme Court refers to the earlier convictions of persons for "criminal contempt." Once the injunction had been originally granted, the plaintiff forest company applied to the court for contempt proceedings against protesters who continued to violate the injunctions. The court agreed with the company that the contempt proceedings should be considered criminal in nature rather than civil and requested the attorney general to intervene and conduct the proceedings (*MacMillan Bloedel Ltd. v. Simpson*, Vancouver Reg. C916306 (August 21, 1992) (BC SC)). As a result, there was a series of "mass trials" involving numerous Clayoquot protesters charged with criminal contempt of court. These trials were indexed under the name *MacMillan Bloedel Ltd. v. Simpson*. The convictions for criminal contempt were based on the courts' findings that the protesters had continually and publicly defied the court order (in the presence of the media, the police and onlookers). This, it was concluded, challenged the

authority of the courts and was designed to diminish public respect. The courts rejected the protesters' defence of necessity and imposed fines and jail terms.

2. Note that *Simpson* involves interim or interlocutory as opposed to permanent injunctions. Much of the discussion is therefore pertinent to chapter 8, "Interlocutory Injunctions."

John P.S. McLaren, "The Common Law Nuisance Actions and the Environmental Battle—Well Tempered Swords or Broken Reeds?"
(1972), 10 *Osgoode Hall Law Journal* 505, at 511-16 (footnotes omitted)

A. An Initial Dilemma—Which Nuisance?

1. Public Nuisance

In terms of litigation strategy the first problem is to determine whether the factual situation falls within the boundaries of public or private nuisance. Given the environmental litigant's concern for championing what he conceives to be the public interest, public nuisance which purports to protect the individual in the exercise of his public rights and which has its genesis in criminal actions to counteract publicly offensive pursuits, such as causing noxious odours, dust, soot and noise, and fouling public thoroughfares and waterways, would seem to be an obvious choice. Superficially, an action which appears to stress the plaintiff's concern for the public interest has obvious attractions for the litigant emphasizing the environmental perspective. Reality, however, is less than kind to the plaintiff in this regard. The courts in recognizing a private action for public nuisance have sought to draw a clear dividing line between its criminal and civil aspects. In brief the civil litigant can only protect his own adversely affected interest. In the absence of facultative legislation he has no inherent standing to sue in the public interest, as a private attorney-general. Well established Canadian authority holds that if the vindication of the public interest is required then the only party who has standing to initiate a prosecution or a civil suit is the governmental representative of that interest, usually the provincial, but on occasion the federal, Attorney-General. Even a municipality, which one might have thought would have a claim to standing as the custodian of the local community interest, has been found impotent in this respect. As action by the Attorney-General is discretionary, there is no guarantee that he will respond affirmatively to complaints and pleas for action by concerned citizens.

The practical effect of this limitation on actionability can best be highlighted by testing the viability of public nuisance in the area of conservation of wilderness and resort areas. The adverse effects of pollution upon our recreational pursuits have become only too obvious in the last decade. Prior to that point in time most urbanites who experienced pollution in their everyday lives could find perhaps some solace in the possibility of vacationing in a clean rural environment. Now in many instances the escape is from one form of pollution to another. With the realization that pollution is no respecter of urban-rural boundaries, and greater citizen sensitivity to the need to protect the natural environment, the question is raised of what the individual can do through the courts to protect the wilderness, the resort area, the provincial or national park from the blight of pollution. The answer, insofar as he seeks to found his claim in tort law solely on the basis of his concern as a member of the public, is nothing. Unless he can tie his action to the infringement of a private right which he possesses, his only resort to remedy the polluted environment is to fall back upon the traditional and often ineffective device of bringing pressure to bear in the political arena, more especially by seeking to goad the Attorney-General into action. The agonizing truth is that the only common law tort action which has its origins in solicitude for the public welfare is of negligible utility in satisfying a growing public concern for the conservation of the country's natural heritage.

In addition to its limited viability as an action for the citizen to protect the public interest, public nuisance has distinct shortcomings as a vehicle for the protection of individual rights. Consonant with their desire to divorce the public and private elements in this action, the courts have sought to limit its application to situations in which the plaintiff can claim damage which is "special," that is different from that which is or could be expected to be suffered by other members of the public. Interpretations of both the terms "the public" and "special damage" rendered by some Canadian courts suggest that counsel for the environmental interest may have to tread with considerable caution in seeking to launch an environmental suit in public nuisance. In the first place there is some doubt as to whether "the public" embraces all those who in a variety of ways do or could make use of the public facility. It has recently been suggested that a plaintiff or group of plaintiffs who make a special use of a public facility in conjunction with others in the neighbourhood are barred from suit, on the ground that their damage in relation to other members of the class is not unique. This was the considered opinion of Furlong CJ of the Newfoundland Supreme Court in *Hickey v. Electric Reduction Co. of Canada*, in which he dismissed the action of a group of commercial fishermen who had claimed to have suffered loss in revenue attributed to the pollution of Placentia Bay by the defendant's plant. If this reasoning is followed, it means that in certain geographical locations, where a significant proportion of the populace engages in a special productive use of public water resources, the special *use* will be the sole frame of reference as to whether the *damage* is special or not. For practical purposes the public equals the special class. Thus counsel who is denied the freedom to sue in the general public interest may now face the further obstacle that he cannot represent that segment of the populace which is most adversely affected by it, if that segment is too large.

Secondly, although it is well accepted that personal injury and property damage fall within the designation "special damage," there is some conflict as to whether it comprehends purely financial loss. The *Hickey* case, which is supported by two earlier decisions relating to commercial benefits derived from fisheries, denies that it does. The rationale for this rather remarkable finding is to be found in a statement of Baxter, J in *Filion v. New Brunswick International Paper Co.*, a case involving an alleged interference with the fishing of a commercial smelt fisherman by waste from the defendant's pulp mill. The judge asserted that since the plaintiff could have no greater rights than other members of the public in fishing, any damage which flowed from pollution of the fishery was by definition merely different in degree from that incurred by others. The decision fails to recognize that uses of public resources vary considerably in incidence and importance, and that this fact is reflected in a wide spectrum of adverse consequences in the event of interference, ranging from minor annoyance to financial ruin. Moreover, the court by divorcing the issue of rights from that of uses suggested another and more far reaching limitation of the anti-pollution suit, that is that whatever the incidence of the special use recovery for financial loss will be barred. The type of victim of pollution who incurs financial loss is the most likely to suffer from its long-term effects because of his permanent interest in the resources and his invest-ment in utilizing it. He therefore has the greatest incentive to remedy it. Accordingly his exclusion from suit would mean the effective submersion of the environmental interest in public nuisance suits. Fortunately there is a countervailing trend in Canadian jurispru-dence. There exists a triad of Ontario appellate decisions which have come to the opposite conclusion in an analogous context. Each of these decisions makes it clear that financial loss incurred by commercial concerns engaged in shipping enterprises on navigable waterways by obstructions to navigation, amounts to "special damage." There is no difference in prin-ciple between financial loss flowing from interference with the commercial uses of the right to navigate and the right to fish in public waters. The nub of the complaint in both cases is the adverse effect upon the use, and upon it alone. Given this equation there is no reason why environmental counsel should not use these latter decisions effectively to counter the arguments of the fishery cases.

The controversy in Canadian jurisprudence over whether financial loss is "special dam-age" does not leave one too sanguine about the possibility of the courts accepting the more general argument that a difference in the degree of damage is sufficient to found a private action in public nuisance. The only decisions which lend support to the argument are three early Ontario cases, one involving obstruction of a highway and the others navigable water-ways, which imply that an aggravated degree of inconvenience (in these instances to plain-tiffs who depended upon the thoroughfares as channels of communication with the outside world) is enough. The utility of these decisions will depend on the willingness of a court to divorce them from their special facts, for it may be argued that the interference in each case came close to being an invasion of the property right of unobstructed ingress and egress, and thus tantamount to a private nuisance. At best their authority as support for a difference in degree as the appropriate criterion may be described as tenuous. In consequence, it is not possible to be confident about using public nuisance [to] inventively protect individuals who are subjected to an aggravated degree of inconvenience for pollution in public places. Thus the worker in a city whose employment is the street or park and who is the victim of constant exposure to noise and air pollution may find that unless his health has as a result of his working conditions perceptibly deteriorated or he can point to property damage he has no standing. His concern to improve his working milieu may be of no avail.

The restrictive nature of the rules surrounding the private action in public nuisance, and the unsatisfactory state of Canadian case authority, suggest that the action has limited po-tential as a means of vindicating the interests of environmentalists. The unfortunate irony of the development of this branch of the law of nuisance is that the chances of the concerned citizen achieving positive results decrease in inverse proportion to the gravity of the offend-ing pollution problem and its adverse consequences. The environmental lawyer is effectively hamstrung in seeking to inject the anti-pollution perspective into the action, because he has to avoid at all costs giving the impression that the defendant's activity is causing a wide-spread common problem. If he does then his client's damage may become indistinguishable from that suffered by the rest of the community, and he will fail to sustain the unique nature of his claim.

The policy reasons underlying these judicial roadblocks are the fear of a multiplicity of claims and the launching of trivial suits. One wonders whether this "floodgates" type of thinking has any more validity here than in other areas of tort law in which it has been utilized to prevent or delay progressive development. It has never been adequately proven that breakthroughs into new areas of liability trigger off large numbers of claims, let alone claims which are trivial. It may of course be argued that with the advent of widespread concern over pollution, that a stimulus to a multiplicity of actions would be provided by a more liberal approach to standing. However, it is the writer's opinion that the more likely result is the coalescence of effort by concerned citizens. There would obviously be suits, but suits involving large numbers of complainants, genuinely launched in the public interest. Furthermore, if there are trivial claims, it is surely not beyond the capacity of the courts to expose and discourage them. The overriding factor in seeking more flexibility here is to circumvent the concern for economic expediency, which may restrain the official protectors of the public interest. However, in the absence of legislation it may be doubted whether there will be any significant judicial movement in the direction of liberalization of standing.

NOTES AND QUESTIONS

1. McLaren refers to cases that appear to provide support for a more liberal approach to standing. See, for example, *Turtle v. City of Toronto* (1924), 56 OLR 252 (AD); *Rainy River Navigation Co. v. Ontario & Minn. Power* (1914), 17 DLR 850 (Ont. SCAD); and *Drake v. Sault Ste. Marie Pulp and Paper Co.* (1898), 25 OAR 251 (CA).

2. The case of *Stein v. Gonzales* (1984), 58 BCLR 110 (SC) has earlier been referred to. There, the plaintiffs were owners of a hotel and apartment building, seeking an injunction (based on public nuisance) in respect of prostitution-related activities on public properties adjacent to their buildings. The plaintiffs alleged that the activities were noisy, bothersome to guests and tenants, and had resulted in a general deterioration of the neighbourhood, causing a significant loss to their businesses and property. While assuming that the activities did amount to a nuisance, the court denied the plaintiffs standing. McLachlin JA stated (at 112-13):

> Public rights, including claims for public nuisance, can be asserted in a civil action by the Attorney General as the Crown officer representing the public. A private person can bring an action for an alleged or anticipated breach of the law only where that breach would constitute a breach of his private rights or would inflict "special" or "peculiar" damage upon him. ...
>
> The policy behind this rule is that the public and criminal jurisdiction of the court is not to be usurped in a civil proceeding. As long as the suffering or inconvenience is general, there is no place for independent intervention by private citizens.

McLachlin J held that the plaintiffs were not suffering a private nuisance since the activities of the defendants were not substantially interfering with the plaintiffs' use of their own property. The nuisance was a public one only. Following the case of *Hickey v. Electric Reduction Co.* (1970), 21 DLR (3d) 368 (Nfld. SC), McLachlin J further held that the plaintiffs did not have standing to sue for the public nuisance because the inconvenience complained of was shared by the public generally. Summarizing the authorities, she stated (at 114-15):

> The common thread which runs through the authorities is that private citizens cannot maintain actions for public nuisance where the suffering and inconvenience complained of is shared by the public or a recognizable class of the public. The ultimate question is simple: is the damage suffered by the plaintiff different from that suffered by other members of the community?

In the case at bar it is not alleged that the defendants are interfering with the plaintiff's use of their property. There is no suggestion that ingress or egress to their property has been blocked. The essence of the plaintiffs' complaint is that the neighbourhood has deteriorated as a result of the defendants' activities in the streets and alleys surrounding their premises, making their premises less desirable to guests and prospective tenants and raising the prospect of financial loss.

Does this constitute damage different from that suffered by other members of the community or a class thereof? I think not. Many other citizens carry on business in the area in which the plaintiffs operate their establishments. There is no suggestion that they, like the plaintiffs, will not suffer losses as a consequence of the increase of prostitution in the neighbourhood. The onus is on the plaintiffs to demonstrate that their loss is special and unique. This they have failed to do. ...

To put the matter another way, different citizens may suffer different injuries as a result of the defendants' conduct, ranging from harassment and annoyance to financial loss. But the injuries suffered, insofar as they are of the same type as those suffered by other members of the public exercising their public rights, remain public injuries in the eyes of the law. ...

While I have arrived at this conclusion on the basis of the authorities, I find it to be supported by important considerations of policy. McEachern CJSC in granting the injunction against activities related to prostitution amounting to a public nuisance west of the area here in question, was careful to state that such relief could be obtained "upon a proper application being made by the Attorney General." There are good reasons, in my view, for maintaining that requirement. First, as a matter of principle, the granting of an injunction to enjoin conduct which is within the purview of the *Criminal Code*, RSC 1970, c. C-34, but not expressly prohibited by the Code is a serious step; it is appropriate that such an incursion into the public domain be supported by the Attorney General who is entrusted and charged with the duty of enforcing public rights. Secondly, it is doubtful whether this problem—essentially a public one—is best regulated by a series of private civil suits.

3. Given the liberalization of claims for economic loss in tort (for example, *Winnipeg Condominium Corp. No. 36 v. Bird Construction Co.*, [1995] 1 SCR 85), can it still be said with confidence that financial losses, such as those alleged to be suffered by the plaintiffs' in *Stein* (and other public nuisance cases, such as *Hickey*) do not count as special damage for the purpose of obtaining standing?

4. Some judges have suggested the need to reconsider the *Hickey* rule. In *Gangier v. Canadian Forest Products Ltd.* (1990), 51 BCLR (2d) 218 (SC), a fisherman brought a private action in public nuisance with respect to the crab industry near the Howe Sound pulp mill. The defendant was in part seeking a ruling that the case should be thrown out under *Hickey v. Electric Reduction Co. of Canada, Ltd.* (1970), 21 DLR (3d) 368 (Nfld. SC) and *Stein v. Gonzales* (1984), 58 BCLR 110 (SC). The court held that the pleadings disclosed arguable causes of action, including that their claim in public nuisance could not be summarily dismissed as it had not been proven whether the plaintiffs had suffered differently from other members of the public. Low J went on to question whether *Hickey* is good law on special damages in *obiter*:

I will go further. Hickey is not binding on this court and I do not see it as having been considered in *Stein* to such an extent that all aspects of it must necessarily apply to the particular facts pleaded in the present case. Also, there is a line of three cases in Ontario which go in a different direction and which were not considered in *Hickey* or in *Stein*. They are: *Crandell v. Mooney* (1878), 23 UCCP 212; *Rainy River Navigation Co. v. Ontario and Minnesota Power Co.* (1914), 26 OWR 752;

and *Rainy River Navigation Co. v. Watrous Island Boom Co.* (1914), 26 OWR 456, all decisions of the Ontario Court of Appeal. These cases all concerned obstructions to navigation and losses amounting to "special damage" caused to shipping enterprises. I think they support the argument that the restriction on private recovery for public nuisance in *Hickey* is far too narrow and that all that should need to be proved is a significant difference in degree of damage between the plaintiff and members of the public generally.

The factual issues were argued in *Gagnier v. Canadian Forest Products Ltd.*, [1991] BCJ no. 2634 (SC), and the case was eventually decided against the plaintiff on the grounds that he had no credible evidence to prove the economic losses he claimed.

5. The Ontario *Environmental Bill of Rights*, SO 1993, c. 28, provides for broader public interest standing:

> 84(1) Where a person has contravened or will imminently contravene an Act, regulation or instrument prescribed for the purposes of Part V and the actual or imminent contravention has caused or will imminently cause significant harm to a public resource of Ontario, any person resident in Ontario may bring an action against the person in the court in respect of the harm and is entitled to judgment if successful.
>
> (2) Despite subsection (1), an action may not be brought under this section in respect of an actual contravention unless the plaintiff has applied for an investigation into the contravention under Part V and,
>
>> (a) has not received one of the responses required under sections 78 to 80 within a reasonable time; or
>>
>> (b) has received a response under sections 78 to 80 that is not reasonable. ...
>
> (6) Subsections (2) and (4) do not apply where the delay involved in complying with them would result in significant harm or serious risk of significant harm to a public resource. ...
>
> 103(1) No person who has suffered or may suffer a direct economic loss or direct personal injury as a result of a public nuisance that caused harm to the environment shall be barred from bringing an action without the consent of the Attorney General in respect of the loss or injury only because the person has suffered or may suffer direct economic loss or direct personal injury of the same kind or to the same degree as other persons.

ADDITIONAL READINGS

T.A. Cromwell, *Locus Standi: A Commentary on the Law of Standing in Canada* (Toronto: Carswell, 1986).

W. Estey, "Public Nuisance and Standing To Sue" (1972), 10 *Osgoode Hall Law Journal* 563.

Law Reform Commission of British Columbia, *Civil Litigation in the Public Interest* (1980).

J.P.S. McLaren, "Nuisance in Canada," in A.M. Linden, ed., *Studies in Canadian Tort Law* (Toronto: Butterworths, 1968), at 320.

Ex Parte Island Records
[1978] Ch. 122 (CA)

LORD DENNING MR: If you would like a caption for this case, I can suggest it. It is "Pop Artists want to stop Bootleggers." It needs explanation for the innocents. Take a popular group who play and sing live in a theatre or in a broadcasting studio. They give an exciting performance. This performance is transmitted on to a tape by a recording company. The company afterwards make records of it and sell them to the public. But there is a person in the audience or beside the wireless set who is listening to the performance. He has in his hand or his pocket one of the latest scientific devices. It is a tiny machine by which he records on tape this exciting performance. It is called a condenser microphone. Having recorded it on the one tape, he then uses the tape to make hundreds of copies and sell them in the form of cassettes and cartridges or gramophone records. Sometimes these are poor in quality. Sometimes they are as good as the records made by the recording companies themselves. They are sold to the public by small shopkeepers at cut prices and eat into the sales of the recording companies. The performers suffer also: because they receive royalties from the recording companies according to the number sold.

The performers, however, have no copyright in their performance: nor have the recording companies. No matter how brilliant the performance—which no one else could rival—nevertheless it is so intangible, so fleeting, so ethereal, that it is not protected by the law of copyright. The actual musical work which they play or sing may itself be the subject of copyright, but the performers have no right in that musical work itself. It may be out of copyright. It may be the work of an old composer who died long ago. Or it may be the copyright of a modern composer or owner, who has already been paid his due. The important thing to notice is that the performers themselves have no copyright.

No matter that the performers have no copyright, nevertheless the making of these secret tapes and records—and the selling of them—is quite illegal if it is done without the written consent of the performers. It is a criminal offence, punishable by fine or imprisonment. Those who engage in this trade are called "bootleggers." That is a term which was coined in the United States 100 years ago. Those engaged in illicit trading in liquor used to hide it in the upper part of their tall boots—the leg of the boot.

We must distinguish these "bootleggers" from the "pirates" in the trade. "Pirates" are different in this way: they do not reproduce live performances. They reproduce existing records. They take the sound records made by the recording companies and reproduce them illicitly on their own tapes and records, and then sell these copies. They can sell them at a very low price, because they have a cheap apparatus for copying, and do not have to maintain studios, or pay artists. They are sold by small shopkeepers in poor surroundings. These copies are not only illegal. They are infringement of copyright. They infringe the copyright of the recording companies in their existing records. These infringers are called "pirates" because "piracy" has long been used to describe the infringement of copyright, as in the phrase "literacy piracy."

These "pirates" used to do an enormous trade in infringing copies of recorded music. It was very difficult to catch them. As soon as one small shopkeeper was sued, he got rid of all infringing material. He passed his stock to a fellow pirate: and then declared that he never had any records except the one which the plaintiffs had discovered. This strategem was, however, defeated by the enterprise of Mr. Laddie. He persuaded the judges of the Chancery Division to make an order—ex parte—on the shopkeeper before the writ is served. This order is served on him, with the writ, in the presence of a solicitor. It catches the pirate unawares—before he has had time to destroy or dispose of his infringing stock or his incriminating papers. It requires him to disclose all relevant material that he has. The order "freezes" the stock which he has and enables the plaintiff to inspect it. The order contained safeguards to see that no injustice was done. The first reported case was the order made by Templeman J in *E.M.I. Ltd. v. Pandit*, [1975] 1 WLR 302 (Ch.). The practice was confirmed and consolidated by the decision of this court in *Anton Piller KG v. Manufacturing Processes Ltd.*, [1976] Ch. 55 (CA). The effect of these ex parte orders has been dramatic. When served with them, the shopkeepers have acknowledged their wrongdoing and thrown their hand in. So useful are these orders that they are in daily use—not only in cases of infringement of copyright, but also in passing-off cases, and other cases. They are called "*Anton Piller*" orders.

Now we have the question whether *Anton Piller* orders can be made against bootleggers. To a layman there would seem no difference between pirates and bootleggers. If an *Anton Piller* order can be made against a pirate, it should be possible, too, against a bootlegger. But there is a difference in law. A "pirate" is guilty of a civil wrong. He is infringing the copyright of the recording companies in their tapes and records. But a "bootlegger" is not guilty of a civil wrong. He is only guilty of a crime. Many of the judges have ignored this difference. They have been granted *Anton Piller* orders ex parte against bootleggers. We are told that Cantley, Plowman, Foster, Whitford, Fox and Slade JJ have granted them. None of those cases has been reported. But three judges have refused them: McCardie J in *Musical Performers' Protection Association Ltd. v. British International Pictures Ltd.* (1930), 46 TLR 485 (Ch.): Megarry V-C in *Apple Corps Ltd. v. Lingasong Ltd.* (1977), 3 FSR 345 (Ch.): and Walton J in this present case on January 3, 1978. This is an appeal from Walton J's decision. It raised a point of such importance—in which the defendant was not represented—that we asked the Attorney-General if he would appoint an *amicus curiae* to help us. He appointed Mr. Gibson, and his assistance has been invaluable.

The Statute

The first point is on the statute. It clearly makes "bootlegging" a crime. But does it confer a civil cause of action on the performers and recording companies?

There have been two main statutes. The first *Dramatic and Musical Performers' Protection Act* in 1925. The second in 1958. There are two additional statutes increasing penalties. One of 1963. The other is 1972. I will read only the material parts of section 1 of the present 1958 statute:

> [I]f a person knowingly—(a) makes a record, directly or indirectly from or by means of the performance of a dramatic or musical work without the consent in writing of the performers, ... he shall be guilty of an offence under this Act, and shall be liable

to a fine of £20 for each record made or punishment of two years or both.

Civil Action for Damages

The courts have discussed on many occasions whether or not the breach of a statute (which prescribes only criminal penalties) also gives a civil action for damages. On this point "the only rule" said Lord Simonds in *Cutler v. Wandsworth Stadium Ltd.*, [1949] AC 398 (HL (Eng.)) at p. 407

> which in all circumstances is valid is that the answer must depend on a consideration of the whole Act and the circumstances, including the pre-existing law, in which it was enacted.

Mr. Laddie submitted that the statutes here were passed for the protection of a particular person or class of persons, namely, the performers. That was seen from the fact that performers could give or refuse their written consent. So this case came, he said, within the pro-cases, such as *Groves v. Lord Wimborne*, [1898] 2 QB 402 (CA); *Monk v. Warbey*, [1935] 1 KB 75 (CA) and *Solomons v. R. Gertzenstein Ltd.*, [1954] 2 QB 243 (CA). But Mr. Laddie's proposition is not universally true. There are numerous penal statutes which could be said to be passed for the protection of a particular class of persons which have been held not to give rise to a civil action for damages. These are the contra-cases, such as *Atkinson v. Newcastle and Gateshead Waterworks Co.* (1887), 2 Ex. D 441 (CA); *Phillips v. Britannia Hygienic Laundry Co. Ltd.*, [1923] 2 QB 832 (CA) and *Cutler v. Wandsworth Stadium Ltd.*, [1949] AC 398 (HL (Eng.)).

The truth is that in many of these statutes the legislature has left the point open. It has ignored the plea of Lord du Parcq in *Cutler's* case (at p. 410). So it has left the courts with a guess-work puzzle. The dividing line between the pro-cases and the contra-cases is so blurred and so ill-defined that you might as well toss a coin to decide it. I decline to indulge in such a game of chance. To my mind, we should seek for other ways to do "therein what to justice shall appertain."

The Protection of Private Rights

The way was pointed out by Mr. Gibson, who was engaged in the recent case of *Gouriet v. Union of Post Office Workers*, [1978] AC 435 (HL (Eng.)). He drew attention to the rule of the Court of Equity in these matters. It intervened to protect a private individual in his rights of property, and in aid of this would grant an injunction to restrain a defendant from committing an unlawful act, even though it was a crime punishable by the criminal court; and would supplement its jurisdiction in this regard by its power under *Lord Cairns' Act* to award damages in lieu of or in addition to an injunction.

The result of *Gouriet's* case may be summarised thus: when a statute creates a criminal offence—prescribing a penalty for the breach of it but not giving any civil remedy—the general rule is that no private individual can bring an action to enforce the criminal law, either by way of an injunction or by damages. It must be left to the Attorney-General to bring an action, either of his own motion or at the instance of a member of the public who "relates" the facts to him.

But there is an exception to this rule in any case where the criminal act is not only an offence against the public at large, but also causes or threatens to cause special damage to a private individual. If a private individual can show that he has a private right which is being interfered with by the criminal act—thus causing or threatening to cause him special damage over and above the generality of the public—then he can come to the court as a private individual and ask that his private right be protected: see *Gouriet's* case by Viscount Dilhorne, at p. 492 by Lord Diplock, at p. 499 by Lord Edmund-Davies, and at p. 518 by Lord Fraser of Tullybelton. The court can, in those circumstances grant an injunction to restrain the offender from continuing or repeating his criminal act. It is no answer then for the defendant to say: "It is a crime which I am about to commit. If an injunction is granted, I shall be in double jeopardy if I break it—on the one hand for contempt of court in the civil jurisdiction—and on the other hand for a penalty in the criminal jurisdiction." The reply to him is simple: "All the more reason why you should not break the law. You will then be in no jeopardy. If you do break it, you will not be punished twice over. Whichever court deals with you, it will take into consideration the punishment which has been, or can be, inflicted by the other."

The exception depends, however, on the private individual having a private right which he is entitled to have protected. That was made clear long ago by Holt CJ in the leading case of *Iveson v. Moore* (1699), 1 L Raym. 486, 91 ER 1224 (CP), when he was considering a public nuisance by stopping up a highway leading to a colliery. It was a criminal act, but it was held that the colliery owner could bring an action against the offender if he could show special damage. Holt CJ said, at pp. 492-93 (p. 1228 (ER)):

[A]ctions upon the case for nuisances are founded upon particular rights; but where there is not any particular right, the plaintiff shall not have an action.

The question, therefore, becomes this: has the plaintiff a particular right which he is entitled to have protected? To this the answer which runs through all the cases is this: A man who is carrying on a lawful trade or calling has a right to be protected from any unlawful interference with it: see *Acrow (Automation) Ltd. v. Rex Chainbelt Inc.*, [1971] 1 WLR 1676 (CA). It is a right which is in the nature of a right of property. Such as a right to have the access to your premises kept clear without being obstructed by nuisance or smells: see *Benjamin v. Storr* (1874), LR 9 CP 400: or a right to run a ferry for profit across the river Mersey without being injured by rail traffic contrary to the penal statute: see *Chamberlaine v. Chester and Birkenhead Railway Co.* (1848), 1 Exch. 870 at pp. 877 and 879; 154 ER 371 at pp. 374-75: or a right to prevent spurious notes being circulated to the damage of the plaintiff's interests: see *Emperor of Austria v. Day and Kossuth* (1861), 3 De GF & J 217 at pp. 251-55; 45 ER 861 at pp. 874-76 (Ch.) or a right to prevent passing-off: see *Levy v. Walker* (1879), 10 Ch. D 436 (CA) at p. 448, by James LJ: or a right to have your servants come unhindered to work, even though it is only made unlawful by a penal statute: see *Springhead Spinning Co. Ltd. v. Riley* (1868), LR 6 Eq. 551 at pp. 561-62: or a right to have your contractual relations maintained inviolate without interference by others, unless there is just cause or excuse: see *National Phonograph Co. Ltd. v. Edison-Bell Consolidated Phonographic Co. Ltd.*, [1908] 1 Ch. 335 (CA) at p. 339; *Torquay Hotel Co. Ltd. v. Cousins*, [1969] 2 Ch. 106 (CA) at p. 138 and the recent cricketers' case *Greig v. Insole*, [1978] 1 WLR 302 (Ch.) at pp. 332-38 by Slade J: or a right in a workman to have his pay slip properly vouched, even though it is only made unlawful by a penal statute: see *Simmonds v. Newport Abercarn Black Vein Steam Coal Co. Ltd.*, [1921] 1 KB 616 (CA) (where a declaration was granted). In all these cases the unlawful interference may be a tort, such as fraud or passing-off; or it may be a crime, such as a public nuisance; or a breach of a statute which imposes only criminal penalties: but whatever be the nature of the unlawful interference, the party concerned is entitled to come himself to the courts of law and to ask to be protected from the unlawful interference. It is no answer for the defendant to say: "It is a crime: and so you cannot sue me." It would be a sorry state of the law if a man could excuse himself by such a plea—and thus cause special damage with impunity. For the fact must be faced: the criminal law is a broken reed in some of these cases. At any rate in this particular case. The police have not the men or the means to investigate the offence or to track down the offenders or to prosecute them. Nor have they the will. Nor has the Attorney-General. He has, we are told, refused his consent to a relator action—presumably because no public rights are involved. So perforce if the law is to be obeyed—and justice be done—the courts must allow a private individual himself to bring an action against the offender—in those cases where his private rights and interests are specially affected by the breach.

This principle is capable of extension so as to apply not only to rights of property or rights in the nature of it, but to other rights or interests, such as the right of a man to his good name and reputation: see *Argyll (Duchess) v. Argyll (Duke)*, [1967] Ch. 302 at p. 344: and his right to the lawful transmission of his mail: see my illustration in *Gouriet's* case, [1977] QB 729 (CA) at pp. 756-57.

The Present Case

In the present case both the performers and the recording companies have, to my mind, private rights and interests which they are entitled to have protected from unlawful interference. The recording companies have the right to exploit the records made by them of the performances. The performers have the right to the royalty payable to them out of those records. Those rights are buttressed by the contracts between the recording companies and the performers. They are rights in the nature of rights of property. Both the recording companies and the performers suffer severe damage if those rights are unlawfully interfered with. Suppose that the bootlegger in the audience had in his hand or his pocket—instead of a recording device—a distorting device: and by it he could introduce a squeak or a screech into the musical performance: and thus ruin its commercial value. No one could doubt that the recording company and the performers could bring action to stop him and claim damages. That illustration shows that they have a private right which they are entitled to have protected: and this is so, no matter whether the interference be by means of a tortious act or a criminal act. The wrongdoer cannot take advantage of his own crime so as to damage a private individual with impunity.

All the cases suggested to the contrary can be distinguished. Thus in *Institute of Patent Agents v. Lockwood*, [1894] AC 347 (HL (Sc.)) the plaintiff had nothing in the nature of a right of property and had suffered no special damages. In the *Musical Performers'* case before McCardie J, and the *Apple Corps* case before Megarry V-C, it was thought that the courts can only give relief in the case of rights of property, strictly so called, whereas the cases I have cited show that the courts give relief whenever there is unlawful interference with the plaintiff's trade or calling.

So my conclusion is that the courts have jurisdiction to grant an *Anton Piller* order in regard to bootleggers, just as they have in regard to pirates. I am confirmed in this view by the fact that it carries out to the full the recommendations of the Committee presided over by Whitford J, 1977 (Cmnd. No 6732), paragraphs 412(iii), 414(iv), 419(iv). The granting of the "Anton Piller" order is subject to the safeguards mentioned in the report of that case. I would, therefore, allow this appeal and remit the case to the judge to deal with bootleggers just as is done in the case of pirates.

SHAW LJ: The world of pop music is in these times richly endowed and prosperous. It is not therefore surprising that it is much afflicted by parasites. Pop stars and the recording companies who are their sponsors and exploiters naturally wish to rid themselves of poachers who prey upon what they properly regard as their preserve.

The question that arises on this appeal is whether the law has adequately provided for the protection of that preserve from the activities of predators who in the pop music scene are described as pirates when they make and sell copies of discs or tapes in breach of copyright and as bootleggers when they make an unauthorised direct recording of a live performance for the purpose of reproducing it for sale to the public.

The essential issue therefore is whether the terms of the section are to be so construed as to bring contraventions of it within the class of case exemplified by *Groves v. Lord Wimborne*, [1898] 2 QB 402 (CA), or whether they give rise to the interpretation and effect demonstrated by *Cutler v. Wandsworth Stadium Ltd.*, [1949] AC 398 (HL (Eng.)). It seems to me to be beyond contention that the section falls within the scope of the later decision. A similar problem fell to be considered in *McCall v. Abelesz*, [1976] QB 585 (CA) in regard to harassment by a landlord in contravention of section 30 of the *Rent Act* 1965. I ventured there in the course of my judgment (at p. 600), to emphasize that the essential requirement for the conferring of a civil remedy by a penal provision was that the offence created must consist of a failure to perform a defined duty which the statute imposes on the potential offender for the benefit of a particular class of person. In a general sense no doubt every penal statute imposes a duty owed to the public not to offend against its provisions. This is very far from a situation in which a duty is defined for the benefit of a particular class. One looks in vain at section 1 of the Act of 1958 for any definition in terms of such a duty. It does no more than provide for the punishment of certain conduct in relation to dramatic or musical works.

To distil from the language of the section a specific duty to performers would involve an illicit process of interpretation. That the product might be potable cannot justify the method or the result.

The decision in *Musical Performers' Protection Association Ltd. v. British International Pictures Ltd.* (1930), 46 TLR 485 was right; and it was affirmed in *Apple Corps Ltd. v. Lingasong Ltd.* (1977), 3 FSR 345.

The first proposition advanced on behalf of the appellants is accordingly, in my view, untenable and should be rejected.

The second proposition was more widely based. It was submitted that performers whose performances were "bootlegged," to use the jargon of the pop world, came within the general rule that

a private person is … entitled to sue in respect of interference with a public right if either there is also interference with a private right of his or the interference with the public right will inflict special damage on him …

per Lord Fraser of Tullybelton in *Gouriet v. Union of Post Office Workers*, [1978] AC 435 (HL (Eng.)) at p. 518, citing *Boyce v. Paddington Borough Council*, [1903] 1 Ch. 109.

Mr. Laddie contended that if on its proper construction section 1 of the Act was only penal in its character and operation, nonetheless a contravention of its provisions inflicted special and particular damage on performers and also on recording companies with whom performers contracted for the exclusive production and reproduction of their performances. Mr. Gibson, who gave a very great assistance to the court in the role of *amicus*, was prepared to concede that having regard to the contractual rights as between recording companies and their performers there might be said to be vested in those parties a special interest in the enforcement of the provisions of the section. In regard to those parties special damage would be suffered by the recording and reproduction of a performance in contravention of the statute. So the argument went. Hence, albeit such a contravention was primarily an interference with a public right, the recording companies and performers might have a title to sue. Mr. Laddie cited in support of this *Arygll (Duchess) v. Argyll (Duke)*, [1967] Ch. 302. That decision, however, was in respect of a special relationship, namely, marriage, and a special quality or obligation which developed from it, namely, confidentiality. These are readily identifiable and definable.

Another authority on which he sought to rely was *Emperor of Austria v. Day and Kossuth* (1861), 3 De GF & J 217; 45 ER 861 (Ch.). Lord Campbell LC in his judgment said, at p. 238 (p. 870 ER):

> Notwithstanding my sincere respect for the authority of that great American jurist, Justice Story, I cannot concur with him in his recommendation of a mysterious obscurity to be pre-served by Courts of Equity respecting special injunctions, and the caution which should make them "decline to lay down any rule which shall limit their power and discretion as to the par-ticular cases in which such injunctions should be granted or withheld." I think that all branches of the law should, if possible, be made clear and simple, and should be defined as accurately as possible.

A little later in his judgment, he said, at p. 240 (p. 870 (ER)):

> I consider that this court has jurisdiction by injunction to protect property from an act threat-ened, which if completed would give a right of action. I by no means say that in every such case an injunction may be demanded as of right, but if the party applying is free from blame and promptly applies for relief, and shows that by the threatened wrong his property would be so injured that an action for damages would be no adequate redress, the injunction will be granted.

As I understand those observations, the interest to be protected must be of a character which is capable of ready recognition and definition.

The contract between a recording company and a performer imposes no obligations on third parties save not to procure a breach by one party or the other. It leaves them under no responsibility but the general one of obeying the law. If they transgress it and are found out they pay the prescribed penalty. I cannot see in what way they invade or impinge directly upon any definable material right vested by law in the contracting parties. Whatever interest there is appears to me too nebulous and amorphous to carry the aspect of a right susceptible of legal protection. It may be that this is why the legislature has not attributed a form of quasi-copyright to performances themselves. In my view the courts cannot make good the hiatus by granting a remedy *in vacuo*. It is not unimportant to remember that a search warrant could not be obtained in a criminal court where a person is suspected of offences under the section. If the claim for relief put forward is well founded, the making of an *Anton Piller* order would be at least a possibility. Thus the civil remedy said to arise collaterally from a penal provision would go beyond what the criminal law permits in the enforcement of that provision. It is not, in my view, a proper function of the courts indirectly to stiffen the sinews of a criminal statute. I much regret, therefore, that I come to a different conclusion from that stated by Lord Denning MR in his judgment and from that which I understand will be expressed by Waller LJ in his judgment. I would dismiss the appeal.

[Waller LJ held that no action could be brought for a simple breach of statutory duty under this section; however, equity does have jurisdiction to grant an injunction where the plaintiff claims special damage to a property interest by a criminal act. The case was then remitted to Chancery Division for determination as to whether on the facts an *Anton Piller* order should be made.]

NOTES AND QUESTIONS

1. What "right" of the plaintiffs is being protected by this decision? Where did that right come from?

2. Parliament decided not to confer copyright protection upon live performances. Does this decision confer that protection? Would the plaintiffs be entitled to damages?

3. If a situation similar to *Island Records* was to occur in Canada today, the law appears to be clearer on the issue of performers' rights. The problem in *Island Records* was that copyright law did not allow a performer to copyright a stage performance. Until recently, the same held true in Canada. While "performing" rights did exist, these rights merely allowed the copyright holder of a musical work to control the public performance of that work. These rights, however, did not protect a performer who did not hold the underlying copyright to the musical work. In other words, these "performing" rights did not allow a performer actually to copyright the "performer's performance." As of January 1996, however, with the coming into force of the *World Trade Organization Agreement Implementation Act*, SC 1994, c. 47, the *Copyright Act*, RSC 1985, c. C-42, as am. now provides protection for a "performer's performance." Under the *Copyright Act*, the "performer's performance" is now a separate and distinct right from the musical work. Thus, if a situation similar to that which occurred in *Island Records* was to occur in Canada, a musical group could have a copyright in their performance, and would have access to the remedies provided under the Act.

4. Some doubt was cast upon the decision in *Island Records* in the later case of *Lonrho v. Shell Petroleum Co. Ltd.*, [1982] AC 173 (HL (Eng.)). See also *RCA Corp. v. Pollard*, [1983] Ch. 135 (CA).

5. In *Pickering v. Liverpool Daily Post and Echo Newspapers Plc*, [1991] 2 AC 370 (HL (Eng.)), the House of Lords reiterated the narrow test for private standing to enforce a statute. Lord Bridge explained that the individual must prove that she or he is a member of a special class of persons intended to be protected by the statute and that the statute reveals an intention "to confer on members of the protected class a cause of action sounding in damages." He

concluded that the private individual must have more than a "sufficient interest" in enforcement of the statute.

> I know of no authority where a statute has been held ... to give a cause of action for breach of a statutory duty when the nature of the statutory obligation or prohibition was not such that a breach of it would be likely to cause a member of the class for whose benefit or protection it was imposed either personal injury, injury to property, or economic loss.

6. In Canada, there is real doubt that statutes that do not expressly create a private cause of action can be used to protect "private rights." In *R v. Saskatchewan Wheat Pool*, [1983] 1 SCR 205, Dickson J stated that there is no tort of breach of statutory duty in Canada. He said (at 215-16), "The pretence of seeking what has been called a 'will o' the wisp,' a non-existent intention of Parliament to create a civil cause of action, has been harshly criticized. It is capricious and arbitrary, 'judicial legislation' at its worst." However, in the later case of *Whistler Cable Television Ltd. v. IPEC Canada Inc.*, [1993] 3 WWR 247 (BC SC), the BC Supreme Court held that *Saskatchewan Wheat Pool* had not eliminated the tort of breach of statute for all purposes. Braidwood J upheld in principle a claim for damages and an injunction for "statutory breach" distinct from negligence, where a private right can be inferred from the statute. The plaintiff brought the action against a competitor who was unlawfully operating a cable television system without a licence. Braidwood J declined to strike out the plaintiff's claim, holding that there still was a tort of statutory breach when the issues were not subsumed in negligence. He held the relevant questions to be:

1. for whose benefit was the Act passed;
2. was it passed in the interest of the public at large, for a particular class of persons, or for both;
3. is the plaintiff within the class of persons the Act was designed to benefit;
4. were the damages suffered by the plaintiff the kind of damage the statute was intended to prevent;
5. are the penalties prescribed in the Act adequate; and
6. does the Act set up a scheme designed to exclusively carry out the objects of the Act?

This case was distinguished and confined in *Mahar v. Rogers Cablesystems Ltd.* (1995), 25 OR (3d) 690 (Gen. Div.).

7. The issue of standing and special damage also arises when a business seeks to restrain a competitor from operating in violation of statutory requirements. See *Shore Disposal Ltd. v. Ed DeWolfe Trucking Ltd.* (1976), 16 NSR (2d) 538 (CA); *Re Swan River-The Pas Transfer Ltd.* (1974), 51 DLR (3d) 292 (Man. CA); *Canada Post Corp. v. G3 Worldwide (Canada) Inc.* (2007), 85 OR (3d) 241; leave to appeal refused [2007] 3 SCR ix; and Robert J. Sharpe, *Injunctions and Specific Performance* (Aurora, ON: Canada Law Book, 2009) (looseleaf), at paras. 3.770-3.840.

For a comment on *Island Records*, see J. Phillips, "Breach of Statutory Duty and Legislative Intent" (1979), 95 *Law Quarterly Review* 179.

PROBLEM

An organization calling itself the "Aryan Solidarity Society" has hired a local hall and advertised a public forum entitled "Dispel the Myth." As its main speaker, the forum features an individual known for his strong views about white supremacy and a supposed world conspiracy of bankers, communists, and Jews. The association plans to march through the streets before the forum.

Another organization, devoted to human rights, has heard of the proposed march and forum and wishes to put a stop to it. Among other things, it claims that the activities will violate s. 319 of the *Criminal Code*, RSC 1985, c. C-46, which provides:

(1) Every one who, by communicating statements in any public place, incites hatred against any identifiable group where such incitement is likely to lead to a breach of the peace is guilty of

(a) an indictable offence and is liable to imprisonment for two years; or

(b) an offence punishable on summary conviction.

(2) Every one who, by communicating statements, other than in private conversation, wilfully promotes hatred against any identifiable group is guilty of

(a) an indictable offence and is liable to imprisonment for a term not exceeding two years; or

(b) an offence punishable on summary conviction.

(3) No person shall be convicted of an offence under subsection (2)

(a) if he establishes that the statements communicated were true;

(b) if, in good faith, the person expressed or attempted to establish by an argument an opinion on a religious subject or an opinion based on a belief in a religious text;

(c) if the statements were relevant to any subject of public interest, the discussion of which was for the public benefit, and if on reasonable grounds he believed them to be true; or

(d) if, in good faith, he intended to point out, for the purpose of removal, matters producing or tending to produce feelings of hatred toward an identifiable group in Canada.

The human rights group nominates two of its members, a local resident who lives on the route planned for the march and another who is Jewish, as plaintiffs. They wish to stop the march and forum from proceeding and seek your advice on the likelihood that a court will issue an injunction. Please advise.

For a similar case, see *Bancroft v. Governing Council of the University of Toronto* (1986), 53 OR (2d) 460 (HC).

CHAPTER EIGHT

Interlocutory Injunctions

INTRODUCTION

The preceding chapter explored how an injunction protects various private or public interests and the rights normally associated with them. It was demonstrated that the exact parameters of an interest and the rights that constitute it are often a function of the type of available remedy. The injunction, being highly coercive, maximizes the vindication of rights. Although many of the cases included in the chapter were interlocutory applications, that designation was not important in the identification of the interests and rights protected.

In this chapter, we focus solely upon interlocutory injunctions from a legal process perspective. The following issues should provide a focus.

Litigation Management

Three essential characteristics ensure the importance of interlocutory injunctions and their influence on litigation management. (1) Speed of application—an interlocutory injunction can be obtained literally at any time of the day; (2) the application can be made *ex parte* (without notice to the defendant); and (3) the injunction can be granted in advance of any final determination of the dispute.

The interplay of these three characteristics results in an applicant having a powerful weapon at his or her disposal. For example, if the element of surprise is important, the application can be made *ex parte*. Alternatively, the applicant may use the injunction to advance his or her settlement prospects by gaining some preliminary judicial recognition of the merits of his or her case. Yet other examples where speed is important are where the injunction is needed to prevent broadcasting of a defamatory program or to prevent picketing in a labour dispute.

Of course, the attributes that make this remedy attractive to the applicant may very well threaten the legitimate interests of the defendant or other third parties. For instance, the surprise visitation of an applicant armed with an injunction granted *ex parte* will reduce the opportunity afforded the defendant to receive legal advice. Preliminary merits adjudication will encourage more interlocutory motions to avoid court delays in hearing cases. An expeditiously gained injunction against broadcasting or primary and secondary picketing will involve the public interest or disturb a sensitive bargaining process without the court necessarily having cognizance of all the parties affected. Thus, the second theme concerns how courts balance the competing interests of litigants and other interested parties.

Balancing Interests

The injunction remedy is one of the most coercive powers a court can exercise. The risk of imprudent use is heightened by the fact that the interlocutory injunction is granted in advance of hearing all the evidence or legal issues. Judicial response to the danger of an unwarranted grant of an interlocutory injunction centres on the appropriate threshold level an application must attain and the degree of irreparable harm that may be occasioned to the applicant should the injunction not be granted. Against the applicant's case the court must balance the potential irreparable harm to the defendant, a particularly onerous task on an *ex parte* application.

Judicial Administration

Separate from the litigants' interests are the courts' overriding concerns with the integrity of the civil litigation process, and maintenance of its authority. The courts must wrestle with two competing principles: (1) that litigants are free to act as they please prior to being adjudged liable for an injury, and (2) the need to provide interim relief to preserve the very essence of the subject matter in dispute. The court must also be concerned with the potentially damaging repercussions if its orders are flouted or appear to impugn its impartiality.

TERMINOLOGY

An interlocutory injunction is an injunction granted before a final determination of the litigants' dispute.

An interim injunction is an interlocutory injunction made for a specified period normally to allow the defendant time to file material in reply or to permit cross-examination on the applicant's affidavit evidence.

Both interim and interlocutory injunctions can be made *ex parte*; that is, without notice to the defendant. An *ex parte* injunction will normally be for a short, specified period. After it is served the applicant normally returns to court to seek its continuance. At this stage, the defendant will usually have notice and can seek its discharge.

In the remainder of this chapter, only reference to interlocutory injunctions will be made.

JURISDICTION

Canadian courts derive their jurisdiction to grant interlocutory injunctions from two sources. Found in all respective provincial courts of justice acts (for example, see Ontario *Courts of Justice Act*, RSO 1990, c. C.43, s. 101) is a provision that empowers a court to grant an injunction where it "appears to a judge of the court to be just and convenient to do so." A second source derives from the fact that all "superior courts of record" hold an inherent jurisdiction to control their own procedure that includes the issuing of injunctions.

One aspect of jurisdiction concerns what a plaintiff must prove to bring his or her case within the "just and convenient" criteria. It is not sufficient for the plaintiff to simply make the argument that he or she needs an injunction because subjectively it would be just and convenient to the plaintiff. What the plaintiff must show is that the interlocutory injunction is necessary to protect an existing recognized legal right that is justiciable. However, we shall see below under the heading "Accessibility Thresholds" that there is flexibility in this concept.

A second aspect of jurisdiction asks whether a plaintiff must have a justiciable substantive claim within the court's jurisdiction before being granted an interlocutory injunction. This is of particular concern where the interlocutory injunction goes beyond mere ancillary support of a substantive legal claim. For example, in the case of a Mareva injunction (a form of injunction that allows a plaintiff to stop the dissipation or removal of assets from the court's jurisdiction pending the hearing of the plaintiff's action) there is no logical connection between the assets being seized and the substantive claim that forms the basis of the plaintiff's action. This has raised the spectre that a plaintiff may well have a substantive cause of action heard in one country but seek a Mareva injunction in the domestic court because that is where the defendant has exigible assets. The plaintiff will seek to gain judgment in a foreign court and then have it entered for enforcement in a domestic court relying upon the prior Mareva injunction. The English courts have vacillated on this issue of jurisdiction, although they have now taken the position that both the substantive cause of action and the Mareva injunction must be justiciable in the court's jurisdiction (see *The Siskina*, [1979] AC 210 (HL), *Channel Tunnel Group Ltd. v. Balfour Beatty Construction Ltd.*, [1993] AC 334 (HL), and *Mercedes-Benz AG v. Leiduck*, [1995] 3 All ER 929 (PC)). In the United Kingdom the ruling in *Mercedes-Benz* has been effectively reversed by provisions enacted as part of the *Civil Jurisdiction and Judgments Act*, 1982 (UK), s. 25. Finally, in *Fourie v. Le Roux*, [2007] 1 WLR 320 (HL), at para. 30, *per* Lord Scott, the House of Lords recognized that the law on jurisdiction had not stood still following *The Siskina* and that

> provided the court has *in personam* jurisdiction over the person against whom an injunction, whether interlocutory or final, is sought, the court has jurisdiction, in the strict sense, to grant it.

The Supreme Court of Canada has addressed the second jurisdictional issue in the context of a labour dispute. In *Brotherhood of Maintenance of Way Employees Canadian Pacific System Federation v. Canadian Pacific Ltd.*, [1996] 2 SCR 495 the Supreme Court had to determine whether the British Columbia Supreme Court had jurisdiction to award an interlocutory injunction to prevent the immediate implementation of a new work schedule that Canadian Pacific Ltd. had imposed while the union was grieving the issue before an arbitrator. Under the applicable labour legislation, the *Canada Labour Code*, there was no interim relief which either the arbitrator, before whom the grievance was heard, or the Federal Labour Relations Board could award to prevent the implementation of the new scheduling pending the decision by the arbitrator on the grievance. Two distinct questions were raised before the Supreme Court. The first dealt with whether a court had jurisdiction to award relief where there was a purported exclusive code of remedies in the applicable legislation. On this issue the Supreme Court reiterated its earlier line of authority, indicating deference, but not servility, to an administrative regime and that where the Code provided "no adequate alternative remedy" the court had a jurisdiction to grant relief. The second question clearly raised the issue whether the BC court had jurisdiction to grant interlocutory injunctions in circumstances where there was no cause of action to which the injunction was ancillary. On this issue, the Supreme Court took the position that a court has jurisdiction "to grant an injunction where there is a justiciable right, wherever that right may fall to be determined."

The Canadian position gives a wide jurisdiction to a court to grant interlocutory relief without the need for it to be ancillary to a substantive cause of action justiciable in the court's own jurisdiction. This position would now appear to be at odds with that practiced by courts in the United Kingdom. In Canada there must still be a justiciable issue but this will go to whether the plaintiff has attained the requisite threshold to support this form of equitable relief. Jurisdiction must also be kept distinct from the exercise of discretion to grant an injunction. Concerns about extra-territorial reach, service, and enforcement go to discretion, not jurisdiction. See also *Canada (Human Rights Commission) v. Canadian Liberty Net*, [1998] 1 SCR 626.

ACCESSIBILITY THRESHOLDS

An "accessibility threshold" describes the minimum level of proof that a substantive legal issue is in dispute and the probability of a successful suit that an applicant must demonstrate before being granted an interlocutory injunction.

"Irreparable harm" refers to the requirement placed on the applicant to prove that without the injunction he or she will suffer loss that cannot be compensated by any other means.

In the following extract, R. Grant Hammond briefly outlines the history of interlocutory injunctions and details the classical model.

R. Grant Hammond, "Interlocutory Injunctions: Time for a New Model?"
(1980), 30 *University of Toronto Law Journal* 241, at 241-44 and 249
(footnotes omitted)

It is not easy to determine how common applications for interlocutory injunctions were prior to the *Judicature Acts*. Kerly considered that the remedy of injunction generally "was wielded by the Court until the nineteenth century with little of its present effect."

By the nineteenth century there were two broad classes of cases in which injunctive relief was, in principle, open: a/ to enable protection of purely equitable rights against infringement by the exercise of a legal title or right in a manner contrary to good faith or inconsistent with purely equitable principles; b/ in aid of legal rights, when the common law remedy of damages was inadequate—as for instance if there was danger of irreparable mischief or where an injunction was required to prevent a multiplicity of actions. In the first class the Court of Chancery was dealing with matters which were entirely within its original and exclusive jurisdiction, and the existence of the right to the injunction claimed depended entirely on the rules of equity. In the second, chancery had no original jurisdiction; its function was simply to grant an injunction in aid of a legal right. Hence it would not (and could not) determine finally a disputed legal right or give the legal remedy of damages. It would interfere only when the legal right was clear or had been established in a court of law, and it then gave its remedy of injunction in extension of the legal remedy and upon an equity founded upon the legal right.

Interlocutory injunctions could be granted in both classes of case, but there is a dispute as to both the standards for relief in the early nineteenth century and the rigour with which they were applied. One commentator has suggested that, even in the pre-*Judicature Act* period, what would today be termed a *prima facie* case had to be made out. Another has viewed the strands of principle as still diffuse and has suggested that formalized standards did not emerge until after the reforms of the 1870s. The better view would appear to be that something less than a *prima facie* case was then required, and that that standard was not then conceived of as a threshold test. Judges typically asserted a broad discretion:

> The Court exercises its jurisdiction not for the purpose of acting upon legal rights, but for the purpose of better enforcing legal rights, or preventing mischief until they have been ascertained. In all cases of injunctions in aid of legal rights—whether it be copyright, patent right, or some other description of legal right which comes before the Court—the office of the Court is consequent upon the legal right; and it generally happens that the only question the Court has to consider is, whether the case is so clear and so free from objection upon the grounds of equitable consideration, that the Court ought to interfere by injunction without a previous trial at law, or whether it ought to wait till the legal title has been established. That distinction depends upon a great variety of circumstances, and it is utterly impossible to lay down any general rule upon the subject, by which the discretion of the Court ought in all cases to be regulated.

But articulated standards were emerging. By mid-century a plaintiff had to demonstrate that there was a "substantial question" to be decided before an interlocutory injunction could issue. This test was espoused by several very experienced appellate judges—Lord Cottenham, Lord Cranworth, and Turner LJ. A real appreciation of the dangers of a hasty and ill-considered grant of the remedy began to be articulated. Yet the language of the cases did not raise a burden of the magnitude which would be prescribed later in the century. This interpretation may be reinforced by the fact that contemporary text writers did not find it necessary to stress, as a preliminary matter, the strength of the plaintiff's case. Indeed, the original text of the work of probably the greatest authority at that time stresses that "the Court does not in general profess to anticipate the determination of rights ... it is enough if [the plaintiff] can show that he has a fair question to raise as to the existence of the right he alleges, and can satisfy the Court that the property should be preserved in its present actual condition, until such questions can be disposed of."

Considered in the abstract, it might be thought that any question of a threshold test for interlocutory injunctive relief would have diminished after the *Judicature Acts*. Law and equity were thenceforth being administered in the High Court of Justice in all its divisions; equity need no longer look quite so nervously over its shoulder at potential allegations of lack of jurisdiction. Yet the standards "firmed up." The model became such that in order to obtain an interlocutory injunction a plaintiff had to establish, as a preliminary matter, a strong *prima facie* case in the sense that if the evidence remained as it was on the affidavits in support of the motion he would in all probability get judgment in his favour. One of the most frequently cited late-nineteenth century cases which illustrates the point was *Challender v. Royal*. In that case the vice-chancellor had granted an interlocutory injunction on a balance of convenience and inconvenience test without any review of the strength of the plaintiff's case. This was expressly and firmly rejected by a strong Court of Appeal, which ruled that the court could not even reach the convenience question unless it was satisfied that the plaintiff had made out a strong *prima facie* case. Once the threshold test had been met, the adequacy of damages and the balance of convenience continued to turn, as always, largely on the facts of the particular case.

Thus, by the close of the century the characteristics of the classical model were established. To state the position that broadly is, however, to gloss over the very real transformation which had come over the remedy; so far as any ultimately discretionary remedy can do, it had formalized. There were probably several reasons for this. First, this remedy, as with so much of the body of judge-made law, was exposed to that particular conservatism which marked the late nineteenth century in Britain—a conservatism which in law no less than in public life demanded prescription, authority, and hierarchy in the organic community. A corollary to that philosophy was the notion of universality—which the classical model fulfilled. The model was compatible, too, with a private law system paying regard essentially only to private interests. That is, the remedy fitted into a litigation model which was characterized by a bipolar dispute of a retrospective and self-contained character wherein the right and the remedy were interdependent and the whole dispute was itself party initiated and controlled.

A model thus conceived and evolved was likely to be put under great stress by several factors. First, if the volume of litigation rose markedly the state of equilibrium the model was supposed to protect might be upset. Second, if the jurisprudence of the particular legal system became more sophisticated and recognized interests of a more diverse and intangible character, both the notion of preserving the status quo in an entirely fluid situation and the "preservation" of that particular interest might require closer and more demanding articulation than had theretofore been required in predominantly proprietary disputes. Third, the notion that the model might serve varying kinds of disputes—the universality of the model—might be called in question. These very factors were to appear in the common law jurisdictions, particularly after World War II. ...

Down to the mid-1960s the principles enunciated in the late nineteenth century did not alter, although greater refinement and articulation took place. As at say, 1965, these principles could have been summarized thus.

1. The necessity to demonstrate a strong *prima facie* case remained a major threshold requirement. This formula really comprehended a double-barrelled test—the requirement was that it had to be demonstrated to the *prima facie* standard both that the right existed and that it had been infringed. Where the likelihood of success was somewhat problematical, for instance if the facts were in serious dispute, an interlocutory injunction was often refused or, alternatively, an early trial ordered. Nothing could have been clearer than the statement by Lord Upjohn in *Stratford and Son v. Lindley* that a plaintiff "must establish a *prima facie* case of some breach of duty ... to him."

2. Having got over the initial hurdle a plaintiff had to demonstrate irreparable damage that could not be compensated if he succeeded at trial. What was meant by "irreparable" in this context was well stated by Lord Wilberforce: "The object of [an interim injunction] is to prevent a litigant, *who* must necessarily suffer the law's delay, from losing by that delay the fruit of his litigation; this is called 'irreparable damage,' meaning that money obtained at trial may not compensate him."

3. Then the plaintiff had to show in addition that the balance of convenience favoured the grant. Often this factor appears to have been the real determinant in borderline cases.

The strictly sequential classical model was overruled by the House of Lords as follows:

American Cyanamid v. Ethicon
[1975] AC 396 (HL (Eng.))

[The appellants (Cyanamid) were the registered proprietors of a patent for absorbable sutures (PHAE) that disintegrated once they had served their purpose and were then absorbed by the body. The respondents (Ethicon) also marketed sutures made from animal tissue called catgut. At the time the appellants introduced their patented product in 1970, the respondents were the dominant suppliers of catgut sutures in the United Kingdom. By 1973, the appellants had succeeded in capturing 15 percent of the suture market. Concerned at this inroad into the suture market, the respondents launched their own absorbable suture (XLG). The appellants alleged the respondents' suture infringed their patent and launched a *quia timet* action for an injunction to restrain the respondents from marketing their absorbable suture in the United Kingdom.]

LORD DIPLOCK stated the facts and continued: My Lords, the question whether the use of XLG as an absorbable surgical suture is an infringement of Cyanamid's patent depends upon the meaning to be given to the three words "a polyhydroxyacetic ester" in the principal claim. Cyanamid's contention is that at the date of publication of the patent those words were used as a term of art in the chemistry of polymerisation not only in the narrower meaning of a homopolymer of which the units in the chain, apart from the end stabilisers, consisted solely of glycolide radicals but also in the broader meaning of a copolymer of which up to 15 per cent of the units in the chain would be lactide radicals; and that what was said in the body of the patent made it clear that in the claim the words were used in this wider meaning.

Ethicon's first contention is that the words "a polyhydroxyacetic ester" in the principal claim bear the narrower meaning only, *viz.* that they are restricted to a homopolymer of which all the units in the chain except the end stabilisers consist of glycolide radicals. In the alternative, as commonly happens where the contest is between a narrower and an wider meaning in a patent specification, they attack the validity of the patent, if it bears the wider meaning, on the grounds of inutility, insufficiency, unfair basis and false suggestion. These objections are really the obverse of their argument in favour of the narrower construction. They are all different ways of saying that if the claim is construed widely it includes copolymers which will not have as surgical sutures the characteristics described in the body of the patent. Ethicon also attack the validity of the patent on the ground of obviousness.

Both Graham J and the Court of Appeal felt constrained by authority to deal with Cyanamid's claim to an interlocutory injunction by considering first whether, upon the whole of the affidavit evidence before them, a *prima facie* case of infringement had been made out.

As Russell LJ put it in the concluding paragraph of his reasons for judgment with which the other members of the court agreed, [1974] FSR 312 (CA) at p. 333:

> [I]f there be no *prima facie* case on the point essential to entitle the plaintiffs to complain of the defendants' proposed activities, that is the end of the claim to interlocutory relief.

"*Prima facie* case" may in some contexts be an elusive concept, but the sense in which it was being used by Russell LJ is apparent from an earlier passage in his judgment. After a detailed analysis of the conflicting expert testimony he said, at p. 330:

> I am not satisfied on the present evidence that on the proper construction of this specification, addressed as it is to persons skilled in the relevant art or science, the claim extends to sterile surgical sutures produced not only from a homopolymer of glycolide but also from a copolymer of glycolide and up to 15 per cent of lactide. That is to say that I do not consider that a *prima facie* case of infringement is established.

In effect what the Court of Appeal was doing was trying the issue of infringement upon the conflicting affidavit evidence as it stood, without the benefit of oral testimony or cross-examination. They were saying:

> If we had to give judgment in the action now without any further evidence we should hold that Cyanamid had not satisfied the onus of proving that their patent would be infringed by Ethicon's selling sutures made of XLG.

The Court of Appeal accordingly did not find it necessary to go into the questions raised by Ethicon as to the validity of the patent or to consider where the balance of convenience lay.

Graham J had adopted the same approach as the Court of Appeal; but, upon the same evidence he had come to the contrary conclusion on the issue of infringement. He considered (at p. 321) that on the evidence as it stood Cyanamid had made out a "strong *prima facie* case" that their patent would be infringed by Ethicon's selling sutures made of XLG. He then went on to deal briefly with the attack upon the validity of the patent and came to the conclusion that upon the evidence before him none of the grounds of invalidity advanced by Ethicon was likely to succeed. He therefore felt entitled to consider the balance of convenience. In his opinion it lay in favour of maintaining the status quo until the trial of the action. So he granted Cyanamid an interlocutory injunction restraining Ethicon from infringing the patent until the trial or further order.

The grant of an interlocutory injunction is a remedy that is both temporary and discretionary. It would be most exceptional for your Lordships to give leave to appeal to this House in a case which turned upon where the balance of convenience lay. In the instant appeal, however, the question of the balance of convenience, although it had been considered by Graham J and decided in Cyanamid's favour, was never reached by the Court of Appeal. They considered that there was a rule of practice so well established as to constitute a rule of law that precluded them from granting any interim injunction unless upon the evidence adduced by both the parties on the hearing of the application the applicant had satisfied the court that on the balance of probabilities the acts of the other party sought to be enjoined would, if committed, violate the applicant's legal rights. In the view of the Court of Appeal the case which the applicant had to prove before any question of balance of convenience arose was "*prima facie*" only in the sense that the conclusion of law reached by the court upon that evidence might need to be modified at some later date in the light of further evidence either detracting from the probative value of the evidence on which the court had acted or proving additional facts. It was in order to enable the existence of any such rule of law to be considered by your Lordships' House that leave to appeal was granted.

The instant appeal arises in a patent case. Historically there was undoubtedly a time when in an action for infringement of a patent that was not already "well established," whatever that may have meant, an interlocutory injunction to restrain infringement would not be granted if counsel for the defendant stated that it was intended to attack the validity of the patent.

Relics of this reluctance to enforce a monopoly that was challenged, even though the alleged grounds of invalidity were weak, are to be found in the judgment of Scrutton LJ as late as 1924 in *Smith v. Grigg Ltd.*, [1924] 1 KB 655 (CA); but the elaborate procedure for the examination of patent specifications by expert examiners before a patent is granted, the opportunity for opposition at that stage and the provisions for appeal to the Patent Appeal Tribunal in the person of a patent judge of the High Court, make the grant of a patent nowadays a good *prima facie* reason, in the true sense of that term, for supposing the patent to be valid, and have rendered obsolete the former rule of practice as respects interlocutory injunctions in infringement actions. In my view the grant of interlocutory injunctions in actions for infringement of patents is governed by the same principles as in other actions. I turn to consider what those principles are.

My Lords, when an application for an interlocutory injunction to restrain a defendant from doing acts alleged to be in violation of the plaintiff's legal right is made upon contested facts, the decision whether or not to grant an interlocutory injunction has to be taken at a time when ex hypothesi the existence of the right or the violation of it, or both, is uncertain and will remain uncertain until final judgment is given in the action. It was to mitigate the risk of injustice to the plaintiff during the period before that uncertainty could be resolved that the practice arose of granting him relief by way on interlocutory injunction; but since the middle of the 19th century this has been made subject to his undertaking to pay damages to the defendant for any loss sustained by reason of the injunction if it should be held at the trial that the plaintiff had not been entitled to restrain the defendant from doing what he was threatening to do. The object of the interlocutory injunction is to protect the plaintiff against injury by violation of his right for which he could not be adequately compensated in damages recoverable in the action if the uncertainty were resolved in his favour at the trial; but the plaintiff's need for such protection must be weighed against the corresponding need of the defendant to be protected against injury resulting from his having been prevented from exercising his own legal rights for which he could not be adequately compensated under the plaintiff's undertaking in damages if the uncertainty were resolved in the defendant's favour at the trial. The court must weigh one need against another and determine where "the balance of convenience" lies.

In those cases where the legal rights of the parties depend upon facts that are in dispute between them, the evidence available to the court at the hearing of the application for an interlocutory injunction is incomplete. It is given on affidavit and has not been tested by oral cross-examination. The purpose sought to be achieved by giving to the court discretion to grant such injunctions would be stultified if the discretion were clogged by a technical rule forbidding its exercise if upon that incomplete untested evidence the court evaluated the chances of the plaintiff's ultimate success in the action at 50 per cent or less, but permitting its exercise if the court evaluated his chances at more than 50 per cent.

The notion that it is incumbent upon the court to undertake what is in effect a preliminary trial of the action upon evidential material different from that upon which the actual trial will be conducted is, I think, of comparatively recent origin, though it can be supported by references in earlier cases to the need to show "a probability that the plaintiffs are entitled to relief" (*Preston v. Luck* (1884), 27 Ch. D 497 (CA) at p. 506, *per* Cotton LJ) or "a strong *prima facie* case that the right which he seeks to protect in fact exists" (*Smith v. Grigg Ltd.* at p. 659 *per* Atkin LJ). These are to be contrasted with expressions in other cases indicating a much less onerous criterion, such as the need to show that there is "certainly a case to be tried" (*Jones v. Pacaya Rubber and Produce Co. Ltd.*, [1911] 1 KB 455 (CA) at p. 457, *per* Buckley LJ) which corresponds more closely with what judges generally treated as sufficient to justify their considering the balance of convenience upon applications for interlocutory injunctions, at any rate up to the time when I became a member of your Lordships' House.

An attempt has been made to reconcile these apparently differing approaches to the exercise of the discretion by holding that the need to show a probability or a strong *prima facie* case applied only to the establishment by the plaintiff of his right, and that the lesser burden of showing an arguable case to be tried applied to the alleged violation of that right by the defendant (*Donmar Productions Ltd. v. Bart (Note)*, [1967] 1 WLR 740 (Ch.) at p. 742, *per* Ungoed-Thomas J, *Harman Pictures N.V. v. Osborne*, [1967] 1 WLR 723 (Ch.) at p. 738, *per* Goff J). The suggested distinction between what the plaintiff must establish as respects his right and what he must show as respects its violation did not long survive. It was rejected by the Court of Appeal in *Hubbard v. Vosper*, [1972] 2 QB 84—a case in which the plaintiff's entitlement to copyright was undisputed but an injunction was refused despite the apparent weakness of the suggested defence. The court, however, expressly deprecated any attempt to fetter the discretion of the court by laying down any rules which would have the effect of limiting the flexibility of the remedy as a means of achieving the objects that I have indicated above. Nevertheless this authority was treated by Graham J and the Court of Appeal in the instant appeal as leaving intact the supposed rule that the court is not entitled to take any account of the balance of convenience unless it has first been satisfied that if the case went to trial upon no other evidence than is before the court at the hearing of the application the plaintiff would be entitled to judgment for a permanent injunction in the same terms as the interlocutory injunction sought.

Your Lordships should in my view take this opportunity of declaring that there is no such rule. The use of such expressions as "a probability," "a *prima facie* case," or "a strong *prima facie* case" in the context of the exercise of a discretionary power to grant an interlocutory injunction leads to confusion as to the object sought to be achieved by this form of temporary relief. The court no doubt must be satisfied that the claim is not frivolous or vexatious; in other words, that there is a serious question to be tried.

It is no part of the court's function at this stage of the litigation to try to resolve conflicts of evidence on affidavit as to facts on which the claims of either party may ultimately depend nor to decide difficult questions of law which call for detailed argument and mature considerations. These are matters to be dealt with at the trial. One of the reasons for the introduction of the practice of requiring an undertaking as to damages upon the grant of an interlocutory injunction was that "it aided the court in doing that which was its great object,

viz. abstaining from expressing any opinion upon the merits of the case until the hearing":
Wakefield v. Duke of Buccleugh (1865), 12 LT 628 (Ch.) at p. 629. So unless the material
available to the court at the hearing of the application for an interlocutory injunction fails
to disclose that the plaintiff has any real prospect of succeeding in his claim for a permanent
injunction at the trial, the court should go on to consider whether the balance of convenience lies in favour of granting or refusing the interlocutory relief that is sought.

As to that, the governing principle is that the court should first consider whether, if the
plaintiff were to succeed at the trial in establishing his right to a permanent injunction, he
would be adequately compensated by an award of damages for the loss he would have sustained as a result of the defendant's continuing to do what was sought to be enjoined between
the time of the application and the time of the trial. If damages in the measure recoverable at
common law would be adequate remedy and the defendant would be in a financial position
to pay them, no interlocutory injunction should normally be granted, however strong the
plaintiff's claim appeared to be at that stage. If, on the other hand, damages would not provide an adequate remedy for the plaintiff in the event of his succeeding at the trial, the court
should then consider whether, on the contrary hypothesis that the defendant were to succeed at the trial in establishing his right to do that which was sought to be enjoined, he would
be adequately compensated under the plaintiff's undertaking as to damages for the loss he
would have sustained by being prevented from doing so between the time of the application
and the time of the trial. If damages in the measure recoverable under such an undertaking
would be an adequate remedy and the plaintiff would be in a financial position to pay them,
there would be no reason upon this ground to refuse an interlocutory injunction.

It is where there is doubt as to the adequacy of the respective remedies in damages available to either party or to both, that the question of balance of convenience arises. It would
be unwise to attempt even to list all the various matters which may need to be taken into
consideration in deciding where the balance lies, let alone to suggest the relative weight to
be attached to them. These will vary from case to case.

Where other factors appear to be evenly balanced it is a counsel of prudence to take such
measures as are calculated to preserve the status quo. If the defendant is enjoined temporarily from doing something that he has not done before, the only effect of the interlocutory
injunction in the event of his succeeding at the trial is to postpone the date at which he is
able to embark upon a course of action which he has not previously found it necessary to
undertake; whereas to interrupt him in the conduct of an established enterprise would cause
much greater inconvenience to him since he would have to start again to establish it in the
event of his succeeding at the trial.

Save in the simplest cases, the decision to grant or to refuse an interlocutory injunction
will cause to whichever party is unsuccessful on the application some disadvantages which
his ultimate success at the trial may show he ought to have been spared and the disadvantages
may be such that the recovery of damages to which he would then be entitled either in the
action or under the plaintiff's undertaking would not be sufficient to compensate him fully
for all of them. The extent to which the disadvantages to each party would be incapable of
being compensated in damages in the event of his succeeding at the trial is always a significant factor in assessing where the balance of convenience lies; and if the extent of the uncompensatable disadvantage to each party would not differ widely, it may not be improper

to take into account in tipping the balance the relative strength of each party's case as revealed by the affidavit evidence adduced on the hearing of the application. This, however, should be done only where it is apparent upon the facts disclosed by evidence as to which there is no credible dispute that the strength of one party's case, is disproportionate to that of the other party. The court is not justified in embarking upon anything resembling a trial of the action upon conflicting affidavits in order to evaluate the strength of either party's case.

I would reiterate that, in addition to those to which I have referred, there may be many other special factors to be taken into consideration in the particular circumstances of individual cases. The instant appeal affords one example of this.

Returning, therefore, to the instant appeal, it cannot be doubted that the affidavit evidence shows that there are serious questions to be tried. Graham J and the Court of Appeal have already tried the question of infringement on such affidavit evidence as was available and have come to contrary conclusions. Graham J has already also tried the question of invalidity on these affidavits and has come to the conclusion that the defendant's grounds of objection to the patent are unlikely to succeed, so it was clearly incumbent upon him and on the Court of Appeal to consider the balance of convenience.

Graham J did so and came to the conclusion that the balance of convenience lay in favour of his exercising the discretion by granting an interlocutory injunction. As patent judge he has unrivalled experience of pharmaceutical patents and the way in which the pharmaceutical industry is carried on. Lacking in this experience, an appellate court should be hesitant to overrule his exercise of his discretion, unless they are satisfied that he has gone wrong in law.

The factors which he took into consideration and in my view properly, were that Ethicon's sutures XLG were not yet on the market; so they had no business which would be brought to a stop by the injunction; no factories would be closed and no work-people would be thrown out of work. They held a dominant position in the United Kingdom market for absorbent surgical sutures and adopted an aggressive sales policy. Cyanamid on the other hand were in the course of establishing a growing market in PHAE surgical sutures which competed with the natural catgut sutures marketed by Ethicon. If Ethicon were entitled also to establish themselves in the market for PHAE absorbable surgical sutures until the action is tried, which may not be for two or three years yet, and possibly thereafter until the case is finally disposed of on appeal, Cyanamid, even though ultimately successful in proving infringement, would have lost its chance of continuing to increase its share in the total market in absorbent surgical sutures which the continuation of an uninterrupted monopoly of PHAE sutures would have gained for it by the time of the expiry of the patent in 1980. It is notorious that new pharmaceutical products used exclusively by doctors or available only on prescription take a long time to become established in the market, that much of the benefit of the monopoly granted by the patent derives from the fact that the patented product is given the opportunity of becoming established and this benefit continues to be reaped after the patent has expired.

In addition there was a special factor to which Graham J attached importance. This was that, once doctors and patients had got used to Ethicon's product XLG in the period prior to the trial, it might well be commercially impracticable for Cyanamid to deprive the public of it by insisting on a permanent injunction at the trial, owing to the damaging effect which this would have upon its goodwill in this specialised market and thus upon the sale of its other pharmaceutical products.

I can see no ground for interfering in the learned judge's assessment of the balance of convenience or for interfering with the discretion that he exercised by granting the injunction. In view of the fact that there are serious questions to be tried upon which the available evidence is incomplete, conflicting and untested, to express an opinion now as to the prospects of success of either party would only be embarrassing to the judge who will have eventually to try the case. The likelihood of such embarrassment provides an additional reason for not adopting the course that both Graham J and the Court of Appeal thought they were bound to follow, of dealing with the existing evidence in detail and giving reasoned assessments of their views as to the relative strengths of each party's case.

I would allow the appeal and restore the order of Graham J.

[Viscount Dilhorne and Lords Cross, Salmon, and Edmund-Davies concurred.]

Appeal allowed.

NOTES AND QUESTIONS

1. *American Cyanamid* lowered the accessibility threshold. In doing so, the House of Lords placed greater attention on the remedial goal of interlocutory injunctions, namely, to maintain the status quo where there is a risk of irreparable harm to the applicant. The apparent reason for lowering the threshold was to avoid courts being required to adjudicate on the merits when the evidence available to them was incomplete and unchallenged. Hammond has suggested another latent explanation (at 250-51):

> Why did such a shift in judicial stance occur? The English chancery bar, despite its formidable talents, has never "worked with its eyes up." It did what it has always done when faced with a pragmatic problem—in this case the specific problem of an overloaded civil litigation system in the 1960s. It devised a procedural solution. Counsel began to use the interlocutory injunction as a means of providing a rapid and relatively cheap method of arbitration of disputes. A motion was filed, often by arrangement with the other party, when a dispute arose. Affidavits in support and opposition would be filed; and since the court had to decide whether a *prima facie* case had been made out, in effect a preliminary trial was gained. More often than not, the defendant, having got an indication of the judge's views, simply abided by the result.
>
> None of this profound movement in the real world appeared on the face of the reports, nor could it; the still strong adherence to precedent under the English common law system required a side-step rather than a head-on charge. The Court of Appeal in particular appears to have been trying to achieve a formula which would accommodate this development in the law yet leave enough room to refuse an injunction where the justice of the case required that the parties be left to the ultimate result at a full trial. Thus, while in form the proceedings were concerned with the desirability of preserving the status quo until the true legal position could be ascertained at trial, in reality the threshold test was used to justify answering the merits, at least in a preliminary way.
>
> This device apparently worked extraordinarily well. The quality of the chancery bench is such that in very few cases was the result at trial (where a trial ultimately resulted) different from the

result on motion. In the decade before *American Cyanamid v. Ethicon*, of "the thousand or so passing off cases [heard] all (or virtually all) of them were 'decided' on motion."

If English trial courts were endeavouring to achieve flexibility in the face of a litigation explosion (and more diverse kinds of claims), it should nevertheless have been predictable that sooner or later questions would be raised as to the desirability of preliminary "mini-trials." It was against this background that *American Cyanamid v. Ethicon* was decided by the House of Lords in 1975.

2. What evidence is offered in *American Cyanamid* to prove that merit adjudication at the interlocutory injunction stage is wrong or inherently unreliable?

3. In *N.W.L. Ltd. v. Woods*, [1979] 1 WLR 1294 (HL (Eng.)), the House of Lords qualified its earlier decision in *American Cyanamid* where the interlocutory injunction application would dispose of the dispute. In *N.W.L. Ltd.*, the applicant, a ship owner operating under a flag of convenience, sought an interlocutory injunction against a trade union that had "blacked" the applicant's ship at all ports in the United Kingdom. The House of Lords declined to issue an injunction because it was "almost certain" that the trade union would have a defence, establishing its right to "black" the ship, pursuant to the then operative *Trade Union and Labour Relations Act*. Lord Diplock dealt with *American Cyanamid* as follows (at 1306):

> My Lords, when properly understood, there is in my view nothing in the decision of this House in *American Cyanamid Co. v. Ethicon Ltd.*, [1975] AC 396 (HL (Eng.)) to suggest that in considering whether or not to grant an interlocutory injunction the judge ought not to give the full weight to all the practical realities of the situation to which the injunction will apply. *American Cyanamid Co. v. Ethicon Ltd.*, which enjoins the judge upon an application for an interlocutory injunction to direct his attention to the balance of convenience as soon as he has satisfied himself that there is a serious question to be tried, was not dealing with a case in which the grant or refusal of an injunction at that stage would, in effect, dispose of the action finally in favour of whichever party was successful in the application, because there would be nothing left on which it was in the unsuccessful party's interest to proceed to trial. By the time the trial came on the industrial dispute, if there were one, in furtherance of which the acts sought to be restrained were threatened or done, would be likely to have been settled and it would not be in the employer's interest to exacerbate relations with his workmen by continuing the proceedings against the individual defendants none of whom would be capable financially of meeting a substantial claim for damages. Nor, if an interlocutory injunction had been granted against them, would it be worthwhile for the individual defendants to take steps to obtain a final judgment in their favour, since any damages that they could claim in respect of personal pecuniary loss caused to them by the grant of the injunction and which they could recover under the employer's undertaking on damages, would be very small.
>
> Cases of this kind are exceptional, but when they do occur they bring into the balance of convenience an important additional element. In assessing whether what is compendiously called the balance of convenience lies in granting or refusing interlocutory injunctions in actions between parties of undoubted solvency the judge is engaged in weighing the respective risks that injustice may result from his deciding one way rather than the other at a stage when the evidence is incomplete. On the one hand there is the risk that if the interlocutory injunction is refused but the plaintiff succeeds in establishing at the trial his legal right for the protection of which the injunction had been sought he may in the meantime have suffered harm and inconvenience for which an award of money can provide no adequate recompense. On the other

hand there is the risk that if the interlocutory injunction is granted but the plaintiff fails at the trial, the defendant may in the meantime have suffered harm and inconvenience which is similarly irrecompensable. The nature and degree of harm and inconvenience that are likely to be sustained in these two events by the defendant and the plaintiff respectively in consequence of the grant or the refusal of the injunction are generally sufficiently disproportionate to bring down, by themselves, the balance on one side or the other; and this is what I understand to be the thrust of the decision of this House in *American Cyanamid Co. v. Ethicon Ltd.* Where, however, the grant or refusal of the interlocutory injunction will have the practical effect of putting an end to the action because the harm that will have been already caused to the losing party by its grant or its refusal is complete and of a kind for which money cannot constitute any worthwhile recompense, the degree of likelihood that the plaintiff would have succeeded in establishing his right to an injunction if the action had gone to trial, is a factor to be brought into the balance by the judge in weighing the risks that injustice may result from his deciding the application one way rather than the other.

4. Subsequent to *N.W.L. Ltd.*, the legislation that gave the trade union its defence was amended. In *Dimbleby & Sons Ltd. v. National Union of Journalists*, [1984] 1 WLR 427 (HL (Eng.)) the injunction was granted.

5. A rearguard action against *American Cyanamid* was mounted by Lord Denning MR in *Fellows and Sons v. Fisher*, [1976] QB 122 (CA). In that case, the applicants were a firm of solicitors seeking to enforce a restrictive covenant in an employment contract that prevented the defendant from working in a legal office within a radius of 12 miles from the applicants for a period of five years after termination of employment. The defendant was in breach of the covenant, although he was not involved in soliciting any of the applicants' clients. The applicants moved for an interlocutory injunction to restrain the defendant. They were unsuccessful at first instance and appealed to the Court of Appeal. Their case was based on the test in *American Cyanamid*. The majority of the court, applying the *American Cyanamid* criteria, declined to issue an injunction on the basis that because no evidence was tendered to show that damages would be an inadequate remedy; therefore, the balance of the convenience lay with the defendant. Lord Denning MR (in a separate judgment) sought to reconcile the competing tests found in *Stratford & Son Ltd. v. Lindley*, [1965] AC 269 (HL (Eng.)) (the classical model) and *American Cyanamid*:

Where then is the reconciliation to be found? Only in this: the House did say, at p. 409:

there may be many other special factors to be taken into consideration in the particular circumstances of individual cases.

That sentence points the way. These individual cases are numerous and important. They are all cases where it is urgent and imperative to come to a decision. The affidavits may be conflicting. The questions of law may be difficult and call for detailed consideration. Nevertheless, the need for immediate decision is such that the court has to make an estimate of the relative strength of each party's case. If the plaintiff makes out a *prima facie* case, the court may grant an injunction. If it is a weak case, or is met by a strong defence, the court may refuse an injunction. Sometimes it means that the court virtually decides the case at that stage. At other times it gives the parties such good guidance that the case is settled. At any rate, in 99 cases out of 100, the matter goes no further.

In support of what I have said, I will give instances from many fields of law. Take industrial disputes, where there is a strike, with picketing, blacking, and the like. The plaintiff's business is being greatly injured. They seek an interlocutory injunction. The courts invariably assess the relative strength of each party's case and grant or refuse an injunction accordingly. They give their reasons and that is the end of the matter. Look at these cases: [He then listed a number of decisions.] All were decided on applications for interlocutory injunctions; and never went to trial.

Similarly with breaches of confidence. If the plaintiff has a strong case, an injunction should be granted: for to postpone it would be equivalent to denying it altogether. But, if the defendant has an available defence, it may be refused: [A further list follows.] [They] were all decided on interlocutory applications and never came for trial.

Likewise with covenants in restraint of trade, and the like. Their validity is frequently discussed on interlocutory applications. If the covenant is *prima facie* valid, an injunction will be granted; but, if not, it will be refused. Once decided, these cases rarely come to trial. [A list again follows.]

So also with passing-off cases: ... It is said that "of the thousand or so passing off cases there have been in the last decade, all (or virtually all) of them were 'decided' on motion": see (1975), 91 LQR 169 and also as to patent cases the article in the *New Law Journal* for March 27, 1975, p. 302.

To which I may add many commercial cases where the granting of an interlocutory injunction virtually decides the action. ...

7. Uncompensatable Disadvantages

There is yet another way out. The House did say, [1975] AC 396, 409:

> if the extent of the uncompensatable disadvantage to each party would not differ widely, it may not be improper to take into account in tipping the balance the relative strength of each party's case ...

There are many cases in which either party could suffer great disadvantages which could not be adequately compensated in damages. In all these it is permissible to consider the relative strength of each party's case.

8. Conclusion

In my opinion this is one of those "individual cases" in which the courts should go by the principles stated by the House of Lords in *J.T. Stratford & Son Ltd. v. Lindley* rather than those stated by them in *American Cyanamid Co. v. Ethicon Ltd.* Applying those principles, I am of opinion that the plaintiffs have not made out sufficiently a *prima facie* case that clause (a) is valid. On the contrary, the defendant has put forward some legitimate reasons for thinking it may be invalid. For that reason alone an injunction should be refused. Apart from this, it is a case of "uncompensatable disadvantages," where damages on either side would not be an adequate remedy. If the clause is valid and yet no injunction is granted, the plaintiff would find it difficult to prove his damages, and if proved, to recover them. If the clause is invalid, and yet an injunction is granted, it would be difficult to assess the damages recoverable by the defendant upon the undertaking in damages. He would have lost a good job with excellent prospects. Even if he gets another job with like wages, it would be difficult to assess the difference in terms of prospects and happiness.

In view of these "uncompensatable disadvantages," the proper course is to have regard to the relative strength of each party's case, and here again, seeing that the clause is of doubtful validity, there should not be an interlocutory injunction.

I would therefore uphold the decision of Donaldson J and refuse an interlocutory injunction.

6. Laddie J has also attempted to reconcile the divergent approaches evident in *Stratford & Son Ltd. v. Lindley* and *American Cyanamid*, in his judgment in *Series 5 Software Ltd. v. Clarke*, [1996] 1 All ER 853 (Ch. D), at 863:

> Accordingly, it appears to me that in deciding whether to grant interlocutory relief, the court should bear the following matters in mind. (1) The grant of an interlocutory injunction is a matter of discretion and depends on all the facts of the case. (2) There are no fixed rules as to when an injunction should or should not be granted. The relief must be kept flexible. (3) Because of the practice adopted on the hearing of applications for interlocutory relief, the court should rarely attempt to resolve complex issues of disputed fact or law. (4) Major factors the court can bear in mind are (a) the extent to which damages are likely to be an adequate remedy for each party and the ability of the other party to pay, (b) the balance of convenience, (c) the maintenance of the status quo, and (d) any clear view the court may reach as to the relative strength of the parties' cases.

In the following extract, Hammond outlines the position in Canada prior to *American Cyanamid*. (See also Robert J. Sharpe, "Interlocutory Injunctions: The Post-American Cyanamid Position," in Eric Gertner, ed., *Studies in Civil Procedure* (Toronto: Butterworths, 1979), chapter 8, at 185.)

R. Grant Hammond, "Interlocutory Injunctions: Time for a New Model?"
(1980), 30 *University of Toronto Law Journal* 241, at 266-67 (footnotes omitted)

Prior to *American Cyanamid* the majority of Canadian cases expressed a need for a plaintiff to demonstrate a *prima facie* case (sometimes with the adjectives "strong" or "fair" added). A lesser number of cases suggested a requirement of a "serious question" to be tried (sometimes coupled with words like "a probability of success"). What was being applied in the majority of cases was the classic sequential model, but one pre-*American Cyanamid* judgment was quite outside the mainstream of authority. Lerner J in a 1973 decision [*Terra Communications Ltd. v. Communicomp Data Ltd.* (1973), 1 OR (2d) 682] held that

> the guidelines to be considered when determining whether an interlocutory injunction should be granted … are (1) that if the plaintiffs' action does not succeed, the plaintiffs will pay any damages suffered by the defendants if they sustain any injury or damage by reason of the order; (2) that the order is necessary to preserve the status quo; (3) that a strong *prima facie* case must be made out that the plaintiffs will succeed; (4) that unless the injunction is granted, the plaintiffs are likely to suffer irreparable injury; (5) that the defendants' interests receive the same consideration as the plaintiffs'; and (6) where the legal right claimed is not sufficiently clear to enable the Court to form an opinion thereon on the application for the interlocutory injunction, the relevant convenience or inconvenience to the parties should be considered.

This judgment could perhaps best be categorized as a "collective effort." To the extent that it does not suggest that the criteria are to be examined in any particular order, it must be assumed that all factors were to be considered both individually and collectively. This would align the Lerner model with the American balancing model evolved through *Virginia Jobbers*, except that there is no mention in the Lerner model of the effect, or potential effect, of the order on third parties and the public generally. This is curious because, like *Virginia*

Jobbers, the dispute in *Terra Communications* arose in an administrative law context. The public interest element might have been expected to weigh heavily in that kind of case. There is no other Commonwealth court which has evolved a model in so open a form as the Lerner model.

NOTE

Although only a decision of the Ontario Divisional Court, *Yule Inc. v. Atlantic Pizza Delight Franchise (1968) Ltd.* (1977), 17 OR (2d) 505 (HC) is consistently cited by later Canadian courts for its exposition of the requisite test for granting an interlocutory injunction.

Yule Inc. v. Atlantic Pizza Delight Franchise (1968) Ltd.
(1977), 17 OR (2d) 505 (HC)

CORY J: This is an appeal by the defendants from the order of the Chief Justice of the High Court granting an interlocutory injunction restraining the defendants, their agents or servants from doing or refusing to do any act with a view to breaching the contract between the plaintiff and the defendant dated August 9, 1975. Leave to appeal the order granting the injunction was granted by Mr. Justice Krever. Some of the facts applicable to the case are set out in the reasons of Evans CJHC as follows:

> James Yule is the president of the plaintiff company and is engaged in the business of selling franchises and food servicing as well as a licensed franchisee of six of the defendants' pizza take-out restaurants. Bernard Imbeault is the president of all three defendant companies. The first named defendant is responsible for the sale and promotion of new franchises. The second is concerned with the servicing and supplying of existing franchises, while the third is a management company which directs the management and operations of the first two defendants.
>
> On August 5, 1975, the plaintiff entered into an agreement executed by the first two defendants giving it the sole and exclusive right to sell franchises in Ontario, subject to the right of the defendants to sell directly. The term of the agreement was for approximately five years with a right of renewal for a five-year term. Pizza Delight Corporation Ltd. was not a party to the agreement but as far as this motion is concerned I propose to make no distinction among the defendant companies as clearly they were all operated and controlled by Mr. Imbeault. Under the terms of the agreement the plaintiff was to receive $6,250 for each franchise sold out of a total franchise fee of $10,000 plus 40% royalties and 2% on gross sales.
>
> It is evident from the material filed that the plaintiff was successful in selling franchises and in opening outlets in Ontario. In addition to opening outlets it had set up a warehousing and distribution system to supply the franchise holders and was also engaged in the construction and supply of equipment to them. Following some complaints from franchise holders the defendants became disenchanted with the plaintiff and on May 27, 1977, informed it by telegram that the agreement was cancelled as of that date. At the same time telegrams were sent to the various franchise holders in Ontario advising them that the plaintiff and its president James Yule, apart from the operation of those take-out restaurants controlled by it, had no other involvement with the defendants. Mr. Yule submits that as a result of these telegrams his reputa-

tion in the franchise field and in the food servicing area has been seriously damaged and his company will suffer severe financial losses since it now holds or is in the process of purchasing real estate and equipment bought specifically for the purpose of carrying out the business generated through his contractual relationship with the defendants.

It may be as well to refer to certain additional matters. Clause 15 of the contract of August 1975 provides for the referral of any dispute between the plaintiff, Yule, Inc., and the franchisees to the two first named defendants. Further references to the contract will be made later in these reasons. The plaintiff deposes that he presently employs 59 people. Twenty-six of those employees do work that flows from the August 1975 contract and would have to be released if the injunction is not granted.

Evans CJHC pointed out in his reasons that the Court is faced here with the situation in which the defendants filed affidavits in which the president of the company recites certain complaints against Mr. Yule and in which two or three franchise holders or former franchise holders express their unhappiness with the treatment accorded them by the plaintiff. In addition the president of the defendant corporation further alleges that James Yule, the president of the plaintiff company engaged in activities outside the scope of the contract and that such activities were and are detrimental to the defendant's business.

The plaintiff, on the other hand, contends that it and Mr. Yule have complied strictly with and carried out all terms of the contract and that its determination by the defendants cannot be supported.

The Chief Justice of the High Court discussed the principles which he felt were applicable to the case and stated:

> The principles which emerge from the cases cited including *American Cyanamid Co. v. Ethicon Ltd.*, [1975] AC 396 (HL (Eng.)) and *Bryanston Finance Ltd. v. de Vries (No. 2)*, [1976] Ch. 63 (CA) make it evident that on an application for an interlocutory injunction the rights of the parties arising out of their contractual relationship are not to be determined by the Court. It is sufficient if the applicant establishes that there is a substantial issue to be tried; that it has demonstrated a *prima facie* case, in the sense that the applicant has a legal right which it is attempting to protect pending trial; that the failure to grant the relief will result in a threatened harm to the applicant which may not be adequately compensable by way of damages and finally, that the preponderance of convenience must be in favour of the applicant if the application for injunctive relief is to succeed.
>
> There is no doubt that litigation which involves the right of the defendant to terminate a contractual relationship formalized between the parties in a written agreement is a serious issue, particularly when there is a definite conflict on the evidence. If one assumes that the plaintiff was not in default under his contract and that his application for an interlocutory injunction is to restrain the defendant from doing acts which would violate the plaintiff's legal right, then following the decision in the *Cyanamid* case in the House of Lords, the applicant would be entitled to the relief sought.
>
> The Court in applications for interlocutory injunctions is always faced with rather inadequate evidence and is forced to consider the results which flow if the injunction is either refused or granted. If in the present case the injunction is refused and the defendants fail at trial, the situation existing prior to the breach by the defendants will be more difficult to reverse and in some respects, for example the reputation of the plaintiff in the franchise trade, may be

irremediable. If the injunction is granted the defendants, under the terms of the written agreement, are in a position to supervise the plaintiff's activities in the franchised outlets. It may be that they will be required to become more concerned in the granting of franchises in Ontario and in their operation if, as they submit, the plaintiff has been delinquent in that respect. In weighing the countervailing propositions, I am satisfies that there is less likelihood that serious inconvenience and loss will result if the injunctive relief sought is granted.

Krever J gave leave to appeal indicating that although he agreed with the result and conclusions of the Chief Justice of the High Court he was of the opinion that the matter was of such importance that it should be referred to this Court.

The appellant contends that the injunction ought not to have been granted for the following reasons:

The learned Chief Justice erred in law in that a Court of Equity will refuse to grant relief to an applicant with unclean hands.

The learned Chief Justice erred in law in formulating the test for the grant of an interlocutory injunction.

The learned Chief Justice erred in law in applying the test for the grant of an interlocutory injunction.

The learned Chief Justice erred in law in granting an injunction to specifically perform a personal service contract in the absence of express negative covenants.

It may be convenient to deal first with the submission that injunctive relief should have been refused because of the unclean hands of the plaintiff. Not any of the alleged misdeeds of the plaintiff appear to be of such a nature that they would disentitle the plaintiff to the relief it sought and that challenge therefore must be disregarded.

Next to be considered is whether the contract in question is one of personal service and whether injunctive relief may be granted to prevent its breach. It must be remembered that the contract of August 1975 was an agreement between corporate entities. It is commercial in its nature. It is not a contract for personal service. Specifically, it is not personal to James Yule and there is no requirement that his services be provided by the plaintiff.

A contract of true personal service or employment will not be enforced at the suit of either party. Courts have been traditionally reluctant to force parties to continue in a personal relationship against the will of either party. That principle has been limited to those situations where the services are of a very personal nature whether they be singing, quarterbacking or managing a musical group. In cases arising out of personal service, injunctions will only issue if there is a specific negative covenant. The Courts have, however, been known to enforce such covenants even though it may thus ensure compliance with the affirmative or positive covenants of the contract.

The approach to contracts that do not provide for such personal service has not been as narrow. For example, the Courts have inferred from a positive covenant granting exclusive and sole authority to sell a product, a negative covenant that such sole and exclusive authority to sell will not be granted to another. The negative covenant so inferred has been enforced by injunctive relief: see A.G. Guest (ed.), *Chitty on Contracts* (London: Sweet & Maxwell, 23rd ed., 1968) at p. 1562.

In this case the contract gives sole and exclusive authority to the plaintiff with regard to certain matters. It would be unduly technical and restricting if the Court were to find that because of the positive wording of the covenant it could not infer the negative. It is eminently sensible and logical to conclude that if an exclusive and sole authority is given the plaintiff that there must be inferred a negative covenant that the defendants will not terminate that authority and grant it to themselves or others. There are a number of authorities with factual situations similar to this case wherein the Courts have inferred and enforced the negative aspect of a grant of sole and exclusive authority: [A list of decisions follows.] The agreement between the parties of August 1975 is not a contract for personal service and injunctive relief is an appropriate remedy.

An argument was raised that the plaintiff had not established that it would suffer irreparable damage if the injunction was not granted. When considering that issue the essential question that the Court must ask itself is, "is it just in all the circumstances that the plaintiff should be confined to a remedy in damages?" The loss here would be difficult to calculate for in effect the plaintiff would be put out of business if the injunctive relief sought is not granted. It would suffer not only loss of profits but also loss of reputation and goodwill. The material of the plaintiff has established that irreparable damage will be suffered by it. On the other hand, if the relief is granted, the defendants are simply required to honour a contract that they entered willingly and which to date has been a successful and profitable one for them. Nor does there appear to be any basis for the submission of the defendants that the contract is based to such an extent on mutual trust and confidence that it should not be specifically enforced.

The final matter to be considered is whether the Chief Justice of the High Court incorrectly stated the test to be applied by the Court in considering interim injunctive release [*sic*]. It could well be inferred that Evans CJHC had concluded that the plaintiff in this case had fulfilled the requirements for all possible tests in that it had demonstrated a strong *prima facie* case as well as showing that there was a substantial issue to be tried. It would appear from the material that the plaintiff has, in fact, met the requirements both of demonstrating a strong *prima facie* case and that there is a substantial issue to be tried. It is, therefore, perhaps unnecessary and unwise to say anything further; however, in deference to the very able and extensive arguments that have been submitted these additional comments are made.

The appellants contended that there are three tests currently in vogue, and that may be applied by Courts when interim injunctions are considered.

The first of these was designated as the multi-requisite test. There, the Courts have held that it is incumbent upon the plaintiff to clear a number of hurdles; the first of the hurdles being that the plaintiff must establish a strong *prima facie* case. If the plaintiff fails in clearing that first obstacle then the application must be dismissed without consideration of any other aspects such as the irreparable damage the plaintiff might suffer, the balance of convenience, or the desirability of maintaining the *status quo*.

The second test was referred to as the multi-factor test. In applying that test the Court will weigh the performance of the plaintiff in a number of categories. The plaintiff might, in fact, fail in one of the categories but by succeeding in others obtain the relief sought. Perhaps this was the test applied by Lerner J in *Terra Communications Ltd. v. Communicomp Data Ltd.* (1973), 1 OR (2d) 682. In that case Lerner J in his well considered and careful reasons set out six factors that the Court should consider on interim injunction applications. One of the factors was that the plaintiff must establish a strong *prima facie* case. However, there was no definite indication that the Court would not consider the other factors if the plaintiff did not first establish a strong *prima facie* case.

The last test has been referred to as the *American Cyanamid* test. That test was set forth in the speech of Lord Diplock in *American Cyanamid Co. v. Ethicon Ltd.* There, it was determined that it was not incumbent upon the applicant to establish a strong *prima facie* case. It was sufficient if the applicant satisfied the Court that his case was not a frivolous one and that there was a substantial issue to be tried. Once the applicant has satisfied that prerequisite then the granting of the relief will be dependent upon a consideration of other matters; including the threatened harm to the applicant which might not be adequately compensable by way of damages; the preponderance of convenience, and, the effect of the injunction upon both parties.

In this case, as in many others where injunctive relief is sought there are difficult questions to be decided at trial. Those questions clearly ought not and cannot be decided upon the conflicting evidence of affidavits and transcripts of cross-examinations, available upon a motion for interim injunction. In such a situation the result ought to be determined on the basis of what has been referred to as the balance of the convenience. That in fact appears to have been the law both in Ontario and in England prior to the *American Cyanamid* decision.

In *Playter v. Lucas* (1921), 51 OLR 492, the headnote which fairly summarizes the decision reads as follows:

> *Held*, upon a motion for an interlocutory injunction, that, there being difficult questions to be decided at the trial, which ought not to be determined in advance, and the material before the Court on the motion not being sufficient to enable the Court to form a satisfactory opinion on the plaintiffs' rights, the disposition of the motion must turn upon the relative convenience or inconvenience which might result to the parties from granting or withholding the injunction; and in this case the balance of convenience was in favour of the defendant, and the injunction should be withheld, on the clear understanding that the defendant was proceeding at his own risk.

That same principle was followed in *Lido Industrial Products Ltd. v. Melnor Manufacturing Ltd.*, [1968] SCR 769. There, Chief Justice Cartwright at p. 771, quoted with approval from 21 Hals., 3rd ed., p. 366, as follows:

> Where any doubt exists as to the plaintiff's right, or if his right is not disputed, but its violation is denied, the Court, in determining whether an interlocutory injunction should be granted, takes into consideration the balance of convenience to the parties and the nature of the injury which the defendant, on the one hand, would suffer if the injunction was granted and he should ultimately turn out to be right, and that which the plaintiff, on the other hand, might sustain if the injunction was refused and he should ultimately turn out to be right. The burden of proof that the inconvenience which the plaintiff will suffer by the refusal of the injunction is greater than that which the defendant will suffer, it if is granted, lies on the plaintiff. ...

R.E. Holland J considered the applicability of the *American Cyanamid* test in *Cradle Pictures (Canada) Ltd. v. Penner* (1975), 10 OR (2d) 444, and determined that it was not the law in Ontario and ought not to be followed. When one considers the very clear and concise reasons of Holland J, it should be remembered that the foregoing authorities do not appear to have been referred to him. Further, the trial of the *Cradle Pictures* action could be heard in St. Catharines within two months of the date of the interim injunction application. Thus, a consideration of the applicability of the *American Cyanamid* test may not have been essential to the decision. To the extent that the reasons for judgment of Holland J could be taken to infer that it should be taken to exclude the application of the *American Cyanamid* test in all types of cases to that extent I respectfully disagree with his reasons.

Similarly, if it is assumed that Lerner J, in *Terra Communications Ltd. v. Communicomp Data Ltd.*, held that the establishment of a strong *prima facie* case is an essential prerequisite condition to the granting of an interlocutory injunction then I must respectfully differ with his conclusion.

In a situation, where, as in this case, there are conflicting affidavits and transcripts of cross-examinations, then the *American Cyanamid* test is an appropriate and proper one to apply. The authorities in Ontario and England referred to earlier support this position.

To determine, on the basis of the material usually appearing before the Court on an interim injunction application whether a strong *prima facie* case has been demonstrated is an exceedingly difficult, if not impossible task. It may be worth recalling the innumerable appellate decisions that emphasize the great advantages afforded to a trial Judge in hearing and seeing the witnesses before making factual findings. Every day throughout the Province juries are instructed that they must make an assessment of the witnesses and in doing so, they should consider among other factors, the appearance and manner of testifying of each witness. In reality it is impossible for a Judge as much as a jury to make a factual assessment without hearing and seeing the witnesses. Although the practice in our jurisdiction may permit more material to be placed before the Court on the motion than is the situation in England, it is still virtually impossible to make a final decision without seeing and hearing the witnesses and parties.

Injunction is a vitally important remedy that must be invoked to protect rights that are considered basic and essential. As a remedy it should remain flexible so as to be applicable to changing times and circumstances. To apply the multi-requisite test would mean that injunctive relief could never be granted in a case such as this where the issues are strongly disputed. It would unduly restrict and fetter the discretion of the Court.

It was argued that to follow the *American Cyanamid* test would increase the frequency of the granting of an interim injunction. That is not likely to be a correct assessment. It must be remembered that the granting of an injunction is a discretionary remedy, subject to the imposition, for the protection of all parties, of appropriate conditions to the granting of the relief. The Court will always recognize that the granting of the remedy may have grave and deleterious consequences for the defendant and thus exercise its discretion with the greatest of care.

It was suggested by the defendants that to consider the economic factors involved as required by the *American Cyanamid* test would be erroneous and dangerous. In truth, however, in most cases such factors are presently considered. It would, in fact, seem to be a sensible, logical and necessary element for consideration on these applications.

As stated earlier, the *American Cyanamid* type of test is, on the authorities, applicable in the situation that pertains in this case. It may be extremely difficult in the face of conflicting material to say a strong *prima facie* case, or even a fair *prima facie* case has been established. In essence all that the Court can truly determine at the interlocutory injunction stage is whether the plaintiff has demonstrated that his case is not frivolous and that there is a substantial issue to be tried. Once a determination has been made on that issue the Court could then well consider the other requisite factors referred to by Lord Diplock. A consideration of the evidentiary problems facing the Courts on interim injunction motions leads to a conclusion that the *American Cyanamid* test is honest in its approach and should be applicable in most cases.

However, it may not be a suitable one in all situations. For example, the highly specialized, technical, and esoteric field of patent law has established a longstanding practice that might be offended by the application of the *American Cyanamid* test: see the judgment of this Court delivered by Griffiths J in *Teledyne Industries Inc. v. Lido Industrial Products Ltd.* (1977), 17 OR (2d) 111 (HC, Div. Ct.).

In the circumstances of this case there was no error made by Evans CJHC in enunciating and applying the *American Cyanamid* test in determining whether to grant the interim injunction.

The appeal is therefore dismissed with costs to the plaintiff in the cause.

Appeal dismissed.

NOTES AND QUESTIONS

1. Recently, on several occasions, the Supreme Court of Canada has had to rule on the appropriate test for an interlocutory injunction, or stay, preventing the enforcement of legislation where its constitutional validity has been challenged. While there are special features to these types of actions, the appropriate test bear marked similarities to that applied in the context of private civil litigation.

In *Attorney General of Manitoba v. Metropolitan Stores (MTS) Ltd.*, [1987] 1 SCR 110 the Supreme Court indicated an appropriate test for interlocutory relief where constitutional validity had been challenged. In that case, the union had applied to the Manitoba Labour Board to have a first contract imposed on the employer. The employer wished to challenge the constitutionality of the statutory power to impose a first contract on the grounds of a violation of the *Canadian Charter of Rights and Freedoms*. The employer sought a stay of proceeding against the Manitoba Labour Board. The trial judge had refused the stay but the Manitoba Court of Appeal then granted the stay.

The Supreme Court of Canada considered that a stay of proceedings and an interlocutory injunction were remedies of the same nature and should be governed by the same rules.

As to what is the appropriate test where constitutional validity is raised, Beetz J, for the court, said (at 127-30):

> The case law is abundant as well as relatively fluid with regard to the tests developed by the courts in order to help better delineate the situations in which it is just and equitable to grant an interlocutory injunction. Reviewing it is the function of doctrinal analysis rather than that of judicial decision-making and I simply propose to give a bare outline of the three main tests currently applied.
>
> The first test is a preliminary and tentative assessment of the merits of the case, but there is more than one way to describe this first test. The traditional way consists in asking whether the

litigant who seeks the interlocutory injunction can make out a *prima facie* case. The injunction will be refused unless he can: *Chesapeake and Ohio Railway Co. v. Ball*, [1953] OR 843, *per* McRuer CJHC, at pp. 854-55. The House of Lords has somewhat relaxed this first test in *American Cyanamid Co. v. Ethicon Ltd.*, [1975] AC 396 (HL (Eng.)), where it held that all that was necessary to meet this test was to satisfy the Court that there was a serious question to be tried as opposed to a frivolous or vexatious claim. Estey J speaking for himself and five other members of the Court in a unanimous judgment referred to but did not comment upon this difference in *Aetna Financial Services Ltd. v. Feigelman*, [1985] 1 SCR 2, at pp. 9 and 10. ...

In the case at bar, it is neither necessary nor advisable to choose, for all purposes, between the traditional formulation and the *American Cyanamid* description of the first test: the British case law illustrates that the formulation of a rigid test for all types of cases, without considering their nature, is not to be favoured (see Jill E. Martin (ed.), *Hanbury and Maudsley's, Modern Equity* (London: Stevens & Sons, 12th ed., 1985) at pp. 736-43). In my view, however, the *American Cyanamid* "serious question" formulation is sufficient in a constitutional case where, as indicated below in these reasons, the public interest is taken into consideration in the balance of convenience. But I refrain from expressing any view with respect to the sufficiency or adequacy of this formulation in any other type of case.

The second test consists in deciding whether the litigant who seeks the interlocutory injunction would, unless the injunction is granted, suffer irreparable harm, that is harm not susceptible or difficult to be compensated in damages. Some judges consider at the same time the situation of the other party to the litigation and ask themselves whether the granting of the interlocutory injunction would cause irreparable harm to this other party if the main action fails. Other judges take the view that this last aspect rather forms part of the balance of convenience.

The third test, called the balance of convenience and which ought perhaps to be called more appropriately the balance of inconvenience, is a determination of which of the two parties will suffer the greater harm from the granting or refusal of an interlocutory injunction, pending a decision on the merits.

I now propose to consider the particular application of the test of the balance of convenience in a case where the constitutional validity of a legislative provision is challenged. As Lord Diplock said in *American Cyanamid* at p. 409:

[T]here may be many other special factors to be taken into consideration in the particular circumstances of individual cases.

It will be seen in what follows that the consequences for the public as well as for the parties, of granting a stay in a constitutional case, do constitute "special factors" to be taken into consideration.

(2) The Balance of Convenience and The Public Interest

A review of the case law indicates that, when the constitutional validity of a legislative provision is challenged, the courts consider that they ought not to be restricted to the application of traditional criteria which govern the granting or refusal of interlocutory injunctive relief in ordinary private or civil law cases. Unless the public interest is also taken into consideration in evaluating the balance of convenience, they very often express their disinclination to grant injunctive relief before constitutional invalidity has been finally decided on the merits. ...

In short, I conclude that in a case where the authority of a law enforcement agency is constitutionally challenged, no interlocutory injunction or stay should issue to restrain that authority from performing its duties to the public unless, in the balance of convenience, the public interest is taken into consideration and given the weight it should carry. Such is the rule where the case against the authority of the law enforcement agency is serious, for if it were not, the question of granting interlocutory relief should not even arise. But that is the rule also even where there is a *prima facie* case against the enforcement agency, such as one which would require the coming into play of s. 1 of the *Canadian Charter of Rights and Freedoms*. ...

The Supreme Court has again addressed this issue in *RJR-MacDonald Inc. v. Canada (Attorney General)*, [1994] 1 SCR 311. There, the court indicated somewhat more definitively that the usual test for interlocutory injunctions in Canada was that of *American Cyanamid*. These two Supreme Court of Canada judgments are extracted in detail in chapter 12, "Charter Remedies." (For those wanting to pursue the special issue of interlocutory injunctions in constitutional litigation at this point, that section of the casebook can be inserted here or later in this chapter.)

2. *Yule* posits three tests for granting an interlocutory injunction. What guidance is offered as to when it is appropriate to use each of the respective tests?

3. One of the reasons for the change in emphasis in *American Cyanamid* was the issue of adjudicating on unchallenged evidence. In Canadian jurisdictions, there is provision for cross-examination on affidavit evidence (see, for instance, Ontario Rules of Civil Procedure, r. 39.02). Should this impact upon the appropriate threshold test chosen by Canadian courts? In *Chitel v. Rothbart* (1982), 39 OR (2d) 513 (CA), MacKinnon ACJO, after quoting from *N.W.L. Ltd. v. Woods, supra*, states (at 522):

It is my view without stating any final opinion on the subject, that the availability of the cross-examination transcript makes more legitimate a preliminary consideration by the motions judge of the merits of the case.

4. Leubsdorf has suggested the following model, which attempts to balance the potential risk of judicial error in granting the interlocutory injunction against the need to minimize irreparable loss of legal rights pending final determination of the litigation: John Leubsdorf, "The Standard of Preliminary Injunctions" (1978), 91 *Harvard Law Review* 524, at 542 (footnotes omitted):

A. The Model and Its Rationale

A court considering a motion for interlocutory relief faces a dilemma. If it does not grant prompt relief, the plaintiff may suffer a loss of his lawful rights that no later remedy can restore. But if the court does grant immediate relief, the defendant may sustain precisely the same loss of his rights.

The dilemma, of course, exists only because the court's interlocutory assessment of the parties' underlying rights is fallible in the sense that it may be different from the decision that ultimately will be reached. The danger of incorrect preliminary assessment is the key to the analysis of interlocutory relief. It requires investigating the harm an erroneous interim decision may cause and trying to minimize that harm. And it decisively distinguishes the preliminary from the final judgment.

The court need not consider every harm resulting from an erroneous preliminary decision, but only harm that final relief cannot redress. If the final judgment can remedy the plaintiff's injuries, there is no occasion to grant immediate protection which may turn out to have been based on error. Likewise, if the defendant's injuries from what turns out to be an erroneous injunction can be redressed later, there is no reason to deny interim relief otherwise warranted. Not even all irreparable harm, but only irreparable harm to legal rights, should count. If the defendant has no right to pasture goats in front of the plaintiff's windows, any harm he suffers from an injunction against doing so comes not from the dangers of interlocutory decision, but from the substantive law.

Leubsdorf's approach has been endorsed in the United States Court of Appeals by (Richard) Posner J in *American Hospital Supply Corp. v. Hospital Products Ltd.* (1985), 780 F2d 589 (7th Cir.). This case involved the breach of a supply agreement for the supply of absorbable surgical staples. The distributor brought an interlocutory injunction action against the supplier to order it to continue honouring the supply agreement. In affirming the lower court's decision in granting the injunction, Posner J remarked:

A district judge asked to decide whether to grant or deny a preliminary injunction must choose the course of action that will minimize the costs of being mistaken. Because he is forced to act on an incomplete record, the danger of a mistake is substantial. And a mistake can be costly. If the judge grants the preliminary injunction to the plaintiff who it later turns out is not entitled to any judicial relief—whose legal rights have not been violated—the judge commits a mistake whose gravity is measured by the irreparable harm, if any, that the injunction causes to the defendant while it is in effect. If the judge denies the preliminary injunction to a plaintiff who it later turns out is entitled to judicial relief, the judge commits a mistake whose gravity is measured by the irreparable harm, if any, that the denial of the preliminary injunction does to the plaintiff.

These mistakes can be compared, and the one likely to be less costly can be selected, with the help of a simple formula: grant the preliminary injunction if but only if $P \times Hp > (1 - P) \times Hd$, or, in words, only if the harm to the plaintiff if the injunction is denied, multiplied by the probability that the denial would be an error (that the plaintiff, in other words, will win at trial), exceeds the harm to the defendant if the injunction is granted, multiplied by the probability that granting the injunction would be an error. That probability is simply one minus the probability that the plaintiff will win at trial; for if the plaintiff has, say, a 40 percent chance of winning, the defendant must have a 60 percent chance of winning $(1.00 - .40 = .60)$. The left-hand side of the formula is simply the probability of an erroneous denial weighted by the cost of denial to the plaintiff, and the right-hand side simply the probability of an erroneous grant weighted by the cost of grant to the defendant.

This formula, a procedural counterpart to Judge Learned Hand's famous negligence formula, see *United States v. Carroll Towing Co.* (1947), 159 F2d 169, 173 (2d Cir.); *United States Fidelity & Guaranty Co. v. Jadranska Slobodna Plovidba* (1982), 683 F2d 1022, 1026 (7th Cir.), is not offered as a new legal standard; it is intended not to force analysis into a quantitative straitjacket but to assist analysis by presenting succinctly the factors that the court must consider in making its decision and by articulating the relationship among the factors. It is actually just a distillation of the familiar four (sometimes five) factor test that courts use in deciding whether to grant a preliminary injunction. The court asks whether the plaintiff will be irreparably harmed if the preliminary injunction is denied (sometimes also whether the plaintiff has an adequate remedy at law), whether the harm to the plaintiff if the preliminary injunction is denied will exceed the harm to the defendant if it is granted, whether the plaintiff is reasonably likely to prevail at trial, and whether the public interest will be affected by granting or denying the injunction (i.e., whether third parties will be harmed—and these harms can then be added to Hp or Hd as the case may be). See, e.g., *Palmer v. City of Chicago* (1985), 755 F2d 560, 576 (7th Cir.). The court undertakes these inquiries to help it figure out whether granting the injunction would be the error-minimizing course of action, which depends on the probability that the plaintiff is in the right and on the costs to the plaintiff, the defendant, or others of granting or denying the injunction. All this is explained at length in *Roland Machinery Co. v. Dresser Industries, Inc.* (1984), 749 F2d 380, 382-88 (7th Cir.), where a panel of this court applied the verbal counterpart to our algebraic formula, as did a different panel in *Maxim's Ltd. v. Badonsky* (1985), 772 F2d 388, 391 (7th Cir.). See also John Leubsdorf, *The Standard for Preliminary Injunctions* (1978), 91 Harv. L Rev. 525. The formula is new; the analysis it capsulizes is standard.

The formula does not depend on the legal basis of the plaintiff's claim, whether it is antitrust law (*Roland*) or trademark law (*Badonsky*) or, as here, the common law of contract, although the nature of the right asserted by the plaintiff may affect the weighting of the harms, see, e.g., *Shondel v. McDermott* (1985), 775 F2d 859, 866-67 (7th Cir.). So may the nature of the permanent remedy to which the plaintiff would be entitled if he prevailed at trial. For example, prevailing parties in breach of contract cases normally are not awarded specific performance, that is, a mandatory injunction to perform. Since many breaches of contract are involuntary, implying that performance would be very costly, routinely ordering specific performance would create situations where the defendant was forced to bargain desperately to buy his way out of the injunction. The high bargaining costs that would result are a deadweight cost of equitable relief. To the extent that those costs attend a preliminary injunction, they are of course relevant to the decision whether to issue such an injunction. But the formula takes account of this; the case we have described would be one where the harm to the defendant from granting the injunction would be very great. Thus the fact that a plaintiff might have no hope of getting specific performance ordered at the conclusion of the trial need not prevent him from obtaining a preliminary injunction. Cf. *Roland v. Dresser Industries, Inc., supra,* 749 F2d at 386. The premise of the preliminary injunction is that the remedy available at the end of trial will not make the plaintiff whole; and, in a sense, the more limited that remedy, the stronger the argument for a preliminary injunction—provided the remedy is not limited for reasons that would make a preliminary injunction equally inappropriate.

As explained in *Roland*, the scope of judicial review of a district judge's decision to grant or deny a preliminary injunction is limited. See 749 F2d at 384-85, 388-91. The usual formulation is that the decision will be reversed only if it is found to be an "abuse of discretion." Unfortunately this phrase covers a family of review standards rather than a single standard, and a family whose members differ greatly in the actual stringency of review. See, e.g., *id.* at 388-91; *Metlyn Realty Corp. v. Esmark, Inc.* (1985), 763 F2d 826, 831-32 (7th Cir.); Henry J. Friendly, *Indiscretion About Discretion* (1982), 31 Emory LJ 747. For example, when we review an order granting or denying a preliminary injunction, we do not do so with as much deference (virtually complete deference) as when reviewing a criminal sentence that is within legal limits but is challenged as too harsh; we do "not simply engage in a perfunctory rubber-stamping of the district court's decision." *Olin Water Services v. Midland Research Laboratories, Inc.* (1985), 774 F2d 303, 307 n. 7 (8th Cir.). But we do give that decision substantial deference, bearing in mind that the district judge had to act in haste, that he had to balance factors which, though they can be related in a neat formula, usually cannot be quantified, and that in dealing with the parties and their witnesses and counsel in the hectic atmosphere of a preliminary-injunction proceeding the judge may have developed a feel for the facts and the equities that remote appellate judges cannot obtain from a transcript. To reverse an order granting or denying a preliminary injunction, therefore, it is not enough that we think we would have acted differently in the district judge's shoes; we must have a strong conviction that he exceeded the permissible bounds of judgment. And although recognizing that the order granting such an injunction must set forth the judge's reasons, see Fed. R Civ. P 65(d), we also recognize that the haste with which the judge must act precludes as full a statement of reasons as could reasonably be demanded of a final decision.

See also Posner's mathematical expression of his approach in R. Posner, *Economic Analysis of Law*, 5th ed. (New York: Aspen Publishers, Inc., 1998), § 21.4.

There is also tacit acceptance of Leubsdorf's approach in *Films Rover International Ltd. v. Cannon Film Sales Ltd.*, [1987] 1 WLR 670, at 680 (Ch.), per Hoffmann J:

> The principal dilemma about the grant of interlocutory injunction, whether prohibitory or mandatory, is that there is by definition a risk that the court may make the "wrong" decision, in the sense of granting an injunction to a party who fails to establish his right at the trial (or would fail if there was a trial) or alternatively, in failing to grant an injunction to a party who succeeds (or would succeed) at trial. A fundamental principle is therefore that the court should take whichever course appears to carry the lower risk of injustice if it should turn out to have been "wrong" in the sense I have described. The guidelines for the grant of both kinds of interlocutory injunctions are derived from this principle.

5. Hammond has suggested the following "variable threshold" model (at 278-81) (footnotes omitted):

> This analysis suggests the following contemporary model with respect to the interlocutory dilemma. A judge should not be deterred by the historical law/equity dichotomy or even by inherited maxims. The contemporary rationale for the remedy can be simply expressed as a vehicle for the preservation of litigation for effective later determination. Given that conceptual purpose for the remedy a variable threshold model could be adopted as a more logical development of existing models. This would require a judge to ask three preliminary questions: 1/ is there a real dispute (in the sense of the claim being nonfrivolous)? 2/ what is the nature of that dispute? 3/ assuming that question 1 is answered affirmatively and after the analysis required in question 2 is undertaken, what threshold test is appropriate for that kind of dispute?
>
> The reasons for question 1 are obvious enough. Frivolous claims should on both efficiency and fairness grounds be tolled at the outset—in the same way as a finding of "no cause of action" on motion tolls an action. But this qualifier should be added to 1. The plaintiff's assertion may be, simply expressed, that although the law does not at present recognize the kind of interest or right or duty being pressed on the court, it ought to. In that kind of case the court should be careful not to equate "no present right" with frivolity. In that situation, the court should simply ask: is this a "real" suit (that is, as far as can now be ascertained is it mounted for objectively arguable reasons on at least plausible grounds)? To adopt, for instance, a threshold test requiring a "*prima facie* case" test in that kind of situation is to adopt a totally static view of the development of the law and, more pointedly, to deprive a plaintiff of the kind of due process protection open to other plaintiffs and to the defendant in the instant case.
>
> Clearly there is some overlap between questions 1 and 2—for instance, analysis of the nature of the dispute will usually also dispose of any issue as to its frivolity—but it is important that both

questions be formally asked because they have functionally different purposes. Once those questions have been answered it should then be a matter of articulating the level of threshold test appropriate to the particular kind of dispute and the sorts of issues at stake in those proceedings. If the dispute is over, say, the potential grounding of all DC-10 aircraft within a particular jurisdiction on account of alleged "unairworthiness," a judge might respond that public safety is an interest which should not lightly be set aside and that therefore a low threshold standard is appropriate in that kind of case. (This notwithstanding that airlines and manufacturers have a substantial economic stake in the outcome which may not be completely recovered by undertaking or bond in the event of the plaintiff ultimately failing on the merits.) Or, adopting standard United States negligence analysis theory, the equation might be put thus: the magnitude of the harm which might result would greatly exceed the temporary costs of avoidance.

If we go to the other end of the legal spectrum, there are interests such as free speech which have traditionally been jealously guarded (for sound policy reasons). It should be difficult to get an interlocutory injunction in a case where free speech is genuinely in issue, and a judge would thus be justified in requiring a showing of a very high degree of probability of success on the merits before the remedy should issue. To take a case in the middle ground—a commercial suit involving pure pecuniary loss—it may be that the appropriate threshold test would be some probability of success but certainly not a *prima facie* case, *strictu sensu*.

Some of the categories where a strong initial showing of probability of right might be anticipated as being required on these preliminary standards of the prospective model are: free speech cases; patents; interlocutory mandatory injunctions in situations where no *restitutio in integrum* could be achieved if the plaintiff ultimately failed on the merits; cases where—for one reason or another—the interlocutory decision must necessarily be dispositive of the whole litigation; cases where the judge would be in as good a position as the trial judge to determine the issue (this category would principally encompass pure questions of construction; swift reviewability on appeal is also a realistic possibility in that kind of case); *quia timet* injunctions.

Of those categories the most difficult is that where the interlocutory application must necessarily be dispositive of the whole litigation. If the outcome of the application will in fact have that result then the court is truly faced with *the* trial, not a trial within a trial. If that is so, the judge should recognize the reality that whilst in form he is confronted with an interlocutory application, it is the ultimate issue—who wins?—which he has presently to resolve. The court would then have two alternatives. First, a procedural solution might be applied (that is, requiring the action to be set down as a matter of urgency, if need be on specific terms). That alternative may not be viable because of the circumstances of the particular case. If it is not (and it should be considered first, because there is an issue of equity towards litigants in other pending suits in crowded civil lists) then the court is faced with the appropriate standards for an interlocutory injunction in that kind of case. There is a logical absurdity in endeavouring to apply the pre-*American Cyanamid* standard. A *prima facie* case that a claim will eventually stand up, or that a party has a claim, is not the same thing as a determination that in fact and law a party does have a sustainable claim. The *prima facie* test would accordingly deprive a defendant of his right to have the ultimate issue decided on the proper standard of proof. The post-*American Cyanamid* test is more plausible but involves dealing with this problem under the head of "balance of convenience"—a curious nomenclature for the appropriate standard of proof, and one that really obscures the problem. The variable threshold model at least requires the judge to ask directly what standard of likelihood of success is appropriate to this kind of case, and the answer must surely be, the full rigour of the civil standard.

Assuming that the necessary identification of a threshold test has been made and met, the court should then consider, as now, the balance of convenience (including any public interest elements) and the adequacy of any other avenues of relief (*not* merely damages). Again, recognition must be made that these questions can overlap both with each other and with the preliminary questions, but they too should be formally posed in so far as they both bear in distinctive ways on the perceived functional purpose of the remedy—the preservation of litigation for an effective later decision.

The reluctance to embrace *American Cyanamid* totally probably stems from the fact that it is difficult to formulate a uniform test for all circumstances. And yet, in the area of interlocutory injunctions which covers a myriad of cases, it is difficult to identify distinguishing characteristics justifying a departure from some normative standards.

In *Cayne and Another v. Global Natural Resources PLC*, [1984] 1 All ER 225 (CA), Kerr LJ suggested that *American Cyanamid* went no further than laying down guidelines when the following prerequisites were present (at 234):

The first, as stated by Lord Diplock, is that the question whether to grant or refuse an interlocutory injunction has been placed into a state of balance to the extent that the court can see that the plaintiffs' case raises a serious issue to be tried. If the plaintiffs fail at that point, then clearly there is no case for an injunction, and obviously the *Cyanamid* guidelines cannot come into play.

The second prerequisite, as it seems to me, is that a trial is in fact likely to take place, in the sense that the plaintiffs' case shows that they are genuinely concerned to pursue their claim to trial, and that they are seeking the injunction as a means of a holding operation pending the trial. It is only in such cases, in my view, that the decision is any guide, though undoubtedly a valuable one, to the problem whether or not the plaintiffs should be protected by an injunction; and it is to be noted that this was indeed the position in the *Cyanamid* case itself. It must also be remembered that the grant or refusal of an injunction is ultimately a matter of statutory discretion, and that the powers of the courts in this regard cannot be fettered by decisions in general terms, when the facts of cases will vary infinitely.

A similar view was taken by the Ontario Divisional Court in *C-Cure Chemical Co. Inc. v. Olympia and York Developments Ltd.* (1983), 71 CPR (2d) 153, at 156, per Reid J for the court, leave to appeal refused (1983), 33 CPC 192 (CA):

In a useful review of the subject the authors of a recent paper observe, I think justly, "Some courts have made the first factor—a strong *prima facie* case—into an initial, or threshold, test, denying the injunction on that basis alone if the test was not met": see Brian MacLeod Rogers and George W. Hately, Q in "Getting the Pre-trial Injunction" (1982), 60 Can. Bar Rev. 1 at p. 9. Yet that view does not appear to me to be at all necessary. I think there is room in our jurisprudence for both. When, because there is no real conflict on the facts, or where, despite a conflict, it is possible to make a reasonable determination of what facts are likely to be proven at trial, the strong *prima facie* case test can be applied. Where that is not so the court may fall back on the *American Cyanamid* test as a reasonable and proper alternative.

That view rests heavily on the impression I have gained from a recent decision of our Court of Appeal. It is to the effect that *American Cyanamid* has not driven out the strong *prima facie* case test, and that there are cases in which the latter is appropriate. The result in that case, *Chitel v. Rothbart* (1982), 39 OR (2d) 513 (CA), proves that point, for there an application for a Mareva injunction was subjected to the strong *prima facie* case test.

Having reviewed this material, perhaps there is some validity to the following quotation from Steele J in *Carlton Realty Co. Ltd. v. Maple Leaf Mills Ltd.* (1978), 22 OR (2d) 198, at 202:

> The Divisional Court in *Yule v. Atlantic Pizza* discussed the various tests in considering the granting of injunctions at p. 510, the first of which was the multi-requisite test and the second was sometimes referred to as the multi-factor test. I will not state them as they are set out therein.
>
> The last test that they referred to was the *American Cyanamid* test. That test was set forth in the speech of Lord Diplock in *American Cyanamid Co. v. Ethicon Ltd.* There it was determined that it was not incumbent upon the applicant to establish a strong *prima facie* case. It was sufficient if the applicant satisfied the Court that his case was not a frivolous one and that there was a substantial issue to be tried. Once the applicant has satisfied that prerequisite then the granting of the relief will be dependent upon a consideration of other matters; including the threatened harm to the applicant which might not be adequately compensable by way of damages; the preponderance of convenience; and, the effect of the injunction upon both parties. The Divisional Court adopted this statement of the *American Cyanamid* test and stated that, in their opinion, Chief Justice Evans was correct. Having been a member of that Court, I adopt this reasoning in principle. I am of the opinion that there is a burden upon the applicant to show to the Court that he has enough of a case—I am adopting Mr. Pepper's word "enough"—that when it comes to trial he will have a reasonable chance of success. Perhaps I am introducing a new term when I use the word reasonable. The cases often refer to a *prima facie* case, a fair *prima facie* case, a strong *prima facie* case, not a frivolous or vexatious case, a chance of success, a probability of success, a serious question to be tried, a substantial issue to be tried. These are only some of the many phrases that have been used in dealing with this matter.
>
> While there are differences in degree in all of these phrases, I do not consider them to be substantially different. Each case must be considered on its own merits and then the discretion of the Court must be exercised. The exercise of a discretion by its nature is not an exact science. Different Judges may come to different conclusions, and provided that they have exercised their discretion within the jurisprudential framework, it is futile to quibble over the semantics of the words they may individually use. The *American Cyanamid* case sets standards that appear in their words to be more lenient than the words "*prima facie* case" or "probability of success." I am of the opinion that there is no serious difference. Surely a serious question to be tried equates to a *prima facie* case. The degree to which a Judge will consider the importance of the nature of the case in coming to his conclusion must be weighed with the knowledge of the other factors which he must consider, such as the question of harm to the parties and damages as an alternative, the balance of convenience to the parties and the need, if any, to maintain the *status quo*.

IRREPARABLE HARM

American Cyanamid places greater attention on the need for the applicant to show "irreparable harm" before being granted an interlocutory injunction. In addition, irreparable harm to the applicant must be weighed against the potential for irreparable harm to the defendant. Only when these are evenly balanced can the court look at the merits.

In *RJR-MacDonald*, [1994] 1 SCR 311, at 341 (see also chapter 12, "Charter Remedies"), the Supreme Court gave its approach to irreparable harm in the following terms:

> "Irreparable" refers to the nature of the harm suffered rather than its magnitude. It is harm that cannot be quantified in monetary terms or which either cannot be cured, usually because one party cannot collect damages from the other.

"Irreparable harm" requires the applicant to prove that damages, being the most common civil law remedy, are inadequate. However, we have seen that courts have never retreated from assessing damages, no matter how problematic their quantification. As the following extract suggests, inadequacy or irreparable harm is a question of degree: Owen M. Fiss, *The Civil Rights Injunction* (Bloomington: Indiana University Press, 1978), at 38 (footnotes omitted).

> I begin with the legacy of the property injunction—the view that in our legal system the relationship among remedies is hierarchical and that in this hierarchy the injunction is disfavoured, ranked low. This hierarchical relationship and the subordination of the injunction is, we recall, primarily the handiwork of the irreparable injury requirement. That requirement makes the issuance of an injunction conditional upon a showing that the plaintiff has no alternative remedy that will adequately repair his injury. Operationally this means that as a general proposition the plaintiff is remitted to some remedy other than an injunction unless he can show that his non-injunctive remedies are inadequate.
>
> There are, to be certain, ambiguities latent in the doctrine. For one thing, inadequacy is not a dichotomous quality, but rather permits of degree, and yet the degree required is never specified. It is not clear how inadequate—whether greatly or slightly—the alternative remedy must be before an entitlement to an injunction is established. Second, there is uncertainty as to which types of inadequacies are to count for the purpose of applying the test. What about the retrospective nature of the damage action, the interposition of the jury, or the future financial unresponsiveness of the defendant? From one standpoint—that of the plaintiff seeking the strongest safeguard of his rights—they are viewed as inadequacies; not so from a more disinterested perspective. Counting the retrospective nature of the damage award as an inadequacy would require a reordering of the hierarchy that would undermine the very doctrine being applied, for that defect is always present. The interposition of the jury also might not count as a defect because the Constitution requires it to be viewed as a virtue. And it might even be argued that the likely financial unresponsiveness of the defendant should not count, because it would strain institutional resources by placing an excessive front load on each individual injunctive lawsuit if an evidentiary inquiry into the present and future financial resources of the defendant were permitted. Third, ambiguities inhere in the irreparable injury requirement because it is not clear which alternative remedies must be shown to be inadequate before the injunction is available. Is it just the damage action or criminal prosecution, or is it also, as the Supreme Court has recently suggested, the criminal defense, *habeas corpus*, removal proceedings, change of venue, disciplinary proceedings, and even appellate review?
>
> These ambiguities permit considerable manipulation of the doctrine. Yet I am concerned with the unmistakable general effect of the doctrine: it creates a remedial hierarchy and relegates the injunction to a subordinate place in that hierarchy. The inadequacy of alternative remedies must

be demonstrated before the injunction can be utilized, but there is no reciprocal requirement on those alternative remedies. The plaintiff in a damage action or a criminal prosecution, for example, need not establish the inadequacy of the injunction before those remedies come available.

See also D. Rendleman, "The Inadequate Remedy at Law Prerequisite for an Injunction" (1981), 33 *U Fla. L Rev.* 346; Douglas Laycock, *The Death of the Irreparable Injury Rule* (Cary, NC: Oxford University Press, 1990); and Douglas Litchman, "Uncertainty and the Standard for Preliminary Relief" (2002), 70 *U Chicago L Rev.* 197.

In the following cases, what influence has inadequacy or irreparable harm had on the court's decision to grant or withhold an interlocutory injunction?

Mott-Trille v. Steed
(1996), 27 OR (3d) 486 (Gen. Div.)

DYSON J: This motion was brought by the plaintiff, Frank Mott-Trille, for an injunction to prevent the defendants from proceeding with a hearing to determine Mr. Mott-Trille's status within the religious group known as the Jehovah's Witnesses.

Background Facts

Mr. Mott-Trille has been both a lawyer and a Jehovah's Witness for approximately 40 years. Over the years, many of his clients have been members of the organization. For example, he has represented Jehovah's Witnesses in matrimonial disputes and in estate matters.

The defendant Watch Tower Bible and Tract Society of Canada ("Watch Tower Society") is an unincorporated association that runs the Jehovah's Witnesses. The defendants John Didur and André Ramseyer are two of the Watch Tower Society's administrators. The defendants W. Glen How, QC, and John Burns are its in-house counsel. The defendant Daryl Harris is the Circuit Overseer for the Jehovah's Witnesses in the area in which Mr. Mott-Trille resides. The defendants Douglas Fraser, Edward Morrison, and Charles Goodvin are members of the church who have been appointed to the "new Judicial Committee" to hear and consider allegations of theft against Mr. Mott-Trille.

In 1993, the Law Society of Upper Canada ("Law Society") launched an investigation into Mr. Mott-Trille's legal practice based on allegations of his misapplication and misappropriation of clients' funds. It is alleged that some members of the Jehovah's Witnesses and the Watch Tower Society itself were affected by Mr. Mott-Trille's mishandling of funds. During the course of its investigation, the Law Society spoke with and obtained information from a number of Jehovah's Witnesses, including Mr. How and Mr. Burns. In July 1994, Mr. Mott-Trille gave an undertaking to the Law Society not to practise law until the resolution of the disciplinary proceedings. The hearings before the Law Society began in June 1995 and are currently adjourned. It is anticipated that the Law Society hearing will resume and be completed within the next few months.

In 1994, the Watch Tower Society conducted its own investigation into whether Mr. Mott-Trille was in violation of any scriptural principles such as to warrant discipline. In April of that year, a Judicial Committee of the Watch Tower Society comprised of three members held a hearing on charges of "theft" against Mr. Mott-Trille. The church's Judicial

Committee decided that Mr. Mott-Trille had committed theft and sentenced him to a reproof, which was subsequently changed to a disfellowship (a "disfellowship" is somewhat analogous to an excommunication in the Roman Catholic Church). Mr. Mott-Trille appealed this decision, according to the Watch Tower Society's procedure, to an Appeal Committee. On April 25, 1994, the Appeal Committee upheld the findings of the first Judicial Committee and the decision to disfellowship Mr. Mott-Trille.

Mr. Mott-Trille had a number of concerns regarding the conduct of the hearings before the Watch Tower Society's first Judicial Committee and the Appeal Committee. He contended that both committees breached the rules of natural justice in that they interviewed witnesses without him being present, limited his right to cross-examination, and prevented him from being represented by legal counsel. Mr. Mott-Trille asserted that the committees applied an incorrect definition of theft in that they had specifically found that he had no intention to steal, yet decided that he had committed theft. He further alleged that Mr. How and Mr. Burns had misrepresented and/or misled all of the tribunals, including the Law Society, with regard to the Jehovah's Witnesses' files carried by Mr. Mott-Trille and their relationship to the Watch Tower Society.

Because of these concerns, Mr. Mott-Trille appealed to the Governing Body of the Jehovah's Witnesses in New York in May 1994. He never heard back directly from the Governing Body. However, in January 1995, the Chair of the first Judicial Committee of the Watch Tower Society phoned Mr. Mott-Trille and informed him that they would be annulling the previous decisions and a new Judicial Committee would be appointed by the church to consider the same charges afresh.

In 1993, the defendant Jeanette Steed sued Mr. Mott-Trille for damages. In 1994, the defendant A.F. Danley also commenced an action against Mr. Mott-Trille. Both Ms. Steed and Mr. Danley were clients of Mr. Mott-Trille and are also Jehovah's Witnesses. These actions were both settled and full and final releases were separately signed on February 7, 1995, by Ms. Steed and August 30, 1995, by Mr. Danley. Both releases included an undertaking of confidentiality by Ms. Steed and Mr. Danley respectively.

The new Judicial Committee of the Watch Tower Society has pressed Mr. Mott-Trille to proceed with the hearing; the last scheduled date was November 9, 1995. In response, Mr. Mott-Trille has issued two statements of claim. The first statement of claim was issued on September 14, 1995 against the same defendants as the within action, except for Ms. Steed and Mr. Danley. As well, the members of the first Judicial Committee were named as defendants. In this action, Mr. Mott-Trille seeks damages and an injunction restraining the hearing of the church's new Judicial Committee until at least the completion of the Law Society disciplinary hearings. The second claim was issued on October 30, 1995. In the second action, Mr. Mott-Trille seeks a declaration that the decisions of the Watch Tower Society's original Judicial Committee and the Appeal Committee and the proceedings of the new Judicial Committee are void and have no legal effect due to breaches of natural justice, lack of jurisdiction and *functus officio*. Mr. Mott-Trille also seeks an injunction restraining the new Judicial Committee of the church from proceeding with any information obtained from Ms. Steed or Mr. Danley, which he claims would be in breach of their confidentiality agreements.

Mr. Mott-Trille subsequently brought this motion for an interim and/or permanent injunction to prevent the new Judicial Committee of the Watch Tower Society from conducting its hearings until the Law Society proceedings and Mr. Mott-Trille's civil actions have concluded. In this motion, Mr. Mott-Trille also requests a declaration that the proceedings of all the ecclesiastical tribunals, including the new Judicial Committee, are void *ab initio* for breaches of the principles of natural justice, bias, errors of law and lack of jurisdiction. Finally, Mr. Mott-Trille seeks an order requiring the production of all documents in the possession and control of the defendants arising out of the matters dealt with by the church's first Judicial Committee, the Appeal Committee, and the second Judicial Committee.

I only propose to deal with the motion as it relates to the application for an interim injunction to enjoin the new Judicial Committee of the Watch Tower Society from conducting its hearings until the Law Society has concluded its proceedings, without prejudice to the plaintiff to reapply for further relief when such hearings have been completed.

Jurisdiction

Courts are justifiably reluctant to interfere with the internal affairs of domestic tribunals, particularly religious organizations such as the Watch Tower Society. However, courts in this province have intervened in the internal affairs of a church where the circumstances warrant. ...

Interlocutory Injunction

In *Yule Inc. v. Atlantic Pizza Delight Franchise* (1977), 17 OR (2d) 505 (Div. Ct.), the Divisional Court adopted the test for interim injunctions formulated in *American Cyanamid Co. v. Ethicon Ltd.*, [1975] AC 396 (HL), and in so doing set down the criteria to be followed in this province. The first issue to be determined on a motion for interlocutory injunction is whether the moving party has presented evidence of a substantial question to be tried. This is a departure from the old rule requiring the moving party to establish a strong *prima facie* case. In *Yule*, Cory J recognized that in cases where there is conflicting affidavit evidence before the court, a determination of the existence of a *prima facie* case is unrealistic. A finding that a serious issue exists is sufficient. Once that determination is made, the court then considers whether the harm may be adequately compensated for by damages and which side the balance of convenience favours. In his review of the law, Cory J quoted from the reasons of the motions judge in the case before him at p. 507:

> The principles which emerge from the cases cited including *American Cyanamid Co. v. Ethicon Ltd.*, [1975] 2 WLR 316, and *Bryanston Finance Ltd. v. de Vries (No. 2)*, [1976] 1 All ER 25, make it evident that on an application for an interlocutory injunction the rights of the parties arising out of their contractual relationship are not to be determined by the Court. It is sufficient if the applicant establishes that there is a substantial issue to be tried; that it has demonstrated a *prima facie* case, in the sense that the applicant has a legal right which it is attempting to protect pending trial; that the failure to grant the relief will result in a threatened harm to the applicant which may not be adequately compensable by way of damages and finally, that the preponderance of convenience must be in favour of the applicant if the application for injunctive relief is to succeed.

Adopting the test in *American Cyanamid*, *supra*, I find that it is clear that there are substantial issues to be tried in this action.

Irreparable Harm

In the case at bar, if the injunction is not granted, the second Judicial Committee of the Watch Tower Society will proceed, likely before the Law Society hearings have completed. Based on the information before the court, and without making a finding as to whether there has been prejudgment by the second Judicial Committee, it is entirely possible that Mr. Mott-Trille will be disfellowshipped by this second Judicial Committee of the church. There was much material put before the court as to the effect of a disfellowship on a member.

The defendants insist that Jehovah's Witnesses are free to interact with a disfellowshipped member in any manner they wish. It is argued that nothing prevents a member from speaking to the disfellowshipped person or giving evidence with respect to that person at a hearing. As a result, the defendants contend that Mr. Mott-Trille will not be impeded in presenting his case before the Law Society and will therefore not suffer any harm that cannot be compensated for by damages.

However, Mr. Mott-Trille has provided the court with contradictory and, in my opinion, convincing evidence in respect of how he might be impeded in communicating with and preparing witnesses for trial or the hearing before the Discipline Committee of the Law Society. The following is a selection of passages taken from various Watchtower magazines:

> Therefore the members of the congregation will not associate with the disfellowshipped one, either in the Kingdom Hall or elsewhere. They will not converse with such one or show him recognition in any way. If the disfellowshipped person attempts to talk to others in the congregation, they should walk away from him. In this way he will feel the full import of his sin. ...
>
> When one ignores the disfellowshipping action and continues his association with the disfellowshipped person, then it shows a bad attitude toward Jehovah's laws. He, in effect, is showing that he upholds the offender and thinks Jehovah's righteous laws are of no account. ... Actually, the one who deliberately does not abide by the congregation's decision puts himself in line to be disfellowshipped for continuing to associate with such one. Since he is classified the same as the one disfellowshipped, "a sharer," then it is reasonable for the same action to be taken against this dissenter. He too can be cut off from Jehovah's favor and from his visible organization.

(The Watchtower, July 1, 1963)

> The situation is different if the disfellowshipped or disassociated one is a relative living outside the immediate family circle and home. It might be possible to have almost no contact at all with the relative. Even if there were some family matters requiring contact, this certainly would be kept to a minimum, in line with the divine principle: "Quit mixing in company with anyone called brother that is a fornicator or a greedy person [or guilty of another gross sin], not even eating with such a man"—1 Corinthians 5:9-11.

(The Watchtower, April 15, 1988)

In my view, it is entirely possible that Mr. Mott-Trille's ability to speak to Jehovah's Witnesses could be severely impaired upon being disfellowshipped and this would have a significant negative impact on his defence before the Law Society. If a potential witness is a Jehovah's Witness and adheres to the dictates of the excerpts cited from the Watchtower as set out, Mr. Mott-Trille or his counsel might well find it impossible to determine what such witness's evidence might be in order to decide whether to call such witness. A person called to testify under such circumstances would be put in an extremely awkward position. Such a person would be caught between their sense of civic duty to fairly impart the facts that they know of the case and the strong belief in their faith, which dictates that they must separate themselves from the outcast member, or risk being contaminated themselves. Mr. Mott-Trille asserts that one person in particular who will be in such a position will be his daughter Sarah, who is an important witness in this case.

If an interim injunction is not granted, there is a very real possibility that Mr. Mott-Trille will be disfellowshipped before the conclusion of the Law Society hearings. As indicated, this could have a significant impact on Mr. Mott-Trille's ability to answer the charges against him at the Law Society.

Mr. Mott-Trille is fighting for the right to continue practising his profession before the Law Society. As indicated, this is a very important right, which the courts have recognized as worthy of protection: see Lee, *supra*; *Kane v. University of British Columbia*, [1980] 1 SCR 1105. In my opinion, Mr. Mott-Trille risks suffering irreparable harm to his ability to earn a livelihood if he is unable to fully and effectively present his case before the Discipline Committee of the Law Society by reason of being a disfellowed Jehovah's Witness.

Disposition

Accordingly, I grant an interim injunction, restraining the defendants from proceeding with the new Judicial Committee hearing of the Watch Tower Society until the Law Society hearings have concluded. It is my view that this order is the least intrusive to the Watch Tower Society's ability to conduct its own affairs, given the circumstances of the case. I make no decision at this time as to whether the breaches of natural justice and other improprieties alleged by Mr. Mott-Trille warrant more serious and permanent intervention by the courts. Mr. Mott-Trille's ability to protect his livelihood before the Law Society should not be hampered by any decision of the second Judicial Committee prior to the Law Society hearing. Mr. Mott-Trille is not a threat to the Watch Tower Society or to Jehovah's Witnesses in general; he can be disciplined as the organization sees fit after the outcome of the Law Society hearings, subject as I have said to Mr. Mott-Trille convincing a court to intervene further.

Motion granted.

David Hunt Farms Ltd. v. Canada (Minister of Agriculture)
(1994), 112 DLR (4th) 181 (FCA)

ROBERTSON JA (for the court): This is an expedited appeal from a decision of a trial judge rendered on January 27, 1994, dismissing the appellant's application for an interlocutory injunction. Given the urgency of the matter the initial application was heard by telephone conference. The trial judge did not offer written reasons and his oral reasons were not recorded. Consequently, we are obliged to assess, as a matter of first impression, whether the trial judge erred in law in applying the well-established tripartite test analyzed in *Turbo Resources Ltd. v. Petro Canada Inc.*, [1989] 2 FC 451 (CA). Pending the disposition of this appeal the respondent agreed not to take the impugned action which the injunction seeks to prohibit. The essence of the dispute may be summarized as follows.

In 1986, a fatal neurological disorder was diagnosed and reported in adult cattle in the United Kingdom. The disease, "Bovine Spongiform Encephalopathy" ("BSE"), is more commonly known as "Mad Cow Disease." It is contracted through contaminated feed and has two distinct attributes. First, the affected animal degenerates rapidly after the first symptoms appear, typically following a several-year incubation period. Second, its presence can only be verified by post-mortem examination of the brain tissue of the deceased animal.

Since BSE was first reported, it has attained epidemic proportions: over 112,000 cases have been tallied in the United Kingdom alone, where approximately one-half of all dairy herds and one-tenth of all beef herds have been affected. In response to these realities, Agriculture Canada discontinued issuing import permits for cattle from the United Kingdom in 1990. It currently requires incidences of the disease to be reported and has instituted an "active surveillance network" to ensure that suspected cases are submitted to a laboratory for confirmation.

In 1988, two years prior to Agriculture Canada's ban on cattle imports, the appellant purchased and imported into Canada two Lincoln Red cattle from the United Kingdom. In November of 1993, a beef cow imported into Canada from the United Kingdom in 1987 by an Albertan farmer was slaughtered after exhibiting neurological symptoms of the kind associated with BSE. In December of 1993, laboratory testing confirmed the preliminary diagnosis of the presence of the disease. Agriculture Canada has subsequently learned that of the 11 United Kingdom herds from which cattle had been exported to Canada between 1982 and 1990, eight had reported their first case of BSE within the preceding 24 months.

In fulfilment of Canada's international obligations, Agriculture Canada notified the Office International des Epizooties, an international health agency, of the Alberta occurrence of BSE in December 1993. That organization had established guidelines for the treatment, diagnosis, and reporting of the disease on a global basis. Agriculture Canada also alerted foreign governmental authorities of the incidence of BSE in Alberta. This information engendered an immediate and negative reaction. Several countries threatened to restrict Canada's access to the export market if it did not take appropriate measures to eliminate the risk of BSE spreading. It is maintained that the Canadian farm economy, both domestic and export, will sustain substantial damage unless all cattle imported from the United Kingdom since 1986, are promptly destroyed. Apparently a failure to take such action, compounded with a second reported incidence of BSE, will result in a revocation by Canada's key trading partners of its recognition as being free of this disease. Under these circumstances, the respondent Minister directed that all cattle imported from the United Kingdom between 1986 and 1990 be destroyed.

On January 10, 1994, a notice was issued under s. 48(1) of the *Health of Animals Act*, RSC 1990, c. 21 ("the Act"), compelling the appellant to deliver the cattle in question for destruction on January 31, 1994. The notice states that the cattle are suspected of either being contaminated by the disease or being in contact with other diseased animals. On January 26, 1994, the appellant initiated an application for judicial review and an interlocutory injunction. The appellant's attack on the validity of the notice hinges on three arguments.

First, the appellant maintains that there is no evidence that its cattle are diseased. It alleges that the cattle did not originate from any of the 11 infected United Kingdom herds and that the cattle's vendor has confirmed that no animal in his herd had contracted the disease or been exposed to contaminated feed. Second, the appellant argues that the belief that the disease is contagious is unsupported. Third, it alleges that the true reason underlying the Minister's decision to destroy cattle imported prior to 1990 was the threat of trade embargoes after the Albertan case was reported. The appellant maintains that if the Minister were truly concerned with the spread of disease, he had within his possession sufficient information as of 1990 to make the decision ultimately made in 1993.

Against this background we now turn to the application of the tripartite test in determining whether the trial judge erred in refusing to exercise his discretion to grant interlocutory relief.

It is common ground that the first prong of the tripartite test has been satisfied. We are told by both parties that the trial judge agreed at the hearing below that the appellant had raised a serious question, at least in part, on the basis of an undertaking made in a similar case which will be heard on March 7, 1994, in Nova Scotia before a trial judge of this court (*Macdonald v. Canada (Minister of Agriculture)*, Court File T-3017-93). In that proceeding, the respondent Minister gave an undertaking that the cattle of the applicant therein would not be destroyed until disposition of the application for judicial review. In return, a consent order expediting the judicial review application was placed before the court and granted by a judge of the trial division.

Apparently, the trial judge below found the respondent's undertaking in the Nova Scotia case persuasive evidence that the "serious issue" test had been satisfied in the case before him. The respondent takes no issue with this finding, although as discussed below he does challenge the relevance of the undertaking when weighing the balance of convenience.

The second prong of the tripartite test is concerned with the issue of irreparable harm. It must be remembered however, that while an applicant may be exposed to irreparable harm if injunctive relief is withheld, so too may a respondent should an injunction be granted. Obviously, the issue of irreparable harm must be addressed from the perspective of both parties. I shall deal first with irreparable harm to the appellant.

In the present case, regulations adopted under the Act require the Minister to pay a maximum compensation of $2,000 per destroyed animal (Maximum Amounts for Destroyed Animals Regulations, 1992, SOR/93-492, s. 3(a)). It is common ground that each of the animals in question is worth substantially more than this amount. The respondent's evidence estimates the value of each animal at $5,000. The appellant believes the value of each to be $7,500. Subject to the submissions discussed below, I think it self-evident that the appellant will suffer irreparable harm if the injunction is refused. It is not the adequacy of the "damages" remedy which is in issue. Rather, it is the adequacy of the "compensation" which is available under the regulations. Where, as in the present case, the amount of the recoverable loss is restricted by statute, and that amount is significantly less than the actual loss to be incurred if the injunction does not issue, irreparable harm is established. I take it to be accepted law that adequate compensation is to be measured in accordance with common law principles: see *American Cyanamid Co. v. Ethicon Ltd.*, [1975] AC 396 (HL).

In anticipation of this finding, the respondent sought to persuade us that in fact and law the appellant will be able to recover compensation exceeding the statutory maximum as fixed by the regulations. He informs us by way of a press release that the Canadian Beef Breeders Council, an agency which represents the interests of beef producers, intends somehow to supplement the regulated maximum to "approach the fair market value" of the cattle.

There are obvious objections to this submission. No mechanism for providing additional compensation is yet in place. Moreover, there is no legal obligation which could be owed by the foregoing agency to the appellant and by which the appellant could enforce payment of full compensation. The appellant is entitled to more than a mere possibility of recovering over and above the prescribed minimum compensation. Finally, the proposed scheme does not embrace the understanding that compensation is intended to approximate those recoverable at common law.

The respondent's alternative submission on this issue is to the effect that if the appellant is not satisfied with the total amount of the compensation, it is free to sue the Minister in tort. This submission invokes s. 50 of the Act, which *prima facie* limits the Minister's liability. That section provides:

> 50. Where a person must, by or under this Act or the regulations, do anything, including provide and maintain any area, office, laboratory or other facility under section 31, or permit an inspector or officer to do anything, Her Majesty is not liable
>
> (a) for any costs, loss or damage resulting from the compliance; or
>
> (b) to pay any fee, rent or other charge for what is done, provided, maintained or permitted.

Ironically, it is the respondent who argues that s. 50 may be interpreted as limiting the liability of the Crown where the Minister acts pursuant to s. 48(1) of the Act. While counsel's interpretation was interesting, I am not persuaded that the appellant has a practical and viable tort remedy in the event it is determined that the animals were wrongfully slaughtered. It is one matter for a party to be able to litigate the actual loss suffered and quite another to prevail in a contested argument that a statute does not immunize the other party (the Minister), from liability. In reaching this conclusion, I could not ignore the fact that the respondent was not able to concede that s. 50 would not present a bar to such an action or indeed that the issue would not be raised. I am satisfied that the appellant will be exposed to irreparable harm if the injunction does not issue. This determination leaves us to consider the irreparable harm from the respondent's perspective.

It would be wrong in law to assume that the respondent cannot sustain irreparable harm. It is equally wrong to assume that a clear finding of irreparable harm to a defendant, such as the respondent Minister, is a condition precedent to deciding whether on a balance of convenience an injunction should issue. Both legal propositions are reflected in the jurisprudence of this court to which I now turn.

The first proposition was firmly established by this court in *Canada (A.-G.) v. Fishing Vessel Owners' Assn. of British Columbia*, [1985] 1 FC 791. In that case, an interlocutory injunction had been granted to prevent the implementation of a government plan to extend the salmon fishing season for vessels using gill nets. Fishing vessels equipped with purse seine nets would have a shorter fishing season. The "seiners" sought an injunction arguing that the decision was discriminatory in that it was premised not on conservation objectives but rather on socio-economic considerations which promoted the interests of "gill netters" at the expense of "seiners."

The trial judge granted the injunction. On appeal, this court held that the trial judge erred in his assumption that the Attorney-General would not suffer irreparable harm if an injunction were issued. Writing for this court, Pratte JA concluded, in part, at p. 795:

[T]he Judge assumed that the grant of the injunction would not cause any damage to the [attorney general]. This was wrong. When a public authority is prevented from exercising its statutory powers, it can be said, in a case like the present one, that the public interest, of which that authority is the guardian, suffers irreparable harm.

It is apparent from the above facts that had the injunction issued, two groups would have been exposed to irreparable harm: "gill netters" who would have been deprived of the opportunity to fish during the extended season and the public interest to the extent that the government plan furthered conservation objectives could not be implemented. I should point out that when determining irreparable harm in the context of a public authority, the issue is not to be decided on the basis of pecuniary considerations alone. The inability of a public authority to carry out its legislated mandate in protecting the public interest is sufficient. The question we must address is whether the public interest will suffer irreparable harm if the appellant is granted injunctive relief. The question is a difficult one.

I am in agreement with Professor Sharpe when he writes that "[i]t is exceptionally difficult to define irreparable harm precisely." (R.J. Sharpe, Injunctions and Specific Performance, 2nd ed. (Toronto: Canada Law Book, 1993), at p. 2-24, para. 440.) To this observation I would add that it is not always self-evident whether the public interest will suffer irreparable harm if injunctive relief is either granted or denied. I am prepared to assume for purposes of the appeal that the public interest will be harmed if the interlocutory injunction issues. In any event, such a finding is not a condition precedent to the application of the third prong of the tripartite test.

The significance of the balance of convenience component of that test was clearly enunciated in *Eng Mee Yong v. Letchumanan*, [1980] AC 331 (PC) at p. 337, per Lord Diplock:

> The guiding principle in granting an interlocutory injunction is the balance of convenience; there is no requirement that before an interlocutory injunction is granted the plaintiff should satisfy the court that there is a "probability," a "*prima facie* case" or a "strong *prima facie* case" that if the action goes to trial he will succeed; but before any question of balance of convenience can arise the party seeking the injunction must satisfy the court that his claim is neither frivolous nor vexatious; in other words that the evidence before the court discloses that there is a serious question to be tried: *American Cyanamid Co. v. Ethicon Ltd.*, [1975] AC 396.

In *Turbo Resources, supra*, Stone JA emphasized the paramountcy of the balance of convenience test while cautioning decision-makers against a purely mechanical application of legal criteria. At p. 20 he observed:

> I should say here that I favour the view that these factors do not constitute a series of mechanical steps that are to be followed in some sort of drilled progression. Professor Robert J. Sharpe cautions against such rigidity of approach in Injunctions and Specific Performance (Toronto, Canada Law Book Ltd., 1983), when he notes that each of the factors should be "seen as guides which take colour and definition in the circumstances of each case." He further observes that they are not to be seen "as separate, water-tight categories," and also that they "relate to each other, and strength on one part of the test ought to be permitted to compensate for weakness in another." In other words, considerable flexibility is called for, *bearing in mind that the balance of convenience is of paramount importance*. [Emphasis added.]

I do not think that it can be doubted that the questions of irreparable harm and balance of convenience are inextricably linked. But it is the balance of convenience which enables a court to take into account diverse factors which cannot be quantified in monetary terms: see Sharpe, *supra*, at p. 2-30, para. 2.530. It is the balance of convenience component of the test which ensures flexibility in the application of equitable principles in diverse factual situations. For example, the likelihood of irreparable harm is but one of the factors that might be weighed when deciding whether to grant an interlocutory injunction: see *Nintendo of America Inc. v. Camerica Corp.* (1991), 44 FTR 80n (CA).

In this case, the respondent has a duty to protect the public interest of all Canadians, not simply those directly affected by notices issued under the Act. Nor can one ignore the substantial financial repercussions which could well follow a second reported case of the disease. We have been told that Canada's beef export business is valued at $1.6 billion. Given the relatively minor financial loss the appellant would suffer coupled with the Minister's efforts toward ensuring adequate compensation, it is arguable that the balance of convenience favours the respondent.

The appellant, however, seeks to inject into the balancing formula an additional factor, namely the Minister's undertaking in the Nova Scotia case not to destroy the cattle until the conclusion of that judicial review hearing scheduled for March 7, 1994. It argues that it is entitled to "equal treatment," to which the respondent counters that the appellant's characterization of the two cases as "equal" is mistaken. The respondent's principal objection to this court considering the Minister's undertaking stems from the supposedly discrete factual circumstances of each case. He argues that it is both inappropriate and wrong in law to tip the balance of convenience in favour of the appellant on the basis of an undertaking rendered within a different factual context.

In my opinion the argument is flawed. The action taken by the respondent in both the case before us and in Nova Scotia was predicated on the same reasoning: that the public interest was best served by destroying all cows imported from the United Kingdom between 1986 and 1990, on the suspicion that they carry BSE. The reason why the respondent seeks to have the appellant's cows destroyed is the selfsame reason that it seeks to have the cattle in the Nova Scotia case destroyed.

The respondent argued that the appellant's cattle were more at risk than those owned by the Nova Scotia farmer because of the precise origin and breed of the respective cattle. That argument must fail for two reasons. First, the evidence does not support the assertion that cattle from one part of the United Kingdom are more at risk of disease than those from another. Second, if the Minister's undertaking in the Nova Scotia decision was based on this criterion, it conflicts with his decision not to treat the disease on a regional or individual basis in Canada because that solution "would not address the demands of our international trade markets."

I cannot accept the respondent's argument that the balance of convenience should be tipped in his favour. The Minister's willingness to permit another case to be decided on the merits, after a short delay, before taking the irreversible action contemplated in the case before us today is decisive of that issue. I therefore conclude that an injunction should issue on the terms appearing below.

During the period of the injunction, which should extend until the judicial review application is finally disposed of by the trial division, the appellant should not sell or otherwise dispose of either of the said cows or otherwise permit either of them to be taken or sent away from the appellant's farm property where they are presently located. The appellant should also be required to keep the said cows in strict quarantine separate or apart from the remainder of its herd. If either of the said cows should manifest any of the symptoms of BSE, the appellant should be required to notify immediately the respondent of the symptoms so observed.

At the hearing of this appeal counsel for the appellant stated that his client would move expeditiously to perfect the judicial review application and to bring it on for hearing in the trial division not later than March 7, 1994, when the Nova Scotia case is set to be heard. Accordingly, the respondent should be at liberty to apply to this court for the dissolution of the injunction upon the ground that the appellant had failed to act bona fide in perfecting the judicial review application or for failure to so act in seeking to have the application heard by the trial division on an urgent basis; that is to say as early as possible, preferably not later than March 7, 1994.

For the foregoing reasons, I would allow the appeal, set aside the order of the trial judge dated January 27, 1994, dismissing the application for an interlocutory injunction and grant the order on the terms outlined above. The appellant is entitled to its costs both here and below. Appeal allowed.

NOTES

1. Where one party is impecunious, should this be a factor in determining whether damages would be an inadequate remedy for the other party? In *Hubbard v. Pitt*, [1976] 1 QB 142 (QB and CA), the plaintiffs, real estate agents, sought an injunction to prevent the defendants from picketing outside their offices. The defendants, a residents' group, were attempting to prevent changes in social composition of an inner city area of London. They attributed blame to the real estate agents who they believed were assisting property developers. The injunction was granted. An appeal was dismissed, Lord Denning MR dissenting. In the course of his judgment, Orr LJ said (at 189):

> The next question to be asked is whether, if the plaintiffs were to succeed at the trial, they would be adequately compensated for the interim continuance of the defendants' activities. In my judgment, the answer is that they plainly would not, because such continuance might well cause very serious damage to their business, and the judge was entitled, on this issue, to have regard to any doubts he might have felt as to the defendants' ability to satisfy any award of damages made against them. Mr. Turner-Samuels has claimed that it would be wrong to do so in the absence of any evidence that the defendants would be unable to pay; but I think that the boot was on the other foot and that in the absence of any evidence as to ability to pay what could amount to very substantial damages the judge would have been entitled to put in the balance any doubts he may have felt as to that matter.

2. See also Paul M. Perell, "The Interlocutory Injunction and Irreparable Harm" (1989), 68 *Can. Bar Rev.* 538; D. Crerar, "'The Death of the Irreparable Injury Rule' in Canada" (1998), 36 *Alberta Law Review* 957; and J. Berryman, "Interlocutory Injunctions and Accessibility Thresholds: Or Once More Round the Mulberry Bush" (1989), 5 *Intellectual Property Journal* 137.

INTERLOCUTORY MANDATORY INJUNCTIONS

Introduction

An interlocutory mandatory injunction requires the defendant to undertake some positive course of action. Where a mandatory injunction is restorative, in effect, the defendant will forgo any benefit of expenditures made prior to the injunction, as well as incur the burden associated with restoring the status *quo ante*. Where a mandatory injunction is purely enforcing an existing duty owed, the defendant will only incur the burden of performing the duty. In both situations, courts are required to weigh the benefits to the plaintiff against the burden to the defendant.

Courts have traditionally been reluctant to award mandatory injunctions because they usually impose substantial inconvenience or hardship on the defendant. In addition, because the damage is likely to have been incurred, there is a justifiable belief that the applicant can be compensated in damages at trial.

This area is further complicated because there is an element of overlap between prohibitive and mandatory injunctions. Often the latter type can be expressed in the former's terms.

Prairie Hospitality Consultants Ltd. v. Renard International Hospitality Consultants Ltd.
(1980), 118 DLR (3d) 121 (BCSC)

LEGG J: The plaintiff brings this application for an interlocutory injunction to restrain the defendant from terminating a franchise agreement executed by the parties on May 2, 1979. It also seeks an interlocutory mandatory injunction requiring the defendant to forward to it certain documents and information to enable it to function as an employment counsellor under the franchise agreement.

The plaintiff's counsel submits that the plaintiff has demonstrated an arguable case that no proper grounds existed for the termination of the franchise agreement by the defendant, that it will suffer irreparable damage if the injunction is not granted and that the balance of convenience lies in favour of granting the injunction. Counsel relies in the main upon *American Cyanamid Co. v. Ethicon Ltd.*, [1975] AC 396 (HL (Eng.)) and *Baxter Motors Ltd. v. American Motors (Canada) Ltd.* (1973), 40 DLR (3d) 450 (BC SC), a decision of Anderson J (as he then was) of this Court that deals with a similar franchise agreement dispute.

A brief examination of the extensive affidavit material filed by each party will explain the reasons for the conclusions I have reached.

The plaintiff operates a personnel placement business in British Columbia. It obtains job orders from clientele for specific positions and also obtains personnel to suit job descriptions. It arranges for interviews, screens applicants and is remunerated on the basis of successfully placing individuals in various positions.

The defendant is a small company which provides employment placement and consulting services in the hotel and catering trade. It employs 13 people. Its head office is in Toronto.

On May 2, 1979, the plaintiff and the defendant executed a franchise agreement made as of September 1, 1978.

Under that agreement the defendant was described as the owner of a system for the promotion and operation of businesses engaged in providing employment consulting and personnel placement services. It granted to the plaintiff an exclusive franchise to use the system in British Columbia. The plaintiff paid the defendant a franchise fee of $10,000 by monthly instalments of $2,000 during the first five months of the agreement. The term of the agreement was for 10 years commencing on September 1, 1979, with a right of renewal for a period of five years.

The main terms and provisions of the agreement may be summarized as follows:

1. The plaintiff agreed to pay a service fee of 10% of its gross income derived from all transactions involving the providing of employment consulting or personnel placement services.

2. The plaintiff agreed to cause its auditors to send a statement directly to the defendant not later than three months after the end of the plaintiff's fiscal year stating that in the opinion of the auditors, the payments made to the defendant for the fiscal year were in compliance with the terms and conditions of the franchise agreement. (The plaintiff's fiscal year end was November 30th.)

3. The plaintiff was to have the use of the Renard name and its trade names, trade marks and trade secrets, and the plaintiff was to give prompt and courteous and efficient service to the public and to comply with Renard policy and procedure memoranda and generally operate the franchise in accordance with the Renard system.

4. The agreement provided for its termination,

    (a) upon mutual written consent, or

    (b) at the option of the defendant if the plaintiff failed to perform any of its obligations under the agreement.

5. If the defendant elected to terminate the agreement, the defendant was required to give the plaintiff ten days' notice in writing setting out the reasons for the termination. The agreement stated that the termination by notice would not be effective if the reasons for termination were completely satisfied and eliminated during the notice period.

On September 26, 1980, the plaintiff received a notice of termination from the defendant dated September 22, 1980, alleging various breaches and defaults by the defendant and stating that the notice was to take effect October 15, 1980. The notice was a detailed one. It listed nine reasons for termination including the failure of the plaintiff to appoint auditors and to provide the defendant with an auditors' statement, the failure to maintain and keep records and reports and to provide copies of these to the defendant, the failure to provide prompt and efficient service to the public, the failure to comply with policy and procedure guidelines required under the agreement and the failure to remit to the defendant proper fees and commissions.

Each of these alleged failures was specifically denied by the vice-president of the plaintiff, Mr. Roth, in his affidavit. Mr. Roth also deposed that if the plaintiff was forced to terminate the agreement it would lose clients and goodwill and cease to function.

Counsel for the defendant submits that the case made out by the plaintiff is tenuous and that the injunction should not be granted because the plaintiff can be compensated in damages. He submits that the plaintiff will not be put out of business by reason of the termination of the franchise agreement and that its remedy, if any, lies in damages. He argues that the plaintiff has not suffered irreparable harm by reason of the termination and that the balance of convenience is not in favour of granting the injunction.

[Legg J applied the test in *American Cyanamid* and concluded that an interlocutory injunction should be granted to restrain the defendant from terminating the franchise agreement.]

In addition to seeking an injunction restraining the defendant from terminating the franchise agreement, the plaintiff also seeks a mandatory injunction that the defendant carry out certain specific matters pursuant to the agreement and in particular to forward copies of job orders, advise the plaintiff in writing of all applicants available for job openings, forward copies of job order lists to the plaintiff and copies of all applicants' résumés relating to job orders of the plaintiff. This relief is claimed in subpara. (c) of the notice of motion.

This claim for relief invites me to make a mandatory order that one party carry out its obligations under the franchise agreement. To a certain extent that agreement is one where confidence and co-operation between the parties is required. A negative injunction in circumstances where confidence and co-operation was required was examined by Sachs LJ in *Evans Marshall & Co. Ltd. v. Bertola SA*, [1973] 1 WLR 349 (CA). At p. 379, after discussing the nature of the agreement, Sachs LJ observed that the fact that some degree of mutual co-operation or confidence is needed does not preclude the Court from granting *negative* injunctions designed to encourage the party in breach to perform his part of the agreement. Later in his judgment Sachs LJ said (at p. 382) that even where specific performance of an agreement would not be ordered, the Court would grant a *negative* injunction to encourage a party in breach to keep his contract.

The *Evans Marshall* case was considered by Anderson J in *Baxter* as authority in support of the proposition that the Court would in exceptional circumstances grant an injunction where it could not enforce performance by the plaintiff of his obligations under the contract.

Are the circumstances in the case at bar sufficiently exceptional to entitle me to grant a mandatory injunction?

Counsel for the defendant urges that a mandatory injunction should only be granted in exceptional circumstances. He referred to *Shepherd Homes Ltd. v. Sandham*, [1970] 3 WLR 348 (Ch.); *Dowty Boulton Paul Ltd. v. Wolverhampton Corp.*, [1971] 1 WLR 204 (Ch.); 24 Hals., 4th ed., p. 534; and *Gravesham Borough Council v. British Railways Board*, [1978] Ch. 379.

The subject-matter of the mandatory injunctions sought in those cases is very different from the subject-matter in respect of which a mandatory injunction is sought in the case at bar. In *Shepherd Homes* the plaintiff sought an injunction to demolish a fence. In *Dowty Boulton Paul* the plaintiff sought an injunction to continue acts of management such as the upkeep of aerodrome runways and buildings. In *Gravesham Borough Council*, the plaintiff sought an injunction against British Railways to direct them to maintain an existing ferry timetable.

By contrast, what the plaintiff seeks in its motion is the forwarding of documents which come into the defendant's possession or are made by it as part of the defendant's continuing business. The duty imposed upon the defendant if the mandatory injunction is granted is thus a very light duty compared with the duty sought to be imposed in those cases cited earlier. Further, the duty sought to be imposed on the defendant is for a limited period of time.

NOTES AND QUESTIONS

1. Given the court's hesitancy about granting the injunction, can you suggest how the defendant's damages would be calculated if it won at trial?

2. In *Films Rover International v. Cannon Film Sales Ltd.*, [1987] 1 WLR 670 (Ch.), the plaintiff sought an interlocutory mandatory injunction to enforce an agreement under which the defendants were obligated to supply films to the plaintiff for distribution in Italy. The defendant wished to renegotiate the contract on more favourable terms. Failing to get the plaintiff's agreement to renegotiate, the defendants sought to terminate the agreement alleging breach of contract by the plaintiff. The following is taken from Hoffmann J's discussion on the granting of an interlocutory mandatory injunction at 679:

The Mandatory Injunction

In the forefront of his argument counsel for Thorn-EMI submitted that the court should not grant an interlocutory mandatory injunction, amounting to specific performance of one of Thorn-EMI's alleged contractual obligations, unless there appeared a high probability that Films Rover would succeed in establishing its legal right at the trial. In this case the Court of Appeal has gone no further than to say that Films Rover has an arguable case and, as I have already said, I propose to treat that as meaning that Films Rover is at least as likely to fail as to succeed. Counsel said that fell well short of the standard of persuasion necessary for the grant of an interlocutory mandatory injunction.

In support of this proposition, counsel for Thorn-EMI relied in particular on the recent decision of the Court of Appeal in *Locabail International Finance Ltd. v. Agroexport, The Sea Hawk*, [1986] 1 WLR 657 (CA) at p. 664 in which Mustill LJ (with whom Balcombe LJ agreed) approved the following passage from the judgment of Megarry J in *Shepherd Homes Ltd. v. Sandham*, [1971] Ch. 340 at p. 351:

> Third, on motion, as contrasted with the trial, the court is far more reluctant to grant a mandatory injunction than it would be to grant a comparable prohibitory injunction. In a normal case the court must, *inter alia*, feel a high degree of assurance that at the trial it will appear that the injunction was rightly granted; and this is a higher standard than is required for a prohibitory injunction.

Mustill LJ went on to say that although this judgment pre-dated *American Cyanamid Co. v. Ethicon Ltd.*, [1975] AC 396 (HL (Eng.)) the statement of principle "in relation to the very special case of the mandatory injunction" was not affected by what had been said in the House of Lords in that case.

I would respectfully agree that there is no inconsistency between the passage from Megarry J and what was said in the *Cyanamid* case. But I think it is important in this area to distinguish between fundamental principles and what are sometimes described as "guidelines," i.e. useful generalisations about the way to deal with the normal run of cases falling within a particular category. The principal dilemma about the grant of interlocutory injunction, whether prohibitory or mandatory, is that there is by definition a risk that the court may make the "wrong" decision, in the sense of granting an injunction to a party who fails to establish his right at the trial (or would fail if there was a trial) or alternatively, in failing to grant an injunction to a party who succeeds (or would succeed) at trial. A fundamental principle is therefore that the court should take whichever course appears to carry the lower risk of injustice if it should turn out to have been "wrong" in the sense I have described. The guidelines for the grant of both kinds of interlocutory injunctions are derived from this principle.

The passage quoted from Megarry J in *Shepherd Homes Ltd. v. Sandham* at p. 351 qualified as it was by the words "in a normal case," was plainly intended as a guideline rather than an independent principle. It is another way of saying that the features which justify describing an injunction as "mandatory" will usually also have the consequence of creating a greater risk of injustice if it is granted rather than withheld at the interlocutory stage unless the court feels a "high degree of assurance" that the plaintiff would be able to establish his right at a trial. I have taken the liberty of reformulating the proposition in this way in order to bring out two points. The first is to show that semantic arguments over whether the injunction formulated can properly be classified as mandatory or prohibitory are barren. The question of substance is whether the granting of the injunction would carry that higher risk of injustice which is normally associated with the grant of a mandatory injunction. The second point is that in cases in which there can be no dispute about the use of the term "mandatory" to describe the injunction, the same question of substance will determine whether the case is "normal" or "exceptional" and therefore requiring special treatment. If it appears to the court that, exceptionally, the case is one in which withholding a mandatory interlocutory injunction would in fact carry a greater risk of injustice than granting it even though the court does not feel a "high degree of assurance" about the plaintiff's chances of establishing his right, there cannot be any rational basis for withholding the injunction.

In *Shepherd Homes Ltd. v. Sandham* Megarry J spelled out some of the reasons why mandatory injunctions generally carry a higher risk of injustice if granted at the interlocutory stage; they usually go further than the preservation of the status quo by requiring a party to take some new positive step or undo what he has done in the past; an order requiring a party to take positive steps usually causes more waste of time and money if it turns out to have been wrongly granted than an order which merely causes delay by restraining him from doing something which it appears at the trial he was entitled to do; a mandatory order usually gives a party the whole of the relief which he claims in the writ and makes it unlikely that there will be a trial. One could add other reasons, such as that mandatory injunctions (whether interlocutory or final) are often difficult to formulate with sufficient precision to be enforceable. In addition to all these practical considerations, there is also what might be loosely called a "due process" question. An order requiring someone to do something is usually perceived as a more intrusive exercise of the coercive power of the state than an order requiring him temporarily to refrain from action. The court is therefore more reluctant to make such an order against a party who has not had the protection of a full hearing at trial.

Megarry J recognised, however, that none of these was a necessary concomitant of a mandatory injunction. For example, there is sometimes a sense in which a mandatory injunction is needed to preserve the status quo. In charterparty withdrawal cases the Commercial Court has frequently granted interlocutory injunctions restraining an owner from using the ship otherwise than in accordance with the terms of the charter (see per Lord Denning MR in *Associated Portland Cement Manufacturers Ltd. v. Teigland Shipping A/S, The Oakworth*, [1975] 1 Lloyd's Rep. 581 (CA)).

Although negative in form, these are (in the case of a time or voyage charter) mandatory in effect because they require the owner to continue to provide the ship. In these cases there is what might (at some risk of oxymoron) be called a "dynamic status quo" which consists in the continuing use of the vessel on the charterer's business. Counsel for the plaintiffs also referred me to *Continental Grain Co. v. Islamic Republic of Iran Shipping Lines and Government Trading Corp of Iran, The Iran Bohonar*, [1983] 2 Lloyd's Rep. 620 (CA) in which the Court of Appeal made a mandatory order requiring owners to direct their vessel to deviate to a safe port and discharge cargo to which the plaintiff claimed title. The order was made because the court considered that there was a serious question to be tried as to whether on the true construction of The Hague Rules the owners were under a contractual obligation to do so. Neither of the Lords Justices (nor for that matter counsel) seem to have suggested that such an order should not be made unless the court felt a high degree of assurance that the plaintiff's construction was right. On the contrary, Ackner LJ said (at 623):

> Whether that argument will succeed or not is another matter. We have had the advantage of [the] submissions [of counsel for the defendants] and it would be churlish to say that they lack force, but speaking for myself I am satisfied that there is a serious question to be argued on this subject.

I would venture to suggest that *The Iran Bohonar* was plainly a case in which, despite the mandatory character of the injunction, the risk of the injustice which would be caused by "wrongly" withholding it was far greater than the risk of injustice if it turned out to have been wrongly granted. It is easy to construct other counterexamples by way of exception to the proposition that mandatory injunctions are more drastic and irreversible in effect and involve greater expense and inconvenience if wrongly granted than prohibitory injunctions.

These considerations lead me to conclude that the Court of Appeal in *Locabail International Finance Ltd. v. Agroexport*, [1986] 1 WLR 657 (CA) at p. 664 was not intending to "fetter the court's discretion by laying down any rules which would have the effect of limiting the flexibility of the remedy," to quote Lord Diplock in the *Cyanamid* case at p. 407. Just as the *Cyanamid* guidelines for prohibitory injunctions which require a plaintiff to show no more than an arguable case recognise the existence of exceptions in which more is required (compare *Cayne v. Global Natural Resources plc*, [1984] All ER 225 (CA)), so the guideline approved for mandatory injunctions in *Locabail* recognises that there may be cases in which less is sufficient. It is significant that both Mustill and Balcombe LJJ did not merely rely on the mandatory nature of the injunction. They went on to explain why in the particular circumstances of the case, the granting of the injunction would give rise to an unacceptable risk of injustice. Mustill LJ said that the injunction would put the defendant "in an irretrievable difficulty," that the defendants appeared unable to comply and would therefore "inevitably be in breach" and that if they failed to comply, they had no officers or assets within the jurisdiction and there was no way in which the injunction could be enforced.

The injunction was granted.

3. In *National Commercial Bank Jamaica Ltd. v. Olint Corp Ltd.*, [2009] UKPC 16, para. 20, Lord Hoffmann, speaking for the Privy Council on an appeal from Jamaica, eschewed the distinction between prohibitory and mandatory orders, suggesting such classification was "barren," and that what mattered were the "practical consequences of the actual injunction." In that case the plaintiff, a customer of the defendant bank, sought to prevent the defendant

from terminating the banking relationship. The defendant had given notice of its intent to terminate offering the plaintiff banking services for fear that the plaintiff's business would attract further unfavourable publicity. It appeared that the plaintiff was engaged in a "Ponzi" investment scheme. See also *Ticketnet Corp. v. Air Canada* (1987), 21 CPC (2d) 38 (Ont. HC).

4. In *Paker v. Canadian Tire Corp.* (1998), 67 OTC 196, Sharpe J stated:

> [I]t is well established that there is a higher standard to be met where interlocutory mandatory relief is sought and, in particular, that the plaintiff must make out a greater likelihood of success.

The threshold test in British Columbia is said to be lower (is there a fair question to be tried?), and the strength of the applicant's case is considered as part of the balance-of-convenience stage. See *RCG Forex Service Corp. v. HSBC Bank Canada*, [2011] BCJ no. 436 (SC).

INTERLOCUTORY INJUNCTIONS AND ENFORCEMENT OF RESTRICTIVE COVENANTS

The enforcement of a restrictive covenant in restraint of trade depends on the reasonableness of the covenant. The potency and effectiveness of the covenant usually diminishes with time. Thus, the timeliness of enforcement is all important. However, enforcement by interlocutory injunction can put the defendant out of employment if in fact the restrictive covenant is being breached. The potential repercussions for the litigants has resulted in some courts insisting upon a *prima facie* case threshold before granting relief. This appears to be justified because there is unlikely to be any more evidence than that which is tendered to gain the interlocutory injunction that the court would need to make a determination of the reasonableness of the restrictive covenant. Again, as in so many other cases there is no consistency amongst courts in the approach that they adopt.

Towers, Perrin, Forster & Crosby Inc. v. Cantin
(1999), 46 OR (3d) 180 (Sup. Ct.)

KITELEY J: This is a request pursuant to s. 101 of the *Courts of Justice Act*, RSO 1990, c. C.43 by the plaintiffs for an injunction until trial against Cantin (a former employee and principal of the plaintiff TPFC) and KPMG (Cantin's current employer) based upon a restrictive covenant not to compete or solicit.

Pitt J made an interim order on September 21, 1999 at which time counsel expected that further affidavits would be submitted and cross-examinations would be conducted. At the time the submissions were made before me, counsel provided 20 volumes of material including hundreds of pages of cross-examinations, facta and books of authorities. The motion had been scheduled to be heard on Friday, November 5. It was adjourned briefly to give Mr. McKee an opportunity to further examine Cantin with respect to undertakings from her cross-examination and the cross-examination of others.

Background

The plaintiff TPFC is the parent corporation of the plaintiff Towers Perrin Inc. Each are part of the Towers Perrin group of companies worldwide. The Tillinghast division of Towers Perrin has two lines of business, the property and casualty insurance practice (the "P and C practice") and the financial services practice. The P and C practice provides actuarial and risk management consulting services to Towers Perrin's clients worldwide in respect of property and casualty insurance issues. Towers Perrin employs approximately 8,000 individuals worldwide of which about 650 are currently principals.

Cantin is 41 years old. She graduated from Laval University in 1980 with a bachelor's degree in Actuarial Science. She became a Fellow of the Casualty Actuarial Society in 1983 and a Fellow of the Canadian Institute of Actuaries in 1984. Between 1980 and 1989, for the most part, she worked as an actuary for Travelers Canada and the Personal Insurance Company. She began employment at Travelers as an actuarial specialist. In 1986, she became an associate actuary in charge of a staff of approximately 12 employees in the actuarial and financial planning area.

Cantin joined as a full-time consultant in the P and C practice in 1989. The P and C practice was divided amongst three lines of business insurance, professional liability and risk management. Cantin worked almost exclusively in the P and C insurance business. In late 1995, Cantin was nominated to become a principal. Cantin accepted. In April 1996, she became manager of the Toronto P and C practice. She remained in that position until she left the firm on June 18, 1999. Immediately prior to her departure, she had managed seven people including two consultants (actuaries), three analysts (actuaries in training) and two administrative staff. She reported to Ollie Sherman who is one of three North American regional managers.

KPMG is a limited partnership which provides accounting and management consulting services in Toronto and throughout the world. As of June 18, 1999, KPMG did not have a P and C practice in Toronto.

On June 7, 1999, Cantin voluntarily announced her intention to resign and join KPMG's Toronto office. Cantin resigned effective on June 18, 1999. On June 21, she joined KPMG for purposes of creating, managing and developing a P and C practice in Toronto. At the time of her termination, Cantin was a shareholder of TPFC. The by-laws of TPFC contained two covenants which the plaintiffs allege have been breached by Cantin, or alternatively, she has breached her fiduciary duty. The plaintiffs seek to enforce the covenants against Cantin. The plaintiffs also allege that KPMG has unlawfully and intentionally interfered with the plaintiffs' economic interests in their relationships with their clients and employees and with Cantin's obligations to the plaintiffs without justification and for its own financial gain. And the plaintiffs allege that KPMG has intentionally and unlawfully induced Cantin to breach her contractual and fiduciary obligations which KPMG knew Cantin owed to the plaintiffs without justification and for its own financial gain.

Test for Granting an Interlocutory Injunction

The plaintiffs must satisfy the court with respect to three elements: the strength of the plaintiffs' case; balance of convenience; and irreparable harm. I will return to the second and third below. In so far as the first element is concerned, Mr. McKee suggests that there are three possible standards: serious issue to be tried (*American Cyanamid Co. v. Ethicon Ltd.*, [1975] AC 396); strong *prima facie* case (*Crain-Drummond Inc. v. Hamel* (1991), 35 CCEL 55 (Ont. Gen. Div.); and *Gerrard v. Century 21 Armour Real Estate Inc.* (1991), 4 OR (3d) 191 (Gen. Div.); and a clear breach of a negative covenant (*Bank of Montreal v. James Main Holdings Ltd.* (1982), 28 CPC 157 (Ont. Div. Ct.)), which is *prima facie* reasonable. Mr. Mulroney agreed that those are the possible standards. What separates counsel is which standard ought to be applied.

Mr. McKee takes the position that his client need not meet the highest standard of strong *prima facie* case. But whichever standard is applied, he asserts that his client has met the standard.

Mr. Mulroney asserts that the plaintiffs must meet the highest standard of strong *prima facie* case, primarily on the basis that the court ought to assume that, since the livelihood of the defendant is at stake, that the highest standard ought to be applied: see *Crain-Drummond, supra*; *Gerrard, supra* and *Jet Print Inc. v. Cohen* (1999), 43 CPC (4th) 123 (Ont. SCJ).

Mr. Mulroney takes the position that the exception in *RJR-MacDonald Inc. v. Canada (Attorney General)*, [1994] 1 SCR 311, 111 DLR (4th) 385 ought to apply, namely where the outcome of the interlocutory injunction motion will have the practical effect of finally determining the rights of the parties, the *prima facie* case standard should apply.

In my view, if the matter could not be brought to trial within two years of Cantin's departure, that argument might have more weight. However, this is a case-managed action. The parties have already exchanged significant documentation and spent days in cross-examinations. Given the advanced state of preparation, I expect that the trial can be heard within one year of Cantin's departure. The *RJR-MacDonald* exception does not apply.

Based on the legal and factual analysis below, I find that the plaintiffs have met even the most onerous standard of proof. Consequently, in this case, other than commenting on the timing issue as it relates to case managed actions, I need not digress into an analysis of which is the applicable standard of proof. ...

[Kiteley J then discussed the applicable tests for determining the enforceability of a restraint of trade clause and determined that the plaintiff had proved to the standard required for an interlocutory injunction that the clause was valid and enforceable. We pick up the judgment on the determination of whether the plaintiff has shown irreparable harm.]

Irreparable Harm

Mr. Mulroney indicated that if I find that the covenant against competition is reasonable, he conceded that the defendants have breached the covenant. He nonetheless relies on *RJR-MacDonald Inc., supra*, and takes the position that the plaintiffs have not established irreparable harm. I agree with Mr. Mulroney that, at the interlocutory stage, "the only issue to be decided is whether a refusal to grant relief could so adversely affect the applicants' own interests that the harm could not be remedied if the eventual decision on the merits does not accord with the result of the interlocutory injunction." Furthermore, the Supreme Court of Canada has defined "irreparable" to mean "the nature of the harm suffered rather than its magnitude. It is harm which either cannot be quantified in monetary terms or which cannot be cured, usually because one party cannot collect damages from the other." Of the examples given by the Supreme Court, the relevant one is where a party will suffer permanent market loss or irrevocable damage to its business reputation.

According to the affidavit of Sherman, Towers Perrin's client base and specifically the client base of the P and C practice in the Toronto office, provides it with a significant profile in the North American market place for actuarial services. Based on his knowledge of the market place, he expressed the belief that the loss of the clients to that point in September 1999 and any loss of additional clients to Cantin would likely result in damage to the profile and reputation of the Toronto office of the Tillinghast division and to the Towers Perrin P and C practice in North America generally. Sherman also deposed that it is unlikely that the plaintiffs can be fully compensated for that loss because one would have to determine not only what work was taken from the plaintiffs in the two years following Cantin's resignation but also what work was taken from the plaintiffs in the years thereafter because of the loss of the client relationships. He asserted that it would be practically impossible to quantify and to compensate the plaintiffs for the whole loss caused to them by Cantin's continued wrongful competition and its effect on their profile and ability to attract new work and new clients. Sherman expressed the view that if the injunction were granted, it would provide Towers Perrin with an opportunity both to re-establish its relationships with the clients and to illustrate to clients who had already left and all other existing clients of Towers Perrin that it continues to have employees and resources in its P and C practice that can provide Canadian clients with the highest calibre of actuarial and other management consulting services and to compete fairly with others in the market place with respect to those clients.

Mr. Mulroney points to the measures which the plaintiffs have initiated to compensate for the conduct of Cantin and KPMG. The plaintiffs have taken important initiatives and have been successful in retaining a substantial amount of their business. However those steps were designed to stem the flow, not reverse the flow. The vigorous steps taken by the plaintiffs reinforce the potentially significant damage to reputation and to revenue which the plaintiffs predict.

I am mindful of the point made in *Bank of Montreal v. James Main, supra*, where at p. 160 the court held that where there has been a clear breach, "courts are inclined to grant injunctions enforcing negative covenants until trial. In such cases the inquiry as to the adequacy of damages as a remedy, and into the balance of convenience, do not have the importance that they otherwise do." Given the admitted breach, any further assessment of this issue is unnecessary.

Balance of Convenience

As indicated above, Mr. Mulroney conceded, in effect, that the defendant Cantin has breached the covenant and that KPMG has induced the breach. It was wise for Mr. Mulroney to have made that concession. Even without an in depth analysis of the conduct of the defendants which was manifested through the cross-examinations and the undertakings arising from the cross-examinations, it is obvious that KPMG took the initiative to have Cantin leave Towers Perrin and join KPMG; that KPMG and Cantin hoped to capitalize on the significant information and influence over clients which Cantin had developed during her tenure at Towers Perrin; that KPMG and Cantin made their own interpretation of the reasonableness of the Towers Perrin covenant against competition; that KPMG and Cantin deliberately conducted themselves in a manner consistent with their interpretation of the Towers Perrin covenant against competition; and that their efforts, which I find to be in violation of the covenant against competition, have paid off. KPMG is earning revenue from Towers Perrin's former clients whom I find fall within the definition of "client." The conduct of the defendants establishes a clear breach of the covenant against competition.

The defendants are the authors of their own misfortune. This was the subject of an observation by Reid J in *Indal Ltd. v. Halko, supra*, at para. 17:

> There appears to be an increasing tendency on the part of businessmen to enter into solemn covenants not to compete and then immediately to embark on the prohibited enterprise. This is done on the basis that a court might find the covenants unenforceable. That is what appears to be the rationale for the behaviour of the Halkos in this case. Whether they are justified in this course of conduct can be determined only at a trial where their action may be vindicated. That notwithstanding, anyone who embarks on such a course of conduct knowingly runs the risk of suffering an interlocutory injunction.

In many cases, the balance of convenience has shifted in favour of permitting the defendant to earn a livelihood while the plaintiff is able to be compensated in damages (*Mercury Marine Ltd. v. Dillion, supra*). However, the ability of Cantin to earn a livelihood has not been made an issue. There is nothing in the record which would persuade me that the balance of convenience favours the defendants. I am reinforced in this conclusion by two points. The first is the answer to an undertaking given by KPMG in which a senior KPMG official recalled

> … that, in the context of presenting the business plan, Mr. Freeborough stated that even if Ms. Cantin was prevented from performing services for any former Tillinghast clients, he still wished to hire Ms. Cantin in order to build a practice.

And second, because Cantin was told repeatedly in writing following her departure that Towers Perrin intended to vigorously pursue compliance with the restrictive covenants. For these reasons, I find that the balance of convenience favours the plaintiffs.

The Remedy

Even if I apply the highest standard of proof, the plaintiffs are entitled to an injunction until trial as follows:

[1] Against Claudette Cantin, an interlocutory injunction restraining her until trial or such other order of this Court from directly or indirectly:

  (a) performing services for, soliciting business from, or participating in client relationship management activities with respect to those clients (or former clients) of Towers Perrin listed in Schedule A to the notice of motion [excepting only the eight corporations listed in paragraph 6 of the affidavit of Sherman sworn October 7, 1999] which would involve Cantin in any capacity or function which is the same as or similar to a capacity or function which she formerly performed for Towers Perrin;

    (b) encouraging, soliciting, or inducing any employee to leave the employ of Towers Perrin, or soliciting for employment, employing or engaging the services of any employee of Towers Perrin or assisting any person, company or entity, including KPMG LLP and KPMG Canada, to engage in any such conduct;

[2] Against KPMG LLP and KPMG Canada, their officers, directors, partners, employees, agents and affiliates until trial or such other order of this Court from direct or indirectly:

    (a) soliciting business from, or performing services for the clients (or former clients) of Towers Perrin listed in Schedule A to the notice of motion [excepting only the eight corporations listed in paragraph 6 of the affidavit of Sherman sworn October 7, 1999] which would involve Cantin in any capacity or function which is the same as or similar to a capacity or function she formerly performed for Towers Perrin;

    (b) soliciting the employment or engaging the services of any employee of Towers Perrin with the assistance of Cantin.

There is one caveat to the injunction. Cantin has already secured the work of 11 corporations. Those corporations were not given notice of this application. They were not represented. At least one of them has engaged Cantin and KPMG on the basis of an indemnity agreement which recognizes the possibility of the enforcement of the covenant against competition. However, none of them should be prejudiced by this order particularly when, as indicated in the affidavit of Gauthier, this order is made at an important point in the fiscal year of most insurers. I doubt that it would be in the interests of any of the parties in this action, that any order I make should prejudice those clients. I am confident that counsel will be able to identify and implement a temporary solution as it affects those 11 clients. I will make a supplementary order if a resolution cannot be achieved by counsel on that subject.

Timetable Until Trial

As indicated above, a significant effort has been expended by all parties since the action was commenced. The parties are not yet ready but counsel have indicated that both sides will prepare expeditiously. The parties in this case were required to mediate pursuant to Rule 24.1. I encourage the parties to resume such efforts. However, failing a resolution of the outstanding issues in the immediate future, steps must be taken to ensure readiness for trial before the end of June 2000. By December 13, 1999, counsel shall submit to me a timetable which will lead to a trial date being set. Counsel will also provide a list of witnesses anticipated at the trial with estimates of time for evidence and submissions in order that the trial length might be assessed.

NOTES

1. The English courts have applied the *American Cyanamid* guidelines to restraint of trade clauses where the action is brought immediately upon the alleged breach occurring as in *Lawrence David Ltd. v. Aston*, [1991] 1 All ER 385 (CA). However, where the action is brought

during the period of restraint and a large part of it had run its course the court will more readily turn to full merit adjudication. See *Lansing Linde Ltd. v. Kerr*, [1991] 1 WLR 251 (CA).

2. See also chapter 9, "Specific Performance."

INTERLOCUTORY INJUNCTIONS PROTECTING INTELLECTUAL PROPERTY AND CONFIDENTIAL INFORMATION

Patent Infringement

There is some authority suggesting that the test in *American Cyanamid* is not applicable to patent actions brought in Canada, and that the applicant must still prove a *prima facie* case. Hammond (at 270-71) summarizes the position as follows (footnotes omitted):

> Although some Canadian courts—perhaps now a majority—have been prepared to utilize *American Cyanamid* either generally or within the framework of the *Yule* model, they have clearly treated patent-related litigation as being excluded from the ambit of the *American Cyanamid* model. The patent situation is always a difficult one: the real question (which is never overtly articulated by the courts) is how much reliance can be placed on the prior patent scrutiny process. The Canadian record, statistically, is bad but not quite in the company of the "leaky sieve" systems. Sixty-nine per cent of patents challenged in the Supreme Court of Canada between 1928 and 1969 were invalid. In all litigation in that period, nearly 40 percent were held invalid. This empirical evidence has to be considered alongside the statutory presumption of validity in section 47 of the *Patent Act*.
>
> In the result, Canadian courts have developed the rather specialized approach described by Brooke JA in the Ontario Court of Appeal:
>
> > I think the practice is no more than this. A recently issued untried patent is deemed to be valid under s. 47 of the *Patent Act*, RSC 1970, c. P-4. When, on a motion for interim injunction for infringement of such a patent, some evidence of infringement is offered and the other general principles applicable to interim injunction are satisfied, if the motion is opposed, although no evidence to the contrary is filed, the rule of practice should be considered. However, in such circumstances I should think it unlikely that, alone, it would tip the scales against the plaintiffs. On the other hand, in cases such as *Aluma, supra*, the presumption of the validity of the patent disappears because of the introduction of evidence to the contrary: *Circle Film Enterprises Inc. v. Canadian Broadcasting Corp.*, [1959] SCR 602 at p. 606. There, the evidence was of such a nature as to raise serious and substantial issues on the question of both infringement and validity of the patent and showed that the defendant had an arguable case. In such circumstances, the rule of practice might well tip the scales of discretion against the issuing of the injunction. The rule of practice must be considered in all such applications but is not an absolute bar to an injunction.
>
> What is more important, from a theoretical standpoint, is that the courts do not appear to have appreciated that what they have really been doing in the patent cases is examining the juristic nature of the rights at stake in the proceedings and asking (somewhat obliquely) how that kind of right should be handled.

The rule of practice enunciated by Brooke JA, *supra*, and taken from *Teledyne Industries Inc. v. Lido Industrial Products Ltd.* (1978), 19 OR (2d) 740 (CA), was done so without regard for *American Cyanamid*. Subsequent decisions endorsing *American Cyanamid* in the Federal Court may have substantially weakened this rule. See, for example, *Apotex Inc. v. Imperial Chemical Industries PLC*, [1989] 2 FC 608 (CA), and *Allergan Pharmaceuticals Inc. v. Bausch & Lomb Inc.* (1985), 7 CPR (3d) 209 (FCTD). However, even if a lower threshold is applied, the need to show irreparable harm is still difficult to surmount in patent infringement where the defendant's undertaking to keep an account of profits will often meet the plaintiff's attempt to show damages as being an inadequate remedy. See also *Merck & Co. v. Apotex Inc.* (1993), 51 CPR (3d) 170 (FCTD); *Cutter (Can.) Ltd. v. Baxter Travenol Laboratories of Can. Ltd.* (1980), 47 CPR (2d) 53 (FCA), leave to appeal to SCC refused (1980), 47 CPR (2d) 53n (SCC); and *Signalsation de Montreal Inc. v. Services de Beton Universels*, [1993] 1 FC 341 (CA).

Trademark Infringement

Where a registered trademark is allegedly being infringed, the Federal Court of Appeal has clearly endorsed *American Cyanamid*. See *Turbo Resources Ltd. v. Petro Canada Inc.*, [1989] 2 FC 451 (CA); *Syntex Inc. v. Novopharm Ltd.* (1991), 36 CPR (3d) 129 (FCA); leave to appeal to SCC refused (1991), 39 CPR (3d) v (note) (SCC); *Hyundai Auto Canada v. Cross Canada Auto Body Supply (West) Ltd.* (2006), 56 CPR (4th) 201 (FC); and Jeffrey Berryman, "Interlocutory Injunctions and Accessibility Thresholds: Or Once More Round the Mulberry Bush" (1989), 5 *Intellectual Property Journal* 137.

Where the action is for passing off, the courts have also applied *American Cyanamid*, although if the matter is likely to be dispositive of the dispute, the courts have placed importance on the strength of the plaintiff's case. See, for example, *Hoffmann-La Roche v. Apotex Inc.* (1982), 72 CPR (2d) 183 (Ont. HC).

Copyright Infringement

Section 34(1) of the *Copyright Act*, RSC 1985, c. C-42 states:

> Where copyright has been infringed, the owner of the copyright is ... entitled to all remedies by way of injunction, damages, accounts, delivery up and otherwise that are or may be conferred by law for the infringement of a right.

The Federal Court has accepted that the appropriate test for considering an interlocutory injunction application for alleged copyright infringement is the same as that applied in *Turbo Resources Ltd. v. Petro Canada Inc.*, *supra*. See *Upjohn Co. v. Apotex Inc.* (1993), 51 CPR (3d) 292 (FCTD). In other courts, where the infringement is clear and blatant, interlocutory injunctions have readily been granted without reference to *American Cyanamid*. In fact many of these cases commence as Anton Piller injunctions (see section titled "Anton Piller Injunctions," below), where a higher threshold has traditionally been demanded. However, proof of irreparable harm is still a necessary requirement. See *Western Steel and Tube Ltd. v. Erickson Manufacturing Ltd.*, [2009] FC no. 1017.

In 1997, the *Copyright Act* was amended to include a "wide injunction" (*Copyright Act*, RSC 1985, c. C-42, s. 39.1, as am. by SC 1997, c. 24, s. 20(4)). This new section allows a copyright owner to seek an injunction enjoining infringement for work in which the plaintiff claims copyright and which is the subject matter of the dispute. However, it also allows the plaintiff to enjoin infringement of other copyright works that the plaintiff may subsequently find in the possession of the defendant and that were not initially in issue, including those for which the plaintiff never held copyright at the time the proceedings were commenced. For the application of this new provision see *Microsoft Corp. v. 9038-3746 Quebec Inc.* (2006), 57 CPR (4th) 204 (FC).

Confidential Information

Outside intellectual property, other trade secrets and confidential information can be protected through an action for breach of confidence. The basis of the cause of action is proof that one party has conveyed to the other information in a fashion to make it clear to the other person that it was communicated in confidence, and that the other person has misused or used the information in an unauthorized manner. See *Cadbury Schweppes Inc. v. FBI Foods Ltd.*, [1999] 1 SCR 142, chapter 11, "Discretionary Reasons for the Denial of Relief."

Confidential information can be divided into two categories. One category involves the privacy interest a person has in keeping from the public personal details of his or her life or other family matters. In this category interlocutory injunctions have been granted to prevent the publication of confidential hospital records that would have identified doctors who had caught the AIDS disease, yet were still carrying on practice in the hospital (see *X. v. Y.*, [1988] 2 All ER 648 (QB)); to prevent the breach of a fiduciary duty (see *Drabinsky v. KPMG* (1998), 41 OR (3d) 565 (Gen. Div.)); to protect the identity of a person who has had a penile implant (see *S.T. v. Stubbs* (1998), 38 OR (3d) 788 (Gen. Div.), but compare with *A.B. v. Stubbs* (1999), 44 OR (3d) 391 (SCJ) (Gen. Div.)); and to prevent the publication of details associated with matrimonial proceedings where the applicant was seeking to divorce her husband, a person who had been convicted of murder and sexual assaults in a high profile case (see *M.E.H. v. Williams* (2011), 105 OR (3d) 344). The jurisprudential underpinning of this action is still a matter of controversy. In the United Kingdom, a right to privacy is built on the action for breach of confidence as well as on the *Human Rights Act 1998* (UK). In *A. v. B. plc*, [2003] QB 195 (CA), Lord Woolfe discussed at length the approach that a trial court judge should take when deciding an interlocutory injunction application alleging an infringement of privacy. While it is usually easy for the plaintiff to establish the existence of a "private fact" that warrants protection and the threshold is thus low for granting an interlocutory injunction, this fact must be balanced against the heightened weight accorded the defendant's public-interest defence to enjoy a right of freedom of expression. As Lord Wolfe concluded:

> The interlocutory injunction can only be justified if a permanent injunction is likely to be the final remedy flowing from the substantive trial.

See also *Campbell v. MGN Ltd.*, [2004] 2 All ER 995 (HL), and *HRH Prince of Wales v. Associated Newspapers Ltd.*, [2008] Ch. 57 (CA). English courts have recently advanced what are called "super injunctions" in which the name of the parties, the fact that the injunction has been sought, and the judge's name are all suppressed. See *LNS v. Persons Unknown*, [2010] EWHC 119 (QB). These orders have become controversial and are the subject of an impending public inquiry. The New Zealand Court of Appeal has recently created a true tort of invasion of privacy in *Hosking v. Runting*, [2005] 1 NZLR 1(CA), although the majority cautioned that "freedom of expression values will ordinarily prevail at the interlocutory stage." For a similar approach, see *Australian Broadcasting Corporation v. Lenah Game Meats Pty, Ltd.* (2001), 208 CLR 199 (HCA). Canadian courts have yet to accept a true tort of privacy and it is still a developing area. See *Nitsopoulos v. Wong* (2008), 298 DLR (4th) 265 (Ont. Sup. Ct.).

The second category involves confidential information concerning trade secrets such as customer lists or particular manufacturing processes. Interlocutory injunctions are readily granted in this category. For example, see *Danik Industries Ltd. v. Just Rite Bumpers & Accessories Ltd.* (1993), 48 CPC (3d) 20, aff'd. (1993), 49 CPC (3d) 204 (BCCA), protecting the plaintiff's specially designed bicycle car-rack, and *Essentially Yours Industries Ltd. v. Infintec Marketing Group*, [2000] 5 WWR 283 (Man. QB); aff'd. on appeal [2000] 7 WWR 297 (Man. CA) protecting the plaintiff's Internet distribution list.

INTERLOCUTORY INJUNCTIONS IN LABOUR DISPUTES

Interlocutory injunctions in labour disputes raise special concerns because the courts often operate in a highly charged political arena where the injunction is likely to be dispositive of the issues in dispute.

In the following, Arthurs et al. outline some of the problems with, and legislative solutions to, court-awarded injunctions in this area.

H.W. Arthurs, D.D. Carter, J. Fudge, H.J. Glasbeek, and G. Trudeau, *Labour Law and Industrial Relations in Canada*
4th ed. (Deventer, the Netherlands: Kluwer Law and Taxation Publishers, 1993), at 309-11 and 313-14 (footnotes omitted)

(a) General

761. The injunction has been by far the most frequently sought remedy in conflict situations. It has the attraction of being available speedily with relatively little formality of proof or pleading, and of stopping illegality and the resulting loss or damage, rather than attempting to compensate for it.

762. On the other hand, the injunction has also given rise to great political and social controversy. First, the very virtues of speed and informality have been seen to involve an undue sacrifice of procedural fairness. Second, the courts' intervention is limited to the suppression of illegality (itself defined according to rather vague common law standards) and is not directed to the underlying causes of conflict. Third, there has been the appearance of anti-unionism in the reaction of some judges to strikes and picketing. As a result, reforms during the 1970's in various Canadian jurisdictions have either entirely displaced the injunction or radically altered the procedure by which it is obtained.

(b) Procedural Problems

763. Injunctions may be granted either temporarily (interlocutory injunctions) or permanently. Permanent injunctions are granted only after a full-scale trial, but because of delays in mounting such trials, they are almost never sought. Temporary injunctions are granted, typically, upon motion, supported only by affidavit evidence, on brief notice or no notice, and on the explicit understanding that they will last only for a fixed period of days, or until the trial of the action. While summary procedures are the key to the usefulness of temporary injunctions, they do undoubtedly pose problems.

764. Where an injunction against picketing is given without notice (*ex parte*) even for a few days, the effect may be to disrupt and demoralize the union's activities. If it should turn out that the injunction was wrongly obtained, and even though it is ultimately dissolved, the employer will still have won a tactical advantage. Even when an injunction is given on notice, typically only of two days' duration, a union's chance to prepare reply evidence is very limited. Moreover, the use of affidavit evidence offers the employer an opportunity for artful equivocation or distortion of the facts in order to elicit the judge's sympathy. It is very difficult, as a practical matter, to either cross-examine or rebut witnesses (deponents) whose affidavits are the only evidence before the court. Because motions are hurriedly scheduled, usually in courts crowded with other business, and heard in an atmosphere of urgency, the opportunity for extended argument and calm deliberation is not easily achieved. And because, in principle, the injunction is only temporary and in prospect of a future full-scale trial (which, however, seldom occurs) rights of appeal against the granting of a temporary injunction are severely limited. Finally, although the plaintiff must promise to indemnify the defendant if it should turn out that the injunction has been wrongly obtained, in practice the defendant almost never has a chance to enforce this promise, since the matter becomes moot after the injunction has run for even a limited period.

765. Added to all of these problems are the facts that courts of general jurisdiction contain relatively few judges who have specialist knowledge of industrial relations or labour law; that such courts lack power to make an independent investigation of the facts or to probe, let alone resolve, the underlying controversies; and that ordinary doctrines of tort, delict or contract administered by them are somewhat obscure and not necessarily consistent with contemporary industrial relations policies and realities.

. . .

(e) Law Reform

775. Given the intensity of resentment against labour injunctions and the apparent validity of some of the criticisms made against them, it is not surprising that several Canadian jurisdictions have adopted reforming statutes.

776. The most far-reaching of these is the Labour Code of British Columbia which specifically deprives the civil courts of the power to issue injunctions against strikes or picketing, except in cases involving immediate and serious danger to individuals, or physical damage to property. In place of the courts' injunction jurisdiction, the labour relations board is given full remedial powers in relation to industrial action, including power to decide whether the case is an appropriate one for subsequent litigation before the courts. The intention of these provisions is to unite within the grasp of a single, knowledgeable tribunal

all aspects of industrial relationships, including that of conflict, and to enable that tribunal to deploy the full range of appropriate responses, described above.

777. Ontario has adopted a more tentative approach. Injunction procedures have been substantially reformed, particularly in relation to problems of proof, notice, and other aspects of fairness. Indeed, there is some suggestion that so long as the controversy involves a "labour dispute," as that term is statutorily defined, no injunction may issue except after unsuccessful recourse to police action. By implication, such a holding would confine the issuance of labour injunctions to cases involving violence and obstruction and other matters of a criminal nature, leaving the remaining aspects of illegality to be dealt with by the labour relations board. The labour relations board, in turn, has acquired extensive new remedial powers in relation to industrial action which is forbidden by the *Labour Relations Act*. However, the *Labour Relations Act* does not purport to be an integrated and complete code, as does the *Labour Code* of British Columbia, and there is conduct to which it is apparently not addressed. It would seem unlikely, therefore, that the courts will ultimately be prepared (in the absence of express legislation such as the *Labour Code* of British Columbia) to concede to the labour relations board plenary and exclusive jurisdiction over industrial action. The present position may be characterized as one of relative equilibrium: the courts are less active and less subject to criticism than formerly; the labour relations board is acquiring experience with its new remedial powers, and gradually extending their reach.

Ontario's legislative solution is now contained in s. 102 of the *Courts of Justice Act*, RSO 1990, c. C.43 (formerly s. 20 of the *Judicature Act*, RSO 1980, c. 223).

Courts of Justice Act
RSO 1990, c. C.43, s. 102

102(1) In this section, "labour dispute" means a dispute or difference concerning terms, tenure or conditions of employment or concerning the association or representation of persons in negotiating, fixing, maintaining, changing or seeking to arrange terms or conditions of employment, regardless of whether the disputants stand in the proximate relation of employer and employee.

(2) Subject to subsection (8), no injunction to restrain a person from an act in connection with a labour dispute shall be granted without notice.

(3) In a motion or proceeding for an injunction to restrain a person from an act in connection with a labour dispute, the court must be satisfied that reasonable efforts to obtain police assistance, protection and action to prevent or remove any alleged danger of damage to property, injury to persons, obstruction of or interference with lawful entry or exit from the premises in question or breach of the peace have been unsuccessful.

(4) Subject to subsection (8), affidavit evidence in support of a motion for an injunction to restrain a person from an act in connection with a labour dispute shall be confined to statements of facts within the knowledge of the deponent, but any party may by notice to the party filing such affidavit, and payment of the proper attendance money, require the attendance of the deponent to be cross-examined at the hearing.

(5) An interim injunction to restrain a person from an act in connection with a labour dispute may be granted for a period of not longer than four days.

(6) Subject to subsection (8), at least two days notice of a motion for an interim injunction to restrain a person from any act in connection with a labour dispute shall be given to the responding party and to any other person affected thereby but not named in the notice of motion.

(7) Notice required by subsection (6) to persons other than the responding party may be given,

(a) where such persons are members of a labour organization, by personal service on an officer or agent of the labour organization; and

(b) where such persons are not members of a labour organization, by posting the notice in a conspicuous place at the location of the activity sought to be restrained where it can be read by any persons affected,

and service and posting under this subsection shall be deemed to be sufficient notice to all such persons.

(8) Where notice as required by subsection (6) is not given, the court may grant an interim injunction where,

(a) the case is otherwise a proper one for the granting of an interim injunction;

(b) notice as required by subsection (6) could not be given because the delay necessary to do so would result in irreparable damage or injury, a breach of the peace or an interruption in an essential public service;

(c) reasonable notification, by telephone or otherwise, has been given to the persons to be affected or, where any of such persons are members of a labour organization, to an officer of that labour organization or to the person authorized under section 89 of the *Labour Relations Act* to accept service of process under that Act on behalf of that labour organization or trade union, or where it is shown that such notice could not have been given; and

(d) proof of all material facts for the purpose of clauses (a), (b) and (c) is established by oral evidence.

(9) The misrepresentation of any fact or the withholding of any qualifying relevant matter, directly or indirectly, in a proceeding for an injunction under this section, constitutes a contempt of court.

(10) An appeal from an order under this section lies to the Court of Appeal without leave.

Much turns on the definition of a "labour dispute." If the defendant can show that his or her activity relates to a labour dispute, the court has a restricted jurisdiction to grant an injunction. However, if the applicant can show that the defendant's activity falls outside the definition of a "labour dispute," the court has its normal jurisdiction to award an injunction. Of particular concern for courts has been the issue of primary and secondary picketing. Contrast the court's approach to this issue in *Alex Henry and Sons Ltd. v. Gale* (1976), 14 OR (2d) 311 with that of the Ontario Labour Relations Board in *Consolidated Bathurst Packaging Ltd. v. Canadian Paperworkers Union Local 343*, [1982] 3 Can. LRBR 324 (Ont.).

In *Ontario (Attorney General) v. Ontario Teachers' Federation* (1997), 36 OR (3d) 367, the attorney general for Ontario brought an action for an interlocutory injunction to restrain teachers from striking. The defendant had organized a series of ongoing province-wide strikes in opposition to legislative changes the government was making to the *School Boards and Teachers' Collective Negotiations Act*. The defendant had described its activities as a "political protest" and not a "labour dispute." When the attorney general brought his action under the general provision for granting interlocutory injunctions, Ontario *Courts of Justice Act*, s. 101, the defendant argued that the attorney general could proceed only by meeting the more stringent requirements laid out in s. 102. On this issue MacPherson J held against the defendant.

> The teachers submit that the Attorney General has proceeded under the wrong section. They say that s. 102 deals with interlocutory injunctions in a "labour dispute" context. There are a number of procedural steps which a moving party must take under s. 102; it is common ground that the Attorney General has not taken some of those steps. Accordingly, the teachers submit, this motion should not be heard.
>
> I do not agree with this submission. The teachers' position on this issue is seriously undercut by the way they have chosen to describe their conduct. In both the public arena and in these court proceedings, they have termed their conduct a political protest, not a labour dispute. It is true that they acknowledge that their conduct is a strike which is, of course, a well-known component of many labour disputes. However, the teachers assert that their conduct is much more than a strike; it is also a political protest directed not against their employers, the school boards, but against the Government of Ontario with respect to the Government's policies and proposed law on various education matters.
>
> In short, the teachers cannot have it both ways. If they want to label their conduct "political protest" and make submissions in court based on that label, they cannot limit the Attorney General's motion to the procedure which governs a labour dispute.
>
> Accordingly, I conclude that the Attorney General is entitled to bring this motion under s. 101 of the *Courts of Justice Act*. I emphasize the word "entitled." On this preliminary issue all that I have decided is that, as between ss. 101 and 102 of the *Courts of Justice Act*, the Attorney General is properly before this court under s. 101. Whether he should be here at all at this juncture, and whether he is entitled to the injunctive relief he seeks, are questions that still need to be addressed.

The residual power held by the courts to intervene in a labour dispute to issue an injunction to prevent an illegal strike has been upheld by the Supreme Court of Canada in *St.-Anne Nackawic Pulp and Paper Co. Ltd. v. Canadian Paper Workers Union, Local 219*, [1986] 1 SCR 704 and *Brotherhood of Maintenance and Way Employees Canadian Pacific System Federation v. Canadian Pacific Ltd.*, [1996] 2 SCR 495.

In *RWDSU Local 558 v. Pepsi-Cola Canada Beverages (West) Ltd.*, [2002] 1 SCR 156, the Supreme Court held that secondary picketing—that is, picketing other than the primary employer—was not generally unlawful unless it involved tortious or criminal conduct. Common law prohibitions against secondary picketing had to be revised to accord to the Charter value given freedom of expression. Balancing an employee's right to expression exercised through secondary picketing against an affected third party could be achieved by insisting on some tortious interference or criminal activity directed against the third party and for whose benefit the injunction could be granted.

Labour Relations Code
RSBC 1996, c. 244

Jurisdiction of Board

136(1) Except as provided in this Code, the board has and must exercise exclusive jurisdiction to hear and determine an application or complaint under this Code and to make an order permitted to be made.

(2) Without limiting subsection (1), the board has and must exercise exclusive jurisdiction in respect of

(a) a matter in respect of which the board has jurisdiction under this Code, and

(b) an application for the regulation, restraint or prohibition of a person or group of persons from

(i) ceasing or refusing to perform work or to remain in a relationship of employment,

(ii) picketing, striking or locking out, or

(iii) communicating information or opinion in a labour dispute by speech, writing or other means.

Jurisdiction of Court

137(1) Except as provided in this section, a court does not have and must not exercise any jurisdiction in respect of a matter that is, or may be, the subject of a complaint under section 133 or a matter referred to in section 136, and, without limitation, a court must not make an order enjoining or prohibiting an act or thing in respect of them.

(2) This Code must not be construed to restrict or limit the jurisdiction of a court, or to deprive a court of jurisdiction to entertain a proceeding and make an order the court may make in the proper exercise of its jurisdiction if a wrongful act or omission in respect of which a proceeding is commenced causes immediate danger of serious injury to an individual or causes actual obstruction or physical damage to property.

(3) Despite this Code or any other Act, a court must not, on an application made without notice to any other person, order an injunction to restrain a person from striking, locking out or picketing, or from doing an act or thing in respect of a strike, lockout, dispute or difference arising from or relating to a collective agreement.

(4) A court of competent jurisdiction may award damages for injury or losses suffered as a consequence of conduct contravening Part 5 if the board has first determined that there has been a contravention of Part 5.

NOTES

1. The exclusive jurisdiction of the British Columbia Labour Relations Board to deal with all matters arising out of a labour dispute has been upheld in *Maz Tudor Inns Ltd. v. Canadian Association of Smelter and Allied Workers* (1985), 68 BCLR 396 (CA).

2. The BC Court of Appeal has indicated that jurisdiction under s. 137 must be exercised with restraint and caution. See *Fletcher Challenge Canada Ltd. v. Local 1092* (1998), 155 DLR (4th) 638 (BCCA).

INTERLOCUTORY INJUNCTIONS IN DEFAMATION ACTIONS

Interlocutory injunctions in defamation actions raise important issues of free speech and prior restraint.

Canada Metal Co. Ltd. v. Canadian Broadcasting Corp.
(1974), 3 OR (2d) 1 (HC)

HOLLAND J: There are two applications presently before me in the above style. The first is an application on behalf of the defendants for an order dissolving or rescinding the *ex parte* injunction granted by Mr. Justice Wilson on January 29, 1974, which restrained the defendants and each of them from alleging or implying by broadcasting on television or otherwise publicizing, that the plaintiffs and/or either of them have brought misleadingly favourable medical evidence and concealed material evidence from medical experts and from misstating the amounts the plaintiffs are spending to install pollution control systems. The second is brought on behalf of the plaintiffs for an order effective until the date of trial or other final disposition of the action, continuing the injunction granted by Mr. Justice Wilson aforesaid and expanding the relief therein granted by restraining the defendants from broadcasting or otherwise disseminating and from advertising or otherwise publicizing any part or portion of a programme entitled "Dying of Lead" or any part or portion of the script thereof or, alternatively, from publicizing certain portions of such script.

Originally, there was a third motion pending before me on behalf of the plaintiffs for an order committing the defendants Mark Starowicz and Max Allen to the common jail for breach of the injunction granted by Mr. Justice Wilson aforesaid and also for an order committing E.S. Hallman, Gary Perly, Graham Fraser and James L. Cooper to jail for knowingly acting in contravention of the said injunction. Mr. Hallman is apparently a vice-president of the Canadian Broadcasting Corporation and general manager of English Language Services for such corporation based in Toronto. Mr. Fraser was apparently the author of a news article appearing in the Globe and Mail, a Toronto newspaper, of which Mr. Cooper is the president and publisher. Mr. Perly apparently is the national chairman of the Canadian Liberation Movement, which published a pamphlet dealing with the subject of the injunction.

The three motions originally came on before me for hearing together and were adjourned to permit Mr. Perly to cross-examine on certain of the affidavits filed on behalf of the plaintiffs. When the motions came on again for hearing an application was made by Mr. Perly for a further adjournment of the third motion so that he could issue a subpoena for the purpose of examining Mr. Outerbridge, who is a solicitor in the office of the solicitors for the plaintiffs, and who also appeared as counsel on behalf of the plaintiffs on the motions. I granted the adjournment of this third motion to permit the issue of the subpoena but without in any way dealing with the propriety of such examination, which matter may well be dealt with by the Master of this Court, I then proceeded with the hearing of the first two motions which are the motion to continue and expand on the one hand, and the motion to dissolve on the other.

The plaintiffs operate secondary lead smelters in the City of Toronto and the activities of the plaintiffs have been the subject of certain publicity in recent months. For example, a stop order was issued by the director of the Air Management Branch of Ontario Ministry of the Environment, dated October 26, 1973, directing the Canada Metal Company Limited to stop their plant from emitting or discharging into the natural environment lead and lead compounds. This order was reviewed under the provisions of the *Judicial Review Procedure Act*, SO 1971, c. 48 by Mr. Justice Keith and at the conclusion of the hearing Mr. Justice Keith made an immediate order setting aside such stop order basically on the ground that the director exercised a power granted to him under the Act arbitrarily and not judicially.

In the morning edition of the Toronto Globe and Mail for Tuesday, January 29, 1974, there appeared an article under the heading "Television" with the subheading "Special on Lead Poisoning Fine Investigative Journalism."

This article read, in part, as follows:

> Tonight at 7, CBC Radio's As It Happens does a one-hour special on lead poisoning which, at least on the basis of reading a transcript, seems to be a definitive and terrifying show—and investigative journalism at its best.
>
> The program was sparked by the controversy over lead emissions and illness around two Toronto smelters. It includes claims that medical experts can be bought to give evidence that favors lead companies and plays down the danger. A doctor from Cleveland says that doctors who minimize the significance of high lead emissions are hired by the firms to say so. …
>
> Doctors on the program claim that excessive lead levels can turn children into vegetables. One doctor says "all they escape is death"—and some do die. The cost of each child turned into a vegetable—just the financial cost and not including emotional torture—was set at $500,000.
>
> The cost of pollution controls at one of the Toronto lead smelters is estimated at $60,000.
>
> A doctor whose evidence helped to get a court to allow a smelter to stay in operation despite apparent lead poisoning in three nearby residents admits on the program that evidence that might have made her change her stand was concealed from her.

On the same day, the plaintiffs issued a writ in this action and applied for an *ex parte* injunction before Mr. Justice Wilson. In support of the application was filed an affidavit sworn by Michael Sigel, secretary-treasurer of the plaintiff Toronto Refiners and Smelters Limited, and an affidavit sworn by Carleton Smith, president and general manager of the Canada Metal Company Limited, by which affidavits the deponents swore that at no time had they or any member of their executive staff, or any other person at their request or with their knowledge, attempted to influence or influenced in any way by money, the expert opinions of Drs. Sachs and Barltrop, who were the two medical experts retained on behalf of their companies. In addition, Mr. Sigel swore that Toronto Refiners and Smelters in now in the final stages of installing a pollution control system at a cost to the company in excess of $150,000 and Mr. Smith swore that Canada Metal Company Limited is now in the final stages of installing a pollution control system at a cost to the company in excess of $300,000.

On the basis of the above affidavits Mr. Justice Wilson granted the *ex parte* injunction above referred to. The defendants were given notice of the injunction after the programme in question had already been broadcast in the Maritime Provinces and a short time before the broadcast was due to commence in Ontario and Quebec.

After consultation with counsel, two portions of the broadcast, which had been carried in the Maritime Provinces, were deleted from the broadcast to the other Provinces and Territories. It is necessary to review the transcript of the broadcast "Dying of Lead" in some detail.

The format of the broadcast appears to be comment by CBC narrators with extracts from tape recorded conversations with various other persons. The transcript of the broadcast is marked ex. "B" to the affidavit of Ira Kaufman and the following are excerpts from such transcript: ...

Defamatory words in a broadcast shall be deemed to be published and constitute libel: the *Libel and Slander Act*, RSO 1970, c. 243, s. 2. In deciding a matter such as this the Court should always bear in mind the principle of freedom of the press. This principle, fortunately, has always existed in Canada, and this existence is specifically recognized by s. 1 of the *Canadian Bill of Rights*. One must bear in mind that this particular programme, a so-called public affairs programme, dealt generally with an area of considerable public concern. This freedom of the press is, of course, a freedom governed by law and is not a freedom to make untrue defamatory statements: see *Reference re Alberta Statutes*, [1938] SCR 100 at p. 133 [aff'd. [1939] AC 117 (PC (Can.))].

The Court in a case of this type will only interfere with a publication of an alleged libel in the very clearest of cases. The Court must be satisfied that the words are beyond doubt defamatory, are clearly untrue so that no defence of justification would succeed, and, where such defence may apply, are not fair comment on true or admitted facts.

The jurisdiction of the Court in cases of this type has been described as "of a delicate nature." The Master of the Rolls in *William Coulson & Sons v. James Coulson & Co.* (1876), 3 TLR 846 (CA) (at p. 846):

> It was for the jury and not for the Court to construe the document, and to say whether it was libel or not. To justify the Court in granting an interim injunction it must come to a decision upon the question of libel or no libel, before the jury decided whether it was a libel or not. ... It ought only to be exercised in the clearest cases, where any jury would say that the matter complained of was libellous, and where if the jury did not so find the Court would set aside the verdict as unreasonable. The Court must also be satisfied that in all probability the alleged libel was untrue. ... It followed ... that the Court could only on the rarest occasions exercise their jurisdiction.

See also *Collard v. Marshall*, [1892] 1 Ch. 571.

Certainly one of the leading cases is *Bonnard v. Perryman*, [1891] 2 Ch. 269 (CA). An alleged defamatory article was printed and an application was brought on behalf of the plaintiffs for an interim injunction restraining the defendants from publishing the article. In support of the application the plaintiffs made affidavits to show that the statements in the article of which they complained were untrue. The defendant made an affidavit in the following terms [at 272]:

> The whole of the allegations in the article entitled "the *Fletcher Mills of Providence, Rhode Island*," complained of by the Plaintiffs, are true in substance and in fact, and I shall be able to prove the same at the trial of this action by subpoenaing witnesses and by cross-examination of the Plaintiffs, and by other evidence which I cannot, and which I submit I ought not to have to, produce on an interlocutory application.

Chief Justice Coleridge gave the majority judgment, in which Lord Esher MR and Lindley, Bowen and Lopes LJJ concurred. Lord Justice Kay dissented but really on the effect of the affidavit and not on the principles of law to be applied to the case. Lord Coleridge, at p. 284, said this:

But it is obvious that the subject-matter of an action for defamation is so special as to require exceptional caution in exercising the jurisdiction to interfere by injunction before the trial of an action to prevent an anticipated wrong. The right of free speech is one which it is for the public interest that individuals should possess, and, indeed, that they should exercise without impediment, so long as no wrongful act is done; and, unless an alleged libel is untrue, there is no wrong committed; but on the contrary, often a very wholesome act is performed in the publication and repetition of an alleged libel. Until it is clear that an alleged libel is untrue, it is not clear that any right at all has been infringed; and the importance of leaving free speech unfettered is a strong reason in cases of libel for dealing most cautiously and warily with the granting of interim injunctions. We entirely approve of and desire to adopt as our own, the language of Lord Esher MR, in *Coulson v. Coulson*, at p. 846—"To justify the Court in granting an interim injunction it must come to a decision upon the question of libel or no libel, before the jury have decided whether it was a libel or not. Therefore the jurisdiction was of a delicate nature. It ought only to be exercised in the clearest cases, where any jury would say that the matter complained of was libellous, and where, if the jury did not so find, the Court would set aside the verdict as unreasonable." In the particular case before us, indeed, the libellous character of the publication is beyond dispute, but the effect of it upon the Defendant can be finally disposed of only by a jury, and we cannot feel sure that the defence of justification is one which, on the facts which may be before them, the jury may find to be wholly unfounded; nor can we tell what may be the damages recoverable. ...

As I see it there are four main areas of complaint concerning the programme, they are:

(1) an allegation that the plaintiffs are polluting the area surrounding their factories with lead and that such pollution is causing lead poisoning with serious risk of illness and even death;

(2) an alleged innuendo that witnesses on behalf of the plaintiffs and in particular Drs. Barltrop and Sachs are prepared to offer their evidence for sale and that they will give untruthfully favourable evidence provided that they are paid;

(3) an alleged innuendo that the plaintiffs or their solicitors have concealed material evidence from a medical expert called on their behalf, and

(4) that the amounts of money, by implication being spent by one or other of the plaintiffs, to combat pollution has been mis-stated.

I will deal with these four allegations in order and in each case must decide whether the allegation or alleged innuendo was clearly defamatory, was clearly untrue and, where such defence may apply, was clearly not fair comment. Before doing so I must decide what effect, in any, I should give to the sworn statements of Starowicz and Allen that they believe all alleged defamatory statements to be true and would seek to prove the truth of such statements in any defamation proceedings. Neither gave any reason for his belief. It is to be noted that Hallman, in his affidavit, did not depose as to his belief as to the truth of the statements but deposes that the defendant Canadian Broadcasting Corporation would seek to prove the truth of such statements in any defamation proceedings. I suppose that Hallman was in no position to depose as to the truth of the statements.

The applications before me are interlocutory motions and as such Rule 292 of the Rules of Practice and Procedure in the Supreme Court of Ontario applies. Such Rule reads as follows:

> 292. Affidavits shall be confined to the statements of facts within the knowledge of the deponent, but, on interlocutory motions, statements as to his belief, with the grounds therefor, may be admitted.

Exception was taken before me to the paragraphs in the affidavits of Starowicz and Allen in question in that the grounds for the belief as to the truth of the facts had not been set out. It has been the practice of the Court when the Rule has not been complied with to disregard the offending paragraph completely: see *Inducon Construction (Eastern) Ltd. v. Vaupere*, [1967] 1 OR 245.

Before simply disregarding the paragraphs in the affidavits I think one should consider the surrounding circumstances. Now, for this purpose I am of opinion that the first area of complaint set out above should be treated on a different footing from the others. That allegation refers to something which, as it appears from the evidence before me, is no simple matter of fact concerning the existence or non-existence of which there can be no room for doubt. Rather, it raises a question which can be answered only after the most detailed and painstaking scientific investigation. Certainly Starowicz and Allen could not swear as to the truth of the allegation because they would have no direct personal knowledge of the truth of such allegation. They would only be in a position to swear as to their belief and their belief must obviously be founded on their opportunity to learn the truth and the investigation that they had made or caused to have been made in this connection. Starowicz was the executive producer of the programme and Allen the story editor. They were the persons responsible for putting the programme together. The programme was based primarily upon tapes of conversations with various persons, including experts in the field of lead pollution, and when all the facts are considered leading up to the swearing of the affidavits the grounds for belief are obvious. In such circumstances, I do not believe it fair to conclude that the defendant is in no position to sustain a plea of justification simply because the affidavits failed to specify the grounds for the belief alleged. Furthermore, in my view, it would be unrealistic to disregard these paragraphs in the affidavits because of a technical non-compliance with Rule 292. I am bearing in mind the wording of the affidavit which was upheld by the Court in *Bonnard v. Perryman*.

I also have regard to *Empire-Universal Films Ltd. et al. v. Rank*, [1947] OWN 725 [rev'd. [1948] OR 235 (CA)], and *Safrance v. Morris*, [1956] OWN 97, cases which, although not directly in point, do indicate that in construing this Rule, regard should be had to the circumstances of the case and the importance of the omission.

The situation is different in respect of the area of complaint No. (4) above. The impugned statement relates to what O'Connor J, in *Cullen v. Stanley*, [1926] IR 73 at p. 85, described as a point "on which there cannot eventually be any room for doubt." It cannot be said that the grounds for belief in the truth of the allegation are obvious, and if the defendant wished to credibly assert a belief in the truth of this allegation the affidavits filed should have specified some basis for that belief. Accordingly, in so far as the paragraphs in the affidavits relate to this allegation I propose to disregard them.

For reasons that will become apparent, the grounds for Starowicz's and Allen's belief in the truth of any allegedly defamatory statements of fact in grounds of complaints Nos. (2) and (3) above are, in my opinion, irrelevant. I must bear in mind, however, that Hallman, Starowicz and Allen all swore that the defendants would seek to prove the truth of all allegedly defamatory statements of fact in the programme in any defamation proceedings.

In coming to my conclusion that I should consider these paragraphs in the affidavits, to the extent I have stated, I bear in mind the heavy responsibility which must rest upon Hallman, Starowicz and Allen as officers of the defendant, the Canadian Broadcasting Corporation. Hallman, in particular, is vice-president of such corporation. The Canadian Broadcasting Corporation was continued under the *Broadcasting Act*, SCR 1967-68, c. 25 [now RSC 1970, c. B-11]. The corporation was established for the purpose of providing the national broadcasting services contemplated by the Act. The services contemplated by the Act include, in part, a requirement that the programming "should be of a high standard," and "should be a balanced service of information, enlightenment and entertainment." The corporation is maintained, in part, by the taxpayers of this country and, as I indicated above, in my view, the responsibility of the officers and servants of such corporation to present broadcasts in a fair way and to deal fairly with issues of public interest is heavy. I assume that Starowicz and Allen had the high standards required of them in their programming in mind when the programme in question was put together and all three deponents had these high standards in mind when they swore that they would seek to justify any defamatory statements.

Dealing then with the first allegation, that is that the plaintiffs polluted the area with lead, which resulted in lead poisoning to individuals, I have no doubt that such an allegation is defamatory. The term defamatory has been defined as any imputation that may tend to lower the plaintiff in the estimation of right-thinking members of society in general or to expose the plaintiff to hatred, contempt or ridicule. Can I be satisfied that such an allegation is clearly untrue? I think not. The material filed before me is in conflict and surely if this were an action for damages for libel the matter would have to be left to the jury.

I now turn to the second allegation which is the alleged innuendo that witnesses on behalf of the plaintiff are prepared to offer their evidence for sale, in that they will give untruthfully favourable evidence provided they are paid. It was argued before me that based upon the transcript of the programme such an innuendo cannot be drawn as against the plaintiffs. In my view, such an innuendo could be drawn from the transcript as against the plaintiffs but not necessarily so. A Judge at a trial in a defamation action might well decide that the words complained of were capable of conveying a defamatory meaning but it would still be a question for the jury whether the words did in fact convey a defamatory meaning. I do not think that a jury would necessarily come to the conclusion that the words complained of were in fact defamatory of these plaintiffs. The fact of the matter is that expert witnesses are paid and the Drs. Barltrop and Sachs were paid. The affidavit material before me indicates that they were paid, or were promised to be paid, their usual fee—whatever that is. The defence of fair comment may also apply in connection with the words complained of in the programme.

I will now deal with the alleged innuendo that the plaintiffs or their solicitors have concealed material evidence from medical experts. On reading the transcript it appears quite clear to me that no such innuendo could be drawn against the plaintiffs. The allegation, if such can be said to have been made, is against the Ministry of the Environment.

I now turn to the fourth allegation which is that the amounts of money, by implication being spent by one or other of the plaintiffs, to combat pollution has been mis-stated. It may be that in the context of the programme such a misstatement would be defamatory. It was argued before me that the reference to the sum of $60,000 was not necessarily in connection with the operation of one or other of the plaintiffs. I would have thought that it was. However, I am of the opinion that there is sufficient doubt about it that again, should there be an action for damages for libel, it would be left to the jury. I do not think that a jury would necessarily find that such a statement was defamatory of the plaintiffs although they could well do so.

I do not think that the fact that there is a pending action for damages against Toronto Refiners and Smelters Company Limited is of any consequence. In the recent case of *Attorney-General v. Times Newspapers Ltd.*, [1974] AC 273 (HL (Eng.)), the House of Lords dealt with newspaper articles which urged a litigant to reconsider its position and which produced evidence to show that the litigant had not exercised due care in the manufacture and sale of thalidomide. The House of Lords held that the article setting out evidence was a clear case of contempt because it created a real risk that the fair trial of the action would be prejudiced and the publication thereof should be restrained by injunction. In the present case, the broadcast was a comment on a matter of general public interest and was not directed toward the litigation in progress. At p. 312 of the judgment in *Attorney-General v. Times Newspapers Ltd.*, Lord Diplock states that discussion, however strongly expressed on matters of general public interest, is not to be stifled merely because there is litigation pending arising out of particular facts to which the general principles being discussed would be applicable. I think that is the rule that should be applied here. It is always open to move to strike out the jury notice in the action pending against one of the present plaintiffs. Lord Reid notes at p. 298 that it can be assumed that a publication of this sort would not affect the mind of a professional Judge.

Therefore, I have come to the conclusion that this is not a case in which the Court should interfere because, as I have said before, the Court will only interfere by way of injunction to prevent publication of alleged libel in the very clearest of cases. There are serious issues of fact which, in my view, could only be satisfactorily resolved by the hearing of evidence before Judge and jury.

It was argued before me that no order should be made for an injunction because damages would be a sufficient remedy. Should the plaintiffs commence an action for damages for libel such damages would be at large, which means, that it would not be necessary for the plaintiffs to prove any particular or special damages: see *South Hetton Coal Ltd. v. North Eastern News Ass'n Ltd.*, [1894] 1 QB 133 (CA) at p. 139. The fact that the defendant, the Canadian Broadcasting Corporation, would be in a position financially to pay any award is certainly a consideration.

The fact that I am ordering that the injunction granted by Mr. Justice Wilson be dissolved should not be taken in any way as being critical of his order. When the application was brought on before him he had only the original article, referred to earlier, appearing in the Globe and Mail and the affidavits deposing that certain of the statements therein were untrue. The programme was about to be broadcast in Ontario and, in fact, had already been broadcast to the eastern Provinces. There was no time to give the defendants notice of the application before him.

For the above reasons the motion to continue and expand the injunction will be dismissed and the motion to dissolve the injunction will be allowed. The injunction granted by Mr. Justice Wilson will therefore be dissolved. In all the circumstances the costs of the application will be costs in the cause in both motions.

Canada Metal Co. Ltd. v. Canadian Broadcasting Corp. (No. 2)
(1975), 7 OR (2d) 261 (HC)

[Note: An appeal from the above judgment of Holland J to the Divisional Court of the High Court of Justice (Stark, Zuber, and Reid JJ) was dismissed with costs to the defendants on May 20, 1975. The following judgment of the court was delivered orally.]

STARK J: This Court is unanimously of the opinion that the appeal from the order of Holland J, must be dismissed for the reasons given by him. We would merely like to add this.

The granting of injunctions to restrain publication of alleged libels is an exceptional remedy granted only in the rarest and clearest of cases. That reluctance to restrict in advance publication of words spoken or written is founded, of course, on the necessity under our democratic system to protect free speech and unimpeded expression of opinion. The exceptions to this rule are extremely rare.

For at least one hundred years and certainly since the leading cases of *William Coulson & Sons v. James Coulson & Co.* (1887), 3 TLR 846 (CA) and *Collard v. Marshall*, [1892] 1 Ch. 571, and perhaps above all, in the leading case of *Bonnard v. Perryman*, [1891] 2 Ch. 269 (CA) it has been universally and consistently held by British and Canadian Courts that such an interim injunction will never be granted where the defendant expresses his intention to justify unless the words in question are so clearly defamatory and so obviously impossible to justify that the verdict of a jury accepting a plea of justification as a defence would of necessity have to be set aside as a perverse finding on appeal. That is not this case. Some of the words in the broadcast here are admittedly capable of defamatory meanings, but they are not all so clearly defamatory that a jury could not decline to accept all or some of the many allegations made by the plaintiff; and certainly the issue of justification in this case is a triable and disputable issue, not one which can be decided at this stage and clearly one which must go to the jury.

I would like to say a word about the effect of Rule 292 which, of course, provides that:

292. Affidavits shall be confined to the statement of facts within the knowledge of the deponent, but, on interlocutory motions, statements as to his belief, with the grounds therefor, may be admitted.

We reject the contention that the grounds referred to in that Rule must themselves be in the form of acceptable evidence. We believe it is sufficient if the grounds suggest or provide information as to the sources from which such evidence might be obtained. It must be remembered that the affidavits of the defendants that are being attacked here on the ground of failure to comply with that Rule do in fact contain the grounds for their belief since the transcript of the broadcast itself is annexed as an exhibit and the transcript contains grounds to enable the defendants to endeavour to justify their statements. Whether the evidence at the time of trial will prove to be adequate, can only be determined at the trial itself. For these reasons, therefore, the appeal is dismissed with costs to the defendants.

Canadian Tire Corp. Ltd. v. Desmond
[1972] 2 OR 60

O'DRISCOLL J: The defendant is an unsatisfied customer of the retail store operated by the plaintiff at 837-857 and 940 Yonge St. in the City of Toronto.

The affidavits filed on this motion, upon which there has been cross-examination, disclose:

(1) On May 7, 1971, the defendant attended at the store operated by the plaintiff at 839 Yonge St., Toronto, and purchased a radio priced at $12.

(2) On September 8, 1971, the defendant states that he returned to the store with the "defective radio."

(3) While in the store on the last-mentioned date, words (and perhaps more) were exchanged between the defendant and the manager of that particular store; the manager told the defendant to leave the store and to stay away from the premises. At this time the defendant alleges that the manager said that the radio had been sold "as is."

(4) The next day, September 9, 1971, the defendant paraded north and south on the sidewalk in front of the plaintiff's store from 7:30 a.m. until 9:30 p.m.; while walking he carried a white sign measuring approximately 3 ft. by 2 ft. with the following words printed thereon:

C.D.N. TIRE

CHEATED

ME

WILL THEY

CHEAT

YOU?

(5) On September 10, 1971, the defendant continued to picket from 8:00 a.m. until 5:00 p.m. when he was served with the writ of summons, notice of motion and affidavit material filed on this motion.

(6) The conduct of the defendant while engaged in the picketing was peaceful, without disturbance; no one was accosted, threatened, obstructed, molested or incommoded; no crowd assembled.

On September 13, 1971, an interim injunction was granted until September 20, 1971; on September 20, 1971, on consent, the injunction was continued until September 27, 1971, and on consents further continued until November 24, 1971, when Osler J, endorsed the notice of motion as follows:

No person appearing, motion is adjourned sine die, to be brought on on 7 days notice; injunction not renewed.

The motion for me was to *continue* the interim injunction until trial: it would appear that the parties were not aware of Osler J's endorsement. However, I shall treat this as an application for an interim injunction.

In my view, the following principles are applicable to the evidence before me:

(a)

The right to peacefully picket or to make a truthful statement is assured and the authorities and statutory provisions deal only with the limitations upon such accepted right. ...

In short, then, the above authorities establish that picketing is only wrongful; (a) If it is featured by *defamatory statements*, or (b) If it is carried on in such manner as to disclose a purpose other than peacefully "obtaining or communicating information," or (c) If it is part of a conspiracy to injure.

(The italics are mine.) *Canada Dairies Ltd. v. Seggie*, [1940] 4 DLR 725 (Ont. HC) at pp. 730 and 733, *per* Mackay J (as he then was).

(b)

[O'Driscoll J quoted from *Bonnard v. Perryman*.]

The cross-examination of the defendant discloses the following questions and answers:

84. Q. This sign that you carried on which was printed the words, "Canadian Tire cheated me" Mr. Desmond, why do you think they cheated you?

A. They took my money and gave me bad merchandise.

85. Q. Can you tell me why you haven't instituted an action in the small claims court for recovery of your money?

A. I don't have that kind of money, you have to have a lawyer.

I would have dismissed this application but for the defendant's use of the words "cheated" and "cheat."

C. Walsh (ed.), Jowitt's Dictionary of English Law (London: Sweet & Maxwell, 1959), vol. 1, p. 359, contains the following:

Cheat. This, in the criminal law, is a generic term for the act of fraudulently obtaining the property of another by any deceitful practice not amounting to felony, but of such a nature that it directly affects or may directly affect the public at large (2 East PC 817; 1 Hawk. 188).

"To cheat is always to defraud": *Hackworth v. Baker*, [1936] 1 WWR 321 (Sask. CA); leave to appeal refused, [1936] 2 WWR 622.

See also: ss. 262-265 of the *Criminal Code*, RSC 1970, c. C-34, where defamatory libel is defined.

Although Kay LJ, dissented in the result in *Bonnard v. Perryman*, he agreed [at 288] that: "... in order to justify the Court in granting an interlocutory injunction in such a case, there must be strong *prima facie* evidence that the statement is untrue."

I hold that there is such evidence here based upon the defendant's answers on cross-examination.

I would therefore grant an interlocutory injunction in the following form:

"The Defendant, his agent, servant or any person acting under his instruction, will be restrained until the Trial or other final disposition of this action from exhibiting any sign or sandwich board, or other printed or written material to the effect that the plaintiff has cheated or defrauded him, or containing any libellous statement of, or concerning the Plaintiff Company or its business, and from molesting, speaking to or approaching any person with a view to dissuading them from working for or from doing business with the Plaintiff by alleging that the Plaintiff cheated or defrauded him or by making any libellous statement of or concerning the Plaintiff Company or dissuading them from observing or performing any existing contract with the Plaintiff."

The writ in this action was issued 5 months ago; no statement of claim has yet been served and filed.

This interim injunction shall be dissolved without further motion or order at 5:00 p.m. EST on March 17, 1972, unless a statement of claim is served and filed prior to that time.

Costs of this motion to be costs in the cause.

NOTES

1. For another case concerning a disgruntled customer wishing to exercise his freedom of expression, this time against a house building company, see *Rosemond Estates Inc. v. Levy* (2003), 65 OR (3d) 79 (SCJ).

2. In *Rapp v. McClelland & Stewart Ltd.* (1981), 34 OR (2d) 452, Griffiths J was of the opinion that the decision in *American Cyanamid* did not change the well-established principles related to the granting of interlocutory injunctions in defamation actions. In *John Doe v. Canadian Broadcasting Corp.* (1993), 86 BCLR (2d) 199 (SC), Boyd J, commenting upon an application for an interlocutory injunction against the CBC prior to its running a program that alleged that the plaintiff had been convicted of drug offences prior to emigrating to Canada, stated (at 214):

> The law provides that where a party seeks to enjoin another's right to publish an alleged defamatory statement, a much higher threshold test is applied by the courts in determining whether injunctive relief (sometimes referred to as "prior restraint") ought to be granted. The traditional balance of convenience is no longer a factor. Prior restraint of speech will only be granted in the "rarest" and "clearest" of cases where "'the Court must be satisfied that any jury would say the matter complained of as libellous'" (*Meier v. Canadian Broadcasting Corp.* (1981), 19 CPC 315, at 317).

3. The paramount importance of free speech has also been asserted by the English Court of Appeal in distinguishing *American Cyanamid* as the applicable standard when considering an interlocutory injunction that sought to prevent the broadcasting of a program allegedly in breach of a contract with the plaintiff concerning the transmission of the program. See *Cambridge Nutrition Ltd. v. British Broadcasting Corp.*, [1990] 3 All ER 523 (CA) and *Holley v. Smyth*, [1998] 2 WLR 742 (CA).

4. Another way of preventing publication of allegedly defamatory material is through the contempt of court powers once litigation has been commenced. An illustration of what was

once called a "gagging writ" is *Attorney-General v. Times Newspapers Ltd.*, [1974] AC 273. The *Sunday Times* had published several articles critical of Distillers, a pharmaceutical company that manufactured thalidomide, a drug used to control morning sickness but which caused birth defects, for its slowness in settling personal injury claims and for the low amounts offered as compensation. Another article was planned, at which time Distillers brought an injunction action to prevent publication. The order was granted on the basis that publication of the article would prejudice the fair outcome of the civil dispute and would constitute a contempt of court in that it would tarnish the administration of justice. The case went on appeal to the European Court of Human Rights ([1979] 2 EHRR 245), which concluded that the applicant's rights of freedom of expression had been violated under article 10 of the European Convention on Human Rights. Subsequently, the UK Parliament enacted the *Contempt of Court Act 1981*. A further transformation of UK law concerning how to balance freedom of expression and the administration of justice has taken place as a result of the enactment in the UK of the *Human Rights Act 1998*. In Ian Cram, ed., *Borrie & Lowe: The Law of Contempt*, 4th ed. (London: LexisNexis, 2010), para. 1.5 (footnotes omitted) the authors have described this new constitutional landscape in the following terms:

> The elevations of rights to (i) freedom of expression (as enshrined in Article 10 of the European Convention on Human Rights ("ECHR")) and (ii) respect for private and family life (under Article 8 of the ECHR) to the status of constitutional values occurred with the passing into law of the Human Rights Act 1998. As a matter of domestic law therefore, the 1998 Act requires some recalibration of the balance that [has] previously been struck at common law and statute between claims to freedom of expression and the interests of administration of justice (including the right to a fair trial which is also expressly protected in Article 6 of the ECHR) and individual privacy. The various ways in which these sometimes conflicting values and interests are being played out in specific contexts features across a number of the chapters in this new edition and gives a particular currency to its contents.
>
> Whilst it is not suggested that domestic law shows signs of moving towards a US-style broad acceptance of court-related speech (and adopting consequently a more obviously remedial focus that seeks to insulate the trial process from external comment and prejudice), it may be instructive in this regard to consider the Canadian experience under the 1982 Charter of Rights and Freedoms. The Canadian settlement of 1982 conferred constitutional status upon freedom of expression and the right to a fair trial. In the context of clashes between freedom of expression and the administration of justice under the pre-1982 common law rules, freedom of expression interests were invariably subordinated to "more pressing" administration of justice claims. According to Lamer CJ in *Dagenais v. Canadian Broadcasting* [Corp.], however, the position after 1982 altered:
>
>> "Like the right of an accused to a fair trial, a fundamental principle of our justice which is now protected by s. 11(d) of the Charter, freedom of expression, including freedom of the press, is now recognised as a paramount value in Canadian society, as demonstrated by its enshrinement as a constitutionally protected right in s. 2(b) of the Charter."
>
> The task of the domestic judiciary (assisted to some extent by rulings from Strasbourg) has been to work through the implications of this new constitutional landscape, assessing *inter alia* the extent to which old, common law restrictions on media reporting and comment are compatible

with the Human Rights Act 1998. At the same time, privacy-based restrictions which may in the past have been supported by reference to a generalised concern to protect the administration of justice, can now be promulgated more firmly by reference to Article 8 and even in extreme cases, Article 2 (right to life).

The Supreme Court of Canada has addressed the criteria to be applied when a court is deciding to issue a publication ban on material that may prejudice a person's right to a fair trial in *Dagenais v. CBC*, [1994] 3 SCR 835. The CBC proposed airing a program titled *The Boys of St. Vincent*, a fictional account of the sexual and physical abuse of students kept in a Catholic boarding school. The respondents were all former or existing members of the Christian Brothers religious order, charged with offences that had taken place in a Catholic training school. They sought an interlocutory injunction restraining the CBC from airing the program. The trial court granted the injunction. The Court of Appeal modified the order, and the Supreme Court set it aside. For the majority Lamer CJ stated:

> A publication ban should only be ordered when:
>
> (a) Such a ban is *necessary* in order to prevent a real and substantial risk to the fairness of the trial, because reasonably available alternative measures will not prevent the risk; and
>
> (b) The salutary effects of the publication ban outweigh the deleterious effects to the free expression of those affected by the ban (at 878).

The right to disseminate judicial proceedings is part of the Supreme Court's developing jurisprudence on the "open court principle" as a part of the right to freedom of expression enshrined in the Charter. See *Canadian Broadcasting Corp. v. The Queen*, [2011] 1 SCR 65.

5. In *Canada (Human Rights Commission) v. Canadian Liberty Net*, [1998] 1 SCR 626 the defendant was operating a voice mail system that promoted anti-Semitic and racist comments. After an investigation the Canadian Human Rights Commission believed such activities were a violation of the *Canadian Human Rights Act* and requested that the Human Rights Tribunal be impanelled to make a final determination. In the interim, the commission sought an interlocutory injunction from the Federal Court to restrain the defendant from continuing its voice mail system pending the tribunal's determination. Neither the commission nor the tribunal had power to give interim orders and thus the commission requested the relief from the Federal Court in reliance of its inherent jurisdiction. In the course of its judgment the Supreme Court indicated that in matters of pure speech the *American Cyanamid* test was inappropriate. In particular, the application of the irreparable harm and balance of convenience criteria were viewed as "grievously undermining" the right of freedom of expression as enshrined in s. 2(b) of the Charter. Both criteria made it practically impossible for the person making the expression ever to satisfy the test because his or her particular interest in speech is unlikely to have a "tangible or measurable interest other than the expression itself." In contrast, the other party will almost always have some interest to benefit from the suppression of speech. The Supreme Court declined to rule on what would be an appropriate threshold test because the issue was moot by the time it came before the court. However, it did comment favourably upon the approach adopted in *Champagne v. Collège d'enseignement général et professionnel (CEGEP) de Jonquière*, [1997] RJQ 2395 (CA) to the effect that prior restraint of allegedly defamatory material will only be justified in the "rarest and clearest of cases" (Jeffrey Berryman, *Equitable Remedies* (Toronto: Irwin Law, 2000), at 47). See also *Canada (Human*

Rights Commission) v. Winnicki (FC), [2006] 3 FCR 446 (TD), restraining the publication of hate speech over the Internet pending a ruling by the Canadian Human Rights Commission.

6. In Manitoba, ss. 57(1) and (2) of the *Court of Queen's Bench Act*, SM 1988-89, c. C280 state:

> 57(1) Subject to subsection (3), the court shall not grant an injunction that restrains a person from exercising the right to freedom of speech.
>
> (2) For the purposes of this section, the communication by a person on a public thoroughfare of information by true statements, either orally or through printed material or through any other means, is an exercise of the right to freedom of speech.

7. The use of the Internet to defame raises new concerns. The fact that it is relatively easy and inexpensive to disseminate defamatory material has meant that courts have been asked to revisit the appropriate test for interlocutory relief. The response of courts has not been to alter the test but to ensure that it is applied in a "careful, considered and appropriate manner." (See *Canadian National Railway Co. v. Google Inc.*, [2010] OJ no. 2230 (Sup. Ct.) and *Barrick Gold Corp. v. Lopehandia* (2004), 71 OR (3d) 416 (CA).)

UNDERTAKINGS

An almost universal requirement placed on an applicant who has been granted an interlocutory injunction will be to give an undertaking as to damages. This undertaking is designed to protect the defendant should he or she be successful at trial.

Rule 40.03 of the Ontario Rules of Civil Procedure states:

> 40.03 On a motion for an interlocutory injunction or mandatory order, the moving party shall, unless the court orders otherwise, undertake to abide by any order concerning damages that the court may make if it ultimately appears that the granting of the order has caused damage to the responding party for which the moving party ought to compensate the responding party.

See also BC r. 45(6), Man. r. 40.03, and NB r. 40.04.

Vieweger Construction Co. v. Rush & Thompkins Construction Ltd.
[1965] SCR 195

[The appellant had entered into an arrangement with Company A to supply equipment and undertake drilling work in connection with a contract which Company A had with the respondents. A subsequent disagreement led to the withdrawal of Company A from the project. The respondents then entered into an arrangement with the appellants whereby they could continue to use the appellant's equipment at the same rent agreed to between appellant and Company A. When the respondent fell into arrears on the rental payments, the appellants sought to remove their equipment. The respondents then obtained an injunction preventing the appellants from removing the equipment. The respondent alleged that the appellants were in a partnership arrangement with Company A and therefore the appellants were contractually bound to complete the project and were not entitled to any rental payments. The injunction was granted with the usual undertaking as to damages.

At trial the appellants succeeded but were not allowed damages attributable to the rent which accrued during the period of the interim injunction. They appealed. On the question of damages pursuant to the undertaking ...]

SPENCE J (at 206): ... I turn now to the appellant company's claim for damages flowing from the interim injunction granted on October 13, 1959, and continued on the motion to vacate. The learned trial Judge in refusing the appellant company's claim for such damages adopted the principle stated by Hyndman J, in *McBrantney v. Sexsmith*, [1924] 3 DLR 84 (Alta. SC) at pp. 87-8, as follows:

> The law is well settled that it does not follow that because an interlocutory injunction is dissolved before or after trial the successful defendant is therefore or in any event entitled to damages. The test is whether the plaintiff, by the suppression of facts, or misrepresentation, or maliciously, improperly obtains the injunction.

It would appear that the proper test was laid down by the Court of Appeal in *Griffith v. Blake* (1984), 27 Ch. D 474 (CA). There, the Court of Appeal was concerned with a dictum of the late Master of the Rolls in *Smith v. Day* (1882), 21 Ch. D 421 (CA), to the effect that the undertaking as to damages only applies where the plaintiff has acted improperly in obtaining the injunction, and all the members of the Court expressed dissent with that view. Baggally LJ said, at p. 476:

> If the defendants turn out to be right, it appears to me that they can, under the undertaking, obtain compensation for all injury sustained by them from the granting of the injunction.

And Cotton LJ said at p. 477:

> But I am of opinion that his *dictum* is not well founded, and that the rule is, that whenever the undertaking is given, and the plaintiff ultimately fails on the merits, an inquiry as to damages will be granted *unless there are special circumstances to the contrary*. (The italics are my own.)

Counsel for the respondent company before this Court agreed to such statement of the principle, but submitted that in this case there were special circumstances as it had not been shown that the respondent company obtained the injunction by any perjury or misrepresentation and that since two Judges in the Trial Division and three Judges in the Court of Appeal were of the opinion that the respondent company was entitled to its injunction, if this Court were of the other view it would be an example of judicial error and not any misrepresentation by the respondent company which caused the injunction to issue.

I am of the opinion that these circumstances do not constitute such "special circumstances" as were in the mind of Cotton LJ. There are examples of plaintiffs who are public bodies and who acted in the public interest to hold the situation *in statu quo* until the rights were determined. There are other cases where the defendant, although he succeeded upon technical grounds, certainly had been guilty of conduct which did not move the Court to exercise its discretion in his favour. In these cases, the Court had found the "special circumstances" which entitled it to refuse a reference as to damages. Here, the respondent company throughout has insisted that very considerable items of heavy construction machinery be held the plaintiff could not use them and therefore make any profit from them, and that situation continued for months until the respondent company's use for the equipment ended.

I am of the opinion that it is an ordinary case of an injunction granted upon a plaintiff's application and upon the plaintiff's undertaking, and that the plaintiff should be required to make good its undertaking. I would, therefore, direct that there be a reference in the ordinary course of procedure in the Province of Alberta to determine such damages and that the appellant company be granted judgment for such damages and the costs of the reference.

It is said that the damages can now be ascertained at the sum of $30,500. Counsel for the respondent, however, submits that there has been no proper proof of damages in that amount and, reading the record, I am of the opinion that under the circumstances in this case this Court would not be entitled to make a specific award of damages upon the evidence set out therein.

In the result, I would allow the appeal, restore the judgment in favour of the appellant company upon the counterclaim for $42,769.64, direct a reference as aforesaid, and allow the appellants its costs throughout.

Appeal allowed.

NOTES

1. Examples of Spence J's "special circumstances" entitling a court to refuse damages after an undertaking is given are found in *A.-G. for Ontario v. Yeotes* (1982), 35 OR (2d) 248 (defendant found loophole in *Planning Act* that allowed him to continue a "checkerboarding" scheme) and in *Capital Regional District v. Heinrich* (1984), 59 BCLR 170 (municipality unsuccessful in enforcing zoning bylaw that prevented auctions on the defendant's premises).

2. An applicant's impecuniosity and, therefore, inability to give a meaningful undertaking should not be used as a barrier against granting relief. See *Allen v. Jambo Holdings Ltd.*, [1980] 1 WLR 1252 (CA). However, in the terms of Dunn J in *Cambridge Credit Corp. Ltd. v. Surfers' Paradise Forests Ltd.*, [1977] Qd. R 261, at 264 (SC), impecuniosity is a "potent factor to take into account when deciding whether to make an order which must be based on a provisional opinion concerning questions of fact and law."

3. In *Delta v. Nationwide Auctions Inc.* (1979), 11 BCLR 346, the plaintiff, Corporation of Delta, which had initially sought specific performance of a land use agreement, was proposing to enact a bylaw to unilaterally cancel the agreement. The defendant moved for an interlocutory injunction to prevent the plaintiff from passing the bylaw. Where the defendant was financially unable to give an undertaking the court exercised its discretion in dispensing with the need for one.

4. A court can require a defendant to give an undertaking to protect the applicant where the interlocutory injunction has been refused. See *Cemasco Management Ltd. v. Analysis Film Releasing Corp.* (1979), 24 OR (2d) 398:

> ANDERSON J: This is a motion for an interlocutory injunction prohibiting the defendant from granting or purporting to grant the distribution rights to the film "L'Innocente" until the trial or other disposition of the action.
>
> I do not propose to discuss the material in detail. I accept that the plaintiff has made out that there is a substantial issue to be tried in the action, but in my view it is not a proper case for an interlocutory injunction.

I do not consider that the plaintiff has shown that irreparable injury or any injury that cannot be adequately compensated in damages will result if the order is not made. In coming to this conclusion, I have not overlooked the submission of counsel for the plaintiff that the film in question is unique.

I am not prepared to give to the word "may" as used by Chief Justice Evans in *Yule Inc. v. Atlantic Pizza Delight Franchise (1968) Ltd.* (1977), 17 OR (2d) 505 (HC, Div. Ct.) at p. 507, when speaking of prospective irreparable injury, the interpretation contended for by counsel for the plaintiff, namely, that all that is required to be shown is a possibility of such injury. To do so would, in my view, fly in the face of the general proposition that the case for an interlocutory injunction must be clear. A real probability of irreparable injury should be shown.

Nor do I consider that the balance of convenience favours the making of the order. If the order is made, the defendant will be precluded from distributing the film which, apart from the claim of the plaintiff, it has a legal right to do. As between permitting the defendant to pursue its legal right or preventing it, on the assertion of the plaintiff's right and until that right can be determined, I see no reason to prefer the latter over the former. On the material before me both parties might lose if distribution of the film were enjoined until trial.

However, in the event that the plaintiff succeeds in the action, the assessment of damages should be facilitated by assuring that proper records are available for that purpose. The defendant, as a term upon which injunction is withheld, should file with the Court an undertaking to make, maintain and keep, until the trial or other final disposition of this action, full and complete records concerning any agreement for distribution in Canada of the motion picture film, "L'Innocente" and of all fees, commissions or other revenue received by or on behalf of the defendant in any way arising from or related to such distribution. The undertaking should be in form satisfactory to the Court and before being filed should be served on the solicitors for the plaintiff, whose right to make submissions to the Court relative to the undertaking is hereby reserved. The undertaking may be executed by the solicitors for the defendant; if by the defendant, the undertaking shall be accompanied by proof of the sufficiency of such execution as binding the defendant.

Upon filing the undertaking in form approved by the Court, an order may issue dismissing this motion with costs in the cause.

If such undertaking has not been filed in due form by Monday, June 11th, the plaintiff may apply *ex parte* for an interlocutory injunction as asked in cls. (c) and (d) of para. 9 of the statement of claim.

The terms of the endorsement made by Hughes J, on April 19, 1979, shall continue until the making of the injunction order.

I shall retain the matter in the meantime.

5. Where an injunction is sought by the Crown to enforce its own proprietary rights, an undertaking in damages will be required. Where the injunction is sought to enforce public rights it is discretionary as to whether an undertaking is required, although normally it is not. In *Hoffmann-La Roche & Co. v. Secretary of State for Trade and Industry*, [1975] AC 295 (HL (Eng.)) the Secretary of State for Trade and Industry sought an injunction to enforce a ruling of the Monopolies Commission which had resulted in an order requiring the plaintiff to lower prices on two drug products. The plaintiff questioned the legality of such an order as having been made in contravention of the rules of natural justice. On the interlocutory injunction

application the trial judge denied the injunction where the Secretary of State refused to give an undertaking as to damages.

In the Court of Appeal, the injunction was granted without requiring an undertaking.

An appeal to the House of Lords was dismissed (Lord Wilberforce dissenting). In the course of his judgment Lord Diplock made the following remarks (at 363):

The right of the Attorney-General, acting on behalf of the Crown as parens patriae, to apply to the court for an injunction to restrain the commission of illegal acts which affect the public was recognised in the 19th century. It was not, however, the practice for the Attorney-General to act on his own initiative. Although this type of action was brought in his name as nominal plaintiff it was brought "on the relation" of a subject and the conduct of the case was undertaken by the "relator." The Attorney-General's function in a relator action was in effect limited to determining, when consent to the use of his name was sought, whether the breach of law alleged by the relator was sufficiently injurious to the public interest to justify its being restrained by injunction. The reason for adopting this device appears to have been that at that time orders for costs could not be made for or against the Crown. The Attorney-General had an undoubted right to sue alone *ex officio* in a law enforcement action (*Attorney-General v. Oxford, Worcester and Wolverhampton Railway Co.* (1854), 2 WR 330 (Ch.)), but in that event the expense incurred by him in doing so would have to be met from public funds win or lose, while the defendant if he lost was out of pocket for the costs of his successful defence. So instead of suing *ex officio* it became the practice for the Attorney-General to sue on the relation of a subject so that orders for costs could be made for and against the relator (*Attorney-General v. Cockermouth Local Board* (1874), LR 18 Eq. 172 at p. 176). For practical purposes once the Attorney-General's consent had been obtained the relator stood in the shoes of a plaintiff in an ordinary suit between subject and subject, and it appears that when the practice was introduced in ordinary suits of making an undertaking as to damages a condition of the grants of interim injunctions a similar undertaking was required in relator actions from the relator, but it was never required from the Attorney-General.

The special position of the Crown with regard to costs was abolished by section 7 of the *Administration of Justice (Miscellaneous Provisions) Act 1933*, but in spite of this the practice of bringing law enforcement actions only on the relation of a subject remained unchanged. So did the practice of requiring undertakings as to damages to be given by relators. Both practices have continued to be followed since the passing of the *Crown Proceedings Act 1947*. This Act, indeed, expressly excludes relator actions from its procedural provisions. It is only in law enforcement actions brought under recent statutes which provide expressly that compliance with some provision of the Act shall be enforceable by civil proceedings by the Crown for an injunction that the Crown sues directly and not by way of a relator action. Three statutes which contain provisions of this kind are the *Monopolies and Restrictive Practices (Inquiry and Control) Act 1948*, the *Wireless Telegraphy Act 1949* and the *Resale Prices Act 1964*.

So even before the passing of the *Crown Proceedings Act 1947* the fact that the suit was brought to enforce jus publicum was not of itself sufficient to displace the ordinary rule that a defendant was entitled to the usual undertaking in damages as a condition of the grant of any interlocutory injunction against him, though the undertaking was exacted from the relator and not from the Crown on whose behalf the Attorney-General was the nominal plaintiff in the suit. I see no reason since the passing of that Act why a rigid rule that the Crown itself should *never* be required to give the usual undertaking in damages should be retained in those law enforcement actions where the Crown now sues without a relator.

Nevertheless, the converse does not follow that in this type of action the court in granting an interim injunction ought *always* to require an undertaking as to damages from the Crown. A relator owes no duty to the public to initiate any law enforcement action. He does not usually do so unless he or a section of the public which he represents has some special interest to protect, in enforcing that particular law, that is not shared by the public at large. Even if he has no special interest—and it is not essential that he should—his action nevertheless is that of an officious, though well-meaning, bystander who is not content merely to stand by. When, however, a statute provides that compliance with its provisions shall be enforceable by civil proceedings by the Crown for an injunction, and particularly if this is the only method of enforcement for which it provides, the Crown does owe a duty to the public at large to initiate proceedings to secure that the law is not flouted, and not simply to leave it to the chance that some relator may be willing to incur the expense and trouble of doing so.

I agree therefore with all your Lordships that the practice of exacting an undertaking in damages from the Crown as a condition of the grant of an interlocutory injunction in this type of law enforcement action ought not to be applied as a matter of course, as it should be in actions between subject and subject, in relator actions, and in actions by the Crown to enforce or to protect its proprietary or contractual rights. On the contrary, the propriety of requiring such an undertaking from the Crown should be considered in the light of the particular circumstances of the case.

See also *Kirklees Metropolitan Borough Council v. Wickes Building Supplies Ltd.*, [1992] 3 All ER 717 (HL) where the House of Lords affirmed its position taken in *Hoffmann-La Roche & Co. v. Secretary of State for Trade and Industry*, above.

6. In *Attorney General for Ontario v. Yeotes* (1980), 28 OR (2d) 577, the Crown gave an undertaking in an action to enforce a provincial planning law. The injunction was granted. On appeal, (1981), 31 OR (2d) 589 (CA), the injunction was dismissed and an order to determine damages was made. At the later hearing (1982), 35 OR (2d) 248 (HC) no damages were assessed. The Crown fell into the category of "special circumstances" justifying the court's refusal to enforce the undertaking. There is no discussion in any of these cases as to the propriety of requiring the Crown to give an undertaking to enforce a public right.

7. In *Church of Jesus Christ of Latter Day Saints v. King* (1998), 41 OR (3d) 389 (CA) the church commenced an action against the defendants alleging fraud in a land deal. In interlocutory proceedings of this action the church had gained both Anton Piller and Mareva injunctions. The church did not prosecute its action and, subsequently, the defendant brought a motion to dissolve the interlocutory injunction and dismiss the action. The defendant also asked for damages, being the solicitor-and-client costs he had incurred in defending himself, pursuant to the undertaking the church had given at the time. Findlayson JA for the Court of Appeal stated:

Analysis

The motions judge proceeded on the basis that he was satisfied that when the statement of claim was issued, the plaintiffs had a reasonable basis to believe that the defendants (the appellants in this hearing) were parties to a dishonest scheme to defraud the Church through a series of land "flips." He acknowledged that the appellants continued to assert their integrity but that a full trial would be necessary to determine this issue between the parties. He found that there were no damages caused by the issue of the interim injunction and therefore no basis to enforce the undertaking as to damages given on the motion to obtain the injunction. He awarded the appellant's party and party costs fixed at $9,950. He awarded to the respondent Church the costs of the motion before him, fixed at $750.

It seems to me, with respect to the motions judge, that he treated the issue of costs solely as an exercise of his discretion in an abandoned action. In this situation, costs follow the event and in the ordinary case they would be restricted to party and party costs. Since the action was justified, in the opinion of the motions judge, there was no basis for imposing an additional sanction on the plaintiffs simply because they had alleged fraud. ...

The result arrived at by the motions judge is not consonant with the critical role played by undertakings made in pursuit of interlocutory relief. They find their origins in equity. It is trite law, but bears repeating here, that a plaintiff's undertaking as to damages reflects the recognition by the court of the risk that a defendant may be wrongfully damaged by an injunction granted on a summary hearing. Courts exercising equitable jurisdiction have long required undertakings before exercising their powers in this regard; rule 40.03 is but the codification of this equitable principle.

The importance of an undertaking is all the more critical when the interlocutory relief sought and granted consists of *Mareva* injunctions and *Anton Piller* orders, as was the case here. In addition, the increasing ease with which plaintiffs may obtain interlocutory relief necessarily requires correspondingly enforced undertakings. In this regard, I adopt the language of Zuber JA, writing in *Nelson Burns & Co. v. Gratham Industries Ltd.* (1987), 23 CPC (2d) 279 at p. 288, 25 OAC 89:

> As a result of a decision of the House of Lords in *American Cyanamid Co. v. Ethicon Ltd.*, [1975] AC 396, [1975] 1 All ER 504, the balance of convenience test has largely displaced an earlier view that an applicant could obtain an interlocutory injunction only if he could show a strong *prima facie* case. Whatever the differences may be between the two standards, it is now plain that in Ontario interlocutory injunctions are easier to obtain than was the case prior to the *American Cyanamid* case.
>
> Because of this change, and because of the number of such injunctions that are sought, it is appropriate to emphasize the serious nature of the undertaking to pay damages which is a condition of the issuance of the interlocutory injunction. In the ordinary course the unsuccessful plaintiff must understand that he is obliged to pay damages in accordance with his undertaking without quibble, and Courts generally will be unsympathetic towards [t]hose who seek to resile from such an obligation.

Although there is discretion, both in equity and in rule 40.03, to excuse a plaintiff of its obligations under an undertaking, there is no reason in this case to excuse the respondents. There is no "special circumstance," to use the language of *Vieweger Construction Co. v. Rush & Tompkins Construction Ltd.*, [1965] SCR 195, 48 DLR (2d) 509, that would lead this court to excuse this plaintiff. Although it is open to a plaintiff to argue that it sought the interlocutory relief in good faith, that is seldom a determinative factor in deciding whether an undertaking will be enforced; see *Wasaga Beach (District) v. Fielding*, [1947] OR 321 (HCJ), affirmed [1947] OR 1012 (CA). ...

I am of the opinion that as rule 40.03 is but the codification of equitable practice, it is to be exercised within the bounds of discretion dictated by equitable principles. Accordingly, in the appropriate case, costs may indeed be awarded under the rubric of damages. This is such a case. The appellants endured, for more than five years, the damage to their professional reputation that flows from the serious allegations made here. In addition, they have borne the expense of defending against the action and the attendant motions. Simply because they had no stake in the substantive issues that were the basis of the action is no reason to conclude that the interlocutory injunction caused them no damage. The only issue that remains is the scale on which the costs should be ordered.

This court has not previously decided the question before us. However, there have been instances where a motions judge, in an exercise of discretion in awarding costs on an abandoned or discontinued action, has decided to elevate the usual scale of costs to solicitor and client based upon the nature of the allegations made in the action. Had this been done in the case in appeal, the cost issue would be academic. While the case law on this question is divided, it is instructive as to the factors that motions judges have looked to in making such an award. Most have found that an award on this scale is appropriate where allegations of fraud and other serious malfeasance are either baselessly made or are never proven at trial; where the effect of the allegations made or of the granting of the interlocutory relief is to seriously affect a defendant's professional reputation; and where a plaintiff fails to retract unmeritorious allegations in a timely fashion. ...

Ordinarily, this court will not interfere with an order of costs. It is a classic exercise of discretion and will not be treated lightly. However, I am not satisfied that the motions judge recognized the significance of the undertaking as to damages given by the defendants in order to obtain this most intrusive injunctive relief against the appellant solicitors. Instead of asking himself if it was reasonable for the plaintiffs to assert fraud, in my opinion he should have addressed the issue of whether the solicitor–client costs incurred by the appellants in order to successfully defend themselves against the serious allegations relating to their practice constituted damages within the meaning of the undertaking. On my reading of the endorsement, he appeared to have accepted the argument of the respondent Church in this court that costs were outside the purview of damages within the meaning of the undertaking.

I want to be clear that I am not suggesting that costs on a solicitor–client basis must always be granted pursuant to the undertaking as to damages given by a plaintiff seeking injunctive relief. But this is not to say that they are not warranted in the particular case. I think the motions judge erred in not taking into consideration whether the full costs of retaining a solicitor fell within the ambit of the undertaking as to damages. That undertaking was given to the court to obtain the injunction.

In my opinion, properly considered, this case more than warranted an award of solicitor and client costs. Since the respondents maintained to the end, including on this appeal, that the allegations were true, such an award is the only public rehabilitation of the appellants' reputation.

8. There is no discretion in Manitoba with respect to an applicant's undertaking. It must be given as a condition of granting the interlocutory injunction. See *Griffin Steel Foundries Ltd. v. Canadian Association of Industrial, Mechanical and Allied Workers* (1977), 80 DLR (3d) 634 (Man. CA).

It is a well established principle of our law that a party who seeks the extraordinary relief of an *ex parte* injunction must make full and frank disclosure of the case. The rationale for this rule is obvious. The judge hearing an *ex parte* motion and the absent party are literally at the mercy of the party seeking injunctive relief. The ordinary checks and balances of the adversary system are not operative. The opposite party is deprived of the opportunity to challenge the factual and legal contentions advanced by the moving party in support of the injunction. The situation is rife with the danger that an injustice will be done to the party. ...

For that reason, the law imposes an exceptional duty on the party who seeks *ex parte* relief. That party is not entitled to present only its side of the case in the best possible light, as it would if the other side were present. Rather, it is incumbent on the moving party to make a balanced presentation of the facts in law. The moving party must state its own case fairly and must inform the court of any points of facts or law known to it which favour the other side. The duty of full and frank disclosure is required to mitigate the obvious risk of injustice inherent in any situation where a judge is asked to grant an order without hearing from the other side.

What is required to meet the obligation of full and frank disclosure has been articulated by Gibson LJ in *Brink's-MAT Ltd. v. Elcombe*, [1988] 3 All ER 188, at 192 (CA), and endorsed by the Manitoba Court of Appeal in *Pulse Microsystems Ltd. v. SafeSoft Systems Inc.* (1996), 134 DLR (4th) 701, at 713:

(i) Disclosure of material facts—those which are material for the judge to know when dealing with the application as made. Materiality is for the court to determine, not the plaintiff's legal advisers.

(ii) The applicant must make proper inquiries before the application is made. This is an objective test and covers facts that the applicant could have known if reasonable steps had been taken over such inquiries.

(iii) The extent of these inquiries must depend on all the circumstances of the case including (a) the nature of the applicant's case, (b) the probable effect on the defendant if the order is granted, and (c) the degree of legitimate urgency at the time of making inquiries.

(iv) If material non-disclosure is proven then the court should ensure that the applicant is deprived of any advantage he or she may have derived from the wrongfully obtained injunction. However, whether the fact not disclosed is of sufficient materiality to justify or require immediate discharge of the order without examination of the merits depends on the importance of the facts to the issues which were to be decided by the judge on the application. The innocence of the applicant in either not perceiving the relevance of the non-disclosed fact or not being aware of the fact itself, is an important but not decisive consideration.

(v) Not every omission to disclose will automatically result in the discharge of the injunction. Ultimately it is a question of how the court should exercise its discretion.

Failure to abide by the duty to make full and frank disclosure will be taken seriously by the court. In addition to the discharge of the injunction it may also lead to an adverse award for solicitor-and-client costs and ultimately an award of punitive damages at the trial of the merits. However, the court always retains a residual discretion not to dissolve the injunction where there has been a failure to make full disclosure and where dissolution would amount to an injustice. See *United States of America v. Yemec* (2003), 67 OR (3d) 394 (SCJ).

Interlocutory Injunctions Against Unknown Persons: John and Jane Doe Orders

In some situations a plaintiff will not know the names of all the potential defendants who are impinging on his or her rights. Common examples are an interlocutory injunction used to prevent protesters picketing a plaintiff's business or from trespassing, or where the plaintiff's intellectual property rights are being violated by unknown street or market vendors. In these types of situations the courts have condoned the use of a John and Jane Doe order. Two distinct questions arise: can an injunction be made against a person who is unknown, and can an injunction be effective against a person who is not a party to the litigation? The Supreme Court of Canada has answered affirmatively to both these questions in *MacMillan Bloedel Ltd. v. Simpson*, [1996] 2 SCR 1048, a judgment considered in chapter 7, "Injunctions."

"John and Jane Doe" has also been authorized by a court as the style of cause where the court has agreed to keep the identity of a litigant hidden from the public. See *John Doe v. Canadian Broadcasting Corporation* (1993), 86 BCLR (2d) 202 and 216 (CA).

The Federal Court of Canada has created a unique form of John and Jane Doe order called a "rolling order." It is a hybrid Anton Piller type of order (a type of civil search warrant and discussed below) designed to deal with counterfeiting and pirating of intellectual property. See the judgment of Reed J in *Fila Canada Inc. v. Doe*, [1996] 3 FC 493 (TD), below in the section on Anton Piller orders.

The ability to enforce injunctions against unknown parties has been discussed in J. Berryman, "Injunctions—The Ability To Bind Non-Parties" (2002), 81 *Can. Bar Rev.* 207.

For an example of an injunction that is truly against all the world, or *contra mundum*, see *Venables v. News Group Papers Ltd.* (unreported, 30/7/2010, Justice Bean, Central Criminal Court, London) available at http://www.judiciary.gov.uk/NR/rdonlyres/3C90FDFC-764E-48D2-920A-45764678615B/0/rvvenablesothersjudgment.pdf.

APPELLATE COURT REVIEW

The granting of an interlocutory injunction is a discretionary matter. In *Hadmor Productions Ltd. v. Hamilton*, [1983] 1 AC 191 (HL (Eng.)), the House of Lords commented upon the function of an appellate court when considering an appeal from a judge with respect to granting an interlocutory injunction, per Lord Diplock (at 220):

> Before adverting to the evidence that was before the judge and the additional evidence that was before the Court of Appeal, it is I think appropriate to remind your Lordships of the limited function of an appellate court in an appeal of this kind. An interlocutory injunction is a discretionary relief and the discretion whether or not to grant it is vested in the High Court judge by whom the application for it is heard. On an appeal from the judge's grant or refusal of an interlocutory injunction the function of an appellate court, whether it be the Court of Appeal or your Lordships' House, is not to exercise an independent discretion of its own. It must defer to the judge's exer-

cise of his discretion and must not interfere with it merely on the ground that the members of the appellate court would have exercised the discretion differently. The function of the appellate court is initially one of review only. I may set aside the judge's exercise of his discretion on the ground that it was based on a misunderstanding of the law or of the evidence before him or on an inference that particular facts existed or did not exist, which, although it was one that might legitimately have been drawn on the evidence that was before the judge, can be demonstrated to be wrong by further evidence that has become available by the time of the appeal, or on the ground that there has been a change of circumstances after the judge made his order that would have justified his acceding to an application to vary it. Since reasons given by judges for granting or refusing interlocutory injunctions may sometimes be sketchy, there may also be occasional cases where even though no erroneous assumption of law or fact can be identified the judge's decision to grant or refuse the injunction is so aberrant that it must be set aside on the ground that no reasonable judge regardful of his duty to act judicially could have reached it. It is only if and after the appellate court has reached the conclusion that the judge's exercise of his discretion must be set aside for one or other of these reasons that it becomes entitled to exercise an original discretion of its own.

This statement of Lord Diplock was approved of by the Supreme Court of Canada in *Vickery v. Nova Scotia Supreme Court (Prothonotary)*, [1991] 1 SCR 671 at [103].

INTERLOCUTORY INJUNCTIONS TO RESTRAIN THE DISPOSITION OF ASSETS PENDING TRIAL: THE MAREVA INJUNCTION

General

The Mareva injunction is a special form of interlocutory injunction that balances two competing interests: (1) that the assets of a defendant are sacrosanct until judgment, commonly referred to as the rule in *Lister v. Stubbs*, (1890) 45 Ch. D 1 (CA) and (2) the need to prevent the defendant from removing assets from the jurisdiction of the court in an attempt to thwart the legitimate claims of the plaintiff.

The Mareva injunction has become a most potent weapon to protect plaintiffs against defendants who seek to take advantage of technology that has allowed the electronic transfer of assets away from the court's jurisdiction. A further innovation has been the worldwide Mareva injunction, which seeks to prevent the defendant from transferring assets from one foreign jurisdiction, where the plaintiff may be able to gain reciprocal enforcement of its judgment, into another foreign jurisdiction where the defendant's assets will be, practically speaking, judgment proof.

Mareva Compania Naviera SA v. International Bulkcarriers SA
[1975] 2 Lloyd's Rep. 509; [1980] 1 All ER 213 (CA)

LORD DENNING MR: This raises a very important point of practice. It follows on a case which we had the other day, *Nippon Yusen Kaisha v. Karageorgis*, [1975] 1 WLR 1093 (CA). The plaintiffs, Mareva Compania Naviera SA, are shipowners who owned the vessel *Mareva*.

They let it to the defendants, International Bulkcarriers SA, on a time charter for a trip out to the Far East and back. The vessel was to be put at the disposal of the defendants at Rotterdam. Hire was payable half monthly in advance and the rate was 3850 dollars a day from the time of delivery. The vessel was duly delivered to the defendants on May 12, 1975. The defendants subchartered it. They let it on a voyage charter to the President of India. Freight was payable under that voyage charter: 90 per cent was to be paid against the documents and the 10 per cent later.

Under that voyage charter the vessel was loaded at Bordeaux on May 29, 1975, with a cargo of fertilizer consigned to India. The Indian High Commission, in accordance with the obligations under the voyage charter, paid 90 per cent of the freight. But paid it to a bank in London. It was paid out to the Bank of Bilbao in London to the credit of the time charterers. The total sum which the India High Commission paid into the bank was £174,000. Out of that the time charterers paid to the shipowners, the plaintiffs, the first two instalments of the half monthly hire. They paid those instalments by credit transferred to the shipowners. The third was due on June 12, 1975; but the time charterers failed to pay it. They could easily have done it, of course, by making a credit transfer in favour of the shipowners. But they did not do it. Telexes passed which make it quite plain that the time charterers were unable to pay. They said they were not able to fulfil any part of their obligations under the charter, and they had no alternative but to stop trading. Their efforts to obtain further financial support had been fruitless.

Whereupon the owners of the vessel treated the defendants' conduct as repudiation of the charter. They issued a writ on June 20. They claimed the unpaid hire which comes to 30,800 US dollars and damages for the repudiation. The total will be very large. They have served the writ on agents here, and they have applied also for service out of the jurisdiction. But meanwhile they believe that there is a grave danger that these moneys in the bank in London will disappear. So they have applied for an injunction to restrain the disposal of those moneys which are now in the bank. They rely on the recent case of *Nippon Yusen Kaisha v. Karageorgis*, [1975] 1 WLR 1093 (CA). Mr. Justice Donaldson felt some doubt about that decision because we were not referred to *Lister v. Stubbs* (1890), 45 Ch. D 1 (CA). There are observations in that case to the effect that the Court has no jurisdiction to protect a creditor before he gets judgment. Lord Justice Cotton said:

> I know of no case where, because it was highly probable that if the action were brought to a hearing the plaintiff could establish that a debt was due to him from the defendant, the defendant has been ordered to give security until that has been established by the judgment or decree.

And Lord Justice Lindley said:

> [W]e should be doing what I conceive to be very great mischief if we were to stretch a sound principle to the extent to which the appellants ask us to stretch it. ...

Mr. Justice Donaldson felt that he was bound by *Lister v. Stubbs* and that he had no power to grant an injunction. But, in deference to the recent case, he did grant an injunction, but only until 17:00 today (June 23, 1975), on the understanding that by that time this Court would be able to reconsider the position.

Now Mr. Rix has been very helpful. He has drawn our attention not only to *Lister v. Stubbs* but also to s. 45 of the *Judicature Act*, which repeats s. 25(8) of the *Judicature Act, 1875*. It says:

> A *mandamus* or an injunction may be granted or a receiver appointed by an interlocutory order of the court in all cases in which it shall appear to the court to be just or convenient.

In *Beddow v. Beddow* (1878), 9 Ch. D 89, Sir George Jessel, the then Master of the Rolls, gave a very wide interpretation to that section. He said:

> I have unlimited power to grant an injunction in any case where it would be right or just to do so.

There is only one qualification to be made. The Court will not grant an injunction to protect a person who has no legal or equitable right whatever. That appears from *North London Railway Co. v. Great Northern Railway Co.* (1883), 11 QBD 30 (CA). But, subject to that qualification, the statute gives a wide general power to the Courts. It is well summarized in Halsbury's Laws of England, vol. 21, 3rd ed., p. 348, par. 729:

> [N]ow, therefore, whenever a right, which can be asserted either at law or in equity, does exist, then, whatever the previous practice may have been, the Court is enabled by virtue of this provision, in a proper case, to grant an injunction to protect that right.

In my opinion that principle applies to a creditor who has a right to be paid the debt owing to him, even before he has established his right by getting judgment for it. If it appears that the debt is due and owing—and there is a danger that the debtor may dispose of his assets so as to defeat it before judgment—the Court has jurisdiction in a proper case to grant an interlocutory judgment so as to prevent him disposing of those assets. It seems to me that this is a proper case for the exercise of this jurisdiction. There is money in a bank in London which stands in the name of these time charterers. The time charterers have control of it. They may at any time dispose of it or remove it out of this country. If they do so, the shipowners may never get their charter hire. The ship is now on the high seas. It has passed Cape Town on its way to India. It will complete the voyage and the cargo discharged. And the shipowners may not get their charter hire at all. In face of this danger, I think this Court ought to grant an injunction to restrain the defendants from disposing of these moneys now in the bank in London until the trial or judgment in this action. If the defendants have any grievance about it when they hear of it, they can apply to discharge it. But meanwhile the plaintiffs should be protected. It is only just and right that this Court should grant an injunction. I would therefore continue the injunction.

ROSKILL LJ: I agree that this injunction should be extended until judgment in the action or until further order. The application to this Court is made *ex parte*, and is necessitated by the fact that the learned Judge, Mr. Justice Donaldson, understandingly in the circumstances, refused to extend the injunction beyond 17:00 this afternoon (June 23, 1975). Though the admirable argument to which we have listened puts the case very fairly both for and against continuing the injunction, the fact remains that we have only heard argument from one side and I do not think it would be right to express any opinion as to what the result would be were this matter hereafter to be argued fully. But, as at present advised, it seems reasonably clear, first, that this Court has jurisdiction to continue this injunction, and, secondly, that the difficult question is whether on the present facts this Court ought at this stage to continue it until judgment or further order. Mr. Justice Donaldson, in his judgment of which we have a full note, has asked a number of other questions of this Court which at present it would be wrong for us to seek to answer. If the defendants were represented, it would no doubt be said on their behalf that the decision of this Court in *Lister v. Stubbs* precludes this Court, not as a matter of jurisdiction but as a matter of practice from granting this injunction.

Indeed it is right to say that, as far as my own experience in the Commercial Court is concerned, an injunction in this form has in the past from time to time been applied for but has been consistently refused. This Court should not, therefore, on an *ex parte* interlocutory application be too ready to disturb the practice of the past save for good reasons. But on the facts of this case, there are three good reasons for granting this injunction. First, this ship was on time charter from the plaintiffs to the defendants on the New York Produce form, which provided, a little unusually, for a daily rate of hire payable half-monthly in advance and only the first two half-monthly instalments have been paid; secondly, there has been what would seem to be a plain and unexcused default in the payment of the third half-monthly instalment, and indeed a repudiation of the time charter by the defendants; thirdly, that third instalment fell due when the ship was under voyage charter from the defendants as time charterers to the President of India as voyage charterers.

On the evidence the defendant time charterers have already received £174,000 from the voyage charterers. Yet they have sent a telex to the plaintiff shipowners in London on June 17 stating that their efforts to raise further financial support have been fruitless and that they have no alternative but to stop trading. If therefore this Court does not interfere by injunction, it is apparent that the plaintiffs will suffer a grave injustice which this Court has power to help avoid—the injustice being that the ship will have to continue on her voyage to India and perhaps—as is not unknown in Indian ports—wait a long time there for discharge without remuneration while the defendants will be able to dissipate that £174,000.

In my judgment it would be wrong to tolerate this if it can be avoided. If it is necessary to find a reason for distinguishing this case from *Lister v. Stubbs*, I would venture to suggest that it is at least arguable that the Court should interfere to protect the shipowners' rights which arise under cl. 18 of the time charter. The relevant part in lines 110 and 111 reads:

> That the Owners shall have a lien upon all cargoes, and all sub-freights for any amounts due under this Charter, including General Average contributions.

There is or may be a legal or perhaps equitable right which the owners may be entitled to have protected by the Court. The full extent and nature of that right has long been a controversial matter and which may have to be resolved hereafter and I therefore say no more about it.

For those rather narrow reasons I should continue this injunction until judgment or further order. It is open to the defendants to apply to discharge the injunction or to apply for a stay under the arbitration clause at any time if they are so advised. I agree with the order proposed by my Lord.

ORMROD LJ: I agree.

In my judgment the plaintiffs here have a very strong case on the merits. We have not heard any argument from the other side because it is an *ex parte* application. In these circumstances I would reserve my own views until I have heard argument from the other side if any such argument is put forward. But in the absence of any such argument, in my view this injunction should be continued.

LORD DENNING MR: So the injunction will be continued from today until the trial of the action or judgment or until further order.

Mr. Rix: Thank you, my Lord. There are two small matters. In the haste to get the matter before Mr. Justice Donaldson, the injunction as asked for was restraining the defendants or agents or otherwise—I wonder if that could be altered to the classic phrase.

LORD DENNING MR: The defendants their agents or servants or otherwise from disposing of the assets or moving them out of the jurisdiction—in case there is any argument.

Mr. Rix: Would your Lordship say with costs here and below?

LORD JUSTICE ROSKILL: It is an *ex parte* application. We do not normally give costs on an *ex parte* application.

LORD DENNING MR: No, I do not think we do. We could make it costs in cause.

LORD JUSTICE ROSKILL: Yes—costs in the cause.

LORD DENNING MR: Yes, costs in cause.

Mr. Rix: Thank you very much, my Lord.

From this decision, the Mareva jurisdiction has blossomed. In the United Kingdom a statutory foundation for Mareva injunctions was introduced in s. 37 of the *Supreme Court Act* 1981 (UK), c. 54. The injunction is now called a "freezing injunction" and can be found in the new Rules of Civil Procedure as r. 25.1(f), introduced as part of the overhaul of civil procedure in the United Kingdom undertaken in 1999. (See *Civil Procedure Act 1997* (UK), c. 12.) The United Kingdom has also issued an extensive practice direction governing the issuance and supervision of "freezing injunctions" found in the Rules of Civil Procedure, CPR Part 25, 6.1, online at http://www.justice.gov.uk/guidance/courts-and-tribunals/courts/procedure-rules/civil/contents/parts/part25.htm.

In Australia the High Court of Australia has recently indicated that the Mareva injunction is not an "injunction" but a "court order." It is issued against parties to a proceeding against whom final relief may be granted, to ensure effective exercise of the court's jurisdiction involved, and against non-parties where those orders are necessary to facilitate the administration of justice. See *Cardile v. LED Builders Pty Ltd.* (1998), 162 ALR 294 (High Ct. of Aust.).

The position throughout the Commonwealth can be contrasted with that adopted by the US Supreme Court in *Grupo Mexicano de Desarrollo v. Alliance Bond Fund Inc.*, 119 S Ct. 1961 (1999). In that case the court held in a close 5 to 4 decision that at the federal level there was no room for a Mareva type of order in the United States. The majority's decision was based on the fact that there had been a longstanding rule that a debtor's assets were sacrosanct before judgment and that the creation of this type of order was better left to the legislature.

The Mareva injunction was considered by the Supreme Court of Canada in the following case. Before reading the case, review the issue of jurisdiction to grant a Mareva injunction discussed at the commencement of this chapter.

Aetna Financial Services Ltd. v. Feigelman
[1985] 1 SCR 2

ESTEY J: The Manitoba Court of Appeal affirmed the trial judge's order granting an injunction which restrained the appellant from transferring certain identified assets out of Manitoba to the appellant's offices in either Toronto or Montreal. This appeal raises squarely and simply the question of the availability of interlocutory orders restraining a defendant in a civil action from disposing of or handling assets in any specific way prior to trial. In England this is said to have originated in a proceeding now identified by the expression "Mareva injunction."

The facts are few and simple. The appellant Aetna Financial Services Limited (for convenience hereinafter called "Aetna") is a company incorporated under the *Canada Business Corporations Act*, 1974-75-76 (Can.), c. 33, with its head office in the City of Montreal and offices in Toronto. At one time it had an office in Manitoba for the promotion of business but not for the processing of business. At the present time the company has contracted its operations largely, if not entirely, to the Montreal office. Its operations consist of the factoring of accounts receivable for its clients on a basis of recourse or non-recourse. In this business Aetna had only two accounts or customers in the Province of Manitoba, one of them being the respondent Pre-Vue Company (Canada) Ltd. The asset in question was acquired from the collection in receivership proceedings concerning the second Manitoba customer Sekine. This realization was in the approximate sum of $270,000 which Aetna was about to transfer to its offices outside Manitoba, either Toronto or Montreal, when these proceedings were commenced.

When the respondent Pre-Vue Company (Canada) Ltd. (for convenience hereinafter called "Pre-Vue") went into default under the debentures issued to and held by Aetna, Aetna appointed a receiver by extra-judicial unilateral action according to an asserted right under the debenture. The appointment of the receiver was subsequently confirmed by the Court of Queen's Bench in Manitoba. The appointment of the receiver was without prejudice to any action by Pre-Vue or its shareholders against Aetna or the receiver. The action against which the present application for injunction rests arose out of this. By statement of claim dated March 30, 1981, Pre-Vue and its shareholders commenced action claiming unliquidated damages, and alleging, *inter alia*, that Aetna, in contravention of the terms of the debenture, failed to give Pre-Vue the allotted time to cure its default, and therefore the appointment of the receiver was improper. There may well be issues arising out of this appointment of the receiver but they are not of concern in the disposition of this appeal dealing as it does with the interlocutory injunction only. Some two years after the confirmation by the court of the appointment of the receiver-manager, the respondents applied for and obtained the injunction in question, wherein it was ordered that the appellant be:

… restrained and enjoined, until the further order of the Court, from removing from Manitoba or otherwise disposing of or dealing with any of its assets within Manitoba, including and in particular any monies paid to or received by the receiver-manager appointed by the Defendant, Aetna Financial Services Limited, to take control and possession of the property and undertaking of Sekine Canada Ltd., save in so far as such assets do not exceed in value the sum of $997,711.21.

In July 1982, an application to set aside the *ex parte* interlocutory order was dismissed. The terms of the injunction were modified, however, so as to restrict the movement of assets by Aetna only to the extent of $250,000.

In the Court of Appeal, the majority determined that an injunction of the type herein issued by the Trial Division was available under the law of the Province of Manitoba and that in the circumstances in the exercise of discretion by the learned trial judge should not be the subject of intervention by the Court of Appeal. The majority varied the judgment of the Trial Division only to the extent of "permitting the discharge of the injunction, on the posting of security by Aetna."

Huband JA dissented, not on the grounds that the so-called Mareva injunction is not available in law in the Province of Manitoba, but that under the circumstances injunctive relief should not have been granted. His Lordship summarized his position [(1982), 19 Man. R (2d) 295, at 319 (CA)]:

It seems to me that a Mareva injunction should be issued in this jurisdiction only where a strong case has been made out that it is necessary to do so to prevent an imminent injustice.

Far from a strong case, I think that the present application for injunctive relief is decidedly weak. It has none of the elements of fraud or sham or movement of assets in order to escape lawful claims which have become part of the jurisprudence justifying Mareva-type injunctions.

There are three threshold issues:

(a) As a matter of law, is this type of injunction available in Manitoba?

(b) Is this type of injunction available in the circumstances revealed in the record on this appeal?

(c) Is the exercise of discretion by the court of first instance properly reviewable on appeal?

The rule as to the availability of an interlocutory injunction generally has been variously stated but, in my view, it is convenient to refer to the succinct description of that order as found in *Chesapeake & Ohio R Co. v. Ball*, [1953] OR 843, where McRuer CJHC stated, at pp. 854-5:

The granting of an interlocutory injunction is a matter of judicial discretion, but it is a discretion to be exercised on judicial principles. I have dealt with this matter at length because I wish to emphasize how important it is that parties should not be restrained by interlocutory injunctions unless some irreparable injury is likely to accrue to the plaintiff, and the Court should be particularly cautious where there is a serious question as to whether the plaintiff would ever succeed in the action. I may put it in a different way: If on one hand a fair *prima facie* case is made out and there will be irreparable damage if the injunction is not granted, it should be granted, but in deciding whether an interlocutory injunction should be granted the defendant's interests must receive the same consideration as the plaintiff's.

Reconsideration of the requirement that the plaintiff must show a "strong *prima facie* case" has come in the wake of the decision of the House of Lords in *American Cyanamid Co. v. Ethicon Ltd.*, [1975] AC 396 (HL (Eng.)). However, the other principles enunciated by McRuer CJHC remain unimpaired. As a general proposition, it can be fairly stated that in the scheme of litigation in this country, orders other than purely procedural ones are difficult to obtain from the court prior to trial. Where the injunction maintains the *status quo* in a way which is fair to both sides, the order is attainable; but, simply because the order would not injure the defendant is not sufficient reason to move the court to grant what is generally regarded as an extraordinary intervention. In *Law Society of Upper Canada v. MacNaughton*, [1942] OWN 551, Rose CJHC stated at p. 551:

> I have always understood the rule to be that the question is not whether the injunction will harm the defendant, but whether it is probable that unless the defendant is restrained, wrongful acts will be done which will do the plaintiff irreparable injury.

A second and much higher hurdle facing the litigant seeking the exceptional order is the simple proposition that in our jurisprudence, execution cannot be obtained prior to judgment and judgment cannot be recovered before trial. Execution in this sense includes judicial orders impounding assets or otherwise restricting the rights of the defendant without a trial. This was enunciated by Cotton LJ in *Lister & Co. v. Stubbs* (1890), 45 Ch. 1 (CA) at p. 13, as follows:

> I know of no case where, because it is highly probable if the action were brought the plaintiff could establish that there was a debt due to him by the defendant, the defendant has been ordered to give a security till the debt has been established by the judgment or decree.

Similarly, the limited availability of an injunction to enjoin a defendant from disposing of his assets was referred to in *Burdett v. Fader* (1903), 5 OLR 532 (affirmed (1904), 7 OLR 72 (Div. Ct.)) at p. 533, by Boyd C:

> The plaintiff may or may not get judgment in this case, but he proposes to restrain the sale or disposition of this stock by the defendant till that is finally determined.
>
> There is no authority for such a course in an action of tort. If the plaintiff is a creditor before judgment, he can sue on behalf of himself and all creditors to attack a fraudulent transfer. If the plaintiff is a judgment creditor, he can proceed by execution to secure himself upon the debtor's property. But if the litigation is merely progressing and the status of creditor not established, it is not the course of the Court to interfere *quia timet* and restrain the defendant from dealing with his property until the rights of the litigants are ascertained.

The principle has been restated in modern times in *Barclay Johnson v. Yuill*, [1980] 1 WLR 1259 (Ch.), where Sir Robert Megarry V-C stated, at p. 1262:

> In broad terms, this establishes the general proposition that the court will not grant an injunction to restrain the defendant from parting with his assets so that they may be preserved in case the plaintiff's claim succeeds. The plaintiff, like other creditors of the defendant, must obtain his judgment and then enforce it. He cannot prevent the defendant from disposing of his assets

pendente lite merely because he fears that by the time he obtains judgment in his favour the defendant will have no assets against which the judgment can be enforced. Were the law otherwise, the way would lie open to any claimant to paralyse the activities of any person or firm against whom he makes his claim by obtaining an injunction freezing their assets.

This problem has been stated and restated many times in this country in the courts of Manitoba and elsewhere: [a list of cases follows].

The general rule in *Lister* has had wide application in the law: see Robert J. Sharpe, *Injunctions and Specific Performance* (Toronto: Canada Law Book Co., 1983), at pp. 94-7. However, the abhorrence which the common law has felt toward allowing execution before judgment has always been subject to some obvious exceptions:

1. For the preservation of assets, the very subject-matter in dispute, where to allow the adversarial process to proceed unguided would see their destruction before the resolution of the dispute: To a large extent this exception to the *Lister* rule has been codified in the various provincial and federal procedural rules. Rule 330(1) of the Queen's Bench Rules (Man.) is typical and provides:

> 330(1) The court may, on the application of any party and on such terms as may be just, make an order for the detention or preservation of property, being the subject of the action … .

See also: Rules of Practice (Ont.), Rule 372; Federal Court Rules, Rule 470(1); Civil Procedure Rules (NS), Rule 43.02; Queen's Bench Rules (Sask.), Rule 389; Rules of Court (Alta.), Rule 468. That the courts had jurisdiction to make an order for the preservation of property pending litigation was, however, recognised even prior to passage of the rules. In *Great Western R. Co. v. Birmingham & Oxford Junction R. Co.* (1848), 2 Ph. 597, 41 ER 1074, Cottenham LC observed, at pp. 602-03 (p. 1076 (ER)), as follows:

> It is certain that the Court will in many cases interfere and preserve property *in statu quo* during the pendency of a suit, in which the rights to it are to be decided, and *that* without expressing, and often without having the means of forming, any opinion as to such rights. It is true that no purchaser *pendente lite* would gain a title; but it would embarrass the original purchaser in his suit against the vendor, which the Court prevents by its injunction. Such are the cases *Echliff v. Baldwin* (16 Ves. 267), *Curtes v. Lord Buckingham* (3 V & B 168), *Spiller v. Spiller* (3 Swan. 556), per Lord Redesdale in Dow. 440. It is true that the Court will not so interfere, if it thinks that there is no real question between the parties; but seeing that there is a substantial question to be decided, it will preserve the property until such question can be regularly disposed of. In order to support an injunction for such purpose, it is not necessary for the Court to decide upon the merits in favour of the Plaintiff.

Although the *Great Western R. Co.* case was decided before *Lister v. Stubbs*, it is none the less still accepted that an injunction to preserve the very subject-matter of the action is not to be equated with an injunction of the Mareva variety. This distinction was recently restated by Craig J in *Rosen v. Pullen* (1981), 126 DLR (3d) 62 (Ont. HC) at pp. 74-5:

> It is unnecessary for the Court to consider the present case on the basis of a *Mareva* injunction because the very subject-matter of the action is the letter of credit in question. It is not a case of an action against a defendant based on a debt where there is a likelihood that the defendant will

remove available assets. See Williston & Rolls, *The Law of Civil Procedure* vol. 2 (1970), p. 585, cited with approval by Lerner J in *OSF Industries Ltd. v. Marc-Jay Investments Inc.* (1978), 20 OR (2d) 566 at p. 567, 88 DLR (3d) 446 at p. 447, 7 CPC 57, as follows:

> (a) An injunction will not be granted to restrain a defendant from parting with or encumbering his property before a creditor has established his right by judgment.

> The result would be entirely different if the property likely to be disposed of is the very subject matter of the litigation.

2. Where generally the processes of the court must be protected even by initiatives taken by the court itself.

3. To prevent fraud both on the court and on the adversary: In *Campbell v. Campbell* (1881), 29 Gr. 252, both the general rule and the exception to it on the basis of fraud, were succinctly stated by Boyd C at pp. 254-5, as follows:

> Where no fraud has been committed the Court will not restrain a defendant from dealing with his property at the instance of a creditor or person who has not established his right to proceed against that property. But where a fraudulent disposal has actually been made of the defendant's property (as is admitted by the demurrer in this case) then the Court will intercept the further alienation of the property, and keep it in the hands of the grantee under the impeached conveyance, until the plaintiff can obtain a declaration of its invalidity, and a recovery of judgment for the amount claimed.

More recent cases in which the fraud exceptions have been applied include *City of Toronto v. McIntosh* (1977), 16 OR (2d) 238 and *Mills v. Petrovic* (1980), 30 OR (2d) 238.

4. *Quia timet* injunctions were generally permitted under extreme circumstances which included a real or impending threat to remove contested assets from the jurisdiction.

Initially the Court of Appeal of the United Kingdom found its jurisdiction to issue this type of *quia timet* order in a section of the judicature legislation that ultimately became s. 45(1) of the *Supreme Court of Judicature (Consolidation) Act, 1925* (UK), c. 49, which authorizes the court to issue an injunction where it appears to the court "to be just or convenient" that the order should be made. In the rise of the Mareva injunction in the Court of Appeal, the source of authority for the Supreme Court was found to reside in this provision which can be traced back through a succession of statutes reaching back to at least the *Common Law Procedure Act, 1854* (UK), c. 125. In later pronouncements concerning this type of injunction, the jurisdiction to do so has been traced even further back into the antiquity of the London Commercial Court. As we shall see, Canadian legislation has followed the same course as s. 45. *Lister, supra,* and many other authorities, notably *Aslatt v. Corp. of Southampton* (1880), 16 Ch. D 143, have made it clear, however, that these words in the statute do not authorize a court to issue an injunction "because the court thought it convenient." Nor in the words of the authors of Halsbury's Laws of England, 4th ed., vol. 24, p. 518, para. 918, has this provision altered the general rules applying to the issuance of interlocutory injunctions.

Section 19(1) of the Ontario *Judicature Act*, RSO 1980, c. 232, is to the same effect as the United Kingdom provision, as are most of the comparable provisions in provincial statutes across the country: *Law and Equity Act*, RSBC 1979, c. 224, s. 36; *Judicature Act*, RSA 1980, c. J-1, s. 13(2); *Queen's Bench Act*, RSS 1978, c. Q-1, s. 45(8); *Queen's Bench Act*, RSM 1970, c. C280, s. 59; *Judicature Act*, RSO 1980, c. 223, s. 19(1); *Judicature Act*, 1972 (NS), c. 2, s. 39(9); *Judicature Act*, RSNB 1973, c. J-2, s. 33 (am. 1981, c. 6, s. 1); *Judicature Act*, RSPEI 1974, c. J-3, s. 15(4); *Judicature Act*, RSN 1970, c. 187, s. 21(m). We are here particularly concerned with s. 59(1) of the *Queen's Bench Act* of Manitoba.

The Quebec *Code of Civil Procedure*, RSQ 1977, c. C-25, provides for interlocutory injunctions in art. 752 "when the applicant appears to be entitled to it." These words, given their plain meaning, clothe the court with at least as much authority and latitude as the jurisdiction to enjoin where it is found "to be just and convenient." The article goes on to provide against the very eventuality contemplated by the application for the Mareva-type of order here:

> 752. … and it is considered to be necessary in order to avoid serious or irreparable injury to him, or a factual or legal situation of such a nature as to render the final judgment ineffectual.

The authority of the Superior Court to respond to an application based on the appropriate facts and demonstrated in the manner prescribed by the Code is at least equal to that of the superior courts of other provinces.

The statutory powers of the courts in Manitoba to issue such injunctive relief is undoubted; the question is, as Hamilton J put it in *Hawes et al. v. Szewczyk*, unreported, noted at [1979] 2 ACWS 274, should the jurisdiction be exercised? This question can only be answered by balancing the principles enunciated in *Lister* on the one hand, and those of *Rasu* on the other.

In *Lister* itself, the issue turned on the narrow distinction on the facts of that case between the debtor-creditor relationship on the one hand (wherein no judicial intervention would be authorized before trial) and the *cestui que trust* relationship on the other hand (where judicial intervention would intervene to protect the trust *res*). *Lister* itself recognized at least three exceptions to the general principle; firstly, where the *res* of the action was demonstrably the property of the claimant; secondly, where the relationship between the adversaries included a condition whereby the defendant-debtor could not, without the acquiescence of the claimant-creditor, defend the claim; and thirdly, the trustee-beneficiary relationship.

While the law has long known exceptions to the *Lister* rule, it was not until a series of Maritime disputes arose that the courts consciously began to build up a special code of rules or subrules for the intervention by the court before judgment, and indeed, before trial, where circumstances warranted such action in the interest of the parties, the community and the law generally. Beginning in 1975, these exceptions to the *Lister* rule came into judicial prominence. They have been grouped by the courts, and legal writers generally, under the new legal generic, the Mareva injunction.

Beginning in early 1975, there were four cases in England arising in the shipping business where the rule in *Lister* was suspended. These are, in their chronological order: *Nippon Yusen Kaisha v. Karageorgis*, [1975] 1 WLR 1093 (CA); *Mareva Compania Naviera SA v. Int'l Bulkcarriers SA*, [1980] 1 All ER 213 (CA); *Rasu Maritima SA v. Perusahaan Pertambangan Minyak Dan Gas Bumi Negara (Pertamina)*, [1978] QB 644 (CA); *Third Chandris Shipping Corp. v. Unimarine SA*, [1979] QB 645 (CA). In the midst of this development process in the

United Kingdom came the Australian case, *Pivovaroff v. Chernabaeff* (1977), 16 SASR 329, which reviewed the English authorities but declined to follow them.

In *Nippon*, the shipowners, being unable to locate the defendant charterers, commenced an action for overdue hire and moved on an *ex parte* basis, as the defendants could not be located, for an order enjoining the defendants from transferring out of the jurisdiction moneys known to be in a London bank account in the name of the defendants. The order was granted as asked, Lord Denning MR stating, at p. 1095:

> It seems to me that the time has come when we should revise our practice. There is no reason why the High Court or this court should not make an order such as is asked for here. It is warranted by s. 45 of the *Supreme Court of Judicature (Consolidation) Act 1925*, which says the High Court may grant a *mandamus* or injunction or appoint a receiver by an interlocutory order in all cases in which it appears to the court to be just or convenient so to do. It seems to me that this is just such a case.

Lane LJ agreed [at 1095] because of the danger of the plaintiff losing money "... to which he is admittedly entitled," although no one made such an admission, as the defendant at no stage of the process appeared.

Mareva followed one month later although it was not reported until 1980. In *Mareva*, the defendant charterers again did not appear and the reference to their argument in Lord Denning's judgment appears to be in error. The ship was out of the jurisdiction, the defendants had disappeared, and the shipowners sought to enjoin the disposal of moneys known to be in a London bank account in the name of the defendants. Because the order in *Nippon* had been made without any reference to the *Lister* case, the High Court, on *ex parte* application, had refused the injunction. In the Court of Appeal the *Lister* case was avoided by reliance upon s. 45 of the *Supreme Court of Judicature (Consolidation) Act, 1925*, mentioned above in the *Nippon* case and upon a commentary on the resultant powers of the court in Halsbury's. Lord Denning then continued, at p. 215 (All ER):

> In my opinion that principle applies to a creditor who has a right to be paid the debt owing to him, even before he has established his right by getting judgment for it.

In explanation of this conclusion, the Master of the Rolls stated on the same page:

> There is money in a bank in London which stands in the name of these charterers. The charterers have control of it. They may at any time dispose of it or remove it out of this country. If they do so, the shipowners may never get their charter hire. The ship is now on the high seas.

Lord Roskill, in concurring [at 216], distinguished the *Lister* case on the basis that by a clause in the charter-party, the shipowners "have a lien upon ... all sub-freights for any amounts due under this charter. ..." The order in *Mareva*, it can be seen, was therefore based on the broad powers given to the court under its jurisdictional statute and in part, at least in the view of one member of the court, on the existence of a contractual lien by the plaintiffs against the prepaid subcharter-party revenues temporarily within the jurisdiction of the United Kingdom court.

In 1977, the Court of Appeal confirmed the denial of such an injunction in *Rasu*. The defendants were clearly outside the jurisdiction but had some assets, or interest in assets, inside the UK. The debt claimed by the plaintiff arose under a charter-party between the plaintiff as a shipowner and the defendants as charterers. Some actions taken by the defendants were capable of interpretation as an effort to transfer or deal with their assets which were in the UK in a manner which would put them beyond the reach of the creditors. The injunction was denied, not because there was not a *prima facie* case of liability, but because the nature of the goods under attack was such that they were wholly unrelated to the action and the claim arising in the plaintiffs, the title to the equipment in question was unclear, the removal of the goods as planned to Germany increased the likelihood of the plaintiffs being able to obtain a *Mareva*-like injunction there, and the seizure and sale of the equipment would realize only a fraction of their true worth as an integral part of a plant being built by the defendants in Indonesia. What is important in the case is the catalogue of matters which Lord Denning set out in his judgment as being those to be taken into consideration by the court in determining whether the exercise of discretion under statute should occur. These matters are:

1. The plaintiff must demonstrate a good arguable case;

2. The assets in question need not be limited to money but could include goods within the jurisdiction;

3. Where the injunction might compel the defendant to provide security, it might tilt the scales in favour of issuance of the injunction.

In justifying the earlier decisions of *Nippon* and *Mareva*, the Master of the Rolls found roots for such an order in the practice in the courts in the City of London, particularly the commercial courts, where the seizure orders, or injunction orders, were issued substantially to compel the defendant to appear and provide bail or security. The historical prerequisite was absence of the defendant from the jurisdiction. Lord Denning noted that the practice, apparently, has long been followed in the United States, except that it has been limited to cases where debt is due from the defendant in a liquidated discernible amount: see *DeBeers v. United States* (1945), 325 US 212 at pp. 222-3. Similar remedies have been, and continue to be, in widespread use in the maritime towns of continental Europe. Accordingly, Lord Denning observed, at p. 658:

Now that we have joined the Common Market it would be appropriate that we should follow suit, at any rate in regard to defendants not within the jurisdiction. By so doing we should be fulfilling one of the requirements of the Treaty of Rome, that is the harmonisation of the laws of the member countries.

He then returned to the theme of the *Lister* principle at p. 659 when he stated:

So far as concerns defendants who are within the jurisdiction of the court and have assets here, it is well established that the court should not, in advance of any order or judgment, allow the creditor to seize any of the money or goods of the debtor or to use any legal process to do so.

There appears to be a discrepancy between these comments of the learned Master of the Rolls and those at p. 663 of the report where His Lordship stated:

I think the courts have a discretion, in advance of judgment, to issue an injunction to restrain the removal of assets, whether the defendant is within the jurisdiction or outside it.

The trial judge in *Rasu* added the further qualification that the plaintiff "has what appears to be an indisputable claim against the defendant" and reference is made with approval to this condition by the Master of the Rolls. In *Rasu*, the turning point in the line of reasoning seems to be reached when the defendants, unlike the defendants in *Mareva* and *Nippon*, appeared in court to defend the claim.

The final dissertation in the Court of Appeal of the United Kingdom on the subject of these injunctions to which I wish, at present, to refer is found in *Third Chandris*, again principally through the judgment of Lord Denning. Here the injunction was issued in the court of first instance and confirmed by the Court of Appeal, apparently because the defendants were outside the jurisdiction, provided no financial returns in the proceedings, or indeed in Panama, the country of registry of the defendants' business, but did have a bank account in London in which had been deposited the proceeds of a subcharter-party entered into after the execution by the defendants of the charter-party from the plaintiff shipowners. The extraordinary factual feature was that the injunction restrained the removal from the jurisdiction of moneys in the defendants' London bank account, although the evidence clearly indicated that the account was in overdraft. Again, the Master of the Rolls catalogued the hurdles which a plaintiff must surmount in order to obtain this type of injunction. They are much the same as in *Rasu* except that (at p. 669) the Master of the Rolls placed more emphasis on the requirement that the plaintiff demonstrate belief in a risk that the assets would be removed before the judgment or award is satisfied. "The mere fact that the defendant is abroad is not, by itself, sufficient." Additionally, a contrast is drawn between a foreign corporation of substance and one operating in a country where no financial disclosure is required and nothing is placed before the court to ascertain the magnitude of the risk of non-payment of any judgment recovered by the plaintiff. In particular, His Lordship went on to observe, at p. 669:

> There is no reciprocal enforcement of judgments. It is nothing more that a name grasped from the air, as elusive as the Cheshire cat.

Lawton LJ referred to the fact that the defendant's assets may be ships flying "the so-called flags of convenience" with little or no trace of substantive worth in the defendant, in or outside the jurisdiction. At p. 671 he expressed the sense of risk which must be found by the court to exist before the issuance of these extraordinary injunctions:

> There must be facts from which the Commercial Court, like a prudent sensible commercial man, can properly infer a danger of default if assets are removed from the jurisdiction.

The mere fact that the defendant was a foreign corporation was not, in the view of Lawton LJ, by itself, sufficient to justify this injunction.

In *Pivovaroff v. Chernabaeff*, Chief Justice Bray, of the Supreme Court of South Australia, set aside the injunction which had been granted to a plaintiff to restrain the defendants from disposing of some real estate which was unrelated to the personal injury claims of the plaintiff. The injunction had been granted on the basis of a belief held by the plaintiff that the defendant, upon the sale of such assets, might leave the country before the trial of the action. The Chief Justice did not follow the *Mareva* cases, largely because the defendant resided in the jurisdiction, but His Lordship added at p. 338:

I am far from satisfied that even in the case of a defendant outside the jurisdiction with assets within it it would be proper to issue an injunction of the type in question here.

The Chief Justice found no escape from the general principle enunciated in *Robinson v. Pickering* (1881), 16 Ch. D 660 (CA): "You cannot grant an injunction to restrain a man who is alleged to be a debtor from parting with his property" (*per* James LJ at p. 661). The Chief Justice then added, at p. 338: "Those cases do not contain any exception for defendants outside the jurisdiction."

The Australian court referred to the judgment of Schroeder JA in *Bradley Bros. (Oshawa) Ltd. v. A to Z Rental Canada Ltd.*, [1970] 3 OR 787 (CA), in the Court of Appeal of Ontario where authorities were applied with the same result. Both courts shied away from the obvious danger of judicial interference with the operations of corporate enterprises where a creditor might see in many management dealings a real risk of loss of assets before the creditor would be able to demonstrate his claim.

The United Kingdom *Mareva* rule might, as Lord Denning observed in *Rasu*, find harmony with the British position in the Common Market, but, as pointed out in *Pivovaroff*, that consideration has no relevancy in Australia, nor indeed would it have any relevancy in any country not bound by the Treaty of Rome.

As for the asserted jurisdiction founded on the judicature legislation in the United Kingdom, Chief Justice Bray described s. 45 as "a machinery section." In the words of the learned authors of Halsbury's Laws of England, 3rd ed., vol. 21, p. 348, para. 729; Halsbury's Laws of England, 4th ed., vol. 24, p. 518, para. 918, s. 45 "did not alter the principles on which courts act in granting injunctions." To the same effect, see *Kerr on Injunctions* (London: Sweet & Maxwell, 6th ed., 1927) at p. 6. Furthermore, Chief Justice Bray in *Pivovaroff*, thought that (at p. 340):

It would seem unlikely that an alternative process of summary execution in anticipation of judgment, available for unliquidated damages as well as for liquidated debts due and payable, should have been slumbering unsuspected for over a century in the interstices of s. 29 and its analogues.

The learned justice was there referring to the Australian counterpart of s. 45 discussed by the Court of Appeal of the United Kingdom in the *Mareva* cases.

What therefore sprung out of the fertile ground of jurisprudence in the mid-1970's in the courts of the United Kingdom as a limited interlocutory injunctive remedy for plaintiffs who were in pursuit of ubiquitous charterers of shipping, has matured into a subprinciple or exception to a general rule of long standing. The plaintiff in the United Kingdom must demonstrate that he has a good arguable case. At least once (*Rasu* at p. 660), the courts have required the plaintiff to show an indisputable claim against the defendant. There must be assets of the defendant within the jurisdiction susceptible to execution. The defendant need not be outside the jurisdiction. There must be a real risk that the remaining significant assets of the defendant within the jurisdiction are about to be removed or so disposed of by the defendant as to render nugatory any judgment to be obtained after trial. *Mareva* injunctions are therefore available not just to prevent the removal of assets from the jurisdiction, but also disposal within the jurisdiction. This has been made certain by the enactment of s. 37(3), *Supreme Court Act, 1981* (UK), c. 54, which reads in part:

37(3) The power of the High Court ... to grant an interlocutory injunction restraining a party to any proceedings from removing from the jurisdiction of the High Court, or otherwise dealing with, assets located within that jurisdiction shall be exercisable in cases where that party is, as well as in cases where he is not, domiciled, resident or present within that jurisdiction.

However, Lord Denning in *Z Ltd. v. A-Z*, [1982] QB 558 (CA) at pp. 571-2, opines that this was the position prior to the enactment. The claim no longer need be limited to debt or liquidated damages. The general rule requiring that the balance of convenience must favour the issuance of the order still exists. The overriding consideration qualifying the plaintiff to receive such an order as an exception to the *Lister* rule is that the defendant threatens to so arrange his assets as to defeat his adversary, should that adversary ultimately prevail and obtain judgment, in any attempt to recover from the defendant on that judgment. Short of that, the plaintiff cannot treat the defendant as a judgment-debtor, the defendant's right to defend the claim may not be impaired, and the defendant in proper circumstances may, within such an order, pay current expenses incurred in the ordinary course of his business.

The gist of the *Mareva* action is the right to freeze exigible assets when found within the jurisdiction, wherever the defendant may reside, providing, of course, there is a cause between the plaintiff and the defendant which is justiciable in the courts of England. However, unless there is a genuine risk of disappearance of assets, either inside or outside the jurisdiction, the injunction will not issue. This generally summarizes the position in this country. [A list of cases follows.]

The harshness of the *Mareva* injunction, issued usually *ex parte*, is relieved against or justified in part by the Rules of Practice which allow the defendant, faced by risk of loss, an opportunity to move against the injunction immediately. On the other hand, the Court of Appeal of England seems to have blessed the practice of using this injunction as a means of coercing a vulnerable defendant into providing security in order to head off irreparable loss from the paralysis which follows the issuance of this type of injunction.

While the *Mareva* injunction is undoubtedly *in personam*, it matters not that on occasion the courts have classified it as *in rem* (see *Cretanor Maritime Co. Ltd. v. Irish Marine Management Ltd.*, [1978] 1 WLR 966 (CA)), because the injunction affords no priority to the potential creditor, for to do so would, in the words of Goff J, "rewrite the ... law of insolvency": *Iraqi Ministry of Defence v. Arcepey Shipping Co. SA*, [1981] QB 65 at p. 71. Unsecured creditors holding a *Mareva* injunction cannot hold a preferred position over other claimants. Hence the practice of including in the order the right to meet legitimate debt payments accruing in the ordinary course of business.

The courts in Canada have given this type of injunction a mixed reception. The earlier decisions in the Ontario courts are reflected in *Bradley Bros.*, where the Court of Appeal continued the principle of *Lister*, Lerner J, in the High Court of Ontario, in a post-*Mareva* decision, maintained the same position: *OSF Industry Ltd. v. Marc-Jay Investments Inc.* (1978), 20 OR (2d) 566 at p. 568. By 1981 the High Court appeared to assume that a *quia timet* jurisdiction was available on a more restricted basis than the *Mareva* formula provided in the United Kingdom: see *Liberty National Bank & Trust Co. v. Atkin* (1981), 31 OR (2d) 715; *Canadian Pacific Airlines Ltd. v. Hind* (1981), 32 OR (2d) 591, where Grange J, as he then was, while raising the question of the existence of the *Mareva* principle in Ontario, found such dishonesty in the defendant's conduct that it was a certainty that he would dispose of all his assets in order to frustrate the plaintiff; and *Quinn v. Marsta Cessian Services Ltd.* (1981), 34 OR (2d) 659, where such an injunction issued on the application of the rules of *Third Chandris Shipping Corp.* The Court of Appeal of Ontario reviewed the conflicting authorities in *Chitel v. Rothbart* (1982), 39 OR (2d) 513, and although it refused the injunction in the circumstances of that case, it recognized in a detailed and comprehensive review of the authorities that the jurisdiction existed in the court to grant such a remedy in a proper case. The test there established is somewhat narrower than that generally applied by the courts in the United Kingdom (*per* MacKinnon ACJO at pp. 532-3):

> The applicant must persuade the court by his material that the defendant is removing or there is a real risk that he is about to remove his assets from the jurisdiction to avoid the possibility of a judgment, or that the defendant is otherwise dissipating or disposing of his assets, in a manner clearly distinct from his usual or ordinary course of business or living, so as to render the possibility of future tracing of the assets remote, if not impossible in fact or in law.

The condition precedent to entitlement to the order is the demonstration by the plaintiff of a "strong *prima facie* case" (at p. 522 OR) and not merely as stipulated in some of the UK authorities, "a good arguable case": *per* Lord Denning in *Rasu*, and *per* Sir Robert Megarry V-C in *Barclay-Johnson v. Yuill*, [1980] 1 WLR 1259 (Ch.) at p. 1265. In summary, the Ontario Court of Appeal recognized *Lister* as the general rule, and *Mareva* as a "limited exception" to it, the exceptional injunction being available only where there is a real risk that the defendant will remove his assets from the jurisdiction or dissipate those assets "to avoid the possibility of a judgment. ..."

In other provinces the courts have reached approximately the same result. The New Brunswick Court of Appeal in *Humphreys v. Buragalia* (1982), 39 NBR (2d) 674 (CA), placed the basis for this kind of injunction on the danger that the defendant will abscond or dispose of his assets so as to prevent realization on any ultimate judgment. The earlier view of the Manitoba Court of Queen's Bench was expressed by Hamilton J in *Hawes v. Szewczyk*, [(1979), 1 Man. R (2d) 226] *supra*, where he concluded that the *Mareva* rule was "a dangerous innovation" and even if technically within the jurisdiction of the court, was one that "should not be exercised." The British Columbia Court of Appeal, in *Sekisui House Kabushiki Kaisha (Sekisui House Co. Ltd.) v. Nagashima* (1982), 42 BCLR 1 (CA) recognized the general principles developed around this interlocutory injunction in the courts of the United Kingdom.

It has been argued by the appellant that the *Mareva* injunction has no place in the laws of this country because provincial legislation has filled the gap by providing statutory remedies. In Manitoba the appellant points to the *Fraudulent Conveyances Act*, RSM 1970, c F160; the *Garnishment Act*, RSM 1970, c. G20; the Court of Queen's Bench Rules, c. XXIV, "Attachment," Rule 582; and Queen's Bench Rule 526, "garnishee" procedures. In other provinces, similar legislation and rules are to be found. In Ontario, for example, there is the *Absconding Debtors Act*, RSO 1980, c. 2, s. 2, which authorizes the seizure of property of a resident of the province who leaves for the purpose of defrauding or defeating creditors; Rule 372 of the present Consolidated Rules of Practice which provides for the preservation of the subject-matter of the proceeding; and the *Fraudulent Conveyances Act*, RSO 1980, c. 176, which authorizes preventive orders where the plaintiff establishes a valid claim and *prima facie* that the conveyance in question was fraudulent. It is said by counsel for the appellant that this type of statute indicates a legislative intent to provide interim relief of a type described in the statutes and no more. On this line of reasoning the courts, it is said, should not "legislate" by adopting the sweeping rules of the *Mareva* line of cases. This should be a matter for the Legislature which is better placed to assess the problem, its incidence in the community and the range of solutions available. One should not assume that the British Legislature has been entirely silent apart from s. 45. See 18 Hals., 4th ed., p. 166, para. 358, where reference is made to statutory authority to set aside fraudulent conveyances. However, the United Kingdom legislation is not as far-reaching as appears to be the case in this country.

The Manitoba Court of Appeal divided on the relevance of these statutes. The majority, speaking through Matas JA, took the view that such legislation and rules of court provide for relief in specific circumstances and do not preclude the invocation by the court of s. 59(1) of the *Queen's Bench Act* for the issuance of a preventive injunction in the nature of the *Mareva* injunction. A similar view has been expressed by Tallis J, now of the Saskatchewan Court of Appeal, in *BP Exploration Co. (Libya) Ltd. v. Hunt* (1980), 23 AR 271 (NWTSC) at p. 306. Huband JA, in dissent, acknowledged that the aforementioned statutes and rules of court do not assist the respondent here as there is no liquidated demand or debt or a conveyance in fraud of creditors. An attaching order might avail but the rule is more precise in its requirements than the *Mareva* rules as they presently stand. As the respondent was "registered to do business in Manitoba" and has an "authorized agent to accept service" (to quote Huband JA), the respondent could not qualify for an attaching order. In the result, the learned justice would preclude recourse to a *Mareva* order where specific remedies are available at law; and if not so available, then "the courts should be cautious to fill the void by an injunction." There are helpful discussions as to the significance of these and other provincial statutes in relation to *Mareva* injunctions in David Stockwood, "Mareva Injunctions" (1980), 3 Advocates' Q 85; Brian M. Rogers and George W. Hately, "Getting the Pretrial Injunction" (1982), 60 Can. Bar Rev. 1 and Debra M. McAllister, "Mareva Injunctions" (1982), 28 CPC 1. Reference is made in the British cases to the availability of bankruptcy legislation which would allow the ultimately successful plaintiff to set aside any disposition made in fraud of creditors by way of preference or improper dealing. The same condition exists in this country where the federal *Bankruptcy Act*, RSC 1970, c. B-3, has uniform application throughout the country.

I do not believe the presence of provincial or federal legislation of the type discussed above can preclude the issuance of a protective injunction or narrow the breadth of expression employed in s. 59(1) of the Manitoba *Queen's Bench Act*. If the court has the authority under such a legislative provision properly construed, then that authority must be expressly reduced by other legislation directed to the problem. Such is not the case here. That answer, of course, does not assist in determining the proper practice of the court when dealing with an application for this type of interlocutory injunction other than to find jurisdiction in the court to respond in a proper case.

Before leaving this aspect of the matter, one should make note of the appellant's submission that the *Bankruptcy Act* of Canada is available to the respondent in the event that improper disposition is made of the appellants' assets followed by an assignment or petition under the *Bankruptcy Act*. This was a consideration in the early *Mareva* judgments in England. It is not decisive on the point of jurisdiction to make, or the propriety in these circumstances to issue, a *Mareva* injunction. The order was not made for the purpose of protecting the respondent from the consequences of any ultimate bankruptcy procedures. The entitlement springs, if it does at all, from the authority of the court at law to make the order and qualification of the respondents under the rules and tests applied by the court in doing so. The *Bankruptcy Act*, which at times may be relevant to the issue presented to the chambers judge on a *Mareva* application, is not a controlling consideration, particularly on the facts in this appeal.

The majority of the Court of Appeal considered that [at 726]:

> One of the factors which is relevant in this case is the clear intention of Aetna to transfer its assets from Manitoba to Montreal, albeit that the intention is openly expressed. And Quebec is not a reciprocating province with respect to enforcement of judgments.

The Manitoba *Reciprocal Enforcement of Judgments Act*, RSM 1970, c. J20, provides the machinery for the enforcement in Manitoba of judgments of the courts in other Canadian provinces which have reciprocal arrangements with the Province of Manitoba. The Act also provides for the entry into such arrangements for the registration in other provinces of judgments of the courts of Manitoba. With the exception of Quebec, all the provinces of Canada, the Northwest Territories and the Yukon Territory have entered into such reciprocal arrangements and have like statutes. Twenty-five per cent of the assets of the appellant are in the Province of Ontario exceeding the value of the assets of the appellant in Manitoba which are affected by the order under appeal. The Manitoba Act and the Ontario Act each require service upon the defendant to have been effected in the province of judgment in order to qualify such judgment for registration and enforcement in the other province (Ontario, in this case). The record here does not expressly show that the appellant was served within the Province of Manitoba with a writ or other originating instrument, or with the notice of motion for this injunction. The respondent is, however, a federal company with an office in Manitoba and was at all relevant times doing business in Manitoba. Under the *Corporations Act* of Manitoba, SM 1976, c. 40 (CCSM, c. C225), such corporations are required to register and to nominate an agent for service, all as noted by Justice Huband in dissent below. More importantly, the appellant appeared in and thereby attorned to the jurisdiction of the court in Manitoba. Thus, any judgment which may arise in these proceedings in Manitoba will qualify for registration enforcement under the Ontario statute and hence could be executed there against the Ontario assets of the appellant in the same manner as though judgment has been issued out of the Supreme Court of Ontario.

In the Province of Quebec, provision is found in the *Code of Civil Procedure* for action upon judgments outside the Province of Quebec:

> 178. Any defence which was or might have been set up to the original action may be pleaded to an action brought upon a judgment rendered out of Canada.
>
> 179. Any defence which might have been set up to the original action may be pleaded to an action brought upon a judgment rendered in any other province of Canada, provided that the defendant was not personally served with the action in such other province or did not appear in such action.
>
> 180. Any such defence cannot be pleaded if the defendant was personally served in such province, or appeared in the original action, except in any case involving the decision of a right

affecting immoveables in this province, or the jurisdiction of a foreign court concerning such right.

In such proceedings reliance may be had upon art. 1220 of the *Civil Code* of the Province of Quebec which supplements the procedure under art. 179, by providing for the proof of judgments from courts outside the Province of Quebec. The *Civil Code* differentiates between foreign judgments and those emanating from the courts of other provinces, and provides in the latter case for a limited process where the defendant in the extra-provincial proceeding was served in the province or appeared in a court of that province. The action in Quebec, upon any judgment later obtained in Manitoba by the respondent, would be a formal process of enforcement not different in substance and execution from the proceedings under the Ontario reciprocal Statute. In the result, Quebec accords a means of enforcement of Manitoba judgments but the converse (which is of no concern in this appeal) is not the case because the reciprocity machinery in the Manitoba statute has not been brought into play. The access to the enforcement procedures under the laws of Quebec renders ineffective, in my view, any argument that the respondent was exposed to some inevitable or irreparable loss if, at the time any judgment issues in the courts of Manitoba, the assets of the appellant have been transferred from Manitoba to Quebec. Furthermore, Ontario is qualified as a "reciprocating state" under the Manitoba legislation, and the appellant, according to the record herein, had assets in that province in excess of the assets impounded in Manitoba by the order under appeal.

A large part of the respondent's factum filed herein, and of argument made in this court, centered upon the winding down of the appellant's business which presumably has created a risk of default by the appellant in meeting its obligations. The factum goes further and says that by reason of this trend, in early 1982, "for all practical purposes, Aetna ceases to exist." The argument is not made that the respondent will go into bankruptcy or be wound up. Essentially, this line of submission must lead to the proposition that while the appellant "will not go into bankruptcy or default" (extract from respondent's factum), there is, in the words of the respondent's factum, "a sufficient risk of Aetna defaulting in its obligations to justify granting of a *Mareva* injunction." Such a default would, of course, invite a petition or force an assignment under the *Bankruptcy Act*. In either case, the respondent has extensive and easily enforceable rights. One right the respondent does not have, with or without the *Mareva* injunction "in aid," is a priority or preference if indeed the appellant has, as the respondent has elaborately calculated in its submissions in this court, become insolvent. It would not appear from the facts revealed on the record that there is any intention on the part of the appellant to default in any obligation to the respondent or to anyone else. An affidavit filed by the appellant states that "... Aetna is currently meeting all its liabilities as they become due." The deponent in this affidavit, Jean-Paul Lafontaine, was cross-examined by counsel for the respondent generally, but no questions were directed to this bald statement which remains uncontradicted in the record. This statement is obviously vital on the key question of the existence of any real risk of loss in the respondent as a basis for the issuance of this exceptional interlocutory order.

However, even assuming the appellant is wound up by its two shareholders, the Traders Group and the Royal Bank of Canada, it is a federal company. If it is solvent, the provisions of the incorporating Act, the *Canada Business Corporations Act*, apply. Dissolution may be effected only on "discharge of any liabilities." Provision is made for notice to creditors and liquidation is conditional upon "adequately providing for the payment or discharge of all its obligations" (s. 204(7)). All of this procedure is made subject to court supervision on the application of the officer designated in the statute or "any interested person," which includes a creditor such as the respondent. The Manitoba *Corporations Act*, ss. 186 and 187, requires a federal corporation to register under the Act and to appoint an agent for service of process in Manitoba. Thus there is a detailed pattern under the combined corporation legislation, provincial and federal, to cover a surrender of charter as a method of avoiding the payment of debts.

On the other hand, if the appellant is insolvent, the remedies under the *Bankruptcy Act* apply and not the procedures under the *Canada Business Corporations Act*. A *Mareva* injunction can neither advance nor interfere with these procedures.

All the foregoing considerations, while important to an understanding of the operation of this type of injunction, leave untouched the underlying and basic question: do the principles, as developed in the United Kingdom courts, survive intact a transplantation from that unitary state to the federal state of Canada? The question in its simplest form arises in the principles enunciated in the earliest *Mareva* cases where the wrong to be prevented was the removal from "the jurisdiction" of assets of the respondent with a view to defeating the claim of a creditor. It has been found by the courts below that there was no such wrongdoing here. An initial question, therefore, must be answered, namely, what is meant by "jurisdiction" in a federal context? It at least means the jurisdiction of the Manitoba court. But is the bare removal of assets from the Province of Manitoba sufficient? The appellant is a federally-incorporated company with authority to carry on business throughout Canada. In the course of doing so, it moves assets in and out of the Provinces of Manitoba, Quebec and Ontario. No breach of law is asserted by the respondent. No improper purpose has been exposed. It is simply a clash of rights: the respondents' right to protect their position under any judgment which might hereafter be obtained, and the appellant's right to exercise its undoubted corporate capacity, federally confirmed (and the constitutionality of which is not challenged), to carry on business throughout Canada. The appellant does not seek to remove the assets in question from the national jurisdiction in which its corporate existence is maintained. The writ of the Manitoba court runs through judgment, founded on service of initiating process on the appellant within Manitoba, into Ontario under reciprocal provincial legislation, and into Quebec by reason of the laws of that province. None of these vital considerations were present in the United Kingdom where *Mareva* was conceived to fend off the depredations of shady mariners operating out of far-away havens, usually on the fringe of legally organized commerce. In the Canadian federal system, the appellant is not a foreigner, nor even a non-resident in the ordinary sense of the word. It is capable of "residing" throughout Canada and did so in Manitoba. It is subject to execution under any Manitoba judgment in every part of Canada. There was no clandestine transfer of assets designed to defraud the legal process of the courts of Manitoba. There is no evidence that this federal entity has arranged its affairs so as to defraud Manitoba creditors. The terminology and trappings of *Mareva* must be examined in the federal setting. In some ways, "jurisdiction" extends to the national boundaries, or, in any case, beyond the provincial boundary of Manitoba. For other purposes, jurisdiction no doubt can be confined to the reach of the writ of the Manitoba courts. These parameters will have to develop in Canada as did the *Mareva* principle in the courts of the United Kingdom. The laws of this country, as developed here from jurisprudence originating in the United Kingdom and variously adopted in some of the provinces, have long included *quia timet* orders when justice and the protection of the judicial process required. "Mareva" is a refinement made necessary to accommodate in the same laws the primary principle of *Lister*. All this is as true in Canada as in the United Kingdom. I conclude that nothing has taken this jurisdiction away from the superior courts in the provinces. In establishing the rules under which superior courts will issue such interlocutory orders in this country, one must not apply *in toto* or verbatim the dicta of the decisions in other legal systems though they may have much in common with those of Canada. The *Mareva* consideration arising in this appeal is the effect of a rightful removal of assets in the ordinary course of business by a resident defendant to another part of the federal system. This by itself will not trigger such an exceptional remedy as it well might do in the United Kingdom where the jurisdiction of the court and the boundaries of the country coincide. Even there, it will be seen in *Rasu Maritima*, an interlocutory injunction was not issued on the removal of assets from the United Kingdom in part because the assets were being moved to another country of the Common Market where the law recognized judgment before trial and indeed execution before judgment. That reasoning is much amplified in its introduction into a federal system. The South Australian court, as we have seen in *Pivovaroff*, has declined to adopt the *Mareva* principles.

Taking this added federal consideration into account, should the injunction have been issued in the first instance and renewed in the Court of Appeal? The *Mareva* rules of the United Kingdom as developed in our courts, do not, in my view of the circumstances here existing, properly reflect the federal concern. The movement of the assets in question was announced in public pronouncements of the two stockholders of the appellant and by the appellant itself. The respondents were expressly made aware of the impending transfer. There is no finding in either court below of any improper motive behind this transfer of assets. The transfer, indeed, was carried out in the ordinary course of business and reflected the history of the conduct of the appellant's business in the past in Manitoba. The appellant never did retain assets in its Manitoba branch operation, either before the appellant commenced dealings with the respondent or thereafter. There is no finding of any intention by the appellant to default on its obligations, either generally or to the respondent, if in law such an obligation is later found to exist. The appellant has not been found to be insolvent and the Court of Appeal expressly ruled this element out as a consideration governing the issuance or denial of the injunction. Finally, there is the federal fact and the procedures of pursuit open to the respondent in tracing these assets through to their destination in Quebec, or in recovering from the assets of the appellant in Ontario.

There is still, as in the days of *Lister*, a profound unfairness in a rule which sees one's assets tied up indefinitely pending trial of an action which may not succeed, and even if it does succeed, which may result in an award of far less than the caged assets. The harshness of such an exception to the general rule is even less acceptable where the defendant is a resident within the jurisdiction of the court and the assets in question are not being disposed of or moved out of the country or put beyond the reach of the courts of the country. The subrule or exception can lead to serious abuse. A plaintiff with an apparent claim, without ultimate substance, may, by the *Mareva* exception to the *Lister* rule, tie up the assets of the defendant, not for the purpose of their preservation until judgment, but to force, by litigious blackmail, a settlement on the defendant who, for any one of many reasons, cannot afford to await the ultimate vindication after trial. I would, with all respect to those who have held otherwise, conclude that the order should not have been issued under the principles of inter-locutory *quia timet* orders in Canadian courts functioning as they do in a federal system.

Finally, there is the question as to whether the appellant tribunal may properly step in and alter a discretionary order, such as an interlocutory order, issued by a court of first in-stance where no sufficient error in law on the part of the courts below has been revealed, or where the order in question was issued based upon a wrong or inapplicable principle of law. Where no significant error of law is revealed, in short, an appellate court should not inter-vene. We do not here have the benefit of reasons from the judge of first instance, Wilson J, issuing the order, but we do have the reasons of the Court of Appeal. That Court, with all respect to those members who confirmed the issuance of the order, did not give due con-sideration and weight to the position of the courts and the position of the parties before those courts when dealing with an interlocutory *quia timet* order in a federal jurisdiction. Though I would have come to the opposite conclusion even aside from that element of the law involved in these proceedings, interference with the exercise of discretion in issuing the order would, apart from this consideration, be unwarranted. It is, however, in my view, an error of law relating to the application of the principles properly governing the execution of the court's discretion in favour of the respondent in issuing the *quia timet* interlocutory order, and accordingly, I would intervene and set aside such order.

I therefore would allow the appeal and set aside the injunction issued in the courts below, with costs to the appellant throughout.

Appeal allowed.

NOTES AND QUESTIONS

1. In *Rasu Maritima SA v. Perusahaan*, [1978] QB 644 (CA) the English Court of Appeal indi-cated that an applicant need only show a threshold level of "good arguable case" consistent with *American Cyanamid*. What threshold test does Estey J choose in *Aetna*? In *R v. Consoli-dated Fastfrate Transport Inc.* (1995), 24 OR (3d) 564 (CA), the court indicated that it was set-tled law in Ontario that the plaintiff had to show a "strong" *prima facie* case before being granted a Mareva injunction. In contrast, British Columbia uses a "good arguable case" (*Tracy v. Instaloans Financial Solutions Centres (BC) Ltd.* (2007), 48 CPC (6th) 157 (BCCA)).

2. Estey J appeared to adopt the criteria of the English courts with respect to the obliga-tions owed by the applicant to the court. Lord Denning MR in *Third Chandris Shipping Corp. v. Unimarine SA*, [1979] QB 645 (CA) listed these as follows:

> Much as I am in favour of the *Mareva* injunction, it must not be stretched too far lest it be en-dangered. In endeavouring to set out some guidelines, I have had recourse to the practice of many other countries which have been put before us. They have been most helpful. These are the points which those who apply for it should bear in mind:
>
> (i) The plaintiff should make full and frank disclosure of all matters in his knowledge which are material for the judge to know: see *Negocios Del Mur SA v. Doric Shipping Corporation SA (The Assios)*, [1979] 1 Lloyd's Rep. 331 (CA).

(ii) The plaintiff should give particulars of his claim against the defendant, stating the ground of his claim and the amount thereof, and fairly stating the points made against it by the defendant.

(iii) The plaintiff should give some grounds for believing that the defendant has assets here. I think that this requirement was put too high in *MBPXL Corporation v. Intercontinental Banking Corporation Ltd.* August 28, 1975; Court of Appeal (Civil Division) Transcript No. 411 of 1975. In most cases the plaintiff will not know the extent of the assets. He will only have indications of them. The existence of a bank account in England is enough, whether it is in overdraft or not.

(iv) The plaintiff should give some grounds for believing that there is a risk of the assets being removed before the judgment or award is satisfied. The mere fact that the defendant is abroad is not by itself sufficient. No one would wish any reputable foreign company to be plagued with a *Mareva* injunction simply because it has agreed to London arbitration. But there are some foreign companies whose structure invites comment. We often see in this court a corporation which is registered in a country where the company law is so loose that nothing is known about it—where it does no work and has no officers and no assets. Nothing can be found out about the membership, or its control, or its assets, or the charges on them. Judgment cannot be enforced against it. There is no reciprocal enforcement of judgments. It is nothing more than a name grasped from the air, as elusive as the Cheshire Cat. In such cases the very fact of incorporation there gives some ground for believing there is a risk that, if judgment or an award is obtained, it may go unsatisfied. Such registration of such companies may carry many advantages to the individuals who control them, but they may suffer the disadvantage of having a *Mareva* injunction granted against them. The giving of security for a debt is a small price to pay for the convenience of such a registration. Security would certainly be required in New York. So also it may be in London. Other grounds may be shown for believing there is a risk. But some such should be shown.

(v) The plaintiff must, of course, give an undertaking in damages—in case he fails in his claim or the injunction turns out to be unjustified. In a suitable case this should be supported by a bond or security: and the injunction only granted on it being given, or undertaken to be given.

3. See also Stanley Sadinsky, "Interlocutory Injunctions and Procedures: The Mareva Injunction," in Jeffrey Berryman, ed., *Remedies: Issues and Perspectives* (Toronto: Carswell, 1991), at 175; A. Zuckerman, "Mareva Injunctions and Security for Judgment in a Framework of Interlocutory Remedies" (1993), 109 *Law Quarterly Review* 432; A. Zuckerman, "Interlocutory Remedies in Quest of Procedural Fairness" (1993), 56 *Modern Law Review* 325; and R. Deane, "Varying the Plaintiff's Burden: An Efficient Approach to Interlocutory Injunctions To Preserve Future Money Judgments" (1999), 49 *University of Toronto Law Journal* 1.

See also the articulation of the criteria applied in *Price v. Canadian Imperial Bank of Commerce* (1988), 81 NBR (2d) 181, at 187 (CA).

4. Although the effect of *Aetna* is to view the issue of "jurisdiction" as applying to moving assets outside Canada, subsequent courts have still granted a Mareva injunction in cases where all the defendant was doing was moving assets into another province. In *Gateway Village Investments Ltd. v. Sybra Food Services* (1987), 12 BCLR (2d) 234 (SC), Southin J granted a Mareva injunction against a defendant who appeared to be closing down its business oper-

ations in British Columbia and returning to Alberta. For Southin J the prospect of seeking reciprocal enforcement of a judgment in another province for a small amount (the amount involved was $65,000) raised significant difficulties of enforcement. In her own words (at 242):

> The blunt reality is that unless there is a great deal of money at stake, the cost of chasing a corporate defendant across Canada is, if not prohibitory, certainly inhibitory.

Southin J indicated that *Aetna* stood for the proposition that "jurisdiction in a federal state is a factor albeit a factor of grave importance."

5. In *Third Chandris, supra*, the English Court of Appeal indicated that there must be a real risk that the defendant may dissipate his or her assets in order to evade judgment. In *Ghoth v. Ghoth*, [1992] 2 All ER 920 (CA) the English Court of Appeal indicated that the Mareva injunction was to "safeguard the plaintiff or petitioner from a situation in which the assets of the opposing party are run down, either with the intention of making that party judgment-proof or at least having that effect without reasonable excuse" (at 922, per Lord Donaldson MR). In *Customs and Excise Commissioners v. Anchor Foods Ltd.*, [1999] 3 All ER 268, the court held that where a transaction has been made in the ordinary course of business that can be characterized as bona fide, it is difficult, although not impossible, to justify a Mareva injunction. In *Chitel v. Rothbart* (1982), 141 DLR (3d) 268 (Ont. CA) the Ontario Court of Appeal indicated that the primary focus was to determine whether the defendant was dealing with his or her assets in a "manner clearly distinct from his usual or ordinary course of business or living." The Federal Court of Appeal has taken a very strict position on proof of dissipation of assets. In *Marine Atlantic Inc. v. Blyth* (1993), 113 DLR (4th) 501 (FCA), the court suggested that there must be actual proof of intent to defeat or frustrate an eventual judgment.

In *Mooney v. Orr* (1994), 100 BCLR (2d) 335 (SC), the plaintiff had brought an action against the defendant to discharge a Mareva injunction. The plaintiff was known as an international deal maker who had structured his deals to maximize income tax, to protect wealth from various attacks (creditors), and to ensure income. The defendant had brought an action against the plaintiff on a counterclaim. The defendant was aware of how the plaintiff had structured his affairs before entering into a business relationship that had soured. The defendant during the course of the original proceedings had sought a Mareva injunction and order to disclose the whereabouts of the plaintiff's assets offshore. The defendant could not show that the plaintiff had removed assets from Canada or that the plaintiff had done anything to make his assets less exigible since entering into the business deal with the defendant. The lack of evidence demonstrating that the plaintiff was doing anything to render impotent the court process was not seen as a barrier to the granting of the injunction. Huddart J allowed the injunction to continue, at least until full disclosure had been given by the plaintiff, at which stage the plaintiff could again seek its discharge. For Huddart J, the guiding principle appears to have been to fashion an order pursuant to the empowering legislation "just and convenient" provision, which shows to the world that the court is not impotent "in the face of those who choose to order their affairs so as to keep all their options open for themselves." The expansionist approach in *Mooney v. Orr* has been endorsed by the BC Court of Appeal in *Silver Standard Resources Inc. v. Joint Stock Co. Geolog*, [1999] 7 WWR 289, at 300 (BCCA), and *Insurance Corp. of British Columbia v. Patko* (2008), 77 BCLR (4th) 254 (CA) at para. 26.

In *R v. Consolidated Fastfrate Transport Inc.* (1995), 24 OR (3d) 564 (CA), the Ontario Court of Appeal divided on the issue of what proof of asset dissipation was required. The Crown was seeking a Mareva injunction to prevent the accused from disposing assets following the windup of its business. The accused had been charged under the *Competition Act* and the Crown feared that if it was successful in its criminal prosecution, and a substantial fine was imposed, the accused would be judgment proof if allowed to dispose of its assets pending the conclusion of the criminal proceedings. Galligan JA (Houlden JA concurring) was of the opinion that the defendant's motive in moving assets out of the court's jurisdiction was decisive. Per Galligan JA (at 578):

> I am not convinced that *Aetna* categorically resolves the question of whether a plaintiff can obtain a *Mareva* injunction on showing either that the defendant has arranged his or her affairs for the purpose of defeating a potential creditor or just that the arrangement might have that effect. However, when I read that judgment and the judgment of this court in *Chitel* together, I am inclined to think that the better view is that the determinative question is the purpose for which the arrangement of assets is made. Thus, I am of the view that there is an improper purpose which will attract *Mareva* relief if the defendant makes an arrangement of its assets with the intention of defeating potential creditors. If, on the other hand, the purpose for the arrangement is a legitimate one in the advance of the defendant's interests, then the fact that the result may defeat potential creditors will not justify the granting of a *Mareva* injunction.
>
> As I said earlier, this is not an ordinary civil case in which the granting of a *Mareva* injunction is under review. If it were, I would have to reach a firm conclusion about whether a plaintiff is entitled to a *Mareva* injunction upon one or other of the alternatives mentioned above or whether the plaintiff can only succeed when the court is persuaded that the defendant acted with the improper purpose of defeating its creditors. Earlier in these reasons, I concluded that the courts must be cautious in the exercise of their jurisdiction to grant injunctions in aid of the criminal law. The exercise of that caution demands, in my view, that when the court adopts principles from the civil law, it acts only upon principles which are certain. It should not act upon principles which are subject to debate.
>
> There can be no doubt that the courts will exercise their jurisdiction to grant *Mareva* injunctions if it is established that the defendant is or has been disposing of its assets for the improper purpose of avoiding a possible judgment. Acting with the caution required when exercising the jurisdiction to issue a civil injunction in aid of the criminal law, I have concluded that a *Mareva* type of injunction can only be issued in aid of the criminal law when the court is persuaded that the accused person is arranging its affairs for the improper purpose of preventing its assets from being available to pay a fine should one be imposed.

Weiler JA was of the opinion that an improper motive requirement was not required and would only operate to hinder the development of the Mareva injunction. In her opinion the key issue was the extent to which the defendant's dealings were outside the ordinary course of business. Per Weiler JA (at 604-5):

> It is relatively easy to draw the inference that a proposed transfer of assets is out of the ordinary course of business, and that a judgment which is likely to be obtained will not be capable of enforcement, where there is evidence that the transfer of assets is for an improper purpose. I believe, however, that other cogent evidence can also meet this two-part requirement. As can be seen from *Aetna, supra*, evidence as to the incorporation of the company is relevant in determining the jurisdiction in which the company is entitled to carry on business. A transfer of assets

within the jurisdiction in which a company is entitled to carry on business would not appear to be a transfer out of the ordinary course of business. Conversely, a transfer of assets to a jurisdiction in which the company is not entitled to carry on business would be some indication of a transfer outside that company's ordinary course of business. As I have already pointed out, a *Mareva* injunction cannot affect the right of a company to pay business debts. While a transfer of assets to pay business debts would not be considered a transfer out of the ordinary course of business, a proposed transfer of assets which is not for the purpose of paying business debts would be some indication that the transfer is out of that company's ordinary course of business. The size of the judgment which would be obtained against the company, the effect it would have on the assets or financial position of the company, as well as the timing of a proposed removal of assets are also, in my opinion, relevant considerations. Finally, the effect of the transfer on the ability to trace assets through a corporate reorganization, and the existence of legislation providing for the reciprocal enforcement of judgments, must be considered in determining the likelihood of enforcing any judgment obtained in the event that an injunction is not granted.

The Manitoba Court of Appeal, in *Clark v. Nucare PLC* (2006), 208 Man R. (2d) 102 (CA), at para. 46, has suggested that the "preponderance of authority supports the view that Mareva injunctions are unavailable against defendants who do not evidence an intention to frustrate the plaintiff's potential judgment."

6. In *Morguard Investments Ltd. v. De Savoye*, [1990] 3 SCR 1077, the Supreme Court of Canada rewrote the rules of private international law with respect to the bringing of an action on a "foreign" judgment. At least where the "foreign" judgment was that of another Canadian court, the basis for an enforcement action was reduced to the question whether the court of the other province had properly taken jurisdiction over the matter. If so, an action for the enforcement of that judgment was appropriate. Does this have any further ramifications for the availability or utility of Mareva injunctions in cases confined to a Canadian setting? (See also *Clarke v. Lo Bianco* (1991), 59 BCLR (2d) 334; *Minkler & Kirschbaum v. Sheppard* (1991), 60 BCLR (2d) 360; and *Federal Deposit Insurance Co. v. Vanstone* (1992), 63 BCLR (2d) 190 where *Morguard* was applied to enforcement actions brought in British Columbia on California, Arizona, and Oklahoma judgments, respectively.)

Mareva Injunctions and Third Parties

While the Mareva injunction is an *in personam* remedy—that is, it is addressed to the person and does not attach directly to his or her assets—it is common to have the order address agents and servants of the defendant. Failure to comply with the order can result in contempt proceedings. Thus, third parties are interested in the obligations the order imposes upon them. These rights and obligations are discussed in the following case.

Z Ltd. v. A-Z and AA-LL Ltd.
[1982] QB 558 (CA)

[In a massive fraud scheme the defendants had defrauded the plaintiffs of £2,000,000. These funds had been paid into several bank accounts and used to acquire other fixed assets. The plaintiffs, upon discovering the fraud, successfully obtained Anton Piller and Mareva injunctions against the defendants. This action continued mainly at the request of five chartered banks who wished elucidation of their responsibilities under a Mareva injunction.

In the course of his judgment Lord Denning MR made the following remarks (at 574-78):]

LORD DENNING MR: …

The Juristic Principle

The juristic principle is therefore this: As soon as the bank is given notice of the *Mareva* injunction, it must freeze the defendant's bank account. It must not allow any drawings to be made on it, neither by cheques drawn before the injunction nor by those drawn after it. The reason is because, if it allowed any such drawings, it would be obstructing the course of justice—as prescribed by the court which granted the injunction—and it would be guilty of a contempt of court.

I have confined my observations to banks and bank accounts. But the same applies to any specific asset held by a bank for safe custody on behalf of the defendant. Be it jewellery, stamps, or anything else. And to any other person who holds any other asset of the defendant. If the asset is covered by the terms of the *Mareva* injunction, that other person must not hand it over to the defendant or do anything to enable him to dispose of it. He must hold it pending further order.

The injunction does not prevent payment under a letter of credit or under a bank guarantee (see *Intraco Ltd. v. Notis Shipping Corporation*, [1981] 2 Lloyd's Rep. 256 (CA) and *Power Curber International Ltd. v. National Bank of Kuwait SAK*, [1981] 1 WLR 1233 (CA)); but it may apply to the proceeds as and when received by or for the defendant. It does not apply to a credit card. The bank must honour all credit cards issued to the defendant and used by him, except when they have been used fraudulently or wrongly. It can debit the amount against the customer's account.

The Things Which Follow

Such being the juristic principle, some things necessarily follow in justice to the bank or other innocent third party who is given notice of the *Mareva* injunction or knows of it.

First, Indemnity

In so far as the bank, or other innocent third party, is asked to take any action—or in the circumstances require him to take any action—and he is put to expense on that account, he is entitled to be recouped by the plaintiff: and in so far as he is exposed to any liability, he is entitled to be indemnified by the plaintiff. This is because when the plaintiff gives notice of the injunction to the bank or innocent third party, he impliedly requests them to freeze the account or otherwise do whatever is necessary or reasonable to secure the observance of the injunction. This implied request gives rise to an implied promise to recoup any expense and to indemnify against any liability; see the notes to *Lampleigh v. Brathwait* (1616), Hob. 105; 80 ER 255 (KB) in *Smith's Leading Cases*, 13th ed. (1929), vol. 1, p. 148. In addition, in support of this implied promise, so as to ease the mind of the third party, the judge, when he grants the injunction, may require the plaintiff to give an undertaking in such terms as to secure that the bank or other innocent third party does not suffer in any way by having to assist and support the course of justice prescribed by the injunction. Such as was done by Robert Goff J in *Searose Ltd. v. Seatrain UK Ltd.*, [1981] 1 WLR 894 (QB) and *Clipper Maritime Co. Ltd. of Monrovia v. Mineral-importexport*, [1981] 1 WLR 1262 (CA).

Second, Precise Notice

The bank or other innocent third party, should be told, with as much certainty as possible, what he is to do or not to do. The plaintiff will, no doubt, obtain his *Mareva* injunction *against the defendant* in wide terms so as to prevent the defendant disposing, not only of any named asset, but also of any other asset he has within the jurisdiction. The plaintiff does this because he often does not know in advance exactly what assets the defendant has or where they are situate. But, when the plaintiff gives notice to the bank or other innocent third party, then he should identify the bank account by specifying the branch and heading of the account and any other asset of the defendant "with as much precision as is reasonably practicable": see *Searose Ltd. v. Seatrain UK Ltd.*, [1981] 1 WLR 894 (QB), at p. 897C.

Third, Search

If the plaintiff cannot identify the bank account or other asset with precision, he may request the bank or other innocent third party to conduct a search so as to see whether he holds any asset of the defendant, provided that he undertakes to pay the costs of the search: see *Searose Ltd. v. Seatrain UK Ltd.*, [1981] 1 WLR 894 (QB) at pp. 896F-G and 897F-G. He may, for example, ask the bank to search the accounts of its branches in inner London to see if the defendant has an account at any of them. The bank may not tell the plaintiff the result of the search, lest it breaks the confidence of the customer. But, if it finds that the defendant has an account, it will freeze it for its own protection: so that it will not be in contempt of court. We are told that in one case the Inland Revenue requested the bank to make a "trawl" of all its branches to see if the defendant had an account at any of them. The bank could not be expected to do this, except on the footing that all the expense was to be paid by the plaintiff.

Fourth, Tell the Judge

In view of the impact of the *Mareva* injunction on banks and other innocent third parties, it is desirable that the judge should be told on the application the names of the banks and third parties to whom it is proposed to give notice: but it should not preclude the plaintiff from giving notice to others on further information being obtained.

Fifth, Maximum Amount

When we first granted *Mareva* injunctions, we did not insert any maximum amount. But nowadays it has become usual to insert the maximum amount to be restrained. The maximum amount is the sum claimed by the plaintiff from the defendant. This is done in case it should be that the defendant has assets which exceed the amount of the plaintiff's claim. If such should be the case, it is not thought right to restrain him from dealing with the excess. That is all very well so far as the defendant is concerned, because he knows, or should know, the value of his assets. But it is completely unworkable so far as the bank or other innocent third party is concerned: because it does not know what other assets the defendant may have or their value.

What then is to be done? In some cases the best course may be to omit the maximum amount altogether: and to make the injunction comprehensive against all the assets of the defendant, as we used to do. This would cause the defendant little inconvenience. Because he could come along at once to the court and ask for the excess to be released—by disclosing the whereabouts of his assets and the extent of them. If he chooses not to do so, it would be because he knows there is no excess. If notice is given to a bank or other third party, they know that they must not deal with any of the assets of the defendant.

In other cases, however, it may still be desirable to insert a maximum amount in the general injunction as against the defendant himself. But, as this is unworkable against a bank, it would at the same time be desirable to add a special injunction restraining the defendant from disposing of any of the sums standing to the credit of the defendant in a specified bank account in excess of the maximum: or from disposing of any item deposited with the specified bank for safe custody. The reason being that every bank or other innocent third party should know exactly what it should or should not do.

Sixth, Normal Living Expenses

Likewise, if in any case it is thought desirable to allow the defendant to have the use of sums for "normal living expenses," or such like, the injunction should specify the sums as figures: without saying what they are to be used for. The bank should not be required to inquire what use is to be made of them. A special account should be opened for such sums.

Seventh, Joint Account

If it is thought that the defendant may have moneys in a joint account, with others, the injunction shall be framed in terms wide enough to cover the joint account—if the judge thinks it desirable for the protection of the plaintiff.

Eighth, Return Day

When granting a *Mareva* injunction *ex parte*, the court may sometimes think it right only to grant it for a few days until the defendant and the bank or other innocent third party can be heard. The injunction is such a serious matter for all concerned that all of them should be given the earliest possible opportunity of being heard. The plaintiff will, of course, in his own interest, give notice to the bank or other innocent third parties at once—either by telephone or telex—and he must follow it up immediately by a written confirmation to be delivered by hand or earliest means. The notice should set out the terms of the injunction, and request that it be observed. The plaintiff should also serve the defendant straight away so that he can apply to discharge it if so advised: see *Negocios Del Mar SA v. Doric Shipping Corporation SA*, [1979] 1 Lloyd's Rep. 331 (CA). But in other cases where service on the defendant is not immediately practicable, for some reason or another, the return day could be later.

Ninth, Undertakings

The plaintiff who seeks a *Mareva* injunction should normally give an undertaking in damages to the defendant, and also an undertaking to a bank or other innocent third party to pay any expenses reasonably incurred by them. The judge may, or may not, require a bond or other security to support this undertaking: but this may not be insisted on when the plaintiff is legally-aided: see *Allen v. Jambo Holdings Ltd.*, [1980] 1 WLR 1252 (CA). But the undertakings only cover damages or expenses reasonably incurred. If the defendant or third party could have reduced it by taking reasonable steps, it is his duty to do so: see *Smith v. Day* (1882), 21 Ch. D 421 (CA) and *Allen v. Jambo Holdings Ltd.* at p. 1256F-H.

Tenth, Discovery

In order to make a *Mareva* injunction fully effective, it is very desirable that the defendant should be required in a proper case to make discovery. If he comes on the return day and says that he has ample assets to meet the claim, he ought to specify them. Otherwise his refusal to disclose them will go to show that he is really evading payment. There is ample power in the court to order discovery: see *A.J. Bekhor & Co. Ltd. v. Bilton*, [1981] QB 923. I am sorry that the majority of the court there reversed Parker J and differed from Griffiths LJ, but it was only on the special facts. I see that the Report of the Committee on the Enforcement of Judgment Debts (1960) (Cmnd. 3909), paragraph 1253, recommended a reform of the law on the lines now embraced by the *Mareva* injunction, and added, in paragraph 1255(v):

> There should be power to order the attendance of the debtor at court and, if need be, to detain him until he has disclosed the whereabouts of the property and lodged it in safe keeping, or otherwise given security as approved by the court.

In lieu of his attendance, it might be a good thing to order him to make discovery on affidavit.

Conclusion

I trust that in this judgment we have set out sufficient guidelines for the banks and other third parties who have notice of *Mareva* injunctions.

NOTES AND QUESTIONS

1. A bank will not be held liable in negligence for failing to comply with a Mareva order. See *Customs and Excise Commissioners v. Barclays Bank Plc*, [2006] 3 WLR 1 (HL).

2. The Ontario Law Reform Commission has recommended in its report on *The Enforcement of Judgment Debts and Related Matters: Part IV* (Toronto: Ontario Ministry of the Attorney General, 1983), at 119-23 to abolish the Mareva jurisdiction. In its place, the commission has proposed the following:

> 2. With the exception of section 22 of the *Family Law Reform Act*, existing provisional remedies should be repealed and replaced by a new prejudgment remedy—to be called "attachment"—the details of which are contained in the following Recommendations. Accordingly, the *Absconding Debtors Act* and the absconding debtors provisions of the *Small Claims Courts Act* should be repealed. In addition, *Mareva* injunctions should no longer be available under section 19(1) of the *Judicature Act*. The only authority for the courts to restrain debtors from dealing with their assets prior to judgment to the detriment of their creditors should be the new prejudgment attachment legislation proposed below.
>
> 3. Prejudgment attachment should be available only in the following circumstances:
>
> (a) where a debtor is about to leave or has left Ontario with intent to defeat, defraud, hinder, or delay his creditors or any of them, or to avoid being served with civil process;
>
> (b) where the debtor conceals himself to avoid service of civil process;
>
> (c) where a debtor has removed or is about to remove his property from the Province, or has assigned, transferred, disposed of, encumbered or secreted his property, or is about to assign, transfer, dispose of, encumber or secrete his property, with intent to defeat, defraud, hinder, or delay any of his creditors, or where the debtor has done or omitted to do any act with respect to his property with intent to frustrate the enforcement of a judgment that might be rendered against him; or
>
> (d) whenever there is a danger that, without such relief, recovery of a debt may be jeopardized.
>
> 4. Prejudgment attachment should not be available only because
>
> (a) the debtor is about to leave or has left the jurisdiction with intent to avoid arrest or to change his domicile;
>
> (b) the debt or liability of the debtor is alleged to have been fraudulently incurred; or
>
> (c) the debtor is not a resident of Ontario. ...
>
> 17. In order to protect debtors, prejudgment attachment should be available only after the creditor has established under oath the existence of one or more grounds for attachment and a strong *prima facie* case on the claim against the debtor, and has affirmed the amount that he seeks to recover from the debtor over and above all setoffs and counterclaims known to him, and that his application for prejudgment attachment is made *bona fide* for the sole purpose of obtaining security for the enforcement of any future judgment in the main action against the debtor.
>
> 18. The jurisdiction to grant prejudgment attachment should be exercised by a judge.
>
> 19(1) Prejudgment attachment should continue to be available upon an *ex parte* application. To provide the debtor with additional protection in such a case, however, the order should be granted for a limited period of time and the attaching creditor should be required to return to court to seek a continuation of the attachment order. On a return of the motion, the onus should

continue to rest upon the attaching creditor to satisfy the court that there are grounds for pre-judgment attachment.

(2) In order to enable the debtor to meet the creditor's claim for a continuation of an attachment order or to challenge the validity of the order, he should be served with a copy of the order together with a copy of the material supporting the creditor's original application.

20(1) In order to safeguard further the interests of the debtor and persons interested in property subject to prejudgment attachment, the issuance of an attachment order should be dependent upon the creditor posting a bond or giving an undertaking in an amount, to be determined by the court, that will cover the plaintiff's probable liability for wrongful attachment (see Recommendations 29-31).

(2) As a precondition to the making of an attachment order, the attaching creditor should also be required to undertake to pay the costs incurred by a third party as a result of the order of attachment.

See also the Alberta Institute of Law Research and Reform Report, *Prejudgment Remedies for Unsecured Claimants* (1988, Report No. 50), at 160 et seq., also recommending abolition of the Mareva jurisdiction in favour of a general pre-judgment attachment order.

3. In New Brunswick, the Code of Civil Procedure incorporates the following provision:

40.03 Injunction for Preservation of Assets (Mareva Injunction)

(1) Where a person claims monetary relief, the court may grant an interlocutory injunction to restrain any person from disposing of, or removing from New Brunswick, assets within New Brunswick of the person against whom the claim is made.

(2) In considering whether to grant an injunction, the court shall take into account the nature and substance of the claim or defence, and consider whether there is a risk of the assets being disposed of or removed from New Brunswick.

(3) Notwithstanding Rule 40.02, an injunction may be granted under this subrule to remain in effect until judgment.

(4) Where an injunction has been granted under this subrule to remain in effect until judgment and the claimant succeeds on his claim for debt or damages, the injunction shall, without further order, continue in effect until the judgment is satisfied.

What impact is the *Aetna* decision likely to have on the concept of "jurisdiction" adopted in the New Brunswick provision?

4. Section 12 of the Ontario *Family Law Act*, RSO 1990, c. F.3, created a form of Mareva injunction for the preservation of property pending its division following separation or divorce:

12. In an application under section 7 or 10, if the court considers it necessary for the protection of the other spouse's interests under this Part, the court may make an interim or final order

(a) restraining the depletion of a spouse's property; and

(b) for the possession, delivering up, safekeeping and preservation of the property.

See similar provisions in the *Family Relations Act*, RSBC 1996, c. 128, s. 67; *Marital Property Act*, RSM 1987, c. M45, s. 21(1), as am. SM 1998, c. 41, s. 31; *Matrimonial Property Act*, RSNS 1989, c. 275, s. 19, as am. 1995-96, c. 13, s. 83; *Family Law Act*, SN 1988, c. 60, ss. 16 and 30; and *Family Law Reform Act*, SPEI 1995, c. 12, s. 12.

An interesting use of a Mareva-type injunction is contained in the *Criminal Code* to restrain the disposal of property where an order for forfeiture is likely to be made.

Criminal Code

RSC 1985, c. C-46, s. 462.33 (as added by RSC 1985, c. 42 (4th Supp.), s. 2; RSC 1993, c. 37, s. 21; RSC 1996, c. 16, s. 60; RSC 1997, c. 18, s. 30; RSC 2001, c. 32, s. 16; RSC 2005, c. 44, s. 4)

462.33(1) The Attorney General may make an application in accordance with subsection (2) for a restraint order under subsection (3) in respect of any property.

(2) An application made under subsection (1) for a restraint order under subsection (3) in respect of any property may be made *ex parte* and shall be made in writing to a judge and be accompanied by an affidavit sworn on the information and belief of the Attorney General or any other person deposing to the following matters, namely,

    (a) the offence or matter under investigation;

    (b) the person who is believed to be in possession of the property;

    (c) the grounds for the belief that an order of forfeiture may be made under subsection 462.37(1) or (2.01) or 462.38(2) in respect of the property;

    (d) a description of the property; and

    (e) whether any previous applications have been made under this section with respect to the property.

(3) A judge who hears an application for a restraint order made under subsection (1) may—if the judge is satisfied that there are reasonable grounds to believe that there exists, within the province in which the judge has jurisdiction or any other province, any property in respect of which an order of forfeiture may be made under subsection 462.37(1) or (2.01) or 462.38(2), in respect of a designated offence alleged to have been committed within the province in which the judge has jurisdiction—make an order prohibiting any person from disposing of, or otherwise dealing with any interest in, the property specified in the order otherwise than in the manner that may be specified in the order.

(3.01) Subsections 462.32(2.1) and (2.2) apply, with such modifications as the circumstances require, in respect of a restraint order.

(3.1) A restraint order may be issued under this section in respect of property situated outside Canada, with any modifications that the circumstances require.

(4) An order made by a judge under subsection (3) may be subject to such reasonable conditions as the judge thinks fit.

(5) Before making an order under subsection (3) in relation to any property, a judge may require notice to be given to and may hear any person who, in the opinion of the judge, appears to have a valid interest in the property unless the judge is of the opinion that giving such notice before making the order would result in the disappearance, dissipation or reduction in value of the property or otherwise affect the property so that all or a part thereof could not be subject to an order of forfeiture under subsection 462.37(1) or (2.01) or 462.38(2).

(6) An order made under subsection (3) shall be made in writing.

(7) Before making an order under subsection (3), a judge shall require the Attorney General to give such undertakings as the judge considers appropriate with respect to the payment of damages or costs, or both, in relation to

    (a) the making of an order in respect of property situated within or outside Canada; and

(b) the execution of an order in respect of property situated within Canada.

(8) A copy of an order made by a judge under subsection (3) shall be served on the person to whom the order is addressed in such manner as the judge directs or as may be prescribed by rules of court.

(9) A copy of an order made under subsection (3) shall be registered against any property in accordance with the laws of the province in which the property is situated.

(10) An order made under subsection (3) remains in effect until

(a) it is revoked or varied under subsection 462.34(4) or revoked under paragraph 462.43(a);

(b) it ceases to be in force under section 462.35; or

(c) an order of forfeiture or restoration of the property is made under subsection 462.37(1) or (2.01), 462.38(2) or 462.41(3) or any other provision of this or any other Act of Parliament.

(11) Any person on whom an order made under subsection (3) is served in accordance with this section and who, while the order is in force, acts in contravention of or fails to comply with the order is guilty of an indictable offence or an offence punishable on summary conviction.

NOTES

1. The Law Reform Commission of Canada has made the following recommendation in its Working Paper No. 30 on *Police Powers: Search and Seizure in Criminal Law Enforcement* (Ottawa: Supply and Services Canada, 1983), at 354, recommendation 39.

39. Where "objects of seizure" are reasonably believed to be in a financial account, the police should be empowered to obtain a warrant to transfer the amount of the seizable funds to an official police account under judicial control. A temporary freezing order on a financial account should be made available where police officers seize financial records that are reasonably believed to contain information that will enable them to apply for a warrant to seize funds in the account. The freezing order should be of fixed duration and limited by the amount of the seizable funds. It should be obtainable from a superior court judge or a judge designated under section 482 of the *Criminal Code*, and subject to an immediate right on the part of the individual concerned to apply for its revocation.

Commentary (at 142) (footnotes omitted):

62. The final component of our recommendation is directed towards clarifying the situation with respect to financial accounts. We begin with the observation that illegally obtained money in tangible form has long been seizable. For example, the 1836 English case of *Burgiss* held that coins found in possession of a prisoner charged with forgery could be retained on the basis that there was reasonable ground to suppose that the coins were proceeds of the crime. Proceeds, of course, may be converted into different forms of property, and Anglo-Canadian courts have recognized the legitimacy of following the money for purposes of restitution insofar as it can be traced through these conversions. Specifically, it has been noted that the mere fact that money has passed through a bank account does not impede the common law right to trace. Moreover, by virtue of the extended definition of "property" in section 2 of the *Criminal Code* so as to include "a right to recover or receive any money or goods," it has been suggested that offences concerning property may cover the possession of funds in accounts. We firmly agree with these positions.

63. The problem with respect to seizing the money in the account under present crime-related law is that subsection 443(1) of the *Criminal Code* refers to seizure of "anything" fitting within the designated classifications, an expression that may not cover intangible forms of obligation represented by a debt or loan. In the recent House of Lords decision in *Cuthbertson*, for example, it was found that a forfeiture provision covering "anything" related to drug offences did not apply to profits of drug trafficking held in bank accounts since these were not "tangible things." While the merits of this decision might be debated and perhaps ultimately resisted by Canadian authority, it would seem prudent to explicitly cover funds in financial accounts in search and seizure provisions intended to apply to them.

2. In *R v. Consolidated Fastfrate Transport Inc.* (1995), 24 OR (3d) 564 (CA), the Ontario Court of Appeal set aside a Mareva injunction that had been obtained by the Crown against the accused. The facts have been set out above. The court held that it had jurisdiction to grant a civil order for the purpose of assisting the criminal law (see generally chapter 7, "Injunctions"). The majority set out the following criteria that the Crown must prove before being granted the injunction. *Per* Galligan JA (at 578-79):

> I have reached the conclusion that the principles upon which civil courts grant *Mareva* injunctions are of help when the court is considering whether to issue a *Mareva* type of injunction in aid of the criminal law. My consideration of the authorities previously referred to has led me to conclude that the following principles apply to the granting of a *Mareva* type of injunction issued in aid of the criminal law:
>
>   (i)   The Crown must demonstrate that the accused person has assets within the jurisdiction of the court;
>
>   (ii)   The Crown must demonstrate a strong *prima facie* case:
>
>   (a)   that the accused person will likely be convicted of the offence with which it is charged, and
>
>   (b)   that the amount of the fine will likely equal or exceed the value of the assets sought to be attached.
>
>   (iii)   The Crown must demonstrate that the accused person is or has been dissipating, removing or disposing of its assets for the improper purpose of making them unavailable to pay a fine in the event of cnnviction.
>
>   (iv)   The Crown must give the usual undertaking respecting damages.

See also *West Mercia Constabulary v. Wagener*, [1982] 1 WLR 127 (QB).

Mareva Injunctions and Extra-Territoriality

In 1990, a series of cases came before the English courts involving disputes justiciable within the English court's jurisdiction, but where the defendants had all or the majority of their assets in other countries. The practice of issuing a worldwide Mareva injunction was approved, although the courts did stress the exceptional circumstances under which these injunctions would be granted and that they still operated *in personam*. See *Babanaft Inter-*

national SA v. Bassatne, [1990] Ch. 13 (CA); *Derby v. Weldon*, [1990] Ch. 48 (CA); and *Derby v. Weldon (No. 3 & 4)*, [1990] Ch. 65 (CA).

Derby v. Weldon (No. 3 & 4)
[1990] Ch. 65 (CA)

[The plaintiff sought a worldwide Mareva injunction against the defendants, otherwise known as C.M.I. This order was sought based on alleged breach of contract, negligence, and breach of fiduciary duty. The plaintiff alleged damages in the vicinity of £25 million. The defendants appeared to have no assets within the United Kingdom. The order was granted and the defendants appealed.]

LORD DONALDSON MR (at 79): In my judgment, the key requirement for any *Mareva* injunction, whether or not it extends to foreign assets, is that it shall accord with the rationale upon which *Mareva* relief has been based in the past. That rationale, legitimate purpose and fundamental principle I have already stated, namely, that no court should permit a defendant to take action designed to frustrate subsequent orders of the court. If for the achievement of this purpose it is necessary to make orders concerning foreign assets, such orders should be made, subject, of course, to ordinary principles of international law. When the Vice-Chancellor said that special circumstances had to be present to justify such an exceptional order, I do not understand him to have been saying more than that the court should not go further than necessity dictates, that in the first instance it should look to assets within the jurisdiction and that in the majority of cases there will be no justification for looking to foreign assets.

I can see neither rhyme nor reason in regarding the existence of some asset within the jurisdiction of however little value as a pre-condition for granting a *Mareva* injunction in respect of assets outside the jurisdiction. The existence of *sufficient* assets within the jurisdiction is an excellent reason for confining the jurisdiction to such assets, but, other considerations apart, the fewer the assets within the jurisdiction the greater the necessity for taking protective measures in relation to those outside it.

The reality is, I think, that it is only recently that litigants have sought extraterritorial relief and that the courts have had to consider whether to grant it and upon what conditions. ...

Enforceability of the Injunctions

First amongst these considerations was that, as he said, "nothing brings the law into greater disrepute than the making of orders which cannot be enforced. The maxim 'equity does not act in vain' is a very sound one." It was suggested in argument that, on the authorities, the maxim referred not to enforceability but to the making of orders with which it was impossible to comply, e.g., to fell a tree which had already been blown down or which lawfully could at once be nullified, e.g., to grant the plaintiff a tenancy at will. However that may be, the Vice-Chancellor was plainly right in his general proposition, although it requires careful examination in the context of particular circumstances.

I find it difficult to believe that, in using the words "cannot be enforced," he meant "cannot be specifically enforced." That that is not the true test is clear, because it is not uncommon for a court to order the disclosure of information which exists only in the mind of an individual. If he is unusually obdurate the order is unenforceable in the sense that the information will not be disclosed. Courts assume, rightly, that those who are subject to its jurisdiction will obey its orders: see *In re Liddell's Settlement Trusts*, [1936] Ch. 365 at p. 374 which, although said in relation to an order affecting wards of court normally resident in this country against a mother normally so resident, is I think of general application. It is only if there is doubt about whether the order will be obeyed and if, should that occur, no real sanction would exist, that the court should refrain from making an order which the justice of the case requires. ...

The Impact of International Law

The third requirement was that the *Mareva* injunction, and indeed any other order of the court, should not conflict with the ordinary principles of international law. This has two aspects. The first is the nature or content of the order itself. The second is its effect upon third parties.

(1) The Nature and Content of the Order

Considerations of comity require the courts of this country to refrain from making orders which infringe the exclusive jurisdiction of the courts of other countries.

A *Mareva* injunction operates solely *in personam* and does not normally offend this principle in any way.

(2) The Effect on Third Parties

Here there is a real problem. Court orders only bind those to whom they are addressed. However, it is a serious contempt of court, punishable as such, for anyone to interfere with or impede the administration of justice. This occurs if someone, knowing of the terms of the court order, assists in the breach of that order by the person to whom it is addressed. All this is common sense and works well so long as the "aider and abettor" is wholly within the jurisdiction of the court or wholly outside it. If he is wholly within the jurisdiction of the court there is no problem whatsoever. If he is wholly outside the jurisdiction of the court, he is either not to be regarded as being in contempt or it would involve an excess of jurisdiction to seek to punish him for that contempt. Unfortunately, juridical persons, notably banks, operate across frontiers. A foreign bank may have a branch within the jurisdiction and so be subject to the English courts. An English bank may have branches abroad and be asked by a defendant to take action at such a branch which will constitute a breach by the defendant of the court's order. Is action by the foreign bank to be regarded as contempt, although it would not be so regarded but for the probably irrelevant fact that it happens to have an English branch? Is action by the foreign branch of an English bank to be regarded as contempt, when other banks in the area are free to comply with the defendant's instructions?

All this was considered in the *Babanaft* appeal [1990] Ch. 13 (CA) and gave rise to what is known as the "*Babanaft* proviso" which was included in the order made by the Vice-

Chancellor. This is not in fact the proviso adopted by the Court of Appeal in the *Babanaft* case itself, but was its preferred solution. As applied by the Vice-Chancellor to the circumstances of the application before him, it read:

> (a) No person other than Rea Bros. Plc., Walsa Nominees Ltd. [C.M.I.] and any officer and any agent appointed by power of attorney of [C.M.I.] and any individual resident in England and Wales who has notice of this paragraph shall as regards acts done or to be done outside England and Wales be affected by the terms of this paragraph or concerned to inquire whether any instruction given by or on behalf of [C.M.I.] or anyone else, whether acting on behalf of [C.M.I.] or otherwise, is or may be a breach of this paragraph save to the extent that this paragraph is declared enforceable by or is otherwise enforced by an order of a court outside England and Wales and then only within the jurisdiction of that other court; ...

The express reason for including such a proviso was that *Mareva* injunctions "have an in rem effect on third parties" and that "*Mareva* injunctions have a direct effect on third parties who are notified of them and hold assets comprised in the order": *per* Kerr LJ in the *Babanaft* case, at p. 25C-E. I know what was meant, but I am not sure that it is possible to have an "in rem effect" upon persons whether natural or juridical and a *Mareva* injunction does not have any in rem effect on the assets themselves or the defendant's title to them. Nor does such an injunction have a *direct* effect on third parties. The injunction (a) restrains those to whom it is directed from exercising what would otherwise be their rights and (b) indirectly affects the rights of some, but not all, third parties to give effect to instructions from those directly bound by the order to do or concur in the doing of acts which are prohibited by the order. Whether any particular third party is indirectly affected, depends upon whether that person is subject to the jurisdiction of the English courts.

I have no doubt of the practical need for some proviso, because in its absence banks operating abroad do not know where they stand and foreign banks without any branch in England who are thus outside the jurisdiction of the English courts may take, and have indeed taken, offence at being, as they see it, "ordered about" by the English courts. All this is recorded in the judgment of Kerr LJ in the *Babanaft* case. However I am not sure that the *Babanaft* proviso is the right answer to this dilemma.

The first objection is that it treats natural persons differently from juridical persons. Why should an English merchant bank which is a partnership, if such there still be, and carries on business abroad as well as in this country be treated differently from a company, yet the proviso does not apply to "any individual resident in England."

The second objection is that it places an English corporate bank in a very difficult position. It may know of the injunction and wish to support the court in its efforts to prevent the defendant from frustrating the due course of justice, but the proviso deprives it of the one justification which it would otherwise have for refusing to comply with his instructions.

The third objection I record without expressing any view on its validity. It is that an order which includes this proviso has ex facie no extraterritorial effect and so is not of a character enabling it to be recognized under the European Judgments Convention and enforced abroad thereunder. In other words, the proviso has a circular effect. This is apparently being argued in the Luxembourg Court of Appeal following an order for the recognition and enforcement of the Vice-Chancellor's order by the Luxembourg court of first instance.

What should be done? I should prefer a proviso on the following lines:

Provided that, in so far as this order purports to have any extraterritorial effect, no person shall be affected thereby or concerned with the terms thereof until it shall be declared enforceable or be enforced by a foreign court and then it shall only affect them to the extent of such declaration or enforcement unless they are: (a) a person to whom this order is addressed or an officer of or an agent appointed by a power of attorney of such a person or (b) persons who are subject to the jurisdiction of this court and (i) have been given written notice of this order at their residence or place of business within the jurisdiction, and (ii) are able to prevent acts or omissions outside the jurisdiction of this court which assist in the breach of the terms of this order.

This seems to me to meet any charge that the court is seeking to exercise an exorbitant jurisdiction, to be even handed as between natural and juridical persons and to avoid any argument based upon circularity.

NOTES

1. In *Mooney v. Orr* (the facts have been outlined above) Huddart J gave a non-exhaustive list of the factors that she took from current authorities, which were influential in determining the exercise of a judicial discretion to grant a Mareva injunction that had extra-territorial effect. The factors were:

   a. the nature of the transaction (local, national, international) giving rise to the cause of action;

   b. the risk inherent in the transaction;

   c. the residency of the defendant;

   d. enforcement rights for judgment creditors in the jurisdiction where the respondent's assets are located;

   e. the amount of the claim; and

   f. the history of the defendant's conduct.

2. The United Kingdom has passed the *Civil Jurisdiction and Judgment Act 1982*, in compliance with the *European Judgment Convention 1968*. This Act allows interlocutory orders from other contracting states' courts to be enforced in the United Kingdom. The Act has also resulted in plaintiffs seeking interim relief in the United Kingdom in support of a substantive claim brought in another jurisdiction. See *Republic of Haiti v. Duvalier*, [1990] Ch. 65 (CA) and *Dadourian Group International Inc v. Simms*, [2006] 1 All ER 709 (CA), providing guidelines for the issuing of worldwide freezing orders. The wide jurisdiction to grant freezing orders under the statute was discussed in *Motorola Credit Corporation v. Uzan*, [2004] 1 WLR 113 (CA), where the court set out five factors to be considered when issuing a freezing order in aid of an action being heard in another jurisdiction. Those factors were:

   a. whether the making of the order will interfere with the management of the case in the primary court—for example, where the order is inconsistent with an order of the primary court or overlaps with it;

b. whether it is the policy in the primary jurisdiction not itself to make worldwide freezing and/or disclosure orders;

c. whether there is a danger that the orders made will give rise to disharmony or confusion and/or risk of conflicting inconsistent or overlapping orders in other jurisdictions, in particular the courts of the state where the person enjoined resides or where assets affected are located; if so, then respect for the territorial jurisdiction of that state should discourage the English court from using its unusually wide powers against a foreign defendant;

d. whether at the time the order is sought there is likely to be a potential conflict as to jurisdiction rendering it inappropriate and expedient to make a worldwide order; and

e. whether, in a case where jurisdiction is resisted and disobedience is to be expected, the court will be making an order it cannot enforce.

This case is discussed in J. Berryman, "Cross-Border Enforcement of Mareva Injunctions in Canada" (2005), 30 *Advocates' Q* 413. The lack of similar legislation in Canada has been commented on by Farley J in *Baur v. Nelvana* (September 1991), [1991] OJ no. 2364 (HC) (unreported).

3. The Supreme Court of Canada has done much to revise the rules on conflict of laws to give more generous rules for the recognition and enforcement of foreign judgments. In particular, the court has encouraged the notion of full faith and credit being given to other courts' judgments and to relying upon a "real and substantial connection" test to determine in which state the action should be brought and, as a consequence, which does not disadvantage either litigant. See *Morguard Investments Ltd. v. De Savoye*, [1990] 3 SCR 1077 and *Hunt v. T & N plc*, [1993] 4 SCR 289. See Vaughan Black and Edward Babin, "Mareva Injunctions in Canada: Territorial Aspects" (1997), 28 *CBLJ* 430. The Supreme Court of Canada has also opened up the possibility that a non-monetary foreign judgment, possibly an interlocutory order, could be enforced by Canadian courts; see *Pro Swing Inc. v. Elta Golf Inc.*, [2006] 2 SCR 612.

4. On the problems for third parties of extra-territorial orders, see A. Malek and C. Lewis, "Worldwide Mareva Injunctions: The Position of International Banks," [1990] *Lloyds Maritime and Commercial Law Q* 88; P. Michell, "The Mareva Injunction in Aid of Foreign Proceedings" (1996), 34 *Osgoode Hall LJ* 741; A. Rogers, "The Extra-territorial Reach of the Mareva Injunction," [1991] *Lloyds Maritime and Commercial Law Q* 231; and David Capper, "*Mareva* Orders in Globalized Litigation," in Jeff Berryman and Rick Bigwood, eds., *The Law of Remedies: New Directions in the Common Law* (Toronto: Irwin Law, 2010), ch. 17.

ANTON PILLER INJUNCTIONS

General

Anton Piller injunctions have been termed civil search warrants. The injunction allows the applicant to seize property or evidence where there is a reasonable belief that the defendant will destroy the same before trial. Anton Piller has become particularly important in the copyright, patent, and trademark areas where modern technology makes the pirating and bootlegging of artistic works easier, as well as in other business using computer recording systems, which can be easily destroyed.

Anton Piller K.G. v. Manufacturing Processes Ltd.
[1976] Ch. 55 (CA)

LORD DENNING MR: During the last 18 months the judges of the Chancery Division have been making orders of a kind not known before. They have some resemblance to search warrants. Under these orders, the plaintiff and his solicitors are authorised to enter the defendants' premises so as to inspect papers, provided the defendant gives permission.

Now this is the important point: The court orders the defendant to give them permission. The judges have been making these orders on *ex parte* applications without prior notice to the defendant. None of the cases have been reported except the one before Templeman J on December 3, 1974, *E.M.I. Ltd. v. Pandit*, [1975] 1 WLR 302 (Ch.). But in the present case Brightman J refused to make such an order.

On appeal to us, Mr. Laddie appears for the plaintiffs. He has appeared in most of these cases, and can claim the credit—or the responsibility—for them. He represented to us that in this case it was in the interests of justice that the application should not be made public at the time it was made. So we heard it *in camera*. It was last Tuesday. After hearing his submissions, we made the order. We now come to give our reasons in public. But at the outset I must state the facts, for it is obvious that such an order can only be justified in the most exceptional circumstances.

Anton Piller KG ("Pillers"), the plaintiffs, are German manufacturers of high repute. They make electric motors and generators. They play an important part in the big new computer industry. They supply equipment for it. They have recently designed a frequency converter specially for supplying the computers of International Business Machines.

Since 1972 Pillers have had, as their agents in the United Kingdom, a company here called Manufacturing Processes Ltd. ("MPL"), which is run by Mr. A.H.S. Baker and Mr. B.P. Wallace, their two directors. These agents are dealers who get machines from Pillers in Germany and sell them to customers in England. Pillers supply MPL with much confidential information about the machines, including a manual showing how they work, and drawings which are the subject of copyright.

Very recently Pillers have found out—so they say—that these English agents, MPL, have been in secret communication with other German companies called Ferrostaal and Lechmotoren. The object of these communications is that MPL should supply these other German companies with drawings and materials and other confidential information so that they can manufacture power units like Pillers. Pillers got to know of these communications through two "defectors," if I may call them so. One was the commercial manager of MPL, Mr. Brian Firth; the other was the sales manager, Mr. Willaim Raymond Knight. These two were so upset by what was going on in MPL that on their own initiative, without any approach by Pillers whatever, on October 2, 1975, one or both flew to Germany. They told Pillers what they knew about the arrangements with Ferrostaal and Lechmotoren. They disclosed also that MPL was negotiating with Canadian and United States firms. In making these disclosures, both Mr. Firth and Mr. Knight were putting themselves in a perilous position, but Pillers assured them that they would safeguard their future employment.

The disclosures—coming from defectors—might have been considered untrustworthy. But they were supported by documents which emanated from both Ferrostaal and Lechmotoren. They showed that MPL was in regular communication with those German companies. They were sending them drawings and arranging for inspection of the Piller machine, for the express purpose that the Lechmotoren company might manufacture a prototype machine copied from Pillers. One of the most telling communications was a telex from a representative of Ferrostaal to Mr. Wallace saying:

It is the opinion of Mr. S. (of Lechmotoren) that the best way to find a final solution for the ... prototype is to send Mr. Beck (also of Lechmotoren) to you as soon as the ... latest design of P. (Piller) has arrived in your factory. In this case it is guaranteed that the Lech prototype will have exactly the same features as the P-type. We hope you will agree to this proposal and we ask you to let us have your telex in order to arrange Mr. Beck's visit accordingly.

On getting this information, Pillers were extremely worried. They were about to produce a fine new frequency converter call the "Silent Block." They feared that MPL, in co-operation with the German manufacturers, would make a copy of their "Silent Block" and ruin the market. They determined to apply to the court for an injunction to restrain MPL and their directors, the defendants, from infringing their copyright on using confidential information or making copies of their machines. But they were fearful that if the defendants were given notice of this application, they would take steps to destroy documents or send them to Germany or elsewhere, so that there would be none in existence by the time that discovery was had in the action.

So, on Wednesday, November 26, 1975, Pillers' solicitors prepared a draft writ of summons and, with an affidavit, they went before Brightman J and asked, first, for an interim injunction to restrain infringement, etc., and, secondly, for an order that they might be permitted to enter the defendants' premises so as to inspect the documents of the plaintiffs and remove them, or copies of them. Brightman J granted an interim injunction, but refused to order inspection or removal of the documents. He said:

There is strong *prima facie* evidence that the defendant company is now engaged in seeking to copy the plaintiffs' components for its own financial profit to the great detriment of the plaintiffs and in breach of the plaintiffs' rights.

He realised that the defendants might suppress evidence or misuse documentary material, but he thought that that was a risk which must be accepted in civil matters save in extreme cases.

Otherwise, [he said] it seems to me that an order on the lines sought might become an instrument of oppression, particularly in a case where a plaintiff of big standing and deep pocket is ranged against a small man who is alleged on the evidence of one side only to have infringed the plaintiffs' rights.

Let me say at once that no court in this land has any power to issue a search warrant to enter a man's house so as to see if there are papers or documents there which are of an incriminating nature, whether libels or infringements of copyright or anything else of the kind. No constable or bailiff can knock at the door and demand entry so as to inspect papers or documents. The householder can shut the door in his face and say, "Get out." That was established in the leading case of *Entick v. Carrington* (1765), 2 Wils. KB 275; 95 ER 807 (CP). None of us would wish to whittle down that principle in the slightest. But the order sought in this case is not a search warrant. It does not authorise the plaintiff's solicitors or anyone else to enter the defendants' premises against their will. It does not authorise the breaking down of any doors, nor the slipping in by a back door, nor getting in by an open door or window. It only authorises entry and inspection by the permission of the defendants. The plaintiffs must get the defendants' permission. But it does do this: It brings pressure on the defendants to give permission. It does more. It actually orders them to give permission—with, I suppose, the result that if they do not give permission, they are guilty of contempt of court.

This may seem to be a search warrant in disguise. But it was fully considered in the House of Lords 150 years ago and held to be legitimate. The case is *United Company of Merchants of England, Trading to the East Indies v. Kynaston* (1821), 3 Bli. (OS) 153; 4 ER 561 (HL (Eng.)). Lord Redesdale said, at pp. 163-64 (p. 564 (ER)):

> The arguments urged for the appellants at the Bar are founded upon the supposition, that the court has directed a forcible inspection. This is an erroneous view of the case. The order is to permit; and if the East India Company should refuse to permit inspection, they will be guilty of a contempt of court. ... It is an order operating on the person requiring the defendants to permit inspection, not giving authority of force, or to break open the doors of their warehouse.

That case was not, however, concerned with papers or things. It was only as to the value of a warehouse; and that could not be obtained without an inspection. But the distinction drawn by Lord Redesdale affords ground for thinking that there is jurisdiction to make an order that the defendant "do permit" when it is necessary in the interests of justice.

Accepting such to be the case, the question is in what circumstances ought such an order be made. If the defendant is given notice beforehand and is able to argue the pros and cons, it is warranted by that case in the House of Lords and by RSC, Ord. 29 r. 2(1) and (5). But it is a far stronger thing to make such an order *ex parte* without giving him notice. This is not covered by the Rules of the Supreme Court and must be based on the inherent jurisdiction of the court. There are one or two old precedents which give some colour for it, *Hennessy v. Rohmann, Osborne & Co.*, [1877] WN 14, and *Morris v. Howell* (1888), 22 LR Ir. 77 (QB) an Irish case. But they do not go very far. So it falls to us to consider it on principle. It seems to me that such an order can be made by a judge *ex parte*, but it should only be made where it is essential that the plaintiff should have inspection so that justice can be done between the parties: and when, if the defendant were forewarned, there is a grave danger that vital evidence will be destroyed, that papers will be burnt or lost or hidden, or taken beyond the jurisdiction, and so the ends of justice be defeated: and when the inspection would do no real harm to the defendant or his case.

Nevertheless, in the enforcement of this order, the plaintiffs must act with due circumspection. On the service of it, the plaintiffs should be attended by their solicitor, who is an officer of the court. They should give the defendants an opportunity of considering it and of consulting their own solicitor. If the defendants wish to apply to discharge the order as having been improperly obtained, they must be allowed to do so. If the defendants refuse permission to enter or to inspect, the plaintiffs must not force their way in. They must accept the refusal, and bring it to the notice of the court afterwards, if need be on an application to commit.

You might think that with all these safeguards against abuse, it would be of little use to make such an order. But it can be effective in this way: it serves to tell the defendants that, on the evidence put before it, the court is of opinion that they ought to permit inspection—nay, it orders them to permit—and that they refuse at their peril. It puts them in peril not only of proceedings for contempt, but also of adverse inferences being drawn against them; so much so that their own solicitor may often advise them to comply. We are told that in two at least of the cases such an order has been effective. We are prepared, therefore, to sanction its continuance, but only in an extreme case where there is grave danger of property being smuggled away or of vital evidence being destroyed.

On evidence in this case, we decided last Tuesday that there was sufficient justification to make an order. We did it on the precedent framed by Templeman J. It contains an undertaking in damages which is to be supported (as the plaintiffs are overseas) by a bond for £10,000. It gives an interim injunction to restrain the infringement of copyright and breach of confidential information, etc. It orders that the defendants do permit one or two of the plaintiffs and one or two of their solicitors to enter the defendants' premises for the purpose of inspecting documents, files or things, and removing those which belong to the plaintiffs. This was, of course, only an interim order pending the return of the summons. It is to be heard, we believe, tomorrow by the judge.

ORMROD LJ: I agree with all that Lord Denning MR has said. The proposed order is at the extremity of this court's powers. Such orders, therefore, will rarely be made, and only when there is no alternative way of ensuring that justice is done to the applicant.

There are three essential pre-conditions for the making of such an order, in my judgment. First, there must be an extremely strong *prima facie* case. Secondly, the damage, potential or actual, must be very serious for the applicant. Thirdly, there must be clear evidence that the defendants have in their possession incriminating documents or things, and that they may destroy such material before any application inter partes can be made.

The form of the order makes it plain that the court is not ordering or granting anything equivalent to a search warrant. The order is an order on the defendant *in personam* to permit inspection. It is therefore open to him to refuse to comply with such an order, but at his peril either of further proceedings for contempt of court—in which case, of course, the court will have the widest discretion as to how to deal with it, and if it turns out that the order was made improperly in the first place, the contempt will be dealt with accordingly—but more important, of course, the refusal to comply may be the most damning evidence against the defendant at the subsequent trial. Great responsibility clearly rests on the solicitors for the applicant to ensure that the carrying out of such an order is meticulously carefully done with the fullest respect for the defendant's rights, as Lord Denning MR has said, of applying to the court, should he feel it necessary to do so, before permitting the inspection.

In the circumstances of the present case, all those conditions to my mind are satisfied, and this order is essential in the interests of justice.

I agree, therefore, that the appeal should be allowed.

SHAW LJ: I agree with both judgments. The overriding consideration in the exercise of this salutary jurisdiction is that it is to be resorted to only in circumstances where the normal processes of the law would be rendered nugatory if some immediate and effective measure was not available. When such an order is made, the party who had procured the court to make it must act with prudence and caution in pursuance of it.

Cases involving Anton Piller injunctions can be grouped into two categories.

J. Berryman, "Anton Piller Orders: A Canadian Common Law Approach"
(1984), 34 *University of Toronto Law Journal* 1, at 7-9 (footnotes omitted)

1. *Cases Which Are Dispositive of the Issues Confronting the Applicant*

Collected under this heading are those cases which, although commenced *ex parte* and still under the cloak of interlocutory proceedings, are for the applicant dispositive. The applicant uses the order to recover property in which he has a proprietary interest, as in confidential papers, or to ensure the withdrawal from sale of commodities which infringe his trade mark, patent, or copyright. The property, that is, a document or infringing article, is the subject matter of the dispute.

The cases grouped in this category primarily concern what is loosely termed industrial property. Within this category an order made pursuant to the Anton Piller injunction bears marked similarities to what is normally available as an interim order in an industrial property action. Logically these should be kept distinct because the grounds upon which they are granted are different. In fact it would be fallacious to suggest that courts grant interim relief to prevent the infringement of copyrights, trade marks, or patents as determinative of the substantive cause of action. As recently reiterated in *American Cyanamid*, that jurisdiction aims only at maintaining the status quo. Courts exercising the Anton Piller jurisdiction have recorded their aversion to dispositive orders by requiring the plaintiff to give an undertaking, if he has not already done so, to issue a writ of summons and to provide a bond against damage should his action be unsuccessful. In this way courts have endeavoured to ensure that the defendant will be given an opportunity to challenge the plaintiff's case in an appropriate forum. However, these requirements ignore some of the realities in which the Anton Piller order operates.

The reason why these cases are considered dispositive when exercising the Anton Piller jurisdiction lies either in the nature of the target subjects or in the type of market in which they operate. Where the applicant participates in a highly volatile market, timing is the decisive factor to ensure profitable organizations. If through utilizing an Anton Piller order the applicant can bring about the withdrawal of the defendant's infringing articles, then it is highly unlikely that he will proceed any further in his cause of action. In essence the applicant is buying time. He is using a most effective and expeditious procedure to safeguard his own lawful business interests and thereby protect his position in an ephemeral market.

In respect to target subjects within this category Anton Piller orders have been directed at defendants operating what could be euphemistically referred to as backroom manufacturing—manufacturing made operational in a short space of time and even more speedily resisted if discovered—and at retailers who form the lower echelons in pyramidal marketing of illicit material. In the case of the latter the Anton Piller order may also seek to elicit information concerning suppliers and customers. For all target subjects the case made against them and implicitly endorsed by the court in granting the applicant's orders appears unanswerable. Nor are they likely to have the resources to continue a prolonged legal action. Under these circumstances this type of case is considered dispositive because probably neither applicant nor defendant has any intention to pursue the substantive cause of action to a further stage. Cases exemplifying this category are *Universal City Studios Inc. v. Mukhtar & Sons Ltd.*, *Vapourmatic Co. Ltd. v. Sparex Ltd.*, *Ex Parte Island Records Ltd.*, and *Bardeau Ltd. v. Crown Food Service Equipment Ltd.*

2. Preservation of Evidence Necessary To Prove a Further Substantive Cause of Action

This category closely resembles the first; however, two features distinguish it as a separate head. First, the plaintiff may have no proprietary interest in the property—usually documents—which is not the subject matter of the dispute. Second, the importance of the documents to the plaintiff is in their evidentiary value to prove a substantive cause of action. Mere recovery alone will not compensate for the plaintiff's injury.

Representative of this category is *Yousif v. Salama*. The plaintiff had entered into a contract which closely resembled an agency commission agreement with the defendant. The plaintiff was owed a considerable sum in commission, which the defendant denied. Records of the transactions were held by the defendant. The court, finding that these documents were essential to the plaintiff's case and being satisfied that there was a strong possibility that they would be destroyed, gave an Anton Piller order instructing the defendant to permit removal of the named documents into the care of the plaintiff's solicitor.

A feature now common to both the above categories, although this was initially not so, is the appendage of interrogatories to the order to elicit information, thereby giving the Anton Piller order all the appearance of a pre-trial discovery and examination. Such an approach was condoned in *Rank Film Distributors Ltd. v. Video Information Centre* by the House of Lords. The appellants (plaintiffs at trial) were owners of copyright films which the respondents were pirating and distributing on video tapes. As part of the court's order the respondents were required to answer interrogatories concerning the parties who supplied them with illicit films to copy and to whom they distributed for resale.

Within each category different issues emerge. Category 1 amounts to an effective way of asserting a proprietary claim. Category 2 is an extension of the present rules of civil procedure relating to the preservation of evidence before trial. The addition of interrogatories to both categories is a significant extension of present pre-trial procedures in that it appears to extend discovery and examination without commensurate extension of the procedural protection normally accorded defendants.

From the time that the above extract was published in 1984, the vast majority of Anton Piller orders are still of the first category; however, a number of additional areas have emerged. They include:

1. Restraint-of-trade clauses upon termination of employment where a fear exists that the defendant has wrongfully removed confidential client lists or other documents.

2. Location and seizure of assets for subsequent judgment as a supplementary feature of a Mareva injunction.

3. Extra-territorial Anton Piller orders where the plaintiff seeks an injunction to gain access to the defendant's premises located in a different jurisdiction. See *Cook Industries v. Galliher*, [1979] Ch. 439 and *Altertext Inc. v. Advanced Data Communications Ltd.*, [1985] 1 WLR 457 (Ch. D).

4. The Anton Piller order as a supplement to the discovery process. See *Profekta International Inc. v. Mai*, [1997] 1 FC 223.

Jurisdictional Base

There are at least three possible sources of the jurisdictional base for Anton Piller orders. One is as a function of the general court's powers to grant injunctions where it is "just and convenient." This type of provision is typically found in the acts establishing superior courts of record. For instance see s. 101 of the *Courts of Justice Act*, RSO 1990, c. C.43. A second jurisdictional base is as a function of the court's inherent jurisdiction to govern its own procedures. All superior courts of record have inherent jurisdiction to create rules and practices to control their own court processes. The Anton Piller order can be seen as an exercise of this power. Indeed, this was the view of the majority of the courts in the United Kingdom before a legislative provision was enacted. Now, under s. 7 of the *Civil Procedure Act 1997* (UK), c. 12 the English courts have power to grant what has been renamed a "Search Order," although this statutory base was not to derogate from the court's pre-existing powers. See M. Dockray and K. Thomas, "Anton Piller Orders: The New Statutory Scheme" (1998), 17 *Civil Justice Quarterly* 272.

A third jurisdictional base, and one that appears to dominate in Canada, is the various practice rules relating to the interim inspection and preservation of property found in all the common law provinces. Ontario's rr. 32.01 and 45.01 are typical.

32.01(1) The court may make an order for the inspection of real or personal property where it appears to be necessary for the proper determination of an issue in a proceeding.

(2) For the purpose of the inspection, the court may,

(a) authorize entry on or into and the taking of temporary possession of any property in the possession of a party or of a person not a party;

(b) permit the measuring, surveying or photographing of the property in question, or of any particular object or operation on the property; and

(c) permit the taking of samples, the making of observations or the conducting of tests or experiments.

(3) The order shall specify the time, place and manner of the inspection and may impose such other terms, including the payment of compensation, as are just.

(4) No order for inspection shall be made without notice to the person in possession of the property unless,

(a) service of notice, or the delay necessary to serve notice, might entail serious consequences to the moving party; or

(b) the court dispenses with service of notice for any other sufficient reason.

> 45.01(1) The court may make an interim order for the custody or preservation of any property in question in a proceeding or relevant to an issue in a proceeding, and for that purpose may authorize entry on or into any property in the possession of a party or of a person not a party.
>
> (2) Where the property is of a perishable nature or likely to deteriorate or for any other reason ought to be sold, the court may order its sale in such manner and on such terms as are just.

There are several problems accommodating the Anton Piller order with the ambit of these rules. (See J. Berryman, *supra*, at 16.)

> It is difficult to avoid the conclusion that all these rules of practice, considered as a whole, have been designed for particular sets of circumstances differing from the modern demands which gave rise to the Anton Piller order. Pursuant to various rules the courts have ordered preservation, detention, or custody of property which is the subject of the action, to ensure that something remains in existence at the determination of the dispute so that an applicant's success will not be hollow. The effect of this order corresponds to category 1 of the Anton Piller order, although it was previously suggested that the rationale for the latter was to prevent abuse of an applicant's proprietary interest.
>
> Assuming that the term "property" encompasses documents, an order which permits the detention of documents or an order for inspection which permits photocopying based on the concept of preserving evidence corresponds with much of category 2 of the Anton Piller order. However, if the order is conditional upon the closing of pleadings, as in Ontario, then it is of little assistance to an applicant who fears the removal of the same documents if notice is given to the defendant. Where the inspection takes on the appearance of a pre-trial discovery and examination—that is, where it includes orders for interrogatories or inspection to determine the contents of documents—then it is very unlikely that the respective rules as currently interpreted would ever operate. Under these rules courts have jealously guarded the discovery process and rebuffed those who have attempted to gain a pre-emptory advantage.

NOTES

1. In *Bardeau Ltd. v. Crown Food Services Equipment Ltd.* (1982), 38 OR (2d) 411 (initial application reported in (1982), 36 OR (2d) 355), Steele J saw the jurisdiction for Anton Piller orders contained in either the rules of civil procedure or the court's inherent jurisdiction.

2. Under the Ontario Rules of Civil Procedure, inspection of property and the interim preservation of property have been separated. Rule 32.01 allowing for inspection and r. 45.01 for interim preservation, are similar to NB's rr. 35.01 and 35.02 respectively. Differences arise in that a slightly conservative nuance colours the Ontario provisions. Instead of New Brunswick's "where inspection … is necessary for the determination of an issue in a proceeding," Ontario has "inspection … where it appears to be necessary for the proper determination of an issue in a proceeding." Again, for interim preservation, New Brunswick's provision address "Preservation of any property in question or relating to an issue," while Ontario's new rules speak of "custody or preservation of any property in question in a proceeding or relevant to an issue." Despite the liberalizing effect of the new Ontario provisions, Anton Piller applicants still have several obstacles to surmount. First, where the applicant is seeking to inspect and photocopy documents rather than merely preserve infringing property, the applicant will have to show that documents are property within the term of r. 32.01. Second, the Ontario

rules are still subject to the courts' attitude that they are applicable only when pleadings have closed, although *Bardeau* may now suggest a change in that attitude. Third, neither of the rules would authorize interrogatories.

Thirty years after its inception, the Supreme Court of Canada finally gained an opportunity to rule on Anton Piller orders in Canada in the following case.

Celanese Canada Ltd. v. Murray Demolition Corp.
2006 SCC 36, [2006] 2 SCR 189

[The plaintiff, Celanese Canada Ltd., is a company that owned and operated a vinyl acetate factory in Edmonton. As part of its corporate restructuring it decided to demolish and sell its Edmonton plant. In order to prepare the site for sale it contracted with the defendant, Murray Demolition Corp., to undertake the demolition. In the course of carrying out that contract, Celanese alleged that Murray Demolition and Canadian Bearings Ltd., an affiliate, secretly copied proprietary and confidential information on the operation of Celanese's plant. Celanese further alleged that this information was being used to construct an unauthorized vinyl acetate facility in Iran.

As part of the litigation, Celanese sought, and obtained, an Anton Piller order against Canadian Bearings. The order made provision for an independent supervising solicitor, as has become the norm in orders given by Ontario courts. The order required the defendant to allow the plaintiff access to search for all documentary evidence touching the substantive dispute, and for its removal. The actual search was undertaken by Eastman, the independent supervising solicitor, and BDO Hayes Smith, an independent accounting firm. At various times, Eastman was in contact with the plaintiff's lawyers, Cassels Brock (CB). Upon service of the order, an executive for the defendant, Canadian Bearings, requested the presence of their solicitors, Borden Ladner Gervais (BLG). The execution of the order took two days, in which over 1,400 electronic documents were downloaded by BDO Hayes Smith and copied to CDs. These were then placed into plastic envelopes and sealed with the signatures of both Eastman and a member of BLG, and given into the custody of BDO Hayes Smith. At this stage, BLG had not had the opportunity to review all the electronic documents copied to determine whether solicitor–client privilege should be claimed.

One day following the seizure of evidence, the plaintiff's lawyers, CB, who were themselves acting as agents of Kasowitz, a Houston-based American law firm responsible for the carriage of the substantive claim, enquired of Eastman the whereabouts of the seized documents, including the records that had been copied and sealed. At this point, Eastman made an error that would prove to be fatal. Believing that there was no agreement between CB and BLG as to how the sealed material was to be handled, and not finding anything in the court order on how to dispose of solicitor–client privilege claims, Eastman instructed BDO Hayes Smith to allow complete access of CB to the sealed material. A lawyer for CB would later admit to having seen a few emails sent between BLG and the defendants, and would write an email confirming that he had reviewed all the electronic documents seized from the defendants. A copy of the sealed material eventually found its way into the hands of Kasowitz, where a lawyer was given instructions to classify the electronic documents into one of four categories—relevant, irrelevant, proprietary, and hot. During this classification, the lawyer also noticed that some of the documents were either addressed to or from BLG, and these he placed into an additional classification of privileged.

Within a few days, and after CB was ordered by the motions judge to furnish a copy of the electronic documents seized, BLG realized that privileged documents had been transferred into the hands of CB and Kasowitz. BLG demanded a return of these documents and to be provided with a list of persons at both firms who had access to the privileged material. CB did not immediately reply to this demand, but later indicated that any privileged material had been deleted from both firms' computing systems. In subsequent litigation, the Ontario Court of Appeal noted that 18 lawyers, clerks, and law students at CB and 12 lawyers at Kasowitz had access to the privileged material over a three-week period.

On the basis of a violation of solicitor–client privilege, BLG moved to have both CB and Kasowitz disqualified from further representing Celanese. This action was dismissed by the motions court, but allowed before the Divisional Court. On further appeal to the Ontario Court of Appeal, the action was remitted back to the motions judge on the basis that both lower courts had misapplied the appropriate test for disqualifying counsel. This judgment was itself appealed to the Supreme Court of Canada. Thus the disputed issue before the Supreme Court was the appropriate test to be used when considering a motion to disqualify counsel of record. However, the Supreme Court took the opportunity to rule on the availability and procedural safeguards that should form part of the standard Anton Piller order in Canada. This part of the judgment is excerpted below.]

[1] BINNIE J: An *Anton Piller* order bears an uncomfortable resemblance to a private search warrant. No notice is given to the party against whom it is issued. Indeed, defendants usually first learn of them when they are served and executed, without having had an opportunity to challenge them or the evidence on which they were granted. The defendant may have no idea a claim is even pending. The order is not placed in the hands of a public authority for execution, but authorizes a private party to insist on entrance to the premises of its opponent to conduct a surprise search, the purpose of which is to seize and preserve evidence to further its claim in a private dispute. The only justification for such an extraordinary remedy is that the plaintiff has a strong *prima facie* case and can demonstrate that on the facts, absent such an order, there is a real possibility relevant evidence will be destroyed or otherwise made to disappear. The protection of the party against whom an *Anton Piller* order is issued ought to be threefold: a carefully drawn order which identifies the material to be seized and sets out safeguards to deal, amongst other things, with privileged documents; a vigilant court-appointed supervising solicitor who is independent of the parties; and a sense of responsible self-restraint on the part of those executing the order. In this case, unfortunately, none of these protections proved to be adequate to protect against the disclosure of relevant solicitor–client confidences. Inadequate protections had been written into the order. Those which had been provided were not properly respected. The vigilance of the supervising solicitor appears to have fallen short. Celanese's solicitors in the aftermath of the search seem to have lost sight of the fact that the limited purpose of the order was to *preserve* evidence not to rush to exploit it. In the result, the party searched (Canadian Bearings) now seeks the removal of Celanese's solicitors (Cassels Brock & Blackwell LLP ("Cassels

Brock")) and to bar Celanese from making further use of their US counsel (Kasowitz, Benson, Torres & Friedman LLP ("Kasowitz")).

. . .

[28] *Anton Piller* orders have been available in Canada for close to 30 years. Unlike a search warrant they do not authorize forcible entry, but expose the target to contempt proceedings unless permission to enter is given. To the ordinary citizen faced on his or her doorstep with an *Anton Piller* order this may be seen as a distinction without a meaningful difference.

[29] Originally developed as an "exceptional remedy" in the context of trade secrets and intellectual property disputes, such orders are now fairly routinely issued in ordinary civil disputes, *Grenzservice Speditions Ges.m.b.H. v. Jans* (1995), 15 BCLR (3d) 370 (SC); in employment law, *Ridgewood Electric Ltd. (1990) v. Robbie* (2005), 74 OR (3d) 514 (SCJ), and *Netbored Inc. v. Avery Holdings Inc.* (2005), 48 CPR (4th) 240, 2005 FC 1405; and even in matrimonial litigation, *Neumeyer v. Neumeyer* (2005), 47 BCLR (4th) 162, 2005 BCSC 1259. In one egregious case, a designated search team attempted to execute an *Anton Piller* order on the 10-year-old son of the defendant at a time when his parents were not at home: *Ridgewood Electric*.

[30] With easier access to such orders, there has emerged a tendency on the part of some counsel to take too lightly the very serious responsibilities imposed by such a draconian order. It should truly be exceptional for a court to authorize the massive intrusion, without advance notice, of a privately orchestrated search on the privacy of a business competitor or other target party. As it was put by Lord Denning MR, in the original *Anton Piller* case:

> We are prepared, therefore, to sanction its continuance [i.e. of the order], *but only in an extreme case* where there is grave danger of property being smuggled away or of vital evidence being destroyed. [Emphasis added.]

(*Anton Piller KG v. Manufacturing Processes Ltd.*, [1976] 1 Ch. 55 (C.A.), at p. 61)

Anton Piller orders, obtained *ex parte*, now regularly permit searches and seizures not only from places of business but from residential premises. While most *Anton Piller* orders are executed properly, they are capable of giving rise to serious abuse, as in *Ridgewood Electric*, mentioned earlier, where Corbett J of the Ontario Superior Court of Justice protested the unacceptable conduct of those executing the order:

> Nigel Robbie arrived home on April 14, 2004, to find a neighbour barricading his front door. His ten-year-old son had been taken to another neighbour's house, distraught. The neighbourhood was in an uproar. A cadre in suits stood at the front of his house brandishing a thick wad of papers, demanding to be let in.
>
> . . .
>
> While everyone is taken to know the law, the Robbies and their neighbours might be excused for not knowing about *Anton Piller* orders. And so the Robbies and their neighbours were left to wonder what kind of country we live in, where one's former employer, acting secretly, may obtain a court order and then enter and search one's private residence. [paras. 1 and 4]

As Sharpe JA, writing in a scholarly mode, has pointed out, "excessive zeal in this area is apt to attract criticism which will impair the ability of the courts to use injunctions in innovative ways in other areas" (R.J. Sharpe, *Injunctions and Specific Performance* (loose-leaf ed.), at para. 2:1300).

[31] The search in the present case was conducted by reputable and responsible people, under the supervision of a senior member of the Ontario bar. The disclosure of solicitor–client confidences came about not by egregious misconduct, but through a combination of carelessness, overzealousness, a lack of appreciation of the potential dangers of an *Anton Piller* order and a failure to focus on its limited purpose, namely the *preservation* of relevant evidence.

[32] Experience has shown that despite their draconian nature, there is a proper role for *Anton Piller* orders to ensure that unscrupulous defendants are not able to circumvent the court's processes by, on being forewarned, making relevant evidence disappear. Their usefulness is especially important in the modern era of heavy dependence on computer technology, where documents are easily deleted, moved or destroyed. The utility of this equitable tool in the correct circumstances should not be diminished. However, such orders should only be granted in the clear recognition of their exceptional and highly intrusive character and, where granted, the terms should be carefully spelled out and limited to what the circumstances show to be necessary. Those responsible for their implementation should conform to a very high standard of professional diligence. Otherwise, the moving party, not its target, may have to shoulder the consequences of a botched search.

. . .

A. *Requirements for an Anton Piller Order*

[35] There are four essential conditions for the making of an *Anton Piller* order. First, the plaintiff must demonstrate a strong *prima facie* case. Second, the damage to the plaintiff of the defendant's alleged misconduct, potential or actual, must be very serious. Third, there must be convincing evidence that the defendant has in its possession incriminating documents or things, and fourthly it must be shown that there is a real possibility that the defendant may destroy such material before the discovery process can do its work: *Nintendo of America, Inc. v. Coinex Video Games Inc.*, [1983] 2 FC 189 (CA), at pp. 197-99; *Indian Manufacturing Ltd. v. Lo* (1997), 75 CPR (3d) 338 (FCA.), at pp. 341-42; *Netsmart Inc. v. Poelzer*, [2003] 1 W.W.R. 698, 2002 ABQB 800, at para. 16; *Anton Piller KG*, at pp. 58-61; *Ridgewood Electric*, at para. 27; *Grenzservice*, at para. 39; *Pulse Microsystems Ltd. v. SafeSoft Systems Inc.* (1996), 67 CPR (3d) 202 (Man. CA), at p. 208; *Ontario Realty Corp. v. P. Gabriele & Sons Ltd.* (2000), 50 OR (3d) 539 (SCJ), at para. 9; *Proctor & Gamble Inc. v. John Doe (c.o.b. Clarion Trading International)*, [2000] FCFCJ No. 61 (QL) (TD), at para. 45; *Netbored*, at para. 39; *Adobe Systems Inc. v. KLJ Computer Solutions Inc.*, [1999] 3 FC 621 (TD), at para. 35.

[36] Both the strength and the weakness of an *Anton Piller* order is that it is made *ex parte* and interlocutory: there is thus no cross-examination on the supporting affidavits. The motions judge necessarily reposes faith in the candour and complete disclosure of the affiants, and as much or more so on the professional responsibility of the lawyers participating in carrying out its terms. We are advised that such orders are not available in the United States (Transcript, at p. 70).

[37] A troubling example in Canada is the *Adobe Systems* case, where a computer software company was tipped off that a small advertising firm in Halifax was using unlicensed versions of some of its software. The affiant swore that, in his opinion, the firm was likely to

destroy its unlicensed copies of the software if it became aware of the pending litigation against it. The target firm was well established and its principals had an excellent reputation in the community. On subsequent cross-examination it was revealed that the source of the informant's opinion that the defendant was likely to destroy unlicensed copies was his "observation of human nature" and not any observation of that particular defendant. Upon a review of the order, Richard ACJ (now CJ of the Federal Court of Appeal) found that the plaintiffs had not made sufficient inquiries of the facts before obtaining the order. Citing *Adobe Systems*, the Federal Court recently reiterated that "[i]n all proceedings taken *ex parte*, and particularly in *Anton Piller* situations, there is a heavy obligation upon the moving party to make full and frank disclosure of all relevant facts to the Court" (*Netbored*, at para. 41).

[38]   At this stage, the challenge to the decision of Nordheimer J to grant the *Anton Piller* order is not before the Court.

B. Terms of the Anton Piller Order

[39]   In *Grenzservice*, a case which dealt with an application to remove counsel who had seen privileged documents in the course of an *Anton Piller* execution, Huddart J (later JA) observed: "This case suggests that safeguards cannot remain implicit in the supervision order. They must be specified" (para. 84). I agree. In *Lavallee, Rackel & Heintz v. Canada (Attorney General)*, [2002] 3 SCR 209, 2002 SCC 61, Arbour J for the majority set out at para. 49 a number of relevant concerns in the criminal law context, which may have some application by analogy. Notwithstanding the general recognition of the need for standard terms, many safeguards which one would expect to have become customary (such as a provision dealing with claims of privilege) are frequently omitted. Corbett J commented in *Ridgewood Electric* that the *Anton Piller* order "has been with us for nearly 30 years, [yet] its 'standard terms' still vary considerably across the province" (para. 3). In the United Kingdom, a set of standardized rules and a model order have been developed. In Australia, Order 25B of the *Federal Court Rules* and Practice Note No. 24 (May 5, 2006) set out a number of standard safeguards for *Anton Piller* orders. See also *Thermax Ltd. v. Schott Industrial Glass Ltd.*, [1981] FSR 289 (Ch. D).

[40]   *Anton Piller* orders are often conceived of, obtained and implemented in circumstances of urgency. They are generally time-limited (e.g., 10 days in Ontario under Rule 40.02 (*Rules of Civil Procedure*, RRO 1990, Reg. 194) and 14 days in the Federal Court, under Rule 374(1) (*Federal Courts Rules*, SOR/98-106)). Despite the urgency, the more detailed and standardized the terms of the order the less opportunity there will be for misunderstandings or mischief. As noted by Lamer J in *Descôteaux v. Mierzwinski*, [1982] 1 SCR 860, at p. 889:

> Searches are an exception to the oldest and most fundamental principles of the common law, and as such the power to search should be strictly controlled.

Unless and until model orders are developed by legislation or recommended by law societies pursuant to their responsibility for professional conduct, the following guidelines for preparation and execution of an *Anton Piller* order may be helpful, depending on the circumstances:

(1) Basic Protection for the Rights of the Parties

(i)   The order should appoint a supervising solicitor who is independent of the plaintiff or its solicitors and is to be present at the search to ensure its integrity. The key role of the independent supervising solicitor was noted by the motions judge in this case "to ensure that the execution of the Anton Piller order, and everything that flowed from it, was undertaken as carefully as possible and with due consideration for the rights and interests of all involved" (para. 20). He or she is "an officer of the court charged with a very important responsibility regarding this extraordinary remedy" (para. 20). See also *Grenzservice*, at para. 85.

(ii) Absent unusual circumstances the plaintiff should be required to provide an undertaking and/or security to pay damages in the event that the order turns out to be unwarranted or wrongfully executed. See *Ontario Realty*, at para. 40; *Adobe Systems*, at para. 43; *Nintendo of America*, at pp. 201-2; *Grenzservice*, at para. 85; *Havana House Cigar & Tobacco Merchants Ltd. v. Jane Doe* (2000), 199 FTR 12, aff'd (2002), 288 NR 198, 2002 FCA 75.

(iii) The scope of the order should be no wider than necessary and no material shall be removed from the site unless clearly covered by the terms of the order. See *Columbia Picture Industries Inc. v. Robinson*, [1987] Ch. 38.

(iv) A term setting out the procedure for dealing with solicitor–client privilege or other confidential material should be included with a view to enabling defendants to advance claims of confidentiality over documents before they come into the possession of the plaintiff or its counsel, or to deal with disputes that arise. See *Grenzservice*, at para. 85; *Ontario Realty*, at para. 40. Procedures developed for use in connection with search warrants under the *Criminal Code*, RSC 1985, c. C-46, may provide helpful guidance. The UK practice direction on this point provides as follows:

> Before permitting entry to the premises by any person other than the Supervising Solicitor, the Respondent may, for a short time (not to exceed two hours, unless the Supervising Solicitor agrees to a longer period)—(a) gather together any documents he [or she] believes may be ... privileged; and (b) hand them to the Supervising Solicitor for [an assessment of] whether they are ... privileged as claimed.
>
> If the Supervising Solicitor decides that ... any of the documents [may be] privileged or [is in any doubt as to their status, he or she] will exclude them from the search ... and retain [them] ... pending further order of the court [(if in doubt as to whether they are privileged), or return them to the Respondent and retain a list of the documents (if the documents are privileged)].
>
> [A] Respondent [wishing] to take legal advice and gather documents as permitted ... must first inform the Supervising Solicitor and keep him [or her] informed of the steps being taken.

(*Civil Procedure*, vol. 1 (2nd Supp. 2005), Part 25, Practice Direction—Interim Injunctions, p. 43, at paras. 11-12)

Experience has shown that in general this is a workable procedure. Counsel supporting the appellants suggested the basic "two-hour" collection period permitted in the UK is too short. This is a matter to be determined by the judge making the order, but it must be kept in mind that unnecessary delay may open the door to mischief. In general, the search should proceed as expeditiously as circumstances permit.

(v) The order should contain a limited use clause (i.e., items seized may only be used for the purposes of the pending litigation). See *Ontario Realty*, at para. 40; *Adobe Systems*, at para. 43; *Grenzservice*, at para. 85.

(vi) The order should state explicitly that the defendant is entitled to return to court on short notice to (a) discharge the order; or (b) vary the amount of security. See *Adobe Systems*, at para. 43; *Grenzservice*, at para. 85; *Nintendo of America*, at pp. 201-2.

(vii) The order should provide that the materials seized be returned to the defendants or their counsel as soon as practicable.

(2) The Conduct of the Search

(i) In general the order should provide that the search should be commenced during normal business hours when counsel for the party about to be searched is more likely to be available for consultation. See *Grenzservice*, at para. 85; *Universal Thermosensors Ltd. v. Hibben*, [1992] 1 WLR 840 (Ch. D).

(ii) The premises should not be searched or items removed except in the presence of the defendant or a person who appears to be a responsible employee of the defendant.

(iii) The persons who may conduct the search and seize evidence should be specified in the order or should specifically be limited in number. See *Adobe Systems*, at para. 43; *Grenzservice*, at para. 85; *Nintendo of America*, at pp. 201-2.

(iv) On attending at the site of the authorized search, plaintiff's counsel (or the supervising solicitor), acting as officers of the court should serve a copy of the statement of claim and the order and supporting affidavits and explain to the defendant or responsible corporate officer or employee in plain language the nature and effect of the order. See *Ontario Realty*, at para. 40.

(v) The defendant or its representatives should be given a reasonable time to consult with counsel prior to permitting entry to the premises. See *Ontario Realty*, at para. 40; *Adobe Systems*, at para. 43; *Grenzservice*, at para. 85; *Sulpher Experts Inc. v. O'Connell* (2000), 279 AR 246, 2000 ABQB 875.

(vi) A detailed list of all evidence seized should be made and the supervising solicitor should provide this list to the defendant for inspection and verification at the end of the search and before materials are removed from the site. See *Adobe Systems*, at para. 43; *Grenzservice*, at para. 85; *Ridgewood Electric*, at para. 25.

(vii) Where this is not practicable, documents seized should be placed in the custody of the independent supervising solicitor, and defendant's counsel should be given a reasonable opportunity to review them to advance solicitor–client privilege claims prior to release of the documents to the plaintiff.

(viii) Where ownership of material is disputed, it should be provided for safekeeping to the supervising solicitor or to the defendant's solicitors.

(3) Procedure Following the Search

(i) The order should make it clear that the responsibilities of the supervising solicitor continue beyond the search itself to deal with matters arising out of the search, subject of course to any party wishing to take a matter back to the court for resolution.

(ii) The supervising solicitor should be required to file a report with the court within a set time limit describing the execution, who was present and what was seized. See *Grenzservice*, at para. 85.

(iii) The court may wish to require the plaintiff to file and serve a motion for review of the execution of the search returnable within a set time limit such as 14 days to ensure that the court automatically reviews the supervising solicitor's report and the implementation of its order even if the defendant does not request such a review. See *Grenzservice*, at para. 85.

See also: *Civil Procedure Act 1997* (UK), 1997, c. 12, s. 7; *Civil Procedure Rules 1998*, SI 1998/3132, r. 25.1(1)(h), and Part 25, Practice Direction—Interim Injunctions; Sharpe, at paras. 2:1100 *et seq.*

[41] It is evident that the draft order placed before the motions judge in this case was deficient in many respects. At issue here is the absence of any provision to deal with solicitor–client confidences. The absence of specific terms in the *Anton Piller* order does not relieve the searching solicitors from the consequences of gaining inappropriate access. Such consequences may include removal. A precisely drawn and clearly thought out order therefore will not only protect the defendant's right to solicitor–client privilege, but also protect the plaintiff's right to continue to be represented by counsel of choice by helping to ensure that such counsel do not stumble into possession of privileged information.

[On the issue of breach of solicitor–client privilege, the court held that Cassels Brock should be removed as solicitors of record to represent Celanese in the proceedings.]

The Supreme Court of Canada has recently had another opportunity to comment upon Anton Piller orders in *British Columbia (Attorney General) v. Malik*, 2011 SCC 18. The province commenced an action against Malik to recover funds ($5.2 million) it had advanced to Malik to pay for his defence in criminal proceedings relating to his alleged involvement in the Air India bombing trial, and for which he had been acquitted. The trial judge had issued the Anton Piller order. The province had used material obtained from Malik's "Rowbotham hearing" (a hearing in which the applicant seeks to secure either funding or a stay of the criminal proceedings on the basis that he cannot afford to retain counsel; an essential requirement to ensure a fair hearing under the Charter) to support its application for the Anton Piller order. Ultimately, the Supreme Court affirmed the trial judge's ruling, holding that the material submitted by the province was admissible before the trial court. The Supreme Court re-affirmed its approach to Anton Piller orders taken in *Celanese*, again stressing the exceptional nature of the relief (*per* Binnie J for the court):

> [5] An *Anton Piller* order is an exceptional remedy and should only be granted on clear and convincing evidence. It is a highly intrusive measure that, unless sparingly granted and closely controlled, is capable of causing great prejudice and potentially irremediable loss. The fact the Province was the applicant here conferred no special Crown privilege or priority. The Province comes before the Court as an ordinary civil litigant and its application should be judged by the same rules as any other litigant, as should be the merits of the position taken by the Malik family respondents.

The Federal Court of Canada has proved to be particularly attractive to litigants requesting Anton Piller orders. The court has a concurrent jurisdiction on intellectual property matters, but has the advantage that its orders are effective across the entire country. Plaintiffs who have been plagued with counterfeit and pirated products that infringe their copyright or trademark have been able to get the Federal Court to issue a "rolling order" against "John and Jane Doe and Persons Unknown." The effect of this order has allowed a plaintiff to sweep down on flea markets and small commercial retailers willing to handle counterfeit goods and seize the infringing material. The seller is then added as a joint defendant to the original action. In the following judgment, Reed J has expressed her concern at the potential abuse of these orders and has crafted what has become a type of standard order.

Fila Canada Inc. v. Doe
[1996] 3 FC 493

REED J: A decision on this motion has been outstanding for a long time. An explanation is required.

Last December 4, the plaintiff brought a motion for an *ex parte, in camera* hearing to obtain an Anton Piller order against Jane Doe and John Doe defendants. It was represented to be a hearing that would require 10 to 15 minutes of the Court's time. On the hearing, a draft order was placed before me for signature. It was represented to be the type of order this Court usually grants. I declined to issue the order in the form in which it was sought. This led to further submissions from counsel and requests from me for various explanations. This dialogue continued for some time, the last being representations I received from counsel on April 26, 1996 and a clarification thereof on May 21, 1996.

The order which is sought is what is known as a "rolling" Anton Piller order. As is obvious from the style of cause, when these orders are obtained from the Court neither the identity nor the address of the persons against whom they will be executed are known. On some occasions one or two persons may be identified as named defendants but they will have no necessary connection to the Jane and John Does against whom the order will also be executed. The unknown defendants are allegedly infringing intellectual property rights belonging to the plaintiff but in different places, at different times and in different circumstances. These "rolling" orders are to be distinguished from defendant-specific Anton Piller orders. While defendant-specific Anton Piller orders may also include Jane Doe and John Doe defendants, in general, the latter will be connected to the named defendants, for example, by being an employee of the defendant or a supplier of the alleged counterfeit goods to the defendant.

The "rolling" orders are executed against street vendors and transient flea market vendors although they are framed in broad enough terms to also encompass the search of retail premises, office premises, vehicles, warehouses, as well as residences. They are usually expressed to last a year subject to being renewed. Careful drafting in this regard is required, otherwise the order may be invalid as a result of the operation of subsections 469(2) and 470(2) of the *Federal Court Rules* [CRC, c. 663]. See also *Société pour l'Avancement des droits en audiovisuel (SADA) Ltée v. Collège Édouard-Montpetit*, [1981] 2 FC 307 (CA).

Anton Piller orders are, in effect, search and seizure orders. The fiction is that the defendant gives permission to the plaintiff to search and seize. The defendant does so under threat of being found in contempt of court if permission is not granted. The penalty for contempt of court, at least theoretically, can be a term of imprisonment. Also, while the theory is that the goods are seized to be retained as evidence for use at trial, the seizures in fact often operate as executions before or sometimes even without judgment. Plaintiffs are using these orders as self-help measures in circumstances in which, in other days, the police may have played a more active role.

Section 8 of the Charter [*Canadian Charter of Rights and Freedoms*, part I of the *Constitution Act, 1982*, RSC 1985, app. II, no. 44] provides that individuals are entitled to be free from unreasonable search and seizures. That section is not confined to search and seizures by police officers or investigators pursuant to statutory powers. It is at least arguable that it applies to the civil search and seizures authorized by order of the Court under an Anton Piller order. An unreasonable search and seizure, as I understand the jurisprudence, encompasses one which has been conducted pursuant to an invalid order, or pursuant to an order which was too broadly drafted, or pursuant to an order which has been unreasonably executed; see *Hunter et al. v. Southam Inc.*, [1984] 2 SCR 145. When Anton Piller orders are sought and obtained from this Court it is important to place them within this context.

I turn, then, to some comments on the practice of seeking these orders. In the first place, motions to obtain such are often brought with the assertion that they are needed urgently. The material in support of the application is filed at the last minute, sometimes only minutes before the application is placed before the judge who is asked to grant it and who is in the midst of a busy motions day. The material is often voluminous. At the same time, the alleged infringers may have been engaging in the activity it is sought to restrain for several months, before counsel brings an application to Court for an Anton Piller order. It is not appropriate for counsel to come to Court, in such circumstances, representing that the matter must be dealt with urgently. As with other motions, the material should be filed at least two clear days before the motion is to be heard, to allow the judge who will hear the application time to review the material before the hearing.

Secondly, there is no need, in many of these cases, for the proceedings to be held *in camera*. In the present case, the order sought is against Jane Doe and John Doe. The identity of the defendants was not even known at the time of the hearing. A review of the file made it clear that there was no reason why an *in camera* hearing should have been requested.

Thirdly, according to the jurisprudence, see *Nintendo of America, Inc. v. Coinex Video Games Inc.*, [1983] 2 FC 189 (CA), before a court grants an Anton Piller order, it must be convinced that the applicant has a *very strong prima facie case*. This means, for example, that the copyright or trade mark rights which are asserted must be clearly identified (e.g., by production of the relevant registration documents, by photocopies of the relevant designs). In the present case, the description of the alleged trade marks and copyrights, which it was sought to protect, contained reference to unperfected applications for trade marks and trade marks for which registrations had never been applied. Indeed, it was in many aspects rather incomprehensible. It was not have given a person executing the order or those against whom it was executed a clear picture of what the order allowed to be seized. This was subsequently corrected.

The applicant's rights to the intellectual property being asserted must also be clearly demonstrated. The application is *ex parte*. Counsel for the applicant has an obligation to explicitly call to the Court's attention any weakness in those rights, of which he or she may be aware. This is a duty owed to the Court. A judge must be convinced that the applicant's apprehension that the counterfeit goods will not be available as evidence for trial if they are not seized, is well founded. If, for example, a representative item could be purchased by plaintiff's investigators and action proceeded with against the vendors, in the normal way, a case has not been made out for an Anton Piller order nor for the execution of it against a given defendant.

I turn then to the need for a supervising solicitor in attendance on all executions of the order. It is on this point that counsel, on behalf of his client, felt most strongly. He argued that such a requirement would make the use of these orders too expensive for his clients, that it is dangerous in some situations because executions of the order can result in physically abusive confrontations, that it is impractical when a number of executions are to take place in different locations simultaneously and, that it is unnecessary because the investigation agency which is employed is knowledgeable in these matters.

I recognize the force of these arguments but I am also mindful of the fact that there is enormous potential for abuse in issuing these orders. The Court is putting in the hands of the plaintiff the power to search the premises and to seize the goods, equipment and records of others. These powers are exercised in each particular situation when the plaintiff determines that particular goods are or relate to an infringement of its intellectual property rights. There is no public official involved in the execution of the order. If the Court is going to assist a plaintiff in the assertion of its rights by giving orders as invasive as Anton Pillers, then, I do not think the cost to the plaintiff should weigh too heavily in the balance when protection for the defendants is the competing consideration. I note costs, in any event, are being spread. It is clear from the pattern of review motions heard by the Court, in Toronto on any given motion day, that activities under these orders are being organized so that the enforcement team searches for and seizes the counterfeit goods pursuant to a number of orders (i.e., on behalf of a number of plaintiffs) at the same time. Counsel refers to these activities as raids.

With respect to the concern that the presence of a solicitor on these raids is not appropriate because the situations may become physically abusive, this is one reason a solicitor should be present. I note that the Anton Piller order requires the person against whom it is being executed *to give permission* for the search and seizure. One has to ask whether permission is really being given if the situation becomes abusive. It sounds as though what may be taking place is a forcible search and seizure. In so far as the impracticability of a solicitor being present when multiple executions are occurring at the same time, in different locations, the example of numerous street vendors appearing around a venue for the one-half hour following a rock concert was given. I do not think it appropriate to deal with that circumstance in the context of a rolling Anton Piller order. It may be that there are situations for which individual Anton Piller orders can be obtained, instead of including them in one of these "rolling" orders, where a solicitorless seizure is justified. Counsel painted a picture of a circumstance in which police officers and the plaintiff's private investigators work together through a crowd. I leave open the question of whether there are situations in which solicitorless search and seizures can be justified. All that it is necessary to say for present purposes is that I am not prepared to provide for such in the present case.

I am asked to put the search and seizure powers into the hands of an investigation agency. The Court has no way of knowing why a particular agency should be granted such authority as opposed to any other. The plaintiff has chosen and pays that agency. The agency's loyalty, in any actions taken by its staff, will naturally be to the plaintiff.

A solicitor attends on the execution of these orders in two capacities: as counsel for the plaintiff and *as an officer of the Court*. It is the plaintiff's solicitor who attends. I accept that this may not be ideal. In the United Kingdom a practice has developed of having licensed Anton Piller officers, independent of the plaintiff, attend and supervise the execution of these orders. This may be a practice that is worth adopting. We do not have it at present, however, and I prefer to have a solicitor present at the execution of these orders, albeit the plaintiff's solicitor, rather than no solicitor at all.

A solicitor, as an officer of the Court, owes duties to the Court as well as to his or her client. Solicitors attend and supervise the execution of these orders to ensure that their boundaries are not exceeded and to be in a position to give the Court an accurate and complete description of what occurred. They have legal expertise and are expected to be able to explain to those enforcing the order and to those against whom it is being executed what is and what is not allowed thereunder. This gives some assurance that the boundaries of the order will not be exceeded. Counsel understand that a misstep or mischaracterization of a situation can lead not only to the particular execution of the order being invalid but also to the vacating of the Anton Piller order itself.

It is argued that the defendant's rights are protected even in the absence of a solicitor because if a search and seizure is improperly conducted, the defendant can always come to Court and have his or her property returned. This is of course the ultimate control. However, the efficiency with which it works will to a considerable extent depend upon the explanation given to the persons against whom the order is executed, as to their rights, the value of the goods seized from any one defendant and the willingness or ability of the individual to obtain independent legal advice. I am not prepared to grant a solicitorless Anton Piller order.

I turn then to what is expected on the motion for review of an execution of the order. In the first place it should be clear that not only the most recent execution of the order is under review but also the continuation of the Anton Piller order itself. The Anton Piller order can be set aside at any time for improper execution or other defect, either by a judge on his or her own motion, or on motion from any of the parties.

Secondly, the motion for review of an execution should include a request that the John Does and Jane Does against whom the order has been most recently executed are added to the statement of claim as named defendants (their identity is no longer unknown). The motion with respect to newly identified defendants will normally contain a request for an interlocutory injunction against them and for an order for the continued detention of the goods and equipment seized pending trial. It is not appropriate to seek release of the property into the hands of the plaintiff without a default judgment having been obtained against the defendant from whom the property has been seized. (I leave open for present purposes the appropriate disposition of goods which have been seized from defendants whose identities have not been ascertained because they have fled during the execution of the order.)

When the order is executed against a person who is already a named defendant and against whom an interlocutory injunction already exists, the motion should be one for a show cause order alleging contempt of court, rather than one to add the person, a second time, as a defendant and the obtaining of a second interlocutory injunction against that person.

The motion for review of an execution of the order must be supported in Court by a full report from the supervising solicitor of the execution or executions to which it relates, including occasions on which the identity of the defendant is not ascertained. This report must include a description of all goods, equipment and records seized, when and from whom they were seized. The most effective and efficient way of providing such, in many cases, will be by photographs coupled with an inventory.

The granting of these orders and the use to which they are being put is a recent evolution of the Anton Piller practice of this Court. Many questions remain unanswered, including some that are of a very fundamental nature. It would be useful to have some Court of Appeal jurisprudence with respect to these types of orders. By their very nature, however, the circumstances under which they are obtained and executed are not conducive to appeals. As counsel is aware, there has been some discussion amongst the judges of this Court with respect to the establishment of a model order. While one judge issues an Anton Piller order, others are called upon throughout the life of the order to approve executions made thereunder and to approve the order's continuation. Thus the development of model orders would serve both the interests of the plaintiffs and of the Court. In the absence of such, however, counsel for the plaintiff asks that I at least issue a "temporary" order so that his client can be placed in somewhat the same position as other Anton Piller "customers" of this Court.

Accordingly, I have decided to issue the plaintiff a rolling Anton Piller order on terms that take account of many of the considerations articulated above. It is significantly different from that which was originally sought. It will carry within it a temporary quality because it will contain a provision allowing for its variation or termination at any time on the Court's motion.

NOTES

1. In *Celanese Canada Ltd. v. Murray Demolition Corp.*, the Supreme Court of Canada did not distinguish between the various types of Anton Piller orders and insisted on an independent supervising solicitor in all cases. The effect of this requirement is to increase the cost of the order, a burden ultimately placed on the defendant should it lose at trial on substantive grounds. Whether Anton Piller orders used in the protection of intellectual properties need this level of supervision is a questionable issue. For a criticism of this aspect of the

court's decision, see Jeff Berryman, "Challenging Shibboleths: Evidence-Based Policy Making, The Supreme Court of Canada, and Anton Piller Orders" (2010), 36 *Adv. Q* 509, and "Anton Piller Orders and the Supreme Court of Canada's New Procedural Guidelines: Celanese Canada Ltd. v. Murray Demolition Corp." (2007), 32 *Adv. Q* 371.

2. It is important for the plaintiff's solicitor to make full and frank disclosure of all material facts that may influence the court in exercise of its discretion. See *BBM Bureau of Measurement v. Cybernauts Ltd.* (1992), 8 CPC (3d) 293 (Ont. Gen. Div.) and *R.S.M.C. Int. Active Wear Inc. v. Quality Goods I.M.D. Inc.* (1994), 57 CPR (3d) 353 (FCTD), where the orders were rescinded for failure to make such disclosure.

The problem with the full and frank disclosure requirement is that it is difficult to determine appropriate sanctions to ensure compliance. In Ontario there is the suggestion that failure to comply must result in setting aside the order (see *United States of America v. Friedland*, [1996] OJ no. 4399 and *Computer Security Products Ltd. v. Forbes*, [1999] OJ no. 4573 (Ont. Sup. Ct.). In other jurisdictions, including the Federal Court, the court maintains its discretion either to set aside or to continue the order where there is sufficient evidence to support the injunction once all the facts are known (*Adobe Systems Inc. v. KLJ Computer Solutions Inc.*, [1999] 3 FC 621). Some courts have suggested that the failure to make full and frank disclosure can result in penalizing the applicant through the imposition of damages, including punitive damages, or through adjustments in costs. See *Pulse Microsystems Inc. v. Safesoft Systems Inc.* (1996), 134 DLR (4th) 701 (Man. CA) and *Columbia Pictures Industries Ltd. v. Robinson*, [1986] 3 All ER 338 (Ch.).

Another problem is the appropriate time to make a determination of a failure to ensure full and frank disclosure. From the time it is given a defendant is obliged to comply with the court's order. Refusing entry and seeking to set the order aside is technically a contempt of court. The courts have indicated that a defendant must obey an injunction, even one wrongfully obtained, although the fact that it has been wrongfully obtained will be taken into account when determining penalty. Nevertheless, a penalty for non-compliance will be leveled. Often this will be in some adverse cost consequences. Practically speaking then, the defendant is compelled to comply. The defendant's protection is in seeking the court to later set aside the order, although by that time the damage is done. In addition, the wrongfulness of the order will usually be determined at the trial rather than on an *inter parte* interlocutory motion. By this time the ability of the defendant to mount a successful objection or to seek damages based on the plaintiff's damage undertaking is compromised. The defendant is unlikely to have the means to take the action or the substantive grounds to object or win at trial. Thus, the defendant is likely to compromise and settle. At the settlement, the plaintiff will extract a promise to withdraw any action against it on the basis of the wrongfully obtained Anton Piller order. The court will never get to scrutinize the order because no full trial will take place.

3. A vital part of Anton Piller orders is the attachment of interrogatories. In *Rank Film Distributors Ltd. v. Video Information Centre*, [1982] AC 380 (HL (Eng.)), the impact of the evidential rule against self-incrimination and, in particular, the interrogatories attached to the order was discussed. See D.M. Paciocco, "Anton Piller Orders: Facing the Threat of the Privilege Against Self-Incrimination" (1984), 34 *University of Toronto Law Journal* 26, at 26-27 (footnotes omitted):

Rank Film involved a copyright dispute. The plaintiffs were the English representatives of the owner of various copyright interests in feature-length films. The defendants were alleged to be "film pirates" who reproduced and distributed unauthorized copies of the movies. In order to maintain the integrity of these copyrights, the plaintiffs realized that it would be necessary to seize all infringing material and to close down the entire operation. That required an order which would not only restrain further contravention and provide for the seizure of contraband held by the defendants but also disclose the extent of the operation and the whereabouts of delivered copies. Only a speedy and unflinching court order could accomplish so much. To that end, they applied *ex parte* and received an Anton Piller order.

There were two elements of the injunction that were controversial. First, the order required the defendants to provide the plaintiffs with the names and addresses of suppliers, receivers, and producers of illicit films. Second, it obliged the defendants to disclose the existence of specified categories of documents and to produce the same. The controversy revolved around the privilege against self-incrimination which the defendants would have been entitled to claim in the face of those demands had they been witnesses in a trial process. Reasoning *sub silentio* that the same right to refuse to answer should apply in the face of forced disclosures attached to an injunction, the majority of the Court of Appeal held that the defendants could refuse to comply with those requirements, and the provisions were struck from the injunction. The plaintiffs appealed in vain to the House of Lords.

The consequences of the dismemberment of the injunction were severe. The plaintiffs lost the ability to gather up distributed contraband films even though the *Copyright Act, 1956* gave them a proprietary interest in these movies. They also lost the ability to trace the chain of supply and the market avenues established by the defendants. Illegal business associates were insulated from discovery.

If the decision applied here in Canada it would not wreak quite as much havoc as it did for the plaintiffs in *Rank Film*. The privilege to refuse to answer is removed by our provincial evidence acts during examinations for discovery. Thus, there would come a time when such defendants would be required to answer. Even granting this, though, the full effectiveness of the remedy depends upon speed and surprise. The prior exchange of pleadings required here and the timing of the discovery process would none the less largely undermine the utility of the injunction. Disclosure would not be compelled until the defendants had had ample time to dispose of secreted copyright material, to warn suppliers, and to destroy documentation not found during the exercise of the injunction. If these consequences occur here, it will be because an exclusionary rule of evidence has seeped from its legitimate confines and because Canadian legislators quite understandably did not anticipate that escape.

J. Berryman, "Anton Piller Injunctions: An Update"
(1985), 2 *Intellectual Property Journal* 49, at 58 (footnotes omitted)

Professor D.M. Paciocco, in his article "Anton Piller Orders: Facing the Threat of the Privilege Against Self-Incrimination," has summarized the state of Canadian authority on self-incrimination into three alternatives.

1. The common law privilege to refrain from answering incriminating questions and to produce incriminating documents extends to Anton Piller respondents and is unaffected by the various evidence acts.

This approach recognizes that the various Evidence Acts deal only with "witnesses" who are "presenting evidence" on "oath or affirmation" in a "judicial proceeding." An Anton Piller defendant satisfies none of these prerequisites to gaining the Acts' protection. It next recognizes that *Rank Film* accurately states the common law privilege and that Canadian courts are likely to follow that decision. Obviously such a result would be to deprive the Anton Piller order of any of its validity in Canada. Professor Paciocco continues:

2(a) The common law privilege to refrain from answering questions has been entirely abrogated in some or in all jurisdictions by a protection against the use of such disclosures in criminal or quasi-criminal prosecutions.

(b)(i) The same scenario applies to documents in Manitoba.

(ii) In British Columbia and Nova Scotia the common law privilege with respect to documents has been abolished and no protection has emerged to replace it. Hence, Anton Piller orders may be made without concern for documentary privileges or protection.

(iii) In the balance of Canadian common law jurisdictions the common law privilege attaches to the production of documents such that Anton Piller orders may not be made requiring the production of documents where to do so would infringe the common law.

This approach requires an extended definition of "witness." For those provinces that have a statutory definition of "witness" extending the protection to the discovery process, then the gap between the language of the statute and the surrounding circumstances of the *Anton Piller* defendant may not be as difficult to bridge. Even if interrogatories are caught, further problems surround disclosure of documents outside the formal discovery process. It would appear, as Professor Paciocco concludes, that the Evidence Acts did not contemplate the *Anton Piller* order.

3. The common law privilege to refrain from answering incriminating questions and to refuse to produce incriminating documents does not extend to Anton Piller respondents.

This alternative would have Canadian courts declining to follow *Rank Film*. Paciocco suggests that this conclusion is supported on four grounds:

1. to follow *Rank Film* would seriously impair the *Anton Piller* order;

2. the trend in Canadian jurisprudence is to curtail exclusionary rules based on the principles against self-incrimination;

3. the underlying rationale for the privilege is not served by an extension to *Anton Piller* defendants. That rationale is to encourage truthfulness and candor in the witness box. Since the *Anton Piller* defendant will always have something to lose even if the answers are not incriminatory, the rule does not encourage candid information. Second, arguments supporting the privilege have more weight when it is the Crown that is pursuing the investigation. Where it is a civil action and the Crown is a mere bystander, the balance is tipped in favour of allowing the plaintiff's action;

4. the plaintiff could proceed to trial and compel the defendant to answer the same questions which the defendant has failed to respond to in the original *Anton Piller* order.

Adoption of the third alternative would result in the defendant being compelled to answer interrogatories and disclose documents that may be self-incriminatory without any of the statutory protections against the subsequent use in other proceedings of these disclosures. For Paciocco, the interests of the *Anton Piller* defendant can be protected by the Court closely scrutinizing the questions that the plaintiff wishes to ask in interrogatories. Only those interrogatories that are in aid of the order should be permissible. While this may not be completely satisfactory, it is better to give the plaintiff effective relief than protect the unmeritorious defendant. Paciocco does point out that the preferred solution would be to compel disclosure and provide protection against use in any subsequent prosecutions. However, this is not a route that has been authorized by statute. This preferred solution has been the one adopted by a majority of the New Zealand Court of Appeal in *Busby v. Thorn E.M.I. Video Programmes Ltd.*, [1984] 1 NZLR 461 (CA).

NOTES

1. The most detailed judicial analysis of Charter issues with respect to Anton Piller orders has been undertaken by Farley J in *Ontario Realty Corporation v. P. Gabriele & Sons Ltd.* (2000), 50 OR (3d) 539 (Sup. Ct.). The defendants mounted a full Charter challenge against the plaintiff's Anton Piller order. The Government of Ontario also intervened, arguing against the challenger. The defendant argued that the *Courts of Justice Act*, the Ontario Rules of Civil Procedure, and the court's inherent jurisdiction did not permit the issuance of an Anton Piller order, which they termed a civil search warrant, and which was in breach of the Charter. In addition, the order violated s. 8 of the Charter because it was not issued in accordance with the procedural elements required by the Supreme Court as set out in *Hunter v. Southam Inc.*, [1984] 2 SCR 145.

With respect to the first argument, much turned on whether the defendant could show that the Anton Piller order did amount to a search warrant. If it did, then it would not be authorized under the *Courts of Justice Act* or Rules of Civil Procedure. On this issue Farley J reviewed the origins of the Anton Piller order and concluded that it clearly originated from the court's inherent jurisdiction. Thus, any further attention to the *Courts of Justice Act* and the Rules was unnecessary. Turning next to the inherent jurisdiction, Farley J pointed to a number of decisions of Canadian courts that reaffirmed, even in a post Charter world, that a court's inherent jurisdiction was alive and well. However, the fundamental flaw in the defendant's argument was the characterization of the Anton Piller order as amounting to a search warrant. The fact that the order is only given after meeting the requisite legal threshold, and then only requires the person served to give permission, coupled with the fact that it is always open for such permission to be refused, determines that the order does not amount to a search warrant.

Farley J also referred to the numerous decisions pointing out that only in exceptional circumstance will a court order be viewed as exercising governmental action. That the plaintiff in this case was a government agency, acting in a private capacity, did not change this conclusion.

Farley J also dealt with the alternative argument. Assuming that s. 8 of the Charter did apply, had the court met the requisite test under *Hunter v. Southam Inc.*, [1984] 2 SCR 145 and *Thomson Newspapers Ltd. v. Canada (Director of Investigations and Research, Restrictive Trade Practices Commission)*, [1990] 1 SCR 425? Those cases require that for a search to be reasonable and pass Charter scrutiny, it must be the product of "prior judicial authorization from an impartial adjudicator acting judicially by reference to objective standards." (D. Mullan, "Anton Piller Orders: Life at the Extremity of the Courts," in J. Berryman, ed., *Remedies: Issues and Perspectives* (Toronto: Carswell, 1991), 189, at 207.) Farley J concluded that the procedural safeguards and substantive test applied for granting an Anton Piller order, met or exceeded all the components of this test.

Finally, Farley J also addressed the question whether, in the case of s. 8 being applicable and violated, an Anton Piller order could be justified under s. 1. On this point, Farley J said (at 558):

> The pressing and substantial objective is the maintenance of the court process from being undermined by those who have demonstrated to be untrustworthy and, therefore, there exists the real possibility that they would suppress evidence. This would not only be to the detriment of the litigant on the other side of the case but it would also tend to destroy the ability of the court to dispense civil justice (and thereby lessen the public's confidence in the court system as a means of resolving disputes).

The defendant's Charter challenge failed on all counts.

2. The temptation for a plaintiff to use this type of order oppressively has been commented upon in *Columbia Pictures Industries Inc. v. Robinson*, [1987] Ch. 38 where damages verging on exemplary in nature were awarded against the plaintiff for high-handed execution of its order. See also J. Berryman, "Anton Piller Injunctions Revisited: Columbia Pictures Industries Inc. v. Robinson" (1987), 3 *Intellectual Property Journal* 317.

3. The issue of interrogatories also arises in the context of Mareva injunctions. See *A.J. Bekhor & Co. Ltd. v. Bilton*, [1981] QB 923 (CA).

ANTI-SUIT INJUNCTIONS

Introduction

Another form of interlocutory injunction that has emerged to manage litigation in courts is the anti-suit injunction. This form of injunction seeks to restrain one of the parties from prosecuting a suit against the other in another jurisdiction. For a variety of reasons, a party may wish to sue in another jurisdiction where that jurisdiction recognizes the claim. For example, the other jurisdiction may have distinct procedural advantages (for example, access to jury trial, different forms of proof, such as strict liability, or access to punitive or triple damages).

Obviously, the advantages that encourage the party to move away from their "natural" jurisdiction are likely to be the very reasons why the other party wishes to have the action heard in the "natural" jurisdiction. The anti-suit injunction restrains the party from prosecuting their suit in other than the "natural" jurisdiction. The issues raised here are usually regarded as ones of conflict of laws. Invariably, the disputes arise between English and Canadian courts on the one hand, and United States courts on the other. A further tension exists on what legal concept is recognized in the respective courts as being determinative of the choice of legal forum.

The leading case in the United Kingdom is *Société Nationale Industrielle Aerospatiale v. Lee Kui Jak*, [1987] AC 871 (PC Brunei). The issue has come before the Supreme Court of Canada on appeal from British Columbia in *Amchem Products Inc. v. British Columbia (WCB)*, [1993] 1 SCR 897.

Amchem Products Inc. v. British Columbia (WCB)
[1993] 1 SCR 897

[The plaintiffs were a number of asbestos companies that had been engaged in the manufacturing and supply of asbestos products for the ship building and construction industry and that did business in the United States, including Texas. The defendants, 194 in number, the majority living in British Columbia, claimed to have been injured through exposure to asbestos while working in British Columbia. The WCB had a subrogated claim from the defendants. The defendants had commenced their suit in Texas for a number of procedural advantages. The plaintiffs had sought to have the action stayed in Texas based on the doctrine of *forum non conveniens*. The Texas courts had rejected the plaintiffs' arguments because that jurisdiction did not recognize any doctrine of *forum non conveniens*. The plaintiffs then brought an interlocutory injunction in British Columbia restraining the defendants from pursuing their suit in Texas. At trial, Esson CJSC had granted the injunction. In the Court of Appeal, the order of Esson CJSC was affirmed and the appeal dismissed.]

SOPINKA J (for the court) [at 911]:

The Issue

The issue to be determined is on what principles should a court exercise its discretion to grant an anti-suit injunction and how these principles apply in this appeal.

Choosing the Forum in Modern Litigation

This Court has not considered this question since its decision in *Antares Shipping Corp. v. The Ship "Capricorn,"* [1977] 2 SCR 422. Meanwhile, the business of litigation, like commerce itself, has become increasingly international. With the increase of free trade and the rapid growth of multi-national corporations it has become more difficult to identify one clearly appropriate forum for this type of litigation. The defendant may not be identified with only one jurisdiction. Moreover, there are frequently multiple defendants carrying on business in a number of jurisdictions and distributing their products or services world wide. As well, the plaintiffs may be a large class residing in different jurisdictions. It is often difficult to pinpoint the place where the transaction giving rise to the action took place. Frequently, there is no single forum that is clearly the most convenient or appropriate for the trial of the action but rather several which are equally suitable alternatives. In some jurisdictions, novel principles requiring joinder of all who have participated in a field of commercial activity have been developed for determining how liability should be apportioned among defendants. In this climate, courts have had to become more tolerant of the systems of other countries. The parochial attitude exemplified by *Bushby v. Munday* (1821), 5 Madd. 297, 56 ER 908, at p. 308 and p. 913, that "[t]he substantial ends of justice would require that this Court should pursue its own better means of determining both the law and the fact of the case" is no longer appropriate.

This does not mean, however, that "forum shopping" is now to be encouraged. The choice of the appropriate forum is still to be made on the basis of factors designed to ensure, if possible, that the action is tried in the jurisdiction that has the closest connection with the action and the parties and not to secure a juridical advantage to one of the litigants at the expense of others in a jurisdiction that is otherwise inappropriate. I recognize that there will be cases in which the best that can be achieved is to select an appropriate forum. Often there is no one forum that is clearly more appropriate than others.

The courts have developed two forms of remedy to control the choice of forum by the parties. The first and more conventional device is a stay of proceedings. This enables the court of the forum selected by the plaintiff (the domestic forum) to stay the action at the request of the defendant if persuaded that the case should be tried elsewhere. The second is the anti-suit injunction, a more aggressive remedy, which may be granted by the domestic court at the request of a defendant or defendants, actual or potential, in a foreign suit. In the usual situation the plaintiff in the domestic court moves to restrain the defendant or defendants from launching or continuing a proceeding in the courts of another jurisdiction. Occasionally, as in this case, the defendants in a foreign jurisdiction who allege that the plaintiff in that jurisdiction has selected an inappropriate forum seek an injunction from the courts of the alleged appropriate forum, in which no proceeding is pending, to restrain continuation of the foreign proceedings. While the restraining order operates *in personam* on the plaintiff in the foreign suit and not on the foreign court itself, it has the latter effect and therefore raises serious issues of comity.

Although both the remedy of a stay and an injunction have as their main objectives the selection of an appropriate forum for the trial of the action, there is a fundamental difference between them which is crucial to the development of the principles which should govern each. In the case of the stay the domestic court determines for itself whether in the circumstances it should take jurisdiction whereas, in the case of the injunction, it in effect determines the matter for the foreign court. Any doubts that a foreign court will not regard this as a breach of comity are dispelled by reading the reaction of Wilkey J of the District of Columbia Circuit of the United States Federal Court of Appeal in *Laker Airways v. Sabena, Belgian World Airlines*, 731 F2d 909 (1984), in which the British courts restrained Laker from continuing an anti-trust suit in United States courts against British airlines. In assessing the role of comity in the formulation of the principles which should inform the exercise of this power, I adopt the definition of comity approved by Justice La Forest J in *Morguard Investments Ltd. v. De Savoye*, [1990] 3 SCR 1077, at p. 1096:

"Comity" in the legal sense is neither a matter of absolute obligation, on the one hand, nor of mere courtesy and good will, upon the other. But it is the recognition which one nation allows within its territory to the legislative, executive or judicial acts of another nation, having due regard both to international duty and convenience, and to the rights of its own citizens or of other persons who are under the protection of its laws. ...

It has been suggested that by reason of comity, anti-suit injunctions should either never be granted or severely restricted to those cases in which it is necessary to protect the jurisdiction of the court issuing the injunction or prevent evasion of an important public policy of the domestic forum. See Richard W. Raushenbush, "Antisuit Injunctions and International Comity" (1985), 71 *Va. Law Rev.* 1039, and *Laker Airlines, supra.* A case can be made for this position. In a world where comity was universally respected and the courts of countries which are the potential fora for litigation applied consistent principles with respect to the stay of proceedings, anti-suit injunctions would not be necessary. A court which qualified as the appropriate forum for the action would not find it necessary to enjoin similar proceedings in a foreign jurisdiction because it could count on the foreign court's staying those proceedings. In some cases, both jurisdictions would refuse to decline jurisdiction as, for example, where there is no one forum that is clearly more appropriate than another. The consequences would not be disastrous. If the parties chose to litigate in both places rather than settle on one jurisdiction, there would be parallel proceedings, but since it is unlikely that they could be tried concurrently, the judgment of the first court to resolve the matter would no doubt be accepted as binding by the other jurisdiction in most cases.

While the above scenario is one we should strive to attain, it has not yet been achieved. Courts of other jurisdictions do occasionally accept jurisdiction over cases that do not satisfy the basic requirements of the *forum non conveniens* test. Comity is not universally respected. In some cases a serious injustice will be occasioned as a result of the failure of a foreign court to decline jurisdiction. It is only in such circumstances that a court should entertain an application for an anti-suit injunction. This then indicates the general tenor of the principles that underlie the granting of this form of relief. In order to arrive at more specific criteria, it is necessary to consider when a foreign court has departed from our own test of *forum non conveniens* to such an extent as to justify our courts in refusing to respect the assumption of jurisdiction by the foreign court and in what circumstances such assumption amounts to a serious injustice. The former requires an examination of the current state of the law relating to the stay of proceedings on the ground of *forum non conveniens*, while the latter, the law with respect to injunctions and specifically anti-suit injunctions.

Forum Non Conveniens

The law of Canada and other common law countries on this subject evolved from the law of England which was most recently restated by the House of Lords in *Spiliada Maritime Corp. v. Cansulex Ltd.*, [1987] AC 460. In setting out the principles which should guide a British court, Lord Goff, who delivered the main judgment, stated at p. 477 that "on a subject where comity is of importance, it appears that there will be a broad consensus among major common law jurisdictions." The English approach has gone through several stages of evolution tending to a broader acceptance of the legitimacy of the claim of other jurisdictions to try actions that have connections to England as well as to such other jurisdictions. Other common law jurisdictions have either accepted the principles in *Spiliada*, or an earlier version of them.

Earlier English cases declined to apply the principle of *forum non conveniens*, which was a Scottish principle, preferring a rule which required a party who had been served within the jurisdiction to establish: (1) that the continuation of the action would cause an injustice to him or her because it would be oppressive or vexatious or constitute an abuse of the process, and (2) that stay would not cause an injustice to the plaintiff. The foundation for this rule was not balance of convenience for the trial of the action but rather abuse of the rights of the parties. A different test applied with respect to cases in which service outside the jurisdiction was necessary. In such a case an order for service *ex juris* was required and the plaintiff had to show that England was the appropriate forum and that the rule authorizing such service was otherwise complied with. In *The Atlantic Star*, [1973] 2 All ER 175, the House of Lords was urged to adopt the principle of *forum non conveniens* from the Scottish law and to discontinue the test which required proof that the action was oppressive or vexatious as a prerequisite to a stay. The House of Lords declined to adopt the Scottish doctrine but opined that since the words "oppressive and vexatious" were flexible (indeed they had never been satisfactorily defined), liberalization of the English rule could be achieved in the application of those terms. In *Rockware Glass Ltd. v. MacShannon*, [1978] 2 WLR 362, those words were discarded in favour of a more liberal and flexible test which required the defendant to establish: (1) that there is another forum to which the defendant is amenable in which justice can be done at substantially less inconvenience or expense, and (2) that the stay did not deprive the plaintiff of a legitimate personal or juridical advantage if the action continued in the domestic court. This was substantially the same as the Scottish rule of *forum non conveniens*.

In *Spiliada, supra*, the House of Lords restated the rule and elaborated on its application. In particular, the court dealt with its application in what it considered two different circumstances. In the "as of right" cases in which the defendant was served in the jurisdiction, the burden of proof that a stay should be granted was on the defendant who was required to show that there is another forum which is clearly more appropriate for the trial of the action. This so-called "natural forum" is the one with which the action has the most real and substantial connection. If this first condition is established, a stay will be granted unless the plaintiff establishes special circumstances by reason of which justice requires that the trial take place in England. Mere loss of a juridical advantage will not amount to an injustice if the court is satisfied that substantial justice will be done in the appropriate forum. In cases in which service is effected *ex juris*, the burden is on the plaintiff throughout and is the obverse of that applicable in cases as of right; that is, the plaintiff must show that England is clearly the appropriate forum. Lord Goff provided some guidance with respect to the relevant factors that determine the appropriate forum. While not intending to provide an exhaustive list, His Lordship referred to the principal factors in his reasons at p. 478:

> So it is for connecting factors in this sense that the court must first look; and these will include not only factors affecting convenience or expense (such as availability of witnesses), but also other factors such as the law governing the relevant transaction (as to which see *Crédit Chimique v. James Scott Engineering Group Ltd.*, 1982 SLT 131), and the places where the parties respectively reside or carry on business. ...

The current state of the law in Canada is summed up adequately by Ellen L. Hayes in "*Forum Non Conveniens* in England, Australia and Japan: The Allocation of Jurisdiction in Transnational Litigation" (1992), 26 *UBC Law Rev.* 41, at pp. 42-43:

> The status of the doctrine of *forum non conveniens* in Canada is unclear. In general terms the Canadian courts have looked to English authorities when considering *forum non conveniens* issues. Their specific approach, however, is not consistent. The most recent cases from the Western provinces refer to the current English test, but at the same time resist adopting a comprehensive test or rule which would result in an "overly legalistic approach." The Ontario courts, on the other hand, have fallen behind the English courts' development of the doctrine and continue to apply a test which has now been replaced by the House of Lords. There is confusion in many of the cases as to whether the test is different when the defendant is served within the jurisdiction rather than *ex juris*, where the burden of proof lies and the weight to be given personal or juridical advantages to the plaintiff of proceeding in the home jurisdiction. …

This review establishes that the law in common law jurisdictions is, as observed by Lord Goff in *Spiliada*, remarkably uniform. While there are differences in the language used, each jurisdiction applies principles designed to identify the most appropriate or appropriate forum for the litigation based on factors which connect the litigation and the parties to the competing fora. A review of the law of Japan by Ellen L. Hayes in the study to which I refer above (*supra*, at p. 63) led her to conclude that similar principles are applied there. Regard for the principles of international comity to which I have referred suggests that in considering an anti-suit injunction the fact that a foreign court has assumed jurisdiction in circumstances which are consistent with the application of the above principles is an important factor militating against granting an injunction.

Anti-Suit Injunctions

England

The English courts have exercised jurisdiction to restrain proceedings in a foreign court and to stay domestic actions since 1821. Leach V-C in *Bushby v. Munday, supra*, at p. 307 and p. 913, stated the rule as follows:

> Where parties Defendants are resident in England, and brought by *subpoena* here, this Court has full authority to act upon them personally with respect to the subject of the suit, as the ends of justice require; and with that view, to order them to take, or to omit to take, any steps and proceedings in any other Court of Justice, whether in this country, or in a foreign country.

The sentiment expressed at that time was that the relief sought, whether an injunction or a stay, operated *in personam* and was not intended to interfere with the other court. Thus viewed, the question to be determined was whether the ends of justice required the issuance of an injunction or a stay. In deciding that an injunction should be granted in *Bushby v. Munday, supra*, the Vice-Chancellor made findings that the English Court was a more convenient jurisdiction; and, that the proceedings in Scotland, due to procedural law, were less likely to elicit the truth. Leach V-C concluded (at p. 308 and p. 913) that the English court should pursue its superior means for determining both law and fact.

The same test evolved for anti-suit injunctions and stays, based on the judgment of Scott LJ in *St. Pierre v. South American Stores (Gath & Chaves), Ltd., supra*. Where these requirements were met, the court would exercise its discretion in granting the stay or enjoining the foreign proceedings. The principles governing the issuance of a stay and an anti-suit injunction remained identical until the House of Lords' decision in *The Atlantic Star, supra*, when the English jurisprudence regarding stays of domestic proceedings underwent the first of the modifications to which I have referred. In *The Atlantic Star*, the House of Lords held that the words "oppressive" and "vexatious" should be interpreted liberally. After the decision in *The Atlantic Star*, it was unclear whether the principles governing the issuance of an anti-suit injunction remained the same or whether they evolved along with the principles governing a stay of domestic proceedings. The House of Lords directly considered this question in *Castanho v. Brown and Root (UK) Ltd., supra*, which involved an application for an anti-suit injunction. Lord Scarman pronounced, at p. 574, that "[t]he principle is the same whether the remedy sought is a stay of English proceedings or a restraint upon foreign proceedings." Lord Scarman approved the reformulation of the principles as set out by Lord Diplock in *The Atlantic Star, supra*, and concluded, at p. 575, that:

> ... to justify the grant of an injunction the defendants must show: (a) that the English court is a forum to whose jurisdiction they are amenable in which justice can be done at substantially less inconvenience and expense, *and* (b) the injunction must not deprive the plaintiff of a legitimate personal or juridical advantage which would be available to him if he invoked the American jurisdiction. [Emphasis in original.]

Lord Scarman emphasized that the "critical equation" in an application for a stay or an anti-suit injunction was between the advantage to the plaintiff and the disadvantage to the defendants. For the purposes of this determination, the prospect of higher damages in the foreign jurisdiction was a legitimate juridical advantage for a plaintiff. The House of Lords applied the law as set out in *Castanho, supra*, in two succeeding cases involving applications to enjoin foreign proceedings (*British Airways Board v. Laker Airways Ltd.*, [1985] AC 53, and *South Carolina Insurance Co. v. Assurantie Maatschappij "De Zeven Provincien" N.V.*, [1987] AC 24).

This test, in so far as it regarded anti-suit injunctions, did not withstand the scrutiny of the Judicial Committee of the Privy Council. In 1987, the Privy Council overturned the liberalized principles that the House of Lords enunciated. The definitive statement of the law was pronounced in *SNI, supra*: an anti-suit injunction will not be issued by an English court unless it is shown that the foreign proceedings will be oppressive or vexatious. It was made clear that the traditional principles as summarized in *St. Pierre v. South American Stores (Gath & Chaves), Ltd., supra*, were to govern applications to restrain foreign proceedings. Thus, the liberalized principles formulated in *Spiliada, supra*, in the context of an application for a stay of domestic proceedings were not to apply to anti-suit injunctions because to do so would be inconsistent with the principles of comity and would disregard the fundamental requirement that an injunction will only be available where it is required to address the ends of justice.

In coming to his conclusion on the law in *SNI*, Lord Goff considered the long history of English law as well as American and Scottish authorities. He stated, at p. 519, that the following basic principles were beyond dispute:

First, the jurisdiction is to be exercised when the "ends of justice" require it. ... Second, where the court decides to grant an injunction restraining proceedings in a foreign court, its order is directed not against the foreign court but against the parties so proceeding or threatening to proceed. ... Third, it follows that an injunction will only be issued restraining a party who is amenable to the jurisdiction of the court against whom an injunction will be an effective remedy. ... Fourth, it has been emphasised on many occasions that, since such an order indirectly affects the foreign court, the jurisdiction is one which must be exercised with caution. ... [Cites omitted.]

In considering the above principles, Lord Goff set out the following test (*SNI, supra*, at p. 522):

In the opinion of their Lordships, in a case such as the present where a remedy for a particular wrong is available both in the English (or, as here, the Brunei) court and in a foreign court, the English (or Brunei) court will, generally speaking, only restrain the plaintiff from pursuing proceedings in the foreign court if such pursuit would be vexatious or oppressive. This presupposes that, as a general rule, the English or Brunei court must conclude that it provides the natural forum for the trial of the action, and further, since the court is concerned with the ends of justice, that account must be taken not only of injustice to the defendant if the plaintiff is allowed to pursue the foreign proceedings, but also of injustice to the plaintiff if he is not allowed to do so. So, as a general rule, the court will not grant an injunction if, by doing so, it will deprive the plaintiff of advantages in the foreign forum of which it would be unjust to deprive him.

This analysis represents the current test for issuance of an anti-suit injunction in England.

The United States of America

Although American courts have exercised the equitable power to restrain parties subject to their jurisdiction from litigating in another forum (see *Cole v. Cunningham*, 133 US 107 (1890)), most American jurisdictions allow parallel foreign proceedings for *in personam* actions. Anti-suit injunctions are used only when "necessary to protect the jurisdiction of the enjoining court, or to prevent the litigant's evasion of the important public policies of the forum" (*Laker Airways v. Sabena, Belgian World Airlines, supra*, at p. 927). As in the case of other jurisdictions, the power to issue such injunctive relief must be exercised with extreme caution because, although in theory the order operates *in personam*, an anti-suit injunction "effectively restrict[s] the foreign court's ability to exercise its jurisdiction" (*Laker Airways, supra*, at p. 927).

In American jurisprudence there are no precise rules governing the issuance of anti-suit injunctions; rather, the equitable circumstances are examined to determine whether the injunction is required to prevent an irreparable miscarriage of justice. A court is to be guided by two tenets. Firstly, the fundamental corollary to concurrent jurisdiction must be respected: parallel proceedings in concurrent *in personam* actions are allowed to proceed simultaneously. Second, impedance of the foreign jurisdiction is to be avoided. (See *Laker Airways, supra*, at pp. 926-27.)

As noted by one author, when faced with foreign courts of concurrent jurisdiction, not all American courts abide by the rule favouring parallel proceedings. Richard W. Raushenbush, "Antisuit Injunctions and International Comity," *supra*, at pp. 1049-50, describes two distinct approaches which have developed. Under the "liberal" approach to anti-suit injunctions, a court will be willing to grant an injunction where the proceedings are duplicative in nature, and they "(1) frustrate a policy of the forum issuing the injunction; (2) [are] vexatious or oppressive; (3) threaten the issuing court's in rem or quasi in rem jurisdiction; or (4) ... prejudice other equitable considerations" (*per Unterweser Reederei, GmbH v. M/S Bremen*, 428 F2d 888 (5th Cir. 1970), at p. 890). The "conservative" approach, as exemplified by Wilkey J in *Laker Airways, supra*, advances the view that issuing anti-suit injunctions to prevent duplicative litigation is inconsistent with the rule permitting parallel proceedings in concurrent *in personam* actions. In the application of the "conservative" approach (at p. 927), anti-suit injunctions are only deployed when it becomes "necessary to protect the jurisdiction of the enjoining court, or to prevent the litigant's evasion of the important public policies of the forum." Often an applicant is additionally required to establish the conventional requirements for issuance of an injunction: a likelihood of success on the merits, a risk of irreparable injury, a lack of significant harm to the defendant, and a public interest in issuing an injunction. (See *Gau Shan Co., Ltd. v. Bankers Trust Co.*, 956 F2d 1349 (6th Cir. 1992).)

As observed by Lord Goff in *SNI*, there is no suggestion in American jurisprudence that applications for stays of proceedings and anti-suit injunctions are governed by the same principles.

Australia

The Federal Court-General Division has discussed the English and American authorities regarding anti-suit injunctions: Gummow J in *National Mutual Holdings Pty. Ltd. v. Sentry Corp.* (1989), 87 ALR 539, at p. 563, concluded that:

> The conduct of foreign proceedings which have a tendency to interfere with the due process of the domestic court may, in the circumstances of a particular case, generate the necessary equity to enjoin those foreign proceedings as vexatious or oppressive. ...

He added three observations. First, "[i]n Australia, there is the further consideration that where a court has begun to exercise the judicial power of the Commonwealth in relation to a particular matter, it has the exclusive right to exercise or control the exercise of the functions which form part of that power or are incidental to it: cf *Pioneer Concrete (Vic) Pty Ltd v Trade Practices Commission* (1982) 152 CLR 460 at 471-3, 474 ... ." Secondly, "[i]t is also to be asked whether effectual relief can be obtained in the courts of the foreign country ... : cf White and Tudor's *Leading Cases in Equity* [9th ed., vol. 1], pp. 635-6." And lastly, "[a] relevant consideration is the existence of substantial reasons of benefit for the plaintiff in bringing the foreign proceedings: [*SNI*] (at 893-4)."

The High Court of Australia has not specifically considered the principles upon which an anti-suit injunction will be granted.

Canada

Canadian jurisprudence is not widely developed on this subject matter. Even the early cases, however, admonished that the power to restrain foreign proceedings should be exercised with great caution and that the strict purpose of such injunctions was to prevent the abuse of the courts by vexatious actions. There is no decision of this Court on the point.

Two recent Nova Scotia decisions dealt with anti-suit injunctions. *Canadian Home Assurance Co. v. Cooper* (1986), 29 DLR (4th) 419 (NSSC App. Div.), predated the English judgment of *SNI*. In that case, an injunction was granted upon MacKeigan JA's findings that the foreign action involving the same parties was of no value to the respondents since, if its resolution was the same as the domestic action, it would not add to the domestic judgment, and, if the judgment were not the same, it would not be recognized in the domestic jurisdiction because of what would be considered to be a jurisdictional error. Without discussion of the governing principles, the injunction was granted. In the later Nova Scotia case of *Rowan Companies, Inc. v. DiPersio* (1990), 69 DLR (4th) 224, which was decided after *SNI*, an anti-suit injunction was refused by the Court of Appeal. Jones JA, delivering the judgment for the court, stated that the balance of convenience favoured the respondent. The factors he relied on were that the action was brought in the *lex loci delicti* which was the appropriate forum and that the applicant carried on business in the foreign jurisdiction where, presumably, some of the witnesses resided. He found, at p. 240, that the action could not be termed "frivolous or vexatious."

In the recent Alberta Queen's Bench decision in *Allied-Signal Inc. v. Dome Petroleum Ltd.* (1988), 67 Alta. LR (2d) 259, Medhurst J purported to apply the English principles enunciated in *SNI* in an action for an anti-suit injunction. He stated, at p. 266:

> After considering all of the submissions that have been made, it is my view that these applications before me should be decided on the basis of which forum is more suitable for the ends of justice in determining the issues in dispute. This includes a consideration of the tripartite test for obtaining interlocutory injunctions in other proceedings.

Medhurst J concluded that on the basis of the *forum non conveniens* test the injunction should be granted. He added that the injunction might also be justified on two further grounds: (1) the foreign action is oppressive due to the risks of inconsistent findings and subsequent actions for contribution and indemnity, and (2) the tripartite test for granting interim injunctions which includes consideration of the public interest and private interests of the parties was satisfied.

Kornberg v. Kornberg (1990), 30 RFL (3d) 238 (Man. CA) (leave to appeal refused, [1991] 1 SCR x), is a case which applied the *SNI* principles. The majority of the Court of Appeal recognized that the principles applicable to an anti-suit injunction were not the same as those applicable to a stay of domestic proceedings. Philp JA, writing for the majority, held that an anti-suit injunction should not be granted unless continuing the foreign proceedings would lead to injustice to the other party or the pursuit of the foreign proceedings was vexatious and oppressive. This decision was in contrast to the Manitoba Court of Appeal decision in *Aikmac Holdings Ltd. v. Loewen*, [1989] 6 WWR 759, which applied the English approach in *Castanho, supra*, which was overruled in 1987 by the Privy Council in *SNI*.

No consistent approach appears to emerge from these cases other than recognition of the principle that great caution should be exercised when invoking the power to enjoin foreign litigation.

The Test

In my view, the principles outlined in *SNI* should be the foundation for the test applied in our courts. These principles should be applied having due regard for the Canadian approach to private international law. This approach is exemplified by the judgment of this Court in *Morguard, supra*, in which La Forest J stressed the role of comity and the need to adjust its content in light of the changing world order. I now turn to the formulation of the test in light of the foregoing.

First, it is useful to discuss some preliminary aspects of procedure with respect to anti-suit injunctions. As a general rule, the domestic court should not entertain an application for an injunction if there is no foreign proceeding pending. While *quia timet* injunctions are granted by the courts, that is done only if the applicant establishes that some threatened action by the defendant will constitute an actionable civil wrong. In general, an injunction is a remedy ancillary to a cause of action. See Case Comment by Elizabeth R. Edinger (1992), 71 *Can. Bar Rev.* 117, at p. 127. In this respect the anti-suit injunction is unique in that the applicant does not have to establish that the assumption of jurisdiction by the foreign court will amount to an actionable wrong. Moreover, although the application is heard summarily and based on affidavit evidence, the order results in a permanent injunction which ordinarily is granted only after trial. In order to resort to this special remedy consonant with the principles of comity, it is preferable that the decision of the foreign court not be pre-empted until a proceeding has been launched in that court and the applicant for an injunction in the domestic court has sought from the foreign court a stay or other termination of the foreign proceedings and failed.

If the foreign court stays or dismisses the action there, the problem is solved. If not, the domestic court must proceed to entertain the application for an injunction but only if it is alleged to be the most appropriate forum and is potentially an appropriate forum. In any case in which an action has been commenced in the domestic forum, it can be expected that the domestic forum is being put forward as an appropriate forum by the plaintiff. In resisting a stay, the plaintiff will also contend that there is no other forum which is clearly more appropriate and that, therefore, the defendant has not complied with the test which I have outlined above. If no action has been commenced in the domestic forum, it has no juridical basis for entertaining an application for an injunction unless it is contended by the applicant that the action should have been commenced in the domestic forum as the more appropriate place of trial and it is potentially an appropriate forum.

The first step in applying the *SNI* analysis is to determine whether the domestic forum is the natural forum, that is the forum that on the basis of relevant factors has the closest connection with the action and the parties. I would modify this slightly to conform with the test relating to *forum non conveniens*. Under this test the court must determine whether there is another forum that is clearly more appropriate. The result of this change in stay applications is that where there is no one forum that is the most appropriate, the domestic forum wins out by default and refuses a stay, provided it is an appropriate forum. In this step of the analysis, the domestic court as a matter of comity must take cognizance of the fact that the foreign court has assumed jurisdiction. If, applying the principles relating to *forum non conveniens* outlined above, the foreign court could reasonably have concluded that there was no alternative forum that was clearly more appropriate, the domestic court should respect that decision and the application should be dismissed. When there is a genuine disagreement between the courts of our country and another, the courts of this country should not arrogate to themselves the decision for both jurisdictions. In most cases it will appear from the decision of the foreign court whether it acted on principles similar to those that obtain here, but, if not, then the domestic court must consider whether the result is consistent with those principles.

In a case in which the domestic court concludes that the foreign court assumed jurisdiction on a basis that is inconsistent with principles relating to *forum non conveniens* and that the foreign court's conclusion could not reasonably have been reached had it applied those principles, it must go then to the second step of the *SNI* test. I prefer the initial formulation of that step without reference to the terms "oppressive or vexatious." At p. 522, Lord Goff states:

> This presupposes that, as a general rule, the English or Brunei court must conclude that it provides the natural forum for the trial of the action, and further, since the court is concerned with the ends of justice, that account must be taken not only of injustice to the defendant if the plaintiff is allowed to pursue the foreign proceedings, but also of injustice to the plaintiff if he is not allowed to do so. *So, as a general rule, the court will not grant an injunction if, by doing so, it will deprive the plaintiff of advantages in the foreign forum of which it would be unjust to deprive him.* [Emphasis added.]

That case was decided on the basis of the injustice to SNI by reason of the loss of juridical advantages in Brunei but not available to it in Texas. The characterization of this loss as oppressive added nothing to the analysis. This is especially so since neither "oppressive" nor "vexatious" was satisfactorily defined in *SNI* nor, from my reading of the cases, anywhere else. If flexibility is the desired objective, it is achieved by the use of the term "injustice" which, in addition, is more in keeping with the language of the statutes which provide for injunctive relief. For example, the British Columbia *Law and Equity Act*, RSBC 1979, c. 224, s. 36, authorizes an injunction when "it appears to the court to be just or convenient."

When will it be unjust to deprive the plaintiff in the foreign proceeding of some personal or juridical advantage that is available in that forum? I have already stated that the importance of the loss of advantage cannot be assessed in isolation. The loss of juridical or other advantage must be considered in the context of the other factors. The appropriate inquiry is whether it is unjust to deprive the party seeking to litigate in the foreign jurisdiction of a judicial or other advantage, having regard to the extent that the party and the facts are connected to that forum based on the factors which I have already discussed. A party can have no reasonable expectation of advantages available in a jurisdiction with which the party and the subject matter of the litigation has little or no connection. Any loss of advantage to the foreign plaintiff must be weighed as against the loss of advantage, if any, to the defendant in the foreign jurisdiction if the action is tried there rather than in the domestic forum. I pointed out in my discussion of the test for determining the *forum non conveniens* that loss of juridical advantage is one of the factors and it will have been considered in step one. It will also be considered in the second step to determine whether, apart from its influence on the choice of the most appropriate forum, an injustice would result if the plaintiff is allowed to proceed in the foreign jurisdiction. The loss of a personal or juridical advantage is not necessarily the only potential cause of injustice in this context but it will be, by far, the most frequent. Indeed most of the authorities involve loss of juridical advantage rather than personal advantage. Nonetheless, loss of personal advantage might amount to an injustice if, for example, an individual party is required to litigate in a distant forum with which he or she has no connection. I prefer to leave other possible sources of injustice to be dealt with as they arise.

The result of the application of these principles is that when a foreign court assumes jurisdiction on a basis that generally conforms to our rule of private international law relating to the *forum non conveniens*, that decision will be respected and a Canadian court will not purport to make the decision for the foreign court. The policy of our courts with respect to comity demands no less. If, however, a foreign court assumes jurisdiction on a basis that is inconsistent with our rules of private international law and an injustice results to a litigant or "would-be" litigant in our courts, then the assumption of jurisdiction is inequitable and the party invoking the foreign jurisdiction can be restrained. The foreign court, not having, itself, observed the rules of comity, cannot expect its decision to be respected on the basis of comity.

Application of Principles to This Appeal

I would allow the appeal on the ground that Esson CJSC (the trial judge) erred in his application of both branches of the rule relating to anti-suit injunctions which I have outlined above. First, with respect to the choice of forum, the first step in the test, having concluded that the Texas court did not apply a *forum non conveniens* test, he failed to consider whether, notwithstanding that fact, the decision was consistent with applicable principles of private international law. Second, although he was of the view that the alleged loss of juridical advantage had little substance, he decided that the Texas proceedings were oppressive. In respect of both branches of the rule he gave undue weight to the absence of a *forum non conveniens* rule in Texas and to the anti-anti-suit injunction granted by the Texas court.

The trial judge found that Texas was not a "wholly inappropriate forum." While he held that British Columbia was a more natural forum than Texas, he also held that the United States was a natural forum and that some state other than Texas was a more natural forum but did not specify which state that was. Indeed, he stated that he would have difficulty in concluding that any particular state was the natural forum. All of the asbestos companies had some connection with Texas and some had a substantial connection. The conclusion is reinforced by reason of the position taken by the respondents in the proceedings before the trial judge that they were not contesting the assumption of jurisdiction over them by the Texas courts. This could only be so if the respondents had a connection to Texas. They had no connection to British Columbia. The acts which were the foundation of the claim took place outside of British Columbia and in the United States. The action had been commenced there and had progressed to the point that a trial date had been set. In finding that both British Columbia and the United States were natural fora, the trial judge must have been of the opinion that an action in the appropriate state in the United States could be justified on the basis of *forum non conveniens* principles. The term "natural forum" is by definition the forum that has the closest connection with the parties and the case. The finding that both the United States and British Columbia were natural fora would suggest that one was not clearly more appropriate than the other. It is not clear that any other state in the United

States was clearly a more appropriate forum and since the case was presented on the basis that it was a contest between Texas and British Columbia, it was not relevant that some other state in the United States was more appropriate. The selection of Texas by the plaintiffs could be justified on the basis that no other forum was clearly more appropriate. As pointed out by the trial judge, Texas might be the natural forum for some of the asbestos companies but not others but neither side was suggesting that the case be decided on an individual basis. In these circumstances, if some weight is given to the choice of forum by the plaintiff in the absence of related litigation pending elsewhere, the decision of the Texas court could be recognized having due regard for the principles of comity to which I have referred above. It appears from the trial judge's reasons that he might have come to this conclusion "on the basis of the facts and submissions *other than those relating to the decisions made in Texas*" (emphasis added). These decisions are respectively the decision as to the application of *forum non conveniens* principles in Texas law and the anti-anti-suit injunction. These decisions in his view disentitled the Texas court to the respect that comity customarily affords. On the basis of the test I have outlined above, this would be sufficient to allow the appeal and dismiss the application for an injunction. In the alternative, however, had I come to the conclusion that the application for an injunction satisfied this part of the test, I would have concluded that it failed the second step of the analysis.

With respect to the second step of the test, I am of the view that the respondents failed to establish that continuation of the proceedings would deprive them of a legitimate juridical advantage of which it would be unjust to deprive them by proceeding in Texas. The principal disadvantages to which reference was made were: (1) the inability to claim over against the appellants Workers' Compensation Board and Cassiar, and, (2) the presence of other actions against some of the respondents brought in British Columbia by other claimants. The trial judge found little substance in these complaints. With respect to the inability to claim over against Workers' Compensation Board, it was based not on any legal impediment but on the inability to gather evidence against them if the action proceeded in Texas. As for Cassiar, the trial judge found that the basis for a possible claim over very tenuous. With respect to (2), he discounted the importance of this because, in light of the enormous scale of the asbestos litigation, there was nothing unusual about the existence of actions in several jurisdictions. In my opinion the trial judge was right to minimize the gravity of these disadvantages. Moreover, these did not represent a loss of advantages that the respondents could reasonably have expected to have, based on their previous connection to British Columbia. As with the first step of the analysis, the trial judge found that the second step was satisfied not by reason of the loss of juridical or other advantages but because the Texas court, by failing to apply the *forum non conveniens* rule and by issuing the anti-anti-suit injunction, rendered the proceedings in Texas oppressive.

With due respect to the trial judge, the principle of comity to which I have referred does not require that the decision of the foreign court be based on the doctrine of *forum non conveniens*. Many states in the United States and other countries do not apply that principle. Indeed, until comparatively recent times, it was not applied in England. Does this mean that a decision of the courts of one of these countries which, in the result, is consistent with the application of our rules would not be entitled to respect? The response must be in the negative. It is the result of the decision when measured against our principles that is important and not necessarily the reasoning that leads to that decision. Moreover, while the Texas courts do not apply a *forum non conveniens* test as such, they are required to comply with Section 1 of the Fourteenth Amendment to the Constitution of the United States which operates to limit the power of a state to assert *in personam* jurisdiction over a non-resident defendant. See *Pennoyer v. Neff*, 95 US 714 (1877). The due process requirements are satisfied when *in personam* jurisdiction is asserted over a non-resident corporate defendant that has "certain minimum contacts with [the forum] such that the maintenance of the suit does not offend 'traditional notions of fair play and substantial justice'": *International Shoe Co. v. Washington*, 326 US 310 (1945), at p. 316, quoting *Milliken v. Meyer*, 311 US 457 (1940), at p. 463. Blackmun J, delivering the opinion of the Court, in *Helicopteros Nacionales de Colombia v. Hall*, 466 US 408 (1984), at p. 414, held that "[e]ven when the cause of action does not arise out of or relate to the foreign corporation's activities in the forum State, due process is not offended by a State's subjecting the corporation to its *in personam* jurisdiction when there are sufficient contacts between the State and the foreign corporation." In the instant case, the Texas court assumed jurisdiction on the basis of the fact that some of the respondents are resident in that state and carry on business or some are not resident but carry on business in that state. The finding of sufficient contact with Texas is supported by the evidence and hence, the jurisdiction in Texas was asserted according to the Due Process Clause. This was conceded by the respondent asbestos companies. In my opinion, the application of this provision, which is a constitutional requirement, is consistent with our rules of private international law relating to *forum non conveniens*. The comments of Vaughan Black in his case comment, "The Standard for Issuing Antisuit Injunctions in Canada" (1991), 44 CPC (2d) 30, at pp. 31-32, are apt:

> The Texas courts, like all American courts, apply the due process clause of the 14th Amendment of the United States Constitution as a check against overbroad "long-arm" jurisdiction. As interpreted, that constitutional provision will not permit a court to assume jurisdiction over a nonresident defendant unless there are minimum contacts between the defendant and the forum. This limitation on territorial jurisdiction is a significant one. Indeed, there are instances where Canadian courts have refused to employ the doctrine of *forum non conveniens* to stay actions brought before them but where, if an analogous suit were brought before an American court, it would almost certainly have been dismissed as lacking the minimum forum contacts required by the US Constitution (e.g. *Robinson v. Warren* (1982), 31 CPC 305, 55 NSR (2d) 147, 114 APR 147 (CA)). In other words, the Texas courts do have a responsible way to ensure that suits brought before them neither encroach on the sovereignty of foreign jurisdictions nor subject out-of-state defendants to a forum which has an insufficient connection to the subject matter of the suit, but this is derived not from the common law doctrine of *forum non conveniens* but rather from the US Constitution. The adjudication of geographically complex cases may require decision makers to be flexible and even imaginative when inquiring into the nature of foreign legal systems.

With respect to the Texas injunction the Texas court was apparently advised that these claimants were not subject to the jurisdiction of the British Columbia court and therefore not bound by the *ex parte* injunction granted by Cowan J. I do not regard this as an attempt to defeat the proceedings in British Columbia and the injunction did not have this effect. It was therefore wrong to visit the conduct of some of the claimants on the entire class so as to enjoin them from proceeding in Texas. In the circumstances, this action on the part of the

Texas court was not a demonstration of disrespect for the British Columbia proceedings so as to disentitle the decision of the Texas court to the ordinary respect which comity affords. Moreover, it had little if any relevance to the issue of injustice which is the second step in the *SNI* analysis. The extent of the disadvantage occasioned by being subject to an action in Texas is not affected by the inability to stop some of the plaintiffs from continuing those proceedings. The issue of injustice is resolved on the assumption that the respondents are subject to those proceedings.

I have concluded therefore that the learned trial judge erred in the exercise of his discretion in respect of the matters that I have outlined above. The court of appeal dismissed the appeal essentially for the reason that in their view the trial judge had properly exercised his discretion and that, therefore, the court of appeal was not permitted to interfere. Many of the principles applied by the trial judge were affirmed by Hollinrake JA with whom McEachern CJBC and Taggart JA agreed. Without intending any disrespect to those reasons, it is not necessary to repeat what I have said with respect to those principles. One matter requires special comment. I do not agree that because an anti-suit injunction does not directly operate on the foreign court but *in personam* on the plaintiff in that court, comity is not involved. The reaction of Wilkey J in *Laker, supra*, and, indeed of Esson CJ in this case demonstrate that, whatever the form of restraint, the court whose proceeding is effectively restrained regards it as an interference with its jurisdiction.

Disposition

I would allow the appeal, set aside the orders below and dismiss the application for an injunction. I see no basis for differentiating between T & N and the other respondents. If the action is to proceed in Texas, it is a proper party to the litigation. It would make little sense to require the claimants to pursue a separate action against one company in British Columbia. The appellants are entitled to costs both here and in the courts below.

NOTES

1. The *forum non conveniens* doctrine had been abrogated by the Texas Supreme Court in *Dow Chemical Co. v. Alfaro*, 786 SW 2d 674 (Texas SC 1990). The doctrine has since been reintroduced in Texas by legislation enacted in 1993, *Texas Civil Procedure and Remedies Code*, s. 71.051.

2. Some provinces have codified the *Amchem* test. See, in British Columbia, the *Court Jurisdiction and Proceedings Transfer Act*, SBC 2003, c. 28; in Saskatchewan, the *Court Jurisdiction and Proceedings Transfer Act*, SS 1997, c. C-41.1; and in Nova Scotia, the *Court Jurisdiction and Proceedings Transfer Act*, SNS 2003 (2nd Sess.), c. 2.

3. For a definitive statement on the applicable test for anti-suit injunctions in the United Kingdom, see the decision of the Court of Appeal in *Deutsche Bank AG v. Highland Crusader Offshore Partners LP*, [2009] 2 All ER (Comm) 987.

4. *Amchem* looks at the issue of comity between the courts of two nation states. In a federal country conflict issues often arise between provinces. In *Aetna, supra*, we saw the Supreme Court of Canada consider the issue of "jurisdiction" with respect to Mareva injunctions and its application in a federal structure. In *Hunt v. T & N plc*, [1993] 4 SCR 289, the

Supreme Court of Canada addressed the issue of how one provincial court should approach legislation of another province which purported to create a barrier preventing one party from making disclosure of documents to the other party. The court held that with respect to the use of these blocking statutes between provinces, such conduct was constitutionally inapplicable. The thrust of the court's decision follows on from *Morguard, supra*, and attempts to provide a minimum standard of order and fairness for the recognition and enforcement of one province's judicial orders by another province.

5. See also V. Black, "The Anti-suit Injunction Comes to Canada" (1988), 13 *Queen's Law Journal* 103; P. Glenn, "The Supreme Court, Judicial Comity and Anti-suit Injunctions" (1994), 28 *University of British Columbia Law Review* 193; J.P. McEvoy, "International Litigation: Canada, Forum Non Conveniens and the Anti-suit Injunction" (1995), 17 *Advocates' Q* 1; and Vaughan Black and Angela Swan, "Concurrent Judicial Jurisdiction: A Race to the Court House or to Judgment? *Lloyds Underwriters v. Cominco Ltd.*" (2008), 46 *CBLJ* 292.

6. The requirement that a domestic court should not entertain an application for an anti-suit injunction before the foreign court has been afforded an opportunity to determine whether it is an appropriate forum has been discussed by the Ontario Divisional Court in *Hudon v. Geos Language Corp.* (1997), 34 OR (3d) 14 (Div. Ct.). The Ontario court took the position that this requirement from *Amchem* was only the "preferable approach" and was not a condition precedent to any anti-suit injunction brought in Ontario.

7. Although the anti-suit injunction appears to have been designed for transnational disputes it has been applied in inter-provincial disputes. See *Gentra Canada Investments Inc. v. Lehndorff United Properties (Canada)* (1995), 34 Alta. LR (3d) 360 (CA).

8. The second part of the *Amchem* test, that the domestic court can consider an anti-suit injunction only if it is the most appropriate forum in which to bring the dispute, has recently been discussed by the English courts. The following excerpt is taken from Jeffrey Berryman, *Equitable Remedies* (Toronto: Irwin Law, 2000), at 101.

> In *Airbus Industrie v. Patel*, [1999] 1 AC 119, the appellant, Airbus Industrie, was the manufacturer of an aircraft in which the respondent, Patel, had been injured when the aircraft crashed while on a domestic flight in India. Patel was an English national who had commenced suit in Texas against Airbus Industrie for negligence. There was no connection to Texas by any of the parties. Airbus had obtained an order from an Indian court preventing Patel from proceeding anywhere other than in India. As a matter of international law this order was not binding on Patel. Airbus had also successfully challenged the Texas court's actions, not on jurisdictional grounds, but on the grounds that as a company which was more than 50% owned by foreign governments it was entitled to claim sovereign immunity under US legislation. The Texas Trial Court had upheld Airbus Industrie's immunity but this had been overturned on appeal. At the time of the present proceedings Airbus was appealing the Texas Court of Appeal's decision to the Texas Supreme Court. While the first appeal had been heard in Texas, Airbus commenced proceedings in the United Kingdom for an anti-suit injunction against Patel. This had been refused by the trial judge but was upheld in the English Court of Appeal, [1997] 2 Ll. Rep. 8 (CA). In granting the injunction the Court of Appeal saw no impediment to its jurisdiction that it was not an appropriate forum to hear the substantive litigation nor that it was acting to protect English jurisdiction. The court saw that it was the only jurisdiction which could control the actions of Patel as a national of the country and amenable to its *in personam* jurisdiction. The court acted under the impression that the Texas

court would not make a ruling on jurisdiction because it did not acknowledge any rules of *forum non conveniens*. The Court of Appeal had concluded that it would be oppressive if Airbus was exposed to liability in Texas, a jurisdiction that was clearly not an appropriate one under any test.

In the House of Lords, the Court of Appeal's decision was overruled. Lord Goff, with whom the other Lords concurred, laid down the general rule:

> [B]efore an anti-suit injunction can properly be granted by an English court to restrain a person from pursuing proceedings in a foreign jurisdiction in cases of the kind under consideration in the present case, comity requires that the English court should have sufficient interest in, or connection with, the matter in question to justify the indirect interference with the foreign court which an anti-suit injunction entails (at 138).

Much of Airbus Industrie's claim for relief had been built upon the inability of the Indian court to enforce its order to prevent Patel from bringing suit in Texas. On this point Lord Goff stated:

> I am driven to say that such a course is not open to the English courts because, for the reasons I have given, it would be inconsistent with comity. In a world which consists of independent jurisdictions, interference, even indirect interference, by the courts of one jurisdiction with the exercise of jurisdiction of a foreign court cannot in my opinion be justified by the fact that a third jurisdiction is affected but powerless to intervene. The basic principle is that only the courts of an interested jurisdiction can act in the matter; and if they are powerless to do so, that will not of itself be enough to justify the courts of another jurisdiction to act in their place (at 141).

The test formulated by Lord Goff is consistent with that articulated in *Amchem*, and was acknowledged as such by Lord Goff.

In Lord Goff's analysis he drew a distinction between "alternative forum" cases and "single forum" cases. The former raises a conflict when two jurisdictions, usually the domestic court and a foreign court, are relevant forums in which to bring the dispute. *Amchem* and *Airbus Industrie* are examples of this type although in *Airbus Industrie* the alternative forums were two foreign courts, India and Texas.

"Single forum" cases arise when the domestic court is asked to grant an anti-suit injunction where the jurisdiction to bring the action only arises in the foreign court. An example of this type is the decision in *Midland Bank Plc. v. Laker Airways Ltd.*, [1986] QB 689 (CA). The plaintiff, an English bank subject to English banking law, was requesting an anti-suit injunction to prevent the defendant, an English air carrier, from pursuing the plaintiff in an anti-trust proceeding commenced in the United States. The defendant had added the plaintiff to the US action on the basis that the plaintiff had withdrawn its financial rescue operation of the defendant in circumstances that suggested the bank conspired with two other English transatlantic air carriers to put the defendant out of business. The court granted the anti-suit injunction. The dealings had all taken place in England and at no stage had the plaintiff subjected itself or its dealings to scrutiny or control by US authorities.

The principles articulated in *Amchem* cannot be applied in single forum cases because there is no issue of disputed appropriate alternative forums. Lord Goff, quoting Judge Wilkey of the United States states the justification for an anti-suit injunction in single forum cases as involving "consideration of the question whether the injunction is required to protect the polices of the English forum." And, an appropriate test would "involve consideration of the extent to which the relevant transactions are connected with the English jurisdiction." Judge Wilkey expressed the rationale for granting an anti-suit injunction as either to "(a) to protect the jurisdiction of the enjoining court, or (b) to prevent the litigant's evasion of the important public policies of the forum." *Laker Airways Ltd. v. Sabena, Belgian World Airlines*, 731 F2d 909 (1984) (US C of A Dist. of Col. Cir.), at 927. As yet there appears to be no reported case of a Canadian court considering the appropriate standard for granting an anti-suit injunction in a single forum case.

9. It is common in international agreements to find either an exclusive or a non-exclusive jurisdiction clause whereby the parties agree to submit to the jurisdiction of a particular court and then waive any rights to object based on *forum non conveniens*. The presence of an exclusive jurisdiction does not always lead to the granting of an anti-suit injunction where one of the signatories to the agreement commences litigation in another jurisdiction. However, in *Donohue v. Armco Inc.*, [2002] 1 All ER 749 (HL), the court, in declining to grant an anti-suit injunction involving a case where the parties had agreed to an exclusive jurisdiction clause favouring the United Kingdom as against the United States, did require the plaintiff in the substantive proceedings brought in New York to give an undertaking not to seek multiple or punitive damages. See also *Royal Bank of Canada v. Coöperatieve Centrale Raiffeisen-Boerenleenbank*, [2004] 1 Ll. R 471 (CA). For the test as to applicability of a forum selection clause in an agreement, see *Z.I. Pompey Industrie v. ECU-Line N.V.*, [2003] 1 SCR 450.

CHAPTER NINE

Specific Performance

GENERAL PRINCIPLES

The equitable remedy of specific performance is an order that a contracting party perform his or her contractual undertakings or else risk being in contempt of court. Like all equitable remedies, specific performance is awarded as a matter of discretion. Moreover, it is awarded only where common law damages are inadequate. As you read the following articles, consider why substitutional relief (common law damages) enjoys priority over specific relief and whether this priority can be justified.

E. Allan Farnsworth, "Legal Remedies for Breach of Contract"
(1970), 70 *Columbia Law Review* 1145, at 1149-56 (footnotes omitted)

The relief available to the promisee is of two main kinds. It is said to be "specific" when it is intended to secure for the promisee the very benefit that he was promised, as where the court confers the promised benefit on the injured party or orders the defaulting promisor to do so. It is said to be "substitutional" when it is intended to provide him with something in substitution for that benefit, as where the court awards the injured party money damages.

Although damages will, in some cases, permit the injured party to arrange an adequate substitute for the expected benefit, specific relief is clearly the form better suited to the objective of putting the promisee in the position in which he would have been had the promise been performed. Of course the passage of time may reduce the effectiveness even of specific relief. The benefit will at best usually be delayed since contract remedies are ordinarily not available until after breach has occurred. And there are some situations in which specific relief is simply not possible at all. For example, the promise may have been one to deliver particular goods which turn out to be defective, or to have been destroyed, or to have been sold to a third person. But there remain many instances in which specific relief will be both timely and feasible. They can be put into two broad categories.

In one category of cases, specific relief does not require the cooperation of the defaulting promisor. If the promise is to deliver goods, an officer of the court may seize and deliver them; if it is to convey land, he may execute a binding conveyance; if it is to pay money, he may seize and sell enough of the promisor's assets to yield the required sum. In this category the practical impediments to specific relief are at a minimum. In the other category of cases, however, specific relief does require the cooperation of the promisor. Consider, for example, a promise to act in a play, to paint a house, or to build a building. To assure specific relief in each of these cases some form of coercion may be needed, so that the practical impediments are substantial.

The civil law systems, i.e., those descended from Roman law, have by and large proceeded on the premise that specific redress should be ordered whenever possible, not only for cases in the first category, but even for those in the second category as well, unless the disadvantages of the remedy outweigh its advantages. As Dawson has said of the German law,

> The main reservations are for cases where specific relief is impossible, would involve disproportionate cost, would introduce compulsion into close personal relationships or compel the expression of special forms of artistic or intellectual creativity. Presumably German courts, like French courts and our own, would not affirmatively order painters to paint pictures or singers to sing.

The logic of the civil law is reinforced by practical considerations in communist countries that lack markets on which aggrieved parties can arrange substitute transactions. The task of manufacture imposed on a state enterprise by a government plan, for example, can only be accomplished if the enterprise receives the specific raw materials that it has been promised for production; money damages are not an adequate substitute.

The common law countries escape both the civil law's doctrinal logic and communism's practical need for compulsion. The early common law courts did know specific relief, for many of the first suits after the Norman Conquest were proprietary in nature, designed to regain something of which the plaintiff had been deprived. Even the action of debt was of this character, since it was based on the notion of an unjust detention of something belonging to the plaintiff. But it became the practice in these actions to allow money damages for the detention in addition to specific relief, and with the development of new forms of action, such as *assumpsit*, that were in no way proprietary, substitutional relief became the usual form.

The typical judgment at common law declared that the plaintiff recover from the defendant a sum of money, which in effect imposed on him a new obligation as redress for the breach of the old. The new obligation required no cooperation on his part for its enforcement since, if the sum was not paid, a writ of execution would issue empowering the sheriff to seize and sell so much of the defendant's property as was required to pay the plaintiff. The proprietary actions remained, so that there were a few instances where relief at common law was specific; for example, in an action by a buyer for replevin of goods sold to him but not delivered, the sheriff might first seize them from the seller and turn them over to the buyer, and the judgment would then declare that the buyer was entitled to them. And, of course, where the claim was to a sum of money that the defendant had promised to pay, the effect, as in the original action for debt, was to give the promisee specific relief; for example, in an action by the seller for the price of goods delivered but not paid for, judgment would be given against the buyer for the full amount of the price. But these instances were the exception rather than the rule, and even where the common law courts granted specific redress, they were unwilling to exert pressure directly on the defendant to compel him to perform. The judgment itself was seen as a mere declaration of rights as between the parties, and the process for its execution was directed not at the defendant but at the sheriff, ordering him to put the plaintiff in possession of real or personal property or to seize the defendant's property and sell such of it as was necessary to satisfy a money judgment.

The enforcement of promises in equity developed along very different lines. Prior to the development of *assumpsit* by the common law courts in the sixteenth century, most of the cases brought before the chancellor were based on promises that would not have been enforceable at common law, and the question was whether they would nevertheless be enforced in equity. After the development of *assumpsit*, equity accepted the test for enforcement that had been developed by the rival common law courts, and refused to enforce simple promises made without "consideration." To this extent its jurisdiction in contract became concurrent with that of the common law courts, and its concern shifted from the enforceability of the promise to the nature of its enforcement.

Under the influence of the canon law (for the early chancellors were usually clerics), decrees in equity came to take the form of a personal command to the defendant to do or not to do something. His cooperation was assumed, and if he disobeyed he could be punished not only for criminal contempt, at the instance of the court, but also for civil contempt, at the instance of the plaintiff. This put into the plaintiff's hands the extreme sanction of imprisonment, which might be supplemented by fines payable to the plaintiff and sequestration of the defendant's goods. So it was said that equity acted *in personam*, against the person of the defendant, while the law acted *in rem*, against his property. But it did not follow that the chancellor stood ready to order every defaulting promisor to perform his promise. Equitable relief was confined to special cases in light of both practical and historical limitations.

The practical limitations grew out of the problems inherent in coercion. Our courts, like those of civil law countries, will not undertake to coerce a performance that is personal in nature—to compel an artist to paint a picture or a singer to sing a song. (They have, to be sure, been ingenious in framing orders enjoining contracted parties from acting inconsistently with their promises as a substitute for orders directing them to perform them—the court that will not order the singer to sing may enjoin him from singing elsewhere.) Our courts have also been reluctant to order specific performance where difficulties of supervision or enforcement are foreseen, e.g., to order a building contractor specifically to perform his contract to repair a house. It has been suggested that "in their origins these ideas carried a load of snobbery, expressed in distaste for menial tasks—'how can a Master judge of repairs in husbandry?'" Today they are more often justified as a means of avoiding conflict and unfairness where no clear standards can be framed in advance. The practical exigencies of drafting decrees to guide future conduct under threat of contempt have also moved courts to require that contract terms be expressed with somewhat greater certainty if specific performance is to be granted than if damages are to be awarded. But these practical limitations are on the whole far less significant than the historical ones.

The most important of the historical limitations derives from the circumstance that, since the chancellor had first granted equitable relief in order to supply the deficiencies of the common law, equitable remedies were readily characterized as "extraordinary." When, during the long jurisdictional struggle between the two systems of courts, some means of accommodation were needed, an "adequacy" test was developed to prevent encroachment by the chancellor on the powers of the common law judges. Equity would stay its hand if the remedy at law was "adequate." To this test was added the gloss that the money damages awarded by the common law courts were ordinarily "adequate"—a gloss encouraged by the philosophy of free enterprise, since in a market economy money ought to enable an aggrieved promisee to arrange a substitute transaction. As one writer put it:

> The law, concerning itself more and more with merchandise bought or sold for money, with things having a definite and calculable exchange value, came to conceive that the money compensation, which was an entirely adequate remedy in the common case, and in many cases the only possible one when once the wrong complained of had been committed, was [generally] the only remedy available for their use. ...

So it came to be that, in sharp contrast to the civil law approach, money damages were regarded as the norm and specific relief as the deviation, even where the law could easily have provided specific relief without any cooperation from the defaulting promisor.

Land, which the common law viewed with particular esteem, was singled out for special treatment. Each parcel, however ordinary, was considered to be "unique," and from this it followed that if a vendor defaulted on his promise to convey land, not even money would enable an injured purchaser to find a substitute. The remedy at law being in this sense "inadequate," a decree of specific performance would ordinarily issue. Although the case for allowing the vendor to have specific performance when the purchaser defaulted was less compelling, equity also granted him relief. But no such reason applied to the contract for the sale of goods, for in a market economy it was supposed that, with rare exceptions for such "unique" items as heirlooms and objects of art, substantially similar goods were available elsewhere. Some attempts have been made to liberalize this restriction. The draftsmen of the *Uniform Commercial Code* state in its Comments that it introduces "a new concept of what are 'unique' goods," and they assert that "where the unavailability of a market price is caused by a scarcity of goods of the type involved, a good case is normally made for specific performance under this Article." But specific performance is still the exception, not the rule, and in contrast to the view held in socialist countries, it is to be justified on the basis of the peculiar needs of the aggrieved party and not the general welfare of society as a whole. Although a court, in determining the adequacy of an award of damages, may take account of such factors as the difficulty of their ascertainment (e.g., under a long-term "output" or "requirements" contract) and the improbability of their collection (e.g., against an insolvent defendant), the typical buyer of goods must still content himself with money as a substitute for the goods in the event of breach.

A second historical limitation, or group of limitations, is premised on the notion that equitable relief is "discretionary." Since the chancellor was to act according to "conscience" (a circumstance that prompted the famous charge that his conscience might vary with the length of his foot), he might withhold relief where considerations of "fairness" or "morality" dictated. Some of the most renowned of these equitable restrictions are embodied in equity's colorful maxims: "he who seeks equity must do equity"; "he who comes into equity must come with clean hands"; and "equity aids the vigilant." One of the most troublesome is the now largely discredited "mutuality of remedy" rule, under which specific performance would not be granted to the aggrieved party unless it would have been available to the other party had the aggrieved party been the one in breach. It is one of the curious inconsistencies to arise out of the dual jurisdiction of law and equity that these restrictions operated to bar only equitable relief and did not prevent the award of damages at law.

The historical development of the parallel systems of law and equity may afford an adequate explanation of the reluctance of our courts to grant specific relief; it is scant justification for it. A more rational basis might be the severity of the sanctions available under the contempt power for their enforcement. In any event, the current trend is clearly in favor of the extension of specific relief. The fusion of law and equity into a single court system at least facilitates a major change in this direction, and commentators have urged such a change.

Why not, as in both French and German law, give specific performance as to any physical object that can be found and is reachable by direct execution? It is true that whenever speed is a factor and markets reasonably organized, promisees will not often ask for it. ... But why not leave this to the promisee's choice?

Still, for the present, the promisee must ordinarily be content with money damages.

Donald H. Clark in his perceptive essay "Rethinking the Role of Specific Relief in the Contractual Setting" argues that if completeness of remedy is the ultimate objective, greater deference should be given to party autonomy in remedy selection and that the historical reluctance to favour substitutional over specific relief is outdated. He forcefully rebuts the traditional arguments that endorsed damages as the presumptive remedy on the basis of adequacy and the difficulty of supervision of awards for specific relief, and he supports arguments for specific relief based on remedial predictability, party autonomy and the completeness of the remedy to the promissee. Excerpts from this essay follow.

Donald H. Clark, "Rethinking the Role of Specific Relief in the Contractual Setting"
in Jeffrey Berryman, ed., *Remedies: Issues and Perspectives* (Toronto: Carswell, 1991), 139 (edited; footnotes omitted)

1. Introduction

An aerial snapshot of private law in Canada substantiates the judgment that we are moving towards a more holistic conception of a law of obligations. ...

Encouraging as are these indicators of some judicial movement towards a more rational and just treatment of rights and obligations, however, conspicuously absent from the examples cited is any sign that in the area of remedy selection the judiciary recognizes a need to reassess the efficacy of the hierarchical relationship of common law and equitable forms of relief. The upholding by the Supreme Court of Canada of an order for the transfer of ownership of the Hemlo gold mine to International Corona Resources, the victim of a breach of confidence, is striking evidence of the continued vitality of the equitable remedial jurisdiction. Yet in the area of contract, damages remains the presumptive remedy, specific relief being assigned an exceptional supplementary role. I am in agreement with Hammond that from the broad perspective of the law of obligations as a whole, the direction to be taken is to break out of the jurisdictional molds forged in distant rivalries between the courts of common law and equity, and purposively to fashion forms of relief that a "context specific evaluation" indicates as being most appropriate. The focus of this paper is, however, a narrower one, that of remedial approaches to the aftermath of contractual breach. In this context I cannot share my colleague's conclusion that "the old hierarchy of remedies is dissolving," notwithstanding Corbin's assertion over 30 years ago that "the impression plainly left by the sum-total of reported cases is that the remedy of specific enforcement is as available as other remedies." The reality is that, in the words of Estey J for a unanimous Supreme Court of Canada in *Asamera Oil Corp. v. Sea Oil & General Corp.*,

> [b]efore a plaintiff can rely on a claim to specific performance ... some fair, real and substantial justification for his claim to performance must be found.

There is one way and one way only to vindicate such a claim. The court has to be persuaded that in the particular circumstances of the case a monetary award would provide inadequate relief. Sporadic instances of specific enforcement of promises outside the categories of contracts for land, unique goods and long-term supply and requirements illustrate nothing more than the will-o'-the-wisp nature of the "inadequacy of damages" yardstick. It is alluring to advocate that the courts abandon their predisposition in favour of damages and make on a case by case basis a remedial choice informed by such factors as economic efficiency, the conduct of the parties and the impact on the defendant of requiring performance. It is the burden of this paper to argue against such a blueprint, and to put forward a model for contract remedies that provides at least a starting point for a principled ordering of this important yet surprisingly inchoate aspect of our legal system.

Relief *in rem*, it will be contended, is presently an underutilized means of protecting legitimate contractual expectations. Foremost among the reasons for its neglect are uncertainty as to its availability, misplaced concern for interests other than those of the promisee, unfounded objections to its practicability, and above all an exaggerated notion as to the capacity of monetary compensation to substitute for contractual performance. At the same time, a lack of coherence in the perceived relationship between specific relief and the principle of mitigation results in some instances in misuse of the specific remedy to the needless detriment of the promisor. ...

4. *Completeness of Remedy*

For many contractual plaintiffs victimized by breach, and looking to the courts for protection of their expectation interest, specific enforcement would be the optimal, in the sense of the most complete form of relief. As has been seen, this ideal is often unattainable. For some it is not even the goal. The most extreme example here would be the party ("victim" would be an inapt label) saved by another's breach from further losses under an improvident contract. Such a plaintiff would be best (and arguably too well) served by a restitutionary money remedy. Where, however, specific relief is both practicable and desired, it should be the law's aim to provide it, a strong justification being necessary for its denial. The presumptive "adequacy" of damages does not represent reality. In its most frequently quoted form, the articulation of the objective of contractual damages concedes the inherent imperfection of the monetary remedy:

> [W]here a party sustains a loss by reason of a breach of contract, he is, *so far as money can do it*, to be placed in the same situation, with respect to damages, as if the contract had been performed.

Some losses are left uncompensated as a matter of policy. Excluded by the remoteness rule, for example, are losses arising from special circumstances either existing but uncommunicated to the defendant before or at the time of contracting, or arising only thereafter. Loss that is notionally compensable is often simply impossible to establish with the necessary degree of probability to meet the requisite burden of proof. Losses of a non-economic nature, where compensated at all, receive only token recognition. They are inherently impossible to quantify on any objectively-defensible basis, and are at the mercy of fluctuating judicial policy concerns. In the last 20 years recovery in contract for mental distress has swung from being completely beyond the pale, to its zenith in the late seventies, and now back to a severely restricted area of availability. ... True, many of the cases that have openly discussed non-economic loss exemplify situations where the damages occasioned by breach could neither have been avoided by a pre-emptive specific remedy nor be repaired by such relief *ex post facto*. Where the contract ties the parties to a continuing relationship, however, as in the employment context, decisions such as *Vorvis* and *Stevenson v. Air Canada* serve only to accentuate the need to make available relief that is restorative in nature.

No less importantly, to focus solely on "mental distress" in evaluating what a contractual plaintiff loses when restrictive remedial rules enable a promisor to deny her performance with only damages as a sanction, is much too narrow. A whole range of intangibles, which the court never considers and which even the plaintiff herself might find difficulty in articulating, risk being left entirely out of account. Variously described by expressions such as "consumer surplus" or "idiosyncratic interests" (Linzer), they are by definition not susceptible to monetary measurement. For this reason they tend to be discounted in the remedial models of Posnerian economic analysts. Harris, Ogus and Phillips, on the other hand, have argued for their quantification, but were driven to the huge concession that

> insofar as [the consumer surplus] is to be reflected in an award of damages, the assessment must proceed on some objective basis (e.g. how would the reasonable man, in the plaintiff's position, have valued the benefit of performance?).

Recognition that the result of such objectification tends toward (at best) undervaluation of the promisee's interests informed Schwartz' and Linzer's advocacy of a much-increased role for specific relief. Kronman's economic analysis took him part way down this path. In his taxonomy a line is drawn between consumer and commercial contracts, specific performance retaining its current exceptional role in the latter context. Is there justification for such a dichotomy? Paradigmatic instances of "idiosyncratic interests," like the aesthetic appreciation of a structure calculated to diminish the market value of a property, certainly will have little place in a business world governed by the bottom line. And Staughton LJ's exaggerated concern in *Hayes v. Dodds* about the potential for a veritable flood of commercial claims for non-economic loss has an air of utter unreality. (Indeed, if the concern had any real substance, it would be material only in relation to monetary, not specific, relief.) Yet it is not fanciful to suggest that even in the context of a commercial contract for a fungible commodity a buyer may well have real, albeit subjective, grounds for preferring specific performance to damages in his particular circumstances. The buyer is, after all, best placed to evaluate the adequacy of an alternative source of supply. As has already been noted, there is a strong natural constraint against insistence without good reason on performance by a recalcitrant promisor.

The nexus between remedies and substantive rights has been the subject of much philo-sophical disputation. For a contractual plaintiff, however, to the extent that specific relief is denied and he is obliged to make do with a less than complete monetary remedy, there is a diminution of the rights for which he bargained and gave value in return. McNeil has de-fined contract in terms of sanctions effective to give substance to interests recognized as entitled to protection:

> The power of contract is the availability to a promisee of legal sanctions adequate to protect his reliance on the promise, to prevent gain by default and to effectuate expectancies where there may be hidden or unprovable reliance.

Yet in relating this concept to the remedy of specific performance, he rationalizes in fam-iliar terms the conventional primacy of monetary relief in the common law world:

> The definition of power of contract leads to the conclusion that, whenever other remedies are adequate to protect the promisee's reliance, restitution and expectancy interests, there is no curtailment of the power of contract in refusing specific performance.

I have sought to demonstrate, first, that damages constitute an *inherently* less complete form of relief than specific enforcement, even though many contractual plaintiffs (doubtless the vast majority in the commercial context) will in any event continue to opt for the money remedy despite its imperfections. Second, "adequacy" is in the eye of the promisee. This is the underlying argument for party autonomy in remedy selection. It is interesting to note that McNeil himself makes a partial concession to this view, albeit in a very limited context:

> [W]hen the parties expressly provide for specific relief, power of contract calls for granting that relief when there is *any doubt* of the efficacy of other available relief.

The central thought of this paper is that it should be accepted that damages are inad-equate for a particular plaintiff if she so adjudges by seeking specific relief. In face of such a remedial preference, it is both presumptuous and productive of injustice to assert, as do Goetz and Scott, that

> [b]reach together with payment of fully compensating damages is properly regarded as alterna-tive performance or "quasi-performance."

My concern in this section has been to indicate the fallacy of the premise of "fully com-pensating damages." Implicit in Goetz and Scott's proposition, however, is acceptance of the notion of "efficient breach" as a justification for permitting the defendant rather than the plaintiff to determine whether damages are to be substituted for performance. This notion will be challenged in the next section of the paper. ...

5. Countervailing Interests

Thus far it has been suggested that the goal of maximizing the completeness of contractual relief militates in favour of promisee autonomy in remedy selection, and the presumptive availability of relief *in specie*. It now becomes necessary to examine the weight to be given to three interests that to a greater or lesser degree might be seen as exerting a countervailing force: those of the defendant promisor, the court (representing the justice system) and third parties.

(a) *The Defendant Promisor*

In Oliver Wendell Holmes' theoretical construct of the nature of the contractual relationship, there is a complete inversion of the postulate of this paper. Under his theory of alternative obligations, according to which the promisor has from the outset the right to opt either to perform or to pay damages in lieu, the promisee's interest in enforcement is at the mercy of the promisor's perceived self-interest:

> The only universal consequence of a legally binding promise is that the law makes the promisor pay damages if the promised event does not come to pass. In every case it leaves him free from interference until the time for fulfilment has gone by, and therefore free to breach his contract if he chooses.

This perspective has already been subjected to critical appraisal by Daniel Friedmann, who concludes that

> the weakness of Holmes' approach lies in its conclusion that the remedy provides a perfect substitute for the right, when in truth the purpose of the remedy is to vindicate that right, not to replace it. Holmes' analysis mistakenly converts the remedy into a kind of indulgence that the wrongdoer is unilaterally always entitled to purchase.

Yet the promisor–conversion thesis here impugned is the very rationale of the resurgence of Holmesian thought in the last 20 years in the guise of the concept of "efficient breach." The argument runs as follows: the promisor should have the right to buy out the promisee's interest in performance, quantified as appropriate at either the expectation or reliance measure, when the result is a net gain to the promisor. Furious has been the battle in the law and economics literature over the relative efficiency of damages and specific performance as contractual remedies. Protagonists of the money remedy, such as Posner and Yorio, have been answered by Schwartz, Friedmann and others. While much of the debate has been conducted in a language shared only by the initiated, two observations are ventured here with the diffidence becoming one who stands outside the charmed circle. First, there seems to be much force in McNeil's position that economic analysis that proceeds on an assumption of zero transaction costs or at best empirically-unsubstantiated hypotheses constitutes merely "circles in the sky." Significantly, after indicating the "broad scope of the inquiry required before even slightly definitive conclusions could be suggested" as to whether a damages rule or a specific performance rule is economically the more efficient, he questions whether it would not be "far better to ignore all the sophistication in favour of historical or more intuitive solutions." And it must surely be allowed that some of the perceived inefficiencies of the specific remedy derive from its present limited and uncertain availability. Birmingham makes a simple yet telling point when he notes that "the availability of the remedy of specific performance might permit achievement of the desired result without the expense of court action by encouraging one contemplating breach to bargain instead to adjust his duties." The second observation is that despite its avowed amorality, the theory of efficient breach has now had to accommodate a major qualification: a promisor should not be permitted to retain gains achieved by "opportunistic behaviour." This is a considerable concession, coming at a time when the courts are increasingly resorting to the principle of unjust enrichment to require disgorgement of the "profit" accruing from "efficient" contractual breach. The judiciary, however, has never overtly espoused the concept of efficient breach. As Lord Wilberforce pithily put it in *Shiloh Spinners Ltd. v. Harding*:

> [E]quity expects men to carry out their bargains and will not let them buy their way out by uncovenanted payments.

There is an undoubted moral underpinning to the notion that *pacta sunt servanda*. Granted that not all who lay emphasis on the moral value of a promise would see it as necessarily requiring specific enforceability at the promisee's election, that emphasis does tend to focus attention at the remedial stage on that party's needs rather than on some ulterior objective of the promisor.

However, while not going so far as to expressly sanction (by setting the price for) a unilateral buy-out by the promisor of the promisee's interest in performance, the courts nevertheless frequently produce the same result by going through an exercise of balancing the interests of the respective parties. The onerousness of performance, in economic terms, is weighed against the benefit to the promisee of specific enforcement. As the test was formulated in a recent English decision: "what are the respective prejudices or hardships that will be suffered by the parties if the order [specific performance] is made or not made?" On the promisee's side this currently involves an examination of the "adequacy" of damages. The countervailing interest asserted by the promisor is that in not being required to live up to an obligation that in most instances will fail to be performed (unless the court grants a release) in an economic environment that has changed for the worse, from the promisor's standpoint, since the date of contract. Such a plea of hardship prevailed in *Weyburn Square Developments Ltd. v. Liggett Drug Ltd.*, where the owner of a shopping mall sought to enjoin the defendant tenant from breaching a lease with seven years still remaining on its term by closing down its drug store. The closure was one of many stemming from a corporate decision to pull out of the unprofitable western Canadian market altogether. Confining the plaintiff to its remedy in damages, Geatros J was influenced by the "extreme harshness on the defendant if required to continue but one outlet in western Canada." Specific relief being equitable in origin, and hence discretionary, its withholding provides a convenient remedial means of tempering the contractual wind to the shorn lamb. But is it defensible? Let us test the issue by supposing that the corporate defendant, in the course of reviewing its business strategy, had been able to seek a judicial ruling (in the form of a reference) on the *legality* of responding to a market downturn by actual or threatened premature termination of the lease. It would have been advised: (i) that even a severe change in economic conditions, however unprofitable it renders performance, does not frustrate a contract. It is incumbent upon a party wishing to have protection against such contingencies to negotiate for it. Should it fail to do so (successfully), it must live with the consequences for good or ill of the risk allocation that is agreed upon; (ii) that if, left unprotected through lack of foresight or negotiating skill, it should attempt to coerce the promisee into submitting to a redrawing of the bargain by use of the leverage of threats of breach, it would risk, though castigation of its conduct as constituting economic duress, the loss of any advantage purportedly gained by this tactic. Is it not bizarre that the lesson of decisions like that in *Weyburn Square* is that the final element of our hypothetical opinion would be: "the best course is to go ahead and breach anyway (preferably showing your reasonableness by making a settlement offer). Then, but only then, will a plea of hardship fall on receptive judicial ears, and a way be found *ex post facto* to shift some part of your risk to the plaintiff promisee."

Deference to the interests of the defendant promisor is also seen in the reasoning frequently advanced for the refusal of specific performance in two particular classes of contract: those involving respectively personal service and protracted performance of complex obligations (typically in construction contracts). In neither context is the rationale convincing. Enforcement *in specie*, against the employee, of the former type of contract would, it is argued, smack of servitude. Linzer speaks of an "odor of peonage" while Schwartz would see it as violating the "liberty interest" of the individual. The result one intuitively feels to be right, but a better basis for withholding specific enforcement is submitted to be the futility of attempting it. There is little practical likelihood of an employer's seeking specific performance of a contract of service (or for services) that does not engage distinctive and subjective attributes and talents of the recalcitrant promisor. Yet if such a party goes through the motions of performance, it would be difficult to bring home any legal sanction if lack of due effort is suspected. How many actions for damages have been brought against a ball player or diva for playing or singing badly? Other, more effective sanctions are employed: the player is traded, the singer not re-engaged. In any event, so formidable would be the task of establishing liability here that litigation is of little use *whatever* the remedy sought. In relation to construction contracts, on the other hand, there is a judicial predilection for the money remedy that reflects a concern not to render the defendant vulnerable to contempt proceedings for non-compliance with an order imprecise in its requirements. The concern is legitimate, but the solution is in the courts' own hands. For there to be binding obligations to be enforced at all, regardless of the form of relief, the parties must have delineated what is required of the contractor with sufficient particularity to pass the test of certainty of terms. That being so, it can hardly be said to be impracticable to frame an order for specific performance with the requisite degree of specificity. Assumptions to the contrary are often veiled in the objection that contracts calling for performance of complex obligations over a period of time are not susceptible to specific enforcement because of the asserted difficulty of supervision. This formulation shifts the focus from the defendant's interests, as a countervailing force in relation to specific relief, to those of the court as representative of the justice system.

(b) The Court

One encounters not infrequently the argument that judicial credibility is on the line when a court orders specific enforcement. Therefore, it is argued, public respect for the legal system should not be put at risk by the making of orders (a) which there is reason to believe the defendant may simply disregard, or (b) compliance with which would require continuing judicial monitoring.

(i) Loss of Dignity

Loss of dignity occurs if an order made *in personam* is ignored by the party to whom it is addressed.

Commentators have inflated this concern. Yorio, for example, has stated that

an order of specific performance requires the court to make certain that its decree is not flouted. Otherwise, the court's prestige may suffer if, having been ordered to perform, the promisor fails to perform or performs badly.

Contrast Lord Wilberforce's sanguinity in *Johnson v. Agnew*:

The factual situation is *commonplace, indeed routine*. An owner of land contracts to sell it to a purchaser, the purchaser fails to complete the contract; the vendor goes to the court and obtains an order that the contract be specifically performed; the purchaser still does not complete.

Respect for the legal system is certainly not enhanced by episodes such as those involving, respectively, Chantelle Daigle and the Baie Comeau PCB's, where injunctions were simply ignored by those against whom they had been issued. But if there is precedential value in these incidents, unedifying examples of justice-on-the-run in contexts where public passions and fears are fanned by the media's insatiable appetite for drama, it is perhaps that they serve to remind us that, Charter or no Charter, legal sanctions are not the universal solvent for the social problems that wrack contemporary society. Even so, and particularly in the field of private law, the proposition that appropriate remedial justice should be denied because of the apprehension of the possibility of non-compliance, is simply untenable. Otherwise, to take but one example, how many spousal maintenance orders would be made?

(ii) Difficulty of Supervision

Where performance of the defendant's obligation would require a complex series of acts or the maintenance of an ongoing relationship, the remedy of specific performance will ordinarily be refused. The reason usually given is that the court will not make an order which would require it to watch over and supervise performance.

Building and construction contracts typify the category of relationships to which Sharpe is here referring. The asserted difficulty of supervision is, however, belied by the ease with which the courts can surmount the supposed obstacle if sufficiently motivated to do so. In a series of nineteenth century cases railway companies which had obtained land on the faith of promises to build railroads were ordered to carry out the promised construction when they reneged on the deal. The courts were affronted by the notion of limiting to a monetary remedy plaintiffs who had on their part given full performance. A pertinent and striking American decision of more recent vintage is *City Stores Co. v. Ammerman*. The plaintiff owner of a department store in Washington DC contracted with the defendant developer of a suburban shopping centre for the "opportunity to accept a lease on terms at least equal to those offered to other major department stores in the center." When the defendant resiled in order to strike a more lucrative deal with Sears, specific performance was ordered on the ground (*inter alia*) that the contract represented for the plaintiff a unique opportunity for expansion into the suburbs of Washington. Even the absence of critical terms of the lease, such as design and construction details, to say nothing of the price of the building, did not deter the judge who, in Linzer's words deemphasized the enforcement problems, finding that rival department stores' leases provided such standards "as to make design and approval of plaintiff's store a fairly simple matter, if the parties deal with each other in good faith and expeditiously, as I shall hereafter order."

On occasion Anglo-Canadian courts, for their part, so far from throwing up their hands at the prospect of retaining oversight of long-term contractual relations, have of their own motion complemented specific enforcement by standards designed to protect the interests of the defendant. *Sky Petroleum Ltd. v. VIP Petroleum Ltd.* was such a case. A 10-year requirements contract was enforced against a gasoline supplier when market conditions in the aftermath of an Arab oil embargo dried up alternative sources of supply at any price. To guard against the risk of stockpiling by the plaintiff, however, Gould J capped the orders that the defendant was enjoined to meet each year, at the contract price, to the average annual volume of the plaintiff's orders prior to the disruption of the market.

Difficulty of supervision is, on any view, a phantom objection to specific relief. It is easily exaggerated, and when the occasion arises for ongoing monitoring of compliance a court appointed master can fulfil this function. In the normal course, however, the judicial role is not to act as a quality controller of the defendant's efforts at performance. Megarry V-C expressed this view of the matter in *Tito v. Waddell (No. 2)*, the monumental saga in which the displaced inhabitants of Ocean Island sought enforcement of the British Phosphate Commissioners' obligation to replant their atoll when mining operations were discontinued:

> [I]t was at one time said that an order for the specific performance of the contract would not be made if there would be difficulty in the court supervising its execution. ... *The real question is whether there is a sufficient definition to what has to be done in order to comply with the order of the court.* That definition may be provided by the contract itself, or it may be supplied by the terms of the order.

Or, it may be added, in light of *Royal Bank of Canada v. Propriétés Cité Concordia Ltée (No. 2)*, the court may be prepared to take a more robust view of the defendant's situation. At issue here was a clause in a long-term lease requiring the bank to keep its premises in the defendant's shopping centre open for business at times consistent with the tenant's normal practice in similar locations. In earlier proceedings, an injunction had been refused following the bank's announced intention to reduce the hours of operation of the branch in question from five full days a week to only a three-hour period on Thursday evenings. It was held to be beyond the Court's capability to supervise an order that, to be effective, would have to ensure that the normal range of banking services were offered by the necessary corps of qualified personnel: "*Le Tribunal n'entend pas ordonner de respecter partiellement l'obligation. Par exemple, ouvrir les portes et y placer un guardien de sécurité ne servirait rien.*" Two years later the bank notified its customers that the branch was to be closed altogether. This time, however, a mandatory injunction *was* granted and the decision was upheld by a unanimous Court of Appeal. The critical question was recognized as being not the feasibility of judicial supervision of the order but, as in Megarry V-C's reformulation, whether the bank had been left in doubt as to what was required in order to comply with it. Conceding that perhaps the injunction did not spell out with full particularity what the bank was being enjoined to do, Montgomery J concluded that the defendant could "live with" the order, given that "[t]he prestige of the Bank is such that I cannot believe that it would wish to keep open a branch at which it did not offer an acceptable level of banking services."

(c) Third Parties

If it is accepted that one of the primary purposes of the law of contracts is to protect the reasonable expectations of the parties engendered by reciprocally assumed binding obligations, it follows that third party interests in performance or non-performance must in general terms be seen as secondary to those of the contracting parties themselves. Broad community concerns are taken into account in the substantive law of contract formation through the concepts of illegality and public policy. While the method of enforcement of contractual obligations not falling outside these bounds may affect third party interests in a vital way, the selection of remedy for breach should not in principle be influenced decisively by those collateral interests when the latter run counter to those of the promisee—*a fortiori* if one accepts the argument advanced above attaching only limited relative weight to the counter-interest of the other contracting party. The one exception, conceded earlier, is the interest of a third party *bona fide* purchaser under a contract executed before he acquires knowledge that the property has already been contractually promised to an earlier buyer. As between the two innocent parties the law protects the interest of the third party by denying the original promisee specific relief and awarding only damages against the contract-breaker. An illustration of a third party interest not entitled to protection against the negative impact of specific enforcement at the instance of the promisee may be found in the context of professional sports. The standard player contract includes a term that while under contract with a particular club the player will not play for any other. If, say, a disgruntled George Bell, while under a long-term contract with the Blue Jays, were to sign to play for the Oakland A's, Toronto might well seek an injunction to prevent his doing so. Putting aside here the supposed obstacle that the two teams in question are not in competition for the same pool of fans, the case for restricting Toronto to the remedy of damages might in part be based on the argument that the granting of an injunction could well result in Bell sitting out the period remaining on his Blue Jay contract (for specific performance is clearly out of the question), thus depriving baseball lovers of the opportunity to enjoy his considerable talents. However well-grounded this fear, the potential negative third-party impact is of no weight as a countervail to the interest of his employer, because the public's "right" to see Bell play baseball is itself derived from Toronto's investment in his services. Had not the Blue Jays (or some other club) initially offered attractive enough terms to induce him to sign, his talents on the diamond would never have been given expression. Bell himself could not have been compelled to put them to use, and it would surely be strange if Toronto's investment were regarded as giving a third party a vested interest capable of fettering the club's ability to enforce the contract it had made. It is possible to argue, however, that as a matter of public policy it should not be open for an employer effectively to contract for a player's exclusive services. Here we encounter another concrete example of the need to address such issues directly, through the substantive law, rather than by manipulation of remedies. In the litigation in the fifties between Ted Dublinski and the Detroit Lions there was a difference of opinion in the Ontario courts as to whether the doctrine of restraint of trade was applicable to a covenant such as that in the Bell example, operative during the currency of an employment contract rather than for a period following its termination. That doctrine entails an evaluation of the reasonableness of a restraint from the standpoint of the public interest as well as that of the parties. A covenant that fails to meet the test is void. If the public's interest in being able to watch George Bell play baseball is thought to outweigh that of his employer in enforcing a bargain freely made, the means to that end should be a delineation of the ambit of permissible contract terms, and not the denial of the most effective form of relief for contractual breach.

The interests of third parties and promisees concerning enforcement of contractual obligations are not always in opposition however. When they are congruent, the thesis of this paper, that wherever practicable specific relief should be available to a promisor desiring it, has the serendipitous effect of vindicating the interests of both. Indeed, in one type of contract the more substantial interest is that of the third party, namely where it is the intended primary beneficiary of the promisee's performance. Protection of that interest, in the form of an annuity for the old coal merchant's widow, was one of the major reasons why specific relief was granted in *Beswick v. Beswick*. The result is laudable, but on the downside the House of Lords' exploitation of the effectiveness of the specific remedy served only to accentuate the need for substantive reform to put the interests of designated third party beneficiaries on a firmer footing. Widow Beswick was a party to the contract between her late husband and his nephew in all but name, yet was enabled to enforce the promise in her favour only because, fortuitously, she happened to be also the promisee's administratrix. Justice was done in the instant case, but the real mischief, the glaringly anachronistic rule of privity, was left uncorrected. Instances of contracts involving such a direct third party interest in performance are very much the exception. Yet a range of such interests, indirect but no less real, may be identified in many contractual settings. Thus, at one end of the scale the interest of a sub-purchaser, who is in contractual relationship to the promisee, corresponds closely to that of the promisee himself. More oblique, and in the nature of a group interest, is that of the customers of the branch that the Royal Bank was threatening to close in *Les Propriétés Cité Concordia*. The broadest, and most amorphous category of third party interest is that of the community. Thus Birmingham concludes his economic analysis of alternative remedial solutions to the problem posed by land restoration clauses, at issue in cases like *Groves* and *Peeveyhouse*, with the following pertinent observation:

> Community interests are not necessarily protected when individuals bargain for personal profit. In both cases under discussion, performance would probably have yielded a social return exceeding the benefit to the contracting parties: Statutes restricting strip mining operations or requiring restorative efforts following exploitation are evidence of public concern to prevent desecration of aesthetically attractive landscapes. A decree directing completion of the work, if obeyed, would increase community welfare when the sum of the resulting gains to the landowner and to individuals other than the contracting parties is greater than the expense of the required performance.

This point must not be pressed too far. To the extent that indirect third party interests are not afforded protection outside the realm of contract (as, for example, by legislation such as that alluded to by Birmingham, or in the law of nuisance), they can have no claim in their own right to be factored in as an influence on remedy selection for contractual breach. Those who would benefit by a free ride are not entitled to dictate the destination. If, however, they happen to desire to move in the same direction as the party (promisee) paying the fare—albeit for differing purposes—their potential serendipitous gain reinforces the case for ensuring that, where practicable, the promisor gets the promisee to the destination that the contracting parties have agreed upon.

6. Conclusion

In the taxonomy of Calibresi and Melemed contract rights in the Anglo-Canadian legal tradition are protected predominantly by a "liability" rather than a "property" rule. That is to say, outside a restricted range of cases there is no enforcement *in specie* of the promisor's obligations and hence, for the promisee, no meaningful entitlement to performance. For the most part, the latter's reasonable substantive expectation may be appropriated by the promisor at a judicial evaluation couched in the form of a compensatory damage award. The primacy of the money remedy, historically rooted in jurisdictional accommodation, is conventionally rationalized on the basis of the adequacy of the monetary substitute to cover the promisee's loss. This is buttressed by solicitude for the promisor's interest in not being coerced into performance and a curial preference for disengagement from soured contractual relationships. Signs of heightened judicial sensitivity to promisees' interest in performance *in specie* are too sporadic to provide the predictability needed for both contract planning and postbreach reaction. In any event, they represent merely conclusions in particular situations as the adequacy of damages, mounting no challenge to the premise that adequacy is objectively determinable.

If completeness of remedy is the goal, as it should be, its attainment so far as practicable requires deference to the promisee's evaluation of whether monetary compensation will suffice. In the vast majority of cases it doubtless will. Where a claim for specific relief is advanced, however, this in itself evidences either the existence of a non-economic interest in performance for which compensation cannot substitute, or an apprehension of under-recovery for economic losses through the operation of the limitative rules governing the awarding of damages. In such circumstances no question of mitigation can arise. Curtailment of promisee autonomy in the selection of specific relief is justifiable, barring highly exceptional circumstances, on only two grounds: (i) futility extrinsic to mere disinclination on the part of the promisor to comply with court-ordered performance. This may arise from legal or factual impossibility, or when the nature of the promisor's obligations is such that it would not be possible to determine whether (enforced) purported performance constituted breach; (ii) the promisee's election is *in substance* for a money payment in circumstances where this would constitute in whole or in part loss reasonably avoidable by the plaintiff without the sacrifice of any intangible benefit. Here mitigation ought to be the determinative concept. Conversely, when the promisor *fails* to elect specific relief while claiming compensable loss exceeding the tangible benefit that performance would yield, it is appropriate to offer the *promisor*, where practicable the option of acceding to an order of specific performance.

NOTES

1. For an influential argument in favour of expanding the use of specific performance, see Alan Schwartz, "The Case for Specific Performance" (1979), 89 *Yale LJ* 271. For an argument

against such an expansion, see Edward Yorio, "In Defense of Money Damages for Breach of Contract" (1982), 82 *Colum. L Rev.* 1366.

2. Much academic writing analyzes the respective merits of specific-performance and damages in economic terms. For a good introduction, see Lewis A. Kornhauser, "An Introduction to the Economic Analysis of Contract Remedies" (1986), 57 *University of Colorado Law Review* 683. For a thorough overview of the literature, see Paul G. Mahoney, "Contract Remedies: General," in Boudewijn Bouckaert and Gerrit De Geest, eds., *Encyclopedia of Law & Economics* (Cheltenham: Edward Elgar, 2000), no. 4600. See also Richard A. Posner, *Economic Analysis of Law*, 6th ed. (New York: Aspen, 2003), chapter 4; A.T. Kronman, "Specific Performance" (1978), 45 *University of Chicago Law Review* 351; J. Berryman, "Specific Performance, Uniqueness, and Investment Contracts: A Canadian Perspective" (1984), 48 *Conveyancing and Property Lawyer* 130; and S. Shavell, "Specific Performance Versus Damages for Breach of Contract: An Economic Analysis" (2006), 84 *Texas L Rev.* 831.

For more general reading, see Robert J. Sharpe, "Specific Relief for Breach of Contract," in Barry J. Reiter and John Swan, eds., *Studies in Contract Law* (Toronto: Butterworths, 1980), at 123; David Cohen, "The Relationship of Contractual Remedies to Political and Social Status: A Preliminary Inquiry" (1982), 32 *University of Toronto Law Review* 31; Donald Harris, Anthony Ogus, and Jennifer Phillips, "Contract Remedies and the Consumer Surplus" (1979), 95 *Law Q Rev.* 581; Ken Cooper-Stevenson, "Principles and Pragmatism in the Law of Remedies" and Grant Hammond, "Rethinking Remedies: The Changing Conception of the Relationship Between Legal and Equitable Remedies," both found in Jeffrey Berryman, ed., *Remedies: Issues and Perspectives*, above; and Benjamin Zarnett, "Specific Performance," [1995] *Law Society of Upper Canada Special Lectures* 193.

A comprehensive historical perspective is provided by Jeffrey Berryman in "The Specific Performance Damages Continuum: An Historical Perspective" (1985), 17 *Ottawa Law Review* 295.

The first few cases in the text are concerned largely with classes of contract where the courts have traditionally been reluctant to award specific performance but where recently there have been some signs of a change of attitude—*viz.*, contracts for the sale of goods and to do work. After considering the traditional law and the wisdom of the modern liberalization, we will then move to the apparent paradox that at the same time specific performance seems to be becoming less readily available for land contracts.

SALE OF GOODS AND SERVICES

General

Falcke v. Gray
(1859), 4 Drewry 651, 62 ER 250 (Ch.)

In this case the bill was filed for a specific performance of a contract entered into between the plaintiff Mr. Falcke and Mrs. Gray, one of the defendants, by which Mrs. Gray had agreed that, at the expiration of a six months' lease to the plaintiff of her furnished house, he should have the option of purchasing two china jars at the price of 40*l*.

In January 1859, the plaintiff, being desirous of finding a furnished house, applied to Mrs. Gray, who was willing to let hers, and on looking over it, he observed the two jars, the subject of the suit. He had for twenty-five years carried on the business of a dealer in curiosities, china, & c., and was eminent in his trade, and was well acquainted with the prices which articles of this kind would fetch.

Shortly afterwards he had an interview with Mrs. Gray at her house; and Mr. Brend, from the office of Boyle and Bryden, estate and house agents, who were Mrs. Gray's agents in the matter, attended to advise Mrs. Gray. A discussion arose as to the terms of letting, and ultimately a rent of seven guineas per week was agreed upon, with an option to the plaintiff that he should at the end of the term be at liberty to purchase certain articles of furniture at a valuation, to be inserted in the agreement, including the two china jars, which were valued at 40*l.*

With regard to the valuation of these jars at 40*l.*, it appeared from the evidence that Mr. Brend told Mrs. Gray that he did not know the value of the jars, but he should think they were worth 20*l.* a-piece; and the agreement was drawn up, putting the value of 40*l.* on the jars, and was signed by Mrs. Gray and the plaintiff.

On the 26th of January the plaintiff went to the house while his agent was taking the inventory, and then the jars had been removed; and on the same day Mrs. Gray came to Mr. Falcke's house, and informed him of the removal of the jars. During the interval between the 19th and the 26th of January Mrs. Gray, having begun to doubt whether the price placed on the jars was fair, was advised that it would be as well to take the opinion of Mr. Watson, also a dealer in curiosities; and, on the 26th, she accordingly went to Mr. Watson, and desired him to come in the evening to value the jars. This he did; and on seeing the jars he was so much struck with their beauty, & c., that he offered Mrs. Gray his cheque for 200*l.* for them at once. Mrs. Gray then asked Mr. Watson if he thought she would be doing anything wrong in so selling them, and he told her it was all right; and she then took his cheque and Mr. Watson took away the jars. Mr. Watson was made a defendant to the bill.

The plaintiff now insisted that he was entitled to a decree for specific performance against Mrs. Gray and to delivery of the jars as against Mr. Watson; and on that part of the case the question was whether the transaction was a *bona fide* one on the part of Watson, or whether he knew of the contract between Mrs. Gray and the plaintiff. The defendant insisted that it was a contract for chattels, and could not be enforced.

The evidence as to the actual value of the vases was conflicting, but putting it at the lowest it greatly exceeded 40*l.*

Mr. Baily and *Mr. Waller* for the plaintiff:

On the question of the jurisdiction of the Court to order delivery of a chattel, the rule to be drawn from all the authorities is this: if you show that the plaintiff cannot have adequate relief by damages the Court will order the chattel to be delivered up. [They cited on this point *Pusey v. Pusey* (referred to in White and Tudor's Leading Cases, at 529), and other cases there referred to, *Fells v. Read* (1796), 3 Ves. 70; 30 ER 899 (Ch.) and *Doloret v. Rothschild* (1824), 1 Sim. & Stu. 590; 57 ER 233 (Ch.).]

Then as to the mode in which the agreement was entered into. Mrs. Gray and Falcke were at arm's length; she thought fit to put her own value on the vases, and she must abide by her own agreement. …

Mr. Glasse and *Mr. Jones Bateman* for Mrs. Gray:

First. This is a hard bargain; the evidence shows that Mrs. Gray's agent was as ignorant of the value of objects of *vertu* as she was herself; she was not, therefore, in fact protected. It may be true that Mr. Falcke did not in terms prevent her from consulting any one else, but practically he did, for he would give her no time; he insisted on the bargain being struck at once or not at all. ...

Mr. Greene and *Mr. Speed* for Mr. Watson. ...

(The Vice-Chancellor intimated to *Mr. Baily* that he need only reply on the question whether the transaction was, having regard to the *res gesta*, such a fair transaction as this Court would assist.)

Mr. Bailey accordingly replied on that point.

(The Vice-Chancellor reserved his judgment, and on the 13th June delivered the following judgment:)

[SIR RICHARD KINDERSLEY VC] (after stating the facts above stated): ... The first ground of defence is, that this being a bill for the specific performance of a contract for the purchase of chattels, this Court will not interfere. But I am of opinion that the Court will not refuse to interfere simply because the contract relates to chattels, and that if there were no other objection, the contract in this case is such a contract as the Court would specifically perform.

What is the difference in the view of the Court between realty and personalty in respect to the question whether the Court will interfere or not? Upon what principle does the Court decree specific performance of any contract whatever? Lord Redesdale in *Harnett v. Yeilding* (1807), 2 Sch. & Lef. 549 (Ire. Ch.) says:

> Whether courts of equity in their determinations on this subject have always considered what was the original foundation for decrees of this nature I very much doubt. I believe that from something of habit, decrees of this kind have been carried to an extent which has tended to injustice. Unquestionably the original foundation of these decrees was simply this, that damages at law would not give the party the compensation to which he was entitled; that is, would not put him in a situation as beneficial to him as if the agreement were specifically performed.

So that the principle on which a court of equity proceeds is this. A court of law gives damages for the non-performance, but a court of equity says: "that is not sufficient—justice is not satisfied by that remedy"; and, therefore, a court of equity will decree specific performance, because a mere compensation in damages is not a sufficient remedy and satisfaction for the loss of the performance of the contract.

Now why should that principle apply less to chattels? If in a contract for chattels damages will be a sufficient compensation, the party is left to that remedy. Thus if a contract is for the purchase of a certain quantity of coals, stock, & c., this Court will not decree specific performance, because a person can go into the market and buy similar articles, and get damages for any difference in the price of the articles in a court of law. But if damages would not be a sufficient compensation, the principle, on which a court of equity decrees specific performance, is just as applicable to a contract for the sale and purchase of chattels, as to a contract for the sale and purchase of land.

In the present case the contract is for the purchase of articles of unusual beauty, rarity and distinction, so that damages would not be an adequate compensation for non-performance; and I am of opinion that a contract for articles of such a description is such a contract as this

Court will enforce; and, in the absence of all other objection, I should have no hesitation in decreeing specific performance.

The next ground of defence is, that the contract in the present case is a hard bargain between the plaintiff and Mrs. Gray; and it is insisted that the inadequacy in price is so great, that on that ground the Court will not decree specific performance. Now the price put on these jars was 40*l.*; what was their actual value? Certainly to talk of their value is to talk of something which is very artificial and fluctuating, depending upon the taste and caprice of the community. But still the jars derive their value from their beauty, distinction and rarity, and those qualities give them a selling value. They have a value in the market. According to the plaintiff's own statement their value would be 100*l.*, or if between persons not brokers 125*l.*; and it is the interest of the plaintiff to represent their value as low as possible. A better test of their value is what Mr. Watson has given for them; and I think I may assume that 200*l.* at least would be a fair price, though I cannot help thinking that their real value rather exceeded than fell short of that sum. But taking 200*l.* as the fair value, the price placed on the jars by Mr. Brend was only one-fifth of their selling value. That this was a hard bargain in the sense of its being for a very inadequate price there can be no doubt; and the defendant insists that, on this ground, the Court will not enforce specific performance.

On the other hand, the plaintiff insists that, although it is true that in hard bargains, using the terms in one sense, the Court will not decree specific performance, still that does not apply to cases of mere inadequacy of price; and this is the question I have now to consider.

The general rule with regard to hard bargains is, that the Court will not decree specific performance, because specific performance is in the discretion of the Court for the advancement of justice; such discretion, indeed, to be exercised, not according to caprice, but on strict principles of justice and equity. In the case of *White v. Damon* (1802), 7 Ves. 30 at p. 35; 32 ER 13 at p. 15 (Ch.), Lord Eldon says, "I agree with Lord Rosslyn that giving a specific performance is matter of discretion; but it is not an arbitrary capricious discretion. It must be regulated upon grounds that will make it judicial." The principle upon which the Court acts with respect to hard bargains appears to me to have been truly expressed by Lord Langdale in the case of *Wedgwood v. Adams* (1843), 6 Beav. 600; 49 ER 958 (Ch.); and the passage in which he enunciates the principle has been quoted with approbation by Lord Justice Turner in *Watson v. Marston* (1853), 4 De GM & G 230; 43 ER 495 (CA). Lord Langdale in *Wedgwood v. Adams* says, that the Court exercises its discretion and decrees specific performance, unless it would be highly unreasonable to do so; and that what is more or less unreasonable cannot well be defined—it must depend on the circumstances of each particular case.

As it is admitted by the plaintiff, that in cases of hard bargains generally the Court will not interfere, it is not necessary to go into any of the cases on the subject other than those which turn more or less on inadequacy of price. And here, I may observe, that in some cases the Court has refused specific performance on the ground of the hardness of the bargain, where there has been not the least impropriety of conduct on the part of the person seeking specific performance. In most of the cases there has been some other ingredient besides mere inadequacy of price; but I will refer to those in which I find the opinion of the Judges express on that particular point. …

The next case I shall mention is *Day v. Newman* (1788), 2 Cox. 77; 30 ER 36 (Ch.). In that case the Court refused to decree specific performance, but left the parties to their remedies at law on the ground of inadequacy in price. That case appears to me to be a distinct decision on the question.

White v. Damon was a case of a purchase at an auction; yet Lord Rosslyn, on the simple ground of inadequacy in price, refused specific performance. This case, therefore shows that inadequacy in price is a sufficient ground for refusing specific performance. Lord Eldon took a different view, but it was on the ground that the sale was by auction.

Now these two last-mentioned cases appear to me to be decisive on the point; and I am of opinion that in the present case I ought to refuse specific performance on the mere ground of inadequacy of price, even if there were none other.

But there is another circumstance in this case besides mere inadequacy. What was the nature of the transaction? It was not the case of a bargain between seller and buyer, the one trying to get the highest, and the other to give the lowest price. The intention of the parties was that a fair and reasonable price should be placed on the articles, and that the plaintiff should have the option of purchasing at such fair and reasonable price. Mrs. Gray, though she was told by Mr. Brend that he was not a judge of the value, thought that the 40*l.* mentioned by him was such a fair price as a competent person would place on the jars; and it was upon that footing that she made the agreement. She was not herself a competent judge, though she knew they were of considerable value. Mr. Falcke knew that she was contracting on that footing, and he knew that the price put upon the jars by Brend was not a fair price. (The Vice-Chancellor, after going through the plaintiff's evidence, from which it appeared that he (knowing that 40*l.* was greatly insufficient, it being only two-fifths of the value, as he said) allowed the contract to be signed on that footing, proceeded:) The question is, whether he can come to the Court to compel Mrs. Gray to sell the jars to him for 40*l.* I admit that this Court is not a court of honour, but it appears to me, that although Mr. Falcke has done nothing he was legally bound not to do, yet, consistently with the authorities and the justice of the case, I must refuse specific performance.

It has, however, been contended that Mrs. Gray, having sold the jars to the defendants the Watsons, should not have been made a defendant. But Mrs. Gray has placed herself in such a position that the suit could not go on without her being made a party. The bill, therefore, must be dismissed without costs as against her.

With regard to the defendants the Watsons, the question is, whether they had notice, when they purchased from Mrs. Gray, that she had entered into an agreement, by virtue of which she could not sell them to another person. Now I cannot help entertaining some suspicion that the Watsons knew something more than that a mere question had arisen as to value. But the *onus* of proving that they had notice lies on the plaintiff, and I think that, although there is some doubt on the evidence, notice to them has not been sufficiently proved. Under all the circumstances, I think the bill, as against the defendants the Watsons, must be dismissed with costs.

NOTES

1. In *Gleason v. Ship Dawn Light et al.* (1997), 130 FTR 284 aff'd. on this point (1998), 223 NR 155 (FCA), the Federal Court of Canada refused to grant specific performance in a case involving the sale of a ship on the grounds that the ship was not unique or irreplaceable and that damages would be an adequate remedy.

2. The uniqueness of the subject matter of a contract is a function not simply of the attributes of the subject matter, but also of the relevance of those attributes to the purchaser. The purchaser of a custom-painted electric guitar will not obtain specific enforcement of the contract because of its one-of-a-kind appearance if he purchased it for its sound quality. In *Wallace v. Allen*, 2009 ONCA 36, 93 OR (3d) 723 the appellant claimed specific performance of an agreement to sell a business. J.L. MacFarland JA wrote:

> The argument can be made that every business is unique. The appellant is an entrepreneur engaged in the acquisition of businesses. His own evidence discloses that he has experience in the sale and purchase of shares of companies. Indeed soon after the respondents refused to close the subject transaction, the appellant bought out a business partner's share in a marina business. While the company itself may be unique in what it does, the appellant's acquisition of the business was not—the appellant acquires businesses for a living. In my view, the trial judge did not err in rejecting the remedy of specific performance.

3. As well as the basic issue of when contracts for the sale of goods will be specifically enforced, *Falcke v. Gray* raises two other difficulties:

   a. the extent to which third party purchasers of property may be affected by a contract of sale such as this, and

   b. the question of whether inadequacy of consideration is itself ever a sufficient ground for refusing specific performance.

These questions will now be considered along with the relationship between the *Sale of Goods Act* and the law of replevin.

Third Parties

Suppose A undertakes to convey property to B, and then later conveys the property to C. B can join C as a defendant in an action for specific performance. Whether B will succeed against C will in general turn on whether C had knowledge of the promised conveyance to A. In *Canadian Long Island v. Irving Wire Products*, [1975] 2 SCR 715, at 737, Martland J adopted the following passage from *Fry on Specific Performance*, 6th ed.:

> If a stranger to the contract gets possession of the subject-matter of the contract with notice of it, he is or may be liable to be made a party to an action for specific performance of the contract upon the equitable grounds of his conscience being affected by the notice.

See also *McLeod v. Castlepoint Development Corp.* (1997), 31 OR (3d) 737 (CA); leave to appeal to the Supreme Court of Canada refused (1997), 34 OR (3d) xv; *Harris v. McNeely* (2000), 47 OR (3d) 161 (CA).

There is some dispute as to the nature of the interest created in the purchaser of personal as opposed to real property. Nevertheless, the law does seem clear that where the contract is capable of specific enforcement, the purchaser acquires an equitable interest as against subsequent transferees unless they are purchasers in good faith. See Andrew M. Tettenborn, "Covenants, Privity of Contract and the Purchaser of Personal Property" (1982), 41 *Cambridge Law Journal* 58; Nili Cohen Grabelsky, "Interference with Contractual Relations and Equitable

Doctrines" (1982), 45 *Modern Law Review* 241, at 243-47, discussing principally *Swiss Bank Corporation v. Lloyds Bank Ltd.*, [1982] AC 584 (CA and HL (Eng.)). Consider s. 39 of the *Conveyancing and Law of Property Act*, RSO 1990, c. C.34:

> It is not necessary, in order to maintain the defence of a purchase for value without notice, to prove payment of mortgage money or purchase money or any part thereof.

The Act applies to transfers by deed of any interest in any form of property in the province. See also *Sutherland Estate v. Dyer* (1991), 4 OR (3d) 168 (Gen. Div.).

In *Taylor v. Eisner* (1993), 105 Sask. R 283, the Saskatchewan Court of Appeal upheld the decision of Kyle J at trial ((1991), 92 Sask. R 39), who refused to order specific performance for the plaintiff purchaser of a herd of elk. While he found that the elk were rare, he concluded that they were not unique. Furthermore, the defendant seller had subsequently sold the herd to third parties who were *bona fide* purchasers without notice and to grant specific performance and direct the third parties to deliver up the animals, would constitute an undue hardship on the third parties. Leave to appeal to the Supreme Court of Canada refused (1997), 158 Sask. R 320.

Inadequacy of Consideration

As we will soon see, one of the maxims of equity is that "equity will not aid a volunteer." For specific performance to be available, therefore, some consideration must be present, even with respect to a deed under seal. Must the consideration be adequate? Does the court in its equitable jurisdiction have authority to consider the equivalence of the considerations exchanged? To what extent does *Falcke* support the view that inadequacy of consideration is itself a sufficient ground for refusing specific performance?

Section 38 of the Ontario *Conveyancing and Law of Property Act*, RSO 1990, c. C.34 provides:

> No purchase made in good faith and without fraud or any reversionary interest in property shall be opened or set aside on the ground of undervalue.

In *Webb v. Dipenta*, [1925] SCR 565, at 574, Rinfret J wrote:

> Any hardship on the defendant which might flow from the specific performance of such an agreement would be merely a consequence of the fact that his speculation proved unfortunate for him. ... [T]he mere inadequacy of the consideration, unaccompanied by any element of fraud or misrepresentation, would hardly afford him a good defence.

See also *Portal Forest Industries Ltd. v. Saunders* (1978), 5 RPR 133, at 145 (BCSC) and *O'Neil v. Arnew* (1976), 16 OR (2d) 549 (HC). Note, however, *Baxter v. Rollo* (or *Bradford*) (1913), 18 BCR 369 (SC and CA) where it is suggested that "if the disparity in price is so great as to shock the conscience and constitute in itself a badge of fraud" (at 370), relief will be denied. In *Baxter*, the court's conscience was not, however, shocked sufficiently by the sale of land worth $6,000 for $180.

However, in *Black v. Wilcox* (1976), 12 OR (2d) 759 (CA), the court set aside an agreement whereby land worth possibly as much as $30,000 was sold for $5,200 and a lifetime right for the vendor and his wife to continue to occupy a house on the farm valued at $250. There the court held that the combination of an improvident bargain plus the overreaching by the defendant should lead to the contract being set aside. This case is fairly typical of a number of decisions where the courts, using the term "unconscionability," have set aside or refused enforcement of improvident bargains where factors such as great age, lack of education, or lack of business acumen have also been present and preyed upon by the other party.

As well as the possibilities raised by unconscionability and extremely gross disparities in the considerations exchanged, there also exist other devices whereby equity has tempered the harshness of bargains. Thus, in *Tamplin v. James* (1880), 15 Ch. D 215 (CA), it was held that situations exist where specific performance will be denied on the grounds of the defendant's mistake albeit that the mistake is not serious enough to justify rescission—that is, the plaintiff would still be left with a common law damages claim. Similarly, the Canadian courts have allowed for hardship existing at the time of entry into the contract as a basis for denying specific performance: for a general discussion and examples, see Norman M. Fera, "Hardship in the Granting of Specific Performance" (1978), 26 *Chitty's Law Journal* 115.

The Sale of Goods Act

Sale of Goods Act
RSO 1990, c. S.1

> 50. In an action for breach of contract to deliver specific or ascertained goods, the court may, if it thinks fit, direct that the contract be performed specifically, without giving the defendant the option of retaining the goods on payment of damages, and may impose such terms and conditions as to damages, payment of the price, and otherwise, as to the court seems just.

See also *Sale of Goods Act*, RSA 2000, c. S-2, s. 51; RSBC, 1996, c. 410, s. 55; RSM 1987, c. S10, s. 53; RSNL 1990, c. S-6, s. 53; RSNB 1973, c. S-1, s. 49; RSNS 1990, c. 408, s. 53; RSPEI 1988, c. S-1, s. 52; and RSS 1978, c. S-1, s. 51; RSY 2002, c. 198, s. 49.

"Specific goods" are defined in the *Sale of Goods Act*, RSO 1990, c. S.1, s.1 as the "goods identified and agreed upon at the time the contract of sale is made." (Equivalent definitions apply in all jurisdictions with a *Sale of Goods Act*.)

There is no statutory definition of "ascertained goods," but it probably refers to goods that have been identified or earmarked by the seller, after the making of the contract, as those he or she intends to supply to the buyer in fulfillment of the contract. See *In re Wait*, [1927] 1 Ch. 606 (CA). How specific this identification must be is not, however, settled. Nor is it settled whether s. 50 comprises a complete code of equitable remedies in relation to sales of goods, or whether a buyer can obtain specific performance outside the circumstances contemplated by that provision. For discussion, see G.H. Treitel, "Specific Performance in the Sale of Goods" (1966), *Journal of Business Law* 211 and *The Law of Contract*, 11th ed. (London: Sweet & Maxwell, 2003), at 1022-26. Cases to note in this area are *Behnke v. Bede Shipping Co.*, [1927] 1 KB 649; *Cohen v. Roche*, [1927] 1 KB 169; *Fraser v. Sam Kee* (1916), 9 WWR 1281 (BC Co. Ct.); *George Eddy Co. v. Noble Corey & Son* (1951), 28 MPR 140 (NBCA); *Cigic v. Mardoon Fabricating Ltd.*, [1969] BCJ no. 92 (BCSC); *In re Wait*, [1927] 1 Ch. 606 (CA); and *Sky Petroleum v. VIP Petroleum Ltd.*, which is extracted below.

The wording of the *Sale of Goods Act*, s. 50 dates from a 19th-century English statute designed in part to expand the availability of specific performance so as to bring English and Scottish law further in line. It has not had that effect. The enactment of this section did not lead to a greater willingness on the part of the courts to award specific performance in sale of goods contracts. Rather, the courts continued to apply the same principles that had evolved at common law prior to the Act enactment of the provision. The discretionary words of the section provided the basis for such an approach—"the court may, if it thinks fit."

The Ontario Law Reform Commission has reported on some of the problems of s. 50 (see the 1979 *Report on Sale of Goods* (Toronto: Queen's Printer, 1979), vol. II, at 436-40).

Professor Grant Hammond, whose writing is referred to above, had an opportunity to deal with the New Zealand counterpart to s. 50 of the Ontario *Sale of Goods Act* following his appointment to the High Court of New Zealand. In the following case, he dealt with the many issues that arise when considering the appropriate remedies that should be available in sale of goods cases and he considered the broad questions of remedial choice that have already been referred to in the articles that introduced this chapter.

Butler v. Countrywide Finance Ltd.
[1993] 3 NZLR 623 (HC)

[As part of an overall agreement to settle a number of outstanding claims, the defendant agreed to sell to the plaintiff certain chattels that were associated with the operation of a motel business. The chattels were not particularly "unique" and could be replaced. A dispute arose between the parties as to what chattels were covered by the agreement and the plaintiff brought an action for specific performance or damages in the alternative.]

HAMMOND J ...

Specific Performance for the Sale of Goods

The general issue of whether, and to what extent a plaintiff should be able to obtain (almost as of right) specific performance in a sale of goods case is a classic problem in commercial law. Counsel for D made no suggestion that the *Sale of Goods Act 1908* does not apply to this case. Section[s] ... 53 of the *Sale of Goods Act 1908* provide[s]:

> 53. Specific Performance—(1) In an action for breach of contract to deliver specific or ascertained goods the Court may, if it thinks fit, on the application of the plaintiff, by its judgment direct that the contract shall be performed specifically, without giving the defendant the option of retaining the goods on payment of damages. ...

Section 53 has its progenitor in s. 52 of the English *Sale of Goods Act 1893*. The section also has counterparts elsewhere in the British Commonwealth.

Some history is necessary. Specific performance is a discretionary, equitable, remedy of considerable antiquity. In some legal systems specific performance is considered the primary remedy, because it enforces the very thing the plaintiff contracted for (performance). In the common law tradition, specific performance has, at least until recently, been regarded as an exceptional remedy. In particular, the availability of specific performance has been conditioned on damages being inadequate.

This traditional approach has, in the last decade or so, come in for increasing criticism. Prior to my appointment to this Bench, I was one of those academics who have been critical of the traditional hierarchy of remedies; see Hammond "The Place of Damages in the Scheme of Remedies" in Finn, *Essays on Damages* (1992) p. 192 *et seq.* The notion that common law remedies have primacy over equitable remedies has been steadily eroded by the New Zealand Court of Appeal; see, in particular *Van Camp Chocolates Ltd. v. Aulsebrooks Ltd.*, [1998] 1 NZLR 354 and *Day v. Mead*, [1987] 2 NZLR 443; and Fisher J in *Newmans Tours Ltd. v. Ranier Investments Ltd.*, [1992] 2 NZLR 68, particularly at p. 96. I have recently also criticised the failure of Courts to liberalise declaratory judgments, as a private law remedy; see *Countrywide Finance Ltd. v. State Insurance Ltd.* (Auckland, CP 792/91, 6 April 1993, Hammond J).

In my view, the law of civil remedies in this country is, as it should be, steadily evolving into a regime in which what is required of a Court is a context specific evaluation of which remedy is most appropriate in the circumstances of a given case, rather than a priori solutions. The problem then becomes one of informed remedial choice.

The factors which, in general, enter into remedial selection are, I suggest, these. It will be recalled that the starting point of any remedial inquiry is the principle of compensation. The principal object of the law of civil remedies is to put the person whose rights have been found to have been violated in the same position—so far as can be done—as if those rights had been observed. This rule finds expression in tort in the proposition that we endeavour to put the plaintiff in the position that person would have been in had the tort not been committed; in contract, the object is to put the plaintiff in the position that person would have been in had the contract been performed according to its terms.

Those general objectives can be achieved in various ways, the most obvious being a choice between some kind of performance-based remedy (for instance, specific performance, or a mandatory injunction); or, by compensatory damages. But, in the most general way, if the adequacy of damages is no longer the watershed (which it has been, based on hopelessly outdated jurisdictional concerns), on what basis are informed judicial choices to be made? The sort of factors I have in mind are these:

1. Plaintiff Autonomy

Generally speaking, assuming a breach of some obligation recognised by the law, a plaintiff should have the "first choice" of remedy. The plaintiff, after all, has been found to have been injured, and where several avenues may redress that injury the plaintiff should, in a very general way, be able to elect her remedy. That, however, must always be subject to the ultimate control of the Court. There may be factors which would make the remedy sought by the plaintiff inappropriate. The simplest example would be over-compensation of a plaintiff by a performance-based remedy.

2. Economic Efficiency

There has been a prolonged and rigorous debate over the last decade as to the relevant efficiency—in economic terms—of common law damages versus equity-based performance remedies ... .

My own view is that that debate is far from conclusive. But what is clear, on any view of the matter, is that the relative efficiencies of possible remedies in a given case is (properly) a relevant factor.

3. *The Relative Severity of the Remedy on the Parties*

A long-standing principle of both moral and legal force is that of proportionality. Possibly the best known example of this in the area of civil remedies is *Boomer v. Atlantic Cement Company Inc.*, 257 NE 2d 870 (1970). In that case a New York Court refused to close down (by injunction) an enterprise worth millions of dollars because of found, but limited, damage to the plaintiffs.

4. *The Nature of the Right Being Supported by the Remedy*

In part, the function of the law of civil remedies is that it should be rights enhancing or rights maximising. To put it another way, remedies realise rights. But, of course, not every "right" has the same strength. Free speech, for instance, is generally heralded in common law jurisdiction as being a nearly absolute right. The stronger the Court's perception of the relevant right, the stronger the remedy which may be required. This is, of course, particularly true of constitutional litigation, but it is also true of private law litigation.

5. *The Moral View To Be Attached to the Interests at Stake*

This is an overtly value-laden question. But the argument for candour on the part of the Court in relation to such questions is overwhelming in the late 20th century. Free speech is again a very good example; routinely such cases involve a higher value, which overrides the plaintiff's particular interest in prior restraint.

6. *The Effect of a Given Remedy on a Third Party (or the Public)*

The older notion that a (private) lawsuit is entirely one between a plaintiff and a defendant is increasingly becoming outmoded. In several areas the older decisions are breaking down. For instance, the classical rule that an injunction will not run in aid of the criminal law is being reassessed.

7. *Difficulties of Calculation*

As I will note hereafter, the general rule is that difficulty of calculation *per se* is no bar to compensatory relief. A Court has to do the best it can, and sometimes what it has to do will be little more than an estimate, though based on articulated grounds. But Courts have increasingly seen difficulties of damages calculations as relevant to the fashioning of remedial relief. Performance remedies may avoid intractable damages problems. A recent example of this is the decision of the Supreme Court of Canada in *LAC Minerals Ltd. v. International Corona Resources Ltd.* (1989), 61 DLR (4th) 14.

8. *The Practicability of Enforcement*

For the sake of the parties concerned, who after all have to live with a performance-type decree; and because no Court should be brought into disrepute by having to attempt to enforce the impossible, and perhaps even the very difficult, this fact is always relevant. But it is not, and should not be, an automatic bar to performance-based relief.

9. *The Conduct of the Parties*

This has, of course, always been one of the great cornerstones of equitable relief. In a system in which common law and equity remedies now inform each other, it is surely also now relevant to a wide range of causes of action.

All of this leads to a conclusion that what is involved in the allocation of the "appropriate" remedy in a given case is a matter of informed choice, bearing in mind the general compensation principle and the factors I have estimated above. These considerations do not lead to a wholesale abandonment of much of the traditional learning. They simply point to a more open remedial system; and a requirement for articulation and candour as to why the relevant choices are being made, rather than the formalistic application of (in many cases) somewhat arid doctrinal rules drawn from some far distant time.

The considerations I have just outlined apply to the general law of civil remedies. It is then necessary to ask, how far, if at all, do those considerations apply to the specialised arena of a sale of goods?

Our s. 52, [*sic*] and its overseas counterparts, goes back (at least) as far as s. 2 of the *Mercantile Law Amendment Act 1856* (UK), which in turn was inspired by a report of the Mercantile Law Commissioners. The commissioners in fact favoured aligning English law with the rather more liberal attitude of Scottish law towards specific performance. It is not at all clear to me that s. 2 as drafted in England fully reflected the commissioners' recommendation. But whether that be so or not, *Re Wait*, [1927] 1 Ch 606, which carried the formidable authority of Atkin LJ within it, held that the section is now the *sole* source of the buyer's right to an order for specific performance. That, in turn, threw up further problems: the meaning of "specific and ascertained goods"; the relationship between rights under that section and a buyer's rights to replevin; and (if one thought this point still to be good law) the lack of mutuality of the remedy of specific performance as between the buyer and seller.

There has been much argument as to whether *Re Wait* was rightly decided.

Atkin LJ suggested that Courts of equity could grant specific performance for the "sale of commodities" in (1) exceptional cases; (2) where the goods could not ordinarily be obtained in the market; and (3) damages were not an adequate remedy. I have already suggested that criterion (3) has much less force today.

His Lordship's view at pp. 635-636 that (whatever the intention may have been) a *narrowing* effect on the remedy was occasioned by the section seems to turn on these considerations:

> It would have been futile in a code intended for commercial men to have created an elaborate structure of rules dealing with rights at law, if at the same time it was intended to leave, subsisting with the legal rights, equitable rights inconsistent with, more extensive, and coming into existence earlier than the rights so carefully set out in the various sections of the Code.

Lord Atkin's decision has been criticised on a number of occasions by thoughtful and careful scholars; see, in particular, Treitel, "Specific Performance in the Sale of Goods," [1966] JBL 211.

In any event the enactment of the section did not, for many years lead to a greater willingness on the part of Courts to award specific performance in sale of goods contracts. As I read them, Courts continued to apply the same sort of principles as had applied prior to the enactment of the section. The section had added the discretionary words "the Court may, if it thinks fit ...," but the invitation seems not to have been taken up; see *Behnke v. Bede Shipping Co.*, [1927] 1 KB 649; *Cohen v. Roche*, [1927] 1 KB 169; and *Sky Petroleum Ltd. v. VIP Petroleum Ltd.*, [1974] 1 WLR 576. ...

The position in the United States is instructive. There the attitude that contracts for the sale of goods are at the opposite end of the spectrum from sales of land was also (quite quickly) remarked. As I have noted, the supposition of the traditional goods rule is that—in a market economy—with rare exceptions (such as heirlooms and objects of art), substantially similar goods are or will be available elsewhere. Even in unusual situations—such as shortages of certain models of cars occasioned by World War II—United States Courts remained as unsympathetic to plaintiffs as their British counterparts. Hence cases such as *Fortner v. Wilson*, 216 P2d 299 (1950), in which it was held that cars "*could* be obtained, by paying an additional amount of money [even] in ... a grey market" (emphasis added).

This harsh attitude influenced the drafters of the *Uniform Commercial Code*. The commentary to that code—drafted by the leading commercial lawyers in the United States at that time—indicated that the code "seeks to further a more liberal attitude than some courts have shown in connection with the specific performance of contracts of sale" and that it introduces "a new concept of what are 'unique' goods." The code provided that the buyer's inability to cover is strong evidence of "the propriety of granting specific performance," and that, "where the unavailability of a market price is caused by a scarcity of goods of the type involved, a good case is normally made for specific performance under this Article"; see UCC 2-716, comments 1, 2 and 3. However, the text of the code, as actually approved by the commissioners, was more circumspect. It provided "specific performance may be decreed where the goods are unique, *or in other proper circumstances*" (emphasis added). The result has been that, in the paradigmatic case, where the seller fails to deliver the goods, the typical buyer must still content himself with money as a substitute, even in the United States. Hence one finds cases such as *Duval & Company v. Malcolm*, 214 SE 2d 356 (1975) where "the mere fact that cotton prices soared after this alleged contract is not in itself adequate to show buyer entitled to specific performance"; see generally Schmitt and Pasterczyk, "Specific Performance under the *Uniform Commercial Code*—Will Liberalism Prevail?" (1976), 26 De Paul L Rev. 54.

On the other hand, United States Courts have shown considerable liberality in granting specific performance of long-term supply contracts. Perhaps the two best known cases are *Kaiser Trading Company v. Associated Metals & Minerals Corporation*, 321 F Supp. 923 (1970) (long-term contract for arjolite, used in aluminium production; world supply limited); and *Eastern Air Lines Inc. v. Gulf Oil Corporation*, 415 F Supp. 429 (1975) (Arab oil embargo; "[breach would cause] chaos and irreparable damage ... . In the circumstances, a decree of specific performance becomes the ordinary and natural relief rather than the extraordinary one," (pp. 442-443).

The most often discussed case in the United States however is *Campbell Soup Co. v. Wentz*, 172 F2d 80 (1948), where an appellate Court found that it would have granted specific performance for the sale of carrots, but declined to do so because the bargain itself was too harsh and oppressive.

Campbell, in my view, demonstrates that (at least in a time of shortage) a plaintiff can properly be awarded specific performance of a contract to sell personal property that would not otherwise be unique.

Contemporary law and economics scholars frequently use *Campbell* as a vehicle for raising an argument that specific performance decrees prevent efficient breaches of contract. But, so far, the law squarely rejects the economic view; in economic terms it is only when goods are unique or in short supply that breach can be efficient, but those are *precisely* the cases in which the Courts *will* grant specific performance.

The questions raised by the issue of specific performance versus damages are in fact central to our jurisprudence, and particularly our contract and commercial law jurisprudence. That is precisely why they are so sharply debated.

These questions are (with respect) routinely asked the wrong way. The first fundamental question is whether we should attribute *any* moral force at all to contract law. If so, we may want the plaintiff to have a right to enforce promises, even if it is inefficient. Alternatively, we may want a plaintiff to have a right to enforce promises *unless* this is clearly and hopelessly inefficient.

The second question is the reverse of the first; why should we *not* attribute moral force to promise? The most extreme answer ever offered on this is Posner's; "the *only* moral value is wealth maximisation" (Posner, "Utilitarianism, Economics, and Legal Theory" (1979), J Legal Stud. 103). A less extreme view—(which I favour) is that, often times, contract breakers are not bad women. Quite often, there is a breakdown of relations with mutual fault and a technical breach on one side; or an inability to perform without hardship; or an inability to perform without the loss of some more valuable opportunity. The conclusions I draw from all of this are these:

1. *Promises* still (thankfully) hold a central position both in the law of contract and sales law (as a specialised branch of contract). The economic viewpoint, which would severely restrict specific performance as a remedy, does not represent the present law anywhere; nor should it.

2. At one time, the specific law relating to sales was more progressive than the general law of civil remedies. Now, sales law remedies, as traditionally conceived, have been overtaken by the general development of remedies law in New Zealand, which has seen a crumbling of the sharp division between law and equity. The traditional sales law thinking on remedies accordingly requires revision. Generally commercial law should be in the van, not the rearguard of legal development, and sales law has some catching up to do in relation to remedies.

3. In that respect, the availability of specific performance around the common law world appears to have been liberalised only slowly in sales law, the most notable extension having been to extend the remedy to long-term supply contracts.

4. What, with respect, needs to be developed further is the notion of commercial uniqueness. By that is meant goods which are, in some sense, essential to the plaintiff's business and for which the procurement of substitutes would cause disruption to that business for some reason or other. Severe delay would be one such reason; lack of expertise would be another; or high transaction costs (to a successful plaintiff) still another. This at least may be a concept which is capable of carrying the law forward, and it has some affinities with the developed North American concept of an "inability to cover." The traditional law has an aesthetic quality (which is appropriate in very particular, but quite rare, cases); commercial uniqueness is a broader concept, and capable of reaching a much wider range of cases.

[After applying the above principles, Hammond J determined that specific performance should not be granted in this case because the description of the chattels in question was too vague. Had this not been the case, he made it clear that if the chattels had been new or in a warehouse, or if they were far fewer and more easily identified, he would not have hesitated to grant the specific relief sought by the plaintiff.]

Replevin

Another possible way to obtain goods that have been sold but not delivered is for the buyer to bring an action for replevin of the goods (considered earlier in chapter 4, "Damages for Invasion of Property Interests").

At common law, an action for replevin was only available when the plaintiff alleged a *wrongful seizure* of goods and did not apply when a seller refused to deliver goods under an agreement of purchase and sale when the goods were lawfully in the seller's possession at the relevant time. By statute in Ontario prior to January 1, 1985 (*Replevin Act*), an action could be taken for the recovery of possession of property when it was alleged that the property had been unlawfully taken from the plaintiff's possession *or* when it was simply alleged that the property was being unlawfully detained by the defendant (including a defendant seller of goods). The *Replevin Act* was repealed and replaced by the *Courts of Justice Act*, SO 1984, c. 11, s. 118 (now RSO 1990, c. C.43, s. 104) and r. 44 of the Ontario Rules of Civil Procedure, reg. 560/84, as amended.

Courts of Justice Act
RSO 1990, c. C.43

104(1) In an action in which the recovery of possession of personal property is claimed and it is alleged that the property,

(a) was unlawfully taken from the possession of the plaintiff; or

(b) is unlawfully detained by the defendant,

the court, on motion, may make an interim order for recovery of possession of the property.

(2) A person who obtains possession of personal property by obtaining or setting aside an interim order under subsection (1) is liable for any loss suffered by the person ultimately found to be entitled to possession of the property.

Rules of Civil Procedure
RRO 1990, reg. 194

Motion for Interim Order

44.01(1) An interim order under section 104 of the *Courts of Justice Act* [1990, RSO 1990, c. C.43] for recovery of possession of personal property may be obtained on motion by the plaintiff, supported by an affidavit setting out,

(a) a description of the property sufficient to make it readily identifiable;

(b) the value of the property;

(c) that the plaintiff is the owner or lawfully entitled to possession of the property;

(d) that the property was unlawfully taken from the possession of the plaintiff or is unlawfully detained by the defendant; and

(e) the facts and circumstances giving rise to the unlawful taking or detention.

(2) The notice of motion shall be served on the defendant unless the court is satisfied that there is reason to believe that the defendant may improperly attempt to prevent recovery of possession of the property or that, for any other sufficient reason, the order should be made without notice.

Order to Contain Description and Value of Property

44.02 An interim order for recovery of possession of personal property shall contain a description of the property sufficient to make it readily identifiable and shall state the value of the property.

Disposition of Motion

Where Made on Notice

44.03(1) On a motion for an interim order for recovery of possession of personal property made on notice to the defendant, the court may,

(a) order the plaintiff to pay into the court as security twice the value of the property as stated in the order, or such other amount as the court directs, or to give the appropriate sheriff security in such form and amount as the court approves, and direct the sheriff to take the property from the defendant and give it to the plaintiff;

(b) order the defendant to pay into court as security twice the value of the property as stated in the order, or such other amount as the court directs, or to give the plaintiff security in such form and amount as the court approves, and direct that the property remain in the possession of the defendant; or

(c) make such other order as is just.

Where Made Without Notice

(2) On a motion for an interim order for the recovery of possession of personal property made without notice to the defendant, the court may,

(a) order the plaintiff to pay into court as security twice the value of the property as stated in the order, or such other amount as the court directs, or to give the appropriate sheriff security in such form and amount as the court approves, and direct the sheriff to take and detain the property for a period of ten days after service of the interim order on the defendant before giving it to the plaintiff; or

(b) make such other order as is just.

Condition and Form of Security

44.04(1) Where an interim order for the recovery of possession of personal property requires either party to give security, the condition of the security shall be that the party providing the security will return the property to the opposite party without delay when ordered to do so, and pay any damages and costs the opposite party has sustained by reason of the interim order.

(2) Where the security is by bond, the bond shall be in Form 44A and shall remain in force until the security is released under rule 44.06.

(3) Where the bond is to be given by a person other than an insurer licensed under the *Insurance Act* to write surety and fidelity insurance, the person giving the bond shall first be approved by the court.

Setting Aside Order

44.05 The court on motion may set aside or vary an interim order for the recovery of possession of personal property or stay enforcement of the order.

Release of Security

44.06 Any security furnished pursuant to an order made under rule 44.03 may be released on the filing of the written consent of the parties or by order of the court.

Duty of Sheriff

44.07(1) Before proceeding to enforce an interim order for the recovery of possession of personal property, the sheriff shall ascertain that any security required by the order has been given.

(2) The sheriff shall serve the order on the defendant when the property or any part of it is recovered or as soon thereafter as is possible.

(3) Where the sheriff is unable to comply with the order, or it is dangerous to do so, the sheriff may move for directions from the court.

(4) The sheriff shall, without delay after attempting to enforce the order and in any event within ten days after service of the order, report to the plaintiff on what property has been recovered and, where the sheriff has failed to recover possession of all or part of the property, on what property has not been recovered and the reason for his or her failure to recover it.

Where Defendant Prevents Recovery

44.08 Where the sheriff reports that the defendant has prevented the recovery of all or part of the property, the court may make an order,

(a) directing the sheriff to take any other personal property of the defendant, to the value of the property that the sheriff was prevented from recovering, and give it to the plaintiff; and

(b) directing the plaintiff to hold the substituted property until the defendant surrenders to the plaintiff the property that the sheriff was prevented from recovering.

See also Alta. Rules of Court, rr. 427-36; BC Rules of Court, r. 46; Man. Queen's Bench Rules, r. 44; Nfld. Rules of the Supreme Court, r. 27; NB Rules of Court, r. 44; NS Civil Procedure Rules, r. 48; PEI Rules of the Supreme Court, r. 44; and Sask. Queen's Bench Rules, rr. 406-10.

NOTES

1. Arguably, the new language contained in s. 104(1)(b) of the *Courts of Justice Act* is narrower than the language that was used in the *Replevin Act* insofar as it might apply to a disappointed buyer of goods. The new language speaks of "recovery of possession." Does this mean that the section is only available if the plaintiff once had but no longer has possession? If so, this provision would not apply to the many cases where a buyer of goods never had possession. On the other hand, the word "recovery" might be given a less technical meaning and refer simply to the obtaining of a thing by an action brought for that purpose.

Following a line of old English cases, the Manitoba Court of Appeal in *Manitoba Agricultural Credit Corp. v. Heaman* (1990), 65 Man. R (2d) 219 (CA), decided that replevin is unavailable if the applicant never had possession. The case, however, did not deal with a sale of goods situation but rather an attempt by a chattel mortgagee to obtain possession of cows from a mortgagor. See also *Sweetripe Drinks Ltd. v. Durabelle Distributors Ltd.* (1996), 112 Man. R (2d) 150 (QB). However, in *Vigro Seed & Supply Ltd. v. Agricultural Development Corp. of Saskatchewan*, [1990] 3 WWR 140 (Sask. CA) the court wrote in *obiter* that in "the case of an unlawful detention (as opposed to unlawful taking) there is not the slightest suggestion in a plain reading of [Saskatchewan Queen's Bench Rules] 406 and 407 that original possession in the claimant is a necessary prerequisite" to a writ of replevin.

In *Karaim (Ed) Trucking Ltd. v. Ducharme* (1996), 111 Man. R (2d) 175 (Master), the plaintiff sold and delivered a trailer to the defendant which was secured by a chattel mortgage. The plaintiff alleged that the defendant had made no payments and did not respond to demands to pay. The plaintiff sought interim recovery of the trailer under Manitoba Queen's Bench Rule 44. The plaintiff sought to distinguish the *Heaman* case on the basis that in this case, the plaintiff did have previous possession of the trailer. The master dismissed the plaintiff's motion on the ground that there was no evidence of an "unlawful detention" by the defendant as the plaintiff had made no demands on the defendant for the return of the trailer.

If the term "recovery" was given a broader meaning, then a disappointed buyer of goods has a choice of remedy against a seller who wrongfully refuses to deliver up possession. If the plaintiff proceeds under s. 50 of the *Sale of Goods Act*, it seems well settled that an order for specific performance of the contract relating to specific or ascertained goods will not be granted if damages are an adequate remedy. This is so notwithstanding that title to the goods may have passed to the plaintiff–buyer.

If the disappointed buyer sues in replevin and it is alleged that the defendant seller of goods refuses to deliver them up and unlawfully detains them, the plaintiff may recover if title has passed (*O'Rourke v. Lee* (1859), 18 UCQB 609).

Accordingly, it seems that an action in replevin is more likely to produce results for the plaintiff than an action under the *Sale of Goods Act*. This is especially so if the plaintiff seeks and obtains an interim order for recovery of possession of the chattels pending the final disposition of the action.

Why is it then that despite the opportunities that replevin appears to provide, it is difficult to find many examples of where it is used? One factor that might dissuade buyers is that if the plaintiff fails to establish his or her right at trial, the defendant is entitled to bring an action against the plaintiff upon the bond and to recover damages—for example, *Van Hull v. Mancer* (1943), 51 Man. R 255 (CA), where the court held that property in goods had not passed from the vendor to the purchaser and the latter had no right to issue a writ of replevin against the former. However, in *Attorney-General of Canada v. Hoverlift Systems Ltd.* (1981), 36 AR 331, Egbert J ordered replevin of goods manufactured under contract for the federal Department of Supply and Services. The contract specifically provided for delivery to the Crown of any partially completed machinery should the Crown exercise its rights to terminate the contract for breach. This had happened here. Without such remedy stipulation, would the result have been the same?

The failure to seek replevin more often may simply result from an unawareness on the part of the bar of its advantages and some shyness because of its procedural detail. In a number of cases, the application was dismissed because the plaintiff had failed to comply with the procedure set out in rules of practice (*Callwood Eng. Co. v. Niagara Finest Poultry Ltd.*, [1963] 2 OR 188 and *Pro-M Inc. v. NR Canada Ltd.* (1978), 20 OR (2d) 168 (Co. Ct.)). For a discussion of the procedural aspects of replevin, see B. Morris, "Replevin" (1980), 2 *Advocates' Q* 188.

However, the remedy remains alive: see *Dresser Industries Inc. v. Vos* (1985), 60 AR 226 (QB, Master) and *Reisner v. World Link Transportation Ltd.*, [2010] AJ no. 1171, in both of which the plaintiffs were successful in seeking return of automobiles in replevin.

2. See L.D. Roebuck, "Where Did Replevin Go? Recovering Possession," Canadian Bar Association—Ontario 1985, Annual Institute on Continuing Legal Education, February 1985 and George R. Stewart, "Enforced Performance of Contracts of Sale on Goods—Towards Greater Flexibility and Usefulness" (1981), 3 *Advocates' Q* 68.

3. Compare art. 2-716 of the *Uniform Commercial Code* with the basic Ontario provision:

> 3. The buyer has a right of replevin for goods identified to the contract if after reasonable effort he is unable to effect cover for such goods or the circumstances reasonably indicate that such effort will be unavailing or if the goods have been shipped under reservation and satisfaction of the security interest in them has been made or tendered.

Long-Term Contracts for the Supply of Goods or Services

In contrast to the discrete, one-time contract of sale (of the kind favoured by textbook writers), many contractual arrangements between commercial parties contemplate ongoing business relationships. Contracts of this sort are referred to in the literature as "relational."

An important class of relational contracts are those that contemplate the repeated or continuous purchase or supply of goods or services over a lengthy period. An auto manufacturer may, for example, agree to purchase its entire requirement of alternators over a period of several years from a particular supplier, who agrees to supply them. (This is known as a "requirements" contract.) Or a garment manufacturer may agree to sell its entire production of men's apparel in a given year to a particular wholesaler, who agrees to purchase it (an "output" contract). The economic advantages of long-term purchase and supply arrangements such as these are evident. They afford suppliers a steady outlet for their products or services or buyers with a guaranteed source of supply, or both. They also eliminate or dampen the effects of price fluctuations by providing both parties with the security of fixed prices or prices that vary according to an agreed index.

Because the quantity and market value of the goods or services to be supplied under these long-term agreements is often highly indeterminate, and because reasonable substitute contracts are often unavailable, damages will frequently be inadequate to fully compensate the victim of a breach. Despite this, courts have traditionally been slow to decree specific performance of these contracts, as the Judicial Committee of the Privy Council's decision in the *Dominion Iron & Steel* case, below, reveals.

Dominion Iron & Steel Co. v. Dominion Coal Co.
(1908), 43 NSR 77 (SC *en banc*)

[Dominion Iron & Steel Co. entered into a long-term requirements contract for the purchase of coal from the Dominion Coal Co. The coal was to come from a mine located near the steel company's foundry and was to be of a certain quality appropriate for the manufacture of steel. The coal company made a number of short deliveries that obliged the steel company to purchase coal elsewhere. They also rejected some of the coal as unfit. Eventually, some three years after entry into the contract, the coal company profitably terminated it. The steel company then commenced an action claiming damages for the losses incurred as a result of the short deliveries and specific performance. Before Longley J the steel company succeeded in obtaining both remedies. The coal company then appealed to the Supreme Court (*en banc*).]

RUSSELL J (at 141-47): ... The defendants complain of the learned judge's finding that the coal delivered was not reasonably free from stone and shale within the meaning of the express stipulation in the contract. With the view that I have taken of the defendants' obligation, I think it would be a waste of time to examine the evidence with reference to this finding. Had the plaintiffs been found in the wrong on their principal contention it would have been necessary to enquire into the validity of this finding for the purpose of determining whether they were not entitled to damages even if the defendants' interpretation were the correct one. The matter has become of relatively trifling importance if the plaintiffs' interpretation of the contract is correct.

Still another point on the question of damages remains to be considered. It is claimed that the plaintiffs have themselves broken the contract by their absolute refusal to accept any coal whatever that was not fit for steel-making purposes. In this connection it is pointed out that part of the plaintiffs' requirements could be supplied with a different character of coal from that required for their steel works. The proportion that this part bore to the rest was stated at the argument as 5 per cent of the whole requirement, but in the findings of the learned trial judge the proportion is differently stated. Taking the daily requirement as 75,000 tons for all purposes, the learned judge finds that 69,000 tons would be required to be free from impurities to the degree demanded by the plaintiff company leaving 6,000 tons that could be properly furnished with a higher percentage of impurities. The rejection of this proportion, if it was rejected, by the Steel Company, may have been without justification and constituted a breach of the contract which would subject them to an action for damages at the suit of the Coal Company, but there is no counterclaim for damages, and the breach was not of such a nature as to entitle the defendants to claim that the contract was discharged, and it may be also, for the reasons stated in the opinion of the learned chief justice, that there was really no breach by the plaintiffs at all, though I do not find it necessary to say yes or no to that question. On the other hand the absolute renunciation by the defendants of their obligations under the contract, as I think the learned trial judge has rightly interpreted it, entitles the plaintiff company to consider itself discharged and to claim damages for the whole period through which the contract was to be operative. Those damages must in my opinion be, among other things, the difference between the agreed price and the market price at the time when the successive deliveries were or will be due. This measure of damages must involve a somewhat speculative assessment, but this difficulty did not prevent the application of the measure in *Roper v. Johnston*, in which the case came on for trial before the last of the instalments was due.

In *Fothergill v. Rowland* also ((1873), 17 Eq. 132 (Eq.) at p. 140), Sir George Jessel scouted the idea that the court could not ascertain the damages for the breaking of a contract for the sale of goods in monthly deliveries extending over three years in the future, and intimated that such a suggestion would rather astonish the gentlemen who practiced on what was called the other side of Westminster Hall.

In the present case the difficulty is immensely greater and may fairly be said to be insuperable. Of what possible value could be any opinion given to-day as to the probable price of coal fifty years from this date? If ever there was a case in which it could be said that the remedy at law by way of damages must be inadequate, surely it is such a case as the present. I must confess that the suggestion of specific performance of such a contract struck me at first as having an air of novelty, and I was greatly surprised to find the question treated so much as a matter of course in the judgment appealed from. It is not the case of a chattel with a *pretium affectionis* such as the Pusey horn or the patera of the Duke of Somerset, and a decree for specific performance involves all or many of the objectionable features pointed out by Lord Cranworth when reversing the Vice Chancellor's decree in *Blackett v. Bates* (1865), LR 1 Ch. App. 117 at p. 124. It involves the performance of continuous acts extending over a long period of time. It was assumed in *Fothergill v. Rowland*, that such acts could not be enforced by a decree of specific performance, and I think that the whole current of modern authority is against the issuing of such a degree. But, on the other hand, I am not aware that any such contract as the present ever came before the court for consideration, or that the court was ever asked for a remedy by parties in the predicament of the present plaintiffs. If we look at the reason of the rule that prevents the specific performance of a contract for chattels, and obliges us to specifically enforce a contract in the exceptional cases in which such relief is afforded, I think we shall agree that these reasons abundantly warrant the court in granting such relief in the present case. The ground, as everybody knows, is the inadequacy of the legal remedy. Here the legal remedy is inadequate for so many and such obvious reasons that it is not necessary to refer to them. The length of time over which the obligations of the defendant extend with the consequent impossibility of ascertaining the damages, the fact that an assessment of damages made in anticipation of the probable conditions of the market at so distant a period in the future, might inflict grievous injustice upon the defendants themselves in the action, the danger that such an assessment followed by an award for damages extending over a period of 90 odd years and payable immediately, would ruin the defendants and render it impossible for them to pay any damages at all, the complexity of the calculations required for such an assessment resulting from the uncertainty of the factors to begin with, and the computation of the discounts required to ascertain the present values of the future obligations—these are only some of the difficulties that stand in the way of giving an adequate remedy at law. Added to these is the circumstance of the proximity of the coal fields to the works of the plaintiff company, which makes it unlikely that any supply derived from other sources can have the same value as that which has been contracted for with the defendant company.

The provision for an arbitration at the end of every five years period does not simplify the matter. On the contrary it seems to me to complicate it by introducing an additional uncertainty into the factors to be considered in assessing the damages because it would be necessary not merely to compare the possible future prices with the ascertained standard of the contract price, but to compare them with a price to be fixed by an arbitration the result of which must be beyond human ken. It may be suggested in answer to this that the price fixed by an arbitration would be presumed to be the same as the future price in the market, and there would therefore be no damages at all after the first five year period had elapsed. This, however, may not be the case. The arbitration would fix the price that the plaintiff should pay for coal from the defendants' mines, which might be, and probably would be, very different from the price which the plaintiffs would have to pay if they had to go into the market. If it were necessary to make a new precedent for a case that is without precedent, I should not hesitate at such a step so long as the precedent is based upon principles already well established. It would not be new law, but simply the application of old and well established law to the circumstances of a novel situation. Happily it is not necessary to make a new precedent. All that is necessary is to revive an old and almost forgotten precedent from the days of Lord Hardwicke. In *Buxton v. Lister* (1746), 3 Atk. 383; 26 ER 1020 (Ch.), the contract was for the sale of timber trees, which was treated (rightly or wrongly is immaterial to the present enquiry) as a contract for chattels. The Lord Chancellor on the opening said he did not know of any instance of a bill of this nature where it was a mere chattel and nothing that affected the realty; that a bill might as well be brought for compelling the performance of an agreement for the sale of a horse or of a stock of any goods or merchandise. But "upon hearing what counsel could allege," the Lord Chancellor saw new light. He proceeded to distinguish between contracts for realty and contracts for chattels, and said that:

> Notwithstanding this general distinction between personal contracts for goods, and contracts for lands, yet there are indeed some cases where persons may come into this court though merely personal, and the plaintiffs' counsel have cited a case in point. *Taylor v. Neville.* That was

for the performance of articles for sale of 800 tons of iron to be paid for in a certain number of years and by instalments, and a specific performance was decreed. Such sorts of contracts differ from those that are immediately to be executed. There are several circumstances which may occur. A man may contract for the purchase of a large quantity of timber, as a ship carpenter, by reason of the vicinity of the timber, and this on the part of the buyer. On the part of the seller suppose a man wants to clear his land in order to turn it to a particular sort of husbandry, there is nothing can answer the justice of the case but the performance of the contract *in specie*.

The necessity for continuous acts and frequent attachments which troubled Lord Cranworth in *Blackett v. Bates* does not seem to have worried Lord Hardwicke in this case. I am well aware that the cases of *Buxton v. Lister* and *Taylor v. Neville* have been adversely criticised by Sir Page Wood VC in *Pollard v. Clayton* (1855), 1 K & J 462 at p. 475; 69 ER 540 at p. 546 (Ch.), but his remarks were only obiter, the bill having in that case been dismissed on the ground of laches. Even as an *obiter dictum* his remarks would be entitled to the highest respect. But I cannot think that he ever had occasion to plough this field of equity jurisprudence as deeply as the work has been done by Mr. Pomeroy, whose note on the subject of these cases is to my mind convincing and conclusive. He says:

> In *Taylor v. Neville* Lord Hardwicke decreed specific performance of a contract for the sale of 800 tons of iron to be delivered and paid for by instalments in a certain number of years. In *Ball v. Coggs* the contract was to pay the plaintiff a certain annual sum for his life and also a certain other sum for every hundred weight of brass wire manufactured by defendant during the life of the plaintiff. A specific performance was decreed by the House of Lords on the ground that the damages would be conjectural and inadequate, and to compel plaintiff to take damages would be to compel him to sell the annual provision during his life secured by the contract for a mere conjectural price.

The reasons given for the decision by the House of Lords as stated by *Pomeroy* are exactly in point in the present case. ...

[These] considerations ... apply to the subject of the special value of this contract to the plaintiffs in view of the proximity of the coal supply to their work. But the other considerations adverted to are, I think, of the greater importance, and the cases cited in reference to them seem to me to fully warrant the statement of *Pomeroy* in his work on specific performance at sec. 15:

> Contracts for the delivery of goods will be specifically enforced when by their terms the deliveries are to be made and the purchase price paid in instalments running through a considerable number of years. Such contracts differ from those that are immediately to be executed. Their profits depending upon future events cannot be estimated in present damages which must of necessity be almost wholly conjectural. To compel a party to accept damages under such circumstances is to compel him to sell his possible profits at a price depending upon a mere guess.

For the reasons given, I think that, subject to some possible modifications of the decree, which can be considered when the rule is moved for, the appeal should be dismissed and the judgment of the learned trial judge affirmed.

Dominion Iron & Steel Co. v. Dominion Coal Co.
[1909] AC 293 (PC (NS))

LORD ATKINSON (at 310-11): According to this view, the coal company were not justified in repudiating their contract, but the steel company are not entitled, at one and the same time, to specific performance of the contract and to damages for the loss of it. Inasmuch, however, as, according to their Lordships' view, this is not a contract of which, on the authorities cited, specific performance would be decreed by a Court of Equity, the plaintiffs are entitled, owing to the wrongful repudiation of the contract by the defendants, to treat the contract itself as at an end and to recover damages in respect of those breaches of it which may have been committed before repudiation. The proper reference should, their Lordships think, be directed to ascertain these damages.

Their Lordships will therefore humbly advise His Majesty that the judgment of the Supreme Court should be affirmed, and that the case should be remitted to that Court to have the damages under the two heads above mentioned assessed in the usual way.

The appellants must pay the costs of the principal appeal. There will be no order as to the costs of the cross-appeal.

NOTE

The Nova Scotia Supreme Court *en banc* in *Dominion Iron* reasons with some care that damages would be an inadequate remedy and that specific performance should be decreed even though the case involved a sale of non-unique goods, and the contract might require extended supervision. It concluded that a proper measure of damages would be difficult, if not impossible, and also that a one-time assessment of damages would bankrupt the defendant. In reversing this decision, the Privy Council stressed the point that "this is not a contract of which, on the authorities cited, specific performance would be decreed by a Court of Equity." Would the Privy Council decide the case the same way today?

Sky Petroleum Ltd. v. VIP Petroleum Ltd.
[1974] 1 WLR 576 (Ch.)

[In March 1970, the plaintiff, Sky Petroleum, entered a contract to purchase all its gasoline and diesel fuel from the defendant, VIP Petroleum, for a period of 10 years at a fixed price. The contract could be terminated on three months' notice by either party. In 1973, during the oil crisis that severely limited oil and gas supplies, the defendant purported to terminate the contract on the ground that the plaintiff had exceeded its allowable credit under the contract. The plaintiff sought an interlocutory injunction to restrain the defendant from witholding supply.]

GOULDING J: This is a motion for an injunction brought by the plaintiff company, Sky Petroleum Ltd., as buyer under a contract dated March 11, 1970, made between the defendant company, VIP Petroleum Ltd., as seller of the one part and the plaintiffs of the other part. ...

After the making of the agreement, it is common knowledge that the terms of trade in the market for petroleum and its different products changed very considerably, and I have little doubt that the contract is now disadvantageous to the defendants. After a long correspondence, the defendants, by telegrams dated November 15 and 16, 1973, have purported to terminate the contract under a clause therein providing for termination by the defendants if the plaintiffs fail to conform with any of the terms of the bargain. What is alleged is that the plaintiffs have exceeded the credit provisions of the contract and have persistently been, and now are, indebted to the defendants in larger amounts than were provided for. So far as that dispute relates, as for the purposes of this motion it must, to the date of the purported termination of the contract, it is impossible for me to decide it on the affidavit evidence. It involves not only a question of construction of the contract, but also certain disputes on subsequent arrangements between the parties and on figures in account. I cannot decide it on motion, and the less I say about it the better.

What I have to decide is whether any injunction should be granted to protect the plaintiffs in the meantime. There is trade evidence that the plaintiffs have no great prospect of finding any alternative source of supply for the filling stations which constitute their business. The defendants have indicated their willingness to continue to supply the plaintiffs, but only at prices which, according to the plaintiffs' evidence, would not be serious prices from a commercial point of view. There is, in my judgment, so far as I can make out on the evidence before me, a serious danger that unless the court interferes at this stage the plaintiffs will be forced out of business. In those circumstances, unless there is some specific reason which debars me from doing so, I should be disposed to grant an injunction to restore the former position under the contract until the rights and wrongs of the parties can be fully tried out.

It is submitted for the defendants that I ought not to do so for a number of reasons. It is said that, on the facts, the defendants were entitled to terminate and the plaintiffs were in the wrong. That, of course, is the very question in the action, and I have already expressed my inability to resolve it even provisionally on the evidence now before me. ...

Now I come to the most serious hurdle in the way of the plaintiffs which is the well known doctrine that the court refuses specific performance of a contract to sell and purchase chattels not specific or ascertained. That is a well-established and salutary rule, and I am entirely unconvinced by Mr. Christie, for the plaintiffs, when he tells me that an injunction in the form sought by him would not be specific enforcement at all. The matter is one of substance and not of form, and it is, in my judgment, quite plain that I am, for the time being, specifically enforcing the contract if I grant an injunction. However, the ratio behind the rule is, as I believe, that under the ordinary contract for the sale of non-specific goods, damages are a sufficient remedy. That, to my mind, is lacking in the circumstances of the present case. The evidence suggests, and indeed it is common knowledge that the petroleum market is in an unusual state in which a would-be buyer cannot go out into the market and contract with another seller, possibly at some sacrifice as to price. Here, the defendants appear for practical purposes to be the plaintiffs' sole means of keeping their business going, and I am prepared so far to depart from the general rule as to try to preserve the position under the contract until a later date. I therefore propose to grant an injunction.

Dealing first with its duration, it will restrain the defendants (in terms I will come to in a moment) until judgment in the action or further order, but not in any event beyond June

30, 1974, without further order of the court. I say that because of a provision in the contract which requires further steps to be taken in relation to the price of supply after that date. The terms which I suggest must, with certain qualifications, follow the notice of motion. If counsel are able to arrive at something more convenient and easier to enforce, they may mention the matter to me at an early date and the wording can be reconsidered, but for the moment I will order that the defendants by themselves, or their servants or agents, in the usual form be restrained from withholding supplies of "motor gasoline and DERV" from the plaintiffs in accordance with the terms of the contract dated March 11, 1970, and such other arrangements, if any, as were agreed between the parties before the issue of the writ in this action. There will be a proviso that the plaintiffs are not to require delivery of more than a specified number of gallons in any one month, and that number is to be ascertained by taking the arithmetical mean of the three months of supply, August, September and October. That will, I hope, prevent any abuse of the injunction by the plaintiffs.

I would be sympathetic to any application by the defendants for the provision of security in some particular sum and form. I do not know whether the plaintiffs can make any specific offer in that respect, or whether the best thing is that all the details should be considered by counsel.

NOTES

1. Review s. 50 of the *Sale of Goods Act*, RSO 1990, c. S.1, above, and the accompanying notes. Does Goulding J in *Sky Petroleum* take (the English counterpart of) this provision to constitute a complete code of equitable relief in sales law? Does it affect your answer that it was an injunction that was granted in *Sky Petroleum*? Compare *In re Wait*, [1927] 1 Ch. 606 (CA), and see also *Re London Wine Co. (Shippers)*, [1986] PCC 121, at 149.

2. Courts have long been willing to specifically enforce contracts for the sale of goods that are physically unique. (See, for example, *Pusey v. Pusey* (1684), 1 Vern 273; *Phillips v. Lamdin*, [1949] 2 KB 33; and the remarks in *Falcke v. Gray*, above, on the potential enforceability of a contract to sell jars of "unusual beauty, rarity and distinction.") However, the uniqueness of a thing need not pertain to its physical features. Under a broader conception, even the most physically ordinary of things might be described as "unique" if there is no ready market in a substitute. Goods that are unique in this sense are often dubbed "commercially unique" (see, for example, the judgment of Hammond J in *Butler v. Countrywide Finance*, above), and commercial uniqueness is sometimes cited as the ground of the decision in *Sky Petroleum*. See, for example, Andrew S. Burrows, *Remedies for Torts and Breach of Contract*, 3d ed. (Oxford: Oxford University Press, 2004), at 462. But compare Stephen M. Waddams, *The Law of Contracts*, 5th ed. (Toronto: Carswell, 2005), at 492, note 49.

3. Shares are often found to be commercially unique. In *UBS Securities Canada, Inc. v. Sands Brothers Canada, Ltd.*, 2009 ONCA 328, 95 OR (3d) 93, E.E. Gillese JA (for the court) wrote:

> Specific performance may be ordered in connection with the shares of a private company because, as in the present case, such shares may not be readily available on the market and valuation can be difficult. Contracts for the sale of publicly traded shares are also candidates for specific performance in circumstances such as those of the present case where the vendor is subject to an injunction restraining it from selling the shares, the purchaser has diligently pursued its

claim for specific performance from the outset, and the plaintiff has entered into additional contracts for the resale of some of the shares .... The uniqueness of the property that is the subject of the contract is one, non-determinative factor in deciding the appropriateness of specific performance. The underlying principle is that if the property is unique, it should be delivered up because damages would not put the party in the position they would have been in but for the breach. The trial judge considered this factor and concluded that the Shares were unique. During the relevant timeframe (i.e. prior to the public listing of the shares in March 2007) there was no readily available substitute for the Shares. In this regard, it is important to note that the time to assess the uniqueness of the property is the date of the anticipatory breach, not the date of trial or judgment: *John E. Dodge Holdings Ltd. v. 805062 Ontario Ltd.* (2002), 63 OR (3d) 304 (CA), at paras. 40 and 43. Furthermore, the Shares were unique because of the special value they had for UBS. In that regard, it will be recalled, UBS had a plan to accumulate as many Bourse shares as possible. Finally, the value and availability of the Shares at the time of breach was not certain.

4. In *Fruits de mer Oceanis Ltée v. Lanteigne et autres* (1995), 163 NBR (2d) 266 (QB), a mandatory interlocutory injunction was granted to a purchaser of a snow crab catch directing the vendor to deliver the catch to it. The defendant had agreed to deliver her entire crab catch to the plaintiff for the 1995 and 1996 seasons at the local market price. The court adopted the following passage from Sharpe, *Injunctions and Specific Performance*, 2d ed., 8-22.

The other important aspect of long-term supply arrangements which may render damage awards less than satisfactory relates to the guarantee of the source of supply. Here, the courts have been more sympathetic. The plaintiff's business or industrial activity may be dependent upon a guaranteed source of supply. If so, the reason for entering the contract extends beyond the desire to cover the risk of price fluctuation and includes the need to ensure a steady supply of the commodity or item in question. Such a plaintiff may have more at stake than could be reflected in a damages award, as his or her entire business may be dependent upon the continuation of performance by the defendant. Again, if an alternative source of supply is available, there is no need and probably no desire on the plaintiff's part to resort to specific performance. On the other hand, if alternative arrangements are not available, it can surely be argued that the chattel or item in question, although ordinary in one sense, when coupled with the element of guaranteed supply over a lengthy period, is sufficiently unique to justify the award of specific relief.

5. See also the injunction cases in chapter 11, "Discretionary Reasons for the Denial of Relief," particularly *Thomas Borthwick & Sons (Australasia) Ltd. v. South Otago Freezing Co. Ltd.*, [1978] 1 NZLR 538 (CA). Is there any difference between specific performance of a long-term exclusive right to export contract and enjoining the defendant from using another company as its exporter?

6. See Peter Linzer, "On the Amorality of Contract Remedies—Efficiency, Equity and the Second Restatement" (1981), 81 *Columbia Law Review* 111 for an outline of the judicial application of s. 2-716(1) of the *Uniform Commercial Code* for long-term supply contracts. Section 2-716(1) provides that

[s]pecific performance may be decreed where the goods are unique or in other proper circumstances

and comment 2 to the section refers particularly to output and requirements contracts involving "a particular or peculiarly available source of market" ("unique") and situations where there is an "inability to cover" ("other proper circumstances").

Ryan v. Mutual Tontine Westminster Chambers Association
[1893] 1 Ch. 116 (CA)

[The defendant agreed to lease to the plaintiff a residential flat for 21 years. A covenant in the lease provided that the landlord would appoint a resident porter for the benefit of the tenants, whose duties were specified in the covenant as follows:

> The general duties of the porter which the tenants are entitled to have performed for them free of extra charge are as follows:
>
>> To be constantly in attendance in the section of the building committed to his charge, either by himself or, in his temporary absence, by some trustworthy assistant.
>>
>> To cleanse every morning before 9 o'clock A.M. the general stairs, passages, lifts, and entrances attached to the section, and to attend to the lighting and extinguishing of the gas therein.
>>
>> To receive and deliver to the several tenants all letters, parcels, and messages, and to receive the keys of the outer doors of the several sets of rooms from the tenants for safe custody, on their leaving for the night.
>>
>> The special services of the porter, which he is bound to render to the several tenants, if required, at a charge of 1s. 6d. per week for each room, comprise the cleaning and arrangement of such room, and the lighting of the several fires whenever required. Any extra services required of the porter by the tenants, and which are not inconsistent with his general duties, are to be the subject of special arrangement between them.
>>
>> Any services rendered by the porter will be rendered by him as the servant of the tenant, and for which, or the consequences whereof, the lessors will not be responsible.

The defendant appointed as a resident porter a man, who was by vocation a cook, who employed boys and cleaning women to perform his duties as porter and who left the premises daily for several hours to act as chef at a neighbouring venue. At trial, Smith J granted a perpetual injunction restraining the defendant from breaching the covenant and, in case he was wrong in giving that decree, he assessed damages at £25. The defendant appealed to the Court of Appeal on the ground that neither an injunction nor specific performance is appropriate in this case.]

LORD ESHER MR: ... It seems to me that this case comes within one or the other, according to the point of view from which it is regarded, of two well-recognised rules of Chancery practice, which prevent the application of the remedy by compelling specific performance. I do not myself put this case as coming within any rule as to contracts to perform personal services. It is not necessary for me therefore to express any opinion as to such a rule. The contract sought to be enforced here is not a contract with a person employed as a servant.

It is a contract between a person who has to employ a servant and a person for whose benefit the employment of such servant is to take place. It is a contract between a landlord and
his tenant, by which the former undertakes to employ a porter to perform certain services
for the benefit of the latter. The contract, therefore, is not merely that the landlord shall
employ a porter, but that he shall employ a porter who shall do certain specified work for
the benefit of the tenant. That is, in my opinion, one indivisible contract. The performance
of what is suggested to be the first part of the contract, *viz.*, the agreement to employ a porter, would be of no use whatever to the tenant unless he performed the services specified.
The right of the tenant under the contract is really an entirety, *viz.*, to have a porter employed by whom these services shall be performed; and the breach of the contract substantially is that these services were not performed. The contract is that these services shall be
performed during the whole term of the tenancy; it is therefore a long-continuing contract,
to be performed from day to day, and under which the circumstances of non-performance
might vary from day to day. I apprehend, therefore, that the execution of it would require
that constant superintendence by the Court, which the Court in such case has always declined to give. Therefore, if the contract is regarded as a whole, there is good ground for
saying that it is not one of which the Court could compel specific performance. It was contended that the Court could grant specific performance of the Defendants' obligation to
appoint a porter. But then the case is brought within another rule, *viz.*, that, when the Court
cannot compel specific performance of the contract as a whole, it will not interfere to compel specific performance of part of a contract. That clearly appears to be a rule of Chancery
practice on the subject. Therefore, if it is urged that what the Judge has ordered to be performed is merely the obligation to appoint a porter, the case falls within that rule, and on
that ground his decision must be reversed. It was argued that the case of *Rigby v. Great
Western Railway Company* (1846), 15 LJ 266 (Ch.), shewed that a contract such as this might
be severed, and that performance of part of it could be enforced. But that is not what the
case appears to have decided. It decided that, where in one contract there were really several
wholly independent stipulations, the Court could grant specific performance of one of
them. It is no authority for the proposition that the Court can separate part of what is really
one single indivisible contract and grant specific performance of that part. Then it was said
that this case fell within the exception which has been established in the railway cases. That
is admitted to be an exception grafted upon the Chancery jurisdiction by decisions, in
which the Court, for the reasons stated, treated cases where railway companies had taken
land on condition of doing works as exceptional, and granted specific performance. But
being admittedly exceptions, these cases do not do away with the general rule, which appears to be applicable to the case before us. The language used by *James* VC, in *Wilson v.
Furness Railway Company* (1869), LR 9 Eq. 28, was cited to us as an authority to shew that
the Court ought in this case to grant specific performance. That language, as applied by the
counsel for the Defendants, is really cited as an authority for the proposition that the Court
of Chancery will always, regardless of any rules, do what the justice of the particular case
requires. But the answer is that the Court of Chancery has never acted on any such proposition. … It appears to me that the appeal must be allowed, and the judgment for the Plaintiff
must stand only for the damages found by the learned Judge.

KAY LJ: I agree. This remedy by specific performance was invented, and has been cautiously applied, in order to meet cases where the ordinary remedy by an action for damages is not an adequate compensation for breach of contract. The jurisdiction to compel specific performance has always been treated as discretionary, and confined within well-known rules.

[After detailing the facts, he continued:]

When one looks at that which was the real gravamen of the action, the contention seems rather odd that we ought to divide the contract into two parts—one that a porter should be appointed, the other that he should perform the duties specified. The lessors' covenant being in substance that the lessee should have the advantage of the performance of certain services by the porter, a covenant which I cannot conceive to be divisible, as was ingeniously suggested, the Plaintiff's claim is shaped thus. It is alleged that the lessee took possession under the lease, but that a proper porter was not appointed, and the lessee does not get the advantage of the performance of the porter's duties. He therefore asks for some remedy by means of which he may have these duties performed. That is really the nature of the action. But now it is sought to overlook that, and to say that, though a contract that the lessee shall have the benefit of the performance by the porter of his duties is not the sort of contract of which the Plaintiff can have specific performance, yet he can claim to have the contract performed specifically to this extent: he can ask the Court to compel the appointment of a proper porter, though, when he is appointed, the Court is not asked to compel performance of his duties. As I have said, the contract is really a single contract—*viz.*, that the Plaintiff shall have the advantage of performance by the porter of his duties; and I dissent entirely from the notion that this contract can be divided into two parts in the way suggested, and the Court asked to grant specific performance of one part, but not of the other.

There are, no doubt, certain cases where a contract may be treated as divisible for the purpose of specific performance. The common case is where there is a contract like that in *Lumley v. Wagner* (1852), 1 DM & G 604; 42 ER 687 (Ch.); in which case the contract was to sing for the plaintiff, and also not to sing for others. The Court says in such cases, though we cannot enforce performance of the contract to sing for a particular person, and so cannot enforce the whole contract; nevertheless, there being the independent negative stipulation against singing for others, we can enforce that by injunction. In the case of *Lumley v. Wagner*, the Lord Chancellor, in the passage which I cited in *Whitwood Chemical Company v. Hardman*, [1891] 2 Ch. 416 (CA), expressly said that, if he had had to deal with the affirmative covenant only, that the defendant would sing for the plaintiff, he would not have granted an injunction. That is one exception to the rule.

There is another exception to the general rules as to specific performance. Ordinarily the Court will not enforce specific performance of works, such as building works, the prosecution of which the Court cannot superintend; not only on the ground that damages are generally in such cases an adequate remedy, but also on the ground of the inability of the Court to see that the work is carried out: *Blackett v. Bates* (1865), LR 1 Ch. App. 117; *Powell Duffryn Steam Coal Company v. Taff Vale Railway Company* (1874), LR 9 Ch. App. 33. An exception to this rule has been established in cases where a railway company has taken lands from a landowner on the terms that it will carry out certain works. In those cases, because damages are not an adequate remedy, the Court has gone to great lengths, and has granted specific performance of the definite works—they must be definite works—which the company that has taken the lands has contracted to do. This case does not come within either of the exceptions to which I have alluded. Therefore, for the reasons stated by the Master of the Rolls, this case is not one in which the Court could compel specific performance.

There appears to me to be also another reason for our decision which is quite sufficient. At the time when the action was brought there had been a breach of covenant. The learned Judge found no difficulty in assessing damages for breach of the contract down to that time. Why should there be any difficulty with regard to future breaches of contract? I have heard no sufficient reason adduced in the argument. If for the breach of contract down to [the] action ... adequate compensation may be given by damages, that appears to me to be a reason for the Court not exercising its extraordinary jurisdiction. A sufficient reply to this argument is not afforded by the mere fact that these damages are not compensation for future breaches of the contract. If that were sufficient, I cannot conceive of any case of a continuing contract where specific performance might not be granted. For these reasons I differ respectfully from the learned Judge, and think that nothing but a judgment for the damages found by him should be given.

[Lopes LJ delivered a separate concurring decision.]

NOTES

1. The "railway cases" referred to by the court in this case are discussed further in *Tanenbaum*, below. Why was this line of cases held to be inapplicable in the *Ryan* case?

2. The availability of damages on a periodic basis for continuing breaches of this contract was obviously a very important consideration of the judgment of the court. How would such damages be assessed? Kay LJ speaks of the trial judge having "no difficulty in assessing damages." How did the trial judge quantify the award down to the time of the action? Is the availability of damages on a periodic basis also an answer to the claim for specific performance in *Dominion Coal*?

3. On January 1, 1985, the following provision came into effect in Ontario:

Courts of Justice Act
RSO 1990, c. C.43

117. Where damages are to be assessed in respect of,
- (a) a continuing cause of action;
- (b) repeated breaches of a recurring obligation; or
- (c) intermittent breaches of a continuing obligation,

the damages, including damages for breaches occurring after the commencement of the proceeding, shall be assessed down to the time of the assessment.

See also Alta. Rules of Court, r. 250; Man. Queen's Bench Rules, r. 52.11; NS Civil Procedure Rules, r. 33; *Supreme Court Act*, RSPEI 1988, c. S-10, s. 45; and Sask. Queen's Bench Rules, r. 262.

4. Did the plaintiff's counsel make a tactical error by including a claim for damages to the date of trial? Presumably, the plaintiff would call evidence to quantify this loss. How could the

plaintiff then argue that for the future, damages are an inadequate remedy? How would you have advised the plaintiff in this regard?

5. In *Posner v. Scott-Lewis*, [1987] Ch. 25, a case dealing with facts that appeared to be similar to those in *Ryan*, the court ordered specific performance of a covenant requiring the landlord to execute an agreement for the provision of the services of a resident porter. The court distinguished the *Ryan* case on the basis that in *Ryan*, the obligations were owed by the porter directly to the residents while in *Posner*, the duties were owed by the lessor to the residents. However, the ratio of the case is arguably found in the willingness of the court to depart from the "usual rule" in contracts involving personal services by applying the following considerations (at 36):

> (a) Is there a sufficient definition of what has to be done in order to comply with the order of the court? (b) Will enforcing compliance involve superintendence by the court to an unacceptable degree? (c) What are the respective prejudices or hardships that will be suffered by the parties if the order is made or not made.

Tanenbaum v. W.J. Bell Paper Co. Ltd.
[1956] OR 278

[The defendant purchased part of a parcel of land owned by the plaintiff, and covenanted to construct a roadway over this land similar to Wicksteed Avenue, a nearby street, to provide access to plaintiff's remaining land and also to lay a watermain connecting with plaintiff's land. After much delay, the defendant did construct a roadway, but of a quality inferior to that of the named street. It also laid the watermain, but of 2-inch pipe rather than 6-inch pipe. It was contemplated in the contract that plaintiff's remaining land might be used for commercial or industrial purposes. The plaintiff brought this action for damages and also for specific performance.]

GALE J: ... The defendant must, therefore, be held accountable for the breach of contract. The plaintiff asks for specific performance of the covenants but the defendant urges that such relief would be inappropriate and too drastic in the circumstances of this case.

Generally the Court will not order a contract to build or to repair to be specifically performed. But an exception to that rule is now recognized and it is my understanding of the authorities that specific performance ought to be decreed where a person undertakes accommodation works on lands possessed by him in consideration for obtaining those lands or in consideration of the purchase-price of other lands sold by him, if the particulars of the work are sufficiently clear and defined and the Court comes to the conclusion that damages will not provide an adequate remedy for the breach of the contract. In *Wolverhampton & Walsall R. Co. v. London & North-Western R. Co.* (1873), LR 16 Eq. 433, Lord Selborne LC acknowledged that modification of the general law. There the plaintiff company agreed to construct a railway-line between certain points. The defendant company agreed to work it and during the continuance of the agreement to develop and accommodate the local and through traffic thereon and to carry over it certain traffic particularly specified. The plaintiff company constructed the line and the defendant company entered into possession of it but diverted a large portion of traffic which ought to have passed over it to other lines belonging to the defendant company. The Lord Chancellor on a demurrer to a bill brought to restrain the defendant company held that the case was one in which the Court could interfere by injunction, that being the type of remedy granted at that time. At p. 441 he said:

> If the Defendants are not using the line as they promised to use it, it appears to me that the other party, who is out of possession by virtue of this Parliamentary agreement, is quite at liberty to come to this Court, and to ask that they may be compelled to use the line as they agreed, provided the Court sees its way to define that which they ought, or ought not, to do. I therefore think this demurrer must be overruled in the usual way.

Mr. McLean suggested that that case, along with several others, should be distinguished as being concerned with the rights and duties of railway companies but there is no reason to think that in proceedings for specific performance or an injunction those companies are to be treated in any different way from individuals. ...

That the Court will enforce building contracts in certain circumstances was firmly established in *Wolverhampton Corp. v. Emmons*, [1901] 1 KB 515 (CA). That was a decision of the English Court of Appeal and may well be regarded as the leading modern authority on the subject. In pursuance of a scheme of improvement the plaintiffs, an urban sanitary authority, conveyed to the defendant some lands abutting on a street. The defendant covenanted that he would erect buildings thereon within a certain time. Subsequently the nature and particulars of the houses to be erected were agreed upon, but the defendant failed to fulfil his covenant to build. The plaintiffs thereupon brought the action and were held entitled to a decree of specific performance. That was not a case involving a railway company. Romer LJ at pp. 524-5 describes the exception to which I have alluded as follows:

> There is no doubt that as a general rule the Court will not enforce specific performance of a building contract, but an exception from the rule has been recognised. It has, I think, for some time been held that, in order to bring himself within that exception, a plaintiff must establish three things. The first is that the building work, of which he seeks to enforce the performance, is defined by the contract; that is to say, that the particulars of the work are so far definitely ascertained that the Court can sufficiently see what is the exact nature of the work of which it is asked to order the performance. The second is that the plaintiff has a substantial interest in having the contract performed, which is of such a nature that he cannot adequately be compensated for breach of the contract by damages. The third is that the defendant has by the contract obtained possession of land on which the work is contracted to be done.

The exception so defined by Romer LJ was considered and expanded somewhat by Farwell J, as he then was, in *Carpenters Estates Ltd. v. Davies*, [1940] Ch. 160. In that case the defendant sold certain land to the plaintiffs for building development and agreed to install roads, mains, sewers and drains on other lands retained by her. The covenant having been broken, the plaintiffs succeeded in an action for specific performance. After setting out, *inter alia*, the passage in the *Emmons* case which I have quoted above, Farwell J seemed to express himself as being of the view that if the conditions as to clarity and inadequacy of damages were present, the plaintiff would be entitled to succeed on his quest for a decree by showing merely that the defendant was in possession of the lands upon which the work was to have been done, and the exception may now perhaps be regarded as being as broad as that. I do not have to settle that question here.

It may be that the learned Judge did not intend to carry the extension of the exception so far because later in his judgment he said at p. 165:

> The defendant has contracted to do the work on her own land in consideration of the purchase price of other land belonging to her, and if the other two conditions are fulfilled, I am unable to see why the Court should be debarred from granting relief by way of specific performance.

He was not, however, prepared to accept as being completely exhaustive the statement of Romer LJ and for the moment, therefore, I prefer to express the exception to the general rule as I have done.

Perhaps it is scarcely necessary to add that the exception which I have outlined has been worked into the fabric of the law of Canada. It was acknowledged and applied by two of the three Judges in *Colton v. Rookledge* (1872), 19 Gr. 121, and was reasserted by Idington J in one of the judgments of the Supreme Court of Canada in *Gross v. Wright*, [1923] SCR 214. In the latter case the litigants entered into a party-wall agreement under which the defendant was to build a wall 2 ft. or more in thickness with its middle line to coincide with the boundary-line. The wall erected by the defendant complied with the agreement to the level of the second storey but was narrowed from there up on the defendant's side, while remaining perpendicular on the plaintiff's side. The latter discovered this situation some years after the wall formed part of the defendant's building and sued for a mandatory injunction to compel the latter to pull down that which had been erected and for specific performance of the agreement. The majority of the Court granted a mandatory injunction on the theory that having obtained a licence to enter on the land for a particular purpose and having breached that licence, the defendant was committing a trespass. However, Idington J expressly awarded the decree which was sought on the ground that the Court had jurisdiction to grant specific performance of the agreement itself. Indeed at p. 219, he stated that in his opinion specific performance was the only appropriate remedy in the circumstances and certainly the other members of the Court did not take the position that the relief being ordered could not have been based on the claim for specific performance of the contract between the parties.

Here the defendant argues that specific performance is not available to the plaintiff, firstly, because the terms of the agreement, ex. 1, as to the road and watermain are not sufficiently explicit, secondly, because the plaintiff can be appropriately compensated in damages if those works do not comply with the provisions of the agreement; and lastly, because the plaintiff has had some performance from the defendant.

As already indicated, I am of the opinion that the road and watermain which were to have been installed by the defendant were sufficiently described by the contract and that the defendant failed to fulfil its obligations in that respect. It is very difficult, if not impossible, to set down a general formula as to what degree of certainty is required in a contract before the Court will enforce its performance, so much depends upon the facts of each case. But I think it may be said with confidence that the certainty which is essential must be a reasonable one, having regard to the nature and subject-matter of the undertaking and the attendant conditions under which and with regard to which it was entered into. The authorities on this point substantiate such a conclusion. ...

All the defendant had to do here was to have copied the essential elements of a named street and to have installed a main which, in view of what must have been in the minds of the parties, would be at least 6 ins. in diameter. There was no room for doubt as to what was to be done and accordingly I hold that the plaintiff is not to be denied his decree by reason of any suggestion of uncertainty or ambiguity as to the nature of the work.

Probably the most serious objection to the granting of specific performance comes from the submission that if the road and watermain do not meet the terms of the agreement, the plaintiff can be properly and sufficiently compensated in damages. Let me say at once, however, that it is my view that such relief, even if capable of being calculated, would be quite inadequate to atone for the inadequacy of the watermain. As long as that pipe remains its sole source of water, parcel "C" cannot be put to its full use and certainly its potential sale value cannot be realized. I suspect that counsel for the defendant was aware of the hopelessness of his arguments that a pecuniary award could counterbalance the lack of a suitable main, because, while stoutly resisting all efforts to have the road replaced, he conceded that the installation of a new watermain would not be a very serious matter.

The question whether damages ought to be substituted for performance with respect to the road has not been easy to decide, but here again I do not subscribe to the idea that an award of damages would give the proper relief. It would be futile to attempt to lay down a general rule as to when damages will be ordered in lieu of enforcing performance. Mr. Weir relied upon the statement of A.L. Smith LJ in *Shelfer v. London Elec. Lighting Co.*, [1895] 1 Ch. 287 (CA) at pp. 322-3, as settling the considerations which bear upon the granting of damages instead of an injunction or specific performance. The Lord Justice of Appeal there said:

> In my opinion, it may be stated as a good working rule that—
>
> (1) If the injury to the plaintiff's legal rights is small,
>
> (2) And is one which is capable of being estimated in money,
>
> (3) And is one which can be adequately compensated by a small money payment,
>
> (4) And the case is one in which it would be oppressive to the defendant to grant an injunction—
>
> then damages in substitution for an injunction may be given.

If that statement is applicable to specific performance cases, then clearly damages are inappropriate here, for none of the elements there mentioned is present. But I am not persuaded that the formula outlined by Lord Justice Smith was meant to extend to cases such as this one. On that occasion the Court was concerned with a continuing nuisance in respect of which the injured party had a *prima facie* right to an injunction, whereas in a case of this kind the onus of showing that he should have a decree requiring performance rests upon the person who seeks it. To my mind that is a vital distinction. ...

The best statement on the subject that I have been able to find appears in *Williston on Contracts* (New York: Baker, Voorhis & Co., rev. ed., 1936), vol. 5, s. 1423, pp. 3976-7, where this appears:

> In contracts other than those ordinarily designated as contracts of service, it is generally true so far as affirmative relief is concerned, that "Equity will not award specific performance where the duty to be enforced is continuous and reaches over a long period of time, requiring constant

supervision by the court." Therefore, "There is no doubt that as a general rule the Court will not enforce specific performance of a building contract." The basis of equity's disinclination to enforce building contracts specifically is the difficulty of enforcing a decree without an expenditure of effort disproportionate to the value of the result. But where the inadequacy of damages is great, and the difficulties not extreme, specific performance will be granted and the tendency in modern times has been increasingly towards granting relief, where under the particular circumstances of the case damages are not an adequate remedy.

In this instance certainly the difficulties which would follow a decree of specific performance would not be extreme. The present roadway would have to be taken up and replaced with what should have been installed there in the first place and that would, of course, be an expensive undertaking. Indeed, the defendant protests strenuously that the cost of having to supplant the present road would not only be substantial but would also be out of all proportion to the advantages to be achieved by doing so. However, in many judgments upon the subject it has frequently been declared that mere hardship on the party in default should not be allowed to overcome the exercise of the Court's discretion in favour of ordering performance. Needless to say, if damages could be easily ascertained and were relatively insignificant in amount, I would pause long before making an order which might seriously prejudice the defendant's existence. Obviously that is not the situation here. As I shall point out in a moment, any attempt to assess damages is likely to prove abortive and the cost of building a proper road, while heavy by some standards, will by no means cripple the defendant company. And it must never be forgotten that if the decree were withheld the Court would, in one sense, be permitting the defendant to take advantage of its own wrong. In that respect I should like to echo other words of A.L. Smith LJ, in the *Shelfer* case, who also said:

> There may also be cases in which, though the four above-mentioned requirements exist, the defendant by his conduct, as, for instance, hurrying up his buildings so as if possible to avoid an injunction, or otherwise acting with a reckless disregard to the plaintiff's rights, has disentitled himself from asking that damages may be assessed in substitution for an injunction.

Certainly the sentiment there expressed should apply to actions for specific performance. If for no other reason, therefore, the conduct of the defendant and its contractor would probably induce me to grant that relief, for, as I have already mentioned, the reckless and almost wilful manner in which the plaintiff's rights were put aside would cause any Court to deal with the defendant quite dispassionately.

It strikes me too that the inadequacy of damages would be of significance here for the added reason that the full enjoyment or worth of the plaintiff's land is permanently impaired while the road is allowed to remain as it is.

However, perhaps the most formidable obstacle to the granting of damages comes from the fact that to try to calculate those damages would be an almost insuperable task. They arise in several ways. The plaintiff should have an amount equivalent to the difference between the estimated cost of repairing the private roadway and that of repairing one like Wicksteed Ave. during the lifespan of the latter. Counsel for the defendant urged that a monetary allowance for that difference would represent the full loss sustained by its adversary, but I do not agree, for clearly the enjoyment of parcel "C" and its disposal-value will continue to be adversely affected so long as the present road is there. I propose to examine those two sources of damages to determine whether either can be properly ascertained.

In the first place, it is questionable who will be making any future repairs. Certainly the defendant has the right to rebuild or repair the road but it is not obliged to do so since the agreement contains no covenant to that effect. Conversely, the plaintiff has no right to alter or rebuild that which is there. But can he repair the road? On behalf of the defendant it was said that Mr. Tanenbaum could enter upon it to make minor repairs at his own expense and counsel for the plaintiff concurred in that suggestion. It is extremely difficult to say, however, to what extent that privilege can be exercised. For example, the plaintiff could not close off the road at any time for that purpose without obtaining permission, for the defendant has already granted further rights of way over it to the Russell company and perhaps to others. It occurs to me, therefore, that it would not be easy to define in advance the scope of the repairs which the plaintiff might make; assuredly he could not make material alterations to that which is there.

Even assuming that the plaintiff is at liberty to mend the surface of the road as it deteriorates, how could the present value of the cost of doing so be reckoned? The evidence proved beyond doubt that Wicksteed Ave. would not require as much in the way of maintenance as the private road but that on occasions when repairs will have to be made the cost of doing so will exceed that which will have to be expended for individual repairs to the private road. That being so, anyone fastened with the unenviable duty of assessing damages would be required to determine the life-expectancy of a cement-based road and then try to estimate what the repairs to this road over that period of time would amount to. I am completely convinced that it would be quite impossible to do that with any degree of accuracy because the extent of future repairs and their frequency will depend on the volume and weight of the traffic the road will be called upon to carry and the speeds at which the vehicles will pass over it. Even if the magnitude and volume of repairs could be predicted, how could anyone come to a conclusion as to what those repairs would cost, bearing in mind that no one can know when they will be needed? Prices ten years hence may bear no relation to to-day's prices. And if all of these data could in some miraculous way be calculated, they would still have to be compared with similar data concerning an imaginary cement-based road.

If the damages relating to the comparative cost of repairs could be determined the struggle would not be over, for there would still have to be a decision as to the amount of damages accruing to the plaintiff because the present road causes and will continue to cause some reduction in the disposal-value of parcel "C." Without doubt, the process of calculating damages in the *Wolverhampton, Emmons* and *Carpenters Estates* cases, and in *Pembroke v. Thorpe* (1704), 3 Swans. 482 (NC), 36 ER 939 (Ch.) and *Price v. Penzance Corp.* (1845), 4 Hare 506, 67 ER 748 (Ch.) was in each instance relatively simple when viewed in the light of what would have to be decided here and yet the Courts trying those cases refused to embark upon such a speculative venture.

The defendant finally contended that specific performance ought not to be granted because the plaintiff has been provided with a hard-surfaced road which can be used. In other words, counsel suggested that since the plaintiff has had some measure of performance, he is precluded from obtaining anything but damages. Once again I do not agree and I am substantiated by the authorities. In *Lane v. Newdigate* (1804), 10 Ves. 192, 32 ER 818 (Ch.)

the decree was made and again in *Gross v. Wright*, the Court, and particularly Idington J, did not hesitate to order the demolition of a substantial part of an existing building and the reconstruction of a wall which had been built but did not comply with the agreement between the parties. If it were otherwise, it would mean that a person who has determined upon non-observance of a contract could arbitrate on what was to be done. I concede, of course that specific performance would probably be refused if the disparity of execution were slight, but that is not the situation here. The differences between the two roads are notable and the fact that the plaintiff will always be out of possession of the lands on which the road is laid and that he has no certain or clear right to effect even minor repairs to it is one which should never be overlooked.

For those reasons I order the defendant to cause to be installed along the westerly boundary of its lands a roadway similar to Wicksteed Ave. and by that I have in mind that there should be laid a road at least 28 ft. wide, having an 8-in. Portland cement base, a 2½-in. asphaltic standard highway hotmix top, two brick gutters 12 ins. in width and consisting of 3 courses of brick and cement curbs. That roadway should extend, of course, from the southerly limit of Wicksteed Ave. to the north rail of the present railway siding. In addition, the defendant must also cause to be installed a 6-in. watermain leading from or close to the defendant's hydrant which is approximately 363 ft. south of the Town main to parcel "C." If the plaintiff desires to have an 8-in. main he will have to pay the difference between the installation of one of that dimension and the 6-in. main I have ordered. I see no reason why both of these works cannot be completed within 4 months from the date of this judgment.

NOTES AND QUESTIONS

1. How would the court supervise the enforcement of its order in this case? What if a dispute arose between the parties as to whether the "asphaltic hot-mix top" used by the defendant met the appropriate standard?

2. Gale J affirms that "[g]enerally, the Court will not order a contract to build or to repair to be specifically performed." According to Gale J, what is the basis of this general principle? Why did it not apply in this case?

3. Suppose a defendant builder is in breach of a promise to effect repairs that will cost the plaintiff owner $64,000 to hire someone else to complete. Will the builder's argument that specific performance should be granted because he can complete the repairs for half that much succeed? See *Chan v. Chadha Construction & Investments Ltd.* (2000), 74 BCLR (3d) 396 (CA).

4. Does the *Tanenbaum* case suggest how far the courts might be prepared to go toward providing specific rather than substitutional relief? In *Dynamic Transport Ltd. v. O.K. Detailing Ltd.*, [1978] 2 SCR 1072, the Supreme Court of Canada went very far indeed in this direction. In this case, the respondent vendor accepted an offer to sell part of its business property to the appellant for $53,000. The vendor refused to convey even before the date for closing arrived. The value of the land had increased to $200,000 as of the date of trial. The Alberta Court of Appeal refused specific performance because it would have been necessary, among other matters, to obtain subdivision approval for the conveyance. In the Supreme Court of Canada, Dickson J (as he then was) dealt with the problem of subdivision approval and made the following order (at 1086-87):

In my opinion, the appellant is entitled to a declaration that the contract between the parties mentioned above is a binding contract in accordance with its terms, including the implied term that the respondent will seek subdivision approval. The appellant is further entitled to an order that the respondent make and pursue a *bona fide* application as may be necessary to obtain registration of the approved plan of subdivision, including registration of the approved plan of subdivision with the Registrar of the North Alberta Land Registration District if approval is obtained. Such application shall be at the expense of the respondent and shall be made within 60 days following delivery of this judgment, or such extended period as may be ordered by a Judge of the Trial Division of the Supreme Court of Alberta in Chambers. In the event that the respondent does not make such application within the time stated, or does not pursue such application with due diligence, the appellant shall be entitled to damages for loss of its bargain in an amount of $147,000. Upon the application for subdivision being successfully made and completed, including registration of the approved plan, the remaining provisions of the agreement, concerning the actual sale and purchase of the land, shall be specifically performed and carried into effect. The date of closing, date of adjustments, and any other matters incidental to closing the transaction shall be as ordered by a Judge of the Trial Division of the Supreme Court of Alberta in Chambers. In the event that the respondent makes and pursues a *bona fide* application as aforesaid, and such application is rejected, then the appellant's claim for specific performance of the provisions concerning sale and purchase stands dismissed, as does the claim for damages in the alternative, and the caveat filed by the appellant shall be discharged. Until that time, the caveat may be maintained.

I would allow the appeal, set aside the judgment of the Appellate Division and substitute therefor an order as aforementioned.

The appellant should have its costs throughout.

5. In the case of *Ludlow v. Beattie* (1978), 20 OR (2d) 363, the court was faced with a situation where the vendor and purchaser had orally agreed that the vendor was to obtain the necessary approval for subdivision, but this was not included in the written agreement. The court ordered the agreement rectified and made a similar order to the one in *Dynamic Transport*.

6. In *B.E.M. Enterprises Ltd. v. Campeau Corporation* (1981), 32 BCLR 116 (CA), it was too late to satisfy the condition. The court awarded damages at the expectation level less 20 percent to reflect the possibility that the condition would not be met. Is the deduction consistent with *Dynamic Transport*?

7. See also *Jordan v. McKenzie* (1985), 3 CPC (2d) 220 (Ont. HC), where the court in giving a plaintiff damages ordered him to transfer shares to the defendant in return.

8. *Dynamic Transport* was not applied in *Wallace v. Allen*, [2007] OJ no. 1074, 85 OR (3d) 88 (aff'd. 2009 ONCA 36, 93 OR (3d) 723). In that case the parties signed a letter of intent for the sale of a business and then, after lengthy negotiations, exchanged a final draft of a share purchase agreement. The seller later refused to complete the transaction. Relying on *Dynamic Transport* the purchaser sought specific performance of the draft agreement. The court held that the parties never concluded a contract because they did not intend to become bound until execution of the final draft agreement, but that it would not have specifically enforced the agreement in any event: "[S]upervision in the present case would far exceed the matters returned to a judge in chambers in the *Dynamic Transport* case. ... [T]here are a host of ... complications and side agreements that the parties have not resolved so the court would have to be an active participant imposing terms." The parties had, for example, agreed that the

vendor would continue to participate in the operation of the business for a period following the sale, but the extent and nature of this involvement had not been worked out in any detail.

9. In considering the adequacy of damages in *Tanenbaum*, Gale J never considers the possibility of measuring damages by reference to the cost of completion. Would this have produced a different view of the question of adequacy?

10. In *Arcadia Marble, Tile & Terrazzo Ltd. v. Oromocto Property Developments Ltd.* (1998), 205 NBR (2d) 358 (CA), a contractor sued a commercial property owner for the balance owing on a contract to replace floor tiles. The owner alleged that there were deficiencies and counterclaimed for, among other things, specific performance. Although the claim for specific performance was ultimately abandoned, the New Brunswick Court of Appeal commented on the availability of specific performance in a building contract case:

> In any event, the time-honoured rule is that specific performance, being an equitable remedy, will not be decreed where common law remedies, such as money damages, are adequate. This rule is deeply rooted in the history of the common law. For a comprehensive historical perspective, see Jeffrey Berryman, "The Specific Performance Damages Continuum: An Historical Perspective" (1985), 17 Ottawa LR 295. Courts have been generally allergic to exceptions to the rule, at least where it is sought to compel performance of a repair contract which has been less than perfectly executed. This judicial aversion to mandatory orders directed at contractors is wise indeed, bearing in mind that damages are invariably an adequate remedy and that very real difficulties inhere to supervision and enforcement of such orders.

11. For a discussion of the proper measure of damages in cases of this kind, see A.M. Tettenborn, "Damages for Breach of Positive Covenants" (1978), 42 *Conveyancer and Property Lawyer (New Series)* 366.

PERSONAL SERVICE CONTRACTS

Giles & Co. v. Morris
[1972] 1 WLR 307 (Ch.)

MEGARRY J: This is a motion by the plaintiff company, for which Mr. Neill appears, to commit three of nine personal defendants, and for leave to sue a writ of sequestration in respect of the tenth defendant, a limited company called Defiance Investments Ltd., which I shall refer to as "Defiance." Mr. Harman appears for all these defendants. The matter arises out of a consent order for specific performance made by Master Dinwiddy on September 8, 1971. The contract in question was made on November 6, 1970, and is of considerable complexity. The defendants between them own all the issued shares in a company called Invincible Policies Ltd., which I shall call "Invincible." Invincible carries on the business of insurance brokers, and has a subsidiary called Trafalgar Insurance Co. Ltd. (which I shall call "Trafalgar") which carries on a motor insurance business: and Invincible owns well over 75 per cent of the shares in Trafalgar. The broad picture is that the moving spirit in Defiance and Invincible was Mr. Arthur Stuart Morris, who for many years had been chairman and managing director of both companies. In 1970 Mr. Morris, who was well on into his sixties and was contemplating ultimate retirement, entered into discussions with a Mr. C.H. Giles, a man in his middle twenties who had experience of lending money on second mortgages, but who seems to have had no experience with motor or other insurance. The upshot of these discussions was the agreement of November 6, 1970. Just over two months later, Mr. Morris died suddenly; and the first and second defendants, against whom orders of committal are sought, are the administrators of his estate.

Under the agreement, Mr. Morris and all the other defendants (save his administrators, who stand in his shoes) are named as the vendors: Defiance, which is also one of the vendors, is named as the second party, the then directors of Invincible as the parties of the third part, Mr. Giles as the fourth party, and Mr. Giles' company, C.H. Giles & Co. Ltd., the plaintiff, as the fifth party. It is the plaintiff in the action who is bringing this motion. The contract provides for Invincible to adopt new articles of association and reorganise its share capital, and also for the sale of certain shares in Invincible to the plaintiff on certain terms, together with a variety of other provisions, filling over 40 pages of foolscap: but I think I need mention only two provisions in any detail.

Clause 2 provides that "On or before completion the vendors will procure the following to be done." Among the seven paragraphs of the clause appears paragraph (f): "Mr. Giles shall enter into a service agreement with [Invincible] in the form of the draft annexed hereto marked 'A.'" The draft marked "A" provides for Mr. Giles to be appointed "as a managing director" of Invincible for five years, and for him to exercise such powers and comply with and perform such directions and duties consistent with his office as "a managing director" in relation to the business and affairs of Invincible "as may from time to time be vested in or given to him by the board of directors of [Invincible] ... ." There is a further provision in the contract, in clause 2(g), that "Mr. Giles shall be appointed a director of Trafalgar." It is from the first of these two provisions that the main difficulty arises. By clause 8 the sale and purchase of the shares was to be completed "as soon as practicable."

After the death of Mr. Morris on January 10, 1971, various discussions took place which all came to nothing. Completion was originally fixed for December 31, 1970, but did not take place. During March and April 1971 various dates for completion were arranged, but still completion did not take place. On March 18, the solicitors for the defendants gave the plaintiff notice to complete within seven days, so that some time after the death of Mr. Morris the defendants, far from resisting completion, were pressing for it. Five of the defendants have for over five months expressed themselves as being willing to comply with the terms of the agreement, and no order is sought against them on this motion; nor is any order sought against the defendant Mr. Tyson, who is abroad and has not been served. The respondents to the motion for committal and sequestration are the defendants Mrs. Morris and Mrs. Matthews, who are the administrators of Mr. Morris; Mr. Thurgood; and Defiance.

The plaintiff's writ claiming specific performance was issued on June 22, 1971; and on September 8, 1971, Master Dinwiddy heard an application by the plaintiff for summary judgment for specific performance under RSC, Ord. 86. The defendants who are willing to perform the contract were represented by solicitors; the first defendant was in person, and the other defendants were represented by counsel. All defendants consented to the master making an order for specific performance; and the order made was for the defendants to procure that various specified acts be done before 4 p.m. on October 4, 1971, or subsequently within four days after service of the order. Two of the acts in question were the execution by Invincible of the service agreement with Mr. Giles, and the appointment of Mr. Giles as a director of Trafalgar.

On October 4, 1971, the board of Invincible met. By then, four additional directors had been appointed; and by six votes to one the board refused to appoint Mr. Giles as a managing director of Invincible on the terms of the service agreement or at all. The board has also expressed its refusal to have Mr. Giles appointed as a director of Trafalgar. The board's objections to Mr. Giles are based on allegations of his inexperience in motor insurance, his conduct while taking part in the running of Trafalgar for a period which began over three months before Mr. Morris's death and continued for some six months in all, and a number of other matters, including the importance to the public of a motor insurance business being conducted on sound financial lines, and allegations of Mr. Giles' intention to adopt policies of which the board does not approve. The board recognises that the agreement is legally binding, and has expressed the willingness of the board to perform the whole of it except the two provisions that I have mentioned; but the board seeks to be released from the order so far as it relates to these two provisions.

As I have mentioned, the order is a consent order. The consent was given on the advice of experienced junior counsel practising in this division. Every objection to performing the two disputed obligations was known to the defendants when they gave their consent to the making of the order. Leading counsel now says on behalf of the defendants for whom he appears that the advice given them by junior counsel was wrong, and that had they put forward the objections which they now urge it is at least highly doubtful whether the order would have been made. That may be so, or it may not. The fact remains that, with no change of circumstances, the defendants are refusing to carry out the order for specific performances to which, on advice, they consented. Mr. Harman says that they are willing to pay damages, but that the court should not use the remedies of committal and sequestration to secure the appointment of Mr. Giles to directorships and a position under a service agreement from which, said Mr. Harman, Mr. Giles would be promptly excluded in breach of contract, thus giving rise to a claim for damages.

It is true that the defendants cannot directly control the directors of Invincible in this respect; but the defendants have sufficient control of Invincible to be able to remove the appointment of a managing director to the company in general meeting, and in that way "procure" the necessary appointment in accordance with the agreement and the order. The plaintiff in fact has put forward a draft special resolution for this purpose in an affidavit sworn over a week before Day 1 of this motion. The defendants have done nothing towards taking this step. Nor have they done anything towards setting aside the judgment. Until in court on Day 1, the defendants had not even mentioned to the plaintiff's solicitors or counsel that they intended to do anything of the kind. There was no more than a part of a single sentence in an affidavit sworn the day before Day 1 by one of the directors of Defiance and Trafalgar who is not a party to these proceedings, respectfully asking on behalf of the board of Invincible that they should be released from any part of the order which would compel them to appoint Mr. Giles a managing director of Invincible. Not only did that request somewhat miss the point, but also it seemed to be advanced merely as part of a defence against the motion for committal and sequestration, on the footing that the order of the court would remain in force but that to this extent the defendants should not be required to obey it.

The course of the proceedings was that on Day 1 Mr. Neill opened the motion, and towards the end of the day Mr. Harman began his reply. Initially, Mr. Harman appeared to be proceeding on the footing of putting forward a defence to the motion based on contentions such as the order for specific performance being an order that never should have been made, the public importance of motor insurance companies being properly conducted by experienced persons, and the futility of procuring the appointment of Mr. Giles as a managing director of Invincible when the board would, he asserted, promptly dismiss him in breach of contract and pay damages. However, Mr. Harman ultimately accepted that there were difficulties in this line of argument so long as the order for specific performance stood, not least in the contention that it was a good defence to a motion for contempt that there was a firm resolution to persist in the contempt. He accepted that it was necessary or at least desirable for him to apply to vary or discharge the consent order.

A weekend happily intervened, and on Day 2, with Mr. Neill not objecting to the shortness of notice, Mr. Harman moved under a cross notice of motion to vary or discharge the consent order. ...

What I have to consider is whether the presence in the agreement of clause 2(f), providing for Mr. Giles to enter into a service agreement with Invincible in the form of the draft annexed to the contract, prevents the court from decreeing specific performance of the entire agreement, including that subclause. It will be observed that there is no question of the plaintiff seeking to enforce any order of the court which will compel any of the defendants to carry out, either as employer or employee, any personal services. The order made is an order to procure "the execution by the company of the engrossment" of the service agreement. The question is whether such an order falls within the principle that the court will not decree specific performance of a contract for personal services.

On the face of it the answer must be No. There is no question of the execution of the decree requiring constant superintendence by the court of a continuous series of acts such as arose in *Ryan v. Mutual Tontine Westminster Chambers Association*, [1893] 1 Ch. 116 (CA), a case that was mentioned but not cited during argument. All that the decree requires in this respect is the procuring of a single act, namely, the execution of the service agreement. When that has been done, the question of any breach of the service agreement and any remedies for that breach is one between Invincible and Mr. Giles, and not between Invincible and the plaintiff. Invincible, too, is a party neither to the contract nor to the action.

The distinction between an order to perform a contract for services and an order to procure the execution of such a contract seems to me to be sound both in principle and on authority. I do not think that the mere fact that the contract to be made is one of which the court would not decree specific performance is a ground for refusing to decree that the contract be entered into. ... [Thus, in *Wilson v. West Hartlepool Railway Co.* (1865), 2 De GJ & S 475; 46 ER 459 (CA)] Knight Bruce LJ said, at p. 488 (p. 464 (ER)):

I agree that there may be and have been cases in which it may well be and has been held that there may, under a bill for specific performance of a contract, be a decree against a defendant to execute a deed containing covenants on his part to do acts of which, from their nature, specific performance could not directly be enforced. But the present I think not a case of that description.

As Turner LJ held not only that the agreement did contemplate the execution of a further deed, but also that the execution of such a deed should be specifically enforced, I think it is clear that both members of the court took the view that specific performance may be decreed of an agreement to execute an instrument even if the obligations under that instrument would not be specifically enforced. ...

That is not the only authority to this effect. Thus there is *Granville v. Betts* (1848), 18 LJ Ch. 32, of which *Fry* says, at p. 389: "The real contract here which the court enforces is a contract to execute the deed"; and see *Stocker v. Wedderburn* (1857), 3 K & J 393 at p. 403; 69 ER 1162 at p. 1166 (Ch.). ... Indeed, were the rule otherwise, I do not see why a lessor could not resist specific performance of a contract to grant a lease if that lease contained any term of which specific performance would not be granted, such a provision like that in *Ryan's* case for the services of a porter, or for repairs; yet he cannot: see *Paxton v. Newton* (1854), 2 Sm. & G 437; 65 ER 470 (Ch.).

There is a further consideration. The obligation to enter into a service agreement is merely one part of a contract which deals with many other matters; and that obligation is the only part of that complex which is said not to be specifically enforceable. Now there is authority for saying that the mere presence in a contract of one provision which, by itself, would not be specifically enforceable (because, for example, it requires the performance of personal services) does not prevent the contract as a whole from being specifically enforced. This is so even if the obligation to perform personal services could be enforced only, for instance, by ordering sequestration: see *Fortescue v. Lostwithiel and Fowey Railway Co.*, [1894] 3 Ch. 621; *Fry on Specific Performance* at p. 53. In such cases, the contract must be regarded as a whole, and the court may refuse to let the disadvantages and difficulties of specifically enforcing the obligation to perform personal services outweigh the suitability of the rest of the contract for specific performance, and the desirability of the contract as a whole being enforced. After all, *pacta sunt servanda*.

One day, perhaps, the courts will look again at the so-called rule that contracts for personal services or involving the continuous performance of services will not be specifically enforced. Such a rule is plainly not absolute and without exception, nor do I think that it can be based on any narrow consideration such as difficulties of constant superintendence by the court. Mandatory injunctions are by no means unknown, and there is normally no question of the court having to send its officers to supervise the performance of the order of the court. Prohibitory injunctions are common, and again there is no direct supervision by the court. Performance of each type of injunction is normally secured by the realisation of the person enjoined that he is liable to be punished for contempt if evidence of his disobedience to the order is put before the court; and if the injunction is prohibitory, actual committal will usually, so long as it continues, make disobedience impossible. If instead the order is for specific performance of a contract for personal services, a similar machinery of enforcement could be employed, again without there being any question of supervision by any officer of the court. The reasons why the court is reluctant to decree specific performance of a contract for personal services (and I would regard it as a strong reluctance rather than a rule) are, I think, more complex and more firmly bottomed on human nature. If a singer contracts to sing, there could no doubt be proceedings for committal if, ordered to sing, the singer remained obstinately dumb. But if instead the singer sang flat, or sharp, or too fast, or too slowly, or too loudly, or too quietly, or resorted to a dozen of the manifestations of temperament traditionally associated with some singers, the threat of committal would reveal itself as a most unsatisfactory weapon: for who could say whether the imperfections of performance were natural or self-induced? To make an order with such possibilities of evasion would be vain; and so the order will not be made. However, not all contracts of personal service or for the continuous performance of services are as dependent as this on matters of opinion and judgment, nor do all such contracts involve the same degree of the daily impact of person upon person. In general, no doubt, the inconvenience and mischief of decreeing specific performance of most of such contracts will greatly outweigh the advantages, and specific performance will be refused. But I do not think that it should be assumed that as soon as any element of personal service or continuous services can be discerned in a contract the court will, without more, refuse specific performance. Of course, a requirement for the continuous performance of services has the disadvantage that repeated breaches may engender repeated applications to the court for enforcement. But so may many injunctions; and the prospects of repetition, although an important consideration, ought not to be allowed to negative a right. As is so often the case in equity, the matter is one of the balance of advantage and disadvantage in relation to the particular obligations in question; and the fact that the balance will usually lie on one side does not turn this probability into a rule. The present case, of course, is a fortiori, since the contract of which specific performance has been decreed requires not the performance of personal services or any continuous series of acts, but merely procuring the execution of an agreement which contains a provision for such services or acts.

It follows that in my judgment the agreement is specifically enforceable, the consent order was properly made, and the advice by junior counsel that there was no defence to the action on this score was sound advice. In those circumstances, I can see no defence to the plaintiff's motion to enforce the order.

NOTES

1. Why have the courts of equity been so reluctant to enforce contracts of personal service?

2. In *Giles v. Morris*, is there any real value to the plaintiffs of an order merely requiring Invincible to execute the service agreement with Giles in light of the fact that Invincible (after executing it) will refuse to perform? What then? If Giles sues Invincible for specific performance, would the court enforce the contract of personal services? Is Megarry J signalling the willingness on the part of modern courts to soften the rule that courts will not specifically enforce a contract of hiring and service? (see *Hill v. Parsons*, below).

Many of the cases relating to contracts of personal service involve claims for injunctions rather than for specific performance. In a typical case where S agrees to become an employee of M and then defaults, counsel for M, the plaintiff, may contemplate suing for specific performance requiring S to serve M for the agreed-upon period. After reviewing the authorities, however, and noting the reluctance of the courts to enforce contracts of personal service, it is more likely that counsel for M will seek another way of accomplishing the same result without asking the courts to undo 150 years of "good law." If, for example, in agreeing to serve M, S also promised not to serve anyone else, counsel for M may seek an injunction to restrain S from working for another in the hope that S will honour his or her contract with M.

We have considered the law of injunctions elsewhere in these materials but it is important to note this inter-relationship between the remedies of specific performance and injunction when dealing with contracts of personal service.

Lumley v. Wagner
(1852), 1 DM & G 604; 42 ER 687 (Ch.)

[Johanna Wagner (niece of Richard) agreed with Benjamin Lumley to sing operatic roles at Her Majesty's Theatre in London for a period of three months from April 1, 1852. Further, she agreed not to "use her talents at any other theatre, nor in any concert or reunion, public or private" without Lumley's consent for that same period.]

[LORD ST. LEONARDS LC:] The present is a mixed case, consisting not of two correlative acts to be done—one by the Plaintiff, and the other by the Defendants, which state of facts may have and in some cases has introduced a very important difference—but of an act to be done by J. Wagner alone, to which is superadded a negative stipulation on her part to abstain from the commission of any act which will break in upon her affirmative covenant; the one being ancillary to, concurrent and operating together with, the other. The agreement to sing for the Plaintiff during three months at his theatre, and during that time not to sing for anybody else, is not a correlative contract, it is in effect one contract; and though beyond all doubt this Court could not interfere to enforce the specific performance of the whole of this contract, yet in all sound construction, and according to the true spirit of the agreement, the engagement to perform for three months at one theatre must necessarily exclude the right to perform at the same time at another theatre. It was clearly intended that J. Wagner was to exert her vocal abilities to the utmost to aid the theatre to which she agreed to attach herself. I am of opinion that if she had attempted, even in the absence of any negative stipulation, to perform at another theatre, she would have broken the spirit and true meaning of the contract as much as she would now do with reference to the contract into which she has actually entered.

Wherever this Court has not proper jurisdiction to enforce specific performance, it operates to bind men's consciences, as far as they can be bound, to a true and literal performance of their agreements; and it will not suffer them to depart from their contracts at their pleasure, leaving the party with whom they have contracted to the mere chance of any damages which a jury may give. The exercise of this jurisdiction has, I believe, had a wholesome tendency towards the maintenance of that good faith which exists in this country to a much greater degree perhaps than in any other; and although the jurisdiction is not to be extended, yet a Judge would desert his duty who did not act up to what his predecessors have handed down as the rule for his guidance in the administration of such an equity.

It was objected that the operation of the injunction in the present case was mischievous, excluding the Defendant J. Wagner from performing at any other theatre while this Court had no power to compel her to perform at Her Majesty's Theatre. It is true that I have not the means of compelling her to sing, but she has no cause of complaint if I compel her to abstain from the commission of an act which she has bound herself not to do, and thus possibly cause her to fulfil her engagement. The jurisdiction which I now exercise is wholly within the power of the Court, and being of opinion that it is a proper case for interfering, I shall leave nothing unsatisfied by the judgment I pronounce. The effect, too, of the injunction in restraining J. Wagner from singing elsewhere may, in the event of an action being brought against her by the Plaintiff, prevent any such amount of vindictive damages being given against her as a jury might probably be inclined to give if she had carried her talents and exercised them at the rival theatre: the injunction may also, as I have said, tend to the fulfilment of her engagement; though, in continuing the injunction, I disclaim doing indirectly what I cannot do directly. …

The authority of *Clarke v. Price* ((1819), 2 Wils. 157; 37 ER 270 (Ch.)) was much pressed upon me by the learned counsel for the Defendants; but that is a case which does not properly belong to their argument, because there there was no negative stipulation, and I quite admit that this Court cannot enforce the performance of such an affirmative stipulation as is to be found in that case; there the Defendant having agreed to take notes of cases in the Court of Exchequer, and compose reports for the Plaintiff, and having failed to do so, the Plaintiff, Mr. Clarke, filed a bill for an injunction, and Lord Eldon, when refusing the injunction, in effect, said, I cannot compel Mr. Price to sit in the Court of Exchequer and take notes and compose reports; and the whole of his judgment shews that he proceeded (and so it has been considered in later cases) on the ground that there was no covenant, on the part of the Defendant, that he would not compose reports for any other person. The expressions in the judgment are:—"I cannot, as in the other case" (referring to *Morris v. Colman* ((1812), 18 Ves. 437; 34 ER 382 (Ch.)), "say that I will induce him to write for the Plaintiff by preventing him from writing for any other person"; and then come these important words "for that is not the nature of the agreement." Lord Eldon, therefore, was of opinion, upon the construction of that agreement, that it would be against its meaning to affix to it a negative quality and import a covenant into it by implication, and he, therefore, very properly, as I conceive, refused that injunction; that case, therefore, in no respect touches the question now before me, and I may at once declare that if I had only to deal with the affirmative covenant of the Defendant J. Wagner that she would perform at Her Majesty's Theatre, I should not have granted any injunction. …

The case of *Hooper v. Brodrick* ((1840), 11 Sim. 47; 59 ER 791 (Ch.)) was cited, as an instance in which the Court had refused an injunction under circumstances like the present; but, in that case, the lessee of an inn had covenanted to use and keep it open as an inn during a certain time, and not to do any act whereby the licence might become forfeited. In point of fact, the application was that he might be compelled to keep it open, and the Vice-Chancellor makes this observation: "The Court ought not to have restrained the Defendant from discontinuing to use and keep open the demised premises as an inn, which is the same in effect as ordering him to carry on the business of an innkeeper; but it might have restrained him from doing, or causing or permitting to be done, any act which would have put it out of his power, or the power of any other person, to carry on that business on the premises. It is not, however, shewn that the Defendant has threatened, or intends to do, or to cause or permit to be done, any act whereby the licences may become forfeited or be refused; and, therefore, the injunction must be dissolved." That, therefore, is an authority directly against the Defendants, because it shews that if there had been an intention to break the negative covenant, this Court would have granted the injunction.

NOTES

1. In *Yule Inc. v. Atlantic Pizza Delight Franchise (1968) Ltd.* in chapter 8, "Interlocutory Injunctions," Cory J notes that an injunction will issue in personal service cases only where there is a specific negative covenant. He notes that the approach of the courts to other contracts is less restrictive.

2. In *Ryan v. Mutual Tontine Westminster Chambers Association*, above, Kay LJ cited *Lumley v. Wagner* and noted the importance of negative covenants in obtaining relief.

3. See Stephen M. Waddams, "Johanna Wagner and the Rival Opera Houses" (2001), 117 *Law Q Rev.* 431.

Warner Brothers Pictures Incorporated v. Nelson
[1937] 1 KB 209

BRANSON J: The facts of this case are few and simple. The plaintiffs are a firm of film producers in the United States of America. In 1931 the defendant, [Bette Davis,] then not well known as a film actress, entered into a contract with the plaintiffs. Before the expiration of that contract the present contract was entered into between the parties. Under it the defendant received a considerably enhanced salary, the other conditions being substantially the same. This contract was for fifty-two weeks and contains options to the plaintiffs to extend it for further periods of fifty-two weeks, at ever-increasing amounts of salary, to the defendant. No question of construction arises upon the contract, and it is not necessary to refer to it in any great detail; but, in view of some of the contentions raised, it is desirable to call attention quite generally to some of the provisions contained in it. It is a stringent contract, under which the defendant agrees "to render her exclusive services as a motion picture and/ or legitimate stage actress" to the plaintiffs, and agrees to perform solely and exclusively for them. She also agrees, by way of negative stipulation, that "she will not, during such time"— that is to say, during the term of the contract—"render any services for or in any other photographic, stage or motion picture production or productions or business of any other person ... or engage in any other occupation without the written consent of the producers being first had and obtained."

With regard to the term of the contract there is a further clause, clause 23, under which, if the defendant fails, refuses or neglects to perform her services under the contract, the plaintiffs "have the right to extend the term of this agreement and all of its provisions for a period equivalent to the period during which such failure, refusal or neglect shall be continued."

In June of this year the defendant, for no discoverable reason except that she wanted more money, declined to be further bound by the agreement, left the United States, and in September entered into an agreement in this country with a third person. This was a breach of contract on her part, and the plaintiffs on September 9 commenced this action, claiming a declaration that the contract was valid and binding, an injunction to restrain the defendant from acting in breach of it, and damages. The defence alleged that the plaintiffs had committed breaches of the contract which entitled the defendant to treat it as at an end. At the trial this contention was abandoned, and the defendant admitted that the plaintiffs had not broken the contract and that she had; but it was contended on her behalf that no injunction could as a matter of law be granted in the circumstances of the case.

At the outset of the considerations of law which arise stands the question, not raised by the pleadings but urged for the defendant in argument, that this contract is unlawful, as being in restraint of trade. The ground for this contention was that the contract compelled the defendant to serve the plaintiffs exclusively, and might in certain circumstances endure for the whole of her natural life. No authority was cited to me in support of the proposition that such a contract is illegal, and I see no reason for so holding. Where, as in the present contract, the covenants are all concerned with what is to happen whilst the defendant is employed by the plaintiffs and not thereafter, there is no room for the application of the doctrine of restraint of trade.

A similar contract came before the Courts in the case of *Guamont-British Picture Corporation, Ltd. v. Alexander* (1936), 2 All ER 1686 (KB), and was upheld by Porter J I respectfully agree with its view. I turn then to the consideration of the law applicable to this case on the basis that the contract is a valid and enforceable one. It is conceded that our Courts will not enforce a positive covenant of personal service; and specific performance of the positive covenants by the defendant to serve the plaintiff is not asked in the present case. The practice of the Court of Chancery in relation to the enforcement of negative covenants is stated on the highest authority by Lord Cairns LC in the House of Lords in *Doherty v. Allman* (1878), 3 App. Cas. 709 (HL (Eng.)). His Lordship said (at p. 719):

> My Lords, if there had been a negative covenant, I apprehend according to well-settled practice, a Court of Equity would have had no discretion to exercise. If parties, for valuable consideration, with their eyes open, contract that a particular thing shall not be done, all that a Court of Equity has to do is to say, by way of injunction, that which the parties have already said by way of covenant, that the thing shall not be done; and in such case the injunction does nothing more than give the sanction of the process of the Court to that which already is the contract between the parties. It is not then a question of the balance of convenience or inconvenience, or of the amount of damage or of injury—it is the specific performance by the Court of that negative bargain which the parties have made, with their eyes open, between themselves.

That was not a case of a contract of personal service; but the same principle had already been applied to such a contract by Lord St. Leonards in *Lumley v. Wagner*. The Lord Chancellor used the following language ((1852), 1 De GM & G 604 at p. 619; 42 ER 689 at p. 693):

> Wherever this Court has not proper jurisdiction to enforce specific performance, it operates to bind men's consciences, as far as they can be bound, to a true and literal performance of their agreements; and it will not suffer them to depart from their contracts at their pleasure, leaving the party with whom they have contracted to the mere chance of any damages which a jury may give. The exercise of this jurisdiction has, I believe, had a wholesome tendency towards the maintenance of that good faith which exists in this country to a much greater degree perhaps than in any other, and although the jurisdiction is not to be extended, yet a Judge would desert his duty who did not act up to what his predecessors have handed down as the rule for his guidance in the administration of such an equity.

… The defendant, having broken her positive undertakings in the contract, without any cause or excuse which she was prepared to support in the witness-box, contends that she cannot be enjoined from breaking the negative covenants also. The mere fact that a covenant which the Court would not enforce if expressed in positive form, is expressed in the negative instead, will not induce the Court to enforce it. That appears, if authority be needed for such a proposition, from *Davis v. Foreman*, [1894] 3 Ch. 654, *Kirchner & Co. v. Gruban*, [1909] 1 Ch. 413 and *Chapman v. Westerby*, [1913] WN 277. The Court will attend to the substance and not to the form of the covenant. Nor will the Court, true to the principle that specific performance of a contract of personal service will never be ordered, grant an injunction in the case of such contract to enforce negative covenants if the effect of so doing would be to drive the defendant either to starvation or to specific performance of the positive covenants ... .

In *Rely-a-Bell Burglar and Fire Alarm Co. v. Eisler*, [1926] Ch. 609 Russell J, as he then was, said at p. 615 ... :

> It was said on the other side that there were points of distinction. It was said that the covenants in those two cases were so framed that the servant, if the covenants were enforced, could make his living neither by serving nor by carrying on business independently, whereas in the present case the covenant only prohibited serving. Therefore, it was said, he was still free to start in business on his own account, and it could not be said, if an injunction were granted in the terms of the covenant, that he would be forced to remain idle and starve. That distinction seems to me somewhat of a mockery. It would be idle to tell this defendant, a servant employed at a wage, that he must not serve anybody else in that capacity, but that the world was still open to him to start business as an independent man. It seems to me that if I were to restrain this man according to the terms of the covenant, he would be forced to remain idle and starve.

Had it not been for that view of the facts, I think that the learned Judge would have granted an injunction in that case.

The conclusion to be drawn from the authorities is that, where a contract of personal service contains negative covenants the enforcement of which will not amount either to a decree of specific performance of the positive covenants of the contract or to the giving of a decree under which the defendant must either remain idle or perform those positive covenants, the Court will enforce these negative covenants; but this is subject to a further consideration. An injunction is a discretionary remedy, and the Court in granting it may limit it to what the Court considers reasonable in all the circumstances of the case.

This appears from the judgment of the Court of Appeal in *Robinson & Co. v. Heuer*. The particular covenant in that case provided that (at p. 452) Heuer

> shall not during this engagement, without the previous consent in writing of the said W. Robinson & Co. Ltd., ... carry on or be engaged either directly or indirectly, as principal, agent, servant, or otherwise, in any trade, business, or calling, either relating to goods of any description sold or manufactured by the said W. Robinson & Co. Ltd. ... or in any other business whatsoever.

[In his judgment, Lindley MR says:]

> When, however, you come to talk about an injunction to enforce it, there is great difficulty. The real difficulty which has always to be borne in mind when you talk about specific performance of or injunctions to enforce an agreement is this—that this Court will never enforce an agreement by which one person undertakes to be the servant of another; and if this agreement were enforced in its terms, it would compel this gentleman personally to serve the plaintiffs for the period of ten years. That the Court never does. Therefore an injunction in those terms cannot be granted, although the agreement to serve the plaintiffs and give his whole care, time, and attention to their business, and not to engage in any other business during his engagement, is valid in point of law. But the plaintiffs do not ask for an injunction in the terms of that agreement.

Before parting with that case, I should say that the Court there proceeded to sever the covenants and to grant an injunction, not to restrain the defendant from carrying on any other business whatsoever, but framed so as to give what was felt to be a reasonable protection to the plaintiffs and no more. The plaintiffs waived an option which they possessed to extend the period of service for an extra five years and the injunction then was granted for the remaining period of unextended time. ...

The case before me is, therefore, one in which it would be proper to grant an injunction unless to do so would, in the circumstances, be tantamount to ordering the defendant to perform her contract, or remain idle, or unless damages would be the more appropriate remedy.

With regard to the first of these considerations, it would, of course, be impossible to grant an injunction covering all the negative covenants in the contract. That would, indeed, force the defendant to perform her contract or remain idle; but this objection is removed by the restricted form in which the injunction is sought. It is confined to forbidding the defendant, without the consent of the plaintiffs, to render any services for or in any motion picture or stage production for anyone other than the plaintiffs.

It was also urged that the difference between what the defendant can earn as a film artist and what she might expect to earn by any other form of activity is so great that she will in effect be driven to perform her contract. That is not the criterion adopted in any of the decided cases. The defendant is stated to be a person of intelligence, capacity and means, and no evidence was deduced to show that, if enjoined from doing the specified acts otherwise than for the plaintiffs, she will not be able to employ herself both usefully and remuneratively in other spheres of activity, though not so remuneratively as in her special line. She will not be driven, although she may be tempted, to perform the contract, and the fact that she may be so tempted is no objection to the grant of an injunction. This appears from the judgment of Lord St. Leonards in *Lumley v. Wagner*, where he used the following language (1 De GM & G at p. 619; 42 ER at p. 693):

> It was objected that the operation of the injunction in the present case was mischievous, excluding the defendant J. Wagner from performing at any other theatre while this Court had no power to compel her to perform at Her Majesty's Theatre. It is true, that I have not the means of compelling her to sing, but she has no cause of complaint if I compel her to abstain from the conclusion of an act which she has bound herself not to do, and thus possibly cause her to fulfil her engagement. The jurisdiction which I now exercise is wholly within the power of the Court, and being of opinion that it is a proper case for interfering, I shall leave nothing unsatisfied by the judgment I pronounce. The effect too of the injunction, in restraining J. Wagner from singing elsewhere may, in the event ... of an action being brought against her by the plaintiff, prevent any such amount of vindictive damages being given against her as a jury might probably be inclined to give if she had carried her talents and exercised them at the rival theatre: the injunction may also, as I have said, tend to the fulfilment of her engagement; though, in continuing the injunction, I disclaim doing indirectly what I cannot do directly.

With regard to the question whether damages is not the more appropriate remedy, I have the uncontradicted evidence of the plaintiffs as to the difficulty of estimating the damages which they may suffer from the breach by the defendant of her contract. I think it is not inappropriate to refer to the fact that in the contract between the parties in clause 22 there is a formal admission by the defendant that her services, being "of a special, unique, extra-ordinary and intellectual character," gives them a particular value "the loss of which cannot be reasonably or adequately compensated in damages" and that a breach may "cost the producer great and irreparable injury and damage," and the artist expressly agrees that the producer shall be entitled to the remedy of injunction. Of course, parties cannot contract themselves out of the law, but it assists, at all events on the question of evidence as to the applicability of an injunction in the present case, to find the parties formally recognizing that in cases of this kind injunction is a more appropriate remedy than damages.

Furthermore, in the case of *Grimston v. Cunningham*, [1894] 1 QB 125 (CA), which was also a case in which a theatrical manager was attempting to enforce against an actor a nega-tive stipulation against going elsewhere, Wills J, granted an injunction, and used the follow-ing language (at p. 139):

> This is an agreement of a kind which is pre-eminently subject to the interference of the Court by injunction, for in cases of this nature it very often happens that the injury suffered in conse-quence of the breach of the agreement would be out of all proportion to any pecuniary damages which could be proved or assessed by a jury. This circumstance affords a strong reason in favour of exercising the discretion of the Court by granting an injunction.

I think that that applies to the present case also, and that an injunction should be granted in regard to the specified services.

Then comes the question as to the period for which the injunction should operate. The period of the contract, now that the plaintiffs have undertaken not as from October 16, 1936, to exercise the rights of suspension conferred upon them by clause 23 thereof, will, if they exercise their options to prolong it, extend to about May 1942. As I read the judgment of the Court of Appeal in *Robinson & Co. v. Heuer*, the Court should make the period such as to give reasonable protection, and no more, to the plaintiffs against the ill-effects to them of the defendant's breach of contract. The evidence as to that was perhaps necessarily some-what vague. The main difficulty that the plaintiffs apprehend is that the defendant might appear in other films, whilst the films already made by them and not yet shown are in the market for sale or hire, and thus depreciate their value. I think that if the injunction is in force during the continuance of the contract, or for three years from now, whichever period is the shorter, that will substantially meet the case.

The other matter is as to the area within which the injunction is to operate. The contract is not an English contract and the parties are not British subjects. In my opinion all that properly concerns this Court is to prevent the defendant from committing the prohibited acts within the jurisdiction of this Court, and the injunction will be limited accordingly.

NOTE

1. On whether a restrictive covenant running with a personal services contract can be held to be illegal for being in restraint of trade, compare *Instone v. Schroeder*, below. See, however, *Detroit Football Co. v. Dublinski*, the next case, for Canadian acceptance of *Warner Brothers v. Nelson* on this issue.

2. *Doherty v. Allman* is discussed briefly in chapter 11.

S.M. Waddams, ed., *Milner's Cases and Materials on Contracts*
4th ed. (Toronto: Emond Montgomery Publications, 1985), at 114

BETTE DAVIS, THE LONELY LIFE. 1962. Chapter eleven and the first part of chapter twelve of this autobiography tell in some detail the story of *Warner Brothers v. Nelson* from Mrs. Nelson's point of view. When she left the United States she had already won an Academy Award, and felt confined by her contract and convinced that Warner Brothers had no serious intention of letting her choose her own parts or find parts she would approve. A few other actors and actresses were also battling the restrictive terms of the standard form of actor's contract. Mrs. Nelson mentions familiar names, James Cagney, Margaret Sullivan, Carole Lombard and Eddie Cantor. In a comparatively new industry, the "stars" were beginning to realize their contribution and were rebelling against the "slavery" of the contract designed to serve the convenience of a more experienced business management. Apparently Mrs. Nelson thought she could not be stopped from working abroad. The litigation cost Mrs. Nelson over $30,000. Sir William Jowitt, retained for the defence, had "recommended" that Mrs. Nelson immediately give him a $10,000 retainer. At this time Mrs. Nelson was, of course, under suspension and receiving no salary. Her decision not to appeal was largely influenced by the actor George Arliss, who had said, "I admire your courage in this affair but now—go back and face them proudly." In fact, Warner Brothers welcomed Mrs. Nelson with open arms and graciously assumed their share of the costs and part of hers. Their standard form had received a shot in the arm that gave assurance to the management side of the whole film industry. In recent years several Hollywood actors have assumed the added role of producer in order to overcome the restraints of the older standard forms.

Detroit Football Co. v. Dublinski; Detroit Football Co. v. Mains
[1955] 4 DLR 176 (Ont. HC)

WELLS J: A motion was made in each of these two actions for an order enjoining the defendant pending the trial of the action from breach of his contract with the plaintiff.

While the facts in each case are not precisely the same they were of sufficient similarity to let the matters be argued together.

What the plaintiff is asking for in each case is an interlocutory injunction enforcing until trial the negative covenants contained in the agreement between the plaintiff company and the defendants Mains and Dublinski respectively. The clause under which the application is brought is para. 5 of the "Standard Players Contract" of the National Football League and is the same in each case. It is as follows:

> 5. The Player promises and agrees that during the term of this contract he will not play football or engage in activities related to football for any other person, firm, corporation or institution except with the prior written consent of the Club and the Commissioner, and that he will not during the term of this contract engage in any game or exhibition of baseball, basketball, hockey, wrestling, boxing or any other sport which endangers his ability to perform his services hereunder, without the prior written consent of the Club. The Player likewise promises and agrees that during the term of this contract, when, as and if he shall receive an invitation

to participate in any All-Star football game which is approved by the League, he will play in said game in accordance with all the terms and conditions relating thereto, including the player compensation therein set forth, as are agreed to between the League and the Sponsor of such game.

Originally the interlocutory injunction was a device used to preserve some property right pending a trial and to maintain matters *in statu quo*. Without going into the matter in detail, the principles on which the Courts acts are succinctly set out in 18 Hals. 2nd ed., p. 27, s. 41, where the learned editor states as follows:

> 41. In cases of interlocutory injunctions in aid of the plaintiff's right, all the Court usually has to consider is whether the case is so clear and free from objection on equitable grounds that it ought to interfere without waiting for the right to be finally established. This depends upon a variety of circumstances, and it is impossible to lay down any general rule on the subject by which the discretion of the Court ought in all cases to be regulated. It is not necessary that the Court should find a case which would entitle the plaintiff to relief at all events: it is quite sufficient if the Court finds a case which shows that there is a substantial question to be investigated, and that matters ought to be preserved *in statu quo* until that question can be finally disposed of.

Section 43 is also of interest and the opening sentence of s. 44 I think has application to the matter before me. They are as follows:

> 43. Where the plaintiff is asserting a right, he should show, at least, a strong *prima facie* case in support of the right which he asserts, but the mere fact that there is a doubt as to the existence of such right is not sufficient to prevent the Court from granting an injunction, although it is a matter for serious attention. Where the application is to restrain the exercise of an alleged right, the plaintiff should show that there are substantial grounds for doubting the existence of such right.
>
> 44. The plaintiff must also as a rule be able to show that an injunction until the hearing is necessary to protect him against irreparable injury; mere inconvenience is not enough. By the term "irreparable injury" is meant injury which is substantial and could never be adequately remedied or atoned for by damages.

The matter was recently discussed in our own Courts by my Lord the Chief Justice of the High Court in *The Chesapeake & Ohio R Co. v. Ball*, [1953] OR 843, where he said at pp. 854-5:

> The granting of an interlocutory injunction is a matter of judicial discretion, but it is a discretion to be exercised on judicial principles. I have dealt with this matter at length because I wish to emphasize how important it is that parties should not be restrained by interlocutory injunctions unless some irreparable injury is likely to accrue to the plaintiff, and the Court should be particularly cautious where there is a serious question as to whether the plaintiff would ever succeed in the action. I may put it in a different way: If on one hand a fair *prima facie* case is made out and there will be irreparable damage if the injunction is not granted, it should be granted, but in deciding whether an interlocutory injunction should be granted the defendant's interests must receive the same consideration as the plaintiff's.

In the case at bar it was argued on behalf of the applicant that irreparable damage would be done it if the negative covenants in para. 5 were not enforced pending the trial of the action. ...

[The] loss to the plaintiff is described in para. 7 in the case of Dublinski and para. 6 in the case of Mains, in Mr. Kerbawy's affidavits, where he says:

> The plaintiff has expended considerable sums in training the said defendant as a professional football player to the standards maintained in the National Football League and as an asset to the said plaintiff. The said expenses include the cost of maintenance of an adequate scouting system to find new players and the maintenance of a training camp and necessary transportation and of providing each player with medical care.

Affidavits were also filed by the defendants in which various facts connected with the alleged breach of contract were set out. ...

Mr. Dublinski, after setting out his negotiations with the plaintiff company, states as follows in para. 14:

> My livelihood is solely dependent on my playing professional football, and if restrained from playing for the Toronto Argonauts, I will be unable to earn a livelihood.

Mains in his affidavit says this in para. 13:

> My livelihood is dependent really on my playing football, and it is only because I am to play for the Toronto Argonauts that I have been given an opportunity to wrestle in Toronto in the off season. If restrained from playing football and wrestling, I will be unable to earn any livelihood.

The defendants were not cross-examined on their affidavits and this evidence, however strange it may seem, stands unimpeached and uncontradicted. It is quite clear on the material that the breach in relation to which the actions are brought took place while the contract between the parties was still in good standing, that is, before May 1, 1955.

A great deal of the argument before me was adduced to distinguishing between the two lines of authorities which are found in the cases, namely, those stemming from the great authority of Lord St. Leonards LC in *Lumley v. Wagner* (1852), 1 De GM & G 604, 42 ER 687, and those cases in which injunctions have been refused. A review of the authorities, of which there are many, leads one to the conclusion which counsel for the defendants stated, that speaking very roughly the guiding principle would seem to be that where a matter of unfair competition is involved or where the services are of a special or unique quality, loss of which cannot be reasonably estimated in damages, negative covenants are frequently enforced, but seldom otherwise. Specific performance of a contract of service cannot be obtained in this way.

It was also argued before me that the clauses in question were void as being in restraint of trade. In respect of that the observations of Branson J in *Warner Bros. Pictures Inc. v. Nelson*, [1937] 1 KB 209, are of value and with respect I follow his reasoning, as he points out at p. 214:

> Where, as in the present contract, the covenants are all concerned with what is to happen whilst the defendant is employed by the plaintiffs and not thereafter, there is no room for the application of the doctrine of restraint of trade. ...

Later on in this very lucid and comprehensive judgment Branson J, after discussing the cases where negative covenants were enforced, observes at pp. 217-9:

The conclusion to be drawn from the authorities is that, where a contract of personal service contains negative covenants the enforcement of which will not amount either to a decree of specific performance of the positive covenants of the contract or to the giving of a decree under which the defendant must either remain idle or perform those positive covenants, the Court will enforce those negative covenants; but this is subject to a further consideration. An injunction is a discretionary remedy, and the Court in granting it may limit it to what the Court considers reasonable in all the circumstances of the case.

[After a lengthy quotation from *Nelson*, Wells J continued:]

It is of course to be noted that in the case just cited there was a formal admission by the defendant that her services were "of special, unique, extraordinary and intellectual character." With great respect, I do not think those words may be used to describe the services which the present defendants contracted to furnish for the plaintiffs.

Mr. Kerbawy was cross-examined on his affidavits in respect of the contracts of both defendants and it is, I think, quite clear from a reading of this cross-examination that the principal injury which the plaintiffs allege they will suffer by reason of the breach of contract is that, having gone to the expense of training and building up the reputation of these defendants, they are now deprived of their services. And in the case of Mains, Mr. Kerbawy, when being re-examined by Mr. Gerity at the end of his cross-examination on his affidavit was asked Q. 69. The question and answer are as follows:

> Q. Mr. Kerbawy, my friend was asking you about the irreparable harm alleged in your affidavit. Can you tell us what will be the position if Mains does not return for the spring training this season?
>
> A. We will have to go to great expense, time and effort to get a replacement for him and then we are not sure that we can secure the lad who has the potentialities and the years' experience with us that we had in Mr. Mains.

With great respect I do not think that that answer disclosed an irreparable injury within the meaning assigned to it by the cases, that is, an injury which may never be adequately remedied or atoned for by damages; it indicates rather a loss which, while it may be difficult of measurement, nevertheless can be adequately measured and compensated for in damages.

There is one further consideration: this is a contract of service, which comes within the words of Lindley MR which have been quoted "that this Court never will enforce an agreement by which one person undertakes to be the servant of another." On the affidavit evidence before me, if the statements made by both defendants which I have already quoted are taken at their face value, it seems to me that the result might be indirectly to grant specific performance of para. 5 of the contract between the parties. It may well be that after investigation at a trial this will be shown not to be the case, but at this stage, this evidence not being contradicted in any way, this consideration should, I think, make me hesitate to grant the interlocutory injunctions asked or exercise my discretion at this time in favour of the plaintiffs.

Under all these circumstances both applications will be dismissed with costs in the cause. ...

Applications dismissed.

NOTE

The remedy being sought in this case was an interlocutory injunction to preserve the status quo pending trial of the main action. Note the principles detailed by Wells J as to when such relief will be granted.

When the case eventually came on for trial, the relevant season had ended as had Dublinski's contract with the plaintiff football club. At trial of the action against Dublinski, [1956] OR 744, McRuer CJHC would not even give damages to the plaintiff for the year in question because he held that the plaintiff had not exercised its option properly in terms of the contract and therefore the defendant was free to play for the Argonauts. He also held that no useful purpose would be served by issuing an injunction. In the alternative, he also held that the clause in question was unenforceable by way of injunction anyway, taking the attitude that the test to be applied to covenants running with the contract was the same as that to be applied to covenants that came into effect after the term of the contract had expired. Here, he felt the covenant, in so far as it applied to Canada as well as to the United States, was more than was reasonably necessary, the CFL in his view being in no way in competition with the NFL. He also noted that as opposed to negative covenants in a contract for the sale of a business, such covenants in a personal services contract had to be proved reasonably necessary by the covenantee. Finally, without finding it necessary to decide in this case whether the clause was void as being in restraint of trade, he disagreed with *Warner Brothers v. Nelson*, where it was held that the restraint of trade doctrine did not apply to covenants running with the contract. (This was also contrary to Wells J in the interlocutory injunction case who agreed with this aspect of *Nelson*.) On appeal, however, McRuer CJHC was reversed ([1957] OR 58 (CA)), the Court of Appeal holding that the plaintiff had properly exercised its option for the 1955 season. This meant that Dublinski was in breach of his contract with the plaintiff and liable to a claim in damages. As with McRuer CJHC, the Court of Appeal treated the question of the injunction as now academic. However, in assessing damages for loss, the Court of Appeal did not say whether it was for breach of the positive or negative covenants in the contract of employment—not that it needed to. There was simply no discussion of the validity or enforceability of the negative covenant. What follows is the Court of Appeal's calculation of the damages to be awarded. Assuming the negative covenant was not subject to a restraint of trade argument, does this damages calculation aid or hinder the argument for an injunction?

Detroit Football Co. v. Dublinski
[1957] OR 58 (CA)

ROACH JA: Professional football in the United States is highly competitive, very popular, and big business. The evidence shows that the defendant was rightly regarded as a star player and would be a valuable asset to any professional football team in the National Football League. As early as 1952 his potentialities as a quarterback had been recognized and he had been acquired by the plaintiff company and over the succeeding years had been trained, and to use the vernacular of the sport, had been "brought along" to eventually fill that vital position on the plaintiff's team. In 1954, he had been chosen to play in the all star game of the season. The loss of his services for the 1955 season was a serious matter for the plaintiff.

Having lost his services for that season, the plaintiff had to look for some outstanding player to take his place and all such players were already under contract with other clubs. The plaintiff eventually purchased another player from the owner of the Washington Red Skins, which is another team in the National Football League. In order to get his services the plaintiff paid $10,000 to that Club and assigned to it the contracts it (the plaintiff) had with two additional players.

There is no evidence on which the then monetary value to the plaintiff or the players it thus traded to the Washington Red Skins can be determined. One of them, although on the roster of the plaintiff Club, was receiving no salary; the other was receiving a salary of $6,500. It is clear, however, that it cost the plaintiff $10,000 capital expenditure to get an outstanding player to take the defendant's place on its team.

The plaintiff paid to the player whom it obtained from the Washington Red Skins a salary of $11,200, which was $3,450 more than the salary which it would have had to pay to the defendant if he had abided by his contract.

The plaintiff, however, in the shuffle saved the salary of $6,500 it would have had to pay to one of the players traded to the Washington Red Skins.

It requires only a mathematical calculation to demonstrate that, leaving out of consideration the value of the players traded to the Washington Red Skins, it cost the plaintiff $6,950 to fill the gap caused by the defendant breaking his contract. That calculation is as follows:

To be paid in acquiring the substitute	$10,000	
To paid salary of substitute.	11,200	
By credit—Salary of defendant		$ 7,750
By credit—Salary of one traded player.		6,500
. . . .	$21,200	$14,250
	14,250	
Net cost to plaintiff	$ 6,950	

It was submitted on behalf of the plaintiff that the foregoing net cost does not represent the total loss suffered by the plaintiff as the result of the contract having been broken. The argument in support of that submission was as follows:

The plaintiff, having recognized the potentialities of the defendant, took him on the club's roster of players looking to the day when those potentialities would have been developed by training and coaching. The plaintiff, like the other clubs in the league, employs professional trainers and coaches. Those employed by it spent time and effort in training the defendant until his playing abilities were such that he was qualified to take his place on the regular lineup and compete with the highly qualified players on the opposing teams. The 1954 season was the first season when, in the opinion of the plaintiff's coaches and trainers, he was thus qualified. That season was the only one during which the plaintiff got any return for the money and time and effort that it had spent on the defendant in bringing him to that degree of efficiency. It was in the nature of a deferred or postponed benefit it then received. Under the renewed contract it was entitled to a similar benefit in the 1955 season.

I think there is merit in the submission. It is very much like the case of the owner of a thoroughbred colt. He recognizes its racing potentialities and spends money in training it and developing those potentialities, looking to the day when it would be fit to be entered in a race, out of which the owner would receive, or at least hope to receive, a prize that would repay him in part for the money spent on the animal. If the animal should break its legs the day before the race, all the money spent on it is a dead loss.

Here, the defendant broke his contract, and it seems reasonable to me that the plaintiff, like the owner of the colt, has suffered some loss.

While the submission is sound, the evidence is lacking that would enable the Court to assess the amount of the loss. If the plaintiff seeks damages on that footing, it should support its claim by the necessary evidence.

It was also submitted on behalf of the plaintiff that the player obtained from the Washington Red Skins was a less efficient and skillful player than Dublinski. There is opinion evidence supporting that submission. In addition to that opinion evidence it would be a reasonable inference that, the defendant having broken his contract the plaintiff, on the threshold of the 1956 season could only get some top ranking player to take his place whom some other competing club in the League would be willing to sell and that no other club in that League would be willing to part with the services of a football player as well qualified and efficient as the defendant. We know also that, while in the 1954 season the plaintiff's team won the championship, in 1955 it finished last. However, in football as in every other sport, there is what is known as the "luck of the game" and it is impossible to say to what extent that luck was a contributing factor to the results in each season. Moreover, there is no evidence that the plaintiff suffered any loss in gate receipts by reason of the absence of the defendant from its team. However, if from that fact it can be assumed that the plaintiff's team was equally as attractive to the devotees of the game without the defendant as with him—the defendant would probably not agree that it was—it cannot be denied that it cost the plaintiff at least $6,950 to make it so.

As indicative of the value the plaintiff placed on the defendant's services is the fact that, before it knew that he had entered into a contract with the Argonaut Club, it offered him an annual salary of $14,000 on a two-year contract covering the 1955 and 1956 season. The defendant rejected that offer; he had already entered into a contract with the Argonaut Club at a salary of $17,500. That indicates the value that the Argonaut Club placed on his services.

For the defendant it was submitted that if the defendant had not broken his contract, he might have been injured even early in the 1955 season and been of diminished or even of no value to the plaintiff for the balance of the season. That is so, but that is a risk that equally applied to the player whom the plaintiff purchased to take the place of the defendant. To put it otherwise, the plaintiff was in no better or worse position, so far as that risk was concerned, by getting the substitute player than it would have been if the defendant had been on its regular line-up in the 1955 season.

Contracts in the field of professional sports stand in no different position than contracts in any other commercial venture. If either of the parties breaks the contract, he becomes liable for such damages as may be proved against him. Here the plaintiff has proved damages amounting at least to $6,950.

It is possible that it suffered a greater loss. The Court however, cannot fix a sum that would amount to perfect compensation and I have concluded that on all the evidence, justice would probably be done by fixing the damages at $6,950.

For the foregoing reasons I would allow the appeal, and direct that judgment be entered for the plaintiff in the sum of $6,950 together with the costs of the trial. The plaintiff is also entitled to the costs of the appeal.

Do the following provisions from the *Competition Act*, RSC 1985, c. C-34, as amended, affect the situation in *Dublinski* or the sample contract that follows?

48(1) Every one who conspires, combines, agrees or arranges with another person

(a) to limit unreasonably the opportunities for any other person to participate, as a player or competitor, in a professional sport or to impose unreasonable terms or conditions on those persons who so participate, or

(b) to limit unreasonably the opportunity for any other person to negotiate with and, if agreement is reached, to play for the team or club of his choice in a professional league, is guilty of an indictable offence and is liable on conviction to a fine in the discretion of the court or to imprisonment for five years or to both.

(2) In determining whether or not an agreement or arrangement contravenes subsection (1), the court before which such a contravention is alleged shall have regard to

(a) whether the sport in relation to which the violation is alleged is organized on an international basis and, if so, whether any limitations, terms or conditions alleged should, for that reason, be accepted in Canada; and

(b) the desirability of maintaining a reasonable balance among the teams or clubs participating in the same league.

(3) This section applies, and section 45 does not apply, to agreements and arrangements and to provisions of agreements and arrangements between or among teams and clubs engaged in professional sport as members of the same league and between or among directors, officers or employees of such teams and clubs where such agreements, arrangements and provisions relate exclusively to matters described in subsection (1) or to the granting and operation of franchises in the league, and section 45 applies and this section does not apply to all other agreements, arrangements and provisions thereof between or among such teams, clubs and persons.

Example of Professional Sports Standard Contract
National Hockey League, Standard Player's Contract (SPC) (2005)

2. The Player agrees to give his services and to play hockey in all NHL Games, All Star Games, International Hockey Games and Exhibition Games to the best of his ability under the direction and control of the Club in accordance with the provisions hereof.

The Player further agrees,

(a) to report to his Club's Training Camp at the time and place fixed by the Club, in good physical condition,

(b) to keep himself in good physical condition at all times during the season,

(c) to give his best services to the Club and to play hockey only for the Club unless his SPC is Assigned, Loaned, or terminated by the Club,

(d) to co-operate with the Club and participate in any and all reasonable promotional activities of the Club which will in the opinion of the Club promote the welfare of the Club and to cooperate in the promotion of the League and professional hockey generally,

(e) to conduct himself on and off the rink according to the highest standards of honesty, morality, fair play and sportsmanship, and to refrain from conduct detrimental to the best interest of the Club, the League or professional hockey generally.

3. In order that the Player shall be fit in proper condition for the performance of his duties as required by this contract, the Player agrees to report for practice at such time and place as the Club may reasonably designate and participate in such Exhibition Games as may be arranged by the Club.

4. The Club may from time to time during the continuance of this SPC establish reasonable rules governing the conduct and conditioning of the Player, and such reasonable rules shall form part of this SPC and the Agreement as fully as if herein written. For violation of any such rules or for any conduct impairing the thorough and faithful discharge of the duties incumbent upon the Player, the Club may impose a reasonable fine upon the Player and deduct the amount thereof from any money due or to become due to the Player. The Club may also suspend the Player for violation of any such rules. When the Player is fined or suspended, he shall be given notice in writing stating the amount of the fine and/or the duration of the suspension and the reason therefor. Copies of the rules referred to herein shall be filed at the main offices of the League and the National Hockey League Players' Association ("NHLPA"). ...

6. The Player represents and agrees that he has exceptional and unique knowledge, skill and ability as a hockey Player, the loss of which cannot be estimated with certainty and cannot be fairly or adequately compensated by damages. The Player therefore agrees that the Club shall have the right, in addition to any other rights which the Club may possess, to enjoin him by appropriate injunctive proceedings without first exhausting any other remedy which may be available to the Club, from playing hockey for any other team and/or for any breach of any of the other provisions of this SPC.

7. The Player and the Club recognize and agree that the Player's participation in other sports may impair or destroy his ability and skill as a hockey Player. Accordingly the Player agrees that he will not during the period of this SPC or during any period when he is obligated under this SPC to enter into a further SPC with the Club engage or participate in football, baseball, softball, hockey, lacrosse, boxing, wrestling or any athletic sport without the written consent of the Club, which consent will not be unreasonably withheld. ...

11. It is mutually agreed that the Club shall have the right to Assign or to Loan this SPC, and the Player agrees to accept and be bound by any such Assignment or Loan, and will faithfully perform and carry out this SPC with the same purpose and effect as if it had been entered into by the Player and such other Club.

It is further mutually agreed that in the event that this SPC is Assigned, or the Player's services are Loaned to another Club, the Club shall by notice in writing ... advise the Player of the name and address of the Club to which he has been Assigned or Loaned, and specify the time and place of reporting. If the Player fails to report to such other club, he may be suspended by such other club and no ... salary shall be payable to him during the period of such suspension. ...

14. The Club may also terminate this Contract upon written notice to the Player (but only after obtaining Waivers from all other Clubs) if the Player shall at anytime:

(a) fail, refuse, or neglect to obey the Club's rules governing training and conduct of players, if such failure, refusal or neglect should constitute a material breach of this SPC;

(b) fail, refuse or neglect to render his services hereunder or in any other manner materially breach this SPC.

In the event of termination under subsection (a) or (b) the Player shall only be entitled to compensation due to him to the earlier of the date such notice is delivered to him or the date of the mailing of such notice to his address as set out below his signature hereto.

In the event this SPC is terminated by the Club while the Player is "away" with the Club for the purpose of playing games the installment then falling due shall be paid on the first week-day after the return "home" of the Club. ...

18. The Club and the Player severally and mutually promise and agree to be legally bound by the League Rules and by any Collective Bargaining Agreement that has been or may be entered into between the member clubs of the League and the NHLPA, and by all of the terms and provisions thereof, copies of which shall be open and available for inspection by the Club, its directors and officers, and the Player, at the main office of the League, the main office of the Club and the main office of the NHLPA. This SPC is entered into subject to the CBA [Collective Bargaining Agreement] between the NHL and the NHLPA and any provisions of this SPA inconsistent with such CBA are superseded by the provisions of the CBA.

The Club and the Player further agree that in case of dispute between them, except as to the compensation to be paid to the Player on a new SPC, the dispute shall be referred within one year from the date it arose to the Commissioner of the League, as an arbitrator and his decision shall be accepted as final by both parties, unless, and to the extent that, other arbitration procedures are provided in any Collective Bargaining Agreement between the member Clubs of the League and the NHLPA to cover such dispute.

The Club and the Player further agree that all fines imposed upon the Player under the Playing Rules, or under the provisions of the League By-Laws, shall be deducted from the ... salary of the Player and be remitted by the Club to the NHL Players' Emergency Assistance Fund.

See also Clifford Ian Kyer, "Case Study in Party Stipulation of Remedy: The NHL Standard Player's Contract" (1981), 39 *University of Toronto Faculty of Law Review* 1.

Page One Records, Ltd. v. Britton
[1967] 3 All ER 822

[By an agreement signed in 1966, the defendants, musicians known collectively as "The Troggs," appointed Page One Records, the first plaintiff, to manage their business affairs for a period of five years. That agreement provided in part that during the period of the contract The Troggs would not "engage any other person firm or corporation to act as managers or agents for [The Troggs] nor act themselves in such capacity." The Troggs also entered, in

1966, a sole agency agreement and a recording agreement with the first plaintiff and, in 1967, a publishing agreement with Dick James Music Ltd., the second plaintiff.

By early 1967, The Troggs had met with considerable success, commanding up to £400 for a single night's engagement, and the evidence was that much of this success was attributable to the skill and effort of the first plaintiff as manager of the group. In June 1967 The Troggs wrote to both plaintiffs alleging that they were in breach of their respective agreements with the group, and purporting to terminate them on that basis. The first plaintiffs sought, *inter alia*, an order that the defendants be restrained until trial from (1) engaging anyone other than the first plaintiff as their manager, and (2) publishing or causing to be published any music performed by them otherwise than through the medium of the first or second plaintiffs.]

STAMP J: ... The defendants have not, in my judgment, established a prima facie case for the view that there were such breaches by the first plaintiff of its duty to The Troggs as to justify The Troggs in repudiating the agreements which they made with the first plaintiff. If all that I had to do was to determine whether the first plaintiff had made out a prima facie case of breach of contract entitling it to damages, I would hold that it had, entitling the plaintiffs to make a heavy claim for damages against the defendants. It does not follow, however, that because the plaintiffs have made out a prima facie case for succeeding in recovering damages in the action, that they have made out a prima facie case, or any case, for an interlocutory or any injunction. ...

Counsel for The Troggs submits that even if the plaintiffs had throughout acted impeccably towards The Troggs, no such injunction as is asked for ought to be granted. He advances three propositions on behalf of The Troggs. (i) That specific performance is never granted to enforce a contract for personal services. (ii) That an injunction is never granted which would have the effect of preventing an employer discharging an agent who is in a fiduciary position vis-à-vis the employer. He emphasises that here the first plaintiff, as manager and agent of The Troggs, is in the position of an employee. (iii) That an injunction is never granted at the suit of the party against whom the party to be restrained could not obtain specific performance. It is urged—and, in my judgment, correctly—that The Troggs could have no action for specific performance of the management or agency agreements against the first plaintiff.

The present case is clearly distinguished, in principle, from such cases as *Lumley v. Wagner*, for there the only obligation on the part of the plaintiffs seeking to enforce the negative stipulation was an obligation to pay remuneration and an obligation which could clearly be enforced by the defendants. Here, however, the obligations to the first plaintiff, involving personal services, were obligations of trust and confidence and were obligations which, plainly, could not be enforced at the suit of The Troggs. Here, indeed, so it seems to me, the totality of the obligations between the parties are more a joint venture almost approaching the relationship of partners than anything else, involving mutual confidence and reciprocal obligations on all sides.

For the purposes of consideration of equitable relief, I must, I think, look at the totality of the arrangements, and the negative stipulations on which the plaintiffs rely, are, in my judgment, no more or less than stipulations designed to tie the parties together in a relationship of mutual confidence, mutual endeavour and reciprocal obligations. These considerations, in the view of Knight Bruce VC in *Johnson v. Shrewsbury and Birmingham Ry. Co.* (1853), 3 De GM & G 914; 43 ER 358 (Ch.), and *Pickering v. Bishop of Ely* (1843), 2 Y & CC 249; 63 ER 109 (Ch.), on which he relied in the former case, distinguish *Lumley v. Wagner.* I quote from the judgment of Knight Bruce VC (at p. 927 (p. 363 (ER)):

> It is clear in the present case that, had the defendants been minded to compel the plaintiffs to perform their duties against their will, it could not have been done. Mutuality therefore is out of the question, and, according to the rules generally supposed to exist in courts of equity, that might have been held sufficient to dispose of the matter; cases however have existed where, though the defendant could not have been compelled to do all he had undertaken to do by the contract, yet as he had contracted to abstain from doing a certain thing the court has interfered reasonably enough.
>
> A case, lately much referred to on this point is that of a German singer, who, having found probably that more could be obtained by breaking her promise than by keeping it, determined to obtain the larger sum and accordingly to break her promise. She could not be compelled to sing as she had contracted to do, but as she had contracted not to sing at any other place than the one specified in the agreement, she was (and very properly in my opinion) restrained from singing at any other place. There all the obligations on the part of the plaintiff could have been satisfied by the payment of money, but not so those of the defendant. Here the parties are reversed. Here all the obligations of the defendants can be satisfied by paying money; but not so the obligations of the plaintiffs, who come here for the purpose in effect of compelling the defendants, by a prohibitory or mandatory injunction, to do or abstain from doing certain acts, while the correlative acts are such as the plaintiffs could not be compelled to do.

Apart altogether, however, from the lack of mutuality of the right of enforcement, this present case, in my judgment, fails on the facts at present before me on a more general principle, the converse of which was conveniently stated in the judgment of Branson J, in *Warner Brothers Pictures Inc. v. Nelson*, [1937] 1 KB 209. Branson J stated the converse of the proposition and the proposition, correctly stated is, I think, this, that where a contract of personal service contains negative covenants, the enforcement of which will amount either to a decree of specific performance of the positive covenants of the contract or to the giving of a decree under which the defendant must either remain idle or perform those positive covenants, the court will not enforce those negative covenants.

In the *Warner Brothers* case Branson J felt able to find that the injunction sought would not force the defendant to perform her contract or remain idle. He said (at p. 219):

> It was also urged that the difference between what the defendant can earn as a film artiste and what she might expect to earn by any other form of activity is so great that she will in effect be driven to perform her contract. That is not the criterion adopted in any of the decided cases. The defendant is stated to be a person of intelligence, capacity and means, and no evidence was adduced to show that, if enjoined from doing the specified acts otherwise than for the plaintiffs, she will not be able to employ herself both usefully and remuneratively in other spheres of activity, though not as remuneratively as in her special line. She will not be driven, although she may be tempted, to perform the contract, and the fact that she may be so tempted is no objection to the grant of an injunction.

So it was said in this case, that if an injunction is granted The Troggs could, without employing any other manager or agent, continue as a group on their own or seek other employment of a different nature. So far as the former suggestion is concerned, in the first place, I doubt whether consistently with the terms of the agreements which I have read, The Troggs could act as their own managers; and, in the second place, I think that I can and should take judicial notice of the fact that these groups, if they are to have any great success, must have managers. Indeed, it is the plaintiffs' own case that The Troggs are simple persons, of no business experience, and could not survive without the services of a manager. As a practical matter on the evidence before me, I entertain no doubt that they would be compelled, if the injunction were granted on the terms that the plaintiffs seek, to continue to employ the first plaintiff as their manager and agent and it is, I think, on this point that this case diverges from the *Lumley v. Wagner* case and the cases which have followed it, including the *Warner Brothers* case: for it would be a bad thing to put pressure on The Troggs to continue to employ as a manager and agent in a fiduciary capacity one, who, unlike the plaintiff in those cases who had merely to pay the defendant money, has duties of a personal and fiduciary nature to perform and in whom The Troggs, for reasons good, bad or indifferent, have lost confidence and who may, for all I know, fail in its duty to them.

On the facts before me on this interlocutory motion, I should, if I granted the injunction, be enforcing a contract for personal services in which personal services are to be performed by the first plaintiff. In *Lumley v. Wagner*, Lord St. Leonards LC, in his judgment, disclaimed doing indirectly what he could not do directly; and in the present case, by granting an injunction I would, in my judgment, be doing precisely that. I must, therefore, refuse the injunction which the first plaintiff seeks. The claim of the second plaintiff seems to me to be inextricably mixed up with the claim by the first plaintiff and no separate argument has really been addressed to me on the basis that the second plaintiff might succeed although the first plaintiff failed to obtain an injunction at the trial.

Motion dismissed.

NOTES

1. For a discussion of the remedial issues raised by these employment cases, see Richard A. Brait, "The Use of Restrictive Covenants in the Employment Contract" (1981), 6 *Queen's Law Journal* 414. Brait also discussed the issue of restraint of trade.

2. See also *Warren v. Mendy*, [1989] 1 WLR 853 (CA) where the plaintiff, Warren, the manager and promoter of the talented boxer Nigel Benn, sought an injunction restraining the defendant from inducing Benn to breach his exclusive management contract with the plaintiff and from acting for Benn in relation to his career. Benn had apparently lost confidence in the plaintiff and sought the services of the defendant. The Court of Appeal confirmed an order discharging an *ex parte* injunction that had been granted preferring the approach taken by Stamp J in *Page One Records, Ltd.* to that of Branson J in *Warner Brothers Pictures*. The court indicated that in cases of contracts for personal services that involved the exercise of special skill or talent and a high degree of mutual trust and confidence between the contracting parties, the court should not enforce negative stipulations under the contract if to do so would likely compel performance of the positive obligations. In this latter respect, the court

was also prepared to be realistic as to the probable effect that any injunction would have on the talented party both from the perspective of his or her needs to maintain their talent or skill in the marketplace and the likelihood that for practical reasons he or she would be forced to abide by the terms of the original agreement. It is interesting to note that notwithstanding the result in this case, Nigel Benn eventually reverted to using Warren as a manager.

3. Alexi Yashin had an exclusive five-year contract to play hockey for the Ottawa Senators. Yashin refused to play in the fifth year unless the Senators increased his salary. The Senators refused, and Yashin sat out the year. When his agreement expired, Yashin would become eligible for free agency. The Senators argued that Yashin's contract would not expire, rendering him eligible for free agency, unless he provided them with an additional season of service to make up for the year he missed. The dispute was submitted to arbitration and the arbitrator was asked to determine when Yashin's contract "expired." Yashin argued that to provide the Senators with another season of service would be tantamount to a mandatory injunction or specific performance, remedies that the courts would not grant in these circumstances. The arbitrator disagreed, and Yashin sought judicial review of that decision.

Mr. Justice Cunningham upheld the arbitrator's decision. Citing *Doherty v. Allman, Warner Brothers Pictures v. Nelson, Detroit Football Co. v. Dublinski,* and *Warren v. Mendy,* he concluded that requiring Yashin to play for the Senators for a further year before being entitled to free agency did not constitute enforcement of the positive covenants in the contract. Yashin had a choice about whether to play, and upholding the arbitrator's decision did not amount to a "round about means of enforcing specific performance." Citing *Warren v. Mendy,* the court stated:

> Compulsion is a question to be decided on the facts of each case with realistic regard for the probable reaction of an injunction on the psychological and material and sometimes the physical need of the servant to maintain the skill or talent.

Following the court's ruling, Yashin decided to return to the Senators and play out his contract. (*Yashin v. The National Hockey League,* [2000] OJ no. 3306 (Ont. Sup. Ct.).)

Hill v. C.A. Parsons & Co. Ltd.
[1972] 1 Ch. 305 (CA)

INTERLOCUTORY APPEAL from BRIGHTMAN J: By writ of August 13, 1971, the plaintiff, John William Hill, claimed against the defendants, C.A. Parsons & Co. Ltd. (1) an injunction restraining the defendants (i) from implementing the notice dated July 31 [*sic*], 1971, addressed to the plaintiffs purporting to determine his employment by the defendants; (ii) from imposing conditions of employment upon the plaintiff other than conditions freely agreed to by him; (iii) from conspiring with others to impose conditions of employment on the plaintiff other than those freely agreed to by him; (2) damages for breach of contract; (3) damages for wrongful conspiracy; (4) further or other relief.

On August 20, 1971, Brightman J made no order upon the plaintiff's motion for an interlocutory injunction to restrain the defendants until trial or further order from implementing the notice of July 30 purporting to determine his employment.

The plaintiff appealed. The grounds of appeal were, *inter alia*, (1) that the judge was wrong in holding that he was precluded by a rule of law from granting the injunction sought, namely the rule that to grant such an injunction would constitute an indirect way of obtaining specific performance of a contract for personal service; (2) that if (which was not admitted) such a rule of law existed an employee had a property right in his contract of employment which the court would protect by way of injunction in a proper case regardless of the existence or otherwise of such a rule of law; (3) the injunction sought was to restrain a future anticipatory breach of contract and as such was outside the scope of the rule of law; (6) [*sic*] the notice purporting to determine the plaintiff's contract of employment was an unlawful act to further a non-existent obligation on the part of the defendants with a third party, namely Draughtsmen's and Allied Technicians' Association ("DATA") to further a common purpose and as such could be restrained.

The facts are stated in the judgments of Lord Denning MR and Sachs LJ.

LORD DENNING MR:

I. Preliminary

In this case a trade union called the Draughtsmen's and Allied Technicians' Association ("DATA") seek to force employers called C.A. Parsons & Co. Ltd. to engage only members of that union. They have extracted an agreement out of the employers to that effect. In pursuance of that agreement, the employers have purported to terminate the engagements of those servants who have not joined the union. The servants have brought this action to test the position. They wish to know whether the conduct of the employers is lawful: and whether it can be stopped.

II. The Facts

Mr. John William Hill is a chartered engineer, now aged 63. He has been employed by C.A. Parsons & Co. Ltd. for the last 35 years, and is due to retire in two years' time when he becomes 65. His salary is £3,000 a year and is soon to be raised. He is a member of their pension scheme. It is important for him to serve till the end of his time, because his pension depends on his average salary for his last three years.

Before 1968 Mr. Hill and other professional engineers were not members of a trade union. But employees of the company of lesser standing, such as draughtsmen and technicians, belonged to one or other of two trade unions. Most belonged to DATA: others belonged to a rival union called ASTMS (The Association of Scientific Technical and Managerial Staffs). DATA then engaged in a vigorous campaign to increase its membership and to gain exclusive negotiating rights. This led to many disputes. The members of DATA "worked to rule" on more than one occasion.

Mr. Hill and other members of the professional staff were disturbed by these inter-union disputes. They joined a union of professional engineers called UKAPE (United Kingdom Association of Professional Engineers). This union has no political objectives and does not seek to use disruptive means of strife.

In March 1970, DATA determined to make all the employees join their union. They called their members out on strike and threatened to "black" the company's products. This placed the company in a critical economic position. Eventually, on May 15, 1970, the company capitulated to the demands of DATA. They agreed to make all their employees join DATA. They signed an agreement with DATA which covered all persons below the heads of departments and assistant heads. It covered, therefore professional engineers like Mr. Hill. (There was to be a list in an appendix of the jobs covered, but this appendix has never been issued.) This agreement contained these clauses:

1. DATA shall have sole negotiating rights for all technical staff covered by this agreement.
2. Membership of DATA will be a condition of service for all new recruits to technical staff.
3. The company will express to all non-union members of the technical staff its strong wish and desire that they should forthwith join DATA. After a period of 12 months from the signing of this agreement, it will be a condition of service for such staff to be members of DATA.

After the 12 months expired, the company sought to comply with the stipulations which DATA had forced upon them. On May 19, 1971, the company wrote to 38 of the professional staff a circular letter. It was in this form:

Dear Mr. Hill,

In accordance with the agreement which the company made with DATA on May 15, 1970, *we hereby give one month's notice of a change in your conditions of employment.*

If you are not already a member of DATA, and prior to May 15, 1970, were not a member of another trade union affiliated to the TUC it will be a condition of employment that you are required to become a member of DATA.

If you have not already done so, you are requested to comply with this condition.

If you wish to have further sight of the company's agreement with DATA, you may do so. ...

Mr. Hill did not agree to the change. He did not become a member of DATA. Nor did the other 37. In consequence, on July 30, 1971, the company gave each one month's notice to terminate his employment. The letter signed by the managing director was as follows:

In a letter to you dated May 19, 1971, the company gave one month's notice of a change in your conditions of employment, that is, that you must become a member of DATA. ...

As far as I am able to ascertain, you have not to date complied with this condition and *are therefore in breach of your contract of employment.*

In view of this, *I regret to have to advise you that your employment with this company will terminate at 5.15 p.m. on Tuesday, August 31, 1971,* unless prior to this date you have taken steps to comply with the condition in your contract of employment regarding DATA membership.

The company is bound to honour its agreement of May 15, 1970, in this matter, and wishes it to be understood that the sole reason for issuing this notice of termination of employment is the fact that you are in breach of your conditions of employment.

Faced with this notice to terminate his employment, Mr. Hill, on August 13, 1971, brought this action against the company. It is a test action to test the position of the 38. He asked for an interim injunction to restrain the company from implementing the notice dated July 30, 1971, purporting to determine his employment. He went before the vacation judge on August 25, but the judge refused the injunction. The judge said:

To my mind there is no doubt whatever that the company will be committing a wrongful act against the plaintiff if it terminates his employment on August 31, as it threatens to do. However, in my judgment, this court has no power to restrain that wrong.

After some discussion, he added: "If I had power to grant an injunction, I would have done so, but I felt constrained by the law."

The plaintiff told the judge that he desired to appeal. The defendants very sensibly agreed that, pending the appeal, they would not implement the notice. So the 38 are still at work.

III. The Letter of May 19, 1971

In the letter of May 19, 1971, the company seemed to think that they could change the conditions of Mr. Hill's employment without his consent. They had no power to do any such thing. Unless he agreed, they would have to terminate his employment by proper notice and then offer him employment on the new conditions. The letter was, therefore, of no effect.

IV. The Letter of July 30, 1971

In the letter of July 30, 1971, the company purported to terminate Mr. Hill's employment by giving one month's notice. They had no power to do any such thing. In order to terminate his employment, they would have to give reasonable notice. I should have thought that, for a professional man of his standing and, I may add, his length of service, reasonable notice would be at least six months, and may be 12 months. At any rate, one month is far too short.

Then comes the important question: what is the effect of an invalid notice to terminate? Suppose the master gives the servant only one month's notice when he is entitled to six? What is the consequence in law? It seems to me that if a master serves on his servant a notice to terminate his service, and that notice is too short because it is not in accordance with the contract, then it is not in law effective to terminate the contract—unless, of course, the servant accepts it. It is no more effective than an invalid notice to quit. Just as a notice to quit which is too short does not terminate a tenancy, so a notice which is too short does not terminate a contract of employment.

Test it this way: take master and servant who are on perfectly good terms and complete confidence in one another. The master decides reluctantly to give the servant notice, but it is too short. The servant can go at once to his master and say: "This is no good: I am entitled to six months' notice." The master, if he is a law-abiding citizen, will look at the contract or take legal advice. He will then say to the servant: "You are quite right. It is too short. Pay no regard to it. I will give you notice of proper length and you can work out your time." In that case the contract clearly continues.

If the servant is entitled thus to put the master right—by telling him the notice is bad—surely the court can do so also. It can say to the master: "Your notice is too short. It does not terminate the contract of employment. You must not act on it." The master, if he is wise, will obey this injunction. The contract of employment will not terminate on the named day, but will continue until determined by a notice of proper length.

V. Suppose the Master Insists on the Named Day

Suppose, however, that the master insists on the employment terminating on the named day? What is the consequence in law? *In the ordinary course of things*, the relationship of master and servant thereupon comes to an end: for it is inconsistent with the confidential nature of the relationship that it should continue contrary to the will of one of the parties thereto. As Viscount Kilmuir LC said in *Vine v. National Dock Labour Board*, [1957] AC 488 (HL (Eng.)), referring at p. 500 to the *ordinary* master and servant case: "if the master wrongfully dismisses the servant, either summarily or by giving insufficient notice, the employment is effectively terminated, albeit in breach of contract." Accordingly, the servant cannot claim specific performance of the contract of employment. Nor can he claim wages as such after the relationship has been determined. He is left to his remedy in damages against the master for breach of the contract to continue the relationship for the contractual period. He gets damages for the time he would have served if he had been given proper notice, less, of course, anything he has, or ought to have earned, in alternative employment. He does not get damages for the loss of expected benefits to which he had no contractual right: see *Lavarack v. Woods of Colchester Ltd.*, [1967] 1 QB 278 (CA).

I would emphasize, however, that that is the consequence in the *ordinary* course of things. The rule is not inflexible. The court can in a proper case grant a declaration that the relationship still subsists and an injunction to stop the master treating it as at an end. That was clearly the view of the Privy Council in the latest case on the subject, *Francis v. Kuala Lumpur Councillors*, [1962] 1 WLR 1411 (PC (Malay.)), where Lord Morris of Borth-y-Gest said, at pp. 1417-18:

> "when there has been a purported termination of a contract of service, a declaration to the effect that the contract of service still subsists will *rarely* be made" adding that "Special circumstances will be required before such a declaration is made."

Let me give an example taken from the decided cases. Suppose that a senior servant has a service agreement with a company under which he is employed for five years certain—and, in return, so long as he is in the service, he is entitled to a free house and coal—and at the end to a pension from a pension fund to which he and his employers have contributed. Now, suppose that, when there is only six months to go, the company, without any justification or excuse, gives him notice to terminate his service at the end of three months. I think it plain that the court would grant an injunction restraining the company from treating the notice as terminating his service. If the company did not want him to come to work, the court would not order the company to give him work. But, so long as he was ready and willing to serve the company, whenever they required his services, the court would order the company to do their part of the agreement, that is, allow him his free house and coal, and enable him to qualify for the pension fund. I take this illustration from the cases of *Ball v. Coggs* (1710), 1 Bro. Parl. Cas. 140; 1 ER 471 (HL (Eng.)); *East India Company v. Vincent* (1740), 2 Atk. 82, 83; 26 ER 451 (Ch.); *Cuckson v. Stones* (1858), 1 E & E 248; 120 ER 902 (KB) and *Warburton v. Co-operative Wholesale Society Ltd.*, [1917] 1 KB 663 (CA).

It may be said that, by granting an injunction in such a case, the court is indirectly enforcing specifically a contract for personal services. So be it. Lord St. Leonards did something like it in *Lumley v. Wagner* (1852), 1 De GM & G 604; 42 ER 689 (Ch.). And I see no reason why we should not do it here.

VI. The Industrial Relations Act 1971

Why does the length of notice matter so much in this case? You might think that, if the first notice is bad, the company would now be able to give another and so get rid of Mr. Hill a few months later.

The answer lies in the *Industrial Relations Act 1971*. It was passed on August 5, 1971. Part II of that Act has not yet been brought into operation, but, when it does, it will confer important rights on workers in respect of membership of trade unions. ...

The net result [of the Act] is this: if the notice given to Mr. Hill is effective to terminate his employment before Part II is brought into operation, he will have to leave his employment and get little compensation. But, if it does not take effect until after Part II is brought into operation, he will not have to leave his employment, nor will he have to join DATA. He will be able to stay on until the normal time for retirement. Hence the importance of this case to Mr. Hill and to the 37 other professional men who stand with him.

VII. Conclusion

In these circumstances, it is of the utmost importance to Mr. Hill and the other 37 that the notices given to them should not be held to terminate their employment. Damages would not be at all an adequate remedy. If ever there was a case where an injunction should be granted against the employers, this is the case. It is quite plain that the employers have done wrong. I know that the employers have been under pressure from a powerful trade union. That may explain their conduct, but it does not excuse it. They have purported to terminate Mr. Hill's employment by a notice which is too short by far. They seek to take advantage of their own wrong by asserting that his services were terminated by their own "say-so" at the date selected by them—to the grave prejudice of Mr. Hill. They cannot be allowed to break the law in this way. It is, to my mind, a clear case for an injunction.

The judge said that he felt constrained by the law to refuse an injunction. But that is too narrow a view of the principles of law. He has overlooked the fundamental principle that, whenever a man has a right, the law should give a remedy. The Latin maxim is *ubi jus ibi remedium*. This principle enables us to step over the trip-wires of previous cases and to bring the law into accord with the needs of today. I would allow the appeal, accordingly, and grant an injunction restraining the defendants from treating the notice dated July 30, 1971, as having determined the plaintiff's employment. ...

SACHS LJ: ... [I]n my judgment the plaintiff is bound to establish at trial that the defendants' primary contention is wrong; that their repudiation of the relevant contract did not in this case terminate that contract in the absence of it being accepted; and that this contract will continue to subsist until the end of the period of any proper notice that the plaintiff may be given by the defendant company. Consequently he will in all probability be found entitled to relief in the shape of such injunctions or declarations as may be appropriate at the date judgment comes to be given. (It is to be noted that Mr. Langdon-Davies inevitably and correctly conceded that at the date of the hearing in this court, if his primary contention was wrong, that contract, under which the plaintiff was still serving, presently subsisted.) The real question is whether the court has power to grant and in its discretion should grant the particular remedy which is claimed by way of interlocutory relief in aid of maintaining the *status quo ante* till trial.

At one stage it seemed that a challenge was being offered to the jurisdiction of the courts to grant an order of the nature sought by the plaintiff: but that suggestion was not pursued—it was bound to fail. Thus in essence the defendants' submission became one that in relation to contracts of service the practice that no such order should be made was so settled that it had by now become an inflexible rule of law which brooked no exceptions. In this behalf the previously mentioned general statements of law in a number of judgments were again relied upon—but the same answer applies as in the case of the primary contention that the contract itself could not subsist after the expiry of an unlawfully short notice. On an examination of the authorities the position in my judgment is that stated by Lord Denning MR: there is no such inflexibility.

It thus becomes relevant first to consider whether an order in the instant case would contravene the main grounds upon which it would be refused in the vast majority of master and servant cases. Foremost amongst the grounds given in George Russell Northcote (ed.), *Fry on Specific Performance* (London: Stevens, 1921) at p. 50 is that it is wrong to enforce a contract which needs personal confidence as between the parties when such confidence may not exist. Here such confidence does exist. Another ground is that common law damages normally provide an adequate remedy. Here they do not. ... A further ground is often the difficulty of reinstatement when the plaintiff's post has been filled. That difficulty does not exist here.

Next one comes to the other previously mentioned factors introduced by the provisions of the *Industrial Relations Act 1971* to which Brightman J was not referred—and which in this particular case produce such an unusual situation.

Looking at the aggregate of the matters just recited it appears to me that this is indeed an exceptional case and that relief should be granted unless there is some good counter argument. For the defendants it was suggested that an order of the court, if made as claimed, would endanger industrial peace as between the defendant company and its employees. I decline to assume that either DATA as an entity or its individual members would in the highly unusual circumstances act in some way that would be unreasonable and incidentally detrimental to their long term interests—far less that they would seek to interfere with an order of the court.

Finally it was urged that any order made would run contrary to the policy or trend of previous practice. At the risk of reiterating views expressed in my judgments on other subject-matters, it seems appropriate to repeat that in matters of practice and discretion it is essential for the courts to take account of any important change in that climate of general opinion which is so hard to define but yet so plainly manifests itself from generation to generation. In that behalf account must, *inter alia*, be taken of the trend of the views of the legislature expressed on behalf of the community in its enactments and also of the trend of judicial decisions.

Over the last two decades there has been a marked trend towards shielding the employee, where practicable, from undue hardships he may suffer at the hands of those who may have power over his livelihood—employers and trade unions. So far has this now progressed and such is the security granted to an employee under the *Industrial Relations Act 1971* that some have suggested that he may now be said to acquire something akin to a property in his employment. It surely is then for the courts to review and where appropriate to modify, if that becomes necessary, their rules of practice in relation to the exercise of a discretion such as we have today to consider—so that its practice conforms to the realities of the day.

It follows that in my judgment there exists no good reason against regarding the instant case as being one in which an order should be made as proposed: so I too would allow the appeal and make that order.

STAMP LJ [dissenting]: For the purposes of this judgment I will assume, without expressing an opinion, that the plaintiff's contract of service is still subsisting, the plaintiff not having accepted the defendants' repudiation of their obligations under it.

Upon this footing an interlocutory injunction in this case could only be granted, if at all, with a view to a specific performance of the contract at the hearing: see *per* Lord Truro L in *Stocker v. Brocklebank* (1851), 3 Mac. & G 250; 42 ER 257 (Ch.); and the propriety or otherwise of granting the interlocutory injunction sought may accordingly be tested by supposing the motion was to be treated as the trial of the action.

The relief sought by the writ, so far as material, is for a perpetual injunction restraining the defendants from implementing the notice dated July 30, 1971, purporting to determine the plaintiff's employment. ... [I]t would be an order that the contract be specifically performed. The defendants would be required to treat the plaintiff as their employee under the terms of his existing contract. The implications of such an order were hardly debated before this court and I only pause to ask the rhetorical question whether it would impose upon the defendants an obligation, enforceable by an order for sequestration, to allow the plaintiff to enter his place of employment and to work there and what the position would be if industrial action by way of lightning strike were taken with a view to his exclusion? Would the order, and I speak of the final order for specific performance or partial specific performance (call it what you will) and not the interlocutory order, be one which could be varied from time to time according to the circumstances? I would venture a tentative answer to such problems by remarking that the plaintiff is either entitled to an order for specific performance or he is not. And what would happen if this plaintiff or some other plaintiff similarly placed misconducted himself or, perhaps because of industrial action or the threat of industrial action, absented himself from his duties?

I would emphasise before going further that whether or not the defendants should, in effect, be restrained from dismissing the plaintiff except after due notice, there is in my judgment no jurisdiction to alter the terms of the plaintiff's employment by requiring the defendants not to dismiss the plaintiff even after due notice. Even if the *Industrial Relations Act 1971* contained a provision enabling that to be done this court could not make an order in anticipation of its provisions coming into force. The most that can in my judgment be done is to decree specific performance of a contract of which it is a term that the plaintiff may be given reasonable notice.

Whatever the position may have been 200 years ago it had by the time of Lord Truro become a principle of the court exercising the equitable remedy of specific performance to refuse it where what was sought to be specifically performed was a contract for personal services. In *Lumley v. Wagner*, the employee not only agreed to perform services for the employer but also, in effect, not to perform them for another. The negative part of the obligation was enforced by the granting of an injunction. That was a much criticised decision and when an attempt was made in *Whitwood Chemical Co. v. Hardman*, [1891] 2 Ch. 416 (CA) to place reliance upon *Lumley v. Wagner* as an exception to the general rule Lindley LJ took the view [at 426-28] that for an injunction to be granted in the case of an agreement for personal services it was for the plaintiff to show that the case fell within some recognised exception to the general rule that the court will not decree specific performance of such a contract.

No authority has been cited to us throwing the slightest doubt upon the statement of principle laid down by Lindley LJ which has always been followed and become deeply embedded in the law. It has been followed again and again … .

I would be far from holding that in a changed and changing world there can be no new exception to the general rule or that in changed circumstances Lindley LJ's statement should be slavishly followed. But the consequences of ordering an employer or employee to perform the contract of service can hardly ever be foreseen and the injustice which may stem from such an order may only become apparent after the order has been made. The court in determining whether to grant or withhold an order for performance of that which has been agreed to be done will not exercise its discretion where the order will be nugatory, uncertain, or as a practical matter impossible to enforce. Nowhere could these considerations be more compelling than where an employee asks for an order upon his employer to continue to employ him.

It is urged on behalf of the plaintiff employee that this is the most exceptional case, justifying and requiring a departure from the general rule because the mutual trust and confidence which ought to exist between employer and employee remains in this case unimpaired. The employers have only been constrained to dismiss the plaintiff by the threat of industrial action. They did not want to dismiss him and under the umbrella of an order of the court in effect restraining them from doing so there is no reason why the happy relationship of employer and employee which hitherto existed should not be continued. On behalf of the defendants it is pointed out, and I think this is a more realistic approach, that it is not correct to say that the defendants are willing to employ the plaintiff but that the true position is that they would be willing to do so but for the fact that they have under pressure entered into an agreement with DATA requiring them to dismiss him and that this agreement cannot be broken without dire consequences. Unless therefore the court is prepared to infer, as I do not think it ought to do, that the defendants' opposition to the making of an order for specific performance is not genuine, it appears to me that the existence of the fears which dictated the dismissal is a strong ground for not making an exception to the general rule that the court will not order specific performance of a contract of employment. I know not what may be the consequence to the defendants of making the order which the court is asked to make or what difficulties may be met in enforcing or giving effect to such an order. The more unwilling they would otherwise be to dispense with the plaintiff's services the more real must be the danger to the defendants' interest in not doing so. …

Nor can I accept that there ought to be a departure from the general rule on the ground that in recent times the practice has been to shield an employee from hardship at the hands of employer or trade union. In its operation the rule is as often as not as beneficial to an employee who by its effect is not to be restrained from leaving his employer and taking his services elsewhere as it is to the employer who at the price of paying damages is not to be required to continue to employ a servant with whose service he wishes for any reason to dispense. In *Lumley v. Wagner*, itself the order enforcing the servant's negative agreement not to perform for another, to the extent that it be regarded as an exception to the general rule, did not operate in the employee's favour. ...

As to the submission founded upon the *Industrial Relations Act 1971*, it would in my judgment be wrong to grant an interlocutory injunction in the hope or belief that the plaintiff may as a result obtain some advantage from the fact that he will still be in the employment of the defendants when the relevant provisions of that Act come into force. I repeat what I said at the outset that an interlocutory injunction could only be granted with a view to a specific performance of the contract at the hearing. No doubt the court could at the hearing make a declaration that the contract was still subsisting; but the fact that such a declaration could be made would be no ground for granting an injunction in the meantime. An interlocutory injunction in the form asked would offer the plaintiff no protection unless it be treated in effect as a declaration of right; and the court cannot make an interlocutory declaration: see *International General Electric Company of New York Ltd. v. Customs & Excise Commissioners*, [1962] Ch. 784 (CA). Indeed it appears to me that what is really being sought on this interlocutory application is a substitute for a declaration of right; and I observe in this connection that if, because the plaintiff has not accepted the defendants' repudiation of the contract it is still on foot, it can, without the aid of an interlocutory injunction, be kept on foot by a continued refusal to accept the repudiation. It would be contrary to the principles upon which the court acts in granting interlocutory injunctions to do so in order to secure to a party some advantage not accorded to him by the contract which he seeks to enforce. Interlocutory injunctions are granted to protect rights sought to be asserted at the trial.

It is also perhaps worth mentioning that despite any change of climate affecting the legal relations between employer and employee the Act contains no provision under which an order on an employer to continue the employment of an employee is contemplated.

Of course, one deplores a situation in which a loyal and good servant may be summarily dismissed at the instance of and under pressure exerted by a third party. That situation may perhaps—I express no opinion—be less likely to arise in the future than is at present the case; but it is not for this court to give him the protection that he would have if the *Industrial Relations Act 1971* had come into operation or to grant him interlocutory relief with a view to preserving his position so that he or his employers may in the future have the advantages which that Act will it is hoped accord.

It may be that as a practical matter damages are not an adequate remedy for the wrongful dismissal in this case; and indeed damages are perhaps never an adequate remedy to a man who is within a few years of his retirement and who hopes to end his working days working. This situation however arises as well where such a man is dismissed after due notice as where he is wrongfully dismissed. I am not persuaded that as a matter of law damages are not an adequate remedy in this case and I do not dismiss the possibility that any loss of pension rights which might have accrued to him had his service been determined by due notice cannot be reflected in an award of damages. ...

I, like Wynn-Parry J in *Keetch v. London Passenger Transport Board*, would follow the sure and safe guide propounded by Lindley LJ in *Whitwood Chemical Co. v. Hardman*.

I think Brightman J came to a correct conclusion and would dismiss the appeal.

NOTES AND QUESTIONS

1. In *Stevenson v. Air Canada* (1981), 126 DLR (3d) 242 (Ont. HC) Henry J referred to *Hill v. Parsons* as a "highly exceptional" case in which the "state of personal confidence between employer and employees … had not ceased to exist."

2. *Hill v. Parsons* was referred to with approval by Anderson J of the British Columbia Supreme Court in *Baxter Motors Ltd. v. American Motors (Canada) Ltd.* (1973), 40 DLR (3d) 450. In that case, he granted an interlocutory injunction to restrain the termination of an auto-mobile franchise agreement and stated "that the Court will, in exceptional circumstances, grant an injunction where it cannot enforce performance by the plaintiff of his obligations under the contract." *Baxter Motors* was subsequently followed in *Prairie Hospitality Consultants Ltd. v. Renard International Hospitality Consultants Ltd.* (1980), 118 DLR (3d) 121 (BC SC) (see chapter 8, "Interlocutory Injunctions") in which the judge took the further step of grant-ing an interlocutory mandatory injunction compelling the defendant to provide documents and information necessary to the operation of the franchise. In this respect, see also *Clitheroe v. Hydro One Inc.*, [2002] OJ no. 4383 (Ont. Sup. Ct.), and the judgment of Megarry J in *Giles v. Morris*, above. What effect does this seemingly changing attitude toward specific perform-ance of contracts of service have on cases that hold that the servant is obliged to accept the master's wrongful termination of a contract and attempt to mitigate immediately? For a thorough discussion of this difficult issue, see John McMullen, "A Synthesis of the Mode of Termination of Contracts of Employment" (1982), 41 *Cambridge Law Journal* 110.

3. In an Ontario case on an unrelated point, the court concluded that it was an error to take judicial notice of and give effect to legislation before it was passed: *Bayshore Trust Co. v. Richardson* (1991), 2 OR (3d) 522 (Gen. Div.).

4. Changing equitable principles relating to specific performance are also being exam-ined in the context of the remedy of "reinstatement" in the area of labour relations. See Kurt H. Decker, "Reinstatement as a Remedy for the Pennsylvania Employer's Breach of a Hand-book or an Employment Policy" (1985), 90 *Dickinson Law Review* 41, at 54-57 and the *Employ-ment Protection (Consolidation) Act, 1978* (UK), c. 44. In Canada, see the *Canada Labour Code*, RSC 1985, c. L-2, s. 242(4)(b); *An Act Respecting Labour Standards*, RSQ, 1997, c. N-1.1, s. 128; and the *Labour Standards Code*, RSNS 1989, c. 246, s. 71.

5. Reinstatement was the issue in *National Ballet of Canada v. Glasco*, a case involving Kimberly Glasco, a principal dancer with the National Ballet. In December 1998, the National Ballet decided not to renew Glasco's contract and she brought a number of proceedings against it including a grievance to the Ontario Labour Relations Board under the collective agreement for reinstatement and a claim in the Superior Court of Justice for damages for wrongful dismissal. The parties subsequently agreed to submit their disputes to binding arbi-tration and Glasco brought an application before the arbitrator for reinstatement until the matter could be fully heard. The arbitrator ordered interim reinstatement and the National Ballet sought to stay that order in the Superior Court. On March 31, 2000, Mr. Justice O'Leary refused to stay the order of the arbitrator ((2000), DLR (4th) 372 (Ont. Sup. Ct. (Div. Ct.))).

The artistic director of the National Ballet, James Kudelka, threatened to quit if he was forced to cast Glasco. The arts community recognized this as a case that raised the funda-mental question as to whether the courts or artistic directors were going to run theatre and dance companies. The National Ballet then returned to court seeking leave to appeal the decision of the arbitrator under the *Arbitration Act* and that application was also dismissed ((2000), 186 DLR (4th) 347 (Ont. Sup. Ct.)). Glasco remained "reinstated" in the interim. The matter was ultimately settled.

If the matter had been before the courts, could the company have resisted a motion by Glasco for an interlocutory injunction restraining the National Ballet from refusing to cast her in the upcoming season?

LAND CONTRACTS

The Traditional Position

At this point, we return to the issue of specific performance of contracts involving an interest in land. Historically, specific performance has been available "as a matter of course" for contracts involving the purchase and sale of land. This special treatment of land transactions is due historically to the importance of land to a person's social and political status during the formative years of English common law:

> [B]argained exchanges of real property were in reality political, legal, and social acts of extraordinary significance. That is, the contractual expectations of purchasers of real property consisted, in whole or in part, of political identity, political authority, a number of legal privileges, and social status, which may or may not have been transferred together with a valuable economic commodity. One may ask, therefore, whether an award of damages which would have enabled the disappointed purchaser to contract for another piece of land—with roughly similar political, cultural, and social attributes—would have constituted adequate compensation.

David Cohen, "The Relationship of Contractual Remedies to Political and Social Status: A Preliminary Inquiry" (1982), 32 *UTLJ* 31, at 39.

In modern times the special treatment of land contracts is usually justified on the basis that land, by its very nature, has a quality of uniqueness that renders damages inappropriate in most cases. This results from the fact that many purchasers of land have selected a particular parcel because it meets their own needs or subjective desires. This is especially so when the purchaser intends to live on the land.

The presumptive approach in favour of specific performance was enunciated by the Supreme Court of Canada in *Kloepfer Wholesale Hardware & Automotive Co. Ltd. v. R.G. Roy*, [1952] SCR 465, at 472, *per* Kerwin J:

> as to the suggestion that damages would be sufficient because it is contended that the plaintiff [purchaser] desired to use the property as an investment, it is sufficient to say that generally speaking, specific performance applies to agreements for the sale of land as a matter of course.

This approach was reaffirmed by the Ontario Court of Appeal in *Bashir v. Koper* (1983), 40 OR (2d) 758. *Bashir v. Koper* was followed in *Citation Realty Inc. v. 463879 Ontario Ltd.* (1989), 72 OR (2d) 440, and in *Coletto Construction Ltd. v. Yongehurst May Developments Ltd.* (1990), 11 RPR (2d) 50 (Ont. HC).

As a result of the "as a matter of course" approach, purchasers were traditionally only rarely denied specific performance because of the fungible nature of the particular land.

Evolving Away from the Traditional Position

The traditional "as a matter of course" approach to the specific enforcement of land contracts had the virtue of certainty and simplicity, but it was unsatisfactory in several respects. Purchasers often purchase land that accords to their peculiar tastes, but it is frequently the case that equally suitable properties are available in the relevant market. Moreover, where the purchaser is a speculator looking for a resale, it is difficult to see why specific performance should inevitably follow and why damages do not offer complete redress.

Furthermore, allowing a plaintiff specific performance has the effect of allowing him or her a risk-free period of speculation at the expense of the vendor between the date of breach and the date of trial. A purchaser will insist on specific performance if the property rises in value after the breach and, insofar as that remedy is routinely awarded, the purchaser cannot be expected to mitigate. There seems to be no good reason why a speculator in real estate should not be subject to the same principle of mitigation as any other purchaser. The disadvantage to the vendor is accentuated if the court permits the purchaser to register a certificate of pending litigation against the title to the property thereby precluding the vendor in most cases from disposing of the property until the litigation is resolved. This may encourage the vendor to settle the claim to its disadvantage. (See "Certificates of Pending Litigation," below.)

Due mainly to concerns like these, a departure from the traditional approach began to gain momentum, as illustrated in the decision of the BC Court of Appeal in *McNabb v. Smith* (1982), 44 BCLR 295, a case decided in the same year as the decision in *Bashir v. Koper*. In *McNabb*, the plaintiff agreed to purchase a residential property from the defendants but prior to closing the transaction, the plaintiff sold the property to a third party for an overall advance in price of $6,200. (The plaintiff "flipped" the property for a quick profit without ever intending to take possession.) The plaintiff's plan was foiled when the defendants refused to complete the first transaction and the plaintiff sued for specific performance. The court held that the plaintiff was a speculator and the property had no particular unique value to her even though she intended to lease the property back from the second purchaser. On this basis, the court concluded that damages were an adequate remedy in the circumstances and it refused to order specific performance. See also *Heron Bay Investments Ltd. v. Peel-Elder Developments Ltd.* (1976), 2 CPC 338 (Ont. HC); *Chaulk v. Fairview Construction Ltd.* (1977), 14 Nfld. & PEIR 13 (Nfld. CA); and *Ansdell v. Crowther* (1984), 11 DLR (4th) 614 (BCCA).

In the following remarkably bold trial court judgment Adams J denied a claim for specific performance on the basis that the plaintiffs had not made out a case for the inadequacy of damages.

Domowicz v. Orsa Investments Ltd.
(1993), 15 OR (3d) 661 (Gen. Div.)

[The plaintiffs, who were experienced investors in apartment buildings, agreed to purchase a 123-suite apartment building in Scarborough from the defendant. The defendant refused to complete the transaction and the plaintiffs sued for specific performance. It took *seven years* to get to trial and Adams J ultimately denied specific performance and directed a further hearing as to damages. He held that the plaintiffs were purchasing the building as an income-producing investment with an intention to improve the building and resell it for a profit. In his decision, the trial judge provided a scholarly analysis of a purchaser's entitlement to specific performance:]

IV Entitlement to Specific Performance

Monetary relief constitutes the normal remedy to redress a breach of contract. Only where this remedy is inadequate will a court decree specific performance: see E. Allan Farnsworth, "Legal Remedies For Breach of Contract" (1970), 70 *Columbia L Rev.* 1145 at p. 1149; Robert J. Sharpe, "Specific Relief for Contract Breach" in B.J. Reiter and J. Swan (eds.), *Studies in Contract Law* (1980); J. Berryman, "The Specific Performance Damages Continuum: An Historical Perspective" (1985), 17 *Ottawa L Rev.* 295; Robert J. Sharpe, *Injunctions and Specific Performance* (1992). While the original reasons for equitable relief being exceptional may relate to a time before the courts of common law and equity merged, Lon L. Fuller and William R. Perdue Jr. gave the classic contemporary foundation for this remedial relationship in their seminal articles "The Reliance Interest in Contract Damages": see L.L. Fuller and William R. Perdue Jr., "The Reliance Interest: 1" (1936), 46 *Yale LJ* 52, and "The Reliance Interest: 2" (1936), 46 *Yale LJ* 373. They did so by developing a powerful policy justification for the granting of "expectation interest" monetary damages to compensate promisees for their "reliance" on failed promises. This justification explained that monetary damages based on the expectation of a party are most consistent with a credit economy and, at the same time, best protect reliance on promises by dispensing with its proof: Fuller and Perdue, "The Reliance Interest: 1," at p. 62.

To this general principle of monetary relief based on a promisee's expectation interest, three important limitations emerged to avoid the possibility that a crushing burden might be imposed on promisors: see E.A. Farnsworth, *supra*, at pp. 1158-59. These limitations are that promisees cannot recover for loss that was avoidable; losses claimed must be foreseeable; and there is no recovery for loss that is too uncertain. For transactions to occur, both promisors and promisees must be encouraged to contract. Rules too solicitous of promisees will deter promisors and *vice versa*. Professor Farnsworth, in a path-breaking article, described the policy of mitigation, one of these limitations, in just such terms at p. 1183:

> Up to this point the discussion has focused on the promisee's interest in his bargain. Yet a society that depends so heavily on private bargains has itself a stake in how bargains fare. And although our legal system does not, as we have already seen, generally regard that stake as sufficient to justify it in compelling parties to perform their promises by penalizing them for failure to perform, it does show concern if adequate attempts are not made to avoid unnecessary waste once a bargain miscarries. In order to encourage the injured party to make reasonable efforts to salvage the transaction, it penalizes him, if his efforts are found wanting, by denying him recovery for loss that he could have avoided through reasonable efforts following breach. As a corollary, it compensates him for the cost of such reasonable efforts as he has made.

Thus, the law does not hold promisors accountable for *all* loss arising from their conduct. Rather, a pragmatic combination of limited monetary relief and substitute transactions has been devised to achieve contract's policy goals. Subject to the inadequacy of money damages in a case of unique goods where there may be no readily available substitute transaction that can meet all the subjective reasons for the promisee entering a contract, money damages will ordinarily be adequate in a market economy to enable an aggrieved promisee to obtain an acceptable substitute. Instead of locking unwilling parties into their failed relationships by requiring specific performance, they are encouraged to do their business with others thereby maximizing economic activity and minimizing economic waste: see A. Kronman, "Specific Performance" (1977), 45 *U Chi. L Rev.* 351. In this respect Robert J. Sharpe has written at pp. 7-7 and 7-8, *Injunctions and Specific Performance, supra*:

> The limiting aspects of contract remedies and the desire to protect the plaintiff's expectation as cheaply as possible is sometimes described as the theory of efficient breach. Where the innocent party's expectation interest can be fully protected by a damages award, damages are to be preferred on this theory. The innocent party is protected and at the same time the party in breach is able to pursue a more profitable or desirable venture. A rule which forced the latter to perform in such circumstances, it is argued by some, would needlessly waste an opportunity for profit.
>
> Granting the plaintiff specific performance in such cases will often go farther than achieving the goal of putting plaintiffs in the position they would have been in had their contracts been performed and may well impose on defendants substantial costs or burdens which might otherwise be avoided. This point turns on the distinction between the plaintiffs' and the defendants' relative costs and advantages of contract breach. By putting plaintiffs in the position they would have been in we mean to ensure that they receive the value to them of the defendant's performance. Where a defendant defaults, it may be assumed that this has been done to gain an advantage or to avoid some hardship in performance. Fulfilling the obligation to the plaintiff may have become a losing proposition. A more attractive and more profitable arrangement with another party may be available. The plaintiff's loss arising on breach is not always a mirror image of the advantage the defendant gains by failing to perform. The accepted view is that contract remedies are not designed to punish the contract breaker and the proper measure for contract damages is compensation for the plaintiff's loss rather than lifting the benefits of breach from the defendant. As it was put in an English case, "[t]he question is not one of making the defendant disgorge what he has saved by committing the wrong, but one of compensating the plaintiff ... [I]t by no means necessarily follows that what the defendant has saved the plaintiff has lost."

The remedy of specific performance, however, is generally seen to be presumptively available to enforce contracts for the purchase and sale of land. Inadequacy of damages is often assumed, possibly because no two properties can be identical ... .

In recent years, however, the Supreme Court of Canada has taken an increasingly principled approach to areas where the rigid application of legal doctrine has sometimes outstripped its true purpose. Land today is no longer tied to the right to vote or to other status attributes which may have driven the almost automatic availability of specific performance in relation to land contracts: see David Cohen, "The Relationship of Contractual Remedies to Political and Social Status: A Preliminary Inquiry" (1982), 32 *UTLJ* 31; see also *A.V.G. Management Science Ltd. v. Barwell Developments Ltd.*, [1979] 2 SCR 43, for related changes in the assessment of loss where title to land cannot be conveyed as promised. This is not to deny that personal or subjective reasons for acquiring land may continue to regularly undermine the adequacy of monetary relief. But as has been suggested, the presence of idiosyncratic reasons for acquiring real property in particular cases does not justify a general rule always entitling a buyer of land to specific performance: see Edward Yorio, *Contract Enforcement, Specific Performance and Injunctions* (1989), at p. 261. Rather, the generally superior efficiencies associated with monetary relief for breach of contract dictate that promisees must have a substantial interest in specific performance before it is awarded. In this respect, Estey J, as he then was, in *Asamera Oil Corp. v. Sea Oil & General Corp.*, [1979] 1 SCR 633 at p. 667-68, stated:

> On principle it is clear that a plaintiff may not merely by instituting proceedings in which a request is made for specific performance and/or damages thereby shield himself and block the court from taking into account the accumulation of losses which the plaintiff by acting with reasonable promptness in processing his claim could have avoided. Similarly, the bare institution of judicial process in circumstances where a reasonable response by the injured plaintiff would include mitigative replacement of property will not entitle the plaintiff to the relief which would be achieved by such replacement purchase and prompt prosecution of the claim. Before a plaintiff can rely on a claim to specific performance so as to insulate himself from the consequences of failing to procure alternate property in mitigation of his losses, *some fair, real and substantial justification for his claim to performance must be found.* Otherwise its effect will be to cast upon the defendant all the risk of aggravated loss by reason of delay in bringing the issue to trial. The appellant in this case contends that it ought to be allowed to rely on its claim for specific performance and the injunction issued in support of it, and thus recover avoidable losses. After serious consideration, I have concluded that this argument must fail.

(Emphasis added.)

Undoubtedly, the purchase of a particular piece of land may *prima facie* suggest the inadequacy of money damages. But if specific performance is truly a discretionary remedy even in cases involving land, the presumption must not be irrebuttable: see *Adderley v. Dixon* (1824), 1 Sim. & St. 607 at p. 610, 57 ER 239, and *Babcock v. Carr* (1982), 34 OR (2d) 65 at p. 70 (HCJ). Indeed, there is ample evidence it is not; see generally, P.J. Brenner, "Specific Performance of Contracts for the Sale of Land Purchased for Resale or Investment" (1978), 24 *McGill LJ* 513; J. Berryman, "Specific Performance, Uniqueness and Investment Contracts: A Canadian Perspective" (1984), 48 *Conveyancing & Property Lawyer* 130; and A. Herschorn, "Specific Performance of Agreements for the Purchase and Sale of Land" (1990), 12 *Advocates' Quarterly* 17. For example, in *Heron Bay Investments Ltd. v. Peel-Elder Developments Ltd.* (1976), 2 CPC 338 (Ont. HCJ) at p. 339 on an application for leave to appeal from an order vacating registration of a certificate of *lis pendens*, Mr. Justice Weatherston stated:

> The remedy of specific performance is one that is peculiar to real estate transactions and is based on the fact that real estate is regarded as unique and of particular importance to the purchaser. Obviously, the purchase of a new house is much different than the buying of a new car, which can be replaced by an almost identical new car. That reasoning does not apply when land is purchased merely as an investment. In the case at bar, the land was purchased as an investment. True it may be a uniquely good investment, but it was not being purchased by the plaintiffs for their own use but only to develop and resell at a profit. Obviously, any loss of profits can be compensated for in damages.

Similarly, in *Chaulk v. Fairview Construction Ltd.* (1977), 14 Nfld. & PEIR 13, the New-foundland Court of Appeal reversed a decree of specific performance where the purchaser had resold two of five duplexes to be conveyed and had plans to sell the remaining three. On behalf of the court, Gushue JA held at pp. 20-21:

> For the various above reasons I would dismiss the appeal as to the enforceability of the contract. As to whether the learned trial Judge properly ordered specific performance of the remainder of the contract, it is my view that this aspect of the appeal must succeed. The remedy of specific performance is an equitable one which should be invoked only if an adequate remedy cannot be found in law, and I do not feel that this situation fits the present case.
>
> This Court is of course a Court of Equity as well as of Law, and has the power to order specific performance of a contract. The above proposition is well-known and accepted, and, insofar as its application to the sale of land is concerned, I can do no better than to quote from the case of *Adderly v. Dixon* (1824), 15 M & St. 607, *per* Sir John Leach VC, who stated:
>
>> Courts of Equity decree specific performance of contracts, not upon any distinction between reality and personality but because damages at law may not, in the particular case, afford a complete remedy. Thus, a Court of Equity decrees performance of a contract for land, not because of the real nature of the land but because damages at law, which must be calculated upon the general money value of the land, may not be a complete remedy to the purchaser to whom the land may have a peculiar and special value.
>
> It is unnecessary for me to say any more about the law, as it is clear. The question here is whether damages would have afforded Chaulk an adequate remedy, and I have no doubt that they could, and would, have. There was nothing whatever unique or irreplaceable about the houses and lots bargained for. They were merely subdivision lots with houses, all of the same general design, built on them, which the respondent was purchasing for investment or re-sale purposes only. He had sold the first two almost immediately at a profit, and intended to do the same with the remainder. It would be quite different if we were dealing with a house or houses which were of a particular architectural design, or were situated in a particularly desirable location, but this was certainly not the case. It is also meaningful that, in paragraph 6 of his Statement of Claim, the respondent states that he "had arranged the re-sale of the three houses in question ... ." It is therefore obvious that damages do afford an adequate remedy to Chaulk, and that these damages should be capable of assessment, with very little difficulty. I would allow this part of the appeal. ...

In *McNabb v. Smith* (1981), 124 DLR (3d) 547 (SC), Bouck J dealt with a claim for specific performance where the purchaser prior to closing made arrangements to "flip" the property to a third party making a substantial profit. In concluding damages would be an adequate remedy the learned trial judge held at p. 552:

> From this discussion, I conclude Mrs. McNabb meant to buy the home from the defendants and sell it to Hrad for the purpose of personal gain. It has no particular unique value to her. Instead, it is an investment. True, she hoped to lease it back from Hrad and remain living there with her husband. But that was not something she bothered to secure through the device of a binding agreement to lease commencing October 1, 1980. Her conduct is ample evidence that the residence was simply used as a means of making a profit. Apart from that, it was of no par-

ticular significance: *Heron Bay Investments Ltd. v. Peel-Elder Developments Ltd.* (1976), 2 CPC 338 at p. 339 (Ont. HC), *per* Weatherston J, *Chaulk v. Fairview Construction Ltd.* (1977), 14 Nfld. & PEIR 13 at pp. 20-21. …

The policy thrust underlying this more principled approach to specific performance is developed by Robert J. Sharpe in his text *Injunctions and Specific Performance, supra,* at pp. 8-4 and 8-5:

> Where the purchaser's interest is investment or resale, the proposition that a substitute could not be found and that therefore damages are inadequate appears even more dubious. Take first the case of the purchaser who intends to use the property as an income-producing asset. Plainly, such a purchaser has no subjective attachment to the particular parcel. It might be argued, however, that the purchaser's own judgment as to the income-producing qualities of this parcel makes it unique. An award of damages, in effect forcing the purchaser back into the market to acquire another parcel in another location, may not offer the same income-producing qualities as the land the purchaser first bargained for. In other words, because no two pieces of land are identical, it could be argued that the purchaser should not be forced to accept the objective judgment of the court as to value. Unless it can be fairly said that the income-producing potential of a given parcel of land is unusually difficult to assess, this argument should be rejected. There is almost inevitably some risk of error in damage assessment and, when that risk becomes significant, specific performance is called for. However, it is not clear that the risks of error inherent in establishing land values for investment purposes are severe.
>
> Similar considerations arise where the purchaser is a speculator acquiring the property for profit on a resale. Land is a fungible good to such a purchaser and the arguments which have been considered elsewhere in this book as to the relative advantages and disadvantages of specific performance and damages apply. Again, it may be argued that since land is so especially difficult to value objectively, a purchaser should not be forced to accept the assessment of others. On the other hand, granting specific performance will often allow such a purchaser, at the expense of the vendor, a risk-free period of speculation between the date of the breach and the date of the trial. There seems to be no reason why a speculator in real estate should not be subject to the same principle of mitigation as the speculator in any other commodity.

I am aware that a rigid rule always requiring specific performance in respect of land contracts has the attraction of remedial certainty which would obviously facilitate planning by litigants. However, the judicial discretion involved in adjudicating equitable claims has always entailed the uncertainty inherent in equity's responsive doctrines: see E. Yorio, "A Defense of Equitable Defenses" (1990), 51 *Ohio State LJ* 1201 at p. 1225. Moreover, as noted by Grange JA in *Bashir* [(1983), 40 OR (2d) 758], the exercise of a court's discretion in equity comes with its own principled considerations. There is no suggestion in the cases reviewed above of remedial anarchy. Rather, there is a conscious effort to explore the real inadequacy of monetary relief in relation to land agreements as well as any failure to mitigate because of the contribution of these twin principles to self-ordering and contract policy. While there is still a presumption that specific performance is appropriate in respect to land interests, these cases show the presumption is rebuttable upon a scrutiny of the transaction. Indeed, a more principled approach to the adequacy of damages may lead to an expansion of the availability of specific performance in relation to contracts where historically it has not been accessible: see David Cohen, *supra*, pp. 69-73; D.M. Beatty, "Labour Is Not a Commodity" (c. 9) and R. Brown, "Contract Remedies in a Planned Economy: Labour Arbitration Leads the Way" (c. 4) in B.J. Reiter and J. Swan (eds.), *Studies in Contract Law, supra*; see also *Beswick v. Beswick*, [1967] 2 All ER 1197 (HL); *Hill v. C.A. Parsons & Co.*, [1972] Ch. 305 (CA); *Sky Petroleum Ltd. v. VIP Petroleum Ltd.*, [1974] 1 All ER 954 (Ch.).

Applying a principled approach to money damages in the instant case, I have come to the conclusion that monetary relief is an adequate remedy for these plaintiffs. While an admirable attempt was made to characterize this apartment building as physically and commercially unique, the evidence in this respect is insufficient. The defendant has demonstrated that other buildings with similar characteristics were on the market during the period in question. Indeed, the purchase of the Parkwoods Village building illustrates the availability of such properties although I accept that the plaintiffs intended to close both transactions on December 15, 1986 and had the money to do so. The plaintiffs were not going to live in the apartment building and its features are representative of many other apartments constructed at about the same time in that neighbourhood and in similar neighbourhoods throughout the Metropolitan area. The subsequent buying pattern of the plaintiffs tends to confirm the entrepreneurial or profit-making purpose of their acquisitions as does the content of their claim for equitable damages. The plaintiffs' purpose in buying was also consistent with the industry practice, in those times, of maximizing a residential apartment building's value by way of rent applications in response to heavy acquisition debt charges. Generally, this value was captured by way of a subsequent resale in the near term. Unfortunately, the plaintiffs' insistence on specific performance has locked the parties into a pathological embrace for the last seven years. The consequent losses to them both illustrates the wisdom of monetary relief in such cases and the value of requiring innocent promisees to mitigate their business losses where reasonably possible.

The plaintiffs argued they acted reasonably in pursuing their equitable remedies to date and rely on the fact that they had obtained a summary judgment for specific performance in May 1987 which was not set aside by the Court of Appeal until April of 1989. However, the plaintiffs were aware from the outset of the defendant's unwillingness to convey the building. Nevertheless, they chose to insist on specific performance while at the same time seizing on a very comparable investment in the form of Parkwoods Village. In May of 1989 they had to revisit their claim for specific performance when the Court of Appeal reversed the summary judgment. Again, they chose to litigate for the property instead of mitigating their losses.

While the duty to mitigate arises on breach, a court will look to the circumstances of each case in determining the precise timing for mitigatory action. For example, in *Asamera, supra*, the plaintiff's reluctance to buy replacement stock in a failing company at the time of breach was accepted as reasonable. However, once the company's future improved this justification for inaction was no longer approved. Unfortunately, this case has been litigated in stages with "common law" damages left to last. The issue of mitigation was only examined in the context of whether Parkwoods Village was in fact a replacement for the subject property. Given the plaintiffs' investment objectives and availability of funds to close both transactions, it is difficult to so characterize the Parkwoods Village property. However, the parties have not directly tackled before me the issue of mitigation on the basis that the plaintiffs are limited to monetary relief. Indeed, the circumstances surrounding the summary judgment application and the related appeal were not developed in evidence. These events were merely mentioned by counsel in argument.

V Conclusion

Accordingly, the plaintiffs' claims for specific performance and equitable damages are dismissed. Counsel are requested to attend on me to speak to the approach now to be taken to the assessment of common law damages and the related issue of mitigation.

NOTE

The decision of Adams J was upheld by the Court of Appeal in a very brief judgment: *Domowicz v. Orsa Investments Ltd.* (1998), 40 OR (3d) 256. The trial judge's assessment of damages in *Domowicz v. Orsa Investments Ltd.* is reported at (1994), 20 OR (3d) 722.

The Modern Position

The halting movement away from the historical "as a matter of course" approach to specific performance of land contracts culminated in the following judgment of the Supreme Court of Canada.

Semelhago v. Paramadevan
[1996] 2 SCR 415

[In August 1986, the purchaser agreed to buy a house from the vendor for $205,000. Prior to the date set for closing the transaction, October 31, 1986, the vendor reneged and subsequently conveyed the house to a third party. The purchaser sued for specific performance or damages in lieu thereof, but because the value of the property had significantly increased to $325,000 as of the date of the trial, the purchaser elected to pursue his claim for damages rather than specific performance. At trial and in the Ontario Court of Appeal, the case was dealt with by the parties on the assumption that specific performance was an appropriate remedy, but, because of the purchaser's election, the case was argued entirely on the issue of the proper measure of damages. This issue was further complicated by the fact that the purchaser had not as yet sold his old house and it too had increased in value from $190,000 in the fall of 1986 to $300,000 at the time of trial. Notwithstanding that the question of entitlement to specific performance was no longer central to the disposition of the case, SOPINKA J (Gonthier, Cory, McLachlin, Iacobucci, and Major JJ concurring) stated:]

While at one time the common law regarded every piece of real estate to be unique, with the progress of modern real estate development this is no longer the case. Both residential, business and industrial properties are mass produced much in the same way as other consumer products. If a deal falls through for one property, another is frequently, though not always, readily available.

It is no longer appropriate, therefore, to maintain a distinction in the approach to specific performance as between realty and personalty. It cannot be assumed that damages for breach of contract for the purchase and sale of real estate will be an inadequate remedy in all cases. The common law recognized that the distinction might not be valid when the land had no peculiar or special value. In *Adderley v. Dixon* (1824), 1 Sim. & St. 607, 57 ER 239, Sir John Leach VC stated (at p. 240):

> Courts of Equity decree the specific performance of contracts, not upon any distinction between realty and personalty, but because damages at law may not, in the particular case, afford a complete remedy. Thus a Court of Equity decrees performance of a contract for land, not because of the real nature of the land, but because damages at law, which must be calculated upon the general money value of the land, may not be a complete remedy to the purchaser, to whom the land may have a peculiar and special value.

Courts have tended, however, to simply treat all real estate as being unique and to decree specific performance unless there was some other reason for refusing equitable relief. See *Roberto v. Bumb*, [1943] OR 299 (CA), at p. 311; *Kloepfer Wholesale Hardware and Automotive Co. v. Roy*, [1952] 2 SCR 465; *Nepean Carleton Developments Ltd. v. Hope*, [1978] 1 SCR 427, at p. 438. Some courts, however, have begun to question the assumption that damages will afford an inadequate remedy for breach of contract for the purchase of land. In *Chaulk v. Fairview Construction Ltd.* (1977), 14 Nfld. and PEIR 13, the Newfoundland Court of Appeal (*per* Gushue JA), after quoting the above passage from *Adderley v. Dixon*, stated, at p. 21:

> The question here is whether damages would have afforded Chaulk an adequate remedy, and I have no doubt that they could, and would, have. There was nothing whatever unique or irreplaceable about the houses and lots bargained for. They were merely subdivision lots with houses, all of the same general design, built on them, which the respondent was purchasing for investment or re-sale purposes only. He had sold the first two almost immediately at a profit, and intended to do the same with the remainder. It would be quite different if we were dealing with a house or houses which were of a particular architectural design, or were situated in a particularly desirable location, but this was certainly not the case.

Specific performance should, therefore, not be granted as a matter of course absent evidence that the property is unique to the extent that its substitute would not be readily available. The guideline proposed by Estey J in *Asamera Oil Corp. v. Seal Oil & General Corp.*, [1979] 1 SCR 633, with respect to contracts involving chattels is equally applicable to real property. At p. 668, Estey J stated:

> Before a plaintiff can rely on a claim to specific performance so as to insulate himself from the consequences of failing to procure alternate property in mitigation of his losses, some fair, real and substantial justification for his claim to performance must be found.

A similar position has been taken by the British Columbia Supreme Court in *McNabb v. Smith* (1981), 124 DLR (3d) 547, at 551:

> The trial judge was of the view in this case that the property was not unique. She stated that, "It was a building lot under construction which would be interchangeable in all likelihood with any number of others." Notwithstanding this observation, she felt constrained by authority to

find that specific performance was an appropriate remedy. While I would be inclined to agree with the trial judge as to the inappropriateness of an order for specific performance, both parties were content to present the case on the basis that the respondent was entitled to specific performance. The case was dealt with on this basis by the Court of Appeal. In the circumstances, this Court should abide by the manner in which the case has been presented by the parties and decided in the courts below. In future cases, under similar circumstances, a trial judge will not be constrained to find that specific performance is an appropriate remedy.

[La Forest J agreed with the proposed disposition of the case by Sopinka J but preferred not to deal with the issue as to the entitlement to specific performance in a case where the matter was not fully argued.]

NOTES

1. In *Corse v. Ravenwood Homes Ltd.* (1998), 226 AR 214, Master Funduk referred to Sopinka J's remarks in *Semelhago* on the availability of specific performance in land contracts as "obiter of the highest order. There is obiter and there is obiter. Some has a lot more weight than others." Indeed, trial courts immediately began to treat this aspect of the judgment in *Semelhago* as law.

2. Following *Semelhago*, it remained to be seen whether any patterns would develop in the case law as to the criteria that would be applied in determining whether a plaintiff has satisfied the onus. Would the courts differentiate between cases involving commercial as opposed to residential property? Would the criteria apply equally to plaintiff purchasers and vendors?

The answers to these questions have enormous practical implications because they determine the advice that is given by lawyers to potential plaintiffs as to whether they should pursue specific performance or abandon that remedy in favour of seeking to mitigate their losses by purchasing a replacement property (if they are disappointed purchasers) or by seeking another buyer (if they are disappointed vendors). Following the wrong path could be disastrous, as was demonstrated in the *Domowicz* decision, extracted above. There, plaintiff purchasers who steadfastly pursued specific performance for some eight years were finally denied that remedy at trial and were faced with an assessment of damages that was considerably reduced because of their failure to mitigate in a timely manner.

3. It was inevitable, in the wake of *Semelhago*, that cases on the specific performance of land contracts would become fact-sensitive. Whether damages are an adequate remedy is, after all, a question about their adequacy to a particular plaintiff. However, while *Semelhago* has dissolved the certainty that once characterized the law in this area, some patterns and principles have emerged from the subsequent case law.

The analysis of the *Semelhago* "uniqueness" criterion in the following lower court decision has been influential.

John E. Dodge Holdings Ltd. v. 805062 Ontario Ltd.
(2001), 56 OR (3d) 341 (SCJ)

[In July 1999, the plaintiff, Dodge, a hotel builder and manager, agreed to purchase 4.12 acres of serviced undeveloped land in the City of Vaughan near Canada's Wonderland from the defendant numbered company (805). The agreement required severance approval from the city in order to proceed. The city approved the severance subject to the condition that, if required, 805 would construct an extension to Calderi Road at a cost of between $350,000 and $500,000 and dedicate it to the city. Neither 805 nor Dodge had any need for the road extension and building it would have been solely for the benefit of other property owners. In May 2000, 805 purported to terminate the agreement. Dodge sued to specifically enforce the agreement.]

LAX J:

Overview

[1] In *Semelhago v. Paramadevan*, [1996] 2 SCR 415 (SCC) the Supreme Court of Canada fundamentally changed the long established rule that specific performance is routinely granted in actions for the purchase and sale of land.

· · ·

[48] This was an arbitrary, capricious and unreasonable breach of a binding contract for the sale of land ... . I conclude that 805 breached the Agreement of Purchase and Sale when it refused to comply with the conditions of severance.

Uniqueness

[49] In *Semelhago v. Paramadevan*, the obiter statement of Justice Sopinka that specific performance should not be granted absent evidence that the property is unique to the extent that its substitute is not readily available sparked a flurry of comment and commentary. It has left trial judges with the difficult task of determining when a property is unique. On this point, there has been little appellate guidance. Nevertheless, the law is developing on a case-by-case basis and some principles are beginning to emerge.

[50] Even before Mr. Justice Sopinka delivered his "critical obiter" in *Semelhago*, courts had begun to move away from granting orders for specific performance where the plaintiff was purchasing land for either income or capital appreciation. *Semelhago* concerned a residential property and as the law develops further, it may turn out to be important to differentiate commercial transactions from residential transactions, which normally include a significant subjective component. However, even in commercial transactions, courts will necessarily have to consider subjectivity and will be confronted with assessing the sincerity and force of the plaintiff's reasons for asserting an interest in the vendor's property rather than its monetary equivalent.

[51] It is worth taking note of two significant pre-*Semelhago* decisions, one concerning realty and the other concerning personalty. I refer to the decisions of Mr. Justice Adams in *Domowicz v. Orsa Investments Ltd.* [above] and Mr. Justice Estey in *Asamera Oil Corp. v. Sea Oil & General Corp.*, [1979] 1 SCR 633. In *Domowicz*, Adams J rejected a claim for specific

performance of a 123-unit apartment building in Scarborough, Ontario finding that the plaintiffs had not proved that the purchase was other than an investment. As the purpose of an investment is to earn profit, damages were an adequate remedy. The decision is important for its very careful and principled analysis of the availability (or more accurately, the unavailability), of the remedy of specific performance.

[52] In *Asamera*, Estey J recognized that a claim for specific performance insulates a plaintiff from the consequences of failing to procure an alternate property in mitigation of his losses, thereby casting upon the defendant all the risk of aggravated loss by reason of delay in bringing the issue to trial. He stated that for this reason there must be "some fair, real and substantial justification for the claim." This was also recognized by Justice Adams in *Domowicz* and by Justice Sopinka in *Semelhago*. Justice Sopinka concluded that as damages is the normal remedy for breach of contract, there is no principled reason to grant a discretionary and extraordinary remedy for breach of contract for the sale of a commodity. Money is both appropriate and adequate compensation.

[53] In a helpful analysis of *Semelhago* by Mr. Paul Perell ["Semelhago v. Paramadevan and the New Paradigm for Specific Performance," in *Gravel to Gavel: Recent Developments in Real Estate Litigation* (Toronto: LSUC, Department of Continuing Legal Education, 1996)], the author argues that Mr. Justice Sopinka actually held an expansive view of the availability of the remedy of specific performance and not a view that is narrowly tied to the availability of a substitute property. He proposes that the key factors for determining uniqueness are (1) that the remedy of damages is comparatively inadequate to do justice, and; (2) that, in the words of Estey J, "the plaintiff show some fair, real and substantial justification for the claim."

[54] These comments echo those of Madam Justice Low in *904060 Ontario Ltd. v. 529566 Ontario Ltd.*, [1999] OJ No. 355 (Ont. Gen. Div.) at para. 14:

> The presumption of uniqueness has not yet been replaced by a presumption of replaceability and that what the Supreme Court did in *Semelhago* was to open the door to a critical inquiry as to the nature and function of the property in relation to the prospective purchaser.

[55] I agree with her comments. As Low J observed, *Semelhago* asks us to examine in each case, the plaintiff and the property. The danger in framing the issue as one of uniqueness (a term that carries with it a pre-*Semelhago* antediluvian aroma) is that the real point of *Semelhago* will be lost. It is obviously important to identify the factors or characteristics that make a particular property "unique" to a particular plaintiff. The more fundamental question is whether the plaintiff has shown that the land rather than its monetary equivalent better serves justice between the parties. This will depend on whether money is an adequate substitute for the plaintiff's loss and this in turn will depend on whether the subject matter of the contract is generic or unique.

[56] What then are those factors that will determine when it is just to order specific performance? The inquiry begins with *Semelhago* by asking if a substitute property is readily available, but it does not end there. The jurisprudence now goes further and I have attempted to summarize below some of the emerging principles.

[57] Uniqueness is a matter of proof and the onus lies on the party seeking the remedy. However, the plaintiff is not required to prove a negative and demonstrate the complete absence of comparable properties. As Mr. Justice Ferrier said in *Greenforco Holding Corp. v.*

Yonge-Merton Developments Ltd., [1999] OJ No. 3232 (Ont. SCJ), this would place an expensive and unacceptable burden on a plaintiff. He also stated that the appropriate time to determine if a substitute property is readily available is at the time of breach. As he explained, this is the time that the innocent party has to assess his position and decide whether to keep the contract alive or to accept the repudiation and sue for damages.

[58] Although a plaintiff may claim specific performance and damages and make an election at trial, as a practical matter, the mitigation principle operates as a powerful disciplining tool. The plaintiff must now carefully and realistically assess if he will succeed in an action for specific performance and this will depend, in part, on whether or not there is a readily available substitute property. If there is, the plaintiff's remedy will be damages and subject to the mitigation principle.

[59] There is both a subjective and objective aspect to uniqueness. While it is difficult to be precise about this, it strikes me that normally, the subjective aspect will be less significant in commercial transactions and more significant in residential purchases, unless the motivation in the latter case is principally to earn profit. In terms of the subjective aspect, the court should examine this from the point of view of the plaintiff at the time of contracting. In some cases, there may be a single feature of the property that is significant, but where there are a number of factors, the property should be viewed as a whole. The court will determine objectively whether the plaintiff has demonstrated that the property has characteristics that make an award of damages inadequate for that particular plaintiff. Obviously, investment properties are candidates for damages and not specific performance.

[60] It is important to keep in mind that uniqueness does not mean singularity. It means that the property has a quality (or qualities) that makes it especially suitable for the proposed use that cannot be reasonably duplicated elsewhere. To put this another way, the plaintiff must show that the property has distinctive features that make an award of damages inadequate. The plaintiff need not show that the property is incomparable.

[61] What then are the factors that led me to conclude that the Magna lands are especially suitable for Dodge's proposed use as a hotel that cannot reasonably be duplicated elsewhere, that damages are an inadequate remedy, and that justice is better served in this case by an order for specific performance?

[62] When Dodge set out to purchase a property for a hotel site, it already owned a hotel property, a few miles south of the Magna lands on the boundary between Vaughan and the City of Toronto. This hotel ... has been a very successful property for Dodge, exceeding both of the typical criteria that are used in the hotel industry to measure a need for expansion. As the site offers no room for expansion, development of a second proximate hotel to capitalize on existing goodwill and to achieve marketing and operational synergies was desirable. ...

[63] ... As the hotel business slows down on weekends, occupancy rates can be improved if there is an incentive for the business client to bring his or her family along. There were two key features to the Magna site that enhanced this opportunity. First, the site is a ten-minute walk from Canada's Wonderland. Second, the site is located at a signaled intersection directly across from the proposed Vaughan Mills Centre development on Jane Street.

[64] Paramount Canada's Wonderland, located 0.6 miles directly north of the proposed hotel site is the largest theme/amusement park in eastern Canada. ... There are no hotels in the vicinity of the park.

[65] The Vaughan Mills Centre is a planned $250 million retail mall to be located directly west of the site … . It is projected to draw 18 million shoppers annually, including over 1,000 tour buses. An interchange on Highway 400 will provide easy access to the mall site as well as to the hotel. Those involved in the construction and development of the Vaughan Mills Centre would logically be attracted to stay at the hotel across the street.

[66] There is other significant development activity in the Vaughan area, which makes this area a particularly suitable one for a hotel. This includes the 60-acre Millennium Campus adjacent and south of the Magna property with 340,000 square feet under construction and an additional 370,000 square feet under development. The Colossus is a 4,800-seat theatre, designed as a replica of the Starship Enterprise, with 19-screens including an IMAX theatre, a game arcade, a lounge and party rooms. As well, a large tract of land between the Vaughan Mills site and Canada's Wonderland is planned for residential development. Vaughan is a growth community and the Jane-Rutherford area is developing at a rapid pace … .

[68] Before purchasing the Magna property, Dodge considered possible hotel sites in Mississauga, Markham and Scarborough, but these did not offer proximity to its other hotel site and for this and other reasons were less attractive to Dodge. After it confined its search to Vaughan, it considered three or four other sites, including hotel sites that were available on the Vaughan Mills property. It rejected locating on the mall site because of concerns about noise, traffic congestion and the use of hotel parking spaces by mall shoppers. The price was also steeper.

[69] The Magna site offers superior access, visibility, traffic patterns and location to each of the other sites that were under consideration. It also has a C7 commercial zoning designation that is more favourable for ancillary uses such as banquet halls and eating establishments. … The ability to have an unrestricted, independent dining facility on the land to accommodate hotel guests, but also to serve patrons in the area, was another distinguishing feature of this site. None of the other sites offered this combination of attractive features at a comparable price. …

[72] The only truly comparable property is located at 350 Caldari Road and was referred to at trial as "the Sorbara property." … There was a great deal of evidence about the Sorbara property, but very little turns on this as the property sold on April 19, 2000 and was therefore not a readily available substitute when 805 breached this Agreement on May 11, 2000.

[73] The defendant argued that the Magna property is unremarkable vacant land. While it is true that it is vacant land, it is not unremarkable land for this plaintiff. This was a contract for the purchase of land that was especially suitable for the kind of hotel that the plaintiff wished to build. …

[74] The plaintiff demonstrated that it was entitled to an order for specific performance and that damages did not adequately compensate it for its loss. For these reasons, Judgment was granted in favour of the plaintiff.

NOTES

1. The judgment of Lax J was upheld by the Ontario Court of Appeal: *John E. Dodge Holdings Ltd. v. 805062 Ontario Ltd.* (2003), 63 OR (3d) 304; leave to appeal to the SCC refused, [2003] SCCA no. 145. In *United Gulf Developments Ltd. v. Iskandar* (2004), 235 DLR (4th) 609, Roscoe JA, speaking for the Nova Scotia Court of Appeal, wrote: "I agree with the statements

of Justice Lax [in *Dodge*] both with respect to the impact of the *Semelhago* decision and the factors relevant to uniqueness in land contract disputes."

2. In his annotation to *Dodge* ("Dodge, Son of Semelhago: Another Guide for the Continually Perplexed" (2001), 46 RPR (3d) 240) Theodore Rotenberg writes:

> *Dodge* is a case about a specialized user of land with commercial business objectives. What makes the remedy of specific performance particularly suitable is that the plaintiff made a rational choice to select a business site, that the future profit stream of the business is related to the site (and therefore difficult to compare to a different site) and that no other comparable land could be found immediately nearby … . The guiding principle for a commercial property which emerges from this [case] is not really a matter of subjective desires ("I like your land, not the land a few kilometres away"), but that the business rationale for the remedy can be objectively evaluated, even if the court categorizes any rationale as "subjective." If a business user of land selects a community and neighborhood in which to locate its enterprise and "substitute" properties are not "readily available," then the court need not and should not question the business decision of a hotelier to locate in Vaughan rather than Mississauga, and should not reject objectively rational business reasons that point to the chosen location rather than another property down the road.

3. In *Cross Creek Timber Traders v. St. John Terminals Ltd.*, (2002) NBR (2d) 201 (QB), specific performance was awarded to the purchaser of 800 acres of vacant heavily wooded land in the Musquash area of New Brunswick. The purchaser's intention was to log the timber and then sell the deforested land. Glennie J held that, although the property

> consists of vacant land, it is not unremarkable land for the purposes of Cross Creek. The volume and species of timber on the property make [it] especially suitable for Cross Creek's proposed use … . I am satisfied [on] the evidence before me that the Lake Retreat property meets the test of uniqueness contemplated by the Supreme Court of Canada in *Semelhago v. Paramadevan*. It cannot be said that the Lake Retreat property is a situation of a mass produced property which can be easily exchanged with any other property. Its substitute is not readily available.

For a useful comment on this case, in which the authors discuss its relation to *Dodge*, see J.W. Lem and G.E. Henderson, "Case Comment: *Cross Creek Timber Traders Inc. v. St. John Terminals Ltd.*" (2002), 49 RPR (3d) 83.

4. In *Earthworks 2000 Design Group Inc. v. Spectacular Investments (Canada) Inc.*, [2005] BCJ no. 8 (SC), Slade J held that a high-exposure commercial property on which the plaintiff planned to build a gas station, a convenience store, and a number of sign structures on which it intended to lease advertising space was not sufficiently unique to ground a claim for specific performance. He characterized as "entirely ordinary" the plaintiff's planned retail use of the property, and was not satisfied that there were no readily available comparable sites on which to carry on a commercial signage business. "There is no connection between the convenience store usage and the use for signage which would establish synergy comparable in quality to that discussed in *John Dodge Holdings Ltd.*, where the court allowed the claim of specific performance." See also *Walker v. Blades*, [2007] BCJ no. 1945 (CA), and *Pioneer Petroleums Limited Partnership v. 2049904 Ontario Inc.*, [2009] OJ no. 518 (CA) (leave to appeal refused [2009] SCCA no. 151).

5. Specific performance has routinely been denied where the purchaser's prospective connection with the land is one of pure investment. In those cases damages have been held

to be the more appropriate form of relief: *Heron Bay Investments Ltd. v. Peel-Elder Developments Ltd.* (1976), 2 CPC 338 (Ont. HC); *Domowicz v. Orsa Investments Ltd.* (1993), 15 OR (3d) 661 (Ont. Gen. Div.); *Tsang v. 853908 Ontario Inc.*, [1995] OJ no. 722 (Ont. Gen. Div.); *Tavares v. Tavares* (2001), 43 RPR (3d) 246 (Ont. SCJ); *Monson v. West Barrhaven Developments Inc.* (2001), 89 BCLR (3d) 104 (SC); *1244034 Alberta Ltd. v. Walton International Group Inc.* (2007), 82 Alta. LR (4th) 259 (CA).

In the following judgment the Saskatchewan Court of Appeal usefully articulates the relationship between the uniqueness criterion from *Semelhago* and the requirement that damages be an inadequate remedy.

Raymond v. Raymond Estate
2011 SKCA 58

CALDWELL JA:

I. Introduction

[1] The appellant, Barry Raymond ("Barry"), appeals from the remedy awarded in his favour by the trial judge, see 2008 SKQB 278. At trial, the judge found that Helen Barbara Raymond and George Alfred Raymond ("Barbara" and "Alfred") had entered into a valid agreement to sell their respective undivided one-quarter interests as tenants in common (the "Parents' Interests") in S ½ 27-7-10 W3M (the "Land") to Barry, their elder son. The judge awarded Barry the remedy of damages on the breach of that agreement by Barbara and Alfred.

[2] For the reasons below, I would set aside the damages award and substitute an order of specific performance requiring the transfer of the Parents' Interests to Barry.

II. Background

[3] Barry is one of three children born to Barbara and Alfred. Barbara and Alfred are deceased but their estates are respondents in this appeal (the "Parents' Estates") and are represented by Beverley Anderson ("Beverley"), their daughter and executrix. Alan Raymond ("Alan") is Barbara and Alfred's younger son. Like their parents, Barry and Alan are farmers and ranchers. Alan is also a veterinarian.

[4] Each of Alfred, Barbara, Barry and Alan are registered owners, as tenants in common, of a one-quarter undivided interest in the Land. The Land includes Barbara and Alfred's home quarter, being SE 27-7-10 W3M (the "Home Quarter"), on which their house, barn and other outbuildings and structures are located. Alan's house and his veterinary clinic are also located on the Home Quarter, but Alan's primary farming and cattle operations are on … the quarter section immediately to the east of the Home Quarter. Barry and his wife, Gladys Raymond ("Gladys"), live and have their farming and cattle operations on the quarter section immediately to the south of the Home Quarter. Both Alan and Barry have used the Land in their respective farming and cattle operations. Alan's son, David Raymond ("David"), currently lives in Barbara and Alfred's house.

[5] This action arose out of a broader dispute between the Raymond brothers as to their succession to the farm land owned by their parents. The dispute arose prior to the deaths of Barbara and Alfred and continues. ...

[6] At trial in this matter, the judge disposed of the question as to whether a sale agreement existed between Barry and his parents and then addressed the appropriate remedy for the breach:

. . .

[87] I am aware of the attachment that farmers have to their land and I have carefully considered the plaintiff's reasons for requesting a transfer of the defendants' interest to him.

[88] Against this I must also consider that Barry has basically not used the property for a number of years and has been able to get along. I feel compelled to take into consideration that Barry is in his late sixties and question the sincerity of his motive to set up his cattle operation on the property. Had Barry pressed his claim in 2002 after the Agreement for Sale was prepared I might have looked at it differently. At this point, six years later, so much has happened between Barry and Alan that I cannot shake the feeling that Barry's motive may not be as genuine as it once was.

[89] In essence, I have not been convinced that the property is unique or irreplaceable in the sense that it cannot be compensated by damages. In my view a damage award will adequately compensate Barry for the purchase. The amount is $70,500.00 which represents one-half the appraised value of the property.

The Parents' Estates do not dispute the finding that a valid and enforceable agreement for the sale of the Land existed between Barry and his parents. This appeal is limited to whether the judge, having found breach of that agreement, properly awarded compensatory damages, not specific performance, as the remedy for that breach. This appeal gives rise to a single question: Did the judge err in finding that compensatory damages was an adequate remedy?

III. Analysis

[7] Until 1996 it had long been a tenet of our law that each parcel of real property was inherently unique. Given this inherent uniqueness, our courts made the equitable remedy of specific performance readily available to a plaintiff purchaser who claimed the vendor had breached a contract for the sale of real property. In 1996, Sopinka J's majority decision in *Semelhago v. Paramadevan*, [1996] 2 SCR 415 ("*Semelhago*"), questioned these longstanding, rudimentary elements of our law of real property. His comments, although *obiter*, were thereafter generally accepted as law. However, Sopinka J did not so much make new law as remind us that a basic legal rationale based on the presumed inadequacy of expectation damages has always underpinned the availability of specific performance as a remedy in cases involving real property. Unfortunately, post-*Semelhago* there has been some confusion as to when the remedy of specific performance will be made available to an aggrieved prospective purchaser of land. For this reason, *Semelhago* has been criticized for founding legal uncertainty in once settled law. This appeal results in part from that uncertainty.

[8] ... It is important to note that the real property at issue in *Semelhago* was a house under construction on a bare lot in Toronto that was "interchangeable in all likelihood with any number of others" (at paras. 7 and 23). Further, at the time, a line of cases had emerged involving aggrieved prospective purchasers who had sought the remedy of specific perform-

ance which distinguished investment properties from other real properties, as examples see: *Heron Bay Investments Ltd. v. Peel-Elder Developments Ltd.* (1976), 2 CPC 338 (Ont. HC) ("*Heron Bay*"); *Chaulk v. Fairview Construction Ltd.*, (1977), 3 RPR 116 (Nfld. CA) ("*Chaulk*"); *McNabb v. Smith* (1981), 124 DLR (3d) 547 (BCSC), aff'd (1982), 132 DLR (3d) 523 (BCCA); and *Domowicz v. Orsa Investments Ltd.* (1993), 36 RPR (2d) 174 (Ont. Gen. Div.).

[9] What *Heron Bay*, *Chaulk*, and *Semelhago* all speak to is the general goal of the law of remedies as it applies to breach of contract, which is to put the plaintiff in the same position that the plaintiff would have been in had the defendant performed under the contract. With this goal in mind, the courts typically awarded a successful plaintiff the common law remedy of compensatory damages. However, where damages will not make the plaintiff whole, the courts may resort to equity and may award a successful plaintiff the discretionary remedy of specific performance. An order for specific performance *requires* the defendant to perform under the contract, thereby making the plaintiff whole. In this context, specific performance is an alternative, equitable remedy made available to a plaintiff only where a common law award of damages would be inadequate. ...

[10] The general approach of courts faced with a breach of contract claim has been to assess the adequacy of damages before resorting to the remedy of specific performance, but then only if compensatory damages proved inadequate. However, prior to *Semelhago*, courts recognized a general exception to this approach when the contract in question involved land and courts understood specific performance to be the primary and accepted remedy in that circumstance. ...

[12] Yet ... even though specific performance was the presumed remedy, underlying that presumption was an acceptance of the *general* inadequacy of damages as a remedy in the circumstances of breach of contract for the transfer of land. Robert J. Sharpe in *Injunctions and Specific Performance*, *supra* describes the rationale underlying that presumption as follows (at para. 7.220):

An award of damages presumes that the plaintiff's expectation can be protected by a money award which will purchase substitute performance. If the item bargained for is unique, then there is no exact substitute. The lack of an available substitute produces two problems. First, it makes the purely monetary loss caused by the defendant's breach very difficult to measure. There are no comparable sales to which reference may be made in order to establish an objective estimate of the value of the promised item or performance. Secondly, even if an objective value of some sort can be found, the effect of denying specific performance and granting damages is to force the plaintiff to settle for some inexact substitute. The plaintiff may, however, have attached to the particular item bargained for a value, sometimes called the "consumer surplus," which is not reflected by objective measurement. In such a case, the value of the item to the plaintiff exceeds the market value (even if it can be established) and it is difficult to justify forcing the plaintiff to accept only the lesser objective value. It might be argued that money relief could also be awarded to compensate the plaintiff for this loss above the market value but, because of its subjective nature, that extra value is extremely difficult to assess. However, if no account is taken of this aspect of the plaintiff's interest in performance, the expectation will not be protected and one of the basic aims of contract remedies will not be fulfilled. By requiring performance of the defendant's obligations *in specie*, the court can avoid the expensive and time-consuming task of translating the effect of the breach into money terms and, more importantly, avoid the risk of inaccurate assessment and thereby achieve a virtual guarantee of remedial adequacy in favour of the plaintiff. [footnotes omitted]

[13] In effect then, Sopinka J's *obiter* reminded us that, notwithstanding the subject matter, the factual circumstances of a thwarted purchase of real property should be examined to see whether the facts are consistent with the assumptions that underpin expectation damages as adequate protection, *i.e.*, do the facts disclose a prospective purchaser whose motivation for purchase is maximization of investment profit and a subject matter that is a fungible for which there is a readily available substitute? And, where the facts are such, *Semelhago* reminded us that damages is the appropriate remedy as it will meet the goal of protecting the prospective purchaser's expectation.

[14] *Semelhago* does not, however, stand for the proposition that the presumption of uniqueness has been supplanted by a presumption of replaceability. See: *904060 Ontario Ltd. v. 529566 Ontario Ltd.*, 1999 CarswellOnt 378 (Gen. Div.) at para. 14, [1999] OJ No. 355 (QL) and *John E. Dodge Holdings Ltd. v. 805062 Ontario Ltd.* (2001), 56 OR (3d) 341 (SCJ) ("*Dodge*"). The only change wrought by *Semelhago* is in the approach of the courts to determining the appropriate remedy; judges must no longer presume the inadequacy of damages as a remedy whenever real property is involved. But, this assessment is not a search for uniqueness. Rather, it is appropriate to characterize a judge's assessment in cases of this nature as an inquiry into whether, in the circumstances, damages would be an inadequate remedy. As Lax J said in *Dodge*:

> [55] … The danger in framing the issue as one of uniqueness (a term that carries with it a pre-*Semelhago* antediluvian aroma) is that the real point of *Semelhago* will be lost. It is obviously important to identify the factors or characteristics that make a particular property unique to a particular plaintiff. The more fundamental question is whether the plaintiff has shown that the land rather than its monetary equivalent better serves justice between the parties. This will depend on whether money is an adequate substitute for the plaintiff's loss and this in turn will depend on whether the subject matter of the contract is generic or unique.

[15] In practical terms, this means the prospective purchaser bears the burden of adducing evidence that the subject property is specially suited to the purchaser and that a comparable substitute property is not readily available. These evidentiary points are necessarily intertwined because, on the basis of the evidence, the prospective purchaser must discharge the overall burden of persuading the judge that the subject property is so different from others that damages is an inadequate remedy and that justice dictates the purchaser should have the subject property. The judge, in turn, must conduct a critical inquiry on the evidence as to the nature and function of the subject property in relation to the prospective purchaser. The evidence and analyses will necessarily overlap, but the overall question the judge must answer is whether the justice of the matter calls for an award of specific performance because damages would be inadequate.

[16] The post-*Semelhago* case law in Saskatchewan has, for the most part, followed the foregoing approach to determining whether compensatory damages is an adequate remedy for breach of an agreement for sale of farm land. …

[19] … [The] cases indicate that specific performance remains the *principal* remedy for breach of contract involving the sale of farm land in Saskatchewan; but, since *Semelhago*, it is neither a presumptive nor automatic remedy.

[20] To bring this back to the matter at hand, the judge summarized Barry's reasons for wanting his Parents' Interests as follows:

> [56] The plaintiff claims that the property in question is unique for the following reasons:
>
> – Barry already has an undivided one-quarter interest in the property;
>
> – the land is also the historical yard-site that Barry has operated his cattle and farming operation on for over 40 years, with his parents;
>
> – Barry has an emotional attachment to the land because he farmed out of the yard-site as did his father and grandfather;
>
> – Barry farmed out of the yard-site with his son Vincent prior to Vincent being accidentally killed. This represents another emotional connection for Barry;
>
> – there are no reasonable yard-sites located in proximity to Barry's home, which is immediately across the road;
>
> – replacement values as to the buildings on the land would make it economically unfeasible to build these facilities on his own property at his age and stage of farming; and
>
> – purchasing land not located within the vicinity of the primary cattle and farming operation would not be a financially viable option for Barry.

The Parents' Estates did not tender much evidence to counter Barry's evidence nor in respect of the existence or availability of farm land comparable to the Land.

[21] As noted at para. 6 above, the judge's assessment of whether damages was an adequate remedy is sparse. I find sufficient error in the judge's assessment to warrant appellate intervention in this matter. Principally, the judge failed to actually assess whether Barry's expectation interest under the agreement for sale could be protected by a monetary award of sufficient value to allow him to purchase substitute performance. This error is comprised of two omissions:

(a) the judge failed to assess whether the Land was specially suited to Barry; and

(b) the judge failed to assess whether a comparable substitute property was readily available.

[22] The judge did acknowledge that farmers have an attachment to their land in general and did say that he had carefully considered Barry's reasons for seeking specific performance. However, the judge failed to conduct a critical inquiry as to the nature and function of the Land in relation to Barry. Rather, the judge focused on Barry's "motive" for pursuing his Parents' Interests, from which I take him to mean an ulterior reason for pursuing specific performance. While a judge's inquiry must involve a critical examination of the motive of the prospective purchaser, "motive" in this sense refers to the *nature* and the *authenticity* or *cogency* of the subjective and objective factors articulated by the prospective purchaser.

Barry's reasons for deciding to acquire his Parents' Interests at the time he entered the agreement for sale are highly material; but a supposed ulterior "motive" for pursuing his claim for breach of that agreement is not. Furthermore, the judge erred by grounding his inquiry into the genuineness of this motive on a misapprehension of the facts dating from a time *after* Barry and his parents had entered the agreement for sale.

[23] The judge erred by relying on Barry's supposed motive for pursuing his claim to ground his conclusion that a damage award would adequately compensate Barry. This approach to determining the appropriate remedy was in error as it did not address Barry's expectation interest in performance under the agreement for sale. In light of this conclusion, it is necessary to consider afresh whether Barry's expectation interest would be adequately protected by an award of damages.

[24] It cannot be said that the Land is, or that Barry treated the Land as, more akin to a commodity than a tract of land having special attributes not found in any other farm land. The Land is immediately across the road from Barry's home quarter. Barry already owns an undivided one-quarter interest in the Land. The Land once belonged to his grandfather and is home to his parents' yard-site. Barry used the Land for over 40 years, with his parents, his brother, and his deceased son. These factors or attributes are cogent and impossible to value precisely. On this basis, I would find that an award of damages cannot restore Barry to the position that he would have been in had the Parents' Estates performed under the agreement for sale of the Parents' Interests. Furthermore, Barry's evidence was also that there are no "reasonable yard-sites" located in close proximity to his home quarter. Whether or not reasonable yard-sites are available, no other yard-site could have the attributes of the Land. In other words, there is no comparable substitute property, let alone one that is readily available. If there is any farm land in respect of which compensatory damages is inadequate, it is typically that farm land which sits directly across the road from a farmer's home quarter. This is especially so where the farmer has an existing legal interest in it, strong emotional and familial ties to it, and sound economic reasons for making it part of his farming operations. Whether pre- or post-*Semelhago*, such farmland is "unique" and the appropriate remedy in such a case is an order for specific performance.

[25] I would, therefore, grant the appeal, set aside the award of damages and substitute therefor an order for specific performance requiring the Parents' Estates to transfer the Parents' Interests to Barry.

W.J. VANCISE JA: I concur.

R.G. RICHARDS JA: I concur.

NOTES AND QUESTIONS

1. In *Erie Sand and Gravel Ltd. v. Seres' Farms Ltd.*, 2009 ONCA 709, 97 OR (3d) 241, the plaintiff sand and gravel company, which had earlier purchased land from the defendant on the north side of a road, contracted to purchase the defendant's lands on the south side of the road. The defendants resisted the plaintiff's claim for specific performance by arguing that its breach deprived the plaintiff only of business profits, so it could be compensated in damages. The Ontario Court of Appeal disagreed:

[106] [T]he trial judge accepted the uncontradicted, uncontested evidence led by Erie that: its financial existence depends on it having an adequate supply of aggregate; aggregate is in scarce supply in Essex County; 50% of the remaining aggregate in Essex County not under Erie's control is located on the subject property; no other lands in the County of Essex containing aggregate are for sale; and, the aggregate on the south side property will supply Erie with sufficient aggregate to meet its needs for a period of between 5 and 10 years.

[107] On these findings, the clear inference is that Erie needs to purchase the south side property so that it will have sufficient aggregate to continue in business. ...

[108] The Koop family has owned and run Erie since 1977. In my view, it is self-evident that loss of a family business represents far more than merely the loss of whatever profits would have been made had it been able to continue in business. For that reason, I reject the foundation on which this ground of appeal rests, namely, that Erie's only harm, should it not be awarded the south side property, is the loss of future profits.

2. As Lax J noted in *Dodge*, where the purchaser intends to occupy the property as a residence, its "uniqueness" is determined mainly by reference to the subjective preferences of the purchaser. Its objective distinctiveness is less relevant than in the case of commercial property. Specific performance is often awarded in these residential cases. See, for example, *Martel v. Mohr*, [2011] SJ no. 258 (QB); *Amar v. Matthew*, [2010] BCJ no. 669 (SC); *Chan v. Tu*, [2006] BCJ no. 1392 (SC); *Van Dyk v. Durno*, [2005] BCJ no. 1052 (SC); *Defranco v. Khatri*, [2005] OJ no. 1890 (SC); *Ali v. 656527 BC Ltd.* (2004), 29 BCLR (4th) 206 (CA); *Holden v. Tanase*, [2002] AJ no. 1424 (QB) (QL); *Taberner v. Ernest & Twins Developments Inc.* (2001), 89 BCLR (3d) 104 (SC); *Cormack v. Hardwardt*, [1998] BCJ no. 2684 (SC) (QL); *Hoover v. Mark Minor Homes Ltd.*, [1998] OJ no. 3259 (Gen. Div.) (QL); *Morsky v. Harris*, [1997] 6 WWR 557 (Sask. QB); rev'd. on other grounds (1998), 168 Sask. R 139 (CA).

3. The following extract from the reasons of Lowry J in *Taberner v. Ernest & Twins Developments Inc.* (2001), 89 BCLR (3d) 104 (SC) gives the flavour of the kind of subjective uniqueness inquiry typical of these residential cases. The property in question was a condominium unit in a building in downtown Vancouver purchased for $389,000:

> The following features, taken in combination, are said to make the subject property unique: it is centrally located with some water view; the condominium is 1600 square feet in size with three bedrooms and two bathrooms; it is on the top floor of an eight story building and there are no immediately adjacent buildings; there are two walls of windows affording good light most of the day; there is a large open living space, minimal hallway space, and good outside deck space; a gas stove or fireplace could be added; and there are two secure parking stalls. Ms. Taberner was in the market looking for a downtown condominium for many months and says that, given the features it has, the subject property is unique in terms of anything else that was available.
>
> The vendor adduces evidence of condominium units that were for sale in the same price range in other buildings which it is said have, or with some renovations could have, many of the same features. But no one unit has the same combination of features. They all differ somewhat either in terms of location in the downtown area, the number of floors the units are above the ground, their size, the number of bedrooms, the parking available, etc. ...
>
> Importance is attached to the fact that Ms. Taberner was looking for an 1800 square foot property, that she was not initially enthusiastic about the subject property, and that she intends to make renovations to it. It is said that, while the property may be desirable from Ms. Taberner's

perspective, there is nothing special about it … . The question, however, is whether it is sufficiently unique. In my view, it is.

Lowry J was also impressed by the fact that the market value of the property had fallen and was at the time of trial about $20,000 less than the purchase price:

> This then is not a case where a plaintiff is seeking a decree of specific performance to acquire a property and, on resale, take advantage of a rising real estate market. It is clear that Ms. Taberner must actually want the property for its own sake. That to my mind is compelling evidence that, at least from her perspective, it is a unique property.

4. Specific performance has occasionally been denied to owner-occupiers. In *Konjevic v. Horvat Properties Ltd.* (1998), 40 OR (3d) 633 (CA), the Ontario Court of Appeal affirmed a judgment refusing specific performance when a purchaser of an expensive residential property in Oakville, Ontario failed to establish that the property was unique in the sense that a substitute would not readily be available. Similarly, in *Corse v. Ravenwood Homes Ltd.*, [1998] AJ no. 509 (QB) (QL) a purchaser of a lot on which his custom home was to be built was denied specific performance on the basis that a number of lots were for sale in the same subdivision and that, accordingly, the lot in question was a fungible asset. See also *Haq v. Grossman*, [1999] OJ no. 4176 (Sup. Ct.) (QL).

5. Courts in England and Australia continue to award specific performance as a matter of course in contracts involving land, though the New Zealand courts may be moving in the direction of *Semelhago*: see S. Mills, "Specific Performance: Sale of Land" (June 2006), *NZLJ* 196.

6. In its 2009 *Final Report on Contract for the Sale and Purchase of Land: Purchasers' Remedies*, the Alberta Law Reform Institute (ALRI) concluded that

> specific performance is fairer as between the vendor and the purchaser; that it is more efficient in the sense that it avoids litigation for the assessment of damages; and that it is more effective than damages because it puts the purchaser in the precise position they would have been in if the contract had been performed, and because damages is not an effective remedy at all if the vendor is judgment-proof due to insolvency.

The ALRI recommended that

> for the purpose of determining whether a purchaser under a contract for the sale of land is entitled to specific performance of the contract, the land that is the subject of the contract be conclusively deemed to be unique at all material times, and legislation should be enacted to that effect.

7. For a comprehensive critical analysis of the decision in *Semelhago*, including discussion of some of the difficulties in assessing damages when a plaintiff pursues specific performance and subsequently elects to abandon that claim and pursue damages, see Clark, "Will That Be Performance … or Cash?: Semelhago v. Paramadevan and the Notion of Equivalence" (1999), 37 *Alta. L Rev.* 589. See also R. Chambers, "The Importance of Specific Performance," in S. Degeling and J. Edelman, eds., *Equity in Commercial Law* (Sydney: Lawbook Co., 2005) 431; Lem, "Blackacre Had No Readily Available Equivalent: Specific Performance and Equitable Damages After Semelhago v. Paramadevan," in Law Society of Upper Canada, *Special Lectures* (2002); LoPresti, "The Evolution of Specific Performance: A Discussion of Specific Performance

and Equitable Damages Before and After Semelhago v. Paramadevan" (2002), 49 RPR (3d) 88; J. Berryman, "Recent Developments in the Law of Equitable Remedies: What Canada Can Do for You" (2002), 33 *VUWLR* 51; Lem, "Annotation: Semelhago v. Paramadevan" (1996), 3 RPR (3d) 3.

8. *Semelhago* did not discuss the availability of specific performance to vendors. In most cases a vendor can be adequately compensated with damages, particularly where the market has declined following the date of the contract. Given, moreover, that a purchaser must now prove uniqueness in order to secure specific performance, the earlier justification for awarding this remedy to a vendor based on the doctrine of mutuality has been considerably eroded. Nevertheless, there are a number of examples of successful claims to specific performance by vendors, including some post-*Semelhago* cases. See *Hoover v. Mark Minor Homes Ltd.*, [1988] OJ no. 3629 (Gen. Div.) (QL); *Landmark of Thornhill Limited v. Jacobson* (1995), 25 OR (3d) 628 (CA); *Taylor v. Sturgeon* (1996), 12 RPR (3d) 107 (NSSC); *Westwood Plateau Partnership v. WSP Construction Ltd.* (1997), 37 BCLR (3d) 82 (SC); *Comet Investments Ltd. v. Northwood Logging Ltd.* (1998), 22 RPR (3d) 294 (BCSC). For analysis and criticism of some of these cases, see Berryman, *The Law of Equitable Remedies* (Toronto: Irwin Law, 2000), at 235-36; and Lem, "Blackacre Had No Readily Available Equivalent: Specific Performance and Equitable Damages After Semelhago v. Paramadevan," above.

9. Saskatchewan has enacted *The Land Contracts (Action) Act*, RSS 1978, c. L-3, as am. SS, 1979-80, c. 92; 1980-81, c. 83; 1982-83, c. 16; 1983-84, c. 42; 2001, cc. 8 and 50; and 2004, c. L-16.1, which provides that prior to a *vendor* suing for specific performance of an agreement for the sale of land, leave of the Court of Queen's Bench must be obtained. On the application for leave, the court is directed to consider, *inter alia*, the value of the land, the state of cultivation, the income and assets of the parties, the prevailing conditions of a local or temporary nature, and all other matters that may appear relevant. Why is the leave requirement limited to actions by vendors? What are the policy reasons behind this provision? See also *Law of Property Act*, RSA 2000, c. L-7, Pt. 5.

10. Further extracts from *Semelhago* on the appropriate principles and quantum of damages can be found in chapter 1, "General Principles of Damages."

Certificates of Pending Litigation

What is to prevent a defendant who is being sued for specific performance from conveying away the property while the litigation is pending? What steps are available to a plaintiff (usually a disappointed purchaser) to protect its interest in the land prior to the final judgment in the action?

A subsequent purchaser of the property for value who acts *bona fide* and without notice of the interest being asserted by the plaintiff in the pending litigation may take title free and clear of the plaintiff's interest. Accordingly, a plaintiff should seek to take steps to put prospective purchasers on notice of its claim. (See "Third Parties," above, under the section "Sale of Goods and Services.")

Actual notice may be provided if the plaintiff becomes aware of who the prospective purchaser might be. Otherwise, registration of "notice" on the title to the property will suffice. Sections 70(1) and 74(1) of the *Registry Act*, RSO 1990, c. R.20 provide:

70(1) After the grant from the Crown of land, and letters patent issued therefor, every instrument affecting the land or any part thereof shall be adjudged fraudulent and void against any subsequent purchaser or mortgagee for valuable consideration without actual notice, unless the instrument is registered before the registration of the instrument under which the subsequent purchaser or mortgagee claims. ...

74(1) The registration of an instrument under this or any former Act constitutes notice of the instrument to all persons claiming any interest in the land, subsequent to such registration, despite any defect in the proof for registration, but nevertheless it is the duty of a land registrar not to register any instrument except on such proof as is required by this Act.

The plaintiff could register a notice of the agreement of purchase and sale, or, better yet, the plaintiff could proceed to obtain a certificate of pending litigation and register it against the title to the land in question.

The present law in Ontario is contained in s. 103 of the *Courts of Justice Act*, RSO 1990, c. C.43 and in r. 42 of the Rules of Civil Procedure:

103(1) The commencement of a proceeding in which an interest in land is in question is not notice of the proceeding to a person who is not a party until a certificate of pending litigation is issued by the court and the certificate is registered in the proper land registry office under subsection (2).

(2) Where a certificate of pending litigation is issued under subsection (1) it may be registered whether the land is registered under the *Land Titles Act* or the *Registry Act*. ...

(4) A party who registers a certificate under subsection (2) without a reasonable claim to an interest in the land is liable for any damages sustained by any person as a result of its registration. ...

(6) The court may make an order discharging a certificate,

(a) where the party at whose instance it was issued,

(i) claims a sum of money in place of or as an alternative to the interest in the land claimed,

(ii) does not have a reasonable claim to the interest in the land claimed, or

(iii) does not prosecute the proceeding with reasonable diligence;

(b) where the interests of the party at whose instance it was issued can be adequately protected by another form of security; or

(c) on any other ground that is considered just,

and the court may, in making the order, impose such terms as to the giving of security or otherwise as the court considers just.

(7) Where a certificate is discharged, any person may deal with the land as fully as if the certificate had not been registered.

Rule 42

Issuing of Certificate
Court Order Required

42.01(1) A certificate of pending litigation (Form 42A) under section 103 of the *Courts of Justice Act* may be issued by a registrar only under an order of the court. ...

Motion Without Notice

(3) A motion for an order under subrule (1) may be made without notice.

Order To Be Served Forthwith

(4) A party who obtains an order under subrule (1) shall forthwith serve it, together with a copy of the notice of motion and all affidavits and other documents used at the hearing of the motion, on all parties against whom an interest in land is claimed in the proceeding.

Discharge of Certificate

42.02(1) An order discharging a certificate of pending litigation under subsection 103(6) of the *Courts of Justice Act* may be obtained on motion to the court.

Prior to 1984, the certificate of pending litigation was called a "*lis pendens.*"

For a plaintiff to be entitled to a certificate of pending litigation, it must establish that an interest in land is in issue. So, for example, an action seeking to set aside a marriage contract that dealt with an interest in the matrimonial home under the *Family Law Reform Act* of Ontario does not raise a question involving an interest in land and no certificate can issue (*McMurdo v. McMurdo Estate* (1988), 26 CPC (2d) 20 (Ont. SC, Master)), or where by virtue of an agreement of purchase and sale, the provisions of the *Planning Act* are violated, no interest in land thereby arises and no certificate of pending litigation is available (*683794 Ontario Ltd. v. Sorrento Developments Ltd.* (1990), 71 OR (2d) 571 (SC, Master), aff'd. (1990), 10 RPR (2d) 145 (Ont. HC)), or where the court determined that a surface oil lease constitutes an interest in land and a caution or caveat may be registered on title (*Garland v. Jones* (1993), 111 Sask. R 134 (QB), aff'd. without reasons (February 19, 1994), CA file no. 1573; *Farm Credit Corp. v. Kerr* (1995), 139 Sask. R 230 (QB), aff'd. (1996), 148 Sask. R 245 (CA)), or where a contractual claim against a corporation for a 50 percent interest in its equity and the land that it owned was limited to a claim against the equity and as no interest in land was in issue, a pending litigation order was not available (*Bruneau v. 2779928 Manitoba Ltd.* (1994), 95 Man. R (2d) 274 (CA)), or where the court supports the registration of a certificate of pending litigation on the basis that the claim involves the tracing of estate funds used to purchase a condominium unit (*LeClair v. LeClair Estate* (1998), 48 BCLR (3d) 245 (CA)).

Because a plaintiff may proceed ex parte to obtain an order permitting the issuance of the certificate, questions of entitlement usually arise after the order has been served on the defendant and the defendant launches a motion for an order discharging the certificate. A defendant that is not content to have its land so encumbered pending the outcome of the litigation may seek to discharge the certificate on the grounds of delay (*Romano v. Ciraco* (1985), 4 CPC (2d) 291 (Ont. SC, Master)), that the action appears to be frivolous or vexatious (*Toronto-Dominion Bank v. Zukerman* (1982), 40 OR (2d) 724), where the registration of the certificate would constitute a breach of an agreement to that effect between the parties (*Greenbaum v. 619908 Ontario Ltd. c.o.b. Green Valley Homes* (1986), 11 CPC (2d) 26 (Ont. HC); *St. Thomas Subdividers v. 639373 Ontario Ltd.* (1988), 29 CPC (2d) 1 (Ont. HC); and *Swallow v. The Midlands Corp.* (1993), 14 OR (3d) 687 (Master)), where damages would clearly provide an adequate remedy in the action (*Earthworks 2000 Design Group Inc. v. Spectacular Investments (Canada) Inc.*, [2005] BCJ no. 8 (SC); *JDM Developments Inc. v. J. Stollar Construction Ltd.* (2004), 24 RPR (4th) 133 (Ont. SC); *Baluster Investments Ltd. v. Iona Corporation* (1987), 21 CPC (2d) 114 (Ont. SC, Master), aff'd. (1989), 37 CPC (2d) 235 (Ont. HC)), and where a plaintiff had failed to make full disclosure in its material supporting the ex parte motion (*Cimaroli v. Pugliese* (1988), 25 CPC (2d) 10 (Ont. HC) and *Passarelli v. DiCienzo* (1989), 34 CPC (2d) 54 (Ont. HC)).

The test for determining whether a certificate should be vacated is similar to the recent law on the test for determining whether an interlocutory injunction should issue (*Chippewas of Kettle & Stoney Point v. Canada (Attorney General)* (1994), 17 OR (3d) 831 (Gen. Div.); chapter 8, "Interlocutory Injunctions," under the section "Accessibility Thresholds"; and *Smart v. Smart Estate et al.* (1993), 86 Man. R (2d) 14 (QB)). The court seeks to determine if there is a substantial issue to be tried and then balances the equities between the parties: *Queen's Court Developments Ltd. v. Duquette* (1989), 36 CPC (2d) 297 (Ont. HC, McNeely LJSC). See also *Kalia v. Landmortgage Corp.*, [2004] OJ no. 4130 (SC, Master). Note also the similarities between the law dealing with undertakings as to damages when interlocutory injunctions are issued (see chapter 8, under the section "Undertakings") and s. 103(4) of the *Courts of Justice Act*.

For similar legislative provisions see, for example, *Court of Queen's Bench Act*, RSM 1987, c. 280, ss. 85-86 and *Queen's Bench Act*, RSS 1978, c. Q-1, ss. 48-49.

See also Ellyn and Goodman, "Certificates of Pending Litigation" (1992), 5 CPC (3d) 65; Zarnet, *Specific Performance* (1995), *Law Society of Upper Canada Special Lectures* 193; and Perell, "Tying Up Land: Certificates of Pending Litigation, Cautions and Registered Agreements" (1989-90), 11 *Advocates' Q* 265.

CHAPTER TEN

Financial Relief in Equity

INTRODUCTION

Although equity has traditionally preferred to award coercive relief (injunctions and specific performance), it also has jurisdiction to award financial compensation. This jurisdiction has two sources. Equity has an inherent jurisdiction to award compensation to redress purely equitable wrongs (such as breach of fiduciary duty) for which the common law offers no remedy. Financial relief awarded under this jurisdiction is known as "equitable compensation."

The second source of equitable jurisdiction to award financial compensation is statutory. Before the merger of the administration of law and equity in the late 19th century, litigants who were refused coercive relief in the courts of Chancery for breach of their common law rights had to bring their actions again in the common law courts—a costly and inefficient practice. In addition, where a plaintiff for equitable relief had in the meantime suffered financial consequences from the wrong in question, the Court of Chancery had no jurisdiction to award damages to the point at which the equitable decree was issued. Here, too, the plaintiff had to resort to the courts of common law to achieve "perfect" relief. A partial antidote to each of these difficulties was provided by the passage of *Lord Cairns' Act* in 1858. This statute was the first enactment on the path to the merger of the courts of common law and equity in England and it created a specific authority for the Court of Chancery to award damages as well as or in substitution for specific performance or an injunction. Despite their statutory basis, damages awarded pursuant to this act and its progeny are known as "equitable damages."

In this chapter, we consider the extent to which equitable damages and compensation still have an independent role to fulfill in our remedial system well over 100 years after the fusion of the courts of common law and equity in England and, in most instances, in Canada as well. To what extent are areas of our law where equitable damages and compensation (along with account* and relief for breach of trust) still necessary because the rights violated are not vindicated at all or inadequately by way of the principles of common law and common law damages? To what extent do these equitable modes of relief provide a potentially more lucrative source of financial relief for plaintiffs and, in particular, are there limitations on the scope of common law damages that are not applied either at all or in quite the same way under equity? For the purposes of equitable damages and compensation, do the principles of causation, foreseeability, contributory negligence, and mitigation, as well as those governing the date at which loss is measured, recovery for non-economic loss, and punitive or exemplary damages work in the same way as they do in the domain of the common law?

---

* For those courses concentrating on equitable remedies, the materials on account in chapter 2, "Awards Measured by Benefit to Defendant," can be integrated usefully within this chapter.

This context will also provide a convenient vehicle for an evaluation of the extent to which the principles and remedies of common law and equity have merged in Canadian law. Is it still appropriate to conceive of common law and equity as separate sources of principle and doctrine? To the extent that it is, what contributions does equity still have to make to the continuing evolution of our remedial system?

Another area where questions of financial compensation have arisen, albeit collaterally in the domain of equity, has been in situations where specific performance is sought subject to an abatement in the contract price. The abatement is meant to reflect the fact that that which the vendor is able to deliver is less than that which has been promised in the contract. That issue is also explored in this chapter and it too has merger dimensions to the extent that the concept has traditionally been viewed as relevant only in equity and the notion of a deduction against common law damages to reflect such a consideration never seriously considered until comparatively recently.

Finally, we use this chapter as a vehicle for exploring the principles governing election of remedies in situations where a plaintiff has sought two mutually exclusive remedies, most commonly specific performance or an injunction in combination with some form of monetary relief, either common law or equitable.

EQUITABLE DAMAGES

Introduction

At a number of points already, we have encountered references to equitable damages. Three examples will suffice. In *Wroth v. Tyler* (chapter 1, "General Principles of Damages"), Megarry J saw equitable damages as providing a way in which losses could be assessed by reference to the value of the land in dispute at the date of trial rather than at the date of breach. In *Hooper v. Rogers* (chapter 7, "Injunctions"), the English Court of Appeal avoided the effects of the principle that common law damages can only be given once harm has occurred by awarding equitable damages instead. In this way, the court was able to put money in the plaintiff's hands for the purposes of restoring land that the defendant had bulldozed and thereby created the risk of the plaintiff's house collapsing in the future. Finally, at the conclusion of the previous chapter, we saw the possibility raised that equitable damages could be awarded in certain situations in substitution for specific performance in the context of a claim based on the doctrine of part performance. However, as was also clear at least historically, there have been limitations on the availability of equitable damages as a substitute for specific performance or an injunction.

In this section of the casebook, we consider the history of equitable damages and the restrictions that the courts have from time to time placed on their availability. More important, however, the objective is to identify more comprehensively than we have done previously the situations in which it is necessary to rely on equitable rather than common law damages as a substitute for or in addition to specific performance or an injunction. In this context, the question is also raised as to why this throwback to the days prior to fusion of the courts of common law and equity is still a matter of concern.

The section starts with the statutory origin of the courts' authority to award such relief.

Lord Cairns' Act
(1858), 21 & 22 Vict., c. 27

2. In all cases in which the Court of Chancery has Jurisdiction to entertain an Application for an Injunction against a Breach of any Covenant, Contract or Agreement, or against the Commission or Continuance of any wrongful Act, or for the specific Performance of any Covenant, Contract, or Agreement, it shall be lawful for the same Court, if it shall think fit, to award Damages to the Party injured, either in addition to or in substitution for such Injunction or specific Performance, and such Damages may be assessed in such manner as the Court shall direct.

J.A. Jolowicz, "Damages in Equity—A Study of Lord Cairns' Act"
(1975), 34 *Cambridge Law Journal* 224, at 224-30 (footnotes omitted)

When, if ever, may a court award damages to a plaintiff whose case sounds only in equity, not in law? In *Hooper v. Rogers* an award of damages in respect of a nuisance which had not yet resulted in any relevant damage was upheld by the Court of Appeal. In *Wrotham Park Estate Co. Ltd. v. Parkside Homes Ltd.* Brightman J awarded substantial damages for breach of a restrictive covenant to the successors in title of the covenantee against the successors in title of the covenantor. In *Wroth v. Tyler* damages for the non-performance of a contract for the sale of a house were assessed by reference to the value of the house at the date of the hearing, not the date of breach. In none of these cases could the decisions have been justified on common law principles alone and all are in fact founded upon the *Chancery Amendment Act 1858*, commonly known as *Lord Cairns' Act*. Yet in *Redland Bricks Ltd. v. Morris*, while the Court of Appeal considered that an elaborate discussion of that Act was necessary and, indeed, differed in opinion as to the result of its application to the circumstances of the case, the House of Lords, through Lord Upjohn, dismissed the matter briefly and categorically with the observation that *Lord Cairns' Act* had nothing whatever to do with the principles of law applicable to the case. The time seems ripe for an examination of the meaning and present status of the Act.

The name of *Lord Cairns' Act* is familiar to every student of the English Legal System as one of the Acts which paved the way to the combined administration of law and equity in a single Supreme Court of Judicature. The *Common Law Procedure Act 1854* had given to the courts of common law a limited power of granting equitable relief as well as damages; *Lord Cairns' Act*, passed on the recommendations of the Chancery Commissioners, gave to the Court of Chancery a parallel power of awarding damages.

The main purpose of the Act was to do away with the necessity for separate proceedings in law and equity in those cases in which a plaintiff could establish his title both to equitable relief in the form of an injunction or decree of specific performance and to damages at common law. It was not the intention of the Act to take away business from the courts of common law nor to give the Court of Chancery concurrent jurisdiction in all cases of tort or breach of contract. The opening words of section 2—the only substantive section—accordingly restrict the Court of Chancery's power to award damages to cases in which it had "jurisdiction to entertain an application" for either an injunction or a decree of specific performance. Within that restriction, however, the Court could, if it thought fit, award damages to the party injured in *addition* to equitable relief and thus do "complete justice" in law as well as in equity.

This provision gave rise to no problems either in Parliament or subsequently in the courts. There is one straightforward example of its application in the Reports in 1860, and the scarcity of cases thereafter indicates that it was absorbed easily into the practice of the Court. The Chancery Commissioners had, however, envisaged a special additional class of case in which they considered that the Court of Chancery should have power to award damages so as to do "complete justice," namely, cases in which the Court, without any default on the part of the plaintiff, found itself unable from special circumstances to grant him "the peculiar equitable relief of specific performance, and in which we think the Court should have jurisdiction to give the plaintiff such other compensation as he ought to have." Power to award damages *in addition* to equitable relief would obviously have been insufficient to meet such a case, and it is almost certainly for this reason that the Act as passed gave to the Court power to award damages "either in addition to or *in substitution* for" an injunction or decree of specific performance.

Cory v. Thames Ironworks & Shipbuilding Co. Ltd. illustrates the kind of situation which the Commissioners probably had in mind. The plaintiff's original claim was for specific performance of a contract for the sale of a ship, delivery of which had been delayed by the default of the seller. After the bill was filed but before the hearing, the sale was completed and the plaintiff then amended his bill so as to ask for a declaration that he had been entitled to a decree when the bill was filed and damages. Wood VC ordered the plaintiff's damages to be assessed and observed that, since the plaintiff was from the first entitled to two different kinds of relief "it would be hard to say that change of circumstances, depriving him of the one, without affecting his right, he should therefore lose the other."

There is no reason to suppose that the plaintiff in this case could not have recovered in a court of common law the damages which he in fact recovered in the Court of Chancery. Wood VC's concern was to relieve him of the need to start fresh proceedings in another court in order to recover damages for the late delivery of the ship. In other words, the Vice-Chancellor considered that the case was one in which the Court of Chancery should do "complete justice" under *Lord Cairns' Act* rather than decline to act on the ground that the plaintiff's claim sounded only in law.

In their historical context, therefore, cases such as this are to be contrasted with others of similar date in which the Court of Chancery demonstrated its anxiety to preserve the division of function between the courts of common law and itself. Wood VC himself, for example, had earlier insisted, in *Wicks v. Hunt*, that it was not the intention of *Lord Cairns' Act* to extend the jurisdiction of the Court of Chancery to cases "where there is a plain common law remedy, and where before the Statute the Court would not have intervened." Even after the Court of Chancery was required by statute in 1862 to determine for itself every question of law or fact cognisable in a court of common law upon which the plaintiff's right to equitable relief depended, the Court continued to insist on its right to send the plaintiff to law. In *Cory's* case the Court was willing to award damages and relieve the plaintiff of the need to take fresh proceedings at law because he had an equitable cause of action when he filed his bill and came very close to making out a complete case for equitable relief. The Court was also willing to make a similar concession where the only impediment to equitable relief, even though occurring before the bill was filed, was attributable to the defendant's default and, thirdly, it would do so in cases in which the plaintiff was prepared to waive performance of those parts of a complex agreement which prevented the agreement as a whole from being susceptible to specific performance. In all these cases, it may be said, the plaintiff had some justification for having started proceedings in equity and it was right, therefore, that a statute designed to enable the Court of Chancery to do "complete justice" should be applied and damages awarded even though, in the result, the plaintiff turned out to be entitled to nothing that he could not have obtained in a court of common law. But where he did not in this way come close to establishing a right to equitable relief—where, it may be said, he showed no equitable cause of action—then his bill would be dismissed and he would be left to bring fresh proceedings in a court of law.

As a statute designed to enable the Court of Chancery to do "complete justice" in law and equity, *Lord Cairns' Act* ceased to have any significance once the *Judicature Acts* had been brought into operation, and the Act was repealed by the *Statute Law Revision and Civil Procedure Act 1883*. Long before then, however, it had been realised that the power to award damages *in substitution* for equitable relief did more than enable the Court to award to deserving suitors the damages that they could otherwise have obtained in a court of common law. Wittingly or unwittingly, through *Lord Cairns' Act*, Parliament had conferred upon the Court of Chancery, and thus in course of time upon the Supreme Court of Judicature, a discretionary jurisdiction to award damages which could not have been awarded at common law. It is with this novel jurisdiction to award "damages in equity" that the remainder of this article is concerned, and it is well to emphasize at the outset that recognition of this novel jurisdiction is equivalent to recognition—to the extent allowed by the Act—of an actual, though limited, fusion of law and equity. It is the characteristic of a cause of action at common law that the plaintiff's typical if not exclusive remedy is an award of damages; it is, or was, characteristic of a cause of action in equity that, whatever the remedy available to the plaintiff, he cannot have damages. To this the combined administration of law and equity makes no difference: all it means is that both kinds of remedy, where appropriate, are available in a single action in a single court. But where damages are available when no cause of action exists at common law, or where, as is commonly the case, damages at common law may be awarded only up to the date of the writ and yet, under *Lord Cairns' Act*, they are awarded "in substitution" for equitable relief to cover the future, then indeed, law and equity have been fused. Before turning to this development, however, it is necessary first to dispose of the technical problem raised by the repeal of *Lord Cairns' Act* in 1883.

The *Statute Law Revision and Civil Procedure Act 1883*, in common with all subsequent *Statute Law Revision Acts* until the *Statute Law Repeals Act 1974*, contained a savings clause preserving, amongst other things, "any jurisdiction or principle or rule of law or equity established or confirmed ... by or under any enactment repealed by this Act." If, therefore, as has been said, the effect of a *Statute Law Revision Act* containing such a savings clause amounts to no more than authorisation for the omission of the repealed enactments from the statute book then, at least until 1974, the jurisdiction created by *Lord Cairns' Act*, in so far as not absorbed by the *Judicature Acts*, survived as statute law. In at least two cases concerned with other legislation, however, the courts have declined to pay so little regard to a repeal, and the true question has been said to be whether a substituted enactment contains anything incompatible with that which was repealed.

In *Chapman, Morsons & Co. v. Guardians of Auckland Union* Lord Esher MR said that the repeal of *Lord Cairns' Act* "was not with the intention of taking away any of the powers given by the Act in a Chancery action, but because it was considered that the *Judicature Acts* re-enacted the powers, and therefore that *Lord Cairns' Act* had become obsolete." This is plausible as a historical explanation of the repeal, but it does nothing to clarify the situation from the technical point of view. If and in so far as *Lord Cairns' Act* did more than anticipate the *Judicature Acts* by creating the novel jurisdiction described above, then Lord Esher says no more than that the Act was repealed under a misapprehension, which is probably true but unhelpful.

Fortunately it is unnecessary to disentangle the statutory confusion for there can be no doubt that the substance of *Lord Cairns' Act* survives, if not with the authority of statute then with the authority of case law. In the first reported case in which the repeal of the Act might have been argued as affecting the result, it was either overlooked or deliberately disregarded by counsel and judge alike, and in no case thereafter has any judge suggested that the substance of *Lord Cairns' Act* is not law. On the contrary, while the formal repeal of the Act has been ignored in the majority of cases, in some the Act's survival has been expressly affirmed. Its continuing legal efficacy was put beyond doubt by the House of Lords in 1924. Delivering the leading speech for the majority in *Leeds Industrial Co-operative Society Ltd. v. Slack* Viscount Finlay voiced his suspicion that the repeal, which he regarded as "unfortunate," had proceeded on some misapprehension, possibly the view that it conferred only the right of giving damages as at common law, and concluded, *Lord Cairns' Act* is one which is continually referred to in English cases, as giving in a convenient form results which it might cost some effort and a good deal of time to work out afresh, and its absence from the Revised Statutes is to be regretted. Though the Act is gone, the law which it laid down still exists, and this case, like many others of the same kind, has throughout, from beginning to end, been dealt with on this view.

So far, at least, as the matters to be discussed here are concerned, the repeal of *Lord Cairns' Act* caused scarcely a ripple on the surface of the law. Some judges have felt obliged to refer to it in order to explain that their powers remained unaffected; no judge has ever held that it made the slightest difference to the substance of the law itself.

NOTE

In Ontario, the relevant provision was for many years a virtual replica of the basic *Lord Cairns' Act* section:

Judicature Act
RSO 1980, c. 223

21. Where the court has jurisdiction to entertain an application for an injunction against a breach of a covenant, contract or agreement, or against the commission or continuance of a wrongful act, or for the specific performance of a covenant, contract or agreement, the court may award damages to the party injured either in addition to or in substitution for the injunction or

specific performance, and the damages may be ascertained in such manner as the court directs, or the court may grant such other relief as is considered just.

In 1984, however, it was repealed and replaced by the *Courts of Justice Act.*

Courts of Justice Act
RSO 1990, c. C.43

99. A court that has jurisdiction to grant an injunction or order specific performance may award damages in addition to, or in substitution for, the injunction or specific performance.

QUESTION

Did this change the law?

In a number of jurisdictions, the basic *Judicature Act* provision was enacted and, even today, either it or a simpler version remains in place. See, for example, *Judicature Act*, RSA 2000, c. J-2, s. 19; *Queen's Bench Act*, SS 1998, c. Q-1.01, s. 66. In others, however, the court's ability to award damages in equity appears to survive by virtue of the express preservation of all the court's equitable jurisdiction. See, for example, *Judicature Act*, RSNS 1989, c. 240, s. 41, referring to the equitable jurisdiction of the Nova Scotia Supreme Court as of October 1, 1884.

The first case that we consider is primarily about the adequacy of pleadings. Indeed, the ratio of the case is almost certainly to the effect that the prayer for relief in the statement of claim contained a sufficiently identifiable pleading for common law damages. However, before reaching that point the Supreme Court also discussed whether the factual situation was one that allowed the court to award equitable damages even though they had not been explicitly sought as an alternative to specific performance. In so doing, the court provides some valuable guidance on the interpretation of the standard *Lord Cairns' Act* provision and the term "jurisdiction" as employed in that Act.

Dobson v. Winton & Robbins Ltd.
[1959] SCR 775

[This case started out principally as a claim by the vendor of property for specific performance against the purchaser who had repudiated its contractual obligations prior to the date of closing. However, a few days prior to the trial of the action, the plaintiff vendor had "mitigated" his losses and sold the property to a third party for some $5,000 below the purchase price of the original contract. This deal closed a few days after the conclusion of the trial. At trial, the plaintiff was therefore no longer seeking specific performance but rather confining himself to a claim in damages. He sought leave to amend his pleadings to this effect but leave was denied, a ruling later sustained on appeal in the Court of Appeal. As a consequence, the principal issues became whether the plaintiff could claim damages in circumstances such as this, whether the pleadings as drafted were adequate to support such a claim, and whether the plaintiff had acted reasonably in selling the property at the time that he had and for the price that he had. The trial court dismissed the plaintiff's claim for damages ((1958), 14 DLR (2d) 110 (Ont. HC)) but disallowed the defendant's counterclaim for a return of the deposit and this judgment was sustained on appeal (unreported). The plaintiff then appealed to the Supreme Court of Canada and the defendant cross-appealed.]

JUDSON J (delivering the judgment of the court): … The difficulty that the learned trial Judge and the Court of Appeal found in this case is largely of historical origin. A plaintiff who elected to issue a bill in Chancery for specific performance could get no damages in that Court until the *Chancery Amendment Act, 1858* (Imp.) c. 27 (*Lord Cairns' Act*), which provided for the award of damages "either in addition to or in substitution for" specific performance. This legislation is still retained in the *Judicature Act*, RSO 1950, c. 190, s. 18. Its application was never as wide in the Court of Chancery as might possibly have been expected. It did not confer upon the Court of Chancery the common law jurisdiction in an action for damages. The prerequisite in the Court of Chancery to the exercise of jurisdiction under this legislation in contract cases was the right to relief by way of specific performance. If, for any reason, a litigant was before the Court without any such right to relief, damages could not be awarded and the plaintiff was still left to his remedy, if any, in a Court of law.

This jurisdictional difficulty disappeared in the *Judicature Act*. The Supreme Court of Ontario has jurisdiction in every legal or equitable claim and the purpose of the legislation as expressed in the concluding words of s. 15(h) of the Act is that "all matters so in controversy between the parties may be completely and finally determined, and all multiplicity of legal proceedings concerning any of such matters avoided." The problem now is not one of jurisdiction or substantive law but the narrow one of pleading, and it is this issue that has been decided in this case adversely to the plaintiff. Both Courts have held that, as pleaded, this case contained nothing more than a claim for specific performance and that with the disappearance of this claim as a result of the second sale, the foundation of the action had gone and the Court could not award damages in addition to or in substitution for specific performance. The submission that an alternative common law claim for damages was pleaded was rejected and the application for amendment refused.

The plaintiff's common law right of action on the facts of this case, as found by both Courts, is clear. On the purchaser's repudiation of the contract, the vendor could have forfeited the deposit and claimed for loss of bargain and out-of-pocket expenses. The *Judicature Act* gives him the right to join this claim with one of specific performance. At some stage of the proceedings he must, of course, elect which remedy he will take. He cannot have both specific performance and a common law claim for loss of bargain. But he is under no compulsion to elect until judgment, and the defendant is not entitled to assume that by issuing the writ for specific performance with a common law claim for damages in the alternative, the vendor has elected at the institution of the action to claim specific performance and nothing else. The present position is clearly summarized in George Russell Northcote (ed.), *Fry on Specific Performance* (London: Stevens, 6th ed., 1921) at p. 604, in these words: "Accordingly, a plaintiff may now come to the Court and say, Give me specific performance, and with it give me damages, or in substitution for it give me damages, or if I am not entitled to specific performance give me damages as at Common Law by reason of the breach of the agreement."

The judgment at trial is based in part upon the proposition that a claim for specific performance must be deleted by amendment before the alternative claim for damages for breach of contract can be considered. The foundation for this theory must be that by issuing a writ for specific performance the plaintiff has elected this remedy and that no other is open to him. *Hipgrave v. Case* (1885), 28 Ch. D 356 (CA), is cited in support of this principle and the plaintiff's action has failed in this case largely because of the construction which the Courts have put upon that decision. There the plaintiff sued for specific performance with a claim in damages under *Lord Cairns' Act* "in addition to or in substitution for specific performance." No common law claim for damages was pleaded in the alternative. By selling the property after the commencement of the action and before judgment, the plaintiff disentitled himself to specific performance and with it fell his claim for damages as framed under *Lord Cairns' Act*. The case is of narrow scope. No application was made at trial to amend the pleadings and the Court of Appeal refused to entertain the application. The case was, therefore, decided on the principles applicable under *Lord Cairns' Act* and the Court of Appeal refused to turn the action into a common law action for damages.

Taken at its face value, the case does emphasize the importance of practice and pleading. If a plaintiff sues in the alternative for specific performance or damages, he must make sure that his claim for damages is identifiable as one at common law for breach of contract. Otherwise he is in danger of having his claim for damages treated as if it were made in substitution for or as an appendage to the equitable remedy of specific performance and then his claim may be defeated by anything which may bar the equitable remedy, unless an amendment is permitted. This is the advice given by the learned editor of *Williams on Vendor & Purchaser*, 4th ed., vol. 2, p. 1025.

The case, however, is not authority for any principle that by issuing a writ for specific performance with an alternative common law claim for damages, the plaintiff has elected his remedy and is bound by the election. If the claim for specific performance alone is made, that constitutes an affirmation of the contract and, to that extent, an election to enforce the contract. But where the alternative common law claim is made, the writ is equivocal and there is no election. The distinction was clearly pointed out by Luxmoore LJ in *Public Trustee v. Pearlberg*, [1940] 2 KB 1 (CA) at p. 19. The matter is summarized in *Williams on Vendor & Purchaser*, 4th ed., p. 1054, as follows:

> Thus, if a purchaser of land makes default in carrying out the contract, and the vendor sues to enforce it specifically, it will be a good defence that the vendor has *subsequently* made some sale or other disposition of the land, which effectually prevents him from completing the contract. This would be no defence to a claim by the vendor for damages for the purchaser's breach of contract.

In view of the character of the pleading in this case, it is unnecessary to say much more about the decision in *Hipgrave v. Case, supra*. It is obviously a case of narrow application and one that should be confined strictly within its limits. Within a few years it was referred to as a "remarkable decision" by Kay J in *Gas Light & Coke Co. v. Towse* (1887), 35 Ch. D 519 at p. 541. It appears to be out of line with the authorities, decided under *Lord Cairns' Act* and referred to in *Elmore v. Pirrie* (1887), 57 LT 333 (Ch.) at p. 335, which held that where there was an equity in the bill at the commencement of the suit, the fact of its disappearance before judgment would not disentitle a plaintiff to relief in damages. *Davenport v. Rylands* (1865), LR 1 Eq. 302 at p. 307, and *White v. Boby* (1877), 26 WR 133 (CA) at p. 134, are to the same effect. Further, it appears to be unduly restrictive of the change brought about by the *Judicature Act*. Both *Elmore v. Pirrie*, and *Tamplin v. James* (1880), 15 Ch. D 215 (CA), held that under the *Judicature Act*, whether or not the Court could in a particular case grant specific performance, it could give damages for breach of the agreement. In *Tamplin v. James*, Cotton LJ at p. 222 stated the effect of the *Judicature Act* as follows:

> It has been urged that if specific performance is refused the action must simply be dismissed. But in my judgment—and I believe the Lord Justice *James* is of the same opinion—as both legal and equitable remedies are now given by the same Court, and this is a case where, under the old practice, the bill, if dismissed, would have been dismissed without prejudice to an action, we should, if we were to refuse specific performance, be bound to consider the question of damages.

I turn now to the prayer for relief, which I set out in full:

> (a) Specific performance of the written contract entered into between the parties dated July 23rd, 1956.
> (b) Damages in the amount of $5,000.00 for delay in the defendant's performance of the contract.
> (c) In the alternative to (a) and (b), forfeiture of its deposit and punitive damages for failure to perform the contract.
> (d) In any event his costs of this section.
> (e) Such further and other relief as this Honourable Court deems meet.

Clause (a) disappears from the action. Clause (b) seems to me equally applicable to a common law claim as to one for specific performance in the circumstances of this case. The plaintiff was selling vacant land and until he was able to mitigate his damages by a resale, he lost the interest on the purchase-price that he should have received and he had to pay taxes that the defendant should have paid. The interest should be calculated at the rate of 5% on $71,000 from the date of closing, September 30, 1956, until October 18, 1957, the date of the resale, and he is entitled to the taxes.

In spite of the obviously untenable claim for punitive damages—a claim that could not mislead any pleader—cl. (c) is clearly identifiable as a common law claim for breach of contract. The measure of damages in this case is the difference between the price provided for in the first contract, $75,000, and the price provided for in the second contract, $70,000. Counsel for the appellant admits that against the difference of $5,000 must be credited the deposit of $4,000: *Mayne on Damages*, 11th ed., p. 234; 29 Hals., 2nd ed., p. 378.

[Judson J here considered the contention advanced by the defendant and accepted both at trial and in the Ontario Court of Appeal that the plaintiff had not proved damages in the sense that evidence had not been adduced establishing that the resale of the house prior to trial was for a fair price and represented acceptable mitigation. Judson J rejected this proposition and held that it was for the defendant to prove that the mitigating steps taken by the plaintiff were unreasonable. As no such evidence had been tendered, that proof had not been entered. The plaintiff was therefore entitled to damages based on the difference between the contract price and the resale price with appropriate adjustments.]

Appeal allowed.

NOTES

1. In addition to providing insights on the relationship between common law and equitable damages and the interpretation of the Canadian equivalents of *Lord Cairns' Act*, *Dobson* also raises the matter of election of remedies, an issue to which we will return shortly.

2. In the course of the article by Professor Jolowicz, he identifies a number of situations in which *Lord Cairns' Act* allowed for an action in damages where no such relief could be obtained at common law. The instance of this that has attracted most attention in recent years is that seemingly provided by *Wroth v. Tyler*, [1974] Ch. 30, already considered in chapter 1, "General Principles of Damages," and noted in the introduction to this chapter. As a substitute for specific performance, equitable damages permitted the courts to measure the extent of the plaintiff's loss by reference to the value of the relevant property at the date of the trial or judgment rather than the normal assessment of common law damages based on the value of the property at the date of breach. In rapidly fluctuating property markets and slow litigation with the possibility of appeals, this offered a singular advantage to specific performance-seeking plaintiffs in certain situations.

However, as seen in chapter 1, the House of Lords, some six years later, in *Johnson v. Agnew*, [1980] AC 367 (HL (Eng.)) made it clear that there was no such advantage to equitable damages over common law damages; common law damages could equally accommodate measurement of loss by reference to the value of the property at the date of trial in appropriate cases. The logic of this position seemed compelling and was quickly embraced by appeal courts in Canada: *306793 Ontario Ltd. in Trust v. Rimes* (1980), 25 OR (2d) 79 (CA) and *Ansdell v. Crowther* (1984), 55 BCLR 216 (CA). Eventually, this position was also explicitly endorsed by the Supreme Court of Canada in *Semelhago v. Paramadevan*, [1996] 2 SCR 415. (For a fuller account of this case, see chapter 1.)

This recognition of *Johnson v. Agnew* raises the question of whether there is any longer a place for equitable (as distinct from common law) damages in the domain of contract law. While they might be seen as still having a role in the domain of tort as a justification for awarding damages once and for all for continuing wrongs or an award of damages as a means of *quia timet* relief, has their life as a separate category of contractual remedy expired?

At present, the answer to this dilemma has to be qualified support of the continued though very limited utility of equitable damages in the domain of contract law and, more specifically, contracts involving an interest in land. To the extent that the common law continues to deny recognition to rights that arise purely in equity, equitable damages may still provide the only route to damages as a substitute for or an addition to specific performance in cases where the plaintiff's claim depends on the doctrine of part performance.

Price v. Strange
[1978] Ch. 337 (CA)

[In this case, the court was confronted by the issue of whether it could order specific performance of an oral contract for an underlease where part of the sublessee's consideration was the performance of work on the premises. This raised a question of whether there was a lack of mutuality of remedies under the oral contract that prevented the plaintiff seeking specific performance. The Court of Appeal held that specific performance was, in fact, available and, in doing so, contributed significantly to the current status of the principle of mutuality. This aspect of the case is reproduced later (chapter 11, "Discretionary Reasons for the Denial of Relief"). However, both Goff LJ and Buckley LJ discussed in the alternative the availability of damages under *Lord Cairns' Act*. Though *dicta*, their elaboration of the meaning of "jurisdiction" is illuminating.]

GOFF LJ: Taking the view I have it is unnecessary for me to decide the other question whether if specific performance were refused damages could be awarded in lieu, but as it was very fully argued I think it right to express my views on it. Having regard to s. 40 of the *Law of Property Act 1925* damages could not be awarded at law, but in my judgment that would not prevent an award of damages in equity under the *Chancery Amendment Act 1858* (*Lord Cairns' Act*). One purpose and a very important purpose of that Act was, of course, to avoid circuity of action by enabling the old Court of Chancery to award damages at law, but the Act clearly went further and enabled that court to give damages where there was no cause of action at law. This was envisaged as early as 1863 in *Eastwood v. Lever* (1863), 4 De GJ & Sm. 114; 46 ER 859 (CA) which was an action for breach of a restrictive covenant where there was no privity at law; and in the like case damages were awarded in *Wrotham Park Estate Co. Ltd. v. Parkside Homes Ltd.*, [1974] 1 WLR 798 (Ch.) at p. 811. That the Act has this wider scope was settled beyond question by the House of Lords in *Leeds Industrial Co-operative Society Ltd. v. Slack*, [1924] AC 851 (HL (Eng.)) a *quia timet* action in respect of a threatened tort.

The absence of a right of action at law in this case is therefore immaterial; nor in my judgment does the case fall within *Lavery v. Pursell*. In that case it was impossible to grant specific performance because it was too late. It was not refused either because of the type of contract involved or in the exercise of discretion, and in my view that case decides nothing more than this, that the court cannot grant damages in lieu of specific performance when it is impossible to effect specific performance.

It was argued, however, that where the court refuses specific performance, not on discretionary grounds, but in accordance with some settled principle, then the court has not jurisdiction to entertain an application for the specific performance of any covenant contract or agreement within the meaning of the 1858 Act. So far as this case turns on want of mutuality that is in my view discretionary, but it was argued that this contract, being for the execution of building repairs, was one of which, in accordance with settled principles, the court could not, or would not, grant specific performance. I suppose that may be true of some contracts, where damages at law are always an adequate remedy and in consequence the old Court of Chancery and modern equity has never interfered, at all events positively, such as a contract for the sale of potatoes, pictures in general, or shares in ICI. If in the future in such a case for some reason or other there is no remedy at law, and damages are sought in equity under the Act, it can be considered on its facts when it comes before the court. It is I think unlikely to arise. The present case, however, is in my judgment not of that character. Although the court does not often order specific performance of a contract to build or do repairs, either because of difficulty in ascertaining precisely what has to be done, or more usually because of the difficulty of supervising performance, still it has jurisdiction to do so, and sometimes does: see A.G. Guest (ed.), *Chitty on Contracts* (London: Sweet & Maxwell, 23rd ed., 1968), Vol. 1 at p. 714, para. 1531:

> Building contracts. The general rule is that a contract to erect a building cannot be specifically enforced. There seem to be three reasons for this rule. First, damages may be an adequate remedy if another builder can be engaged to do the work. Secondly, the contract may not specify the work to be done with sufficient certainty. And thirdly specific performance may require "constant supervision." But specific performance of a contract to build will be decreed if (i) the work is precisely defined; (ii) damages will not adequately compensate the plaintiff; and (iii) the defendant is in possession of the land on which the work is to be done.

Even in a case of a contract for personal services in which the court is still more chary of granting specific performance. Megarry J said this (with which I entirely agree) in *C.H. Giles & Co. Ltd. v. Morris*, [1972] 1 WLR 307 (Ch.) at pp. 318-19:

> In general, no doubt, the inconvenience and mischief of decreeing specific performance of most of such contracts will greatly outweigh the advantages, and specific performance will be refused. But I do not think that it should be assumed that as soon as any element of personal service or continuous services can be discerned in a contract the court will, without more, refuse specific performance. Of course a requirement for the continuous performance of services has the disadvantage that repeated breaches may engender repeated applications to the court for enforcement. But so may many injunctions; and the prospects of repetition, although an important consideration, ought not to be allowed to negative a right. As is so often the case in equity, the matter is one of balance of advantage and disadvantage in relation to the particular obligations in question; and the fact that the balance will usually lie on one side does not turn this probability into a rule.

Therefore, if it were necessary to decide the point I would allow the appeal on the second limb and award damages under *Lord Cairns' Act*, but it is not necessary, since for the reason I have already given I would allow the appeal on the first point and order specific performance on the term as to compensation which I have indicated.

BUCKLEY LJ: I now come to the point on *Lord Cairns' Act*. The learned judge, having held that he could not decree specific performance on the ground of lack of mutuality, held that it followed that he could not award damages under *Lord Cairns' Act*. As I have reached the contrary conclusion on specific performance, it is not necessary for the decision of this appeal that I should consider the position under the Act, but as it has been argued I will state my opinion on it. The learned judge posed this question:

> If specific performance should not be decreed because of lack of mutuality, is the plaintiff nevertheless entitled to damages in lieu of specific performance?

It would, I think, have been more accurate to ask whether, if specific performance should not be decreed because of lack of mutuality, the court could nevertheless grant damages to the plaintiff in lieu of specific performance, for it is clear that the Act gives no entitlement to damages: it confers a discretion on the court to award damages.

Section 2 of the Act provides as follows so far as is relevant to specific performance:

In all cases in which the court of Chancery has jurisdiction to entertain an application … for the specific performance of any covenant contract or agreement it shall be lawful for the same court, if it shall think fit, to award damages to the party injured, either in addition to or in substitution for such … specific performance and such damages may be assessed in such manner as the court shall direct.

Two points are clear. First, the court is invested with the discretion whenever it has jurisdiction to entertain a claim for specific performance, but not otherwise. Secondly, the discretion is not confined to cases in which damages could be recovered at law (*Leeds Industrial Co-operative Society Ltd. v. Slack*, [1924] AC 851 (HL (Eng.)), and see *Eastwood v. Lever* (1863), 4 De GJ & Sm. 114; 46 ER 859 (Ch.) and in particular per Turner LJ (at p. 128 (p. 865 (ER))). There are, of course, classes of contracts of which the court acting on accepted principles will not in any circumstances decree specific performance. Contracts for the sale and purchase of any commodity readily available on the market at an ascertainable market price and contracts for personal services are examples. In the case of any such contract it would, I think, be correct to say that the court has no jurisdiction to entertain an application for the specific performance of the contract. Can there be circumstances in which the court has no such jurisdiction in respect of a contract for a sale and purchase of land or for the grant of an estate or interest in land? In this court Mr. Jaques has conceded that, if the court has a discretion whether to grant or to refuse specific performance, the section applies. So, if I am right on specific performance, the discretion under the section is available, but the plaintiff does not seek its exercise. I will return in a moment to the position if the conclusion I have reached on specific performance is wrong. The learned judge relied on a statement in Fry (George Russell Northcote (ed.), *Fry on Specific Performance* (London: Stevens, 6th ed., 1921) at pp. 283-84 (para. 594)), which is in these terms:

It has been further held that the doctrine of part performance does not extend to enable the Court to award damages on a parol contract of which specific performance could not have been granted.

That statement is, perhaps, rather misleading. The decision in *Lavery v. Pursell*, which is cited as authority for it, did not depend on the fact that the contract in that case was an oral agreement on which damages could not have been recovered at law on account of the *Statute of Frauds*; it depended on the fact that specific performance had became impracticable. The time within which the subject-matter of the sale, which consisted of materials to be recovered by the demolition of a house, was to be removed from the site, had run out.

If I am right in my conclusion on the specific performance point it is, in my judgment, clear that considerations of mutual performance do not bear on the jurisdiction of the court to entertain a claim to specific performance but on the exercise of its discretion in granting or withholding that remedy. If I am wrong in my conclusion on the specific performance point and the Fry proposition is correct, I remain of the opinion that considerations of mutuality go to discretion, not to jurisdiction. If lack of mutuality at the date of the contract were to deprive the court of jurisdiction to decree specific performance, I find it difficult to see how subsequent events could confer jurisdiction; and yet it is clear that a vendor of land who at the date of the contract of sale has a defective title, but subsequently perfects it before the purchaser has repudiated the contract, can sue the purchaser for specific performance.

Moreover if want of title at the date of contract deprives the court of jurisdiction, what need could a purchaser have to repudiate the contract on discovering the defect? Why should he not rely on the lack of jurisdiction? In *Halkett v. Dudley*, [1907] 1 Ch. 590 Parker J described the act of repudiation as giving rise to an equitable right affecting the equitable remedy by way of specific performance. This assumes that the remedy was at least potentially available before the act of repudiation, which could not be the case if initial lack of mutuality had deprived the court of jurisdiction to grant the remedy.

In *Murrell v. Goodyear* (1860), 1 De GF & J 432; 45 ER 426 (Ch.) the plaintiff contracted to sell the fee simple in land but had a defective title, having only a limited estate in the land. The fee simple in remainder was outstanding in the heir of a previous owner. In that state of affairs the plaintiff could not have claimed specific performance successfully. The defendant purchaser purported to repudiate the contract and at about the same time bought up the estate of the heir. The vendor was granted specific performance against the purchaser with an allowance to the purchaser of the cost of getting in the estate outstanding in the heir. It was held that the purchaser, having by his own act cured the defect in the title, could not avail himself of this to destroy the original contract. It will be observed that the purchaser had by his transaction with the heir put it out of the power of the vendor to remedy the defect in his title. I find it easy to explain this decision on the basis that the court in the exercise of its discretion was achieving justice between the parties, but I cannot explain it on the basis that the acquisition by the purchaser of the outstanding estate invested the court with a jurisdiction which theretofore it had not had.

These considerations lead me to the conclusion that if, contrary to my own view, the relevant date as at which mutuality must be ascertained is the date of the contract, lack of mutuality at that date does not result in the court being without jurisdiction to entertain a claim to specific performance but it is a matter to be taken into account by the court in deciding whether to exercise its discretion in favour of granting specific performance or refusing it.

On this view of the law the court had at all relevant times jurisdiction to entertain a claim to specific performance of the contract between the parties, and consequently had at all relevant times a discretion under the section to award damages in addition to, or in substitution for, specific performance. Whether, if I am wrong on specific performance, the court should have made any such award is a question on which I express no opinion.

NOTES AND QUESTIONS

1. What if specific performance is impossible at the date of the commencement of the action either because the property has been destroyed or has come into the hands of a *bona fide* purchaser for value without notice? Should this be affected by whether the plaintiff knew or should have known of the impossibility?

2. As already noted, the making of a claim for damages without an alternative plea for specific performance in *Dobson v. Winton & Robbins Ltd.*, above, constitutes a binding election. However, questions also arise as to whether other conduct on the part of the plaintiff should be viewed as constituting an election of remedies. That issue is developed further in the section, "Election of Remedies," below.

3. Consider also the impact of s. 99 of the Ontario *Courts of Justice Act*, above, and, in particular, whether it diminishes further the need to be concerned about the extent to which a

plaintiff has a basis for claiming specific performance or an injunction before being entitled to claim equitable damages.

SPECIFIC PERFORMANCE WITH AN ABATEMENT IN THE PURCHASE PRICE

Introduction

If the vendor of an interest in land is unable to comply strictly with the contract, it may, in some circumstances, nevertheless be specifically enforced as far as possible with an abatement of the purchase price to compensate for the failure to comply with the contract (*In re Contract between Fawcett and Holmes* (1889), 42 Ch. D 150 (CA); and *Mason v. Freedman*, [1958] SCR 483). This doctrine may apply where there is a defect in title—that is, where the vendor does not possess the entire estate he or she has contracted to convey (*Mason v. Freedman*) or where the land does not comply with the description in the contract (*Bowes v. Vaux* (1918), 43 OLR 521). The rules of equity governing this situation vary depending on whether the vendor or the purchaser is applying for specific performance, with it being much easier for purchasers to secure relief on such terms. See, generally, Charles Harpum, "Specific Performance with Compensation as a Purchaser's Remedy—A Study in Contract and Equity" (1981), 40 *Cambridge Law Journal* 47.

If it is the vendor who is asking for specific enforcement with abatement of the price, the courts have felt that it is inequitable that the purchaser should be required to take something less than that which has been bargained for (*Bowes v. Vaux*). Thus, such an order will be made only if the purchaser obtains substantially what was bargained for—that is, if the defect is of a minor nature (*Rutherford v. Acton-Adams*, [1915] AC 866 (PC (NZ)). *Le Mesurier v. Andrus* (1986), 54 OR (2d) 1 (CA), leave to appeal to SCC refused 63 OR (2d) x represents one of the rare cases in which a vendor obtained relief, notwithstanding an inability to convey all that was promised in the contract of purchase and sale. It also represents a continuation in the evolution of the law governing the links between equitable remedies and damages at common law. Grange JA (for the court) wrote:

> Whatever the original intention of the Legislature, the fusion of law and equity is now real and total … [W]here specific performance with an abatement is available to a vendor, he must equally be entitled to the common law remedy of damages with an "abatement" or reduction in those damages for the deficiency of title.

This suggestion that common law remedies should be available in aid of purely equitable rights and entitlements depends on a fuller version of the fusion of common law and equity than we have encountered to this point.

For discussions of *Le Mesurier v. Andrus* and the whole issue of the extent to which law and equity have fused in Ontario and generally, see Paul M. Perell, "A Legal History of the Fusion of Law and Equity in the Supreme Court of Ontario" (1988), 9 *Advocates' Q* 972 and *The Fusion of Law and Equity* (Toronto: Butterworths, 1990).

Another example of the fusion of common law and equity can be found in *BICC Plc. v. Burndy Corporation*, [1985] Ch. 232 (CA), where the court found that a set-off arising at law (as opposed to equity) could be a complete defence to a claim for specific performance.

Note the following three cases dealing with the purchaser's claim to specific performance with an abatement in the purchase price:

Ontario Asphalt Block Company v. Montreuil

In *Ontario Asphalt Block Company v. Montreuil* (1916), 52 SCR 541, the plaintiff had entered into a 10-year lease ($1,000 per year) with the defendant lessor, who believed he owned the fee simple whereas in fact he had a life estate. The lease provided that on performance of the terms and the giving of six months' notice that the lessee could purchase the premises for $22,000. Plaintiff relied on the lease and spent considerable money ($300,000) improving the property. Plaintiff gave notice and tendered the money but defendant refused to convey. The Supreme Court of Canada gave judgment decreeing specific performance of the agreement and an abatement in the purchase money based upon the difference in value of an estate in fee simple and an estate for life. The court applied the rule in *Bain v. Fothergill* and would not award damages for loss of bargain. In a subsequent action between the plaintiff and the re-maindermen, the Supreme Court of Canada imposed a lien on the property for the amount by which lasting improvements made during the term of the lease had enhanced the value of the property (*Montreuil v. The Ontario Asphalt Company* (1922), 63 SCR 401).

Ruskowsky v. Palechek

In *Ruskowsky v. Palechek* (1978), 13 AR 21, neither the plaintiff purchaser nor the vendors knew at the time the offer was signed and accepted that subdivision approval was necessary for the vendors to sell one of their two adjoining lots. Subdivision approval required that 20 percent of the land be reserved for the community. Specific performance was allowed with a 10 percent abatement of the purchase price so that the cost of the reserve would fall equally on both lots.

Di Cenzo Construction Co. Ltd. v. Glassco

In *Di Cenzo Construction Co. Ltd. v. Glassco* (1978), 21 OR (2d) 186 (CA), it was stressed that the purchaser's position after closing is very different than it was before closing. Prior to closing the vendor (who does not rely on a contractual provision to rescind the contract) may be required to accept an abatement in the purchase price if he or she lacks good title to part of the land. After the closing, the rule *caveat emptor* applies and, unless the purchaser comes within one of the following four exceptions: (1) fraud, (2) error in *substantialibus*, (3) a con-tractual condition (for example, a compensation clause), or (4) a warranty collateral to the contract that survives the closing, there cannot at that point be a claim for an abatement in the purchase price.

An important qualification on a purchaser's right to seek specific performance and abate-ment is the presence of an annulment clause in the contract of sale and purchase. This clause is designed to preclude the right of the purchaser to seek abatement. The effect of the clause is to entitle a vendor to terminate the contract if he or she is unable or unwilling to lift a defect in title as requested by the purchaser. In such a case, the purchaser is only entitled to the return of the deposit. However, a vendor cannot rely on this clause to excuse his or her own arbitrary or capricious actions, or deliberate failure to do what an ordinary prudent person would do to ensure the contract's fulfillment. See *Mason v. Freedman*, [1958] SCR 483.

The Nature of the Abatement

One issue that is the subject of some uncertainty is the nature of the abatement or compensation, as it is sometimes called. In *Grant v. Dawkins*, [1973] 1 WLR 1406 (Ch.), Goff J held that the purchase price marked the limit of any abatement and that, thereafter, the plaintiffs had to look to *Lord Cairns' Act* for further recovery. Harpum, above, disagrees with this and suggests that compensation may go as far as full expectation damages to the extent that the rule in *Bain v. Fothergill* does not apply. He bases this argument, *inter alia*, upon the ability of the courts of equity, even before *Lord Cairns' Act*, to award full damages in some cases along with specific performance and the parallels between this and the award of compensation along with specific performance. Indeed, he goes on to argue that, with the enactment of *Lord Cairns' Act* in 1858, it became appropriate to regard damages and compensation at equity as assimilated.

This matter is explored in the following judgment, one that also serves as a useful link to the next section on the remedy of compensation:

Sokoloff v. 5 Rosehill Avenue Developments Ltd.
(1998), 21 RPR (3d) 176 (Ont. Gen. Div.)

[The plaintiffs bought two contiguous apartments off the plans. The defendant vendor then built them with lower ceilings than appeared on the plans. The plaintiff purchasers elected to take specific performance with an abatement in the purchase price and an issue arose as to how that abatement was to be calculated.]

GANS J: ...

Damages

The more vexing question to be answered at this juncture is the amount of compensation the Sokoloffs are otherwise entitled to as a result of the problems with which they are beset. While I find the article by Charles Harpum, "Specific Performance with Compensation as a Purchaser's Remedy—A Study in Contract and Equity" (1981), 40 *Cambridge Law Journal* 47-82, of assistance in describing the legal foundation for an award of compensation, theory and practice do not admit of easy reconciliation. I have nevertheless drawn the following from the material provided:

1. Assessing compensation is, for all intents and purposes, the same task as assessing damages for breach of contract.

2. In instances involving specific performance, a purchaser, in so far as such is possible, is to be placed in the same position as if the contract had been performed—in this respect, the purchaser can recover damages for loss of bargain.

3. Damages for loss of bargain can be established by:

   (a) providing the purchaser with a rateable reduction from the purchase price without regard to the actual value of the land,

   (b) reimbursing the purchaser for the cost of remediation,

   (c) providing the purchaser with the difference between the value of the land without the defect and with the defect,

   (d) providing the purchaser with the difference between the purchase price and the value of the land without the defect.

4. In cases of this nature, the court is not wedded to any particular methodology so long as it has regard to the material circumstances, including the intention of the parties, in determining the purchase price at first instance.

In the instant case, unlike [claims for the cost of remediation], I am left with the difficult task of having to assess the negative effect of the bulkheads and the drop ceiling. In some cases, this task is accomplished by calculating the proportion of the defect to the property as a whole. (*Le Mesurier v. Andrus* (1986), 25 DLR (4th) 424 (Ont. CA).) While I was told that the "defect" covers something in the area of 40% of the apartment, that number does not take into account the amount of the lowered ceilings the Sokoloffs expected in any event, the exact percentage of which was not led in evidence. I was told, however, that one might reasonably expect bulkheads to occupy something in the order of 5 to 10 percent of an apartment condominium.

I was also provided with evidence of an experienced real estate agent who went through several scenarios based upon her assessment of the "feel" of the apartment from a square footage point of view. Thereafter, she attempted to multiply her sense of the size of the unit, namely a unit of 1500 square feet as opposed to the contract size of 1900 square feet, by various prices per square foot, the latter of which numbers were extracted from the initial price of the unit and recent resales of other units in the building of differing size. Needless to say, this analysis was not all that precise for a variety of reasons, including the fact that there were no comparables to underscore the cost per square foot utilized by the witness. After undertaking all kinds of machinations, the witness, Ms. Goodchild, fell back to her basic instincts as an agent in suggesting that the initial price of the unit ($409,000) should be reduced by 12-15%, yielding an abatement range between $49,000 and $61,000. (It is interesting to note, however, that Ms. Goodchild thought the defect so severe she would have advised her clients against closing.)

The Sokoloffs bought this unit as their "final" home, a fact which is more than a little significant. They are so unhappy about the situation, they are now contemplating selling the suite, which is perhaps a little inconsistent with their not having sought rescission at first instance. Having regard, however, to the evidence, including the photos which graphically describe the situation (particularly of the master bedroom), I do not think the diminution in value described by Ms. Goodchild is so out of line to warrant adjustment, but for a little tinkering. I assess the value of the defect to be 13.5%, or $55,215. I therefore find that the Sokoloffs are entitled to specific performance with compensation fixed at that amount. Counsel have advised that they will be able to affect a reconciliation of this amount with the adjustments required on closing, had such taken place on the original date set for same. I leave it to them to arrive at those numbers absent my involvement.

Ms. Conway but briefly attempted to argue that under the circumstances of this case, the Sokoloffs are entitled to punitive damages and damages for mental distress. She abandoned the latter claim after being reminded that no evidence was led on the subject. She reluctantly gave up on the former having had her attention directed to the decision of the Supreme Court of Canada in *Wallace v. United Grain Growers Ltd.*, [1997] 3 SCR 701. As I indicated to her during the course of argument, while I was not happy with the apparent rancour that developed between the Developer and Mr. Sokoloff after the litigation was first threatened, such behaviour is not so malicious, reprehensible or contemptible as to warrant rebuke from the court.

The counterclaim of the Developer will also be dismissed, as will the application filed under the *Landlord and Tenant Act*. As previously indicated, during the course of the trial, the Developer, with the Sokoloffs' consent, purported to amend its defence and counterclaim by abandoning its claim for possession and damages occasioned as a result of the Sokoloffs' alleged breach of contract in not closing when and as specified. At the conclusion of trial, I asked counsel for further submissions on the amendment and the effect of same because of the defendants' actions at first instance in accepting the Sokoloffs' repudiation and then commencing suit for damages and possession. Such a course of action has been held in many cases to constitute an "election," in which case the party so electing is precluded from then changing direction and asserting a claim for specific performance, as in the matter before me.

Mr. Justice Sharpe, in his book *Injunctions and Specific Performance*, questions the otherwise blind adherence to the "rather strict and inflexible language" of the rule. He postulates there is good reason to reconsider this intractable position (para. 10.820). He suggests that in instances where there has not been any prejudice arising from the election or that the election does not give rise to the notion of estoppel, a party should be permitted to alter its position, which might have been created through inadvertence or precipitous or bad advice. In my view, this formulation by Mr. Justice Sharpe makes eminent sense, particularly when one has regard to Rule 26 (amendment to pleadings), where a court is obliged to permit an amendment unless irreparable prejudice would result. Furthermore, I have never been able to understand why one is entitled to advance inconsistent claims to judgment "without recrimination," but not entitled to change an election if in such latter instance the party opposite is not prejudiced in the slightest.

Therefore, but for my finding that the Sokoloffs are entitled to specific performance with compensation, under the circumstances of this case I would have permitted the Developer to argue that it was entitled to specific performance without abatement.

COMPENSATION

Introduction

Until recently, few Canadian examples of the award of the equitable remedy of compensation existed. Now, as well as having a role to play in the abatement context, it has become a very prominent remedy in cases of breach of trust and fiduciary duty as well as the misuse or appropriation of confidential information. As such, it provides an alternative in certain situations to two other equitable remedies: account whereby a faithless trustee or fiduciary or the abuser of a confidence may be required to disgorge profits obtained at expense of the plaintiff (see chapter 2, "Awards Measured by Benefit to Defendant") and restitutionary orders requiring the repayment of moneys belonging in equity to the plaintiff. Where, however, the trustee, fiduciary, or abuser of confidence has not benefitted from the breach or where the harm to the plaintiff is greater than any such benefit, the plaintiff will want to look to another remedy. In this regard, compensation at equity provides a possible avenue of recourse. Indeed, it may allow greater scope for financial relief than that provided at common law under either contract or tort principles on the basis that it may not be constrained by or as constrained by many of the principles that limit the availability of traditional common law and tort damages and, in particular, the principles of foreseeability, causation, and contributory negligence. Two groundbreaking and excellent discussions of these dimensions of compensation are provided by Ian E. Davidson, "The Equitable Remedy of Compensation" (1982), 13 *Melbourne Univ. L Rev.* 349 and the Honourable Mr. Justice Gummow, "Compensation for Breach of Fiduciary Duty," in T.G. Youdan, ed., *Equity, Fiduciaries and Trusts* (Toronto: Carswell, 1989), at 57. For more recent discussions, see John D. McCamus, "Prometheus Unbound: Fiduciary Duties in the Supreme Court of Canada" (1997), 28 *Can. Bus. LJ* 107; Jeff Berryman, "Equitable Compensation for Breach by Fact-Based Fiduciaries: Tentative Thoughts on Clarifying Remedial Goals" (1999), 37 *Alta. L Rev.* 95; Paul M. Perell, "Compensation and the Scope of Equity's Remedial and Restitutionary Generosity" (1999), 37 *Alta. L Rev.* 114; and C. Rickett, "Equitable Compensation: Toward a Blueprint?" (2003), 25 *Sydney L Rev.* 31.

The scope of the remedy also provides an excellent vehicle for a reassessment of the extent of the merger of the principles and remedies of common law and equity. Indeed, both the remedy and the issue of fusion as well as the articles referred to are highlighted dramatically in the following landmark judgment.

Canson Enterprises Ltd. v. Boughton & Co.
[1991] 3 SCR 534

[At issue here was the liability of a solicitor for breach of fiduciary duty owed to clients. The breach in question involved failing to inform client purchasers and developers of his involvement on behalf of other clients with a particular transaction. As a result, the clients believed that they were purchasing land directly from particular vendors when, in fact, there was an intermediate purchaser who was making a profit of $115,000 on the intervening flip of the land. Subsequently, the clients lost a considerable amount of money on the land in question through the negligence of a soil engineer and a firm hired to drive pilings for a building to be erected on the land, only part of which loss was able to be recovered from the tortfeasors.

Once the full involvement of the solicitor and the other relevant facts came to light, the clients sued for both the secret profit and also for the losses suffered on the development of the land. In the context of these proceedings, a special case was stated to the BC Supreme Court on the basis that the facts alleged against the solicitor were true and that the clients would never have bought the property had they known of the intermediate transaction.

In the Supreme Court of Canada, the attention of the court focused on whether the solicitor could be held responsible for the losses on the development, with the clients arguing that such a loss came within the ambit of the equitable remedy of compensation.]

LA FOREST J (Sopinka, Cory, and Gonthier JJ concurring): ...

Analysis

The appellants, we saw, firmly base their claim in equity for breach of a fiduciary duty. Although they could pursue various claims at common law, they maintain that they can seek equitable remedies concurrently and may choose the remedy most advantageous to them. The respondents do not contest this and, in my view, quite properly concede this point. The appellants' position is fully supported so far as torts and contracts are concerned by this court's decision in *Central Trust Co. v. Rafuse*, ... [[1986] 2 SCR 147], and so far as claims in law and equity are concerned by the House of Lord's decision in *Nocton v. Lord Ashburton*, [1914] AC 932 (HL (Eng.)). ...

The nature of the remedy of compensation for breach of an equitable obligation, except as it applies to property held in a fiduciary capacity, is rather obscure; for an excellent discussion, see Ian E. Davidson, "The Equitable Remedy of Compensation" (1982), 3 Melbourne UL Rev. 349. There are not many cases on the issue. None the less, the inherent jurisdiction of equity to compensate for a breach of a fiduciary duty cannot be denied. It is at times used where the exercise of another equitable jurisdiction, for example rescission of contract, has become impossible: see *McKenzie v. McDonald*, [1927] VLR 134. But, as already mentioned, it has also been used independently of other remedies where there was a misstatement by a fiduciary or other persons in special circumstances. Certain developments before the *Supreme Court of Judicature Act, 1873* (UK), c. 66, held the promise of providing a means of dealing with situations now dealt with at common law as negligent misstatement under the principles expounded in *Hedley Byrne & Co. v. Heller & Partners Ltd.*, [1964] AC 465 (HL (Eng.)). For an account of this development, see Davidson, *op. cit.*, especially at pp. 357 *et seq*. The cases of *Burrowes v. Lock, supra* [(1805), 10 Ves. Jun. 450; 32 ER 927 (Ch.)], and *Slim v. Croucher, supra* [(1860), 1 DF & J 518; 45 ER 462 (Ch.)], discussed in *Nocton v. Lord Ashburton* are instructive on this point. However, *Derry v. Peek* (1889), 14 App. Cas. 337 (HL (Eng.)), where it was held that actual fraud was necessary to ground an action for deceit, was for a time thought to have more extensively limited remedies for loss for misrepresentation both at common law and in equity. In that climate, *Burrowes v. Lock* was explained on the basis of estoppel and *Slim v. Croucher* was held to be wrongly decided: see *Low v. Bouverie*, [1891] 3 Ch. 82 (CA). None the less, the judges in *Nocton v. Lord Ashburton* subsequently appear to have at least approved of the principle underlying both these cases: see also *Davidson, op. cit.*, who (at p. 368) cites a comment of Lord McNaghten in argument in *Balkis Consolidated (Ltd.) v. Tomkinson* (1893), 42 WR 204 at p. 205 (HL (Eng.)) (a comment not found in the "official" report, [1893] AC 396), which would suggest that he thought *Slim v. Croucher* was good law.

However that may be, the remedy of compensation in cases like the present is not likely to be resorted to frequently. The tort of deceit has long provided a convenient common law remedy that makes resort to the equitable remedy infrequent in cases of fraud, and with the development of the principle in *Hedley Byrne & Co. v. Heller & Partners Ltd.*, *supra*, it is unlikely to be used often in cases of negligent misstatement. None the less, it may at times be of utility; for an example, see *McKenzie v. McDonald, supra*, where on the facts a remedy in negligence was held to be unavailable. There may, as well, be other situations where equity may make use of the remedy in its traditional role of filling gaps in the law or improving the remedies available for a breach of duty: see *Davidson, op. cit.*

The simple fact is, however, that there is a paucity of cases where compensation has been awarded for breach of fiduciary duty in a context such as the present. More particularly, apart from the present case and *Jacks v. Davis, supra* [[1980] 6 WWR 11 (BCSC), aff'd. (1982), 39 BCLR 353 (CA)], upon which it is based, only a few cases have anything to say regarding the effect of the intervening fault of a third party on compensation and not much more about the related issue of mitigation. The most elaborate judicial discussion appears in the New Zealand case of *Day v. Mead*, [1987] 2 NZLR 443 (CA), where the court addressed the issue of contributory negligence in connection with a solicitor's breach of duty. I shall return to *Day v. Mead* later.

I shall begin by attempting to describe the nature of compensation and, more particularly, what it means in the present context. The appellants strongly emphasized that the courts of equity had, before the *Judicature Act*, no power to award damages, this being the exclusive domain of the common law, and the only statutory change to this régime was made by *Lord Cairns' Act* and its successors. Equity, they assert, was concerned with restoring a plaintiff to the position he or she was in before the breach of duty calling upon equity's intervention. The situation, they argued, was not changed by the *Judicature Act*, which was aimed largely at providing for the enforcement of law and equity in the same courts, not in altering the jurisdiction exercisable under each system.

There can be little doubt that damages come within the province of the common law (see, for example, *Todd v. Gee* (1810), 17 Ves. Jun. 273; 34 ER 106), although some early transgressions appear to have taken place where equity awarded damages (see R.P. Meagher, W.M. Gummow and J.R.F. Lehane, *Equity, Doctrines and Remedies* (Sydney: Butterworths, 2nd ed., 1984) at §2304). Damages are a monetary payment awarded for the invasion of a right at common law. Equity aimed at restoring a person to whom a duty was owed to the position in which he or she would have been had the duty not been breached. This it did through a variety of remedies, including compensation.

The difference between damages and restitution was abundantly clear in cases of breaches of trust, and in that context the following statement of James and Baggallay LJJ in *Ex p. Adamson* (1878), 8 Ch. D 807 (CA) at p. 819, appears unexceptionable:

> The Court of Chancery never entertained a suit for damages occasioned by fraudulent conduct or for breach of trust. The suit was always for an equitable debt or liability in the nature of debt.

It was a suit for the restitution of the actual money or thing, or value of the thing, of which the cheated party had been cheated.

But while the same approach of restitution or restoration applied in the case of simple compensation not involving the restoration of property, the difference in practical result between compensation and damages is by no means as clear. All that Lord Haldane tells us about this (at p. 958) is that "[t]he measure of damages [he was there speaking in a generic and not in a technical sense] may not always be the same as in an action of deceit or for negligence," and in the case before him he was content to say that it was a mere matter of form. On this matter, I fully agree with Cooke P in *Day v. Mead, supra,* at p. 451, that in many cases it is "a difference without a distinction." The question is whether, like the case before him, this is one of them.

The appellants urged us to accept the manner of calculating compensation adopted by the courts in trust cases or situations akin to a trust, and they relied in particular on the *Guerin* case, *supra.* I think the courts below were perfectly right to reject that proposition. There is a sharp divide between a situation where a person has *control* of property which in the view of the court *belongs* to another, and one where a person is under a fiduciary duty to perform an obligation where equity's concern is simply that the duty be performed honestly and in accordance with the undertaking the fiduciary has taken on: see L.S. Sealy, "Some Principles of Fiduciary Obligation," [1963] Camb. LJ 119; L.S. Sealy, "Fiduciary Relationships," [1962] Camb. LJ 69. In the case of a trust relationship, the trustee's obligation is to hold the *res* or object of the trust for his *cestui que trust,* and on breach the concern of equity is that it be restored to the *cestui que trust* or, if that cannot be done, to afford compensation for what the object would be worth. In the case of a mere breach of duty, the concern of equity is to ascertain the loss resulting from the breach of the particular duty. Where the wrongdoer has received some benefit, that benefit can be disgorged, but the measure of compensation where no such benefit has been obtained by the wrongdoer raises different issues. I turn then specifically to that situation.

McKenzie v. McDonald, supra, usefully sets the stage for discussion. There the plaintiff, a widow, had approached the defendant real estate agent advising him she wished to sell her farm for £4.5s. per acre. The defendant inspected the property and was advised by an experienced land valuer that it was worth the price asked. He, however, persuaded the plaintiff that it was not worth that price and later proposed an arrangement, which she accepted, whereby she would convey it to him in exchange for property he owned plus an amount to make up the difference between the value of her land and his. He, however, undervalued her farm (at £4 per acre) and overvalued his land. The court found the defendant liable for breach of a fiduciary duty. Since third parties had acquired the farm, the court could not order rescission, so it ordered the defendant to pay the plaintiff compensation for the undervaluation of the farm and the overvaluation of his land. It is important to observe that, although the defendant had subsequently sold the farm for £4.10s. an acre on extended terms, the court assessed the value of the farm in terms of the initial sale price, £4.5s., not its value at the time of judgment. That was the loss the defendant suffered because she would have sold the land for the initial sale price.

The case thus demonstrates that, while compensation is designed to put the plaintiff in as good a position pecuniarily as before the injury, as Lord Haldane put it in *Nocton v. Lord*

Ashburton, supra, "it is imperative to ascertain the loss resulting from breach of the relevant equitable duty": see Davidson, *op. cit.* The case also illustrates that compensation is not the same for every equitable remedy. Had this been an action for an account, the value would have been determined at the time of judgment.

An award of compensation is no less that because the amount recovered in a particular case is the same as would have been awarded in an action at common law. It was not felt necessary in *McKenzie v. McDonald* to bring in common law concepts to arrive at the same result as would have been obtained in a common law action. There were no issues of remoteness, or intervening cause, as arose here, however, and the appellants, we saw, strongly maintained that doctrines like remoteness and mitigation have no place in equity.

I should first of all say that the fact that such limitations may not have been developed before the *Judicature Act* is no ground for saying there is no room for further development of equitable principles to deal with the situation. We have it on high authority that equitable principles were not frozen in time: see *United Scientific Holdings Ltd. v. Burnley Borough Council*, [1978] AC 904 (HL (Eng.)). As Lord Diplock put it, at p. 926: "Nor did the coming into force of that Act bring to a sudden halt the whole process of development of the substantive law of England that had been so notable an achievement of the preceding decades." We have been given no case where the principles applicable to trusts have been applied to a breach of a fiduciary duty of the type in question here, and for reasons already given, I see no reason why they should be transposed here. The harshness of the result is reason alone, but apart from this, I do not think that the claim for the harm resulting from the actions of third parties can fairly be looked upon as falling within what is encompassed in restoration for the harm suffered from the breach. That is the view taken by all the Canadian courts that have dealt with the issue. In addition to *Jacks v. Davis* and the present case, reference may also be made to *Laskin v. Bache and Co., supra* [[1972] 1 OR 465 (CA)], and *Burke v. Cory, supra* [[1959] OWN 129 (CA)], both in the Ontario Court of Appeal.

I have no doubt that policies underlying concepts like remoteness and mitigation might have developed from an equitable perspective. However, given the paucity of authority in the field, it is scarcely surprising that courts will deal with a case falling properly within the ambit of equity as if it were a common law matter or as justifying the use of its mode of analysis. This can be seen from *Burke v. Cory*, and *Laskin v. Bache*. In *Cory*, a broker induced a client to purchase certain stocks after gaining his confidence by emphasizing the broker's qualifications and his possession of private information regarding the stocks and then making false representations about the company. The court held that apart from the action of deceit, which requires an allegation of fraud, liability for the misrepresentation could be rested on the existence of a fiduciary relationship. The amount of compensation (which the court there referred to as the measure of damages) was calculated in terms of the loss at the time of the allotment.

In *Cory*, and for that matter in *Laskin*, the court was also willing to apply the concept of mitigation of damages. Mitigation in equity was also found to be appropriate in *Le Mesurier v. Andrus* (1986), 54 OR (2d) 1 (CA), and it seems to be implicit in this court's decision in *Asamera Oil Corp. v. Sea Oil & General Corp.*, [1979] 1 SCR 633. This is consistent with the fact that equity acted on the basis of fairness and justice. The truth is that barring different policy considerations underlying one action or the other, I see no reason why the same basic claim, whether framed in terms of a common law action or an equitable remedy, should give rise to different levels of redress.

[La Forest J here made reference to *United Scientific Holdings* and *Le Mesurier v. Andrus*, quoting the same passage from Lord Diplock's judgment in the former that Grange JA had relied on in *Le Mesurier*.]

The most dramatic example of this approach is the New Zealand case of *Day v. Mead* to which I have previously referred. Mead, Day's solicitor, acted for him for many years in connection with land subdivision projects and other ventures. None of the investments could fairly be described as speculative until those that gave rise to the litigation. These concerned a newly formed company, Pacific Mills Ltd., of which Mead was a director and shareholder. The investment and the decision of the trial judge are conveniently set forth in the headnote to the case, at p. 443, as follows:

> In July 1977, acting on Mead's advice, Day purchased 20,000 shares, at $1 per share, in Pacific Mills, knowing that Mead was a shareholder and that his firm's nominee company had lent money to Pacific Mills. After this initial investment of $20,000, Day took an interest in the company's business, regularly visiting its paper-mill factory and attending a couple of directors' meetings as an onlooker. Then, in December 1977, once again acting on Mead's advice, Day subscribed for a further 80,000 shares in the company at a cost of $80,000. In March 1978 the company went into receivership, and Day lost both investments. He sued Mead for his loss plus interest, claiming breach of fiduciary duty. The High Court Judge held that Mead was in breach of his fiduciary duty to Day in failing to refer Day to an independent solicitor and in failing to inform him of the management and financial difficulties facing the company. The Judge further held that Day was entitled to full compensation for his first investment, but, as Day was equally to blame for the loss of his second investment due to his business experience and his involvement with the company between July and December 1977, he was entitled to compensation for only half that investment. The Judge awarded Day damages of $60,000, but refused interest on the grounds of Day's delay in bringing the case to trial.

The Court of Appeal affirmed the decision of the trial judge except as to the matter of interest, an issue I need not discuss here. It agreed that Mead, though he acted quite innocently, was, having regard to the circumstances, in breach of fiduciary duties. In the absence of complete disclosure of the various conflicts of interest, he should have referred Day to an independent adviser and should have informed him of the problems faced by the company.

What is important for our purposes is the manner in which the Court of Appeal dealt with compensation, and in particular the question whether the compensation could be reduced in respect of the second investment in 1977 because of Day's contributory negligence. Like the trial judge, it concluded that it was proper to apportion the loss. In its view, not only was this justifiable on the basis of equitable principles, but law and equity had become so merged in this area that the principles of contribution should apply. As well, judge-made law was quite properly affected by legislative action, there the *Contributory Negligence Act*, and by other current trends. Having reviewed a number of cases where there was an intermingling of common law and equitable principles, Cooke P continued, at p. 451:

These developments accord with what is probably the most authoritative modern exposition of the effect that should be accorded to the *Judicature Acts* in England, namely the speech of Lord Diplock in *United Scientific Holdings Ltd. v. Burnley Borough Council*, [1978] AC 904 (HL (Eng.)) at pp. 924-927. As Lord Diplock put it, law and equity have mingled now; the Acts did not bring to a sudden halt the whole process of development of the common law of England that had been so notable a feature of the preceding decades; the legislation placed no ban upon further development of substantive rules by judicial decision. I respectfully subscribe to such views, as will be apparent from *Hayward v. Giordani*, [1983] NZLR 140 at p. 148.

Compensation or damages in equity were traditionally said to aim at restoration or restitution, whereas common law tort damages are intended to compensate for harm done; but in many cases, the present being one, that is a difference without a distinction. There is, however, the more significant historical difference that Courts of equity were regarded as having wider discretions than common law Courts. Equitable relief was said to be always discretionary. Its grant or refusal was influenced by ideas expressed in sundry maxims. He who seeks equity must do equity. He who seeks equity must come with clean hands. Delay defeats equity. These are merely examples. Further, relief could be granted on terms or conditions.

Whether or not there are reported cases in which compensation for breach of a fiduciary obligation has been assessed on the footing that the plaintiff should accept some share of the responsibility, there appears to be no solid reason for denying jurisdiction to follow that obviously just course, especially now that law and equity have mingled or are interacting. It is an opportunity for equity to show that it has not petrified and to live up to the spirit of its maxims. Moreover, assuming that the *Contributory Negligence Act* does not itself apply, it is nevertheless helpful as an analogy, on the principle to which we in New Zealand are increasingly giving weight that the evolution of Judge-made law may be influenced by the ideas of the legislature as reflected in contemporary statutes and by other current trends: compare *Dominion Rent A Car Ltd v. Budget Rent a Car Systems (1970) Ltd.*, [1978] 2 NZLR 395, citing *Erven Warnink v. J. Townend & Sons (Hull) Ltd.*, [1979] AC 731 (HL (Eng.)) at p. 743 *per* Lord Diplock.

I agree with this approach. As I have attempted to demonstrate, it would be possible to reach this result following a purely equitable path. I agree with Cooke P that the maxims of equity can be flexibly adapted to serve the ends of justice as perceived in our days. They are not rules that must be rigorously applied but malleable principles intended to serve the ends of fairness and justice. Lord Haldane reminded us in *Nocton v. Lord Ashburton* of the elasticity of equitable remedies. But in this area, it seems to me, even the path of equity leads to law. The maxim that "equity follows the law" (though I realize that it has traditionally been used only where the Courts of Chancery were called in the course of their work to apply common law concepts) is not out of place in this area where law and equity have long overlapped in pursuit of their common goal of affording adequate remedies against those placed in a position of trust or confidence when they breach a duty that reasonably flows from that position. And, as I have indicated, willy-nilly the courts have tended to merge the principles of law and equity to meet the ends of justice as it is perceived in our time. That, in effect, is what was done in *Jacks v. Davis, supra*, and by the courts below in the instant case. As I see it, this is both reasonable and proper. It is worth observing that while the breakthrough in *Hedley Byrne, supra*, took place in a common law context, it finds its roots in equitable principles: see Gummow in Youdan, *op. cit.*, at p. 60; Davidson, *op. cit.*, at pp. 370-1.

Lord Diplock's remark to the effect that the two streams of common law and equity have now mingled and interact are abundantly evident in this area. That is as it should be, because in this particular area law and equity have for long been on the same course and whether one follows the way of equity through a flexible use of the relatively undeveloped remedy of compensation, or the common law's more developed approach to damages is of no great moment. Where "the measure of duty is the same," the same rule should apply: see Somers J in *Day v. Mead, supra*, at p. 457. Only when there are different policy objectives should equity engage in its well-known flexibility to achieve a different and fairer result. The foundation of the obligation sought to be enforced, Somers J notes, is "the trust or confidence reposed by one and accepted by the other or the assumption to act for the one by that other." That being so, it would be odd if a different result followed depending solely on the manner in which one framed an identical claim. What is required is a measure of rationalization. I fully concur with the following statement of Somers J, at p. 458:

> I am disposed to think that the equitable and common law obligations as to disclosure, use of confidential information, and want of care discernible in the cases are now but particular instances of duties imposed by reason of the circumstances in which each party stands to the other and that while the particular remedy for breach of duty may depend upon the way the case has developed, equity and the law are set upon the same course.

I am aware that reservations have been expressed in some quarters about this fusion or, perhaps more accurately, mingling of law and equity: see Jill E. Martin (ed.), *Hanbury's Modern Equity* (London: Stevens, 12th ed., 1985) at pp. 22-6. But no case was brought to our attention where it has led to confusion, and there are many cases, some of which I have discussed, where it has made possible a just and reasonable result. It simply provides a general, but flexible, approach that allows for direct application of the experience and best features of both law and equity, whether the mode of redress (the cause of action or remedy) originates in one system or the other. There might be room for concern if one were indiscriminately attempting to meld the whole of the two systems. Equitable concepts like trusts, equitable estates and consequent equitable remedies must continue to exist apart, if not in isolation, from common law rules. But when one moves to fiduciary relationships and the law regarding misstatements, we have a situation where now the courts of common law, now the courts of equity moved forward to provide remedies where a person failed to meet the trust or confidence reposed in that person. There was throughout considerable overlap. In time the common law outstripped equity and the remedy of compensation became somewhat atrophied. Under these circumstances, why should it not borrow from the experience of the common law? Whether the courts refine the equitable tools such as the remedy of compensation, or follow the common law on its own terms, seems not particularly important where the same policy objective is sought.

Where a situation requires different policy objectives, then the remedy may be found in the system that appears more appropriate. This will often be equity. Its flexible remedies such as constructive trusts, account, tracing and compensation, must continue to be moulded to meet the requirements of fairness and justice in specific situations. Nor should this process be confined to pre-existing situations. Lord Diplock has reminded us that the régime of conjoint application of law and equity introduced by the *Judicature Act* must not be seen as bringing to a halt the process of development of substantive law in both great systems of judicially created law. And this court in cases such as *Canadian Aero Service Ltd. v. O'Malley, supra* [[1974] SCR 592], and *Lac Minerals, supra* [[1989] 2 SCR 574], to name but two, has not been slow to accept this counsel.

But, as these cases underline, equity cannot be rigidly applied. Its doctrines must be attuned to different circumstances. Quite obviously not all fiduciary obligations are the same. It would be wholly inappropriate to interpret equitable doctrines so technically as to displace common law rules that achieve substantial justice in areas of common concern, thereby leading to harsh and inequitable results. I wholeheartedly reject the notion advanced by the appellants that the Court of Appeal "fell into error because of a misplaced concern with concepts of common sense and reasonableness." I would have thought these concerns were central to both common law and equity.

It was said, however, that the approach is necessary to sustain fiduciary relationships. I do not accept that there is need to strengthen the fiduciary position to the point of unnecessary harshness. Both the common law and equity sufficiently support the fiduciary position by compensating the victim of the breach of confidence. Damages equivalent to those for deceit would seem sufficient to meet both these ends. That was the level of compensation awarded by the courts below and neither party contested its appropriateness.

Disposition

I would dismiss the appeal with costs.

McLACHLIN J (Lamer CJC and L'Heureux-Dubé J concurring): ... My first concern with proceeding by analogy with tort is that it overlooks the unique foundation and goals of equity. The basis of the fiduciary obligation and the rationale for equitable compensation are distinct from the tort of negligence and contract. In negligence and contract the parties are taken to be independent and equal actors, concerned primarily with their own self-interest. Consequently, the law seeks a balance between enforcing obligations by awarding compensation and preserving optimum freedom for those involved in the relationship in question, communal or otherwise. The essence of a fiduciary relationship, by contrast, is that one party pledges herself to act in the best interest of the other. The fiduciary relationship has trust, not self-interest, at its core, and when breach occurs, the balance favours the person wronged. The freedom of the fiduciary is diminished by the nature of the obligation he or she has undertaken—an obligation which "betokens loyalty, good faith and avoidance of a conflict of duty and self-interest": *Canadian Aero Service Ltd. v. O'Malley*, [1974] SCR 592. In short, equity is concerned, not only to compensate the plaintiff, but to enforce the trust which is at its heart.

The trust-like nature of the fiduciary obligation manifests itself in characteristics which distinguish it from the tort of negligence and from breach of contract. Thus, Wilson J in *Frame v. Smith*, [1987] 2 SCR 99 at p. 136 (approved by Sopinka and La Forest JJ, in *Lac Minerals Ltd. v. International Corona Resources Ltd.*, [1989] 2 SCR 574 at pp. 599 and 646), attributed the following characteristics to a fiduciary obligation: (1) the fiduciary has scope for the exercise of some discretion or power; (2) the fiduciary can unilaterally exercise that power or discretion so as to affect the beneficiary's legal or practical interests; (3) the beneficiary is pecuniarily vulnerable or at the mercy of the fiduciary holding the discretion or power. ...

These differences suggest that we cannot simply assume that an analogy with tort law is appropriate. And even if we could, the analogy would not be of great assistance. For tort offers different measures of compensation, depending on the nature of the wrong. The measure for deceit, for example, is more stringent than for negligence. So adoption of a tort measure does not solve the problem. The further question arises: which tort measure? One might argue that the appropriate analogy is with the tort of deceit, since both deceit and breach of fiduciary obligation involve wrongful acts with moral overtones. But the better approach, in my view, is to look to the policy behind compensation for breach of fiduciary duty and determine what remedies will best further that policy. In so far as the same goals are shared by tort and breach of fiduciary duty, remedies may coincide. But they may also differ.

The danger of proceeding by analogy with tort law is that it may lead to us to adopt answers which, however easy, may not be appropriate in the context of a breach of fiduciary duty. La Forest J has avoided one such pitfall in indicating that compensation for a breach of fiduciary duty will not be limited by foreseeability, but what of other issues? For instance, the analogy with tort might suggest that presumptions which operate in favour of the injured party in a claim for a breach of fiduciary duty will no longer operate; for example, the presumption that trust funds will be put to the most profitable use. And it is clear that tort law is incompatible with the well developed doctrine that a fiduciary must disgorge profits gained through a breach of duty, even though such profits are not made at the expense of the person to whom the duty is owed. La Forest J allows that benefits may be disgorged, but addresses only the case where no such benefit was obtained (at p. 146). From this it appears that he would treat benefit to the fiduciary on the basis of equitable principles, and losses to the plaintiff on the basis of common law. In my view it is preferable to deal with both remedies under the same system—equity. Rather than begin from tort and proceed by changing the tort model to meet the constraints of trust, I prefer to start from trust, using the tort analogy to the extent shared concerns may make it helpful. This said, I readily concede that we may take wisdom where we find it, and accept such insights offered by the law of tort, in particular deceit, as may prove useful.

My second concern with proceeding by analogy with tort is that it requires us to separate so called "true trust" situations, where the trustee holds property as agent for the beneficiary, from other fiduciary obligations. This distinction is necessary if one proceeds by analogy with tort because the tort analogy cannot apply in the former category (see La Forest J, pp. 145-6). In my view, however, this distinction is artificial and undercuts the common wrong embraced by both categories—the breach of the obligation of trust and utmost good faith which lies on one who undertakes to control or manage something—be it property or some other interest—on behalf of another. Nor do the cases support the distinction, as illustrated by the analysis which follows of *R v. Guerin*, [1984] 2 SCR 335.

Differences between different types of fiduciary relationships may, depending on the circumstances, dictate different approaches to damages. This may be significant as the law of fiduciary obligations develops. However, such differences must be related in some way to the underlying concept of trust—the notion of special powers reposed in the trustee to be exercised exclusively for the benefit of the person who trusts. The distinction between the rights of a claimant in equity for maladministration of property as opposed to wrongful advice or information, resides in the fact that in the former case equity can and does require property wrongfully appropriated to be restored to the *cestui que trust* together with an account of profits. Where there is no property which can be restored, restitution in this sense is not available. In those cases, the court may award compensation in lieu of restitution. This is a pragmatic distinction in the form of the remedy which must not obscure the fact that the measure of compensation remains restitutionary or "trust-like" in both cases. Any further distinction is difficult to support. Why in principle, should a trustee's abuse of power in relation to tangible property attract less compensation than a trustee's abuse of power in relation to a lease or a mortgage or the purchase of a business or a home? The goals of equity in the latter category of case, as asserted in *Nocton v. Ashburton, supra*, are not only to compensate the plaintiff but to deter fiduciaries from abusing their powers. Whence then the difference in compensation?

Having concluded that equitable compensation should not be determined by the simple expedient of resorting to tort, I come to the central question in this case. What is the ambit of compensation as an equitable remedy? Proceeding in trust, we start from the traditional obligation of a defaulting trustee, which is to effect restitution to the estate. But restitution *in specie* may not always be possible. So equity awards compensation in place of restitution *in specie*, by analogy for breach of fiduciary duty with the ideal of restoring to the estate that which was lost through the breach.

The restitutionary basis of compensation for breach of trust was described in *Ex p. Adamson* (1878), 8 Ch. D 807 (CA) at p. 819:

> The Court of Chancery never entertained a suit for damages occasioned by fraudulent conduct or for breach of trust. The suit was always for an equitable debt or liability in the nature of debt. It was a suit for the restitution of the actual money or thing, or value of the thing, of which the cheated party had been cheated.

It has been widely accepted ever since. As Professor Davidson states in his very useful article "The Equitable Remedy of Compensation" (1982), 13 Melbourne UL Rev. 349 at p. 351, "the method of calculation [of compensation] will be that which makes restitution for the value of the loss suffered from the breach." ...

While foreseeability of loss does not enter into the calculation of compensation for breach of fiduciary duty, liability is not unlimited. Just as restitution *in specie* is limited to the property under the trustee's control, so equitable compensation must be limited to loss flowing from the trustee's acts in relation to the interest he undertook to protect. Thus, Davidson states "it is imperative to ascertain the loss *resulting from breach of the relevant equitable duty*" (at p. 354, emphasis added).

The need for a link between the equitable breach and the loss for which compensation is awarded is fair and sound in policy and is supported in *Guerin*. The trial judge in *Guerin* did not measure damages as the difference between the lease which was entered into and that which the band was prepared to authorize, because the golf club would not have entered into a lease at all on the terms sought by the band, and it could not therefore be said that the breach had caused the band to lose the opportunity to enter a lease on the authorized terms. Nor did the trial judge simply assess damages as the difference between the value of the lease actually entered into and the amount that the land was worth at the time of trial, which would be the result if causation were irrelevant. Rather, he concluded that had there been no breach, the band would have eventually leased the land for residential development. He allowed for the time which would have been required for planning, tenders and negotiation, and he also discounted for the fact that some of the then current value of the surrounding developments was due to the existence of the golf course. In other words, he assessed, as best he could, the value of the actual opportunity lost as a result of the breach.

The requirement that the loss must result from the breach of the relevant equitable duty does not negate the fact that "causality" in the legal sense as limited by foreseeability at the time of breach does not apply in equity. It is in this sense that I read the statement of Street J in *Re Dawson, supra* [(1966), 84 WN (Pt. 1) 399 (NSW)], that "causality, foreseeability and remoteness do not readily enter into the matter" (quoted in *Guerin* at p. 360), and the broad language of *Caffrey v. Darby* (1801), 6 Ves. Jun. 488; 31 ER 1159 (relied on by Street J), where in fact a causal link between the breach and the loss was found, the court stating that had the trustees adhered to their duty "the property would not have been in a situation to sustain that loss" (at p. 404) (appropriation by a third party). ...

In summary, compensation is an equitable monetary remedy which is available when the equitable remedies of restitution and account are not appropriate. By analogy with restitution, it attempts to restore to the plaintiff what has been lost as a result of the breach, *i.e.*, the plaintiff's lost opportunity. The plaintiff's actual loss as a consequence of the breach is to be assessed with the full benefit of hindsight. Foreseeability is not a concern in assessing compensation, but it is essential that the losses made good are only those which, on a common sense view of causation, were caused by the breach. The plaintiff will not be required to mitigate, as the term is used in law, but losses resulting from clearly unreasonable behaviour on the part of the plaintiff will be adjudged to flow from that behaviour, and not from the breach. Where the trustee's breach permits the wrongful or negligent acts of third parties, thus establishing a direct link between the breach and the loss, the resulting loss will be recoverable. Where there is no such link, the loss must be recovered from the third parties.

I come finally to the application of these principles to this case. The breach of fiduciary duty is conceded, as is the fact that the plaintiffs would not have bought an interest in the property and the joint venture had there been no breach. This establishes that the breach of fiduciary duty resulted in the acquisition of this interest. The question is whether, applying a common sense view of causation, the further losses sustained in the course of construction can be said to have resulted or flowed from the breach of fiduciary duty.

In my view, the answer to this question is no. The construction loss was caused by third parties. There is no link between the breach of fiduciary duty and this loss. The solicitor's duty had come to an end and the plaintiffs had assumed control of the property. This loss was the result, not of the solicitor's breach of duty, but of decisions made by the plaintiffs and those they chose to hire. To put in the terms of Wilson J in *Guerin*, what the plaintiffs lost as a result of the breach of fiduciary duty was the opportunity to say no to acquisition of the property represented by the joint venture. The difference in the price represented by the secret profit, together with expenditures incidental to the acquisition, restores that lost opportunity. (The trial judge awarded what he termed consequential damages. It is not clear what these consist of and whether they could be said to flow from the breach itself. As the point was not argued, I would not disturb this award.) Thereafter, recourse does not lie in equity against the solicitor, whose duty and control had ended, but against others.

This result accords with common sense and policy. If fiduciaries on land transactions who breach their fiduciary duty were responsible not only for losses flowing from the fiduciary breach, but for all wrongful acts associated with the property thereafter which cause loss to the plaintiff, they would not only be deterred from breach of duty, but rendered impotent. Insurance rates for solicitors would rise (if insurance could be obtained) and the costs of providing the services would increase accordingly. If such a result were necessary to protect innocent purchasers or deter misconduct, perhaps a case could be made for it. But it is not necessary as a policy of the law. The law gives a plaintiff other remedies. It is fairer that losses arising from construction on the property after the purchase be borne by those who assume responsibility for the construction rather than by the solicitor who acted in the purchase transaction. Where construction is concerned, it is their negligent conduct—not the solicitor's—which the law should seek to deter.

For these reasons I would dismiss the appeal.

STEVENSON J: I have read the draft judgment of my colleague, La Forest J, and agree with his conclusion and am in substantial agreement with his reasoning.

I part company with his reasoning on two points.

(1) Compensation as a Remedy

Firstly, while I am in agreement that compensation here should not be determined in the same way as a court of equity would determine compensation in the case of a claim against a trustee, I would not define compensation in equity as merely putting the plaintiff in as good a position as the plaintiff was before the breach. In *McKenzie v. McDonald*, [1927] VLR 134, the defendant actually took title to the principal's property and I would have been inclined to make him disgorge the profit. This case is not one of profit making and restitutionary concepts do not fit.

On the other hand, I think Viscount Haldane was correct in *Nocton v. Lord Ashburton*, [1914] AC 932 (HL (Eng.)) at p. 958, when he says that the measure of damages in a compensation claim may not always be the same as in an action of deceit or negligence. The thrust of the article by Davidson in the University of Melbourne Law Review ["The Equitable Remedy of Compensation" (1982), 3 Melbourne UL Rev. 349] is that compensation in equity differs from damages, particularly, of course, where equity is looking at restitution. The difference is also helpfully discussed by Gummow J, writing extra-judicially, in "Compensation for Breach of Fiduciary Duty," in T.G. Youdan, ed., *Equity, Fiduciaries, and Trusts* (Toronto: Carswell, 1988).

In my view, a court of equity, applying principles of fairness, would and should draw the line at calling upon the fiduciary to compensate for losses arising as a result of the unanticipated neglect of the engineers and pile-driving contractor. The fiduciary had nothing to do with their selection, their control, their contractual or bonding obligations. It follows that I agree with the trial judge and the British Columbia Court of Appeal that these losses are too remote, not in the sense of failing the "but for" test, but in being so unrelated and independent that they should not, in fairness, be attributed to the defendant's breach of duty.

(2) The Fusion of Law and Equity

I do not think that the so-called fusion of law and equity has anything to do with deciding this case. If it did, the rules of equity would prevail. I greatly fear that talk of fusing law and equity only results in confusing and confounding the law. I do agree that equity is not frozen at the time of the *Judicature Acts*. But the *Judicature Acts* were not a new *Statute of Uses*.

Nor do I agree that principles of contributory negligence were introduced by fusion. This subject is addressed in the article of Gummow J, to which I referred. Common law contributory negligence was a complete bar to the action which it would be if equity adopted the common law. Moreover, this court has held that contributory negligence legislation does not apply in a claim for breach of trust: *Carl B. Potter Ltd. v. Mercantile Bank of Canada*, [1980] 2 SCR 343 (cited by Gummow J). The beneficiary is under no duty to the trustee any more than the plaintiff here was under any duty to the defendant solicitor. I do not say that a court of equity might not find some losses to be caused by a plaintiff rather than a defendant, and to be too remote in that sense, but it would not do so because of the fusion of law and equity.

Appeal dismissed.

[Wilson J took no part in the judgment.]

NOTES AND QUESTIONS

1. For commentary on *Canson*, see Paul M. Perell, "The Aftermath of Fusion: Canson Enterprises v. Boughton & Co." (1992), 14 *Advocates' Q* 488 and, for more general modern writing on the issues of fusion and liability raised in this case, see Sir Anthony Mason, "The Place of Equity and Equitable Remedies in the Contemporary Common Law World" (1994), 110 *Law Q Rev*. 238; Charles Rickett and Tim Gardner, "Compensating for Loss in Equity: The Evolution of a Remedy" (1994), 24 *VUWLR* 19; and John D. Heydon, "Causal Relationships Between a Fiduciary's Default and the Principal's Loss" (1994), 110 *Law Q Rev*. 328. See also *Target Holdings Ltd. v. Redferns (a firm)*, [1996] 1 AC 921 (HL (Eng.)), in which *Canson* is discussed, and *O'Halloren v. RT Thomas Family Properties* (1998), 45 NSWLR 212 (CA), in which *Canson* was also cited in a case involving a company director abusing his power in dealing with the assets of the company. In dealing with causation, the New South Wales Court of Appeal asked whether the loss would have occurred even if there had been no breach. The awarding of these types of damages as part of equitable compensation is controversial in Australia and has reactivated a debate about the role of modern equity. See M. Tilbury, "Fallacy or Furphy?: Fusion in a Judicature World" (2003), 26 *UNSW LJ* 357; D. Morgan, "Harris v. Digital Pulse: The Availability of Exemplary Damages in Equity" (2003), 29 *Monash UL Rev*. 377; and G. Davis, "The Flowering of Equitable Compensation in Australian Remedial Law: The Underrated Case of *Biala Pty. Ltd. v. Mallina Holdings Ltd*" (2008), 42 *Loy. LA L Rev*. 271.

2. Given that La Forest and McLachlin JJ reached the same conclusion on the issue of liability, the question arises as to whether the exercise in which they engaged was merely a classification game or dispute with no practical consequences. That the debate might not be purely theoretical is, however, suggested strongly by the next case in which the differences between these two judges surfaced, the famous case of *Norberg v. Weinrib*, [1992] 2 SCR 226. This involved the liability of a physician for, *inter alia*, engaging in sexual relations with a drug-dependent patient. In that context, La Forest J (Gonthier and Cory JJ concurring) and McLachlin J (L'Heureux-Dubé J concurring) differed as to the nature of the wrong and the

resulting award of damages. La Forest J classified the wrong as a battery and awarded $20,000 general damages and $10,000 punitive damages. In contrast, McLachlin J, treating the wrong as a breach of fiduciary duty, awarded $20,000 for the plaintiff's drug addiction, $25,000 for sexual exploitation, and $25,000 punitive damages. Sopinka J did not see the doctor's conduct as involving either battery or breach of fiduciary duty but was prepared to award the plaintiff $20,000 to compensate her for the doctor's failure to treat her drug addiction but no punitive damages. Stevenson J took no part in the judgment with the consequence that the appeal was allowed on the terms of the La Forest judgment. On its face, this suggests that there are at least some situations where the categorization of a wrong as arising in equity under the rubric of breach of fiduciary duty may have an impact on both the available heads of damage and quantum.

Subsequently, the issue resurfaced in *M.(K.) v. M.(H.)*, [1992] 3 SCR 6, a case involving a claim by a daughter against her father for damages and/or compensation for incest based on both battery and breach of fiduciary duty. Here, too, there was discussion of whether the level of damages would be the same or different, depending on whether the cause of action was in battery or for breach of fiduciary duty. McLachlin J referred back to her judgment in *Canson Enterprises* to the effect that damages for the tort of battery might not necessarily produce the same results as compensation in equity for breach of fiduciary duty. However, in this case, she concurred with La Forest J when he held that, on the facts, the quantum should be the same whether the award was treated as damages for battery or compensation for breach of fiduciary duty. The two categories of wrong were concerned with the same policy objectives, according to La Forest J. At the very least, this amounts to an indirect acknowledgment of the availability of compensation in equity for breach of fiduciary duty for non-pecuniary losses or, putting it another way, of breach of fiduciary duty extending to conduct compromising physical integrity. At the same time, La Forest J also expressly reaffirmed the capacity of the courts to award punitive damages in equity to punish the father for breach of fiduciary duty, thereby creating a majority of the court in favour of that aspect of McLachlin J's judgment in *Canson Enterprises*.

Since then, the scope of the equitable remedy of compensation has come to the fore yet again in the following judgment, one in which the "roles" of La Forest and McLachlin JJ were reversed with the former delivering the judgment of the majority of the court sustaining the award of compensation in equity for breach of fiduciary duty and McLachlin J delivering a joint judgment with Sopinka J (in which Major J concurred) against the availability of that relief.

Hodgkinson v. Simms
[1994] 3 SCR 377

[The plaintiff, Hodgkinson, while a stockbroker by profession, was unfamiliar with the intricacies of tax planning. He therefore sought out the defendant, Simms, an accountant and tax consultant. His purpose in doing so was to obtain independent investment advice for tax planning and sheltering purposes. This led to a relationship of trust as between the two, a relationship that was cultivated by the defendant. The concrete result of this relationship was investment by the plaintiff in four Multiple Unit Residential Buildings (MURBs), tax-sheltered real estate investments. Unbeknownst to the plaintiff, the defendant was in fact a "promoter" of these developments in the sense that he was working on a commission basis for the developers of the MURBs. Had he been aware of this fact, the plaintiff would not have invested in the MURBs.

Despite the interest of the defendant in the projects in question, the price that the plaintiff paid for his investments was a fair one. However, after purchase, their value fell dramatically during a period of heavy decline in the real estate market, and the plaintiff sued the defendant for the losses that he had sustained. He alleged negligence, breach of contract, and breach of fiduciary duty.

In the British Columbia Supreme Court ((1989), 43 BCLR (2d) 122), the action in negligence was dismissed and not thereafter pursued. However, the plaintiff was successful in recovering his losses on the basis of breach of both contract and fiduciary duty. The failure of the defendant to disclose his conflict of interest was held to give rise to an action in both contract and fiduciary duty. On appeal ((1992), 65 BCLR (2d) 264), the British Columbia Court of Appeal reversed the trial judge's holding of breach of fiduciary duty and, while sustaining the finding of breach of contract, reduced the damages to a prorated proportion of the commissions that the defendant had received from the developers for his part in the four projects.]

LA FOREST J (L'Heureux-Dubé and Gonthier JJ concurring):

[The majority found that the defendant had breached his fiduciary duty to the plaintiff. In so doing, La Forest J made reference to the following, *inter alia*, policy justification.]

The desire to protect and reinforce the integrity of social institutions and enterprises is prevalent throughout fiduciary law. The reason for this desire is that the law has recognized the importance of instilling in our social institutions and enterprises some recognition that not all relationships are characterized by a dynamic of mutual autonomy, and that the marketplace cannot always set the rules. By instilling this kind of flexibility into our regulation of social institutions and enterprises, the law therefore helps to strengthen them. ...

[He then turned to the question of damages:]

The trial judge assessed damages flowing from both breach of fiduciary duty and breach of contract. She found the quantum of damages to be the same under either claim, namely the return of capital (adjusted to take into consideration the tax benefits received as a result of the investments), plus all consequential losses, including legal and accounting fees. As I stated at the outset, I cannot find fault with the trial judge's disposition of the damages question.

It is useful to review some key findings of fact that bear on the issue of damages. The trial judge found the appellant paid fair market price for each of the four investments. However, she found that throughout the period during which the appellant was induced by the respondent's recommendations into making the investments, the respondent was in a financial relationship with the developers of the projects. In short, the trial judge found the respondent stood to gain financially if the appellant invested according to his recommendations. She further found that if the appellant had known of the true relationship between the respondent and the developers, he would not have invested. She also found that had the parties turned their minds to the potential consequences of the respondent's relationship with the developers it would have been reasonably foreseeable that the appellant would not have invested.

I turn now to the principles that bear on the calculation of damages in this case. It is well established that the proper approach to damages for breach of a fiduciary duty is restitutionary. On this approach, the appellant is entitled to be put in as good a position as he would have been in had the breach not occurred. On the facts here, this means that the appellant is entitled to be restored to the position he was in before the transaction. The trial judge adopted this restitutionary approach and fixed damages at an amount equal to the return of capital, as well as all consequential losses, minus the amount the appellant saved on income tax due to the investments.

The respondent advanced two arguments against the trial judge's assessment of damages for breach of fiduciary duty. Both raise the issue of causation, and I will address these submissions as they were argued.

The respondent first submitted that given the appellant's stated desire to shelter as much of his income as possible from taxation, and his practice of buying a wide variety of tax shelters, the appellant would still have invested in real-estate tax shelters had he known the true facts. The main difficulty with this submission is that it flies in the face of the facts found by the trial judge. The materiality of the non-disclosure in inducing the appellant to change his position was a live issue at trial which the judge resolved in the appellant's favour, a finding accepted by the Court of Appeal. For reasons given earlier, I agree with this finding.

What is more, the submission runs up against the long-standing equitable principle that where the plaintiff has made out a case of non-disclosure and the loss occasioned thereby is established, the onus is on the defendant to prove that the innocent victim would have suffered the same loss regardless of the breach; see *London Loan & Savings Co. v. Brickenden*, [1934] 2 WWR 545 (PC (Can.)) at pp. 550-51; see also *Huff v. Price* [(1990), 51 BCLR (2d) 282 (CA)] at pp. 319-20; *Commerce Capital Trust Co. v. Berk* (1989), 57 DLR (4th) 759 (Ont. CA) at pp. 763-64. This Court recently affirmed the same principle with respect to damages at common law in the context of negligent misrepresentation; see *Rainbow Industrial Caterers Ltd. v. Canadian National Railway Co.*, [1991] 3 SCR 3 at pp. 14-17. I will return to the common law cases in greater detail later; it suffices now to say that courts exercising both common law and equitable jurisdiction have approached this issue in the same manner. In *Rainbow*, Sopinka J, on behalf of a 6-1 majority of this Court, had this to say, at pp. 15-16:

> The plaintiff is the innocent victim of a misrepresentation which has induced a change of position. It is just that the plaintiff should be entitled to say "but for the tortious conduct of the defendant, I would not have changed my position." A tortfeasor who says, "Yes, but you would have assumed a position other than the *status quo ante*," and thereby asks a court to find a transaction whose terms are hypothetical and speculative, should bear the burden of displacing the plaintiff's assertion of the *status quo ante*.

Further, mere "speculation" on the part of the defendant will not suffice; see *ibid.*, at p. 15; *Commerce Capital, supra*, at p. 764. In the present case the respondent has adduced no concrete evidence to "displac[e] the plaintiff's assertion of the *status quo ante*," and this submission must, therefore, be dismissed.

The respondent also argued that even assuming the appellant would not have invested had proper disclosure been made, the non-disclosure was not the proximate cause of the appellant's loss. Rather, he continued, the appellant's loss was caused by the general econom-ic recession that hit the British Columbia real estate market in the early 1980s. The respond-ent submits that it is grossly unjust to hold him accountable for losses that, he maintains, have no causal relation to the breach of fiduciary duty he perpetrated on the appellant. …

Contrary to the respondent's submission, this result is not affected by the ratio of this Court's decision in *Canson Enterprises, supra*. *Canson* held that a court exercising equitable jurisdiction is not precluded from considering the principles of remoteness, causation, and intervening act where necessary to reach a just and fair result. *Canson* does not, however, signal a retreat from the principle of full restitution; rather it recognizes the fact that a breach of a fiduciary duty can take a variety of forms, and as such a variety of remedial con-siderations may be appropriate; see also *McInerney v. Macdonald*, [[1992] 2 SCR 138] at p. 149. Writing extra-judicially, Huband JA of the Manitoba Court of Appeal recently re-marked upon this idea, in "Remedies and Restitution for Breach of Fiduciary Duties" in The 1993 Isaac Pitblado Lectures, [*Fiduciary Duties/Conflicts of Interest* (Winnipeg: Law Society of Manitoba, Manitoba Bar Association, and University of Manitoba Faculty of Law, 1993)] 21-32 at p. 31:

> A breach of a fiduciary duty can take many forms. It might be tantamount to deceit and theft, while on the other hand it may be no more than an innocent and honest bit of bad advice, or a failure to give a timely warning.

Canson is an example of the latter type of fiduciary breach, mentioned by Huband JA. There, the defendant solicitor failed to warn the plaintiff, his client, that the vendors and other third parties were pocketing a secret profit from a "flip" of the subject real estate such that the property was overpriced. See also *Jacks* [*v. Davis*, [1983] 1 WWR 327 (BCCA)]. In this situation, the principle of full restitution should not entitle a plaintiff to greater com-pensation than he or she would otherwise be entitled to at common law, wherein the limit-ing principles of intervening act would come into play.

Put another way, equity is not so rigid as to be susceptible to being used as a vehicle for punishing defendants with harsh damage awards out of all proportion to their actual behav-iour. On the contrary, where the common law has developed a measured and just principle in response to a particular kind of wrong, equity is flexible enough to borrow from the com-mon law. As I noted in *Canson*, at pp. 587-88, this approach is in accordance with the fusion of law and equity that occurred near the turn of the century under the auspices of the old *Judicature Acts*; see also *M. (K.) v. M. (H.), supra*, at p. 61. Thus, properly understood *Canson* stands for the proposition that courts should strive to treat similar wrongs similarly, regardless of the particular cause or causes of action that may have been pleaded. As I stated in *Canson* at p. 581:

> [B]arring different policy considerations underlying one action or the other, I see no reason why the same basic claim, whether framed in terms of a common law action or an equitable remedy, should give rise to different levels of redress.

In other words, the courts should look to the harm suffered from the breach of the given duty, and apply the appropriate remedy.

Returning to the facts of the present case, one immediately notices significant differences from the wrong committed by the defendant in *Canson* as compared to the character of the fiduciary breach perpetrated by the respondent. In *Canson* there was no particular nexus between the wrong complained of and the fiduciary relationship; this was underlined, at p. 577, by my colleague, McLachlin J, who followed a purely equitable route. Rather, the fiduciary relationship there arose by operation of law, and was in many ways incidental to the particular wrong. Further, the loss was caused by the wrongful act of a third party that was unrelated to the fiduciary breach. In the present case the duty the respondent breached was directly related to the risk that materialized and in fact caused the appellant's loss. The respondent had been retained specifically to seek out and make independent recommendations of suitable investments for the appellant. This agreement gave the respondent a kind of influence or discretion over the appellant in that, as the trial judge found, he effectively chose the risks to which the appellant would be exposed based on investments which in his expert opinion coincided with the appellant's overall investment objectives. In *Canson* the defendant solicitor did not advise on, choose, or exercise any control over the plaintiff's decision to invest in the impugned real estate; in short, he did not exercise any control over the risks that eventually materialized into a loss for the plaintiff.

Indeed, courts have treated common law claims of the same nature as the wrong complained of in the present case in much the same way as claims in equity. I earlier referred to *Rainbow Industrial Caterers*. The plaintiff there had contracted to cater lunches to CN employees at a certain price per meal. The price was based on the estimated number of lunches the defendant would require over the period covered by the contract. This estimate was negligently misstated, and the plaintiff suffered a significant loss. The Court was satisfied that but for the misrepresentation, the plaintiff would not have entered into the contract. The defendant, however, alleged that much of the loss was not caused by the misrepresentation but rather by certain conduct of CN employees, *e.g.*, taking too much food. This argument was rejected by the Court in the following terms, at p. 17:

> ... CN bore the burden of proving that Rainbow would have bid even if the estimate had been accurate. That was not proved, and so it is taken as a fact that Rainbow would *not* have contracted had the estimate been accurate. The conduct referred to in para. 49 [that is, the conduct of the CN employees] would not have occurred if there had been no contract, and therefore the loss caused thereby, like all other losses in the proper execution of the contract by Rainbow, is directly related to the negligent misrepresentation. [Emphasis in original.]

Thus, where a party can show that but for the relevant breach it would not have entered into a given contract, that party is freed from the burden or benefit of the rest of the bargain; see also *BG Checo International Ltd. v. British Columbia Hydro and Power Authority*, [1993] 1 SCR 12 at pp. 40-41 (per La Forest and McLachlin JJ). In short, the wronged party is entitled to be restored to the pre-transaction *status quo*. ...

The respondent points to a number of cases in which courts have refused to compensate plaintiffs for losses suffered owing to general market fluctuations despite the existence of "but for" causation; *Waddell v. Blockey* (1879), 4 QBD 678 (CA); *Huddleston v. Herman & MacLean*, 640 F2d 534 (5th Cir. 1981), aff'd. in part 459 US 375 (1983); *McGonigle v. Combs*, 968 F2d 810 (9th Cir. 1992).

The respondent placed considerable reliance on the *Waddell* case. There the defendant sold rupee paper of his own to the plaintiff on the fraudulent basis that the paper belonged to persons other than the defendant. After the purchase the rupee paper rapidly fell in value owing to an unrelated decline in the market for such paper. The plaintiff eventually sold the paper five months later at a loss of £43,000. The English Court of Appeal, reversing, held that despite the proven fraudulent misrepresentation, the plaintiff was not entitled to any damages on the grounds that there was "no natural or proximate connection between the wrong done and the damage suffered"; *per* Thesiger LJ at p. 682.

[La Forest J then proceeded to both marginalize and reject the approach of the English Court of Appeal in *Waddell* and made reference to the seemingly conflicting judgment of the BC Court of Appeal in *Allan v. McLennan* (1916), 31 DLR 617. Then, after an extensive canvassing of relevant US authority, he continued:]

From a policy perspective it is simply unjust to place the risk of market fluctuations on a plaintiff who would not have entered into a given transaction but for the defendant's wrongful conduct. I observe that in *Waddell, supra,* Bramwell LJ conceded, at p. 680, that if *restitutio in integrum* had been possible, the plaintiff could probably have recovered in full. Indeed counsel for the appellant argued that the proper approach to damages in this case was the monetary equivalent of a rescissionary remedy. I agree. In my view the appellant should not suffer from the fact that he did not discover the breach until such time as the market had already taken its toll on his investments. This principle, which I take to be a basic principle of fairness, is in fact reflected in the common law of mitigation, itself rooted in causation; see S.M. Waddams, *The Law of Contracts* ([Aurora, ON: Canada Law Book,] 3rd ed., 1993), at p. 515. In *Asamera Oil Corp. v. Sea Oil & General Corp.,* [1979] 1 SCR 633, this Court held that in an action for breach of the duty to return shares under a contract of bailment, the obligation imposed on the plaintiff to mitigate by purchasing like shares on the open market did not commence until such time as the plaintiff learned of the breach or within a reasonable time thereafter.

There is a broader justification for upholding the trial judge's award of damages in cases such as the present, namely the need to put special pressure on those in positions of trust and power over others in situations of vulnerability. This justification is evident in American caselaw, which makes a distinction between simple fraud related to the price of a security and fraudulent inducements by brokers and others in the investment business in positions of influence. In the case at bar, ... the wrong complained of goes to the heart of the duty of loyalty that lies at the core of the fiduciary principle. In redressing a wrong of this nature, I have no difficulty in resorting to a measure of damages that places the exigencies of the market-place on the respondent. Such a result is in accordance with the principle that a defaulting fiduciary has an obligation to effect restitution *in specie* or its monetary equivalent. ... I see no reason to derogate from this principle; on the contrary, the behaviour of the respondent seems to be precisely the type of behaviour that calls for strict legal censure. Mark Ellis puts the matter in the following way in *Fiduciary Duties in Canada* [Don Mills, ON: Richard DeBoo, 1989], at pp. 20-2:

> [T]he relief seeks primarily to protect a party owed a duty of utmost good faith from deleterious actions by the party owing the fiduciary duty. The vehicles by which the Court may enforce that duty are diverse and powerful, but are premised upon the same desire: to strictly and jeal-

ously guard against breach and to redress that breach by maintenance of the pre-default *status quo*, where possible.

The remedy of disgorgement, adopted in effect if not in name by the Court of Appeal, is simply insufficient to guard against the type of abusive behaviour engaged in by the respondent in this case. The law of fiduciary duties has always contained within it an element of deterrence. ... In this way the law is able to monitor a given relationship society views as socially useful while avoiding the necessity of formal regulation that may tend to hamper its social utility. Like-minded fiduciaries in the position of the respondent would not be deterred from abusing their power by a remedy that simply requires them, if discovered, to disgorge their secret profit, with the beneficiary bearing all the market risk. If anything, this would encourage people in his position to in effect gamble with other people's money, knowing that if they are discovered they will be no worse off than when they started. As a result, the social benefits of fiduciary relationships, particularly in the field of independent professional advisors, would be greatly diminished.

In view of my finding that there existed a fiduciary duty between the parties, it is not in strictness necessary to consider damages for breach of contract. However, in my view, on the facts of this case, damages in contract follow the principles stated in connection with the equitable breach. The contract between the parties was for independent professional advice. While it is true that the appellant got what he paid for from the developers, he did not get the services he paid for from the respondent. The relevant contractual duty breached by the respondent is of precisely the same nature as the equitable duty considered in the fiduciary analysis, namely the duty to make full disclosure of any material conflict of interest. This was, in short, a contract which provided for the performance of obligations characterized in equity as fiduciary.

Further, it remains the case under the contractual analysis that but for the non-disclosure, the contract with the developers for the MURBs would not have been entered into. The trial judge found as a fact that it was reasonably foreseeable that if the appellant had known of the respondent's affiliation with the developers, he would not have invested. This finding is fully reflected in the evidence I have earlier set forth. Put another way, it was foreseeable that if the contract was breached the appellant would be exposed to market risks (*i.e.*, in connection with the four MURBs) to which he would not otherwise have been exposed. Further, it is well established that damages must be foreseeable as to kind, but not extent; as such any distinction based on the unforeseeability of the extent of the market fluctuations must be dismissed; see *H. Parsons (Livestock) Ltd. v. Uttley Ingham & Co.*, [1978] QB 791, at p. 813; *Asamera, supra*, at p. 655. See also S.M. Waddams, *The Law of Damages* ([2d ed. (Aurora, ON: Canada Law Book)] 1991), at paras. 14.280 and 14.290.

The Court of Appeal's approach to contractual damages is puzzling in that it seemed to accept the finding that if the contractual duty had not been breached the investments would not have been made, yet it proceeded to award damages in proportion to the amounts paid by the developer to the defendant. It is clear, however, that there would have been no such fees had the investments not been made. In short, I am unable to follow the Court of Appeal's reasoning on the issue of damages for breach of contract, and I would restore the award of damages made by the trial judge. ...

SOPINKA and McLACHLIN JJ (Major J concurring):

[According to the minority, no breach of fiduciary duty was present on the facts, only a breach of a contractual obligation to disclose the conflict of interest. The minority then proceeded to consider the extent of the defendant's liability for damages for that breach. Included in their identification of the relevant principles, was the following elaboration.]

(a) Causation

The appellant in this case does not allege that the losses which he incurred were caused directly by the respondent's breach of contract. Instead, he claims that "but for" the respondent's breach of the first contract, the appellant would not have entered into subsequent investment contracts which, due to an economic downturn, were significantly devalued. A literal application of the "but for" approach to causation has been rejected in British, Canadian and American case law, in the context of both equitable and common law claims.

In *Waddell v. Blockey* (1879), 4 QBD 678, a case involving an action for fraudulent misrepresentation, the Queen's Bench Division ordered damages in the amount of the difference between the price paid by the individual represented by the plaintiff and the fair market value of the item sold. Although the rupee paper would not have been purchased had the defendant made full disclosure of the fact that he owned the paper which he sold to the purchaser, the defendant was not held liable for the resulting losses sustained by the purchaser due to devaluation of the item. Thesiger LJ reasoned as follows in this regard at pp. 682 and 684:

> There is [in this case] no natural or proximate connection between the wrong done and the damage suffered. ...
> But the present case is complicated by the circumstance of the defendant's fiduciary position in the matter of the purchase, and by the fact that the fraud did not touch the value of the article sold ... . *It would seem, however, strange if under such circumstances a plaintiff who has got the article he bargained for, upon whom no fraud as regards its value has been practised, could, after the article has been depreciated and resold at a loss owing to a cause totally unconnected with the fraud, claim to recover all the loss which he has thereby sustained. I cannot see upon what principle such a claim could be based.* [Emphasis in original.]

Similarly, in *Canson Enterprises Ltd. v. Boughton & Co.*, [1991] 3 SCR 534 at p. 580, this Court recognized that the results of supervening events beyond the control of the defendant are not justly visited upon him/her in assessing damages, even in the context of the breach of an equitable duty. ...

C. Application to the Case at Bar

In assessing the damages for respondent's breach of contract it is necessary to ask whether the loss sustained by the appellant arose naturally from a breach thereof or whether at the time of contracting the parties could reasonably have contemplated the loss flowing from the breach of the duty to disclose. In the event that either criterion is satisfied, the respondent should be held liable for that loss. Finally, the damage assessment as a whole must represent a fair resolution on the facts of this case.

(a) Causation

In our view, it cannot be concluded that the devaluation of the appellant's investments arose naturally from the respondent's breach of contract. The loss in value was caused by an economic downturn which did not reflect any inadequacy in the advice provided by the respondent. We would reject application of the "but for" approach to causation in circumstances where the loss resulted from forces beyond the control of the respondent who, the trial judge determined, had provided otherwise sound investment advice. Therefore, the respondent cannot be held liable for the appellant's losses under the first arm of the test set out in *Hadley* [*v. Baxendale* (1854), 9 Ex. 341; 156 ER 145].

(b) Reasonable Contemplation

Turning to the second arm of the *Hadley* test, the trial judge made certain findings of fact as to what the reasonable contemplation of the parties had been at the time of contracting. With respect to the first contract, between the appellant and the respondent, the trial judge concluded that the respondent fulfilled his requirement to give sound investment advice to the appellant and found that there had been no negligent misrepresentation with respect to the quality of the investments in question. The trial judge also concluded that if the parties had turned their minds to the potential consequences of the respondent's failure to make full disclosure to the appellant under the first contract, they would have contemplated that the appellant would not have entered the subsequent investment contracts and that a change in the economy could adversely affect any investment.

However, the material question to be considered is whether the parties would reasonably have contemplated the losses associated with an economic downturn as liable to result from the respondent's breach of his duty to make full disclosure: *Victoria Laundry* [*(Windsor) Ltd. v. Newman Industries Ltd.*, [1949] 2 KB 528 (CA)]. This question can only be answered in the negative. It would simply not be reasonable for the parties to have contemplated that the respondent's failure to make full disclosure was likely to result in devaluation of the investment due to an economic downturn. As indicated previously, the two events were in no way causally related. The answer might have been different had the respondent's services been defective with respect to assessing the likelihood of economic downturn or the likely effect of an economic downturn on the future value of the investments. However, no such defects were revealed in this case.

Moreover, the fact that the breach of the duty to disclose was a continuing one does not affect our conclusion in this regard. The factual finding was that the investments were sound ones, but for the economic downturn, and there is no evidence to indicate that, had the respondent disclosed his conflicting interests prior in time to the economic downturn, the appellant would have sold his interest in the investments. In fact, it would be unreasonable to infer that he would have done so, given that the investments were sound ones.

In situations involving breach of a duty to disclose, courts have consistently recognized the right of plaintiffs to compensation for losses equivalent to the difference between the price which they paid for a particular investment and the actual value of the investment purchased: *Waddell, supra,* and *Canson, supra.* In the case at bar, the trial judge concluded that there was no evidence to indicate that the appellant had paid anything more than the fair market value for the investments which he made. Therefore, it would appear that no damages should have been assessed. However, McEachern CJ in the Court of Appeal concluded, at p. 280, that "the law so dislikes a failure of disclosure of material facts that it assumes the value of the investment was less than the amount paid, at least to the extent of the amounts paid by the developer to the defendant." There was no cross-appeal from the judgment of the Court of Appeal. In these circumstances we are not entitled to reduce the award of damages made by the Court of Appeal. ...

[Iacobucci J concurred with La Forest J subject to one reservation not relevant in the present context.]

Appeal allowed. Judgment of Prowse J reinstated.

NOTES AND QUESTIONS

1. The majority judgment spends considerable time identifying why damages based on restoring the plaintiff to the position he was in prior to the purchase of the MURBs is justified by reference to the nature of the fiduciary relationship between the parties. It then asserts that even if the claim had been confined to one of breach of contract, the quantum of damages would still have been the same. The minority disagrees. In cases of collateral reliance (as here), what are the principles that the courts have normally followed in awarding contractual damages to compensate for that reliance? Do these principles more closely accord with the majority's or the minority's view of this case? Should plaintiffs be able to assert an entitlement to the costs of collateral reliance in situations where a claim based on expectation damages would produce a lower award? Should it matter whether or not the case is one involving breach of fiduciary duty as well as or instead of breach of contract? Is this case distinguishable from *Canson* on the issues of causation and foreseeability (as asserted by the majority) or not (the minority)?

2. Incidentally, the minority position that the facts were indistinguishable from those in *Canson* seems to suggest that even had the minority found a breach of fiduciary duty, they would not have awarded damages at the level accepted by the majority. Does this indicate that both the majority and the minority accept that the principles governing the award of damages or compensation in a case such as this are the same whether the plaintiff is proceeding in contract or breach of fiduciary duty and that their real disagreement is over the relevant measurement or assessment principles?

3. Writing of the differences in approach between La Forest J and McLachlin J in *Canson*, Berryman made the following statement:

> There is great attraction in La Forest J's approach to equitable compensation which requires articulation of what particular policy is being pursued to justify exceeding the cautious and developed approach of common law damages assessment. The difficulty with McLachlin J's position is that it does not give hortatory guidance on when it is appropriate to impose the full rigours which accompany equitable compensation. The justification that a fiduciary relationship differs appreciably from similarly placed common law duties is more an argument for the imposition of punitive damages to deter or punish than a reason to move to different forms of compensatory assessment [footnote omitted].

See Jeffrey Berryman, "Some Observations on the Application of Equitable Compensation in WA: Dempster v. Mallina Holdings Ltd." (1995), 25 *UWA L Rev.* 317, at 327.

Whether one agrees or disagrees with Berryman's preference for the position of La Forest J over that of McLachlin J, the utility of pleading breach of fiduciary duty as a means of securing punitive damages in a situation that also involves a breach of contract is clear under current Canadian law. In *Vorvis v. Insurance Co. of British Columbia*, [1989] 1 SCR 1085 (see chapter 1, "General Principles of Damages") and *Wallace v. United Grain Growers Ltd.*, [1997] 3 SCR 701, the Supreme Court held that for punitive and aggravated damages to be available in a breach of contract situation that breach must be associated with another independent actionable wrong. One way of setting up such an independent actionable wrong is to establish a parallel breach of fiduciary duty: see, for example, *Mustaji v. Tjin* (1995), 24 CCLT (2d) 191 (BCSC), aff'd. (1996), 25 BCLR (2d) 220 (CA). Would this species of "avoidance" of the contractual ban ever be justifiable under the La Forest J theory in *Canson*?

4. Proceeding by way of breach of fiduciary duty rather than breach of contract might also be advantageous in situations where the losses in question were not foreseeable at the time of the contract but had become so at the date of breach. Customary contract law would suggest no recovery. However, foreseeability in breach of fiduciary duty actions (as in tort) appears to be related to the date of the breach of duty. (Note, however, *Murano v. Bank of Montreal* (1995), 20 BLR (2d) 61 (Ont. Gen. Div.), aff'd. in part but without resolution of this issue (1998), 163 DLR (4th) 21 (Ont. CA), where Adams J holds that the more limiting contract foreseeability rule is not an invariable one.)

5. The principles of causation applicable to claims for equitable compensation are illustrated by the judgments in *Martin v. Goldfarb* (1998), 41 OR (3d) 161 (CA), leave to appeal to SCC refused (February 18, 1999); and *Crescent Restaurants Ltd. v. ICR Brokerage Inc.*, 2010 SKCA 92, 359 Sask. R 149.

Computing the Level of Compensation

Cadbury Schweppes Inc. v. FBI Foods Ltd.
[1999] 1 SCR 142

[Cadbury Schweppes lawfully cancelled a licence that a company had to manufacture and market "Clamato Juice." Thereafter, in breach of the obligations that survived the cancellation of the licence, the company in collaboration with FBI Foods went to market with a product called "Caesar Cocktail." It was made from the same recipe as Clamato Juice, save that it did not contain clam juice or that of any other seafood. For five years, Cadbury Schweppes did nothing about this, believing that the only restraint on the company and FBI Foods was not to manufacture anything with clam juice in it for five years. In 1988, however, Cadbury, having received new advice, commenced an action in the British Columbia Supreme Court in which it sought to secure an injunction restraining FBI Foods (the other company having gone out of business) from continuing to market Caesar Cocktail and for damages or compensation for the losses it had suffered in the meantime. The basis of this action was a claim that FBI had used wrongfully confidential information when it and the other company based the new product on the recipe for Clamato Juice albeit without clam juice.

In the Supreme Court of Canada, there was no longer any issue as to liability and the case turned on whether or not the British Columbia Court of Appeal ((1996), 138 DLR (4th) 682) had been correct in awarding a permanent injunction and an award of compensation to be measured by the profits Cadbury Schweppes would have made on selling an additional amount of Clamato Juice equivalent to the volume of Caesar Cocktail that FBI had sold during the 12 months following the termination of the original licence. The theory of this award was that it would have taken 12 months for the company and FBI to have developed the recipe had they acted alone and without access to the recipe for Clamato Juice and that Cadbury Schweppes would have sold additional Clamato Juice in exactly the same quantities as FBI had sold its product.]

BINNIE J (delivering the judgment of a Court otherwise consisting of L'Heureux-Dubé, Gonthier, McLachlin, Iacobucci, Major, and Bastarache JJ): ...

[In considering the nature of the claim, Binnie J noted that, in the domain of unauthorized use or disclosure of confidential information, the equitable right potentially ran alongside a number of other possible causes of action—actions sounding in tort, contract, and property law. He then stated that this was not a situation where there was a fiduciary relationship and that any characterization of the plaintiff's right as one sounding in property was controversial and, in particular, did not amount to the equivalent of a true patent claim. Nevertheless, while also accepting that equitable rules could provide a higher level of recovery in some instances than that provided under tort law, he held that there were no reasons in this instance that compensation should exceed tort law's normal level of recovery based on the concept of what the plaintiff would have earned "but for" the defendant's wrong.]

Relevance of Lord Cairns' Act 1858 to Jurisdiction To Award Financial Compensation

There appears to be a continuing controversy over the extent to which, if at all, the award of financial compensation is affected by the historic complexities of the *Chancery Amendment Act, 1858* (*Lord Cairns' Act*) and its modern progeny.

The origins of this particular controversy predate the merger of law and equity. The concept of damages is a creature of the common law. The passage of *Lord Cairns' Act* in 1858 conferred on the Courts of Equity a jurisdiction to award damages in addition to or in lieu of an injunction or other specific equitable relief. ...

The practical implication of resting compensation on *Lord Cairns' Act* would be to substitute monetary compensation for injunctive restraint but not necessarily to make compensation available for losses suffered prior to the application for an injunction. In addition, where as in this case, the trial judge held the plaintiffs to be disentitled to an injunction, the jurisdiction to award damages would be open to challenge. There might in fact be a jurisdictional problem in cases where there is "nothing to injunct the defendant against" (D. Capper, "Damages for Breach of the Equitable Duty of Confidence" (1994), 14 *Legal Stud.* 313, at p. 314).

In *Nichrotherm Electrical Co. v. Percy*, [1957] RPC 207, the English Court of Appeal expressed some doubt about the availability of financial compensation in equity outside *Lord*

Cairns' Act. In *English v. Dedham Vale Properties Ltd.*, [1978] 1 WLR 93 (Ch. D), Slade J, at p. 111, attributed the award of compensation in *Seager v. Copydex Ltd. (No. 2)* [[1969] 2 All ER 718 (CA)] to *Lord Cairns' Act*, although Lord Denning nowhere mentioned it. As recently as 1979, Vice-Chancellor Megarry suggested in *Malone v. Commissioner of Police of the Metropolis (No. 2)*, [1979] 2 All ER 620 (Ch. D), at p. 633, that:

> [I]f there is no case for the grant of an injunction, as when the disclosure has already been made, the unsatisfactory result seems to be that no damages can be awarded under this head. ...

See also the *Spycatcher* case [*Attorney-General v. Guardian Newspapers (No. 2)*, [1990] AC 109 (HL (Eng.))] *per* Lord Goff of Chieveley, at p. 286; *Ben-Israel v. Vitacare Medical Products Inc.* [(1997), 78 CPR (3d) 94 (Ont. Gen. Div.)] *per* Beaulieu J, at p. 109; *Pharand Ski Corp. v. Alberta* (1991), 80 Alta. LR (2d) 216 (QB) *per* Mason J, at p. 257, para. 180, *et seq.*; and J. D. McCamus, "Equitable Compensation and Restitutionary Remedies: Recent Developments," *Special Lectures of the Law Society of Upper Canada 1995: Law of Remedies: Principles and Proofs*, 295, at p. 330.

There are English decisions that award financial compensation for breach of *fiduciary* duty in the absence of any claim for an injunction or other equitable relief. See, e.g., *Nocton v. Lord Ashburton*, [1914] AC 932 (HL), where Viscount Haldane LC observed (at p. 952) that the Court of Chancery, operating on "the conscience" of the delinquent solicitor,

> could order the defendant, not ... to pay damages as such, but to make restitution, or to compensate the plaintiff by putting him in as good a position pecuniarily as that in which he was before the injury.

Although *Nocton v. Lord Ashburton* was a case of a faithless fiduciary, the decision in *Lac Minerals* [*v. International Corona Resources*, [1989] 2 SCR 574], as already discussed, is authority for the proposition that the availability of equitable remedies in a breach of confidence action does not now turn on the presence or absence of a fiduciary duty. Other Canadian cases which have based an award of financial compensation for breach of confidence in the exercise of a general equitable jurisdiction without trying to find a fiduciary duty or worrying about the restrictions buried in the modern successors of *Lord Cairns' Act* include *Apotex Fermentation Inc. v. Novopharm Ltd.* [(1998), 80 CPR (3d) 449 (Man. CA)]; *Recovery Production Equipment Ltd. v. McKinney Machine Co.*, [1998] AJ No. 801 (QL) (CA); *Treadwell v. Martin* (1976), 67 DLR (3d) 493; *Planon Systems Inc. v. Norman Wade Co.*, [1998] OJ No. 3547 (QL) (Ont. Gen. Div.); *Z Mark International Inc. v. Leng Novak Blais Inc.* (1996), 12 OTC 33 (Ont. Gen. Div.). See also L. Tsaknis, "The Jurisdictional Basis, Elements, and Remedies in the Action for Breach of Confidence—Uncertainty Abounds" (1993), 5 *Bond L Rev.* 18 at pp. 46-47.

Equity, like the common law, is capable of ongoing growth and development: *Canson Enterprises, supra, per* La Forest J at p. 580; *United Scientific Holdings Ltd. v. Burnley Borough Council*, [1978] AC 904 (HL (Eng.)), *per* Lord Diplock, at p. 926. In my view, therefore, having regard to the evolution of equitable principles apparent in the case law, we should clearly affirm that, in this country, the authority to award financial compensation for breach of confidence is inherent in the exercise of general equitable jurisdiction and does not depend on the niceties of *Lord Cairns' Act* or its statutory successors. This conclusion is fed, as well, by the *sui generis* nature of the action. The objective in a breach of confidence case is to put the confider in as good a position as it would have been in but for the breach. To that end, the Court has ample jurisdiction to fashion appropriate relief out of the full gamut of available remedies, including appropriate financial compensation.

H. *The Subject Matter of the Compensation*

In the present case, the trial judge found, and the Court of Appeal agreed, that the Clamato formula and related processes, insofar as they had been disclosed to the appellants, constituted a unique *combination* of elements, notwithstanding that some or all of the constituent elements were themselves widely known within the juice industry. It is to be emphasized that this is a case of unauthorized use as opposed to unauthorized disclosure. The information passed to Caesar Canning was found to satisfy the requirements of being inaccessible to the uninitiated, and to constitute an identifiable and distinct source of information which Caesar Canning wrongfully used for its own commercial advantage. As such, it was worthy of protection, but what, in dollar terms, did its misuse cost the respondents?

In the respondents' view their Clamato information is, literally, priceless. They say its continued use must be forever enjoined. It is only past misuse which, being now incurable, will have to be compensated in mere dollars and cents. In the appellants' view, on the other hand, the Court should focus on what the trial judge found was the peripheral importance of the information actually used. Caesar Cocktail, in one formulation or another, would have been on the market. The processing and other details, however confidential, did not add to its market potential. In other words, the appellants' position is that the use of confidential information may have been an actionable wrong but it did not cause any monetary loss to the respondents.

I. *Measure of the "Lost Opportunity"*

The applicable concept of restoration was set out in the reasons of McLachlin J in *Canson Enterprises* as follows at p. 556:

> In summary, compensation is an equitable monetary remedy which is available when the equitable remedies of restitution and account are not appropriate. By analogy with restitution, *it attempts to restore to the plaintiff what has been lost as a result of the breach; i.e., the plaintiff's lost opportunity.* The plaintiff's actual loss as a consequence of the breach is to be assessed with the full benefit of hindsight. Foreseeability is not a concern in assessing compensation, but it is essential that the losses made good are only those which, on a common sense view of causation, were caused by the breach. [Emphasis added.]

The concept of the "lost opportunity" is particularly apt here. The respondents' real complaint is not that the appellants manufactured Caesar Cocktail at a particular temperature or atmospheric pressure. Production details are a means to an end. The respondents' "lost opportunity" was that the appellants, using these confidential production techniques, entered the marketplace with Caesar Cocktail a year earlier than would otherwise have been the case. The respondents were not entitled to be free of competition from the appellants. Apart from the clam juice limitation, they were only entitled to be free of the appellants' competition which used the respondents' confidential information. The respondents argue that no consultant could duplicate "precisely" the Clamato production details. This may be true, but the trial judge reasoned that it would not be necessary for the appellants or their consultants to discover independently the *actual* Clamato details within that year. Juice formulation is not rocket science. A consultant skilled in the art and deploying a variety of techniques could have come up with a plausible clam-free copycat product within 12 months to bring the respondents' commercial "opportunity" to a close. Moral indignation is not a factor that is to be used to inflate the calculation of a compensatory award. The respondents' entitlement is to no more than restoration of the full benefit of this lost but time-limited opportunity.

J. The Trial Judge Found the Confidential Information To Be "Nothing Very Special"

The trial judge [(1994), 93 BCLR (2d) 318] awarded the respondents the equivalent of the consulting fee it would have cost Caesar Canning to develop Caesar Cocktail without improper use of the respondents' confidential information ... . The "consulting fee" approach uses the putative development costs (in this case, of Caesar Cocktail) as a *proxy* for the *market value* of the confidential information. In adopting this approach the trial judge relied on the analysis of Lord Denning in *Seager v. Copydex Ltd. (No. 2), supra*, already discussed, who for the purposes of assessing equitable compensation divided confidential information into three categories: "nothing very special," "something special" and "very special indeed," as follows, at pp. 719-20:

> The difficulty is to assess the value of the information taken by the defendant company. ... The value of the confidential information depends on the nature of it. [1] If there was *nothing very special* about it, that is, if it involved no particular inventive step but was the sort of information which could be obtained by employing any competent consultant, then the value of it was the fee which a consultant would charge for it; because in that case the defendant company, by taking the information, would only have saved themselves the time and trouble of employing a consultant. But, on the other hand, [2] if the information was *something special*, as, for instance, if it involved an inventive step or something so unusual that it could not be obtained by just going to a consultant, then the value of it is much higher. It is not merely a consultant's fee, but the price which a willing buyer—desirous of obtaining it—would pay for it. It is the value as between a willing seller and a willing buyer. [3] ... if the plaintiff is right in saying that the confidential information was *very special indeed*, then it may well be right for the value to be assessed on the footing that, in the usual way, it would be remunerated by a royalty. The court, of course, cannot give a royalty by way of damages; but it could give an equivalent by a calculation based on a capitalisation of a royalty. Thus it could arrive at a lump sum. Once a lump sum is assessed and paid, then the confidential information would belong to the defendant company in the same way as if they had bought and paid for it by an agreement of sale. [Emphasis added.]

The trial judge clearly consigned the trade secrets which the respondents had confided to the appellants to the "nothing very special" category, as she awarded Lord Denning's measure of compensation applicable to the lowest level of importance, a mere consulting fee to represent the avoided cost of in-house development. The respondents complain that no consultant could exactly replicate the magic of Clamato, and certainly could not do so in 12 months. The trial judge's view, however, was that it would not be necessary for the appellants to discover and replicate *exactly* the respondents' production techniques. They would be competitive using substitute techniques that produced any sufficiently close copycat tomato-based product to satisfy the ordinary customer. If the market value of the confidential information is the proper measure of compensation in this case, I would accept the assessment of the trial judge. My quarrel is not with her calculation but with the underlying premise that market value is the appropriate approach on the facts of this case.

K. The Springboard Doctrine

The trial judge acknowledged that the breached confidences had acted as a "springboard" to enable the appellants to bring Caesar Cocktail to market 12 months earlier than would otherwise have been the case. The "springboard" or "head start" concept descends from the judgment of Roxburgh J in *Terrapin Ltd. v. Builders' Supply Co. (Hayes) Ltd.* (1959), [1967] RPC 375 (Ch. D), aff'd. [1960] RPC 128 (CA) at p. 391:

> As I understand it, the essence of this branch of the law, whatever the origin of it may be, is that a person who has obtained information in confidence is not allowed to use it as a spring-board for activities detrimental to the person who made the confidential communication, and spring-board it remains even when all the features have been published or can be ascertained by actual inspection by any member of the public. ...

The respondents contend that the trial judge erred in her measure of equitable compensation for two reasons. Firstly and most importantly, they were not in the business of selling their trade secrets to competitors, and therefore the "market value" of the information is irrelevant. There is some support for this in the reasons of Sir Edward Eveleigh in *Dowson & Mason Ltd. v. Potter*, [1986] 2 All ER 418 (CA), where at p. 422 he rationalized *Seager v. Copydex Ltd. (No. 2)*, on the basis that in that case the plaintiff "would have sold [the] information; that was his line of business." There is also some support for this view in *Coco v. A.N. Clark (Engineers) Ltd.* [[1969] RPC 41 (Ch. D)] *per* Megarry J at p. 50.

Secondly, the respondents say the "springboard" cases are inapplicable because, properly understood, they presuppose that at the end of the "head start" period, the defendants would in fact have discovered the actual secrets they earlier misappropriated. In fact, they say, Clamato has been often emulated but never precisely copied.

In my view the respondents' argument reads the jurisprudence too narrowly. The unique features of the respondents' manufacturing process, and its alleged lack of replicability, do not necessarily establish a causal relationship to a financial loss. The respondents were not in the business of selling information, and I therefore agree with them that the "market value" of the confidential information is not the appropriate measure of compensation in this case.

That having been said, the respondents *were* in the business of exploiting commercial opportunities, and their ability to make a profit from Clamato was limited by the acknowledged entitlement of the appellants to market a similar product without clam juice. The assessment of compensation has therefore to address the value of the lost market opportunity and, in particular, the lost advantage of being able to market Clamato free of the appellants' competition for 12 months, and not be diverted to a valuation of the confidential information itself.

The trial judge held that the appellants were able to approximate the taste of Clamato without ever having had access to the secret "dry mix," and that this approximation was sufficient for commercial purposes. While the details of the respondents' particular combination of manufacturing process might have remained undiscovered forever, she found that there are different substitute ways to produce the desired result. As the trial judge observed, Clamato had a certain identity of taste and texture and "considerable changes can be made to the ingredients and process of a food product without the product identity being changed" (p. 329). For that reason, the precision of a few degrees temperature here or a few pounds pressure there, and the other details imparted in confidence to the appellants, were found to be "nothing very special." These findings are important because they show that while Clamato is unique, its uniqueness is not a condition of exploiting (nor an assurance of defending) the commercial opportunity.

The respondents complain that the trial judge's analysis was hypothetical, because the appellants have never in fact reproduced Clamato using non-confidential technology. However, the Court is free to draw inferences from the evidence as to what would likely have happened "but for" the breach: *Lac Minerals*, *per* Sopinka J, at pp. 619-20, and *per* La Forest J, at pp. 668-69; *Rainbow Industrial Caterers Ltd. v. Canadian National Railway Co.*, [1991] 3 SCR 3, at p. 15; … . In the case of *Coco v. A.N. Clark (Engineers) Ltd.*, *supra*, on which they rely so strongly, Megarry J, at p. 49, pointed to the artificiality of actually requiring the confidant to discover "independently" the information of which he or she is already aware.

In my view, the key to the assessment of equitable compensation in this case is the expected duration of the respondents' "lost opportunity," i.e., the economic advantage they would have enjoyed after the cancellation of the licence "but for" the breach. It would be inequitable to protect the respondents' interest in a commercial opportunity they never enjoyed by invoking undue solicitude for their "nothing very special" information.

There is a further more general objection to the respondents' formalistic approach. Equity has set a relatively low threshold on what kinds of information are *capable* of constituting the subject matter of a breach of confidence. In *Coco v. A.N. Clark (Engineers) Ltd.*, *supra*, Megarry J, at p. 47, considered that "some product of the human brain" applied to existing knowledge might suffice. A similarly expansive concept was adopted in *Lac Minerals* at p. 610 by Sopinka J, quoting Lord Greene MR in *Saltman Engineering Co. v. Campbell Engineering Co.* (1948), 65 RPC 203 (CA), at p. 215. Gurry in *Breach of Confidence* [Oxford: Clarendon Press, 1984], gives instances of information which were protected from disclosure because they were otherwise inaccessible, despite the fact that they possessed little or no actual value, including the commercially disastrous invention for rearing pigs at issue in *Nichrotherm Electrical Co. v. Percy*, *supra*. He concludes, at p. 82:

> It would seem, therefore, that the nonsensical nature of information is not to be regarded as a barrier to confidentiality, but, rather, as a factor which the court will take into account in the exercise of its discretion whether to grant equitable relief, *or as a factor affecting the quantum of any damages* which may be in question. [Emphasis added.]

While equity is thus quick to protect confidences, it cannot be blind to the nature of the opportunity lost to the respondents, or the value of their information, when consideration turns to remedies. Equity will avoid unjustly enriching the confider by overcompensating for "nothing very special" information just as it will avoid unjustly enriching the confidee by awarding less than realistic compensation for financial losses genuinely suffered. Characterizing the action as "*sui generis*" does not alter the relevance of this equitable principle.

It seems to me that the respondents' arguments for exclusivity relate at bottom to their claim for injunctive relief. The information may be nothing very special, they say, but it is ours, and the appellants have no right to its use, with or without payment. Refusal of an injunction, they say, would be equivalent to the grant of a compulsory licence. I think it is therefore convenient to turn at this stage to the claim for injunctive relief, and in light of the decision reached under that head, I will then complete the consideration of financial compensation.

[At this point, the court held on the basis of the plaintiff's delay in asserting its rights, the not very special nature of the information, the balance of competing equities, and the adequacy of monetary relief that this was not an appropriate case for the issuing of a permanent injunction.]

M. The Measure of Financial Compensation

The respondents, thus denied an injunction, must look entirely to dollars and cents for their restoration. I think, as stated, the Court of Appeal was correct to reject the trial judge's "consulting fee" approach in this case. The award would not restore the respondents to the position they would have been in but for the breach. The respondents did not lose a consulting fee. They were not in that business.

This case is closer to *Dowson & Mason Ltd. v. Potter, supra*, where the plaintiff, as here, was a manufacturer, not a seller of information. In that case, the court affirmed the trial judge's view (at p. 424) that:

> ... the proper basis for the assessment of damages is the loss suffered by the plaintiffs according to their *loss of profits* resulting from the assumed wrongful disclosure and use of the confidential information. ... [Emphasis added.]

In my view, however, the British Columbia Court of Appeal erred in being prepared to assume, for purposes of achieving an equitable result, that if Caesar Cocktail had been kept off the market because of its unconscionable origins, the respondents would have filled the void with sales of Clamato juice. The respondents' damages, on this assumption, would be their lost profit on the *assumed* sales of Clamato juice. While this approach puts the focus where it belongs, on the financial position of the respondents, it makes a number of unjustified assumptions. There is as yet no precise evidence that the sales of Clamato juice were affected by the marketing of Caesar Cocktail, and if so to what extent. The compensation order of the Court of Appeal raises issues of causation that concerned the courts as long ago as 1895 in *Robb v. Green*, [1895] 2 QB 1, *per* Hawkins J, at pp. 19-20:

> It is impossible with mathematical accuracy to ascertain [the loss]. It would be unjust to saddle the defendant with every loss of custom the plaintiff has sustained, for that cannot all be reasonably attributed to the unlawful action of the defendant. The specific instances as yet traced to the defendant's action are, it is true, but few; but still their loss does not form the limit of the injury to the plaintiff, for the wholesale canvass of his customers was likely to influence many and to diminish permanently his receipts and profits. On the other hand, fluctuation of business, bad times, and many other circumstances may possibly have contributed to the loss. I cannot, therefore, award the plaintiff an indemnity against the whole diminution of his trade.

In *Canson Enterprises, supra,* McLachlin J emphasized, at p. 556, that "[t]he plaintiff's actual loss as a consequence of the breach is to be assessed with the full benefit of hindsight … but it is essential that the losses made good are only those which, on a common sense view of causation, were caused by the breach."

The reference directed by the Court of Appeal should therefore continue, but on somewhat modified terms. Firstly, the mandate is to assess the loss attributable to the breach of confidence, if any, sustained by the respondents during the 12-month period following the termination. For this purpose, some guidance may be taken from the discussion of compensation for breach of trade secrets outlined in the *American Restatement (Third) of Unfair Competition,* ch. 4, at §45, p. 516:

> e. *Relief measured by plaintiff's loss.* A frequent element of loss resulting from the appropriation of a trade secret is the lost profit that the plaintiff would have earned in the absence of the use by the defendant. The plaintiff may prove lost profits by identifying specific customers diverted to the defendant. The plaintiff may also prove lost profits through proof of a general decline in sales or a disruption of business growth following the commencement of use by the defendant, although the presence of other market factors that may affect the plaintiff's sales bears on the sufficiency of the plaintiff's proof. If the evidence justifies the conclusion that the sales made by the defendant would have instead been made by the plaintiff in the absence of the appropriation, the plaintiff may establish its lost profits by applying its own profit margin to the defendant's sales.

The respondents led some evidence of a general nature that Clamato's national market share dropped from 83.1 percent to 77.8 percent in the 12 months after termination, and that Caesar Cocktail picked up 7.1 percent of the national market in its first year of sales. The respondents will no doubt lead evidence that their loss of market share can be linked to evidence of sales that were in fact diverted to Caesar Cocktail or its derivatives in that period. The task of the Referee is to get as good an approximation as is possible at this late date of the magnitude of the respondents' loss. In pursuing this inquiry, the Referee ought not to demand from the respondents a level of proof that is greater than the subject matter permits. See, e.g., *Planon Systems Inc. v. Norman Wade Co., supra, per* Spence J, at paras. 72-75.

Secondly, the compensable period is the 12 months following termination, as directed by the Court of Appeal. The appellants argue that the 12-month period ought to begin with the date of the notice of April 15, 1982 and point out that the trial judge said the appellants *could* have developed a Caesar Cocktail-like tomato juice without using the Clamato manufacturing information "within the 12-month notice period." The fact is, however, that on April 15, 1983, the date when the licence expired, the appellants did not have a formulation for Caesar Cocktail that complied with their legal obligations to the respondents. They had in fact taken no steps to produce a product that complied. I see no reason to "backdate" the fiction of their hypothetical research to the notice period. The appellants did not begin to sell a product in breach of the confidence until April 15, 1983. Thus began the period of unfair competition which turned the respondents' "opportunity" into a "lost opportunity." I therefore believe that the Court of Appeal was correct to start the compensable period on April 15, 1983. The trial judge found that the competition would have ceased to be unfair once the appellants could reasonably have been expected to come up with a tomato juice product independently of the confidential information. The trial judge fixed that period at 12 months. Accordingly, the respondents' argument to extend the compensation period beyond April 14, 1984 should also be rejected. As the market advantage created by the "nothing very special" information lapsed at the end of the 12-month period, an award that continued the compensable period beyond that date would benefit the respondents to an extent which the courts below found would be unjust.

Thirdly, the Referee may think it proper to have regard to the "other market factors" mentioned in the *American Restatement*. It must be remembered that, at the time of the termination, Caesar Canning and FBI Foods had built up a business infrastructure to which the respondents denied themselves access by their notice of termination, and which the appellants were perfectly entitled to utilize to advance their own economic interests thereafter. As counsel for the respondents acknowledged in oral argument, the appellants "had the distribution system, they had the experience, they'd built up the market and they had the contacts. Why did they have to take this [trade secret] as well?" His point was to emphasize the vulnerability of his clients to a breach of confidence. However, if in fact the sales of Clamato dropped in the 12 months following termination, as appears to be the case, it may be that at least some of the drop was caused by the self-inflicted deprivation of this business infrastructure, and was not causally related to the existence of Caesar Cocktail.

Fourthly, the assessment of the respondents' loss of profit may include consideration of the royalties otherwise payable under the Licence Agreement for the 12-month compensable period. While it is true the respondents intended to exit the licensing business and to confine themselves thereafter to manufacturing and distribution, it is also true that the appellants frustrated that intention by continuing to use at least part of what was licensed. The Referee may, therefore, as part of the assessment of the respondents' loss of profit, consider whether all or a portion of the licence fees otherwise payable (which represented the parties' own evaluation of the income stream attributable to the subject matter), should fairly be included in the calculation.

Fifthly, the Referee will have to keep in mind that the objective is a broadly equitable result. Mathematical exactitude is neither required nor obtainable. In *United Horse-Shoe and Nail Co. v. Stewart* (1888), 13 App. Cas. 401 (HL (Eng.)), Lord Watson, admittedly in a patent case, said, at p. 413, that estimating the loss to the plaintiff's trade "must always be more or less a matter of estimate, because it is impossible to ascertain, with arithmetical precision, what in the ordinary course of business would have been the amount of the [plaintiffs'] sales and profits." The Referee will have to operate by analogy with the principle expressed in *Wood v. Grand Valley Railway Co.* (1915), 51 SCR 283, *per* Davies J, at p. 289:

> It was clearly impossible under the facts of that case [*Chaplin v. Hicks*] to estimate with anything approaching to mathematical accuracy the damages sustained by the plaintiffs, but it seems to me to be clearly laid down there by the learned judges that such an impossibility cannot "relieve the wrongdoer of the necessity of paying damages for his breach of contract" and that on the other hand the tribunal to estimate them whether jury or judge must under such circumstances do "the best it can" and its conclusion will not be set aside even if the amount of the verdict is a matter of guess work.

This principle was quoted and applied in *Penvidic Contracting Co. v. International Nickel Co. of Canada*, [1976] 1 SCR 267, *per* Spence J, at pp. 279-80. See also *Apotex Fermentation Inc. v. Novopharm Ltd.*, *supra*, where the Manitoba Court of Appeal states, at p. 512:

> Where injury has been suffered in a complex commercial setting, a "flexible and imaginative approach" to the assessment of the damages may be required.

These considerations are not, of course, exhaustive. I mention them because they arose out of the argument before us, and it is devoutly to be hoped that they may save the parties some time and money at the next stage of their 16-year long wrangle. ...

Appeal allowed with costs. Cross-appeal dismissed with costs.

QUESTIONS

Given that it appears that the court is relying primarily upon normal principles governing the award of damages in tort in this instance, what purpose, if any, is served by treating the cause of action here as one arising in equity rather than tort and producing an entitlement to equitable compensation, rather than common law-based tort damages? Does the retention of these distinctions, at least in cases such as this, perpetuate undue complexity and mystification in legal principles and rules?

The following important case illustrates the relatively unconstrained approach of modern Canadian courts to the assessment of equitable compensation as contrasted with the more rule-laden approach to assessment of common law damages.

Whitefish Lake Band of Indians v. Canada (Attorney General)
(2007), 87 OR (3d) 321 (CA)

LASKIN JA (for the court):

A. *Overview*

[1] The Crown breached its fiduciary duty to the Whitefish Lake Band of Indians 120 years ago. The issue on this appeal is whether the trial judge erred in his assessment of compensation for that breach. The facts of this case are straightforward. Its resolution is not.

[2] Whitefish occupies a reserve near Sudbury. In 1886, Whitefish surrendered the timber rights on its reserve to the Crown, which then sold these rights for $316. In 2002, Whitefish sued the Crown for damages for an improvident sale. Shortly before the trial, the Crown admitted that it breached its fiduciary duty by failing to obtain a fair value for Whitefish's timber rights.

[3] The trial judge, Blenus Wright J, was then asked to assess Whitefish's compensation for the Crown's admitted breach. To do so, he had to determine two issues: first, what was the fair value of the timber rights in 1886; and second, how is that fair value to be assessed in 2005, the date of trial.

[4] On the first issue, the trial judge valued Whitefish's timber rights in 1886 at $31,600. He did so by choosing the highest price paid for comparable timber at a public auction. On the second issue, the trial judge assessed Whitefish's compensation at $1,095,888. In doing so he took into account that the Crown had not profited from its breach of duty and that it had no legal obligation to pay prejudgment interest until 1992. He adjusted the fair value of the timber rights for inflation between 1886 and 1992, and awarded simple interest on that adjusted amount from 1992 to 2005.

[5] Whitefish appeals the trial judge's valuation on the first issue and the Crown cross-appeals. Whitefish contends that the trial judge erred by failing to accept reliable evidence from its own expert, who placed the value of the timber rights in 1886 at $50,000. The Crown contends that the trial judge erred by failing to use a weighted average of the valuations of its expert, which would have produced a figure of $16,000.

[6] On the second issue, Whitefish, supported by the intervenors, contends that the trial judge erred in three related ways. First, it says that the trial judge erred by failing to compensate it in equity for its lost opportunity to have the $31,600 invested for its benefit, and to have the use of the investment income; second, it says that the trial judge erred in law by holding that he could not include compound interest as an element of equitable compensation; and, third, it says that the trial judge's finding that the sale proceeds would have been "dissipated" is contrary to the terms of the surrender, the provisions of the *Indian Act*, RSC 1886, c. 43, and the principles of equitable compensation, and is unsupported by the evidence. Whitefish claims that an award that fairly compensates it for the Crown's breach of fiduciary duty would be in the range of $23 million. The Crown contends that the trial judge's use of inflation and simple prejudgment interest achieved a "fair, equitable and proportionate award" of compensation in an historical claim.

[7] On the first issue, I would not give effect either to Whitefish's appeal or the Crown's cross-appeal. The trial judge did not err in principle in valuing the timber rights in 1886 at $31,600 and I would defer to his valuation. On the second issue, however, I agree with Whitefish's three arguments. I would allow the appeal on this issue and set aside the trial judge's award. Because the record is insufficient, this court cannot substitute its own award for that of the trial judge. I would order a new hearing to determine the equitable compensation to which Whitefish is entitled. ...

C. Analysis

First issue: Did the trial judge err in determining that the fair value of Whitefish's timber rights in 1886 was $31,600? ... I would not give effect to the appeal or the cross-appeal on the first issue.

Second issue: Did the trial judge err in his assessment of Whitefish's compensation?

(a) The trial judge's award and the parties' positions on appeal

[33] At trial, Whitefish sought equitable compensation for the loss of its opportunity to invest the fair value of its timber rights. It contended that the court should presume the sale proceeds would have been invested in the Whitefish trust account maintained by the government, where it would have earned compound interest. It relied on an expert's report, which, based on an 1886 valuation of $31,600 for its timber rights, assessed the band's com-

pensation in 2005 at approximately $23 million. The Crown contended that Whitefish would be fairly compensated by awarding it in 2005 the amount of money it should have been paid in 1886 adjusted for inflation.

[34] The trial judge substantially accepted the Crown's contention. He adjusted the figure of $31,600 for increases in the Consumer Price Index between 1887 and 1992. In 1992, amendments to the *Crown Liability and Proceedings Act*, RSC 1985, c. C-50 obligated the Crown to pay prejudgment interest on money that it owed in accordance with provincial legislation. The trial judge therefore took the 1992 inflation adjusted figure and on that amount allowed simple prejudgment interest of five per cent per year to the date of trial. The total compensation he awarded equalled $1,095,888 plus costs.

[35] The trial judge rejected Whitefish's claim for unrealized investment income for three reasons. First, he rejected Whitefish's position that the $31,600 would have been deposited in the trust account and remained there. In his view, that position was "highly improbable" and "not realistic." Instead he found it likely that the $31,600 would have been deposited in the trust account and then "dissipated" within a reasonable time.

[36] Second, the trial judge concluded that the payment of compound interest before 1992 was precluded by the Crown's historical immunity from paying interest.

[37] Third, the trial judge concluded that compound interest in equity was not available because the Crown did not wrongly convert trust funds for its own use and did not benefit from any breach of its duty. In the trial judge's words, "it simply failed to perform its duty."

[38] In this court, Whitefish submits that each of the three reasons the trial judge gave for denying it equitable compensation reflects an error in principle. Whitefish acknowledges that the court should award an amount that is "fair and proportionate," but says that, as a starting point, it should use the amount generated by investing $31,600 in the trust account at compound rates of interest. That starting point, Whitefish argues, gives effect to the provisions of the *Indian Act*, the Treaty and the surrender, to the government's practice, and to equity's presumption that the money Whitefish should have been paid would have been put to the most profitable use. If this court agrees that the trial judge committed a reviewable error, Whitefish asks us to fix the compensation to which it is entitled, rather than send its claim back for a new trial or an assessment. ...

(b) My approach

[40] For reasons that I will elaborate on, I agree that Whitefish is entitled to equitable compensation for the Crown's breach of fiduciary duty. It is entitled to be put in the position it would have been in but for the Crown's breach. Had the Crown fulfilled its fiduciary duty, it would have invested 90 per cent of the $31,600 in the Whitefish trust account. That money would have earned investment income, which would have been available for Whitefish and its members.

[41] The trial judge's award does not fairly compensate Whitefish for the money the Crown failed to obtain, invest and hold for Whitefish and its members. It does not do so because it is tainted by the three errors Whitefish alleges. ...

[42] Ordinarily, the appropriate remedy is a new hearing or a reference on compensation. Neither side, however, wants a new hearing, and both have urged us to fix compensation doing the best we can with the available evidence.

[43] If the evidentiary record and the expert reports provided an adequate footing to fix an appropriate award, I would attempt what the parties have asked us to do. However, the record is either silent or inadequate on so many considerations relevant to a "fair and proportionate" award, that to do justice to both parties a new hearing is required. ...

(c) Whitefish is entitled to equitable compensation for its lost opportunity to invest the fair value of its timber rights and receive the investment income

[47] Whitefish submits that it is entitled to equitable compensation for the Crown's breach of fiduciary duty. Whitefish further submits that an award of equitable compensation should recognize its lost opportunity to have the fair value of its timber rights invested for its benefit, and to receive the investment income for its use and the use of its members. It contends that the trial judge erred in principle by failing to award any compensation for this lost opportunity caused by the Crown's breach of fiduciary duty.

[48] Equitable compensation is equity's "counterpart" to common law damages. Its quantum is "determined by analogy with the principles of trust law": see *Guerin v. The Queen*, [1984] 2 SCR 335 at p. 390 SCR, Dickson J. Its aim is compensatory. Its object is to restore the plaintiff to the position that the plaintiff would have been in had the fiduciary not breached its duty. See *Canson Enterprises Ltd. v. Boughton Co.*, [1991] 3 SCR 534, [1991] SCJ No. 91, at pp. 578-79 SCR; *Guerin* cited to CNLR at p. 121. See also Oosterhoff et al., *Oosterhoff on Trusts*, 6th ed. (Scarborough, Ont.: Carswell, 2004) at 1044, 1047; Donovan W.M. Waters, ed., *Waters' Law of Trusts in Canada*, 3rd ed. (Toronto: Carswell, 2005) at 1215-1217; Peter D. Maddaugh and John D. McCamus, *The Law of Restitution*, looseleaf (Aurora, Ont.: Canada Law Book, 2004) at 5-50-5-56.

[49] Equitable compensation and common law damages differ in three important ways bearing on this appeal: first, while the purpose of equitable compensation is to put the plaintiff in the position it would have been in but for the breach, the purpose of common law damages is to restore the plaintiff to its original position; second, equitable compensation is assessed at the date of trial while common law damages are assessed at the date of the breach; and third, equity presumes that the trust funds will be invested in the most profitable way or put to the most advantageous use. See Oosterhoff, *supra*.

[50] Here, as I have said, Whitefish submits that an award of equitable compensation should recognize its lost opportunity to have invested the asset it was deprived of—the fair value of its timber rights—and to receive the income on that investment. It contends that the trial judge erred in principle by failing to award any compensation for this lost investment opportunity, and therefore did not restore it to the position it would have been in if the Crown had fulfilled its fiduciary duty. I agree.

[51] In my view, this is an appropriate case to award equitable compensation. Modern jurisprudence of the Supreme Court of Canada has emphasized that remedies for breaches of fiduciary duty should be flexible. Not every breach of fiduciary duty attracts the remedy of equitable compensation: see *Canson* at pp. 574-75 SCR. The remedy chosen should be the most appropriate one on the facts of the case. In considering the appropriate remedy, the court should look at the harm suffered from the breach: see *Hodgkinson v. Simms*, [1994] 3 SCR 377, [1994] SCJ No. 84. Or, in the words of Binnie J in *Cadbury Schweppes Inc. v. FBI Foods Ltd.*, [1999] 1 SCR 142, [1999] SCJ No. 6, at para. 26, the remedy must meet "underlying policy objectives."

[52] In my view, there are two compelling, and indeed, unanswerable justifications for awarding Whitefish equitable compensation, measured by its lost opportunity to have the fair value of its timber rights invested by the government and to receive the investment income. The first is the Supreme Court of Canada's holding in *Canson* that a fiduciary's discretionary control of a beneficiary's property attracts an award of equitable compensation. The second is the Supreme Court of Canada's affirmation of an award of equitable compensation in *Guerin* on facts similar to those in the present case.

[53] Under *Canson*, when a fiduciary who has discretionary control of a beneficiary's property breaches its duty to the beneficiary, an award of equitable compensation is justified. Thus, here, the Crown's breach of fiduciary duty when it had discretionary control over the sale of Whitefish's timber rights and the sale proceeds rightfully attracts an award of equitable compensation. Moreover, the appropriateness of equitable compensation is reinforced by two related considerations: the nature of the fiduciary duty that was breached, and the nexus between the breach and the loss.

[54] In his majority judgment in *Canson* at p. 578 SCR, La Forest J drew a distinction—a "sharp divide"—between two classes of fiduciary duties. In one class are cases where the property in question belongs to the beneficiary but is controlled by the fiduciary. In the other class are cases where the fiduciary is merely required to perform its duty honestly and in accordance with its undertaking. La Forest J stressed that these two classes of cases engage different policy objectives. Only in the first class of cases where the fiduciary controls the property of the beneficiary and equity's concern is to compensate for what the property would be worth, should equity use its well recognized flexibility to achieve a different and fairer result.

[55] Whitefish can legitimately claim the benefit of equity's remedial flexibility because the Crown directed the sale of the band's timber rights and had discretionary control over the sale proceeds. Both the *Indian Act, 1886* and the Treaty prohibited Whitefish from selling its timber rights directly to a third party. The Crown was interposed between Whitefish and the purchaser for the historical purpose of preventing the band from being exploited.

[56] Thus, once it agreed to sell its timber rights, Whitefish surrendered those rights to the Crown. Under the Treaty, the Crown was obliged to sell these rights to "the best advantage." The Crown sold the rights to Robillard and received the sale proceeds. Section 70 of the *Indian Act, 1886* and the surrender similarly obliged the Crown to invest the proceeds for the benefit of the band members and their descendants. The Crown met this obligation by depositing the proceeds in a trust account, which it maintained and controlled for the benefit of Whitefish. Unquestionably, the Crown had discretionary control over the sale of Whitefish's timber rights and the proceeds received from that sale.

[57] The Crown's fiduciary duty to our Aboriginal people is of overarching importance in this country. One way of recognizing its importance is to award equitable compensation for its breach. The remedy of equitable compensation best furthers the objectives of enforcement and deterrence. It signals the emphasis the court places on the Crown's ongoing obligation to honour its fiduciary duty and the need to deter future breaches.

[58] The nexus between the Crown's breach and Whitefish's loss also supports an award of equitable compensation. In some breach of fiduciary duty cases—*Canson* is an example—equitable compensation will not be warranted because there is no direct connection between the breach and the loss. In this case, however, the Crown's discretionary control over

the sale and the sale proceeds led directly to the Whitefish's loss. Equitable compensation is thus the appropriate remedy.

[59] The second justification for an award of equitable compensation is the Supreme Court of Canada's decision in *Guerin*. In *Guerin*, the most directly applicable case, the Supreme Court of Canada affirmed the trial judge's application of trust principles in awarding an Aboriginal band equitable compensation for the Crown's breach of fiduciary duty. The facts giving rise to the Crown's breach were straightforward. The Crown leased surrendered reserve land to a golf club on terms less favourable than those authorized by the band. The trial judge, Collier J, then had to decide the band's compensation for the Crown's breach.

[60] He concluded that the band should be compensated for its lost opportunity to develop the surrendered land in the most advantageous way, which in his view was as a residential subdivision. His award of $10 million was upheld by the Supreme Court of Canada. In his majority decision at p. 386 SCR, Dickson J said that although the Crown was not a trustee, its fiduciary duty to the Aboriginal people was "trust-like." Thus, compensation for a breach of its duty should be measured by principles similar to those that govern the law of trusts. And, in her concurring reasons, at pp. 361-63 SCR, Wilson J endorsed the compensatory nature of the remedy given by the trial judge—the lost opportunity for residential development because of the Crown's breach.

[61] *Guerin* concerned land and Whitefish concerns timber rights. But, in substance, Whitefish's claim in this case is no different from the band's claim in *Guerin*. Each band sought equitable compensation measured by the lost opportunity to use its asset because of the Crown's breach of fiduciary duty. In *Guerin*, the lost opportunity was the opportunity to develop its land. In *Whitefish*, the lost opportunity was the opportunity to sell its timber rights at market value, to have the proceeds of the sale invested by the government in an interest bearing trust account, and to receive the investment income. Equitable compensation was awarded to the band in *Guerin*. It should be awarded to Whitefish in this case as well.

[62] In failing to apply the principles from *Canson* and *Guerin*, the trial judge committed a fundamental and reviewable error. Even so, the Crown argues, we should not disturb the trial judge's award for two reasons: first, even in equity, the Crown cannot be liable for compound interest; and, second, the trial judge's finding of "dissipation" is reasonable. Therefore, the Crown submits, the trial judge's award of approximately $1 million is a generous award for the Crown's breach. I will deal with these two issues raised by the Crown.

(d) Equitable compensation for the Crown's breach can include the payment of compound interest

[63] Whitefish argues that its lost opportunity was the opportunity to have the $31,600 invested in the trust account maintained by the government for its benefit. It submits that investment would have earned compound interest at rates prescribed by successive Orders-in-Council. Whitefish says that at least as a starting point, the accumulated amount of capital and interest is the equitable compensation to which it is entitled. In other words, Whitefish is not seeking merely the money that it should have had in 1886, which is substantially what the trial judge awarded. Instead, it claims the amount that the money, if invested at compound rates of interest, would have generated with the passage of time.

[64] Of course, both compound interest and simple interest account for the time value of money. The difference between the two is this: compound interest is interest on the accumulated principal and interest; simple interest is interest on the principal alone. See *Bank of America Canada v. Mutual Trust Co.*, [2002] 2 SCR 601, [2002] SCJ No. 44, at paras. 23-24.

[65] The Crown argues that an award of equitable compensation cannot include compound interest. It makes two points in support of its position. First, it says Whitefish is not entitled to compound interest in equity because, as the trial judge found, the Crown did not deliberately breach its fiduciary duty and it did not profit from its breach.

[66] Second, the Crown says Whitefish's lost opportunity was the loss of use of the money ($31,600) in 1886. Ordinarily, a plaintiff is compensated for loss of use of money by an award of prejudgment interest on that money. However, because of the Crown's common law and historic immunity from paying interest, such an award—whether simple interest or compound interest—was not available against the Crown until 1992. Therefore, by law, the trial judge was limited to awarding Whitefish compensation equivalent to what $31,600 was worth in 2005.

[67] I will first discuss why I accept—with qualifications—Whitefish's position. I will then address the Crown's contrary arguments.

(i) Whitefish's compensation is determined by asking what likely would have happened if the Crown had not breached its duty

[68] To compensate Whitefish for its lost opportunity, the key question the court must answer is what likely would have happened if the Crown had acted as it should have and had not breached its fiduciary duty. The answer lies partly in the obligations imposed on the Crown by statute and the surrender, in the way the Crown managed money derived from the sale of reserve land or timber rights on reserve land, and in the principles of equitable compensation.

[69] The Crown's statutory and surrender obligations dictate the starting point for fixing Whitefish's compensation. Both obligated the Crown to invest 90 per cent of the $31,600 for the benefit of Whitefish and its members. The court should presume that the Crown would have honoured its legal obligations.

[70] Under s. 70 of the *Indian Act, 1886* the Crown was required to invest at least 90 per cent of any money obtained from the sale of timber on an Indian reserve. "How and in what manner" it invested the money was within its discretion. ...

[72] The Crown's practice in managing Indian money also dictates where it likely would have invested the money obtained from the sale of Whitefish's timber rights. It was the Crown's practice to invest the proceeds of sale of timber rights on reserve land in a trust account it maintained and controlled for the band's benefit. That is what the Crown did with the $316 it received from the sale of Whitefish's timber rights to Robillard. ...

[73] To give effect to what likely would have happened, I think it fair to assume that money in the Whitefish account would have earned interest at rates prescribed by successive Orders-in-Council and compounded for some, if not all, of the 120-year period. The evidence to support this assumption comes from the Manual for the Administration of Band Moneys, prepared by the federal government's Indian Moneys Directorate and produced as an exhibit at trial. ...

[76] However, the position that Whitefish urges on us must be qualified in two ways. These qualifications are among the reasons why a new hearing is necessary.

[77] The first qualification concerns whether the Crown paid compound interest on money in band trust accounts between 1886 and 1969. The Manual itself does not address how interest was calculated before April 1, 1969. … Whether the Crown paid or should have paid compound interest on band accounts for some or all of the period 1886-1969 is a matter that should be clarified at the new hearing.

[79] The second qualification concerns whether the annual interest that would have been earned on the invested sale proceeds of Whitefish's timber rights would have stayed in the account to be compounded or would have been paid out to the band and its members. … [W]e cannot tell what likely would have happened over time because neither side filed Whitefish account records for the period 1891-2005. This too is a matter that should be clarified at a new hearing.

[80] Subject to these two qualifications, however, I think it fair to conclude that if the Crown had fulfilled its fiduciary duty in 1886, it would have received $31,600 for the sale of Whitefish's timber rights; it would have deposited 90 per cent of that amount ($28,440) in Whitefish's capital account; it would have paid interest on whatever money was in Whitefish's account at rates stipulated by successive Orders-in-Council; and at least it would have compounded the interest annually between April 1, 1969 and March 31, 1980, and semi-annually afterwards.

[81] This likely scenario is also consistent with the principles of trust law, which, according to *Guerin*, govern Whitefish's claim in equity. It establishes a framework for restoring Whitefish to the position it would have been in but for the Crown's breach of fiduciary duty. It results in an assessment of Whitefish's compensation at the date of trial, not at the date of breach.

[82] Whitefish also argues this scenario is consistent with equity's presumption that the proceeds of sale of Whitefish's timber rights would have been invested in the most profitable way or put to their most advantageous use. This presumption, however, does not come into play because we know what the Crown would have done with the fair value of these rights. It would have invested 90 per cent in the trust account it maintained for the band and distributed the rest to the band members. …

(ii) *An award of equitable compensation that includes compound interest is not barred*
by the nature of the Crown's breach or the Crown's historic immunity from
paying interest

[83] I turn now to the Crown's two submissions on why, even in equity, the court cannot award compound interest. First, the Crown submits that compound interest is not available in equity because, as the trial judge found, it did not deliberately breach its fiduciary duty, convert Whitefish's money for its own use, or profit from its breach. Second, the Crown submits that compound interest cannot be awarded as an element of equitable compensation because of the Crown's historic immunity from paying interest.

[84] On the first issue, Whitefish challenges the findings of the trial judge and asks us to substitute a finding that the Crown's breach was "wilful, egregious and unconscionable." I see no basis to do so. The trial judge's findings are entitled to deference, and on the record before him, were reasonable.

[85] Nonetheless, I do not think that the trial judge's findings assist the Crown in avoiding an award of compound interest as an element of equitable compensation. Entitlement to equitable compensation does not require the Crown to have profited from its breach or to have intentionally conducted itself wrongfully. Equity is engaged because the Crown had discretionary control over the sale of Whitefish's property and over the sale proceeds, which it was required to invest for the band's benefit. See *Canson* at pp. 573-74 SCR. The nature of the Crown's breach of duty does not afford a defence to an award of equitable compensation that includes compound interest, if compound interest is required to restore Whitefish to the position it would have been in had the Crown fulfilled its duty.

[86] The Crown's second submission on why the court cannot award compound interest as an element of equitable compensation rests on its historic immunity from paying interest. ...

[87] In his award for compensation, the trial judge relied on the Crown's immunity from paying prejudgment interest before 1992. For the period from 1992 to the date of trial, the trial judge awarded prejudgment interest under s. 128 of the *Courts of Justice Act*, RSO 1990, c. C.43.

[88] Whitefish submits that this immunity does not prevent the court from awarding compound interest as an element of equitable compensation. The Crown submits that Whitefish cannot avoid the Crown's immunity by re-characterizing its claim as one for equitable compensation. In effect, the Crown says that the court cannot do indirectly what it is prohibited from doing directly.

[89] I agree with Whitefish's submission and would hold that the Crown's common law and statutory immunity from paying interest does not preclude the inclusion of compound interest as an element of an award of equitable compensation. An award of equitable compensation that includes compound interest differs fundamentally from prejudgment interest on a damages award. ...

[90] Equitable compensation differs from prejudgment interest. In equity, compensation is assessed, not calculated, and it is assessed at the date of trial, not the date of injury or breach. In an appropriate case, compound interest may form part of that assessment. The assessment does not necessarily involve a mathematical calculation. But to give effect to equity's objective of putting the beneficiary in the position it would have been in but for the fiduciary's breach of duty, equity's assessment may take compound interest into account. For example, in this case an award that takes compound interest in account may be needed to fairly compensate Whitefish for its lost opportunity caused by the Crown's improvident sale of the band's timber rights.

[91] By contrast, prejudgment interest—under, for example, the *Courts of Justice Act*—is a straight, linear calculation. It is added to a successful party's claim, virtually as of right, at a rate specified in advance and calculated from the date of injury or breach to the date of judgment. Prejudgment interest does not form part of the court's assessment of an appropriate damages award. In short, a claim for compound interest as an element of equitable compensation is not a claim for prejudgment interest, and therefore is not barred by the Crown's pre-1992 immunity. ...

[96] In *Guerin*, at (1981), 127 DLR (3d) 170, [1982] 2 FC 445 (TD), after Collier J ordered compensation, the plaintiff brought a motion for prejudgment interest on the amount that he had awarded. He refused to allow prejudgment interest, holding that s. 35 of the

Federal Court Act or the common law barred the claim. The Supreme Court agreed. In her concurring reasons at p. 364 SCR, Wilson J expressly approved Collier J's denial of prejudgment interest.

[97] However, the trial judge's ruling in *Guerin* does not assist the Crown. Collier J had already awarded the band equitable compensation assessed at the date of trial. To award prejudgment interest on that amount would have violated s. 35 of the *Federal Court Act*, and as important, would have amounted to overcompensation. Indeed, if anything, the court's ruling in *Guerin* affirms the distinction between an assessment of compensation in equity and an award of prejudgment interest.

[98] In the case before us, Whitefish seeks only what was granted in *Guerin*, an award of equitable compensation assessed at the date of trial. Unlike the plaintiff in *Guerin*, Whitefish does not ask for prejudgment interest on that award. Thus, the ruling in *Guerin* relied on by the Crown does not apply to this case. …

(e) The trial judge's finding that the $31,600 would have been "dissipated" within a reasonable time is unsupportable

[101] The trial judge concluded that Whitefish's claim was not justified because the band unreasonably assumed the fair value of its timber rights would have been deposited in the trust account and remained there earning compound interest until 2005. In his view, at para. 29, "on the principle of 'first in, first out,'" the money "would likely have dissipated within a reasonable time." The Crown made the same point in this court. It contended that Whitefish's claim fails to take into account "the virtual certainty" the bonus payment would not have sat untouched in the band's account for 120 years.

[102] I disagree. The trial judge's holding, echoed by the Crown, is unsupportable because it is contrary to one of equity's presumptions, is entirely speculative and is inconsistent with the terms of the surrender. In the absence of evidence to the contrary—and there is virtually none—equity presumes that the defaulting fiduciary must account to the beneficiary on a basis most favourable to the beneficiary. The trial judge's finding presumes exactly the opposite—that the Crown will account to Whitefish on a basis most favourable to the Crown. See Oosterhoff, *supra*, at 1047.

[103] However, this does not mean that Whitefish is entitled to 120 years of accumulated capital and interest. That too is unsupportable. Instead, I would adopt the approach used by Collier J in *Guerin*, which was later approved by the Supreme Court of Canada, and discount Whitefish's award to reflect realistic contingencies.

[104] Unfortunately, we have an unsatisfactory record on which to make an informed judgment about Whitefish's annual expenditures, either out of its revenue account or its capital account. This unsatisfactory evidentiary record is a principal reason why a new hearing is needed to determine a fair and proportionate award of equitable compensation. …

D. Conclusion

[130] There are two issues on this appeal: first, did the trial judge err in his determination of the fair value of Whitefish's timber rights in 1886; second, did the trial judge err in his assessment of Whitefish's compensation, and if so, what is a "fair and proportionate" assessment?

[131] On the first issue, Whitefish appealed and the Crown cross-appealed from the trial judge's finding that the fair value of Whitefish's timber rights in 1886 was $31,600. In my view, the trial judge's finding is reasonable and is not tainted by any error in principle. Therefore, I would not give effect to the appeal or to the cross-appeal on this issue.

[132] On the second issue, Whitefish appealed the trial judge's finding that it was entitled to compensation in the amount of $1,095,888. I would allow the appeal on this issue. In my view, the trial judge erred in principle by failing to award Whitefish equitable compensation for its lost investment opportunity caused by the Crown's breach of fiduciary duty. Whitefish is entitled to compensation measured by the amount the fair value of its timber rights would have earned in the Whitefish trust account maintained by the government for its benefit, but discounted to reflect realistic contingencies. Because the deficiencies in the record prevent this court from assessing Whitefish's compensation, I would order a new hearing on this issue. ...

Appeal allowed in part; cross-appeal dismissed.

NOTES AND QUESTIONS

1. Laskin JA wrote that "while the purpose of equitable compensation is to put the plaintiff in the position it would have been in but for the breach, the purpose of common law damages is to restore the plaintiff to its original position." How does a plaintiff's "original position" differ from the position it would have occupied absent the wrong? What was Whitefish's "original position"?

2. Suppose that the Crown had owed Whitefish a contractual obligation to obtain a fair value for its timber rights. Would Whitefish have been awarded compound interest as part of its damages for breach of that obligation? If not, which of the three differences between equitable compensation and common law damages identified by Laskin JA would explain this different outcome? Would this difference be justified in your view? (The leading Canadian case on the availability of compound interest at common law is *Bank of America Canada v. Mutual Trust Co.*, [2002] 2 SCR 601.)

ELECTION OF REMEDIES

Introduction

In many instances, the plaintiff's claim will be formulated in the alternative as a plea for equitable relief—for example, specific performance or an injunction—or damages. As *Dobson* exemplifies, such pleadings are not generally seen by the courts as claims for contradictory relief. However, issues do arise as to when a plaintiff must elect as between the two remedies and what constitutes an election for these purposes.

As we have seen already, the general rule seems to be that the plaintiff claiming equitable relief or damages can wait until judgment before choosing. Moreover, if the plaintiff then chooses damages, that constitutes an irrevocable election. (Indeed, that is also true if a plaintiff seeks damages without pleading for specific performance in the alternative.) What if, on the other hand, the plaintiff chooses specific performance (or an injunction)? Are there circumstances in which the plaintiff can still revert to a claim for damages? An affirmative answer was given to that question in *Johnson v. Agnew*, [1980] AC 367 (HL (Eng.)), the relevant parts of which may be found in chapter 1, "General Principles of Damages." Reread that aspect of Lord Wilberforce's judgment.

NOTES

1. For commentary on this decision, see Marion Hetherington, "Keeping the Plaintiff Out of His Contractual Remedies: The Heresies That Survive Johnson v. Agnew" (1980), 96 *Law Q Review* 403, at 408-11. The author argues against the necessity for a court order discharging the decree of specific performance before the plaintiff can assert a claim to damages. If the decree is disobeyed, then the plaintiff should be able to rely on his common law rights which come into existence on non-performance of a contract. Would this be a better solution?

2. Subsequently, this aspect of *Johnson v. Agnew* has been applied in *Gaspari v. Creighton Holdings Ltd.* (1984), 52 BCLR 30.

3. Sometimes, of course, the possibility of specific performance not working can be anticipated. In this respect, see the note on *Dynamic Transport v. O.K. Detailing Ltd.* in chapter 9, "Specific Performance," under the heading "Long-Term Contracts for the Supply of Goods or Services." However, in *MacLauchlan v. Ferrier (In Trust)* (1993), 33 RPR (2d) 248 (Ont. Gen. Div.), Chapnik J in *dicta*, relying on *Dobson*, stated that once a plaintiff elected at judgment for specific performance with an abatement in the purchase price, that election was binding short of the court itself determining (as in *Johnson v. Agnew*) that the plaintiff should no longer be held to her or his choice.

4. For an interesting twist on the timing of an election, see *Island Records Ltd. v. Tring International plc*, [1995] 3 All ER 444 (Ch.). Here, the plaintiff was seeking either damages or an account for copyright infringement. The plaintiff moved for summary judgment on the issue of liability to be followed by an inquiry as to financial consequences. While willing to submit to summary judgment, the defendant argued that the plaintiff was obliged on summary judgment being entered to elect as between damages and an account. This was rejected by the court. Lightman J held that such an election could be postponed until such time (such as after discovery) as the plaintiff had sufficient information and time to make an informed choice.

5. Another issue that arises where the plaintiff seeks specific performance and damages in the alternative is whether the plaintiff then has control as to which of those remedies he or she ultimately elects or whether the defendant can submit to judgment for the remedy of his or her choice.

Beauchamp v. Coastal Corporation
[1986] 2 FC 298 (CA)

[Proceedings were initiated against the appellants when they failed to complete a contract for the sale of a vessel. The respondents sought in the alternative specific performance or damages and the seizure of the vessel (the sole asset of the appellants) *in rem*. During the course of setting a trial date, the respondents informed the appellants by letter that they only intended to pursue their claim for damages. The appellants brought a motion to strike the claim for specific performance which was resisted by the respondents and ultimately dismissed. (The appellants were questioning the court's jurisdiction *in rem* if the claim for specific performance was removed.)

The appellants brought a further motion seeking to confess to judgment in favour of the respondents for the specific performance of the contract. To this end, documents required to complete the transaction were tendered on the respondents' solicitors. The respondents' solicitors did not accept the tender and the motion was dismissed. At trial the respondents were awarded damages for breach of contract. The appellants were appealing that decision.

The judgment of the court was delivered by MacGuigan J.]

MacGUIGAN J: ...

[After stating the facts, he continued:]

The principal issue pressed by the appellants in oral argument related to the effect of their tender of March 9th, which they contended "cured" their original failure to complete on November 16th. More fully stated, the appellants' argument is that, there having been no election by the respondent to retract the claim for specific performance, the contract was still open for completion, on the basis of the general contract principle that where a party continues to treat a contract as outstanding and is seeking its performance, the other party may proceed to perform his part of the bargain; the respondent's refusal to complete was a repudiation of the contract, which until that time had continued to exist; in this situation it was then the respondent rather than the appellants that was in breach of contract, and the appellants were entitled to sue for damages for this breach. ...

In support of their contention the appellants cite the following passage from Halsbury's Laws of England, 4th ed., vol. 44, p. 383:

> 561. *Election between remedies*. A plaintiff claiming specific performance or damages in the alternative may before the trial elect to accept the repudiation of the contract by the defendant and abandon the claim to specific performance, by communicating his election to the defendant or by other acts showing an unequivocal election to terminate the contract. The right of election will cease, however, if the defendant remedies the breach before the plaintiff accepts the repudiation and the defendant is able and willing to perform his part of the contract ...

The case relied on by Halsbury for the effect of remedying a breach of contract is *Frost v. Knight* (1872), LR 7 Ex. 111 at p. 112. However, the reference in that case to keeping the contract alive for the benefit of the other party as well as for his own is strictly related to an anticipatory breach of contract, where the promisee's decision to treat the breach as inoperative has the effect of keeping the contract alive until its original date of completion. It has no precedential value for a case of actual breach of contract as here.

The respondent also relies on a statement in Robert J. Sharpe, *Injunctions and Specific Performance* (Toronto: Canada Law Book, 1983), at pp. 398-99:

> The other option is to insist upon further performance. This usually involves suing for specific performance, but a similar issue arises where the innocent party is able to perform his side of

the contract without further co-operation from the repudiating party other than payment. The effect of suing for specific performance is to keep the contract alive. The obligation to perform remains for both parties, and certain important implications follow. The promisee must remain ready, willing and able to complete his side of the contract. … If the innocent party does choose to keep the contract alive, he must take care not to put himself in breach by failing to meet his own obligations. In the often-quoted language of Asquith LJ: "An unaccepted repudiation is a thing writ in water and of no value to anybody: it confers no legal rights of any sort or kind." The risk the promisee takes in keeping the contract alive, although usually slight, is that he keeps the contract alive for both parties, and if subsequent events arise which excuse the defendant from performing, the defendant will be excused despite his earlier breach. … Similarly, the innocent party who decides to pursue performance must himself be careful to avoid committing an act which will put him in breach of the sort to excuse performance by the defendant, as the contract is said to be alive for all purposes.

The quotation from Asquith LJ, which was much used by counsel for the appellant, is from *Howard v. Pickford Tool Co. Ltd.*, [1951] 1 KB 417 (CA) at p. 421, a case in which the court refused to entertain a claim for a declaration that a six-year contract for personal services of the plaintiff had been repudiated by the conduct of the defendants since the fact that the plaintiff was continuing to perform his part of the contract in the particular situation rendered the problem academic.

The other authority relied upon by Sharpe, in addition to *Frost v. Knight* was *Goldenberg v. Lieberman*, [1951] OWN 405 at p. 406, where McRuer CJHC declared:

> Where a plaintiff sues for specific performance with an alternative claim for damages it is always open to a defendant at any time before judgment to accept the plaintiff's election to treat the contract as subsisting and himself elect to carry it out, thereby relieving him of any liability on the alternative claim for damages.

Although I reserve for a moment whether a suit for specific performance can be said to be an election for any purpose, and although this statement is in any event an *obiter dictum*, nevertheless I believe the meaning of the distinguished Chief Justice is clear and must be treated with respect. McRuer CJHC in fact repeated his views, again by way of an *obiter dictum*, in *Dobson v. Winton & Robbins Ltd.*, [1958] OWN 57 at p. 59:

> The plaintiff by his pleading came into Court stating that he was ready and willing to carry out the contract. The defendant might have at any time elected to abandon its defence and carried out the contract. In that case the plaintiff would have been entitled to his costs and any damages sustained by reason of the delay in carrying out the contract.

The same view was expressed by Reid J in *Lyew v. 418658 Ontario Ltd.* (1982), 35 OR (2d) 241. However, this latter decision was reversed by the Ontario Court of Appeal at (1982), 134 DLR (3d) 384n, 26 RPR 213. Lacourcière JA said for the court [at 384]:

> The summary judgment is based on the proposition that a plaintiff who claims specific performance is subject to specific performance at any time that the defendant elects to submit it. We do not accept that proposition as clear law: see *Dobson v. Winton & Robbins Ltd.*, [1959] SCR 775, particularly at p. 781, which casts some doubt on the *dicta* relied upon by the Motions

Court Judge. Accordingly, the matter should proceed to trial where the matter will be determined on all of the equities.

The *Dobson* case cited by the Ontario Court of Appeal, which was the appeal from the judgment of McRuer CJHC, as affirmed by the Ontario Court of Appeal [unreported], is the authority most directly on point. It was an action for specific performance of an agreement for the sale of land, which the purchaser had repudiated. Because the vendor closed another transaction for the sale of the same land to a third party while the trial was pending, the question was whether the vendor, by selling as he did, could go on with a claim for damages and whether his pleading was adequate for this purpose. The dismissal of the claim for damages by McRuer CJHC was reversed by a unanimous Supreme Court. Judson J wrote for the court ([1959] SCR 775 at pp. 779-81):

> The plaintiff's common law right of action on the facts of this case, as found by both Courts, is clear. On the purchaser's repudiation of the contract, the vendor could have forfeited the deposit and claimed for loss of bargain and out-of-pocket expenses. The *Judicature Act* gives him the right to join this claim with one of specific performance. At some stage of the proceedings he must, of course, elect which remedy he will take. He cannot have both specific performance and a common law claim for loss of bargain. But he is under no compulsion to elect until judgment, and the defendant is not entitled to assume that by issuing the writ for specific performance with a common law claim for damages in the alternative, the vendor has elected at the institution of the action to claim specific performance and nothing else. ...
>
> The judgment at trial is based in part upon the proposition that a claim for specific performance must be deleted by amendment before the alternative claim for damages for breach of contract can be considered. The foundation for this theory must be that by issuing a writ for specific performance the plaintiff has elected this remedy and that no other is open to him. *Hipgrave v. Case* (1885), 28 Ch. D 356, is cited in support of this principle and the plaintiff's action has failed in this case largely because of the construction which the Courts have put upon that decision. ...
>
> The case, however, is not authority for any principle that by issuing a writ for specific performance with an alternative common law claim for damages, the plaintiff has elected his remedy and is bound by the election. If the claim for specific performance alone is made, that constitutes an affirmation of the contract and, to that extent, an election to enforce the contract. But where the alternative common law claim is made, the writ is equivocal and there is no election. The distinction was clearly pointed out by Luxmoore LJ in *Public Trustee v. Pearlberg*, [1940] 2 KB 1 (CA) at p. 19. The matter is summarized in *Williams on Vendor & Purchaser*, 4th ed., p. 1054, as follows: "Thus, if a purchaser of land makes default in carrying out the contract, and the vendor sues to enforce it specifically, it will be a good defence that the vendor has *subsequently* made some sale or other disposition of the land, which effectually prevents him from completing the contract. This would be no defence to a claim by the vendor for damages for the purchaser's breach of contract."

As the Supreme Court here indicates, the theory espoused in the *Dobson* case by McRuer CJHC and in the instant case by the appellants is that a claim for specific performance amounts to an election of that remedy. The Supreme Court strongly rejects this proposition. The claim for specific performance in the present case, even as reaffirmed in

February 1984, is, therefore, not an election of that remedy alone. It was always accompanied by the alternative claim for damages.

Further, the effect of bringing an action for specific performance is not, as the appellants contend, to retain the contract in effect and enforceable at any time at the instance of either. The bringing of such an action with an alternative clause for damages invokes the jurisdiction of the court to enforce the contract, if it can be equitably enforced, and otherwise to award damages for its breach. If the contract can be equitably enforced it is for the court to determine when and on what terms it is to be completed and what adjustments are to be made for losses resulting from the breach. Thus in *Public Trustee v. Pearlberg*, [1940] 2 KB 1 (CA) at p. 19, a case referred to by Judson J in the *Dobson* case, Luxmoore LJ observed:

> Where (as in the present case) time for completion is not of the essence of the contract, it is always open to a vendor to fix a reasonable time for completion and so make time of the essence, but *where a vendor starts an action for specific performance it appears to me that the issue of a writ is equivalent to a notice to the purchaser that he must complete his purchase at a time which will be fixed by the Court if the vendor succeeds in his action.* Having given notice of this fact it seems to me to be impossible, while the action is pending, for the vendor to fix some other and shorter time for completion under some provision of the contract.

(Emphasis added.)

In *Johnson v. Agnew*, [1980] AC 367 (HL (Eng.)) at p. 398, Lord Wilberforce wrote:

> A vendor who seeks (and gets) specific performance is merely electing for a course which may or may not lead to implementation of the contract; what he elects for is not eternal and unconditional affirmation, but a continuance of the contract under control of the court which control involves the power, in certain events, to terminate it. If he makes an election to all, he does so when he decides not to proceed under the order for specific performance, but to ask the court to terminate the contract (see the judgment of Greene MR in *Austins of East Ham Ltd. v. Macey*, [1941] Ch. 338 (CA) at p. 341).

It seems to me to follow that until the innocent party makes an unequivocal election against specific performance the effect of his having claimed it and of having asserted his readiness, willingness and ability to perform the contract cannot be, as the appellants contend, to retain the contract as in effect for all purposes and enforceable at the instance of either party. That would deprive the innocent party of his election, which he alone has as the result of the other party's original default. As the election to forego specific performance in favour of damages can be made at any time during the litigation, it existed and was exercisable at the moment when the appellants made their tender of performance, if indeed the respondent's equitable right to specific performance had not already been irrevocably foregone by what had occurred earlier when the letters of January 5, 1984 and February 2, 1984 (pp. 143 and 145 of the case), were written. Persisting in keeping the claim for specific performance in the statement of claim is itself of little significance. It asks for the relief but the claim can be withdrawn at any moment. If a tender of performance by the party in default could cure his breach he would have, simply because of a claim for specific performance, after breaking the contract, as much right to enforce it as the innocent party has. Even if, with McRuer CJHC in the *Dobson* case, the innocent party were allowed "his costs and any damages sustained by the delay in carrying out the contract" he would still be allowed only the specific performance option and not the right to withdraw the claim and take his alternative common law remedy of damages.

This would not be equity, because it would not be fair, in relation to a contract of which time was of the essence, to abrogate the distinction between the wronged and the wronging party. The election of remedies must remain at the option of the innocent party, and to that extent, the contract will be alive in an unequal way, or, more accurately, it will remain alive but will be enforceable, if at all, only by the originally non-defaulting party on such terms as to compensation as a court of equity may prescribe.

The other points raised by counsel for the appellant were dealt with at the hearing and counsel for the respondent was not called on to answer them.

The appeal accordingly fails and I would dismiss it with costs.

Appeal dismissed.

QUESTIONS

1. When a party is seeking an alternative remedy in specific performance or damages, is it preferable to view this as:
   a. a claim for either specific performance or damages, with the choice being the plaintiff's or
   b. a claim for specific performance, but, if this is refused, then damages?
On which of these bases has the court in this case made its decision?

2. From this case, what do you conclude about the principle of mutuality? Is it appropriate to distinguish between situations involving anticipatory repudiation and those of repudiation at the time at which performance becomes due in terms of the entitlement of the person repudiating to resile and again express a willingness to perform? For an example of the contrary position, see *Carma Developers v. Groveridge Imperial Properties* (1985), 36 Alta. LR (2d) 355 (QB) and see also the theory advanced by Sopinka J delivering the judgment of the Supreme Court of Canada in *Semelhago v. Paramadevan*, [1996] 2 SCR 415:

> Moreover, the claim for specific performance revives the contract to the extent that the defendant who has failed to perform can avoid a breach if at any time up to the date of judgment, performance is tendered. [Where] the injured party ... continue[s] to insist on performance ... the contract continues in force and neither party is relieved of their obligations under the agreement.

Does this suggest that *Beauchamp* was decided wrongly or can no longer be regarded as good law? Should the situation differ as between a claim with respect to a chattel (as in *Beauchamp*) and a claim with respect to realty as in *Semelhago* and *Carma*?

3. Is it appropriate in an action for breach of contract to use language such as "innocent party," and "distinction between wronged and the wronging"?

4. The case cites an excerpt from Sharpe which speaks of the risks of keeping the contract alive. Do you think that these risks are removed if a claimant seeks damages as an alternative remedy?

5. As we have seen already in chapter 9, "Specific Performance," Canadian courts have now moved away from the notion that specific performance is the invariable remedy in contracts involving a contract for the disposition of an interest in land. Because of this, as suggested

earlier in this chapter, there will undoubtedly be occasions on which the question of mitigation will arise. Should the plaintiff have pursued her or his claim for specific performance to trial or should he or she have realized that such relief was impossible or not feasible? In the latter event, damages may not be measured by reference to the value of the property at the date of trial but at the date on which mitigation could reasonably have been effected. Fairly obviously, such an outcome should not be affected by the election of the plaintiff to abandon a claim for specific performance immediately before or during the trial. For an affirmation of this approach, see *Garbens v. Khayami* (1994), 17 OR (3d) 162 (Gen. Div.), though compare *Carma*, above, which might be read as suggesting the contrary.

CHAPTER ELEVEN

Discretionary Reasons for the Denial of Relief

INTRODUCTION

As is already apparent, equitable remedies are seldom if ever available as of right; rather, they are subject to the discretion of the court. Indeed, the study of equitable remedies is in very large measure the study of judicial discretion. In particular, we have spent much time examining the various nuances of the most significant factor bearing on judicial discretion over equitable remedies, the adequacy of damages. We have also seen how judicial discretion in this domain is affected by the court's perception of whether it can adequately supervise the implementation of the remedy that is being sought. In addition, though often controversially, parties on either side of a dispute where equitable relief is being sought will seek to appeal to the public interest as a factor bearing on the availability of a remedy.

Cutting across all these factors, the nature of the interest that is the subject of the litigation will often have an impact on the extent to which the court will see itself as having discretion either generally or in relation to particular considerations. Recollect the rather more stringent attitude that the courts have taken when an injunction is being sought to restrain a trespass as opposed to a nuisance. In the domain of contract, specific performance has come closest (at least until recently) to being seen as a remedy of right, rather than discretion, when the disposition of an interest in land is involved. Conversely, the courts have consistently recognized very broad discretion to deny enforcement of personal service contracts against employees.

The principal reason for the reluctance of the court to grant equitable relief in the domain of personal services contracts is its sense that to do so will in many instances be oppressive. Injunctions against working elsewhere will be denied even in the face of the clearest of negative covenants if the impact will be to force the defaulting employee to return to work with the plaintiff "or starve." In other domains as well, the oppressive or disproportionate impact of the remedy being sought will bear upon the court's discretion. Recall *Dempsey v. J.E.S. Developments Ltd.* (1976), 15 NSR (2d) 448 (TD) (chapter 7, "Injunctions"), where the court refused to award a mandatory injunction compelling the demolition of the trespassing portion of a building constructed with willful disregard for the plaintiff's rights. Notwithstanding the nature of the violation of the plaintiff's rights, the impact of the relief sought when measured against the extent of the violation of the plaintiff's interest indicated a money remedy, albeit accompanied by punitive damages. We have also seen how in *Falcke v. Gray* (chapter 9, "Specific Performance"), the court appealed to considerations remarkably similar to modern conceptions of unconscionability as a reason for the denial of relief in the case of default in a contract to sell unique chattels. Similarly, in *Cadbury Schweppes Inc. v. FBI Foods Ltd.* (chapter 10, "Financial Relief in Equity"), the Supreme Court of Canada took into account a range of factors in exercising its discretion against the grant of a permanent injunction to restrain the marketing of "Caesar Cocktail." Included among these considerations was the fact that the plaintiff had delayed some five years in the taking of proceedings, albeit under the mistaken assumption that it had no cause of action.

In this chapter, we have two principal objectives. First, largely in the context of cases in which specific performance is being sought for breach of contract, we want to examine in somewhat greater depth the use of judicial discretion over equitable relief on the basis of factors such as the ones identified in the preceding paragraph—those that often have colourful maxims of equity attached to them and are concerned with the relative substantive and remedial rights of the parties under the contract, the conduct of the parties, and the practical impact of the grant of the remedy being sought. Second, we want to return to a theme explored in a preliminary fashion in the cases on injunctions in personal services contracts—namely, the question of the extent to which the courts should recognize party autonomy in the stipulation of contractual objectives. Are there circumstances where the courts should accept a drastic limitation, if not total exclusion, of their normal remedial discretions because of the way in which the parties have expressed their intentions in a contract? We will examine this question in two interrelated contexts—first, by returning to a more general examination of the phenomenon of express negative covenants as well as strongly worded positive obligations and, second, by considering the rather sparse law on even more direct attempts to control judicial discretion by the use of "remedy stipulation" clauses.

EQUITY WILL NOT AID A VOLUNTEER

Equity will not aid a volunteer. As the following case illustrates, courts have traditionally taken this to imply that gratuitous promises will not be specifically enforced, even if they are under seal and binding at common law.

Riches v. Burns
(1924), 27 OWN 203

[An action to enforce specific performance of a contract.]

RIDDELL J in a written judgment, said that in July 1911, the plaintiff bought from the defendant a parcel of land with a house on it for $8,500. Later in the same month, he obtained from the plaintiff (*sic*) an option to purchase a parcel of land of 50 feet frontage. The learned Judge was unable to find that these dealings were part of the same transaction or that they had any connection with each other—the plaintiff asserted the affirmative, the defendant was negative. There appeared to be no reason for crediting one party rather than the other, and, there being conflict, the Judge proceeded on the onus of proof.

The document evidencing the option was under seal, and read, "This option is given in consideration of the sum of $1," but no money was in fact paid or intended to be paid. It was to continue

until the said Burns commences to build upon the said land or sells the said land or part of it ...
after his having given the said Riches notice for three days addressed to his office ... when, unless he exercised the option in writing ... within the said three days, it will cease and have no
force or effect.

Notice was sent to the plaintiff on the 28th May, 1914, that the plaintiff (*sic*) proposed to sell, and giving him three days to exercise his option. No notice was taken by the plaintiff of this. The defendant did not sell. The notice had, in itself, no effect upon the plaintiff's rights.

The option was to continue until sale or commencement of building; and, if it should be considered that the final words of the paragraph quoted contained a provision inconsistent with the earlier provision, the earlier provision must prevail, the document being under seal.

The option was without consideration in fact. A seal imports consideration; but that does not assist the plaintiff in his action for specific performance: George Russell Northcote (ed.), *Fry on Specific Performance* (London: Stevens, 6th ed., 1921) at p. 53, para. 116; *Savereux v. Tourangeau* (1908), 16 OLR 600 (Div. Ct.).

It does not seem to have been decided that in actions for specific performance, as in other cases, evidence is admissible to prove that there was in fact valuable consideration, although only a nominal consideration is recited; but, in the learned Judge's opinion, such evidence is admissible, *Leifchild's case* (1865), LR 1 Eq. 231; cf. *Llanelly Railway and Dock Co. v. London and North-Western Railway Co.* (1873), LR 8 Ch. 942. It was open to the plaintiff to prove, if he could, *aliunde*, that there was good and valuable consideration; and, if his evidence were accepted as against that of the defendant, he would succeed. But it could not be accepted, and the option must be taken as it read.

The claim for specific performance failed.

Semble, that the lapse of time would also furnish an answer.

Action dismissed with costs.

NOTES

1. *Riches v. Burns* was followed in *Rapattoni v. McDonald*, [1988] OJ no. 1461. See also *Jefferys v. Jefferys* (1841), Cr. & Ph. 138; and *Cannon v. Hartley*, [1949] Ch. 213. Compare the decision in *Riches v. Burns* with that of the Supreme Court of Canada in *Davidson v. Norstrant* (1921), 61 SCR 493, where specific performance was ordered in favour of a purchaser who exercised an option under seal that provided it was given in return for a sum of $100 "now paid," even though this sum was not, in fact, paid.

2. Riddell J does not discuss whether the $1 consideration would have supported a decree of specific performance if it had actually been paid to the defendant. We saw in chapter 9, "Specific Performance," that the inadequacy of consideration alone is not a bar to specific performance. However, nominal consideration is arguably not merely inadequate—it is unreal: it is consideration "in name only." In *Mountford v. Scott*, [1975] Ch. 258 (Ch. & CA) the defendant granted the plaintiffs a six months' option to purchase his house for £10,000 in

consideration of the sum of £1. In upholding the trial judge's decree of specific performance, Russell LJ said (at 265):

> [I]t appears to me irrelevant to the question of remedy under the contract for sale and purchase that the valuable consideration can be described as a token payment and so also if the option agreement can be under seal with no payment.

Note that the decree of specific performance granted in *Mountford v. Scott* required the defendant to perform his promise to convey the property, a promise for which the defendant paid £10,000. The option, which was purchased for nominal consideration, was held by Russell LJ to be "valid" in the sense that a purported withdrawal of the offer by the defendant during the period of the option would be "ineffective." Is *Mountford* authority for the proposition that nominal consideration will support a decree of specific performance? Compare G.H. Treitel, *The Law of Contract*, 11th ed. (London: Sweet & Maxwell, 2003), at 1037 with J.B. Berryman, *The Law of Equitable Remedies* (Toronto: Irwin Law, 2000), at 200. See also G. Jones and W. Goodhart, *Specific Performance*, 2nd ed. (London: Butterworths, 1996), at 24-25.

LACK OF MUTUALITY

Hanbury, *Modern Equity*
8th ed. (London: Stevens & Sons, 1962), c. 23, at 547-50 (footnotes omitted)

In Claims for Specific Performance, Equity Will Insist on the Principle of Mutuality

Is there such a rule? Fry lays down that specific performance will not, as a rule, be granted of a contract which is not obligatory on both parties, in the sense that, at the time at which it was executed, both had the right to come to equity to have it specifically enforced. But we are on debatable ground, for the exceptions are so numerous and so weighty that it has been argued, not merely that they eat up the rule, but that the rule never was on their plates. On the other hand, it is undoubtedly a convenient formula under which a certain line of decisions can find common shelter.

Fry's proposition is attacked by Ashburner, who refuses to give "want of mutuality" a place among the defenses to a suit for specific performance. On this matter Maitland, for once, is not so clear as he might be. He tells us that "Chancery came to the doctrine ... that 'remedies should be mutual,'" but yet follows Ashburner in his condemnation of want of mutuality as a defence. He seems to think that equity laid down in a general way that remedies *should* be mutual, without being willing to commit himself to saying that remedies *must* be mutual. In fairness to Fry it must be pointed out that Maitland argues from one particular case, which Fry admits to be an exception. But the most vigorous objector to the rule was Ames. He begins his famous article on the subject with an enumeration of no less than eight exceptions. The most obvious concerns the *Statute of Frauds*. A plaintiff may obtain specific performance of a contract which the defendant has, but he himself has not, signed. Leach MR in *Flight v. Bolland* attributed this exception to two causes:

(a)   that the statute requires an agreement to be signed only by the party to be charged,

(b)   that the plaintiff, by the very fact of filing the bill, has in effect rendered the remedy mutual.

In that case it was held that an infant cannot sustain a suit for specific performance, because a suit for specific performance could not be maintained against him.

It has been pointed out that this is the first case in England in which so wide a principle was laid down, though Leach MR was forestalled by Lord Redesdale in Ireland. The formula is a convenient vehicle for the rule that equity will not order specific performance of a gratuitous promise, even though it be under seal. It will carry also the rule that an employer will not be forced to keep a servant. Further, it provides an explanation of the converse phenomenon that in cases in which the court grants specific performance to one party as a matter of course, it will grant it to the other, although such a concession might, in another class of contract, be highly anomalous. In contracts for the sale or lease of land, equity, in order that its remedies may be mutual, will grant to the lessor or vendor specific performance of the contract of the lessee or purchaser to pay rent or purchase-money, though these demands are purely pecuniary, and as a rule equity will not deal with a mere money claim.

Ames' attack on the supposed rule. Legal science provides many illustrations of the commonplace, that a generality may be a good servant, but a bad master. In other words, it is one thing to refuse specific performance on the ground that the remedy is not, in the particular case, mutual, and quite another to lay down, as a universal principle, that without mutuality the remedy of specific performance will never be granted. Ames shows that this supposed general principle of mutuality simply has not the capacity to contain the cases, and if applied with rigorous consistency, would lead to absurd results. Moreover, it would make nonsense of old authorities, whose correctness has never been questioned. Fry insists that the element of mutuality must have been present at the time at which the parties entered into the contract. *Flight v. Bolland* bears out this view in that it decides that an infant cannot succeed if he files his bill before majority. But it was decided in *Clayton v. Ashdown* that if he files his bill after attainment of majority, he is entitled to succeed, though he would himself continue to have a defence for a reasonable time after the arrival of that period. Again, the rigid application of Fry's principle would have demanded a different decision in *Wilkinson v. Clements* from that at which the Lords Justices of Appeal in Chancery arrived.

> A had agreed to lease to B several plots of land, on the terms that B should build houses on all the plots. B mortgaged the contract to C, who built houses on two of the plots, and demanded leases of these. Here we have a contract for a lease of land, which equity will enforce, set against a contract for personal services, which equity will not enforce. A sought to resist a decree for specific performance except on the terms that C would assume liability to build on the virgin plots, but it was held that C, having fulfilled the conditions of the contract as regards two plots at the time at which he filed his bill, was entitled to a lease of those two plots, without undertaking any liability as to the other plots.

The most powerful weapon, however, in Ames' armoury is supplied by *Hoggart v. Scott*, where Leach MR, the very judge who decided *Flight v. Bolland*, on which Fry's generality so largely rests, laid down that in a contract for the sale of land, the vendor is entitled to specific performance if, *at the hearing*, he can show a good title, though he had not such a title at the time of the contract. All these cases go to swell the flood that well nigh engulfs the supposed rule of mutuality. But Ames is far too conscientious a critic to confine himself to mere iconoclasm. He has a very constructive suggestion, in the shape of a substituted formula, which will satisfactorily cover both *Flight v. Bolland* and the numerous cases which are usually called "exceptions" to the principle applied in it. He works out the result that the crucial factor is, not the availability of specific performance to the defendant *at the time of the contract*, but the assurance to the defendant, by some means other than the common law remedy of damages, that, *after performance*, the plaintiff's side of the contract will be carried out. This assurance was present in *Hoggart v. Scott*, absent in *Flight v. Bolland*. The extent of the respect shown in America for Ames' views may be measured by the fact that what is, to all intents and purposes, his doctrine, is incorporated into the *Restatement of the Law of Contracts*. In England Fry's rule dies hard, making repeated appearances in the *dicta* of judges. But it is dangerous in that, though it will explain some cases, there are more which it cannot explain. Though there is hardly such a thing known to English law as a rule without exceptions, yet a rule which is overloaded with exceptions may perhaps be said to lose its claim to be a rule.

Price v. Strange
[1978] Ch. 337 (CA)

[As noted already in the context of a previous extract from this judgment in chapter 10, "Financial Relief in Equity," this case made a significant contribution to the evolution of the law governing mutuality. The judge at first instance dismissed the action on the grounds that specific performance of an oral contract of lease could not be granted, since at the time the contract was entered into, it was not capable of mutual enforcement. The principal basis for that holding was that the oral contract called for the tenant to do work on the relevant premises.

On appeal, the plaintiff argued on the issue of mutuality that "(1) the judge erred in law in holding that the defendant was entitled to resist by way of specific performance of the oral agreement on the ground that the remedies of the parties were not mutual by reference only to the facts which had occurred at or prior to the formation of the agreement; [and] (2) the judge erred in law in failing to hold that if the defence of lack of mutuality had been a good defence to relief by way of specific performance of the oral agreement the defendant had lost the right to insist on such defence by the trial of the action."]

GOFF LJ: … The judge accepted as good law certain statements in George Russell Northcote (ed.), *Fry on Specific Performance* (London: Stevens, 6th ed., 1921), and quoting from *Fry* he said:

My understanding of the law is that it is correctly stated in *Fry on Specific Performance*, at pp. 219 and 222, and also p. 223. *Fry* says, at p. 219: "A contract to be specifically enforced by the court must, as a general rule, be mutual,—that is to say, such that it might, at the time it was entered into, have been enforced by either of the parties against the other of them." At p. 222 in paragraph 463 he says: "The mutuality of a contract is, as we have seen, to be judged of at the time it is entered into." At p. 223 *Fry* says: "From the time of the execution of the contract being the time to judge of its mutuality it further follows, that the subsequent performance by one party of terms which could not have been enforced by the other will not prevent the objection which would arise from the presence of such terms." ... I hold accordingly.

... The plaintiff's main case is that the statement in *Fry on Specific Performance* that mutuality has to be determined at the date of the contract is not good law, and that on the contrary the question of mutuality is simply one of the factors, which like hardship, mistake and delay has to be considered in the exercise of a judicial discretion when the court is considering whether or not to order specific performance, and, therefore, the relevant time is that of the hearing, and, he argues, if that be the proper rule, then having regard to all the circumstances this is a proper case for an order, especially as the work has now been finished and complete justice can be done by a monetary adjustment.

I must return to consider that in detail, but first Mr. Brodie made an alternative submission that even if Sir Edward Fry were right, and if the plaintiff had not been allowed to do any of the work, still the court would have granted an adjournment to give him an opportunity of doing it, or else would have made a conditional order or have granted an injunction to restrain the defendant from preventing him from doing the work on the principle laid down in *Lumley v. Wagner* (1852), 1 DGM & G 604; 42 ER 687 (Ch.) and other reports.

For my part, I do not think that the court would have granted any such relief before any of the work had been done, and, as I see it, the contrary was expressly decided in *Peto v. Brighton, Uckfield & Tunbridge Wells Railway Co.* (1863), 1 Hem. & M 468; 71 ER 205 (Ch.). Different considerations might apply after part performance. However, in my judgment, it is unnecessary for us to reach any conclusion on these alternative submissions. No application for an injunction was in fact made, and the time for an application had long since passed when it came to the trial.

I turn, therefore, to the question whether Sir Edward Fry was right or wrong. In the first part of paragraph 463, on p. 222, he was dealing with the defence of mutuality in a very different context, namely, that a party cannot rely on a want of mutuality which has arisen from his own post contract default.

The second part of paragraph 463 of *Fry on Specific Performance*, on which the judge relied, is of course a categorical statement of the defendant's case and has the authority of Sir Edward Fry himself to back it.

[After a detailed consideration of case law, commentary and principle, Goff LJ concluded ultimately:]

In my judgment, therefore, the proposition in *Fry* is wrong and the true principle is that one judges the defence of want of mutuality on the facts and circumstances as they exist at the hearing, albeit in the light of the whole conduct of the parties in relation to the subject matter, and in the absence of any other disqualifying circumstances the court will grant specific performance if it can be done without injustice or unfairness to the defendant. In *Ogden v. Fossick* (1862), 4 DGF & J 426; 45 ER 1249 (Ch.) specific performance was refused, but in that case there were continuing obligations of service on the part of the plaintiffs commensurate with the whole term of the lease contracted to be granted.

If, therefore, the plaintiff had been allowed to finish the work and had done so, I am clearly of opinion that it would have been right to order specific performance, but we have to consider what is the proper order, having regard to the fact that he was allowed to do an appreciable part and then not allowed to finish. Even so, in my judgment, the result is still the same for the following reasons.

First, the defendant by standing by and allowing the plaintiff to spend time and money in carrying out an appreciable part of the work created an equity against herself. This is supported, first, by *Hart v. Hart* (1881), 18 Ch. D 670 at p. 685 and *Parker v. Taswell* (1858), 2 DG & J 559, at p. 571; 44 ER 1106 at p. 1111 (Ch.) which show that where there has been part performance the court will struggle against difficulties to secure total performance, but much more strongly by the principles laid down in *Chalmers v. Pardoe*, [1963] 1 WLR 677 (PC (Fiji)) at p. 681. That case shows that where A encourages or permits B to build on or improve A's land on the faith of an understanding or assurance, short of a binding contract, that he will permit him to have it or use it for B's own benefit, equity will in a proper case not merely give B a lien for recovering his expenditure but compel A to implement the understanding. *A fortiori* must it be so where, as here, the plaintiff was allowed to start work on the defendant's property on the faith of an actual contract which, notwithstanding the want of writing, was by the very act of part performance made enforceable in equity.

Secondly, the work has in fact been finished. The court will not be deterred from granting specific performance in a proper case, even though there remain obligations still to be performed by the plaintiff if the defendant can be properly protected: see *Langen & Wind Ltd. v. Bell*, [1972] Ch. 685 which concerned a sale of shares where the purchase price could not be ascertained for two years, and where the defendant was ordered to execute transfers and deliver them and the certificates to stakeholders. See also *C.H. Giles & Co. Ltd. v. Morris*, [1972] 1 WLR 307 (Ch.) where Megarry J said, at p. 318:

> [T]he court may refuse to let the disadvantages and difficulties of specifically enforcing the obligation to perform personal services outweigh the suitability of the rest of the contract for specific performance, and the desirability of the contract as a whole being enforced. After all, *pacta sunt servanda*.

Still more readily should it act where the work has been done so that the defendant is not at risk of being ordered to grant the underlease and having no remedy except in damages for subsequent non-performance of the plaintiff's agreement to put the premises in repair.

Thirdly, the defendant can be fully recompensed by a proper financial adjustment for the work she has had carried out.

I am fully satisfied that the law is as I have stated it to be, but, even if I were wrong and the defence of mutuality ought to be considered according to the position at the date of the contract, still it is conceded, and, in my judgment, unquestionably correctly, that such a defence may be waived. *Halkett v. Dudley*, [1907] 1 Ch. 590 is alone sufficient authority for that proposition. Then on the facts of this case the defence clearly was waived. Not only did the defendant permit the plaintiff to start upon the work which would of itself be sufficient, in my view, but she also accepted the increased rent payable under the contemplated under lease and went on doing so after her purported repudiation.

For these reasons I would allow this appeal and order specific performance but upon terms that the plaintiff do pay to the defendant proper compensation for the work done by her. As a matter of strict right that must take the form of an inquiry as to what it would have cost the plaintiff to complete the works himself, with an order that he do pay or allow the defendant the amount certified with a set-off against any costs payable by the defendant, the costs of the inquiry being reserved. The plaintiff has however offered, subject to any question whether the expense incurred by the defendant was unnecessary or extravagant, to compensate her more handsomely by paying or allowing the actual cost to her, and it may well be possible, and certainly in the best interests of the parties, for them to agree [to] a figure and so obviate proceeding with the inquiry, which could well involve them in further considerable litigation and expense.

BUCKLEY LJ: ... I will deal first with the question of mutuality. It is easy to understand that as the equitable jurisdiction to enforce specific performance of contractual obligations developed it should have become an accepted rule that equity would not compel one party to perform his obligations specifically in accordance with the terms of the contract unless it could also ensure that any unperformed obligations of the other party would also be performed specifically. For breaches of some kinds of contract, pre-eminently contracts for the sale of land, the common law remedy of damages was inadequate. The courts of equity consequently supplemented the common law by introducing the equitable remedy of specific performance, compelling the defendant to carry out his contract instead of penalising him in damages for failing to do so.

Considering the position *a priori* and apart from authority, it would seem that the questions which should be asked by any court which is invited to enforce specific performance of a contractual obligation should be: (1) is the plaintiff entitled to a remedy of some kind in respect of the alleged breach of contract? (2) If so, would damages be an adequate remedy? (3) If not, would specific performance be a more adequate remedy for the plaintiff? (4) If so, would it be fair to the defendant to order him to perform his part of the contract specifically? The first question goes to the validity and enforceability of the contract. Only if it is answered affirmatively do the subsequent questions arise. If the second question is answered affirmatively there is no occasion for equity to interfere, so that again the subsequent questions do not arise. If the second question is answered in the negative it will not necessarily follow that the third question must be answered affirmatively. For instance, the circumstances may not be such as to admit of specific performance, as where the subject matter of the contract no longer exists. Only in the event of the third question arising and being answered in the affirmative can the fourth question arise. It is here, as it seems to me, that the alleged principle of mutuality comes in.

If one party were compelled to perform his obligations in accordance with the terms of the contract while the obligations of the other party under the contract, or some of them, remained unperformed, it might be unfair that the former party should be left to his remedy in damages if the latter party failed to perform any of his unperformed obligations. This is a consideration which bears upon the appropriateness of specific performance as a remedy in the particular case: it has no bearing on the validity or enforceability of the contract, that is to say, upon whether the plaintiff has a cause of action. A contract of which mutual specific performance cannot be enforced may yet afford a good cause of action for a remedy in damages at law. It would seem, therefore, that the appropriate time at which to consider the fourth question, and the appropriate circumstances to consider, must be the date of judgment and the circumstances then existing. And yet Sir Edward Fry said in very clear terms *Specific Performance* (London: Stevens, 3rd ed., 1892) p. 215 (6th ed., p. 219):

> A contract to be specifically enforced by the court must, as a general rule, be mutual, that is to say, such that it might, at the time it was entered into, have been enforced by either of the parties against the other of them.

[At this point, Buckley LJ considered criticism of Fry's position as well as American and Australian caselaw, before continuing:]

These judicial views are all at variance with the Fry proposition. The *American Restatement* (1932), Contracts, para. 373, contains the following formulation:

> Specific performance may properly be refused if a substantial part of the agreed exchange for the performance to be compelled is as yet unperformed and its concurrent or future performance is not well secured to the satisfaction of the court.

We have been referred to a large number of English decisions, in none of which has the Fry proposition been commented on but which nevertheless have a bearing upon its correctness. It may be convenient if I collect them into three categories. First, cases of contracts for sale where at the date of the contract the vendor was unable to show a good title to the property agreed to be sold. [A list of cases follows.]

Secondly, cases in which the consideration on one side consisted of an obligation to perform services or carry out works. [A list of cases including *Maddison v. Alderson* follows.]

Thirdly, cases in which the obligation of one party was not to be performed until the obligation of the other party had been performed. [A list of cases including *Maddison v. Alderson* follows.]

Unless there is something particular about contracts for the sale of land as for instance that neither party is bound to complete immediately—and I am not aware of any case in which such an argument has been considered—there was lack of mutual availability of the remedy of specific performance at the date of the contract in all the cases of the first class because of the vendor's initial inability to convey what he had contracted to sell. At law this does not affect the validity of the contract, for the vendor's obligation is to convey a good title at completion. If a purchaser becomes aware that in some material respect the vendor has not the title he contracted to sell he may, if he acts promptly, repudiate the contract in the sense of saying that he will not complete it. This will afford him a good defence to a claim by the vendor to specific performance, but, if the vendor can cure the defect in his title before completion becomes due, the purchaser will, notwithstanding his repudiation, be liable in damages for breach of contract: see *Halkett v. Dudley*, [1907] 1 Ch. 590. Yet in none of the cases of the first category except *Joseph v. National Magazine Co. Ltd.*, [1959] Ch. 14 was it suggested that the lack of initial mutuality afforded a defence to the claim to specific performance; and in the last-mentioned case, although specific performance was not ordered because the exact terms of the article which was the subject matter of the contract had never been agreed between the parties, Harman J, at p. 20, expressly declined to accept an argument based on lack of mutuality at the date of the contract.

A vendor who cannot convey what he has contracted to sell cannot, of course, rely upon the fact as a defence to a claim by the purchaser for specific performance. This would be to allow him to rely on his own fault. Where a purchaser sues for specific performance the court does not inquire whether the vendor has a good title before making its order. The usual specific performance order includes a direction of an inquiry whether the vendor can make a good title in accordance with the contract. If it is found that he cannot, the purchaser can either insist upon performance to the extent of the vendor's ability with an appropriate abatement in the purchase price or be relegated to his remedy in damages, *faute de mieux*, not on any ground of lack of mutuality. Lack of mutuality is only of significance where the defendant from whom specific performance is sought can show that at whatever may be the relevant date the plaintiff cannot be, or, if a past date is relevant, could not have been, ordered to perform his unperformed obligations specifically.

Initial mutuality was lacking in the cases of the second category because the services to be rendered or the works to be done were such as the court would not order to be specifically performed; but where ... the plaintiff had fully performed or carried out those services or works, the court ordered specific performance of the other party's obligations which were of kinds the specific performance of which the court could enforce. In *Kirkland v. Bird* (1968), 112 SJ 440 (Ch.), Cross J said that where the plaintiff had fully carried out his obligations it was "hard to see how the mutuality principle came in at all."

Mr. Jaques, for the defendant, has submitted that the principle of mutuality has no relevance to the third category of cases, in which he says that the obligation of one party is conditional on the prior performance of the other party's obligation. Such contracts are not truly conditional—and Mr. Jaques does not, I think, suggest that they are—in the sense that the bargain is intended to have contractual effect only if a precedent condition is satisfied, e.g. a contract to assign and to accept assignment of a lease if the landlord's consent can be first obtained. In the class of case now under consideration there are mutual binding obligations from the start, but the terms of the contract are such that the obligation of one party does not fall to be performed until the other party has performed his obligation or some specified part of it.

[Buckley LJ here considered cases in the third category and rejected the defendant's argument that they were not relevant.]

Although the point about mutuality seems not to have been taken in the English authorities I have mentioned, except before Harman, Cross and Stamp JJ, their trend is clearly inconsistent with the Fry proposition. Indeed, those cases in the second category in which specific performance was decreed could not have been decided as they were if the Fry proposition were correct. In my opinion, Lord Cranworth stated the true position succinctly and clearly in *Blackett v. Bates* (1865), LR 1 Ch. App. 117 when he said, at p. 124, that "the court does not grant specific performance unless it can give full relief to both parties." I think that it is also worth recalling what Knight Bruce V-C said in *Salisbury v. Hatcher* (1842), 2 Y & C Ch. Cas. 54, at pp. 63-64; 63 ER 24 at p. 28:

> In cases of specific performance the want of mutuality is a consideration generally material, but it is contrary to principle and authority to say that perfect mutuality is requisite in order to call a court of equity into action. There are cases in which plaintiffs have had a decree of specific performance against defendants, who, when the bill was filed, were not in a condition to enforce

specific performance in their own favour. Where no legal invalidity affects the contract, the enforcement of it in this court is a matter of judicial discretion. In this case it has not been contended that there is any legal invalidity. Suppose Mrs. Salisbury to have obtained a legal conveyance of the fee before the time fixed for completion of the contract, and to have done and tendered all other things requisite to be done and tendered. If this were done in sufficient time she would, I apprehend, have been entitled to recover, at law, on the contract. The contrary, indeed, has not been argued, and I do not understand that on that point the counsel for the defendant desire a case for the opinion of a court of law. If so, this becomes a case for the judicial discretion of the court of equity to which application for specific performance is made.

I can discover nothing in principle to recommend the Fry proposition and authority seems to me to be strongly against it. Accordingly, in my judgment, it should be regarded as wrong. The time at which the mutual availability of specific performance and its importance must be considered is, in my opinion, the time of judgment, and the principle to be applied can I think be stated simply as follows: the court will not compel a defendant to perform his obligations specifically if it cannot at the same time ensure that any unperformed obligations of the plaintiff will be specifically performed, unless, perhaps, damages would be an adequate remedy to the defendant for any default on the plaintiff's part.

Upon the judge's findings of fact in the present case the defendant's obligation to grant a sublease to the plaintiff was immediate. The case consequently falls into my second category. The plaintiff remained in occupation of the *maisonette* but, as from February 10, 1974, at the increased rent. The defendant however repudiated the agreement before the plaintiff had completed the repairs and without having executed a new sublease. She has subsequently completed the agreed repairs at her own expense.

The present case differs from any decided case to which I have referred in this respect, that, although all the agreed repairs have been done, they have not all been done by the plaintiff. In my judgment, however, this is no bar to the plaintiff's right to a grant of a sublease in accordance with the contract. That the plaintiff did not do all the work was not due to any default of his: it was due to the defendant's unjustified repudiation of the contract. She was, in my opinion, clearly under an implied obligation not to prevent the plaintiff from performing his part of the contract, but she did so. This was an incident of her wrongful repudiation of her obligation to grant him a sublease. The financial consequences of the defendant's having carried out at her own expense work which under the contract should have been done by the plaintiff at his expense could be adjusted by appropriate accounts, inquiries and adjustments under the court's order. If, as Goff LJ has said, this part of the case can be dealt with by agreement, so much the better.

Buckley LJ also then proceeded to consider whether damages could have been awarded under *Lord Cairns' Act* should specific performance not have been available. This portion of his judgment has been reproduced in chapter 10, "Financial Relief in Equity."

NOTES

1. For Canadian acceptance of this aspect of *Price v. Strange*, see *Holden Corp. v. Gingerfield Properties Ltd.* (1987), 59 OR (2d) 304 (HC) and *Higginbotham v. IFC Holdings Ltd.*, [1985] BCJ no. 1232 (SC) (QL).

2. Mutuality and the case of *Price v. Strange* were considered in the following article: Gregory Burton and Judith I. Winton, "Specific Performance: Mutuality: Damages in Lieu: A Question of Jurisdiction or Discretion" (1979), 8 *Sydney Law Review* 716.

3. Specific performance was denied for want of mutuality in *Politzer v. Metropolitan Homes Ltd.*, [1976] 1 SCR 363, on facts that revealed a complete absence of mutuality. Laskin CJ wrote:

> I regard the agreement of sale and purchase as illusory. I see no binding contract supported by consideration in an agreement under which the purchaser may choose to perform or not, without liability if he decides not. Certainly there is no mutuality of obligation; and without necessarily saying that this is in all cases necessary to support an action for specific performance it is plain to me that such relief cannot be successfully sought by the purchaser in the present case.

The following familiar case brings together a number of important issues relating to the availability of specific performance—adequacy of damages, availability of the remedy with respect to promises to pay money, and also mutuality. Consider whether the result would have been the same had old Peter Beswick agreed to work for his nephew for 20 hours a week.

Beswick v. Beswick
[1966] Ch. 538 (CA)

[P.B. sold his business to his nephew. The consideration was that the nephew would employ P.B. as a consultant for the rest of P.B.'s life at £6.10 per week, then on P.B.'s death would pay his widow £5 per week as a charge on the business. P.B. died but after one payment to Mrs. B., the nephew refused to pay any more. Mrs. B. sued for specific performance of the agreement. She did this in both her personal capacity and as administratrix of P.B.'s estate.]

DANCKWERTS LJ (at pp. 560-61): … The arguments in favour of specific performance are attractive. They might not be applicable in cases where the only plaintiff was the beneficiary; but where the party to the agreement or his personal representative is a plaintiff, the situation is different. The deceased sold the business to the defendant and the defendant has the complete benefit of the contract and complete performance of the deceased's obligations under the contract. The payment of £5 a week to the widow by the defendant was part of the consideration for the sale, and justice and equity demand that the defendant should perform his part of the bargain.

Mutuality is the essence of specific performance … . There is no doubt that if the deceased or the widow had died before the business had been transferred, the defendant would have been entitled to specific performance of the contract for the sale of the business to him. Where a contract has been partly performed, the court tries to see that the rest of the contract is duly performed … .

There are additional reasons which make the remedy of specific performance appropriate: (1) The remedy at law is plainly inadequate if only nominal damages can be recovered, and (2) anyhow, in order to recover damages in an action at law on a continuing obligation it may be necessary to bring a series of actions. So specific performance is a more effective and convenient remedy. [A list of authorities follows.]

It was suggested that equity would not give the remedy of specific performance of a contract to make a money payment. This contention is quite untenable. A purchaser of land is frequently compelled to pay the price by specific performance at the instance of a vendor; and the same principle must apply to the price of a business: see *Palmer v. Lark*, [1945] Ch. 182 where the form of order settled by Vaisey J will be found, providing for delivery by the vendor of the conveyance and documents of title, and payment of the purchase-money by the purchaser. The steps that are taken in such a case are illustrated in *Morgan v. Brisco* (1885), 31 Ch. D 216; (1886), 32 Ch. D 192.

Beswick v. Beswick
[1968] AC 58 (HL)

LORD UPJOHN (at pp. 96-102): My Lords, to return to this case. Admittedly A1 can sue from time to time for damages at common law on failure to pay each instalment of the annuity. But surely on a number of grounds this is a case for specific performance.

First, here is the sale of a business for full consideration wholly executed on A's part who has put C into possession of all the assets. C is repudiating the obligations to be performed by him. To such a case the words of Kay J in *Hart v. Hart* (at p. 685) are particularly appropriate:

> [W]hen an agreement for valuable consideration between two parties has been partially performed, the court ought to do its utmost to carry out that agreement by a decree for specific performance.

The fact that A by the agreement was to render such services as consultant as he might find convenient or at his own absolute discretion should decide may be ignored as *de minimis* and the contrary was not argued. In any event the fact that there is a small element of personal service in a contract of this nature does not destroy that quality of mutuality (otherwise plainly present) want of which may in general terms properly be a ground for refusing a decree of specific performance.

In the courts below, though not before your Lordships, it was argued that the remedy of specific performance was not available when all that remained was the obligation to make a money payment. Danckwerts LJ rightly demolished this contention as untenable for the reasons he gives (CA), [1966] Ch. 538 at pp. 560-61.

But when the money payment is not made once and for all but in the nature of an annuity there is an even greater need for equity to come to the assistance of the common law. Equity is to do true justice to enforce the true contract that the parties have made and to prevent the trouble and expense of a multiplicity of actions. This has been well settled for over a century: *Swift v. Swift* (1841), 3 Ir. Eq. R 267. In that case an annuity of £40 p.a. was payable to a lady quarterly and Lord Plunket LC enforced specific performance of it. He said (at pp. 275-76):

It is said she has a complete remedy at law for the breach of this contract, and that, therefore, this court should not interfere. Now, the remedy at law could only be obtained in one of two ways, either by at once recovering damages for all the breaches that might occur during the joint lives of herself and the defendant, or by bringing four actions in each year, and recovering in each the amount of a quarterly payment of the annuity. Those are the two modes of redress open to the plaintiff at Law. And I am called on to refuse relief here on the ground that such remedies are equally beneficial and effectual for the plaintiff as that which this court could afford. To refuse relief on such a ground would not, in my opinion, be a rational administration of justice. I do not see that there is any authority for refusing relief, and certainly there is no foundation in reason for doing so.

Then, after referring to the case of *Adderley v. Dixon* (1824), 1 Sim. & St. 607; 57 ER 239 (Ch.) he continued (at pp. 276-77):

Applying this to the present case, leaving the plaintiff to proceed at law and to get damages at once for all the breaches that might occur during the joint lives of her and the defendant, would, in effect, be altering the entire nature of the contract that she entered into; it would be compelling her to accept a certain sum, a sum to be ascertained by the conjecture of a jury as to what was the value of the annuity. This would be most unreasonable and unjust: her contract was for the periodical payment of certain sums during an uncertain period; she was entitled to a certain sum of money, and she agreed to give up that for an annuity for her own and the defendant's lives, and to insist on her now accepting a certain sum of money in the shape of damages for it, would be in effect to make her convert into money, what she, having in money, exchanged for an annuity. As to her resorting four times every year to a Court of Law for each quarterly payment of this annuity, it is a manifest absurdity to call that a beneficial or effectual remedy for the plaintiff; and resting the case on that ground alone, I think I am warranted by the highest authority in granting the relief sought.

It is in such common sense and practical ways that equity comes to the aid of the common law and it is sufficiently flexible to meet and satisfy the justice of the case in the many different circumstances that arise from time to time.

To sum up this matter: had C repudiated the contract in the lifetime of A the latter would have had a cast iron case for specific performance. Can it make any difference that by the terms of the agreement C is obliged to pay the annuity after A's death to B? Of course not. On the principle I have just stated it is clear that there can be nothing to prevent equity in A's specific performance action making an appropriate decree for specific performance directing payment of the annuity to A but during his life and thereafter to B for her life.

There is abundant authority to support that proposition. The first is *Keenan v. Handley* (1864), 12 WR 930 (Ch.) and on appeal (1864), 2 De GJ & Sm. 283; 46 ER 384 (Ch.), the facts of which are sufficiently set out in the judgment of Lord Denning MR. That case seems to me dead in point and I do not accept the argument that the mother, Ellen Keenan, was contracting as trustee for her child; such a relationship cannot be spelt out of Captain Handley's letter. As one of the contracting parties she was suing to enforce her rights under the letter, as later modified by agreement for payment of £100 a year to herself for her life and £50 a year to the child and after Ellen Keenan's death £150 a year to the child for her life. True it is that no point was taken either at first instance or in the Court of Appeal that the infant could not sue but, as *Tweddle v. Atkinson* (1861), 1 B & S 393; 121 ER 762 (QB) had only been decided some three years before, that point cannot have been overlooked. I draw the inference that it never occurred to those distinguished equity judges who tried that case that there could be any difficulty in making an order upon C at the instance of A to pay B. That is made clear by the order in that case which is to be found in that great book of authority, Arthur Robert Ingpen (ed.), Seton on Judgments and Orders (see London: Stevens, 7th ed., 1912, vol. 3 at p. 2212). That was followed by *Peel v. Peel* (1869), 17 WR 586 (Ch.) also discussed by Lord Denning MR. Then came the Irish case of *Drimmie v. Davies*, [1899] 1 IR 176 (Ch.) a very familiar type of case where the parties in a firm agreed together to pay annuities to the dependants of a partner when he should die. The executors of a deceased partner brought an action to enforce payment of the annuities and succeeded. Although my noble and learned friend, Lord Pearce, has set out the observations of Holmes LJ in that case in his speech, it so exactly expresses my own view that I set it out again. Holmes LJ said at p. 190:

> In this case Davies, junior, covenanted for valuable consideration with Davies, senior, that in certain events he would pay annuities to the children of the latter. If such annuities had become payable in the life of the covenantee, and they were not paid, what legal obstacle would there be to his suing the covenantor? Indeed, I believe that it is admitted that such an action would lie, but that it would only result in nominal damages. A result more repugnant to justice, as well as to legal principle, I can hardly imagine. The defendant would thereby escape from paying what he had undertaken to pay by making an illusory payment never contemplated by either party. Well, if Davies, senior, would have been entitled to sue in his lifetime if the annuities were then payable, his executors would have the same right of action after his death. As I have already said, the question is elementary.

Finally there was the rather unusual case of *Hohler v. Aston*, [1920] 2 Ch. 420 also mentioned by Lord Denning MR who quotes the relevant passage from the judgment of Sargant J (as he then was). This again shows the extent of the power of equity to assist the common law, limited only by canons of common sense and the practical limitations on the power to oversee and administer specific performance decrees. So the power and indeed duty, in proper cases, of the court of equity to make specific performance orders in favour of third parties at the instance of one of the contracting parties is not in doubt.

But when A dies and his rights pass to A1, it is said that the remedy of specific performance is no longer appropriate against C. The argument was first that the estate of A suffered no damages by reason of C's failure to pay B; so A1 is entitled to nominal damages but as she is not otherwise interested in the agreement as such it would be wrong to grant specific performance; for that remedy is available only where damages will be an inadequate remedy. Here nominal damages are adequate. Further, it was argued, to do so would really be to confer upon B a right which she does not have in law or equity to receive the annuity. Then, secondly, it was said that if the remedy of specific performance is granted it might prejudice creditors of A so that the parties ought to be left to their strict rights at law. Thirdly, it is said that there are procedural difficulties in the way of enforcing an order for specific performance in favour of a third party. I will deal with these points, though in reverse order.

As to procedural difficulties, I fear I do not understand the argument. The point if valid applies to an action for specific performance by A just as much as by A1 yet in the authorities I have quoted no such point was ever taken; in *Drimmie v. Davies* indeed the action was by executors. Further, it seems to me that if C fails to obey a four-day order obtained by A1, B could enforce it under the clear and express provisions of RSC, Ord. 45, r. 9 (formerly Ord. 42, r. 26). Alternatively A1 could move for and obtain the appointment of a receiver of the business upon which the annuity is charged and the receiver would then be directed by the Court to pay the annuity to B out of the profits of the business. Finally, A1 could issue a writ of *fi. fa.* under Ord. 45, r. 1, but as A1 would then be enforcing the contract and not modifying or compromising it the court would obviously in executing its order compel her to carry out the contract in toto and hand the proceeds of execution to B. This point is entirely without substance.

Then as to the second point. Let me assume (contrary to the fact) that A died with substantial assets but also many creditors. The legal position is that *prima facie* the duty of A1 is to carry out her intestate's contracts and compel C to pay B; but the creditors may be pressing and the agreement may be considered onerous; so it may be her duty to try and compromise the agreement with C and save something for the estate even at the expense of B. See *Ahmed Angullia v. Estate & Trust Agencies (1927), Ltd.*, [1938] AC 624 (PC (Singapore)) at p. 632 *per* Lord Romer. So be it, but how can C conceivably rely upon this circumstance as a defence by him to an action for specific performance by A1? Of course not; he, C, has no interest in the estate; he cannot plead a possible jus tertii which is no concern of his. It is his duty to fulfil his contract by paying C. A1 alone is concerned with the creditors, beneficiaries or next of kin of A and this point therefore can never be a defence by C if A1 in fact chooses to sue for specific performance rather than to attempt a compromise in the interest of the estate. This point seems to me misconceived. In any event, on the facts of this case there is no suggestion that there are any unpaid creditors and B is sole next of kin, so the point is academic.

Then, as to the first point. On this question we were referred to the well-known *dictum* of Lush LJ in *Lloyd's v. Harper* (1880), 16 Ch. D 290 (CA) at p. 321:

> I consider it to be an established rule of law that where a contract is made with A for the benefit of B, A can sue on the contract for the benefit of B and recover all that B could have recovered if the contract had been made with B himself.

While in the circumstances it is not necessary to express any concluded opinion thereon, if the learned Lord Justice was expressing a view on the purely common law remedy of damages. I have some difficulty in going all the way with him. If A sues for damages for breach of contract by reason of the failure to pay B he must prove his loss; that may be great or nominal according to circumstances.

I do not see how A can, in conformity with clearly settled principle in assessing damages for breach of contract, rely at common law on B's loss. I agree with the observations of Windeyer J in *Coulls v. Bagot's Executor and Trustee Co. Ltd.* (1967), 119 CLR 460 in the High Court of Australia. But I note, however, that in *Lloyd's v. Harper* (at pp. 315-17) James and Cotton LJJ treated A as trustee for B and I doubt whether Lush LJ thought otherwise.

However, I incline to the view that on the facts of this case damages are nominal for it appears that A died without any assets save and except the agreement which he hoped would keep him and then his widow for their lives. At all events let me assume that damages are nominal. So it is said nominal damages are adequate and the remedy of specific performance ought not to be granted. That is, with all respect, wholly to misunderstand that principle. Equity will grant specific performance when damages are inadequate to meet the justice of the case.

But in any event quantum of damages seldom affects the right to specific performance. If X contracts with Y to buy Blackacre or a rare chattel for a fancy price because the property or chattel has caught his fancy he is entitled to enforce his bargain and it matters not that he could not prove any damage.

In this case the court ought to grant a specific performance order all the more because damages *are* nominal. C has received all the property; justice demands that he pay the price and this can only be done in the circumstances by equitable relief. It is a fallacy to suppose that B is thereby obtaining additional rights; A1 is entitled to compel C to carry out the terms of the agreement. The observations of Holmes LJ already quoted are very much in point.

My Lords, in my opinion the Court of Appeal were clearly right to grant a decree of specific performance. ...

NOTES

1. S.M. Waddams, *The Law of Damages*, 2d ed. (Aurora, ON: Canada Law Book, 1991), at 5.150-5.190 (footnotes omitted) contains a useful analysis of the adequacy of damages aspect of this case:

2. Third Party Beneficiary Contracts

Where one person makes a promise to another for the benefit of a third, the promise is enforceable at the suit of the promisee, but not, according to current law, at the suit of the beneficiary. Ultimately, it seems desirable and likely that the law of contracts will be altered to permit an action to be brought by the beneficiary. The precise form of such a change raises complex questions and falls outside the scope of this work. The only question addressed here is the proper scope of the promisee's remedy.

It has been recognized since the decision in *Beswick v. Beswick* in 1968 that the promisee may sue for specific performance of the contractual obligation. However the view was then expressed, by four of the five law lords, that in an action for damages the promisee would recover only nominal damages. If the beneficiary has no remedy, and the promisee can recover only nominal damages, it is no exaggeration to describe the result, as Lord Reid did, as "grossly unjust."

The injustice was avoided in *Beswick v. Beswick* by granting a decree of specific performance, chiefly because damages were inadequate. There is an oddity in the reasoning here. If nominal damages are appropriate because the plaintiff really has suffered no loss, it follows that no compensation is deserved. Damages in that case are not "inadequate": they fully meet the justice of the plaintiff's claim. On the other hand if, as the court held, the promisee is entitled to specific performance, that must be because the promisee has bought the benefit of the promised performance and is therefore entitled to compel a performance that has been paid for. It seems odd, in those circumstances, to say that the promisee suffers no loss if the performance is not rendered.

There are arguments, however, that substantial damages are appropriate in such a case. One argument is that the promisee will lose the satisfaction of benefiting the third party, a satisfaction that is presumably worth to the promisee what otherwise could have asked of the promisor. Another argument is that the promisee's right to have performance rendered in accordance with the promise is a valuable right that could be compromised for a cash payment; a rational promisor would pay up to the full cost of performance for release from the obligation. If the promisor breaks the promise, and specific enforcement is not decreed, there would seem to be a case for an award of damages in lieu of specific enforcement, and there is ample reason for measuring such damages by the price that a rational promisor would have paid for release from the obligation. It is suggested in a later chapter that this measure of damages is defensible on compensatory principles, for the promisor, by breaking the promise in such circumstances as to preclude an actual decree of specific performance, deprives the promisee of a valuable right, namely the right to bargain with the promisor for release. Against this argument can be made the accusation of circularity. It is only where a contract is specifically enforceable that damages in lieu of specific performance can properly be measured by the defendant's gain from breach, but the third party beneficiary contract is said to be specifically enforceable only because damages are nominal, and therefore, inadequate. So if a persuasive case is made for substantial damages the case for specific enforcement disappears. A possible answer to this point is that an injunction restraining breach could be granted to the promisee even though damages were considered to be adequate, inadequacy of damages not being a requirement for an injunction. Substantial damages could then be defended on the basis of an award in lieu of an injunction.

These complexities indicate, it is submitted, that the only ultimately satisfactory solution will be the recognition of a right of action in the third party, either directly or by some such device as trust. In the absence of such recognition, however, it is not alien to the traditions of the common law to use such devices as are available to achieve just results.

2. In the course of his judgment, Lord Hodson notes that there may be other reasons for not making an order of specific performance in favour of an executor(rix) or administrator(rix):

It is true that specific performance would not be ordered so as to disregard the fiduciary position which the appellant occupies as administratrix. Situations might arise in the administration of an estate when there might be conflicting claims between creditors and persons entitled beneficially otherwise, but this is not such a case. There was in the agreement reference to creditors but there was no evidence directed to this matter and no reason to assume the existence of conflicting claims at the present day.

Waugh v. Slavik
(1975), 62 DLR (3d) 577 (BCSC)

[A father and his nine-year-old son died in a plane crash, and it was uncertain who had died first. The will of the deceased father had left a bequest to his parents, and the residue to his son. However, he had given instructions for the preparation of a new will, which had never been executed. The intended beneficiaries under this instrument signed an agreement providing that the estate was to be divided up in accordance with the deceased's instructions. Later the defendant Slavik, who was the former wife of the deceased and mother of the deceased's son, repudiated the agreement as she believed she would receive the entire residue of the estate from the intestacy of the son. The judge decided that the agreement was supported by consideration on the part of the defendant Slavik and one of the plaintiffs, Waugh, who had given up a claim under the *Administration Act*, RSBC 1960, c. 3, ss. 91 and 92, as the common law spouse of the deceased. The issue was then one of whether Waugh could sue to enforce the agreement given that some of the beneficiaries under it had not provided consideration; that is, they were not giving up any claim by entering into the agreement with Slavik and Waugh.]

BOUCK J: ... *Beswick v. Beswick* decided that specific performance of a contract can be ordered where the persons between whom consideration passed or their personal representatives are parties to the action. This is so despite the fact that strangers to the contract who have not given consideration may benefit from the decree. The minority came to the same conclusion in *Coulls*. The reasoning from these two authorities is attractive and I can see no reason why it should not be applied in Canada. It will do justice between the parties in this action by holding them to their bargain.

Furthermore a decree of specific performance meets other tests the law imposes to determine whether it should be granted. First there is a mutuality between Dianne Waugh and Ann Slavik. Each could have sued the other for specific performance. Secondly, Ann Slavik repudiated the agreement. Dianne Waugh could have chosen to treat the agreement as at an end and sued for damages. Alternatively she could have disregarded the repudiation, treated the contract as if it still existed and sued for specific performance. This is precisely the procedure she chose to follow.

By ordering specific performance the equitable machinery of the law is available to the co-plaintiffs following the reasoning of the House of Lords in *Beswick v. Beswick*. The end result will be the sharing of the estate of Paul Bowers in accordance with the agreement of 22nd March 1974.

THE "CLEAN HANDS" DOCTRINE

Cerilli v. Klodt
(1984), 48 OR (2d) 260

[Klodt agreed to sell a house to Cerilli for $50,000—$4,800 in cash and $45,200 by certified cheque on closing. This agreement was subject to the agreement of Klodt's estranged wife who had a half-interest in the property. She refused to go ahead with the deal at what she assumed was a purchase price of $45,200. However, when she learned of the under the table payment to her husband, which would bring the price up to $50,000, she was willing to proceed with the deal at that price. The Klodts did not complete, Cerilli sued for specific performance, and Mrs. Klodt did not defend against the action.]

SOUTHEY J: [After concluding that Cerilli knew of the reason for the cash payment of $4,800, he continued.] This scheme, in my judgment, was clearly fraudulent, and the result in law is that the agreement between the plaintiff and Robert Klodt is void and unenforceable in the courts. I think it is necessary to refer only to the passage from the decision of the Court of Appeal in England in *Alexander v. Rayson*, [1936] 1 KB 169, which was quoted and applied by the Supreme Court of Canada in *Zimmermann v. Letkeman*, [1978] 1 SCR 1097 at p. 1101. Mr. Justice Martland, delivering the judgment of the court, quoted from the decision of Lord Justice Romer in the *Alexander v. Rayson*, [[1936] 1 KB 169, at 182 (CA)] case as follows:

> It is settled law that an agreement to do an act that is illegal or immoral or contrary to public policy, or to do any act for a consideration that is illegal, immoral or contrary to public policy, is unlawful and therefore void. But it often happens that an agreement which in itself is not unlawful is made with the intention of one or both parties to make use of the subject matter for an unlawful purpose, that is to say a purpose that is illegal, immoral or contrary to public policy. The most common instance of this is an agreement for the sale or letting of an object, where the agreement is unobjectionable on the face of it, but where the intention of both or one of the parties is that the object shall be used by the purchaser or hirer for an unlawful purpose. In such a case any party to the agreement who had the unlawful intention is precluded from suing upon it. *Ex turpi causa non oritur actio.* The action does not lie because the Court will not lend its help to such a plaintiff. Many instances of this are to be found in the books.

Although the agreement was originally intended to defraud Mrs. Klodt, she assented to the sale at a price of $45,200 in a letter from her solicitor, Mr. Rivard, to Mr. Zito dated March 14, 1984. That letter states that Mrs. Klodt has instructed Mr. Rivard to accept the offer to purchase at $45,200. Subsequently, when the fact that Mr. Cerilli had agreed to pay a total of $50,000 became known, Mrs. Klodt, through her solicitor, Mr. Rivard, confirmed that she was prepared to sell her one-half interest in the matrimonial home to Mr. Cerilli on a basis of a purchase price of $50,000. This was in a letter dated May 8, 1984. Mrs. Klodt did not file a statement of defence, and pleadings were noted closed against her.

Mr. Pharand contended that to dismiss the action would do an injustice to Mrs. Klodt in that she would be denied the specific performance of the agreement to sell the property at $50,000, she having indicated her consent to such a decree by her failure to plead.

It is clear from the authorities to which Mr. Humphrey referred, however, that the court is under an obligation to refuse to give effect to an illegal agreement whenever the illegality comes to the attention of the court, even though the parties do not raise it. See the judgment of Mr. Justice Krever in *Menard v. Genereux* (1982), 39 OR (2d) 55 at p. 64, where he quotes from a decision of the Court of Appeal of Saskatchewan in *Williams v. Fleetwood Holdings Ltd.* (1973), 41 DLR (3d) 636 at p. 640 [quoting from *Alexander v. Rayson*, at 190]:

> The moment that the attention of the Court is drawn to the illegality attending the execution of the lease, it is bound to take notice of it, whether such illegality be pleaded or not.

There is another fundamental difficulty with the position of Mrs. Klodt as put forward by Mr. Pharand. It is not the same thing, in my view, to decline to defend an action for specific performance as it is to sue for specific performance and ask the court to enforce the agreement that the party has entered into. If Mrs. Klodt had brought an action for specific performance, it would be apparent that there was, in fact, no agreement having the terms on which she is willing to sell her house. She would not be willing to sell the house for $50,000 with $4,800 going directly to her husband without her having the opportunity of participating in that part of the purchase price. On the other hand, the only basis on which Robert Klodt was willing to sell the house for $50,000 was on the basis that he received $4,800 under the table. There is no agreement for the sale for $50,000 with the full purchase price to be divided between the vendor joint tenants in accordance with their interests.

Furthermore, to permit judgment to go in favour of Mr. Cerilli against Mrs. Klodt because of her failure to plead would be to put the court in the position of enforcing this illegal and dishonest contract to the advantage of one of the wrongdoers. The courts may not be used in that way, and the agreement will not be enforced for the benefit of anyone.

The action for specific performance will be dismissed for these reasons.

NOTES

1. An appeal from *Cerilli* was dismissed on the basis of minutes of settlement: (1986), 55 OR (2d) 399n (CA).

2. Just as the parties cannot consent to judgment for an equitable remedy which is based on a fraud and thereby oust the supervisory role of the courts, rules of civil procedure dealing with default proceedings also provide that a party who claims equitable relief cannot simply sign a default judgment in the registrar's office when the defendant is in default. Instead, that party must move before a judge for judgment. In this manner, the court retains the opportunity to exercise a discretion when granting an equitable remedy even when a party is in default. See, for example, Ontario Rules of Civil Procedure, rr. 19.04-05.

3. *Cerilli* may be contrasted usefully with the following judgment where knowledge that a transaction was in breach of another contract proved insufficient for the invocation of the "clean hands" doctrine. The judgment is also instructive on the nature of the remedy of a declaration as well as the requirement that unclean hands be related directly to the impeached transaction as well as to the party actually seeking equitable relief.

Hong Kong Bank of Canada Ltd. v. Wheeler Holdings Ltd.
[1993] 1 SCR 165

[Respondents Town House and Wellington were "limited-dividend" companies statutorily described as being incorporated to hold and manage low-rental housing and subject to a restriction in their charters to a maximum annual dividend. CHMC loaned both money to build and operate low rental housing for a forty-year term starting on the completion date. The mortgages provided that their terms were in addition to those granted or implied by statute and that they were made pursuant to the *National Housing Act*. Both companies entered into operating agreements with CMHC that prohibited the mortgage or sale of the projects without CMHC approval. The mortgages adopted the terms of the operating agreements as part of the mortgage and stipulated that breach of the operating agreements constituted breach of the mortgages.

A loan made by the Bank of British Columbia to Town House and Wellington, along with the respondent Wheeler Holdings, was secured by second mortgages on the projects and was personally guaranteed by the personal respondents. CMHC did not consent to the second mortgages. This mortgage was among the assets purchased by the respondent Hongkong Bank of Canada ("Hongkong") from the Bank of British Columbia in 1986.

In 1988, Town House and Wellington agreed to sell the projects ("1988 sales") to the respondents 375069 Alberta Ltd. and 386360 Alberta Ltd. ("1988 purchasers"). The 1988 sale agreements provided that title would be given to the 1988 purchasers free and clear of obligations under the CMHC operating agreements, and provided for liquidated damages if such title could not be given. These sale agreements also contained a provision expressly negating and rejecting the covenants implied by s. 62(1) of the *Alberta Land Titles Act* with the result that the transferees did not assume the obligations under the mortgage.

In 1989, Hongkong began an action to foreclose on its second mortgages. Hongkong proposed a judicial sale of the projects ("1989 sale") to yet another numbered company—376491 Alberta Ltd. ("1989 purchaser")—owned by owner of the other two numbered companies. The 1989 sale agreement provided that the 1989 purchaser would get title subject to the CMHC mortgages but free and clear of the terms of the CMHC operating agreements.

Hongkong sought approval of the 1989 sale from the Alberta Court of Queen's Bench, but a Master refused this approval. Hongkong appealed this finding to a chambers judge, and the 1988 purchasers commenced an action seeking a declaration that they were owners of the projects under the 1988 sale agreements and that they were not bound by the CMHC operating agreements. The appeal and the actions were heard together by the chambers judge. The 1989 sale was approved by the chambers judge and the 1988 purchasers were granted the declaration they requested. Appeals were launched by CMHC in respect of each proceeding. CMHC's appeal to the Alberta Court of Appeal was dismissed [(1990), 75 DLR (4th) 307 (Alta. CA)]. The main issue here was whether the appellant mortgagee can successfully impeach a subsequent mortgage and sale on the basis of statutorily mandated contractual terms prohibiting a sale or disposition of the mortgaged property. Issues arose as to the applicability of the equitable "clean hands" doctrine, the alleged illegality of the second mortgages and the 1988 and 1989 sales, the vires of the corporate powers of Town House and Wellington, and the respondents' right to redeem the properties on payment of the amounts outstanding under the first mortgages.]

SOPINKA J (delivering the judgment of the Court): ...

1. Clean Hands

CMHC argues that the respondents should be denied the relief they seek because they are guilty of misconduct such as to disentitle them from equitable relief. Assuming for the moment that Town House and Wellington were legally capable of granting the second mortgage to the Bank of British Columbia (Hongkong Bank) and of disposing of the projects via the agreements for sale, it is evident that they have committed a flagrant breach of their contracts with CMHC. However, it is not Town House and Wellington who seek relief from the court in this action. With respect to the parties who are seeking relief from the court, I am not convinced that the remedies sought constitute equitable relief in every case or that there is in any event sufficient evidence before the court to conclude that these respondents have unclean hands. There is accordingly no equitable ground upon which to deny relief to the respondents.

In determining whether the respondents are entitled to equitable relief, it is important not to paint all the respondents with the same brush. As was noted in *Moody v. Cox*, [1917] 2 Ch. 71 (CA), at pp. 87-88, "equity will not apply the principle about clean hands unless the depravity, the dirt in question on the hand, has an immediate and necessary relation to the equity sued for." CMHC seeks to paint all respondents with the same brush, arguing that equity should deny all relief in this case because Town House and Wellington are seeking to escape obligations to CMHC. However, an entire transaction does not become tainted merely because certain parties to the transaction may have unclean hands. Town House and Wellington may be seeking to escape obligations to CMHC, but this does not taint all transactions involving properties subject to those obligations. It is necessary to show that the respondents actually seeking relief from the court are in fact seeking equitable relief and are guilty of wrongdoing amounting to unclean hands.

The two numbered companies who are the purchasers under the 1988 sale agreements seek a declaration that they are the beneficial owners of the properties in question pursuant to these agreements. There has been significant debate in the literature and jurisprudence as to whether a declaration constitutes equitable relief or is a *sui generis* remedy and, if it is the latter, whether equitable principles should bar relief. The Chancery Courts of England had long exercised a limited jurisdiction to grant declaratory judgments, which power was expanded by the *Chancery Act* of 1850. With the merging of the two court systems under the *Judicature Act, 1873*, declaratory jurisdiction was also assumed by the courts of common law. If one categorizes remedies by virtue of their origin in the Court of Chancery or the courts of common law, then, the declaratory judgment would seem to be an equitable remedy.

However, starting with the English case of *Chapman v. Michaelson*, [1909] 1 Ch. 238 (CA), a number of courts have held that the declaratory judgment does not constitute equitable relief. In *Chapman*, the Court of Appeal distinguished the granting of a declaration that security documents were invalid from the more common equitable remedy of delivering up of the unenforceable security documents. In the latter situation, relief was always made subject to equitable conditions of repayment being imposed on the borrower, but the court refused to impose similar conditions on a borrower granted a declaratory remedy on the grounds that the declaration "is not equitable relief" (p. 242). Although some English decisions have taken a different approach in the intervening years, the *Chapman* approach was reiterated in *Tito v. Waddell (No. 2)*, [1977] Ch. 106, in which Megarry V-C stated that the remedy is "neither a legal nor an equitable remedy, but statutory" (p. 259).

This view as to the nature of the declaratory remedy has largely prevailed in Australia and New Zealand. Similarly, the consensus in Canada seems to be that the remedy is *sui generis* rather than wholly equitable. Sarna in *The Law of Declaratory Judgments* (2nd ed. 1988), for example, states at p. 216 that "the development of Canadian case law has seen little or no reference to the equitable nature of the remedy."

However, a number of Canadian judgments at the lower levels have applied equitable principles to those who seek a declaration. For example, in *Sara v. Sara* (1962), 36 DLR (2d) 499, the British Columbia Court of Appeal refused to grant a declaration that a marriage was void to a man who had polygamously married his Canadian wife in order to be admitted to the country, and then been supported by her for a number of years after his arrival, on the basis *inter alia* that the husband had unclean hands. *Re Morris and Morris* (1973), 42 DLR (3d) 550 (Man. CA) and *Re MacDonald and Law Society of Manitoba* (1975), 54 DLR (3d) 372 (Man. QB) also take the view that the declaratory remedy is an equitable one. At least some American decisions are to the same effect, such as *Campbell v. Campbell*, 300 NYS 760 (Sup. Ct. 1937) and *Mills v. Mills*, 179 A 5 (Conn. 1935), in which the plaintiffs were held to be disentitled to declaratory relief on the basis of unclean hands and *laches*, respectively.

While the above decisions all seem to have been based, expressly or impliedly, on the view that declaratory relief was equitable in nature, it appears that even if the remedy is seen to be *sui generis*, equitable principles such as clean hands can play a role in the exercise of the court's discretion whether or not to grant the remedy. As Zamir states in *The Declaratory Judgment* (1986), at p. 191:

> This discretion is employed, as discretion was originally employed in respect of all equitable remedies, primarily to do justice in the particular case before the court. It is wide enough to allow the court to take into account virtually all objections and defences possible in equitable proceedings.

Zamir goes on to cite various English cases in which the motives of the plaintiff were taken into account, the claim was dismissed on the basis of *laches*, and inequitable behaviour on the part of the plaintiff was considered to be a defence to a declaratory judgment.

Some other authors take a different approach. In *Equity—Doctrines and Remedies* (2nd ed. 1984), at p. 466, Meagher, Gummow and Lehane review a number of decisions and conclude that on both authority and principle, the traditional equitable barriers to relief do not apply to declaratory relief. Likewise, Sarna, *supra*, at p. 216, states that "there has yet to appear a serious proposal that the exercise of discretion on declaratory proceedings be confined to the general principles governing equity."

While it may be that certain equitable restrictions such as the requirement that legal remedies be insufficient and that there be a probability of irreparable or at least very serious damage should not be applied to declaratory remedies, I would conclude that in the exercise of the discretion whether or not to grant a declaration, the court may take into account certain equitable principles such as the conduct of the party seeking the relief. In the context of this case, then, the allegation that the 1988 purchasers have unclean hands should be addressed.

The only real evidence before this Court with regard to the alleged misconduct of the 1988 purchasers is that they knew that the 1988 sale agreements constituted a breach of the CMHC mortgages and in fact agreed to pay a higher price for the land if the Operating Agreements could be successfully breached. As well, there is the fact that shortly after the execution of the sale agreements, the sole director and shareholder of the numbered companies married the sister of the directors of Town House and Wellington. In my view, this evidence is too tenuous a foundation for the application of the principle. Absent a finding of collusion, knowledge by a purchaser that the vendor is breaching a contractual provision would be insufficient to disentitle the purchaser to equitable relief. This conclusion applies with greater force to the exercise of discretion to refuse declaratory relief in which the "unclean hands" doctrine is applied in a less structured manner and is but one of the factors to be considered. With respect to the family connection, no finding was made by the courts below with respect to any scheme between the parties to defeat the rights of CMHC. Without such a finding, this fact alone is of little importance.

The only party unquestionably seeking equitable relief in this case is Hongkong, which is seeking a judicial sale in its mortgage foreclosure action. There is no evidence that Hongkong was guilty of any misconduct. Hongkong seems particularly free of suspicion of misconduct because it was not even the original mortgagee. It purchased a mortgage acquired by its predecessor in title. If Hongkong were the original mortgagee, there might be suspicion that the second mortgages had been made with the intention of intentionally defaulting in order to escape obligations to CMHC. Here there can be no such suspicion because Hong-kong purchased the mortgages some five years after they were first made. There is no evidence of a plot to enter into second mortgages as part of a scheme to escape obligations to CMHC, but even if there was such a scheme Hongkong could not have been a participant. The mere fact that the relationship among the numbered companies, Town House and Wellington may arouse suspicions is not a sufficient basis upon which to deny an equitable remedy to Hongkong.

With respect to the numbered company which seeks to purchase under the judicial sale in the foreclosure action, CMHC argues that all participants in a foreclosure action, including the prospective purchasers at a court-conducted sale, must be governed by equitable principles. In this case, it is evident that the 1989 purchaser knew of the provisions of the Operating Agreement, and in fact the Offer to Purchase is expressly stated to be contingent on a declaration by the court that the terms, conditions and obligations in the Operating Agreement will not be binding on the purchaser. Nonetheless, aside from the relationship of the 1989 purchaser to the other numbered companies and to Town House and Wellington, which will be discussed below, there does not appear to be evidence of wrongdoing on the part of the 1989 purchaser which would warrant a finding of unclean hands. As is the case with the 1988 purchasers, mere knowledge that one is participating in a transaction which constitutes a breach of a contract to which one is not a party does not seem to me to be sufficient to constitute unclean hands. Further, a review of the jurisprudence in this area fails to reveal any cases in which a judicial sale has been disallowed on the basis of the unclean hands of the proposed purchaser, which may well be a result of the fact that, as here, it is not the purchaser but the mortgagee who seeks relief from the court, even though the purchaser stands to benefit from the relief.

CMHC relied on *Re Valley Vu Realty (Ottawa) Ltd. and Victoria & Grey Trust Co.* (1984), 44 OR (2d) 526 (H.C.), aff'd. (1984), 47 OR (2d) 544n (CA), and *Colonial & Home Fuel Distributors Ltd. v. Skinners' Ltd.* (1963), 39 DLR (2d) 579 (Man. QB), aff'd. (1963), 46 DLR (2d) 695 (Man. CA), aff'd. [1964] SCR v, in support of its contention that relief should be denied on equitable grounds. In my view, both cases are distinguishable because in both cases there was direct evidence that the very parties who were seeking equitable relief were guilty of misconduct in that they were parties to a breach of contract.

In *Re Valley Vu, supra,* the court refused to assist a mortgagor in obtaining a discharge of a mortgage through prepayment because the mortgagor had intentionally breached the terms of the mortgage, including a provision restraining alienation. In this case, neither Hongkong nor the numbered companies is party to a breach of contract. The only parties in breach are Town House and Wellington. In *Colonial,* the court refused to allow a party to use a company which was his alter ego to circumvent a restrictive covenant. In this case, there is no clear evidence and no finding that either Hongkong or any of the numbered companies were the alter egos of Town House and Wellington. I agree with Lieberman JA's assessment of the respondents' relationship (at p. 168):

> One can, of course, speculate about the motivation behind the parties entering into the agreements for sale and its connection or otherwise with the relationship of those parties, but without evidence to substantiate such a speculation the appellant's submission falls far short of establishing a common operating mind behind the respondent companies. There is in my view

no direct evidence to establish an intention to circumvent the contractual liability of the original mortgagors, and I cannot infer such an intention. This is not a case justifying the piercing of the corporate veil.

The relationship between the numbered companies and Town House and Wellington is undoubtedly suspicious, but without direct evidence it is impossible to conclude that they jointly acted to free Town House and Wellington of their obligations towards CMHC.

The numbered companies do seek to avoid the CMHC operating agreement but in so far as the terms of the operating agreement are incorporated into the mortgages, which is the extent the statute contemplates, CMHC retains the right to accelerate the loan or increase the interest rates. Thus even if Hongkong is granted the equitable relief which it seeks, CMHC is not left without a remedy for breach of its operating agreements.

I therefore conclude that there is no basis for refusing equitable relief or declaratory relief to the respondents on the "clean hands" principle.

[The court went on to hold that the statutorily mandated contract provisions could not operate independently to prevent or invalidate the transactions in question; they did not apply as against strangers to that contract. In so doing, the court relied variously on the fact that the legislation did not outlaw such transactions but rather confined itself to requiring CMHC to include such terms in the relevant agreements. It also was influenced by the bar against restraints on alienation. However, it was not prepared to go as far as the chambers judge and make an order to the effect that the respondents were entitled to redeem the properties by paying the money due under the first mortgage held by CMHC. The relevant provisions respecting redemption were not a sufficient clog on the equity of redemption to justify such an order.]

Appeal allowed in part.

Bolianatz Estate v. Simon
2006 SKCA 16, 275 Sask. R 170

[Irving Simon, a beneficiary under a will, had originally been named executor, but he renounced his position when it came to light that he had stolen some $19,000 from the testator. The estate sought to have Simon's inheritance denied. Lane and Richards JJA, in separate judgments, refused to deny Simon's bequest. Cameron JA dissented.]

[1] LANE JA:

[Lane JA held that a bequest could not be denied unless the legatee had committed fraud for the purpose of acquiring it, and unless the bequest would not have been made but for the testator's perception of the good character of the legatee—neither of which was made out on the facts.]

. . .

[38] RICHARDS JA: ... I agree with the conclusion of Justice Lane and his reasons for reaching it but wish to set out my own views on three points: (a) the question of whether the Testator would have denied the bequest to Mr. Simon had he known of the fraud; (b) the application of the clean hands maxim; and (c) the application of the *ex turpi causa* principle.

[39] Overall, I believe that allowing this appeal would effectively open the door to a system whereby beneficiaries can be assessed to determine if they are morally worthy of receiving their bequests. This is problematic because the principles on which such assessments could be made are not apparent. Secondarily, a move in that direction would tend to create undesirable uncertainty in relation to wills and, as a result, would tend to impose the expense and delay of litigation on many estates.

I. Factual Matters

[Richards JA suggested that very clear evidence would be required to show that the testator would have discontinued the bequest had he known of the theft, and that no such evidence had been proved.]

. . .

II. The Clean Hands Maxim

[48] In any event, and more fundamentally, I also have concerns about the application of the clean hands maxim to the facts of this case. In my opinion, it does not apply in the circumstances at hand for two reasons.

[49] First, one of the most basic features of the maxim is that it engages in circumstances where a plaintiff in equity approaches the court for relief. That, of course, is reflected in the standard formulation of the maxim itself: "He who comes into equity must come with clean hands" and, I note, it is deeply rooted in the case law back to the earliest decisions. In other words, the very nature of the clean hands principle is that it operates against a plaintiff to deny him or her relief in equity which would otherwise be available. See: Spry, *The Principles of Equitable Remedies*, 6th ed. (Agincourt: Carswell, 2001) at p. 169; Denis Browne, *Ashburner's Principles of Equity*, 2nd ed. (London: Butterworth & Co., 1933) at p. 465; John McGhee, QC, *Snell's Equity*, 31st ed. (London: Thomson Sweet and Maxwell, 2005) at p. 98. The maxim is not a broad instrument which is used in a general or open-ended way to see that justice is done or to sanction wrongdoing. I am aware of no situation where it has been applied other than as a response to a claim advanced by a plaintiff.

[50] This basic reality is significant in this case. These proceedings were initiated by Mr. Bolen, the administrator of the Testator's estate pursuant to Queen's Bench Rule 452(d)(i) for the determination of a question related to the administration of the estate. No equitable relief is being sought by any party. More to the point, no equitable relief is being sought by Mr. Simon. It seems to me, therefore, that the basic prerequisite for the application of the clean hands maxim is simply not met. Mr. Simon is not a plaintiff in equity seeking a remedy from the court. I also observe, parenthetically, that there is no apparent precedent for invoking the clean hands maxim on the theory that Mr. Simon might have become a plaintiff if the administrator had refused to pay out his legacy and Mr. Simon had then chosen to sue for it.

[51] My second concern about the application of the clean hands maxim in this appeal is that, on the basis of the existing authorities, there is not a sufficiently close connection between Mr. Simon's crime and his legacy to engage the maxim. The fact Mr. Simon took the funds near the time the will was executed and that some of those funds might ultimately have found their way into his hands as an inheritance does not create a sufficient link between the fraud and the bequest.

[52] *Halsbury's Laws of England*, 4th ed., vol. 16(2), (London: LexisNexis UK, 2003) at pp. 240-241 describes the nature of the necessary connection between wrong doing in issue and the equitable relief being sought in order to make the clean hands principle applicable:

> A court of equity refuses relief to a claimant whose conduct in regard to the subject matter of the litigation has been improper. ...
>
> *The maxim does not mean that equity strikes at depravity in a general way; the cleanliness required is to be judged in relation to the relief sought, and the conduct complained of must have an immediate and necessary relation to the equity sued for.* [Emphasis added, cite omitted]

[53] The much cited decision in *Moody v. Cox and Hatt*, [1917] 2 Ch. 71 illustrates the point. In that case, a solicitor for one party accepted a bribe (without notifying his clients) during contract negotiations. His clients decided not to rescind the entire contract as a consequence of the bribe, but contended that the other side (which had offered the bribe) was barred from any equitable remedy in relation to the contract. In rejecting this contention, Lord Scrutton wrote at pp. 87-88:

> ... I think it is quite clear that the passage in *Dering v. Earl of Winchelsea*, 1 Cox 318 which has been referred to shows that *equity will not apply the principle about clean hands unless the depravity, the dirt in question on the hand, has an immediate and necessary relation to the equity sued for.* In this case the bribe has no immediate relation to rectification, if rectification were asked or to rescission in connection with a matter not in any way connected with the bribe. [Emphasis added]

See also: *HongKong Bank of Canada v. Wheeler Holdings*, [1993] 1 SCR 167 at paras. 32-33.

[54] All of this is directly applicable here. There is no suggestion that Mr. Simon was included in the Testator's will because of some illegal action on the part of Mr. Simon and there is self-evidently no direct connection between the fraud itself and the Testator's bequest to Mr. Simon. Thus, putting aside the basic point that he is not making a claim in equity in these proceedings, Mr. Simon's criminal conduct does not have "an immediate and necessary relation to the equity sued for" within the meaning of the long-standing line of cases in this area.

[55] In my opinion, therefore, the authorities indicate that the clean hands maxim, as generally understood and applied, cannot be used to deny Mr. Simon his inheritance. He is not a plaintiff in equity seeking the assistance of the court. In addition, there is not a sufficient connection between his crime and the legacy.

[56] As a result, it strikes me that the real question in this appeal concerning the clean hands maxim is whether the Court should push past the precedents and extend the law of wills by taking an expanded view of the maxim. Perhaps put more accurately, the real question is whether the Court should take the position that immoral or illegal conduct by a beneficiary, not directly connected to the making of a bequest, can defeat that bequest.

[57] In answering this question, it is helpful to consider the broader pattern of the law in this field. In that regard, the authorities appear to have recognized only a limited number of very particular situations where the conduct of a beneficiary, in and of itself, will invalidate an inheritance. The first of these is where the beneficiary perpetrates a fraud on the testator and obtains the legacy by virtue of that fraud. See: *Kennell v. Abbott*, 31 ER 416. The second is where the testator is coerced by the beneficiary into a bequest he or she does not want to make. See: *Hall v. Hall* (1868), LR 1 P & D 481; J. Martyn et al., *Theobald on Wills*, 16th ed. (London: Sweet & Maxwell, 2001) at 3-27. The third is where the beneficiary kills the testator. In such circumstances he or she is de-barred from taking under the will or intestacy of the victim. See: *Cleaver v. Mutual Reserve Fund Life Association*, [1892] 1 QB 147; *In the Estate of Hall v. Knight and Baxter*, [1914] P. 1.

[58] Aside from such exceptions, the general orientation of the law is very much against involving the courts in superintending the question of whether particular beneficiaries merit their inheritances. Bequests are not denied because a beneficiary is of bad character, has behaved immorally or has been involved in criminal activity.

[59] In terms of general principle, this recommends itself as a sound approach. It fits with the basic assumption that individuals are entitled to dispose of their property as they see fit. It promotes certainty and efficiency in the handling of wills by avoiding costly and protracted disputes over the proper allocation of testators' assets. And finally, it recognizes and avoids the deep problems involved in attempting to identify the particular kinds of behaviour which should deny an inheritance.

[60] The significance of this last consideration is readily illustrated by simple variations on the facts of this case. For example, what would the result of this appeal be if Mr. Simon had stolen only $200? What if he had stolen just $10 but had assaulted the Testator in the process? What if he had stolen the $19,000 but the Testator, on his deathbed, appeared to forgive the crime? What if he had stolen nothing but, assuming such a property existed, had negligently burned down an uninsured house comprising the bulk of the estate? Finally, what if he had stolen nothing but, unknown to the Testator, had slandered the Testator by falsely and publicly accusing him of serious moral misconduct?

[61] These questions show that broadening the situations where an inheritance can be denied on the basis of a beneficiary's conduct would involve a host of difficult inquiries which do not lend themselves to any sort of principled response. Simply stated, how could the law make meaningful distinctions between the fact patterns in the preceding paragraph in order to determine which of them should lead to the inheritance being denied? The difficulty in answering that question suggests there are good reasons for continued travel on the path the law has followed to date, i.e. the path which restricts judicial intervention in this area to limited and specific situations such as where a testator acts fraudulently, exercises coercion or kills the testator.

[62] On the specific facts of this case, I am not persuaded that there is a way to both grant Mr. Bolen the relief he seeks and to confine the rationale for any such decision in a way which avoids drawing the courts into a realm where there is no principled basis for making decisions. ...

[63] In sum, I believe the application of the clean hands maxim, or of some equivalent approach, on the facts of this case would necessarily engage a principle which would tend to create undesirable uncertainty in relation to wills. It would open the door to litigation

which would involve the adjudication of questions which do not yield to principled resolution and, as a secondary consequence, would increase expense and delay in the distribution of estates.

III. Ex Turpi Causa

[64] I am also not persuaded that the doctrine of *ex turpi causa non oritur actio* has any application to this appeal.

. . .

[72] CAMERON JA (dissenting):

[The following extract from the judgment of Cameron JA deals with the application of the "clean hands" doctrine:]

. . .

[134] ... I am of the respectful opinion ... that Mr. Simon is not entitled to the legacy, which is to say he is in no position to successfully lay claim to it because his fraud and theft are so closely related to the legacy as to make it unconscionable for him to do so. That relationship is such, in my view, as to invite the application of the equitable doctrine of clean hands.

[135] Before elaborating upon this, I should like to make the point that contentious business involving the administration of the estates of deceased persons traditionally fell within the jurisdiction of the Court of Chancery as a court of equity. The point does not have the significance it once did, since the administration of law and equity has been fused, and since the Court of Queen's Bench is expressly directed to administer concurrently all rules of equity and the common law. Still, the point is worth making, for the doctrine of clean hands is an equitable doctrine, open to be invoked by the Court in the exercise of its equitable jurisdiction.

[136] There is a companion point I should also like to make, and this has to do with the nature of a claim by a legatee seeking to enforce payment of a testamentary gift. A residuary legatee does not have a beneficial ownership in the assets of the estate and does not, on the death of the testator, become equitable owner of any part of the unadministered estate. The executor takes full title to the testator's property, and a residuary legatee has only an equitable chose in action, a right to compel the administration of the estate. Once the residue of the estate is allocated by the executor on completion of the residuary accounts, however, the executor becomes the trustee, and the interest of the residuary legatee then becomes that of a beneficiary under a trust. (See, Harold Greville Hanbury & Jill E. Martin, *Modern Equity*, 16th ed. (London: Sweet & Maxwell Ltd., 2001) at pp. 59-62.)

[137] The significance of these two points is this: Suppose Mr. Simon were before the Court of Queen's Bench claiming the legacy. His would be a claim for relief in the nature of an order compelling the administration of the estate or enforcing the trust in his favour. Such claims engage the jurisdiction of the Court in relation to the administration of estates and trusts, including its equitable jurisdiction in that regard. That being so, the door would be open for the administrator to rely on the doctrine of clean hands in defence of the relief sought by Mr. Simon. In this connection I note that *The Queen's Bench Act, 1998*, states in section 55 that, "The rules of equity may be relied on by way of defence." The door would

also be open for the Court to apply the doctrine of clean hands and deny the relief sought by Mr. Simon if satisfied that his fraud and theft had the requisite "immediate and necessary relation" to the sought-after relief as to make it unjust to grant that relief.

[138] While perhaps self-evident I should add that I think it appropriate, for the purpose of addressing the issue of Mr Simon's entitlement to the legacy, to suppose he were before the Court lying claim to it. I say this in light of the question placed before the Court: Is Mr. Simon entitled to the legacy in view of his conduct? He is entitled to the legacy if he is in a position to claim it; otherwise he is not. That being so, I think the question is best approached from the perspective of a claim by Mr. Simon to recover the legacy.

[139] On this approach, the critical issue is whether there exists a sufficient nexus between Mr. Simon's fraud and theft, on the one hand, and the legacy and his claim to it, on the other, so as to make it unjust to order payment of the legacy at his instance.

[140] This much is clear. Mr. Simon's fraud is not connected to the legacy in the most direct sense, that is in the sense the legacy was obtained by fraud. Were it necessary for the connection to be that direct, as a prerequisite to invoking the equitable doctrine of clean hands, his claim to the legacy could not be denied, even though the legacy is tainted by fraud and would not have been given to him had the testator been aware of the fraud.

[141] In my judgment, however, the nexus need not be this direct. Were it otherwise, resort to the general principle lying at the core of the doctrine of clean hands would be thus confined, which is to say confined to those instances in which the general principle has crystallized into more specific and precise principles in relation to transactions procured by fraud, misrepresentation, undue influence, and so on. In other words the general principle would, as such, cease to have any but rhetorical value. But that is not the case. The general principle remains operative, as such, notwithstanding its crystallization into more specific principles regarding the effects of fraud and its like on transactions of one kind or another and the availability of remedies of one kind or another.

[142] And it is here where my opinion comes to rest, for I am of the view that Mr. Simon's fraud and theft are so closely connected to the legacy in *time* and *effect* and *substance* as to make it unconscionable for him to receive the legacy.

[143] The legacy consists of a third of the estate, which in turn consisted of money in the bank, the bulk of which was attributable to the money the testator had received from his sister's estate. Mr. Simon's fraud in gaining access to the testator's bank account and stealing a good part of the money in the account occurred at the very time the testator was conferring the legacy. That is the connection *in time*. The connection *in effect* is that the testator, had he known of Mr. Simon's fraud and theft, would not have conferred the legacy and, had he been capable of doing so, would have revoked the legacy on discovery of Mr. Simon's actions. That leaves the connection *in substance*. Mr. Simon stole the amount of the legacy and more. Indeed, he stole more than half the corpus of the estate and as much as two thirds of the money the testator had received from his sister's estate, the receipt of which had prompted the testator to make his Will.

[144] In these circumstances, I cannot accept the notion that a court, charged with the adminstration of the rules of equity, would allow Mr. Simon to successfully lay claim to the legacy. The only basis upon which a court might allow him to do so is this: While his hands are so legally, morally, and distressingly dirty, this counts for nothing because the dirt upon his hands and the relief he seeks lack "the immediate and necessary relation" required of the

doctrine of clean hands. Even if I should think—as I do not—that this test is that narrow, which is to say that it demands a connection equivalent to the direct connection associated with a legacy procured by fraud, or obtained, maintained, or assisted through fraud, I should look to broaden the test or its application in keeping with the nature of equitable principles as flexible, as capable of direct application rather than by analogy, and as resistant to ossification. I simply cannot see equity allowing Mr. Simon to successfully lay his hands on the gift in light of the close connection in time and effect and substance between the making of the gift and his unconscionable conduct.

[145] On this basis alone I would hold that Mr. Simon is not entitled to the legacy. ...

Appeal dismissed.

[Leave to appeal to the Supreme Court of Canada was refused: [2006] SCCA no. 222.]

LACHES

As we saw much earlier in dealing with damages, delay in the institution and prosecution of proceedings may have a dramatic effect upon the amount of damages awarded to a successful plaintiff. At equity, however, the consequences of delay or "*laches*" may go further and result in the total denial of equitable relief. "A court of equity," said Lord Camden in *Smith v. Clay* (1767), 2 Amb. 645, 3 Brown, Ch. 639, "has always refused its aid to stale demands, where the party slept upon his rights, and acquiesced for a great length of time. Nothing can call forth this court into activity but conscience, good faith, and reasonable diligence; where these are wanting, the court is passive, and does nothing. Laches and neglect are always discountenanced, and therefore, from the beginning of this jurisdiction, there was always a limitation to suits in this court."

At one stage, it was thought that equity demanded promptness of litigants and that unreasonable delay irrespective of any other considerations would defeat a plea for equitable relief. However, the better view is that it's necessary that the plaintiff has by the delay either acquiesced in the defendant's conduct or prejudiced the defendant. In the leading case of *Lindsay Petroleum Co. v. Hurd* (1874), LR 5 PC 221, it was held that:

> The doctrine of laches in courts of equity is not an arbitrary or a technical doctrine. Where it would be practically unjust to give a remedy, either because the party has, by his conduct, done that which might fairly be regarded as equivalent to a waiver of it, or where, by his conduct and neglect he has, though perhaps not waiving that remedy, yet put the other party in a situation in which it would not be reasonable to place him if the remedy were afterwards to be asserted, in either of these cases lapse of time and delay are most material. But in every case if an argument against relief, which otherwise would be just, if founded upon mere delay, that delay of course not amounting to a bar by any Statute of Limitations, the validity of that defence must be tried upon principles substantially equitable. Two circumstances always important in such cases are the length of the delay and the nature of the acts done during the interval, which might affect either party and cause a balance of justice or injustice in taking the one course or the other, so far as relates to the remedy.

In *Erlanger v. New Sombrero Phosphate Co.* (1878), 3 AC 1218, Lord Blackburn cited the above passage from *Lindsay Petroleum* and then wrote:

> I have looked in vain for any authority which gives a more distinct and definite rule than this; and I think, from the nature of the inquiry, it must always be a question of more or less, depending on the degree of diligence which might reasonably be required, and the degree of change which has occurred, whether the balance of justice or injustice is in favour of granting the remedy or withholding it. The determination of such a question must largely depend on the turn of mind of those who have to decide, and must therefore be subject to uncertainty; but that, I think, is inherent in the nature of the inquiry.

These passages from *Lindsay Petroleum* and *Erlanger* were cited with approval by the Supreme Court of Canada in *Harris v. Lindeborg*, [1931] SCR 235. In *M.(K.) v. M.(H.)*, [1992] 3 SCR 6 La Forest J wrote (at para. 98):

> [T]here are two distinct branches to the laches doctrine, and either will suffice as a defence to a claim in equity. What is immediately obvious from all of the authorities is that mere delay is insufficient to trigger laches under either of its two branches. Rather, the doctrine considers whether the delay of the plaintiff constitutes acquiescence or results in circumstances that make the prosecution of the action unreasonable. Ultimately, laches must be resolved as a matter of justice as between the parties, as is the case with any equitable doctrine.

The following case provides an example of a situation where a lengthy delay did not prevent the assertion of a claim.

Grauer Estate v. Government of Canada
(1986), 1 FTR 51

[The plaintiffs were seeking a declaration that a Crown expropriation in 1954 had been "made without or in excess or jurisdiction"—that is, was a nullity. (Land had been expropriated to build an addition to Vancouver International Airport but was never built because plans changed.) At a hearing in 1954, a price was fixed for compensation and a declaration made to the effect that the property in question vested in the Crown. The plaintiffs did not ever accept the compensation or sign any release in favour of the Crown. However, the Crown refused to abandon the expropriation.]

COLLIER J: [After considering a number of arguments and finding for the plaintiff, the court considered the final defence, that of *laches*.] ... I was referred, by counsel for the defendants, on this point, to what I wrote in *Guerin v. The Queen*, [1982] 2 FC 385 at pp. 428-29, concerning that legal defence:

> The law, as to the operation and effect of the doctrine of *laches* is, to my mind, accurately set out in *Halsbury's Laws of England*, [4th ed., vol. 16; see also R.E. Megarry and P.V. Baker, eds., *Snell's Principles of Equity*, 27th ed. (London: Sweet & Maxwell, 1973), 35], at paragraph 1476:
>
> > 1476. *The defence of laches.* A plaintiff in equity is bound to prosecute his claim without undue delay. This is in pursuance of the principle which has underlain the Stat-

utes of Limitation, *vigilantibus et dormientibus lex succurrit*. A court of equity refuses its aid to stale demands, where the plaintiff has slept upon his right and acquiesced for a great length of time. He is then said to be barred by his *laches*.

[A]nd, at paragraph 1477:

In determining whether there has been such delay as to amount to *laches*, the chief points to be considered are (1) acquiescence on the plaintiff's part, and (2) any change of position that has occurred on the defendant's part. Acquiescence in this sense does not mean standing by while the violation of a right is in progress, but assent after the violation has been completed and the plaintiff has become aware of it.

[A]gain, at paragraph 1478:

1478. *Acquiescence as an element in laches.* The chief element in *laches* is acquiescence, and sometimes this has been described as the sole ground for creating a bar in equity by the lapse of time. Acquiescence implies that the person acquiescing is aware of his rights and is in a position to complain of an infringement of them.

Hence acquiescence depends on knowledge, capacity and freedom. As regards knowledge, persons cannot be said to acquiesce in the claims of others unless they are fully cognisant of their right to dispute them. Where a plaintiff is kept in ignorance of his cause of action through the defendant's fraud, time will only begin to run from the time when the plaintiff discovers the truth or ought reasonably to have done so. It is not necessary, however, that the plaintiff should have known the exact relief to which he was entitled; it is enough that he knew the facts constituting his title to relief. As regards capacity, there is no acquiescence, and *laches* is not imputed, while the party is a minor or is mentally disordered.

[A]nd, at paragraph 1480:

1480. *Change in defendant's position.* Regard must be had to any change in the defendant's position which has resulted from the plaintiff's delay in bringing his action. This may be, for instance, because by the lapse of time he has lost the evidence necessary for meeting the claim. A court of equity will not allow a dormant claim to be set up when the means of resisting it, if it turns out to be unfounded, have perished.

[A]nd, finally, at paragraph 1481:

Apart from statute, time alone was no bar to an action in a case of express trust. Time still is no bar in certain cases of breach of trust, although, where there is no statutory bar, an action for breach of trust, like any other equitable claim, may be barred by acquiescence, whether this consists in assent to the breach of trust or in subsequent condonation, or by other circumstances which, combined with delay, make it inequitable to allow the action.

This action was commenced in 1974. The defendants contended the plaintiffs have waited too long to bring suit. Reference was made to a number of possible witnesses, all now dead. Those witnesses might, in my view, have been able to testify on the issue of the dealings with de Havilland, and as to whether or not there was invalidity, as alleged by the plaintiffs in respect of that matter. The defendants also referred to the facts that documents have been lost or destroyed.

I have found, on the evidence of witnesses still remaining and on the documentary evidence tendered, in favor of the defendants on that particular issue: against invalidity.

I am unable to see there has been any deterioration, or change, in the defendant's position, attributable to delay in bringing this action.

I point out the expropriation took place in 1954. The evidence discloses no serious effort; by Transport, to discuss compensation was made until 1957. The information proceedings were not commenced until 1959, and not disposed of until 1962. The plaintiffs have remained in occupation since the taking. A demand for possession was made in 1974, but not followed up.

The defence of *laches* fails.

In contrast, in the next case, the Supreme Court of Canada regarded delay (when combined with other factors) as fatal to the plaintiff's claim for a permanent injunction though not, as seen already in chapter 10, "Financial Relief in Equity," to the equitable remedy of compensation.

Cadbury Schweppes Ltd. v. FBI Foods Ltd.
[1999] 1 SCR 142

[The relevant facts appear in the earlier extract in chapter 10.]

BINNIE J: ...

L. Award of a Permanent Injunction

Injunctive relief, whether interim, interlocutory or permanent, is available in appropriate circumstances to restrain the apprehended or continued misuse or disclosure of confidential information. The problems here were, firstly, the delay of the respondents in asserting their rights coupled with the appellants' change of circumstances in the interim, relying at least in part on the respondents' inactivity; secondly, the trial judge's finding that the protected information was "nothing very special"; and thirdly, the conclusion of the trial judge that any loss could be adequately remedied by financial compensation.

(1) Delay Coupled with Change in Circumstances

The trial judge considered this objection to be virtually conclusive. "This is not a case for an injunction," she wrote (at p. 347), "and has not been since mid-1983, if it ever was." The respondents were slow to assert their rights against the appellants, and, once asserted, were slow in pressing ahead with the action. Caesar Cocktail entered the market on April 15, 1983. The respondents knew then that the appellants were selling a copy of Clamato juice minus the clam broth. The fact the respondents may have delayed action under a misapprehension of their legal rights was certainly a consideration relevant to the defence of acquiescence raised against them, but the delay thus explained away may nevertheless be taken into consideration when weighing the equities of a permanent injunction. On January 10, 1985 the appellants paid $955,000 for the assets of the bankrupt Caesar Canning influenced, at least in part, by the continuing lack of action on the part of the respondents.

It was not until June 19, 1987 that the respondents wrote a "cease and desist" letter to the FBI companies threatening litigation. An action was commenced about a year later. The appellants sought further particulars of the statement of claim, and a further year passed before the plaintiffs filed their notice of intention to proceed. The courts below found that the plaintiffs had allowed some six years to elapse after the termination of the Licence Agreement before they got serious with their action against the appellants.

In R.J. Sharpe, *Injunctions and Specific Performance* (loose-leaf), numerous cases are cited at para 1.840 for the proposition that "a combination of delay and prejudice to the defendant is required to deprive the plaintiff of a specific remedy to which he or she is otherwise entitled." This combination, often considered as a second branch of the doctrine of *laches*, may deny injunctive relief even where the plaintiff's conduct does not amount to acquiescence in the correctness of the defendant's position under the first branch of that doctrine. The distinction is noted at pp. 76-78 by La Forest J in *M. (K.) v. M. (H.)*, [[1992] 3 SCR 6]. A good example of this principle in action is *Institut national des appellations d'origine des vins et eaux-de-vie v. Andres Wines Ltd.* (1987), 40 DLR (4th) 239 (Ont. HC), *per* Dupont J, at p. 297, affirmed by the Ontario Court of Appeal (1990), 71 DLR (4th) 575n, leave to appeal to the Supreme Court of Canada refused, [1991] 1 SCR x. In that case, the French wine authority and French champagne producers sought to restrain Canadian wineries from associating the name "champagne" with their products. There was no suggestion that the French plaintiffs had ever acquiesced in the correctness of the legal position advanced by the Canadian defendants. Nevertheless, apart from everything else, the Court held that during the period of delay (much longer than here) the Canadian wineries had invested large amounts of money in the research and development of "domestic champagne," and had carved out a domestic market. The injunction was refused, and for these and other reasons the action was wholly dismissed.

However, as the authors of Sharpe, *Injunctions and Specific Performance, supra,* also point out at para 1.870, delay plus detriment do not necessarily bar the action entirely. There may be delay combined with prejudice which "has less drastic effect and which is relevant to the issue of remedial choice, that is, delay sufficient to deprive the plaintiff of specific relief but not to bar action altogether." In *Stephenson Jordan & Harrison Ltd. v. MacDonald & Evans* (1951), 69 RPC 10 (CA), at p. 16, it was considered relevant to the grant of an injunction that the third party sought to be enjoined (as the appellants are in this case) had not been alerted to the alleged breach of confidence "before they had ... incurred any substantial expense." The plaintiff was left to its claim for financial compensation. In this case, the delay of the respondents, combined with the ongoing investment and commercial activity of the appellants based on Caesar Cocktail in the interim, argued powerfully against the grant of injunctive relief.

(2) The "Nothing Very Special" Nature of the Information

As to the trial judge's view that the "nothing very special" quality of the information militated against the grant of a permanent injunction, support is found in the discussion of La Forest J in *Lac Minerals* [*v. International Corona Resources*, [1989] 2 SCR 574], at p. 643:

> Imposing a disability on a party in possession of confidential information from participating in a market in which there is room for more than one participant may be unreasonable, such as *where the information relates to a manufacturing process or a design detail*. In such cases, it may be that the obligation on the confidee is not to use the confidential information in its possession *without paying compensation for it* or sharing the benefit derived from it. [Emphasis added.]

The Court of Appeal in this case nevertheless reversed the trial judge's ruling and granted a permanent injunction. Newbury JA thought it inequitable to subject the defendant, in effect, to a forced sale of the confidences. She preferred the approach of Lord Evershed MR in *Terrapin* [*Ltd. v. Builders' Supply Co. (Hayes) Ltd.*, [1960] RPC 128 (CA)], at p. 135, where he doubted that the misappropriation of confidential information by a competitor should be regarded as "merely a matter of compensation in pounds, shillings and pence." Newbury JA also quoted, at p. 349, the statement of Smith LJ in *Shelfer v. City of London Electric Lighting Co.*, [1895] 1 Ch. 287 (CA), at p. 322, that

> a person by committing a wrongful act (whether it be a public company for public purposes or a private individual) is not thereby entitled to ask the Court to sanction his doing so by purchasing his neighbour's rights, by assessing damages in that behalf. ...

The law would lose its deterrent effect if defendants could misappropriate confidential information and retain profits thereby generated subject only to the payment of compensation if, as and when they are caught and successfully sued.

I think, however, that one's indignation in this case has to be tempered by an appreciation of the equities between the parties at the date of the trial. Eleven years had passed since Caesar Cocktail went into production, using "nothing very special" information that could promptly have been replaced (had the respondents made a timely fuss) by substitute technology accessible to anyone skilled in the art of juice formulation. At the date of trial, it would have been manifestly unfair to allow information of peripheral importance to control the grant of injunctive relief. The equities in favour of the respondents' claim for an injunction to put Caesar Cocktail off the market rightly yielded to the appellants' equities in continuing a business to whose success the confidential information had so minimally contributed.

(3) Adequacy of a Monetary Remedy

The present case essentially involves the settlement of financial accounts between business entities. The injunction, if granted, would have inflicted damage on the appellants disproportionate to the legitimate interest of the respondents: see, e.g., the *Spycatcher* case [*Attorney-General v. Guardian Newspapers Ltd. (No. 2)*, [1990] AC 109 (HL (Eng.))], *per* Lord Goff, at p. 290:

> But the [*Spycatcher* disclosures in the newspaper] were very short: they gave little detail of the allegations: a number of the allegations had been made before: and in so far as the articles went

beyond what had previously been published, I do not consider that the judge erred in holding that, in the circumstances, the claim to an injunction was *not proportionate* to the legitimate aim pursued. [Emphasis added.]

An injunction in the circumstances of the present case would inflict competitive damage on the appellants in 1999 far beyond what is necessary to "restore" the respondents to the competitive position they would have enjoyed "but for" the breach 16 years ago on April 15, 1983.

As in *Schauenburg Industries Ltd. v. Borowski* (1979), 101 DLR (3d) 701 (Ont. HC), *per* Craig J, at p. 712, the blow to the respondents, whatever it may be, can be adequately compensated by money.

In these circumstances, the trial judge was correct to refuse a permanent injunction, and the permanent injunction issued by the British Columbia Court of Appeal should be vacated.

NOTES

1. To what extent, if at all, should delay in a situation such as this be relevant to the availability and extent of the alternative remedy (*compensation in equity*) sought by the plaintiff?

2. The defence of *laches* has been held not to apply to defeat a claim where a statutory limitation period applies, expressly or by analogy, to that claim. See *Re Pauling's Settlement Trusts*, [1961] 3 All ER 713 (Ch. Div.), aff'd. (1963), [1964] 1 Ch. 303 (Ch. Div.), at 735, *per* Lord Wilberforce; *Deschenes Drilling Ltd./Les Forages Deschenes Ltée v. Mallet* (1996), 175 NBR (2d) 233 (CA), referring to *Nepean Hydro-Electric Commission v. Ontario Hydro*, [1982] 1 SCR 347 (SCC), at 379, *per* Dickson J (as he then was), dissenting; *Rio Alto Exploration Ltd. v. White* (1990), 104 AR 84 (QB) (QL); and *Weicker v. Weicker*, [1986] AJ no. 705 (QB) (QL). See also Graeme Mew, *The Law of Limitations* (Toronto: Butterworths, 1991), at 22–23.

However, this position is now doubtful. In British Columbia, Alberta, Saskatchewan, and Newfoundland the legislatures have expressly preserved the doctrine of laches in their limitations statutes: *Limitations Act*, RSBC 1996, c. 266, s. 2; *Limitations Act*, RSA 2000, c. L-12, s. 10; *The Limitations Act*, SS 2004, c. L-16.1, s. 22; *Limitations Act*, SNL 1995, c. L-16.1, s. 3. See, on the BC provision: *Roberts v. The Queen* (2002), 220 DLR (4th) 1 (SCC), at para. 108; and *Rhyolite Resources Inc. v. CanQuest Resource Corp.* (1999), 64 BCLR (3d) 80 (CA). The general limitations statutes in all other common law jurisdictions except Ontario expressly preserve the operation of "any rule of equity in refusing relief on the ground of acquiescence, or otherwise, to any person whose right to bring an action is not barred by virtue of this Act." See *Limitation of Actions Act*, RSNB 1973, c. L-8, s. 65; *The Limitation of Actions Act*, RSM 1987, c. L150, s. 59; *Limitation of Actions Act*, RSNWT 1988, c. L-8, s. 49; *Limitation of Actions Act*, RSNS 1989, c. 258, s. 31; *Statute of Limitations*, RSPEI 1988, c. S-7, s. 51. The Supreme Court of Canada has recently held that such a provision will permit the doctrine of laches to apply even if a claim is not barred by statute: *Roberts v. The Queen* (2002), 220 DLR (4th) 1 (SCC), at para. 108. In Ontario, the relevant saving provision is found in the *Real Property Limitations Act*, RSO 1990, c. L.15, s. 2.

HARDSHIP

Patel v. Ali
[1984] Ch. 283

[The Patels were seeking specific performance of a contract entered into in 1979 for the sale of a house owned by Mrs. Ali and Mr. Ahmed. Initially, completion of the transaction was delayed because of an injunction secured by the trustee in bankruptcy of Mr. Ali, Mrs. Ali's husband. Then there were difficulties in serving Mr. Ahmed, who had returned to Pakistan. Eventually, when these difficulties had been surmounted, the Patels made an application for summary judgment in July 1983.]

GOULDING J: ...

[After recounting the history of the matter, he continued.]

Meanwhile, the circumstances of the defendant had changed disastrously. At the date of the contract she had one child who was still a baby; and, so far as she knew, she was in good health. She was about 23 years old. She spoke and still speaks, in the words of her solicitor's affidavit, "virtually no English at all." In the summer of 1980 she was found to have a bone cancer in her right thigh. On 24 July 1980, that is three days after the order of Fox J in the bankruptcy proceedings, her right leg was amputated at the hip joint. She was then in an advanced state of pregnancy and gave birth to her second child on 31 August 1980. In the spring of 1981 her husband went to prison and remained there until mid-summer 1982. After his release she became pregnant again and her third child was born in August 1983.

The defendant has been fitted with an artificial leg. She is able to walk about the house and dress herself, but not to do shopping, and she needs help with household duties and with the children. She is greatly dependent on friends and relations to enable her to keep her home going and to look after her children, especially on her sister who, I was told, lives only a few doors away, and on a friendly neighbour, Mrs. Dhillon.

It is in these circumstances that the defendant asks the court to refuse specific performance of the contract and to leave the plaintiffs to their remedy in damages. Her advisors recognise that the court must be satisfied that the legal remedy will be effective, and there is evidence that sympathetic persons in the Muslim Community in which she lives are willing to put up money for that purpose.

That the hardship to the defendant of enforced removal from the property would be great is, on the evidence, beyond doubt. Any accommodation which the local authority could immediately provide for the defendant is likely to deprive her of the daily assistance on which she relies, or at least greatly to diminish it. The move would necessarily cause much more severe disturbance to the lives of the children, now aged five years, three years and four or five months, than a family removal does in ordinary cases, and might even make it impossible for the defendant to keep them with her, handicapped as she is by her physical disability.

The hardship which would be caused to the plaintiffs if specific performance were refused and adequate pecuniary compensation were available is not, so far as the evidence reveals, greater than what is necessarily involved in being disappointed of the purchase after so long a delay. Since the contractual date for completion in 1979 the plaintiffs have lived in accommodation rented from their local authority, Brent London Borough Council.

It is not in dispute that, like other equitable relief, the specific performance of contracts is a discretionary remedy; but, in the ordinary case of a sale of land or buildings, the court normally grants it as of course and withholds it only on proof of special facts. The textbooks and reported decisions have long recognised hardship as one ground on which, in a proper case, a purchaser or vendor may be refused specific performance and be left to his right to damages for breach of contract at law. The difficulty is to determine within what limits hardship to a defendant can properly be said to justify this exercise of judicial discretion. There is no doubt that, in the majority of cases, the hardship which moves the court to refuse specific performance is either a hardship existing at the date of the contract or a hardship due in some way to the plaintiff. In the present case, neither of those conditions being satisfied, the plaintiffs rely strongly on that principle or practice, which is stated in varying terms in all the well-known textbooks. It is sufficient for me to cite a passage from *Fry on Specific Performance* (6th ed., 1921) at p. 199:

> It is a well-established doctrine that the court will not enforce the specific performance of a contract, the result of which would be to impose great hardship on either of the parties to it; and this although the party seeking specific performance may be free from the least impropriety of conduct. The question of the hardship of a contract is generally to be judged of at the time at which it is entered into: if it be then fair and just and not productive of hardship, it will be immaterial that it may, by the force of subsequent circumstances or change of events, have become less beneficial to one party, except where these subsequent events have been in some way due to the party who seeks the performance of the contract. For whatever contingencies may attach to a contract, or be involved in the performance of either part, have been taken upon themselves by the parties to it. It has been determined that the reasonableness of a contract is to be judged of at the time it is entered into, and not by the light of subsequent events, and we have already seen that the same principle applies in considering the fairness of a contract.

However, the principle so stated cannot be erected into a fixed limitation of the court's equitable jurisdiction. It is recognised, both by Fry LJ in his book and in the argument of Mr. Simpkiss for the plaintiffs in the present action, that the court has sometimes refused specific performance because of a change of circumstances supervening after the making of the contract and not in any way attributable to the plaintiff. One such case is *City of London v. Nash* (1747), 1 Ves. Sen. 11 at p. 12; 27 ER 859 at p. 859 (Ch.) where Lord Hardwicke LC refused specific performance of a contract which required the demolition of houses and building of new ones, because he thought that the demolition would be a public loss and no benefit to the plaintiffs, who would be sufficiently compensated by damages at law. This seems a strong case, because the difficulties were due to breaches of contract by the defendant himself. The fuller report of the case in 3 Atk. 511 at p. 517 shows, however that Lord Hardwicke LC was also influenced by *laches* on the part of the City of London. Another relevant case is *Webb v. Direct London and Portsmouth Railway Co.* (1852), 1 De. GM & G 521; 42 ER 654 (CA) where the Court of Appeal refused specifically to enforce a purchase of land by the company after it had abandoned its proposed enterprise of constructing a railway from Epsom to Portsmouth. Similar in principle are the cases where the court has refused injunctions to compel specific performance of restrictive covenants by reason of a change in the character of the neighbourhood, even where the plaintiff and his predecessors in title have in no way contributed thereto: see *Sobey v. Sainsbury*, [1913] 2 Ch. 513 at p. 529. Thus, I am satisfied that the court's discretion is wide enough, in an otherwise proper case, to refuse specific performance on the ground of hardship subsequent to the contract and not caused by the plaintiff.

Another limitation suggested by Mr. Simpkiss was that, in the reported cases, as he said, hardship successfully relied on has always related to the subject matter of the contract and has not been just a personal hardship of the defendant. Certainly, mere pecuniary difficulties, whether of purchaser or of vendor, afford no excuse from performance of a contract. In a wider sense than that, I do not think the suggested universal proposition can be sustained. In *Webb's* case, the hardship in no way affected the title to the property or its physical condition. It was a hardship to the railway company to be compelled to pay for land it could never use, just as it is a hardship to the defendant here to be compelled to convey a house she cannot now well do without.

The important and true principle, in my view, is that only in extraordinary and persuasive circumstances can hardship supply an excuse for resisting performance of a contract for the sale of immovable property. A person of full capacity who sells or buys a house takes the risk of hardship to himself and his dependants, whether arising from existing facts or unexpectedly supervening in the interval before completion. This is where, to my mind, great importance attaches to the immense delay in the present case, not attributable to the defendant's conduct. Even after issue of the writ, she could not complete, if she had wanted to, without the concurrence of the absent Mr. Ahmed. Thus, in a sense, she can say she is being asked to do what she never bargained for, namely to complete the sale after more than four years, after all the unforeseeable changes that such a period entails. I think that in this way she can fairly assert that specific performance would inflict upon her "a hardship amounting to injustice" to use the phrase employed by James LJ, in a different but comparable context, in *Tamplin v. James* (1880), 15 Ch. D 215 (CA) at p. 221. Equitable relief may, in my view, be refused because of an unforeseen change of circumstances not amounting to legal frustration, just as it may on the ground of mistake insufficient to avoid a contract at law.

In the end, I am satisfied that it is within the court's discretion to accede to the defendant's prayer if satisfied that it is just to do so. And, on the whole, looking at the position of both sides after the long unpredictable delay for which neither seeks to make the other responsible, I am of opinion that it *is* just to leave the plaintiffs to their remedy in damages if that can indeed be effective.

I have come to this conclusion without taking into account the welfare of the defendant's children except as involved in her own personal hardship. I much doubt whether, even in the present atmosphere of opinion on which Mr. Briggs dwelt in his address, the interests of the children are material in their own right, though he did derive some support from the obiter observations of Isaacs J in the High Court of Australia in *Gall v. Mitchell* (1924), 35 CLR 222 at p. 230:

> Hardships of third persons entirely unconnected with the property are immaterial. But I do not think that rule excludes the case of third persons so connected with the defendant that, by reason of some legal or moral duty which he owes them, it would be "highly unreasonable" for

the court actively to prevent the defendant from discharging his duty. The circumstances of such a case might, in my opinion, be properly weighed for the purpose of determining the discretion of the court.

On the other hand, I am not persuaded by Mr. Simpkiss's suggestion that the refusal of specific performance may not be of value to the defendant because of the still undetermined claim of her husband's trustee in bankruptcy. It seems not unlikely that, if she can succeed in keeping possession of the house here, she may also keep it in the bankruptcy court, at any rate for a period of some years, even if the trustee's claim is well-founded: cf. *In re Holliday (A Bankrupt)*, [1981] Ch. 405 (CA).

I will hear counsel on the precise form of order. What I have in mind is this. The order will recite the parties' agreement to treat the hearing of the appeal as the trial of the action as between the plaintiffs and the defendant. I will direct that, if within a specified period—I suggest on or before 29 February next—a certain sum is paid into court to the credit of the action, or otherwise secured to the satisfaction of the plaintiffs, then the master's order will be discharged. Instead, an inquiry will be ordered what damage the plaintiffs have suffered by reason of the breach of contract by Mr. Ahmed and the defendant. The defendant will be ordered to pay the amount found due on the inquiry and the plaintiffs' taxed costs of the action, including this appeal, the costs of the inquiry being reserved. I have heard argument regarding the sum to be paid in, and I fix it at £10,000. If the money is not provided by the date specified, the appeal is to stand dismissed with costs. In either event, there will be a legal aid taxation of the costs (so far as not previously dealt with) of those parties who have been legally aided incurred during the respective periods when they have been so aided. I perceive that the order may confer a benefit on Mr. Ahmed, though absent from the appeal, but that seems to me inevitable in the circumstances.

Order accordingly.

NOTES

1. This decision should be contrasted with the Ontario decision of *Stewart v. Ambrosina* (1975), 10 OR (2d) 483, aff'd. (1977), 16 OR (2d) 221 (CA) where the hardship relied upon to resist specific performance of a contract for the sale of a family home was a combination of continuing matrimonial difficulties, the eventual suicide of the husband, and Mrs. Ambrosina being left with six children to raise and little from her husband's estate. After rejecting the argument that the matrimonial difficulties at the time of the contract were sufficient, Cory J (in a judgment approved by the Court of Appeal) proceeded to deal with the present state of affairs:

> Even if it is assumed that undue hardship is a ground for refusing specific performance, such hardship must have existed at the time the contract was made and cannot be hardship that has arisen subsequently from a change of circumstances: see 36 Hals., 3rd ed., p. 301. That proposition would seem to be fair and well founded. If there is to be any certainty of contracts, the law must deal with the situation as it existed at the time of the formation of the contract. If that were not the case, then difficult problems arise. How long after the contract, for example, should the Court look at the circumstances of the parties to determine if there is undue hardship? Is the time to extend for one month or one year after the date of the contract, or date for its performance?

The more extended the time for considering undue hardship may be the more the defendant raising such a defence benefits from a delay in the trial of an action based on his breach, for a subsequent illness or accident may give rise to a hardship that could be considered undue.

I have researched as diligently as I could and I have regretfully reached the conclusion that I cannot on the basis of hardship arising subsequent to the date of the contract and its date for performance, refrain from granting specific performance.

More recently, in *Bowser v. Prager* (1999), 95 OTC 302 (SCJ) (QL), Weekes J stated (at para. 14) that, while "[g]enerally speaking, that assessment is made as of the time the agreement is entered into, … post contract factors are sometimes taken into consideration." In so doing, he made reference to Sharpe, *Injunctions and Specific Performance*, 2nd ed. (Aurora, ON: Canada Law Book, 1992) (looseleaf updated November 1998), at para. 10.370.

2. For a Canadian example of hardship existing at the time of the contract contributing to the denial of relief, see *1110049 Ontario Ltd. v. Exclusive Diamonds* (1995), 25 OR (3d) 417 (CA). Here, the defendant had agreed to sell a family business at a time when he was consumed with grief over the death of his wife with whom he had operated the business for a number of years. Though unwilling to attribute improper pressure to the plaintiff company, the court nevertheless referred to the manifest nature of the defendant's vulnerability at the time of the contract and the hardship that would be occasioned by now compelling him to sell the business. His period of intense grief had ended and he now wanted to resume the running of his business. When this was linked with an argument based on the adequacy of damages, the court set aside the judgment at first instance, denied specific performance, and directed an assessment of damages by the master. See also *Bowser v. Prager*, above, where the court denied specific performance on the basis of hardship in a situation where the vendor was taking medication for depression in the aftermath of release from involuntary commitment to a psychiatric facility. In so doing, the court, as well as emphasizing the defendant's medical condition, took account of the fact that he had debts, was on social assistance, and would not be able to afford similar accommodation. More particularly, the judge referred to the "spectre of homelessness." Nonetheless, the plaintiff recovered damages in excess of $12,000.

3. For further discussion of this issue, see Jacqueline A. Priest, "Hardship and Specific Performance," [1984] *New Law Journal* 927 and 949 and Norman M. Fera, "Hardship in the Granting of Specific Performance" (1978), 26 *Chitty's Law Journal* 115.

NEGATIVE COVENANTS

It has traditionally been held that courts have little discretion to deny an injunction to restrain a party from breaching an express negative covenant, except where this would be tantamount to specifically enforcing a contract that cannot be specifically enforced (such as a personal service contract—see *Lumley v. Wagner* and its progeny, in chapter 9). The classic statement of this position occurs by way of obiter in the judgment of Lord Cairns in *Doherty v. Allman* (1878), 3 App. Cas. 709 (HL (Ire.)). In that case, the owner of the reversionary interest in a farm sought to restrain the tenant under a 999-year lease from converting a barn into six dwellings to be rented. The lease contained no promise by the tenant not to modify the property in this manner. Lord Cairns held, however, that if it had contained such a negative covenant he would have been compelled by authority to enforce it by injunction:

My Lords, if there had been a negative covenant, I apprehend, according to well-settled practice, a Court of Equity would have had no discretion to exercise. If parties, for valuable consideration, with their eyes open, contract that a particular thing shall not be done, all that a Court of Equity has to do is to say, by way of injunction, that which the parties have already said by way of covenant, that the thing shall not be done; and in such case the injunction does nothing more than give the sanction of the process of the Court to that which already is the contract between the parties. It is not then a question of the balance of convenience or inconvenience, or of the amount of damage or of injury—it is the specific performance, by the Court, of that negative bargain which the parties have made, with their eyes open, between themselves.

NOTES

1. Lord Cairns's obiter was applied by the English Court of Appeal in *Araci v. Fallon*, [2011] EWCA Civ 668. The plaintiff, Ibrahim Araci, owned the horse "Native Khan," one of the favourites to win the Epsom Derby in 2011. Araci entered a contract with the defendant Kieren Fallon under which Fallon was paid £10,000 in return for undertaking (1) to ride Native Khan whenever requested by Araci to do so, and (2) not to ride the horse of any rival in any race in which he was asked by Araci to ride Native Khan. Araci asked Fallon to ride Native Khan in the 2011 derby. Fallon declined. He planned to ride a rival horse named "Recital" instead. Araci sued, not to compel Fallon to ride Native Khan (he had lost trust in the jockey), but for an interim injunction to restrain Fallon from riding Recital. The judge at first instance declined to grant the injunction, holding that damages were an adequate remedy. Despite only rarely interfering with the discretion of judges regarding interlocutory relief, the Court of Appeal granted the injunction. After setting out and approving the above passage from *Doherty*, Lord Justice Jackson wrote:

> Where the defendant is proposing to act in clear breach of a negative covenant, in other words to do something which he has promised not to do, there must be special circumstances (e.g. restraint of trade contrary to public policy) before the court will exercise its discretion to refuse an injunction.

Native Khan finished fifth in the Derby, just ahead of Recital.

2. For another interesting modern application of Lord Cairns's statement that the court has no discretion to exercise where a contract contains an express negative covenant against the doing of something, see *Attorney General v. Barker*, [1989] 3 All ER 257 (CA). This involved the award of a worldwide injunction against a former employee of Buckingham Palace enjoining the publication of a book in which a range of palace "secrets" were to be revealed. As part of Barker's contract of employment, he had entered into an express negative covenant not to author reminiscences of this sort and, in issuing an injunction against Barker, one of the judges made express reference to Lord Cairns's statement as the governing rule in such matters.

Fothergill v. Rowland
(1873), 17 LR Eq. 132

Demurrer

The Plaintiffs in this case, *Richard Fothergill* and *Ernest Thomas Hankey*, were ironmasters, carrying on the *Aberdare Ironworks*. The Defendant, *Richard Rowland*, was lessee of the *Newbridge Colliery*.

The bill alleged that the Plaintiffs had for some time been accustomed to purchase coals of the Defendant *Rowland*, and that at the time of making the agreement hereinafter mentioned there was a subsisting contract, under which *Rowland* was supplying the Plaintiffs from 1871 to the 4th of January 1872 with a quantity of coal from the said colliery:

That at the time of the making of the agreement of the 6th of December 1871, the *Newbridge Colliery* was only opened upon one seam of coal, called "the No. 3 seam," and was only partially opened on that seam: that *Rowland* was anxious to extend the openings in the seam, and had made representations to that effect to the Plaintiffs, and that he (*Rowland*) was short of capital for extending his works, and that, with a comparatively small outlay, the colliery would produce nearly 300 tons of coal a day, and that if a siding could be had on the *Taff Vale Railway*, near the *Taff Vale Ironworks*, he (*Rowland*) would be able to deliver the coals with greater facility and a considerable reduction of cost:

That the Plaintiffs were then in a position to consume at the ironworks a much larger quantity of coal then they had previously taken, and were disposed to make an arrangement with *Rowland* to supply him with capital to enable him to extend his colliery, and also to make an arrangement with the *Taff Vale Railway Company* for the construction of a siding, provided that *Rowland* would enter into a contract of sale to the Plaintiffs of all the coal which the said colliery would produce, for a lease of five years, provided that the quantity then supplied should not be less than a stated minimum:

That negotiations for an arrangement upon this footing resulted in an agreement, come to at a meeting between the Plaintiffs and *Rowland* on the 6th of December, 1871, by which they agreed that *Rowland* should sell to the Plaintiffs, and that the Plaintiffs should buy the whole of the get of the coal of the No. 3 seam of the said colliery for five years, the quantity not to be less than that then delivered to the *Taff Vale Ironworks*, unless the coal should fail, at 6*s.* per ton, provided that the *Taff Vale Railway Company* would provide a siding to which *Rowland* should forthwith make a road, and that the Plaintiffs should lend to *Rowland* £1000 to aid him in opening the colliery, and that this agreement was reduced to writing in the form of a pencil memorandum signed by *Rowland*, and about the same time the Plaintiffs agreed with *Rowland*, that, besides the coal of the said No. 3 seam, another vein should be included in the contract, and, at the option of the Plaintiff *Fothergill*, any other vein of coal within the colliery should be included:

That the said agreements were reduced to writing by a memorandum in the form of a letter of the 4th of January 1872, addressed to *Rowland* and confirmed by him in writing, and another memorandum subscribed thereto of the 5th of January 1872, which were as follows:

Dear Sir—I have been excessively occupied since our interview last month, and have not found time to sit down and write in detail that which we mutually agreed upon beyond the simple sale of coal described in the pencil memorandum we drew up together in the following terms:

6 Dec. 1871

Sold *R.F.*, Esq., M.P., the whole of the get of the No. 3 coal out of the *Newbridge Colliery* property for five years, the quantity, not to be less than at present delivered to his *Taff Vale* works, unless the coal should fail, at 6*s.* per ton payment as usual.

To which I desire now to add that we arranged, when so required, that you would deliver the said coal into our wagons on a siding of the *Taff Vale Railway* at such a reduction in price as you could obtain off the cost in comparison with the delivery into the *Taff Vale* works, provided that the *Taff Vale Railway Company* would provide such siding (which you had not been able to obtain), and to which you would forthwith make a road; in reference to which I am glad to inform you that I have seen Mr. *Fisher*, and obtained his consent to his company providing the needful siding, a most valuable concession in prospect of the possibly very large quantities of coal you talked of flooding me with. I also promised to lend you £1000, to aid you in opening and developing the said colliery at the rate of 5 per cent per annum interest, to be taken in such proportions monthly as you require in exchange for your acceptances at six months' date, all which please confirm, and I remain,

Yours faithfully,
Rich. Fothergill.

5th Jan. 1872.

It is understood between us that besides the No. 3 coal named herein that the *Forest Vach Vein* is included in the foregoing contract, and, further, that any other vein of coal worked shall be included at the option of Mr. *Fothergill* or representatives.

Rich. Fothergill.
Richd. Rowland.

That in part performance of the said agreement *Rowland* had commenced to deliver coal from the said colliery to the ironworks; that the Plaintiffs had advanced to him the sum of £1000, which he had employed in extending the colliery; and that the siding was constructed by the *Taff Vale Railway Company* under the arrangement made with them by one of the Plaintiffs:

That after January 1872, coal of the description yielded by the colliery increased very much in value, and that *Rowland* had appealed to the Plaintiffs to make some modification in the contract, which they had refused, though they had made an allowance by way of gift to the amount of one-third of the contract price; but that no variations in the contract had been assented to by the Plaintiffs:

That coal of the description yielded by the colliery had advanced from 6*s.* to 13*s.* per ton:

That the Plaintiffs had discovered that *Rowland*, in violation of the terms of his agreement, was selling coal from the said No. 3 seam to other persons than the Plaintiffs; and that the deliveries were greatly below the minimum quantities specified in the contract:

That in August 1873, the Plaintiffs discovered that *Rowland* had entered into an agreement with the Defendants *Spickett, Price, Bassett,* and *Meyer,* for the sale to them of the colliery; and that such agreement was entered into for the purpose of evading the performance on the part of *Rowland* of the agreement between the Plaintiffs and himself, and of depriving the Plaintiffs of their rights in the premises.

The Plaintiffs prayed, first, for an injunction to restrain the Defendants from selling, assigning, or disposing of or interfering with the colliery, except subject to the agreement between the Plaintiffs and *Rowland*; and from selling, disposing of or interfering with any coal gotten or to be gotten out of the said colliery, except for the purpose of the performance of the agreement; and, secondly, that it might be declared that the Plaintiffs were entitled to the whole of the get of the seam of coal No. 3, and of the *Forest Vach Vein* of the colliery, and also, at the option of the Plaintiffs, to the whole of the get of any other seam of coal worked at the colliery during the period of five years, upon the terms of the said agreement embodied in the memoranda of the 6th of December 1871, and the 4th and 5th of January 1872.

The Defendants demurred to the bill.

SIR G. JESSEL MR: ... The question is one which I am sorry to have to decide against the Plaintiffs. No honest man, whether on the Bench or off it, can approve of the conduct of the Defendants. The first Defendant, *Rowland*, has entered into a contract *bona fide* for valuable considerations to sell a quantity of coal to be raised from his mine to the Plaintiffs. He has received the advantages of the contract, and because coal has risen in value and he can get a better price elsewhere, he does not choose to perform his contract. Such conduct ought not to meet with the approval of anybody. Then the question I have to determine is, whether the Plaintiffs have come to the right Court to obtain that which the law will undoubtedly give them, namely, compensation in some shape or other for the loss they have sustained by his breach of contract. It appears to me, as the law now stands, a Court of Equity cannot give them any relief.

The first question is, what is the contract for? In my view of the contract it is one for the sale of coals, that is, coals gotten, the get of coal, the severed chattel, and it has no relation whatever to a contract for real estate. That point really was not argued by Mr. *Fry*, although Mr. *Marten* did touch upon it. I think it must be assumed, therefore, to be a simple contract for the sale of a chattel of a very ordinary description not alleged to be a peculiar coal, or coal that cannot be got elsewhere. On the contrary, as I read the bill, there is coal that can be got elsewhere of the same description, only at a higher price. The result is that the Plaintiffs will incur an amount of damage to be measured by the market price which they may have to pay for the coal of the same description as the coal agreed to be supplied by the Defendant *Rowland*.

It is said, however, that, although you can ascertain the market price as regards all the past non-delivery, you cannot ascertain exactly the market price as to future deliveries. To say that you cannot ascertain the damage in a case of breach of contract for the sale of goods, say in monthly deliveries extending over three years (which is the case here, for there are three years unexpired of the contract), is to limit the power of ascertaining damages in a way which would rather astonish gentlemen who practise on what is called the other side of *Westminster Hall*. There is never considered to be any difficulty in ascertaining such a thing, therefore I do not think it is a case in which damages could not be ascertained at law.

That being so, what is there to distinguish this from any ordinary contract for the sale of goods? We have been told it has some connection with the colliery. I suppose coals must necessarily have connection with a colliery, and it happens that the person who sold the coal to be produced from a given colliery was also at that time the owner of the colliery. I apprehend there is no difficulty about entering into a contract for the sale of coal coming from a particular colliery by persons not owners of that colliery; that is the common practice. The coals not being delivered, and there being no means of obtaining their delivery without compelling the Defendant *Rowland* to raise them, it has been admitted before me that this is a contract of which you cannot obtain a specific performance in a Court of Equity.

Therefore any relief to be obtained by the Plaintiffs in the shape of compensation must be obtained at law, and I do not understand that the Plaintiffs, coming here for an injunction which they ask, are willing to abandon their claim to compensation at law in the shape of damages.

Then it is said, assuming this contract to be one which the Court cannot specifically perform, it is yet a case in which the Court will restrain the Defendants from breaking the contract. But I have always felt, when at the Bar, a very considerable difficulty in understanding the Court on the one hand professing to refuse specific performance because it is difficult to enforce it, and yet on the other hand attempting to do the same thing by a roundabout method. If it is right to prevent the Defendant *Rowland* from selling coal at all—he not having stipulated not to sell coal, but having stipulated to sell all the coal he can raise to somebody who has promised valuable consideration—why is it not right to compel him to raise it and deliver it? It is difficult to follow the distinction, but I cannot find any distinct line laid down, or any distinct limit which I could seize upon and define as being the line dividing the two classes of cases—that is, the class of cases in which the Court, feeling that it has not the power to compel specific performance, grants an injunction to restrain the breach by the contracting party of one or more of the stipulations of the contract, and the class of cases in which it refuses to interfere. I have asked (and I am sure I should have obtained from one or more of the learned counsel engaged in the case every assistance) for a definition. I have not only been able to obtain the answer, but I have obtained that which altogether commands my assent, namely, that there is no such distinct line to be found in the authorities. I am referred to vague and general propositions—that the rule is that the Court is to find out what it considers convenient, or what will be a case of sufficient importance to authorize the interference of the Court at all, or something of that kind.

That being so, and not being able to discover any definite principle on which the Court can act, I must follow what Lord *St. Leonards* says, in *Lumley v. Wagner* (1852), 1 De GM & G 604; 42 ER 687 (Ch.), is the proper conduct for a Judge, in not extending this jurisdiction. I am not, however, entirely without assistance from authority, because it appears to me that this very case has been put, though only by way of illustration, by a very great Judge, Lord *Cottenham*, in *Heathcote v. North Staffordshire Railway Company* (1850), 2 Mac. & G 100 at p. 112; 42 ER 39 at p. 44 (Ch.), where he says: "If *A.* contract with *B.* to deliver goods at a certain time and place, will Equity interfere to prevent *A.* from doing anything which may or can prevent him from so delivering the goods?" That is the exact case I have to deal with, because I have decided that the contract is a contract for the delivery of goods. Finding the *dictum* of Lord *Cottenham* express on the subject, and the Plaintiffs' counsel not having been able to produce to me any authority in which there has been such an injunction granted on the sale of goods or any chattel, in a case in which specific performance could not be granted, I think I shall do right in following that authority; and I say, although I say it with much regret, that it is a case in which Equity can afford no relief. ...

[Demurrer allowed.]

Metropolitan Electric Supply Co. Ltd. v. Ginder
[1901] 2 Ch. 799

The plaintiffs were a company who supplied electricity in a large district in London, and this was a motion by them to restrain the defendant from taking the electric energy required for his licensed public-house, known as the Red Lion, No. 72, High Holborn, from any person, firm, or company other than the plaintiffs, in breach of an alleged agreement.

On November 16, 1898, the defendant had signed what was called a contract, but in point of fact was a statutory form of request to the plaintiffs, as follows:

> I the undersigned request you to supply electric energy as specified below, and I agree to take all such electric energy subject to such of the clauses of the *Electric Lighting Acts* and the company's provisional orders as relate to the supply of electricity for the parish in which the premises to be supplied are situate, and also subject to the following terms and conditions, *viz.*: (1.) the consumer agrees to take the whole of the electric energy required for the premises mentioned below from the company for a period of not less than five years; (2.) the charge for electric energy to be $4\frac{1}{2}$ *d*. per Board of Trade unit.

Then followed provisions for registering the supply by meter, power of lamps, repairs, & c., but there was no covenant by the company to supply energy, nor by the defendant to take any. The final clause was as follows:

> In the event of the company's standard rate of charges being reduced below the price herein quoted during the continuance of this agreement the consumer is to have the benefit of such reduced rate.

Similar forms of request had been signed by other persons for different terms of years, and in one case at the rate of 4*d*. per unit.

In February 1901, the defendant gave notice to the plaintiffs to disconnect his premises from their system, and made arrangements to get a supply from a rival company, on the ground, as he alleged, that the energy supplied by the plaintiff was insufficient.

The plaintiffs thereupon commenced this action against the defendant, and moved for an interim injunction.

The motion was not heard out, but the hearing of the action was accelerated and the case was heard with witnesses upon the issues raised in the affidavits. ...

BUCKLEY J stated the facts, and held in the evidence that the energy supplied by the plaintiffs was reasonably such as the defendant was entitled to receive, and continued: One of the first defences which is raised is this: it is said that the language of the contract is affirmative and not negative, and that the Court is asked to grant an injunction upon the footing that there is a negative covenant, when in point of fact there is none. Now, in dealing with that contention it appears to me that my first duty is to construe the contract, and that, for the purpose of arriving at the true construction of the contract, I must disregard what would be the legal consequences of my construing it in the one way or the other way. I must first find out what it means; and when I have found out what it means, then I must apply proper legal principles to the contract as construed. There is a passage in the judgment of Lord Selborne in *Wolverhampton and Walsall Ry. Co. v. London and North Western Ry. Co.* (1873), LR 16 Eq. 433 at p. 440 which I desire to read on this part of the case. Referring to *Lumley v. Wagner* (1852), 1 De. GM & G 604; 42 ER 687 (Ch.), Lord Selborne said:

> With regard to the case of *Lumley v. Wagner*, to which reference was made, really when it comes to be examined it is not a case which tends in any way to limit the ordinary jurisdiction of this Court to do justice between parties by way of injunction. It was sought in that case to enlarge the jurisdiction on a highly artificial and technical ground, and to extend it to an ordinary case of hiring and service, which is not properly a case of specific performance: the technical distinction being made, that if you find the word "not" in an agreement—"I will not do a thing"— as well as the words "I will," even although the negative term might have been implied from the positive, yet the Court, refusing to act on an implication of the negative, will act on the expression of it. I can only say that I should think it was the safer and the better rule, if it should eventually be adopted by this Court, to look in all such cases to the substance and not to the form. If the substance of the agreement is such that it would be violated by doing the thing sought to be prevented, then the question will arise whether this is the Court to come to for a remedy. If it is, I cannot think that ought to depend on the use of a negative rather than an affirmative form of expression.

The cases since that, I think, have gone to shew that that which Lord Selborne says would be the true principle if it should eventually be adopted by this Court, has really now been adopted by this Court. The language here is that the consumer agrees to take the whole of the electric energy required for his premises from A. The company was bound to supply under the statute if asked. The consumer asks. The result is that he thereupon had a right as against the plaintiffs to be supplied. The only question for bargain then was the price, which was fixed at $4\frac{1}{2} d$. They were contracting, not affirmatively for the supply of something, but negatively that the defendant would not take from somebody else. There is no affirmative contract here to take anything at all. Ginder does not agree that he will take any energy from the plaintiffs. He says he will take the whole of the electric energy required. It is competent to him to burn gas if he likes, and require no energy. The only thing he was contracting to do was that if he took electric energy he would take it from the plaintiffs. It seems to me the whole essence of that contract is that which is not expressed in words, I agree, but which by implication is really the only thing existing, a contract that he will not take from somebody else. He agrees to take the whole from A, which necessarily implies that he will not take from B. As matter of construction therefore, not by express words but by necessary implication, I think there is here an agreement not to take from others. In that state of things, how do the authorities stand? In the first place, it is said that in the recent case of *Whitwood Chemical Co. v. Hardman*, [1891] 2 Ch. 416 (CA), the language was that A would give the whole of his time to the company's business, which implied that he would not give any to anybody else. I agree that is exactly similar to this in the sense that here it is an agreement that he will take the whole of his required supply, and in *Whitwood Chemical Co. v. Hardman* it was that he would give the whole of his time. But when I read the judgments in that case it appears to me that the Lords Justices founded themselves entirely on this—that what they were dealing with was a contract for personal service, which of course this Court will not in general specifically perform. What they pointed out was that the parties were not thinking of contracting there about excluding the manager from acting for another: that was not in their contemplation. What was in their contemplation was that they should enjoy his whole time—that he should give them his service without reservation, but they did not contemplate the negative stipulation that he should not serve others. It being a contract of personal service, it is quite plain, I think, that the Court of Appeal were not prepared to extend the doctrine of *Lumley v. Wagner* as to contracts of personal service beyond the case where there exists, as there did in *Lumley v. Wagner*, express negative words. But, on the other hand, there is *Catt v. Tourle* (1869), LR 4 Ch. App. 654, a case equally on all fours with the present as regards the expression, but not a case of personal service. There the words were that the plaintiff should have the exclusive right of supplying all ale, and he asked for an injunction to restrain a person from supplying the ale himself or obtaining it from another person; and succeeded in getting it. ...

The contract really is a contract, the whole of which is in substance the negative part of it, that he will take the whole from them, involving that he will not take any from anybody else. I therefore think that the fact that the contract is affirmative in form and not negative in form is no ground for refusing an injunction. ...

It seems to me that this is a contract which it was competent for the plaintiffs to make, and that they are entitled to succeed in the action.

I must, therefore, grant an injunction to restrain the defendant, during the residue of the term of five years which is mentioned in the contract of November 16, 1898, from taking the electric energy required for his premises from any person other than the plaintiffs; but I think I must reserve liberty to the defendant to apply, by which I mean this—that if at any time the plaintiffs are not prepared to supply the energy which he wants, or if they supply an energy which is not an efficient supply such as they are bound to give by the Act of Parliament, then I think he ought to be at liberty to apply to be relieved from the operation of the injunction.

[Part of the judgment of Buckley J is omitted.]

Thomas Borthwick & Sons (Australasia) Ltd. v. South Otago Freezing Co. Ltd.
[1978] 1 NZLR 538 (CA)

[The plaintiff ("Borthwicks") and the defendant ("Sofco") had been in the contractual relationship of exporter and freezing company (that is, slaughterhouse) respectively since 1946. Their current contract was to run for 20 years from October 1968, with each party having the right to submit amendments to arbitration at three-year intervals. In 1974, the defendant was taken over and in 1976 the new management purported to repudiate the contract on three days' notice. A clause of the contract provided that the defendant freezing company would only handle stock (that is, buy, kill, and process) for the plaintiff. The plaintiff sought an injunction to restrain the defendant from breaching the provisions. At trial, Wild CJC, [1977] 1 NZLR 366 granted the injunction. The defendant appealed.

The judgment of the court was delivered by Cooke J, who briefly reviewed the facts, stated that Borthwicks were entitled to refuse the repudiation and treat the contract as still in force, and concluded that the court had jurisdiction to grant an injunction in a sale of goods situation. He continued:]

COOKE J: … Turning to the second question, that the jurisdiction is *discretionary* can hardly be doubted. It is true that there are general *dicta* of Lord Cairns LC in *Doherty v. Allman* (1878), 3 App. Cas. 709 (HL (Eng.)) at pp. 719-720, to the effect that on breach of an express negative covenant entered into for valuable consideration the court of equity would have no discretion to exercise. But these have to be compared with Lord Blackburn's more guarded observations at p. 730. Lord Blackburn discounted "the mere technical differences between negative words and affirmative words in a covenant" and said, "As long as it is fair and right and proper that the Court should enforce the bargain which is made, the Court does enforce it. …" With the fusion of law and equity long since accomplished, the Lord Chancellor's especial familiarity with equity practice need not prevent us from obtaining some guidance from Lord Blackburn also. Moreover Lord Cairns may well not have had in mind contracts for personal services. A line of authorities has developed showing that a negative covenant will not be enforced by injunction if the effect will be that the defendant must either remain idle or serve the plaintiff. They were reviewed in *Warner Bros. Pictures Inc. v. Nelson*, [1937] 1 KB 209. If the present case falls in principle within that line, or is sufficiently analogous, there would be strong reason for withholding an injunction.

There does not appear to be any authority binding this court to attach magic importance to the presence or absence of an express negative covenant. We are free, and would prefer, to adopt the approach which Fry J said he would have favoured in *Donnell v. Bennett* (1883), 22 Ch. D 835 if not fettered by authority binding on him, and which Lord Selborne L favoured in *Wolverhampton & Walsall Railway Co. v. London and North-Western Railway Co.* (1873), LR 16 Eq. 433. In *Donnell v. Bennett* Fry J said:

> The question which arises is by no means an easy one. It is difficult because of the state of the authorities upon the point. It appears to me that the tendency of recent decisions, and especially the cases of *Fothergill v. Rowland* (1873), LR 17 Eq. 132 and of the *Wolverhampton and Walsall Railway Company v. London and North Western Railway Company* (1873), LR 16 Eq. 433, is towards this view—that the Court ought to look at what is the nature of the contract between the parties; that if the contract as a whole is the subject of equitable jurisdiction, then an injunction may be granted in support of the contract whether it contain or does not contain a negative stipulation; but that if, on the other hand, the breach of the contract is properly satisfied by damages, then that Court ought not to interfere whether there be or be not the negative stipulation. That, I say, appears to me to be the point towards which the authorities are tending and I cannot help saying that in my judgment that would furnish a proper line by which to divide the cases. But the question which I have to determine is not whether that ought to be the way in which the line should be laid down, but whether it has been so laid down by the authorities which are binding on me (at pp. 837-38).

In the *Wolverhampton* case Lord Selborne said:

With regard to the case of *Lumley v. Wagner* (1852), 1 DM & G 604; 42 ER 687 (Ch.), to which reference was made, really when it comes to be examined it is not a case which tends in any way to limit the ordinary jurisdiction of this Court to do justice between parties by way of injunction. It was sought in that case to enlarge the jurisdiction on a highly artificial and technical ground, and to extend it to an ordinary case of hiring and service, which is not properly a case of specific performance: the technical distinction being made, that if you find the word "not" in an agreement—"I will not do a thing"—as well as the words "I will," even although the negative term might have been implied from the positive, yet the Court, refusing to act on an implication of the negative, will act on the expression of it. I can only say, that I should think it was the safer and the better rule, if it should eventually be adopted by this Court, to look in all such cases to the substance and not to the form. If the substance of the agreement is such that it would be violated by doing the thing sought to be prevented, then the question will arise, whether this is the Court to come to for a remedy. If it is, I cannot think that ought to depend on the use of a negative rather than an affirmative form of expression. If, on the other hand, the substance of the thing is such, that the remedy ought to be sought elsewhere, then I do not think that the forum ought to be changed by the use of a negative rather than an affirmative (at p. 440).

And again:

But here you have an agreement confirmed by statute, in other words an Act of Parliament, vesting practically for ever (for 999 years), the line of the Plaintiff company, on certain terms, in the Defendants. The Defendant company are in possession; nothing whatever remains to be done to complete their railway, nor can they be ousted from it. The only question is, whether, being in possession under that Act of Parliament for that period of time, they are or are not at liberty to depart from the terms on which it was stipulated that they should have that possession. I do not think that any of the questions, or any of the difficulties which arose in those other cases, at all apply to a case like this. If the Defendants are not using the line as they promised to use it, it appears to me that the other party, who is out of possession by virtue of this Parliamentary agreement, is quite at liberty to come to this Court and to ask that they may be compelled to use the line as they agreed, provided the Court sees its way to define that which they ought, or ought not, to do. I therefore think this demurrer must be overruled in the usual way (at p. 441).

The *Wolverhampton* case is striking. As the passage just quoted indicates, the agreement confirmed by statute was no short-term one. The company in possession of the line was bound to work and manage it and carry local and through traffic, the obligation being imposed in comprehensive and somewhat general terms. It is noteworthy that there was provision for annual arbitration. Part of the argument in support of the demurrer to the bill claiming an injunction was:

[H]ow could the Court ascertain here whether, for example, the Defendant company was properly developing the local traffic? If the Court attempted this, it would have to superintend the working of the line for 999 years (at p. 437).

Lord Selborne did not accede to this argument, though his decision may do no more than establish that an injunction *could* be granted in such a case. It should be added that the first of the passages quoted above from his judgment was approved by the Privy Council in

Lord Strathcona Steamship Co. v. Dominion Coal Co., [1926] AC 108 (PC (NS)) at p. 121. The High Court of Australia likewise preferred his views in *Pakenham Upper Fruit Co. Ltd. v. Crosby* (1924), 35 CLR 386.

The approach advocated in *Corbin on Contracts* (St. Paul: West Pub. Co., 1950 *ff.*), sec. 1206, is in harmony with that of Lord Selborne and Fry J and we find it helpful:

> There are two kinds of cases in which an injunction has been granted to prevent the breach of a negative promise. In one of these the injunction is merely an indirect mode of specifically enforcing an accompanying affirmative promise. There is no reason why it should not be used for such a purpose if it will probably be effective and if the only reason for not enforcing the affirmative promise by a decree for specific performance in affirmative form is that there are mere practical difficulties in the enforcement of such an affirmative decree. An injunction should never be used for this purpose if the affirmative promise is one that for substantial reasons ought not to be specifically enforced.

From that passage and the rest of the section it is apparent that Professor Corbin regarded a need for continual supervision of operations by the court as the sort of practical difficulty which might rule out specific performance, yet to be no valid objection to a restraining injunction; whereas he thought that such an injunction was undesirable and should be refused for "substantial reasons" if in effect it would compel personal services or the like. As an instance of the latter class of case his work cites *People's Savings Bank v. First National Bank* (1918), 173 P 52 (Wash. Sup. Ct.), a case about a clearing house association, which was the agent and fiduciary representative of all the member banks.

As we see it, the main significance of an express negative covenant (such as is found here in cl. 10) is twofold. It enables the court readily to define what the defendant may be enjoined from doing; and it emphasises that the defendant has unequivocally accepted this obligation, thus tending to make it more difficult for him to set up hardship. As Dixon J said in *J.C. Williamson Ltd. v. Lukey and Mulholland* (1931), 45 CLR 282:

> If ... a clear legal duty is imposed by contract to refrain from some act, then, *prima facie*, an injunction should go to restrain the doing of that act (at p. 299).

After a review of the authorities, in which he finds "many inconsistencies" of statement, Mr. I.F. Spry comes to substantially that conclusion in his book on *Equitable Remedies* (London: Sweet & Maxwell, 1971) at p. 509.

In applying to the present case the principles to which we have referred, the first point to be noted is that the central feature of this contract is the sale of goods. Certainly it is much more comprehensive than that, as the Chief Justice said; but the core of it is in the recital that "... subject to the terms of this agreement the exporting company shall purchase (from the freezing company) the entire available exportable output (excluding offal) of the said works ... ." Sofco has the right to retain up to 20 percent of its exportable stock to export on its own account. And cls. 3 and 10 result in a further exception to Borthwicks' exclusive rights, for the contract is subject to the statutory obligations owed to producers by Sofco as licensee of an export slaughterhouse: see the *Meat Act 1964*, s. 34 as substituted in 1976, embodying the so-called "open door" policy. Subject to these exceptions, in essence the contract is an exclusive selling agreement, within the classification in A.G. Guest (ed.), *Chitty on Contracts* (London: Sweet & Maxwell, 23rd ed., 1968) at para. 891, with various ancillary provisions. The most important of the latter are the obligation of Sofco to buy stock at the current prices for export of meat and skins as notified to it from time to time by Borthwicks, called in the contract "the schedule prices," and to kill, freeze and process the same at the works; and the corresponding obligation of Borthwicks to notify the schedule prices from time to time so as to enable Sofco to buy stock during the whole of the season.

Notwithstanding the exceptions to Borthwicks' exclusive rights under the contract, we are prepared to assume that counsel for Sofco are right in saying that Borthwicks are seeking specific performance in a roundabout way: that the injunction means that Sofco could use its works to fulfil the contract or not at all. Still, for the reasons already indicated, that is not per se an objection to an injunction. Nor does it matter much that the contract has at its heart the sale of goods. A contract for the sale of goods obtainable on the market will not normally be specifically enforced; but s. 53 of the *Sale of Goods Act* allows even a formal decree for specific performance—a jurisdiction which is exercised if damages would clearly be an inadequate remedy, as when the goods have exceptional value. In *Dougan v. Lee* (1946), 71 CLR 142 the High Court of Australia accepted the principle that the court of equity can intervene where chattels are of special value to a person in order to carry on his business. We have no doubt on that point.

What we were told from the Bar suggests that the formula for the calculation of damages laid down by cl. 20, in the event of termination of the agreement, might produce an unrealistically low figure by comparison with present-day prices. Be that as it may, it is obvious that for a company such as Borthwicks, aiming to export to and develop worldwide markets, an assurance of continuity of supply from a source over which the exporter has some control may well be of much more value than cash in hand. It is a form of tied house, a traditional commercial advantage. Mr. Norman's oral evidence confirms this. What he said justifies the conclusion that, at a price, Borthwicks could obtain elsewhere alternative supplies to an extent sufficient to enable them to fulfil their current contractual commitments, and probably more. But it would be unreal to suggest that a lump-sum award under cl. 20 after a rescission of the contract, or a series of awards in annual actions for damages while the contract is kept on foot, would necessarily be an adequate substitute for the exports themselves at prices regulated under the contract. On the evidence as a whole, and bearing in mind particularly the subject-matter of this contract, we do not regard damages as an adequate remedy.

There remains perhaps the most difficult point in the case. It did not figure at all prominently in the initial submissions for Sofco in this court—nor, apparently, in the Supreme Court—but it received somewhat more emphasis as the argument progressed; though possibly in consequence of questions from the Bench. Are the relations which an injunction seems likely to compel the parties to maintain such as to make the remedy undesirable in principle? This is the kind of point which troubled Sugerman J in a case to which we referred counsel, *Atlas Steels (Australia) Pty. Ltd. v. Atlas Steels Ltd.* (1948), 49 SR (NSW) 157. There an injunction was sought to restrain a Canadian company from breaches of a negative covenant in a yearly agreement appointing a New South Wales company its sole distributor and agent in an extensive territory. The judge refused the remedy, assimilating the case to one of a contract for personal service: not merely in that it was a contract of agency but also in that it involved specific services and personal relationships between the parties of a close and continuing kind.

In England Stamp J applied similar reasoning in *Page One Records Ltd. v. Britton*, [1968] 1 WLR 157 (Ch.) when refusing an interlocutory injunction which would have compelled a group of musicians to employ the plaintiff as their manager. The judge spoke of personal services, obligations of trust and confidence, and "more a joint venture almost approaching the relations of partners than anything else. ..." And in *Evans Marshall & Co. Ltd. v. Bertola*, [1973] 1 WLR 349 (Ch.), which was rather closer on the facts to the present case, Kerr J refused an interlocutory injunction to prevent breaches of a contract for sole agency and distribution rights for a Spanish company's sherry in the United Kingdom, that company having tried to extricate itself from the contract, which had 14 years to run, on being taken over by another company. He thought that an injunction might well be refused at the trial. Among the grounds of his decision were that no case had been cited where a permanent injunction had been granted in respect of such an agreement for that length of time; and that the agreement was not merely an agreement to sell and buy sherry but was in the nature of a joint venture requiring co-operation and confidence between the parties. But the Court of Appeal reversed that decision and granted an interlocutory injunction to preserve the status quo until trial. Sachs LJ with whom the other members of the court agreed, said (at p. 379):

Length of Injunction

On the question of length of injunction we had cited to us *Lord Strathcona Steamship Co. Ltd. v. Dominion Coal Co. Ltd.*, [1926] AC 108 (PC (NS)). There the Privy Council upheld a first instance injunction granted in 1922 restraining for 10 years any dealing with "The Lord Strathcona" inconsistent with a 1914 charterparty granted by the previous owners of the vessel.

Moreover, we have properly been reminded of a much-cited passage in the speech of Lord Cairns LC in *Doherty v. Allman* (1878), 3 App. Cas. 709 (HL (Eng.)) at p. 720. This makes it plain that there can and, indeed, should be taken into account as a cogent factor that the court is being asked to do no more than what the parties have previously freely agreed.

It seems to me that the judge gave rather over great weight to the potential length of the injunction sought by the plaintiffs and may also have overlooked the possibility that at trial the court might merely grant an injunction for a lesser term, for instance of sufficient length to enable an orderly winding-up of the existing arrangements, or for the duration of the plaintiffs' current agreement with sub-agents.

The Nature of the Agreement

Next I turn to the weight to be given to the nature of the relations between the parties which the judge likened to that of a joint venture where confidence and co-operation between the parties is required. I am not at all sure that the analogy is quite correct. This is a commercial agreement between trading companies that can be implemented to the profit of both parties, if each conforms with its express and implied terms. As in a great many commercial contracts consultation between the parties as to implementation is desirable: but that does not necessarily turn them into joint ventures.

But in any event, the fact that some degree of mutual co-operation or confidence is needed does not preclude the court from granting negative injunctions designed to encourage the party in breach to perform his part. Examples are to be found in cases such as *Warner Brothers Pictures Inc. v. Nelson*, [1937] 1 KB 209, a film producer and film artist case, and *Decro-Wall International*

SA v. Practitioners in Marketing Ltd., [1971] 1 WLR 361, which concerned a sole distributor agreement.

Having been only at an interlocutory stage, the *Evans Marshall* case is of limited weight. Yet it does suggest that a party who deliberately sets out to destroy a long-term commercial contract should not lightly be allowed to escape an injunction on the joint venture ground. And the reminder about the *Strathcona* case is valuable. In the present case the contract had nearly 12 years to run when the Chief Justice granted the injunction. On the hearing of the appeal counsel were not able to refer us to any case of an injunction of comparable length in respect of a commercial contract. The *Strathcona* charterparty provided that the charterers should have the vessel for seasons of about six months in each year; and, as Sachs LJ mentions, it was to last another ten years at the date of the injunction. The report does not show which party had to provide the crew, and evidently no point was taken as to whether the closeness of relations might in itself tell against an injunction; but the decision at least suggests that the long duration of commercial relations need not be a reason for refusing an injunction. We add a reference to *Dietrichsen v. Cabburn* (1846), 2 Ph. 52; 41 ER 861 (Ch.), where Lord Cottenham L held that the court would restrain by injunction breach of a covenant not to employ any other wholesale agent for the sale of a certain patent medicine, the agreement apparently having 15 years to run.

In relation to the remedy we attach some importance also to the absence of any suggestion in this case that the 1970 contract is void as being in unreasonable restraint of trade. The *Esso* case [*Esso Petroleum Co. Ltd. v. Harper's Garage (Southport) Ltd.*] in the House of Lords has brought out the flexibility and vitality of the restraint of trade doctrine. Passages in the speeches confirm that the doctrine can apply to contracts to sell the whole output of a business to one buyer—at all events if there is some exorbitance as to the term of the contract or otherwise, or some other special feature: see for instance [1968] AC 269 (HL (Eng.)) at pp. 296 and 298, per Lord Reid, and pp. 333 and 337, per Lord Wilberforce. The doctrine had indeed been applied to that type of case in *McEllistrim v. Ballymacelligott Co-op Agricultural and Dairy Society*, [1919] AC 548 (HL (Ire.)). And, quite apart from the restraint of trade doctrine, if there appeared to be anything seriously unfair on unreasonable about this long-term contract, we would be most reluctant to support an injunction. Accepting as we do, however, that it is in substance a fair and reasonable contract—a view strengthened by the provision for amendment by arbitration at intervals—it would *prima facie* be in the public interest for the court to uphold and enforce such a contract by granting the most effective available remedy.

At first sight the contract is quite complicated and no doubt sensible co-operation and mutual confidence are needed if it is to operate with maximum efficiency. But that is not unusual in trading contracts. Most of the ancillary machinery, such as the notification by Borthwicks of schedule prices and the furnishing by Sofco of killing details, involves mainly matters of a routine kind. Nor is it at all likely that the personnel concerned in the day-to-day carrying out of the contract would be influenced by this litigation or by the change in the ultimate control of Sofco. Killing operations in a freezing works follow a uniform pattern and are basically the same, no matter whether the stock is subject to some contract or received under statutory obligation. The affidavit and oral evidence for Sofco does not show that the buying part of the contract, under cl. 3, has caused or is expected to cause any particular problems. It is significant that there is no evidence of practical difficulties in the working of the contract in the past. There has been a consensual change to the charge relating to sheep and lambs under cl. 9(b). It was not submitted in this court that the litigation commenced in Dunedin in 1976 is directly relevant to the present case; indeed Sofco expressly contended that it is irrelevant. We are not concerned with that dispute. What does stand out from the evidence in the present case is that all the troubles between the parties seem to have emerged after the change of control of Sofco. This cannot be allowed to help Sofco resist an equitable remedy.

We agree with the Chief Justice that cl. 17 means that the property passes at scale. As to the evidence for Sofco that in practice that company has not allocated the carcases until a later stage, evidently that practice has been followed without inconvenience to either party; but there seems to be no valid reason why Sofco should not comply with the contract more strictly if Borthwicks insist. If unfairness did arise in the operation of the contract, it might well be within the scope of the triennial arbitration clause, which has some importance in this part of the case also. Borthwicks acknowledge the width of that clause and in particular accept—rightly, we think—that changed economic circumstances may justify amendments under it even if the changes are not confined to the freezing industry. Moreover, although the injunction has been granted for the duration of the contract, the court would have jurisdiction to dissolve or modify it if, for instance, new circumstances could be shown to be making its operation truly oppressive. As stated in Spry's *Equitable Remedies* at pp. 515-516, an express reservation of leave to apply is probably unnecessary; but in view of the long term of this injunction we think that the formal order of the Supreme Court should be supplemented by expressly reserving such leave to each party.

The Chief Justice recognised that he had a discretion. In all the circumstances he saw no reason why he should not exercise it in favour of Borthwicks. Taking into account the various matters just traversed, and encouraged by the *Dietrichsen, Wolverhampton, Strathcona*, and *Evans Marshall* cases, we have come to the conclusion that there are not sufficiently substantial reasons against the granting of the injunction to which Borthwicks are *prima facie* entitled. We think that the Chief Justice was abundantly justified in his decision and is certainly not shown to have been wrong in the way he exercised his discretion.

Accordingly, subject to the reservation of leave to apply, the injunction will stand and the appeal will be dismissed.

Appeal dismissed.

COVENANTS TO KEEP OPEN A BUSINESS

When the New Zealand Court of Appeal sustained the injunction in *Borthwick*, it did not directly force Sofco to stay in business. Rather, as in the personal service contract injunction cases, it told Sofco that, if it was to remain in business, it had to fulfill its contractual obligations to Thomas Borthwick and to work exclusively for it. Obviously, in most instances, the practical effect of such an order will be the indirect enforcement of the principal contractual obligations; Sofco will stay in business and work exclusively for the plaintiff. It will be as though specific performance of those principal contractual obligations had been granted.

There are, however, situations of long-term commercial contracts where only specific performance or a mandatory injunction will protect the interests of the plaintiff. In recent times, this has been exemplified by cases in which the objective has been to restrain an anchor or cornerstone tenant in a shopping or commercial complex from closing its business at that location. In these situations, the tenant may often be willing to pay the rent for the balance of the term of the lease on the basis of a calculation that this will ultimately cost it less than staying open at an unprofitable location. However, as far as the owner of the complex is concerned, the continued payment of rent is not perceived as adequate. Frequently, the rent that the anchor tenant is paying will be below what was the market rate at the time of its entry into the lease because the owner of the complex was anxious to provide an incentive to secure such a desirable tenant. Moreover, the payment of even the whole of that rent for the balance of the life of the lease will not reflect the losses suffered by the owner of the complex if it affects the ability to attract and retain other tenants in the balance of the complex. With the departure of the anchor tenant, the commercial desirability of the overall location may be diminished considerably. Indeed, depending on the terms of the lease with other existing tenants, the departure of the anchor tenant may put the owner in breach of its contractual obligations to those tenants. A further dimension is added where the situation does not involve a surrender of the lease but a mere cessation of operations with the premises simply going "dark." In such cases, there is not even the possibility of mitigation.

Thomas Borthwick might help in situations where the tenant in question has only one operation. Given an appropriately worded contractual provision, a court might conceivably award an injunction ordering the tenant not to carry on business save at that location. An example of this is afforded by *Edmonton Northlands v. Edmonton Oilers Hockey Corp.* (1993), 15 Alta. LR (3d) 179 (QB), aff'd. (1994), 17 Alta. LR (3d) 382 (CA), in which the applicant secured interlocutory relief restraining the hockey club from decamping and playing its home games elsewhere in breach of a 15-year licensing agreement. However, in most instances, the lessor is confronted with a tenant that operates many branches and that is simply making an economic decision to close an unprofitable one or one that no longer fits within its overall business plan. This suggests a major impediment to a *Thomas Borthwick*-type remedy. Only direct relief will seemingly do in most of these cases—either a decree of specific performance or a mandatory injunction enjoining the defendant from closing out its operation at the relevant location. Unfortunately for lessors, the bulk of the Canadian jurisprudence is against the award of such relief in these circumstances. See A.M. Kaufman, "Operating Clauses in Shopping Centre Leases: Lights Out for the Vacating Tenant" (1991), 18 *Can. Bus. LJ* 245. See, as well as the case excerpted here, *Bramalea Ltd. v. Canada Safeway Ltd.* (1985), 4 CPC (2d) 144 (Ont. HC); *Lundrigan Group Ltd. v. Lawton's Drug Stores Ltd.* (1985), Nfld. & PEIR 22 (Nfld. Dist. Ct.); *Weyburn Square Developments v. Liggett Drug Ltd.*, [1988] 6 WWR 401 (Sask. QB); *Islington Village Inc. v. Citibank Canada* (1992), 27 RPR (2d) 100 (Ont. Gen. Div.), aff'd. (November 23, 1992) [1992] OJ no. 2953 (CA); *Lackner Centre Developments Inc. v. TD Bank* (1993), 32 RPR (2d) 204 (Ont. Gen. Div.); *Chatham Centre Mall v. New Miracle Food Mart Inc.* (1994), 40 RPR (2d) 129 (Ont. Gen. Div.); *566719 Ontario Ltd. v. New Miracle Food Mart Inc.* (1994), 41 RPR (2d) 22 (Ont. Gen. Div.); *Toulon Development Corporation v. Loblaws* (1995), 161 NBR (2d) 313 (QB); *Centre City Capital Ltd. v. Bank of East Asia (Canada)*, [1997] OJ no. 5218 (Gen. Div.) (QL); *West Nipissing Economic Development Corp. v. Weyerhaeuser Co.*, [2002] OJ no. 4731 (Sup. Ct.); *Vista Sudbury Hotel Inc. v. Oshawa Group Ltd.*, [2004] OJ no. 2206 (QL); and *Longwood Station Ltd. v. Coast*

Capital Savings Credit Union, [2007] BCJ no. 2300 (SC). Indeed, outside of Quebec, there seems to have been only one successful application for this kind of relief: *Bentall Properties Ltd. v. Canada Safeway Ltd.*, [1988] BCJ no. 775 (SC) (QL) and this was in the context of interlocutory, not final, relief. Subsequently, the BC Court of Appeal distinguished *Bentall* but remarked:

> Some academic commentators have suggested that the cases have given inadequate weight to the equitable nature of the remedy and the potential unfairness to the landlord and other tenants of allowing the tenant to "turn out the lights." I should not be taken as saying that it is the law of British Columbia that an order of that kind cannot be granted.

See *A.L. Sott Financial (Newton) Inc. v. Vancouver City Savings Credit Union* (2000), 72 BCLR (3d) 383 (CA).

S.B.I. Management Ltd. v. Wabush (Carol) Co-op Society Ltd.
(1985), 51 Nfld. & PEIR 257 (Nfld. SC)

STEELE J: This is an application by S.B.I. Management Limited (S.B.I.) the owner and lessor of Carol Lake Shopping Center at Labrador City, for an injunction prohibiting the defendant, Carol Wabush Co-op Society Limited (Co-op) from vacating the leased premises in the shopping center and ceasing to carry on its supermarket business. The plaintiff relies on clauses 5.01 and 5.03 of the lease between the parties.

> 5.01 The Tenant will not use or occupy the Leased Premises or any part thereof for any purpose other than the operation of the business of a supermarket under the name of "Co-op."
>
> 5.03 The Tenant shall not leave said Leased Premises unoccupied or vacant, but shall continuously during the entire Term of his Lease conduct and carry on in the Leased Premises the type of business for which the Leased Premises are leased, keep in stock in said store a full and ample line of merchandise for the purpose of carrying on its retail business therein, maintain an adequate sales force to serve properly all customers and operate said business in an efficient and diligent manner.

The Co-op takes the position that the supermarket is no longer financially viable and that economic hardship will continue if operations at that particular shopping center do not cease. On January 21, 1985, the directors of the Co-op decided to discontinue the supermarket operation as of the end of February, "because of declining sales and mounting business losses." It intends to continue its supermarket business at another long established outlet in the Town of Labrador City approximately two miles away. Counsel for the Co-op states emphatically that the defendant will continue to pay the basic rent of $50,000.00 per annum together with the additional rent of $1,250.00. The Co-op is willing and indeed anxious to co-operate with any intended subtenant permitted to take over with the consent of S.B.I. It says it will remain liable to the plaintiff-landlord for any breaches of the lease by any sub-tenant.

S.B.I. claims that if the Co-op is permitted to breach the lease (clauses 5.01 and 5.03 in particular) that it will suffer irreparable harm and immeasurable damages. Counsel for the plaintiff points out, firstly, that there will be a reduction in consumer traffic in the shopping center as a whole; that they will lose their right and expectancy to receive percentage rental from the Co-op; and thirdly, that they will lose the benefit of percentage rental from certain other tenants in the shopping center that are now obligated to pay percentage rental. Counsel for S.B.I. maintains that the court is obligated to prevent the anticipated breach of the lease announced by the Co-op by the issuing of a mandatory injunction prohibiting the Co-op from ceasing to carry on its supermarket operations. S.B.I. insists that the Co-op be compelled by injunction to honour the terms of the lease.

Counsel for the Co-op says that the order requested is essentially an order of the court directing the Co-op to continue to carry on a supermarket business.

A mandatory injunction is one which requires a party to act positively. It looks into the future and requires a party to carry out a duty that it is obligated to perform. The granting of a mandatory injunction is governed by the general principles for the granting of injunctive relief but there are, as we shall see, certain special problems. ...

In my opinion the granting of a mandatory injunction as requested in this case would not be appropriate and in fact be contrary to long established policy that the court ought not to order specific performance of an obligation involving continuous acts requiring supervision by the court, as for example, the carrying on of a business or a service contract. As we shall see the order requested could not possibly be enforced. In short, it involves the performance of a duty under a lease (contract) that necessitates continuous acts in the future making inevitable supervision by the court.

In the text by Robert J. Sharpe, *Injunction on [sic] Specific Performance* (Toronto: Canada Law Book Co., 1983), the learned author states at page 13:

> It is often said that where the obligation of the defendant requires performance of an ongoing or complex nature, the court will not grant an injunction, thereby undertaking the task of supervision.
>
> The difficulty of supervision and the court's reluctance to make an order which will require further judicial direction or intervention is a familiar theme, especially in mandatory injunction cases.

In *Dowty Boulton Paul Ltd. v. Wolverhampton Corp.*, [1971] 1 WLR 204 (Ch.) at pp. 211-12, Pennycuick V-C stated:

> It is very well established that the court will not order specific performance of an obligation to carry on a business or, indeed, any comparable series of activities. See in this connection 30 Halsbury's Laws (3rd Ed.), pp. 267-69, paras. 365-366:
>
> > The court does not enforce the performance of contracts which involve continuous acts and require the watching and supervision of the court. ...
> >
> > A judgment for specific performance is not pronounced, either at the suit of the employer or the employee, in the case of a contract for personal work or service. ... This principle applies not merely to contracts which involve the rendering of continuous services by one person to another, as, for instance, a contract to work a railway line.
>
> The cases cited in the note under that last sentence are a number of cases in the middle of the last century. It would not be useful to refer to them. The principle is established, I should have thought, beyond argument. For this purpose there is no difference between an order for

specific performance of the contract and a mandatory injunction to perform the party's obligation under the contract.

In *Attorney General v. Colchester Corporation*, [1955] 2 QB 207, Lord Goddard CJ, at p. 217 observed:

> No authority has been quoted to show that an injunction will be granted enjoining a person to carry on a business, nor can I think that one ever would be, certainly not where the business is a losing concern. ...

No doubt the general rule is that the court is reticent and cautiously shies away from a mandatory injunction or an order of specific performance in circumstances that require a defendant to perform continuous acts of a complex nature in the future and by their nature requiring surveillance and supervision from the court. However, as pointed out by Sharpe at pages 14-23 and 285-286 the tendency to avoid injunctions or orders necessitating supervision is not absolute. At page 286 Sharpe observed:

> The supervision concern has already been examined in the context of injunctions. There it was observed that while there is a preference for orders which do not require subsequent litigation to test the adequacy of the defendant's compliance, such orders will be made where justice requires. Similarly, with specific performance, there has never been an absolute refusal to award the remedy in cases which might require supervision where the plaintiff is able to demonstrate sufficient need for it. In fact, the principle is a flexible one.

In recognizing the flexibility of the principle or rule avoiding orders that require supervision I am on the facts of this case satisfied that the granting of the injunction requested would not be appropriate. Apart from the likelihood of supervision the order could never be satisfactorily enforced.

I have discussed the authorities that support the principle that the court does not willingly grant orders that require supervision of continuous acts. Coupled with that rule is the requirement that a mandatory injunction ought to be granted in such terms that the person against whom it is granted must know exactly what he is required to do. It is a matter of clearly understanding the court's direction.

Counsel for S.B.I. requests an order that the Co-op be restrained from ceasing to carry on its business operations on the leased premises and in particular demands compliance with article 5.03 of the lease. In this respect I agree with counsel for the Co-op that what is asked for is in actuality an order directing the Co-op to continue to carry on a supermarket business at the shopping center. What immediately arises is the definition of "supermarket"; when is a supermarket no longer a supermarket? It is a matter of interpretation and definition. The problem is twofold: firstly, we have the carrying on of a supermarket business on a day to day basis that would in due course require the court's intervention and oversight, and secondly, the more basic question of what is required to constitute a business a supermarket.

The problems of complying with such an order are overwhelming: Can staff be reduced? Can certain products, lines or commodities be curtailed or discontinued? What must the magnitude and size of the operation be in order to be a "supermarket"? How many days or nights a week must the operation be open without being in breach of the condition? The questions and problems are numerous. It is equally obvious that the answers do not immediately spring to mind. It is apparent that any injunction or order that directs compliance with article 5.03 of the lease cannot define or establish with any degree of accuracy a standard or qualification to make a business a supermarket; secondly, even if such an order were possible, it would require superintendence by the court. It would be an order that could not be enforced. It is for these reasons that I conclude in the exercise of my discretion that the injunction requested must be refused.

In the event that the defendant breaches the lease, as it has threatened to do, the plaintiff's remedy is in damages. Admittedly vexed questions may arise on any assessment of damages. However, difficulty in assessing damages is not necessarily synonymous with irreparable harm or immeasurable damages. These questions are problems for another day.

The plaintiff's summons is dismissed. In the exercise of my discretion I order that costs be costs in the cause.

NOTES AND QUESTIONS

1. Obviously, one of the primary concerns identified by the court in this case is a perceived difficulty of supervision of any decree of specific performance or of a mandatory injunction. How can the court judge whether the defendant is continuing to operate the business in a manner consistent with the spirit of the contract and in such a way as to maintain the image and reputation of the complex? Is this an impediment to such relief in all cases of this kind? Can these problems be avoided by the fashioning of a sufficiently precise decree or by the inclusion of a sufficiently precise clause in the relevant contract? In this latter respect, how might one improve on the clause in *Wabush*?

2. Assuming that securing a mandatory injunction is impossible or virtually so in such cases, how would you proceed to develop a claim for damages to reflect the full extent of the lessor's interest in the performance of the contract?

3. In his article, extracts from which are reproduced early in chapter 9, Donald H. Clark adverts to the slight possibility that the situation might be more favourable to the lessor if there was a clause in the contract stipulating the availability of specific performance or a mandatory injunction as the remedy that would flow from breach. How, if at all, should this change the situation? According to Gotlib J in *Tritav Holdings Ltd. v. National Bank of Canada* (1996), 47 CPC (3d) 91 (Ont. Gen. Div.), it should make no difference: "Whether or not the landlord comes to this court with clean hands, I express the view that the parties cannot contract out of the law as it exists." Do you agree? Incidentally, what is the law that cannot be contracted out of: the law on the availability of mandatory injunctions in cases of this kind, or the more general discretion of the courts over the grant of equitable remedies?

4. For another dimension of the anchor tenant problem, see *Gateway Realty Ltd. v. Arton Holdings Ltd.* (1991), 106 NSR (2d) 163 (TD).

5. This domain may perhaps provide one example of the civil law's greater willingness than the common law to provide specific relief. Recall the Quebec case noted by Clark in his article where Montgomery JA, in sustaining the award of a mandatory injunction to prevent a bank from closing its doors at a particular location, posited that it was not in the bank's interests to offer inferior service at that location in response to the order to remain open: *Royal Bank of Canada v. Propriétés Cité Concordia Ltée (No. 2)*, [1983] RDJ no. 524 (CA). More recently, a court in another civil law jurisdiction, Scotland, has responded in much the same

way. In *Retail Parks Investments Ltd. v. Royal Bank of Scotland*, [1996] SLT 669, an Extra Division of the Inner House of the Court of Session issued a decree ordering the bank to stay in business during normal working hours at a particular location until August 17, 2002. The court held that the obligations of the bank were set out with sufficient precision in the relevant lease and the enforcement difficulties could too easily be exaggerated in such cases. Subsequently, in *Highland and Universal Properties Ltd. v. Safeway Properties Ltd.*, [2000] Sessions Cases 297, [2000] SLT 414, the Scottish Court of Sessions decreed performance of a covenant in a lease requiring the tenant supermarket to remain open for trade during normal business hours until March 24, 2009. Both these cases stand in stark contrast to the decision of the House of Lords in the following case.

Co-operative Insurance Society Ltd. v. Argyll Stores (Holdings) Ltd.
[1996] Ch. 286

[The plaintiff had leased a unit in a shopping centre to the defendant for the operation of a Safeway supermarket. The lease was to run for 35 years from August 1974 and the supermarket was an anchor or key tenant. In April 1995, having incurred operating losses of £70,300 in the previous year, the defendant gave notice that it was closing the store (along with 26 others throughout the country). The plaintiff responded by offering to allow the defendant to remain at a decreased rent until such time as a suitable assignee could be found, assignment being permitted under the lease. The defendant did not respond but instead stripped the store of fixtures and fittings and closed it.

The relevant provisions of the lease were to the effect that the tenant would not use the "premises for any purpose other than as a retail store for the sale of food, groceries, provisions and goods" and that it would

> keep the demised premises open for retail trade during the usual hours of business in the locality and the display windows properly dressed in a suitable manner in keeping with a good class parade of shops.

The plaintiff sought specific performance of these covenants in the lease and/or damages. On a motion for summary judgment, the judge refused to order specific performance but instead granted an order for damages. The plaintiff appealed to the Court of Appeal.]

ROCH LJ: One matter that has been quite apparent in this appeal is that the defendants have behaved very badly. In 1982 they entered into a lease of the premises for a term of 35 years from 4 August 1979, the term expiring in the year 2014. They knew that they were the tenants of the anchor unit at this shopping centre, and that the presence of a supermarket would attract other small businesses to the centre, which in many cases, without a supermarket being there, would not be viable. They entered into covenants under which they undertook to operate and keep open the demised premises as a supermarket. No doubt the rent they paid was lower because of the obligations that they had assumed under those covenants. The defendants were not bound themselves to maintain a supermarket at this shopping centre for 35 years because they had the power to sublet the premises or assign the remainder of their lease.

In April 1995 the defendants wished to cease operating a supermarket at the Hillsborough Shopping Centre. They communicated their intention to close their supermarket to the plaintiffs on 11 April by letter.

[The plaintiffs responded on April 12. After setting out the terms of that letter, Roch LJ continued:]

The defendants deliberately did not answer or acknowledge that letter. Instead they proceeded, starting on 6 May, to strip out the fixtures and fittings of the premises and to close the supermarket, completing this process of 19 May, despite being sent a further letter by the plaintiffs' solicitors dated 11 May requiring them to comply with their covenants. When this process had been completed the defendants were able to say that an order by the court requiring them to comply with their covenant would involve them in an expenditure estimated to exceed £1m. to refit the premises so that they would be suitable for use as a supermarket.

We therefore have the unedifying spectacle of a large commercial company seeking to rely on its own wanton and quite unreasonable conduct as one argument against the making of an order for specific performance. The purpose of the civil law is not to punish, save in certain limited and narrowly defined circumstances, but to compensate. The basic issue in this case, in my opinion, is whether damages are an adequate remedy. If they are, then no order for specific performance could be made. If they are not, there is the further question whether the judge was right to exercise his discretion to refuse an order for specific performance by the defendants of their covenants. It is not in my view helpful to ask whether a covenant in a lease sounds only in damages. Nor is it consistent with respect for the law to say that a clear undertaking freely entered into can be disregarded when that suits the covenantor on the payment of money, despite the effect that the breach may have on the covenantee and others, when the covenantor would know that the covenantee and others would rely on the fulfilment of the covenant.

In my judgment, damages are not an adequate remedy. Damages will not compensate the plaintiffs for the disappearance of the supermarket, or for the effect of that on the other businesses in the shopping centre. The plaintiffs' claim for damages cannot include compensation for their loss of revenue from other units in the shopping centre, because the tenants of those other units have contractual obligations to pay their rents which will survive the closure of the supermarket. More importantly, those involved in the other businesses, who assumed obligations under their leases in reliance on there being a supermarket in the shopping centre and who will be adversely affected, have no remedy against the defendants.

[Roch LJ here dealt with the question of whether there was a rule to the effect that specific performance or a mandatory injunction would not be granted in cases such as this. After referring, *inter alia*, to *Giles & Co. v. Morris* in chapter 9, "Specific Performance," and *Redland Bricks v. Morris* in chapter 7, "Injunctions," he concluded that the time had come "for rethinking the rationale for the rule or practice whichever it may be." He then continued:]

Damages not being an adequate remedy for the plaintiffs, should the court nevertheless have declined to grant specific performance? There was nothing in the conduct of the plaintiffs which could lead a court to decline to grant this equitable remedy. The plaintiffs were not guilty of delay nor had they behaved in any way in which it could be said that they did not come to court with clean hands.

Was this an order which should not be made because it was either indefinite in time or an order the terms of which could not be sufficiently precise? In my view, neither of those considerations represented in this case a reason for withholding the remedy. Specific performance would require the defendants to operate a supermarket at the premises until the year 2014 or until such time as they obtained a subtenant or assignee willing and capable to operate a supermarket at the Hillsborough Shopping Centre. Further it is, in my opinion, possible to define with sufficient certainty the obligations which the order would enjoin the defendants to meet in carrying on the business of a supermarket: the order would simply repeat the terms of the covenants into which the defendants had entered. There has been no suggestion in this case, any more than there was in the *Braddon Towers* case ([1987] 1 EGLR 209), that the terms of such covenants were so uncertain that the covenants were void. Further, if the defendants are ordered to continue the operation of a supermarket at the premises, it is inconceivable that they would not operate the business efficiently. To do otherwise would damage their commercial reputation. Day-to-day supervision by the court or by the plaintiffs would be unnecessary.

The second matter on which the judge relied when exercising his discretion not to grant specific performance was:

> The situation with which the court is now presented is one in which a vastly disproportionate amount of costs would be incurred if the order was made at this stage. It is of course the case that the defendants closed the store, in deliberate and knowing breach of its covenant. However, it did so openly and in the light of the settled practice of the court to award damages. That, of course, is a further good reason for me to follow that practice and not to depart from it.

Here, in my opinion, the judge misdirected himself. In *Morris's* case ([1970] AC 652, at p. 666) Lord Upjohn said:

> Unlike the case where a negative injunction is granted to prevent the continuance or recurrence of a wrongful act the question of the cost to the defendant to do works to prevent or lessen the likelihood of a future apprehended wrong must be an element to be taken into account: (a) where the defendant has acted without regard to his neighbour's rights, or has tried to steal a march on him or has tried to evade the jurisdiction of the court or, to sum it up, has acted wantonly and quite unreasonably in relation to his neighbour he may be ordered to repair his wanton and unreasonable acts by doing positive work to restore the status quo even if the expense to him is out of all proportion to the advantage thereby accruing to the plaintiff. ... (b) but where the defendant has acted reasonably, though in the event wrongly, the cost of remedying by positive action his earlier activities is most important for two reasons. First, because no legal wrong has yet occurred (for which he has not been recompensed at law and in equity) and, in spite of gloomy expert opinion, may never occur or possibly only upon a much smaller scale than anticipated. Secondly, because if ultimately heavy damage does occur the plaintiff is in no way prejudiced for he has his action at law and all his consequential remedies in equity. So the amount to be expended under a mandatory order by the defendant must be balanced with these considerations in mind against the anticipated possible damage to the plaintiff and if, on such balance, it seems unreasonable to inflict such expenditure upon one

who for this purpose is no more than a potential wrongdoer then the court must exercise its jurisdiction accordingly.

In the present case the defendants fall clearly within category (a) as being persons who have acted wantonly and quite unreasonably in ignoring the plaintiffs' letters and in removing from the premises all the fixtures and equipment necessary for them to be operated as a supermarket, despite the fact that the loss made at that supermarket was considerably less than the annual rental payable, and the plaintiffs had indicated a willingness to adjust the rent in the event of the defendants continuing to operate their supermarket until such time as they could find a subtenant or assignee.

[In concurring with Roch LJ, Leggatt LJ dealt in greater detail with the argument that the court should not grant relief because of the "settled practice" of the courts not to exercise their discretion in favour of plaintiff in this kind of case. He was clearly of the view that any reliance by the defendant on that "settled practice" should not get in the way of the court granting relief in a situation such as this. In contrast, the dissenting judge placed great store on the "settled practice."]

Appeal allowed with costs.
Order for specific performance of terms of lease suspended until March 4, 1996.

NOTE

On appeal, the House of Lords unanimously reversed the Court of Appeal. In so doing, it did not place great emphasis on the "settled practice" and reliance induced by that. Rather, as in *Wabush*, above, the court's major concern was the traditional one of difficulty of supervision and the associated prospect of contempt proceedings. The extract from the principal judgment of Lord Hoffmann that follows also identifies another reason for denying relief as well as the court's direct critique of the majority reasoning in the Court of Appeal.

Co-operative Insurance Society Ltd. v. Argyll Stores (Holdings) Ltd.
[1998] AC 1 (HL (Eng.))

LORD HOFFMANN: ... There is a further objection to an order requiring the defendant to carry on a business, which was emphasised by Millett LJ in the Court of Appeal. This is that it may cause injustice by allowing the plaintiff to enrich himself at the defendant's expense. The loss which the plaintiff may suffer through having to comply with the order (for example, by running a business at a loss for an indefinite period) may be far greater than the plaintiff would suffer from the contract being broken. As Professor R.J. Sharpe explains ("Specific Remedies for Contract Breach" in *Studies in Contract Law* (eds. Reiter and Swan) at p. 129):

> In such circumstances, a specific decree in favour of the plaintiff will put him in a bargaining position vis à vis the defendant whereby the measure of what he will receive will be the value to the defendant of being released from performance. If the plaintiff bargains effectively, the

amount he will set will exceed the value to him of performance and will approach the cost to the defendant to complete.

This was the reason given by Lord Westbury LC in *Isenberg v. East India House Estate Co. Ltd.* (1863), 3 De GJ & S 263 at p. 273 for refusing a mandatory injunction to compel the defendant to pull down part of a new building which interfered with the plaintiff's light and exercising instead the Court of Chancery's recently-acquired jurisdiction under *Lord Cairns' Act, 1858* to order payment of damages:

> ... I hold it ... to be the duty of the court in such a case as the present not, by granting a mandatory injunction, to deliver over the defendants to the plaintiff bound hand and foot, in order to be made subject to any extortionate demand that he may by possibility make, but to substitute for such mandatory injunction an inquiry before itself, in order to ascertain the measure of damage that has been actually sustained.

It is true that the defendant has, by his own breach of contract, put himself in such an unfortunate position. But the purpose of the law of contract is not to punish wrongdoing but to satisfy the expectations of the party entitled to performance. A remedy which enables him to secure, in money terms, more than the performance due to him is unjust. From a wider perspective, it cannot be in the public interest for the courts to require someone to carry on business at a loss if there is any plausible alternative by which the other party can be given compensation. It is not only a waste of resources but yokes the parties together in a continuing hostile relationship. The order for specific performance prolongs the battle. If the defendant is ordered to run a business, its conduct becomes the subject of a flow of complaints, solicitors' letters and affidavits. This is wasteful for both parties and the legal system. An award of damages, on the other hand, brings the litigation to an end. The defendant pays damages, the forensic link between them is severed, they go their separate ways and the wounds of conflict can heal.

The cumulative effect of these various reasons, none of which would necessarily be sufficient on its own, seems to me to show that the settled practice is based upon sound sense. Of course the grant or refusal of specific performance remains a matter for the judge's discretion. There are no binding rules, but this does not mean that there cannot be settled principles, founded upon practical considerations of the kind which I have discussed, which do not have to be re-examined in every case, but which the courts will apply in all but exceptional circumstances. As Slade J said in the passage which I have quoted from *Braddon Towers Ltd. v. International Stores Ltd.*, [1987] 1 EGLR 209, at p. 213, lawyers have no doubt for many years advised their clients on this basis. In the present case, Leggatt LJ remarked that there was no evidence that such advice had been given. In my view, if the law or practice on a point is settled, it should be assumed that persons entering into legal transactions will have been advised accordingly. I am sure that the learned Lord Justice would not wish to encourage litigants to adduce evidence of the particular advice which they received. Indeed, I doubt whether such evidence would be admissible.

5. The Decision of the Court of Appeal

I must now examine the grounds upon which the majority of the Court of Appeal thought it right to reverse the judge. In the first place, they regarded the practice which he followed as outmoded and treated Lord Wilberforce's remarks about relief against forfeiture in *Shiloh Spinners Ltd. v. Harding*, [1973] AC 691, at p. 724 as justifying a rejection of the arguments based on the need for constant supervision. Even Millett LJ, who dissented on other grounds, said that such objections had little force today. I do not agree. As I have already said, I think that Lord Wilberforce's remarks do not support this proposition in relation to specific performance of an obligation to carry on an activity and that the arguments based on difficulty of supervision remain powerful.

The Court of Appeal said that it was enough if the contract defined the tenant's obligation with sufficient precision to enable him to know what was necessary to comply with the order. Even assuming that this to be right, I do not think that the obligation in clause 4(19) can possibly be regarded as sufficiently precise to be capable of specific performance. It is to "keep the demised premises open for retail trade." It says nothing about the level of trade, the area of the premises within which trade is to be conducted, or even the kind of trade, although no doubt the tenant's choice would be restricted by the need to comply with the negative covenant in clause 4(12)(a) not to use the premises "other than as a retail store for the sale of food groceries provisions and goods normally sold from time to time by a retail grocer food supermarkets and food superstores." This language seems to me to provide ample room for argument over whether the tenant is doing enough to comply with the covenant.

The Court of Appeal thought that once Argyll had been ordered to comply with the covenant, it was, as Roch LJ said, "inconceivable that they would not operate the business efficiently." Leggatt LJ said that the requirement "was quite intelligible to the defendants, while they were carrying on business there … . If the premises are to be run as a business, it cannot be in the defendants' interest to run it half-heartedly or inefficiently … ." This treats the way the tenant previously conducted business as measuring the extent of his obligation to do so. In my view this is a non sequitur: the obligation depends upon the language of the covenant and not upon what the tenant has previously chosen to do. No doubt it is true that it would not be in the interests of the tenant to run the business inefficiently. But running the business efficiently does not necessarily mean running in the way it was run before. Argyll had decided that, from its point of view, the most efficient thing to do was to close the business altogether and concentrate its resources on achieving better returns elsewhere. If ordered to keep the business open, it might well decide that the next best strategy was to reduce its costs as far as was consistent with compliance with its obligations, in the expectation that a lower level of return would be more than compensated by higher returns from additional expenditure on more profitable shops. It is in my view wrong for the courts to speculate about whether Argyll might voluntarily carry on business in a way which would relieve the court from having to construe its order. The question of certainty must be decided on the assumption that the court might have to enforce the order according to its terms.

The respondent argued that the court should not be concerned about future difficulties which might arise in connection with the enforcement of the order. It should simply make the order and see what happened. In practice Argyll would be likely to find a suitable assignee (as it in fact did) or conduct the business so as to keep well clear of any possible enforcement proceedings or otherwise come to terms with the CIS. This may well be true, but the likelihood of Argyll having to perform beyond the requirements of its covenant or buy its way out of its obligation to incur losses seems to me to be in principle an objection to such an order rather than to recommend it. I think that it is normally undesirable for judges to make orders in terrorem, carrying a threat of imprisonment, which work only if no one inquires too closely into what they mean.

The likelihood that the order would be effective only for a short time until an assignment is an equivocal argument. It would be burdensome to make Argyll resume business only to stop again after a short while if a short stoppage would not cause any substantial damage to the business of the shopping centre. On the other hand, what would happen if a suitable assignee could not be found? Would Argyll then have to carry on business until 2014? Mr. Smith who appeared for the CIS, said that if the order became oppressive (for example, because Argyll were being driven into bankruptcy) or difficult to enforce, they could apply for it to be varied or discharged. But the order would be a final order and there is no case in this jurisdiction in which such an order has been varied or discharged, except when the injuncted activity has been legalised by statute. Even assuming that there was such a jurisdiction if circumstances were radically changed, I find it difficult to see how this could be made to apply. Difficulties of enforcement would not be a change of circumstances. They would have been entirely predictable when the order was made. And so would the fact that Argyll would suffer unquantifiable loss if it was obliged to continue trading. I do not think that such expedients are an answer to the difficulties on which the objections to such orders are based.

Finally, all three judges in the Court of Appeal took a very poor view of Argyll's conduct. Leggatt LJ said that they had acted "with gross commercial cynicism"; Roch LJ began his judgment by saying that they had "behaved very badly" and Millett LJ said that they had no merits. The principles of equity have always had a strong ethical content and nothing which I say is intended to diminish the influence of moral values in their application. I can envisage cases of gross breach of personal faith, or attempts to use the threat of non-performance as blackmail, in which the needs of justice will override all the considerations which support the settled practice. But although any breach of covenant is regrettable, the exercise of the discretion as to whether or not to grant specific performance starts from the fact that the covenant has been broken. Both landlord and tenant in this case are large sophisticated commercial organisations and I have no doubt that both were perfectly aware that the remedy for breach of the covenant was likely to be limited to an award of damages. The interests of both were purely financial: there was no element of personal breach of faith, as in the Victorian cases of railway companies which refused to honour obligations to build stations for landowners whose property they had taken: compare *Greene v. West Cheshire Railway Co.* (1871), LR 13 Eq. 44. No doubt there was an effect on the businesses of other traders in the Centre, but Argyll had made no promises to them and it is not suggested that CIS warranted to other tenants that Argyll would remain. Their departure, with or without the consent of CIS, was a commercial risk which the tenants were able to deploy in negotiations for the next rent review. On the scale of broken promises, I can think of worse cases, but the language of the Court of Appeal left them with few adjectives to spare.

It was no doubt discourteous not to have answered Mr. Wightman's letter. But to say, as Roch LJ did, that they had acted "wantonly and quite unreasonably" by removing their fixtures seems to me an exaggeration. There was no question of stealing a march, or attempting to present CIS with a fait accompli, because Argyll had no reason to believe that CIS would have been able to obtain a mandatory injunction whether the fixtures had been removed or not. They had made it perfectly clear that they were closing the shop and given CIS ample time to apply for such an injunction if so advised.

Appeal allowed.

NOTES

1. Which court has the better argument?

2. The judgment of the House of Lords was referred to and applied by the General Division of the Ontario Court in *Centre City Capital Ltd. v. Bank of East Asia (Canada)*, above. However, in *A.L. Sott Financial (Newton) Inc. v. Vancouver City Savings Credit Union*, 2000 BCCA 143, 72 BCLR (3d) 383, the BC Court of Appeal stated that it would be open to applying the Scottish authority, *Retail Parks Investments Ltd. v. Royal Bank of Scotland*, above, instead of *Argyll Stores* in an appropriate case.

3. In *Highland and Universal Properties Ltd. v. Safeway Properties Ltd.*, above, Lord Kingarth, of the Scottish Court of Sessions, wrote:

> One factor referred to specifically [by Lord Hoffmann in *Argyll Stores*] was the need for constant supervision by the court—in the sense of the court having to give an indefinite series of rulings in applications made by the parties in order to ensure the execution of the order. In Scotland, however, any practical difficulties in policing compliance with an order of the type in question can be exaggerated. As Lord McCluskey indicated in [*Retail Parks Investments Ltd. v. Royal Bank of Scotland (No. 2)*, 1996 SC 227; 1995 SLT 1156 (Outer House)]:
>
>> The possible difficulties for the debtor in the obligation in knowing what is required of him should be considered against the background of the enforcement procedures available if a breach of the order is alleged. Thus, if the pursuers were to allege a breach they would require to proceed by petition and complaint and, unless a breach were to be admitted, the court would then have to determine whether or not any breach of the order had occurred and, before imposing a penalty, would have to be satisfied that the defenders had acted or were acting in wilful disobedience of the court's order: these procedures would diminish the risk of a person's being punished for, or even found in breach of, a court order which turned out to be lacking in precision. Furthermore, if the court, after the matter has been brought to its attention in a petition and complaint, were to hold that the defenders had not complied with the order but that the non-compliance was not a wilful defying of the court's order, the court could, without proceeding to punishment, give the defenders a further opportunity to comply in the light of the court's pronouncement that the order has been breached by the defenders' previous acts or omissions. Accordingly there should be no insuperable difficulty in policing compliance with an order of the court pronounced in suitable terms.
>
> The history in Scotland since ... orders, at least ad interim, have routinely been granted ... has not, it seems, given rise to any obvious difficulties in enforcement or supervision. Another factor referred to in [*Argyll Stores*] was the difficulty of drawing an order, reflecting the terms of the obligation, with sufficient precision. In Scotland, however, if the particular order sought was one which passed what Lord McCluskey described as "the usual and familiar tests of precision, speci-

fication, definition and notice" (*Retail Parks Investments* at p 242) (and thus if the position was that the order sought was prima facie competent) it would be difficult to see how similar considerations would arise at the stage when the court's discretion was considered. In any event, contrary to the defenders' submissions in this case, many of the difficulties said to be inherent in the looseness of the language of such clauses would, on the face of it, still require to be confronted in any claim for damages where loss fell to be measured against the performance which could have been expected if there had been no breach.

4. In *Nickel Developments Ltd. v. Canada Safeway Ltd.* (2001), 199 DLR (4th) 629 (Man. CA), the owner of a shopping centre sued for a declaration that its anchor tenant, Safeway, was in breach of a covenant requiring that the leased premises be used "only as a supermarket and for no other purpose." With five years remaining in the lease, Safeway, which had opened another supermarket elsewhere in the same small city, had ceased operations in the shopping centre while remaining in occupation and continuing to pay rent so as to prevent a competitor from taking its place. The majority of the court (Twaddle J dissenting) held that the undertaking to "use the leased premises only as a supermarket and for no other purpose" not only limited Safeway's use of the premises but moreover required it to use them for that purpose continuously. The court granted the declaration (this was not an action for specific performance). In the course of their majority judgment, Kroft and Monnin JJA emphasized that the "stay open" covenant was central to the bargain between the parties:

> The Westwood Shopping Centre has provided significant and intended advantages to Safeway. These include the construction in accordance with its specifications and non-competition protection during its term. For these and other benefits received, Safeway assumed obligations including the undertaking to continue to operate a supermarket in the shopping centre that would attract clientele to the premises as a whole. That theme is central to the lease and to this judgment.

5. For a critical analysis of the decision of the House of Lords in *Argyll Stores*, see Andrew M. Tettenborn, "Absolving the Undeserving: Shopping Centres, Specific Performance and the Law of Contract" (1998), *The Conveyancer and Property Lawyer* 23. See also D. Pearce, "Remedies for Breach of a Keep-Open Covenant" (2008), 24 *J Contract L* 199.

REMEDY STIPULATION

One potential way of limiting the discretion of the court over the grant and extent of remedies under a contract is by way of contractual provision specifying the nature and limits of recourse available where it is alleged that the contract has been breached. As reflected in arbitration clauses, such attempts at remedy stipulation may be directed to control over the forum that will adjudicate disputes. They may also purport to specify whether or not a specific remedy will be available in the event of breach, such as in the abortive provision for specific performance in *Tritav*, above. Commonly, contracts will also involve attempted regulation of the types and amount of damages available in the event of breach ("liquidated damages" clauses). We commence in this last domain before returning to more general questions about the legitimacy of remedy stipulation.

Elsley v. J.G. Collins Insurance Agencies Limited
[1978] 2 SCR 916

[The plaintiff purchased a general insurance business of a competitor, D.C. Elsley Ltd., owned by the defendant, Elsley. The agreement contained a restraint of trade clause preventing Elsley for a period of ten years from working in the general insurance business within the vicinity of the business. The parties further agreed to include a liquidated damages clause in which the vendor would pay $1,000 for each and every breach. Following the sale of the insurance business, the plaintiff employed Elsley to manage the general insurance business of his former company. Under the employment agreement a further restraint of trade clause was inserted in which Elsley agreed not to take part in the general insurance business for a period of five years following termination of employment within the vicinity of the business. A similar liquidated damages clause was inserted into this agreement. Elsley worked for the plaintiff for 17 years under the terms of the employment agreement, following which, after giving appropriate notice, he left the plaintiff's employment and commenced his own general insurance business, taking over half the plaintiff's clients with him. The plaintiff then commenced an action for damages for breach of the restraint of trade clause and for an injunction. The trial court allowed the action, granted the injunction, and awarded the plaintiff damages for the loss of premiums paid by the plaintiff's clients that had taken their business to the defendant. The defendant appealed. Before the Ontario Court of Appeal, the appeal was dismissed save one variation: that the damages should be assessed on the basis of all the commissions earned by the defendant from selling general insurance contracts down to the date of the granting of the injunction. The defendant appealed.]

DICKSON J [After concluding for the court that the covenant was enforceable, he continued:] The only other question is as to damages. The injunction granted at trial and continued by the Court of Appeal ceased to have effect with the death of Elsley, after the judgment of the Court of Appeal. Proceedings in this court were continued by his widow as executrix of his estate.

The damage issue is one of some importance and difficulty. It subsumes two questions: (i) the right of a plaintiff enforcing a restrictive covenant to claim both an injunction and damages: (ii) whether the quantum is, or is limited to, the amount stipulated as liquidated damages in the covenant. In other words, can Collins claim *any* damages; and if so, is the amount limited to $1,000? I would answer both of these questions in the affirmative.

The Court was referred to a number of authorities. The first, in time, was *Jones v. Heavens* (1877), 4 Ch. D 636. In that case, the covenant precluded the carrying on of the business of a saddler under penalty of 100 pounds to be paid by way of liquidated damages for each such offence. A motion was made for an injunction. It was argued that the plaintiff's remedy was by action for recovery of the sum named as liquidated damages. An injunction was granted. Thus, even where there is provision for liquidated damages, the plaintiff may elect instead to ask for an injunction to prevent breach.

In the later case of *National Provincial Bank of England v. Marshall* (1888), 40 Ch. D 112 (CA), the defendant, on entering the service of the plaintiffs, a banking company, had executed a bond in the penal sum of 1,000 pounds a condition of which was that he should pay this sum to the plaintiffs as liquidated damages if he should within a limited period after leaving the service of the plaintiffs accept employment in any other bank. The defendant accepted other employment in breach of the bond and the plaintiffs brought an action claiming an injunction. In response to the claim the defendant offered to pay the penal sum of 1,000 pounds. The Court held that he could not purchase his liberty to do the proscribed act. Lord Justice Cotton said that if the obligee brings an action at law he can recover damages, but (p. 116) "… if he comes into a Court of Equity the agreement will be enforced, if no action for damages has been brought, and an injunction will be granted." This case illustrates the principle that if the plaintiff is entitled to an injunction, the defendant cannot deprive him of this remedy by paying damages. The plaintiff may pursue whatever remedy is his due, even though it clearly affords him wider relief than another remedy open to him. Cotton LJ, added that if the Bank had brought an action they were not obliged to prove the damage they had suffered, but would be entitled without proof of damage to recover 1,000 pounds as liquidated damages. Lindley LJ, in the same case spoke of the plaintiffs having an alternative remedy by way of injunction to enforce the agreement if they do not bring an action.

An early Canadian case, *Snider v. McKelvey* (1900), 27 OAR 339, dealt also with the matter. The defendant, who had sold his medical practice, acted in defiance of the sale agreement by which he had bound himself in the sum of $400 to be paid if he set up in practice within a defined time and area. Robertson J granted an injunction and awarded damages of $100. On appeal, the Court held that the plaintiff must elect whether to take judgment for the $400 or for the injunction. The plaintiff insisted that the $400 was a penalty and, if such, he could have damages assessed for the breach of the condition as well as the injunction to restrain further breaches. Osler JA, in the leading judgment, rejected this argument. He declined to recognize any distinction between the case of bond with a penalty and an agreement to pay liquidated damages, because the plaintiff would, if the equitable remedy by injunction were enforced, be obtaining performance of the agreement *in specie* and also what he was only entitled to recover in the case of its non-performance. He was of opinion that the $400 was intended to be payable as liquidated damages. After referring to the passage of *Lord Cairns' Act*, 21-22 Vict., ch. 27, the learned judge of appeal had this to say, p. 344:

> It is clear that the Act did not enable the Court to give the plaintiff a double remedy where before the Act his right was in the alternative—either at law or in equity, but not in both: *Sainter v. Ferguson* (1849), 7 CB 716; 1 Mac. & G 286; 41 ER 1275 (Ch.).

The following passage from the judgment of Osler JA, is of particular interest because of the distinction made in respect of those cases concerning the sale of goodwill where there was no valid covenant or bond for the breach of which the plaintiff could have sued at law, and therefore no choice available between a suit at law and injunction in equity (pp. 344-5):

> The learned trial Judge relied upon the case of *Mossop v. Mason* (1869), 16 Gr. 302; (1870), 18 Gr. 360; (1871), 18 Gr. 453 (in appeal), where damages were awarded as well as an injunction. But that case is quite distinguishable. There the defendant had sold to the plaintiff *inter alia* the goodwill of the business of an innkeeper carried on by him, and the bill was filed to restrain him from resuming the business he had sold and for damages sustained in consequence of his having done so. There was, as the Court held, no valid covenant or bond for the breach of which the plaintiff could have sued at law. The plaintiff had, therefore, no alternative remedy, and his right to recover rested solely upon the defendant's equitable obligation, implied in the sale of the goodwill, not to hold out in any way that he was carrying on business in continuation of, or in succession to,

the business formerly carried on by him, the goodwill of which he had sold. See *Labouchere v. Dawson* (1872), LR 13 Eq. 322; approved in *Trego v. Hunt*, [1896] AC 7 (HL (Eng.)).

There was, therefore, nothing to prevent the Court from directing a reference to ascertain what damages the plaintiff had sustained consequent upon the breach of the equitable obligation.

We are, of course, not dealing here with a sale of goodwill but with an agreement for employment. McLennan JA shared the opinion of Osler JA that the $400 was clearly liquidated damages and he regarded it as clearly settled that in the case of liquidated damages the plaintiff must elect between the damages and an injunction. This case emphasizes that the basic principle being applied is the prohibition against double recovery. The agreed liquidated damages sum is to be a complete remedy for the entire breach specified. Once this sum has been awarded, to grant an injunction for even part of the breach would be to have overlapping remedies.

A year later, Wright J, in *General Accident Assurance Corporation v. Noel*, [1902] 1 KB 377, concluded that the current of authority in England was such that if the plaintiffs elected to take an injunction they could not have judgment as well for the liquidated damages for which the employment agreement in the case provided.

The British Columbia case of *Campbell, Imrie and Shankland v. Park*, [1954] 2 DLR 170 (BCSC) was cited in argument. In that case a restrictive covenant had been given by a chartered accountant engaged to serve as branch manager by a firm of accountants. The agreement was silent as to the payment of a stated amount for breach. The plaintiffs sought both injunction and damages. The defendant, relying on *General Accident Assurance Corporation v. Noel*, [1902] 1 KB 377 said they could not have both. Wilson J, as he then was, had this to say in respect of that contention, p. 183:

> The plaintiffs have asked for an injunction and for damages. The defendant, relying on *Gen'l Accident Ass'ce Corp. v. Noel*, [1902] 1 KB 377, says they cannot have both, but must elect. The case referred to is one in which the restrictive agreement contained a clause requiring the covenantor, in case of breach, to pay 100 pounds as liquidated damages. Very reasonably, the covenantee was required to elect. The sum of 100 pounds had been agreed to by the parties as being the total amount of damage which the covenantee would suffer by a breach. If he were paid this sum, he could not reasonably ask for an injunction to prohibit the doing of something in respect of which he had already collected full damages. But here the plaintiffs cannot say what their full damage may be i.e. the defendant is allowed to continue to attract their clients, they can only tell me what damage they have suffered to date, and ask me to prevent the defendant from inflicting on them further damage. I have no doubt that it is my right and duty so to do. I refer to *Garbutt Business College Ltd. v. Henderson*, [1939] 4 DLR 151 (Alta. SC), as a case in which both forms of relief were granted.

The judge fixed damages at $1,000 and granted an injunction.

In the recent case in this Court, *H.F. Clarke Limited v. Thermidaire Corporation Limited*, [1976] 1 SCR 319, the claim was for damages for breach of a restrictive covenant contained in a distributorship agreement. The question of injunction was not in issue. The agreement provided that the defaulting party would be required to pay as liquidated damages the gross profit realized from the sale of competitive products. The issue was whether the plaintiff could recover this amount or only provable damages. A majority of the Court held in favour of the latter disposition. In the majority judgment the Chief Justice in *obiter dicta* had this to say, p. 335:

> There is no doubt that a covenantee cannot have both an injunction during the covenant period and damages based on a breach of covenant for the entire period where they are based on a formula. There is case law holding that where a fixed sum is stipulated as the liquidated damages upon a breach, the covenantee cannot have both the damages and an injunction but must elect between the two remedies: see *General Accident Assurance Corp. v. Noel*, [1902] 1 KB 377; *Wirth and Hamid Booking Inc. v. Wirth* (1934), 192 NE 297 (CANY). I do not however read these cases as excluding damages for past loss by reason of the breach, but only as precluding recovery of the liquidated amount referable to breach in the future which that amount was designed to cover and against which an injunction has been granted.

The *Campbell, Imrie and Shankland* case, as well as the passages quoted above from *Snider* and *H.F. Clarke*, in my opinion, point up the fact that a plaintiff may have a right to damages in equity in addition to an injunction if he can establish his entitlement under the appropriate equitable considerations. In Ontario, the Court's power to award damages in equity is founded on what is now s. 21 of the *Judicature Act*, RSO 1970, c. 228, which is derived from *Lord Cairns' Act* of 1858. Section 21 provides as follows:

> 21. Where the court has jurisdiction to entertain an application for an injunction against a breach of a covenant, contract or agreement, or against the commission or continuance of a wrongful act, or for the specific performance of a covenant, contract or agreement, the court may award damages to the party injured either in addition to or in substitution for the injunction for specific performance, and the damages may be ascertained in such manner as the court directs, or the court may grant such other relief as is considered just.

It should be remembered that if a plaintiff is entitled to an injunction to restrain breach of a restrictive covenant, he is entitled to prevent the entire breach, not just part of it. Thus, for any part not restrained, he may be entitled to unliquidated damages in equity. There would be no double recovery provided the damages were not referable to any period during which breach was restrained by the injunction. This right to damages would not be based on the liquidated damages clause, but on the right under s. 21 to damages in equity in substitution for an injunction in respect of the period of breach prior to the granting of the injunction. A plaintiff, of course, cannot delay seeking an injunction in order to inflate his damages. He would not be entitled to damages past the time when he should have sought the injunction.

How then should the measure of such damages be determined? It will generally be appropriate to adopt in equity rules similar to those applicable at law: I.C.F. Spry, *Equitable Remedies* (Sydney Law Book Co., 1971), at pp. 552-4. This is so not because the Court is obliged to apply analogous legal criteria, but because the amount of compensation which would satisfy the loss suffered, and which the Court considers it just and equitable be paid, usually happens to be equivalent to the amount of legal damages which would be appropriate. The award is still governed, however, by general equitable considerations which would not apply if the plaintiff were seeking damages at law rather than in equity. These considerations might serve, for example, to reduce the amount, due to such factors as delay or acquiescence. In addition, if the parties have agreed on a set amount of damages at law, or a maximum amount, it would be unconscionable, in my opinion, to allow recovery of a greater amount of damages in equity.

In the case of a gross underestimate of damages as, presumably, in the present case, the plaintiff may receive an amount equivalent to the liquidated damages sum, plus an injunction, and therefore appear to have double relief. But such is not the case. The injunction relates to the latter part of the period in respect of which the restrictive covenant imposes restraint, the damages (not exceeding the stipulated liquidated damages) relate to the period prior to the granting of the injunction and are in substitution for injunctive relief during that period.

V

The matter of the right of a plaintiff to recover legal damages for actual loss sustained where a lesser stipulated amount is mentioned was considered in the House of Lords decision in *Cellulose Acetate Silk Company Limited v. Widnes Foundry (1925) Limited*, [1933] AC 20 (HL (Eng.)). The amount stipulated was 20 pounds for each week of delay in the erection of an acetone recovery plant. The contractors were thirty weeks late. The actual loss suffered was 5,850 pounds. The case is of interest in two respects. First, the recovery was limited to 600 pounds, the agreed damages. Second Lord Atkin, delivering judgment, said that he found it unnecessary to consider what would be the position if the stipulated 20 pounds per week were a penalty, adding at p. 26:

> It was argued by the appellants that if this were a penalty they would have an option either to sue for the penalty or for damages for breach of the promise as to time of delivery. I desire to leave open the question whether, where a penalty is plainly less in amount than the prospective damages, there is any legal objection to suing on it, or in a suitable case ignoring it and suing for damages.

There is authority indicating that a penalty clause is ineffective even where it is less than the actual loss suffered (see *Hals.* (4th Ed.), vol. 12, para. 118, p. 422 and the authorities cited therein). The result would be that actual damages could be recovered which exceeded the amount stipulated as a penalty. To that extent, the proposition appears to me to be contrary to principle and productive of injustice. The foundation of relief in equity against penalties is expressed in Story, *Equity Jurisprudence* (14th ed.) at section 1728, as follows:

> Where a penalty or forfeiture is designed merely as a security to enforce the principal obligation, it is as much against conscience to allow any party to pervert it to a different and oppressive purpose as it would be to allow him to substitute another for the principal obligation.

The operation of this relief in the face of contrary agreement by the party is also explained in this section:

> If it be said that it is his own folly to have made such a stipulation, it may equally well be said that the folly of one man cannot authorize gross oppression on the other side.

It is now evident that the power to strike down a penalty clause is a blatant interference with freedom of contract and is designed for the sole purpose of providing relief against oppression for the party having to pay the stipulated sum. It has no place where there is no oppression. If the actual loss turns out to exceed the penalty, the normal rules of enforcement of contract should apply to allow recovery of only the agreed sum. The party imposing the penalty should not be able to obtain the benefit of whatever intimidating force the penalty clause may have in inducing performance, and then ignore the clause when it turns out to be in his advantage to do so. A penalty clause should function as a limitation on the damages recoverable, while still being ineffective to increase damages above the actual loss sustained when such loss is less than the stipulated amount. As expressed by Lord Ellenborough in *Wilbeam v. Ashton* (1807), 1 Camp. 78 at p. 78; 170 ER 883 at p. 883 (*Nisi Prius*): "Beyond the penalty you shall not go; within it, you are to give the party any compensation which he can prove himself entitled to." Of course, if an agreed sum is a valid liquidated damages clause, the plaintiff is entitled at law to recover this sum regardless of the actual loss sustained.

In the context of the present discussion of the measure of damages, the result is that an agreed sum payable on breach represents the maximum amount recoverable whether the sum is a penalty or a valid liquidated damages clause.

It should be noted that the above principles concern only the situation where there is a single sum specified for breach of the agreement, or a single breach. Where there are different breaches and the agreement provides for a particular sum of liquidated damages to be payable for each and every breach, there is no bar to awarding the liquidated damages amount for each breach which has occurred to date of trial, and also awarding an injunction to restrain future breaches. In *Imperial Tobacco v. Parslay*, [1936] 2 All ER 515, the Court of Appeal held that an agreed sum payable on every breach of a covenant was a recoverable amount of liquidated damages for past breaches, even though an injunction had also been granted to prevent future breaches. In principle, this result is correct. There is no double recovery because the liquidated damages award and the injunction are referable to different breaches.

To summarize:

1. Where a fixed sum is stipulated as and for liquidated damages upon a breach, the covenantee must elect with respect to that breach between these liquidated damages and an injunction.

2. If he elects to take the liquidated damages stipulated he may recover that sum irrespective of his actual loss.

3. Where the stipulated sum is a penalty he may only recover such damages as he can prove, but the amount recoverable may not exceed the sum stipulated.

4. If he elects to take an injunction and not the liquidated sum stipulated, he may recover damages in equity for the actual loss sustained up to the date of the injunction or, if tardy, up to the date upon which he should have sought the injunction, but in either case, not exceeding the amount stipulated as payable upon a breach.

5. Where a liquidated damages sum is stipulated as payable for each and every breach, the covenantee may recover this sum in respect of distinct breaches which have occurred and he may also be granted an injunction to restrain future breaches.

Applying these propositions to the present case, in my view the plaintiff was entitled to an injunction and such damages as he could prove to date of trial but not to exceed the sum of $1,000.

I would accordingly dismiss the appeal and direct the payment of such damages, not to exceed $1,000, as the respondent can establish in respect of the period from June 1, 1973 to date of trial, for the loss of commission on all contracts of general insurance sold by Elsley during that period, after taking into account expenses incurred in securing and servicing the contracts.

Success has been divided. The respondent sustained the validity of the covenant; the appellant succeeded in limiting damages to the stipulated amount. I would not award costs to either party.

Appeal allowed in part.

NOTES AND QUESTIONS

The principal issue raised by the penalty clause-liquidated damages cases is the extent to which the courts are prepared to recognize attempts by the parties to stipulate the remedies that will be available in the event of breach of contract. There seem, in fact, to be two bases for the courts' general antipathy toward penalty clauses. First, they represent an early example of the courts being willing to interfere in contractual situations where they felt that one of the parties had overreached or taken advantage of a superior bargaining position. Second, the 19th century courts were anxious to prevent parties contracting out of their ability to take private law disputes to the regular courts. Behind this attitude appear two predominant concerns—the first, a desire for self-preservation on the part of the courts and the second, a paternalistic concern to prevent the parties from a course of action that they may shortly come to regret.

To what extent these same factors influence the courts today is somewhat unclear. Suffice it to say that the Supreme Court of Canada in cases such as *Elsley* and, more particularly, *H.F. Clarke Ltd. v. Thermidaire Co. Ltd.*, [1976] 1 SCR 319, have continued to deal with this issue from the perspective that penalty clauses are simply unenforceable though it is fair to say that Canadian courts nowadays show a greater inclination to respect party stipulation by being more liberal in their concept of what constitutes a liquidated damages clause. However, this traditional approach to the problem has come under increasing criticism. First, it is argued by some that the penalty clause issue should simply be treated as another example of "unconscionability" and treated under that general rubric rather than *sui generis*—that is, abandon any jurisdiction preservation basis for the doctrine and not treat penalties as automatically offensive. Beyond this, there has been much debate, in the United States particularly, about the economic basis of the penalty clause doctrine with some commentators arguing that penalty clauses are generally entitled to protection by the courts from an economic efficiency perspective. See, for example, Charles J. Goetz and Robert E. Scott, "Liquidated Damages, Penalties and the Just Compensation Principle: Some Notes on an Enforcement Model and a Theory of Efficient Breach" (1977), 77 *Columbia Law Review* 554; Kenneth W. Clarkson, Roger Leroy Miller, and Timothy J. Muris, "Liquidated Damages v. Penalties: Sense or Nonsense?" [1978] *Wisconsin Law Review* 351; Peter Linzer, "On the Amorality of Contract

Remedies—Efficiency, Equity and the Second Restatement" (1981), 81 *Columbia Law Review* 111; and Ian R. Macneil, "Efficient Breach of Contract: Circles in the Sky" (1982), 68 *Virginia Law Review* 947; and see also *Meuiner v. Clouthier* (1984), 46 OR (2d) 188.

Of course, the issue of remedy stipulation is not confined to the arena of penalty clauses. As a cursory reading of a collective agreement or a university tenure document will reveal, parties will frequently stipulate specific performance in the form of reinstatement in the case of wrongful or unfair dismissals and, of course, this will generally be for the direction of an arbitrator or other stipulated adjudicative body rather than the courts. In a somewhat different context, injunctions to be issued by the regular courts will sometimes be stipulated as the relief to be available in support of a restrictive covenant in the sale of a business or the termination of an employment arrangement. Surprisingly, these situations have seldom been dealt with by the Canadian courts. In addition to *Tritav*, above, see *Psenica v. Dee-Zee Construction Ltd.*, [1999] SJ no. 749 (QB) (QL). In *Psenica* the plaintiff snow removal company sought an interim injunction to restrain a former employee, Psenica, and his company from breaching provisions in his employment contract prohibiting him from, *inter alia*, engaging in the snow removal business or soliciting the plaintiff's clients. One term of the employment agreement provided: "The employee acknowledges that in addition to any and all rights of the Employer, the Employer shall be entitled to injunctive relief in order to protect the Employer's rights and property." Scheibel J held that the non-competition clause in the agreement was overly broad and unenforceable. Regarding the remedy stipulation, he wrote:

Even though the contract provides that the applicant shall be entitled to injunctive relief, the issue of a contractual right to have injunctive relief is not conclusive. It is only one factor, albeit an important one, in the exercise of the discretionary power of the court. This issue is discussed in S.M. Waddams, *The Law of Contracts*, 4th ed. (Toronto: Canada Law Book Inc., 1999), at §695, 512 and 13, where the author states:

Where a contract expressly provides that the promisor will submit to specific remedies, the court's attitude has been to take account of the provision, as relevant to the exercise of judicial discretion, but not to admit the parties' agreement as controlling. In the Alabama case of *Stokes v. Moore* [77 So. 2d 331 (1955)], the Supreme Court of Alabama said:

We do not wish to express the view that an agreement for the issuance of an injunction, if and when a stipulated state of facts arises in the future, is binding on the court to that extent. Such an agreement would serve to oust the inherent jurisdiction of the court to determine whether an injunction is appropriate when applied for and to require its issuance even though to do so would be contrary to the opinion of the court.

The court went on to say, however, that "[t]he Provision for an injunction is important in its influence upon an exercise of the discretionary power of the court to grant a temporary injunction." A similar view was taken by Branson J, in *Warner Bros. Pictures Inc. v. Nelson* [[1937] 1 KB 209], where the express agreement of a movie actress that the contract should be enforceable by injunction was held to be relevant and persuasive, though not determinative. It is appropriate in this way to give weight to the parties' agreement, but altered circumstances may give to a decree of specific enforcement an effect that had not been anticipated and might be oppressive, and consequently the court, which has to make and enforce the order, can never relinquish ultimate control of it and responsibility for it.

This aspect of *Psenica* was approved by the Manitoba Court of Appeal in *Horizon Custom Builders Ltd. v. Behrens*, 2001 MBCA 198, 160 Man. R (2d) 296 (at para. 12). See also *Dragon Systems Inc. v. Kolvox Communications Inc.*, [1995] OJ no. 3715 (Gen. Div.).

See Clifford Ian Kyer, "Case Study in Party Stipulation of Remedy: The NHL Standard Players Contract" (1981), 39 *University of Toronto Faculty of Law Review* 1.

In your view, should the courts continue to assert their overall discretion over the availability of equitable relief? Would it be possible for the courts to attribute some, if not conclusive, effect to clauses stipulating specific performance or an injunction as being the remedy available in the event of breach? If so, by what standards should the court decide whether or not to give effect to the remedy stipulation in any particular case?

CHAPTER TWELVE

Charter Remedies

INTRODUCTION

In this chapter, we turn to the question whether the advent of the *Canadian Charter of Rights and Freedoms* has had an impact on the availability and scope of the remedies covered in the previous chapters of this casebook. Has the Charter led to any reconceptualization of the nature and purpose of the various remedies? Has it caused any re-evaluation of traditional limits on their availability either generally or within the domain affected by the Charter?

The Charter speaks explicitly to relief in s. 24(1), which provides:

> Anyone whose rights or freedoms, as guaranteed by this Charter, have been infringed or denied may apply to a court of competent jurisdiction to obtain such remedy as the court considers appropriate and just in the circumstances.

On its face, this provision can be seen as providing the courts with a very broad discretion in the crafting of remedies, a discretion potentially untrammelled by previous common law and equitable limits—for example, ordering an apology: *Perera v. Canada*, [1998] 3 FC 381 (CA). Indeed, it has been argued that the scope of s. 24(1) of the Charter should not be restricted by the corrective mission of the historic range of common law and equitable remedies. Rather, as a remedial provision within a constitutional enactment, it should be viewed as having important regulatory objectives and as authorizing remedies that have as their primary objective not the rectification of or provision of compensation for past injustices but the achievement of future compliance with the Constitution by the ordering of remedies that

> respond to harms and conditions that may not be causally connected to proven violations and also to balance all the interests affected by the remedy.

Kent Roach, *Constitutional Remedies in Canada* (Aurora, ON: Canada Law Book, 1994) (serial), para. 3.40, and see the review of this book by Jamie Cameron, "The Charter and Remedial Choice" (1995), 45 *University of Toronto Law Journal* 525.

There are a wealth of remedial issues under the Charter, including many issues related to remedies for unconstitutional legislation, such as reading down, reading in, severance, and delayed or suspended declarations of invalidity. There are also complex issues relating to jurisdiction to order remedies and to apply the Charter. See Peter Hogg, *Constitutional Law of Canada*, 5th ed. (Toronto: Carswell, 2007) (serial), cc. 37, 38, and 55; R.J. Sharpe and K. Roach, *The Canadian Charter of Rights and Freedoms*, 4th ed. (Toronto: Irwin Law, 2009), c. 17; Constitutional Law Group, *Canadian Constitutional Law*, 4th ed. (Toronto: Emond Montgomery, 2010), c. 25.

This chapter focuses on jurisprudence in which the courts, within an essentially public law conception of the Charter, have considered the availability of damages and injunctive relief (both final and interlocutory) for Charter violations, and the choice between declarations and injunctions as a final remedy under s. 24(1) of the Charter. What are the principles on which the courts have based their remedial choices in such cases? Are they principles that really have relevance only in the domain of the Charter or, more generally, public law litigation; or do they have something to offer for the development of remedial law in the private law domain? What is the value added when damages or injunctions are sought under the Charter as opposed to under the private law doctrines studied in previous chapters? Of necessity, this involves a consideration of the extent to which public and private law litigation have varying objectives.

The remedial regime envisaged by the Charter may be conditioned by very different goals and conceptions of the role of the courts than is the case under the classical vision of remedies, a vision developed largely within the setting of the resolution of private disputes between discrete parties.

However, what is also apparent is that the discretion to do what is "appropriate and just" has the potential to be conditioned or controlled by the very factors and considerations that have contributed to the evolution of the general remedial regime. Moreover, similar issues concerning the nature and conceptualization of remedial discretion may be at play under both s. 24(1) and private law remedies. Obviously, any assessment of the use of s. 24(1) has to be focused on this interplay between, on the one hand, an ostensibly wide discretion located within the potentially broader litigation framework of many constitutional disputes and, on the other, the restraining hand of existing jurisprudential principles. How have the courts interpreted their mandate? Where has the balance between creativity and restraint been struck?

The Nature of Remedial Discretion Under the Charter

The following extract outlines different ways to conceptualize remedial discretion under the Charter. As you read it, think about the extent to which remedial discretion under the Charter is both distinct from and similar to remedial discretion in private law.

Kent Roach, "Principled Remedial Discretion Under the Charter"
(2004), 25 *Supreme Court Law Review* (2d) 101, at 106-13
(footnotes incorporated into text)

I. *Remedial Discretion Under the Charter*

A. *The Importance of Remedial Discretion*

Remedial discretion is an important feature of the Charter. Section 24 was placed in the Charter in no small part because Canadian courts refused to exercise discretion under both the *Canadian Bill of Rights* [see *Hogan v. The Queen*, [1975] 2 SCR 574] and the common law to award remedies, such as the exclusion of improperly obtained evidence [*Wray v. The Queen*, [1971] SCR 272] or a stay of proceedings [*Osborn v. The Queen*, [1971] SCR 184]. Remedial discretion is specifically provided in s. 24(1) of the Charter, which contemplates such remedies being ordered "as the court considers appropriate and just." As Justice McIntyre observed in *Mills v. The Queen* [[1986] 1 SCR 863, at 965], "it is difficult to imagine language which could give the court a wider and less fettered discretion. It is impossible to reduce this wide discretion to some sort of binding formula for general application in all cases, and it is not for appellate courts to pre-empt or cut down this wide discretion." More recently, Chief Justice McLachlin [in *R v. 974649 Ontario Inc.*, [2001] 3 SCR 575, at para. 18] has similarly observed that s. 24(1) "appears to confer the widest possible discretion on a court to craft remedies for violations of Charter rights." ...

B. Types of Remedial Discretion

Although remedial discretion seems at one level to be an undeniable fact under the Charter, it is one that requires justification. The ambiguous nature of the trial judge's remedial discretion is demonstrated in the jurisprudence concerning appellate deference to issues of remedial choice. Appellate courts will not generally evaluate a remedy on a *de novo* basis. At the same time, they will intervene if the trial judge erred in setting out the relevant legal test, was clearly wrong or gave reasons that were "so brief and conclusionary that it is difficult to say whether other errors were made" [*R v. Feeney*, [1997] 2 SCR 13, at para. 84] . ... In *Doucet-Boudreau* [2003 SCC 62, at para. 87], the majority emphasized that in evaluating s. 24(1) remedies "reviewing courts ... must show considerable deference to trial judges' choice of remedy, and should refrain from using hindsight to perfect a remedy. A reviewing court should only interfere where the trial judge has committed an error of law or principle."

Recent debates among scholars of private law remedies about the degree to which equitable remedies are discretionary or rule-based may be helpful in clarifying the nature of remedial discretion, as well as the controversial nature of the enterprise. Professor Peter Birks has argued that remedial decision-making must be ruled-based in order to promote certainty in the law and accord with the ideal of the rule of law. [See Peter Birks, "Rights, Wrongs, and Remedies" (2000), 20 *OJLS* 1, at 36-37; Peter Birks, "Three Kinds of Objections to Discretionary Remedialism" (2000), 29 *W Aust. L Rev.* 1; and Darryn Jenson, "The Rights and Wrongs of Discretionary Remedialism" (2003), *Sing. J of Legal Studies* 178.] Others, however, defend so-called "discretionary remedialism" [see Simon Evans, "Defending Discretionary Remedialism" (2001), 23 *Sydney L Rev.* 463, at 480*ff.*; and Patricia Loughlan, "No Right to a Remedy? An Analysis of Judicial Discretion in the Imposition of Equitable Remedies" (1989), 17 *Melb. L Rev.* 132] on the basis of the impossibility of avoiding the need for judgment and flexibility in remedial decision-making. Although proponents of rule-based remedial decision-making raise the spectre of unfettered remedial decision-making, many of the advocates of discretionary remedialism support a more restrained and less positivistic form of discretion. They advocate what Ronald Dworkin describes as a "weak" form of discretion that is governed by legal principles as opposed to a "strong" form of discretion that applies "when a judge runs out of rules." Professor Dworkin sees principles as "standards that reasonable men can interpret in different ways" [Ronald Dworkin, *Taking Rights Seriously* (Cambridge: Harvard University Press, 1977), at 69, 34] and contrasts them with rules, which in his view have a more self-executing or categorical nature. Multiple principles can be relevant to a judicial decision and must be weighed by the judges whereas a legal rule as conceived by Dworkin either applies or it does not apply. To be sure, Dworkin's distinctions

between weak and strong forms of discretion and between rules and principles are controversial and they may discount the need for interpretation in applying rules. Nevertheless, as
will be seen, they provide a helpful guide to conceptualizing remedial discretion under the
Charter.

1. Strong Remedial Discretion

The idea of strong discretion is based on a positivistic sense that at some point the rules run
out and that this gives the judge unconstrained freedom to make a decision by exercising
discretion. Such a discretion seems anomalous in a legal regime committed to the rule of
law and the protection of rights. Peter Birks [in "Three Kinds of Objections to Discretionary
Remedialism," above, at 15], for example, has argued that "the whole point of the rule of
law" is to avoid rule on the basis of "the wills and whims of a person or a group of people.
The blessings of this commitment [to the rule of law] have been overlooked by the discretionary remedialists who suddenly suppose that the judges should be the one group answerable only to God." To be sure, the idea of strong discretion sits uneasily with the ideals of the
rule of law and the concept that where there is a right, there is a remedy. [Professor Birks
argues that "discretionary remedialism cannot allow the plaintiff to have rights. To make
room for the discretion, it has to reduce the plaintiff to a supplicant seeking the exercise of
a discretion in his favour. He cannot be heard to demand rights." Birks, ibid., at 13.] At the
same time, it is perhaps unfair to castigate strong discretion as simply a matter of will and
whim. Remedial discretion is, at the end of the day, exercised by judges who are constrained
by their institutional role to act in an impartial manner. A judge who exercises strong discretion is not necessarily immune from criticism that the discretion has been exercised
unfairly or unwisely. [See Dworkin, *Taking Rights Seriously*, above, at 33.]

As will be seen, there are some areas of constitutional remedies that at present seem to
be exercised on the basis of strong discretion. Examples might include the discretion of a
judge not to award an equitable remedy [see *Chippewas of Sarnia Band v. Ontario* (2000),
195 DLR (4th) 135 (Ont. CA). But for a discussion on the basis on which this discretion
should be exercised and the need to relate the exercise of the discretion to legal principles,
see my "Remedies in Aboriginal Litigations," in Magnet and Dorey, eds., *Aboriginal Rights
Litigation* (Toronto: Butterworths, 2003), at 323-26]. ... One of the hallmarks of pure discretion is that it need not be accompanied by reasons. Reasons are generally seen as means to
relate a legal decision to some applicable rule or principle and are superfluous when there
are no such standards.

2. Rule-Based Remedial Discretion

Rule-based discretion can be seen as an (over)reaction to the dangers of pure or strong
discretion. The idea behind rule-based discretion is that appellate courts should formulate
rules that will outline the circumstances in which trial judges should exercise their remedial
discretion. Dworkin defines rules as "applicable in an all-or-nothing fashion." This means
that "if the facts a rule stipulates are given" and the rule is validly on point then "the answer
it supplies must be accepted" [Dworkin, *Taking Rights Seriously*, above, at 24]. His example
of a rule is that a will must be witnessed by three persons to be valid. Dworkin may lean

towards something of a caricature of rules, but as will be seen, there are some examples of courts taking such a seemingly categorical approach to issues of remedial discretion.

One value of rules is that they can promote certainty about the law, provided that it is clear what rule applies and the judge is faithful to the result required by the rule. Unlike strong discretion, the application of rules also often invites and requires reasons from the judge. The reasons, however, will be focused on whether the conditions precedent to the rule apply or perhaps whether a conflicting rule applies. In some cases, reasoning about whether a rule applies will cause greater reflection about the purposes and principles that are at stake, but often reasons will end at the issue of whether the case at hand is sufficiently analogous to the cases contemplated by the rule that the rule should apply ... .

Resistance to inflexible rules may produce a situation that gravitates towards strong discretion. The reason for this is that rules often focus on particular factual conditions precedent and not the underlying reasons why the conditions should have those consequences. Both strong discretion and rule-based discretion can be united by relative inattention to underlying principles ... .

3. *Principled Remedial Discretion*

An alternative to either strong or rule-based remedial discretion is principled remedial discretion. Dworkin's account of principles suggests that they are more general and in some ways more controversial than rules. Dworkin's theory is best known for its distinction between rights-based principles and collective policies and the demanding obligation to seek right answers in hard cases. What is perhaps less well known is his sense that there are multiple principles and policies that can be considered in a particular case and that judges must decide the weight of any principle in a particular case. Dworkin has a more modest description of principles, not as full-blown right answers, but as something "which officials must take into account, if it is relevant, as a consideration inclining in one direction or another." On this account, a judge is "required to assess all of the competing and conflicting principles" that bear on a case and "make a resolution of these principles rather than identifying one among others as 'valid'" [Dworkin, *Taking Rights Seriously*, above, at 26, 72]. This account of multiple principles, though perhaps not entirely consistent with Dworkin's ultimate aspiration for a right answer through adjudication, allows for a more meaningful distinction between rule-based and principled remedial discretion. It opens up the space for judges to consider multiple principles—such as the need for an effective remedy and the need to respect the institutional role of the judiciary—when deciding questions of remedies without attempting to formulate particular rules about the circumstances in which one of these principles will have greater weight or when particular remedies should be ordered.

The idea that even the exercise of remedial discretion under the Charter can be principled is a compelling aspiration. It promises that something of the same methodology that is applied to determining the content of the rights and the justification of any limit on the right can also be applied to remedial decision-making. In this sense, it unites the process of determining rights and remedies. At the same time, it allows us to make sense of the fact that trial judges have a discretion to formulate appropriate and just remedies in particular circumstances.

There are some areas of constitutional remedies that gravitate towards a principled approach to Charter remedies. In *R v. Gamble* [[1988] 2 SCR 595], Justice Wilson stressed the connections between the process of interpreting rights and devising remedies when she stated that "a purposive approach should, in my view, be applied to the administration of Charter remedies as well as to the interpretation of Charter rights .... Charter relief should not be denied or 'displaced by overly rigid rules.'" At various junctures, the Supreme Court has stressed that remedies should vindicate the purposes of particular Charter rights. In *Osborne v. Canada* [[1991] 2 SCR 69], the Court expressed the importance of selecting a remedy that would vindicate the values of freedom of expression. In *Schachter v. Canada* [[1992] 2 SCR 679], the Court indicated that "the absolute unavailability of reading would mean that the standards developed under the Charter would have to be applied in certain cases in ways which would derogate from the deeper social purposes of the Charter." In that case, the Court took a principled approach to the remedial choice between reading in and a declaration of invalidity by basing it on the general principles of the need to respect the role of the legislature and the purposes of the Charter. To be sure, these general principles require further interpretation and application, but they provide a better and more general framework than the rule-based approach taken in *Schachter* to the separate question of when a declaration of invalidity should be suspended.

A principled approach to the exercise of remedial discretion might be impractical if it demanded that only one principle was relevant to any particular exercise of remedial discretion. Fortunately, it is easier to accept the idea of multiple and competing purposes and policies than it is multiple and competing rules. Once it is accepted that a principled approach can implicate more than one principle, it is possible to see the Court's frequent attention to the need to respect the proper role of legislatures, the executive and the judiciary, to balance competing interests, and to provide effective remedies as a principled approach to remedial decision-making. [See *Schachter v. Canada*, [1992] 2 SCR 679; and *Mahe v. Alberta*, [1990] 1 SCR 342. On the multiple purposes and principles that courts consider when ordering constitutional remedies, see my *Constitutional Remedies in Canada*, above, c. 2.]

A principled and purposive approach to the exercise of remedial discretion does not necessarily mean that the court will select the remedy that maximizes the relevant right in all cases. Rather it requires that judges consider all of the relevant and at times competing principles and attempt to order the best remedy possible. It also requires that judges attempt to justify their selection of remedies in a manner that fits with the general interpretative approach taken to determining the scope of rights and reasonable limits under the Charter.

Summary

The three approaches to the exercise of remedial discretion outlined above can be seen as a spectrum.

Rule   Principle   Strong Discretion

Although a rule-based and strong-discretion approach are set at the opposite end of the spectrum because they recognize the extremes of either control or freedom of the trial judge, they also are united by their relevant neglect of the issue of general principles. ... [A] frequent reaction to the inflexibility of rule-based discretion is to exercise strong discretion by ignoring the rules. The spectrum approach is also helpful because it demonstrates that particular decisions may lie at the borderline of the categories. For example, a rule-based approach may lean towards principle to the extent that interpretation and application of the rules engages broader and more general questions about the purposes of the rules. A principled approach may lean towards strong discretion to the extent that it emphasizes appellate deference to the trial judge's choice of remedy.

The Nature of Charter Litigation

As already noted, Charter litigation raises issues and problems quite different from those encountered in private law litigation, and these differences will often be significant at the remedial stage.

As Dickson J (as he then was) explained in an extrajudicial comment ("The Public Responsibility of Lawyers" (1983), 13 *Manitoba Law Journal* 175, at 187 (footnote omitted)):

> The remedial powers contained in s. 24 of the Charter will also offer a test of the creativity of the legal mind. The section provides that anyone whose rights and freedoms have been infringed or denied may apply to the court to obtain such remedy as the court considers appropriate and just in the circumstances. The outer limits of s. 24 have yet to be tested but American experience teaches us that the remedial aspects of constitutional rights litigation will often be the most difficult and most important. In a very real sense the 1954 decision by the United States Supreme Court in *Brown v. Board of Education of Topeka* that racially segregated schools were a denial of equal protection of the laws was the easy part. Almost thirty years later problems of how to enforce desegregation are still being sorted out. Similarly, American judges have been expected to run railroads and preside over state prison systems. Where the vindication of constitutional rights simply involves the nullification of past wrongs, the remedial options are quite straightforward. But where positive action is needed to correct the denial of constitutional rights, the remedial questions become more vexing. The protection of equality rights is especially amenable to such complexities, so that the coming into force of s. 15 of the Charter in 1985 may provide further perplexity in the fashioning of remedies.

A.M. Chayes, "The Role of the Judge in Public Law Litigation" (1976), 89 *Harvard Law Review* 1281, at 1281-83 and 1302 discusses, contrasts, and summarizes the characteristics of private and public law litigation in the United States as follows:

> In our received tradition, the lawsuit is a vehicle for settling disputes between private parties about private rights. The defining features of this conception of civil adjudication are:
>
> (1) The lawsuit is *bipolar*. Litigation is organized as a contest between two individuals or at least two unitary interests, diametrically opposed, to be decided on a winner-take-all basis.
>
> (2) Litigation is *retrospective*. The controversy is about an identified set of completed events: whether they occurred, and if so, with what consequences for the legal relations of the parties.
>
> (3) *Right and remedy are interdependent.* The scope of the relief is derived more or less logically from the substantive violation under the general theory that the plaintiff will get compensation measured by the harm caused by the defendant's breach of duty—in contract by giving plaintiff the money he would have had absent the breach; in tort by paying the value of the damage caused.

(4)   The lawsuit is a *self-contained* episode. The impact of the judgment is confined to the parties. If plaintiff prevails there is a simple compensatory transfer, usually of money, but occasionally the return of a thing or the performance of a definite act. If defendant prevails, a loss lies where it has fallen. In either case, entry of judgment ends the court's involvement.

(5)   The process is *party-initiated* and *party-controlled*. The case is organized and the issues defined by exchanges between the parties. Responsibility for fact development is theirs. The trial judge is a neutral arbiter of their interactions who decides questions of law only if they are put in issue by an appropriate move of a party. ...

The public law litigation model portrayed in this paper reverses many of the crucial characteristics and assumptions of the traditional concept of adjudication:

[a]   The scope of the lawsuit is not exogenously given but is shaped primarily by the court and parties.

[b]   The party structure is not rigidly bilateral but sprawling and amorphous.

[c]   The fact inquiry is not historical and adjudicative but predictive and legislative.

[d]   Relief is not conceived as compensation for past wrong in a form logically derived from the substantive liability and confined in its impact to the immediate parties; instead, it is forward looking, fashioned *ad hoc* on flexible and broadly remedial lines, often having important consequences for many persons including absentees.

[e]   The remedy is not imposed but negotiated.

[f]   The decree does not terminate judicial involvement in the affair: its administration requires the continuing participation of the court.

[g]   The judge is not passive, his function limited to analysis and statement of governing legal rules; he is active, with responsibility not only for credible fact evaluation but for organization and shaping the litigation to ensure a just and viable outcome.

[h]   The subject matter of the lawsuit is not a dispute between private individuals about private rights, but a grievance about the operation of public policy.

Choice of Remedies in Charter Cases

Consider the framework for analysis of remedial choice offered in the following extract.

M.L. Pilkington, "Monetary Redress for Charter Infringement"
in Robert J. Sharpe, ed., *Charter Litigation* (Toronto: Butterworths, 1987), 308-10
(footnotes omitted)

In determining what remedy is appropriate and just, I suggest a three-pronged inquiry.

1. Effective Redress for the Victim's Infringement

First, from the point of view of the victim of the infringement, what remedy or remedies would most effectively redress the wrong he has suffered, putting him in the position he would have been in had his rights not been infringed?

Section 24 relies upon those whose rights have been infringed to take the initiative to enforce Charter guarantees. The effectiveness of this enforcement mechanism will depend on whether the available remedies provide the victim of a Charter infringement with sufficient incentive to take action. A person charged with an offence or otherwise defending or resisting a government claim likely has sufficient incentive to assert Charter infringements as a basis for seeking a defensive remedy such as exclusion of evidence, stay of proceedings, dismissal of charges or declaration of invalidity. Where the only available remedy depends upon the victim of the infringement taking affirmative action (such as claiming monetary redress or seeking an injunction), the infringement may go unredressed unless the victim has sufficient incentive to seek the remedy.

With respect to monetary redress for Charter infringement, this first line of inquiry raises three issues which will be examined below: (a) where the victim of a Charter infringement has suffered actual injury resulting from the infringement, is it sufficient to leave the victim to his ordinary remedies, or should he be entitled to a remedy pursuant to section 24(1)? (b) should monetary redress for Charter infringement be limited to compensation for actual injury or be available to redress the infringement of a right *per se*? and (c) if monetary redress is available to redress the infringement *per se*, on what basis should the quantum of the award be assessed?

2. Implementation of the Charter and the Effective Operation of Government

The second line of inquiry in determining what remedy is appropriate and just is from the point of view of the public role of the Charter: what remedy would most effectively foster the implementation of the Charter by deterring future infringements and ensuring future compliance without interfering unduly with the effective operation of government and the implementation of legitimate government policy?

As others have argued, the primary role of a court in constitutional litigation is different from its role in conventional litigation. The emphasis shifts from dispute resolution to the articulation and enforcement of constitutional values. With respect to the appropriateness of monetary redress as a remedy, this second line of inquiry raises four more issues, which will be addressed below: (d) do monetary awards have a deterrent effect? (e) are punitive damages appropriate to remedy Charter infringements? (f) on what basis is it appropriate and just to protect defendants from monetary liability for constitutional infringements? and (g) to what extent should courts award monetary redress as an alternative to defensive remedies?

3. Capacity of Courts To Implement Remedies

The third line of inquiry in determining what remedy is appropriate and just is from the point of view of the court as an institution: can the remedy be effectively implemented by a court? There are two problems here. First, a court has "the power of neither the sword nor the purse" to implement its decisions. To the extent that a court compels a government to

take action to rectify constitutional wrongs, it has only the contempt power and the legitimacy of its decisions to rely upon. Where a court seeks to enforce minority rights against a
majority which controls the government, it must depend on the majority's acceptance of the
legitimacy of the court's decision even though it may not agree with the decision itself. A
court which seeks to implement rights through large-scale reforms which the public is not
prepared to accept (as in the school busing cases in the United States), places its effectiveness at risk.

The second related problem a court must address in assessing its capacity to implement
a remedy is the degree to which the remedy requires the court to assume what are otherwise
legislative and executive functions and the extent to which the court can equip itself to do
so effectively. The remedies available to redress constitutional wrongs vary in the degree to
which they intrude on the legislative and executive spheres.

For the most part, the least intrusive remedies are those which operate by nullification:
e.g. where evidence is held inadmissible, charges are dismissed, legislation is declared to be
of no force or effect or government is prohibited from doing something because of Charter
infringement. These remedies are the least intrusive because they are limited to telling legislatures and governments what they cannot do. This may cause the legislature or government to change its conduct or policies, or redirect its expenditures, but the actual decision
as to how this should be done is left to the legislature or government.

Affirmative remedies for unconstitutional action, which would include damages, mandatory injunctions and structural injunctions, are each successively more intrusive. The damages remedy may result in the reallocation of substantial resources from public expenditure
to private redress. The mandatory injunction, by directing the government to act, limits the
government's range of choice. The structural injunction, in which the court prescribes and
supervises the reform of institutions which are found in contravention of guaranteed rights,
interferes extensively with legislative and executive discretion. The processes involved in
determining and implementing most affirmative remedies may be analogous to those employed by courts exercising ordinary remedial jurisdiction, but the structural injunction
raises problems of policy making and enforcement which do not lend themselves to being
resolved through ordinary litigation procedures. Since courts are well-suited to and experienced at assessing monetary awards, this third line of inquiry creates no difficulties for determining whether monetary redress is appropriate and just.

Just as determining whether a guaranteed right has been infringed involves balancing
between protected interests and the needs of a free and democratic society, so the assessment of an appropriate remedy requires the balancing of a number of competing interests
and factors.

DAMAGES AS A CHARTER REMEDY

As suggested by Pilkington, the issue of the scope of damages as a remedy for violation of
the Charter is a complex one. It depends in part upon the extent to which the making of such
awards should, in Roach's terms, be seen as having regulatory as opposed to corrective objectives, as being more concerned with the deterrence of future unconstitutional behaviour
than with the compensation of individual victims. However, as the following extract makes
clear, there are many more dimensions to the issue.

David J. Mullan, "Damages for Violation of Constitutional Rights—
A False Spring?"
(1995), 6 *National Journal of Constitutional Law* 105, at 114-19 (footnotes omitted)

In terms of the extent of governmental liability, the most extreme position would be one in which all violations of the *Charter* were actionable simply on proof of a breach or *per se* and also that there would be a claim to substantial damages in all such cases, a claim that did not depend upon establishing that the violation had manifested itself in quantifiable harm. Indeed, there is some academic as well as judicial support for such a position. …

However, without necessarily challenging the policy bases of this position, I believe it is necessary to take into account the ramifications of supporting it. As already noted, it would mean that, in all cases, liability would flow directly from the breach and, in its strongest form, that substantial damages would be available independently of any proof of actual loss. Moreover, this would be so irrespective of the provision of the *Charter* which had been breached and the character of the government authority responsible for perpetrating the breach. Also, there would be no limitations on either the reach of the tort or exposure to a substantial damages judgment based on an inquiry into the existence of malice, bad faith, or negligence; save perhaps in the consideration of whether to also impose punitive, exemplary or moral damages, these would be irrelevant matters. Given the reluctance of the Canadian courts to impose common law liability in damages on those exercising legislative, law enforcement, prosecutorial, and judicial and quasi-judicial powers or, more generally, to treat liability in tort as springing automatically from the mere existence of an *ultra vires* decision or action, acceptance of this form of *per se* liability for any species of *Charter* violation would involve the adoption of very different principles of official liability in the context of *Charter* litigation than our law has countenanced to this point.

In fact, the Supreme Court of Canada has already hinted strongly that the association of damages claims with direct challenges to the validity of primary legislation will not be entertained readily [*Schachter v. Canada*, [1992] 2 SCR 679, at 720]. In other words, the Court appears to have asserted that the mere fact that legislation is contrary to the *Charter* will not generate a damages claim against the government on the part of those who have been injured at least in the context of proceedings where the legislation is attacked directly by reference to section 52 of the *Constitution Act, 1982*. Moreover, it is difficult to see the Court taking a different stance in cases where the validity of the legislation is challenged collaterally, either in the form of an action framed simply as a claim for damages or by way of a challenge to official implementation of or action under the impugned legislation with an associated claim for damages. This suggests that it is likely that there will either be an absolute immunity in such contexts or, as at least one court has suggested, an immunity defeated only by proof of wilful infringement of *Charter* rights by the legislature either in the original enactment of the legislation or, perhaps somewhat more realistically, by a failure on the part of the legislature to repeal or amend a regime in the face of consistent advice that it is contrary to the *Charter*.

Further in the domain of "legislative" action, it is also difficult to envisage the courts taking too different a posture in relation to subordinate legislators such as the Governor in Council. Absent proof of malice or deliberate infringement of constitutional rights, it would be surprising if the courts imposed damages liability on those making orders-in-council, regulations, or by-laws and, of course, this would mean little or no difference between damages claims based on *Charter* violations and damages claims based on assertions of other forms of *ultra vires* argument.

Undoubtedly, there will also be pressures for maintenance of similar immunities in the arena of judicial and quasi-judicial functions. Without going through all the possible contexts in which this question might arise, it is worth reflecting upon tribunal denial of procedural rights. Is it likely that the courts will move to automatic liability in situations where that denial, in addition to being a violation of common law natural justice or procedural fairness rights, constitutes an infringement of the principles of fundamental justice by reference to section 7 of the *Charter* and the rights enshrined in that section? What seems more probable is that the courts will either adopt the common law immunities for such conduct, immunities which adhere unless there is proof of malice; or, at most, may move to a somewhat less extreme form of immunity (*e.g.* no liability absent negligence) in recognition of the importance of the nature of the constitutional interests at stake and perhaps as a form of deterrence. Putting it another way, the constitutional tort which emerges is likely to be defined in terms of either the malicious or negligent denial of the principles of fundamental justice. In any event, the case for automatic liability is not self-evident and one can envisage a lengthy battle in the courts before the relevant principles are refined sufficiently.

In the law enforcement field, similar considerations will also undoubtedly intrude in the elaboration of the principles of liability. However, to the extent that some of the standards of conduct imposed by the *Charter* on law enforcement agencies are both specific and have close connections with known or existing torts with particular relevance to the law enforcement process (such as false arrest, false imprisonment, malicious prosecution, assault, as well as property-based suits springing from illegal searches and seizures), the principles that emerge when *Charter* violations are also pleaded in such cases may well be ones that involve liability by reference simply to the *Charter* breach. Nonetheless, it is unlikely that the reasons or bases for that will be a general judicial commitment to *per se* liability for *Charter* violations. Rather, the major influence will be the qualified or trespass and *per se* nature of the analogous common law torts. Moreover, even here, the issue of whether there are classes of perpetrator who are entitled to at least some form of immunity is clearly going to remain an issue.

Indeed, in terms of the potential of the *Charter* to create a rather different configuration of liability for damages than exists under current common law and statutory regimes, one of the most likely possibilities for significant change would seem to rest in a reevaluation of certain species of statutory and, perhaps even, common law immunity. To the extent that statutory immunities may be more extensive than provided for by the common law, there may be an inclination on the part of the courts to see them as being *ultra vires* at least where they have the impact of depriving citizens of any cause of action for *Charter* violations. Even in the domain of common law immunities, there may be reasons for reevaluation of their application when the context is the violation of rights and freedoms enshrined in the *Charter*.

Evaluate the following early Charter damages case in the light of the considerations raised above.

Crossman v. The Queen
[1984] 1 FC 681 (TD)

[The plaintiff was arrested by the police, taken to the station, and told he could contact his lawyer. He was, however, not permitted to speak to the lawyer until an officer had questioned him for approximately one hour. No statement was taken, but the plaintiff subsequently pleaded guilty and was sentenced to a term of imprisonment. The plaintiff brought this action for damages, claiming that he had been denied his right to retain and instruct counsel without delay, contrary to s. 10(b) of the Charter.]

WALSH J [Having found that there was a Charter infringement and that the conduct of the police constituted a tort]: Having decided that a tort was committed the next question is what sanction or remedy can the court impose? This is not a case involving admissibility of a statement improperly taken from an accused; in fact no such statement was taken. Neither is it a case where as a result of the interview without counsel being allowed to be present, plaintiff suffered actual damage since, in due course, he pleaded guilty in any event. However, the failure to impose some sanction would be to condone the unfair, and in my opinion, illegal conduct of the police officer in question. Plaintiff cited the case of *Paragon Properties Ltd. v. Magna Envestments Ltd.* (1972), 24 DLR (3d) 156 (Alta. SC, AD), as authority for the proposition that although exemplary or punitive damages were not claimed in the prayer for relief in a counterclaim, they may properly be awarded in answer to a claim for general damages. In the case of *Kingsmith v. Denton* (1977), 3 AR 315, dealing with damages against a police officer for unjustifiable assault, $1,500 was awarded as exemplary damages. The conduct of the defendant was found reprehensible and offensive to the ordinary standards of morality or decent conduct in the community. This is somewhat akin to s. 24(2) of the *Canadian Charter of Rights and Freedoms* which excludes the admissibility of evidence obtained in a manner that infringed or denied any rights or freedoms guaranteed by the Charter if it is established that having regard to all the circumstances the admission of it in the proceedings "would bring the administration of justice into disrepute." In the present case we are not dealing with the admissibility of any statement made but the circumstances in which the interview took place would itself bring the administration of justice into disrepute. It is by s. 24(1) that the court may apply such remedy as it considers appropriate and just in the circumstances.

In commenting on the enforcement of the *Charter of Rights and Freedoms*, Walter S. Tarnopolsky, in his text *Canadian Charter of Rights and Freedoms Commentary* (Toronto: Carswell, 1982) at p. 502, states that the remedy available in s. 24(1) would clearly include damages where suitable. At p. 503 he states that the power to award damages would, where suitable, cover exemplary, punitive or moral damages as well as the strictly compensatory type. He refers to the judgment of Lord Devlin in *Rookes v. Barnard*, [1964] AC 1129 (HL (Eng.)) at p. 1226, where he states that exemplary damages are appropriate in cases of "oppressive, arbitrary or unconstitutional action by servants of the government."

Defendant, on the question of damages, referred, *inter alia*, to the case of *R v. Vermette (No. 4)* (1982), 1 CCC (3d) 477 (Qué. SC) at p. 495, in which it is stated:

> We are of the view that when a court is required to grant a remedy under s. 24(1) of the Charter, that remedy, in addition to being appropriate and just, must also be effective.

and also referred to the case of *Re Ritter and The Queen* (1983), 3 DLR (4th) 321 (BCSC) at p. 335, in which it is stated:

> I have therefore concluded that in so far as any right or freedom guaranteed to the accused by the Charter might be said to have been breached on the facts as described to be, the only relief which the accused seek could not, in my view, possibly be considered an appropriate remedy, nor am I able in the circumstances to suggest any course which, at this point, would serve to remedy any such alleged breach.

These are both cases with very unusual facts which it is not necessary to go into here as they are not really applicable. The case of *R v. Esau* (1983), 20 Man. R (2d) 230 (CA) at p. 236, dealing with an alleged improper search held:

> Apart from the issue as to the admissibility of illegally obtained evidence, anyone who has been subjected to unreasonable search and seizure is entitled to apply to a court of competent jurisdiction for remedial relief. In an instance where the search is abortive, the damages might be substantial, particularly if force were used against an innocent citizen. In a case such as this, however, where evidence of illicit drugs is revealed, and where no force was exercised against the accused, I would hazard the guess that the remedy would be modest indeed.

Although counsel for plaintiff argued that it is improper to take into consideration the fact that plaintiff eventually pleaded guilty to the charge for which he was arrested, which has nothing to do with exemplary or punitive damages to be awarded for preventing his counsel from being present during his interview, I do not believe this can be altogether ignored in fixing the amount of damages to be allowed.

Defendant's counsel suggests that a simple declaration that the police officer committed an error would be sufficient to act as a deterrent to similar conduct by police officers in future. I do not agree. The damages to be awarded should be sufficiently punitive as to act as a deterrent, but on the other hand the fault is not as serious as it would have been had plaintiff been refused altogether the right to retain or instruct counsel without delay or had not been informed of that right in direct contravention of s. 10(b) of the Charter. Since the present case deals with a question which does not appear to have been directly decided before and is not specifically spelled out in the Charter, so that the infringement of plaintiff's rights must be based by inference on the intention of the Charter considered in the light of the particularly objectionable conduct of the police officer with respect to the right which I have found plaintiff had to have his counsel, who was ready and available, with him during his interview, this must be considered in mitigation of damages.

Under the circumstances damages will be awarded in the amount of $500 and costs.

Judgment for plaintiff.

NOTES

1. In *R v. Hamill* (1984), 13 DLR (4th) 275, at 297-98 (BCCA), Esson JA made the following observation:

> It is arguable that, in granting civil remedies for Charter breaches, courts should assess damages at more substantial levels than have prevailed for trespasses arising out of illegal entry. If the more substantial assessment is necessary in order to make the remedy effective, it would be just and appropriate to make such an assessment.

2. Compare *Vespoli v. The Queen*, 84 DTC 6489 (FCA) dismissing a claim for damages for a violation of the s. 8 guarantee against unreasonable search and seizure on the grounds that the court could "find in the record no solid evidence that the appellants really suffered as a consequence of the illegal seizures."

3. Should proof of actual loss be an essential ingredient to a claim for damages under the Charter? If not, what factors should govern the quantification of an award? The following case now provides a structure for Charter damage claims. It stresses that Charter damages can serve the remedial purposes of compensation (including for non-pecuniary loss), deterrence, and vindication of rights. To what extent do these purposes diverge from the award of damages under the common law? This case also recognizes an open-ended category of countervailing factors against the award of damages. How should courts approach this category? Think about whether the quantum of damages awarded in this case ($5,000) makes Charter damage litigation by individuals economically viable. Finally, how does this case fall under the spectrum of approaches for the exercise of remedial discretion discussed above? Does it provide workable principles to govern the exercise of remedial discretion?

Vancouver (City) v. Ward
2010 SCC 27, [2010] 2 SCR 28

The CHIEF JUSTICE (for the Court)

I. Introduction

[1] The *Canadian Charter of Rights and Freedoms* guarantees the fundamental rights and freedoms of all Canadians and provides remedies for their breach. The first and most important remedy is the nullification of laws that violate the *Charter* under s. 52(1) of the *Constitution Act, 1982*. This is supplemented by s. 24(2), under which evidence obtained in breach of the *Charter* may be excluded if its admission would bring the administration of justice into disrepute, and s. 24(1)—the provision at issue in this case—under which the court is authorized to grant such remedies to individuals for infringement of *Charter* rights as it "considers appropriate and just in the circumstances."

· · ·

[2] The respondent Ward's *Charter* rights were violated by Vancouver and British Columbia officials who detained him, strip searched his person and seized his car without cause. The trial judge awarded Mr. Ward damages for the *Charter* breaches, and the majority of the Court of Appeal of British Columbia upheld that award.

[3] This appeal raises the question of when damages may be awarded under s. 24(1) of the *Charter*, and what the amount of such damages should be. Although the *Charter* is 28 years old, authority on this question is sparse, inviting a comprehensive analysis of the object of damages for *Charter* breaches and the considerations that guide their award.

[4] I conclude that damages may be awarded for *Charter* breach under s. 24(1) where appropriate and just. The first step in the inquiry is to establish that a *Charter* right has been breached. The second step is to show why damages are a just and appropriate remedy, having regard to whether they would fulfill one or more of the related functions of compensation, vindication of the right, and/or deterrence of future breaches. At the third step, the state has the opportunity to demonstrate, if it can, that countervailing factors defeat the functional considerations that support a damage award and render damages inappropriate or unjust. The final step is to assess the quantum of the damages.

[5] I conclude that damages were properly awarded for the strip search of Mr. Ward, but not justified for the seizure of his car. I would therefore allow the appeal in part.

II. Facts

[6] On August 1, 2002, Prime Minister Chrétien participated in a ceremony to mark the opening of a gate at the entrance to Vancouver's Chinatown. During the ceremony, the Vancouver Police Department ("VPD") received information that an unknown individual intended to throw a pie at the Prime Minister, an event that had occurred elsewhere two years earlier. The suspected individual was described as a white male, 30 to 35 years, 5' 9", with dark short hair, wearing a white golf shirt or T-shirt with some red on it.

[7] Mr. Ward is a Vancouver lawyer who attended the August 1 ceremony. On the day, Mr. Ward, a white male, had grey, collar-length hair, was in his mid-40s and was wearing a grey T-shirt with some red on it. Based on his appearance, Mr. Ward was identified—mistakenly—as the would-be pie-thrower. When the VPD officers noticed him, Mr. Ward was running and appeared to be avoiding interception. The officers chased Mr. Ward down and handcuffed him. Mr. Ward loudly protested his detention and created a disturbance, drawing the attention of a local television camera crew. The television broadcast showed that Mr. Ward had a "very agitated look on his face," "appeared to be yelling for the benefit of the onlookers" and was "holding back" as he was being escorted down the street.

[8] Mr. Ward was arrested for breach of the peace and taken to the police lockup in Vancouver, which was under the partial management of provincial corrections officers. Upon his arrival, the corrections officers instructed Mr. Ward to remove all his clothes in preparation for a strip search. Mr. Ward complied in part but refused to take off his underwear. The officers did not insist on complete removal and Mr. Ward was never touched during the search. After the search was completed, Mr. Ward was placed in a small cell where he spent several hours before being released.

[9] While Mr. Ward was at the lockup, VPD officers impounded his car for the purpose of searching it once a search warrant had been obtained. VPD detectives subsequently determined that they did not have grounds to obtain the required search warrant or evidence to charge Mr. Ward for attempted assault. Mr. Ward was released from the lockup approximately 4.5 hours after he was arrested and several hours after the Prime Minister had left Chinatown following the ceremony.

. . .

VI. Analysis

A. When Are Damages Under Section 24(1) Available?

(1) The Language of Section 24(1) and the Nature of Charter Damages

[16] Section 24(1) empowers courts of competent jurisdiction to grant "appropriate and just" remedies for *Charter* breaches. This language invites a number of observations.

[17] First, the language of the grant is broad. As McIntyre J observed, "[i]t is difficult to imagine language which could give the court a wider and less fettered discretion": *Mills v. The Queen*, [1986] 1 SCR 863, at p. 965. The judge of "competent jurisdiction" has broad discretion to determine what remedy is appropriate and just in the circumstances of a particular case.

[18] Second, it is improper for courts to reduce this discretion by casting it in a straitjacket of judicially prescribed conditions. To quote McIntyre J in *Mills* once more, "[i]t is impossible to reduce this wide discretion to some sort of binding formula for general application in all cases, and it is not for appellate courts to pre-empt or cut down this wide discretion": *Mills*, at p. 965.

[19] Third, the prohibition on cutting down the ambit of s. 24(1) does not preclude judicial clarification of when it may be "appropriate and just" to award damages. The phrase "appropriate and just" limits what remedies are available. The court's discretion, while broad, is not unfettered. What is appropriate and just will depend on the facts and circumstances of the particular case. Prior cases may offer guidance on what is appropriate and just in a particular situation.

[20] The general considerations governing what constitutes an appropriate and just remedy under s. 24(1) were set out by Iacobucci and Arbour JJ in *Doucet-Boudreau v. Nova Scotia (Minister of Education)*, 2003 SCC 62, [2003] 3 SCR 3. Briefly, an appropriate and just remedy will: (1) meaningfully vindicate the rights and freedoms of the claimants; (2) employ means that are legitimate within the framework of our constitutional democracy; (3) be a judicial remedy which vindicates the right while invoking the function and powers of a court; and (4) be fair to the party against whom the order is made: *Doucet-Boudreau*, at paras. 55-58.

[21] Damages for breach of a claimant's *Charter* rights may meet these conditions. They may meaningfully vindicate the claimant's rights and freedoms. They employ a means well-recognized within our legal framework. They are appropriate to the function and powers of a court. And, depending on the circumstances and the amount awarded, they can be fair not only to the claimant whose rights were breached, but to the state which is required to pay them. I therefore conclude that s. 24(1) is broad enough to include the remedy of damages for *Charter* breach. That said, granting damages under the *Charter* is a new endeavour, and an approach to when damages are appropriate and just should develop incrementally. *Charter* damages are only one remedy amongst others available under s. 24(1), and often other s. 24(1) remedies will be more responsive to the breach.

[22] The term "damages" conveniently describes the remedy sought in this case. However, it should always be borne in mind that these are not private law damages, but the distinct remedy of constitutional damages. As Thomas J notes in *Dunlea v. Attorney-General*, [2000] NZCA 84, [2000] 3 NZLR 136, at para. 81, a case dealing with New Zealand's *Bill of*

Rights Act 1990, an action for public law damages "is not a private law action in the nature of a tort claim for which the state is vicariously liable but [a distinct] public law action directly against the state for which the state is primarily liable." In accordance with s. 32 of the *Charter*, this is equally so in the Canadian constitutional context. The nature of the remedy is to require the state (or society writ large) to compensate an individual for breaches of the individual's constitutional rights. An action for public law damages—including constitutional damages—lies against the state and not against individual actors. Actions against individual actors should be pursued in accordance with existing causes of action. However, the underlying policy considerations that are engaged when awarding private law damages against state actors may be relevant when awarding public law damages directly against the state. Such considerations may be appropriately kept in mind.

(2) Step One: Proof of a Charter Breach

[23] Section 24(1) is remedial. The first step, therefore, is to establish a *Charter* breach. This is the wrong on which the claim for damages is based.

(3) Step Two: Functional Justification of Damages

[24] A functional approach to damages finds damages to be appropriate and just to the extent that they serve a useful function or purpose. This approach has been adopted in awarding non-pecuniary damages in personal injury cases (*Andrews v. Grand & Toy Alberta Ltd.*, [1978] 2 SCR 229), and, in my view, a similar approach is appropriate in determining when damages are "appropriate and just" under s. 24(1) of the *Charter*.

[25] I therefore turn to the purposes that an order for damages under s. 24(1) may serve. For damages to be awarded, they must further the general objects of the *Charter*. This reflects itself in three interrelated functions that damages may serve. The function of *compensation*, usually the most prominent function, recognizes that breach of an individual's *Charter* rights may cause personal loss which should be remedied. The function of *vindication* recognizes that *Charter* rights must be maintained, and cannot be allowed to be whittled away by attrition. Finally, the function of *deterrence* recognizes that damages may serve to deter future breaches by state actors.

[26] These functions of s. 24(1) damages are supported by foreign constitutional jurisprudence and, by analogy, foreign jurisprudence arising in the statutory human rights context.

[27] Compensation has been cited by Lord Woolf CJ (speaking of the *European Convention of Human Rights*) as "fundamental." In most cases, it is the most prominent of the three functions that *Charter* damages may serve. The goal is to compensate the claimant for the loss caused by the *Charter* breach; "[t]he applicant should, in so far as this is possible, be placed in the same position as if his Convention rights had not been infringed": *Anufrijeva v. Southwark London Borough Council*, [2003] EWCA Civ 1406, [2004] QB 1124, at para. 59, *per* Lord Woolf CJ Compensation focuses on the claimant's personal loss: physical, psychological and pecuniary. To these types of loss must be added harm to the claimant's intangible interests. In the public law damages context, courts have variously recognized this harm as distress, humiliation, embarrassment, and anxiety: *Dunlea*; *Bivens v. Six Unknown Named Agents of Federal Bureau of Narcotics*, 403 US 388 (1971); *Taunoa v. Attorney-General*,

[2007] NZSC 70, [2008] 1 NZLR 429. Often the harm to intangible interests effected by a breach of rights will merge with psychological harm. But a resilient claimant whose intangible interests are harmed should not be precluded from recovering damages simply because she cannot prove a substantial psychological injury.

[28] Vindication, in the sense of affirming constitutional values, has also been recognized as a valid object of damages in many jurisdictions: see *Fose v. Minister of Safety and Security*, 1997 (3) SA 786 (CC), at para. 55, for a summary of the international jurisprudence. Vindication focuses on the harm the infringement causes society. As Didcott J observed in *Fose*, violations of constitutionally protected rights harm not only their particular victims, but society as a whole. This is because they "impair public confidence and diminish public faith in the efficacy of the [constitutional] protection": *Fose*, at para. 82. While one may speak of vindication as underlining the seriousness of the harm done to the claimant, vindication as an object of constitutional damages focuses on the harm the *Charter* breach causes to the state and to society.

[29] Finally, deterrence of future breaches of the right has also been widely recognized as a valid object of public law damages: e.g., *Attorney General of Trinidad and Tobago v. Ramanoop*, [2005] UKPC 15, [2006] 1 AC 328, at para. 19; *Taunoa*, at para. 259; *Fose*, at para. 96; *Smith v. Wade*, 461 US 30 (1983), at p. 49. Deterrence, like vindication, has a societal purpose. Deterrence seeks to regulate government behaviour, generally, in order to achieve compliance with the Constitution. This purpose is similar to the criminal sentencing object of "general deterrence," which holds that the example provided by the punishment imposed on a particular offender will dissuade potential criminals from engaging in criminal activity. When general deterrence is factored in the determination of the sentence, the offender is punished more severely, not because he or she deserves it, but because the court decides to send a message to others who may be inclined to engage in similar criminal activity: *R v. B.W.P.*, 2006 SCC 27, [2006] 1 SCR 941. Similarly, deterrence as an object of *Charter* damages is not aimed at deterring the specific wrongdoer, but rather at influencing government behaviour in order to secure state compliance with the *Charter* in the future.

[30] In most cases, all three objects will be present. Harm to the claimant will evoke the need for compensation. Vindication and deterrence will support the compensatory function and bolster the appropriateness of an award of damages. However, the fact that the claimant has not suffered personal loss does not preclude damages where the objectives of vindication or deterrence clearly call for an award. Indeed, the view that constitutional damages are available only for pecuniary or physical loss has been widely rejected in other constitutional democracies: see, e.g., *Anufrijeva*; *Fose*; *Taunoa*; *Smith*; and *Ramanoop*.

[31] In summary, damages under s. 24(1) of the *Charter* are a unique public law remedy, which may serve the objectives of: (1) compensating the claimant for loss and suffering caused by the breach; (2) vindicating the right by emphasizing its importance and the gravity of the breach; and (3) deterring state agents from committing future breaches. Achieving one or more of these objects is the first requirement for "appropriate and just" damages under s. 24(1) of the *Charter*.

(4) Step Three: Countervailing Factors

[32] As discussed, the basic requirement for the award of damages to be "appropriate and just" is that the award must be functionally required to fulfill one or more of the objects of compensation, vindication of the right, or deterrence of future *Charter* breaches.

[33] However, even if the claimant establishes that damages are functionally justified, the state may establish that other considerations render s. 24(1) damages inappropriate or unjust. A complete catalogue of countervailing considerations remains to be developed as the law in this area matures. At this point, however, two considerations are apparent: the existence of alternative remedies and concerns for good governance.

[34] A functional approach to damages under s. 24(1) means that if other remedies adequately meet the need for compensation, vindication and/or deterrence, a further award of damages under s. 24(1) would serve no function and would not be "appropriate and just." The *Charter* entered an existent remedial arena which already housed tools to correct violative state conduct. Section 24(1) operates concurrently with, and does not replace, these areas of law. Alternative remedies include private law remedies for actions for personal injury, other *Charter* remedies like declarations under s. 24(1), and remedies for actions covered by legislation permitting proceedings against the Crown.

[35] The claimant must establish basic functionality having regard to the objects of constitutional damages. The evidentiary burden then shifts to the state to show that the engaged functions can be fulfilled through other remedies. The claimant need not show that she has exhausted all other recourses. Rather, it is for the state to show that other remedies are available in the particular case that will sufficiently address the breach. For example, if the claimant has brought a concurrent action in tort, it is open to the state to argue that, should the tort claim be successful, the resulting award of damages would adequately address the *Charter* breach. If that were the case, an award of *Charter* damages would be duplicative. In addition, it is conceivable that another *Charter* remedy may, in a particular case, fulfill the function of *Charter* damages.

[36] The existence of a potential claim in tort does not therefore bar a claimant from obtaining damages under the *Charter*. Tort law and the *Charter* are distinct legal avenues. However, a concurrent action in tort, or other private law claim, bars s. 24(1) damages if the result would be double compensation: *Simpson v. Attorney-General*, [1994] 3 NZLR 667 (CA), at p. 678.

[37] Declarations of *Charter* breach may provide an adequate remedy for the *Charter* breach, particularly where the claimant has suffered no personal damage. …

[38] Another consideration that may negate the appropriateness of s. 24(1) damages is concern for effective governance. Good governance concerns may take different forms. At one extreme, it may be argued that any award of s. 24(1) damages will always have a chilling effect on government conduct, and hence will impact negatively on good governance. The logical conclusion of this argument is that s. 24(1) damages would never be appropriate. Clearly, this is not what the Constitution intends. Moreover, insofar as s. 24(1) damages deter *Charter* breaches, they promote good governance. Compliance with *Charter* standards is a foundational principle of good governance.

[39] In some situations, however, the state may establish that an award of *Charter* damages would interfere with good governance such that damages should not be awarded unless

the state conduct meets a minimum threshold of gravity. This was the situation in *Mackin v. New Brunswick (Minister of Finance)*, 2002 SCC 13, [2002] 1 SCR 405, where the claimant sought damages for state conduct pursuant to a valid statute. The Court held that the action must be struck on the ground that duly enacted laws should be enforced until declared invalid, unless the state conduct under the law was "clearly wrong, in bad faith or an abuse of power": para. 78. The rule of law would be undermined if governments were deterred from enforcing the law by the possibility of future damage awards in the event the law was, at some future date, to be declared invalid. Thus, absent threshold misconduct, an action for damages under s. 24(1) of the *Charter* cannot be combined with an action for invalidity based on s. 52 of the *Constitution Act, 1982*: *Mackin*, at para. 81.

[40] The *Mackin* principle recognizes that the state must be afforded some immunity from liability in damages resulting from the conduct of certain functions that only the state can perform. Legislative and policy-making functions are one such area of state activity. The immunity is justified because the law does not wish to chill the exercise of policy-making discretion. As Gonthier J explained:

> The limited immunity given to government is specifically a means of creating a balance between the protection of constitutional rights and the need for effective government. In other words, this doctrine makes it possible to determine whether a remedy is appropriate and just in the circumstances. Consequently, the reasons that inform the general principle of public law are also relevant in a *Charter* context. [para. 79]

[41] The government argues that the *Mackin* principle applies in this case, and, in the absence of state conduct that is at least "clearly wrong," bars Mr. Ward's claim. I cannot accept this submission. *Mackin* stands for the principle that state action taken under a statute which is subsequently declared invalid will not give rise to public law damages because good governance requires that public officials carry out their duties under valid statutes without fear of liability in the event that the statute is later struck down. The present is not a situation of state action pursuant to a valid statute that was subsequently declared invalid. Nor is the rationale animating the *Mackin* principle—that duly enacted laws should be enforced until declared invalid—applicable in the present situation. Thus, the *Mackin* immunity does not apply to this case.

[42] State conduct pursuant to a valid statute may not be the only situation in which the state might seek to show that s. 24(1) damages would deter state agents from doing what is required for effective governance, although no others have been established in this case. It may be that in the future other situations may be recognized where the appropriateness of s. 24(1) damages could be negated on grounds of effective governance.

[43] Such concerns may find expression, as the law in this area matures, in various defences to s. 24(1) claims. *Mackin* established a defence of immunity for state action under valid statutes subsequently declared invalid, unless the state conduct is "clearly wrong, in bad faith or an abuse of power" (para. 78). If and when other concerns under the rubric of effective governance emerge, these may be expected to give rise to analogous public law defences. By analogy to *Mackin* and the private law, where the state establishes that s. 24(1) damages raise governance concerns, it would seem a minimum threshold, such as clear disregard for the claimant's *Charter* rights, may be appropriate. Different situations may call for different thresholds, as is the case at private law. Malicious prosecution, for example,

requires that "malice" be proven because of the highly discretionary and quasi-judicial role of prosecutors (*Miazga v. Kvello Estate*, 2009 SCC 51, [2009] 3 SCR 339), while negligent police investigation, which does not involve the same quasi-judicial decisions as to guilt or innocence or the evaluation of evidence according to legal standards, contemplates the lower "negligence" standard (*Hill v. Hamilton-Wentworth Regional Police Services Board*, 2007 SCC 41, [2007] 3 SCR 129). When appropriate, private law thresholds and defences may offer guidance in determining whether s. 24(1) damages would be "appropriate and just." While the threshold for liability under the *Charter* must be distinct and autonomous from that developed under private law, the existing causes of action against state actors embody a certain amount of "practical wisdom" concerning the type of situation in which it is or is not appropriate to make an award of damages against the state. Similarly, it may be necessary for the court to consider the procedural requirements of alternative remedies. Procedural requirements associated with existing remedies are crafted to achieve a proper balance between public and private interests, and the underlying policy considerations of these requirements should not be negated by recourse to s. 24(1) of the *Charter*. As stated earlier, s. 24(1) operates concurrently with, and does not replace, the general law. These are complex matters which have not been explored on this appeal. I therefore leave the exact parameters of future defences to future cases.

[44] I find it useful to add a comment on the judgment of our Court in *Béliveau St-Jacques v. Fédération des employées et employés de services publics inc.*, [1996] 2 SCR 345. *Béliveau St-Jacques* is not determinative of the availability of the public law remedy of damages under s. 24(1). The judgment raised specific issues concerning the interpretation of ss. 49 and 51 of the Quebec *Charter of human rights and freedoms*, RSQ, c. C-12, and its interaction with the statutory regime set up under the *Act respecting industrial accidents and occupational diseases*, RSQ, c. A-3.001.

[45] If the claimant establishes breach of his *Charter* rights and shows that an award of damages under s. 24(1) of the *Charter* would serve a functional purpose, having regard to the objects of s. 24(1) damages, and the state fails to negate that the award is "appropriate and just," the final step is to determine the appropriate amount of the damages.

(5) Step Four: Quantum of Section 24(1) Damages

[46] The watchword of s. 24(1) is that the remedy must be "appropriate and just." This applies to the amount, or quantum, of damages awarded as much as to the initial question of whether damages are a proper remedy.

[47] As discussed earlier, damages may be awarded to compensate the claimant for his loss, to vindicate the right or to deter future violations of the right. These objects, the presence and force of which vary from case to case, determine not only whether damages are appropriate, but also the amount of damages awarded. Generally, compensation will be the most important object, and vindication and deterrence will play supporting roles. This is all the more so because other *Charter* remedies may not provide compensation for the claimant's personal injury resulting from the violation of his *Charter* rights. However, as discussed earlier, cases may arise where vindication or deterrence play a major and even exclusive role.

[48] Where the objective of compensation is engaged, the concern is to restore the claimant to the position she would have been in had the breach not been committed, as

discussed above. As in a tort action, any claim for compensatory damages must be supported by evidence of the loss suffered.

[49] In some cases, the *Charter* breach may cause the claimant pecuniary loss. Injuries, physical and psychological, may require medical treatment, with attendant costs. Prolonged detention may result in loss of earnings. *Restitutio in integrum* requires compensation for such financial losses.

[50] In other cases, like this one, the claimant's losses will be non-pecuniary. Non-pecuniary damages are harder to measure. Yet they are not by that reason to be rejected. Again, tort law provides assistance. Pain and suffering are compensable. Absent exceptional circumstances, compensation is fixed at a fairly modest conventional rate, subject to variation for the degree of suffering in the particular case. In extreme cases of catastrophic injury, a higher but still conventionally determined award is given on the basis that it serves the function purpose of providing substitute comforts and pleasures: *Andrews v. Grand & Toy*.

[51] When we move from compensation to the objectives of vindication and deterrence, tort law is less useful. Making the appropriate determinations is an exercise in rationality and proportionality and will ultimately be guided by precedent as this important chapter of *Charter* jurisprudence is written by Canada's courts. That said, some initial observations may be made.

[52] A principal guide to the determination of quantum is the seriousness of the breach, having regard to the objects of s. 24(1) damages. The seriousness of the breach must be evaluated with regard to the impact of the breach on the claimant and the seriousness of the state misconduct: see, in the context of s. 24(2), *R v. Grant*, 2009 SCC 32, [2009] 2 SCR 353. Generally speaking, the more egregious the conduct and the more serious the repercussions on the claimant, the higher the award for vindication or deterrence will be.

[53] Just as private law damages must be fair to both the plaintiff and the defendant, so s. 24(1) damages must be fair—or "appropriate and just"—to both the claimant and the state. The court must arrive at a quantum that respects this. Large awards and the consequent diversion of public funds may serve little functional purpose in terms of the claimant's needs and may be inappropriate or unjust from the public perspective. In considering what is fair to the claimant and the state, the court may take into account the public interest in good governance, the danger of deterring governments from undertaking beneficial new policies and programs, and the need to avoid diverting large sums of funds from public programs to private interests.

[54] Courts in other jurisdictions where an award of damages for breach of rights is available have generally been careful to avoid unduly high damage awards. This may reflect the difficulty of assessing what is required to vindicate the right and deter future breaches, as well as the fact that it is society as a whole that is asked to compensate the claimant. Nevertheless, to be "appropriate and just," an award of damages must represent a meaningful response to the seriousness of the breach and the objectives of compensation, upholding *Charter* values, and deterring future breaches. The private law measure of damages for similar wrongs will often be a useful guide. However, as Lord Nicholls warns in *Ramanoop*, at para. 18, "this measure is no more than a guide because ... the violation of the constitutional right will not always be coterminous with the cause of action at law."

[55] In assessing s. 24(1) damages, the court must focus on the breach of *Charter* rights as an independent wrong, worthy of compensation in its own right. At the same time, damages

under s. 24(1) should not duplicate damages awarded under private law causes of action, such as tort, where compensation of personal loss is at issue.

[56] A final word on exemplary or punitive damages. In *Mackin*, Justice Gonthier speculated that "[i]n theory, a plaintiff could seek compensatory and punitive damages by way of 'appropriate and just' remedy under s. 24(1) of the *Charter*": para. 79. The reality is that public law damages, in serving the objects of vindication and deterrence, may assume a punitive aspect. Nevertheless, it is worth noting a general reluctance in the international community to award purely punitive damages: see *Taunoa*, at paras. 319-21.

[57] To sum up, the amount of damages must reflect what is required to functionally serve the objects of compensation, vindication of the right and deterrence of future breaches, insofar as they are engaged in a particular case, having regard to the impact of the breach on the claimant and the seriousness of the state conduct. The award must be appropriate and just from the perspective of the claimant and the state.

(6) Forum and Procedure

[58] For a tribunal to grant a *Charter* remedy under s. 24(1), it must have the power to decide questions of law and the remedy must be one that the tribunal is authorized to grant: *R v. Conway*, 2010 SCC 22, [2010] 1 SCR 765. Generally, the appropriate forum for an award of damages under s. 24(1) is a court which has the power to consider *Charter* questions and which by statute or inherent jurisdiction has the power to award damages. Provincial criminal courts are not so empowered and thus do not have the power to award damages under s. 24(1).

[59] As was done here, the claimant may join a s. 24(1) claim with a tort claim. It may be useful to consider the tort claim first, since if it meets the objects of *Charter* damages, recourse to s. 24(1) will be unnecessary. This may add useful context and facilitate the s. 24(1) analysis. This said, it is not essential that the claimant exhaust her remedies in private law before bringing a s. 24(1) claim.

B. Application to the Facts

[60] At trial, Justice Tysoe held that the provincial correction officers' strip search and the Vancouver Police Department's vehicle seizure violated Mr. Ward's right to be free from unreasonable search and seizure under s. 8 of the *Charter*. There are thus two distinct claims to consider.

(1) Damages for the Strip Search

[61] The first question is whether Mr. Ward has established entitlement to the s. 24(1) remedy of damages. This requires him to show: (1) a breach of his *Charter* rights; and (2) that an award of damages would serve a functional purpose in the circumstances, having regard to the objects of s. 24(1) damages. If these are established, the burden shifts to the state (step 3) to show why, having regard to countervailing factors, an award of damages under s. 24(1) of the *Charter* would be inappropriate. If the state fails to negate s. 24(1) damages, the inquiry moves to the final step, assessment of the appropriate amount of the damages.

[62] Here the first step is met. Justice Tysoe found that the strip search violated Mr. Ward's personal rights under s. 8 of the *Charter*. This finding is not challenged on this appeal. Nor is it suggested that the British Columbia Supreme Court is not an appropriate forum for the action.

[63] The second question is whether damages would serve a functional purpose by serving one or more of the objects of s. 24(1) damages—compensation, vindication and deterrence.

[64] In this case, the need for compensation bulks large. Mr. Ward's injury was serious. He had a constitutional right to be free from unreasonable search and seizure, which was violated in an egregious fashion. Strip searches are inherently humiliating and degrading regardless of the manner in which they are carried out and thus constitute significant injury to an individual's intangible interests: *R v. Golden*, 2001 SCC 83, [2001] 3 SCR 679, at para. 90.

[65] The corrections officers' conduct which caused the breach of Mr. Ward's *Charter* rights was also serious. Minimum sensitivity to *Charter* concerns within the context of the particular situation would have shown the search to be unnecessary and violative. Mr. Ward did not commit a serious offence, he was not charged with an offence associated with evidence being hidden on the body, no weapons were involved and he was not known to be violent or to carry weapons. Mr. Ward did not pose a risk of harm to himself or others, nor was there any suggestion that any of the officers believed that he did. In these circumstances, a reasonable person would understand that the indignity resulting from the search was disproportionate to any benefit which the search could have provided. In addition, without asking officers to be conversant with the details of court rulings, it is not too much to expect that police would be familiar with the settled law that routine strip searches are inappropriate where the individual is being held for a short time in police cells, is not mingling with the general prison population, and where the police have no legitimate concerns that the individual is concealing weapons that could be used to harm themselves or others: *Golden*, at para. 97.

[66] In sum, the *Charter* breach significantly impacted on Mr. Ward's person and rights and the police conduct was serious. The impingement on Mr. Ward calls for compensation. Combined with the police conduct, it also engages the objects of vindication of the right and deterrence of future breaches. It follows that compensation is required in this case to functionally fulfill the objects of public law damages.

[67] The next question is whether the state has established countervailing factors that would render s. 24(1) damages inappropriate or unjust.

[68] The state has not established that alternative remedies are available to achieve the objects of compensation, vindication or deterrence with respect to the strip search. Mr. Ward sued the officers for assault, as well as the City and the Province for negligence. These claims were dismissed and their dismissal was not appealed to this Court. While this defeated Mr. Ward's claim in tort, it did not change the fact that his right under s. 8 of the *Charter* to be secure against unreasonable search and seizure was violated. No tort action was available for that violation and a declaration will not satisfy the need for compensation. Mr. Ward's only recourse is a claim for damages under s. 24(1) of the *Charter*. Nor has the state established that an award of s. 24(1) damages is negated by good governance considerations, such as those raised in *Mackin*.

[69] I conclude that damages for the strip search of Mr. Ward are required in this case to functionally fulfill the objects of public law damages, and therefore are *prima facie* "appropriate and just." The state has not negated this. It follows that damages should be awarded for this breach of Mr. Ward's *Charter* rights.

[70] This brings us to the issue of quantum. As discussed earlier, the amount of damages must reflect what is required to functionally fulfill the relevant objects of s. 24(1) compensation, while remaining fair to both the claimant and the state.

[71] The object of compensation focuses primarily on the claimant's personal loss: physical, psychological, pecuniary, and harm to intangible interests. The claimant should, in so far as possible, be placed in the same position as if his *Charter* rights had not been infringed. Strip searches are inherently humiliating and thus constitute a significant injury to an individual's intangible interests regardless of the manner in which they are carried out. That said, the present search was relatively brief and not extremely disrespectful, as strip searches go. It did not involve the removal of Mr. Ward's underwear or the exposure of his genitals. Mr. Ward was never touched during the search and there is no indication that he suffered any resulting physical or psychological injury. While Mr. Ward's injury was serious, it cannot be said to be at the high end of the spectrum. This suggests a moderate damages award.

[72] The objects of vindication and deterrence engage the seriousness of the state conduct. The corrections officers' conduct was serious and reflected a lack of sensitivity to *Charter* concerns. That said, the officers' action was not intentional, in that it was not malicious, high-handed or oppressive. In these circumstances, the objects of vindication and deterrence do not require an award of substantial damages against the state.

[73] Considering all the factors, including the appropriate degree of deference to be paid to the trial judge's exercise of remedial discretion, I conclude that the trial judge's $5,000 damage award was appropriate.

(2) Damages for the Car Seizure

[74] As with the strip search, we must determine whether Mr. Ward has established entitlement to the s. 24(1) remedy of damages to compensate for the constitutional wrong he suffered due to the City's seizure of his vehicle. Again, this requires determining: (1) breach of *Charter* right; (2) whether an award of damages would serve a functional purpose, having regard to the objects of s. 24(1) damages; (3) whether the state has established countervailing factors negating an award of s. 24(1) damages; and (4) quantum, if the right to damages is established.

[75] The trial judge found that the seizure of the car violated Mr. Ward's rights under s. 8 of the *Charter*. This finding is not contested and thus satisfies the first requirement.

[76] The next question is whether Mr. Ward has established that damages under s. 24(1) for the car seizure are appropriate and just from a functional perspective.

[77] The object of compensation is not engaged by the seizure of the car. The trial judge found that Mr. Ward did not suffer any injury as a result of the seizure. His car was never searched and, upon his release from lockup, Mr. Ward was driven to the police compound to pick up the vehicle. Nor are the objects of vindication of the right and deterrence of future breaches compelling. While the seizure was wrong, it was not of a serious nature. The police officers did not illegally search the car, but rather arranged for its towing under the impres-

sion that it would be searched once a warrant had been obtained. When the officers determined that they did not have grounds to obtain the required warrant, the vehicle was made available for pickup.

[78] I conclude that a declaration under s. 24(1) that the vehicle seizure violated Mr. Ward's right to be free from unreasonable search and seizure under s. 8 of the *Charter* adequately serves the need for vindication of the right and deterrence of future improper car seizures.

VII. *Disposition*

[79] The appeal is allowed in part. The award against the City in the amount of $100 is set aside, substituted by a declaration under s. 24(1) that the vehicle seizure violated Mr. Ward's right to be free from unreasonable search and seizure under s. 8 of the *Charter*. The award of damages against the Province in the sum of $5,000 for breach of Mr. Ward's s. 8 *Charter* rights is confirmed.

[80] We have been informed of a pre-existing agreement between Mr. Ward and the Province regarding costs and, as such, no cost order is made between Mr. Ward and the Province. No costs are awarded to or against the City.

NOTES AND QUESTIONS

1. *Ward* does not require the proof of negligence or some other form of fault in addition to the violation of Charter rights as a prerequisite to awarding damages under the Charter. At the same time, it does not require that damages be awarded for every violation of the Charter. Does this set the appropriate balance between strong, rule-based, and principled discretion as discussed by Roach in the extract above?

2. *Ward* recognizes compensation, deterrence, and the vindication of Charter rights as the main purposes served by Charter damages. How do these purposes compare with the purposes served by common law damages? How do they compare with those advocated by Pilkington in the extract above? Vindication of Charter rights is obviously a purpose that is particular to the Charter, but what role should deterrence play in awarding Charter damages? What is the relevance that the defendant in the case was the city of Vancouver and the province of British Columbia and not, as in some of the tort actions dismissed in the case, the individual officers who conducted the search? Does the court's recognition of deterrence as a purpose of Charter damages mean that exemplary or punitive damages should not be awarded under the Charter?

3. Has the court created a distinct form of public law liability for damages tied to the applicability of the Charter to governments under s. 32(1) of the Charter and the recognition of remedial discretion under s. 24(1)? If so, what, if any, influence should private law concepts have on the awarding of Charter damages?

4. The court in paragraph 43 of the *Ward* judgment suggests that private law concerning damages may "embody a certain amount of 'practical wisdom' concerning the type of situation in which it is or is not appropriate to make an award of damages against the state." How does this compare with the suggestions made by Mullan in the above extract?

5. The court also suggests in the same paragraph that "private law thresholds and defences" may have some relevance under the open-ended category of good governance concerns that might prevent the award of damages even when they are required to compensate, vindicate, and deter Charter violations. The court warns, however, that these "are complex matters which have not been explored on this appeal" and that "the exact parameters of future defences" will have to be decided in future cases. Is this a strong form of remedial discretion as discussed by Roach, or is it simply a recognition of the limits of a particular case that did not claim damages from, for example, the exercise of prosecutorial, judicial, or legislative functions? Is there a risk that the "practical wisdom" of private law restrictions on damages might frustrate the purposes of the Charter and Charter damages?

6. Although it was not an issue in *Ward*, it appears that Charter damages are subject to normal statutes of limitations: *Ravandahl v. Saskatchewan*, [2009] 1 SCR 181; however, for an earlier contrary position that held that Charter damage claims were immune from a short limitation period that benefited public authorities, see *Prete v. Ontario (Attorney-General)* (1993), 110 DLR (4th) 94 (Ont. CA). Is it consistent with the public law and constitutional premises of *Ward* to subject damages to statutes of limitations? What would be the effect of a statute that purported to provide good faith or absolute immunity to restrict the award of Charter damages?

7. For a more detailed assessment of damages as a remedy for Charter violations, see Marilyn L. Pilkington, "Damages as a Remedy for Infringement of the Canadian Charter of Rights and Freedoms" (1984), 62 *Canadian Bar Review* 517; Ken Cooper-Stephenson, *Charter Damages Claims* (Toronto: Carswell, 1990); and Kent Roach, *Constitutional Remedies in Canada* (Toronto: Canada Law Book), c. 11 (looseleaf); and Kent Roach, "A Late Spring: Charter Damages After *Ward v. Vancouver*" (2011), 29 NJCL (forthcoming).

8. One of the reasons why there has not been all that much litigation involving claims for damages for s. 15 violations by state officials may be the availability of recourse for such wrongs under human rights statutes. There may also be a sense that *Seneca College of Applied Arts and Technology v. Bhadauria*, [1981] 2 SCR 181 precludes the making of such claims. There, it was held that the existence of a complaint mechanism under the Ontario *Human Rights Code* precluded the evolution of a common law tort of discrimination. It is, however, an open question whether the same argument for the exclusivity of human rights statute processes applies to preclude the recognition of a constitutional tort based on violations of s. 15. See *Perera v. Canada* (1998), 158 DLR (4th) 341 (FCA), sustaining a refusal of the trial division judge ([1997] FCJ no. 199 (TD) (QL)) to strike out a statement of claim on this basis. For further elaboration of this whole issue, see Tamar Witelson, "Retort: Revisiting Bhadauria and the Supreme Court's Rejection of the Tort of Discrimination" (1999), 10 NJCL 149, at 181-83 and David J. Mullan, "Tribunals and Courts: The Contemporary Terrain—Lessons from Human Rights Regimes" (1999), 24 *Queen's Law Journal* 643.

Another reason, as discussed in Mullan, above, is that courts may be reluctant to award damages if the officials relied on legislation or regulations. *Mackin v. New Brunswick*, [2002] 1 SCR 405, at para. 82, indicated that "absent conduct that is clearly wrong, in bad faith or an abuse of power, the courts will not award damages for the harm suffered as a result of the mere enactment or application of a law that is subsequently declared to be unconstitutional." Does this form of good-faith immunity strike the appropriate balance between what the Supreme Court called "the protection of constitutional rights and the need for effective government" (*Mackin*, at para. 77)? The court distinguished this form of qualified immunity in *Ward* because the state did not rely on specific statutory authority for the strip search that violated the Charter, but is the approach in *Ward*, which stresses the responsibility of governments under the Charter, in tension with the approach in *Mackin*, which provides good-faith immunity for Charter violations authorized by legislation? Is it also in tension with the court's decision in *Kingstreet Investments Ltd v. New Brunswick (Finance)*, [2007] 1 SCR 3, which ruled that money collected under a tax subsequently found to be unconstitutional should be repaid and which rejected immunities as inconsistent with the supreme law of the constitution?

In *Canada v. Hislop*, [2007] 1 SCR 429, the court held that while those who successfully challenge a law under the Charter should generally receive full retroactive relief, departures from the rule could be justified in cases where (1) the court made a substantial change in the law; (2) the government reasonably relied in good faith on the law as previously stated; (3) a retroactive remedy would unduly interfere with the role of government, especially in allocating public resources; and (4) the departure from the norm of fully retroactive relief would not be unfair to the successful Charter applicants. The court held on the facts that full retroactive repayment of spousal benefits to same-sex partners was not warranted from 1985 (when Charter equality rights came into force).

Where the order to make payments comes not as a result of a finding that a statute is invalid but in response to an executive or administrative decision that is held to be contrary to the Charter, should the court have the same concern with the financial consequences of a mandatory order? See, for example, *Conseil des Écoles Separées Catholiques Romaines de Dufferin et Peel v. Ontario (Ministre de l'Éducation et de la Formation)* (1996), 30 OR (3d) 681 (Div. Ct. and CA), *per* Hawkins J, with the Court of Appeal simply refusing to reverse an associated order denying the province a stay of the order pending the outcome of its appeal. Here, the court ordered the Ontario government to pay more than $10 million toward the construction of a French-language school in order to effectuate the Charter rights of French-speaking students in the district. This created an exception to the government's moratorium on new capital projects.

Subsequently, there have been other examples where the Supreme Court of Canada has approved orders having financial consequences in situations where administrative discretion has been exercised in a way that violated Charter rights. See, for example, *Eldridge v. British Columbia (Attorney General)*, [1997] 3 SCR 624 (mandating the provision of translation services to the hearing-impaired in hospitals and under the province's medical services program) and *New Brunswick (Minister of Health and Community Services) v. G. (J.)*, [1999] 3 SCR 46 (ordering that the province provide legal assistance to a woman resisting the renewal of an order placing her children in the custody of the state).

INJUNCTIONS AS A CHARTER REMEDY

Injunctions and Crown Immunity

Before we consider the principles governing the availability of interlocutory injunctions in Charter litigation, one matter should be cleared. Often, a party seeking an injunction as a Charter remedy will be suing the Crown or a Crown servant. Crown liability legislation in all provinces (except Quebec) confirms the common law doctrine that an injunction cannot issue against the Crown itself, but provides that a declaration in lieu of an injunction can be made. The federal *Crown Liability Act*, RSC 1985, c. C-50 has also been amended to include a similar provision (SC 1990, c. 8, s. 28, amending s. 22). Declaratory relief is usually a satisfactory substitute at the final judgment stage, but is not available as an interim measure. However, interlocutory injunctions have often been granted against government officials on the ground that, where they act beyond their powers, they are not entitled to the protection of the statute: see *MacLean v. Liquor Licence Board of Ontario* (1975), 9 OR (2d) 597 (HC) and Robert J. Sharpe, *Injunctions and Specific Performance*, 3rd ed. (Aurora, ON: Canada Law Book, 2000), chapter 3. More important, it now seems accepted that provisions prohibiting the award of injunctive relief against the Crown do not and, indeed, constitutionally could not apply to prevent the award of such relief as a remedy in constitutional (including Charter) cases. See Peter W. Hogg and Patrick Monahan, *Liability of the Crown*, 3rd ed. (Toronto: Carswell, 2002), citing *Van Mulligen v. Saskatchewan Housing Corporation* (1982), 23 Sask. R 66 (QB) and, subsequently, *Prete v. Ontario* (1993), 16 OR (3d) 161 (CA) and *Liebman v. Canada (Minister of National Defence)*, [1994] 2 FC 3 (TD). See also Roach, above, paragraphs 13.90-13.160.

In *Doucet-Boudreau v. Nova Scotia*, [2003] 3 SCR 3, the entire Supreme Court assumed that an injunction could be issued and enforced against Nova Scotia under s. 24(1) of the Charter. Iacobucci and Arbour JJ stated, at para. 51:

> The power of the superior courts under s. 24(1) to make appropriate and just orders to remedy infringements or denials of *Charter* rights is part of the supreme law of Canada. It follows that this remedial power cannot be strictly limited by statutes or rules of the common law. We note, however, that statutes and common law rules may be helpful to a court choosing a remedy under s. 24(1) insofar as the statutory provisions or common law rules express principles that are relevant to determining what is "appropriate and just in the circumstances."

In their dissent, Lebel and Deschamps JJ also assumed that an injunction could be enforced, and enforced though contempt proceedings (*Doucet-Boudreau*, at para. 136).

Interlocutory Injunctions

We have already seen in the general chapter on interlocutory injunctions that it has sometimes been suggested that, where the principal claim is one affecting constitutional rights and freedoms, the standards for obtaining such relief should be modified. Thus, Hammond has asserted in "Interlocutory Injunctions: Time for a New Model?" (chapter 8, "Interlocutory Injunctions") that it "should be difficult to get an interlocutory injunction in a case where free speech is genuinely in issue." Presumably, he was speaking to an interlocutory injunction that is aimed at restricting speech—for example, preventing an alleged defamation—and the corollary should be that interlocutory injunctions should be easier to obtain when sought in support of free speech rights—for example, temporarily enjoining the enforcement of publication bans issued by an inferior court or tribunal.

On the other hand, we have also noted in that same chapter examples of acceptance of the proposition that where the validity of a statute (including subordinate legislation) is at stake, despite the fact that Charter or other constitutional rights appear to be raised genuinely, there is a tendency to support the *status quo* as reflected in the law as it presently appears on the books; see, for example, *Morgentaler v. Ackroyd* (1983), 42 OR (2d) 659 (HC), referred to and applied in *Municipality of Metropolitan Toronto v. N.B. Theatrical Agencies* (1984), 44 OR (2d) 574 (HC). Indeed, this sense of preserving the *status quo* even in the face of a serious constitutional challenge was also relied upon by the Ontario High Court in the interlocutory proceedings in the Charter mandatory retirement litigation: *Bregzis v. Governing Council of the University of Toronto* (1985), 53 OR (2d) 348 (HC). However, the BC Court of Appeal adopted a rather different posture in sustaining the grant of an interlocutory injunction in that same context: *Vancouver General Hospital v. Stoffman* (1985), 68 BCLR 230 (CA).

What this superficial survey of material already covered suggests is that there may be no simple answer to the question: what is the appropriate posture for a court to take in interlocutory proceedings where Charter and other constitutional rights and freedoms are at stake? Much may depend on the nature of the particular right or freedom being asserted, the context in which that assertion is taking place, and, more particularly, whether the principal litigation involves a challenge to legislation, an order or action of an administrative or executive nature, or, perhaps now, the actions or threatened actions of a private person. As the first case in this section suggests, it may also depend in large measure on the nature of what is required by the interlocutory relief with mandatory or structural interlocutory remedies being just as difficult to obtain in this domain as they are in essentially private law litigation.

Since the coming into force of the Charter, the Supreme Court of Canada has had a number of opportunities on which to develop operating principles for lower courts in making decisions on whether to grant an interlocutory injunction in cases involving Charter challenges. Assess whether the court has provided a clear roadmap for first instance judges who represent the first and often only effective line of recourse in this domain. Also, consider the extent to which such judgments are affected by the factors or considerations outlined in the previous paragraph.

Attorney General of Manitoba v. Metropolitan Stores (MTS) Ltd.
[1987] 1 SCR 110

[The respondent had commenced proceedings to have a provision in the Manitoba *Labour Relations Act* empowering the Manitoba Labour Board to impose a first contract declared contrary to the Charter. The respondent sought a stay of the union's application to the board pursuant to the impugned provision of the Act, pending final determination of the Charter challenge. The Queen's Bench judge refused a stay, but the Manitoba Court of Appeal allowed an appeal and granted a stay.]

BEETZ J: ... A stay of proceedings and an interlocutory injunction are remedies of the same nature. In the absence of a different test prescribed by statute, they have sufficient characteristics in common to be governed by the same rules and the courts have rightly tended to apply to the granting of interlocutory stay the principles which they follow with respect to interlocutory injunctions: [authorities omitted].

The case-law is abundant as well as relatively fluid with regard to the tests developed by the courts in order to help better delineate the situations in which it is just and equitable to grant an interlocutory injunction. Reviewing it is the function of doctrinal analysis rather than that of judicial decision-making and I simply propose to give a bare outline of the three main tests currently applied.

The first test is a preliminary and tentative assessment of the merits of the case, but there is more than one way to describe this first test. The traditional way consists in asking whether the litigant who seeks the interlocutory injunction can make out a *prima facie* case. The injunction will be refused unless he can: *Chesapeake & Ohio R. Co. v. Ball*, [1953] OR 843, *per* McRuer CJHC, at pp. 854-5. The House of Lords has somewhat relaxed this first test in *American Cyanamid Co. v. Ethicon Ltd.*, [1975] AC 396 (HL (Eng.)) where it held that all that was necessary to meet this test was to satisfy the court that there was a serious question to be tried as opposed to a frivolous or vexatious claim. ...

In the case at bar, it is neither necessary nor advisable to choose, for all purposes, between the traditional formulation and the *American Cyanamid* description of the first test: the British case-law illustrates that the formulation of a rigid test for all types of cases, without considering their nature, is not to be favoured: see Jill E. Martin (ed.), *Hanbury and Maudsley's Modern Equity* (London: Stevens & Sons, 12th ed., 1985) at pp. 736-43. In my view, however, the *American Cyanamid* "serious question" formulation is sufficient in a constitutional case where, as indicated below in these reasons, the public interest is taken into consideration in the balance of convenience. But I refrain from expressing any view with respect to the sufficiency or adequacy of this formulation in any other type of case.

The second test consists in deciding whether the litigant who seeks the interlocutory injunction would, unless the injunction is granted, suffer irreparable harm, that is harm not susceptible or difficult to be compensated in damages. Some judges consider at the same time the situation of the other party to the litigation and ask themselves whether the granting of the interlocutory injunction would cause irreparable harm to this other party if the main action fails. Other judges take the view that this last aspect rather forms part of the balance of convenience.

The third test, called the balance of convenience and which ought perhaps to be called more appropriately the balance of inconvenience, is a determination of which of the two parties will suffer the greater harm from the granting or refusal of an interlocutory injunction, pending a decision on the merits.

I now propose to consider the particular application of the test of the balance of convenience in a case where the constitutional validity of a legislative provision is challenged. As Lord Diplock said in *American Cyanamid*, at p. 409: "... there may be many other special factors to be taken into consideration in the particular circumstances of individual cases."

It will be seen in what follows that the consequences for the public as well as for the parties, of granting a stay in a constitutional case do constitute "special factors" to be taken into consideration.

The Balance of Convenience and the Public Interest

A review of the case-law indicates that, when the constitutional validity of a legislative provision is challenged, the courts consider that they ought not to be restricted to the application of traditional criteria which govern the granting or refusal of interlocutory injunctive relief in ordinary private or civil law cases. Unless the public interest is also taken into consideration in evaluating the balance of convenience, they very often express their disinclination to grant injunctive relief before constitutional invalidity has been finally decided on the merits.

The reasons for this disinclination became readily understandable when one contrasts the uncertainty in which a court finds itself with respect to the merits at the interlocutory stage, with the sometimes far-reaching albeit temporary practical consequences of a stay of proceedings, not only for the parties to the litigation but also for the public at large.

(i) Difficulty or Impossibility To Decide the Merits at the Interlocutory Stage

The limited role of a court at the interlocutory stage was well described by Lord Diplock in the *American Cyanamid* case, at p. 407:

> It is no part of the court's function at this stage of the litigation to try to resolve conflicts of evidence on affidavit as to facts on which the claims of either party may ultimately depend nor to decide difficult questions of law which call for detailed argument and mature considerations. These are matters to be dealt with at the trial.

The *American Cyanamid* case was a complicated civil case but Lord Diplock's *dictum*, just quoted, should *a fortiori* be followed for several reasons in a Charter case and in other constitutional cases when the validity of a law is challenged.

First, the extent and exact meaning of the rights guaranteed by the Charter are often far from clear and the interlocutory procedure rarely enables a motion judge to ascertain these crucial questions. Constitutional adjudication is particularly unsuited to the expeditious and informal proceedings of a weekly court where there are little or no pleadings and submissions in writing, and where the Attorney General of Canada or of the Province may not yet have been notified as is usually required by law: see *Home Oil Distributors Ltd. v. A-G BC* (1939), 53 BCR 355; *Weisfeld v. The Queen* (1985), 16 CRR 24 (FC, TD); and, for an extreme example, *Turmel v. CRTC* (1985), 16 CRR 9 (FC, TD).

Still, in Charter cases such as those which may arise under s. 23 relating to minority language educational rights, the factual situation as well as the law may be so uncertain at the interlocutory stage as to prevent the court from forming even a tentative opinion on the case of the plaintiff: *Marchand v. Simcoe County Board of Education* (1984), 10 CRR 169 (Ont. HC) at p. 174.

Furthermore, in many Charter cases such as the case at bar, some party may find it necessary or prudent to adduce evidence tending to establish that the impugned provision, although *prima facie* in violation of a guaranteed right or freedom, can be saved under s. 1 of the Charter. But evidence adduced pursuant to s. 1 of the Charter essentially addresses the merits of the case.

This latter rule was clearly stated in *Re A-G Can. and Gould*, [1984] 2 SCR 124, aff. [1984] 1 FC 1133, setting aside [1984] 1 FC 1119.

Such cautious restraint respects the right of both parties to a full trial ... . Also, it is consistent with the fact that, in some cases, the impugned provision will not be found to violate a right or freedom protected by the Charter after all and thus will not need to be saved under s. 1: see *R v. Jones*, [1986] 2 SCR 284.

In addition, to think that the question of constitutional validity can be determined at the interlocutory stage is to ignore the many hazards of litigation, constitutional or otherwise.

A plaintiff may fail for lack of standing, lack of adequate proof, procedural or other defect. As was correctly put by Professor J.E. Magnet (J.E. Magnet, "Jurisdictional Fact, Constitutional Fact and the Presumption of Constitutionality" (1980), 11 *Man. LJ* 21 at p. 29):

> Unconstitutionality cannot be understood as an unqualified condition. It has to be understood in light of the plaintiff's ability to bring to fruition judgment in his favour.

However, the principle I am discussing is not absolute. There may be rare cases where the question of constitutionality will present itself as a simple question of law alone which can be finally settled by a motion judge. A theoretical example which comes to mind is one where Parliament or a legislature would purport to pass a law imposing the beliefs of a State religion. Such a law would violate s. 2(a) of the *Canadian Charter of Rights and Freedoms*, could not possibly be saved under s. 1 of the Charter and might perhaps be struck down right away: see *A-G Que. v. Quebec Ass'n of Protestant School Boards*, [1984] 2 SCR 66 at p. 88. It is trite to say that these cases are exceptional.

Most of the difficulties encountered by a trial judge at the interlocutory stage, which are raised above, apply not only in Charter cases but also in other constitutional challenges of a law. I therefore fully agree with what Professor Robert J. Sharpe wrote in *Injunctions and Specific Performance* (Toronto, Canada Law Book, 1983), at p. 177, in particular with respect to constitutional cases that "the courts have sensibly paid heed to the fact that at the interlocutory stage they cannot fully explore the merits of the plaintiff's case." At this stage, even in cases where the plaintiff has a serious question to be tried or even a *prima facie* case, the court is generally much too uncertain as to the facts and the law to be in a position to decide the merits.

(ii) The Consequences of Granting a Stay in Constitutional Cases

Keeping in mind the state of uncertainty above referred to, I turn to the consequences that will certainly or probably follow the granting of a stay of proceedings. As previously said, I will not restrict myself to Charter instances. I also propose to refer to a few Quebec examples. In that province, the issuance of interlocutory injunctions is governed by arts. 751 and 752 of the *Code of Civil Procedure*, RSQ 1977, c. C-25:

> 751. An injunction is an order of the Superior Court or of a judge thereof, enjoining a person, his officers, agents or employees, not to do or to cease doing, or, in cases which admit of it, to perform a particular act or operation, under pain of all legal penalties.
>
> 752. In addition to an injunction, which he may demand by action, with or without other conclusions, a party may, at the commencement of or during a suit, obtain an interlocutory injunction.
>
> An interlocutory injunction may be granted when the applicant appears to be entitled to it and it is considered to be necessary in order to avoid serious or irreparable injury to him, or a factual or legal situation of such nature as to render the final judgment ineffectual.

While these provisions differ somewhat from the English law of injunctions, they are clearly inspired by and derived from this law and I do not think that the Quebec cases I propose to refer to turn on any differences between the English law and the Code.

Although constitutional cases are often the result of a *lis* between private litigants, they sometimes involve some public authority interposed between the litigants, such as the board in the case at bar. In other constitutional cases, the controversy or the *lis*, if it can be called a *lis*, will arise directly between a private litigant and the State represented by some public authority: *Morgentaler v. Ackroyd* (1983), 42 OR (2d) 659 (HC).

In both sorts of cases, the granting of a stay requested by the private litigant or by one of them is usually aimed at the public authority, law enforcement agency, administrative board, public official or Minister responsible for the implementation or administration of the impugned legislation and generally works in one of two ways. Either the law enforcement agency is enjoined from enforcing the impugned provisions in all respects until the question of their validity has been finally determined, or the law enforcement agency is enjoined from enforcing the impugned provisions with respect to the specific litigant or litigants who request the granting of a stay. In the first branch of the alternative, the operation of the impugned provisions is temporarily suspended for all practical purposes. Instances of this type can perhaps be referred to as suspension cases. In the second branch of the alternative, the litigant who is granted a stay is in fact exempted from the impugned legislation which, in the meanwhile, continues to operate with respect to others. Instances of this other type I will call exemption cases.

Whether or not they are ultimately held to be constitutional, the laws which litigants seek to suspend or from which they seek to be exempted by way of interlocutory injunctive relief have been enacted by democratically elected legislatures and are generally passed for the common good, for instance, the providing and financing of public services such as educational services, or of public utilities such as electricity, the protection of public health, natural resources and the environment, the repression of what is considered to be criminal activity, the controlling of economic activity such as the containing of inflation, the regulation of labour relations, etc. It seems axiomatic that the granting of interlocutory injunctive relief in most suspension cases and, up to a point, as will be seen later, in quite a few exemption cases, is susceptible temporarily to frustrate the pursuit of the common good.

While respect for the Constitution must remain paramount, the question then arises whether it is equitable and just to deprive the public, or important sectors thereof, from the protection and advantages of impugned legislation, the invalidity of which is merely uncertain, unless the public interest is taken into consideration in the balance of convenience and is given the weight it deserves. As could be expected, the courts have generally answered this question in the negative. In looking at the balance of convenience, they have found it necessary to rise above the interests of private litigants up to the level of the public interest, and, in cases involving interlocutory injunctions directed at statutory authorities, they have correctly held it is erroneous to deal with these authorities as if they have any interest distinct from that of the public to which they owe the duties imposed upon them by statute.

The following provide examples of the concern expressed by the courts for the protection of the common good in suspension and exemption cases. I will first address the suspension cases.

Société de dévelopement de la Baie James v. Kanatewat, [1975] Que. CA 166, is a striking illustration of interlocutory relief which could have compromised the common good of the public as a whole. In that case, the Quebec Court of Appeal, reversing the Superior Court,

[1974] RP 38, dismissed an application for interlocutory injunction which would have required the appellants to halt the James Bay project authorized by the *James Bay Region Development Act*, 1971 (Que.), c. 34, the constitutional validity of which had been challenged by the respondents. Crête JA, as he then was, wrote what follows in looking at the balance of convenience at p. 182 [translation]:

> … I am not convinced that the actual or perceived inconvenience to the respondents was of the same order of magnitude as the growing energy requirements of Quebec as a whole.

Turgeon JA reached the same conclusions at p. 177 [translation]:

> It is important to note at the outset that hydro-electric power is Quebec's only primary energy resource. With the current world oil crisis, this resource has become of paramount importance in ensuring the economic future and the well-being of our citizens. *The interests of the people of Quebec are represented in this case by the principal appellant companies.*
>
> The evidence indicates that it is imperative for Hydro-Quebec to implement its programme in order to meet the growing demand for electricity up to 1985 … . A work stoppage would have disastrous consequences since it would necessitate setting up a substitute programme to produce electricity by means of thermal or nuclear power stations.

(Emphasis added.) (Leave to appeal was granted by this court on February 13, 1975, but a declaration of settlement out of court was filed on January, 1980, further to which, on the same date, Chief Robert Kanatewat and others discontinued their appeal.)

In *A-G Que. v. Lavigne*, [1980] Que. CA 25, the Quebec Court of Appeal, again reversing the Superior Court, [1980] Que. SC 318, dismissed an application for interlocutory injunction enjoining the Attorney-General, the Minister of Education, the Minister of Municipal Affairs and others from temporarily enforcing certain provisions of the *Act respecting municipal taxation and providing amendments to certain legislation*, 1979 (Que.), c. 72. The statute in question provided for school financing through a system of grants; taxation became a complementary method subject to new conditions. The scheme allegedly violated the constitutional guarantees of s. 93 of the *Constitution Act, 1867*, an allegation which was later sustained by this court in *A-G Que. v. Greater Hull School Board*, [1984] 2 SCR 575.

The Superior Court had granted an interlocutory injunction for the following reasons, *inter alia*, at pp. 323-4:

> We should make clear from the outset that the case before us does not present the *ordinary* constitutional issue: this is not the usual case of conflict between jurisdiction of the federal government and one of the provinces, a jurisdictional conflict between two provinces, or of a province which is said to have legislated beyond the scope of the powers granted by s. 92 of the BNA Act.
>
> This is a *very special case* (like s. 133 of the *BNA Act*) where it is alleged that the legislation under attack violates a *constitutional guarantee.*
>
> The case does not, therefore, simply raise a constitutional issue, but rather a guaranteed right, like the language right (s. 133).
>
> In the case of a constitutional guarantee like language or religion, where it is apparent that a right has been infringed, the litigant has an absolute right to the recourse of injunction. This

flows from the very nature of the constitutional guarantee. *When a right is constitutionally guaranteed, whatever the dimensions of the consequences, its immutable nature remains.* ...

(Emphasis added.)

The Quebec Court of Appeal reversed the Superior Court, holding as follows at p. 26:

> The judge of the Superior Court, in giving reasons for issuing the injunctions, concludes that the impugned provisions, on their very face, violate the constitutional guarantees contained in s. 93 of the *British North America Act*, that it is sufficient in this case that a right be infringed to give rise to an absolute right to the recourse of injunction, without requiring proof of harm or the balance of convenience.
>
> After studying the record and considering the arguments presented by counsel for both parties with regard to the Superior Court decisions, we are of the view that the right upon which the plaintiffs, applicants for the interlocutory injunction, based their claim is not clear, and that the issues in dispute are very complex. The scope of the constitutional guarantees which were invoked is not free from doubt and *the effect of injunctions is to suspend the operation of an important part of the Act, throughout the Province of Quebec.* In the circumstances, at this stage in the proceedings, the presumption that the Act is valid must prevail over the prospect of an uncertain right.

(Emphasis added.)

It can be seen that, apart from the presumption of the constitutionality, the Court of Appeal took into consideration the paralyzing impact of the injunction which would have suspended the operation of an important part of the impugned legislation throughout the province.

A somewhat similar situation arose in *Metro. Toronto School Board v. Minister of Education* (1985), 53 OR (2d) 70 (HC, Div. Ct.). Interim measure regulations which provided for the funding of separate schools were challenged as being *ultra vires* by the school board and the teacher's federation in an application for judicial review. The Divisional Court vacated an order of a single judge prohibiting the expenditure of funds pursuant to the regulations, pending a decision of the Divisional Court on the main application. The following words reflect the interest shown by the court in the preservation of the educational system (at p. 81):

> On the evidence before this court as between the applicants, on the one hand, and the Roman Catholic separate school boards, teachers, students and parents on the other, the balance of convenience overwhelmingly is in the latter's favour. *The disruption of the educational system and its interim funding is, in the opinion of this court, a matter to be avoided at all costs.*

(Emphasis added.)

Reference can also be made to *Pacific Trollers Ass'n v. A-G Can.*, [1984] 1 FC 846, where the Trial Division of the Federal Court declined to grant an interlocutory injunction restraining certain Fisheries Officers from enforcing amendments made to the *Pacific Commercial Salmon Fishery Regulations*, the validity of which had been attacked. And see *A-G Can. v. Fishing Vessel Owners' Ass'n of BC*, [1985] 1 FC 791, where the Federal Court of Appeal, reversing the Trial Division, dismissed an application for interlocutory injunction restraining fisheries officers from implementing the fishing plan adopted under the *Fisheries Act*, RSC 1970, c. F-14, and the *Pacific Commercial Salmon Fishery Regulations*, CRC 1978,

c. 823. The plan in question was alleged to be beyond the legislative power of Parliament and beyond the powers conferred by the *Fisheries Act*. The court noted at p. 795:

> [T]he Judge assumed that the grant of the injunction would not cause any damage to the appellants. This was wrong. When a public authority is prevented from exercising its statutory powers, it can be said, in a case like the present one, that the public interest, of which that authority is the guardian, suffers irreparable harm. …

These words of the Federal Court of Appeal amplify, somewhat broadly perhaps, the idea expressed in more guarded language by Browne LJ in *Smith v. Inner London Education Authority*, [1978] 1 All ER 411 (CA) at p. 422:

> He [the motion judge] only considered the balance of convenience as between the plaintiffs and the authority, but I think counsel for the authority is right in saying that where the defendant is a public authority performing duties to the public one must look at the balance of convenience more widely, and take into account the interests of the public in general to whom these duties are owed. I think this is an example of the "special factors" affecting the balance of convenience which are referred to by Lord Diplock in *American Cyanamid Co. v. Ethicon Ltd.*

Similar considerations govern the granting of interlocutory injunctive relief in the context of exemption cases.

Ontario Jockey Club v. Smith (1922), 22 OWN 373 (HC), is the earliest example I know of an exemption case. The plaintiff club sought an interim injunction restraining the Provincial Treasurer and the Provincial Police Commissioner from collecting from it a provincial tax which was allegedly indirect and *ultra vires* of the province, or in the alternative, from closing the club's race-track, until a decision was rendered on the merits. Middleton J, concerned with the protection of the public interest, issued the injunction subject to an undertaking by the club to pay into court from time to time the amount payable in respect of the taxes claimed.

In *Campbell Motors Ltd. v. Gordon* (1946), 62 BCR 481 (SC and CA) the appellant company sought a declaration that the *National Emergency Transitional Powers Act*, 1945 (Can.), c. 25, and certain regulations made thereunder for the purpose of [s. 2(1)(c)] "maintaining, controlling and regulating supplies and services, prices, transportation … to ensure economic stability and an orderly transition to conditions of peace" were *ultra vires* on the ground that the war had come to an end. That appellant company was a used car dealer. It had been convicted four times for contravention to the regulations further to which its licence had been cancelled by the Wartime Prices and Trade Board, three of its motor vehicles had been seized together with certain books and records and it had been prohibited from selling any motor vehicles except with the concurrence of the representative of the board in Vancouver. By a majority decision, the British Columbia Court of Appeal, confirming the motion judge, refused to continue an *ex parte* interim injunction restraining members of the board from prosecuting the company for doing business without a licence and also refused to order the return of the company's seized property. Sydney Smith JA, who gave the reasons of the majority, wrote at p. 501:

> If this injunction were to stand there would be a risk of confusion in the public mind which, in the general interest, should not without good reason be authorized.

Robertson JA, who agreed with the reasons of Sydney Smith JA, added at p. 500:

> Subsection (c) of s. 2 quoted above, showed the extent of the economic affairs of Canada, to which the legislation applies. If an injunction were to be granted, no one can tell the result it might have on the economic position of Canada, as many persons might, in consequence, refuse to obey the law and, when proceeded against, apply for and obtain injunctions and proceed to do as they wish, thus resulting in economic confusion and ultimately in inflation.

A more recent example can be found in *Black v. Law Society of Alberta* (1983), 24 Alta. LR (2d) 106 (QB), and *Law Society of Alberta v. Black* (1983), 29 Alta. LR (2d) 326 (CA). The Law Society had adopted two rules, one of which prohibited members from being partners in more than one law firm; the other rule prohibited members residing in Alberta from entering into partnerships with members residing outside Alberta. This latter rule was challenged as being inconsistent with s. 6(2) of the Charter. The Alberta Court of Queen's Bench granted an interlocutory injunction restraining the Law Society from enforcing the two rules against the plaintiff solicitors pending the trial of the action. The Law Society only appealed the order granting the interlocutory injunction with respect to the first rule. In allowing the appeal, Kerans JA, who delivered the reasons of the court, wrote at p. 329:

> It is correct … that the fact that the injunction is sought against a public authority exercising a statutory power is a matter to be considered when one comes to the balance of convenience. However, we do not agree that the *Cyanamid* test simply disappears in such a case.

The *Morgentaler* case, *supra*, is an exemption case involving the Charter which has been quoted and relied upon several times. The plaintiff applicants had opened a clinic offering abortion services, which was not an "accredited hospital" within the meaning of s. 251 of the *Criminal Code*, RSC 1970, c. C-34. They commenced an action claiming that s. 251 was inconsistent with the *Canadian Charter of Rights and Freedoms* and an interim injunction and a permanent injunction. Pending the hearing and disposition of the interim injunction, they sought an "interim interim" injunction restraining the Chief of the Metropolitan Toronto Police Force, the Commissioner of the Ontario Provincial Police, and their servants, agents or any persons acting under their instruction, from investigating, inquiring into, reporting and otherwise acting upon the activities of the plaintiffs referable only to s. 251 of the *Criminal Code*. Linden J, of the Ontario High Court, dismissed their application and expressed the following opinion on the balance of convenience at p. 666:

> The third matter that must be demonstrated is that the balance of convenience in the granting of an interim injunction favours the applicants over the respondents. If only these two sets of parties were involved in this application it might well be that the convenience of the applicants would predominate over that of the respondents, since the applicants have much to lose while the respondents do not. However, this is not an ordinary civil injunction matter; it involves a significant question of constitutional law and raises a major public issue to be addressed—that is, what may law enforcement agencies do pending the outcome of constitutional litigation challenging the laws they are meant to enforce?
>
> It is contended in this application that the courts should halt all prosecution (and even investigation) of alleged offences under s. 251 pending the final resolution of the constitutional issue. Such a step would grant to potential offenders an immunity from prosecution in the

interim and perhaps forever. In the event that the impugned law is ultimately held to be invalid, no harm would be done by such a course of conduct. But, if the law is ultimately held to be constitutional, the result would be that the courts would have prohibited the police from investigating and prosecuting what has turned out to be criminal activity. This cannot be.

For example, let us assume that someone challenged the constitutional validity of the *Narcotic Control Act*, RSC 1970, c. N-1, and sought an injunction to prevent the police from investigating and prosecuting that person for importing and selling narcotics pending the resolution of the litigation. If the court granted the injunction, the sale of narcotic drugs would be authorized by court order, which would be most inappropriate if the law is later held to be valid. ...

In my view, therefore, the balance of convenience normally dictates that those who challenge the constitutional validity of laws must obey those laws pending the court's decision. If the law is eventually proclaimed unconstitutional, then it need no longer be complied with, but until that time, it must be respected and this court will not enjoin its enforcement. Such a course of action seems to be the best method of ensuring that our society will continue to respect the law at the same time as it is being challenged in an orderly way in the courts. This does not mean, however, that in exceptional circumstances this court is precluded from granting an interim injunction to prevent grave injustice, but that will be rare indeed.

The principles followed in the above-quoted cases have been summarized and confirmed for the greater part by this court in *Gould, supra*.

The same principles have been followed recently in *Re Bregzis and Governing Council of University of Toronto* (1985), 53 OR (2d) 348 (HC), where the applicant, an associate librarian was retired involuntarily from his employment with the university, when he reached the age of 65, in accordance with the university's mandatory retirement policy. He challenged the legality of the retirement policy as well as s. 9(a) of the *Human Rights Code, 1981* (Ont.), c. 53, on the ground that they offended s. 15 of the *Canadian Charter of Rights and Freedoms*. In his reasons, Osborne J of the Ontario Supreme Court referred to judgments in both *Morgentaler, supra*, and *Gould, supra*, and agreed that "the spectrum of concern on the balance of convenience issue must be wider than the issue joined by the parties themselves" (p. 352).

Another case involving facts somewhat similar to *Bregzis* is *Vancouver General Hospital v. Stoffman* (1985), 68 BCLR 230 (CA), where the plaintiffs, 15 doctors with active medical practices, contested the validity of a hospital regulation approved by the Minister of Health pursuant to the *Hospital Act*, RSBC 1979, c. 176, and under the authority of which their admitting privileges had been terminated because they were over the age of 65. The regulation allegedly constituted discrimination based on age in violation of s. 15(1) of the *Canadian Charter of Rights and Freedoms*. In a unanimous judgment, the British Columbia Court of Appeal confirmed the judgment of the Supreme Court of British Columbia which had granted the doctors an interlocutory injunction restraining the hospital from interfering with their privileges pending termination of the issue. While the Court of Appeal did not explicitly refer to the public interest, it nevertheless showed its concern for the safety of the 15 respondents' patients in holding that "All of the doctors were in good health at the material time" (at p. 231).

Finally, in *Re Rio Hotel Ltd. and Liquor Licence Board; A-G NB, Intervenant*, SCC, July 31, 1986, granting leave to appeal and staying proceedings before the Liquor Licensing Board, Dickson CJC, Beetz, McIntyre, Chouinard and Lamer JJ (unreported [now reported 72 NBR

(2d) 180n]), Rio Hotel Ltd., which had admittedly violated the conditions of its liquor permit relating to the presence of nude dancers on the premises, challenged the validity of those conditions on the basis of the Charter as well as of ss. 91 and 92 of the *Constitution Act, 1867*. It had lost in the New Brunswick Court of Appeal [(1986), 69 NBR (2d) 20] and was threatened with the cancellation of its permit when, in a judgment dated July 31, 1986, this court granted it leave to appeal as well as a stay of proceedings before the Liquor Licensing Board, pending the determination of its appeal. The stay was granted subject to compliance with an expedited schedule for filing the materials and for hearing the appeal. No reasons were given by this court but those who were present at the oral argument of the application for leave to appeal and for a stay could easily infer from exchanges between members of the court and counsel that the Court was alive to the enforcement problems created for the New Brunswick Liquor Licensing Board with respect to licence holders other than the Rio Hotel.

(iii) Conclusion

It has been seen from what precedes that suspension cases and exemption cases are governed by the same basic rule according to which, in constitutional litigation, an interlocutory stay of proceedings ought not to be granted unless the public interest is taken into consideration in the balance of convenience and weighted together with the interest of private litigants.

The reason why exemption cases are assimilated to suspension cases is the precedential value and exemplary effect of exemption cases. Depending on the nature of the cases, to grant an exemption in the form of a stay to one litigant is often to make it difficult to refuse the same remedy to other litigants who find themselves in essentially the same situation, and to risk provoking a cascade of stays and exemptions, the sum of which make them tantamount to a suspension case.

The problem had already been raised in the *Campbell Motors* case, *supra*, where Robertson JA wrote at p. 500 in the above-quoted passage:

> If an injunction were to be granted, no one can tell the result it might have on the economic position of Canada, as many persons might, in consequence, refuse to obey the law and, when proceeded against, apply for and obtain injunctions and proceed to do as they wish. …

In a case like the *Morgentaler* case, *supra*, for instance, to grant a temporary exemption from the provisions of the *Criminal Code* to one medical doctor is to make it practically impossible to refuse it to others. This consideration seems to have been very much in the mind of Linden J in that case where, passing from the particular to the general, he wrote at p. 667:

> It is contended in this application that the courts should halt all prosecution (and even investigation) of alleged offences. … Such a step would grant to potential offenders an immunity from prosecution in the interim and perhaps forever.

This being said, I respectfully take the view that Linden J has set the test too high in writing in *Morgentaler* that it is only in "exceptional" or "rare" circumstances that the courts will grant interlocutory injunctive relief. It seems to me that the test is too high at least in exemption cases when the impugned provisions are in the nature of regulations applicable to a relatively limited number of individuals and where no significant harm would be suffered by the public; it does not seem to me, for instance that the cases of *Law Society of Alberta v. Black*, *supra*, and *Vancouver General Hospital v. Stoffman*, *supra*, can be considered as exceptional or rare. Even the *Rio Hotel* case, *supra*, where the impugned provisions were broader, cannot, in my view, be labelled as an exceptional or rare case.

On the other hand, the public interest normally carries greater weight in favour of compliance with existing legislation in suspension cases when the impugned provisions are broad and general and such as to affect a great many persons. And it may well be that the above mentioned test set by Linden J in *Morgentaler* is closer to the mark with respect to this type of case. In fact, I am aware of only two instances where interlocutory relief was granted to suspend the operation of legislation and, in my view, these two instances present little precedent value.

One of these instances is *Home Oil Distributors Ltd. v. A-G BC* (1938), 53 BCR 355 (CA), where the majority of the British Columbia Court of Appeal confirmed the granting of an interlocutory injunction restraining the enforcement of the *Coal and Petroleum Products Control Board Act, 1937* (BC), c. 8, pending final determination of the validity of this statute which regulated the price at which gasoline could be sold in the province. The impugned legislation was *intra vires* on its face. The sole ground invoked against it was that it constituted a colourable attempt to regulate the international oil industry and to foster the local coal industry at the expense of that of foreign petroleum. And the sole evidence of this colourable intent was the interim report of a Royal Commission made prior to the passing of the statute. In *Home Oil Distributors Ltd. v. A-G BC*, [1940] SCR 444, this court looked at the report of the Royal Commission but it upheld the validity of the legislation. The granting of an interlocutory injunction by the motion judge, confirmed by the Court of Appeal, in a case of this nature, is an early and perhaps the first example where this was done in Canada. In a strong dissent, McQuarrie JA was the only judge who dealt at any length with the public interest aspect of the case and underlined the one million dollars a year cost of the injunction to the public. The decision seems to have been regarded as an isolated one in the *Campbell Motors* case, *supra*, at p. 501, in a passage that may amount to a veiled criticism. In my view, the *Home Oil Distributors* decision of the British Columbia Court of Appeal constitutes a weak precedent.

The other instance is *Société Asbestos Ltée v. Société nationale de l'amiante*, [1979] Qué. CA 342, where the Quebec Court of Appeal, reversing the Superior Court, issued an interlocutory injunction restraining the Attorney-General and any other person, physical or corporate, from enforcing any right conferred upon them by Bill No. 70, *Act to establish the Société nationale de l'amiante, 1978* (Que.), c. 42, and by Bill No. 121, the *Act to amend the Act to establish the Société nationale de l'amiante, 1979* (Qué.), c. 44, pursuant to which the appellant's property could be expropriated and the constitutional validity of which had been challenged in a declaratory action. The two statutes in question had been enacted in the French language only, in violation of s. 133 of the *Constitution Act, 1867*, and the Court of Appeal immediately came to the firm conclusion that, on that account, they were invalid. This is one of those exceptional cases where the merits were in fact decided at the interlocutory stage.

In short, I conclude that in a case where the authority of a law enforcement agency is constitutionally challenged, no interlocutory injunction or stay should issue to restrain that authority from performing its duties to the public unless, in the balance of convenience, the public interest is taken into consideration and given the weight it should carry. Such is the rule where the case against the authority of the law enforcement agency is serious, for if it were not, the question of granting interlocutory relief should not even arise. But that is the rule also even where there is a *prima facie* case against the enforcement agency, such as one which would require the coming into play of s. 1 of the *Canadian Charter of Rights and Freedoms*.

I should point out that I would have reached the same conclusion had s. 24 of the Charter been relied upon by counsel. Assuming for the purpose of the discussion that this provision applies to interlocutory relief in the nature of the one sought in this case, I would still hold that the public interest must be weighed as part of the balance of convenience: s. 24 of the Charter clearly indicates that the remedy sought can be refused if it is not considered by the court to be "appropriate and just in the circumstances."

On the whole, I thus find myself in agreement with the following excerpt from Sharpe, *supra*, at pp. 176-7:

> Indeed, in many situations, problems will arise if no account is taken of the general public interest where interlocutory relief is sought. In assessing the risk of harm to the defendant from an interlocutory injunction which might later be dissolved at trial, the courts may be expected to be conscious of the public interest. Too ready availability of interlocutory relief against government and its agencies could disrupt the orderly functioning of government.

I would finally add that in cases where interlocutory injunction issues in accordance with the above-stated principles, the parties should generally be required to abide by the dates of a preferential calendar so as to avoid undue delay and reduce to the minimum the period during which a possibly valid law is deprived of its effect in whole or in part: see in this respect *Black v. Law Society of Alberta*, *supra*, at p. 119, and the *Rio Hotel* case, *supra*. ...

I am of the view that [Krindle J, the judge who heard the motion for a stay] applied the correct principles. More particularly, at p. 154, she looked at the public interest and at the inhibitory impact of a stay of proceedings upon the board, in addition to its effect upon the employer and the union:

> It would seem to me that the granting of a stay in this case would invite the granting of stays in most other cases of applications for first agreements or applications involving the mandatory inclusion of sections within negotiated agreements. In effect, for a two or three year period, prior to any finding of invalidity of those sections, their operation would be suspended, suspended in circumstances where the *status quo* cannot, practically speaking, be maintained.
>
> In my opinion, in both the circumstances of this particular case and more generally, the balance of convenience favours proceeding as though the sections were valid unless and until the contrary is found.

While this is an exemption case, not a suspension case, and each case, including *a fortiori* an exemption case, turns on its own particular facts, yet, the inconvenience suffered by the parties is likely to be quite similar in most cases involving the imposition of a first collective agreement. Accordingly, the motion judge was not only entitled to but required to weigh the precedential value and exemplary effect of granting a stay of proceedings before the Board. I have not been persuaded that she committed reversible error in concluding that "the granting of a stay in this case would invite the granting of stays in most other cases of applications for first agreements." ...

The judgment of the Court of Appeal could be construed as meaning that an interlocu-tory stay of proceedings may be granted as a matter of course whenever a serious argument is invoked against the validity of legislation or, at least, whenever a *prima facie* case of vio-lation of the *Canadian Charter of Rights and Freedoms* will normally trigger a recourse to the saving effect of s. 1 of the Charter. If this is what the Court of Appeal meant, it was clearly in error: its judgment is in conflict with *Gould, supra*, and is inconsistent with the principles set out herein.

I would allow the appeal and set aside the stay of proceedings ordered by the Manitoba Court of Appeal.

There should be no order as to costs.

NOTE

For discussion of *Metropolitan Stores*, see Jamie Cassels, "An Inconvenient Balance: The In-junction as a Charter Remedy," chapter 11 in Jeffrey Berryman, ed., *Remedies: Issues and Per-spectives* (Toronto: Carswell, 1991), at 271.

RJR-MacDonald Inc. v. Canada (Attorney General)
[1994] 1 SCR 311

[The applicant, RJR-MacDonald, was seeking an interlocutory stay against the enforcement of the Tobacco Products Control Regulations, which had placed controls on tobacco adver-tising. In the Quebec Superior Court, the *Tobacco Products Control Act*—the legislative au-thority to make the regulations—had been held to be *ultra vires*. In the Quebec Court of Appeal, the legislation was upheld as being valid. We pick up the judgment of Sopinka and Cory JJ, delivering the judgment of the court, after the determination that the courts had jurisdiction to consider such interlocutory relief.]

V. *Grounds for Stay of Proceedings*

The applicants rely upon the following grounds:

1. The challenged *Tobacco Products Control Regulations, amendment* were promulgated pursuant to ss. 9 and 17 of the *Tobacco Products Control Act*, SC 1988, c. 20.

2. The applicants have applied to this Court for leave to appeal a judgment of the Que-bec Court of Appeal dated January 15, 1993. The Court of Appeal overturned a de-cision of the Quebec Superior Court declaring certain sections of the Act to be be-yond the powers of the Parliament of Canada and an unjustifiable violation of the *Canadian Charter of Rights and Freedoms*.

3. The effect of the new regulations is such that the applicants will be obliged to incur substantial unrecoverable expenses in carrying out a complete redesign of all its packaging before this Court will have ruled on the constitutional validity of the enabling legislation and, if this Court restores the judgment of the Superior Court,

will incur the same expenses a second time should they wish to restore their packages to the present design.

4. The tests for granting of a stay are met in this case:

(i) There is a serious constitutional issue to be determined.

(ii) Compliance with the new regulations will cause irreparable harm.

(iii) The balance of convenience, taking into account the public interest, favours retaining the *status quo* until this court has disposed of the legal issues. ...

B. The Strength of the Plaintiff's Case

Prior to the decision of the House of Lords in *American Cyanamid Co. v. Ethicon Ltd.*, [1975] AC 396 (HL (Eng.)), an applicant for interlocutory relief was required to demonstrate a "strong *prima facie* case" on the merits in order to satisfy the first test. In *American Cyanamid*, however, Lord Diplock stated that an applicant need no longer demonstrate a strong *prima facie* case. Rather it would suffice if he or she could satisfy the court that "the claim is not frivolous or vexatious; in other words, that there is a serious question to be tried." The *American Cyanamid* standard is now generally accepted by the Canadian courts, subject to the occasional reversion to a stricter standard: see Robert J. Sharpe, *Injunctions and Specific Performance* (2nd ed. 1992), at pp. 2-13 to 2-20.

In *Metropolitan Stores*, Beetz J advanced several reasons why the *American Cyanamid* test rather than any more stringent review of the merits is appropriate in *Charter* cases. These included the difficulties involved in deciding complex factual and legal issues based upon the limited evidence available in an interlocutory proceeding, the impracticality of undertaking a s. 1 analysis at that stage, and the risk that a tentative determination on the merits would be made in the absence of complete pleadings or prior to the notification of any Attorneys General.

The respondent here raised the possibility that the current status of the main action required the applicants to demonstrate something more than "a serious question to be tried." The respondent relied upon the following *dicta* of this Court in *Laboratoire Pentagone Ltée v. Parke, Davis & Co.*, [1968] SCR 269, at p. 272:

> The burden upon the appellant is much greater than it would be if the injunction were interlocutory. In such a case the Court must consider the balance of convenience as between the parties, because the matter has not yet come to trial. In the present case we are being asked to suspend the operation of a judgment of the Court of Appeal, delivered after full consideration of the merits. It is not sufficient to justify such an order being made to urge that the impact of the injunction upon the appellant would be greater than the impact of its suspension upon the respondent.

To the same effect were the comments of Kelly JA in *Adrian Messenger Services v. The Jockey Club Ltd. (No. 2)* (1972), 2 OR 619 (CA), at p. 620:

> Unlike the situation prevailing before trial, where the competing allegations of the parties are unresolved, on an application for an interim injunction pending an appeal from the dismissal

of the action the defendant has a judgment of the Court in its favour. Even conceding the ever-present possibility of the reversal of that judgment on appeal, it will in my view be in a comparatively rare case that the Court will interfere to confer upon a plaintiff, even on an interim basis, the very right to which the trial Court has held he is not entitled.

And, most recently, of Philp J in *Bear Island Foundation v. Ontario* (1989), 70 OR (2d) 574 (HC), at p. 576:

> While I accept that the issue of title to these lands is a serious issue, it has been resolved by trial and by appeal. The reason for the Supreme Court of Canada granting leave is unknown and will not be known until they hear the appeal and render judgment. There is not before me at this time, therefore, a serious or substantial issue to be tried. It has already been tried and appealed. No attempt to stop harvesting was made by the present plaintiffs before trial, nor before the appeal before the Court of Appeal of Ontario. The issue is no longer an issue at trial.

According to the respondent, such statements suggest that once a decision has been rendered on the merits at trial, either the burden upon an applicant for interlocutory relief increases, or the applicant can no longer obtain such relief. While it might be possible to distinguish the above authorities on the basis that in the present case the trial judge agreed with the applicant's position, it is not necessary to do so. Whether or not these statements reflect the state of the law in private applications for interlocutory relief, which may well be open to question, they have no application in *Charter* cases.

The *Charter* protects fundamental rights and freedoms. The importance of the interests which, the applicants allege, have been adversely affected require every court faced with an alleged *Charter* violation to review the matter carefully. This is so even when other courts have concluded that no *Charter* breach has occurred. Furthermore, the complex nature of most constitutional rights means that a motions court will rarely have the time to engage in the requisite extensive analysis of the merits of the applicant's claim. This is true of any application for interlocutory relief whether or not a trial has been conducted. It follows that we are in complete agreement with the conclusion of Beetz J in *Metropolitan Stores*, at p. 128, that "the *American Cyanamid* 'serious question' formulation is sufficient in a constitutional case where, as indicated below in these reasons, the public interest is taken into consideration in the balance of convenience."

What then are the indicators of "a serious question to be tried"? There are no specific requirements which must be met in order to satisfy this test. The threshold is a low one. The judge on the application must make a preliminary assessment of the merits of the case. The decision of a lower court judge on the merits of the *Charter* claim is a relevant but not necessarily conclusive indication that the issues raised in an appeal are serious: see *Metropolitan Stores*, *supra*, at p. 150. Similarly, a decision by an appellate court to grant leave on the merits indicates that serious questions are raised, but a refusal of leave in a case which raises the same issues cannot automatically be taken as an indication of the lack of strength of the merits.

Once satisfied that the application is neither vexatious nor frivolous, the motions judge should proceed to consider the second and third tests, even if of the opinion that the plaintiff is unlikely to succeed at trial. A prolonged examination of the merits is generally neither necessary nor desirable.

Two exceptions apply to the general rule that a judge should not engage in an extensive review of the merits. The first arises when the result of the interlocutory motion will in effect amount to a final determination of the action. This will be the case either when the right which the applicant seeks to protect can only be exercised immediately or not at all, or when the result of the application will impose such hardship on one party as to remove any potential benefit from proceeding to trial. Indeed Lord Diplock modified the *American Cyanamid* principle in such a situation in *N.W.L. Ltd. v. Woods*, [1979] 1 WLR 1294 (HL (Eng.)), at p. 1307:

> Where, however, the grant or refusal of the interlocutory injunction will have the practical effect of putting an end to the action because the harm that will have been already caused to the losing party by its grant or its refusal is complete and of a kind for which money cannot constitute any worthwhile recompense, the degree of likelihood that the plaintiff would have succeeded in establishing his right to an injunction if the action had gone to trial is a factor to be brought into the balance by the judge in weighing the risks that injustice may result from his deciding the application one way rather than the other.

Cases in which the applicant seeks to restrain picketing may well fall within the scope of this exception. Several cases indicate that this exception is already applied to some extent in Canada.

In *Trieger v. Canadian Broadcasting Corp.* (1988), 54 DLR (4th) 143 (Ont. HC), the leader of the Green Party applied for an interlocutory mandatory injunction allowing him to participate in a party leaders' debate to be televised within a few days of the hearing. The applicant's only real interest was in being permitted to participate in the debate, not in any subsequent declaration of his rights. Campbell J refused the application, stating at p. 152:

> This is not the sort of relief that should be granted on an interlocutory application of this kind. The legal issues involved are complex and I am not satisfied that the applicant has demonstrated there is a serious issue to be tried *in the sense of a case with enough legal merit* to justify the extraordinary intervention of this court in making the order sought without any trial at all. [Emphasis added.]

In *Tremblay v. Daigle*, [1989] 2 SCR 530, the appellant Daigle was appealing an interlocutory injunction granted by the Quebec Superior Court enjoining her from having an abortion. In view of the advanced state of the appellant's pregnancy, this Court went beyond the issue of whether or not the interlocutory injunction should be discharged and immediately rendered a decision on the merits of the case.

The circumstances in which this exception will apply are rare. When it does, a more extensive review of the merits of the case must be undertaken. Then when the second and third stages of the test are considered and applied the anticipated result on the merits should be borne in mind.

The second exception to the *American Cyanamid* prohibition on an extensive review of the merits arises when the question of constitutionality presents itself as a simple question of law alone. This was recognized by Beetz J in *Metropolitan Stores*, at p. 133:

> There may be rare cases where the question of constitutionality will present itself as a simple question of law alone which can be finally settled by a motion judge. A theoretical example

which comes to mind is one where Parliament or a legislature would purport to pass a law imposing the beliefs of a state religion. Such a law would violate s. 2(a) of the *Canadian Charter of Rights and Freedoms*, could not possibly be saved under s. 1 of the *Charter* and might perhaps be struck down right away; see *Attorney General of Quebec v. Quebec Association of Protestant School Boards*, [1984] 2 SCR 66, at p. 88. It is trite to say that these cases are exceptional.

A judge faced with an application which falls within the extremely narrow confines of this second exception need not consider the second or third tests since the existence of irreparable harm or the location of the balance of convenience are irrelevant inasmuch as the constitutional issue is finally determined and a stay is unnecessary.

The suggestion has been made in the private law context that a third exception to the *American Cyanamid* "serious question to be tried" standard should be recognized in cases where the factual record is largely settled prior to the application being made. Thus in *Dialadex Communications Inc. v. Crammond* (1987), 34 DLR (4th) 392 (Ont. HC), at p. 396, it was held that:

> Where the facts are not substantially in dispute, the plaintiffs must be able to establish a strong *prima facie* case and must show that they will suffer irreparable harm if the injunction is not granted. If there are facts in dispute, a lesser standard must be met. In that case, the plaintiffs must show that their case is not a frivolous one and there is a substantial question to be tried, and that, on the balance of convenience, an injunction should be granted.

To the extent that this exception exists at all, it should not be applied in *Charter* cases. Even if the facts upon which the *Charter* breach is alleged are not in dispute, all of the evidence upon which the s. 1 issue must be decided may not be before the motions court. Furthermore, at this stage an appellate court will not normally have the time to consider even a complete factual record properly. It follows that a motions court should not attempt to undertake the careful analysis required for a consideration of s. 1 in an interlocutory proceeding.

C. Irreparable Harm

Beetz J determined in *Metropolitan Stores*, at p. 128, that "[t]he second test consists in deciding whether the litigant who seeks the interlocutory injunction would, unless the injunction is granted, suffer irreparable harm." The harm which might be suffered by the respondent, should the relief sought be granted, has been considered by some courts at this stage. We are of the opinion that this is more appropriately dealt with in the third part of the analysis. Any alleged harm to the public interest should also be considered at that stage.

At this stage the only issue to be decided is whether a refusal to grant relief could so adversely affect the applicants' own interests that the harm could not be remedied if the eventual decision on the merits does not accord with the result of the interlocutory application.

"Irreparable" refers to the nature of the harm suffered rather than its magnitude. It is harm which either cannot be quantified in monetary terms or which cannot be cured, usually because one party cannot collect damages from the other. Examples of the former include instances where one party will be put out of business by the court's decision (*R.L. Crain Inc. v. Hendry* (1988), 48 DLR (4th) 228 (Sask. QB)); where one party will suffer permanent market loss or irrevocable damage to its business reputation (*American Cyanamid, supra*); or where a permanent loss of natural resources will be the result when a challenged activity is not enjoined (*MacMillan Bloedel Ltd. v. Mullin*, [1985] 3 WWR 577 (BCCA)). The fact that one party may be impecunious does not automatically determine the application in favour of the other party who will not ultimately be able to collect damages, although it may be a relevant consideration (*Hubbard v. Pitt*, [1976] QB 142 (CA)).

The assessment of irreparable harm in interlocutory applications involving *Charter* rights is a task which will often be more difficult than a comparable assessment in a private law application. One reason for this is that the notion of irreparable harm is closely tied to the remedy of damages, but damages are not the primary remedy in *Charter* cases.

This Court has on several occasions accepted the principle that damages may be awarded for a breach of *Charter* rights: (see, for example, *Mills v. The Queen*, [1986] 1 SCR 863, at pp. 883, 886, 943 and 971; *Nelles v. Ontario*, [1989] 2 SCR 170, at p. 196). However, no body of jurisprudence has yet developed in respect of the principles which might govern the award of damages under s. 24(1) of the *Charter*. In light of the uncertain state of the law regarding the award of damages for a *Charter* breach, it will in most cases be impossible for a judge on an interlocutory application to determine whether adequate compensation could ever be obtained at trial. Therefore, until the law in this area has developed further, it is appropriate to assume that the financial damage which will be suffered by an applicant following a refusal of relief, even though capable of quantification, constitutes irreparable harm.

D. The Balance of Inconvenience and Public Interest Considerations

The third test to be applied in an application for interlocutory relief was described by Beetz J in *Metropolitan Stores* at p. 129 as: "a determination of which of the two parties will suffer the greater harm from the granting or refusal of an interlocutory injunction, pending a decision on the merits." In light of the relatively low threshold of the first test and the difficulties in applying the test of irreparable harm in *Charter* cases, many interlocutory proceedings will be determined at this stage.

The factors which must be considered in assessing the "balance of inconvenience" are numerous and will vary in each individual case. In *American Cyanamid*, Lord Diplock cautioned, at p. 408, that:

> [i]t would be unwise to attempt even to list all the various matters which may need to be taken into consideration in deciding where the balance lies, let alone to suggest the relative weight to be attached to them. These will vary from case to case.

He added, at p. 409, that "there may be many other special factors to be taken into consideration in the particular circumstances of individual cases."

The decision in *Metropolitan Stores*, at p. 149, made clear that in all constitutional cases the public interest is a "special factor" which must be considered in assessing where the balance of convenience lies and which must be "given the weight it should carry." This was the approach properly followed by Blair J of the General Division of the Ontario Court in *Ainsley Financial Corp. v. Ontario Securities Commission* (1993), 14 OR (3d) 280, at pp. 303-4:

> Interlocutory injunctions involving a challenge to the constitutional validity of legislation or to the authority of a law enforcement agency stand on a different footing than ordinary cases involving claims for such relief as between private litigants. The interests of the public, which the

agency is created to protect, must be taken into account and weighed in the balance, along with the interests of the private litigants.

1. The Public Interest

Some general guidelines as to the methods to be used in assessing the balance of inconvenience were elaborated by Beetz J in *Metropolitan Stores*. A few additional points may be made. It is the "polycentric" nature of the *Charter* which requires a consideration of the public interest in determining the balance of convenience: see Jamie Cassels, "An Inconvenient Balance: The Injunction as a Charter Remedy," in J. Berryman, ed., *Remedies: Issues and Perspectives* (1991), 271, at pp. 301-5. However, the government does not have a monopoly on the public interest. As Cassels points out at p. 303:

> While it is of utmost importance to consider the public interest in the balance of convenience, the public interest in *Charter* litigation is not unequivocal or asymmetrical in the way suggested in *Metropolitan Stores*. The Attorney General is not the exclusive representative of a monolithic "public" in *Charter* disputes, nor does the applicant always represent only an individualized claim. Most often, the applicant can also claim to represent one vision of the "public interest." Similarly, the public interest may not always gravitate in favour of enforcement of existing legislation.

It is, we think, appropriate that it be open to both parties in an interlocutory *Charter* proceeding to rely upon considerations of the public interest. Each party is entitled to make the court aware of the damage it might suffer prior to a decision on the merits. In addition, either the applicant or the respondent may tip the scales of convenience in its favour by demonstrating to the court a compelling public interest in the granting or refusal of the relief sought. "Public interest" includes both the concerns of society generally and the particular interests of identifiable groups.

We would therefore reject an approach which excludes consideration of any harm not directly suffered by a party to the application. Such was the position taken by the trial judge in *Morgentaler v. Ackroyd* (1983), 150 DLR (3d) 59 (Ont. HC), per Linden J, at p. 66.

> The applicants rested their argument mainly on the irreparable loss to their potential women patients, who would be unable to secure abortions if the clinic is not allowed to perform them. Even if it were established that *these women* would suffer irreparable harm, such evidence would not indicate any irreparable harm to *these applicants*, which would warrant this court issuing an injunction at their behest. [Emphasis in original.]

When a private applicant alleges that the public interest is at risk that harm must be demonstrated. This is since private applicants are normally presumed to be pursuing their own interests rather than those of the public at large. In considering the balance of convenience and the public interest, it does not assist an applicant to claim that a given government authority does not represent the public interest. Rather, the applicant must convince the court of the public interest benefits which will flow from the granting of the relief sought.

Courts have addressed the issue of the harm to the public interest which can be relied upon by a public authority in different ways. On the one hand is the view expressed by the Federal Court of Appeal in *Attorney General of Canada v. Fishing Vessel Owners' Association of BC*, [1985] 1 FC 791 (CA), which overturned the trial judge's issuance of an injunction restraining Fisheries Officers from implementing a fishing plan adopted under the *Fisheries Act*, RSC 1970, c. F-14, for several reasons, including, at p. 795:

> (b) the Judge assumed that the grant of the injunction would not cause any damage to the appellants. This was wrong. When a public authority is prevented from exercising its statutory powers, it can be said, in a case like the present one, that the public interest, of which that authority is the guardian, suffers irreparable harm.

This dictum received the guarded approval of Beetz J in *Metropolitan Stores* at p. 139. It was applied by the Trial Division of the Federal Court in *Esquimalt Anglers' Association v. Canada (Minister of Fisheries and Oceans)* (1988), 21 FTR 304.

A contrary view was expressed by McQuaid JA of the PEI Court of Appeal in *Island Telephone Co., Re* (1987), 67 Nfld. & PEIR 158, who, in granting a stay of an order of the Public Utilities Commission pending appeal, stated at p. 164:

> I can see no circumstances whatsoever under which the Commission itself could be inconvenienced by a stay pending appeal. As a regulatory body, it has no vested interest, as such, in the outcome of the appeal. In fact, it is not inconceivable that it should welcome any appeal which goes especially to its jurisdiction, for thereby it is provided with clear guidelines for the future, in situations where doubt may have therefore existed. The public interest is equally well served, in the same sense, by any appeal. ...

In our view, the concept of inconvenience should be widely construed in *Charter* cases. In the case of a public authority, the onus of demonstrating irreparable harm to the public interest is less than that of a private applicant. This is partly a function of the nature of the public authority and partly a function of the action sought to be enjoined. The test will nearly always be satisfied simply upon proof that the authority is charged with the duty of promoting or protecting the public interest and upon some indication that the impugned legislation, regulation, or activity was undertaken pursuant to that responsibility. Once these minimal requirements have been met, the court should in most cases assume that irreparable harm to the public interest would result from the restraint of that action.

A court should not, as a general rule, attempt to ascertain whether actual harm would result from the restraint sought. To do so would in effect require judicial inquiry into whether the government is governing well, since it implies the possibility that the government action does not have the effect of promoting the public interest and that the restraint of the action would therefore not harm the public interest. The *Charter* does not give the courts a licence to evaluate the effectiveness of government action, but only to restrain it where it encroaches upon fundamental rights.

Consideration of the public interest may also be influenced by other factors. In *Metropolitan Stores*, it was observed that public interest considerations will weigh more heavily in a "suspension" case than in an "exemption" case. The reason for this is that the public interest is much less likely to be detrimentally affected when a discrete and limited number of applicants are exempted from the application of certain provisions of a law than when* the application of the law is suspended entirely. See *Black v. Law Society of Alberta* (1983), 144 DLR (3d) 439 (Alta. QB); *Vancouver General Hospital v. Stoffman* (1985), 23 DLR (4th) 146 (BCCA); *Rio Hotel Ltd. v. Commission des licences et permis d'alcool*, [1986] 2 SCR ix.

Similarly, even in suspension cases, a court may be able to provide some relief if it can sufficiently limit the scope of the applicant's request for relief so that the general public interest in the continued application of the law is not affected. Thus in *Ontario Jockey Club v. Smith* (1922), 22 OWN 373 (HC), the court restrained the enforcement of an impugned taxation statute against the applicant but ordered him to pay an amount equivalent to the tax into court pending the disposition of the main action.

2. The Status Quo

In the course of discussing the balance of convenience in *American Cyanamid*, Lord Diplock stated at p. 408 that when everything else is equal, "it is a counsel of prudence to … preserve the *status quo*." This approach would seem to be of limited value in private law cases, and, although there may be exceptions, as a general rule it has no merit as such in the face of the alleged violation of fundamental rights. One of the functions of the *Charter* is to provide individuals with a tool to challenge the existing order of things or *status quo*. The issues have to be balanced in the manner described in these reasons.

E. Summary

It may be helpful at this stage to review the factors to be considered on an application for interlocutory relief in a *Charter* case.

As indicated in *Metropolitan Stores*, the three-part *American Cyanamid* test should be applied to applications for interlocutory injunctions and as well for stays in both private law and *Charter* cases.

At the first stage, an applicant for interlocutory relief in a *Charter* case must demonstrate a serious question to be tried. Whether the test has been satisfied should be determined by a motions judge on the basis of common sense and an extremely limited review of the case on the merits. The fact that an appellate court has granted leave in the main action is, of course, a relevant and weighty consideration, as is any judgment on the merits which has been rendered, although neither is necessarily conclusive of the matter. A motions court should only go beyond a preliminary investigation of the merits when the result of the interlocutory motion will in effect amount to a final determination of the action, or when the constitutionality of a challenged statute can be determined as a pure question of law. Instances of this sort will be exceedingly rare. Unless the case on the merits is frivolous or vexatious, or the constitutionality of the statute is a pure question of law, a judge on a motion for relief must, as a general rule, consider the second and third stages of the *Metropolitan Stores* test.

At the second stage the applicant must convince the court that it will suffer irreparable harm if the relief is not granted. "Irreparable" refers to the nature of the harm rather than its magnitude. In *Charter* cases, even quantifiable financial loss relied upon by an applicant may be considered irreparable harm so long as it is unclear that such loss could be recovered at the time of a decision on the merits.

The third branch of the test, requiring an assessment of the balance of inconvenience, will often determine the result in applications involving *Charter* rights. In addition to the damage each party alleges it will suffer, the interest of the public must be taken into account. The effect a decision on the application will have upon the public interest may be relied upon by either party. These public interest considerations will carry less weight in exemption cases than in suspension cases. When the nature and declared purpose of legislation is to promote the public interest, a motions court should not be concerned whether the legislation actually has such an effect. It must be assumed to do so. In order to overcome the assumed benefit to the public interest arising from the continued application of the legislation, the applicant who relies on the public interest must demonstrate that the suspension of the legislation would itself provide a public benefit.

We would add to this brief summary that, as a general rule, the same principles would apply when a government authority is the applicant in a motion for interlocutory relief. However, the issue of public interest, as an aspect of irreparable harm to the interests of the government, will be considered in the second stage. It will again be considered in the third stage when harm to the applicant is balanced with harm to the respondent including any harm to the public interest established by the latter.

VII. Application of the Principles to These Cases

A. A Serious Question To Be Tried

The applicants contend that these cases raise several serious issues to be tried. Among these is the question of the application of the rational connection and the minimal impairment tests in order to justify the infringement upon freedom of expression occasioned by a blanket ban on tobacco advertising. On this issue, Chabot J of the Quebec Superior Court and Brossard JA in dissent in the Court of Appeal held that the government had not satisfied these tests and that the ban could not be justified under s. 1 of the *Charter*. The majority of the Court of Appeal held that the ban was justified. The conflict in the reasons arises from different interpretations of the extent to which recent jurisprudence has relaxed the onus fixed upon the state in *R v. Oakes*, [1986] 1 SCR 103, to justify its action in public welfare initiatives. This Court has granted leave to hear the appeals on the merits. When faced with separate motions for interlocutory relief pertaining to these cases, the Quebec Court of Appeal stated that "[w]hatever the outcome of these appeals, they clearly raise serious constitutional issues." This observation of the Quebec Court of Appeal and the decision to grant leaves to appeal clearly indicate that these cases raise serious questions of law.

B. Irreparable Harm

The applicants allege that if they are not granted interlocutory relief they will be forced to spend very large sums of money immediately in order to comply with the regulations. In the event that their appeals are allowed by this Court, the applicants contend that they will not be able either to recover their costs from the government or to revert to their current packaging practices without again incurring the same expense.

Monetary loss of this nature will not usually amount to irreparable harm in private law cases. Where the government is the unsuccessful party in a constitutional claim, however, a plaintiff will face a much more difficult task in establishing constitutional liability and obtaining monetary redress. The expenditures which the new regulations require will therefore impose irreparable harm on the applicants if these motions are denied but the main actions are successful on appeal.

C. Balance of Inconvenience

Among the factors which must be considered in order to determine whether the granting or withholding of interlocutory relief would occasion greater inconvenience are the nature of the relief sought and of the harm which the parties contend they will suffer, the nature of the legislation which is under attack, and where the public interest lies.

The losses which the applicants would suffer should relief be denied are strictly financial in nature. The required expenditure is significant and would undoubtedly impose considerable economic hardship on the two companies. Nonetheless, as pointed out by the respondent, the applicants are large and very successful corporations, each with annual earnings well in excess of $50,000,000. They have a greater capacity to absorb any loss than would many smaller enterprises. Secondarily, assuming that the demand for cigarettes is not solely a function of price, the companies may also be able to pass on some of their losses to their customers in the form of price increases. Therefore, although the harm suffered may be irreparable, it will not affect the long-term viability of the applicants.

Second, the applicants are two companies who seek to be exempted from compliance with the latest regulations published under the *Tobacco Products Control Act*. On the face of the matter, this case appears to be an "exemption case" as that phrase was used by Beetz J in *Metropolitan Stores*. However, since there are only three tobacco producing companies operating in Canada, the application really is in the nature of a "suspension case." The applicants admitted in argument that they were in effect seeking to suspend the application of the new regulations to all tobacco producing companies in Canada for a period of one year following the judgment of this Court on the merits. The result of these motions will therefore affect the whole of the Canadian tobacco producing industry. Further, the impugned provisions are broad in nature. Thus it is appropriate to classify these applications as suspension cases and therefore ones in which "the public interest normally carries greater weight in favour of compliance with existing legislation."

The weight accorded to public interest concerns is partly a function of the nature of legislation generally, and partly a function of the purposes of the specific piece of legislation under attack. As Beetz J explained, at p. 135, in *Metropolitan Stores*:

> Whether or not they are ultimately held to be constitutional, the laws which litigants seek to suspend or from which they seek to be exempted by way of interlocutory injunctive relief have been enacted by democratically-elected legislatures and are generally passed for the common good, for instance: … *the protection of public health* … . It seems axiomatic that the granting of interlocutory injunctive relief in most suspension cases and, up to a point, as will be seen later, in quite a few exemption cases, is susceptible temporarily to frustrate the pursuit of the common good. [Emphasis added.]

The regulations under attack were adopted pursuant to s. 3 of the *Tobacco Products Control Act* which states:

> 3. The purpose of this Act is to provide a legislative response to a national public health problem of substantial and pressing concern and, in particular,
>
> (a) to protect the health of Canadians in the light of conclusive evidence implicating tobacco use in the incidence of numerous debilitating and fatal diseases;

(b) to protect young persons and others, to the extent that is reasonable in a free and democratic society, from inducements to use tobacco products and consequent dependence on them; and

(c) to enhance public awareness of the hazards of tobacco use by ensuring the effective communication of pertinent information to consumers of tobacco products.

The Regulatory Impact Analysis Statement, in the *Canada Gazette*, Part II, Vol. 127, No. 16, p. 3284, at p. 3285, which accompanied the regulations stated:

> The increased number and revised format of the health messages reflect the strong consensus of the public health community that the serious health hazards of using these products be more fully and effectively communicated to consumers. Support for these changes has been manifested by hundreds of letters and a number of submissions by public health groups highly critical of the initial regulatory requirements under this legislation as well as a number of Departmental studies indicating their need.

These are clear indications that the government passed the regulations with the intention of protecting public health and thereby furthering the public good. Further, both parties agree that past studies have shown that health warnings on tobacco product packages do have some effects in terms of increasing public awareness of the dangers of smoking and in reducing the overall incidence of smoking in our society. The applicants, however, argued strenuously that the government has not shown and cannot show that the specific requirements imposed by the impugned regulations have any positive public benefits. We do not think that such an argument assists the applicants at this interlocutory stage.

When the government declares that it is passing legislation in order to protect and promote public health and it is shown that the restraints which it seeks to place upon an industry are of the same nature as those which in the past have had positive public benefits, it is not for a court on an interlocutory motion to assess the actual benefits which will result from the specific terms of the legislation. That is particularly so in this case, where this very matter is one of the main issues to be resolved in the appeal. Rather, it is for the applicants to offset these public interest considerations by demonstrating a more compelling public interest in suspending the application of the legislation.

The applicants in these cases made no attempt to argue any public interest in the continued application of current packaging requirements rather than the new requirements. The only possible public interest is that of smokers' not having the price of a package of cigarettes increase. Such an increase is not likely to be excessive and is purely economic in nature. Therefore, any public interest in maintaining the current price of tobacco products cannot carry much weight. This is particularly so when it is balanced against the undeniable importance of the public interest in health and in the prevention of the widespread and serious medical problems directly attributable to smoking.

The balance of inconvenience weighs strongly in favour of the respondent and is not offset by the irreparable harm that the applicants may suffer if relief is denied. The public interest in health is of such compelling importance that the applications for a stay must be dismissed with costs to the successful party on the appeal.

NOTES AND QUESTIONS

1. One of the questions left over from the Supreme Court of Canada's judgments in these cases is the extent to which they are relevant in other non-Charter contexts. For example, is the test developed by the Supreme Court appropriately deployed in nuisance and trespass cases where the public interest is advanced as a relevant consideration to the availability of injunctive relief? On an application for interlocutory relief in the context of an administrative law, a judicial review application, would the approach of the court have been exactly the same if, for example, the applicants in *Metropolitan Stores* had been challenging the labour board imposition of a first contract on the basis that the board had made a patently un-reasonable decision or, if in *RJR-MacDonald*, the regulations had been attacked as *ultra vires* of the scope of the empowering statute? In *Sobeys Inc. v. UFCW, Local 1000A* (1993), 12 OR (3d) 157 (Gen. Div.), it was held that, as opposed to the situation in Charter cases (where the stan-dard of review is that of correctness), the applicant for a stay of proceedings in relation to decisions that were protected by a privative clause, and where the resulting standard of ju-dicial review was that of patent unreasonableness, had to establish that it had a strong *prima facie* case on the merits, not just a serious issue to be tried.

2. What is to be made of the court's assertion in *RJR-MacDonald* of the proposition that, because of the uncertain state of the law governing the recovery from governments of com-pensation for the consequences of complying with legislation that is contrary to the Charter, the applicants in such cases should always be considered as suffering potentially irreparable harm should the interlocutory relief be denied? Given that the occasions on which financial compensation is available for unlawful administrative action are very few, should the oppos-ite apply in that realm or does the proposition hold with even greater force in the purely administrative law realm? (Of course, that assumption did the applicants little good in *RJR-MacDonald*—despite it, they failed to obtain a stay of the operation of the legislation pend-ing disposition of their appeal to the Supreme Court of Canada. Moreover, with their ultimate success in the Supreme Court on the merits of the constitutional challenge (*RJR-MacDonald Inc. v. Canada (Attorney General)*, [1995] 3 SCR 199), the question is raised as to whether they then had any entitlement to damages for whatever losses they incurred as a result of comply-ing with the law in the meantime and, if so, how those losses should be computed.) The court's decision in *Mackin v. New Brunswick (Minister of Finance)*, [2002] 1 SCR 405, discussed above, suggests that RJR-Macdonald Corp. would not automatically be entitled to damages caused by the unconstitutional limitation on its ability to advertise, but would have to estab-lish that the law was enacted with some degree of fault by the government such as an abuse of process, lack of good faith, or perhaps negligence.

3. For a more recent application of this aspect of *RJR-MacDonald*, see *Ontario Federation of Anglers & Hunters v. Ontario (Minister of National Resources)* (1999), 43 OR (3d) 760 (SCJ). However, there too the applicants lost. They were seeking an interim injunction suspending the operation of a regulation cancelling the annual spring bear hunt in Ontario. Do the same considerations that favour the government position in attempts to suspend the operation of primary legislation apply in the instance of subordinate legislation?

4. What if the government had lost in the Quebec Court of Appeal; should it be able to make an application to the Supreme Court of Canada for an order continuing the effective-ness of the legislation pending the disposition of its appeal?

Permanent Injunctions

Prohibitory Injunctions

Where constitutional rights are being violated, there is obviously jurisdiction in the courts to grant an injunction or its prerogative equivalent, an order in the nature of prohibition, enjoining or prohibiting the continuation of the violation. Thus, in *Howard v. Stony Mountain Institution* (1985), 19 DLR (4th) 502 (FCA), the Federal Court of Appeal made an order in the nature of prohibition preventing the continuation of penitentiary disciplinary proceedings that were in violation of Howard's s. 7 right to the protection of the principles of fundamental justice where his "life, liberty and security of the person" were at stake.

So far, the jurisprudence in this domain has not really explored the issue of whether the courts' discretion over the grant of such relief should be more constrained than in the case of violation of statutory, non-constitutional rights. Generally, however, it should be kept in mind that judicial discretion over permanent injunctive relief in the domain of public law has seldom, if ever, been tied to the adequacy of damages. This situation is explained in part by the severe limitations on the availability of damages for unlawful administrative action and also one suspects by a sense that, even if damages might be available after the event, it does not become a statutory authority to plead the adequacy of damages as a justification for continuing with the violation of a statutory right or entitlement. It would be surprising if that position were to alter in the domain of Charter rights even with the acceptance of a form of direct *per se* liability in damages for constitutional violations.

Where, however, the issue might arise is whether the courts should be less inclined in the case of Charter violations to listen to the other kinds of appeal to their discretion that surface quite frequently in public law cases: availability of alternative remedies, delay, unclean hands, no useful purpose. Does the fact that a Charter right or freedom is in jeopardy lessen the claims of the defending government agency to resist the award of relief on the basis of such discretionary considerations?

One domain where the Supreme Court seemingly has not accepted that the standards should be the same as apply in the domain of private litigation is that of *quia timet* injunctions. In *Operation Dismantle v. Canada*, [1985] 1 SCR 441, the plaintiff was seeking both declaratory and injunctive relief with respect to the testing over Canada by the United States of cruise missiles with nuclear warheads. The basis for this challenge was the alleged threat that such testing posed to "life, liberty and security of the person" in part by reason of the threat to peace posed by the build up of a nuclear arsenal. Dickson CJC (delivering the judgment of the majority) dealt with the plea for injunctive relief on the basis that it was *quia timet* in nature and, in so doing, referred to the private law test of "a very strong probability" of the feared harm occurring as the touchstone for determining whether such relief should be granted. He then moved on, however, to speak in terms of demonstrating "future probable harm," a seemingly less stringent standard. Roach has criticized the court for this arguing that, where Charter rights are at stake, the test should be even less restrictive and based on "reasonable possibility" (above, at para. 13.390). Do you agree?

A further question arises in situations where the grant of an injunction in vindication of Charter rights and freedoms flies in the face of existing legislation. Should this also be seen as affecting the courts' discretion over relief? We explore that issue in the next section on mandatory injunctions.

Mandatory Injunctions

In the case of mandatory injunctions or the prerogative equivalent of relief in the nature of *mandamus*, an important question is whether the concern from private law litigation that the court should take account of the more intrusive nature of such relief and the problems of fashioning a sufficiently clear decree should also influence the granting of an injunction under s. 24(1) of the Charter. In many Charter cases, the Supreme Court expressed a clear preference for declaratory relief as more flexible than the use of mandatory injunctions. For example, in the minority language case of *Mahe v. Alberta*, [1990] 1 SCR 342 at 393, Dickson CJC stated:

> I think it best if the Court restricts itself in this appeal to making a declaration in respect of the concrete rights which are due to the minority language parents in Edmonton under s. 23. Such a declaration will ensure that the appellants' rights are realized while, at the same time, leaving the government with the flexibility necessary to fashion a response which is suited to the circumstances. As the Attorney General for Ontario submits, the government should have the widest possible discretion in selecting the institutional means by which its s. 23 obligations are to be met; the courts should be loath to interfere and impose what will be necessarily procrustean standards, unless that discretion is not exercised at all, or is exercised in such a way as to deny a constitutional right. Once the Court has declared what is required in Edmonton, then the government can and must do whatever is necessary to ensure that these appellants, and other parents in their situation, receive what they are due under s. 23. Section 23 of the *Charter* imposes on provincial legislatures the positive obligation of enacting precise legislative schemes providing for minority language instruction and educational facilities where numbers warrant. To date, the legislature of Alberta has failed to discharge that obligation. It must delay no longer in putting into place the appropriate minority language education scheme.

In an equality rights case involving the need to provide the deaf with sign language interpreters for medically essential treatment, the court similarly concluded that a "declaration, as opposed to some kind of injunctive relief, is the appropriate remedy in this case because there are myriad options available to the government that may rectify the unconstitutionality of the current system. It is not this Court's role to dictate how this is to be accomplished." *Eldridge v. British Columbia*, [1997] 3 SCR 624 at para. 96.

The preference for declaratory relief is variously based. Among the arguments accepted have been the following or a combination thereof: (1) the legislature should have an opportunity to decide whether it wants to limit the protections provided by the Charter by recourse to the "notwithstanding" clause; (2) the courts are not in a position to fashion an order that would specify how the effectuation of the right should take place; (3) the immediate effectuation of the right was not feasible given the proximity of the election; (4) mootness; and (5) mandatory relief was not necessary because courts could rely on administrative officials to respond to declaratory relief. Which of these grounds have analogues in private litigation? Which of them are distinct public law justifications? And which are rooted in the

Charter? Having regard to the purposes of the Charter, are any of them legitimate restrictions on the availability of mandatory relief? See Kent Roach, "Remedial Consensus and Dialogue Under the Charter" (2002), 39 *UBC Law Rev.* 211.

In *Canada (Prime Minister) v. Khadr*, [2010] 1 SCR 44, the Supreme Court reversed a mandatory order that Canada request Omar Khadr's repatriation from the United States. Khadr was detained at Guantanamo Bay, the US detention camp in Cuba. The court entered a declaration that Canada had violated Khadr's rights when it had sent officials to Guantanamo Bay to interrogate him in 2003 and 2004. The court stated:

> [39] Our first concern is that the remedy ordered below [the mandatory order] gives too little weight to the constitutional responsibility of the executive to make decisions on matters of foreign affairs in the context of complex and ever-changing circumstances, taking into account Canada's broader national interests. For the following reasons, we conclude that the appropriate remedy is to declare that, on the record before the Court, Canada infringed Mr. Khadr's s. 7 rights, and to leave it to the government to decide how best to respond to this judgment in light of current information, its responsibility for foreign affairs, and in conformity with the *Charter*.

The court also justified its use of a declaration as opposed to a mandatory order by expressing concerns about the adequacy of the record:

> [42] The record before us gives a necessarily incomplete picture of the range of considerations currently faced by the government in assessing Mr. Khadr's request. We do not know what negotiations may have taken place, or will take place, between the US and Canadian governments over the fate of Mr. Khadr. As observed by Chaskalson CJ in *Kaunda v. President of the Republic of South Africa*, [2004] ZACC 5, 136 ILR 452, at para. 77: "The timing of representations if they are to be made, the language in which they should be couched, and the sanctions (if any) which should follow if such representations are rejected are matters with which courts are ill-equipped to deal." It follows that in these circumstances, it would not be appropriate for the Court to give direction as to the diplomatic steps necessary to address the breaches of Mr. Khadr's *Charter* rights.

Canada issued a diplomatic note requesting that the United States not use the fruits of interrogation by Canadian officials in Omar Khadr's subsequent military commission proceedings after the court's declaration that Khadr's rights had been violated and no effective remedy provided. The United States declined to honour this request.

In subsequent litigation, a trial judge found that Khadr has still not received an effective remedy and that Canada had breached the common law duty of procedural fairness and the doctrine of fair expectations by not consulting Khadr and his lawyers before issuing the diplomatic note. This part of the decision is innovative and potentially places common law obligations on how governments should respond to declarations. The trial judge in this case also retained jurisdiction and required Canada to propose another remedy. Khadr would then be allowed to comment on its adequacy: *Khadr v. Canada (Prime Minister)*, 2010 FC 715. Note that retention of jurisdiction will be discussed in the next part of this chapter. The government was able to have this judgment stayed, pending appeal with the Federal Court of Appeal, applying the tests from the *Metropolitan Stores* and *RJR-MacDonald* cases, discussed above. It also expressed doubts about whether courts could require the government to make diplomatic representations as a remedy under s. 24(1): *Canada v. Khadr*, 2010 FCA 199. The appeal was subsequently declared moot in the light of Khadr's guilty plea in a military commission held at Guantanamo: *Canada v. Khadr*, 2011 FCA 92.

The Supreme Court's preference for declarations over mandatory orders as constitutional remedies is not, however, absolute. In *Canada (Attorney General) v. PHS Community Services Society*, 2011 SCC 44 (better known as the Insite case), the court ordered a mandamus to require the minister of health to issue an exemption under the *Controlled Drugs and Substances Act* (CDSA) to allow the continued operation of a safe injection site in downtown Vancouver. The court concluded that the minister's refusal to grant the exemption violated s. 7 of the Charter because it was arbitrary and grossly disproportionate to the purposes of the Act in protecting public safety and health—the trial judge had found that the safe injection site had prevented the transmission of disease by the use of dirty needles and had not increased crime in the neighbourhood. The court justified the choice of a mandatory order in the form of a mandamus over a declaration as follows:

> [146] One option would be to issue a declaration that the Minister erred in refusing to grant a further exemption to Insite in May 2008, and return the matter to the Minister to reconsider the matter and make a decision that respects the claimants' *Charter* rights.
>
> [147] However, this remedy would be inadequate.
>
> [148] The infringement at stake is serious; it threatens the health, indeed the lives, of the claimants and others like them. The grave consequences that might result from a lapse in the current constitutional exemption for Insite cannot be ignored. These claimants would be cast back into the application process they have tried and failed at, and made to await the Minister's decision based on a reconsideration of the same facts. Litigation might break out anew. A bare declaration is not an acceptable remedy in this case. ...
>
> [150] In the special circumstances of this case, an order in the nature of mandamus is warranted. I would therefore order the Minister to grant an exemption to Insite under s. 56 of the *CDSA* forthwith. (This of course would not affect the Minister's power to withdraw the exemption should the operation of Insite change such that the exemption would no longer be appropriate.) On the trial judge's findings of fact, the only constitutional response to the application for a s. 56 exemption was to grant it. The Minister is bound to exercise his discretion under s. 56 in accordance with the *Charter*. On the facts as found here, there can be only one response: to grant the exemption. There is therefore nothing to be gained (and much to be risked) in sending the matter back to the Minister for reconsideration.

These two recent cases raise the remedial question: what justifies the decision to rely on a declaration in the Omar Khadr case, but use a more intrusive mandatory order in the Insite case? Can the difference be adequately explained by the court's deference to the state's foreign affair duties in *Khadr*? Do differences in the adequacy of the record in the cases also help explain the different remedial choices? Do they suggest that remedies are a matter of strong discretion as discussed in the preliminary reading?

Among the other possibilities for responding to concerns about the intrusiveness of a mandatory injunction is the use of a device that sometimes is deployed in both private law (*Stollmeyer v. Trinidad Lake Petroleum Co. Ltd.*, [1918] AC 485 (PC (Trin.))) and public law cases not raising constitutional issues (*Sparvier v. Cowessess Indian Band No. 73* (1993), 13 Admin. LR (2d) 266 (FCTD)): the postponement of the operation of the order gives the defendant an opportunity to respond effectively or to remove the conditions giving rise to the need for the order. The most prominent examples of this expedient in a constitutional setting have been *Schachter*, above, and *Reference re Manitoba Language Rights*, [1985] 1 SCR 721, in which the entire statutes of Manitoba were held to be unconstitutional and of no force and effect because they had not been enacted in both English and French. At the initial stage, the Supreme Court made the following order:

Conclusions

(i) Section 133 of the *Constitution Act, 1867*, and s. 23 of the *Manitoba Act, 1870*, are mandatory.

(ii) All Acts of the Manitoba Legislature that were not printed and published in both the English and French languages are, and always have been, invalid and of no force and effect.

(iii) The Acts of the Manitoba Legislature which would currently be in force were it not for their constitutional defect (*i.e.*, current Acts) are deemed to have temporary validity and force and effect from the date of this judgment to the expiry of the minimum period required for translation, re-enactment, printing and publishing.

(iv) Rights, obligations and any other effects which have arisen under current Acts, and purportedly repealed or spent Acts, of the Legislature of Manitoba, which are not saved by the *de facto* doctrine or doctrines such as *res judicata* and mistake of law, are deemed temporarily to have been, and to continue to be, valid, and of force and effect until the expiry of the minimum period required for translation, re-enactment, printing and publishing.

(v) The court will, at the request of either the Attorney-General of Canada or the Attorney-General of Manitoba, made within 120 days of the date of this judgment, establish the minimum period necessary for translation, re-enactment, printing and publishing of (1) unilingual Acts of the Legislature of Manitoba which would be currently in force were it not for their constitutional defect, and (2) the unilingual repealed and spent Acts of the Legislature of Manitoba. Following such a request, a special hearing will be set and submissions will be accepted from the Attorney-General of Manitoba and the other intervenors.

(vi) *"An Act respecting the Operation of Section 23 of the Manitoba Act in regard to Statutes,"* 1980 (Man.), c. 3, is invalid and of no force and effect in its entirety if it was not enacted, printed, and published in both official languages. In any event, ss. 1 to 5 are invalid and of no force and effect.

After a further "special hearing to establish the minimum period necessary for translation, re-enactment, printing and publishing of" the affected legislation, the court made the following order ([1985] 2 SCR 347):

In The Matter Of: Section 55 of the *Supreme Court of Canada Act*, RSC 1970, c. S-19;
    And In The Matter Of: A Reference by the Governor in Council concerning language rights under s. 23 of the *Manitoba Act, 1870*, and s. 133 of the *Constitution Act, 1867*, and set out in Order in Council P 1984-1136 dated the 5th day of April 1984;

And In The Matter Of: A special hearing to establish the minimum period necessary for translation, re-enactment, printing and publishing of:

1. unilingual Acts of the Legislature of Manitoba which would be currently in force were it not for their constitutional defect: and

2. the unilingual repealed and spent Acts of the Legislature of Manitoba;

pursuant to the opinion of the Supreme Court of Canada dated the 13th day of June, 1985.

This special hearing having come on this date for the determination of the minimum period necessary for translation, re-enactment, printing and publishing of:

1. unilingual Acts of Legislature of Manitoba which would currently be in force were it not for their constitutional defect; and

2. the unilingual repealed and spent Acts of the Legislature of Manitoba;

pursuant to the opinion of this Court dated the 13th day of June, 1985.

And after the hearing from the applicant (the province of Manitoba) that the Continuing Consolidation of the Statutes of Manitoba and Regulations, and Rules of Court and Administrative Tribunals will appear in bilingual, parallel column format when printed and published.

And after hearing from the parties hereto:

This Court:

1. Gives effect to the commitment of the province of Manitoba that the Continuing Consolidation of the Statutes of Manitoba, and Regulations, and Rules of Court and Administrative Tribunals will appear in bilingual, parallel column format when printed and published.

2. Orders that the period of temporary validity for the laws of Manitoba will continue as follows:

(a) to 31st December 1988 for:

(i) the Continuing Consolidation of the Statutes of Manitoba; and

(ii) the Regulations of Manitoba; and

(iii) Rules of Court and of Administrative Tribunals;

(b) to the 31st of December 1990 for all other laws of Manitoba.

3. Any of the parties hereto, may, in the case of necessity upon further application, supported by such evidence as may be required, return to this court for such further determination as this court may decide.

Order granted.

Thereafter, a further dispute arose as to the range of instruments covered by the initial order. This too was referred to the Supreme Court of Canada, which, in conjunction with a further order clarifying the scope of its judgment, granted further extension of time for compliance: see [1992] 1 SCR 212.

NOTES AND QUESTIONS

Would it have been appropriate for the court to have simply declared the statutory law of Manitoba to have been of no force and effect? What would have been the consequences of this? Another alternative is suggested by Denise Réaume in "Language Rights, Remedies and the Rule of Law" (1988), 1 *Canadian Journal of Law and Jurisprudence* 35, at 55*ff*.: selective refusal of enforcement against Franco-Manitobans of untranslated laws. What are the advantages of this solution? For further detail and discussion, see Roach, above, at para. 13.420*ff*.

Structural Injunctions

The *Manitoba Language Rights* judgment has been regarded by many as the first example of a structural injunction issued by a Canadian court. However, as Roach points out, it is more in the nature of a reparative injunction in that the order focuses on "repairing a past wrong by mandating the performance of a specific legal duty, rather than reorganizing an ongoing social institution to benefit a disadvantaged group" (above, at para. 13.420). Nonetheless, as he also acknowledges (ibid.), the order made contains some of the significant features of structural injunctions as developed in the context of US constitutional litigation:

> The court's retention of jurisdiction …, its sanction of remedial delay and its commitment to ensure eventual compliance all resemble the American experience with structural injunctions.

To the extent that the structural injunction is primarily concerned with the mandating of conditions under which constitutional rights will be respected in the future, it, of course, is primarily a regulatory (as opposed to a corrective) form of relief. As such, it represents a significant deviation from the traditional remedial norms of private law litigation. As the following materials make clear, however, its entry into the panoply of public law remedies is not without its critics.

Robert J. Sharpe, "Injunctions and the Charter"
(1984), 22 *Osgoode Hall Law Journal* 473, at 476-79 (footnotes omitted)

II. The American Experience

A. Models of Constitutional Injunctions

In his important monograph, *The Civil Rights Injunction*, Owen Fiss identifies three models of constitutional injunction. Each model corresponds with an evolutionary phase in American constitutional litigation. The first and most familiar is the preventative injunction. This model operates as a kind of scaled-down criminal statute, prohibiting named parties from engaging in defined behaviour which has been found to violate a constitutional principle or guarantee. Similar decrees are common in the realm of private law. As remedial decrees, they are relatively uncontroversial in the constitutional setting. The second model is the reparative injunction. This too has its parallel in the private law mandatory injunction. Like its private law cousin, it requires that positive steps be taken by the defendant to repair the effects of past wrongs or to carry out some affirmative legal duty. In the constitutional setting, the reparative injunction is typically designed to correct the effects of past wrongs, often in cases of racial discrimination.

The third model, the structural injunction, Fiss calls a "truly unique legal instrument." Although he admits that it has as distant cousins decrees reorganizing railways or ordering divestitures on antitrust grounds, its distinctive feature is that it amounts to "a declaration that henceforth the court will *direct* or *manage* the reconstruction of the social institution, in order to bring it into conformity with the Constitution." By issuing structural injunctions, judges immerse themselves in the details of the organization and administration of important public agencies. Decrees of this kind are not issued except as a last resort. It is only where preventative or reparative measures fail to bring about the state of affairs promised by the Constitution, that judges will jump the usual institutional barriers and become, in effect, school board trustees, prison wardens and hospital administrators. Only when the agency in question has failed to live up to its constitutional obligations, will the injunction be justified. However, when such institutions do fail, Fiss argues that the courts have no real choice but to interfere.

There can be little doubt as to the availability and appropriateness of prohibitive injunctions to restrain the enforcement of unconstitutional laws or practices. Such orders were a feature of pre-Charter law in Canada and will surely continue to provide appropriate remedial relief for unconstitutional action. More controversial are orders which mandate a positive course of action, designed to bring about a state of affairs in compliance with constitutional guarantees. In such cases, the court steps beyond merely striking down or stopping an unconstitutional law or practice and engages in reparative measures required to remedy the effects of past wrongs. In the private law area, mandatory relief is seen as more difficult to justify than negative order, primarily because of problems in defining the actual obligation, and because such orders carry the risk that the court may be undertaking a continuing supervisory role. If the defendant is recalcitrant, the court may find itself faced with the choice of either backing down and allowing the wrong to go unremedied or becoming immersed in the details of the defendant's activity and having to entertain repeated applications for enforcement. In the American constitutional experience, this has meant courts' involvement in the "structural" reform of powerful public agencies seemingly incapable of constitutional behaviour.

B. The Evolution of Structural Injunctions

I certainly do not suggest that it would be appropriate to decree a "structural" injunction as the first response to a constitutional violation. Judges and courts suffer obvious institutional disadvantages when engaging in this sort of activity. It is important to emphasize that American courts do not issue structural injunctions except as a last resort. In the modern water-shed constitutional decision of *Brown v. Board of Education*, the Supreme Court rejected the "separate but equal" doctrine and held that the practice of maintaining racially segregated schools violated the equal protection guarantee of the 14th Amendment. Initially, the Court merely proclaimed the right it found, and required re-argument on remedy. Although the Court clearly saw the right to be protected, it perceived from the start that the elaboration of appropriate remedial measures would be a delicate and difficult task. A negative decree, prohibiting school boards from operating racially segregated schools, was plainly not enough. The effects of past discrimination were such that a mere prohibition against future discrimination would be insufficient. The effects of the past had to be attacked: some form of positive action was called for. Thus, in *Brown v. Board (II)* the Court fashioned a remedy to meet the right which had been found. The Court explicitly drew upon the traditions of equity:

> In fashioning and effectuating the decrees, the courts will be guided by equitable principles. Traditionally, equity has been characterized by a practical flexibility in shaping its remedies and by a facility for adjusting and reconciling public and private needs. These cases call for the exercise of these traditional attributes of equity power.

This initial response was cautiously innovative. School boards were required to submit plans for approval. The courts would retain jurisdiction to review these plans, but the onus to make school administration comply with the demands of the constitution rested with the school boards.

The decision represented a departure from the traditional model of "one-shot, once-and-for-all" adjudication in which the court does not expect to be called upon to make further decisions or orders upon the final judgment. While the Court explicitly refrained from engaging in school reform on its own motion, it equally explicitly retained a supervisory role to ensure the defendants lived up to their positive obligations. It was only after years of delay by local boards that the Court resorted to more intrusive means. In a 1971 decision, the Court dealt with a case in which, despite lengthy and protracted proceedings, the schools in the defendant's district remained segregated. The Board's plan was rejected as inadequate and the Court appointed its own expert to design an appropriate plan for desegregation, including busing. Further plans were also invited from minority members of the school board and from the Department of Health Education and Welfare. Ultimately, the Court accepted its own expert's plan and ordered the implementation by injunction. Despite the novelty of this "structural" decree, the court used the language of traditional equity jurisprudence to justify its action:

> If school authorities fail in their affirmative obligations under these holdings, judicial authority may be invoked. Once a right and a violation have been shown, the scope of a district court's equitable powers to remedy past wrongs is broad, for breadth and flexibility are inherent in equitable remedies.

It is significant that traditional language is used to justify non-traditional behaviour. Can orders of this kind be justified as a logical or appropriate extension of traditional principles? Should similar measures be taken by Canadian courts?

NOTES

1. Estey J, in an extrajudicial remark, *New Developments in the Law of Remedies,* "The Law of Remedies—An Overview," [1981] *Law Society of Upper Canada Special Lectures* 1, at 18-19 (Don Mills, ON: Richard De Boo, 1981) (footnotes omitted), answered these questions in the negative:

> The American parallel in the field of remedies leaves Canadian lawyers breathless. Take, for example, the *Boston School Desegregation* cases of 1974 and 1975, *Morgan v. Hennigan* and *Morgan*

v. Kerrigan. In the American vernacular, this type of constitutional litigation is divided into three phases. In *Phase 1*, the judges perform the task traditional to our courts, namely, they find whether or not liability resides in the defendants. The parties in that case included a cast of thousands commencing with the complaining class and ending with the mayor of the City. The District Court found liability in the defendants, which was confirmed in the Circuit Court of Appeals. In *Phase 2*, the trial court then resumed its operations, created a plan for desegregation, held hearings on the plan, and finally approved it. The hearing included evidence from court-appointed experts, citizens committees, and anyone else who apparently desired to come in off the streets and take part. The President of the Court of Appeals, in writing about this case, stated:

> All of these issues ordinarily would be appropriate grist for the relevant educational policy-making body, here the Boston School Committee. Indeed the function is very close to legislative decision-making. Because the legislative authorities would not act however, the District Judge was forced to move beyond the traditional judicial role and into Phase 3 where he fashioned his own remedy.

In *Phase 3*, the Court set deadlines, directed the contracts and purchases to be made, and even placed a high school into receivership.

This line of remedy is wholly foreign to us, so far, and I would suggest that no amount of prodding by our law schools, professors, and commentators will bring this kind of litigation through the doors of our court-rooms. The court in that process actively directed the expenditure of tax money leaving the raising of such revenues to the Legislative Branch.

We have no doubt failed to learn from our American brothers, as for example when we adopted the 1972 *Income Tax Act*, having watched the Internal Revenue Code engage the energies of a significant part of professional life in the US. We have also witnessed the log-jams in American courts caused by people in search of remedies. Indeed we have threatened to follow the American medical litigation practices in the field of damages and evidence. All of this is discussed from the American viewpoint in a recent article in 1979 in the *Harvard Law Review* by one Fiss. My only comment is that we should thank the Almighty that the common law developed before the law reviews came along.

2. Note that the use of structural injunctions by US courts is well known; however, they have also been used in India, Germany, and South Africa. See *Minister of Health v. Treatment Action Campaign (No. 2)*, 2002 (5) SA 721 (S. Afr. Const. Ct.) for a survey of comparative law and a conclusion that courts can order mandatory relief and retain supervisory jurisdiction.

The next case is arguably the most important Charter remedy case yet decided by the Supreme Court. Although it affirms that injunctions and the retention of jurisdiction can be used as a Charter remedy, the court was divided 5:4 on whether such a remedy accorded with the separation of powers between the judiciary and the elected branches of governments and was procedurally fair to the government.

Doucet-Boudreau v. Nova Scotia (Minister of Education)
[2003] 3 SCR 3, 2003 SCC 62

[1] The judgment of McLachlin CJ and Gonthier, Bastarache, and Arbour JJ was delivered by IACOBUCCI and ARBOUR JJ: This appeal involves the nature of remedies available under s. 24(1) of the *Canadian Charter of Rights and Freedoms* for the realization of the minority language education rights protected by s. 23 of the *Charter*. The specific issue is whether a trial judge may, after ordering that a provincial government use its best efforts to build French-language school facilities by given dates, retain jurisdiction to hear reports on the progress of those efforts. The issue of broader and ongoing judicial involvement in the administration of public institutions is not before the Court in this case.

I. Background and Judicial History

[2] The appellants are Francophone parents living in five school districts in Nova Scotia (Kingston/Greenwood, Chéticamp, Île Madame-Arichat (Petit-de-Grat), Argyle, and Clare) and Fédération des parents acadiens de la Nouvelle-Écosse Inc., a non-profit organization that monitors the advancement of educational rights of the Acadian and Francophone minority in Nova Scotia. The Attorney General of Nova Scotia is the respondent, acting on behalf of the Department of Education of Nova Scotia.

[3] Apart from the specific facts of the case, it is most important to note the historical context on which this dispute is centred. As we will discuss below, French-language education in Nova Scotia has not had an enviable record of success. While the situation improved over the rather dismal record of the previous centuries, the twentieth century left much to be achieved. Section 23 of the *Charter* has been the hope of the French-speaking minority of Nova Scotia to redress the linguistic failings and inequality of history. ...

[5] The application was heard before LeBlanc J in October 1999. LeBlanc J declared that the applicants were entitled parents under s. 23 of the *Charter* and that the number of students warranted the provision of French homogeneous secondary school facilities in Chéticamp, Île Madame-Arichat (Petit-de-Grat), Argyle, and Clare: (2000), 185 NSR (2d) 246. He noted, however, that the real issue was not the existence and content of the applicants' s. 23 rights, but the date on which the programs and facilities would finally be made available.

[6] LeBlanc J found that the respondents had not given sufficient attention to the serious rate of assimilation among Acadians and Francophones in Nova Scotia. The Province treated s. 23 rights as if they were but one more demand for educational programs and facilities, and failed to accord them due priority as constitutional rights. Meanwhile, assimilation continued. LeBlanc J stated that "[i]t is beyond any doubt that it is time that homogeneous programs and facilities be provided to s. 23 students" (para. 206).

[7] LeBlanc J considered the state of school programs and facilities, including the progress that had already been made toward complying with s. 23 of the *Charter*, in each of the five school districts at issue. He directed the Province, which, through the Department of Education, is responsible for providing school facilities, and the Conseil, which is responsible for program provision, to build schools and provide programs by more and less specific deadlines. LeBlanc J required that the respondents use their "best efforts" to comply with

his order. Finally, he retained jurisdiction to hear reports from the respondents on their compliance. The precise wording of the order was as follows:

[1] In Kingston/Greenwood, the entitled parents under Section 23 have a right to a homogeneous French program from grades Primary to 12 and the entitled parents have a right to a homogeneous French facility for grades Primary to 12 by September 2000.

[2] In Cheticamp, the entitled parents under Section 23 have a right to a homogeneous French secondary program in a homogeneous French facility by September 2000.

[3] In Île Madame-Arichat (Petit-de-Grat), the Respondent CSAP shall use its best efforts to provide a homogeneous French program for grades 9 through 12 by September 2000 and the Respondent Department of Education shall use its best efforts (a) to provide a homogeneous French facility (on an interim basis) for grades 9 through 12 by September 2000 and (b) to provide a permanent homogeneous French facility by January 2001.

[4] In Argyle, the Respondent CSAP shall use its best efforts to provide a homogeneous French program for grades Primary through 12 by September 2000 and the Respondent Department of Education shall provide a homogeneous French facility for grades Primary through 12 by September 2001.

[5] In Clare, the Respondent CSAP shall provide a homogeneous French program for grades Primary through 12 by September 2000 and the Respondent Department of Education shall take immediate steps to provide homogeneous French facilities for grades Primary through 12 by September 2001.

[6] The Respondents shall use their best efforts to comply with this Order.

[7] The Court shall retain jurisdiction to hear reports from the Respondents respecting the Respondents' compliance with this Order. The Respondents shall report to this Court on March 23, 2001 at 9:30 a.m., or on such other date as the Court may determine.

[8] The reference to "the Court" in the final paragraph was interpreted by LeBlanc J, and the parties, as a reference to himself sitting as a judge of the provincial supreme court, rather than to the Supreme Court of Nova Scotia generally, which, as a court of first instance, would be competent to hear applications relating to any failure by the respondents to comply with LeBlanc J's order and would require no express retention of jurisdiction. LeBlanc J presided over several of these "reporting hearings" between July 27, 2000, and March 23, 2001. Prior to each reporting session the trial judge directed the Province to file an affidavit from the appropriate official at the Department of Education, setting out the Department's progress in complying with the trial judge's decision. The trial judge permitted the respondent and Conseil to adduce evidence, including rebuttal evidence on various matters relating to compliance with the best efforts order. The Attorney General of Nova Scotia, on behalf of the Department of Education, appealed the part of the order in which LeBlanc J retained his jurisdiction to hear reports.

[9] The majority at the Nova Scotia Court of Appeal allowed the appeal before the final scheduled reporting hearing took place ((2001), 194 NSR (2d) 323, 2001 NSCA 104). Flinn JA, writing for the majority, emphasized that the declaration of the parents' rights and the order to provide programs and facilities were not in issue in the appeal (para. 6). Only the trial judge's retention of jurisdiction to hear reports was challenged. Flinn JA held that the trial judge, having decided the issue between the parties, had no further jurisdiction to re-

main seized of the case. This opinion was based on the common law principle of *functus officio* and Flinn JA's view that the *Judicature Act*, RSNS 1989, c. 240, not only fails explicitly to authorize the retention of jurisdiction by a trial court after it has decided the issues before it and provided a remedy, but also precludes a trial judge from retaining jurisdiction to determine whether there is compliance with the order ... . He concluded that, while it is true that courts have broad ranging powers under s. 24(1) to fashion remedies, and are encouraged to be creative in so doing, the *Charter* does not extend a court's jurisdiction to permit it to enforce its remedies. Finally, Flinn JA expressed a reluctance to open the door to American jurisprudence on the enforcement of mandatory injunctions and a fear that post-trial intervention by trial judges in the enforcement of remedies would undermine the tradition of co-operation between the judiciary and the other branches of government.

[10] Freeman JA dissented. In his view, LeBlanc J's order was not final and the judge was not *functus officio* until the continuing supervision was completed; the trial judge was able to keep his decision from being final simply by declaring that he was doing so. Freeman JA referred to the order as a "creative blending of declaratory and injunctive relief with a means of mediation" and found it to be "of the very essence of the kind of remedy courts are encouraged to seek pursuant to s. 24(1) to give life to *Charter* rights" (para. 70). He noted that requiring fresh applications by the parties each time the Province or the Conseil appeared not to be using its best efforts could have dragged matters out interminably, and would have left the matter to a judge with less familiarity with the issues and legal principles involved. Freeman JA concluded that the order, meant to "head off the potential for an enforcement nightmare," "got the job done, virtually on time, with a minimum of inconvenience or unnecessary cost" (para. 84). ...

B. *The Retention of Jurisdiction*

(1) *The Importance of Context: Sections 23 and 24 of the Charter*

[23] It is well accepted that the *Charter* should be given a generous and expansive interpretation and not a narrow, technical, or legalistic one (*Hunter v. Southam Inc.*, [1984] 2 SCR 145; *R v. Big M Drug Mart Ltd.*, [1985] 1 SCR 295; *Re BC Motor Vehicle Act*, [1985] 2 SCR 486; *Reference re Prov. Electoral Boundaries (Sask.)*, [1991] 2 SCR 158; *Vriend v. Alberta*, [1998] 1 SCR 493). The need for a generous interpretation flows from the principle that the *Charter* ought to be interpreted purposively. While courts must be careful not to overshoot the actual purposes of the *Charter*'s guarantees, they must avoid a narrow, technical approach to *Charter* interpretation which could subvert the goal of ensuring that right holders enjoy the full benefit and protection of the *Charter*. In our view, the approach taken by our colleagues LeBel and Deschamps JJ which appears to contemplate that special remedies might be available in some circumstances, but not in this case, severely undervalues the importance and the urgency of the language rights in the context facing LeBlanc J.

[24] The requirement of a generous and expansive interpretive approach holds equally true for *Charter* remedies as for *Charter* rights (*R v. Gamble*, [1988] 2 SCR 595; *R v. Sarson*, [1996] 2 SCR 223; *R v. 974649 Ontario Inc.*, [2001] 3 SCR 575, 2001 SCC 81 ("*Dunedin*")). In *Dunedin*, McLachlin CJ, writing for the Court, explained why this is so. She stated, at para. 18:

[Section] 24(1), like all *Charter* provisions, commands a broad and purposive interpretation. This section forms a vital part of the *Charter*, and must be construed generously, in a manner that best ensures the attainment of its objects ... . Moreover, it is remedial, and hence benefits from the general rule of statutory interpretation that accords remedial statutes a "large and liberal" interpretation ... . Finally, and most importantly, the language of this provision appears to confer the widest possible discretion on a court to craft remedies for violations of *Charter* rights. In *Mills* [[1986] 1 SCR 863], McIntyre J observed at p. 965 that "[i]t is difficult to imagine language which could give the court a wider and less fettered discretion." This broad remedial mandate for s. 24(1) should not be frustrated by a "(n)arrow and technical" reading of the provision ... . [Reference omitted.]

[25] Purposive interpretation means that remedies provisions must be interpreted in a way that provides "a full, effective and meaningful remedy for *Charter* violations" since "a right, no matter how expansive in theory, is only as meaningful as the remedy provided for its breach" (*Dunedin, supra*, at paras. 19-20). A purposive approach to remedies in a *Charter* context gives modern vitality to the ancient maxim *ubi jus, ibi remedium*: where there is a right, there must be a remedy. More specifically, a purposive approach to remedies requires at least two things. First, the purpose of the right being protected must be promoted: courts must craft responsive remedies. Second, the purpose of the remedies provision must be promoted: courts must craft effective remedies.

[26] The purpose of s. 23 of the *Charter* is "to preserve and promote the two official languages of Canada, and their respective cultures, by ensuring that each language flourishes, as far as possible, in provinces where it is not spoken by the majority of the population" (*Mahe v. Alberta*, [1990] 1 SCR 342, at p. 362).

[27] A further aspect of s. 23 of the *Charter* is its remedial nature (see, for example, *Mahe* [[1993] 1 SCR 839], at p. 363; *Schools Reference* [[1993] 1 SCR 839], at p. 850; *Arsenault-Cameron v. Prince Edward Island*, [2000] 1 SCR 3, 2000 SCC 1, at para. 26). The section is designed to correct past injustices not only by halting the progressive erosion of minority official language cultures across Canada, but also by actively promoting their flourishing (*Mahe, supra*, at p. 363; *Schools Reference, supra*, at p. 850). Section 23 must therefore be construed "in recognition of previous injustices that have gone unredressed and which have required the entrenchment of protection of minority language rights" (*Schools Reference*, at p. 850; see also *Arsenault-Cameron, supra*, at para. 27). ...

[28] The minority language education rights protected under s. 23 of the *Charter* are unique. They are distinctively Canadian, representing "a linchpin in this nation's commitment to the values of bilingualism and biculturalism" (*Mahe, supra*, at p. 350). Section 23 places positive obligations on governments to mobilize resources and enact legislation for the development of major institutional structures (*Mahe*, at p. 389). While the rights are granted to individuals (*Schools Reference*, at p. 865), they apply only if the "numbers warrant," and the specific programs or facilities that the government is required to provide varies depending on the number of students who can potentially be expected to participate (*Mahe, supra*, at p. 366; *Schools Reference, supra*, at p. 850; *Arsenault-Cameron, supra*, at para. 38). This requirement gives the exercise of minority language education rights a unique collective aspect even though the rights are granted to individuals.

[29] Another distinctive feature of the right in s. 23 is that the "numbers warrant" requirement leaves minority language education rights particularly vulnerable to government delay or inaction. For every school year that governments do not meet their obligations under s. 23, there is an increased likelihood of assimilation which carries the risk that numbers might cease to "warrant." Thus, particular entitlements afforded under s. 23 can be suspended, for so long as the numbers cease to warrant, by the very cultural erosion against which s. 23 was designed to guard. In practical, though not legal, terms, such suspensions may well be permanent. If delay is tolerated, governments could potentially avoid the duties imposed upon them by s. 23 through their own failure to implement the rights vigilantly. The affirmative promise contained in s. 23 of the *Charter* and the critical need for timely compliance will sometimes require courts to order affirmative remedies to guarantee that language rights are meaningfully, and therefore necessarily promptly, protected (see, for example, *Marchand v. Simcoe County Board of Education* (1986), 29 DLR (4th) 596 (Ont. HC); *Marchand v. Simcoe County Board of Education (No. 2)* (1987), 44 DLR (4th) 171 (Ont. HC); *Lavoie v. Nova Scotia (Attorney-General)* (1988), 47 DLR (4th) 586 (NSSCTD); *Conseil des Écoles Séparées Catholiques Romaines de Dufferin et Peel v. Ontario (Ministre de l'Éducation et de la Formation)* (1996), 136 DLR (4th) 704 (Ont. Ct. (Gen. Div.)), aff'd (1996), 30 OR (3d) 681 (CA); *Conseil Scolaire Fransaskois de Zenon Park v. Saskatchewan*, [1999] 3 WWR 743 (Sask. QB), aff'd [1999] 12 WWR 742 (Sask. CA); *Assoc. Française des Conseils Scolaires de l'Ontario v. Ontario* (1988), 66 OR (2d) 599 (CA); *Assn. des parents francophones de la Colombie-Britannique v. British Columbia* (1998), 167 DLR (4th) 534 (BCSC)).

[30] To put the matter of judicial remedies in greater context, it is useful to reflect briefly on the role of courts in the enforcement of our laws.

[31] Canada has evolved into a country that is noted and admired for its adherence to the rule of law as a major feature of its democracy. But the rule of law can be shallow without proper mechanisms for its enforcement. In this respect, courts play an essential role since they are the central institutions to deal with legal disputes through the rendering of judgments and decisions. But courts have no physical or economic means to enforce their judgments. Ultimately, courts depend on both the executive and the citizenry to recognize and abide by their judgments.

[32] Fortunately, Canada has had a remarkable history of compliance with court decisions by private parties and by all institutions of government. That history of compliance has become a fundamentally cherished value of our constitutional democracy; we must never take it for granted but always be careful to respect and protect its importance, otherwise the seeds of tyranny can take root. ...

[34] [I]n the context of constitutional remedies, courts must be sensitive to their role as judicial arbiters and not fashion remedies which usurp the role of the other branches of governance by taking on tasks to which other persons or bodies are better suited. Concern for the limits of the judicial role is interwoven throughout the law. ...

[36] Deference ends, however, where the constitutional rights that the courts are charged with protecting begin. As McLachlin J stated in *RJR-MacDonald Inc. v. Canada (Attorney General)*, [1995] 3 SCR 199, at para. 136:

> Parliament has its role: to choose the appropriate response to social problems within the limiting framework of the Constitution. But the courts also have a role: to determine, objectively

and impartially, whether Parliament's choice falls within the limiting framework of the Constitution. The courts are no more permitted to abdicate their responsibility than is Parliament.

Determining the boundaries of the courts' proper role, however, cannot be reduced to a simple test or formula; it will vary according to the right at issue and the context of each case.

[37] Returning to this appeal, we believe that LeBlanc J was duly guided by historical and contextual factors in crafting a remedy that would meaningfully protect, indeed implement, the applicants' rights to minority official language education for their children while maintaining appropriate respect for the proper roles of the executive and legislative branches.

[38] As indicated earlier, the history of French-language education in Nova Scotia has been disappointing, resulting in high rates of assimilation that have continued well into the period when this litigation began. While the situation is not what it was in the eighteenth and nineteenth centuries when French-language education in Acadia was for the most part either expressly prohibited or unavailable, the promise of s. 23 had yet to be fulfilled in the five school districts at issue in this appeal when the appellants brought their application demanding homogeneous French-language facilities before the Supreme Court of Nova Scotia in 1998. Through the mid-1990s, s. 23 parents had pressured the government to provide homogeneous French-language facilities in presentations to Legislative Committees and in written and oral submissions to Ministers of Education. They had submitted petitions, letters, and expert analyses on assimilation to the Province. In 1996, amendments to the *Education Act* provided for a French-language school board, the Conseil scolaire acadien provincial, geared toward the fulfilment of the Province's s. 23 obligations. The school board then decided to provide the facilities at issue in this appeal. From 1997 to 1999, the provincial government announced the construction of homogeneous French-language schools in Petit-de-Grat, Clare, and Argyle. The schools were never built, and the construction projects were officially put on hold in September 1999.

[39] The reason for the delay, broadly speaking, was the government's failure to give due priority to s. 23 rights in educational policy setting. Indeed, LeBlanc J observed that the real issue between the parties by the time of trial was the date on which the programs ought to be implemented, rather than any question as to whether they were required in the first place. The government cited a lack of consensus in the community, a consequent fear that enrollment would drop, and lack of funds as reasons for its decision to place the previously announced school construction projects on hold pending cost-benefit reviews. LeBlanc J rightly concluded that none of these reasons justified the government's failure to fulfill its obligations under s. 23. He found that the government had been treating the provision of s. 23 schools no differently from programs or facilities generally, without attention to purposes of s. 23 of the *Charter* and the role that homogeneous schools play in French linguistic and cultural preservation and flourishing (para. 205). Meanwhile, assimilation continued (para. 210) and enrollment in the Conseil's schools was dropping. Programs were in jeopardy (paras. 229-30).

[40] It is in this urgent context of ongoing cultural erosion that LeBlanc J crafted his remedy. He was sensitive to the need for timely execution, the limits of the judicial role, and the desirability of allowing the government flexibility in the manner of fulfilling its constitutional obligations when he ordered the government to make best efforts to provide facilities by particular dates and retained jurisdiction to hear progress reports. However, the

urgency of the context does not by itself create jurisdiction in a superior court to issue a remedy of unlimited scope under s. 24(1) of the *Charter*. We now turn to the question of whether LeBlanc J's order was within the jurisdiction of a superior court.

(2) The Jurisdiction of a Superior Court To Issue a Remedy Under Section 24(1) of the Charter

[41] Section 24(1) entrenches in the Constitution a remedial jurisdiction for infringements or denials of *Charter* rights and freedoms. The respondent makes various arguments suggesting that LeBlanc J exceeded his jurisdiction by violating constitutional norms, statutory provisions, and common law rules. We will first deal with the extent of the remedial jurisdiction in s. 24(1) and the constitutional limits to that jurisdiction proposed by the respondent. Later we will discuss how statutes and common law rules might be relevant to the choice of remedy under s. 24(1).

[42] Clearly, if there is some constitutional limit to the remedial power either in s. 24(1) or in some other part of the Constitution, the judge ordering a remedy must respect this boundary. As a basic rule, no part of the Constitution can abrogate or diminish another part of the Constitution (*New Brunswick Broadcasting* [[1993] 1 SCR 319], at p. 373, McLachlin J citing *Reference re Bill 30, An Act to amend the Education Act (Ont.)*, [1987] 1 SCR 1148). For example, a court could not compel a provincial government to do something pursuant to s. 24(1) which would exceed the jurisdiction of the province under s. 92 of the *Constitution Act, 1867*.

[43] A remedy under s. 24(1) is available where there is some government action, beyond the enactment of an unconstitutional statute or provision, that infringes a person's *Charter* rights (see *Schachter v. Canada*, [1992] 2 SCR 679, at pp. 719-20). In the present appeal, the difficulty does not lie with the legislation: no provision or omission in the *Education Act* prevented the government from providing minority language education as required by the *Constitution Act, 1982*. On the contrary, the *Education Act*, as amended in 1996, establishes a French-language school board to provide homogeneous French-language education to children of s. 23 entitled parents. Neither is the problem rooted in any particular government action; rather, the problem was inaction on the part of the provincial government, particularly its failure to mobilize resources to provide school facilities in a timely fashion, as required by s. 23 of the *Charter*. Section 24(1) is available to remedy this failure.

[44] To repeat its text, s. 24(1) of the *Charter* provides:

> Anyone whose rights or freedoms, as guaranteed by this *Charter*, have been infringed or denied may apply to a court of competent jurisdiction to obtain such remedy as the court considers appropriate and just in the circumstances.

[45] The purposive reading of s. 24(1) and also the ordinary meaning of the drafter's language make it clear that s. 24(1) guarantees that there must always be a court of competent jurisdiction to hear anyone whose rights or freedoms have been infringed or denied (see *Nelles v. Ontario*, [1989] 2 SCR 170, at p. 196, and *Mills, supra*, at p. 881). The default court of competent jurisdiction is a superior court established under s. 96 of the *Constitution Act, 1867*. It is also plainly contemplated in s. 24(1) that a court of competent jurisdiction will have the authority to grant a remedy that it considers appropriate and just in the circumstances. ...

[50] The nature and extent of remedies available under s. 24(1) remain limited by the words of the section itself and must be read in harmony with the rest of our Constitution. As McIntyre J wrote in *Mills, supra*, at p. 965:

> What remedies are available when an application under s. 24(1) of the *Charter* succeeds? Section 24(1) again is silent on the question. It merely provides that the appellant may obtain such remedy as the court considers "appropriate and just in the circumstances." It is difficult to imagine language which could give the court a wider and less fettered discretion. It is impossible to reduce this wide discretion to some sort of binding formula for general application in all cases, and it is not for appellate courts to pre-empt or cut down this wide discretion.
>
> McLachlin CJ recently endorsed this passage in *Dunedin, supra*, at para. 18. Consequently, a party seeking to challenge a *Charter* remedy ordered by a s. 96 court must show that the order is not "appropriate and just in the circumstances."

[51] The power of the superior courts under s. 24(1) to make appropriate and just orders to remedy infringements or denials of *Charter* rights is part of the supreme law of Canada. It follows that this remedial power cannot be strictly limited by statutes or rules of the common law. We note, however, that statutes and common law rules may be helpful to a court choosing a remedy under s. 24(1) insofar as the statutory provisions or common law rules express principles that are relevant to determining what is "appropriate and just in the circumstances."

(3) The Meaning of "Appropriate and Just in the Circumstances"

[52] What, then, is meant in s. 24(1) by the words "appropriate and just in the circumstances"? Clearly, the task of giving these words meaning in particular cases will fall to the courts ordering the remedies since s. 24(1) specifies that the remedy should be such as the court considers appropriate and just. Deciding on an appropriate and just remedy in particular circumstances calls on the judge to exercise a discretion based on his or her careful perception of the nature of the right and of the infringement, the facts of the case, and the application of the relevant legal principles. Once again, we emphasize McIntyre J's words in *Mills, supra*, at p. 965:

> It is difficult to imagine language which could give the court a wider and less fettered discretion. It is impossible to reduce this wide discretion to some sort of binding formula for general application in all cases, and it is not for appellate courts to pre-empt or cut down this wide discretion.

[53] With respect, the approach to s. 24 reflected in the reasons of LeBel and Deschamps JJ would tend to pre-empt and reduce this wide discretion. Their approach would also, in this case, pre-empt and devalue the constitutional promise respecting language rights in s. 23. In our view, judicial restraint and metaphors such as "dialogue" must not be elevated to the level of strict constitutional rules to which the words of s. 24 can be subordinated. The same may be said of common law procedural principles such as *functus officio* which may to some extent be incorporated in statutes. Rather, as LeBel and Deschamps JJ appear to recognize at paras. 135 and following, there are situations in which our Constitution requires special remedies to secure the very order it envisages.

[54] While it would be unwise at this point to attempt to define, in detail, the words "appropriate and just" or to draw a rigid distinction between the two terms, there are some broad considerations that judges should bear in mind when evaluating the appropriateness and justice of a potential remedy. These general principles may be informed by jurisprudence relating to remedies outside the *Charter* context, such as cases discussing the doctrine of *functus* and overly vague remedies, although, as we have said, that jurisprudence does not apply strictly to orders made under s. 24(1).

[55] First, an appropriate and just remedy in the circumstances of a *Charter* claim is one that meaningfully vindicates the rights and freedoms of the claimants. Naturally, this will take account of the nature of the right that has been violated and the situation of the claimant. A meaningful remedy must be relevant to the experience of the claimant and must address the circumstances in which the right was infringed or denied. An ineffective remedy, or one which was "smothered in procedural delays and difficulties," is not a meaningful vindication of the right and therefore not appropriate and just (see *Dunedin, supra*, at para. 20, McLachlin CJ citing *Mills, supra*, at p. 882, *per* Lamer J (as he then was)).

[56] Second, an appropriate and just remedy must employ means that are legitimate within the framework of our constitutional democracy. As discussed above, a court ordering a *Charter* remedy must strive to respect the relationships with and separation of functions among the legislature, the executive and the judiciary. This is not to say that there is a bright line separating these functions in all cases. A remedy may be appropriate and just notwithstanding that it might touch on functions that are principally assigned to the executive. The essential point is that the courts must not, in making orders under s. 24(1), depart unduly or unnecessarily from their role of adjudicating disputes and granting remedies that address the matter of those disputes.

[57] Third, an appropriate and just remedy is a judicial one which vindicates the right while invoking the function and powers of a court. It will not be appropriate for a court to leap into the kinds of decisions and functions for which its design and expertise are manifestly unsuited. The capacities and competence of courts can be inferred, in part, from the tasks with which they are normally charged and for which they have developed procedures and precedent.

[58] Fourth, an appropriate and just remedy is one that, after ensuring that the right of the claimant is fully vindicated, is also fair to the party against whom the order is made. The remedy should not impose substantial hardships that are unrelated to securing the right.

[59] Finally, it must be remembered that s. 24 is part of a constitutional scheme for the vindication of fundamental rights and freedoms enshrined in the *Charter*. As such, s. 24, because of its broad language and the myriad of roles it may play in cases, should be allowed to evolve to meet the challenges and circumstances of those cases. That evolution may require novel and creative features when compared to traditional and historical remedial practice because tradition and history cannot be barriers to what reasoned and compelling notions of appropriate and just remedies demand. In short, the judicial approach to remedies must remain flexible and responsive to the needs of a given case.

(4) Application to This Case: The Remedy Ordered by the Trial Judge Was Appropriate and Just in the Circumstances

(a) The Reporting Order Effectively Vindicated the Rights of the Parents

[60] LeBlanc J exercised his discretion to select an effective remedy that meaningfully vindicated the s. 23 rights of the appellants in the context of serious rates of assimilation and a history of delay in the provision of French-language education in Kingston (Greenwood, Chéticamp, Île Madame-Arichat (Petit-de-Grat), Argyle, and Clare). The facts as found by LeBlanc J disclosed that continued delay could imperil the already vulnerable s. 23 rights, their exercise depending as it does on the numbers of potential students. As Freeman JA noted in dissent in the Court of Appeal, the reporting hearings were aimed at identifying difficulties with the timely implementation of the trial judge's order as they arose, instead of requiring fresh applications by the appellants every time it appeared that a party was not using its best efforts to comply with the judge's order.

[61] In the absence of reporting hearings, the appellant parents would have been forced to respond to any new delay by amassing a factual record by traditional means disclosing whether the parties were nonetheless using their best efforts. A new proceeding would be required and this might be heard by another judge less familiar with the case than LeBlanc J. All of this would have taken significant time and resources from parents who had already waited too long and dedicated much energy to the cause of realizing their s. 23 rights. The order of reporting hearings was, as Freeman JA wrote "a pragmatic approach to getting the job done expeditiously" (para. 74). LeBlanc J's order is a creative blending of remedies and processes already known to the courts in order to give life to the right in s. 23.

[62] In assessing the extent to which LeBlanc J's remedy was appropriate and just in the circumstances, it is useful to examine the options before the trial judge. In doing so we are not intending to usurp the role and discretion of the trial judge but only to gain a fuller understanding of the situation he faced. LeBlanc J could have limited the remedy to a declaration of the rights of the parties, as the Court considered prudent in *Mahe, supra*, at pp. 392-93. In *Mahe*, however, the primary issues before the Court concerned the scope and content of s. 23 of the *Charter*, including the degree of management of control of schools to be accorded to s. 23 parents, and the determination of when the numbers are sufficient to warrant given programs and facilities. After clarifying the content and scope of the s. 23 rights at issue, the Court chose the remedy of ordering a declaration of those rights. It did so to allow the government the greatest flexibility to fashion a response suited to the circumstances (p. 393). The assumption underlying this choice of remedy is that governments will comply with the declaration promptly and fully.

[63] After *Mahe*, litigation to vindicate minority language education rights has entered a new phase. The general content of s. 23 in many cases is now largely settled (*Mahe, Schools Reference, Arsenault-Cameron*, all *supra*). In the present case, for example, it was clear to and accepted by the parties from the start that the government was required to provide the homogeneous French-language facilities at issue. The entitled parents sought the assistance of the court in enforcing the full and prompt vindication of their rights after a lengthy history of government inaction.

[64] Our colleagues LeBel and Deschamps JJ state at para. 140 of their reasons that the trial judge was not faced with a government which had understood its obligations but re-

fused to comply with them. Our colleagues suggest that there was some issue as to what s. 23 demanded in the situation. With respect, this portrayal is directly at odds with the findings of fact made by the trial judge. At para. 198 of his reasons, the trial judge wrote:

> It is apparent that the real issue between the parties is the date on which these programs and facilities are to be implemented. The Department, in its submissions, does not challenge the applicants' right and entitlement to these programs and facilities but point [*sic*] to a number of factors which ought to satisfy the applicants. The Conseil opposes the applicants' claim for an earlier implementation of the transition plan but supports the applicants in its [*sic*] demand for declaration that the Department ought to be directed to provide homogeneous facilities.

[65] LeBlanc J further noted that the Department of Education did not provide either statistical or financial evidence with respect to the "numbers warrant" test and that, in any case, the number of children of s. 23 parents were greater than the number in the case of *Mahe, supra*, decided by this Court (paras. 200-201). Instead, the government argued at trial that it should be allowed to delay its obligations because of a lack of consensus in the Acadian and Francophone communities (para. 202) and because the political compromise in s. 23 required a "go-slowly approach" (para. 214). According to the trial judge, the government did not deny the existence or content of the s. 23 rights of the parents but rather failed to prioritize those rights and delayed fulfilling its obligations. The government "did not give sufficient priority to the serious rate of assimilation occurring among Acadians and Francophones in Nova Scotia and the fact that rights established in s. 23 are individual rights" (para. 204) despite clear reports showing that assimilation was "reaching critical levels" (para. 215). These are the findings of fact which can only be made by a judge who has heard all the evidence at trial. These findings are not on appeal and it is not open for appellate judges to reverse these findings without proper justification. LeBlanc J properly took account of the factual circumstances within which he exercised his discretion to select a remedy which was appropriate and just.

[66] LeBlanc J obviously considered that, given the Province's failure to give due priority to the s. 23 rights of its minority Francophone populations in the five districts despite being well aware of them, there was a significant risk that such a declaration would be an ineffective remedy. Parents such as the appellants should not be forced continually to seek declarations that are essentially restatements of the declaration in *Mahe*. Where governments have failed to comply with their well-understood constitutional obligations to take positive action in support of the right in s. 23, the assumption underlying a preference for declarations may be undermined. In *Mahe, supra*, at p. 393, Dickson CJ recognized this possibility:

> As the Attorney General for Ontario submits, the government should have the widest possible discretion in selecting the institutional means by which its s. 23 obligations are to be met; the courts should be loath to interfere and impose what will be necessarily procrustean standards, *unless that discretion is not exercised at all, or is exercised in such a way as to deny a constitutional right*. Once the Court has declared what is required in Edmonton, then the government can and must do whatever is necessary to ensure that these appellants, and other parents in their situation, receive what they are due under s. 23. [Emphasis added.]

This Court's judgment in *Mahe* speaks to all provincial and territorial governments. LeBlanc J was entitled to conclude that he was not limited to declaring the appellant parents' rights and could take into consideration that the case before him was different from those in which declarations had been considered appropriate and just.

[67] Our colleagues LeBel and Deschamps JJ suggest that the reporting order in this case was not called for since any violation of a simple declaratory remedy could be dealt with in contempt proceedings against the Crown. We do not doubt that contempt proceedings may be available in appropriate cases. The threat of contempt proceedings is not, in our view, inherently more respectful of the executive than simple reporting hearings in which a linguistic minority could discover in a timely way what progress was being made towards the fulfilment of their s. 23 rights. More importantly, given the critical rate of assimilation found by the trial judge, it was appropriate for him to grant a remedy that would in his view lead to prompt compliance. Viewed in this light, LeBlanc J selected a remedy that reduced the risk that the minority language education rights would be smothered in additional procedural delay.

(b) The Reporting Order Respected the Framework of Our Constitutional Democracy

[68] The remedy granted by LeBlanc J took into account, and did not depart unduly or unnecessarily from, the role of the courts in our constitutional democracy. LeBlanc J considered the government's progress toward providing the required schools and services (see, e.g., paras. 233-34). Some flexibility was built into the "best efforts" order to allow for unforeseen difficulties. It was appropriate for LeBlanc J to preserve and reinforce the Department of Education's role in providing school facilities as mandated by s. 88 of the *Education Act*, as this could be done without compromising the entitled parents' rights to the prompt provision of school facilities.

[69] To some extent, the legitimate role of the court *vis-à-vis* various institutions of government will depend on the circumstances. In these circumstances, it was appropriate for LeBlanc J to craft the remedy so that it vindicated the rights of the parents while leaving the detailed choices of means largely to the executive.

[70] Our colleagues LeBel and Deschamps JJ appear to consider that the issuance of an injunction against the government under s. 24(1) is constitutionally suspect and represents a departure from a consensus about *Charter* remedies (see para. 134 of the dissent). With respect, it is clear that a court may issue an injunction under s. 24(1) of the *Charter*. The power of courts to issue injunctions against the executive is central to s. 24(1) of the *Charter* which envisions more than declarations of rights. Courts do take actions to ensure that rights are enforced, and not merely declared. Contempt proceedings in the face of defiance of court orders, as well as coercive measures such as garnishments, writs of seizure and sale and the like are all known to courts. In this case, it was open to the trial judge in all the circumstances to choose the injunctive remedy on the terms and conditions that he prescribed.

(c) The Reporting Order Called on the Function and Powers of a Court

[71] Although it may not be common in the context of *Charter* remedies, the reporting order issued by LeBlanc J was judicial in the sense that it called on the functions and powers known to courts. In several different contexts, courts order remedies that involve their continuing involvement in the relations between the parties (see R.J. Sharpe, *Injunctions and Specific Performance* (2nd ed. (loose-leaf)), at paras. 1.260-1.490). Superior courts, which

under the *Judicature Acts* possess the powers of common law courts and courts of equity, have "assumed active and even managerial roles in the exercise of their traditional equitable powers" (K. Roach, *Constitutional Remedies in Canada* (loose-leaf), at para. 13.60). A panoply of equitable remedies are now available to courts in support of the litigation process and the final adjudication of disputes. For example, prejudgment remedies developed in such cases as *Mareva Compania Naviera S.A. v. International Bulkcarriers S.A.*, [1975] 2 Lloyd's Rep. 509 (CA), and *Anton Piller KG v. Manufacturing Processes Ltd.*, [1976] 1 Ch. 55 (CA), involve the court in the preservation of evidence and the management of parties' assets prior to trial. In bankruptcy and receivership matters, courts may be called on to supervise fairly complex and ongoing commercial transactions relating to debtors' assets. Court-appointed receivers may report to and seek guidance from the courts and in some cases must seek the permission of the courts before disposing of property (see *Bennett on Receiverships* (2nd ed. 1999), at pp. 21-37, 443-45). Similarly, the courts' jurisdiction in respect of trusts and estates may sometimes entail detailed and continuing supervision and support of their administration (see D.W.M. Waters, *Law of Trusts in Canada* (2nd ed. 1984), at pp. 904-9; *Oosterhoff on Wills and Succession* (5th ed. 2001), at pp. 27-28). Courts may also retain an ongoing jurisdiction in family law cases to order alterations in maintenance payments or parenting arrangements as circumstances change. Finally, this Court has in the past remained seized of a matter so as to facilitate the implementation of constitutional language rights: see *Reference re Manitoba Language Rights*, [1985] 1 SCR 721; *Re Manitoba Language Rights Order*, [1985] 2 SCR 347; *Re Manitoba Language Rights Order*, [1990] 3 SCR 1417; *Reference re Manitoba Language Rights*, [1992] 1 SCR 212. Lower courts have also retained jurisdiction in s. 23 cases: *British Columbia (Association des parents francophones) v. British Columbia* (1996), 139 DLR (4th) 356 (BCSC), at p. 380; *Lavoie, supra*, at pp. 593-95; *Société des Acadiens du Nouveau-Brunswick Inc. v. Minority Language School Board No. 50* (1983), 48 NBR (2d) 361 (QB), at para. 109.

[72] The difficulties of ongoing supervision of parties by the courts have sometimes been advanced as a reason that orders for specific performance and mandatory injunctions should not be awarded. Nonetheless, courts of equity have long accepted and overcome this difficulty of supervision where the situations demanded such remedies (see Sharpe, *supra*, at paras. 1.260-1.380; *Attorney-General v. Birmingham, Tame, and Rea District Drainage Board*, [1910] 1 Ch. 48 (CA), aff'd [1912] AC 788 (HL); *Kennard v. Cory Brothers and Co.*, [1922] 1 Ch. 265, aff'd [1922] 2 Ch. 1 (CA)).

[73] As academic commentators have pointed out, the range of remedial orders available to courts in civil proceedings demonstrates that constitutional remedies involving some degree of ongoing supervision do not represent a radical break with the past practices of courts (see W.A. Bogart, "'Appropriate and Just': Section 24 of the Canadian *Charter of Rights and Freedoms* and the Question of Judicial Legitimacy" (1986), 10 *Dalhousie L J* 81, at pp. 92-94; N. Gillespie, "Charter Remedies: The Structural Injunction" (1989-90), 11 *Advocates' Q* 190, at pp. 217-18; Roach, *Constitutional Remedies in Canada, supra*, at paras. 13.50-13.80; Sharpe, *supra*, at paras. 1.260-1.490). The change announced by s. 24 of the *Charter* is that the flexibility inherent in an equitable remedial jurisdiction may be applied to orders addressed to government to vindicate constitutionally entrenched rights.

[74] The order in this case was in no way inconsistent with the judicial function. There was never any suggestion in this case that the court would, for example, improperly take

over the detailed management and co-ordination of the construction projects. Hearing evidence and supervising cross-examinations on progress reports about the construction of schools are not beyond the normal capacities of courts.

[75] The respondent argues that the reporting order issued by LeBlanc J violated the common law doctrine of *functus officio*. As we have said, statutes or common law rules cannot strictly pre-empt the remedial discretion in s. 24(1). Nonetheless, the doctrine of *functus officio* properly speaks to the functions and powers of courts. Therefore, an examination of the *functus* question is useful in deciding whether LeBlanc J issued an order that is appropriately judicial.

[76] Flinn JA for the majority in the Court of Appeal decided that the trial judge, having issued the best efforts order, had no further jurisdiction with respect to the parties and was therefore precluded from retaining jurisdiction to hear reports on its implementation (para. 21). This view is based on a mis-characterization of the reporting portion of the order as somehow separate from and additional to the best efforts injunctions. On the contrary, in our view, the reporting sessions formed an integral part of the remedy fashioned by LeBlanc J. Moreover, the *functus* doctrine has no application where the trial judge does not purport to alter a final judgment. There was no indication that the retention of jurisdiction included any power to alter the disposition of the case.

[77] A closer examination of the doctrine is helpful. The *Oxford Companion to Law* (1980), at p. 508, provides the following definition:

> *Functus officio* (having performed his function). Used of an agent who has performed his task and exhausted his authority and of an arbitrator or judge to whom further resort is incompetent, his function being exhausted.

[78] But how can we know when a judge's function is exhausted? Sopinka J, writing for the majority in *Chandler v. Alberta Association of Architects*, [1989] 2 SCR 848, at p. 860, described the purpose and origin of the doctrine in the following words:

> The general rule that a final decision of a court cannot be reopened derives from the decision of the English Court of Appeal in *In re St. Nazaire Co.* (1879), 12 Ch. D 88. The basis for it was that the power to rehear was transferred by the *Judicature Acts* to the appellate division.

[79] It is clear that the principle of *functus officio* exists to allow finality of judgments from courts which are subject to appeal (see also *Reekie v. Messervey*, [1990] 1 SCR 219, at pp. 222-23). This makes sense: if a court could continually hear applications to vary its decisions, it would assume the function of an appellate court and deny litigants a stable base from which to launch an appeal. Applying that aspect of the *functus* doctrine to s. 23(1), we face the question of whether the ordering of progress reports denied the respondents a stable basis from which to appeal.

[80] In our view, LeBlanc J's retention of jurisdiction to hear reports did nothing to undermine the provision of a stable basis for launching an appeal. He did not purport to retain a power to change the decision as to the scope of the s. 23 rights in question, to alter the finding as to their violation, or to modify the original injunctions. The decision, including the best efforts order and the order to appear at reporting sessions, was final and appealable.

[81] In any case, the rules of practice in Nova Scotia and other provinces allow courts to vary or add to their orders so as to carry them into operation or even to provide other or

further relief than originally granted (Nova Scotia *Civil Procedure Rules*, Rule 15.08(d) and (e); Ontario *Rules of Civil Procedure*, RRO 1990, Reg. 194, Rule 59.06(2)(c) and (d); *Alberta Rules of Court*, Alta. Reg. 390/68, Rule 390(1)). This shows that the practice of providing further direction on remedies in support of a decision is known to our courts, and does not undermine the availability of appeal. Moreover, the possibility of such proceedings may facilitate the process of putting orders into operation without requiring resort to contempt proceedings.

[82] The respondent relies on the Nova Scotia's *Judicature Act* to support its argument that the ordered reporting hearings were improper. However, even if that Act could have the effect of limiting the jurisdiction granted by s. 24(1) of the *Charter*, nothing in the *Judicature Act* appears to remove from a trial judge the power to hear reports on the implementation of his or her order. Section 33 of the *Judicature Act* provides that proceedings in the Supreme Court of Nova Scotia shall be "heard, determined and disposed of" by a single judge, but this does not limit the powers of the court to order reporting hearings. Section 34(d) of the *Judicature Act* allows a presiding judge to reserve judgment for a maximum of six months, but in our view, judgment was not reserved in this case since LeBlanc J delivered his judgment within the six-month period. Section 38 of the *Judicature Act* provides that "an appeal lies to the Court of Appeal from any decision, verdict, judgment or order" of a judge of the Supreme Court of Nova Scotia. LeBlanc J did nothing that would preclude the appeal of his decision or choice of remedy.

(d) The Reporting Order Vindicated the Right by Means That Were Fair

[83] In the context, the reporting order was one which, after vindicating the entitled parents' rights, was not unfair to the respondent government. The respondent argues that it was subject to an overly vague remedy. In our opinion, the reporting order was not vaguely worded so as to render it invalid. While, in retrospect, it would certainly have been advisable for LeBlanc J to provide more guidance to the parties as to what they could expect from the reporting sessions, his order was not incomprehensible or impossible to follow. In our view, the "reporting" element of LeBlanc J remedy was not unclear in a way that would render it invalid.

[84] Doubtless, as LeBel and Deschamps JJ point out, the initial retention of jurisdiction by LeBlanc J could have been more specific in its terms so as to give parties a precise understanding of the procedure at reporting sessions. Nonetheless, the respondent knew it was required to present itself to the court to report on the status of its efforts to provide the facilities as ordered by LeBlanc J. LeBlanc J's written order is satisfactory and clearly communicates that the obligation on government was simply to report. The fact that this was the subject of questions later in the process suggests that future orders of this type could be more explicit and detailed with respect to the jurisdiction retained and the procedure at reporting hearings.

[85] It should be remembered that LeBlanc J was crafting a fairly original remedy in order to provide flexibility to the executive while vindicating the s. 23 right. It may be expected that in future cases judges will be in a better position to ensure that the contents of their orders are clearer. In addition, the reporting order chosen by LeBlanc J is not the only tool of its kind. It may be more helpful in some cases for the trial judge to seek submissions

on whether to specify a timetable with a right of the government to seek variation where just and appropriate to do so.

[86] Once again, we emphasize that s. 24(1) gives a court the discretion to fashion the remedy that it considers just and appropriate in the circumstances. The trial judge is not required to identify the single best remedy, even if that were possible. In our view, the trial judge's remedy was clearly appropriate and just in the circumstances.

(5) Conclusion

[87] Section 24(1) of the *Charter* requires that courts issue effective, responsive remedies that guarantee full and meaningful protection of *Charter* rights and freedoms. The meaningful protection of *Charter* rights, and in particular the enforcement of s. 23 rights, may in some cases require the introduction of novel remedies. A superior court may craft any remedy that it considers appropriate and just in the circumstances. In doing so, courts should be mindful of their roles as constitutional arbiters and the limits of their institutional capacities. Reviewing courts, for their part, must show considerable deference to trial judges' choice of remedy, and should refrain from using hindsight to perfect a remedy. A reviewing court should only interfere where the trial judge has committed an error of law or principle.

[88] The remedy crafted by LeBlanc J meaningfully vindicated the rights of the appellant parents by encouraging the Province's prompt construction of school facilities, without drawing the court outside its proper role. The Court of Appeal erred in wrongfully interfering with and striking down the portion of LeBlanc J's order in which he retained jurisdiction to hear progress reports on the status of the Province's efforts in providing school facilities by the required dates.

V. Disposition

[89] In the result, we would allow the appeal, set aside the judgment of the Court of Appeal, and restore the order of the trial judge.

[90] We would award full costs to the appellants on a solicitor–client basis throughout, including the costs for the reporting hearings. The appellants are parents who have, despite their numerous efforts, been consistently denied their *Charter* rights. The Province failed to meet its corresponding obligations to the appellant parents despite its clear awareness of the appellants' rights. Accordingly, in looking at all the circumstances, our view is that solicitor–client costs should be awarded.

LEBEL and DESCHAMPS JJ (dissenting) (Major and Binnie JJ concurring):

I. Introduction

[91] The devil is in the details. Awareness of the critical importance of effectively enforcing constitutional rights should not lead to forgetfulness about the need to draft pleadings, orders and judgments in a sound manner, consonant with the basic rules of legal writing, and with an understanding of the proper role of courts and of the organizing principles of the legal and political order of our country. Court orders should be written in such a way

that parties are put on notice of what is expected of them. Courts should not unduly encroach on areas which should remain the responsibility of public administration and should avoid turning themselves into managers of the public service. Judicial interventions should end when and where the case of which a judge is seized is brought to a close.

[92] In our respectful view, without putting in any doubt the desire of the trial judge to fashion an effective remedy to address the consequences of a long history of neglect of the rights of the Francophone minority in Nova Scotia, the drafting of his so-called reporting order was seriously flawed. It gave the parties no clear notice of their obligations, the nature of the reports or even the purpose of the reporting hearings. In addition, the reporting order assumed that the judge could retain jurisdiction at will, after he had finally disposed of the matter of which he had been seized, thereby breaching the constitutional principle of separation of powers. The order did so by reason of the way it was framed and the manner in which it was implemented. In our opinion, the reporting order was void, as the Court of Appeal of Nova Scotia found, and the appeal should be dismissed.

II. The Nature of the Issues

[93] This appeal raises the sole question of the validity of the reporting order made by LeBlanc J ((2000), 185 NSR (2d) 246). In this context, we do not intend to engage in a full review of the factual background and of the judicial history of this case. For the purposes of our reasons, we are content to rely on their extensive review in the reasons of our colleagues. We will only add such details about the reporting order and its implementation as might be of assistance to our analysis of the legal questions at stake in this appeal.

[94] At the outset, we wish to emphasize that we fully agree with our colleagues in their analysis of the nature and fundamental importance of language rights in the Canadian Constitution, as well as on the need for efficacy and imagination in the development of constitutional remedies. Indeed, we dissent because we believe that constitutional remedies should be designed keeping in mind the canons of good legal drafting, the fundamental importance of procedural fairness, and a proper awareness of the nature of the role of courts in our democratic political regime, a key principle of which remains the separation of powers. This principle protects the independence of courts. It also flexibly delineates the domain of court action, particularly in the relationship of courts not only with legislatures but also with the executive branch of government or public administration.

[95] As to the other issues such as mootness, immunities and mandatory injunctions, we are in broad agreement with our colleagues and do not intend to comment any further on them. We turn now to an analysis of the issues which lie at the root of our disagreement with the majority as to the final disposition of this appeal.

[96] In this analysis, we will first review the nature of the reporting order and we will determine whether it can be considered consistent with the principle of procedural fairness. We will then discuss the principles of separation of powers and *functus officio*; we will demonstrate that the question of whether the trial judge had jurisdiction to issue the order is germane to the determination of whether the trial judge breached the separation of powers. In both discussions, the appropriateness of the remedy will be called into question. In the former, we will assess the appropriateness of the order for reporting hearings from the perspective of the parties subject to it, while in the latter, we will analyse the appropriateness of

the order, by taking into consideration the proper role of courts within our constitutional order.

III. The Drafting of the Order and the Principle of Procedural Fairness

[97] The drafting of applications asking for injunctive relief, or of orders granting such remedies, can be a serious challenge for counsel and judges. The exercise of the court power to grant injunctions may lead, from time to time, to situations of non-compliance where it may be necessary to call upon the drastic exercise of courts' powers to impose civil or criminal penalties, including imprisonment (R.J. Sharpe, *Injunctions and Specific Performance* (2nd ed. (loose-leaf)), at p. 6-7). Therefore, proper notice to the parties of the obligations imposed upon them and clarity in defining the standard of compliance expected of them must be essential requirements of a court's intervention. Vague or ambiguous language should be strictly avoided (*Sonoco Ltd. v. Local 433* (1970), 13 DLR (3d) 617 (BCCA), at p. 621; *Sporting Club du Sanctuaire Inc. v. 2320-4365 Québec Inc.*, [1989] RDJ 596 (Que. CA)).

[98] Unfortunately, the drafting of the present reporting order was anything but clear. Its brevity and apparent simplicity belie its actual complexity and the state of confusion and uncertainty in which it left not only all of the parties, but the trial judge himself at times. This order was final, not interim, and it was tied to the "best efforts order," which was not couched in terms liable to shed much light on the nature of the obligations of the respondents. Given that this part of the order was not challenged on appeal, we will not discuss it at length, but instead, will focus exclusively on the reporting order which is the object of this appeal.

[99] At first, when judgment was rendered, the reporting order read, at para. 245:

> The applicants have requested that I should maintain jurisdiction. I agree to do so. I am scheduling a further appearance for Thursday, July 27, 2000 at 1:30 p.m., and at that time the respondents will report on the status of their efforts. I am requesting the respondents to utilize their best efforts to comply with this decision.

This drafting was slightly modified in the final order, dated December 14, 2000:

> The Court shall retain jurisdiction to hear reports from the respondents respecting the respondents' compliance with this Order. The respondents shall report to this Court on March 23, 2001 at 9:30 a.m., or on such other date as the Court may determine.

[100] As Flinn JA observed in his reasons in the Court of Appeal ((2001), 194 NSR (2d) 323, 2001 NSCA 104), nobody knew the exact nature of these reports. Their form and content were undefined. There was no indication as to whether they should be delivered orally or in writing or both nor as to how detailed they should be and what kind of supporting documents, if any, would be needed. The order also provided for hearings, but again, it left the parties in the dark as to the procedure, purpose or nature of these sessions of the court. The parties learned only shortly before these hearings that affidavits needed to be filed and deponents made available for cross-examination. Further, there seemed to be little direction, if any at all, as to what sort of evidence was required to be included for the purpose of the hearings. The nature of these hearings, as the process developed, appeared to become a cross between a mini-trial, an informal meeting with the judge and some kind of mediation

session, for the purpose of monitoring the execution of the school-building program for Francophone students.

[101] The trial judge himself seemed unsure about the nature of the hearings he had ordered and of the process he had initiated. At first, he appeared to lean towards the view that those hearings were regular sessions of the court, that he had not issued a final order and that additional relief could be requested. For example, in the July 27, 2000 hearing, the trial judge stated that in the hearings, he "would have the opportunity to determine if the Respondents were indeed making every or best efforts to comply" (appellants' record, at p. 762). This was a reiteration of a claim made earlier in that hearing (appellants' record, at p. 720). Similarly, in the August 9, 2000 hearing, the trial judge stated: "the amount of room I have with respect to a decision or direction or comment is very limited" (appellants' record, at pp. 997-98); this statement implies that the trial judge had the power, albeit limited, to make orders. However, after the setting down of his formal order, at the last hearing in March 2001, he commented that he could not grant further relief, that he had fully disposed of the matter in his order and accompanying reasons, which were released the previous summer. He added that the sessions had a solely informational purpose.

[102] In the meantime, schools were built or renovated and made available to Francophone students. It is difficult to determine whether those sessions accomplished anything in this respect. What these sessions certainly did was sow confusion, doubt and uncertainty about the obligations of the respondents and about the nature of a process that went on over several months. The trial judge appeared to view this process as open ended and indeterminate, with more sessions being scheduled as he wished. Nobody really knew when it all would come to an end.

[103] The uncertainty engendered by the reporting order was not merely inconvenient for the parties. In our view it amounted to a breach of the parties' interest in procedural fairness. One essential feature of a fair procedural rule is that its contents are clearly defined, and known in advance by the parties subject to it (*Supermarchés Jean Labrecque Inc. v. Flamand*, [1987] 2 SCR 219, at pp. 233-36; see also: D.J. Mullan, *Administrative Law* (2001), at p. 233; R. Dussault and L. Borgeat, *Administrative Law: A Treatise* (2nd ed. 1990), vol. 4, at pp. 279-82; S.A. de Smith, H. Woolf and J.L. Jowell, *Judicial Review of Administrative Action* (5th ed. 1995 & Cum. Supp. 1998), at pp. 432-36).

[104] Moreover, as we noted above, the trial judge in his initial characterization of the order seemed to believe, and certainly gave the impression, that he had the power to make further orders based on what was presented to him at the reporting sessions. In other words, he purported to have available the coercive power of the state to compel the parties to act, and suggested that he could do so based on conclusions that he would draw from the evidence placed before him. In the result, the parties found themselves before a trial judge who purported to exercise judicial functions and powers, and who provided almost nothing by way of procedural guidelines. The parties were denied notice which, as L'Heureux-Dubé J has noted, is a rule "so fundamental in our legal system that I do not think there is any necessity to discuss it at length" (*Supermarchés Jean Labrecque, supra*, at p. 233). For this reason alone, the trial judge's order can be found to be inappropriate under s. 24(1) of the *Canadian Charter of Rights and Freedoms* and therefore void. Nonetheless, we turn now to a discussion of the principles of separation of powers and *functus officio*. Consideration of

these principles will aid in assessing the appropriateness of the remedy, in light of the judiciary's proper role within our constitutional order.

IV. The Appropriate Role of the Judiciary

[105] While superior courts' powers to craft *Charter* remedies may not be constrained by statutory or common law limits, they are nonetheless bound by rules of fundamental justice, as we have shown above, and by constitutional boundaries, as we shall see below. In the context of constitutional remedies, courts fulfill their proper function by issuing orders precise enough for the parties to know what is expected of them, and by permitting the parties to execute those orders. Such orders are final. A court purporting to retain jurisdiction to oversee the implementation of a remedy, after a final order has been issued, will likely be acting inappropriately on two levels. First, by attempting to extend the court's jurisdiction beyond its proper role, it will breach the separation of powers principle. Second, by acting after exhausting its jurisdiction, it will breach the *functus officio* doctrine. We will look at each of these breaches in turn.

1 The Separation of Powers

[106] Courts are called upon to play a fundamental role in the Canadian constitutional regime. When needed, they must be assertive in enforcing constitutional rights. At times, they have to grant such relief as will be required to safeguard basic constitutional rights and the rule of law, despite the sensitivity of certain issues or circumstances and the reverberations of their decisions in their societal environment. Despite—or, perhaps, because of—the critical importance of their functions, courts should be wary of going beyond the proper scope of the role assigned to them in the public law of Canada. In essence, this role is to declare what the law is, contribute to its development and to give claimants such relief in the form of declarations, interpretation and orders as will be needed to remedy infringements of constitutional and legal rights by public authorities. Beyond these functions, an attitude of restraint remains all the more justified, given that, as the majority reasons acknowledge, Canada has maintained a tradition of compliance by governments and public servants with judicial interpretations of the law and court orders. ...

[110] [T]he principle of separation of powers has an obverse side as well, which equally reflects the appropriate position of the judiciary within the Canadian legal system. Aside from their duties to supervise administrative tribunals created by the executive and to act as vigilant guardians of constitutional rights and the rule of law, courts should, as a general rule, avoid interfering in the management of public administration.

[111] More specifically, once they have rendered judgment, courts should resist the temptation to directly oversee or supervise the administration of their orders. They should generally operate under a presumption that judgments of courts will be executed with reasonable diligence and good faith. Once they have declared what the law is, issued their orders and granted such relief as they think is warranted by circumstances and relevant legal rules, courts should take care not to unnecessarily invade the province of public administration. To do otherwise could upset the balance that has been struck between our three branches of government.

[112] This is what occurred in the present case. When the trial judge attempted to oversee the implementation of his order, he not only assumed jurisdiction over a sphere traditionally outside the province of the judiciary, but also acted beyond the jurisdiction with which he was legitimately charged as a trial judge. In other words, he was *functus officio* and breached an important principle which reflects the nature and function of the judiciary in the Canadian constitutional order, as we shall see now.

2 Functus Officio

. . .

[114] The existence and scope of a right of appeal has often been made the focus of analytical attention in applying the *functus* doctrine. Such was the case when the power of the Court of Chancery to rehear cases was extinguished by the *Judicature Acts* in 1873 by fusing common law and equity jurisdictions into one court and providing for a single appeal to a newly created Court of Appeal (*In re St. Nazaire, supra*). Originally, this was also the focus of the *functus* analysis for administrative tribunals that had rights of appeal tightly constrained by statute (see *Grillas v. Minister of Manpower and Immigration*, [1972] SCR 577). However, the underlying rationale for the doctrine is clearly more fundamental: that for the due and proper administration of justice, there must be finality to a proceeding to ensure procedural fairness and the integrity of the judicial system. The point is plainly made by Sopinka J in *Chandler, supra*, at pp. 861-62:

> As a general rule, once … a tribunal has reached a final decision in respect to the matter that is before it in accordance with its enabling statute, that decision cannot be revisited because the tribunal has changed its mind, made an error within jurisdiction or because there has been a change of circumstances. …
>
> To this extent, the principle of *functus officio* applies. It is based, however, on the policy ground which favours finality of proceedings rather than the rule which was developed with respect to formal judgments of a court whose decision was subject to a full appeal.

[115] If a court is permitted to continually revisit or reconsider final orders simply because it has changed its mind or wishes to continue exercising jurisdiction over a matter, there would never be finality to a proceeding … .

[117] In addition to this concern with finality, the question of whether a court is clothed with the requisite authority to act raises concerns related to the separation of powers, a principle that transcends procedural and common law rules. In our view, if a court intervenes, as here, in matters of administration properly entrusted to the executive, it exceeds its proper sphere and thereby breaches the separation of powers. By crossing the boundary between judicial acts and administrative oversight, it acts illegitimately and without jurisdiction. Such a crossing of the boundary cannot be characterized as relief that is "appropriate and just in the circumstances" within the meaning of s. 24(1) of the *Charter*.

V. Application of the Relevant Principles to the Present Case

[118] When the above principles are applied to the present facts, it is evident that McIntyre J's admonition in *Mills v. The Queen*, [1986] 1 SCR 863, that s. 24(1) "was not intended to turn the Canadian legal system upside down" is apropos (p. 953). In our view, the

trial judge's remedy undermined the proper role of the judiciary within our constitutional order, and unnecessarily upset the balance between the three branches of government. As a result, the trial judge in the present circumstances acted inappropriately, and contrary to s. 24(1).

[119] As we noted above, the trial judge equivocated on the question of whether his purported retention of jurisdiction empowered him to make further orders. Regardless of which position is taken, the separation of powers was still breached. On the one hand, if he did purport to be able to make further orders, based on the evidence presented at the reporting hearings, he was *functus officio*. We find it difficult to imagine how any subsequent order would not have resulted in a change to the original final order. This necessarily falls outside the narrow exceptions provided by *functus officio*, and breaches that rule.

[120] Such a breach would also have resulted in a violation of the separation of powers principle. By purporting to be able to make subsequent orders, the trial judge would have assumed a supervisory role which included administrative functions that properly lie in the sphere of the executive. These functions are beyond the capacities of courts. The judiciary is ill equipped to make polycentric choices or to evaluate the wide-ranging consequences that flow from policy implementation. This Court has recognized that courts possess neither the expertise nor the resources to undertake public administration. In *Eldridge v. British Columbia (Attorney General)*, [1997] 3 SCR 624, at para. 96, it was held that in light of the "myriad options" available to the government to rectify the unconstitutionality of the impugned system, it was "not this Court's role to dictate how this is to be accomplished."

[121] In addition, if he purported to adopt a managerial role, the trial judge undermined the norm of co-operation and mutual respect that not only describes the relationship between the various actors in the constitutional order, but defines its particularly Canadian nature, and invests each branch with legitimacy. In *Vriend v. Alberta*, [1998] 1 SCR 493, Iacobucci J noted that "respect by the courts for the legislature and executive role is as important as ensuring that the other branches respect each others' role and the role of the courts" (para. 136). He discussed the wording of provisions of the *Charter* that expressed this norm of mutual respect (para. 137), and remarked that this norm has "the effect of enhancing the democratic process" (para. 139).

[122] Similarly, McLachlin J (as she then was) in the 1990 Weir Memorial Lecture reviewed the elements of our legal culture—including our political climate, our tradition of judicial restraint, and the system of references—that have contributed to a spirit of co-operation, rather than confrontation among the branches of government (B.M. McLachlin, "The Charter: A New Role for the Judiciary?" (1991), 29 *Alta. L Rev.* 540, at pp. 554-56). Moreover, referring to her reasons in *Dixon v. British Columbia (Attorney-General)* (1989), 59 DLR (4th) 247 (BCSC), she spoke to the importance of considerations of institutional legitimacy for a court crafting a remedy (at p. 557):

> It was not for me, I felt, to dictate to the Legislature what sort of law they should enact; that was the responsibility of the elected representatives. But, again following a time-honoured judicial tradition, I offered advice on what limits on the principle of one person–one vote, might be acceptable.

[123] McLachlin J expressed this concern for the principle of democratic legitimacy in respect of the relationship between the judiciary and the legislature, but the principle ex-

tends to that between the judiciary and the executive. This Court has recognized that in the Canadian parliamentary system, the executive is inextricably tied to the legislative branch. The Court in *Attorney General of Quebec v. Blaikie*, [1981] 1 SCR 312, at p. 320, observed that "[t]here is thus a considerable degree of integration between the Legislature and the Government." In *Wells v. Newfoundland*, [1999] 3 SCR 199, at para. 53, the Court held: "On a practical level, it is recognized that the same individuals control both the executive and legislative branches of government."

[124] Therefore, just as the legislature should, after a judicial finding of a *Charter* breach retain independence in writing its legislative response, the executive should after a judicial finding of a breach, retain autonomy in administering government policy that conforms with the *Charter*. In our constitutional order, the legislature and the executive are intimately interrelated and are the principal *loci* of democratic will. Judicial respect for that will should extend to both branches.

[125] Thus, if the trial judge's initial suggestion that he could continue to make orders, and thereby effectively engage in administrative supervision and decision making accurately characterizes the nature of the reporting sessions, the order for reporting sessions breached the constitutional principle of separation of powers. Since no part of the Constitution can be interpreted to conflict with another, that order cannot be considered appropriate and just in the circumstances, under s. 24(1). The trial judge's order for reporting sessions should also be considered inappropriate because it put into question the Canadian tradition of mutual respect between the judiciary and the institutions that are the repository of democratic will.

[126] If, however, the trial judge's statement in the last session that he could not make further orders correctly characterized his remedial order, then he breached the separation of powers in another way. When considered in light of this constitutional principle and applied to the present facts, McLachlin CJ's proposition that "s. 24 should not be read so broadly that it endows courts and tribunals with powers that they were never intended to exercise" (*R v. 974649 Ontario Inc.*, [2001] 3 SCR 575, 2001 SCC 81 ("*Dunedin*"), at para. 22) leads to the conclusion that the trial judge's remedy was not appropriate and just in the circumstances.

[127] The appellants argued that the trial judge retained jurisdiction only to hear reports, and that these hearings had purely "suasive" value. They also argued that the hearings were designed to hold "the Province's feet to the fire" (SCC hearing transcripts). They further suggested that the threat of having to report to the trial judge functioned as an incentive for the government to comply with the best efforts order. In the words of the appellants:

Is it a coincidence that, after a nine month delay (October 1999 to July 2000) the Province called for tenders eight days before the reporting hearing and "fast tracked" the school? The Province knew that it would have to report on July 27. The Province ensured that a call for tenders and a construction schedule were in place for July 27.

[128] If this characterization of the trial judge's activity is accurate, then the order for reporting sessions did not result in the exercise of adjudicative, or any other, functions that traditionally define the ambit of a court's proper sphere. Moreover, it resulted in activity that can be characterized as political. According to the appellants' characterization, a primary purpose of the hearings was to put public pressure on the government to act. This kind of pressure is paradigmatically associated with political actors. Indeed, the practice of publicly

questioning a government on its performance, without having any legal power to compel it to alter its behaviour, is precisely that undertaken by an opposition party in the legislature during question period.

[129] In the above, we reasoned that the trial judge, by breaching the separation of powers, would have put in question the norm of co-operation that defines the relationship between the branches of government in Canada. We will presently demonstrate how the trial judge, by improperly altering the relationship between the judiciary and the executive, would have breached the separation of powers. ...

[131] With the reporting hearings, the trial judge may have sought to exert political or public pressure on the executive, and at least appeared to do so. In our view, such action would tend to politicize the relationship between the executive and the judiciary.

[132] If the reporting hearings were intended to hold "the Province's feet to the fire," the character of the relationship between the judiciary and the executive was improperly altered and, as per the *Provincial Court Judges Reference*, the constitutional principle of separation of powers was breached. Once again, since no part of the Constitution can conflict with another, the trial judge's order for reporting hearings cannot be interpreted as appropriate and just under s. 24(1).

[133] We would reiterate, at this point, the importance of clarity and certainty in the provisions of a court order. If the trial judge had precisely defined the terms of the remedy, in advance, then the ensuing confusion surrounding his role may not have occurred. Moreover, by complying with this essential element of fair procedure, he may have been able to avoid the constitutional breach of the separation of powers that followed.

VI. Neither a Breach of Procedural Fairness nor of the Separation of Powers Was Appropriate

[134] We noted above that this Court in *Eldridge* recognized the appropriateness of judicial restraint in issuing a remedy under s. 24(1), given the variety of choices open to the executive in administering policy. Implicit in the declaratory remedy ordered in that case was the presumption that the government will act in good faith in rectifying *Charter* wrongs and the recognition that legislatures and executives, not the courts, are in the best position to decide exactly how this should be done. Turning to the present case then, the trial judge's decision to provide injunctive relief already represented a departure from the cooperative norm that defines and shapes the relationships among the branches of the Canadian constitutional order. We do not deny that in the appropriate factual circumstances, injunctive relief may become necessary. However, the trial judge's order for reporting sessions then purported to go even further, and breached both a fundamental principle of procedural fairness and the constitutional principle of separation of powers.

[135] One might argue that such a breach is appropriate where it is the only way that a claimant's rights can be vindicated. Alternatively, one might suggest that if a government has ignored previous, less intrusive judicial measures, and thereby put into question their efficacy, a court might be justified in abandoning the presumption of governmental good will that we referred to above. In our view, the present case gave rise to neither of these arguments.

[136] Turning to the first argument, if the hearings were aimed at ensuring the vindication of the claimants' rights by providing them with the opportunity to enforce or alter the

remedy, there were alternatives available. If the claimants felt that the government was not complying with any part of the order, then they could have brought an application for contempt. The majority seems to suggest that contempt proceedings would have been less effective in this case in ensuring timely performance of the order, without being any more respectful of the separation of powers. However, we would note that expedited applications are possible in Nova Scotia and other jurisdictions to deal with cases quickly and efficiently. In addition, the reporting order at issue in this case precluded applying to any other judge for relief and was, in this way, even more limiting than a contempt proceeding. Most importantly, contempt proceedings are more consistent with our adversarial system, which is based on the common law norm of giving the parties primary control over the proceedings (see J.I.H. Jacob, *The Fabric of English Civil Justice* (1987), at p. 13). In contrast, the present order for reporting sessions placed the trial judge in an inappropriate, ongoing supervisory and investigative role despite the availability of the equally effective, well-established, and minimally intrusive alternative of contempt relief.

[137] Consequently, it is clear that the order for reporting hearings was not the only means of vindicating the claimants' rights, and that recourse to a readily available alternative would have been consistent with a defining feature of our legal system. Recourse to this alternative would not have resulted in an interpretation of the court's remedial powers that was so broad as to purport to endow the court with powers that it was "never intended to exercise" (*Dunedin, supra*, at para. 22). It is important to stress that in the present case, it is not clear that actual recourse to a contempt application would have been necessary. The point is simply that if judicial enforcement of the deadlines in question were necessary, recourse to this alternative would not have overextended the court's powers.

[138] On a last note, we find it difficult to imagine circumstances where a breach of one party's fundamental right to notice would aid in the vindication of another's *Charter* rights. In any event, the present facts do not present such a case. The intrusiveness of the trial judge's order was in no way necessary to secure the claimants' s. 23 interests. Given the absence of any causal connection between the breach of the parties' right to notice and the effectiveness of the purported remedy, we would conclude that the breach cannot be considered appropriate for the purposes of s. 24(1).

[139] The second argument is simply not applicable in this case. The facts here do not require us to decide whether previous government non-compliance can ever justify remedial orders that breach principles of procedural fairness and the separation of powers. The Government of Nova Scotia did not refuse to comply with either a prior remedial order or a declaration with respect to its particular obligations in the fact-situation at hand. No such order was made and it is impossible to determine whether the government would have responded in the present case to either a declaration of rights, or the injunction to meet the deadline as these measures were combined with the order purporting to retain jurisdiction to oversee the reporting sessions. Therefore, it cannot be asserted that the trial judge's order has succeeded where less intrusive remedial measures failed.

[140] Moreover, what was required by the Government of Nova Scotia to comply with its obligations pursuant to s. 23 was not self-evident at trial. The trial judge was not faced with a government which was cognizant of how it should fulfill its obligations, but refused to do so. Indeed, at issue before the trial judge was precisely the question of what compliance with s. 23 involved. The present order, therefore, did not overcome governmental recalcitrance in

the face of a clear understanding of what s. 23 required in the circumstances of the case. Remedies must be chosen in light of the nature and structure of the Canadian constitutional order, an important feature of which is the presumption of co-operation between the branches of government. Therefore, unless it is established that this constitutional balance has been upset by the executive's clear defiance of a directly applicable judicial order, increased judicial intervention in public administration will rarely be appropriate.

[141]   In choosing and reviewing s. 24(1) remedies, it is important to remember that the inquiry into the appropriateness of a remedy should be undertaken from an *ex ante* perspective. The simple fact that a desired result occurs after a remedial order is issued is not relevant to determining the question of the order's appropriateness. In our view, an adequate *ex ante* assessment must consider the risks that attend a given remedy. In the present case, as Freeman JA noted in dissent, if the trial judge "misread the degree of co-operation he could expect from the players, there was a risk of failure" (para. 84). That the present remedy's susceptibility to failure was tied to the capacities of a particular judge should in itself give pause. In our view, whether a remedy is appropriate should be assessed with reference to the remedy itself and not the particular capacities of a given judge to manage that remedy. More importantly, where a thorough *ex ante* assessment of a remedy reveals that it will certainly be inconsistent with basic legal principles and constitutional doctrines, such a remedy should not be considered appropriate. Available remedies that do not result in such breaches should, *a contrario*, be considered to be more appropriate. ...

[143]   In the present case, refusing superior courts the power to order reporting hearings clearly would not deny claimants' access to a recognized *Charter* remedy, as such an order is entirely idiosyncratic. More importantly, refusing superior courts this power would not deprive claimants of access to that which they are guaranteed by s. 23, namely, the timely provision of minority language instruction facilities. Indeed, if the appellants' characterization of the reporting hearings' purpose is correct, it is difficult to see how they could have been more effective than the construction deadline coupled with the possibility of a contempt order. In our view, the availability of this legal sanction for non-compliance with the order to meet the construction deadline would have provided at least as much incentive for the government to remedy the s. 23 breach as would have reporting hearings, in which the presiding judge was without the power to make further orders. Moreover, at the level of constitutional principle, because this incentive is legal in nature, it would not have led to the improper politicization of the relationship between the judiciary and the executive.

[144]   Also, it should be noted that the trial judge's order was not consistent with this Court's retention of jurisdiction in the *Reference re Manitoba Language Rights*, [1985] 1 SCR 721. Far from purporting to supervise compliance with a remedy, the Court in that case retained jurisdiction to ask for the government's assistance in fashioning it. The Court did not thereby exceed its constitutional role by purporting to oversee administrative action. The Court was ultimately respectful of the executive's capacity to make the policy choices necessary to comply with constitutional requirements.

VII. Conclusion

[145]   In the result, the trial judge breached both a principle of procedural fairness and the constitutional principle of separation of powers, and it is not clear that alternative, less-

intrusive remedial measures, would not have achieved the ends sought. While a trial judge's decisions with respect to remedies are owed deference, we believe that this must be tempered when fundamental legal principles are threatened. In light of these principles, and in the presence of untested alternative remedies, we would find that the present trial judge's retention of jurisdiction was not appropriate and just under s. 24(1). The Court of Appeal was correct in declaring that the order to retain jurisdiction for the purposes of reporting sessions was of no force and effect. ...

[147] The proper development of the law of constitutional remedies requires that courts reconcile their duty to act within proper jurisdictional limits with the need to give full effect to the rights of a claimant. To read into s. 24(1) a judicial *carte blanche* would not only "turn the Canadian legal system upside down," but would also be an injustice to the parties who come before the court to have their disputes resolved in accordance with basic legal principles. In our view, proper consideration of the principles of procedural fairness and the separation of powers is required to establish the requisite legitimacy and certainty essential to an appropriate and just remedy under s. 24(1) of the *Charter*.

NOTES AND QUESTIONS

1. What judgment do you find persuasive—the majority's reliance on the remedial discretion of the trial judge and the principle of effective remedies, or the minority's reliance on respect for institutional roles?

2. Is the reliance that the majority places on the use of complex remedies in private law appropriate, or does the case raise concerns about the separation of powers and the role of the judiciary in relation to the legislature and the executive that are specific to public law?

3. Is the minority persuasive when it distinguishes the court's decision in the *Manitoba Language Rights* judgment, above, as one in which the court "retained jurisdiction to ask for the government's assistance in fashioning it"? Do you agree that the court "did not thereby exceed its constitutional role by purporting to oversee administrative action"? Was Leblanc J not asking for the government's assistance, as well as the assistance of other parties, in this case?

4. Would the case have been more appropriately handled if, as suggested by the minority, the trial judge's "best efforts" order was enforced by means of contempt? Was the order specific enough to be enforceable by contempt?

5. The majority suggests that the trial judge's order could have been improved by greater specificity. Is this a good thing? Will judges be in a position to make more specific orders? Would more specific orders increase concerns about the judiciary invading governmental functions?

6. Do the majority and the minority have different perceptions about the willingness of the Nova Scotia government to comply with s. 23 of the Charter? For an argument that declarations may be appropriate when a government has simply ignored an issue, but that injunctions and supervisory injunctions may be appropriate in cases in which governments both defy Charter rights or do not have the competence necessary to implement them, see Roach and Budlender, "Mandatory Relief and Supervisory Jurisdiction" (2005), 122 *South African Law Journal* 325.

7. The majority stresses the specific context of minority language rights. Would similar structural remedies and the retention of supervisory jurisdiction be appropriate in other institutional contexts—for example, in a custodial institution where conditions of confinement might result in cruel and unusual punishment; or in a health system where people may die because of excessive wait times? For a prediction that trial judges will "think twice" and may well be reluctant to exercise supervisory jurisdiction in health care cases arising out of *Chaouli v. Quebec*, [2005] 1 SCR 791, see Kent Roach, "The Courts and Medicare: Too Much or Too Little Judicial Activism?" in Flood, Roach, and Sossin, eds., *Access to Care, Access to Justice* (Toronto: University of Toronto Press, 2005). But for two cases where judges retained jurisdiction to ensure that the government complied with the Charter in the sensitive national security context, see *Abdelrazik v. Canada*, 2009 FC 580, at paras. 167-168 (retaining jurisdiction and right to order further remedies until travel documents issued to a Canadian citizen listed by the UN Security Council as associated with al-Qaeda and citizen returned to Canada); *Khadr v. Canada (Prime Minister)*, 2010 FC 715, stayed pending appeal 2010 FCA 199; appeal declared moot 2011 FCA 92 (retaining jurisdiction until Canada proposes an effective remedy and allowing applicant to comment on adequacy of proposed remedies).